The ENCYCLOPEDIA
of CHRISTIANITY

Volume 3
J–O

The

of

Volume 3

editors

translator and English-language editor

statistical editor

WILLIAM B. EERDMANS PUBLISHING COMPANY

BRILL

ENCYCLOPEDIA CHRISTIANITY

J–O

Erwin Fahlbusch
Jan Milič Lochman
John Mbiti
Jaroslav Pelikan
Lukas Vischer

Geoffrey W. Bromiley

David B. Barrett

GRAND RAPIDS, MICHIGAN / CAMBRIDGE, U.K.
LEIDEN / BOSTON

Originally published in German as
Evangelisches Kirchenlexikon, Dritte Auflage (Neufassung)
© 1986, 1989, 1992, 1996, 1997
Vandenhoeck & Ruprecht, Göttingen, Germany

English translation © 2003 by
Wm. B. Eerdmans Publishing Company

Published jointly 2003 by
Wm. B. Eerdmans Publishing Company
255 Jefferson Ave. S.E., Grand Rapids, Michigan 49503
and by
Koninklijke Brill NV
Leiden, the Netherlands

Printed in the United States of America

09 08 07 06 05 04 03   10 9 8 7 6 5 4 3 2 1

Library of Congress Cataloging-in-Publication Data

Evangelisches Kirchenlexikon. English.
    The encyclopedia of Christianity / editors, Erwin Fahlbusch . . . [et al.];
translator and English-language editor, Geoffrey W. Bromiley;
statistical editor, David B. Barrett; foreword, Jaroslav Pelikan.
        p.   cm.
    Includes index.
    Contents: v. 3. J–O.
    ISBN 0-8028-2415-3 (cloth: v. 3: alk. paper)
    1. Christianity — Encyclopedias.   I. Fahlbusch, Erwin.
II. Bromiley, Geoffrey William.   III. Title.
BR95.E8913   2003
230′.003 — DC21   98-45953
                                                CIP

Brill ISBN 90 04 12654 6

Contents

List of Entries

LIST OF ENTRIES

LIST OF ENTRIES

Introduction

This introduction provides a brief guide to the editorial conventions followed throughout the *Encyclopedia of Christianity,* as well as to the statistical information specially prepared for the *EC* by David Barrett.

ALPHABETIZATION

Articles are arranged alphabetically word by word (not letter by letter), with hyphens and apostrophes counted as continuing the single word; all commas are ignored. For example:

> Antiochian Theology
> Anti-Semitism, Anti-Judaism
> . . .
> Augsburg Confession
> Augsburg, Peace of
> . . .
> Calvin, John
> Calvinism
> Calvin's Theology
> . . .
> Church Year
> Churches of Christ

STATISTICS

The *EC* includes separate articles for each of the six major areas (formerly "continents") currently recognized by the United Nations (i.e., Africa, Asia, Europe, Latin America and the Caribbean, Northern America, and Oceania). It also presents separate articles for all independent countries of the world, omitting only those whose population, according to U.N. estimates for 1995, is less than 200,000 (e.g., Andorra, Nauru).

Accompanying each country article is a standard statistical box with the following format:

Argentina

	1960	1980	2000
Population (1,000s):	20,616	28,094	37,032
Annual growth rate (%):	1.55	1.51	1.19
Area: 2,780,400 sq. km. (1,073,518 sq. mi.)			

A.D. *2000*
Population density: 13/sq. km. (34/sq. mi.)
Births / deaths: 1.90 / 0.78 per 100 population
Fertility rate: 2.44 per woman
Infant mortality rate: 20 per 1,000 live births
Life expectancy: 74.2 years (m: 70.6, f: 77.7)
Religious affiliation (%): Christians 92.9 (Roman Catholics 90.2, Protestants 5.9, indigenous 5.4, marginal 1.4, unaffiliated 1.1, other Christians 0.6), nonreligious 2.2, Muslims 2.0, Jews 1.5, other 1.4.

The demographic information in these boxes is taken from the *World Population Prospects: The 1996 Revision* (New York [United Nations], 1998). Depending on the presentation in U.N. tables, figures for 1960, 1980, and 2000 are either for that year alone or for a five-year period beginning with that year. In each case where the United Nations provides three estimates, the medium variant estimates are cited. Information on country area is taken from the *1996 Britannica Book of the Year* (Chicago, 1996). For countries like Argentina, where the birth rate minus the death rate (1.12 per 100 population) does not equal the annual growth rate (1.19), the difference is due to migration — in this case, *into* the country.

David Barrett, editor of the *World Christian Encyclopedia* (2d ed.; 2 vols.; New York, 2001) and president of Global Evangelization Movement, Richmond, Virginia, has provided all the information on religious affiliation in the statistical boxes. In the first place, the boxes present the breakdown of overall religious affiliation for each country, using the following sixteen categories:

atheists — persons professing atheism, skepticism, or disbelief, including antireligious (opposed to all religion)

Baha'is — followers of the Baha'i World Faith, founded in the 19th century by Bahā' Allāh

Buddhists — followers of any of the branches of Buddhism; worldwide, 56 percent are Mahayana (northern), 38 percent Theravada (Hinayana, or southern), 6 percent Tantrayana (Lamaism)

Chinese folk religionists — followers of the traditional Chinese religion, which includes local deities, ancestor veneration, Confucian ethics, Taoism, divination, and some Buddhist elements

Christians — followers of Jesus Christ, either affiliated with churches or simply identifying themselves as such in censuses or polls

Confucianists — non-Chinese followers of Confucius and Confucianism, mostly Koreans in Korea

Hindus — followers of the main Hindu traditions; worldwide, 70 percent are Vaishnavas, 25 percent Saivas, 3 percent Saktas, 2 percent neo-Hindus and reform Hindus

Jews — adherents of Judaism

Muslims — followers of Islam; worldwide, 83 percent are Sunnites, 16 percent Shiites, 1 percent other schools

new religionists — followers of Asian 20th-century new religions, new religious movements, radical new crisis religions, and non-Christian syncretistic mass religions, all founded since 1800 and most since 1945

nonreligious — persons professing no religion, nonbelievers, agnostics, freethinkers, dereligionized secularists indifferent to all religion

Shintoists — Japanese who profess Shinto as their first or major religion

Sikhs — followers of the Sikh reform movement arising out of Hinduism

spiritists — non-Christian spiritists, spiritualists, thaumaturgists, medium-religionists

Taoists — followers of the religion developed from the Taoist philosophy and from folk religion and Buddhism

tribal religionists — primal or primitive religionists, animists, spirit-worshipers, shamanists, ancestor-venerators, polytheists, pantheists, traditionalists, local or tribal folk-religionists

The country boxes list each religious group that numbers at least 1.0 percent of the population of that county; any groups that number 0.9 percent or less of the population are grouped together under "other." Because of rounding, the totals of all the religious groups in a country may not equal 100.0 percent.

Second, for the category "Christians," the information in the boxes shows in parentheses the break-down by ecclesiastical bloc, using the following seven categories:

Anglicans — persons in a church that is in fellowship with the archbishop of Canterbury, especially through its participation in the Lambeth Conference; Episcopalians

indigenous — Christians in denominations, churches, or movements who regard themselves as outside of mainline Anglican/Orthodox/Protestant/Roman Catholic Christianity; autonomous bodies independent of foreign origin or control (e.g., Independent Charismatic Churches [Braz.], house church movement [China], isolated radio believers [Saudi Arabia], Zion Christian Church [S.Af.], Vineyard Christian Fellowship [U.S.])

marginal — followers of para-Christian or quasi-Christian Western movements or deviations out of mainline Protestantism, not professing Christian doctrine according to the classic Trinitarian creeds (i.e., Apostles', Nicene) but often claiming a second or supplementary or ongoing source of divine revelation in addition to the Bible (e.g., Christian Scientists, Jehovah's Witnesses, Mormons, Unitarians)

Orthodox — Eastern (Chalcedonian), Oriental (Pre-Chalcedonian, Non-Chalcedonian, Monophysite), Nestorian (Assyrian), and nonhistorical Orthodox

Protestants — persons in churches that trace their origin or formulation to the 16th-century Reformation and thus typically emphasize justification by faith alone and the Bible as the supreme authority, including (1) churches in the Lutheran, Calvinistic, and Zwinglian traditions; and (2) other groups arising before, during, or after the Reformation (e.g., Waldenses, Bohemian Brethren, Baptists, Friends, Congregationalists, Methodists, Adventists, Pentecostals, Assemblies of God)

Roman Catholics — persons in a church that recognizes the pope, the bishop of Rome (with the associated hierarchy), as its spiritual head

unaffiliated — professing Christians not associated with an church

As with the different religions, so for the different types of Christians, any group that numbers at least 1.0 percent of the population of the country is listed. Any groups of Christians that number 0.9 percent or less of the population are included together under "other Christians." Because of rounding, the totals of all the individual Christian groups may not equal the total percentage of

Christians. Furthermore, where persons affiliate themselves with, or are claimed by, two Christian groups at once, the total of the percentages of the individual Christian groups in a country may exceed the countrywide percentage of Christians. This problem of double counting (evident, for example, in the Argentina box on p. xi) is left unresolved in the *EC*.

Accompanying each major area article are three tables that list most of the information appearing in the individual country statistical boxes. The first table displays demographic information; the second, data on overall religious affiliation; the third, data on church affiliation. The religion tables list separately the 12 most popular religions worldwide (i.e., the above list of 16 minus Baha'is, Confucianists, Shintoists, and Taoists), with all the others accounted for under "Other." In the tables showing ecclesiastical breakdown, all Christians are counted in one of the seven categories (or, in cases of double counting, in more than one category). The tables of religion and of Christianity report country by country all adherents of a religious position or Christian grouping that total at least 0.1 percent of the population. In addition, all tables present totals for the major area as a whole, as well as for each region that U.N. statistics distinguish within the major area. (The tables accompanying "Africa," for example, show totals for the whole continent; for the regions of eastern, middle, northern, southern, and western Africa; and also for each country that has a separate article in the *EC*.) Finally, for purposes of comparison, relevant figures for the whole world appear as the top row of each major area table.

CROSS-REFERENCES

A variety of cross-references aid the reader in locating articles or specific sections of articles. One type appears as a main title, either (1) making clear where a subject is treated or (2) indicating the exact article title. For example:

(1) **Aid** → Christian Development Services; Development 1.4

 Anathema → Confessions and Creeds

(2) **Ancient Church** → Early Church

 Ancient Oriental Churches → Oriental Orthodox Churches

Other cross-references appear within the text of articles. Those referring to other sections of the present article have the form "(see 1)," "(see 3.2)."

Cross-references to other articles cited as such appear (3) within parentheses in the text, following a cross-reference arrow and using the exact spelling and capitalization of the article title, and (4) on a separate line after the text proper and before the bibliography. In both cases, multiple cross-references are separated by semicolons, and only a single, initial arrow is used. Items cross-referenced within the text of an article normally do not also appear following the text of the article.

(3) In the latter part of the 20th century some churches in the United States and Europe have tried to revive the right of church asylum for some refugees whom the government refused to recognize as political refugees (→ Sanctuary 1; Resistance, Right of, 2).

 As such, dance rejects an antibiblical dualism (→ Anthropology 2.3 and 3.2; Soul).

 The Roman Catholic Church reacted negatively, placing Beccaria's book on the Index (→ Censorship; Inquisition 2). Then in the 19th century F. D. E. Schleiermacher (1768-1834; → Schleiermacher's Theology) criticized theologically the theory of retribution.

(4) → Anglican Communion 4; Clergy and Laity; Consensus 4; Councils of the Church

 → Catholicism (Roman); Church 3.2; Lay Movements

 → Communities, Spiritual; Ethics 2; Monasticism 3.2.2; Property, esp. 3.2-3

Finally (5), cross-references also appear within the flow of the text, with an arrow appearing before a word or phrase that points clearly (but not necessarily exactly) to the title of another article. Specific sections referred to are indicated by section marks and numbers in parentheses. Normally (6), the exact name of an article is used if a specific section is cited.

(5) The extension of the problem to political matters makes it necessary to define the relations between the obedience of → faith (§3), → freedom (§2), and → reason.

 In the controversy with the → Pelagians Augustine's main concern was to show that grace is not limited to external aids like the →

law (§§3.1-2) or the teaching and example of Christ.

Jewish → proselyte baptism incorporates the baptized not only into the religious fellowship but also into God's → covenant → people. This matter is relevant in the dialogue between Israel and the → church (§§1.4.1.3, 2.1, 5.5.3).

(6) . . . the 19th-century → apocalyptic movement in the United States.

vs. . . . the 19th-century apocalyptic movement (→ Apocalypticism 3) in the United States.

BIBLIOGRAPHIES

Within a bibliography (or separate section of a bibliography), entries are ordered first by author, then by title (disregarding an initial article in any language). Successive articles by the same author(s) are separated by semicolons.

In individual bibliographic entries, the names of series are included only if the title is omitted (typically only for biblical commentaries). For works appearing both in a non-English language and in English translation, normally only the English title is cited.

Consulting Editors

Ulrich Becker *Education*
Eugene L. Brand *Liturgy; Worship*
Faith E. Burgess *Women's Studies/Issues*
Carsten Colpe *Religious Studies*
Hans-Werner Gensichen† *Asia; Mission Studies*
Martin Greschat *Biographies; Church History*
Heimo Hofmeister *Philosophy*
Hubertus G. Hubbeling† *Philosophy*
Anastasios Kallis *Orthodoxy*
Leo Laeyendecker *Sociology*

Ekkehard Mühlenberg *Church History*
Hans-Jürgen Prien *Latin America*
Dietrich Ritschl *Systematic Theology; Ethics*
Jürgen Roloff *New Testament*
Joachim Scharfenberg† *Practical Theology; Psychology*
Traugott Schöfthaler *Sociology*
Rudolf Smend *Old Testament*
Albert Stein† *Law; Church Law*

Contributors

Andreas Aarflot, *Oppegård, Norw.*
  Norway

Adolf Adam, *Mainz, Ger.*
  Liturgy 3

Edgar G. Adams, *Richmond, Va.*
  Military Chaplaincy 2.2

Ruth Albrecht, *Hamburg*
  Martyrs; Martyrs, Acts of the

James N. Amanze, *Gaborone, Botswana*
  Malawi

Charles Arian, *Baltimore*
  Jewish-Christian Dialogue

Susan Asch, *Paris*
  Kimbanguist Church

E. Theodore Bachman†, *Princeton Junction, N.J.*
  Lutheran Churches

Kenneth Baker†, *Bradford, Eng.*
  Lesotho

Michael Barkun, *Syracuse, N.Y.*
  Oneida Community

Jean-Pierre Bastian, *Strasbourg, Fr.*
  Mexico

Arnulf Baumann, *Wolfsburg, Ger.*
  Jewish Christians 2; Jewish Mission

Jörg Baur, *Göttingen, Ger.*
  Orthodoxy 1

Tina Mary Beattie, *Bristol, Eng.*
  Mary, Devotion to, 2

Uwe Becker, *Göttingen, Ger.*
  Judges, Book of

José Oscar Beozzo, *São Paulo, Braz.*
  Latin American Council of Bishops

CONTRIBUTORS

HERBERT FROST†, *Cologne*
Moderator

CLAUDE GEFFRÉ, *Paris*
Nouvelle théologie

HANS-WERNER GENSICHEN†, *Heidelberg, Ger.*
Mission 3

UWE GERBER, *Darmstadt, Ger.*
Kenosis

WOLFGANG GERN, *Mainz, Ger.*
Laos; Myanmar

FRIEDRICH WILHELM GRAF, *Munich*
Liberal Theology

ROBERT M. GRANT, *Chicago*
Montanism

JAY D. GREEN, *Lookout Mountain, Ga.*
Lausanne Movement

JOEL B. GREEN, *Wilmore, Ky.*
Mary in the New Testament

HANS-JÜRGEN GRESCHAT, *Marburg, Ger.*
Kitawala

MARTIN GRESCHAT, *Münster, Ger.*
Modern Church History 1

GEORGE GRIMA, *Msida, Malta*
Malta

HEINER GROTE†, *Bensheim, Ger.*
Lourdes; Offices

ALBRECHT GRÖZINGER, *Basel, Switz.*
Miracle 3

JOHANNES GRÜNDEL, *Munich*
Moral Theology

GABRIEL HABIB, *Vienna, Va.*
Middle East Council of Churches

GERT HAENDLER, *Bad Doberan, Ger.*
Keys, Power of the

WOLFGANG HAGE, *Marburg, Ger.*
Nestorians 2-3

JOE HALE, *Lake Junaluska, N.C.*
Methodist Churches

WOLFGANG HARNISCH, *Marburg, Ger.*
Kerygma

PETER HAUPTMANN, *Überlingen, Ger.*
Old Believers

WOLF-DIETER HAUSCHILD, *Münster, Ger.*
Lutheranism

RÜDIGER HAUTH, *Witten, Ger.*
Mormons

ROBERT D. HAWKINS, *Columbia, S.C.*
Oratorio; Organ, Organ Music

JOHN H. HAYES, *Atlanta*
Masorah, Masoretes

MARKKU HEIKKILÄ, *Helsinki, Fin.*
Military Chaplaincy 1–2.1

SCOTT HENDRIX, *Princeton*
Luther's Theology

WILLI HENKEL, *Munich*
Latin American Councils 1

JOHANNES HENSCHEL, C.S.SP., *Cologne*
Kenya

PETER HERTEL, *Ronnenberg, Ger.*
Opus Dei

KLAUS HESSE, *Berlin*
Mongolia

MARY HINKLE, *St. Paul, Minn.*
Mary Magdalene

NORMAN A. HJELM, *Wynnewood, Pa.*
Lutheran Churches; Lutheran World
Federation; Lutheranism; Marxism and
Christianity

HARRY C. HOEBEN, *Cadier en Keer, Neth.*
Liberia

HEIMO HOFMEISTER, *Heidelberg, Ger.*
Metaphysics 1-2; Moralism; Motive, Ethics of

KARL HOHEISEL, *Bonn*
Occultism

E. BROOKS HOLIFIELD, *Atlanta*
North American Theology

TRAUGOTT HOLTZ, *Halle, Ger.*
James; Jesus

VICTOR W. C. HSU, *Waldwick, N.J.*
Mauritius

WOLFGANG HUBER, *Berlin*
Legitimation

HANS HÜBNER, *Göttingen, Ger.*
Justification 1; Law 2

ARLAND J. HULTGREN, *St. Paul, Minn.*
Jude, Epistle of; Lord's Prayer; Mark, Gospel of;
Nazirites

HANS INEICHEN, *Nürnberg, Ger.*
Linguistics 1-3

LOUIS JACOBS, *London*
Jewish Theology

PAUL JENKINS, *Basel, Switz.*
Mali

JOHN A. JORGENSON, *Wayne, Pa.*
Old Age

ERIC JUNOD, *Lausanne, Switz.*
Origenism

OTTO KAISER, *Marburg, Ger.*
Lamentations, Book of

ANASTASIOS KALLIS, *Münster, Ger.*
Orthodox Church

MARTIN KARRER, *Wuppertal, Ger.*
Millenarianism

KAROL KARSKI, *Warsaw*
Mariavites

VOLKER KASCH, *Stuttgart, Ger.*
Malaysia

CONTRIBUTORS

RUDOLF WOLFGANG MÜLLER, *Freiburg, Ger.*
Money

JENS MÜLLER-KENT, *Berlin*
Military Chaplaincy 3

HUBERTUS MYNAREK, *Odernheim, Ger.*
New Thought

PETER NAGEL, *Halle, Ger.*
Mandaeans; Manichaeanism; Nag Hammadi

STANISŁAW CELESTYN NAPIÓRKOWSKI, *Lublin, Pol.*
Mariology 2.1-6

WALTER NEIDHART†, *Basel, Switz.*
Occasional Services 2-4

ANGELIKA NEUWIRTH, *Berlin*
Mosque

LEOPOLDO NIILUS, *Washington, D.C.*
Middle East Council of Churches

ENGELHARD !NÔABEB, *Karibib, Namibia*
Namibia

MARK A. NOLL, *Wheaton, Ill.*
Northern America

EDWARD NOORT, *Hamburg*
Joshua, Book of

CHRISTIAN OEYEN, *Siegburg, Ger.*
Old Catholic Churches

PETER VON DER OSTEN-SACKEN, *Berlin*
New Testament Era, History of

RICHARD S. OSTRANDER, *Siloam Springs, Ark.*
Moody, Dwight L.

KLAUS OTTE, *Mehren, Ger.*
Last Judgment

ECKART OTTO, *Munich*
Jerusalem

JOHN W. PADBERG, S.J., *St. Louis, Mo.*
Jesuits

HENNING PAULSEN†, *Hamburg*
Literature, Biblical and Early Christian, 2

JAEL B. PAULUS†, *Karlsruhe, Ger.*
Jewish Practices

ALBRECHT PETERS†, *Ziegelhausen, Ger.*
Law 3

HEINRICH PETRI, *Regensburg, Ger.*
Mary, Devotion to, 1

PHILIP H. PFATTEICHER, *Pittsburgh, Pa.*
Liturgy 5; Occasional Services 1

PETER C. PHAN, *Washington, D.C.*
Missio canonica

CRAIG A. PHILLIPS, *Arlington, Va.*
Language; Literary Criticism

GREGORY F. AUGUSTINE PIERCE, *Chicago*
Lay Apostolate

PAUL E. PIERSON, *Pasadena, Calif.*
Mission Schools

DAFNE SABANES PLOU, *Buenos Aires, Arg.*
Latin American Council of Churches

GÜNTHER PÖLTNER, *Vienna*
Ontology

JEAN PORTER, *Notre Dame, Ind.*
Natural Law 6

MARK ALLAN POWELL, *Columbus, Ohio*
Jesus Seminar

HANS-WERNER PRAHL, *Kiel, Ger.*
Leisure

WILHELM PRATSCHER, *Vienna*
Kingdom of God 2

HANS-JÜRGEN PRIEN, *Cologne*
Latin America and the Caribbean 1; Nicaragua

BRUNO PRIMETSHOFER, *Vienna*
Observance

MURIEL M. RADTKE, *Ipswich, Mass.*
Kindergarten; Moral Education

HANS-DIETHER REIMER†, *Stuttgart, Ger.*
Jehovah's Witnesses

INGRID REIMER, *Stuttgart, Ger.*
Moral Rearmament

HELMUT REINALTER, *Innsbruck, Aus.*
Josephinism; Masons

JOHN D. REMPEL, *New York*
Mennonites

JOHN REUMANN, *Philadelphia*
Kerygma; Koinonia

DIETRICH RITSCHL, *Reigoldswil, Switz.*
Libertinism; Marriage and Divorce 1; Mediating Theology; Medical Ethics; Middle Axioms; Office of Christ

ROBERT B. ROBINSON, *Philadelphia*
Narrative Theology

JÜRGEN ROLOFF, *Erlangen, Ger.*
Joseph

MICHAEL ROOT, *Columbus, Ohio*
Joint Declaration on the Doctrine of Justification

A. JAMES RUDIN, *New York*
Oberammergau

WILLIAM G. RUSCH, *New York*
Leuenberg Agreement; Mott, John R.

HORACE O. RUSSELL, *Radnor, Pa.*
Jamaica

WALTER SAFT, *Bad Kissingen, Ger.*
Meditation

WALTER SAWATSKY, *Elkhart, Ind.*
Kazakhstan; Kyrgyzstan; Moldova

CARL SCHALK, *Melrose Park, Ill.*
Motet

JOACHIM SCHARFENBERG†, *Kiel, Ger.*
Libido; Narcissism

LEO SCHEFFCZYK, *Munich*
Neoscholasticism

CONTRIBUTORS

James A. Scherer, *Oak Park, Ill.*
Missiology; Mission 3; Missionary; North American Missions

Theo Schiller, *Marburg, Ger.*
Liberalism 1-3

Johannes Schilling, *Kiel, Ger.*
Monastery

Annemarie Schimmel, *Bonn*
Number

Günther Schiwy, *Wörthsee, Ger.*
New Age

Margarete Schlüter, *Frankfurt*
Midrash; Mishnah

Hans-Christoph Schmitt, *Uttenreuth, Ger.*
Literature, Biblical and Early Christian, 1

Thomas Martin Schneider, *Koblenz, Ger.*
Niemöller, Martin

Thaddeus A. Schnitker, *Münster, Ger.*
Litany

Wolfgang Schoberth, *Bayreuth, Ger.*
Nature

Walter Schöpsdau, *Bensheim, Ger.*
Kolping Society; Mixed Marriage

Willy Schottroff†, *Kassel, Ger.*
Ordeal

Caroline Schröder, *Bonn*
King, Martin Luther, Jr.; Niebuhr, Reinhold

Thomas L. Schubeck, S.J., *University Heights, Ohio*
Latin American Theology; Liberation Theology

Hartwig von Schubert, *Hamburg*
Life 2

Werner Schwartz, *Speyer, Ger.*
Meaning; Norms

Elisabeth Schwarz, *Vienna*
Metaphor

Joachim Schwarz, *Lindau, Ger.*
Love; Oath

Steven S. Schwarzschild†, *St. Louis, Mo.*
Judaism

Juan Schwindt, *Buenos Aires, Arg.*
Latin American Council of Churches

Bob Scott, *Auckland, N.Z.*
Marginalized Groups

R. Kevin Seasoltz, O.S.B., *Collegeville, Minn.*
Liturgical Movement

Frank C. Senn, *Evanston, Ill.*
Kiss of Peace; Laying on of Hands; Liturgical Vessels

Klaus Seybold, *Basel, Switz.*
Monarchy in Israel

Stanley H. Skreslet, *Richmond, Va.*
Mission 1-2

Michael Slusser, *Pittsburgh, Pa.*
Justin Martyr

Rudolf Smend, *Göttingen, Ger.*
Moses

J. Alberto Soggin, *Rome*
Leviticus, Book of; Numbers, Book of

Renate Söhnen-Thieme, *Tübingen, Ger.*
Mahabharata

Aidan W. Southall, *Madison, Wis.*
Madagascar

Walter Sparn, *Erlangen, Ger.*
Neology; Orthodoxy 1

Hermann Spieckermann, *Göttingen, Ger.*
Josiah; Kingdom of God 1; Noah

Peter Staples, *Utrecht, Neth.*
Oxford Movement

Ekkehard Starke, *Duisburg, Ger.*
Life 1; Marxism 2; Marxism and Christianity

Albert Stein†, *Brühl, Ger.*
Lay Preaching; Official Principal

Jürgen Stein, *Bremen, Ger.*
Optimism and Pessimism

Peter Steinacker, *Darmstadt, Ger.*
Kingdom of God 3

Friedrich Stentzler, *Berlin*
New Religions

Fritz Steppat, *Berlin*
Lebanon

Kenneth W. Stevenson, *Fareham, Eng.*
Marriage and Divorce 3.6

Eberhard Stock, *Gladenbach, Ger.*
Logic and Theology

Philipp Stoellger, *Zurich*
Linguistics

Dietrich Stollberg, *Marburg, Ger.*
Lifestyle

Georg Strecker†, *Göttingen, Ger.*
James, Epistle of; John, Epistles of

Maria-Barbara von Stritzky, *Münster, Ger.*
Light

Gerlinde Strohmaier-Wiederanders, *Berlin*
Minster; Oratory

Holger Strutwolf, *Pirmasens, Ger.*
Origen

David L. Stubbs, *Holland, Mich.*
Obedience

Jouko Talonen, *Helsinki, Fin.*
Latvia

Rudolf von Thadden, *Göttingen, Ger.*
Kulturkampf

Evangelos Theodorou, *Athens*
Liturgy 4

WINFRIED THIEL, *Bochum, Ger.*
Joel, Book of; Jonah, Book of; Malachi, Book
of; Micah, Book of; Nahum, Book of; Obadiah,
Book of

HANS-JOACHIM THILO, *Lübeck, Ger.*
Old Age 1

NORMAN E. THOMAS, *Penney Farms, Fla.*
Medical Missions; Missionary Conferences;
Missionary Training

NIKOLAUS THON, *Bochum, Ger.*
Modern Church History 3

HARTWIG THYEN, *Neckargemünd, Ger.*
John the Baptist

MICHAEL TRESCHOW, *Kelowna, B.C.*
Knox, John

PAUL-ANDRÉ TURCOTTE, *Paris*
Nation, Nationalism

WOLFGANG ULLMANN, *Berlin*
Nicaea, Councils of; Niceno-
Constantinopolitan Creed

HANS G. ULRICH, *Erlangen, Ger.*
Neighbor

JAKOB M. M. DE VALK, *Rotterdam, Neth.*
Manipulation

LUKE VERONIS, *Tiranë, Alb.*
Orthodox Missions

JÜRGEN VIERING, *Bovenden, Ger.*
Modernity

HANS VÖCKING, *Frankfurt*
Libya

FALK WAGNER†, *Vienna*
Modern Period

HERIBERT WAHL, *Munich*
Neurosis

GEOFFREY WAINWRIGHT, *Durham, N.C.*
Lux Mundi; Methodism; Newbigin, J. E. Lesslie

JOHN WALL, *Camden, N.J.*
Marriage and Divorce 4

ANDREW F. WALLS, *Edinburgh*
New Zealand

REGINA WEGEMUND, *Hamburg*
Mauritania

RUDOLF WEILER, *Vienna*
Natural Law 1-5

ERIKA WEINZIERL, *Vienna*
Modernism

DOROTHEA WENDEBOURG, *Tübingen, Ger.*
Monasticism

FRITZ WEST, *Marine on St. Croix, Minn.*
Lector

PAUL WESTERMEYER, *St. Paul, Minn.*
Mass, Music for the

THEO WETTACH, *Würzburg, Ger.*
Missionary Conferences

GERNOT WIESSNER†, *Göttingen, Ger.*
Mongolian Mission

KLAUS WINKLER†, *Hannover, Ger.*
Joy; Laughing and Crying

JOHN WITTE JR., *Atlanta*
Law and Legal Theory

ERNST WÜRTHWEIN†, *Marburg, Ger.*
Kings, Books of; Law 1

DIETMAR WYRWA, *Berlin*
Old Roman Creed

WALTHER C. ZIMMERLI†, *Brunswick, Ger.*
Kantianism

Abbreviations

Abbreviations generally follow those given in the *Journal of Biblical Literature* "Instructions for Contributors." For those not listed there, the abbreviations in the second edition of S. M. Schwertner's *Internationales Abkürzungsverzeichnis für Theologie und Grenzgebiete* (Berlin, 1992) are used; for works of theology or related fields not listed in either source, new abbreviations have been formed.

Writings listed below under the section "Early Church Writings" include those of writers through Augustine.

BIBLICAL BOOKS, WITH THE APOCRYPHA

Gen.	Genesis	Zeph.	Zephaniah
Exod.	Exodus	Hag.	Haggai
Lev.	Leviticus	Zech.	Zechariah
Num.	Numbers	Mal.	Malachi
Deut.	Deuteronomy	Add. Est.	Additions to Esther
Josh.	Joshua	Bar.	Baruch
Judg.	Judges	Bel	Bel and the Dragon
Ruth	Ruth	1-2 Esdr.	1-2 Esdras
1-2 Sam.	1-2 Samuel	4 Ezra	4 Ezra
1-2 Kgs.	1-2 Kings	Jdt.	Judith
1-2-3-4 Kgdms.	1-2-3-4 Kingdoms	Ep. Jer.	Epistle of Jeremiah
1-2 Chr.	1-2 Chronicles	1-2-3-4 Macc.	1-2-3-4 Maccabees
Ezra	Ezra	Pr. Azar.	Prayer of Azariah
Neh.	Nehemiah	Pr. Man.	Prayer of Manasseh
Esth.	Esther	Sir.	Sirach / Ecclesiasticus / Wisdom of Jesus, Son of Sirach
Job	Job		
Ps.	Psalms	Sus.	Susanna
Prov.	Proverbs	Tob.	Tobit
Eccl.	Ecclesiastes	Wis.	Wisdom of Solomon
Cant.	Canticles / Song of Solomon / Song of Songs	Matt.	Matthew
		Mark	Mark
Isa.	Isaiah	Luke	Luke
Jer.	Jeremiah	John	John
Lam.	Lamentations	Acts	Acts of the Apostles
Ezek.	Ezekiel	Rom.	Romans
Dan.	Daniel	1-2 Cor.	1-2 Corinthians
Hos.	Hosea	Gal.	Galatians
Joel	Joel	Eph.	Ephesians
Amos	Amos	Phil.	Philippians
Obad.	Obadiah	Col.	Colossians
Jonah	Jonah	1-2 Thess.	1-2 Thessalonians
Mic.	Micah	1-2 Tim.	1-2 Timothy
Nah.	Nahum	Titus	Titus
Hab.	Habakkuk	Phlm.	Philemon

Heb.	Hebrews	1-2-3 John	1-2-3 John
Jas.	James	Jude	Jude
1-2 Pet.	1-2 Peter	Rev.	Revelation

OLD TESTAMENT PSEUDEPIGRAPHA

2-3 Apoc. Bar.	Syriac, Greek *Apocalypse of Baruch*	Ep. Arist.	*Epistle of Aristeas*
1-2-3 Enoch	Ethiopic, Slavonic, Hebrew *Enoch*	Jos. As.	*Joseph and Aseneth*
		Pss. Sol.	*Psalms of Solomon*

EARLY CHURCH WRITINGS, WITH NAG HAMMADI TRACTATES

Ap. Jas.	*Apocryphon of James*	Dial. Sav.	*Dialogue of the Savior*
Apoc. Paul	*Apocalypse of Paul*	Did.	*Didache*
Athanasius		Did. apos.	*Didascalia apostolorum*
Ep. mon.	*Epistula ad monachos*	Eusebius	
Ep. Serap.	*Epistula ad Serapionem*	Hist. eccl.	*Historia ecclesiastica*
Augustine		Gos. Thom.	*Gospel of Thomas*
C. Jul.	*Contra Julianum*	Gregory of Nazianzus	
Conf.	*Confessions*	Or. theol.	*Orationes theologicae*
De civ. Dei	*De civitate Dei*	Herm. Sim.	*Hermas, Similitude(s)*
De doc. Christ.	*De doctrina Christiana*	Ign. [Ignatius]	
De Gen. ad litt.	*De Genesi ad litteram*	Smyrn.	*Letter to the Smyrnaeans*
De grat. et lib. arb.	*De gratia et libero arbitrio*	Irenaeus	
De pecc. mer.	*De peccatorum meritis et remissione et de baptismo parvulorum*	Adv. haer.	*Adversus omnes haereses*
		Justin Martyr	
De praed. sanct.	*De praedestinatione sanctorum*	1-2 Apol.	*1-2 Apologia*
De spir. et litt.	*De spiritu et littera*	Dial.	*Dialogue with Trypho*
De Trin.	*De Trinitatae libri quindecim*	Lactantius	
Ench.	*Enchiridion ad Laurentium de fide spe et caritate*	De mort. pers.	*De mortibus persecutorum*
		Div. inst.	*Divinae institutiones*
Serm.	*Sermones*	Origen	
Barn.	*Barnabas*	C. Cels.	*Contra Celsum*
1-2 Clem.	*1-2 Clement*	Comm. in Rom.	*Commentarii in Romanos*
Clement of Alexandria		Pap. Eger.	*Egerton Papyrus*
Protr.	*Protrepticus*	Tertullian	
Cyril of Jerusalem		Adv. Marc.	*Adversus Marcionem*
Cat.	*Catecheses*	Adv. Prax.	*Adversus Praxeam*
		De praescr. haeret.	*De praescriptione haereticorum*

DEAD SEA SCROLLS

| 1QH | *Hôdāyōt (Thanksgiving Hymns)* | 1QS | *Serek hayyaḥad (Rule of the Community, Manual of Discipline)* |
| 1QM | *Milḥāmāh (War Scroll)* | | |

ABBREVIATIONS

CLASSICAL TARGUMS AND RABBINIC WRITINGS

b.	Babylonian Talmud	*Ber.*	*Berakot*
m.	Mishnah	*Gen. Rab.*	*Genesis Rabbah*
t.	Tosefta	*Meg.*	*Megilla*
y.	Jerusalem Talmud	*Ned.*	*Nedarim*
ʿAbod. Zar.	*ʿAboda Zara*	*Sanh.*	*Sanhedrin*
ʾAbot	*ʾAbot*	*Šeqal.*	*Šeqalim*
B. Bat.	*Baba Batra*	*Soṭa*	*Soṭa*

OTHER ANCIENT, MEDIEVAL, AND EARLY MODERN WRITINGS

CA	Confessio Augustana (Augsburg Confession)
CA Apol.	Apology of the Confessio Augustana
Calvin, J.	
Inst.	*Institutes of the Christian Religion*
Dionysius the Pseudo-Areopagite	
Mys. theol.	*Peri mystikēs theologias*
Formula of Concord	
Ep.	Epitome
SD	Solid Declaration
Gertrude "the Great"	
Leg.	*Legatus . . . divinae pietatis*
Hugh of St.-Victor	
Quaest. in ep. Pauli	*Quaestiones et decisiones in epistolas D. Pauli*
John of Damascus	
De fide orth.	*De fide orthodoxa*
Josephus	
Ag. Ap.	*Against Apionem*
Ant.	*Jewish Antiquities*
J.W.	*Jewish War*
Maximus the Confessor	
De eccl. hier.	Scholium on Dionysius's *De ecclesiastica hierarchia*
Melanchthon, P.	
Treatise	*Treatise on the Power and Primacy of the Pope*
Peter Lombard	
Sent.	*Sentences*
Plato	
Par.	*Parmenides*
Phd.	*Phaedo*
Plt.	*Politicus*
Plotinus	
Enn.	*Enneades*
Schmalk. Art.	Schmalkaldic Articles
Strabo	
Geog.	*Geography*
Suetonius	
Claud.	*Divus Claudius*
Tacitus	
Ann.	*Annales*
Thomas Aquinas	
De pot.	*De potentia Dei*
Summa theol.	*Summa theologiae*

MODERN PUBLICATIONS AND EDITIONS

AA	I. Kant, *Gesammelte Schriften* (Berlin, Akademie Ausgabe)
AAS	*Acta apostolicae sedis*
AB	Anchor Bible
ABD	*Anchor Bible Dictionary*
AbNTC	Abingdon NT Commentaries
ACO	*Acta conciliorum oecumenicorum*
ACW	Ancient Christian Writers
AEcR	*American Ecclesiastical Review*
AGLB	Aus der Geschichte der lateinischen Bibel
AHSJ	*Archivum historicum Societatis Jesu*
AnBoll	*Analecta Bollandiana*
ANET	*Ancient Near Eastern Texts*
ANF	The Ante-Nicene Fathers: Translations of the Writings of the Fathers down to A.D. 325 (ed. A. Roberts and J. Donaldson)
Ang.	*Angelicum. Periodicum internationale de re philosophica et theologica*
ANRW	*Aufstieg und Niedergang der römischen Welt*
ApF(L)	*Apostolic Fathers* (trans. K. Lake)
ARSP	*Archiv für Rechts- und Sozialphilosophie*

AsbTJ	Asbury Theological Journal	DSp	Dictionnaire de spiritualité, ascétique et mystique
ATD	Das Alte Testament Deutsch		
BBKL	Biographisch-bibliographisches Kirchenlexikon	dü	Der Überblick. Zeitschrift für ökumenische Zusammenarbeit und weltweite Begegnung
BerOl	Berit Olam: Studies in Hebrew Narrative and Poetry		
		EAT	Die El-Amarna Tafeln
BFA(C)	Bulletin of the Faculty of Arts, University of Egypt, Cairo	EDNT	Exegetical Dictionary of the New Testament
BgMiss	Bibliografia missionaria	EeT(O)	Eglise et théologie (Ottawa)
BHH	Biblisch-Historisches Handwörterbuch	EKKNT	Evangelisch-katholischer Kommentar zum Neuen Testament
Bib	Biblica		
BibRev	Bible Review	ELC	Encyclopedia of the Lutheran Church
BiPa	Biblia patristica	EMQ	Evangelical Missions Quarterly
BJRL	Bulletin of the John Rylands University Library of Manchester	EncDSS	Encyclopedia of the Dead Sea Scrolls
		EncEC	Encyclopedia of the Early Church
		EncJud	Encyclopaedia Judaica
BJS	British Journal of Sociology	EncRel(E)	The Encyclopedia of Religion (ed. M. Eliade)
BKAT	Biblischer Kommentar: Altes Testament		
BNTC	Black's New Testament Commentaries	EncTal	Encyclopedia talmudica
BoA	M. Luther, Luthers Werk in Auswahl (Bonn)	ER	Ecumenical Review
		ERT	Evangelical Review of Theology
BPat	Biblioteca patristica	ETL	Ephemerides theologicae Lovanienses
Cath(M)	Catholica (Münster)	EvQ	Evangelical Quarterly
CBC	Cambridge Bible Commentary	FC	Fathers of the Church
CBQ	Catholic Biblical Quarterly	FirstT	First Things
CCH	Central Church History	FOTL	Forms of the Old Testament Literature
CChr.CM	Corpus Christianorum, Continuatio mediaevalis	GCS	Die griechischen christlichen Schriftsteller der ersten drei Jahrhunderte
CChr.SL	Corpus Christianorum, Series Latina		
CD	K. Barth, Church Dogmatics	GK	Gestalten der Kirchengeschichte
CDP	Cambridge Dictionary of Philosophy	Greg.	Gregorianum
CH	Church History	HAT	Handbuch zum Alten Testament
CIC	Codex Iuris Canonici	HCE	Handbuch der christlichen Ethik
CIDoc.D	Centro Intercultural de Documentación–documentos	HCH	Handbook of Church History
		HCOT	Historical Commentary on the Old Testament
CPL	Clavis patrum Latinorum		
CR.BS	Currents in Research: Biblical Studies	HDThG	Handbuch der Dogmen- und Theologiegeschichte
CRINT	Compendia rerum Iudaicarum ad Novum Testamentum		
		HibJ	Hibbert Journal: A Quarterly Review of Religion, Theology, and Philosophy
CSCO	Corpus scriptorum Christianorum orientalium		
		HIsl	Handwörterbuch des Islam
CSEL	Corpus scriptorum ecclesiasticorum latinorum	HistCh	History of the Church (Jedin)
		HKKR	Handbuch des katholischen Kirchenrechts
CT	Concilium Tridentinum (13 vols.; Freiburg, 1963-76)	HNT	Handbuch zum Neuen Testament
		HNTC	Harper's New Testament Commentaries
CTJ	Calvin Theological Journal	HO	Handbuch der Orientalistik
DArt	Dictionary of Art (Grove's)	HÖ	Handbuch der Ökumenik
DEM	Dictionary of the Ecumenical Movement	HR	History of Religions
DH	Denzinger-Hünermann, Enchiridion symbolorum (37th ed., 1991)	HRG	Handbuch der Religionsgeschichte
		HTKNT	Herders theologischer Kommentar zum Neuen Testament
Dialog	Dialog: A Journal of Theology		
DMiss	Dictionary of Mission: Theology, History, Perspectives	HWP	Historisches Wörterbuch der Philosophie
		IBC	Interpretation: A Bible Commentary for Teaching and Preaching
DPL	Dictionary of Paul and His Letters		
DSB	Daily Study Bible		

ABBREVIATIONS

IBMR	*International Bulletin of Missionary Research*	*MECW*	Karl Marx and Friedrich Engels, *Collected Works*
ICC	International Critical Commentary	*MennEnc*	*Mennonite Encyclopedia*
IDB	*Interpreter's Dictionary of the Bible*	*MennQR*	*Mennonite Quarterly Review*
IEJ	*Israel Exploration Journal*	*MethH*	*Methodist History*
IJPR	*International Journal for Philosophy of Religion*	MHSJ	Monumenta historica Societatis Jesu
		Miss.	*Missiology*
IJST	*International Journal of Systematic Theology*	*MisSt*	*Mission Studies*
		MNTC	Moffatt New Testament Commentary
IKZ	*Internationale kirchliche Zeitschrift*	*MTZ*	*Münchener theologische Zeitschrift*
IRM	*International Review of Missions*	*MySal*	*Mysterium salutis*
ISBE	*International Standard Bible Encyclopedia* (rev. ed.)	*NBl*	*New Blackfriars*
		NCB	New Century Bible
ITC	International Theological Commentary	NCBC	New Century Bible Commentary
IThQ	*Irish Theological Quarterly*	*NCE*	*New Catholic Encyclopedia*
JBL	*Journal of Biblical Literature*	*NDCST*	*New Dictionary of Catholic Social Thought*
JbM	*Jahrbuch Mission*		
JChS	*Journal of Church and State*	*NDSW*	*New Dictionary of Sacramental Worship*
JEH	*Journal of Ecclesiastical History*	NEB	New English Bible
JGNKG	*Jahrbuch der Gesellschaft für Niedersächsische Kirchengeschichte*	*NEBrit*	*New Encyclopaedia Britannica*
		NEchtB	Neue Echter Bibel
JMS	*Journal of Mennonite Studies*	*NGDMM*	*New Grove Dictionary of Music and Musicians*
JPC	*Journal of Pastoral Care*		
JPS	Jewish Publication Society Holy Scriptures (1917)	*NHL*	*Neues Handbuch der Literaturwissenschaft*
JPsHF	*Jahrbuch für psychohistorische Forschung*	*NHP*	*Neue Hefte für Philosophie*
JPST	Jewish Publication Society Tanakh (1985)	NIB	New Interpreter's Bible
		NIBC	New International Biblical Commentary
JPSTC	Jewish Publication Society Torah Commentary	NICNT	New International Commentary on the New Testament
JR	*Journal of Religion*	NICOT	New International Commentary on the Old Testament
JRA	*Journal of Religion in Africa*		
JRH	*Journal of Religious History*	*NIDNTT*	*New International Dictionary of New Testament Theology*
JTS	*Journal of Theological Studies*		
JWCI	*Journal of the Warburg and Courtauld Institutes*	NIGTC	New International Greek Testament Commentary
KAI	H. Donner and W. Rollig, *Kanaanäische und aramäische Inschriften*	*NJBC*	*New Jerome Biblical Commentary*
		NRSV	New Revised Standard Version
KAT	Kommentar zum Alten Testament	*NTD*	Das Neue Testament Deutsch
KHC	Kurzer Hand-Commentar zum Alten Testament	*NTS*	*New Testament Studies*
		NTSR	New Testament for Spiritual Reading
KJV	King James Version	*NuMu*	*Nuevo mundo. Revista de teología latinoamericana*
LARR	*Latin American Research Review*		
LMTG	*Lexikon missionstheologischer Grundbegriffe*	*NWDLW*	*New Westminster Dictionary of Liturgy and Worship*
LPGL	G. W. H. Lampe, *Patristic Greek Lexicon*	*NZM*	*Neue Zeitschrift für Missionswissenschaft*
LQ	*Lutheran Quarterly*	*OCCT*	*The Oxford Companion to Christian Thought*
LTK	*Lexikon für Theologie und Kirche*		
LuJ	*Luther-Jahrbuch*	*OEMIW*	*Oxford Encyclopedia of the Modern Islamic World*
LuthW	*Lutheran World*		
LW	*Luther's Works*, "American Edition" (55 vols.; St. Louis and Philadelphia, 1955-76)	*OiC*	*One in Christ: A Catholic Ecumenical Review*
		OR	*L'osservatore romano*
LWI	*Lutheran World Information*	OTGu	Old Testament Guides

OTL	Old Testament Library	ThRev	Theological Review of the Near East School of Theology (Beirut)
OTS	Oudtestamentische Studiën	TLZ	Theologische Literaturzeitung
PBSer	People's Bible Series	TOTC	Tyndale Old Testament Commentaries
PG	Patrologia Graeca	TPQ	Theologisch-praktische Quartalschrift
PhEW	Philosophy East and West	TRE	Theologische Realenzyklopädie.
PhSt(B)	Philosophische Studien (Berlin)	TRu	Theologische Rundschau
PL	Patrologia Latina	TS	Theological Studies
PO	Patrologia orientalis	TUAT	Texte aus der Umwelt des Alten Testaments
ProcC	Proclamation Commentaries		
ProEcc	Pro Ecclesia	TynBul	Tyndale Bulletin
PRSt	Perspectives in Religious Studies	TZ	Theologische Zeitschrift
Psy.	Die Psyche	VD	Verbum Domini
RAC	Reallexikon für Antike und Christentum	VF	Verkündigung und Forschung
RE	Realencyklopädie für protestantische Theologie und Kirche	VT	Vetus Testamentum
		VTSup	Vetus Testamentum Supplements
REJ	Revue des études juives	WA	M. Luther, Werke. Kritische Gesamtausgabe (Weimarer Ausgabe)
RelW	Religions of the World (5 vols.; Santa Barbara, Calif., 2002)		
		WA.TR	— Tischrede
REPh	Routledge Encyclopedia of Philosophy	WBC	Word Biblical Commentary
RGG	Religion in Geschichte und Gegenwart	WCE	World Christian Encyclopedia (2d ed., 2 vols., 2001)
RLAT	Revista latinoamericana de teología		
RSE	Revue des sciences ecclésiastiques	WestBC	Westminster Bible Companion
RSR	Recherches de science religieuse	WPKG	Wissenschaft und Praxis in Kirche und Gesellschaft
RSV	Revised Standard Version		
RTL	Revue théologique de Louvain	WuA(M)	Wort und Antwort. Zeitschrift für fragen des Glaubens. Mainz
RTP	Revue de théologie et de philosophie		
SacPa	Sacra pagina	WW	Word and World
SC	Sources chrétiennes	ZAW	Zeitschrift für die alttestamentliche Wissenschaft
SecCent	Second Century		
SocComp	Social Compass	ZBK	Zürcher Bibelkommentar
Spec.	Speculum: A Journal of Mediaeval Studies	ZdZ	Die Zeichen der Zeit
StLi	Studia liturgica	ZEvKR	Zeitschrift für evangelisches Kirchenrecht
Str-B	H. L Strack and P. Billerbeck, Kommentar zum Neuen Testament aus Talmud und Midrasch	ZKT	Zeitschrift für katholische Theologie
		ZMR	Zeitschrift für Missionskunde und Religionswissenschaft
SVTQ	St. Vladimir's Theological Quarterly		
SWJT	Southwestern Journal of Theology	ZNW	Zeitschrift für die neutestamentliche Wissenschaft
TDNT	Theological Dictionary of the New Testament		
		ZPE	Zeitschrift für Papyrologie und Epigraphik
TDOT	Theological Dictionary of the Old Testament	ZPhF	Zeitschrift für philosophische Forschung
		ZRGG	Zeitschrift für Religions- und Geistesgeschichte
TGI	Textbuch zur Geschichte Israels		
Theol.	Theology: A Journal of Historic Christianity	ZTK	Zeitschrift für Theologie und Kirche

STATES AND PROVINCES

Ala.	Alabama	D.C.	District of Columbia
Ark.	Arkansas	Del.	Delaware
Calif.	California	Fla.	Florida
Colo.	Colorado	Ga.	Georgia
Conn.	Connecticut	Ill.	Illinois

ABBREVIATIONS

Ind.	Indiana	N.Y.	New York
Kans.	Kansas	Okla.	Oklahoma
Ky.	Kentucky	Ont.	Ontario
Man.	Manitoba	Oreg.	Oregon
Mass.	Massachusetts	Pa.	Pennsylvania
Md.	Maryland	R.I.	Rhode Island
Mich.	Michigan	S.C.	South Carolina
Minn.	Minnesota	Tenn.	Tennessee
Mo.	Missouri	Tex.	Texas
Mont.	Montana	Va.	Virginia
N.C.	North Carolina	Vt.	Vermont
Nebr.	Nebraska	Wash.	Washington
N.H.	New Hampshire	Wis.	Wisconsin
N.J.	New Jersey	W.Va.	West Virginia
N.M.	New Mexico		

GENERAL

acc.	accusative	e.g.	*exempli gratia*, for example
A.D.	*anno Domini*, in the year of the Lord	EKD	Evangelische Kirche in Deutschland
adv.	adverb	emp.	emperor
Akkad.	Akkadian	Eng.	England, English
Alb.	Albania	*ep.*	*epistula(e)*, letter(s)
aor.	aorist	esp.	especially
Arab.	Arabic	est.	estimated, estimate
Aram.	Aramaic	ET	English translation
Arg.	Argentina	et al.	*et alii*, and others
art(s).	article(s)	etc.	*et cetera*, and so forth
Aus.	Austria	exp.	expanded
Austral.	Australia	f	females
b.	born	fac.	facsimile
B.C.	before Christ	fem.	feminine
B.C.E.	before the Common Era	ff.	and following
bk(s).	book(s)	Fin.	Finland
Braz.	Brazil	fl.	*floruit*, flourished
c.	*corpus articuli*, the body of the article (Thomas Aquinas)	Fr.	France, French
		FS	Festschrift
ca.	circa	ft.	foot, feet
can(s).	canon(s)	Ger.	Germany, German
C.E.	the Common Era	Gk.	Greek
cent(s).	century, centuries	Heb.	Hebrew
cf.	*confer*, compare	ibid.	*ibidem*, in the same place
chap(s).	chapter(s)	i.e.	*id est*, that is
comp(s).	compiler(s), compiled (by)	J	Yahwist source
cond.	condensed	Jam.	Jamaica
D	Deuteronomic source	Jpn.	Japan, Japanese
d.	died	km.	kilometer(s)
Den.	Denmark	L	material in Luke not found in Matthew or Mark
diss.	dissertation		
dist.	distinction	Lat.	Latin
E	Elohistic source	lect.	lecture
ed(s).	edited (by), edition, editor(s)	lit.	literal(ly)

LLat.	Late Latin		to Matthew and Luke but not found in
LXX	Septuagint		Mark
M	material in Matthew not found in Mark	q(q).	question(s)
	or Luke	repr.	reprinted
m	males	rev.	revised (by, in), revision
m.	meter(s)	Russ.	Russian
Mal.	Malawi	S.Af.	South Africa
masc.	masculine	s.c.	*sed contra*, on the contrary (Thomas
Mex.	Mexico		Aquinas)
mi.	mile(s)	Scot.	Scotland
MLat.	Middle Latin	ser.	series
Moz.	Mozambique	sess.	session
Msgr.	Monseigneur	sing.	singular
MS(S)	manuscript(s)	Skt.	Sanskrit
MT	Masoretic Text	Slav.	Slavic
n(n).	note(s)	Sp.	Spanish
NATO	North Atlantic Treaty Organization	sq.	square
Neth.	Netherlands	SSR	Soviet Socialist Republic
NGO(s)	nongovernmental organization(s)	St.	Saint
no.	number	supp(s).	supplement(s), supplementary
Norw.	Norway, Norwegian	Swah.	Swahili
n.s.	new series	Swed.	Sweden, Swedish
NT	New Testament	Switz.	Switzerland
N.Z.	New Zealand	Syr.	Syriac
OEng.	Old English	trans.	translated by, translator(s), translation
OHG	Old High German	Turk.	Turkey, Turkish
OPer.	Old Persian	U.K.	United Kingdom
orig.	original(ly)	U.N.	United Nations
OT	Old Testament	UNESCO	United Nations Educational, Scientific,
P	Priestly source		and Cultural Organization
p(p).	page(s)	U.S.	United States
par.	parallel(s), parallel to	USSR	Union of Soviet Socialist Republics
par(s).	paragraph(s)	v(v).	verse(s)
Ph.D.	*philosophiae doctor*, doctor of philosophy	Vg	(Latin) Vulgate
Pi.	Piel	v.l.	*varia lectio*, variant reading
pl.	plural	vol(s).	volume(s)
Pol.	Poland, Polish	vs.	versus
pop.	population	WCC	World Council of Churches
P.R.	Puerto Rico	YMCA	Young Men's Christian Association
pseud.	pseudonym	YWCA	Young Women's Christian Association
pt.	part	→	cross-reference to another article
pub.	published, publication	*	passim
Q	hypothetical source of material common	§	section

The ENCYCLOPEDIA
of CHRISTIANITY

Volume 3
J–O

— J —

Jacob

1. Biblical Evidence
2. History of Scholarship
3. Jacob in the NT

1. Biblical Evidence
Apart from the mention of Jacob in the Joseph stories, the Jacob traditions are found in Genesis 25–35. Although these stories can be attributed largely to J, some material from P (esp. in chaps. 25 and 35) and E (esp. in chaps. 28; 30–33; 35) is also present. Genesis 35 can be ascribed almost entirely to E and P (→ Pentateuch).

Jacob deceives his older twin, Esau, and must flee. He acquires wives in Paddan-aram and attains considerable prosperity. After fleeing Laban, his father-in-law, he is reconciled with Esau, encounters God in Bethel just as he did earlier, and receives the new name "Israel." The promises to → Abraham and → Isaac are fulfilled in him (→ Promise and Fulfillment).

2. History of Scholarship
The most satisfying explanation for Jacob is that involving tribal history. In this regard, Genesis 34 best suits the notion of such a history with its singling out of Levi and Simeon. Jacob's 12 "sons" represent the → tribes of Israel. Jacob himself personifies the overriding unity of Israel, whence his new name. H. Seebass suggests that Jacob as the "father" of the 12 tribes represents a historical Jacob and a historical "Israel," both of whom were clan leaders who entered Canaan and established their own tribal cults in connection with the cults of Canaanite sanctuaries.

Jacob founded a cult associated with the "God of the Fathers" (A. Alt, M. Noth). He is the wandering or homeless Aramean mentioned in the "shorter creed" (Deut. 26:5; see G. von Rad), and he was the first patriarch to attain pan-Israelite status in Shechem (Noth). He belongs to the earliest developmental stage of the Pentateuch traditions, a stage during which central Palestinian tribes were still shaping these traditions. The incorporation of the promised land into the theme of promise did not occur until the connection was made with the Jacob traditions themselves.

3. Jacob in the NT
The only important mention of Jacob in the NT is found in Rom. 9:10-13, where → Paul associates the secret of election and rejection with Jacob and Esau. Although both are Rebekah's children and Isaac's sons, the younger is given preference over the older; God loves the one and hates the other.

→ Israel 1

Bibliography: T. E. FRETHEIM, "Genesis," NIB 1.319-674 • H. GAMBERT, *Isaac and Jacob, God's Chosen Ones* (New York, 1969) • L. MEIER, *Jacob* (Lanham, Md.,

1994) • S. E. PORTER, "Jacob," *ABD* 3.599 • G. VON RAD, *The Problem of the Hexateuch, and Other Essays* (Edinburgh, 1966) • J. A. SANFORD, *The Man Who Wrestled with God: Light from the OT on the Psychology of Individuation* (New York, 1981) • H. SEEBASS, *Der Ervater Israel* (Berlin, 1966) • H. M. WAHL, *Die Jakobserzählungen. Studien zu ihrer mündlichen Überlieferung, Verschriftung und Historizität* (Berlin, 1997) • S. D. WALTERS, "Jacob Narratives," *ABD* 3.599-608.

WILLIAM McKANE

Jacobites → Syrian Orthodox Church

Jainism

Jainism, like → Buddhism, is an anti-Brahmanic Indian religion that stresses salvation but is without an ultimate personal God and without an impersonal universal soul (→ Hinduism; Mysticism). Its founder, Vardhamāna, known as Mahāvīra (i.e., Great Hero), was an itinerant teacher in Bihar (northern India) contemporaneous with the Buddha (d. ca. 400 B.C.). Vardhamāna is presumed to have been the successor of Pārśvanātha, or Pārśva, although nothing is known about the latter's life; he allegedly died 250 years before Mahāvīra.

Jainism is a → monastic religion with strong lay participation and a community divided into three or four parts: monks, sometimes also nuns, lay brothers, and lay sisters. The tendency is to accommodate the life of the laity as much as possible to that of the monks, with the exception of celibacy. Ethical principles emphasize especially the notion of *ahiṁsā* (nonviolence, esp. nonkilling), fasting (even to death), → celibacy, and renunciation of possessions (→ Asceticism). The *ahiṁsā* is first and foremost a corpus of dietary regulations involving the use of water, prompted by the conviction that the entire cosmos is filled with life that may not be destroyed through use. The four elements of earth, water, fire, and air are all "alive" or "animated" insofar as they not only harbor small living beings but also themselves consist hypothetically of discrete, infinitesimally small living beings. Monks are therefore generally permitted to eat and drink only after laypersons have destroyed the living beings in these foods through cooking, whence also the absolute dependence of monks on the laity.

Through an endless cycle of rebirth (→ Reincarnation), unredeemed souls traverse the various forms of existence of those in → hell, of nonhuman earthly life forms (elements, plants, animals), of human beings, and of gods. Such rebirth is generally viewed as the highest misfortune; escaping it presupposes adherence especially to the ethical principles mentioned above. This ethical behavior is augmented by mental processes the Jains describe in exacting complexity in their doctrine of → salvation. The heart of what is generally called the theory of → karma is the conviction that karmic particles of a material nature become associated with the human soul through the four passions of anger, pride, deceit, and greed (the so-called mechanism of bondage). To rid itself of the burden of its karma, each individual soul must gain control over its passions. Once freed, the soul hastens upward to the sphere of the saved at the summit of the cosmos, from which no more rebirths are possible. The Jain → worldview is thus mechanistic.

The detailed description of the cosmos with its various hells and other spheres is complemented by an extensive → mythology concerned with, among other things, the religion's founders, the 24 chronologically sequential Tirthankaras (Skt. *tīrthaṅkara,* "ford maker," one preparing the way). Of the 24, only the last 2 — Pārśva and Mahāvīra — were genuine historical figures, the remainder being products of mythology. The various Tirthankaras have been protrayed and worshiped in countless representations, which are venerated as divine portrayals, largely reminiscent of the Buddha type (the Jain → Bhakti). Jain temples are found in most parts of India and attest the considerable influence the religion once enjoyed.

During the first to the fifth centuries A.D., the Jain community split into two groups: the Svetambaras (Skt. *śvetāmbara,* "white-clad") and the Digambaras (*digambara,* "sky-clad," i.e., naked). While the former include both monks and nuns, the Digambaras do not include nuns in the strict sense as adherents with a status comparable to that of monks; indeed, the devaluation of women, already widespread in India in early times, is more pronounced among the Digambaras than among the Svetambaras. Since the split the two groups have constituted separate denominations with distinct religious literary traditions. Over the course of time Jainism as a whole was increasingly influenced by Hindu religious culture, seen, for example, in the veneration of Jain versions of female Hindu deities.

Within the Svetambara area of western India (esp. the states of Gujarat and Rajasthan) and at the initiative of a certain Lonka Shah, a thoroughly reformed, nonidolatrous version of Jainism has developed since the 15th century. This version itself split into the rather loosely organized Sthānakvāsīs (beginning the first half of the 17th cent.) and the more tightly organized Terāpanthīs (community constituted in 1760; the best-known Terāpanthā leader was Acharya Tulsi [1913-97]).

In 1991 there were 3.4 million Jains in India, or less than half of 1 percent of the country, a slight drop in percentage when compared with figures for 1961. Jain laypersons are nowadays mainly traders and industrialists, and many are quite wealthy, having embraced "lay prosperity" rather than renouncing possessions.

Bibliography: K. Bruhn, "Five Vows and Six *Avashyakas:* The Fundamentals of Jaina Ethics," http://www.here-now4u.de/eng/contents.html • M. Carrithers and C. Humphrey, eds., *The Assembly of Listeners: Jains in Society* (Cambridge, 1991) • J. E. Cort, ed., *Open Boundaries: Jain Communities and Culture in Indian History* (Albany, N.Y., 1998) • P. Dundas, *The Jains* (London, 1992) • H. von Glasenapp, *Jainism: An Indian Religion of Salvation* (Delhi, 1999; orig. pub., 1925) • C. Humphrey and J. Laidlaw, *The Archetypal Actions of Ritual: A Theory of Ritual Illustrated by the Jain Rite of Worship* (New York, 1994) • H. Jacobi, trans., *Jaina Sutras* (2 vols.; New York, 1968; orig. pub., 1884-95) • P. S. Jaini, *Gender and Salvation: Jaina Debates on the Spiritual Liberation of Women* (Berkeley, Calif., 1991); idem, *The Jaina Path of Purification* (Delhi, 1979) • P. Pal, *The Peaceful Liberators: Jain Art from India* (Los Angeles, 1994) • W. Schubring, *The Doctrine of the Jainas* (2d ed.; Delhi, 2000; orig. pub., 1935).

Klaus Bruhn

Jamaica

	1960	1980	2000
Population (1,000s):	1,629	2,133	2,587
Annual growth rate (%):	1.55	1.60	0.95
Area: 10,991 sq. km. (4,244 sq. mi.)			

A.D. 2000

Population density: 235/sq. km. (609/sq. mi.)
Births / deaths: 1.91 / 0.54 per 100 population
Fertility rate: 2.27 per woman
Infant mortality rate: 10 per 1,000 live births
Life expectancy: 75.5 years (m: 73.2, f: 77.8)
Religious affiliation (%): Christians 84.1 (unaffiliated 39.1, Protestants 25.9, indigenous 9.1, Roman Catholics 4.5, Anglicans 4.1, marginal 1.3, other Christians 0.1), spiritists 10.1, nonreligious 3.7, Hindus 1.2, other 0.9.

1. General Situation
2. Christians
   2.1. Roman Catholics
   2.2. Anglicans
   2.3. Baptists
   2.4. Presbyterians and the United Church
   2.5. Methodists
   2.6. Other Protestant Bodies
3. Other Living Faiths

1. General Situation

The island of Jamaica is the third largest island of the Caribbean archipelago. A parliamentary democracy, Jamaica was given autonomy by the United Kingdom in 1959 and won its full independence in 1962. The great majority of its inhabitants are of African descent. The nation's economy, dependent mainly on tourism and also on bauxite mining, has stagnated since 1995. Between 1996 and 2000 employment fell by roughly a sixth (→ Unemployment).

Before Europeans arrived, Jamaica was inhabited by Amerindians. The Tainos occupied the island from the middle of the first millennium, with evidence of their culture and beliefs surviving to the present day. Christopher Columbus, the first European to come to Jamaica, landed on the shores of the island on May 4, 1494. With Columbus came the → Roman Catholic Church. Both the church and the Spanish government maintained their dominance until the British conquest in 1655 (→ Colonialism). The advent of the Europeans had disastrous consequences for the Tainos, most of whom had perished from disease and cruelty by 1600.

Spanish colonization in the Caribbean was driven primarily by a search for precious metals. Jamaica actually produced very little such metals, but it was arable and fruitful, and agriculture developed well. To satisfy domestic as well as foreign needs for food, the local population was pressed into farming. When their numbers declined, Africans were brought in to take their place. The Africans came as slaves, and a lucrative trade in human cargo developed that supplied the sugar, coffee, and tobacco plantations. The practice of → slavery was rationalized on two religious grounds: since the Africans had largely become obedient to → Islam, they were regarded as apostate and in need of → evangelism; second, it was necessary for such apostates to be kept in the company of Christians if they were to acquire a true knowledge of the faith.

Spanish colonial rule reproduced the political and religious structures and the culture of Spain in the West Indies. The arrival of the English in 1655 under Admiral William Penn and General Robert Venables changed little at first, but in time Jamaica adopted the Cromwellian structures of Commonwealth England as laid down by the poet John Milton. These structures of English → Protestantism continue to have great influence in present-day Jamaica. Unfortunately, the competing interests of Catholic Spain and Protestant England left the Church of England more associated in people's minds with buccaneering and booty than with piety.

The Quakers, who arrived in Jamaica shortly after the British, soon began erecting meetinghouses in Port Royal. George Fox (1624-91), the founder of the Society of → Friends, visited the island in 1672. Quakers have given enduring leadership to the Jamaican community in social work, education, art, and religion.

→ Moravian missionaries first came to Jamaica in 1754. They provided considerable impetus in the struggle to abolish slavery, as did the 18th-century evangelical revival. Abolition, which was decreed in 1833 and implemented in 1838, was followed by widespread → poverty and frequent periods of social unrest.

2. Christians
2.1. *Roman Catholics*
With the arrival of the British, Roman Catholics were officially proscribed and forced underground. This restriction lasted until 1837, when → Jesuits were allowed to come to the island. By the 1870s Roman Catholics had again become a significant presence in Jamaica and were granted freedom to worship in public. This new freedom enabled Catholics to evangelize, especially in the parishes of Kingston and St. Andrew, as well as in areas where the church had ancient land rights. This evangelization was aided by a series of politically caused migrations of Roman Catholics from Haiti.

Since the 19th century the Roman Catholic Church in Jamaica has never been large, but it has maintained an important place in national life. Its work has been concentrated in urban centers, and its leadership has consistently engaged in vigorous efforts on behalf of the poor and immigrants. Since the Second → Vatican Council (1962-65), Catholics in Jamaica have been very active in → ecumenism. The Roman Catholic Church was a founding member of the Caribbean Council of Churches (1973), and the archbishop of Kingston has often served as president of the Jamaican Council of Churches. Four Jamaicans have been consecrated → bishops, one of whom serves in the Bahamas, and one in Antigua.

2.2. *Anglicans*
When Jamaica was taken by the British in 1655, the Church of England became the church of the state, quickly establishing itself across the island. Anglicans remained dominant both as an evangelizing force and as a political force well into the 19th century. In the early 1800s there was a concerted effort to make the Church of England the Church of Jamaica; after 1870, however, all efforts at establishment were abandoned.

Church personnel continued to be drawn from England, and not until the 1940s was a Jamaican consecrated suffragan bishop. Since then a succession of Jamaican bishops has transformed the church into a truly Jamaican institution. The Anglican Church in Jamaica is now part of the Church in the Province of the West Indies. This church holds pride of place in Jamaican society, being known for its educational system, for its provision of → chaplains for the armed services and the constabulary, and for its community services.

2.3. *Baptists*
George Lisle (or Liele, ca. 1750-1828), a former slave in the American colonies, founded the Baptist church in Jamaica, a church that ultimately became the source of two of the largest church bodies in the island today — the Jamaica Baptist Union and Revival Zion, a charismatic Baptist church. The Jamaica Baptist Missionary Society, formed in 1842, trained ministers for both local and overseas service, with an emphasis on African missions, initially in the Cameroons. The society helped spur the growth of → Baptists in Jamaica in the 19th century. Even though the national leadership of the Baptists had become thoroughly Jamaican by the 1860s, however, class and social barriers still were tolerated in the community.

Only in the 1950s did some white Baptist churches open their pulpits to black Jamaicans. With considerable help from the U.S. Southern Baptist Convention, structures for church growth and nurture have been created with considerable success among Jamaican Baptists.

2.4. *Presbyterians and the United Church*
Scottish Presbyterians first came to Jamaica in 1824. Their situation was somewhat similar to that of the Anglicans from England, since their church was the established church of Scotland (→ Presbyterianism). At times, Presbyterians were recognized as the established church in Kingston, though its early work was largely limited to labor in plantations owned by persons who had ties to Scotland. It was not influenced by evangelical movements, and only the formation of the Scottish Mis-

sionary Society (1796) led to a modest presence in Jamaica. Significantly, when a Jamaican Presbyterian synod was formed, one of its first acts was to decide to start a mission in Africa, which led to the evangelization of Port Harcourt and the Ibo people in eastern Nigeria.

In 1956 Presbyterians, → Congregationalists, and the → Christian Church (Disciples of Christ) merged to form the United Church in Jamaica and the Cayman Islands, one of the early united churches formed as a result of the modern ecumenical movement (→ United and Uniting Churches). The Congregationalists had come to Jamaica under the impetus of the London Missionary Society (formed in 1795). The Disciples came to Jamaica in the 1890s.

2.5. Methodists

Methodists were first organized in Jamaica in 1789 with the arrival and preaching of Thomas Coke (1747-1814). Their early appeal was primarily to British migrants, merchants, and sailors, as well as to freed slaves who had escaped from Cuba and the United States and developed small businesses. Over the years this church has had considerable influence in the creation of educational institutions and, not least, in the fostering of significant political and social movements through which Jamaican national aspirations have been formulated and expressed.

2.6. Other Protestant Bodies

Another Protestant body active in Jamaica is the Seventh-day Adventist Church (→ Adventists), whose work began toward the end of the 19th century and which grew considerably in the 20th century. Many → Pentecostal-type churches with roots in the United States are also strong in Jamaica, including the New Testament Church of God (Cleveland, Tenn., begun in Jamaica in 1917), Church of God of Prophecy (1923), Church of God in Jamaica (1907, Anderson, Ind.), and the United Pentecostal Church (1933, Jesus Only movement).

3. Other Living Faiths

A variety of other religious groups exists in Jamaica, some of which offer unique national expressions. The Universal Negro Improvement Association, founded in 1914 by the Jamaican-born Marcus Garvey (1887-1940) as a movement to end discrimination against African people, inspired an emphasis on the African heritage of Jamaicans, especially that associated with Ethiopia. Although this movement led in part to expressions of the → Ethiopian Orthodox tradition, in Jamaica the most celebrated Ethiopian movement has been → Rastafarianism (→ Latin America and the Caribbean 2.6). This

movement, an expression both of confidence in a coming redemption of Africans in the West and of interpretations of several biblical prophecies, has become internationally known for its hairstyle (dreadlocks), use of marijuana (ganja), and popular musical style (reggae).

West African religions, some with a Christian overlay, are also present in Jamaica, notably Kumina, Obeah (lit. "sorcery"), and Pocomania, groups that mix African, Roman Catholic, and Protestant elements (→ Spiritism).

The Jewish community in Jamaica, the United Congregation of Israelites, dates from Spanish times and consists today of Sephardic and Ashkenazic Jews (→ Judaism). A mosque serves African, Indian, Pakistani, Syrian, and Egyptian adherents of Islam. Followers of the Baha'i faith are also found in Jamaica. Small groups of Hindus found among East Indian residents are present on the island, as are certain new religious movements such as the Church of Scientology and the Unification Church.

Bibliography: Jamaican Christianity: A. DAYFOOT, *The Shaping of the West Indian Church, 1492-1962* (Gainesville, Fla., 1999) • S. C. GORDON, *God Almighty Make Me Free: Christianity in Preemancipation Jamaica* (Bloomington, Ind., 1996) • D. A. McGAVRAN, *Church Growth in Jamaica* (Lucknow, India, 1961) • F. J. OSBORNE, *History of the Catholic Church in Jamaica* (Chicago, 1988) • H. O. RUSSELL, *The Missionary Outreach of the West Indian Church: Jamaican Baptist Missions to West Africa in the Nineteenth Century* (New York, 2000).

Other topics: B. CHEVANNES, *Rastafari: Roots and Ideology* (Syracuse, N.Y., 1994) • E. DE SOUZA, *United Congregation of Israelites* (Kingston, Jam., 1995) • E. B. EDMONDS, *Rastafari: From Outcasts to Culture Bearers* (Oxford, 2003) • R. LEWIS and P. BRYAN, eds., *Garvey: His Work and Impact* (Trenton, N.J., 1991) • J. G. MELTON and M. BAUMANN, eds., "Jamaica," *Religions of the World: A Comprehensive Encyclopedia of Beliefs and Practices* (Santa Barbara, Calif., 2002) 2.713-15 • K. E. A. MONTEITH and G. RICHARDS, eds., *Jamaica in Slavery and Freedom: History, Heritage, and Culture* (Kingston, Jam., 2002) • I. MOORISH, *Obeah, Christ, and Rastaman: Jamaica and Its Religion* (Cambridge, 1982) • P. SHERLOCK and H. BENNETT, *The Story of the Jamaican People* (Princeton, 1998) • G. E. SIMPSON, *Black Religions in the New World* (New York, 1978); idem, *Religious Cults of the Caribbean: Trinidad, Jamaica, and Haiti* (3d ed.; Rio Piedras, P.R., 1980) • R. J. STEWART, *Religion and Society in Post-emancipation Jamaica* (Knoxville, Tenn., 1992).

HORACE O. RUSSELL

James

The NT mentions several men called James.

James the son of Zebedee and brother of John. He seems to have been an early disciple of → Jesus (Mark 1:19 and par., cf. Luke 5:10) and was one of the → Twelve (Mark 3:17 and par.; Acts 1:13). With his brother and → Peter (and sometimes Andrew), he was one of the inner circle of Jesus' → disciples (Mark 1:29; 5:37 and par.; 9:2 and par.; 10:35-41; cf. Matt. 20:20-24; also John 21:2). According to Mark 3:17, Jesus gave him and his brother the nickname "Boanerges" (meaning "Sons of Thunder"), thus indicating their calling as preachers. James was martyred under Agrippa I (41-44; → Herod, Herodians; Martyr). With Peter and John he no doubt played a prominent part in the early post-Easter community (→ Primitive Christian Community).

James the brother of Jesus (Mark 6:3 and par.; Gal. 1:19). This James evidently recognized the claim of Jesus only after meeting the risen Lord (→ Resurrection 1; see 1 Cor. 15:7; also John 7:5; Mark 3:21, 31-35). He quickly attained to a prominent position in the community (Gal. 1:19; 2:9; Acts 12:17; 15:13) and ultimately became the leader in Jerusalem (Gal. 2:12; Acts 21:18). Around A.D. 62 he was stoned to death under the → high priest Ananus (Josephus *Ant.* 20.200; → Persecution of Christians 2). His leadership role was due not merely to his relationship with Jesus but to his own significance. At the apostolic council (Acts 15; Gal. 2:1-10), in the Antioch affair (Gal. 2:11-14), and in → Paul's last visit to Jerusalem (Acts 21:18-25), James maintained fellowship with uncircumcised → Gentile Christians so long as → Jewish Christians were not forced to live contrary to the → law. He himself lived as a strict Jew, as may be seen from his nickname "The Just" (*Gos. Thom.* 12; Hegesippus in Eusebius *Hist. eccl.* 2.23.4-7, etc.) and from the opposition of the Pharisees to his execution (Josephus *Ant.* 20.201). Later he became a leading figure in Jewish Christianity, with some sharply anti-Pauline views. The Epistle of James, traditionally ascribed to him, is an indication of his significance. Jude highlights the authority of his own letter by calling himself (v. 1) a brother of James.

James the son of Alphaeus. This James was one of the Twelve (Mark 3:18 and par.; Acts 1:13; see also Mark 2:14 v.l.).

James the father of Judas (Luke 6:16; Acts 1:13; also John 14:22).

James the younger. He was the son, father, or husband of a Mary who was a witness of the crucifixion (Mark 15:40 and par.) and of the empty tomb (16:1 and par.).

Bibliography: R. BAUCKHAM, *Jude and the Relatives of Jesus in the Early Church* (Edinburgh, 1990) 5-44 • B. CHILTON and C. A. EVANS, *James the Just and Christian Origins* (Boston, 1999) • M. HENGEL, "Jakobus der Herrenbruder–der erste 'Papst'?" *Glaube und Eschatologie* (Tübingen, 1985) 71-104 • K. NIEDERWIMMER, "'Ιάκωβος," *EDNT* 2.167-69 • W. PRATSCHER, *Der Herrenbruder Jakobus und die Jakobustradition* (Göttingen, 1987) • W. SCHMITHALS, *Paul and James* (Naperville, Ill., 1965) • H.-J. SCHOEPS, *Jewish Christianity* (Philadelphia, 1969).

TRAUGOTT HOLTZ

James, Epistle of

The Epistle of James is one of the → Catholic Epistles. Apart from its simple introductory greeting, it lacks the basic characteristics of letters and does not seem to be written with a specific situation in view; even the admonitions regarding wealth and poverty (1:9-11; 2:1-7; 5:1-6) relate to no particular circumstances in the church. The work is more in the nature of a tractate with exhortation as its goal (→ Parenesis). It strings together admonitory proverbs and didactic passages (2:1-13, 14-26; 3:1-12) in no special order. The recipients are "the 12 tribes in the Dispersion" (1:1) — that is, the whole → church. The book's date and place of composition are uncertain (but probably ca. A.D. 100).

Although the author calls himself → James (1:1), several factors argue against this claim. The main point is that the Greek is better than one would expect from a strict Jewish Christian. Its literary style seems modeled on the LXX, and reference is lacking to the problem of Jewish Christians and → Gentile Christianity or to the ceremonial law. The tradition of Jesus attested in the letter points to a later date; the authenticity of the work was under debate into the fourth century. Similarly, some scholars argue that points of contact with 1 Peter and the → Apostolic Fathers (esp. Hermas) indicate a later stage of early Christianity (→ Primitive Christian Community).

The purpose of the Epistle of James is to give authoritative ethical instruction to the new Israel of the → diaspora and to summon believers to a concrete realization of the Christian life. The author draws on the broad tradition of the → ethics of antiquity, the Jewish Wisdom tradition (→ Wisdom Literature), the popular ethics of Hellenistic Judaism and Cynic → Stoicism, apocalypse, and the early Christian tradition.

The discussion of → faith and works in 2:14-26

is theologically significant. It is directed less against Paul than against a misunderstanding of his doctrine of → justification that leaves no place for works. It additively relates faith and works (→ Synergism), the main parenetic interest being in the latter. In an anti-Pauline fashion, works rather than faith alone are understood as the essential condition of → salvation. The demand for works rules out criticism of the law and implies continuity between the OT → Torah and "the perfect law, the law of liberty" (1:25; 2:12; cf. 2:8).

Objection is sometimes made that this position brings irresolvable tension with Paul's doctrine of → grace and faith. Other signs of the difference between this letter and Paul are that no mention is made of the → cross and → resurrection, that it replaces the relation of indicative and imperative with direct ethical demand, that it no longer takes into adequate account the radical power of → sin, and that it misses the dialectic of the Christian life. None of these criticisms is unanswerable, however, and a summary rejection of the epistle as mere moralism fails to do justice to perhaps its real concern, namely, to correct a faith that is no longer oriented to works.

Bibliography: Commentaries: C. Burchard (HNT; Tübingen, 2000) • P. H. Davids (NIBC; Peabody, Mass., 1989) • M. Dibelius and H. Greeven (Hermeneia; Philadelphia, 1976) • R. P. Martin (WBC; Waco, Tex., 1988) • F. Mussner (HTKNT; 5th ed.; Freiburg, 1987) • W. Schrage (NTD; 13th ed.; Göttingen, 1985) 5-59.

Other works: R. J. Bauckham, *James: Wisdom of James, Disciple of Jesus the Sage* (London, 1999) • T. B. Cargal, *Restoring the Diaspora: Discursive Structure and Purpose in the Epistle of James* (Atlanta, 1993) • R. Hoppe, *Der theologische Hintergrund des Jakobusbrief* (2d ed.; Würzburg, 1985) • M. A. Jackson-McCabe, *Logos and Law in the Letter of James: The Law of Nature, the Law of Moses, and the Law of Freedom* (Leiden, 2001) • T. C. Penner, *The Epistle of James and Eschatology: Re-reading an Ancient Christian Letter* (Sheffield, 1996) • W. Popkes, *Adressaten, Situation und Form des Jakobusbrief* (Stuttgart, 1986) • W. H. Wachob, *The Voice of Jesus in the Social Rhetoric of James* (New York, 2000).

Georg Strecker†

Jansenism

1. Doctrine of Grace
2. Controversy
3. Impact
4. Evaluation

1. Doctrine of Grace

Jansenism takes its name from Cornelius Jansen the Younger (1585-1638), who gave the movement its theological basis with his *Augustinus* (published posthumously in Lyons in 1640). As a student and professor at the University of Lyons, and later as bishop of Ypres, Jansen was in continual conflict with the → Jesuit-scholastic doctrine of → grace (→ Scholasticism). In the Lyons tradition he focused on the anti-Pelagian writings of → Augustine (354-430; → Augustine's Theology) and methodologically, with an antischolastic bias, developed a pessimistic → anthropology. Already in 1514 John Eck (1486-1543), in answer to late medieval Augustinians, had rejected this view as an excessive interpretation of Augustine. Similarly, the Council of → Trent (1545-63), along with the condemnation in 1567 of the Lyons professor Michael Baius (1513-89, in the → bull *Ex omnibus afflictionibus* of Pius V; DH 1901-80), repudiated it, finding in it the basis of the Reformation doctrine of → justification.

On Jansen's view the so-called state of grace enjoyed by the first pair is a natural endowment and not a superadded gift *(donum superadditum)*, the loss of which at the fall meant that → Adam and the race lost completely the ability to restore a positive relationship with God. The work of Christ alone avails to salvation. In Augustinian fashion the idea is rejected that this work simply gives sufficient grace *(gratia sufficiens),* which we must freely accept if it is to become effective grace *(gratia efficiens).* Any good impulse is divine grace, but the grace of justification is overcoming grace *(gratia victrix).* Unconditional infralapsarian → predestination encompasses the whole way of salvation, especially the gift of perseverance. This rigorous rejection of → synergism made inevitable a conflict with the Jesuits, whose counterposition was radically presented by Luis de Molina (1535-1600) in his work *Concordia liberi arbitrii cum gratiae donis* (1588) and maintained in a moderated form against the → Dominicans in the "congruism" of R. → Bellarmine and F. Suárez. Conflict with the → teaching office followed quickly and inevitably.

2. Controversy

The Jesuit College at Lyons replied to Jansen's *Augustinus* with six countertheses. In 1641 the → Inquisition forbade both. In 1642 Urban VIII (1623-44) issued the bull *In eminenti*, which declared *Augustinus* heretical. The University of Lyons refused to be silenced, however, rejecting the bull as a Jesuit fabrication.

This conflict in France, however, did not remain

one of theological faculties. Jean Duvergier de Hauranne (1581-1643), known as Saint-Cyran, had been in contact with Jansen since 1605. Carrying out reforms in the church and aiming to deepen → piety by self-responsible spiritual direction, Saint-Cyran had close links to the → Cistercian convent of Port-Royal (located originally 29 km. / 18 mi. from Paris), which became the center of Jansenism. After Saint-Cyran's death Antoine Arnauld (1612-94) took up both the dogmatic defense of the *Augustinus* and the related → spirituality. Against the → casuistry and laxity of the Jesuits in preparation for Communion, he wrote his work *De la fréquente communion* (1643), which the Jesuits rightly saw as an attack on their priestly position in the church's sacramentalist system. For its part, the government saw in Jansenism a threat to religious unity. With the question of the place of the Inquisition in France and the independence of the French clergy and French policy, the controversy quickly assumed political dimensions for both → church and state.

In 1653 Rome condemned five propositions taken from Jansen's *Augustinus* (DH 2001-7). In his response Arnauld recognized the → infallibility of the papacy and accepted the charge that the propositions were heretical (the *quaestio iuris,* i.e., as a matter of law, the pope was always correct). Arnauld argued, however, that in the sense condemned, the propositions were in fact not in the *Augustinus* (the *quaestio facti,* or factual question). This evasion was possible because only the first proposition appears word-for-word in the *Augustinus.*

In 1656 Blaise → Pascal (1623-62), one of the most brilliant and uncompromising of the Jansenists, who came to know Jansenism through the sisters at Port-Royal, published his *Lettres à un provincial* (Provincial letters), in which he sharply attacked the Jesuits and the Thomists (→ Thomism). Along with Pascal's literary successes there was a miraculous healing of a niece of his at Port-Royal, whose influence was then at its height.

For reasons of state Louis XIV (1643-1715) took the side of the Jesuits. With the support of Rome, in 1660 he set out to destroy Jansenism. In 1669, after sharp debate, the resistance of several French bishops forced Clement IX (1667-69) to provisionally relent from the anti-Jansenist efforts (the so-called Clementine Peace). When the Jansenists took the papal side in the → Gallican controversies, however, and when Arnauld furnished Rome with evidence of laxness in Jesuit morality (the "laxism" system, which in fact was ultimately condemned; DH 2101-67), the king renewed the attack on Jansenism. Leading Jansenists fled to the Spanish Netherlands

(P. Quesnel in 1678, Arnauld in 1679, D. Gerberon in 1682).

The profound spirituality of the Jansenists came to expression in a translation of the NT, with commentary, by Pasquier Quesnel (1634-1719) — his *Réflexions morales* — leading to the winning of new adherents and increasing the confusion and persecution in France. The rigorism of Jansenism seemed to be a threat to the church system, on which the state relied, with Jesuit help.

In 1701 a conflict arose among the Jansenists themselves concerning the *quaestio facti.* The renewed condemnation of the five propositions by Clement XI (1700-1721) in the bull *Vineam Domini Sabaoth* (1705, DH 2390), backed by Louis and by Spain, led to the dissolution of Port-Royal and the destruction of the convent (1710) because the nuns refused to accept it. In 1713 the bull *Unigenitus* (DH 2400-2502), which became state law in France, condemned 101 propositions of Quesnel, many of which enshrined church tradition. Against this measure many French bishops appealed, unsuccessfully, for the calling of a general council (the so-called Appellants vs. the Acceptants).

Under severe persecution popular enthusiasm mounted, and devout fanaticism recorded → miracles and martyrdoms (→ Martyr), culminating in the question whether or not help *(secours)* should be given to ecstatics by blows on the breast (hence the Securist and Antisecurist parties). When, under Jesuit influence, the archbishop of Paris declared that penance administered by an Appellant priest was invalid (→ Penitence), a last controversy arose between king, Parliament, and church, which ended with the banning and overthrow of the archbishop. The banishing of the Jesuits in 1764 and the shadow of the revolution finally ended the conflict.

3. Impact

The Jansenist heritage is preserved in the Church of Utrecht (→ Old Catholic Churches), which was influenced by the Jansenist refugees Quesnel, Arnauld, and Gerberon; in the intellectual history of France (J. B. Racine, Père Grégoire, the French → Revolution); and, as a result of increasing French influence, in Italy (S. de Ricci, D. Palmieri) and Austria, where it pioneered → Josephinism. It could gain no foothold in Germany.

4. Evaluation

On the basis of a strict Augustinianism directed against synergism, Jansenism, which was often denounced as conservative and rejected as heretical by the → Roman Catholic Church, developed into a reforming movement with a theological, moral, and political impact. It stands opposed to the secularized optimistic anthropology of the → Enlightenment and the → baroque lifestyle. Basic theological and ethical questions, to which different answers were given in different countries, combine in it with ecclesiastical issues and matters relating to the state church. Questions of power politics were also involved; some Jansenists even took part in the French Revolution. A notable phenomenon, not explicable merely in terms of philosophical interest, is the energy with which Europe, then struggling with absolutism and the Enlightenment, discussed and thought through the issues.

In spite of Roman Catholic suspicions, the ontology of Jansenism is not compatible with that of the → Reformation. The "experience of the heart," focused on personal passion and → righteousness, hides the Reformation message of the "alien righteousness" *(iustitia aliena)* that Christ alone gives us. Jansenism gave some support to the → Huguenots and in some cases showed a strong affinity to Gallicanism, being very critical of the absolutism of the French monarchy. In its → asceticism and ecclesiology, however, it was always closely related to the → early church.

→ Modern Church History; Molinism

Bibliography: J. van Bavel and M. Schrama, eds., *Jansenius et la jansénisme dans les Pays-Bas* (Louvain, 1982) • C. Bentivoglio, *Istoria della Costituzione Unigenitus* (3 vols.; Bari, 1968) ed. of the 18th-cent. MS by Raffaele Belvederi • P. R. Campbell, *Power and Politics in Old Regime France* (London, 1996) • L. Ceyssens, *Jansenistica* (4 vols.; Mechelen, 1950-59); idem, *Jansenistica minora* (11 vols.; Mechelen and Amsterdam, 1951-79); idem, *La seconde période du jansénisme* (2 vols.; Brussels and Rome, 1968-74); idem, *Sources relatives à l'histoire du jansénisme et de l'antijansénisme des années 1677-1679* (Louvain, 1974) • R. Clark, *Strangers and Sojourners at Port Royal: Being an Account of the Connections between the British Isles and the Jansenists of France and Holland* (New York, 1972) • W. Doyle, *Jansenism: Catholic Resistance to Authority from the Reformation to the French Revolution* (New York, 2000) • D. van Kley, *The Jansenists and the Expulsion of the Jesuits from France, 1757-1765* (New Haven, 1975) • L. Kolakowski, *God Owes Us Nothing: A Brief Remark on Pascal's Religion and on the Spirit of Jansenism* (Chicago, 1995) • B. R. Kreiser, *Miracles, Convulsions, and Ecclesiastical Politics in Early Eighteenth-Century Paris* (Princeton, 1978) • C. H. O'Brien, "Jansenists on Civil Toleration in Mid-Eighteenth Century France," *TZ* 37 (1981) 71-93 • M. R. O'Connell, *Blaise Pascal: Reasons of the Heart* (Grand Rapids, 1997) • A. Sedgwick, *Jansenism in Seventeenth-Century France: Voices from the Wilderness* (Charlottesville, Va., 1977) • F. E. Weaver, *The Evolution of the Reform of Port-Royal* (Paris, 1978).

Manfred Biersack

Japan

	1960	*1980*	*2000*
Population (1,000s):	94,096	116,807	126,428
Annual growth rate (%):	0.99	0.68	0.12
Area: 377,835 sq. km. (145,883 sq. mi.)			

A.D. *2000*

Population density: 335/sq. km. (867/sq. mi.)
Births / deaths: 1.03 / 0.91 per 100 population
Fertility rate: 1.48 per woman
Infant mortality rate: 4 per 1,000 live births
Life expectancy: 80.3 years (m: 77.3, f: 83.3)
Religious affiliation (%): Buddhists 54.5, new religionists 26.2, nonreligious 10.4, Christians 3.6 (indigenous 1.1, other Christians 2.5), atheists 3.0, Shintoists 2.0, other 0.3.

Overview
1. Earliest Christian Mission
2. Second Christian Period
3. Christianity after 1945
   3.1. Rebuilding
   3.2. Nonchurch Christianity
   3.3. Ecumenical Relations
4. Religious Freedom
5. Other Religions
   5.1. Shinto and Buddhism
   5.2. New Religions

Overview

In what has been a generally vigorous globalization of world economy, Japan has stood out as a giant in the Pacific Asian theater, and indeed the world. After the United States, it has the most technologically powerful economy in the world. Economic decline threatened in the late 1990s, but Japan maintains an enormous trade surplus with the world. According to U.N. figures for 1996, Japan's infant mortality rate (4 per 1,000 live births) was lower than that of any other country, and its average life expectancy (80.3 years) was higher than that of any other. Such data suggest a healthy society of high achievers dedicated to continuing their national and personal success.

In its long history Japan has had three encounters with Christianity, before which it embraced →

Confucianism and → Buddhism. The last two — one a philosophy of life, the other a religion — were syncretistically united in → Shinto, the popular religion of Japan (→ Syncretism).

1. Earliest Christian Mission
In the history of Christian → mission (§3), the work in Japan has often been dramatic. Begun in 1549 by F. → Xavier (1506-52), an original member of the → Jesuits, it developed with astonishing speed. Arriving soon after the Jesuits, the → Franciscans, → Augustinians, and → Dominicans did successful work in the southwest island of Kyūshū and the center of the main island, Honshū. At the beginning of the 17th century there were an estimated 750,000 Christians.

From that time, however, the church came under long and severe persecution. The leaders of Japan saw Christian → mission (§§1-2) as a bridgehead for Western conquest and reacted accordingly. The obvious difference between the old religions and the associated popular customs, on the one side, and, on the other, the Christian lifestyle also provoked a reaction. Christianity was assailed by Shinto, Confucianism, and Buddhism. Many people who remained faithful, especially farmers, had to leave their homes, and many suffered a → martyr's death by crucifixion. The final act was a farmers' revolt in Shimabara in 1637, a social rather than religious protest, which ended with the brutal massacre of 37,000 Christians. The Tokugawa Shogunate (1603-1867) then engaged in further severe persecution, subjected believers to refined → torture, and closed the country to foreigners. Only the Dutch and Chinese were allowed to trade, and only in Nagasaki. The introduction of Christian symbols was strictly forbidden. Nevertheless, Christianity survived, though the faith became mixed with popular practices.

2. Second Christian Period
The second period in the history of Christianity in Japan began with the opening of the country to the West, which dates from 1853 and the arrival from the United States of Commodore Matthew Perry. In 1868 Emperor Meiji (1852-1912) ended the Tokugawa Shogunate. Under him Japan began to develop politically and culturally into a modern → state. Diplomatic pressure from countries that regarded → religious liberty as one of the basic principles of a modern state led to the lifting of the ban on Christian mission.

Roman Catholicism returned in 1859 in the person of the Paris Foreign Society priests. In 1865 a group of descendants of Japan's first Christians contacted Bernard Petitjean in his church in Nagasaki, and thus began a search for more *kakure* (hidden) Christians, who had kept the faith alive underground for over 200 years. Of the 60,000 hidden Christians, about half listened to the teachings of the French priests, while the other half chose to continue their practice in secret, as they had been taught by their ancestors.

The first American Protestant → missionary also came in 1859 (→ North American Missions). Other missionaries included the Anglican C. M. Williams (1829-1910), the Presbyterian J. C. Hepburn (1815-1911), and the Dutch Reformed S. R. Braun (1810-80) and G. F. Verbeck (1830-98). Then came Methodists (→ Methodist Churches), → Baptists, Lutherans (→ Lutheran Churches), and the → Salvation Army from the United States, Canada, and the United Kingdom (→ British Missions). The Russian → Orthodox Church began work in Hokkaidō and then in Tokyo.

The new mission work met with rapid success. Christian witnesses included the Samurai Knights, a spiritual rather than a political knighthood, suppressed under the Meiji rule. In 1872 M. Uemura (1858-1925), later the leader of the Japanese church, formed some secretly baptized believers into the first Protestant church at Yokohama. Other centers of Christian mission were Kumamoto, where the Kumamoto Band was formed under the leadership of the American teacher L. L. Janes (1839-1909), and Sapporo, where W. S. Clark (1826-86) founded the Sapporo Band.

At first, Japanese Christians tried to preserve → unity and to avoid splitting up into → denominations. Christianity was viewed as having an inner relation to the democratic movement for human and civil → rights, and the church attained great influence in both urban and rural areas. Christian schools were founded, including the first Japanese school for girls — a vital step in education for women. Especially well known was the Doshisha English School in Kyoto, founded by J. Niijima (1843-90), which in 1876 enrolled 30 young men of the Kumamoto Band. Christian missionaries, including Roman Catholic women religious, also founded hospitals, orphanages, retirement communities, leper colonies, and clinics.

The 1889 constitution publicly recognized religious freedom for the first time in Japan, but the educational rescript of 1890 put emperor worship, which was firmly linked to state Shinto, at the spiritual center of Japan. Growing nationalism abated the enthusiasm for Western culture, which resulted in a decline in the number of Christians. Japan's military victories in wars with China (1894-95) and Russia (1904-5) gave the people greater confidence in the empire. In this nationalistic atmosphere the church accommodated itself to emperor worship and the state ideology. Also, Japanese government officials began to link Christianity with socialism, further tarnishing its reputation.

After World War I the Christian politician S. Yoshino (1878-1933) opposed the antidemocratic tendency of the government. At a time of economic recession and social misery, T. Kagawa (1888-1960), a Christian evangelist and reformer, worked for the improvement of conditions among workers in the poorer sections of the cities. Kagawa helped found the Federation of Labor (1918) and the Farmers' Union (1921).

Imperial → fascism came to Japan when the military seized power. Especially after conquests in China and Southeast Asia in the 1930s, emperor worship became the basis of the Japanese → worldview, and the emperor increasingly became the object of worship as a living deity. Direct and indirect persecution of Christians recommenced. At this time the Vatican gave Japanese Roman Catholics permission to visit Shinto shrines in order to avoid conflict with Japanese nationalism (→ Nation, Nationalism). Then the Protestant Church reluctantly came together as Nippon Kirisuto Kyodan (United Church of Christ in Japan) and adjusted itself to the war policy. Unity had been the ideal of Japanese Christians from the very first. The absolute deifying of the emperor was now pushed to such an extreme that the proclamation of the parousia by the Holiness Church was regarded as hostile to the state. Many Christians were imprisoned, and some were martyred.

3. Christianity after 1945
3.1. *Rebuilding*
After Japan's defeat in 1945 the emperor publicly renounced his claim to deity. State Shinto was abandoned under pressure from the United States as the occupying power. The new (and present) constitution of 1947, which is based on the principles of sovereignty of the people, respect for human rights, and pacifism, separated the state and religion (→ Church and State), granting religious liberty in the true sense. A second opening up of the country followed, as political and intellectual obstacles to mission were removed. Overseas churches and missionary societies gave decisive help to the churches, which had been shattered by the war.

In 1951 the Anglicans, Baptists, Methodists, Lutherans, part of the Reformed and Presbyterians,

and part of the Holiness Church left Kyodan. Many new denominations were formed, and various missionary projects were planned and executed. Kyodan broke free from state interference and set up a new constitutional order. In 1967, in the name of its → moderator, Kyodan publicly confessed its war guilt after the model of the Stuttgart Declaration of Guilt. Inside and outside Kyodan this step provoked vigorous discussion.

When the period of interest in Christianity and enthusiasm for American culture ended, missionary work became less intense. Missionary work in the 20th century focused on the cities, and work in small towns and rural areas declined. Overall, the church became more intellectual, with most new members coming from the educated middle class.

One positive feature has been the historic commitment of Japanese Christians to education and social welfare, as well as to the development of a democratic society. Such efforts have tended to give Christianity a national prominence much greater than might be expected from the relatively small number of Christians currently in Japan.

3.2. *Nonchurch Christianity*
The Mukyokai (lit. "nonchurch") movement, or nonchurch Christianity, is significant in Japan. It was started at the beginning of the 20th century by K. Uchimura (1861-1930), who argued that the Japanese churches were making a vital mistake by imitating the Western churches in → theology, → liturgy, and orders (→ Church Orders). His aim was to bring the gospel to the Japanese without the garb of Western church institutions. His association has no pastors; it is run by the laity on the principle of the priesthood of all believers. It is no accident that some of its leaders and adherents bravely and resolutely opposed Japanese militarism during World War II. After the war T. Yanaihara and S. Nambara also played a leading role as → pacifists. Japanese churches should see in the Mukyokai movement a question put to themselves regarding their role within Japanese society.

3.3. *Ecumenical Relations*
The National Christian Council in Japan, founded in 1923, promotes communication between the denominations in Japan and churches abroad. The council, which has made some initial attempts at interreligious dialogue, organizes working parties for → peace and human rights. The educational and social work of the → YMCA and YWCA is also effective. The Roman Catholic group Justitia et Pax makes contributions along similar lines. This approach by Christians who previously were very conservative is arousing new attention in serious circles.

4. Religious Freedom

Article 20 of the constitution guarantees religious freedom to all citizens and bars state interference with, or support for, religious organizations. It also bars religious organizations from exercising any political authority. It bans coerced religious activity and prohibits the state from sponsoring religious education or other religious activity. It has reduced the dominant role of Shinto as the imperial cult.

Registered religious groups are exempt from taxes on land purchase or construction of religious buildings. They must supply annual reports and may be inspected. The education curriculum is prescribed by the government for public schools, but in addition private schools may include courses of religious instruction. Ecumenical organizations continue to thrive in the new environment thus provided.

5. Other Religions

5.1. *Shinto and Buddhism*

There has been an obvious shift in Japanese politics. Shintoists, who are becoming increasingly nationalistic, want the government to safeguard the position of the Shinto Yasukuni shrine. Long a symbol of Japanese militarism, this shrine is regarded as the site of the souls of the war dead, which are regarded as hero gods who will eternally protect the kingdom of Japan. The Shinto Political Union, which was founded to restore emperor worship, is seeking political influence. A Buddhist counterpart is the Komei Party within the new religion Soka Gakkai. This party has pursued a zigzag course between the Right and the Left.

The activities of other Buddhist orders are restricted almost entirely to celebrations of the dead as popular practices. Yet there are impulses of renewal within Buddhism. Convinced pacifist Buddhists oppose Yasukuni nationalism and act together with critical Christians.

5.2. *New Religions*

The events of World War I, the rise of fascism, and Japan's defeat in World War II combined to spawn several so-called new religions in Japan, some that have experienced astonishing rates of growth and worldwide influence. Although difficult to characterize generally, these religions all offer salvation, often with the theme of Japan's role as bearing a spiritual message to the rest of the world. They often involve magic and miracles, have an eclectic range of spirits and deities, and address the personal, social, and national concerns experienced by modern-day Japanese citizens.

The largest of the new religions is Soka Gakkai (Jap. for "value creation society"), founded in 1930. With legal recognition in over 150 countries and appealing especially to the lower classes, in 2000 its worldwide membership numbered upwards of 20 million persons. Stemming from Buddhist roots, it sees fundamental unity between religion and politics and has founded the political party Komeito ("clean government party") to express its views. Since 1970 it has been marked by virulent anti-Christian efforts.

Rissho Koseikai ("society for the establishment of righteousness"), with 5 million adherents, is a modern Buddhist folk movement based on the teachings of the Japanese Buddhist leader Nichiren (1222-82). Founded in 1938 by Niwano Nikkyo, it teaches members to pursue their own enlightenment in fellowship with others.

Reiyukai ("friends of the spirit association") follows a lay Buddhist tradition and combines temporal concerns with ancestor worship. Developed in the 1920s from the teaching of K. Kakutaro (d. 1944), it had approximately 3 million adherents in 2000. It was perhaps the most successful new religion before and during World War II, when, unlike most other religions, it was free of government control. It has been weakened by frequent defections (e.g., Niwano Nikkyo left it to form Rissho Koseikai).

Another new religion with approximately 3 million adherents is Seicho-No-Ie ("truth of life"), which began in 1930 with the publication of a magazine of this name by M. Taniguchi (d. 1985). Teaching that mind is the sole reality and that faith and mental purification can heal the body, this group resembles Christian Science.

Tenrikyo ("religion of divine wisdom") was founded in 1838 by N. Miki (d. 1887); in 2000 it had over 2 million members. Developed as a protest against the feudal order, Tenrikyo at first was recognized as a branch of Shinto, later changed its affiliation to Buddhism (1880), and finally became an official Shinto group (1908). It has adopted three collections of Miki's revelations as its central scriptures, which feature teachings on oracles, shamanistic practices, and ecstatic dances.

The Japanese new religion most publicized in the West has been Aum Shinrikyo ("supreme truth"; "aum" is a form of the Skt. sacred syllable *om*), infamous because of its nerve-gas attack in the Tokyo subway system in 1995. In January 2000 the Public Security Commission ruled that the group, which has changed its name to Aleph, continued to pose a threat to society and would be held under scrutiny for up to three years.

→ Asian Theology; Biblical Theology 2.4

Bibliography: P. B. CLARKE, ed., *Japanese New Religions in Global Perspective* (Richmond, Surrey, 2000) • R. H. DRUMMOND, *A History of Christianity in Japan* (Grand Rapids, 1971) • C. B. FRANCIS and J. M. NAKAJIMA, *Christians in Japan* (New York, 1991) • Y. FURUYA, ed., *A History of Japanese Theology* (Grand Rapids, 1997) • A. HARRINGTON, *Japan's Hidden Christians* (Chicago, 1993) • A. H. ION, *The Cross and the Rising Sun* (2 vols.; Waterloo, Ont., 1990-93) • J. M. KITAGAWA, *On Understanding Japanese Religion* (Princeton, 1987) • A. LANDE, *Meiji Protestantism in History and Historiography: A Comparative Study of Japanese and Western Interpretation of Early Protestantism in Japan* (New York, 1989) • K. S. LEE, *The Christian Confrontation with Shinto Nationalism: A Historical and Critical Study of the Conflict of Christianity and Shinto in Japan in the Period between the Meiji Restoration and the End of World War II* (Philadelphia, 1966) • M. MIYATA, *Mündigkeit und Solidarität: Christliche Verantwortung in der heutigen japanischen Gesellschaft* (Gütersloh, 1984); idem, "The Politico-Religion of Japan–the Revival of Militarist Mentality," *Bulletin of Peace Proposals* 13 (1982) 12-17 • I. READER and G. J. TANABE JR., *Practically Religious: Worldly Benefits and the Common Religion of Japan* (Honolulu, 1998) • A. M. SUGGATE, *Japanese Christians and Society* (New York, 1996) • G. J. TANABE JR., ed., *Religions of Japan in Practice* (Princeton, 1999) • S. TURNBULL, ed., *Japan's Hidden Christians, 1549-1999* (2 vols.; Surrey, 2000).

MITSUO MIYATA

Jehovah's Witnesses

1. Background
2. Beliefs
3. Organization

1. Background

Jehovah's Witnesses were organized as a missionary "service corporation." The parent organization is the Watch Tower Bible and Tract Society (1881, WTS) in Brooklyn, New York, with branch offices around the world. Leadership is vested in the lifelong president and (as of the year 2000) a corporation of 13 members, through which "God himself" rules (→ Theocracy). The worldwide field in which preachers are gathered and commissioned is divided into branches, districts, circuits, and congregations, under the care of district and circuit overseers and congregational elders. Only a few full-time workers with a half-year training at the Gilead School in Brooklyn are appointed by the WTS for a modest salary.

Every Witness has a preaching ministry in the form of conversations, letters, and silent street witness with the publications *Watchtower* and *Awake!* as well as house-to-house visits with literature or longer home → Bible study with those who are interested. There are also public addresses and conferences. Five gatherings a week serve for training.

The functional structure and beliefs of Jehovah's Witnesses have historical roots. In 1872 Charles Taze Russell (1852-1916), a young Pittsburgh merchant, came into contact with an Adventist splinter group. In 1879 he began to publish the paper *Zion's Watch Tower.* He had obviously adopted the ideas of the original → Adventists (the Millerite movement) and refashioned them as principles of belief and structure that are still basic for Jehovah's Witnesses.

2. Beliefs

The first principle is *radical separation from the churches* (which are tools of Satan, the whore of Babylon, Revelation 17–18), from their theologians ("servants of religion"), from their teachings (e.g., the → Trinity, the immortal → soul, the torments of → hell), and from their ceremonies and practices, → baptism being replaced by dedication to obedient service "in the name of Jehovah," and the → Eucharist (called the Lord's evening meal, or memorial of Christ's death) being celebrated once a year, after sundown on the 14th of Nisan. Jehovah's Witnesses do not want an organized religion with a name, church buildings, ceremonies, or congregational life. They prove their loyalty to Jehovah God and his earthly fellowship by voluntary missionary service.

The second principle is *lay Bible study* on the basis of a strict → fundamentalism and an attitude of exclusive obedience. The exposition is legalistic and is centrally controlled. The drinking of blood and blood transfusions are prohibited, for example, on the basis of Acts 15:29.

The third point is an *apocalyptic plan of redemption,* with constant recalculation of the time when this era will end and the kingdom of Jehovah (the millennium; → Millenarianism) will be set up. Russell prophesied that the end would come in 1874, then 1878, finally 1914. His successor, Joseph F. Rutherford (1869-1942), later explained that 1914 was the date of the invisible establishment of Christ's kingdom in heaven. Jehovah's Witnesses have since proclaimed "the good news of the established kingdom." The generation that lived in 1914 with believing hearts will live on until everything is manifest. Next, 1925 was proclaimed as the climax and conclusion of the great tribulation, and 1975 as the end of the 6,000 years of human history.

The fourth principle is the *dualistic conflict between two kingdoms* (→ Dualism). Satan is the lord of this world and has a large following, including all organized religion. → Religion is of pagan origin, and to be infected by → paganism is a serious sin. Customary feasts and holidays are rejected as pagan (e.g., → Christmas, → Easter, and birthdays). The whole political system also belongs to Satan's realm, and Jehovah's Witnesses must steer clear of it. They refuse military and civilian service, do not take → oaths, will not salute flags, do not take part in elections, reject appointments, and engage in no social action. The result is that they are proscribed in many countries and suffer persecution. During World War II some 6,000 were imprisoned by the National Socialists, and 800 were put to death. All those who oppose Jehovah's Witnesses and reject their message belong to Satan's kingdom. Their destruction in the bloody battle of Harmagedon (Rev. 16:16) is a central point in WTS teaching.

Finally, the Jehovah's Witnesses set their *hope on a new → paradise*, rather than strictly on the return of Christ. The true worshipers of Jehovah will live in peace on a purified earth. The 144,000 (understood literally), of whom only a small remnant is still alive, will reign with Christ in heaven. There is thus a two-class system. → Jesus Christ himself has only a subordinate role in the WTS doctrinal system. He is the mediator in a more formal sense (by his sacrificial death) and is also Jehovah's regent.

3. Organization

The Watch Tower organization is a closed system that isolates its members and makes them dependent by authoritarian leadership, indoctrination, and a demand for total commitment. This atmosphere results in conflicts of faith, disillusionment, distrust of social forces outside the group, and difficulties in relating to others. There is a rapid turnover in membership; in some places as many as one-third of those who join each year leave the organization. Worldwide in 2001 the Witnesses reported 6.1 million members in 235 countries.

→ Sect

Bibliography: M. ALFS, *The Evocative Religion of Jehovah's Witnesses: An Analysis of a Present-Day Phenomenon* (Minneapolis, 1991) • J. A. BECKFORD, *The Trumpet of Prophecy: A Sociological Study of Jehovah's Witnesses* (New York, 1975) • J. BERGMAN, *Jehovah's Witnesses and Kindred Groups: An Historical Compendium and Bibliography* (New York, 1984) • H. D. H.

BOTTING and G. N. A. BOTTING, *The Orwellian World of Jehovah's Witnesses* (Toronto, 1984) • A. HOLDEN, *Jehovah's Witnesses: Portrait of a Contemporary Religious Movement* (London, 2002) • M. J. PENTON, *Apocalypse Delayed: The Story of Jehovah's Witnesses* (Toronto, 1985) • S. F. PETERS, *Judging Jehovah's Witnesses: Religious Persecution and the Dawn of the Rights Revolution* (Lawrence, Kans., 2000) • D. A. REED, *Blood on the Altar: Confessions of a Jehovah's Witness Minister* (Amherst, N.Y., 1996) • H.-D. REIMER and O. EGGENBERGER, *. . . neben den Kirchen. Gemeinschaften, die ihren Glauben auf besondere Weise leben wollen; Informationen, Verständnishilfen, kritische Fragen* (6th ed.; Constance, 1986) 218-52 • A. ROGERSON, *Millions Now Living Will Never Die: A Study of Jehovah's Witnesses* (London, 1969) • WATCHTOWER BIBLE AND TRACT SOCIETY OF NEW YORK, *Did Man Get Here by Evolution or by Creation?* (Brooklyn, N.Y., 1967).

HANS-DIETHER REIMER†

Jeremiah, Book of

1. Content
2. Criticism and Composition
   2.1. Criticism
   2.2. Composition
3. Jeremiah the Prophet
   3.1. Life and Ministry
   3.2. The Suffering Prophet

1. Content

Chaps. 1–25 of the Book of Jeremiah consist largely of poetic oracles of doom directed against Judah, interspersed with longer and shorter prose sections (e.g., chaps. 7 and 11). The prose has → Deuteronomistic characteristics and has commonly been distinguished from the prose in which the so-called Baruch biography of Jeremiah is written. According to W. Rudolph, the latter is represented in 1–25 by 19:1-10, 14-15 and 20:1-6, although it is principally located in the second half of the book (26; 28; 29; 34:1-7; 36; 37–45; 51:59-64). A particular category of poetic material is constituted by the "laments" or "complaints" of Jeremiah, whether those that explore Jeremiah's hard lot as a → prophet (8:18–9:1; 12:1-5; 15:10-21; 17:9-18; 20:7-9) or those where he appears as an intercessor in a communal context (e.g., 14:2-10; 14:17–15:4). Poetry is also employed in oracles against foreign nations, which are differently located in the Hebrew and Greek texts (25:15-38; 46–51 in the Hebrew, and 25:15–31:44 in the LXX).

The passage 25:1-13, regarded as a conclusion of the preceding part of the book, has been drawn into discussions about the contents of the two scrolls mentioned in chap. 36 (vv. 1-8, 27-32). The phrase *bassēper hazzeh*, "in this book" (25:13), has been taken as a reference to either the first or the second scroll, rather than to a book containing the oracles against foreign nations. The contents of the scrolls have been variously identified with the oracles of doom against Judah (although some prose is included in Rudolph's definition of the contents of the scrolls), along with oracles against foreign nations. O. Eissfeldt has supposed that the scrolls were made up of the prose that principally appears in chaps. 1–25 and constituted a considered retrospect of the oracles that Jeremiah had delivered over a 23-year period (25:3).

2. Criticism and Composition
2.1. *Criticism*
Three differing critical appreciations of the contents of the Book of Jeremiah may be considered.

2.1.1. The first view is the source theory of S. Mowinckel (1914), which has been adopted and modified by Rudolph. The three sources are given as A, B, and C, and the contents of the B source (the so-called Baruch biography) have been given above. Rudolph describes the A source as constituted by poetic sayings of the prophet Jeremiah, which are to be identified, for the most part, with the oracles delivered against Judah in 1–25. The C source mostly consists of the prose that is interspersed with the poetry in 1–25 (7:1–8:3; 11:1-14 [17]; 16:1-13 [18]; 17:19-27; 18:1-12; 21:1-10; 22:1-5; 25:1-14) and otherwise only 34:8-22 and chap. 35. Thus the C source is mainly located in the first half of the book, and the B source in the second. The B source, attributed to Baruch, Jeremiah's scribe, has been widely regarded as a contemporary historical source; it is different in this respect from the C source, which is taken as an interpretation of Jeremiah's prophetic activity shaped by exilic conditions and perspectives.

The validity of this distinction has been challenged by E. W. Nicholson and others, who have urged that the element of exilic reinterpretation of Jeremiah's ministry is as much present in the one as in the other. The advantages of supposing (as Rudolph does) that the postulated C-source passages are parts of a once-continuous source that has been chopped up and distributed among the poetry are not obvious. A different kind of conclusion is that these poetic pieces have severally and separately attracted ad hoc exegetical comment in prose and that this prose itself has been subject to further pro-

cesses of expansion. Rudolph does not pursue the rearticulation of his postulated C source, apart from a proposal that 22:1-5 is a continuation of 7:1–8:3.

2.1.2. The view that the Book of Jeremiah has received a thoroughgoing Deuteronomistic expansion and that the relation of the poetry to the prose of Rudolph's source C is best understood on this assumption has been argued in great detail by W. Thiel. An important aspect of this method is the view that the prose compositions attributed to a Deuteronomistic redactor (D) have a kernel in relation to which they cohere. The kernel may be poetry, or poetry that Thiel critically reconstructs, but it may also be prose. The compositions may be small, medium, or large, for Thiel supposes that the work of D has an all-embracing and systematic character. The question to be asked is whether the book overall has as high a degree of literary and theological organization as Thiel maintains.

2.1.3. H. Weippert has argued that the prose of the Book of Jeremiah should be regarded as the product of the prophet himself and that the parallels that scholars have formulated between (1) the prose of Deuteronomy and the Deuteronomistic literature and (2) the prose of the Book of Jeremiah are insufficiently refined. When they are subjected to closer scrutiny, whether statistical or semantic, it emerges (so Weippert) that the differences between (1) and (2) are more significant than their affinities.

2.2. *Composition*
Weippert's view of the prose foreshortens the processes of composition, since it implies that the book may be regarded as having more or less achieved its extant shape in the lifetime of the prophet Jeremiah. There is a similarity and a difference between Weippert and Rudolph. Rudolph's interest is also focused on the historical Jeremiah, but he does not suppose that the prose of his source C is Jeremiah's prose. Nevertheless, this prose, although it comes to us in Deuteronomic/Deuteronomistic dress, does give us access (so Rudolph) to the historical Jeremiah and preserves the sense of his preaching.

Thiel's assumptions remove us from the historical context of Jeremiah's ministry to later times. His view that the processes involved in the growth and composition of the book are long and complicated, carrying us into exilic and postexilic times, is a realistic one.

3. Jeremiah the Prophet
3.1. *Life and Ministry*
Jeremiah, who was of a priestly family located in Anathoth, received his call in 626 B.C. in the reign of → Josiah and continued through the reigns of

Jehoiakim and Zedekiah until the exile in 587 B.C. (1:1-3). The date 626 is usually associated with an assumption that there was a period of silence between 621 and 609, and some argue that a later date (609) for Jeremiah's call is a more economical hypothesis.

The description of Jeremiah as a prophet to the nations in the call narrative (1:4-10) has troubled commentators, and it may be that the extant book is presupposed by the call narrative and that "prophet to the nations" (v. 5) is a reference to the oracles against foreign nations. It has been supposed that Jeremiah was a nationalistic prophet before becoming a doom prophet and that the oracles against foreign nations are attributable to the nationalistic phase of his activity. A more probable conclusion, however, is that these oracles are not attributable to the prophet Jeremiah.

3.2. *The Suffering Prophet*

Although H. Reventlow has argued to the contrary, the individual laments should be regarded as giving us access to the interior life of the prophet. His vocation is full of → suffering and contradiction; he feels the bitterness of his condition and cannot desist from attaching blame to → Yahweh and charging him with deceit (e.g., 20:7-9). Jeremiah is foredoomed to be rejected because the falsehood that defeats the truth of God's word is installed as religious orthodoxy. The people are deceived by words of peace spoken by prophets who have an impeccable religious legitimacy, and Jeremiah asks Yahweh whether he is not responsible for deceiving them (4:10; cf. 6:14 = 8:11). Jeremiah cannot reach the people with the truth of God's word and suffers pain in his estrangement and rejection. In this respect he is a forerunner of the One who "came to what was his own, and his own people did not accept him" (John 1:11); it is understandable that Jeremiah was identified with the Suffering Servant of Isaiah 40–55.

By the Jews who experienced the exile, Jeremiah is acknowledged as a true prophet whose witness was vindicated. Since, in their view, effective intercession was part of the equipment of a prophet, they explained the case of Jeremiah by holding that Yahweh had forbidden him to exercise his power as an intercessor. In this way they solved a theological problem that their understanding of the prophetic office created for them (7:16-20; 11:14; 14:2-10, 11-16; 14:17–15:4).

→ Israel 1

Bibliography: Commentaries: D. BERRIGAN, *Jeremiah: The World, the Wound of God* (Minneapolis, 1999) • J. BRIGHT (AB; Garden City, N.Y., 1965) • W. HOLLADAY (Hermeneia; 2 vols.; Philadelphia and Minneapolis, 1986-89) • D. R. JONES (NCBC; Grand Rapids, 1992) • G. L. KEOWN, P. J. SCALISE, and J. G. SMOTHERS (WBC; Waco, Tex., 1995) on chaps. 26–52 • W. McKANE (ICC; Edinburgh, 1986) on chaps. 1–25 • W. RUDOLPH (HAT; 3d ed.; Tübingen, 1968).

Other works: M. P. KNOWLES, *Jeremiah in Matthew's Gospel: The Rejected Prophet Motif in Matthean Redaction* (Sheffield, 1993) • J. R. LUNDBLOM, "Jeremiah, Book of," *ABD* 3.706-21 • S. MOWINCKEL, *Zur Komposition des Buches Jeremia* (Oslo, 1914) • E. W. NICHOLSON, *Preaching to the Exiles* (Oxford, 1970) • K. M. O'CONNOR, *The Confessions of Jeremiah: Their Interpretation and Role in Chapters 1–25* (Atlanta, 1988) • G. H. PAUKE-TAYLOR, *The Formation of the Book of Jeremiah: Doublets and Recurring Phrases* (Atlanta, 2000) • H. G. REVENTLOW, *Liturgie und prophetisches Ich bei Jeremia* (Gütersloh, 1963) • W. THIEL, *Die deuteronomistische Redaktion von Jeremia 1–25* (Neukirchen, 1973); idem, *Die deuteronomistische Redaktion von Jeremia 26–45* (Neukirchen, 1981) • H. WEIPPERT, *Die Prosareden des Jeremiabuches* (Berlin, 1973).

WILLIAM McKANE

Jerome

Jerome (ca. 345-420), born Eusebius Hieronymus (perhaps as early as 333), was an outstanding translator, exegete, and theologian of the early church. He was the son of a well-to-do Christian family that owned property in Strido (near Emona, or modern Ljubljana, Slovenia). He was educated in → Rome, and his teachers included, until 363, the famous grammarian Aelius Donatus (though not Marius Victorinus, neither does Jerome seem to have been closely acquainted with Ambrose in Rome; he did, however, study together with Rufinus). Jerome's student years in Rome deeply influenced him and seem to have been the source of his interest in biblical philology. The time in Rome was also the beginning of his orientation toward several of the empire's significant political and religious centers.

Jerome traveled first (367/68?) to Trier, in Gaul, where Emperor Valentinian I (364-75) resided. Presumably the acquaintance with monasticism he made there prompted him to lead a communal life for several years (until 371?) in Strido, Emona, and Aquileia. He then left rather suddenly for Syria, one of his main goals being to become acquainted with monasticism in Antioch and Khalkís (on the Greek island Euboea) and to live an ascetic life himself, albeit in the form of a relatively comfortable "desert" sojourn (S. Rebenich). Here Jerome laid the foundation (ca. 375-77) for the linguistic expertise for which he became well known even during late antiquity itself (learning Greek, Hebrew, a bit of Arabic and Punic, naturally also Aramaic and Syrian). At the same time, his attitude toward his classical Roman education changed, which he later (384?) articulated as a change "from a Ciceronian to a Christian." Jerome's pronounced orientation toward the bishop of Rome is already noticeable in Syria. He inquired with Damasus of Rome (pope 366-84) about the Trinitarian conflicts and was ordained as a priest by the Antiochian bishop Paulinus, who was closely allied with Rome.

From 379/80 Jerome was in Constantinople, where one of his major contacts was Gregory of Nazianzus (329/30-389/90), to whom he owed especially his acquaintance with the works of → Origen (ca. 185-ca. 254), which would prove to be of such significance. After Gregory's unexpected resignation as bishop of Constantinople, Jerome went back to Rome and lived among the urban aristocracy. Here he began his groundbreaking and important revisions of the Latin Bible, initially according to the Greek text, which led ultimately to the Vg, the Latin version of the Bible most widely used in the West. Scholars do not agree whether during this period he also actually served as secretary to Damasus. In any event, some in Rome seem to have favored him as the successor to Damasus. When Siricius (384-99) was elected instead, Jerome found himself in an untenable situation.

In 386 Jerome moved to Bethlehem, where he was followed by Paula, a Roman matron dedicated to a life of devotion, and her daughter St. Eustochium. After various academic journeys, including to various locales associated with Egyptian → monasticism and to Didymus the Blind (ca. 313-98), Jerome intensively pursued his scholarly projects. In Bethlehem he also engaged in what were in part extremely hateful literary controversies with contemporary theologians (Ambrose, John of Jerusalem, and his former fellow student Rufinus) and became entangled in the dispute regarding Origen and Pelagianism. His ten-year correspondence with → Augustine (394-404) was also burdened by considerable tension. Jerome died in 420 and was eventually canonized (feast day, September 30).

After Augustine, Jerome was the most productive Latin theologian of antiquity, though the chronology of his works can be reconstructed only indirectly. His earliest writings include the *Vita Pauli*, the first Latin monastic legend. Beginning with the Constantinople period, Jerome produced editions and translations of scholarly and exegetical works from the Greek (e.g., the chronicle of Eusebius and exegetical homilies of Origen; → Exegesis, Biblical). In Bethlehem he produced independent works on biblical interpretation (*Quaestiones hebraicae in Genesim* plus commentaries on Isaiah, Ezekiel, Daniel, Galatians, Ephesians, Philippians, and Titus). After the fashion of Suetonius, he also wrote a kind of bibliography of ecclesiastical writers, *De viris illustribus* (with chap. 85 on himself). His voluminous correspondence (150 letters among those he wrote and received have survived) provides a unique look at the → theology and daily life of his time. As the large number of → pseudepigrapha show, Jerome's translations of the Bible (→ Bible Versions 2.3) and his exegetical works exerted an almost incalculable influence on Western theological history.

Primary sources: AGLB 23, 27 • BPat 12 • CChr.SL 72-80 • *The Correspondence (394-419) between Jerome and Augustine of Hippo* (trans. C. White; Lewiston, N.Y., 1990) • *CPL* 580-621 • CSEL 49 • D. ERASMUS, *The Edition of St. Jerome* (ed. and trans. J. F. Brady and J. C. Olin; Toronto, 1992) • GCS 6, 11/1, 33, 47, 49 • *PL* 23-26 • SC 242, 323, 386 • *Select Letters of St. Jerome* (trans. F. A. Wright; Cambridge, Mass., 1963).

Secondary works: J. D. ADAMS, *The Populus of Augustine and Jerome: A Study in the Patristic Sense of Community* (New Haven, 1971) • D. BROWN, *Vir trilinguis: A Study in the Biblical Exegesis of St. Jerome* (Kampen, 1992) • A. FÜRST, *Augustins Briefwechsel mit Hieronymus* (Münster, 1999) • A. KAMESAR, *Jerome, Greek Scholarship, and the Hebrew Bible: A Study of the "Quaestiones hebraicae in Genesim"* (Oxford, 1993) • J. N. D. KELLY, *Jerome: His Life, Writings, and Controversies* (New York, 1975) • F. X. MURPHY, "Jerome, St.," *NCE* 7.872-74 • S. REBENICH, *Hieronymus und sein Kreis. Prosopographische und sozialgeschichtliche Untersuchungen* (Stuttgart, 1992) • E. F. RICE, *St. Jerome in the Renaissance* (Baltimore, 1985) • A. DE VOGÜÉ, *Histoire littéraire du mouvement monastique dans l'antiquité*, vol. 4, *Sulpice Sévère et Paulin de Nole (393-409), Jérôme, homéliste et traducteur des "Pachomiana"* (Paris, 1997).

CHRISTOPH MARKSCHIES

Jerusalem

1. Topography
2. Pre-Israelite
3. Preexilic
4. Persian
5. Hellenistic

6. Roman
7. Judaism, Christianity, and Islam

1. Topography

Jerusalem is situated immediately west of the Mount of Olives (790-820 m. / 2,600-2,700 ft. above sea level), at the junction of northern and southern → Palestine, on the Cisjordan highlands. Up to the last century it was bordered on the east by the Kidron Valley (2 Sam. 15:23; John 18:1) and on the west and south by the Hinnom Valley (Josh. 15:8; 18:16). It is divided by the Cross Valley, a central valley that runs from north to south (Josephus *J.W.* 5.140), separating a western hill from one on the east. Settlement began on the south side of the southeast hill, close to the source of the Gihon (1 Kgs. 1:33 etc.) in the Kidron Valley, with protection from all sides but the north.

2. Pre-Israelite

The oldest traces of settlement in Jerusalem consist of Chalcolithic ceramics from the fourth millennium B.C. The earliest architecture is a fragment of an Early Bronze Age house from the third millennium on the southeast hill. The history of the city begins in the Middle Bronze Age (18th cent. B.C.) with the construction of a fortress uncovered by K. M. Kenyon (pp. 76-97) and Y. Shilo (p. 12) above the source of the Gihon.

Egyptian texts of the time refer to *ʒwš ʒmm* (= Heb. *yěrûšālēm*, "foundation [*yrh* I] of [the god] *šālēm*"). During the Late Bronze Age (14th/13th cent.), terracing was introduced above the Gihon spring on the east slope of the southeast hill, probably as the podium of an acropolis. The Amarna Letters (*EAT* 285-90) show that Jerusalem (Akkad. *uruú-ru-sa-lim*) was the urban center of the central hill-country, close to Shechem, which was a threat to it.

3. Preexilic

In the 11th century B.C. Jerusalem was a Canaanite enclave between the northern and southern tribes of → Israel (§1). → David captured it (2 Sam. 5:6-9) and made it the metropolis of his kingdom (→ Monarchy in Israel). He renewed the terracing (v. 9) and built a palace (v. 11), but his building program was modest compared to that of → Solomon, who extended the city to the north by building the → temple (→ Sanctuary) and palace (1 Kings 6–7).

With the division of Israel into North and South (1 Kings 12), Jerusalem lost some of its importance, since it was now only the capital of little Judah. It was under threat from the empires of Egypt and Mesopotamia, Palestine being the boundary be-

tween them. When Assyria conquered the northern kingdom in 722/721 B.C., refugees fled to Judah and were perhaps the reason for the extension of the city to the southwest hill (see 2 Kgs. 22:14; Zeph. 1:10-11). A slum area developed on the southeast hill (Shilo, 28). Strengthening of the defenses there (2 Chr. 32:5) was no doubt connected with Hezekiah's defiance of Assyria. To prepare Jerusalem for a siege Hezekiah built a tunnel 512 m. (1,680 ft.) long, ending in the pool of Shiloah (2 Kgs. 20:20; 2 Chr. 32:2-4, 30 [= Gk. *Silōam*, John 9:7]; *KAI* 189). The tunnel provided increased access to a spring and, during a siege, could replace the undefended aqueduct through the Kidron Valley (Isa. 8:6).

With the decay of Assyrian power → Josiah built a wall to defend the southwest hill (see N. Avigad, 46-49). Josiah's political measures were accompanied by cultic reforms that culminated in centralization, which, in exilic interpretation (2 Kings 22–23), made Jerusalem the only legitimate place at which to worship → Yahweh. After Josiah's fall (609 B.C.) Jerusalem came for a time under Egyptian and then under Babylonian influence. It was taken by the Babylonians in 597 (2 Kgs. 24:10-17) and then again, in response to Zedekiah's revolt, in 586, when the temple was destroyed (25:8-21).

4. Persian

The rebuilding of the temple and the work of Nehemiah marked Jerusalem in the Persian period. At the urging of the prophets Haggai and Zechariah, the rebuilding of the temple was begun under Zerubbabel in 520 B.C. and completed in 515. The southwest sector was unoccupied during the Persian period, and settlement on the southeast hill was limited to the ridge. The east slope was bordered by the wall that Nehemiah built in 545 (Neh. 2:11–3:32; 7:1-3). This fortification was part of a reform that made Jerusalem the capital of the Persian province of Judah, now detached from Samaria.

5. Hellenistic

Transition from Persian to Ptolemaic rule produced little construction. When Jerusalem became a Seleucid polis (2 Macc. 4:9), a gymnasium was built west of the temple, and in the final Seleucid phase the fortress Acra was built south of the temple (1 Macc. 1:33-35).

In the → Hasmonaean period the southwest hill was brought into the system of fortifications and resettled (the "first wall," *J.W.* 5.136, 142-45). A royal Hasmonaean palace was built on the east slope, and the eastern section of Nehemiah's wall was renewed on the southeast hill (Shilo, 30; cf. 1 Macc. 12:36-37).

6. Roman

Greater changes came with → Herod the Great (ruled 37-4 B.C.). From 20 B.C. to A.D. 63 the temple precincts were extended (Josephus *Ant.* 15.398-402), with the fortress Antonia being constructed at the northern edge of the precincts. If indeed the Antonia is no longer to be associated with the materials from the period of Hadrian found in the convent Notre Dame de Sion and in the Convent of Flagellation, then it is to be associated instead with the rock plateau north of the present temple precinct, a plateau severely reduced during the Muslim period. If the Antonia guarded the precincts, then these structures dominated the lower city on the southeast hill, the southern part of which was a slum area, but the northern part a district much favored by devout Jews because of its proximity to the temple. In this northern district were the palace of Adiabene (*J.W.* 5.252) and the Theodotus → synagogue of Greek-speaking Jews (Jeremias, 75-76), from which might well have come the Hellenistic circle to which Stephen belonged (Acts 6–7).

The upper city on the southwest hill was dominated by the palace and citadel of Herod. The palace was built in the Persian-Hellenistic pavilion style in a garden setting (*J.W.* 5.176-81), on an artificial platform. Under Pilate it served as the Roman praetorium (Mark 15:16), though in the fourth century the hearing before Pilate was linked to the Hagia Sophia church in the area of the Hasmonaean palace (CSEL 39.62 etc.). North of the palace the southwest hill was defended by the citadel with the named towers Mariamne, Hippicus, and Phasaelus (*J.W.* 5.161-71); the foundations of the last of these still remain. In front of the palace was the agora, or place of assembly (Mark 15:8-15), the central point of a quarter in which the house of Caiaphas was located (Matt. 26:57; Mark 14:53-54). North of the Cross Valley was the section for handworkers and merchants (*J.W.* 5.331), which under Herod had been brought into the defensive system by a second north wall (5.146).

More recent burials in the present-day Muristan (Otto, 154-59) show that the area of the Church of the Holy Sepulchre, which is linked to the death and burial of Christ, was outside this second wall. Only under Herod Agrippa I (A.D. 41-44), with the extending of the "new city" to the north, was this area defended by a third wall that stretched northward to the present Damascus Gate.

7. Judaism, Christianity, and Islam

7.1. Jerusalem was taken by Titus (39-81, emperor from 79) in A.D. 70 after a six-month siege. He destroyed the city, including the temple. Hadrian (emperor 117-38) rebuilt it as a city for Roman veterans and a garrison town, dedicating it in 135 to Jupiter Capitolinus and renaming it Aelia Capitolina. These and earlier developments led to a rebellion under Simeon bar Kokhba (132-35) in the hope that God would not allow a final desecration of the temple and the Holy City and that, with the expulsion of the Romans from Jerusalem, he would set up his messianic kingdom. Only at the end of the third century, on the ninth day of the month Ab, supposedly the day of the destruction of the temple, were the Jews permitted to mourn at a part of the western wall of the temple that had not been destroyed. This practice started the tradition of the Wailing Wall.

→ Judaism is irrevocably linked to Jerusalem in its bemoaning of → sin and the → wrath of God; in its scribal preoccupation with the temple and the cult, which seeks to replace the expiatory function of the cult; and finally in the eschatological expectation of the building of a new temple as the initiation of the messianic kingdom (→ Eschatology 1; Kingdom of God).

7.2. After the destruction of Jerusalem by Titus, Christian → apocalyptic circles awaited the descent of the heavenly Jerusalem (Revelation 21). Representing the new earth, this renewed Jerusalem was the antithesis of → Rome, the representative of the old world (chaps. 17–18). The heavenly Jerusalem would belong to the Christians (21:2), who would be the new Israel and the new temple in the holy city (3:12). Hence there would be no need for the building of a new temple.

As apocalyptic expectation waned, Christian piety began to focus on the earthly Jerusalem as the place of the death and → resurrection of Christ (→ Christology 1) and of the early church (→ Primitive Christian Community). Already in the second century, Christian pilgrims were coming to Jerusalem from western parts of the empire and venerating the tomb of Christ. The early Byzantine Church of the Holy Sepulchre, built near the pagan temple, symbolized Titus's destruction of the temple of the old → covenant. In the Byzantine period the temple square was a sign of the judgment of God on the ruined city.

7.3. Under Jewish influence Jerusalem became important for Muḥammad (ca. 570-632) in the early stages of → Islam. In Medina he prayed toward Jerusalem and only later toward Mecca (Qur'an 2:143-45). After the Muslim conquest of Jerusalem (638), the Umayyads built the Dome of the Rock (685-91) and the Al-Aqsa → Mosque (early 8th cent.), thus forging a direct link with the Israelite-Jewish temple tradition, giving it an Islamic form.

Qur'an 17:1 relates the night ascension of the Prophet from the Holy Rock, which we may relate to the → ascension of Christ from the nearby Mount of Olives. For Muslims, Jerusalem ranks only after Mecca and Medina as a place of heavenly → revelation.

Relations between the three → monotheistic world religions — Judaism, Christianity, and Islam — are now regulated by the guarantee of unconditional → religious liberty in Jerusalem (→ Israel 3), a guarantee often sorely tested by the vagaries of Israeli-Palestinian disagreements.

Bibliography: N. Avigad, *Discovering Jerusalem* (Oxford, 1984) • M. Barker, *On Earth as It Is in Heaven: Temple Symbolism in the NT* (Edinburgh, 1995) • B. Chilton and C. A. Evans, *Jesus in Context: Temple, Purity, and Restoration* (Leiden, 1997) • C. Coüasnon, *The Church of the Holy Sepulchre in Jerusalem* (London, 1974) • A. Elad, *Medieval Jerusalem and Islamic Worship: Holy Places, Ceremonies, Pilgrimage* (Leiden, 1995) • O. Grabar, M. al-Asad, A. Audeh, and S. Nuseibeh, *The Shape of the Holy: Early Islamic Jerusalem* (Princeton, 1996) • L. J. Hoppe, *The Holy City: Jerusalem in the Theology of the OT* (Collegeville, Minn., 2000) • A. Houtman, M. Poorthuis, and J. Schwartz, eds., *Sanctity of Time and Space in Tradition and Modernity* (Leiden, 1998) • T. A. Idinopulos, *Jerusalem Blessed, Jerusalem Cursed: Jews, Christians, and Muslims in the Holy City from David's Time to Our Own* (Chicago, 1991) • J. Jeremias, *Jerusalem in the Time of Jesus* (Philadelphia, 1969) • K. M. Kenyon, *Digging Up Jerusalem* (London, 1974) • B. Mazar, *The Mountain of the Lord* (Garden City, N.Y., 1975) • E. Otto, *Jerusalem–die Geschichte der Heiligen Stadt. Von den Anfängen bis zur Kreuzfahrerzeit* (Stuttgart, 1980) • N. Rosovsky, *City of the Great King: Jerusalem from David to the Present* (Cambridge, Mass., 1996) • Y. Shilo, *Excavations of the City of David I, 1978-1982* (Jerusalem, 1984) • J. Z. Smith, *To Take Place: Toward Theory in Ritual* (Chicago, 1992) • A. D. Tushingham, *Excavations in Jerusalem, 1961-1967* (vol. 1; Toronto, 1985) • Y. Yadin, ed., *Jerusalem Revealed: Archaeology in the Holy City, 1968-1974* (Jerusalem, 1976).

Eckart Otto

Jesuits

1. Establishment and Purpose
2. Constitutions
3. Founding (1540) to Suppression (1773)
4. Restoration (1814) to the Present
5. Statistics
6. Current Activities

1. Establishment and Purpose

The Society of Jesus (*Societas Jesu*, S.J.), officially established in 1540, traces its origin to the coming together of → Ignatius of Loyola (1491-1556) and six of his companions who had been influenced by his *Spiritual Exercises:* Nicolás Bobadilla (1507-90), Pierre Favre (1506-46), Diego Laínez (1512-65), Simão Rodrigues (d. 1579), Alfonso Salmerón (1515-85), and Francis → Xavier (1506-52). At Montmartre in Paris on August 15, 1534, these men took a → vow of poverty and chastity and also vowed that, if possible, they would go on a → pilgrimage to → Jerusalem to visit the sites of Jesus' life and preach Christianity. By 1536 Paschase Broët (1500-1562), Jean Codure (1508-41), and Claude Jay (1504-52), similarly influenced, had joined the group. These ten made up the first members of the society. Prevented from going to Jerusalem in 1537, these men, by now all ordained priests, offered their services to the → pope in Rome in 1538 for → preaching, hearing confessions (→ Confession of Sins), catechetical instruction (→ Catechesis), and social work.

Early in 1539 this group resolved to found an order and drew up *Prima formula instituti*, which with few alterations was incorporated into the → bull *Regimini militantis ecclesiae*, by which Paul III (1534-49) approved the order on September 27, 1540. The society set itself the goal of "helping souls to progress in Christian life and doctrine and the propagation of the faith" under the banner of the cross "in service of the Lord and the Roman pope, his vicar on earth." Members of the order took the customary religious vows of poverty, chastity, and obedience, as well as a fourth vow of → obedience to the pope, thus expressing a readiness to undertake without hesitation any papal mission that was for the salvation of souls and the propagation of the faith. In 1541 Ignatius was elected the order's general superior. From then until his death 15 years later, he oversaw the development of the society and, most important, engaged in writing its constitutions.

2. Constitutions

In writing the → constitutions, Ignatius received much help from Juan de Polanco (1516-77), his secretary. Promulgated in trial form by Jerónimo Nadal (1507-80), one of the early Jesuits and a trusted collaborator of Ignatius, the constitutions were put into force by the first General Congregation (1558). New features as compared with other, earlier orders were the *Spiritual Exercises* as the primary personal formative experience of the members, the absence of a specific garb and choral prayer, the centralization of leadership in general and provincial superiors, a variety of "experiments" undertaken in the novitiate, a long period of probation, and different grades of membership. After two years novices — both those intending to be priests ("scholastics") and those who become lay brothers — take the three simple vows, from which the order can release them for cause. The "scholastics" (i.e., students) then study the humanities, philosophy, and theology, interrupted by a period of apostolic work, especially teaching.

After the completion of these studies and priestly → ordination, the members engage in a period of formation analogous to the novitiate. They then take final vows as spiritual coadjutors, or as professed of final vows. The structure is strongly monarchical but with ample provision for consultation. The general, advised by a group of assistants, has absolute power and appoints all the leaders. The General Congregation, the ultimate governing body of the society, which the assistants, provincial superiors, and elected representatives from each province attend, elects the general for life. This centralization is designed to make the order efficient in serving the cause of the church. The obedience is a full spiritual, sometimes called ascetic, obedience (→ Asceticism). Although the constitutions provide the order with its structure, the *Spiritual Exercises* shapes its inner spiritual principles and its external apostolic activities.

3. Founding (1540) to Suppression (1773)

The Society of Jesus grew rapidly. By 1615 it had 37 provinces (i.e., regional groupings), with total membership between 15,000 and 16,000. Although not established explicitly as a teaching order, the founding in 1547-48 of its first school specifically for lay students inaugurated education as a main focus of its work in secondary schools and → universities according to the principles laid down in *Ratio studiorum* (1599). These schools increasingly required teachers who were experts in fields beyond → philosophy and → theology, the disciplines customary for → priests, which led to Jesuits' becoming engaged in teaching and scholarship in almost every field of Western intellectual life.

The Jesuits also served as confessors to princes in the major courts of Europe, a role that often led to political involvement (→ Church and State). Pasto-

ral care was a major concern, especially in giving the *Spiritual Exercises,* in encouraging the sacrament of penance (now called → reconciliation) and frequent reception of the → Eucharist, in personal spiritual direction, and in the Marian congregations, which were started around 1565 for both → clergy and laity. With the aim of providing instruction and formation for the Christian life, P. Canisius (1521-1608) and R. → Bellarmine (1542-1621) wrote → catechisms that enjoyed widespread and long-lasting popularity.

Although the society had not been founded in opposition to the → Reformation, the range of its activities led naturally to its involvement in the Counter-Reformation. In addition to strengthening the Roman Catholicism of the Council of → Trent (→ Catholic Reform and Counterreformation), where several Jesuits took prominent parts as theological advisers, it also entered vigorously into theological controversies and pastoral initiatives, which the Protestant churches quite understandably regarded as adversarial. With these activities and their engagement in schools and universities, the Jesuits helped to shape the spirit of the post-Tridentine → Roman Catholic Church.

Jesuit → missionary work started by Xavier in the 1540s spread in the 17th century to Japan, China, and Latin America. In the age of Spanish and Portuguese conquest, Jesuits went as missionaries to newly opened overseas territories and made up for losses in Europe by successes based on the principles of accommodation and inculturation. In Latin America they brought social and cultural development, as well as conversion, by means of → reductions (i.e., Indian settlements) under missionary leadership. From around 1600 controversy and bloody persecution followed initial success in Japan. The Jesuits' acceptance of Chinese religious customs and their regard for Chinese culture involved them in the Rites Controversy of the late 17th and 18th centuries. The rejection of inculturation in the 1742 papal resolution of this controversy greatly impeded subsequent missionary work in China and to an extent also in India (→ Acculturation).

The Roman College, founded by Ignatius in 1551 and later known as the Gregorian University, became a major center of academic work, especially in philosophy and theology. In these disciplines the Jesuits largely adhered to → Thomistic → Scholasticism as it had blossomed afresh in 16th-century Spain under F. Suárez (1548-1617). The Jesuits also staffed several of the national colleges in Rome, among them the German and the English colleges, with the aim of training a cadre of learned and devout priests for their native lands. Bellarmine devoted himself to elaborating systematic theology, as well as controversial theology with Protestant orthodoxy.

From the middle of the 17th century, the society also came into conflict with → Jansenism. In the debates concerning the capacity or incapacity to perform good works with or without → grace and in conflicts concerning the quality of the contrition preceding the sacrament of penance, they took a less rigorous view than the Jansenists. B. → Pascal (1623-62), himself a Jansenist, heaped scorn on the Jesuits in his *Provincial Letters.*

The Jansenist and Rites controversies, the Jesuits' single-minded obedience to the pope, their various political entanglements, and the international character of the society aroused resentment against the order at the time of the → Enlightenment. A tendentious interpretation of the principle that the end justifies the means and a view of tyrannicide as legitimate were attacked as Jesuitical. From the middle of the 18th century, Enlightenment governments expelled the Jesuits from many European countries and their colonies. Portugal did so in 1759, France in 1764, Spain in 1767, Naples and Sicily in 1767 and 1768, and Parma in 1768. Under intense pressure from those governments, Pope Clement XIV (1769-74) finally felt compelled to disband the order, as he said, "for the peace of the church," doing so in 1773 in his papal brief *Dominus ac Redemptor noster.*

Frederick II (1740-86) in Prussia, however, as well as Catherine II (1762-96) in White Russia, who was keeping an eye on her recently annexed part of Poland, opposed the measure. They refused to promulgate the brief in their territories, which allowed the Jesuits to survive regionally, at first with tacit, and then with explicit, papal permission.

4. Restoration (1814) to the Present

Pius VII (1800-1823) restored the Jesuits universally on August 7, 1814, in his bull *Sollicitudo omnium ecclesiarum.* The society soon made up for its reverses, although various edicts and persecutions continued to limit its work in some countries. France in particular often impeded that work. Russia restricted the order and expelled the Jesuits in 1820, as also, for various periods, did Portugal, Spain, Switzerland, and several Latin American countries, often in reaction to the society's support of a developing → Ultramontanism. That circumstance and the society's championing of Vatican I led to the temporary banning of the Jesuits in Germany during the → Kulturkampf.

From the restoration until almost the middle of the 20th century, the Society of Jesus was much more conservative in thought and activity than it had been before it was suppressed. In the time immediately before and after World War II, however, Jesuits increasingly enlarged — both in breadth and in depth — the boundaries of their research, speculation, and activities. Exemplifying this change were several Jesuit scholars of the latter half of the 20th century, most notably Pierre Teilhard de Chardin of France in paleontology and spirituality; Karl → Rahner of Germany, John Courtney Murray of the United States, and Bernard Lonergan of Canada in → systematic theology; Henri de Lubac of France in → patristics; and Walter Ong of the United States in cultural studies.

As was true of the Roman Catholic Church in general, so in particular the Society of Jesus was greatly influenced by the Second → Vatican Council, at which several of its members played important parts as *periti* (i.e., expert theological advisers). The General Congregations since 1965 have responded vigorously and positively to the council.

The 31st General Congregation (1965-66), which took place during and after the last session of Vatican II, sought to adapt the internal life and external apostolic activity of the society to the visions of church and world that the council had developed. It elected as superior general Pedro Arrupe, a Spaniard who had spent years in Japan. The 32d (1974-75) specified the perennially central mission of the society in its contemporary circumstances to be the service of faith, of which the promotion of justice was an absolute requirement (→ Righteousness, Justice).

The 33d General Congregation (1983) confirmed the orientations of the previous two congregations and elected as general Peter-Hans Kolvenbach, a native of the Netherlands who had long worked in the Middle East. The 34th (1995) authoritatively annotated the original Jesuit constitutions, giving them a set of complementary norms as a current expression of the spirit of the original constitutions. It also situated the mission and ministries of the society, the service of faith and its integrating principle, the justice of the → kingdom of God, in the context of sympathetic engagement with other cultures and dialogue with other Christians, with members of other religious traditions, and with nonbelievers. Along with their attention to external apostolic works, these congregations have shown a renewed and explicit awareness of, and emphasis on, personal interior relationships with God and practices of spiritual discernment.

The first Jesuits to settle permanently in the United States came in 1634 as members of the Roman Catholic colonizers of Maryland, which was intended to be a haven for persecuted English Catholics. Only with the American Revolution, however, did Jesuits in the United States enjoy full religious toleration (→ Tolerance). At the restoration in 1814 there were 20 Jesuits in the United States. In the 19th century a good number came from Europe as missionaries; more important, the United States proved to be an extraordinarily fertile field for Jesuit vocations.

5. Statistics

Jesuit piety and activities have always attracted followers. There were 1,000 members when Ignatius died, and 22,601 at the suppression in 1773. On its restoration the society had 674 members, which rose to 15,073 in 1900, doubled to 30,579 in 1950, and reached its peak — 36,038 — in 1965.

In 2000 the society had 21,354 members living and working in 127 countries around the world, 8 of them having the presence of only a single Jesuit. Africa was home to 1,295 members (with the largest single contingent — 299 — in the Democratic Republic of the Congo), Asia and Oceania had 5,493 (India the largest with 3,766 members in 16 provinces), Europe had 7,170 (Spain the largest with 1,808 members), Latin America had 3,308 (Brazil the largest with 814), and North America had 4,088 (3,635 in the United States).

The greatest proportionate growth in number and geographic spread of the Society of Jesus since World War II has been in the → Third World. Between the years 1965 and 2000 the percentage of Jesuits in Africa increased from 1 to 6 percent of the worldwide total. In 2000 Jesuits were active there in 21 countries, including (besides Congo-Kinshasa) Madagascar (233 members) and Zambia (174). For the 38 countries in Asia with a Jesuit presence, the percentage of Jesuit membership doubled during the same period, from 13 percent to 26 percent. After India, the largest Asian provinces were the Philippines (367), Indonesia (305), and Japan (261). In Latin America, where the Society of Jesus began its service in the 16th century, Jesuit membership since 1965 has modestly increased its worldwide proportion from 12 percent to 15 percent of the total. In contrast, the number of Jesuits in Europe decreased during the same 35-year period from 47 percent to 34 percent of the total society membership, and in North America from 27 percent to 19 percent.

6. Current Activities

Several pontifical institutes in Rome are under Jesuit direction: the Gregorian University, the Biblical Institute, the Oriental Institute (→ Orthodox Church), the Vatican Observatory, and Vatican Radio. The society also continues to staff national colleges in Rome, residences for seminarians who are attending ecclesiastical universities.

Presently the activities of the Jesuits range from higher and secondary → education to parish ministry, from research institutes to spiritual centers, from programs of the fine and performing arts to agricultural stations, from justice advocacy to publishing houses. Jesuits publish more than 1,000 periodicals in 50 languages, including *America* and *Theological Studies* in the United States, *Stimmen der Zeit* in Germany, *Civiltà cattolica* in Italy, *Études* in France, *Razón y fe* in Spain, and *The Way* in England (→ Christian Publishing).

Education is the best known and most widespread work of the Jesuits in the United States, where they sponsor 46 secondary schools and 28 colleges and universities. Georgetown University, founded in 1789, was the first of its institutions of higher education, followed by St. Louis University in 1818 and then by 20 more colleges and universities in the 19th century, with 6 others added in the 20th century. Two national theological centers complete the roster of American Jesuit institutions of higher education. In 2000 these schools, which together had more than a million living alumni, enrolled 183,099 students and conferred 45,201 academic degrees. Other major Jesuit works in the United States include retreat houses and spiritual centers, a large number of parishes, and a great variety of social initiatives committed, especially in urban locations, to the service of the poor and the → marginalized. The 450 members of the two Canadian Jesuit provinces, anglophone and francophone, engage in similar works across that country.

Jesuits in Africa are heavily engaged in the seminary training of the native diocesan clergy, which is also growing rapidly. Jesuit education in general is a major commitment in African and Asian countries, with the most concentrated effort being made in India. There the society has more than 30 university colleges, 5 graduate faculties of theology and philosophy, almost 100 secondary schools, 10 technical/professional schools, and many primary schools connected with parishes. The promotion of justice and commitment to the poor and the marginalized in India has most conspicuously involved assistance to the Dalits.

As in the Third World developing countries, so

in Latin America the society is heavily engaged both in educational work and in social action projects. The latter have been undertaken in response to widely perceived structural inadequacies in Latin American political and social circumstances. That involvement has given the society a high and somewhat controversial profile, and at the same time it has encouraged an increase in → vocations since approximately 1970.

→ Religious Orders and Congregations; Spirituality; Theological Education

Bibliography: Documents of the General Congregations: D. R. Campion and A. C. Louapre, eds., *Documents of the Thirty-third General Congregation of the Society of Jesus* (St. Louis, 1984) • J. L. McCarthy, ed., *Documents of the Thirty-fourth General Congregation of the Society of Jesus* (St. Louis, 1995) • J. W. Padberg, ed., *Documents of the Thirty-first and Thirty-second General Congregations of the Society of Jesus: An English Translation of the Official Latin Texts* (St. Louis, 1977) • J. W. Padberg, M. D. O'Keefe, and J. L. McCarthy, *For Matters of Greater Moment: The First Thirty Jesuit General Congregations. A Brief History and a Translation of the Decrees* (St. Louis, 1994).

Other works: AHSJ • A. de Backer and C. Sommervogel, eds., *Bibliothèque des écrivains de la Compagnie de Jésus* (11 vols.; Paris, 1890-1932) with *Supplément au "de Backer–Sommervogel"* (2 vols.; ed. E. Rivière; Toulouse, 1911-30) • W. V. Bangert, *A History of the Society of Jesus* (rev. ed.; St. Louis, 1986) • D. L. Fleming, *Draw Me into Your Friendship: The Spiritual Exercises, a Literal Translation and a Contemporary Reading* (St. Louis, 1996) • J. de Guibert, *The Jesuits: Their Spiritual Doctrine and Practice* (St. Louis, 1964) • Ignatius of Loyola, *The Constitutions of the Society of Jesus* (St. Louis, 1970); idem, *A Pilgrim's Testament: The Memoirs of St. Ignatius of Loyola* (St. Louis, 1995); idem, *Spiritual Exercises and Selected Works* (New York, 1991) • D. Letson and M. Higgins, *The Jesuit Mystique* (Chicago, 1995) • D. Lonsdale, *Eyes to See, Ears to Hear: An Introduction to Ignatian Spirituality* (London, 1990) • MHSJ • J. W. O'Malley, *The First Jesuits* (Cambridge, Mass., 1993) • J. W. O'Malley, J. W. Padberg, and V. J. O'Keefe, *Jesuit Spirituality: A Now and Future Resource* (Chicago, 1990) • C. O'Neill and J. Domínguez, eds., *Diccionario histórico de la Compañía de Jesús* (4 vols.; Rome and Madrid, 2001) • J. W. Padberg, ed., *The Constitutions of the Society of Jesus and Their Complementary Norms* (St. Louis, 1996) • L. Polgár, *Bibliographie sur l'histoire de la Compagnie de Jésus, 1901-1980* (3 vols. in 6; Rome, 1981-90) • P. Vallin, "Jésuites," *DSp* 958-1065.

John W. Padberg, S.J.

Jesus

1. Sources
2. Origins
3. Jesus' Life
   3.1. Public Ministry
   3.2. Passion
4. Jesus' Mission
   4.1. Preaching
   4.2. Deeds
5. Messianic Self-Understanding
6. Message in the Church

1. Sources

The sources for an account of Jesus, both secular and Christian, are complex.

1.1. Ancient histories contain no direct references. The so-called *testimonium Flavianum* (Josephus *Ant.* 18.63-64) refers to Jesus as "a wise man, if indeed one ought to call him a man. . . . He was the Messiah." This passage, however, seems at least to have undergone Christian revision. In his account of the execution of → James, Josephus (*Ant.* 20.200) identifies James as the brother of Jesus, "the so-called Christ."

Suetonius (ca. 69-after 122) takes us back furthest. Then comes Tacitus (ca. 55-ca. 120). According to them, during the 40s in → Rome there were disturbances in the → synagogue regarding "Chrestus" (i.e., Christ; Suet. *Claud.* 25.4), and the fire of Rome led to a → persecution of Christians in A.D. 64 (Tac. *Ann.* 15.44; see also Suet. *Nero* 16.2). Whether Nero (54-68) knew that Christians derived their name from the Christ who had been executed under Pontius Pilate in the reign of Tiberias, or whether it was Tacitus who noted this information, we cannot tell.

Most of the rabbinic testimonies are worthless, being polemical and legendary. → Judaism largely avoided any direct naming of Jesus because he was deemed a heretic by the rabbis.

1.2. The earliest Christian sources are Paul's letters (→ Paul). They contain confessional formulas and statements (Rom. 1:3; 1 Cor. 11:23-25; 15:3-5) that presuppose wider knowledge.

The most important sources are the Gospels (→ Gospel 1). Most scholars think that the Gospels rely in part on older traditional materials, both oral and written. Matthew and Luke seem to share a common sayings tradition. Mark also seems to have had before him a → passion story, though it is arguable where it begins and ends. Mark also seems to have been the first to offer a connected account (ca. A.D. 70). Matthew and Luke followed the same outline;

John took an independent course and used material that came from a different stream or streams of tradition.

The depiction in the Gospels is not strictly historical but is much influenced by available traditions. The original tradition seems to have circulated in Aramaic among Jewish members of the Jesus movement in Palestine. In the NT, though, traditions about Jesus appear, except for isolated words, only in Greek. The authors passed down only the material that seemed important to them, and even then only in a form shaped by their own interests. Belief in the identity of the earthly Jesus and the risen Lord promoted further development of the tradition, but the Evangelists still aimed to give a historical account.

The history of Jesus can be deduced only through a critical analysis of the form and content of the individual pieces of tradition. But it is misleading to suggest, as some scholars have, that genuine Jesus material is to be found only in traditions that are distinct from first-century Jewish notions and from later Christian ideas. This so-called criterion of dissimilarity is unreliable (→ Jesus Seminar 3). Stated negatively, the primary concern for the historian is to determine whether a given tradition is unsuitable. Stated positively, the historian's aim is to demonstrate the coherence of traditions judged on other grounds to be authentic. Although the details of such an analysis are often uncertain, it can still yield positive results. What cannot be changed is the fact that our picture of Jesus is necessarily shaped by the choice of certain traditions.

2. Origins
The ancient tradition begins with the → baptism of Jesus by → John the Baptist (see also Acts 1:22; 10:37-38; 13:23-25; John 1:29-34). Although the traditions about the birth and infancy in Matthew and Luke do not supply information that rigorous analysis would find historical, they nonetheless do provide information about Jesus' origin and early life. He was brought up in Nazareth of Galilee (Mark 1:9; 6:3; John 1:45; 7:41-42), apparently in a family conscious of Jewish tradition (he and his brothers had biblical names, Mark 6:3). → David was allegedly his ancestor (Rom. 1:3; Eusebius *Hist. eccl.* 3.19-20). The year of his birth is not known for certain. He was about 30 years old when he began his ministry (Luke 3:23). His father was a carpenter, and he may have been one as well (Mark 6:3; Matt. 13:55).

Jesus' geographic and social background possibly gave him a certain breadth of outlook, but it was of no particular importance. He may have come under Pharisaic influence (→ Pharisees). The style of his preaching and disputing gives evidence of some theological training. He may have mastered Hebrew but usually spoke Aramaic. It is difficult to determine the extent to which he was literate. He left no written remains, but the Gospels portray him as very adroit in his appropriation of the Hebrew Bible.

Jesus was baptized by John. Jesus may have regarded his baptism as the sign and place of his calling, though in a way that we cannot determine in detail. It was undoubtedly of decisive importance, since the whole Christian tradition understood it as the beginning of his public ministry.

Jesus' message was closely akin to that of the Baptist. Its core was the urgent proximity of the → kingdom of God and an ensuing call for repentance (Mark 1:14-15 and par.). Along the lines of early Jewish → eschatology, his message took up that of the prophets. The Baptist had made this connection clear with his manner of life (Mark 1:6; Matt. 11:18). Judgment was accordingly John's predominant theme, though with individual application in distinction from the → Prophets. In this regard, as also in lifestyle, Jesus differed fundamentally from the Baptist. At least some of his disciples may have been former disciples of John (John 1:35-40). The kinship with John was obvious to outsiders (Mark 2:18; 6:14-16), and Jesus himself bore witness to it (Matt. 11:18-19; Mark 11:29-30; also Matt. 21:32).

Jesus clearly regarded John as a prophet. How John regarded Jesus is harder to tell. The fact that a Baptist community existed alongside the church for a time (e.g., Acts 19:1-7) might suggest that John did not fully acknowledge him. The question of Jesus' mission obviously occupied John in prison (Matt. 11:2-6 and par.). The public emergence of Jesus and John's imprisonment were close together in time (Mark 6:17, 14, 16). Mark 1:14 sees the relation in terms of salvation history, whereas John 3:22-30 stresses the function of John as an eyewitness.

3. Jesus' Life
3.1. *Public Ministry*
Galilee was the center of Jesus' ministry, → Jerusalem the place of the crucifixion. Mark focuses on the ministry in Galilee and surrounding areas to the north and east, the only mention of Jerusalem being in relation to Jesus' trip to celebrate → Passover and his ensuing passion there. The → Synoptic gospels give the impression that Jesus' ministry lasted only a year.

The fourth gospel, however, depicts Jesus' ministry taking place both in Jerusalem and in Galilee, which must have lasted two to four years, according to the feasts mentioned. Galilee around Lake Gennesaret and Capernaum was doubtless the center of his work, and his disciples were Galileans (Mark 14:70; John 7:52; Acts 1:11). Yet a longer ministry is far more likely, and the rich Jerusalem traditions in John could hardly fit into the shorter span suggested by Mark. Dovetailing the accounts into a detailed itinerary, however, is hardly possible, nor is the portrayal of any inner development.

3.2. Passion

Although the passion is the best-attested part of the story, considerable problems remain. A question arises whether the Friday crucifixion was on the 14th of Nisan (John) or the 15th (Synoptics). The account in John is probably secondary and has probably been influenced by John's understanding of Jesus as the true Passover Lamb (John 1:29; 19:36). The exact year is also debatable, but A.D. 30 or 31 is likely. The total ministry of Jesus was the ground of the complaint. This situation complicated prosecution by the Romans, but Jewish circles sharply opposed him. The tetrarch of Galilee, → Herod Antipas, was disturbed by his ministry (Mark 6:14-16; Luke 13:31).

At first the Pharisees were not opponents, and the Gospels' portrayal of them as such contains a fair amount of (anachronistic) inaccuracy (see Luke 7:36; 13:31a). The Pharisees were linked to Jesus by concentration on a life under God's eschatological will embracing all → Israel. Conflict arose over definition of this will. For the Pharisees it meant → sanctification in terms of the → Torah (→ Law); for Jesus it meant trust and devotion (to the fulfillment of Scripture).

The messianic claim of Jesus was the main thing that separated him from the Jewish groups of his day. This claim inevitably challenged those who were responsible for the Torah, and it could also have unsettled the Romans. The entry into Jerusalem had a marked impact, and the cleansing of the temple might well have been the decisive factor. The opportunity came with the offer of Judas to locate and identify Jesus. If it was desired to eliminate him as a deceiver of the people, crucifixion on a feast day was very appropriate. Jewish leaders handed him over to Pilate, who condemned and executed him. Whether there was a formal hearing before the Sanhedrin or, more likely, only a kind of preliminary investigation is not wholly clear. An important point for the Jewish authorities was the saying about the destroying and eschatological rebuilding of the temple (Mark 14:58; John 2:19; Acts 6:14).

As the inscription on the → cross shows (Mark 15:26; John 19:19), Pilate executed Jesus as a political rebel, indicating Roman concerns for violent upheaval and revolt. No doubt Pilate did not take Jesus seriously theologically, but he was more than willing to meet the demands of the Jewish leaders. Not surprisingly, he did not hunt down the followers of Jesus. As expected, they had left Jesus in the lurch (Mark 14:50), many of them returning disillusioned to Galilee (see Deut. 21:23; 17:13 [t. Sanh. 11:7]).

Nevertheless, a following quickly reassembled, convinced by Christophanies that Jesus had risen from the dead and received the life of the coming kingdom of God (→ Resurrection). This experience led to a new understanding of his end and ministry, and it was in this light that the story was remembered and transmitted.

4. Jesus' Mission

4.1. Preaching

The preaching of Jesus was shaped by the nearness of the kingdom of God, a notion that makes the present a time of urgent decision (→ Apocalypticism 3.2). Mark 1:15, although secondary, offers a good summary of the message. In the kingdom of God it is God himself who acts.

Jesus preferred to describe God's reality in → parables. In this way he made God immediately perceptible without making him an object. Judaism expounded the Torah in parables; Jesus set forth God himself in parables (Mark 1:22). The God whom Jesus proclaimed is the God who wills our → salvation. He is like the man who invites people to a feast (Matt. 22:1-14), the → father who joyfully welcomes back the son who has gone astray (Luke 15:11-32), and the master who pays full wages to all who work for him (Matt. 20:1-16). He is the God who will as surely complete his work as leaven will leaven the whole lump (Matt. 13:33 and par.), as the tiny seed will produce a great plant (Matt. 13:31-32 and par.), and as the seed will bear fruit (Mark 4:26-29). We must accept the invitation, or the divine offer, and return to God. The kingdom of God is → life (Mark 9:43-45), to which Jesus calls us.

The God who through Jesus will bring salvation to the world in the last time demands unconditional commitment. This God of whom Jesus spoke is the God of Israel, who through → Moses made his will authoritatively known. Jesus summoned people to do God's will totally (Matt. 5:17, an essentially authentic passage). As Jesus intended them, the antitheses of the → Sermon on the Mount (Matt. 5:21-48) do not annul the law but give the law its true function. In the teaching of Jesus, people must be ready for unconditional commitment to God, which includes love of one's → neighbor. The climax of the Torah is the twofold commandment of → love (Mark 12:28-34). A test of personal salvation is the giving or withholding of compassion (Matt. 25:31-46).

Unconditional dedication to God leads to unconditional salvation, for salvation is the sole will of God. In keeping with one strand in the Hebrew prophets, Jesus set the cult below commitment to God and neighbor (see Matt. 5:23-24; Luke 10:30-37; Matt. 9:13; 12:7). He promised salvation especially to "tax gatherers and sinners." This schematic phrase denotes those who by choice or due to circumstances were outside the religiosocial community in Judaism and hence had no → hope of salvation. God would accept them, as he would accept followers of the Torah who did not base their life on legal observance but on God's turning to the world (→ Kerygma).

4.2. Deeds

The work of Jesus consisted of acts as well as preaching. As the word expounds the act, so the act is the basis of the word. The promise of salvation corresponds to the fellowship that Jesus depicted by common meals. In this elementary gesture he turned especially to those not integrated into society in the usual way.

His → miracles in particular gave striking expression to his saving action. There can be no doubt that he did things that those around him regarded as miracles, even though individual accounts may be secondary (see Mark 3:22; Matt. 11:4-5; 12:28). The reply to the question of the Baptist in Matt. 11:3-6 shows the intended purpose of miracles: in them Jesus was fulfilling prophetic promises of the final age of salvation. Those who had been excluded from the religious or social community on physical grounds were made whole and reintegrated into the life of the people. He enacted what he proclaimed. He accepted outcasts. Some of the saving acts of Jesus took place on the → Sabbath, perhaps for the sake of demonstration.

Jesus expressed the purpose and significance of his mission by other symbolic acts as well. From among his followers he chose the → Twelve as representatives of the restored Israel, the end-time people of God (see Matt. 19:28). He also sent them out as his messengers to prepare the land of Israel symbolically for the coming of the end (Mark 6:7-13; Matt. 10:5-15).

Finally, he invaded the → temple precincts in a public act. He banished commercial dealings from the → sanctuary and thus achieved proleptically the eschatological purity of the place of worship. (Other interpreters have understood the act as his symbolically destroying the temple to make way for a new, eschatological temple made by God.)

5. Messianic Self-Understanding

The work of Jesus reflects a special sense of mission. As in the case of the Baptist, the prophetic elements in Jesus' ministry are unmistakable. But in the antitheses and in the relating of the parables to his own work there emerges a self-understanding that must be called messianic (→ Messianism).

According to the Gospels the term he most used was "Son of Man" (→ Christological Titles 2). This term occurs in all layers of the Jesus tradition, but in the NT it is restricted almost exclusively to his own sayings and is not used in early confessions. Scholars have long debated whether the Son of Man sayings go back to Jesus or are the product of early Christian reflection or at least development of the sayings tradition. But many of them probably do reflect his messianic self-understanding. The saying about confessing or denying Jesus and the corresponding action of the Son of Man at his coming (Mark 8:38; Luke 12:8-9) presuppose functional identity between Jesus and the Son of Man. Jesus evidently expected exaltation as Son of Man and believed that even in his public ministry he represented the coming Son of Man. Being God's representative in the world, he would be so in the coming world as well. This understanding explains the juxtaposition in the Gospels of statements attributed to Jesus that stress the urgently imminent future of salvation and those that emphasize its presence in his present work (e.g., Luke 11:20).

Many sayings relate the Son of Man to → suffering (Mark 9:31; Luke 17:24-25; see also John 3:14; 12:34). The Son of Man title also plays a role in the passion narratives (Mark 14:21, 62). Jesus possibly expected to be exalted as the Son of Man through suffering. He almost certainly had to reckon with the prospect of his own suffering and → death. This possibility became more of a certainty in his last days and hours (see already Luke 13:31-33). For this reason he linked the distributed bread and cup to his approaching death. He understood the elements to represent the life that he was about to offer up for many (→ Eucharist 2). In keeping is the saying that the Son of Man will give his life a ransom for many (Mark 10:45). Jesus regarded his approaching death as a final offering for a world that would not respond to the urgent summons of God made through him.

6. Message in the Church

The limitations of all historical writing affect the literary depiction of Jesus in the Gospels as well. This depiction seeks to understand him, but understanding is itself a historical process that links those who understand to the one they understand (→ Hermeneutics). The → primitive Christian community necessarily related its faith in the risen Lord to Jesus, who thereby became identified as the risen Lord. Christians today also understand Jesus only within their own historical horizons.

The name "Jesus Christ" proclaims the significance of Jesus for faith. God's action in Christ is set forth in the history of Jesus. The history of Jesus is essentially grasped when it is seen as God's action in Christ. The question of the continuity between Jesus and the developing → church arises in this regard. It exists when the church knows that in the historical development of its faith and life, it is being shaped by the → God who has definitively revealed himself in the Christ-history of Jesus (→ Christology 1). Jesus understood himself as God's last and authoritative messenger. He put not merely his word but his person, including his end, in this service. Accordingly, the messenger had to become the message.

→ Agrapha; Discipleship; Golden Rule; Incarnation; New Testament Era, History of; Parousia; Peter; Q; Sadducees; Scribes; Zealots

Bibliography: D. ALLISON, *Jesus of Nazareth: Millenarian Prophet* (Minneapolis, 1998) • M. BORG, *Jesus: A New Vision* (San Francisco, 1987) • G. BORNKAMM, *Jesus of Nazareth* (Minneapolis, 1995; orig. pub., 1956) • R. E. BROWN, *The Birth of the Messiah: A Commentary on the Infancy Narratives in the Gospels of Matthew and Luke* (New York, 1993); idem, *The Death of the Messiah: From Gethsemane to the Grave. A Commentary on the Passion Narratives in the Four Gospels* (New York, 1994) • R. BULTMANN, *The History of the Synoptic Tradition* (rev. ed.; New York, 1976); idem, *Jesus and the Word* (New York, 1989; orig. pub., 1926); idem, *Theology of the NT* (2 vols.; New York, 1951-55) • B. CHILTON and C. A. EVANS, eds., *Studying the Historical Jesus: Evaluations of the Current State of Research* (Leiden, 1994) • J. D. CROSSAN, *The Historical Jesus: The Life of a Mediterranean Jewish Peasant* (San Francisco, 1992) • G. W. DAWES, ed., *The Historical Jesus Quest: Landmarks in the Search for the Jesus of History* (Louisville, Ky., 2000) • M. DIBELIUS, *Jesus* (Philadelphia, 1949; orig. pub., 1939) • B. D. EHRMAN, *Jesus: Apocalyptic Prophet of the New Millennium* (New York, 1999) • P. FREDRIKSEN, *From Jesus to Christ: The Origins of the NT Images of Jesus* (New Haven, 1988); eadem, *Jesus of Nazareth, King of the Jews* (New York, 1999) • J. P. MEIER, *A Marginal Jew: Rethinking the Historical Jesus* (3 vols.; New York, 1991-2001) • N. PERRIN, *Rediscovering the Teaching of Jesus* (New York, 1967) • E. P. SANDERS, *The Historical Figure of Jesus* (London, 1993); idem, *Jesus and Judaism* (Philadelphia, 1985) • A. SCHWEITZER, *The Quest of the Historical Jesus: A Critical Study of Its Progress from Reimarus to Wrede* (New York, 1968; orig. pub., 1906) • G. VERMES, *Jesus the Jew: A Historian's Reading of the Gospel* (London, 1973) • N. T. WRIGHT, *Jesus and the Victory of God* (Minneapolis, 1996).

TRAUGOTT HOLTZ

Jesus People

1. Origins
2. Characteristics
3. Growth and Decline
4. Implications

1. Origins

The Jesus People were theologically conservative → youth in the United States who emerged as a group distinct from the hippie → counterculture during the late 1960s and early 1970s. Initially the product of attempts by a few evangelical pastors and youth workers to evangelize hippies, the movement spread and began to attract a following among church youth. After a period of intense media publicity, the movement's style and jargon were widely adopted by evangelical young people across the nation, who used the Jesus People as a basis to create a parallel evangelical version of the larger youth culture.

The beginnings of the Jesus People movement can be traced to the San Francisco Bay area, where in 1965 a group of young bohemian converts began to gather within John MacDonald's First Baptist Church in Mill Valley, California. As thousands of seekers and troubled youth descended upon San Francisco during 1967's "Summer of Love," the Mill Valley group persuaded MacDonald of the physical and spiritual needs of the growing hippie population. MacDonald in turn appealed to several Bay Area Baptist leaders, who provided funds for the group to establish the Living Room Coffeehouse in the middle of the Haight-Ashbury district. At about the same time Kent Philpott, a young seminarian at the Southern Baptist's Golden Gate Seminary, opened the Soul Inn Coffeehouse in the basement of the Lincoln Park Baptist Church to feed and shelter hippie youth. Together, the two establishments made contact with thousands of young people before they closed in late 1968.

While San Francisco was the home of the movement's first stirrings, its early stronghold was farther to the south in and around the Los Angeles area. There, on the Sunset Strip, the His Place of Southern Baptist youth worker Arthur Blessitt achieved considerable success working with drug addicts and runaways (→ Substance Abuse). Meanwhile Don Williams, First Presbyterian of Hollywood's youth pastor, had begun the Salt Company Coffeehouse, which attracted high school age youth interested in the counterculture. Most successful of all was Calvary Chapel in Costa Mesa, where Pastor Chuck Smith led his small congregation in reaching out to the local hippie population. Smith oversaw the establishment of a string of communal houses and allowed folk and mild rock music styles into the churches' worship services and Bible studies; by 1969 the church was bursting at the seams. While these most successful examples of the nascent movement had direct ties to the evangelical mainstream (→ Evangelical Movement), other very visible groups that emerged in the Los Angeles area, such as Moses David Berg's radically separatist Teens for Christ (later, the → Children of God) and Tony and Susan Alamo's ultrafundamentalist Alamo Foundation, represented a cultic, authoritarian underside of the Jesus People (→ Fundamentalism).

By 1969 and 1970 the movement was in evidence outside southern California. The Christian World Liberation Front (CWLF) had been established in the radical hotbed of Berkeley. The Shiloh network of communes maintained a number of communal houses and farms in and around Portland, Oregon. In Washington State Linda Meissner's Jesus People Army had established a number of communal houses and coffeehouses throughout the state, as well as a branch in Vancouver, British Columbia. Elsewhere, Jesus People communes, coffeehouses, and fellowships sprang up in a number of places across North America, including Kansas City, Cincinnati, Milwaukee, Toronto, Buffalo, rural upstate New York, Norfolk, and Atlanta.

2. Characteristics

Although the combination of counterculture and evangelical religion that produced the Jesus People was utterly unexpected, the two subcultures manifested a number of affinities. First, the exuberant style of Pentecostal worship (→ Pentecostal Churches) was attractive to hippies, who tended to be interested in the mystical (→ Mysticism) and who valued spontaneity and emotional openness. Second, the black and white churches of the South were the musical roots of the rock music that played such a central role

within the counterculture. Third, the evangelical emphasis on the end times — particularly as characterized in this period by the popularity of books like Hal Lindsey's *Late Great Planet Earth* (1970) — mirrored hippie perceptions of the → apocalyptic direction of modern America. Fourth, evangelicalism's traditional associations with rural America, its primitivist tendencies, and its outsider status fitted nicely with countercultural sensibilities and nostalgia for simpler times. Finally, evangelical views about → sin and the need for → salvation seemed convincing as dreams of a hippie utopia unraveled amid evidence of the physical, psychological, and social pathologies of permissive sex and drug use.

Because of the unorganized nature of the overall movement, local circumstances and personalities played important roles in shaping the nature and direction of various Jesus People groups. Nonetheless, there was a general pervading ethos that characterized the larger movement. True to their countercultural roots, beards for men, long hair for both sexes, and hippie fashions were the defining couture of the Jesus People. Their → worship services were emotional and often characterized by the display of the Pentecostal gifts of the Spirit (→ Charisma 1). Most of the movement maintained a general distrust of the religious establishment, which could mean anything from a disapproval of "cold" non-evangelical congregations to viewing all established churches with disdain (as was the case with the Children of God). They venerated the Bible, devoting hours to reading, memorizing, and "rapping" about its meaning. For the most part the Jesus People were very literalistic in their understanding of the Scriptures (→ Exegesis, Biblical), which fed their penchant for the apocalyptic. This factor also contributed to a vital emphasis on → evangelism.

While the Jesus People commune was perhaps the purest distillation of the movement, its predominant institution was the coffeehouse, which served as gathering place, evangelistic center, and communication point for groups in different locales. One of the strongest factors binding together the sprawling movement was its adaptive use of popular culture. Jewelry, posters, buttons, and bumper stickers emblazoned with slogans and symbols provided a visible means of self-identification. Underground "Jesus papers" such as the *Hollywood Free Paper* and the CWLF's *Right On!* enjoyed regional and, at times, national circulation within the movement. Most important, however, was "Jesus music," a hybrid of folk, pop, country, gospel, and rock styles that served as an omnipresent vehicle for worship, evangelism, and entertainment. Through exposure on the coffeehouse circuit and through a growing number of regional "Jesus festivals," a market arose for recordings by popular Jesus music singers and bands.

3. Growth and Decline

The year 1971 marked a floodtide of publicity as the Jesus People were "discovered" by America's leading periodicals and broadcast networks. Much of this coverage was undoubtedly triggered by the controversy that swirled around the November 1970 release of the British rock opera *Jesus Christ Superstar*. Certainly, the cultural dissonance of the combination of hippie music and fashions with the "old-time religion" also played a role in its becoming a major story. Perhaps even more important, the Jesus People made for an upbeat, reassuring "youth angle" after several years of stories about rioting youth, draft dodgers, drug use, and the sexual revolution. Coverage in the secular press triggered an outpouring of interest in the religious press as well, particularly within evangelical circles, where the Jesus People were looked upon as evidence of the enduring cultural relevance of Christianity and as a harbinger of a coming national → revival.

With media exposure (→ Mass Media) the Jesus People movement exploded across North America during 1971 and 1972, fueled by a torrent of evangelical youth eager to identify with the movement. Existing groups like the Shiloh communities and the Children of God attracted numerous recruits, while hundreds of new communes, fellowships, and coffeehouses sprang up. Just as important, Jesus People themes, music, and jargon were incorporated into the existing youth programs of churches, high school–based groups like Campus Life, and successful youth evangelism programs such as the Spiritual Revolution Now campaigns among Southern Baptist young people in the southwestern United States (→ Youth Work).

The high-water mark of the Jesus People movement came in June 1972 with Campus Crusade for Christ's EXPLO '72 in Dallas, Texas. The weeklong event, which attracted 80,000 young people, was both a convincing demonstration of the Jesus movement's strength and its absorption by mainstream evangelicalism. Following EXPLO, however, the secular press paid little attention to the movement, and by mid-1973 it had become old news in the religious press as well.

Despite this lack of publicity, the Jesus People movement held forth at the grassroots level well into the late 1970s. That it finally began to fade partly reflected the fact that its adherents were growing older and making life decisions that took them away from an active role in the movement. Probably an even more significant factor, however, was the changing direction of the youth culture. As the counterculture receded and new musical styles and the subcultures that surrounded them grew in popularity, the style of the hippie-based Jesus People was increasingly out of step with the times. The up-and-coming cohort of evangelical youth, attracted to new music, clothing, and hairstyles, sought new ways to relate to a rapidly fragmenting set of youth cultures.

4. Implications

Although the Jesus People movement lasted only about a decade, its influence upon the larger evangelical subculture was profound. Thousands of movement converts entered seminary or moved into positions in various evangelical parachurch ministries, and tens of thousands more blended into local congregational life and ministry. A number of parachurch organizations (e.g., Jews for Jesus), the multimillion-dollar contemporary Christian music industry, and some of America's fastest-growing denominations of the late 20th century (including Calvary Chapel, Hope Church, and the → Vineyard) trace their roots directly back to the Jesus People. On a more general level, the informality of the Jesus movement's music and worship altered the practices of nearly all evangelical churches. It also paved the way for the "seeker-friendly" phenomenon as embodied in congregations such as Willow Creek Community Church of South Barrington, Illinois.

Clearly, however, the most important result of the Jesus People movement was its direct impact upon the evangelical youth scene. The Jesus People served as a bridge back to the American mainstream for many of the countercultural youth who joined the movement during the 1960s and 1970s. For the evangelical youth caught up in its enthusiasm, it provided a way to negotiate the boundaries between family religious loyalties and their peer group. As such, the Jesus People persona provided a means by which youth could maintain their religious identity during adolescence. Overall, evangelicalism's adaptation of the Jesus People movement was the culmination of a trend (traceable back to the Youth for Christ movement of the 1940s) that gradually accepted the validity of an evangelical equivalent to the larger, overarching youth culture.

Bibliography: D. DiSabatino, *The Jesus People Movement: An Annotated Bibliography and General Resource* (Westport, Conn., 1999) • R. S. Ellwood, *One Way:*

The Jesus People Movement and Its Meaning (Englewood Cliffs, N.J., 1973) • R. M. Enroth, E. E. Erickson, and C. B. Peters, *The Jesus People: Old-Time Religion in the Age of Aquarius* (Grand Rapids, 1972) • L. Eskridge, "'One Way': Billy Graham, the Jesus Generation, and the Idea of an Evangelical Youth Culture," *CH* 67 (1998) 83-106 • G. D. Kittler, *The Jesus Kids and Their Leaders* (New York, 1972) • C. McDannell, *Material Christianity: Religion and Popular Culture in America* (New Haven, 1996) esp. chap. 8, "Christian Retailing" • D. E. Miller, *Reinventing American Protestantism: Christianity in the New Millennium* (Berkeley, Calif., 1997) • J. T. Richardson, M. W. Stewart, and R. B. Simmonds, *Organized Miracles: A Study of a Contemporary, Youth, Communal, Fundamentalist Organization* (New Brunswick, N.J., 1979) • C. Smith, with H. Steven, *The Reproducers: New Life for Thousands* (Glendale, Calif., 1972).

Larry Eskridge

Jesus Seminar

1. Founding
2. Results
    2.1. Jesus' Sayings
    2.2. Jesus' Deeds
3. Evaluation
4. Significance

The Jesus Seminar is a consultation of historical scholars that meets regularly in America. They are best known for a project undertaken from 1985 to 1996, when they considered the historical authenticity of sayings and deeds attributed to → Jesus in all documents before A.D. 300. They published their findings in two major works, *The Five Gospels* (1993) and *The Acts of Jesus* (1998). The work was controversial in that it challenged or denied the historicity of many biblical traditions, and the ensuing scandal was heightened by the group's facility at attracting attention in the popular realm. Through frequent interaction with print and television media (→ Mass Media), the Jesus Seminar brought the quest for the historical Jesus into the homes of average Americans, and its work was discussed in congregational and civic settings that bypassed the usual conventions of academia.

1. Founding

The Jesus Seminar was founded by Robert W. Funk and officially sponsored by the Westar Institute, a California-based nonprofit educational foundation directed by Funk. The latter, a scholar of international renown and author of several books on the literary interpretation of the Gospels, was for a time executive director of the Society of Biblical Literature. John Dominic Crossan, also a widely published and highly regarded scholar, served as cochair of the seminar.

Membership was open to all persons with academic credentials and a willingness to suspend personal religious convictions in order to consider matters on the basis of historical evidence alone. The group met twice a year, with 30-40 scholars in attendance at each session. Over 200 persons were associated with the group at one point or another, with 74 signing the roster for *The Five Gospels,* and 79 for *The Acts of Jesus.*

2. Results

2.1. *Jesus' Sayings*

In the first phase of its work, the seminar reviewed a database of sayings attributed to Jesus in various sources. After circulating papers and hearing arguments regarding the authenticity of each saying or group of sayings, members voted on the degree of authenticity they thought could be attributed to the material. Such votes were color-coded: *red* indicated a high likelihood of authenticity, *black* a low likelihood, with *pink* and *gray* showing relative degrees of moderate uncertainty. The results were tabulated in *The Five Gospels,* which printed the texts of the four canonical gospels and that of the apocryphal *Gospel of Thomas* (→ Nag Hammadi) with the words of Jesus printed in red, pink, gray, or black as indicated by weighted averages of the seminar's voting. In the seminar's findings, the Gospel of Mark contained only 1 red saying and 234 black ones. John contained no red sayings (and only 1 pink), with 134 black. Matthew and Luke, with 11 and 14 red sayings, respectively, fared only slightly better.

The results were thus overwhelmingly negative. Most of the sayings deemed authentic, furthermore, were generic moral or philosophical observations that were not particularly religious (e.g., Matt. 5:39-42; Mark 12:17; Luke 10:30-35). Most of the red and pink sayings are in fact ones believed to derive from the → Q source used by Matthew and Luke in composition of their gospels. Well-known Bible verses classified as black sayings include Jesus' words regarding the salt of the earth (Matt. 5:13), bearing the cross (Mark 8:34), and being born again (John 3:3). All seven of Jesus' words from the cross are regarded as inauthentic (Mark 15:34; Luke 23:34, 43, 46; John 19:26-30), as are most of his sayings about himself, including both his claim to be the Messiah (Mark 14:62) and his assertion about being "the way, and the truth, and the life" (John 14:6). All sayings in which Jesus spoke of the end of the world or a final judgment are black. Monologues by Jesus to which there could have been no witnesses are considered to be counterfeit, as are all verses in which Jesus expresses foreknowledge of events after his death. By contrast, three sayings in the *Gospel of Thomas* were accorded red status, including two parables of Jesus not found in the canonical texts.

2.2. *Jesus' Deeds*

The seminar next considered deeds attributed to Jesus, with similar results. Out of 176 reported events, the seminar selected only a handful that could be deemed probably or even possibly authentic. The seminar affirmed that Jesus was baptized by → John and became an itinerant teacher in Galilee, proclaiming the → kingdom of God and conducting a ministry that involved curing sick people and → exorcizing those who thought they were demon possessed. He also consorted with social outcasts, told parables, and inspired hostility in some who thought he was mad or an agent of Beelzebub. He was crucified during the prefecture of Pontius Pilate. The seminar soundly rejected, however, the historicity of Jesus' birth to a virgin, the notion that he worked miracles other than possibly psychosomatic healings, and the claim that his body came back to life after he was put to death.

The portrait of Jesus that emerged from these studies was that of a secular folk hero who was not given to making theological statements about God. He styled himself not as a prophet but as a popular social critic, ridiculing what he considered to be the empty values of his society. Favorite targets of his wit were reliance on wealth, uncritical respect for blood relatives, and the pomposity of religion. He put forward no program of his own beyond what he regarded as commonsense observations about life. Thus, he encouraged communal sharing, radical compassion, and inclusive hospitality. Jesus described the kingdom of God as a present reality, visible in an egalitarian community life in which he called all people to participate.

Journalists found the image of scholars "blackballing Jesus" to be irresistible, and for over a decade the group's findings were regularly reported in newspapers with sensationalist headlines (e.g., "Scholars Determine Jesus Did Not Teach the Lord's Prayer"). Every major newsmagazine in America did at least one cover story on the Jesus Seminar during the 1990s, and members of the group were frequently featured on television programs. Funk himself argued for a "new reformation" in Christianity that would reject a "creedalism" built around

nonhistorical supernatural events (esp. the virgin birth, miracles, and the resurrection). He encouraged Christians to practice the inclusivity and reciprocal forgiveness that Jesus favored, while rejecting most of the historic doctrines that churches have taught concerning Jesus.

3. Evaluation

Evaluation of the Jesus Seminar has often been emotional. Luke Timothy Johnson (Emory University), for example, attacks it in *The Real Jesus.* Howard Clark Kee (Boston University) called the group "an academic disgrace," and Richard Hays (Duke University) accused the seminar of "reprehensible deception" for presenting conjectural ideas to the public as though they were assured results of scholarship. More pointed criticisms have focused on methods of research, the credibility of the group's findings, and on how its results are to be interpreted.

A related critique, probably the single greatest objection to the seminar's published work, is that it reports as historically inauthentic what is in fact only unverifiable: proving that there is no historical evidence to substantiate the claim that Jesus was born of a virgin, for example, is not equivalent to establishing that it did not happen (→ Historiography). The Jesus Seminar, in the mind of many observers, moves too quickly from the one claim to the other.

Methodologically, many critics charge that the seminar gave too much weight to the criterion of dissimilarity, which holds that reported items about Jesus are more likely to be authentic when they present him in ways that differ from what was commonplace for Palestinian Judaism, as well as from what became normative for early Christianity. When such a criterion is pushed too far, it can prejudice inclusion of data that would present Jesus as the necessary link between Palestinian Judaism and the → early church (→ Jewish Christians), predetermining a portrait of a generic figure who is not very Jewish and who has little in common with his followers.

In broader terms, the question has been raised whether individual traditions can legitimately be evaluated in piecemeal fashion apart from an overall hypothesis. The assumption implied by such a question is that the seminar members must have had some such vision (e.g., → secularization) that guided them in their deliberations and predetermined the results. Likewise, the group's supposed neutrality has been challenged, insofar as "lack of commitment to a faith perspective" can be construed as constituting an → ideological orientation in its own right.

Some of the seminar's findings were received — at least initially — as implausible. The Jesus Seminar maintains that Jesus had no recognizable → eschatological vision, and thus members generally take all material that presents him as speaking in → apocalyptic language about the future (e.g., the fate of Israel, the final judgment, or the imminent end of the age) to be inauthentic. Is this conclusion really credible, some ask, when both John the Baptist, Jesus' mentor, and the apostolic community of his followers, including → Paul, clearly entertained notions along these lines?

Furthermore, some wonder, if Jesus was basically just a witty spouter of aphorisms who befriended peasants and reached out to the → marginalized, why would he have been regarded as dangerous? Unless he was thought to be some kind of prophet, even a → messiah, why would powerful authorities unite in seeking his execution? The seminar's response to the latter point is to deny that there was any focused attempt to eliminate him. Contrary to the biblical accounts, Jesus was allegedly caught up in some cavalier pogrom of potential troublemakers. If perhaps he staged some kind of symbolic demonstration in the temple court during the Passover feast, he might have caught the attention of the Romans, who did not distinguish between social critics and political revolutionaries, and simply been executed without trial.

Such a construal of Jesus' death, however, requires that the → passion narratives of the Gospels be regarded as almost totally fictive, which illustrates another hurdle the seminar has encountered in convincing people of their minimalist conclusions. At least the first three gospels were written within two decades of the deaths of people who knew Jesus well and who died as a result of their loyalty to him (→ Synoptics). Within such a short span of time, and given such intense commitment, is it really likely that those responsible for these gospels would have gotten so much so wrong so quickly?

Finally, even those who do accept the Jesus Seminar's findings differ somewhat in their interpretation of the research. Marcus Borg, a prominent member of the seminar, has indicated that the large amount of "gray" material should not be deemed "probably inauthentic" but, rather, "inconclusive." Often, says Borg, pink and black votes would cancel each other out, so that material deemed gray was that over which there had been sharp division.

4. Significance
Although it has had minimal impact in the rest of the world, the Jesus Seminar was enormously influential on late-20th-century NT scholarship in the United States. Several persons associated with the seminar have continued to be influential participants in Jesus studies, including Funk, Crossan, Borg, Kathleen Corley, Gerd Lüdemann, and Stephen J. Patterson. Other scholars — including Dale Allison and N. T. Wright — have articulated their views in conscious distinction to those of the Jesus Seminar, reflecting in a negative way the range and impact of the group's work. By the turn of the 21st century the Jesus Seminar had become a force to be reckoned with in historical Jesus studies (at least in its homeland); whether building on its claims or discounting them, no Jesus scholar could afford to ignore them.

→ Liberal Theology; Literature, Biblical and Early Christian, 2; New Testament Era, History of; Sociohistorical Exegesis

Bibliography: M. J. Borg, *Jesus in Contemporary Scholarship* (Valley Forge, Pa., 1994) • R. W. Funk, *Honest to Jesus: Jesus for a New Millennium* (San Francisco, 1996) • R. W. Funk, R. W. Hoover, and the Jesus Seminar, eds., *The Five Gospels: The Search for the Authentic Words of Jesus* (New York, 1993) • R. W. Funk and the Jesus Seminar, eds., *The Acts of Jesus: The Search for the Authentic Deeds of Jesus* (San Francisco, 1998) • L. T. Johnson, *The Real Jesus: The Misguided Quest for the Historical Jesus and the Truth of the Traditional Gospels* (San Francisco, 1996) • R. J. Miller, *The Jesus Seminar and Its Critics* (Sonoma, Calif., 1999) • M. A. Powell, *Jesus as a Figure in History: How Modern Historians View the Man from Galilee* (Louisville, Ky., 1998) • M. J. Wilkins and J. P. Moreland, eds., *Jesus under Fire: Modern Scholarship Reinvents the Historical Jesus* (Grand Rapids, 1995).

Mark Allan Powell

Jewish Christians

1. Biblical and Patristic Period
  1.1. Term
  1.2. Sources and Spread
  1.3. Theology
2. Historical Development to the Present
  2.1. Development since Antiquity
  2.2. Today
  2.3. Theological Questions

1. Biblical and Patristic Period
1.1. *Term*
The loose term "Jewish Christians" takes on sharp contours only when it is used in agreement with patristic sources. It is used for Christians who link

their confession of Christ to a theology and lifestyle of Jewish structure (M. Simon, G. Strecker).

1.2. *Sources and Spread*

The early Christian fathers from the time of → Irenaeus (d. ca. 200) describe Jewish Christians. There are quotations from perhaps three Jewish-Christian gospels (→ Apocrypha 2.1.2), and there is a reference to Jewish Christians in the Pseudo-Clementines (→ Pseudepigrapha 2).

Jewish Christians lived in → Jerusalem up to its destruction in A.D. 70. We have testimony to their presence in → Alexandria and → Rome in the third century. From archaeology it has been learned that they survived in northern and eastern Palestine up to the fourth century. They were strong in Syria up to the fifth century.

1.3. *Theology*

The → primitive Christian community was a Jewish eschatological conversion movement. Notwithstanding its rite of → initiation and its fellowship meal, it was part of → Judaism. Criticism of the cult by Hellenists (Acts 6–8; 11) who were driven out of Jerusalem and who accepted pagans in → Antioch prepared the way for → Paul, who, on the basis of the → cross and → resurrection of → Jesus Christ, denied that the → law can save (→ Salvation). At the apostolic council (A.D. 48; → Acts of the Apostles §8), it was recognized that → Gentile Christians need not keep the law. Jewish Christians, however, were still to be bound by it. The Jewish-Christian mission was committed to → Peter.

→ James, head of the community from 49, laid strong emphasis on observance of the law (Gal. 2:11-13; Acts 21:20-26). Radical Jewish Christians wanted to bind Gentile Christians to it as well (see Galatians and Philippians 3). After the slaying of James in A.D. 62 by the Jews, the movement separated from Judaism, a division sealed by the historically debated flight of Jewish Christians to Pella in Transjordan (A.D. 66) and the reference to them in the Eighteen Benedictions (ca. A.D. 90).

In the days of → Justin Martyr (ca. 100-ca. 165), Jewish Christians were still tolerated in the church. The Gospel according to the → Ebionites and the Gospel of the → Nazarenes are based on the Synoptic tradition. The Ebionites observed both the → Sabbath and the Lord's Day. Because the Jewish Christians tended to be anti-Pauline, the canonizing of Paul's epistles (→ Canon 2.2) was divisive, as were also the → Gnostic inclinations of Jewish Christians. Even more difficult was the fact that the Jewish Christians, apart from the Nazarenes, could accept Christ only as a prophet or an angel (→ Christology). Hence the judgment of → Jerome: "They want to be both Jews and Christians, but they are neither Jews nor Christians" (*Ep.* 112.13).

→ Early Church

Bibliography: J. Daniélou, *The Theology of Jewish Christianity* (Chicago, 1964) • J. D. G. Dunn, ed., *Jews and Christians: The Parting of the Ways, A.D. 70 to 135* (Grand Rapids, 1999) • M. Hengel, "Between Jesus and Paul," *Between Jesus and Paul: Studies in the Earliest History of Christianity* (Philadelphia, 1983) 1-29 • F. S. Jones, "Jewish Christians," *Eerdmans Dictionary of the Bible* (ed. D. N. Freedman; Grand Rapids, 2000) 709-10 • G. Luedemann, *Opposition to Paul in Jewish Christianity* (Philadelphia, 1989) • H.-J. Schoeps, *Jewish Christianity: Factional Disputes in the Early Church* (Philadelphia, 1969) • M. Simon, *Verus Israel: A Study of the Relations between Christians and Jews in the Roman Empire, 135-425* (New York, 1986) • G. Strecker, *Das Judenchristentum in den Pseudoklementinen* (2d ed.; Berlin, 1981); idem, "Judenchristentum und Gnosis," *Altes Testament, Frühjudentum, Gnosis* (ed. K.-W. Tröger; Gütersloh, 1980) 261-82 • P. Vielhauer and G. Strecker, "Jewish Christian Gospels," *NT Apocrypha* (rev. ed.; 2 vols.; ed. W. Schneemelcher; Philadelphia, 1991) 1:134-78.

Helmut Merkel

2. Historical Development to the Present

2.1. *Development since Antiquity*

The development of Christianity into a state religion with toleration for → Judaism changed the situation of Jewish Christians for the worse. The last remnants of their communities were either absorbed into the larger church by the sixth century or were opposed as heretical. Jews converting to Christianity (→ Jewish Mission) now joined the dominant church, which recognized them only if they gave up their previous identity. In point of fact the → baptism of all Jews was decreed in Spain in 613, and in the Byzantine Empire and France in 632. Although these decrees did not lead to the permanent elimination of Jews in those countries, it is clear that their position was made increasingly difficult. Nevertheless, in the → Middle Ages Jewish Christians were often called, with a hostile purpose, to represent Jewish teachings (e.g., in formal disputations). At times they were able to render valuable service in mediation between Jews and Christians.

From the Jewish standpoint Jewish Christians were suspected of → conversion only for base motives, such as fear of martyrdom, apostasy, or career advancement. Conversely, coerced conversion, as in Spain and Portugal in the 14th and 15th centuries, raised the suspicion of crypto-Judaism. As renegades, Jewish Christians were viewed as dead by the Jews and with enduring suspicion by Christians. Such suspicion led to increasing discrimination and, as in the → Inquisition, to outright persecution.

Since the 19th century the question of Jewish-Christian congregations and → identity has been posed afresh. In 1884 J. Rabinowitz founded a Jewish-Christian congregation in Kishinev, Bessarabia (now Chişinau, Moldova), and the International Jewish Christian Alliance was founded in 1925. The persecution of Jews in the Third Reich (→ Holocaust) made many Christians of Jewish or Jewish-Christian descent come to terms with the question of their identity. Not being Aryans, they could be persecuted no less than Jews. After the founding of the State of Israel in 1948, Jewish-Christian congregations came together there, and since about 1970 there have been several in the United States and Canada.

2.2. Today

There are still Jewish Christians who hide their Jewish descent. Increasingly, however, converted Jews stress their Jewish identity. Jewish-Christian congregations are gaining in importance. In Israel such congregations are found in the confessional churches, but they also exist as independent and strongly evangelical messianic assemblies (→ Evangelical Movement). From just a handful in the 1970s, their number grew to over 35 by 1999.

Common to all Jewish Christians is the search for a liturgical life that will express their identity (including → Sabbath worship, the → Hebrew language, use of the Psalms, celebration of the → Passover, and other biblical-Jewish customs). The title "Messianic Jew" has increasingly come into use, stressing as it does both adherence to the Messiah → Jesus (→ Messianism) and the preservation of Jewish identity.

In the United States and Canada, as a result of the 1967 Six Day War and the → Jesus People movement, there has been, among both Jews and Christians, an increasing awareness of a Jewish-Christian presence. The group Jews for Jesus, under M. Rosen, using unconventional evangelistic methods especially among urban young people, is very strictly organized but for the most part refrains from forming its own congregations. In 2003 the Union of Messianic Jewish Congregations under D. Juster, founded in 1979, comprised 84 congregations in the United States, plus 8 in five other countries. The → worship of these congregations is oriented strongly to the model of the → synagogue. The Fellowship of Mes-

sianic Congregations under A. Fruchtenbaum is more traditionally Christian. In 1998 the U.S. Center for World Mission (Pasadena, Calif.) estimated that there were 132,000 Jews worldwide who see Jesus as their Messiah and Savior; messianic congregations or synagogues exist in approximately 15 countries.

2.3. Theological Questions

At the present time there are only the beginnings of an independent Jewish-Christian theology. The main issue is how to preserve Jewish identity within Christianity. The adoption of → Jewish practices presupposes biblical roots. At times, however, the adoption of rabbinic rules (e.g., Juster's suggestion to use the 613 commands and prohibitions of the → Torah) is also considered.

Jews for the most part do not accept the separate existence of Jewish Christians. A person born of a Jewish mother is a Jew (see Gal. 4:4), but the Supreme Court of Israel has ruled that conversion to another religion cancels one's existence as a Jew. Nevertheless, there are some Israelis who do not rule out the future recognition of Jewish Christians.

On the Christian side the starting point is that Acts 15 does not exclude the preservation of Jewish identity within Christianity. Gal. 3:28 ("there is no longer Jew or Greek") is not opposed to this preservation. Jewish Christians can serve Christianity as a whole by helping it to rediscover its Jewish roots. Their existence also constitutes a warning against all → anti-Semitism.

　　　→ Jewish-Christian Dialogue

Bibliography: A. BAUMANN, Judenchristen heute (Hannover, 1988) • D. BERGER and M. WYSCHOGROD, Jews and "Jewish Christianity" (New York, 1978) • A. FRUCHTENBAUM, Hebrew Christianity: Its Theology, History, and Philosophy (Grand Rapids, 1974) • D. JUSTER, Jewish Roots: A Foundation of Biblical Theology for Messianic Judaism (Rockville, Md., 1986) • K. KJÆR-HANSEN, Joseph Rabinowitz and the Messianic Movement (Grand Rapids, 1995); idem, ed., Jewish Identity and Faith in Jesus (Jerusalem, 1996) • P. VON DER OSTEN-SACKEN, Christian-Jewish Dialogue: Theological Foundations (Philadelphia, 1986) • S. PINES, The Jewish Christians of the Early Centuries of Christianity according to a New Source (Jerusalem, 1966) • D. A. RAUSCH, Messianic Judaism: Its History, Theology, and Polity (New York, 1982) • H.-J. SCHOEPS, Jüdisch-christliches Religionsgespräch in neunzehn Jahrhunderten (Frankfurt, 1949) • D. W. TORRANCE, The Witness of the Jews to God (Edinburgh, 1982).

　　　　　　　　　　　　　　　　ARNULF BAUMANN

Jewish Mission

1. Biblical Foundations
2. Historical Development
   2.1. Protestant Churches
   2.2. Roman Catholic and Orthodox Churches
3. Continuing the Mission
4. From Mission to Dialogue

1. Biblical Foundations

Jewish mission does not have merely an abstract basis (e.g., Christianity's claim to absoluteness or the universal nature of → salvation) but rests partly on the concrete experiences of earliest Christianity. → Jesus was aware of being sent to "the lost sheep of the house of Israel" (Matt. 15:24), and it was to them that he symbolically sent out the → Twelve (Mark 6:7-13). Furthermore, the message of Jesus as Messiah spread first "in Jerusalem, in all Judea and Samaria" (Acts 1:8), and then in other places to Jews and various God-fearers. In the initial stages it was not clear that the message concerning Christ was also for → Gentiles (Matt. 15:21-28; Acts 10). It was also debated whether → baptism should not be linked to conversion to → Judaism (Acts 15). The question of Christian Gentiles engaging in missions to the Jews hardly arose in the NT, since there were Jews and → Jewish Christians in every place (1 Cor. 12:13; Gal. 3:28). The fundamental NT position is that the → gospel is for everyone, but for Jews first (Rom. 1:16), since without them there would be no Christianity.

2. Historical Development

On the basis of biblical experience there have always been Jewish conversions. However, all attempts of state churches from the time of Constantine (306-37) to force → conversion (§1) upon the Jews (e.g., through compulsory baptism, forced disputations, the → Crusades, the → Inquisition, pogroms) must be regarded as denying the basic NT position.

2.1. *Protestant Churches*

The → Reformation did not at first greatly change the attitude shaped by the early church's anti-Judaism. According to that position, the regnant church is justified in exploiting its own position of → power to impose Jewish integration. Although new approaches were anticipated by later Protestant → orthodoxy (§2; e.g., the federal theology of J. Cocceius of Leiden and E. Edzard's proselytizing work in Hamburg), → Pietism was the first to renounce force in favor of → proclamation to individuals. The Jewish mission now began in the strict sense.

In 1728 J. H. Callenberg founded the Institutum Judaicum et Muhammedicum in Halle, which produced writings and sent out → missionaries who claimed no privileges but engaged in conversations with Jews on the same social level. → Revivals, with their enthusiasm for → mission, brought a new thrust. The London Society for Promoting Christianity among the Jews was founded in 1808, and similar societies followed in Berlin (1822), Basel (1830), Cologne (1843), and Leipzig (1871). Functioning like other mission endeavors, these societies aimed at individual conversion, to this end sending out missionaries to the centers of Jewish population in eastern Europe. The names of these groups testify to a sense of material distinction from Gentile mission. Many individual missionaries, serving apart from organized societies, were also at work.

The Jewish mission could count on a certain measure of goodwill but hardly exerted much influence on the churches or aroused any great love for the Jewish people. The number of conversions was relatively small. Leading representatives such as F. Delitzsch in Leipzig and H. L. Strack in Berlin opposed → anti-Semitism, though the Jewish mission itself was not entirely free from the idea of assimilation or from anti-Jewish thinking. National Socialism brought Jewish missions to a halt in Germany just as they were coming into increased dialogue with Jews (1930-33), though there was solidarity with the persecuted in, for example, Austria and Romania.

The shattering experience of the → Holocaust led many Jewish mission societies to give up their work (e.g., in Holland, Cologne, and Berlin) and, under new names, to turn to → Jewish-Christian dialogue (as happened, e.g., in Sweden, Switzerland, Great Britain, and East Germany; see 4).

2.2. *Roman Catholic and Orthodox Churches*

In the → Roman Catholic Church the brothers Alphonse and Theodore Ratisbonne, converted Jews who had become priests, founded the Fathers and Sisters of Our Lady of Zion in 1843, orders for Jewish mission. After → Vatican II redefined the relation between Christianity and Judaism (*Nostra aetate* 4), these orders rejected the aim of conversion, reorienting themselves instead to the "friendly discussions" specified in *Nostra aetate*. Still, however, individual conversions of Jews continued.

The older attitude may still be found in the → Orthodox Church and the → Oriental Orthodox Churches. Individual conversions take place, but there is no organized Jewish mission.

3. Continuing the Mission

There has been an unbroken tradition of Jewish mission in Scandinavia, the Church of England, the

Reformed Church in England, the U.S. Lutheran Church–Missouri Synod, and many evangelical church bodies. Work also continues in Germany with new emphasis upon the need for → dialogue, upon the overall relationship to Judaism, and upon support for Jewish Christian congregations.

A new thrust came with the → Lausanne movement (beginning with the 1974 Lausanne Covenant; → Evangelical Movement), from which the Lausanne Consultation on Jewish Evangelism arose in 1980. The consultation, which held its sixth international conference in New York in 1999, promotes the Jewish mission worldwide (→ Evangelical Missions).

Arising in San Francisco in 1973 out of the → Jesus People movement, the evangelical group Jews for Jesus conducts an aggressive, confrontational style of → evangelism in the United States and several other countries, arguing that acceptance of faith in Jesus does not entail rejection of one's Jewish heritage. It faces vigorous opposition from the group Jews for Judaism and from current Judaism generally (but see recent work by D. Cohn-Sherbok), which maintains that one cannot both be a Christian convert and be considered a Jew.

4. From Mission to Dialogue

Since World War II a bifurcation of Christian thought regarding the Jewish mission has widened and deepened. Recent studies, such as the widely read work of J. Carroll, have sensitized many in and out of churches to the intolerance and arrogance that have marked Christians in their attitudes toward Jews throughout the two millennia just past. While missions to the Jews remain active in conservative church circles, the mainline denominations have moved from mission to dialogue, often decrying the forms of Christian triumphalism that have nourished the Jewish mission in the past. The work of Y. S. Ariel offers a comprehensive discussion of past and present activities of this mission in the United States (→ Proselytism).

Those preferring to emphasize dialogue point to the enrichment possible in the present global village when Christians view positively the broad spectrum of religious life existing throughout the world. A proper entry to any fellowship is the stance of authentic dialogue, which identifies common points (e.g., among Judaism, Christianity, and → Islam) but also seeks to understand the differences in respect to presuppositions, basic tenets, and the various doctrinal, liturgical, and social consequences of the respective faith commitments. Such dialogue greatly facilitates coming to points of mutual agreement, common experience in → worship, and joint ethical expression in the face of social injustice.

Bibliography: Y. S. Ariel, *On Behalf of Israel: American Fundamentalist Attitudes toward Jews, Judaism, and Zionism, 1865-1945* (Brooklyn, N.Y., 1991); idem, *Evangelizing the Chosen People: Missions to the Jews in America, 1880-2000* (Chapel Hill, N.C., 2000) • A. Brockway, ed., *The Theology of the Churches and the Jewish People: Statements by the World Council of Churches and Its Member Churches* (Geneva, 1988) • J. Carroll, *Constantine's Sword: The Church and the Jews. A History* (Boston, 2001) • D. Cohn-Sherbok, *Messianic Judaism* (London, 2000) • Consultation on World Evangelization, "Christian Witness to the Jewish People," *How Shall They Hear?* (Wheaton, Ill., 1980) • K. Kjær-Hansen, ed., *Jewish Identity and Faith in Jesus* (Jerusalem, 1996) • A. Sovik, ed., *Christian Witness and the Jewish People* (2d ed.; Geneva, 1977) • D. W. Torrance, ed., *The Witness of the Jews to God* (Edinburgh, 1982) • H. Ucko, *Common Roots, New Horizons: Learning about Christian Faith from Dialogue with Jews* (Geneva, 1994) • G. Wigoder, *Jewish-Christian Relations since the Second World War* (Manchester, 1988).

Arnulf Baumann and Roger S. Boraas

Jewish Philosophy

1. Definition
2. Biblical Period and Antiquity
3. Middle Ages
4. Jewish Mysticism
5. The Enlightenment to Hermann Cohen
6. Franz Rosenzweig to the Contemporary Period

1. Definition

Jewish philosophy is the development by Jewish thinkers, in general conceptual terms, of what it means to be a Jew. One commonly used medieval triad defines the main subjects of Jewish thought as → God, → Torah (including revelation, the process by which it came to be), and the people of → Israel (§1). Topics like creation, redemption, life after death, the land of Israel, and prayer are often also part of comprehensive Jewish philosophies.

Each philosophy of → Judaism is written by a particular person in a specific time and place, and thus it is not surprising that each philosophy responds to its age and environment both in the topics on which it focuses and in its approach to those topics. Moreover, Jewish philosophy has been influenced by dominant trends in the larger intellectual world. Since Jews have lived virtually everywhere in the world, Jewish history is entangled with universal history. Sometimes Jews have readily assimilated the thought of others and in some way made it Jewish, and sometimes they have simply rejected other views. Most often, however, Jews have been eclectic, adopting some points from non-Jewish philosophers while rejecting others.

As in other traditions, the distinction between Jewish philosophy and → Jewish theology is not a sharp one, especially since some thinkers write what they themselves have termed "theology" in some of their works and "philosophy" in others. In general, however, → theology is an exploration of ideas by people who themselves are committed to their tradition and are speaking to an audience who is likewise within that particular tradition. → Philosophy, in contrast, may be written by persons committed to a given tradition, but it is addressed to those both within and outside that tradition, and so its criteria for acceptable argumentation must satisfy the perhaps more stringent intellectual standards of outsiders who have no vested interest in accepting the tradition's claims.

2. Biblical Period and Antiquity

The biblical period extends from → Abraham (ca. 1700 B.C.E.) to Daniel (ca. 160 B.C.E.), and the classical rabbinic period extends from about 200 B.C.E. to 500 C.E. While the Bible and rabbinic literatures of the → Mishnah, → Talmuds, and → Midrash contain a plethora of important ideas, systematic philosophy among the Jews did not develop until Philo of Alexandria (b. 15-10 B.C.E., d. C.E. 45-50), or arguably not until Sa'adia ben Joseph (882-942, sometimes known by his title *gaon,* "head [of an academy]"). Thus while many of the books of the Bible, the Apocrypha, and rabbinic literature affirm some ideas and deny others, sometimes even with rudimentary argumentation, none presents an extended, reasoned approach to these issues that is intended for both non-Jewish and Jewish audiences.

Biblical writers were clearly interested in affirming the Jewish → covenant with God, which would continue from Abraham through all generations. The land of Israel and progeny would be Israel's primary rewards for observing the covenant, while God would gain a people who would be "a priestly kingdom and a holy nation" (Exod. 19:6), whose task it was to be "a light to the nations" (Isa. 49:6), a model of the kind of life that God really wanted people to live. Biblical authors thus rail in particular against idolatry and immorality, the cultic and moral opposites of the covenantal ideals. God created the world and will ultimately bring a → mes-

siah to make it ideal (Isa. 2:2-4; 10:27–12:6, esp. 11:1-12); in the meantime, Israel's job is to obey God's commandments so as to be God's partners in making this a better world.

When the Jews came into contact with the Persians in the sixth century B.C.E. and then later with the Greeks in the fourth century B.C.E., they assimilated some of the ideas of these people and resisted others. The task that Jewish philosophy set itself in Hellenistic Roman antiquity was not so much that of wrestling with popular → polytheistic religions and the → emperor worship that was cultivated as an ideology of → state. It was rather that of gaining victory in the competition with Greek philosophical → monotheism and its related → ethics (→ Hellenism; Hellenistic-Roman Religion). It had to show that Jewish monotheism was the pure and untainted model.

With the help of Stoic terms, God was thought of as ruling the cosmos with his power (Wis. 1:7; *Ep. Arist.* 132; Josephus *Ant.* 8.107 and *Ag. Ap.* 2.184-85), which goes along with the teleological argument (Wis. 13:5, 9; *Ant.* 1.155-56; → God, Arguments for the Existence of). The law leads to → virtues (*Ep. Arist.* 144-51, 168; 4 Macc. 1:17-18; 5:22-24; *Ag. Ap.* 2.146; *Gen. Rab.* 44:1), which culminate in the four cardinal virtues: prudence, justice, fortitude, and temperance (Wis. 8:7; 4 Macc. 1:6, 18). Aristobulus (3d-2d cent. B.C.E.), whom Eusebius (ca. 260-340) and Clement of Alexandria (ca. 150-ca. 215) wrongly regarded as a Peripatetic, held the same doctrine of God. Extant fragments show that he dealt with the problem posed by biblical anthropomorphism. Popular philosophical ideas of the last three centuries B.C.E. and the first century of the Common Era are articulated in the biblical books of Ecclesiastes and Daniel, in the didactic poem of Pseudo-Phocylides, the *Epistle of Aristeas,* the Wisdom of Solomon, 4 Maccabees, and the works of Josephus (ca. 37-ca. 100 C.E.).

Rabbinic literature also manifests Persian, Greek, and Roman influence. While the rabbis primarily continued and developed earlier biblical themes, they also borrowed from Greek and Roman thought, just as they borrowed from Greek and Roman law. The wording of the Torah, however, often stood in the way of commitment to any specific school. Those who have the promise that God will bless the fruit of their body, land, and cattle (Deut. 28:4) could not agree with → Stoicism that health, well-being, and children are → adiaphora, or matters of indifference. Agreeing, however, with Alexandrian philosophy in a resultant eclecticism, the rabbis adopted elements of Plato (427-347 B.C.E.; →

Platonism) — particularly his *Timaeus* and *Laws* — and Stoicism. At the same time, the → rabbis stereotyped Epicurus (341-270 B.C.E.) and his followers as the absolute enemies of God who deny fundamental principles of Jewish faith.

Philo of Alexandria is the only Jewish thinker before Saʿadia Gaon who approaches systematic thought. Thanks to the early church, which saw in him a kind of → church father, most of his writings have survived, from which his approach clearly emerges. By absorbing theology into ethics, Philo could view the Torah as the supreme philosophical system. He methodically arranged the individual commands, including narrative portions, and related them to virtues. The commands oriented to God relate to intellectual virtues, which contain true theology. Those oriented to people relate to ethical virtues, headed by the four cardinal virtues. They are the basis of → happiness *(eudaimonia),* which consists, to the extent possible, of the *imitatio Dei* (imitation of God).

Influential in the further development of the concept of God was Philo's interpretation of the uniqueness of God, whose existence is proved cosmologically and ontologically, and also the simplicity of God. God is simple, without admixture or confusion, and is self-sufficient. To create and govern the world, this God needs intermediate beings in a hierarchy of being. To avoid a danger that is immanent in the → philosophy of religion, namely, that of losing Jewish distinctiveness, Philo stressed theologically the priestly and prophetic task of the Jewish people in relation to humanity as a whole, a thought that often recurred in the period that followed. While Philo's approach is thus coherent and well integrated, he developed much of it in the standard rabbinic mode of commentaries on biblical texts; not until Saʿadia was the form of the thought, as well as its substance, clearly systematic.

3. Middle Ages

After the model of Arab philosophy, which for its part rested on → Greek philosophy as mediated by Syrian Christians, Jewish philosophy in the Middle Ages worked out its own systematic presentations. It was mostly written in Arabic, but Hebrew translations followed and gave us the titles that are usually cited today. We may distinguish four groups: followers of the eclectic school known as kalam (Arab. *kalām,* "speech"), Neoplatonists, Aristotelians, and critics of → Aristotelianism. Yet there is also a good deal of overlapping. These approaches reflect various differences, yet they share in a common battle to uphold the unity of God. On the one hand, this

unity was thought to be threatened by the Christian doctrine of the → Trinity; on the other, the divine attributes might be misunderstood as hypostatizations. → Islam and Christianity also challenged the claim to absoluteness of the revelation in the Torah.

3.1. With his definition of the close relation between → reason and → revelation, Saʿadia ben Joseph was perhaps the true founder of Jewish philosophy. His main work was *Sefer emunot ve-deʿot* (Book of beliefs and opinions). In content, he argued, reason and revelation (i.e., the Torah) are the same, and thus reason on its own can know the truth of revelation. Revelation is for the purpose of instruction. It helps those who cannot think for themselves to acquire the truth, protects thinkers from error, and promotes the identity of reason and revelation. It also specifies the particulars of commandments, for which reason can give only a general rationale. He divides the commandments into those of reason, which for the avoidance of error repeat what reason may know, and those of → obedience, which God in his goodness and wisdom has revealed in order to make observance of the commandments of reason easier. God is the Creator God, whose nature is known in his acts but who, on account of the inadequacy of language, we describe by the terms "life," "power," and "wisdom." Strictly, however, God possesses only two formal attributes: unity and uniqueness.

3.2. The first medieval Jewish Neoplatonist was Isaac ben Solomon Israeli (ca. 850-ca. 950). He further developed Philo's concept of God's → emanations to explain not only how God rules the world without becoming tainted or limited by it but also how God creates it. From the first matter and form God creates only intellect, from which emanates → soul. As in Aristotle, soul for Israeli is rational, animal, and vegetative. The aim of philosophy is *imitatio Dei* by achieving the highest virtues.

The most significant and original representative of Jewish Neoplatonism, however, came a century later in the figure of the Spaniard Solomon Ibn Gabirol (ca. 1020-ca. 1057). Ibn Gabirol proposed a fully developed series of emanations. God is the first substance, followed by divine will, universal matter, universal form, intellect, soul, nature, and the world of the senses. Ibn Gabirol bridged the gulf between simple uncreated being and the multiplicity of the created — between God and the world — by his doctrine of matter and form. Matter is basic and general. The divine will stamps form upon it as that which is specific and supported. Individual being is thus given to matter. In contrast to God, who is necessary, matter is only possible, although it makes possible and determines the multiplicity of → creation. The act of creation is God's affair. Since we possess very little of this tradition, it is not surprising that the authorship of Ibn Gabriol's book *Fons vitae* (Fountain of life; Heb. *Maqor ha-hayyim*), which is completely extant only in Latin translation, was misattributed to either a Muslim or a Christian philosopher (called Avicebron or Avencebrol) as late as the 19th century.

Bahya ben Joseph ibn Pakuda (11th cent.), in his *Duties of the Heart* (ca. 1080), focuses on describing a life of → piety. He contrasts the commands of reason and revelation, which are combined as external → duties, to the duties of the heart, which have as their object the relationship to God. At their head, as the presupposition, is the duty of knowing God. In the familiar proof of the kalam, namely, from creation to a Creator, we also find teleological features. The unity of God is discussed in Neoplatonic terms. The stress falls on understanding all the attributes relating to God's work only as the negation of their opposites, which is true even of such formal attributes as existence, unity, and eternity (→ Negative Theology [Western]). For followers of the Torah, Bahya commends an asceticism that seeks a middle way.

The 12th century saw a series of Neoplatonists like the mathematician and astronomer Abraham bar Hiyya, who wrote the first philosophical works in Hebrew; Joseph ibn Tzaddik; the poet Moses Ibn Ezra; the grammarian Abraham Ibn Ezra; and Judah ha-Levi (ca. 1075-1141), perhaps the most famous representative of this school. Ha-Levi's *Sefer ha-Kuzari* (Book of the Khazar) is a warm defense of Judaism. In it the king of the Khazars puts questions to a philosopher, a Christian, and a Muslim, but he finds the answers of a Jewish scholar so satisfying that he, together with his whole realm, converts to Judaism. Very much in contrast to the → rationalists of his time, ha-Levi places the locus of religious authority not in reason but in revelation. He then argues that ultimately the Christian and Muslim revelations depend on the veracity of the Jewish revelation, which alone was attested by 600,000 people standing at Mount Sinai. Unlike many of the rationalist philosophers who focus on the experience of the individual, ha-Levi emphasizes the idea of God's election of the people of Israel as a whole. This election is a specific prophetic endowment of the people that the full development of the Torah makes possible in the land of Israel. The → salvation of the world comes through the people of Israel.

3.3. The first Jewish representative of Aristotelianism was Abraham Ibn Daud of Toledo (d. ca. 1180), who borrowed from Ibn Sīnā, and whose major philosophical work, *Sefer ha-emuna ha-rama* (Book of sublime faith), is extant only in two Hebrew translations. He did not use Aristotle's proof from the moved to the first mover but argued from the possible, which is caused, to the necessary, which is not caused, and which must be one, infinite, and incorporeal — that is, God. He avoided attributing positive attributes to God. The Torah, which he considered the perfect practical philosophy, includes ethics, economics, and politics and is the way to the perfection of practical reason. The nonrational cultic commandments support the rational commandments, and the doctrines of faith lead to the perfection of theoretical reason. Since God as their author is immutable, so too the Torah is immutable. It cannot be abolished, nor can it be corrupted, as Christians and Muslims have done. As in the thought of Judah ha-Levi, for Ibn Daud Israel has a prophetic task that is tied to the land.

Jewish philosophy in the Middle Ages reached its climax with Maimonides (Moses ben Maimon, Maimuni, 1135-1204) in his systematic work *More nevukhim* (The guide of the perplexed). Here God is proved by arguing from movement to the first mover, from moved movers to the unmoved mover, from corruptible being to eternal being, from potentiality to pure actuality. God has no positive attributes, for his absolute unity and simplicity transcend such attributes, even those of relation, since he is the only one to exist necessarily. There is a place, however, for negative attributes, which uphold God's uniqueness, and also for positive attributes of action, which point to the pure causality of God. The positive attributes that we find in the Bible are strictly negations of privations.

Maimonides holds firmly to the creation of the world, viewing it as a world that went forth from God; he uses the testimony of the Torah to decide what he claims Aristotle found inconclusive, namely, whether the world existed eternally or was created. The intellectual commandments of the Torah mediate perfect knowledge, which leads to love of God and immortality. The ethical commandments lead to the perfection of virtues. The knowledge of God and ethics come together in the *imitatio Dei* insofar as it is made possible by knowledge. It consists of being like God in his deeds. Only philosophers know the whole law, but the one immutable and inalienable Torah communicates to the people the basic truths that Maimonides had summed up in his "Thirteen Basic Doctrines" (→ Jewish Theology 2), part of his *Mishneh Torah* (The Torah reviewed), an earlier code of Jewish law.

Thanks to Maimonides, Aristotelianism flourished within Judaism, but there was also debate as to the orthodoxy of his school. The last significant Aristotelian was a scholar from the south of France, Gersonides (Levi ben Gershom, 1288-1344). We know his practical philosophy chiefly from his biblical commentaries. His ideas about God and the world are found in his main work, which was written in Hebrew, *Sefer milḥamot Adonai* (Book of the wars of the Lord). God is supreme thought; for him there is no distinction between thought and → nature, which includes existence and unity. Unlike Maimonides, Gersonides found a place for positive attributes, since conceptual differentiation does not imply multiplicity, and since the qualities ascribed to other beings all derive from the divine attributes. He argued teleologically for the creation of the world.

3.4. Although no enemy of philosophy, Ḥasdai ben Abraham Crescas of Gerona (1340-1410) opposed the predominance of reason that philosophy had accorded to Judaism. In his *Or Adonai* (The light of the Lord, 1410), he developed the basic doctrines of Judaism in an ascending series:

1. the basic presuppositions of all religion: God's existence, unity, and incorporeality;
2. the six presuppositions of revelation: God's knowledge, → providence, and omnipotence; also prophecy, human → freedom, and → teleology in the Torah and the world;
3. eight obligatory doctrines that are independent of specific commandments: the creation of the world, the → immortality of the soul, reward and → punishment, the → resurrection of the dead, the eternality of the Torah, the supremacy of → Moses as a prophet, the ability of the Urim and Thummim to foretell the future (e.g., Exod. 28:30), and the coming of the Messiah; also three obligatory doctrines that are directly rooted in specific commandments: the efficacy of prayer and of the priestly benediction, God's readiness to accept the penitent, and the spiritual value of the High Holidays and the festivals; and
4. thirteen nonobligatory doctrines (e.g., concerning paradise and hell [no. 9]; concerning the impossibility of knowing God's essence [no. 13]).

Proof of God involves deduction from things that might exist to that which necessarily exists. Positive attributes can be ascribed to God because they are not the nature whose presupposition is existence but are only inseparably linked to it and to one another. The Torah, which is the reward for faithfulness and suffering prior to the Sinai revelation, redeems from the powers that sway people to do wrong; in all its commandments the Torah aims at → love of God and eternal felicity.

Crescas's pupil Joseph Albo (ca. 1380-ca. 1444), in his popular work *Sefer ha-ʿiqqarim* (Book of principles), works out a system of Judaism on the basis of the three basic doctrines of the existence of God, revelation, and reward and punishment. With fear of God, → joy, and love, the Torah mediates a disposition to happiness in this world and to eternal life in the world to come. It also gives the knowledge that we need to reach this goal.

4. Jewish Mysticism

While the roots of Jewish → mysticism go back to the 2d century C.E., the major works of Jewish mysticism were written in the 13th century and thereafter. This mysticism comes in two forms: → cabalism and → Hasidism.

4.1. Cabalism is largely the product of Spanish Jewish intellectuals, including a number of rabbis. They wrote in Spain or, when Jews were expelled from Spain during the Inquisition in 1492, in Israel. This form of mysticism was strongest between the 13th and 16th centuries. Mystical works of this type were committed to writing, and they reinforced the necessity to obey Jewish → law by giving it new meaning.

The first major work of this type of mysticism, the *Sefer ha-zohar* (Book of splendor) was written in the 13th century by Moses de León (1250-1305). Other important authors of this school include Moses Cordovero (1522-70; see his *Tomer Devorah* [Palm tree of Deborah]) and Isaac Luria (1534-72), who introduced several significant changes in Jewish mysticism. Joseph Karo (or Caro, 1488-1575), author of *Shulḥan ʿarukh* (Prepared table), an authoritative code of Jewish law, was also a mystic whose work graphically illustrates the commitment of this school to Jewish law.

In part a reaction to Christian persecution of Jews in the → Crusades and → Inquisition, medieval Jewish mysticism encouraged Jews to look inward for meaning rather than at the hostile world in which they lived. God created the world using the Torah as his blueprint, and so Jews could discover the inner workings of the world and how they should act in it by studying the Torah and obeying its precepts. They needed to recognize, however, that the Torah has four different levels of meaning (→ Hermeneutics): the "simple," contextual meaning *(peshat)*, the interpreted meaning *(derash)*, intimated meanings hinted at by the text *(remez)*, and secret meanings *(sod)*. Only those who could fathom the Torah's esoteric meanings would be privy to God's plans. The *Zohar* and subsequent texts of this school sought to unpack those secret meanings in order to know how to set aside the troubles of this world by recognizing the world's temporary significance and unifying one's body (and not just one's will) with God. Study of the Torah, particularly its secret teachings, and observing its commandments would enable a person to escape this world and unite with God, as long as one had that purpose in mind.

Luria added several important features to earlier Jewish mysticism. In creating the world, God had tried to infuse it with too much of his presence, and so the finite vessels of the world shattered (the *shevirat ha-kelim*). This is a powerful metaphor for the brokenness of life, its pain, moral → evil, and physical limitations. Our task is to help God put the world back together again, and so unification and unity are major themes in Luria's thought. We accomplish that end through mystical study and through observing the commandments. In Luria's view, these acts literally construct the world anew. Sexual intercourse between husband and wife, for example — in particular on Friday evening, the eve of the → Sabbath, when God and the people of Israel come together as husband and wife — not only gives the couple pleasure and fulfills the Torah's commandments to satisfy each other's sexual desires (Exod. 21:10) and possibly procreate (Gen. 1:28), but their union also helps God to unify and repair the brokenness of the world. Luria's theory gave renewed meaning and motivation to observing the commandments.

4.2. The other major form of Jewish mysticism, Hasidism, is a product of the lower socioeconomic classes of eastern Europe. It began in the 18th century with Israel ben Eliezer, known as Ba'al Shem Tov (Master of the Good Name, the "Besht," ca. 1700-1760). In its origins this movement was expressly antiestablishment, that is, antirabbinic and anti-intellectual. It concentrated instead on the power of any untutored individual to cleave to God (*devekut*, "meditative attachment to God") through song, → dance, individual → prayer, and even wordless hymns and whistles. Traditional, legally defined forms of → worship, according to this view, are not only unnecessary but insufficient, for intentionality in prayer and in action is the key.

This form of Jewish mysticism accordingly did not produce philosophical theories, as did cabalism. Rather, it produced collections of stories and songs. In a somewhat later form of Hasidism, the *tsaddiq*, or totally righteous person, could intercede with God on another's behalf. Dynasties of Hasidic rab-

bis developed, each with his own disciples and modes of thought and behavior, but even those that retained the emphasis on song and dance have ironically adopted very strict forms of Jewish practice and typical modes of rabbinic study.

5. The Enlightenment to Hermann Cohen

With the → Enlightenment and emancipation in the late 18th century and thereafter, the Torah came under attack as a self-evident order of life among those Jews living in the areas affected by these new ideas — namely, central and western Europe and North America. Spurred on by Christian polemics, Moses Mendelssohn (1729-86) maintained in his book *Jerusalem; or, On Religious Power and Judaism* (1783) that Judaism was in accord with the rational religion of the pre-Kantian Enlightenment; its uniqueness, therefore, had to be defined. The truths of reason that are generally accessible are subject to corruption, so that a place is needed where they can be kept pure and uncorrupted. This place is the Jewish nation, which alone teaches, proclaims, preaches, and seeks to uphold those truths by its very existence, which is safeguarded by the Torah, the revealed law that relates solely to action. The law is a necessary supplement for the religion of reason. Traces of Mendelssohn's thinking remain to this day in the slogan "orthopraxis."

→ Idealism brought new blossoming to Jewish philosophy, only a few of whose representatives can be mentioned in this context. Adopting the system of F. W. J. Schelling (1775-1854), Solomon Formstecher (1808-89) defined Judaism as the religion of the spirit (the title of his book published in 1841), which knows the world soul as the transcendent God. Since the aim of life is *imitatio Dei* through moral acts, in content Judaism is ethical monotheism. In → paganism, the religion of nature, nature is the world soul. → Aesthetics thus replaces ethics. Christianity and Islam have the role of promoting the religion of spirit in the regions of the earth they control, and they will lose their inevitable tendency to accommodate to natural religion when Judaism has completed its development from objectivity to → subjectivity.

In his work *Religious Philosophy of the Jews* (1842), the → Hegelian Samuel Hirsch (1815-89) sought to demonstrate the unity of religious truth, which for him is the Hebrew Bible plus philosophical truth. Nature and freedom are posited with humanity. If nature triumphs over freedom, it becomes a divine principle, the result of which is the passive religion of paganism. If freedom triumphs over nature, abstract freedom becomes concrete freedom. Not just freedom, but its content, moral action, is then given by God, and we have the active religion embodied in Judaism. As in Formstecher, Christianity is in the middle so as to lead to concrete freedom. The task of the Jewish people is to bear witness to the truth by its life.

Despite an irrationalist impulse, Solomon Steinheim (1789-1866) was a rationalist in his wide-ranging *Revelation according to the Teaching of the Synagogue* (4 vols., 1835-65), which he could not have written as he did apart from Immanuel Kant. Viewing the → antinomy of reason and revelation as a special instance of the antinomy between reason and → experience, he thought that reason is defined by necessity and revelation by freedom, so that divine and human freedom can be disclosed only by revelation that comes from without and is accessible to all. In the knowledge that religious truth must be the content of revelation, critical reason subjects itself to revelation. Revelation is imparted to the Jewish people in order that this people may preserve it and make it known to the world. Christianity has the same task as in Formstecher.

In Hermann Cohen (1842-1918), founder of the neo-Kantian school at Marburg, the idea of God initially did no more than guarantee the unending actualizing of the moral demand. But in his Berlin period, especially in the posthumous *Religion of Reason from Jewish Sources* (1919), he supplemented the God of ethics with the loving God of religion, with whom we may have a personal relation. God alone makes it possible for us to achieve humanity and redemption from → sin. The general aim of the law as the form of correlation with God is that we should become more human. Its specific aim is that Jewish nationality should endure as the carrier of the religion of pure monotheism.

6. Franz Rosenzweig to the Contemporary Period

Franz Rosenzweig's (1886-1929) religious → existentialism in *The Star of Redemption* (1921) begins with the givenness of God, the world, and humanity, and their mutual relations. The divine-human relation is revelation as the spontaneous act of divine love for the individual in which God's nature as a loving Father and almighty Creator is known. It presupposes the God-world relation of creation and leads to our own relation to the world as cosmic redemption, and hence the six-pointed star formed by the superimposition of the triangle creation-revelation-redemption on the triangle God-world-humanity. The law must become a command that we each may fulfill today; it must not remain merely a set of externally imposed obligations. No Jew

should therefore say that he or she does not observe Jewish law, but only that he or she does not do so *yet*, indicating a readiness to engage in a stronger relationship with God when it will become possible for the person to observe more of God's commandments.

In keeping with his understanding of Hasidism, especially in his work *I and Thou* (1923), Martin Buber (1878-1965) found revelation in the I-Thou relation. Unlike the I-It relation, which is structured by space, time, and → causality, the I-Thou relation is totality, immediacy, presence, love, reciprocity, exclusiveness, and freedom. An I-Thou relation with anything (a pet, a tree) can lead to a meeting with God, the eternal Thou, but encounter with a → person is the true likeness. The I-Thou relation with God is unique in that it can never sink to the level of an I-It relation. → Dialogue takes place best in community, as Judaism, with its strongly communal modes of study, practice, and organization, should illustrate. The Torah is simply teaching, not authoritative command.

Mordecai M. Kaplan (1881-1983) created Reconstructionism, an approach to Judaism that emphasizes Judaism as not only a religion but a full civilization with a specifically Jewish land (Israel), language (Hebrew), song, art, dance, and even culinary patterns, in addition to beliefs and rituals (*Judaism as a Civilization* [1934]). Jewish civilization is eternally evolving, and → religion is at its center. Its ideas and practices must therefore be reconstructed to capture ancient concerns in modern form. God, for Kaplan, is deistic — specifically, "the power that makes for salvation," the power in nature that actualizes all potential for good. As a result, God has no will and cannot command; Jewish law consists of universal moral demands and folkways. Salvation is in this life, as we seek to overcome the moral and physical limitations of life. Kaplan is almost unique in the history of Jewish philosophy in his → deism, and that part of his philosophy has not won much adherence among Jews. His view of Judaism as an evolving, religious civilization, however, has been adopted by almost all streams of Judaism.

In Abraham Joshua Heschel's (1907-72) philosophy of religion (*Man Is Not Alone* [1951], *God in Search of Man* [1955]) the reality of God, to which all reality refers, precedes all inquiry into God. God is the God of feeling, of concern for us in creation, revelation, and redemption. We react to the experience of this concern by making it our own. The Torah is the sign of the love of God that calls for response.

In the second half of the 20th century Jewish

philosophers continued to write on the critical issues of God, prayer, revelation, law, covenant, good and evil, and redemption, but many focused on two critical events of the 1940s — the threat to the very existence of the Jewish people that reached a climax in the National Socialist → Holocaust, and the establishment of the State of Israel in 1948 after almost 1,900 years of Jewish statelessness.

On the former issue in particular, theological aspects gained the upper hand. The frank paganism of Richard L. Rubenstein in *After Auschwitz* (1966), the first philosophical treatment of those horrific events, was rooted in the Holocaust as the ultimate disproof of a theistic, morally good God. For Eugene Borowitz, though, to deduce the death of God from the Holocaust is to grant the victory to evil. According to Borowitz, two criteria to which the idea of God must measure up are that he makes life possible and that he safeguards his people's existence. The → diaspora reminds the State of Israel of its religious roots. According to Emil L. Fackenheim (*God's Presence in History* [1970]), Jews cannot escape their destiny of living with the → absolute. Even nonreligious Jews, by the fact of their survival as Jews, bear witness against idolatry, death, and delusion, and for humanity, health, and life.

The establishment of the State of Israel has given birth to a number of new Zionist theories. For example, Arthur A. Cohen (*The Natural and Supernatural Jew* [1962]) maintains that the contradiction located in history is overcome by redemption. Hence the founding of the State of Israel could not end the exile. For him it is an eschatological principle that makes understanding and patience possible for believers. It is also a universal category wherein judgment is passed on history. In overstressing pure existence, Judaism is not missing its supernatural calling to bear witness to the imperfect sanctity of the natural order. For Mordecai M. Kaplan, Israel is the place where Jewish life in all of its civilizational aspects can best flourish. David Hartman (*A Living Covenant* [1986]), an Orthodox rabbi, holds a similar view. For Hartman, while current events in nature or history, including the establishment of the State of Israel, are not direct expressions of God's will or design, Israel has religious significance because of its potential for the full realization of the Torah as a way of life.

For Abraham Isaac Kook (1865-1935), first chief rabbi of modern Israel (1921-35), Israel does indeed have divine significance. Unlike the connection of every other people with its homeland, the Jews' connection to the land of Israel was created by God's gift to Abraham and his descendants, and so the establishment of the modern state of Israel is the beginning of the era of Jewish redemption. In contrast, for Yeshayahu Leibowitz (*Judaism, Human Values, and the Jewish State* [1992]), another Orthodox rabbi, → Zionism is not motivated by religious concerns at all; rather, it is "the program for the attainment of political and national independence" after centuries of being ruled by others.

Of the more traditional subjects of Jewish philosophy, contemporary Jewish scholars have advanced Jewish thought most in the field of ethics. With an absolute explosion in the late 20th century of human ability to control nature through → technology, moral questions about what we *should* do abound. Moreover, since the tradition could not have even contemplated some of the moral issues that now face humanity in such areas as medicine (→ Medical Ethics), let alone ruled on them, the methodological question of how to gain moral guidance from the Jewish tradition on these new matters has become critical. Contemporary Jewish philosophers like David Ellenson, Louis Newman, Elliot Dorff, and Aaron Mackler have proposed varying theories as to how to discern the moral meaning of the Jewish tradition in the face of these new challenges, and writers adopting the approaches of all modern movements in Judaism have articulated their interpretations of how Judaism would have us respond to specific moral questions in our time.

→ Anti-Semitism, Anti-Judaism; Jewish Practices; Spinozism

Bibliography: Premodern: H. A. FISCHEL, *Rabbinic Literature and Greco-Roman Philosophy* (Leiden, 1973) • L. E. GOODMAN, *Jewish and Islamic Philosophy: Cross-pollinations in the Classic Age* (New Brunswick, N.J., 1999) • J. GUTTMANN, *Philosophies of Judaism: The History of Jewish Philosophy from Biblical Times to Franz Rosenzweig* (New York, 1964) • I. HUSIK, *A History of Mediaeval Jewish Philosophy* (Philadelphia, 1958; orig. pub., 1916) • A. HYMAN, *Eschatological Themes in Medieval Jewish Philosophy* (Milwaukee, Wis., 2002) • H. KASSIM, *Aristotle and Aristotelianism in Medieval Muslim, Jewish, and Christian Philosophy* (Lanham, Md., 2000) • J. NEUSNER, *Jerusalem and Athens: The Congruity of Talmudic and Classical Philosophy* (Leiden, 1997) • T. RUDAVSKY, *Time Matters: Time, Creation, and Cosmology in Medieval Jewish Philosophy* (Albany, N.Y., 2000) • G. SCHOLEM, *Sabbatai Sevi: The Mystical Messiah* (Princeton, 1973) • K. SEESKIN, *Searching for a Distant God: The Legacy of Maimonides* (New York, 2000).

Modern: E. B. BOROWITZ, *Choices in Modern Jewish*

Thought (2d ed.; New York, 1995) • M. Buber, *I and Thou* (New York, 1996; orig. pub., 1923) • A. A. Cohen, *The Natural and Supernatural Jew* (New York, 1962) • E. N. Dorff and L. E. Newman, eds., *Contemporary Jewish Ethics and Morality: A Reader* (New York, 1995); idem, eds., *Contemporary Jewish Theology: A Reader* (New York, 1999) • E. L. Fackenheim, *Encounters between Judaism and Modern Philosophy* (New York, 1973); idem, *God's Presence in History* (New York, 1970) • A. J. Heschel, *God in Search of Man: A Philosophy of Judaism* (New York, 1955); idem, *Man Is Not Alone: A Philosophy of Religion* (New York, 1951) • M. M. Kaplan, *Judaism as a Civilization: Toward a Reconstruction of American-Jewish Life* (rev. ed.; New York, 1957; orig. pub., 1934) • S. Kepnes, P. Ochs, and R. Gibbs, *Reasoning after Revelation: Dialogues in Postmodern Jewish Philosophy* (Boulder, Colo., 1998) • M. L. Morgan, *Beyond Auschwitz: Post-Holocaust Jewish Thought in America* (Oxford, 2001); idem, ed., *A Holocaust Reader: Responses to the Nazi Extermination* (New York, 2001) • F. Rosenzweig, *The Star of Redemption* (New York, 1971; orig. pub., 1921).

Survey and general history: J. B. Agus, *The Evolution of Jewish Thought* (London, 1959) • J. L. Blau, *The Story of Jewish Philosophy* (New York, 1971) • D. H. Frank, O. Leaman, and C. H. Manekin, eds., *The Jewish Philosophy Reader* (London, 2000) • S. T. Katz, ed., *Jewish Ideas and Concepts* (New York, 1977); idem, ed., *Jewish Philosophers* (New York, 1975) • J. Maier, *Geschichte der jüdische Religion* (rev. ed.; Freiburg, 1992) • K. Seeskin, *Autonomy in Jewish Philosophy* (New York, 2001) • S. Spero, *Holocaust and Return to Zion: A Study in Jewish Philosophy of History* (Hoboken, N.J., 2000).

Günter Mayer and Elliot N. Dorff

Jewish Practices

1. Worship
   1.1. Times of Prayer
   1.2. Liturgy
   1.3. Ritual Garments
   1.4. History
2. Festivals
   2.1. Sabbath
   2.2. Pilgrimage Festivals: Passover, Weeks, Tabernacles
   2.3. Days of Awe: Rosh Hashanah, Yom Kippur
   2.4. Minor Festivals: Hanukkah, Purim, Yom Ha-Atzma'ut
3. Fast Days and Days of Commemoration
   3.1. Ninth of Av
   3.2. Yom Hashoah
4. Home and Table Rituals
   4.1. Grace after Meals
   4.2. Mezuzah
5. Life-Cycle Ceremonies
   5.1. Birth
   5.2. Bar and Bat Mitzvah
   5.3. Marriage
   5.4. Death and Mourning

1. Worship

With the Roman destruction of the second → temple in 70 c.e., the biblically mandated covenantal sacrificial worship ceased. Rabbinic leaders decreed that → prayer, along with study of → Torah and charitable deeds, fills the void. They consequently developed the mechanisms of a new verbal system of → worship. These prayers, while often located in a → synagogue, may be recited virtually anywhere. The most important prayers are recited facing the Temple Mount in → Jerusalem, and the architectural focus of the synagogue is its Jerusalem-facing wall, which houses the Torah scroll(s).

Any gathering of ten adult Jews (traditionally only men), a *minyan,* forms a quorum for public prayer that can be led by any participant. In the absence of this quorum, Jews still recite most of the service privately, but the ideal setting is communal, as indicated by the formulation of virtually all prayer texts in the plural. The → rabbi's primary function is to teach and decide matters of law; a professional *hazan* (cantor) may be engaged to lead the prayers.

1.1. *Times of Prayer*

The rabbis decreed three fixed times of weekday congregational prayer: morning, afternoon, and evening. On most holidays, including the Sabbath, an additional service follows the morning prayers to correspond to that day's special offering in the temple. Other prayers accompany home rituals, especially meals.

1.2. *Liturgy*

The traditional language of prayer is → Hebrew, with a scattering of Aramaic; vernacular prayer is common today in nontraditional settings. By the medieval period, and perhaps earlier, fixed prayers dominated the service. The primary rubrics of the service are the recitation of the Shema, Deut. 6:4-9, the biblical declaration of faith in God's unity, and related passages with the → blessings surrounding it; the Amidah, the prayer of between 7 and 19 blessings that substitutes for the sacrificial offerings and offers praise, petition, and thanksgiving to God; and the reading of → Torah, accompanied by a selection from the Prophets on Sabbaths and holidays. These items are all enriched by the recitation of psalms, supplicatory prayers, and various calendrically determined rituals, many of which had their origins in the temple. Regional variations create minor differences in fixed texts but significant differences in the choices and placement of liturgical poetry and in the musical settings of the prayers. The fundamental global unity of Jewish worship ensures, though, that any Jew can enter any synagogue and participate fully.

1.3. *Ritual Garments*
Ritual garments include the requirement of a head covering for all males and for married females, especially during prayer and study. Most often, men wear a *kipah* or *yarmulke* (skullcap). During morning prayers, men traditionally wear a *tallit* (prayer shawl with ritually knotted fringes at the four corners) and, on weekdays only, *tefillin* (phylacteries, small leather boxes on the forehead and upper arm containing slips of parchment on which are written the relevant biblical commandments, like the passage containing Deut. 6:8).

1.4. *History*
Fixed prayers challenge the principle expressed in *m. Ber.* 4:3 that the worshiper must pray with intentionality and concentration *(kavvanah)*. Answers to this challenge have varied over the years, beginning with the introduction of liturgical poetry and continuing with rich traditions of mystical → meditation on the fixed prayer texts. Beginning in 19th-century Germany and spreading quickly to the rest of western Europe and especially America, Reform Judaism challenged the necessity of fixed prayer texts, revising and abbreviating the liturgy and introducing vernacular prayer. Consequently, today's communities exhibit an enormous spectrum of practices.

2. Festivals
2.1. *Sabbath*
The Jewish calendar is lunar-solar, meaning that the regular addition of a leap month preserves the 12-month lunar year's ties with the agricultural seasons. The new moon of each month is a minor holiday. The other important (and independent) marker of time is the seven-day week. The weekly → Sabbath is the most important holiday, shaping the life patterns of the Jewish world and considered a marker of God's → covenant with Israel. From sundown Friday through dark on Saturday, observant Jews abstain from all work, as decreed in the Bible, in imitation of God's rest on the seventh day of creation and in commemoration of the exodus from Egypt.

The rabbis carefully defined what constitutes work, collecting these rules into a significant section of their legal literature, first in the → Mishnah, then in the → Talmud, and eventually into medieval codes like the *Shulḥan ʿarukh* (→ Jewish Philosophy 4.1). Less traditional Jews do not consider these codes binding and develop their own interpretations of Sabbath rest.

2.2. *Pilgrimage Festivals: Passover, Weeks, Tabernacles*
The three biblical pilgrimage festivals are Pesach (→ Passover), Shavuot (Feast of Weeks/Pentecost), and Sukkot (Feast of Tabernacles). Before the destruction of the temple, these were festivals of → pilgrimage to Jerusalem. These festivals came to combine agricultural celebrations with historical commemorations. After the weekly Sabbath, they constitute the most important cycle of the Jewish year. All are joyous occasions, celebrated today by family gatherings, synagogue prayers, and special rituals. Modified rules of Sabbath rest also apply to the first and last days of the festivals.

Pesach, a weeklong festival beginning on the 15th of Nisan, at the time of the early spring barley harvest, commemorates the exodus from Egypt. As a reminder of the Israelites' hasty escape into the wilderness, Jews eat *matzah,* unleavened bread, during the entire festival, entirely removing all leavened foods from their homes. On the first (and, outside Israel, the second) evening of the festival, an elaborate home table ritual called the *seder* centers on the recitation of the Passover → Haggadah, which remembers the redemptive events of the exodus and the observance of the holiday in the temple and, after a sumptuous meal, looks to the future messianic redemption. Many elements of this ritual are designed to engage the children, including symbolic foods, beloved songs, and a requirement that the children ask questions.

Shavuot comes seven weeks after Passover, on the 6th of Sivan, timed to correspond to the wheat harvest and the completion of the Omer, the period of bringing ceremonial sheaves of grain to the temple. It is a two-day feast in the → diaspora, a one-day feast in Israel. By the rabbinic period, it was understood also to correspond to the day of the → revelation at → Sinai when Israel received the Torah from God. Commemoration of this latter event has become its dominant meaning. Mystical traditions of learning Torah for the entire first night of the festival, followed by morning prayers at dawn, are popular.

Sukkot, on the 15th of Tishri, was originally the weeklong fall → harvest festival, incorporating prayers and rituals for plentiful winter rains. It also commemorates the Israelites' 40 years of wandering in the wilderness, when the people lived dependent entirely on God's mercy. As a reminder of both these themes, and of the shelter, protection, and peace that God provides even in the worst of times, Jews dwell for this festival in a *sukkah,* or booth with a flimsy roof, at least eating and sometimes sleeping there too. Other symbols of the holiday are the *lulav* (a palm branch bound together with myrtle and willow) and *etrog* (citron), used in the prayers. The festival concludes with an additional gathering, called Shemini Atzeret (the eighth day of assembly). Its second day became, in the diaspora, Simchat Torah, the day of rejoicing in the Torah, the day on which the annual cycle of Torah readings is completed and immediately begun again. This day, which concludes the fall holiday season, is marked by extensive dancing with the Torah scroll and generally festive behavior.

2.3. *Days of Awe: Rosh Hashanah, Yom Kippur*
The Days of Awe, or High Holy Days, precede Sukkot in the fall, beginning with Rosh Hashanah, the New Year, on the 1st and 2nd of Nisan, and concluding with Yom Kippur, the Day of → Atonement, on the 10th. These are the most solemn days of the Jewish year, a time of → penitence during which all must ask → forgiveness from each other and then from God for all sinful behavior. The ancient understanding is that on Rosh Hashanah God opens the Book of Life and inscribes the fate of each individual for the coming year. On Yom Kippur, at the close of the day, the book is sealed. The liturgical line "Prayer, penitence, and charity avert the evil decree" guide actions leading up to and during this period.

The most important symbol of this period is the *shofar,* the ram's horn, recalling the ram → Abraham sacrificed instead of → Isaac. The shofar is blown as a warning daily in the synagogue in the month preceding Rosh Hashanah. On Rosh Hashanah 100 blasts are incorporated into elaborate prayers. Yom Kippur concludes this period with a 25-hour total → fast spent in intensive communal prayer, formal confession to God, and introspection, concluded with the blast of the shofar. Proper participation in the process guarantees God's forgiveness of sin.

2.4. *Minor Festivals: Hanukkah, Purim, Yom Ha-Atzma'ut*
Hanukkah (lit. "dedication"), or Lights, beginning on the 25th of Kislev, is an eight-day festival approximately at the time of the winter solstice. It commemorates the victory of the Maccabees (→

Apocrypha 1.3.3) over the Assyrians and their rededication of the defiled Jerusalem temple in 165 B.C.E. According to rabbinic myth, although the → priests found only enough consecrated oil to last one day, it lasted eight days. Hence, each night an additional light on an eight-branched *menorah* (candelabra) is lit. Because these lights may not be used for illumination, an additional candle must always be present. Since no → work should be done while the candles burn, various games developed around the holiday. To commemorate the miracle of the oil, eating fried foods like potato pancakes or doughnuts is customary.

Purim, or Lots, on the 14th of Adar (15th in ancient walled cities like Jerusalem), always falls a month before Pesach. It celebrates the deliverance of the Jews of Persia through Queen Esther. Its observance includes the reading of Esther from a handwritten parchment scroll, giving gifts to the poor, giving gifts of food to friends, wearing costumes, and engaging in general merriment. Many communities and families celebrate additional "Purims" during the year in celebration of their own deliverances from disaster.

Yom Ha-Atzma'ut, Israeli Independence Day, falls on the 5th of Iyar, between Pesach and Shavuot. It is increasingly celebrated by Jews around the world as part of their ritual calendar.

3. Fast Days and Days of Commemoration
The Jewish calendar also contains a cycle of fast days, commemorating and mourning for disasters that afflicted the people throughout its history. In early rabbinic times these fasts were much more numerous, and some, like fasts for rain during droughts in Israel, apply only there. Beyond those discussed below there are also various minor fasts.

3.1. *Ninth of Av*
Ninth of Av, called by its date, which falls in high summer, is the day on which, according to Jewish tradition, both the first and second temples were destroyed. Other disasters of Jewish history also occurred on or around this date and are also commemorated at this time, the most famous being the → Crusaders' destruction of the Rhineland Jewish communities in 1096 and the expulsion of the Jews from Spain in 1492. Some Jews include the → Holocaust on this list. Like Yom Kippur, this day is observed by a 25-hour total fast. Rituals include the reading of Lamentations and special poems of lament and symbols of mourning like sitting on the floor or low chairs, wearing no leather, and abstaining from Torah study except passages related to the day.

3.2. *Yom Hashoah*

Yom Hashoah, Holocaust Memorial Day, is observed on the 29th of Nisan, a week before Yom Ha-Atzma'ut. Rituals for this day are still evolving but do not include fasting. In Israel, air-raid sirens go off simultaneously in the morning, and the entire country stops for a few minutes. The same occurs a week later on the day before Yom Ha-Atzma'ut in commemoration of Israel's fallen soldiers.

4. Home and Table Rituals

Rabbinic Judaism's ideal is to imbue every action with an acknowledgment of God's presence and of its consequent intrinsic holiness. Many actions, then, including significant aspects of → everyday life, are accompanied by a corresponding *berakah,* or blessing. In addition, the rabbis elaborated on the biblical dietary laws, allowing consumption of some meat, but only if the animals are ritually slaughtered and the meat prepared in ways that are humane and that acknowledge that a life is being taken. Fundamental to this process is the removal of all blood. Kosher food, in addition, rigidly separates meat from the milk created to sustain its life.

4.1. *Grace after Meals*

Deut. 8:10 commands, "When you have eaten your fill, give thanks to the Lord your God" (JPST). Consequently, the primary Jewish grace follows the meal. Its full form occurs only after a formal meal, established by the inclusion of bread and the blessing over it. This liturgy contains a series of four blessings: for God as a provider of food; for the land, especially Israel, as a source of food; for the rebuilding of Jerusalem; and an effusive acknowledgment of God's goodness. This ritual is incumbent upon the individual but is ideally recited with a table fellowship of three men or three women, or with a minyan. This liturgy marks especially the feasts that accompany each festival discussed above and the life-cycle rituals discussed below.

4.2. *Mezuzah*

The Jewish home is itself a holy space. This holiness is marked ritually by the placement of a *mezuzah,* a parchment containing the words of the Shema with its declaration of God's unity and subsequent command to "write them on the doorposts of your house and on your gates" (Deut. 6:9), at every entrance door. The cases protecting the parchment can be quite beautiful.

5. Life-Cycle Ceremonies

Jewish life-cycle ceremonies need not take place in the synagogue, although they often do. The primary locus of most is the home and the feast organized around the family table to acknowledge the moment.

5.1. *Birth*

A boy is → circumcised on the eighth day as Abraham circumcised his son Isaac on the eighth day. This act marks the boy's entry into Israel's covenant with God. He also receives his name as part of the ceremony. The festive meal following the ceremony is considered part of it, and an elaborated grace after meals is traditional.

Ceremonies for girls were very simple until recently, with the new father, after being called to the Torah, asking for the recitation of a blessing in which she receives her name, often without being present. Today, many elaborate on this recognition creatively and include a festive meal in their ceremonies.

5.2. *Bar and Bat Mitzvah*

Children achieve adult status in the Jewish community automatically when they reach the age of religious responsibility, known as *bar* or *bat mitzvah* (son or daughter of the commandment), at age 13 for a boy or, traditionally, 12 for a girl. Any ceremony simply acknowledges this change in status by celebrating the adolescent's first fulfillment of public adult roles. For boys, and for girls in nontraditional settings, this recognition usually means at least being called to the Torah during public prayer and often involves leading much of the day's services, including delivering a *devar Torah* (words of Torah), or sermon. A festive meal is also part of the celebration.

5.3. *Marriage*

Today's → marriage ceremony combines two discrete elements: the formal betrothal ceremony, which legally binds the couple (after which, religious divorce would be required), and the wedding proper. Both take place today under a *huppah,* a canopy symbolizing the couple's new home. The *sheva berakot* (seven blessings), which constitute the second part of the ceremony and which are repeated at festive meals as part of the grace after meals for the following week, connect this couple's wedding both to → Adam and Eve in the Garden of Eden and to the future messianic joy of Jerusalem. Recitation of these blessings requires a minyan, indicating Judaism's stress on the communal role of marriage and procreation.

5.4. *Death and Mourning*

→ Funeral rituals developed around two poles: honor to the dead and comfort to the mourners. The funeral service consists primarily of psalms and eulogies. Burial occurs as quickly and simply as possible; traditionally only burial in the ground using linen shrouds and a simple casket or bier is allowed. Formal mourning — the *shivah* — lasts a week, beginning with the "meal of consolation" (also with a special grace after meals) served to the mourners upon return from the cemetery. During this time, mourners may neither work nor leave their home; the community cares for their needs and helps them to mourn, holding services in the house. In the Middle Ages, the *kaddish,* an ancient doxological praise of God, became the mourner's prayer, recited by children for 11 months after a parent's death, and thereafter on the *yahrzeit* (anniversary) of the death.

→ Cabala; Halakah; Jewish Theology; Midrash; Salvation 2

Bibliography: W. D. Dosick, *Living Judaism: The Complete Guide to Jewish Belief, Tradition, and Practice* (San Francisco, 1995) • R. M. Geffen, ed., *Celebration and Renewal: Rites of Passage in Judaism* (Philadelphia, 1993) • R. Hammer, *Entering Jewish Prayer: A Guide to Personal Devotion and the Worship Service* (New York, 1994); idem, *Entering the High Holy Days: A Guide to Origins, Themes, and Prayers* (Philadelphia, 1998) • I. Klein, *A Guide to Jewish Religious Practice* (New York, 1979).
Ruth Langer and Jael B. Paulus†

Jewish Theology

1. Rabbinic Period
2. Medieval Thought
3. Cabala and Hasidism
    3.1. Cabala
    3.2. Hasidism
4. Modern Jewish Thought
    4.1. Key Thinkers
    4.2. Issues

1. Rabbinic Period

The thinking of the biblical authors and of the Talmudic rabbis has rightly been described as organic, that is, responsive to the concrete situations of human → life in all its variety. In the Bible, for instance, God is ever present, making demands on his people and on all humanity. He is the Controller and Governor of the universe. But no attempt is made to consider how God is said to create ex nihilo, how divine → providence operates in detail. That there is → evil in the universe is taken for granted, and there are mighty probings both in the Bible (esp. the Book of Job) and in rabbinic literature as to why the righteous → suffer and the wicked prosper. But there is hardly any treatment in these sources as to why there should be evil at all in a world created by the All Good. Not until the → Middle Ages were such questions raised or, for that matter, the question of what is meant by describing God as good.

If we bear in mind what has been said about the organic, nonsystematic nature of rabbinic thought — as well as of the Bible, on which such thought is based — it can be seen how uncertain are the efforts of modern scholars such as G. F. Moore (1851-1931), Solomon Schechter (1850-1915), and E. E. Urbach (1912-91) to delineate rabbinic theology. As these scholars have themselves admitted, the very attempt to present themes in a systematic manner imposes a thought pattern on the material that is not really there, with the inevitable distortion that results from an ordered arrangement of basically disorganized, dynamic responses to particular challenges.

Insofar as one can speak of a theological scheme in rabbinic literature, it consists of three great ideas and their interrelations: → God, the → Torah, and Jewish peoplehood. The key verse for the rabbis, and also for → Judaism as a whole, is the Shema (lit. "hear"): "Hear, O Israel: The Lord our God, the Lord is One" (Deut. 6:4 JPS). For the → rabbis the statement that God is one means that there are no other gods and that to worship idols is a heinous → sin; rather than worship idols, the Jew must be prepared to suffer martyrdom. God is omnipotent and omniscient, though these terms are too abstract and too foreign to the thought patterns of the rabbis actually to have been used by them. Nothing is hidden from God's vision. He knows the future as well as the past. His eyes are open to all human deeds, rewarding the good and → punishing the wicked, and yet human beings have free will, and hence it makes sense for God to give us commandments and hold us responsible for obeying them. As God says in the Torah, "I have put before you life and death, blessing and curse. Choose life — if you and your offspring would live — by loving the Lord your God, heeding His commands, and holding fast to Him" (Deut. 30:19-20 JPST). Later the rabbis would say, "Everything is in the hands of Heaven except for fear of Heaven [i.e., human free will]" (*b. Ber.* 33b).

God's will is revealed in the Torah (lit. "teaching"). The Torah is twofold: the written Torah (the Pentateuch and, by extension, the rest of the Hebrew Scriptures) and the oral Torah, conceived originally as the body of doctrine and practice given by God to → Moses at Sinai and then extended to embrace all the explanations and elaborations of the Jewish sages throughout Jewish history. The Torah embraces the precepts — the *mitzvot,* that is, practical rules and regulations, commands and prohibitions. By carrying out the mitzvot, the Jew does God's will. But there is a Torah for the non-Jewish world as well in the form of the seven Noachian laws: (1) not to murder, (2) not to steal, (3) not to worship idols, (4) not to commit adultery or incest, (5) not to blaspheme, (6) not to eat flesh torn from an animal while the animal is still alive, and (7) to have an adequate system of justice in society (t. 'Abod. Zar. 8:4; b. Sanh. 56a-b, 60a). Thus the Torah is given to → Israel (§1) but through Israel to all humanity.

With only minor differences, the rabbis believed in a personal → Messiah, a human being, scion of the House of David, who will be sent by God at "the end of days" to restore the Jewish people to their ancient homeland. With the coming of the Messiah, the temple will be rebuilt, the sacrificial system will be reintroduced, and from Zion the Torah will go forth to bring all people to → worship the one true God.

Sometime after the advent of the Messiah, the → resurrection of the dead will occur; the righteous, including "the righteous of the nations of the world," will then enjoy the nearness of God, "basking in the radiance of the Shekinah" (God's earthly dwelling) for all eternity. This state is known in the rabbinic literature as the world to come (Olam ha-Ba), though occasionally this term refers also to the blissful state of the individual → soul after the death of the body. The more usual term for the latter, however, is "the Garden of Eden," the place or state in which righteous souls enjoy the proximity of the Shekinah while awaiting reunion with the body at the resurrection. The souls of the wicked are punished in Gehenna for a maximum of 12 months. Both Josephus (ca. 37-ca. 100) and the → Talmud inform us that the → Sadducees, unlike the → Pharisees, denied altogether the existence of another world, since there is no explicit reference to this concept in the Scriptures.

2. Medieval Thought

Jewish theologians of the Middle Ages, like their Christian counterparts and the Arabic mutakallimun, were obliged to face squarely the challenge of → Aristotelian philosophy to traditional religion. The problem of → faith versus → reason, unknown in the earlier rabbinic period, now loomed large. The "God of the philosophers," the unmoved, ineffable first cause, seemed to be sharply opposed to the "God of Abraham, Isaac and Jacob," in the famous distinction drawn by Blaise → Pascal (1623-62). The attempt at reconciling the two conceptions, so at variance with one another, demanded a complete rethinking of the doctrine of divine attributes.

Moses Maimonides (1135-1204), the greatest of the medieval Jewish theologians, developed further the earlier idea of negative attributes. According to Maimonides, we can speak of God's essential attributes — his existence, unity, and wisdom — only in negative terms. When it is said that God exists, this word has no reference to God's true nature, which is beyond all human comprehension, but means only that God is not in a state of nonexistence. Similarly, when it is said that God is one, the meaning is that there is no multiplicity in his being, and when it is said that God is wise, it means that he is never ignorant. With regard to the attributes of action, however, a positive understanding is allowed, but only because such attributes (e.g., God's justice and goodness) are consciously adopted from the human condition (→ Negative Theology [Western]).

For all his → rationalism, Maimonides admits that reason must come to a halt when faced with the apparently insoluble problem of how to reconcile the doctrine of divine foreknowledge with human free will (→ Freedom). According to Maimonides, both horns of the dilemma must be seized. God does know all the future deeds of humans, and yet humans have freedom of choice. Gersonides (Levi ben Gershom, 1288-1344) and Ḥasdai Crescas (1340-1410) sense a real contradiction in the two concepts. Gersonides is moved to qualify severely the doctrine of divine foreknowledge, while, according to Crescas, human beings only appear to have freedom of choice.

Maimonides was not the first to draw up a list of basic principles of the Jewish faith, but his listing became the standard and accepted formulation for subsequent Jewish thought, at least for Orthodox Jewish belief. Maimonides' 13 principles are (1) the existence of God, (2) God's unity, (3) God's incorporeality, (4) God's eternity, (5) the need to worship God alone, (6) the → prophets as true prophets of God, (7) Moses as the greatest of the prophets, (8) God's giving the Torah to Moses, (9) the immutability of the Torah, (10) God's knowing all human deeds, (11) reward and punishment, (12) the coming of the Messiah, and (13) the resurrection of the dead.

Little imagination is required to see that behind this and similar formulations by Jewish theologians lie the challenges presented to Judaism by its daughter religions, Christianity and → Islam. A major thrust in the thought of Jewish theologians in this period is to demonstrate that the Torah given by God to the people of Israel is eternal and has not been superseded by other religions.

Although Maimonides lists the resurrection of

the dead as a basic principle of Judaism, he is at pains to point out that although the dead will be resurrected, they will eventually die again — only the soul is immortal. Naḥmanides (ca. 1195-1270) takes strong issue with Maimonides, holding that the resurrected body will live forever, albeit in a very refined state.

Joseph Albo (ca. 1380-ca. 1444), in his popular work *Sefer ha-ʿiqqarim* (Book of principles), provides a summary of the views of his predecessors on the question of → dogma in Judaism, discussing in the process what constitutes a religion and how religions differ from one another. Albo naturally stresses the superiority of Judaism over all other religions, while tacitly admitting that there is a central core common to all religions. Judah ha-Levi (ca. 1075-1141) similarly engages in dialogue with → Greek philosophy, Christianity, and Islam.

In some Jewish-Christian disputations theologians on the Jewish side took issue especially with the claim that a new Israel had been chosen by God to take the place of the old. For a majority of the medieval Jewish theologians, Christianity is less than a pure → monotheism because of its doctrines of the → incarnation and the → Trinity. All agree that Islam is a pure monotheistic faith, although a false religion from the Jewish standpoint.

3. Cabala and Hasidism

3.1. *Cabala*

The mystical meditations current in 12th- and 13th-century Provence and Spain culminated in the theosophical system known as the → cabala, whose classic text is the *Zohar*. It received considerable elaboration in 16th-century Safed (also known as Zefat, one of the four Jewish holy cities of Palestine) by Moses Cordovero (1522-70) and especially Isaac Luria (1534-72), whose disciples produced virtually a new cabalistic system.

Central to every version of the cabala is the idea that there are two aspects to the divine nature. The theology of the cabala is thus radical in two respects. On the one hand, the ultimate ground of being, God as he is in himself, known as En Sof (without end, limitless), is beyond all human comprehension. Going beyond the medieval thinkers, the cabalists do not permit even negative attributes to be used of En Sof. This aspect of deity is not even referred to in the Bible, except by an occasional, very obscure hint (e.g., Eccl. 3:11).

The Godhead in manifestation, on the other hand, is conceived of in dynamic terms, controlling the universe by means of ten powers, or potencies, known as the *sefirot* (numbers, divine emanations).

Thus there is a *sefira* of judgment and another of mercy, the one male and active, the other female and passive. Moreover, the biblical idea of man and woman created in God's image means, for the cabalists, that the human person is a mirror of the sefirotic realm.

By a process of → emanation the power of En Sof manifests itself in the sefirotic realm, whence it descends, in a great chain of being, throughout all the lower worlds. Human beings, at the end of the chain, can exert an influence on the worlds above. Every virtuous human deed or thought sends beneficent impulses on high to promote harmony among the sefirot and thus to render possible the flow of divine → grace to all the worlds. Conversely, every vicious deed or thought sends baneful impulses on high, causing the flow of divine grace to be arrested. The Godhead is thus dependent, in a sense, on human conduct.

Furthermore, the cabala contains the notion of a demonic side to existence known as the Sitra Achra (the other side) with its own sefirot, an unholy parody of the sacred realm. Although the cabalists never tire of stressing the complete unity between En Sof and the sefirot, and although they conceive of the Sitra Achra as ultimately controlled fully by God ("like a vicious dog at the end of a long leash"), the more traditional theologians considered the cabala to have come dangerously close to → dualistic heresy. Nevertheless, the cabala eventually became theologically respectable in most Jewish circles, even to the extent that a denial of the cabala was occasionally seen as heresy.

3.2. *Hasidism*

→ Hasidism has been described as mysticism for the masses. Its basic ideal is that of *devekut*, "cleaving," that is, a perpetual being with God in the mind. In this respect Hasidism is somewhat averse to theological speculation, since such speculation is seen to be a hindrance to the devekut ideal.

Some Hasidic masters, however, such as Shneur Zalman of Liady (1745-1813), did endeavor to develop a complete theological system based on the cabala. For these thinkers the finite universe enjoys no ultimate existence at all. The cosmos is real only from the human point of view; from God's point of view, as it were, there is no universe, and there are no creatures to inhabit the universe. It is only because the divine energy is screened from human gaze that the universe and its creatures appear to have an independent existence. This acosmic theology is read into the word "one" in the Shema. God is not only unique, as the medieval thinkers affirmed, but is the sole ultimate being, a doctrine that has been called panentheistic (i.e., all is in God). Traditional theologians took strong issue with Hasidic panentheism on the ground that it tends to obliterate the dividing line between God and his creatures, the infinite and the finite, the holy and the unholy, good and evil.

4. Modern Jewish Thought
4.1. *Key Thinkers*
With the beginnings of Jewish emancipation at the end of the 18th century and the emergence of the Jew into Western society, the main theological issues centered on the question of → universalism and particularism in Judaism. The pioneer of the new thinking, Moses Mendelssohn (1729-86), argued that although Judaism holds fast to the laws revealed at Sinai, the basic beliefs of religion — the existence of God and the → immortality of the soul — were nevertheless universal truths to be apprehended by all through the use of unaided reason.

The tension between the particularism prevalent in the preemancipation period and the wider horizons that were opening up resulted in the emergence in Germany of the movement known as Reform Judaism. Theologians of reform like Abraham Geiger (1810-74) and Samuel Holdheim (1806-60) tried to distinguish the immutable central core, or essence, of normative Judaism — conceived in terms of the prophetic call to a life of justice, righteousness, and holiness — from the allegedly inessential rituals and practices that differ from age to age. Samson Raphael Hirsch (1808-88) was the foremost exponent, in contrast, of a neoorthodoxy in which the traditional practices were preserved intact but now were wedded to a "Western" approach. In the words of Hirsch's famous slogan, the ideal for the Jew was to be an "Israel-Mensch," that is, a full member of Western society appreciating the values of Western culture and, at the same time, intensely loyal to the mitzvot.

The advance of science and the challenges presented to the tradition by the new worldview that it brought resulted in the adoption by some modern Jewish theologians of naturalistic → philosophies of religion in general and of Judaism in particular. The most determined Jewish naturalist was Mordecai M. Kaplan (1881-1983) who, in his very long life and many activities, reinterpreted the concept of God. God, for Kaplan and his disciples, is not a divine person but the power in the universe that makes for righteousness. Faith in God, on this view, means an attitude affirming that the universe is so constituted that righteousness will ultimately win out. Kaplan held, moreover, that such an attitude has always

been that of Jewish believers, that — at least for the sophisticated — the term "God" has been a kind of shorthand. Religious supernaturalists have had no difficulty in refuting this view.

Martin Buber (1878-1965), in contrast, stressed the personalistic aspects of religion (→ Person). In Buber's "I and Thou" philosophy we do not meet God by talking about him, as the medieval thinkers were wont to affirm, even when formulating their doctrine of negative attributes. God is to be encountered, rather, in → dialogue, by the meeting of the Thou that is behind all particular thous.

Franz Rosenzweig (1886-1929), the other most famous Jewish religious → existentialist (see his *Star of Redemption*), describes Judaism as based on the three ideas of → creation, → revelation, and redemption. For Rosenzweig the mitzvot are not to be seen as a kind of package either to be accepted in toto or to be discounted. On the contrary, each of the mitzvot should be accepted as significant only when it has awakened the urge for acceptance in the heart and mind of the believer; then it must be embraced wholeheartedly. Rosenzweig, in his approach to Christianity, was prepared to admit that non-Jews could come to God only through → Jesus, but he held that Jews had no need of a Son to bring them to the Father, since, because of the Torah, they were already with the Father.

4.2. *Issues*
Specific events, movements, and issues of the 20th century caused Jewish theologians to reevaluate and reinvigorate their theological traditions. These issues include especially the → Holocaust, → Zionism and the establishment of the State of Israel, Jewish → feminism, ethical questions raised by → technology and medical developments, the nature of Jewish → law, and postmodern theologies.

4.2.1. The Nazi Holocaust has caused some contemporary Jewish theologians to reflect upon this frightful catastrophe using traditional terms like "sin," "guilt," "punishment," and "collective responsibility." Since the dead included many religious people and innocent children, most believers have been inclined to use the biblical metaphor of God's hiding his face during that time. Such a position leaves unsolved the tormenting problem why he was silent before immense, unjustified, and excruciating human suffering.

Some have explored the idea that God is limited by given factors, a strain of Jewish theology developed in different ways by the classical rabbis and by Maimonides. Still others have maintained that the Holocaust has shown once and for all that the idea of a personal God must be abandoned.

To regard the establishment of the State of Israel as divine compensation for the Holocaust is hardly a satisfying → theodicy, for why should so many have to suffer in order to bring it about? Nevertheless, some religious Jews believe that the Holocaust provided the birth pangs that enabled the State of Israel to be born in what is now a partially realized → eschatology.

Finally, most Jews return to themes in the Book of Job and in the Talmud, according to which human beings cannot fathom God's justice. They hold that we can and should question God about his role in the Holocaust, even castigating God, as → Abraham did long ago, for his apparent injustice, but that nevertheless we must dedicate ourselves to the holy tasks of perpetuating and enhancing Judaism, preserving the Jewish people, and fixing the world through acts of kindness and social action. Some do so in terms of classical Jewish theology, discounting the problems that the Holocaust raises as insoluble; some maintain that we must believe in God and carry out his commandments, despite the problems of theodicy that the Holocaust raises, because the Holocaust and Stalin's Russia showed what avowedly secular regimes produce without God; and others, most notably Emil Fackenheim, claim that through the Holocaust God revealed a new commandment, beyond the 613 in the Torah, namely, "that we not give Hitler a posthumous victory" by abandoning Judaism, as Hitler wanted us to do.

4.2.2. The establishment of the State of Israel has also been a major theme in modern Jewish theology. Already in the 19th century Moses Hess, Heinrich Graetz, Zvi Hirsch Kalischer, and Theodor Herzl advocated the reestablishment of a Jewish state in Palestine. They were followed in the early 20th century by Ahad Ha-am (the pen name of Asher Ginzberg), Judah Leib Gordon, Beryl Katznelson, and many others. The rationale for a Jewish effort to establish a new Jewish state differed among these various Zionist thinkers, as did the methodology proposed for doing so and the kind of state to be created. Still, these writers — theologians and nontheologians alike — all sought a Jewish state for political or cultural reasons.

Among religious thinkers, most Orthodox Jews opposed Zionism on the grounds that Jews needed to wait for God to send the Messiah to bring his people back to Israel and that any human effort along those lines would be a violating of God's will and thus destined to fail.

Classical Reform thinkers in the 19th and early 20th centuries (e.g., Abraham Geiger, Isaac Meir Wise, Kaufman Kohler) also opposed Zionism, but for very different reasons. They maintained that Jews should not isolate themselves in any land; they should rather, in fulfillment of Mic. 5:7, spread themselves "surrounded by many peoples [and] shall be like dew from the LORD." Thus could they truly be "a light to the nations" (Isa. 49:6) in modeling ethical monotheism. Moreover, for such Reform thinkers, nationalism of any sort was counterproductive (→ Nation, Nationalism); one should instead aim for universalism. This view was adopted as the official statement of the Reform position in the Pittsburgh Platform of 1885.

Other religious writers, though, found religious grounds for such a human effort as Zionism, beginning with Zvi Hirsch Kalischer in the 19th century and including in the 20th century such others as the Conservative rabbi Solomon Schechter, Mordecai Kaplan, and the Orthodox mystic Abraham Isaac Kook. As different as their general theologies and Zionist theories were, these religious writers drew on a long history of Jewish identification with the land of Israel, beginning with God's promise of the land to Abraham, Isaac, and Jacob and continuing through the ages in Jewish → prayers recited several times each day asking God to return his presence and the Jews to the homeland.

Ultimately the secular and religious exponents of Zionism carried the day — so much so that the Reform movement has now established a Zionist party of its own. At the same time, thinkers in Israel and abroad are now facing the major theoretical problem inherent in Zionism — namely, how Israel can be both a → democracy with legal guarantees of freedom of religion and a distinctly Jewish state.

4.2.3. The → women's movement that began in earnest in the 1960s has had a noted effect on Jewish theology. Female images of God embedded in traditional texts — in particular, God as Presence (shekinah) — have been explored, and Jewish feminist understandings of Jewish law and practice have been developed by such American thinkers as Judith Plaskow, Rachel Adler, Ellen Umansky, and Blu Greenberg (→ Feminist Theology).

In addition, the emerging equality of women in society generally has had an immense effect on Jewish life as well as Jewish thought. Beginning with Mordecai Kaplan's daughter in 1922, the first girl to have a Bat Mitzvah ceremony to mark Jewish adulthood, women have increasingly become part of Jewish liturgical life. Already at the beginning of the 20th century, virtually all Conservative and Reform synagogues had mixed seating (rather than men and women sitting in separated sections), and by the 1980s all Reform synagogues and more than 90 percent of Conservative synagogues were fully egalitarian. In addition, girls and women have increasingly received the same levels of formal Jewish education as boys and men have, culminating in the ordination of women as rabbis in the Reform (1973) and Conservative (1985) movements.

4.2.4. In the late 20th and early 21st centuries, new attention has been focused on Jewish → ethics as technology has provided new powers with their attendant moral questions about when and how to use them. The theoretical problem of how to access the tradition to gain moral guidance from it has been given new attention in current times when significant numbers of Jews no longer presume that it can easily be determined what classical Jewish law says about such questions. Because much of the new technology was not even contemplated in times past, let alone dealt with, even those in the Orthodox and Conservative movements in Judaism who wish to rely on Jewish law must search for underlying concepts and values, since there are no immediately discernible precedents.

Modern Jewish ethicists often consider Jewish law, Jewish theological beliefs, and Jewish moral values in addition to socioeconomic factors and the science of the day to determine what a reasonable reading of the Jewish tradition should be on any given issue. The various approaches to Judaism embodied in the theological stances of the several movements in modern Judaism have produced a lively discussion on specific contemporary issues such as stem cell research and privacy in Internet communications — often, surprisingly, with more agreement in the results than the diversity in assumptions and methodologies might lead one to expect.

4.2.5. Jewish law itself has undergone a thoroughgoing theological analysis in recent times. As → Enlightenment ideas pervaded central and western Europe and America, Jews living in those lands no longer were forced by governmental officials to abide by Jewish law. Jews then needed either fresh rationales to abide by such law without enforcement or a new form of Judaism without law. Thinkers in each of the movements in American Judaism created such theologies of law to explain what parts of it to obey and why. In the process, the understanding of God's revelation of Jewish law at Mount Sinai in discreet Hebrew words, of which we have an accurate record in hand, became only one possible theory.

With strong roots in the thinking of Franz Rosenzweig and later Abraham Joshua Heschel, other thinkers (e.g., Robert Gordis, Ben Zion Bokser) see revelation as a process of inspiration by which God inspired and continues to inspire people to rule in certain ways. Yet other modern thinkers (Elliot Dorff, David Lieber) understand revelation as the product of human beings aspiring to discern what God is and what God wants of them. Finally, some (Harold Schulweis, Harold Kushner, Eugene Borowitz), following the lead of Mordecai Kaplan, understand the Torah to be totally a human product, albeit one that seeks to mark the religious moments of life.

4.2.6. In recent years, → postmodern theologies of Judaism have also emerged. Abandoning the modern attempt to put religious experience into categories of reason or experience, postmodern theologians like Emanuel Levinas, Peter Ochs, and Laurie Zoloth seek rather to find both God and the good through telling and reinterpreting stories of the tradition and new stories of the lives of contemporary Jews.

In one oft-quoted passage in *m. 'Abot* 5:25, Ben Bag Bag says of the Torah, "Turn it over and turn it over again, for everything is in it." All of these modern and postmodern Jewish theologies are the product of Jewish thinkers examining and reformulating Jewish concepts — sometimes in very new ways and sometimes in very old ways — to make them live in the present time.

→ Jewish Philosophy

Bibliography: Rabbinic and traditional theology: D. HARTMAN, *A Living Covenant: The Innovative Spirit in Traditional Judaism* (Woodstock, Vt., 1997) • N. LAMM, *Faith and Doubt: Studies in Traditional Jewish Thought* (New York, 1971) • E. LEVINAS, *Nine Talmudic Readings* (Bloomington, Ind., 1990) • G. F. MOORE, *Judaism in the First Centuries of the Christian Era* (3 vols. in 2; Peabody, Mass., 1997; orig. pub., 1927-30) • S. S. SCHECHTER, *Aspects of Rabbinic Theology* (New York, 1965; orig. pub., 1909) • G. SCHOLEM, *Kabbalah* (Jerusalem, 1974) • E. E. URBACH, *The Sages: Their Concepts and Beliefs* (2d ed.; Jerusalem, 1979).

Women's issues: S. GREENBERG, ed., *The Ordination of Women as Rabbis: Studies and Responsa* (New York, 1988) • P. NADELL, *Women Who Would Be Rabbis: A History of Women's Ordination, 1889-1985* (Boston, 1998) • J. PLASKOW, *Standing Again at Sinai: Judaism from a Feminist Perspective* (San Francisco, 1990).

Other: E. BOROWITZ, *Renewing the Covenant: A Theology for the Postmodern Jew* (Philadelphia, 1991) • M. BUBER, *I and Thou* (New York, 1996; orig. pub., 1923) • E. N. DORFF, *Conservative Judaism: Our Ancestors to Our Descendents* (New York, 1996); idem, *Knowing God: Jewish Journeys to the Unknowable* (Northvale, N.J., 1992); idem, *Matters of Life and*

Death: A Jewish Approach to Modern Medical Ethics (Philadelphia, 1998); idem, *To Do the Right and the Good: A Jewish Approach to Modern Social Ethics* (Philadelphia, 2002) • E. N. DORFF and L. E. NEWMAN, eds., *Contemporary Jewish Ethics and Morality: A Reader* (New York, 1995); idem, eds., *Contemporary Jewish Theology: A Reader* (New York, 1999) • E. L. FACKENHEIM, *God's Presence in History* (New York, 1970) • N. GILLMAN, *The Death of Death: Resurrection and Immortality in Jewish Thought* (Woodstock, Vt., 1997); idem, *Sacred Fragments: Recovering Jewish Theology for the Modern Jew* (Philadelphia, 1990) • A. GREEN, ed., *Jewish Spirituality* (2 vols.; New York, 1987) • L. JACOBS, *The Book of Jewish Belief* (New York, 1984); idem, *A Jewish Theology* (London, 1973) • M. M. KAPLAN, *Judaism as a Civilization: Toward a Reconstruction of American Jewish Life* (rev. ed.; New York, 1957; orig. pub., 1934) • K. KOHLER, *Jewish Theology* (New York, 1968) • E. LEVINAS, *Difficult Freedom: Essays on Judaism* (Baltimore, 1990) • F. ROSENZWEIG, *The Star of Redemption* (New York, 1971; orig. pub., 1921) • H. SCHULWEIS, *For Those Who Can't Believe: Overcoming the Obstacles to Faith* (New York, 1994).

LOUIS JACOBS and ELLIOT N. DORFF

Jewish-Christian Dialogue

Overview
1. Rethinking Origins
2. Overlapping Histories and Divergent Memories
3. Theological Developments
    3.1. Christian Supersessionism
    3.2. Understandings of God
    3.3. Interpretation of Sacred Texts
    3.4. Religious Significance of the State of Israel
    3.5. Mission and Witness in a Religiously Plural World
4. Organizational Strategies

Overview

For almost 2,000 years Christians and Jews have assigned one another inconsequential roles in the master narratives that they each have handed on from one generation to another. From a traditional Jewish perspective the covenantal relationship between → God and → Israel (§1) determines the ultimate welfare of the world. The destiny of the nations depends upon Israel's realization of its sacred obligations. Although non-Jews may serve as God's instruments to remind Israel of its duties, most Jews have historically maintained that they have little or nothing of theological or spiritual substance to learn from non-Jews, including Christians. The question why God needed, or even bothered, to create so many Christians may have confounded some Jews, but it has not provoked serious and sustained attention over the centuries.

Christians have had greater difficulty ignoring → Judaism, since → Jesus and his earliest disciples were Jewish. The question how one can follow the path of Jesus without remaining faithful to his Jewish tradition vexed the early church and required considerable ingenuity to answer. The responses that coalesced by the third century were built on the logic of Christian supersessionism. According to this view, God sent Jesus to the Jewish people, but his own people failed to embrace his message; God thus rejected the Jews, thereby rendering the → covenant with the Jewish people obsolete. In its place stood a new covenant made known in the person of Jesus Christ, through whom alone people could come into right relationship with God. The historical catastrophes that befell the Jewish nation, especially the destruction of the second temple in 70 C.E., were interpreted as a divine judgment on Judaism, a reading of events that served to bolster the exclusivity of Christian truth claims. Arnold Toynbee epitomized a pervasive bias by dismissing Judaism as "fossilized religion." According to some traditional renderings of ancient history, the Jewish people merely served as a negative witness to anyone who denied Jesus Christ as Lord and Savior.

The ongoing and often creative interplay of Christians and Jews over the centuries belies the caricatures etched into their inherited scripts. Neither Christians nor Jews have been able to avoid dealing with the other, for they each have had to negotiate unavoidable economic, political, and social entanglements, which has left deep impressions on both religious traditions. Increasingly, historical scholarship demonstrates that the borders separating Jews and Christians in centuries past have been far more open to a profound exchange of ideas than either community has publicly acknowledged.

Since roughly 1950, however, Christians and Jews have begun to reckon openly with the profound interweaving of their traditions and with the fact that this interconnection can no longer be suppressed without imperiling the moral credibility of Christianity and the physical survival of the Jewish people. The imperative to confront the legacy of Jewish-Christian relations has become inescapable in the light of two epoch-making events of the 20th century: the → Holocaust, often called the Shoah (from Heb. *šô'â*, "calamity, catastrophe"), and the rebirth of → Israel (§2). The challenges posed by these landmark events have triggered a revolution in Christian self-understanding that touches the very foundations of the → church. In the wake of these developments, Jews are also finding themselves challenged to reexamine some of their most fundamental assumptions about themselves, the world, and God.

The changing dynamics of Jewish-Christian dialogue are difficult to chart in detail, but four central markers will serve to organize this evolving landscape.

1. Rethinking Origins

Jews and Christians both lay claim to a sacred heritage that flows in an unbroken stream from → Abraham into their distinct religious traditions. Both Christians and Jews insist that they are the true extension of Israelite religion, and they evoke this ancient connection to establish their authority and to justify their singular status as God's covenantal partners. According to the majority of Jews past and present, the followers of Jesus, most especially the apostle → Paul, deviated from the chain of → tradition. A movement that sprouted on Jewish soil became an altogether different religion with the influx of nonobservant → Gentiles. Jews saw themselves as the true and only legitimate offspring of ancient Israel, and the peculiar spin that followers of Jesus put on their scriptures was the work of interlopers who could not even engage the text in its original Hebrew.

In contrast, Christians characteristically regarded second-temple Judaism as a legalistic and spiritually depleted tradition that Jesus and his followers were unable to salvage. By means of a supersessionist theology of displacement, Christians maintained that the church was organically connected to "the Scriptures" (i.e., the OT) and could rightfully trace its lineage through Israel's kings, priests, and prophets back to Abraham. According to this theological schema, God had reconstituted a new Israel, composed of all people who placed their → faith in Jesus Christ. The ancient promises found their fulfillment in Christ, and thereby the church eclipsed the → synagogue as the locus of covenantal life. Jews were condemned as blind to the inner truth and meaning of their own scriptures. Rabbinic Judaism was written off as a deviant movement stubbornly marching down a dead-end street.

Since at least the 1970s Jewish and Christian scholars have overturned these historical constructs and exposed the polemical purposes that these portraits served. Jesus and his followers are increasingly repositioned within the matrix of Palestinian Juda-

ism, a context far more varied and complex than once acknowledged. The → Pharisees, routinely dismissed by Christian scholars in the 19th and early 20th centuries as the impoverished inhabitants of a religious wasteland, have reemerged as the architects of a spiritual revolution with antecedents as far back as the Elohist contribution to the → Torah (ca. 850 b.c.e.). It is becoming clear that both Jews and Christians are profoundly indebted to a religious movement that helped to shift the locus of authority from the → priesthood to the → rabbinate, from the → temple in → Jerusalem to synagogues in local communities, and, most important, from the written Torah to a more open and adaptive tradition of interpretation, known as the oral Torah, a vast corpus that was subsequently redacted into the → Mishnah and → Talmud.

The significance of this legacy is etched into the foundations of both the Jewish and the Christian traditions. Whereas the priesthood was open only to males born within a priestly family, any Jewish man could become a rabbi on the basis of his learning. New methods of → interpretation enabled any Jew to participate in the ritual and liturgical practices once confined to the temple and limited to the priesthood. Every Jewish home could reflect the sacred rhythms of the temple, for the dinner table was transposed into an altar, and the fellowship of friends and family constituted an alternative concept of priesthood. A way of living was developed that sacralized daily routines and enabled Jews to sanctify life in all its ordinary wonders. These innovations both democratized and universalized Torah observance, in the process cultivating the intellectual and spiritual ground on which both Christianity and rabbinic Judaism could take root.

As a result of this reappraisal of second-temple Judaism, scholars such as E. P. Sanders have reexamined the polemical battles between Jesus and his Jewish contemporaries, concluding that almost every argument in the Gospels fell within the spectrum of Jewish debate. Current studies (e.g., J. P. Meier's *Marginal Jew: Rethinking the Historical Jesus*) seek to locate Jesus in the Judaism of his time and to shed more light on his actions, his teaching, and the diverse gospel accounts interpreting his life. Moreover, not only has the Jewishness of Jesus become a touchstone for NT scholarship, but the deep linkages that bind Paul to the complex of Jewish belief and practice have also emerged as a critically important (albeit sorely neglected) dynamic. The logic of Paul's arguments and the theological trajectories of his thought are increasingly recognized as deeply shaped by the rabbinic imagination.

If the early followers of Jesus and the → early church were enmeshed in the turbulent struggles of the Jewish community, then historians are compelled to reexamine the development of messianic claims attached to Jesus (→ Messianism). How did Christians traverse the distance from Jesus to Christ and from Christ to God? Furthermore, the entanglements suggest that the partings of the ways took place over a much longer period of time and over a greater variety of disputes than previously believed. The old similes that compare the relationship of Jews and Christians to that of parents and children lose their explanatory appeal. Instead, scholars such as Alan Segal suggest that both rabbinic Judaism and early Christianity are more accurately represented as rival siblings. Both traditions were compelled to take radical leaps to adapt to the trauma generated by the destruction of the second temple. Both traditions were forced to reenvision their identities and to redefine the basis of covenantal loyalty as they were catapulted into new settings and attracted new constituencies. The reexamination of Jewish and Christian origins thus provides a fresh angle of vision into the content and character of religious identity-formation.

2. Overlapping Histories and Divergent Memories

While the legacy of anti-Judaism is indelibly etched in Jewish memories, Christians are in large measure oblivious to this anguished past. Christian memories of missionary triumph and compassionate global outreach conceal a foul underbelly of Christendom. The history of Jewish-Christian encounter demonstrates that a gospel of → love can be inverted and placed in the service of hate. Indifference, ignorance, and contempt for the Jewish people and Judaism have repeatedly found sanctuary in the hearts and minds of Christians — → Roman Catholics, → Orthodox, and → Protestants alike. With very few exceptions, the greatest Christian thinkers and the most pious Christian saints mirrored or even magnified the anti-Jewish bias of the surrounding culture. The prospects of a new relationship depend upon the willingness of Jews and Christians to examine their overlapping histories and their divergent memories and to pursue this inquiry rigorously together.

The question of the relation of traditional Christian anti-Judaism and modern → anti-Semitism continues to ignite explosive debates. Some scholars maintain that the Christian tradition supplied an arsenal of toxic images of the Jewish people. The mythological underpinnings of modern anti-Semitism are the secularized versions of ancient and medieval fantasies in which the Jewish people are imagined as demonic agents, hell-bent on taking over the world. These fantasies were popularized and disseminated in the art, literature, music, and theater of the medieval era, and they provided a basis for the conspiratorial worldview of Nazi ideology.

Other scholars insist that there is a sharp distinction between Christian anti-Judaism and modern anti-Semitism. While Christians with an apocalyptic mind-set shared an expectation that the Jewish people would either perish or convert during the trials and tribulations of the → last judgment, this transformation depended on God; in the meantime, the church had an obligation to preserve the Jewish people as a negative witness. Their degradation was highlighted as an irrefutable demonstration of the consequences that flow from the rejection of Jesus Christ. Official ecclesiastical policies are thereby understood to offer significant protections against the eliminationist strategies that grew out of late 19th-century anti-Semitism. In contrast to the pseudo-science of Nazism, Christians envisioned the church as a corporate reality that could successfully absorb the Jewish people.

Scholars will doubtless long continue debating the level of Christian complicity in the Shoah. Modern anti-Semitism, however, is indisputably linked to the resilience and adaptability of Christian anti-Judaism. Christian and Jewish historians largely agree that the Nazi policies against the Jews could not have taken root without the previous centuries of Christian hatred and violence. As a result, Christians and Jews have inherited a vexed history that threatens to assign them fixed roles. Upon the discovery of the depth and breadth of Christian contempt for the Jews, many Christians are thrust into a narrative in which they are destined to play the part of persecutors and bystanders. Jews in turn find themselves scripted in the role of passive victims and deprived of any significant role in shaping their own destiny. The guilt and defensiveness that come from this representation of the past offer a precarious psychological foundation upon which to build a new relationship.

Making progress requires a far subtler reading of the Jewish-Christian encounter. Historians are increasingly calling into question what Salo Baron has characterized as the lachrymose conception of Jewish-Christian history (i.e., as an endless recitation of catastrophes). The significant fluctuations in the Jewish-Christian encounter bespeak a complex relationship that includes not only massacres and expulsions but ongoing and creative interactions. Legislation developed and implemented by → church and state often sought to isolate Jews and push them to the margins of the society, yet the implementation of these legal codes varied from region to region. Civil authorities repeatedly revived these proscriptions because the social and economic interplay of Jews and Christians was difficult to suppress.

Historians have begun to note the cross-pollination between Jews and Christians in the fields of biblical → exegesis and interpretation, art, → liturgy, → philosophy, and → theology. Although practitioners were often prompted to conceal such interconnections, a mutual invigoration did occur in past centuries, against all odds. The creative genius of both traditions is found not in the reactive habits of withdrawal and disengagement but in the arduous struggle with the other. Religious identities take shape in the dialectical process of resistance and accommodation, and the creative tensions within and between these religious communities have given rise to some great intellectual and spiritual achievements. The retrieval of this historical legacy holds the promise of mutual enrichment in the future.

The leap from disputation to → dialogue is in large measure a bequest of the → Enlightenment, an inheritance that has proved both a blessing and a curse to modern Jews and Christians. The initial dialogues that emerged in Europe and North America during the late 19th and 20th centuries were built on the shaky premise that religious differences do not make much difference; what matters is what is held in common. Interfaith dialogues were animated by the hope that Jews and Christians could outgrow their idiosyncratic beliefs and rituals. Once they relinquished their doctrinal attachments and tribal loyalties, they could espouse moral principles and embrace spiritual sentiments that both parties would eventually discover to be interchangeable.

Interfaith dialogues that merely homogenize spiritual, ethical, and theological distinctions continue to attract the more secular members of both communities. Advocates of this version of the Jewish-Christian dialogue share the vague conviction that it does not really matter whether one is a Christian or a Jew as long as one is sincere and tolerant. These dreams, however, of a harmonious convergence have foundered on the Shoah and the establishment of the modern state of Israel. In the shadow of these events, the ethnic/cultural as well as spiritual and theological distinctions between Jews and Christians turn out to be far more resilient than once imagined. More significantly, any agenda that imperils the ongoing integrity of Judaism and the Jewish people must now be considered suspect on

ethical, spiritual, and theological grounds. In the shadow of Auschwitz, any conversation that collapses the boundaries between Jews and Christians is monologue masquerading as dialogue.

A series of landmark documents by Roman Catholics and Protestants redefined the terms of Christian theological engagement and demonstrated an unprecedented resolve to confront the Christian legacy of anti-Judaism. A pronouncement by the → World Council of Churches at its First Assembly, in Amsterdam in 1948, classifying anti-Semitism as a sin against God and humanity and, even more significantly, *Nostra aetate,* the Declaration of the Relation of the Church to Non-Christian Religions (1967), from → Vatican II, signaled the beginning of a major theological reversal. By retrieving Paul's thought at Rom. 11:29 and insisting that God's covenant with the people Israel has never been revoked, the Roman Catholic Church set a cornerstone for a nonsupersessionist understanding of the Christian relationship with Judaism. Since the late 1960s Christians have begun to work through the theological implications of this affirmation. The process of forging a constructive partnership with the Jewish people has proceeded with grand bursts of creativity and demoralizing fits of frustration.

Briefly stated, Christians and Jews have frequently come to the table with different agendas. Christians have been habitually fascinated with the recovery of their Jewish roots. They have wanted to understand the Jewishness of Jesus and to discover common theological ground so that Christians and Jews might stand together and be reconciled. In contrast, many Jews have been committed to the dialogue as a means of dismantling Christian anti-Semitism, neutralizing Christian evangelistic outreach in the Jewish community (→ Evangelism), and building a broader base of support for the State of Israel in the face of the largely hostile secular and liberal Christian media.

The future of Jewish-Christian relations demands a reshuffling of this lopsided conversation. The prospects of a constructive encounter in large measure turn on the ability of Christians and Jews to frame a theological agenda in which there is genuine mutuality and a disciplined receptivity to the wisdom of the other. Reciprocity requires the active participation of both communities, and here the demographic imbalances between Christians and Jews present a major obstacle. Without a robust Jewish community, confident in its ability to negotiate the tensions of living in a religiously plural world and observant enough to respond to the challenges of a secular society, Christians will find themselves standing alone before shattering memories or forced to substitute an unapproachable abstraction for the living reality of the Jewish people.

The demographic asymmetry may severely limit the possibilities of dialogue, with North America and Israel serving as the primary hubs, and Europe and Australia as secondary centers. The very limited opportunity that Christians in Africa, Asia, and Latin America have to engage Jews and actively participate in a searching exchange is an enormous stumbling block. The temptations to slip into supersessionist patterns and/or lapse into a Marcionite version of Christianity may prove irresistible without corrective encounters with knowledgeable and committed Jews. If the vitality and coherence of Christianity and Judaism are interconnected, then one of the most daunting challenges will be the dissemination of theological insights that emerge from the Jewish-Christian encounter to populations with few Jewish conversation partners.

The publication of *Dabru Emet: A Jewish Statement on Christians and Christianity* in September 2000 demonstrated a commitment on the part of a significant number of scholars and rabbis from the Reconstructionist, Reform, Conservative, and modern Orthodox movements to enter into a new relationship with Christians. This overture dared to place theology at the center of the conversation, in consequence of which growing numbers of Jewish scholars and clergy are beginning to realize that an encounter with the most foundational truth claims, practices, and beliefs of their Christian neighbors can function as the catalyst for greater understanding of their own tradition as well as the other's.

3. Theological Developments

Although the Jewish-Christian dialogue is opening up a wide range of theological issues, five items in particular will continue to receive attention: Christian supersessionism, contrasting understandings of God, the interpretation of sacred texts, the religious significance of the State of Israel, and mission and witness in a religiously plural world.

3.1. *Christian Supersessionism*

The legacy of supersessionism disfigures the ethical and theological core of Christianity. When Christian affirmations are built upon the negation of Judaism and the Jewish people, the moral content of the gospel is betrayed. This adversarial construction of Christian identity has precipitated downward spirals. A people who stand in opposition to the truth do not warrant civil → rights. Such people are regarded not only as outsiders but as dangerous agents of an alien and disruptive power. The Shoah

has shown us clearly that when the spiritual integrity of a people is attacked, their physical survival is also put in jeopardy. Supersessionism undercuts the promises of the gospel by reducing the boundaries of compassion so that they extend no further than the Christian's own faith community. As a consequence of massive ethical failures, Christians can no longer evaluate the moral content of their tradition on the basis of its treatment of fellow members or potential converts. The ethical character of a religious tradition is embodied in the community's response to the stranger. The virtue of hospitality, so pivotal in the ancient world, has reemerged as a vital gauge of the church's moral character, and this generosity of spirit calls for a nonsupersessionist worldview.

Christian supersessionism not only shrinks the ethical base of the tradition but also erodes the church's theological foundation. If the God of Israel decided that the Jewish people had failed and as a result God decided to abandon the covenantal commitment with the Jewish people, on what basis can Christians have confidence that God will not give up on the church? Supersessionism generates a theological portrait of an untrustworthy God who does not keep promises, who inspires terror but not confident and loving fidelity.

3.2. *Understandings of God*

Efforts to correct the inadequacies of supersessionism generate serious theological questions about the nature of God. The most vexing question revolves around a nonsupersessionist → Christology. A number of scholars have noted that the Jewish concept of the Messiah was far more fluid and arguably far less central than earlier generations imagined. They have also pointed out that Christians gave this category a whole new range of meanings when they applied this title to Jesus (→ Christological Titles). Christians and Jews thus often speak past one another when they use the same term. Furthermore, when the conception is transposed into a Greek idiom and comes to function as the proper name "Christ," the word is freighted with content that has little in common with past or present Jewish notions.

Far more problematic are the Christological formulations that evolved into such central Christian doctrines as the → incarnation and the → Trinity. Jewish avoidance and resistance to theological discourse that appears to compromise the integrity of → monotheism presents Christians with an important challenge. A vast range of competing Christological notions have accumulated in the church over the ages, and the encounter with Jews is prompting Christians to examine critically how Christian God-talk can misrepresent the God of Israel and promote a noxious triumphalism. Rather than flatten the particular texture of these doctrines, a growing number of Christian theologians are exploring their traditions and retrieving ancient ways of speaking of the dynamic and relational character of God without lapsing into supersessionism.

Christian doctrines of God often register as unintelligible or even idolatrous in the minds and hearts of Jews. Over the centuries, a majority of Jewish scholars have maintained that these formulations deliver a portrait of God that they must not only reject but pronounce theologically false. Increasing numbers of Jewish theologians are beginning to reappraise this reflexive dismissal of Christian God-talk. They are reexamining how this language shapes the imagination of Christians and wondering anew what impact these truth claims have on the Jewish people and Judaism. The revelation to which Christian doctrine points will no doubt lie outside the experience of Jews, most especially those who are Torah observant. Some Jewish scholars are finding, however, that Christian theological discourse is not as alien or as irrelevant as once believed. In a secular age when membership within a religious community is increasingly an act of choice, both Jews and Christians need to acquire the ability to name their core affirmations and to articulate their own dynamics of belonging.

This creative interplay is evoked when Christians turn their attention to Jewish understandings of God and scrutinize the Jewish emphasis on the transcendence and the radical otherness of a God beyond mediation (→ Immanence and Transcendence). The theological language used by many Jews seems to render God so remote as to become irrelevant. How is one to encounter God if there is nothing that can mediate or make God's reality known? If Trinitarian and incarnational language runs the risk of overdetermining our images of God's immanence, are there not also dangers in at least some formulations of God's oneness? Is oneness primarily about number, a fixed and static formula about God's unknowability, or is oneness more about the uniqueness and unconditional loyalty of the covenantal partnership?

The question of God's oneness has given rise to an array of understandings over the centuries within both the Jewish and the Christian communities. If the dialogue entails genuine reciprocity, then Christians and Jews may prompt one another to survey their own traditions and to reclaim neglected voices that will deepen each community's spiritual reservoir. The dialogue flourishes not through the exchange of vague affirmations but in encounters where Christians and Jews challenge one another to articulate their core religious convictions, to discover the distinctive character of each tradition, and to recognize the inscrutable domains where language and experience fail to penetrate the depths of the other's religious life.

3.3. *Interpretation of Sacred Texts*

The same scriptures that bind Christians and Jews together also set them apart. In the encounter with one another and the text, however, a door opens onto an unfamiliar domain where new ways of reading and interpreting Scripture become possible. It is difficult to exaggerate the importance of this development. Christians today (and to a lesser extent Reform and Conservative Jews) are tempted to subscribe to methods of reading that flatten their sacred writings. Historical criticism has certainly provided essential insights into the struggles behind and within the Bible, but this approach has also constricted its significance by insisting that the truth of the text is determined solely by the author's original intent and/or its reception by an original community.

In the 20th century, historical criticism trumped all other literary approaches (→ Literary Criticism), yielding in the process an empty-hearted notion of the "living Word." Increasingly, the professionals subdued the Bible and, knowingly or not, restricted access to the laity. A different kind of literalism won the day, which proved no less confining than the plain and simple readings of the fundamentalists. Scholars assumed that they were the only legitimate authorities who could expound Scripture's truth and fix its meaning. By and large, the public learned to defer to the experts and, as a result, forfeited a once common biblical literacy.

A number of cultural pressures, some associated with → postmodernism, have broken the stranglehold of the historical-critical method and unleashed new and fruitful ways of reading and interpreting the Bible. According to the Jewish tradition, serious engagement with a sacred text entails a performance that is comparable to striking a hammer against a rock — the act of study cracks the text into 70 pieces, and the inquirers must scramble to collect the sacred fragments. No one person alone can collect all the splinters, and thus serious engagement with sacred writings requires a community. In virtue of individual experience everyone is endowed with special sight, since each can notice and recover fragments that might have escaped the notice of others.

Beneath this metaphor lies an approach that democratizes access to the Bible and finds within it unbounded textual treasures. The Jewish tradition maintains that sacred texts harbor multiple layers of meaning. The Bible does not offer a fixed → truth that applies to all people at all times but speaks a fresh word to each generation. The right meaning of the Bible is discerned as the community struggles with the multitude of readings that have accumulated within the tradition. Wisdom does not arise from the Scriptures apart from a spirited encounter with the discoveries of earlier generations of readers. The discipline of reading the Bible develops in the process of learning how to join a raucous debate that extends from ancient times into an uncertain future. To participate in this study one must learn to listen and respond to the voices of the entire community, and study is thus understood as a sacred duty binding the individual to the people of Israel.

Dialogue with the Jewish people has inspired a growing number of Christians to develop some new habits of reading. By surveying the hermeneutical practices of each community and noting modulations in different times and places, Jews and Christians are discovering a range of meanings within, as well as between, their respective traditions. One Protestant tendency is to attempt a leap over almost 2,000 years of tradition in the hopes of making direct contact with the Word. This proclivity can dislodge individuals from the larger community of readers, the living and the dead, and imprison them within their own peculiar circumstances. A plunge into the plurality of understandings within the Bible as well as within our respective traditions is far more invigorating, precisely because the reader is invariably pulled into the thick of competing, if not contradictory, claims. Those who dare to enter into serious study of the Bible are thrown into a textual tug-of-war, which requires interpretive daring and even playfulness.

If the Scriptures pull communities in different directions with extravagant promises of undiscovered riches, there is a kind of indeterminacy that raises unsettling questions about the Bible's truth. How is the community to decide which interpretation is authoritative? Or, differently stated, given the multitude of possible readings, how do we constitute a cohesive community that is bound and guided by its scriptural tradition? This conundrum is evoking heated debate among Jews as well as Christians. If a community cannot nail down the truth of the Scriptures, then — according to some Jews and Christians — the issue of justice must serve as the governing criterion (→ Righteousness, Justice). The community is called to decide which

interpretation of Scripture promotes a just ordering of society, and in light of the history of both Jewish and Christian communities, special attention must center on the implications of any given interpretation concerning the vulnerable outsider. Others privilege different criteria, opting for readings that protect the boundaries of the community or preserve doctrinal deposits from the past. In the ensuing battles over the Bible, Christians and Jews will notice that the most ferocious campaigns are fought within their respective camps. Yet they do well to examine how the struggles within each community are conducted. Each community has its distinctive style of wrestling with its sacred writings, and each can learn something from the other. In fact, one could say that, to preserve the integrity of their scriptural legacies, Jews and Christians must open themselves to the discovery of new meanings.

3.4. *Religious Significance of the State of Israel*
The establishment of the State of Israel in 1948 has raised new issues in the Christian-Jewish dialogue. Christians had historically seen both the destruction of the Jerusalem temple and the rise of the Jewish → diaspora as confirmation of God's rejection of Judaism and the Jewish people. It is thus no accident that Emperor Julian the Apostate (361-63) sought to undermine the basic self-understanding of Christians by attempting to rebuild the Jerusalem temple.

The significance of the land of Israel remains a matter of some controversy among Christians. One strain of thought has historically seen the land itself as having sacramental value, both because it is the place where Jesus lived, died, and was resurrected and because Christians affirm an organic connection to the biblical people of Israel. A continuing Christian presence there has provided an ongoing witness that many Christians regard as indispensable to the proclamation of the gospel. Other Christians have insisted that God's promises are not tied to a specific piece of real estate; any theological attachment to a specific land can be too easily politicized and thus lead to idolatrous justifications of unjust actions and policies.

While this debate over the status of the land of Israel is bound to continue, there is no escape from the need of Christians to relate to the theological, political, and economic claims of the Jewish people to the land and the State of Israel. The refusal of the Vatican to exchange ambassadors with the Jewish state at its establishment in 1948 was a sore point in Roman Catholic–Jewish relations. Thus the Fundamental Agreement between Israel and the Vatican, signed in 1993, was an event of major significance, removing a significant obstacle to Roman Catholic–Jewish rapprochement.

The State of Israel is both a subject and a locus for Christian-Jewish dialogue. The dialogue takes on a different aspect in Israel, where a sovereign Jewish majority governs Christian as well as Muslim minorities. The moral and ethical issues raised by a Jewish government ruling Gentiles are of concern to Israeli and diaspora Jews alike. In Israel and in the diaspora political issues can overshadow theological considerations. Christians are striving to balance their recognition of Jewish claims with their concern for the rights of the Palestinian Arabs, many of whom are Christian (→ Israel 3). In the face of Christian criticism of Israeli policies, Jewish organizations have frequently assumed a defensive posture. Their responses, however, raise a fundamental question for the dialogue: when does legitimate criticism of Israeli policies cross the line into anti-Zionism, and then from anti-Zionism into anti-Semitism?

The outbreak of the second intifada in September 2000 has led to new tensions among Christians and Jews. Liberal Christians remain troubled by the unconditional religious attachment of Jews to the land of Israel, maintaining that Jewish claims to the land and its resources often obscure the legitimate demands of the Palestinians. A number of Protestant groups have issued statements on the Middle East that many Jews have considered inimical to the well-being of the State of Israel. At the same time, many conservative and evangelical Christians, who have often stood on the margins of the dialogue, have gained new Jewish allies through their firm support of Israel.

This shifting of alliances is compounded within Israel itself, as the divide between secular and ultra-Orthodox Jews grows deeper. This internal debate is further intensified as Jews in the diaspora struggle to determine what place the State of Israel should play in the formation of their own religious identity. Finally, the complexity and instability of the situation are magnified by the increase in religious militancy and the inescapable challenge of responding to → Islam and the growing Muslim population. The destinies of these disparate groups are intricately interwoven, and the impact of these tangled relationships will influence for better or worse the future of Jewish-Christian relations.

3.5. Mission and Witness in a Religiously Plural World

The Christian-Jewish encounter compels both communities to reconsider the narrative arc of their sacred stories. In some of its forms the familiar Christian plot that moves from creation to fall to Jesus'

redemptive death and → resurrection deletes the people of Israel from its own story and undermines hope for the future restoration and consummation of the entire created order. When Christians proclaim that the prophetic → promises have been fulfilled in Christ, the Jewish rejection of these claims serves as a valuable reminder of the unfinished condition of God's → creation. In light of the dialogue, many Christians are discovering that any construal of the Christian story that maintains that the battle is over and the victory done substitutes a spiritual abstraction for the collaborative struggle to transform the world. Some forms of → apocalyptic thought tend to blind churches to the immediate responsibilities of a healing ministry. The desperation of a world split into warring social, economic, ethnic, and religious factions demands that Christians reexamine the purposes of the Christian → mission.

In assessing the mission of the church, Christians affirm that Jesus Christ is the Savior of the world. If the Jewish people do not experience Jesus as the true way into relationship with God, does that mean that Jews are self-deceived and clinging to a failed covenant? On the one hand, a supersessionist answer to this question underscores the need to bring the world's lost souls to Christ. The end that defines this expression of Christian hope is a → kingdom where religious differences are overcome in and through Christ, a vision of triumph that in fact fertilizes seeds of contempt for all those who dwell in other religious traditions.

On the other hand, a nonsupersessionist rendering of this universal claim will need to move in different directions. Some Christians will argue, along the lines of Paul van Buren, that this statement is part of the doxological language of the church. The assertion that Jesus Christ is the Savior of the world corresponds to the language of love used by a spouse (e.g., "she is the most beautiful woman in the world" or "he is the only one"). Others such as Mark Heim maintain that Jesus Christ is indeed the only way to → salvation as defined within the Christian tradition. People in other religious traditions, however, have different ends for which they strive, and their participation within these communities may guide them to their ultimate goals. The goal of salvation to which Jesus Christ points differs from the salvations articulated within other religious communities. Nirvana is not the same goal envisioned by Jews or Christians, and so the varied topography of religious faiths underscores the need to speak of different salvations.

The call to witness will surely continue to direct Christians into the world, although whether such witness surrenders its bid for universal dominance and redefines the nature of its cosmic relevance remains an open question. The Christian claim that the church alone provides access to God's truth will prove increasingly difficult to maintain in a religiously plural world. The response to the disorienting array of religious alternatives will reveal the moral and theological character of Christian communities. To argue that God wants Christians to dissolve all religious differences speaks forcefully about the God Christians → worship. How can Christians maintain the exclusivity of their universal claims without simultaneously restricting the freedom and sovereignty of God? In conversation with others — and especially with Jews — this question assumes urgency and importance.

Religious → pluralism also presents the Jewish community with a daunting challenge. If Judaism is constituted by a revelatory truth that defies translation, what have Jews to say to non-Jews? What does it mean to be a "chosen people" who are nonetheless called to be "a light to the nations"? The Jewish tradition divides humanity in two: Jews and Gentiles. Gentiles are recognized and affirmed as righteous insofar as they conform to the dictates of the Noachian laws. On close inspection, the legal requirements that apply to non-Jews appear as a somewhat reduced version of the Torah. Righteous Gentiles are deemed worthy in virtue of their approximation of a Torah-observant life. In some sense, their conformity to these legal standards makes them "anonymous Jews." Consequently, the insistence that righteous Gentiles also have a place in → heaven is not as magnanimous an affirmation as it first appears. Furthermore, to squeeze all non-Jews into one massive human lump fails to recognize the distinctive character of each faith community. Whether Jews have a sacred story that can accommodate the reality of religious pluralism remains an open question. Jews no less than Christians must make significant theological refinements within their traditions if they are to welcome others in all their particularity as a source of blessing.

Fruitful theological encounter requires a level of → humility that has not been the hallmark of either the Christian or the Jewish tradition. The grammar of each tradition is confusing and may prove beyond the outsider's mastery. Yet, the benefits of striving to become religiously bilingual in a secular culture are enormous. In learning the language of the other's tradition, Jews and Christians gain insights into their own traditions that they otherwise could not achieve. Furthermore, when Christians and Jews struggle to articulate their core affirma-

tions in terms comprehensible to the other, they acquire a greater ability to bring the distinctive wisdom of their own tradition to bear on the larger society.

In the future, theological dialogue will require Christians and Jews to explore the communal practices that shape their respective communities, for significant struggles are being waged within each tradition, and the outcome of these conflicts remains uncertain. The most fruitful prospects do not lie in a romantic quest to overcome all differences. Theological dialogue at its best will lead Christians and Jews to a deeper understanding of their own irreducible singularity and in the process illuminate the underlying mystery of the other, a mystery that neither tradition can contain but both must honor.

4. Organizational Strategies

Since 1970 a variety of interfaith councils, institutes, and coalitions have emerged. Some are agencies designed to combat prejudice, others are community councils that champion greater tolerance and civility, and some are institutes that design and implement educational programs for the promotion of interfaith understanding.

In the United States the National Conference of Christians and Jews (NCCJ) was founded in 1928, largely to combat the anti-Catholic prejudice that came to the fore during the 1928 campaign of Al Smith, the first Roman Catholic presidential candidate from a major political party. The NCCJ's focus gradually broadened beyond the Jewish-Christian sphere, and it is today known as the National Conference for Community and Justice.

In Europe the → International Conference of Christians and Jews was founded in the wake of World War II and the Shoah. Today it is headquartered in Germany (in the former home of Jewish philosopher Martin Buber) and has 36 constituent organizations in 32 countries. In the United Kingdom the Council of Christians and Jews was formed in 1947. Its honorary patron is the queen, and its honorary chairs are the chief rabbi, the Anglican archbishop of Canterbury, and the Roman Catholic archbishop of Westminster.

Particularly in the last 30 years Christian denominations, most especially the Roman Catholic Church, have taken critically important steps to form and disseminate new understandings for Christians of Judaism and the Jewish people. The Evangelical Lutheran Church in America, further, has also taken a critical step in officially repudiating the anti-Semitic writings of Martin → Luther.

There has also been an encouraging proliferation

of Jewish studies programs in colleges and universities in North America and parts of Europe. New initiatives in and between Christian and Jewish theological seminaries are haltingly being developed. Students in various settings can cross-register and encounter faculty from the other tradition. The combined impact of these recent developments in academic institutions has placed the Jewish-Christian dialogue on the horizon of both communities.

The terms of engagement are shifting, and the most promising prospects for Jewish-Christian dialogue entail educational endeavors that move vital scholarship out of academic isolation into the community at large. In a culture infatuated with a spirituality that is freed of institutional entanglements, there is a growing need for educational experiences that connect people both to the rigors of learning and to living within a particular religious tradition. The prevailing assumption is often that such work requires Christians and Jews to make an inward turn that avoids the difficulty of interfaith encounter. Given the understandable apprehension that an open society poses a greater risk to the survival of Judaism (e.g., in respect to intermarriage) than did the closed and restricted social ordering of the past, Jews are especially nervous about welcoming overtures from Christians to serious encounter.

Organizations that advance Jewish-Christian dialogue must shape initiatives that deepen the understanding and commitment of the participants to their own religious communities. Also, however — since most Christians and Jews find themselves in a world where they live, work, and play side by side — both the church and the synagogue must equip their members to engage their neighbors in conversation about the things that matter most. If Jews and Christians do not learn how to discuss and debate the issues of the day, and if they are unable to tap the wellsprings of their respective traditions, then neither community will have anything of substance to offer the world at large. To meet the challenges of living in religiously plural societies, Jewish-Christian institutes will need to mediate educational encounters that bridge the academy and congregation, the seminary and discussion group, the school and the community center. If the destinies of Christianity and Judaism are interwoven, then the future of both may depend on their willingness to enter into a new conversation and respond to a new set of circumstances.

→ Jewish Mission; Jewish Philosophy; Jewish Theology

Bibliography: *The emergence of Christianity and rabbinic Judaism:* P. VAN BUREN, *According to the Scriptures: The Origins of the Gospel and of the Church's OT* (Grand Rapids, 1998) • A. DAVIES, ed., *Anti-Semitism and the Foundations of Christianity* (New York, 1979) • J. D. G. DUNN, *The Partings of the Ways: Between Christianity and Judaism and Their Significance for the Character of Christianity* (Philadelphia, 1991) • L. FELDMAN, *Jew and Gentile in the Ancient World* (Princeton, 1993) • P. FREDRIKSEN, *From Jesus to Christ: The Origins of the NT Images of Jesus* (2d ed.; New Haven, 2000) • J. GAGER, *The Origins of Anti-Semitism* (New York, 1983) • J. P. MEIER, *A Marginal Jew: Re-thinking the Historical Jesus* (3 vols.; New York, 1991-2001) • R. RUETHER, *Faith and Fratricide* (New York, 1974) • E. P. SANDERS, *Jesus and Judaism* (Philadelphia, 1985) • A. SEGAL, *Rebecca's Children: Judaism and Christianity in the Roman World* (Cambridge, Mass., 1986).

From anti-Judaism to anti-Semitism: D. BERGER, ed., *History and Hate* (Philadelphia, 1986) • R. CHAZAN, *Medieval Stereotypes and Modern Antisemitism* (Berkeley, Calif., 1997) • J. COHEN, *The Friars and the Jews: The Evolution of Medieval Anti-Judaism* (Ithaca, N.Y., 1982) • M. R. COHEN, *Under Crescent and Cross: The Jews in the Middle Ages* (Princeton, 1994) • E. FLANNERY, *The Anguish of the Jews* (New York, 1965) • D. I. KERTZER, *The Popes against the Jews* (New York, 2001) • G. I. LANGMUIR, *History, Religion, and Antisemitism* (Berkeley, Calif., 1990); idem, *Toward a Definition of Antisemitism* (Berkeley, Calif., 1990) • F. E. MANUEL, *The Broken Staff: Judaism through Christian Eyes* (Cambridge, Mass., 1992) • H. OBERMAN, *The Impact of the Reformation* (Grand Rapids, 1994); idem, *The Roots of Anti-Semitism in the Age of Renaissance and Reformation* (Philadelphia, 1984) • M. SAPERSTEIN, *Moments of Crisis in Jewish-Christian Relations* (Philadelphia, 1989).

Theological resources for the Jewish-Christian encounter: T. FRYMER-KENSKY, D. NOVAK, P. OCHS, D. SANDMEL, and M. SIGNER, eds., *Christianity in Jewish Terms* (Boulder, Colo., 2000) • M. GOLDBERG, *Jews and Christians: Getting Our Stories Straight* (Valley Forge, Pa., 1991) • W. HARRELSON and R. M. FALK, *Jews and Christians: A Troubled Family* (Nashville, 1990) • S. M. HEIM, *The Depth of the Riches: A Trinitarian Theology of Religious Ends* (Grand Rapids, 2001); idem, *Salvations: Truth and Difference in Religion* (Maryknoll, N.Y., 1995) • D. NOVAK, *Jewish-Christian Dialogue: A Jewish Justification* (New York, 1989) • J. PAWLIKOWSKI, *Jesus and the Theology of Israel* (Wilmington, Del., 1989) • D. SANDMEL, R. CATALANO, and C. LEIGHTON, eds., *Irreconcilable Differences?* (Boulder, Colo., 2001) • R. K. SOULEN, *The God of Israel and Christian Theology* (Minneapolis, 1996) • C. M. WILLIAMSON, *A Guest in the House of Israel: Post-Holocaust Church Theology* (Louisville, Ky., 1993) • M. R. WILSON, *Our Father*

Abraham: Jewish Roots of the Christian Faith (Grand Rapids, 1989).

CHRISTOPHER M. LEIGHTON and
CHARLES ARIAN

Job, Book of

1. The Book and the Man
2. Prologue and Epilogue
3. Poem and Problems
    3.1. Job and His Friends
    3.2. Yahweh and the Whirlwind
    3.3. Text
    3.4. Wisdom and Influences
    3.5. Interpolations
    3.6. Wisdom Crisis
4. Parallels

1. The Book and the Man

At the heart of the Book of Job is a preeminently righteous man named Job (Heb. *'iyyôb*). An account is given of his thoughts and conduct when faced with extraordinary misfortune and → suffering. The book is a poem (3:1–42:6) with a prose prologue (1:1–2:13) and epilogue (42:7-17).

2. Prologue and Epilogue

The prologue and epilogue are a Wisdom story (1:1-5, 13-22; 42:11-15). In the face of his loss of wealth and children, Job suffers patiently. Ultimately, his fortunes are restored by → Yahweh (42:12-15) after visits of sympathy from relatives and acquaintances (v. 11). According to an expansion in 1:6-12; 2:1-13; 42:7-10, 16-17, → "Satan" is the one who brings on Job's afflictions and an additional plague. Job passes this test as well. Three friends come to comfort him, but according to 42:7 they do not speak what is right; they are saved from the wrath of Yahweh by Job's intercession (vv. 7-9).

Yahweh restores Job's health (42:10a) and gives him twice as much as before (vv. 10b, 12). In the long run, then, the righteous are protected and rewarded. Mention of the righteous Job in Ezek. 14:14, 20 shows that the story was a familiar one. The reference to Satan (like the mention of Satan in Zech. 3:1) belongs to the (early) postexilic period.

3. Poem and Problems

3.1. *Job and His Friends*

The poem presents a more complex Job. After Job's elaborate self-cursing in chap. 3, the text consists first of three rounds of dialogue between Job and his friends (4–14; 15–21; 22–27). The basic problem

here is the Wisdom doctrine that righteousness brings good and wickedness evil, and that Yahweh causes both to happen (→ Wisdom Literature). Both sides begin here but argue along different lines. The friends conclude from Job's misfortunes that he must have sinned, hence he ought to confess his → guilt to God and in this way regain his favor (5:8, 17-26; 11:13-20; 22:21-23, 26-30). Job, as the prologue intimates, although recognizing that he may not be perfect, is not aware of any sin that would account for the extraordinary afflictions that have overtaken him. He thus thinks that God has treated him unjustly and doubts whether God is just (9:22-24, 28b-31; 10:6-7; 16:9, 12-17; 19:6-7). The friends perceive God's justice (→ Righteousness, Justice) in his visiting of evil on evildoers (15:20-35; 18:5-21; 20:4-29). Job thinks that God tolerates evildoers and even prospers them (21:6-33). As the friends see what they think is stubbornness in Job, their pastoral concern in the first round turns to accusation of specific faults in the third (e.g., 22:4-11).

Job, having first wished that God might slay him (6:8-13), increasingly asks for dialogue with God, for a trial, in which he might present his case and make his complaint against God (10:2; 13:3, 18-27; 23:3-6), confident that he will prevail (23:7). In God himself and not in another Job expects to find a witness (16:19), a deliverer or advocate (19:25). The dialogue ends with a monologue by Job (29–31) in which he wishes that he might regain his former honorable estate (chap. 29), complains of his present plight (chap. 30), expresses his general sense of innocence in the form of an oath (31:1-34), which both ends the conversation with the three friends and prepares the way for an encounter with God, and flings against God his final challenge (31:35-37).

3.2. *Yahweh and the Whirlwind*

The encounter with God takes the form of a theophany. Yahweh appears in a whirlwind and addresses Job (38:1–39:12, 19-30; 40:8-14), and Job replies (40:3-5 and 42:2, 3aβ, 5, 6). (The Wisdom expansion in 39:13-18; 40:1-2; 40:15–41:34 results in a doubling of the divine discourse and Job's response.) Yahweh's questions regarding the Creator and creation of the world and his challenge to Job to perform similar acts of power leave Job no option but to acknowledge the omnipotence and omniscience of Yahweh and to confess his own impotence and ignorance. In the process Job learns to know God existentially and not just intellectually.

3.3. *Text*

The tension between chap. 3 and 1:22; 2:10, and also between 42:7 and the speeches, has led to the view that the poem has supplanted an earlier text between 2:13 and 42:7.

3.4. Wisdom and Influences

In form and content the book gives evidence of various influences. The speeches of Job and his friends are Wisdom debates. The friends admonish and teach. Also from Wisdom comes the teaching about nature in God's speech. Elements from the Psalms (e.g., in the hymnic parts; → Hymn 1) may be seen in Job's varied complaint, but not in his self-cursing in chap. 3 or in his accusing God. Various legal forms and terms occur in the debate with God. The relation between God's speech in chaps. 38–41 and Job's challenge in (29–)31 may not be compared with psalms of complaint, which do not put a statement of innocence before an oracle from Yahweh, or with court procedure, in which there is no divine verdict after an oath of purification, but with Pss. 15; 24; Isa. 33:14b-16; Mic. 6:6-8, and the Egyptian Book of the Dead 125. The work dates to the fifth century B.C.

3.5. Interpolations

Two interpolations have been discerned from a later hand. The ode to wisdom in chap. 28 anticipates God's speech with its thesis that wisdom is accessible only to God. In chaps. 32–37 a fourth friend, Elihu, otherwise not mentioned in the book, takes up Job's words and in four speeches tries to show Job that his sufferings are educational.

3.6. Wisdom Crisis

With Ecclesiastes, the Book of Job gives evidence of a crisis in Israelite Wisdom. The Job of the poem, and with him its author, is troubled by the problem that contrary to Wisdom teaching, the righteous must undergo great sufferings. The solution, even without a direct answer from God, is that Job must submit to the divine omnipotence and omniscience that manifest themselves to him.

Job's accusation in 9:24 — that "the earth is given into the hand of the wicked" and that God "covers the eyes of its judges" — suggests that God has turned demonic, a most serious theological challenge to the prevailing doctrine of the One who rewards righteousness and punishes wickedness. The exchange in 42:1-6 culminates in Job's comment, "I despise myself, and repent in dust and ashes." The difficulties with this statement are immense.

The Heb. verb šûb, normally used for "repent," is not used here. Rather, it is a form of nḥm, involving an action best translated as "comfort myself." That Job should be shown to "repent" after the whole volume of protests of his innocence and righteousness from the initial characterization through the entire poem makes little sense, even if the normal verb had been used. Once the idea was suggested, however, a zealous devotee of Deuteronomic orthodoxy apparently picked it up and wrote an epilogue, making things turn out the way they were supposed to, according to the three friends, with Job receiving more than he had before his tragic losses. The ending thus seems to reveal a rather shallow orthodoxy that could not accept the difficult poetic conclusion.

4. Parallels

Literary works with similar forms and motifs occur elsewhere in the ancient Near East. The dialogue form and nature lists (note Job 38–41) occur both in Egypt and in Mesopotamia. Mesopotamian texts from the first and second millennium deal with the problem of the righteous suffering in the form of laments, with restoration as a solution (*ANET* 589-91, 596-604; W. Beyerlin, 157-65). There is little reason to suppose, however, that the Book of Job borrows much from such parallels.

→ Theodicy

Bibliography: Commentaries: G. FOHRER (KAT; Gütersloh, 1963) • N. HABEL (OTL; Louisville, Ky., 1985) • F. HESSE (ZBK; Zurich, 1978) • F. HORST (BKAT; 4th ed.; Neukirchen, 1983) chaps. 1–19 • C. NEWSOM (NIB; Nashville, 1996) • M. H. POPE (AB; Garden City, N.Y., 1965) • R. D. SACKS (Atlanta, 1999) • A. DE WILDE (OTS; Leiden, 1981).

Other works: D. BERRIGAN, *Job: Death and No Dominion* (Franklin, Wis., 2000) • M. CHENEY, *Dust, Wind, and Agony: Character, Speech, and Genre in Job* (Stockholm, 1994) • Y. HOFFMAN, *A Blemished Perfection: The Book of Job in Context* (Sheffield, 1996) • W. E. HULME, *Christian Caregiving: Insights from the Book of Job* (St. Louis, 1992) • E. KUTSCH, "Unschuldsbekenntnis und Gottesbegegnung. Der Zusammenhang zwischen Hi 31 und 38ff.," *Kleine Schriften zum Alten Testament* (Berlin, 1986) 308-35 • B. MCKIBBEN, *The Comforting Whirlwind: God, Job, and the Scale of Creation* (Grand Rapids, 1999) • L. G. PERDUE, *Wisdom in Revolt: Metaphorical Theology in the Book of Job* (Sheffield, 1991) • L. G. PERDUE and W. C. GILPIN, eds., *The Voice from the Whirlwind: Interpreting the Book of Job* (Nashville, 1992) • C. WESTERMANN, *The Structure of the Book of Job: A Form-Critical Analysis* (Philadelphia, 1981).

ERNST KUTSCH

Joel, Book of

The Book of Joel has a strong liturgical orientation. A serious plague of locusts and drought (chap. 1) signifies the threatening proximity of the day of → Yahweh (2:1-11). This setting issues in a proclamation of a day of lamentation and → fasting (2:12-17), which brings about a turn to → salvation (2:18-32). The day of Yahweh becomes a day of judgment on foreign peoples, while → Jerusalem and Judah experience deliverance and paradisiacal fruitfulness (chap. 3).

The date of the book is contested, though it may be the beginning of the fourth century B.C. (a different view is taken by W. Rudolph). The author was perhaps a temple → prophet from Jerusalem. Some scholars question the literary unity of the work, viewing it rather as a redactional composition around the theme of the day of Yahweh.

Joel uses prophetic materials to explain the given situation in relation to the → future. Conversion (expressed liturgically) is crucial.

Bibliography: Commentaries: E. ACHTEMEIER (NIB; Nashville, 1996) • J. L. CRENSHAW (AB; Garden City, N.Y., 1995) • A. DEISSLER (NEchtB; Würzburg, 1981) • W. RUDOLPH (KAT; Gütersloh, 1971) • A. WEISER (ATD; 7th ed.; Göttingen, 1979) • H. W. WOLFF (Hermeneia; Philadelphia, 1977).

Other works: G. W. AHLSTRÖM, *Joel and the Temple Cult of Jerusalem* (Leiden, 1971) • S. L. COOK, *Prophecy and Apocalypticism: The Postexilic Social Setting* (Minneapolis, 1995) • J. JEREMIAS, "Joel / Joelbuch," *TRE* 17.91-97 (extensive bibliography) • O. PLÖGER, *Theokratie und Eschatologie* (3d ed.; Neukirchen, 1968) 117-28.

WINFRIED THIEL

John, Epistles of

1. 1 John
2. 2-3 John

1. 1 John

1.1. Although 1 John is included among the → Catholic Epistles, along with 2 and 3 John, it does not have the essential marks of a letter. When, though, the author calls his readers "children" and "beloved," it shows that he was addressing specific people in a community (e.g., 2:7, 12-14). These people "believe in the name of the Son of God" (5:13). The entire church is in view, not just a single → congregation. The work is thus a homily in which an introduction (1:1-4) is followed by sections that are alternately hortatory (1:5–2:17; 2:28–3:24; 4:7–5:4a; 5:13-21; → Parenesis) and dogmatic (2:18-27; 4:1-6; 5:4b-12).

The aim of the book is to confirm the church in true faith and in responsible and loving conduct in the face of the seductions of false teachers (2:18-27; 4:1-6; 5:6). Teaching a → Docetic → Christology (4:2), they have come forth from, and have departed from, the community itself (2:19), yet they claim to be → prophets (4:1). By destroying the → unity of the church, they cause offense over against mutual Christian → love *(agapē)* and fulfill the prophecy of the coming of the → antichrist in the last days (2:18; → Last Judgment). Only by standing fast in the → tradition to which the author bears witness (1:1-3) and by observing the old and new commandment of → love can the readers abide in the Father and the Son (2:6; 4:16).

Gnostic elements (in the sense of → gnosis as an original experience of God) and a futurist eschatological sense (→ Eschatology 2) come to expression in dualistic language (2:15-17). Determination and ethical responsibility intertwine dialectically. Indicative and imperative are related as cause and effect (4:11).

1.2. It is commonly held that the three Johannine letters were written as pastoral letters sometime after the Gospel of John, and by the same author. Against that position, the priority of the gospel cannot so easily be presupposed. Moreover, the linguistic and material similarities between the letters and the gospel (emphasis on truth, love, etc.) but differences in theological outlook (in eschatology, pneumatology, and → atonement), as well as the ecclesiological, rather than Christological, orientation of the letters, might better be explained by asserting independent authorship within a Johannine school. The differences would not then have to be traced to different literary sources but could point to oral tradition that resulted in discussion within the school.

Patristic witness locates 1 John and the whole Johannine tradition in Asia Minor. The date of composition of the letters was the late first century or the early second.

2. 2-3 John

These short epistles are actual letters. If their common author ("the elder," or presbyter, mentioned in 2 John 1 and 3 John 1) is the basic authority for the Johannine circle, they record early Johannine theology: an → apocalyptic outlook (antichrist, rewards), realistic expectation of the → parousia, an explicit incarnational Christology (i.e., that Christ has "come in the flesh," 2 John 7; cf. 1 John 4:2), an incipient → dualism, and Christian teaching characterized by a stress on the community of God and a striving for truth and love (2 John 5-6, 9). Concerning John the elder, note the witness of Papias (ca. 60-130), as recorded in the fourth century by Eusebius (*Hist. eccl.* 3.39.3).

The purpose of 2 John is to oppose false teachers and to announce the elder's coming visit, whereas 3 John records the reaction to the sending of itinerant preachers. Above all, the influential Diotrephes opposes the authority of the elder and will not welcome the messengers (3 John 9-10). W. Bauer concluded that the elder was a champion of orthodoxy and Diotrephes a heretic representing the majority in the congregation. E. Käsemann advanced the theory that there was a conflict here between office and spirit, with Diotrephes standing for church order and the elder for a free charismatic outlook (→ Charisma). Another theory is that emerging chiliastic features within the Johannine school in Asia Minor placed the author outside the mainstream of doctrinal development, even though — as its founder — he occupied an important place in it for a time.

→ Incarnation; John, Gospel of

Bibliography: Commentaries: R. E. BROWN (AB; Garden City, N.Y., 1982) • R. BULTMANN (Hermeneia; Philadelphia, 1973) • C. H. DODD (MNTC; London, 1946) • J. L. HOULDEN (HNTC; New York, 1973) • I. H. MARSHALL (NICNT; Grand Rapids, 1978) • R. SCHNACKENBURG (New York, 1992) • S. S. SMALLEY (WBC; Waco, Tex., 1984) • D. M. SMITH (IBC; Louisville, Ky., 1991) • G. STRECKER (Hermeneia; Minneapolis, 1996).

Other works: W. BAUER, *Orthodoxy and Heresy in Earliest Christianity* (Philadelphia, 1971) • R. E. BROWN, *The Community of the Beloved Disciple* (New York, 1979) • E. KÄSEMANN, "Ketzer und Zeuge. Zum johanneischen Verfasserproblem," *ZTK* 48 (1951) 291-311.

GEORG STRECKER†

John, Gospel of

1. Structure and Contents
2. Sources and Message
3. Composition
4. Background
5. Place and Time

1. Structure and Contents

The main body of the Gospel of John comprises two sections: the public ministry of Jesus (2:1–11:54) and the parting discourses and the passion (11:55–19:42). The prologue, with the story of John the Baptist and the calling of the → disciples, forms the introduction (chap. 1), and the resurrection stories form the conclusion (20). Chap. 21 is an addition.

The first section contains narratives, which are often combined with dialogues: the wedding at Cana (chap. 2), the interview with Nicodemus (3), the Samaritan woman (4:1-42), the healing of the official's son (4:43-54), the healing at the pool (5), the feeding and the storm (6), the healing of the blind man (9), and the raising of Lazarus (11). Discourses detached from narratives occur in chap. 10 (the Good Shepherd) and chaps. 7–8. (The story of the woman taken in adultery [7:53–8:11] is found only in later MSS.)

The passion story (→ Passion, Accounts of) begins with the anointing at Bethany and the entry into Jerusalem (12:1-19) and the Last Supper (13:1-11, with foot washing instead of the words of institution). It ends with the arrest, trial, crucifixion, death, and burial (18–19). Between the beginning and the end come the parting discourses (13:12–17:26), of which only the High Priestly Prayer (chap. 17) forms a self-contained unit.

2. Sources and Message

The passion story in John is closely related in detail to that in the → Synoptics and perhaps comes from the source used in Mark. A difference is that the hearing before Pilate is more expansive (18:28-38; 19:6-12). Older reports are better presented in John than in Mark, including anointing in Bethany *before* the entrance into Jerusalem (12:1-19) and crucifixion on the day *before* the Passover (18:28).

The *sēmeia* (signs) source used in the first section is closely related to the sources used by the Synoptics in their accounts of → miracles (cf. John 6:1-21; 9:1-7 with Mark 4:35-41; 6:30-51; 8:22-26; also John 4:43-54 with Matt. 8:5-13). In the *sēmeia* source the miraculous elements seem to be emphasized, but John warns against a mere belief in miracles (2:23-24; 4:48, etc.) and points to the speeches for an understanding of the mission of Jesus. Jesus' words are "spirit and life" (6:63); the miracles should be understood symbolically. The miracle of feeding shows that Jesus is the Bread of Life (6:35), and the giving of sight to the blind man makes the point that the coming of faith is a "seeing" (9:35-39). The dialogue inserted into the raising of Lazarus shows again that Jesus himself is life already (11:25-26). A mere belief in Jesus as wonder-worker is responsible for his death (11:45-54).

The revelatory speeches in which the revealer introduces himself as "I am" (4:26; 6:35; 8:12, etc.) are without parallel in the Synoptics. R. Bultmann's (1884-1976) theory that John used a Gnostic sayings source has not gained acceptance. Parallels in the Nag Hammadi texts (esp. *Dialogue of the Savior*), however, show that the speeches and dialogues rest on pieces of source material that were developed out of sayings of Jesus and out of → kerygmatic and liturgical material. There are parallels for these sayings in the Synoptics (e.g., John 13:16 = Matt. 10:24; John 8:19 = Matt. 11:27) and also in the Apocrypha (e.g., John 5:39, 45-47 = Pap. Eger. 2; John 4:14 and 7:37-38 = *Gos. Thom.* 13; John 3:3, 5 = Justin Martyr *1 Apol.* 61; John 14:2-12 = *Dial. Sav.* 132.2-19).

3. Composition

Many sections of John seem to be worked out with great care (e.g., chaps. 6; 9; 11), whereas others seem to put together materials of different kinds (esp. chaps. 7–8). Passages often appear to be in the wrong place. Thus 3:31-36 interrupts the sequence of 3:23-30 and 4:1-3; similarly, 14:31 would seem to lead directly to 18:1, but chaps. 15–17 come between. Many times the flow is broken by what seem to be irrelevant interruptions (e.g., 5:28-29; 6:52-59). But Bultmann's attempt to achieve a clear connectedness by larger or smaller rearrangement and elimination of some glosses hardly does justice to the development of the work and does not explain how the assumed confusion arose.

Probably the text was not written all at once but over a longer period of time in the Johannine school (E. Haenchen, R. E. Brown). A combination of *sēmeia* material and the passion story formed the original gospel, which, like Mark, contained only some sayings material. Unlike Matthew and Luke, which introduced sayings material from new sources into the Markan framework, John further expounded the original sayings material and turned it into dialogues and speeches. Analogies are found in the → Gnostic writings *(Gos. Thom., Dial. Sav., Ap. Jas.)*. Also originating from a Gnostic context is the Prologue of John (1:1-18), which assumes a Christian-Gnostic adaptation of the Jewish Wisdom myth (→ Wisdom Literature). The precursors of the speeches and dialogues of John thus originated in the preaching and teaching of the Johannine congregation. Strong polemic is directed against the Jews, not referring to unbelieving Israel as a whole, but to the leading elites in Jerusalem and their successors who initiated the reconstitution of Judaism after the Jewish War (D. Boyarin). The controversy with a gnosticizing interpretation of Jesus' sayings rests on debates within the Johannine community (note the numerous parallels to Johannine sayings in *Gos. Thom.*). In chap. 17 a Gnostic speech is taken up unaltered.

An ecclesiastical redaction coincided with the composition of 1 John. It brought the work into line with early Catholic → eschatology and sacramental teaching (5:28-29; 6:39b, 40b, 52-59; 19:26) and reconciled the tradition of the Beloved Disciple with the → Peter tradition of → early Catholicism (chap. 21). While the Gospel of John gained acceptance in the Catholic Church only with difficulty, it was highly valued by the Christian Gnostics. (The oldest commentaries on John come from the school of Valentinus.)

4. Background

A leading element in the background of the Johannine school was exclusion from the synagogue (9:22). As a result, "the Jews" became a symbol of the hostile world, although → Israel, the → Law, and the Prophets were not rejected. The antithesis to the world, often with appeal to → Abraham and → Moses, is depicted in → dualistic categories (light and darkness) that have parallels in the → Qumran texts (6:39-47; 8:33-40; 9:29-34). The concept of the Paraclete (14:16, 26; 15:26; 16:7) also has an analogy in the Qumran texts in the figure of the heavenly advocate, the "Spirit of truth" (15:26). In the interpretation of the sayings of Jesus, however, use is also made of the → metaphors and mythical language of Gnosis as a hermeneutical principle: the antithesis of heavenly and earthly, above and below, and the understanding of Jesus as the revealer who is sent down from → heaven. Thus in the later stage of the experience of the Johannine community, a defense against a Gnostic-spiritualizing understanding of the Savior (→ Soteriology) is decisive. The heavenly revealer, in whose message eternal life is present, is none other than the earthly Jesus, who was glorified in his death on the cross.

5. Place and Time

The close relationship of the Johannine milieu with the *Odes of Solomon,* as well as with the writings of Nag Hammadi that likewise originated in Syria, leads to a Syrian origin of the Gospel of John. The final version must have been made shortly before the end of the first century. Manuscript evidence shows that the gospel was familiar in Egypt quite early (the oldest fragment comes from the first half of the second century).

In the middle of the second century this gospel arrived in Asia Minor, where it became associated with the tradition of John of Ephesus, author of the Apocalypse of John (→ Irenaeus is the first witness), and thus subsequently won acceptance even in early Catholicism, in spite of serious resistance. Perhaps the name "John" was first attached to the gospel in this time, while the original authority was the unnamed disciple "whom Jesus loved" (13:23; also 19:26). In the supplementary chapter this disciple is expressly designated as a guarantor of the tradition preserved in the gospel (21:20, 24).

→ Apocalyptic; New Testament Era, History of

Bibliography: Commentaries: C. K. BARRETT (2d ed.; Philadelphia, 1978) • R. E. BROWN (AB; 2 vols.; Garden City, N.Y., 1966-70) • R. BULTMANN (Philadelphia, 1971) • E. HAENCHEN (Hermeneia; 2 vols.; Philadelphia, 1984) • R. SCHNACKENBURG (3 vols.; New York, 1968-82) • D. M. SMITH (AbNTC; Nashville, 1999).

Other works: J. ASHTON, Interpretation of John (2d ed.; Edinburgh, 1997); idem, Understanding the Fourth Gospel (New York, 1991) • P. BORGEN, Logos Was the True Light, and Other Essays on the Gospel of John (Trondheim, 1983) • R. E. BROWN, The Community of the Beloved Disciple (New York, 1979) • R. A. CULPEPPER, Anatomy of the Fourth Gospel: A Study in Literary Design (Philadelphia, 1983) • C. H. DODD, The Interpretation of the Fourth Gospel (Cambridge, 1953) • D. J. HARRINGTON, John's Thought and Theology: An Introduction (Wilmington, Del., 1990) • M. HENGEL, The Johannine Question (Philadelphia, 1989) • E. KÄSEMANN, The Testament of Jesus: A Study of the Gospel of John in the Light of Chapter 17 (Philadelphia, 1966) • R. KYSAR, The Fourth Evangelist and His Gospel: An Examination of Contemporary Scholarship (Minneapolis, 1975); idem, "The Fourth Gospel: A Report on Recent Research," ANRW 2.25.3.2389-480 • J. L. MARTYN, History and Theology in the Fourth Gospel (2d ed.; Nashville, 1979) • D. M. SMITH, Johannine Christianity: Essays on Its Setting, Sources, and Theology (Columbia, S.C., 1984); idem, John among the Gospels: The Relationship in Twentieth-Century Research (2d ed.; Columbia, S.C., 2001).

HELMUT KOESTER

John of Damascus

St. John of Damascus, also known as John Damascene, was born into an affluent Christian family known as Mansour about the year 676, not long after the city's capture by Muslims (though some date his birth to as early as 655). An adviser to Caliph Abdul Malek, John's father, Sergius, was well respected and influential in the city's government. As a young man, John received the best education available, much of it coming from the tutoring of Cosmas, a Sicilian monk who had been captured by pirates and was destined for slavery. Recognizing both the faith and the learning of the elderly monk, John's father interceded with the caliph for his freedom. Cosmas then tutored John in both the classics and Christian theology. With the death of his father, John accepted a position as chief councillor to the caliph.

Perhaps because of growing hostilities between Christians and Muslims, however, John resigned his civil service position about 700 and went to the historic Mar Saba lavra (→ Monasticism 4.1), near → Jerusalem in the Judean desert. There Patriarch John V of Jerusalem (705-35) ordained him a → priest. According to a biography dating from the tenth century, John spent the rest of his life in either Jerusalem or the → monastery, preaching and writing on issues facing the church. He died between 749 and 753.

John's early reputation as a theologian and devoted priest was directly related to the → heresy of iconoclasm, which he forcefully opposed. The Roman-Byzantine Emperor Leo III (717-41) issued an edict in about 726 forbidding the venerations of → icons, despite the vigorous protests of Patriarch Germanos of Constantinople (715-30). The emperor's action created a storm affecting both those Christians within the Roman-Byzantine Empire and those beyond it. Living beyond the reach of the government and church in Constantinople, John was in a position both to respond in writing to the iconoclasts and to rally the local Christian population to oppose their actions. His opposition intensified after Leo issued a second edict in 730 prohibiting the public display of icons. John wrote two more theological treatises in which he continued his defense of the use and veneration of icons with a thoroughgoing refutation of the iconoclastic positions. John was able to provide a theological defense of the use of icons with reference both to Scripture and to earlier patristic teachings. Widely circulated, these three letters became powerful tools in the hands of the opponents of the imperial policy of iconoclasm.

With support from Emperor Constantine V (741-75), the son and successor of Leo, a group of iconoclastic → bishops convened a council in Hieria near Constantinople in 754. The council defended the iconoclasts and anathematized those who opposed them. Particular attention was paid to John of Damascus, who, now only a few years after his death, was castigated as a "teacher of impiety" and a "worshiper of images." This attack, however, did not deter other opponents of iconoclasm such as Theodore of Studios (759-826), who later relied upon John's theological insights.

After a debate that lasted eventually more than a hundred years, the theological position of the iconophiles, those in favor of icons, eventually predominated. With the support of Empress Irene, another council met in → Nicaea in 787, formally repudiated the decision of the earlier council, and affirmed the value of icons and their veneration. Recognized as the Seventh Ecumenical Council by many, this synod also formally honored John. He eventually came to be known as the Chrysorrhoas (golden stream) because of his oratorical skills. A brief resurgence of iconoclasm in the Byzantine world was ended by another council in Constantinople in 843, an effort supported by Empress Theodora.

John was a prolific writer who addressed many of the critical theological challenges facing the church in his time. A number of his treatises examined contemporary heresies afflicting the church in his region. He included early → Islam in their number, viewing it as a form of Christian heresy. He also produced numerous sermons and → hymns, many of which continue to be used in the liturgical services of the → Orthodox Church. His three homilies on the dormition of Mary are especially noteworthy.

Next to his writings against iconoclasm, John's best-known and most important work is *Pēgē gnōseōs* (Fount of knowledge), which some church historians have called the first Christian → *Summa theologica*. The text is divided into three distinct parts. The first, known as "Philosophical Chapters" and commonly called "Dialectics," deals with → philosophy and makes special reference to the works of Aristotle (→ Aristotelianism). The second part, "Concerning Heresy," is a updating of the writings of the fourth-century bishop Epiphanius. The third part, "An Exact Exposition of the Orthodox Faith," is an extensive presentation of Christian theology with rich reference to Scripture, the writings of the early Eastern fathers, and conciliar decisions. This part of his work had great value for subsequent theologians in both the Christian East and the Christian West.

In some Roman Catholic writings John is referred to as the last great father of the East. In 1890 the → Roman Catholic Church designated him a doctor of the church. The Orthodox Church views John as an important theologian within the ongoing patristic tradition. He is honored as a saint in both the West and the East, with feast day on December 4 (formerly in the West, March 27).

→ Church Fathers; Councils of the Church; Images 3.2; Mary, Devotion to

Bibliography: Primary sources: On the Divine Images: Three Apologies against Those Who Attack the Divine Images (trans. D. Anderson; 2d ed.; Crestwood, N.Y., 1994) • *On the Dormition of Mary: Early Patristic Homilies* (trans. B. E. Daley; Crestwood, N.Y., 1988) • *Writings: The Fount of Knowledge* (trans. F. H. Chase; New York, 1958).

Secondary work: J. Meyendorff, *Christ in Eastern Christian Thought* (Washington, D.C., 1969).

Thomas FitzGerald

John the Baptist

John the Baptist is mentioned over 90 times in the canonical gospels and Acts. The only other reference of note is in Josephus *Ant.* 18.116-19. The accounts in the Slavonic translation of Josephus *J.W.* 2.110 and 168 and the Mandaica are apocryphal expansions of the Christian tradition.

Luke 3:1-3 tells us that in the 15th year of the reign of Tiberius (i.e., A.D. 28/29), John came on the scene with his call for "a baptism of repentance for the forgiveness of sins" (Mark 1:4 and par.; → Penitence). If, according to the Gospels of Matthew (cf. Matt. 3:11 and 26:28 and par.) and John, John's → baptism does not confer forgiveness, and if Josephus plays down his apocalyptic significance (*Ant.* 18.116-19; cf. Matt. 3:2, 7-12 and par.), his original summons shows that John's baptism had an eschatological character (H. Thyen).

Jewish washings (also in → Qumran) and the baptisms of the early → Mandaeans did not need a baptizer. Even when they served as rites of → initiation, as at Qumran or in the case of proselyte baptism (→ Proselytism), which is not attested before John the Baptist, they were constantly repeated. They all aimed at ritual cleanness (→ Cultic Purity), as we see from the Jewish understanding of the baptism of John in Josephus. Within the movement itself John's baptism is without analogy inasmuch as it carries a promise of remission of sins and deliverance in the imminent judgment (→ Last Judgment). The priestly descent of John and his withdrawal to the desert (Luke 1:5-25, 57-80) suggest that his baptismal practice stood in some tension with the official expiatory cult in the → temple. In this respect there is some likeness to Qumran, although any idea of closer connection to this community is purely imaginary.

The execution of John the Baptist by Herod Antipas (4 B.C.–A.D. 39) shows that John worked in Herod's tetrarchy, and his beheading at Macherus (*Ant.* 18.119) points to the mouth of the Jordan in Perea. John's baptism, preaching, and way of life, however, had an influence far beyond Perea, as may be seen from the fact that → Jesus and other Galileans came to him. Matt. 11:7-15, Mark 11:29-

32, and *Ant.* 18.119 show that John was held in high regard by the people. The masses viewed the defeat of Herod in battle against the Nabateans as a divine punishment for his execution of John. Messianic expectations (Luke 3:15; John 1:19-22) clustered around him.

Many of the followers of John the Baptist became members of the emerging → church, which then preserved the memory of John and his baptism (cf. Luke 1 and Matt. 3:13-15 as the account of the installation of Christian baptism). The saying about the "more powerful than I" who would baptize "with the Holy Spirit and fire" (Matt. 3:11 and par.) was related to Jesus. Mark and Matthew portray John as Elijah redivivus, as the one who prepares the way for the messianic Son of Man (Mark 9:9-13). In Luke and John he is more a faithful witness of Jesus and the model of a Christian → martyr.

The widespread hypothesis that John the Baptist's followers, as a messianic → sect rivaling the church, made him posthumously a cultically venerated redeemer, as supposedly documented in the Benedictus (Luke 1:67-79), the Magnificat (1:46-55), and the Johannine Prologue (John 1:1-18), is highly improbable. Acts 19:1-5 hardly offers support to the theory, for Paul here seeks to confirm former disciples of John in their messianic faith in Jesus rather than polemicizing against a Baptist sect.

→ Kingdom of God

Bibliography: S. BULGAKOV, *The Friend of the Bridegroom: On the Orthodox Veneration of the Forerunner* (trans. B. Jakim; Grand Rapids, 2003) • P. HOLLENBACH, "Social Aspects of John the Baptizer's Preaching Mission in the Context of Palestine Judaism," *ANRW* 2.19.1.850-75 • J. REUMANN, "The Quest for the Historical Baptist," *Understanding the Sacred Text* (ed. J. Reumann; Valley Forge, Pa., 1972) 183-99 • W. SCHENK, "Gefangenschaft und Tod des Täufers," *NTS* 29 (1983) 453-83 • C. H. H. SCOBIE, *John the Baptist* (Philadelphia, 1964) • M. STOWASSER, *Johannes der Täufer im Vierten Evangelium. Eine Untersuchung zu seiner Bedeutung für die johanneische Gemeinde* (Klosterneuburg, 1992) • W. B. TATUM, *John the Baptist and Jesus: A Report of the Jesus Seminar* (Sonoma, Calif., 1994) • J. E. TAYLOR, *The Immerser: John the Baptist within Second Temple Judaism* (Grand Rapids, 1997) • H. THYEN, "Baptisma metanoias eis aphesin hamartiōn," *Zeit und Geschichte* (Tübingen, 1964) 97-125 • M. TILLY, *Johannes der Täufer und die Biographie der Propheten. Die synoptische Täuferüberlieferung und das jüdische Prophetenbild zur Zeit des Täufers* (Stuttgart, 1994) • R. L. WEBB, *John the Baptizer and Prophet: A Socio-historical Study* (Sheffield, 1991) • W. WINK, *John the Baptist in the Gospel Tradition* (Cambridge, 1968) • G. YAMASAKI, *John the Baptist in Life and Death: Audience-Oriented Criticism of Matthew's Narrative* (Sheffield, 1998).

HARTWIG THYEN

Joint Declaration on the Doctrine of Justification

1. Background
2. Development and Ratification
3. Content
4. Debate and Criticism

The Joint Declaration on the Doctrine of Justification (JDDJ) is an official statement of the → Roman Catholic Church and the churches of the → Lutheran World Federation (LWF) affirming that a → consensus exists between them on "basic truths of the doctrine of justification" and thus that the condemnations relating to → justification contained in the documents of each church no longer apply to the other. It was developed between 1993 and 1997 and was signed by representatives of the two communions in 1999.

1. Background

Lutheran-Catholic dialogues in the decades prior to the JDDJ repeatedly affirmed a consensus on the doctrine of justification (→ Ecumenical Dialogue). The 1972 report *The Gospel and the Church* by the international Joint Lutheran–Roman Catholic Study Commission affirmed that "a far-reaching consensus is developing in the interpretation of justification" (§26). The commission, however, did not elaborate the detailed content of this consensus.

Greater detail came from national dialogues during the 1980s. The lengthy report of the Lutheran-Catholic dialogue in America, *Justification by Faith* (1983), stated the belief that "a fundamental consensus on the gospel" had been achieved (§164). A German dialogue between representatives of the Evangelical Church in Germany, including Lutheran, Reformed, and United churches, and the Roman Catholic Church did not speak of consensus in its 1985 report, *Condemnations of the → Reformation Era: Do They Still Divide?* but it did state that the mutual 16th-century condemnations relating to justification need no longer apply to the churches today in a sense that could divide them.

These statements, however convincing their arguments, spoke only for the dialogue participants, who could not commit their churches to these conclusions. The reception of these conclusions required some action by the churches themselves.

2. Development and Ratification

At the request of the Evangelical Lutheran Church in America, the Lutheran World Federation in 1993 committed itself to a process, in coordination with the Roman Catholic Church, to consider declaring nonapplicable the mutual condemnations dealing with justification. During 1994 a first draft of a statement was developed that both declared the condemnations nonapplicable and laid out the agreement on justification behind such a declaration. On the basis of responses from Lutheran and Catholic authorities, revisions of the text occurred until a final draft was produced in January 1997 and submitted for approval to the Vatican and to the member churches of the LWF. (All drafts were composed in German, the original language of the JDDJ.)

In June 1998 the Council of the LWF affirmed the JDDJ on the basis of positive responses by 81 churches, representing 84 percent of the Lutherans in the LWF. A response from the Roman Catholic Church appeared open to differing interpretations and necessitated further discussions and the development of an "annex" to the JDDJ that alleviated remaining concerns. An Official Common Statement affirming the JDDJ "in its entirety" was signed by representatives of the Vatican and the LWF in Augsburg, Germany, on October 31, 1999.

3. Content

After a brief introduction, the JDDJ contains five major sections, further divided into 44 numbered paragraphs. The first section lays out the biblical basis of the agreement, while the second briefly states the way in which justification constitutes an ecumenical problem. The third and fourth sections are the JDDJ's heart. The third section states the common understanding of justification and culminates in the following common confession: "By → grace alone, in → faith in Christ's saving work and not because of any merit on our part, we are accepted by → God and receive the → Holy Spirit, who renews our hearts while equipping and calling us to good works" (§15).

Section 4 elaborates this common understanding in relation to seven traditionally controversial issues: → sin and human cooperation with God's justifying act, justification as → forgiveness and renewal, the place of faith in justification, the justified as sinner, → law and gospel, the → assurance of salvation, and the good works of the justified. In each case, a statement of agreement is followed by spe-

cific Lutheran and Catholic affirmations that, while divergent, "do not destroy the consensus regarding the basic truths" (§40). The JDDJ thus claims what has been called a differentiated consensus, that is, a consensus on basic truths that still permits more detailed differences. These differences, however, "are no longer the occasion for doctrinal condemnations" (§5).

A final section states the significance and scope of the JDDJ. Most significantly, it states that "a consensus in basic truths of the doctrine of justification" exists (§40) and that the relevant doctrinal condemnations from the → Reformation era thus do not apply today (§41; → Catholic Reform and Counterreformation). These conclusions were emphasized in the Official Common Statement ratifying the JDDJ. Further paragraphs note, however, that this agreement "must come to influence the life and teachings of our churches" and that "questions of varying importance still need further clarification" (§43). Questions relating to ecclesiology, → ministry, and → sacraments are explicitly mentioned.

4. Debate and Criticism

The JDDJ was affirmed in many Lutheran churches without extensive debate. In Germany, however, home to the largest national body of Lutherans, a vehement debate developed in both the church and the secular press. In all, 151 university theology professors (a significant minority) called for the rejection of the JDDJ. Central to the debate was the question whether the JDDJ adequately reflected the Lutheran understanding of justification as not simply one doctrine among others but as the interpretive key and criterion for understanding and judging all aspects of Christian thought and life. Although only one of the German Lutheran regional churches (and the Lutheran section of one united church) rejected the JDDJ, many of the affirming German churches included in their answers extended elaborations of the very same Lutheran assertions about justification that some critics had claimed were compromised by the JDDJ.

Roman Catholic criticism of the JDDJ was infrequent before its signing, partly because the Catholic decision-making process did not involve public debate. In addition, drafts of the JDDJ were not widely circulated in Catholic circles. Some critical Catholic voices were raised after the signing of the JDDJ, contending that certain Catholic convictions (e.g., the cooperation of the justified within justification itself and the role of created grace in justification) were not adequately reflected in the JDDJ.

→ Ecumenism, Ecumenical Movement

Bibliography: H. G. ANDERSON, T. A. MURPHY, and J. BURGESS, eds., *Justification by Faith* (Minneapolis, 1985) • A. DULLES, "Two Languages of Salvation: The Lutheran-Catholic Joint Declaration," *FirstT* 10 (December 1999) 25-30 • FACULTY OF THEOLOGY, GEORGIA AUGUSTA UNIVERSITY, GÖTTINGEN, *Outmoded Condemnations? Antitheses between the Council of Trent and the Reformation on Justification, the Sacrament, and the Ministry–Then and Now* (trans. O. K. Olson; Fort Wayne, Ind., 1992) • G. FORDE, "The Critical Response of the German Theological Professors to the Joint Declaration on the Doctrine of Justification," *Dialog* 38 (1999) 71-72 • E. JÜNGEL, "Um Gottes willen–Klarheit! Kritische Bemerkungen zur Verharmlosung der kriteriologischen Funktion des Rechtfertigungsartikels– aus Anlaß einer ökumenischen 'Gemeinsamen Erklärung zur Rechtfertigungslehre,'" *ZTK* 94 (1997) 394-406 • K. LEHMANN and W. PANNENBERG, eds., *The Condemnations of the Reformation Era: Do They Still Divide?* (Minneapolis, 1989) • K. LEHMANN, M. ROOT, and W. G. RUSCH, eds., *Justification by Faith: Do the Sixteenth-Century Condemnations Still Apply?* (New York, 1997) • THE LUTHERAN WORLD FEDERATION and THE ROMAN CATHOLIC CHURCH, *Joint Declaration on the Doctrine of Justification* (Grand Rapids, 2000) • H. MEYER, "Ecumenical Consensus: Our Quest for and the Emerging Structures of Consensus," *Greg.* 77 (1996) 213-25 • W. G. RUSCH, ed., *Justification and the Future of the Ecumenical Movement: The Joint Declaration on the Doctrine of Justification* (Collegeville, Minn., 2003) • D. YEAGO, "Lutheran–Roman Catholic Consensus on Justification: The Theological Achievement of the 'Joint Declaration,'" *ProEcc* 7 (1998) 449-70.

MICHAEL ROOT

Jonah, Book of

The Book of Jonah is the only part of the → Minor Prophets that consists of a prophet story in which a psalm (2:1-9) has been inserted. The work tells of the prophet's attempt to evade a divine commission, the miraculous way in which God brought him back, his proclamation of judgment upon Nineveh, the → penitence of Nineveh, which moves God to withhold his judgment, and the anger of Jonah that God spared the city upon its conversion, to which God responds with instruction.

The main character, Jonah, is taken from a note in 2 Kgs. 14:25, referring to a → prophet who proclaimed a message of → salvation in the eighth century B.C. However, the work was probably written later (4th or even 3d cent.), constituting a literary unity (apart from 2:1-9; a different view is taken by L. Schmidt) but integrating various folkloric elements and other materials, including the great fish (2:1, 10), which figures largely in Christian → iconography and may go back to a tradition in Jaffa. Many quotations and allusions show familiarity with the mainstream biblical tradition.

The Jonah story is a novelette with didactic intention. It demonstrates the sovereign freedom of God's gracious action (→ Grace), especially to alien peoples who, by their fear of God and readiness for conversion, put → Israel and its representative, Jonah, to shame.

Bibliography: Commentaries: A. DEISSLER (NEchtB; Würzburg, 1984) • W. RUDOLPH (KAT; Gütersloh, 1971) • J. M. SASSON (AB; Garden City, N.Y., 1990) • P. TRIBLE (NIB; Nashville, 1996) • A. WEISER (ATD; 7th ed.; Göttingen, 1979) • H. W. WOLFF (BKAT; Neukirchen, 1977).

Other works: T. M. BOLIN, *Freedom beyond Forgiveness: The Book of Jonah Reexamined* (Sheffield, 1997) • K. M. CRAIG, *A Poetics of Jonah: Art in the Service of Ideology* (Columbia, S.C., 1993) • A. LACOCQUE and P. E. LACOCQUE, *Jonah: A Psycho-religious Approach to the Prophet* (Columbia, S.C., 1990) • D. MARCUS, *From Balaam to Jonah: Anti-prophetic Satire in the Hebrew Bible* (Atlanta, 1995) • R. F. PERSON, *In Conversation with Jonah: Conversation Analysis, Literary Criticism, and the Book of Jonah* (Sheffield, 1996) • P. TRIBLE, *Rhetorical Criticism: Context, Method, and the Book of Jonah* (Minneapolis, 1994).

WINFRIED THIEL

Jordan

	1960	1980	2000
Population (1,000s):	1,695	2,923	6,330
Annual growth rate (%):	2.93	5.42	3.04
Area: 89,246 sq. km. (34,458 sq. mi.)			

A.D. *2000*

Population density: 71/sq. km. (184/sq. mi.)
Births / deaths: 3.47 / 0.43 per 100 population
Fertility rate: 4.70 per woman
Infant mortality rate: 25 per 1,000 live births
Life expectancy: 71.0 years (m: 68.9, f: 73.3)
Religious affiliation (%): Muslims 92.3, Christians 5.3 (Orthodox 2.8, indigenous 1.7, other Christians 0.8), nonreligious 1.8, other 0.6.

1. Geography and Economy
2. Population

74

1. Geography and Economy

The Hashemite Kingdom of Jordan is poor in resources, with desert occupying most of its area. Only phosphate and potash are of economic significance, followed by → tourism and light industries. Although for a time Jordan could not support itself agriculturally because of low and irregular precipitation, yet with modern → technology it somehow overcame its lack of water and is producing a variety of vegetables and fruits. Getting enough water, however, remains one of the chief problems threatening economic development. Jordan is working hard to develop a viable economy, which is presently dependent on foreign aid.

2. Population

The population of Jordan is 97.8 percent Arab, most of whom are Jordanian (32.4 percent), Palestinian (32.2 percent), Iraqi (14.0 percent), or Bedouin (12.8). Among Christian groups, 1.7 percent of the population is Armenian. Of the nearly 1.5 million Palestinian → refugees registered with the United Nations Relief and Works Agency, almost 275,000 live in camps. Another 210,000 live in Jordan under displacement status. Ethnic minorities consist of immigrants from the Caucasus in the 19th century, for example, Armenians and Kurds, but especially Circassians (ca. 25,000).

3. Religions

Almost all Jordanian Muslims are → Sunnites (→ Islam). The → Shiites are a very small minority, as are also the Druze and the → Bahais.

The percentage of Christians is declining, since the population growth is higher among Muslims and since many Christians emigrate, mainly to the United States, Europe, and Australia. There are a fair number of Christians among the Palestinian refugees. They live in such cities as Amman, Ma'dabā, Al Karak, As Salṭ, and 'Ajlūn.

About half the Christians belong to the Greek → Orthodox Church. The next largest community is composed of the Greek Catholic Church (Melkite-Uniate) and the smaller Latin (Roman) Catholic Church of Jerusalem, who have together about 16,000 members. The → Syrian Orthodox Church of Antioch and the → Armenian Apostolic Church count about 5,000 affiliates. There are also about 4,000 members related to the Episcopal and Lutheran Churches.

4. Political Development

Jordan came into being with the collapse of the Ottoman Empire at the end of World War I. It was first under British mandate and then became independent in 1946. After the division of Palestine in 1948, Jordanian troops remained in the West Bank to keep law and order. In 1950 the West Bank was annexed to the East Bank of Jordan, and in the June war of 1967 it was occupied by Israel along with the old city of → Jerusalem. The Palestinian refugees became both an economic and a political responsibility for Jordan and a challenge to its security. In October 1994 Jordan signed a formal peace agreement with Israel.

5. Religious Policy

Islam is the state religion of Jordan, but the constitution grants freedom of religion and conscience and forbids discrimination for religious reasons. This provision is observed to a large degree (→ Church and State).

The relatively liberal policy of the Jordanian government also gives Christians plenty of scope in the Jordanian society. They have some seats in Parliament: 11 of 80 in the lower house and around 4 of 40 in the upper house. From one to three Christians of Transjordanian or Palestinian descent are usually given a place in the cabinet, but Christians, unlike Circassians, may not hold the highest office in the state or the army.

Bibliography: M. BOULBY, *The Muslim Brotherhood and the Kings of Jordan, 1945-1993* (Atlanta, 1999) • B. MacDONALD, R. ADAMS, and P. BIENKOWSKI, eds., *The Archaeology of Jordan* (Sheffield, 2001) • H. C. METZ, *Jordan, a Country Study* (4th ed.; Washington, D.C., 1991) • B. MILTON-EDWARDS and P. HINCHCLIFFE, *Jordan: A Hashemite Legacy* (London, 2001) • M. MOADDEL, *Jordanian Exceptionalism: A Comparative Analysis of State-Religion Relationships in Egypt, Iran, Jordan, and Syria* (New York, 2002).

THOMAS KOSZINOWSKI

Joseph

Joseph is a common name in the Bible. It means "may he [God] add [more sons]" (Gen. 30:23).

1. The patriarch Joseph was the son of → Jacob and Rachel. Tradition locates his grave at Shechem (Josh. 24:32; Gen. 50:25). He was the tribal head of the central Palestinian tribes of Ephraim and Manasseh, generally referred to as the house of Joseph (Deut.

33:13-17; Judg. 1:22-23). He was also the hero of the Joseph story in Genesis 37 and 39–47, 50, which differs considerably, both materially and formally, from the other patriarchal narratives (→ Patriarchal History), and in which some see Wisdom influence (→ Wisdom Literature). Sold by his brothers into Egypt, Joseph experienced many difficulties but finally rose to power and was reconciled to his brothers. → Diaspora Judaism saw him as an ideal of young Israelite manhood and also as an example of obedience to the faith in an alien land (see *Jos. As.*; also Acts 7:9-16).

2. "Joseph" was the name of the father of Jesus. Reliable tradition has it that he was of the house of David, a carpenter in Nazareth in Galilee (Matt. 13:55; Luke 4:22; John 1:45; 6:42). The Jewish-Christian tradition of the → virgin birth, attested in the NT only in Matt. 1:18-25 and Luke 1:34-35, is to be viewed primarily as the result of Christological reflection (→ Christology 1), whereas its value as a historic witness is questionable. According to this tradition, Joseph was only legally Jesus' father (cf. Matt. 1:16 with Luke 3:23). The later idea of → Mary's perpetual virginity would have it that the brothers of Jesus (Matt. 13:55; Luke 8:20; Acts 1:14) were Joseph's children by a former marriage, so that he came to be thought of as an old man.

Though second to Mary, Joseph as the legal father of Jesus is one of the most important → saints for the → Roman Catholic Church. He has recently been made the patron of manual workers, with May 1 as his feast day.

3. Joseph the son of Jonam (Luke 3:30) and Joseph the son of Mattathias (v. 24) were ancestors of Jesus.

4. Joseph the brother of Jesus (Matt. 13:55; Mark 6:3) was Joses, according to the Galilean form of the name.

5. Joseph of Arimathea (Mark 15:43, 45 and par.) was a prominent member of the Sanhedrin who saw to the burial of Jesus.

6. Joseph Barsabbas was the other candidate for election to the → Twelve when Matthias was chosen (Acts 1:23).

7. Joseph, a Levite of Cyprus whom the apostles named Barnabas (Acts 4:36), sponsored → Paul and later accompanied him on his first missionary journey.

Bibliography: On 1: G. W. Coats, "The Joseph Story and Ancient Wisdom," *CBQ* 35 (1973) 285-97 • H. Donner, *Die literarische Gestalt der alttestamentlichen Josephsgeschichte* (Heidelberg, 1976) • R. S. Kraemer, *When Asenath Met Joseph: A Late Antique Tale of the Biblical Patriarch and His Egyptian Wife, Reconsidered* (New York, 1998) • M. Niehoff, *The Figure of Joseph in Post-biblical Jewish Literature* (Leiden, 1992) • C. Westermann, *Joseph: Eleven Bible Studies on Genesis* (Minneapolis, 1996).

On 2: J. Blinzler, "Joseph," *LTK* (2d ed.) 5.1129-30 • R. E. Brown, *The Birth of the Messiah* (2d ed.; New York, 1993) • D. B. Howell, *Matthew's Inclusive Story: A Study in the Narrative Rhetoric of the First Gospel* (Sheffield, 1990) • G. Schneider, "Ἰωσήφ," *EDNT* 2.214-16.

JÜRGEN ROLOFF

Josephinism

1. Meaning
2. Origin
3. Growth
4. Limits

1. Meaning

The term "Josephinism" denotes the extension of the absolute authority of the state to all church matters other than doctrine. Flourishing particularly in Austria under Joseph II (Holy Roman emperor 1765-90), it entailed the full subjection of the church and its institutions to the interests and control of the autonomous → state (→ Church and State). Along with dominant → Enlightenment ecclesiastical policies, including religious toleration, it also contained strong reforming elements.

2. Origin

Already under Joseph's mother, Maria Theresa (succeeded to the Hapsburg dominions 1740, coregent in Austria with Joseph 1765-80), various intellectual movements existed that decisively influenced Josephinism, including → Jansenism, reform Catholicism, Catholic Enlightenment, and Febronianism. Influential, too, was a church-and-state tradition in Europe that reached back into the Middle Ages. We might refer also to dominant Enlightenment trends, such as embodied in the teachings of G. W. Leibniz (1646-1716), L. A. Muratori (1672-1750), P. Giannone (1676-1748), and C. Wolff (1679-1754), as well as those of the French rationalists.

3. Growth

Joseph II, though personally a believing Roman Catholic, was rigorous in setting up an Enlightenment state church system. He first formed a strictly bureaucratic and centralized state, and then organized a territorial church system with a new diocesan structure (→ Diocese). The most significant aspect of the policy was that correction of church abuses was not a matter for the → pope, since the pope no longer had jurisdiction in the state. Dealings with the → curia would be at the court level.

Josephinism especially affected → monasticism, for the jurisdiction of monasteries passed from the pope to the local diocesan bishops, and some religious orders were suppressed (→ Religious Life). The resources of disbanded → monasteries were put into a religious fund. To achieve uniformity, the training of the clergy was standardized by the establishment of general seminaries under state control. When the emperor tried to regulate religious practice directly, however, thereby offending the sensibilities of many sectors of the population, Pius VI (1775-99) visited Vienna in 1782. This visit resulted in the adoption of a → concordat that sanctioned the new diocesan system but that in effect protested the other measures. Noteworthy proponents of Josephinism were W. A. Kaunitz (1711-94) and G. van Swieten (1700-1772) in the field of educational and cultural reform.

4. Limits

The Toleration Edict of 1781 gave to members of the Evangelical Church of the Augsburg and Helvetic Confession and the Greek Orthodox Church (→ Orthodox Church) full civil → rights and a limited measure of freedom of worship. Josephinism was still influential up to the days of Francis Joseph I (emperor 1848-1916), although the concordat of 1855 officially ended the state church system. In both Austria and Germany in the 19th century Josephinism opened the door to liberal trends. Liberal influence was especially strong in the popular political Josephinism of Germany.

→ Modern Church History

Bibliography: P. P. BERNARD, *Jesuits and Jacobins: Enlightenment and Enlightened Despotism in Austria* (Urbana, Ill., 1971) • M. C. GOODWIN, *The Papal Conflict with Josephinism* (New York, 1938) • H. KLUETING, ed., *Der Josephinismus. Ausgewählte Quellen zur Geschichte der theresianisch-josephinischen Reformen* (Darmstadt, 1995) • E. KOVAĆS, ed., *Katholische Aufklärung und Josephinismus* (Vienna, 1979) • F. MAASS, *Der Frühjosephinismus* (Vienna, 1969); idem, *Der Josephinismus. Quellen zu seiner Geschichte* (5 vols.; Vienna, 1951-61) •

S. K. PADOVER, *The Revolutionary Emperor, Joseph II of Austria* (rev. ed.; Hamden, Conn., 1967) • H. REINALTER, ed., *Der Josephinismus. Bedeutung, Einflüsse und Wirkungen* (Frankfurt, 1993).

HELMUT REINALTER

Joshua, Book of

1. The Man and His Work
2. Structure and Redaction
3. Relation to the Pentateuch

1. The Man and His Work

Joshua (Heb. *yĕhôšuaʿ*, also *yĕhôšûaʿ*, *yēšuaʿ*, *hôšēaʿ*, Num. 13:8, 16; LXX *Iēsous*), the son of Nun, was originally an Ephraimite. Although different locations have been proposed for Timnath-heres, his burial place (Judg. 2:9), all the traditions are inclined to locate it somewhere in the hill country of Ephraim. His name means "Yahweh helps."

According to the reconstruction of A. Alt (1883-1956), the land conquest actually consisted of various processes of internal restructuring and of military skirmishes on a smaller scale (→ Israel 1). Joshua probably represents a military leader who was initially involved only in the conflicts in central Palestine but then came to be viewed by later tradition as the central figure of the land conquest as a whole. As a result of this development, Joshua's final stature is thus considerably enhanced. He is closely associated with → Moses, first as his assistant (Exod. 33:11), then as a spy (Num. 13:8, 16), and finally as Moses' successor (Num. 27:18-23), who was already present when Moses received the commandments (Exod. 24:13; → Decalogue).

2. Structure and Redaction

The Book of Joshua can be divided into three parts. The first deals with the seizure of West Jordan (chaps. 1–12). The second tells of the dividing up of the land (13–21). The third gives instructions relating to settlement (22–24). One noteworthy feature is that chaps. 2–9 focus on central Palestine.

Although attempts have frequently been made to discern the literary sources of the → Pentateuch in Joshua as well, the main features of M. Noth's (1902-68) addendum, or completion, hypothesis have generally proved to be sound. The etiologically focused traditions in Joshua 2–9 were combined during the early monarchy with chaps. 10 and 11. Archaeological evidence (→ Archaeology 1) does not yet enable us to decide either for (thus the evidence from Hazor) or against (thus that from Jericho) the historicity of events in the Book of Joshua.

Some of the texts were subjected to an initial Deuteronomistic redaction (1:1ff.; 8:30-35; 12; 21:43–22:6; 24; → Deuteronomistic History), and a second round of Deuteronomistic editing is discernible in 1:7-9, 13:2-6, and chap. 23, linking the theme of disobedience to the → law (§1) with that of the incomplete land conquest and the remaining population there. Evidence of Priestly redaction is similarly evident in a whole series of passages. The geographic lists in 13–21 are cast in narrative form and are based on a system of tribal boundaries (→ Tribes of Israel) from the period predating nationhood and from a territorial description that Alt dates to the time of → Josiah (Josh. 15:21-52; 18:21-28; 19:41-46). Discussion regarding the dating of these lists has not yet reached a definitive conclusion.

3. Relation to the Pentateuch

The idea that the land conquest fulfills the earlier land promise links the Book of Joshua with the Pentateuch. In the theological reflection of the Deuteronomistic historian, the loss of the land comes to mean that the land has in fact been taken away. Here Joshua is the opposite pole, and the land conquest constitutes especially → Yahweh's gift.

→ Covenant 1

Bibliography: Commentaries: R. G. Boling and G. E. Wright (AB; New York, 1982) • R. B. Coote (NIB; Nashville, 1998) • A. H. Curtis (OTGu; Sheffield, 1998) • H. W. Hertzberg (ATD; Göttingen, 1953) • R. D. Nelson (OTL; Louisville, Ky., 1997) • M. Noth (HAT; 2d ed.; Tübingen, 1953) • J. A. Soggin (OTL; Philadelphia, 1972).

Other works: A. Alt, "Judas Gaue unter Josia" (1925), *Kleine Schriften zur Geschichte des Volkes Israel* (vols. 1-2; Munich, 1953) 2.276-88; idem, "Das System der Stammesgrenzen im Buche Josua" (1927), ibid. 1.193-202 • A. G. Auld, *Joshua, Moses, and the Land: Tetrateuch-Pentateuch-Hexateuch in a Generation since 1938* (Edinburgh, 1980) • M. Gordon, *Together in the Land: A Reading of the Book of Joshua* (Sheffield, 1993) • E. Otto, *Das Mazzotfest in Gilgal* (Stuttgart, 1975) • L. L. Rowlett, *Joshua and the Rhetoric of Violence: A New Historicist Analysis* (Sheffield, 1996) • R. Smend, "Das Gesetz und die Völker," *Die Mitte des Alten Testament* (Munich, 1986) 124-37 • J. Svensson, *Towns and Toponyms in the OT: With Special Emphasis on Joshua 14–21* (Stockholm, 1994) • N. Winther-Nielsen, *A Functional Discourse Grammar of Joshua: A Computer-Assisted Rhetorical Structure Analysis* (Stockholm, 1995).

Edward Noort

Josiah

Josiah, king of Judah (639/638-609 b.c.), was the last significant ruler on the throne of → David. The sources tell us more about what he stood for than about himself. During his reign a book of the law (probably identical with the core of Deuteronomy) was found in the → temple at Jerusalem, which Josiah pledged himself and his people to keep. Cultic reform meant exclusive worship of → Yahweh (Deut. 6:4-25; → Monolatry) and centralization of worship (chap. 12) in → Jerusalem. (Authentic material strongly shaped by Deuteronomistic redaction appears in 2 Kings 22–23; a wholly tendentious parallel account is 2 Chronicles 34–35.) This reform took place in the 18th year of his reign (621/620), and it marks a turning point in the history of OT religion. In spite of some subsequent reverses (e.g., Jer. 44:15-19; Ezekiel 8), the exclusive claim of Yahweh and the restriction to one site of worship at Jerusalem were undisputed after the sixth century in Judah.

Little is known about Josiah prior to the reform. As a result of the assassination of his father, Amon (641/640), he came to the throne when only eight years of age; at the earliest, he could have an influence on politics only a decade later. The basic problem was the fact that since the days of Ahaz (742/741-725), Judah had been a vassal of Assyria and had suffered economic burdens and religious and political restrictions and humiliations. The reform might have brought confrontation with Assyria, but its rapid decline spared Josiah such a test. He did, though, run into opposition from the Egyptians, heirs of the claim to lordship over Palestine. Since Josiah's reform demanded national independence, it was logical — though strategically unwise — for Josiah to do battle with Pharaoh Neco (609-595) at Megiddo (609). Josiah was killed in the hopeless fight, but he has been remembered in the hearts of Judeans and Jews as a national hero and reformer (2 Kgs. 22:2; 23:25; Jer. 22:10, 15-16; 2 Chr. 35:25).

→ Israel 1; Monarchy in Israel

Bibliography: G. W. Ahlström, *Royal Administration and National Religion in Ancient Palestine* (Leiden, 1982) • J. H. Hayes and J. M. Miller, *Israelite and Judean History* (Philadelphia, 1977) esp. 458-69 • A. Laato, *Josiah and David Redivivus: The Historical Josiah and the Messianic Expectations of Exilic and Postexilic Times* (Stockholm, 1992) • E. W. Nicholson, *Deuteronomy and Tradition* (Philadelphia, 1967) • H. Spieckermann, *Juda unter Assur in der Sargonidenzeit* (Göttingen, 1982).

Hermann Spieckermann

Journalism, Ecclesiastical → Church
Communications

Joy

1. Infants and small children express joy in life by
spontaneous movements and cries. Adults gradually
become aware that a feeling of delight corresponds
to happy situations, not only in the physical sphere,
but also intellectually and spiritually. It must be
learned that the state of joy is only one very limited
state alongside other possible feelings (→ Childhood; Adulthood).

For some individuals the dealings with various
spiritual states in the course of life that affect attitudes and conduct are joyless and frustrating. Thus
in the history of philosophy and theology one
must discuss the affections in order to have a relevant → anthropology that is true to experience. In
this context joy shows itself to be directly dependent on relations with others. Emotional states like
pleasure and joy, as well as pain, anger, and →
grief, are experienced unrestrictedly and totally in
early childhood. Increasingly in social relations,
however, possibilities arise of ambivalent experience in connection with different and mixed emotions (→ Laughing and Crying). This development
finally leads to the ability, in joy and sorrow, to
maintain a sustainable feeling of → identity in social relations.

2. In theology joy can be a constitutive element in
the relationship with → God. God is the origin of
joy as he protects his people (as the OT makes clear)
and promises them deliverance in time and space.
He is also the guarantor of everlasting joy (as Jesus
Christ says afresh and uniquely represents in the
NT). He is thus the focus of all earthly hopes of redemption from pain and the fear of being
relationally unconnected (→ Anxiety; Hope). The
whole Christian assurance of hope is based on eschatologically anticipatory joy (→ Eschatology) that
in the face of every experience of sorrow and destruction, we still have a → future.

3. To grasp this joy here and now presupposes an
ability to differentiate modes of experience and to
focus on those that really count. Over against the joy
of the senses stands the joy of the spirit or joy in the
beautiful (→ Aesthetics). This latter joy in turn constantly demands a relation that satisfies impulses, is
worthy of humanity, and is in keeping with one's
age.

In a Christian → lifestyle joy is an expression of a
special quality of being that can be gained and
brought to our awareness from a trust in God and
→ love for others. To do so, we must differentiate
the illusory joy of mere pleasure or enjoyment,
which is fleeting, from true joy.

Individuals, however, can also lose joy in life by
trying to keep it to themselves. A privatized joy that
is no longer shared alienates us from reality and becomes mere gloating. Shared joy, however, is doubled joy, for the exchanging with others of events
that produce joy expresses a hope for common →
happiness and is oriented to the future. From a
Christian standpoint the special quality of this future is that in it, as pain and → suffering are removed, the experience of (present) reality coincides
with unlimited joy, just as God has willed.

4. Meantime, in → everyday life we can find forms
of expressing joyous experiences that correspond to
the future hope. Festivals and gatherings for joyful
occasions such as anniversaries can be shaped in
such a way that they assume a symbolic character
and point beyond themselves.

Bibliography: G. ANDERSON, *A Time to Mourn, a Time
to Dance: The Expression of Grief and Joy in Israelite
Religion* (University Park, Pa., 1991) • W. G. MORRICE,
Joy in the NT (Grand Rapids, 1984) • E. OTTO and
T. SCHRAMM, *Fest und Freude* (Stuttgart, 1977) •
C. SAMRA, *The Joyful Christ: The Healing Power of Hu-
mor* (San Francisco, 1986) • H. SCHRÖER, L. STEIGER,
and A. B. DU TROIT, "Freude," *TRE* 11.584-90.

KLAUS WINKLER†

Jubilee Year → Holy Year

Judaism

1. Definition

Judaism is a live historical phenomenon that has extended over more than 3,000 years and manifested itself in just about every spot on earth. To describe a phenomenon of this magnitude is obviously impossible even in many volumes (indeed, the literature on the subject is virtually unlimited) — much more so in a brief overview. All that one can hope to do is to select a few essential characteristics that seem to define Judaism and to observe their temporal and geographic development. The selection itself must be made on the basis of an understanding of the phenomenon that is determined by three factors: as much empirical knowledge as one can gather, a theory that does the greatest possible justice to the facts, and a consciously normative element — that is, what about the phenomenon is believed to account at least in part for its endurance and that may even justify its future existence.

The normative factor may be taken from a number of perspectives. One taken by outsiders to Judaism (sometimes themselves Jews) is what Salo W. Baron, an important 20th-century historian of the Jewish people, pejoratively called "lachrymose history" — that is, Jews have always been a small people who have been victimized by their much more powerful political and religious hosts and neighbors. Their history, seen from this perspective, is therefore a history of reactions, rather than actions, toward the non-Jewish world around and above them.

Another such perspective is the classically Christian view that the religion of Israel was a preparation for the coming of the Messiah (i.e., a *praeparatio evangelica*), and that since the rise of Christianity Judaism is then at best not important anymore or even a living corpse (e.g., Ahasver, the legendary → wandering Jew; Arnold Toynbee describing the Jews as a "fossil" civilization). The evolutionary schema of especially 19th-century biblical criticism and the periodization of the so-called religion of Israel, then "prophetic religion," followed by *Spätjudentum* (i.e., "late Judaism," from the beginnings of rabbinic Judaism after the Babylonian exile to the early strata of the → Talmud) are extant instances of this latter perspective, for what can come after "late"? Contrary to such theories as these that undermine the integrity, significance, and prospects of Judaism, an accurate perspective must encompass the entire sweep of Jewish history, and a sympathetic one will even hope for its future growth.

Judaism, then, is best described as the religious culture of radical, ethical → monotheism perpetuated by the Jewish people. Or as the American Jewish thinker Mordecai Kaplan formulated it, Judaism is the religious civilization of the Jewish people from biblical times to the present, together with their aspirations for the future.

2. Core Doctrines

2.1. *Covenant*

Such a definition of Judaism implies that there is a necessary relationship between people and religion or religious culture. The entrenched term for that relationship from biblical times to today is the → "covenant" (Heb. *běrît*) between God and Israel. Anyone who adopts the religion also automatically becomes a member of the people. The biblical models for this connection are Abraham's household and Ruth, and by the second century of the Common Era, specific procedures for → conversion to Judaism had been developed. Conversely, anyone born into the people is, according to Jewish religious law (the → Halakah), obligated to obey the laws of the religion and, in a looser sense, to learn and practice elements of Jewish culture. Those outside the covenant of God with Israel are part of the broader covenant of God with → Noah and all his descendants, which, according to the → rabbis, binds all people to establish rules of justice and to shun murder, idolatry, adultery/incest, blasphemy, eating a limb from a living animal, and theft.

These traditional concepts establish the inherent dialectical tension in Judaism between its → universalism and its particularism. Ethical monotheism, especially when expanded into a full culture, obviously casts a universal net over all humankind, while the peoplehood of Israel is clearly a particularistic, ethnic entity. The point in Judaism is that these two dimensions are always kept in an often difficult and differently balanced unity. In contrast, Christianity has in theory discarded the ethnic-historical moment.

2.2. *Torah*

The historically favored term for what is here called "the culture of radical, ethical monotheism" is → "Torah." This term, when fully explicated, may be taken to be the common thread that binds into one entity the long and variegated history of Judaism. Etymologically, it means "[divine, revealed] teaching." In the Septuagint translation it is often rendered *nomos*, "law," which is also reasonably valid in view of the centrality of → law in the Bible, the Talmud, in all of medieval Judaism, and even in the significantly secularized culture of many modern Jews. The expanding semantic significance of the word "Torah" itself tells the story: Most narrowly it refers to the → Pentateuch; more broadly it denotes all of the Hebrew Bible, not including the → Apocrypha; more broadly still, it refers not only to the written Torah but also to the oral Torah, Jewish → tradition transmitted by word and practice through the generations; and most broadly it refers to any teaching based on the tradition.

A bibliographic note will be helpful here. The Hebrew Bible consists of stories, laws, sermons, history, poetry, and other types of materials that undoubtedly first appeared in oral form and only later were written down. It is divided into three parts — Torah (Pentateuch), Prophets, and Writings. The first postbiblical collection of oral traditions is the → *Mishnah,* a relatively compact code compiled by Rabbi Judah, president of the Sanhedrin, in about 200 C.E. Other materials collected in the first and second centuries C.E. (the Tannaitic period) became part of another work, the *Tosefta,* edited by Rabbis Hiyya and Oshaiah, and yet others are known through reports in the later *Talmud* (lit. "instruction").

In the next several hundred years (the Amoraic, or Talmudic, period), rabbis in Palestine and Babylonia used the Mishnah as the base for their legal discussions, since it articulated the traditional view of how the written and oral Torah were to be interpreted and integrated. A record of the discussions and expansions of the Mishnah that took place in Palestine was edited in about the year 400 in what is known as the *Palestinian* (or Jerusalem) *Talmud;* the longer, better-known, and therefore more authoritative *Babylonian Talmud,* recording the discussions and expansions of the Mishnah in Babylonia, was edited around 500. In addition, theological, homiletical, and moral exegeses of the Bible were collected in books of such interpretations (a midrash), including, for example, *Genesis Rabbah* (the expanded Genesis), *Exodus Rabbah,* and so forth, beginning in the fifth century.

The classical rabbis, those who forged the distinctively Jewish interpretation and application of the Bible and hence Judaism itself, were the people whose sayings and logic appear in these works — the Mishnah, Tosefta, Talmuds, and → Midrash. Medieval and modern rabbis continue the substance and methodology of Judaism that the → Pharisees in the first century B.C.E. and C.E. began and that the classical rabbis carried on. In addition, rabbinic rulings on specific legal questions, called

responsa or *teshuvot* (answers), have been written from the early → Middle Ages to our own time; similarly, homiletical, moral, and theological commentaries on the Bible and Talmud have continually appeared throughout Jewish history and are being produced today.

Through such works the Judaism of the Pharisaic rabbis overarched, as the German-Jewish philosophical theologian Franz Rosenzweig (1886-1929) pointed out, the single most traumatic caesura in Jewish history prior to the Nazi → Holocaust — the destruction of the second temple and therewith the transformation of Judaism from a religion centered on that → temple to a religious culture centered on "the small sanctuary," that is, the family and the prayer-and-study hall (i.e., → synagogue). In the subsequent two millennia and today, both the Bible and the Talmud are almost always disseminated with numerous and exhaustive commentaries, appendixes, updatings, and so forth, all of which become Torah in the larger sense of the word.

Until the Western emancipation of Jewry, beginning about 1760, and among religious Jewry to this day, this widening culture of Torah was further extrapolated in many forms: commentaries; legal responsa and codes; homiletical, philosophical, mystical, and literary interpretations, and more. Even in significantly secularized and assimilated modern Jewish societies, the forms of thought and the values of this historic culture continue to exercise their power, both in the → diaspora and in the State of Israel. Thus one may indeed speak of Judaism as one religious culture, however differentiated and complex, that looks like an inverted pyramid, with the fundamental document, the Bible, at its narrow base and ever wider and higher levels as the centuries pass. It is a strongly literary and verbal culture, with law the plumb line from its original angle to the hypotenuse, and the whole, still widening, growing triangle is, as it were, self-consciously historical/traditional. Sa'adia Gaon, the founder of mainline → Jewish philosophy in Moslem Babylonia (ca. 900), then will have had in mind what we are calling the Jewish culture of ethical monotheism when he defined the Jewish people as constituted by its *tôrôt,* or Torahs.

The substance of Torah, from the Bible on, includes laws, theological doctrines, stories, and hopes for the future. The law spells out rituals for the → worship of God, which traditional Jews do three times each day, involving the → Sabbath each week and the seasonal holy days, including the three pilgrimage festivals (→ Passover, Shavuot, Sukkot) and the High Holy Days (Rosh Hashanah and Yom Kippur); rituals marking life's passages of birth, adolescence, marriage, and death; → dietary laws (revolving around *kashrut*, "keeping kosher"); family law (engagement, → marriage, divorce, inheritance); and the full gamut of civil and criminal law (→ Jewish Practices). Throughout all of these elements, since biblical and rabbinic literature depicts God as moral and as demanding morality of humanity, much of the substance of Judaism consists of moral → norms.

2.3. *Ethical Monotheism*
In addition to covenant and Torah, Judaism affirms ethical monotheism. This element also unifies the historical phenomena of Judaism over space and time. "Ethical monotheism" is a term put forward especially in modern Judaism, particularly in 19th-century Germany, but it may be taken to summarize correctly the primary thrust of Judaism from its biblical and rabbinic roots to modern times. Monotheism means belief in one and, more important, a unique → God, who is absolutely transcendent to the universe (→ Immanence and Transcendence), just as what "ought" to be is necessarily and in kind different from what "is." Monotheism is therefore inherently ethical (→ Ethics), for it addresses the world, and especially humankind in the world, with the regulative ideals (norms, imperatives, commands, etc.) that issue forth from their Maker. This is the essential meaning of belief in → creation. Thus it is universally acknowledged that the word *mitzvah*, "commandment," is the single most central notion in historic Judaism.

2.4. *Return*
Another central notion in historic Judaism is *teshuvah*, usually translated simply "repentance" but in fact meaning more broadly "return [to the proper path of moral action]." The Jewish people, defined as the community of adherents of Judaism, is the bearer of a radical monotheism, whose function in history is to embody, explore, and establish its truth as widely as possible until, in the messianic consummation, humankind as a whole will live by that truth. (Emphasis on ethical monotheism will tend toward Jewish universalism, as put forward, for example, in medieval Jewish Spain and in the West in the 19th century; in contrast, a dialectical emphasis on its bearer, the Jewish people, as especially emphasized in the present period, will tend toward Jewish particularism. Whether a fully stable and healthy balance has ever been achieved in Jewish history between these two poles is open to debate.) The vast body of accumulated Jewish literature and experience must then, if one attempts to understand its essential thrust systematically, be selected, interpreted,

and extrapolated in the light of this ethicism, which again illustrates the pairing of ethos and ethnos.

3. Historical Overview of Classical Judaism
Once the outlook outlined here is adopted, one can beneficially interpret the periods of Jewish history as intellectual, social, and cultural exfoliations of the essential religious and ethical spirit of Judaism. Throughout the biblical age the unity of the people and the religion of Israel were being forged, the former as the carrier of the latter, and the latter as the expression of the will of God not only for the Jewish people but through them also for all other nations. Therefore the encounters between Israel and Egyptians, Assyrians, Persians, and other groups were in some part used for the enrichment of the core religious cognition of the Bible of ethical monotheism — that is, that individuals and societies are to relate to one another in the manner demanded by the God of morality; conversely, this contact was understood in part as the perennial struggle against immoral → paganism.

3.1. *Hellenistic and Rabbinic Ages*
In the Hellenistic age (→ Hellenism), which overlapped in its beginning with the biblical age and in its end with the classical rabbinic age, the first great encounter took place between Judaism and a high → culture of the West. Here the very word "Judaism" was first coined. This attempt at a symbiosis of Jewish philosophy with Hellenistic cosmopolitanism was crafted during a period in which Jews also experienced → anti-Semitism and ideological schisms.

In the more self-enclosed circles of Jewish society in Palestine and then particularly in Babylonia, the so-called rabbinic age interpreted and expanded the meaning of the Bible through the techniques of midrash, converted biblical law into the much broader Halakah based on it, and transformed biblical doctrine into a vast and multisided structure of → Haggadah (nonlegal or supralegal formulations of beliefs, morals, opinions, culture, → mysticism, etc.). In these rabbinic genres of literature, the general doctrines and prescriptions of biblical religion were specified for all the details of daily individual and social life (religious, civil, economic, criminal, etc.), and at the same time they were expanded to deal with new questions and circumstances.

The relatively cosmopolitan character of Hellenistic Jewish culture proved to be untenable, both practically and conceptually, and was in fact absorbed and transformed in nascent Christianity. The Talmud, in contrast, ever since Jewishly understood as the canonical interpretation of biblical religion, became and has remained the essence of historic Judaism.

3.2. *Gaonic Age*

In the subsequent Gaonic (from *gaon*, or religious head of the organized, largely autonomous community) age in Babylonia, which lasted about 650-1050, Talmudic law continued to be applied and expanded in responsa literature and began to be structured in codes. In addition, systematic → philosophy and mysticism, mutually related and intertwined, arose as new genres of Jewish literature, the latter in no small measure in response to interaction with Moslem culture and to the first great schism in Judaism since Christianity, Karaism, an anti-Pharisaic biblicism that rejected rabbinism and talmudism.

3.3. *To 1800*

In the last thousand years, Jews lived primarily in Europe and the Mediterranean basin. Two major forms of Judaism developed in its two primary centers: *Sephardic*, in the Mediterranean rim and especially Spain, and *Ashkenazic*, in northern Europe. These two forms of Judaism were felicitously described by Leo Baeck, German rabbi and theologian of the 20th century, as, respectively, "religion of culture" and "culture of religion." While Jewish religion and especially its law always remained central in both communities, and while there was always some interaction between them, the two formed importantly different cultural matrices, with different non-Hebrew, though Jewish, languages and even different liturgies and legal tendencies.

The more liberal societies of → Islam exercised a great deal of influence on Jewish thinking and culture. → Linguistics, belles lettres, and especially philosophy and mysticism were produced, and they made a significant impact on the religious core. In fact, to this very day the Spanish-Jewish Middle Ages have been most determinative in forming the basic core of the Jewish philosophico-theological tradition, from the → Platonist Isaac Israeli (ca. 850-ca. 950), through its permanent peak in the → Aristotelian Maimonides (1135-1204), down to the more eclectic Joseph Albo (ca. 1380-ca. 1444) and the Abarbanel (or Abrabanel) family, especially Isaac (1437-1508) and Judah (ca. 1460-ca. 1521), a core developed during the very death throes of Jewish Spain under its unification and Christianization by Ferdinand and Isabella. In this culture, too, Jewish mysticism acquired its classic, canonical form in the *Zohar*, the so-called Bible of → Cabala, which imprinted its seal on subsequent Jewish culture as much as the great rationalist strain. Both conceptually and historically, the two tended to interact and mutually to nurture the centrality of religious eth-

ics. Politically, Jews sometimes experienced serious strains under Muslim rule, but often they managed to create a positive symbiosis with their Muslim rulers.

Christian Europe, in contrast, was marked by → ghettos, crusades, pogroms, and expulsions. There Jews tended more to "work their own vineyards." Intense exegetical and post-Talmudic extrapolations were pursued, and the movement of "Ashkenazic pietism" in the High Middle Ages, stressing individual → piety and mystical → devotion, produced a → lifestyle and literature of its own. In the meantime, Jewish economic and political life was squeezed into very delimited areas. When Christian rulers conquered Spain and Portugal and forced Jews either to convert to Christianity or to leave, Iberian Jews were either forced into pretended → baptism (→ Marranos) or had to move to other parts of the world. Lurianic Cabala, which strengthened millenarian tendencies, was at least in part their religious reaction to their fate. The rest had to leave to join Sephardic Jewish communities in the eastern Mediterranean, particularly Turkey, or the more numerous Ashkenazic Jewish communities of Europe.

Here again the conventional periodization of Western → historiography makes no sense. Despite some repercussions of the → Renaissance among the relatively small Jewish community of Italy, on the whole the Middle Ages extended for Jewry until at least the end of the 18th century. Expulsions from France, Spain, Portugal, and Germany in the 14th and 15th centuries moved the center of gravity of Ashkenazic Jewry to Poland, where Halakic Judaism was again extended, deepened, and strengthened. In the later 18th century, though, an antirabbinic, populist, and pietist movement arose in the southern regions of eastern Europe in the form of → Hasidism.

4. Features of Classical Judaism

At least four general features of Judaism up to the last two centuries can be discerned.

4.1. *Centrality of the Moral Life*

The first such feature is that the central concern of classical (i.e., biblical and Talmudic) Judaism — moral life under and for the sake of God — was consistently the all-consuming enterprise. Under many and different circumstances the broad laws and doctrines of classical Judaism were always essentially preserved, used as the foundation for further developments, translated both linguistically and conceptually in order to expand their viability, and, most particularly, always brought to a high degree of specificity. Jewish law thus became a gigantic body of common law (precedents on the basis of a divine "constitution").

The joke about the rabbi who was not at all worried about the spiritual problems of a man in his congregation as long as the man continued to observe all required practices, though ostensibly advocating a mindless ritualism, in fact touches on a pervasive truth of Judaism, namely, its primacy of praxis and its endless concern with a religiously humane life. Even highly abstract theoretical concerns in philosophy, theology, and mysticism were bound to the law that orders daily life, so that they are typically — in a tradition from Maimonides to Rabbi J. B. Soloveitchik (1920-92) — a philosophy/theology/mysticism of the law, and certainly always within its bounds. Finally, then, seemingly theoretical concerns lead in Judaism to a philosophy/theology/ mysticism of the good life.

4.2. *Absence of Politics*

Second, connected with this positive feature of historic Judaism is what may appear to be a negative feature, namely, the large-scale absence of → politics. Deprived of their own polity and having no immediate place for a politics of their own, individual Jews and Jewish communities had to seek a modus vivendi within the political systems in which they found themselves, both theoretically and practically, legally and conceptually. They were thus led to conclude that politics was the strange enterprise of strangers (the Heb. term for "idolatry" lit. means "strange service"), which Jews had to work through in order to be able to face the real business of life — God and daily living in community. How much a pound of potatoes cost or what → prayer to say when one could feed one's family was the concrete human activity they dealt with, living in a world different from that in which kings and noblemen, bishops and sultans waged war with one another.

4.3. *Messianism*

Third, the one perennial political dimension of Judaism has always been → messianism. The Jewish polity-to-come, the only one worth being morally and humanly concerned about, is the messianic → kingdom of God on earth, which will bring the Jewish people together again in their land under the rule of divine law. In this kingdom, as Maimonides formulated it, there will be enough economic and social affluence for Jews and, in their wake, all humankind to devote themselves with undivided attention to the knowledge and works of God. The details of messianic theology and history have therefore always been in the foreground for Judaism, even though much controverted.

Historically, there has not been a single generation in which somewhere a pseudomessiah has not arisen to a greater or lesser welcome, so strong has been the religiously and metaphysically felt need for "the end of exile." All who claimed to be the Messiah failed to institute such a kingdom, but their failure and death have not sufficed to extinguish the flame of yearning for the Messiah to come. Furthermore, when such yearnings linked themselves to particular people, schisms — otherwise strikingly absent in the history of classical Judaism — typically ensued (e.g., Christianity, Shabbethaianism). Such schismatic movements also have typically divested themselves of the Halakah as the one firm anchor of normal premessianic Judaism, even though much controverted by their current circumstances.

4.4. *Persecution*

So far in this bird's-eye view of the history of Judaism from the perspective of ethical monotheism, the usual tale of persecution has been avoided. It comes last here, for it is possible, and indeed it may be correct, to understand Judaism as having developed in its chief lines according to its own inner dynamic and not primarily as a reaction to outside forces. For example, during the first four centuries of the Common Era, which saw both the peak of rabbinic productivity and also the massive rise of Christianity, rabbinic literature alludes to Christianity and takes its claims seriously, but in the end the rabbis discussed it only rarely. Christianity has typically not been a relevant problem for Judaism, until Jews were forced in medieval and modern Europe to defend themselves against physical and religious violence. Additionally, it is clear that in this period the relationship of Judaism to Islam was both intellectually and historically much more positive, if only because the kinship between these two religious cultures is much more solid. To be sure, persecutions, expulsions, restrictions, and forcible (and typically unsuccessful) conversions always played an important, lamentable role in the life of Jewry.

While Jewish religious culture was deeply affected by such continual experiences, the millennia-long history of Judaism was nevertheless essentially determined by its basic character as a culture of ethical monotheism. This culture, for itself and for the world, consistently endeavored to moralize human life under unaccountably many and different circumstances and frequently in the teeth of great hostility. The obverse of such adversity was the ultimately helpful historical status of Judaism as a powerless → minority, which was deprived by history of not only the opportunities but also the temptations of worldly rule.

5. Judaism in the Nineteenth and Twentieth Centuries

Worldliness — or to use another term, → secularism — has been the growing social and cultural condition with which Judaism and the Jewish people, together with the rest of the world, have had to cope, both negatively and positively, in the last two centuries. The democratic revolutions of the 18th and subsequent centuries, first in the West and then spreading southward and eastward, offered the prize of political emancipation to Jewry. The → Enlightenment completed the shift from → metaphysics and traditional → religion to → science and technology, from → revelation to → reason, and from inherited class to individual effort. On the whole, the convergence of the historic Jewish esteem for practical rationality and similar tendencies in → modernism did not remain unnoticed; indeed, enemies of modernization quite commonly have identified it as Jewishly inspired and called it Judaization. Still, for all its openness to science and practicality, Judaism clearly embodies a religious and moral perspective on the world that is at root very different from a secular perspective. Thus, as scientific advances exploded and science became more and more respected, advocates of Judaism, like those of other religions, had to fight to convince adherents that one could and should be religious as well as scientific. Moreover, Judaism's focus on the community has had to be defended against the rampant → individualism inherent in Enlightenment doctrines.

The first significant encounter between Judaism and modernism unfolded in Germany, and the forms of that conflict manifested themselves over time elsewhere as well. Jews sought to integrate their Jewish identity with → modernity on cultural, political, economic, and social levels without excessive loss of authenticity, although this approach also produced a backlash among those who thought that modernity threatened Judaism and Jewish identity. Religious forms of this modern metamorphosis included liturgical, linguistic, legal, and ideological changes by those fostering liberalism in the name of Reform Judaism as distinguished at first from traditional orthodoxy and then also from a kind of neoorthodoxy. On the level of "high culture" the medieval Spanish tradition of philosophy, theology, and critical, historical scholarship was resumed very productively under the title "science of Judaism" (*Wissenschaft des Judentums*). A middle movement then emerged among those who sought truly to integrate tradition with modernity; in America it was called Conservative Judaism, and in Israel *Masorti* (traditional) Judaism. Liberalism, old and new orthodoxies, and the emerging middle movement each changed with the passage of time and according to social settings as these new developments spread from Germany to the United States, where the earlier developments reached their hitherto fullest realizations, and eventually also to the State of Israel.

In the late 20th century, a significant minority of Jews in the United States embraced forms of secularism while maintaining a Jewish ethnic consciousness, while the majority continued to affirm one or another of the religious forms developed earlier, with by far most Jews identifying as either Reform or Conservative. In Israel the spectrum spread from official nationalist-secular ideology to its own radical opponents among the so-called anti-Zionist ultraorthodox. While the various forms of Judaism live together in relative harmony in the Jewish diaspora, in Israel the secular/religious divide is exacerbated by government funding of religious institutions and exemptions for Orthodox students from army service.

Apart from the Nazi destruction of European Jewry and with it European Jewish culture, clearly the most important events in modern Judaism are the immigration to North America of millions of eastern European Jews in the early decades of the 20th century and the establishment of the State of Israel in 1948. What the long-range effects of these events will be on Judaism as a religious culture has yet to be determined. A few preliminary symptoms, however, have already appeared. The Holocaust has raised major questions for → Jewish theology and philosophy, and it has given Jews a sense not only of the depravity of evil but also of the need to make sure that Jews are never again made victims. That conviction indeed continues to be a motivating factor for Jews worldwide, but especially in Israel, to defend themselves.

The North American experience has contributed to the ability of Jews to live together while practicing plural forms of Judaism. Indeed, never before has the largest Jewish community in the world been so diverse in its thought and practice. In addition, Mordecai Kaplan's concept of Judaism as not only a religion but also a civilization has shaped all forms of American Judaism and contributed to its richness. This concept includes ever-evolving forms of Jewish art, music, dance, and drama. Institutionally, furthermore, Kaplan's idea of the synagogue-center has taken root, so that synagogues now house not only worship and Jewish education but also Jewish social, cultural, social action, and even athletic activities.

The State of Israel has, above all, rejuvenated the → Hebrew language, the historical vehicle of Judaism. Now that it is again a living tongue, all of Jewish classical resources and values have been revived both for scholarship and for daily use. Also, what had for 2,000 years been at most academic topics — Jewish political, civil, and even some ritual law — are now being confronted again as live, albeit problematic, options.

As for institutional religion, in the beginning of the Zionist resettlement of "the holy land," Jews brought their eastern-European forms along: rabbinic and Hasidic orthodoxy (most of it opposed to → Zionism as a social movement) and their antithesis — secular, nationalist → socialism. With the mass immigration to Israel of western-European Jews just before World War II and after it because of the impact, both personal and political, of American Jewry, a small but effective sector of religious → liberalism (Reform Judaism, Conservative Judaism, etc.) has arisen. Even in the kibbutzim, the most significant social product of the earlier waves of settlement, various elements of historical Judaism seem to have emerged from the secular-socialist foundations. The impact of the reality of the State of Israel on all aspects of the rest of Jewry and Judaism in the world is, in any case, overwhelming.

Two chief characteristics may be noted from this overall phenomenon of Jewish modernization — one historical, the other axiological. The historical characteristic is the full and horrific backlash against Jews and Judaism even in polite American society of the 1930s and 1940s, but more egregiously in Stalinist Russia and most especially in Nazi Germany, where "the final solution of the Jewish problem" was concocted with, it must be added, substantial historical and ideological aid from within Christian Europe. While we have argued, then, that the lachrymose theory of Jewish history is faulty, we must acknowledge that Judaism and Jews have been greatly affected by anti-Jewish propaganda and activities foisted on Jews by Christians and, in recent decades, by Muslims.

The axiological characteristic is that even in sometimes radical Jewish secularism, some of the basic values of historical Jewish culture have been perpetuated and have even extrapolated themselves. Jewish literariness, cosmopolitanism, and historical self-consciousness, Jews' focus on law and social reform, Jews' heavy involvement in medicine and education, and even the sense of Jewish alienation among the long-since totally assimilated and historicist "conservatives" — all find their roots in classical Judaism. After the onslaught on Judaism and the Jewish people by Nazis, Fascists, Bolsheviks, and others (exponentializing many centuries of reli-

gious, political, and ideological enmity), in the 20th century since World War II and now in the 21st century a Jewish counterreaction is unmistakable: Jews are reasserting their historical identity, most eminently in the form of a sovereign state; they are insisting on their own physical and socioeconomic security; and they are even returning to traditional forms of religion. A sign of the last point is the 1999 platform statement of the American Reform rabbinate, which emphasizes the importance to Reform Jews of learning about traditional Judaism and practicing as much of it as they can. How Jewish radical, ethical monotheism will fare from here on is perhaps the ultimate question about Judaism.

Bibliography: Popular sources: E. B. Borowitz and F. W. Schwartz, *The Jewish Moral Virtues* (Philadelphia, 1999) • L. Jacobs, *The Book of Jewish Beliefs* (New York, 1984); idem, *The Book of Jewish Practice* (West Orange, N.J., 1987) • H. Kushner, *To Life! A Celebration of Jewish Being and Thinking* (Boston, 1993) • D. Orenstein and J. R. Litman, eds., *Lifecycles: Jewish Women on Biblical Themes in Contemporary Life* (Woodstock, Vt., 1997) • L. Trepp, *The Complete Book of Jewish Observance* (New York, 1980) • E. M. Umansky and D. Ashton, eds., *Four Centuries of Jewish Women's Spirituality: A Sourcebook* (Boston, 1992).

Academic sources: L. Baeck, *The Essence of Judaism* (rev. ed.; New York, 1948) • S. W. Baron, *A Social and Religious History of the Jews* (18 vols.; Philadelphia and New York, 1952-83) • J. Carroll, *Constantine's Sword: The Church and the Jews, a History* (Boston, 2001) • A. A. Cohen and P. Mendes-Flohr, eds., *Contemporary Jewish Religious Thought* (New York, 1987) • E. N. Dorff, *Matters of Life and Death: A Jewish Approach to Modern Medical Ethics* (Philadelphia, 1998); idem, *To Do the Right and the Good: A Jewish Approach to Modern Social Ethics* (Philadelphia, 2002) • E. N. Dorff and L. Newman, eds., *Contemporary Jewish Ethics and Morality: A Reader* (New York, 1995); idem, eds., *Contemporary Jewish Theology: A Reader* (New York, 1999) • M. Elon, *Jewish Law: History, Sources, Principles* (4 vols.; Philadelphia, 1988) • *EncJud* • *EncTal* • L. Ginzberg, *The Legends of the Jews* (7 vols.; Baltimore, 1998; orig. pub., 1909-38) • M. M. Kaplan, *Judaism as a Civilization: Toward a Reconstruction of American-Jewish Life* (rev. ed.; New York, 1957; orig. pub., 1934) • S. S. Schwarzschild, *The Pursuit of the Ideal: Jewish Writings of Steven Schwarzschild* (ed. M. Kellner; Albany, N.Y., 1990) • R. Seltzer, *Jewish People, Jewish Thought: The Jewish Experience in History* (New York, 1980) • J. B. Soloveitchik, *Halakhic Man* (Philadelphia, 1983; orig. pub., 1944).

Steven S. Schwarzschild†
and Elliot N. Dorff

Jude, Epistle of

The author of the Epistle of Jude calls himself "a servant of → Jesus Christ" and "brother of → James" but does not tell us to whom he is writing (vv. 1-2). The cause of writing is the intrusion of false teachers into an unknown community. These teachers promote licentiousness and, in fact, deny Christ (vv. 3-4). Their judgment is depicted (vv. 5-19) in terms taken from examples in the OT and the → Apocrypha (vv. 5-7, 9, 11) and by means of pre-Christian and early Christian prophecy (vv. 14-18). The recipients are admonished to cling to their "most holy faith" (v. 20), the faith "once for all entrusted to the saints" (v. 3). They are told how to care for persons affected by false teaching (vv. 22-23, although these verses are textually uncertain at points). A → doxology, but no final greeting, closes the letter (vv. 24-25).

Authorship by the Lord's brother (cf. Mark 6:3) is unlikely, since the writer has composed Greek well, and the → pseudepigraphic *1 Enoch* is quoted as authoritative (vv. 14-15). Various elements suggest that it was composed during the postapostolic period: the appeal to the → apostles as the standards of tradition (v. 17), the understanding of faith as a formally and substantively fixed entity (vv. 3, 20), the typological characterization of false teachers (possibly representing an early form of → gnosis; see vv. 4b, 8b, 10a, 19), and the decision not to engage in any dispute with them. The Epistle of Jude derives from Hellenistic Jewish Christianity (→ Jewish Christians 1).

Although some scholars suggest an earlier date, the late first century is more plausible. Since the author of 2 Peter appears to have drawn upon portions of Jude, the writing of 2 Peter would be the terminus ante quem for the writing of Jude. The place of writing cannot be determined.

→ Catholic Epistles

Bibliography: R. J. Bauckham, *Jude, 2 Peter* (WBC; Waco, Tex., 1983); idem, *Jude and the Relatives of Jesus in the Early Church* (Edinburgh, 1990) • E. M. Sidebottom, *James, Jude, 2 Peter* (NCBC; Grand Rapids, 1982).

Helmut Merkel and Arland J. Hultgren

Judges, Book of

1. Title and Office
2. Contents
3. Origin
4. Theological Intention

1. Title and Office
The Book of Judges (Heb. *šōpĕṭîm*) derives its title from the charismatic tribal heroes (→ Tribes of Israel) who, during the period preceding the monarchy, repeatedly rescued → Israel (§1) during times of extreme distress. At the same time, they occupied a temporally restricted office of leadership.

2. Contents
Three major parts can be discerned. The *introduction* (1:1–2:5) offers a retrospective on the ongoing land conquest of the tribes west of the Jordan (in the form of a "negative account of occupation").

The *main section* (2:6–16:31) contains the actual stories. Judg. 2:11-19 interprets theologically the history (→ Historiography 1) of the period of the judges, suggesting that because of its apostasy to other gods, Israel falls into the hands of its enemies. When it cries out for help, → Yahweh awakens judges, who rescue Israel. The book develops this schema in the colorful stories of Othniel, Ehud, Deborah and Barak, Gideon (= Jerubbaal, father of Abimelech), Jephthah, and Samson. Judg. 3:31, 10:1-5, and 12:8-15 also contain brief, enumerative remarks about the judges Shamgar, Tola, Jair, Ibzan, Elon, and Abdon. The episode about the city kingship of Abimelech in Shechem, which constitutes a separate piece, is critical of kingship (chap. 9; cf. 8:22-23)

Finally, the *addenda* consist of the stories of the founding of the sanctuary at Dan (chaps. 17–18) and the disgraceful deed of the Benjaminites and its punishment (19–21). A refrain throughout these chapters bemoans the lack of a king (17:6; 18:1; 19:1; 21:25), substantiating, by default, the necessity of kingship.

3. Origin
The period of judges extended from the death of → Joshua (Judg. 2:8-10) to the accession of → Saul (1 Sam. 7:15-17). M. Noth (1902-68) ascribed the composition of the Book of Judges basically to the author of the → Deuteronomistic history. This author allegedly drew from various stories about local tribal heroes ("great judges"), whom he integrated into his schema (Judg. 2:11-19) as pan-Israelite leaders of a war of Yahweh (→ Holy War), and from a fragmentary list of "lesser judges" (10:1-5; 12:8-15).

Recent scholars go beyond Noth in discerning more complex stratification, suggesting, for example, that the work of the Deuteronomistic historian was reworked and augmented in several places by late-Deuteronomistic editors (e.g., 1:27–2:5; 2:17;

17–18). Chaps. 19–21, together with the refrains advocating kingship, were added even later (4th cent. b.c.?).

4. Theological Intention

One important leitmotiv permeating the various literary strata is the legitimacy of the → monarchy in Israel. While the Deuteronomistic historian basically contests this legitimacy (see 8:22-23), the editor who added the refrains positive toward kingship views the period of judges as one of hopeless chaos moving of necessity toward monarchy.

→ Pentateuch

Bibliography: Commentaries: R. G. BOLING (AB; Garden City, N.Y., 1975) • K. BUDDE (KHC; Tübingen, 1897) • H. W. HERTZBERG (ATD; 6th ed.; Göttingen, 1985) • D. T. OLSON (NIB: Nashville, 1998) • T. J. SCHNEIDER (BerOl; Collegeville, Minn., 2000) • J. A. SOGGIN (OTL; 2d ed.; London, 1987).

Other works: S. ACKERMAN, *Warrior, Dancer, Seductress, Queen: Women in Judges and Biblical Israel* (New York, 1998) • R. BARTELMUS, "Forschung am Richterbuch seit Martin Noth," *TRu* 56 (1991) 221-59 • U. BECKER, *Richterzeit und Königtum* (Berlin, 1990) • A. BRENNER, ed., *A Feminist Companion to Judges* (Sheffield, 1993) • M. NOTH, *The Deuteronomistic History* (Sheffield, 1981; orig. pub., 1943) • W. RICHTER, *Traditionsgeschichtliche Untersuchungen zum Richterbuch* (2d ed.; Bonn, 1966) • G. YEE, ed., *Judges and Method: New Approaches in Biblical Studies* (Minneapolis, 1995).

UWE BECKER

Judgment → Last Judgment

Julian of Norwich

1. Julian of Norwich (ca. 1342–after 1416) was an English anchoress, visionary, spiritual guide, and theologian. In 1373, at the age of 30, she suffered a grave illness. Lying on her bed in the expectation of death, Julian had a series of → visions that became the basis for her composition of theological texts. Little else is known of her life, although tradition has it that by 1394 she was an anchoress, probably at St. Julian's church, Norwich (→ Anchorites).

The MSS of Julian's work transmit two different but related texts, which scholars refer to as the Short and the Long Text of *The Revelation of Love*. In the Long Text, Julian describes subsequent experiences of 1388 and 1393 that suggest her dissatisfaction with the Short Text and develop a crucial insight

that led to the dramatic revision of that earlier work. Julian testifies that she spent two decades — there is evidence to suggest as much as 40 years — pondering the content of her experience.

Like many late medieval women who wrote religious works, Julian was concerned about her theological authority. Unlike many of those women, however, she did not describe herself as divinely commissioned to write but instead emphasized her own certainty that her visions had universal value. In the Short Text she assured her readers that she was not a teacher, for she was "a woman, ignorant, weak and frail," yet even this fact was not sufficient cause for her to be silent about the goodness of God. In the Long Text the explicitly gendered reference has been replaced by her description of herself as "a simple, unlettered creature." Omitting the gendered aspect of inadequacy has been attributed to Julian's matured confidence in her role as a teacher, but both passages still raise the question of Julian's education, specifically her acquaintance with the theological currents of late medieval Christianity, and more generally, her literacy. Even if Julian had little formal education as a child, throughout her adult life she developed a theological sensibility and the literary skills to create a complex treatise addressing fundamental aspects of Christian belief.

The Revelation of Love (also later known as *The Revelations of Divine Love* or *Book of Showings*) begins with Julian's assertion that she had long desired "three graces": to have a recollection or physical sight of Christ's passion, to have a severe physical illness, and to be wounded with contrition, compassion, and longing for God. The first grace reflects Julian's familiarity with the medieval practices of → meditation that encourage the individual to create an imaginative experience of presence at the site of Christ's suffering and death. The second would allow her to receive the last rites, the richest benefit offered by the church's sacramental system. And the third echoes the common devotional theme of feeling the stabbing pain of sorrow for → sin, loving identification with God, and longing for deeper connection to God (→ Mysticism).

Julian then turns to the pivotal scene of her illness, when her curate tells her to look at the → cross he had brought. While focusing on the cross, she suddenly saw blood trickling down from the crown of thorns. Further visualizations of the physicality of the passion ensue, as well as verbal and visual expressions of theological points not at first glance linked directly to the passion. Julian declares that the revelations were communicated to her by physical vision, by words formed in her understanding, and by spiritual vision, a threefold distinction that suggests Julian's familiarity with late medieval contemplative theory.

2. The first revelation of the Short Text introduces themes that occupied Julian throughout her life. For Julian, a vision of the copious outpouring of Christ's blood was a testimony to the divinity and humanity of Christ suffering for her, which comforts her. This physical sight was accompanied by a spiritual sight of God's → love, which two of her most characteristic images convey. She declares that the Lord "is our clothing, for he is the love that wraps and enfolds us, embraces us and guides us, hangs about us in tender love, that he may never leave us." And she describes seeing "something small, no bigger than a hazelnut, lying in the palm of my hand." The smallness of this image taught her that everything has being only through God's love. Next, a vision of the befouling of Christ's body and his face caking with blood is complemented by a vision of God "in a point," which she understands to mean that God is everywhere and does everything.

This insight triggers a major question: If God does everything, what is sin? In the Augustinian, Christian Neoplatonic tradition, Julian asserts that sin is nothing, no-thing, having no kind of substance or existence. Yet she is keenly aware of → evil and → suffering in the world, in the face of which she declares that the Lord consoled her, saying, "All will be well, and every kind of thing will be well." Her reflections on the ostensible → paradox of sin as causing palpable suffering yet being nonexistent, and on a divine assurance of universal well-being, lead to → anthropological insights. Julian declares that "in each soul that will be saved there is a good will that never assented to sin and never will." She also sees the Lord sitting in her soul, a vision that is interpreted to mean that the Lord dwells permanently within the human soul. The Short Text ends on a pastoral note without fully resolving the theological questions about sin and human nature.

3. In the Long Text, Julian greatly expands upon these reflections and organizes the visions and insights into an account of 16 initial, plus 2 later, revelations. She also acknowledges anxiously that her revelations contradict the church's teachings about sin and damnation, thus raising the issue of dogmatic → authority.

The resolution of the fundamental tension about sin and the nature of → God is expressed in a story about a lord who issues a command to a loyal servant. The servant "starts off at once, running with all speed, in his love to do what his master wanted. And without warning he falls headlong into a deep ditch and injures himself very badly." The details of this story are then analyzed as a revision of the fall of → Adam. Here the fall — literally a fall into a ditch — is due to no fault of the servant but rather to "his own good will and great longing." Yet the consequence of the fall is genuine suffering caused by the pain of his injuries and his separation from his lord.

The story is then retold with the loyal servant as the second person of the Trinity, who fell when Adam fell, taking upon himself all blame. He fell when Adam fell because of the absolute unity between human nature and his divine nature, a unity not ruptured by the violence of the fall. Julian thus clarifies her earlier anthropological insights: a substantial part of the human being is always essentially united to God and never sins; that is, God is part of the human being. And her image of God is expressed in a new way: God is Father who creates, Mother who redeems, and Holy Spirit who perfects. The effect of → atonement is a loving, maternal reformation or rebirthing of the human being that integrates the essential, divine part of the self with the created part of the self. Thus Julian's visions in the Short Text that link the passion of Christ with → creation, the nonexistence of sin, and divine love as the sustaining force of all existence are finally resolved in these last chapters in the Long Text in a profoundly optimistic vision of universal salvation as the ultimate incorporation of all life into a loving God.

4. Julian had a local reputation in her own day, and there was a revival of interest in *The Revelation of Love* in the 17th century. Her work is also having a major modern revival, as seen in numerous translations now available, "Julian prayer groups," and popular publications, Web sites, and retreats dedicated to using the insights of Julian for reflection on theological and pastoral questions. The Order of Julian of Norwich, a contemplative, semienclosed monastic order of the Episcopal Church, was founded in 1985.

→ Devotional Literature; Middle Ages; Theosis

Bibliography: Primary sources: F. BEER, ed., *Julian of Norwich's "Revelations of Divine Love": The Shorter Version Ed. from B. L. Add. MS 37790* (Heidelberg, 1978) • E. COLLEDGE and J. WALSH, eds., *A Book of Showings to the Anchoress Julian of Norwich* (2 vols.; Toronto, 1978) • G. R. CRAMPTON, ed., *The Shewings of Julian of*

Norwich (Kalamazoo, Mich., 1993) • M. GLASSCOE, ed., *A Revelation of Love* (2d ed.; Exeter, 1986).

Translated sources: E. COLLEDGE and J. WALSH, trans., *Showings* (New York, 1978) • E. SPEARING, trans., *Revelations of Divine Love* (London, 1998).

Secondary works: D. N. BAKER, *Julian of Norwich's Showings: From Vision to Book* (Princeton, 1994) • G. JANTZEN, *Julian of Norwich: Mystic and Theologian* (New York, 1988) • B. PELPHREY, *Love Was His Meaning: The Theology and Mysticism of Julian of Norwich* (Salzburg, 1982) • F. RIDDY, "Julian of Norwich and Self-Textualization," *Editing Women* (ed. A. M. Hutchison; Toronto, 1998) 101-24 • N. WATSON, "The Composition of Julian of Norwich's Revelation of Love," *Spec.* 68 (1993) 637-83.

ANNE L. CLARK

Jurisdiction → Polity, Ecclesiastical

Justice → Righteousness, Justice

Justification

1. NT
   1.1. Proclamation and Theology of Justification
   1.2. Modern Research
   1.3. Paul's Theology of Justification
   1.4. Forensic and Participatory Categories
   1.5. Effective History of Paul's Theology in the NT
   1.6. The Proclamation of Jesus and Paul's Theology of Justification
   1.7. Significance of Justification
2. Historical and Systematic Theology
   2.1. Concept
   2.2. History of Theology and Doctrine
   2.3. Systematic Issues
   2.4. Ecumenical Theology

Words from both the Lat. *iustitia* (justice, justification, justify) and the Anglo-Saxon *rightwise(n)* (righteousness, declare or make righteous) are available in English to render terms from the single root *ṣdq* in Hebrew and the *dikaio-* word family in Greek. Accordingly, in English there are often separate treatments of "justification" and "righteousness" (e.g., R. B. Hays, J. Reumann). In German, as in many languages, the relevant terms *Rechtfertigung* and *Gerechtigkeit* are more closely related. This article treats the → theology and → proclamation of the doctrine in the NT and in later → systematic theology. For fuller OT and NT background, see "Righteousness, Justice."

1. NT

1.1. *Proclamation and Theology of Justification*
It is the task of systematic theology to reflect on the doctrine of justification (see 2); only with reservations, therefore, can we speak of a NT doctrine of justification. → Paul, preeminently the NT theologian of justification, brought it to expression theologically, not as abstract doctrine, but in proclamation. In Galatians and Romans he presented justification in frameworks that differ in their theological conceptions because of different situations. The constant element is justification by → faith. The variable element is the theological system of coordinates within which Paul reflects on the subject.

1.2. *Modern Research*
Modern research has questioned whether "justification by faith and not by works of the law" really occupies so high a place. If for the → Reformers it was central to NT theology, W. Wrede (1859-1906) and A. → Schweitzer (1875-1965) argued that it was only a polemical doctrine, conditioned by specific situations, or a "secondary crater," compared to the volcanic peak of "in Christ" mysticism. More recently, E. P. Sanders has in particular denied its central importance in Pauline theology, giving primacy to participatory categories ("eschatological participation" in Christ's death and life for God) over forensic categories. F. Watson, on the basis of his sociological interpretation of Pauline theology, contested the understanding of Paul that we find in R. Bultmann (1884-1976), E. Käsemann (1906-98), and other adherents of → dialectical theology along the lines of M. Luther's doctrine of justification (→ Luther's Theology). G. Strecker, among others, argued that, in the course of Paul's theological development, it was first in Galatians that he began to present his doctrine of justification.

There are important elements of truth in what these exegetes say. Overall, however, there are insufficient reasons for disputing the central position of the proclamation of justification in Pauline thought.

1.3. *Paul's Theology of Justification*
To understand justification in Paul, we need to consider his → biography in correlation with various situations of the addressees of his letters (see J. Becker). Theological reflection on the → law played a role of considerable importance in this regard. We can adequately interpret what he has to say about law and justification in Galatians and Romans (→ Law and Gospel) only if we keep in mind his call. He himself tells us in Gal. 1:13-14 that he had

been a fanatical rigorist for the law who had persecuted the church of God. Apparently he had persecuted → Jewish Christians for their criticism of the law and their partial freedom from it. Hence his calling as an → apostle must have involved the startling recognition that God was on the side of these Christian lawbreakers! If so, he had to begin a decisive rethinking of the law and consequently of justification, already in the period shortly after his Damascus experience.

This new insight was by no means purely theoretical. It was also existential, since for Paul the Jew there had to be, along with his changed view of the law, a changed view of existence. Coming as he did from the OT, Paul meant by existence his *existence before God,* a fundamentally forensic existence: we stand responsible before God. Paul spoke clearly of this existence before God or Christ in 1 Thess 1:3; 2:19; 3:9, 13. Since, however, this letter was written after the mission synod (the so-called apostolic council in Acts 15), at which Paul believed he had succeeded in contending for freedom in principle from the law, it follows that already at this time two constituent features were present that would be given literary expression in Galatians and Romans: a sense of the basic forensic character of human existence (the OT legacy) and freedom from the law as the decisive new element over against the OT. That the formula "justification by faith and not by works of the law" is not encountered in 1 Thessalonians is explained by the situation of the addressees.

Whether this formula played a role at the mission synod can be answered, if at all, only from Galatians. The *argumentatio* in Galatians 3 and 4 — that "being-in-Christ," or being saved, is incompatible with being unsaved under the law (functionally the same as being under → sin!), and therefore that the Galatians should not submit to → circumcision because, by so doing, they would bring themselves under bondage to the law — really precedes the *narratio* (biographical account) that Paul provides in chaps. 1 and 2. In that account Paul brings in the council to show that even the Jerusalem "pillars" had recognized his law-free gospel; he then moves on, by way of the incident at Antioch, to the *propositio* of the letter (→ Rhetoric 1). We find this element in the formula about justification ("A person is justified not by the works of the law but through faith in Jesus Christ," 2:16) as an answer about the attitude of → Peter ("we know . . ."; see J. Becker, 283, on Rom. 3:28; M. Theobald, "Der Kanon," argues that this verse presents "communal property," a church statement from Antioch not peculiar to Paul). Already at this period, then, "justifi-

cation on the basis of faith and not on the basis of works of the law" would be a conviction shared by Paul and the Jerusalem leadership. Nevertheless, Paul was perhaps reading rather too much into what was agreed upon at the council, for it is hard to think that those at Jerusalem would have fully accepted the critical attitude toward the law that we find in Galatians 3–5 and on behalf of which Paul appeals to them as witnesses.

To all appearances, Paul later had to come to the realization that his theology of the law in Galatians was diametrically opposed to the theological convictions of the Jerusalem leaders. In Romans, it seems, we have a line of argument that has → Jerusalem in view. It does not abandon in the slightest Paul's conviction that justification is by faith, but it is no longer integrated in the theological coordinate system of a well-nigh absolute criticism of the law. Paul clung to his basic theological conviction but was flexible enough intellectually to set it in a new system of coordinates. In this setting, the law, while it cannot justify (Rom. 3:20), has a positive side. Its commands are "holy and just and good" (7:12). It is itself "spiritual" (*pneumatikos,* 7:14). Perhaps it is even more important that Paul now makes "the righteousness of God" (*dikaiosynē theou,* 1:17; 3:21, 22; → Righteousness 2.3), to which he does not refer in Galatians, a key concept. (Phil 3:9, a reference difficult to date, has acc. + art.: *tēn ek theou dikaiosynēn,* "righteousness from God.")

In Galatians, righteousness is entirely a gift in the process of justification; in Romans, the righteousness of God is not only God's gift to us (Bultmann) but also the power of God (Käsemann). In Galatians, to be sure, Paul does speak of spheres of power, including destructive spheres (law, → sin, elements of the world, 4:3, 9), but in Romans the power of God's righteousness stands opposed to that of sin; the law, in spite of 6:14, is no longer a destructive power, and no mention is made of the elements of the world. Justification, in consequence, is not only a forensic event but also a matter of being set in a different sphere of power; the justified are placed by God in another "space," they are "in Christ," "in the Spirit." The Spirit dwells in them (Romans 8). Thus an ontic presupposition is provided for the → parenetic exhortation (chaps. 12–15, though cf. earlier Gal. 5:16–6:10).

The special theological achievement of Paul was that with the concept of the righteousness of God, he could bring together the "subjective" element of faith (Rom. 1:16-17; 3:21-22) and the "objective" element of God's atoning act in Christ (3:24-25; → Atonement). Furthermore, by adopting and applying a specific variation of → apocalyptic thought, he could expound the righteousness of God as the cosmic event of its → revelation (*apokalyptetai*, "is revealed," 1:17; *pephanerōtai*, "has been disclosed," 3:21) and at the same time as the ever new event in its individual application to believers. New also in Romans is the way in which in chaps. 9–11, within the framework of a theology of justification, seen in terms of election and the righteousness of God, Paul presents the → salvation of Israel (11:26; → People of God), which differs from what we find in 1 Thess. 2:14-16 and Gal. 4:21–5:1.

This analysis assumes a difference in Paul's view of the law between Galatians and Romans. Others would hold to a consistency that does not permit any variation in Paul's views. Some condemn Paul to inconsistency, if not self-contradiction (H. Räisänen).

1.4. *Forensic and Participatory Categories*

The relative correctness in the thesis of E. P. Sanders that participatory categories are decisive for the doctrine of justification is that, according to Paul, the justified do "participate" in the world of God. In reality, however, Sanders falls into the old error of → liberal theology by seeing a material difference between juridical-forensic justification and the new creation (R. A. Lipsius, H. Lüdemann, O. Pfleiderer, H. J. Holtzmann; → New Self).

In Pauline theology, however, the verdict of God that pronounces a person righteous has effective power (K. Kertelge), for, as an existential thinker, Paul experiences existence both as one who is pronounced righteous and as one who is set in the sphere of the righteousness of God and of God's liberating Spirit. The two things are experienced as a single totality. He may speak of this one existence "in two different circles of thought" (Lüdemann), for the terminology of pneumatological expression in Romans 8 (→ Holy Spirit) is different from that of the forensic statements in chap. 3. But though the concepts differ, the existential reality is inseparable. The complex character of the life of faith, which we cannot understand in separate units, may be seen also in 2 Corinthians 3, with its climax in v. 18.

1.5. *Effective History of Paul's Theology in the NT*

In the effective history of Pauline theology in the NT, Paul's theology of justification is, to be sure, taken up in the Deutero-Pauline writings (e.g., Col. 2:6-15; Eph. 2:4-10; 1 Tim. 2:3-6; Titus 2:11-14). It is modified considerably, however, in what it intends to assert through its arrangement in a different theological horizon.

James 2:14-26 is directed against Paul. Clearly James does not understand faith the way Paul does,

as a total existential reality. He is therefore forced to make his own coordinate of faith and works (not "of the law") and, as a result, to postulate justification by both faith and works. Unlike Paul, James does not have any pneumatic dimension to his presentation.

1.6. *The Proclamation of Jesus and Paul's Theology of Justification*

E. Jüngel has shown that Paul's proclamation of justification had its roots in Jesus' proclamation of the reign of God. "Rom. 14:17 [gives us] the right to maintain that Paul replaced the concept of the *basileia* [→ kingdom of God] with that of *dikaiosynē* [the righteousness of God]" (*Paulus*, 267).

1.7. *Significance of Justification*

We are essentially forensic beings. Hence we always must justify ourselves before some court or other, whether it be our fellow humans, ourselves, or God. This basic existential reality of human existence has significance for → hermeneutics. The church's proclamation ought to recognize justification as a point of contact and, in → preaching, bring out the liberating implications of justification. The theology of justification is not outdated. It gives proclamation its opportunity.

Bibliography: On 1.1-2: R. BULTMANN, "Δικαιοσύνη θεοῦ," *JBL* 83 (1964) 12-16 • R. B. HAYS, "Justification," *ABD* 3.1129-33 • H. HÜBNER, "Pauli theologiae proprium," *NTS* 26 (1980) 445-73 (on Sanders); idem, "Die paulinische Rechtfertigungstheologie als ökumenisch-hermeneutisches Program," *Worum geht es in der Rechtfertigungslehre? Das biblische Fundament der "Gemeinsamen Erklärung" von katholischer Kirche und Lutherischem Weltbund* (ed. T. Söding; Freiburg, 1999) 76-105 • E. KÄSEMANN, "The Righteousness of God" (1961), *NT Questions of Today* (Philadelphia, 1969) 168-82 • K.-W. NIEBUHR, "Die paulinischen Rechtfertigungslehre in der gegenwärtigen exegetischen Diskussion," *Worum geht es in der Rechtfertigungslehre?* ed. Söding, 106-30 • J. REUMANN, "Righteousness (NT)," *ABD* 5.745-73 • E. P. SANDERS, *Paul and Palestinian Judaism: A Comparison of Patterns of Religion* (Philadelphia, 1977) • G. STRECKER, "Befreiung und Rechtfertigung," *Rechtfertigung* (FS E. Käsemann; Tübingen, 1976) 497-508 • F. WATSON, *Paul, Judaism, and the Gentiles: A Sociological Approach* (Cambridge, 1986).

On 1.3-4: J. BECKER, *Paul, Apostle to the Gentiles* (Louisville, Ky., 1993) • J. D. G. DUNN, *The Theology of the Apostle Paul* (Grand Rapids, 1998) • O. HOFIUS, *Paulusstudien* (Tübingen, 1989) • H. HÜBNER, *Biblische Theologie des Neuen Testaments,* vol. 1, *Prolegomena;* vol. 2, *Die Theologie des Paulus* (Göttingen, 1990-93) esp. 1.227-39; idem, *Law in Paul's Thought* (Edinburgh, 1977) • K. KERTELGE, *Grundthemen paulinischen Theologie* (Freiburg, 1991); idem, "Paulus zur Rechtfertigung allein aus Glauben," *Worum geht es in der Rechtfertigungslehre?* ed. Söding, 64-75; idem, *"Rechtfertigung" bei Paulus* (2d ed.; Münster, 1971) • H. RÄISÄNEN, *Paul and the Law* (Philadelphia, 1986) • J. REUMANN, "Justification by Faith in Pauline Thought: A Lutheran View," *Rereading Paul Together* (Notre Dame, Ind., forthcoming) Notre Dame conference, 2002 • H. SCHLIER, *Grundzüge einer paulinischen Theologie* (Freiburg, 1978) • U. SCHNELLE, *Gerechtigkeit und Christusgegenwart* (Göttingen, 1983); idem, *Wandlungen im paulinischen Denken* (Stuttgart, 1989) • T. SÖDING, "Kriterium der Wahrheit? Zum theologischen Stellenwert der paulinischen Rechtfertigungslehre," *Worum geht es in der Rechtfertigungslehre?* ed. Söding, 193-246 • P. STUHLMACHER, *Gerechtigkeit Gottes bei Paulus* (Göttingen, 1965); idem, *Reconciliation, Law, and Righteousness* (Philadelphia, 1986) • M. THEOBALD, "Der Kanon von der Rechtfertigung (Gal 2,16; Röm 3,28)–Eigentum des Paulus oder Gemeingut der Kirche?" *Worum geht es in der Rechtfertigungslehre?* ed. Söding, 131-92; idem, "Rechtfertigung und Ekklesiologie," *ZTK* 95 (1998) 103-17.

On 1.5-7: R. GYLLENBERG, *Rechtfertigung und Altes Testament bei Paulus* (Stuttgart, 1973) • E. JÜNGEL, *Justification: The Heart of the Christian Faith* (Edinburgh, 2001); idem, *Paulus und Jesus* (3d ed.; Tübingen, 1979) • H. MERKLEIN, *Studien zu Jesus und Paulus* (Tübingen, 1987) • H. GRAF REVENTLOW, *Rechtfertigung im Horizont des Alten Testaments* (Munich, 1971). See also the bibliographies in "Christology," "Galatians, Epistle to the," "Holy Spirit," "Law," "Righteousness, Justice," and "Romans, Epistle to the."

HANS HÜBNER

2. Historical and Systematic Theology

2.1. *Concept*

In modern → systematic and → ecumenical theology, the term "justification" is used in two different ways. In a broad sense "justification" functions as a covering term for the entire saving action of God and its appropriation by human beings, serving to bring out the centrality of → righteousness or justice in the saving relationship between God and sinful humanity. In a narrower sense the term refers to a particular way of understanding the relationship, event, or process of → salvation: in traditional → Protestantism, one that accords primary or exclusive importance to a legal, forensic, or declarative understanding of the way in which human beings become righteous or just before God; in Roman → Catholicism after the 16th century, to a causal un-

derstanding in which the ideas of infused → grace and merit are indispensable. Taken in its broad sense (as it usually will be here), justification has been a topic of the highest importance virtually throughout the Christian tradition. Taken in either of its narrower senses, much of the tradition is silent about justification.

2.2. *History of Theology and Doctrine*

2.2.1. From the second to the fourth centuries, theologians often discussed justification, especially in exegetical contexts. Interpreting passages like Rom. 3:28, *1 Clement,* → Irenaeus, → Tertullian, and → Origen all emphasize that justification is for Jew and Greek alike, by → faith and apart from the works of the → law (see K. H. Schelkle, 108-21). Origen argued that "justification by faith alone suffices, so that a person is justified only by believing, even if he had done no work" (*Comm. in Rom.* 3.9.2), taking "work" in a broad sense: not only conformity to the OT law but any deed done outside of faith is only apparently good and fails to justify the doer. About the relation between divine and human agency in salvation, there was little controversy in the → early church, and texts that speak in openly juridical ways of justification by faith regularly stand side by side with passages of great moral and ascetic rigor, or alongside texts that speak of salvation as a deifying participation in God (→ Theosis). The early church saw no problem here, and the Eastern Orthodox theological tradition ever since has generally found these juxtapositions untroubling (→ Orthodox Church).

2.2.2. When the British monk Pelagius (ca. 354-after 418) came to Rome in the late fourth century, he was scandalized by the moral laxity he found there, including that of many Christians. Pelagius offered a theology of moral renewal that appealed especially to aristocratic Christians dismayed by the decay of Roman society. In human nature created good, in free will, and in the law's instruction, God has graciously given us all that we need to lead a disciplined and obedient life, worthy of our high calling as Christians. → Augustine (354-430) himself had rightly said, Pelagius thought, that → sin is corrupt habit (*Conf.* 8.5.12). Having freely fallen into evil habits, we can freely, if arduously, dig our way out of them. For Pelagius, Paul's remarks about justification by faith apart from the works of the law are easily subject to abuse and should be taken only as a rejection of justification by specifically Jewish observances, not as a suggestion that faith without "works of righteousness" is sufficient for justification (T. de Bruyn, 83).

In response to Pelagius, Augustine developed an

increasingly comprehensive and rigorous account of salvation by grace alone *(sola gratia)*. "What do you have that you did not receive?" (1 Cor. 4:7), Augustine asks the Pelagians, and argues that all our good works must themselves be free gifts of God. The faith by which Christians believe, without which there can be no true justice or virtue (*C. Jul.* 2.3.17-33), must also be wholly a gift of grace (*De praed. sanct.* 2.7). Any form of pride or boasting before God is thereby excluded. Sinful human beings have no power to escape their lost condition by their own efforts, but God's grace makes good every human lack: "Unless he rules, you fall; unless he lifts you up, you are down" (*Serm.* 156.10). Any "merit" on our part is therefore itself a gift of grace (*De grat. et lib. arb.* 6.15). Grace is thus strictly prevenient; it precedes and brings about any human action pertinent to salvation. For this reason, Augustine argues in his last writings, salvation must find its ultimate basis in God's predestinating will.

Grace is, moreover, interior; God works faith and → love by his own direct action upon the human mind and will, and not only by exterior inducement. Christ is the source of grace and the sole justifier of human beings (*De pecc. mer.* 1.3.18), but the immediate agent of divine grace is the indwelling → Holy Spirit (Rom. 5:5), who, as God's love in person, enables us to love God in the only way God is fit to be loved: with his own love. Perfect love and righteousness are, however, never realized in this life. Remission of sins in → baptism and daily → prayer for the → forgiveness of sin remain necessary for all. For Augustine, God justifies primarily by making us genuinely just or righteous, though the element of forgiveness or "nonreckoning" of sins must also have a place (*De spir. et litt.* 7.11; 13.22). "The righteousness of God" is chiefly God's transformation of sinners into those who love him and obey his commands, those who live to praise his undeserved generosity (ibid., 11.18).

Augustine's teaching on grace and justification received strong endorsement at the Council of Carthage in 418 (DH 225-30) and later, against "semi-Pelagian" resistance, at the Second Council of Orange (529; DH 373-97), although → predestination, except for a brief repudiation of the thought that God preordains any evil act (DH 397), is passed over in silence. Much of the subsequent Western debate about justification takes the form of a struggle over what to make of the Augustinian inheritance (→ Augustine's Theology).

2.2.3. Early → Scholasticism (11th-12th cents.) made two particularly important contributions to the theology of justification. First, new ways of thinking about the saving significance of the → cross (→ Theologia crucis) clarified the Christological basis of justification. Scholastic theologians after → Anselm of Canterbury (1033-1109) saw the cross in good part, though not exclusively, within the framework of a juridical relationship between God and humanity. Especially by way of the concept of satisfaction, they attempted to show how the cross enacts God's justice toward both humanity and himself, and they saw the forgiveness of sins, and not only the grace that makes righteous, as the direct accomplishment of the cross (in contrast to ancient → Christologies, where God's justice toward the → devil plays a key role, and redemption from captivity to the devil rather than the forgiveness of sins is the chief outcome of Christ's passion). From Anselm through the → Reformation and beyond, theologians worked out the notion of satisfaction in many different ways, not always linked to substitution and still less to penalty, but the basic effect was to tie the forgiveness of sins, and so justification, closely to the cross.

Second, when he treats the sacrament of penance (→ Penitence) in book 4 of his *Sentences* (dist. 17.1), Peter Lombard (ca. 1100-1160), citing a passage from Ambrose, characterizes the outcome of this → sacrament, in particular the forgiveness of sins, as "being justified." Because of the enormous influence of the *Sentences,* "the justification of the ungodly" subsequently became a standard topic in medieval theology. Lombard's move also helped cement the close relationship between the theological problem of justification and the practice of the sacrament of penance. The connection between the two played a central role in the controversies about justification at the time of the Reformation.

2.2.4. Of the many theologies of grace and justification developed in the Middle Ages, that of → Thomas Aquinas (ca. 1225-74) has been the most influential. Aquinas puts conceptual tools adapted from Aristotle in the service of a theology of justification that follows Augustine in vigorously affirming salvation *sola gratia*. But he accords a central place to forgiveness and defines justification specifically as the remission of sins (*Summa theol.* I of II, q. 113, art. 1, s.c.). So understood, justification is "a transformation from a state of unrighteousness to a state of righteousness," an act by which God not only declares, but makes, sinners just or righteous (I of II, q. 113, art. 1, c.; art. 2, ad 2).

Justification depends from first to last on the grace of God, which itself effects the free human response of faith and cannot be acquired or merited by any human act. Grace is both the gift of the Holy

Spirit in the deepest interior of the soul and the inevitable created effect of the Spirit's immediate presence, a "form" (specifically a dispositional quality) by which the human being is re-created (I of II, q. 110, art. 2, ad 3) in conformity to Christ and begins, as the Father's adopted child, to share in Christ's own love for the Father.

In "the order of nature" — from God's point of view, as it were — justification thus begins with the infusion of grace and is completed by the forgiveness of sins. But from the sinner's own point of view, the perspective is reversed: justification begins with the unmerited forgiveness of sins, from which the gift of interior grace follows (I of II, q. 113, art. 8, ad 1). Aquinas thus denies that a person can know with certainty that he or she has grace (I of II, q. 112, art. 5) but nonetheless holds that we can have certainty of salvation, though he assigns this certainty primarily to the theological virtue of → hope rather than to that of faith (II of II, q. 18, art. 4; → Assurance of Salvation).

2.2.5. Later Scholasticism includes a complex variety of views on justification, ranging from the strict Augustinianism of Gregory of Rimini (ca. 1300-1358) to proposals (particularly following the rejection of Averroistic determinism in the bishop of Paris's condemnation of 1277) that ascribe a considerable role to unaided human → freedom in justification. Theologies of the latter sort — of which Gabriel Biel's (ca. 1420-95), inspired by William of Ockham (ca. 1285-1347), is sometimes taken to be a particularly clear example (see H. A. Oberman) — typically hold that human beings can in fact merit the initial gift of grace and remission of sins without special divine aid; to those who do their moral best by their own natural powers (facit quod in se est), God will not deny grace. Having received the gift of created grace, human beings can further apply themselves to a level of moral accomplishment beyond their natural powers — namely, love of God in fulfillment of the Great Commandment — and so merit salvation.

This position is not → Pelagianism. In his influential theory of divine "acceptation," Duns Scotus (ca. 1265-1308) had argued that no created reality can impose any obligation upon God. Human action under grace, let alone prior to it, has no intrinsic claim upon divine reward. Thus for a theology like Biel's, God gives grace and eternal life as rewards for human acts because he has freely decided, in his "ordained power" (potentia ordinata), to regard these acts as meritorious, not because their inherent worth requires God to value them. In his "absolute power" (potentia absoluta) God could have set up an

entirely different relationship to creation than the saving order upon which he has contingently, though wisely, decided. This qualification undercuts (partly in criticism of Aquinas) the thought that even the most graced human act can be intrinsically meritorious. But it has the practical effect of forcing sinners, desperate for surety about their own destiny before God, back upon their own uncertain resources.

2.2.6. For Martin → Luther (1483-1546; → Luther's Theology) God justifies sinners by reckoning or imputing to them the righteousness of Christ. Justification thus has an irreducibly forensic character: it is God's declaration or promise of forgiveness and righteousness for the sake of Christ, who by his cross has won for us the favor of God and defeated sin, → death, and the devil, the "monsters" that threaten to destroy us (LW 27.10). The righteousness that justifies is thus outside us and "alien" to us. For this reason, Luther holds, when we look to Christ, we may be completely confident of God's mercy, despite our own sinful lack of good works without and love within (thus Luther's claim that the believer is simul iustus et peccator, "at once justified and a sinner," against the introspective uncertainty and despair fostered, in his view, by late medieval theologies of justification and penitential practices). Justifying faith is this reliant apprehension of Christ bearing the sins of the world. Justification is therefore not only by grace alone but "by faith alone" (sola fide); when it comes to justification, faith cannot be supplemented by works or merits.

At the same time, Luther declines to understand justification as exclusively forensic. Rather, in the faith that clings to Christ, we become joined to him "like one person" (quasi una persona, LW 26.168), and this union with Christ by faith is basic to Luther's understanding of justification (see 26.129-30). Relying on Christ outside ourselves, we become new selves; indeed, faith "creates divinity, not in the substance of God, but in us" (WA 40/1.360.24-25; cf. LW 26.227). For Luther, justification thus includes a "real-ontological" transformation of the believer (C. E. Braaten and R. W. Jenson).

Luther insists on a forensic dimension to justification not in order to exclude human transformation from justification but to clarify where we must ultimately look for salvation, against the backdrop of the impending → last judgment. Before the bar of divine justice even the greatest → saints can rely not on the works grace has wrought within them but on Christ alone (see LW 32.190). Understood in this way, justification is "the article by which the church stands or falls" (WA 40/3.352.3) because on it the church's → proclamation of the → gospel depends, although Luther also ascribes to the → Trinity, the → incarnation, and the → resurrection, among others, the status of "the chief article" (*LW* 24.7-8; 28.94).

2.2.7. John → Calvin's (1509-64; → Calvin's Theology) theology of justification is close to Luther's in most particulars: the centrality of the forensic aspect, the importance of faith's union with Christ, justification by faith alone without works or merits, certainty of salvation through faith in Christ. In the *Institutes*' sequence of topics Calvin assigns to justification a distinctive location (*Inst.* 3.11-16). Between his treatment of faith and justification he presents a section on → sanctification and rebirth. He does so not in order to make sanctification a condition for justification but to block any → antinomian inferences from the doctrine of justification, against which he thought Lutheran theology insufficiently guarded.

Luther and early Lutheran theology make no systematic distinction between justification and sanctification but view justification as itself transformation and rebirth (see CA Apol. 4.72, 117-18, 313). Subsequent disputes led to the standardization of a sharp distinction between the two in much Protestant theology, with the aim of keeping renewal of life out of justification, for fear of imperiling the believing sinner's certainty of salvation in Christ. (For a Lutheran version of this distinction, see → Formula of Concord, SD 3.38-41, 54.)

2.2.8. In its Decree on Justification (DH 1520-83) the Council of → Trent (1545-63) outlines the basic contours of subsequent Roman Catholic reflection on justification. For Trent no purely forensic understanding of justification can be sufficient. Justification is not only forgiveness of sins and the imputation of Christ's righteousness (DH 1561) but also the genuine transformation of the sinner into a righteous person through the Holy Spirit's gift of interior grace and love (DH 1528-29). Faith does not give certainty of salvation and does not by itself entitle us to suppose that our sins are forgiven (DH 1533-34, 1562-65); it cannot be said that we are justified by faith alone, without the engagement of our own will (DH 1559). At the same time (against the dominant late medieval position represented by Biel), nothing on our part that precedes the grace of justification can merit justification (DH 1532). Our merits are rather themselves the gifts of God, the fruits of the free grace of God in Christ within us (DH 1545-49, 1582). Trent thus aims at a doctrine that sees justification as at every

point dependent on the prior grace of God and at the same time that upholds the transforming power of God's saving love in Christ, embodied in the moral striving of God's faithful people (→ Devotion, Devotions).

2.2.9. In the wake of the Reformation controversies, justification became a standard topic in every theological system and dogmatic manual within the divided Western confessions, and the subject of continuous debate between Lutherans, Calvinists, Anglicans, and Roman Catholics. This debate has produced highly nuanced and conceptually sophisticated treatments of justification on all sides, and to some extent it still does.

These accounts of justification have regularly been undertaken, however, on the assumption that a proper theology of justification must vindicate the position of one or another of the divided Western → denominations and refute the rest. A narrow understanding of the term (see 2.1) has thus been taken for granted and used as a polemical tool; theologies of justification that fail to use the favored concepts of one confession (→ Confession of Faith) or school are assumed to repudiate the most basic claims of Christian faith about justification. That they might instead make the same claims — or at least compatible ones — in different terms is a possibility that this long history of denominational polemic has often not entertained (see 2.4).

2.3. *Systematic Issues*
Although the theology of justification since the 16th century has been preoccupied on all sides with the Reformation problematic, modern theology has at the same time been engaged in a debate about the context of justification. Protestant theology after the Reformation generally assumed that every new question must be handled in a way that squares with, if it does not directly express, the truth of justification by faith alone. As a result, the 16th-century language about justification recurs constantly in modern Protestant thought, but the issues actually under discussion are often far removed from those in dispute at the time of the Reformation. This disparity has in turn given rise to a question about the basic Protestant discourse itself: What is the relevance of justification? The truth of justification by faith cannot be doubted, lest Protestant Christianity and the culture it has fostered renounce their reason for being. But in what context can talk of justification be relevant and meaningful for a modern world far removed from the confessional and theological conflicts of the 16th century — to say nothing of the 1st century? To this question modern Protestant thought has of-

fered three kinds of answers, in two of which it has been joined by Roman Catholic theology.

2.3.1. After the German → Enlightenment justification by faith, along with the larger network of Christian doctrine to which it belongs, was sometimes taken to be the exoteric form of a philosophical truth properly conceived in some other way. Immanuel Kant (1724-1804; → Kantianism), for example, argued that the intelligibility of radical moral → conversion depends upon the idea of justification. In the forum of divine justice moral guilt can be made good only by the vicarious suffering of another, whose merit is graciously reckoned to the guilty. But here each of us must be his or her own redeemer. In the moment where one becomes morally a new person by the radical exercise of one's own freedom, the → new self willingly takes on the misery due to the guilt of the old — although we may find it necessary to represent this moral atonement to ourselves in personified form, as the act of the Son of God, whose suffering merits justification for all (AA 6.71-79).

In the context of quite different philosophical projects, J. G. Fichte, G. W. F. Hegel, F. Schelling, and others put justification by faith to similarly revisionary use. Since these philosophical quests for what Kant called the "rational meaning" (see AA 6.83) of traditional Christian doctrines often end up (as in Kant's own treatment of justification) rejecting the chief claims of the traditional doctrine, theologians have typically been wary of them. In the case of justification (among others), however, they have influentially served both as a challenge that Protestant theology had to meet and as a testimony to the cultural potency of the doctrine.

2.3.2. While committed to the substance of the traditional doctrine of justification (against the views in 2.3.1), modern Protestant dogmatic and systematic theology has often reconceptualized it and tried to extend its reach, hoping to uphold the relevance of justification in the face of distinctively modern problems. For Friedrich → Schleiermacher (1768-1834; → Schleiermacher's Theology), redemption belongs in the sphere of human experience or consciousness, as a change from the suppression to the dominance of our ever-present "God-consciousness." Justification expresses a crucial point about this experience of redemption or rebirth: it originates entirely in divine causality, not in human spontaneity.

By contrast, Albrecht Ritschl (1822-89) understood redemption chiefly in terms of the spirit's ascent to ethical mastery over the conditions of nature. Justification, however, is the necessary experi-

ential basis of redemption, since it involves the awareness of a new relationship to God (forgiveness) in which we find ourselves receptive to the divine impulse for ethical transformation.

Using the early Heidegger's philosophy (→ Existentialism), Rudolf Bultmann (1884-1976) viewed justification as articulating the gospel's offer of authentic existence in the face of anxiety and death (→ Existential Theology). He interpreted his → demythologizing project in → hermeneutics as an epistemological extension of the Reformation doctrine of justification. Paul → Tillich (1886-1965) understood justification in psychological terms, as acceptance that one is accepted, against all temptations to secure our finite existence by our own efforts. While reluctant to equate justification before God with justice among human beings, recent theologies have sometimes been concerned to show the social and political relevance of justification.

Whatever concepts they use, theologies that proceed in this way assume that justification by faith can be meaningful or relevant only if it (1) answers a universal human question or perhaps (2) expresses some basic truth about human existence. Liberal Protestant theologians have not been alone in following this pattern. Conservative Lutherans like Paul Althaus (1888-1966) and Werner Elert (1885-1954), much concerned to defend the traditional Lutheran doctrine against various revisionist conceptualities, nonetheless insist that justification can be meaningful only against the background of a primordial human experience of lawlike constraint and implicit divine judgment. Since → Vatican II Roman Catholic theology has sometimes followed this pattern as well, perhaps most often along the lines of (2): justification is a way, for example, of expressing our necessary basic trust in the worthwhileness of existence. Liberal or conservative, Protestant or Catholic, theologies of this type have sought for justification by faith something of the immediate significance it had for European humanity in an earlier time.

2.3.3. Against this pattern some modern theologians have argued that justification can be understood only in the context of the biblical narrative of → creation, fall, redemption in Christ, and final consummation yet to come. The meaningfulness or relevance of justification stands or falls with the meaningfulness of this narrative and of the ongoing effort of the Christian community to interpret it. John Henry → Newman's (1801-90) theology of justification embodies this approach and also anticipates later ecumenical developments by arguing that "there is little difference but what is verbal in the various views on justification, found whether among Catholic or Protestant divines" (p. ix). Karl → Barth (1886-1968) locates justification in the context of a thoroughly Christocentric account of → reconciliation, arguing that we can grasp neither our sin nor our justification apart from the apprehension of Jesus Christ as he is depicted in Scripture. Some Lutheran theologians argue that the impending last judgment has particular weight in the scriptural and narrative context necessary for understanding justification (e.g., Peter Brunner, Albrecht Peters). Much modern Roman Catholic theology of justification, especially before Vatican II, also assumes some narrative and dogmatic context of this kind.

The compatibility of the forensic and transformative dimensions in the believer's relation to God — of God's consoling declaration of righteousness to sinners (e.g., Rom. 4:5) and the requirement that our inmost being must be renewed (e.g., Eph. 4:23) — has proved to be the most persistent conceptual challenge in the theology of justification. Some theologies argue that this problem can best be handled by placing justification clearly in the context of the church's ancient faith in the Trinity; this approach both follows Reformation precedent and holds out the most ecumenical promise.

2.4. Ecumenical Theology

The → Joint Declaration on the Doctrine of Justification (JD) between the → Roman Catholic Church and the → Lutheran World Federation (1999) marks the most important ecumenical development on justification. The JD does not claim theological originality but, rather, intends to summarize and apply the results of several generations of official interchurch conversations about justification, in particular those of the American Lutheran–Catholic dialogue (H. G. Anderson, T. A. Murphy, and J. Burgess), the Ecumenical Working Group in Germany (K. Lehmann and W. Pannenberg), and the international Lutheran–Roman Catholic Joint Commission (esp. "All under One Christ"; → Ecumenical Dialogue). These dialogues in turn draw on extensive ecumenical scholarship on justification, beginning before Vatican II (e.g., H. Küng; S. Pfürtner; O. H. Pesch; K. Lehmann, M. Root, and W. G. Rusch).

2.4.1. According to the JD, the Lutheran and Catholic churches have reached "a consensus on basic truths" concerning justification (§13; see also §§5, 14, 40, 43). Lutherans and Catholics officially agree that justification "is the work of the triune God," based on Christ's saving death and resurrection alone, so that God accepts us and we receive the Holy Spirit "by grace alone, in faith" (§15). Thus: "as

sinners our new life is solely due to the forgiving and renewing mercy that God imparts as a gift and we receive in faith, and never can merit in any way" (§17; see also the annex to JD, 2C: justification is "by faith alone").

The two churches also agree that the doctrine of justification has a unique status. All the truths of Christian faith are "internally" connected to it, so that this doctrine is "an indispensable criterion that constantly serves to orient all the teaching and practice of our churches to Christ" (§18; thus "no teaching may contradict this criterion," annex 3). In light of this basic consensus on justification, each side can recognize that the doctrinal condemnations historically leveled at the other on justification do not in fact apply to each other's teaching as presented in the JD itself (§§5-7, 13, 41-42).

2.4.2. This consensus on justification does not claim to eliminate all of the historic differences between Lutheran (and other Protestant) and Roman Catholic views of justification. The differences can, however, be handled in several different ways.

Sometimes the traditional difference is not a genuine disagreement because the crucial concepts are different on each side. When, for example, Protestants historically claim that justification is by faith alone and Catholics historically deny this claim, they seem not to succeed in actually disagreeing. By "faith" Catholic teaching generally means assent to the truths that God reveals. Protestants have never claimed that we are justified by faith alone in this sense. When Protestants speak of faith, they mean the grace-wrought trust of the whole self in God's mercy in Christ. Catholics have not intended to deny that we are justified by faith alone in this, quite different, sense (§§25-27). On this basis the apparent disagreement about certainty of salvation also turns out to be more verbal than substantive. Catholic teaching endorses this certainty when "faith" is understood in the characteristically holistic Protestant sense (§36).

Sometimes the traditional conflict chiefly reflects a difference of emphasis or underlying concern. Thus, for example, the Catholic affirmation of cooperation and merit in the justified person's relation to God is meant to uphold the genuinely transformative character of God's justifying grace in Christ, not to claim that any human action can acquire this grace. The Lutheran denial of merit and cooperation in regard to justification is meant to uphold the complete reliability of God's mercy toward sinners in Christ, not to deny that justification necessarily involves a transformed life of love and good works (§§19-24, 31-33, 37-39). Differences of this kind represent mutually complementary, rather than incompatible, teachings.

Finally, the traditional difference sometimes represents a real disagreement, but not one significant enough to be regarded as church dividing. The most likely case in point is the debate over the sinfulness of the justified. Catholic teaching holds that the continuing "contradiction to God" of the justified is not, strictly speaking, sin but, rather, "concupiscence," which becomes sin when the will assents to and pursues it. Lutherans hold that this "contradiction to God" is genuinely sin and so claim that the Christian is *simul iustus et peccator* (see 2.2.6). This point may turn out to be a difference in concept rather than judgment, but both sides seem willing to grant that it represents a genuine disagreement in teaching. But this disagreement extends only along a narrow conceptual front and has few practical consequences: both sides reject any complacency about sin on the part of the justified and agree that believers must daily pray for the forgiveness of sin and look to God's grace in Christ alone for justification (§§28-30). As such, this sort of disagreement is not a fundamental difference in faith, sufficient to divide churches, but a difference in theological interpretation, of a sort always found in the church (e.g., in the varying interpretations of the councils of → Nicaea or → Chalcedon) and compatible with unity in faith and ecclesial life.

2.4.3. Though officially approved by the Lutheran and Roman Catholic churches, the modern ecumenical consensus on justification summarized in the JD remains controversial. On the Lutheran side some argue that there is no consensus and assume that any agreement between Lutherans (or other Protestants) and Catholics, especially on this issue, must conceal a deeper "fundamental difference" that validates established denominational divisions (see 2.2.9).

On both sides others argue that the proposed → consensus is genuine as far as it goes but that its significance depends on whether it leads to agreement on a variety of other contested issues (emphasizing a point made in the JD itself, §43). Chief among the latter is a series of ecclesiological questions centering on → ministry, → episcopacy, and → church order. Here especially Protestants have wanted to see the doctrine of justification exercise its critical function as "the article by which the church stands or falls," while Catholics have insisted that the legitimate correction of abuses not become indifference to God's own good gifts in the establishment and ordering of the church (see *Church and Justification*). Ecumenical progress on these issues between Protestants and Catholics has been elusive, though it may yet prove possible.

The difficulty on all sides in knowing what to make of the hard-won ecumenical agreement on justification may owe much to the way in which it, like most modern ecumenical agreements, was reached. Perhaps inevitably, the dialogues from which these agreements originate have been structured by the assumption that each → denomination is doctrinally self-sufficient. As a result, the possibility that any side might have to change its doctrinal mind — repent — has been excluded, and the thought that much has really changed has naturally been difficult to justify.

Bibliography: On 2.1-3: C. E. BRAATEN and R. W. JENSON, eds., *Union with Christ: The New Finnish Interpretation of Luther* (Grand Rapids, 1998) • T. DE BRUYN, trans., *Pelagius's Commentary on St. Paul's Epistle to the Romans* (Oxford, 1993) • W. ELERT, *The Structure of Lutheranism* (St. Louis, 1962) • E. JÜNGEL, *Justification: The Heart of the Christian Faith* (Edinburgh, 2001) • H. KÜNG, *Justification: The Doctrine of Karl Barth and a Catholic Reflection* (New York, 1964) • B. LOHSE, *Martin Luther's Theology: Its Historical and Systematic Development* (Minneapolis, 1999) • A. E. McGRATH, *Iustitia Dei: A History of the Christian Doctrine of Justification* (Cambridge, 1986) • B. MARSHALL, "Justification as Declaration and Deification," *IJST* 4 (2002) 3-28 • J. H. NEWMAN, *Lectures on the Doctrine of Justification* (1838) (3d ed., London, 1874; repr., Westminster, Md., 1966) • H. A. OBERMAN, *The Harvest of Medieval Theology* (3d ed.; Durham, N.C., 1983) • O. H. PESCH, *Die Theologie der Rechtfertigung bei Martin Luther und Thomas von Aquin* (2d ed.; Mainz, 1985) • O. H. PESCH, F.-L. HOSSFELD, and M. THEOBALD, "Rechtfertigung," *LTK* (3d ed.) 8.882-902 • O. H. PESCH and A. PETERS, *Einführung in die Lehre von Gnade und Rechtfertigung* (Darmstadt, 1981) • A. PETERS, *Rechtfertigung* (2d ed.; Gütersloh, 1990) • S. PFÜRTNER, *Luther and Aquinas on Salvation* (New York, 1965) • K. H. SCHELKLE, *Paulus, Lehrer der Väter. Die altkirchliche Auslegung von Römer 1–11* (2d ed.; Düsseldorf, 1959) • H. SPIECKERMANN, K. KERTELGE, W. DETTLOFF, and G. SAUTER, "Rechtfertigung," *TRE* 28.282-364 • B. STUDER, *The Grace of Christ and the Grace of God in Augustine of Hippo: Christocentrism or Theocentrism?* (Collegeville, Minn., 1997).

On 2.4: "All under One Christ" (1980), *Growth in Agreement* (ed. H. Meyer and L. Vischer; New York, 1984) 241-47 • H. G. ANDERSON, T. A. MURPHY, and J. BURGESS, eds., *Justification by Faith* (Minneapolis, 1985) • K. LEHMANN and W. PANNENBERG, *The Condemnations of the Reformation Era: Do They Still Di-*

vide? (Minneapolis, 1990) • K. LEHMANN, M. ROOT, and W. G. RUSCH, eds., *Justification by Faith: Do the Sixteenth-Century Condemnations Still Apply?* (New York, 1997) • LUTHERAN–ROMAN CATHOLIC JOINT COMMISSION, *Church and Justification: Understanding the Church in the Light of the Doctrine of Justification* (Geneva, 1994) • THE LUTHERAN WORLD FEDERATION and THE ROMAN CATHOLIC CHURCH, *Joint Declaration on the Doctrine of Justification* (Grand Rapids, 2000) • W. G. RUSCH, ed., *Justification and the Future of the Ecumenical Movement: The Joint Declaration on the Doctrine of Justification* (Collegeville, Minn., 2003).

BRUCE D. MARSHALL

Justin Martyr

Justin (d. ca. 165) was a Christian teacher from Flavia Neapolis (modern Nablus) in the Roman province of Syria. He tells us that his people were the Samaritans (*Dial.* 120.6) and that his father was Priscus, his grandfather Bacchus (*1 Apol.* 1.1); these names and the fact that he was not → circumcised (*Dial.* 28.2) suggest that he was quite assimilated to Greco-Roman customs. He traveled as a teacher and spent at least two periods of time in → Rome, where he was martyred under the prefect Rusticus.

Some important writings by Justin have been preserved: *Dialogue with Trypho,* which presents arguments in favor of Christian faith in contrast to → Judaism, and two *Apologies* (the second probably an addendum to the first) addressed to Emperor Antoninus Pius (138-61) and his sons, Marcus Aurelius and Commodus. The *Apologies* can be dated to the early 150s; the *Dialogue* adds a warning about → Gnostic groups (35.6) to the denunciation of → Marcion in the *Apologies* (*1 Apol.* 26.5), which suggests that it is later. Lost are a *Syntagma* (Compilation) against the → heresies (*1 Apol.* 26.8) and — if it is not the same text under a different title — one against Marcion (→ Irenaeus *Adv. haer.* 4.6.2 and 5.26.2). Eusebius mentions other writings (*Hist. eccl.* 4.18), but the texts with those titles that survive are not thought to be by Justin, nor are the other works found in the only main MS of his works.

The *Dialogue* as we have it supposes a debate spread over two days; unfortunately, a large amount of text seems to be missing from the discussions of the second day. It is not known who Trypho might have been or whether the debate directly reflects an actual experience. At places in the *Dialogue* the Jewish teacher is given an active role with strong lines to speak, and his companions, who are perhaps Gentiles considering → conversion (§1) to Judaism, are occasionally allowed to speak. Justin attempts to show that Christianity, not Judaism, is the way for Gentiles to be saved.

If we possessed only the *Dialogue,* we would think of Justin as a teacher who expounded the sacred books of the Jews. He credits an old man with persuading him that the Hebrew prophets knew a purer and earlier form of truth than the → Greek philosophers and that Christ could enlighten him (*Dial.* 7–8). Justin employs most books of the LXX version of the OT, drawing especially on Psalms, Isaiah, and the patriarchal narratives of Genesis. He shows some knowledge of post-Septuagint translations and a willingness to argue details of the Greek text (43.8; 84; 131.1; 137.3), but not a familiarity with Hebrew. The main phases of the debate concern the characteristics of the Messiah, whether Scripture permits speaking of a second divine being, whether Jesus is that being and the Messiah (→ Christology), and whether → Gentiles are to be saved by becoming Jews or by becoming Christians. While the tone of the discourse is generally civil, Justin at times uses extremely insulting language in referring to the Jews.

The *Apologies* appeal to the Roman emperor to stop the practice of executing Christians simply for bearing the name of Christian. In the *First Apology* Justin not only argues that the practice is unreasonable but also tries to improve the Christian image: he summarizes Jesus' moral teaching (14–17), defends the credibility of the Christian account of Jesus (18–22), shows how the Hebrew prophets support that account at all points (23–53), ascribes the ideas of the Greeks to a copying from those same prophets, garbled by demons in the process (54–60), and describes and explains the rituals of → baptism and the → Eucharist (61–67), in what are the fullest descriptions of Christian rituals in second-century texts. The *Second Apology* (which seems to be a follow-up to the first, precipitated by the outbreak of fresh → persecution under the prefect Urbicus) contains some of the same themes.

If only these *Apologies* had survived, Justin would be viewed mainly as a philosopher with a conventional second-century background. While many of his ideas are typically Stoic, he criticizes the Stoics for believing in fate (→ Chance). He is most famous for defending the worship of Jesus Christ by identifying him with the divine Logos, who animates the universe and holds it together, and who makes human beings rational by sowing in them a share in himself (hence the term *logos spermatikos,* "seed-logos"; *2 Apol.* 8.3; 13.3). The Spirit of God is identified especially as the source of prophecy. God the Creator is distinct from the world and so far transcends creation as to have no proper name (*1 Apol.* 61.11; *2 Apol.* 6[5].1-2). Since humans are rational, they have free will and thus can expect to be judged after death.

The *Acts* of the martyrdom of Justin and several of his students *(Martyrium S. Iustini et sociorum)* is preserved in three related recensions and is believed to have a historical basis. It portrays Justin as a teacher in Rome whose students visit him at his lodgings in order to study the Christian faith. There is no evidence that Justin held any rank or office in the church apart from his teaching activities. One student of Justin's, Tatian the Syrian, has left us a writing of his own, *Oratio ad Graecos* (Discourse against the Greeks), and Irenaeus of Lyons cites Justin in a way suggesting that Irenaeus also may have studied with him (*Adv. haer.* 4.6.2).

Justin deserves credit not only as a → martyr for the Christian faith but also as a teacher who knew how to use both Scripture and → philosophy. In order to explain and defend Christianity, he creatively appropriated the cultural traditions of the society in which he lived, showing how those traditions could serve as a providential preparation for understanding divine → revelation.

Bibliography: Primary sources: L. W. BARNARD, trans., *The First and Second Apologies* (New York, 1997) • T. B. FALLS, trans., *St. Justin Martyr: The First Apology, The Second Apology, Dialogue with Trypho, Exhortation to the Greeks, Discourse to the Greeks, The Monarchy; or, The Rule of God* (New York, 1948) • M. MARCOVICH, ed., *Dialogus cum Tryphone* (Berlin, 1997); idem, ed., *Iustini Martyris Apologiae pro Christianis* (Berlin, 1994) • H. MUSURILLO, ed., *The Acts of the Christian Martyrs* (Oxford, 1973) • A. L. WILLIAMS, trans., *The Dialogue with Trypho* (Providence, R.I., 1975; orig. pub., 1930).

Secondary works: H. CHADWICK, *Early Christian Thought and the Classical Tradition* (Oxford, 1966) • E. R. GOODENOUGH, *The Theology of Justin Martyr* (Amsterdam, 1968; orig. pub., 1923) • E. F. OSBORN, *Justin Martyr* (Tübingen, 1975) • W. A. SHOTWELL, *The Biblical Exegesis of Justin Martyr* (London, 1965) • O. SKARSAUNE, *The Proof from Prophecy: A Study in Justin Martyr's Proof-Text Tradition* (Leiden, 1987) • T. STYLIANOPOULOS, *Justin Martyr and the Mosaic Law* (Missoula, Mont., 1975) • D. TRAKATELLIS, *The Pre-Existence of Christ in the Writings of Justin Martyr* (Missoula, Mont., 1976) • J. C. M. VAN WINDEN, *An Early Christian Philosopher: Justin Martyr's Dialogue with Trypho* (Leiden, 1971).

MICHAEL SLUSSER

K

Kabbala → Cabala

Kampuchea → Cambodia

Kantianism

1. Kant's Philosophical Achievement
2. Reactions to Kant's Philosophy
3. Neo-Kantianism and Other Developments

1. Kant's Philosophical Achievement

The thought of Immanuel Kant (1724-1804) is central to modern → philosophy in two respects. First, it is a definitive synthesis of → rationalism and → empiricism, the two main strands of early modern thought. Second, it became the basic position to which all subsequent philosophies were more or less explicitly related.

Kant's writings are customarily divided into two periods, *precritical* and *critical.* The second began in 1781 with publication of the first edition of the *Critique of Pure Reason,* which lays out the basic elements of his theoretical philosophy, which were also presented in a popular version in the *Prolegomena to Any Future Metaphysics* (1783). He followed these works with a parallel treatment of moral philosophy in the *Fundamental Principles of the Metaphysic of Morals* (1785) and the *Critique of Practical Reason*

(1787). The third domain of reason he covered in the *Critique of Judgment* (1790), which elucidates the nature and status of → aesthetics and of → teleological reasoning as applied to organic (as contrasted with mechanical) causation and to consideration of the order of nature as a whole. Kant's critical writings delineate the nature and limits of theoretical knowledge, distinguishing it clearly from speculation (metaphysics) on the one hand and from → faith (morality) on the other. His *Religion within the Limits of Reason Alone* (1793) sets forth a moral and rational version of Protestant Christianity.

Kant's great significance lies in the critical-transcendental turn of his thought, which completes the endeavor of modern philosophy to provide a nontranscendent grounding for both the → truth of our knowledge and the → norms governing our actions. With the skepticism and empiricism of David Hume (1711-76) as its point of departure, Kant's first *Critique* modified the rationalist doctrine of innate ideas by the empiricist doctrine that our knowing is necessarily conditioned by our sense experience.

Kant's solution, beyond the capability of either school on its own, delimits the domain of knowledge possible for theoretical reason in such a way that the pure forms of intuition (space and time) and the pure → categories of the understanding, which are generated a priori by the mind, can find legitimate application only within the bounds of possible sense → experience. Any employment of theoretical → reason apart from its application to sense experience is speculative → metaphysics, which leads one into all sorts of fallacies. They include the rational psychology that seeks to prove the soul's → immortality, the rational cosmology that seeks a theoretical grasp of the order and origin of the world as a whole, and the rational → theology that attempts proofs for God's existence (→ God, Arguments for the Existence of) — a false use of theoretical reason that does not work because proofs for God cannot be a part of scientific knowledge.

The intellectual landscape is different for practical reason. Here the → categorical imperative provides the form of the absolutely valid moral law, the universal basis, legislated by reason itself, for the norms that ought to govern human actions. Necessarily presupposed as the postulates of this practical reason are God, → freedom, and immortality. As the → Enlightenment drew to a close, Kant thus completed the basic program of modern philosophy without resorting to "onto-theology." Also, by separating faith (practical reason) from knowledge in theology, he opened the door to a new foundation for the philosophy of religion.

2. Reactions to Kant's Philosophy

Kantian philosophy was rapidly disseminated and widely discussed, in Germany and abroad, by both critics and advocates. K. L. Reinhold (1758-1823) expounded the Kantian philosophy in a series of writings during the 1780s and so helped to popularize it. F. Schiller (1759-1805) combined Kant's ethics and aesthetics with his own concept of moral education (influenced by J.-J. Rousseau) in his influential essays, plays, and poetry.

Especially noteworthy are three others who took issue in various ways with Kant's opposition of faith to knowledge. Fellow Königsberger and early supporter J. G. Hamann (1730-88), an antirationalist religious thinker influenced by Hume, criticized Kant's distinction of "pure" reason from sense experience in a "metacritical" essay withheld from publication until after his own death. J. G. → Herder (1744-1803), like Hamann at first a disciple, later turned away from Kant to a version of → Spinozism and attacked the first Critique. F. H. Jacobi (1743-1819) dismissed the Kantian restriction of knowledge to the finite, sensory realm by championing instead the "leap of faith" to apprehension of God. Each of this trio developed his position with reference to the implications of Kantianism for philosophy of religion.

The philosophies of the main German idealists — J. G. Fichte, F. W. J. Schelling, and G. W. F. Hegel — could not have developed as they did without their Kantian roots. All three reacted directly to Kant's theory of knowledge. The essay Human Freedom (1809) by Schelling (1775-1854) is an explication of the theme from Kant, among others, that freedom is the potentiality for either → good or → evil. A. Schopenhauer (1788-1860) also fixed on the Kantian view of will, in that for him will underlies all phenomena or representations of the world as knowable; in his philosophy will occupies the place of God. In → Romanticism and theology, F. D. E. → Schleiermacher (1768-1834) espoused the autonomy of religious feeling by following the precedent of Kant's segregating into separate domains the theoretical, practical, and aesthetic dimensions of our mental life.

The empiricist side of Kant had an advocate in J. F. Fries (1773-1843) of Jena, whose philosophy nevertheless found a place for aesthetic and religious meaning; it continued into the 20th century in the neo-Friesian school headed by L. Nelson (1882-1927) of Göttingen. Also in the empiricist camp, J. F. Herbart (1776-1841), a self-proclaimed "nonidealist Kantian," envisaged the goal of → education as ethical character formation of the individual in parallel with formation of an ethical community in the political realm (→ Politics).

3. Neo-Kantianism and Other Developments

A return to Kant followed the decline of Hegelianism after the failed revolution of 1848 and also ensued from the turn to thought forms of the natural sciences on the part of German academic philosophy after 1860. The German idealist philosophers came to be portrayed as inferior imitators of Kant rather than promoters of his heritage. The prominent scientist Hermann von Helmholtz (1821-94) criticized the new and crudely materialistic metaphysics of his colleagues, which seemingly flew in the face of the critical philosophy.

The Marburg school of neo-Kantianism, headed by Jewish ethical idealist Hermann Cohen (1842-1918) and Plato scholar Paul Natorp (1854-1924), advanced a critical theory of natural science focused not on physical nature as such but instead on the methods of scientists. Like Kant it reduced religion to morality, replaced the religious community with the social community, and in Cohen's case emphasized personal "I-Thou" relations in which love transcends social morality. Ernst Cassirer (1874-1945), with his Philosophy of Symbolic Forms (1923-29), is the best known of the school in the English-speaking world. In criticizing Hegelianism and in stressing justice, Marburg neo-Kantianism became the main political philosophy of → socialism and had many exponents in Germany, Italy, France, and Russia.

Another important example of the varieties of neo-Kantianism, the Baden school, was led by the historian of philosophy Wilhelm Windelband (1848-1915) and the philosopher Heinrich Rickert (1863-1936). It sharply distinguished natural sciences (as nomothetic, dealing in facts and general laws) from historical and cultural sciences (as idiographic, concerned with values and interpretation of unique events). Wilhelm Dilthey (1833-1911) reflected this perspective in his writings on the *Geisteswissenschaften* (human sciences) and the problems of historicism.

Even after the waning of neo-Kantianism as such, and indeed apart from it, Kant's influence continued unabated. Nearly all philosophers of the 20th century had to contend with Kant. The Munich school (H. Krings, H.-M. Baumgartner) systematized a new form of Kantianism. The religious philosophy of Martin Buber (1878-1965) was indebted to Cohen's neo-Kantianism. Protestant theologians Albrecht Ritschl (1822-89) and Ernst → Troeltsch (1865-1923) were also influenced by Kant, Ritschl in making ethically self-conscious life central to Christian theology and practice, and Troeltsch as theological heir to Dilthey's struggles with → historicism. Roman Catholic theology, in the neo-Thomism of Joseph Maréchal (1878-1944) and the "transcendental" Thomism of Karl → Rahner (1904-84), confronted the implications of Kant's transcendental method, as also have Gerhard Ebeling (1912-2001) and other Protestants.

Bibliography: Primary source: I. KANT, *Religion and Rational Theology* (ed. A. W. Wood and G. di Giovanni; Cambridge, 1996).

Secondary works: H. ALLISON, *Kant's Theory of Freedom* (Cambridge, 1990); idem, *Kant's Transcendental Idealism* (New Haven, 1983) • E. CASSIRER, *Kant's Life and Thought* (New Haven, 1981) • R. HANNA, *Kant and the Foundations of Analytic Philosophy* (Oxford, 2001) • K. KÖHNKE, *The Rise of Neo-Kantianism: German Academic Philosophy between Idealism and Positivism* (Cambridge, 1991) • P. PARRINI, ed., *Kant and Contemporary Epistemology* (Dordrecht, 1994) • B. SASSEN, ed., *Kant's Early Critics: The Empiricist Critique of the Theoretical Philosophy* (Cambridge, 2000) • S. SEDGWICK, ed., *The Reception of Kant's Critical Philosophy* (Cambridge, 2000) • T. WILLEY, *Back to Kant: The Revival of Kantianism in German Social and Historical Thought,* *1860-1914* (Detroit, 1978) • A. WOOD, *Kant's Ethical Thought* (Cambridge, 1999).

WALTHER C. ZIMMERLI† and ROBERT F. BROWN

Karma

Karma (Skt. *karma,* act [noun]) denotes in the Vedic period a special sacrificial act, then, from the time of the Śatapatha Brāhmaṇa and the early → Upanishads, all the actions in life that carry directly in themselves their own material and moral effect. Karma is one of the basic ideas of all Indian religions (→ Buddhism; Hinduism; Jainism) but is variously interpreted. It signifies universal interdependence and thus transcends a → causality that is merely material, subjecting also the psychological, moral, and mental levels of existence to a strict law of cause and effect. Karma is a principle that affects the subject of an act by creating formative or habitual structures ("Whatever we do we become," Bṛhadāraṇyaka Upanishad 4.4.5). Karma is thus the basis of cosmic order and individual responsibility.

In Buddhism karma is the sole principle of the genesis and order of the world. In Hinduism, however, though it is without beginning and the basis of time, it can be limited or compensated by God's action or the human practice of penance (→ Penitence). It does not entail determinism but underlies the specifically human → freedom for decision, though this relation is conditioned by earlier karma and is thus relative. Therefore, and since there can be no full compensation in one life, the doctrine of karma is associated with the originally independent doctrine of → reincarnation, which links → suffering and compensatory justice and thus makes → theodicy unnecessary.

The criticism that belief in karma leads inevitably to social and ethical lethargy is unjust, even though members of higher → castes have justified the oppression of others by misuse of the doctrine. In fact, people in free decision can use their lives to generate positive karma and thus break through the cycle of suffering and achieve openness to the future or a historical relation to karma. Especially in neo-Hinduism (e.g., illustrated by Vivekananda, Gandhi, and Aurobindo), karma is well interpreted in terms of its social and political implications. Since it is impossible to clearly differentiate one's own karma from that of others, karma can be an important integrative factor in social interpretation, and one that takes the ecological nexus into account.

→ Anthropology; Ecology

Bibliography: S. Bercholz and S. C. Cohn, eds., *Entering the Stream: An Introduction to the Buddha and His Teachings* (Boston, 1993) • A. S. Dalal, ed., *A Greater Psychology: An Introduction to Sri Aurobindo's Psychological Thought* (New York, 2001) • M. K. Gandhi, *Book of Prayers* (Berkeley, Calif., 1999); idem, *The Essential Writings of Mahatma Gandhi* (Delhi, 1993) • P. Heehs, ed., *The Essential Writings of Sri Aurobindo* (New York, 1998) • A. L. Herman, *The Problem of Evil and Indian Thought* (New Delhi 1976) • C. F. Keyes and E. V. Daniel, *Karma: An Anthropological Inquiry* (Berkeley, Calif., 1983) • K. K. Mittal, ed., *Perspectives on Karma as Rebirth* (Delhi, 1990) • W. D. O'Flaherty, ed., *Karma and Rebirth in Classical Indian Traditions* (Berkeley, Calif., 1980) • R. Pannikar, "The Law of Karma and the Historical Dimension of Man," *PhEW* 22 (1972) 25-43 • B. R. Reichenbach, *The Law of Karma: A Philosophical Study* (Honolulu, 1990) • S. Vivekananda, *Karma-yoga and Bhakti-yoga* (rev. ed.; New York, 1973).

MICHAEL VON BRÜCK

Kazakhstan

	1960	1980	2000
Population (1,000s):	9,996	14,919	16,928
Annual growth rate (%):	3.50	1.18	0.45

Area: 2,717,300 sq. km. (1,049,200 sq. mi.)

A.D. *2000*

Population density: 6/sq. km. (16/sq. mi.)
Births / deaths: 1.69 / 0.84 per 100 population
Fertility rate: 2.10 per woman
Infant mortality rate: 31 per 1,000 live births
Life expectancy: 69.2 years (m: 64.8, f: 73.4)
Religious affiliation (%): Muslims 39.3, nonreligious 29.5, Christians 20.7 (Orthodox 16.5, Roman Catholics 2.1, unaffiliated 1.1, other Christians 1.0), atheists 10.0, other 0.5.

1. General Situation
2. Nestorian History
3. Russian and Soviet Eras
4. Current Tensions for Christianity and Islam

1. General Situation

In the fifth century A.D. the territory now called Kazakhstan was part of Transoxiana, or the region north of the Oxus (modern Amu Dar'ya) River, an area north of the Himalayas along the middle of the famous Silk Road, which extended from the eastern coast of the Mediterranean Sea to China. The population changed several times as Asiatic tribes migrated westward. The Kazakhs are now traced to → nomads who were part of a Turkic khanate in the sixth century.

In the modern era Russian and Soviet policy sought to make the nomadic Kazakhs sedentary by fostering agricultural and industrial development (→ Soviet Union). The population became very mixed over the past 130 years, however, when central Asia and Siberia functioned as the settlement frontier for Slavic and other nationalities seeking land. Still larger population movements resulted from the forced deportation of peoples under Stalinism.

Kazakhstan became an independent country for the first time in 1991. Although heir to a very long tradition (President Nursultan Nazarbayev claimed continuity with the Turkic khanate of the 6th-8th cents.), its present condition is quite catastrophic. After initial optimism about economic and cultural → development, both the policies of the international community, which treated central Asia as a sphere of influence for one of the great powers, and the internal shift toward severe authoritarianism, religious intolerance, and corruption in every sphere have resulted in a very bleak picture. A recent book declared that "Kazakhstan has been descending into an abyss, it has moved from being a Second World country to a Third World country . . . all the parameters point to genocide by one man [Nazarbayev] against his people" (A. George, xiv).

To fathom the dimensions of such an "abyss" requires us to recall the drastic transformations of the past century. Thus we associate notions of a new breadbasket for the USSR with N. Khrushchev's Virgin Land program (1958-59), which, however, resulted in undercutting the nomadic cattle-grazing economy and in excessive erosion. By the end of the USSR in 1991, the Aral Sea had shrunk to a third of its former size, and the salt flats had blown over large sections of that "virgin land," one of the worst environmental catastrophes of the 20th century (→ Environmental Ethics). We also associate the Baikonur Cosmodrome, the oldest and largest Soviet missile- and rocket-testing facility, with Kazakhstan. Much more negatively, the Semey (formerly Semipalatinsk) region served as a nuclear testing ground (479 tests in the period 1949-89) and included a major nuclear accident. Finally, over 70 forced labor camps were located in Kazakhstan.

Kazakhstan is the largest of the central Asian post-Soviet states, covering a land mass of up to 3,000 km. (1,875 mi.) east to west, and 2,000 km. (1,250 mi.) north to south. Its population density is the lowest of all Asian nations except Mongolia. Ethnic Kazakhs constitute only 46 percent of the population, with Russians 35 percent; in 1991 there were still one million Germans in Kazakhstan. Indeed, over 100 nationalities were identified in 1991. Between 1930 and 1991 the → literacy rate rose from 2 to 98 percent.

Other statistics reveal a dark side of Kazakhstan's history. Forced collectivization during the 1930s resulted in the death of 1.75 million Kazakhs, which then represented 42 percent of the population. A further 350,000 Kazakhs died during World War II at the European front. Finally, since 1991 there has been a mass exodus of about 3 million Russians, Ukrainians, Germans (750,000), and Jews, representing a severe loss of skilled labor. In the Qostanay (formerly Kustanay) region, once heavily German, there is now an 80 percent → unemployment rate, with not one factory in operation.

The Kazakhs, also referred to during the Middle Ages as White Huns, are a Turkic people. During the Soviet period the Kazakh language was written in the Cyrillic alphabet, and the present literary intelligentsia was trained in Russian. Indeed, many Kazakhs came to view Russian as the lingua franca of the USSR, and Kazakhstan delayed declaring Kazakh the official language till the mid-1990s. A kind of linguistic war involves Iranians (and other Islamic countries), who urge adoption of the Arabic alphabet in writing Kazakh, whereas the Turks (who are a major trading partner) support use of the Latin alphabet.

2. Nestorian History

Because the → Nestorians were long thought to have been heretical, not recognizing the Christological formula of the Council of → Chalcedon (451; → Oriental Orthodox Churches), and because they existed primarily outside the → Roman Empire, little was known in the West about their church. Recent scholarship has confirmed its essentially orthodox Christianity and has drawn special attention to its missionary character and the major role that → monasteries played in the geographic spread of Nestorian Christianity. The Nestorian church became a major, though minority, church in Persia, and its → missionaries reached as far away as India and China, communicating in Syriac. Although separate from the Syriac church, the Nestorians adopted Syriac as the language of worship wherever they went.

After the Persian (East Syrian) national church was granted toleration (in an edict by Persian shah Yazdegerd I in 409), two synods were held that in-

cluded representatives from central Asia. At the synod of Patriarch Isaac (410), the record shows that → bishops attended from as far away as Samarqand (now in Uzbekistan), north of the Oxus River in central Asia. Indeed, the next synod, called by Patriarch Dadyeshu in 424, even included bishops from what is now Afghanistan.

When Persian shah Kavadh I fled into exile (497-501), he went north to the White Huns, also called Turks, and was joined by two Nestorian laymen. Karaduset, Nestorian bishop of Arran, west of the Caspian Sea, and four priests soon joined them. The bishop sought to minister to Byzantine Christian captives among the Huns and to evangelize the captors. The clergy stayed for 7 years, but the laymen remained for 30 years. Later too a → Monophysite Armenian bishop joined the missionaries and taught agriculture to the nomads. The mission, which involved preaching, baptizing, and reducing the language of the Huns to written form, was a success. The contemporary account of the mission reveals that the missionaries gladly accepted hardship for the cause of Christ; that there was little conflict between the Nestorian, Byzantine, and Armenian traditions; and that there was a "full-rounded blend of spiritual and practical missionary methods — evangelism, → education, and agriculture" (S. Moffett, 209).

Patriarch Timothy of the Persian church (served 780-823) left behind letters that indicate another mission to north-central Asia, the region of Kazakhstan. By then there were a half dozen bishops along the northeastern frontier of Persia, and the episcopal see of Samarqand had been elevated to metropolitan status, giving it administrative oversight of surrounding bishops. The "king of the Turks," according to one letter, requested that Patriarch Timothy send bishops and priests to his land. This group is believed to have comprised the Turkic peoples and Huns living as nomads north of Persia. Present-day Baptists in Zhambyl, in southern Kazakhstan, claim that in their city (then called Taraz) along the Silk Road there were many Christians, with a congregation lasting till 940. Later letters during the 40-year ministry of Timothy reveal his interest in assisting the growing number of churches, monasteries, and bishoprics across what are now the nations of Uzbekistan, Kazakhstan, and Tajikistan. By the tenth century monasteries could be found across central Asia linked to the trade route from Persia to China. Such monasteries served not only for → worship and → evangelism but also as inns for the Christian merchants traveling through; also they provided medical care and ran schools. In this way Christianity "began to seep into the local life of central Asia" (D. T. Irvin and S. W. Sunquist, 305).

According to one estimate, there were 32 million Christians within the Byzantine and Western Holy Roman Empires by A.D. 1000, plus 12 million Nestorians in Asia. By that date, however, the Nestorians had already passed their zenith. The following centuries were a time of numerical decline because of extreme and long-term → persecution. There was sustained social and political repression under Islamic dominance from the 8th century onward, although only in the 14th century did → Islam become the official religion in central Asia. Indeed, Islam was influential in the southern parts, so that Bukhara (now in Uzbekistan) became known as third in importance to Mecca and Medina, but in the northern (i.e., Kazakhstan) area it managed only a weak hold, with no important centers of learning. The wholesale massacres of Timur (Tamerlane) "the exterminator" at the beginning of the 15th century dealt Asian Christianity its fatal blow.

3. Russian and Soviet Eras

3.1. When Roman Catholic missionaries launched new missions to India and China in the 16th century (→ Catholic Missions), they followed sea routes rather than the Silk Road. The Russian Orthodox reached central Asia and Kazakhstan primarily in the 17th and 18th centuries as the Russian Empire extended eastward. There were occasional links in the intervening years because the tribes of Rus had been paying tribute to the Golden Horde in Astrakhan, but the rise of Muscovy till it became the Russian Empire under Peter the Great (czar 1682-1725), with its efforts to link with western Europe, made eastern adventures rare. Russian assimilation of the Kazakh steppe, where there were a number of Kazakh khanates, became more extensive only in the 19th century.

In 1860 Kazakhstan became part of the Russian Empire, and by 1890 more than 500,000 settlers (primarily Russians and Ukrainians) had arrived. During the agricultural reforms of Prime Minister Pyotr Stolypin (1906-11), 438,000 peasants were settled in the Akmolinsk, Turgay, Uralsk, and Semipalatinsk provinces of Kazakhstan. German colonists from the established colonies in European Russia also sought new land. By World War I they numbered 63,000, only 0.5 percent of the population but representing half of the most educated. The kulakization drive brought more Germans, to which were added 462,000 Germans exiled to Kazakhstan after 1941.

Through immigration and forced resettlement, members of the → Russian Orthodox Church and Lutherans (→ Lutheran Churches), Roman Catholics, → Mennonites, and → Baptists thus became part of the Kazakhstan religious scene. During the first third of the 20th century, there were some mission efforts to convert the Kazakhs and other nationalities in the region, some by the → Orthodox Missionary Society, others by the Mennonites and Baptists, including some initial attempts to translate the Scriptures.

3.2. From 1929 till the end of the USSR in 1991, Kazakhstan was shaped by the official policy of combating religion. Churches, mosques, and religious schools were mostly closed by the early 1930s. In 1917 there were 26,000 mosques in central Asia; by 1942 only 1,312 remained open. The ideological program to foster → atheism proceeded in tandem with what was happening elsewhere in the USSR, since it was guided by the center. As was true elsewhere, during World War II the pressure on religious practice eased, and the first years after the war were a time of reopening of churches and mosques, though in quite limited number.

In 1943 the Religious Board of Central Asia and Kazakhstan (SADUM) was established to oversee religious life, including the appointment of mullahs and teachers. Yet by 1985 there were fewer than 100 registered mosques throughout the USSR, and for all of central Asia only two madrasahs (Muslim educational institutions). The mufti heading the SADUM had Soviet support but lacked popular Muslim support. But already in 1989 then party secretary Nazarbayev removed Kazakhstan from the jurisdiction of SADUM, appointing a Kazakh, Ratbek Nysanbayev, as mufti of Kazakhstan. Most of the actual mosques (perhaps 100 times the official number) had functioned without registration, with leaders who lacked formal training. These illegal mosques have been the home of a number of Islamic fundamentalists.

When the Russian Orthodox Church emerged after the war, it had a bishopric in Alma-Ata, then the capital of Kazakhstan. In 1958, before new closures of churches and mosques, there were 60 congregations within the Kazakhstan diocese, but by 1966 this number had dropped to 46. During the perestroika years this pattern changed, and the number of congregations increased to 57 by 1986, then serving about 127,000 faithful, and then to 80 in 1991, and 102 in 1994. Indeed, according to a 1984 general report by K. M. Kharchev of the USSR Council for Religious Affairs, although the number of Orthodox congregations was still declining in the USSR as a whole, within the Kazakh SSR there was pressure to register 242 religious associations. Many of these were mosques and churches of the Baptists and Mennonites, but there were also many congregations of Orthodox. In 1991 Patriarch Aleksei II established three independent dioceses within the new state of Kazakhstan, with Archbishop Aleksei of Almaty (new designation) and Semipalatinsk heading an intereparchial commission. That is, the church remained fully under the Moscow Patriarchate, since its faithful were for the most part Russians and Ukrainians living in Kazakhstan.

For the official All-Union Council of Evangelical Christians–Baptists (AUCECB), its churches in Kazakhstan were a mix of peoples, many having been sent to the coal mines in Karaganda (now Qaraghandy) Oblast, or to labor camps in western and northeastern Kazakhstan, who then started new churches. Some of the earliest churches began in the early 20th century, and by 1930 there was a Central Asian Union of Baptists. In Kazakhstan the Mennonites and German Baptists soon represented 30-40 percent of the membership and often provided leadership, since in the prewar years they had received better education (including theological) than had been possible for the Evangelical Christians and the Baptists, who had been hunted down as sectarians before 1917. By 1988 there were 152 congregations and groups, 108 of them officially registered, 9 of them having more than 500 adult members each. Yet there were only 56 ordained presbyters, as shortage of clergy remained a severe problem.

During the Khrushchev attack on religion (1959-64), many Baptist congregations split over the question of whether to submit to state restrictions. In 1962 reformers managed to organize the unregistered churches into the Council of Churches of Evangelical Christians/Baptists (CCECB), which was quite successful in its resistance. There were numerous arrests, but the Council of Prisoners' Relatives, a women's organization, kept the issue alive through the circulation of its *Bulletin* between 1960 and 1988. The Central Asian department of the CCECB became one of the better organized, overseeing several of the secret printing presses. When German activists from Tselinograd (now Astana, since 1998 the capital) immigrated to Germany, they quickly organized Friedensstimme (Voice of peace), a mission society that sent relief and published religious literature that was smuggled back into the country.

Although statistical data are less readily available for other Protestant groups, there were congregations of Lutherans, → Pentecostals, → Adventists, and Mennonites, with nearly half their number registered by 1984. In general these groups were treated as local religious associations with no union structure, although the Lutherans finally received a superintendent after 1980 who was able to visit some of the congregations. In an official report Kharchev noted a large number of registrations by Pentecostals and Mennonites (1979-84) and pointed out that half of the Muslim mosques were unregistered, as were 41 percent of the Mennonites, 61 percent of the Molokans (or "Spiritual Christians," an offshoot of Doukhobors), and 71 percent of the Pentecostals. He also reported a 12 percent increase in clergy and mullahs. In his eyes a greater problem was the unregistered "cult servants" (so the officialese), 45 percent of whom, or 2,436, were active in Kazakhstan and central Asia; about half of this number were Muslims.

4. Current Tensions for Christianity and Islam

The pressure for greater religious freedom for both Muslims and Christians had become evident by 1984, when Kharchev, who represented a new Soviet professional, urged less restrictive registration as preferable to the presence of many illegal groups. The government of Nazarbayev initially attempted a policy of tolerance, with a new law on religion (1992) granting full religious freedom. The exceptions were restrictions on some independent Pentecostals, the → Unification Church of Sun Myung Moon (which had initiated a missionary program), and the Deva Maria cult (originating in Kiev). By 2000, however, there were new restrictions, especially on Muslim missionaries from abroad.

Even more so than in Russia and Ukraine, Kazakhstan experienced economic chaos in the early 1990s. One response was the emergence of charitable associations for emergency services. Foreign donations, many from religious bodies, accounted for major efforts, one specialist speaking of "the great donor tsunami of 1994-96." A new Law of Associations (May 1996) continued to regulate all nongovernmental organizations (NGOs), including religious associations. That year there was an explosion of new registrations — 3,050 NGOs during 1996 alone, compared with only 559 total in the previous five years. In essence, nonprofits were providing services in all areas of life that the government was finding itself increasingly unable to supply. As in Russia and Ukraine, the new registrations included many parachurch organizations with ties to America, Korea, or western Europe (→ Relief and Development Organizations).

One new phenomenon was the emergence of Christian communities among Kazakh and other traditionally Muslim peoples. When the Baptist Union of Kazakhstan met for a missionary conference in 1999, it counted 70 of its 500 participants who were of central Asian nationality, many of them from local, self-governing congregations that conducted their meetings in Kazakh or other Turkic languages.

Following passage of the 1992 legislation on → religious liberty, Kazakhstan experienced a surge in religious activity. In 1998 the Kazakh legislature began considering numerous drafts of much more restrictive legislation, and finally in early 2002 a new law was ready for signature by the president. Its key features were to require all missionaries to be registered with a local religious entity, to enable the banning of unregistered groups (some of whom resisted registration because of the costs), and in particular to deny legal registration to all Muslim organizations outside the framework of the Spiritual Administration of Muslims of Kazakhstan. Increasingly, the government claimed that the Shymkent region of southern Kazakhstan was a hotbed of religious fundamentalism that posed a threat to national security. What they had in mind was the fact that the majority of the 350,000 Uzbeks living in that region are typically more devout in their practice of Islam than are the Kazakhs. Civil rights groups have continued to challenge the restrictions as unwarranted.

Bibliography: F. CORLEY, ed., *Religion in the Soviet Union: An Archival Reader* (New York, 1996) • N. DAVIS, *A Long Walk to Church: A Contemporary History of Russian Orthodoxy* (Boulder, Colo., 1995) • A. EHTESHAMI, ed., *From the Gulf to Central Asia: Players in the New Great Game* (Exeter, 1994) • A. GEORGE, *Journey into Kazakhstan: The True Face of the Nazarbayev Regime* (Lanham, Md., 2001) • D. T. IRVIN and S. W. SUNQUIST, *History of the World Christian Movement,* vol. 1, *Earliest Christianity to 1453* (Maryknoll, N.Y., 2001) • *Istoriia evangel'skikh Khristian–Baptistov v SSSR* (Moscow, 1989) • KESTON INSTITUTE, *Keston News Service* (Oxford, 1971-) • D. C. LEWIS, *After Atheism: Religion and Ethnicity in Russia and Central Asia* (New York, 2000) • S. H. MOFFETT, *A History of Christianity in Asia,* vol. 1, *Beginnings to 1500* (2d ed.; Maryknoll, N.Y., 1998) • M. B. OLCOTT, *Kazakhstan: Unfulfilled Promise* (Washington, D.C., 2002) • S. P. RAMET, *Nihil Obstat: Religion, Politics, and Social Change in East-Central Europe and Russia* (Durham, N.C., 1998) • A. RASHID, *The Resurgence of Central Asia: Islam or Nationalism?* (London, 1994) • M. H. RUFFIN and D. WAUGH, eds., *Civil Society in Central Asia* (Seattle, Wash., 1999) • W. SAWATSKY, *Soviet Evangelicals since World War II* (Scottdale, Pa., 1981).

WALTER SAWATSKY

Kenosis

1. Background
2. Reformation and Orthodoxy
3. Neo-Lutheranism
4. Radical Views

1. Background

Kenosis (i.e., "emptying," Phil. 2:5-11, esp. v. 7) is a concept used in elucidation of the relation of the earthly → Jesus to the Logos as the second person of the → Trinity during his earthly life. In the → early church it was equated with the assuming of human nature by the Logos in the → incarnation. There have been three interpretations in Protestant theology.

2. Reformation and Orthodoxy

At the → Reformation the Reformed → extra calvinisticum could view the incarnation and humiliation as one and the same act of the Logos (→ Calvin's Theology), but the Lutherans taught an exchange of the properties of the divine and human natures (*communicatio idiomatum* with *genus maiestaticum*), and hence they had to explain whether or how, for example, Jesus' thirst relates to his deity (→ Luther's Theology). The kenosis has to do with him who became man — but did this step involve a concealing (*krypsis*) of the exercise of the divine attributes, as taught by the Tübingen theologian J. Brenz (1499-1570), or did it refer instead to their partial renunciation (*kenōsis*), as taught by M. Chemnitz (1522-86)? Support for both views could be found in the → Formula of Concord (SD 8.73, 75 and 8.26, 65).

A debate thus arose in 1616 between Giessen (B. Mentzer) and Tübingen (M. Hafenreffer), and in 1624 the Decisio Saxonica decided in favor of kenosis. Emergent → Christology was critical of the → dogma (Jesusology), thus forcing Lutheranism to make a clear distinction between the two states of *exinanitio* (self-emptying, self-renunciation) and *exaltatio* (exaltation) as regards the participation of the humanity in the divine nature. Kenosis as a logical adjustment to real communication of the attributes threatened to burst through the limits of the two-natures teaching on the incarnation. Split into a human nature and an effectively emptied-out divine nature, so that only at the → resurrection would he again be the whole Logos, Jesus threatened to become a creature of fable. The criticism of Giessen was that separate activities meant separate persons.

3. Neo-Lutheranism

In the 19th century → Lutheranism had to face the even more radical question of bridging the gulf between the Jesus of history and the Christ of dogma. The neo-Lutheranism of Erlangen now applied Phil. 2:6-7 to the preexistent Logos. The Logos limits his deity to the bearer of a developing human life. The inner-Trinitarian relation changes to the extent that the Logos renounces divine self-awareness (G. Thomasius, F. H. R. Frank, W. F. Gess). There is a negative reciprocal relation between the deity and humanity of the Mediator.

This polarity between pre- and postexistent deity on the one side and a humanity that develops in normal human fashion on the other, as an application of the difference between the two kingdoms (→ Two Kingdoms Doctrine) to two-natures Christology, reflects contemporary problems in adjusting theology to the bourgeois world of the time (→ Theology in the Nineteenth and Twentieth Centuries). Deity is also claimed for the humiliated one (with K. → Barth, E. Jüngel, J. Moltmann, et al. speaking of condescension), or else kenosis takes the more radical, atheistic form of the death of God (→ God Is Dead Theology).

4. Radical Views

Radical kenosis takes Philippians 2 to imply the total self-giving of God. God is Jesus, "the man for others," in a totally kenotic movement (T. J. J. Altizer). The modern godless world is again defined by the God from whom it turns. The theology of the death of God (W. Pannenberg) and the *etsi Deus non daretur* (as if God were not, D. → Bonhoeffer), which appeals to G. W. F. Hegel (1770-1831), tries to take the experience of kenosis that we have daily in the absence of God and to show that it is a modern way of experiencing God in the → discipleship of Jesus Christ (D. Sölle).

→ Soteriology

Bibliography: T. J. J. ALTIZER, *The Contemporary Jesus* (Albany, N.Y., 1997) • K. BARTH, "The Doctrine of Reconciliation," *CD* IV/1, 128-54, 179-210 • R. BAUCKHAM, *The Theology of Jürgen Moltmann* (Edinburgh, 1995) • D. BONHOEFFER, *Christ the Center* (New York, 1966) • M. CHEMNITZ, *Ministry, Word, and Sacraments: An Enchiridion* (ed. L. Poellot; St. Louis, 1981) • J. COBB, C. IVES, and M. ABE, *The Emptying God: A Buddhist-Jewish-Christian Conversation* (Maryknoll, N.Y., 1990) • U. GERBER, *Christologische Entwürfe* (vol. 1; Zurich, 1970) • D. L. GUDER, *The Incarnation and the Church's Witness* (Harrisburg, Pa., 1999) • E. JÜNGEL, *Theological Essays* (trans. J. B. Webster; Edinburgh, 1989) • J. MOLTMANN, *Experiences in Theology: Ways and Forms of Christian Theology* (Minneapolis, 2000); idem, *History and the Triune God: Contributions to*

Trinitarian Theology (New York, 1992); idem, *The Trinity and the Kingdom of God* (London, 1981) • W. PANNENBERG, *Jesus, God and Man* (Philadelphia, 1968) 307-23; idem, *Systematic Theology* (vol. 2; Grand Rapids, 1994) 377-79; idem, ed., *Die Erfahrung der Abwesenheit Gottes in der modernen Kultur* (Göttingen, 1984) • W. M. PORTIER, *Tradition and Incarnation: Foundations of Christian Theology* (New York, 1994) • T. M. SNIDER, *The Divine Activity: An Approach to Incarnational Theology* (New York, 1990) • D. SÖLLE, *Stellvertretung. Ein Kapitel Theologien nach dem "Tode Gottes"* (2d ed.; Stuttgart, 1982) • T. F. TORRANCE, *Preaching Christ Today: The Gospel and Scientific Thinking* (New York, 1990) • G. WAINWRIGHT, *For Our Salvation: Two Approaches to the Work of Christ* (Grand Rapids, 1997) • C. WEISSMANN, *Die Katechismen des Johannes Brenz* (Berlin, 1990) • C. WELCH, *God and Incarnation in Mid-Nineteenth Century German Theology: G. Thomasius, I. A. Dorner, A. E. Biederman* (New York, 1965) • V. WHITE, *Atonement and Incarnation: An Essay in Universalism and Particularity* (Cambridge, 1991).

UWE GERBER

Kenya

	1960	1980	2000
Population (1,000s):	8,332	16,632	30,340
Annual growth rate (%):	3.14	3.56	2.55
Area: 582,646 sq. km. (224,961 sq. mi.)			

A.D. 2000

Population density: 52/sq. km. (135/sq. mi.)
Births / deaths: 3.53 / 0.98 per 100 population
Fertility rate: 4.30 per woman
Infant mortality rate: 57 per 1,000 live births
Life expectancy: 57.4 years (m: 56.1, f: 58.6)
Religious affiliation (%): Christians 79.4 (Roman Catholics 25.1, indigenous 24.7, Protestants 20.9, Anglicans 6.3, unaffiliated 4.1, Orthodox 3.0, other Christians 0.2), tribal religionists 11.2, Muslims 7.3, Baha'is 1.2, other 0.9.

1. General
2. History, State, Society, Economy
3. Religious Situation

1. General

The Republic of Kenya, an East African nation on the Indian Ocean, is bordered by Somalia, Ethiopia, Sudan, Uganda, and Tanzania. It includes a coastal region, the hinterland, and a highland region with the volcanic Rift Valley, which is very fertile. A prominent feature is Lake Victoria; there are deserts in the north and northeast.

The population of Kenya consists of many ethnic groups, including Gikuyu (or Kikuyu, 22 percent), Luhya (14 percent), Luo (13 percent), Kalenjini (12 percent), Akamba (11 percent), Kisii (6 percent), and Meru (6 percent), with much smaller percentages of other African peoples, Arabs, Asians, and Europeans. Intermarriages increasingly take place across ethnic and language groups. About 30 percent of the population is urban.

2. History, State, Society, Economy

The country has been settled since Paleolithic times. By the 10th century A.D. peoples of the Niger-Congo language family had occupied all of East Africa. Other ethnic groups migrated later. Structured societies, as well as towns, developed on the coast. Iron and ivory were important early exports. From 1735 to the end of the 19th century, the slave trade (→ Slavery) disrupted tribal structures.

After the Berlin Congo Conference of 1884-85, Lord Salisbury, British prime minister and foreign minister (1882-92), secured Kenya and Uganda (→ Colonialism). In 1895 the British government took over political power from the Imperial British East Africa Company. Construction work on a railroad from coastal Mombasa inland to Lake Victoria brought Indian workers to the country, and settlers from Europe and South Africa occupied much productive land and organized agricultural and industrial development. The British introduced an indirect form of rule in 1900 that allowed a limited place for African authority.

A first independence movement started in 1921 with the founding of the Young Kikuyu Association, renamed the Kikuyu Central Association in 1925. Colonial subjugation led to the Mau Mau uprising from 1952 until the end of the decade. Subsequent elections gave Africans a limited right of participation. After the 1961 election, in which Africans won a majority, the leader of the Kenya African National Union, Jomo Kenyatta (ca. 1894-1978, imprisoned 1953-61 because of the Mau Mau revolt), joined the government. In 1963 Kenyatta became the first prime minister of Kenya and then, from 1964 until his death in 1978, its president. He was succeeded by his vice-president, Daniel arap Moi.

Between 1982 and the reestablishment of a multiparty system in December 1991, Kenya was a one-party state. Moi has remained in office continuously since 1978, though his presidential elections in 1992 and 1997 were plagued by irregularities. The difficult question facing Moi at the turn of the millen-

nium is how to mediate between centralism and tribal federalism.

Kenya society consists of over 50 ethnolinguistic groups. The Gikuyu, who are numerically the largest, are primarily an agricultural people, though from colonial times they have included a growing middle and even upper class. Most Kenyans belong to the traditional structure of society, which rests on a sense of belonging and mutual responsibility. Since independence (1963), however, a bureaucracy has developed, as well as a merchant and trading class that is becoming strongly oriented to Western values. Within this group the *watajiri* (Swah. "capitalist, employer, the rich"), or rich upper class, is overtaking Indians from the middle and upper echelons of the business community.

Economically, the country relies mainly on the marketing of coffee, corn, and tea, with → tourism also playing an important part. Kenya has undergone some industrialization but is still mainly agrarian, with most of the people living by subsistence farming. After an initial emphasis on "African socialism" (1965), the trend is now toward developing a market economy. An economic union with Tanzania and Uganda broke up in 1977 but now has been replaced by a new and wider union with other countries in eastern and central Africa.

3. Religious Situation

3.1. Portuguese Catholic missionaries brought the first contacts with Christianity in 1498 (→ Catholic Missions; Mission 3). The first missionary period ended in the 17th century; the second began in the middle of the 19th, with the arrival of J. L. Krapf (1810-81) of the Anglican Church Missionary Society in 1844 (→ British Missions). British Methodists (→ Methodist Churches) followed in 1862, Roman Catholic Holy Ghost Missionaries in 1889, Scottish Presbyterians (→ Reformed and Presbyterian Churches) in 1891, and other denominations later.

3.2. In 2000 the → Roman Catholic Church in Kenya was organized in 18 → dioceses and was seeing an increasing number of national priests and bishops. The Association of Member Episcopal Conferences in Eastern Africa sponsors a pastoral institute in Eldoret that is important for all East Africa, where participants are trained in the → acculturation or incarnation of the gospel in an African context, developing → theology, → liturgy, rites, and → symbols that are truly African.

The Anglican Church (→ Anglican Communion), represented throughout Kenya, became independent of Canterbury in 1960 and is now the Church of the Province of Kenya. The interdenominational Africa Inland Mission began work in 1895; in 2000 its daughter body, the Africa Inland Church, had over 5,400 congregations.

Other important churches in 1995 included the African Orthodox Church of Kenya (from 1928, with 560,000 adherents), overseen by the Patriarchate of Alexandria; the Presbyterian Church of East Africa, which became fully independent in 1943 (600,000 adherents); the Kenya Assemblies of God (560,000), arising in 1968 from a split from the International Pentecostal Assemblies; the Pentecostal Assemblies of God (500,000), a work of Canadian Pentecostals from 1910; and the Seventh-day Adventists (263,000), from 1906. The Pentecostal Evangelistic Fellowship of Africa (→ Pentecostal Churches) exerts great influence. The → Salvation Army has also been active since 1921. All the churches do valuable charitable and social work.

The first African Independent Church developed among the Luo as early as 1914 (Nomiya Luo Church). In 1995 there were an estimated 731 Independent Churches in Kenya. The largest two were the African Independent Pentecostal Church of Africa (founded 1925, with 1.2 million persons affiliated in 1995) and the New Apostolic Church (founded 1973, with 1.0 million affiliated). The largest split off Roman Catholicism in Africa is the Kenyan group Mario Legio of Africa (separated in 1962), which had 385,000 adherents in 1995.

There is a balanced relation between → church and state. The 1969 constitution guarantees → religious liberty. The state took over all church schools in 1968 but allows the churches a right of participation that gives them influence at every level. On the Joint East African Religious Education Committee, the government and churches develop common curricula and textbooks for → religious education. Teachers of religion are trained at the University of Nairobi and Kenyatta University.

3.3. There is increasing ecumenical cooperation. The → All Africa Conference of Churches and the Association of Evangelicals of Africa and Madagascar cover several African countries, the former comprising 147 Protestant, Anglican, Orthodox, and Independent churches and councils (1994). There is also a National Council of Churches of Kenya (NCCK), founded in 1943 (with roots back to 1913), with 27 religious organizations and denominations as full members and 14 with observer status (2000). Protestants and Anglicans also work together in the Christian Churches Educational Association. There is also a Protestant Churches Medical Association and, for Independent Churches, the East African Christian Alliance (1965) and the United Orthodox Independent Churches of East Africa (1971).

All the churches have a concern for Africanization in theology and liturgy. Ecumenical activity is also important in radio and television, as the churches sponsor regular programs in several languages. The communication arm of the Catholic Bishops' Conference sponsors several broadcasts a month in Swahili, Meru, Gikuyu, and English, and there are also radio and television programs in Nairobi. Protestant churches also have an active broadcast schedule.

Notwithstanding financial problems, publications are also increasing. The Roman Catholic Church publishes the important *African Ecclesial Review* and *Catholic Mirror,* the Africa Inland Church *Kesho* and *Today,* and the NCCK *Beyond.* Reference should also be made to ongoing translation of the Bible (→ Bible Versions) in the different languages of Kenya.

Bibliography: D. B. BARRETT et al., eds., *WCE* (2d ed.) 1.425-31 • D. B. BARRETT, G. K. MAMBO, J. MACLAUGHLIN, and M. J. MCVEIGH, eds., *Kenya Churches Handbook: The Development of Kenya Christianity, 1498-1973* (Kisumu, Kenya, 1973) • M. CROUCH, ed., *A Vision of Christian Mission: Reflections on the Great Commission in Kenya, 1943-1993* (Nairobi, 1993) • M. N. GETUI and P. KANYANDAGO, *From Violence to Peace: A Challenge for African Christianity* (Nairobi, 1999) • F. K. GITHIEYA, *The Freedom of the Spirit: African Indigenous Churches in Kenya* (Atlanta, 1997) • K. KYLE, *The Politics of the Independence of Kenya* (New York, 1999) • M. M. MAXON and T. P. OFCANSKY, *Historical Dictionary of Kenya* (Lanham, Md., 2000) • A. ODED, *Islam and Politics in Kenya* (Boulder, Colo., 2000) • A. M. B. RASMUSSEN, *Modern African Spirituality: The Independent Holy Spirit Churches in East Africa, 1902-1976* (London, 1996) • M. A. WILSON, ed., *Modern Kenya: Social Issues and Perspectives* (Lanham, Md., 2000) • Z. WINSLOW, *Kenya* (Philadelphia, 2000).

JOHANNES HENSCHEL, C.S.Sp.

Kerygma

1. NT Usage and Background
2. Summarizing the NT Gospel Proclamation
3. Bultmann and Kerygmatic Theology
4. Subsequent Concerns

1. NT Usage and Background

The Gk. noun *kērygma* means "proclamation, what is heralded aloud." There are eight occurrences in the NT, six of them in → Paul (1 Cor. 1:21, → preaching, the apostle's priority; 2:4, Christ crucified; 15:14; Rom. 16:25; 2 Tim. 4:17; Titus 1:3) and two in the → Synoptics, plus "the sacred and imperishable proclamation of eternal salvation" in the shorter ending of Mark. Some scholars stress not just what is preached but the dynamic action of proclaiming (C. F. Evans; R. H. Mounce, *Essential Nature,* 64, "content in the act of being proclaimed"). The verb *kēryssō,* "announce, proclaim aloud," is much more common (61 times in the NT, esp. in the Gospels and Paul).

The practice is rooted in the institution of the herald *(kēryx)* in the Greek world, going back to Homer. Heralds appeared in the city-state, athletic games, diplomatic missions, and cult life; the (Stoic) philosopher could be a herald for the god(s). No figure in the OT, even the → prophet, is comparable; *kēryssō* vocabulary is rare in the Septuagint (G. Friedrich, 683-94, 697-702, 714-15; L. Coenen, 48-52).

In the NT the noun *kērygma* is used of Jonah (Matt. 12:41 par. Luke 11:32 Q; Jonah 3:2 LXX, overthrow of Nineveh); the verb often, of John the Baptist (Mark 1:4, 7; Acts 13:24, *prokēryssō,* "proclaim publicly"), → Jesus (Mark 1:38, 39; Matt. 4:17, 23; 9:35, etc.; Luke 4:18-19, 44), his disciples (Matt. 10:7, 27), those healed by Jesus (Mark 1:45; 5:20) — but especially of, and by, Paul (Acts 9:20; 19:13; 20:25; 28:31; 1 Thess. 2:9; 1 Cor. 1:23; Gal. 2:2; 5:11), as well as for other Christian evangelists (Acts 8:5; 10:42; 1 Cor 15:11). The noun *kēryx* occurs at 1 Tim. 2:7 and 2 Tim. 1:11 for Paul, and at 2 Pet. 2:5 for Noah. (See Friedrich, Coenen, and O. Merk, 292, on how *kērygma* as "the message of Christ is transformed into a [missionary] preaching concerning existence.") The terminology is often interrelated with the → gospel and with preaching "good news" (Luke 8:1; 1 Thess. 2:9; 1 Cor. 15:1, 11; Rom. 10:8-17; J. Roloff, 83-93, the apostolic gospel as *paradosis,* material handed on orally, and *kērygma).* But proclamation may be about doom as well as salvation (Jonah, Noah, 1 Pet. 3:19; cf. 4:6). There can also be Jewish preaching of the commandments (Rom. 2:21).

2. Summarizing the NT Gospel Proclamation
Attempts have often been made to summarize the early Christian message or kerygma. A. Harnack (78) put together "the common proclamation" about Jesus in the first generation of believers. A. Seeberg outlined a *Glaubensformel,* or creedal formula, used for missionary preaching, → catechesis, and → confession of the faith (p. 85).

Of great influence in the English-speaking world was C. H. Dodd's reconstruction in 1936 of a "Jerusalem kerygma" (from sermons in Acts 2, 13, 10:34-43, and shorter passages in chaps. 3, 4, and 5) and a "Pauline kerygma" (from pre-Pauline passages in his letters, e.g., 1 Cor. 15:3b-5; Rom. 1:3-4). Dodd then compared and amalgamated these two into "the apostolic preaching," which was public, to the non-Christian world, and which he distinguished sharply from *didachē,* or ethical teaching, indeed as "gospel" and "law" respectively, although scarcely in a → Reformation sense (1951; see also J. I. H. McDonald, F. B. Craddock, 453).

Variations and corrections on Dodd's kerygma were proposed by T. F. Glasson, B. Reicke, and others. Some regarded the Acts sermons as late or even Lukan creations, not from Aramaic sources, and preferred to treat the confessional formulas in the Epistles (the so-called *homologiae)* less rigidly (H. Conzelmann, 62-71, 87-89). For summaries and critique, see K. Goldammer ("kerygma" is a modern concept), W. Baird (Dodd and Bultmann [see 3] are mutually corrective), J. Reumann, C. Brown.

Dodd's application of his kerygma to Mark (providing the outline, so that this first gospel became "the kerygma with commentary"), as well as to other NT books, provided a unifying trend in biblical studies, indeed a centripetal movement back to Jesus. Articles on "the kerygma" in NT and OT books and authors became common. H. W. Wolff, as part of the "kerygmatic theology" movement, produced studies on the kerygma of the Yahwist and the Deuteronomist. The journal *Interpretation* ran a series that included "the kerygma of" the Deuteronomistic historian (by W. Brueggemann, in 22 [1968] 387-402), the Chronicler (J. M. Myers, 20 [1966] 259-73), Proverbs (R. E. Murphy, 20 [1966] 3-14), Jonah (G. M. Landes, 21 [1967] 3-31), Luke (O. Betz, 22 [1968] 131-46), John (R. E. Brown, 21 [1967] 387-400), Romans (J. P. Martin, 25 [1971] 303-28), Galatians (M. Barth, 21 [1967] 131-46), Hebrews (F. F. Bruce, 23 [1969] 3-19), and Revelation (M. Rissi, 22 [1968] 3-17).

3. Bultmann and Kerygmatic Theology
R. Bultmann (1884-1976) gave the concept of kerygma programmatic significance. He laid the foundations in his early work, but the roots in the history of → theology became apparent only with his stress on the term from 1929 onward (e.g., "Significance," esp. 241, "Jesus Christ confronts people in the kerygma and nowhere else"). The concept corresponds, on one side, with the interest of → dialectical theology in the category of the → Word of

God, but it does justice, on the other side, to the insight from form criticism that the smallest units in the Synoptic tradition are controlled by the purpose of → proclamation (→ Literary Criticism).

In contrast to liberal "life of Jesus" research, Bultmann claimed that the significance of Jesus comes to light only by way of the message about Christ. Christian → faith, which consists in the assurance of the → forgiveness of sins, rests on the declaration that Jesus is God's eschatological act of → salvation. Because it owes its assurance to the NT kerygma, it does not need certainty through historical data. For Bultmann the "new quest" for the historical Jesus remained under suspicion for setting aside the offense of the message about Christ and trying to evade the venture of faith by a dubious orientation to what may be seen (→ Demythologizing). On Bultmann's view, only the post-Easter kerygma is relevant, though we cannot reduce it to a specific formula, and many kerygmatic formulations are possible (G. Ebeling). Others argued, however, for greater emphasis on precrucifixion events and the character of Jesus (G. N. Stanton, E. E. Lemcio).

4. Subsequent Concerns

The intense interest in "kerygma theology" from the 1930s to the 1960s, whether in the form of Bultmann or Dodd, was diminished by the New Hermeneutic and the (new) quests for the historical Jesus; the trends toward variety, rather than unity, in the NT (hence the pl. *kērygmata*, J. D. G. Dunn, *Unity*, 11-32, xxii-xxiii); and debate over whether the Christian → revelation should be seen against the horizon of history (W. Pannenberg, including → apocalypticism) or of → experience (E. Herms, the tip of the iceberg of subsequent ahistorical approaches to the NT, emphasizing the literary side and the responses of varied readers today and their experiences, including feminist, African, etc.).

"Kerygma" remains a part of Pauline preaching (Craddock) and theology (e.g., J. A. Fitzmyer, §§16-20; Mounce, "Preaching"; Dunn, *Theology*, §7.3). The dogmatic questions raised by Bultmann continue to appear with regard to "Word," proclamation, and faith (I. A. McFarland).

Bibliography: On 2.1: L. COENEN, "Proclamation, Preach, Kerygma: Κηρύσσω," *NIDNTT* 3 (1978) 48-57 • C. F. EVANS, "The Kerygma," *JTS* 7 (1956) 25-41 • G. FRIEDRICH, "Κῆρυξ κτλ.," *TDNT* 3.683-718 • O. MERK, "Κηρύσσω κτλ.," *EDNT* 2.288-92 • R. H. MOUNCE, *The Essential Nature of NT Preaching* (Grand Rapids, 1960) • J. ROLOFF, *Apostolat–Verkündigung–Kirche* (Gütersloh, 1965).

On 2.2: W. BAIRD, "What Is the Kerygma? A Study of 1 Cor 15:3-8 and Gal 1:11-17," *JBL* 76 (1957) 181-91 • C. BROWN, "Proclamation, Preach, Kerygma: The Structure and Content of the Early Kerygma," *NIDNTT* 3.57-67 • H. CONZELMANN, *An Outline of the Theology of the NT* (New York, 1969) • F. B. CRADDOCK, "Preaching," *ABD* 5.451-54 • C. H. DODD, *The Apostolic Preaching and Its Developments* (London, 1936); idem, *Gospel and Law: The Relation of Faith and Ethics* (New York, 1951) • T. F. GLASSON, "The Kerygma: Is Our Version Correct?" *HibJ* 51 (1953) 129-32 • K. GOLDAMMER, "Der kerygma-Begriff in der ältesten christlichen Literatur," *ZNW* 48 (1957) 77-101 • A. VON HARNACK, *History of Dogma* (New York, 1961; Ger., 1885; ET from 3d ed., 1900) • J. I. H. MCDONALD, *Kerygma and Didache: The Articulation and Structure of the Earliest Christian Message* (Cambridge, 1980) • B. REICKE, "A Synopsis of Early Christian Preaching," *The Root of the Vine* (London, 1953) 128-60 • J. REUMANN, "The Kerygma and the Preacher," *Dialog* 3 (1964) 27-35 • A. SEEBERG, *Der Katechismus der Urchristenheit* (Leipzig, 1903) • H. W. WOLFF, "The Kerygma of the Yahwist" (1964) and "The Kerygma of the Deuteronomistic Historical Work" (1975), *The Vitality of the OT Traditions* (ed. W. Brueggemann and H. W. Wolff; Atlanta, 1975) 41-66 and 83-100.

On 2.3: R. BULTMANN, "The Concept of the Word of God in the NT" (1933), *Faith and Understanding* (trans. L. P. Smith; New York, 1969) 286-312; idem, "NT and Mythology" (1948), *NT and Mythology and Other Writings* (ed. S. Ogden; Philadelphia, 1984) 1-44; idem, "On the Problem of Demythologizing" (1952), *NT and Mythology*, ed. Ogden, 95-130; idem, "The Primitive Christian Kerygma and the Historical Jesus" (1961), *The Historical Jesus and the Kerygmatic Christ* (ed. C. E. Braaten and R. A. Harrisville; Nashville, 1964) 15-42; idem, "The Significance of the Historical Jesus for the Theology of Paul" (1929), *Faith and Understanding*, trans. Smith, 220-46; idem, *Theology of the NT* (2 vols.; New York, 1951-55) esp. 1.33-183, 2.239-41 • G. EBELING, *Theology and Proclamation: Dialogue with Bultmann* (Philadelphia, 1966) • E. E. LEMCIO, *The Past of Jesus in the Gospels* (Cambridge, 1991) • G. N. STANTON, *Jesus of Nazareth in NT Preaching* (Cambridge, 1974).

On 2.4: J. D. G. DUNN, *The Theology of Paul the Apostle* (Grand Rapids, 1998); idem, *Unity and Diversity in the NT: An Inquiry into the Character of Earliest Christianity* (2d ed.; London, 1990) • J. A. FITZMYER, "Pauline Theology," *NJBC* 1382-1416 • E. HERMS, *Theologie–eine Erfahrungswissenschaft* (Munich, 1978) • I. A. MCFARLAND, "Kerygma II: Dogmatisch," *RGG* (4th ed.) 4.936-38 • R. H. MOUNCE, "Preaching, Kerygma," *DPL* 735-37 • W. PANNENBERG, ed., *Revelation as*

History (New York, 1968) • G. Schunack, "Kerygma I: Neutestamentlich," *RGG* (4th ed.) 4.935-36.

Wolfgang Harnisch and John Reumann

Keys, Power of the

1. Systematic Introduction
2. In Church History

1. Systematic Introduction

The power of the keys (Lat. *potestas clavium*) is the power to open or close entry to the → kingdom of God, to bind or loose (Matt. 16:19; 18:18). It includes pastoral authority (→ Pastoral Care) to pronounce → forgiveness of → sin, or absolution (→ Penance), and gives validity to acts of binding, disciplining, and ordering in → excommunication, the imposing of penalties or remedial measures, and → church discipline (→ Indulgences). It underlies authoritative → proclamation and doctrinal decisions (→ Teaching Office). From these angles it describes the commission and functions of the church or congregation.

According to Reformation conviction, every church member has a share in the power of the keys by passing on the → gospel of the rule of God and the message of → justification, by leading on to confession of sin, by exhorting to repentance, and by encouraging → confession of faith. The primary obligation, however, rests on authorized persons (i.e., church officeholders). The power of the keys takes on practical significance in pastoral practice, while we find its ecclesiological dimension in the ordained → ministry. In Protestant churches it forms a part of church government along with the → preaching of the Word and administration of the → sacraments. On a Roman Catholic view it is a comprehensive term for the ecclesiastical power that is exercised by the → pope, the → bishops, and their delegates in the ministry of teaching, consecrating, and ruling (→ Church Government 5.1).

Today the office of absolving has largely lost its predominant position in favor of other tasks and functions of the → church (§1). In contrast to what takes place in many → free churches, little prominence is given to the pronouncing or denying of personal → salvation in what the mainline churches say and do.

2. In Church History

In the → early church → Cyprian of Carthage (d. 258) argued that only the → bishop has the power of the keys for the forgiveness of sins (→ Penitence 1.2). He saw in bishops the successors of → Peter, for whose primacy he found a basis in Matt. 16:18-19, Luke 22:32, and John 21:15-17. → Jerome (d. 420) advocated the relating of this primacy only to the bishop of Rome, an idea promoted by → Leo I (440-61). In practice, however, others continued to exercise the power of the keys of Matt. 16:19: bishops, → priests, even monks at times (→ Monasticism).

In the early Middle Ages the power of the keys found expression in penitential books, which became unified in the ninth century. → Gregory VII (1073-85) claimed in *Dictatus papae* (1075; → Middle Ages 2.3.3) that, in view of the power of loosing granted to Peter in Matt. 16:19, the pope had the right to release people from oaths they had taken. Peter Lombard (ca. 1100-1160) systematically discussed the power of the keys in *Sent.* 4.18. → Thomas Aquinas (ca. 1225-74; → Thomism) defined the power of the keys as the authority to bind and to loose that church judges may exercise (*Summa theol.* III supp., qq. 17-20).

M. → Luther (1483-1546; → Luther's Theology), in early works on penitence and penance, asked whether the pope has the power to command. His later work "The Keys" (1530) criticized the pope for basing salvation "on his keys, upon our own works, and not upon the grace of God" (*LW* 40.330). Luther firmly believed that a right use of the power is a mark of the church, along with the Word, → baptism, and the → Eucharist (*LW* 41.153-54 and Schmalk. Art. 3.7 [1537]). P. → Melanchthon (1497-1560; → Reformers 2.1.1) dealt with the matter in CA 28 and his *Treatise on the Power and Primacy of the Pope* (1537). J. → Calvin (1509-64; → Calvin's Theology) understood the power of the keys in terms of spiritual proclamation of the Word and church discipline, which he established in Geneva (e.g., *Inst.* 3.4.12-15, 20-23; 4.1.22; 4.2.10; 4.12.1-7, 10; → Church Discipline 1). In 1551 the Council of Trent rejected these Reformation views.

With the → Enlightenment and → Pietism the importance of the issue declined, although neo-Lutheranism took it up in the 19th century (esp. T. Kliefoth, J. Löhe, and A. Vilmar). → Vatican I cited Matt. 16:19 in the dogmatic constitution *Pastor aeternus*, on the church of Christ, but did not pursue the matter. → Vatican II texts and the 1983 → Codex Iuris Canonici (can. 988.1) have simple references to the keys. Though of less significance today, the power of the keys is still the basis of ongoing ministries and institutions.

Bibliography: F. Büchsel, "Δέω (λύω)," *TDNT* 2.60-61 • J. Jeremias, "Κλείς," ibid. 3.744-53 • M. Luther, "The Keys" (1530), *LW* 40.325-77; idem, "On the Councils and the Church" (1539), ibid. 41.9-178 • O. Michel, "Binden und Lösen," *RAC* (2d ed.) 2.374-80 • E. Schlink, *Theology of the Lutheran Confessions* (Philadelphia, 1961) • H. Vorgrimler, "Das 'Binden und Lösen' in der Exegese nach dem Tridentinum bis zu Beginn des 20. Jahrhunderts," *ZKT* 85 (1963) 460-77 • D. S. Yeago, "The Office of the Keys: On the Disappearance of Discipline in Protestant Modernity," *Marks of the Body of Christ* (ed. C. E. Braaten and R. W. Jenson; Grand Rapids, 1999) 95-122.

GERT HAENDLER

Kierkegaard, Søren

Søren Aabye Kierkegaard (1813-55), Danish philosopher of religion and critic of → rationalism, can be viewed as one of the founders of → existentialism. The seventh child of a well-to-do wool merchant, he attended secondary school and studied → theology and → philosophy in his hometown, Copenhagen. He successfully concluded these studies in 1840 with his theological examinations and in 1841 with a master's degree in philosophy (a degree equivalent to today's Ph.D.). His dissertation, "The Concept of Irony, with Continual Reference to Socrates," introduced several themes that were present throughout his life, including a preoccupation with the role of the individual, the importance of irony and what may be called "negativity" in human life, and the significance of Socrates as a model human. The decade between 1830 and 1840, however, was overshadowed by the death of his mother, five of his siblings, and finally of his father (1838) and profoundly affected his spiritual disposition. After becoming engaged to Regine Olsen in September 1840, he brought the engagement to an end a year later amid dramatic inner struggles. From that point on, he lived on his inheritance and as a freelance writer, composing works in a yearly rhythm and publishing them with self-financing.

Kierkegaard's works were of two types. Many of his best-known works, such as *Either/Or* (1843), *Fear and Trembling* (1843), *The Concept of Anxiety* (1844), *Philosophical Fragments* (1844), and *Concluding Unscientific Postscript* (1846), are attributed to pseudonyms. The purpose was not to escape responsibility for the works; rather, the pseudonyms are like fictional characters whom Kierkegaard creates, who have their own viewpoints on life.

Through this practice, Kierkegaard hoped to engage his readers and force them to think for themselves about existence. The other stream in his authorship was "upbuilding" and religious works published under his own name. This stream includes such works as *Eighteen Upbuilding Discourses* (1843-45), *Upbuilding Discourses in Various Spirits* (1847), and *Christian Discourses* (1848).

Kierkegaard rarely left the immediate surroundings of his hometown. In 1840 he visited Jutland, his family's place of origin, and in the winter of 1841-42 he attended F. Schelling's lectures for several months in Berlin, which he visited again on shorter trips in 1843 and 1846. Kierkegaard died at only 42 years of age in a Copenhagen hospital, in the midst of the storm he created by a public attack on the → state church, an attack made both in the name of "New Testament Christianity" and simple "human honesty," which Kierkegaard believed compelled him and his contemporaries to admit that they were not living in accordance with the NT. At his death he was almost destitute financially, though his published works amount to 26 volumes in the latest English edition of *Kierkegaard's Writings*.

Kierkegaard was never able to escape entirely the influence of his father's overwhelming personality and of the latter's melancholic → piety. His father combined a strict, orthodox Lutheranism (→ Orthodoxy 1) with an enthusiasm for → logic and formal argumentation, and this combination was at odds with a → curse the father had leveled at God in the face of financial distress even before Søren's birth. Kierkegaard became convinced that as a result, the family itself was cursed, a conviction the many deaths in his immediate family certainly seemed to confirm. The psychological and emotional disposition resulting from this conviction may have prompted the forced end to his engagement. He believed firmly that marriage required open communication and honesty but felt that he could not explain himself to Regine without disclosing secrets about his father that he had a duty not to divulge.

Kierkegaard's difficult childhood and youth decisively influenced his philosophical view of things. The poetic character of his philosophical work also lends expression to his basic conviction that genuine philosophical truth about morality and religion is not the same as objective truth, which can be communicated directly as a body of knowledge. Kierkegaard believed rather that in a philosophical discussion about existence, similar to the Socratic dialogue, it was necessary to entangle one's dialogue partner in a sequence of questions and reflection through which the latter then found the way to his or her own truth. It is not that Kierkegaard did not believe there were moral and religious truths that could be stated. Rather, the problem is that the truths in question concern life and thus require a "double reflection" in which the recipient of the truth not only understands the truths but can apply them to his or her own life.

Human existence is for Kierkegaard an unfinished process, and no "system" of existence is possible for finite persons (though this limitation does not hold for God). A person's existence as a self is a process, a sequence of moments in which that person effects the synthesis of infinitude and finitude represented by the fulfilled moment. On this view, the individual appears as a profoundly historical being, and for Kierkegaard this status means that beyond the crowd and the → masses, people become individuals again, albeit not individuals in and for themselves, but rather before God. Kierkegaard sees the new foundation of → faith and religion, and specifically of the Christian religion, not in the performance of external Christian rituals but in a radical and complete surrender of the self to God. During the last two years of his life, this conviction came to expression in Kierkegaard's vehement attacks against the circumstances of official Christianity as represented by the official church in his hometown.

Kierkegaard's philosophy influenced the theology of K. → Barth, F. Gogarten, and R. Bultmann. Existential philosophy and fundamental → ontology are inconceivable without him.

→ Anxiety; Dialectical Theology; Existential Theology; Paradox; Religion, Criticism of

Bibliography: Primary sources: Journals and Papers (7 vols.; ed. H. V. Hong and E. H. Hong; Bloomington, Ind., 1967-78) • Kierkegaard's Writings (26 vols.; ed. H. V. Hong et al.; Princeton, 1978-2000) • The Parables of Kierkegaard (ed. T. Oden; Princeton, 1978) • The Prayers of Kierkegaard (ed. P. Lefevre; Chicago, 1956).

Secondary works: C. S. EVANS, Kierkegaard's "Fragments" and "Postscript": The Religious Philosophy of Johannes Climacus (2d ed.; Amherst, N.Y., 1999; orig. pub., 1983); idem, Søren Kierkegaard's Christian Psychology: Insight for Counseling and Pastoral Care (Grand Rapids, 1990) • M. J. FERREIRA, Love's Grateful Striving: A Commentary on Kierkegaard's "Works of Love" (Oxford, 2001) • D. J. GOUWENS, Kierkegaard as Religious Thinker (New York, 1996) • A. HANNAY, Kierkegaard: A Biography (New York, 2001) • J. LIPPITT, Humour and Irony in Kierkegaard's Thought (New York, 2000) • H. C. MALIK, Receiving Søren Kierkegaard: The Early Impact and Transmission of His Thought (Wash-

ington, D.C., 1997) • P. MINEAR, The Bible and the Historian (Nashville, 2002) • T. H. POLK, The Biblical Kierkegaard: Reading by the Rule of Faith (Macon, Ga., 1997) • M. A. RAE, Kierkegaard's Vision of the Incarnation: By Faith Transformed (Oxford, 1997) • A. RUDD, Kierkegaard and the Limits of the Ethical (Oxford, 1993) • M. WESTPHAL, Becoming a Self: A Reading of Kierkegaard's "Concluding Unscientific Postscript" (West Lafayette, Ind., 1996); idem, Kierkegaard's Critique of Reason and Society (Macon, Ga., 1987).

MICHAEL LÖBL

Kimbanguist Church

1. History
2. Teaching
3. Spread

1. History

The Kimbanguist Church takes its name from Simon Kimbangu (1889?-1951). A native of the Lower Congo, he was a catechist of the Baptist Missionary Society (→ Baptists; British Missions) in the Ngombe Lutete region. Performing miracles of → healing, he drew thousands of pilgrims to his hometown of Nkamba. They left plantations, factories, churches, and hospitals to hear the good news of → salvation and liberation that the *ngunza* (prophet) proclaimed from April 6, 1921.

Kimbangu's activities soon concerned the authorities, who were fearful of nationalistic rebellion. On the prompting of the → Roman Catholic Church and the merchants of Thysville (present-day Mbanza-Ngungu), the colonial government of the Belgian Congo (later Zaire, now the Democratic Republic of Congo) ordered the arrest of Kimbangu in June 1921 on a charge of disturbing the public peace. Avoiding capture, Kimbangu and some of his followers visited the villages of the Lower Congo, but then in September — after a brief public ministry of only a few months — he and his followers gave themselves up. After a short trial Kimbangu was condemned to death, but on the plea of the public prosecutor, supported by the Baptist Mission, the sentence was commuted to life imprisonment. He was taken to Elisabethville (Lubumbashi), where after 30 years in prison he died on October 12, 1951.

Simon's wife, Muilu Marie, preserved the tradition by keeping in contact secretly with her imprisoned husband. Of the original 37,000 adherents (by the church's count, not statistically confirmed), fewer than 3,000 still survived at the time of his death. → Persecution of the movement was the reason for its spread beyond the limits of the Lower Congo and for the multiplication of parallel movements (Ngunzism, Mpadism, Matswanism, Nzambi Malembe, etc.).

Shortly before Congo gained its independence, and after a hard fight for the free exercise of faith led by Lucien Luntadila Ndala (b. 1934), who later became secretary general, the Église du Jésus Christ sur la terre par le prophète [later changed to "par son envoyé spécial"] Simon Kimbangu (EJCSK, Church of Jesus Christ on earth by the prophet [later: "by his special messenger"] Simon Kimbangu) was officially recognized in December 1959 under the spiritual leadership of Diangienda Kuntima Joseph (1918-92), the youngest son of the prophet. At Diangienda's death, leadership passed to his older brother Dialungana Kiangani Salomon (1916-2001), and then in 2001 to Simon's grandson Simon Kimbangu Kiangani (b. 1951). Main tenets of the church include the doctrine of the → Trinity, the missionary command, respect for → authority, abstention from politics, hierarchical organization, and renunciation of → force, → fetishism, → racism, and polygamy. For much of the church the role of the → prophet is that of the promised Comforter of John 14, but the official belief is that he was simply the *ntumwa*, Christ's African messenger or witness.

For some years there were rifts in the EJCSK, with rival claims to leadership. A serious problem was that the EJCSK was not the only group of Kimbanguists appealing to Kimbangu. But it prevailed, thanks to its acceptance into the → World Council of Churches in August 1969 (the first African → Independent Church so accepted) and into the → All Africa Conference of Churches in May 1974, and also thanks to a law forbidding → sects (and therefore rival groups) passed in December 1971. The EJCSK thus achieved the same rank as the Roman Catholic Church and the Protestant Église du Christ au Zaire. It was recognized to be the third religious force in Congo and the official representative of Kimbanguism.

2. Teaching

According to Diangienda's *Essence de la théologie kimbanguiste,* the church's doctrines are as follows: one trinitarian God, salvation solely by → grace, → faith and good works, → baptism by the → Holy Spirit and by → laying on of hands at the age of discretion, and the → Eucharist three times a year (April 6, the beginning of Kimbangu's ministry; October 12, his death; and December 25, Jesus' birth), with honey and cakes.

Of greater practical significance than these doctrines are the principles and methods (*Statutes* [1959]), which enjoin the duties of respecting authority, paying taxes, mutual → love, and mutual confession, and which forbid alcohol and tobacco (→ Substance Abuse), bathing or sleeping naked, dancing, quarreling, and returning to fetishism. Women also must wear head scarves, ornaments must not be worn at → prayer, shoes must be removed upon entering church, and there must be obeisance to the so-called spiritual leaders.

At the head of the international, national, and regional hierarchy are the pastors, → deacons, deaconesses, and catechists, who watch over believers at the local level, where there is an intensive community life. We also find trumpet blowers, who lead the *nsinsani* (ritually based collections according to groups/congregations); choral members, who lead cultic activities (with spontaneous → hymns); monitors, who serve in green and white uniforms; and women, or *mamas*, who are the backbone of the EJCSK and active in all the church's development projects.

Thanks to the generous offerings of the members and to *salongo* (unpaid work), the EJCSK has built three large → temples (in Nkamba [called New Jerusalem by members], in Kinshasa-Matete, and in Matadi), the "House of the People" (its administrative building), and a reception center. It has also built dozens of clinics for the poor and a large network of schools. Support from abroad has also enabled it to set up a theological faculty, a large agricultural center in Lutendele, a hospital, social centers, and other facilities.

3. Spread

In the 1990s the Kimbanguist Church was one of the fastest-growing religious bodies in the world. In 2000 it had upwards of 6.5 million adherents in the Democratic Republic of Congo, 500,000 in Angola, and 150,000 in Congo (Brazzaville). It is active also in Burundi, Central African Republic, Gabon, Kenya, Zambia, Belgium, France, and Portugal.

→ Acculturation; African Theology; Black Theology; Charismatic Movement; Contextual Theology

Bibliography: S. Asch, *L'église du prophète Kimbangu. De ses origines à son rôle actuel au Zaïre, 1921-1981* (Paris, 1983) • K. Diangienda, *L'histoire du Kimbanguisme* (Kinshasa and Lausanne, 1984) • A. Droogers, "An African Translation of the Christian Message: Changes in the Concept of Spirit, Heart, and God among the Wagenia of Kisangani, Zaire," *Man, Meaning, and History* (ed. R. Schefold et al.; The Hague,

1980) 300-331; idem, "Kimbanguism at the Grass Roots: Beliefs in a Local Kimbanguist Church," *JRA* 11 (1980) 188-211 • H. E. HEIMER, "The Kimbanguists and the Bapostolo: A Study of Two African Independent Churches in Luluabourg, Congo" (Diss., Hartford, Conn., 1971) • W. J. HOLLENWEGER, *Marxist and Kimbanguist Mission: A Comparison* (Birmingham, Eng., 1973) • J. M. JANZEN and W. MACGAFFEY, eds., *An Anthology of Kongo Religion: Primary Texts from Lower Zaïre* (Lawrence, Kans., 1974) • W. MACGAFFEY, *Modern Kongo Prophets* (Bloomington, Ind., 1983) • D. J. MACKAY, "The Once and Future Kingdom: Kongo Models of Renewal in the Church at Ngombe Lutete and in the Kimbanguist Movement" (Diss., Aberdeen, 1985) • M.-L. MARTIN, *Kimbangu: An African Prophet and His Church* (Grand Rapids, 1976) • S. S. SIMBANDUMWE, *A Socio-Religious and Political Analysis of the Judeo-Christian Concept of Prophetism and Modern Bakongo and Zulu African Prophetic Movements* (Lewiston, N.Y., 1992); idem, "Understanding the Role of a Modern Prophet in Kimbanguist Hymns," *HR* 32 (1992/93) 165-83 • W. USTORF, *Afrikanische Initiative. Das aktive Leiden des Propheten Simon Kimbangu* (Frankfurt, 1975).

SUSAN ASCH

Kindergarten

1. History
   1.1. Roots
   1.2. U.S. Movement
2. Young Children with Disabilities
3. Current Situation

Kindergarten is an educational program, either all-day or half-day, for the year preceding entrance into the first grade in public schools. The kindergarten experience is part of early → childhood education, which encompasses educational experiences from birth through age eight.

1. History

1.1. *Roots*

Early childhood education in the 21st century can trace its roots to several early thinkers. Martin → Luther (1483-1546) advanced the then radical idea that all boys should be educated and that music and physical education should be part of that education. The Bohemian churchman and educator Johannes Comenius (1592-1670) proposed that all children — both girls and boys — go to school and that → education include "learning by doing" (e.g., learning to speak by speaking).

Also making significant contributions to early childhood education were Jean-Jacques Rousseau (1712-78) and Johann Pestalozzi (1746-1827). Rousseau, who assumed that children were "naturally" good, proposed that they be allowed to learn by following their natural instincts without restraint. He insisted on the use of concrete learning materials in the classroom in order to assist the children during extended periods of free play. Pestalozzi, a Swiss educator, was also a strong advocate for child-centered learning, as well as for an integrated curriculum. Teachers would plan a variety of sensory experiences in separate interest centers in the classroom, from which each child could then choose his or her own learning experiences. He also encouraged placing young children in groups for instruction and outlined teaching procedures for mothers to use at home with their children.

In colonial New England, primary schools were mandated by churches to teach reading so that children would be able to read the Holy Scriptures. After the Revolutionary War (1785-83) the U.S. Constitution, which established a separation of → church and state, left to the states the responsibility for educating their own citizens. From the very first the primary school was charged by parents with teaching the basic skills of reading, writing, and arithmetic, which involved even very young students. In 1826, for example, public schools were enrolling up to 20 percent of all three-year-olds; in that year, 5 percent of all public school children were below the age of four (B. Spodek and O. N. Saracho). By 1835, however, enrollment of young children had begun to decline because of a concern for the balanced development of the young child. Taking the child out of the home and away from the influence of the mother came to be seen as developmentally inappropriate.

1.2. *U.S. Movement*

The kindergarten movement in the United States has direct roots in the ideas promulgated by the disciples of Friedrich Froebel (1782-1852), a German educator. Rejecting the conventions of the orthodox, subject-centered German schools, Froebel created a school (or *Garten*, "garden") in which young children could grow through a series of ordered activities. These play activities were to demonstrate that everything in the universe functions in relationship to God and has a specific purpose in life. Froebel's idea that young children were to be educated outside the home was considered revolutionary in its time.

The first private kindergarten in the United States was established in 1856 by Margarethe Schurz in her own home in Watertown, Wisconsin. Schurz, a Froebelian-trained German kindergarten teacher, conducted her class in German. Between 1850 and 1870 at least ten other German-speaking kindergartens were founded in New York, Detroit, Milwaukee, and elsewhere.

In 1860 Elizabeth Peabody opened a similar, but English-speaking, kindergarten in Boston, and she went on to become the principal promoter of the English-speaking kindergarten movement in the United States. Froebel's philosophy was compatible with New England → transcendentalism, which provided intellectual support for the establishment of kindergartens in America. Milton Bradley, a toy and educational materials manufacturer, began to produce learning materials that enhanced the teaching of Froebel's theories in the kindergartens of America. By the latter years of the 19th century, most American cities had private kindergartens, including some conducted in homes.

In 1873 in St. Louis, Missouri, Susan E. Blow, with the support of William T. Harris, superintendent of schools, founded the first U.S. public kindergarten. When Harris later became U.S. commissioner of education, he encouraged further development of Froebelian principles in early childhood education in order to prepare immigrant and poor children for the American → industrial society.

Alice Putnam, an ardent advocate for changing the methods used in the kindergarten, worked with progressive reformers in the Chicago area, including Jane Addams (1860-1935) and John Dewey (1859-1952), to refine her ideas. Her training sessions for teachers were largely influential in convincing teachers to modify Froebel's methods.

Patty Smith Hill, professor at Columbia University Teachers College (1906-35), modified Froebel's methodology by including more free activities in the curriculum. She advocated sand and water play, housekeeping corners, and building with large building blocks, believing that the curriculum of the kindergarten ought to reflect the children's current life rather than that of another culture and another generation. Today's kindergarten classrooms reflect many of Hill's ideas regarding the curriculum.

The work of Maria Montessori (1870-1952) further influenced the kindergarten curriculum. A physician working in Italy, Montessori developed a unique educational philosophy as a result of her work with children with mental disabilities, stressing in particular the child's initiative and → freedom. Montessori hallmarks include a set of carefully crafted learning materials, the breaking up of practical skills (e.g., for cleaning a table) into se-

quential steps for learning, and careful preparation of the school environment for orderly learning. Several Montessori nursery schools were begun in the 1920s in the United States but lost popularity in the ensuing decades. During the 1960s, however, Montessori methodologies again became popular in the United States and have been incorporated into nursery schools, kindergartens, and the primary grades.

In recent years the thinking of early childhood educators has been influenced by the Reggio Emilia community preschools of northern Italy. Hallmarks of the Reggio schools include teachers staying with the same children for many years, documenting learning experiences, and encouraging the children to learn from their → environment, or "third teacher" (J. Brewer).

Various religious groups have often sponsored kindergartens for poor, immigrant, and minority children. Jewish support for kindergartens has been strong, except among the Orthodox Jewish communities. Before the 1980s few → Roman Catholic schools had kindergartens. Orthodox and fundamentalist groups have been less likely to support kindergartens because of the perceived liberal nature of the curriculum, the focus on play activities, and the lack of any creed or dogma.

2. Young Children with Disabilities

Although in the United States the private education of children with disabilities began in the 18th century, the field remained poorly supported until the 1970s (→ Persons with Disabilities). With the enactment in 1975 of the Education for All Handicapped Children Act and subsequent laws, federal money became available to support the education of disabled children, beginning at age three. Also authorized are intervention services for preschoolers with disabilities, ages three to five, and for infants and toddlers, from birth through age two. (In 1990 the name of the law was changed to the Individuals with Disabilities Education Act.)

Worldwide, only a minority of countries subscribe to an integration philosophy that provides services to special-needs children in regular classrooms or in close proximity to regular classrooms. In many of these countries (e.g., Austria), integration is a relatively new phenomenon, with programs typically offered in separate facilities. Most of the world's disabled children have limited educational opportunities of any kind.

3. Current Situation

The largest professional organization of early childhood educators in the United States is the National

Association for the Education of Young Children, which in 1985 established the National Academy of Early Childhood Programs to accredit early childhood programs, including kindergartens. The association advocates a developmentally appropriate curriculum for the kindergarten. Many parents today, however, as at the beginning of the movement in the 19th century, want their children to attend a kindergarten where the emphasis is on academics, believing that an early start will better prepare their children for success in school and the work world.

Most U.S. parents send their children to kindergarten, since publicly supported programs are now available in almost all states. As recently as 1993 kindergarten was mandated in only seven states. Enrollment in all preprimary programs has grown substantially in the decade beginning in 1987, when enrollment of children between ages three and five rose by 33 percent. About 50 percent of this enrollment was in full-day programs, as compared with 35 percent in 1987 (T. D. Snyder).

Today's kindergarten curriculum is diverse and may include — besides play, music, art, and introductory reading and counting activities — field trips, an artist-in-residence program, use of computer programs, environmental education, and sign language.

The Association for Childhood Education International, which has consultative status with the → United Nations as a nongovernmental organization, promotes appropriate educational conditions, programs, and practices for children through the elementary grades and includes provincial and state associations. The World Organization for Early Education (Organisation Mondiale pour l'Éducation Prescolaire, OMEP) promotes the study and education of young children and shares information on education, development, health and nutrition, playgrounds, and toys in reference to young children all over the world. UNESCO and OMEP, which publishes the *International Journal of Early Childhood Education* and holds a biennial international assembly, work jointly on projects of mutual concern.

→ Moral Education

Bibliography: B. BEATTY, "'The Letter Killeth': Americanization and Multicultural Education in Kindergartens in the United States, 1856-1920," *Kindergartens and Cultures: The Global Diffusion of an Idea* (ed. R. Wollons; New Haven, 2000); idem, *Preschool Education in America: The Culture of Young Children from the Colonial Era to the Present* (New Haven, 1995) • K. J. BREHONY, ed., *The Origins of Nursery Education: Friedrich Froebel and the English System* (New York, 2001) • J. BREWER, *Early Childhood Education: Preschool through Primary Grades* (Boston, 2001) • E. G. HAINSTOCK, *The Essential Montessori: An Introduction to the Woman, the Writings, the Method, and the Movement* (rev. ed.; New York, 1997) • S. L. KROGH, *Educating Young Children: Infancy to Grade Three* (New York, 1994) • G. S. MORRISON, *Early Childhood Education Today* (6th ed.; Englewood Cliffs, N.J., 1995) • T. D. SNYDER, *Digest of Education Statistics, 1998* (Washington, D.C., 1998) • B. SPODEK and O. N. SARACHO, *Right from the Start: Teaching Children Three to Eight* (Boston, 1994) • R. WOLLONS, ed., *Kindergartens and Cultures: The Global Diffusion of an Idea* (New Haven, 2000) • G. A. WOODILL, J. BERNHARD, and L. PROCHNER, *International Handbook of Early Childhood Education* (New York, 1992).

MURIEL M. RADTKE

King, Martin Luther, Jr.

Martin Luther King Jr. (1929-68) was an American civil rights worker and theologian. As a representative of the → peace movement, a gifted preacher, and an intellectual, King drew from the Bible and from the American founding documents in becoming a leader of nonviolent resistance to institutionalized → racism.

King was born on January 15, 1929, in Atlanta, Georgia. A Baptist preacher since 1947 — like his father and grandfather before him — he began his theological studies at the Crozer Theological Seminary in Chester, Pennsylvania. There he became familiar with Walter → Rauschenbusch's → Social Gospel, was impressed by the teachings and work of Gandhi, and read, among others, Reinhold → Niebuhr, Paul → Tillich, and Henry David Thoreau. He concluded his studies with honors in 1951. At Boston University, where he studied with advocates of philosophical personalism (→ Person), he received his Ph.D. in 1955. He had already returned to the South the year before to become → pastor at the Dexter Avenue Baptist Church in Montgomery, Alabama. Also in Boston he had met Coretta Scott; the two married in 1953.

In 1955 King became involved in the Montgomery bus strike, which began without any clue of its significance but then turned into an increasingly organized movement of noncooperation. When the Montgomery Improvement Association was founded, a citizens' committee for the improvement of relationships between the races, King was elected chair. After the bus strike ended successfully, the Southern Christian Leadership Conference was founded, with its headquarters in Atlanta, Georgia. King became its first president and also worked as the assistant pastor at the Ebenezer Baptist Church in Atlanta alongside his father.

A high point of the protest movement was the May 1963 agreement in Birmingham, Alabama, to abolish segregation, an agreement preceded by demonstrations in which African-American schoolchildren also participated. During these disputes King composed his "Letter from a Birmingham Jail," which became a classic of protest literature. On August 28, 1963, an estimated 200,000 persons converged on the capital city in the March on Washington, the highlight of which was King's "I Have a Dream" speech, which some have called the most powerful public address in the United States in the 20th century. Drawing on the second paragraph of the Declaration of Independence (affirming the inalienable → rights of "life, liberty, and the pursuit of happiness" for "all men"), King confronted the nation with his compelling dream of the full equality of rights among the races. To improve voter registration of African American citizens, King led a march from Selma, Alabama, to Montgomery in March 1965.

King and his family were the targets of several attacks, and he was repeatedly arrested. The resistance he encountered in his own home contrasted starkly with the national and international acknowledgment he received, including a state visit to Ghana in 1957, an invitation to Bombay by the Gandhi Peace Foundation in 1959 for talks with Nehru and Indira Gandhi, and an honorary doctor of laws degree from Yale University, as well as the Nobel Peace Prize in 1964.

Not everyone interested in improving the legal position of African Americans shared King's views. Some objected especially to the policy of nonviolent protest. In 1965 the Black Power movement initiated by Malcolm X became more influential, and in the northern big cities African-Americans tended to react negatively to the message of the preacher.

To the extent that King found the interests of the → civil rights movement coupled with those of the peace movement, he also began to question the politics of the federal government. It was not enough, he thought, merely to expose the discrepancies between the laws of the individual states and the unrealized promises of the U.S. Constitution; one must also view institutionalized racism in connection with American economic realities and foreign policy. King's critical position in opposition to the Viet Nam War led to tensions with the White House, not only for him personally, but also for the entire civil rights movement.

The last project King worked on was the planning of the Poor People's Campaign in Washington, which was held after his death in May 1968. On April 4, 1968, he was shot to death on a motel balcony in Memphis, Tennessee, by James Earl Ray. Since 1986 King's birthday has been observed as a public holiday in the United States.

→ Black Theology; Economic Ethics; Peace; Poverty

Bibliography: Primary sources: The Autobiography of Martin Luther King, Jr. (ed. C. Carson; New York, 1998) • *The Papers of Martin Luther King, Jr.* (ed. C. Carson; 4 vols.; Berkeley, Calif., 1992-2000) 10 more vols. in preparation • *A Testament of Hope: The Essential Writings of Martin Luther King, Jr.* (ed. J. M. Washington; San Francisco, 1986).

Secondary works: C. CARSON, comp., *A Guide to Research on Martin Luther King, Jr., and the Modern Black Freedom Struggle* (Stanford, Calif., 1989) • R. LISCHER, *The Preacher King: Martin Luther King, Jr., and the Word That Moved America* (New York, 1995) • S. B. OATES, *Let the Trumpet Sound: The Life of Martin Luther King, Jr.* (New York, 1982) • G. PRESLER, *Martin Luther King* (12th ed.; Reinbek, 2002).

CAROLINE SCHRÖDER

Kingdom of God

1. OT
2. NT
3. History of Theology
   3.1. Dogmatic Range
   3.2. Development
      3.2.1. Early Fathers
      3.2.2. Augustine
      3.2.3. Middle Ages
      3.2.4. Reformers
      3.2.5. Cocceius, Pietism, Enlightenment
      3.2.6. Nineteenth Century
      3.2.7. Twentieth Century
   3.3. Systematic Theology

1. OT

The OT contains only a few late references to the kingdom of God. The terms used — Heb. *mĕlûkâ, malkût, mamlākâ;* Aram. *malkû, šolṭān,* all meaning "kingdom," "kingly rule," or "empire" — show that what is meant is God's royal rule or dominion. None of these well-attested terms, however, is primarily theological. For the most part, they refer to earthly kingdoms and empires, whether Israelite, Babylonian, or Persian. There is certainly unanimity that

God gives and takes away earthly dominion (see 2 Sam. 16:8; 1 Chr. 10:14, etc.), but this conviction did not at first give rise to any more profound theological reflection.

The theological basis of the idea of the kingdom of God is to be found, rather, in the preexilic theology of the Jerusalem → temple, which viewed God as King. This idea was strongly influenced by Canaanite religion, which found concrete expression by way of the → Ugaritic texts. At the heart of the Jerusalem theology stood "the LORD of Hosts" (YHWH ṣĕbā'ôt), present on Zion, as the personal God of each Israelite; as the protector of the Davidic dynasty, the city, and the land; and finally as God of the whole world, with a claim to praise in heaven and on earth (see Isa. 6:3; Pss. 2; 24; 29; 48; 93, etc.; → Monotheism; Yahweh). Nowhere in this temple theology, however, do we read of a kingdom of God, although the world is his, and heaven and the Jerusalem temple on Zion are his home.

This theology suffered a deep crisis when the Jerusalem temple of God the King, Yahweh Sabaoth, was reduced to dust and ashes in 587/586 B.C., and the city and land lost both their king and his dominion and came under subjection to Nebuchadnezzar II (ruled 605-562) and his empire. Under the impact of Deuteronomic theology, however, the loss was seen as a failure, not of God, but of the kings of → Israel (§1) and Judah (→ Deuteronomistic History). From this theologically uncompromising standpoint Israel's desire for an earthly king came to be seen as a rejection of the divine dominion (see Judg. 8:22-23; 1 Sam. 8:5-7; 12:12). The divine pardon, which became evident in the foundation of the postexilic temple community in Jerusalem, opened the door for a revival of the idea of divine kingship in the postexilic period, initially at a time of political dependence, but then of religious autonomy under Persian rule. The divine kingship could now be understood in terms of the kingdom of God.

Against the background of Deuteronomic and Priestly theology (→ Pentateuch), a hierocratic concept developed, with Israel initially being to God "a priestly kingdom [mamleket kōhănîm] and a holy nation [gôy qādōš]" (Exod. 19:6). But when this approach proved ineffective on account of its inward orientation, a theocratic conception such as we find in Chronicles and Daniel proved to be more fruitful, reflecting as it did the situation in the Persian Empire and allowing at the same time for a reconsideration of Israel's own history.

The rule of God there is a reality on earth, and therefore every earthly kingdom that God protects and that will guarantee the temple and the → law has a share in God's own rule. On the commission of God Nathan could promise → David a successor who, in God's own words, would endure forever "in my house and in my kingdom" (1 Chr. 17:14; cf. 2 Sam. 7:16). → Solomon was chosen to sit "upon the throne of the kingdom [malkût] of YHWH" and to rule over Israel (1 Chr. 28:5). The kingdom (mamleket) was put in the hands of the house of David (2 Chr. 13:8). Darius ordered that in his kingdom (malkû) the God of Daniel should be worshiped, whose kingdom (malkû) would never perish (Dan. 6:26; 2 Chr. 36:22-23 par. Ezra 1:1-3).

In the Hellenistic and Maccabean parts of the Book of Daniel, the theocratic concept became eschatological or apocalyptic in an early form (→ Eschatology; Apocalyptic 2). The kingdom of God breaks in now, in discontinuity with previous history, though no uniform picture may be presented. Along with the handing over of God's eternal dominion to the Son of Man (Dan. 7:13-14), it is also handed over to "the holy ones of the Most High" (vv. 18, 22) or "the people of the holy ones of the Most High" (v. 27). God no longer entrusts his kingship to an alien people (2:44). Messianic expectation does not arise as such in this connection (→ Messianism).

The theocratic concept of the kingdom of God still persisted. After the pattern of Dan. 4:3, 34 and 1 Chr. 29:11-12, in later texts it usually took a hymnic form (→ Hymn 1) that stressed the universality of the divine dominion (Ps. 22:28; 103:19; 145:11-13; also Obad. 21). The Tannaite invitation to both Jews and → proselytes to take upon themselves "the yoke of the kingdom of heaven" agrees fully with this presentation.

→ Historiography; Jerusalem; Monarchy in Israel; Theology of History

Bibliography: J. GRAY, *The Biblical Doctrine of the Reign of God* (Edinburgh, 1979) • R. G. KRATZ, *Translatio imperii* (Neukirchen, 1991) • H. S. KWON, *The Zion Traditions and the Kingdom of God: A Study on the Zion Traditions as Relevant to the Understanding of the Concept of the Kingdom of God in the NT* (Jerusalem, 1998) • J. NEUSNER and B. CHILTON, *Jewish-Christian Debates: God, Kingdom, Messiah* (Minneapolis, 1998) • H. SPIECKERMANN, *Heilsgegenwart. Eine Theologie der Psalmen* (Göttingen, 1989) 165-225 • E. E. URBACH, *The Sages* (Cambridge, Mass., 1994; orig. pub., 1975) 400-419 • R. I. VASHOLZ, *Pillars of the Kingdom: Five Features of the Kingdom of God Progressively Revealed in the OT* (Lanham, Md., 1997) • R. O. ZORN, *Christ Triumphant: Biblical Perspectives on the Church and the Kingdom* (Edinburgh, 1997).

HERMANN SPIECKERMANN

2. NT

The concept of the kingdom of God (Gk. *basileia tou theou*) appears throughout the NT but most of all in the Jesus tradition. Similar terms are simply "kingdom," "kingdom of the heavens," or "kingdom of the Father." After Easter we also read of the kingdom of Christ. The term has both a local and a functional aspect.

2.1. Central to the message of → *Jesus,* even where the phrase does not occur, is the imminent kingdom of God. As in Jewish parallels, this kingdom is something future as regards its full actualization (cf. → John the Baptist in Luke 3:9). In the first → beatitude in Luke 6:20, the kingdom of God is promised to the poor, which would be absurd were there not to be a complete restructuring of earthly relations. Jesus assumes that the kingdom will be future also in the → Lord's Prayer (Luke 11:2 and par.), at the Last Supper (Mark 14:25 and par.), in what is said about entry into it (Mark 9:47; 10:15 and par.), and in three growth → parables: the seed that grows of itself (Mark 4:26-29), the mustard seed (4:30-32 and and par.), and the leaven (Matt. 13:33 and par.), in which the unassuming start is contrasted with the overwhelming conclusion. Jesus presupposes the nearness of the kingdom of God in Mark 9:1 and par. when he emphasizes that some present will see the coming of the kingdom of God "with power" *(en dynamei),* that is, in its full realization. The → future is always an imminent future. (The → Jesus Seminar has addressed the question of future eschatology.)

Jesus, however, typically focuses on the beginnings of the actualization of the kingdom of God. In distinction from what we find in → apocalyptic, the → Zealots, and the → Qumran community, there is a certain place for the present divine rule in Pharisaic → Judaism, as may be seen in the confession (→ Confession of Faith) and in observance of the Torah (Str-B 1.172-84). Nevertheless, this theme is not so important there as it is in Jesus, who saw the future kingdom of God as already a present reality in his → exorcisms (Luke 11:20 and par., where the kingdom of God *ephthasen* [aor.], "has come"). As distinct from many apocalyptists who tried to fix dates and times for the incursion of the kingdom, Jesus stresses its presence "among you" (Luke 17:20-21). Even the debated reference to storming the kingdom, which seems to mean that the resolute will win it, presupposes realization in the present (Matt. 11:12 and par.). Its presence is not known by all but only by those who see in Jesus of Nazareth the end-time representative of God, or, after Easter, only by those who believe in him.

The inbreaking rule of God may be perceived in God's unconditional turning to us. In meeting us without prejudice, Jesus demonstrates the unsurpassable and underived → love of God, which evidences the eschatological quality of the coming reign (→ Eschatology 2). Beggars will be blessed (Luke 6:20), the despised will be invited to the great banquet (14:16-24 and par.), the lost will be sought (15:1-7 and par.), and → forgiveness will be pronounced (Matt. 18:21-22; John 7:53–8:11). The sovereign God gives the kingdom (Luke 12:32). This motif is strong in Revelation and at the same time has anti-Zealot and anti-Pharisee components inasmuch as one cannot achieve the kingdom by force or by Torah observance. The kingdom can be had only with the openness of a child (Mark 10:15 and par.).

In the message of Jesus the promise of salvation predominates, and the thought of judgment is less prominent (e.g., as compared with Luke 3:7-9). Nevertheless, the thought of rule is stressed in all seriousness. As God turns unconditionally to us, so we must yield unconditionally to him. The greatness of the gift means logically the surrender of all that goes before (Matt. 13:44-46, 47-50). We must not have a care for worldly things but seek first the kingdom of God, and then we shall find all else (Luke 12:31 and par.). To enter the kingdom we must let go of all that would impede us (Mark 9:47). Sayings about → discipleship that stress this kind of readiness clarify the human aspect of the actualizing of God's rule, which involves service, not earthly dominion (Mark 10:42-45 and par.).

2.2. In the early post-Easter period the → *Q source* shows that the authority of the → disciples to engage in saving acts is linked to their proclamation of the imminent divine rule, so that they in their situation are continuing the work of Jesus (Luke 10:9 and par.). In contrast to the followers of the Baptist, the first → primitive community has a sense of eschatological motivation that comes to light here (Luke 7:28 and par.).

2.3. In 1:14-15 *Mark* uses the phrase "the kingdom of God has come near" *(ēngiken hē basileia tou theou)* to sum up the message of Jesus. According to 4:10-12, Jesus discloses to the disciples, not to those outside, the "secret," or "mystery" *(mystērion),* of the kingdom by interpreting the parables of the kingdom. Here again the kingdom of God is the core of Jesus' → proclamation, the future aspect being in this case central.

2.4. We find plainer emphases on the kingdom in *Matthew.* The references to the *basileia tōn ouranōn* (lit. "kingdom of the heavens") stand under the influence of Jewish usage, but "kingdom of God" is also found in 12:28, 19:24, and a few other places. The mention of heaven perhaps stresses the universal character of the kingdom. The concept characteristically takes an ethical turn in Matthew, which is very clear in 5:20, where a better → righteousness than that of the Pharisees is required for entrance into the kingdom (see 6:33). Doing the Father's will is a prerequisite in 7:21 (cf. 6:10). Along similar lines the thought of judgment receives stronger emphasis, as in 22:11-14. Matthew has a concern for one's concrete → lifestyle and its mastering. In this regard, for all the differences, there is some similarity to Pharisaic → Judaism.

Other aspects of the kingdom that are important in Matthew are as follows. It is a universal blessing of → salvation that is open to all who do God's will (21:43; 25:34). The → church (§2.1) is closely connected with the kingdom, though not identical; it has the keys of the kingdom (cf. 18:18; 16:19; → Keys, Power of the). The Son of Man has a present kingdom in the world (13:41; cf. the post-Easter references to the kingdom of Christ), yet the kingdom of the Son of Man is also still future (16:28; cf. Mark 9:1). There is a presence of the kingdom in the exorcisms of Jesus (12:28), as later the risen Lord will have present dominion in 28:18, though the term "kingdom" does not occur here. This dominion is seen dialectically, for it finds expression in the preaching of the → gospel of the kingdom (= engaging in → mission, 4:23-25; 9:35) and also in the proclaiming of judgment (5:20).

2.5. *Luke* accentuates the traditional concept of the kingdom of God on the basis of his view of history (→ Historiography 2). Delay of the → parousia means that as regards the future kingdom of God, the thought of imminence is less to the fore (21:31; 22:16-18; cf. the motif of the Spirit in Acts 1:6-8). Talk about the presence of the kingdom of God also receives a new stress. The kingdom is certainly present in the saving acts of Jesus, but it is also described spatially as present in → heaven (Luke 23:42-43; cf. 16:19-31).

As in Matthew, so in Luke the kingdom of God is the content of post-Easter proclamation. Note the link between *euangelizomai* (proclaim the good news of) in 4:43 (also Acts 8:12), *kēryssō* (proclaim) in 8:1 (also Acts 20:25), and *laleō* (speak) in 9:11 and elsewhere. The presence of the kingdom is concealed in missionary → preaching (→ Mission), and we must pass through great tribulation to enter it (Acts 14:22). Luke also refers to the kingdom of Christ, which is future in 22:29-30, although already present in heaven in 23:42-43.

2.6. *John*, with his distinctive → Christology (§1), pays less attention to the kingdom of God. We find mention of it only in 3:3, 5, where being born of water and the Spirit (→ Baptism) is required for entry into it. John uses "life" *(zōē)* instead of "kingdom." In 18:36 we find a reference to the kingdom of Christ, which is now present in heaven.

2.7. After Easter the investing of the risen Lord with divine power means that we hear more of the kingdom of Christ. There are references to this kingdom already in the Gospels, for the Crucified bears the title of *basileus* (king) in Mark 15:2, 9 and parallels, but we find many more such references in the rest of the NT, especially in the *Pauline corpus,* the *Deutero-Paulines,* and the *later epistles.* The present kingdom of God is mentioned in 1 Cor. 4:20 and Col. 4:11 in a context of missionary ecclesiology, and in Rom. 14:17 in an ethical context. The future aspect of the kingdom, however, predominates. The kingdom of God is a future gift of salvation in 1 Thess. 2:12; 1 Cor. 6:9-10; 15:24, 50; Gal. 5:21; Jas. 2:5 (see also Heb. 12:28).

Eph. 5:5 directly links the kingdom of God to the kingdom of Christ. The trend is clear: the kingdom of God is future but will be manifested at the parousia. The kingdom of Christ may also be seen as future (2 Tim. 4:1, also 2 Pet. 1:11) but is mostly seen as present, as clearly in 1 Cor. 15:24-25 (also Col. 1:13, with ecclesiological accents) and Heb. 1:8.

The universal aspect of the preaching of the kingdom of God by Jesus is still intact, though the typical view of the kingdom in Jesus is quantitatively less prominent in view of experiences with the risen Lord (his being invested with heavenly glory and power) and the → Holy Spirit (§1) and the new presentation demanded by the increasing number of Gentile believers in the churches.

2.8. The Book of *Revelation* stands apart inasmuch as it has its own decisive emphases. In 1:6 and 5:10 (cf. 1:9) Christ has made believers a kingdom for God, and even if we have here only a proleptic actualizing of the kingdom, the link between kingdom and church is stronger than elsewhere. Again, 11:15 and 12:10 equate the kingdom of God and the kingdom of Christ. Christ exercises divine rule to the comfort of believers. Finally, 20:4 speaks of a future interim messianic kingdom.

2.9. The NT references to the kingdom of God display a thrust toward uniformity but still defy systematization. The kingdom of God stands related to the kingdom of Christ and the church and evidences the tension between present and future eschatology that is a mark of Christian proclamation and → theology.

Bibliography: J. Awwad, "The Kingdom of God and the State," *ThRev* 22 (2001) 35-60 • G. R. Beasley-Murray, *Jesus and the Kingdom of God* (Grand Rapids, 1986) • J. A. Brooks, "The Kingdom of God in the NT," *SWJT* 40 (1998) 21-37 • G. W. Buchanan, *Jesus, the King and His Kingdom* (Macon, Ga., 1984) • B. Chilton, "The Kingdom of God in Recent Discussion," *Studying the Historical Jesus* (ed. B. Chilton and C. A. Evans; Leiden, 1994) 255-80; idem, *Pure Kingdom: Jesus' Vision of God* (Grand Rapids, 1996); idem, ed., *The Kingdom of God in the Teaching of Jesus* (Philadelphia, 1984) • H. M. Evans, "Current Exegesis on the Kingdom of God," *PRSt* 14 (1987) 67-77 • L. Guy, "The Interplay of the Present and Future in the Kingdom of God (Luke 19:11-44)," *TynBul* 48 (1997) 119-37 • M. Hengel and A. M. Schwemer, eds., *Königsherrschaft Gottes und himmlischer Kult im Judentum, Urchristentum und in der hellenistischen Welt* (Tübingen, 1991) • W. H. Kelber, *The Kingdom in Mark* (Philadelphia, 1974) • J. M. McDermott, "Jesus and the Kingdom of God in the Synoptics, Paul, and John," *EeT(O)* 19 (1988) 69-91 • M. Öhler, "The Expectation of Elijah and the Presence of the Kingdom of God," *JBL* 118 (1999) 461-76 • M. Pamment, "The Kingdom of Heaven according to the First Gospel," *NTS* 27 (1981) 211-32 • N. Perrin, *The Kingdom of God in the Teaching of Jesus* (London, 1963) • T. Pippin and G. Aichele, eds., *Violence, Utopia, and the Kingdom of God* (London, 1998).

Wilhelm Pratscher

3. History of Theology

3.1. *Dogmatic Range*

Though the kingdom of God was central in the → proclamation of Jesus, over the centuries it has not remained so in → theology and the → church. It becomes less prominent even in the NT, as we see in Paul and John (see 2). As problems arose in the course of dealing with history, however, the concept came to the fore again. Its pictorial and symbolic content varies enormously (C. McDannell and B. Lang). Dogmatically, it embraces the doctrine of → God, → Christology, ecclesiology (→ Church), → eschatology, → ethics, and → piety.

3.2. *Development*

3.2.1. *Early Fathers*

In the → Apostolic Fathers eschatological and moral emphases are always present in discussions of the kingdom of God, though with variations. The eschatology, however, is governed less by → assurance of salvation than by anxiety lest one be unable to meet the entrance requirements.

The early → apologists expected the kingdom of God as the millennium after Christ's return (→

Millenarianism 2). This view faded with the *Chronicles* of Hippolytus (d. ca. 236). → Irenaeus (d. ca. 200), in opposition to → Gnosticism, saw the church as a type of the kingdom of God, which in the church embraces → paradise on earth. → Tertullian (ca. 160-ca. 225) saw in the kingdom a reward for the merits won by → asceticism. Millenarian hopes were a kind of compensation for → Jerusalem, which was despised and lost in the world.

After the rule of Constantine (306-37), whom the Eastern church hailed as one raised up by God, attempts were made to link the empire to the kingdom of God, as in the → political theology of Eusebius of Caesarea. In the West the church was still relatively critical of the state, though naturally → bishops were Romans. The kingdom of God was still an end-time entity, and the empire was integrated into salvation history (Prudentius).

3.2.2. *Augustine*

→ Augustine (354-430; → Augustine's Theology) dealt with the theme of the kingdom of God in the context of his theology of history and → theodicy. He saw two different, interfused societies that are distinguished from one another by God's → grace and judgment: the earthly commonwealth (*civitas terrena* or *civitas diaboli*) and the city of God (*civitas Dei*). Different concepts of → love and of → peace distinguish them. In the former, love is oriented to humans; in the latter, to God. Earthly peace is the absence of → war, while heavenly peace is rest and unending enjoyment of God.

After initial millenarian notions Augustine saw the church as a kingdom that is fighting against evil, with membership in the kingdom gained by → baptism. There is no visible kingdom of God on earth. A link between the religious idea of the kingdom and the political remains as long as the church or → state orients itself in some form to the concept of "eternal Rome" and ceases to look at the eschatological Jerusalem. This orientation developed in both East and West, though with different accents (caesaropapism, spiritualists, and the → Investiture Controversy). Glowing millenarian hopes, however, resisted the equation of either state or church with the kingdom of God and served to restrain the church's shortcomings.

3.2.3. *Middle Ages*

Joachim of Fiore (ca. 1135-1202) related the doctrine of the Trinity to the course of history. First is the kingdom of the Spirit (identified as the millennium that begins with Christ), then the overcoming of antichrist and the judgment, and finally the transcendental kingdom of God. Joachim's prophecies reinforced the Franciscan Spirituals (esp. Fra Dolcino), who envisioned an eschatological social utopia that would shortly be achieved.

The messianic concept of the *imperium Romanum* also lived on. Frederick II (ruled 1215-50) called himself the leader and messiah of the new age, and as world emperor he sought to establish the Christian *imperium* and a kingdom of peace. In the Middle Ages the idea of the kingdom of God split into two varieties, the one political and ecclesiological (the social utopias), the other spiritual.

The mystical identification of the ground of the soul with God himself (→ Mysticism 2) made possible an understanding of the kingdom of God that contained the true human nature, which is already present and imperishable (M. → Eckhart).

3.2.4. Reformers

In the theology of M. → Luther (1483-1546; → Luther's Theology), Augustinian traditions of the two cities link up with medieval traditions of the two kingdoms. Luther's ambivalent view of the kingdom of God is connected with his concept of the two kingdoms. First, the kingdom of God stands in antithesis to the kingdom of the world, of the devil. The theater of the battle between God and Satan is the present world, where the gospel stirs up strife because it seeks the world's renewal. Since we are purely passive in the event of → justification, before God we can belong to only one of the two kingdoms. Second, as the kingdom of Christ, the kingdom of God stands opposed to that of Adam (i.e., the *regnum rationis*, "rule of reason"). God as Creator and Lord of all things, even of the → devil, rules over both. In the kingdom of Christ, where Christ is King and Lord, God heals the world, and his kingdom is spiritual. But God's rule is both spiritual and secular, and Christians belong to both spheres. The two spheres have unity in God but must not be intermixed. This position is the basis of the later → two-kingdoms doctrine, which, in contrast to the view of Luther, postulates an autonomy of the secular order. The consequences of Luther's teaching are (1) a socioethical sanctification of the world as God's world, (2) the separation of clerical and secular power, and (3) the nonconsideration of eschatological perspectives of accomplishment as norms of existing orders.

U. → Zwingli (1484-1531; → Zwingli's Theology) gave supremacy to the Bible, but with a partially humanistic understanding. His concept of the kingdom of God included features of the *civitas Christiana*. That which the Holy Spirit does in us is also of benefit to the state, hence that state is most blessed in which true religion also dwells. The kingdom of God has an external aspect, and it is thus advanced when Christians hold positions in government. Both secular rulers and those who discharge a spiritual office (esp. prophets) are God's representatives, though the prophets take precedence.

The view of J. → Calvin (1509-64; → Calvin's Theology) has three features. First, the kingdom of God is expressed in creation, in his rule over → nature and history (*ordo naturae, providentia specialis*; see *Inst.* [1559] 1.6.3). Second, the kingdom of God is the restitution of fallen → creation; it is built up as the true knowledge of God is implanted in us by Christ, and it breaks in with Christ's kingdom (i.e., the church). Third, the kingdom of God is the endtime consummation of God's exercise of power, when he will be King of the world (*Inst.* 3.20.43).

In the → Anabaptist world and among the Spiritualists, the kingdom of God became a dominant motif in criticism of institutions, states, and churches. Separation was a reason for equating the → congregation with the otherworldly kingdom, which is here given a social form. The Spiritualists left the natural world to its own devices and to its inevitable destruction (→ Spiritualism). The kingdom of God belongs to the heavenly order and has no place in history. The more violent radicals predicted an imminent overthrow of the present order (M. Hoffmann), which, in the unfortunate Münster episode, they attempted to hasten (J. Matthys, John of Leiden).

3.2.5. Cocceius, Pietism, Enlightenment

J. Cocceius (1603-69) sketched stages in → salvation history, and millenarianism and eschatology now took a missionary turn. These ideas influenced → Pietism, which hoped for a transforming of the world into the kingdom of God (J. A. Bengel, J. M. Hahn, F. C. Oetinger, P. J. Spener), for which we may become workers (A. H. → Francke). By way of Pietism the idea of the kingdom of God came into the → metaphysics and philosophy of history of → idealism (F. W. J. Schelling, G. W. F. Hegel), which, as distinct from I. Kant (1724-1804; → Kantianism), did not see the kingdom of God merely ethically. Finally, the concept became the secular one of a kingdom of freedom with which true history begins (K. → Marx). The idea of the kingdom became a disputed issue between → fascism and socialism.

In the meantime the → Enlightenment had related the concept of the kingdom to education and to the idea of → progress (G. E. Lessing). Kant gave precision to this philosophical millenarianism with his hope of eternal peace in a republican union of nations (→ Disarmament and Armament 2). Morality here is to act in a way consonant with the kingdom of God.

3.2.6. Nineteenth Century

F. D. E. → Schleiermacher (1768-1834; → Schleiermacher's Theology) also had a moral view of the kingdom of God. For him, the basis of moral action was Christ as model. Jesus founded the kingdom of God, which unleashes Christ's redeeming activity and which itself is a miracle performed by Christ. Seeking the kingdom of God comes with regeneration, and morality derives from a consciousness of God. The heavenly kingdom of philosophical ethics and the kingdom of God are materially one and the same.

In the train of Schleiermacher the later 19th century took up the difficult problem of the relation between the kingdom of God and → culture (A. Ritschl, R. Rothe, T. Kliefoth, W. Löhe). Movements of awakening (→ Revivals) tracing back to Pietism reacted to the → industrial society, mass poverty, and a Eurocentric outlook influenced by → colonialism (→ Dependence). Intensive worldwide → mission took place, sponsored by the expanding countries of Europe and North America. The idea of sending linked up with the thought of spreading, gathering, and announcing the coming kingdom of God. The task of saving souls became fused with the bringing of culture and the establishing of human → rights. The concept of the kingdom of God now became a synthesis of the apocalyptic ending of the world and its present-day betterment. The saying "Jesus is Victor" (J. C. and C. F. Blumhardt) came to express a cosmological view of the kingdom of God.

3.2.7. Twentieth Century

The reformulation of eschatology (J. Weiss, A. → Schweitzer), the early → dialectical theology, and P. → Tillich's (1886-1965) culture theology were all still oriented to the problems raised by Schleiermacher. They mostly agreed that the kingdom of God is a transcendent entity that God alone can introduce. The dogmatic implications were diverse. At first P. Althaus (1888-1966) shared, as → Barth did, Schleiermacher's skepticism regarding all visions of consummation. K. Barth (1886-1968) made eschatology total but avoided all apocalyptic. He integrated the idea of the kingdom of God into the dialectic of → time and eternity and thereby "ontologized" eschatology (S. Hjelde, 369-70). Tillich opposed mythological ideas of the kingdom of God. For him the kingdom embraced all that takes place as its transcendental meaning, as the consummation posited in the event (Gesammelte Werke 6.80). R. Bultmann (1884-1976; → Existential Theology) existentialized the concept by arguing that for Jesus the imminence of the kingdom of God is the situation of decision, in which it is our absolute destiny to stand.

The → Barmen Declaration (1934) marked a turning point. Here the kingdom of God gives ethical orientation to both rulers and ruled, independently of faith (thesis 5), but it also sets eschatological limits to the state's sphere of competence. In the background is the concept of the royal dominion of Christ (thesis 2) as the basis of → ethics. This concept makes it clear that the kingdom of God is not just otherworldly, and in this way it rejects the totalitarian claims of all ideologies and opposes any granting of autonomy to secular orders.

This approach, along with the criticisms of society offered by the → Social Gospel (→ North American Theology 7-8) and the works of the brothers → Reinhold (1892-1971) and H. Richard Niebuhr (1894-1962), greatly influenced the ecumenical movement (→ Ecumenism, Ecumenical Movement). The kingdom of God now became a standard by which to criticize social conditions. It is a ground of hope and the goal of processes of revolutionary change. The existing church of Christ is in some sense its sign (affirmed at the 1966 Geneva World Conference on Church and Society, the 1968 Uppsala Assembly of the → World Council of Churches [WCC], and the 1968 Medellín conference of the Latin American Council of Bishops; → Theology of Revolution). The WCC (1983 Vancouver Assembly) views the church as a witness to the kingdom of God in its solidarity with the poor. Practice thus anticipates the → future. Christians may not be building up the kingdom of God, but they are building up human society, and there are signs of the kingdom in every culture. Theologically (→ Mission 1-2), the church can be seen as a sacrament of the kingdom (1980 Melbourne World Mission Conference).

J. Moltmann's reformulating of Christ's sovereignty has been influential. Inheriting the vocabulary of the Blumhardts and adopting the social criticism of the kingdom-of-God tradition that was central for Swiss → religious socialism, Moltmann thus came to see Jesus' victory in the resurrection as the basis of political practice. In the light of the relations between God and the earth, institutions must be changed in orientation to the kingdom of God.

The concept of the kingdom of God also permeated the American → civil rights movement, spearheaded by M. Luther → King Jr. (1929-68; → Black Theology), as it has done many other religious and social movements in the United States (→ Modern Church History 2.4-7). Latin American → liberation theology describes the kingdom of God in terms of an eschatological deepening of the process of liberation. For people living in the context of "structural sin," the kingdom empowers for self-liberation and is the goal of integral (i.e., historical and redemptive) liberation.

Official Roman Catholic theology finds difficulty with an eschatological understanding of the kingdom of God. In the 19th century the Tübingen School (J. S. Drey, J. B. Hirscher) tried to uphold an equation of church and kingdom by means of the idea of development. At → Vatican II, however, the image of the church as the pilgrim people of God at last made it possible to think of the kingdom of God as the goal of the pilgrimage, the consummation. Also, however, the church represents "the kingdom of Christ already present in mystery" (*Lumen gentium* 3; see also 9, 35-36).

Millenarian views have survived, enjoying some revival among 17th-century Puritans, then emerging with even greater strength in the 19th and 20th centuries. A common belief within the → evangelical movement, advanced with variations in detail, is that when world evangelization is complete, Christ will come again to establish his millennial kingdom (Matt. 24:14). Then, after a final conflict with evil, the kingdom of God will be established forever with the new heaven and the new earth, in which righteousness alone dwells and the will of God is perfectly done.

3.3. *Systematic Theology*

In systematic theology the point is made that God is the Lord of the world and that everything is subject to his lordship. This lordship has a soteriological aspect, its presupposition being the experience of a world that is hopelessly disrupted through original → sin. The fundamental fault rests on the premise that we have → freedom to sin, and therefore God's lordship as Creator must leave room for the sinful misuse of our freedom. Account must be taken of the fact that → evil may be present. The kingdom of God then has the task of overcoming evil, a task that God in Christ takes up redemptively in love.

With Christ the kingdom of God is present insofar as Christ himself is the King. This event of the kingdom, however, took place in the *absconditas* (C. H. Ratschow), the hidden manner in which God is now present in the world; hence we can only believe the kingdom of God, not see it. It is future in the sense that only then can we imagine the presently hidden nature of blessedness being transcended. The kingdom of God is God's free act, not the result of development or of human activity. Nevertheless, it is the basis and goal of human action inasmuch as faith, as a form of life grounded in Jesus, owes its creative impulse to him. We cannot establish specific directions for action by way of → analogy, but we can find perspectives and options that affect individuals, society, and the cosmos.

Bibliography: AUGUSTINE, *The City of God* (New York, 1994) • R. BARBOUR, ed., *The Kingdom of God and Human Society* (Edinburgh, 1993) • P. J. BRENNAN, *Reimagining Evangelization: Toward the Reign of God and the Communal Parish* (New York, 1995) • B. GOUDZWAARD, *Globalization and the Kingdom of God* (Washington, D.C., 2001) • S. HJELDE, *Das Eschaton und die Eschata* (Munich, 1987) • H. P. KAINZ, *Democracy and the Kingdom of God* (Dordrecht, 1993) • C. McDANNELL and B. LANG, *Heaven: A History* (New Haven, 1988) • B. J. MALINA, *The Social Gospel of Jesus: The Kingdom of God in Mediterranean Perspective* (Minneapolis, 2001) • J. MOLTMANN, *The Trinity and the Kingdom: The Doctrine of God* (Minneapolis, 1993; orig. pub., 1980) • H. R. NIEBUHR, *The Kingdom of God in America* (Middletown, Conn., 1988; orig. pub., 1937) • W. PANNENBERG, *Theology and the Kingdom of God* (Philadelphia, 1969) • C. H. RATSCHOW, "Eschatologie VIII," *TRE* 10.334-63 • W. RAUSCHENBUSCH, *The Righteousness of the Kingdom* (Lewiston, N.Y., 1999).

PETER STEINACKER

Kings, Books of

1. Contents
2. Origin
3. Theological Intention
4. Historical Place

The two Books of Kings were originally one. The LXX divided them and put them with the two Books of Samuel to form the four books *Basileiōn* (of kingdoms, of reigns) dealing with the monarchy. The Vg followed this arrangement with its four books *Regum* (of kings). The division came into the Hebrew Bible in the 15th and 16th centuries.

1. Contents

Kings may be divided into three parts:

1. 1 Kings 1–11, the age of Solomon;
2. 1 Kings 12–2 Kings 17, the age of the divided kingdoms; and
3. 2 Kings 18–25, Judah after the fall of Israel.

The books assemble materials from many kinds of sources. On the one hand, especially recognizable in the last two parts, a succinct chronological record gives statistics on the kings of Israel and Judah (→ Monarchy in Israel). On the other hand, interwoven in this framework are prophetic stories (→ Elijah;

Elisha), political accounts (1 Kings 12; 2 Kgs. 8:28–10:17), stories of wars (1 Kings 20; 22; 2 Kgs. 18:17–19:36; → Holy War), and theological appraisals and interpretations of important historical events (1 Kgs. 11:1-13, 29-39; 2 Kgs. 17:7-41; 21:2-16). In connection with the story of → David's dynasty, the books begin with an account of the ascent of → Solomon to the throne (1 Kings 1–2).

2. Origin

2.1. The text refers to three sources that the writer has drawn on: the Book of the Acts of Solomon (1 Kgs. 11:41), the Book of the Annals of the Kings of Israel (1 Kgs. 14:19; 15:31, and 16 additional appearances), and the Book of the Annals of the Kings of Judah (1 Kgs. 14:29; 15:7, and 13 other references).

M. Noth (1902-68) theorized that the Books of Kings were compiled by the author of the → Deuteronomistic history, who set older materials, such as the prophetic cycles of the Elijah, Elisha, and Isaiah stories, plus other traditions, in his own chronological framework and added theological reflections (e.g., 2 Kgs. 17:7-8).

2.2. Modern students prefer a more complex thesis, namely, that the works took their present shape only over a longer period and through the activity of various Deuteronomistic groups. First came a historical sketch with the chronology of the kings of Israel and Judah and some isolated older materials, especially from the age of Solomon. In this account the kings of Judah were censored by the Deuteronomistic redaction according to the political situation of their day, but all Israel's kings were assessed negatively (with reference to "the sin of Jeroboam," 2 Kgs. 3:3). To a large extent this basic Deuteronomistic document is thought to be the same as Noth's framework.

At a second stage prophetic Deuteronomists introduced the figures and sayings of the prophets, which explain the collapse of the two kingdoms as punishment from → Yahweh for religious offenses (see 1 Kgs. 11:29-33; 14:7-10*, 14; 16:2-4; 2 Kgs. 21:10-13; 22:15-17). Older, Deuteronomistically edited narratives about Elijah and Isaiah were also added. On this view the last stage was that of nomistic redactions that stressed the obligation of the → law (Deuteronomy; 2 Kings 22–23) and its significance for the history of Israel and Judah (2 Kgs. 17:7-20; 21:2b-9).

Finally, post-Deuteronomistic additions were made, especially in the first part, to the stories of Solomon and Elisha. These additions include an incident relating Solomon's wisdom in judgment (1 Kgs. 3:16-28) and the story of the visit of the queen of Sheba (10:1-13; 2 Kgs. 2:1–8:15; 13:14-21).

3. Theological Intention

Religious and theological tendencies are discernible in all strata. Special emphasis lies on the connection between act and consequence. Such tendencies are less evident in the earliest strata, which are concerned more with national and religious matters and provide a retrospective on a long series of kings. In the prophetic and nomistic strata, however, these tendencies become considerably more pronounced. Here the disasters that befall the two kingdoms are clearly related to disobedience to Yahweh and therefore to obedience to the law as the condition of future prosperity. This thesis provided a way to come to terms with the disastrous history and points the way to survival in the existing situation. We thus have more historical interpretation than historical presentation.

4. Historical Place

The Books of Kings took their present shape after the destruction of → Jerusalem in 587 B.C. The Deuteronomistic history dates from before the middle of the sixth century, with the Deuteronomistic prophetic and nomistic parts beginning from the middle to the last third of the sixth century onward for a considerable period. The books were probably written in → Palestine, perhaps in the neighborhood of Mizpah. It is less likely that they were compiled by exiles.

→ Historiography

Bibliography: Commentaries on 1 and 2 Kings: T. E. FRETHEIM (WestBC; Louisville, Ky., 1999) • J. GRAY (OTL; 3d ed.; London, 1977) • G. HENTSCHEL (NEchtB; 2 vols.; Würzburg, 1984-85) • J. A. MONTGOMERY and H. S. GEHMAN (ICC; Edinburgh, 1951) • M. NOTH (BKAT; vol. 1; Neukirchen, 1968) • M. REHM (2 vols.; Würzburg, 1979-82) • C. L. SEOW (NIB; Nashville, 1999) • D. J. WISEMAN (TOTC; Leicester, 1993) • E. WÜRTHWEIN (ATD; 2 vols.; Göttingen, 1977-84).

Commentaries on 1 Kings: G. RICE (ITC; Grand Rapids, 1990) • J. WALSH (BerOl; Collegeville, Minn., 1996).

Commentaries on 2 Kings: M. COGAN and H. TADMOR (AB; Garden City, N.Y., 1988) • R. L. COHN, D. W. COTTER, J. T. WALSH, and C. FRANKE (BerOl; Collegeville, Minn., 1999).

Other works: C.-J. AXSKJÖLD, *Aram as the Enemy Friend: The Ideological Role of Aram in the Composition of Genesis–2 Kings* (Stockholm, 1998) • P. DUTCHER-WALLS, *Narrative Art, Political Rhetoric: The Case of*

Athaliah and Joash (Sheffield, 1996) • H. D. HOFF-MANN, *Reform und Reformen* (Zurich, 1980) • A. JEPSEN, *Die Quellen des Königsbuches* (2d ed.; Halle, 1956) • M. NOTH, *The Deuteronomistic History* (Sheffield, 1981; orig. pub., 1943) • R. F. PERSON, *The Kings-Isaiah and Kings-Jeremiah Recensions* (Berlin, 1997) • W. SPIECKERMANN, *Juda unter Assur in der Sargonidenzeit* (Göttingen, 1982) • T. VEIJOLA, *Die ewige Dynastie* (Helsinki, 1975).

ERNST WÜRTHWEIN†

Kirchenkampf → Church Struggle

Kiss of Peace

Paul's instruction to "greet one another with a holy kiss" (Rom. 16:16; 1 Cor. 16:20; 2 Cor. 13:12; see also 1 Pet. 5:14) may have been based on a practice in Greco-Roman clubs, in which new members were received with a kiss. A kiss of greeting concluded Christian initiation and served as the welcome to the → Eucharist in → Justin Martyr's (d. ca. 165) *1 Apol.* 65 and the *Apostolic Tradition,* attributed to Hippolytus (d. ca. 236).

The kiss of peace came to conclude the synaxis, or → liturgy of the Word (→ Worship). Then, in the light of Jesus' command to be reconciled with one's brother before offering one's gift at the → altar (Matt 5:23-24), it became more closely associated with the offertory. This was the liturgical position of the kiss of peace in all but the Roman Rite, in which it was located just before the administration of the Communion. This unique location in the Roman → Mass may reflect the Roman practice of the fermentum, in which portions of the consecrated elements from the pope's Eucharist were sent to other eucharistic celebrations around the city.

The kiss of peace became the "Pax Domini sit semper vobiscum" (The peace of the Lord be with you always; *response:* And with your spirit) in the Western medieval Mass. It retained this position in Reformation-era Lutheran, Anglican, and post-Tridentine Roman liturgies.

Recent American Lutheran, Anglican, Methodist, and Presbyterian liturgies (1978, 1979, 1989, 1993) provide the option of exchanging the greeting of peace before the offertory, as in the Eastern liturgies. Since the 1970s it has also been customary to accompany the greeting of peace with a gesture such as a handshake, an embrace, or an actual kiss. Initiated by the presiding minister (→ Pastor, Pastorate),

the peace is shared by all worshipers and is now seen as an act of hospitality.

Bibliography: G. DIX, *The Shape of the Liturgy* (2d ed.; London, 2001; orig. pub., 1945) • J. A. JUNGMANN, *The Mass of the Roman Rite: Its Origins and Development (Missarum sollemnia)* (rev. ed.; New York, 1959) • L. E. PHILLIPS, *The Ritual Kiss in Early Christian Worship* (Cambridge, 1996).

FRANK C. SENN

Kitawala

The Kitawala movement arose in 1911 in what was then British Nyasaland (now Malawi). The Briton Joseph Booth (1851-1932), a free-lance → missionary working for many new Christian groups, directed it from outside. The African Elliott Kenan Kamwana (1872-1956), a student of Booth's, preached the good news inside the country. The American Charles Taze Russell (1852-1916) inveighed in his writings against church and government, which would be eliminated at the return of Christ. Kamwana adapted this teaching to the → colonial situation, preaching that the British would disappear and give place to an African kingdom of peace (→ Crisis Cult). His success was sensational. Between December 1908 and March 1909 he baptized over 9,000 people. Missionaries lobbied the governor, who banned Kamwana (as he had previously done Booth). Kamwana was allowed to return only in 1937.

Meanwhile, migrant laborers from Nyasaland carried the message to the mines in the copper belt and to Katanga (now the province of Shaba in the Democratic Republic of the Congo). The publications of the Watch Tower Society (→ Jehovah's Witnesses), soon translated into African languages, were brought from South Africa. This connection explains the name: "tawa" is a variation of "tower," and "ki-" and "-la" were added from Bantu.

Kitawala finally spread across the two Rhodesias (now Zambia and Zimbabwe), as well as parts of the former Belgian Congo and Mozambique. There was no outstanding prophet, central leadership, or uniform message. Those who were dissatisfied joined for longer or shorter periods. Wherever there was a strike or unrest or resistance, the whites saw Kitawala at work. The result was that it was closely watched, and in the Congo banned and persecuted. Orthodox Jehovah's Witnesses tried in vain to control the movement. Today only remnants of it remain. In Malawi it is no more tolerated than Jehovah's Witnesses are.

Kitawala stirred the masses for various reasons.

Earlier in Nyasaland the Calvinist missionaries had baptized only catechumens (→ Catechesis) who were trained and morally upright (according to Scottish standards). Kamwana, however, baptized all comers, for → Jesus himself had accepted the unlearned and sinners. In some circles it was also hoped that Kitawala would cleanse the land of → magic and → witchcraft, which the Westerners would not stop or suppress. Other adherents of Kitawala set their hopes on "Ba-america," former slaves now far superior to the Westerners in cleverness and goodness. As bringers of salvation, these preachers represented the returning Christ.

→ Cargo Cult

Bibliography: H.-J. GRESCHAT, Kitawala (Marburg, 1967) • R. I. ROTBERG, The Rising of Nationalism in Central Africa: The Making of Malawi and Zambia, 1873-1964 (Cambridge, Mass., 1967).

HANS-JÜRGEN GRESCHAT

Knowledge → Epistemology

Knox, John

The prominent Scottish reformer John Knox (ca. 1513-72) came from a lower-class family in Giffordgate, Scotland, and probably studied at St. Andrews. Although he did not earn any academic degrees, he became a → priest in 1536 and worked till 1543 as a notary in Haddington, then as a private tutor to sons of the Protestant nobility. In 1546 the Protestant preacher George Wishart, whom Knox had tried to protect during his own preaching itinerancy (albeit to no avail), was burned as a heretic by the archbishop of St. Andrews. This event deeply affected Knox because shortly before his arrest Wishart had advised Knox to return to his students (allegedly advising Knox, "Return to your bairns and God bless you. One is sufficient for a sacrifice").

Knox went to St. Andrews, where the Protestants had murdered the archbishop and had now barricaded themselves. When he finally managed to get into the besieged city in 1547, he was offered the "public office and task of → preaching." Although plagued by self-doubt that brought him to tears, when he finally put on "Wishart's cloak," he discovered his calling as "God's trumpeter."

St. Andrews was taken by the French in June, and Knox was captured and had to serve 19 months as a galley slave. The English finally freed him and allowed him to continue propagating the Reforma-

tion in northern England. He was made chaplain to Edward VI (1547-53) and also helped compose the articles of the second edition of the → Book of Common Prayer, especially the so-called Black Rubric regarding the reception of the → sacrament. He also urged the Church of England to undertake a Calvinist reform.

In 1553 Knox fled from the new government of Roman Catholic Mary Tudor (1553-58) and soon was preaching that women regents endangered the state and violated God's commandments. He also emphasized that believing citizens were permitted to engage in armed → resistance against regents who perverted true faith. He supported English → Puritanism and worked from 1554 as a preacher among the English and French refugees in Frankfurt and Geneva, where he was profoundly influenced by John → Calvin and his teachings. In 1555 Knox returned to Scotland for a brief period, married, and continued to advance the cause of the → Reformation. In 1556 he accepted a call to return to Geneva, where he served as pastor of the English church for three years. In Geneva he published The First Blast of the Trumpet against the Monstrous Regiment of Women (1558), targeting the regent, Mary of Guise (1554-59), and Mary Tudor.

In 1559 Knox returned to Scotland once and for all to counter the threat to the Reformation presented by the regent Mary of Guise. His militant and violent preaching ignited a civil war. After Mary died in 1560, Parliament adopted Knox's Reformed confession (Confessio Scotica, 1560; → Confession of Faith) and his → liturgy but rejected his plans for social reform. Knox then held a position at St. Giles, Edinburgh.

From the pulpit and before a royalist public, Knox decried the queen, Mary Stuart, who returned from France in 1561 to win back her kingdom for Roman Catholicism. He preached violent sermons against the celebration of masses for the queen, as well as against the worldliness of her court. Although Knox was hoping for a final victory when she abdicated in 1567, the minority around James VI (1567-1625) continued the partisan rebellion. Knox was quick to make enemies, but at the end of the day he had effectively claimed Scotland for the Reformed faith.

In September 1572, when news of the slaughter of French Protestants at the massacre of St. Bartholomew's Day reached Scotland, Knox suffered a stroke, an event that did not, however, prevent him from continuing to preach violently about the Catholic threat. He died in Edinburgh on November 24, 1572.

→ Calvinism; Reformation Principles; Reformers

Bibliography: Primary sources: History of the Reformation in Scotland (2 vols.; ed. W. C. Dickinson; London, 1949; orig. pub. 1587, 1644) • *Works* (6 vols.; ed. D. Laing; Edinburgh, 1846-64; repr., New York, 1966).

Secondary works: R. G. KYLE, *The Mind of John Knox* (Lawrence, Kans., 1984) • R. K. MARSHALL, *John Knox* (Edinburgh, 2000) • W. S. REID, *The Trumpeter of God* (New York, 1974) • J. G. RIDLEY, *John Knox* (New York, 1968) • H. R. SEFTON, *John Knox: An Account of the Development of His Spirituality* (Edinburgh, 1993).

MICHAEL TRESCHOW

Koinonia

1. Biblical Foundations
   1.1. Terms
   1.2. Paul
   1.3. Other NT
2. Applications through the Centuries
   2.1. Patristic
   2.2. The Fellowship versus the Papal Church
   2.3. Protestant Gemeinschaft, Diakonia
   2.4. Other Uses
3. Ecumenical Developments
   3.1. ARCIC
   3.2. Zizioulas
   3.3. Tillard
   3.4. Lutherans and Free Church
   3.5. World Council of Churches

1. Biblical Foundations

1.1. *Terms*

The Gk. noun *koinōnia* and related words — with the root meaning "(have in) common, communal; have a share or part (in something); go partners in" — occurs some 119 times in the Bible (J. Reumann). There is no corresponding term in Hebrew, little of significant use in the LXX, and no use by Jesus. The background of this word lies in secular Greek, where it meant, for example, "(business) partner" (Luke 5:10) or "possessions held in common" (see Acts 2:44-45; 4:32).

In Latin, *communio,* with its many meanings, was the usual equivalent of *koinōnia,* although sometimes *societas* was used. English renderings vary. For just the last sentence of 2 Corinthians, two versions use four different terms in the text and margin: "fellowship" and "participation in" (13:14 RSV), and "communion" and "sharing in" (13:13 NRSV). The terms always had a certain currency in biblical stud-

ies (F. Hauck) and theology, but a complete history of usages remains to be written.

1.2. *Paul*

Koinonia comes into prominence in the letters of → Paul. The reference to "sharing in the blood of Christ . . . sharing in the body of Christ" (1 Cor. 10:16) occurs in the epistolary context of believers, whom God has called "into the fellowship of his Son" (1 Cor. 1:9; see also 2 Cor. 1:7 and Phil. 3:10 and 4:14, amid sufferings; Phil. 1:5, sharing the gospel in → evangelism; Phlm. 6). More broadly, in the triadic benediction at 2 Cor. 13:13, this fellowship involves "the communion of the Holy Spirit" (i.e., sharing by all Christians in the Spirit; less likely, an association formed by the Spirit); see also Phil. 2:1. Paul also employed "koinonia" in connection with the collection for the poor saints in → Jerusalem (2 Cor. 8:4; 9:13; Rom. 15:26-27) and the support of teachers in a → congregation (Gal. 6:6). The "right hand of fellowship" (Gal. 2:9) pledges mission, unity, and response financially in faith. With infidelity, however, there can be no koinonia (2 Cor. 6:14).

1.3. *Other NT*

While 2 John 11 warns that one can "participate in the evil deeds" of false teachers by welcoming them, 1 John 1:2-7 uses "koinonia" for the relation of believers vertically with the Father and the Son, and horizontally with each other. Heb. 2:14 ("share flesh and blood," with *koinōneō* paralleled by *metechō;* cf. 7:13) refers to Christ's → incarnation, and 13:16 to sharing possessions. The references in 1 Pet. 4:13 and 5:1 are to sharing Christ's suffering and glory; 2 Pet. 1:4 looks toward becoming (future) "participants of the divine nature" by escape from the world.

2. Applications through the Centuries

2.1. *Patristic*

From this biblical base the Greek fathers used koinonia terms in a great variety of ways. They could refer to (1) associations of various sorts; a relationship between persons, even sexual intercourse; or fellowship of human beings with God; (2) the act of sharing — at table fellowship, or between the Father and the Son; of the Logos, in a human body; or the union of the faithful with Christ; (3) the → Eucharist; and (4) distribution of alms (*LPGL* 762-64).

2.2. *The Fellowship versus the Papal Church*

In 1921 C. A. A. Scott touched off a controversy when he argued that *hē koinōnia* at Acts 2:42 referred specifically to "the Fellowship," a technical self-designation for what existed under the Spirit before "the organised Ecclesia" and the later congregational, presbyterial, and episcopal forms of organization (pp. 158-69; → Church Government). In 1943 L. Hertling emphasized *koinōnia/communio* as a key idea in the → early church, which he conceived of as "a network of sacramentally focused local churches bound together ultimately by the mutual openness of their eucharistic celebrations" (ET 4-5), with the bishop of Rome as focal point (2; cf. 58, 65-66). This view was intended as a contrast to juridically oriented understandings of the church. Note the connections and contrasts with → Vatican II sketched in J. Wicks's introduction to the English translation.

2.3. Protestant Gemeinschaft, Diakonia

In Germany a volume on church fellowship among Lutheran, Reformed, and Union churches and on the nature of the Evangelical Church in Germany appeared with the title *Koinonia* (Berlin, 1957). An address by J. G. Davies to the Division of Interchurch Aid and Service to Refugees of the → World Council of Churches (WCC) highlighted money and fraternal aid as legitimate NT expressions of koinonia. Thus koinonia has often been paired with → diakonia as well as with discussion of the nature of the → Trinity, → worship (§2.1), ecclesiology (→ Congregation 2.3.2-3), and → proclamation (§3.3).

2.4. Other Uses

Reflections of increased interest in koinonia include works by J. Hamer, G. Panikulam, and J. Hainz. The term has also been used widely for small groups and for fellowship and → Bible study, in parishes and among youth and students. It is also used in connection with the → base community movement and in → ethics (e.g., in America in the work of Paul Lehmann; → Social Ethics 2.1).

3. Ecumenical Developments

Long and widely known from its use in small-group settings and in Eastern Orthodox thought (→ Orthodoxy 3.8), "koinonia" has come increasingly to be used in bilateral → dialogues and by the WCC itself (→ Ecumenical Theology 2; Heresies and Schisms 2.6).

3.1. ARCIC

An early example is the *Final Report 1981* of the Anglican–Roman Catholic International Commission (ARCIC; see H. Meyer and L. Vischer, 61-129). Here "koinonia" was employed to unify work on the Eucharist and on ministry and → authority. The report of ARCIC II, in 1990, was entitled "Church as Communion" (J. Gros, H. Meyer, and W. G. Rusch, 328-43).

3.2. Zizioulas

Particular impetus came from the treatment of the topic in a series of studies by John D. Zizioulas (later

Metropolitan John of Pergamum), especially *Being as Communion*. Involved are a Trinitarian theology from the → Cappadocian Fathers, stressing the interrelatedness as communion of Father, Son, and Spirit and a corresponding ecclesiology under the → bishop in the local church (which is not the parish but the → diocese). Egalitarian unity of bishops, in the Eucharist, is the result in Zizioulas's neo-patristic synthesis.

3.3. Tillard

Closely related has been the approach of J.-M. R. Tillard, O.P., in a series of treatments, notably *Église d'églises* (an English translation appeared in 1992 but was withdrawn by the publisher for inaccuracies). Koinonia ecclesiology stresses salvation as ecclesial, with the church in God's plan (see Ephesians) as a zone for reconciled humanity. Dioceses have local identity but are in communion with other dioceses through the bishops; there is thus synodality, "a church of churches."

3.4. Lutherans and Free Church

Lutherans made use of koinonia as a concept in moving toward a constitutional understanding of the → Lutheran World Federation in 1990 as a communion of churches (J. H. Schjørring, P. Kumari, and N. A. Hjelm, chap. 5 and throughout). A continuing quest for definition of the term is reflected in a statement and essays found in a volume edited by H. Holze.

The fruitfulness of the theme for → free church thought is suggested by Miroslav Volf's volume *After Our Likeness*. Against a background of proposals by Zizioulas and Joseph Ratzinger (summarized 29-123), Volf takes up the church as image of the Trinity, ecclesially reflecting concepts of Trinitarian personhood, in ways congruent with radical Baptist and other ideas of the church as gathered community.

3.5. World Council of Churches

In the WCC as "a fellowship of churches," and particularly in its → Faith and Order Commission, the theme of koinonia has received major attention. The final report from the WCC 1991 Canberra Assembly was entitled "The Unity of the Church as Koinonia: Gift and Calling" (M. Kinnamon, 172-74; Gros, Meyer, and Rusch, 936-38). The theme of the Fifth World Conference on Faith and Order (Santiago de Compostela, 1993) was "Towards Koinonia in Faith, Life, and Witness." The treatment of this theme, drafted over the previous two years, became a position paper in the official report, *On the Way to Fuller Koinonia* (Kinnamon, 263-95; see also section reports on pp. 228-62, esp. "The Understanding of Koinonia" and "Message to the Churches," Gros,

Meyer, and Rusch, 939-41). This position paper exhibits both valuable insights and unsolved problems, as well as revealing how elastic the term has become. Does a relational ecclesiology suffice, or should koinonia also encompass all humanity, creation, and justice issues?

Analysis of bilateral dialogues (S. Wood) and other proposals shows how widespread among the churches koinonia is, and in how many areas, especially church and ministry, the term appeared in the late 20th century. See "Perspectives on Koinonia" (Pentecostal–Roman Catholic dialogue, 1989) and "The Church as Communion in Christ" (Disciples of Christ–Roman Catholic dialogue, 1992), in Gros, Meyer, and Rusch, 735-52 and 386-98. The U.S. Lutheran–Roman Catholic dialogue, beginning in 1998, has made koinonia ecclesiology its topic for a tenth round of dialogue.

Bibliography: T. F. Best and G. Gassmann, eds., *On the Way to Fuller Koinonia: Official Report of the Fifth World Conference on Faith and Order* (Geneva, 1994) • A. Birmelé, *La communion ecclésiale. Progrès oecuméniques et enjeux méthodologiques* (Paris, 2000) • J. G. Davies, *Members of One Another: Aspects of Koinonia* (London, 1958) • N. J. Duff, *Humanization and the Politics of God: The* Koinonia *Ethics of Paul Lehmann* (Grand Rapids, 1992) • J. Gros, H. Meyer, and W. G. Rusch, eds., *Growth in Agreement II: Reports and Agreed Statements of Ecumenical Conversations on a World Level, 1982-1998* (Grand Rapids, 2000) • J. Hainz, *Koinonia. "Kirche" als Gemeinschaft bei Paulus* (Regensburg, 1982); idem, "Κοινωνία κτλ.," *EDNT* 2.303-5 • J. Hamer, *Church Is a Communion* (London, 1964) • F. Hauck, "Κοινός κτλ.," *TDNT* 3.789-809 • L. Hertling, *Communio: Church and Papacy in Early Christianity* (Chicago, 1972; orig. pub., 1943) • H. Holze, ed., *The Church as Communion: Lutheran Contributions to Ecclesiology* (Geneva, 1997) • M. Kinnamon, ed., *Signs of the Spirit: Official Report [of the] Seventh Assembly, Canberra, Australia* (Geneva, 1991) • P. L. Lehmann, *Ethics in a Christian Context* (New York, 1963) • H. Meyer and L. Vischer, eds., *Growth in Agreement: Reports and Agreed Statements of Ecumenical Conversations on a World Level* (New York, 1984) • G. Panikulam, *Koinōnia in the NT* (Rome, 1979) • J. Reumann, "Koinonia in Scripture: Survey of Biblical Texts," Best and Gassmann, *On the Way to Fuller Koinonia,* 37-69 • J. H. Schjørring, P. Kumari, and N. A. Hjelm, eds., *From Federation to Communion: The History of the Lutheran World Federation* (Minneapolis, 1997) • C. A. A. Scott, *Christianity according to St. Paul* (Cambridge, 1927) • J.-M. R. Tillard, *Église d'églises. L'ecclésiologie de communion* (Paris, 1987) •

M. Volf, *After Our Likeness: The Church as the Image of the Trinity* (Grand Rapids, 1998) • S. Wood, "Ecclesial Koinonia in Ecumenical Dialogues," *OiC* 30 (1994) 124-45 • J. Zizioulas, *Being as Communion: Studies in Personhood and the Church* (Crestwood, N.Y., 1985).

John Reumann

Kolping Society

The Kolping Society, which grew out of the "Kolping Families" founded from 1849 in Cologne by Adolph Kolping (1813-65) for young men working in large cities, is a family-oriented Roman Catholic social society (→ Societies and Associations, Ecclesiastical). By the time of Kolping's death, there were 418 Kolping societies in many countries of the world. In the United States the first Kolping societies were organized in 1859. Presently they are organized as the Catholic Kolping Society of America (1923).

The distinctive feature of this movement is the local community centered on "Kolping houses," which are variously residences, centers, or parish facilities. Some groups are formed for young adults, others for senior citizens or for sports or community service. Mainly they offer educational and → leisure programs to meet the needs of workers, all in line with Kolping's concern for social renewal through religious → education, vocational training, and instruction in the → family and social involvement. Membership is now open to people in every type of vocation. The broader organization is according to area, diocese, and nation, with a spiritual leader as well as a president.

In its work of development the Kolping Society seeks to foster and promote international cooperation and solidarity. In the → Third World it aims to train skilled workers and to help create a middle class. Constant expansion (e.g., to Portugal, Kenya, Uganda, India, Bolivia, Chile, Colombia, Peru, and Mexico since 1980) shows how relevant its goal is of bringing about social change by individual and social development (→ Social Ethics), by the kindling of personal responsibility, by granting opportunities for education, and by the practicing of communal democratic life in a family fellowship.

Worldwide, the movement is based in Cologne. In 1999 it had 450,000 members in 53 countries, organized in more than 5,000 families. Germany had the largest membership with (as of 30 June) 276,042 members in 2,774 families.

→ Catholicism (Roman); Labor Movement; Labor Unions, Christian; Lay Movements

Bibliography: S. BERGEN, *Social Democracy and the Working Class in the Nineteenth and Twentieth Century Germany* (New York, 2000) • C. FELDMANN, *Adolph Kolping. Für ein soziales Christentum* (2d ed.; Freiburg, 1991) • H. GRANVOGL, *Adolph Kolping und die christlich-soziale Bewegung. Eine regionalgeschichtliche Untersuchung zum Verhältnis zwischen Kirche und Arbeitnehmer in den Jahren 1830-1866* (Augsburg, 1987) • H.-J. KRACHT, *Adolph Kolping. Priester, Pädagoge, Publizist im Dienst christlicher Sozialreform* (Freiburg, 1993) • H. A. KREWITT, "Kolping Society, Catholic," *NCE* 8.248 • F. LÜTTGEN, *Johan Gregor Breuer und Adolph Kolping. Studien zur Frühgeschichte des Katholischen Gesellenvereins* (Paderborn, 1997) • H. A. RAEM, *Katholischer Gesellenverein und Deutsche Kolpingsfamilie in der Ära des Nationalsozialismus* (Mainz, 1982) • P. STEINKE, *Leitbild für die Kirche. Adolph Kolping, Sendung und Zeugnis seines Werkes heute* (Paderborn, 1992).

WALTER SCHÖPSDAU

Koran → Qur'an

Korea → North Korea; South Korea

Krishna Consciousness, International Society for

1. Founder
2. As Western Movement of Spiritual Awakening
3. Prehistory
4. Indian Sources
5. Historical Evaluation

1. Founder

Abhay Charan De (1896-1977), founder of the International Society for Krishna Consciousness (ISKCON), was born in Calcutta, where he received university training in philosophy, English, and economics. In 1922 he came in contact with the Vishnu Gaudiya Mission (→ Hinduism 3.3), whose founder, Bhaktisiddhanta Sarasvati Thakura (d. 1937), had prepared the way for the worldwide work of the 32d guru in a succession that had begun with the prehistorical avatars, or "descents," of the gods (see 3). In 1933 De became a formal disciple of Bhaktisiddhanta, who in late 1936, just before his death, commissioned De to spread Krishna consciousness in English to the West.

Later De embraced the call under the name of A. C. Bhaktivedanta Swami Prabhupada and in 1959

became a sannyasin, one who accepted the renounced order of life. Prabhupada traveled to the United States in 1965 to preach Krishna consciousness, and in 1966 he founded ISKCON in New York City. By the time of his death in Vrindavan, south of New Delhi, he had supported the spread of ISKCON (from 1968 onward) to Great Britain, Netherlands, and Germany.

2. As Western Movement of Spiritual Awakening

ISKCON temples and places of instruction and → meditation have been set up throughout the world in cities, in railroad stations, and in castles. These efforts are supported by a very productive and scholarly press with many branches, the Bhaktivedanta Book Trust. The term "order" might be used to describe the organization of devotees (mostly male), who meet daily for five-hour services of → worship but do not live a community life. In 1998 there were about 3,000 core members of ISKCON in the United States, 8,000 worldwide, with up to 250,000 "congregational," or lay, members. The number of unorganized adherents is greater and amounts to millions in India, where the movement had its origins.

3. Prehistory

The original movement, which has now been strengthened, consisted and consists of followers of the Bengal Brahman mystic and philosopher Visvambhara Misra (1485-1533), who was born in Navadvīpa on the Ganges, 80 km. (50 mi.) north of what is now Calcutta. Under the name "Caitanya" (or "Krishna Caitanya"), he brought about a reformation of the older Vishnu Mādhva movement through → Bhakti piety. This movement included a communication from the god Krishna, which became canonical along with the → Bhagavad Gita, and the story of the → love of shepherdesses for their hero Krishna, which rests on a very different tradition centered on the town of Mathura.

Krishna, an avatar of Vishnu, identified with Vishnu as his representative and thus stood at the start of a chain of tradition, at the beginning of which Vishnu's power as creator merely followed Krishna as a personal Brahma (i.e., creator). At the center of this tradition the fervent admirers of Caitanya could even exalt him above Krishna. And at the end of the chain Prabhupada bore witness to the mystically erotic love of the → soul for the absolute deity that is both identical with it and different from it, and he also offered a scholarly summary of the related written tradition of the Vedas.

4. Indian Sources

By grammatical and lexical exegesis, English translation, and verse-by-verse commentary, Prabhupada gave prominence to the longest, finest, and best known of the 18 → Puranas, which gathered up Vedic Vishnu tradition in the period from the eighth to the tenth century and which, in virtue of its tenth canto, became the starting point for a new Bhakti-Krishna piety, thus taking on the name "Bhagavata Purana" (i.e., "Story of the followers of the Exalted One"). In a way that is related to the interpretation of the Bhagavad Gita by Rāmānuja (ca. 1017-1137, but see also the philosophy of Śankara [700?-?750]), this work stresses from the classical tradition the idea of a gracious god, namely, Krishna, with his eternally beloved Rādhā.

Of the 20 biographical works of the disciples of Caitanya and their students, Prabhupada then canonized the most authentic and the best thought out metaphysically (→ Metaphysics), the *Nectar of the Glorious Deeds of Caitanya* (see *Śrī Caitanya-Caritāmṛta*). This work, composed in Bengali between 1608 and 1615/17, relates the three stages of the life of Caitanya, the "first, middle, and last game" (*Ādi, Madhya, Antya Līlā*), to those in which Krishna unfolds himself in his dealings with the world, dancing, loving, and having no specific goal in mind.

Prabhupada's commentary applies the cosmic game of unfolding, which was brought to earth with the descent of Krishna and other masters, including Caitanya, to the feeling, spirit, and bodily movement of individuals. Individuals can achieve this unfolding only by the trancelike recitation of the mantra "Hare Krishna." ("Hare" is the vocative of *hari*, "the fire-colored," another name for Vishnu or Krishna.) This recitation makes unnecessary the reading of holy scripture or consideration of a system of universal redemption. The recitation involves the 16-fold repetition of a "rosary" of 108 pearls, and therefore 1,728 utterances in all. The first two words of this 16-word mantra give ISKCON its unofficial name: the Hare Krishna movement.

5. Historical Evaluation

The longing for redemption into which the worshiping legacy of the Vishnu → sects transformed itself under the oppressive Muslim occupation of North India (Bengal under the Delhi sultans from 1211 and under the Mongols from 1529) could take the new form of a readiness for loving surrender (*bhakti*), for nonviolence (*ahiṁsā*), and for divine → grace (*prasāda*). Furthermore, as Krishna Consciousness it could accommodate alternative movements with a spiritual basis in modern → industrial

societies, especially when incorporating Mahatma Gandhi's (1869-1948) description of the poor as *harijan*, or children of Hari.

The resultant missionary success of ISKCON is countered by the fact that Caitanya's work has helped to give the striving for freedom concrete form in Bengal nationalism (which the relatively new state of Bangladesh hardly expresses). We do not find this element in Prabhupada, which has been a hindrance to ISKCON and helped to keep its membership small. At the same time, Western and Eastern admirers must wrestle with the implications of this most impressive contemporary achievement of Indian thought.

→ Mysticism; New Religions; Youth Religions

Bibliography: Commentaries on primary sources: Bhagavad-gītā as It Is (New York, 1983) • *Śrī Caitanya-Caritāmṛta of Kṛṣṇadāsa Kavirāja Gosvāmī* (3 *līlās* [episodes] in 17 vols.; New York, 1973-75) • *Śrī Īśopaniṣad* (New York, n.d.) • *Śrīmad-Bhāgavatam of Kṛṣṇa-Dvaipāyana Vyāsa* (12 cantos in 48 vols.; New York, 1972-86).

Original works of Swami Prabhupada: Dialectic Spiritualism: A Vedic View of Western Philosophy (Moundsville, W.Va., 1985) posthumously published writings • *Krsna: The Supreme Personality of Godhead* (3 vols.; Los Angeles, 1970) • *Teachings of Lord Caitanya: The Golden Avatara* (Los Angeles, 1988) • *Varṇāśrama Dharma* (New York [after 1973]) on the caste system.

ISKCON publications: Back to Godhead (1944-) • SATSVARŪPA DĀSA GOSWAMI, *Prabhupāda. Der Mensch, der Weise, sein Leben, sein Vermächtnis* (Vaduz, 1984; ET *Prabhupada: He Built a House in Which the Whole World Can Live* [cond. ed.; Los Angeles, 1996]) • *Origins: Higher Dimensions of Science* (Los Angeles, 1984) • *Songs of the Vaisnava Acaryas* (trans. A. C. B. S. Prabhupada; Los Angeles, 1974) • HARIKEŚA SWAMI VIṢṆU-PĀDA, *Handbuch des Kṛṣṇa-Bewußtseins* (n.p., 1985); idem, *Varṇāśrama: Manifesto for Social Sanity* (New York, 1981).

Secondary works: D. G. BROMLEY and L. D. SHINN, eds., *Krishna Consciousness in the West* (Lewisburg, Pa., 1989) • J. A. B. VAN BUITENEN, *Rāmānuja on the Bhagavadgītā* (Delhi, 1968) • J. B. CARMAN, *The Theology of Rāmānuja: An Essay in Interreligious Understanding* (New Haven, 1974) • W. EIDLITZ, *Kṛṣṇa-Caitanya. Sein Leben und seine Lehre* (Stockholm, 1968) • S. P. HUYLER, *Meeting God: Elements of Hindu Devotion* (New Haven, 1999) • E. B. ROCHFORD JR., *Hare Krishna in America* (New Brunswick, N.J., 1985) • E. WEBER and T. RAJ CHOPRA, eds., *Shri Krishna Caitanya and the Bhakti Religion* (Frankfurt, 1988).

CARSTEN COLPE

Kulturkampf

1. Term and Historical Situation
2. Course
3. End and Result

1. Term and Historical Situation

The liberal R. Virchow (1821-1902) first used the term "Kulturkampf" in an 1873 address to describe the conflict between the new German Empire (from 1871) and the → Roman Catholic Church. The state effort to extend control over the church was part of the wider sociopolitical struggle between the modern → state and the traditional 19th-century church (→ Church and State; Tradition). A new order of relationship between the church and the world was coming into being with the process of → secularization. The conflict was by no means restricted to the German Empire of O. von Bismarck (1815-98). In various forms and with varying degrees of vehemence, it affected many other European countries (e.g., Switzerland and Austria). Somewhat later and with a different accent it also affected the French Third Republic.

The specific background of the Kulturkampf was the reaction of the → pope to 19th-century → liberalism and its deconfessionalizing of public life from the time of the 1848 → revolution. Increasingly during this period civil society was attempting to break free from the influence of the church, which for its part was making renewed efforts to exert ecclesiastical → authority (see esp. the encyclical *Quanta cura* of 1864, with its attached → Syllabus of Errors, which championed the complete independence of the church, denounced secular education, and demanded the subjection of all scholarly research to the church). Then at → Vatican I (1870) the church elevated papal → infallibility in matters of doctrine and morals to the rank of a dogma. Given these tensions, it is not surprising that conflict arose in fields in which the church and the modern state both had an interest, especially education.

A new political edge was given to the issue when the papacy saw its power basis in Rome diminished by the completion of Italian unification and the ending of the → Papal States, and when German unification under the leadership of Prussia caused German Roman Catholics to feel that they had been pushed to the very margin of developments. In the Center Party (i.e., the Catholic bloc), then, forces came together that felt doubly threatened by the new situation, that is, by the rise to power of the Protestant Prussian monarchy and by the claim of the modern secular state to sovereignty.

2. Course

Open conflict between state and church came directly after the successful ending of the Franco-Prussian War (1870-71), when the archbishop of Cologne took ecclesiastical measures against Bonn professors of theology who were not ready to accept the decisions of Vatican I. When the bishop of East Prussian Ermeland then withdrew the → missio canonica from a religious teacher in Braunsberg (Pol. Braniewo) who had repudiated Vatican I, Bismarck, who later linked the beginning of the Kulturkampf to the problem of the Polish → minority in East Prussia, reacted in July 1871 by abolishing the Catholic department in the Prussian Ministry of Religion.

Logically the conflict came to a head in the field of education. In March 1872 a law was passed regarding inspection of schools that gave the church only a limited and revocable right of inspection. In June Prussia forbade monks and nuns to teach in the schools, and then in July an imperial law banished the → Jesuits from the country. Earlier, in December 1871, an addition had been made to the penal code on the prompting of Bavaria — the so-called Pulpit Paragraph — which imposed penalties for misusing the spiritual office to disturb the public peace.

The Kulturkampf reached its climax with the so-called May laws of 1873, which A. Falk (1827-1900), a radically liberal minister of religion, introduced to define more sharply the limits of the church's disciplinary power and to regulate the training and placement of pastors, who now were allowed to study only at state universities. These laws and their penalties produced an intolerable situation involving vacant bishoprics, imprisonment of priests, lack of teachers, and so forth. Measures were also introduced to make civil → marriage (§1) compulsory in Prussia (1874) and then in the empire (1875).

The Kulturkampf left its mark on the Protestant church as well. The school inspection law affected confessions and evoked Protestant protest. Civil marriage was less troubling to Protestants because they were less firmly attached to the church. The Kulturkampf weakened the bond between the state and the Protestant church and released energies that went to the formation of a synodical constitution for Prussia (→ Synod) in the years 1875 and 1876.

3. End and Result

The end of the 1870s saw the conclusion of the Kulturkampf as new circumstances brought a new orientation in ecclesiastical politics. At the Vatican Leo XIII (1878-1903) was less uncompromising than → Pius IX (1846-78), and Bismarck, in a change of domestic policy, turned from the liberals and sought support from the Catholic Center Party and the conservatives as the battle against the Social Democrats became his main concern. With a series of mitigating laws (1880-87) the more extreme positions enforced during the Kulturkampf were abandoned, and procedures were established for the filling of vacancies. Yet the central laws that asserted the authority of the modern secular state remained in force, including school inspection, registering, and notification of religious appointments. Parts of the Roman Catholic population also remained uneasy about the new German Empire.

→ Modern Church History

Bibliography: M. L. ANDERSON, "The Kulturkampf and the Course of German History," *CCH* 19 (1986) 82-115 • E. L. EVANS, *The German Center Party, 1870-1933: A Study in Political Catholicism* (Carbondale, Ill., 1981) • R. LILL, *Die Wende im Kulturkampf. Leo XIII, Bismarck und die Zentrumspartei, 1878-80* (Tübingen, 1973) • R. LILL and W. ALTGELD, eds., *Der Kulturkampf* (Zurich, 1997) • R. J. ROSS, *The Failure of Bismarck's Kulturkampf: Catholicism and State Power in Imperial Germany, 1871-1887* (Washington, D.C., 1998) • H. W. SMITH, *German Nationalism and Religious Conflict: Culture, Ideology, Politics, 1870-1914* (Princeton, 1995) • R. VON THADDEN, "Bismarck—ein Lutheraner?" *Weltliche Kirchengeschichte* (Göttingen, 1989) 146-63; idem, "Die Geschichte der Kirchen und Konfessionen," *Handbuch der Preussischen Geschichte* (ed. W. Neugebauer; Berlin, 2001) 3.566-606.

RUDOLF VON THADDEN

Kurds

1. Names
2. Identity
3. History
4. Religion
5. Present-Day Problems

1. Names

Kurdistan, originally a term for "steppe country" and later for the land of the Kurds, was the term given by the Seljuk government of Iran (1092-1194) to a region that must have stretched from between Lakes Van (in present-day western Turkey) and Urmia (in eastern Iran) south to the Zagros Mountains (extending along the Iran-Iraq border). The basic word came to be used, as in Arabic, as a collective and denoted "tiller of the field" or "shepherd."

Today some scholars identify the Kurds as the Karduchoi of Xenophon's *Anabasis* (3.5.15–4.1.11), a group living east of the Upper Tigris, those whom Strabo called the Gordyaioi (*Geog.* 16.1.24). This identification would presuppose a self-designation of Iranian origin that might have been borne by the successors of the Medes who had moved westward beginning in the fifth century.

2. Identity

After these obscure beginnings, relative to which the arguments are largely politically motivated, the ethnogenesis came to end at the latest in resistance against marauding Arabs in either A.D. 637 or 651. From this point on, the identity of the Kurds is clearly established by the fact that their language, folklore (legends, style of clothing), social structure (→ marriage of cousins, property rights displaying either agreement or competition between feudal aristocrats and economically independent farmers and → nomads), and moral code (graded loyalties to and between the agas of families, clans, and tribes — and between these secular leaders and the sheikhs of religious orders and their followers) are all Northwest Iranian.

3. History

The Kurds were conquered by the Arabs in the 7th century. The region was held by the Seljuk Turks in the 11th century, by the Mongols from the 13th to the 15th centuries, and then by the Safawid and Ottoman Empires. Having been decimated by the Turks in the years between 1915 and 1918 and then having struggled to free themselves from Ottoman rule, the Kurds were encouraged by the Turkish defeat in World War I and by subsequent pleas for self-determination for non-Turkish nationalities in the empire. The Treaty of Sèvres (1920), which ended the Ottoman Empire, provided for the creation of an independent Kurdish state. After Turkey's military revival under Kemal Atatürk, however, the Treaty of Lausanne (1923), which superseded Sèvres, failed to mention the creation of a Kurdish state.

These basic ethnic realities have repeatedly given rise to historical movements, including the founding of independent principalities and of dynasties outside Kurdistan (both up to the 16th cent.). In modern times, either of their own volition or through ruling or interested powers (Turks, Europeans, etc.), the Kurds related to social and political entities by which or against which they have had to define themselves as a people, a → nation, or a → minority. Often they have sought by revolt to move on from the last status to the first or second, but they have never been able to achieve the intended result of maintaining their own state.

With the end of the Persian Gulf War in 1991, another Kurdish uprising against Iraq was crushed; nearly 500,000 Kurds fled to the Iraq-Turkey border, and more than one million fled to Iran (→ Refugees). Thousands subsequently returned to their homes under U.N. protection. In 1992 the Kurds established an "autonomous region" in northern Iraq and held a general election. Their community was badly divided, however, into two opposing groups that engaged in sporadic warfare with each other. In 1999 the two groups of Iraqi Kurds ceased hostilities.

4. Religion
Reconstructing the original religion and → mythology of the Kurds from their neighbors and from modern folklore might seem possible, but it has not yet been done with any success. Subsequent to their origins, the varied orientation of the Kurds made them receptive to → syncretism (via the Ahl-e-Haqq, Alawites, and Yezidis). The need to overcome diversity, however, led a few to become Islamic Shiites (the dervish orders of the Naqshbandīyah and Qādirīya; → Shia, Shiites), but more than two-thirds became → Sunnis (of the Shafiʿite law school). Christians who live in the Kurdish territory — persons belonging to the → Syrian Orthodox Church, the Assyrian or → Nestorian Church, or the → Armenian Apostolic Church — are not seen as authentically Kurdish, even though in some cases they have adopted the language and customs of the Kurds.

5. Present-Day Problems
Since World War I the Kurds have suffered discrimination at the hands of newly created states. They have been the victims of social → prejudice and disparagement, have been denied the → rights promised by the Iranian revolution of 1979, and have been exposed to open → genocide by Iraq during its war with Iran (1980-88).

Attempts at a Kurdish federation, even in light of the great freedom movements of 1989, have made no headway against prevailing political orders, despite the large number of Kurds (estimates range from a conservative 11 million, through 14 million posited by sociologists, to a figure of 18-20 million used by nationalists), the wide extent of their language (three main groups, with two dialects), and the scope of the territory in which they live (in all, 410,000 sq. km. / 158,000 sq. mi., an area between

the size of France and Germany, covering 194,400 sq. km. in Turkey, 124,950 sq. km. in Iran, 72,000 sq. km. in Iraq, and 18,300 sq. km. in Syria). Several political parties in countries of the region, Kurdish academies and academics, and various friendly exile groups and organizations have been at work on behalf of the Kurds, but thus far in uncoordinated fashion.

Bibliography: W. BEHN, The Kurds in Iran: A Selected and Annotated Bibliography (London, 1977) • M. VAN BRUINESSEN, Agha, Shaikh, and State: The Social and Political Structures of Kurdistan (London, 1992) • N. ENTESSAR, Kurdish Ethnonationalism (Boulder, Colo., 1992) • D. McDOWALL, A Modern History of the Kurds (2d ed.; London, 2000) • L. I. MEHO and K. L. MAGLAUGHLIN, comps., Kurdish Culture and Society: An Annotated Bibliography (Westport, Conn., 2001) • R. W. OLSON, Turkey's Relations with Iran, Syria, Israel, and Russia, 1991-2000: The Kurdish and Islamist Questions (Costa Mesa, Calif., 2001) chap. 4; idem, ed., The Kurdish Nationalist Movement in the 1990s: Its Impact on Turkey and the Middle East (Lexington, Ky., 1996) • Ö. WAHLBECK, Kurdish Diasporas: A Comparative Study of Kurdish Refugee Communities (New York, 1999).
CARSTEN COLPE

Kuwait

	1960	1980	2000
Population (1,000s):	278	1,375	1,966
Annual growth rate (%):	10.53	4.48	2.18
Area: 17,818 sq. km. (6,880 sq. mi.)			

A.D. 2000

Population density: 110/sq. km. (286/sq. mi.)
Births / deaths: 1.93 / 0.24 per 100 population
Fertility rate: 2.44 per woman
Infant mortality rate: 12 per 1,000 live births
Life expectancy: 76.7 years (m: 74.9, f: 79.0)
Religious affiliation (%): Muslims 89.9, Christians 8.0 (Roman Catholics 4.2, indigenous 3.3, other Christians 0.5), other 2.1.

1. Geography and Economy
2. Political Development
3. Religions
4. Religious Policy

1. Geography and Economy
The economy of the State of Kuwait is based on oil, which in 2000 accounted for nearly 75 percent of government income. In the same year Kuwait main-

tained an average production of 2.1 million barrels of crude oil per day and had 10 percent of the world's oil reserves.

In 2000 Kuwaiti Arabs constituted only 37 percent of the total population. The rest were Arabs from other places (24.6 percent, esp. from Egypt, Syria, Lebanon, and Palestine); Bidoon (lit. "without"), or stateless Arab refugees struggling to gain recognition within Kuwait (6.4 percent); and non-Arabs (32.0 percent, esp. guest workers from the Philippines, Pakistan, India, and Iran, with a few also from Europe). In 2000 almost all of the population (97 percent) lived in metropolitan areas.

2. Political Development

From 1546 to 1918 Kuwait was under the sovereignty of the Ottoman Empire. The Al-Sabah ruling family, which came to Kuwait in the early 18th century, began its autonomous rule in 1756. In 1899 the emir of Kuwait made a treaty with Great Britain, by the terms of which Kuwait maintained control over its internal affairs, with Great Britain assuming responsibility for the country's security and foreign relations (→ Colonialism). The British also provided advisers to staff the country's nascent modern → bureaucracy.

Kuwait became independent from Great Britain in June 1961, taking the form of a constitutional monarchy. (With its Bedouin traditions, however, it might also be called a tribal → democracy.) Later that year it formed a freely elected parliament, called the National Assembly, with 50 members. Only literate males over 21 have voting rights. Because of differences in opinion with the ruling emir, the assembly was dissolved in July 1986. Political parties are not allowed, although many nonofficial political groups and forums operate within Kuwait. In 1981 Kuwait joined the Gulf Cooperation Council. In August 1990 Iraq invaded Kuwait, which remained under Iraqi occupation until it was liberated in February 1991 (→ War).

3. Religions

According to the 1962 constitution, Kuwait is an → Islamic state, and the → Shariʿa is considered a main source of legislation. Nearly 90 percent of the population is Muslim, with → Sunnis in the majority, but with a large minority of → Shiites. The non-Muslim population consists mainly of Christian, Hindu, and Farsi foreign workers.

In 2000 the largest Christian groups were the → Roman Catholics (75,000 persons affiliated) and the → Coptic Orthodox (60,000). The several smaller groups (numbering no more than a few thousand adherents each) included Catholic → Melchites of Antioch, → Anglicans or Episcopalians, the → Armenians of the Apostolic Church, and the Arabs of the Eastern Orthodox and → Oriental Syrian (Syriac) Orthodox Churches of Antioch.

4. Religious Policy

The Kuwaiti government is relatively tolerant in religious matters. Although → proselytism of Moslems is illegal, immigrant religious minorities are permitted some worship facilities.

Under the influence of the Ayatollah Khomeini's (1900?-1989) Islamic revolution in Iran, → fundamentalist forces, mainly of Iranian Shiite origin, strengthened their call for a stricter application of Islamic laws in all Muslim nations. For this reason, Iran supported the movement of opposition inside Kuwait in order to exert pressure on the Kuwaiti regime to reduce its aid to Iraq in Iraq's war against Iran (1980-88). Fear of being swamped by foreigners and of having reduced revenues from oil sharpened internal division and offered fruitful soil for the growth of fundamentalist ideas.

→ Islam and Christianity

Bibliography: G. E. FULLER and R. R. FRANCKE, *The Arab Shiʿa: The Forgotten Muslims* (New York, 1999) 155-78 • H. A. HASSAN, *The Iraqi Invasion of Kuwait: Religion, Identity, and Otherness in the Analysis of War and Conflict* (London, 1999) • M. JOYCE, *Kuwait, 1945-1996: An Anglo-American Perspective* (London, 1998) • A. N. LONGVA, *Walls Built on Sand: Migration, Exclusion, and Society in Kuwait* (Boulder, Colo., 1997) • H. MUGHNI, *Women in Kuwait: The Politics of Gender* (London, 2001) • B. J. SLOT, *The Origins of Kuwait* (2d ed.; Kuwait City, 1998) • M. TETREAULT, *Stories of Democracy: Politics and Society in Contemporary Kuwait* (New York, 2000) • K. L. VAUX, *Ethics and the Gulf War: Religion, Rhetoric, and Righteousness* (Boulder, Colo., 1992).

THOMAS KOSZINOWSKI

Kyrgyzstan

1. General Situation
2. Ancient Christian History
3. Modern Imperial and Soviet Periods
4. Contemporary Crisis for Islam and Christianity

1. General Situation

The present independent state of Kyrgyzstan was established in 1991 when the USSR ceased to exist (→ Soviet Union). Thereafter the former Kirgiz Soviet Socialist Republic began a process of transformation

	1960	1980	2000
Population (1,000s):	2,173	3,628	4,543
Annual growth rate (%):	3.39	2.02	0.86

Area: 198,500 sq. km. (76,600 sq. mi.)

A.D. 2000

Population density: 23/sq. km. (59/sq. mi.)
Births / deaths: 2.31 / 0.69 per 100 population
Fertility rate: 2.84 per woman
Infant mortality rate: 35 per 1,000 live births
Life expectancy: 69.2 years (m: 65.3, f: 73.1)
Religious affiliation (%): Muslims 65.8, nonreligious 18.5, Christians 9.2 (Orthodox 6.4, unaffiliated 1.6, other Christians 1.3), atheists 5.5, other 1.0.

into a secular Islamic state. Kyrgyzstan is located on the western end of the Tian Shan mountain range (which extends into northwestern China), and 85 percent of its land is higher than 1,500 m. (5,000 ft.) above sea level. Ethnic Kyrgyz (also Kirghiz, Khirgiz, or Qyrgyz) total close to 60 percent of the total population, and Russians, 22 percent, with smaller percentages of Uzbeks (esp. in the west in the Fergana Valley), Ukrainians, Tatars, Chinese, Germans, and Tungans (Dungans). A further 120,000 Kyrgyz live in neighboring Uzbekistan, Tajikistan, and Kazakhstan. Another group of approximately 110,000 Kyrgyz moved to Xinjiang Uighur Autonomous Region of China in 1930 to avoid the antireligious policies of the Soviets.

When the new Kyrgyz state was declared, it was announced that Kyrgyz, a Turkic language, would be the sole official language in all administrative offices by 1994. The language is closely related to Kazakh, with many Mongolian and Altai-Turkic elements. It was written in Arabic script until 1920, when Cyrillic became required. From 1920 till 1991 the Kirgiz SSR, like all other parts of the USSR, used Russian as its official language, which many people in rural areas failed to learn. The government now is interested in undoing the legacy of Russian and then Soviet imperial control, but because a large part of the population is not Kyrgyz, Russian still serves as a lingua franca. A constitutional amendment in 1996 permitted the further official use of Russian.

When the new Kyrgyzstan emerged, there was talk of its becoming a central Asian Switzerland, for it has a strong agricultural tradition, formerly producing enough buttermilk, yogurt, and cheese to supply the entire Soviet Union. Known also for political and religious tolerance, it was thought that prospects for a transformation into a modern → democracy were good. Just a few years earlier, Soviet leaders had acted to remove key members of the ad-

ministration who were charged with corruption, and the new party secretary Askar Akayev, now president of Kyrgyzstan (since October 1990), had long headed the Academy of Sciences. But then a drift began into authoritarianism and economic decline.

New nongovernmental organizations (NGOs) began proliferating in Kyrgyzstan in the mid-1990s, with 700 having registered by January 1998; many of them have religious ties. Most of these groups are "grant based" — that is, local organizations of professionals and people of goodwill, with little grassroots support, disbursing aid from foreign foundations or → relief organizations. A continuing problem is inadequate cooperation between such NGOs and the Kyrgyz government, especially given the increasingly authoritarian regime of Akayev.

Kyrgyzstan slipped into serious poverty between 1991 and 1995, the gross domestic product dropping by 75 percent, and a large percentage of the working population suffered from wage arrears. According to the World Bank, 62.5 percent of the population was below the poverty line in 1996 (set at $40, or 716 som, per month), and 18.2 percent was below the extreme poverty line (221 som). For the needed turnaround, both the government and the NGOs must demonstrate a new level of fiscal transparency and must make a new commitment to the basic goal of alleviating → poverty.

2. Ancient Christian History

Some sources claim that as early as A.D. 90 Christians were already present in the city of Osh, and archaeological discoveries point to the early presence of Christianity near Issyk-Kul (lit. "warm lake") and the Talass Valley. Other sources tell of Christian → bishops from the regions of central Asia extending from Samarqand (now in Uzbekistan) to the Afghan cities of Rayy (near modern Tehran), Neyshābūr (Nishapur), Mary (Merv), and Herāt who attended the → synods of the East Syrian church (in the Persian Empire) in 410 and 424. The Kazakh and Kyrgyz regions were then part of the silk trade route, which explains the existence of Christian churches. There are also tombstone inscriptions in Syriac and Turkic that prove that from 1249 to 1345 a sizable community of Turkic → Nestorian Christians existed in what was then known as Chagatai territory, near present-day Bishkek (Frunze under the Soviets, earlier Pishpek), the Kyrgyzstan capital.

This presence of Christianity for more than a millennium virtually disappeared from popular memory because of the entrance of other religions and conquerors, especially the eventual triumph of

→ Islam. There were large communities of Zoroastrians (Zoroaster was born in central Asia; → Iranian Religions 6-7), as well as Buddhists, but it was Islam that made the major impression. In 713, during their second wave of expansion, the Islamic Arabs conquered and ruled over the Fergana Valley. Before long, Bukhara (now in Uzbekistan) had become second only to Mecca as a center of Islamic religiosity and learning. Five centuries later the Mongol Genghis Khan conquered Bukhara (1220), killing 30,000 and burning the city. Later, in 1380, Tamerlane invaded, even capturing Baghdad in 1393. He proceeded to make Samarqand into what was called the grandest capital city of ancient Asia, resettling there the intelligentsia and artisans from the territories he conquered.

Central Asia, and Kyrgyzstan in particular, also contributed to the development of Islam itself. The mystical and ecstatic tradition known as → Sufism was born there, before spreading widely in Africa and Asia. Along the Silk Road numerous → monasteries were important to the preservation of Christianity, providing rest for the traveler, encouraging the copying of sacred texts, and fostering theological debate. The word "sufi" (Syr. "wool") no doubt refers to the rough wool clothing worn by monks and nuns.

There were also Christians present during the major invasions that ultimately destroyed Syriac and Nestorian Christianity. The Kerait Turks as far east in Siberia as Lake Baikal had become Christian. The son of Genghis Khan took a Christian wife from the Keraits, and many of the prominent military officers ruling central Asia in the 13th century were Christian. Then Maḥmūd Ghāzān, ruler of the Golden Horde, converted to Islam in 1295, which marked the end of → toleration of Christianity in central Asia and Persia. Ghāzān ordered the destruction of churches, synagogues, and temples throughout his domain.

3. Modern Imperial and Soviet Periods

3.1. Christianity was introduced from Russia to Kyrgyzstan as a result of the expansion of the Russian Empire and the resultant immigration (voluntary and involuntary) of numerous nationalities. Various Kyrgyz tribes began creating an independent khanate during the 15th century with a distinctive Kyrgyz language. Though many Kyrgyz were subject to passive Chinese rule in the mid-18th century, by 1830 all Kyrgyz were paying tribute to the Khanate of Qŭqon (Kokand), and most were Muslim, though only limited religious practice was allowed. During the following century various Kyrgyz

tribes began appealing to Russians, especially the governorship in Siberia, for help against the Khanate of Qŭqon.

In 1876 the Russians finally destroyed the khanate and brought all Kyrgyz into submission. Russian administration varied between attaching the region to the Semireche Oblast of Turkestan, then to the Steppe Administration, and back again to Turkestan. Beginning in the 1880s there were immigrations by Ukrainians to the Fergana Valley, with larger-scale immigration following after 1905. → Orthodox churches emerged, administered from Tashkent (Uzbekistan) or from Kazakhstan. When the Russian imperial government tried to mobilize the local population during 1916, there was a revolt of 10,000 Kyrgyz gathering in Osh. This incident ended with several thousand Russian settlers being killed and 100,000 Kyrgyz deaths at the hands of the Russians and the flight to China of a third of the population.

3.2. The advent of Soviet power began with General M. V. Frunze, who was born in Bishkek, making concessions to end the terror, and finally in 1936 the Kyrgyz became a Soviet republic. A remaining problem was the division of the Fergana Valley between Kyrgyz SSR and Uzbek SSR.

The Soviet antireligion campaign began in 1929, primarily against Muslims in the southern region, especially in the Fergana Valley. Religious life gradually resumed after World War II, and the campaign by Premier N. Khrushchev against religion (1959-64) was less effective in Kyrgyzstan than elsewhere. For example, a 1984 report about religion within the USSR showed that in only one year the number of clergy and mullahs in the Kirgiz SSR (many of them unregistered) had jumped by 76 percent.

It was also in this region that → Mennonite adherents of the millenarian leader Abram Peters finally settled in 1882, after having attempted a settlement in Aulie Ata (now Zhambyl, Kazakhstan). They first located in Leninpol (formerly Nikolaipol), not far from Fergana. As late as 1988 there were still 500 adult members in this congregation.

As more settlers followed, congregations of → Baptists, Evangelical Christians (mostly indigenous believers, including many converts from Molokans in Caucasia, similar to → Plymouth Brethren), Pentecostals, and Mennonites were formed. Having together shared the antireligious persecutions under Stalin, they resumed worship after 1944 in united congregations as part of the All-Union Council of Evangelical Christians–Baptists, the Mennonites representing about half the entire membership. Other Mennonites were among the first to register independent churches after 1967, especially in Tokmak and Krasnaya Rechka, near Frunze. The split in the Evangelical Christian and Baptist community during the Khrushchev campaign also resulted in very active churches of the groups known as Initsiativniki (Initiators) or Reformers, who eventually formed the Council of Churches of Evangelical Christians–Baptists.

Although a number of leaders were imprisoned, including women active in illegal Sunday schools, the level of persecution suffered by Kyrgyz believers was less than that endured by believers in other Soviet republics. This relatively relaxed climate, in fact, attracted religious activists from elsewhere.

From this evangelical community, increasingly of mixed nationality, leaders of Mennonite origin initiated → missionary work with Kyrgyz and other Turkic nationalities. The first attempts at Scripture translation began in the 1920s but were stopped by the religious persecution. These translation projects were resumed in the late 1970s through the initiative of several individuals who had spent years of their childhood in Kyrgyz families and learned the language. Those children had been separated from their parents who had earlier been deported (as Soviet Germans) to this region in 1941. Later, when restrictions were eased, the children were able to return to Soviet German Mennonite and Baptist homes in Kyrgyzstan, where bonds of friendship with their Kyrgyz hosts developed.

Once the USSR collapsed in 1991, the Ray of Hope Mission, the mission arm of the Kyrgyzstan Baptist Union, launched programs that included summer camps, weekly Bible clubs for children, relief, and radio programs. As Kyrgyzstan slipped into serious economic crisis, their work, heavily supported by recent Soviet German emigrants in Germany, turned also to addressing the drug problem and providing job training for street children (an increasing problem). Although the union's membership began slipping following massive emigration to Russia and Germany, independent Kyrgyz-speaking congregations provided new growth.

4. Contemporary Crisis for Islam and Christianity

President Akayev initially worked with reformers, supported Boris Yeltsin during the attempted coup in 1991, and encouraged the market and democratic reforms. Numerous religious movements also sought haven in Kyrgyzstan, and Bishkek became a center for → Jehovah's Witnesses, → Baha'is, and others. Then came missionaries, especially evangelical Protestants, from America, western Europe, and

Korea (Presbyterians), who seemed to favor large, high-publicity events in sports arenas. Muslim missionaries, the most active coming from Dagestan, a republic in southern Russia, also arrived and saw the Protestants as harmful and the Akayev regime as too secular. The Kyrgyz Muftiate began urging that all Kyrgyz should be Muslim, just as all Russians should be Orthodox.

Late in 1995 Kyrgyz security forces began warning about foreign groups encouraging Islamic → fundamentalism in the southern regions. By mid-1996 a government body to monitor religious activity was again established, and religious education was banned from state schools. At the end of 1996 the Ministry of Justice required the reregistration of all religious groups, and there was soon talk of a new law on religion.

At the end of 2001 the Kyrgyzstan legislature indeed passed a new religion law that enlarged state controls over religion. The new law, going into effect with President Akayev's signature in 2002, made the registration of religious organizations compulsory, required that religious educational activity be licensed, and banned all missionary activity not first registered (*how* was left to the discretion of authorities). Some of the initial attempts at enforcement suggested serious trouble for all religious groups, especially for the more extremist movements. In the southern region the Muslim call to prayer via loudspeakers was banned. Adherents of the Reform Evangelical Christians–Baptists, who refused to register on principle, began experiencing harassment. One young Baptist refusing to swear the military oath and bear arms was declared ineligible for alternative service because his church was not registered. It should be noted that registered Baptists are now allowed to perform alternative service (→ Conscientious Objection).

Tensions remain for Muslims, since only 931 of the 2,000 mosques are registered, and Kyrgyz authorities are becoming more concerned about the political loyalty of activist Muslims. They are aware that a high proportion of those who attend mosques regularly are Uighurs, who are generally more religious than the Kyrgyz.

Bibliography: J. Anderson, *Kyrgyzstan: Central Asia's Island of Democracy?* (Amsterdam, 1999) • F. Corley, ed., *Religion in the Soviet Union: An Archival Reader* (New York, 1996) • N. Davis, *A Long Walk to Church: A Contemporary History of Russian Orthodoxy* (Boulder, Colo., 1995) • D. T. Irvin and S. W. Sunquist, *History of the World Christian Movement,* vol. 1, *Earliest Christianity to 1453* (Maryknoll, N.Y., 2001) • *Istoriia evangel'skikh Khristian–Baptistov v SSSR* (Moscow, 1989) • Keston Institute, *Keston News Service* (Oxford, 1971-) • W. Klein, *Das nestorianische Christentum an den Handelswegen durch Kyrgyzstan* (Turnhout, 2000) • D. C. Lewis, *After Atheism: Religion and Ethnicity in Russia and Central Asia* (New York, 2000) • S. H. Moffett, *A History of Christianity in Asia,* vol. 1, *Beginnings to 1500* (2d ed.; Maryknoll, N.Y., 1998) • J. S. Olsen, *An Ethnohistorical Dictionary of the Russian and Soviet Empires* (Westport, Conn., 1994) esp. 416-23 • M. H. Ruffin and D. Waugh, eds., *Civil Society in Central Asia* (Seattle, Wash., 1999) • W. Sawatsky, *Soviet Evangelicals since World War II* (Scottdale, Pa., 1981).

Walter Sawatsky

Kyrie → Mass

L

Labor → Social Partnership; Work

Laicization

In Roman Catholic → canon law "laicization" denotes the removal of the spiritual status that is conferred by → ordination (→ Clergy and Laity). The legal consequence is the loss of the rights and duties associated with clergy status (e.g., → Missio canonica). On the basis of 1983 → CIC 290-93, laicization may take place by an invalidation of ordination, in punishment for an offense, or as an act of grace. A distinction must be made between the loss of clergy status and the setting aside of the obligation of → celibacy, which is an obstacle to marriage.

In the case of invalidation a judgment or an administrative declaration gives automatic effect to the legal consequences (can. 1712). If the ordination is valid, laicization is either by a judgment in a church trial or, should there be serious grounds in the case of a → deacon or very serious grounds in that of a → priest, by rescript of the apostolic see. The obstacle to marriage can be overcome only by an additional → dispensation from the vow of celibacy, which the papacy alone may issue. The laicization of a validly ordained priest that makes possible a dispensation from celibacy presupposes not only the meeting of the criteria for loss of status but also the presence of special grounds for the dispensation.

Today, in consequence of the restrictive new order of conduct, only the originally defective sanctioning of ordination to the priesthood and the longtime and unchangeable abandonment of the priestly life are legally permissible reasons for laicization by the diocesan bishop. Under the influence of the papal policy on dispensations, which is governed by the Roman ideal of the priesthood, the Congregation of the Faith (→ Curia) has the competence to issue rulings that both in fact and in law supplement the coded regulations.

A cleric who has been laicized may be reinstated by rescript of the apostolic see.

→ Vow

Bibliography: Laicization procedures: CONGREGATION FOR THE DOCTRINE OF THE FAITH, "De modo procedendi in examine et resolutione petitionum quae dispensationem a caelibatu respiciunt," *AAS* 72 (1980) 1132-35; idem, "Normae procedurales de dispensatione a sacerdotali caelibatu," ibid. 1136-37.

Other: H. HEIMERL, *Der laisierte Priester. Seine Rechtsstellung* (Graz, 1973); idem, *Der Zölibat. Recht und Gerechtigkeit* (Vienna, 1985) 47-88 • H. SCHMITZ, *Kleriker- und Weiherecht* (2d ed.; Trier, 1977) • F. P. SWEENEY, "Laicization (Canon Law)," *NCE* 8.325-26; idem, *The Reduction of Clerics to the Lay State* (Washington, D.C., 1945).

BERND T. DRÖSSLER

Laity → Clergy and Laity

Lamaism → Tibetan Religions

Lamentations, Book of

1. Name, Place in Canon, Authorship
2. Form and Genre
3. Message
4. Origin
5. Liturgical Use

1. Name, Place in Canon, Authorship

The Book of Lamentations consists of five songs. The book's usual name in modern → Bible versions comes, by way of the Vg *(Lamentationes)* and the LXX *(Thrēnoi [Ieremiou]),* from Jewish tradition, in which it is called *qînôt,* "laments for the dead" *(b. B. Bat.* 15a). In Hebrew MSS and printed copies it is usually named after the first word: *'êkâ,* "alas, how."

Though Lamentations is placed among the → Megilloth (i.e., festal scrolls), the LXX, followed by dependent and modern versions, inserts it after the Book of Jeremiah on the basis of the Jewish tradition that Jeremiah composed Lamentations after the destruction of → Jerusalem in 587 B.C. According to one view already attested probably in 2 Chr. 35:25 and followed by the Targum (→ Bible Versions 2), the laments refer in part to the death of King → Josiah in 609 B.C. (see 4:20). Neither view is tenable.

2. Form and Genre

The alphabetic character of the first four laments, enhanced to a triple alphabetic acrostic in the third, with a similar trend in the fifth, shows at once that these are literary compositions. This conclusion is confirmed by the songs' transcending the normal genre of individual or national complaint. They manifest a → kerygmatic and didactic purpose that governs their structure.

3. Message

The deliberate arrangement of the laments gives evidence of their primarily literary and didactic significance. The third lament forms the core. By reminding the survivors of the disaster both of the sound of their complaint and of God's omnipotence, the poet seeks to lead them to repentance (→ Penitence) and conversion, which are necessary for renewing their relation to God and experiencing liberation.

The second and fourth songs form the inner frame, and the first and fifth the outer frame (R. Brandscheidt). The second stresses the severity of God's wrathful judgment and cautiously asks whether it was appropriate (→ Wrath of God). The fourth describes the wrenching → sufferings of Jerusalem during the siege and capture but at the end promises absolution. The first emphasizes that Zion's sufferings were without parallel and asks that its foes receive similar treatment. The fifth describes the wretched conditions under the occupation and the barbarities experienced, praying that → Yahweh will lead the people back to himself. Several verses acknowledge that the disaster was deserved (1:8, 14, 18; 2:14; 3:39-42; 4:6, 13; 5:21).

4. Origin

Since the second song portrays the disaster most vividly, it is often regarded as the oldest. In view of its basic agreement with this song and its verbal borrowings, the first is thought to be dependent on it. For similar reasons the second and presumably also the first were known to the fourth, while the fifth in its present form (with possibly an earlier version, without vv. 6-7, 18?) was influenced by the fourth, so that the same sequence emerges for songs 1-2 and 3-5 together.

Lamentations cannot have been written before 587 or after the devastation of Edom in the fifth century B.C. (cf. 4:21 with Mal. 1:2-5). The development of the theology of guilt and conversion shows parallels to the theology of the → Deuteronomistic school. Familiarity with the language of the lament psalms and with the court theology of monarchy (see 4:20), borrowings from Jeremiah, and the didactic interest that makes use of the forms of → Wisdom literature suggest that the songs or their author originated in Jerusalem.

5. Liturgical Use

It is generally agreed that shortly after they were written, the songs were used in exilic and early postexilic mourning festivals (see Zech. 7:1-7; 8:18-19). After the destruction of the second temple in A.D. 70 and the imperial rebuilding of Jerusalem as Aelia Capitolina in 135, Lamentations was used in private reading on the anniversary of the temple's destruction. Only in early medieval times did it come to be read publicly in the synagogue on the same day (→ Worship 1).

→ Literature, Biblical and Early Christian 1

Bibliography: Commentaries: H. J. BOECKER (ZBK; Zurich, 1985) • D. M. GOSDECK (PBSer; Milwaukee, Wis., 1994) • D. R. HILLERS (AB; Garden City, N.Y., 1972) • O. KAISER (ATD; Göttingen, 1992) • O. PLÖGER (HAT;

Tübingen, 1969) • I. W. PROVAN (NCBC; Grand Rapids, 1991) • A. WEISER (ATD; 2d ed.; Göttingen, 1967).

Other works: R. BRANDSCHEIT, *Gotteszorn und Menschenleid* (Trier, 1983) • T. LINAFELT, *Surviving Lamentations: Catastrophe, Lament, and Protest in the Afterlife of a Biblical Book* (Chicago, 2000) • J. NEUSNER, *Lamentations Rabbah* (Atlanta, 1997) • W. D. REYBURN, *A Handbook on Lamentations* (New York, 1992) • C. WESTERMANN, *Lamentations: Issues and Interpretation* (Minneapolis, 1994).

OTTO KAISER

Language

1. General Definitions
2. Language in Greek Philosophy
3. Language in the Bible
4. Medieval and Early Modern Theories of Language
5. Modern Linguistics

1. General Definitions

Language is a cognitive faculty and behavior that is central to human life. Languages are complex systems that communicate knowledge, information, thoughts, ideas, and human → experience. There are many kinds of languages, ranging from the speech of concrete human communities to elaborate symbolic, mathematical, musical, and computational systems. Although researchers continue to question and investigate the possibility of language in nonhuman populations, it is still clear that language separates human beings from all other species.

Language is a social and biological process that arises in concrete human social groups, which means that language is always subject to historical change and development. The study of language has developed within a variety of academic fields, including → linguistics, → philosophy, and → literary criticism.

The field of linguistics investigates how language works, that is, how sounds and extralinguistic gestures and movements are formed by the human body, how these sounds and gestures are organized, and the process by which they are interpreted and understood. Linguistics thus overlaps with disciplines such as semiotics, or the study of → sign systems. The term "philology" is often used interchangeably with "linguistics," sometimes to refer to the discipline of linguistics in general but more often to refer to the study of literary texts or to historical linguistics.

Languages or linguistic systems contain their own inherent structures, whether in their respective rules and grammars or in their various performatives, pragmatics, or gestures. The study of linguistics can be divided into three broad categories. *Syntax* studies the overall structure of a particular language and investigates how expressions, such as phrases and sentences, are properly constructed within that language. *Semantics* investigates how these linguistic units function to convey → meaning. *Pragmatics* studies the ways in which the language is practiced or used.

In addition, *morphology* analyzes the structure of words within a particular language or language family. Morphological analyses investigate the formation of words in relation to their *phonology,* the organization of sounds in spoken languages, and their syntax along with the lexicon available to the practitioners of those languages.

Historical or comparative linguistics investigates the change and development within particular languages or language families, tracing the historical development of particular languages or the interrelationship between languages that share a similar, or related, structure, syntax, morphology, phonology, or semantics.

The purview of the philosophy of language often overlaps with that of linguistics, particularly when the issue of the meaning of language and its own possibility are investigated. For this reason, for some philosophers the philosophy of language is integrally connected to issues in the philosophy of the mind, particularly when philosophers investigate how linguistic structures and practices are interpreted and understood by the human being.

In the 20th century, linguistic theory began to be employed increasingly to investigate, and in some cases to resolve, long-standing questions in the philosophy of language. As a result, the concerns of these two disciplines have often converged.

2. Language in Greek Philosophy

The earliest theories of language focus on naming. In these theories words are understood to be names for objects. In the *Cratylus* Plato (427-347 B.C.; → Platonism) argues that the words employed within a language are not directly related to the object named by a word in any natural manner but rather are social conventions.

Aristotle (384-322 B.C.; → Aristotelianism) develops his philosophy of language primarily in the separate treatises *De interpretatione* and *Poetics.* He divides the study of language into three disciplines: → logic, → rhetoric, and poetics. While Aristotle's study of language makes a number of refinements on the linguistic theory of Plato, it continues to focus primarily on the identification and classification of speech units.

The → Stoics, dating from about 300 B.C., divide the discipline of philosophy into three parts: logic, → ethics, and physics. Their study of language, undertaken under the category of logic, is based on the assumption that human rational discourses reflect the activity of cosmic → Reason itself. Their logic pays particular attention to the meaning of an expression (the signified) and the expression itself (the signifier).

3. Language in the Bible

In the opening verses of Genesis God speaks and breathes on the waters covering the earth, and → life emerges. Testimony to the fecundity of God's → word (*dābār*) in the Hebrew tradition is found in Isa. 55:10-11, where the creative activity of God is described in terms of a linguistic utterance.

Ancient Hebrew theology identified naming as a central function of language. In the OT the archetypal human being, Adam (Heb. *'ādām*, Gen. 2:7), is created from the dust of the "ground" (*'ădāmâ*) in the "likeness" (*děmût*, Gen. 1:26; 5:1) of God. There is a reference also to a "stream" (*'ēd*, 2:6) that flowed through the Garden of Eden. The assonance of these four words in this passage suggests that in some way the name given to an object relates to its nature. In Gen. 2:9-20 Adam is allowed to name the created things of the earth. One of the descendants of Adam, Noah's son, is named Shem, meaning "name."

Genesis 11 tells the Hebrew myth of the origins of the variety of human languages. The people of the earth, according to the story, were originally one people with one language. They began to build a tower in their city on the plain of Shinar, an act that God saw as evidence of their pride. God then confused their language so that they could no longer understand one another's speech (Gen. 11:7). The tower was "called Babel [from Heb. *bālal*, confuse], because there the Lord confused the language of all the earth; and from there the Lord scattered them abroad over the face of all the earth" (v. 9).

The NT story of → Pentecost in Acts 2 tells how "devout Jews from every nation under heaven" (v. 5), through the descent of the → Holy Spirit upon the → apostles, were able to understand the apostles, each in their own native language. For the writer of Luke/Acts this incident demonstrates the reversal of the division brought about by Babel by the renewing and life-giving presence in the newly founded Christian community.

In the Gospel of John the divine Word, described as an activity of the divine being in Isaiah 55:10-11, becomes incarnate in the person of Jesus. Early Christians began to understand → Jesus to be an incarnation of the divine Word, or as an embodied utterance of the divine being.

4. Medieval and Early Modern Theories of Language

In the opening book of his *Confessions,* → Augustine of Hippo (354-430) develops the classical theory of language that words essentially name objects. According to this denotative theory, every word names something, and therefore each word has a particular meaning. A sentence is merely a combination of such names. While Augustine made no attempt to formulate a systematic theory of language, these reflections on the role of language as naming reveal the continuity of his thought with earlier Platonic theories of language.

The question of whether and how language names things arose again within medieval philosophy in the disputes between scholastic thought and → nominalism. The central question raised by William of Ockham (ca. 1285-1347) and other nominalists was whether universals had any real existence apart from being thought and apart from the act of their naming (→ Universalism and Particularism).

In the 17th century the Jansenists Antoine Arnauld (1612-94) and Pierre Nicole (1625-95), with the possible help of Blaise → Pascal (1623-62), collaborated on *La logique, ou l'art de penser* (1662), commonly referred to as the Port-Royal logic. The Port-Royal grammarians developed a systematic logic that paid careful attention to the definition and use of terms and concepts. Their logic laid an important foundation for the development of modern linguistics. The discussion of protospeech and the origin of language inaugurated by G. W. Leibniz (1646-1716) was given further attention in the writings of T. Hobbes (1588-1679), J.-J. Rousseau (1712-78), E. B. de Condillac (1715-80), and J. G. → Herder (1744-1803).

Modern historical linguistics owes its origins in England to the work of the Orientalist scholar W. Jones (1746-94), and in Germany to the work of F. Bopp (1791-1867), W. von Humboldt (1767-1835), and J. Grimm (1785-1863). In his 1786 presidential address to the Bengal Asiatic Society, Jones noted the linguistic relationship between Sanskrit, Greek, and Latin and on that basis postulated the existence of what is now called the Indo-European language family.

5. Modern Linguistics

The most influential work in the modern study of language is Ferdinand de Saussure's *Cours de linguistique générale* (1916). Saussure (1857-1913) coined the term "semiology" to describe his method of linguistic analysis. He distinguished between language as it is used *(parole)* and language as the system *(langue)*. Contrasting the synchronic (parole) and the diachronic (langue), his method focused primarily on the synchronic functioning of language.

Saussure's distinction between langue and parole finds a parallel in the later distinction of Noam Chomsky (b. 1928) between linguistic competence and linguistic performance, that is, the knowledge a speaker has of the language itself and the way he or she employs it in speaking or other specific uses of the language.

C. S. Peirce (1839-1914) also developed a complex theory of linguistic signs that he called the semiotic. This theory distinguishes between (1) the representamen, or linguistic sign itself; (2) the object to which the sign refers; and (3) the interpretant, the idea or meaning that is entailed from this process. Peirce maintained that this semiotic process never comes to an end but contains a built-in dynamism that allows it to continue ad infinitum.

Following World War II verificationist and naming theories of language were for the most part set aside in favor of smaller, more piecemeal studies of language and its particular usages.

Much of 20th-century philosophy centered on the belief that language and its usage lies at the heart of many problems and issues in philosophy. L. Wittgenstein (1889-1951) maintained that much of philosophy comes as a result of mistakes about how language actually functions. In his *Philosophical Investigations* Wittgenstein rejects denotative theories of language. Language, he argues, has no central essence but rather is composed of a variety of different "language games" that overlap and operate simultaneously (§§65-66, 92). The meaning of a word therefore cannot be separated from its usage within a particular language game or games. The study of the actual working of a language receives further development in the speech-act semantics of J. L. Austin (1911-60) and J. R. Searle (b. 1932). These studies of "ordinary language" are to be contrasted with the large-scale universal theory of language developed by Chomsky (→ Linguistics 2.2).

Some approaches to linguistic theory have been offered by scholars within the fields of literary theory and analysis rather than from the field of linguistics itself. Linguistics and various approaches within literary theory converge in the analysis of discourse (i.e., the communication between the speaker/writer and the hearer/reader).

The movement commonly referred to as Russian formalism arose from a number of different academic groups. In 1915 R. Jakobson (1896-1982) founded the Moscow Linguistic Circle. The St. Petersburg Society for the Study of Poetic Language (OPOIaZ) was founded by V. Shklovsky (1893-1984) and Y. Tynyanov (1894-1943) in the following year. In 1926 Jacobson moved from Moscow to Prague, where he joined V. Mathesius (1882-1945) in founding the Prague Linguistic Circle. This circle included the phonologist N. S. Trubetzkoy (1890-1938).

The formalists made numerous contributions to the study of phonology and to the development of structuralist approaches to literary criticism. Shklovsky, V. Propp (1895-1970), and other formalists focused on the analysis of narrative, plot, and literary devices, tending to view literary texts as a self-contained system comprising an assemblage of literary devices.

In 1928 M. Bakhtin (1895-1975) and P. N. Medvedev (1891-1938) laid the foundation for a sociological poetics created in response to the literary approaches and methods of various Russian formalists. Central to the method of Bakhtin and other members of his circle is the historical and sociological analysis of the "utterance," which includes its extralinguistic elements. This approach is extended in V. N. Voloshinov's (1895-1936) *Marxism and the Philosophy of Language* (1930), which recognizes that ideological investments are always contained within language. This position is paralleled by present-day sociolinguistics, an approach that examines the usage of language in determinative sociopolitical contexts and investigates the relation of class, race, gender, ethnicity, and power on actual language use.

In reaction to structuralist linguistics, J. Derrida (b. 1930) has outlined a method for the "deconstruction" of Western → metaphysics, particularly in its "logocentrism." For Derrida, deconstruction demands the abandonment of reference to any center of meaning. Within language, therefore, meaning is always deferred *(différence)*. In *Writing and Difference* (1967) Derrida also criticized the metaphysical concepts employed within structuralist linguistics. In his deconstructive methods Derrida has placed a greater emphasis on the signifier than on the signified, arguing for the indeterminacy, even the arbitrariness, of the signifier's meaning.

Bibliography: J. L. AUSTIN, *How to Do Things with Words* (Oxford, 1962) • S. BLACKBURN, ed., *The Oxford Dictionary of Philosophy* (Oxford, 1996) • N. CHOMSKY, *Aspects of the Theory of Syntax* (Cambridge, Mass., 1965); idem, *Syntactic Structures* (The Hague, 1957) • D. CRYSTAL, *A Dictionary of Language* (Chicago, 2001) • J. DERRIDA, *Writing and Difference* (Chicago, 1978; orig. pub., 1967) • A. FLEW, ed., *A Dictionary of Philosophy* (2d ed.; New York, 1984) • R. HALE and C. WRIGHT, eds., *A Companion to the Philosophy of Language* (Oxford, 1997) • J. KRISTEVA, *Language the Unknown: An Initiation into Linguistics* (New York, 1989) • P. LUDLOW, ed., *Readings in the Philosophy of Language* (Cambridge, Mass., 1997) • F. DE SAUSSURE, *Cours de linguistique générale* (Paris, 1916; 3d ed., 1949; ET *Course in General Linguistics* [New York, 1959]) • V. N. VOLOSHINOV, *Marxism and the Philosophy of Language* (Cambridge, Mass., 1986; orig. pub., 1930) • G. WARD, *Barth, Derrida, and the Language of Theology* (Cambridge, 1999) • L. WITTGENSTEIN, *Philosophical Investigations* (3d ed.; Oxford, 2001).

CRAIG A. PHILLIPS

Language and Theology

1. Basic Dimensions of Human Life
    1.1. The Ability to Speak
    1.2. Language Systems
    1.3. Oral and Written Speech
2. Forms of Faith and Religion (Religious Language)
    2.1. Religion and Language
    2.2. Prayer
    2.3. Myth and Mythical Language
    2.4. Historical and Theological Narratives
    2.5. Spoken and Written Word
3. Place of Revelation (Word of God)
    3.1. The Trinity
    3.2. Christology
    3.3. Linguistic Models
4. Medium and Material of Theological Reflection (Theological Language)
    4.1. Understanding Scripture
    4.2. Interpretation of Scripture
    4.3. Theory of Reason and Language
5. Medium of Religious Communication

In many respects → language is an area of focus in theology: anthropologically as a basic dimension of human life (→ Anthropology), phenomenologically as a form of faith and religion (→ Phenomenology of Religion), theologically as the place and means of revelation (→ Revelation; Word of God), method-ologically as the medium and material of theological reflection (→ Exegesis, Biblical; Hermeneutics), and practically as the instrument and medium of religious communication. Theories of theological language may focus on one or more of these aspects and thus take a specific turn, but in what follows several central areas are considered.

1. Basic Dimensions of Human Life

Anthropologically, language may be described as the human ability to speak and use (linguistic) signs, as the plurality of specific cultural language systems, or as concrete spoken or written language.

1.1. *The Ability to Speak*

Given the doctrine of creation in the divine likeness (→ Anthropology 3), the human ability to speak is a result of the divine address to us that calls us into fellowship with God, either as individuals or as a species (→ Promise and Fulfillment), makes possible our own answer, and gives us the power to articulate and thus disclose all reality (Gen. 2:19-20). We may say with M. Luther (1483-1546; → Luther's Theology) that it is also, soteriologically, a divinely constituted condition for communicating and hearing the proclamation of the gospel: "None of us knows why God gave us languages until we see that it is for the proclamation of the gospel" (BoA 2.450-51). A Trinitarian theology connects these two approaches, for as the Word, the Son is both mediator of creation and Redeemer. God constitutes us by the same Word by which he saves us. The ability to speak implies the ability to talk to God and with God. This basic facility, however, is used properly only when faith frees us to respond concretely to God in worship, thanksgiving, and petition — that is, only when it frees us to speak not just *about* God but also *to* → God (§7; → Prayer).

1.2. *Language Systems*

Individual language systems interest theology both negatively (to overcome them) and positively (to establish them). The plurality of languages does not prevent but, in the → Holy Spirit (§1.2), makes possible a unity of experience within the Christian community. Conviction regarding the divine origin of language and the related unity raises three additional problems.

1.2.1. A first question is that of the *origin of languages*. In Christian tradition, allegedly confirmed by James IV of Scotland in the 15th century, the original language was Hebrew. Beginning at the end of the 18th century, however, the natural explanation of human language (advanced by J. G. Herder, W. von Humboldt, and F. D. E. Schleiermacher) helped to make this historical question obsolete (see 4.3.1.3).

1.2.2. A further question was that of the *multiplicity of languages*. Following Gen. 11:1-9, Jewish (→ Cabala) and Christian tradition traced it to human pride and regarded it as a symptom of the sinfulness of human existence (→ Sin 3). By contrast, the experience at → Pentecost (§3) and → glossolalia in the Christian church were understood as an eschatological manifestation of the final overcoming of sin.

1.2.3. Finally, biblical traditions and Neoplatonic convictions (→ Platonism 3) took the view that God's original speech and the language of angels are pure forms, as are numbers (the book of nature being composed in the language of mathematics, which is the same for all peoples). This view led to the attempts to construct a *universal grammar or language* that would restore the unity of human speech. Noteworthy efforts in this direction were made by R. Bacon (ca. 1220-92), R. Llull (ca. 1233-ca. 1315; → Llullian Method), and G. W. Leibniz (1646-1716).

It was not until J. G. Hamann (see 4.3.1.2), Herder, and Schleiermacher, when the constitutive relationship between the multiplicity of languages and human individuality was understood, that the traditional topos connecting the multiplicity of languages with sin was revised and the efforts at creating a universal language were judged to be not only impracticable but philosophically and theologically undesirable. Not a single language but unceasing and irreducible many-sided conversations in the Christian community will further a new creation. In postmodern theology (e.g., M. C. Taylor and D. Klemm; → Postmodernism), such insights into the fundamentally irreducible nature of the multiplicity of languages have demonstrated the necessarily deconstructive consequences for efforts at theological unity (see J. Derrida and G. Deleuze).

1.3. *Oral and Written Speech*

Our main concern in theological and religious reflection on language (→ Philosophy of Religion 3) must be, not just the human ability to speak and the cultural phenomena of linguistic systems, but the forms of oral and written speech and the accompanying problems regarding understanding and exposition of faith and religion — in short, the phenomenon of religious discourse. Because there can be language without religion but not religion and faith without language, the religiosity of these phenomena does not constitute one of their linguistic characteristics; it refers instead to the life and practices of the religious community that uses them (L. Wittgenstein, I. Dalferth).

Because the religious use of language is always multifarious and concrete and is variously related to the other ways language is used in any given cultural context, religious language exists only in a multiplicity of linguistic phenomena such as in → metaphors in mutual interaction with the linguistic and conceptual traditions of a given culture (B. H. Blumenberg, P. Stoellger). Yet this interrelationship does not rule out the possibility that in every religious community typical modes of language use do indeed emerge that establish the phenomenon of religious discourse and ultimately develop a specific network of language and speaking that can be articulated and analyzed as the religious language of a particular community.

2. Forms of Faith and Religion (Religious Language)

Phenomenologically, it is possible to describe typical basic forms of religious language. Following the discussion by E. Husserl, M. Heidegger, or E. Lévinas (H. Adriaanse, J. L. Marion, B. Casper), these religious phenomena are to be distinguished from the problems attaching to the phenomenology of philosophical-theological language (B. Welte, E. Biser).

2.1. *Religion and Language*

From the beginnings of cultural development religion and language have been closely associated, although semantically we cannot differentiate between language and what is discussed (→ Symbol) or pragmatically between the divine and the human speaker (H. Usener). Language is originally understood and experienced as the actualization, rather than as the symbolizing, of reality. Language is creative. It produces and orders reality, and its most basic performance is thus the utterance and articulation (hence integrated order) of reality.

2.1.1. In the *Bible* this original function of language is restricted to the divine word of creation (Genesis 1; Rom. 4:17); only in a derived sense is it applied to the human speech that also embraces reality (Gen. 2:19-20) and that mediates truth (Rom. 10:14-17). Yet in the use of names, magic formulas (→ Magic), and → blessing and → cursing as powerful phenomena, we can see how language invokes and affects reality.

2.1.2. → *Mysticism, ecstasy, and charismatic traditions* cultivate participation in the creative power of divine language. Authentic divine speech occurs within the silent self-immersion in the divine discourse that cannot be perceived aurally (mysticism), though it can also be found in unintelligible glossolalia, which requires → interpretation, and in prophetic speech, in which divine speech interprets itself for human beings. The ability to participate in this original "divine" language either meditatively, ecstatically, or prophetically can be cultivated by individuals or groups by training and tradition, using the appropriate techniques. It can also lead to the development of a special sacred language (the language of worship) in which this speech occurs. Or the recollection of such speech is transmitted or evoked, whose contrast with daily speech underscores the special efficacy of religious language.

This form of participation in divine speech became theologically significant especially through its association with Neoplatonic and Augustinian efforts at attaining inner *illuminatio* in the tradition of Christian mysticism and in the theosophical tradition extending from J. Böhme and F. C. Öttinger to F. W. Schelling. Since the 19th century such efforts at participation have become variously associated with non-Christian, especially Indian and Asian traditions (→ Theosophy), though in the 20th century they have also experienced a remarkable renaissance in the various charismatic movements within Christianity.

2.1.3. In a different way the mainline churches have kept in view the *creative power of the divine word* as is seen in the theological distinction given to the office of → priest or pastor, in the binding power of the word of absolution (→ Penitence), and in the reality of the proclamation of the Word and the → sacraments. Even though distinctions do obtain in the theological rationale employed in the various traditions of Roman Catholicism (ecclesiology, doctrine of the sacraments), the Eastern church (new creation, earthly reflection of the eternal worship service), Lutheranism (promise, effectual Word), and the Reformed churches (constitutive community memorial), all these traditions nonetheless understand the "speaking" that takes place in these liturgical events to be an efficacious act that itself constitutes reality and that acquires legitimation through a special divine institution.

More recent attempts to characterize such speaking as a performative speech act (following the lead of J. L. Austin's speech-act analysis; see also O. Bayer, H. Luther, R. Wonneberger, and H. P. Hecht) are problematic to the extent that the reality of performative speech depends on the existence of certain social conventions, while the efficacy of the divine word precisely does not. Although such performative analyses can indeed explicate ecclesiological matters, they thus cannot explicate the efficacy of God's Word.

2.2. *Prayer*
The more clearly a distinction is observed, in speaking, both between language and world and between God and humanity, the more plainly can prayer be seen as a basic religious endeavor in which humans converse linguistically with the (divine) ground of → meaning. Prayer may take many different forms (petition, thanksgiving, praise, confession, promises, sayings, hymns, songs, free forms). It may be individual or collective, extemporaneous or cultically regulated. The biblical tradition understands all such processes as a turning to the God who has made his own prior pronouncements. It is in a consciousness of the fundamental distinction between Creator and creature, though also in an awareness of God's helping proximity and patriarchal concern for his creatures, that the entirety of life, in all its dimensions, can be brought before God in language and thus provide a point of orientation for human life and action.

Christian discourse with God is fundamentally based in prayer, something not only long known to the theology of the Eastern church (→ Doxology) but also acknowledged in hermeneutical theology (G. Ebeling), in more recent theologies of the Trinity (H. M. Barth), and in transcendental-hermeneutical (R. Schaeffler) and analytic (D. Z. Phillips, V. Brümmer) philosophy of religion.

2.3. *Myth and Mythical Language*
Myth and mythical language involve a rationalizing of speech insofar as they observe the differences between symbol and symbolizing, on the one side, and, on the other, divine and human speech (E. Cassirer, Blumenberg; → Symbol 2). Not a mythical narration as such, which articulates narratively the collective experience of a given orientation in the world, but its dramatic, ritual presentation in the cult gives force to what is said. A distinction thus arises in mythical language between word and action that leads to the liberation of myth from its religious use and on to an aesthetic use.

2.4. *Historical and Theological Narratives*
Notwithstanding several mythical elements and recollections, mythical speech plays more of a background role in the Jewish-Christian tradition. Because God is experienced, confessed, and addressed not only as Creator but also as a savior who continues to create ever anew within his creation, basic religious experiences are recounted and transmitted not in mythical accounts but in basic historical and theological narratives (→ Theology of History; Exodus, Book of; Sinai; Passion, Accounts of; Salvation History). Within linguistically disclosed reality religious language thus acquires the function of distinguishing between life that is commensurate with and life that is contrary to God.

Through this distinction between being and

promise, condition and future, factual reality and future hope, and the old and the new in the process of history, religious language orients the life of both the community and the individual ontically and ethically ever anew toward God. Such distinctions can be found in various guises in Israel's awareness of election (→ Israel 1), in the stories of the exodus and the → covenant (§1), in the distinctions made in the → law, in prophecy (→ Prophet, Prophecy), in the confessions of guilt and sin, in cultic sacrificial and atonement rituals, in narratives, and in songs and psalms. Such distinctions then culminate in → apocalypticism.

In the light of the cross and → resurrection of → Jesus Christ (→ Theologia crucis), the Christian faith confesses that this eschatological turn in time has already occurred. Christian speech thus combined the orientation achieved by distinguishing between the old and the new with the eschatological distinction (→ Eschatology) between the "already" and the "not yet" and proclaimed the past history of Jesus Christ as the ultimate truth of the history of the entire world. To this end, it created the speech form of the → gospel, which proclaims as → hope to the entire world that God's promise was fulfilled in Jesus Christ; that is, it no longer propagates the arrival of the new within the horizon of the old; rather, it announces its universal implementation within the horizon of the new.

The NT distinction between the life that has already appeared in Christ (→ Faith) and its universal actualization (in the → last judgment and in hope in eternal life) replaces the OT distinction between actual life and the life desired by God. The basic principle moving history is seen no longer in the vertical distance between Creator and creation, which is perverted by sin, but in the horizontal expansion of divine love, which integrates creaturely life into the divine life. The basic forms of Christian speech that developed were accordingly confession of this eschatological event (talk *about* God's → love; → Confession of Faith), its → proclamation as salvation for all humankind (talk *of* God's love), and prayer (talk directed *to* God's love) as doxology, thanksgiving, petition, and intercession. From the outset, each of these forms emerged in a contextually concrete, functional multiplicity, yet they always took their cue and standard from the gospel of Jesus Christ.

A contextual network of Christian language and life soon emerged through the semantic and pragmatic association of these speech forms. This network provided a binding standard in Scripture. It combined the gospel (God's speech) with confession (talk about God), prayer (talk directed to God), and proclamation (talk of God) in an exemplary fashion in → liturgy, and did so, through repetition, in a fashion capable of imitation and inviting participation. It reflected critically in → theology on this combination and its contents within the context of the cultural life of a given time. And, finally, it formulated the grammar of Christian speech in → dogma.

2.5. *Spoken and Written Word*

A decisive consolidating factor was the admixture of the spoken and the written word — of the word as it was spoken and lived out, on the one side, and, on the other, of Scripture written, read, and finally printed.

2.5.1. To be sure, literary communication was common in the days of Jesus, and he himself could read and write (John 8:6, 8; Luke 4:16, though cf. Matt. 13:54 and Mark 6:2). Yet the presentation of the imminent kingdom of God demanded a situation in which the word was *both spoken and lived out at one and the same time.* The eschatological nearness of God was present and direct and could not be communicated in written form at a distance. Its presence and proximity intended to provoke repentance, to make people in an immediate fashion either accept or reject salvation in view of the in-breaking kingdom of God. This news thus had to be spoken and lived rather than merely written and read. Moreover, because its claim was to alter a person's entire life rather than merely to address one's thinking or feeling, Jesus presented this news in person. Accordingly, it was genuinely understood only where it resulted in personal discipleship to Jesus.

2.5.2. The Christian community never forgot that the gospel was originally communicated by a combination of speaking and living. In the liturgy of its services it preserves this relation. Yet what Jesus had originally spoken and lived now had to be transmitted in a form that could be written, read, and ultimately printed. Development of the communication of the gospel from a lived-out word to *Scripture* and *the book of the Bible* fundamentally altered the thought and life of Christians.

Christianity originated in the semiliterate culture of the Roman Empire, and from the very outset not only oral tradition but also literate communication by means of letters, preaching, and gospel texts played an essential role. Gnostic speculation and the Marcionite rejection of many sacred writings quickly forced early Christianity to preserve its own identity by establishing a canon of authoritative texts. Because of its continued dealings with these texts, Christianity flourished after the waning of antiquity in the manuscript culture of the monastic Middle Ages, which in the midst of a semi-illiterate or illiterate world constituted an island of written culture that also initiated the beginnings of science.

During the Reformation era Christianity eagerly embraced the possibilities offered to it by the mechanization of writing and the accompanying possibilities of mass producing written texts. Here it not only exerted considerable influence on the development of modern written culture but also simultaneously encouraged the → Enlightenment to the extent that printed books promoted the phenomenon of the individual reader, the attendant emergence of a reading public capable of evaluation and judgment as well as of the superindividual phenomenon of "public opinion," and finally the critical and comparative access to stored information of the most varied kind over the distances of space and time.

Today Christianity participates much less persuasively in the transition to a culture of electronic communication in which not only texts but increasingly pictures and other graphics are playing a central role. This development has doubtless led to an enormous increase in the capacity to store information and make that information accessible. Yet the technical expansion of video communication systems has also combined various aspects of both oral and literate communication, while simultaneously preserving the possibilities for individual distance and interruption, such that the merely hermeneutical interpretive multiplicity of what is written and printed (an interpretive multiplicity quite characteristic of modernity) is now transitioning into the concrete variety of a multiplicity of simulated realities. That is, we are not only reading texts in a variety of ways, we are also living in a variety of realities (Blumenberg, N. Goodman). The consequences of these developments for Christian life and thought can hardly be overestimated.

The growing dominance of the written and printed word over against what is heard, lived, and experienced has also multiplied the possibilities for individuals to distance themselves from community. It has hastened the transition of Christianity from a life praxis guided by conviction to a system of beliefs regulated by dogma. It has also made possible the development of a critically thinking theology with its own methods, problems, and skills, and it has obscured the distinction between the interior and exterior reflection of Christian faith. Although Christianity is not a religion of the book, without the book its modern development is both inconceivable and incomprehensible.

2.5.3. The importance of the → *mass media* and of forms of communication and interaction has found a place on the agenda of practical theological reflection from the days of Schleiermacher (→ Practical Theology), but their systematic significance for the formation of the contents of Christian proclamation and theology and for the shaping of Christian consciousness has not yet been sufficiently investigated. Only more recently has the problem of the media (of communication) begun to concern practical, exegetical, and → systematic theology (Taylor, K. J. Kuschel, G. Thomas, W. Nethöfel, R. Volp).

3. Place of Revelation (Word of God)

Theologically, language serves as a model for thinking about God (→ Word of God). In controversy with Jewish and Hellenistic → monotheism, the doctrine of the Logos (Philo; → Platonism 2.2), → Gnosticism, and popular mythological religion produced the Trinitarian and Christological dogmas (→ Christology; Trinity). God's Word, the second person of the Trinity, is that particular self-distinction within God that makes it possible for God to enter into creation, without suspending the distinction between Creator and creature, and to liberate the creature for creaturely life with God; to accomplish this liberation, God becomes a mortal human being in Jesus. Where Christology reflects on what this incarnation means for Jesus and for us, the doctrine of the Trinity reflects on what it means for God. Both doctrines are soteriologically motivated, and both raise fundamental problems whose solution has been sought in specifically theological theories of language.

3.1. *The Trinity*

In regard to the Trinity, these questions focus primarily on how to preserve the unity and oneness of God when we speak of the Father, Son, and Spirit, or about God, God's Word, and God's Spirit. Another question involves how to guarantee the concreteness of references to the Father, Son, and Spirit, given the predicative structure of our own speech, or how to understand the relationship between inner-Trinitarian specificity, on the one hand, and, on the other, the salvific economic acts of God or the experience of God. Answers are sought in the doctrines of the one essence in three persons and in an examination of several key issues, including (1) the aseity of the Father's *archē;* (2) the analogical nature of the concept of person and of all other Trinitarian definitions with regard to the Father, Son, and Spirit; (3) the relationality of the understanding of person; (4) the correspondence, within the Augustinian tradition, between the inner-Trinitarian, differentiated relationships and the external-Trinitarian, undifferentiated relationships; and (5) and the relationship, in the Palamite tradition, between God's spirit and God's energies.

3.2. *Christology*

The questions with which Christology is concerned similarly address the unity of Jesus Christ, who is defined, according to the doctrine of the dual natures (→ Chalcedon, Council of), as "true God" *(vere Deus)* and "true man" *(vere homo)*. Christology also examines the following topics: (1) his full divinity and unmixed combination of the two natures in the unity of his person *(communicatio idiomatum);* (2) his full humanity accompanied by a preservation of God's own prerogative, in terms of his *assumptio* (assumption [of flesh]), *anhypostasis* (non-self-subsistence, or personality, i.e., Christ's human nature subsisting in the person of the Word), and *enhypostasis* (in-personality, i.e., Christ's subsistence as the eternal person of the Word); (3) the unity of the person and the work or office of Jesus Christ (priest, prophet, and king); (4) the integration of this history into God's life (self-disenfranchisement, exaltation, doctrine of "state" [*status*]); and (5) the conceivability of the divinity of Jesus Christ under the conditions of his earthly existence (doctrine of kenosis, or self-emptying). Concerning all these problems, theology crafts linguistic formulations intended to ensure not only the intelligibility of the Christian faith but also its proclamation and identity within history.

3.3. *Linguistic Models*

The Christological and Trinitarian grammar of faith influences the language of every aspect of Christian life and thought. Beyond this influence, in the doctrine of God and in Christology and ecclesiology, it also combines with linguistic figures that emerged through discussions during the various phases of the church's existence (early church, Middle Ages, Reformation, modernity) with Greco-Hellenistic → ontology, physics, and metaphysics (→ Greek Philosophy).

3.3.1. Negative and mystical theology (→ Apophatic Theology) cast basic doubts on the ability to speak about God at all. Ontological exegesis of Exod. 3:14 (LXX), however, made possible a definition of God as the origin of all being, whose attributes, on the basis of our experience of life and being, could be expressed along the three lines of the Areopagite: the way of negation, of eminence, and of causality (*via negationis, eminentiae, causalitatis;* → Negative Theology 2). In 1215 the Fourth Lateran Council explicitly stated that this definition merely makes God's essence expressible rather than actually comprehending it and that, despite any similarity between the Creator and the creature, a yet greater dissimilarity was ultimately to be acknowledged.

On the basis of this thinking, High Scholasticism (→ Thomism; Scotism) acknowledged the presence of grace that completes rather than denies nature and developed (various) ontologically based doctrines regarding *analogical reference to God* (→ Analogy) by associating analogies of proportionality with those of attributes in a specific way. The result was a theological-philosophical hybrid discourse that made natural speech about our world of experience into a basis for speaking analogically about God.

3.3.2. I. Kant (1724-1804) destroyed this analogical approach by eliminating its ontological basis. Luther had already insisted that in theological usage every word takes on a new meaning, and so the dialectic of *two different worlds of discourse* replaced an analogical mixed discourse (→ Philosophy and Theology). The dialectic of "revealed God" *(Deus revelatus)* and "hidden God" *(Deus absconditus)* in the model of law and gospel thus replaces analogical reference to God in the model of nature and grace. Correspondingly, natural reference to the human being as *animal rationale* is replaced by the dialectic of the one who is in need of being justified *(homo iustificandus),* who is both a creature and a sinner, or "at once righteous and a sinner" *(simul iustus et peccator).*

3.3.3. Enlightenment → theism renewed analogical thinking in → physicotheology until D. Hume (1711-76) and Kant epistemologically destroyed it. In the *19th century* the dialectic of Reformation thinking is additionally incorporated into an overall incarnational-pneumatological model (G. W. F. Hegel, J. R. Illingworth) in which God's spirit is articulated in the dialectical transition through the heterogeneity of the world process itself until the divine ultimately becomes completely transparent.

3.3.4. In the *20th century* → neoscholasticism has revived the ontological doctrine of analogy in the *analogia entis* (analogy of being; E. Przywara, O. Söhngen). It has also found reformulation in → transcendental theology as the subject's fundamental structure of correspondence or operation (K. Rahner, B. L. Lonergan), or it has been corrected and replaced as the *analogia imaginis* of symbolic talk about being (P. Tillich).

K. Barth, however, took the dialectical components of the Reformation tradition to form an absolute separation between God and the world, but he combined them and incarnational components of revelation theology to produce a Christological analogy of faith (*analogia fidei*) anchored in an inner-Trinitarian analogy of relation (*analogia relationis*; see 4.3.2.2). E. Jüngel developed this notion into a consistent analogy of advent from the perspective of God's coming in Jesus Christ, in which God is expressed as the mystery of the world.

The → analytic philosophy of religion describes analogy, on the one hand, as a semantic operation that characterizes every language when it discusses something new and, on the other, as a specific rule of theological language that always allows it to control terminologically what in religion must be the metaphoric and symbolic way of speaking. Religious language uses images (Wittgenstein), stories (R. B. Braithwaite), models (I. T. Ramsey), and rhetorical figures that include the speakers (D. Evans), figures whose rules can be articulated theologically and formulated as (Trinitarian) grammar (A. Farrer) applicable to talk about God.

→ Feminist theology has shown how one-sidedly patriarchal many of these images, metaphors, and analogies have been. Its question regarding the (un)avoidable anthro- or andro-centricity of talk about God has raised the debate concerning metaphor and analogy out of the sphere of theoretical reflection and made it the subject of analysis of concrete linguistic practice, with sociological and psychological consequences.

4. Medium and Material of Theological Reflection (Theological Language)

Methodologically, Christian theology must confront the problem of language not only with regard to talk about God in the larger sense but also because of its use of Scripture. Here language as the concrete medium of scriptural expression (i.e., the original biblical languages) first presents a specialized philological problem. In connection with the question of the correct understanding of Scripture within the framework of scriptural doctrine, it is also a specialized hermeneutical problem (*hermeneutica sacra*). In the 20th century, philosophical hermeneutics shifted its focus from understanding the text to understanding the notion of understanding itself. Theological hermeneutics followed suit by shifting its focus from understanding Scripture to understanding the notion of understanding God. As a result of these shifts, language itself became a fundamental issue of theology. The problem of language confronts theology methodologically not only in connection with work on scriptural texts but also in connection with scriptural doctrine and as a basic problem of the theological enterprise in the larger sense.

4.1. *Understanding Scripture*

Dealing with scriptural texts in connection with exegesis, translation, and transmission of their original version (→ Origen) confronted theology from the very outset with philological and hermeneutical problems.

4.1.1. The question of correct exegesis was answered first with a specific combination of typological and allegorical interpretation allowing the text to be understood on several different levels of meaning (the threefold or fourfold meaning of Scripture). In his doctrine of signs *Augustine* (354-430; → Augustine's Theology) developed a semiotic theory of language that was determinative for the Christian West up to the Reformation. According to this theory, not only Scripture but the whole reality of creation is a network of signs, or a book, that, when it is read, will lead by a right use of signs and things signified (*signa, res*) to ultimate truth, which alone is worthy not only to be used (*uti*) but also to be enjoyed (*frui*).

4.1.2. The Augustinian tradition understood the book of Scripture as a key to the book of nature, and the book of nature as the expository framework for the book of Scripture. By contrast, R. *Descartes* (1596-1650) and *Galileo* (1564-1642) advocated an independent understanding of the book of nature. With this emancipation of the book of nature from the book of Scripture, they introduced the modern notion of a scientific investigation of the world (see Blumenberg).

4.1.3. *Luther,* in contrast, focused on the power of self-disclosure inherent in God's word and in Scripture itself. Scripture must be its own interpreter (*sui ipsius interpres*) in its literal sense (*sensus literalis*), even without recourse to allegory, as long as one focuses on its real theme (*res*), namely, Jesus Christ. On this view, theology becomes scriptural exegesis and grammar, with a focus on the Christ-theme of biblical texts. Its basic insights no longer derive from the (metaphysical) analysis of nature but from a study of Scripture itself in the original languages.

4.1.4. The renaissance of exegesis resulting from the Reformation concentration on Scripture led to a rediscovery of the importance of *linguistic knowledge, grammar, and rhetoric* in theological learning (P. Melanchthon, P. Ramus). The accompanying emphasis on the uniqueness of God's salvific actions in Jesus Christ, however, a uniqueness that cannot be generalized, simultaneously introduced a fundamental distinction between theology and modern science, which focused on the disclosure of predictable universal laws (Galileo, Descartes). This distinction also presaged the later distinction between the humanities and natural sciences in the 19th century and the gradual drifting apart of theology and the (natural) sciences, as well as the dominance of historical queries in theology since the Enlightenment.

Only recently has this one-sided neo-Protestant view been overcome, following the dissolution of the modern scientific paradigm in physics, cosmology, and biology, and since the discovery, within postmodern discussion, of the fundamental cultural significance of → rhetoric and of the irreducible variety of linguistic play within language. This development has shown that the historical-critical orientation of theology, despite all its successes, was a temporally determined, negative product of the scientific reason of the Enlightenment, with its focus on universality and on universal unity, and has thus opened up that orientation to criticism.

4.2. *Interpretation of Scripture*

Scriptural doctrine thus became the main focus of methodological discussion within modern Protestant theology, including (1) within Protestant orthodoxy itself in its confessional dispute with Rome, (2) within Pietism in its inner-Protestant dispute with orthodoxy, (3) within the Enlightenment in its criticism of all separate denominational theology in the name of universal reason and reproducible experience, (4) in the 19th century in the historical criticism of reason and in the historical-critical examination of biblical texts, and finally (5) in the 20th century in the multifarious attempts to regain theological access to Scripture beyond the aporias of both historical-critical and ahistorical-dogmatic methods. Orthodoxy interpreted Scripture within the dogmatic doctrinal context of law and gospel, Pietism within the practical life context of the believer, the Enlightenment within the theoretical and moral context of universal reason and scientific experience, the 19th century within the framework of historical reason and historical-religious academic questions, and the 20th century within the context of several different perspectives: psychological and sociological, phenomenological and existential-ontological, hermeneutical, political and sociological, linguistic, analytic philosophical, and deconstructionist.

During the 20th century the constant and bewildering increase in methodologies for dealing with Scripture caused fundamental communication problems between lay Christians and academic theology and generated fundamentalist reactions, but also an acknowledgment that there really can be no linear exegetical articulation of the contents of faith based on Scripture or any unequivocal theological transference of faith into reason. As a text, Scripture is not in any unequivocal sense to be understood as the self-interpretive word of God. This admission indeed does not mean that we can read Scripture arbitrarily according to our own context. It does mean, however, that Scripture does not have only one sense. It speaks in different ways, and there is no one reason by which it can be understood.

4.3. *Theory of Reason and Language*

The doctrine of Scripture now rests on a nuanced theory of reason and language. This fact has become increasingly clear from the end of the 18th century. Theological and philosophical sketches concentrate typically on three concretely interrelated approaches that analyze the linguistic problem of the subject, that of the object, and especially the religious use of language.

4.3.1. *Subject-oriented approaches* usually follow Kant's transcendental, Hamann's reproductive-poetic, Schleiermacher's discursive hermeneutical, or M. Buber's dialogic way.

4.3.1.1. Transcendental approaches (→ Transcendental Philosophy) begin with the subject and try to trace back language and understanding to a network of cognitive conditions and basic semiotic operations that make possible experiential and interpretive dealings with the world and ourselves (Lonergan, Rahner, and J. B. Lotz). Such approaches, however, can also begin with the language community and explicate the conditions for successful speaking and understanding as necessary prerequisites for a community that manifests transcendent communication (K. Apel, J. Habermas). Roman Catholic thinkers have been especially inclined to adopt such transcendental-theological premises in defining God as the ultimate ground of reality and possibility both of the cognitive operations constituting our speaking and understanding (self) and of that which is understood (the world) and of the community of those who are thereby capable of understanding (Lonergan, Rahner, Lotz; → Theology). Religious reflection (→ Philosophy of Religion) appeals to transcendental structures of language, experience, and understanding (Schaeffler, H. Krings) and thus posits a controversial plurality of actual experience with language and reality in unified, universally applicable rational conditions.

4.3.1.2. Against the rationally abstract emphasis of the Enlightenment and Kant's transcendental criticism and reconstruction, J. G. Hamann (1730-

88) claimed that the wealth of human knowledge rests on a concrete exchange of words. Poetry, not a transcendent pure reason, is the "mother tongue of the human race." Concrete language cannot be circumvented with the critique of reason; in all its variety, language is a gift God gives for human use, and God is accordingly understood as an author and writer. His writing is understood and interpreted within the horizon of the multiplicity of human language and should be productively adopted and developed in each individual life.

4.3.1.3. In opposition to Hamann's thesis that speech had a divine origin, J. G. Herder (1744-1803) argued that even as animals, human beings had speech. Human speech is embedded in natural speech common to all living creatures and is distinguished only by the fact that humans are not led by instinct. Human → freedom rests on our speech-relation to the world. We acquire this relationship and are able to use it because we are always involved in concrete speech relations. W. von Humboldt (1767-1835) adopted this approach in regard to the role of individual education and the spiritual development of humanity.

F. D. E. Schleiermacher (1768-1834; → Schleiermacher's Theology) developed Herder's basic thought theologically and made of it an embracing general hermeneutic on the basis of an understanding of language as concrete communicative action. All speaking takes place within a relationship to something that has already been spoken and already been thought; as such, it is a specific connection between the universal (language) and the individual (thinking) in (written) texts within the framework of a specific context of both communication and action (the "doctrine of goods"). Understanding texts thus demands that one interpret them within the various contexts in which they function(ed): grammatically within their language contexts, psychologically within the authors' life context, and thematically within the larger communication context. The meaning of texts then emerges to the extent that the interplay between what has gone before and what emerges or is created anew becomes clear within precisely these three contexts.

Because this process of articulation is infinite, the meaning of a given text can never be exhausted once and for all; rather, its interpretation has arrived at its goal when it in its own turn provides the impetus for continuing the dialogue in yet new texts. Scripture, too, should accordingly be interpreted with reference to the Christian context of communication in the light of general historical, philological, and hermeneutical queries and is understood

only to the extent that it provides the impetus for continuing Christian-religious discourse. The exposition of texts and transcendental speech reflection thus lead us on to the hermeneutic of concrete communication.

4.3.1.4. In a different way M. Buber (1878-1965) claimed that language, true humanity, and individuality all develop out of → dialogue (§1; → Jewish Philosophy 5). Not in speech about something but in addressing and being addressed by someone (the Thou) lie the origin and process of language. By basing his own view in God's dialogue with human beings, Buber thus provided a starting point for philosophical and theological personalism in religion (e.g., as developed by F. Ebner, F. Rosenzweig, M. Scheler, G. Marcel, and E. Brunner; → Person).

Rosenzweig (1886-1929) was especially effective in going beyond this premise. In his *Star of Redemption* he understands all processes of thinking as grammatical and from this perspective then reassesses Jewish, Christian, and Muslim theology. The emphasis on the "other" in Lévinas and in the (linguistic) phenomenological philosophy of religion (B. Casper, J. Möller, J. L. Marion) continues this discussion with a focus on ethics.

4.3.2. The religious philosophy of Hegel (1770-1831; → Hegelianism) and the theology of Barth (1886-1968; → Dialectical Theology) are more oriented to the *object*.

4.3.2.1. Hegel's theory of the → absolute seeks to protect the truth content of religion and the unity of reason by expounding the variety of religious communication as different elements in the development of the absolute spirit, which attains to itself in the process of history through the views, ideas, and concepts of others. Religion takes the form of imagination, but its truth content becomes a concept that philosophy may develop (F. Wagner, J. Dierken).

Hegel's insight into the intrinsically representational character of religious utterances was understood and developed in extremely different ways. It was developed anthropologically from the perspective of the representing or conceptualizing religious subject, logically from the perspective of the religious content thus represented or conceptualized, and semiotically from the perspective of the actual medium of representation constituted by religious concepts. This insight prompted D. F. Strauss to analyze the original church's production of myths in the NT, L. Feuerbach to understand religion in terms of its anthropological roots, and K. Marx and F. Engels to examine the reflection of concrete economic and social relationships in religious concepts. Schelling incorporated the same insight in a revelatory-realistic philosophical model, and F. C. Kreutzer used it in a speculative theory of symbols.

These models provided points of departure for theories of symbols all the way up to Tillich, for whom religious language symbolized the deeper dimension of reality as that which concerns us unconditionally. Finally, C. S. Peirce transcended this insight in a general, pragmatically based theory of signs from which he developed a semiotically nuanced tool for analyzing religious speech and thought, a tool whose significance has only recently been acknowledged (H. Deuser).

4.3.2.2. Whereas Hegel started with the process of the spirit's coming to itself in history, Barth began with the event of the self-revealing Word of God. In contrast to attempts that demanded a more historical method of exegesis over against the Hegelian tradition, and a more pneumatic one over against the Schleiermacherian tradition, Barth brought the understanding of Scripture and proclamation into a comprehensive understanding of the Word of God. After originally contrasting sharply the Word of God and the human word in his commentary on Romans (1922), Barth developed in *CD* I/1 a doctrine of the three forms of God's Word as proclaimed, written, and revealed (in Israel and Jesus Christ), all of which in *Scripture and Proclamation* he defined as particular forms of God's Word.

Realizing the danger of an unnuanced identifying of God's Word with human speech, in *CD* IV Barth argued (with the first Barmen thesis) that Jesus Christ alone is the one Word of God, "whom we are to trust and obey in life and in death," while Scripture and proclamation are human witnesses that respond to that Word and point to it. On the one hand, human talk (the church) can indeed witness to God's Word; yet because it cannot do so in any self-evident or instinctively appropriate way, it is absolutely necessary for theology to exert a measure of critical control over it. On the other hand, God's Word is so inextricably identified with Jesus Christ that Barth ultimately rejects in principle all natural theology and any fundamental revision of the Reformational order of law and gospel.

E. Jüngel has shown what the implications of Barth's approach are for the theology of language. By bringing himself to expression, God fundamentally interrupts our human speech and life. The consequences of this interruption for language can be seen in the NT parables and in the irreducibly metaphoric and narrative basic structure of the language of faith. The cross of Christ reveals the character and ground of this interruption to be God's love, and the theological explication of this event requires

the Trinitarian development of this expression of love (in language) that God is.

4.3.3. Twentieth-century analytic, phenomenological, and hermeneutical approaches focus on the aspect of the *religious use of language*.

4.3.3.1. The critical turn in analytic philosophy (G. E. Moore, B. Russell, Wittgenstein) as directed toward language led in logical → positivism (R. Carnap, A. J. Ayer, A. Flew) to the charge that religious language is meaningless because it cannot be verified or falsified. This charge is answered neither by eschatological verification beyond this life (J. Hick) nor by religious → experience in this life (J. B. Wilson, H. D. Lewis, N. Smart). Such responses merely displaced the problem altogether or, because of the irreducibly personal reference attaching to all religious experience, were able to demonstrate the cognitive validity of religious statements only in terms of transcendental philosophy on the basis of experience as such rather than empirically with regard to religious experience.

In contrast to a one-sided empirical focus on the cognitivity of religious statements (i.e., their capacity for articulating truth), more exact analyses of religious usage have been undertaken (→ Cognition 1). It is expressive, emotive, and conative (R. M. Hare, R. B. Braithwaite, R. Hepburn), or interpretative, symbolic, and expressive of reality. The role of images, parables, metaphors, and myths is examined (I. M. Crombie, F. Ferré, I. T. Ramsey). The logical status of God as a name, concept, or description is analyzed (E. L. Mascall, M. Durrant, P. Geach). The problem of analogy (J. M. Bocheński, H. Palmer, J. F. Ross), of metaphor (I. G. Barbour, M. Hesse, J. Soskice), and of the religious use of images (Wittgenstein, W. D. Hudson, D. Z. Phillips) is discussed.

The need to move from a syntactic-semantic to a pragmatic analysis of religious language becomes clearer in relation to the analysis of human speech (J. L. Austin, J. R. Searle) and with reference to the function of religious language in acts such as confession, consoling, and praying (D. D. Evans, J. W. McClendon, M. Mananzan; see also O. Bayer, H. Luther, R. Wonneberger, and H. P. Hecht). This approach involves not just approximation to a linguistic theory (W. A. de Pater, E. Güttgemanns) but insight into the way religious language and action is interwoven into the overall cultural interaction (Dalferth). The same result is reached in analyses of religious language based on the later philosophy of Wittgenstein (1889-1951) that interrelate speech and life, language games and forms of life, and that explain theology as the grammar of religious language that cannot be thought of simply in terms of the rational criteria of scientific speech (N. Malcolm, P. L. Holmer, P. Winch, Phillips).

The ensuing charge of fideism (K. Nielsen) fails to see that the thesis of the intrinsically internal nature of all criteria of rationality and reality implies a fundamentally new orientation for the question of reality. Reality itself is unavoidably plural in nature, and its unity applies only within the linguistically articulated transition between life-forms whose understandings of reality exhibit only family resemblances. At this point the postmodern discussion can begin (J.-F. Lyotard).

4.3.3.2. In its orientation toward the actual use of religious language, the methods of analytic philosophy of religion resemble those of the phenomenological analyses of language and religion. If understanding is a linguistic and socially mediated interpretive stance toward reality in which we see, construe, interpret, and experience something *as* something, then such understanding always takes place within the intersubjective framework of a social form of life mediated by language, since there can be no merely "private language" or a speaker who is wholly detached socially.

The existential-ontological premise of M. Heidegger (1889-1976) overcame the subject-oriented phenomenology of E. Husserl (1859-1938) by postulating an even more fundamental relationship between understanding and self-understanding. Heidegger defined understanding as the basic ontological structure of existence within the actual world. The historical hermeneutic of dialogue of H. G. Gadamer (1900-2002) developed this original relationship more precisely through an analysis of the context of linguistic tradition of which every person engaged in understanding is already a part. This view suggested the existence of promising relationships between phenomenological and hermeneutical traditions, on the one hand, and, on the other, analytic traditions of the other, relationships being variously analyzed in today's discussion (P. Ricoeur, H. Jauss, G. Lindbeck, W. G. Jeanrond, Blumenberg, Dalferth).

The phenomenological traditions of Husserl and Heidegger are being productively continued not only within the French cultural sphere but elsewhere as well (Lévinas, A. T. Peperzak, X. Tilliette, K. E. Løgstrup, H. Adriaanse, J. L. Marion). Moreover, linguistic-phenomenological descriptions of religion, as well as religiohistorical language research, continues to play an important role in religious studies (G. Mensching, F. Melzer, U. Mann).

4.3.3.3. A hermeneutical theology (R. Bultmann,

E. Fuchs, Ebeling) on the basis of the theology of the Word of God of Luther and Barth, and under the influence of the later Heidegger, had already addressed the problem of speech (→ Hermeneutics 3.2 and 3.3). Like dialectical theology, it began with the impossibility of continuing to speak about God in the traditional way, given past experiences. Bultmann countered the theology focused on the facts of salvation by focusing instead on the salvific event of the kerygma and its capacity to illuminate existence and by implementing this view methodologically in his program of → demythologization and existential interpretation. At the same time, the salvation-event was shown to be a language-event. It thus took into account both the linguistic nature of human existence (Fuchs) and the word-event of the whole Christ-happening (Ebeling; → Existentialism).

Language is here a self-exposition of being that comes to expression in speech, in and through us. In it we must distinguish between the authentic self-exposition of being and our own inauthentic statements and expressions. The criterion is the Word of God. The only usage that is authentic is that which sees us as God sees us — as justified sinners (→ Justification). Authentic language thus takes place as a word-event whose basic structure is "I say something to you" (Ebeling) and that discloses our true situation as human beings.

The categories of word-event or speech-event are not just pragmatic or existential; they are also theological, implying a Christological (Fuchs, Jüngel) or sacramental (Ebeling) understanding of language. Problems with this view are (1) its isolation from linguistic research and theory (Güttgemanns); (2) subjection to political, ideological (→ Ideology), and sexist misuse (→ Sexism 1); (3) a sometimes uncritical absolutizing of the category of word-event; and (4) blindness to new hermeneutical discussions based on the contributions of poststructuralism and deconstructionism (→ Structuralism).

All these faults are consequences of the basic difficulty of mediating the thesis of the priority of the linguistic self-exposition, not only of God, but of being, with conceptions of language that follow Schleiermacher or Gadamer in focusing on dialogue and communication. If the model of the word-event is consistently limited to the self-exposition of God and not of being (Jüngel), then there can be a fruitful sensitivity to metaphoric and narrative language in the biblical tradition (H. Weder, W. Harnisch), in systematic theology (Jüngel, G. Bader), and in practical theology (A. Grözinger), with varied links to the thought of Ricoeur and to Blumenberg's view of metaphor (Stoellger).

5. Medium of Religious Communication

Practically, language is an express theme in practical theology (H. Fischer). Relevant discussions are problems of Bible translation (E. Nida; → Bible Versions); the homiletic rediscovery of narrative and rhetoric (Grözinger, G. Otto; → Preaching 4.3.2); the significance of narrative, poetic, and fictional language in → religious education (G. Baudler, W. Neidhart); the problem of inclusive language in the liturgy and church; the role of depth psychology in interpreting Scripture (E. Drewermann; → Depth-Pychological Exegesis); and sociolinguistic research into religious language, including holy silence and glossolalia (W. J. Samarin). In sum, we can say that by a change in the paradigm of language, theology has become more sensitive, both theoretically and practically, to the as yet unforeseeable consequences of the broadened and deepened understanding of religious language.

→ Linguistics

Bibliography: Language, religion: W. P. ALSTON, *Divine Nature and Human Language: Essays in Philosophical Theology* (Ithaca, N.Y., 1989) • I. U. DALFERTH, *Theology and Philosophy* (2d ed.; Eugene, Oreg., 2001) • N. K. FRANKENBERRY, ed., *Language, Truth, and Religious Belief: Studies in Twentieth-Century Theory and Method in Religion* (Atlanta, 1999) • A. GRÖZINGER, *Die Sprache des Menschen* (Munich, 1991) • R. P. SHRIVASTAVA, *Language, Meaning, and Religion* (Delhi, 1990) • R. SWINBURNE, *The Coherence of Theism* (rev. ed.; Oxford, 1993); idem, *Faith and Reason* (2d ed.; Oxford, 1983).

Religious language: H.-C. ASKANI, *Das Problem der Übersetzung. Dargestellt an Franz Rosenzweig* (Tübingen, 1997) • I. G. BARBOUR, *Myths, Models, and Paradigms: The Nature of Scientific and Religious Language* (London, 1974) • M. KAEMPFERT, ed., *Probleme der religiösen Sprache* (Darmstadt, 1983) • M. M. OLIVETTI, ed., *Religione, parola, scrittura* (Padua, 1992) • D. Z. PHILLIPS, *Wittgenstein and Religion* (New York, 1993) • J. F. A. SAWYER, *Sacred Languages and Sacred Texts* (London, 1999) • D. R. STIVER, *The Philosophy of Religious Language: Sign, Symbol, and Story* (Cambridge, Mass., 1996) • H. TONKIN and A. A. KEEF, eds., *Language in Religion* (Lanham, Md., 1989).

Language in theology: R. BERNHARDT and U. LINK-WIECZOREK, eds., *Metapher und Wirklichkeit. Die Logik der Bildhaftigkeit im Reden von Gott, Mensch und Natur* (Göttingen, 1999) • M. BUNTFUSS, *Tradition und Innovation. Die Funktion der Metapher in der theologischen Theoriesprache* (Berlin, 1997) • G. H. CLARK, *Language and Theology* (2d ed.; Jefferson, Md., 1993) • I. U. DALFERTH, *Religiöse Rede von Gott* (Munich, 1981) • I. T. RAMSEY, *Religious Language* (London, 1993; orig. pub., 1957) • P. RICOEUR and E. JÜNGEL, *Metapher. Zur Hermeneutik religiöser Sprache* (Munich, 1974) • P. STOELLGER, *Metapher und Lebenswelt* (Tübingen, 2000) • G. WARD, *Barth, Derrida, and the Language of Theology* (Cambridge, 1995) • H. WEDER, ed., *Die Sprache der Bilder. Gleichnis und Metapher in Literatur und Theologie* (Gütersloh, 1989) • N. WOLTERSTORFF, *Divine Discourse: Philosophical Reflections on the Claim That God Speaks* (Cambridge, 1995).

Theological language: G. EBELING, *Introduction to a Theological Theory of Language* (Philadelphia, 1973) • S. GÄRTNER, *Gottesrede in (post)-moderner Gesellschaft. Grundlagen einer praktisch-theologischen Sprachlehre* (Paderborn, 2000) • W. A. DE PATER, *Theologische Sprachlogik* (Munich, 1971) • D. Z. PHILLIPS, *Faith after Foundationalism: Plantinga–Rorty–Lindbeck–Berger. Critiques and Alternatives* (2d ed.; Boulder, Colo., 1995) • W. SCHNEEMELCHER, ed., *Das Problem der Sprache in Theologie und Kirche* (Berlin, 1959) • M. C. TAYLOR, *Erring: A Postmodern A/theology* (Chicago, 1984) • R. VOLP, ed., *Zeichen. Semiotik in Theologe und Gottesdienst* (Munich, 1982).

Practical matters: P. HÜNERMANN and R. SCHAEFFLER, *Theorie der Sprachhandlungen und heutige Ekklesiologie* (Freiburg, 1987) • J. KIRCHBERG, *Theologie in der Anrede als Weg zur Verständigung zwischen Juden und Christen* (Innsbruck, 1991) • T. LUKSCH, *Predigt als metaphorische Gott-Rede. Zum Ertrag der Metaphernforschung für die Homiletik* (Würzburg, 1998) • G. RAMSHAW, *God beyond Gender: Feminist Christian God-Language* (Minneapolis, 1995) • D. TRACY, *Plurality and Ambiguity: Hermeneutics, Religion, Hope* (San Francisco, 1987) • R. J. VANDER MEY, *God Talk: The Triteness and Truth in Christian Clichés* (Downers Grove, Ill., 1993) • R. ZERFASS, ed., *Erzählter Glaube, erzählende Kirche* (Freiburg, 1988) • J. A. ZIMMERMAN, *Liturgy as Language of Faith: A Liturgical Methodology in the Mode of Paul Ricoeur's Textual Hermeneutics* (Lanham, Md., 1988).

INGOLF U. DALFERTH

Laos

1. Geography and Demographics

Laos — in full, the Lao People's Democratic Republic — is a landlocked nation in Southeast Asia domi-

	1960	*1980*	*2000*
Population (1,000s):	2,177	3,205	5,693
Annual growth rate (%):	2.22	2.29	2.80

Area: 236,800 sq. km. (91,429 sq. mi.)

A.D. *2000*

Population density: 24/sq. km. (62/sq. mi.)
Births / deaths: 3.95 / 1.16 per 100 population
Fertility rate: 5.92 per woman
Infant mortality rate: 76 per 1,000 live births
Life expectancy: 56.0 years (m: 54.5, f: 57.5)
Religious affiliation (%): Buddhists 48.2, tribal religionists 41.3, nonreligious 4.6, Christians 2.7 (Roman Catholics 1.0, other Christians 1.7), Chinese folk religionists 1.5, atheists 1.2, other 0.5.

nated by jungles, with high mountains along its eastern border. Its longest borders are with Viet Nam to the east and Thailand to the west, with shorter borders also with China (north), Cambodia (south), and Myanmar (west). Ethnically, the largest groups in 2001 were the Lao Loum (or Valley Lao, 68 percent), Lao Theung (Hill Lao, 22 percent), and Lao Soung (Mountain Lao, which includes Hmong and Yao, 9 percent). There are also Vietnamese and Chinese → minorities. Four-fifths of the labor force is engaged in subsistence agriculture; in 1999 the literacy rate was estimated to be only 57 percent. Laos is one of the poorest countries in Asia.

2. History

The Lao, a Thai people, came to Laos from northern Viet Nam in the 11th century, becoming part of the Khmer kingdom ruled from Angkor. The rise of several small Laotian states led to a West Laos and East Laos. The princes of East Laos established the tradition of modern Laos. Under Fa Ngum in the 14th century, Theravada → Buddhism became the state religion. In the early 16th century spirit cults were banned, and their shrines destroyed. Rivalries for the throne and foreign incursions (e.g., by the Annam from Viet Nam) led to division into three kingdoms: Vientiane, Luang Prabang, and Champassak. With the conquering of Vientiane by Siam in 1778, all Laos became Siamese.

In 1893 Siam withdrew from the west bank of the Mekong River and recognized Laos as a French protectorate. The French did not infringe on the privileges of the Laotian crown (→ Colonialism), but they showed little interest in the development of Laos. After a brief occupation by Japan a movement for Laotian sovereignty declared independence from France in 1945. France restored its control in 1946.

The mainly rural resistance groups under Prince

Souphanouvong founded the movement Lao Issara (Free Laos). They first withdrew to Thailand but then returned to Laos as the Pathet Lao (National Lao movement). The 14-nation Geneva Conference of 1954 established Laos as a unified, independent buffer state between Thailand and North Viet Nam. When the Pathet Lao did not secure recognition at the conference, however, civil war ensued, which lasted until 1975. During this period the rightist royalist government of Laos received massive aid from the United States and Thailand, as did the Communist Pathet Lao from North Viet Nam, but neither side was able to dislodge the other. Between 1964 and 1973 the United States, helped by the Hmong mountaineers, heavily bombed Laos. The Paris Peace Conference of 1973 restored the Pathet Lao under Souphanouvong, who in 1975 became president of the newly established Lao People's Democratic Republic.

Before easing foreign investment laws in 1988, Laos relied almost exclusively on Viet Nam for military and financial aid and policy direction. Although Laos still had a Communist government in 2001, it was pursuing economic liberalization. In 1997 it joined the Association of Southeast Asian Nations.

3. Buddhism and Phi Cult

Buddhism came relatively late to the small Laotian states. The domestic situation, including the instability and final overthrow of the partial monarchies, contributed to its success. At the same time, belief in a spirit religion, or *phi* worship, spread widely. The *phi* were venerated as protective spirits, but especially as the *khwan* (soul-substances) of those who had died by accident or who had been possessed; they were also feared as spirits that had not become ancestral spirits (→ Ancestor Worship). In village ceremonies the *khwan* are summoned back by village elders, who have the name *pham* (related to "Brahman," the highest, priestly class). Buddhism never mixed with the *phi* cult, but there are points of contact.

Buddhist culture decayed under foreign influence from the 18th century, but the French protectorate helped to strengthen it. The Buddhist monastic orders and school system were reorganized in 1951. The education of conservative politicians in the West during the 1960s and 1970s, which influenced their lifestyle, had a shattering effect on Laotian Buddhism. Some monks are critical of the consumer society, but others have accepted uncritically a reduced role for themselves. Many Pathet Lao are convinced Buddhists, but in the first years after 1975 the → bureaucracy regimented the work of the → monasteries.

After a volatile history Buddhism now enjoys recognition as an integral part of Lao culture. Buddhist monks and nuns, living in 2,800 monasteries and village temples, are united in the Lao Buddhist Fellowship, a member of the Asian Buddhist Conference for Peace. They also belong to the comprehensive Laotian Front for National Reconstruction. The Department of Religious Affairs oversees the teaching of Buddhism, making sure that it conforms to Marxist principles.

4. Churches

4.1. *Roman Catholic*

The → Roman Catholic Church owes the beginnings of its missionary history in Laos to the → Jesuits, who reached Laos from Tongking in approximately 1630 (→ Mission 3). The Société des Missions Étrangères de Paris followed in 1750. Missionary work intensified after 1876, with the first mission set up on the island of Don in the Mekong River (1885) and an apostolic vicariate established in Vientiane (1899). The Oblates of the Immaculate Virgin Mary (O.M.I.) came to northern Laos in 1935, while the Société des Missions Étrangères was based in the south of the country in Savannakhet, where an apostolic vicariate was established in 1958. The first Laotian → priest was ordained in 1963, the first Laotian → bishop consecrated in 1974. In 1997 there were four Laotian bishops and 18 diocesan priests. After 1975 the flight of many Roman Catholic Vietnamese families to Laos led to a sense of greater independence for the church. The work currently focuses on lay instruction and the promotion of rural → base communities.

4.2. *Protestant*

The first Protestant missionary to Laos was Daniel McGilvary (1828-1911), who, commissioned by the Presbyterian Church, U.S.A. (→ Reformed and Presbyterian Churches), came first to northern Thailand, then in 1868 to Luang Prabang, where he worked among the rural Khmer mountaineers. Approximately 500 Khmu were baptized in the years that followed.

The first Protestant church in Laos was founded by Darbyite missionaries from Switzerland working in the Missionaire Évangélique (→ Darbyites). Their work, which was oriented to Bible translation, began among the Lao Loum of southern Savannakhet (1902). The Overseas Missionary Fellowship came in 1957. Independent local churches have been formed, and lay preachers and catechists trained.

In 1929 the → Christian and Missionary Alliance began work among the mountain tribes of the north. The Laotian Evangelical Church (LEC), founded in about 1970 as the fruit of mission work, had strong ties to the rightist regime before 1975. After the Communists took control, some 5,000 Protestant Christians left the country. In 2000 the LEC had 22,000 members, and there were perhaps 10,000 other Christians in 500 independent groups. The LEC belongs to the → Christian Conference of Asia and the Evangelical Fellowship of Asia (→ Evangelical Movement). By participating in the Lao Front for National Reconstruction, the church hopes for better chances of → dialogue and public sharing in national life, as well as for ecumenical encounter (→ Ecumenical Dialogue).

The missions mentioned had to leave Laos after 1975, but the Mennonite Central Committee (→ Mennonites) and the → Friends, with North American workers, took up a ministry of reconciliation. The evangelical aid organization World Concern also entered Laos in 1981. From 1984 onward most of the Christian aid societies operating in Laos merged into Laos Christian Services.

The constitution of 1991 guarantees religious freedom and welcomes religious-based humanitarian organizations, yet the government restricts this liberty in practice. In some cases, Christian groups have suffered persecution on the basis of laws against causing "social turmoil."

→ Asian Theology

Bibliography: D. B. BARRETT et al., eds., *WCE* (2d ed.) 1.438-41 • Y. BOURDET, *The Economics of Transition in Laos: From Socialism to ASEAN Integration* (Northampton, Mass., 2000) • G. EVANS, *The Politics of Ritual and Remembrance: Laos since 1975* (Honolulu, 1998); idem, ed., *Laos: Culture and Society* (Chiang Mai, 1999) • C. J. IRESON, *Field, Forest, and Family: Women's Work and Power in Rural Laos* (Boulder, Colo., 1996) • D. MCGILVARY, *A Half Century among the Siamese and the Lao* (New York, 1912) • W. SAGE and J. HENCHY, eds., *Laos: A Bibliography* (Singapore, 1986) • B. L. SMITH, *Religion and Legitimation of Power in Thailand, Laos, and Burma* (Chambersburg, Pa., 1978) • M. STUART-FOX, *Buddhist Kingdom, Marxist State: The Making of Modern Laos* (Bangkok, 1996); idem, *Historical Dictionary of Laos* (2d ed.; Lanham, Md., 2001); idem, *A History of Laos* (New York, 1997) • M. THAN and J. L. H. TAN, eds., *Laos' Dilemmas and Options: The Challenge of Economic Transition in the 1990s* (New York, 1997) • J. J. ZASLOFF and L. UNGER, eds., *Laos: Beyond the Revolution* (New York, 1991).

WOLFGANG GERN

Lapsi

The lapsi were apostates from the Christian faith during the → persecution under Decius (249-51). An edict of the emperor in February 250 ordered the whole population to show loyalty to the gods of the → Roman Empire by an act of → sacrifice (→ Roman Religion). Local commissions supervised the execution of the edict and gave a certificate *(libellus)* for compliance.

A shocking number of Christians yielded. Since the edict applied only for a set time, however, many sought readmission to the church's fellowship. As might be expected, the question of readmission gave rise to controversy. On the one side were those who, during this early period of Christianity, viewed idolatry, like murder and adultery, as a → sin for which there was no forgiveness. On the other side were those who, from the beginning of the third century, saw → penitence and the → authority of the church to forgive as occasionally applying to such sins (see Ps. 6:5).

Important decisions were taken by → Cyprian, bishop of Carthage (248/49-58), at two → synods (251 and 252) vis-à-vis the opposing parties. Cyprian's view was complicated by the fact that among his radical opponents were heroes of the faith, whereas Cyprian himself had evaded the authorities by flight. The attitude and situation of Dionysius, bishop of Alexandria (248-64), were similar. Among those who refused compliance and had been imprisoned, being honored as confessors (almost as highly as → martyrs), were the rigorists, who called for a pure → church and rejected any reconciliation with the lapsi. This position led them into schism (→ Heresies and Schisms) in Rome (and beyond) under Novatian (a rival bishop of Rome from 251) against Cornelius (pope 251-53). The same thing happened later amid the tetrarch persecutions in Egypt (306) under Melitius (d. ca. 325) against Peter of Alexandria (d. 311), then yet again in Carthage at the time of the → Donatist schism. But the confessors also had a laxer wing consisting of those who, on the strength of their → charism of a strong faith, immediately gave letters of peace to lapsi seeking readmission.

Against the two fronts Cyprian strengthened and extended the institution of episcopal penance (→ Bishop, Episcopate), which was received by the *ecclesia catholica* at Arles (314) and → Nicaea (325). Cyprian distinguished the lapsi into those certified as having sacrificed — either *sacrificati* (full sacrifice) or *turificati* (incense sacrifice) — and then additionally the group of *libellatici* (those with a certificate, gained through bribery or a surrogate, who did not make an offering). The severity of → guilt and extenuating circumstances were weighed by the bishop, and the penitential period before readmission was fixed accordingly. No penitent lapsi, however, were to be left in fear of eternal damnation.

The acute problem of the lapsi thus led to episcopal usurpation of the authority to remit sins, though in the light of the historical alternative, we see that the bishops used it pastorally (see Luke 15:3-7) and with Christian mercy.

Bibliography: H. von Campenhausen, *Ecclesiastical Authority and Spiritual Power in the Church of the First Three Centuries* (Peabody, Mass., 1997; orig. pub., 1953) • Cyprian, *The Lapsed: The Unity of the Catholic Church*, ACW 25 • W. H. C. Frend, *Martyrdom and Persecution in the Early Church: A Study of a Conflict from the Maccabees to Donatus* (Oxford, 1965) • J. Grotz, *Die Entwicklung des Bußstufenwesens in der vornicänischen Kirche* (Freiburg, 1955) • J. D. Laurance, *Priest as Type of Christ: The Leader of the Eucharist in Salvation History according to Cyprian of Carthage* (New York, 1984) • A. D. Lee, *Pagans and Christians in Late Antiquity: A Sourcebook* (London, 2000) • B. Poschmann, *Paenitentia secunda* (Bonn, 1940) • H. Rahner, *Church and State in Early Christianity* (San Francisco, 1992) • J. J. Sebastian, ". . . *Baptisma unum in sancta ecclesia . . .*": *A Theological Appraisal of the Baptismal Controversy in the Work and Writings of Cyprian of Carthage* (Delhi, 1997) • R. Selinger, *Die Religionspolitik des Kaisers Decius. Anatomie einer Christenverfolgung* (New York, 1994).

Ekkehard Mühlenberg

Last Judgment

1. Term
2. Bible
3. History of Dogma
4. Relevance and Discussion Today

1. Term

The term "last judgment," based on the "last times" of 2 Esdr. 7:73, is used for the last and definitive consummation of history. It is also called the universal judgment, for it pertains to all, both good and bad. It is the judgment of Christ insofar as it brings into play his nature and his action. Since the last judgment is not the mere completion of an immanent process but is subject primarily to the sovereignty of God, it is also called the judgment of God.

2. Bible

2.1. There is as yet no monographic account of the last judgment in the OT. Exposition of the OT tries to bring together under the term the many different aspects in the different traditions and complexes. The early period bases the last judgment on the kingship of God (e.g., see 1 Sam. 24:15; Ps. 82:2-4). We then have prophecies of judgment (→ Prophet, Prophecy), which include announcement of judgment, reasons for judgment, complaint, proof of → guilt, and pleas. In this structured presentation the concept is eschatological and apocalyptic. The prophets await the disruptive action of God in judgment. As Judge, he will prevail over all foes and all opposing powers and bring the history of the world to its consummation (2 Esdr. 7:70-74; Dan. 12:2; Joel 3:14, etc.).

2.2. There is also no comprehensive monograph on the last judgment in the NT. The preaching of both → John the Baptist and → Jesus is governed by the thought of judgment (Matt. 3:7-12; 10:28, etc.). Jesus' concept of judgment is individualistic, not national. The command of → love will be the standard (Matt. 25:31-46). Jesus is Judge (Mark 14:62), but the verdict also depends on one's attitude to him.

→ Paul has a rich vocabulary of judgment. In him the last judgment is the coming day of wrath (1 Thess. 1:10; 5:9). God is Judge (2 Thess. 1:5; Rom. 2:2-3), and so is Christ (2 Cor. 5:10). The judgment is universal; all must give account (Rom. 14:10-12). Both pessimistic features and assurance of salvation characterize the judgment (Rom. 5:9).

→ John speaks of the traditional last judgment in which the Son will judge the living and the dead (John 5:27-30). The typical Johannine view, however, is that the coming of Christ into the world means judgment already (9:39).

Hebrews includes the last judgment in the list of basic teachings of the Christian → faith (6:2). Revelation tells the great drama of the last judgment, in which the enemy of God is defeated and → salvation is granted to the elect (esp. 20:11-15).

3. History of Dogma

With its acceptance into the → Niceno-Constantinopolitan Creed, the last judgment became part of the church's ecumenical legacy of faith, even though there was no consensus about the details of the judgment. In → Alexandrian theology, for example, it was a spur to moral action, while in the Latin church it was the place of legal reward and punishment. → Augustine (354-430) stressed the significance of the returning Christ as Judge (*De civ. Dei* 20.30; → Augustine's Theology). → Scholasti-

cism was interested in the sequence of events (see the *Sentences* of Peter Lombard), for which popular and ecclesiastical art supplied illustrations. There were also dramas of the last judgment in which Christ figured almost solely as the stern Judge (→ Iconography).

The → Reformers stressed the importance of Christ as Judge, but M. → Luther (1483-1546) freed himself from the works righteousness of papal teaching, which ignores the significance of Christ's pardon in judgment (WA 47.310.7ff.; → Luther's Theology). U. → Zwingli (1484-1531) thought that there will be manifested at the last judgment that which is decided immediately at physical death (*Exposition and Defense of the Theses*, art. 57; → Zwingli's Theology). J. → Calvin (1509-64) especially emphasized justification by grace alone, even in judgment (*Inst.* 3.11.13-23; 3.12; → Calvin's Theology). The Council of → Trent clung to traditional teaching.

4. Relevance and Discussion Today

Today there is some uncertainty as to the function of the last judgment, now that the importance of judgment by works has been diminished by Reformation theology. History as an anticipation of the last judgment can itself be viewed as world judgment (J. Moltmann). On this view history is a permanent crisis. The last judgment retains its significance as a consummation of what is necessarily provisional in time. It is the manifestation of that which essentially and basically constitutes and conditions our space-time reality here and now.

The hermeneutical problem in talking about the last judgment is that of coordinating divine and human action. Can human action be adequate to God's judging and assessing action in such a way that the last judgment can be a theme of theological reflection? Sermons on judgment (→ Preaching) among the → sects and in the churches for the most part give a positive answer either by presenting the last judgment as a threat or by seeing it as executed in some historical event.

→ Apocalypticism; Apocatastasis; Assurance of Salvation; Death; Eschatology; Forgiveness; Grace; Hope; Parousia; Predestination; Reconciliation; Resurrection; Righteousness, Justice; Soteriology; Time and Eternity; Wrath of God

Bibliography: T. AONO, *Die Entwicklung des paulinischen Gerichtsgedankens bei den Apostolischen Vätern* (Vienna, 1979) • G. BORNKAMM, "Die Offenbarung des Zornes Gottes. Röm 1–3," *Das Ende des Gesetzes. Gesamte Aufsätze* (vol. 1; 5th ed.; Munich, 1966) 9-33 •

E. Brunner, *Eternal Hope* (Philadelphia, 1954) • M. Bull, ed., *Apocalypse Theory and the Ends of the World* (Oxford, 1995) • A. Y. Collins, *Cosmology and Eschatology in Jewish and Christian Apocalypticism* (Leiden, 1996) • C. E. Evans and P. W. Flint, eds., *Eschatology, Messianism, and the Dead Sea Scrolls* (Grand Rapids, 1997) • R. Guardini, *Eternal Life: What You Need to Know about Death, Judgment, and Life Everlasting* (Manchester, N.H., 1998; orig. pub., 1940) • G. D. Kaufman, *Systematic Theology* (New York, 1968) chap. 22 • P. Lehmann, *The Transfiguration of Politics* (New York, 1975) • J. Macquarrie, *Principles of Christian Theology* (New York, 1966) chap. 15 • J. Moltmann, *Theology of Hope* (Minneapolis, 1993; orig. pub., 1964) • R. Niebuhr, *Beyond Tragedy: Essays on the Christian Interpretation of History* (Freeport, N.Y., 1971; orig. pub., 1937) • W. Pannenberg, *Theology and the Kingdom of God* (Philadelphia, 1969) • K. Rahner, *On the Theology of Death* (New York, 1962) • H. G. Reventlow, ed., *Eschatology in the Bible and in Jewish and Christian Tradition* (Sheffield, 1997) • P. Tillich, *Systematic Theology* (3 vols. in 1; Chicago, 1967) 3.398-401 • K. L. Yinger, *Paul, Judaism, and Judgment according to Deeds* (New York, 1999).

Klaus Otte

Latin America and the Caribbean

In current U.N. usage the "major area" (i.e., continent) "Latin America and the Caribbean" includes the entire continental landmass south of the United States, plus the collection of islands roughly enclosing the Caribbean Sea. Besides the Caribbean (also called the West Indies), this major area comprises the regions of Central America (here referring to the eight countries from Mexico south to Panama) and South America.

1. Latin America

1.1. *Term*

"Latin America" was from the beginning a cultural-historical rather than a geographic term. Although the origin of this term is disputed, Mónica Quijada has shown that it has roots in Spanish America, where it came into use beginning in the 1850s. Hence the previously widespread thesis that the term reflects exclusively the expansionist French politics of Napoléon III must be revised. In the following discussion the term "Latin America" is also used anachronistically in reference to the colonial period and geographically in the larger sense.

1.2. *Indigenous Religions*

Even though the developmental stages of the neo-evolutionist model as represented since Julian H. Stewart are disputed, its three-part schema does help in distinguishing broadly the cultural forms and their attendant religious developments that the European conquerors found when they first came to the New World.

1.2.1. At the *least-developed cultural stage* were hunters, fishers, and gatherers, with or without the beginnings of agriculture. On their arrival the earliest Europeans found marginal tribes, as well as tropical forest tribes with developed agriculture, the cultivation of tropical roots, and such achievements as river navigation, hammocks, and ceramics.

Among virtually all the tribes we find the idea of a supreme god, a creator god, and a tribal father. This cultic hero might be worshiped directly or in magic and cultic rites. Hunters typically worshiped animal deities, and farmers, vegetation deities. The → myth of spirits in the form of the human head was common, originating generally among hunters. The corresponding cultic instrument, the pumpkin rattle, was found mainly among farmers, who worked out the association between the head and the hollowed out pumpkin.

Shamans, who used the rattle as their main instrument, derived from the religious sphere of hunters. The → shaman had influence over wilderness spirits, which allowed hunters, after appropriate → sacrifices and on threat of → punishment, only a limited number of animals. As long as they were undisturbed by whites, these tribes thus maintained the ecological balance (→ Ecology). The shaman had important functions relating to the origination of the → soul in the newborn and the destruction of the dangerous animal soul of humans after death.

The burial practices of the tropical tribes also pointed to a link between → human sacrifices, fertility, and a belief in → resurrection. The common

Latin America and the Caribbean in A.D. 2000: Demography

	Population (1,000s)	Annual Growth Rate (%)	Population Density (per sq. km. / mi.)	Births / Deaths (per 100 pop.)	Fertility Rate (per woman)	Infant Mortality Rate (per 1,000 live births)	Life Expectancy (years)
World total	6,091,351	1.27	45 / 116	2.13 / 0.86	2.66	51	66.9
Latin America	514,688	1.41	25 / 65	2.13 / 0.64	2.48	32	70.7
Caribbean[a]	37,757	1.05	162 / 419	2.00 / 0.76	2.52	37	70.1
Bahamas	302	1.39	22 / 56	1.72 / 0.52	1.95	12	74.8
Barbados	264	0.32	615 / 1,592	1.34 / 0.85	1.73	8	77.1
Cuba	11,201	0.30	101 / 262	1.16 / 0.72	1.55	8	76.7
Dominican Republic	8,495	1.43	175 / 454	2.18 / 0.52	2.57	30	72.2
Haiti	7,817	1.84	282 / 731	3.29 / 1.19	4.40	73	55.7
Jamaica	2,587	0.95	235 / 609	1.91 / 0.54	2.27	10	75.5
Trinidad and Tobago	1,341	0.99	261 / 677	1.72 / 0.61	2.10	12	74.6
Central America	135,497	1.66	55 / 141	2.40 / 0.52	2.75	29	72.7
Belize	242	2.26	11 / 27	2.75 / 0.39	3.14	27	75.7
Costa Rica	3,798	1.84	74 / 192	2.24 / 0.40	2.78	11	77.3
El Salvador	6,319	1.92	300 / 778	2.50 / 0.58	2.76	35	70.7
Guatemala	12,222	2.68	112 / 291	3.39 / 0.60	4.43	34	69.0
Honduras	6,485	2.49	58 / 149	3.00 / 0.51	3.72	31	71.0
Mexico	98,881	1.42	50 / 131	2.22 / 0.51	2.49	28	73.4
Nicaragua	4,694	2.41	36 / 92	3.02 / 0.53	3.35	39	69.7
Panama	2,856	1.43	38 / 98	2.03 / 0.51	2.42	19	74.8
South America[b]	341,434	1.35	19 / 50	2.03 / 0.67	2.37	33	70.2
Argentina	37,032	1.19	13 / 34	1.90 / 0.78	2.44	20	74.2
Bolivia	8,329	2.15	8 / 20	3.05 / 0.82	3.92	56	63.6
Brazil	169,202	1.18	20 / 51	1.89 / 0.72	2.10	38	68.3
Chile	15,211	1.18	20 / 52	1.82 / 0.57	2.35	12	76.0
Colombia	38,905	1.47	34 / 88	2.13 / 0.55	2.51	30	72.1
Ecuador	12,646	1.74	46 / 120	2.32 / 0.58	2.76	41	70.8
Guyana	874	0.98	4 / 11	1.88 / 0.70	2.10	52	66.2
Paraguay	5,496	2.46	14 / 35	2.96 / 0.51	3.84	37	70.8
Peru	25,662	1.60	20 / 52	2.26 / 0.62	2.64	37	69.8
Suriname	452	1.00	3 / 7	1.84 / 0.54	2.10	20	72.7
Uruguay	3,274	0.55	19 / 48	1.64 / 1.04	2.19	16	73.3
Venezuela	24,170	1.82	27 / 69	2.28 / 0.47	2.72	19	73.7

Note: Because of rounding, population figures for the regions and the major area as a whole may not equal the sum of their constituent parts.
[a]Figures include Anguilla (U.K.), Antigua and Barbuda, Aruba (Neth.), British Virgin Islands, Cayman Islands (U.K.), Dominica, Grenada, Guadeloupe (Fr.), Martinique (Fr.), Montserrat (U.K.), Netherlands Antilles, Puerto Rico (U.S.), St. Kitts and Nevis, St. Lucia, St. Vincent and Grenadines, Turks and Caicos Islands (U.K.), United States Virgin Islands. [b]Figures include Falkland Islands (U.K.), French Guiana.

tasting of the ashes of the dead (i.e., endocannibalism) among agrarian tribes was a resurrection ritual within a → worldview that viewed the process of becoming and decaying after the model of plants. Material concepts of supernatural beings were rare in these cultures.

1.2.2. Tribes at the *intermediate cultural stage* were found in the Caribbean and the sub-Andes. Their cultural level was similar to that of formative phases of higher cultures. Distinctive features were class distinctions in → society, supraregional → organization, war for religious and political purposes, tombs and → temples, and improved technology.

The religious ideas of the hunters and farmers still had an impact but, in these tribes, were supplemented by a differentiated cult after the higher cultural pattern with the trinity of temples, → priests, and idols. In case the supreme god was considered an inactive god who did not interfere in worldly affairs, lesser deities were at work. The cult was a response to their activities, for example, in the form of sacrifice. The idea of the unity of all living things (→ Life 2) was prominent, so that the border between gods, humans, and → animals was fluid. The idea of transformations of personal numina — depicted variously as people, animals, or trees — was the source of all → totemistic phenomena. Ancestor worship was usually linked to → animism,

Latin America and the Caribbean in A.D. 2000: Religious Affiliation (as percentage of population)

	Christians	Muslims	Hindus	Non-religious	Chinese Folk Religionists	Buddhists	Tribal Religionists	Atheists	New Religionists	Sikhs	Jews	Spiritists	Other
World total	33.1	20.0	12.8	12.7	6.3	5.9	4.1	2.4	1.6	0.4	0.2	0.2	0.3
Latin America	92.6	0.3	0.2	3.1	—	0.1	0.2	0.5	0.1	—	0.2	2.3	0.4
Caribbean[a]	78.9	0.3	1.0	9.8	0.1	—	—	2.3	—	—	—	7.2	0.4
Bahamas	92.7	—	—	5.1	0.1	—	—	—	—	—	0.3	1.4	0.4
Barbados	97.0	0.8	0.3	0.5	—	—	—	—	—	—	—	—	1.4
Cuba	45.2	0.1	0.2	28.9	0.2	0.1	—	7.3	—	—	—	17.9	0.1
Dominican Republic	95.4	—	—	1.7	0.1	—	—	0.5	—	—	—	2.2	0.1
Haiti	95.9	—	—	1.3	—	—	—	—	—	—	—	2.6	0.2
Jamaica	84.1	0.1	1.2	3.7	0.3	—	—	—	—	—	—	10.1	0.5
Trinidad and Tobago	65.3	7.1	22.1	2.1	0.4	0.3	—	—	—	—	0.1	1.3	1.3
Central America	96.2	0.3	—	2.7	—	—	0.1	0.2	—	—	0.1	0.1	0.3
Belize	90.7	0.6	2.5	0.8	—	0.4	0.1	—	—	—	1.0	0.8	3.1
Costa Rica	96.4	—	—	1.7	1.1	0.1	—	0.2	—	—	0.1	0.1	0.3
El Salvador	97.6	—	—	1.4	—	—	0.3	0.1	—	—	—	—	0.6
Guatemala	98.0	—	—	1.0	—	—	—	0.5	—	—	—	0.2	0.3
Honduras	97.2	0.1	—	0.8	—	0.1	0.1	0.2	—	—	—	1.1	0.4
Mexico	96.0	0.3	—	3.3	—	—	0.1	0.1	—	—	0.1	—	0.1
Nicaragua	96.2	—	—	1.5	0.1	0.1	0.4	0.1	—	—	—	1.4	0.2
Panama	88.2	4.4	0.3	2.4	0.1	0.8	0.7	0.6	0.6	—	0.1	0.5	1.3
South America[b]	92.7	0.3	0.1	2.6	—	0.2	0.3	0.5	0.2	—	0.3	2.6	0.2
Argentina	92.9	2.0	—	2.2	—	0.1	0.2	0.8	0.1	—	1.5	0.2	—
Bolivia	94.4	—	—	1.0	—	0.1	0.7	0.4	—	—	—	—	3.4
Brazil	91.3	0.1	—	2.6	—	0.3	0.1	0.4	0.3	—	0.2	4.7	—
Chile	89.0	—	—	7.2	—	—	0.9	2.5	—	—	0.2	—	0.2
Colombia	96.7	0.1	—	1.2	—	—	0.6	0.2	—	—	—	1.0	0.2
Ecuador	97.5	—	—	1.5	0.1	0.1	0.5	0.1	—	—	—	—	0.2
Guyana	51.3	8.0	32.4	1.5	0.3	0.3	2.1	0.6	—	—	—	1.7	2.0
Paraguay	97.7	—	—	1.2	—	0.2	0.5	0.2	0.1	—	0.1	—	—
Peru	97.2	—	—	1.2	0.1	0.3	0.6	0.2	0.3	—	—	—	0.1
Suriname	50.9	13.1	18.3	4.8	0.2	0.4	1.8	0.1	4.9	—	0.2	3.7	1.7
Uruguay	65.3	—	—	26.9	—	—	—	6.2	—	—	1.2	0.2	0.2
Venezuela	94.9	0.3	—	2.0	—	0.1	0.6	0.2	—	—	0.2	1.1	0.6

Note: A dash represents a value of less than 0.05 percent. Because of rounding, horizontal totals may not equal 100.0.

[a]Figures include Anguilla (U.K.), Antigua and Barbuda, Aruba (Neth.), British Virgin Islands, Cayman Islands (U.K.), Dominica, Grenada, Guadeloupe (Fr.), Martinique (Fr.), Montserrat (U.K.), Netherlands Antilles, Puerto Rico (U.S.), St. Kitts and Nevis, St. Lucia, St. Vincent and Grenadines, Turks and Caicos Islands (U.K.), United States Virgin Islands. [b]Figures include Falkland Islands (U.K.), French Guiana.

the idea that all nature has a soul, the spirits being good or evil in their relation to humans.

1.2.3. At the stage of *developed culture* were the Chibchas in what is now central Colombia and more strictly the Mayas and Aztecs (to name only the best known) in Mesoamerica (i.e., the area from the central valley of Mexico to the center of Costa Rica) and the Incas in South America. Class distinctions became more rigid, and we find political organization into → states and empires, with war for the purpose of conquest or exacting tribute. For the temple cult there was a special priestly class distinct from shamanism. Agriculture was made more productive by irrigation, and settlements could now become regular urban centers.

Artistically, we find ceramics (though no potter's wheels), painting, sculpture, and weaving that can stand comparison with those of antiquity. The Andes tribes excelled in metallurgy (silver, gold, bronze), as well as in weaving, irrigation systems, terracing, and political and economic development (Incas). The Mayas took the lead in developing mathematics (inventing zero and calculating in blocks of 20), which they used in the calendar and in astronomy. They were also advanced in writing systems, today mostly deciphered, which reveal nearly 1,000 years of history.

The religion of the higher cultures was complex, since it incorporated earlier features. In the Inca Empire we find the cult of the sun god Inti, whose

Latin America and the Caribbean in A.D. 2000: Church Affiliation (as percentage of population)

	Total Christians	Roman Catholics	Indigenous	Protestants	Orthodox	Unaffiliated	Anglicans	Marginal
World total	*33.1*	**17.6**	**6.2**	**5.8**	**3.7**	**1.5**	**1.0**	**0.5**
Latin America	*92.6*	**88.5**	**8.3**	**10.1**	**0.1**	**1.1**	**0.2**	**1.5**
Caribbean[a]	*78.9*	**62.7**	**3.7**	**11.4**	—	**3.9**	**1.6**	**1.3**
Bahamas	*92.7*	16.9	6.6	59.6	0.1	7.1	8.9	2.2
Barbados	*97.0*	4.4	7.1	33.3	0.2	21.2	28.1	2.7
Cuba	*45.2*	41.3	1.4	2.2	—	—	—	1.1
Dominican Republic	*95.4*	88.6	1.9	4.9	—	0.1	0.1	0.8
Haiti	*95.9*	83.2	5.5	21.1	—	2.9	1.5	0.7
Jamaica	*84.1*	4.5	9.1	25.9	0.1	39.1	4.1	1.3
Trinidad and Tobago	*65.3*	30.5	3.3	14.2	0.8	3.0	12.1	1.5
Central America	*96.2*	**91.4**	**4.3**	**5.9**	**0.1**	**2.1**	**0.1**	**2.1**
Belize	*90.7*	66.1	2.4	19.1	—	1.5	3.9	2.3
Costa Rica	*96.4*	93.0	2.3	10.5	—	0.3	—	2.4
El Salvador	*97.6*	91.0	11.1	10.3	—	0.5	—	2.5
Guatemala	*98.0*	79.4	9.9	17.4	—	12.0	—	2.0
Honduras	*97.2*	91.3	3.4	8.6	0.1	1.1	0.1	1.5
Mexico	*96.0*	93.0	3.3	3.1	0.1	1.2	—	2.2
Nicaragua	*96.2*	92.0	3.9	15.1	—	0.5	0.2	1.3
Panama	*88.2*	84.4	2.5	13.7	0.1	2.0	0.8	1.8
South America[b]	*92.7*	**90.2**	**10.4**	**11.7**	**0.1**	**0.5**	**0.1**	**1.3**
Argentina	*92.9*	90.2	5.4	5.9	0.5	1.1	0.1	1.4
Bolivia	*94.4*	90.7	1.9	7.4	0.1	0.6	—	1.8
Brazil	*91.3*	89.8	16.1	19.0	0.1	0.1	0.1	1.0
Chile	*89.0*	76.0	27.9	3.0	0.2	1.1	0.1	3.3
Colombia	*96.7*	96.3	1.6	2.8	—	—	—	0.9
Ecuador	*97.5*	94.5	2.1	2.1	—	0.3	—	2.0
Guyana	*51.3*	9.5	3.3	22.6	1.1	6.0	7.8	1.0
Paraguay	*97.7*	94.6	1.3	3.7	0.2	2.5	0.3	0.6
Peru	*97.2*	92.0	1.8	7.0	—	1.0	—	1.8
Suriname	*50.9*	23.5	0.8	17.6	—	7.6	0.2	1.2
Uruguay	*65.3*	78.7	1.5	3.8	0.9	0.5	—	3.8
Venezuela	*94.9*	92.7	1.7	2.3	0.1	1.3	—	1.8

Note: A dash represents a value of less than 0.05 percent. Because of rounding, horizontal totals of the individual Christian groups may not equal the total percentage of Christians. Also, Christians in some countries are counted in more than one category, in which case the total of the individual groups may exceed the overall percentage of Christians.

[a]Figures include Anguilla (U.K.), Antigua and Barbuda, Aruba (Neth.), British Virgin Islands, Cayman Islands (U.K.), Dominica, Grenada, Guadeloupe (Fr.), Martinique (Fr.), Montserrat (U.K.), Netherlands Antilles, Puerto Rico (U.S.), St. Kitts and Nevis, St. Lucia, St. Vincent and Grenadines, Turks and Caicos Islands (U.K.), United States Virgin Islands. [b]Figures include Falkland Islands (U.K.), French Guiana.

son the ruling Inca was believed to be, as well as the pre-Inca god Viracocha, who created the sun and later was assimilated into the Inca pantheon. This cult represented the imperial religion, but subject states worshiped other gods, as the tribes worshiped their respective ancestral and protective spirits. Important for Christian → mission were the → ethics, the idea of → sin, and → penance and absolution, both among the Incas and elsewhere. Blood was also a factor, since by means of it humans cooperated with the gods in maintaining cosmic order. There is a connection here with human sacrifices, which assumed central significance among the Toltecs and

Aztecs. In the higher religions the idea that the dead have a part in the acts of the living played a role, but belief located them in specific spheres.

1.3. *Colonialism and Mission*

1.3.1. After Portugal had secured its own maritime expansion in 1454 through a donation of Pope Nicholas V (1447-55), the Catholic monarchs Isabella of Castile (1474-1504) and Ferdinand of Aragon (1479-1516) also received a donation in 1493 from Alexander VI (1492-1503), after the discoveries of Columbus (1451-1506), giving them the right to take possession of islands and coastal areas on the way to India, albeit with the obligation to support missionary work as well (→ Colonialism; Colonialism and Mission). As the landmass of the American continent became evident, the Spanish monarchs reinterpreted the → bulls dealing with land on the way to Asia as applying to land on the way to America (L. Weckmann).

In the Treaty of Tordesillas with Portugal (1494), the Spanish monarchs agreed on a line of demarcation between their respective discoveries in the New World at approximately 46° West of Greenwich (the Portuguese with rights to the east of this line, the Spanish to the west). Soon after its discovery of the coast of Brazil in 1500, however, Portugal ceased to recognize the boundary, which could not be precisely measured before the 18th century in any case, as the limit of its expansion in Brazil. The other European sea powers — England, Holland, and France — never did recognize the treaty.

1.3.2. In the summons *(requerimiento)* of the Spanish monarchs of 1514, which was to be read to the Indian tribes before their military subjugation, it was stated that the pope had given the New World to the Spanish kings, who now demanded the people's subjection to Spanish rule and their acknowledgment of the pope as the vicar of Christ, refusal being legitimate grounds for their enslavement (→ Slavery). The Spaniards interpreted even the appearance of resistance or lack of cooperation as the crime of lèse-majesté and therefore automatically also as an insult to God, which justified enslavement. Even this pretext was not used in many instances in Brazil, where the Paulists took slaves as they fancied. Although the Portuguese legislation generally focused more on the settlers' interests than did the corresponding Spanish legislation, it was implemented less effectively.

In general, though the missions were not always conducted with the military protection of the conquerors, the goal was always the incorporation of the indigenous peoples into the colonial sphere of power. Such was the case even when the voluntary nature of the proclamation enjoined by the gospel was not misused, for example, in the Jesuit → reductions from Paraguay to northern Mexico during the 17th century, a process that also served to secure boundaries. This view by no means intends to ignore the enormous missionary accomplishments — often at the cost of great personal renunciation — of the → Franciscans, → Dominicans, → Augustinian Hermits, Mercedarians, and Jesuits, to mention but the most important.

Especially with regard to the Paraguay reductions, the relative independence and isolation from the colonial sphere was so great that it also served as

an excuse for the expulsion of the Jesuits in 1767. Earlier, in 1759, they had been expelled from Brazil, partly because of the resistance of the Guaraní against the boundary shift at the Uruguay River (1754-56) and the desire of Sebastião de Carvalho, marqués of Pombal, to assert a Portuguese trade monopoly over the missionary villages along the Amazon.

For a long time there was no alternative to Christianity, which at first practiced mass → baptisms. Indian religion was suppressed, and the original cultic sites were destroyed. The Europeans set up churches, chapels, wayside crosses, and figures of the saints, in addition to instituting many Christian feasts. Attendance at → catechism and → mass was enforced, at times by corporal punishment. Millions of African slaves were also brought to the Caribbean and the Atlantic seaboard. They were branded by the state and baptized with no great preparation by the church, being placed under canon law and the → Inquisition. → Pastoral care of the Africans was even worse than that of the Indians, so that among them, as among the Indians, a syncretistic → popular religion developed that enabled them to maintain their own → identity (→ Afro-American Cults; Syncretism).

The economic interests of the upper classes and settlers could be satisfied only with the help of slaves or with quasi-feudal dependence in the form of the encomienda (a grant of Indians to serve a colonist with tribute and labor) or repartimiento (a grant of adult male Indians forced to work in rotation throughout the year). Irresolvable opposition thus arose between these interests and the church's missionary goals, and also between the transplanted structures of the church of the Portuguese-Spanish settlers and the missionary church, something that became ever more clear in the 18th century in the light of enlightened absolutism, with the increased emphasis on the economic and mercantile interests of the monarchies.

Another factor was the increasing emphasis on the monarchy, involving the complete subordination of the church under the Crown. Examples include the Concordat of 1753, which gave to the Spanish crown universal church patronage throughout its empire but which Charles III (1759-88) construed such that he himself represented the "vicar and legate of the Apostolic See." In the patronage dispute from 1727 onward, the Portuguese crown had to be satisfied with what amounted to merely a decorative elevation of the royal chapel to the Patriarchate of Lisbon (1737) and the bestowal of the title *rex fidelissimus* (1748). Under Joseph I (1750-77), however, the Portuguese crown, through Carvalho, ruthlessly imposed its will on the church as well.

1.3.3. During the 16th century various → bishops, members of orders (→ Religious Orders and Congregations), and even laypersons recognized the opposition between the mission church and the settlers' church and tried to intervene on behalf of the Indians (perhaps less so on behalf of the blacks); such intervention took place much more vigorously in the Hispano-American sphere than in the Portuguese-Brazilian sphere. Such protest, however, could always be silenced by the patronate church, in which even bishops were quasi–state officials (→ Patronage, Ecclesiastical); in extreme cases, the silencing could include expulsion from the Americas. Bishops who tried to overcome this opposition by intervening on behalf of the Indians included Toribio de Mogrovejo, formerly inquisitor of Granada, who as the archbishop of Lima (1580-1606) was the great organizer of the Peruvian church; Vasco de Quiroga, the bishop of Michoacán, Mexico (1537-65), who established villages where Indians could receive medical care plus training in work skills; and Juan del Valle, bishop of Popayán, Colombia (1548-60), who condemned the encomienda at his second synod in 1558.

Bishop Antonio de Valdevieso (León, Nicaragua) was the only bishop murdered during the colonial period because of his decisive intervention on behalf of the Indians (d. 1549/50). His murderers were two sons of the governor Rodrigo Contreras. In his sermons under the auspices of the Dominicans in Santo Domingo in December 1511, Antonio de Montesinos (ca. 1486-ca. 1540) was the first to condemn the enslavement of the Indians as being irreconcilable with the gospel; an uncertain tradition suggests he may have died violently at the hands of German mercenaries in Venezuela because of his role as *protector de indios.*

The secular priest and occasional military chaplain Bartolomé de Las Casas (1484-1566) took up the cause of the repressed, gave up his encomienda in Cuba, joined the Dominicans, and fought at court for laws protecting the Indians. He then found that not even as the bishop of Chiapas (Mexico) was he able to get his "New Laws of the Indies" (1542) passed against the interests of colonial society, laws that among other things provided for the abolition of the encomienda. Although papal decrees on behalf of the Indians' human → rights (e.g., *Sublimus Deus* [1537] of Paul III; *Commissum nobis* [1639] of Urban VIII) contributed to raising consciousness of the Indians' plight, they were unable to effect any substantive change in social and economic structures.

1.4. Roman Catholicism and Protestantism in the Nineteenth and Twentieth Centuries

The cooperation of the authorities, the church, and the Inquisition largely protected the Spanish and Portuguese colonial sphere from any enduring influence from Protestant merchants and sailors, and Protestantism was thus able to acquire a foothold only where the Protestant powers themselves — namely, England, the Netherlands, and Denmark — were securely established in the Caribbean sphere. It is equally important to remember, however, that Protestantism itself indirectly shaped Catholicism insofar as the initially late-medieval character of Catholicism was quickly overcome by the Tridentine spirit of Counter-Reformation Christendom. In Latin America and the Caribbean, however, where the challenge of a Protestant opponent was absent or only vaguely a peripheral issue, a religious society emerged that was more uniform than in Europe and that constituted what was in part a distinctly external, cultural Catholicism.

The Enlightenment and, even more, the disputes generated during struggles for political independence had plunged this Catholicism into its most profound crisis yet in Latin America. It was structurally weakened because most of its bishoprics were unoccupied and its regular clergy were largely in a state of dissolution. As a result, the Roman Catholic Church found itself bullied about by the young states through the continued maintenance of the right of patronage and found its own privileges under attack by Freemasons and liberals (→ Masons). Whereas it was initially a state church, it now had to accept a more general atmosphere of freedom of conscience and religious choice, albeit to various degrees in the various states, and in the second half of the 19th century even the separation of church and state (in Mexico, Colombia, and Brazil).

From the mid-19th century the church was able somewhat to recover, thanks to deeply rooted popular piety under the auspices of the Romanization favored by → Ultramontanism and with the help of foreign entities and new orders, which established educational and social institutions. Although it tried to preserve its special privileges through → concordats and to protect itself against the spread of Protestantism, it had only temporary success. The opening of the subcontinent to global trade and the accompanying influx of merchants, technicians, and scientists from Protestant countries, along with waves of immigrants, especially to Brazil, Argentina, Uruguay, Paraguay, and Chile, which especially the liberal elite viewed as necessary elements of modernization, increased the demands for religious freedom.

During the first half of the 19th century, initial contacts with Protestantism often took the form of itinerant salesmen associated with the Bible societies, who were hoping to initiate church reforms by the dissemination of Bibles translated into the language of the people, generally in recognized Catholic translations. The Scottish Baptist James Thomson (1788-1854) was simultaneously an agent of the British and Foreign School Society and also influenced educational reforms by advocating the pedagogical method of the Quaker Joseph Lancaster, which made extensive use of biblical texts (without commentary) in encouraging literacy. Congregations of aliens and immigrants were formed independently. To some extent one can see in the second half of the 19th century a certain synchronism between the rise of liberal, anticlerical regimes and the beginning of missionary work by Anglo-Saxon → denominations (esp. Presbyterian, → Methodist, and → Anglican). The → missionaries of these bodies also acted as Bible colporteurs and in some cases made contact with the Freemasons in order to influence society, at times being Masons themselves.

Then followed the → free church missions of the → Baptists, Disciples of Christ (→ Christian Church [Disciples of Christ]), → Salvation Army, → Adventists, and Church of the Brethren (→ Brethren Churches), which had been at work since 1734 in the non-Spanish Antilles, Suriname, Guyana, and the Mosquito Coast of Nicaragua. At the turn of the 20th century came the → faith missions, nondenominational bodies patterned on the → China Inland Mission. We also find nondenominational youth groups (e.g., the → YMCA). Up to World War I there were four → synods of German immigrant congregations in Brazil, which united after World War II as the Evangelical Church of the Lutheran Confession in Brazil, numerically the strongest mainline Protestant church. Protestants were most active in Brazil, Mexico, the Caribbean, Argentina, Uruguay, and Paraguay. In the Andes region only Chile was a focal point. The → Pentecostal churches, which before World War I had a footing only in Chile as a split from the Methodists, spread rapidly after 1930 during the world economic crisis and made Protestantism, which hitherto had attracted only the middle classes, a genuine lower-class mass religion in Chile, Brazil, Guatemala, Mexico, and Haiti.

Two new phenomena have come on the scene since the 1950s. First, we find a number of small or very small churches and → sects from the United States, in part neo-Pentecostals. In Guatemala, for example, there are now more than 200 Protestant groups. Then there are several major multinational religious enterprises, such as Evangelism in Depth, the → church growth (§5) movement, the mass → evangelism of Billy Graham or Luis Palau, Bill Bright's Campus Crusade for Christ, and World Vision, with its programs of aid and development (→ Relief and Development Organizations). The number of Protestants is rising steadily, though at a different pace in the different countries. Protestants constitute about 10 percent of the total population of Latin America and the Caribbean, with 20 percent or more in a few countries.

Protestantism came to Latin America as immigrants arrived when slave labor gave way to that of free farm workers and artisans, and also as missionaries came, who were often hailed as the representatives of the → work ethic and who up to the end of the 19th century maintained this sense in accordance with their North American sense of mission. In this regard we should not overlook the link to the economic expansion of the United States. To some degree many of the missionaries from → fundamentalist churches and sects, with their noncontextual proclamation, consciously or unconsciously have supported North American socioeconomic interests that favor maintaining the status quo in Latin America. The same comment applies to conservatives in the Roman Catholic → hierarchy.

1.5. *Christianity and Modern Challenges*
The ecumenical demand for cooperation, first within the Roman Catholic and Protestant camps, then between them (→ Ecumenism, Ecumenical Movement), has also helped the churches to better face the socioeconomic and political challenges of the Latin American situation. In Roman Catholicism cooperation began in 1899 with the Latin American Plenary Council at Rome. After World War II bishops' conferences were founded nationally, followed by the → Latin American Council of Bishops (CELAM) in 1955 and the Latin American Confederation of Religious (CLAR) in 1959.

In 1968 at Medellín, Colombia, the impulses deriving from → Vatican II found creative expression in Latin America at the second bishops' conference (→ Latin American Councils 2.4). Supported by the inner renewal of the → base communities, the Roman Catholic Church, with its understanding of → peace as social justice, has become a factor in sociopolitical renewal, though naturally to differing degrees from diocese to diocese and country to country. During the pontificate of John Paul II (1978-), → liberation theology has been increasingly marginalized, with conservative or even reactionary candidates favored in episcopal appointments. Whereas the third Latin American Bishop's

Conference (Puebla, 1979) still emphasized the basically Catholic substratum of society, in view of the continuing expansion of Protestantism in the 1980s the pope demanded new efforts at evangelization, making such efforts also the theme of the fourth General Assembly of the Latin American bishops (Santo Domingo, 1992).

At three Congresses on Christian Work in Latin America (meeting in Ancon, Panama, in 1916, in Montevideo in 1925, and in Havana in 1929), and by the formation of → national councils of churches, Protestant missionary work has attempted cooperation, although it has hardly achieved more than orderly coexistence. After World War II only a minority of Protestants belonged to the → World Council of Churches. The Conferencia Evangélica Latinoamericana (Latin American Evangelical Conference), meeting at Buenos Aires in 1949, Lima in 1961, and Buenos Aires in 1969, promoted the struggle for unity with the participation now of the immigrant churches. It also wrestled more seriously with the realities of life in Latin America, helped in this regard by the commissions on church and society (ISAL) and on Christian education (CELADEC), each founded in 1961. Nevertheless, the conferences attracted only one segment of Protestantism, since a lack of minimal theological consensus regarding the new sociopolitical challenges meant that cooperation simply led to the strengthening of existing divisions.

More recent attempts at unification led to the continental institutionalization of the polarization between the ecumenically open branch of Protestantism engaged in social criticism, which between 1978 and 1982 convened as the → Latin American Council of Churches (CLAI) and sought the cooperation of the Roman Catholic Church, and the evangelical-fundamentalist branch, which convened in 1982 as the Latin American Evangelical Fellowship (CONELA) in conscious delimitation over against the WCC. Since the waning of the East-West conflict, however, it has become increasingly evident that a consciousness of social criticism can emerge despite fundamentalist theology.

In Brazil in 1982 the founding of the National Council of Christian Churches (CONIC) gave institutional form for the first time to cooperation between Protestants and Roman Catholics. Such cooperation, though, does occur informally in many other places, especially among the advocates of liberation theology.

In the 1970s and 1980s the churches became increasingly aware of the grave structural problems in Latin America that came to expression in the flight from the land, mass → unemployment or underemployment, hunger, homelessness, malnutrition, illiteracy, family disruption, and vagrant children. In response to these problems most states were resorting to military dictatorships, which, appealing to national security, quelled social unrest by forcibly silencing opponents by every possible means, including → torture and murder. Over 1,000 Christians were killed in the 1970s because of their work on behalf of social justice (→ Persecution of Christians).

The problems have their roots in a corrupt ruling class that has become the national class; in a misuse of world trade, which results in the ruthless exploitation of peripheral economic systems (→ Dependence); and in false concepts of development that are governed by the interests of industrialized states (→ Industrial Society) and that have led to monstrous debts, which have brought Mexico, Brazil, and Argentina to the brink of bankruptcy. Development has also been hindered by an educational system that is as little oriented to the needs of Latin America as are industry and agriculture, with their excessive fixation on the land and on exports instead of engaging in land reform, which would make possible the means of subsistence for most of the population and meet domestic demands.

The middle classes and oligarchy, which pursue the European or North American lifestyle, often block any possibility of development for the masses, which have little share in the process of forming political public opinion, even though a facade of democracy might suggest that they do. The same criticism applies in even greater measure to the Indian → minorities, who are becoming increasingly conscious of their ethnic identity. Ever since the Cuban revolution (1958/59), the rigidity of structures representing institutional injustice, which are defended with repressive force from above, has repeatedly generated guerrilla movements, most recently in Peru and currently also in Colombia, which in their own turn hinder development and recently have been financed through drug smuggling.

1.6. Sects, Syncretism, and Other Religions

Indian religious life continues both in microgroups that have remained isolated and in the form of parallel cults among formally Christianized macrogroups, such as in Bolivia or Guatemala. → Popular Catholicism has also been affected to a large degree by Indian or Afro-American → piety (→ Syncretism). Afro-American religions are strong in the Caribbean, as illustrated by → voodoo in Haiti, the Maria Lionza cult in Venezuela, and → Umbanda (in symbiosis with → spiritism) in Brazil. Indepen-

175

dently, many spiritist societies (→ Occultism) play an important role in Brazil and Argentina. Other world religions entered Latin America in the 20th century from the Near East, India, China, and Japan.

Of the sects the → Mormons and → Jehovah's Witnesses are the most active. Since the masses are still much more religious and much less affected by → secularization than the people of Europe, Latin America also provides fertile soil for new religious movements, whether imported like the → Unification Church International (which has made headway with its pronounced opposition to Communism and which has enormous financial resources, having become an important force in Uruguay with its purchase of businesses and communication media) or native groups, like the Valley of the Dawn cult in Brazil.

→ Development 1; Latin American Theology; Third World

Bibliography: History, culture, politics: C. I. ARCHER, ed., The Wars of Independence in Spanish America (Wilmington, Del., 2000) • L. BETHEL, ed., The Cambridge History of Latin America (11 vols.; Cambridge, 1984-96) • D. A. BRADING, The First America: The Spanish Monarchy, Creole Patriots, and the Liberal State, 1492-1867 (Cambridge, 1991) • A. BRYSK, From Tribal Village to Global Village: Indian Rights and International Relations in Latin America (Stanford, Calif., 2000) • J. C. CHASTEEN, Born in Blood and Fire: A Concise History of Latin America (New York, 2001) • H. J. DOMNICK, J. MÜLLER, and H.-J. PRIEN, eds., Interethnische Beziehungen in der Geschichte Lateinamerikas (Frankfurt, 1999) • I. E. FEY and K. RACINE, eds., Strange Pilgrimages: Exile, Travel, and National Identity in Latin America, 1800-1990s (Wilmington, Del., 2000) • M. S. GRINDLE, Audacious Reforms: Institutional Invention and Democracy in Latin America (Baltimore, 2000) • R. HARVEY, Liberators: Latin America's Struggle for Independence, 1810-1830 (Woodstock, N.Y., 2000) • R. S. HILLMAN, ed., Understanding Contemporary Latin America (Boulder, Colo., 1997) • J. W. HOPKINS, ed., Latin America: Perspectives on a Region (2d ed.; New York, 1998) • J. E. KICZA, ed., The Indian in Latin American History: Resistance, Resilience, and Acculturation (rev. ed.; Wilmington, Del., 2000) • J. KINSBRUNER, Independence in Spanish America: Civil Wars, Revolutions, and Underdevelopment (2d ed.; Albuquerque, N.M., 2000) • F. W. KNIGHT, Race, Ethnicity, and Class: Forging the Plural Society in Latin America and the Caribbean (Waco, Tex., 1995) • J. LARRAÍN, Identity and Modernity in Latin America (Oxford, 2000) • L. A. PAYNE, Uncivil Movements: The Armed Right Wing and Democracy in Latin America (Baltimore, 2000) •

M. QUIJADA, "Sobre el origen y difusión del nombre 'América Latina,'" Revista de Indias 58 (1998) 595-616 • A. J. R. RUSSEL-WOOD, The Portuguese Empire, 1415-1808 (Baltimore, 1998) • J. W. SHERMAN, Latin America in Crisis (Boulder, Colo., 2000) • T. E. SKIDMORE and P. H. SMITH, Modern Latin America (5th ed.; New York, 2001) • S. M. SOCOLOW, The Women of Colonial Latin America (New York, 2000) • H. VELTMEYER and J. PETRAS, The Dynamics of Social Change in Latin America (New York, 2000) • L. WECKMANN, Constantino el Grande y Cristóbal Colón. Estudios de la supremacía papal sobre islas (1091-1493) (Mexico City, 1992) • E. WILLIAMSON, The Penguin History of Latin America (New York, 1992) • T. C. WRIGHT, Latin America in the Era of the Cuban Revolution (rev. ed.; Westport, Conn., 2001).

Religion: M. P. AQUINO, Our Cry for Life: Feminist Theology from Latin America (trans. D. Livingstone; Maryknoll, N.Y., 1993) • L. BOFF, New Evangelization: Good News to the Poor (trans. R. R. Barr; Maryknoll, N.Y., 1991) • B. BOUDEWIJNSE, A. DROOGERS, and F. KAMSTEEG, eds., More than Opium: An Anthropological Approach to Latin American and Caribbean Pentecostal Praxis (Lanham, Md., 1998) • E. L. CLEARY and H. STEWART-GAMBINO, Conflict and Competition: The Latin American Church in a Changing Environment (Boulder, Colo., 1992) • G. COOK, ed., Crosscurrents in Indigenous Spirituality: Interface of Maya, Catholic, and Protestant Worldviews (Leiden, 1997) • J. I. DOMÍNGUEZ, ed., The Roman Catholic Church in Latin America (New York, 1994) • E. DUSSEL, ed., The Church in Latin America, 1492-1992 (Maryknoll, N.Y., 1992) • I. ELLACURÍA and J. SOBRINO, eds., Mysterium liberationis: Fundamental Concepts of Liberation Theology (Maryknoll, N.Y., 1993) • V. GARRARD-BURNETT, ed., On Earth as It Is in Heaven: Religion in Modern Latin America (Wilmington, Del., 2000) • A. J. GILL, Rendering unto Caesar: The Catholic Church and the State in Latin America (Chicago, 1998) • G. H. GOSSEN, with M. LEÓN-PORTILLA, eds., South and Meso-American Native Spirituality: From the Cult of the Feathered Serpent to the Theology of Liberation (New York, 1993) • D. IRARRÁZAVAL, Inculturation: New Dawn of the Church in Latin America (trans. P. Berryman; Maryknoll, N.Y., 2000) • J. L. KLAIBER, The Church, Dictatorships, and Democracy in Latin America (Maryknoll, N.Y., 1998) • E. LANGER and R. H. JACKSON, eds., The New Latin American Mission History (Lincoln, Nebr., 1995) • D. LEHMANN, Struggle for the Spirit: Religious Transformation and Popular Culture in Brazil and Latin America (Cambridge, 1996) • M. LÖWY, The War of Gods: Religion and Politics in Latin America (London, 1996) • D. R. MILLER, ed., Coming of Age: Protestantism in Contemporary Latin America (Lanham, Md., 1994) •

C. Parker, *Popular Religion and Modernization in Latin America: A Different Logic* (trans. R. R. Barr; Maryknoll, N.Y., 1996) • H.-J. Prien, *Das Evangelium im Abendland und in der Neuen Welt. Studien zu Theologie, Gesellschaft und Geschichte* (Frankfurt, 2000); idem, *Formação da Igreja Evangélica no Brasil* (São Leopoldo, 2002); idem, *La historia del Cristianismo en América Latina* (Salamanca, 1985); idem, ed., *Religiosidad e historiografía. La irrupción del pluralismo religioso en América Latina y su elaboración metódica en la historiografía* (Frankfurt, 1998) • J. I. Saranyana, ed., *Teología en América Latina* (vol. 1; Madrid, 1999) covers 1493-1715 • J. F. Schwaller, ed., *The Church in Colonial Latin America* (Wilmington, Del., 2000) • B. H. Smith, *Religious Politics in Latin America, Pentecostal vs. Catholic* (Notre Dame, Ind., 1998) • D. Stoll, *Is Latin America Turning Protestant?* (Berkeley, Calif., 1990) • K.-W. Westmeier, *Protestant Pentecostalism in Latin America: A Study in the Dynamics of Missions* (Madison, N.J., 1999).

Hans-Jürgen Prien

2. The Caribbean

Although traditionally associated in many respects with Latin America, the Caribbean — which, according to current U.N. usage, comprises the islands roughly enclosing the Caribbean Sea — is a very heterogeneous area. It includes the islands of the Greater Antilles (Cuba, Hispaniola [Haiti and the Dominican Republic], Jamaica, and Puerto Rico), the Lesser Antilles (the Virgin Islands, the Windward and Leeward Islands, and the islands north of Venezuela, including Trinidad and Tobago), and the Bahamas. (Outside of the current U.N. usage, the term "Caribbean" commonly also includes Belize, Guyana, Suriname, each with a non-Spanish colonial history.)

The Caribbean produced the first black republic (Haiti) in 1804. In 1959 Cuba achieved a second independence. But there are still British, Dutch, French, and U.S. colonies in the region (→ Colonialism). For all the differences in the region, the Caribbean has had common historical experiences, including Spanish colonialism (16th cent.), → slavery (17th-19th cent.), and U.S. involvement (20th cent.).

2.1. Spanish Colonization

When the Spaniards arrived in 1492, Caribbean history started anew, now written by the Europeans. Christopher Columbus (1451-1506) became lost in the Caribbean, convinced that he had discovered the coast of Asia, and without hesitation took possession of the Caribbean islands, populated by Caribs, Arawaks, and Tainos, in the name of the Catholic

kings of Spain. The Spaniards considered themselves the legitimate owners of the New World, thanks to a papal donation in 1493 by Alexander VI, who authorized the Catholic kings to exploit the islands and the continent under the condition that they would work for the conversion of the natives to the Catholic faith. Christianization thus became an essential part of Western colonialism.

In *Universalis ecclesiae* (1508) Julius II granted the *patronato* (patronage) to the Catholic kings, who organized the Caribbean ecclesiastically, creating the first three dioceses in 1511: Santo Domingo, Concepción de la Vega, and San Juan de Puerto Rico, which belonged to the Archdiocese of Seville. The Caribbean, however, witnessed no "spiritual conquest" of the Indians, only military conquest and extermination. (The original Indian population has survived only in Suriname and along the coast of Guyana, where a few thousand Indians still cling to their own culture.)

With the arrival of the Dominicans in Hispaniola about 1510, the first complaints were voiced regarding the ill treatment of the Indians. According to Bartolomé de Las Casas (1484-1566), the Dominicans made the first serious attempt to preach the gospel and to criticize the exploitation of the Indians. He mentioned specifically a sermon of Pedro de Córdoba (ca. 1482-1525), the superior of the Dominican community. In 1511 Antonio de Montesinos (ca. 1486-ca. 1540) delivered a famous sermon in defense of the rights of the Indians in which he asked with what right or justice the Indians were held in such dreadful and abhorrent slavery: "How you oppress and exploit them, or, more accurately, put them to death, merely to gain and send home a daily quota of gold! Are they not human beings?"

The lifestyle and the sermons of the Dominicans in defense of the voiceless influenced Las Casas's decision in 1514 to become a protector of the Indians and a member of the Dominican community. His social thought displays a definite radicalization. In his first Memorial de Remedios (1516) he suggested the idea of bringing slaves from Africa as laborers for the colonial economy in the Caribbean in order to liberate the Indians from this obligation. In 1540 he still believed that the slaves from Africa were criminals or prisoners of war. Finally in his *Historia de las Indias* (1552-61) he condemned the capture of slaves in Africa and the trans-Atlantic slave trade, as well as the poor treatment of the black slaves in the sugar plantations of the Caribbean. Las Casas eventually started to doubt the legitimacy of the papal donation of 1493. For Las Casas the only right action would be to return the properties and lands to the Indians. He even considered that the Indians had the right to start a just war against the Spanish dominion. At the end of his life he considered the whole circle of conquest from 1492 to 1561 as a history of robberies, assassinations, and oppression.

2.2. *Slavery*

At the beginning of the 16th century the Spanish introduced the cultivation of sugarcane within the plantation system. The Caribbean islands did not have gold or silver, so sugarcane became the source of wealth for Spain and western Europe. Its production, however, depended on the availability of cheap labor. Since the Indians were quickly decimated by exploitation and disease, the only alternative seemed to be to bring slaves directly from Africa. This institution of slavery had the greatest impact on the development of the Caribbean.

The first slaves from Africa began arriving in Hispaniola in 1505. From the outset the church was entangled in the slavery system and thus could not protest against the injustice. Many clergy themselves owned slaves, and monasteries used slave labor to run their sugar factories. The church treated slaves as its members but did little for them pastorally and even began a policy of suppressing their culture.

Spain began losing its hegemony over the Caribbean when the British first entered the region in 1624, followed by the Dutch in 1634 and the French a year later. Throughout the 17th century the Caribbean became divided into various colonies, with many of the smaller ones undergoing several changes of ownership. The result was that a single colony might develop a variegated culture. St. Martin, for example, today is partly French and partly Dutch, but the people speak English.

Between the 16th and 19th centuries more than nine million Africans were forcibly brought to the New World, with the peak of the slave trade in the 17th and 18th centuries. In the Spanish and French colonies the slaves were integrated into the Roman Catholic Church through their receiving baptism and other sacraments. We know of no prophetic voice defending the African slaves, such as Las Casas did for the Indians.

Slavery in the Caribbean was abolished first in Haiti in 1804, achieved there by the slaves themselves, who fought at the same time against colonialism (→ Haiti 1). In 1833 slavery was abolished in the British colonies, in 1848 in French colonies, in 1863 in Dutch colonies, in 1873 in Puerto Rico, and in 1880 in Cuba.

2.3. *Protestant Mission*

The churches varied according to the confessional traditions of the colonial masters, and thus several varieties of → Protestantism came into the Caribbean. The Anglicans (→ Anglican Communion) first came to the Barbados in 1626, the Reformed (→ Reformed and Presbyterian Churches) to Curaçao in 1650, the Lutherans (→ Lutheran Churches) to the Virgin Islands in 1666, the Society of → Friends to Jamaica in 1671, the → Moravians to St. Thomas in 1732, the Methodists (→ Methodist Churches) to Antigua in 1760, the Congregationalists (→ Congregationalism) to Tobago in 1808, the Presbyterians to Jamaica in 1813, the → Baptists to Jamaica in 1814, and the → Salvation Army to Jamaica in 1887.

In many areas taken over by the Protestant powers, most of the inhabitants were Roman Catholic (e.g., Jamaica in 1655, where England forbade Roman Catholicism). Roman Catholicism was revived in Jamaica only with the coming of the → Jesuits in 1837 but then became so strong that the → Roman Catholic Church is now the largest single church on the island. Of the total population in the Caribbean, approximately 24 million (63 percent) were Roman Catholic in the year 2000.

Although Protestantism was present in the Caribbean from the 17th century, only in the 19th century did it begin generally to penetrate the black population. (In the previous century the Moravians and Methodists had actually been the first to work directly with blacks, a decision that the ruling classes often opposed.) In general, Protestant missionaries did not involve themselves in the sociopolitical question of slavery and thus in effect condoned the system.

During the 19th century, however, the colonial powers began to fear a "new Haiti" in the Caribbean and realized that it might be more dangerous if its slaves were not Christianized. Religious indoctrination thus became an important weapon in the hands of the dominant class, who were facing the challenge of emancipation but had no intention of abolishing the colonial order. The first Anglican bishop of Barbados, W. Hart Coleridge (bishop 1824-42), received full cooperation from the British government and the local authorities in granting religious education to the slaves.

In one instance the slaves themselves saw political fruit from their accepting the message. On Jamaica in 1783 the Native Baptist Church was founded by George Liele (ca. 1750-1820), who, born a slave in the United States, became the first black Baptist to be ordained pastor and then was the first black missionary in Jamaica. In 1831 the so-called Baptist War started, a slave revolt that used this church to organize active resistance to slavery. The dominant class suppressed the revolt and curtailed Baptist missions in British colonies. The Baptist missionaries, however, then realized that there was no way forward without the abolition of slavery. William Knibb (1803-45), for example, a Baptist pastor active in Jamaica, told the 1832 annual meeting of the Baptist Missionary Society in London, "God is the defender of the oppressed and will not forget the African." Knibb prayed for his brethren in Jamaica, saying that if he died before the emancipation of his brothers and sisters in Christ was achieved, in heaven he would fall down before God and beseech him to open the eyes of Christians in England to the scandal of slavery.

2.4. *U.S. Involvement*

A new era in the Caribbean began with the U.S. occupation of Cuba and Puerto Rico in 1898. By the Treaty of Paris of 1898, which formally ended the Spanish-American War, Spain ceded Puerto Rico, Guam, and the Philippines to the United States and renounced all claim to Cuba, thus ending its more than four centuries of direct involvement in the Caribbean. U.S. troops left Cuba in 1902, but Puerto Rico became in effect a U.S. colony. In 1917 the Puerto Ricans officially became American citizens.

The Americanization of Puerto Rico went hand in hand with the introduction of numerous Protestant churches, which typically defended the status quo. From the 1930s Puerto Rican Protestantism became primarily Pentecostal; culturally, it has been indifferent toward the island's economic, social, and political problems. Pentecostals are the fastest-growing Christian group in Puerto Rico, where approximately 30 percent of the traditionally Catholic population is now Protestant.

In subsequent years the United States sometimes worked through local strongmen to maintain its interests in the Caribbean. One example was Rafael Trujillo (1891-1961), the often brutal president/dictator (1930-61) of the Dominican Republic. His government granted special privileges to the Roman Catholic Church, which maintained silence, despite rampant human rights violations in the country. Finally, in 1960 the Catholic bishops issued a pastoral letter against Trujillo. In 1965 U.S. Marines intervened to avoid the return to power of Juan Bosch, elected president in 1963 but forced into exile by a coup. The United States prepared the way for Joaquín Balaguer, formerly Trujillo's figurehead president, to remain in power until 1978.

With the fall of Cuban dictator Fulgencio Batista (1901-73, ruled 1952-59), the revolutionary movement in Cuba under Fidel Castro gained independence. When the new government turned to → so-

cialism and failed to restore promised liberties, some 700,000 Cubans fled the country, most to the United States. In 1961 an invasion of Cuba backed by the U.S. Central Intelligence Agency was crushed by Castro's forces. A decades-long U.S. embargo of Cuba, begun in 1962, has severely damaged the Cuban economy.

From 1958 to 1966 Haitian dictator François ("Papa Doc") Duvalier (1907-71) silenced or expelled religious leaders who refused to legitimate his power. In 1966 Duvalier reached an agreement with the Vatican that created the conditions for the total submission of the Catholic Church to his regime. In 1971 Duvalier was succeeded by his son Jean-Claude, who continued his father's policies. For the first time in 1980 the Bishops' Conference of Haiti criticized the Duvalier regime. In 1986 Jean-Claude fled Haiti aboard a U.S. Air Force jet. Since that time the government has been largely ineffective, with the U.S. military intervening in 1994 to reinstall President Jean-Bertrand Aristide, a liberation theologian, in the presidency.

In 1979 a revolutionary process in Grenada, a member of the British Commonwealth, was directed against dictator Eric Gairy. This process was guided by the New Jewel movement and the popular leader Maurice Bishop. When the United States withdrew economic aid and supported Gairy, Bishop made an alliance with Cuba and the USSR. The argument that Grenada was now a threat to U.S. security was used to justify President Reagan's invasion in 1983, which produced no evidence in support of the contention. Local and regional leaders were divided on the issue. The bishop of Grenada, Sidney Charles, supported the invasion, but Roy Neehall, the general secretary of the → Caribbean Conference of Churches (CCC), supported the revolutionary process already in place in Grenada.

2.5. *Ecumenism*

The ecumenical movement is more active in the Caribbean than in Central or South America. The Ecumenical Council of Cuba and the Jamaican Council of Churches were each founded in 1941, with other councils of churches arising in the Bahamas (1948), Puerto Rico (1954), Curaçao (1958), Antigua (1964), Trinidad and Tobago (1967), and St. Vincent (1969). Many of these include the Roman Catholic Church as a full member.

In 1973 an important regional ecumenical achievement was the founding of the CCC, which began with the joining of 18 churches representing 12 Christian traditions, including the Roman Catholic. This act was the climax on the road to closer church cooperation within the region. The impulse came from new local leaders who were independent of the main city churches. The CCC strongly defends → human dignity and makes a significant contribution to development in the Caribbean. Another body, the Antilles Episcopal Conference, includes 16 Roman Catholic → dioceses.

Another unique ecumenical achievement in the Caribbean was the establishment in 1970 of the United Theological College of the West Indies, a joint effort of 11 churches. Located in Jamaica, it is the theological training institute of their leaders.

Two Orthodox churches have established a presence in the Caribbean. In 1970 the → Ethiopian Orthodox Church, which has joined the CCC, arrived in Jamaica and in Trinidad and Tobago. The Greek → Orthodox Church was first established in the Bahamas.

The Caribbean embraces various cultures. Native languages such as Papiamento in the Lesser Antilles and Creole in Haiti illustrate the cultural diversity. The mainline churches like the Anglican, Lutheran, Presbyterian, and Roman Catholic have a European stamp. Only in the later 20th century was there any serious attempt, particularly by Roman Catholicism, to adjust to local culture, especially in the spheres of → liturgy and → church music. Charismatic churches like the Pentecostals (→ Pentecostal Churches), as well as the Baptists, are more open to the contribution that popular culture can make.

2.6. Religious Pluralism

Though Christianity has been predominant in the Caribbean, especially since the 19th century, it is not the only religion. When the slaves joined the churches, they did not give up their African beliefs (→ Guinea 2). In the 17th and 18th centuries, when the ruling classes regarded Christian teaching as dangerous and thus not to be shared with the slaves, the latter were under little religious influence, which explains the development of African types of religion in the Antilles. We find → voodoo in Haiti, Santería in Cuba, Shango in Trinidad and Tobago, Gagá in the Dominican Republic, Obeah in Jamaica, and Brúa in Curaçao (→ Afro-American Cults). While the churches were hostile to African religious values, the slaves had no alternative but to make use especially of public Catholic symbols to guarantee the survival of their African soul. Syncretism became a general practice, which drew on African as well as Western Christian sources.

In the mid-17th century a Jewish community established itself in Curaçao, building what is now the oldest → synagogue in use in the Americas. Since then, Judaism has been present in the Caribbean.

→ Hinduism and → Islam have become major religions in some countries of the area. After the ending of slavery new immigration was needed to keep the plantations going, which led to the arrival of many Asian workers in the 19th century. Today their descendants make up one-third or more of the population of Trinidad and Tobago and, in South America, of Suriname and Guyana. These Hindus and Moslems have retained their original religious observances. There is a general spirit of tolerance of these religions, as shown by the recognition of religious feast days of the various religions as national holidays. Still, however, there is no regular → dialogue between these religions and the Christian churches.

The last decades of the 20th century witnessed a mosaic of new religious movements taking shape in the Caribbean, some imported and some native. Of the imported ones, the Seventh-day Adventists, Jehovah's Witnesses, and the Pentecostal churches, all from the United States, have spread throughout the region. Since the 1970s the Pentecostal or charismatic movement has also successfully penetrated the mainstream churches, with its practices of healing and trances, which are viewed (and promoted) as signs of the Holy Spirit.

The best-known native religious movement is the → Rastafarian, which originated in Jamaica in the early 1930s and is now present throughout the region. On Puerto Rico the Mita movement, which resembles Pentecostalism, arose in 1940 and spread to the Dominican Republic and Haiti. Basic to it is possession by the → Holy Spirit. The revivalist movement in Jamaica is similar. Palma Sola, a mixture of traditional Catholic symbols and voodoo practices, arose in the Dominican Republic in 1961.

These movements tend to have the following common features: they involve the lower class and develop best in the context of economic crises; they react conservatively to the ruling system; and they are a revival of Afro-Antilles traditions, thus helping to revive Afro-Antilles identity. They provide the best evidence that the peoples of the Caribbean continue to seek their own identity.

Bibliography: History, culture, politics: B. BRERETON and K. A. YELVINGTON, eds., *The Colonial Caribbean in Transition: Essays on Postemancipation Social and Cultural History* (Gainesville, Fla., 1999) • A. T. BRYAN and A. SERBIN, eds., *Distant Cousins: The Caribbean-Latin American Relationship* (Coral Gables, Fla., 1996) • R. D. E. BURTON, *Afro-Creole: Power, Opposition, and Play in the Caribbean* (Ithaca, N.Y., 1997) • M. CRATON, *Empire, Enslavement, and Freedom in the Caribbean* (Kingston, Jam., 1997) • R. S. DUNN, *Sugar and Slaves:*

The Rise of the Planter Class in the English West Indies, 1624-1713 (Chapel Hill, N.C., 2000) • P. C. EMMER, ed., *General History of the Caribbean* (vol. 2; London, 1999) • J. FERGUSON, *The Story of the Caribbean People* (Kingston, Jam., 1999) • C. FRASER, *Ambivalent Anticolonialism: The United States and the Genesis of West Indian Independence, 1940-1964* (Westport, Conn., 1994) • J. GILMORE, *Faces of the Caribbean* (London, 2000) • W. HOOGBERGEN, ed., *Born out of Resistance: On Caribbean Cultural Creativity* (Utrecht, 1995) • D. Y. KADISH, ed., *Slavery in the Caribbean Francophone World* (Athens, Ga., 2000) • F. W. KNIGHT, ed., *General History of the Caribbean* (vol. 3; London, 1999) • F. W. KNIGHT and C. A. PALMER, eds., *The Modern Caribbean* (Chapel Hill, N.C., 1989) • J. R. MANDLE, *Persistent Underdevelopment: Change and Economic Modernization in the West Indies* (Amsterdam, 1996) • J. ROGOZINSKI, *A Brief History of the Caribbean: From the Arawak and the Carib to the Present* (rev. ed.; New York, 1999) • K. A. SANDIFORD, *The Cultural Politics of Sugar: Caribbean Slavery and Narratives of Colonialism* (New York, 2000) • A. O. THOMPSON, *The Haunting Past: Politics, Economics, and Race in Caribbean Life* (Armonk, N.Y., 1997) • E. WILLIAMS, *From Columbus to Castro: The History of the Caribbean, 1492-1969* (New York, 1984; orig. pub., 1970) • S. M. WILSON, ed., *The Indigenous People of the Caribbean* (Gainesville, Fla., 1997).

Religion: D. J. AUSTIN-BROOS, *Jamaica Genesis: Religion and the Politics of Moral Orders* (Chicago, 1997) • D. B. BARRETT et al., eds., *WCE* (2d ed.) • D. BISNAUTH, *History of Religions in the Caribbean* (Trenton, N.J., 1996) • G. BRANDON, *Santería from Africa to the New World: The Dead Sell Memories* (Bloomington, Ind., 1993) • CEHILA, *Historia general de la iglesia en América Latina*, vol. 4, *Caribe* (Salamanca, 1995) • A. C. DAYFOOT, *The Shaping of the West Indian Church, 1492-1962* (Gainesville, Fla., 1999) • L. G. DESMANGLES, *The Faces of the Gods: Vodou and Roman Catholicism in Haiti* (Chapel Hill, N.C., 1992) • E. DUSSEL, ed., *The Church in Latin America, 1492-1992* (Tunbridge Wells, Eng., 1992) • R. GÓMEZ TRETO, *The Church and Socialism in Cuba* (Maryknoll, N.Y., 1988) • H. GOSSAI and N. S. MURRELL, eds., *Religion, Culture, and Tradition in the Caribbean* (New York, 2000) • A. LAMPE, *História do Cristianismo no Caribe* (Petrópolis, 1995); idem, *Mission or Submission? Moravian and Catholic Missionaries in the Dutch Caribbean during the Nineteenth Century* (Göttingen, 2000); idem, ed., *Christianity in the Caribbean: Essays on Church History* (Kingston, Jam., 2001) • J. M. MURPHY, *Working the Spirit: Ceremonies of the African Diaspora* (Boston, 1994) • M. F. OLMOS and L. PARAVISINI-GEBERT, eds., *Sacred Possessions: Vodou, Santería, Obeah, and the Caribbean* (New Brunswick, N.J., 1997) • F. J. OSBORNE, *History of the Catholic Church in Jamaica* (Chicago, 1988) • S. SILVA GOTAY, *Protestantismo y política en Puerto Rico, 1898-1930* (San Juan, 1997) • R. J. STEWART, *Religion and Society in Post-emancipation Jamaica* (Knoxville, Tenn., 1992).

ARMANDO LAMPE

Latin American Council of Bishops

1. Origin
2. Nature
3. Structure
4. Development
5. Publications
6. History

1. Origin

The idea of founding the Consejo Episcopal Latinoamericano (CELAM, or Latin American Council of Bishops) was proposed at the first General Conference of Latin American Bishops, held at Rio de Janeiro, July/August 1955. Leading concerns of the → Roman Catholic Church that led to the founding were the shortage of → priests and the need to take steps against "the Protestant threat." On September 24, 1955, Pope Pius XII (1939-58) founded CELAM for the purpose of coordinating the various bishops' conferences of Latin America. Headquarters would be Bogotá, Colombia. Corresponding bodies in Rome are the Pontifical Commission for Latin America (CAL, since 1958) and the General Council for Latin America (COGECAL, since 1963).

2. Nature

CELAM sees itself today as an organization to foster → communication, reflection, and cooperation among the conferences. It coordinates initiatives and enterprises of common interest and prepares the conferences summoned by the papacy.

3. Structure

The statutes were altered pursuant to → Vatican II. CELAM now consists of the presidents of the 22 bishops' conferences of Latin America and the Caribbean, one delegate selected by each conference, the → bishops of the executive board, and the presidents of the various divisions, sections, and secretariats of CELAM. These persons make up the full assembly, which elects the president, two vice-presidents, and the general secretary for four-year terms. The general secretary coordinates all the organs and ministries of CELAM, especially the divisions (→ catechesis, church → offices, → education, laity, lifestyle, → liturgy, missions, → pastoral care, social communication, and → vocations), sections (→ culture, → ecumenism and religious dialogue, family counseling, and → youth), and secretariats (holy sites, → military chaplaincy, movements of population, and unbelievers).

4. Development

In addition to the work done and the conferences held by the various divisions, CELAM has a working group for theological and pastoral reflection (since 1969) and has founded the following institutes: the ILP (Institute for Pastoral Liturgy), in Medellín, Colombia, in 1965; the ICLA (Latin American Institute for Cathechetics), in Manizales, Colombia, in 1966; and the IPLA (Latin American Pastoral Institute) in Quito, Ecuador. In 1972 these institutes were fused into a single organization in Medellín, since 1978 called the ITL (Theological Pastoral Institute). In 1989 its center was moved to Bogotá.

5. Publications

Every two months CELAM issues a bulletin, a collection of documents with over 100 titles, and, through ITL, the journal *Medellín* (since 1975). It has three ongoing editorial projects: a collection of basic texts for Latin American seminaries; a collection for the 500th anniversary of evangelization, with some 30 or more works already in print; and a Latin American church history.

6. History

In 1955 CELAM embraced 350 ecclesiastical jurisdictions (archdioceses, dioceses, prelatures, vicariates, and others), with 150 million inhabitants. In 1990 there were 430 million inhabitants in almost 700 jurisdictions, and by 1998 there were 500 million inhabitants, with 860 bishops for 705 jurisdictions.

A very fruitful period followed the founding (1962-72), marked by the collegial and ecumenical experience during Vatican II, which more than 600 Latin American bishops attended. CELAM devoted itself to church reform and to applying the decisions of Vatican II to Latin America. This process culminated in the second bishops' conference, held at Medellín in August 1968 (→ Latin American Councils 2.4).

The concern to bring the conclusions of Medellín into the life of the church led to a climate of increasing tension among bishops and clergy and to conflict with state organs that were defending "national security." A further period (1972-83) was marked by Vatican pressure for centralization. It led on the one hand to plans for global action and on the other to clashes with many of the ecclesiastical and theological movements stemming from Medellín. Students and → liberation theology played an important role at this juncture. The third bishops' conference took place in this climate in January/February 1979 at Puebla, Mexico. It reiterated, however, the options for the poor, for youth, and for a total liberation of the oppressed.

After 1984 the election of new leaders and John Paul II's summoning of a novenarium (i.e., a nine-year period of preparation for the next conference, each year being dedicated to a special theme) for the 500th anniversary claimed a good deal of energy. The fourth General Conference of the Latin American bishops was held in October 1992 in Santo Domingo, Dominican Republic. This conference emphasized the call to evangelize cultures, including modern culture, as well as the cultures of the marginalized peoples of Latin America, especially Afro-Americans, Amerindians, and women.

→ Development 1; Latin America and the Caribbean; Latin American Councils 2.3-6; Latin American Theology; Marginalized Groups; Theology of Revolution

Bibliography: L. BETHELL, *Latin America since 1930: Economy, Society, and Politics* (Cambridge, 1994) • CELAM, *The Church in the Present-Day Transformation of Latin America in the Light of the Council: Second General Conference of Latin American Bishops, Bogotá [and] Medellín . . . Colombia, 1968. Position Papers* (Bogotá, 1970); idem, *Elementos para su história, 1955-1980* (Bogotá, 1982) • E. L. CLEARY, *Born of the Poor: The Latin American Church since Medellín* (Notre Dame, Ind., 1990); idem, ed., *Path from Puebla: Significant Documents of the Latin American Bishops since 1979* (Washington, D.C., 1989) • A. J. GILL, *Rendering unto Caesar: The Catholic Church and the State in Latin America* (Chicago, 1998) • A. T. HENNELLY, ed., *Santo Domingo and Beyond: Documents and Commentaries from the Fourth General Conference of Latin American Bishops* (Maryknoll, N.Y., 1993) • C. NÚÑEZ, *Crisis and Hope in Latin America: An Evangelical Perspective* (Pasadena, Calif., 1996) • S. R. PATTNAYOK, ed., *Organized Religion in the Political Transformation of Latin America* (Lanham, Md., 1995) • PONTIFICIA COMMISSIO PRO AMERICA LATINA, *Los últimos cien años de la evangelización en América Latina. Centenario del Concilio Plenario de América Latina, simposio histórico* (Vatican City, 2000) • H.-J. PRIEN, "Puebla," *Lateinamerika. Gesellschaft–Kirche–Theologie* (ed. H.-J. Prien; Göttingen, 1981) 2.61-208.

José Oscar Beozzo

Latin American Council of Churches

1. History
2. Present Directions

The Consejo Latinoamericano de Iglesias (CLAI), or Latin American Council of Churches, is an ecumenical body covering the continent and including Latin America and the Hispanic Caribbean. It consists of 150 churches and ecumenical organizations. The latter are associate or fraternal members. Its headquarters is in Quito, Ecuador.

1. History

The Panama Conference (1916) is traditionally recognized as the starting point of the ecumenical movement in Latin America. That conference was convened as a Latin American response to the great Edinburgh → missionary conference of 1910, at which Protestant missions working in Latin America were not included, since it was considered that this region was Roman Catholic territory that had already been evangelized (→ Mission; North American Missions; Catholic Missions). In Panama, Protestant → missionaries met to discuss questions of relations and strategies, including → evangelism and mission, secular → education, and the training of ministers (→ Theological Education).

Since 1916 a number of conferences and consultations have brought Protestant Christians in Latin America and the Caribbean closer together. Several bodies came into existence for cooperation and study, among them the Latin American Union of Protestant Youth (ULAJE, founded in 1941), → World's Student Christian Federation in Latin America (MEC, 1954), Church and Society in Latin America (ISAL, 1961), and Latin American Protestant Commission for Christian Education (CELADEC, 1962). In 1964 the Protestant "Pro-Unity" Commission in Latin America (UNELAM) came into existence. UNELAM soon saw the need for Protestant churches to adopt a more realistic position in relation to the ecumenical question and resolved to invite the churches to a continental assembly to decide on the possibility of setting up an ecumenical council. The theme of that assembly would be "Unity and Mission in Latin America."

This assembly of churches met at Oaxtepec, Mexico, in September 1978 and approved the setting up of a Latin American council of churches. It also decided that a constituent assembly should be convened within four years to discuss all the relevant ecclesiological and constitutional points. The called-for assembly in fact met at Huampaní, Peru, in 1982, when the constitution of CLAI was promulgated and its standing orders were approved. Subsequent assemblies were convened at Indaiatuba, São Paulo, Brazil (1988), Concepción, Chile (1995), and Barranquilla, Colombia (2001).

2. Present Directions

CLAI includes Anglicans, Baptists, Disciples of Christ, Lutherans, Methodists, Moravians, Orthodox, Pentecostals, Presbyterians and Reformed, Waldensians, as well as united churches and independent churches. In ecumenical fellowship all these churches and the associated or fraternal bodies recognize the doctrinal basis of CLAI. As in the basis of the → World Council of Churches, so CLAI confesses "Jesus Christ as God and Savior according to the Holy Scriptures"; in unity, its members are trying to "fulfill together their common calling and mission to the glory of God, Father, Son, and Holy Spirit."

The main object of CLAI is to promote the "unity, solidarity and cooperation of the people of God in Latin America as a local expression of the universal church of Christ and as a testimony and contribution to the → unity of the Latin American people." The ecumenical purpose of CLAI is indissolubly linked to the great political, economic, social, and religious issues and the hopes of the peoples of this continent. CLAI is governed by an assembly that meets every four to six years. Between assemblies the council is managed by a board that consists of a president and 16 members. In this board a balanced denominational and regional representation is sought, including representatives of the neglected sectors (indigenous peoples, women, blacks, young people, etc.).

The priorities of CLAI have been determined by the various demands and challenges coming from the most deprived sectors of Latin American society and the churches. Its eight program areas are women, children, and family; pastoral work with indigenous peoples and blacks; → pastoral care, → solidarity, and human → rights; evangelization, → spirituality, and → worship; → communications; health and environment; education for → peace and ecumenical peace efforts; and → ecumenical dialogue. The Liturgy Network created by CLAI connects over 1,000 ministers, theologians, liturgists, and church members all over the region by the Internet (see www.clai.org.ec); its work has renewed worship and has strengthened Latin America identity at local church services.

The work for peace and human rights has been very strong. In the early 1990s it focused on Central America. At the end of the decade three countries

— Guatemala, Peru, and Colombia — were selected as focal points to develop a peace program involving churches, the organizations of civil society, and the people. This program includes peace actions, education, and theological reflection (→ Peace Education; Peace Research).

CLAI has also endorsed joint work among theological institutes and seminars, seeking to promote ecumenical thinking and exchanges. → Dialogue with the new, fast-growing Pentecostal independent movements in the region is one of its main concerns (→ Pentecostal Churches). With its work centered in the churches, CLAI promotes practical participation; the training and enabling of leaders; the contribution of women, youth, and indigenous and → black theology to the ecumenical movement; common celebration; and dialogue and cooperation among its member churches and bodies.

CLAI publishes books and two periodicals: a quarterly magazine *Signos de vida* (Signs of life) and a monthly newspaper *Nuevo siglo* (New century).

→ Contextual Theology; Ecumenical Association of Third World Theologians; Ecumenical Theology; Ecumenism, Ecumenical Movement; Latin American Theology; National Councils of Churches

Bibliography: C. L. Berg Jr. and P. Pretiz, *Spontaneous Combustion: Grass Roots Christianity in Latin American Style* (Pasadena, Calif., 1996) • B. Campos, *Debate sobre el Pentecostalismo en América Latina* (Quito, 1998) • G. Cook, *The New Face of the Church in Latin America: Between Tradition and Change* (Maryknoll, N.Y., 1994) • E. Langer and R. H. Jackson, eds., *The New Latin American Mission History* (Lincoln, Nebr., 1995) • D. Lehmann, *Democracy and Development in Latin America: Economics, Politics, and Religion in the Post-War Period* (Philadelphia, 1990) • H.-J. Prien, *Die Geschichte des Christentums in Lateinamerika* (Göttingen, 1978) 914ff.

Juan Schwindt, Sergio Marcos Pinto Lopes, and Dafne Sabanes Plou

[*Note:* The above article has been adapted, with permission, from the 2d ed. of the *Dictionary of the Ecumenical Movement* (World Council of Churches Publications, 2002).]

Latin American Councils

1. Colonial Period
   1.1. Significance
   1.2. Church Organization
   1.3. Mexican Juntas
   1.4. First Mexican and Lima Councils
   1.5. Second Mexican and Lima Councils
   1.6. Junta Magna
   1.7. Third Mexican and Lima Councils
   1.8. San Salvador Synods
2. Nineteenth and Twentieth Centuries
   2.1. Latin American Plenary Council
   2.2. Brazilian Plenary Councils
   2.3. Rio de Janeiro Conference
   2.4. Medellín
   2.5. Puebla
   2.6. Santo Domingo

1. Colonial Period

1.1. *Significance*

Soon after their arrival in Latin America in the 15th century, → missionaries from Europe met together to seek common answers to their problems. Thus some ten *juntas* (i.e., high-level meetings) took place in Mexico that one might call forerunners of the Latin American councils. Technically, councils involve the participation of several → bishops. The Latin American councils dealt with the introduction of Indians to the Christian → faith, the administration of the → sacraments in the context of → mission, entry into the Christian life, and the preparation of → catechisms and → liturgical books.

1.2. *Church Organization*

In 1511 the first three → dioceses in Latin America were established: Santo Domingo (in present-day Dominican Republic), Concepción de la Vega (Dominican Republic), and San Juan de Puerto Rico. Santa María la Antigua del Darién (Panama) followed in 1513. Up to 1546 all New World dioceses were under the Seville metropolitan. In that year Paul III (1534-49) set up three church provinces in Latin America. The first was Santo Domingo, with Concepción de la Vega, San Juan de Puerto Rico, Coro (Venezuela), and Cartagena (Colombia) as suffragans. The second was Mexico, with the dioceses of Guatemala (1531), Oaxaca, Tlaxcala (Puebla de Los Angeles, 1519), Chiapas, Michoacán, and Guadalajara (1548). The third was Lima, with the dioceses of Cuzco (1534), Quito, Panamá, Nicaragua (1527), and Popayán. At the time of the third Lima council, this province also included Charcas (La Plata), Tucumán, Asunción (Paraguay), Santiago de Chile, and La Imperial. The Diocese of San Salvador de Bahia was set up in Brazil in 1550, which in 1676 became an archdiocese comprising the dioceses of Rio de Janeiro and Olinda.

1.3. *Mexican Juntas*

Several bishops participated in the Mexican juntas (1524-46), which we thus must describe as → synods. In the collegial exercise of their pastoral mission, they issued binding decrees. They dealt with prerequisites for → baptism, marital questions (→ Marriage) among new Christians, and admission to the → Eucharist. In the baptismal debate between the orders, an important role was played by the → bull *Altitudo divini consilii* (1537) of Paul III.

The first bishop (and later first archbishop) of Mexico, Juan de Zumárraga (1468-1548), was commissioned to prepare two catechisms. The *Doctrina breve,* issued in his name in 1543/44, was based on the catechism of Pedro de Córdoba (ca. 1482-1525). The second catechism drew on Spanish reformer Constantino Ponce de la Fuente in the first part and on the work of → Erasmus (1469?-1536) in the second. The antithesis between colonizing and evangelization (→ Colonialism; Colonialism and Mission; Evangelism) was already becoming apparent (esp. through the writing of B. de Las Casas).

1.4. *First Mexican and Lima Councils*
Whereas Zumárraga contemplated attending the Council of → Trent (1545-63), his successor, Alonso de Montúfar (d. 1569), paid more attention to local demands, which did not permit any lengthy absence as archbishop. He asked for → dispensation from the *ad limina* visit, requiring his presence in Rome. No Latin American bishop was present at Trent.

The first councils of Mexico City (1555) and of Lima (1552) drew up a → church order regulating rights, duties, personnel, and business. They also prescribed → punishments. Time-consuming consultation with Spain and Rome was decreed to be no longer necessary.

1.5. *Second Mexican and Lima Councils*
With a *cédula real* (royal letters patent) on July 12, 1564, King Philip II (1556-98) of Spain ordered the enforcement of Trent by the Latin American councils. This decree was accepted by the second council of Mexico (1565) and of Lima (1567). The second Lima council devoted itself to the duties of bishops as elucidated by Trent. It demanded permanent residence for bishops, regular → visitations, the founding of seminaries, and the establishment of parishes with approximately 400 members. Bishops and priests were to preach on → Sundays and holy days (→ Preaching). Pagan cults were opposed, and a uniform catechism was called for.

1.6. *Junta Magna*
The Junta Magna of 1568, a high-level meeting of churchmen and royal officials, including Francisco de Toledo, the newly named viceroy of Peru, and presided over by Cardinal Diego de Espinoza, the president of the Council of Castile, established →

patronage and restricted the influence of Rome. The Indian church now became the Spanish colonial church. Anything besmirching the conquest must be suppressed, conflicts with the secular authorities were to be avoided, and the Indians had to be portrayed as an uncultured race on the lowest level (J. Beckmann, *HistCh* 5.257ff.). After 1587 Rome insisted on ratifying all individual synods, but then in 1590 Philip decreed that no synodal rulings should be promulgated without the consent of the Council of the Indies.

1.7. *Third Mexican and Lima Councils*
Under Archbishop Toribio de Mogrovejo (1538-1606, later canonized) of Lima, the third Lima council (1582/83) called for the use of native languages in religious instruction and for a four-week catechumenate. Polygamy had to be renounced before baptism. Idolatry was forbidden, which included visiting pagan places of prayer, singing pagan hymns, and participating in pagan games and → dances. Christian songs, games, and dances were to replace pagan ones. A serious weakness was the failure to set up a national clergy.

Bartolomé de Las Casas (1484-1566) had an unmistakable influence on the third Mexican council (1585), which took up some major questions of → ethics. In a letter to Philip II dated October 16, 1585, the bishops opposed war against the Indians and their enslavement (→ Slavery). They criticized the feudal labor practices of the encomienda and repartimiento. Even after finally securing approval from Rome in 1622, however, the catechism of the third Mexican council did not come into use.

1.8. *San Salvador Synods*
The constitutions of the Synod of San Salvador de Bahia (1707) contained a catechism for slaves. Though the institution of slavery was presupposed, the decrees give evidence of religious concern, addressing issues of food, clothing, free marital choice, and participation in → worship and instruction.

Bibliography: Acta et decreta concilii plenarii Americae Latinae (Vatican City, 1999) fac. ed. with Lat. and Sp. text • "Diocesan Synods and Provincial Councils (1524-1907)," *BgMiss* 9 (1946) 118-35 • W. HENKEL, *Die Konzilien in Lateinamerika,* vol. 1, *Mexiko, 1555-1897* (Paderborn, 1984) • PONTIFICIA COMMISSIO PRO AMERICA LATINA, *Los últimos cien años de la evangelización en América Latina. Centenario del Concilio Plenario de América Latina, simposio histórico* (Vatican City, 2000) • J. F. SCHWALLER, ed., *The Church in Colonial Latin America* (Wilmington, Del., 2000) • R. VARGAS UGARTE, *Concilios Limenses (1551-1772)* (3 vols.; Lima, 1951-54).

WILLI HENKEL

2. Nineteenth and Twentieth Centuries

During the colonial period we find only a peripheral Christianity in Latin America, emerging from the end of the 15th century and limited to diocesan, archdiocesan, and provincial councils. The first truly continental council was held in 1899.

In the 20th century the → bishops began meeting in national councils called conferences. The → Codex Iuris Canonici does not use this term, and in this way, at the express wish of Pius XII (1939-58), these manifestations of the synodical spirit of the Latin American church were deprived of legal standing. Conferences took place at Rio de Janeiro in 1955, Medellín, Colombia, in 1968, Puebla, Mexico, in 1979, and Santo Domingo, Dominican Republic, in 1992.

2.1. *Latin American Plenary Council*

The Latin American Plenary Council took place in 1899. In 1890 Leo XIII (1878-1903) had set up the Latin American Plenary Committee to prepare for the council in Rome, which reveals a desire to Romanize the Latin American church. In 998 canons questions regarding paganism, → superstition, religious ignorance, → socialism, Freemasonry, the press, and other matters were all dealt with — questions that suggest in general the exporting of European and especially Roman problems to Latin America. Of the 104 members of the episcopate, 13 archbishops and 41 bishops took part in the council, but it did not have the significance of the 16th-century councils, nor can it be compared with the 20th-century conferences.

2.2. *Brazilian Plenary Councils*

Two plenary councils were held in Brazil — the first in 1890, the second in 1939. At the instigation of Cardinal Sebastião Leme (1882-1942), the latter attempted, in a spirit of triumphalism, to show the power of the church against the populism of Brazilian president/dictator Getúlio Vargas (1883-1954), with a view to upholding the interests of the church vis-à-vis the state.

2.3. *Rio de Janeiro Conference*

Of special importance was the founding of the → Latin American Council of Bishops (CELAM) pursuant to the first General Conference of Latin American Bishops, held at Rio de Janeiro from July 25 to August 8, 1955. With the creation of CELAM this conference succeeded in setting up the first truly continental organization for the coordination of pastoral work over a whole region. In this regard it preceded similar organizations later formed in Africa, Asia, and Europe.

2.4. *Medellín*

In all, 601 Latin American bishops took part in → Vatican II (1962-65). There was a great need to take a fresh look at Latin America in the light of Vatican II, especially given the reality of a dependent and impoverished continent. After an initial attempt to do so at a gathering of CELAM at Mar del Plata in 1966, the second bishops' conference took place at Medellín from August 26 to September 6, 1968, inaugurated by Paul VI (1963-78). This conference, which was even more important than the famed third Lima council (1582/83; see 1.7), must be seen as the most significant conciliar event in the history of the Latin American church. The church as a whole made a fundamental pastoral option in favor of the → base communities, liberating → education, liturgical renewal, and → solidarity with the poor. → Liberation theology influenced many of its conclusions. Even more important than the initial impetus was the later impact on the clergy and laity, on religious orders and congregations, on bishops, and on social, political, academic, and student movements, as well as on workers and peasants.

2.5. *Puebla*

In contrast, the third conference, held at Puebla from January 27 to February 13, 1979, showed a church full of serious tensions. CELAM itself had caused these tensions when the general secretary, Alfonso López Trujillo, repudiated the basic principles of Medellín. A conservative trend (→ Conservatism) limited the church's capacity to respond to the many military dictatorships that dominated Latin America during the next decade. A short time later the ideology of "national security" would lead to thousands of → martyrs, among them priests, members of orders, and even bishops, including the archbishop of San Salvador, Oscar Arnulfo Romero (1917-80).

A process of "restoration" had begun in the church, which led to the persecution of liberation theologians, the questioning of base communities, and the discrediting of revolutionary political involvement. A few months later, on July 19, the Sandinista → revolution triumphed in Nicaragua. In this context a radically new relation between faith and politics became possible. A new era had begun in Latin American history in which Christians could again struggle on the people's behalf as they had done in the battle for the first emancipation from Spain and Portugal. Events would later prove, however, that the Sandinistas could neither live up to the initial promises nor retain popular support, so that the church was wise not to commit itself to overly naive solidarity with them.

2.6. *Santo Domingo*

From October 12 to 28, 1992, following its inauguration by John Paul II, the fourth general bishops' conference was held at Santo Domingo. The conference marked the 500th anniversary of the discovery and evangelization of America. The two major themes discussed by the 356 bishops, theologians, and lay participants were the evangelization of cultures and human development as a dimension of the "new evangelization" (John Paul II's term; → Evangelism). The final document praises the church's role in defending the Indians but does not criticize any of its past actions, such as legitimizing black slavery. Unlike the previous three conferences — Rio de Janeiro, Medellín, and Puebla — the Santo Domingo conference was highly controlled by Rome and conservative groups in Latin America.

→ Acculturation; Culture and Christianity; Latin American Council of Churches; Latin American Theology

Bibliography: *Acta et decreta concilii plenarii Americae Latinae* (Vatican City, 1999) fac. ed. with Latin and Spanish text • M. R. CANDELARIA, *Popular Religion and Liberation: The Dilemma of Liberation Theology* (Albany, N.Y., 1990) • *The Church in the Present-Day Transformation of Latin America in the Light of the Council: Second General Conference of Latin American Bishops, Bogotá [and] Medellín . . . Colombia, 1968. Position Papers* (Bogotá, 1970) • CONFERENCIA GENERAL DEL EPISCOPADO LATINOAMERICANO, *New Evangelization, Human Development, Christian Culture: Fourth General Conference of Latin American Bishops* (Washington, D.C., 1993) • G. COOK, *The New Face of the Church in Latin America: Between Tradition and Change* (Maryknoll, N.Y., 1994) • E. DUSSEL, *Die Geschichte der Kirche in Lateinamerika* (Mainz, 1988) • G. GUTIÉRREZ et al., *Santo Domingo and After: The Challenges for the Latin American Church* (London, 1993) • A. T. HENNELLY, ed., *Santo Domingo and Beyond: Documents and Commentaries from the Fourth General Conference of Latin American Bishops* (Maryknoll, N.Y., 1993) • C. ROWLAND, *The Cambridge Companion to Liberation Theology* (Cambridge, 1999) • P. E. SIGMUND, *Liberation Theology at the Crossroads: Democracy or Revolution* (New York, 1990); idem, ed., *Religious Freedom and Evangelization in Latin America: The Challenge of Religious Pluralism* (Maryknoll, N.Y., 1999) • W. URANGA, *Para interpretar Santo Domingo* (Buenos Aires, 1992).

ENRIQUE DUSSEL

Latin American Theology

1. Origins
2. Colonial Christendom (1492-1808)
   2.1. Spiritual Conquest
   2.2. Spiritual Decline
3. Christendom in Crisis (1808-1930)
   3.1. Liberalism and Wars of Independence
   3.2. Rupture between Church and State (1850-1929)
4. New Christendom (1930-62)
5. Liberationist and Pentecostal Christianity (1962-present)

1. Origins

For most of their 500-year presence in Latin America, Roman Catholic theologians and missionaries have employed methods and concepts taken largely from Western European theology. Most missionaries who came to Latin America had been previously schooled in scholastic theology, principally in the theological and philosophical writings of → Augustine (354-430; → Augustine's Theology), → Thomas Aquinas (ca. 1225-74; → Scholasticism), and the Dominican theological school at Salamanca, Spain, founded by Francisco de Vitoria (ca. 1480-1546). Scholastic theology predominated throughout most of Latin American history, being embodied until the 20th century in an ecclesial-societal model called Christendom, then in a derivative form known as New Christendom, created around 1930. → Liberation theology and Pentecostalism emerged later in the 20th century with new theological emphases.

This article reviews these theologies within the historical context of social forces at work during the conquest, colonization, and neocolonization of Latin America. It highlights church-state relationships, how the churches understood → salvation or redemption, and how churches related a person's or a people's final destiny to the gospel's imperatives to → love one's neighbor and to act justly. "Church" here refers mainly to the → Roman Catholic Church, but in later historical periods it includes also Protestant churches, especially Pentecostals.

The taproot of Christendom was Augustinian theology. Augustine taught that the → state was founded upon justice and that justice would be realized only in the commonwealth, the founder and ruler of which is Jesus Christ. Augustine called the community of the redeemed and elect "the City of God," an eschatological reality to be fully revealed in the final consummation of the world. The church, he said, is a mixture of the redeemed and the nonredeemed, and it prefigures the City of God, even as it labors in the Earthly City to bring more souls into God's City. In the late medieval period, the Augustinian school took this doctrine a momentous step further, teaching that the → pope as Christ's vicar ruled the commonwealth, which became in effect a → theocracy encompassing both church and state. Gradually the church came to understand itself both as the exclusive channel of salvation *(extra ecclesiam nulla salus)* and as a civilizing teacher in → society.

Thus the Roman Catholic Church throughout the Middle Ages and during most of Latin American history claimed for itself the highest authority in both the terrestrial and celestial cities, proclaiming its mission assertively, and sometimes aggressively, to all peoples in every land (→ Catholic Missions). Catholic → missionaries in Latin America followed quite aggressively the gospel command "Go therefore and make disciples of all nations . . ." (Matt 28:19), with some missionaries justifying the use of force if necessary. The proselytizers tried to be both universal, by trying to convert and baptize all people, and comprehensive, by influencing all sectors and institutions of society, including the state.

Neither theologians nor bishops distinguished clearly between the temporal and spiritual spheres, the → sacred and the profane. They often confused and reversed the roles of → clergy and laity (e.g., clergy became involved in politics, and governors acted like bishops). In its pastoral practice, the church simply appropriated the two roles of Christianizing and civilizing members of society. To accomplish this twofold mission, the church recognized the need for a Christian ruler to allow missionaries to preach the gospel and, once the people accepted the faith, to see that they obeyed civil and church laws. As for the state, it expected that the church would in turn support its political-military agenda as part of the pact. This symbiotic relationship flourished until the late 18th century, when it began to decay.

The seeds of Christendom were first sown in Latin American soil in the late 15th century. It flourished until the end of the 17th century, began to wither in the 18th, and finally died in the early 20th. From its ashes arose New Christendom in the early 20th century. Its chief theoretician was the French philosopher Jacques Maritain (1882-1973), who modified the traditional architectonic using the theology of Thomas Aquinas. The church of New Christendom, like its predecessor, tries to exert influence over all sectors of society. Unlike Christendom, however, it recognizes the state's autonomy and so tries to influence the state's public policy indirectly by means of its social doctrine. It also tries to influence society through laypersons, who are encouraged by the hierarchy to live out Catholic social principles in the marketplace.

Working within the frameworks of Christendom and New Christendom, theologians have assumed →

Anselm's classic definition of → theology as "faith seeking understanding." They probed the meaning of → faith through rational knowledge and optimistically sought to create through → reason a conceptual synthesis of → salvation history. This theological method paid scant attention to → culture or the people's faith experience. Catholic missionaries who followed this approach generally ignored or were highly critical of the beliefs, rituals, and experiences of the native peoples, dismissing them as superstitious and idolatrous. This mode of proselytizing followed a theological method that contemporary theologians call "theology from above," that is, doctrine presented to the → masses without taking into account their reality and religious experience.

Another theological school that influenced missionary work in Latin America was Christian utopianism. Its missionaries attended to the faith, culture, and experiences of the people, while drinking from the wells of theologians and the 16th-century humanist-utopian thinkers → Erasmus (1469?-1536) and Thomas More (1478-1535). Erasmus and More made a powerful impact on Spain and, through missionaries like Bartolomé de Las Casas (1484-1566), on Latin American missionary development. Other humanist-utopians include Vasco de Quiroga and the Jesuit missionaries, who took into account the language, beliefs, rituals, and behavior of the indigenous people in their work of evangelization (→ Evangelism). Today's liberation theologians have related their own work to this utopian school, which they call "theology from below," a type of theological reflection that accounts for people's faith, culture, struggles, and human → rights.

European Protestant missionaries brought to Latin America their own theological traditions, distinctively different from Iberian Catholicism (→ Evangelical Missions). Arriving throughout Latin America in the mid-19th century, evangelical Protestantism began slowly. By the end of World War I, there were about 200,000 Protestants. → Protestantism grew more rapidly in the 1930s and, with the arrival of the Pentecostals in the 1960s, began a period of very rapid growth. Evangelical Protestant missionaries emphasized the Word of God, → justification by faith, culture, → democracy, → progress, and the God of freedom. Evangelical theology also underscored individual freedom and a work ethic that supported the capitalist free enterprise system and Western democracy in Latin America (J. Míguez Bonino, *Doing Theology*, 11).

These theologies, both Catholic and Protestant, have influenced and, in varying degrees, continue to influence the way the church in Latin America interacts with the state, how the church has sought to convert indigenous people to Christianity, and how it understands salvation in relation to one's social responsibility.

2. Colonial Christendom (1492-1808)

Led by their Roman Catholic monarchs, Portugal and Spain from the 8th to the 15th centuries employed force through the → Inquisition and the → Crusades to convert or drive off Muslims and Jews from the Iberian Peninsula. When that task was completed at Granada in 1492, Spanish and Portuguese missionaries and conquistadores employed the same theology, ethos, institutions, strategy, and military might in the Americas, where they converted pagan nations to the Catholic faith and vanquished those who resisted. The Spanish came first (1492), then the Portuguese (1510), carrying cross and sword to establish Christianity.

Before the encounters with the indigenous peoples, popes — especially Alexander VI (1492-1503) and Leo X (1513-21) — had issued a number of → bulls that gave the Portuguese and Spanish rulers patronage, or jurisdiction, over the Americas. The bulls authorized the rulers to found churches and to appoint → bishops in the Americas. In the New World → church and state would work together both to Christianize and to civilize people. But because the state, not the church, possessed → patronage, the former was the dominant partner in the Americas, especially so in Brazil, where the governor exercised almost absolute power over the church.

In the Latin American colonies for the first 350 years, the state wielded far more authority in religious affairs than did the papacy, having the power to establish bishoprics and seminaries, appoint bishops, exact → tithes, and veto papal bulls. In fact, however, the state created few bishoprics and seminaries in Latin America. Even though the church worked as the junior partner, it nonetheless possessed considerable authority, especially in Spanish America, where it exercised its influence by directly shaping and informing civil law, → education, and governmental structures. These institutions in turn supported the church's → teaching, → preaching, and sacramental life. The extensive institutional impact of Catholic Christendom is still evident today in Latin American politics, education, and culture, although competing ecclesial models (e.g., ecclesial → base communities and → Pentecostal churches) have significantly reduced its influence.

2.1. *Spiritual Conquest*

Christian → proselytism in the Americas was an ambiguous process because the priest's proclama-tion of the cross of Christ often accompanied or followed the conquistador's brandishing of the sword. This conjunction of cross and sword, with all its tensions and inconsistencies, appears in three early stages of missionary activity.

2.1.1. The first stage of evangelization took place in the Caribbean region between 1492 and 1519. The earliest missionaries, who were largely from religious orders (→ Dominicans, → Franciscans, and Carmelites), sought to convert the indigenous people, called *Indios,* by peaceful means, though some missionaries under certain conditions justified the use of → force. Many missionaries believed that unless the Indians were converted and baptized, they would not be saved. Spiritual → conversion aimed at the salvation of individuals, or "saving their souls," and involved a twofold process of rooting out false beliefs (e.g., → animism and → polytheism) and practices (human sacrifice and polygamy) and replacing them with Christian truths, participation in the → sacraments, and life in accordance with the commandments.

The attempt to convert the indigenous Caribs, Arawaks, and Tupis met with little success. The Spanish incursion, swayed far more by the conquistadores' desire for precious metals than by zeal for helping missionaries convert the people, led to the destruction of these peoples, most of them dying from diseases carried from Europe or from harsh treatment by their conquerors. Few among the survivors were evangelized in this stage.

Spaniards, both at home and in the New World, were disturbed by their Christian militia slaughtering masses of non-Christian people and by other atrocities that seemed totally inconsistent with Spain's evangelical aims. Denunciations of the conquerors' conduct led to debates that produced condemnations of conquistador philosophy, just-war arguments and counterarguments, and the passage of more humane laws. Ultimately, however, the conquest received official approval.

An early attempt to justify the violent conquest was *el Requerimiento,* a notification read to the indigenous people demanding that they recognize the authority of the church, pope, and monarchy or else suffer the consequences (G. Gutiérrez, *Las Casas,* 109-13). The latter involved physical subjugation, confiscation of property, and punishment appropriate to traitors (i.e., execution). The public reading of the Requirement, not always with translation into local languages, began with a summary of Christian history from the creation story to the Alexandrine bulls. The reading was believed to absolve the conquerors from moral culpability for inflicting punishment on the native people, should they refuse to concede, and to place the blame on the Indians for the conquistadores' use of force (C. Gibson, 38-39).

Both outside observers and Spaniards alike raised questions about the justice of Spain's conquest, its coercive practices, and its right to rule the new lands. A Scottish Franciscan asked eight preachers employed by the Spanish monarch, "With what justice are the Spaniards able to enter the Indies as they are now doing?" (L. Hanke, 149). European justice was Aristotelian justice (rendering to each person what is due), guided by charity (love directed to God and neighbor). Francisco de Vitoria argued that the papal grant given to the Spanish Crown had no temporal value and that the Indian refusal to recognize this authority was no reason for waging war against them or for seizing their land (pp. 239-64).

The early Dominicans, → Augustinians, Franciscans, and later the → Jesuits frequently raised issues of justice with respect to the conquest, treatment of the Indians, and the encomienda (an institution in which groups of indigenous people were legally "entrusted" to the conquistador, to whom they paid tribute or labor). The encomienda and the church became rival institutions. The issue concerning who should have control over the Indians and how the latter ought to be treated erupted in 1511 in Santa Domingo, where Dominican friar Antonio de Montesinos (ca. 1486-ca. 1540) denounced from the pulpit the *encomenderos'* harsh treatment of the Indians, calling their practices unjust and grievously sinful.

"What constituted justice and how could it be achieved were questions raised with every important step Spaniards took" (Hanke, 1). Churchmen and colonists argued with each other about the right to wage → war against the native people. Vitoria and many other missionaries and theologians strongly opposed forced conversion, enslavement, and the encomienda. Dominican Bartolomé de Las Casas and Jesuit António Vieira (1608-97) expressed their opposition on the basis of God's justice revealed in Scripture, human justice rooted in natural law, and their own outrage over the mistreatment of the people.

2.1.2. In the second stage of evangelization (1519-51), Spanish missionaries entered Mexico and Peru on the heels of Hernando Cortés's (1485-1547) conquest of the Aztecs in the central valley of Mexico (1519-21) and Francisco Pizarro's (ca. 1475-1541) vanquishing the Inca Empire near Cuzco, Peru (1533). The Franciscan missionaries moved throughout Mexico, including lands now part of southern California and Texas, converting the people to Chris-

tianity en masse. The church quickly organized itself, setting up bishoprics in Mexico City, center of the Aztec Empire, and in Lima, where the missionaries established great universities and printing presses. In both regions the indigenous population rapidly declined because of disease, the spread of alcoholism, fierce battles waged by the conquistadores, and repression.

The person speaking most strongly on behalf of the peasants was Bishop Bartolomé de Las Casas, who debated Juan Sepúlveda, in Valladolid, Spain (1550-51), on whether the encomienda was just. Las Casas had earlier argued that it was unjust and had helped convince Spain to pass the so-called New Laws of the Indies (1542-43), which prohibited Indian enslavement and called upon church officials and royal officers to relinquish their encomiendas. Actually carrying out the New Laws, however, was another matter. Bishop Antonio de Valdivieso of Nicaragua, who tried to enforce the abolition of → slavery as the New Laws required, was assassinated in 1550. Latin American theologians today regard the first missionaries who protested against the repression of indigenous peoples as the forerunners of contemporary liberation theology.

Not all missionaries opposed the coercive institutions like the encomienda. Defenders, like the renowned Franciscan Toribio de Benavente (ca. 1490-1569), better known by his Indian name Motolinía, held that the encomienda, if carefully regulated to safeguard the people's welfare, was necessary for the good of the Indians. In a letter to Emperor Charles V (1555) expressing his disagreement with Las Casas on the use of force, Motolinía argued, "They who do not wish to hear the holy gospel of Jesus Christ of their own free will should be forced; here the proverb applies, 'Better forced to be good than free to be bad'" (Gutiérrez, *Las Casas*, 137). Motolinía and others justified the encomienda on the grounds that it allowed greater control over the converts, which was judged necessary for ridding the people of their idolatrous practices.

What sort of theology supported such absolute authority and coercive measures over the indigenous people? A fully satisfying answer is difficult to give, but the theology seems to have emerged from convictions that because salvation could be achieved only within the church and because human sacrifice and idolatry would lead the unfaithful baptized Indians to perdition, military force was justified to stop such practices.

How essential were → baptism and explicit faith in Christ in order that non-Christians be saved? A number of views existed among theologians in the

16th century. On one end of the spectrum, some held that salvation was not possible without baptism and explicit → confession of faith. The priest John Trithemius stated that apart from Christian faith, "there will be no Indians in heaven" (Gutiérrez, *Las Casas*, 243). At the other end of the spectrum were the humanists, who held that those who have not heard of Jesus Christ but have kept the two great love commands are saved. In a middle position Domingo de Soto (1494-1560) argued that implicit faith in Christ is sufficient for salvation; although the people of the Indies have lived in total ignorance of Christian truths, still they may be saved. The Inquisition, however, would reject his view.

Many theologians and missionaries understood redemption as the attaining of eternal bliss because → Jesus, born without sin, offered his life as satisfaction for the sins of humankind. Salvation as satisfaction consists in God pardoning sins by means of the crucifixion of Jesus. This theology, however, isolates Jesus' death from the rest of his life, and it gives the impression that the Father arbitrarily chose the → cross of Jesus to make up for our sins. As the Salvadoran theologian Jon Sobrino has noted, such a total focus on the death of Jesus ignores "the intrinsic relationship that exists between Jesus' proclamation of liberation, his denunciation of oppression, and his historical death on the cross" (*Christology*, 193). This theology of redemption urges persons to do penance for their sins rather than proclaim the values of God's reign. If one worships God, confesses one's sins, and does penance, one is saved. T. Matt Garr shows in a study of popular religion among the Quechuans in Peru that the people have established a relationship with God on a quid pro quo basis: "If you honor God, God will bless you; if you do not, God will punish" (A. McGovern, 90). Little emphasis is given to God's gratuitous love, imitating the life of Jesus, or being just.

Although some missionaries, such as the Dominicans and Jesuits, taught that acting justly on the basis of the gospel teaching was necessary for salvation, most simply emphasized participation in the sacraments. Referring to the majority perspective of this period, Gutiérrez has noted that "eternal life was seen exclusively as a future life and not as present in an active and creative form within our concrete historical involvement as well" (*Theology of Liberation*, 39). D. Brackley nicely sums up the prevailing → eschatology that conditioned proselytizing the indigenous people and African slaves: "Christ did not come to bring social justice before we die; he came to bring happiness with God after we die" (pp. xxi-xxii).

2.1.3. The third stage of evangelization (1551-1620) included the systematic establishment of the church. Early in this stage the church's best missionary practice was carried out by Antonio Valdivieso, Manuel da Nóbrega, and Francisco José Jaca de Aragón. Jaca, a Capuchin who worked with black slaves in Cartagena, Colombia, later wrote an important document questioning the subjugation of blacks to slavery and protesting the heavy burden placed on the Indians. These missionaries and their communities respected the indigenous tribes and black slaves as full human beings, teaching that they had basic rights that must never be violated. Some missionaries learned the native languages and culture in order to evangelize more effectively, thus following Augustine's teaching that faith presupposes understanding. These missionaries would administer baptism only after the people were properly instructed and had expressed a desire to be baptized. This emphasis on understanding was resisted by many → priests, who supported quick and mass baptisms of the people "without too many questions asked or catechisms learned" (Hanke, 74).

Missionaries also established schools and other social structures, as well as political-cultural-economic systems, notably the Jesuit → reductions in Paraguay and Bolivia, which began in 1609. The reductions, numbering about 30 and involving up to 300,000 Indians at the height of the experiment, were enclosed villages with fully controlled institutions that protected the Guaraní from being enslaved and afforded them opportunities for education and evangelization. The reductions were praised in Europe for their economic creativity and for their educating the people in culture and music and forming them in spiritual values.

In Spanish America clergymen such as Juan de Zumárraga (1468-1548), archbishop of Mexico, Vasco de Quiroga (1470-1565), and Las Casas introduced the utopian ideals of Erasmus and More. Following More's *Utopia*, Quiroga created Michoacán, a community in Santa Fe (present-day New Mexico) that held common ownership of property. Laborers, women as well as men, worked a six-hour day, and the fruits of their collective labor were distributed according to need. Quiroga envisioned a cooperative life in the midst of the exploitative encomiendas and haciendas, but his dream was never realized. The Christian-humanist utopian movement ended in the late 16th century partly because the *encomenderos* strongly opposed it, and partly because the Council of → Trent (1545-63) associated Erasmus's writings with Protestantism. This development gave license to the Spanish Inquisition to censor what it judged to be the unorthodox views of these humanist-utopian missionaries in the New World.

Although the missionaries baptized large numbers of people during this period, some observers have questioned the lasting success of the conversions because the indigenous people and African slaves, even after accepting Catholic teaching and baptism, continued to celebrate their own traditional rites and festivals. Their songs and dances possessed hidden, non-Christian religious meanings. Certain symbols (the cross), practices (→ fasting and → confession of sins), and creator myths suggested a similarity of these native religions to Christianity. Yet things did not always mean to the newly converted people what they appeared to mean to the missionaries. The Mayan epic *Popol Vuh,* for example, presents classic Jewish-Christian themes of → creation, rebellion-fall, destructive flood, and a hero-savior born of a virgin who dies for his followers and then rises. The Mayans melded the worship of the Virgin → Mary with the ritual of their own deities, such as Pachamama, or Earth Mother. Roman Catholic theology was itself influenced and altered by Native American religious practice, becoming syncretistic in practice if not in doctrine. Black Africans, transported to the Americas in chains, brought with them stories, folk songs, plays, and religious festivals that they integrated into the Catholic faith imposed on them by the colonists.

Yet while evangelization in certain areas may have been superficial or inauthentic, in other areas it was effective, alive even today in syncretistic forms of folk religion or popular religiosity. The indigenous people accepted → Catholicism, but on their own terms. By giving special meanings and nuances to Christian religious symbols, the indigenous people have been able to cope with their oppressive colonial situation for over 500 years, to continue to believe in God, and to seek final justice (→ Colonialism; Colonialism and Mission).

2.2. *Spiritual Decline*

The decline of the church in the Americas began with the political-economic demise of Bourbon Spain in the early 1700s and with both Spain and Portugal losing their dominance of the seas to the English, who themselves were beginning to exert control over Latin America. As the homelands grew less stable, factions within the colonial church between secular clergy and the → religious orders, and between the Creoles (persons of Spanish descent born in the New World) and the *peninsulares* (recent arrivals from the Iberian Peninsula), became more polarized. The Council of Trent appointed secular clergy, who were fully subordinate to the local bishop, to replace priests from religious orders as the pastors of parishes. The latter then moved to the frontiers and worked with indigenous people.

This secular-religious tension came to a climax during the last quarter of the 18th century following the expulsion of the Jesuits. The minister of Portugal, the marquis of Pombal, falsely accused the Jesuits of supporting a Guaraní rebellion against the Treaty of Madrid (1750) and had them expelled from Portugal and all its American colonies in 1759 — a total of 2,200 Jesuits, first from Brazil (1759) and then elsewhere (1769). The expulsion of the Jesuits, who had contributed greatly to the church's prosperity, brought about a severe shortage of priests and a loss of intellectual and spiritual leadership. As a consequence, many native Americans left the church. The church became increasingly controlled by the state. Spain, exhausted by wars and badly governed by Bourbon kings, was losing its grip on the colonies.

3. Christendom in Crisis (1808-1930)

As tensions mounted between the colonial governments and the Iberian monarchies, liberal Creoles publicly protested Iberian trade restrictions. Influenced by the → Enlightenment's emphasis on reason, freedom, and nationalism, the Creoles began to think of independence in the early 1800s, encouraged by the revolutions in the United States and France. These tensions led to wars of independence, victory for the Creoles, and subsequently a rupture between church and state.

3.1. *Liberalism and Wars of Independence*

In the struggle between the colonies and the homelands, the conservative bishops aligned themselves with Spain to oppose the Creoles' movement for independence. Other than the bishops, most clergy, who were generally upper- and middle-class Creoles, threw their lot in with the independence movement. Indeed, some clergy even took up arms and organized armies. A Mexican guerrilla group of militant priests, both mestizo and Creole, identified with the indigenous people and envisioned a radical → revolution that would bring greater equity for the majority. The war in Mexico (1810-15), led by Father Miguel Hidalgo, was a call to Indians and mestizos alike, not only to reject Spanish rule but also to crush the injustices that exploited the Mexican lower classes. For the most part, however, the wars were waged by Creoles to liberate themselves from Spain's imperialism and not for justice for the indigenous people. Independence, in fact, benefited neither the poor majority nor the church. Before independence, the Creole oligarchy had dominated the impoverished people, and they continued to do so after independence.

Spain responded with military force to these stirrings and regained much of its control, except for the Río de la Plata region, which resisted successfully and remained independent. The transition to independence took place in opposition to a basic ecclesial framework of Catholic → conservatism. There was no major change in culture or theological breakthrough during this crisis. Although some bishops and many upper-class priests favored the movement, most of the Latin American hierarchy, especially the *peninsulares*, were royalists who opposed independence largely for political and economic reasons.

The wars of independence shattered the fundamental structure of Christendom. As the colonial armies did battle with Spain, the liberal and conservative clergy took opposite sides, and the ensuing battle splintered the church. Once the ties between the colonies and the homelands were broken, Spain and Portugal ceased sending seminarians and priests, which in turn led to many vacancies in church offices. Consequently, the state began to fill the vacuum, assuming greater power over ecclesial offices and moving toward a state-controlled church.

Independence for the Brazilians followed a nonviolent route. By the beginning of the 19th century, Brazil had become many times larger and wealthier than Portugal. Moreover, Brazil gained even more credibility and authority as a nation when the Portuguese king John VI, together with his royal family and government, fled to Rio de Janeiro when Napoleon invaded Portugal in 1807. There they remained until 1821, when John was pressured to return home. Brazil, being unwilling to part with the new status that it had enjoyed during the exiled king's presence, declared its independence and installed John's son Dom Pedro as emperor of Brazil (1822-31). Yet the Roman Catholic Church in Brazil, never as strong as the church in Spanish America, hit its nadir in the 19th century. The number of priests and religious decreased significantly. The clergy had families and gave little attention to their ministry. Brazil's Dom Pedro II (emperor 1840-89), the titular head of the church, was a tepid Catholic and communicated poorly with the Vatican.

In liberating themselves from Spain and Portugal, the newly independent nations soon came under the thumb of the British. As the Argentine Methodist theologian José Míguez Bonino has observed, "Our political emancipation from Spain was — however justified and necessary — a step in the Anglo-Saxon colonial and neocolonial expansion" (*Doing Theology*, 14). Spain had dominated colonial Christendom for over 300 years. It had given wine and oil for gold and silver. England began its neocolonial dominance by trading its manufactured products in return for Latin America's raw materials and cheap labor.

3.2. *Rupture between Church and State (1850-1929)*

Independence meant the end of the system of patronage, which also meant that missionaries would no longer be coming from Spain or Portugal, no seminaries would be established, and no priests would be ordained. The state's rupture with the church began after 1850. The first liberal constitution was promulgated in Colombia in 1849, which proposed the separation of church and state. The church began to fade out of the picture, though it continued to have sociopolitical importance and to wield some power in civil matters. Most Latin Americans were still Christians, except for the elite Creole oligarchy. Christendom was not dead, but it was dying. The death knell came to Colombia in 1849 when the government declared itself anti-Christian and anti-Catholic, repudiating its Spanish past. So did Argentina in 1853 and much of Latin America in the 1850s. The church in Brazil also lost influence in the second half of the 19th century.

From 1850 to 1929 a new political project unfolded as the liberal oligarchy began to replace the conservative one and to do battle with the conservative church. Liberal politicians looked to France for their cultural ideals and to the United States for their technological ideals. In Mexico in the late 1850s President Benito Juárez confiscated all the church's wealth, suppressed → monasteries, and declared freedom of religion. The liberal government drove a thick wedge between church and state. Virtually everywhere in Mexico the → Ultramontane church declined. Yet the rural masses, steeped in popular syncretistic religiosity, remained faithful to the traditional church. When Mexican president Plutarco Elías Calles tried to implement the antireligious articles of the 1917 Constitution, the bishops responded by suspending all religious services. The church's interdict moved a grassroots guerrilla army (the Cristeros) to revolt militarily against the government's action. In June 1929 church and state were forced to come to an interim agreement, with religious services allowed to resume. Christendom was dead, but traditional Christianity flourished among the peasants.

Christendom began to unravel for a number of

reasons: the Latin American church lost resources (books and personnel) from the former homelands, liberal and conservative clergy became embroiled in conflicts, and there was an absence of bishops and seminaries. A hostile, anti-Catholic oligarchy assumed rule over most of the former colonies. The 19th-century church possessed little theology and an inadequate → Christology. Protestant theologian John Mackay (1889-1983), a missionary in Latin America toward the end of this period (1916-32), observed that the Creole Catholics had a devotion to the dead Christ, who was for them an expiatory victim. They ignored the historical Jesus, who preached the good news of the → kingdom of God to the poor (→ Poverty), healed the sick, raised the dead, warned the rich, and denounced hypocrites. The humanity of Jesus offered little appeal to the South American worshipers. "He is regarded as a purely supernatural being, whose humanity, being only apparent, has little ethical bearing upon ours. This docetic Christ died as the victim of human hate, and in order to bestow → immortality, that is to say, a continuation of the present earthly, fleshly existence" (Mackay, 98). This theology of Christ as a supernatural expiatory victim led to a focus on individual repentance (→ Penitence) while ignoring → ethics and the corporate life of the church.

Christendom in this period ran aground for another reason. The Christendom church, while regarding itself as the exclusive depository of salvation, failed to respect secular institutions as having their own distinctive ends and used the state for the direct and immediate benefit of the church. Following the wars of independence, the new republican states reversed the roles and now used the church to impose their rule over the people. Colonial Christendom thus became republican regalism, wherein the state ran the church. Then for about a hundred years the disfranchised church found itself isolated from mainstream society.

In an unsuccessful attempt to rescue Christendom, the church in Rome around the middle of the 19th century sent religious teaching orders to Latin America as part of a systematic effort to "Romanize" the Catholic Church (i.e., make it accountable directly to the Vatican). Before the church would have any impact, however, it would first have to change its theology of church and state, its mode of evangelizing, and its ministry to the poor.

4. New Christendom (1930-62)

New Christendom was the church's theological attempt to revive Roman Catholicism in Latin America — first by distinguishing, and then by integrat-

ing, the spiritual and temporal realms that had been split asunder over the previous century. Whereas in colonial Christendom the church sought to transform the world by direct political action in cooperation with the state, New Christendom tried to better the world, first, by respecting the state's distinctive ends, which were to maintain the peace and to promote the common good, and, second, by interacting only indirectly with the state.

The year 1930 marks the turning point. The church gained breathing space when the anti-Catholic liberal class lost power, which happened largely because of the economic crisis of 1929. The church came charging back, but this time it took a new tack. Rather than trying directly to form an alliance with the state to increase its influence, the church sought to increase its power by working with various private organizations. The church believed that, after it had achieved sufficient power, the state would then be forced to acknowledge its political and social rights. The success of the new Christendom strategy was most visible in Argentina and Brazil. Before 1930 the Argentine church reorganized itself and gained a stronger position in society. It eventually developed a doctrine called integration, which looked for answers to family, social, and political problems exclusively in the faith. When Juan Perón came to power in the mid-1940s, he succeeded in getting a stronger church to support him by guaranteeing its rights (P. Richard, 93-94). In the 1930s Getúlio Vargas, president of Brazil, recognizing a well-organized church led by Cardinal Sebastião Leme, who had mobilized the laity, created a corporatist state that made the church an integral part of the republic (T. Bruneau, 43-45).

This new approach to Christianizing society was given legitimacy first in *Rerum novarum* (1891), where Pope Leo XIII (1878-1903) distinguished between public and private societies within the overall society and recognized the viability of a political yet private movement called Christian Democracy. The latter involved lay Catholics in social and civic organizations during the 1930s and 1940s in Brazil, Chile, Venezuela, Ecuador, and El Salvador. Pius XI (1922-39) further defined and defended New Christendom's program, called → Catholic Action (1931). Like Christian Democracy, Catholic Action called upon lay leaders to learn Catholic social principles, which they would apply in the workplace, private business, labor unions, and universities.

Jacques Maritain, the major theorist of New Christendom in the late 1920s and 1930s, developed a conceptual framework that detailed how the church should relate to the state. He first made a fundamental distinction between the temporal and the spiritual orders, arguing that neither order can be negated, reduced to, or separated from the other. Even though the temporal order refers to the whole of civilization and the spiritual order transcends the institutional church, in actuality they apply to the state and to the church respectively. The spiritual order is the order of → grace, and the temporal order is the order of → nature, which includes culture, the state, and the laws of justice. Each order must work toward its own end. The spiritual order must "vivify and superelevate the temporal order," enabling the secular society to reach the temporal common good (p. 98). Why is superelevation necessary? Building on Aquinas's theological presupposition that grace builds on, or "fulfills," nature, Maritain argued that the church, a graced institution, accomplishes its spiritual mission when it grows within a well-ordered and just society governed by the state, a natural institution. The state, wounded by its own selfishness, cannot achieve its natural ends alone but needs God's grace. And thus it requires the church's indirect intervention to help it realize its natural ends.

Maritain also argued that God's redemptive work cannot be realized within the temporal sphere. The state's efforts to promote the common good, to bring about → peace, and to ensure human rights in society thus do not usher in God's reign. In working toward these ends, the state establishes the conditions for the possibility of salvation for persons, disposing them for personal encounter with God. Working for justice, in other words, does not effect salvation for the workers. There is no cause-and-effect relationship between working for the social good in history and life hereafter. Achieving heavenly bliss is essentially a solitary quest. Gutiérrez, as we shall see below, disagreed with Maritain on this point.

In Latin America, Maritain's theory had a significant impact in the Roman Catholic Church, but it was not faithfully or uniformly followed. Once the church had amassed bargaining power by building a strong social base, it began to make deals with the state. The Catholic Action program in Brazil led in many cases to a radicalizing of Catholics who saw the need to become more directly involved in political action. In other countries, such as Chile and Peru, participants in Catholic Action experienced an identity crisis. Some laypersons became conservative apologists in defense of the church; others became radicals working to transform society. Gutiérrez, who learned his theology within the context of New Christendom, pinpointed other deficiencies in Maritain's approach: it lacks an adequate Christology, a social-scientific analysis of problems, and a method for relating Scripture to pastoral practice.

5. Liberationist and Pentecostal Christianity (1962-present)

Latin Americans suffered severe repression, civil war, and social upheaval during military dictatorships that began in the late 1950s and that continued into the 1980s. In this period two new religious movements and theologies arose: first, a radical liberationist movement in the early 1960s that directly addressed sociopolitical and economic problems that exploited the poor; second, an evangelical Pentecostal movement that came from North America and that broke through social barriers, cultural traditions, and a church caste system. It evangelized individuals, both rich and poor, Indian, black, mestizo, and Creole. Both movements and their corresponding theologies have challenged traditional Catholic and Protestant churches in many ways and have drawn Christians away from the mainline Protestant and Catholic institutions.

5.1. The liberationist movement attracted laypersons from Catholic Action who had become radicalized by their earlier involvement with the poor and with workers' unions. It also appealed to university students, educators in the adult → literacy programs created by Paulo Freire (1973), Protestants and Catholics involved in leftist movements, and priests and women religious who were working directly with the poor. → Pastors and → catechists organized the people into small groups that came to be called ecclesial → base communities. Small groups of 15-25 persons learned to reflect critically on economic, social, and other problems affecting their neighborhood and region in light of the → Word of God. Base communities and the movement as a whole instilled in the people a deeper understanding of the gospel's relevance for everyday life and gave them greater awareness of their role of responding as Jesus did to the call of the kingdom of God.

The theology of liberation began by reflecting on themes and issues arising from the people's grassroots movement. Arising at the dawn of the Second → Vatican Council (1962-65) and mediated by an analysis of the structural conditions that are shown to impoverish or oppress the people, this radical theology reflects systematically on questions arising out of the experience of the people. Its insights are funneled into the communities as a guide for community action.

The liberationist movement conceives of a

church, for example, different from the Christendom model, which forms alliances with the state in its efforts to proclaim its mission and to gain protection. Instead, it views the church as prophetic, a body that listens critically to the voices of the poor before it speaks. It identifies causes of oppression, takes stands on injustices, imagines new patterns of human relationships, and envisions a brand new society. The church invites more active participation from laypersons, and it likewise calls the clergy and religious to accompany the poor as they struggle to improve their situation and to stand in solidarity with them as they encounter violent reprisals for initiatives taken. Liberation theology thus rejects the New Christendom model, which insists on keeping the clergy out of politics. The Vatican, however, largely continues to support this model.

Gutiérrez and Míguez Bonino offer Catholic and Protestant perspectives of this radical theology, both of which stand in marked contrast to the theologies of Christendom and of New Christendom. Gutiérrez defines theology as "a critical reflection, in the light of the Divine Word received in faith, on the presence of Christians in the world" ("Liberation Theology," 548). Critical reflection means probing deeply, with the aid of social scientists, into human experience, which sometimes requires searching for the underlying causes of social problems. This reflection may generate a theological question that voices a concern of the oppressed (e.g., "Is our God a God of justice?"). Using the Bible, Gutiérrez and others search for theological understanding on the difficult question of how to proclaim God's love to the exploited.

Faith is described as an encounter with God that impels persons and the community to commit themselves to the liberation of others. Faith has a transformative element aimed at liberating the whole human being. Liberation is a single, salvific process that involves different levels of meaning: the political-economic, the human, and the spiritual. To be genuinely free, a person and a community must cooperate with God's active presence and love in all these dimensions of existence. Unlike Maritain's theology, which sees constructive social involvement as preparatory for salvation but not redemptive in itself, Gutiérrez regards the creative and liberating work of human beings as salvific whenever Christ is the driving force — alike in political encounter, psychological growth, and spiritual → reconciliation. He speaks of liberating events as the growth of God's reign, though he is careful not to identify the reign of God with any single event.

Míguez Bonino, like Gutiérrez, begins with the people's reality, undertakes a social analysis as part of his method, and then reflects on the situation in light of Scripture. His sociohistorical analysis of violence from the conquest to contemporary times reveals how long-standing oppression eventually led to resistance and liberation movements today. He also locates himself within the prophetic theological tradition in which God's reign is a prime metaphor for upholding love, justice, and freedom as supreme values. He defines justice as fidelity to the exclusive claims of God within a covenantal relationship that includes a special partiality for the poor and the downtrodden. For him, the church should determine its priorities by asking, "Which order of society is compatible with the exercise of justice?" not "What degree of justice is compatible with maintaining the basic order of society?" The Spirit of God instructs persons to exercise their power for the liberation of others rather than using power to impose one's will. Yet Míguez Bonino does not speak of human participation in response to God's initiative as the "work" of God's reign, as Gutiérrez does. Rather, he describes the praxis of Christians as anticipating God's reign. Although he emphasizes the importance of human agency in the struggle toward liberation, he avoids discernment language that tries to figure out what must be done in the situation. Safeguarding the primacy of God's initiative, Míguez Bonino's ethics calls upon Christians to listen to what the Spirit prompts in light of sacred Scripture.

For liberation theologians as well as for the people at large, the concept of → solidarity is key and counters the → individualism of neoliberalism. Solidarity captures a people's own sense of working together for justice, and it serves as the nucleus of an ethic that integrates human rights and other values. Feminist liberation theologians (→ Feminist Theology), who have made many important contributions to this theology, have raised important questions about solidarity, asking, for example, whether solidarity with the poor encompasses the concerns of women and people of color. Protestant theologian Elsa Tamez of Costa Rica and Catholic theologian Yvone Gebara of Brazil have in their own analysis unmasked structural injustices against women within Latin American society.

5.2. The second major religious movement with a distinctive theology in modern Latin America is Pentecostalism, which arose from late-19th-century evangelicals. Today it is the largest and the most rapidly growing Christian tradition in Latin America. It shares with the evangelical churches certain core beliefs about the Trinitarian God, the divinity of Jesus,

→ sin and redemption, eternal life, and the Bible as the inspired Word of God. The baptism of the Holy Spirit is its most distinctive teaching. Pentecostals emphasize → sanctification and not simply justification, thus distinguishing themselves from Reformation theology. Whereas justification involves God's forgiveness and a person's sorrow and renunciation of sin, sanctification moves on to eradicate not only one's personal sin but one's sinful root.

As liberation theology focuses on the basic ecclesial community as an object of reflection, Pentecostal theology concentrates on the weekly Pentecostal service as the locus of its theologizing. At a typical service, the pastor calls people to conversion through Jesus, instructing those assembled that accepting the Lord calls for stopping their drinking, cheating, and lying. "As the leaders pray, the people start falling down — 'slain in the Spirit' — the outward expression of the Holy Spirit comes into their lives" (P. Moreno, 65). People return week after week, even after being slain in the Spirit, seeking the ultimate goal — the final rapture in which they are to be taken up to heaven before the premillennial second coming of Christ.

Joining a Pentecostal community requires a twofold movement of pulling away from one's sinful past (e.g., forsaking drunkenness and marital infidelity) and embracing a new future centered in Jesus' call to be baptized in the → Holy Spirit. Roman Catholic pastors indeed preach against alcoholism, for example, but Pentecostal pastors and the supporting community go on to effectively insist that one renounce it. In one typical conversion account, a Pentecostal reports: "I liked to drink. I was a womanizer. My home was going down the tubes. I was destroying myself. I didn't even think about my kids. On 12 June 1979, God had mercy on me. He called me. I felt God's touch. I accepted Christ into my life. Afterwards I felt His strength" (P. Berryman, 149-50).

Critics differ in their assessment of whether preaching the gospel and striving for personal holiness move Latin American Pentecostal Christians to go beyond personal transformation and to participate in sociopolitical activity. Based on his study of Pentecostals in Brazil and in other regions of the world, theologian Harvey Cox has made a strong case that Pentecostals often take prophetic stances on social issues. Taking the opposite view, historian Jean-Pierre Bastian contends that Pentecostals in Latin America have actually been very similar to traditional rural Catholics, practicing a kind of "Catholicism without priests" that reinforces the status quo rather than protests against it. Pedro Moreno, a Latin American Pentecostal, says that Pentecostal churches and their leaders present a "positive and integrated view of faith and the world," but then he questions "whether the explosive growth of Pentecostalism will bring forth the long-awaited and much needed economic and social transformation of Latin America" (p. 65). He notes that the Pentecostals' emphasis on salvation, combined with a belief that the second coming is close at hand, tends to diminish their interest in social transformation. In his view, the idea of the immediacy of God's reign has caused many to stay aloof from politics, economics, and engineering.

5.3. Both liberation theology and Pentecostalism have had a major impact on Roman Catholics and Protestants who have played key roles in the revolutionary drama of Latin America. In certain ways the two → denominations are similar. Both have made a deliberate outreach to the poor, to different classes and castes, to laypersons, and to women. Both are strongly biblical, appealing to the Word of God as the highest authority for ordering their lives and their priorities, and placing strong emphasis on Jesus, who leads persons to undergo a conversion. Finally, both see their theology and → spirituality as prophetic in the biblical sense.

Yet the two theologies differ in key points. First, liberation theology, even though it is dedicated to working for justice especially on behalf of the poor, labors within a church that is a hierarchically organized institution. The Pentecostals are much more decentralized and localized and allow for a greater equality among their lay membership. Second, each tradition has a markedly different eschatology that shapes its stance toward politics, political regimes, and socioeconomic change. For the Pentecostals, conversion to the new future and to Christ's premillennial return involves an interim period of living within a new community where people are healed, God is praised, and some people speak in tongues (→ Glossolalia). They are called to lead a holy life centered in the Spirit and to evangelize by preaching the gospel to others. Though there are many exceptions, the Pentecostals' striving for personal holiness and evangelizing others does not generally move the members to participate in sociopolitical transformation. For adherents of liberation theology, God's reign is both a future and a present reality. While the good news points toward what is yet to come, the promise of that reality gives meaning to, and is present in, historical reality. The reign of God, which calls all human beings to love, justice, freedom, and peace, is the driving force urging believers to transform the whole human being as well as the conditions that impede that transformation.

Christians influenced by liberation theology undergo a conversion experience. Like Pentecostalism, liberation theology speaks about a double movement of breaking with one's sinful past and entering into a new life in Christ. Unlike Pentecostal theology, however, this theology describes conversion as involving sociohistorical as well as interpersonal concerns. Growth in solidarity with other victims accompanies the personal transformation. Breaking with sin means repenting from personal sins — including personal betrayals, acts of cowardice, and selfish and underhanded actions — but people also mention recognizing and rejecting their own complicity in or tolerance of social sin, such as cooperating with the military or discriminating against people of a lower caste. Holiness for the liberationist Christian means loving one's neighbor and living in solidarity with → marginalized and oppressed groups. Sobrino refers to this kind of love as political holiness because it calls the disciple of Jesus to join in solidarity with one's suffering brothers and sisters (*Spirituality,* 80-81).

Latin American theology today is in transition, mirroring the reality of nations that have undergone revolutionary turmoil over the last half-century. Given the major differences and the history of acrimony between Roman Catholic and Protestant theologies and their subsets, liberation and Pentecostal theologies, it seems that the next major step must involve → ecumenical dialogue among all parties.

Bibliography: On 1: Augustine, *The City of God* (trans. M. Dods; New York, 1950) • D. Brackley, *Divine Revolution: Salvation and Liberation in Catholic Thought* (Maryknoll, N.Y., 1996) • D. Martin, *Tongues of Fire: The Explosion of Protestantism in Latin America* (Oxford, 1990) • J. Míguez Bonino, *Doing Theology in a Revolutionary Situation* (Philadelphia, 1975).

On 2-4: S. Abou, *The Jesuit "Republic" of the Guaranís (1609-1768) and Its Heritage* (New York, 1997) • L. Bethell, ed., *The Cambridge History of Latin America* (vol. 1; Cambridge, 1984) • D. Brackley, *Divine Revolution: Salvation and Liberation in Catholic Thought* (Maryknoll, N.Y., 1996) • T. Bruneau, *The Political Transformation of the Brazilian Catholic Church* (London, 1974) • E. Dussel, *History and the Theology of Liberation: A Latin American Perspective* (Maryknoll, N.Y., 1976); idem, ed., *The Church in Latin America, 1492-1992* (Kent, 1992) • C. Gibson, *Spain in America* (New York, 1966) • G. Gutiérrez, *Las Casas: In Search of the Poor of Jesus Christ* (Maryknoll, N.Y., 1993); idem, *The Power of the Poor in History: Selected Writings* (Maryknoll, N.Y., 1983); idem, *A Theology of Liber-*

ation: History, Politics, and Salvation (Maryknoll, N.Y., 1988; orig. pub., 1973) • L. Hanke, *The Spanish Struggle for Justice in the Conquest of America* (Boston, 1965; orig. pub., 1949) • A. Hastings, "Latin America," *A World History of Christianity* (ed. A. Hastings; Grand Rapids, 1999) chap. 9 • B. Keen, *A History of Latin America,* vol. 1, *Ancient America to 1910* (Boston, 1991) • J. Klaiber, *The Catholic Church in Peru, 1821-1985* (Washington, D.C., 1992); idem, "Peru: Evangelization and Religious Freedom," *Religious Freedom and Evangelization in Latin America* (ed. P. Sigmund; Maryknoll, N.Y., 1999) chap. 15 • A. McGovern, *Liberation Theology and Its Critics* (Maryknoll, N.Y., 1989) • J. Mackay, *The Other Spanish Christ* (New York, 1933) • S. Mainwaring, *The Catholic Church and Politics in Brazil, 1916-1985* (Stanford, Calif., 1986) • J. Maritain, *Integral Humanism: Temporal and Spiritual Problems of a New Christendom* (Notre Dame, Ind., 1973) • J. L. Mecham, *Church and State in Latin America* (Chapel Hill, N.C., 1966; orig. pub., 1934) • J. Míguez Bonino, *Doing Theology in a Revolutionary Situation* (Philadelphia, 1975) • A. Morán, "El Popol Vuh, expresión y sumario de sentido ético fundamental," *RLAT* 52 (2001) 49-64 • R. Poblete, "The Church in Latin America: A Historical Survey," *The Church and Social Change in Latin America* (ed. H. Landsberger; Notre Dame, Ind., 1970) chap. 3 • P. Richard, *The Death of Christendoms, Birth of the Church: Historical Analysis and Theological Interpretation of the Church in Latin America* (Maryknoll, N.Y., 1987) • W. E. Shiels, *King and Church: The Rise and Fall of the Patronato Real* (Chicago, 1961) • J. Sobrino, *Christology at the Crossroads: A Latin American Approach* (Maryknoll, N.Y., 1976) • F. de Vitoria, *Political Writings* (ed. A. Pagden and J. Lawrance; Cambridge, 1991).

On 5 (Liberationist Christianity): L. Boff, *Passion of Christ, Passion of the World* (Maryknoll, N.Y., 1987) • D. Brackley and T. Schubeck, "Moral Theology in Latin America," *TS* 62 (2002) 123-60 • P. Freire, *Education for Critical Consciousness* (New York, 1973) • G. Gutiérrez, "Liberation Theology," *NDCST* 548-53; idem, *A Theology of Liberation: History, Politics, and Salvation* (Maryknoll, N.Y., 1988; orig. pub., 1973) • J. Míguez Bonino, *Christians and Marxists: The Mutual Challenge to Revolution* (Grand Rapids, 1976); idem, *Toward a Christian Political Ethics* (Philadelphia, 1983) • T. Schubeck, *Liberation Ethics: Sources, Models, and Norms* (Minneapolis, 1993).

On 5 (Protestant and Pentecostal Christianity): J.-P. Bastian, "The Metamorphosis of Latin American Protestant Groups: A Sociohistorical Perspective," *LARR* 28 (1993) 33-61 • P. Berryman, *Stubborn Hope: Religion, Politics, and Revolution in Central America* (Maryknoll, N.Y., 1994) • H. Cox, *Fire from Heaven:*

The Rise of Pentecostal Spirituality and the Reshaping of Religion in the Twenty-first Century (Reading, Mass., 1994) • P. DAMBORIENA, *Tongues as of Fire: Pentecostalism in Contemporary Christianity* (Cleveland, 1969) • D. DAYTON, *Theological Roots of Pentecostalism* (Grand Rapids, 1987) • G. GUTIÉRREZ, *We Drink from Our Own Wells* (Maryknoll, N.Y., 1984) • P. MORENO, "Evangelical Churches," *Religious Freedom and Evangelization in Latin America* (ed. P. Sigmund; Maryknoll, N.Y., 1999) chap. 3 • J. SOBRINO, *Spirituality of Liberation: Toward Political Holiness* (Maryknoll, N.Y., 1985).

THOMAS L. SCHUBECK, S.J.

Latter-day Saints → Mormons

Latvia

	1960	1980	2000
Population (1,000s):	2,129	2,529	2,397
Annual growth rate (%):	1.26	0.51	−0.83

Area: 64,610 sq. km. (24,946 sq. mi.)

A.D. *2000*

Population density: 37/sq. km. (96/sq. mi.)
Births / deaths: 1.01 / 1.42 per 100 population
Fertility rate: 1.40 per woman
Infant mortality rate: 14 per 1,000 live births
Life expectancy: 69.6 years (m: 64.0, f: 75.1)
Religious affiliation (%): Christians 67.2 (Orthodox 25.0, Protestants 21.7, Roman Catholics 20.0, indigenous 6.3, other Christians 0.2), nonreligious 26.4, atheists 5.4, other 1.0.

1. General Situation
2. Churches
   2.1. Lutheran
   2.2. Roman Catholic
   2.3. Orthodox
   2.4. Old Believers
   2.5. Baptist
   2.6. Others
3. Interchurch Relations
4. Other Religions
5. Church and State

1. General Situation

Latvia, the central country of the Baltic States (Estonia to the north, Lithuania to the south), is bordered by Russia and Belarus on the east. A democratic parliamentary republic, Latvia is a member of the → United Nations, the World Trade Organization, the Council of Europe, and the Organization for Security and Cooperation in Europe. In 2001 the six largest ethnic groups were the Latvians (57.6 percent, vs. 75.5 percent in 1935), Russians (29.6 percent, vs. 10.6 percent in 1935), Belorussians (4.1 percent), Ukrainians (2.7 percent), Poles (2.5 percent), and Lithuanians (1.4 percent).

In 1998 Latvia's major exports were wood and paper products (34 percent), textiles and clothing (16 percent), food and beverages (10 percent), and base and fabricated metals (10 percent). Chief recipients of these exports were Germany (16 percent), the United Kingdom (14 percent), Russia (12 percent), Sweden (10 percent), and Lithuania (7 percent).

As a result of the activities of German missionaries and an invasion of German merchants and knights (the Knights of the Sword, later the Teutonic Order), the Latvians were brought under German rule at the turn of 13th century. In 1282 Riga (founded in 1201) and other towns were included in the Hanseatic League, a northern German trading organization. Later, all or part of what is today Latvia was ruled by Sweden, Poland, or Russia. Even with the various ruling powers, however, the Baltic German elite played a dominant role in Latvian social life until the end of the 19th century.

The Latvian national awakening began in the 1860s, with the country gaining independence in November 1918. The period 1918-40 saw the establishment of the socioeconomic and cultural institutions of the new republic. In 1934 Kārlis Ulmanis, leader of the Latvian Farmers' Union, declared a state of siege and instituted authoritarian rule because of the unstable political situation. The normal life of people was still quite peaceful, however, and by the late 1930s the living standard was relatively high.

Soviet troops occupied Latvia in 1940-41 and again from 1944 to 1991. During 1941-43 the country was occupied and ruled by Nazi Germany as a part of the province of Ostland. The Communist and Nazi terrors have left stinging memories in the minds of Latvian people, for whom the Soviet deportations to Siberia in 1941 and 1949 were especially terrible. Since August 1991, when Latvia finally regained its independence, it has initiated democratic reforms and adopted a market economy. Latvia is interested in membership in both the European Union and NATO. Modern Latvian society continues to struggle with many social and economic problems.

2. Churches

Christianity came to Latvia from the east early in the second millennium. After the Russian → conversion to Orthodox Christianity in 988, the eastern part of present-day Latvia had contacts with Russian Christianity. According to Henrik's *Chronicle of Livonia* (1226), German crusaders destroyed several Orthodox churches in Jersika (Livonia). Not until the 1840s, when social conditions were favorable, did great numbers of Latvians ever convert to Orthodoxy.

The most significant contribution to the Christianization of the Baltic region came from Germany in the 12th century. The pioneer → missionary to the Latvian area was Meinhard (d. 1196), a monk from Holstein. Western Christianity made little progress, however, until the third bishop of Riga, Albert of Buxhoevden (served 1199-1229), arrived in the country with ships and German soldiers. Riga became an archbishopric in 1282, and by the end of the 15th century 70 churches were serving the land. Until the 20th century the ecclesiastical life of what is today Latvia was determined mostly by German clergy, although the Christian influence was not very deep among the people, especially in the countryside. As late as the 18th century ancient songs, tales, and pagan traditions were significant spiritual influences on the Latvians.

The → Reformation was brought to Riga in 1521 by Andreas Knopken, a pupil of Martin → Luther and pastor of Riga's St. Peter's Church. During Swedish rule the ecclesiastical order was firmly in the hands of Lutheran → orthodoxy (§1), with Swedish → church law in force from the 1690s to 1832. The first translation of the NT into Latvian (also known as Lettish) was published in 1685, followed by the OT in 1689. The very beginning of the 1740s and the beginning of the 19th century were times of considerable spiritual awakening.

In 1729 Christian David, a → Moravian, came with other brethren from Herrnhut to Riga and Valmiera (Ger. Wolmar). Herrnhutism was a large and popular movement that had a great influence on social and cultural life in the Baltic region, most notably in the Baltic singing festivals, which began in Latvia in 1873, and in the Latvian national awakening of the 19th century.

2.1. *Lutheran*

During the nation's first period of independence, 1918-40, the Evangelical Lutheran Church of Latvia (ELCL) enjoyed the status of a national, or → people's, church. The first Latvian bishop was Karlis Irbe (served 1922-31), a strong personality who maintained many foreign contacts. Especially during the 1920s theological debates flared between the more liberal theological faculty of the University of Latvia and the more conservative leadership of the

church. In 1935 over 68 percent of ethnic Latvians (and 55 percent of the entire population) were Lutheran. Throughout the period of independence the activities of the ELCL deeply involved all aspects of Latvian life. In 1938, for example, between 40 and 50 percent of all → baptisms, → marriages, and → funerals in the country were performed under the auspices of the ELCL.

Irbe's successor, Archbishop Teodors Grünbergs, led the church during the difficult war years, 1939-44, but then was expelled from the country. In exile, Grünbergs was influential in organizing his fellow expatriate Latvians into the Evangelical Lutheran Church of Latvia in Exile, which he headed until his death in 1962. This church, which in 1989 became the Latvian Evangelical Lutheran Church Abroad (LELCA), has its headquarters in Esslingen-Berkheim, Germany. Over the years it has helped to sustain Latvian national awareness in Germany and other European countries, the United States, Canada, and Australia. According to Lutheran World Federation (LWF) statistics, in 2002 the LELCA had a membership of 40,000.

Under Communism the ELCL lost its status as a national church. In 1944-45 it lost over half its → clergy to exile, and until 1950 it was subject to strict limitations pursuant to Soviet laws concerning religion. By 1987 it was estimated that there were only 25,000 active Lutherans in Soviet Latvia.

The theological and spiritual influence of theology professor Roberts Feldmanis (1910-2002) has been significant, especially from the beginning of the 1980s. And since 1987 a spiritual awakening in the Mezaparks (Forest Park) Parish in Riga has had a special role in the rebuilding of the church.

During glasnost and perestroika a group of active, mostly young pastors organized the Atdzimšana un Atjaunošana (rebirth and renewal) movement to defend the rights of Christians. Some of the movement's members helped to found the Popular Front of Latvia, a party that played an active role in regaining Latvian independence in 1991. The rebirth and renewal movement was active in extending a Christian influence into Soviet Latvian society. Accordingly, Latvia was the first Soviet republic in which the Christian message was broadcast on public radio and TV and in which religious instruction was provided in public schools. In 1990 the education of clergy was resumed at the University of Latvia.

In 1995 the ELCL expanded its education activities with the founding of St. Gregor's School in Saldus, and in 1997 it opened the Luther Academy in Riga. In 2002, according to LWF figures, the ELCL had 250,000 members. The exact number could be considered higher, however, for perhaps at least twice that many Latvians regard themselves as Lutherans. The great majority of the nearly 300 ELCL parishes have between 20 and 100 registered members.

The ELCL is marked by a broad spectrum of theological positions. The liberal heritage from the interwar period has decreased, while → biblicism and Lutheran confessionalism have increased among the clergy. Contacts with the conservative American Lutheran Church–Missouri Synod are quite extensive. The ELCL has also received considerable attention because of its debates over the → ordination of women. The present archbishop, Jānis Vanags, is opposed to the ordination of women and is widely supported throughout the church, although some women pastors, ordained before 1993, are still serving.

Two other small Lutheran groups active in Latvia are German Lutherans, since 2001 in fellowship with the ELCL, and the Confessional Lutheran Church. The latter, which arose from a schism within the ELCL in 1996, has a close relation with two conservative groups in the United States: the Wisconsin Evangelical Lutheran Synod and the Evangelical Lutheran Synod (→ Lutheran Churches; Lutheranism).

2.2. Roman Catholic

The → Jesuits were active in Latvia as far back as the 16th-century Polish occupation. The → Roman Catholic Church has been an important factor in Latvian life, especially in Latgale, a region in the southeastern part of the country, where during the first period of national independence it was the established church. A → concordat between the Vatican and Latvia (1922) gave Latvian Catholics privileged status. In 1935 a quarter of all Latvians were Roman Catholic. The Roman bishop, Jazeps Rancans, was one of the best-known personalities in Latvian politics, representing his party (Latvian Christian Farmers and Catholics' Party) in the Saeima, or Latvian Parliament. There was a Roman Catholic theological faculty at the University of Latvia in 1938-40.

During the Communist regime the Roman Catholic Church occupied a stronger position than the ELCL. Its theological seminary began work in Riga in 1946, nine years before Lutherans were allowed to educate future clergy. Catholics were encouraged in 1983 when the Communist regime permitted Bishop Julijans Vaivods to be elevated to cardinal. A visit of John Paul II to Latvia (and the other Baltic countries) in 1993 received considerable attention in the → mass media.

In 2000 Latvian Roman Catholics had over 250 parishes served by four bishops. There are upwards of a half million baptized Roman Catholics in Latvia, with half of them active members of the church. A Roman Catholic charismatic movement called Effata is also very active, especially among young people.

2.3. Orthodox

During the period 1721-1917, when the Russians ruled Latvia, Orthodoxy was "the religion of the czar." Especially in the 1840s large numbers of ethnic Latvians joined the → Orthodox Church. In 1925 the church included 104,000 Russians and 53,000 Latvians. The first Latvian archbishop, Jānis Pommers, was a widely regarded leader of the Orthodox Church during the first period of independence, serving as a member of the national Parliament. In 1937-40 there was also a special institute of Orthodox theology at the University of Latvia.

In 1936 the Orthodox community in Latvia placed itself under the jurisdiction of the ecumenical patriarch of Constantinople, but in 1940 Soviet church politics led the Orthodox Church to be reunited with the Patriarchate of Moscow (→ Russian Orthodox Church). During the later Soviet Russian occupation, 1944-91, the church was under the strict control of Moscow. In 1992 after Latvia regained its independence, the church was granted autonomy, but it remains canonically linked to the Moscow Patriarchate.

An Orthodox theological seminary operates in Riga, as well as → monasteries in Riga and Jēkabpils. In 2000 the 114 parishes of the Orthodox Church were served by 64 priests. The Riga Cathedral, a remarkable structure, was used as a planetarium under Communist rule but has recently been restored. The Latvian Orthodox Church plays an important role in unifying ethnic Russians and Latvians in today's frequently difficult sociopolitical circumstances.

2.4. Old Believers

The → Old Believers, a very traditional Orthodox group, have their roots in a Russian movement of the 17th century. In order to avoid → persecution in Russia, many from this group fled to Latvia while it was under Swedish and Polish control. Old Believers enjoyed a golden age in the first period of Latvian independence; at the end of the 1930s there were 100,000 Old Believers in Latvia.

The process of democratization and glasnost at the end of the 1980s provided new possibilities for Old Believers. In 2000 they had 66 parishes in Latvia, one of which — the Grebenshchikov congregation — was the largest parish of Old Believers in the world. In and near Riga there are 20,000 people who share this spiritual heritage, and they are joined by

50,000 others in the rest of Latvia, mostly in Latgale. New church buildings have been dedicated during recent years. Latvian Old Believers maintain close contacts with related communities in the United States and other countries.

2.5. *Baptists*

The Baptist movement in Latvia, which began in 1860 in Courland (the historical name of a region on the eastern Baltic shore), later played an influential role in the social and political life of that area. → Baptists were the most active element in the Christian Workers' Society political party.

During the Communist period the Baptist church continued to function, a small branch of it surviving as an underground church. The Latvian Baptists now have their own bishop, and many Baptist pastors use vestments associated with the more liturgical denominations. In 2000 the Baptists had 85 parishes served by 75 pastors. There is a Baptist theological seminary in Riga. In 1999 Baptists joined Lutherans and Pentecostals in an → evangelism campaign.

2.6. *Others*

In 2000 there were altogether about 170 different denominations and religious groups, Christian and non-Christian, in the Latvian republic. Besides the five groups discussed above in this section, the largest Christian bodies were the → Pentecostals and related charismatic groups. The Pentecostal movement was active already during the first period of Latvian independence. After World War II it was not accepted as an official religious organization by the Communists, and its members were forced to join the Baptists; when they refused to obey this order, all of the Pentecostal pastors were arrested and deported. After Stalin's death they came back to Soviet Latvia, but they had no opportunity to serve legally. Like some of the Baptists, Pentecostals survived in Latvia during the Soviet period only as an underground church. A new period began in 1989 when the Association of Latvian Pentecostal Congregations was founded. This movement, which is presently quite active, in 2000 numbered 79 parishes and almost 7,000 members.

Other charismatic groups are spiritually related to the Pentecostals. One is the Latvian group Jaunā Paaudze (New generation), which in 2000 had as many as 6,000 members. Another branch of the Latvian → charismatic movement is connected to the movement associated with the so-called Toronto Blessing.

Also in Latvia are the Seventh-day → Adventists (since 1896), with fewer than 4,000 members, and the Latvian → Methodist Church (founded 1921),

with fewer than 1,000 members. Other smaller Christian groups include the → Armenian Apostolic Church in Latvia (founded 1993), the Neo-Apostolic Church, the → Salvation Army, the → YMCA, the → YWCA, and the Latvian Bible Society. Most of these last groups were founded or refounded after the Soviet Russian occupation ceased in 1991.

There are also some unregistered religious groups. Many nonconfessional → house churches and prayer groups are also working in Latvia. Marginal Christian groups are present in Latvia in small numbers. In 2000 → Jehovah's Witnesses claimed about 2,000 members; the → Mormon Church, 200.

3. Interchurch Relations

The two Latvian Lutheran churches, the ELCL and the LELCA, are both members of the → World Council of Churches, the → Lutheran World Federation, and the → Conference of European Churches. In addition, the ELCL has joined in the → Leuenberg Agreement, and it participated in the deliberations between Nordic and Baltic Lutheran churches and the Anglican churches of the United Kingdom that led to the → Porvoo Declaration of communion between those bodies, although it has not signed the declaration. Traditionally, the ELCL has had close ties with the Church of Sweden, but because of some theological differences, these contacts are not as deep today as they were during the interwar period. Since 1992 its ties with the Lutheran Church–Missouri Synod have become increasingly important. In June 2001 delegates to the official ELCL synod overwhelmingly approved "pulpit and altar fellowship" with this U.S. group, as well as cooperative activity with the conservative Selbständige Evangelisch-Lutherische Kirche (Independent Evangelical Lutheran Church) of Germany.

Despite theological differences between the ELCL and the LELCA, the two churches have been able to cooperate in a common → hymnal published in 1992 and in a common yearbook that has been published annually since 1993. The theological influence of the LELCA has been significant in Latvia, especially on the Department of Theology of the University of Latvia.

Other Latvian Protestant groups are also members of international associations and have many foreign contacts. The relationship between the five largest churches in Latvia are positively expressed in cooperation on practical questions as well as in politics and in sociopolitical dicussions concerning Latvian society. This → ecumenism is more practical than dogmatic or confessional in nature.

4. Non-Christian Religions

Although the Jewish community of Latvia has its roots in the 17th century, the first Jewish congregation was founded only in 1764. Before 1940 Latvia was home to 100,000 Jews, half of them in Riga, worshiping in 300 synagogues and prayer houses. Three-quarters of Latvia's Jews did not survive the Nazi occupation. In 2001 there were 15,000 Jews in Latvia, 93 percent of them in Riga (→ Judaism).

Since the 1980s religious pluralism has greatly increased in Latvia. New non-Christian groups registering with the government include a Hare Krishna group, the Islamic community (→ Islam), a → Baha'i assembly, a Buddhist society (→ Buddhism), and a → Shinto group. Among new religions and cults one finds → New Age, → Christian Science, the → Unification Church, Scientology, the so-called Last Testament Church, a group called the Family, and even Satanism. The relation of such groups to the state has raised many questions. Additionally, Dievturība, or Latvian indigenous → paganism, has been active; in 2000 it had 550 members in 13 parishes.

5. Church and State

Between the two world wars the ELCL was a national church, as was the Roman Catholic Church in Latgale. → Religious education had a strong position in public schools, especially after 1934.

During the Soviet period property was nationalized, many pastors were arrested, and church activities were restricted. During the premiership of Nikita Khrushchev (1958-64), → atheism was actively promoted, and many church buildings were closed. Despite such persecution, the Christian churches survived. During the last years of Mikhail Gorbachev, especially after 1988, the growing Latvian independence provided impetus to → religious liberty.

Although → church and state are separate in Latvia, the five main Christian denominations have a special status in relation to the state. Official services on November 18, the Day of Independence, as well as on other special days, are reminders of the traditional links between the Latvian Republic and its Christian heritage. Moreover, many people who no longer participate in parish activities consider themselves Lutheran, and in this sense Lutheranism is still Latvia's principal denomination.

These five denominations have the right to provide religious instruction in public schools, although in practice such education is very much dependent on the availability of finances in particular local schools. The University of Latvia has a non-confessional theological faculty. In hospitals, prisons, armed forces, and other public institutions, guidance of a spiritual nature can be offered as long as it is received voluntarily. The state pays the salaries of → military chaplains.

Bibliography: C. von Aderkas, "Gemeinschaft des Schicksals und des Glaubens—die evangelisch-lutherische Kirche Lettlands," Lutherische Kirche im baltischen Raum (ed. W. Kahle; Erlangen, 1985) • A. R. Aklaev, From Confrontation to Integration: The Evolution of Ethnopolitics in the Baltic States (Frankfurt, 2001) • R. Balodis, ed., State and Church in the Baltic States: 2001 (Riga, 2001) • A. Cherney, The Latvian Orthodox Church (Welshpool, U.K., 1985) • F. Gordon, Latvians and Jews between Germany and Russia (rev. ed.; Stockholm, 2001) • M. Mickelsen, City of Life, City of Death: Memories of Riga (Boulder, Colo., 2001) • A. Pabricks, Latvia: The Challenge of Change (London, 2001) • G. Philipp, Die Wirksamkeit der Herrnhuter Brüdergemeine unter den Esten und Letten zur Zeit der Bauernbefreiung (Cologne, 1974) • J. Talonen, Church under the Pressure of Stalinism: The Development of the Status and Activities of the Soviet Latvian Evangelical Lutheran Church during 1944-1950 (Jyväskylä, Fin., 1997) • E. Vebers, ed., The Integration of Society in Latvia: A Framework Document (Riga, 1999) • I. Zalite, "Evangelisch-Lutherische Kirche Lettlands, 1944-1990," Geblieben ist, was lebt und trägt. Stimmen aus der Evangelisch-Lutherischen Kirche Lettlands (ed. J. Junker; Gross Oesingen, Ger., 2000).

Jouko Talonen

Laughing and Crying

Laughing and crying reveal a person's inner feelings and emotional capacities. It is not surprising, then, that from antiquity they have been the theme of philosophical reflection and adduced in interpretation of what is human. In keeping with modern differentiation of the academic disciplines, they have been taken up in interdisciplinary studies making use of → philosophy, → theology, → aesthetics, literary studies, → psychology, and → sociology. They bring out both the comic and the tragic aspects of human life.

In all the detailed inquiries the main concern must be to see in laughing and crying important marks of the human ability to master and shape existence and thus to achieve a relevant → anthropology. On the philosophical side H. Plessner (1892-1985) must count as the classic representative of this endeavor. For him laughing and crying are a human monopoly. They bear witness to our "eccentric position" as being in the body yet also relating to it. In contrast to gestures and verbal communications (→ Language), laughing and crying as expressive bodily manifestations respond to the limits of human → behavior and precisely in this way evade the limits. Both are forms of emotional expression in which control over the body is lost. There are many occasions for them, and they are triggered by various factors. Ambivalent situations with many meanings, but posing no direct threat to existence, are met with laughing. But when we meet a situation in which we find that the usual ways of dealing with life mean disorganization and are suddenly swept from under us, we begin to cry. In laughing, we no longer control our relation to the body; in crying, we ourselves abandon it (Plessner, 122).

Alongside this philosophical and anthropological approach empirical studies of behavior raise the question of the relation of the laughing and crying to individual → development. Here laughing as compared to crying is described (in terms of developmental psychology) as a prelinguistic possibility of giving direct expression to feelings. These are the emotional states that correspond to restricted emotional, cognitive, and social development (→ Socialization) and that then structure interpersonal communication. In this regard great stress is laid on the function of the human face as a means of expressing relational attitudes. These data find confirmation in studies of → narcissism (H. Kohut), that is, in the question as to the conditions of a feeling of self-worth.

Biblically, laughing and crying are an expression of feelings of superiority or abandonment to circumstances (or even to God). Sarah, furthermore, responded with an inward (sarcastic?) laugh when she first heard the promise of a son (Gen. 18:12). Luke 6:21, 25 reflect in particular the opposing possibilities of attitude toward the → dialectic of existence in this world, which undergo reversal under the divine judgment that overturns this world. At any rate, the experience of both → autonomy and painful visitation (→ Suffering) has a provisional character vis-à-vis the eschatologically determined (→ Eschatology) → freedom from all tension and emotional dependence. Within the community, rejoicing and weeping are to be noticed and reflected (Rom. 12:15).

Dealing with interpersonal → conflicts in → pastoral care can be an occasion to promote, as the situation demands, laughing and crying, which frequently have been held in check by role clichés or exaggerated educational ideals. Such response will give increased emotional security and work against behavioral disturbances. In this respect debate with the findings of → psychoanalysis, → group dynamics, and → humanistic psychology in the school of C. R. Rogers (1902-87) can offer valuable stimulation toward developing a new culture of feelings.

→ Anxiety; Depression; Despair; Fear; Grief; Joy

Bibliography: I. S. GILHUS, *Laughing Gods, Weeping Virgins: Laughter in the History of Religion* (London, 1999) • C. R. GRAVES, *The Game of Humor: A Comprehensive Theory of Why We Laugh* (New Brunswick, N.J., 1997) • H. KOHUT, *Narzißmus* (Frankfurt, 1973) • T. LUTZ, *Crying: The Natural and Cultural History of Tears* (New York, 1999) • B. J. OROPEZA, *A Time to Laugh: The Holy Laughter Phenomenon Examined* (Peabody, Mass., 1995) • R. PIDDINGTON, *The Psychology of Laughter: From Plato to Freud* (New York, 1933) • H. PLESSNER, "Lachen und Weinen," *Philosophische Anthropologie* (ed. G. Dux; Frankfurt, 1970) 11-171 • R. R. PROVINE, *Laughter: A Scientific Investigation* (New York, 2000) • K. H. RENGSTORF, "Γελάω, καταγελάω, γέλως," *TDNT* 1.658-62; idem, "Κλαίω, κλαυθμός," ibid. 3.722-26 • D. WICKBERG, *The Senses of Humor: Self and Laughter in Modern America* (Ithaca, N.Y., 1998).

KLAUS WINKLER†

Lausanne Movement

1. Background
2. Lausanne Congress and Covenant
3. Results

The Lausanne movement is an international, transdenominational movement of evangelicals associated with the Lausanne Committee for World Evangelization and dedicated to the study, promotion, and fulfillment of cooperative → evangelism worldwide. The movement derives its name and spirit from the International Congress on World Evangelization, held at Lausanne, Switzerland, in July 1974.

1. Background
The history of the Lausanne movement must be understood in the context of attempts to build a global strategy for evangelism before 1974. Since World War II the only remotely unified voice of international Christian action among Protestants had come from mainline moderates and liberals in the ecumenical or conciliar movement embodied in the → World Council of Churches (WCC). From an evangelical perspective, the WCC is often perceived as

upholding interchurch and interfaith → unity at the expense of doctrine, social ministry to the detriment of the individual and spiritual claims of the → gospel, and → universalism over the exclusive demands of Christ. The disorganized and scattered voices of evangelicalism, however, could hardly muster a coherent perspective, let alone a strategy, for promoting their understanding of global Christianity and the practice of evangelism (→ Evangelical; Evangelical Movement).

The 1966 Berlin World Congress on Evangelism began to turn the tide for evangelicals. With the international recognition, financial support, and organizational acumen of the Billy Graham Evangelistic Association, congress participants joined the worldwide conversations about the nature and prospect of global evangelism. In an era of rapid cultural change, the cold war, and mass communications (→ Mass Media), evangelicals put forth a strong effort at Berlin to strike a confident note on behalf of biblical evangelism in a manner that seemed to take seriously at least some of what conciliar Christians had long argued about unity and even social ministry. The commitments of the Berlin congress, however, did not go far enough. In 1967 Carl F. H. Henry commented that the Berlin Congress had "brought the evangelical movement to a brink of decision over three major concerns that impinge upon its evangelistic task in the world . . . theological, socio-political and ecumenical" (p. 1). The 1974 Lausanne Congress clearly pushed evangelicals beyond this brink.

2. Lausanne Congress and Covenant

The Lausanne Congress drew roughly 2,700 participants (nearly 4,000 total, including guests, observers, and media) from 150 countries and 135 Protestant denominations who met to network, mutually encourage, pray, and plan a unified strategy for global evangelism. Appropriate in light of the congress theme, "Let the Earth Hear His Voice," the gathering was heralded as the most globally distributed and representative conference on evangelism ever held to date.

The greatest single legacy of this ten-day event is the Lausanne Covenant. This 2,700-word, 15-point document asserts clearly that → salvation is personal and only through → faith in Jesus Christ. Unlike previous evangelical affirmations, however, the covenant carefully balances an uncompromising commitment to biblical → authority and doctrinal → orthodoxy with recognition of the need for interfaith → dialogue, ecumenical cooperation, non-Western participation, and sociopolitical action on

a global scale. It addresses honestly, and with genuine evangelical conviction, the cultural moment. The covenant, which contains a pledge of commitment to the task of world evangelization, was signed by a large majority of congress participants. It has been translated into many different languages and remains an indispensable guide for the movement nearly 30 years later. In several important respects, the Lausanne Congress and its covenant mark an important turning point for modern evangelicalism's sense of Christian mission.

First, the Lausanne Congress broadened traditional evangelical ideas about evangelism to include a wider range of concerns than just "soul winning." The opening paragraph of the covenant speaks of being "moved to penitence by our failures," a reference to the general lack of social concern and responsibility emblematic of traditional evangelical notions of Christian mission. Past evangelical preaching that emphasized only spiritual aspects of salvation and that neglected social and political concerns were roundly criticized at the congress, especially by its non-Western participants. The Lausanne Covenant, in the words of René Padilla, shows that "biblical evangelism is inseparable from social responsibility, Christian discipleship, and church renewal" (p. 11). While the covenant did not reduce evangelism to social ministry, it questioned any suggestions that evangelists could effectively express the gospel without attending to social, economic, and political needs (par. 5).

Second, though organized and largely dominated by American and British evangelicals (notably Billy Graham and John Stott), the 1974 congress was attended by hundreds of Christian leaders from the → Third World (nearly one-third of the participants), whose concerns were heard and heeded to an unprecedented degree. The Third World began to emerge less exclusively as *objects* of evangelism and much more as *partners* in ministry. Coming near the end of the age of decolonization (→ Colonialism and Mission), Lausanne importantly acknowledged the legitimacy and dignity of indigenous cultures and churches, giving credence to Third World Christian leaders. By affirming Third World Christians and acknowledging past failures, evangelicals at Lausanne opened the door to a kind of cross-cultural dialogue that would later attune Western ears to rethinking aspects of the gospel when seen in light of non-Western cultures.

Third and closely related, the congress affirmed what might be legitimately described as a *thick* sense of culture, taking seriously at least some insights of modern-day cultural anthropology. A humble, even penitent, tone characterizes the Lausanne Covenant on the question of → culture. "Missions have all too frequently exported with the Gospel an alien culture, and churches have sometimes been in bondage to culture rather than to the Scripture" (par. 10). The covenant declares that "a new missionary era has dawned," conceding that "the dominant role of western missions is fast disappearing" (par. 8). Prior conferences had generally taken the Western-oriented definition of Christian → mission for granted. Lausanne would signal a new day for evangelicals, who would thereafter pursue strategies for evangelization that endeavored to speak the gospel in ways that were both transcultural and sensitive to local contexts (→ Evangelical Missions).

Finally, the congress affirmed that Christian unity and cooperation across denominational and (within some limits) theological boundaries would be imperative for world evangelization. The covenant went as far as to call on all Christians to "break out of our ecclesiastical ghettos and permeate non-Christian society" (par. 6). It went on to proclaim "unity" as a necessary virtue rather than something to fear, admitting that past expressions of disunity ultimately weakened the church's witness (par. 7). Lausanne boldly answered any lingering question about whether mainstream evangelicals were moving to shed the → separatism of their → fundamentalist forebears.

3. Results

Missiologist Peter Beyerhaus has argued that the real significance of the Lausanne Congress has not been the concepts and strategies it endorsed but rather the energy it spawned and the missionary consciousness it raised. As he saw it, "Small rivers, some of which had been rather unnoted before [Lausanne,] became confluent, and by their union formed one mighty stream, which was deep enough to carry a fleet of evangelistic fisherboats, and which had water enough spiritually to fertilize the dried soil of latter 20th century christendom" (p. 170). In the months following Lausanne, this "stream" began to take shape as a group of 50 men and women — the Lausanne Continuation Committee for World Evangelizaion — convened to organize an assortment of conferences, symposia, and consultations. The group's name was later changed to the Lausanne Committee on World Evangelization (LCWE). Their charge was simple: to preserve the spirit of Lausanne by supporting all international and regional efforts consistent with the covenant. From these meetings and other less formal developments, the Lausanne movement was born.

Significantly, leaders of the Lausanne movement determined to maintain a decentralized, even nonlocalized, focus so as avoid becoming too closely tied to any particular culture or national identity (a feature of the WCC that some have criticized). The LCWE resisted a merger with the World Evangelical Fellowship (→ World Evangelical Alliance) for this reason, and the suggestion of building a center for world evangelization was also dismissed on similar grounds. As a result, the movement has been able to shape a wide-ranging, multidimensional ministry. Lausanne had a hand, directly or indirectly, in nearly every formal evangelistic initiative undertaken around the world during the last quarter of the 20th century, apart from those associated with the → Roman Catholic Church, Pentecostalism (→ Pentecostal Churches), or the WCC. LCWE has acted as an umbrella agency, sounding board, and resource for countless churches, denominations, mission societies, theological seminaries, colleges, and parachurch organizations in support of many different tasks and issues related to evangelism.

Global missionary strategy has remained the central concern and area of expertise for the LCWE. In conjunction with the Mission Advanced Research and Communication Center, the Strategy Working Group of the LCWE annually publishes *World Christianity,* a presentation of social statistics on unreached or newly evangelized people groups as a way of tracking the growth of Christianity in countries around the world. LCWE has been especially sensitive to the ways that unique cultures and worldviews receive the gospel and how Christians might be more sensitive to working with these groups. At the Lausanne-sponsored Consultation on World Evangelization held at Pattaya, Thailand, in June 1980, participants identified 17,000 population groups with no indigenous core of Christian believers. At this consultation 17 miniconsultations also worked to develop evangelism strategies relevant to particular groups, including Marxists, Jews, Muslims, secularized peoples, Hindus, Buddhists, the urban poor, and Chinese.

In 1989 a second Lausanne congress convened in Manila, involving 3,500 people from 170 countries. Lausanne II sparked the AD 2000 Movement, which developed a series of specific strategies for completing world evangelization in Africa, Asia, and Latin America, plus several major initiatives in the areas of prayer (esp. in what has been called spiritual warfare), social concern, and Bible translation. The Lausanne Women's International Network was formed soon after Lausanne II as a way to address the needs and problems faced by women around the world.

The congress produced the Manila Manifesto, a document similar to the Lausanne Covenant in tone and content, with a few exceptions. For instance, it addresses with greater bluntness "the failures in Christian consistency which we see in both Christians and churches" (§7), and it admits that non-Christian religions "sometimes contain elements of truth and beauty," even while rejecting any sense that they might somehow constitute "alternative gospels" (§3). A third major world congress is being planned for the fall of 2004 in Thailand.

Since Lausanne has always been considered an idea-oriented movement, strategy has never been limited to mere tactical concerns. The Theological Committee of the LCWE, led for many years by John Stott, has consistently spoken to theological issues and problems in contemporary global ministry in an effort to maintain its doctrinal integrity, to address newly emergent issues, and to educate those serving. One matter the Theological Committee has faced, though not satisfactorily clarified, has been the doctrine of the → church, an issue on which Lausanne 1974 and its covenant has been consistently criticized for being too vague and even undermining the authority of the institutional church. Furthermore, during the 1990s alone, LCWE sponsored international consultations on numerous theological matters, issuing substantial statements on topics ranging from Christian → nominalism to the role of Scripture, spiritual warfare to the unique theological challenges of Jewish evangelism (→ Jewish Mission).

Finally, the LCWE has been active in aiding, financing, and encouraging national churches in the Third World, as well as Third World missionaries, whose numbers have grown more than 15-fold since 1974. While the Lausanne Covenant had taken important steps toward dealing with the knotty questions of Christianity and culture, much further work needed to be done. A theological consultation, "Gospel and Culture," held at Willowbank, Bermuda, in January 1978 drew together dozens of the world's leading missiologists, anthropologists, church leaders, and theologians to think more carefully and deliberatively about the transmission of the gospel and the relationship between faith and culture.

One of the most substantial and concentrated efforts in this vein has been the Chinese Coordination Center of World Evangelization (CCCWE), an initiative begun in 1976 and devoted to organizing Chinese Christians around the world as a way of aiding the evangelization of China. In the summer of 2001 CCCWE sponsored a congress on evangelization in Malaysia where 1,600 Chinese delegates from around the world identified practical problems in China and strategies for more effective transmission of the gospel.

The Lausanne Movement has not lacked for critics. From the Left, it is no surprise that mainline Protestants (esp. those associated with the WCC) have found Lausanne's theologically conservative sense of mission too narrow, and its refusal to conflate evangelism with social concern, inadequate and unholistic (see H. Berkhof). Criticisms from the Right have been perhaps even more pointed. In 1978 evangelical missiologist Arthur Johnston argued that the Lausanne vision for world evangelization was theologically soft, overly concerned with social and political issues, and fraught with compromise in the name of cooperation. What others recognized as long-overdue changes for the better, Johnston feared as an evangelical forfeiting of the essence of the Great Commission (pp. 358-60). While ultimately more affirming, Peter Beyerhaus has voiced other concerns about Lausanne. He has criticized the Lausanne movement for its lack of developed theologies of non-Christian religions. Like Johnston, he has also warned that the Lausanne vision can easily lapse into a new form of social gospel. Finally, Beyerhaus wonders if Lausanne's continual projections of a progressive, almost unstoppable movement toward world evangelization represents a dangerously naive optimism. Rather than emphasizing only confidence, he cautions that the path of gospel obedience will inevitably provoke resistance, hatred, and persecution (pp. 182-83).

While hardly perfect, the Lausanne movement has been providing a guiding light for millions on countless issues that have arisen in the course of pursuing world evangelization. It would be difficult to overstate the significance of the Lausanne movement for setting a global agenda for evangelical Christian ministry during the last quarter of the 20th century. One would be hard pressed to locate an evangelical seminary curriculum, a Christian world → relief organization, a denominational missions agency, or even an inner-city ministry that has been untouched by the vision, instruction, or far-reaching spirit of Lausanne. Well into the 21st century, it seems, the Lausanne movement will continue to play a defining role in the endeavors of global Christianity.

→ Ecumenism, Ecumenical Movement; Missionary Conferences 3

Bibliography: H. BERKHOF, "Berlin versus Geneva: Our Relationship with the 'Evangelicals,'" *ER* 28 (1976) 80-86 • P. BEYERHAUS, "Evangelicals, Evangelism, and Theology: A Missiological Assessment of the Lausanne

Movement," *ERT* 11 (1987) 169-85 • K. Bockmuehl, *Evangelicals and Social Ethics: A Commentary on Article 5 of the Lausanne Covenant* (trans. D. T. Priestley; Downers Grove, Ill., 1975) • R. T. Coote and J. Stott, eds., *Down to Earth: Studies in Christianity and Culture. The Papers of the Lausanne Consultation on Gospel and Culture* (Grand Rapids, 1980) • J. D. Douglas, ed., *Let the Earth Hear His Voice: International Congress on World Evangelization, Lausanne, Switzerland* (Minneapolis, 1975) • C. F. H. Henry, *Evangelicals at the Brink of Crisis: Significance of the World Congress on Evangelism* (Waco, Tex., 1967) • A. P. Johnston, *The Battle for World Evangelism* (Wheaton, Ill., 1978) • A. Kirk, *The Good News of the Kingdom Coming: The Marriage of Evangelism and Social Concern* (Downers Grove, Ill., 1983) • "Lausanne '74–an Overview," *EMQ* 10 (1974) 259-320 • J. Matthey, "Milestones in Ecumenical Missionary Thinking from the 1970s to the 1990s," *IRM* 88 (1999) 291-303 • C. R. Padilla, *The New Face of Evangelicalism: An International Symposium on the Lausanne Covenant* (Downers Grove, Ill., 1976) • J. Stott, "The Significance of Lausanne," *IRM* 64 (1975) 288-94; idem, "Twenty Years after Lausanne: Some Personal Reflections," *IBMR* 19 (1995) 50-55; idem, ed., *Making Christ Known: Historic Mission Documents from the Lausanne Movement, 1974-1989* (Grand Rapids, 1997) • E. S. Utuk, "From Wheaton to Lausanne: The Road to Modification of Contemporary Evangelical Mission Theology," *Miss.* 14 (1986) 205-20.

Jay D. Green

Law

1. OT

1.1. Term

The idea of law has many nuances in the OT, which we see from the different words used for it. Thus we have *mišpāṭîm* (ordinances), *huqqîm* (statutes), *miṣwôt* (commandments), *děbārîm* (words), and others. These terms cover civil and criminal law and both the ethical and the cultic sphere.

More comprehensively after Deuteronomy we find *tôrâ*, which originally denoted only the direction of the → priest in cultic, legal, and moral questions (Deut. 33:10; Hos. 4:6; Mic. 4:2; Jer. 18:18; Ezek. 7:26; Mal. 2:6-7) but in Deuteronomy is used for the whole revelation of the will of → Yahweh to → Israel. After Deuteronomy *tôrâ* came to signify the whole → Pentateuch (at the latest by the 2d cent. b.c., but probably earlier). Since the Pentateuch is a narrative work with laws interposed, "law" is perhaps not the most suitable rendering of *tôrâ* in this case. "Instruction" or "teaching" would be better.

1.2. Book of the Covenant

The oldest collection of laws is in the → Book of the Covenant (Exod. 20:22–23:19). Probably dating from before the state or from the early state period, this document shows that Israel, like any human society, possessed binding → norms (surely only a selection here) in written form. Israelite law is heavily indebted, both in concepts and in particular regulations, to law codes developed in various ancient Near East societies, going back to Sumer and subsequent national entities (see esp. V. H. Matthews and D. C. Benjamin, M. T. Roth). Various types may be noted.

Casuistic laws (→ Casuistry) come first. They follow a pattern common in antiquity. Introduced by *kî* (when) or *'im* (if), these declarations first state the law and then give the penalty (e.g., Exod. 21:2-11, 18-35). Using precedents, and perhaps borrowing forms found in Canaan, they offer legal guidance to a judiciary made up of tribal elders and later of full citizens called together to handle legal cases in the various regions or localities (see Ruth 4). The OT presents them as statutes given by Yahweh (Exod. 21:1).

Then we should note *capital offenses* (Exod. 21:12, 15-17; 22:18). A participial form is used (in 21:12, lit. "one striking a person mortally"), and then the death penalty follows (lit. "shall surely be put to death"). The listing of many cases with the identically worded threat of death is surely meant as the sternest warning to offenders that will establish valid norms in the community. We have here what A. Alt (1883-1956) called apodictic law.

Next we find *prohibitions* in the strongest grammatical form. They generally appear in similarly structured series focusing on specific areas; for example, the ten prohibitions in Exod. 23:1-3, 6-9 have to do with antisocial conduct. The arrangement in uniform series, as well as the number ten, suggests they were intended for use in proclamation and teaching. These prohibitives define incorrect conduct and, in so doing, also establish an ethical norm (or group ethos). Within the Book of the Covenant see also Exod. 22:17, 20, 21, 27, as well as the → Decalogue (Exod. 20:2-17; Deut. 5:6-21, in the present form influenced by Deuteronomic/Deuteronomistic thinking).

These texts, to which one might add the prohibitions in Lev. 18:7-16 (i.e., of unchastity in the extended family) and the cursings (→ Curse) of Deut. 27:15-26 (i.e., of offenses committed mostly in secret), show that even at an early time, if only selectively, it was laid down what must not be done in Israel. An order of life was thus set up that came from Yahweh, the God to whom they owed their deliverance from Egypt. With the gift comes the task of living according to God's will.

1.3. Prophets

The question whether the → prophets, in unmasking the → sins of their day, refer back to such laws has been given various answers. Many of them are negative after the example of J. Wellhausen (1844-1918), for express references are lacking. But from the many parallels that we find in the reasons that the prophets give for announcing disaster, one may conclude that they presupposed a knowledge of the order of life required and regarded breaches of this order as calamitous. Their proclamation was undoubtedly of great importance in the further development of law. Wellhausen even called them the founders of the religion of law, an expression that is true only with reservations.

1.4. Deuteronomy

What Wellhausen had in mind was especially the development of law in Deuteronomy. This book expands what is present in core in the earlier laws. As the tôrâ or sēper hattôrâ (book of → Torah), it brings together the various types. In particular, it brings to light as nowhere else the theological basis of law. Israel, as the people whom God has chosen in his love, has been given the law along with the land promised to the patriarchs (→ Promise and Fulfillment). By their attitude to it, obedience or disobedience, will be decided the people's → life or → death, their weal or woe (Deut. 30:15). Constantly, then, there is an urgent summons to → obedience, with an emphasis on the goodness and clarity of the law, and how easy it is to keep it (30:11-14). → Covenant

and law go together. As Yahweh has stated that he will be Israel's God, Israel states that it will be his people. But this relationship means hearkening to Yahweh's voice (26:16-19). Promise and obligation are indissolubly related. In content the law of Deuteronomy relates especially to cultic unity and purity. The place that Yahweh has chosen is the only cultic site (e.g., 16:2, 6, 11, 15, 16; → Temple), and all foreign religious influences must be kept out.

Worth noting is the → parenetic reshaping of older laws and the humane element in individual and social ethics (21:15–25:16). Born out of national and religious threats, the law helps the people of Yahweh to achieve and maintain their own identity. We can see this purpose in the Deuteronomistic interpretation of its historical experience after the collapse of 587 B.C. (see the Books of Kings). Israel and Judah lost the land because they did not keep the law of Yahweh. But they are summoned to do so in the existence that remains for them and in this way to see their way through to a new future.

1.5. Postexilic Period

In the postexilic period the law (Deuteronomy? the whole Pentateuch?) was recognized by the Persians and declared to be obligatory for the Jews (Ezra 7). The earlier thesis that in postexilic time the law became detached from the covenant as an independent entity (M. Noth), thus giving rise to extreme legalism, has now come into question in the light of such references as Psalms 1, 19B, 119 (joy in the law) and Sirach (e.g., 2:16; 15:15; 24:23-29; 45:5, etc.).

As regards the understanding of the law in → Judaism, one may say with A. Nissen (43) that the Torah does not remove access to God but creates it, that it does not take God away but makes him present, that it is God himself who is close. An important point in the Judaism of the → Pharisees and → rabbis is that the Torah of → Sinai is believed to be handed down in oral as well as written tradition, so that the link with God is preserved through all of life's changing scenes.

→ Dietary Laws; Ethics; Halakah; Hammurabi, Code of; Holiness Code; Jewish Theology; Law and Legal Theory; Moses; Punishment

Bibliography: A. Alt, "The Origins of Israelite Law," *Essays in OT History and Religion* (Oxford, 1966) 81-121 • H. J. Boecker, *Law and the Administration of Justice in the OT and Ancient East* (London, 1980) • B. Halpern and D. W. Hobson, eds., *Law, Politics, and Society in the Ancient Mediterranean World* (Sheffield, 1993) • C. van Houten, *The Alien in Israelite Law* (Sheffield, 1991) • E. Kutsch, *Verheißung und Gesetz. Untersuchungen zum sogenannten "Bund" im Alten Testament* (Berlin,

1973) • V. H. Matthews and D. C. Benjamin, *OT Parallels: Laws and Stories from the Ancient Near East* (rev. ed.; New York, 1997) • Y. Muffs, *Love and Joy: Law, Language, and Religion in Ancient Israel* (Cambridge, Mass., 1992) • J. Neusner, *The Halakhah: An Encyclopaedia of the Law of Judaism* (5 vols.; Leiden, 2000) • A. Nissen, *Gott und der Nächste im antiken Judentum* (Tübingen, 1974) • M. Noth, *The Laws in the Pentateuch, and Other Studies* (Philadelphia, 1967) • M. T. Roth, *Law Collections from Mesopotamia and Asia Minor* (2d ed.; Atlanta, 1997) • J. A. Sanders, *Torah and Canon* (Philadelphia, 1972) • E. Würthwein and O. Merk, *Verantwortung* (Stuttgart, 1982) • W. Zimmerli, *The Law and the Prophets* (Oxford, 1965).

Ernst Würthwein†

2. NT

A much-debated exegetical question is that of the importance and function of the law in the NT. The theological implications of the answer given are highly relevant to determining the relation between the OT and the NT. The NT presents no single view of the law, which reflects the church's struggle to define itself in relation to Israel.

2.1. Jesus

We know the attitude of → Jesus to the law only from the → Synoptics, which were influenced and fashioned by the Easter faith. The Synoptic tradition contains sayings of Jesus that are conformable with the law and others that are critical of it. We are thus tempted to expound his view in terms of prior theological convictions. If we accept the tested but not undisputed criterion that the greatest authenticity lies where we can relate the sayings neither to a genuinely Jewish nor to a genuinely Christian theological outlook, the authentic tradition may well be found in sayings that are critical of the law.

In Mark 7:15 Jesus basically abolishes the OT → dietary laws by anchoring the concept of purity in the ethical rather than the cultic sphere (→ Cultic Purity). There is no reason to suppose that he did not mean the saying as radically as it is formulated (U. Luz). In Mark 10:2-12 and parallels he sets aside the provision of Deut. 24:1-4 for a certificate of divorce (→ Marriage 3), which made it possible for a husband to divorce his wife. In Mark 2:27 he redefined the role of the → Sabbath. Though his statement has its roots in the Sabbath commandment, it transcends OT thinking. Whether the abrogation of the OT *lex talionis* in Matt. 5:38-39 is authentic is contested by some scholars.

Nevertheless, Jesus in no way totally abrogates the law in an antinomianism of principle. His message, which even in this area is an intimation of the rule of God, often relates positively to the → Decalogue. In Matt. 5:21-30 he radicalizes the sixth and seventh commandments. In Mark 7:9-13 he interprets the fifth commandment in support of the first: we must not play off God against parents or others. The authenticity of the twofold command of love in Mark 12:28-34 and parallels has been disputed. The proclamation of a Torah of Zion in contrast to that of Sinai (P. Stuhlmacher) rests on an untenable differentiation within the OT law (H. Gese). Yet there is a certain fundamental element of negation of the law's validity that only those can dismiss who deny its presence in the saying about the taking of the kingdom by violence (Matt. 11:12-13; Luke 16:16).

2.2. The Hellenists

Debate rages concerning the attitude taken to the law by the Hellenists, that is, Greek-speaking → Jewish Christians in Jerusalem (Acts 6). As distinct from the Hebrews, they were probably critical of the law to a degree that we cannot now determine (vv. 13-14). Against the thesis that in this regard they stood in the tradition of Jesus, the objection might be made that the Hebrews and consequently the → Twelve were not persecuted like the Hellenists for transgressing the law (Acts 6:9–9:2). But the ambivalent attitude of Jesus adequately explains why there should be differences in the Christian community itself during the early years. There is no proof that the Hellenists engaged in circumcision-free mission to the Gentiles, but it is likely enough.

2.3. Paul

In his zeal for the law → Paul at first persecuted the Jewish-Christian Hellenists on account of their critical attitude to it (Gal. 1:13-14). His calling as an → apostle to the Gentiles thus necessarily involved a radical change in his understanding of the law. This change did not have to mean at once the developed doctrine of → justification that we find for the first time in Galatians. Yet it is unlikely that his new view would not have a soteriological component (contra G. Strecker), for otherwise the forensic dimension that is so decisive in his thinking would have been irrelevant for him in face of the Galatian confusion. We are thus to reject any idea that in the doctrine of justification we have only a situational "polemical doctrine" (W. Wrede) or a "secondary crater" (A. → Schweitzer) of his theology (note the influential variant in E. P. Sanders).

In Galatians Paul leaves the impression that at the apostolic council (or, more precisely, the Gentile mission synod; → Acts of the Apostles §8) he established freedom in principle from the law in his negotiation with the "pillars" (Gal. 2:1-10). But the theological exposition (esp. the argument in 3:1–5:12) does not express any agreement with Jerusalem. Paul views the law as an enslaving power, not given directly by God but by → angels (3:19), provoking acts of sin. Christian life, however, is life in → freedom; being bound by the law is its negation. Those who pledge themselves by → circumcision to keep "the entire law" (holon ton nomon) have "fallen away from grace" (5:3-4). Paul knows no one who has observed all the law's commands (3:10). Thus the reference to fulfilling "the whole law" (ho pas nomos) in love (5:14) is ironic. Full observance of the whole law is not possible.

No doubt the synod allowed Paul (and Barnabas) to pursue a circumcision-free Gentile mission, and Paul took this concession to mean that it accepted his view of a law-free Gentile mission. Possibly the believers in Jerusalem saw in uncircumcised Gentile Christians a Christian parallel to the so-called God-fearers.

Paul did not maintain a strict → antinomian position. He is more conciliatory in 1 Corinthians 8–9, and finally in Romans he says that the law is holy (7:12) and spiritual (v. 14), and he now relates its fulfilling in → love to the commands of the law (13:8-10). Yet the irrelevance of the cultic commands still stands (14:14, 20). As in Galatians, Paul also still argues that there can be no justification by way of the law. The only point is that he now sets his theology of justification in the context of the righteousness of God (not mentioned in Galatians) and the law of God. Sin manifests itself not merely in transgression of the law but more subtly in misuse of the law for self-justification by its works and the resultant self-boasting (Rom. 3:27; 10:2-4). Nevertheless, the law itself bears witness to justification without the works of the law (3:20; chap. 4, in which the law is clearly more than the → Pentateuch). A new and positive understanding of Israel corresponds to this new and positive view of the law (9–11).

The attempt of H. Räisänen to portray Paul as self-contradictory because of his different statements about the law, and on this ground to say that he is no theologian, must be regarded as unsuccessful, for we must compare the undisputed differences between Galatians and Romans with tensions even within the same letter that Paul intentionally introduced for reasons of composition.

2.4. Post-Pauline Theology
Alongside several passages in Colossians and Ephesians (Col. 2:16; Eph. 2:15), Hebrews and James are of particular interest with regard to the subsequent history and influence of Pauline theology. Hebrews independently modifies Paul's idea of the end of the law, taking "law" almost exclusively in the cultic sense. The bloody → sacrifices ordained by the law have been replaced definitively by the once-for-all bloody sacrifice of Christ (7–10). Yet the OT law was God's law, and it thus contained "a shadow of the good things to come" (10:1). Christ is presented as the → high priest in cultic terms taken from the law, yet there is a radical break with cultic thinking. Hence the accent is more on discontinuity than continuity. In the new → covenant, which has definitively replaced the old, God writes his laws (note the pl. in Jer. 38:33 LXX; cf. the sing. in 31:33 MT) on our hearts (Heb. 8:10; 10:16). These laws, however, are not the same as the cultic laws of the old covenant. The fact that they are the same as the moral commands of the Mosaic law is not taken into account.

James refers to "the perfect law, the law of liberty" (1:25) and "the royal law" (2:8), which is not simply identical with the OT law but accords with its moral demands (Lev. 19:18 in Jas. 2:8). Jas. 2:14 takes polemical aim at the Pauline doctrine of justification without works of the law, asserting that no one is justified without works (though the author does not say "works of the law," referring instead to works of love); that is, there is no justification by faith alone. Here James opposes a misunderstood Paul or Paulinism. Jas. 2:10 reiterates the notion articulated in Gal. 3:10; 5:3, though with reverse argumentation: one must keep the whole law (holon ton nomon).

2.5. Synoptists
Mark does not use the word "law" but preserves important sayings of Jesus that are critical of the law (2:27; 7:15; 10:5-9).

Despite much effort, researchers have not fully determined the attitude of Matthew toward the law. In view of material discrepancies, even basic questions in interpretation of Matthew are still debated, for example, whether it is a Jewish-Christian or, less likely, a Gentile-Christian gospel. According to Matt. 5:18 (Q), not one iota or dot will pass from the law (see also 23:23) until all is accomplished. If the apocalyptic end-time event is in view (but cf. 24:35), 5:18 seems to clash with the antitheses of 5:21-48 if they abrogate and do not merely radicalize the commandments of the law. V. 17, which seems to work over an older topos (Rom. 13:8-10), might be harmonized with abolition, for in this view, as in radicalizing, there takes place fulfillment of the law and the prophets. The redacted version of Mark 12:28-31 in Matt. 22:34-40 presents the twofold commandment of love as the epitome of the law (see also 7:12).

Luke's view of the relation between Jesus and the law is understandable only if we look at Acts as well. Luke's version of the saying about taking the kingdom by violence (16:16 Q) has it that before the Baptist there were "only" the law and the prophets, but now there is "also" the preaching of the kingdom (H. Conzelmann). In keeping is the dropping of Mark 7:1-23 with its abrogation of Leviticus 11. Partial abolition of the statutes of the law comes after → Pentecost. The cultic dietary laws are set aside in Acts 10–11 (esp. 10:15), as is the law of circumcision in Acts 15. But Gentile Christians have to keep the so-called apostolic decree of 15:20, 28-29 (see also 21:25). For Luke the law not only imposes demands and prohibitions but also has a prophetic function. What is written in it (and also in the Prophets and the Psalms) concerning the death and → resurrection of Jesus has to be fulfilled (Luke 24:44-49; see also Acts 28:23).

2.6. John

Also for John the law has the positive function of bearing witness to Jesus, the law in this case being equated with Scripture (e.g., John 10:34 and 15:25, which are sayings from the Psalms as "law"). The Scriptures bear witness to Jesus (5:39). Moses accuses unbelieving Jews, for he wrote about Jesus (5:45-46). But Moses can also stand for the law in the narrower sense (7:23). At the same time, Jesus also speaks of "your law" (8:17; 10:34; see also 15:25). Notwithstanding the positive function of the law, its day is over; → grace and → truth are opposed to the law (1:17). → Revelation has now become a reality in Jesus, whereas previously it could not occur in the true sense.

→ Ethics 2; Gospel 1

Bibliography: H. CONZELMANN, Gentiles, Jews, Christians: Polemics and Apologetics in the Greco-Roman Era (Minneapolis, 1992) • A. A. DAS, Paul, the Law, and the Covenant (Peabody, Mass., 2001) • W. D. DAVIES, "Paul and the Law: Reflections on Pitfalls in Interpretation" and "Law in the NT," Jewish and Pauline Studies (Philadelphia, 1984) 91-122 and 227-42 • S. K. DAVIS, The Antithesis of the Ages: Paul's Reconfiguration of Torah (Washington, D.C., 2002) • C. H. DODD, Gospel and Law (Cambridge, 1951) • J. D. G. DUNN, ed., Paul and the Mosaic Law (Grand Rapids, 2001) • E. D. FREED, The Apostle Paul, Christian Jew: Faithfulness and Law (Lanham, Md., 1994) • H. HÜBNER, Das Gesetz in der synoptischen Tradition (2d ed.; Göttingen, 1986); idem, Gottes Ich und Israel. Zum Schriftgebrauch des Paulus in Römer 9–11 (Göttingen, 1984); idem, Law in Paul's Thought (Edinburgh, 1984) • V. KOPERSKI, What Are They Saying about Paul and the Law? (New York, 2001) • K. KUULA, The Law, the Covenant, and God's Plan (Helsinki, 1999) • W. LOADER, Jesus' Attitude towards the Law: A Study of the Gospels (Grand Rapids, 2002) • C. M. PATE, The Reverse of the Curse: Paul, Wisdom, and the Law (Tübingen, 2000) • H. RÄISÄNEN, Paul and the Law (2d ed.; Tübingen, 1986); idem, The Torah and Christ: Essays in German and English on the Problem of the Law in Early Christianity (Helsinki, 1986) • R. K. RAPA, The Meaning of "Works of the Law" in Galatians and Romans (New York, 2001) • E. P. SANDERS, Paul and Palestinian Judaism: A Comparison of Patterns of Religion (Philadelphia, 1977); idem, Paul, the Law, and the Jewish People (Philadelphia, 1983) • G. STRECKER, The Sermon on the Mount (Nashville, 1988) • P. STUHLMACHER, Reconciliation, Law, and Righteousness: Essays in Biblical Theology (Philadelphia, 1986) • L. THURÉN, Derhetorizing Paul: A Dynamic Perspective on Pauline Theology and the Law (Tübingen, 2000) • S. WESTERHOLM, Israel's Law and the Church's Faith: Paul and His Recent Interpreters (Grand Rapids, 1988).

HANS HÜBNER

3. Dogmatics
3.1. Early Eastern Church

Taking up such Pauline antithetical constructions as "law of Christ" (Gal. 6:2; 1 Cor. 9:21), "law of faith" (Rom. 3:27), and "law of the Spirit" (Rom. 8:2), along with "the perfect law, the law of liberty" of James (1:25; 2:12) and the "new commandment" of John (13:34; 1 John 2:8), the → Apostolic Fathers insisted on "the new law of our Lord Jesus Christ" (Barn. 2.6), who as a new Moses had opened up the "ways of life" (Herm. Sim. 5.6.3). Although the law was a way of → salvation for Jewish Christians and apostasy for → Paul, Marcion (d. ca. 160) proclaimed a purified Pauline → gospel in opposition to the jealous creator-god of the Sinai law (→ Marcionites).

→ Irenaeus (d. ca. 200) integrated the law into a "universal education of the human race" by the God-Logos, equating the → natural law (→ Stoicism), which had been set in the hearts of the patriarchs, with the → Decalogue and finding its culmination in the new commandment of the gospel. Clement (ca. 150-ca. 215) and → Origen (ca. 185-ca. 254) oriented the triadic law of nature, Moses, and Christ to union with God. The → Cappadocian Fathers worked the biblical figures into this ascetic ideal of instruction or discipline (paideia). For them → Jesus is the model of true knowledge of God and pure striving after virtue. The Eastern Church (→

Orthodox Christianity) to this day does not make a theme of the distinction between → law and gospel.

3.2. Western Church and Roman Catholicism

3.2.1. In the West → Tertullian (ca. 160-ca. 225) developed a judicial ethics with emphasis always on the harder commandment. → Cyprian (ca. 200-258) stressed the sacramental aspects, and Lactantius (ca. 250-ca. 325) began with natural law. Ambrose (ca. 339-97) integrated the law into the rule of faith seen in terms of → salvation history. Expositors of Romans took note of the tension between law and gospel.

Against the background of the eternal law (*lex aeterna*) of Cicero (106-43 B.C.), → Augustine (354-430; → Augustine's Theology) worked out a schema of law and → grace that became normative in the West. The law is given that we might strive after grace; grace is given that we might fulfill the law (*De spir. et litt.* 34; *Ep.* 145.1). There are thus four steps in salvation history: before the law, under the law, under grace, and at eternal peace (*Ench.* 31.118). The law covers original → sin but cannot overcome it. To this end there is need of the grace, mediated by the church, in which Christ becomes both the mediator of salvation (*sacramentum*) and our example (*exemplum*).

3.2.2. Concentration on the twofold commandment and the → Golden Rule (Matt. 7:12) is reflected in the struggle with → Judaism. Origen (→ Origenism) points out the different OT semantic fields and stresses three: the ritual law, which allegorically prefigures Christ and the community (→ Allegory; Congregation); the mandates summed up in the Decalogue, which also apply to Christians; and things that we must observe (e.g., monogamy) as well as interpret allegorically (→ Allegory). Ambrose and Augustine adopted a similar structure. Ambrosiaster found doctrines of faith, commands of natural law, and sacramental symbols. The medieval disputes regarding → tithes and interest directed attention to legal statutes.

By 1300, then, we find the triad of moral commandments, cultic regulations, and legal statutes (William of Auxerre and William of Auvergne). Along the lines of the *Summa Halensis* of John of Rupella, → Thomas Aquinas (ca. 1225-74; → Thomism) structured the tractate on law in his *Summa theologiae* in this way. The Decalogue unfolds natural law. God gave the ritual regulations to → Israel to preserve them for the → Messiah. With the coming of the Messiah, the → sacraments have been transposed. Along the lines of the *Politics* of Aristotle (384-322 B.C.; → Aristotelianism), the legal statutes offer a model of true life in society.

3.2.3. The Middle Ages linked Augustine's doctrine of grace more closely to the sacraments and softened the anti-Pelagian and predestinarian elements (→ Pelagianism; Predestination). A distinction was made between the old law and the new in terms of the OT promises (Jer. 31:31-34; Ezek. 11:19; 36:26-27) and Paul's antithesis of letter and spirit (2 Cor. 3:6). According to Thomas the former is imposed from outside, the latter is primarily given by the → Holy Spirit and only secondarily embodied in Scripture (*Summa theol.* I of II, q. 106, art. 1). Hence the participation of the → new self in Christ's paschal mystery is no longer under the law. Yet the gospel has not yet achieved autonomy; it is still ordered to the new law.

G. Seripando (1492/93-1563), general of the → Augustinians (1539-51), strove in vain to persuade the Council of → Trent to accept the Reformation relationship between law and promises (*CT* 5.822) and the role of the law in awakening a knowledge of → sin. Misunderstanding the → Reformation along antinomian lines, Trent insisted on the freedom of the will, on the fulfillment of the law as a condition of salvation, and on Christ as a lawgiver (DH 1536-39, 1568-76).

→ Vatican II rediscovered the gospel and proclaimed the church as an institution of freedom (→ Church 3.2). Roman Catholic theologians, however, have hardly yet discussed the theme of law and gospel (G. Söhngen, O. H. Pesch, P. Knauer).

3.2.4. Already in the early church the distinction between the old law of bondage and the new law of the freedom of children, along with the ascetic ideal of angel-like conformity to God, led to graduations in fulfillment of the commandments (→ Ethics). This approach finally took the sharper form of differentiation between commandments and counsels, adumbrated in the NT duality of → household rules and a pilgrim ethos.

Only at Vatican II did taking monastic → vows cease to be regarded as a second baptism (as it did esp. for → Jerome and → Bernard of Clairvaux) and come to be integrated into the universal calling to → sanctification. Yet → monasticism still means particular closeness to the poor and celibate Jesus, who was obedient even unto death.

3.3. Reformation

Following J. → Wycliffe (ca. 1330-84), the Bohemian Reformation asserted the unconditional and exclusive authority of the law of Christ. Adopting Scripture as a norm, it read the OT in terms of the NT: *lex Dei = lex Christi = lex evangelica*. Pledged solely to their Master, Christ, the later → Bohemian

Brethren called themselves brothers of the law of Christ (J. A. Comenius).

The 16th-century Reformers, however, took over the medieval structure of the law and radicalized the Augustinian relating of law and grace and Thomas's thesis of the old and new law, finding a distinction between law and gospel as the "twofold Word or preaching of God" (WA 10/1/2.155.22). They rejected a two-stage ethics. In encounter with the gospel message of victory, the many directions become "one law which runs through all ages, is known to all men, is written in the hearts of all people, and leaves no one from beginning to end with an excuse" (*LW* 27.355). All the Reformers moved within the triangle of the will of God that is engraved on every human → conscience (Rom. 2:14-15); of the Decalogue, as summed up in the twofold commandment; and of the spiritual exposition and physical fulfillment of this commandment by Jesus himself.

Various uses of the law are delineated. The unconditional self-giving of Jesus to God and others points up the convicting use of the law (*usus elenchticus,* the refutational use), which points to Christ. For M. → Luther (1483-1546) this use of the law joins with the powers of death in attacking Christ and our conscience. Another use of the law is civil or political (*usus civilis vel politicus),* which serves to ward off external chaos, for God is ruler as well as judge. Beyond these two uses that Luther expressly stresses, all the Reformers note the distinctive nature of NT exhortations, which they call either the third use of the law (P. → Melanchthon and J. → Calvin) or the practical fulfillment of the gospel (*usus practicus evangelii,* so Luther; W. Joest). A final use (overlapped by the third) involves training in the Decalogue and ceremonies within catechetical instruction in a manner appropriate to children (*sensus puerilis decalogi et ceremoniarum;* see WA 11.31.10).

Within the common factors Luther stressed the eschatological dialectic of law and grace (→ Luther's Theology). Melanchthon (1497-1560) introduced the natural law of antiquity and the Middle Ages with an orientation to piety and education. There thus emerged the contours of the "natural systems" of the 17th and 18th centuries (W. Dilthey). As U. → Zwingli (1484-1531; → Zwingli's Theology) had already opposed God's Word to human statutes, so Calvin (1509-64; → Calvin's Theology) insisted on the unity of the → covenant above all differences in its administration.

J. Agricola (1494-1566), in contrast, differentiated Christ's call to → conversion (§1) from the law

of Moses, which had failed as a way of salvation. In the debate stirred up by the Eisenach Synod of 1556 concerning the function of the law for Christians, A. Poach (1516-85), A. Otho (1505-83), M. Neander (1525-95), and A. Musculus (1514-81) pleaded for direct leading by the Spirit, the new self being above the heteronomous schema of requirement and achievement (→ Antinomian Controversies). The → Formula of Concord (1577) points to the danger of self-chosen divine service (Ep. 6.4) and, along with obedience "from a free and merry spirit" (SD 6.17), insists on the need for specific directions. Even as the new self, the Christian lives, not above, let alone without, but "in the law of the Lord" (SD 6.18).

3.4. *Modern Period*

3.4.1. With the help of the Decalogue and the three estates, Lutheran → orthodoxy (§1) developed a theonomous ethos. Reformed theologians turned more to the triad of the covenant of nature, Moses, and Christ, which persisted also in English and American → Puritanism. → Pietism stressed the law of sanctification set forth in the life of Jesus.

3.4.2. The → Enlightenment presented Jesus as a teacher of virtue comparable with Socrates. With → modernity, however, many competing spheres of life with their own historical, social, economic, biological, and psychological laws broke free from the basic Christian orientation. To confront this → emancipation, Lutheran theologians in the 19th century, in → catechesis and → pastoral care, returned to the distinction between law and gospel (esp. F. A. Philippi, A. von Harless, T. Harnack, C. A. G. von Zezschwitz, and the Missouri Synod theologian C. F. W. Walther).

With the revolution in theology after World War I, the theme of law and gospel figured in the conflict regarding God's → revelation in the orders of creation, that is, in → marriage, → family, people, → state, race, and → class. In the doctrine of *Volksnomoi* (laws of the Volk [a National Socialist position], W. Stapel, F. Gogarten, E. Hirsch) and also in the "socialist decision" (P. → Tillich), the law is freed from its reference to Christ and given a historical setting. In W. Elert (1885-1954) it takes the dark form of an order of force and death in God's wrathful judgment (→ Wrath of God). Christians, too, are "kairologically" caught in the interplay of judging law and saving gospel. The NT imperatives of grace replace the third use of the law.

3.4.3. K. → Barth (1886-68) at first opposed the synthesis of → culture Protestantism with a radical separation of God and humankind and therefore of judgment and grace, of law and gospel (→ Dialectical Theology). But then he and E. Thurneysen (1888-1974) sought to link a "cliff fortress" of ethics to that of → Christology. With the *Fides quaerens intellectum* (Faith in search of understanding) of his book on → Anselm, Barth worked out a relationship between promise and claim, between gospel and law, that influenced the → Barmen Declaration (1934). The thesis that the law is a "necessary form of the gospel, whose content is grace" (E. Kinder and K. Haendler, 13) now became part of the "basic substance" of Barth's dogmatics (*CD* IV/3, 370). There are no autonomous orders; we learn God's will as a most concrete command in analogy to Christ. The institutional bond of human life is dissolved into the ordered relationship of men and women, parents and children, near and distant neighbors.

3.4.4. After World War II F. Gogarten (1887-1967) pressed on to a distinction between true → secularization and false → secularism. God's personal summons in the command brings trust in the gospel and thus frees the world for responsibility. G. Ebeling found in the distinction between law and gospel "the logic of the substance of theology" (*Dogmatik* 3.289). Along these lines he tried to show that the basic human situation is a "situation of the word."

Harking back to I. Kant and F. D. E. → Schleiermacher, Tillich (1886-1965) drew the law into the universal interpenetration of spirit and nature, ultimately making it personal. First, along with symbols like "form" and "structure," the law was for him an indication of "the structural determinateness of things and events" (*Systematic Theology* 1.186). Then, in the context of personal responsibility, it takes on the purely obligatory dimension of the → categorical imperative in its many demands. Finally, with the inner conflict of will, it proves to be the judgment of true essence on our alienated existence. In the dynamic of "love, power, and justice" (*Main Works* 3.583-650), the third use of the law has the form of a → righteousness that is quantitatively evaluating, qualitatively judging, and creatively transforming.

3.4.5. Various attempts have been made to mediate between the Lutheran order "law and gospel" and Barth's sequence "gospel and law" (esp. by P. Althaus, H. Asmussen, E. Schlink, H. J. Iwand, E. Wolf, H. Gollwitzer, H. Vogel, H. Thielicke, E. Brunner, W. Joest, and B. Klappert; cf. G. Wingren, "Barth's Conception"). Schlink (1903-84) evolved his "ecumenical dogmatics" from the gospel. In the discussion of ecumenical bodies Barth's sequence constantly appears, but there are also signs of a new legalism, for example, in some → fundamentalist trends in → Third World churches (→ Third World Theology).

3.5. *Problems*

In a survey it is best to orient oneself to the Reformers, using the thread of Romans. The gospel of Christ passes the judgment of law on Gentiles and Jews, but it does so under the richly developed grace of Christ. There thus results a strict confrontation of law and gospel. The indicative of salvation, however, also carries with it the imperatives of grace. This combination results in a second reordering of the relationship between law and gospel. The chapters on Israel (Romans 9–11) stress the ongoing possibility of eschatological flight from the holy God to the merciful God.

These concurrent schemata may be transposed from Christology to human existence, which gives us the sequence "gospel and law." Only those who are themselves accepted can accept others. Achievement follows gift. The sequence "law and gospel" points to the mystery. A breakthrough to final → freedom presupposes the harnessing of all our powers, but this achievement cannot be forced. First comes the descent of self-knowledge, then the ascent of knowledge of God (J. G. Hamann, A. Tholuck).

The debated schemata, then, relate to different religious → experiences. They take on their full biblical and Reformation meaning only when they are firmly anchored Christologically and consciously oriented eschatologically.

Bibliography: On 3.1-3: G. EBELING, "On the Doctrine of the *Triplex Usus Legis* in the Theology of the Reformation" and "Reflexions on the Doctrine of the Law," *Word and Faith* (Philadelphia, 1963) 62-78 and 247-81 • W. JOEST, *Gesetz und Freiheit. Das Problem des Tertius usus legis bei Luther und die neutestamentliche Parainese* (4th ed.; Göttingen, 1968) • P. KNAUER, *Die Glaube kommt von Hören. Ökumenische Fundamentaltheologie* (6th ed.; Freiburg, 1991) • O. H. PESCH, *Theologie der Rechtfertigung bei Martin Luther und Thomas von Aquin* (Mainz, 1967) • O. H. PESCH and A. PETERS, *Einführung in die Lehre von Gnade und Rechtfertigung* (Darmstadt, 1981) • G. SÖHNGEN, *Gesetz und Evangelium. Ihre analoge Einheit; theologisch, philosophisch, staatsbürgerlich* (Freiburg, 1957) • J. WITTE JR., *Law and Protestantism: The Legal Teachings of the Lutheran Reformation* (Cambridge, 2002).

On 3.4-5: K. BARTH, *Anselm: Fides quaerens intellectum* (London, 1960; orig. pub., 1931) • G. EBELING, *Dogmatik des christlichen Glaubens* (3 vols.; Tübingen, 1979) • G. O. FORDE, *The Law-Gospel Debate* (Minneapolis, 1968) • E. KINDER and K. HAENDLER,

eds., *Gesetz und Evangelium* (Darmstadt, 1968) •
B. Klappert, *Promissio und Bund. Gesetz und Evangelium bei Luther und Barth* (Göttingen, 1976) • A. Peters, *Gesetz und Evangelium* (Gütersloh, 1981) •
E. Schlink, "Law and Gospel as a Controversial Theological Problem," *The Coming Christ and the Coming Church* (Edinburgh, 1967) 144-85; idem, *Ökumenische Dogmatik* (Göttingen, 1961) 211-51, 310-20, 456-70 •
P. Tillich, *Main Works = Hauptwerke* (6 vols.; Berlin, 1987-92); idem, *Systematische Theologie* (vol. 1; 4th ed.; Stuttgart, 1973) • G. Wingren, "Barth's Conception of 'the Word,' *Theology in Conflict: Nygren, Barth, Bultmann* (Philadelphia, 1958) 108-28; idem, *Creation and Law* (Philadelphia, 1961).

Albrecht Peters†

Law and Gospel

1. Luther's and Melanchthon's Distinction
2. Use of the Distinction in Lutheranism
3. Law and Gospel in Other Traditions
4. Twentieth-Century Discussion

1. Luther's and Melanchthon's Distinction

1.1. The concepts of → law and → gospel, each with a wide range of definitions and theological functions in the Bible, assumed a distinctive use within the theology of reformers Martin → Luther (1483-1546; → Luther's Theology) and Philipp → Melanchthon (1497-1560) as a dialectical description of God's judgment on sinners and his restoration of life for his elect children. Though the two colleagues placed different accents on elements of this → dialectic, the use each made of it remained much alike. The concept of their proper distinction in pastoral practice became for the Wittenberg → Reformation a primary hermeneutical guide for the interpretation and application of the biblical message. Integral to their understanding of how God works with sinners to restore them to his kingdom, the distinction between law and gospel and proper use of each within this dialectical tension provided Luther and Melanchthon the key to proper proclamation of God's Word and to effective → pastoral care.

1.2. Luther's distinction between law and gospel arose out of his wrestling with the paradox involved in the biblical definition of the relationship between the Creator God and the human creature. Luther strove to take seriously both the biblical affirmation that as Creator, God is totally sovereign and responsible for all in his → creation and the parallel assumption that individual human creatures are to-

tally responsible for all that the Creator has placed at their disposal. In struggling with this paradox of two → responsibilities, Luther formulated his → anthropology of a distinction of "two kinds of human righteousness."

This distinction posited, on the one hand, that in God's sight human creatures attain → righteousness (true humanity) only passively, through God's mercy, by the unconditioned creative or re-creative act of his Word. On the other hand, they are actively righteous in relationship to others through new → obedience, which produces good works in line with God's commands. Luther analyzed the Christian life through another and corollary distinction between two spheres of life (sometimes called → two kingdoms), one relating to God through trust in him, the other relating to his creation through acts of → love.

The distinction of law and gospel is a third corollary drawn from the paradox of total divine and total human responsibility (within their respective domains). It describes the interaction between God's gift of human identity as children of God through Christ's work to sinners (gospel) and the expectations he has for the behavior or performance of his children as a result of this gift of their identity (law).

Melanchthon differentiated three uses of the law. First, it curbs wanton sinfulness and compels or allures sinners into proper behavior. Second, under the law the burden of God's expectations crushes sinners, producing repentance by accusing them of failing to perform God's will and, above all, by accusing them of failing to trust in him and receive his gift of identity as God's children. The gospel comes to repentant sinners with the restoration of life, won by Christ's assumption of the death pronounced on all sin by the judgment of the law. Therefore, third, believers turn to the law for guidance in choosing what to do as children of God.

1.3. The proper distinction of law and gospel takes place, according to Luther and Melanchthon, in the face of the mystery of continued → evil in the lives of God's chosen children, who have received the gift of → faith in Christ through his Word in oral, written, or sacramental form (the → means of grace). Luther believed that God's Word actually has the power to kill and make alive: in the form of the law it carries out God's judgment upon sin; in the form of the gospel it effects death to sin and resurrection to new life in Christ because of Christ's work.

Luther taught that law and gospel bring about a turning from sinfulness to trust in Christ and the new obedience that flows from that trust in the daily struggle of the Christian life. The law addresses sinners who are serving false gods, while the gospel brings the promise of redemption and life to those broken by the law's crushing power. Because Christians are righteous and sinful at the same time (*simul iustus et peccator*) — totally righteous because God's re-creative Word has made them so, totally touched by their sinfulness through the mystery of evil's continuing presence in their lives — the dialectic of law and gospel must continue throughout the believers' life on earth.

1.4. Law and gospel are not respectively to be equated precisely with → sanctification and → justification, for the law's call to repentance creates the situation in which justification takes place, when God gives the gift of faith in Christ to the sinner. Living by faith in the sanctified life is a life motivated by Christ's love (gospel) to fulfill God's commands. The precise relationship between the accusing law, the life-restoring gospel, and the fulfillment of these commands has been much disputed in Luther interpretation, in both the 16th and the 20th centuries.

2. Use of the Distinction in Lutheranism

2.1. Most of Luther's and Melanchthon's students used their teachers' distinction of law and gospel in preaching and in theological writings. Matthias Flacius Illyricus (1520-75) placed it at the basis of his hermeneutics, in his *Clavis Scripturae sacrae* (Key to sacred Scripture, 1567). Through this oft-reprinted work the distinction influenced the proclamation and teaching of Lutheran → orthodoxy (§1).

Because the law-gospel distinction functions not as one doctrine among many but rather as a presupposition for teaching all doctrines or topics, its role in 17th-century Lutheran public teaching changed. It did so because the Melanchthonian system had no place for analyzing presuppositions and conceptual frameworks. Presented as one topic among others in the → Formula of Concord (1577), law and gospel continued to be mentioned prominently by most Lutheran orthodox theologians but without the dialectical tension vital for Luther and Melanchthon.

2.2. → Pietist theologians also continued to use the connection of law and gospel as a key for Christian living. For Philipp Jakob Spener (1635-1705) and August Hermann → Francke (1663-1727), the gospel empowered believers to live and walk according to God's law in daily life. Pietist authors generally avoided the sharp confrontation with God's → wrath against sin so important for the early → reformers and focused more on the use of both law and gospel as media of instruction for faith and life. Early modern anthropology enabled Pietists to concentrate on psychological aspects of the effects of law and gospel that Luther implicitly addressed but was not able to explain. This new emphasis arose, however, without the discipline of the dialectical tension between God's mercy and his demands because Luther's sense of the mystery of the continuation of evil, of the believer's simultaneous righteousness and sinfulness, had been lost. Therefore, some Pietist writers accented the behavior of the Christian more than God's mercy and trust in that mercy.

2.3. In the → Enlightenment, Lutheran thinkers tended to avoid topics such as the wrath of God and the atoning death and resurrection of Christ (→ Atonement), thus leading to the abandonment of the formerly widely used distinction between law and gospel. Theologians in the 19th century from F. D. E. → Schleiermacher (1768-1834; → Schleiermacher's Theology) to Albrecht Ritschl (1822-89), for differing reasons, ignored or dismissed the distinction.

It gained new currency, however, in the Lutheran confessional revival, particularly in Erlangen in the works of Adolf von Harless (1806-79) and others, and in St. Louis in C. F. W. Walther's (1811-87) posthumously published lectures on the topic, lectures that became a standard textbook for homiletics and → dogmatics in his own Missouri Synod and in other North American Lutheran churches.

3. Law and Gospel in Other Traditions

3.1. Other Christian theological traditions have generally not used the terms "law" and "gospel" in this dialectical tension as a formal hermeneutic. When they have paid attention to this distinction, the treatments have often reflected a direct interaction with the Lutheran concept. Eastern Orthodox theologians generally resolve the paradox of divine and human responsibility with the doctrine of → synergy, in which God's grace and human works mutually enable each other so that a person attains salvation from death and sin (→ Orthodox Church).

Though differing accents can be found in Roman Catholic treatments of salvation, theological systems influenced by → Thomas Aquinas (ca. 1225-74; → Thomism) and the Council of → Trent focus first of all on God's grace but assess human righteousness from the standpoint of the grace-assisted merit won by human performance of God's law. The gospel of Christ's atoning work is thus understood within a framework determined by God's expectations for human performance.

3.2. Protestant thinkers have addressed the paradox of divine and human responsibilities in a variety of ways. John → Calvin (1509-64; → Calvin's Theology) stressed divine responsibility with his doctrine of double → predestination, which indeed played a more prominent role in later Calvinist → orthodoxy (§2; → Calvinism) than in his own thought. In his *Institutes* Calvin treats God's promise in Christ as the basis of the relationship between the gospel of free → forgiveness of sins through Christ and the good works produced by faith. These works, he taught, have no merit in themselves but bestow on those elected by God without condition temporal and heavenly rewards because of God's gracious concession. For Calvin gospel and law do not stand in dialectical tension, as for Luther, but rather work together in producing the Christian life. Later Calvinist theologians particularly accented God's gift of distinct covenants of law and gospel to his people. Some covenantal theologians placed emphasis on human performance, the lack of which in sinners is covered by Christ's atoning work; others rooted God's entire relationship with human creatures in his mercy and defined works as only the result of faith.

Crucial for some 16th-century → Anabaptist teachers and their successors in subsequent centuries was the human behavior that God's grace produced. This approach gave the law the more prominent place in daily Christian living.

John → Wesley (1703-91) highlighted God's grace but placed critical emphasis on human acceptance of that grace. Against the immoral lifestyle of 18th-century England, he waged a campaign that urged strict adherence to God's law on the basis of faith in Christ.

4. Twentieth-Century Discussion

4.1. Out of the Calvinist tradition came Karl → Barth's (1886-1968) polemic against the Lutheran distinction of law and gospel that he encountered in early 20th-century Germany. Several prominent mid-20th-century German theologians, including Friedrich Gogarten (1887-1967), Werner Elert (1885-1954), Hans-Joachim Iwand (1899-1960), and Gerhard Ebeling (1912-2001), attempted to accent the relevance of the distinction of law and gospel, in part in exchanges with Barth. For Elert, whose influence also spread to North American → Lutheranism, the accusing law is always in sharp opposition to the gospel of Christ. Opposing the teaching of the Formula of Concord, Elert asserts that the law cannot be used positively in the Christian life (i.e., in its "third use"); rather, the gospel

moves believers to follow its own imperatives, which are not to be viewed as commands but as God's gracious offers for proper human living.

4.2. Gustaf Wingren (1910-2000), professor at Lund in Sweden, also used law and gospel as the framework for his presentation of the biblical message, but with a higher appreciation of the positive aspects of the law in the Christian life. Swedish bishop Bo Giertz (1905-98) emphasized the use of the distinction in pastoral care; he composed a fictional exposition of the proper distinguishing of law and gospel, *The Hammer of God* (1973), that concretizes its use in critical pastoral situations.

In their broader definitions the concepts of law and gospel remain at the center of ecumenical discussion. In the narrower Lutheran definition the hermeneutical principles expressed in the proper distinction of law and gospel, with corollaries in theological anthropology (two kinds of righteousness) and in → ethics and social theory (two realms), will certainly be represented in continuing application of the biblical message to the situations of church and world in the 21st century.

Bibliography: G. L. Bahnsen, W. C. Kaiser Jr., D. J. Moo, W. G. Strickland, and W. A. VanGemeren, *Five Views on Law and Gospel* (Grand Rapids, 1996) • H.-M. Barth, "Gesetz und Evangelium I," *TRE* 13.126-42 • K. Barth, *Evangelium und Gesetz* (Munich, 1935) • C. H. Dodd, *Gospel and Law: The Relation of Faith and Ethics in Early Christianity* (New York, 1951) • G. Ebeling, *Luther: An Introduction to His Thought* (Philadelphia, 1970) • W. Elert, *Law and Gospel* (Philadelphia, 1967) • G. O. Forde, *The Law-Gospel Debate: An Interpretation of Its Historical Development* (Minneapolis, 1969); idem, *Theology Is for Proclamation* (Minneapolis, 1990) • B. Giertz, *The Hammer of God* (Minneapolis, 1973) • L. Haikola, *Gesetz und Evangelium bei Matthias Flacius Illyricus* (Lund, 1952) • A. Peters, *Gesetz und Evangelium* (2d ed.; Gütersloh, 1994) • *The Promising Tradition: A Reader in Law-Gospel Reconstructionist Theology* (St. Louis, 1972) • C. F. W. Walther, *The Proper Distinction between Law and Gospel* (St. Louis, 1929; orig. pub., 1897) • G. Wingren, *Creation and Law* (Philadelphia, 1961); idem, *Gospel and Church* (Philadelphia, 1964).

Robert Kolb

Law and Legal Theory

1. Definition
2. Pre- and Post-Christian Rome
3. The Papal Revolution
4. The Protestant Reformation

5. The Enlightenment
6. Law and Religion Today

1. Definition

The term "law" does not admit of easy or universal definition. Viewed in its broadest social terms, law consists of all norms that govern human conduct — moral commandments, state statutes, church canons, family rules, commercial habits, communal customs, and others — and all actions taken to formulate and respond to those norms. Viewed in narrower political terms, law consists of the social enterprise by which certain → norms are formulated by legitimate political authorities and actualized by persons legitimately subject to those political authorities. The process of legal formulation involves legislating, adjudicating, administering, and other conduct by legal officials. The process of legal actualization involves obeying, negotiating, litigating, and other conduct by legal subjects.

Most Western nations today are dedicated to the rule of law and have constitutions that define the powers and provinces of political authorities and the rights and duties of citizens and subjects. Most nations make formal distinctions between the executive, legislative, and judicial powers of government and functions of law. Most distinguish between bodies of criminal law, public law (constitutional and administrative law), and private law (on contracts, torts, property, inheritance, and others). Most have sophisticated rules and procedures to facilitate the legal transactions and interactions of their citizens and subjects and to resolve disputes among citizens and between citizens and the government. Most recognize multiple sources of law — constitutions, treaties, statutes, regulations, judicial precedents, customary practices, and more. Of increasing importance to many nations today are public international laws (on diplomacy, warfare, humanitarian aid, human rights, and → environmental protection) and private international laws (on global economics, trade, → communications, and dispute resolution).

Many of the legal ideas and institutions that prevail among Western nations today are parts and products of a long and venerable Western legal tradition. This legal tradition was born out of the ancient civilizations of Israel, Greece, and Rome and was nurtured for nearly two millennia by Christianity and for more than two centuries by the → Enlightenment. The Western legal tradition has embraced enduring postulates about justice and mercy, rule and equity, nature and custom, principle and precept. It has featured recurrent ideas about → authority and → power, → rights and liberties, indi-

viduals and associations, public and private. It has developed distinctive methods of legislation and adjudication, of negotiation and litigation, of legal rhetoric and interpretation, of juridical science and systematics.

The precise shape and balance of the Western legal tradition at any period have been determined, in part, by the Western religious tradition. When the dominant ideas, officials, symbols, and methods of the Western religious tradition have changed, the shape and balance of the Western legal tradition have often changed as well.

Four major shifts in the Western religious tradition, discussed in the sections below, have triggered the most massive transformations of the Western legal tradition: (1) the Christianization of the → Roman Empire in the 4th through 6th centuries, (2) the papal revolution of the late 11th to 13th centuries, (3) the Protestant → Reformation of the 16th century, and (4) the Enlightenment movements of the 18th and 19th centuries. The Western legal tradition was hardly static between these four watershed periods, but these were the critical civilizational moments and movements that permanently redirected the Western legal tradition.

2. Pre- and Post-Christian Rome

The first watershed period came with the Christian conversion of the Roman emperor and empire in the fourth through sixth centuries. Before that time, Roman law reigned supreme throughout much of the West, defining the status of persons and associations and the legal actions and procedures available to them. Roman law proscribed delicts (torts) and crimes, protected the public property and welfare of the Roman state, and regulated private property, commerce, → slavery, inheritance, and the household.

Roman law also established the imperial cult (→ Roman Religion). Rome was to be revered as the Eternal City, ordained by the gods and celebrated at its altars and basilicas. The Roman emperor was to be worshiped as a god and king in the rituals of the imperial court and in the festivals of the public square. Roman law itself was viewed as the embodiment of an immutable divine law, appropriated and applied through the sacred legal science of imperial pontiffs and jurists.

A refined legal theory emerged after the first century b.c., built in part on Greek prototypes. Cicero, Seneca, and other Roman philosophers cast in legal terms Aristotle's topical methods of reasoning, rhetoric, and interpretation, as well as his concepts of natural, distributive, and commutative justice (→

Aristotelianism). Gaius, Ulpian, and other Roman jurists drew what would become classic Western distinctions between (1) → civil law *(ius civile)*, the statutes and procedures of a particular community, to be applied strictly or with equity; (2) common law *(ius gentium)*, the principles and customs common to several communities and often the basis for treaties; and (3) → natural law *(ius naturale)*, the immutable principles of right reason that are supreme in authority and divinity and must prevail in cases of conflict with civil or common laws.

The early Christian church stood largely opposed to this Roman legal system, as had the Jewish communities in which the church was born. Christians could not accept the imperial cult or readily partake of the pagan rituals required for participation in commerce, the military, litigation, and other public forums and activities. The → early church thus organized itself into separate communities, largely withdrawn from official Roman society. Early church constitutions, such as the *Didache* (ca. 100) and *Didascalia apostolorum* (ca. 250), set forth internal rules for church organization and offices, clerical life, ecclesiastical discipline, charity, education, → family, and property relations. Early Christian leaders, building on the injunctions of → Jesus and → Paul, generally taught → obedience to the political authorities up to the limits of Christian → conscience. The clergy also urged upon their Roman rulers political and legal reforms consonant with Christian teachings. Such legal independence and legal advocacy by the church brought forth firm imperial edicts from the mid-first century onward, condemning Christians to intermittent waves of brutal → persecution.

The conversion of Emperor Constantine to Christianity in 312 and the formal establishment by law of Trinitarian Christianity as the official religion of the Roman Empire in 380 ultimately fused these Roman and Christian laws and beliefs. The Roman Empire was now understood as the universal body of Christ on earth, embracing all persons and all things. Viewed as both pope and king, the Roman emperor reigned supreme in spiritual and temporal matters. Roman law was viewed as the pristine instrument of natural law and Christian morality.

This new → syncretism of Roman and Christian beliefs allowed the Christian church to imbue Roman law with a number of its basic teachings and to have them enforced throughout much of the empire — notably and most brutally against such heretics as the → Arians, Apollinarians, and → Manichaeans. Particularly in the great synthetic texts of Roman law, the Codex Theodosianus (438) and the Corpus Iuris

Civilis (565), Christian teachings on the → Trinity, the → sacraments, → liturgy, holy days, → Sabbath observance, → sexual ethics, → charity, → education, and much else were copiously defined and regulated. This firm legal establishment of Trinitarian Christianity contributed enormously both to its precocious expansion throughout the West and to its canonical preservation for later centuries.

This new syncretism of Roman and Christian beliefs, however, also subordinated the church to imperial rule. Christianity was now, in effect, the new imperial cult of Rome, presided over by the Roman emperor. The Christian clergy were, in effect, the new pontiffs of the Christian imperial cult, hierarchically organized and ultimately subordinate to imperial authority. The church's property was, in effect, the new public property of the empire, subject both to its protection and to its control. Thus Roman emperors and other political rulers convoked many of the church → councils and major synods; appointed, disciplined, and removed the higher clergy; administered many of the church's parishes, → monasteries, and charities; and legally controlled the acquisition, maintenance, and disposition of church property.

This so-called caesaropapist pattern of substantive influence but procedural subordination of church to state, and of the Christian religion to law, was largely accepted in the → Orthodox churches of the Byzantine Empire and its successor polities. Following the → political theology of John → Chrysostom (ca. 347-407), Gregory of Nyssa (ca. 330-ca. 395; → Cappadocian Fathers), and others, Eastern Orthodox clerics readily merged Christian and secular law and life, leaving legal and political matters primarily to the emperor or magistrate as vicars of Christ and devoting themselves primarily to Christian liturgy and teaching. This pattern sometimes met with more resistance in the West as strong clerics such as Gelasius I (492-96) and → Gregory the Great (590-604) insisted on a sharper separation of spiritual and secular law and authority. But with the rise of the great Germanic kings in the eighth and ninth centuries, notably Charlemagne of France and Alfred the Great of England, the Western church was also subjected to firm political rule and control. This pattern was often exacerbated by the growing practice in the West of placing church properties under feudal tenure and thus placing their clerical occupants under the control of local feudal lords (→ Feudalism).

3. The Papal Revolution
The second watershed period of the Western legal tradition came with the papal revolution, or Grego-

rian Reform, of the late 11th through 13th centuries. Beginning in 1075, the Roman Catholic clergy, led by → Gregory VII (1073-85), threw off their civil rulers and established the church as an autonomous legal and political corporation within Western Christendom. The church now claimed new jurisdiction (from Lat. *ius dico,* lit. the power to "speak the law") for the West. The church claimed personal jurisdiction over clerics, pilgrims, students, the poor, heretics, Jews, and Muslims. It claimed jurisdiction over the content of doctrine and liturgy; over ecclesiastical property, polity, and patronage; over sex, → marriage, and family life; over education, charity, and inheritance; and over oral promises, → oaths, various contracts, and all manner of moral, ideological, and sexual crimes. The church predicated these jurisdictional claims on its traditional authority over the Christian sacraments. It also predicated these claims on the papal power of the → keys, bequeathed by Christ to → Peter (Luke 22:32; Matt. 16:18-19) — a key of knowledge to discern God's word and will, and a key of power to implement and enforce that word and will throughout Christendom.

The church developed an elaborate pan-Western system of → church laws, called → canon law, to support these jurisdictional claims. Thousands of legal and ethical teachings drawn from the *Apostolic Constitutions,* patristic writings, and Christianized Roman law were collated and synthesized in the famous Decretum Gratiani (ca. 1140), the anchor text of medieval canon law. The Decretum was then heavily supplemented by papal and conciliar legislation and juridical glosses and commentaries, which were later integrated in the five-volume → Corpus Iuris Canonici. A vast hierarchy of church courts and officials administered this canon law in accordance with sophisticated new rules of procedure and evidence. A network of ecclesiastical officials presided over the church's executive and administrative functions. The medieval church registered its citizens through → baptism, taxed them through → tithes, conscripted them through the → Crusades, educated them through the church schools, and nurtured them through the cloisters and monasteries. The medieval church was, in F. W. Maitland's famous phrase, the first true → state in the West, and medieval canon law became the first → international law since the eclipse of classical Roman law half a millennium before.

This complex new legal system of the church attracted sophisticated new legal and political theories. The most original formulations came from such medieval jurists as Hostiensis (ca. 1200-1271),

Gandinus (ca. 1245-1311), Bartolus (1314-57), and Baldus (ca. 1327-1400), and from such medieval theologians as → Anselm (1033-1109), Abelard (1079-1142), Hugh of St.-Victor (1096-1141), and → Thomas Aquinas (ca. 1225-74). These writers reclassified the sources and forms of law, ultimately distinguishing (1) the eternal law of the creation order; (2) the natural laws of the Bible, → reason, and conscience; (3) the positive canon laws of the church; (4) the positive civil laws of the state; (5) the common laws of all nations and peoples; and (6) the customary laws of local communities. They developed enduring rules for the resolution of → conflicts among these types of laws, as well as for resolving contests of jurisdiction among their authors. They developed refined concepts of legislation, adjudication, and executive administration, as well as core constitutional concepts of sovereignty, election, and representation. They developed a good deal of the Western theory and law of chartered corporations, private associations, foundations, and trusts.

The medieval canon law developed sophisticated theories and forms of individual and corporate rights. Canon law defined the rights of the → clergy to their liturgical offices and ecclesiastical benefices, their exemptions from civil taxes and duties, and their immunities from civil prosecution and compulsory testimony. It defined the rights of ecclesiastical organizations like parishes, monasteries, charities, and guilds to form and dissolve, to accept and reject members, to establish order and discipline, to acquire, use, and alienate property. It defined the rights of church councils and synods to participate in the election and discipline of → bishops, abbots, and other clergy. It defined the rights of the laity to worship, evangelize, maintain religious symbols, receive the sacraments, travel on religious → pilgrimages, and educate their children. It defined the rights of the poor, widows, and needy to seek solace, succor, and sanctuary within the church. To be sure, such rights were not unguided by duties, nor were they available to all parties. Only the Catholic faithful — and notoriously not Jews, Muslims, or heretics — had full protection of rights, and their rights were to be exercised with appropriate ecclesiastical and sacramental constraints. But the formulations of basic medieval rights regarding exemptions, immunities, privileges, and benefits, as well as religious worship, travel, speech, and education, have persisted, with ever-greater inclusivity, to this day.

Medieval canon law also developed a sophisticated theory of canonical equity. The jurists referred to canon law variously as the mother of exceptions, the epitome of the law of love, and the mother of justice. As the *mother of exceptions,* canon law was flexible, reasonable, and fair, capable either of bending the rigor of a rule in an individual case through → dispensations and injunctions, or of punctiliously insisting on the letter of an agreement through orders of specific performance or reformation of documents.

As the *epitome of the law of love,* canon law afforded special care for the disadvantaged — widows, orphans, the poor, the handicapped, abused wives, neglected children, maltreated servants, and the like. It provided them with standing to press claims in church courts, competence to testify against their superiors without the permission of the latter, methods to gain succor and shelter from abuse and want, and opportunities to pursue pious and protected careers in the cloister.

As the *mother of justice,* canon law provided a method whereby the individual believer could reconcile himself or herself at once to God and to neighbor. Church courts treated both the legality and the morality of the conflicts before them. Their remedies enabled litigants to become righteous and just, not only in their relationships with opposing parties and the rest of the community, but also in their relationship to God. These features of canon law were all critical reasons for the enormous popularity and success of church courts in much of medieval Christendom.

4. The Protestant Reformation

The third watershed period in the Western legal tradition came with the transformation of canon law and civil law, and of church and state, in the Protestant Reformation. The Reformation was inaugurated by Martin → Luther (1483-1546) of Wittenberg in his famous posting of 95 theses in 1517 and his burning of the canon law and the papal bull *Exsurge, Domine* (1520), which condemned his views. The 16th-century Reformation, however, was the culmination of more than two centuries of dissent within the → Roman Catholic Church against some of its sacramental theology, liturgical practice, canon law, and ecclesiastical administration. The Reformation ultimately erupted in various quarters of western Europe in the early 16th century, settling into Lutheran, Calvinist, → Anabaptist, → Anglican, and → free church branches.

The early Protestant reformers — including Luther, John → Calvin (1509-64), → Menno Simons (1496-1561), and Thomas → Cranmer (1489-1556) — taught that salvation comes through faith in the gospel, not by works of law. Individuals stand directly before God, seek God's gracious for-

giveness of sin, and conduct life in accordance with the Bible and Christian conscience. To the reformers, Roman Catholic canon law obstructed the individual's relationship with God and obscured simple biblical norms for right living. The early Protestant reformers further taught that the church is at heart a community of saints, not a political corporation. Its cardinal signs and callings are to preach the Word, administer the sacraments, catechize the young, and care for the needy. To the reformers, the Catholic clergy's legal rules obstructed the church's divine mission and usurped the state's role as God's vice-regent. To be sure, the church must have internal rules of order to govern its own polity, teaching, and discipline (→ Church Government), and it must critique legal injustice and combat political illegitimacy. According to classic Protestant thought, however, law is primarily the province of the state not of the church, of the magistrate not of the minister.

These Protestant teachings helped to transform Western law in the 16th and 17th centuries. The Protestant Reformation permanently broke the international rule of the Roman Catholic Church and its canon law, splintering Western Christendom into competing nations and regions, each with its own religious and political ruler. The Protestant Reformation also triggered a massive shift of power and property from the church to the state. State rulers now assumed jurisdiction over numerous areas previously governed by the church and its canon law, including marriage and family life, property and testamentary matters, charity and poor relief, contracts and oaths, and moral and ideological crimes. Particularly in Lutheran and Anglican polities, the state also came to exercise considerable control over the clergy and over the polity and property of the church, in part in self-conscious emulation of the laws and practices of Christianized Rome.

These massive shifts in legal power and property from cleric to magistrate, from church to state, did not suddenly deprive Western law of its dependence upon → religion. Roman Catholic canon law remained an ineradicable part of the common law of the West in Catholic and Protestant polities alike. It was readily used both by church officials to govern their internal religious affairs and by civil authorities to govern matters of state. Moreover, in the Catholic polities of France, Spain, Portugal, and Italy, as well as in their many Latin American and African colonies, the legal and moral pronouncements of the Catholic episcopacy still often had a strong influence on the content of state law, and Roman Catholicism was the de facto, if not de jure, established and protected religion of many of these communities until the 20th century.

In Protestant polities of early modern Europe and the North American colonies (→ Colonialism), many new Protestant theological views came to direct and dramatic legal expression. For example, Protestant theologians replaced the traditional sacramental understanding of marriage with a new idea of the marital household as a "social estate" or "covenantal association" of the earthly kingdom. On that basis, Protestant jurists developed a new state law of marriage, featuring requirements of parental consent, state registration, church consecration, and peer presence for valid marital formation, as well as a law of absolute divorce on grounds of adultery, desertion, and other faults, with subsequent rights to remarry, at least for the innocent party. Protestant theologians replaced the traditional understanding of education as a → teaching office of the church with a new understanding of the public school as a "civic seminary" for all persons to prepare for their respective → vocations. On that basis, Protestant magistrates replaced clerics as the chief rulers of education, state law replaced church law as the principal law of education, and the general callings of all Christians replaced the special calling of the clergy as the raison d'être of education. Some Protestant theologians introduced a view of "three uses" of the law — political, theological, and didactic — particularly the → Decalogue. On that basis, Protestant jurists developed arresting new theories of natural law and equity, introduced sweeping changes in civil laws of social welfare and moral discipline, and developed an integrated theory of the retributive, deterrent, and rehabilitative functions of criminal law and ecclesiastical discipline.

Luther and Calvin emphasized that a person is at once saint and sinner (simul iustus et peccator). This anthropology, which later Protestants worked out in detail, became a firm foundation for later Western theories of → democracy and human rights. On the one hand, Protestants argued, every person in Christendom is created in the image of God and justified by → faith in God. Every person is called to a distinct vocation, which is equal in dignity and sanctity to all others. Every person is a prophet, priest, and king and is responsible to exhort, minister, and rule in the community. Every person thus stands equal before God and before his or her neighbor (→ Equality). Every person is vested with a natural liberty to live, to believe, and to love and serve God and neighbor. Every person is entitled to the vernacular Scripture, to education, to work in a vocation.

On the other hand, Protestants argued, every person is also sinful and prone to → evil and egoism. People individually need the restraint of the law to deter them from evil and to drive them to repentance, and they need the association of others to exhort, minister to, and rule them with law and with → love. Every person, therefore, is inherently a communal creature, belonging to a family, a church, and a political community.

These social institutions of family, church, and state, later Protestants argued, are divine in origin and human in organization (→ Social Systems). They are created by God and governed by godly ordinances. They stand equally before God and are called to discharge distinctive godly functions in the community. The family is called to rear and nurture children, to educate and discipline them, to exemplify love and cooperation. The church is called to preach the Word, administer the sacraments, educate the young, aid the needy. The state is called to protect order, punish crime, promote community. Though divine in origin, these institutions are formed through human covenants. Such covenants confirm the divine functions and the created offices of these institutions. Such covenants also organize these offices so that they are protected from the sinful excesses of the officials who occupy them. Family, church, and state are thus organized as public institutions, accessible and accountable to each other and to their members. Calvinists especially stressed that the church is to be organized as a democratic congregational polity, with a separation of ecclesiastical powers among → pastors, → elders, and → deacons; election of officers to limited tenures of office; and ready participation of the → congregation in the life and leadership of the church.

By the later 16th century, Protestant groups began to recast these theological doctrines into democratic norms and forms. Protestant doctrines of the → person and → society were cast into democratic social forms. Since all persons stand equal before God, they must stand equal before God's political agents in the state. Since God has vested all persons with natural liberties of life and belief, the state must ensure them of similar civil liberties. Since God has called all persons to be prophets, priests, and kings, the state must protect their constitutional → freedoms to speak, to preach, and to rule in the community. Since God has created persons as social creatures, the state must promote and protect a plurality of social institutions, particularly the church and the family.

Protestant doctrines of → sin, in turn, were cast into democratic political forms. The political office must be protected against the sinfulness of the political official. Political power, like ecclesiastical power, must be distributed among self-checking executive, legislative, and judicial branches of government. Officials must be elected to limited terms of office. Laws must be clearly codified, and discretion closely guarded. If officials abuse their office, they must be disobeyed. If they persist in their abuse, they must be removed, even if by revolutionary force or regicide. These Protestant teachings were among the driving ideological forces behind the revolts of the French → Huguenots, Dutch → Pietists, and Scottish Presbyterians against their monarchical oppressors in the later 16th and 17th centuries. They were critical weapons in the arsenal of the revolutionaries in England and America, and likewise were important sources of inspiration and instruction during the late 18th and 19th centuries, the great age of democratic construction in North America and western Europe.

5. The Enlightenment

The fourth watershed period in the Western legal tradition came with the 18th- and 19th-century Enlightenment. The Enlightenment was no single, unified movement but a series of diverse ideological movements in various academic disciplines and social circles of western Europe and North America. Enlightenment philosophers, such as David Hume (1711-76), Jean-Jacques Rousseau (1712-78), and Thomas Jefferson (1743-1826), offered a new secular theology of → individualism, → rationalism, and nationalism (→ Nation, Nationalism) to supplement, if not supplant, traditional Christian beliefs. The individual was no longer viewed primarily as a sinner seeking salvation in the life hereafter. To Enlightenment exponents, every individual was created equal in virtue and dignity (→ Human Dignity), vested with inherent rights of life, liberty, and property, and capable of choosing his or her own means and measure of → happiness. Reason was no longer the handmaiden of revelation, rational disputation no longer subordinate to homiletic declaration. The rational process, conducted privately by each person and collectively in the open marketplace of ideas, was considered a sufficient source of private morality and public law. The nation-state was no longer identified with a national church or a divinely blessed covenant people but was to be glorified in its own right. Its constitutions and laws were sacred texts reflecting the morals and mores of the collective national culture; its officials were secular priests representing the sovereignty and will of the people.

Such sentiments were revolutionary in their time and were among the driving forces of the national → revolutions in America and France and a principal catalyst for the reformation of many Western legal systems. They inspired sweeping legal changes in the late 18th and 19th centuries, including new constitutional provisions for limited government and ample civil liberties, new injunctions to separate → church and state, new criminal procedures and methods of criminal → punishment, new commercial, contractual, and other laws of the private marketplace, new laws of private property and inheritance, shifts toward a fault-based law of delicts and torts, the ultimate expulsion of slavery in America, and the gradual removal of discrimination based on race, religion, culture, and gender. Many Western nations also developed elaborate new codes of public and private law, transformed the curricula of their faculties of law, and radically reconfigured their legal professions.

The secular theology of the Enlightenment penetrated Western legal philosophy. Spurred on by Hugo Grotius's (1583-1645) famous statement that "natural law can exist even without the existence of God," jurists offered a range of secular legal philosophies, often abstracted from earlier Christian and Greco-Roman teachings. Writers from John Locke (1632-1704) to Thomas Paine (1737-1809) postulated a mythical state of nature that antedated and integrated human laws and natural rights. Nationalist myths were grafted onto this paradigm to unify and sanctify national legal traditions: Italian jurists appealed to their utopian Roman heritage; English jurists to their ancient constitution and Anglo-Saxon roots; French jurists to their Salic law; German jurists to their ancient constitutional liberties.

As these secular myths dissipated under the hot lights of early modern philosophical → skepticism, a triumvirate of new legal philosophies came to prominence in the later 18th and 19th centuries. *Legal → positivists,* such as Jeremy Bentham (1748-1832) and John Austin (1790-1859), contended that the ultimate source of law lies in the will of the legislature, and its ultimate sanction in political force. *Natural law theorists,* most notably Immanuel Kant (1724-1804), sought the ultimate source of law in pure reason and conscience, and its ultimate sanction in moral suasion. *Historical jurists,* such as Friedrich Karl von Savigny (1779-1861) and Otto von Gierke (1741-1921), contended that the ultimate source of law is the → custom and character of the *Volk,* and its ultimate sanction is communal condemnation (→ Historicism). These juxtaposed positivist, naturalist, and historicist legal philosophies have persisted in legal academies to this day, now heavily supplemented by an array of realist, socialist, feminist, and other schools of legal thought and with a growing number of interdisciplinary approaches that study law in interaction with the methods and texts of → theology, economics (→ Economy), → science, literature, → psychology, → sociology, and → anthropology.

The secular theology of the Enlightenment also transformed and secularized modern legal institutions. The cardinal secular beliefs of the Enlightenment came to prominent legal expression in the 20th century — individualism in constitutional doctrines of privacy; rationalism in the doctrines of freedom of speech, press, and assembly; nationalism in the totalitarian laws and polities of democracy, → fascism, and → socialism. In socialist polities, ambitious interpretation of the Enlightenment doctrine of separation of church and state led to campaigns to eradicate theistic religion altogether, a policy often manifest in the brutal martyrdom of the faithful and massive confiscations of religious property. In democratic polities, ambitious interpretation of the same separation of church and state doctrine has served to privatize theistic religion and to drive many religious communities from active participation in the legal and political process.

6. Law and Religion Today

Though these recent secular movements have removed traditional forms of religious influence on Western law, contemporary Western law still retains important connections with Christian and other religious ideas and institutions.

Even today, law and religion continue to cross over and cross-fertilize each other in a variety of ways. Law and religion are conceptually related. They both draw upon prevailing concepts of the nature of being and order, the person and community, knowledge and truth. They both embrace closely analogous doctrines of sin and crime, covenant and contract, → righteousness and justice, which invariably bleed together in the mind of the legislator, judge, and juror. Law and religion are methodologically related in that they share overlapping hermeneutical methods of interpreting authoritative texts, casuistic methods of converting principles to precepts, systematic methods of organizing their subject matters, pedagogical methods of transmitting the science and substance of their craft to students. Law and religion are institutionally related through the multiple relationships between political and religious officials and the multiple institutions in which these officials serve.

Even today, the laws of the secular state retain strong moral and religious dimensions. These dimensions are reflected not only in the substantive doctrines of private and public law that are derived from earlier Christian theology and canon law but also in the characteristic forms of contemporary legal systems. Every legitimate legal system has what Lon L. Fuller calls an inner morality — a set of attributes that bespeak justice and fairness. Its rules are generally applicable, publicly proclaimed and known, uniform, stable, understandable, nonretroactive, and consistently enforced. Every legitimate legal system has what Harold J. Berman calls an inner sanctity, a set of attributes that command the obedience, respect, and fear of both political authorities and their subjects. Like religion, law has authority — written or spoken sources, texts or oracles, that are considered to be decisive or obligatory in themselves. Law has → tradition — a continuity of language, practice, and institutions. Law has liturgy and ritual — the ceremonial procedures and words of the legislature, the courtroom, and the legal document that reflect and dramatize deep social feelings about the value and validity of the law.

Even today, religion maintains a legal dimension, an inner structure of legality, that gives religious lives and religious communities their coherence, order, and social form. Legal habits of the heart structure the inner spiritual life and discipline of religious believers, from the reclusive hermit to the aggressive zealot. Legal ideas of justice, order, atonement, restitution, responsibility, obligation, and others pervade the theological doctrines of countless religious traditions. Legal structures and processes — the Christian canon law, the Jewish → Halakah, the Muslim → Shari'a — continue to organize and govern religious communities and their distinctive beliefs and rituals, mores and morals.

In recent years the interaction of law and religion has attracted a considerable body of historical and theoretical scholarship. These interdisciplinary studies will be of vital importance as we continue the struggle to understand the concepts and commandments of law, justice, and order, and as we prepare Western law and Western culture for the emergence of a common law of all humanity in the new millennium.

Bibliography: C. K. Allen, *Law in the Making* (6th ed.; Oxford, 1958) • E. Barker, ed., *Social and Political Thought in Byzantium* (Oxford, 1957) • H. J. Berman, *Faith and Order: The Reconciliation of Law and Religion* (Atlanta, 1993); idem, *Law and Revolution: The Forma-*

tion of the Western Legal Tradition (Cambridge, 1983) • L. L. FULLER, *The Morality of Law* (rev. ed.; New Haven, 1969) • R. H. HELMHOLZ, *The Spirit of the Classical Canon Law* (Athens, Ga., 1996) • O. O'DONOVAN and J. L. O'Donovan, eds., *From Irenaeus to Grotius: A Sourcebook in Christian Political Thought, 100-1625* (Grand Rapids, 1999) • R. POUND, *Jurisprudence* (5 vols.; St. Paul, Minn., 1959) • G. TELLENBACH, *Church, State, and Christian Society at the Time of the Investiture Conflict* (London, 1959) • B. TIERNEY, *The Idea of Natural Rights: Studies on Natural Rights, Natural Law, and Church Law, 1150-1625* (Atlanta, 1997); idem, *Religion, Law, and the Growth of Constitutional Thought, 1150-1625* (Cambridge, 1982) • L. VALLAURI and G. DILCHER, eds., *Christentum, Säkularisation und modernes Recht* (2 vols.; Baden-Baden, 1981) • K. VOIGT, *Staat und Kirche von Konstantin dem Grossen bis zum Ende der Karolingerzeit* (Stuttgart, 1936) • J. WITTE JR., *Law and Protestantism: The Legal Teachings of the Lutheran Reformation* (New York, 2002); idem, *Religion and the American Constitutional Experiment: Essential Rights and Liberties* (Boulder, Colo., 2000).

JOHN WITTE JR.

Law, International → International Law

Law, Natural → Natural Law

Lay Apostolate

1. History
2. Use Today

1. History

For many centuries in Europe, the church (both Roman Catholic and eventually also Protestant, depending on the country) was closely intertwined with secular social structures. On matters of public policy, for example, church officials would regularly consort with the monarchy or the local lord or ruler, and religious holy days were celebrated as secular holidays. Likewise, the early guilds were organized as much around religious affiliation as they were around specific occupations.

As → society began to separate from the → church, becoming more and more autonomous, the nature of the relationship changed. The idea of the lay apostolate, which emerged in the late 19th century, was part of the → Roman Catholic Church's new strategy for influencing the world. The term itself was first associated with the Society of St. Vincent de Paul in France from as early as the 1860s.

Church leaders were aware that in the modern era → clergy could not easily enter factories, union halls, health and welfare facilities, nonparochial schools, government offices, and other centers of power. The lay apostolate was conceived, as Pius XI (1922-39) expressed it in his "Discourse to the Catholic Associations of Rome" (1931), as "participation of the laity in the apostolate of the → hierarchy." It was seen as a way of encouraging the laity to bring the gospel to a pluralistic world in which the church was just one social institution among many.

In particular, the lay apostolate movement offered Roman Catholics in Europe's → industrial centers an alternative to the Communist and Socialist movements, which were attracting considerable support among the working classes. The various lay apostolate organizations commissioned groups of "like-to-like" Catholics to bring about social change in their "special milieu," or specific situations. These groups would meet regularly for mutual support and to plan modest actions under the formula "see, judge, act." A priest would usually act as chaplain for each such group.

For example, Msgr. (later Cardinal) Joseph Cardijn of Belgium started small groups of young miners and other workers in his hometown in the 1920s. From the mid-1930s until the late 1950s, he served as general chaplain for the Young Christian Workers, which at one time had chapters in 64 countries around the world, including the United States and Canada. The lay apostolate movement was also the catalyst behind the Young Christian Students and the Christian Family Movement and was closely associated with the Christian Democratic political parties in Europe.

2. Use Today

The meaning and practice of the lay apostolate were debated at the Second → Vatican Council, which led to fundamental changes in how the vocation of the laity is perceived in the Roman Catholic Church. The council stressed → baptism, not priestly → ordination, as the foundation for the church's mission. The laity were no longer to be seen as merely participating in the mission of the clergy and hierarchy but rather as having a → vocation of their own in the workplace, family life, and community affairs. They "seek the → kingdom of God by engaging in temporal affairs and directing them according to God's will. They live in the world, that is, they are engaged in each and every work and business of the earth and in the ordinary circumstances of social and family life. . . . [They] contribute to the sanctification of the world, as from within like leaven, by fulfilling their own particular duties" (*Lumen gentium* 31).

The actual term "lay apostolate" is not used in a precise way today and in fact is falling into disuse. It is sometimes used to mean the opposite of lay ministry, which is usually defined as Christian service explicitly designated or commissioned by a parish or diocese, such as reading the Scriptures at mass, distributing communion, teaching religion classes, or performing acts of charity like feeding the hungry or caring for the homeless under the auspices of a church program.

Among Roman Catholics, at least, there is no consensus on what term to use for the apostolic activity Christians perform in the world, especially if it has not been chartered or organized by the church itself. Some Protestant denominations speak of "ministry in daily life," and some Catholics and others refer to "the spirituality of work." Still, the idea of laypeople connecting their faith with their daily life in real and meaningful ways continues to grow in all Christian denominations.

→ Clergy and Laity

Bibliography: T. BOKENKOTTER, *Church and Revolution* (New York, 1998) • Y. CONGAR, *Lay People in the Church* (Westminster, Md., 1965); idem, *Priests and Laymen* (London, 1966) • W. DROEL, *Full-Time Christians: The Real Challenge from Vatican II* (Mystic, Conn., 2002) • G. F. A. PIERCE, *Spirituality at Work: Ten Ways to Balance Your Life on-the-Job* (Chicago, 2001) • K. RAHNER, "Notes on the Lay Apostolate," *Theological Investigations* (vol. 2; Baltimore, 1963) 319-52 • M. WALSH and B. DAVIES, *Proclaiming Justice and Peace: Papal Documents from "Rerum novarum" through "Centesimus annus"* (rev. ed.; Mystic, Conn., 1991) • R. J. WICKS, ed., *Handbook of Spirituality for Ministers* (New York, 1995).

WILLIAM DROEL and
GREGORY F. AUGUSTINE PIERCE

Lay Movements

Overview
1. Key Developments in Christian History
    1.1. From the NT to the Council of Nicaea
    1.2. The Constantinian Era
    1.3. The Sixteenth Century
    1.4. From the Wars of Religion to World War I
2. The Twentieth-Century Advance
    2.1. Ecumenical Organizations
    2.2. Protestantism
    2.3. Eastern Orthodoxy
    2.4. Roman Catholicism
    2.5. The Century's Legacy

Overview

Until recently, the Christian laity has tended to be defined simply as the nonordained church membership. The long-standing second-class status of the laity within the churches has been reinforced by society's low opinion of nonprofessional laity in all fields.

Developments within the churches and society alike have led to a more positive view. Today Christian laity are increasingly regarded as baptized followers of Christ who are endowed with gifts of the Holy Spirit that fit them for service both within the church, where they labor together with → clergy, and within the world, where they bring the gospel to bear on the family, the workplace, and the community.

This momentous shift has occurred chiefly because of the power of lay movements — periodic efforts of Christians to recover a proper recognition of the role to which God calls the laity in fulfillment of the divine intention for the church and the world. Lay movements accelerated throughout the 20th century, assuming an unprecedented variety of institutional expression and generating an expanded volume of scholarship.

1. Key Developments in Christian History

1.1. *From the NT to the Council of Nicaea*

Across the centuries Christians have typically looked to the NT for understanding the divinely intended role of laypeople in the life and mission of the church. There they have discovered no separate prescription for either lay or clerical conduct. Indeed, *laïkos* (Gk. "of/from the people"), from which the word "laity" derives, does not appear, and *klēros* ("lot, allotment, inheritance"), the source of words such as "cleric" and "clergy," refers not to a single group but to the whole of the believing people (Col. 1:12; → People of God). Throughout, NT authors stress a single pattern of Christian life applicable to everyone who follows Christ. All are called to be → disciples and saints; each is linked with others by the power of the Spirit in bonds of → faith, → hope, and → love.

The first appearance of *laïkos* among Christian authors is in *1 Clem.* 40.5 (written ca. A.D. 95), referring to the ordering of Jewish → worship reflected in the OT. It appears to have had no influence upon subsequent authors, however, for the term does not occur again for approximately 100 years, appearing next in the writings of such leaders as → Tertullian, Clement of Alexandria, → Origen, and → Cyprian. Its usage among them was infrequent and varied. The term was likely taken from the secular Greek-speaking world, where laïkos refers to the local population, in contrast to the civil administration.

During the century before the First Council of → Nicaea (325), as the role of the clergy became increasingly elevated in authority and sanctity, the body constituting the laity was correspondingly viewed as occupying an inferior position. A main reason for this development was the church's gradual adoption of the deeply entrenched Greco-Roman sociopolitical pattern, in which civil authorities occupied a superior position (ordo) over the people.

The growing inequality of clergy and laity is evident, for example, in the statement that a → bishop is to love his laity like children, and they are to love him as "a father, a lord and God, after the almighty God" (Did. apos. 1.20, written ca. 230). In the same period Origen showed the influence of an antecedent practice within the Jewish community by teaching that the Christian clergy, like priests and Levites in the Hebrew Scriptures, must be free from material cares so that they can attend properly to the "law of God." Origen thus proposed that the chief "ministry of the laity" (the first appearance of this phrase) is to provide clerics with the material resources necessary for their upkeep.

The trend toward lay subordination was moderated in this period by the patent faithfulness and courage of countless numbers of rank-and-file Christian men and women who bore witness to their Lord amid the → persecutions inflicted by Roman authorities. This faithfulness was also evident in the persistence with which many "ordinary" Christians taught the gospel and reached out in compassion to the needs of their non-Christian neighbors. Never was the NT teaching about the → discipleship of all Christians entirely forgotten.

Nevertheless, the prevailing currents in the church and the world were moving in a different direction. It is not surprising that the pivotal Council of Nicaea, convened by Emperor Constantine, made only two passing mentions of the laïkos (cans. 5 and 19). Reflecting the widespread view of the inferior position of laypeople relative to that of the ordained, canon 19 refers to laity simply as those on whom hands have not been laid (→ Laying on of Hands).

1.2. The Constantinian Era
With the embrace of Christianity by Constantine (ruled 306-37), the stage was set for profound changes in the now imperially favored religion, including changes involving the continued ascent of the clergy and descent of the laity. A major early step came with Constantine's conferral of civil responsibilities and privileges upon bishops and other clergy. Clergy, for instance, were not required to pay taxes or perform military service, and some bishops developed such a taste for temporal power that in 343 the Council of Sardica chastised African bishops who were concerned only with their "dignity and profane affairs" and did not "help the poor, the laity, and the widows." The distinction between the two classes of Christians was further heightened by the gradual adoption of → celibacy as a sign of the clergy's complete dedication to Christ's service; the "inferior way" of family life was left to the laity. The clericalization of the church received significant philosophical and theological grounding by the teaching of → Gregory I (ca. 540-604) and Dionysius the Pseudo-Areopagite (ca. 500) that the hierarchical ordering within the church between those who lead and those who are led is God-given, reflecting the pattern woven by the Creator into → creation.

With the breakup of the → Roman Empire and the attendant social and cultural decline in Europe, the clergy's elevated position in → church and → society made them the chief recipients and custodians of → education. Laypeople, now largely blocked from the privilege of learning, bore for centuries the burdens of illiteracy (→ Literacy). This development went hand in hand with a new emphasis on the role of the → sacraments in human salvation, in the dispensing of which the clergy were the critical agents. The laity were thus reduced to the role of passive observers in the church's worship.

During the → Middle Ages the disempowering of the laity came to be more pronounced in Western Christendom than in Eastern Christendom. In the East the laity had continuing access to education and played an active role in theological reflection, the → liturgy, the training of clergy, and decision-making processes in general (→ Church Government). Lay Christian rulers in the East were not subject to anything like the Western popes, who argued forcefully for the superiority of the spiritual order over the temporal. For the → Orthodox the way was thus open for emergence of a harmony between the spiritual and the temporal, between clergy and laity, that has been evident in modern times.

Movement in the West toward a challenge of the laity's subordination began in the 11th century, a primary catalyst for which was the revival of schools and the increased availability of education to growing numbers of people. The rise of commerce was a further stimulus. Christian laypeople now were acquiring the ability to read the Bible and a mind-set to think for themselves.

Beginning in the first half of the 11th century and continuing into the 15th, these new forces contributed to the rise of numerous reform efforts, notably by the Albigenses and → Waldenses in France, the → Hussites in Bohemia, and the Lollards in England. These four groups, which made recovery of the role of the laity a significant objective and may themselves thus be considered lay movements, were rejected as heretical by church authorities. Other groups more acceptable to Rome sought a return to simple, Christlike forms of life and service that they hoped would be embraced by the laity. Some within this latter number, notably the → Franciscans, were soon integrated into the prevailing clergy-dominated church structures. Others, however — particularly the → Brethren of the Common Life, a movement that arose in the Netherlands as part of a trend toward mystical expressions of Christianity, and a comparable group for women, the Sisters of the Common Life — managed to maintain a lay focus.

1.3. *The Sixteenth Century*

The climax of reform initiatives that had been building for generations occurred in 16th-century Europe. The laity were not the major focus of the controversies of this tumultuous time, but the changes promoted by the → Reformers included a new understanding of the role of the laity and new expressions of their role in everyday life.

Although different forms of → Protestantism emerged during the → Reformation, to varying extents they each embraced certain key insights that led to the ground-breaking changes initiated by Martin → Luther (1483-1546) in Germany. Luther taught that all Christians, laity and clergy alike, have equal standing before God in that all are joined by → baptism and faith to Christ and thus share in his priesthood. Moreover, all Christians have access to the Word and are called to serve God. Luther's energy and creativity led to a rich implementation of these core theological convictions. He translated the Bible into German (→ Bible Versions), the language of the people, and prepared vernacular liturgies, → hymns, and → catechisms for the use of laypeople.

Ordinary Christian people now had a clarity about their faith, and an eagerness to express it, which had not been present since the early centuries of the church. In many parts of Europe, Christian laymen and laywomen came into a new prominence within the Protestant churches, and large numbers of them were energized by their faith to implement the gospel message in all areas of their lives. Protestantism thus became the first great lay movement in Christian history.

Coexisting with the changes were important continuities with the past. For example, the need was widely recognized for having special ministers set apart for leadership within the church. This practice, however, was never developed in a way that generated a subordination of laity as complete as that which had existed in medieval Europe. Nevertheless, a distancing between clergy and laity began to be apparent within the Lutheran churches in Germany before the end of the 16th century. The → pastor's learning and his responsibility for knowing and communicating biblical truth so elevated his role that it tended to diminish the laity. This trend grew stronger and spread to other Protestant churches.

During the 16th century, powerful reforming currents continued to flow within the → Roman Catholic Church. Some of this energy was spent countering Protestant theological claims, and some of it was directed at seeking new forms of Christian understanding and life that better reflected the gospel. Like the Catholic reform effort generally, the Council of → Trent, convened in 1545 by Paul III (1534-49), became so intent on differentiating Catholic positions from those of Protestants that it contributed substantially to a reassertion of many traditional positions. One of the council's major achievements was to set in motion the founding of diocesan seminaries, which eventually gave effective attention to the training of men for the priesthood (→ Theological Education). Also, an important catechism from this period, the → Catechismus Romanus (1566), noted that the church can be understood as "prelates and pastors of the church." This picture of a clergy-centered church (not others more reflective of Scripture, also noted in the catechism) subsequently became a central theme in the teaching of such influential leaders as Robert → Bellarmine and Peter Canisius.

1.4. *From the Wars of Religion to World War I*

As religious outlooks hardened among Protestants and Roman Catholics in the 16th and 17th centuries, theological polemics came to be linked with social and political divisions, which led to bloody wars between embittered European Christians (→ Thirty Years' War). Soon, in reaction against this degrading of the religious spirit, some in both Catholic and Protestant camps sought to recover the gospel in a way that allowed hearts and minds to be freshly nourished and enlivened. The result was a steady stream of new expressions of Christian faith, most of which led to a rise of a sense of responsibility among the laity for the church's life and mission.

The writings of Francis de Sales (1567-1622), the Roman Catholic bishop of Geneva (from 1602), played a formative role. Francis found a ready audience for his claims that all Christians, not just the clergy, are called to holiness and that religion must be related to every aspect of life. Gaston de Renty (1611-49), a French Catholic layman, took this message to heart and expressed it in a variety of ways; his widely read biography, translated into German by Lutherans and into English by an Anglican, gave his life far-reaching influence. One of Renty's friends, a master shoemaker named Henry Michel Buch (1598-1666), was inspired to establish the Frères Cordonniers (Shoemakers' brotherhood), a lay Catholic society whose purpose was to promote holiness among the members in the exercise of their craft (→ Sanctification). Similar developments continued and expanded among Roman Catholics throughout much of Europe.

A comparable development occurred among Lutherans in Germany, as → Pietist leaders such as Philipp Jakob Spener (1635-1705) and August Hermann → Francke (1663-1727) came to recognize that the NT call to discipleship applies to every Christian. Especially crucial was the Pietists' conviction that Christian witness is to be carried out by laypeople, not only in the everyday routines of family and work, but also among people in faraway places who have not yet heard the gospel message. So strong did this conviction become that Pietist influence, together with that of English-speaking Evangelicals, was a major force stimulating the global missionary outreach that arose in the 18th and 19th centuries among Protestants in both Europe and North America (→ British Missions; North American Missions).

Not just to Asia, Africa, and Latin America did awakened Protestants seek to impart the gospel. Many saw firsthand that people in so-called Christian Europe were being battered by the new forces of industrialization and urbanization (→ Industrial Society); large numbers too were being turned away from the churches and Christian values by a rising tide of secularist ideology (→ Secularism). In response, numerous fresh initiatives were taken in the 19th century, often under the leadership of Christian laymen and laywomen, to bring the gospel to bear on these situations and among these people. For many of the leaders, such as the Anglican Evangelicals who formed the Clapham Sect in England, the way forward was via a voluntary society (→ Voluntarism), through which like-minded individuals could collaborate in a common task. For others,

such as leaders of the → Inner Mission in Germany and their counterparts among Protestants in many countries around the world, it was preferable to create institutions such as schools and hospitals where dedicated, trained laypeople would take responsibility for administering tangible expressions of Christian service (→ Medical Missions).

This accelerating demonstration of Christian laypeople's concern to implement the church's mission in the world was accompanied by a comparable, though usually more muted, expression of growing lay responsibility for the internal life of the church. It was evident especially among churches in Great Britain and the United States, where the presence both of a democratic-type church polity and of egalitarian social currents was strongest. This development was seen, for example, in the prominence of the lay preacher and the class meeting within → Methodism, and in the governance role played by laypeople among Baptists in such matters as selecting their preacher, owning church property, and managing budgets.

In the Roman Catholic Church the → pope, bishops, and other clergy proved far less willing to concede a place for lay leadership. A small though significant step in this direction was taken in 1905, however, when Pius X (1903-14), in his decree *Sacra Tridentina Synodus,* called for a more active and informed participation of Catholic laity in the → mass. It was a harbinger of later changes.

2. The Twentieth-Century Advance

The 20th century began with people in many parts of the world unusually optimistic about the → progress they believed human inventiveness would now achieve. As decades passed, however, this → optimism was chastened by a series of crises, and it became evident that the emerging global civilization was imperiled by grave threats of human making. Nevertheless, through all the crises, people in every land continued to work with hope for change, realizing that the times required new patterns of thought and action.

The churches were influenced by this climate, often being represented in creative vanguards that made a mark upon the century. This accomplishment was due largely to the more active part played by Christian laypeople in the affairs of both the church and the world. So substantial was this lay engagement that the 20th century has been aptly called the century of the laity.

2.1. *Ecumenical Organizations*

During much of the 20th century a striking leadership role on behalf of lay renewal was played by a variety of ecumenical organizations that now, as never before, drew Christians together across denominational and national boundaries. One of the most powerful of these ecumenical lay movements consisted of associations of university students, present in countries around the world. Starting in the latter part of the 19th century with such organizations as the Student Volunteer Movement, the → YMCA and → YWCA, and the → World's Student Christian Federation, the university Christian movement grew steadily to include large numbers of young men and women who were gripped by a new vision of the gospel's demands upon the church and the world.

Two of the young people decisively shaped by their involvement in the ecumenical student associations were John R. → Mott (1865-1955) and Joseph H. Oldham (1874-1969). Each of these laymen gave extraordinary leadership to the emerging ecumenical movement, and each contributed significantly to keeping the rediscovery of the laity before this movement in its formative years. Oldham, as a leader of the Universal Christian Council on → Life and Work, nudged that pioneering ecumenical organization, at its 1937 Oxford conference, to recognize the critical role of laypeople's → vocations in closing the gap between the church and the secular world. "Nothing could be plainer," he wrote in a preparatory volume for the conference, "than that if the Christian faith is in the present and future to bring about changes, as it has done in the past, in the thought, habits and practices of society, it can only do this through being the living, working faith of multitudes of lay men and women conducting the ordinary affairs of life" (W. A. → Visser 't Hooft and J. H. Oldham, 117).

Oldham also played a major role in shaping the → World Council of Churches (WCC), launched formally in Amsterdam in 1948, and in turning its attention to lay witness in the world. Other early leaders of the WCC shared his passion and helped give it institutional expression. Under the leadership of Dutch lay theologian Hendrik Kraemer (1888-1965) and French lay theologian Suzanne de Diétrich (1891-1981), the laity's role became a principal issue in the early programs of the Ecumenical Institute, established by the WCC at the Château de Bossey, near Geneva. Hundreds of laity and clergy from churches around the world were moved by their experience at Bossey to carry its founding vision back to their homelands.

In 1954 the Second Assembly of the WCC affirmed that "as Christ came to minister, so must all Christians become ministers of his saving purpose

according to the particular gift of the Spirit which each has received." It implemented this theological conviction by creating a Department on the Laity within its administrative structures. The department's staff leader, Swiss pastor Hans-Ruedi Weber, together with others such as British layman Mark Gibbs, were effective emissaries of the lay cause.

By the late 1960s, however, it was evident that growing numbers of church leaders active in WCC circles from developing nations were not as attracted to this way of approaching Christian discipleship as was the earlier generation of ecumenical leaders. For them, chronic problems within their lands (esp. poverty, injustice, and marginalization) required urgent attention, and they successfully pushed for a recasting of WCC programs and organizational structures so as to focus on these problems. By 1971 the Department on the Laity no longer existed as a distinct office, and lay issues retreated to a secondary importance. Concurrently, the council's → Faith and Order section, which had long addressed divisive ecclesiological issues, published a major consensus statement named *Baptism, Eucharist, and Ministry* (1982). The document showed significant progress among theologians and churches toward agreement on these three issues, but it gave only scant attention to their bearing on the laity. By the last decades of the 20th century, the WCC was no longer the leader it had once been in focusing the churches' attention on recognizing and ending the subordination of the laity.

2.2. Protestantism

During the decades following World War II, Protestants in many lands undertook fresh initiatives that affirmed the laity's role in the church's mission to the world. Many were stimulated by exposure to the WCC's activity in this field; others derived inspiration from different sources. Though they typically had little contact with each other, virtually all shared a lively awareness of God's calling to Christians to serve the divine purposes in the world at a time of far-reaching global change. Together their efforts constituted a multifaceted lay movement surpassing any that had previously appeared among Protestants.

One strand of this prodigious effort was the appearance of a substantial body of literature whose authors probed major issues regarding the laity's role in church and world. The most influential volumes included H. Kraemer's *Theology of the Laity* (1958), which argues that any lasting lay renewal must be grounded in a reconceptualization of the church that recognizes the centrality of the church's mission in the world and the place of laypeople on the leading edge of this mission. *The Layman in Christian History* (1963), a collection of 16 essays edited by Stephen C. Neill and H.-R. Weber, explores the historical ebb and flow of lay renewal with a comprehensiveness never before attempted. In their book *God's Frozen People* (1964), Mark Gibbs and T. Ralph Morton probe the numerous ways that centuries of clericalization continue to affect the churches. And William Diehl proposes in *The Monday Connection* (1991) that Christians seek to make their impact upon work, home, and community through a deliberate, five-pronged ministry of competency, presence, → ethics, change, and → lifestyle.

Two important expressions of the 20th-century Protestant lay movement first appeared in Germany. Reinold von Thadden-Trieglaff (1891-1976) led the way by organizing a church conference known as Kirchentag, a weeklong gathering of German Protestants for the deepening of their faith and the exploration of its relevance to issues confronted in daily life. Begun in 1949 and held every two years, the Kirchentag typically has brought together well over 100,000 people in major German cities. For layman von Thadden, a principal reason for this endeavor was his conviction that it is "the crucial task of our generation to enable the laity to witness to the Christian faith in economics, in their jobs, and in → politics" (415).

Other German Protestants took steps to bring together small groups known as evangelical academies for intense dialogue about the relevance of Christian faith to contemporary social problems. By 1980 there were 19 such academies, most of them in West Germany. A special feature of their programs has been the bringing together of people active in the church with others who are not. Both the Kirchentag and the academy initiatives attracted favorable attention among Protestants in other countries, and soon comparable efforts were under way elsewhere. Especially striking has been the spread of lay academies and retreat centers in other countries; by the 1990s several hundred were to be found around the world, on all six continents, with programs involving a wide range of topics and participants.

Among Protestants in the United States, three other features of the lay movement have received especially notable expression. The national governing bodies of most major denominations incorporated statements affirming the ministry of the laity within their charter documents, and some also established national agencies to encourage implementation of denominational positions in congregations across the country. Second, some theological seminaries have inaugurated programs aimed both at working directly with laypeople to strengthen their ministries and at helping future clergy recognize that lay empowerment is a critical part of their ordained ministries. Finally, scores of small independent organizations have been established to encourage and strengthen laypeople's witness in the world. Many of them, such as the InterVarsity Christian Fellowship's Marketplace Ministry and the Fellowship of Companies for Christ International, are directed by, and appeal to, Christians primarily within conservative, evangelical expressions of Protestantism (→ Evangelical Movement). Such lay initiatives as these have also appeared, in varying forms, in other countries.

2.3. *Eastern Orthodoxy*

The 20th century also saw a resurgence of lay activity within the Eastern Orthodox churches. Through much of this period, traditional patterns of Orthodox life were disrupted by the rise of Communist governments in Eastern Europe. With the crushing burden of persecution often placed upon priests and bishops, laypeople took ever more responsible leadership roles within their churches. They thus built upon foundations of ecclesial communion established in earlier centuries, and they became eager participants in the rediscovery of the laity occurring within ecumenical organizations.

A notable early instance of Orthodox lay renewal was the Russian Student Christian Movement, founded in 1923 by Russian émigrés in Czechoslovakia. Engaging the participation of leading Russian theologians, this student venture, like counterparts within Protestantism, contributed significantly to the invigoration of Orthodoxy within both Europe and North America. Another important example of lay initiative, formed 12 years earlier in Greece, is the Zoë (Life) Brotherhood. Its members, all theologically educated, commit themselves to spending part of the year living in community, then to serving churches throughout Greece, usually as preachers and teachers.

A third, more comprehensive lay venture within the Orthodox churches is Syndesmos (Bond of unity), the World Fellowship of Orthodox Youth. Established in 1953 to foster communication between Orthodox youth organizations in Western Europe and the Middle East, Syndesmos grew into an association of some 70 youth organizations and theological schools in 32 nations. Its members have been especially active in the revival of → Orthodox missions, the encouragement of Orthodox involvement in the ecumenical movement, the pursuit of Orthodox unity, and the promotion of eucharistic renewal within the Orthodox churches.

2.4. *Roman Catholicism*

Roman Catholic laity were encouraged to play a more active role in both church and world by most 20th-century popes. A major step came during the pontificate of Pius XI (1922-39), who in 1931 gave fresh impetus to the involvement of laypeople in the hierarchically controlled network of organizations called → Catholic Action. Through participation in such diverse organizations as Young Christian Students, the Legion of Decency, and the Christian Family Movement, Catholic laymen and laywomen took an increasingly active part in this papal-inspired initiative to rebuild Christian foundations for Western society. The growth of the Catholic lay movement was also actively promoted by Pius XII (1939-58), who in 1951 and 1957 convened world congresses on the → lay apostolate in Rome.

The next two popes, John XXIII (1958-63) and Paul VI (1963-78), encouraged the epochal Second → Vatican Council to make lay issues a prominent part of its agenda. Lay renewal, in fact, was a major consequence of the council's actions. This came partly through particular lay-focused pronouncements made on such matters as the active role laypeople should play in parish councils, worship, and outreach; it came partly, too, in the way the laity's status was upgraded through pronouncements on more fundamental theological themes such as those which viewed the church as consisting of all the baptized and as called by God to seek the transformation of the world through involvement in the ordinary routines of daily life. During the pontificate of John Paul II (1978-) the renewing momentum generated by the council was at times slowed, but it continued in such initiatives as John Paul's 1981 encyclical *Laborem exercens*, on human work, and his convening in 1987 of the World Synod on the Laity.

Initiatives for lay renewal, though frequently directed by the → hierarchy, also increasingly came from Roman Catholic laypeople themselves. Within their worldwide communion, perhaps the most striking new manifestation of lay responsibility was the proliferation of small groups of laypeople called → base communities, which began in Brazil in the 1950s and spread widely in Latin America, as well as in Africa and Asia. Functioning usually without priests, these groups met regularly for worship, Bible study, and mutual support; a prime objective was to discover the gospel's relevance for personal life and for broader social, political, and economic problems (→ House Church).

In North America and Europe a variety of Roman Catholic organizations emerged in the post-conciliar period to implement the council's encouragement of an active lay apostolate in secular life. Two of the most prominent were in the United States. The Woodstock Business Conference, sponsored by the Jesuit-led Woodstock Theological Center in Washington, D.C., convened Catholic business executives in metropolitan areas across the country for periodic discussion of ways to bring Christian values into their organizations. And the National Center for the Laity, created in 1977 in Chicago, sought to counterbalance what it considered a too-great concentration by clerical leadership on recruiting laypeople for the performance of parish roles traditionally filled by priests. Center leaders believed — like their counterparts in some Protestant organizations — that dwindling supplies of clergy should not be allowed to become the occasion for slighting the laity's primary calling to be the church in the world. The center's concern was effectively served by publication of a series of booklets exploring how Christians can practice their spirituality in such vocational realms as business, farming, law, nursing, and military service.

2.5. *The Century's Legacy*

By the end of the 20th century, lay movements had brought an extraordinary surge of Christian lay involvement in the life and mission of the churches. It was also clear, however, that the massive weight of the past still kept multitudes of Christians tied to familiar patterns of lay subordination and passivity. Even when individual clergy and laypeople wished to break from the old ways, they often found themselves unwittingly repeating them, so strong was the power of habit and the lingering force of long-standing theological and institutional traditions.

Nevertheless, the most important legacy from 20th-century lay movements was a recognition that the grip of the old ways can be broken and that a different, more faithful pattern is possible for the whole Christian community. Never before has the time seemed so propitious for mounting a sustained effort among all the churches to understand the laity's integral place in all aspects of the churches' life and mission and to implement that vision with bold new action and enduring institutional reform.

Some of the possibilities for the 21st century can be suggested in the form of three questions:

1. Has not the time come for all Christians to reclaim the NT vision and name lay subordination and passivity as a grave aberration?
2. Has not the time come to gather the widely diverse, largely isolated groups seeking lay renewal into regular communication and fellowship, so

that mutual learning and collaborative action can occur?

3. Has not the time come for a larger portion of the theological and institutional resources of the churches to be deployed in addressing both the conceptual and practical issues that impede full-scale lay renewal?

If such questions are pursued with patience and persistence, a far-reaching change, now only barely perceived, may well occur.

→ Ecumenism, Ecumenical Movement

Bibliography: N. APOSTOLA, ed., *A Letter from Christ to the World: An Exploration of the Role of the Laity in the Church Today* (Geneva, 1998) • Y. CONGAR, *Lay People in the Church: A Study for a Theology of Laity* (London, 1985) • W. DIEHL, *The Monday Connection: On Being an Authentic Christian in a Weekday World* (San Francisco, 1993) • L. DOOHAN, *The Laity: A Bibliography* (Wilmington, Del., 1987) • A. FAIVRE, *The Emergence of the Laity in the Early Church* (New York, 1990) • M. FRAKES, *Bridges to Understanding: The "Academy Movement" in Europe and North America* (Philadelphia, 1960) • M. GIBBS and T. R. MORTON, *God's Frozen People: A Book for and about Christian Laymen* (Philadelphia, 1965) • H. KRAEMER, *A Theology of the Laity* (Philadelphia, 1958) • S. NEILL and H.-R. WEBER, eds., *The Layman in Christian History* (Philadelphia, 1963) • K. B. OSBORNE, *Ministry: Lay Ministry in the Roman Catholic Church; Its History and Theology* (New York, 1993) • *Reopening the Ecumenical Discussion of the Laity* (= ER 45/ 4 [1993]) • R. STEVENS, *The Other Six Days: Vocation, Work, and Ministry in Biblical Perspective* (Grand Rapids, 1999) • R. VON THADDEN-TRIEGLAFF, "The Kirchentag and the Renewal of the Church," *ER* 9 (1956/57) 410-18 • W. A. VISSER 'T HOOFT and J. H. OLDHAM, *The Church and Its Function in Society* (London, 1937) • H.-R. WEBER, *A Laboratory for Ecumenical Life: The Story of Bossey, 1946-1996* (Geneva, 1996) • WORLD COUNCIL OF CHURCHES, *Laici in Ecclesia: An Ecumenical Bibliography on the Role of the Laity in the Life and Mission of the Church* (Geneva, 1961).

PAUL M. MINUS

Lay Preaching

The obvious meaning of the phrase "lay preaching" is church proclamation by members of the congregation who are not ordained. The → primitive Christian community was acquainted with speaking at worship as the Spirit freely prompted (1 Corinthians 14). In the → early church, however, speaking was by right of office.

The wandering preachers of the → Waldenses and mendicant orders encountered prohibitions from the 12th century onward. The → Reformation allowed lay preaching in case of need. Martin → Luther (1483-1546) and article 14 of the → Augsburg Confession put increasing stress on orderly calling as opposed to preaching without qualifications. The Reformed confessional writings allowed lay preaching by → elders and → deacons when no pastors were available. → Pietism and revivalism encouraged free personal testimonies. J. H. Wichern (1808-81), founder of the German → Inner Mission, wanted the lay preaching of trained assistants of pastors in his mission to the people. In the German → church struggle during World War II, lay preaching provided an emergency ministry in fraternal orders. Contemporary church orders provide for lay preaching by elders, assistants, or → lectors, whose task is to supplement the preaching of theologians, a practice that will continue even when shortages of ministers end.

→ Baptists, Lutherans (at least in theological education for clergy), and others like → Methodist churches provide for a great deal of supervised lay preaching. Lay preachers with or without some kind of certification officiate at prayer times and at → worship in discharge of the duty of proclamation that Methodism, for example, has always seen to be that of all church members. This practice relaxes the distinction between → clergy and laity and has made a special impact upon the Reformation churches in America. The → Anglican Communion and → Lutheran churches have lay readers for liturgical and pastoral duties. Roman Catholic → canon law in its new form allows episcopally sanctioned lay preaching at worship in exceptional cases but not at the celebration of the → Eucharist, at least in the form of the homily, which only a → priest or deacon may give. The lay preaching that has developed in many countries since → Vatican II rests on a liberal interpretation of these rules and has been reinforced, as in other ecclesial bodies, by the shortage of clergy that began in the 1980s.

Bibliography: P. W. CHILCOTE, *John Wesley and the Women Preachers of Early Methodism* (Metuchen, N.J., 1991) • N. FOLEY, *Preaching and the Non-ordained: An Interdisciplinary Study* (Collegeville, Minn., 1983) • G. MILLBURN and M. BATTY, eds., *Workaday Preachers: The Story of Methodist Local Preaching* (Peterborough, 1995) • P. A. PARACHINI, *Lay Preaching: State of the Question* (Collegeville, Minn., 1999).

ALBERT STEIN†

Laying on of Hands

The gesture of laying hands on or over a person or an object conveys varied significance as an act of blessing, confirming, consecrating, commissioning, ordaining, setting apart for special use, absolving, → healing, and other related uses. The act is understood to convey the transmission of authority, special grace, or spiritual power from someone recognized as specially authorized or charismatically endowed.

In the OT, laying on of hands is used to transmit a vital force (Gen. 48:14-20), to identify the offerer (Leviticus 1–8) or the transfer of → sin (Lev. 16:21) in the sacrificial cult (→ Sacrifice), and to transfer the charisma of office from an incumbent to a successor (Num. 27:18-23; Deut. 34:9).

In the NT, laying on of hands is used as a gesture of → blessing (Mark 10:16), a therapeutic action (Mark 6:5; 8:23-25; Luke 4:40), an imparting of the Spirit (Acts 8:14-19; 19:5-6), a setting apart of public ministers (Acts 6:1-6; 13:1-3), and for the purpose of → ordination to office (1 Tim. 4:14; 5:22).

The laying on of hands played an important role in rites of Christian → initiation in the ancient church. It was used to → exorcise and to bless catechumens when they were dismissed from the assembly after the liturgy of the Word and to receive the newly baptized into the eucharistic assembly. From this latter use laying on of hands evolved into the distinctive gesture of the rite of → confirmation. In postbaptismal ceremonies, the gesture was often used in conjunction with → anointing and signified the imparting of the gift of the → Holy Spirit.

Laying on of hands is also the central gesture in rites of → ordination. Semikahs, or rabbinic ordinations in early Judaism, almost certainly included the laying on of hands, but it is debatable whether this → Jewish practice influenced Christian ordination, was influenced by Christian ordination, or developed independently of Christian ordination. In the *Apostolic Tradition*, attributed to Hippolytus (ca. 170-ca. 236), the laying on of hands was applied to → bishops, presbyters (→ Elder), and → deacons. In ordination the gesture occurs in conjunction with a prayer for the bestowal of the Holy Spirit. The traditions that believe in the apostolic succession of bishops regard the laying on of hands on a new bishop by those who have been similarly ordained as bishops to be an essential sign. The laying on of hands often occurs in acts of blessing at installations of bishops and pastors, for the → consecration of deaconesses, and for the commissioning of → missionaries.

Laying on of hands is used to convey the promise of God in absolution, acts of healing, and marriages.

In liturgical orders of individual or corporate confession, those who confess sins may receive the laying on of hands in conjunction with the declaration of absolution (→ Confession of Sins). The laying on of hands has accompanied anointing in rites of → pastoral care of the sick and dying. While Reformation churches abolished extreme unction, rites of healing with → anointing and the laying on of hands are being renewed in many traditions today. Laying on of hands is commonly used in → marriage services to apply the blessing of God on marriage in general to the newly wedded couple, although in the Roman tradition the nuptial blessing was given only to the bride.

Laying on of hands may be used as a general act of blessing. Raising one's hands in → benediction is a general blessing of the assembly. Newly ordained → Roman Catholic priests often give a blessing to those who attend their ordination or first mass. In → monasteries the gesture is used for those going on a journey.

Laying on of hands may be applied to material elements in the blessing of water in → baptism and over the bread and wine of the → Eucharist at the epiclesis. It is also used in Roman Catholicism in the blessing of holy → water and other → sacramentals.

→ Liturgy

Bibliography: H. BANTING, "Imposition of Hands in Confirmation: A Medieval Problem," *JEH* 7 (1956) 147-59 • C. HARRIS, "Visitation of the Sick: Unction, Imposition of Hands, and Exorcism," *Liturgy and Worship* (ed. W. K. Lowther Clarke; New York, 1932) 472-540 • L. A. HOFFMAN, "Jewish Ordination on the Eve of Christianity," *StLi* 13 (1979) 11-41 • A. KAVANAGH, *Confirmation: Origins and Reform* (New York, 1988) • E. J. KILMARTIN, "Ministry and Ordination in Early Christianity against a Jewish Background," *StLi* 13 (1979) 42-69 • P. PFATTEICHER, *Commentary on the Occasional Services* (Philadelphia, 1983) • B. POSCHMANN, *Penance and the Anointing of the Sick* (New York, 1964) • R. W. QUERE, "The Spirit and the Gifts Are Ours: Imparting or Imploring the Spirit in Ordination Rites," *LQ* 27 (1975) 322-46 • K. W. STEVENSON, *Nuptial Blessing: A Study of Christian Marriage Rites* (New York, 1983).

FRANK C. SENN

Lebanon

1. General Situation
2. Christian Churches
3. Muslim and Jewish Communities
4. Religion and State

	1960	1980	2000
Population (1,000s):	1,857	2,669	3,289
Annual growth rate (%):	2.94	−0.01	1.45
Area: 10,230 sq. km. (3,950 sq. mi.)			

A.D. 2000

Population density: 321/sq. km. (833/sq. mi.)
Births / deaths: 2.06 / 0.62 per 100 population
Fertility rate: 2.41 per woman
Infant mortality rate: 25 per 1,000 live births
Life expectancy: 71.0 years (m: 69.1, f: 72.9)
Religious affiliation (%): Christians 52.9 (Roman Catholics 42.4, Orthodox 15.9, indigenous 4.3, other Christians 1.2), Muslims 42.6, nonreligious 3.4, atheists 1.0, other 0.1.

1. General Situation

The modern state of Lebanon was created by declaration of France, which held a mandate over it when the Ottoman Empire collapsed in 1920. It was first called Grand Liban, but in 1926 the constitution named it the Republic of Lebanon.

Apart from coastal states that were occupied by the Crusaders in the 12th and 13th centuries, this area of the Near East had been under Muslim rule for almost 1,300 years. Because of the inaccessibility of the high parts of Lebanon and the politics of the Muslim rulers, the communities of the Christians and the Druze (an Islamic sect) were able to survive and even, after 1861, to enjoy some measure of autonomy in the separate district of Mount Lebanon.

In 1932 Christians made up 50 percent of the population, which was then 785,000 (Maronites composed 29 percent of the population, Greek Orthodox 10 percent, Greek Catholics 6 percent, with the remaining 5 percent a mixture of Assyrians of the East, evangelicals, and others). The Muslims then numbered 49 percent (Sunni 22 percent, Shiite 20 percent, and Druze 7 percent). Since then, the population has multiplied over fourfold. Although there are varying reports of the relative Muslim-Christian balance, according to the national constitution the population continues to be considered 50 percent Christian and 50 percent Muslim.

2. Christian Churches

2.1. At the Council of → Chalcedon in 451, the Maronite Church decided against the so-called → Monophysites and thus came into conflict with the → Syrian Orthodox Church of Antioch. At the same time, it retained its independence from the Greek → Orthodox Church of Antioch, of Byzantine tradition, and continued its use of the Syriac liturgical tradition. In 685 it chose its first patriarch, whose

seat is presently in Bkerke, north of Beirut. Originally, the Maronites had moved from their first home on the Orontes in Syria to northern Lebanon, where they had developed as an agricultural community on the Kadisha River. When the Maronites made contact with Rome during the → Crusades, they started to be influenced by Latin culture and theology. Union with Rome, however, was sealed only in 1736 (→ Uniate Churches).

The Maronites also settled in other parts of Lebanon and achieved considerable influence in the government and economy of the country. They played a leading role in the struggle for a special status within the Ottoman Empire, and then, with the help of France, they made the biggest contribution to the formation of the Lebanese state.

2.2. The other Christian churches, which are widely dispersed across Lebanon, did not identify themselves as much with Lebanese nationalism as the Maronites did. They are centered for the most part in the cities, apart from some Orthodox Christians who settled in the rural area of Al-Koura in northern Lebanon. The site of the Patriarchate of the Orthodox Church of Antioch is Damascus.

After the conquest of Constantinople in 1453, the Ottoman Empire granted those Orthodox Christians, as the leading religious minority, an official status. When some of them opted for union with Rome and founded the Greek Catholic Church of Antioch in 1724, they also claimed for themselves the older Byzantine title of → Melchites. The Muslim government took the side of the Orthodox Christians in the ensuing conflicts. Many Greek Catholics had moved from neighboring countries into Lebanon, even though Damascus was the seat of their patriarch.

2.3. After World War I many refugees settled in Lebanon, where are now found, among others, the → Armenian Apostolic Church (Gregorians) and their Catholicossate, or Patriarchate, of Cilicia (Sis). Other smaller Christian communities were established by Western Catholic missions and belong to the Syrian Catholic Church, whose patriarchate is in Beirut; the Chaldean Catholic Church, whose patriarchate is in Iraq; and some Catholics of the Latin Rite, whose patriarchate is in → Jerusalem. An annual Assembly of Catholic Patriarchs and Bishops of Lebanon has been established to coordinate the ministries of the Maronite and the five other Roman Catholic churches in Lebanon.

Since 1823 European and American Protestant → missionaries have also been at work in Lebanon and have established Protestant churches, whose members are largely former Orthodox and Catholic

Christians. Most of these Protestant congregations belong to the National Evangelical Synod of Syria and Lebanon, which was founded in 1924. Another related umbrella organization was founded in 1936, the Supreme Council of the Evangelical Fellowship of Lebanon and Syria.

2.4. Historically derived tensions between these many Christian churches are numerous and sharp. Yet ecumenical relations do exist, initially in an Ecumenical Pastoral Group (founded 1968) and the Near East Council of Churches, with roots back to 1927, composed initially of only Protestant churches. The latter was replaced in 1974 by the → Middle East Council of Churches (MECC), comprising Eastern and → Oriental Orthodox, as well as the Catholic and Protestant churches. The regional headquarters of the MECC is in Beirut.

3. Muslim and Jewish Communities

With the establishment of the state of Lebanon immediately after World War I, the → Sunni Muslims lost the privileged status they had enjoyed under Ottoman rule. Whereas Christian groups could now draw on their churches, Sunni organizations had to be created anew. They included the office of republican mufti and a representative system. Only gradually did the Sunni upper, middle, and lower classes accept the new state.

In contrast to the Sunni, the → Shiite Muslims are mostly farmers in the Bekáa Valley and South Lebanon. They are strongly dependent on their land and are the group that has contributed least to the social and economic development of the country. In the past they were judged to be heterodox and suffered at the hands of the Sunni rulers. They received official religious recognition only in 1926. In 1967 a special law granted them a Supreme Shiite Islamic Council, whose first president initiated a movement aiming at fighting for the general improvement of their situation.

The Druze confess an esoteric religion that developed out of Shiite Islam in the 11th century but have since parted company with it. Like the Shiites, they were formerly the victims of Sunni oppression. Today they have become part of the national Islamic Council in Lebanon. They are mostly hill-farmers in south-central Lebanon and in parts of Syria and Israel. Since feudal families of Druze affiliation have played an important part in the history of Lebanon, they early became a recognized religious community; in the 19th century they shared with the Maronites in the autonomous District of Mount Lebanon. Their institutions were regulated by national law in 1962.

For centuries small Jewish communities have existed in the cities of Lebanon. In 1932 there were 3,500 Jews. Their number grew to 10,000 in 1956, but after a period of hostilities against Israeli civilians, by 2000 fewer than 2,000 remained.

4. Religion and State

4.1. Subsequent to the special 19th-century regulations for Mount Lebanon, a political, social, and legal confessionalist system developed with religious communities as the constitutive element. Under the French mandate this sociopolitical arrangement continued, and under an independent Lebanon it was confirmed in 1943 by an unwritten agreement between national leaders known as the National Pact. Accordingly, the religious communities and individuals belonging to them have equal political and civil rights. They regulate their domestic affairs themselves, however, and individual special religious or ecclesiastical courts act on the basis of their own laws of family and inheritance. Consequently, there is no civil → marriage.

Furthermore, parliamentary deputies, though representing the whole nation, are grouped according to the religious communities on the basis of 50 percent Muslims and 50 percent Christians. More particularly, the president is a Maronite, the prime minister is a Sunni, and the president of Parliament a Shiite. This proportion is adhered to in public services. With regard to external affairs, the National Pact specifies that Lebanon belongs to the League of Arab States but enjoys full sovereignty, so that it can neither be absorbed into an Arab union nor come under any Western protectorate.

4.2. The aim of the National Pact, for at least some of its authors, was gradually to overcome confessional divisions by creating a state that all the communities involved could recognize as their own. In fact, the pact made possible both peaceful coexistence and economic → development, along with progress toward a national integration that fostered common interests among entrepreneurs and intellectuals and helped civil organizations and political parties rise above the confessional structure.

Working against integration, however, was the fact that broad masses of the people did not share in the common progress. Also adverse in its effects was an unsettled international situation with the intervention of foreign forces (i.e., other Arab states, Israel, Iran, and the Western powers).

4.3. In 1975 civil war broke out. Lasting until 1990, it involved local forces (Lebanese parties and the army), neighboring states (esp. Syria and Israel), and international organizations (the Arab League and the United Nations). The cause of the war was not religious, but since the state failed to provide order and integration, the political role was assumed by the different religious communities. All sides soon became aware that there was no easy way out of the crisis. A proposed system of small religious states or cantons was rejected as an inadequate basis for the peaceful coexistence of the various components of Lebanese society.

The war was ultimately ended by the Taif Agreement, which the Lebanese Chamber of Deputies ratified in 1989 and which, in 1990, became an integral part of the constitution in the newly proclaimed Second Republic of Lebanon. The agreement formally abolished confessionalism as the aim of the Lebanese state, established a more equal distribution of public offices and mandates between Christians and Muslims, and legalized the (temporary) stationing of Syrian armed forces in Lebanon.

The problems involved are very complex, and the interests of the participants very antithetical, which has so far prevented any comprehensive solution. The dangers of further civil war have become clear, however, which has promoted a willingness for compromise and an interest in examining thoroughly the points of conflict. For example, concepts relating to secularism that traditionalists previously found offensive are no longer excluded from open-minded discussion. Furthermore, the development of modern schools in Lebanon represents reason for hope.

→ Church and State; Islam; Islam and Christianity

Bibliography: L. Abul-Husn, *The Lebanese Conflict: Looking Inward* (Boulder, Colo., 1998) • D. B. Barrett et al., eds., *WCE* (2d ed.) 1.444-48 • R. B. Betts, *The Druze* (New Haven, 1988) • C. Dagher, *Bring Down the Walls: Lebanon's Postwar Challenge* (New York, 2000) • F. El-Khazen, *The Breakdown of the State in Lebanon, 1967-1976* (Cambridge, Mass., 2000) • M. S. Kramer, *Arab Awakening and Islamic Revival: The Politics of Ideas in the Middle East* (New Brunswick, N.J., 1996) esp. 209-44 • W. Phares, *Lebanese Christian Nationalism: The Rise and Fall of an Ethnic Resistance* (Boulder, Colo., 1995) • A. Saad-Ghorayeb, *Hizbullah: Politics and Religion* (London, 2001) • W. A. Semaan, *Aliens at Home: A Socio-religious Analysis of the Protestant Church in Lebanon and Its Backgrounds* (London, 1986) • T. Tschuy, *Ethnic Conflict and Religion: Challenge to the Churches* (Geneva, 1997) • A. Wessels, *Arab and Christian? Christians in the Middle East* (Kampen, 1995).

Fritz Steppat

Lectionary → Readings, Scripture

Lector

1. Jewish Setting
2. Christian Setting
   2.1. Early Church
   2.2. To the Middle Ages
   2.3. Reformation to the Present

The office of lector (Lat. "reader") is necessitated by the public reading of Scripture, an essential element in both Jewish and Christian → worship. The development of the role of lector in these two religious traditions exhibits striking similarities.

1. Jewish Setting

By the fourth century B.C. the Israelites knew the public reading of the → law (§1; Neh. 7:73b–8:12). The worship of the → synagogue, however, provides the first evidence for lectors as a regular feature of Jewish prayer life. Both the → Torah and the haftarah were read in the → liturgy of the synagogue, at least from the time of Jesus (Luke 4:16-21), with the reader of the Torah pericope occupying a position of particular honor. Originally only one person read the whole Torah pericope (→ Readings, Scripture), but later the practice evolved of having the worship leader "call to the Torah" members of the congregation, the number increasing with the sanctity of the day.

At first any member of the community could be summoned to read, including women, minors, and slaves. Over time, however, those eligible to read came to be restricted. Women were excluded in Tannaitic times, as were boys when reading became an initiatory → rite for those celebrating their Bar Mitzvah. Eventually only adult men were allowed to read, no more than three for each Torah reading. While originally called up to read in any order, lectors came to be ranked by honor.

The difficulty of finding persons capable of reading the Torah led to its professionalization, even in Hebrew-speaking synagogues, which often lacked enough literate members to rotate the task. Furthermore, since the Hebrew text was unpunctuated and written with no division between words, the Torah was difficult to read and came to be cantillated. Increasingly over the first millennium in the Christian era, the responsibility for reading the Torah fell to professionals: the → rabbi, a designated reader, or a cantor. Although members of the congregation were still called to the Torah, their active role was limited to offering → blessings before and after its reading.

2. Christian Setting

2.1. *Early Church*

The early church adapted the role of lector from the synagogue, along with other patterns in the liturgy of the Word. Reading is mentioned as a liturgical act in Col. 4:16, 1 Tim. 4:13, and → Justin Martyr *1 Apol.* 67.3-4; reference to the role of lector is found in Rev. 1:3, *2 Clem.* 19:1, and the writings of → Tertullian (*De praescr. haeret.* 41).

A century ago the charism of the reader in the → early church was a matter of dispute. Hans Achelis counted lectors, along with → prophets and evangelists, among the leaders of the church possessing gifts of the → Holy Spirit. Against this view, Adolf von Harnack argued that readings and the office of lector evolved after the original intensity of the prophets' inspiration, their direct witness to the Holy Spirit, had weakened. We lack sufficient evidence to resolve this debate. We do know that lectors in the first two centuries read all the readings and that their role was in some ways similar to that of synagogue lectors. While anyone was eligible to read, the requirements of literacy and the difficulty of deciphering the unspaced and unpunctuated text limited the number of persons capable of performing the task. Accordingly, the skills that the task required lent importance to the role of lector.

By the third century, again emulating developments in the synagogue, the church was establishing a lectorate. In his *Apostolic Tradition,* Hippolytus noted, "The reader is appointed by the bishop giving him a book, for he is not ordained." Fourth-century references to the office of lector are found for Asia Minor, Cappadocia, Syria, Palestine, and Africa. There are references to lectors in Spain from the sixth century. In the Roman West, lectors were counted among the lower or minor orders of clergy, along with doorkeepers, exorcists, and acolytes.

2.2. *To the Middle Ages*

As Christian worship moved from homes to church buildings, the lector read from the ambo the selections of Scripture to be proclaimed in the assembly and later sang some elements of the liturgy, notably psalms and versicles. Soon the lector's responsibility for all of the readings began to erode. After the reading of the Gospel was taken over by → deacons in the fourth century, the lector read only the Epistle. This situation pertains even today in the → Orthodox Church, where the Epistle is still read by a lector, ordained or lay, and the Gospel by the deacon. In the West, however, the lector was denied even the responsibility for reading the Epistle, a task passed in the ninth century to the subdeacon. Thus, as in the synagogue of the same period, the liturgical role of lector in the Western church of the → Middle Ages became largely symbolic.

As the importance of the lector in the liturgy of the church waned, that of the lectorate in the order of the church waxed. Originally open to all males capable of reading in the assembly, it came to serve as a probationary stage for those launching ecclesiastical careers. Eventually, in both East and West, the lectorate became a stage preparatory to ordination to the → priesthood. In the fourth century in the West, children intended for service in the church were admitted to the lectorate, which typically involved training at home by mentors. When numbers warranted, as in Rome and Lyons, lectors were trained in special episcopal schools (the *scholae lectorum*). After the sixth century they served parochial clergy as altar boys or choirboys. Eventually the lectorate, devoid of all responsibility, became merely a status conferred upon men headed for → ordination.

2.3. *Reformation to the Present*

The → Reformation expanded the responsibilities of the position of reader. Protestant churches discarded the lectorate as an anachronism and revived the ancient tradition of having laypersons read Scripture in worship. Simultaneously, however, pastoral need required the creation of a Protestant office of reader, with responsibility for performing some clerical functions, either assisting ordained clergy or serving in their absence, including reading the whole service of worship aloud.

This office first emerged in the Church of Scotland in the mid-16th century and survived for 100 years. It became more widespread in modern times, initiated in the Church of England in 1866 and the Church of Scotland in 1918 and used by Lutherans on the American frontier in the 19th century and in Germany during the → church struggle and following World War II. While the office was instituted to alleviate a shortage of clergy, the activities of persons serving in it were typically restricted, for example, from celebrating the Lord's Supper or granting absolution after the → confession of sin. Whether the right to preach should be granted to this office is a matter of debate. Women in Protestant churches have been allowed to serve as readers since the last third of the 20th century.

Following the Second → Vatican Council, the → Roman Catholic Church shaped a similar office of reader. In the apostolic letter *Ministeria quaedam,* issued as a → motu proprio in August 1972, Paul VI suppressed the ancient minor order of lector and established, as one of two forms of lay ministry universal in the Roman Catholic Church, a new ministry of reader. In addition to reading the OT and Epistle lections, the reader is also permitted to lead the assembly in psalm, song, and prayer. The ministry of reader is not limited to candidates for the diaconate or priesthood.

Apart from the office or ministry of reader, laypersons today in both Roman Catholic and Protestant churches, liturgical and nonliturgical, commonly read lections in worship without the requirement of formal licensing. Liturgical churches refer to this individual as lector; nonliturgical churches prefer the term "reader." Training manuals and programs have been developed to deepen understanding and hone the skills of persons serving in this ministry.

→ Ministry, Ministerial Offices

Bibliography: History: H. ACHELIS, "Lector," RE 11 • M. ANDRIEU, "Les orders mineurs dans l'ancien rite romain," RSE 5 (1925) 232-74 • A. CHUPUNGCO, "Diaconate (Minor Ministries)," EncEC 1.232-33 • J. G. DAVIES, "Deacons, Deaconesses, and the Minor Orders in the Patristic Period," JEH 14 (1963) 1-15 • I. ELBOGEN, Jewish Liturgy: A Comprehensive History (Philadelphia, 1993) 129-49 • A. VON HARNACK, "On the Origin of the Readership and Other Lower Orders," Sources of the Apostolic Canons (London, 1895) 54-92 • P. DE PUNIET, The Roman Pontifical: A History and Commentary (London, 1932) 122-40.

Roman Catholic: NATIONAL CONFERENCE OF CATHOLIC BISHOPS, BISHOPS' COMMITTEE ON THE LITURGY, Ministries in the Church: Commentary on the Apostolic Letters "Ministeria quaedam" and "Ad pascendum" (Washington, D.C., 1974) • The Rites of the Catholic Church (vol. 2; Collegeville, Minn., 1991) 97-106.

Protestant: G. FUHRMANN, Grenzgänger. Lectoren im Dienst der Verkündigung (Hanover, 1987) • C. HEADLEY, Readers and Worship in the Church of England (Bramcote, 1991) • T. G. KING, Readers: A Pioneer Ministry (London, 1973).

Practical: J. DUCHARME and G. DUCHARME, Lector Becomes Proclaimer (San Jose, Calif., 1985) • A. R. ROSSER, A Well-Trained Tongue: Formation in the Ministry of Reader (Chicago, 1996).

FRITZ WEST

Legate → Nuncio

Legislation → Church Law 6

Legitimation

Those who can accredit themselves, or who have letters of accreditation, can command legitimation. In this sense legitimation means justification before others or → institutions by appeal to an authority that is recognized on both sides (→ Law and Legal Theory). In a narrower sense the term denotes the justification of a social order, especially of a legal type. In the → modern period this focus has given rise to the problem that classic ideals of legitimation have lost their obvious cogency. As long as the office of a monarch rested on the grace of God, social → hierarchies on the will of God, and the legal order on unchanging → natural law, no problem of legitimation could arise. The problem became acute only when the modern sense of → autonomy gave human beings themselves control over social structures (→ Enlightenment). The question of legitimation then had to be put in a new way. Legitimacy now came to mean that a political order is worthy of recognition (J. Habermas; → State; State Ethics). The question of legitimation is thus a central consequence of the modern process of → secularization (→ Secularism).

For earlier ideas oriented to natural law, there could be no separating of legality and legitimacy. Valid law represented only the rules of law that agreed with the principles of natural law; in this view, unjust law was no law at all. As the concept of natural law increasingly came into question, however, legality and legitimacy broke apart. As I. Kant (1724-1804; → Kantianism) sharply put it, legality, as distinct from morality, means compliance or noncompliance with the law, irrespective of motive (Metaphysik der Sitten AB 15). Legality is thus distinct from legitimacy.

The consequences of the new situation found formulation as early as the late 18th century. C.-M. Talleyrand's (1754-1838) concept of legitimacy attempted to renew the traditional and religious justification of political rule. During the same period, however, legal → positivism in its first classic forms in J. Bentham (1748-1832) and J. Austin (1790-1859) advanced a contrary view of legitimacy. On this view the validity of the legal order does not rest on a superpositive legitimacy but solely on the positive nature of law itself. Simply the fact that law is promulgated by a competent → authority determines its legitimacy.

The rule of law thereby established forms the basis of rational government, a type of legitimation that M. → Weber (1864-1920) distinguished from that of traditional and charismatic government (→

Charisma). The differentiation of legitimation from legality is a valuable one for secular and pluralistic societies. The consequences of its forfeiture may be seen in a shocking way in states that appeal to a purely religious or revolutionary legitimacy (→ Revolution).

At the same time, experience of the excesses of legal injustice in the 20th century has called into acute question the positivist answer to the problem of legitimation. It has compelled us to look again at the question of the legitimation of legal rule. The new insight is that it belongs to a mature → democracy to be able to raise the question of the legitimacy of its decisions, even though they have been reached by a formally correct, majority vote. The extreme case of civil disobedience, which raises the question in vivid form, is thus a constituent element in democracy (→ Resistance, Right of).

An understanding of the criteria of legitimation is decisive. Attempts to answer this question point, on the one hand, to the development of international standards of human → rights — preeminently the U.N. Universal Declaration of Human Rights (1948) — and, on the other hand, to the elementary principles of political justice that must be respected if political government and legal order are not to lose their legitimation.

The question of legitimation does not arise merely in the political sphere but specifically also ecclesiastically. What we need here are criteria by which to assess the legitimacy of what the church says and does. Possible criteria of this kind are conformity to Scripture, agreement with a specific confession (→ Confession of Faith), relevance, and orientation to human justice. In a given case each of these criteria may be challenged, and the criteria may be in tension with one another. For this reason theological work needs to be done with reference to the legitimacy of what the church says and does.

If theology abandons its independent critical role and simply serves existing interests of legitimation, however, it runs the risk of becoming no more than a science of legitimation. As D. → Bonhoeffer (1906-45) said of this kind of theology, it is a science in which we have learned both to excuse everything and to justify everything (*Gesammelte Schriften* 5.404). The problem of legitimation thus confronts theology with the task of fundamental distinction, that is, of → criticism.

Bibliography: J. HABERMAS, *Justification and Application: Remarks on Discourse Ethics* (Cambridge, Mass., 1993); idem, *Legitimation Crisis* (Cambridge, 1988; orig. pub., 1973) • S. M. LIPSET, *Political Man: The Social Bases of Politics* (Baltimore, 1988; orig. pub., 1960) • T. PARSONS, "Authority, Legitimation, and Political Action," *Structure and Process in Modern Societies* (Glencoe, Ill., 1960) 170-98 • J. RAWLS, *A Theory of Justice* (rev. ed.; Cambridge, Mass., 1999) • A. J. SIMMONS, *Justification and Legitimacy: Essays on Rights and Obligations* (Cambridge, 2001) • M. WEBER, *Economy and Society: An Outline of Interpretive Sociology* (2 vols.; Berkeley, Calif., 1978; orig. pub., 1922).

WOLFGANG HUBER

Leisure

1. History
2. Concepts
3. Use
4. Issues

1. History

Like Fr. *loisir*, the Eng. term "leisure" derives from Lat. *licere*, "be permitted." In the ancient Greek polis the political and literary ruling class evolved the idea of *scholē* (rest, leisure), a period of freedom from work so as to make possible personal development, with a view to political and social office. The work of citizens was *a-scholia* (busyness, lack of leisure), whereas that of slaves was *ponos* (labor, toil).

Ancient Rome put up huge buildings in which people could pass the time together. Under Constantine the Circus Maximus, the largest Roman hippodrome, could seat up to 250,000 spectators, and public baths were built to hold up to 60,000. Leisure (Lat. *otium*, "free time, leisure") was a cultural ideal, as distinct from work (*neg-otium*, "busyness, absence of leisure"), which was disparaged.

Only in the Christian → Middle Ages did → work come to be viewed positively and leisure retreat into the background. In the agrarian → feudal economy and in joint manual work, the time spent in labor was structured by the natural cycles of day and night, summer and winter, and leisure time was spent socially, with no separation between work and the home. Up to the 18th century the numerous secular and ecclesiastical feasts provided freedom from work for as many as half the normal working days. With the coming of industrialization, many of these feasts were abolished.

Manufacturing and industry began driving a wedge between work and the home from the 17th century, made production independent of natural cycles, strengthened a linear and measurable understanding of → time, and led to opposition between work and leisure time (→ Industrial Society). The hours of work were steadily extended, and only with the labor movement and government action were they finally reduced — to an 80-hour-week in 1860, a 48-hour-week in 1920, and a 40-hour-week in 1980. By 2000 the workweek in France and Germany had been shortened to 35 hours. Whereas the middle class still viewed leisure along classical lines as an opportunity for culture, the labor movement sometimes demanded leisure time to promote political education.

After 1920 leisure time became important as a time of → consumption. The National Socialists (1933-45) promoted leisure for political mobilization and control (their motto: Strength through Joy). Today the overall leisure time has increased through reduced working hours, more holidays, and a longer period of retirement.

2. Concepts

There is no single view of leisure time. Its primary meaning is variously (1) what is left of the day when work, travel, sleep, meals, and other necessary activities are subtracted; (2) a time of recuperation of forces spent on work, school, and other tasks; (3) freedom from the pressures of work, family, and social and political responsibility; (4) the time at our own disposal to do with as we please; or (5) time for personal development, self-fulfillment, or culture.

According to the definition, leisure time is the opposite of work, the prolongation of work experience, or a learning product. When the importance of work decreases (→ Vocation), so does its impact on leisure time.

3. Use

The use of leisure time is strongly influenced by age, education, and job (esp. for women who are housewives); less so by sex, type of job, position in the life cycle, and place of residence; and least of all by income or possession of an automobile. Different traditions, climates, and infrastructures also have an impact. Privileged groups (e.g., officials, teachers, students) have more leisure time; the disadvantaged (e.g., farmworkers, the self-employed, working women) have less.

The use of leisure time has been increasingly commercialized (→ Capitalism; Consumption) and made more passive (esp. through the dominance of the → mass media), trends resisted by active educational and ethical programs. The churches are similarly concerned about these trends and offer considerable personal and material resources in urging a

better use of leisure. Increase in the availability of leisure time calls for new standards of conduct so as to strike a balance in its use between the demands of others and one's → autonomy.

4. Issues

Liberation from demanding physical labor and increasing psychological and ecological pressures affect the use of leisure time. Sports and self-regulated forms of activity offer new bodily experiences. The dominance of the media with their offering of distractions produces passivity and dictation by others. The stylizing of new → norms of achievement and status symbols leads to rivalry and uncertainty as to status. Unpaid work in leisure time results in a shadow economy. Travel as an important use of leisure has opened up new spheres of experience.

Changes in personality result as leisure time becomes a lifestyle. For younger, highly qualified urban groups in our postmaterial society, leisure style and the quality of life are more important than vocation. When → unemployment is high, however, people typically value the chance to find and keep a job far more than they do leisure time. The unemployed, whose lives are not structured by their jobs, view enforced leisure negatively. High unemployment works against the experience and understanding of leisure.

→ Everyday Life; Tourism

Bibliography: C. AITCHISON, N. E. MacLEOD, and S. J. SHAW, *Leisure and Tourism Landscapes: Social and Cultural Geographies* (London, 2000) • S. M. GELBER, *Hobbies: Leisure and the Culture of Work in America* (New York, 1999) • J. GERSHUNY, *Changing Times: Work and Leisure in Postindustrial Society* (Oxford, 2000) • D. A. KLEIBER, *Leisure Experience and Human Development: A Dialectical Interpretation* (New York, 1999) • H. W. OPASCHOWSKI, *Psychologie und Soziologie der Freizeit* (Opladen, 1988) • H.-W. PRAHL, *Soziologie der Freizeit* (Munich, 2000).

HANS-WERNER PRAHL

Lent → Church Year

Leo I

Leo I (d. 461), known as Leo the Great, was → pope beginning in the summer of 440. Not much is known about Leo's early years. Suggestions that he was born in Tuscany remain improbable as long as other signs point to an urban Roman origin. Before becoming pope, he was (arch)deacon at the papal court, and as early as 440 Empress Galla Placidia entrusted him with a political mission to Gaul. Leo devoted a great deal of energy to his urban Roman congregation, particularly through his sermons, and encouraged the production of narrative and pictorial cycles as wall frescoes or mosaics in the → basilicas of Paul and Peter. Leo's ecclesiastical work focused on delimitation; he directed antiheretical measures first against the → Manichaeans, who had fled to → Rome, and then also against → Pelagians and Priscillians.

One traditional theme affecting Roman ecclesiastical leadership was the question of the date of → Easter (§4). Leo argued, for example, with → Cyril and Dioscorus, patriarchs of → Alexandria, against the Alexandrian date. In debates with the churches of Africa, Gaul, Italy, and Illyria, Leo also insisted on Roman primacy, or universal Roman → authority, in questions of church order and doctrine, carrying on an extraordinarily vehement dispute with Hilary of Arles. Such work on the organizational and theological unity of the church also had significant political implications in Italy, where state power in its previous form was rapidly collapsing. The bishop of Rome and his administration assumed an increasing number of state responsibilities. Leo was able to acquire from the Western emperor Valentinian III (423-55) a rescript recognizing Leo's claims to authority and legislative powers.

Especially in his letter of June 13, 449, to Patriarch Flavian of Constantinople, Leo tried to influence developments at the Council of Ephesus (449), which he called *Latrocinium* (i.e., the Robber Council). His articulation of several central formulas regarding the theory of the two natures of Christ profoundly shaped subsequent developments, both pro and con (→ Christology), though → Monophysite circles did accuse the pope of → Nestorianism.

It was not until after the death of the Eastern emperor Theodosius II in 450, when the climate of ecclesiastical politics changed with the new rulers Marcian and Pulcheria, that the so-called Tome of Leo was received at a synod dominated by Eastern views, the Council of → Chalcedon (451). Although Leo had originally demanded such an assembly (albeit in Italy), he now followed its developments with concern, and his influence both on this council and on its doctrinal decisions are interpreted differently. In any event, a distinction must be made between the rhetoric favorable to Leo and his actual theological significance at the council. The council's acts do show that Cyril through his writings played a considerable role in demonstrating Leo's orthodoxy. Despite the obvious "Cyrillization" (A. de Halleux)

of Leo's theology in the synod's doctrinal results, the citation of the *salva igitur* section (DH 293) did preserve one of his central formulas. It was all the easier for the council's Western legates to agree with the *hena kai ton auton* (one and the same) in the final synodal statement because Leo himself had used the expression in the Tome to Flavian ("We must say this again and again: one and the same is truly Son of God and truly son of man," §4).

At the same time, however, Leo's claim to universal authority at the Council of Chalcedon was rejected, for the council granted the patriarch of Constantinople virtually complete equality with his Roman colleague (can. 28). Leo confirmed the results of the council (excepting, of course, can. 28) with appropriate delay (not until March 453). In the subsequent disputes regarding the results of Chalcedon, Leo tried to defend and secure his Christology among Palestinian monks and Egyptian bishops and with Eastern emperor Leo I (457-74). In what is known as the *Tomus secundus,* Leo articulated and secured the older theology with a new vocabulary, largely avoiding the problematic formula regarding the two natures. Unfortunately, none of these efforts was able to heal this first great church schism (→ Heresies and Schisms).

When Rome was threatened during the great fifth-century movement of Teutonic peoples into southern and western Europe, Leo met with the Huns under Attila in 452 at the behest of Valentinian III and in 455 with the Vandal king Genseric (ruled 428-77). Leo was able to persuade the Huns not to attack Rome and the Vandals to spare the city's inhabitants when they occupied Rome. Leo died in 461 and is buried in St. Peter's. He was canonized; his feast day is November 10 in the West, February 18 in the East.

In all, 96 of Leo's sermons and 173 letters (143 by Leo himself) have been preserved.

→ Roman Empire

Bibliography: Primary sources: ACO 2.2, 2.3, 2.4 • CChr.SL 138 • *CPL* 1656-61 • *PL* 54-56 • *SC* 22, 49, 74, 200 • N. P. TANNER, ed., *Decrees of the Ecumenical Councils* (2 vols.; London, 1990) 1.77-82 (Eng. trans. of Tome of Leo).

Secondary works: H. ARENS, *Die christologische Sprache Leos des Großen. Analyse des Tomus an den Patriarchen Flavian* (Freiburg, 1982) • J. M. ARMITAGE, *The Economy of Mercy: The Liturgical Preaching of St. Leo the Great* (Durham, N.C., 1997) • A. DE HALLEUX, "La définition christologique à Chalcédoine," *RTL* 7 (1976) 3-23, 155-70 • S. O. HORN, *Petrou Kathedra. Der Bischof von Rom und die Synoden von Ephesus (449) und Chalcedon* (Paderborn, 1982) • T. G. JALLAND, *The Life and Times of St. Leo the Great* (London, 1941).

CHRISTOPH MARKSCHIES

Lesotho

	1960	1980	2000
Population (1,000s):	870	1,367	2,294
Annual growth rate (%):	2.01	2.69	2.46

Area: 30,355 sq. km. (11,720 sq. mi.)

A.D. 2000

Population density: 76/sq. km. (196/sq. mi.)
Births / deaths: 3.41 / 0.95 per 100 population
Fertility rate: 4.51 per woman
Infant mortality rate: 63 per 1,000 live births
Life expectancy: 60.8 years (m: 59.4, f: 62.2)
Religious affiliation (%): Christians 92.6 (Roman Catholics 41.4, unaffiliated 18.7, Protestants 14.4, indigenous 13.1, Anglicans 4.7, other Christians 0.3), tribal religionists 6.3, other 1.1.

1. General Situation
2. Religious Situation

1. General Situation

The Kingdom of Lesotho, an enclave within the Republic of South Africa, is a small constitutional monarchy. Its capital is Maseru. The chief crops are corn, wheat, sorghum, and barley, with herding also important. Water is its most important natural resource, which, after completion of a major hydropower plant in 1998, it has been selling to South Africa. Other exports are clothing, footwear, wool, and mohair. South Africa employs large numbers of mine workers, whose earnings in 1996 accounted for one-third of Lesotho's gross domestic product.

During the early 19th century the young Sotho king Mshweshwe (or Moshoeshoe, ca. 1786-1870) brought together the speakers of Sotho (or Basuto or Basotho) in southern Africa. By 1868 he had secured British protection to counteract dangers created by Boer expansion. In 1884 Basutoland, as it was then called, became a crown colony (→ Colonialism).

In 1966 Lesotho became an independent kingdom within the British Commonwealth. The first king was Paramount Chief Motlotheli (Moshoeshoe II [1938-96]), the first prime minister Chief Leabua Jonathan. In 1970 Jonathan suspended elections in which the opposition party claimed victory. He ruled as a dictator with a coopted parliament, ignoring the constitution, repressing opposition, and

having the king arrested. When the Evangelical Church engaged in opposition, it was persecuted, with the editor of the church paper being murdered, the vice-president exiled, and others being imprisoned and → tortured. In 1986 officers under General Justinus Lekhanya seized power with South African help, reinstalling Moshoeshoe II as head of state. The constitution remained suspended, and all political activity was forbidden. A fresh coup overthrew the king in February 1990.

Further coups and changes in the monarchy occurred throughout the 1990s. In 1998 South Africa and Botswana sent troops into Lesotho to help suppress antigovernment protests. All sides agreed to hold elections in 2000, but disagreements caused further delays.

2. Religious Situation

In 1833 the Paris Mission (→ French Missions), from which the Lesotho Evangelical Church traces its origins (→ Reformed and Presbyterian Churches), began work in Lesotho, with the cooperation of Moshoeshoe I. The → missionaries engaged in both missionary and educational activity, and from the very first the church has seen itself as a kind of territorial church with social and political responsibilities. In 1862 the first Roman Catholic priests arrived, followed in 1875 by the first Anglicans. The impact of → mission has been strong, although an appreciable minority continue to practice their tribal religions (→ Guinea 2).

In the year 2000 the → Roman Catholic Church was the largest single Christian group. Among non-Catholics, the two largest groups were the Lesotho Evangelical Church and the Anglican Church (in the Anglo-Catholic tradition; → Anglican Communion). There were also about 30 much smaller Protestant denominations, plus over 200 separate → Independent Churches. There are also a small number of → Bahais, Hindus (→ Hinduism), and Muslims (→ Islam). With the growth of the Roman Catholic population, Lesotho became an archdiocese in 1961 and was honored by a visit from Pope John Paul II in 1988.

There are good interdenominational relationships. The Christian Council of Lesotho (→ National Councils of Churches) was formed in 1964 and is a member of the → All Africa Conference of Churches. The churches also show a constructive interest in the affairs of state (→ Church and State). The three main churches have a special interest in education, operating most of the country's schools (with the help of a government subsidy). In 2000 the literacy rate was estimated to be 71 percent. The autonomous National University of Lesotho, which had its beginnings in the Catholic University College, opened in 1945 at Roma, Lesotho.

→ African Theology

Bibliography: J. E. Bardill and J. H. Cobbe, *Lesotho: Dilemmas of Dependence in Southern Africa* (Boulder, Colo., 1985) • D. B. Barrett et al., eds., *WCE* (2d ed.) 1.448-51 • E. A. Eldredge, *A South African Kingdom: The Pursuit of Security in Nineteenth-Century Lesotho* (Cambridge, 1993) • F. D. Ellenberger, *History of the Basuto, Ancient and Modern* (Morija, Lesotho, 1992) • M. Epprecht, *"This Matter of Women Is Getting Very Bad": Gender, Development, and Politics in Colonial Lesotho* (Pietermaritzburg, 2000) • D. Johnston, comp., *Lesotho* (rev. ed.; Oxford, 1996) • P. Letuka, *Women in Lesotho* (Maseru, Lesotho, 1997) • L. B. B. J. Machobane, *Government and Change in Lesotho, 1800-1966: A Study of Political Institutions* (New York, 1990) • W. C. M. Maqutu, *Contemporary Constitutional History of Lesotho* (Mazenod, Lesotho, 1990) • M. Nthunya, *Singing Away the Hunger: The Autobiography of an African Woman* (Bloomington, Ind., 1997).

Kenneth Baker†

Leuenberg Agreement

1. History
2. Content and Method
3. Results
4. Ongoing Work

The Leuenberg Agreement is a statement resulting mainly from theological conversations between Lutheran and Reformed churches in Europe. The drafting process was completed on March 16, 1973, and the agreement came into effect on October 1, 1974. The churches that officially subscribe to the Leuenberg Agreement grant to each other pulpit and table/altar fellowship and commit themselves to common witness and service on the basis of the agreement. Since 1974 over 100 European → Lutheran, Reformed, United, → Methodist, → Hussite, → Waldensian, and Czech Brethren churches have signed the agreement or accepted the basis of the "Joint Declaration of Church Fellowship," which appears in the final sections (29-48) of the agreement. In addition, five South American Protestant churches have signed the agreement.

1. History
The drafting process that was completed in 1973 concluded a → dialogue between European

churches begun after the Second World War, which included the → Arnoldshain and the Schauenburg Conferences. In its initial stages between 1956 and 1960, this dialogue addressed theological questions, but there was then no intention either of building a process of → reception or of changing the relations between churches.

In 1962 a new stage was begun when the dialogue was transferred to the Commission on → Faith and Order of the → World Council of Churches. The new agenda started in 1963 sought to identify an explicit theological → consensus, call the churches to binding decisions, and result in concrete actions. This work continued until 1967, when four series of theses were presented to the churches for their comments. These theses addressed God's Word and God's presence, the law, → confession of faith, and the boundaries of the → church. After encouraging responses from many churches, the dialogue continued in 1969-70 with official delegates from the churches considering the topic "Church Fellowship and Church Division." In 1970 the idea of an agreement first surfaced. In the following year the first draft was prepared; the final draft was completed at Leuenberg, near Basel, Switzerland.

2. Content and Method
The Leuenberg Agreement contains 49 articles. After an introductory word to the participating churches, the first two sections indicate that it is a common understanding of the → gospel that allows the churches to declare and to realize church fellowship. Sections 3-5 describe the road to fellowship; sections 6-16, the common understanding of the gospel shared by the signing churches. Sections 17-28 are devoted to an accord on the doctrinal condemnations of the Reformation era, including such topics as the Lord's Supper (→ Eucharist), → Christology, and → predestination. The final sections, 29-48, take up the declaration and realization of church fellowship. Section 49 expresses the hope that the agreement and achievement of fellowship will be an encouragement to other churches.

The methodology of the agreement is based on four points. First, the stress is more on a joint presentation of the current situation facing these churches in Europe than only on overcoming theological differences. Second, there is a clear recognition that the agreement is not a new confession of faith; it does not replace earlier confessions. Rather, while it acknowledges that theological conversations should continue, the Leuenberg Agreement bears witness to the central core of the gospel, with the result that both the Lutheran and Reformed traditions can be seen as witnessing to the same truth. Third, the problem of the condemnations that marked the 16th-century Reformation is addressed under the rubric "nonapplicability." Those condemnations were not necessarily wrong, but they no longer apply to the present churches. Fourth, attention is given to the legal aspects of the agreement: It does not create church union or unification as the Prussian Union had attempted in1817, yet it is also more than a theological consensus. The Leuenberg Agreement is seen to have consequences for fellowship among the churches.

The special importance of the agreement for ecumenical methodology lies in its acceptance of "differentiated consensus." To overcome the historic doctrinal differences between the Lutheran and Reformed traditions, a distinction is made between the common understanding of the gospel, which is sufficient for unity, and divergent views that can be held between and within churches if they do not challenge the basic common understanding of the gospel. On this point the methodology of the Leuenberg Agreement is similar to that of the → Joint Declaration on the Doctrine of Justification (1999) between the member churches of the → Lutheran World Federation and the → Roman Catholic Church.

3. Results

The goal of the Leuenberg Agreement is that the signing churches live in fellowship and engage in common witness and service. It is clear that in a number of places relations between the churches have changed. The agreement by its methodology did contribute to the Formula of Agreement of 1997 in the United States, which provided for full communion between the Evangelical Lutheran Church in America and the Presbyterian Church (U.S.A.), the Reformed Church in America, and the United Church of Christ.

Common witness by the Reformation churches in Europe, however, is at a preliminary stage. There has been an asymmetry in the reception process. For the Reformed side there seems to be an attitude of acceptance of Leuenberg as a natural step, and the Reformed wish to follow up the agreement with attention to current issues. For the Lutheran side, in contrast, the approach seems to be one of minute inspection of the agreement and of a stress on continuing doctrinal conversations.

Open questions remain about the wider influence of the Leuenberg Agreement. What are the effects of the agreement on Lutheran, Reformed, and United traditions worldwide? Can the agreement be applied

beyond these churches and the pre-Reformation churches related to them? Through the Leuenberg Fellowship (see 4) the Leuenberg churches have maintained working contacts with the → Anglican Communion and the European Baptist Federation. It is not clear, however, how far these relations can be extended.

4. Ongoing Work

The Leuenberg Agreement itself provides (esp. §§38-39) for ongoing theological conversation and study. Thus since its signing theological work has continued in a series of conversations concerning the teachings of the participating churches. The topics discussed have included "The Church of Jesus Christ"; "Sacraments, Ministry, and Ordination"; "Ethical Decision Making"; "Leuenberg, Meissen, and → Porvoo — A Comparison of Three Ecumenical Proposals"; "The Christian Witness on Freedom"; "The Church and Israel"; and "Church — People — State — Nation." The findings of these theological conversations, which have been published in the series Leuenberg Documents (in English and German), are viewed as a contribution to wider → ecumenical dialogue among the churches. The report of the conversations entitled "The Church of Jesus Christ" has been adopted by a General Assembly of the Leuenberg Fellowship. It is of special note as an expression of a common understanding of Protestant churches on ecclesiology.

The commitments of the Leuenberg Agreement also find continuing expression in the Leuenberg Fellowship. This fellowship seeks to promote the unity and community of the Protestant churches that have signed the agreement or the "Joint Declaration of Church Fellowship." The Leuenberg Fellowship is a modest organization, holding a General Assembly about every six years. Such assemblies took place in Sigtuna, Sweden, in 1976; Driebergen, Netherlands, in 1981; Strasbourg in 1987; Vienna in 1994; and Belfast in 2001. Assemblies elect an executive committee that is led by a presidium of three persons and is responsible for the ongoing work of the fellowship between General Assemblies. A secretariat, headed by a director with a small staff, is located in Berlin.

The fellowship regards itself as one of the steps on the way to the unity of the church of Jesus Christ and thus maintains relations with the World Council of Churches, the → Conference of European Churches, the Lutheran World Federation, and the → World Alliance of Reformed Churches, as well as with the Anglican World Communion and the European Baptist Federation.

→ Reformed and Presbyterian Churches; United and Uniting Churches

Bibliography: Primary texts: W. Hüffmeier and C.-R. Müller, eds., *Versöhnte Verschiedenheit–der Auftrag der evangelischen Kirchen in Europa. Texte der 5. Vollversammlung in Belfast, 2001* (Frankfurt, 2002); idem, eds., *Wachsende Gemeinschaft in Zeugnis und Dienst. Texte der 4. Vollversammlung in Wien, 1994* (Frankfurt, 1995) • Leuenberger Texte, *Sakramente, Amt, Ordination* (1995); *Die Kirche Jesu Christi* (1996); *Leuenberg, Meissen und Porvoo* (1996); *Evangelische Texte zur ethischen Urteilsfindung* (1997); *Das christliche Zeugnis von der Freiheit* (1999); *Kirche und Israel* (2001); *Kirche–Volk–Staat–Nation* (2002) (Frankfurt).

Secondary works: H.-J. Luibl, C.-R. Müller, and H. Zeddies, eds., *Unterwegs nach Europa. Perspektiven evangelischer Kirchen–ein Lesebuch* (Frankfurt, 2001) • W. G. Rusch and D. F. Martensen, eds., *The Leuenberg Agreement and Lutheran-Reformed Relationships* (Minneapolis, 1989) includes English text of the agreement • E. Schieffer, *Von Schauenberg nach Leuenberg. Entstehung und Bedeutung der Konkordie reformatorischer Kirchen in Europa* (Paderborn, 1983) • L. Vischer, ed., *Rowing in One Boat: A Common Reflection on Lutheran-Reformed Relations Worldwide* (Geneva, 1999).

WILLIAM G. RUSCH

Levites → Priest, Priesthood

Leviticus, Book of

1. Title
2. Contents
3. Place in Pentateuch

1. Title

"Leviticus" is the title of the third book of the → Pentateuch. It comes from the Gk. *Leuïtikos* by way of the Lat. *Leviticus.* The term offers no guidance as to the contents, for any supposed reference to the Levites is off the mark. The Hebrew title is simply *wayyiqěrā*, "and he [the Lord] called," from the opening word.

2. Contents

In content, Leviticus first presents the laws of → sacrifice, in two sequences (chaps. 1–5 and 6–7), including burnt offerings, grain offerings, sacrifices of well-being (or "peace offerings," RSV), sin offerings, and guilt offerings. Next are laws pertaining to the priesthood (8–10), dealing with the → ordination

and institution of the → priests and their rights. The laws of purity (11–15; → Cultic Purity) are aimed at fashioning a pure → Israel (§1) free from every spot or stain. The law regarding the Day of → Atonement (16) presents the earliest version of this still-central observance of Israelite → piety (→ Jewish Practices 2.1).

The → Holiness Code (chaps. 17-26; → Sacred and Profane) deals, among other things, with ethical issues. Scholars differ as to whether we originally have here a single corpus. Links to the Book of Ezekiel have long been noted, and A. Cholewiński has drawn attention to features in common with Deuteronomy. Most scholars view the code as a later redaction, though with some preexilic elements (M. Haran).

3. Place in Pentateuch

Leviticus is a product of a Priestly school whose work appears in a new introduction to Genesis (1:1–2:4a) and in other places throughout the Pentateuch. Leviticus is the most substantial contribution of this school.

Bibliography: Commentaries: E. S. Gerstenberger (ATD; 6th ed.; Göttingen, 1993) • J. E. Hartley (WBC; Dallas, 1992) • W. C. Kaiser Jr., (NIB; Nashville, 1994) • G. A. F. Knight (DSB; Edinburgh, 1981) • J. Milgrom (AB; Garden City, N.Y., 1991) • M. Noth (OTL; 2d ed.; Philadelphia, 1977) • J. R. Porter (CBC; Cambridge, 1976) • N. H. Snaith (NCB; London, 1967) • G. J. Wenham (NICOT; Grand Rapids, 1992; orig. pub., 1979).

Other works: A. Cholewiński, *Heiligkeitsgesetz und Deuteronomium* (Rome, 1976) • M. Haran, *Temples and Temple-Service in Ancient Israel* (Oxford, 1978) • K. Koch, *Die Priesterschrift. Von Exodus 25 bis Leviticus 16* (Göttingen, 1959) • J. Neusner, *Leviticus Rabbah* (Atlanta, 1997) • R. Peter-Contesse and J. Ellington, *A Translator's Handbook on Leviticus* (New York, 1990) • G. von Rad, *Die Priesterschrift im Hexateuch* (Stuttgart, 1934) 30-57 • J. F. A. Sawyer and M. Douglas, *Reading Leviticus: A Conversation with Mary Douglas* (Sheffield, 1996).

J. Alberto Soggin

Liberal Theology

1. Term
   1.1. In Modern Judaism and Christianity
   1.2. As a Doctrine of Faith
   1.3. As a Polemical Concept
2. National Developments
   2.1. England and Scotland

1. Term

The term "liberal theology" is widely used in modern → Protestantism and → Judaism, but only marginally in 19th- and early 20th-century Roman → Catholicism. It shares the imprecision of the concept of → liberalism in politics and culture. Three aspects of its usage call for consideration: in modern Judaism and Christianity, as a doctrine of faith, and as a polemical concept.

1.1. *In Modern Judaism and Christianity*

In modern Judaism and Christianity theologians are called liberal who view the → Enlightenment and modern → culture as legitimate expressions of the Judeo-Christian tradition and who, in contrast to religious → conservatism and orthodoxy, try to reformulate the traditional faith in a way that is open to → modernity. In this modernist orientation liberal theology has been strongly influenced by the efforts of the liberal middle classes (→ Bourgeois, Bourgeoisie) to achieve political and social → emancipation.

In Protestantism the term became an influential one in Britain and the United States. In keeping with the strong political and social impact exerted by a reform-oriented middle class, Anglo-American Protestantism has had a clearly identifiable liberal tradition with an uncontested canon of classic liberal writers, including J. Locke (1632-1704), D. Hume (1711-76), and J. S. Mill (1806-73). In close connection with the securing of individuals against the → state and their participation in the state, liberals in the churches postulated the religious maturity of individuals (→ Adulthood) and, in many cases, the autonomy of local → congregations (→ Congregationalism). By church reforms they sought to strengthen the power of the laity (→ Lay Apostolate; Lay Movements).

In Germany, however, where the middle class was politically weak, there was no clear identification of liberal theology with a religiopolitical program. From the later Enlightenment the establishment of modern → autonomy was at the center of liberal theology, and many liberal German theologians also supported political liberalism, yet the relation of individual → freedom to both → church and state and the connection between political and ecclesiastical liberalism were both contested.

In Switzerland, Holland, and other European countries, especially Czechoslovakia, the traditions of liberal democracy greatly influenced Protestantism. In these places, then, liberal theology expressly espoused political liberalism.

In Roman Catholicism and also in Judaism, middle-class emancipation formed the context of liberal theology. In the former, where there was aloofness from middle-class reforming movements until well into the 20th century, some British and German university theologians carefully adopted the term after 1890 but then dropped it again early in the 20th century when the → teaching office took disciplinary measures in its battle against → modernism (→ Antimodernist Oath).

In European Judaism the concept had a broad history following the period from 1815 to the March 1848 → revolution, which has been little investigated. In connection with emancipation and assimilation a self-conscious Jewish middle class came into being that, if it did not secure entry into middle-class society by → baptism (H. Heine), sought a new Jewish identity appropriate to cultural modernity and was thus very open to the liberal theology of Protestantism. This reform Judaism wholly supported political liberalism. The strength of the liberal tradition in German Judaism before 1933 meant that the theological work of the World Union for Progressive Judaism (founded 1926) was, and continues to be, decisively influenced by classic representatives of German Reform Judaism like A. Geiger (1810-74) and H. Cohen (1842-1918).

1.2. *As a Doctrine of Faith*

Openness to the Enlightenment and rejection of a religious traditionalism that criticized modernity found expression in the liberal theology of both Judaism and Protestantism. Specifically, it included → criticism of → authority, historicocritical revision of the traditional → confessions (→ Apostles' Creed 4), recognition of religious → pluralism within the fellowship of faith, and a vision of the practice of → piety that is no longer defined dogmatically (→ Dogma) but rationally, that is, in humanitarian or ethical terms (→ Humanity; Ethics). The basic elements of this liberal theology focus on concern for individual religious self-determination.

A liberal theology is thus not a → dogmatics but a doctrine of faith. The normative exposition of an accepted doctrine involves reflection of religious → experience and expressed piety. From the days of the Enlightenment the dogmatic definition of the identity of one's own → denomination gives place to a presentation, grounded in the → philosophy of religion (i.e., in a general concept of → religion), of the supraconfessional essence of Christianity or, for

Jews, of the essence of Judaism. Along these lines, together with the distinctives of one's own → tradition, it is assumed that the basic agreement of all piety shaped by → monotheism will be demonstrated.

Features of liberal theology, then, are (1) criticism of the dogmatic claims of one's own fellowship of faith to absolutism and (2) openness to other religions. For modern Protestantism, however, this position does not mean renouncing the view that Christianity (or Protestantism) is culturally the supreme religion. Because Protestantism is the religion of → freedom and personality, it is destined to become the religion of the modern culture of → individualism.

The theologians of neo-Protestantism thought in terms of culture theologies as distinct from church theologies. They did not aim to strengthen the doctrinal homogeneity of a confessional church but to integrate modern social pluralism religiously. The more modern → society divides into competing ideological camps (→ Ideology; Worldview), the more it needs a fundamental religious → consensus, which can be found only on the basis of a rational Christian belief in humanity. The Protestant tradition is what decisively defines rational Christianity. Thus liberal culture theologians, despite their → tolerance for other opinions and openness to them, tend toward a structural illiberalism, showing intolerance toward other theological schools and Roman Catholicism.

1.3. *As a Polemical Concept*
From as early as the latter part of the 18th century, liberal theology in both Christianity and Judaism encountered the argument that its dedogmatizing destroyed the essence of the faith tradition, that tolerance led to unrestricted → relativism, and that the postulate of the maturity of individuals sanctioned an → individualism that loosened established ties to the church or → synagogue. Liberal theology became a battle cry in ecclesiastical politics that denoted a theological error that had long since been perceived and overcome (H. J. Birkner, 34). For conservative theologians in Protestantism, Roman Catholicism, and orthodox Judaism, the term "liberal" came to be seen as the epitome of theological illegitimacy. It meant the dissolving of binding ideals, the individualistic disruption of the fellowship of faith, and assimilation to the middle-class → optimism of → progress.

This type of attack itself reflected the various historicopolitical contexts of theological thought. In 19th-century Germany, under the impact of an authoritarian state and the alliance of the ecclesiastical elite with political conservatism, the polemical use of the term "liberal theology" was much stronger than in western Europe and the United States. The same applied to the partly socialist (→ Socialism) and partly conservative antiliberal movements of the early 20th century. In all → industrial societies there has been since 1890, and even more so since 1918, an anti-middle-class protest against the relativistic historical thinking of liberals and a search for a new binding authority.

In German Protestantism this theological antiliberalism was much more aggressive and politicized than in western Europe and the United States. With few exceptions (e.g., R. Bultmann [1884-1976]), the Luther renaissance, → dialectical theology, conservative-revolutionary neo-Lutheranism, and → religious socialism combined their criticism of liberal theology with a radical repudiation of party political liberalism. In Germany these politically and theologically opposing syntheses of the theological and political criticism of liberalism strengthened the rejection of the Weimar Republic, with its liberal and welfare-state traditions.

2. National Developments
2.1. *England and Scotland*
Liberal theology in England and Scotland was strongly influenced at first by the → free churches deriving from the radical wing of the → Reformation and from 16th- and 17th-century → Unitarian circles. Yet with the Broad Church party in the early 19th century, a tradition of liberal theology also came into the English national church (→ Anglican Communion).

In the Unitarian tradition three elements are central: (1) rejection of the doctrine of the → Trinity and stress on the full humanity of Jesus (→ Christology), who is seen primarily as an ethical model and a guarantee of moral perfectibility; (2) a close connection, influenced by → deism, between religion and morality, according to which a virtuous life is the most important expression of piety; and (3) an emphasis on the freedom of the will and a moralistic understanding of → sin, with belief in the possibility of active → penitence and expiation.

Of great influence in this regard was J. Priestley (1733-1804), who emigrated to the United States because of violent attacks on his → "Arianism" and his support for the French Revolution. His pupil T. Lindsey (1723-1808) privately founded in London the first Unitarian chapel (1774), which soon had many successors. The Unitarian Society for Promoting Christian Knowledge (1791) numbered some 300 congregations even before it received official recognition in 1844. Under the influence of the critical theology of F. C. Baur (1792-1860) and D. F. Strauss (1808-74), T. S. Smith (1788-1861) and J. Martineau (1805-1900) combined a Unitarian → creation → mysticism and ethicist view of Jesus with a → universalism of grace according to which the divine goodness requires the eschatological salvation of all things (→ Apocatastasis; Eschatology; Life 1).

In the Anglican Broad Church party enlightened criticism of dogma was less prominent than a romantic belief in a new unity of religion (→ Romanticism), the history-shaping individual, and national society. Influenced by S. T. Coleridge (1772-1834), T. Arnold (1795-1842), T. Carlyle (1795-1881), and C. Kingsley (1819-75), liberals used the existing journal *Modern Churchman* to promote church reform, the adjustment of the faith tradition to modern science (→ Science and Theology), including Darwinism (→ Evolution), and the social reforms evoked by poverty, industrialization, and urbanization. This focus on ethics, which found expression in the central position granted to the idea of the → kingdom of God and to belief in a movement toward this kingdom in history, was powerfully represented by F. D. Maurice (1805-72), who, with Kingsley and in the teeth of strong resistance, developed a Christian socialism and popularized his "free Christianity" by founding institutions for popular education. Maurice's battle for a new reformation, which M. Arnold (1822-88) and others supported, was later continued by modernist Roman Catholics like F. von Hügel (1852-1925) and G. Tyrrell (1861-1909) and by the more orthodox Congregationalist P. T. Forsyth (1848-1921).

In the main, liberal theology in England and Scotland had a strong orientation to social reform. In contrast to liberal theology on the Continent, it was closer to the labor movement, related more firmly to the churches and → universities, and less radical in its criticism of the Bible and dogma, so that often a naive Bible piety might also be called liberal. The basic orientation to practical matters and to the people made possible a broad circulation of liberal theology in every denomination after 1945, though the controversies surrounding J. A. T. Robinson's *Honest to God* (1963), J. Hick's *Myth of God Incarnate* (1977), and D. Cuppit's *Christ and the Hiddenness of God* (1971; 2d ed., 1985) showed how strong the resistance was to this form of criticism.

2.2. North America

2.2.1. In North America liberal theology developed among substantially different intellectual and political circumstances. Again, no single definition of the term covers all its implications and usages.

"Liberal," indeed, has as often been a pejorative term adopted by conservatives for their opponents as it has been the self-designation of any particular group. American appropriations of the views of European thinkers (as in the case of Karl → Barth and others) have at times strongly influenced the landscape. Theological phenomena that historians of doctrine may now call liberal were not always originally designated by that term.

Early appearances in America of a theology of the liberal sort emerged in protests against the → Puritan orthodoxy of Massachusetts Bay Colony by such figures as R. Williams (ca. 1603-83), A. Hutchinson (1591-1643), and the Quaker Mary Dyer (d. 1660) and the work of her successors such as W. Penn (1644-1718) in Pennsylvania and the itinerant Quaker preacher J. Woolman (1720-72). Liberal opposition to a dominant → Calvinism (esp. as opposed to the revivalist → orthodoxy [§2] of the New England interior and to the continued Calvinist influence at Yale) began to take hold at Harvard and in the Boston area with 18th- and early 19th-century figures such as C. Chauncy (1705-87) and J. Mayhew (1720-66), known for their → Arminian or Socinian views.

2.2.2. Unitarianism properly so-called, brought to the United States by Priestley and Lindsey, soon became the most influential tradition of liberal theology in that country. Under the influence of W. E. Channing (1780-1842), the first Unitarian congregation, which had been founded in Boston in 1775, openly called itself Unitarian for the first time in 1819. In Channing's → biblicist supernaturalism we find a combination of radical repudiation of the inherited doctrine of satisfaction (→ Justification), diaconal involvement (→ Diakonia) on behalf of the oppressed, and a social-reforming fight for legal equality for blacks.

R. W. Emerson (1803-82), the founder of → transcendentalism, which was so influential in the United States, also expressed his mystically → pantheistic and radically individualistic belief in personality by action on behalf of the emancipation of slaves (→ Slavery). Emerson's pupil T. Parker (1810-60) agreed that the romantically idealistic belief in the divinity and → immortality of the individual must be given concrete form in → love of one's → neighbor, social reform, and the battle against → racism.

By means of the American Unitarian Association, founded by Channing, Emerson, and Parker, which was the most important organization for Protestant liberal theology in the United States, and then also by means of the social theology of

H. Bushnell (1802-76), which reminds us of the views of F. D. E. → Schleiermacher (1768-1834; see 2.4.2), liberal theology in North America (→ North American Theology) was strongly characterized by a belief in the kingdom of God that focused on the mission of the American nation and by a humanitarian Jesus piety that saw Jesus primarily as a moral example and that regarded approximation to the unity of love of God and neighbor lived out by him as the essence of successful Christianity. In the 19th century the most important academic training center for Unitarians was Harvard Divinity School, which promoted a so-called progressive orthodoxy in opposition to revivalism and the new confessional → fundamentalism.

2.2.3. Along with the Unitarians and Bushnell, the → Universalists also helped to form the new tradition. Influenced theologically by Chauncy, J. Murray (1741-1815), and H. Ballou (1771-1852), they formed a church in 1790 and conveyed to liberal Protestantism in the United States the view that God in his universal love wills the → happiness of all people. Thus even the active promotion of one's own well-being ranks as approximation to the kingdom of God.

2.2.4. Liberal theology along such lines lived reasonably peacefully alongside more conservative tendencies until the controversy over Darwin's *Origin of Species,* which began in the early 1860s. From then until the celebrated 1925 "Monkey Trial" in Dayton, Tennessee, and beyond, American Christianity became polarized to an unprecedented degree. In the face of a dominant anti-Darwinist orthodoxy, a relatively small group of thinkers maintained their belief that Christian faith need not stand in opposition to reason and the findings of science. At the same time, a few Americans in the universities and theological faculties were bringing home from Germany the fruits of historical-critical study of the Bible. Among the most prominent of the latter was C. A. Briggs (1841-1913) of Union Seminary in New York, condemned for his views by the General Assembly of the Presbyterian Church. A generation later Harry Emerson Fosdick (1878-1969) was preaching a liberal gospel intellectually compelling to many who could not accept → evangelical orthodoxy.

2.2.5. North American liberal theology has also been very sensitive to the problems created by capitalist industrialization (→ Capitalism). This concern is evident in Bushnell's pupil W. Gladden (1836-1918) and the Baptist W. → Rauschenbusch (1861-1918), the most important advocates of the → Social Gospel. Strongly influenced by A. Ritschl (1822-89), Rauschenbusch took the liberal belief that individuals must contribute actively by their moral lifestyle to redemption and the setting up of God's kingdom and expanded it into a full-blown social theology that argues that individuals cannot be redeemed if society is left unredeemed. Jesus was thus stylized into a social reformer who offers appropriate and binding directions for the overcoming of the problems of social integration in modern society. This thesis explains the rapid onset of criticism of liberal theology in the 1920s.

Much more strongly than in Germany, the new orthodoxy and new realism remained basic elements in North American liberal theology in virtue of the close connection between the → theology of history, the belief in progress, and the high valuation of the American → nation. The ethnic and religious → pluralism of the United States also demanded a constant wrestling with the classic problems of liberal theology, namely, the question of an essence of Christianity that transcends the confessions, or that of the relation between Christian claims to truth and religious experience in other religions. For this reason liberal theology had a greater impact in academic discourse in North America than in Europe, even though the religiopolitical situation was marked by abiding and deepening differences between liberal and fundamentalist Protestantism. At the same time, liberal theology could so profoundly affect Roman Catholicism in North America that many of the clergy found themselves in ongoing opposition to the Vatican (→ Roman Catholic Church).

Of great significance, finally, for the promotion of liberal religious discourse in the United States was the Reformed synagogue, which — as distinct from strict orthodoxy, the most centrist Conservative Judaism, and the Reconstructionists around M. Kaplan (1881-1983) — rejected the absolute obligatoriness of the → Halakah and stressed the universally valid elements in the ethical monotheism of Judaism. Partly as a result of the destruction of Judaism in central Europe during the → Holocaust, there has been intensive theological exchange between the Reformed synagogue and liberal Protestantism in the United States.

2.3. *France, Holland, Switzerland, and Czechoslovakia*

Protestantism in France, Holland, Switzerland, and Czechoslovakia, as well as Roman Catholicism in France and Holland, were also strongly influenced by liberal traditions. Despite profound differences in social and religiopolitical context, liberal theology in these countries had a substantially similar program, namely, the exposition of the Christian tradition against the background of the political and cultural emancipation of the middle class.

In *France* theology became middle class by means of the overcoming of denominational antagonisms. The Christian tradition was to promote the integration of a society that had been deeply divided since 1789. Influential in French liberal theology were A. Vinet (1797-1847, who taught at Lausanne), J.-E. Renan (1823-92), P. Sabatier (1858-1928), and M. Goguel (1880-1955).

In *Holland* we find instead an openness to historical criticism represented, for example, by A. Kuenen (1828-91). Then, after the dissolving of the denominationally related faculties in 1870, there was a stress on the → history of religion.

In *Switzerland* a strong ecclesiastical tradition of liberal theology was initiated in the 19th century in connection with German → idealism. In this regard H. Lang (1826-76) and A. E. Biedermann (1819-85) played a mediating role that still exerts an influence.

In *Czechoslovakia* the tight link between liberal theology and middle-class emancipation may be seen clearly in T. Masaryk (1850-1937), who, after converting from Roman Catholicism to the Reformed Church, taught in Prague, interpreted the Bohemian Reformation as the basic datum of the history of Czechoslovakian freedom, and, as president of the Czechoslovak Republic, proclaimed his humanitarian faith as primarily ethical discipleship of Jesus, but also in criticism of traditional Christological dogma. In the struggle against confessionalism his many followers were able to effect a union between the Lutherans and the Reformed (1918). In the resulting Evangelical Church of Czech Brethren, liberal theological influences were strong at first, but soon, under the impact of J. L. Hromádka (1889-1969) and his followers, who were close to Barth, they ceased to direct the theological course of the young church. Strong modernist tendencies affected the Czechoslovak Hussite Church, however, which came into being in 1919 with powerful nationalist feelings in a movement to break away from Rome. Both churches helped the middle class in the new republic to achieve a self-conscious liberal and social democratic identity when the middle classes in other countries such as France and Germany were for the most part supporting the new antiliberalism.

2.4. Germany

2.4.1. Thus far the history of liberal theology in German Protestantism has not been adequately researched. In 1774 J. S. Semler (1725-91) used the term *liberalis theologia* for a strictly historical investigation of the NT with no dogmatic presupposi-

tions. In distinction from ecclesiastical Christianity this theology was meant to serve the perfecting of Christianity and the justification of a rational and practical "private Christianity." In the battle for the legitimacy of the Enlightenment, liberal theology became a party name for the neologists (→ Neology) and rationalists (→ Rationalism), who fought for doctrinal freedom in the church and sought to replace a faith centering on original sin, → predestination, and Christ's vicarious penal suffering with a universally rational belief in the Creator God, moral → autonomy, and the → immortality of the soul. After 1789 this emancipatory concept took on a political dimension. Those who fought against the bondage of the letter and the compulsion of dogma must also be advocates of political freedom and human → rights.

2.4.2. Neither Schleiermacher (→ Schleiermacher's Theology), who later came to be known as the → church father of "free Protestantism," nor the followers of G. W. F. Hegel (1770-1831; → Hegelianism) called themselves liberal theologians. The title was adopted in the early 19th century, however, by later rationalists like H. G. Tzschirner (1778-1828), W. T. Krug (1770-1842), and K. G. Bretschneider (1776-1848), who played a considerable role in setting up the early liberal political opposition in Germany. Their aim was to establish in both church and state the so-called principle of Protestantism, that is, criticism of the → hierarchy, independent thinking, and individual freedom. They distinguished this Protestant freedom both from the Roman system of authority and from the terrorist → anarchy (→ Terrorism) of the revolutionary democrats, so that liberal theology expressed the hope of achieving revolutionary change by rational reform. After 1840, however, the phrase also took on a tendentiously revolutionary content. Radical democratic Lichtfreunde (Friends of light) and "German Catholics" (who rejected the pope and many Catholic dogmas and rites), as well as left-wing Hegelians like D. F. Strauss, conceived of liberal theology as a transformation of Christianity into belief in the divinity of the human species (→ Anthropology).

2.4.3. After the 1848 → revolution the Tübingen school of F. C. Baur, Der deutsche Protestantenverein (German Protestant union, 1863), and the *Protestantische Kirchenzeitung* (Protestant church newspaper, 1854) made liberal theology into a polemical concept opposed to the dominant alliance of confessional Lutheran orthodoxy and the restorationist police state. In so doing, they stressed the basic harmony between ecclesiastical and political liberalism. For prominent theologians of the Protestant Union like R. Rothe (1799-1867), liberal theology meant, on the one hand, the battle against dogmatic compulsion, doctrinal authority, church control of schools, and the clericalizing of → politics and, on the other hand, the vision of a national church analogous to a smaller German nation that, as a true → people's church, embracing all sectors of the population, would effect the national religious integration of the new state. Jews and Roman Catholics would attain to full civic rights only when converting to this national Protestant church.

The religious cultural ideal of the Protestant Union was thus marked less by pluralism and tolerance than by high expectations of homogeneity, that is, by the hope of a new religious unity of culture. As opposed to contemporary Roman Catholic and conservative Protestant concepts of culture, this religious integration of society did not demand for its achievement the church's authoritarian control over the state but the religious permeation of all political institutions, or strengthening of the unity between national culture and the church. The fact that after 1880 liberal theologians like O. Pfleiderer (1839-1908) and A. Bonus (1864-1941) could call for a Germanizing of Christianity and a continuation of the → Kulturkampf shows how politically illiberal this → Culture Protestantism really was. Even liberal theologians who organized a left wing commonly expounded Protestant freedom in sharp opposition to Romanism. Yet they had a liberal cultural ideal inasmuch as they advocated the separation of church and state.

2.4.4. A. Ritschl, the → history-of-religions school, and those who wrote for M. Rade's (1857-1940) *Christliche Welt* (Christian world) did not call themselves liberal theologians. Criticizing the Protestant Union and appealing to the British social liberalism of Carlyle and Kingsley (also Channing), Rade, F. Naumann (1860-1919), E. → Troeltsch (1865-1923), O. Baumgarten (1858-1934), and W. Bousset (1865-1920) used "liberal theology" after 1890 primarily as a synonym for a naive, optimistic, cultural middle-class theology that did not do justice to such critical cultural experiences of the time as the rise of proletarian (→ Proletariat) socialism and the threat posed to free persons by the autonomies of capitalist modernization. Only in the early 20th century, when the church authorities in Prussia took repressive measures against religiously liberal pastors, were alliances made between the older liberals of the Protestant Union and the Freunden der *Christlichen Welt* (i.e., the theologians who wrote for Rade's journal), so that even before 1914 both Ritschlians and members of the history-

of-religions school like Troeltsch could at times be described as liberal theologians.

The extremely polemical use made of the term by conservative Lutherans before 1914 is consistent with this view. These Lutherans found in liberal theology a politically and theologically false synthesis of nonchurchly neo-Protestantism and Liberal Party reforming politics. For them, this combination offered the empire Western enlightenment, democratism, and individualism. With its relativizing of the churches, however, it dissolved the only solid basis of true authority and morality.

Conservative criticism of liberal theology was directed especially against Troeltsch, who, with A. von Harnack (1851-1930), was seen as its classic representative in the early 20th century. Troeltsch's great international impact was due primarily to his readiness, under the pressure of the modern sense of history, to take seriously the particularity of Christianity in religious history and to withdraw its traditional claim to dogmatic absolutism in favor of the view that it was supreme only in a temporally and spatially relative sense. As he saw it, Christian faith was simply a central force of cultural synthesis within European and American culture. It was designed to safeguard the claims of personality over against depersonalizing trends in modern society. Troeltsch thus demanded that the → sects with their productivity in social reform and the mystical tradition with its individualism (→ Mysticism) should be integrated into a dogmatically ossified church.

2.4.5. Already before the beginning of World War I, younger representatives of a new antiliberalism linked rejection of party political liberalism with a fundamental criticism of liberal theology. In "antiliberal harmony" (K. Tanner) with the nontheological battle against all "liberalist thinking," liberal theology was dehistoricized into a concept that denotes the principially false orientation of all neo-Protestant theology. At the same time, theologians organized into liberal Protestant associations — including, for example, H. Mulert (1879-1950), M. Rade, O. Baumgarten, E. Foerster (1865-1945), and H. von Soden (1881-1945) — claimed the term programmatically so that, on behalf of a democracy under threat, they might forge a new alliance between liberal piety and liberal democratic politics.

After 1933 K. Barth (1886-1968) and theologians of the → Confessing Church engaged in the → church struggle as a war of principle against all liberal theology, since by its criticism of the Christ → revelation and church doctrine, this theology had prepared the way for the → German Christians to postulate the presence of God in the national revolution. The German Christians, however, argued that the Confessing Church was simply following the liberal line in its battle for the inner autonomy of the church (→ Natural Theology).

Champions of liberal Protestant organizations such as H. Weinel (1874-1936) thought that the definitive end of the age of middle-class liberalism had come with National Socialism (→ Fascism) and thus programmatically abandoned the slogan "liberal theology." Others, especially Mulert, regarded it as a symbol of political resistance. If Protestantism did not want to repress its liberal traditions in conformity with the spirit of the age, it must aggressively defend such basic principles of the Enlightenment as tolerance, constitutionalism (→ Law and Legal Theory), the rights of → minorities, and the equality of the Jews. This stand explains why the National Socialists either suppressed liberal Protestant organizations and publications or forced them to dissolve themselves.

3. Recent Tendencies

Karl Barth's growing influence in America generalized the just-described experience with the German Christians in such a way that liberal theology came to mean not so much a theology of the Left — Barth's own theology, politically speaking, was precisely that — as any theology seeking to marry the spirit of its age in such a way as to become dependent on nonbiblical categories of thought. Barth saw this tendency not only in his own German university teachers who, he saw, had supported German aspirations in World War I but also in the several generations of German thinkers from Schleiermacher to von Harnack. This pejorative perspective on liberalism accompanied the strong influence of dialectical theology in American theological schools. Although the liberal theology of the theology-and-culture correlation remained identifiably alive in certain sectors, it also took on dialectical clothing in the work of such scholars as Bultmann, widely translated and read in America, and P. → Tillich (1886-1965).

American neoorthodoxy, as propounded especially by Reinhold → Niebuhr (1892-1971), identified liberal theology pejoratively not so much as a matter of trimming the gospel to the spirit of the age as a refusal to take seriously the realities of sin and → evil and therefore becoming overly optimistic or sentimental in confronting realities such as → war and economic greed. Social Gospel optimism suffered Niebuhr's severe criticism, but also the → pacifist and isolationist attitudes held by many American Christians as World War II drew near, and even after the beginning of American involvement in the war.

The decline of dialectical or neoorthodox theology in North America after the mid-1960s was not followed by a swing of the pendulum toward a new, coherent liberal theology in any sense recognizable from the previously defined meanings of the term. Harvey Cox's celebrated *Secular City* (1965) represented a new form of theological optimism, but Cox did not found a consistent or lasting school of thought. The U.S. → civil rights and anti–Vietnam War movements attracted participants of many theological persuasions, including those who espoused a North American version of Latin American → liberation theology, albeit a position with a very different intellectual pedigree. Dialectical and neoorthodox positions gave way to a variety of contextual positions — African American, Hispanic, feminist, Asian, and others — as well as to the so-called death of God position (→ God Is Dead Theology).

The failure of persons of classic liberal sentiment, including political liberals, to produce or gather around any new form of liberal theology has been striking. Perhaps the → secularization and fragmentation of late 20th-century American life so diluted a formerly "Christian" culture that a liberal interpretation of tradition within that culture is seen by many to produce not an alternative expression of faith but rather the risk of dissolution of identifiable faith itself.

The fundamental renaissance of liberal political theory in the West German constitution was not accompanied by a programmatic readoption of the concept of liberal theology. The situation was different in German-speaking Switzerland, where, on the basis of an intensive adoption of the ethical theology of A. → Schweitzer (1875-1965), M. Werner developed a liberal history of dogma (→ Dogma, History of), and F. Buri and U. Neuenschwander founded a new liberal theology (1953). During the 1950s in the United States, however, no one espoused a program of postdialectical liberal theology. It is the more surprising, then, that in West Germany prominent representatives of the theological antiliberalism of the 1920s relaxed their basic criticism of liberal theology and, in close connection with political changes, sought to prevent the repudiation of liberal piety from also acting as criticism of liberal parliamentary democracy. This liberal profile of what had once been dialectical theology received particularly influential emphasis from R. Bultmann with his disputed program of → demythologization.

In connection with the social upheavals of the 1960s, postdialectical theologians achieved significance in West Germany, giving new application to such representatives of neo-Protestantism as Schleiermacher and Troeltsch. Similarly among followers of dialectical theology older models of thought oriented to the antithesis between liberal culture theology and church theology yielded to new theologies of experience. How far this new situation in the discussion may be seen as a transformation of the tradition of liberal theology it is impossible as yet to say. A strange contradiction seems to mark liberal theology today. Organizationally, the Protestant liberal social milieu of 1933-45 has largely vanished. Yet after the late 1960s the liberal culture and pluralism of West German society came into public discussion in the church. Thus T. Rendtorff's ethical theology shows that liberal theology no longer stands in antithesis to church theology. Conversely, E. Jüngel's hermeneutical theology of experience makes it plain that the basic insights of liberal Protestantism can be taken up implicitly in the medium of dogmatic language games. This change might be explained as follows. If the Protestant church is not to fall behind the democratic constitutional state and pluralist society, with their developed liberalism of outlook, it seems to need liberal theology.

The North American situation was quite different. By the late 20th century the word "liberal" had become most prominent as an imprecation of the Right toward the whole range of positions outside self-named "evangelical" culture, rather than a name chosen for themselves by holders of a coherent theological position on the Left. Conservatives could organize around disciplined perspectives, while liberals preferred to argue with one another. Those of liberal persuasion were and are united mainly by their resistance to the growing political power of the Right, by their attraction to positions favoring "choice" (as opposed to "right to life"), the ordination of gay persons, opposition to capital punishment, internationalism, → ecumenism, and interreligious → dialogue. In this general camp (even if not precisely agreeing on every issue) one finds writers such as Gordon Kaufman, Diana Eck, and David Tracy, as well as the journals *Christian Century, Tikkun,* and others. One also sees in certain writers — as, for example, George Lindbeck, John Howard Yoder, and Stanley Hauerwas — a significant combination of strong attention to Bible, tradition, and church, with relatively liberal social positions on certain issues.

Liberal theology in this range of senses is now to be found, usually in a minority position, in most American denominations, including the Roman Catholic Church. It remains the majority view in groups such as the Quakers (→ Friends, Society of) and Unitarian-Universalists, and in progressive issue-oriented groups uniting Christians of various confessional loyalties.

→ Idealism; Theology in the Nineteenth and Twentieth Centuries

Bibliography: H. J. BIRKNER, "Liberale Theologie," *Kirchen und Liberalismus im 19. Jahrhundert* (ed. M. Schmidt and G. Schwaiger; Göttingen, 1976) 33-42 • C. A. BRIGGS, *Theological Symbolics* (New York, 1914) • R. BULTMANN, *Faith and Understanding* (Philadelphia, 1987) • K. CAUTHEN, *The Impact of American Religious Liberalism* (New York, 1962) • C. CHAUNCY, *The Benevolence of the Deity, Fairly and Impartially Considered* (Boston, 1784) • G. J. DORRIEN, *The Making of American Liberal Theology: Imagining Progressive Religion, 1805-1900* (Louisville, Ky., 2001) • H. E. FOSDICK, *As I See Religion* (Westport, Conn., 1975; orig. pub., 1932) • F. W. GRAF, *Theonomie. Fallstudien zum Integrationsanspruch neuzeitlicher Theologie* (Gütersloh, 1987); "What Has London (or Oxford or Cambridge) to Do with Augsburg? The Enduring Significance of the German Liberal Tradition in Christian Theology," *The Future of Liberal Theology* (ed. M. D. Chapman; Aldershot, 2002) 18-38; idem, ed., *Profile des neuzeitlichen Protestantismus* (3 vols.; Gütersloh, 1990-93) • W. R. HUTCHISON, *The Modernist Impulse in American Protestantism* (Durham, N.C., 1992; orig. pub., 1976); idem, ed., *American Protestant Thought: The Liberal Era* (New York, 1968) • G. KAUFMAN, *God, Mystery, Diversity: Christian Theology in a Pluralistic World* (Minneapolis, 1996) • M. J. LANGFORD, *A Liberal Theology for the Twenty-first Century: A Passion for Reason* (Burlington, Vt., 2001) • R. S. MICHAELSEN and W. C. ROOF, ed., *Liberal Protestantism: Realities and Possibilities* (New York, 1986) • D. E. MILLER, *The Case for Liberal Christianity* (San Francisco, Calif., 1981) • J. J. OWEN, *Religion and the Demise of Liberal Rationalism* (Chicago, 2001) • D. PHILIPSON, *The Reform Movement in Judaism* (New York, 1967; orig. pub., 1907) • M. RUMSCHEIDT, ed., *Adolf von Harnack: Liberal Theology at Its Height* (San Francisco, 1989) • F. SCHLEIERMACHER, *On Religion: Speeches to Its Cultured Despisers* (trans. R. Crouter; Cambridge, 1996; orig. pub., 1799) • P. TILLICH, *The Protestant Era* (Chicago, 1948).

FRIEDRICH WILHELM GRAF and LEWIS S. MUDGE

Liberalism

Overview
1. Theoretical Roots
2. Relation to Religion and the Church
3. Political Development
4. In the United States

Overview

Liberalism is one of the great political and ideological trends of the last three centuries (→ Ideology; Politics), its high point being in the 19th century, when it had two rivals, → conservatism (after the French Revolution) and → socialism (in the course of industrialization). Socialism was weakened by → fascism and German National Socialism, but after 1945 it revived both ideologically and structurally in the rivalry between Western → democracy and Soviet Communist party dictatorship (→ Marxism 1).

At the heart of liberal thinking stands the individual, who in virtue of the gift of → reason enjoys free self-determination (→ Freedom) and can accord moral and legal respect to others, but who needs the secure legal framework of the state (constitution, basic rights, parliamentary → representation) to be able to develop freely. In particular, the freedom of economic self-regulation by the market (→ Economy; Economic Ethics) and competition (→ Achievement and Competition) and the clash of opinions and ideas link individual development to historical → progress.

The main agent of liberalism is the middle class (→ Bourgeois, Bourgeoisie). This class, however, has increasingly inclined to use political measures to protect the interests and possessions (→ Property) that go along with liberal principles and to ignore the social inequalities introduced and protected by → capitalism.

1. Theoretical Roots

Liberalism had its theoretical roots in → natural law and → Enlightenment philosophy, especially in Britain and France (J. Locke, D. Hume, J.-J. Rousseau), but also in the German → idealism of I. Kant (1724-1804; → Kantianism) and, in part, G. W. F. Hegel (1770-1831; → Hegelianism), along with the classic middle-class economic and social theories of A. Smith (1723-90), J. Bentham (1748-1832), D. Ricardo (1772-1823), and J. S. Mill (1806-73). Influential constitutional thinkers were Montesquieu (1689-1755), A. de Tocqueville (1805-59), and, in Germany, W. von Humboldt (1767-1835), R. von Mohl (1799-1875), and the parliamentarians and publicists K. von Rotteck (1775-1840) and K. T. Welcker (1784-1868).

In the later 19th century there were only isolated developments (e.g., by L. Brentano and I. Hobhouse). Max → Weber (1864-1920) was no longer motivated by any attempt to construct a system but by critical sociological reflection on modern capitalist and bureaucratic civilization (→ Bureaucracy; Sociology).

2. Relation to Religion and the Church

As regards → religion and the → church, liberalism from the outset stood at a relativizing and secularizing distance (→ Secularization). Its demand for → religious liberty and → tolerance was always its basic paradigmatic value. Sharp conflicts often arose with the claim of the → Roman Catholic Church to all-embracing authority, especially in Spain, Italy, and France, but also in the Benelux countries, and in Germany in the case of the → Kulturkampf.

Liberalism had certain points of contact with → Protestantism (e.g., dissenting churches, the individual relationship to God, the work ethic in the sense of Max Weber; → Dissenters). A point of particularly hot debate was the denominational influence on educational policy (→ Denomination; School and Church), as might be seen in West Germany even up to 1960.

Specific ethical issues still arise today (→ Social Ethics), such as → abortion as a punishable offense (→ Punishment 2). But with the separation of → church and state that became the rule in the 20th century, the traditional laicism of liberalism has largely lost its significance.

3. Political Development

Politically, liberalism developed in various ways in Europe. It established itself as one of the two great parties in Britain. It was very influential in republican strands in France. It took roots in the farming community in Denmark. It was split even in the organizing phase in Germany after the unsuccessful 1848 revolution. In 1867 the National Liberals favored O. von Bismarck (1815-98) and unification, while the Progressives (later the Liberal Party) opposed the empire and clung to left-wing constitutionalism. In Italy a small middle-class liberal group was dominant up to 1914, but it could not stand before a politically organized → Catholicism (the Partito Popolare) or finally before fascism. Reforming developments in favor of social liberalism gained a foothold only with broad party support (e.g., in Britain and France). The Protestant social movement in Germany (F. Naumann, first president of the National Social Union) attempted something along these lines but could only marginally influence the consolidated left-wing liberalism, which existed in the Fortschrittliche Volkspartei (Progressive people's party, 1910-18).

From 1929 in the United States, with the depression and New Deal, a welfare-state liberalism emerged (mainly connected with the Democratic Party) that is often polemically attacked as left wing (see 4).

Democratization of the franchise, the rise of labor parties, and economic problems after World War I undermined liberal parties on every hand. After World War II, under U.S. leadership, liberal political and economic systems were reestablished, but liberal parties, like the German Free Democrats, could survive only as tiny minorities. Even modern attempts at reorientation (e.g., R. Aron, R. Dahrendorf) vacillate painfully between ordoliberalism, neoliberalism, and neoconservatism (→ Economy 3.2). They also encounter → pragmatism and vested interests in political practice.

Bibliography: R. DAHRENDORF, Die Chancen der Krise. Über die Zukunft des Liberalismus (Stuttgart, 1983) • L. GALL, ed., Bürgertum und bürgerlich-liberale Bewegung in Mitteleuropa seit dem 18. Jahrhundert (Munich, 1997) • A. C. GOULD, Origins of Liberal Dominance: State, Church, and Party in Nineteenth-Century Europe (Ann Arbor, Mich., 1999) • K. HOLL, G. TRAUTMANN, and H. VORLÄNDER, eds., Sozialer Liberalismus (Göttingen, 1986) • E. J. KIRCHNER, ed., Liberal Parties in Western Europe (Cambridge, 1988) • H. J. LASKI, The Rise of European Liberalism (New Brunswick, N.J., 1997; orig. pub., 1936) • R. LATHAM, The Liberal Moment: Modernity, Security, and the Making of Postwar International Order (New York, 1997) • G. M. LUEBBERT, Liberalism, Fascism, or Social Democracy: Social Classes and the Political Origins of Regimes in Interwar Europe (New York, 1991) • T. SCHILLER, Liberalismus in Europa (Hannover, 1978).

THEO SCHILLER

4. In the United States

Developments in the United States in many ways paralleled, yet in certain particulars departed from, the European experience. The → individualistic, tolerant tenets of the 18th-century European → Enlightenment quickly caught on in America, influencing the founders of the nation and the character of the U.S. Constitution. The same assumptions translated into optimistic views associated with the educated middle class, including belief in the essential goodness of human beings, in individual property rights, and in limitations on the powers of government. Such convictions went together with laissez-faire economics, claims of → freedom to adopt self-chosen directions in life, confidence in the inevitability of social progress, and resistance to all externally imposed dogmas, whether of church or state. Some of these positions paradoxically became tenets of 20th-century → conservatism, and some liberals of the same period allied themselves with forces wishing to change the social status quo.

Specific liberal programs have differed according to time, place, and situation. Late 19th- and early 20th-century industrialization and unregulated "robber baron" capitalism threw many into poverty (→ Industrial Society), demonstrating the failure of liberal principles to provide a good life for everyone. Many liberals began to recognize a need for social reform. Some began to look to the state to guarantee basic conditions of economic life, a minimum wage, and social security. Many favored a new idea: the progressive taxation of incomes. Socialists also supported such causes but favored more total government control of the economy. Liberals continued to uphold ideals of individual → autonomy, now combined with enlightened social goals. Liberal opinion after World War I added internationalism to its agenda, among other things supporting Woodrow Wilson and his proposal for the League of Nations.

An influential liberal social philosopher of this period was John Dewey (1859-1952), who propounded an instrumentalist form of → pragmatism. In this view, → truth partook of no transcendent reality but varied in its formulation with the problem at hand. Dewey stood for social experimentation as opposed to abstract reasoning, favored → democracy not only as a political system but also as a locus of moral value, and supported various forms of social reform, including women's suffrage.

The economic boom of the late 1920s reinforced liberal confidence in the compatibility of individual autonomy with social progress. Such hopes were dashed at the end of the decade by the coming of the Great Depression, a disastrous downturn not resolved until the onset of World War II. The establishment in the 1930s under Franklin Roosevelt of what amounted to a liberal welfare state brought with it both a redefinition of liberalism and its relocation to the moderate left wing of the Democratic Party. The most influential liberal intellectual of this period may well have been essayist and editor Walter Lippmann (1889-1974), whose early books championed the changes brought about under the rubric of Roosevelt's New Deal.

The period following World War II brought with it new expressions of liberal → optimism as well as a new level of participation by Roman Catholic figures such as John Courtney Murray (1904-67), whose book We Hold These Truths (1960) contributed to the electoral success of John F. Kennedy in 1960. A more secular and leftward-tending version of liberalism emerged after the war in the writings of urban public intellectuals such as Hannah Arendt, Alfred Kazin, Norman Podhoretz, Norman Cousins, and Bayard Rustin in journals such as Commentary, Partisan Review, New Republic, and

Nation. A centrist, if elitist, liberalism continued in the editorial pages of the *New York Times* and the *Washington Post.*

Many features of the → civil rights and antiwar movements of the 1960s conformed to a broadly liberal agenda, now increasingly expressed in antiestablishment and sometimes civilly disobedient terms. A radical belief in → progress — indeed, a belief in the socially transformative power of popular movements — appears in such works as Theodore Roszak's *Making of a Counter-Culture* (1969) and *Where the Wasteland Ends* (1972) and Charles Reich's *Greening of America* (1970). Both intellectual and practical leadership of a liberal theological bent came from Martin Luther → King Jr.

Few of the just-named writers and movements particularly claimed the title "liberal," but they nonetheless represented what this tradition stood for in their time. As liberal expressions became still more diverse, beginning to represent a wide array of specific communities and interests, the term itself came less and less to denote any single definable philosophy. Rather, it found itself co-opted as a term of reproach aimed by conservatives at the Left.

It has been increasingly difficult to identify liberalism with any one set of tenets or fundamental principles. Perhaps it has been easier to identify typically 20th-century liberal causes, especially integration of the races, sexual equality, environmentalism, the eradication of → poverty, abolition of capital punishment, defense of → abortion rights, internationalism, and support for the → United Nations. Such views are associated with educated classes of the Northeast, the upper Midwest, and the West Coast. They are not the platform of any one political party — both major American parties are home to a wide range of attitudes and interests — but "liberals" do tend to vote Democratic.

Meanwhile, a more technical sense of this term, rooted in Enlightenment principles, has developed among academics, particularly political philosophers. This usage currently centers upon the view that the public world should be ruled by minimalist shared convictions about justice, leaving to individuals and voluntary communities the responsibility for defining and living out their different notions of the → good. Here liberalism is the alternative, not to conservative philosophies in general, but to communitarianism, as championed by such figures as Michael Sandel and Amitai Etzioni.

The most influential expression of liberalism in this philosophical sense has been that of John Rawls, who argues for a theory of justice as fairness, elaborating what might be concluded by reasoners

dialoguing in good faith behind a "veil of ignorance" separating them from knowledge of their actual social identities and interests. The Rawlsian view, at least in its original form, implied a claim to have articulated an ideal form of public life, in contrast to the opinion — held, for example, by the British writer Isaiah Berlin — that liberalism at best calls for a tolerant modus vivendi among competing values in a radically → pluralistic world.

Liberalism in America today appears increasingly to be the view of many, but certainly not all, members of the educated classes, of university professors, and of many media figures and commentators. It is a tolerant, well-meaning, "decent," and scientifically literate worldview, held with or without any particular partisan political application or detailed conceptual justification.

Bibliography: C. W. ANDERSON, *A Deeper Freedom: Liberal Democracy as an Everyday Morality* (Madison, Wis., 2002) • H. ARENDT, *The Human Condition* (2d ed.; Chicago, 1998; orig. pub., 1958) • I. BERLIN, *Four Essays on Liberty* (London, 1969) • T. W. BOXX and G. M. QUINLIVAN, eds., *Public Morality, Civic Virtue, and the Problem of Modern Liberalism* (Grand Rapids, 2000) • H. W. BRANDS, *The Strange Death of American Liberalism* (New Haven, 2001) • N. COHEN, *The Reconstruction of American Liberalism, 1865-1914* (Chapel Hill, N.C., 2002) • G. CROWDER, *Liberalism and Value Pluralism* (London, 2002) • J. DEWEY, *A Common Faith* (New Haven, 1934) • T. R. HURTGEN, *The Divided Mind of American Liberalism* (Lanham, Md., 2002) • M. L. KING JR., *A Testament of Hope: The Essential Writings of Martin Luther King, Jr.* (ed. J. M. Washington; San Francisco, 1991) • W. LIPPMANN, *Essays in the Public Philosophy* (Boston, 1955) • K. MATTSON, *Intellectuals in Action: The Origins of the New Left and Radical Liberalism, 1945-1970* (University Park, Pa., 2002) • J. RAWLS, *Political Liberalism* (New York, 1993); idem, *A Theory of Justice* (Cambridge, Mass., 1997; orig. pub., 1971) • M. J. SANDEL, *Liberalism and the Limits of Justice* (2d ed.; New York, 1998; orig. pub., 1982).

LEWIS S. MUDGE

Liberation Theology

1. Origin and Development
    1.1. Gestation and Birth (1962-71)
    1.2. Maturation and Repression (1972-78)
    1.3. Consolidation amid Controversy (1979-92)
    1.4. Shifts in Response to Global Change
        (1993-present)
2. Themes

1. Origin and Development

The seeds of liberation theology were sown on Latin American soil in the early 1960s. Young Catholic and Protestant theologians reflected on the people's life of faith within the context of the people's resistance to oppressive living and working conditions. Shortly after the birth of liberation theology in 1968, similar types of theologies arose in other regions of the world, from North America (black liberation theology), Africa (South African liberation theology), India, Southeast Asia (Korean minjung theology), and the Philippines (Christians for National Liberation). Each emerged from its own cultural-political context, developed its own distinctive method, and addressed unique regional problems. These liberation theologies speak of God and Jesus as liberators of the poor and oppressed and insist that justice and spirituality work hand in hand. They also reflect on the experiences of women and men who assume coresponsibility with God for their liberation. This article concentrates on Latin America but also indicates links with parallel theologies elsewhere.

1.1. *Gestation and Birth (1962-71)*

The idea for a new theology emerged gradually from meetings of a small group of young Roman Catholic and Protestant theologians who initially came together to discuss the situation of the poor in Latin America and how they and the churches might address the misery and oppression of the people. Gathering about the time of the beginning of the Second → Vatican Council (1962-65), these theologians discussed issues such as the relation of → faith and → poverty, the → gospel and social justice, and new models of → church. They developed their perspectives on such issues during and following the close of the council. In a meeting of theologians at Petrópolis, Brazil, in 1964, this emerging theology was described as "critical reflection on praxis" (A. McGovern, 8).

Vatican II inspired and gave guidance to these theologians. It outlined, for example, new models of church, including the prophetic or servant model, which the theologians developed in relation to the Latin American pastoral situation. The conciliar Decree on the Apostolate of Lay People, *Apostolicam actuositatem* (§8), encouraged this new wave of Latin American theologians to consider the faith community's works of charity and justice as a source for theology. The document's stress on →

Catholic Action also reinforced the laypeople's involvement in the ecclesial base communities. The council's emphasis on love and justice on behalf of the poor led to the theologians' creating what has become liberation theology's bedrock principle: the option for the poor. This option involves a free choice or commitment by individuals or groups both to resist exploitation of the poor and oppressed and to work proactively to change social structures to new ones that protect the dignity and rights of the poor. Most important for liberation theology, the council urged the whole church and its theologians to read the signs of the times in light of the gospel. Since reading these signs calls for examining concrete situations, the Latin American theologians took as their point of departure for doing theology the reality of those who are poor and oppressed.

The "theology of liberation" (*teología de la liberación*) was born and christened in 1968. In that year Gustavo Gutiérrez, widely recognized as the leader of this movement, introduced the term in a major address to theologians and pastoral workers at Chimbote, Peru. A few months later Roman Catholic bishops convened at Medellín, Colombia, for the Second Conference of Latin American Bishops (hereafter "Medellín"). Advised by this new wave of theologians, the bishops produced important documents on → peace, justice, → family, → education, and → youth that provided theological grounding, sociological analysis, and pastoral guidelines for how Latin Americans might transform → society in light of the Second Vatican Council.

The bishops at Medellín applied and even advanced the principles and concepts of Vatican II. Whereas the council called merely for renewing the temporal order, Medellín spoke of transforming deficient and sinful social structures within that order, which in large part brought about "institutionalized violence." Moreover, the bishops at Medellín defined → solidarity with the poor as a firm commitment; it means that "we make ours their problems and their struggles" ("Poverty of the Church," §10). Finally, the bishops expanded the meaning of "reading the signs of the times." Whereas the council described this mode of discernment as "seeing, judging, and acting," the Latin American bishops called upon both rich and poor to commit themselves to this process of seeing, judging, and acting *on behalf of the poor*. They also emphasized that the "seeing" requires social analysis in order to uncover the root causes of exploitative institutional practice. In short, while Vatican II called generically for reform,

Medellín called more specifically for transformative social action.

A few years after Medellín, Gutiérrez defined liberation theology as "a critical reflection on Christian praxis in the light of the Word" (*Theology,* 11). Furthermore, for him and many of his colleagues, Christian praxis is "transformative activity that is influenced and illumined by Christian love" (*Truth,* 99). The praxis component in this theology refers both to people's protest against the status quo and to pastoral activity that creates new structures. In this first stage of development, groups of Christians in Brazil, Paraguay, and Guatemala began to organize resistance to repressive military governments and to the miserable economic conditions that the majority of the people endured daily. Praxis also encompassed apostolic movements involving university students, peasants trying to improve working conditions, the radical wing of the Workers' Catholic Action organizing labor, and radical members of leftist movements, galvanized by Fidel Castro and Che Guevara's socialist → revolution in Cuba, building resistance movements. Praxis also included the reflective activity of Catholic clergy and women religious as well as ministers and lay leaders in evangelical churches, who often questioned their own churches' alliances with the unjust political order (C. L. d'Épinay, 6; R. Alves, 242-48; → Clergy and Laity; Lay Movements).

A key resource for this new theology is the ecclesial → base community, which consists of 15-25 people who meet weekly to discuss a biblical passage and its relevance for their lives. In light of Scripture, participants talk about issues, for example, that involve unemployment, medical care, clean drinking water, or housing. As people organized themselves and took action, they often encountered severe repression at the hands of the national police and the rich landowners. Even though they faced reprisals, hundreds of base communities and other grassroots organizations emerged, including mothers' clubs, youth groups, and nutrition centers. Together they formed part of the popular movement on which theologians reflected and wrote.

These political, educational, and ecclesial activities, as well as perspectives from Medellín, reports from lay organizations, and theological symposia, all provided the context and the material from which this theology grew. Liberation theologians are fond of saying that the first act of their theology, or the material object of theological reflection, is the commitment to work for the liberation of the poor under God's inspiration and power. The actual theologizing on this material object constitutes the second act.

1.2. *Maturation and Repression (1972-78)*

In the second stage of development, liberation theologians published many systematic works that refined their methodology, and they developed new Christologies, ecclesiologies, and spiritualities that spoke directly to the problems of the poor. These writings expanded and systematized the earlier perspectives that called for an integral liberation of the people. Such liberation is a single process involving many dimensions. At the basic level, liberation means transforming material conditions so that the poor can have their basic needs met for food, shelter, and health care. At a deeper level, it means having the opportunity to make one's own decisions. At a deeper level yet, liberation gives individuals and groups the capacity and freedom to make decisions. At the deepest level, liberation means communion with God and neighbor, which brings peace and happiness. While many theologians (H. Assmann, L. Boff, and L. Gera) concentrated on the faith and → spirituality of the poor and on activity aimed at structural change, others (E. Dussel, I. Ellacuría, and J. L. Segundo) analyzed and critiqued the traditional → Latin American theology that supported the status quo.

Also during this time the euphoria initially felt by theologians, pastoral workers, and the people began to diminish as they encountered opposition to programs of liberation within the church and repression from military dictatorships and right-wing military governments. The military governments made arbitrary arrests, seized and tortured suspected leftists (most of whom were never seen again), set off bombs in universities, and executed tens of thousands of men, women, and children. Dictators, who had been in power for many years in Brazil, Guatemala, Haiti, Nicaragua, and Paraguay, persecuted people who sought social change, labeling them subversives and Communists. The title of José Míguez Bonino's book *Doing Theology in a Revolutionary Situation* (1975) hints at the risks of doing liberation theology in this stage of its growth.

In this repressive political context, theologians hammered out the essential elements of liberation theology. They include (1) a dialogic method that involves analysis and reflection on the existential situation in light of God's Word, (2) concentration on the faith life of the poor and the oppressed, (3) the use of social-scientific analysis as a theoretical instrument to understand institutions and public policies, (4) a praxeological element aimed at transforming human and social relationships as well as theology itself, and (5) an integral perspective that sees God's reign permeating every dimension of human existence, including the political, the human, and the spiritual (→ Kingdom of God). To gain greater insight into the various dimensions of integral liberation, liberation theologians use "mediations" (i.e., theoretical studies in any relevant field) to illuminate reality. These mediations include social sciences to understand institutions, biblical and theological resources to interpret the → Word of God, and practical orientations that provide guidelines for action (C. Boff).

Several events helped expand and enrich liberation theology during this period, including a meeting at El Escorial near Madrid in 1972 at which Latin American theologians exchanged ideas with European theologians over the direction and method of their respective theologies. In 1975 Latin American and European theologians met again in Mexico City to address methodology in different areas of theology, including exegetical, systematic, historical, and philosophical. The theme of the conference, "Captivity and Liberation," reflected the repression that was then occurring as a backlash to this new theology. In same year North American and Latin American theologians met in Detroit, where theologians from Canada and the United States became acquainted with the reality and the theology of their colleagues from the south. In 1976 theologians from Third World nations met at Dar es Salaam, Tanzania, to share ideas and to create the → Ecumenical Association of Third World Theologians (EATWOT), which subsequently held an annual event that would eventually involve female as well as male theologians from Africa, Asia, Europe, Latin America, and North America.

1.3. *Consolidation amid Controversy (1979-92)*

The third stage of the development of liberation theology began at the dawn of the Third Conference of Latin American Bishops, or CELAM III, held at Puebla, Mexico, in 1979 (hereafter "Puebla"). Preparatory deliberations for Puebla included opposition to the theology of liberation by reactionary bishops and theologians, who threatened to undo Medellín's strong commitment to the poor. Despite resistance by the conservatives, however, the majority of bishops at Puebla declared in their documents a strong continuity with the perspectives of Medellín. They reinforced the importance of solidarity and espoused the option for the poor, calling it now a "preferential option," meaning that people should make a conscious and free commitment to work with the poor, although not to the exclusion of the nonpoor. In addition, the Puebla bishops labeled structural situations and policies that oppress the poor as "institutionalized injustice" and "institu-

tionalized violence" (CELAM III, no. 1259). The church's mission, they said, calls for the practice of liberation in the spirit of Jesus.

In light of Puebla, liberationists began to consolidate their theological perspectives, elaborating the biblical, theological, and ethical implications of their principles of solidarity and preferential option for the poor. As this integrating process was unfolding, certain church officials both within Latin America and within the Vatican began to criticize some liberation theologians for holding positions that were allegedly contrary to Roman Catholic doctrine.

In the 1980s, at the insistence of female theologians, the theology of liberation began to widen its focus to include women and people of color as groups in Latin America among the poor and oppressed who have special concerns that need to be addressed. In this manner liberation theology, which had previously focused almost exclusively on political-economic types of oppression, began to pay attention to the rampant → sexism and → racism that made poor women doubly oppressed and poor women of color triply oppressed. Women liberation theologians thus expanded the meaning of solidarity with the poor.

Theologians Elsa Tamez of Costa Rica, Ivone Gebara of Brazil, and María Pilar Aquino of Mexico focused on the machismo pervading Latin American culture and on violence against women. Tamez has shown in her studies of Latin American myths, songs, and dance how machismo attitudes have degraded women by reinforcing negative stereotypes. She urges theologians who work in cultures within and beyond Latin American borders to expose oppressive stereotyping. Aquino has analyzed the root causes of → war, especially of those not formally declared, which wreak terrible violence against women. In a similar vein, female theologians from other Third World countries have also focused on how wars have hurt women. Theologian Mercy Amba Oduyoye of Ghana, for example, has shown how wars, coupled with political-economic mismanagement, have forced women to assume the role of parenting alone after losing their home and country. Single mothers, she says, "give until they have nothing more to share but their poverty" (p. 126).

As the horizons of liberation theology expanded and became consolidated, liberation theologians drew criticism from clergy and theologians from Latin America, Europe, the United States, and most especially from the Vatican. The more prominent critics included Cardinal Alfonso López Trujillo of Colombia, a former president of CELAM; Cardinal

Joseph Ratzinger, head of the Vatican Congregation for the Doctrine of the Faith; European theologians of the International Theological Commission, appointed by the Vatican; and U.S. theologians Michael Novak and James Gustafson. These and other opponents have attacked liberation theology on many fronts, including theological, ethical, social-scientific, and epistemological.

In the area of → theology, critics have charged that liberation theology reduces faith to politics by emphasizing earthly transformation over transcendent reality and spiritual growth (A. López Trujillo, 79). Second, critics such as Gustafson, a theologian and ethicist, have found fault with the principle of the preferential option for the poor because it seems to limit God's universal love by implying that God loves the poor more than the nonpoor (p. 25). Third, adversaries have complained that liberation theologians uncritically employ Marxist concepts, especially that of class struggle, which pits the poor against the rich (Congregation for the Doctrine of the Faith, pt. 9, no. 10). Fourth, critics have suggested that the notion of a preferential option for the poor fosters an unjust partiality, or a kind of reverse discrimination. (For response to these critiques, see esp. McGovern, *Liberation Theology and Its Critics;* T. Schubeck, *Liberation Ethics;* and Segundo, *Theology and the Church.*)

1.4. *Shifts in Response to Global Change (1993-Present)*

The fourth developmental stage involves the response of liberation theology to global changes. It has shown more awareness of patriarchal and machismo culture (including the violence this culture generates), the inequalities of medical care, ecological problems (e.g., destruction of rain forests; → Environmental Ethics), and the cultures of feminist, Afro-American, and indigenous theologies. Liberation theologians have paid special attention as well to the role of rapid → communication in intensifying the consciousness of the world as a whole; the failure of revolutionary movements in Latin America (notably in Chile, Nicaragua, and El Salvador); social disintegration, crime, and → terrorism; the collapse of the Soviet bloc in 1991; the strengthening of neoliberal → capitalism, with its structural → unemployment; and the mounting external debt of many Third World countries.

The theology of liberation has undergone parallel shifts. First, theologians today pay greater attention to how globalization of the economy has intensified and worsened the problems of the poor. With respect to the Latin American economy, liberation theologians today are analyzing the severe problems of poverty and structural inequality brought on by the new liberal economy and the globalization of market relations. All Latin American theologians see poverty as a grave moral issue, but their responses promote either a radical or a moderate mode of action. The radical response comes from theologians who do more systems analysis, are more critical of the market, and offer alternatives that are influenced by Marxist and critical social science. This group includes Enrique Dussel (Mexico), Jung Mo Sung (Brazil), and Franz Hinkelammert (Costa Rica). The moderate liberationist group is less critical of market forces, makes more use of Roman Catholic social teaching, and envisions transformation as reform of the system. This group includes Tony Mifsud (Chile) and Juan Carlos Scannone (Argentina). Radicals and moderates concur that the market must be guided and limited by juridical instruments that insist on some democratic accountability and that ensure the meeting of basic needs.

Second, as the new millennium and the jubilee year 2000 were approaching, certain liberation theologians argued that the enormous external debt of nations such as Argentina, Brazil, and Mexico should be forgiven. They held that servicing the debt was fundamentally unjust and was hurting the poor.

Third, theologians have used the concept of solidarity both to counter the neoliberal → individualism that erodes the foundations of group action and to form the nucleus of an → ethics that integrates the common good and human → rights.

Fourth, feminist liberation theologians through their international networking, their analysis of → culture, and their insistence on integrating experience with theory have enriched liberation theology (→ Feminist Theology).

Finally, liberation theologians have contributed greater social depth to ethics, particularly to → ecology and bioethics. In bioethics, for example, a liberationist perspective urges bioethicists to reread the principles of autonomy, beneficence, and paternalism in light of what groups want and not simply because of individual needs or desires.

2. Themes

Liberation theologians have introduced or fostered discussion on a number of themes, some of which have already been mentioned: option for the poor, consciousness raising, liberation of women, and ecclesial base communities. Two theological themes central to the entire enterprise, however, are God as liberator and solidarity with the poor.

2.1. *God as Liberator*

Liberation theologians speak about → God and → Jesus as liberator and about God's salvific work as liberation. Even though the terms "liberator" and "liberation" in reference to God appear rarely in the Bible, these theologians rightly point out that the action of God and Jesus on behalf of others demonstrates God's concern to liberate God's people. God acts in history to free people, as in the exodus, as well as for individuals like Job. In the Book of Exodus God hears the cry of the poor and sends Moses to Pharaoh, demanding that he let the people leave Egypt (Exod. 3:9-10). In the Book of Job God does not crush Job, even though Job questions the justice of God; instead, God enlightens him and calls the lonely Job to the fullness of communion and freedom (chap. 42).

Gutiérrez maintains that in the NT "the Bible presents liberation — salvation — in Christ as the total gift, which . . . gives the whole process of liberation its deepest meaning and its complete and unforeseeable fulfillment" (*Theology,* xiv). In writing to the Romans, Paul speaks of Christ Jesus liberating Christians "from the law of sin and of death" (Rom. 8:2).

Biblical theologians Severino Croatto of Argentina and Jorge Pixley of Nicaragua show that the exodus experience illuminates how God through Moses frees a people from political-economic bondage while at the same time transforming the consciousness of the people from a slave mentality to a new awareness that enables them to take risks and accept the responsibility of freedom. They are further inspired to care for poor, vulnerable, and marginal persons in society, as spelled out in the covenant.

Croatto applies this liberating experience of exodus to contemporary Latin America. He argues that just as God worked through Moses to free the Hebrew people from enslavement, so God acts in a similar manner today by calling upon Moses figures to help free the oppressed.

Pixley, like Croatto, assumes the validity of the analogy of exodus. The liberation that God accomplished for the Hebrews in the exodus is an authoritative precedent for liberation movements in our day. He points to many similarities between the Hebrew and Latin American peoples. First, liberation involves a movement from oppression in Egypt to freedom in the promised land, a movement marked by a class struggle. Second, both the Hebrews yesterday and the Latin Americans today resist powerful oppressors who exploit → religion in order to justify the prevailing order and to crush the resistance of the poor. Third, both groups have accepted the same God as their liberator. God, for Pixley, is the "universal instigator of the new and the better" (Schubeck, *Liberation Ethics,* 14). By actualizing the maximum potential of human beings, God brings about newness and greater freedom and also insists that the people keep free from future dominators.

As for Jesus, liberation theologians are keenly aware of how certain images of Christ and their corresponding Christologies have played an alienating role in the 500-year history of Christian Latin America (e.g., the vulnerable and helpless baby Jesus in the arms of Mary, the suffering-dying-dead-defeated Christ who reinforces the people's → fatalism, and the Christ as celestial monarch who is used to legitimate the earthly monarch's policies). By presenting Jesus as Liberator who actively resists the unjust status quo, liberation theologians direct the people toward a new, freeing image of Christ and also toward a self-image that helps them become active subjects in determining their own histories.

2.2. *Solidarity with the Poor*

From the 1960s to the present day, the theme of solidarity with the poor has been an essential element of liberation theology. First, theologians use it to counter the neoliberal individualism that pervades political-economic structures in Latin America. Some neoliberals oppose the concept of solidarity because they fear it will upstage individual rights. Second, it has inspired the formation of new relationships and communities. Tony Mifsud thinks of solidarity as a communitarian vision of the person in a network of human relationships. The "I," he says, implies a "we"; conversely, the "we" permits the authentic realization of the "I" (p. 62). Third, this theme has served as a root concept that integrates love, justice, freedom, and human rights. Maria Clara Bingemer identifies love and justice as the core meaning of solidarity — love moves a person to commitment in friendships, while justice helps the person to respect the others as equals.

This theme of solidarity has helped theologians to raise their own level of awareness about who are to be included under the banner of the poor. Specifically, Latin American women liberation theologians have asked whether solidarity with the poor includes the concerns of women and people of color. In the first stages of development, liberation theology regarded the poor as a homogenous group until feminist and black theologians showed that poverty and oppression degrade people in different ways. Solidarity with poor women and with black women, however, calls for different analyses, theological perspectives, and action.

Elsa Tamez, who regularly and closely collaborates with African and Asian theologians, has discovered patterns that both positively shape the identity of women and that, as imposed by foreign patriarchal elements, exploit women. She has shown how machismo and the violence that it engenders (expressed in sexual aggression and in traditional music and dance) demean women. She suggests several strategies for resisting and finally overcoming these various forms of cultural violence.

3. Reception

Liberation theology has exerted an enormous influence on the conscience of the world. Karl → Rahner praised liberation theology because it "has opened our eyes to structural injustice" (P. Imhof and H. Biallowons, 64). Richard McCormick has spoken of liberation theology as one of the significant developments in → moral theology over the last half of the 20th century.

Although liberation theology is not simply moral theology, its creative method has demonstrated a new way of addressing ethical problems, as well as thinking critically about biblical → hermeneutics, → Christology, spirituality, and ecclesiology. Whatever the specific focus, this theology has fought against the separatist mentality that dichotomizes reality into the → sacred and the profane, or into the individual and the social. Countering that dualism, liberation theology presents a perspective that sees Christ's action as permeating every dimension of human existence.

Liberation theology rapidly spread to other continents, creating mutually enriching dialogue among theologians, pastoral workers, educators, and students, especially in North America, Africa, and Asia. Through the organizing efforts of Sergio Torres of Chile, liberation theology began to develop with many diverse groups in the United States, groups including Asians, African Americans, Latinos, and Native Americans. These groups shared with Latin American theology certain methodological perspectives, including the process of reflecting on lived experience and the use of social analysis.

Within the → Roman Catholic Church liberation theology has also influenced the pastoral letter on the economy, *Economic Justice for All* (1986), issued by the National Conference of Catholic Bishops. In this letter the bishops adopted a modified form of the preferential option for the poor as a criterion for evaluating national economic policies.

In summary, liberation theology has exerted international influence on the Roman Catholic Church. It has shaped Christian theologies in Third World countries, largely because of its commitment to the poor and because of its methodology. In contrast to pre–Vatican II Roman Catholic theology, which separated theory from practice, liberation theology has concentrated on developing its theory and principles from practice and even challenging its theoretical claims on the basis of the people's lived experience. In short, liberation theology's contribution involves an integration of theology and lived faith, contemplation and action.

→ Latin American Council of Bishops

Bibliography: Classic liberationist works: C. Boff, "Epistemology and Method of the Theology of Liberation," *Mysterium liberationis: Fundamental Concepts of Liberation Theology* (ed. I. Ellacuría and J. Sobrino; Maryknoll, N.Y., 1993) 57-85 • L. Boff, *Church, Charism, and Power* (New York, 1985); idem, *Ecclesiogenesis: The Base Communities Reinvent the Church* (Maryknoll, N.Y., 1986) • L. Boff and C. Boff, *Introducing Liberation Theology* (Maryknoll, N.Y., 1987) • D. Ferm, *Third World Liberation Theologies: An Introductory Survey* (Maryknoll, N.Y., 1986) • G. Gutiérrez, *A Theology of Liberation: History, Politics, and Salvation* (Maryknoll, N.Y., 1988; orig. pub., 1973); idem, *The Truth Shall Make You Free* (Maryknoll, N.Y., 1990) • J. Míguez Bonino, *Doing Theology in a Revolutionary Situation* (Philadelphia, 1975); idem, *Faces of Jesus: Latin American Christologies* (Maryknoll, N.Y., 1984); idem, *Toward a Christian Political Ethics* (Philadelphia, 1983) • J. L. Segundo, *The Community Called Church* (Maryknoll, N.Y., 1973); idem, *The Liberation of Theology* (Maryknoll, N.Y., 1976); idem, *Theology and the Church* (Minneapolis, 1985).

Roman Catholic works: M. C. L Bingemer, "Solidarities or Conflict? Possibilities of Dialogue between Catholic Social Thought and Liberation Theology," *SEDOS Bulletin* 23 (1991) 309-13 • CELAM II, *The Church in the Present-Day Transformation of Latin America in the Light of the Council*, vol. 2, *Conclusions* (Bogotá, 1970) • CELAM III, "Evangelization in Latin America's Present and Future," *Puebla and Beyond* (ed. J. Eagleson and P. Scharper; Maryknoll, N.Y., 1979) 194, 278-79 • Congregation for the Doctrine of the Faith, *Libertatis nuntius* (Vatican City, 1984) • National Conference of Catholic Bishops, *Economic Justice for All: A Pastoral Letter on Catholic Social Teaching and the U.S. Economy* (Washington, D.C., 1986) • Paul VI, "Octogesima adveniens," *Catholic Social Thought: The Documentary Heritage* (ed. D. J. O'Brien and T. A. Shannon; Maryknoll, N.Y., 1992) 265-86.

History: E. Dussel, *A History of the Church in Latin America: Colonialism to Liberalism (1492-1979)* (Grand

Rapids, 1981) • A. López Trujillo, *De Medellín a Puebla* (Madrid, 1980) • R. A. McCormick, "Moral Theology, 1940-1989: An Overview," *TS* 50 (1989) 3-24 • S. Mainwaring, *The Catholic Church and Politics in Brazil, 1916-1985* (Stanford, Calif., 1986) • R. Oliveros, "History of the Theology of Liberation," *Mysterium liberationis: Fundamental Concepts of Liberation Theology* (ed. I. Ellacuría and J. Sobrino; Maryknoll, N.Y., 1993) 3-32 • P. Richard, *The Death of Christendoms, Birth of the Church: Historical Analysis and Theological Interpretation of the Church in Latin America* (Maryknoll, N.Y., 1987).

Ethical and feminist works: M. P. Aquino, "Justice Upholds Peace: A Feminist Approach," *The Return of the Just War* (ed. M. P. Aquino and D. Mieth; London, 2001) 102-10 • D. Brackley and T. Schubeck, "Moral Theology in Latin America," *TS* 62 (2002) 123-60 • J. Gustafson, *Ethics from a Theocentric Perspective,* vol. 1, *Theology and Ethics* (Chicago, 1981) • T. Mifsud, "La cultura de la solidaridad como proyecto ético," *NuMu* 54 (1997) 345-56 • M. A. Oduyoye, "Poverty and Motherhood," *The Power of Naming* (ed. E. Schüssler Fiorenza; Maryknoll, N.Y., 1996) 124-31 • T. Schubeck, "Ethics and Liberation Theology," *TS* 56 (1995) 107-22; idem, *Liberation Ethics: Sources, Models, and Norms* (Minneapolis, 1993) • E. Tamez, "Cultural Violence against Women in Latin America," *Women Resisting Violence* (ed. M. J. Mananzan et al.; Maryknoll, N.Y., 1996) chap. 1.

Other works: R. Alves, "El protestantismo como una forma de colonialismo," *Perspectivas para el diálogo,* no. 38 (November 1968) 242-48 • J. S. Croatto, *Exodus: A Hermeneutics of Freedom* (Maryknoll, N.Y., 1981) • G. Cummings, *A Common Journey* (Maryknoll, N.Y., 1993) • A. Dawson, "The Origins and Character of the Base Ecclesial Community: A Brazilian Perspective," *The Cambridge Companion to Liberation Theology* (ed. C. Rowland; Cambridge, 1999) 109-28 • C. L. D'Épinay, "La iglesia evangélica y la revolución latinoamericana," *CIDoc.D* 78 (1968) 6 • D. Dorr, "Poor, Preferential Option for," *NDCST* 755-59 • P. Imhof and H. Biallowons, eds, *Faith in a Wintry Season: Conversations and Interviews with Karl Rahner in the Last Years of His Life* (New York, 1990) • A. McGovern, *Liberation Theology and Its Critics* (Maryknoll, N.Y., 1989) • G. V. Pixley, *On Exodus: A Liberation Perspective* (Maryknoll, N.Y., 1987) • C. Rowland, ed., *The Cambridge Companion to Liberation Theology* (Cambridge, 1999) • R. J. Schreiter, *The New Catholicity: Theology between the Global and the Local* (Maryknoll, N.Y., 1997).

Thomas L. Schubeck, S.J.

Liberia

	1960	1980	2000
Population (1,000s):	1,039	1,876	3,256
Annual growth rate (%):	2.79	3.17	3.25

Area: 99,067 sq. km. (38,250 sq. mi.)

A.D. 2000

Population density: 33/sq. km. (85/sq. mi.)
Births / deaths: 4.40 / 1.16 per 100 population
Fertility rate: 5.86 per woman
Infant mortality rate: 101 per 1,000 live births
Life expectancy: 59.5 years (m: 58.0, f: 61.0)
Religious affiliation (%): tribal religionists 42.5, Christians 39.5 (indigenous 13.5, Protestants 12.3, unaffiliated 8.9, Roman Catholics 4.6, other Christians 1.2), Muslims 16.0, nonreligious 1.7, other 0.3.

1. General Situation
2. Religious Situation
   2.1. Non-Christians
   2.2. Protestants
   2.3. Roman Catholics
   2.4. Ecumenical Relations

1. General Situation

The Republic of Liberia was founded as a colony in 1822 (→ Colonialism) in order to serve as a settlement for former American slaves (→ Slavery). American and British warships brought increasing numbers of freed slaves to it, ignoring the rights of 16 native peoples (including the Kpelle, Gio, Mano, and Loma from the Mande language family; and the Bassa, Grebo, and Klao from the Kru language family). In 1847 Liberia became an independent republic, with a constitution modeled on that of the United States. After 1870 political power was in the hands of the True Whig (We Hope in God) Party. The most important presidents were W. V. S. Tubman (d. 1971) and W. R. Tolbert (d. 1980).

In April 1980 a coup ended the dominance of Liberians of U.S. origin, with the army under Samuel Doe coming to power. After years of increasing instability, a civil war broke out in 1989 led by Charles Taylor. The following seven years were disastrous for the country, as three rival armies contended for power, in the process destroying much of the country's economy. In 1997 Taylor was elected president in the first national election in 12 years.

Liberia has rich resources of iron, diamonds, gold, and timber, the development of which has been severely hindered by the destruction of the country's infrastructure in the civil war. By occupation, 70 percent of the labor force is engaged in agriculture. In 1999 the estimated unemployment rate was 70 percent. Most of the country's foreign exchange earnings come from revenues generated by its maritime registry.

2. Religious Situation

2.1. *Non-Christians*

Overall, almost half of the people of Liberia belong to traditional African religions (→ Tribal Religions; Guinea 2). In the interior a much higher percentage adhere to traditional religions and engage in → ancestor worship. Secret societies (Poro for men, Sande for women), with their distinctive → initiation rites, play a dominant role throughout the country. Islam, spread mainly by Mandigo traders, has adherents mostly among the Vai, more than 90 percent of whom are now Muslim. Beginning in the 1950s, Muslim Ahmadīya missionaries arrived from Pakistan and Egypt.

2.2. *Protestants*

Historically, Liberia is built on the Christian principles with which the American Colonization Society tried to solve the problems of the Afro-American population in the United States. The first leaders of Liberia came from the American Protestant churches. The 1847 constitution, which is still valid, recognizes → religious liberty and liberty of conscience. Though Liberia calls itself a Christian society, it protects all religions (→ Church and State).

Among indigenous churches the first was the Providence Baptist Church in Monrovia, followed by other Baptist churches. Today they all belong to the Liberian Baptist Convention (→ Baptists), which in 1995 was Liberia's largest Christian group.

Pentecostal missionaries from the United States began work in 1908 (→ Pentecostal Churches). Full self-government characterizes this church. It embraces several related groups, including the Liberia Assemblies of God and the United Pentecostal Church.

The → Lutheran Church started with the arrival of Lutheran missionaries in the interior in 1860. Success came slowly, and the Evangelical Lutheran Church in Liberia was founded only in 1947. This church changed its name to the Lutheran Church in Liberia in 1965. Most of its members live in rural areas. It belongs to the → World Council of Churches (WCC), the → Lutheran World Federation, and the → All Africa Conference of Churches.

Methodists were among the first settlers in 1822, and a Methodist church was founded after the coming of the first missionary in 1833. For the Methodists a major concern was the development of their own schools.

The Episcopal Church of Liberia (→ Anglican Communion) derives from the Protestant Episcopal Church of the United States. Its first indigenous bishop was consecrated in 1885. Its strong orientation to the United States stopped it from joining the Anglican Province of West Africa until 1975, when it became more open to African sister churches. It too belongs to the WCC.

Church structures in the United States plainly influenced the rise of the African Methodist Church (1873), the African Methodist Episcopal Zion Church (1876), and the Pentecostal Assemblies of the World (1919). Independent churches from other parts of Africa also spread to Liberia. From Nigeria came the Church of the Lord (Aladura) in 1947, which rapidly increased its membership with the help of its message of sanctification (→ Independent Churches).

2.3. *Roman Catholics*

The → Roman Catholic Church has a longer history. The Portuguese reached the coast of Liberia in 1462, and the region was placed under the Diocese of Cape Verde in 1533. Real missionary work, however, began only much later. In 1841 the U.S. bishops tried to set up a mission in Monrovia (→ North American Missions), but without success. A second effort in 1848 was ultimately thwarted by strong opposition in 1887. Finally, in 1906 the Society of African Missions began work in Monrovia and Kakata. When the Kru proved receptive, the work focused on this people. It met with increasing success, and now there are three dioceses with national bishops. Monrovia is the seat of the Catholic Bishops' Conference of Liberia.

2.4. *Ecumenical Relations*

The mainline churches all belong to the Liberian Council of Churches (→ National Councils of Churches). Their main concern is to separate ecclesiastical and political interests. Since Tubman and Tolbert were both church officeholders, serious tensions arose between church and state as regards human and civil → rights. The statements of the churches on this theme developed into open protest. Nor did this attitude change with the excesses of the military regime. At the end of 1984 the council came into direct confrontation with this regime, which was trying to block a return to civil government by its secret and arbitrary arrests and → tortures. The military rulers accused the church leaders of acting like politicians and threatened to treat them as such. Underlying the present troubles is the legacy of the first immigrants and their leaders with their close intertwining of religious and political thinking.

→ African Theology

Bibliography: D. E. Dunn, *Historical Dictionary of Liberia* (2d ed.; Lanham, Md., 2001); idem, *A History of the Episcopal Church in Liberia, 1821-1980* (Metuchen, N.J., 1992) • S. Ellis, *The Mask of Anarchy: The Destruction of Liberia and the Religious Dimension of an African Civil War* (New York, 1999) • P. Gifford, *Christianity and Politics in Doe's Liberia* (Cambridge, 1993) • A. F. Kulah, *Liberia Will Rise Again: Reflections on the Liberian Civil Crisis* (Nashville, 1999); idem, *Theological Education in Liberia: Problems and Opportunities* (Lithonia, Ga., 1994) • I. A. Nass, *A Study in Internal Conflicts: The Liberian Crisis and the West African Peace Initiative* (Enugu, Liberia, 2000) • L. Sanneh, *West African Christianity: The Religious Impact* (Maryknoll, N.Y., 1983) • P. L. N. Seyou, *Quick-Fixing the State in Africa: The Liberian Case* (Boston, 1998).

HARRY C. HOEBEN

Libertinism

This broad term denotes deviation from an accepted → norm, doctrine, or morality. Its use is for the most part derogatory. Libertines include the following:

1. In Acts 6:9 the members of a synagogue who had been slaves abroad and were now freedmen (KJV: "libertines"). They promoted the persecution of Stephen.
2. The Genevan patriots who had fought for the city's independence and who at first supported J. → Calvin but then (as Perrinists) opposed his strict church order (→ Church Discipline) and the French influx.
3. A movement of spiritualists (Loists) in Antwerp against whom M. → Luther warned in a 1525 letter.
4. The related supporters (opposed by Calvin in 1545) of the Dutch Quintin (Quintinists). In 1546 Quintin was executed at Tournay in France for immorality and → heresy. The Quintinists were → quietist and → pantheistic mystics (→ Mysticism).

The term is occasionally used today for moral laxity in general, but mostly in the historical sense.

Bibliography: J. Calvin, *Treatises against the Anabaptists and against the Libertines* (Grand Rapids, 1982) • B. J. Kaplan, *Calvinists and Libertines: Confession and Community in Utrecht, 1578-1620* (Oxford, 1995) • D. Wetsel, *Pascal and Disbelief: Catechesis and Conversion in the Pensées* (Washington, D.C., 1994).

DIETRICH RITSCHL

Libido

For centuries theologians used the term "libido" to refer to the largely evil element of desire. During the 19th century A. Moll (1862-1939) introduced it to the field of medicine, and S. Freud (1856-1939) eventually made it the central concept in his doctrine of desire (→ Psychoanalysis). Freud distinguished between the *source,* partially from impulses in erogenous zones in the body, and the *goal,* a release of libidinous energy, though with a possible switch from activity to passivity. The *object* of libido is a variable entity that constitutes what Freud called the destinies. At first Freud developed his theory dualistically (→ Dualism) in terms of the antithesis between object-oriented libido and the instinct of self-preservation. But when it appeared that sexual impulses (→ Sexuality) manifest themselves in → narcissism and make the self the object (→ Ego Psychology) instead of something outside, he gave up that concept and theorized instead a → conflict between the object libido and the ego libido.

Not least under the influence of his theological friend O. Pfister (1873-1956), Freud gradually broadened his originally biologically conceived notion of the libido to embrace both Platonic eros (→ Platonism) and Pauline → love. In a later work he could then call it the thrust toward ever greater unity, which shows a tendency to preserve and develop life. Over against libido Freud set the death instinct, or thanatos — the urge to return to matter. He thus ended with yet another dualistic theory.

In this regard Freud was coming closer to C. G. Jung (1875-1961), who espoused a single primal libido that can be either sexualized or desexualized and that is similar to the general concept of energy of → soul. At the time of his break with Jung, Freud regarded this concept as too undifferentiated.

When P. → Tillich (1886-1965) found in the teaching of Freud the possibility of an existential interpretation of human life, what had been the dominant influence of the Swedish theologian A. Nygren (1890-1978) and his strict separation between eros and agape could be overcome. Not least under the impact of the empirical research of A. Kinsey (1894-1956), American → pastoral psychology, especially in S. Hiltner (1909-84) and A. C. Outler (1910-89), took up Freud's concept into the theory and practice of Christian → ethics and → pastoral care and recognized theologically the development of the libido in early childhood (→ Development 2).

In Anglican theology we also find a kind of post-Freudian integration of the libido concept into religious practice. R. S. Lee saw it first in sensually joyous worship, while R. Green set it in a framework of pastoral psychology. In Roman Catholic → moral theology A. Grabner-Haider formulated it as a right to desire.

Still to be worked on and clarified is the question raised by the early Frankfurt school (→ Critical Theory) as to the relation between the structure of → society and the libido structure.

→ Aggression; Identity; Psychology

Bibliography: S. Freud, "Psychoanalyse" und "Libidotheorie" (1923), *Gesammelte Werke* (vol. 13; 9th ed.; Frankfurt, 1987) 211-33; idem, "Triebe und Triebschicksale" (1915), ibid. (vol. 10; 7th ed.; Frankfurt, 1981) 210-33 • A. Grabner-Haider, *Recht auf Lust?* (Vienna, 1970) • R. Green, *Only Connect: Worship and Liturgy from the Perspective of Pastoral Care* (London, 1987) • E. Grosz and E. Probyn, eds., *Sexy Bodies: The Strange Carnalities of Feminism* (London, 1995) • S. Hiltner, *Sex Ethics and the Kinsey Reports* (New York, 1953) • E. M. Jones, *Libido Dominali: Sexual Liberation and Political Control* (South Bend, Ind., 2000) • C. J. Jung, *Psychology of the Unconscious: A Study of the Transformations and Symbolisms of the Libido: A Contribution to the History of the Evolution of Thought* (Princeton, 1991) • R. S. Lee, *Psychology and Worship* (London, 1955) • A. Lingis, *Libido: The French Existential Theories* (Bloomington, Ind., 1985) • A. Moll, *Untersuchungen über der Libido sexualis* (Leipzig, 1898) • H. Nagera, *Basic Psychoanalytic Concepts on the Libido Theory* (London, 1990) • A. Nygren, *Agape and Eros* (Philadelphia, 1953; orig. pub., 1930) • A. C. Outler, *Psychotherapy and the Christian Message* (New York, 1954) • P. Tillich, *Love, Power, and Justice* (New York, 1954).

JOACHIM SCHARFENBERG†

Libya

	1960	1980	2000
Population (1,000s):	1,349	3,043	6,387
Annual growth rate (%):	3.70	4.37	3.20
Area: 1,757,000 sq. km. (678,400 sq. mi.)			

A.D. 2000

Population density: 4/sq. km. (9/sq. mi.)
Births / deaths: 3.79 / 0.60 per 100 population
Fertility rate: 5.44 per woman
Infant mortality rate: 45 per 1,000 live births
Life expectancy: 67.6 years (m: 65.9, f: 69.8)
Religious affiliation (%): Muslims 95.4, Christians 3.9 (Orthodox 2.4, Roman Catholics 1.0, other Christians 0.5), other 0.7.

1. General Situation
2. Religious Situation

1. General Situation

Libya, or the Socialist People's Libyan Arab Jamahiria, is the easternmost of the four Maghreb countries in northwest Africa. Tunisia and Algeria are neighbors to the west, the Mediterranean to the north, Niger and Chad to the south, and Egypt and the Sudan to the east. Settled first by Berbers, Libya was ruled successively by Carthage, Rome, the Vandals, and the Ottomans. Italy ruled the country from 1911 to 1943, then the British and French military governors until Libya became a constitutional monarchy in 1952. A military junta led by Colonel Muammar al-Qaddafi seized power in 1969. Qaddafi continued in power through the turn of the millennium.

In 2001 approximately 97 percent of the population was Berber or Arab. Also in 2001 there were over 600,000 nonnationals, an estimated 500,000 of whom were Africans from surrounding countries.

Libya's socialist-oriented economy depends primarily upon revenues from the oil sector, which, since the discovery of oil in 1959, has financed revolutionary movements and the promotion of Islam in many other countries. Current oil resources provide 68 percent of Libya's annual revenue, plus 63 percent of its exports. The government has been ineffective in channeling this income to its own people. With desert and semidesert regions covering 92 percent of the land and only 1 percent of the land under permanent cultivation, Libya must import about 75 percent of its food requirements. In 2000 unemployment stood at 30 percent.

2. Religious Situation

In the first centuries A.D. Libya was evangelized from Egypt (→ Mission), and as in most of the → Roman Empire in North Africa, Christianity spread rapidly in the cities. From the seventh century onward, however, Libya gradually came under the sway of → Islam. Since the completion of Islamization in 1067, the country has had virtually no Christian influence.

Article 2 of the Constitutional Proclamation of December 11, 1969, makes → Sunni Islam the state religion. Most Muslims in Libya belong to the tradition of the Hanafite or Shafi'ite law schools. Only the tribal Sanusi in the province of Cyrenaica belong to the Malikites. Article 2 also guarantees → religious liberty as long as there is conformity to "traditional practices." Here is the legal basis for the toleration of Christians, who come under the Ministry of Unity and Foreign Affairs. Most of the

Christians of various → denominations are foreign workers, teachers, and technicians who are in Libya only for a limited period and who have little communication with Libyans.

In October 1970 the → Roman Catholic Church gave up its property and endowments, in return for which the state gave it two buildings for assembly and worship in Tripoli and Benghazi and allowed the bishop to stay in Tripoli with the title "apostolic administrator." This bishop is also in charge of the apostolic vicariates of Benghazi and Darnah and the apostolic prefecture of Misrāta. Ten priests were also allowed to do pastoral duty, raised to 12 in 1985. In 1989, at the request of the government, the → Vatican was also able to send 100 sisters to work in state hospitals and social centers. Libya established diplomatic relations with the Vatican in 1997.

Since 1889 the → Free Church North African Mission has been active in Libya. Its Arabic radio transmissions from Monte Carlo can be heard all over North Africa. From 1900 onward there was also an Anglican congregation (→ Anglican Communion), but it lasted only to 1936, when the Italian colonial authority (→ Colonialism) expelled all non–Roman Catholic → missionaries.

In Tripoli, the capital, there is a → Union Church, an Anglican Church, a Baptist Church (→ Baptists), and a Church of Christ. As a result of the oil boom the influx of Egyptian workers increased the number of Coptic Christians (→ Coptic Orthodox Church), who in 2000 were the largest Christian group (85,000 adherents). The government first allowed local Coptic congregations after a visit to Libya by Patriarch Shenouda in 1971.

→ African Theology; Islam and Christianity

Bibliography: G. ARNOLD, *The Maverick State: Gaddafi and the New World Order* (New York, 1997) • D. B. BARRETT et al., eds., *WCE* (2d ed.) 1.455-57 • V. CHRISTIDES, *Byzantine Libya and the March of the Arabs toward the West of North Africa* (Oxford, 2000) • *Coexistence between Religions: Reality and Horizons. A Consultation between Pontifical Council for Interreligious Dialogue and World Islamic Call Society* (Vatican City, 1990) • J. GURNEY, *Libya: The Political Economy of Oil* (Oxford, 1996) • H. MATTES, *Die innere und äußere islamische Mission Libyens* (Mainz, 1986) • T. NIBLOCK, *"Pariah States" and Sanctions in the Middle East: Iraq, Libya, Sudan* (Boulder, Colo., 2001) • R. B. ST. JOHN, *Historical Dictionary of Libya* (3d ed.; Lanham, Md., 1998) • G. L. SIMONS, *Libya: The Struggle for Survival* (2d ed.; New York, 1996) • D. J. VANDEWALLE, *Libya since Independence: Oil and State-Building* (Ithaca, N.Y., 1998).

HANS VÖCKING

Life

1. Bible and Theology
   1.1. OT
   1.2. NT
   1.3. Developments
2. Science and Ethics
   2.1. Science
   2.2. Systematic Theology
      2.2.1. Reverence for Life
      2.2.2. Peace in Nature
      2.2.3. Integrity of Creation
   2.3. Ethics

1. Bible and Theology
1.1. *OT*
1.1.1. In the OT → Yahweh is consistently the source of life (e.g., Ps. 36:9; Jer. 2:13; 17:13; Job 33:4). He is the one who gives life to all creatures (see Gen. 1:1–2:4a or 2:4b-25) and also the one who takes it away (Ps. 104:29). Thus all life stands related to God as Lord of life and → death. He himself is "the living God" (e.g., Deut. 5:26; Josh. 3:10; also Ps. 18:46 etc.). In → oaths in Israel we find the formula "as the LORD lives" (Judg. 8:19; Ruth 3:13, etc.). Life is the supreme good that nothing can surpass or relativize. As Ecclesiastes says, "Whoever is joined with all the living has hope, for a living dog is better than a dead lion" (9:4).

Life is concrete in the OT (→ Anthropology 1). It shows no trace of the Hellenistic → dualism of perishable body and imperishable → soul (→ Greek Philosophy), nor does it have an expectation of individual → resurrection. Instead, long life is the reward for following the divine and wise commands (Exod. 20:12; Lev. 18:5; Deut. 5:16; 16:20; 30:19; Prov. 10:27, etc.; → Decalogue; Wisdom Literature), and early death is a → punishment (1 Sam. 2:32; Jer. 28:16-17; Ps. 55:23). The → prophet Ezekiel radicalizes the view that the righteous will live and that the unrighteous must die (8:7-18; 14:12-20; 18:1-29; 32:1-32).

1.1.2. The equation of → obedience with (long and happy) life and disobedience with (early and dishonorable) death developed into a relation between action and condition that may still be found in some forms of the doctrine of → predestination. The blessings of God may be seen in earthly prosperity and his curse in misfortune.

The Book of Job, however, sharply disrupts this schema with its theme of the suffering and complaint of an innocent righteous person. The despairing questioning of God's justice by Job (→ Theodicy) finds no answer in the sovereignty of God, which Job does not doubt but presupposes. His objections are simply silenced by his recognition of God's sovereignty (42:1-6). Ecclesiastes contains an even more radical sense of the futility of all human action (1:2-18) and of the obvious injustice of life (4:1-8). The result in this case is a radical → skepticism.

These experiences of unremedied individual injustice, along with the national calamities of exile, destruction, and persecution, led in postexilic → Judaism to the development of a national, and later a personal, → eschatology (see Isaiah 24–27, the so-called Apocalypse of Isaiah), according to which the righteous would rise again on "the day of Yahweh" and sinners would be led away to eternal punishment. This expectation of eternal life came to full flower in Hellenistic Judaism (*TDNT* 2.857-61; → Hellenism).

1.2. NT

1.2.1. The NT has many ways of speaking about life. In distinction from the life (*bios*) indwelling all organic entities, human life is identified as *zōē*.

In the proclamation of → Jesus as we find it in the → Synoptics, life is in general a spontaneous expression of existence that, after the manner of birds, focuses on the present and does not fall victim to anxiety about the → future (Matt. 6:25-34 and par.; → Sermon on the Mount). Yet *zōē* is related to the concept of future eternal life, since Jesus in his preaching was not yet looking back on his own death and → resurrection (e.g., see Mark 10:30 and par.; Matt. 7:14; Mark 9:43, 45).

In John Jesus gives life through his word; indeed, he *is* life (11:25; 14:6; also 6:35). This designation is theologically possible because Jesus, in the Johannine understanding, is the incarnate, but from the very beginning divine, Logos (10:30), and the earthly Jesus is always at the same time the exalted Christ (→ Incarnation; Christology 1). With his coming into the world, Jesus offers the presence and lordship of God in his → proclamation (5:39). New (or eternal) life is experienced by believing acceptance of the word of Jesus (8:12; → Word of God 2). It shows itself to the world in → love (1 John 4:9-12) and to God in → obedience (John 13:15; *TDNT* 2.871). In this sense the resurrection from the dead is itself an event that breaks into the present (8:51), since the final power of death is broken (10:27-29). Judgment, then, takes place when we deny the love of God declared in the proclamation of Jesus, not at the last judgment or in a remote hereafter (12:44-50).

John presents a radical realized eschatology that is marked by the absence of any speculation or expectation in terms of → salvation history. The new life that has broken in with the presence of Jesus, which is offered in his preaching, *is* eternal life.

1.2.2. The theology of → Paul stands under the sign of eschatological tension between the "already" and the "not yet." The foundation stone of new life has been laid in the death and resurrection of Jesus, but Christ is the first fruits of those who rise again. All → creation is still waiting longingly for redemption (Rom. 8:22-23; → Soteriology). The presupposition of Christian participation in the new life is the → forgiveness of → sin promised in → baptism. Eternal life is still the content of Christian → hope, but it is also anticipated by believers in the concrete working out of their lives.

The hermeneutical key (→ Hermeneutics) to understanding this thinking is Paul's theology of the cross (→ Theologia crucis). The old, sinful I is crucified with Christ, so "it is no longer I who live, but it is Christ who lives in me" (Gal. 2:20). M. → Luther calls this experience the crucifixion of the I, which means that the Christian is set in suffering. With a clearly antienthusiast purpose, Paul stresses this connection. As an → apostle he testifies, "I carry the marks [*stigmata*] of Jesus branded on my body" (Gal. 6:17). The new life — as the correspondence of faith that is active in love (E. Jüngel; see Phlm. 5-7) — is thus essentially a → discipleship of the cross. In spite of proclamation, however, we may constantly fall short in this regard, as the example of the Galatians shows (1:6-8; 3:1-5). This discipleship is inseparably bound up with suffering under the conditions of existence on earth, yet it also involves protest against the causes of suffering where they can be eliminated. All life is thus oriented to "the → freedom of the glory of the children of God" (Rom. 8:21), to unveiled glory (2 Cor. 4:6 etc.), but first it must reveal itself with all its works before the judgment seat of Christ (2 Cor. 5:10).

Both exegetically and theologically, there is debate about the degree to which one may deduce from the apostle's promises of universal salvation a universal redemption of all life (i.e., all creation; → Apocatastasis).

1.3. Developments

In later NT writings, often reflecting the survival or consolidation of primitive churches, and again in early Christian tradition (→ Ignatius), the concept of life tends to have less theological depth and to carry more moral features (e.g., Eph. 4:18), being oriented to a future life in the hereafter (Col. 3:3) or dualistically spiritualized (→ Dualism; Gnosis).

→ Anthropology; Literature, Biblical and Early Christian, 1-2; Israel 1; Parousia

Bibliography: K.-H. BERNHARDT, J. BERGMAN, and H. RINGGREN, "הָיָה *hāyāh*," *TDOT* 3.369-81 • R. BULTMANN, G. VON RAD, and G. BERTRAM, "Ζάω, ζωή, κτλ.," *TDNT* 2.832-75 • E. JÜNGEL, *Death, the Riddle and the Mystery* (Philadelphia, 1974) • E. KÄSEMANN, "The Saving Significance of the Death of Jesus in Paul," *Perspectives on Paul* (Philadelphia, 1971) 32-59 • C. F. D. MOULE, "The Meaning of 'Life' in the Gospel and Epistles of St. John," *Theol.* 78 (1975) 114-25 • R. TAYLOR, "The Eschatological Meaning of Life and Death in the Book of Wisdom," *ETL* 42 (1966) 72-137 • C. WESTERMANN, *Elements of OT Theology* (Atlanta, 1982) 85-102 • H. W. WOLFF, *Anthropology of the OT* (Philadelphia, 1974).

EKKEHARD STARKE

2. Science and Ethics

2.1. *Science*

The attempt to describe life with the methods of physics and chemistry has had some success in biology, yet it can hardly be claimed that biology offers an explanation of the phenomenon of life. It does not seek to define life but merely to describe organic systems and processes scientifically. But what or how much of life can science control and → manipulate? We cannot separate biology from its technological derivatives; biotechnology, for instance, increasingly offers means of extending more broadly the knowledge gained in biology. Like biology, it has the task of showing in what context and to what end life is to be disclosed, described, and directed.

The fact that "life" can denote either biological or → biographical life means that there can be different ways of approaching it and interpreting it philosophically. As regards the understanding of the term *bios,* there is debate between the biology that views itself as the independent knowledge of living bodies (from the time of K. F. Burdach and J.-B. Lamarck), the philosophy of life that trusts intuitive experience (W. Dilthey, F. → Nietzsche, G. Simmel, H. Bergson), and finally biologism, which is politically influential.

According to biologism, all of human → behavior (esp. social behavior) can be fully explained in terms of biology or biological principles. Unlike biology, it is thus a → worldview. We do not yet have biologism when biologists apply their wealth of theories to all living things, including human beings, but only when the claim is made that such theories are not just hypotheses but definitive → truth. This claim may be made gently, but we see its full harshness when it aggressively represses interpretations and practices that have other than a biological basis, such as in → pedagogics, medicine, → psychotherapy, or → politics. Biologism was actually operative as → eugenics and → racism in Germany, the United States, and other places during the late 19th century and first half of the 20th century. It may be asked today whether the development of modern agricultural, medical, and biological technology does not promote the seeking of a totally materialistic view of all life.

2.2. *Systematic Theology*

To depict the relation of the Christian community to organic → nature, Protestant theology has recently found three symbolic formulas (→ Symbol 4) that increasingly give centrality both to the preservation of individual life and to its natural foundations.

2.2.1. *Reverence for Life*

The phrase "reverence for life" is the basis of many attempts in Protestant theology to understand life. → Reverence or respect is a kind of interhuman relation, but also one that is religious and → aesthetic. The corresponding relation to nature transcends natural science. Yet although we cannot link this formula to a scientific view, it does have an impact.

A. → Schweitzer (1875-1965) commented that reverence for life provided him with a basic principle of morality: the → good consists in preserving, promoting, and enhancing life; evil, then, is destroying, damaging, or obstructing life. Schweitzer did not demand a blind affirmation of life, as though as many creatures as possible were to be produced. His point is that we are to value and conserve life as a qualified totality.

Schweitzer's approach, which is a step toward acceptance of the will for life, requires further elaboration. The appeal to revere life, though, ought to have an effect on us. It involves the acceptance of → death as the price of life, yet not cynically but sorrowfully (→ Grief). The scientific analysis and economic use of life must not lead to brutalization but must be done cautiously and in solidarity with one's fellow creatures.

2.2.2. *Peace in Nature*

Another formula is "peace in nature," which carries over ideas from a policy of security into relations with nature. Forerunners were → Francis of Assisi (1181/82-1226) and Berthold von Regensburg (ca. 1220-72). In his "Canticle of the Sun" Francis called all living creatures and even the heavenly bodies, the forces of nature, and death itself his brothers and sisters. He would neither extinguish fire nor fell trees, neither slaughter → animals nor so much as cross out letters on a page. Berthold found in every living creature a natural inclination toward → peace.

The starting point of modern talk about peace in nature is the ecological crisis (→ Ecology), which theologians relate to the sighing of the creature and the groaning of the Spirit in Romans 8:18-26 and to the early creation stories in Genesis 1–11 (→ Primeval History [Genesis 1–11]). In this crisis the experience of meaninglessness overshadows the original goodness of every creature.

We must follow the original will of God and find satisfaction in our creatureliness. If we try to master the whole, we will finally have to rule ourselves as subjects, and there would be total violence (→ Force, Violence, Nonviolence). If our relation to nature is seen solely from the angle of self-preservation, it can only be one of → conflict. We must take into account the requirements of the rest of nature if we are to have the means to make it serviceable to us. We must guard against the devastating consequences of our own enormous technological powers as well as against natural forces. From a Christian perspective the reduction of violence against nature is the decisive criterion of our relation to it. The resultant → categorical imperative is that we should act in such a way that the effects of our actions are consonant with the ongoing multiplicity of life and the permanence of human freedom (W. Huber and H.-R. Reuter, 243ff.).

2.2.3. Integrity of Creation

Behind the slogan "integrity of → creation," which had such a widespread impact on the ecumenical movement in the 1980s (→ Ecumenism, Ecumenical Movement), stands the biblical symbol of the Garden of Eden, in which God set Adam "to till it and keep it" (Gen. 2:15). In this formula the term "creation" does not mean the original act of creating, for in this respect we can neither preserve nor destroy anything. Nor can "creation" here be synonymous with the universe. In that sense the formula would be meaningless, for we cannot preserve the universe. Rather, the term stands for a certain relation to the world, to which the slogan urges due attention. The relation is to the totality that lies before us and limits us (T. Rendtorff, 1.33-49). We are to accept this reality with trust in God, and we are to give it back into God's hands. In so doing, we manifest the exoneration of life that finds expression in the symbols of eternal life, new life in Christ, and the new creation (→ Eschatology; New Self; Time and Eternity).

The eschatological horizon of life, however, does not merely exonerate but also has a critical impact. The → parables of the kingdom of heaven set the things of earth in new and redemptive relations. It is debated how far one may meaningfully posit a →

hierarchy of lower and higher forms of life (see M. Welker; → Process Theology). The standards and models that are constantly found in nature do not offer the basis for a statistical → natural law (K. Demmer, 43-53), nor are they arbitrary. Their acceptance depends on whether experience takes the path of conceptual communication and focuses on abiding structures or whether it chooses the path of an elementary encounter with the lilies of the field, which bloom today and tomorrow are thrown into the oven (C. Link, 194). In the first case there is only a direct relation between subject and object. In the second the relation is part of the embracing history of God with his creation, wherein the direct relation is broken off and reopened in a new way. The subject-object relation is set in a new light and loses the absoluteness with which one thing is put above another. Success and failure, life and decay — each has its criterion and content in the free election of God.

2.3. Ethics

Determining the development, decline, and limitation of life cannot be done within absolute limits but only as there is participation in life and regard and respect for fellow creatures. Each speaks in its own way for itself, and living rightly is the art of listening and paying attention to one's own voice and also to that of others.

The three symbolic statements all run up against the one important question, How does the value of all forms of life relate to → human dignity? Some Protestant writers tend to equate the two. They may even demand that we pay all forms of life the respect that the Kantian categorical imperative (→ Kantianism) requires of us when it forbids total exploitation. Others contrast human dignity with the value of animals (→ Values, Ethics of), speaking of phenomena of natural law rather than principles of natural law, or mentioning the teleonomy, versus the teleology, of → evolution (§7, M. Honecker). With the help of the concept of human dignity — or, theologically, of the divine likeness — an answer can be given to the general questions of rules for living and to the specific questions of → medical ethics pertaining, for example, to the beginning and end of life (see S. E. Lammers and A. Verhey, E. E. Shelp).

→ Organism; Power 2; Science and Theology; Sin 3

Bibliography: D. P. BARASH, *Ideas of Human Nature: From the Bhagavad Gita to Sociobiology* (Upper Saddle River, N.J., 1998) • K. DEMMER, *Leben in Menschenhand. Grundlagen des bioethischen Gesprächs* (Freiburg, 1987) • P.-M. EMONET, *The Greatest Marvel of Nature: An In-*

troduction to the Philosophy of the Human Person (New York, 2000) • F. FRANCK, J. ROZE, and R. CONNOLLY, ed., *What Does It Mean to Be Human? Reverence for Life Reaffirmed by Responses from around the World* (New York, 2000) • A. J. HESCHEL, *Who Is Man?* (Stanford, Calif., 1968) • M. HONECKER, *Einführung in die theologischen Ethik* (Berlin, 1990) • W. HUBER and H.-R. REUTER, *Friedensethik* (Stuttgart, 1989) • S. E. LAMMERS and A. VERHEY, eds., *On Moral Medicine* (Grand Rapids, 1987) • C. LINK, "Die Transparenz der Natur für das Geheimnis der Schöpfung," *Ökologische Theologie. Perspektiven zur Orientierung* (ed. G. Altner; Stuttgart, 1989) 166-95 • J. C. POLKINGHORNE and M. WELKER, eds., *The End of the World and the Ends of God: Science and Theology on Eschatology* (Harrisburg, Pa., 2000) • T. RENDTORFF, *Ethics* (2 vols.; Philadelphia and Minneapolis, 1986-89) • J. R. RICHARDS, *Human Nature after Darwin: A Philosophical Introduction* (London, 2000) • A. SCHWEITZER, *Civilization and Ethics* (London, 1929); idem, *Reverence for Life* (New York, 1969); idem, *The Teaching of Reverence for Life* (New York, 1965) • E. E. SHELP, ed., *Theology and Bioethics: Exploring the Foundations and Frontiers* (Dordrecht, 1985) • M. WELKER, *Universalität Gottes und Relativität der Welt. Theologische Kosmologie im Dialog mit dem amerikanischen Prozeßdenken nach Whitehead* (2d ed.; Neukirchen, 1988) • WORLD COUNCIL OF CHURCHES, *Creation and the Kingdom of God* (Geneva, 1988).

HARTWIG VON SCHUBERT

Life and Work Movement

1. Background
2. Stockholm, 1925
3. Oxford, 1937
4. Legacy of Social Responsibility in the WCC
   4.1. The WCC in Process of Formation
   4.2. Since 1948
5. Conclusion

1. Background

From the beginning, the exercise of Christian obedience through social → responsibility has been one of the key features of the worldwide ecumenical movement. Indeed, Christians have often found it easier to respond to the needs of contemporary society than to resolve the internal divisions within what the Holy Spirit founded at Pentecost as the one → church of Jesus Christ.

The flagship of this movement has been the → World Council of Churches (WCC), though it is far from being the only significant instrument of the ecumenical movement. At every level of the human community, from the most local to the most deliberately universal, there exist associations, councils, congresses, and organizations contributing to the movement. The WCC puts much effort into supporting these efforts and forming appropriate networks among them. Some of these groups explicitly bring Christians together to discover how they can reconcile their still-divided churches; others emphasize enabling Christians to serve in effective partnership the people and communities given to them as neighbors across whatever barriers (esp. language, politics, class, ethnicity, race, and religion) now divide the human community. The Life and Work movement was the first effort seeking to galvanize the whole church to work practically toward the latter goals.

2. Stockholm, 1925

The First World War was the catalyst for much devoted work among Christians throughout Europe and North America to find new ways of contributing to → peace and social health. Already in the long years of growing rivalry between Germany, on the one hand, and France and the United Kingdom, on the other, many Christians were becoming gravely concerned at the prospect of historically "Christian nations" going to war with one another. What had been at first purely national bodies — such as the Interdenominational Social Service Council in the United Kingdom, Le Christianisme Social in France, the Evangelisch-Sozialer Kongress in Germany, and the Federal Council of Churches in the United States, with its links to the → Social Gospel movement — all started to turn their attention also to the wider international scene. The Fellowship of Reconciliation, for instance, was founded by pacifists in 1914 (→ Pacifism) and then grew into an international fellowship in 1919. All of these published, before the war, notable manifestos about the "social principles" or the "public social and moral witness" Christians should be following. But they found it difficult to know what to do once war had broken out.

Leaders, including the British-Canadian Quaker J. Allen Baker, the German pastor Friedrich Siegmund-Schulze, and Charles McFarland of the U.S. Federal Council (for the peace work of whose churches Andrew Carnegie gave a gift of $2 million in 1914), had taken steps to offer a memorandum to the Hague Peace Conference of 1907 "expressing the Christian conviction that arbitration should be used as the means of settling conflicts between the nations." In 1908 and 1909 large interdenominational parties of German and British Christians visited each other's country to encourage the striving for peace. These efforts led to the founding of what became the World Alliance for Promoting International Friendship through the Churches, whose first attempt to hold a founding assembly, in Konstanz, Germany, in August 1914, was broken up by the outbreak of the very war they were gathering to prevent.

Nonetheless, the concern for peace dominated the hearts and prayers of many Christians throughout the war, and still more in the months after its end, when international meetings became possible once more. Some envisioned a fellowship or council of churches that would take a more aggressive role in working together to promote world peace and address human needs.

The lead was clearly taken by Nathan Söderblom (1866-1931), who became archbishop of the Church of Sweden shortly before the war broke out. He had previously lived in Germany and in France and had taken part in many of the early meetings for peace and social witness in both countries. Already in the first weeks of the war, he endeavored to persuade church leaders in various countries to join him in an appeal for peace and Christian fellowship. He felt it to be the urgent duty of the church's servants to keep the idea of peace alive so as to proclaim the Christian's faith in God's sovereignty, in which alone the destiny of all peoples could be fulfilled.

As the end result of a long process that had become for many "a deeply spiritual pilgrimage" (Nils Karlström, 541), Söderblom was finally able to invite to Stockholm, and himself chair, the Universal Christian Conference on Life and Work, which met August 19-30, 1925. His 1924 letter of invitation spelled out its aim in these words: "We hope, under the guidance of God and through the counsel of all, to be able to formulate programs and devise means for making them effective, by which the fatherhood of God and the brotherhood of all peoples will become more completely realized through the Church of Christ."

The conference, attended by more than 600 delegates from 37 countries, addressed six main topics:
1. the purpose of God for humanity and the duty of the church;
2. the church and economic and industrial problems;
3. the church and social and moral problems;
4. the church and international relations;
5. the church and → Christian education; and
6. methods of promoting cooperation among the churches and their closer association on federal lines.

The gathering was much enriched by a strong Orthodox delegation, headed by the patriarchs of Alexandria and Jerusalem (→ Orthodox Church). In 1921 the → Roman Catholic Church had been invited to send delegates to the conference then being planned, but it ignored the invitation, although a few Roman Catholic observers were present as individuals. The mission countries were represented, though just barely — two delegates each were present from India, China, and Japan. Despite these limitations, we can still characterize the conference as ecumenical in motive and operation. Indeed, some observers remarked that this conference was the most representative gathering of Christians since the Council of → Chalcedon in 451.

As a practical matter, under the slogan "Doctrine divides, service unites," the conference sought to emphasize areas of practical service and to shun theological debate. Addresses on the first day of the conference, however, revealed how unrealistic such a distinction was. English bishop F. Theodore Woods of Winchester argued that the God-given sovereignty of Jesus Christ and the human striving to serve the coming of the → kingdom of God on earth were linked within the efforts of Christians at any given time. Later in the same program, German bishop Ludwig Ihmels of Saxony clearly disagreed, rejecting outright any idea that mere humans could establish God's kingdom in this world.

Nils Ehrenström lists three significant achievements of this first Life and Work conference (pp. 548-50). It was the first truly ecumenical gathering in modern times, engaging not just interested individuals but churches, for almost all of those attending came as appointees of their respective communions. Second, the conference promoted a new theological and personal openness among participants, even in the face of the stresses and tensions that delegates predictably experienced so soon after the armistice of 1918. Finally, the meeting ended with a clear sense that the churches were responsible for the whole of human life and that Christians should and could unite in serving their → neighbors of any kind. It witnessed to the shared conviction that the sovereignty of God extended over the entire life of the world and therefore "demanded the unconditional acceptance of principles which even churches that nominally accepted them had too often allowed to remain a dormant part of their creed."

3. Oxford, 1937

The hopeful enthusiasm Stockholm generated was, however, to prove short-lived. With the crash of the

New York stock market in 1929, → unemployment soared throughout North America and Europe; with the rise of → fascism in Italy and Germany, in violent confrontation with the Communism based in Russia, all other → social systems looked horribly fragile; with the invasion of Ethiopia by Italy (1936) and of China by Japan (Manchuria in 1931, China proper in 1937), the impotence of the League of Nations was exposed. These threats deeply challenged those searching for appropriate Christian responses. No naive → optimism for a better future could provide an adequate basis for the costly and long-term → obedience that was being required. Rather, it was the uncomfortably stern theology of Karl → Barth (1886-1968; → Dialectical Theology) that compelled radical new thinking, such as the single-minded insistence of Dietrich → Bonhoeffer (1906-45), who declared in an address to a Life and Work meeting in 1934 at Fanø, Denmark, "Peace means to give oneself altogether to the law of God, wanting no security, but in faith and obedience laying the destiny of the nations in the hand of Almighty God, not trying to direct it for selfish purposes."

As was Stockholm, so the Oxford Conference was ecumenical, though again without official Roman Catholic participation, and again with relatively small representation from the Orthodox churches (40 delegates out of 425) and from churches of the Third World (30 delegates). The total delegates were divided into official representatives of the churches (300 delegates), experts in one or another academic or practical field relevant to the conference (100), and "fraternal delegates and ecumenical officers" (25). In addition, several hundred invited observers and youth representatives were present (Ehrenström, 588).

This second — and, by its own decision, final — major Life and Work conference met on July 12-26, 1937. The overall theme was "Church, Community, and State," with deliberations taking place in five sections:
1. church and community;
2. → church and state;
3. church, community, and state in relation to the economic order;
4. church, community, and state in relation to education; and
5. the universal church and the world of nations.

The essential tone of this conference was stated by its chief architect, J. H. Oldham (1874-1969), following the Roman Catholic writer Christopher Dawson, as "the life and death struggle between Christian faith and the secular and pagan ideologies of our time" (Ehrenström, 587).

The conference is remembered for (1) firm words relativizing the role of the → state ("we do not consider the state as the ultimate source of law but as its guarantor. . . . There can be for the Christian no ultimate authority but very God"); (2) the slogan "Let the church be the church" (i.e., nothing less than what God has called into being and can empower); and (3) the decision to invite the → Faith and Order conference in Edinburgh that would begin that summer on August 3 to join Life and Work in creating a "World Council of Churches" that would embrace the two movements.

At their conference the Faith and Order delegates agreed to the proposal to found a world council. Accordingly, a Life and Work meeting that was to be held in May 1938 in Utrecht became a meeting of the new Provisional Committee of the → World Council of Churches in Process of Formation. At that meeting the committee invited W. A. → Visser 't Hooft to become general secretary of the new council and planned the inaugural assembly for August 1941. World events would postpone formal beginning until 1948.

Since the Universal Christian Council on Life and Work had explicitly handed its role over to the WCC in 1938 and then disbanded itself, the expectation of all concerned was that it would now be up to the assemblies of the council to reach major decisions and arrange the necessary staff work for whatever was to be done in the field of social responsibility. Whereas Faith and Order continued on as a discrete department, subunit, or subcluster within the WCC, the entity known as Life and Work no longer existed per se; its programs and concerns were assumed by the new council in process of formation.

The remainder of this article highlights the major efforts the WCC has undertaken since 1938 in pursuit of the goals that originally animated the Life and Work movement.

4. Legacy of Social Responsibility in the WCC
4.1. *The WCC in Process of Formation*
Even before the world council could be formally launched, the coming of World War II thrust upon it a plethora of Life and Work concerns. One direct effect of the war was the creation of a large new organ of mutual aid. The incipient WCC had collaborated during the war with the Central Bureau for Interchurch Aid in Europe, led since 1922 by a Swiss, Adolf Keller, in Zurich and cosponsored by the U.S. Federal Council of Churches. In 1944 this bureau integrated itself into the WCC to launch a new department — the Department of Reconstruction and

Interchurch Aid — wholly devoted to reconstruction in Europe through the sharing of all available humanitarian aid with the shattered communities throughout the continent. It soon gathered a staff of 67 people in the international office in Geneva, with a constantly growing number of national ecumenical bodies being created to take responsibility for such interchurch aid. (This effort did not include the Roman Catholic Church, which worked within its own agencies.) Thus began what was to become by far the best funded and most extensive, possibly also most effective, social program of the council, facilitating "the sharing of resources — spiritual, personal, material, and financial — by the ecumenical fellowship to help meet needs on behalf of humanity, and without distinction of creed, caste, race, nationality, or politics" (Geoffrey Murray, 201).

Within a few months, the same department in the WCC was also given responsibility for doing whatever could be done for the millions of → refugees adrift on the Continent. This work provided many lessons for the comparable, if longer-term, work with migrants in Europe that the successor department began in 1961. Back in 1948, as the → United Nations struggled to cope with the effects of the fighting in Palestine, Interchurch Aid was authorized by the WCC's founding assembly in Amsterdam to extend its services to the Middle East, where there were then 660,000 Arab refugees from Palestine.

This work involved close relationships with the services undertaken by the United Nations, at whose founding conference at San Francisco in mid-1945 the WCC had already been represented, foreshadowing yet another vast area of social responsibility: concern for peace and human → rights. The ecumenical movement was to make a vital contribution to this work through a new Commission of the Churches on International Affairs (CCIA), established at a meeting in Cambridge in 1946 to serve both the WCC and the → International Missionary Council (IMC). Accomplishments of the CCIA include 21 instances in the years from 1954 to 1965 when it made representations on behalf of the churches to the relevant political powers.

4.2. Since 1948

The Life and Work story since the founding of the WCC in Amsterdam in 1948 includes an impressive number of programs and initiatives that have developed and extended Archbishop Söderblom's original vision. The following paragraphs identify some of the highlights of the churches' continued efforts to express practically "the fatherhood of God and the brotherhood of all peoples."

Amsterdam, 1948. The WCC's first assembly, in Amsterdam, considered the theme "Man's Disorder and God's Design," with the third section addressing "The Church and the Disorder of Society," and the fourth "The Church and the International Disorder." Section 3 provided a thoughtful, brief chapter entitled "The Responsible Society," emphasizing that a society, like all human beings, is responsible primarily to God and then to the neighbor; thus "it is required that economic justice and provision of equality of opportunity be established for all the members of society" (*Report*, 78). Section 4 is remembered especially for its declaration on → religious liberty, which contributed several key points to the U.N. Universal Declaration of Human Rights, adopted and proclaimed later that year.

Evanston, 1954. At the second assembly, held in Evanston, near Chicago, fresh attention was drawn to the large field of racial and ethnic relations, with a resolution declaring the assembly's conviction that "any form of segregation based on race, color, or ethnic origin is contrary to the Gospel, and is incompatible with the Christian doctrine of man and with the nature of the Church of Christ" (*Evanston Speaks*, 96; → Racism). This statement proved of crucial importance in the bitter controversies regarding South Africa and race relations in the United States in the 1960s.

Department of Church and Society. In 1954 the WCC established Church and Society, with an American economist, Paul Abrecht, as its secretary. This department soon realized that the most urgent issues in the world concerned the revolutionary social pressures and changes then occurring in the new nations of the South. It took note of an ecumenical study conference for East Asia held in 1952 in Lucknow, India, that had proposed action in regard to radical reform of land tenure systems, planned economic → development, support of the struggle for freedom and self-determination in East Asia, and the development of new policies by Western nations to support political and economic change.

Geneva, 1966. The Lucknow conference opened the way to a program called the Common Christian Responsibility towards Areas of Rapid Social Change. This initiative ran from 1955 until 1961, when discussions at the 1961 New Delhi Assembly suggested a world conference to be entitled "Christians in the Technical and Social Revolutions of Our Time," which was held at Geneva in July 1966. This conference was significant for including equal numbers of participants from the nations of the South and from North America and Europe. The presence of a strong team of Roman Catholic observers, making constant reference to the Second → Vatican Council's Pastoral Constitution on the Church in the Modern World, *Gaudium et spes*, was also a new experience for the WCC. Overall, the conference made a ringing call for justice within and among the nations, and for justice not just in the economic and political spheres but also in international commercial and cultural relationships. It provoked fierce argument in some circles, especially in North America, foreshadowing an era of controversy.

Uppsala, 1968. Building on the recent Geneva conference, Church and Society work broadened enormously at the fourth WCC assembly, held in Uppsala, Sweden. This assembly, the most activist and politically oriented of all assemblies, led to the formation of several new programs dealing with Life and Work themes.

One such program was the *Commission on the Churches' Participation in Development* (CCPD), with "development" encompassing social justice, self-reliance, and economic growth; throughout, people, not statistics, were to receive the emphasis. This focus led to an enduring priority of responding to the views and wishes of those who are → marginalized and impoverished by the wider society, which was to become virtually a trademark for the WCC in many of its programs — in mission, education, and health, no less than in politics and development. The CCPD appealed to the churches to set aside 2 percent of their income for development purposes, to be channeled in ways decided by the groups who received the funds.

A second program was the *Christian Medical Commission.* Over the years this initiative has focused especially on preventive and primary health care, looking away from large, hi-tech hospitals to the potential skills of ordinary people in ordinary places, not forgetting the knowledge of traditional medicine and the social patterns of a healing community (→ Medical Missions).

A third program was the → *Program to Combat Racism,* which included a special fund, undergirded by a proportion of the WCC's own financial reserves, that was to be used for grants without strings to organizations of people oppressed on account of their race. In 1970 this approach provoked a storm of protest in certain quarters in the North, whipped up by Prime Minister John Vorster of South Africa, when he responded swiftly to news of grants to freedom movements that were taking up arms against the remaining white rulers in Southern Africa by accusing the WCC of paying for "guns to guerrillas."

SODEPAX, 1968-80. The new attitudes of the Roman Catholic Church arising from Vatican II led in 1968 to a promising agreement with the WCC to create a joint committee on Society, Development, and Peace, known widely as → SODEPAX. Enjoying a large budget in its early years, this group produced an impressive body of work in the early 1970s, including the report of a study conference on the theology of development to which Gustavo Gutiérrez from Peru contributed a draft of his book *A Theology of Liberation,* a work that opened a whole new chapter in global theology led by Latin America (→ Liberation Theology; Latin American Theology). Other large international conferences that SODEPAX organized addressed the role of the → communications media in development and peace (1970), peace and the international community (1970), the churches' role in the development of Asia (1970), and peace in Northern Ireland (1973). Before long, however, perhaps influenced by all the tensions the Vatican had to face in the aftermath of Paul VI's decision on contraception, support for SODEPAX ebbed, and it was reduced to a shadow of its initial flowering before collapsing in 1980.

MIT, 1979. The many questions also being raised, especially in the less advanced South, about the astonishing advances in → science and → technology converged in the Church and Society world conference "Faith, Science, and the Future," held at the Massachusetts Institute of Technology in Cambridge, Massachusetts. This conference brought together an impressive cross-section of Christians working in science and technology with theologians and others concerned about the effects of new technological advances on the sustainability of human civilization itself. Once again, the difficulty of reaching real mutual understanding between those from the North and those from the South provided the most memorable moments.

Vancouver, 1983. At the Sixth Assembly of the WCC, in Vancouver, Canada, a new momentum for holding together what had often appeared to be separate programs of the WCC took effect as the assembly voted in favor of a "conciliar process of mutual commitment and covenant to justice, peace and the integrity of all creation" (JPIC). This initiative advanced the earlier attempt to codify the overall goals of Christian social responsibility in terms of "a just, participatory and sustainable society," now in explicit challenge to the "demonic powers" of economic oppression, militarism, and the ever-increasing waste, pollution, and exhaustion of the natural resources of the planet for the selfish purposes of the rich. This process was eagerly taken up in some quarters, especially in the South, but notably also in both Germanys, where it was widely seen as the long-awaited successor to the kind of "peace council" for which Dietrich Bonhoeffer had pleaded between the two world wars.

Ecumenical Decade of Churches in Solidarity with Women, 1988-98. Approved by the WCC Central Committee in 1987, this decade was a call to churches to review their structures and make whatever changes necessary so that women might share power equally with men at all levels. Over the decades the WCC has initiated many studies of the role of women in church and society and has constantly prodded and challenged the churches to open greater opportunities to their women members. It has insisted on complementarity of status, rooted in the conviction that women and men are created by God for mutual relationship with one another, even as they remain distinct and often differing in perspective, yet equal, with no necessary priority for either sex. One of the weightiest findings of the ecumenical decade was the shocking extent of domestic violence inflicted on women in virtually every sort of community and culture, not excluding the churches.

Seoul, 1990. A world convocation on JPIC gathered nearly a thousand people in Seoul, South Korea, and issued an "Act of Covenanting." The act began with ten affirmations, including "We affirm that all exercise of power is accountable to God" and "We affirm God's preferential option for the poor." The final report identified four large "concretizations" for action by Christians and churches: "(1) for a just economic order, and liberation from the bondage of foreign debt that affects the lives of hundreds of millions of people; (2) for the true security of all nations and peoples, and the demilitarization of international relations, and for a culture of non-violence as a force for change and liberation; (3) for preserving the gift of the earth's atmosphere to nurture and sustain the world's life, and for building a culture that can live in harmony with creation's integrity (→ Environmental Ethics); and (4) for the eradication of racism and discrimination on national and international levels for all people, and for the breaking down of walls which divide people because of their ethnic origin."

Canberra, 1991. The realities of war dominated the seventh WCC assembly, held in Canberra, Australia, just as the standoff over Iraqi-invaded Kuwait flamed into the Gulf War. The war preoccupied much of the assembly's time and energies, not least on account of the ambiguities of the oil trade, the threat posed by nuclear weapons, and the sensitivity of relations between Christians, Jews, and Muslims in the Middle East and elsewhere — all complicating yet further an already tangled situation. Few present felt that the long resolution emerging from a full day's debate in plenary session could actually make much difference to what was happening, yet the attempt to face this vast tragedy together as a single, hugely diverse Christian community, with participants from many of the warring countries and with sympathies leaning toward both sides, was itself a landmark in the growth of awareness of the world citizenship — and therefore world responsibility — that arises from shared allegiance to the risen Christ.

Jubilee 2000. The major justice issue of the growing economic gap between rich and poor was brought to the foreground in the later 1990s by the global Jubilee 2000 campaign. This effort sought to apply the biblical teaching in Leviticus 25 and 27 of a "Sabbath year of jubilee" (when goods and land lost by whatever means would be restored to the family of the original owner) to the enormous international debt that saddled many poorer countries of the South. Eagerly supported by nongovernmental organizations, among them many churches and Christians, and warmly encouraged by the WCC at its eighth assembly in Harare, Zimbabwe, in December 1998, the Jubilee campaign created a whole new global climate of opinion, perhaps more successfully than any other in the 20th century. Since the goal of debt cancellation was only in small part achieved by the end of 2000, this effort will surely continue to play a high-profile role in the 21st century. Christians, among others, have tried to show that this opportunity is nothing less than a call from God for each and every sector of humanity to rise to a new level of respect and generosity toward all its neighbors. Only daring obedience along such lines will empower the human race also to resolve the enormous environmental problems ahead and the common expectation that violence can solve tensions and disputes.

5. Conclusion

From this evolving story of Life and Work, under its various names and titles, it is readily apparent that all attempts to bring Christians together from different backgrounds to exercise their common social responsibility soon run into tensions. As Paul Abrecht wrote, "Despite the achievements in recent years, ecumenical social thinking remains a precarious enterprise. A substantial number of Christians in our Churches are probably still very much opposed to the directions it takes. . . . As the pressures for rapid social change in society increase, the polarization of opinion in our Churches on basic social questions will undoubtedly become greater rather than diminish . . . ecumenical witness will become more difficult in the future" ("Development," 259).

This story of Life and Work has included antagonisms between warring nationalisms in World War I, between the two sides of the cold war from the late 1940s to the tearing down of the Berlin Wall in 1989, between the competing hopes for empire and for independence in the years soon after World War II, between the apostles of the free market in the later 20th century and those marching with Jubilee 2000 to demand the cancellation of the unpayable debts of the poor.

Within the life of the churches, as well as within and between the different great faiths, there are constant areas of tension because of differing histories, cultures, expectations, and senses of identity. There are also lasting tensions between those who embody → tradition, → authority, and power in a church and those who, in institutional terms, are simply ordinary members.

There have also been — and remain — major differences in theology within the total ecumenical movement, for instance between those who see the → salvation available in Christ as a matter for individual decision and those who see that salvation primarily in terms of corporate or community relationships, or between those who believe that Jesus, in speaking of the kingdom of God, was pointing to something beyond earthly history and those who believe he was pointing to signs and realities we can begin to know and receive as God's gifts even now.

Such tensions, in each sphere, will always be present. The story of Life and Work and its successors in no way encourages any expectation of a smooth, readily popular, and unfailingly successful exercise of social responsibility. It will remain a difficult, though always worthwhile, path of obedience. The all-important question, as in the 1930s, remains, To whom are we as Christians responsible? In the ecumenical movement, Christians of every background learn that their disagreements and tensions are to be subordinated to their common and shared accountability to God. In the presence of God, all stand together. No claim to be necessarily more right than one's neighbor is accepted. For in the cross of Christ, as the WCC World Mission Conference at Melbourne in 1980 put it, "The eye of faith discerns the embodiment of a God who out-suffers, out-loves and out-lives the worst that worldly powers can do." With such a perspective, human diversities and differences are best viewed as

learning opportunities, giving all parts of the church the chance to grow in their sensitivities and sympathies.

→ Ecumenism, Ecumenical Movement

Bibliography: Reports of world conferences: G. K. A. BELL, ed., *The Stockholm Conference, 1925: The Official Report of the Universal Christian Conference on Life and Work Held in Stockholm, 19-30 August, 1925* (London, 1926) • G. H. DUNNE, ed., *In Search of a Theology of Development: A SODEPAX Report* (Geneva, 1970) • J. H. OLDHAM, ed., *The Churches Survey Their Task: The Report of the Conference at Oxford, July 1937, on Church, Community, and State* (London, 1937; repr. as *Foundations of Ecumenical Social Thought: The Oxford Conference Report* [Philadelphia, 1966]) • R. L. SHINN, *Faith and Science in an Unjust World: Report of the WCC Conference on Faith, Science, and the Future* (2 vols.; Geneva and Philadelphia, 1980) • SODEPAX, *World Development: The Challenge to the Churches. The Conference on World Cooperation for Development, Beirut, Lebanon, April 1968* (Geneva, 1968) • M. M. THOMAS and P. ABRECHT, eds., *World Conference on Church and Society, Geneva, July 15-26, 1966: Christians in the Technical and Social Revolutions of Our Time* (Geneva, 1967) • WORLD COUNCIL OF CHURCHES, *Statements of the World Council of Churches on Social Questions* (Geneva, 1956).

Surveys: P. ABRECHT, "The Development of Ecumenical Social Thought and Action," *The Ecumenical Advance: A History of the Ecumenical Movement,* vol. 2, *1948-1968* (2d ed.; ed. H. E. Fey; Geneva, 1986) 233-59 • A. VAN DER BENT, *Commitment to God's World: A Concise Critical Survey of Ecumenical Social Thought* (Geneva, 1995) • R. DICKINSON, "Diakonia," *A History of the Ecumenical Movement,* vol. 3, *1968-2000* (ed. J. Briggs, M. Oduyoye, and G. Tsetsis; Geneva and Grand Rapids, forthcoming) • E. DUFF, *The Social Thought of the World Council of Churches* (New York, 1956) • N. EHRENSTRÖM, "Movements for International Friendship and Life and Work, 1925-1948," *A History of the Ecumenical Movement: 1517-1948* (3d ed.; ed. R. Rouse and S. C. Neill; Geneva, 1986) 543-96 • M. ELLINGSEN, *The Cutting Edge: How Churches Speak on Social Issues* (Grand Rapids, 1993) • D. HUDSON, *The Ecumenical Movement in World Affairs* (London, 1969) • N. KARLSTRÖM, "Movements for International Friendship and Life and Work, 1910-1925," *History of the Ecumenical Movement,* ed. Rouse and Neill, 507-42 • P. LODBERG, "Peace and Justice," *History of the Ecumenical Movement,* ed. Briggs, Oduyoye, and Tsetsis • L. MUDGE, "Ecumenical Social Thought," *History of the Ecumenical Movement,* ed. Briggs, Oduyoye, and Tsetsis • G. MURRAY, "Joint Service as an Instrument of Renewal," *Ecumenical Advance,* ed. Fey, 199-231 • O. F. Nolde, "Ecumenical Action in International Affairs," *Ecumenical Advance,* ed. Fey, 261-85.

Specific topics: P. Abrecht, *The Churches and Rapid Social Change* (New York, 1961) • R. H. Bainton, *Christian Attitudes towards War and Peace: A Historical Survey and Critical Reevaluation* (London, 1961) • G. Baum and H. Wells, eds., *The Reconciliation of Peoples: Challenge to the Churches* (New York, 1997) • A. F. Carrillo de Albornoz, *Religious Liberty* (New York, 1967) • T. Derr, *Barriers to Ecumenism: The Holy See and the World Council on Social Questions* (New York, 1983) • R. van Drimmelen, *Faith in a Global Economy: A Primer for Christians* (Geneva, 1998) • U. Duchrow, *Alternatives to Global Capitalism: Drawn from Biblical History, Designed for Political Action* (Amsterdam, 1995) • R. M. Fagley, *The Population Explosion and Christian Responsibility* (New York, 1960) • D. Gosling, *A New Earth: Covenanting for Justice, Peace, and the Integrity of Creation* (London, 1992) • D. Hallman, ed., *Ecotheology: Voices from South and North* (Geneva, 1994) • G. Jacques, *Beyond Impunity: An Ecumenical Approach to Truth, Justice, and Reconciliation* (Geneva, 2000) • M. May, "The Kingdom of God, the Church, and the World: The Social Gospel and the Making of Theology in the Twentieth-Century Ecumenical Movement," *The Social Gospel Today* (ed. C. H. Evans; Louisville, Ky., 2001) 38-52 • C. D. Moe-Lobeda, *Healing a Broken World: Globalization and God* (Minneapolis, 2002) • P. Niles, comp., *Between the Flood and the Rainbow: Interpreting the Conciliar Process of Mutual Commitment (Covenant) to Justice, Peace, and the Integrity of Creation* (Geneva, 1992) • K. Nürnberger, *Prosperity, Poverty, and Pollution: Managing the Approaching Crisis* (Pietermaritzburg, 1999) • J. H. Oldham, *Christianity and the Race Problem* (London, 1924) • K. Raiser, *For a Culture of Life: Transforming Globalization and Violence* (Geneva, 2002) • L. Rasmussen, *Earth Community, Earth Ethics* (New York, 1996) • J. de Santa Ana, ed., *Sustainability and Globalization* (Geneva, 1998).

MARTIN CONWAY

Lifestyle

1. Place
2. Themes
3. Significance of the Church
4. Helps

1. Place

Christian → ethics and → moral theology each deal with the shaping of → life, individual as well as communal. Yet the whole practice of the church is an expression of the Christian lifestyle. Lifestyle is therefore also a central theme in → pastoral theology.

→ Religious instruction and → pastoral care especially help to shape a lifestyle that is consonant with faith, adapted to the individual, related to society, and in keeping with the situation. This lifestyle does not have to be equated with middle-class convention or with what is generally accepted and morally desirable in → society. We must also avoid the misunderstanding that the → gospel contains in essence the introduction to a Christian lifestyle and that it is particularly of a social nature (as in love of neighbor).

An authoritarian attitude, rules of conduct viewed as → norms, subjection, and immaturity on the one side contrast with loving → tolerance, → freedom of decision, independence, and → autonomy on the other in much the same way as → law and gospel or the striving for security and → faith. In the cohuman reality of society and within the individual psyche, these contrasts often seem to be radical alternatives, but in fact we cannot differentiate them sharply or relate them along the lines of tension and ambivalence.

Hence it is not the task of the → church to preach a correct lifestyle but to awaken independence, freedom of decision, the courage to be, a readiness for risks — in short, faith. At the same time, the church, as an organized Christian community, is the place where this community speaks about a lifestyle that is in keeping with its faith.

2. Themes

2.1. Basic questions of lifestyle include the relation between faith and → everyday life, between the Christian and the civil community, between ecclesiastical and political practice. At issue is the mutual relation between the individual (→ Individualism) and society, the tension between the traditional norm and life as it is now lived, the possibility and limit of personal freedom, truthfulness, → love, and → piety. → Asceticism and → hedonism might be seen as the two extremes of a lifestyle that is appropriate to faith, of one that stands between → fasting and feasting. A shadow rests over every lifestyle variation — that of anxious denial of the world over asceticism, that of avarice and the fear of missing something (→ Anxiety) over joy in life.

A problem arises with talk about the model character or credibility of the Christian lifestyle, for such talk is never according to the gospel. By reversing the Pauline relation between indicative and imperative, gospel and law, this kind of talk can lead to self-deception, living out a lie, and sham holiness. In pastoral care especially it comes clearly to light that our efforts to achieve a lifestyle in keeping with faith constantly fail and that we are thus to see in the church a fellowship of failures in → solidarity with one another (→ Justification).

2.2. Pastoral care often comes up against the following lifestyle themes: love and partnership in → marriage and → family but also in relations between unmarried partners, including → homosexuals; new forms of communal life that seek to make good the isolation of the nuclear family and the loss of clan, village society (→ City), and neighborhood; competition or cooperation, solidarity or rivalry in education and → vocation; alienation and the need to repersonalize → work; new → technologies; a healthier → environment (→ Ecology); the quality of life; the ideology of growth, coupled with excessive pressure (not least, moral pressure) on and by people; mobility and continuity (→ Tradition); commitment and freedom; reliability (→ Faithfulness) and → emancipation; desires for independence and a caring mentality; and addiction and drug problems (→ Substance Abuse). Other themes are the medicalizing of society; new evaluations of → suffering, sickness (→ Health and Illness), → grief and → death, fortune and destiny, justice and → peace in both individual and political life (→ Politics); the rediscovery of → spirituality and piety; the longing for participation and integration, that is, for society, and at the same time the fear of incorporation and tutelage, and hence the rejection of what is viewed as the church.

2.3. In the debate about a natural lifestyle, which again distinguishes Creator and creature (→ Creation) by means of reverence for life (A. → Schweitzer), there also develops a feeling for the sacramental character of the world (→ Sacramentality) and the holiness of the profane (→ Sacred and Profane). Life's rhythms are accepted again, and the → church year achieves new relevance. A sense of the need for a politically responsible lifestyle (→ Responsibility) that posits the relevance of the creed (→ Confession of Faith) to public life is increasing. The separation of the place of work from the place of residence and of work from → leisure raises new problems of lifestyle and forces the church to face the question of how it sees itself. Is it to compete with the leisure industry and caring agencies?

3. Significance of the Church

The significance of the church for lifestyle naturally cannot be restricted to the leisure sphere or the car-

ing sector of a society. As a Christian lifestyle that is consistent with faith may be necessary as divine service (→ Worship) in everyday life (see Rom. 12:1), and every Christian may represent the church in a specific place, so the church as an organized society of believers cannot be involved for its part merely in social → diakonia. Yet it may be overextended as the "church for others."

Individual Christians are also overextended in the two spheres of church and world if they are expected to be totally engaged with each of them. Hence there is a need for a precise definition of the meaning and goal of the church as an → institution. As the communion of saints, it promotes faith and adoration (CA 7, 8) and, to that extent, is a decisive factor in the lifestyle of Christians. The setting of this lifestyle, though, is the whole world. A separate congregational life must therefore be regarded as questionable. It cannot be seen as the preferred setting of a Christian lifestyle, even though it necessarily is so for full-time church workers.

4. Helps

As aids in the search for a lifestyle that is consonant with both the situation and faith, the church offers pastoral → counseling, facilities for public addresses and discussions (→ Church Conference Centers), public comments, and other contributions to the shaping of opinion and the making of decisions. These efforts are all attempts to expound for our own day the church's tradition of faith in Holy Scripture and creed.

The so-called counsels of perfection (or "evangelical counsels" or monastic ideals; → Monasticism) of → poverty, chastity, and → obedience (Matt. 16:24; 19:12) do not do justice to the wealth of this tradition, nor do other attempts to give the Christian lifestyle legal codification. No Christians can escape the responsibility, in each critical situation, of deciding for themselves, with reference to others, what their faith specifically demands in terms of lifestyle. The church to which they belong can support them in the decision, but it should not decide for them.

→ Behavior, Behavioral Psychology; Creativity; Despair; Development 2; Experience; Fear; Identity; Psychotherapy; Sexuality; Socialization; Trust

Bibliography: S. Bobert-Stützel, *Frömmigkeit und Symbolspiel. Ein pastoralpsychologischer Beitrag zu einer evangelischen Frömmigkeitstheorie* (Göttingen, 2000) • R. Bohren, *Lebensstil, Fasten und Feiern* (Neukirchen, 1986) • D. B. Gutknecht and E. W. Butler, eds., *Family, Self, and Society: Emerging Issues, Alternatives, and*

Interventions (Lanham, Md., 1985) • C. Hakim, *Work-Lifestyle Choices in the Twenty-first Century: Preference Theory* (Oxford, 2000) • S. Katz, *Old Age as Lifestyle in an Active Society* (Berkeley, Calif., 1999) • H. Maddox, *Happiness, Lifestyle, and Environment* (Daylesford, Austral., 1982) • K. E. Nipkow, "Christlicher Glaube als Lebensgestaltung," *WPKG* 76 (1987) 297-319 • M. E. Sobel, *Lifestyle and Social Structure: Concepts, Definitions, Analyses* (New York, 1981) • D. Stollberg, "Der verborgene und der offenbare Gott," *Der Glaube der Christen* (vol. 1; ed. E. Biser et al.; Munich, 1999) 424-42 • P. Teilhard de Chardin, *The Phenomenon of Man* (New York, 1961).

Dietrich Stollberg

Light

1. General
2. Antiquity
   2.1. Near East and OT
   2.2. Greek Philosophy
3. Christianity
   3.1. NT
   3.2. Fathers
   3.3. Middle Ages

1. General

On the basis of observation that the sun's light makes → life and development possible by its brightness and warmth, light in human thought and religion has become a → symbol for life, → happiness, fame, deliverance (→ Soteriology), and → salvation.

2. Antiquity

2.1. *Near East and OT*

In the Near East and Egypt light religions arose through cultic veneration of light, which in the form of the sun, moon, and stars was viewed as a symbol or manifestation of deity (e.g., Re in Egypt, Shamash in Babylon, Sin in Ur, El and Baal in Canaan).

In contrast, the OT sees the sun and moon only as lights that the Creator God (→ Creation) set in the vault of heaven (Gen. 1:14-18). In the OT "light" denotes the saving action of God as an expression of his goodness and → grace (Ps. 89:15; 112:4). Furthermore, the → law as the → Word of God means light, that is, direction for → Israel (Ps. 19:1-8; Prov. 6:23) and for the → Gentiles (Isa. 42:6; 49:6). In Hellenistically influenced Wisdom speculation (→ Wisdom Literature), wisdom is light surpassing all created light (Wis. 7:10, 24-26).

2.2. *Greek Philosophy*

In the didactic poem of Parmenides (ca. 540-after 480 b.c.; → Greek Philosophy), light for the first time is mentioned as the symbol of → truth and being. A high point of Greek light speculation is the sun similitude of Plato (427-347; → Platonism) in *Plt.* 6.507B–509C, in which he compares the supreme principle — the idea of the good, as the cause of being — to the light of the sun, the visible copy of the invisible original.

The Neoplatonism of Plotinus (ca. a.d. 205-70) extended the Platonic view into a light → metaphysics. As essentially light, the One — the supreme and absolutely transcendent hypostasis — can impart itself to all else. In a shining forth of light, the One can produce lesser hypostases, spirit and → soul, as light from light, without diminishing itself (*Enn.* 4.3.17.13). Conversely, the One as it is present in different degrees in being enables each hypostasis to return to itself.

3. Christianity

3.1. *NT*

In the NT, light symbolism, which is oriented to Christ's saving act (→ Christology), is developed most clearly in the Johannine writings. The Prologue to John calls the Logos the life that is our light (1:4). The Logos → incarnate in Jesus (1:14) is the light of the world (8:12; 9:5), the dispenser of divine light, the source of life (1:9), which makes it possible for us to be God's children (12:36). From the statement that God is light (1 John 1:5), it is deduced that fellowship with him shows itself by our walking in light and truth.

3.2. *Fathers*

In theological wrestling with the relation between Jesus Christ and God the Father, light symbolism, anchored in the tradition of antiquity and the Bible, helped to safeguard the unity of God and to prevent any thought of a diminution of his deity by the proceeding of the Son from the Father (so → Justin Martyr, Tatian, → Tertullian, → Origen, Dionysius of Alexandria). The symbolism made its way into the Nicene Creed in the formula "light from light" (→ Nicaea, Councils of; Niceno-Constantinopolitan Creed).

In a modified adoption of the light metaphysics of Neoplatonism, → Augustine (354-430) stressed the essential unity of divine light in the → Trinity, of which we may have a vision on the basis of our divine likeness. Grounded in Logos speculation, this light symbolism became a doctrine of illumination in which, with an appeal to biblical → authority, the symbolism of light and that of Word were related and even exchangeable (*De Trin.* 4.2.4).

Following Gregory of Nyssa (ca. 330-ca. 395), the future aspect of light symbolism became mystical obscurity in Dionysius the Pseudo-Areopagite (ca. 500; → Mysticism). In the overfulness of light the knowledge of God, reinterpreted as → ecstasy, takes place beyond all intellectual apprehension (*Mys. theol.* 1.1; [*PG* 3.997D–1000A]).

3.3. *Middle Ages*

In the West the speculative line of light symbolism deriving from Augustine, which sees a link between illumination and → grace, led to the light metaphysics of Robert Grosseteste (ca. 1170-1253) and the light speculation of Bonaventure (ca. 1217-74), who viewed divine grace as the living shining of the divine light in us. It then led to the light → ontology of Albertus Magnus (ca. 1200-1280). The light mysticism of Dionysius was promoted by the Latin translation of Erigena (ca. 810-ca. 877), and then by way of Meister → Eckhart (ca. 1260-ca. 1328), John Tauler (ca. 1300-1361), Henry Suso (ca. 1295-1366), and Jan van Ruysbroeck (1293-1381). Finally it influenced Nicholas of Cusa (1401-64; → Mysticism 2).

In the East the mysticism of Dionysius the Pseudo-Areopagite also made an impact through the commentary of Maximus the Confessor (ca. 580-662), according to whom the supraessential in God can be reached only in a dark ray. Light mysticism reached its peak in → Hesychasm, which is traced back to Simeon the New Theologian (949-1022) and which grants us experience of union with God in light visions. To support this mysticism, which was cultivated at Mount → Athos from the time of Gregory of Sinai (d. 1346), Gregory Palamas (ca. 1296-1359; → Palamism), in debate with the monk Barlaam the Calabrian (ca. 1290-ca. 1350), developed his Cappadocian-related theological system (→ Cappadocian Fathers), in which he defined light as divine energy and uncreated grace, but not as the divine essence, which is wrapped in darkness. Significant for → anthropology is the imparting of this light, along the lines of biblical → monism, to the whole person, both soul and body, so that → *theōsis,* or filling with uncreated light, is not just an individual spiritual event but a manifestation of common edification.

→ Babylonian and Assyrian Religion; Egyptian Religion; Enlightenment; Orthodoxy 3, Starets

Bibliography: H. CONZELMANN, "Φῶς κτλ.," *TDNT* 9.310-58 • L. DUPRE and J. WISEMAN, eds., *Light from Light: An Anthology of Christian Mysticism* (2d ed.; New York, 2001) • V. LOSSKY, *The Mystical Theology of the Eastern Church* (2d ed.; Crestwood, N.Y., 1976) • MECHTHELD OF MAGDEBURG, *The Flowing Light of the Godhead* (ed. F. Tobin; New York, 1998; orig. written, ca. 1250-82) • J. MEYENDORFF, "Palamas," *DSp* 12.81-107 • G. THIESSEN, *Traces of Light: Sermons and Bible Studies* (London, 1996).

MARIA-BARBARA VON STRITZKY

Linguistics

1. Language as a Theme
2. Linguistics and Grammar
3. Language in Philosophy
4. Language and Theology

1. Language as a Theme

Language is a theme in various disciplines. In addition to → philosophy, especially the philosophy of language, a number of empirical disciplines focus on → language as a topic of research — traditional philology, linguistics, and related disciplines such as sociolinguistics and psycholinguistics. We are familiar with language in everyday use, in conversation and agreements. Linguistics and the philosophy of language take ordinary speech as the starting point of their deliberations.

Linguistics directs its interest to the structure of language as a human capacity, its inner coherence, its functions in society and culture, and the relations between specific languages. Linguistics is empirical in describing the actual use of natural languages, theoretical in developing an explanatory theory of language. Language is a many-sided structure at all levels, and thus linguistics embraces phonology (the study of speech sounds and their distribution), morphology (the study of meaningful units — esp. words — and their formation), syntax (the study of the arrangement of meaningful units to form constituents [phrases, sentences, etc.]), and, more recently, the relations of text, context, and cultural cotext.

With the growing interest in linguistics, additional areas have been brought into its domain since the 1970s, especially the theory of signs (semiotics), sociology (sociolinguistics and cultural linguistics), code theory (pragmalinguistics), psychology (psycholinguistics), hermeneutics and rhetoric, the universality of language (universal grammar), and → communication, media, and information technology (computer linguistics). The limits of linguistics thus cannot be defined precisely. It is, on the one hand, an academic discipline in its own right; on the other, a transdisciplinary aspect of research in socio-, psycho-, and neurolinguistics, as well as in → pragmatism, semantics, hermeneutics, and many other fields. It is used in various methodological disciplines (e.g., exegetics) but also more generally in the philosophy of language and in → theology.

2. Linguistics and Grammar

2.1. Linguistics had its essential beginning in the 19th century with the works of F. Bopp (1791-1867), J. Grimm (1785-1863), and W. von Humboldt (1767-1835). By historical comparison the laws of language were to be grasped and described according to their historical development.

2.2. The *Cours de linguistique générale* (1916) of F. de Saussure (1857-1913) marked the beginning of the modern study of linguistics. Language *(langage)* as the totality of linguistic phenomena was here distinguished as the system of language *(langue)*, in contrast to its actual use *(parole,* "speech") in specific situations. Unlike previous linguists, Saussure dealt with the ordering of the system of language synchronically, not diachronically (as historical language change). He described linguistic → signs (§1) as the union of signifier *(signifiant)* and signified *(signifié)*. Language was understood as an immanent system of relations, or structure, whose elements stand in relations of opposition (→ Structuralism). In the structuralist linguistics developed by Saussure, we can distinguish three main directions: the Prague school of N. S. Trubetzkoy (1890-1938) and R. Jakobson (1896-1982), the Copenhagen school of L. Hjelmslev (1899-1965), and the American structuralists, notably L. Bloomfield (1887-1949) and Z. S. Harris (1909-92).

2.2.1. In the Prague school Trubetzkoy developed phonology as a doctrine of sounds, defining them not by their physical quality but by their function of distinguishing words within the system of a given language. Jacobson projected an inventory of 12 binary phonological features, in terms of which the sounds of all languages could be analyzed.

In Hjelmslev's theory of "glossematics," the Copenhagen school generalized the method of phonological analysis, seeking to describe the structure and relationship of the two levels of expression (phonology) and content (grammar). At both levels linguistic units are related to each other syntagmatically (in their actual linear sequence) and paradigmatically (in units that can be substituted for each other in the actual sequence).

In American descriptivism, Bloomfield tied behaviorism to linguistics, seeking to describe linguistic units without regard to considerations of → meaning. Harris developed distribution analysis, which analyzes linguistic elements from their context and distribution within sentences. He filtered out by segmentation the smallest units addressed by linguistic research (phonological and morphological), classified the segments by distribution analysis, and finally determined the relations between the distribution classes.

2.2.2. N. A. Chomsky (b. 1928) changed distribution analysis into transformational, or generative, grammar. Linguistic analysis is to distinguish grammatical from nongrammatical sentences. An adequate grammar of a language "generates" all the grammatical sentences of that language, making clear the structure of each. Generative grammar is no longer just a classification of parts of sentences but seeks to be an axiomatic characterization of our language intuition, which generates all the sentences of our language. In his *Aspects of the Theory of Syntax* (1965), Chomsky divided the syntax of language into deep and surface structure. Surface structure, which derives from deep structure, is the basis of phonological structure. Deep structure forms the semantic basis of a sentence. Similar to Saussure's distinction between langue and parole, Chomsky distinguished competence (the knowledge of a language as a dynamic system of rules) from performance (the realizing of this competence in actual speech).

2.3. Unlike structural linguistics, a grammar related to content must consider meaning. L. Weisgerber (1899-1985) (and J. Trier) went back to the linguistic philosophy of Humboldt with his reference to language (the mother tongue) as power *(energeia)* and not as work *(ergon)*. It carries with it a worldview and is characterized by an inner form. Weisgerber was interested in the relation between the approaches of Humboldt and Saussure. He criticized structural linguistics for focusing only on the outer form of language, rather than on the inner form, that is, on language as a formative intellectual capacity. Humboldt's interest was not primarily in the study of languages but in language itself as a means of philosophical argument and knowledge, as a worldview.

3. Language in Philosophy

3.1. In antiquity Plato (427-347 B.C.; → Greek Philosophy 5; Platonism) in the dialogue *Cratylos* had asked whether the association between a word and its referent is based on nature *(physei),* or whether it is based only on agreement or convention *(homologia,* later *thesei)*. According to his view, names are not wholly capricious but are also conditioned by the function of naming something. The relation between a name and the thing named is not naturally determined.

3.2. Aristotle (384-322; → Aristotelianism; Greek Philosophy 6) did not develop an explicit philosophy of language or propose a single concept of language, although he did comment on language throughout his works. Well-known is his list of → categories, or basic structures of thought, which can be interpreted as semantic, logical, or ontological. In *De interpretatione* he deals with the *logos apophantikos* (assertion, judgment), stating that nouns differ from verbs and predicates, and each of them from the whole sentence. In *Poetica* the parts of speech are divided into sounds, letters, and sentence (logos).

Language is also brought into Aristotle's biological and psychological writings. The ethical and rational contents seem to distinguish human speech from animal speech, which has only emotional content. The sound of speech itself is conventional. Aristotle singled out the pragmatic aspects of speech when in his → *Rhetoric* he distinguished advisory, judgmental, and celebratory speech. Only judgments, not petitions or commands or other types, have truth-value. A familiar passage in *De interpretatione* (16a3-8) contains the elements of a semantic theory with the distinction of linguistic signs into writing, sound, psyche, and thing.

The theses of Aristotle, with their complex theory of signs known as the *scientia sermocinalis,* had a long history and, with → Stoicism, were one of the main sources of medieval linguistics (→ Middle Ages 1.4.4). Overall, this linguistics viewed language, as defined by the *grammatica speculativa* (i.e., theoretical, philosophical, or universal grammar), as mirroring reality.

3.3. G. W. Leibniz (1646-1716) was one of the founders of the modern philosophy of language and → logic and, with I. Newton (1642-1727), is credited with discovering calculus. Leibniz investigated natural languages and developed artificial languages, using a three-stage semantic scheme of speech, idea, and thing. Ideas, or the contents of the consciousness, are articulated or grasped in thinking and speaking; their understanding is false if there is a false correlation of words and ideas. Signs are thereby not just "mirrors" of the world but a way to come to (self-)consciousness. In his theory of signs Leibniz worked out the program of a universal science that includes a universal notation (*characteristica universalis*) and a formal system of reasoning (*calculus ratiocinator*). According to Leibniz, language competence is a clear, distinct, but inade-

quate knowledge *(cognitio clara distincta inadaequata),* that is, a kind of technical knowledge.

3.4. In its study of human beings and their place in nature and history (→ Anthropology 4), the → Enlightenment and early Romanticism had a comprehensive interest in language as a medium of rationality. Language divides humans from → animals. Thoughts on language were worked out by J. G. Hamann (1730-88) and J. G. → Herder (1744-1803). In his discussion of the origin of language, Herder pointed to its national character and its historical and cultural variety.

Humboldt understood language as worldview (today known as the linguistic relativity principle; cf. the Sapir-Whorf hypothesis), with the plurality of the one implying the plurality of the other. Although reality may be unified, the power of the human mind is shown by the variety of worldviews it constructs, explicitly known through the different languages.

F. D. E. → Schleiermacher (1768-1834) developed the first modern hermeneutics, which encompasses both psychological aspects and linguistic, or grammatical, aspects. The latter, stemming from his studies in Plato and in the NT, represent the beginning of textual and linguistic emphases. W. Dilthey (1833-1911) followed Schleiermacher in his hermeneutics and textual studies in founding the modern *Geisteswissenschaften* (human sciences).

3.5. Modern linguistics, pioneered by G. Frege (1848-1925), has significantly shaped our view of language. Frege tried to show that arithmetic derives with strict logic from a small number of basic principles (→ Axiom) and deductive rules. The defects of everyday speech ought to be remedied by a precise artificial language of concepts that observes syntactic and semantic rules, much as in mathematics. He thus founded the logic of predicates and statements (→ Logic 2.2). His insights led also to analysis of ordinary language and thus became a theme in analytic linguistics (→ Analytic Philosophy 2.3).

The difference between the linguistics of formal speech and that of everyday speech still plays a role in the discussion of the philosophy of language. B. Russell (1872-1970) showed how philosophical difficulties in statements that have no meaning (e.g., "the present king of France") can be removed by translation into formal speech, that is, by strictly distinguishing everyday speech from ideal language. He thus incisively advanced the notion of language philosophy as criticism. Russell's main contribution was the idea of logical atomism as the principle of a philosophical grammar.

G. E. Moore (1873-1958) extended critical linguistics to the language of ethics (→ Analytic Ethics 2.1). He developed a commonsense model for the analysis of meaning, where analysis involves a reductive, defining translation. Attempts at mediation between formal language (L. Wittgenstein 1921, R. Carnap, A. Tarski, S. Kripke, P. F. Strawson, E. Tugendhat, J. Hintikka) and everyday language (Wittgenstein 1953, G. Ryle, J. L. Austin, J. R. Searle, D. Wunderlich, J. Schulte, N. Malcolm, B. McGuinness, E. von Savigny) appear in the works of W. Quine, D. Davidson, M. Dummett, N. Goodman, H. Putnam, and others.

3.6. Linguistics has been expanded by speech-act theory (Searle, Austin), which focuses not so much on grammar and sentences as on the "act of speech," thus viewing language as agency. It studies articulation in its context (as in pragmatism), analyzes conversation and discourse (Wunderlich), and studies the socially and individually determined variations of language (esp. in sociolinguistics and psycholinguistics).

Searle distinguishes philosophy of language, linguistic philosophy, and linguistics. The first deals with general questions of reference and meaning; the third, with questions of the phonology, syntax, and semantics of natural languages; and the second, with the relation between the other two. Following what has been called the linguistic turn (after a book of that title edited by R. Rorty), or the whole movement of linguistic philosophy, Searle thus confronts the classic analytic approach (e.g., that of Carnap), that is, logical atomism and the ideal of a formal or ideal (meta)language; his orientation, rather, is to ordinary language or speech to solve, explicate, or eliminate philosophical problems.

The question then arises of the difference between linguistics and linguistic philosophy. While the latter does not approach its questions empirically, linguistics objects to a lack of empirical proof or verification and also to a lack of a fitting underlying system. W. P. Alston accepted the linguistic objections but distinguished the aims of describing a language and of making theoretical concepts precise. Rorty searches for descriptions (as indeed linguistics does), in particular, those that function to eliminate certain philosophical problems. Searle sees the aim as formulating the rules of speech acts as they apply universally, not those of a single natural language (unlike the interest of linguistics generally in both universal grammar and individual grammars).

3.7. Despite the lack of any generally accepted distinction of linguistic philosophy from linguistics,

the latter has been a main paradigm in philosophy ever since the linguistic turn. (Before the 20th-cent. paradigm shift from language to pictures, or the so-called iconic turn, one could say that linguistics was *the* main paradigm.) This linguistic paradigm has been held in philosophy implicitly since → F. Nietzsche, M. Heidegger, and L. Wittgenstein, explicitly so since Rorty's volume appeared in 1967. The linguistic turn is as well a turn away from a classic analytic approach (such as structuralism) to postanalytic philosophy (and poststructuralism), for example, in Rorty, N. Goodman, or J. Derrida. We thus note a diversification of language-oriented approaches in philosophy, as also in theology. Reasons for this diversity include the lack of a single linguistic method and the limited scope of any theory of meaning in classic analytic philosophy or in structuralism, which prevents it from dealing with broader questions of diachrony, perspectivity, and actual performance.

Currently vying for attention are many different approaches: ordinary-language philosophy, pragmatism, semiotics, hermeneutics, (new) rhetoric, and speech-act theory. In each, philosophy deals with its problems and questions by way of their representation in language in an everyday, social, and cultural context.

This horizon of language, expanding through the awareness of society and culture, is explored in different methods and paradigms of language research: *pragmatically* since the later Wittgenstein by Austin, Searle, Putnam, Rorty, M. Jung, and F. Fellmann; *semiotically* since C. S. Peirce, W. James, and C. W. Morris by A. J. Greimas, K. O. Apel, U. Eco, K. Oehler, J. Trabant, and H. Pape; *by a semiotic theory of interpretation* since Nietzsche by J. Simon, W. Stegmaier, H. Lenk, and G. Abel; *postanalytically* by Goodman and others; and *poststructurally* by Derrida, M. Foucault, and P. de Man.

A distinct field of language-oriented research, sometimes integrating the former aspects, is the *phenomenological and hermeneutical school*. One branch, led by E. Cassirer (who speaks of language as a symbolic form), deals with the → phenomenology of symbolic forms and culture. The other, which deals with hermeneutics in a stricter sense, is represented by Heidegger, H.-G. Gadamer, J. Grondin, G. Figal, and especially the Husserlian phenomenology of P. Ricoeur, H. Blumenberg, and B. Waldenfels, as well as by the group Poetik und Hermeneutik (led by Blumenberg and H. R. Jauss and oriented to the new rhetoric and W. Iser's "reception aesthetics" [*Rezeptionsästhetik*]). Another field of philosophy of language is the Jewish → philosophy of religion, as developed by F. Rosenzweig and M. Buber (see also F. Ebner, E. Rosenstock-Huessy, E. Lévinas, and H.-C. Askani).

Bibliography: On 1: T. G. Bever, J. J. Katz, and D. T. Langendoen, eds., *An Integrated Theory of Linguistic Ability* (New York, 1976) • R. E. Butts and J. Hintikka, eds., *Basic Problems in Methodology and Linguistics* (Dordrecht, 1977) • R. Hausser, *Foundations of Computational Linguistics: Human-Computer Communication in Natural Language* (2d ed.; Berlin, 2001) • J. F. Ihwe, ed., *Literaturwissenschaft und Linguistik. Ergebnisse und Perspektiven* (3 vols.; Frankfurt, 1971-72) • T. Sebeok, ed., *Current Trends in Linguistics* (14 vols.; The Hague, 1963-76) • D. Wunderlich, *Foundations of Linguistics* (New York, 1979).

On 2: L. Bloomfield, *Language* (rev. ed.; New York, 1933; orig. pub., 1914); idem, "A Set of Postulates for the Science of Language," *Readings in Linguistics* (vol. 1; 4th ed.; ed. M. Joos; Chicago, 1966) 26-31 • N. Chomsky, *Aspects of the Theory of Syntax* (Cambridge, Mass., 1965); idem, *New Horizons in the Study of Language and Mind* (New York, 2000) • E. Coseriu, *Textlinguistik* (3d ed.; Tübingen, 1994) • A. J. Greimas, *On Meaning: Selected Writings in Semiotic Theory* (Minneapolis, 1987); idem, *Structural Semantics* (Lincoln, Nebr., 1984) • Z. S. Harris, *Methods in Structural Linguistics* (Chicago, 1951) • L. Hjelmslev, *Prolegomena to a Theory of Language* (rev. ed.; Madison, Wis., 1961; orig. pub., 1943) • E. L. Keenan and L. M. Faltz, *Boolean Semantics for Natural Language* (Dordrecht, 1985) • C. Lévi-Strauss, *Structural Anthropology* (2 vols.; New York, 1963-76) • J. A. Lucy, *Language Diversity and Thought: A Reformulation of the Linguistic Relativity Hypothesis* (New York, 1992) • S. Peters and E. Saarinen, eds., *Processes, Beliefs, and Questions: Essays on Formal Semantics of Natural Language and Natural Language Processing* (Dordrecht, 1982) • F. de Saussure, *Cours de linguistique générale* (Paris, 1916; ET *Course in General Linguistics* [New York, 1959]) • N. S. Trubetzkoy, *Principles of Phonology* (Berkeley, Calif., 1969; orig. pub., 1939) • B. L. Whorf, *Language, Thought, and Reality: Selected Writings* (Cambridge, Mass., 1956).

On 3: J. Derrida, *Limited Inc.* (Evanston, Ill., 2000) • U. Eco, *A Theory of Semiotics* (Bloomington, Ind., 1976) • G. Frege, *Collected Papers on Mathematics, Logic, and Philosophy* (Oxford, 1984; orig. pub., 1967) • I. Hacking, *Why Does Language Matter to Philosophy?* (New York, 1975) • R. Harré and R. Harris, eds., *Linguistics and Philosophy: The Controversial Interface* (Oxford, 1993) • C. O. Hill, *Word and Object in Husserl, Frege, and Russell: The Roots of Twentieth-Century Philosophy* (Athens, Ohio, 1991) • W. v. Humboldt, *Werke,* vol. 3, *Schriften zur Sprachphilosophie* (8th ed.; Darmstadt, 1996) • M. Jung, *Erfahrung und Religion. Grundzüge einer hermeneutisch-pragmatischen Religionsphilosophie* (Freiburg, 1999) • J. J. Katz, ed., *The Philosophy of Linguistics* (New York, 1985) • A. P. Martinich, ed., *The Philosophy of Language* (4th ed.; New York, 2001) • K. Murasugi and R. Stainton, eds., *Philosophy and Linguistics* (Boulder, Colo., 1999) • W. V. O. Quine, "Methodological Reflections on Current Linguistic Theory," *Semantics of Natural Language* (ed. D. Davidson and G. Harman; Dordrecht, 1972) 442-54; idem, *Word and Object* (Cambridge, Mass., 1960) • R. Rorty, ed., *The Linguistic Turn* (Chicago, 1967) • F. D. E. Schleiermacher, *Hermeneutik und Kritik, mit einem Anhang sprachphilosophischer Texte Schleiermachers* (ed. M. Frank; 8th ed.; Frankfurt, 1999; orig. pub., 1838) • L. Wittgenstein, *Philosophical Investigations* (2d ed.; Oxford, 1997; orig. pub., 1953); idem, *Tractatus Logico-Philosophicus* (London, 1974; orig. pub., 1921).

Hans Ineichen and Philipp Stoellger

4. Language and Theology

4.1. Theology is a matter of words. It presents words about the Word, or even about God, yet it uses language not only as an instrument but also as a medium, and thus we can speak of language as the way of → theology. For this reason theology — if it is self-reflective — necessarily involves a theory of language that must encompass both *langue* and *parole*, Scripture and religious language, "the Word of God" and ordinary language.

A significant difference exists, however, between receiving guidance from Scripture and receiving it from speech (in using religious language or, especially, hearing the → kerygma, or the "living word of the gospel") — that is, between being oriented to the signs in Scripture (and their reference and → meaning) and focusing on the spoken language as in → rhetoric (and its effects, forms, and performance). Linguistics relates to the former in text theories (see U. Eco and W. G. Jeanrond) and also in → structuralism and classic analytic theory. To the latter, linguistics relates via speech-act theory, → pragmatism, and hermeneutics or rhetoric.

Because → religion begins with religious speech, and grows and lives by it as well, issues arise of "competence" and "performance." We can thus see that an orientation in theology merely to propositions misses the dimensions of perspectivity, the media used, pragmatics, and facticity (e.g., the factor of the individual or the actual historical horizon of one's perspective), which are clarified by hermeneutics, media theory, pragmalinguistics, and → phenomenology. For this reason both the classic approaches of language, such as rhetoric and hermeneutics, and the late or postmodern approaches, such as (new) pragmatism, poststructuralism, and postanalytic symbol theory, are helpful for theology.

Linguistics in theology has different fields of attention: Scripture, religious language, and the various symbolic forms. The basic element for theology is not the concept or the term (as it is in classic analytic theory) but the → metaphor (which stands for tropes generally), for religious language, as well as the language of theology (e.g., in its treatment of "incarnation," "the word of the cross," even "Jesus Christ" and "resurrection"), is basically metaphoric.

4.2. The history of these questions begins in Christian theology with → Jesus preaching the → kingdom of God in → parables and with Paul's main topic, the → cross. Both are key matters of → exegesis in a linguistic perspective. The idea of a theology of language arises from the tradition of the prophetic theology of God's Word (marked by "thus says the Lord").

The Greek tradition is quite different, for it is directed not by a revealed → word of God but by the rational Logos (thus "theology" from *theos,* "God," and *logos,* "word, thought, reason").

Especially in regard to Scripture, linguistics is used in exegesis as an instrument of text analysis. The same application occurs in the analysis of theological texts in patristics, the mystics, the → Reformation, and all others.

Beginning with → Origen, the Jewish-Hellenistic exegesis of the Septuagint, the rabbinic schools of the → Masorah, and patristic biblical exegesis all had linguistic foundations. A premodern version of linguistics (and hermeneutics) was rhetoric, and thus we see the rhetorician → Augustine (354-430) dealing with the meaning of life and of everything by the basic distinction of → sign *(signum)* and thing *(res).* His thesis is that everything is sign at least for God, who is the final and ultimate *res* (see *De doc. Christ.*).

The mystics, especially Meister Eckhardt, J. Tauler, and Henry Suso, were innovative for theology in the Middle Ages. They used language in inventive ways, later prompting linguistic and semiotic research on their usage (see R. Margreiter and A. M. Haas).

M. → Luther's theology of language and the rhetorical theology of P. → Melanchthon are of central interest for → Protestantism (esp. in the mystical and humanistic traditions). Since the Luther renaissance around 1900, they have been widely explored

by E. Bizer, G. Ebeling, O. Bayer, J. Ringleben, and others. Connected to this tradition is the "poetological theology" of H. Timm, K. Huizing, and G. Bader.

Since Protestant theology has been oriented to Scripture, exegetics is theologically fundamental, as we see, for example, in R. Bultmann, E. Fuchs, G. v. Rad, and Hans Weder. Linguistics has broadened the diachronic historical-critical method to include synchronic aspects as well, notably in the work of K. Berger, E. Güttgemanns, H. Schweizer, and J. Barr.

Besides exegetics, → systematic theology and the → philosophy of religion have taken the linguistic turn, most clearly so as they follow → analytic philosophy and pragmatism (I. U. Dalferth, J. Track, H. Deuser, D. Z. Phillips, V. Brümmer, H. Vroom, H. G. Hubbeling, and M. Sarot). Current developments, however, are oriented also to semiotics, interpretation theory, theory of → culture, phenomenology, postanalytic philosophy, and poststructuralism. Linguistics will clearly remain key for exegetics and one aspect of the philosophy of religion, but its role has been widened by the other approaches to language currently adopted in theology.

Bibliography: Exegesis: W. BADER, *Simson bei Delila. Computerlinguistische Interpretation des Textes Ri 13–16* (Tübingen, 1991); idem, ed., *"Und die Wahrheit wurde hinweggefegt." Daniel 8 linguistisch interpretiert* (Tübingen, 1994) • J. BARR, *The Semantics of Biblical Language* (London, 1961) • O. DANGL, *Methoden im Widerstreit. Sprachwissenschaftliche Zugänge zur deuteronomischen Rede von der Liebe Gottes* (Tübingen, 1993) • D. JOBLING and S. MOORE, eds., *Poststructuralism as Exegesis* (Atlanta, 1992) • B. MEALAND, "On Finding Fresh Evidence in Old Texts: Reflections on Results in Computer Assisted Biblical Research," *BJRL* 74 (1992) 67-87 • D. PATTE, *Structural Exegesis for NT Critics* (Minneapolis, 1990) • W. SCHENK, *Die Sprache des Mattäus. Die Text-Konstituenten in ihren makro- und mikrostrukturellen Relationen* (Göttingen, 1987) • H. SCHWEIZER, *Computerunterstützte Textinterpretation. Die Josefsgeschichte beschrieben und interpretiert im Dreischritt: Syntax–Semantik–Pragmatik* (3 vols.; Tübingen, 1995).

Metaphor: D. H. AARON, *Biblical Ambiguities: Metaphor, Semantics, and Divine Imagery* (Leiden, 2001) • T. LUKSCH, *Predigt als metaphorische Gott-Rede. Zum Ertrag der Metaphernforschung für die Homiletik* (Würzburg, 1998) • P. STOELLGER, *Metapher und Lebenswelt. Hans Blumenbergs Metaphorologie als Lebenswelthermeneutik und ihr religionsphänomenologischer Horizont* (Tübingen, 2000).

Religious language: G. BADER, *Symbolik des Todes*

Jesu (Tübingen, 1988) • I. U. DALFERTH, *Religiöse Rede von Gott* (Munich, 1981); idem, ed., *Sprachlogik des Glaubens. Texte analytischer Religionsphilosophie und Theologie zur religiösen Sprache* (Munich, 1974) • G. EBELING, *Introduction to a Theological Theory of Language* (London, 1973); idem, *Word and Faith* (London, 1984); idem, *The Word of God and Tradition: Historical Studies Interpreting the Divisions of Christianity* (London, 1968) • A. JEFFNER, *The Study of Religious Language* (London, 1972) • J. LOSEE, *Religious Language and Complementarity* (Lanham, Md., 1992) • T. MICHELS, ed., *Sprache und Sprachverständnis in religiöser Rede. Zum Verhältnis von Theologie und Linguistik* (Salzburg, 1973) • D. R. STIVER, *The Philosophy of Religious Language: Sign, Symbol, and Story* (Cambridge, Mass., 1996).

Other: W. ENGEMANN, *Semiotische Homiletik. Prämissen, Analysen, Konsequenzen* (Tübingen, 1993) • A. GRÖZINGER, *Die Sprache des Menschen. Ein Handbuch. Grundwissen für Theologinnen und Theologen* (Munich, 1991) • E. GÜTTGEMANNS and U. GERBER, eds., *Linguistische Theologie* (Bonn, 1972) • A. M. HAAS, *Mystik als Aussage. Erfahrungs-, Denk- und Redeformen christlicher Mystik* (Frankfurt, 1996) • K. HUIZING, *Ästhetische Theologie*, vol. 1, *Der erlesene Mensch. Eine literarische Anthropologie*; vol. 2, *Der inszenierte Mensch. Eine Medien-Anthropologie*; vol. 3, *Jesus am Kamener Kreuz. Würzburger Poetikvorlesungen. Ein Theaterstück* (Stuttgart, 2000-2004) • W. G. JEANROND, *Theological Hermeneutics: Development and Significance* (New York, 1991) • I. LAWRENCE, *Linguistics and Theology: The Significance of Noam Chomsky for Theological Construction* (Metuchen, N.J., 1980) • R. MARGREITER, *Erfahrung und Mystik. Grenzen der Symbolisierung* (Berlin, 1997) • D. Z. PHILLIPS, *Faith and Philosophical Enquiry* (London, 1970); idem, *Religion and Understanding* (Oxford, 1967); idem, *Religion without Explanation* (Oxford, 1976).

PHILIPP STOELLGER

Litany

"Litany" (Gk. *litaneia,* "entreaty"), a term for petitionary → prayer, denotes a whole literary genus in the → history of religion in which one or more petitions or invocations of persons or gods are presented by one or several people, and the other participants answer with a set refrain (e.g., Psalm 136). The Kyrie of the → Mass is the relic of a litany. The All Saints Litany is another form of the genus, which M. → Luther (1483-1546) used as the basis of his Latin Litany (1529).

In the Roman Catholic → liturgy litanies are sung on certain occasions. Anglican churches (→ Anglican Communion) have an extended litany similar to Luther's. T. → Cranmer's (1489-1556) litany of 1544 was the first service to be introduced in English. The → Orthodox Church also uses litanies, called ektenes (Gk. *ekteneia,* "earnestness [in prayer]").

→ Worship

Bibliography: C. JONES, G. WAINWRIGHT, E. YARNOLD, and P. BRADSHAW, eds., *The Study of Liturgy* (rev. ed.; London, 1992) • J. A. JUNGMANN, *The Mass of the Roman Rite* (vol. 1; New York, 1951) 333-46 • E. C. RATCLIFF, "The Choir Offices: The Litany," *Liturgy and Worship* (ed. W. K. L. Clarke and C. Harris; New York, 1933) 282-87 • L. D. REED, *The Lutheran Liturgy* (Philadelphia, 1947) • F. C. SENN, *Christian Liturgy: Catholic and Evangelical* (Minneapolis, 1997) • R. F. TAFT, *The Great Entrance: A History of the Transfer of Gifts and Other Preanaphoral Rites of the Liturgy of St. John Chrysostom* (2d ed.; Rome, 1978) 311-73.

THADDEUS A. SCHNITKER

Literacy

1. Agents
2. Methods
3. Literacy and the Ecumenical Movement

According to the UNESCO "Monitoring Report on Education for All" (October 2001), nearly 900 million adults worldwide are illiterate, and there are fears that the number may soon reach a billion people. Illiteracy affects men and women in both individual and social life, hinders the development of both the → person and → society, and represents a denial of the right to education (→ Rights, Human and Civil).

1. Agents

In the 19th century, workers' unions and political groups began to teach workers to read and write with a view to enabling them to exercise their political rights and thereby to change the conditions of their life and work. In the 20th century, nations and international organizations, especially those of the → United Nations, sponsored programs of mass literacy. Groups connected with churches, trade unions, and social movements have also become increasingly important in these efforts. Many countries of the → Third World have organized campaigns against illiteracy, albeit with varying results.

One of the most important nongovernmental

organizations at work in the field of literacy is the International Council for Adult Education, founded in 1973. The council, which represents the global interests of many institutions devoted to the cause of adult → education and especially to the cause of literacy, oversees both regional and national structures.

2. Methods

The methods used in the pursuit of literacy might be described according to underlying pedagogical principles and political goals. They fall into three groups.

The *traditional* method of dealing with questions of literacy, which predominated in the past, is to teach reading and writing without relating these skills to → everyday life. Though there have been improvements in practice, the principles and aims of this method remain unchanged.

A *functional* method regards itself as an instrument of → development and thus tries to relate the teaching of reading, writing, and mathematics to everyday life so as to contribute to the solution of people's problems, particularly those in the areas of production and health (→ Public Health). UNESCO has propagated this method since 1964 and has used it in many Third World countries, although not always with encouraging results.

The method that could be called *liberating* sets for itself a higher goal, without neglecting the traditional and functional approaches: to view literacy as a practice of liberation in all areas of life, especially areas such as → politics, economics, and health. The needs of people are the starting point for this method as it seeks to develop programs of instruction, including the production of teaching materials (→ Didactics). The people themselves must play an active role, taking education into their own hands.

This liberating method presupposes that literacy is an open process, that it must lead to a postliteracy that changes the lives of former illiterates and thus produces changes in society. The fact that people's actual interests have not always been considered has often caused illiterate persons to resist participating in literacy campaigns. The antithesis between a written and an oral culture has also often contributed to this resistance. Respecting local languages and cultures, paying heed to the vital everyday problems of people, and enlisting their active participation in the work of teaching all help to overcome such resistance. Those concerned must learn to see in literacy an instrument that will help change the actual living conditions of persons, groups, and societies.

3. Literacy and the Ecumenical Movement

The ecumenical movement follows the method of dealing with illiteracy that aims at liberation (→ Ecumenism, Ecumenical Movement). From its beginnings, this movement has attached great importance to education and especially to literacy. The World Council for Christian Education and later the → World Council of Churches (WCC) and many of its member churches and affiliated organizations have seen the importance of the problem and made considerable efforts to contribute to the overcoming of illiteracy. By creating elementary educational programs, the WCC has encouraged the churches to take up this task, putting Christian ideas into practice pedagogically, aiming at a society of justice, → solidarity, and peace.

Bibliography: E. CUSHMAN et al., eds., *Literacy: A Critical Sourcebook* (Boston, 2001) • V. DAVID, *The Rise of Mass Literacy: Reading and Writing in Modern Europe* (Cambridge, 2000) • P. FREIRE, *Pedagogy of the Oppressed* (New York, 1972) • P. FREIRE and D. MACEDO, *Literacy: Reading the Word and the World* (South Hadley, Mass., 1987) • F. C. LAUBACH and R. S. LAUBACH, *Toward World Literacy: The Each One Teach One Way* (Syracuse, N.Y., 1960) • M. DE LA LUZ REYES and J. J. HALCÓN, eds., *The Best for Our Children: Critical Perspectives on Literacy for Latino Children* (New York, 2001) • R. P. MOSES and C. E. COBB JR., *Literacy and Civil Rights* (Boston, 2001) • P. ROBERTS, *Education, Literacy, and Humanization: Exploring the Work of Paulo Freire* (Westport, Conn., 2000) • B. V. STREET, ed., *Literacy and Development: Ethnographic Perspectives* (London, 2001) • R. YAGELSKI, *Literacy Matters: Writing and Reading the Social Self* (New York, 2000).

ANTONIO FAUNDEZ

Literary Criticism

1. Origins
2. Medieval and Reformation Methods
3. Early Modern Literary Criticism
4. Literary Criticism and Biblical Studies
5. Formalist Methods
6. Critical Social Theory
7. Modern Criticism in English Literature
8. Structuralist Literary Theories
9. Psychoanalytic Literary Theories
10. Marxist Literary Criticism
11. Reader-Response, or Reception, Aesthetics
12. Poststructuralist and Deconstructionist Literary Theory
13. Postcolonial Theory

Literary criticism seeks to appraise the value, quality, form, or meaning of literary and other artistic productions or cultural artifacts. "Criticism" is derived from the Gk. verb *krinō*, "discern, judge." In some cases literary criticism is synonymous with hermeneutics or other methods of → interpretation. In other cases such → criticism focuses on more formal issues, including an investigation of the text or artifact's lexicography, form, plot, or structure. In the latter decades of the 20th century the discipline of literary theory expanded the purview of literary criticism to include many divergent approaches designed to assist the literary critic, including methods used in history, → linguistics, → philosophy, → theology, → sociology, → anthropology, → psychology, and → hermeneutics.

1. Origins

The origin of Western literary criticism is rooted in the ancient Greek study of grammar and → rhetoric and in discussions of beauty and → aesthetics. Aristotle's (384-322 B.C.) *Poetics* is an early critical literary investigation of both the literary forms and the devices employed within the genre of Greek dramatic production known as tragedy. In his discussion of catharsis in this study, Aristotle also investigated the effects of tragedy on the audience.

Literary criticism in the ancient world often focused on the interpretation of sacred texts or scriptures. This interest is evident in ancient Greek commentaries on the Homeric corpus and in Jewish commentaries on the Holy Scriptures. The need for targums — translations and brief commentaries on selected passages from Hebrew scriptures into Aramaic or Greek — arose in the second-temple period, when Hebrew no longer served as a spoken language for many Jews. Targums often contained comment on the textual variants, lexicography, grammar, or → meaning of the particular passages under investigation. This tradition received further expansion and codification in the emergence of the → Mishnaic and → Talmudic texts in the third century A.D.

In the late Hellenistic period two schools of biblical interpretation emerged centered in → Antioch and → Alexandria, although the lines between them are blurred. The Antiochean school favored more literal and historical interpretation of biblical texts over the more allegorical interpretations of the Alexandrian school. Christian writers including → Origen (ca. 185-ca. 254), → Chrysostom (ca. 347-407), and → Augustine (354-430) wrote extensive commentaries on the Scriptures, employing at times both literal and historical methods of interpretation, as well as allegorical methods.

2. Medieval and Reformation Methods

Medieval methods of literary criticism employed a fourfold schema that investigated the literal, allegorical, tropological (moral), and anagogical (mystical) meanings of the text. With the rediscovery of the writings of Aristotle and Plato from the middle of the 12th century to the middle of the 13th, medieval exegetes incorporated the ideas and methods of these newly found texts into their existing studies of language, grammar, and rhetoric.

Martin → Luther's (1483-1546) methods, focusing on the "plain sense" of the Scripture and his doctrine of *sola Scriptura*, shifted literary criticism from the fourfold medieval methods of interpretation to a more historical and theological (i.e., doctrinal) approach. Luther's method was adopted in the biblical commentaries of John → Calvin (1509-64).

3. Early Modern Literary Criticism

Modern literary criticism finds its roots in the → Enlightenment rejection of the supernatural in favor of the rational. The term "aesthetics" was first used in the modern sense by A. Baumgarten (1714-62), who contrasted masculine reason with its "handmaid," aesthetics. Immanuel Kant's (1724-1804) use of aesthetic discourse, more specifically artistic judgments, in his *Critique of Judgment* (1790) to bridge the chasm between the noumenal and phenomenal realms (the subjects of his two earlier critiques, *Critique of Pure Reason* [1781] and *Critique of Practical Reason* [1788]) placed literary criticism and aesthetic judgment at the forefront of 18th-century European philosophy (→ Kantianism).

The intermingling of aesthetic and artistic judgments, philosophy, and theology was further developed in the German idealist tradition by Friedrich Schiller's *Aesthetic Education of Man*, in the Romantic tradition by Friedrich von Schlegel (1772-1829), and in the emphasis on feeling or emotion in the theological and hermeneutical work of Friedrich → Schleiermacher (1768-1834; → Schleiermacher's Theology).

4. Literary Criticism and Biblical Studies

Historical repetitions and narrative inconsistencies in the → Pentateuch led to the suggestion in the 17th century that Moses was likely not the author of the entire Pentateuch. Thomas Hobbes (1588-1679) and Baruch Spinoza (1632-77) both suggested that the person most likely responsible for the Pentateuch was Ezra. The beginning of "source criticism" of the Pentateuch is found in the work of J. Astruc

(1684-1766), who in 1753 published an anonymous work that identified two strands of narrative organized around the divine Hebrew names for God, Elohim and → Yahweh. At the time, however, Astruc did not question the Mosaic authorship of the Pentateuch. Source criticism of the Pentateuch found further expansion in the 18th century in J. G. Eichhorn's (1752-1827) three-volume *Introduction to the OT* (1781-88) and in the 19th century in Julius Wellhausen's (1844-1918) two-volume *History of Israel* (1878).

In contrast to the examination of longer narrative strands or traditions, the "form criticism" of Herman Gunkel (1862-1932) examined smaller pieces of biblical narrative organized by their literary genre or form. Such forms include myth, saga, law, and folktale. The term *Formgeschichte* to describe this method was first employed in its later technical sense by NT scholar Martin Dibelius (1883-1947). The central aim of form criticism is to examine the prehistory of a literary text and to ascertain the particular historical context, or *Sitz im Leben,* that gave rise to the later written form of the narrative (→ Literature, Biblical and Early Christian, 1).

"Redaction criticism" *(Redaktionsgeschichte)* is the term coined by Willi Marxsen (1919-93) to refer to the literary method that recognizes that each biblical author not only inherits a preliterary tradition but shapes it according to that author's theological or narrative interests. Important early redaction-critical works on the NT texts include Marxsen's *Mark the Evangelist* (1956; ET 1969); Günther Bornkamm, Gerhard Barth, and Hans Joachim Held's *Tradition and Interpretation in Matthew* (1963); and Hans Conzelmann's *Theology of St. Luke* (1954; ET 1960). Norman Perrin also employed this method throughout his work, not least in his influential *The NT: An Introduction* (1974). Perrin also explicated the method in *What Is Redaction Criticism?* (1969).

Biblical criticism in the 20th and 21st centuries has employed methods derived from a wide variety of discourses. Most significant are structuralist, psychoanalytic, poststructural, feminist, womanist, gay, lesbian, Marxist, race-oriented, and postcolonial theories.

5. Formalist Methods
In his *Cours de linguistique générale,* published posthumously in 1916, Ferdinand de Saussure (1857-1913) laid the foundation not only for the study of → language and linguistics in the 20th century but also for what later was to be called → structuralism.

Saussure distinguished between language as it was spoken *(parole)* and language as an abstract system *(langue).* This method contrasted the synchronic (parole) with the diachronic (langue), or the signifier with the signified. The distinction Saussure had drawn between langue and parole was taken in a different direction by C. S. Peirce (1839-1914), who called his interpretive method semiotics, or the study of signs (→ Sign).

Russian formalism adopted methods first devised for the study of language and applied them to an analysis of literary productions. Formalists understood a literary work to be largely an assemblage of literary devices. In his *Theory of Prose* (1925) V. Schlovsky coins the term for a literary device he calls estrangement *(ostraniene),* which makes an object or image stand apart from, or "outside," of its immediate literary context. Vladimir Propp's (1895-1970) *Morphology of the Russian Folktale* (1958) focuses on an analysis of the basic forms, particularly in terms of plot, that characterize the folktale.

In reaction to the limitations of Russian formalism, Mikhail Bakhtin (1895-1975) developed in his *Problems of Dostoevsky's Poetics* (1929) a "dialogic" method that focused on the multiplicity of characters' voices ("polyphony") in Dostoevsky's novels that are not restrained or controlled by the author. His term "heteroglossia" describes the multifaceted meanings that arise from all utterances.

6. Critical Social Theory
Literary criticism after Kant has continually returned to the question of the role of the human subject in the process of interpretation and to the question of the nature and identity of the human subject itself. Where premodern theories of interpretation placed the focus on the object of interpretation seen as separate from the interpreting subject, Kant's → metaphysics placed this task of interpretation within the thought of the interpreting subject, who thus constructed an interpretation of the object.

Sigmund Freud's (1856-1939) recognition of the overdetermination of human consciousness — that is, no one cause of consciousness can be identified, and the unconscious can uncontrollably spill into conscious thought — opened new avenues for the investigation of the identity of human subjects within literary and artistic texts. Because literature, in every genre and form, brings to expression both the dominant and repressed ideas of a particular culture, the study of literature often allows the critic or theorist to identify broader social, ideological, political, and psychological themes within the culture in which the text or work of art was produced.

Because human identities are forged within particular cultures, literature is a place where such questions about identity are often discussed or elaborated.

With the failure of the general → revolution in Europe after 1848, many Western Marxists turned their attention to cultural criticism, because, as Karl → Marx (1818-83) dialectically noted, artistic expression, in much the same way as religious expression, contains the kernel of protest against societies structured by capitalist market relations and thus could be harnessed for social or political revolution. Because their work was articulated within or alongside academic institutions, these Western Marxist theorists often refrained from direct political engagement.

The most influential of the early Marxist critics was the Hungarian Georg Lukács (1885-1971). Before his conversion from neo-Kantian philosophy to Marxism, Lukács published *The Theory of the Novel* (1920). In 1923, after his conversion, Lukács published *History and Class Consciousness*, in which he developed an interpretive approach that provided the basis for later "standpoint theory," arguing that the → proletariat held a unique position within capitalist societies that allowed them, and them only, not only to see but also to resolve the long-standing antinomies inherent in capitalist economies but also in the philosophical theories developed within these economies.

The Institut für Sozialforschung, or Institute of Social Research, was founded in Frankfurt in 1923. By the 1930s, when Max Horkheimer (1895-1973) was the director, the school produced a variety of interdisciplinary academic studies, including the philosophical and cultural studies of Theodor Adorno (1903-69) and the psychological studies of Erich Fromm (1900-1980) and Herbert Marcuse (1898-1979). The "critical social theory" of the Frankfurt School (→ Critical Theory) was broadly sociological in the Marxist tradition. Their investigation of "mass culture," employing psychological, economic, philosophical, and literary methods, was directed particularly to the question of how → fascism came to power in Germany after World War I. In their *Dialectic of Enlightenment* (1944; ET 1972), Adorno and Horkheimer analyze the phenomenon of mass culture and the regression of civilization, even while many were speaking of "progress" and "enlightenment."

The literary-critical methods developed by Walter Benjamin (1892-1940) and later employed by Adorno attacked the valorization of the interpreting subject within cultural and literary theory since Kant, over and against the object of interpretation itself. Benjamin envisioned a method of "profane illumination" by which a work of art might be allowed to "speak for itself" without the conceptual violence inherent in many philosophical literary critical methods, namely in the imposition of the interpreter's own meaning onto the object of interpretation.

7. Modern Criticism in English Literature

The rise of modern literary and cultural studies in English can be traced to Matthew Arnold's (1822-88) *Essays in Criticism* (1865), in which criticism itself is elevated to the status of literature, and to his *Culture and Anarchy,* first published in journal form between 1867 and 1868. For Arnold, the end and aim of all literature is → truth. Literature, he hoped, not religion, would be the means to civilize the middle classes in England. The ideological use of literature in the English language incorporated nationalist concerns such as the formation of "Englishness" and, particularly in the work of T. S. Eliot, an emphasis on → tradition.

American New Criticism, taking its name from the 1941 book of John Crowe Ransom (1888-1974) *The New Criticism,* flourished from the late 1930s to the 1950s. The movement can be described as formalist, given its attention to the study of the text, most often poems, as a self-contained whole, which was to be investigated apart from the intentions of the text's author or the interpretive actions of the reader. Ransom's 1937 essay "Criticism Inc." valorized the role of the professional academic literary critic, whose task in the face of the vulgar culture and crass commercialism of capitalist societies was to ward off the moral decline of Western civilization through the study of literature. In his 1943 *Education and the University,* F. R. Leavis (1895-1978) propounded the education of highly trained experts in the study of literature, particularly within academic English departments, who would be able to preserve and transmit the truths of literature within a society threatened by the cultural disintegration brought on by → mass media, advertising, and emerging technologies.

8. Structuralist Literary Theories

Structuralist methods of literary criticism owe a large debt to the linguistic theories of Saussure and the early anthropological work of Émile Durkheim (1858-1917). Claude Lévi-Strauss (b. 1908) developed an anthropological theory, shaped by the linguistic theories of Roman Jacobson (1896-1982) and the work of Durkheim, that sought to describe the entire structure or totality of human societies. His anthropological method, as a result, focused on how the overall societal or cultural structure formed, shaped, and produced the thoughts and actions of human subjects, who were constitutively structured by this larger social whole. Structuralist theorists, in other words, applied the distinction Saussure drew between langue and parole to objects and human activities, always seeking to discover the more comprehensive structure, or "langue," of the object or activity under investigation.

Structuralist literary theories are characterized by the priority given to the analysis of the system of a literary work — that is, the overall work — over and against an analysis of its constitutive elements. They usually are characterized by the adoption of methods developed within linguistics or the study of language to literature and the desire to formulate general rules about how literary texts function. This tendency is evident in A. J. Greimas's *Structural Semantics* (1966), in which he develops a model to show how the structure of narratives, not the content of selected narrative elements as in Propp's study of the Russian folktale, makes meaning possible. Gérard Gennette's *Narrative Discourse* (1972) examines the function of narrative and how the narrator functions in relation to other elements, including characters, of literary texts. This area of investigation is commonly called narratology.

9. Psychoanalytic Literary Theories

In the 1950s Jacques Lacan (1901-81), a renegade Freudian theorist, began to develop his own psychoanalytic theories based on the work of Freud read alongside structuralist linguistics and anthropology. For Lacan the ego is an illusion that can never take the place of the unconscious because the ego itself is the product of the unconscious, the ground of all being. Lacan's psychoanalytic theory is "poststructuralist" in its recognition that the process of identity formation is never complete, because the subject never comes to a final understanding or interpretation of the self. The subject, for Lacan, is an effect of language.

In *Revolution in Poetic Language* (1984), Julia Kristeva focuses her attention on what lies beyond language, calling her method "semanalysis," a term derived from the "semiology" (or semiotics) of Saussure and the "psychoanalysis" of Freud, as interpreted through Lacan. For Kristeva, what is repressed can find expression in the language of poetry or in the language of mental illness.

Since the time of the Frankfurt school, literary criticism has been marked by the cross-fertilization of many fields of academic inquiry. This interconnectedness is evident, for example, in the work of Louis Althusser (1918-90). In his attempt to remove the Hegelian and idealist categories from Marxist discourses, Althusser employs structuralist insights derived from Saussure's linguistic studies and the structuralist anthropological work of Lévi-Strauss, alongside the psychoanalytic theories of Lacan, placing them within a Marxist framework in which the distinction is made between the economic base and cultural superstructure.

10. Marxist Literary Criticism

Written within the confines of a Western Marxist cultural theory, R. William's (1921-88) *Keywords* (1976) investigates the historical changes in the meaning and usage of English words that are particularly relevant to social, political, and literary theory. From a similar Marxist perspective, Terry Eagleton's *Literary Theory* (1983) surveys and critiques a wide variety of literary theories, grouped within general categories, propounded from the late 19th century to the last decades of the 20th century.

In *Criticism and Ideology* (1976) Eagleton develops a method of Marxist literary criticism that focuses on the function and effects of ideology in literary texts. Eagleton's theory is developed in response to the theory of ideology outlined in Pierre Macherey's *Theory of Literary Production* (1966). For Macherey the task of criticism focuses on the incompleteness of the text, that is, what because of ideology the text cannot say. The object of literary criticism is therefore the unconsciousness of the text, namely that of which the text is not, and cannot be, aware. For Eagleton, Macherey's formalist (structuralist) method is not able to account for the real historical and material contradictions that underlie the production of every text and therefore provide insufficient grounds for a "science of the text." In *Walter Benjamin; or, Towards a Revolutionary Criticism* (1981), Eagleton moves from textual criticism toward a method that focuses on the "problems of cultural production and the political use of artifacts" (p. x).

In his publications during the late 1980s and 1990s on → postmodernism, particularly in *Postmodernism; or, The Cultural Logic of Late Capitalism* (1991), Fredric Jameson maintains that postmodernism is correlative with the historical manifestation of global → capitalism in much the same way that → modernism was correlative with commodity capitalism. In *The Political Unconscious* (1981), also shaped by Macherey's theory of unconsciousness of the text, Jameson develops a political theory of narrative, understood as an → epistemology, structured around the problematics of ideology, desire, representation, and history.

11. Reader-Response, or Reception, Aesthetics

Reader-response theories developed with the phenomenological tradition of Edmund Husserl (1859-1938; → Phenomenology). They seek to analyze how a text is interpreted by the reader and how the meaning of that text is produced by the reader within his or her consciousness. H. R. Jauss developed his theory of "aesthetic reception" in reaction both to formalist theories of literature, which tended to ignore the history of a text, and to interpretations shaped explicitly by a desired political outcome. Jauss employs the concept of a text's "horizons of expectation" to describe the information that might be helpful to the reader — the historical context and expectations of the text at the time it was produced — but leaves the reader with the ultimate decision about the meaning of the text.

Stanley Fish's (b. 1938) theory of "affective stylistics" emerged as a reaction to the emphasis within the New Criticism, which insisted that the meaning of a text came from within the text itself. For Fish, the response of the reader to the text is more important than the formal text. Fish's interpretive method thus radically sunders the reader from any intention of the text or its author, focusing instead on the subjective experience of the reader, whose interpretation may nonetheless be guided by one or more "interpretive communities."

12. Poststructuralist and Deconstructionist Literary Theory

One of the goals of any deconstructive theory is to demonstrate that the "given" is not natural but always a construction, produced by the very discourse that constitutes it. Poststructuralist, or deconstructionist, theory in the1980s and 1990s was primarily influenced by the work of two theorists, Michel Foucault (1926-84) and Jacques Derrida (b. 1930). Foucault wrote what he called genealogies (not histories) of prisons, psychiatry, sexuality, and a variety of other developments in 18th- and 19th-century European societies. In these studies Foucault analyzes the particular relations of power and knowledge that produced the "discourses," that is, the definitions and categories that organize and regulate human behavior and action, often without explicit human knowledge or consent. These discourses, Foucault argues, in fact create the objects or categories they purport to study.

Derrida's philosophical theories seek the deconstruction of the binary and hierarchical oppositions in Western philosophical thought, which include mind/body, presence/absence, and inside/outside. Derrida destabilizes the relationship between the signifier and the signified. Within language, meaning is always deferred (différence). Deconstruction therefore demands the abandonment of any stable or fixed reference to any given center of meaning (the signified).

Feminist theorists employ a wide variety of literary methods and approaches. Some feminists challenge and subvert discourses that exclude or marginalize women, others investigate and celebrate the identities of women, and still others examine the expression of women and their experiences in literature (→ Feminism).

Following the decentering actions of deconstructive theory and the work of Foucault, gay and lesbian theorists have turned their attention to the cultural construction of heterosexual normativity (→ Homosexuality). In Gender Trouble (1990) Judith Butler employs Foucault's understanding of discourse, read alongside Derrida's deconstructive methods and J. L. Austin's (1911-60) understanding of language as performative, to argue that gender itself is performative, that is, it is not constituted essentially but rather by its continual, repeated performance; in other words, for Butler gender is culturally constructed. Her overall aim is to deconstruct the idea that human beings have fixed identities. As is the case with feminist theories, so gay and lesbian theorists have embraced a wide diversity of theoretical and literary approaches.

13. Postcolonial Theory

The most formative book in postcolonial literary theory is Edward Said's work Orientalism (1978). "Orientalism" describes how Western texts represented the "East." For Said, this representation is a Western production of academic knowledge by means of "dominating, restructuring, and having authority over the Orient" (p. 3). Postcolonial theories, following Foucault, investigate the "discourse" of → colonialism and the relationships of power and knowledge that underlie the production and reproduction of those colonialist discourses. Postcolonial methods often focus on the eclectic, multicultural, cross-disciplinary, and the hybridized.

By the last decade of the 20th century, literary theory had been employed within almost every field of academic study in the humanities or the liberal arts, from history, philosophy, and religion to cultural studies, film studies, and studies of gender, → sexuality, and race.

Bibliography: Overview: H. BERTENS, *Literary Theory: The Basics* (New York, 2001) • J. CULLER, *Literary Theory: A Very Short Introduction* (Oxford, 1997) • M. MCKEON, ed., *Theory of the Novel: A Historical Approach* (Baltimore, 2000) • R. SELDEN, P. WIDDOWSON, and P. BROOKER, *A Reader's Guide to Contemporary Literary Theory* (4th ed.; London, 1997) • L. TYSON, *Critical Theory Today: A User-Friendly Guide* (New York, 1999).

Antiquity to early modern: J. BARTON, ed., *The Cambridge Companion to Biblical Interpretation* (Cambridge, 1998) • H. DE LUBAC, *Medieval Exegesis: The Four Senses of Scripture* (2 vols.; Grand Rapids, 1998-2000) • S. L. MACKENZIE and S. R. HAYNES, eds., *To Each Its Own Meaning: An Introduction to Biblical Criticisms and Their Applications* (Louisville, Ky., 1999) • E. V. MCKNIGHT, *Meaning in Texts: The Historical Shaping of a Narrative Hermeneutics* (Philadelphia, 1978) • J. NEUSNER, *Introduction to Rabbinic Literature* (New York, 1994) • N. PERRIN, *The NT, an Introduction: Proclamation and Parenesis, Myth and History* (New York, 1974); idem, *What Is Redaction Criticism?* (Philadelphia, 1969) • I. WATT, *The Rise of the Novel: Studies in Defoe, Richardson, and Fielding* (Berkeley, Calif., 1957).

Formalism to Marxist theories: L. ALTHUSSER, *Lenin and Philosophy, and Other Essays* (London, 1971) • L. ALTHUSSER and E. BALIBAR, *Reading "Capital"* (New York, 1971) • P. ANDERSON, *Considerations on Western Marxism* (London, 1985) • M. ARNOLD, *Culture and Anarchy: An Essay in Political and Social Criticism* (Indianapolis, 1971) • T. EAGLETON, *Criticism and Ideology: A Study in Marxist Literary Theory* (London, 1976); idem, *Literary Theory: An Introduction* (Minneapolis, 1983); idem, *Walter Benjamin; or, Towards a Revolutionary Criticism* (London, 1981) • T. HAWKES, *Structuralism and Semiotics* (London, 1977) • D. HELD, *Introduction to Critical Theory* (Berkeley, Calif., 1980) • F. JAMESON, *The Political Unconscious: Narrative as a Socially Symbolic Act* (Ithaca, N.Y., 1981); idem, *Postmodernism; or, The Cultural Logic of Late Capitalism* (Durham, N.C., 1991); idem, *The Prison-House of Language: A Critical Account of Structuralism and Russian Formalism* (Princeton, 1972) • J. KRISTEVA, *Revolution in Poetic Language* (New York, 1984) • J. LACAN, *Écrits: A Selection* (New York, 1977) • C. LÉVI-STRAUSS, *Structural Anthropology* (London, 1958) • G. LUKÁCS, *The Theory of the Novel: A Historico-Philosophical Essay on the Forms of Great Epic Literature* (London, 1971) • P. MACHEREY, *A Theory of Literary Production* (London, 1978; orig. pub., 1966) • H. MARCUSE, *Eros and Civilization: A Philosophical Inquiry into Freud* (Boston, 1955).

Recent theories: J. BUTLER, *Gender Trouble: Feminism and the Subversion of Identity* (New York, 1990) • J. DERRIDA, *Of Grammatology* (Baltimore, 1998); idem, *Writing and Difference* (Chicago, 1980) • J. DOLLIMORE, *Sexual Dissidence: Augustine to Wilde, Freud to Foucault* (Oxford, 1991) • S. FISH, *Is There a Text in This Class? The Authority of Interpretive Communities* (Cambridge, Mass., 1982) • M. FOUCAULT, *The History of Sexuality: An Introduction* (New York, 1990) • H. L. GATES, ed., *"Race," Writing, and Difference* (Chicago, 1987) • R. C. HOLUB, *Reception Theory: A Critical Introduction* (London, 1984) • J.-F. LYOTARD, *The Postmodern Condition: A Report on Knowledge* (Minneapolis, 1984) • E. SAID, *Orientalism* (New York, 1978) • G. C. SPIVAK, *In Other Worlds: Essays in Cultural Politics* (New York, 1998) • R. S. SUGIRTHARAJAH, *Postcolonial Criticism and Biblical Interpretation* (Oxford, 2002).

CRAIG A. PHILLIPS

Literature, Biblical and Early Christian

1. OT

1.1. *Task*

Viewing the OT as literature means engaging in critical literary analysis (→ Exegesis, Biblical) of the individual books. There is then an attempt to achieve a synthetic picture of the development of the entire literature of Israel from its early beginnings to the age of the Maccabees. This study will also take account of Israel's life settings. First, however, this endeavor must survey the forms and genres of the preliterary tradition.

1.2. History of Research

H. Gunkel (1862-1932) initiated this kind of study, at least in outline (*Die israelitische Literatur* [1906]). Earlier works by G. Wildeboer and K. Budde did little more than present the results of → literary criticism and date the texts accordingly. In contrast, Gunkel was less interested in giving dates. A history of literature that takes seriously the way in which the OT texts, like all texts of antiquity, relate conventionally to life deals more with the types underlying what is individual. It will thus be more a history of literary genres. Gunkel thus saw the history of Israel's literature, on the one hand, from the standpoint of the requirement of the → history-of-religions school for an understanding of biblical religion within Near Eastern culture and its social institutions and, on the other hand, under the influence of J. G. → Herder (1744-1803), from the standpoint of an aesthetic interest in OT literature in connection with the laws of form and style that are found in folk poetry. For Gunkel, genres were shaped by a common life setting (*Sitz im Leben*), a common treasury of thoughts and feelings, and a common form of speech (see Gunkel and J. Begrich, 22-23).

Gunkel's own execution of this program suffered from weaknesses. His arrangement of the material — (1) popular literature preceding the emergence of the great authors, up to about 750 B.C.; (2) the great authors, approximately 750-540; and (3) imitators — did not do justice to the significance of the exilic and postexilic epochs. His theory that shorter and stylistically purer forms indicate an earlier period, while longer, reworked, and mixed forms betray a later origin, contradicts the findings of folklore research both within and outside the OT. There was also more oral tradition at a later period than Gunkel allowed for (note the criticism of Gunkel by recent scholars of folklore such as P. G. Kirkpatrick).

Along the same lines as Gunkel's work, we might mention J. Hempel's (1891-1964) *Handbuch* of 1930. Unlike Gunkel, however, Hempel separates the account of forms from that of the course of history. R. Smend's contribution to the new edition of this *Handbuch* (1978) also calls for notice. In the English-speaking world we should refer to N. K. Gottwald's socioliterary introduction (1985), though here Israel's → social history underlies the arrangement.

Most OT introductions simply put brief notes on the genres before analysis of the works (see O. Eissfeldt, as early as 1934).

1.3. Preliterary Forms and Genres

For the most part the OT is simply the written form of an oral tradition, of which the following are the most important genres. Comparative studies have shown the relation of various genres used by biblical writers to Sumerian, Akkadian, Babylonian, Assyrian, Canaanite (Ugaritic), and Egyptian literatures then available.

1.3.1. First, we have *songs*, which, with Gunkel, we may classify as private secular poems, political poems, and liturgical songs. The Song of the Well in Numbers 21:17-18 belongs to the first class (perhaps a work song sung at the digging of a well). To this class also belong love songs (see Canticles) and funeral dirges (e.g., 2 Sam. 1:19-27, called *qînâ*, "lamentation," in v. 17). Political poems include secular victory songs (see 1 Sam. 18:6-7), mostly sung by women to the accompaniment of instruments and dancing (→ Dance). Songs of taunt directed toward enemies belong in the same class (e.g., Num. 21:27-30*). Poetic evaluations of political events might be transmitted by tribal oracles (see the blessings by Jacob in Genesis 49 and by Moses in Deuteronomy 33; → Blessing). The Song of Deborah in Judges 5, however, is liturgical, at least in its present form.

The most important liturgical songs, according to Gunkel and Begrich, are hymns (e.g., Psalm 96; → Hymn 1), songs of national complaint (Psalm 80), songs of individual complaint (Psalm 3), and songs of individual thanksgiving (Psalm 30). We must also include royal → psalms (Psalm 2), for despite considerable formal differences, they had a common setting at liturgical royal ceremonies (R. Rendtorff). How far Wisdom psalms (e.g., Psalm 1) had a cultic setting is debated. Also unclarified is the question how far personal → piety, which had a significant role in → Israel (§1), might count as a life setting alongside the official cult.

1.3.2. For the OT *narrative tradition* we find life settings both in popular tradition, through a class of storytellers, and in the court and Wisdom tradition. In classifying the former, Gunkel referred to sagas (i.e., stories), fables, → myths, and fairy tales, though it is only in terms of motifs that the OT retains myths and fairy tales (e.g., Gen. 6:2 and Num. 22:28-30). Plant fables occur in Judg. 9:8-15 and 2 Kgs. 14:9. As regards "sagas," Gunkel differentiates prehistorical sagas, patriarchal sagas, and folk-hero sagas (stories of great political and religious leaders like → Moses, → David, or → Elijah). Many sagas are for him etiologies or contain subsequent etiological motifs. He distinguishes ethnological (Gen. 9:20-27), geological (chap. 19), and etymological (11:9) etiologies. Especially important for him in the OT are cultic etiologies (see 28:10-22*; one should avoid the designation "cultic legends" because of the ambiguous nature of the term "legend").

In the court and Wisdom tradition (→ Wisdom Literature), which took written form from the very first, we find short stories (Genesis 37–50*) and historical narratives (2 Kings 9–10*) covering a long span of time and set in many different places. Government interests account for the annals (1 Kgs. 9:26-28) and lists (2 Sam. 8:16-18).

1.3.3. Like their counterparts in surrounding countries, the OT *proverbs* also have their setting in court wisdom (see Prov. 25:1). They must have been written down by scribes and a broader educated class. How far the OT also contains a popular tribal wisdom is open to debate. As in other countries we may distinguish in Israel between nature wisdom and practical wisdom. There are few examples of the former in the OT (e.g., some number proverbs, Prov. 30:15-31*; cf. 1 Kgs. 4:33). As regards the latter, we find many admonitory proverbs (some positive, e.g., 19:20; others negative, 22:22). Other types are pronouncement proverbs (O. Kaiser, "Wahrsprüche," e.g., 18:3) and didactic speeches (chaps. 1–9).

1.3.4. Among the *statutes* handed down in the OT (→ Law 1) are the casuistic rulings (*mišpāṭîm*, "ordinances," Exod. 21:1, e.g., vv. 18-19), which served as standards for the administration of justice by elders at the gate of each community (see Ruth 4). A. Alt differentiated between these rulings and the people-related and Yahweh-related apodictic law that he found in three forms in the OT, namely, prohibitions (e.g., Exod. 23:1-9* and the → Decalogue), legal statutes stating the consequence *môt yûmāt* ("shall be put to death," e.g., Exod. 21:12-17*), and curses (Deut. 27:15-26, esp. against those who offend secretly).

Alt thought that the setting of this legislation was one of liturgy (→ Worship) rather than ordinary jurisprudence, but modern research has found instances of apodictic law outside Israel as well. It has also pointed to the head of the family rather than → Yahweh as the original authority behind such law. It suggests that there might have been different settings for the various legal forms, but the debate continues. Especially debated is whether we have in the *môt yûmāt* statements of casuistic law in apodictic form (G. Fohrer) or the setting of limits that must not be passed, quite apart from actual cases (H. J.

Boecker). Another persuasive theory is that the prohibitions were originally practical didactic directions, more ethos than law (W. H. Schmidt).

1.3.5. The earliest forms of *prophetic speech* (→ Prophet, Prophecy) in the OT are thought to come from the written prophetic books (the prophetic sayings of the → Deuteronomistic history were probably already formulated under this influence). Hence only the rhetorical forms of the written prophets can be reconstructed with any certainty, though even here the original sayings might well have undergone some alteration when put in written form.

From the days of Gunkel four basic forms of prophetic speech have been discerned: threat (C. Westermann), accusation (Westermann, K. Koch, often the basis of the threat), → promise, and admonition. The recipients might be Israel, foreign countries, or individuals. Prophetic sayings, especially threats and promises, often have the form of sayings of Yahweh, especially the introductory "Thus says Yahweh," or the intermediate or concluding "says [*nĕ'um*] Yahweh." Prophecy also borrows forms, including laments based on funeral dirges (e.g., Amos 5:1-24; 6:1-8), love songs (Isa. 5:1-10), disputations (Amos 3:3-8), historical surveys (Amos 9:7), judgments (Jer. 2:5-13), and the priestly → Torah (Hag. 2:10-13).

Much of the prophetic material, especially that relating to preclassical prophecy, also takes a narrative form written either by the prophet or by another (Jer. 13:1-11; Amos 7:10-17). Common in this class are accounts of → visions (Amos 7–9*), symbolic actions (Isaiah 20; 2 Kgs. 13:14-19), and calling (Isaiah 6; Jer. 1:4-19; 1 Kgs. 19:19-21).

1.4. *OT Writings and Theological Tradition*
How the OT writings came into being is much debated. As regards the → Pentateuch and the Prophets, sharply divergent theories have been advanced in recent decades. The criteria that have been used thus far for dating are now regarded as inadequate. We do best, then, not to see the works primarily in terms of date but as expressions of typical groupings in Israel's religious and cultural life. O. H. Steck has suggested five streams of tradition: the Wisdom tradition (originally related to the Jerusalem court), the priestly tradition, the cultic tradition of the Jerusalem temple singers, the prophetic tradition, and the Deuteronomic/Deuteronomistic tradition. The institutional background of these five streams, however, is still obscure (e.g., whether rural Levites or rather scribes who devoted themselves to the interpretation of the prophetic and legal tradition).

We will try to show from the example of the Pentateuch how the literature of the OT might have been shaped by the traditions named. Texts like Genesis 37–50* suggest that individual blocks of Wisdom tradition were first put in written form even before the emergence of the Pentateuch sources. Strata such as the Elohistic and Yahwistic, encompassing several different Pentateuchal themes and discernible by the consistent use of "Elohim" or "Yahweh," seem to presuppose a combination of Wisdom and prophetic traditions. For this reason they are often not dated before the writing prophets. The priestly sections then come from a specific priestly Pentateuchal tradition probably associated with the Babylonian exile. The merging of the prophetic-Wisdom traditions with the priestly materials then took place within Deuteronomic-Deuteronomistic circles (Genesis 15, Exodus 16, Leviticus 17–26, and Deuteronomy 34 all suggest postpriestly Deuteronomistic redaction). Finally, the addition of the Deuteronomistic history created a work encompassing Genesis 1 through 2 Kings 25. The fact that the priestly, theocratic rival account in Chronicles used materials from this sequence supports the view that it must have been in existence even in the late postexilic years. During the early Hellenistic period and under priestly influence (Smend), the Pentateuch then received a status of its own. It would owe its special position to the fact that it included every basic theological tradition apart from that of the Jerusalem temple singers, which probably played a determinate role in the rise of most of the prophetic books.

→ Apocrypha; Book of the Covenant; Canon; Historiography; Holiness Code; Masorah, Masoretes; Megilloth; Patriarchal History; Priest, Priesthood; Primeval History (Genesis 1–11); Pseudepigrapha

Bibliography: Y. AMIT, Hidden Polemics in Biblical Narrative (Leiden, 2000) • H. J. BOECKER, Law and the Administration of Justice in the OT and Ancient East (London, 1980) • J. H. CHARLESWORTH, ed., The Hebrew Bible and Qumran (North Richland Hills, Tex., 2000) • J. L. CRENSHAW, OT Wisdom: An Introduction (rev. ed.; Louisville, Ky., 1998) • O. EISSFELDT, The OT: An Introduction (New York, 1965; orig. pub., 1934) • G. FOHRER, Introduction to the OT (Nashville, 1968) • A. GIBSON, Text and Tablet: Near Eastern Archaeology, the OT, and New Possibilities (Aldershot, 2000) • N. K. GOTTWALD, The Hebrew Bible: A Socio-Literary Introduction (Philadelphia, 1985) • H. GUNKEL, Die israelitische Literatur (Leipzig, 1906; repr., Darmstadt, 1963) • H. GUNKEL and J. BEGRICH, Einleitung in die Psalmen (Göttingen, 1933; ET Introduction to Psalms [Macon, Ga., 1998]) • P. D. HANSON, The Dawn of Apocalyptic (Philadelphia, 1975) • O. KAISER, Einleitung in das Alte Testament (Gütersloh, 1969; ET Introduction to the OT [Minneapolis, 1975]) • P. G. KIRKPATRICK, The OT and Folklore Study (Sheffield, 1988) • R. KNIERIM, "Criticism of Literary Features, Form, Tradition, and Redaction," The Hebrew Bible and Its Modern Interpreters (ed. D. A. Knight and G. M. Tucker, eds.; Philadelphia, 1985) • K. KOCH, The Growth of the Biblical Tradition (New York, 1969) • R. E. MURPHY, The Tree of Life: An Exploration of Biblical Wisdom Literature (3d ed.; Grand Rapids, 2002) • A. NAHKOLA, Double Narratives in the OT: The Foundations of Method in Biblical Criticism (New York, 2001) • D. L. PETERSEN, The Prophetic Literature: An Introduction (Louisville, Ky., 2002) • G. VON RAD, Wisdom in Israel (London, 1972) • R. RENDTORFF, The OT: An Introduction (Philadelphia, 1986) • W. SCHMIDT, OT Introduction (2d ed.; New York, 1999) • R. SMEND, "Die altisraelitische Literatur," NHL 1.273-323 • O. H. STECK, "Strömungen theologischer Traditionen im Alten Testament," Wahrnehmungen Gottes im Alten Testament (Munich, 1982) 291-317 • S. TERRIEN, The Psalms: Strophic Structure and Theological Commentary (Grand Rapids, 2003) • C. WESTERMANN, Basic Forms of Prophetic Speech (Cambridge, 1991; orig. pub., 1960).

HANS-CHRISTOPH SCHMITT

2. NT

2.1. Tasks and Problems

The history of the literature of the NT describes the circumstances and conditions under which the literature of the first churches arose (→ Primitive Christian Community). It needs to consider the origin of the forms and genres and the changes that took place in them. We cannot understand the development without insight into the sociocultural and socioeconomic conditions that seem to be aesthetically transmitted in the texts (i.e., the Sitz im Leben). Yet we must also pay attention to the history of the impact and reception of the NT in church history. To study primitive Christianity on its literary side necessarily forces us to study its actual history. We must trace the path that the forms and genres and texts took throughout primitive Christianity. When we also take into account the contents and theological topics, then matters of tradition and redaction (i.e., the mutual relations of author and community) also call for consideration. The literature of primitive Christianity bears witness to its material and aesthetic interaction with the age in which it was set. Note must therefore be taken of its contacts with the literature of early Judaism and → Hellenism and its connection with the history of → religion in general.

A task of this kind raises material and methodological problems. Materially, it is by no means easy to demarcate a sphere of "NT literature." Orientation to the limits of the → canon is not very meaningful, and most scholars have abandoned it. Instead, they speak of early Christian literature and include the → Apostolic Fathers and NT → apocrypha. There is also an openness to the literature of early → Judaism and Hellenism. Only thus, it seems, can we speak of a literature of primitive Christianity. At the same time, we must not ignore the specific distinctives of this literature but must give it its own profile and assessment.

The methodological problems are closely related to considerations of content. A review of primitive Christian literature must be historical and diachronous. It is bound by its own views of the development and history that prevail in its own day. Yet in its description it must draw close to the forms, genres, and texts at issue. In terms of the criticism of style and form, it must be synchronous. The two approaches are complementary, but adopting them together is difficult.

Another point is that the transition from oral to written literature has not yet been really clarified, and the equation of the oral with the preliterary can hardly be sustained. A result is the debatability of the concept of *Sitz im Leben*. It is true enough that when a form or genre develops, it always relates to a specific social and historical situation. At the same time, however, forms and genres exhibit aesthetic resistance in the face of changing historical situations (→ Aesthetics).

The demarcation of primitive Christian literature is methodologically open to question. The transition to the → early church took place on many different literary planes and terminated only with the completion of the canon. Again, only partially can we establish the beginnings denoted theologically by → Easter. Along with new features it is hard to detect in primitive Christian literature the prior history or parallels to the literature of the age. For that reason, trying to put this literature in periods will always give rise to methodological debate (e.g., the issue of → early Catholicism). There are breaks as well as continuity.

2.2. *History of Research*
In 1882 F. Overbeck (1837-1905) became the first to articulate the task and program of a history of primitive Christian literature. According to him, such a history must deal with the first writings of Christianity, writings Christianity created from within its own means and whose history is found in its forms. Its texts will reflect exclusively the interests of the Christian community and its refusal to intermingle with the Hellenistic world. Only with the → apologists do we find adoption of the forms of secular literature, which marks the end of the primitive literature, ratified by the canon. Overbeck's wide-ranging discussions in differentiation of the primary literature and its ideological presuppositions have been taken up, but only with reservations.

We find the first beginnings in the methodological reflections of the → history-of-religions school, added strength being given by form criticism. In *From Tradition to Gospel* (1935) M. Dibelius (1883-1947) linked the question of the development of forms to an attempt to describe the individual forms and genres. P. Vielhauer (1975) gave depth to his methodological discussion by differentiating between literary and preliterary texts. If the premises of Overbeck and the work of Dibelius still dominate modern research, interest now focuses on redefining the genres and synchronous description (K. Berger). At the same time, more attention is paid to the theoretical and sociological aspects related to hermeneutical considerations (→ Hermeneutics) and insight into reception theory. Thus far, however, there has been no methodological synthesis.

2.3. *Rise and Development*
2.3.1. In the first post-Easter beginnings of Christian literature, many genres were potentially present. We may not learn much from distinguishing between the literary and oral, but a wealth of forms characterizes the epoch, even though there may be methodological debate when an attempt is made to relate them to specific texts. We might mention → doxologies (e.g., Eph. 3:20-21), liturgical pieces (Rom. 1:3-4; 1 Tim. 3:16), confessions (Eph. 4:4-6; 1 Tim. 2:5-6; 1 John 4:2; → Confession of Faith), and kerygmatic formulas (1 Cor. 15:3-7; → Kerygma) in the earliest stages (see Vielhauer).

Then we find formulas of sending, commitment, death, resurrection, and exaltation, which may be combined and which in their language, theology, and aesthetics, though Christologically focused, bear witness to the legacy of OT and early Jewish theology. In them, therefore, the → Christology is part of the statement about God and is formulated as a truth. At the same time, such formulas are understandable only if they are read against the background of early theological efforts. They are indissolubly linked to the history of the first churches, though we cannot in every case describe the socioeconomic and sociocultural context (nor should the cultic background be neglected).

Along with these formulas another feature influencing this first literature is the broad stream of the → Jesus tradition, which R. Bultmann, Vielhauer, and Berger have tried to categorize. It includes the diverse sayings traditions: → Wisdom sayings (e.g., Matt. 11:25-26; Mark 13:23, 37), "I" sayings (Mark 2:17; Luke 10:3; 12:49-53), admonitions (Matt. 6:2-13, 16-18; Luke 17:3-4), and → parables (Matt. 25:14-46; Luke 15:3-32). Although the details of this tradition cannot be sorted out unequivocally, it does attest the renewing power of Jesus' sayings. If we then differentiate the stories, the lines of demarcation are not rigid (note the debate between Bultmann and Dibelius about apophthegms vs. paradigms). A narrative unit can end with a saying, and many sayings are embedded in stories. For the more specific narrative tradition we turn to the → miracles traditions (e.g., Mark 1:21-28; 3:1-6; Luke 5:1-11), which are clearly akin to Hellenistic texts. The wealth of the total Jesus tradition relates not merely to that of Jesus' → proclamation but also to the variety of church situations (reassurance, internal discussion, apologetics, and → mission), though in many cases we can only make hypotheses about these situations. The tradition clearly had a formally persistent power, and social conditions were surely mediated and not merely reflected both aesthetically and theologically.

With the Pauline Epistles we have the first intensive use of letters in primitive Christian history. At many points we see kinship to the texts and topics of Hellenistic letters (note the arguments and rhetorical structuring of the Pauline texts; → Rhetoric). Yet there are also considerable differences as the forms and features are adopted in altered ways. The modifications reflect the power of apostolic theology, but the manner of reception also points to the need for communication among widely scattered communities. We see from 1 Thess. 4:13-18 that apocalyptic forms and genres found early adoption (→ Apocalypticism). We finally see at this phase the beginnings of → parenesis (e.g., Phil. 4:8; 1 Thess. 5:14-22), which will take many forms and go beyond immediate needs. Wisdom and Hellenistic-Stoic elements appear (→ Stoicism), but the social setting is that of catechetical instruction.

2.3.2. In the second period of the history of primitive Christian literature, we do not find new forms or genres but a strengthening of the possibilities found already at the first stage. This development is necessarily connected with the fact that writing is the mode. Thus kerygmatic forms are fused and form a new and characteristic unity. Hymns also integrate many formulaic elements but become a genre of their own (Phil. 2:6-11; Col. 1:15-20; 2 Tim. 2:11-13; → Hymn 2). Similar processes apply to apocalyptic and the modified use of the epistle (in the Deutero-Paulines, the → Catholic Epistles, and the → pseudepigrapha).

The further development of form-critical processes that were already in motion applies also to the Jesus tradition with new stories and historical narratives and more miracle stories. In this connection we have the first collections (e.g., the pre-Markan collections, the emergence of a complete → passion narrative, and early forms of the Synoptic apocalypse). → Q is also usually put in this period, though its actual scope is a matter of hypothesis, as is its exact genre, apart from some connection with collections of Wisdom sayings. We certainly cannot say with certainty what groups were behind it or what its actual setting was (→ missionaries? → catechesis?).

As regards the → gospel as a genre, we find parallels in Hellenism and early Judaism, although the gospel stands as a unique form. It cannot be explained merely in terms of the immanent development or kerygmatic structuring of the tradition. It is a sum of accepted traditions. For this reason special importance attaches to the author of Mark and to the theology received by him.

2.3.3. The concluding period of the history of early Christian literature (see also the Apostolic Fathers) influenced the emergence of → John (using extant traditions) and Revelation, as well as the incipient collection of Pauline epistles. Although the initial forms and genres continued, they now became apocryphal. As the churches grew and turned increasingly to the world, however, new forms emerged (e.g., the early apologies), which in their themes and structuring reflect the early Jewish tradition. The same applies to the complex emergence of the Acts of the Apostles, which resembles the Gospels inasmuch as it incorporates formal elements from Hellenistic literature but overall serves only Luke's theological interest.

2.4. Impact

In the transition from the history of primitive Christianity to that of the early church, the literature also underwent some characteristic changes. As the first writings acquired increased authority and a canonical claim was made for them, a need for commentaries on them arose. This development is a first example of the impact (including an aesthetic one) of the primitive literature. With the undisputed presence of the first texts, no new genres developed, but the old forms continued in the form of the apocryphal writings. The process of reception underwent a decisive change with the canon. There was a strong literary trend and a corresponding changed relation between the literature and the social context of the churches.

→ Agrapha; Exegesis, Biblical, 2; Historiography 2; Household Rules; Lord's Prayer; New Testament Era, History of; Pastoral Epistles; Sermon on the Mount

Bibliography: D. E. AUNE, *The NT in Its Literary Environment* (Philadelphia, 1987) • J. L. BAILEY and L. D. VANDER BROEK, *Literary Forms in the NT* (Louisville, Ky., 1992) • W. A. BEARDSLEE, *Literary Criticism of the NT* (Philadelphia, 1970); idem, "Recent Literary Criticism," *The NT and Its Modern Interpreters* (ed. E. Epp and G. W. MacRae; Atlanta, 1989) 175-98 • K. BERGER, *Formgeschichte des Neuen Testaments* (Heidelberg, 1984) • R. E. BROWN, *An Introduction to the NT* (New York, 1997) • R. BULTMANN, *The History of the Synoptic Tradition* (2d ed.; New York, 1968) • M. DIBELIUS, *A Fresh Approach to the NT and Early Christian Literature* (New York, 1936); idem, *From Tradition to Gospel* (New York, 1935) • B. GERHARDSSON, *The Origins of the Gospel Traditions* (Philadelphia, 1979) • E. GÜTTGEMANNS, *Candid Questions concerning Gospel Form Criticism* (Pittsburgh, 1979) • A. J. HULTGREN, *The Parables of Jesus: A Commentary* (Grand Rapids, 2000) • D. H. JUEL, *An Introduction to NT Literature* (Nashville, 1978) • W. H. KELBER, *The Oral and the Written Gospel* (Philadelphia, 1983) • H. KOESTER, *Ancient Christian Gospels: Their History and Development* (Philadelphia, 1990); idem, *Introduction to the NT,* vol. 2, *History and Literature of Early Christianity* (Philadelphia, 1982) • E. McKNIGHT, "Form and Redaction Criticism," *NT and Its Modern Interpreters,* ed. Epp and MacRae, 149-74 • F. OVERBECK, *Über die Anfänge der patristischen Literatur* (Darmstadt, 1966; orig. pub., 1882) • J. M. ROBINSON, *The Critical Edition of Q* (Minneapolis, 2000) • J. T. SANDERS, *The NT Christological Hymns* (Cambridge, 1971) • G. STRECKER, *History of NT Literature* (Harrisburg, Pa., 1997) • G. THEISSEN, *The Miracle Stories of the Early Christian Tradition* (Philadelphia, 1983) • P. VIELHAUER, *Geschichte der urchristlichen Literatur* (Berlin, 1975).

HENNING PAULSEN†

3. Early Church
3.1. *Christian Literature and the Tradition of Antiquity*

This section deals with the religious literature composed by Christians in the period of the → early church. Secular works by Christian authors belong here only in an extended sense. Early Christian writings are the main source of our knowledge of the history and teaching of the early church. As part of the literature of late antiquity, these writings document historically the momentous synthesis between antiquity and Christianity.

In a way that is hard to imagine, the Greek and Latin literature of the imperial period (→ Roman Empire) was tied to conventions in genre, style, and vocabulary. Classicism was dominant and supplied models from the past. Education was primarily in the art of → rhetoric (§1) and was accordingly offered by the schools dedicated to that art. Authors and readers alike were brought under the same formal claims. From the second century on, Christian literature adjusted to this situation for two reasons. First, it had to meet the standards if it was to be read by the upper classes of the empire, that is, senators, the elite in the cities, and officials. Second, Christian writers were trained in the same schools and naturally wrote in the forms they had learned. Up to the sixth century the church did little to change the schools of antiquity, with their pagan norms. The church might criticize the literary and rhetorical arts used by pagans and heretics, but it also accepted them in the service of its own → truth.

3.2. *The Special Language of the Bible and the Early Church*

The Greek and Latin Bible constituted a special problem, since it seemed to be a literary monstrosity that put off educated readers. The church found two different solutions to the problem. On the one hand, the argument ran that the divine Word has no need of literary forms, as the success of missions showed. On the other hand, an effort was made to show that all the genres and styles of Greek and Roman literature are present in the Bible, as argued by → Jerome and → Augustine.

The orientation to the Bible and its literary form is the most important element common to all early Christian literature. The influence of the Bible, along with many new semantic coinings, led to the development of a special early Christian language. Greek loanwords were another special feature in Latin Christianity (C. Mohrmann).

3.3. *Christian Literature in the Second and Third Centuries*
3.3.1. *Greek*

In keeping with the course of Christian → mission (§3), Greek was the first language used in Christian literature. Even in the West Greek was used, since there too Christianity came first to groups that spoke Greek. A Christian Latin literature developed only toward the end of the second century. Though this literature had many original features, by and large it was still dependent on the Greek and achieved its prime only in the fourth century.

Primeval Christian literature (F. Overbeck) — that is, the NT writings and those of the older → Apostolic Fathers — had a subliterary character, judging by the standards of antiquity. Yet one should not simply describe them as popular. One may detect influences on this literature from Hellenistic Judaism and also some efforts toward literary stylization.

The second-century → apologists were the first to direct their works to pagan readers. They presented divine truth and the moral blamelessness of Christians in a language that educated readers would find familiar. To this end they used different genres, including petition to the emperor, legal pleas, exhortation, teaching, debate, and dialogue. Stylistically, the range covers the simple diction of the philosopher → Justin Martyr (d. ca. 165) in his two apologies (ca. 155 and 161), the lofty prose of Tatian (*Oratio ad Graecos* [ca. 165]) and Athenagoras (*Supplication* [ca. 177]), and the brilliant, exhortatory style of the so-called *Epistle to Diognetus* (ca. 200). → Apologetics reached a scholarly climax with the work of Origen (*C. Cels.* [after 245]).

The first to achieve a lofty literary style, to judge from extant Greek fragments, were educated → Gnostics who wrote tractates, sermons, letters, and poems in classical meters, as well as the first exegetical works on NT texts (e.g., Heracleon's *Commentary on John*). → Preaching gradually took rhetorical form, but the oldest surviving sermon, the so-called *2 Clement* (ca. 150; → Apostolic Fathers 2.3.2.) is a simple work. The Easter Sermon of Melito of Sardis (d. ca. 190) is already, however, a brilliant piece of "Asian" rhetoric.

New demands in the second century gave rise to new forms. The martyr literature used either the form of narrative, often in letters, or the mostly fictitious record (→ Martyrs, Acts of the). Writings against → heresies range from the short list of errors after the model of the philosophical doxography (the oldest example is Justin's lost *Tractate against All Heresies*) to the more explicit refutation in several books, which also contain positive expositions of the church's teaching (→ Irenaeus, *Adversus omnes haereses* [ca. 180/190], and Hippolytus, *Refutatio omnium haeresium* [after 222]). Doctrinal and edifying tractates cover some of the same ground as sermons and letters. The letters of important personalities were collected and handed down, including the seven epistles of → Ignatius of Antioch (d. ca. 107; → Apostolic Fathers 2.4). The collec-

tions of the letters of Dionysius of Corinth (second half of the 2nd cent.) and Origen have been lost.

Easter epistles became a practice in Alexandria from the third century onward. The → bishop would announce the date of → Easter to the churches in Egypt and take a position on disputed issues. → Church orders with legal and liturgical rulings have come down from, for example, Syria and Egypt. From the time of the *Didache* (→ Apostolic Fathers 2.1), claims were laid to apostolic sanction, the most extensive text being the *Apostolic Constitutions* of the late fourth century. Hippolytus of Rome (d. ca. 236), however, issued his *Apostolic Tradition* (ca. 215) in his own name.

The beginnings of Christian universal histories may be seen in the *World Chronicles* of Julius Africanus (d. ca. 250) and Hippolytus (d. ca. 236). Christian novels served to edify and entertain. Along with apocryphal acts (→ Apocrypha 2.2) we might mention the Clementine literature, including *Recognitions* in Latin and *Homilies* in Greek (both 4th cent.).

The first author to attain eminence as a writer and philosopher was Clement of Alexandria (d. ca. 215; → Alexandrian Theology). His *Protrepticus* is a summons, in the style of philosophical persuasion, to his readers to become Christians. His *Paedagogus* is a hortatory work with directions for a Christian → lifestyle. The *Stromateis* (Miscellanies), written in a style common to antiquity, offers philosophical and antiheretical teaching for advanced Christians. The Christian hymn at the end of the *Paedagogus* is the oldest surviving Christian poem in classical style apart from those written by Gnostics.

As a scholar Clement was surpassed by Origen (d. ca. 254; → Origenism). Origen wrote shorter and longer Bible commentaries that satisfied every philological demand. His exegetical homilies are more spiritual in character. His *De principiis* works out a system of Christian doctrine on the basis of the → rule of faith. Obviously made up of a series of tractates, it can hardly be called a dogmatics or a systematic theology. He wrote in a scholarly prose appropriate to his subjects, without embellishments.

Unlike Origen, who was first an independent teacher and only later a presbyter (→ Elder), his pupil Dionysius of Alexandria (d. ca. 265) represents the educated, literary, and ecclesiastically active bishop who came increasingly to dominate the field. The remains of his writings and letters on questions of philosophy, exegesis, church law, and the doctrine of the Trinity show him to have been a writer of high rank.

The most important critic of Origen in the third century was Methodius of Olympus (d. ca. 311). Of literary importance was his *Symposium*. In this work, which is a counterpart to Plato's dialogue of the same name, 12 virgins extol the ascetic life.

3.3.2. *Latin*

Latin Christian literature was inaugurated by the work of → Tertullian (d. ca. 225). His 31 extant writings contain apologetic, antiheretical, dogmatic, hortatory, and polemical tractates. They are in rhetorical style and are composed in a virtuoso, highly original, literary language. We might mention his *Apology*, which is given the form of a judicial plea to the provincial rulers of the Roman Empire. Tertullian's literary individuality protected him from imitation. His turning to → Montanism (ca. 207) also weakened his influence. Minucius Felix (d. ca. 250), who was clearly dependent on Tertullian, followed a Ciceronian model in his apologetic dialogue *Octavius*.

The writings and letters of → Cyprian of Carthage (d. 258) made a great impact on the church. They gave his opinion on pastoral, legal, and ecclesiological matters, arising out of the Decian → persecution, the Novatian schism, and → heretical baptism (→ Lapsi; Baptism). Special mention must be made of his classic ecclesiological work *De ecclesiae catholicae unitate*. Cyprian was trained in rhetoric but set it aside in favor of a biblical vocabulary. He avoided classical reminiscences. His style has been described as curial. The Pseudo-Cyprianic *De aleatoribus* (On dice players) was probably a sermon, the oldest extant in Latin. Though it echoes Cyprian, its language is popular.

The presbyter and later rival bishop Novatian (d. 257/58) was the first Roman Christian to write a theological work in Latin: *De Trinitate*. The oldest biblical commentary in Latin, an exposition of Revelation, was by Victorinus of Pettau (d. ca. 304). Latin martyr literature resembles Greek. *Acts of the Scillitan Martyrs* was written in the protocol form (North Africa, ca. 180). The *Passion of Perpetua and Felicity* (an account of the martyrs, ca. 203) and Cyprian's *Acta proconsularia* (258) are in narrative style. Pontius (d. ca. 260) wrote a life of Cyprian, the first Christian biography. It begins only with Cyprian's baptism and gives most space to his martyrdom. The most important ante-Nicene translation in the West was that of the Greek Bible into Latin, the *Vetus Latina* (→ Bible Versions 2.3).

3.4. *Christian Literature in the Fourth and Fifth Centuries*

3.4.1. *Greek*

The change in relations between → church and state that came with Emperor Constantine (306-37) led to an upsurge in Christian literature. In the fourth century works of both academic and artistic brilliance abounded. Variations on traditional genres accompanied the use of new ones.

The learned Eusebius of Caesarea (d. ca. 340) wrote a world history, the *Chronicles*, preserved in Syriac, Armenian, and Latin translations, which as a result of translation and continuation by Jerome (ca. 345-420), was very influential in the West as well. Eusebius also wrote the first church history, best known as *Ecclesiastical History*. In this work's last edition (324), it led up to the sole rule of Constantine. Divine promises were seen to come to fulfillment in the peace between church and empire. The work combines rhetorical stylization according to the rules of the historiography of antiquity with invaluable quotations from older works, so that the style resembles that of a learned collection of documents. This history became the basis and model for all later church histories (→ Historiography 3.2), of which we might mention those of Socrates (d. 450), written after 439, Sozomen (fl. early 5th cent.), and Theodoret of Cyrrhus (ca. 393-ca. 460). With his *Life of Constantine* (after 337), a panegyric to the Christian emperor, Eusebius founded the Christian ruler-ideology of the Byzantine Empire (→ Byzantium; Emperor Worship).

Apologetics in the fourth century took the form of learned debate with pagan philosophy (→ Greek Philosophy) and religion. An outstanding example is the double work of Eusebius, *Preparation for the Gospel* and *Demonstration of the Gospel*. Along similar lines are *Against the Gentiles* and *Incarnation of the Word* (ca. 335/37) by → Athanasius (ca. 297-373). The climax here was the classic presentation of the → incarnation. The most significant Greek apology of the fifth century was *Graecarum affectionum curatio* (Healing of Greek diseases), by Theodoret.

Preaching involved a revival of the rhetoric of antiquity, since it offered possibilities no longer at the command of pagan orators under the dictatorship of the late Roman Empire. The great → Cappadocians and John → Chrysostom (ca. 347-407) were equal if not superior to the great pagan orators. The three main types of sermons were the hortatory, the exegetical, and the panegyric (on feast days). Clarity and simplicity were the rule (→ Rhetoric 2). As the church calendar developed in the fourth and fifth centuries, occasions for the panegyric sermon increased, which gave more scope for the adornment of rhetoric. Exegetical preaching had some affinity to the biblical commentary; series of exegetical sermons might often be published as extended exposition. The great theologians of Antioch, Diodore of Tarsus (d. ca. 390) and Theodore of Mopsuestia (ca. 350-428), composed grammatical-historical commentaries (→ Antiochian Theology).

There were many special works of theology and parenesis. Letters were collected and published for both their ecclesiastical importance and their literary quality (e.g., the collections of the letters of Basil of Caesarea [ca. 330-79], Gregory of Nazianzus [329/30-389/90], and Synesius of Cyrene [ca. 370-ca. 413]). The Arian controversy (→ Arianism; Trinity) and the Christological controversies (→ Christology 2) gave rise to many dogmatic and polemical works from the early fourth century onward. Preaching and exegetical literature might also have a polemical purpose (→ Polemics). Arius (ca. 280-336) composed his *Thaleia* (Banquet) in what seems to be a mixture of prose and verse. Dialogue was also a common polemical form (→ Cyril of Alexandria [ca. 375-444], Theodoret). The church's dogma took shape in this literature. In the fourth century we must mention especially the classic *Orations against the Arians*, written between 340 and 346 by Athanasius. He also created a new form of polemical treatise with official documents appended to them (see, e.g., *On the Rulings of the Synod of Nicaea* [350/51] and his *Second Apology* [357]).

The great Cappadocians — Basil, Gregory of Nazianzus, and Gregory of Nyssa (ca. 330-ca. 395) — wrote in the final phase of the Arian controversy. From the standpoint of both thought and literature, their work is the high point of the Greek literature of the early church. Basil's work *On the → Holy Spirit* (375) rounds off the doctrine of the Trinity by teaching the full deity of the Spirit. Its combination of careful theological argument and personal religious statement makes this work one of the most important early dogmatic writings. Gregory of Nazianzus, a master of rhetoric, gave classical expression to the orthodox doctrine of the Trinity in his five *Theological Orations* (380). Gregory of Nyssa, finally, demolished all the devices of the Arians in his *Books against Eunomius*.

The learned and very productive Apollinaris the Younger of Laodicea (ca. 310-ca. 390) fought the Arians but himself became a heretic with his bold attempt to solve the problem of the incarnation theoretically. His main work was his *Exposition of the Divine Incarnation* (→ Incarnation 2.2.3). Bishop Epiphanius of Salamis (ca. 315-403) continued the tradition of listing heresies. In his comprehensive but clumsy *Panarion* (Medicine chest) he refuted 80 heresies, including from his own time those of the Arians, Apollinarians, and Messalians (an ascetic re-

vival movement; → Monasticism 4.2). The value of this work lies in its quotations.

In the theological controversies of the fifth century, the appeal to past authority became increasingly important. The patristic appeal played a significant part, and the dogmatic florilegium emerged as a literary genre. The → catena (or collection of traditional exegesis) was an exegetical parallel from the end of the fifth century onward.

As the church received state recognition, confessions (→ Confession of Faith), doctrinal writings, and synodical rulings (→ Councils of the Church) took on an official character. Synodical acts and canons were collected, often with a particular ecclesiastical goal in mind.

A special position was occupied by the writings appearing at the end of the fifth century under the name of Dionysius the Areopagite (see Acts 17:34), now known most commonly as Dionysius the Pseudo-Areopagite. These works fused the Neoplatonic and Christian traditions (→ Platonism), making a great impact in both the East and, as a result of translation in the ninth century, the West (→ Church 2.2.6).

Monasticism, which developed in the fourth century, contributed many works and forms. The sayings of the Desert Fathers were handed down quite early in collections (*Apophthegmata Patrum*). Writings on the ascetic life range from rules and practical directions to the speculative theory of the mystical ascent of the soul to God (→ Mysticism). Special note should be taken of the rule of Pachomius (ca. 290-346) and the *Asketikon* of Basil of Caesarea (with longer and shorter rules for Eastern monasticism). We should mention, too, the *Spiritual Homilies* possibly written by the Messalian, Simeon of Mesopotamia (5th cent.), and the many works of Evagrius Ponticus (346-99), who adopted the form of the "sentences" of popular philosophy and espoused an Origenist theology. Monastic writings could also verge on hagiography (→ Saints, Veneration of).

A pioneering work in this regard was Athanasius's *Life of Anthony*, which depicted the hermit life as the path to true holiness, helped to promote monasticism, and became a model for later lives of the saints. Along with the lives of martyrs these works increasingly took on legendary features. In addition to individual lives we find accounts of ascetics (→ Asceticism) over whole regions, such as *History of the Monks in Egypt* (ca. 400), the *Historia Lausiaca* of Palladius (419/20, d. between 420 and 430), and the *Religious History* of Theodoret.

Christian poetry took two forms: poetry in classical meters (Gregory of Nazianzus, Synesius) and singable liturgical poetry (→ Liturgy). The latter, taking its rhythm from word accents rather than the quantity of syllables, found its models in the Bible and the synagogue. This liturgical poetry reached an artistic climax in the works of Romanos Melodus, who was perhaps a conflation of two persons.

3.4.2. Latin

Latin Christian literature developed astonishingly in the fourth century. Already by the end of the century, it was at least equal in quality to pagan literature. Traditional genres were consciously adopted, and with a Christian orientation, works rivaling the pagan were produced. A biblically based literary aesthetics found theoretical defenders in Jerome (*Ep.* 53 and 58) and Augustine (*De doc. Christ.* 4). Lactantius (ca. 250-ca. 325), who was an admirer of Cicero (106-43 B.C.), pioneered this development. He addressed educated pagans both in a philosophical apology, *The Divine Institutions,* and in his work of historical apologetics, *The Deaths of Persecutors.* Hilary of Poitiers (ca. 315-ca. 367) wrote biblical commentaries and also took part in the Arian controversy. Typical of the age was the conversion of the rhetorician and philosopher Marius Victorinus Afer (4th cent.), who wrote commentaries on Paul and made a philosophically significant contribution to Trinitarian teaching.

Ambrose of Milan (ca. 339-97) was a brilliant preacher and expositor and also a defender of Nicene orthodoxy (→ Nicaea, Councils of). His work on the ministry *De officiis ministrorum,* a kind of ethics for clergy, was written after the model of Cicero's *De officiis.* Jerome combined asceticism with writing. He was an exegete and Bible translator who also wrote edifying and polemical works and has left behind what are from a literary standpoint brilliant letters. In exegesis we should note the commentaries on Paul written 360-80 by the so-called Ambrosiaster (or Pseudo-Ambrose). The expositions of Paul by Marius Victorinus, Pelagius (who taught in Rome in the late 4th and early 5th cents.; → Pelagianism), and Augustine offer testimony to the fourth-century Pauline renaissance, which had such an influence on Western theology.

For all its high formal quality, the pre-Augustinian Christian literature of the West was intellectually still indebted to Greek theology. We see this connection in the active work of translation that became necessary as Greek was less well known. Especially Rufinus of Aquileia (ca. 345-411) and Jerome provided important Greek texts for the Western Middle Ages with their renderings of Origen, Eusebius, and monastic writings. From a philological and literary standpoint Jerome's translation of the Bible (known since the 13th cent. as the Vulgate) is an outstanding achievement.

Among hagiographic and monastic works we may mention not only the lives of Jerome and the edifying and partly fictional life of Anthony by Athanasius but also the *Life of Martin of Tours* and the *Dialogues of Martin* by Sulpicius Severus (ca. 360-ca. 430). Practical and spiritual questions of the monastic life constitute the substance of the main works of John Cassian (ca. 360-after 430), his *Institutes* and *Collations of the Fathers.* A mature summary of early Christian monastic experience may be found in the *Rule* of → Benedict of Nursia (ca. 480-ca. 547; → Benedictines).

In the fourth century the rapid development of → pilgrimages to Palestine produced a practical travel literature. The *Itinerarium Egeriae* has particular charm. It is a lively account of the pilgrimage to the Holy Land undertaken by the lady Egeria (ca. 381-84), written in good popular style.

Augustine (354-430) stands out above almost every other early theologian as a philosophical and theological thinker (→ Augustine's Theology). As a writer, too, he is a master of educated rhetoric. Cicero is the model for his early writings. His immense output as presbyter and bishop makes sparing use of the rhetorical arts at his disposal. In his sermons, including *Enarrationes in Psalmos* and *In Evangelium Iohannis Tractatus,* he employs simple rhetorical devices (even rhyme on occasion) to attract his readers. His *Confessions* (ca. 400) is a masterpiece of world literature. Written in the form of prayer, it describes Augustine's life as an example of God's gracious working within the framework of his creative action. The work smoothly fuses together biblical terminology and rhetorical style; there is no literary model for it. Augustine's erudite *City of God* (413-26) addresses the Christian and pagan elite. Begun as an apology, it surpasses all previous efforts in this direction with its sketch of a → theology of history. It thus became the basis of the medieval understanding of history and the cosmos.

Stimulated by Augustine, Orosius (early 5th cent.) wrote a world history (417/18) along similar lines, *Historiae adversus paganos.* Salvian of Marseilles (ca. 400-ca. 480) wrote a theological interpretation of the history of the time. In the political upheavals caused by the barbarian invasions, he found a divine judgment (*De gubernatione dei* [440]).

After modest beginnings, with Commodian (fl. middle 3d cent.), Christian poetry underwent expansive development in the 4th century. Epic paraphrases of biblical books were written for readers familiar with Virgil (70-19 B.C.). Juvencus (early 4th cent.) wrote a paraphrase of the Gospels. The *Cento* (ca. 360) of Proba, a "patchwork poem" composed of verses from Virgil, dealt with prehistory and redemption. Sedulius wrote an Easter poem (*Carmen Paschale* [ca. 450]). Hilary of Poitiers and especially Ambrose composed hymns in classical meter for congregational use. Pope Damasus I (366-84) extolled the Roman martyrs in epigrams. The supreme Christian poet of the fourth century was Prudentius (348-ca. 410). His poems, in almost all the classical genres, seem to have followed a master plan. They were to be the Christian counterpart to the poetry of antiquity. Outstanding is the *Psychomachia*, the first Christian allegorical poem (→ Allegory). It depicts the battle between personified → virtues and vices.

The political and philosophical victory of Christianity made it possible for one and the same author to follow both Christian and pagan literary traditions. Most impressive in this regard was Boethius (ca. 480-524), who wrote philosophical and theological works and translated Aristotle (→ Aristotelianism) and Porphyry (d. ca. 303). Condemned to death by Theodoric (471-526) for high treason, Boethius composed in prison his *Consolation of Philosophy*, a dialogue with personified philosophy written for his own comfort. Showing full mastery of ancient literary tradition, the work also contains many poems, but the author's Christianity emerges only in veiled form. In the Middle Ages Boethius was honored as a martyr, and his *Consolation* was read as a work of Christian edification (→ Devotional Literature).

3.5. *Christian Literature in the Near East*
In the territories on both sides of the eastern frontier of the Roman Empire, Christian literature developed in popular form (in Syriac, Armenian, Georgian, Coptic, Ethiopian, and Arabic). Usually, Bible translation formed the starting point, and there were also translations of Greek literature.

An original Christian literature of a high level emerged in, especially, Syria. Its national and religious individuality was strengthened by the decision the Syrians made for → Nestorianism and → Monophysitism. Authors included Bardesanes (Bar-Daisan) of Edessa (154-222), Aphrahat (early 4th cent.), and Ephraem Syrus (ca. 306-73), who was equally significant as an exegete, a writer against heresy, and a poet.

3.6. *Transmission*
In virtue of the importance attached to orthodox theologians of the past (→ Church Fathers) in both Byzantium and the West, their works were continu-

ally copied. Priority was often given, however, to contemporary interests, with the result that many significant works were lost. Much of the literature of the past, including from before Nicaea, was either not handed down at all or only partially so. Thus most of the second-century Greek apologetic writings that we have, we owe to only one codex, that which was prepared in 914 for the learned Bishop Arethas of Caesarea (ca. 850-944; Codex Parisinus Graecus 451). From the fourth century, heretical works were destroyed, and their possession was forbidden. Consequently, we know this literature only from quotations in works written against it or from its being handed down under orthodox names. Many works of authors who were declared heretics (e.g., Origenists, Nestorians, Monophysites) have been preserved in Near Eastern translations.

3.7. *Research*
Scholarly interest in early Christian literature began in the → modern period with the humanists in the 15th and 16th centuries (→ Humanism). Finding in the church fathers an ideal synthesis of antiquity and Christianity, they published the first printed editions of the Greek and Latin writers. From the days of the → Reformation, both polemics and efforts at reunion have had recourse to the early Christian texts (→ Ecumenism, Ecumenical Movement). In the 17th and 18th centuries Roman Catholic and Anglican scholars prepared monumental editions and historical interpretations, some of which are still in use today.

Modern historical and philological research began in the 18th century. Traditional positions were critically examined, chronology was amended, new texts were discovered and published, many critical editions came out, and several important collections (esp. CSEL, GCS, PO, and CSCO) were initiated. Protestants set out to publish all early authors, including heretics, in contrast to dogma-oriented patrology (→ Patristics). Classical philologists fostered the integration of Christian literature into that of antiquity.

Gaps remained, however. On the one hand, theological research often neglected questions of style and genre. On the other, classical philologists disparaged everything Christian and the supposedly decadent late antiquity. In the 20th century parties and programs came closer together. It was seen that simple interpretive models like "antique form" and "Christian content" are inadequate. Theological and philological scholars are now studying together both the innovations of Christian authors and the ways in which they adopted and transformed classical styles and genres.

Bibliography: B. ALTANER, *Patrology* (New York, 1960) • O. BARDENHEWER, *Geschichte der altkirchlichen Literatur* (5 vols.; Freiburg, 1902-32) • P. M. BLOWERS, A. R. CHRISTMAN, D. G. HUNTER, and R. D. YOUNG, eds., *In Dominico Eloquio–In Lordly Eloquence: Essays on Patristic Exegesis in Honor of Robert Louis Wilken* (Grand Rapids, 2002) • H. VON CAMPENHAUSEN, *The Fathers of the Greek Church* (London, 1963); idem, *The Fathers of the Latin Church* (London, 1964) • F. L. CROSS, *The Early Christian Fathers* (London, 1960) • W. H. C. FREND, *The Rise of Christianity* (Philadelphia, 1984) • E. J. GOODSPEED, *A History of Early Christian Literature* (Chicago, 1966) • R. M. GRANT, *Greek Apologists of the Second Century* (Philadelphia, 1988) • P. J. HAMELL, *Introduction to Patrology* (Cork, Ire., 1968) • C. MOHRMANN, *Études sur le latin des chrétiens* (4 vols.; Rome, 1958-77) • J. PELIKAN, *The Christian Tradition: A History of the Development of Doctrine,* vol. 1, *The Emergence of the Christian Tradition (100-600)* (Chicago, 1971) • J. QUASTEN, *Patrology* (3 vols.; Westminster, Md., 1950-60) • W. G. RUSCH, *The Later Latin Fathers* (London, 1977) • O. DE URBINA, *Patrologia Syriaca* (Rome, 1965) • F. YOUNG, *From Nicaea to Chalcedon: A Guide to the Literature and Its Background* (Philadelphia, 1983) • N. ZERNOV, *Eastern Christendom: A Study of the Origin and Development of the Eastern Orthodox Church* (London, 1961).

GERHARD MAY

Lithuania

	1960	1980	2000
Population (1,000s):	2,779	3,421	3,690
Annual growth rate (%):	1.34	0.78	−0.24

Area: 65,301 sq. km. (25,213 sq. mi.)

A.D. *2000*

Population density: 57/sq. km. (146/sq. mi.)
Births / deaths: 1.08 / 1.21 per 100 population
Fertility rate: 1.50 per woman
Infant mortality rate: 11 per 1,000 live births
Life expectancy: 71.3 years (m: 65.8, f: 76.8)
Religious affiliation (%): Christians 87.7 (Roman Catholics 82.4, Orthodox 3.1, Protestants 1.4, other Christians 1.0), nonreligious 11.1, other 1.2.

1. Historical Overview
2. Current Situation
3. Religious Situation

1. Historical Overview

Ancient Baltic culture can be traced to around 2500 B.C., when local cultures began to merge with newly arrived Indo-Europeans. The pre-Christian religion, largely known from a few shrines still being uncovered by archaeologists, was Indo-European in origin and, while it changed considerably over time, had a certain correspondence to the pantheons of other religions (→ Paganism).

In about A.D. 1240 Mindaugas (d. 1263) became the ruler of Lithuania and was able to unite the unruly duchies of the area. In 1251 he was, largely for political reasons, baptized and received the title of king from the → pope, although most of the dukes and the people retained the indigenous non-Christian religion. The official Christianization of Lithuania began in 1387 under the grand duke of Lithuania, Jogaila (1351-1434), who confederated his country with Poland and ultimately became King Władysław II of Poland. For several centuries the history of Lithuania was bound up with the history of Poland; through the Union of Lublin (1569) the two states were merged as equal partners in a Polish-Lithuanian confederation.

As the Polish-Lithuanian government collapsed in the 1700s, the Russian Empire moved in, annexing most of Lithuania by 1795. The people rebelled against Russian rule in 1831 and again in 1863 but failed to gain independence. The Russians repressed the people, prohibiting the printing of books in Lithuanian and closing their schools. During this period there was a significant emigration to the United States.

In 1905 a conference of elected representatives demanded self-government for the Lithuanian people within the Russian state, but this demand was rejected. During World War I the country was occupied by Germany. At its first opportunity, on February 16, 1918, Lithuania declared independence from both Russia and Germany and established a democratic system of government, the first of the Baltic States to do so (→ Nation, Nationalism).

Its independence, however, was short-lived, as the country was threatened by its several neighbors. After the end of the war Russia attempted to overtake the country but was defeated by the Lithuanians in 1920. That same year Poland occupied Vilnius, the capital city, holding it until 1939. Germany seized part of Lithuania in March 1939. Then, after a German-Russian agreement later that year gave Russia control of the Baltic region, the Russians occupied all of Lithuania in 1940 and made it a Soviet republic with a Communist government.

After the Germans invaded Russia, the Lithuanians revolted against the Soviets and again established their own government. Soon, however, the Germans once more conquered the country, occupying it until 1944, when the Russians again took over. Lithuania existed as a Soviet state until 1990 when, as Eastern Europe became free, it became the Republic of Lithuania.

2. Current Situation

The present-day Lithuania is the southernmost of the three Baltic States, all lying along the eastern shore of the Baltic Sea. The countryside is predominantly low lying, with many lakes and swamps. Forests cover 30 percent of Lithuania; 54 percent of the land is devoted to agriculture. Ethnically, 81 percent of the people in the year 2001 were Lithuanian, 9 percent Russian, 7 percent Polish, and 2 percent Belorussian.

Relations with Russia have improved, though unresolved issues remain. The last Russian troops withdrew from Lithuania in 1993. A border agreement with Russia was signed by both presidents in October 1997. In June 2000 Parliament passed a de-Sovietization law, and a delegation was authorized to negotiate with Russia for reparations for the 50 years of Soviet occupation.

Since gaining its independence, Lithuania has actively pursued closer ties with the West. In January 1994 it joined NATO's Partnership for Peace program, and in June of that year it became an associate partner of the European Union (EU). February 2000 saw the first formal accession negotiations to join the EU, and in May 2000 Lithuania led the prospective members of the second wave of enlargement of NATO.

In the 1990s the political development of independence and the forging of closer political ties to the West had parallel features in Lithuania's economic progress. The main feature has been a move toward a private economic structure from the state-regulated regime known during the Soviet occupation. By 2000 the economic situation, rocky throughout the 1990s, improved somewhat. The gross domestic product grew by more than 2 percent in 2000, and that year and the next saw healthy increases in both imports and exports. Such factors fueled hopes for success in Lithuania's EU application process.

3. Religious Situation

Until the 13th century Christianity was prevented from spreading in Lithuania by the country's weak ties with Christian lands, by the absence of a strong national state, and by confrontation with German crusaders, the Teutonic Knights. At the time of Jogaila the country began to become Christian when the official pagan cult was destroyed.

The → Reformation of the 16th century made a significant impact in Lithuania through the efforts of nobles who had studied at universities in Wittenberg and Leipzig, where → Lutheranism was strong. A weak → Roman Catholic Church made the spread of the Reformation possible, and by midcentury Lithuania was predominantly Protestant.

In 1564, however, the king of Lithuania and Poland, Sigismund II Augustus (1520-72), undertook to implement the decisions of the Council of → Trent (1545-63), both to reform the Roman Catholic Church and to stop the spread of → Protestantism. In 1570 the → Jesuits established a college in Vilnius that King Stephen Báthory transformed into a university in 1579, which became a significant educational institution in the region. The growth of Roman Catholicism led inexorably to the weakening of Protestant influence.

During periods of Russian dominance there were serious efforts to assimilate Lithuania culturally and religiously, which meant making the country → Orthodox. Such attempts, however, ultimately proved unsuccessful.

When Lithuania gained its independence in 1918, it granted equal rights to all religious confessions. A → concordat with the Vatican in 1926, however, established the privileged position of that church and gave to it the dominant religious position. Only about 5 percent of the country was Lutheran or Reformed. There were also small representations of → Baptists, → Methodists, Seventh-day → Adventists, → Pentecostals, the New → Apostolic Church, and the → Jehovah's Witnesses — all established in the latter 19th and early 20th centuries. In addition, the internationally famous Lithuanian philosopher Vilius Storosta (1868-1953), known as Vydunas, was influential in advocating a return to the indigenous Lithuanian pagan religion, called Romuva.

The present post-Soviet religious situation is built on the effects of recent history, not least the prolonged occupations both by Nazi Germany and the Soviet Union. Since the breakup of the Soviet Union and subsequent moves to independence, major dark shadows remain in the background, most vivid of which was the destruction of the Jewish → ghetto in Vilnius, now marked only by a simple plaque and countless clouds of memories in the minds of → Holocaust survivors (→ Judaism). Currently the Jewish community represents only 0.2 percent of the population.

Of the confessing Christian population, the dominant community is Roman Catholic. With the annexation of Lithuania by the Soviet Union, the Roman Catholic Church became a vital element in the resistance movement through the 1940s. Despite severe repression during the Soviet era, in 1995 it comprised two archdioceses based in Vilnius and Kaunas. In the four diocesan entities there were 715 congregations, two theological seminaries, and a few convents and monasteries.

The next largest Christian communities in 2000 were → Russian Orthodox, → Old Believers (Bezpopovtsy, or priestless, sect), and Protestants, including Lutherans and Reformed. A small Muslim community remains (→ Islam), having descended from Tatars who settled in the 14th century. They too suffered severely under the 50 years of Communist domination. In the 1990s the number of Pentecostals and charismatics grew to over 50,000 adherents, many drawn from existing church memberships.

Relations between → church and state have been transformed since the departure of the Soviet influence in 1989. There is current recognition of rights for all religious groups, although there are two levels of legal status for religious communities. The Law on Religious Communities and Associations (1995) recognizes nine "traditional" religious communities that have formed a part of the Lithuanian cultural, social, and spiritual heritage: Roman Catholics, Greek Catholics (→ Uniate Churches), Evangelical Lutherans, Evangelical Reformed, Russian Orthodox, Old Believers, Jews, Sunni Muslims, and Karaites (a Jewish movement accepting only the Hebrew Bible, not the Talmud). Other religious groups are eligible for state recognition after 25 years of official registration in Lithuania. State recognition provides for some tax privileges, permission to teach religion in public schools, and time on national television. These opportunities have resulted in a renewal of growth for Roman Catholics in particular. The new freedom has also given hope for both the Muslim and the Jewish communities.

Bibliography: R. ABDELAL, "Lithuania: Toward Europe and the West," National Purpose in the World Economy: Post-Soviet States in Comparative Perspective (Ithaca, N.Y., 2001) chap. 4 • M. ALISAUSKIENE and D. GLODENIS, "Lithuania," RelW 3.794-96 • A. ASHBOURNE, Lithuania: The Rebirth of a Nation, 1991-1994 (Lanham, Md., 1999) • M. BOURDEAUX, Land of Crosses: The Struggle for Religious Freedom in Lithuania, 1939-1978 (Devon, U.K., 1979) • R. BUTTERWICK, ed., The Polish-Lithuanian Monarchy in European Context, c. 1500-1795 (New York, 2001) • R. J. KRICKUS, Showdown: The Lithuanian Rebellion and the Breakup of the Soviet Empire (Washington, D.C., 1997) • A. T. LANE, Lithuania Stepping Westward (London, 2001) • J. RIMAITIS, Religion in Lithuania (Vilnius, 1971) • S. SUZIEDELIS, The Sword and the Cross: A History of the Church in Lithuania (Huntington, Ind., 1988).
                                                        THE EDITORS

Liturgical Books

1. Development and Types
2. Roman Catholic Church
3. Eastern Churches
4. Protestant Churches
5. North America
6. Third World Churches in North America

1. Development and Types

1.1. The *Bible* is the oldest and most basic liturgical book for Christian → worship. With the OT the first churches took over from the → synagogue the liturgical reading of Scripture, a practice that is inseparably linked to the formation of the NT → canon. Just as the Hebrew Scriptures and then the Greek translation of those Scriptures were the primary books to be read in the assembly, so the churches began to assemble lists of books and collections of books, later included in the full NT, that could be regarded as having the authority necessary for communal reading. The NT itself already evidences this growing process of collection with its references to the early uses of the letters of Paul (Col. 4:16; 1 Thess. 5:27).

The canon was first of all a list of books for the assembly. As these books were brought together in collections, Christians most frequently favored the use of the *codex,* the bound, hand-copied volume that could easily be carried and used from house assembly to house assembly, rather than the scroll, which required a treasury and a special building.

1.2. At first the one who presided at worship selected the passages that were to be read, but soon it became a habit to mark off the readings in → Bible MSS. Regular lectionaries then developed (→ Readings, Scripture). The origins and early contents of these lectionaries, understood as lists of readings, remain largely inaccessible to us, but we do have such lists from fourth-century → Jerusalem and from eighth-century → Rome. Subsequently, actual liturgical books containing only these readings would sometimes be prepared: *evangelaries,* containing the appointed readings from the Gospels; *epistolaries,* containing readings from the apostolic letters; or full *lectionaries,* containing all the readings for celebrations of the → Eucharist.

1.3. At first the president had the task of formulating many of the → prayers, especially the great prayer of the Eucharist. Themes, texts, and models were available, as we see from early *church orders* such as the *Didache* and the *Apostolic Tradition.* These → church orders themselves, however, which were not actual liturgical books but essays on communal life including patterns for the communal → liturgy, represented the beginning of a tendency to enforce certain patterns of prayer in regional churches. In the end, written prayers began to be circulated. In the West, *libelli* (sheets with eucharistic formularies) were then an early stage of the *sacramentaries,* which provided full texts.

These texts traveled north in Carolingian times and were part of a massive Germanic inculturation of Christian liturgy. They returned to Rome as a Frankish-Germanic-Roman mix that was subsequently regarded as the "Roman liturgy." Important types or families of sacramentaries include the Old Gelasian, the eighth-century Frankish Gelasian, the Gregorian (including the 8th-cent. Hadrianum), and the mixed Gelasian-Gregorian of the ninth and tenth centuries.

1.4. Besides the sacramentaries, an important series of liturgical books was the *Ordines Romani,* books of ceremonies that describe worship according to the Roman and the Germano-Roman use or give rules for liturgical practice. The oldest examples come from the late seventh and early eighth centuries. These books, the core of which involves descriptions of the papal → Mass, formed the basis for the later *pontificals,* the liturgical books for episcopal functions. A definitive *Pontificale Romanum* was published in 1485 and again in 1596, and the *Ceremoniale Episcoporum* in 1600.

1.5. While music in worship is mentioned in very early sources, and while the *Psalter* and some ancient → hymnals (see *Odes of Solomon*) probably formed the earliest actual liturgical books for singing, the oldest Western written sources for music in the liturgy include the *tonare* (a listing of the beginning of hymn texts according to the eight tones, 8th cent.), the *books of antiphons* (at first texts without notation, 9th cent.), and the books for cantors (with notes, 9th and 10th cents.). The terminology is not uniform. The *graduale* (Frankish) or the *cantatorium* (Roman), supplemented by the *responsoriale,* contains the songs between the readings in the Western Mass (the "gradual," the "tract," and the "alleluia"). The *antiphonary* (Roman) contains the processional songs (entrance, offertory, and communion). In the Frankish sphere, the book of antiphons embraces all these songs (→ Church Music).

1.6. As regards the Liturgy of the → Hours, at first several liturgical books were used. In addition to the Bible and antiphons, we find *hymnals,* psalms, *books of homilies* (with extracts from the Fathers), and *martyrologies* (→ Church Fathers; Martyrs). When traveling friars were interested in carrying what they needed for the Divine Office with them, these many books came to be reduced to the single volume of a *breviary.* Even so, originally these books simply set out the order of prayers for the → church year and quoted the first words of the relevant texts. The development toward a single volume now indicated an individualization of the celebration of the hours, exactly the opposite of the original Christian purpose in the use of the codex. There were diverse Western patterns of daily prayer. When the Roman Breviary was published in 1568, some monastic orders and friars retained their own usages.

1.7. The original liturgical books were usually the Bible and some loose papers designed for the hands of the presider or other liturgical ministers, which then developed into a whole library of books needed for the celebration of a single service. The increasing tendency in the West, however, was to create liturgical books that would contain all the necessary texts and rubrics in a single volume. This development, unfortunately, coincided with the increasing clericalization of the liturgy and even the emergence of the silent Mass, in which only a single priest needed the texts.

By the end of the 13th century, we find the *plenary missal,* which carries the readings, as well as the prayers and the songs for the Mass. The subsequent Roman Missal of Pius V in 1570 stands in this tradition. The *rituale* (together with the *agenda,* the *manuale,* the *obsequiale,* the *sacerdotale,* the *pastorale,* etc.) contains texts necessary for the celebration of other → sacraments and → sacramentals. The question raised by this development is whether a liturgical book can genuinely serve the goals of the liturgy, whether privatization and a mistaken sense that the book "contains the liturgy" are not its inevitable implications.

2. Roman Catholic Church

The development toward a single book underwent some reversal in the contemporary → Roman Catholic Church with the liturgical reforms after the Second → Vatican Council (1962-65; → Liturgy 3). The new sacramentary no longer contains all the needed texts and music. It requires supplementing by many other books — lectionary and hymnal, for example — and envisions that the liturgy is the celebration of the entire participating community, each according to one's order and ministry. The lectionary itself will usually be a full collection of the readings, based upon the list published as *Ordo lectionum* (1969; 2d ed., 1981).

Since broad scope is now allowed for accommodating national and cultural differences (→ Acculturation; Culture and Christianity), the official Roman publications *(editiones typica)* have only limited practical significance, ideally offering instead patterns and texts for translation and local adaptation. Of these, the missal was published in Rome in 1970, the Liturgy of the Hours beginning in 1971, and the revised pontifical and ritual in fascicles from 1968 onward.

3. Eastern Churches

3.1. In contrast to recent developments in the West, the churches of the East (→ Orthodox Church) have shown little change in their liturgical books since the early → Middle Ages. Most commonly, several books are required for the celebration of a liturgy in the Eastern churches. The central book in the Byzantine Rite (→ Liturgy 4), for example, is probably the *euchologion,* which is somewhat akin to a Western sacramentary. It contains the texts needed by the → priest and the → deacon at a celebration of the Divine Liturgy or at other sacraments and blessings.

Partial editions are the *little euchologion,* the *hierodiakonikon,* the *hagiasmatarion,* and the *archieratikon* (for the → bishop). In addition, the *typicon* regulates the calendar and the rubrics. The *doxastarion* and the *kondakarion* are for choir leaders, and the *antiphonarion* for the responsive singing of the choirs. Texts and music for the shifting yearly cycle, which depends upon the date of → Easter (§4), are contained in special books for the fasts, for Easter *(pentekostarion),* for the Sundays through the year, utilizing the eight tones *(oktoechos),* and for fixed observances all through the 12 months of the year *(menaion).*

A liturgical celebration involves many people, drawing on resources found in all of these liturgical books. The basic order for the Liturgy of the Hours, also drawing on many of these resources, is set out in the *horologion.*

3.2. There are also many liturgical books for the reading of Scripture. The Gospels are found either in the *tetraevangelion,* which contains the four gospels divided into pericopes in the ancient fashion, or the *aprakos,* which organizes the pericopes according to the liturgical year. The *apostolos* contains the Acts and the NT letters. There are also books containing OT readings (called proverbs) and 20 ex-

tracts from the Psalter, as arranged in the Septuagint and with added prayers and hymns for daily worship *(psalterion).* The *menologion* and *synaxarion* contain shortened lives of the → saints for edifying reading.

4. Protestant Churches

4.1. The earliest contributions to the tradition of liturgical books in the churches of the → Reformation were essays on the evangelical use of the already existing and diverse medieval materials. Such essays were written by Martin → Luther in 1523 *(Formula missae et communionis)* and 1526 *(Deutsche Messe)* and also made up a large part of the *visitation articles* (i.e., instructions for the visitors of parishes) of the early 16th century. Luther's essays and these articles then became the models for the subsequent church orders (Ger. *Kirchenordnungen*) found throughout Lutheran Germany and the Nordic countries. These orders were not liturgical books as such but, like the ancient church orders, officially authorized directions for the ordering of the churches, for their schools and ministries, and for care of the poor — but also for their public worship.

At first, local parishes continued to use medieval books but tried to follow the proffered advice in adapting them to an evangelical meaning. Early on, however, these books were supplemented by the new hymnals for congregational song (after the Bible, the most basic evangelical liturgical book) and then by the *cantionales* for choral use. Slowly, the new evangelical patterns for the liturgy, now placed in the language of the people, appeared as actual liturgical books, especially collections of texts for the liturgies called agendas. Sometimes further help was offered to the preachers in the form of *postils,* or collections of sermons on the texts of the classic Western lectionary.

4.2. Some early reformers published full texts for the liturgy as they envisioned it, aiming to supplant the medieval books immediately. Most notable were efforts by Thomas → Müntzer (1523), Ulrich → Zwingli (1523-25), and John → Calvin (1542). After some time, this model was also followed in Lutheran territories, though always with considerable unease about making a "new law" out of the books (→ Lutheranism). Nonetheless, Protestant liturgical books widely appeared: agenda in Germany, *liturgie* or *ordre du culte* in Switzerland and France, *kyrkohandbok* in Scandinavia, *dienstboek* or *orden voor de eredienst* in the Netherlands, the → *Book of Common Prayer* in England, and the *Book of Common Order* in Scotland.

4.3. In Protestantism the development of new liturgical books slowed considerably with the close of the 16th century. If we ignore the books of devotion that → Pietism produced for individual and public → edification (→ Devotional Literature), and if we set aside some interesting experiments by rationalist Christians (→ Enlightenment), it remained for the work of 18th- and 19th-century immigrants to North America and for the → liturgical movement of the 19th and 20th centuries to resume the creation of liturgical books.

Henry Melchior Muhlenberg's "liturgy" of 1748, actually (like Luther's early work) an essay on the use of available books and materials for a classic liturgy in a new land, and Wilhelm Löhe's *Agenda* of 1844 can be regarded as precursors of this work. The American revision of the Book of Common Prayer (1977), the *Lutheran Book of Worship* (1978), the American Presbyterian *Book of Common Worship* (1993), and the English Anglican *Common Worship* (2000) can be seen as its harvest and fruition. Many other liturgical books lie between these markers.

4.4. The search for recovery of the Bible as the principal liturgical book of the Christian assembly and the question of the appropriate use of other liturgical books in renewed Christian worship remain quite alive. One important development in respect to current liturgical books is the resurgence of the idea that liturgy is a communal action that has a shape, an "order." Books, then, are taken in hand only as they are needed to enact that shape. This idea is present in the recurrent "outline of the rite" found in almost all contemporary Western liturgical books, Protestant and Roman Catholic.

Bibliography: "Books, Liturgical," *NWDLW* 96-114 • D. M. Hope and G. Woolfenden, "Liturgical Books," *The Study of Liturgy* (rev. ed.; ed. C. Jones, G. Wainwright, E. Yarnold, and P. Bradshaw; London, 1992) 96-101 • E. Palazzo, *A History of Liturgical Books* (Collegeville, Minn., 1998) • K. Parry et al., eds., *The Blackwell Dictionary of Eastern Christianity* (Oxford, 1999) • L. D. Reed, *The Lutheran Liturgy* (Philadelphia, 1947) • A. Schmemann, *Introduction to Liturgical Theology* (Crestwood, N.Y., 1986) • F. C. Senn, *Christian Liturgy: Catholic and Evangelical* (Minneapolis, 1997) • L. C. Sheppard, "The Liturgical Books," *Twentieth Century Encyclopedia of Catholicism* (New York, 1962) 109 • C. Vogel, *Medieval Liturgy: An Introduction to the Sources* (Washington, D.C., 1986; orig. pub., 1966) • H. Wegman, *Christian Worship in the East and West* (New York, 1985).

Karl-Heinrich Bieritz and
Gordon W. Lathrop

5. North America

Protestant churches in North America can be described as preferring a small number of liturgical books and as placing greater emphasis on the hymnal than do other Christians. Many → denominations (e.g., the → Lutheran Churches) combine their liturgical book and hymnal; others that profess themselves nonliturgical have responsive readings and traditional liturgical texts placed in their hymnals as "worship resources."

Episcopalians, with the most complex set of books, include all major public services and most pastoral offices in *The Book of Common Prayer*. Minor services, usually in the form of modules to be inserted into principal liturgies, are found in *The Book of Occasional Services*. The hymnal contains both hymns and liturgical music; collects, lectionary, and capsule biographies for the commemorations of the calendar are found in *Lesser Feasts and Fasts*.

Lutherans in the United States include public services in their hymnal *The Lutheran Book of Worship*, and private and special services in → *Occasional Services*. Each successive Lutheran hymnal has included more liturgical material, which corresponds to the trend throughout American Protestantism.

In the rest of American → Protestantism liturgical texts are matters of indifference, and pastors choose from materials included in the hymnal, draw on denominational resources, or borrow from other ecclesial bodies. In the 19th century Protestants issued optional directories, or outlines, for worship services. Presbyterians, Methodists, and the United Church of Christ have produced elaborate resources. Commercially produced resources, often called minister's manuals, have been widely used in the denominations where the pastor must create orders of service. Through these books the influence of the liturgical churches has been strong, if unnamed, on the worship of most Protestantism.

Many groups in the United States use no printed resources at all, notably the Quakers (→ Friends, Society of), where silence plays a larger part, and the → Pentecostal churches, where informality, emotionalism, and spontaneity are valued. While the flow of events in these services is quite predictable, no texts are consulted in the ordering of their specific content.

6. Third World Churches in North America

Because the United States is heavily Spanish-speaking, most denominations have translated their materials into Spanish for home use in conjunction with the Hispanic churches, producing joint texts that are also put to use in Latin America. Along with these texts, indigenous practices survive, usually originating in Latin American Roman Catholicism, which are usually alive in oral → tradition.

Cooperative translation is true to a lesser extent for Asian churches, for they are often of nonliturgical wings of Protestantism. The Asian branches of the liturgical bodies, in contrast, show less interest in indigenous practice than do Hispanic Christians.

Bibliography: A. J. Chupungco, *Liturgies of the Future: The Process and Methods of Inculturation* (New York, 1989) • F. Kabasele Lumbala, *Alliances avec le Christ en Afrique* (2d ed.; Paris, 1994) • A. C. Piepkorn, *Profiles in Belief: The Religious Bodies of the United States and Canada* (4 vols. in 3; New York, 1977-79) • J. F. White, *Protestant Worship: Traditions in Transition* (Louisville, Ky., 1989).

Paul V. Marshall

Liturgical Movement

1. Background
2. Nineteenth Century
   2.1. The Continent
   2.2. United Kingdom
   2.3. United States
   2.4. Scandinavia
3. Church Architecture
4. Twentieth Century
   4.1. The Continent
   4.2. United Kingdom
   4.3. United States
   4.4. Ecumenical Efforts

The modern liturgical movement involved an effort to enrich the experience and appreciation of the → liturgy among baptized Christians. Although its foundations were laid in the 18th and 19th centuries, as an organized movement it took shape in the 20th century in various Western countries and passed through phases with varying purposes and tactics. Liturgical scholars generally consider that it ended in the late 1960s, following the Second → Vatican Council. It was a movement in the sense that it gathered people around a cause, namely, the active participation of all baptized Christians in the church's → worship. Aimed at changing the patterns of worship, it was led by charismatic leaders who promoted change through publications and conferences. As a movement it should be distinguished from the scholarly work that put it on a firm foundation and also from the actual reforms of the lit-

urgy that were either mandated or allowed by officials of the various churches. Throughout history there have been various organized attempts to reform the churches' liturgies. The expression "liturgical movement" in the modern sense, however, first appeared in Germany in 1894 with the publication of *Vesperale Romanum,* edited by Anselm Schott.

1. Background

In a sense the modern movement simply developed themes that arose in the 18th century. Although liturgy in the → Enlightenment was generally either rationalistic or pietistic, the awakenings in Great Britain and America promoted several liturgical exceptions. Growing out of the First Great Awakening were the Methodist societies founded by the Wesley brothers, → John (1703-91) and Charles (1707-88). Their worship was countercultural in that it was sacramental, emphasizing → baptism and the Lord's Supper, as well as demonstrating a commitment to practical works of mercy among the poor and → marginalized. It was enthusiastic in that it appealed to the emotions through both the singing of → hymns and a style of → preaching directed at personal → conversion (§1). This emphasis on revivalistic preaching affected the design of church buildings, as the pulpit received increased prominence (→ Church Architecture).

Another important movement was the High Church party of late 17th- and 18th-century → Anglicanism in England and Scotland. Refusing to take the Oath of Allegiance and Supremacy to William and Mary, these Anglicans emphasized the apostolic succession of the episcopate, the catholicity of each episcopal church, and the authority of the → church fathers for the interpretation of Scripture. These concerns surfaced again in the 19th-century → Oxford Movement.

In many ways the 19th-century liturgical developments were a romantic reaction to the → rationalism of the Enlightenment. This romantic revivalism emphasized the → Middle Ages or the → Reformation as the great ages of Christian faith, although efforts to retrieve historical liturgies often resulted merely in a concentration on the externals of such earlier periods.

2. Nineteenth Century
2.1. *The Continent*
In the 19th century Roman Catholicism was to some extent still reacting to the Protestant Reformation, as it was also to the French Revolution, during which many church buildings were demolished or turned over to other uses. Consequently (in the

spirit of medieval Catholicism), the papacy was widely given greater status than national churches. This → Ultramontane movement involved in part the restoration of → monasteries. Dom Prosper Guéranger (1805-75) thus restored the Benedictine abbey of Solesmes and implemented a liturgy that was more pleasing than the → baroque theatricalism that had preceded it. Although scholars disagree in evaluating Guéranger's project, it is generally acknowledged that it was an antiquarian reconstruction that tended to be out of touch with the majority of lay Christians. At Solesmes, → Gregorian chant was restored, there was a scrupulous observance of rubrics, and the liturgy was celebrated in an austere manner. Unlike the 20th-century liturgical movement, however, the abbey did not succeed in bringing the liturgy to the → masses.

Solesmes, though, did share its spirit with other Benedictine foundations in the second half of the 19th century, the most important of which was Beuron, a German monastery formed in 1863 by Maurus and Placidus Wolter that became well known for its pseudo-Romanesque art. In 1872 Beuron founded Maredsous in Belgium, where the rector of the abbey school, Dom Gerard van Caloen, published the first French-Latin missal in 1882. Maria Laach, a German monastery in the Rhineland, was taken over by monks from Beuron in 1893, and in 1899 monks from Maredsous founded Mont César in Belgium. These monasteries produced distinguished liturgical scholars in the 20th century.

The French Revolution and the Napoleonic Wars also resulted in a reorganization of church life in Germany. Frederick William III sought to impose the liturgical order of the 16th century on the provinces of Prussia, but the areas unaffected by the king's directives, such as Mecklenburg and Bavaria, introduced a High Church Lutheran liturgy somewhat similar to the liturgy of the Tractarian movement in England.

Mention should be made of the contributions of Wilhelm Löhe (1808-72), whose primary concerns were ecclesiological, although his neo-Lutheranism was considered confessionally rigid and pietistic. When he was sent as pastor to a small town in northern Bavaria where he was free from close supervision, he established an "evangelical catholic" form of worship that provided for frequent celebrations of the Holy Communion and also for the practice of private confession and absolution as an independent → means of grace (→ Confession of Sins). Like the Tractarians, Löhe saw important links between the church, the liturgy, and social

ministry. He was a leader in establishing the deaconess movement in Germany and was also instrumental in sending missionary pastors to care for immigrants to America.

2.2. *United Kingdom*

In Great Britain the 19th century was marked by the industrial revolution. The established Church of England, with its dry rationalism, found that it had little appeal to the new working class created by this → revolution. Evangelicals were more successful in reaching out to the poor, but despite the growth of Nonconformist churches, many people were left untouched by any church. Constitutional changes were enacted to effect a partial disestablishment of the Church of England, but church leaders and Oxford University opposed these measures largely because they provided for the suppression of bishoprics by Parliament. In this situation the Oxford and Cambridge Movements were born.

John Keble (1792-1866), John Henry → Newman (1801-90), Edward B. Pusey (1800-1882), and their fellow Oxonians sought the independence of the church and its right to regulate its own life. These Tractarians (so-called because of the series of 90 tracts they produced from 1833 to 1841) emphasized the → sacraments as instruments of spiritual power. This view set them at odds with Evangelicals, who felt that viewing baptism in this light undermined the doctrine of → justification by -> faith. The Tractarians also developed a clearer understanding of the presence of Christ in the → Eucharist. Robert Wilberforce (1802-57), in *The Doctrine of the Holy Eucharist,* emphasized that while faith is necessary to perceive the grace of the sacrament, spiritual gifts are communicated at God's initiative and not simply through subjective religious feelings. Although the Tractarians, or Anglo-Catholics, are sometimes accused of importing the Roman rite into Anglican worship, they were not deeply concerned about ceremonial details; they simply desired to properly observe the rubrics of the → Book of Common Prayer. It was more important to them that the Eucharist be celebrated regularly than that it be celebrated with splendor.

It was the Cambridge Camden Society that was primarily concerned with the externals of liturgical worship. John Mason Neale (1818-66) and the members of the Cambridge Ecclesiological Society, the name taken by the Camden Society after its move to London in 1846, were devoted to improving the aesthetic environment in which the liturgy was celebrated. Accordingly, they took a special interest in the construction of the many new churches erected in the 19th century to accommodate the exploding British urban population. Both Neale and Augustus Welby Pugin (1812-52) felt that Gothic architecture was the best expression of Catholic faith and worship. These ritualists emphasized the importance of → vestments and other appurtenances of liturgical celebration. Since the neo-Gothic churches had chancels and divided → choir stalls, surpliced choirs took up the singing of choral liturgies, thus replacing the more boisterous singing that took place in the west galleries of traditional Anglican churches.

2.3. *United States*

Confessional and liturgical developments in Germany influenced church life in the United States not only among Lutherans but also among the members of Reformed churches. Philip Schaff (1819-93) left Germany to become a professor at the German Reformed Seminary in Mercersburg, Pennsylvania. Inspired by the theological writings of Friedrich → Schleiermacher (1768-1834; → Schleiermacher's Theology) and his emphasis on feeling as the basis of religion, Schaff envisioned the development of an evangelical catholic church in America rooted in the spirit that permeated much German theology of the time.

2.4. *Scandinavia*

In Scandinavia what might be called a folk church developed (→ People's Church [Volkskirche]). For example, in Sweden there were revivals under the leadership of Henrik Schartau (1757-1825), who placed great emphasis on confessional worship and catechetical instruction. Throughout the 20th century the Church of Sweden was marked by a strong liturgical consciousness, associated with movements such as the Society of St. Birgitta, centered in the medieval town of Vadstena, and the charismatic influence of persons such as the parish priest Gunnar Rosendal.

Somewhat similar developments occurred in Norway and Finland. In Norway a basically lay movement was established under the leadership of Hans Nielsen Hauge (1771-1824), and in Finland under the leadership of the lay preachers Paavo Ruotsalainen (1777-1852) and Lars Levi Laestadius (1800-1861). These movements, which were reactions against the Enlightenment, viewed the → church as a community of faithful disciples.

This model of folk church took shape above all in Denmark under the inspiration of Nikolai Fredrik Severin → Grundtvig (1783-1872). Grundtvig, truly a giant of the 19th century, was a student of Anglo-Saxon literature, theologian, author of more than 1,500 hymns, and founder of the Danish *Folkehøjskoler* (folk high school) movement. At about age 40

he experienced conversion (his "matchless discovery"), which led him away from rationalism and toward a more classic, sacramental Lutheran theology. Grundtvig's influence resulted in a movement in the Church of Denmark marked by a high ecclesiology and an emphasis on the importance of the sacraments for the Christian life. His emphases were similar to those of the Oxford Movement in England, although he rejected any kind of clerical elitism. A distinctive aspect of Grundtvig's ecclesiology is its emphasis on the → Apostles' Creed as the → confession of faith, affirmed by the individual and the congregation at baptism, which expresses a word of → salvation coming from God. He argued that the principles of the Christian life are based on this confession by the congregation, on the → proclamation of the gospel, and on songs of praise. He refused to emphasize the individual, solitary appropriation of faith that was so central to his contemporary, Søren → Kierkegaard (1813-55).

3. Church Architecture

Although the revival of Gothic architecture was a hallmark of → Romanticism, in America the neo-Gothic church was not the only kind of church building being constructed. Liturgical restoration there was forced to take into consideration the revival movement arising from the Great Awakenings, a movement that affected most aspects of American Protestantism. → Preaching was central to revival meetings, and the personality and enthusiasm of the preacher were central to revivalist effectiveness. Preachers thus preferred a small desklike pulpit only large enough to hold their notes, but they relished a large platform on which to move back and forth as they called for personal conversions. Since the goal was to make an impact on the worshipers, elements that had previously been eschewed in Reformed and Puritan churches were restored, including → organs, stained glass, and choirs. The result was a concert-hall arrangement for churches, especially those of the Methodist and Baptist traditions, where the congregation became less an assembly and more an audience. In these churches the role of the sacraments tended to be minimal, so → altars and fonts were diminutive.

The triumph of the Gothic revival in America was manifest in the work of the Anglo-Catholic architect Ralph Adams Cram (1863-1942). At first he was so convinced that the Gothic style was best suited to Roman Catholic worship that he was reluctant to design churches for Protestants. Eventually, however, his Gothic churches with large chancels were also constructed for Methodists, Presbyterians, Congregationalists, and Unitarians, as well as Episcopalians and Lutherans.

4. Twentieth Century

4.1. *The Continent*

The important liturgical scholars of the first half of the 20th century were primarily historians: the Roman Catholic Josef Jungmann, S.J., the Anglican Gregory Dix, the Lutheran Luther D. Reed, the Reformed William D. Maxwell, and the Methodist J. Ernest Rattenbury. Their historicocritical study of the Christian tradition led to the idealization of the patristic period as the golden age for liturgists.

Among European Roman Catholics in the early years of the 20th century, the liturgical movement assumed a popular character. In November 1903 Pope Pius X issued a → motu proprio on sacred music that also pleaded for a general return to the liturgy as the primary source of Christian life. Those who were imbued with Guéranger's spirit emphasized only the aesthetic restoration of sacred music found in this letter, with the consequence that Solesmes became the center for the study of Gregorian chant.

It was above all Dom Lambert Beauduin (1873-1960), a monk of Mont César at Louvain, who understood the full significance of Pius X's exhortation on the liturgy and → church music. In 1909 at a conference in Mechelen, he proposed a practical program for liturgical renewal that included a translation of the Roman missal and its promotion as the principal prayer book for all Roman Catholics. He called for a liturgical orientation of all → piety based on the → Mass and the Liturgy of the → Hours and advocated the special formation of choirs through retreats at liturgical centers. Beauduin realized that priests must first of all be won over to the liturgical movement if they were to apply its principles on a pastoral level. Following this conference, Mont César became the center for carrying out Beauduin's program. Two organs were developed through which the monks of Mont César propagated their ideas: the review *Questions liturgiques et paroissiales* and conferences of the newly established Semaines Liturgiques.

Not until the 1940s did France become a dynamic center of liturgical renewal, although the academic study of the liturgy had been developing there since the beginning of the century. The *Dictionnaire d'archéologie chrétienne et de la liturgie* was begun in 1903 by Fernand Cabrol and Henri Leclercq and ultimately completed in 1947 through the labors of Henri Marrou. In 1943 the Centre de Pastorale Liturgique was established under the direction of the French Dominicans. Two years later that center began the publication of *La Maison-Dieu,* which from its start has been a key liturgical journal. Also in 1945 the first annual national French liturgical congress was held.

In 19th-century Germany the pastoral aspects of the liturgical movement were absent, with the result that the liturgy was the concern only of an elite rather than of the whole Christian people. However, using the profound historical insights of Abbot Ildefons Herwegen of Maria Laach (1874-1946), Dom Odo Casel of Maria Laach (1886-1948), and Monsignor Romano Guardini (1885-1968), the German movement soon departed from the Solesmian tradition, taking on an academic, speculative character. In 1918 the Ecclesia Orans series was initiated at Maria Laach with the publication of Guardini's slender volume *Vom Geist der Liturgie* (ET *The Spirit of the Liturgy* [1930, 1998]). The → monastery established the Verein zur Pflege der Liturgiewissenschaft for the publication of academic studies on the liturgy, and in 1921 Casel, together with Anton Baumstark and Guardini, founded the *Jahrbuch für Liturgiewissenschaft.* In this annual Casel developed a perspective on the theological understanding of the liturgy based on the theology of the church fathers and the history of religions (emphasizing the *Kultmysterium*).

Mention should also be made of the work of Pius Parsch (1884-1954), an Augustinian canon of Klosterneuburg near Vienna. In two journals he edited, *Lebe mit der Kirche* (1928-52) and *Bibel und Liturgie* (since 1926), Parsch emphasized the important link between liturgy and the Bible. In 1936 Josef Jungmann published *Die Frohbotschaft und unsere Glaubensverkündigung* (ET *The Good News Yesterday and Today* [1962]), which exerted a decisive influence on the development of both the catechetical and the liturgical movements by providing a basis of sound scholarship for the increasing demands of both reforms. Between 1939 and 1945 Jungmann wrote his major work on the liturgy, the two-volume *Missarum sollemnia,* published in 1948 (ET *The Mass of the Roman Rite* [1950]).

In 1940 the Roman Catholic hierarchy took over the leadership of the liturgical movement in Germany by appointing a liturgical commission with representatives from Maria Laach, Beuron, Klosterneuburg, and the → Oratory at Leipzig. In 1943 the German bishops sent a report to Pope Pius XII on the movement in Germany, requesting a number of indults, including a reform of both the breviary and the ritual itself.

Since liturgical reformers, both Protestant and

Catholic, have often found themselves at odds with the leadership of their churches and also in conflict with popular piety, and since these reformers have often issued a negative critique of Western society, the liturgical movement has sometimes been regarded as dangerous and out of hand. Such opposition was reflected in the attitude of both Roman officials and some of the most ardent Protestant pastors. It was important, then, that in 1943 Pius XII issued his encyclicals *Mystici corporis Christi,* which deals with the church and its worship, and *Divino afflante Spiritu,* which deals with the study of Scripture. Both documents are generally positive toward what the liturgical reformers were trying to accomplish, providing a firm biblical and ecclesiological foundation for their efforts.

Following World War II, liturgical congresses were held annually in Europe. In 1947 the Liturgical Institute of Trier was founded, with Johannes Wagner as director. Three years later it began publishing *Liturgisches Jahrbuch.* At the same time the Herwegen Institute for the Promotion of Liturgical Studies at Maria Laach was established and commenced publication of *Archiv für Liturgiewissenschaft.* From 1947 the Vatican began to take charge of the liturgical movement among Roman Catholics. That year Pius XII issued his → encyclical *Mediator Dei,* which contained sharp criticisms of abuses of the movement, as well as praise for its positive elements. In point of fact, this encyclical introduced a period of concrete changes in the liturgical celebration of the Mass and other sacramental rituals.

4.2. *United Kingdom*

In the United Kingdom there was no 20th-century liturgical movement comparable to what occurred on the Continent. For Roman Catholics the traditional Tridentine liturgy was a primary expression of pre-Reformation Christianity. Among Roman Catholics James G. Crichton played a significant role in his efforts to translate Continental liturgical reforms into practice in the British Isles. In Ireland annual liturgical conferences with an ecumenical emphasis have been held since World War II by the → Benedictines at Glenstal Abbey.

Anglicans who were interested in liturgical renewal moved into Anglo-Catholicism, embracing a pre-Reformation style of worship similar to that of Roman Catholics. Nevertheless, within the Church of England the Alcuin Club and the Henry Bradshaw Society have made important scholarly contributions to liturgical renewal. Probably the most important contribution to reform in England came from Dom Gregory Dix, an Anglican Benedictine

from Nashdom Abbey, most notably in his *Shape of the Liturgy* (1945).

Protestants, who often harbored intense anti-Catholic feelings, generally hindered liturgical renewal, even in the Church of England. It should be noted that in the United Kingdom Nonconformist churches of → Puritan background have typically been unsympathetic toward the liturgical movement in any of its forms.

4.3. *United States*

The liturgical movement in the United States was inaugurated by Virgil Michel, a Benedictine from St. John's Abbey in Collegeville, Minnesota. In the early 1920s he was sent to Europe to study and came under the influence of Lambert Beauduin at the Collegio di Sant'Anselmo in Rome. Michel returned to the United States committed to the European liturgical movement, but he was able to give it a distinctly American character. His vision was solidly grounded in the doctrine of the mystical body of Christ and in a firm conviction that the liturgy belongs to the entire church and not simply to → clergy and religious. Michel's horizons were broad: he knew that the liturgical, social, educational, and biblical dimensions of the church's life must be carefully interrelated and that regional and national political issues must also be discussed in a liturgical context. In effect, he knew that everything that touches the mystical body should be of concern to every worshiping Christian. In 1926 he founded both the journal *Oratre fratres,* which later became *Worship,* and the Liturgical Press.

After Michel's sudden death in 1938 his work was taken up by his fellow Benedictine Godfrey Diekmann. In 1927 a group of Roman Catholic laymen — artists, architects, and draftsmen from the Boston and New York area — established the Liturgical Arts Society (1928-72) and its publication *Liturgical Arts,* edited for many years by Maurice Lavanaux.

Among Roman Catholics in the United States liturgical changes were promoted by events such as liturgical days and weeks. The first such day was held at St. John's Abbey in Collegeville in 1929. This event was expanded into the national Liturgical Week, the first of which was held in Chicago in 1940 under the sponsorship of the Benedictine Liturgical Conference. In 1943 the Benedictines passed the planning of such weeks to an independent board that came to be known as the Liturgical Conference. These weeks attracted thousands of participants, especially during the 1960s. In 1979 the conference became ecumenical when it merged with the Lutheran Society for Worship, Music, and the Arts.

The liturgical movement in the United States was

given academic recognition through the development of programs in liturgical studies. In 1941 Reynold Hillenbrand, a priest of the Archdiocese of Chicago, organized a summer school in liturgical studies at St. Mary of the Lake Seminary in Mundelein, Illinois, where the teachers included Godfrey Diekmann, Gerard Ellard, Martin Hellriegel, and A. R. Reinhold. In the summer of 1947 the first actual graduate degree program in liturgical studies was established at the University of Notre Dame by Michael Mathis, C.S.C. (1885-1960), leading to the establishment of a doctoral program in 1965. Other graduate programs in liturgical studies were developed at the Catholic University of America in Washington, D.C., and at St. John's University in Collegeville, Minnesota.

In 1958 North American Lutherans produced the *Service Book and Hymnal,* a liturgical book that reflected a 100-year effort in American Lutheranism to recover the heritage of Reformation → church orders. It was considered a high mark in the effort of liturgical renewal. This book gave back to the congregation what was sung by choirs in classic Lutheran church orders, thereby implementing a view of liturgy, espoused in the modern liturgical movement, as the work of the people. The liturgical order included a full → eucharistic prayer, with the option of simply using the *verba,* or Words of Institution, alone. The book was authentically American in that alongside European chorales and Roman Catholic plainsong, it included Anglo-American → hymnody.

4.4. *Ecumenical Efforts*

The Second Vatican Council, convened by Pope John XXIII in 1962, issued its Constitution on the Sacred Liturgy, *Sacrosanctum concilium,* in 1963. This document mandated liturgical changes in Roman Catholic liturgical books and inspired leaders of the Anglican and mainline Protestant churches to institute major programs of liturgical reform and renewal. Official ecumenical liturgical consultations were organized, beginning in 1969 with the International Consultation on English Texts. Common texts were published as *Prayers We Have in Common* (1970; rev. 1972, 1975).

Perhaps most valuable ecumenically has been the work done by churches on *Common Lectionary* (1983, rev. 1992). These efforts reflect the significant ecumenical consensus on liturgical matters that has been achieved since 1969. This consensus is further reflected in official orders and hymnals of churches, such as the *Lutheran Book of Worship* (1978), the revised Episcopal *Book of Common Prayer* (1979), the *United Methodist Hymnal* (1989), and *The Presbyterian Hymnal* (1990). At the start of the 21st century,

many of the mainline churches are again revising their liturgical books in the light of pastoral experience, theological and ecclesiological reflection, and ecumenical advances gained since earlier revisions.

Scholarly and pastoral liturgical work continues to be carried out in the United States by various institutes and learned societies. Among them are Associated Parishes, an Episcopal fellowship based in Washington, D.C.; the Order of St. Luke, a liturgical society within the United Methodist Church dating from 1948; the United Methodist Society for Worship, founded in 1974; the Church Service Society within the Presbyterian Church (U.S.A.); and the National Association of Pastoral Musicians, based in Washington, D.C. Of signal importance for the liturgical movement in the United States and Canada is the thoroughly ecumenical North American Academy of Liturgy, begun in 1974 and officially founded in 1975 at a meeting at the University of Notre Dame.

Bibliography: B. Botte, *From Silence to Participation: An Insider's View of Liturgical Renewal* (Washington, D.C., 1988) • L. Brinkhof, "Chronicle of the Liturgical Movement," *Liturgy in Development* (ed. L. G. M. Alting von Geusau; Westminster, Md., 1966) 40-67 • J. D. Crichton, *Light in the Darkness: Forerunners of the Liturgical Movement* (Collegeville, Minn., 1996) • V. C. Funk, "Liturgical Movement, The (1830-1969)," *NDSW* 695-715 • K. Hughes, *How Firm a Foundation: Voices of the Early Liturgical Movement* (Chicago, 1990) • C. Jones, G. Wainwright, E. Yarnold, and P. Bradshaw, eds., *The Study of Liturgy* (rev. ed.; London, 1992) • E. Koenker, *The Liturgical Renaissance in the Roman Catholic Church* (St. Louis, 1966) • P. Marshall, *Anglican Liturgy in America* (3 vols.; New York, 1989-90) • O. Olson, "Contemporary Trends in Liturgy Viewed from the Perspective of Classical Lutheran Theology," *LQ* 26 (1974) 110-57 • K. Peckler, *The Unread Vision: The Liturgical Movement in the United States of America, 1926-1955* (Collegeville, Minn., 1998) • L. Reed, *The Lutheran Liturgy* (Philadelphia, 1947) • O. Rousseau, *The Progress of the Liturgy* (Westminster, Md., 1951) • F. Senn, *Christian Liturgy: Catholic and Evangelical* (Minneapolis, 1997) • L. Shepherd, *The People Worship: A History of the Liturgical Movement* (New York, 1967) • B. Spinks and I. Torrance, *To Glorify God: Essays in Modern Reformed Liturgy* (Grand Rapids, 1999) • M. Taylor, *Liturgical Renewal in the Christian Churches* (Baltimore, 1967) • R. Tuzik, *How Firm a Foundation: Leaders of the Liturgical Movement* (Chicago, 1990) • J. White, *A Brief History of Christian Worship* (Nashville, 1993); idem, *Christian Worship in Transition* (Nashville, 1976).

R. Kevin Seasoltz, O.S.B.

Liturgical Vessels

1. Vessels of the Word
2. Vessels of the Lord's Supper
3. Other Sacramental Vessels
4. Other Liturgical Vessels

Liturgical vessels are containers used to hold materials that are essential to liturgical celebrations, such as scrolls and books (→ Liturgical Books), bread and → wine, → water and oil, candles and → incense. These vessels often acquire an ornate design that reflects the sanctity lent to them by their sacred contents. Some vessels, like the → ark of the covenant in ancient Israel, acquire a holiness of their own (→ Sacred and Profane).

1. Vessels of the Word

The *ark of the* → *synagogue* is a recess or closet in which are kept the scrolls of the Torah used in public worship. This was originally a portable wooden chest, like the ark of the covenant. Subsequently, it was a recess built into the wall of the synagogue toward which the people turn for prayer (usually east). It came to be regarded as symbolic of the Holy of Holies in the → temple, and the parocheth, or curtain, was hung in front of it. On the festival of Simhath Torah (lit. "Rejoicing of the Torah"), when all scrolls are taken out, a lighted candle is placed in the ark.

The scrolls of the Torah are covered with a wrapping called *mappah* (from Lat. *mappa,* "napkin"). This "mantle of the law" is made in the form of a bag to fit the scroll after it has been rolled up. It is open at the bottom and closed at the top except for two openings to allow the scroll handles to pass through. The mantle is made of expensive materials that should never have been used for any other purpose.

Books used in Christian worship have also received ornamental covers. The *Ordo Romanus Primus* (ca. 700) refers to a *capsa* (case) in which the gospel book is stored when not used in the liturgy.

2. Vessels of the Lord's Supper

The bread of the Lord's Supper (→ Eucharist) is placed on and distributed from a plate called the *paten.* In the first millennium of Christianity the use of leavened bread was common and patens were quite large, often like trays. They became smaller when the Latin West began using unleavened wafer-bread from the end of the 9th century. The consecrating paten was circular in shape and, by the end of the Middle Ages, was fitted onto the top of the cup, or chalice. A larger paten was used for the ministration of Holy Communion.

The wine of the Lord's Supper is contained in a cup called *calix* in Latin (Eng. chalice). Ancient communion cups had two handles and were usually made of base metals such as pewter. The official recognition of Christianity gave impetus to the use of silver or gold-gilt cups, although Boniface was familiar with wooden cups in the 8th century. The *Ordo Romanus Primus* specified that a large two-handled cup called the *scyphus* be used to contain the wine supplied by the people, while a smaller cup is used on the → altar for the consecration. Before the communion of the people, wine from the consecrated cup was poured into the scyphus and people drank from it with a tube called a *fistula*. Fistulas received their widest use during the 11th and 12th centuries. The pope still receives communion in this way at pontifical masses. This manner of imbibing wine, which remained in some Lutheran churches until the 18th century, was defended on grounds of practicality and decorum.

With the withdrawal of the cup from the laity after the 12th century, the cups became smaller. The restoration of the cup to the laity in the → Reformation churches necessitated larger cups. Among the Reformed they were usually wooden or pewter, but among Lutherans and Anglicans (→ Lutheran Churches; Anglican Communion) cups of silver or gold-gilt were common. In the → Orthodox Church, where the cup was never withheld from the laity, communion cups have remained larger in size. However, communicants are given both bread and wine together from a spoon on which the bread has been dipped into the cup.

At the beginning of the 20th century, concerns of hygiene prompted the use of individual cups or glasses for the ministration of the wine. This practice was never adopted in Europe as much as in North America. In order to retain the symbolism of the common cup, statements concerning communion practices have recommended that chalices be fitted with a pouring lip and that the wine be poured from the chalice into the individual glasses, rather than having the glasses prefilled before the consecration.

Vessels have been needed to store bread and wine used for Holy Communion. A chalicelike vessel fitted with a lid called a *ciborium* has been used to store wafer-breads. This lid may have evolved from the *pyx,* which was a receptacle used to store consecrated bread. Such vessels go back to the early centuries, when the → sacrament was reserved for the communion of the sick and those prevented from attending the Sunday Eucharist. Toward the end of the Middle Ages, with the development of the cult of veneration of the sacrament, pyxes were sometimes contained in a steeplelike tower called a sacrament house or suspended under a canopy or given a pedestal. A vessel called a *monstrance* was designed for the purpose of showing the consecrated host to the people. It assumed the form of a circular window surrounded by a silver or gold frame. Monstrances arose first in Holland and Germany in connection with the Feast of Corpus Christi, but in the → baroque period exposition of the host became more frequent and widespread in the devotion called the benediction of the Blessed Sacrament (→ Eucharistic Spirituality)

Wine and water were stored in a vessel called the *cruet* (Fr. *cruette*), which in the Middle Ages was made of base or precious metals, although today it is usually made of glass. *Flagons,* or communion pitchers, came into use in the Reformation churches because of the need for larger supplies of wine to commune the people. In the 16th century they were usually cylindrical, but in the 17th and 18th centuries they became pear shaped and were richly ornamented.

3. Other Sacramental Vessels

Baptismal basins are containers within → baptismal fonts that hold the water. They are usually made of bronze or silver and are conformed to the base of the font. In the post-Reformation period the basin was not always a part of the font and could be placed on a stand or table when baptisms were celebrated. These basins tended to be very small, marking the end of the practice of immersion (→ Baptistery). The Byzantine churches also used basins, but of much larger dimensions than those used in Roman Catholic and Protestant churches.

Chrismatories, or oil stocks, are metal caskets designed to hold the three sacramental oils that have been used since the second century: the oil of the catechumens, for prebaptismal rites; the oil used for the anointing of the sick; and the chrism used for postbaptismal anointings, confirmation, and coronations.

4. Other Liturgical Vessels

An *aspergillum* (Lat. *aspergo,* "spray, sprinkle") is a container filled with water from the baptismal font and is used to sprinkle the congregation at times when the rite of asperges is used as a reminder of → baptism. The practice developed from the medieval rite of → blessing the → monasteries on Sundays. In the reformed Roman Catholic liturgy of 1969, the sprinkling of the assembly is the first option in the introductory rite of the Mass. Sprinkling the congregation at the renewal of baptismal vows in the Easter Vigil is now practiced in several traditions, although often evergreen boughs are used for this purpose rather than an aspergillum.

A *thurible,* or censer, is a metal pot with a perforated lid used to hold burning coals on which grains of incense are placed for incensing. Censers usually are equipped with chains for swinging them in processions or toward objects and people. Sometimes today clay pots are used for burning incense.

A *lavabo* (= Lat. "I shall wash") is a small finger bowl into which water is poured from a cruet so that the presiding minister at the Eucharist may wash his or her fingers before handling the bread. In earlier times the bowl was large enough for celebrants to wash their hands. It is a hygienic practice that commends itself today.

A *reliquary* is a receptacle used for storing and sometimes exposing the → relics or remains of the body of a saint or an object associated with the life of Christ or the → saints, such as a fragment of the cross or a piece of a saint's clothing. Reliquaries have assumed various sizes and shapes, including caskets, crosses, rings, and even shapes of parts of the body. They are often richly ornamented.

An *ambry* (Lat. *armarium*) is a cabinet, cupboard, or chest used to store consecrated elements used in Christian worship, such as eucharistic bread and oils. It was sometimes placed in a sacristy or in a niche in the wall of the sanctuary. Since the 13th century ambries have been kept locked. The eucharistic ambry developed into a *tabernacle* in the 16th century and was usually placed on or above the mensa of the main, or high, altar. Portions of the consecrated bread from the Eucharist were stored or reserved in an ambry or tabernacle to be taken to the sick. Today the ritual guidelines of the → Roman Catholic Church discourage placing the tabernacle on the altar, which may be freestanding. A burning lamp or votive light near the tabernacle or ambry indicates the presence of the consecrated elements within it.

Bibliography: J. G. Davies, *The Architectural Setting of Baptism* (London, 1962) • *Eucharistic Vessels of the Middle Ages* (Cambridge, Mass., 1975) • J. Gilchrist, *Anglican Church Plate* (London, 1967) • A. Kass, "Torah Ornaments," *EncJud* 15.1255-58, 1261 • A. A. King, *Eucharistic Reservation in the Western Church* (New York, 1964) • G. Müller-Jürgens, "Communion Vessels," *ELC* 1.545-47 • National Conference of Catholic Bishops, *Environment and Art in Catholic Wor-*

ship (Washington, D.C., 1978) • R. Wischnitzer, "Ark," *EncJud* 3.450-58.

Frank C. Senn

Liturgics

1. Theological Place
2. Subject Matter
3. Task
4. Method
5. History
    5.1. Primary Sources
    5.2. Scholarly Publications
6. Concerns

1. Theological Place

How one defines the proper place of liturgics within the spectrum of theological disciplines depends on how one understands → liturgy and what significance one attributes to it in the life of the → church. If one sees *leitourgia* as a fundamental and central function of ecclesial existence, then scholarly reflection on liturgy has its rightful place both within theology proper, especially ecclesiology, and also within the practical theological disciplines, where liturgics has mostly been located since it emerged as a separate discipline. Ultimately, liturgics exists at the intersection of scholarly theological reflection and the concrete realities of liturgical life.

2. Subject Matter

The subject matter of liturgics is as broad as are the manifold ways in which Christians give liturgical expression to their lives together. Liturgics is thus much more than the study of ecclesially approved rites and texts, since it encompasses the breadth of the liturgical lives of Christians through the centuries, including the porous boundaries of those lives, for example, with practices of popular religiosity or with nonauthorized forms of liturgical experimentation. Liturgics is not primarily devoted to ritual minutiae but to liturgy as a key site of communal, grace-full encounter with the Holy One. Such encounter always takes place within material reality, and liturgics therefore best defines its subject matter not as a separatist endeavor devoted to "sacred space" but as a study of the sacred as always in relation to wider cultural materials. While the subject matter of liturgics is concretely embodied in particular communities, the discipline likewise reflects on the (liturgical) reality of the whole → people of God both present in and transcending particular ritual performances.

There are differing views on the content of liturgics, but most liturgical scholarship covers the following themes: the material reality of liturgical celebration (→ anthropological, cultural, social, etc.), fundamental ritual patterns (whether defined as shape or as order), key celebrations and liturgical rhythms (e.g., the → sacraments and the → church year), and the theological meaning of liturgy.

3. Task

The task of liturgics is to interpret and thereby to enable the flourishing of the liturgical practices of the people of God so that these practices indeed will be sites of grace-full encounter with the Holy One. The task of liturgics, thus understood, necessitates attention to historical development, to present-day realities, and to future possibilities, which arise, not least of all, out of prophetic criticism of existing forms. Liturgics thus has a critical function, often exercised in → dialogue with other theological disciplines but also with critical theories emerging elsewhere, such as theories attentive to gender and race.

4. Method

Methodologically, liturgics ranges broadly. In the past, three key interpretive lenses have shaped the discipline, namely, historical, theological, and pastoral approaches. Historically, liturgics has drawn especially on disciplines such as philology and history, as well as adjacent theological disciplines such as → theology proper, homiletics (→ Preaching), → hymnology, and → pastoral care. In recent decades, other interpretive lenses such as those offered by → hermeneutics, semiotics, → sociology, and cultural theories have become increasingly important.

5. History

A history of the discipline has not been written, although historical narratives of the development of → worship abound, each authorizing particular versions of the liturgical past. Since facts are always theory-specific, each construction of the liturgical past also involves a struggle over meaning today. A history of theological and scholarly reflection on liturgy, however, still awaits the light of day, even if recent years have seen a welcome increase in studies of earlier exponents of the discipline.

In the first centuries of the church, reflection on worship — in the form of pastoral and spiritual expositions of liturgy — took place within the rites of → initiation. In the Middle Ages → allegorical interpretations of the liturgy flourished, in the East, for example, in the *Exposition of the Divine Liturgy* of Nikolaos Kabasilas (ca. 1320-71).

In the → Reformation, worship became a critical theological concern, mostly in relation to concrete liturgical practices. The Renaissance brought the first sustained wave of interest in primary sources and in their publication. Humanistic scholarship (→ Humanism), which opened the doors in the West for a better knowledge of Eastern liturgies, introduced into its ecclesial language the term "liturgy." Within the → Anglican Communion, the Caroline Divines and Nonjurors deserve special mention for their marked interest in matters liturgical.

In the 18th century liturgics began to emerge as a separate theological discipline. The → Enlightenment fostered criticism of existing liturgies and worship practices; it also furthered a decidedly historical orientation of the discipline, which largely dominated the 19th century. Within Roman Catholicism, a focus on rubrics narrowly defined liturgics. Within Protestantism F. D. E. → Schleiermacher (1768-1834; → Schleiermacher's Theology), with his liberal-theological focus on the self and its religious consciousness, decisively shaped Protestant liturgics.

In the 20th century the → liturgical movement rediscovered the liturgy as a fundamental site of ecclesial existence and brought a renewed insistence on the role of the ecclesial community as the bearer of the liturgy. One of the results of this movement within Roman Catholicism was that, after → Vatican II, liturgics became a mandatory discipline in its own right in Roman Catholic theological faculties.

5.1. *Primary Sources*

The primary source of liturgics is the liturgical event itself. Since as a performance, however, this event is not stable and possesses no continuous site and since it is an open question where the "meaning" of this liturgical event might be located, liturgics has historically relied on textual and material witnesses to liturgical events for its work, especially → liturgical books, sermons, → church music, architecture (→ Church Architecture), art, and seasonal rhythms — in short, the material realities that witness to the always-elusive liturgical event. Scripture, as the supreme liturgical book, claims a special place.

Since the time of the Enlightenment there has developed a rich tradition of editions of liturgical sources, and the 20th century saw a decisive deepening of the study and interpretation of these sources. Recent years have brought about an important broadening of the traditional canon of liturgical sources, for example, in relation to women's ways of worship. (For example, women's diaries and popu-

lar writings provide crucial insights into the liturgical lives of people who never had access to the elite clerical power of the pen.) Many writings of religious women on worship exist, especially in convent archives all over the world.

5.2. *Scholarly Publications*

Editions of primary liturgical sources are complemented by scholarly publications that shape the contours of the discipline. Mention may be made of the current liturgical journals *Archiv für Liturgiewissenschaft, Ephemerides liturgicae, Maison-Dieu, Studia liturgica* (organ of the international ecumenical Societas Liturgica), and *Worship*. A number of important series also shape the field, including Alcuin Club Collections, Bibliotheca Ephemerides Liturgicae, and Liturgiewissenschaftliche Quellen und Forschungen. Modern standard works include *The Study of Liturgy, L'Église en prière, Gottesdienst der Kirche, Handbuch der Liturgik,* and *Handbook for Liturgical Studies.* Digital resources are increasingly important in the field.

6. Concerns

In addition to the continuing historical, pastoral, and theological work of liturgics, the following currently are urgent concerns: (1) a liturgical theology able to incorporate theoretically the multiple facets of life in the 21st century so as to make the meaning of liturgy not outside of material realities — including issues of gender, class, race, and geopolitical location — but within them; (2) a liturgical theology attentive to the provocative mappings of recent theories of culture, from notions of the global (and its challenges, e.g., to liturgical ways of conceiving of inculturation) to the impact of information technologies and the rise of Web-based liturgical sites; and (3) a liturgics able to create a liturgical imagery focused on the flourishing of all in the worshipful encounter with the living and lifegiving God.

Bibliography: A. J. CHUPUNGCO, ed., *Handbook for Liturgical Studies* (5 vols.; Collegeville, Minn., 1997-2001) • G. W. LATHROP, *Holy People: A Liturgical Ecclesiology* (Minneapolis, 1999); idem, *Holy Things: A Liturgical Theology* (Minneapolis, 1993) • B. T. MORRILL, ed., *Bodies of Worship: Explorations in Theory and Practice* (Collegeville, Minn., 1999) • B. NICHOLS, *Liturgical Hermeneutics: Interpreting Liturgical Rites in Performance* (Frankfurt, 1996) • F. C. SENN, *Christian Liturgy: Catholic and Evangelical* (Minneapolis, 1997) • R. F. TAFT, *Beyond East and West: Problems in Liturgical Understanding* (2d ed.; Rome, 1997) • D. W. VOGEL, ed., *Primary Sources of Liturgical Theology: A Reader*

(Collegeville, Minn., 2000) • R. VOLP, *Liturgik. Die Kunst Gott zu feiern* (2 vols.; Gütersloh, 1992-94) • G. WAINWRIGHT and K. W. TUCKER, eds., *The Oxford History of Christian Worship* (New York, forthcoming).

TERESA BERGER

Liturgy

1. Term and Development
   1.1. Term
   1.2. Development
      1.2.1. Judaism
      1.2.2. NT and Patristic
2. Churches of the Reformation
   2.1. The West on the Eve of the Reformation
   2.2. Luther and Lutheranism
   2.3. Reformed
   2.4. Anglican
   2.5. Free Churches
3. The Roman Catholic Church after the Reformation
   3.1. Council of Trent
   3.2. Vatican II
4. Orthodox Church
   4.1. Byzantine Liturgy
   4.2. Liturgies Used
   4.3. Structure and Sequence
   4.4. Characteristics
   4.5. Other Rites
5. Congregation-Specific Liturgies
6. Feminist Liturgy

1. Term and Development

1.1. *Term*

In the pagan world, "liturgy" (Gk. *leitourgia,* from *leïtos,* "concerning the public," plus *ergon,* "work") originally had an entirely secular use, connoting the service owed to the public by persons of means; in addition, philanthropists took on additional service, also called liturgy. The basic meaning was thus "service for the people."

A secondary, cultic usage developed for the term, perhaps because ultimately the public was to benefit from the service rendered to the gods. This cultic meaning was adopted in the LXX and in Hellenistic → Judaism for a number of Hebrew terms involving the service of God, and ultimately for priestly service, but the two strands of meaning appear to be mixed. At the time of the birth of Christianity, the Jewish world understood the term as meaning "service to God for the good of the people."

The NT reflects all of these uses, with additional emphasis placed on the sacrificial significance of Christ's death. Only in postapostolic times, however, was the term *leitourgia* routinely applied to worship, with *leitourgos* (the person performing the liturgy) applied to clergy. In the → Orthodox Church "liturgy" came to mean exclusively the celebration of the → Eucharist (§2), while in the medieval West it indicated the whole system of worship. In classic Protestantism, "liturgy," when used, generally meant public worship of all kinds.

In the 1970s the Greek roots of the word "liturgy" were wrongly combined in popular literature to redefine the word as "what the people do," a meaning often put forward in support of radical liturgical change. Philological or historical-theological basis is lacking, however, for such a reading.

1.2. *Development*

1.2.1. *Judaism*

The three centers of Jewish worship in the first century were the home, the → temple, and the → synagogue. From the home Christianity inherited the berakah, or blessing, a major influence in the development of the → eucharistic prayer. From the synagogue came the basic pattern of the eucharistic liturgy, the concept of a lectionary, and the shape of daily services of → prayer. The temple was organized around → sacrifice, so last of all, Christian liturgy adopted some of its terminology and accoutrements, usually in a highly allegorical sense (→ Worship 1.2-3).

1.2.2. *NT and Patristic*

The Christian scriptures were written in an already worshiping church and thus do not set out to prescribe liturgical rubrics, with the exception of → Paul's disjunction of the Lord's Supper from the communal meal (1 Cor. 11:34). The NT clearly shows a church that not only met for worship and instruction but administered → baptism and the Eucharist, believing both actions to be of dominical command. There is also evidence for → anointing of the sick (Jas. 5:14-16) and for → laying on of hands on neophytes and those set apart for certain kinds of → ministry (Acts 6:6; 8:17; 13:3, etc.).

By the end of the first century, → Justin Martyr *(1 Apol.)* and the *Didache* (→ Apostolic Fathers 2.1) attest to structured local liturgy. By the beginning of the third century, the existence of nearly fixed texts and rubric control is attested to by the *Apostolic Tradition* of Hippolytus (d. ca. 236). The so-called peace of the church under Constantine (306-37) provided a matrix in which rich textual and ceremonial growth could occur.

2. Churches of the Reformation

2.1. *The West on the Eve of the Reformation*

Developments during the Middle Ages led to a situation in which liturgical rites were complicated, clericalized, and practiced in what to the laity was an inaccessible language — Latin. This inaccessibility contributed to a wide variety of lay devotions (→ Piety) that could be performed at the hours of prayer and during the celebration of the → Mass. → Preaching, including lay preaching, usually took place outside the liturgy. The offering of masses, particularly for the dead (→ Worship 2.1-2), had great economic importance because of the considerable payments that were often involved.

In the early 16th century the Renaissance had just begun to produce the scriptural, historical, and linguistic learning that would create formal liturgical study, but the → Reformers were almost all in their graves before the results of such study were available. The consequence of this vacuum of information was that when the great Reformers approached liturgical revision, two factors dominated their efforts: their reading of Scripture and their personal outlook. Except in Anglicanism, Protestants gained and expressed a new freedom for the creation of local rites. By and large they preferred the didactic to the affective elements of worship, and the verbal to the visual and kinesthetic.

2.2. *Luther and Lutheranism*

Martin → Luther (1483-1546; → Luther's Theology) did not attempt to use Scripture for detailed prescriptions for worship, since he considered liturgical forms to be in themselves → adiaphora, or not essential to the gospel, and he resisted attempts at → biblicism in liturgy. His reading of Scripture, however, led him to reject in particular any sacrificial language in the Eucharist, along with the invocation of → saints and veneration of their → relics. Alone among the Reformers, Luther retained aural confession as of value to those who chose it. In common with others, however, Luther returned the sermon to a prominent role in the service. He emphasized congregational song, and he himself wrote hymns and liturgical music (→ Church Music). In general, Luther and Lutheranism retained more visual and kinesthetic richness in worship than did other Protestants, a situation that existed until the Anglican revival of the 19th century.

Luther's first great liturgical creation, the *Formula Missae et Communionis* (1523), was a conservative revision of the Mass that retained the Latin language and much traditional text and ceremony. It became the principal liturgical model for the "Common Service" of some German-speaking and most English-speaking Lutherans in North America (→ Liturgical Books). Luther's *German Mass* of 1526 replaced Latin with German, paraphrased the ordinary of the Mass, and further simplified ceremonies. This liturgy is the model for much contemporary European Lutheran worship and was originally used in some German-speaking congregations in North America.

2.3. *Reformed*

Much more radical than Luther's changes were the reforms of text and ceremonial initiated by Ulrich → Zwingli (1484-1531; → Zwingli's Theology) in Zurich and John → Calvin (1509-64; → Calvin's Theology) in Geneva, each showing strong biblical and didactic emphases. Zwingli's *Epicheiresis* (1523) was a completely new eucharistic liturgy, almost a systematic prayer, although retaining some traditional features. Preaching was not linked to a lectionary, and all music was forbidden.

Calvin's *Form of Church Prayers* (1542) survives in Directories of worship in → Reformed and Presbyterian churches, which provide service directions but not texts. In this tradition the Eucharist was celebrated quarterly, although Calvin himself recommended weekly observance. Geneva is recalled mostly for the methods of psalm singing that developed there, even though hymns and → organs were forbidden.

Geneva influenced Presbyterian worship in Scotland, England, and North America. Particularly in America, present-day Reformed worship is moving from Directories to optional fixed texts. Hymns have largely replaced psalms, and instrumental music is the norm.

2.4. *Anglican*

The chief distinction between Anglican and other Protestant worship is the concept of uniformity, by which → consensus in worship provides ecclesiastical cohesion in the absence of more precise doctrinal agreement. Anglican worship centers on the use of the Book of Common Prayer (BCP), first issued in 1549 and revised in 1552, largely the work of Thomas → Cranmer (1489-1556). The prayer book provided complete texts of daily, Sunday, and occasional services, and its use was mandatory. Historically, the BCP is Lutheran in its liturgical conservatism and ceremonial richness, but Calvinistic in its theology. All editions provide daily and eucharistic lectionaries. The English revision of 1662 formed the basis of development in all the daughter churches, although the church in the United States was heavily influenced by that of Scotland. Hymnody was generally accepted only in the 19th century.

Contemporary Anglicanism has benefited from Third World experimentation, especially that of the churches of South Africa and South India, whose rites have influenced revisions in England and North America (Mass 2; Worship 2.3).

2.5. Free Churches

The term "free churches" includes particularly → Baptists, → Brethren groups, Congregationalists (→ Congregationalism), → Mennonites, Methodists (→ Methodism), → Moravians, plus the myriad denominations of North America. Emphasis is placed on preaching, the → pastor's prayer, and congregational singing. With some exceptions, sacraments are infrequently celebrated.

The American experience is also influenced by black worship (→ Black Theology; Black Churches), and the "camp meeting" and "revival" services of the frontier days. Worship in the black and → revival traditions is quite emotional; in the latter it often comes to a climax with converts or penitents publicly acknowledging their → conversion (§1; → Worship 4).

→ Easter

Bibliography: D. Adams, From Meeting House to Camp Meeting (Saratoga, Calif., 1981) • G. Cumming, A History of Anglican Liturgy (London, 1982) • C. Jones, G. Wainwright, E. Yarnold, and P. Bradshaw, eds., The Study of Liturgy (rev. ed.; London, 1992) • I. Pahl, Coena Domini (Freiburg, 1983) • F. C. Senn, Christian Liturgy: Catholic and Evangelical (Minneapolis, 1997); idem, Protestant Spiritual Traditions (New York, 1986) • B. Thompson, ed., Liturgies of the Western Church (Philadelphia, 1980) • V. Vajta, Luther on Worship: An Interpretation (Philadelphia, 1958) • R. Wallace, Calvin's Doctrine of the Word and Sacrament (Edinburgh, 1953) • J. F. White, A Brief History of Christian Worship (Nashville, 1993); idem, Protestant Worship (Louisville, Ky., 1989).

PAUL V. MARSHALL

3. The Roman Catholic Church after the Reformation

3.1. Council of Trent

The Council of → Trent (1545-63) realized that renewal of the liturgy was bound up with reform of the → church (→ Catholic Reform and Counterreformation). It thus formally asked the → pope to republish all liturgical books and to make them binding for all → dioceses and orders that did not have their own ancient uses for at least 200 years. Thus appeared the Roman Breviary (1568), Missal (1570), Pontifical (1596), Ceremonial (1600), and Ritual (1614; → Mass 2.3). The Congregation of Rites was set up in 1588 (combined with another

congregation in 1975 as the Congregation for Divine Worship and the Discipline of the Sacraments; → Curia 1.2.2) to supervise observance. In consequence, a uniform Roman liturgy was established, which led to the study of rubrics and an emphasis on → casuistry.

The age of the → baroque gave the liturgy visual and audible embellishment, and → popular religion also had a fresh impact. The age of church → Enlightenment sought greater simplicity and rationality and faced the danger of making liturgy an instrument of pastoral → pedagogics.

The Catholic restoration of the 19th century sought a closer link with Rome and the Middle Ages. The 20th century → liturgical movement sought a better understanding and more active celebration of liturgy, while recognizing that the liturgy itself stands in urgent need of renewal.

3.2. Vatican II

In Sacrosanctum concilium, the Constitution on the Sacred Liturgy, → Vatican II addressed and developed the concerns of the liturgical movement.

3.2.1. In its interpretation it argued that the liturgy "is rightly seen as an exercise of the priestly office of Jesus Christ. . . . In it full public worship is performed by the Mystical Body of Jesus Christ, that is, by the Head and his members. From this it follows that every liturgical celebration, because it is an action of Christ the Priest and of his Body, which is the Church, is a sacred action surpassing all others. No other action of the Church can equal its efficacy by the same title and to the same degree" (7).

The subjects of liturgy are therefore Christ, who sanctifies (→ Sanctification) believers by Word and → sacrament, and the church, which responds with gratitude and praise. Liturgy thus has a structure that is both descending (katabatic) and ascending (anabatic), that is, a dialogic character. It would be wrong to equate liturgy and cult, for the latter has only the ascending side. The liturgy is not identical with the sum of → rites and ceremonies, nor is it just a cloak of → prayer thrown over the church's acts of ministry.

3.2.2. As a result of the new understanding of liturgy, Sacrosanctum concilium demands active participation (14), regard for → liturgics and liturgical instruction (15-19), and renewal in parts that can be changed. The biblical readings should be increased, the element of communion stressed, the national languages given a larger role, and the liturgy better adapted to national and local contexts (→ Acculturation; Culture and Christianity).

Paul VI established the Consilium for the Implementation of the Constitution on the Sacred Liturgy (1964) to see to the carrying out of these directives. In quick succession new liturgical books and approved translations appeared. A remaining pastoral task is to promote the intelligent and active participation of all members.

→ Baptism; Easter; Eucharist; Funeral 2.2-3; Holy Water; Hours, Canonical; Incense; Marriage; Ordination; Priest; Religious Orders and Congregations; Worship 2

Bibliography: B. BOTTE, From Silence to Participation: An Insider's View of Liturgical Renewal (Washington, D.C., 1988) • INTERNATIONAL COMMISSION ON ENGLISH IN THE LITURGY, Documents on the Liturgy, 1963-1979: Conciliar, Papal, and Curial Texts (Collegeville, Minn., 1982) • E. B. KOENKER, The Liturgical Renaissance in the Roman Catholic Church (St. Louis, 1966) • F. R. MCMANUS, Sacramental Liturgy (New York, 1967) • B. G. MEEKS, ed., The Landscape of Praise: Readings in Liturgical Renewal (Valley Forge, Pa., 1996) • D. N. POWER, The Sacrifice We Offer: The Tridentine Dogma and Its Reinterpretation (Edinburgh, 1987) • J. H. P. REUMANN, The Supper of the Lord: The NT, Ecumenical Dialogues, and Faith and Order on Eucharist (Philadelphia, 1985) • J. F. WHITE, Christian Worship in Transition (Nashville, 1976).

ADOLF ADAM

4. Orthodox Church

In the → Orthodox Church, "liturgy" covers all cultic activity (→ Worship), and especially its main act, the → Eucharist, which is commonly referred to as the Divine Liturgy.

4.1. Byzantine Liturgy

The most important Orthodox liturgy is the Byzantine, which comes from → Antioch and is thus close to the ancient rite of Syrian Antioch. It adopted features of its own in Constantinople (→ Byzantium), and some also from Cappadocia. Patristic teaching, especially in → Christology and pneumatology, provided the occasion for this development. Connected with the concentration on Trinitarian and pneumatological elements is the epiclesis, or invoking of the → Holy Spirit over the sacrificial gifts of the Eucharist. Also apparent in the further development of liturgical forms is the influence of Byzantine liturgical commentaries and their symbolic interpretations (→ Trinity).

4.2. Liturgies Used

The Byzantine → anaphora, the main part of the Divine Liturgy, is fixed, although the rite includes other anaphoras. The Liturgy of Basil, used today only ten times each year, apparently goes back to Basil of Caesarea (ca. 330-79; → Cappadocian Fathers), whose name it bears.

The so-called Liturgy of Chrysostom is the most common. It is celebrated almost exactly as in the time of Justinian II (685-95, 705-11). The prayers of the priest distinguish it from the Liturgy of Basil. The ascription to John → Chrysostom (ca. 347-407) perhaps indicates its origin in Antioch and an early use possibly going back to Chrysostom himself. Its kinship to the Syrian Anaphora of the Twelve Apostles has often been noted.

On days when there is no full anaphora, the Liturgy of Presanctified Gifts is used. The so-called Liturgy of St. Peter is not an authentic Byzantine liturgy; in it the Roman canon replaces the Byzantine anaphora.

4.3. Structure and Sequence

A characteristic of the structure of the Byzantine liturgy is that the so-called Liturgy of the Catechumens (the service of the Word) follows the preparation of the gifts (the Proskomodia, or offering). The former prepares the way for the Lord's coming in his Word with → psalms, → hymns, and prayers. The coming is symbolized by the solemn Little Entrance with the Gospel Book.

The Liturgy of the Faithful follows the Scripture readings. After the Great Entrance, or the procession with the sanctified bread and wine, come the → kiss of peace, the saying of the creed (→ Confession of Faith), and the anaphora. The anaphora itself includes dialogue between the priest and the congregation, the prayer of thanksgiving, the "Holy, Holy, Holy" of Isaiah 6:3 (or Sanctus), the words of institution and anamnesis, and the consecration with the epiclesis. Finally come the intercessions, the → Lord's Prayer, communion, and dismissal.

4.4. Characteristics

The Orthodox liturgy is viewed as an earthly copy of the heavenly liturgy and a depiction of the decisive events in Christ's saving work — → incarnation, passion, burial, → resurrection, → ascension, and sending of the Holy Spirit. It brings together in some sense the mysterium fascinosum with the mysterium tremendum (the mystery that causes both fascination and trembling). Concelebration has continued without a break; the → deacon has an important role to play, and the congregation also participates intensively. The liturgy is anchored in the life of the people; in the Near East it did much to maintain and preserve Christianity in the period of Turkish occupation. The rite has been translated into various languages and may readily be put into new ones.

The Byzantine Liturgy is marked by the veneration of → icons and by a richly developed → hymnology, both of which have their source in the conviction that the eucharistic liturgy, as well as daily prayers, is at the center of the → church year, where the → sacraments and the → sacramentals are to be found.

4.5. Other Rites

The Byzantine Liturgy is the liturgy of all Orthodox → autocephalous churches. Each of the other ancient Near Eastern churches, including the → Oriental Orthodox churches, has its own special liturgical forms, which depend on the family to which it belongs. The so-called Antioch group includes the West Syrian Rite (Jacobites, Uniate Syrians, Malankars, Marcionites, Armenians) and the East Syrian Rite (Nestorians, Chaldeans, Malabar Church). In this group intercessions for the living and the dead conclude the anaphora.

In the so-called Alexandrian group, which includes the Coptic and Ethiopian Rites, the intercessions come directly before the first part of the thanksgiving and after the Sanctus. In the first group, too, the epiclesis follows the words of institution and the anamnesis, while the second group has a double epiclesis — the first before the words of institution, the second after the anamnesis. There are also differences in the number of anaphoras, the calendar, the prayers of intercession, the hymns, the veneration of icons, and other details.

→ Baptism; Easter; Funeral 3; Liturgics; Marriage; Ordination; Orthodoxy 3; Prayer 4; Priest

Bibliography: J. F. BALDOVIN, The Urban Character of Christian Worship: The Origins, Development, and Meaning of Stational Liturgy (Rome, 1987) • F. HEILER and H. HARTOG, Die Ostkirchen (ed. A. M. Heiler; Munich, 1971) • A. SCHMEMANN, Introduction to Liturgical Theology (Crestwood, N.Y., 1966) • H.-J. SCHULZ, The Byzantine Liturgy: Symbolic Structure and Faith Expression (New York, 1986) • R. F. TAFT, The Byzantine Rite: A Short History (Collegeville, Minn., 1992); idem, The History of the Liturgy of St. John Chrysostom (5 vols.; Rome, 1975-2000) • H. WYBREW, The Orthodox Liturgy: The Development of the Eucharistic Liturgy in the Byzantine Rite (Crestwood, N.Y., 1990).

EVANGELOS THEODOROU

5. Congregation-Specific Liturgies

One of the glories of liturgy is its ability to bring together diverse groups and give them a common voice and expression. Sometimes, however, certain liturgies are devised to meet the needs of specific groups or persons. Some of these services are aspects of pastoral ministry. The reconciliation of penitents, sometimes called private confession (→ Confession of Sins; Penitence), usually follows a

prescribed form. Orders for the visitation of the sick and the commendation of the dying have long been part of Anglican and Lutheran service books.

Another traditional way in which the church extends its liturgical ministry into the life of individual families is the → blessing of houses. The practice is very old, going back at least into the late Middle Ages, and was an aspect of the celebration of the Epiphany (January 6), when the Magi entered "the house" where the holy family was residing (Matt. 2:11). Chalk was blessed so that congregants or the priest could mark the lintels of houses with the numerals of the year and the initials of the three Magi — Kaspar, Melchior, and Balthasar. In some places the blessing of houses occurred at → Easter.

Within the context of the Christian year (→ Church Year), various occupations have sometimes been given particular focus and attention: farmers on the Rogation Days before Ascension Day; ordinands at the Ember Days; mariners on the fourth Sunday after the Epiphany in the former calendar, when the Gospel was Matt. 8:23-27; families on the first Sunday after → Christmas (the Feast of the Holy Family); young people on the first Sunday after the Epiphany, when the Gospel used to be the story of the boy Jesus in the temple (Luke 2:41-52); mothers on "Mothering Sunday," the fourth Sunday in Lent (called mid-Lent), when the Epistle was Gal. 4:21-31 (Jerusalem, "the mother of us all"); and the newly baptized on the second Sunday of Easter. Similarly, German Lutherans on the last Sunday of the church year remembered those of the parish who had died during the year past.

The → Roman Catholic Church has provided "Eucharistic Prayers for Masses with Children." The title is carefully chosen: the Masses are not "for" children, as if they were directed specifically to them, nor are they "children's Masses," as if they belonged to children. The → Mass is the Mass, but it may upon occasion be celebrated with specific groups, one of which may be an assembly of children.

All of these services and rites are aspects of the larger liturgy of the church. Certain other rites have been created for use in specific situations and on transitory occasions. The Lutheran Book of Worship (1978), for example, provides an order for corporate confession and forgiveness. The uses of this form include the → reconciliation of those who are estranged from each other, such as families or factions within the congregation; the acknowledgment of a share in corporate wrongs or → guilt, such as participating in repressive actions toward outcasts, lack of openness to strangers in the community, or supporting industries that destroy the environment or contribute to dictatorial governments; and response to a time of civic tension and strife in a community.

In their desire to minister to all within their congregations, several denominations (e.g., Episcopal, Lutheran, Methodist, and Presbyterian) have attempted to devise some form or rite for use by a couple who are about to divorce. These attempts have generally been unsuccessful, however, because if a couple could be brought together for prayer, they probably ought not to be getting divorced. Moreover, it has proved difficult to find biblical texts or warrant to endorse such a liturgy. The Lutheran *Occasional Services* (1982) provides not a service as such but resources and suggestions for use in counseling called "Prayers during the Time of Separation or Divorce" (→ Marriage and Divorce).

At the present time, it would be possible to gather a great many texts of liturgical forms and orders that have been composed within congregations for specific groups such as altar guilds, young people, couples on retreat, and retired persons. With no common heritage or form, these orders are ad hoc creations, often intended for single-use only. None would be common to several › congregations or → denominations and would thus be instructive or particularly helpful for others only insofar as they provide suggestions for some things that might be said or done on a similar occasion in a different place.

These forms cannot be said to be liturgies in the best sense of the word, for they are not services of the whole church, transcending denominational divisions. Rather, they are an assemblage of readings and prayers, the chief purpose of which is to instruct, commend, or otherwise recognize a specific group of people in a specific place. The most comprehensive collection of such rites and forms is the English translation of the Roman Catholic *De benedictionibus,* supplemented with 42 prayers and blessings for use in the United States and published under the title *Book of Blessings* (1989).

→ Pastoral Care; Pastoral Care of Children; Pastoral Care of the Sick; Youth Work

Bibliography: Book of Blessings (New York, 1989) • P. H. PFATTEICHER, *Commentary on the Occasional Services* (Philadelphia, 1983).

PHILIP H. PFATTEICHER

6. Feminist Liturgy

Throughout Christian history women have been liturgical practitioners, even if often neither in their own right nor in their own rite. What has come to be authorized as liturgical tradition, however, has largely left invisible both the multifaceted agency and the manifold marginalizations of women within the → worship life of the churches. Feminist liturgies first emerged as a response to a liturgical tradition that was perceived as thoroughly androcentric. These liturgies arose in the context of the 1960s and their women's liberation movements, profound cultural shifts in the lives of women, and ecclesiological and theological reorientations (e.g., provided by → Vatican II and the emergence of → feminist theology). From the early 1970s onward, feminist liturgies have been celebrated in growing numbers. These women-identified celebrations have thrived in parish women's groups, adult education centers, divinity schools, independent feminist communities, and a variety of other ecclesial and nonecclesial settings.

In the early 1980s an avalanche of publications of feminist liturgies began, and by the 1990s there was a clearly established tradition of services of worship by and for women, or, more precisely, a feminist liturgical tradition. By the present time, feminist liturgies have become a global phenomenon, being celebrated in women's groups and feminist liturgical communities all over the world. These new liturgical traditions are supported by an unparalleled explosion of religious material by and for women, such as new women-identified songs, → prayers, → litanies, → meditations, and → creeds.

6.1. The initial theoretical starting point of feminist liturgies was the claim that both the liturgical tradition and the existing worship life of the churches were deeply androcentric and therefore hardly life-giving for women. While early feminist critiques centered on problems such as male leadership and exclusively masculine language, more nuanced criticism soon appeared as more complex examples surfaced of the liturgical marginalization of women, of silencing, and of misnaming. A growing feminist awareness brought the recognition of wide-ranging gender asymmetry for women at worship: liturgical androcentricity marks not only liturgical language (Scripture and → liturgical books, esp. → hymnals) but also liturgical performance (e.g., the male preacher and presider in a congregation mostly made up of women). Androcentricity marks the liturgical tradition actualized in → worship (e.g., the underrepresentation of women in lectionary readings or in cycles of saints-day festivals) and is embodied in the exclusion of women from specific liturgical tasks (e.g., presiding at key ritual moments, at least in the more traditional but also in many evangelical and fundamentalist congregations).

In contradistinction, feminist liturgies, arising out of criticism of this liturgical androcentricity, make the liberation and the flourishing of women central to liturgical celebration. Some of these celebrations have involved a ritual exodus from the traditional worship life of the churches and the creation of feminist liturgical → base communities, or "women church" communities.

6.2. Most feminist liturgies share a certain style, clustering around the following characteristics. Liturgical production and leadership are squarely in the hands of women, and leadership is often shared rather than in the hands of one celebrant. Feminist liturgies prize nontraditional worship space, and the circle is generally preferred as the gathering form. Liturgical traditions are treated with freedom. Liturgical → dance has been rediscovered, and new rituals created (e.g., a → rite of washing and → anointing after a rape). Feminist liturgies show a predilection for → symbols such as water, candles, and flowers, as well as the symbolic world of women's lives, so often subject to trivialization. In respect to content, feminist liturgies emphasize women-identified materials in language, readings, prayers, worship themes, and images. Ecofeminist sensibilities abound. Almost always, feminist liturgies are ecumenically oriented; some are also interreligious celebrations. Dividing lines between churches and faiths recede into the background in light of the stark divide between women's suffering and women's liberation (→ Feminism; Women's Movement). Feminist liturgies thus render visible a liturgical space in the borderlands of traditional ecclesiological demarcations.

In recent years recognition has grown of the dividing lines between women themselves, especially along markers such as race, class, sexual orientation, and geopolitics. Recognition of such differentiations has both complicated and enriched the ways in which women's lives come to be represented in feminist liturgies.

6.3. Feminist liturgical concerns have been taken up to some extent in the official liturgical life of the churches, especially on the level of language. This change is evident in more recent worship books, lectionaries, psalters, and hymnals, which attempt to leave exclusive language behind, at least as it pertains to human beings. Not all of these liturgical texts have secured official approval, however, and many such texts continue to be used only in more unofficial and local ways. Official liturgical reception of women-identified concerns has been slow, and there are strong denominational and regional differences as well as various forms of liturgical backlash.

6.4. In the last few decades, both the checkered reception of feminist concerns in the official worship of the churches and the rise of distinct feminist liturgical practices can be seen as part of a larger women-identified → liturgical movement that has profoundly (re)shaped the relationship of many women to worship. Despite earlier embodiments of women-identified liturgical practices (e.g., the Women's World Day of Prayer), the movement in the late 20th century birthed something new: with a feminist theological vision it has become possible to name both the constraints and silences that have historically surrounded women as liturgical agents and to recover and reinvent the liturgy as a site of struggle for women's flourishing. The final goal of this women-identified liturgical movement is a liturgy that is life-giving and does justice to all, including all of creation and the One named and worshiped as source of all creation.

Bibliography: N. E. BECKMAN, "Mrs. Murphy's Arising from the Pew: Ecclesiological Implications," *ER* 53 (2001) 5-13 • T. BERGER, ed., *Dissident Daughters: Feminist Liturgies in Global Context* (Louisville, Ky., 2002) • D. J. J. DIJK, *Een beeld van een liturgie. Verkenningen in vrouwenstudies liturgiek met bijzondere aandacht voor het werk van Marjorie Procter-Smith* (Gorinchem, 1999) • L. A. NORTHUP, *Ritualizing Women: Patterns of Feminine Spirituality* (Cleveland, 1997) • M. PROCTER-SMITH, *In Her Own Rite: Constructing Feminist Liturgical Tradition* (Akron, Ohio, 2000; orig. pub., 1990) • M. PROCTER-SMITH and J. WALTON, eds., *Women at Worship: Interpretations of North American Diversity* (Louisville, Ky., 1993) • S. A. ROSS, *Extravagant Affections: A Feminist Sacramental Theology* (New York, 1998) • R. R. RUETHER, *Women-Church: Theology and Practice of Feminist Liturgical Communities* (San Francisco, 1985).

TERESA BERGER

Lives of the Saints

The imprecise phrase "lives of the saints" describes works in the genre of hagiography. Veneration of → saints has always produced descriptions of their lives presupposed by stories about them. The forms of such lives range from popular narratives and legends to more stylized literary biographies. The aim of creating historically verifiable accounts is a purely academic ideal. Only the → Roman Catholic Church has a legally defined concept of saints (through its canonization process), though the understanding of the → Orthodox Church is very similar.

Along with apocryphal acts of the apostles we

find stories of the final hours of → martyrs, told because of their witness unto blood, first in letters, then in accounts of trials, which provided opportunity for apologetic dialogues (→ Martyrs, Acts of the). Quite early such accounts were extended, and martyrdom became the crowning achievement of an exemplary life of devotion (e.g., *Vita Cypriani*). The universal custom of commemorating the dead provided a liturgical anchor for public reading. Eusebius of Caesarea (d. ca. 340) made the first collection of martyr stories (which unfortunately has not survived).

After the period of Christian → persecution the lives of monks (e.g., *Vita Antonii* by → Athanasius) offered instruction in piety. Edited collections appeared by the end of the fourth century (e.g., *Historia monachorum,* translated from Greek into Latin by Rufinus). There were also the various collections of the lives of the Fathers (→ Monasticism). Local calendars (e.g., in Rome, North Africa, and Egypt) corresponded to the collections, adding local traditions. In the Middle Ages legendary additions and reconstructions abounded (e.g., Simeon Metaphrastes in the 10th cent. for the Greek church, *Legenda aurea* [Golden legend] by James of Voragine at the end of the 13th cent.). The Eastern churches sought to order the tradition liturgically in menologions and → synaxaria.

There was some realization that nonhistorical legends were being created. Protestant criticism of veneration of the saints strengthened this sense, and → humanism provided it with philological weapons. After the → Reformation efforts were made to publish old and reliable lives of the saints. Following the plan drawn up by the → Jesuit Heribert Rosweyde (1569-1629), John van Bolland (1596-1665) authored *Acta sanctorum,* a hagiographic → encyclopedia arranged according to calendar dates and claiming to meet the demands of historical criticism. The Bollandists in the Jesuit order continued this work and still follow the original edition (now covering January 1 to November 10 [Antwerp, 1643-1940] 68 vols.). Among rival enterprises one might mention that of the Benedictine Jean Mabillon (1632-1707), who collected accounts of early Benedictines, and that of Thierry Ruinart (1657-1709), who collected the earliest acts of martyrs.

In the Protestant churches examples of the saints were already being collected from tradition at the time of the Reformation, purged of legendary elements (e.g., by Georg Major and Hermann Bonnus). In persecuted churches there were also accounts of Protestant martyrs (e.g., Jean Crespin, *Le livre des martyrs* [Geneva, 1554], and John Foxe, *Acts and Monuments of Matters Happening in the Church* [London, 1563; orig. pub. in Latin, Strasbourg, 1554], commonly known as *Foxe's Book of Martyrs;* also similar works in the Anabaptist tradition, e.g., *Het Offer des Heeren* [The sacrifice to the Lord, 1562] and Tieleman Jansz van Braght, *Martelaersspiegel* [Martyrs' mirror, 1660]).

→ Pietism was interested in the witness of the lives of saintly persons (e.g., see works by Gottfried Arnold and Gerhard Tersteegen). Revivalism continued this trend in tracts and also in church histories (e.g., by J. August Neander; → Historiography 3). Today, after a fixation on sociological structures, the theological task of → biography has again gained recognition.

→ Literature, Biblical and Early Christian 3

Bibliography: AnBoll • G. ASHTON, *The Generation of Identity in Late Medieval Hagiography: Speaking the Saint* (London, 2000) • *Bibliotheca hagiographica Graeca* (3d ed.; Brussels, 1957; orig. pub., 1895) • *Bibliotheca hagiographica Latina antiquae et mediae aetatis* (2 vols.; 2d ed.; Brussels, 1911; orig. pub., 1898-1901) • *Bibliotheca hagiographica orientalis* (Brussels, 1970; orig. pub., 1910) • P. BROWN, *The Cult of the Saints: Its Rise and Function in Latin Christianity* (Chicago, 1981) • L. L. COON, *Sacred Fictions: Holy Women and Hagiography in Late Antiquity* (Philadelphia, 1997) • H. DELEHAYE, *The Work of the Bollandists through Three Centuries, 1615-1915* (Princeton, 1922) • D. H. FARMER, *The Oxford Dictionary of Saints* (4th ed.; Oxford, 1997) • F. HAUSS, *Väter der Christenheit* (3 vols.; Wuppertal, 1976; orig. pub., 1957-59) • F. G. HOLWECK, *A Biographical Dictionary of the Saints, with a General Introduction on Hagiology* (Detroit, 1969; orig. pub., 1924) • H. L. KELLER, *Reclams Lexikon der Heiligen und der biblischen Gestalten. Legende und Darstellung in der bildenden Kunst* (8th ed.; Stuttgart, 1996; orig. pub., 1968) • W. NIGG, *Great Saints* (London, 1948) • T. F. X. NOBLE and T. HEAD, eds., *Soldiers of Christ: Saints and Saints' Lives from Late Antiquity and the Early Middle Ages* (University Park, Pa., 1995) • W. SMITH and H. WACE, eds., *A Dictionary of Christian Biography, Literature, Sects, and Doctrines* (4 vols.; New York, 1984; orig. pub., 1877-87) • S. STICCA, ed., *Saints: Studies in Hagiography* (Binghamton, N.Y., 1996).

EKKEHARD MÜHLENBERG

Llullian Method

"Llullian method" denotes the overall approach of Ramón Llull (ca. 1233-ca. 1315) — Catalan writer, Scholastic, polymath, adviser of popes and princes,

Islamic and Jewish scholar and → missionary — whose basic goal in his writings was to see Jews and Muslims converted. Of his 263 writings, 36 contain the word *ars* (method, way, art) in the title. Llull called this literary work, and especially the summary of it, *Ars generalis ultima* (1305-8), or *Ars magna*.

This title, similar to the *Ars maior* and *Ars minor* of Roman grammarian Aelius Donatus (4th cent. A.D.), whose influence extended throughout western Europe into the Middle Ages, came to be used for the combination of logical predicates that can underlie any subject. This method, called the Ars Llulliana as well as the Ars Magna, was followed across the centuries in → alchemy, → ethics, → ontology, doctrine, and even algebra as a means of calculating the interaction of the principles of a discipline and arriving at true propositions. The involved formalizing made possible mechanisms that can be applied both to groups of predicates and to the basic elements in machines. By regularly combining irreducible units of meaning, Llull set up a model for an intensional → logic that is highly significant for both the verification and the production of meaningful statements, in fields as diverse as interfaith → dialogue and universal sign language.

→ Cabala; Mysticism

Bibliography: Primary sources: Blanquerna: A Thirteenth-Century Romance (trans. E. A. Peers; London, 1926) • *The Book of the Beasts* (trans. E. A. Peers; Westport, Conn., 1978) • *The Book of the Lover and the Beloved* (trans. M. D. Johnston; Warminster, Wiltshire, 1995) • *Opera Latina*, CChr.CM 32-39, 75-80, 111-15, 180A-C • *Selected Works of Ramón Llull (1232-1316)* (2 vols.; trans. A. Bonner; Princeton, 1985).

Secondary works: M. D. JOHNSTON, *The Evangelical Rhetoric of Ramon Llull* (New York, 1996); idem, *The Spiritual Logic of Ramon Llull* (Oxford, 1987) • E. W. PLATZECK, *Raimund Lull. Sein Leben, seine Werke, die Grundlagen seines Denkens* (2 vols.; Düsseldorf, 1962-64) • F. A. YATES, *The Art of Memory* (Chicago, Ill., 1966) 173-98; idem, "The Art of Ramon Lull," *JWCI* 17 (1954) 115-73; idem, "Ramon Lull and John Scotus Eriugena," ibid. 23 (1960) 1-44.

CARSTEN COLPE

Local Ecumenism

The term "local ecumenism" may be used with reference both to informal cooperative activities among → congregations and → dioceses and to the historic ecumenical concern for the more formal unity of "all in each place." Local ecumenism may be distinguished (though not separated) from efforts to realize unity and shared → mission at national, regional, and global levels.

"The ecumenical movement is not alive," said delegates to the Lund Conference on → Faith and Order (1952), "unless it is local." Nine years later, this conviction was amplified by the → World Council of Church's New Delhi Assembly in its famous definition of Christian → unity: "We believe that the unity which is both God's will and his gift to his church is being made visible as all in each place who are baptized into Jesus Christ and confess him as Lord and Savior are brought by the Holy Spirit into one fully committed fellowship, holding the one apostolic faith, preaching the one Gospel, breaking the one bread, joining in common prayer, and having a corporate life reaching out in witness and service to all." According to the assembly report, "Being one in Christ means that unity among Christians must be found in each school where they study, in each factory or office where they work, and in each congregation where they worship, as well as between congregations." This profile of local unity continues to inform → ecumenical dialogues.

Initiatives for local ecumenism, formal and informal, have so proliferated in the past half century that even a representative listing is nearly impossible. In England there are hundreds of Local Ecumenical Projects, in which congregations from different → denominations enter into written agreements to share ministry, buildings, and congregational life. In the United States Ecumenical Shared Ministries (ESMs) have grown rapidly in recent years, often without much denominational support. ESMs include yoked parishes, in which congregations of different denominations share a → pastor and programs, and federated churches, in which persons holding membership in two or more denominations form a single congregation. In Latin America church → base communities — groups of lay Christians, generally poor, who meet regularly to reflect on Scripture, build community, and plan for social action in their neighborhoods — reflect a spirit of local ecumenism.

Other expressions of local ecumenism, found in many parts of the world, include local councils of churches, common → worship on such occasions as the Week of Prayer for Christian Unity, and shared service through groups such as Habitat for Humanity. It is no longer unusual for congregations to develop common educational programs, to pray for neighboring congregations of other traditions, or to invite ecumenical participation in their baptisms, installations, and other celebrations.

At times, local ecumenical efforts are ahead of denominational agreements. It can also happen, however, that congregations or dioceses fail to "receive" (i.e., act on) the results of national or global → dialogues (→ Reception). Effective local ecumenism draws support from wider ecumenical arenas, even as it contributes to them.

While it is hard to generalize, local ecumenism often manifests several characteristics: concern for practical issues (e.g., → mixed marriage), a greater focus on cooperative service than on theological reconciliation, and lay leadership (→ Lay Movement). A single key leader, lay or ordained, can have significant impact on local ecumenism, either as catalyst or deterrent.

→ Ecumenism, Ecumenical Movement

Bibliography: A. BIRMELÉ, ed., *Local Ecumenism: How Church Unity Is Seen and Practised by Congregations* (Geneva, 1984) • M. CONWAY, "Local Ecumenism," *DEM* 629-33.

MICHAEL KINNAMON

Logic

1. General Data
2. Historical Data
   2.1. Aristotelian Approach
   2.2. Stoic Approach

1. General Data

1.1. The term "logic," coming from Gk. *logos,* has many meanings and is used in various ways. Even logicians dispute the subject matter and tasks of the discipline. When it is simply a matter of exactly following rules and principles, we do not have logic in the strict sense. Themes like "transcendental logic" in I. Kant (1724 1804; → Kantianism; Transcendental Philosophy), really an → epistemology, and the supposed logic of G. W. F. Hegel (1770-1831; → Hegelianism) and German → idealism (a kind of metaphysical speculation; → Metaphysics) do not properly belong in logic.

As a discipline, logic primarily tries to establish the most general conditions on which an argument is cogent, helping to detect and remove faults in the line of thinking. In this sense logic is a basic discipline of → philosophy but also a tool in all academic work. Early attempts to present it in formulas after the manner of mathematics, and thus to make its application more secure, made great strides, especially in the 19th and 20th centuries, and greatly reduced purely philosophical preoccupation with it.

Logic is a particularly general and presupposi-

tionless discipline. All other disciplines are subject to its → criticism as regards the cogency of their arguments, their contradictions, their use of empty terms, and so on. This role is true of mathematics, → theology, and → philosophy. Only historically may logic be regarded as a part of philosophy. Formally, it may today resemble mathematics, an even more specialized discipline, but it is not a part of mathematics, even though the two disciplines owe much to one another.

1.2. Human thinking as such hardly follows the rules of logic. Logic arises only when thinking has taken place and what has been thought is stated and presented in some natural or artistic → language. Logic must be as pure as possible, that is, free from the influences and tasks of other disciplines. From the time of E. Husserl's (1859-1938) *Logische Untersuchungen,* psychologism (→ Psychology), or the overemphasis on the psychological side of thinking, has been generally recognized as a mistake. But the mistake of what we could call linguism is still often made when abstraction is made from, for example, the grammatical features of the natural language that is used.

Very common is ontologism, the mistaken introduction of ontic presuppositions, which is appropriate in → ontology but not in logic. A hidden form of ontologism is what has been called gnoseologism, the overhasty introduction of the standpoint of → truth into formal logic. Truth presupposes existence, and decision regarding truth or falsehood is a matter for epistemology or gnoseology, which for its part needs ontology, as well as logic.

Before one applies the rules of logic, in order to stress and if possible isolate what is really relevant logically, one must often first translate into a more or less artificial language resembling that of mathematics. This process can be difficult, not merely because an express appeal to logic is unpopular, but because there can be no protest against the mistakes in logic that are uncovered thereby. One can redress a logical error only by admitting and retracting it. Adding new assertions can only make it worse. To judge from present-day development of the discipline, use of logic is only in its beginnings. In the future, use of the computer in logic is expected to increase (→ Technology).

2. Historical Data

Like the concept of logic, so the history of logic is much debated. The basic work of C. Prantl (1820-88) covered only up to the year 1500 and has not yet been adequately continued. W. Risse gathered rich materials for the task. Good arguments may be advanced in objection to the credibility of more recent sketches (W. Wieland, G. Jacoby). We still await a reliable history free from party prejudice.

2.1. *Aristotelian Approach*

Apart from problematic beginnings in the pre-Socratics (→ Greek Philosophy), the Sophists, and Plato (427-347 B.C.; → Platonism), as well as forms of logic in ancient India and China that have not yet been thoroughly researched, most historians find the start of logic in the logical works of Aristotle (384-322; → Aristotelianism) that were gathered together in the *Organon*. Aristotle expounded his system in an astonishingly complete way. His work has continually influenced the European sphere, especially during the → Middle Ages, but right up to our own time. Not enough is yet known about its important history in the Arab world. For its reception and perfecting we should also take note of Galen (129-ca. 199), Michael Constantine Psellus (1018-ca. 1078), Peter of Spain (= John XXI, d. 1277), and many others.

This classical Aristotelian logic, often unjustly criticized today, was highly valued, cultivated, and developed in → Scholasticism as a tool of disputation (→ Rhetoric 1). It underwent simplification in the famous and brilliant logic of Port-Royal (*La logique, ou l'art de penser* [1662], by A. Arnauld, P. Nicole, B. → Pascal, C. Lancelot, et al.), and it prevailed generally in this form until the 19th century.

On the doctrine of the concept or term, Aristotelian logic built the doctrines of judgment and conclusion. The term is the simplest formal element. It has only to be identical with itself *("A is A")* and distinct from everything else *("A is not not-A")*. This principle is that of identity or noncontradiction. It also involves the principle of excluded middle ("either *A* or not-*A*"). We have here the axioms of the Aristotelian doctrine of the term or concept. Concepts are joined by what was later called the copula into a sentence as subject and predicate. When a sentence raises a claim to truth, it is a judgment. Its quality and quantity, however, the copula fixes more precisely as the logical connection, which may be positive or negative, universal or particular.

At the heart of this type of logic are the so-called syllogisms, which were long considered as prototypes of the only valid conclusions. A syllogism consists of two premises, or statements, that are related by a term that is common to both as subject or predicate. In a valid syllogism a third statement follows as the conclusion, which sets the concepts of the premises in a logical relation of subject and predicate. Thus one might argue:

1. All people are mortal.
2. All Athenians are people.
3. Therefore all Athenians are mortal.

The middle term (here "people") determines what "figure" of syllogism we have. The quality and quantity of the two premises determine the "mood" (or "mode").

Aristotle disregarded the order of premises and thus found only three figures, with 15 moods. Scholasticism knew four figures and as many as 19 moods. As a mnemonic device, it invented names for these moods (the most famous is "Barbara," for the above argument form). The system underwent many refinements. One of the 19 moods (Bamalip) is now seen to be a combination and is thus viewed as superfluous. With three others (Darapti, Felapton, and Fesapo), it leads to a conclusion only on a presupposition additional to the middle term. A. Menne and E. W. Platzeck developed the system of moods in its most refined form. Now that Aristotelian logic is depicted in a way that is radically freed from linguistic considerations, development of the system of figures and moods is at an end.

2.2. *Stoic Approach*

Aristotle and his followers also dealt with nonsyllogistic conclusions, including hypotheticals ("if . . . then") and disjunctives ("either . . . or"). Today these and similar conclusions have again come to be seen as basic. Already in antiquity thinkers of mostly the → Stoic school, in competition with the Megarians (or Megarics, esp. Diodorus Cronos [fl. 300 B.C.]), initiated a different structure of logic, known to us fragmentarily from Sextus Empiricus (fl. early 3d cent. A.D.), which takes as its basis, not the term or concept, but the statement, which is accepted or known as true or untrue. Chrysippus (ca. 280-ca. 206 B.C.) also took this approach (he is said to have taught 20,000 valid conclusions), as later did Philo (d. A.D. 45-50) and others. Because of its uncertain foundations, however, this approach did not get far at the time and lost its way.

The enterprise was again pursued seriously only in 19th-century Europe. Gottlob Frege (1848-1925), Giuseppe Peano (1858-1932), Alfred North Whitehead (1861-1947), Bertrand Russell (1872-1970), Jan Łukasiewicz (1878-1956), Ludwig Wittgenstein (1889-1951), Alfred Tarski (1901-83), and others pioneered various systems along such lines. Forerunners were Augustus De Morgan (1806-71) and George Boole (1815-64), who rather too slavishly took algebra as a model. Ernst Schröder (1841-1902) was the first to note the distinctive nature and symmetrical structure of the algebra of logic and to give it its own definitive form.

The computer today uses the Boole-Schröder algebra. It combines Aristotelian and Stoic logic and completes the theory of definition that is only fragmentary in Aristotle. In this sense it is a part of Aristotelian logic. But it can also do the calculation of statements, which is basic to Stoic logic. Most of the modern symbolic systems of logic work along lines suggested by Philo and the Stoics. Yet, with the further development of the Aristotelian type, it has become apparent again that the approach of Aristotle is the more universal and can be translated without problems into structures that work out in computer-supported applications. The future of applied logic, then, may well lie in the Aristotelian direction.

→ Analytic Philosophy; Categories; Deontology; God, Arguments for the Existence of; Logic and Theology; Nominalism

Bibliography: A. Arnauld, *Logic; or, The Art of Thinking; being the Port Royal Logic* (Edinburgh, 1850) • J. M. Bocheński, *A History of Formal Logic* (2d ed.; New York, 1970) • G. Boole, *An Investigation of the Laws of Thought, on Which Are Founded the Mathematical Theories of Logic and Probabilities* (London, 1854; repr., New York, 1961) • B. B. von Freytag Löringhoff, *Neues System der Logik. Symbolisch-symmetrische Rekonstruktion und operative Anwendung des aristotelischen Ansatzes* (Hamburg, 1985) • E. Husserl, *Logical Investigations* (London, 1970; orig. pub., 1900-1901) • G. Jacoby, *Die Ansprüche der Logistiker auf die Logik und ihre Geschichtsschreibung. Ein Diskussionsbeitrag* (Stuttgart, 1962) • J. Lear, *Aristotle and Logical Theory* (Cambridge, 1980) • C. Prantl, *Geschichte der Logik im Abendlande* (4 vols.; Leipzig, 1855-70; repr., Graz, 1955) • W. V. Quine, *Methods of Logic* (4th ed.; Cambridge., Mass., 1982); idem, *Philosophy of Logic* (Englewood Cliffs, N.J., 1970) • W. Risse, *Die Logik der Neuzeit* (2 vols.; Stuttgart, 1964-70) • A. Tarski, *Logic, Semantics, and Metamathematics* (2d ed.; Indianapolis, 1983) • A. N. Whitehead and B. Russell, *Principia Mathematica* (3 vols.; Cambridge, 1910-13; 2d ed., 1925) • W. Wieland, "Zur Problemgeschichte der formalen Logik," *ZPhF* 6 (1958) 71-93.

Bruno Baron von Freytag Löringhoff†

Logic and Theology

1. History of the Relation
2. Current Issues and Relation

1. History of the Relation
In the course of its history → theology has constantly debated its relation to → logic. We find both basic rejection of logic and its consistent defense and application. It should be stressed, however, that the positive investigation and development of logic easily prevailed. Radical opponents of logic like Peter Damian (1007-72) were marginal figures, not least because they faced the dilemma that they had to presuppose and use logic in their criticism of it, or that in a way that was ruinous for theology, they had to introduce a distinction between divine logic and human logic.

The tradition of a mutually respectful and enriching relation has been followed in Roman Catholic theology and in the → philosophy of religion in the Scandinavian, Anglo-American, and Dutch spheres. In German Protestant theology (→ Theology in the Nineteenth and Twentieth Centuries), the influence of → dialectical theology and of an arbitrary acceptance of S. → Kierkegaard's thought (→ Existentialism), a polemical rejection of logic, gained a footing. Only gradually, with the growing reception of → analytic philosophy, did it lose its hold.

2. Current Issues and Relation
To reconstruct the structure of the relation between logic and theology, we must first distinguish the different forms of logic.

2.1. Logic may be distinguished into *general logic*, which deals with universal, objective structures (rather than with the "laws of thinking") and is related to → language, and *applied logic*, which presupposes the validity of general logic but applies its rules in a specific area. Different relations between logic and theology result from this distinction.

2.2. In the debate about the scientific character of theology (→ Science; Philosophy of Science), the problem of logic in theology involves the binding nature of general logic. In this regard it is clear that scientific theology, like any other form of rational argumentation, must follow the basic rules of general logic (→ Rhetoric 1), since this limitation is a necessary (if not totally adequate) condition of being scientific. If theology claims to be scientific, then there can be no "theological logic" that contradicts the basic → axioms of general logic, such that theological statements might ever be characterized as such by their contradictory nature.

2.3. If we presuppose the validity of general logic, it is both meaningful and necessary to investigate the logic of theology, that is, to work out, in the mode of reflection on the axioms and methodology of the discipline, the specific and characteristic rules that distinguish theology from all other sciences (A. Jeffner, D. Ritschl).

2.4. The relation also comes into view when we inquire about the logic of → religion. Here we find two opposing positions. As a champion of the first position, J. M. Bocheński (1902-95) distinguishes sharply between the logic of religion, which has the status of applied logic, and that of theology, which can use the logic of religion as an aid but is not identical with it.

In the opposing tradition of the philosophy of religion, which the later philosophy of L. Wittgenstein (1889-1951) adopted (N. Malcolm, W. D. Hudson, D. Z. Phillips, et al.), theology itself is defined as the logic of religion, or, more exactly, as the grammar of religious language. On the ground that every language game is logically autonomous, external criteria for the analysis and verification of the religious language game are rejected.

2.5. Formal systems of logic are only beginning to be used to give precision to theological arguments, though the effectiveness of the logic of declarative statements, predicates, and moods, at least as regards proofs of God, has already been demonstrated (H. Scholz, C. Hartshorne, A. Plantinga, H. G. Hubbeling).

2.6. The relations depicted have crowded out interest in the possibility of a theological basis for logic along the lines of → Augustine (354-430), G. W. Leibniz (1646-1716), B. Bolzano (1781-1848), and H. Scholz (1884-1956). This neglect, however, means that the question of knowing the → truth of the basic axioms of logic and their ultimate basis remains unanswered. Similarly, no use is made of an important point of contact for the deepening of the relation between logic and theology, and no work is being done on what is a central task for theology that sees itself as transcendental (→ Transcendental Philosophy; Transcendental Theology).

→ Analytic Ethics; Antinomy; Aristotelianism 1.2; Language and Theology; Nominalism; Ontology; Reason; Scholasticism

Bibliography: J. M. BOCHEŃSKI, *The Logic of Religion* (New York, 1965) • I. U. DALFERTH, ed., *Sprachlogik des Glaubens* (Munich, 1974) • R. M. HARE, *Freedom and Reason* (Oxford, 1963) • C. HARTSHORNE, *The Logic of Perfection* (La Salle, Ill., 1962) • H. G. HUBBELING, *Einführung in die Religionsphilosophie* (Göttingen, 1981) • W. D. HUDSON, ed., *The Is-Ought Question* (London, 1969) • H. O. JONES, *Die Logik theologischer Perspektiven* (Göttingen, 1985) • A. PLANTINGA, *The Nature of Necessity* (Oxford, 1978) • A. N. PRIOR, *Logic and the Basis of Ethics* (Oxford, 1949) • I. T. RAMSEY, *Religious Language: An Empirical Placing of Theological Phrases* (London, 1957) • D. RITSCHL, *The Logic of The-ology* (Philadelphia, 1987) • H. SCHOLZ, *Concise History of Logic* (New York, 1961; orig. pub., 1931) • E. STOCK, *Die Konzeption einer Metaphysik im Denken von Heinrich Scholz* (Berlin, 1987) • L. WITTGENSTEIN, *Philosophical Investigations* (3d ed.; Oxford, 2001).

EBERHARD STOCK

Logos → Christological Titles 3.4

Lord's Prayer

1. The Different Versions
2. Tradition and Redaction
3. Use

1. The Different Versions

1.1. The NT contains two versions of the Lord's Prayer. The form used in most → liturgies is that of Matt. 6:9b-13, which begins with the invocation "Our Father, [you] who are in the heavens" (lit. trans.). Three petitions follow in reference to God ("your name . . . your kingdom . . . your will"), and four in reference to those who are praying ("our bread . . . our debts . . . lead us not . . . deliver us"). The oldest MSS omit the → doxology. The shorter form in Luke 11:2b-4 opens with the simple address "Father." It has two you-petitions ("your name . . . your kingdom") and three we-petitions ("our bread . . . our sins . . . lead us not").

The first, second, and sixth petitions in Matthew's version are also in Luke's. The fourth and fifth in Matthew's version are different in Luke's, and Luke lacks Matthew's third and seventh. In the fourth petition in Matthew we pray for bread "this day," but in Luke we ask for the repeated giving of the bread "each day." In the first half of the petition for → forgiveness, Matthew has "debts," but Luke has "sins." In the second half of the same petition Matthew uses a verb in the aorist tense, by which the forgiveness of others is declared by the one praying (a "performative utterance") in conjunction with divine forgiveness; Luke's version at this place uses a verb in the present tense to declare a constant readiness to forgive.

Yet another version of the Lord's Prayer appears in *Did.* 8.2 (→ Apostolic Fathers 2.1). It has three minor deviations from Matthew and closes with a two-part doxology.

1.2. The close agreement between Matthew and Luke suggests to many scholars that the original might have been taken from → Q (→ Synoptic Gospels); other scholars have concluded that the two versions represent two independent traditions (M and L, respectively), which have been highly stable in this instance. In either case, it is commonly thought that Luke's version is closer in scope and content to its source. That version can be translated back into Aramaic (→ Aramaeans) rather easily. Moreover, it has the rhythm and rhymes of Aramaic poetry, even with the uncertainty of back translation. This factor probably shows that → Jesus formulated the prayer using everyday Aramaic, not sacral → Hebrew. The first and second petitions parallel the Kaddish prayers that concluded synagogue → worship (§1.2), and the second and fifth resemble those in the Prayer of Eighteen Benedictions. Jesus was rooted in → Judaism, even though he made his own contribution.

1.3. One immediately notices that the Lord's Prayer is short and is bare of liturgical adornment. This characteristic is evident especially in the invocation → "Father" (Aram. *abba*), which addresses → God (§5.2) in familiar, colloquial terms. God can also be called Father in Hebrew prayers, but other titles are always added to denote distance ("our Father, our King," or "my Father, my Lord").

The first petition presupposes the sanctity of God's name (Ps. 105:3; 106:47, etc.; Ezek. 36:23) and asks God to demonstrate this sanctity in the world.

The second petition presupposes belief in God's royal power as the source of a new future for → Israel (Ezek. 20:33-34; Isa. 52:7-10). As distinct from the Kaddish, however, Jesus does not ask God to act hastily or to work only on behalf of Israel. The work that he has begun is to be definitive and universal.

The fourth petition, for bread, contains the difficult Gk. word *epiousios*, which is used nowhere else in the NT or in Greek literature generally, except in patristic commentaries on the Lord's Prayer. Various proposals (*italicized* in the following phrases) have been made concerning the meaning of this word:

1. "our bread [= the necessities of life] *for existence*";
2. "our bread *for the existing* [day]";
3. "our bread *for the coming* [day]" (prayed in an evening or early morning prayer);
4. "our bread [in a spiritual sense] *for the coming* [day]" (with an eschatological orientation, signifying fulfillment in the final kingdom with Christ); and
5. "our bread *that comes to us*" (i.e., that which comes to us from God).

English versions of the Bible, at least since the time of Tyndale (1525; → Bible Versions), have actually translated the term as "daily" from Old Latin versions of the NT (*cotidianum*, "daily," which is also in the Vg at Luke 11:3, but Matt. 6:11 has *supersubstantialem*, "supersubstantial"), thus "our daily bread" (see M. → Luther's *täglich*, 1522), even though the Greek term, notoriously ambiguous, does not have that sense, strictly speaking. In any case, the petition shows unqualified trust in the fatherly goodness of God and liberation from self-seeking anxiety.

The fifth petition is the only one consisting of two phrases, and for lack of Jewish parallel, we may suspect that the second phrase has been added. Yet the parable in Matt. 18:23-34 shows that God's readiness to forgive should give rise to a corresponding human readiness.

Within its eschatological frame of reference, the sixth petition is a cry of need in the face of end-time testing (→ Temptation), though this interpretation is not without theological problems (e.g., that God would lead one into it). The Gk. word *peirasmos*, "testing" or "temptation," is used elsewhere in the NT to signify end-time testing, when many will actually fall away (Matt. 26:41; Luke 22:40; 1 Pet. 4:12; Rev. 3:10). In this present world the disciples of Jesus (→ Discipleship), who often have only a minimal or frugal existence and are frequently → persecuted, undergo testing. God is close but also distant, so that their faithfulness is tested constantly. One should not weaken this petition along the lines of Jas. 1:13. Unlike the righteous of the OT (Ps. 139:23 etc.), the disciples of Jesus do not ask to be tested. They are always petitioners, rather than persons who seek merit through accomplishments.

2. Tradition and Redaction

The shorter version can be traced back to Jesus without difficulty. It is in keeping with the total proclamation of → Jesus (§4) and might be seen as a key to it. Considerations regarding the original source militate against Luke's having derived it from Matthew; why would he have cut short the original? The we-petitions show that the Lord's Prayer was not meant for individual piety but for common use among Jesus' disciples or followers. The Lukan context (11:1-28) suggests a recollection of baptism, and Paul also uses "Abba" within a baptismal framework (Gal. 4:6; Rom. 8:15). Perhaps in early days the Lord's Prayer was used by the newly baptized (note the direct reference of Cyril of Jerusalem [ca. 315-386?]; → Baptism 1).

Instruction on → prayer was already provided in Q (Luke 11:9-13 par. Matt. 7:7-11). Luke adds the parable of the friend (11:5-8) to show his → Gentile

Christian readers that they may pray with confidence. His use of "sins" in place of "debts" in the fifth petition was also helpful for them, and he formulated the petitions for bread and forgiveness so that they presuppose the regularity of daily life. Two later minuscules make Luke's second petition a prayer for the → Holy Spirit, but in spite of the support of Gregory of Nyssa (ca. 330-ca. 395; → Cappadocian Fathers), this reading can hardly have been the original.

Matthew makes more drastic changes. Writing perhaps for Jewish Christians, he replaces the encouragement to pray (which was unnecessary for → Jewish Christians) with a warning against inappropriate prayers (6:5-8). He offers a liturgically more stylized version. The invocation is like that of Jewish prayers. The three you-petitions and four we-petitions are also liturgical. In content the third petition is an extension of the first two. The second half of the fifth petition is recast to relate divine and human forgiveness along the lines of Sir. 28:2 (see Matt. 6:14-15). With regard to the sixth petition, the seventh explains that temptation comes from the evil one or (less likely) from → evil rather than from God. The Father is to protect us from it. The prayer has no liturgical conclusion. Only later majuscules and most of the minuscules offer a three-membered doxology along the lines of 1 Chr. 29:11-13, which does not occur in the early Latin and Vg versions.

3. Use

The *Didache* tells Christians to pray the Lord's Prayer three times daily (8.3). → Tertullian (ca. 160-ca. 225), → Cyprian (ca. 200-258), and → Origen (ca. 185-ca. 254) were early expositors of the prayer, often construing it ethically. The invocation and the first three petitions are viewed as a call to a sanctified life, with the third teaching us to put God's will first. The petition for bread is sometimes extended so as to cover all human needs, though often allegorized with an eye on the Eucharist along the lines of John 6. The seventh petition teaches that God will free us from every possible evil.

From the days of Charlemagne (ruled 768-814), children have been taught the Lord's Prayer. The → rosary extended its use. It even became a magical formula in medieval folk piety. The Middle Ages associated various external rites with the Lord's Prayer, such as the lifting up of the cup and the Host, the → sign of the cross, and the kissing of the paten at the embolism.

The Lord's Prayer became a fixed part of the liturgy (→ Worship 1.4) only at the time of Cyril of Je-

rusalem. In Eastern → liturgies (§4) it is prayed before the breaking of the consecrated bread; in the Roman → Mass, immediately after the consecratory prayer known as the canon of the Mass. Usually a more generalizing addition to the seventh petition is recited (the embolism, or insertion). In his *Formula missae* (1523), → Martin Luther (1483-1546; → Liturgy 2.2) omitted the canon but put the Lord's Prayer just before Communion. His *Deutsche Messe* (1526) places a paraphrase of the Lord's Prayer after the sermon. Lutheran liturgical orders place the Lord's Prayer either before or after Communion.

The Lord's Prayer, generally in its Matthean version with doxology, has been included in the → Catechismus Romanus (1556) and in most → catechisms from the → Reformation. It is included in both the Small and Large Catechisms of Martin Luther (1529), the Anglican Church Catechism (1553/ 1572), the Presbyterian Westminster Catechisms (1647; → Westminster Assembly and Confession), the Standard Catechism of the Methodist Episcopal Church (1905; this church merged with others in 1968 to form the United Methodist Church), and the → Old Catholic Catechism (1972).

The → Reformers gave the Lord's Prayer a prominent place not only in their catechisms but also in catechetical sermons. → Pietism taught it as an introduction to prayer in catechetical instruction (→ Catechesis 1.4), though rating spontaneous prayer more highly. The → Enlightenment used it as a substitute for the → creed, as we can see from many sermons, → devotional literature, and poetic renditions. Along with other liturgical texts (e.g., the → Apostles' and Nicene Creeds, the Gloria in Excelsis, canticles), the ecumenical International Consultation on English Texts has proposed a version of the Lord's Prayer in revised English that is increasingly used in many ecclesial traditions.

There has been some discussion of whether the Lord's Prayer might become a common prayer of both Jews and Christians, though the → theodicy question and especially feminist criticism of the patriarchal imagery (→ Feminist Theology) have raised objections.

→ Sermon on the Mount

Bibliography: R. E. BROWN, "The Pater Noster as an Eschatological Prayer," *TS* 22 (1965) 175-208 • J. H. CHARLESWORTH, ed., *The Lord's Prayer and Other Prayer Texts from the Greco-Roman Era* (Valley Forge, Pa., 1994) • C. F. EVANS, *The Lord's Prayer* (London, 1963) • M. D. GOULDER, "The Composition of the Lord's Prayer," *JTS* 14 (1963) 32-45 • A. J. HULTGREN, "The Bread Petition of the Lord's Prayer," *Christ and*

His Communities (ed. A. J. Hultgren and B. Hall; Cincinnati, 1990) 41-54 • INTERNATIONAL CONSULTATION ON ENGLISH TEXTS, *Prayers We Have in Common*, (2d ed.; Philadelphia, 1975) • J. JEREMIAS, *The Lord's Prayer* (Philadelphia, 1964) • J. M. LOCHMAN, *The Lord's Prayer* (Grand Rapids, 1990) • E. LOHMEYER, *"Our Father": An Introduction to the Lord's Prayer* (New York, 1965) • W. RORDORF, "The Lord's Prayer in the Light of Its Liturgical Use in the Early Church," *StLi* 14 (1980/81) 1-19 • N. T. WRIGHT, "The Lord's Prayer as a Paradigm of Christian Prayer," *Into God's Presence: Prayer in the NT* (ed. R. N. Longenecker; Grand Rapids, 2001) 132-54.

HELMUT MERKEL and ARLAND J. HULTGREN

Lord's Supper → Eucharist

Lourdes

Lourdes, France, is a place of pilgrimage on the western slopes of the Pyrenees in the valley of the Gave du Pas River (→ Mary, Devotion to; Pilgrimage). There in February 1858 the 14-year-old Bernadette Soubirous (1844-79, canonized in 1933), a day laborer's daughter, had a vision of a woman in a niche of the grotto of Massabielle. The woman told her, "Que soy era Immaculada Councepciou" (I am the Immaculate Conception). She told Bernadette and the worshipers soon assembled with her to pray the → rosary, do penance (→ Penitence), convert sinners, walk in → processions, drink from the spring in the grotto and wash in its water (which was declared to have miraculous qualities), and found a church. In all, between February and July 1858 Bernadette had 18 such visions.

Against considerable initial resistance from both church and state, episcopal approval of the apparitions was secured in 1862. Papal recognition followed on the part of → Pius IX (1846-78) and Leo XIII (1878-1903). In 1907 Pius X (1903-14) made the day of the first vision (February 11) a feast day for the whole → Roman Catholic Church.

Visions of Mary in France and other countries from the beginning of the 19th century confirmed the devout understanding of simple folk and children (→ Popular Religion). Lourdes was also seen as strong support for the recently declared dogma of the Immaculate Conception (1854; → Mariology). If the church vouched for the appearances, then even though they did not become an article of faith, believers had to regard them highly.

Lourdes became a manifesto against laicizing (→ Church and State) and a place of pilgrimage for all France. The Diocese of Tarbes was renamed the Diocese of Tarbes and Lourdes (1912). The French bishops' conferences now meet at Lourdes. Internationally, Lourdes has also begun to work integratively on behalf of → Catholicism. With a new railroad, cheap fares, an airport, and good roads, it is now one of the most visited of all places of pilgrimage. It has its own staff of monastic assistants and volunteers to aid the sick and handicapped.

Most pilgrims (over five million in 2000) do not stay more than two days. They engage in → prayer, the singing of → hymns to Mary, silence in the grotto, the lighting of candles, drinking the water, bathing for some of the sick, blessings of the sick, masses, processions, and the evening praying of the rosary (often in several languages). They can use the rock basilica of 1876, the rosary church of 1889, or the huge underground Church of Pius X, consecrated in 1958, which has a capacity of 20,000 persons. At times → indulgences are available. → Healings are sought, but more often → suffering is accepted or even offered up as a → sacrifice to God. The Bureau Médical de Lourdes and the Comité Médical International de Lourdes report on healings that cannot be explained by natural causes. Through February 1999 the church has officially recognized 66 cases of healing (→ Miracle). The statue at Lourdes set up on Bernadette's instructions is one of the best examples of a Madonna without child.

A sore point for Protestants is that more and more Protestant charismatics are said to be taking part in the pilgrimages.

Bibliography: S. BEAUMONT, *Histoire de Lourdes* (Toulouse, 1993) • R. HARRIS, *Lourdes: Body and Spirit in the Secular Age* (New York, 1999) • R. LAURENTIN, *Bernadette of Lourdes: A Life Based on Authenticated Documents* (Minneapolis, 1979) • R. LAURENTIN et al., eds., *L'histoire authentique des apparitions* (4 vols.; Paris, 1961-64) • P. MARNHAM, *Lourdes: A Modern Pilgrimage* (London, 1981) • A. NEAME, *The Happening at Lourdes: The Sociology of the Grotto* (New York, 1968).

HEINER GROTE†

Love

1. Roots
2. Human Models
3. Platonic Ascent
4. The Election of Israel

1. Roots

Modern scholarship deals with love primarily in → psychology and → sociology. As regards the roots of love, we are referred to → ethnology and the study of → behavior. Living creatures develop behavior patterns that foster their survival as individuals and species. Members of a group reject nonmembers as strangers or → enemies. The coupling of sexually different beings involves a positive choice to the exclusion of others. Raising young creates a relation between generations that involves care and the warding off of dangers. Self-preservation is a lifelong task and helps to preserve the species, yet it may be sacrificed in natural → death or in defense of group members, especially descendants.

The common feature in all these forms of behavior is an impulse of turning to and the unavoidable turning from, which is the cost of love. The value of love is that it serves the safeguarding of the development of → life, both quantitatively and qualitatively.

2. Human Models

From the roots mentioned, models develop in human beings that carry the typical features of loving relationships and that, in complex psychological, social, and cultural forms, become that which is called love in → society:

- sexual love (→ Sexuality), consisting of the coming together of two individuals who merge into one or whose cells merge, with attendant issues of the choice of partner, the surrender or maintaining of the individual, and the demand for, or making of, sacrifice;
- relation of parent to child, which involves the concerns of care and giving, forbidding and permitting, accepting and rejecting, and reproaching and → forgiving;
- relation of child to parent, with its problems of breaking free, opposing, → trust, → anxiety, and respect;
- sibling relations, with the issues of struggling for parental love and for ranking, mutual support, scattering and coming together again, and conflict and reconciliation; and
- self-love or self-reference, with the problems of self-confidence and self-despising, the punishment and rewarding of self, and the loss, surrender, and gaining of → self.

3. Platonic Ascent

Love in all its forms has been institutionalized (→ Institution) and ritualized (→ Rite). It has been a deity in different ways in the religions, although there has not necessarily been any common concept. → Greek philosophy tried to find such a concept, and after many attempts Plato (427-347 B.C.; → Platonism) achieved a synthesis that is still influential today. Eros is the demand or longing for the perfect, which is beauty. Hence eros is always a lack. It is always seeking, finding the beautiful in beautiful things and persons. The beautiful itself is unmoved and unchanging. Eros, then, presupposes an abstract process of thought as well as an ethical process of purification free of all things transitory. For this reason art, like → pedagogy and → politics, could be called erotic. The value of what is always higher directs and qualifies eros.

Aristotle (384-322 B.C.; → Aristotelianism) carries the thought further and makes it cosmic and universal. By its perfection pure form attracts matter by awakening its eros. The divine is the unmoved mover. In ethics Aristotle also speaks of → friendship *(philia, amicitia)*, which Scholasticism opposed to *concupiscentia*.

Neoplatonism, especially Plotinus (ca. A.D. 205-70), added to the ascent a preceding descent, but the divine as eros remains perfect love. Proclus (410 or 412-85), whose ideas gained great influence through Dionysius the Pseudo-Areopagite (ca. 500), still allows the One to be identical with itself, but he also has it proceed out of itself and then return. Eros forms a chain of love that purifies and illumines what has fallen and reunites it with the One.

4. The Election of Israel

A feature of Israel's religion (→ Israel 1) is election by one God. The motif of → Yahweh in love choosing a people and binding himself to it in → faithfulness runs through the patriarchal tradition (→ Primeval History [Genesis 1–11]) by way of the → exodus, → Sinai, and Deuteronomy to the present self-understanding of the Jewish people (→ Judaism). Sexual love, the love of parents and children, and friendship all naturally occur, but they are never hypostatized. The patriarchal society knows a relationship with God as child to father, but the dominant model is that of lover and beloved.

Hosea, Jeremiah, and Ezekiel confront a faithless people with a passionate lover. The models of father, mother, and ruler are more prominent in the → creation and Zion traditions. Deutero-Isaiah (Isaiah 54) carries the thought of love a step further. The one who has been betrayed forgives the one who is unfaithful. The suffering of the lover finds personification in the Suffering Servant, and it has atoning power. In Job human → suffering constitutes a reason to doubt God's love. The demand of the → Torah in Deut. 6:4-5 and Exod. 20:6 involves the focusing of human life on a relationship of love. Present misfortune may be a reason for despair, but it is also a reason for reassurance of God's love in the whole history of the Jewish people.

5. God as Love (NT)

5.1. The → Synoptic tradition tells us that in the name of a merciful God, → Jesus eliminates barriers between the righteous and sinners (Mark 15), friends and foes (Luke 6:27), and Jews and → Gentiles (Matt. 8:5-13 and par.). Naturally, this overleaping love creates new divisions between those who accept it and those who reject it and exclude themselves from the feast. We thus find the community ethic of love of neighbor (Luke 6:36-42 and Matt. 25:31-46). As you love, so you will be loved, and vice versa. The → healings are depicted as witness to God's turning to us. The one who loves ventures life itself. Only by giving is life won (Mark 8:34-37 and par.). The stories of the birth, → baptism (§1), intimations of the passion, transfiguration, passion, and resurrection (→ Easter) present Jesus as the beloved Son in whom the Father manifests himself, in whom he suffers, and whom he raises again as the victory of love. Love is here a life story that can be told.

For → Paul this story has universal significance (Rom. 5:12-21, comparing Adam and Christ). He asks how Jews and Gentiles can participate in it. In faith we find ourselves broken and loved by the same inseparable love of God that is in Christ (Rom. 8:29-39). Love is a feature of the union of the members of Christ's body (1 Corinthians 13). It is the practice of faith (Gal. 5:6, 13-15). It is a gift that is dearly bought.

In Johannine theology (→ John, Gospel of) the world is about to perish (John 3:16-18), and only love can free it from its anxiety. Love consists in the fact that God gives his only Son so that all will be won. Hence John can say that "God is love, and those who abide in love abide in God, and God abides in them" (1 John 4:16b).

5.2. The doctrine of the → Trinity represents the conceptual attempt to combine the God of Israel with the history of Jesus and with the ancient Greco-Roman understanding of the world. Its logic consists in an explication of love. The lover invokes or calls into existence a beloved, namely, the world. Because God loves, he grants freedom. Anxiety within that freedom, however, leads to selfishness; love is lost, the integrity of life is threatened, and natural death now becomes something frightening.

God's love, however, holds firm to the beloved as the Son, and he elects the Son in the human being Jesus, who voluntarily suffers the death of the separated human being. In that death and in God's own loyalty to his chosen one, love is revivified. The spirit of love and of freedom now reigns between the lover and the beloved; that spirit opens itself up to the world, and the world itself can now participate in the history of reconciliation. Because life rather than death is now our future, the former selfishness and anxiety of existence are overcome. Fear is no longer found within love (1 John 4:17).

As Albert → Schweitzer (1875-1965) demonstrated, love in the NT remains oriented toward its eschatological (→ Eschatology) fulfillment. Once the initial feeling of near expectation has waned, however, this eschatological qualification is dropped, and love oscillates between nomistic and moral praxis within the church community, on the one hand, and Neoplatonic or → Gnostic speculation, on the other.

6. European Tensions

6.1. The first Christian centuries had the task of merging the biblical and Hellenistic legacies regarding love. → Augustine (354-430; → Augustine's Theology), whose concept became normative for the West, chose *caritas* as the key word. It is implanted in us by the Creator to direct us to God, but we misuse it in our craving to achieve earthly goals. The love of God must help us, then, lest we fall victim to *cupiditas.*

A century later Dionysius gave lasting impact to the thinking of Proclus. God, who is the One, the → good, the fullness, reaches out and gathers in. Love of self, neighbor, and God is one and the same.

→ Monasticism cultivated renunciation of the world for the sake of closeness to God. In it mercy became → asceticism. The decline of morals at the collapse of the → Roman Empire was met with the effort to free love from everything carnal and earthly and to make it heavenly alone. This focus provides the context of discussion of the new medieval myths of Tristan and Iseult (also Isolde) or Perceval, and the theme of inevitably unlucky love (→ Middle Ages 1). But the other side is also present. Dante's (1265-1321) heavenly Beatrice is followed by Boccaccio's (1313-75) earthy *Decameron,* though Boccaccio felt no opposition to Dante. The high minnesingers of the 12th and 13th centuries scorned → marriage and physical love. The revered woman and the heavenly Virgin merged into one another. Ordinary people, however, sought more immediate satisfaction.

Passion mysticism constituted a special form. It sought union with Christ by killing off the self ($\to$ Mysticism 2; Discipleship 2). In such mysticism imitation of Christ was a way of suffering and of mystical union in love (e.g., $\to$ Bernard of Clairvaux, Henry Suso, J. Tauler). Something similar may be seen in Islamic mysticism ($\to$ Mysticism 1) and later in Protestant $\to$ piety (e.g., Count N. L. von $\to$ Zinzendorf; $\to$ Moravian Church).

The $\to$ Renaissance discovered Greek antiquity, especially Plato. For Michelangelo (1475-1564), however, the ideal was flesh-and-blood humanity, not the divine soul.

Martin Luther's (1483-1546; $\to$ Luther's Theology) Reformation was only in apparent contradiction, since it sought religious depth for the new human self-awareness. Love as infinite longing is simply the vain attempt at self-redemption. God is love as both Creator and Redeemer, hence he is already with the sinner ($\to$ Sin), who must simply accept this love in $\to$ faith. $\to$ Luther found the loving presence of God in the Lord's Supper ($\to$ Eucharist 3). Once Christ says, "This is my body," his body is present through the Word and power of the Holy Spirit. This presence gives faith its assurance and its freedom to love. Unbelief, however, turns love into $\to$ wrath (§§2-3). Luther saw the distinction in terms of $\to$ law and gospel, from which he deduced his $\to$ two-kingdoms doctrine.

6.2. From the time of the troubadours the great writers on love oriented themselves to the inevitable destruction of perfect love. Don Quixote loves in knightly fashion a coarse village maiden. Romeo and Juliet pay for their violation of barriers with death. Don Juan's eros is unsatisfied. Marquis de Sade (1740-1814) makes a martyr of pure love, and Richard Wagner (1813-83) makes death of love the only redemption. The middle-class world vacillates between the superficial desire for a happy ending and the deeper search for sacrifice.

G. W. F. Hegel (1770-1831; $\to$ Hegelianism) attempted a synthesis. The presence of God is love, and in the death of Christ, love takes the negative to itself and transforms it.

The congregation represents this love in faith. If the $\to$ church wants to dominate, however, it becomes secular. Love, then, must pass over into society, which is possible only through the medium of $\to$ reason. The moral $\to$ state is thus the goal of God's love.

The church, the visible and social actualization

of love, also has the task of standing with those who are closest to infinite pain. K. $\to$ Marx (1818-83) gave this mission to the $\to$ proletariat, which cannot be fulfilled without dictatorship ($\to$ Marxism 1).

S. $\to$ Kierkegaard (1813-55) set the risk of faith before love. Love must therefore be grasped by faith, for experience of it is always ambivalent.

7. High Points of Debate

Since the 18th century the intimacy of *marriage* has been the model of love. Love as passion, though, claims that it can violate $\to$ norms, yet when norms lose their force, only pure feeling remains. Love without conditions or ends, and therefore without cost, is unstable. Therapeutic writings ($\to$ Psychoanalysis) and practice view the relationship of husband and wife as an opportunity for learning throughout life and all its stages.

In the United States a socioreligious movement emerged during the second half of the 19th century that understood God's kingdom simultaneously as both a religious and a political task and Jesus especially as a social reformer. The preeminent representative of this Social Gospel movement was W. $\to$ Rauschenbusch (1861-1918). Although similar thinking also emerged in Europe, this insistence on bringing or incorporating love into society itself typifies more the spirit of democracy in America (A. de Tocqueville) and the attempts to establish a social balance between various population groups ($\to$ Martin Luther King Jr.).

A new mysticism involves the evolutionary thinking ($\to$ Evolution) of P. Teilhard de Chardin (1881-1955) regarding the cosmic Christ, as well as the $\to$ New Age search for harmony, which may perhaps testify to a global common understanding that seeks to free love of every restriction. If it is not put into practice, however, this kind of attitude results in self-deception. $\to$ Feminist theology seeks to reactivate the mother-child model in the relationship to God, and in this way it responds to the search for security. At the same time it fights for a symmetrical relation between the sexes ($\to$ Sexism), an aspect of the relationship to God yet to be fully developed theologically.

8. Hinduism and Buddhism

The history and variety of the religious culture of $\to$ Hinduism and $\to$ Buddhism between India and Japan defy summary. The gods of Indian religion are sexually differentiated, and their mutual relations and relations with their worshipers are also erotic. Hindu Gods like Siva and Kali are both kind and fearsome. The approach of believers to the gods is one of *bhakti* (devoted surrender). Personal relations are built up, overlaid, and even fully replaced in a universal order, *dharma*. Throughout the course of life, or → karma, individuals must follow this order, for good and evil bring ineluctable fruits. Strict order becomes *saṁsāra* (the cycle of rebirth), from which *mokṣa* (release, redemption) is sought, which is achievable through meritorious acts, asceticism, and trustful surrender.

The life and teaching of Buddha (ca. 563-ca. 483 B.C.) were devoted to redemption. Neither meritorious acts nor asceticism, he taught, can help a person out of the cycle, for the will and the thirst for life keep it intact. By the exercise of kindness, pity, rejoicing with others, and equanimity, one can break free from willing and therefore from the compulsion to be a separate self. In Mahayana Buddhism the idea developed that human beings themselves could become bodhisattvas and give themselves enlightenment. Since in this religious framework the individual was felt to be a burden or at least transitional, love became something fluid and suprapersonal and came into tension with the social order. This conclusion applies also to Zen Buddhism in China and Japan, with its practice of *bushidō* (a code of chivalry valuing honor above life).

9. Islam

The → Qur'an and early → Islam present no special religious relation to love. They presuppose natural loving relations and prescribe them in religious legal statutes that are close to human needs, especially rules of marriage and divorce. According to Qur'an 3:31, when you love Allah and follow his commandments, Allah will love you and pardon your sins. In the ninth century, at a time of great political expansion for the Islamic kingdoms, → Sufism arose. This doctrine and practice of mental concentration was ascetic, mystical, pantheistic (→ Pantheism), and loving. The Sufi master al-Ḥallāj (ca. 858-922) said of the relation between God and the self, "I am he whom I love, and he whom I love is I."

Al-Ghazālī (1058-1111) succeeded in reconciling Sufism with the orthodox tradition in a way similar to that employed by Christian Scholasticism, namely, with the help of Plato and Aristotle. At the first stage love is self-preservation; at the second it is gratitude to those who do us good or from whom we expect good. At a higher stage it turns to others because they are good. Then it turns to the beautiful. At the highest stage of love the relation is to God, a truth resting on God's having made us in his image. He does not love us out of any lack but out of his own → perfec-

tion so as to kindle love in us. This responsive love finds expression as love of neighbor and also as immersion in the love of God, even to the point of dissolution in it. Because historically Islam never developed a notion of duality between church and state, it views itself as the direct legislative power within society, a position irreconcilable with the pluralism of values characteristic of Western societies.

Hans Küng's idea of inviting all the world's religions to come to an understanding regarding a common or shared "world ethos" is certainly worthy of our most serious efforts.

Bibliography: H. ARENDT, *Love and St. Augustine* (Chicago, 1996) • M. BALINT, *Primary Love and Psychoanalytic Technique* (London, 1985; orig. pub., 1952) • T. J. VAN BAVEL, "Love," *Augustine through the Ages: An Encyclopedia* (ed. A. D. Fitzgerald; Grand Rapids, 1999) 509-16 • L. BOFF, *Church: Charism and Power. Liberation Theology and the Institutional Church* (New York, 1985); idem, *Jesus Christ Liberator: A Critical Christology for Our Times* (Maryknoll, N.Y., 1978) • V. BRÜMMER, *The Model of Love: A Study in Philosophical Theology* (New York, 1993) • E. FROMM, *The Art of Loving* (New York, 2000; orig. pub., 1956) • J. B. LONG, "Love," *EncRel(E)* 9.31-40 • N. LUHMANN, *Love as Passion: The Codification of Intimacy* (Stanford, Calif., 1998; orig. pub., 1982) • J. A. MAGNO, *Self-Love: The Heart of Healing* (Lanham, Md., 2000) • J. MOLTMANN, *The Crucified God: The Cross of Christ as the Foundation and Criticism of Christian Theology* (New York, 1974) • F. J. NOCKE, *Liebe, Tod und Auferstehung* (3d ed.; Munich, 1993) • A. NYGREN, *Agape and Eros* (New York, 1969) • J. PIEPER, *Faith, Hope, Love* (San Francisco, 1997) • W. C. PLACHER, *Narratives of a Vulnerable God: Christ, Theology, and Scripture* (Louisville, Ky., 1994) • G. PORTELE, *Autonomie, Macht, Liebe. Konsequenzen der Selbstreferentialität* (Frankfurt, 1988) • D. DE ROUGEMENT, *Love in the Western World* (rev. ed.; Princeton, 1983) • P. SCHMIDT, *Vater, Kind, Bruder. Biblische Begriffe in anthropologischer Sicht* (Düsseldorf, 1978) • W. TRILLHAAS, *Sexualethik* (2d ed.; Göttingen, 1970).

JOACHIM SCHWARZ

Loyalty → Faithfulness

Luke, Gospel of

5. Genre and Style
6. Theology

1. Author

As the language of the Gospel of Luke indicates, its author came from educated pagan circles, probably in the North Aegean. At the time of writing he had become a Christian and belonged to a group of missionaries a generation after the death of → Peter and → Paul. His work, which may date to about 80-90, is evidently that of a historian of the day (→ Historiography 2), a convert (→ Conversion 1) anxious to defend the faith, and an evangelist with a zeal to impart it. The author aimed his work at → Gentiles in his own circle, at cultivated Jews, and at Christians who had perhaps been unsettled by conflicting reports (note Luke 1:4; Acts 22:30; 25:26). Theophilus, to whom he dedicated the work (Luke 1:3; Acts 1:1), might well have belonged to the third group, unless he was simply a God-fearer who had as yet moved into neither → Judaism nor Christianity.

2. Structure

Luke divided his work into two parts, the gospel and Acts. The first part opens with a prologue in the secular manner (1:1-4) and then offers accounts of the birth of → John the Baptist and the birth of → Jesus. The story of the work of the Baptist reaches a climax in the → baptism of Jesus (3:21-22).

The → messianic ministry of Jesus takes place first in Galilee (4:1–9:50). Jesus shows himself to be the Messiah with the features of a man of God, that is, of a → prophet and healer. The second part of the gospel, announced with the account of the transfiguration, stands under the sign of the → suffering and → death of the Messiah (9:51–19:27). This journey to Jerusalem offers the occasion for instruction of the → disciples and for many addresses. The entry into Jerusalem introduces the third and last part of the gospel, which focuses on the final teaching in the temple, the → passion, and the → resurrection (19:28–24:53).

3. Sources

In his use of sources, Luke, an accomplished author, obliterates traces of these documents like all the historians of his time. He may have used different sources, alternating them in blocks. The sources include stories of the births of John and Jesus, → Q, Mark, material peculiar to Luke, and perhaps a passion story similar to that in John's gospel. The special Lukan material has some individual features (e.g., breadth of narration, dramatic beauty, and good characterization).

4. Texts

In addition to the late Byzantine text, textual criticism distinguishes (more clearly in Acts) the so-called Egyptian and Western texts. The former is generally to be preferred to the latter, which contains additional episodes (e.g., in Luke 6:5 v.l.) and divergent readings. The Egyptian, however, is not more neutral than the Western. Both give us insight on the situation of the text in the second century, without allowing us to go back to the first.

5. Genre and Style

The work of Luke claims to be historical but aims to convince or reassure rather than to instruct. It may be viewed as a monograph (→ Gospel) oriented toward individuals rather than peoples or cities. The personages involved in historical situations are guided by the will of God. In the gospel, which narrates the life of Jesus, God reveals his victory in the direction of events. The resurrection of Jesus transcends human acts of violence. The Book of Acts then offers, as it were, the history of a philosophical movement, accounts of the disciples succeeding that of the founder. The mission of Peter and Paul is here oriented to the fact of the resurrection and receives its efficacy from the → Holy Spirit.

Luke achieved a higher literary level than his predecessors. In his work Christian literature ceased to be merely popular propaganda, though without becoming secularized. The selected vocabulary, however, has nothing of the artificiality or preciosity of the reactionary movement of Atticism. It is the koine of the day (→ Greek Language), inspired by the LXX (→ Literature, Biblical and Early Christian, 2).

6. Theology

For Luke the Christian God is the Creator and the Redeemer of → Israel, although the saving purpose that God pursues is constantly thwarted by his own people (→ Salvation; People of God). The intervention of Jesus is the expression of the final effort of the divine goodness to arouse Israel. When, according to Luke, the majority of the Jews rejected the divine offer, it is made (in Luke's day) to the Gentiles (Acts 28:28). Christianity for Luke is a universal religion.

Although Christianity is seen as the goal for all nations, it does not cast off Israel's past. According to Luke's exegesis, the Scripture that the Holy Spirit once dictated and now expounds is in full agreement with the apostolic witness (Acts 15:14-15; 28:25). Christian → lifestyle, however, is shaped by the commands of → love in the gospel rather than by the precepts of the → law. Though Luke puts the divine intervention first, he does not neglect the need for human response (*metanoia;* → Penitence), which must be maintained in the form of lasting commitment.

Luke bears witness to the standardizing of Petrine and Pauline theologies toward the end of the first century. Yet a more optimistic view of humanity softens the Pauline picture of the radical alienation of sinners (Romans 1–3). The → cross, then, is less the expression of a curse than the result of the commitment of Jesus and an expression of human violence.

Like others of his time, Luke understands the → parousia to be delayed. The present is not the end time in the sense of → apocalyptic but the last portion of the history of salvation and perdition (→ Salvation History). There are two main historical periods: that of → promise and that of fulfillment. The latter begins with John the Baptist, culminates in Jesus, and continues in the age of the witnesses and Luke himself. It is not yet the age of the → kingdom of God, but various factors advance the kingdom, such as Jesus' presence, mutual love in the → primitive community, missionary successes, and martyrdom (→ Martyrs).

→ New Testament Era, History of; Synoptics

Bibliography: Commentaries: F. Bovon (EKKNT; 3 vols.; Neukirchen, 1989-2001; ET Hermeneia; Minneapolis, 2002-) • R. A. Culpepper (NIB; Nashville, 1995) • J. A. Fitzmyer (AB; 2 vols.; Garden City, N.Y., 1981-85) • J. B. Green (NICNT; Grand Rapids, 1997) • T. L. Johnson (SacPa; Collegeville, Minn., 1991).

Other works: F. Bovon, *Luke the Theologian: Thirty-three Years of Research (1950-1983)* (Allison Park, Pa., 1987) • H. J. Cadbury, *The Making of Luke-Acts* (2d ed.; London, 1958) • H. Conzelmann, *The Theology of St. Luke* (Philadelphia, 1982; orig. pub., 1960) • M. D. Goulder, *Luke: A New Paradigm* (Sheffield, 1989) • H. Hendrickx, *The Third Gospel for the Third World* (Collegeville, Minn., 1996) • J. Jeremias, *Die Sprache des Lukasevangeliums* (Göttingen, 1980) • J. Jervell, *Luke and the People of God: A New Look at Luke-Acts* (Minneapolis, 1972) • L. E. Keck and J. L. Martyn, *Studies in Luke-Acts* (Philadelphia, 1980) • J. D. Kingsbury, *Conflict in Luke: Jesus, Authorities, Disciples* (Minneapolis, 1991) • R. Maddox, *The Purpose of Luke-Acts* (Edinburgh, 1982) • J. H. Neyrey, ed., *The Social World of Luke-Acts: Models for Interpretation* (Peabody, Mass., 1991) • P. Pokorný, *Theologie der lukanischen Schriften* (Göttingen, 1998) • G. Schneider, *Lukas, Theologe der Heilsgeschichte* (Bonn, 1985) • R. J. Swanson, *NT Greek Manuscripts: Variant Readings Arranged in Horizontal Lines against Codex Vaticanus. Luke* (Sheffield, 1995) • R. C. Tannehill, *The Narrative Unity of Luke-Acts* (2 vols.; Philadelphia, 1986, and Minneapolis, 1990) • D. L. Tiede, *Prophecy and History in Luke-Acts* (Philadelphia, 1980).

François Bovon

Luther, Martin

Overview
1. Birth, Education, and Early Career
2. The Evangelical Breakthrough and Early Conflict with Rome
3. Conflict among the Reformers
4. The Reformation Established
5. Final Years

Overview

Martin Luther (1483-1546) was the leading figure of the → Reformation era, itself an age of outsized personalities. While there were other "evangelical" or "Protestant" reform movements in the 16th century, Luther's was first both in time and influence.

An erudite scholar, impassioned polemicist, formidable opponent in debate, expert in Hebrew and Greek, and a masterly writer in both Latin and German, Luther was the most widely published author of his time. His immense literary output included theological treatises and disputations, Bible translations and commentaries, sermons, → hymns, liturgies, → catechisms, devotional writings, and an extensive correspondence, both private and public.

It is clear that Luther's reformatory work was inseparable from his several roles or vocations: as an Augustinian friar and ordained priest of the Church of Rome (until 1521); as a university professor and a parish pastor and preacher; as a counselor to urban magistrates and territorial rulers, as well as to fellow clerics and churchmen; as a husband and father; and as a shaper of the emerging "Lutheran" church and defender of its faith.

Luther's career was marked by antinomies. Himself trained in the theologies of medieval → Scholasticism, he became a relentless critic of the Scholastics as exponents of a piety of "works righteousness" (i.e., doing one's moral best with the aid of divine grace) that militated against the gospel's unconditional promise of → salvation by God's mercy alone, for the sake of Christ's merits alone, through → faith (trust of the heart) alone. Himself religiously formed as a monk of strict observance, he came to reject → monasticism's claim to be the authentic life of Christian "perfection," which he now located, rather, in the ordinary Christian's life of unfeigned love to God and the neighbor within the circumstances of daily life in the world. Himself a Catholic → priest, set apart from the laity by his capacity to offer the propitiatory sacrifice of the → Mass on behalf of the living and the dead, he came to affirm the priesthood of all believers by virtue of their baptism and, therewith, their privilege and obligation to intercede before God in → prayer for all persons and to render to God their perpetual sacrifice of praise and thanksgiving.

Condemned and excommunicated by the → Roman Catholic Church, outlawed by the emperor and estates of the Holy Roman Empire, Luther became — not by intention or personal design, but in consequence of the course of events in both church and state — a primary agent in the dividing of Western Christendom into competing confessions ("denominations"), a fateful development that, after his death, issued in an age of devastating religious wars.

1. Birth, Education, and Early Career

Martin Luther's life ended where it began: in the town of Eisleben, in the county of Mansfeld, in electoral Saxony. There he was born on November 10, 1483, the son of strict, frugal, pious parents. And there he died, of heart failure, on February 18, 1546, while on a diplomatic mission to reconcile the feuding counts of Mansfeld. Educated, until age 18, at schools in Mansfeld, Magdeburg, and Eisenach, Luther matriculated at the University of Erfurt in 1501, where he studied the writings of Aristotle and was schooled in the late medieval → nominalist tradition of philosophy and theology associated with William of Ockham and his heirs. After graduating with an M.A. in early 1505, Luther began the study of law, which soon came to an abrupt end. Moved by religious anxiety about his soul's salvation and terrified by a near encounter with death in a violent thunderstorm, he vowed to become a monk and, in July 1505, entered the Erfurt cloister of the Observant → Augustinian Hermits. In 1507 he was ordained priest, celebrated his first Mass, and began the study of → theology, devoting himself with special fervor to → meditation on Scripture. Later in life he could justly claim that he was a monk "without reproach," a self-estimate that finds confirmation in his election, in 1515, as district vicar in charge of ten monasteries, including his own motherhouse at Erfurt.

In the winter of 1510-11 Luther traveled to Rome on business of his order. Upon his return he was transferred to the cloister in Wittenberg at the directive of Johann von Staupitz, the head of the German Augustinian Observants, who was also Luther's father confessor and theological mentor. After receiving the doctor of theology degree in 1512, Luther succeeded Staupitz as professor of Bible at the recently founded (1502) University of Wittenberg, where he remained until his death. In 1514 he was also appointed preacher at the parish church of St. Mary. Meanwhile, in 1513, he had launched his pioneering exegetical lectures on the Psalms (1513-15), Romans (1515-16), Galatians (1516-17), and Hebrews (1517-18), after which he returned to the Psalms (1519-21).

2. The Evangelical Breakthrough and Early Conflict with Rome

During the course of these lectures, and drawing upon his study of → Augustine, especially Augustine's anti-Pelagian writings (→ Augustine's Theology), Luther arrived at his evangelical breakthrough, or reformational discovery. This insight afforded him a new understanding of the biblical "righteousness of God" as the spotless righteousness of Christ himself that a merciful God freely imputes and imparts to sinful human beings apart from works of law, so that they are "justified," or made right with God, by faith alone in the gospel promise of this inestimable gift. The precise date and, indeed, the specific content of this discovery remain controverted among scholars, not least because one can observe significant shifts of emphasis in Luther's developing theology of → justification during these same years (→ Reformation Principles).

With the declaration that "the whole Aristotle is to theology as darkness is to light," Luther in September 1517 advanced 97 theses against scholastic theology. These were followed, in October, by his 95 theses "on the power and efficacy of → indulgences," which were soon disseminated throughout the empire. Focusing on the church's pivotal sacrament of penance, and touching as they did on sensitive issues of papal authority, the theses became the proximate occasion for charges of heresy and proceedings against Luther in Rome, which ultimately led to two bulls by Leo X condemning his teachings (*Exsurge Domine,* June 15, 1520) and excommunicating him (*Decet Romanum Pontificum,* January 3, 1521). On December 10, 1520, Luther himself in effect excommunicated Leo by publicly burning the bull of condemnation and the book of church law.

As early as July 1519, at the Leipzig debate with Johann Eck, Luther had asserted that → popes and church councils could (and did) err, hence supreme authority in the church resided solely with the Word of God in Scripture. And by late 1519 he had also concluded that the papacy was a veritable → anti-christ. During the course of 1520 Luther set forth the main components of his reform program in his German tract *To the Christian Nobility of the German Nation,* and in his Latin treatise *On the Babylonian Captivity of the Church* he criticized the medieval church's entire sacramental system as either lacking biblical foundation altogether or contravening Christ's original institution of the two genuine sacraments, → baptism and the → Eucharist.

At the Diet of Worms in April 1521, appearing before Emperor Charles V and the assembled estates, Luther refused to recant his teachings unless "convinced by the testimony of the Scriptures or by clear reason," declaring, "My conscience is captive to the Word of God." The ensuing Edict of Worms imposed the imperial ban on Luther and proscribed his writings. On his return journey home he was taken into protective custody by order of his prince, Elector Frederick III, "the Wise," and housed at the castle Wartburg, where he remained presumably in hiding from early May 1521 until early March 1522. A period of intense literary activity, these months witnessed Luther's translation of the NT directly from the Greek text. This translation was published in September 1522, that of the whole Bible in 1534. Distinguished by its lively, vernacular German, the "Luther Bible" became a genuine people's Bible and a principal means of spreading the evangelical message, as well as a major factor in shaping the modern German language (→ Bible Versions 4.2).

3. Conflict among the Reformers

Luther's return to Wittenberg in early 1522 was prompted by the turbulence attending efforts there to introduce reforms (e.g., lay communion in both bread and wine, clerical marriage) with which he agreed in principle but whose hasty implementation he disavowed as lacking due solicitude for timid consciences, thus as failing to join faith with love. Luther quickly succeeded in quelling the tumult by preaching against any form of compulsion in matters of belief, in the process alienating his colleague Andreas Carlstadt (ca. 1480-1541, also spelled Karlstadt), who saw reform as mandated by God's clear, unequivocal commands and whose theology, in any case, was by 1523 profoundly at odds with Luther's.

Other divisions in the movement followed in 1524-25: the break with Thomas → Müntzer (ca. 1489-1525) and the rebellious peasants, who in Luther's judgment had confused Christian freedom with sociopolitical liberation; and, not least, the break with the renowned Dutch humanist Desiderius → Erasmus (1469?-1536), whose defense of

"free will" (i.e., moral cooperation) in the matter of the sinner's salvation impressed Luther as nothing but a latter-day species of → Pelagianism. The former break, however, did not mark the end of the Lutheran Reformation as a popular movement, nor did the latter sever Lutheranism from → humanism as such. In June 1525, in the midst of these conflicts, Luther married Catherine von Bora (1499-1552), a former Cistercian nun. Their union issued in six children, and the hospitable Luther home in Wittenberg (in the former Augustinian cloister) came to serve as a model for the Protestant parsonage.

The most serious and far-reaching schism in the ranks of the Reformation transpired during the years 1525-29, when Luther and his Wittenberg colleagues became embroiled in a bitter controversy with the Swiss and South German reformers over the Lord's Supper. The controversy was actually initiated by the Zurich reformer Ulrich → Zwingli (1484-1531), who insisted that Christ could be present only spiritually, not physically or bodily, in the supper. The Lutheran doctrine — that Christ's true body and blood are really in, and distributed with, the consecrated elements of bread and wine — was repudiated as "absurd" and "neopapist." The conflict failed of resolution at the Marburg Colloquy of 1529, whose sponsors had hoped to effect a united Protestant theological and political front. In 1536, however, the Wittenbergers and the Strasbourg reformers Martin → Bucer (1491-1551) and Wolfgang Capito (1478-1541) achieved "concord" in the dispute.

4. The Reformation Established

During the 1520s Luther was also engaged in crafting new orders of → worship and church organization (→ Church Government), including his revisions in the traditional liturgies of baptism and the Latin Mass (1523); his new German Mass and Order of Baptism (1526); his many contributions to evangelical → hymnals (beginning in 1524); and, of particular import, his two catechisms (1529): the Small Catechism, designed for the laity, and the Large Catechism, for the → clergy and heads of households. The development of a Lutheran territorial church was furthered by the "visitation" of parishes in electoral Saxony, for which Luther drafted instructions in 1528. One result was the ruler's assumption of episcopal powers as an "emergency bishop," an outcome that Luther himself considered but a temporary expedient.

Throughout the 1520s, especially up to 1525, Luther's widely broadcast message enjoyed a cordial, even enthusiastic reception in leading towns and cities of the empire and the Swiss Confederation, as well as in various princely territories and rural communes. The reasons for this response continue to be pondered and debated by historians. The remarkable transition from Luther's own religion to the Lutheran Reformation as a popular, mass movement admits of no easy explanation. Certainly many factors were involved, political and economic no less than religious in nature. One may conjecture, however, that Luther's resolution of his personal quest for a merciful God and for → assurance of salvation was one that resonated with countless persons who, like him, were beset by doubts that they could ever hope to satisfy the holy law of God out of their own resources, even if assisted to that end by God's sacramental graces. For the inescapable question remained: how can I be confident that I have done enough to stand accepted before God at the → last judgment and so to receive eternal life as a due reward?

5. Final Years

Luther's later years were troubled by physical exhaustion, serious illness, and many disappointments over what seemed the tardy pace of authentic reform. They were also a time of unabated productivity, as evident in his important lectures on Galatians (1531, published 1535) and his decade-long lectures on Genesis (1535-45); his Schmalkaldic Articles (1537), composed as a summary and defense of evangelical doctrine for use at a projected general council of the church; his treatise *On the Councils and the Church* (1539), which identified the essential "marks" *(notae),* or attributes, of the true church; his vitriolic attack *On the Jews and Their Lies* (1543), accusing the Jews of perverting the Scriptures and blaspheming Christ and the Virgin Mary, a tract strikingly at variance with an earlier, compassionate essay *That Jesus Christ Was Born a Jew* (1523); and his final blast, *Against the Roman Papacy: An Institution of the Devil* (1545), evoked by the emperor's declared intention to proceed against the true (i.e., Protestant) church by force of arms.

Martin Luther did not regard "reformation of the church" as a human act or accomplishment, much less his own private undertaking. Such renewal was God's work alone, to be realized only at the end of time. Luther thus viewed himself as God's unworthy instrument for the present proclamation of the newly recovered gospel as "the power of God for salvation" (Rom. 1:16) in a world ever beset by the terrible powers of sin, death, and the devil. It remained for later Lutheran-Protestant hagiography

to transform the steadfast preacher of faith into the superlative hero of faith, and therewith to elevate the earthbound Luther into the timeless realm of metahistory and myth.

Bibliography: R. H. BAINTON, *Here I Stand: A Life of Martin Luther* (Nashville, 1950) • H. BORNKAMM, *Luther in Mid-Career, 1521-1530* (Philadelphia, 1983) • M. BRECHT, *Martin Luther* (3 vols.; Philadelphia and Minneapolis, 1985-93) • M. U. EDWARDS JR., *Luther's Last Battles: Politics and Polemics, 1531-1546* (Ithaca, N.Y., 1983) • H. JUNGHANS, ed., *Leben und Werk Martin Luthers von 1526 bis 1546. Festgabe zu seinem 500. Geburtstag* (2 vols.; Berlin, 1983) • J. M. KITTELSON, *Luther the Reformer: The Story of the Man and His Career* (Minneapolis, 1986) • B. LOHSE, *Martin Luther's Theology: Its Historical and Systematic Development* (Edinburgh, 1999) • M. LUTHER, *Luther's Works* (56 vols.; ed. J. Pelikan and H. Lehmann; St. Louis and Philadelphia, 1955-86) • H. A. OBERMAN, *Luther: Man between God and the Devil* (New Haven, 1986) • E. G. RUPP, *Luther's Progress to the Diet of Worms* (Chicago, 1951).

DAVID W. LOTZ

Luther Research

1. German
2. International
3. Nontheological Research
4. Luther Texts, Congresses

1. German

The history of Luther research in Germany in the 19th century begins with L. von Ranke (1795-1886) and his six-volume *Deutsche Geschichte im Zeitalter der Reformation* (1839-47; ET *History of the Reformation in Germany* [1845-47]). Though tinged with → Romanticism, this work puts Martin → Luther (1483-1546; → Luther's Theology) squarely in the setting of the 16th-century → Reformation. J. Köstlin, G. Kawerau, O. Scheel, H. Boehmer, and R. and E. Seeberg continued along these lines in the late 19th and early 20th centuries.

Theologically, A. Ritschl (1822-89) in his three-volume *Die Christliche Lehre von der Rechtfertigung und Versöhnung* (1870-74; ET *The Christian Doctrine of Justification and Reconciliation* [1966]) aimed to situate Luther ethically in the middle-class society of his time. W. Herrmann (1846-1922) followed Ritschl, as did E. → Troeltsch (1865-1923) with his distinction between old and new → Protestantism and between → Lutheranism and → Calvinism. Against Ritschl's ethicizing of Luther,

T. Harnack (1817-89) in his two-volume *Luthers Theologie* (1862-86, repr., 1927) stressed the tension between God's → wrath and his → love in Luther's → Christology, which is determinative for human → salvation. But Harnack's picture of Luther was still confessional, like that of P. Althaus and W. Elert, on the basis of the 19th-century Erlangen school (→ Conservatism; Theology in the Nineteenth and Twentieth Centuries).

The understanding of Luther in the → liberal theology of Ritschl (→ Culture Protestantism) was overcome only by the new orientation of → dialectical theology to the Reformation teaching of the → Word of God (K. → Barth, F. Gogarten, G. Merz, W. von Loewenich) and by the Luther renaissance. Beginning early in the 20th century with K. Holl (1866-1926), this movement confronted the historical Luther with modern questions, defining his → religion as a religion of → conscience. Holl's students, including E. Hirsch (1888-1972), H. Bornkamm (1901-77), and H. Rückert (1901-74), followed this latter course.

Debate with the polemical Roman Catholic picture of Luther, especially as painted by H. Denifle (1844-1905) and H. Grisar (1845-1932), as well as the publication for the first time of Luther's lectures on the Psalms (1876) and Romans (1908) and the postscripts to the lectures on Galatians and Hebrews (1918 and 1929), led to intensive research into the date and content of Luther's Reformation discovery. The first phase of this research put the discovery of → righteousness by → faith (from Rom. 1:17) in 1514/15 (E. Hirsch, E. Vogelsang, R. Prenter [who argued for 1512], H. Bornkamm, G. Ebeling). A second phase, beginning in 1958, dated the Reformation turning point in 1518 with the discovery of the Word as the means of → grace by which faith receives righteousness (K. Aland, O. Bayer, M. Brecht). Meanwhile, research into the movement in Luther's early theology away from medieval theology (L. Grane, Ebeling, H. A. Oberman, B. Lohse, R. Schwarz, K.-H. zur Mühlen; → Middle Ages) made it less necessary to fix precisely the date of the Reformation discovery, which seemed to be clear at least in the Romans lectures (1515/16).

Roman Catholic Luther research participated in this discussion. With J. Lortz's (1887-1975) two-volume *Die Reformation in Deutschland* (1939-40; ET *The Reformation in Germany* [1968]), this → dialogue became more constructive and less polemical (→ Ecumenism, Ecumenical Movement). Although Lortz did not fully accept Luther's theological criticism of the Middle Ages, he saw the necessity for the Reformation. According to E. Iserloh, Luther combated a nonbiblical, semi-Pelagian (→ Pelagianism) → nominalism (G. Biel) and rediscovered primal Catholicism in → Augustine and → Thomas Aquinas (→ Augustine's Theology; Thomism).

Over against this theological relativizing of the Reformation, O. H. Pesch argued for open dialogue because Luther's discovery of righteousness by faith was territory that Roman Catholic theology (e.g., when oriented to Thomas) could enter. For P. Manns Luther was a common father in the faith who became a "heretic" (→ Heresies and Sects) for the sake of the → truth.

2. International

On the international scene the Swedes in particular (G. Aulén, A. Nygren, R. Bring, G. Wingren, B. Hägglund) took up Luther's theology of → creation and the motif of struggle in Luther's thinking (between God and the → devil, flesh and spirit, eros and agape). The Finns (L. Pinomaa, T. Mannermaa) focused on Luther's concept of God and his → anthropology, arguing for a union between Christ and the believer, while the Danes turned to Luther's doctrine of the → Holy Spirit (R. Prenter) and his relation to the Middle Ages (L. Grane). In Norway Luther's doctrine of the church was an issue (I. Lønning).

American Luther research concentrated on Luther's relation to the late Middle Ages (H. A. Oberman, D. Steinmetz, S. Hendrix, K. Hagen), to the → Renaissance, to → humanism, and to the radicals (J. Pelikan, G. W. Forell, L. W. Spitz, E. W. Gritsch, M. U. Edwards), while English Luther research devoted itself to Luther's concept of righteousness (G. E. Rupp, P. Watson). Themes in France were Luther's Christology (M. Lienhard) and his relation to medieval → Catholicism (D. Olivier).

3. Nontheological Research

Nontheological Luther research has investigated the distinctive features of Luther's German and its significance in the history of the language (G. Bebermeyer, H. Bluhm, J. Erben, B. Stolt, H. Wolf; → Language). The psychological and relational aspects of Luther's emergence as a reformer have also called for study (E. Erikson, Hendrix; → Psychoanalysis).

In Luther's humanistic liberation of his age from the spiritual tutelage of the medieval church, Marxist Luther research found the beginnings of the "early bourgeois" → revolution (→ Marxism and Christianity 2), which was completed in the Reformation era by T. → Müntzer (1489-1525; G. Zschäbitz, G. Brendler). There has also been special interest in Luther's → biography (R. Bainton, H. Bornkamm,

M. Brecht, R. Schwarz). Efforts have been made to shed light on Luther's theology by investigating the tension between the historical Luther and his reception in later history, especially in the → church struggle (H. Iwand, R. Herrmann, W. Joest, Ebeling).

4. Luther Texts, Congresses

After the first translations of Luther's Latin texts (1740ff.) and the Erlangen edition (1826ff.), the Weimar (1883ff.) edition has now critically edited over 100 volumes of Luther's work in four parts: writings, letters, table talk, and German Bible. Work still proceeds on indexes to the writings. For students there are critical editions of selected works, for example, by O. Clemen (4 vols.; Bonn, 1912-13; and 8 vols.; Berlin, 1930-35), the American *Luther's Works* (55 vols.; 1955-86), and the Berlin edition (6 vols.; 1979-99). K. Aland's *Hilfsbuch zum Lutherstudium* offers easier access to Luther's works.

General aids to Luther research include the *Luther-Jahrbuch*, the *Lutherbibliographie*, which lists over 1,000 titles a year, and the *Luther Digest*, an annual abridgment of Luther studies, published in the United States. Meeting every four to six years, the International Congress for Luther Research, which has gathered in Århus (1956), Münster (1960), Jarvenpaa (1966), St. Louis (1971), Lund (1977), Erfurt (1983), Oslo (1988), St. Paul (1993), Heidelberg (1997), and Copenhagen (2002), helps to coordinate worldwide research.

Bibliography: H. BOEHMER, *Luther im Lichte der neueren Forschung* (Leipzig, 1906; 5th ed., 1918) • H. BORNKAMM, *Luther's World of Thought* (St. Louis, 1965) • C. BRAATEN and R. JENSON, eds., *Union with Christ: The New Finnish Interpretation of Luther* (Grand Rapids, 1998) • M. EDWARDS, "Luther's Biography," *Reformation Europe: A Guide to Research* (vol. 2; ed. W. S. Maltby; St. Louis, 1992) 5-20 • S. HENDRIX, "American Luther Research in the Twentieth Century," *LQ,* n.s., 15 (2001) 1-23 • H. JUNGHANS, "Lutherbiographien zum 500. Geburtstag der Reformators 1983," *TLZ* 110 (1985) 491-514 • J. KITTELSON, "Luther the Theologian," *Reformation Europe,* ed. Maltby, 21-46 • W. VON LOEWENICH, "Zehn Jahre Lutherforschung in Deutschland (1938-48)," *Von Augustin zu Luther* (Witten, 1959) 307-78 • P. MANNS, ed., *Zur Bilanz des Lutherjahres* (Wiesbaden, 1986); idem, ed., *Zur Lage der Lutherforschung heute* (Wiesbaden, 1982) • K.-H. ZUR MÜHLEN, "Die Erforschung des 'jungen' Luthers seit 1876," *LuJ* 50 (1983) 48-125; idem, "Das Lutherjahr 1983 und die Lutherforschung," *VF* 34 (1989) 3-23 • O. H. PESCH, "Twenty Years of Catholic Luther Research," *LuthW* 13 (1966) 303-16; idem, "Zur Frage nach Luthers reformatorischer Wende. Ergebnisse und Probleme der Diskussion um Ernst Bizer, *Fides ex auditu*," *Cath(M)* 20 (1966) 216-43, 264-80.

KARL-HEINZ ZUR MÜHLEN

Lutheran Churches

1. General Characteristics and Statistics

Confessional bonds, provided mainly by the → Augsburg Confession and Martin → Luther's (1483-1546; → Luther's Theology) Small → Catechism and in many instances the entire Book of Concord (1580), distinguish the Lutheran churches. These churches allow for variety in constitution and organization, whether as territorial churches or as small → minority churches (→ Diaspora). Ways of → worship derive from the → early church (→ Liturgy). Polity may be episcopal (→ Bishop, Episcopate), synodical (→ Synod), congregational (→ Congregationalism), or a combination of such forms. State or → people's churches continuous from the → Reformation era and new churches stemming from migration or missionary endeavor are on the same ecclesial level.

In 2002 the number of Lutherans in the world exceeded 65 million (or 3.2 percent of the world's 2.06 billion Christians). The Lutheran totals compare with 246 million worldwide in the → Orthodox Church and 1.02 billion in the → Roman Catholic Church. While world population has more than doubled since 1960, the Lutheran total during that same time has remained about the same. Redistribution has been going on among Lutherans, with declining numbers in Europe and considerable growth in the → Third World, most notably in Africa.

2. Europe
2.1. *Germany*

The external status of Lutheran churches in Germany reflects centuries of intertwined relations with temporal territories and political → power (§3). While Reformation teaching distinguished between the nature of the church and the role of the state (→ Church and State; Two Kingdoms Doctrine), an ecclesial territorialism peculiar to Germany has prevailed. The religious equality characteristic of modern secular states, however, ended the old territorial government and opened the way to an independent development of organized churches. Yet elements of the old order remain (e.g., the boundaries of the *Landeskirchen,* or territorial churches). In legal matters church and state cooperate. Lutheran territorial and free churches throughout Germany have some 13.6 million members (2002). When added to the estimated 9 million Lutherans in the territorial Union churches, the total represents 35 percent of the world's Lutherans.

In Germany 11 Lutheran territorial churches are members of the Evangelische Kirche in Deutschland (EKD, Evangelical Church in Germany) and the → Lutheran World Federation (LWF); the Lutheran classis of the Reformed territorial Church of Lippe is also a member of the LWF. Eight of these Lutheran churches also compose the Vereinigte Evangelisch-Lutherische Kirche Deutschlands (VELKD, United Evangelical Lutheran Church in Germany, organized in 1948): Bavaria (2.75 million members), Brunswick (440,000), Hannover (3.3 million), Mecklenburg (230,000), North Elbia (2.2 million), Oldenburg (484,000), Saxony (937,000), Schaumburg-Lippe (66,000), and Thuringia (514,000). The other three LWF member churches are Oldenburg (484,000 members), Pomerania (130,000), and Württemberg (2.45 million). The six member churches of the Evangelische Kirche der Union (EKU, Evangelical Church of the Union) also respect the confessional status of their Lutheran parishes: Berlin-Brandenburg, Pomerania, Saxony, Silesia, Rhineland, and Westphalia. This respect also holds true in the federatively united Church of Hesse-Nassau, as well as in Anhalt, Bremen, and Electoral Hesse-Waldeck (Lutheran Parish Association).

German Lutheran → free churches originated from protest against the Union churches or dissatisfaction over the political or territorial character of the mainline churches. The Selbstständige Evangelisch-Lutherische Kirche (SELK, Independent Evangelical Lutheran Church, with 37,700 members), a 1972 merger, comprises several formerly separate free churches. It has elements of episcopal, synodical, and congregational polities. Although it has no fellowship with the Lutheran territorial churches or with the LWF, the SELK does maintain ties with the Lutheran Church–Missouri Synod (LC-MS) and the Wisconsin Lutheran Synod in the United States, as well as with similar Lutheran bodies in Australia and Great Britain.

2.2. *Northern Europe*

Shortly after the Reformation had begun in Germany and → Lutheranism began to spread abroad, the Nordic countries became a second large Lutheran bloc. Scholars from Wittenberg led the way, and in time entire populations responded. Elements of these beginnings remain evident in today's public worship and in the establishment of national or folk churches.

The Church of *Sweden* (7.4 million members) claims nearly 85 percent of the population. In January of 2000 the centuries-long identity of this church as a state church came to an end. With freedom to determine much of its own life, the Church of Sweden now defines itself as an "open folk church" and is gradually finding its way toward new patterns of mission, education, and stewardship. Uppsala, the first among 13 → dioceses, is the seat of the archbishop. Historic episcopal succession (→ Episcopacy) enables the Swedish church to cherish continuity, to see the Reformation not as a break but as a renewal, and to provide creative ecumenical leadership.

The Church of *Norway* (3.8 million members), like the Church of Sweden, claims nearly 85 percent of the population. The king is titular head of this state church, and Parliament its final legislative body. Since 1984 a national synod has handled church affairs with a national church council as its executive unit. The 11 dioceses are equal, and their bishops form a national bishops conference, with one of their number elected chairperson. Of the three theological schools the Congregational Faculty (Menighetsfakultetet) in Oslo — independent, pietistic in spirit (→ Pietism), and confessionally Lutheran — trains most of the pastors. The Evangelical Lutheran Free Church of Norway, an associate member church of the LWF with 30,000 members, has represented since 1877 the ongoing struggle for separation of church and state. At present, major discussions between church and state are pursuing new forms of relation between the two (→ Norway 1.2.1).

The Evangelical Lutheran Church in *Denmark* (4.53 million members) claims 84 percent of the population. The governmental Ministry of Church Affairs is the highest authority in practical church matters. Bishops of the ten dioceses usually consider the bishop of Copenhagen as first among equals. As heads of their separate dioceses, which are considered independent entities, the bishops together cannot legally speak for the church. The parishes are self-governing. The Church of Denmark also includes in its number Lutherans on the Faeroe Islands and in Greenland, each of which is a vice-diocese of the Diocese of Copenhagen.

The Evangelical Lutheran Church of *Finland* (4.61 million members), until 1809 part of the Church of Sweden (currently 6 percent of the population remain Swedish-speaking), retains marks of a state church, despite the religious neutrality of the Finnish Republic. Turku (Åbo), one of eight dioceses, is the seat of the archbishop. This church is noted for its influential pietistic movements (→ Revivals). Few people have left the church (→ Church Membership 5), despite the freedom to do so.

The Evangelical Lutheran Church of *Iceland* (227,000 members) includes the large majority of the people of that country. An independent republic from 930 to 1262, and then since 1941, Iceland and its mother country, Norway, came under Danish rule in 1380. Finally in 1918 Denmark recognized Iceland's independence, and in 1940 the German occupation of Denmark completed the separation. The church is now a single diocese, and its ties with the state remain close. Its spiritual life includes a distinctive vein of passion → mysticism.

2.3. Western Europe

Outside Germany and the Nordic countries Lutheran churches are minorities (→ Diaspora). Some, however, retain national features (in Alsace, Austria, Hungary, Romania, and countries in the former Czechoslovakia and Yugoslavia). There are Lutheran congregations, some linked to the Evangelical Church in Germany, in all countries of western and southeastern Europe.

The *United Kingdom* has three Lutheran associations. The Lutheran Council of Great Britain (100,000 members), a council recognized by the LWF, links some very old Lutheran congregations (as early as 1669) to newer ones formed after World War II by immigrant Germans, Poles, Balts, Hungarians, Slovaks, and Scandinavians. The Evangeli-

cal Lutheran Synod of German Language in the United Kingdom, formed in 1956, comprises congregations supported by the EKD and VELKD. The Lutheran Church in Great Britain (2,750 members) was formed in 1961 and since 1988 has been a member of the LWF.

The Evangelical Lutheran Church in the Kingdom of the *Netherlands* (15,000 members) has a long history and a distinctive confessional identity. Since the 1920s its membership has declined by two-thirds. Since 1986 this church has been involved, with the Netherlands Reformed Church and the Reformed Churches in the Netherlands (→ Reformed and Presbyterian Churches), in a process of church unification called Samen op Weg, "Together on the Way." There is a present commitment to form a new church from these three bodies, the Protestant Church in the Netherlands, to begin functioning in 2004.

In *France* the Alliance Nationale des Églises Luthériennes de France includes the Church of the Augsburg Confession in Alsace and Lorraine (210,000 members), as well as the Evangelical Lutheran Church of France (40,000). The latter body is concentrated in the regions of Paris and Montbéliard. Since 1913 Lutherans and Reformed have been partners in the Protestant Federation of France. The small Malagasy Protestant Church in France (8,000) is a member of both the LWF and the World Alliance of Reformed Churches.

The Evangelical Lutheran Church in *Italy* (7,000 members) is of 19th-century origin. It has mainly German membership, with Italian accessions. It maintains formal relations with the EKD and VELKD.

Lutheran congregations in *Switzerland* comprise the Federation of Evangelical Lutheran Churches in Switzerland and the Principality of Liechtenstein (Basel, Bern, Zurich, Fribourg, Neuchâtel, Vaduz), which reports a membership of 6,500. These churches, along with the multilingual Evangelical Lutheran Church in Geneva, which dates to 1707, have ties with the EKD and VELKD. The Regional Association of Swedish Congregations (five parishes in Switzerland with 6,000 members) centers in the Lausanne area.

2.4. Southeastern Europe

Lutheran churches in southeastern Europe, mainly in the former Austro-Hungarian Empire, have their roots in the Reformation, and Germans participated in their establishment. Their growth, however, was not a matter of spreading German folkways, and since World War II the ethnic German element in these churches has sharply diminished, if not disappeared.

An exception is the Evangelical Church of the Augsburg Confession in *Austria*. After World War II ethnic German refugees swelled its membership to 400,000, a number now reduced to 341,000. Protestantism had survived underground until the Edict of Toleration (→ Tolerance) in 1781 and full → religious liberty in 1861 — two dates with meaning for churches in the southeast. For purposes of legal recognition by the government, the Lutheran church and the smaller Reformed body comprise an ecclesiastical entity called the Evangelical Church of the Augsburg and Helvetic Confessions, a designation that allows for cooperation in certain areas but leaves the two groups fully independent in respect to confessional identity and governance. Austrian Lutherans are members of the LWF.

In *Hungary* the Magyar Evangelical Lutheran Church of the Augsburg Confession (430,000 members, as compared with over 1.5 million Reformed) is a product of dispersion. Planted in Reformation times, it increased under persecution.

Among the Slavic peoples, two Lutheran churches in what was formerly Czechoslovakia represent the largest grouping of Lutherans in southeastern Europe. The Evangelical Church of the Augsburg Confession in the *Slovak Republic* (372,000 members) is historically linked to Hungarian Lutherans. Its former Czech counterpart, under Austria, in 1918 joined the Evangelical Church of → Moravian Brethren. The ensuing Evangelical Church in Bohemia Moravia, and Silesia (134,000) disappeared after World War II. Lutheran Poles in the Teschen region of what is now the *Czech Republic* continue as the Silesian Evangelical Church of the Augsburg Confession (40,000).

Three ethnically separate Lutheran churches in what was formerly Yugoslavia, established after 1918 from fragments of the Austro-Hungarian era, include the Slovak Evangelical Church of the Augsburg Confession in the Republic of *Serbia and Montenegro* (50,000 members), the Evangelical Church of the Augsburg Confession in *Slovenia* (20,000), and the Evangelical Church in the Republic of *Croatia* (4,500).

In *Romania* the Reformation took hold among the German and Hungarian inhabitants of Transylvania. Descendants of 12th-century German settlers, the Siebenbürger Sachsen (i.e., Transylvania Saxons), retain their Evangelical Church of the Augsburg Confession, but with only 16,400 members, much reduced — by emigration back to Germany — from the 400,000 of the German-style *Landeskirche* earlier in the 20th century. Hungarians in Romania have a shrinking Evangelical Lutheran

Church of the Augsburg Confession in Romania (32,000).

2.5. *Eastern and Northeastern Europe*

In eastern and northeastern Europe Germans brought the Reformation, and indigenous Lutheran churches resulted.

In *Poland* the Counter-Reformation (→ Catholic Reform and Counterreformation) eliminated most of earlier Lutheran gains. During the 19th century German immigration and assimilation with the Poles created several Lutheran and United churches. The one remaining after 1945 is the Evangelical Church of the Augsburg Confession in Poland (80,000 members, down from a membership before the war of 500,000, mostly Germans).

After independence from the former Soviet Union, Lutheran churches in the Baltics and in the trans-Ural region have come alive. The resettlement of ethnic Germans from the Ukraine and Volga regions of the Soviet Union during World War II led eventually to the formation of over 500 Lutheran congregations. These German-speaking churches were, in the time of the Soviet Union, supervised at a distance from Riga, Latvia. Lay leadership by both women and men was invaluable, and duly appointed deans supervised the districts into which the congregations were divided. The Evangelical Lutheran Church in *Russia, Ukraine, Kazakhstan, Belarus, Central Asia, and Transcaucasia* is now a body of 250,000 members with a resident archbishop in St. Petersburg. A second Lutheran church in Russia, the Evangelical Lutheran Church of Ingria in Russia (16,000 members), is of Finnish background and is also centered in St. Petersburg.

German elements left the Baltic lands during World War II, and Lutheran relations now stem largely from Sweden and Finland. In the Baltic region are remnants of once much larger churches: the *Estonian* Evangelical Lutheran Church (now with 200,000 members), the Evangelical Lutheran Church of *Latvia* (250,000), and the Evangelical Lutheran Church of *Lithuania* (30,000). These churches have seen a modest but steady growth as their countries have been reconstructed after Soviet occupation. Baltic churches "in exile" also continue in Germany, Sweden, Great Britain, Canada, the United States, Australia, and Latin America.

3. North America

In North America, the *United States* and *Canada* should be seen together, since the same Lutheran churches have had activity in both nations. In 1985 the Evangelical Lutheran Church in Canada (ELCIC, 189,000 members) united two-thirds of

Canada's Lutherans, and in 1987 the Evangelical Lutheran Church in America (ELCA, 5.125 million) brought together two-thirds of the Lutherans in the United States. In both countries the other third adheres mainly to the LC-MS (2.6 million U.S. members) and the Lutheran Church–Canada (LC-C), which is part of the LC-MS (82,000). The 8.23 million Lutherans in the United States amount to 2.8 percent of the population, while in Canada the 280,000 Lutherans amount to 0.9 percent.

Among non–Roman Catholic Christians in America, Lutherans are the third largest group after → Baptists and Methodists (→ Methodist Churches). Had the approximately 3 million Europeans arriving as Lutherans in the period from 1820 to 1940 remained so, the Lutherans perhaps would have become the largest non–Roman Catholic denomination in America. All Lutheran newcomers were from non-English-speaking backgrounds and consequently faced "the language question." In time, English replaced the rich diversity of original mother-tongues, and for the first time the Lutheran churches gained a sure presence in the anglophone world. This presence was a matter of critical importance because no major confession was more deeply torn by the two world wars of the 20th century than the Lutheran. Yet this very fact aroused American Lutherans to ecumenical and global activity, not least in helping to form the Lutheran World Convention in 1923 and the LWF in 1947.

3.1. The organizing principle for Lutherans in America was not territorial, as in much of Europe, but ethnic, linguistic, or doctrinal. After the founding of the first permanent synod (1748), what was initially called the Ministerium of North America became, largely through the work of Henry Melchior Muhlenberg (1711-87), the Ministerium of Pennsylvania, as other synods were formed. From the Muhlenberg line came the General Synod (1820), then two more confessionally conservative offshoots — the United Synod, South (1862), and the General Council (1866). In 1918 these three synods merged, with others, into the United Lutheran Church in America (ULCA), representing one-third of the Lutherans in North America.

The other two-thirds were found in Lutheran churches of various sizes, churches that were themselves often the product of mergers — from the Evangelical Lutheran Church (ELC, formed in 1917 with 1 million members, Norwegian in origin), the American Lutheran Church (ALC, 1845, 973,000, German), and the Augustana Evangelical Lutheran Church (1860, 557,400, Swedish), to the small United Evangelical Lutheran Church (UELC, 1896,

62,000, Danish), Suomi Synod (1890, 36,000, Finnish), and American Evangelical Lutheran Church (AELC, 1872, 23,000, → Grundtvigian Danish). These bodies or their predecessors, and the Lutheran Free Church (1897, 73,000, Norwegian), joined with the ULCA in 1918 to form the National Lutheran Council (NLC). A common service agency, also for postwar relief work in Europe, the NLC aided the rise of the Lutheran World Convention and later the LWF.

Experience in the NLC fostered union at home. In 1960 a new American Lutheran Church with 2.4 million members was formed by the ELC, the older ALC, the UELC, and the Lutheran Free Church. Then in 1962 the Lutheran Church in America (LCA, 3.2 million) united the ULCA, Augustana, AELC, and Suomi groups. Other advances followed.

The Synodical Conference (1872-1964), led by the LC-MS, broke up over doctrinal issues as the Wisconsin Evangelical Lutheran Synod (formed in 1917 as the merger of synods from Wisconsin [organized in 1850], Minnesota [1860], and Michigan [1860], now with 414,000 members) and the Evangelical Lutheran Synod (1918, 24,000 members, Norwegian) went their own ways. The Synod of Evangelical Lutheran Churches (1959, 21,000, Slovak) joined Missouri. In 1966 the churches in the NLC and the LC-MS combined to create the Lutheran Council in the U.S.A. Former cooperative services were supplemented with theological studies at the insistence of LC-MS.

The early years of this council (to 1971) marked a high point of American Lutheran unity. Yet while the LC-MS and ALC had attained pulpit and table fellowship, for the LCA such fellowship existed only with the ALC. Internal controversy led by traditionalists subsequently fractured the LC-MS, and advocates of a new order left the LC-MS and in 1977 organized the Association of Evangelical Lutheran Churches (AELC, 94,500 members). This AELC influenced further church union. In 1987 the ALC, LCA, and AELC merged, forming the current ELCA. The Lutheran Council in the U.S.A. was dissolved, although agencies such as Lutheran World Relief (1946) and the Lutheran Immigration and Refugee Service (1939) continue inter-Lutheran tasks.

3.2. The Evangelical Lutheran Church in Canada, mentioned above, was formed by a merger of the LCA Canada Section (former ULCA and Augustana) and the Evangelical Lutheran Church of Canada (ALC Canada District, Norwegian and old ALC). As a northern accompaniment of the Lutheran advance in the United States, the ELCIC, tracing its roots to 18th-century Nova Scotia, concentrated its work in Ontario and later spanned the western provinces to the Pacific. A complete merger of Canada's Lutherans seemed possible on grounds of common → conservatism, but then the Missouri Synod Districts formed the LC-C (1987, 79,600 members). Canadian Lutheran World Relief (1946) gained prominence by resettling Baltic and German refugees. The Lutheran Council in Canada (1967) continues, much reduced, as the Lutheran contact with the national government.

3.3. Independence has been cherished up to the point where joining a larger body is a matter of survival, as in the case of the Icelandic Synod (1881, 7,100 members), which years ago came into the ULCA. But the Eielsen Synod (1846, Norwegian) continues alone with but 50 members. Other small groups might be mentioned, each determined to hold fast to something precious, though not so grasped by others. The Latvian, Estonian, and Lithuanian Lutheran Churches in Exile in Canada and the United States repeat the old epic of costly freedom.

4. Latin America

In Latin America and the Caribbean the 1.12 million Lutherans (83 percent of them in Brazil) are distinctive amid the region's 48 million Protestants and a heavily Roman Catholic population of 481 million. Springing mainly from evangelical Europeans, the Lutheran churches have not been perceived by other Protestants as missionary bodies but, rather, as churches preserving the confession of the 16th-century Reformation. The → Pentecostal churches, in contrast, appear as Latin America's modern Reformation. In point of fact, however, during the 20th century the missionary task did come alive among Lutherans. Lutheran membership in Latin America may thus be seen as deriving from three sources: diaspora, descendants, and converts.

4.1. Diaspora

The Lutheran diaspora in Latin America, which includes diplomatic officials, businesspeople, seamen, and others, is reminiscent of earlier times when the first Lutheran churches were planted — by Danes in the Danish West Indies in 1666 (since 1917 the U.S. Virgin Islands), by the Dutch in Suriname in 1741, and by diverse ethnic groups in Guyana in 1743.

In the 1920s and especially the 1940s, the two world wars spurred emigration to Latin America. German, Hungarian, Slovak, and Baltic refugees, along with Scandinavians, formed multilingual congregations of a new type in Argentina, Peru, Ecuador, Colombia, and Venezuela (five languages in Caracas), and also in other capital cities, for example,

in Mexico, Costa Rica, and Bolivia. Pastors were sent from Germany, Scandinavia, and elsewhere. The Latin American Area Desk in the LWF Department for Mission and Development (Geneva) has kept these and other immigrant congregations in touch with one another and with larger churches, largely through the periodic All Latin American Lutheran Conferences that it sponsors.

4.2. Descendants

Descendants, the second group, consist of approximately one million Lutherans in Brazil, Argentina, and Chile. Mainly of German origin, their first ancestors were pioneer colonists in Brazil's Rio Grande do Sul (1824). The Evangelical Church of Lutheran Confession in *Brazil* (formed in 1959 with 714,000 members), based in Pôrto Alegre, has its theological school in São Leopoldo. The Evangelical Lutheran Church in Brazil (1904, 220,000) has LC-MS ties and operates its own high schools.

In *Argentina* the first German congregation (1843) led to the Evangelical Church of the River Plate (1899, 47,000), a united church 90 percent of whose members are Lutheran, with congregations also in Uruguay and Paraguay. The Missouri Synod–related Evangelical Lutheran Church of Argentina (1905, 1928, 30,000), largely of Ukraine and Volga German origin, has its own theological school.

In *Chile* the 15,000 Lutherans, mainly of German descent, formed the Evangelical Lutheran Church in Chile (1904, 1937, from United to Lutheran in 1959, 3,000 members). A 1975 schism over questions of human rights, reflecting the general social and political crisis in Chile, led to the formation in that year of the Lutheran Church in Chile (12,000 members); both of these churches are members of the LWF.

4.3. Converts

Latin American Lutherans of the third type, converts, have come largely from mission activities supported since 1898 by North American Lutherans. They include English-, Spanish-, and Portuguese-speaking whites, Indians, and blacks. In addition to Lutherans in *Puerto Rico*, where there are Spanish-speaking churches affiliated with the Caribbean Synod of the Evangelical Lutheran Church in America, and the Lutheran Church in *Guyana* (1743, 1943, 11,000 members), the formation of the United Evangelical Lutheran Church in Argentina (1908, 1948, 7,000) marked a new day. Mission work also extended to Mexico and later to Chile and Peru. An independent Lutheran society, the World Mission Prayer League, began work in Colombia (1936), Bolivia (1938), and Ecuador (1951). Its largest result is the *Bolivian* Evangelical Lutheran Church (18,000 Aymara Indians). The Evangelical Lutheran Church in *Suriname* (1743, 4,000) retains a Dutch connection.

All these and other churches have links to the Latin American Area Desk of the LWF's Department for Mission and Development, some also to the ELCA Division for Global Mission (Chicago). Additionally, it should be noted that in *El Salvador* the Salvadoran Lutheran Synod (1977, 12,000), which joined the LWF in 1983, has borne an enormous burden for its nation in times of civil war and abuse of human → rights.

5. Africa

The classic missions lands of Africa, Asia, and the Pacific (→ Mission 3) now claim approximately 700 million Christians. Among them are an estimated 19 million Lutherans (2.7 percent of the total): Africa has 11.95 million, Asia 6.1 million, the Pacific 996,000. A unifying process has been gathering separate groups into synods and missions into ecclesial bodies. Changes so prominent from the late 1940s to the 1970s continue to rearrange the way mission work relates to national or local churches.

Africa has several German-language Lutheran churches linked with mission and immigration since the colonial period (from 1780). Mergers led to the United Evangelical Lutheran Church in Southern Africa (1981). This church is actually a council of Lutheran churches that includes the Evangelical Lutheran Church in Southern Africa (Cape Church) (formed in 1961 with 4,250 members), the Evangelical Lutheran Church in Southern Africa (Natal-Transvaal) (1981, 11,000), and the German Evangelical Lutheran Church in Namibia (1960, 7,000). The early links of these churches were with churches and mission bodies in Germany — Hannover (Cape), Hermannsburg and Berlin Mission (Natal-Transvaal), and Rhenish Mission (Namibia). It is to be noted that the largest Lutheran church in South Africa, the Evangelical Lutheran Church in Southern Africa, does not belong to the United group. The Lutheran Church in *South Africa* (32,000) and the Free Evangelical Lutheran Synod of South Africa (3,048) relate to Lutheran Free Churches in Germany and the LC-MS. Independent Swedish and Norwegian congregations, and a few using English, strengthen the foreign links of Lutherans in South Africa.

Throughout Africa, missions — German, Scandinavian, American, and Free Lutheran — have joined with nationals in establishing national churches, once but no longer referred to as younger churches. The largest is the *Ethiopian* Evangelical Church Mekane Yesus (formed in 1866, organized

in 1959, now with 3.36 million members). Next in size are the Evangelical Lutheran Church in *Tanzania* (1890, 1963, 2.5 million), the Malagasay Lutheran Church in *Madagascar* (1866, 1975, 2.25 million), the Evangelical Lutheran Church in Southern Africa (1834, 1975, 769,000), and, in *Namibia,* the Evangelical Lutheran Church in Namibia (1883, 1954, 580,000) and the Evangelical Lutheran Church in the Republic of Namibia (1842, 1957, 300,000). In these five countries the major mission efforts in the formative years were respectively from Sweden, Germany and Sweden, Norway, Sweden, and Finland, and Germany (→ Scandinavian Missions). Later, American participation became strong, especially in aiding German missions that were "orphaned" after the two world wars.

Self-governing Lutheran churches have also been formed in 17 other African countries: *Angola* (formed in 1979, now with 22,000 members), *Botswana* (1986, 20,000), *Cameroon* (3 church bodies, total membership of 230,000), *Central African Republic* (1974, 55,000), *Chad* (1964, 21,500), *Democratic Republic of Congo* (136,000), *Eritrea* (1926, 12,000), *Ghana* (1966, 26,000), *Kenya* (two church bodies with a total membership of 85,000), *Liberia* (1947, 71,000), *Malawi* (1982, 25,000), *Mozambique* (1988, 1,250), *Nigeria* (two Lutheran bodies formed in 1954 and 1963 with a total membership of 1.25 million), *Senegal* (3,100), *Sierra Leone* (2,150), *Zambia* (3,320), and *Zimbabwe* (1962, 110,000).

In the 1970s and 1980s two white African churches — the Evangelical Lutheran Church in Southern Africa (Cape Church) and the German Evangelical Lutheran Church in South West Africa (now Namibia) — were subjects of extremely important ecclesiological, theological, and ethical debates within the LWF, regarding apartheid within the two churches. In 1984 at the Eighth Assembly of the LWF, held in Budapest, the membership of these two churches in the LWF was suspended, since no grounds could be found that these churches had "publicly and unequivocally" rejected the system of apartheid; they had failed to end the division of the church on racial grounds (→ Racism). In this unprecedented action the LWF viewed apartheid as a matter of faith, a *status confessionis.* Only in 1991, after lengthy theological, pastoral, and ecclesial deliberation leading to rejection of apartheid, was the membership in the LWF of these two churches restored.

6. Asia and Oceania

In Asia and Oceania, whose total population in 2000 was 3.7 billion, the number of Christians is estimated as upwards of 330 million. Of this total about 7.15 million, or a little more than 2 percent, are Lutheran. Virtually all of the approximately 55 self-governing Lutheran church bodies in this region are members of the LWF.

6.1. Middle East

The Middle East claims few Lutherans, perhaps only 3,500. The largest number are in the Evangelical Lutheran Church in *Jordan* (3,000 members). This church includes the West Bank and Jerusalem Old City, with its landmark German Evangelical Redeemer Church (1898), which ministers in German, Arabic, and English and has ties with German and American Lutherans. Separate congregations in Haifa and Tel Aviv relate to the Norwegian mission. There is a German congregation in Beirut (1860) that relates to the EKD, as does a congregation in Syria. Swedish schools around Jerusalem, Danish work in Arab lands as far away as Aden (1903), and newer Finnish work in Israel illustrate Lutheran diversity.

Since 1948, work with Palestinian refugees in Israel and the Palestinian territories by the Lutheran World Service, a department of the LWF often cooperating with other nongovernmental organizations, has won distinction. The Augusta Victoria Hospital, originally built in the late 19th century at the behest of Kaiser Wilhelm II of Germany at the Mount of Olives in Jerusalem, came under operation by the LWF in the early 1950s. It has remained one of the few medical centers available to the Palestinian people. In 2003, however, the Israeli government began to make unprecedented tax demands that threaten the continued work and even existence of the hospital. The distressing threats to this institution illustrate the difficult role of churches and church agencies in the complex and dangerous environment of Israel and the Palestinian territories.

6.2. South-Central Asia

In *India,* now with a population of more than one billion persons, the 62 million Christians include 1.65 million Lutherans. For the most part, they exist in nine church bodies that together form the United Evangelical Lutheran Church in India (UELCI), which was established in 1975 to succeed the former Federation of Evangelical Lutheran Churches (1926).

The roots of one of the constituent bodies — the Tamil Evangelical Lutheran Church (1919, now with 103,600 members) — go back to 1706 and the work of Bartholomew Ziegenbalg (1682-1719) and Heinrich Plütschau (1677-1752), the first Protestant missionaries to India. In 1956 Rajah B. Manikam became the Tamil church's first Indian bishop. The two largest UELCI bodies are the Andhra Evangelical

Lutheran Church (begun 1842, constituted 1927, 700,000 members) and Gossner Evangelical Lutheran Church (1844, 1919, 380,100). The other six in order of size are the Jeypore Evangelical Lutheran Church (1882, 1954, 140,000), Northern Evangelical Lutheran Church (1864, 1950, 80,000), India Evangelical Lutheran Church (1895, 1958, 56,500), Arcot Lutheran Church (1863, 1913, 35,000), South Andhra Lutheran Church–Telegu (1865, 1945, 45,500), and Evangelical Lutheran Church in Madhya Pradesh (1877, 1949, 13,500). A group not affiliated with the LWF or the UELCI is the North Western Gossner Evangelical Lutheran Church (100,100 members). These churches are located in the eastern part of India, from the southern tip to the far north.

Doctrinal agreement achieved with the → Church of South India after 1947 led to joint theological education in Madurai, Bangalore, and Secunderabad (although the Lutheran churches did not become part of the Church of South India). Separate Lutheran seminaries continue elsewhere, and a graduate school in Chennai (formerly Madras), Gurukul Lutheran College and Research Institute, is supported by the UELCI. The India Evangelical Lutheran Church, linked both to the LWF and to the LC-MS, trains its pastors at Nagercoil.

Lutherans in *Pakistan* have affiliated with the Church of Pakistan (1.16 million members), which was formed in 1970 by Anglican, Methodist, Scottish Presbyterian, and Lutheran churches. In *Bangladesh* there are two Lutheran churches: the Bangladesh Lutheran Church (2,800 members) and the Bangladesh Northern Evangelical Lutheran Church (8,600). The small Lanka Lutheran Church (1,200) in *Sri Lanka* is related to the India Evangelical Lutheran Church.

6.3. Eastern and Southeastern Asia

In the People's Republic of *China* the former Lutheran Church of China (1920-58) once claimed approximately 100,000 members. Initiated by Basel and Rhenish missionaries in 1846, Lutheran activity in China peaked in the 1920s, when there were some 600 Scandinavian, American, and German church workers in the country (→ China Inland Mission). Many Chinese Lutherans fled during the 1949 revolution and the subsequent Cultural Revolution, but many more have remained. Lutherans are now numbered in the nonconfessional China Christian Council, which reportedly includes some 15 million Protestants (→ China 3).

Especially after the mainland revolution of 1949, → *Hong Kong,* now a "special administrative region" of China, became a new center for Lutherans, complete with schools, two theological seminaries (one affiliated with the LC-MS), and an inclusive LWF-led relief program. The five Hong Kong churches are of mainland origin: the Chinese Rhenish Church, Hong Kong Synod (begun 1847, constituted 1949, now with 12,000 members); Evangelical Lutheran Church of Hong Kong (a remnant of the Lutheran Church of China, constituted 1955, 12,800); Lutheran Church, Hong Kong Synod (related to the LC-MS, 1917, 1977, 8,100); Tsung Tsin Mission of Hong Kong (1847, 1929, 7,500); and Hong Kong and Macao Lutheran Church (2,300). These bodies form the Hong Kong Lutheran Federation, Ltd. All except the Lutheran Church, Hong Kong Synod are member churches of the LWF.

Taiwan has had Lutherans only since refugees fled there from the Chinese mainland as a result of the 1949 revolution. The Taiwan Lutheran Church was constituted in 1954 (8,220 members, LWF). Other Lutheran churches in Taiwan are the China Evangelical Lutheran Church (affiliated with the Missouri Synod, constituted 1966, 2,620), Chinese Lutheran Brethren Church (1957, 3,000), Lutheran Church of Taiwan (Republic of China) (1977, 1,600, LWF), and Lutheran Church of the Republic of China (1,200, LWF).

In *Malaysia* and *Singapore* the 89,500 Lutherans are mainly in Sabah (North Borneo) in the Basel Christian Church of Malaysia (begun 1886, constituted 1925, 45,000 members) and the Protestant Church in Sabah (1953, 1966, 32,500). In the peninsula cities are found the Chinese-speaking Lutheran Church in Malaysia and Singapore (1907, 1963, 6,000 members) and the Tamil (India)-speaking Evangelical Lutheran Church in Malaysia (1951, 1963, 5,300). In 1977 these four bodies formed the Federation of Evangelical Lutheran Churches in Malaysia and Singapore. Only the Protestant Church in Sabah is not in the LWF. The Lutheran Church in Singapore, a member of the LWF, has 3,000 members.

Indonesia, strongly Muslim, is home to the largest Lutheran constituency outside Europe and North America (4.26 million). Eight church bodies, found largely in North Sumatra but also in other parts of Indonesia, are widely known by their acronyms. They stem from the work of the Rhenish Mission (1861), the eventually patriarchal role of Ludwig Nommensen (1834-1918), and the confessional identity gained through Luther's Small Catechism. In the order of their appearance as self-governing churches, these bodies are the GPKB (Batak Christian Community Church, Java, 1927, 20,000 members), HKI (Indonesian Christian Church, 1927,

350,000), HKBP (Protestant Christian Batak Church, 1930, 3 million), GKPS (Simalungun Protestant Christian Church, 1963, 198,500), GKPI (Christian Protestant Church in Indonesia, 1964, 255,600), GKLI (Indonesian Christian Lutheran Church, 1965, 16,900), GKPM (Protestant Christian Church in Mantawai, 1973, 22,300), and GKPA (Christian Protestant Church of Angkola, 1974, 27,500). All churches except the GKLI are in the LWF. Three other Lutheran churches in Indonesia, all members of the LWF, are the Nias Protestant Christian Church (334,000 members), the Pakpak Dairi Christian Protestant Church (30,500), and the United Protestant Church (10,000).

Of singular interest in connection with the Indonesian Lutheran churches is the fact that their Lutheran identity and membership in the LWF is based not on confessional documents from the 16th century but on the original Confession of Faith of the Huria Kristen Batak Protestan of 1951. This indigenous confession, which is biblically, creedally, and contextually based, was deemed to be in conformity with historic Lutheranism by the churches of the LWF, even though it does not mention classic Lutheran documents. It has been recognized as a confession parallel to, and consistent with, the Augsburg Confession of 1530.

In *Papua New Guinea,* where Johannes Flierl (1858-1947) of the Neuendettelsau Mission Society began work in 1886, and where German, American, and Australian efforts combined after 1920, the Evangelical Lutheran Church of Papua New Guinea was constituted in 1956. It is presently a church of 815,000 members. To the west lies the Gutnius ("good news" in pidgin) Lutheran Church–Papua New Guinea (begun in 1949 by the Missouri Synod, constituted 1961, 95,000 members). Both churches are in the LWF, and the former is also ecumenically active. Both churches also have strong ties to Australia.

In *Japan* Lutheran mission work began in 1892. The Japan Evangelical Lutheran Church (1922, 22,000 members, LWF) grew following World War II, especially when former China missionaries came after 1949. Four newer bodies are the Japan Lutheran Church (linked to the Missouri Synod, associate member of LWF, begun 1948, constituted 1969, 2,800 members), Japan Lutheran Brethren Church (1949, 1,250), Kinki Evangelical Lutheran Church (1950, 1961, 2,600, LWF), and West Japan Evangelical Lutheran Church (1949, 1962, 3,560). Major ties exist with America and Scandinavia.

In *Korea,* work supported by the LC-MS began in 1958. The Lutheran Church in Korea (1971, 3,125 members) is active in the LWF and is a significant minority in a heavily Presbyterian Protestantism (→ Presbyterianism).

As in Latin America and Africa, so in Asia the LWF, through the Asia Area Desk of its Department for Mission and Development, assists the scattered churches in many ways. The first All-Asia Lutheran Conference, at Madras in 1956, set the pattern for regular regional conferences of these churches.

In the predominantly Roman Catholic *Philippines,* Lutheran work began in 1957. The Lutheran Church in the Philippines (1967, 27,000 members) is linked both to the LC-MS and to the LWF.

6.4. *Australia and New Zealand*

In *Australia* Lutherans are a tiny minority among the 6.7 million Anglicans and Protestants. The Lutheran Church of Australia (85,000 members) is a 1966 union of two long-separated churches descended from German immigrants (1839 and 1841) who were opposed to the Evangelical Church of the Old Prussian Union. A schism in 1846 led eventually to the United Evangelical Lutheran Church in Australia, active in the LWF until 1966, and to the Evangelical Lutheran Church of Australia, which was related to the LC-MS. Although since the merger of 1966 the former connections have officially ceased, the new church body opted in 1991 for associate membership in the LWF. Scandinavian and German congregations exist in Sydney, Melbourne, and elsewhere.

In *New Zealand* congregations of the Lutheran Church of New Zealand (1,200 members) comprise a district of the Lutheran Church of Australia.

7. Lutheran Churches Today

What is basically a statistical review of Lutheran churches throughout the world — 133 of which are affiliated with the LWF, representing 61.7 million persons in 73 countries — scarcely illuminates the life and mission of those churches. Stories of the roles of these churches in theological reflection, in → relief and humanitarian service, in mission in a globalized world, and in peacemaking are told in other places. Three areas of Lutheran life, however, require brief mention in this section.

7.1. *Lutheran Churches in Communion*

Initially, Lutheran churches saw the global LWF as "a free association of Lutheran Churches." This definition promoted a view of individual churches, self-governing and autonomous in all respects. After more than 40 years of working and living together, however, these churches came to see this definition as representing a strikingly weak ecclesiology. In 1950, at the Eighth Assembly of the LWF, held in

Curitiba, Brazil, it was agreed that the self-understanding of the LWF is now, in the words of its present constitution, to be "a communion of churches which confess the triune God, agree in the proclamation of the Word of God and are united in pulpit and altar fellowship. The LWF confesses the one, holy, catholic, and apostolic Church and is resolved to serve Christian unity throughout the world." This *communio* (→ Koinonia) ecclesiology (which is not necessarily shared by Lutherans who have remained outside the LWF) is increasingly seen as binding churches throughout the world in new and indissoluble ways. Its full depth is being discovered only as new and sometimes uncertain steps are taken together.

7.2. *Lutheran Churches in Transition*

A realistic vision of *communio* is requiring Lutheran churches throughout the world to view their lives within particular and sometimes unique contexts. This perspective involves a continuing quest both for an awareness of identity and for relevance in society. Lutheran churches are beginning to realize the need to take active part in seeking a more just society, but there is not yet a clear or differentiated appreciation of the key role that theological understandings — such as the traditional Lutheran hallmark of → justification by → grace through → faith, or the newly found ecclesiology of *communio* — can have in this pursuit. Links to the state and to ethnicity, tribal and national, are still far too strong, and calls for mission are often merely hollow statements. Visions of *communio* are still weak and sometimes misunderstood, and the lack of eschatological awareness is remarkable. Yet there is within the Lutheran churches of the world a growing sense that the church's being is for the people.

7.3. *Lutheran Churches in the Church Catholic*

For most Lutheran churches, the search for identity and relevance in society is a calling common to all churches. Visible unity is necessary if that calling is to shape the churches' life and witness in the world.

After generations of separation and isolation, Lutheran churches in the latter part of the 20th century exhibited a growing commitment to → ecumenical dialogue and decision. In many cases concrete steps were taken, often after years of study and dialogue:

Leuenberg Agreement (1973), between Lutheran, Reformed, and, later, Methodist churches on the European continent;

Meissen Agreement (1988), between the Church of England and the Evangelical Churches in Germany;

Porvoo Common Statement (1996), between Nordic and Baltic Lutherans and the Anglican churches of the United Kingdom and Ireland;

Formula of Agreement (1997), between the American member churches of the World Alliance of Reformed Churches and the ELCA;

Joint Declaration on the Doctrine of Justification (1999), between the LWF and the Roman Catholic Church; and

Called to Common Mission (2001), between the Episcopal Church, U.S.A., and the ELCA.

In addition, concrete steps have been taken toward communion between Anglicans and Lutherans in Southern Africa. And countless other national and international bilateral dialogues have occurred between Lutherans and other churches. In many cases these efforts have led to theological and ecclesiological breakthroughs.

Yet even as new forms of unity in faith are declared, many steps toward the realization of that unity in life and witness are yet to be taken. The future of Lutheran churches throughout the world clearly lies, to use the → Faith and Order phrase, in fuller "*communio* in faith, life, and witness" with all churches.

→ Ecumenism, Ecumenical Movement

Bibliography: Statistics: D. B. BARRETT et al., eds., *WCE* (2d ed.) • *Directory Lutheran World Federation / Handbuch Lutherischer Weltbund* (Geneva, 2001) • "The Lutheran World Federation 2001 Membership Figures" and ". . . Membership Details," *LWI*, July 2002, 4-12.

Other works: E. T. BACHMANN and M. B. BACHMANN, *Lutheran Churches in the World: A Handbook* (Minneapolis, 1989) • W. ELERT, *The Structure of Lutheranism* (St. Louis, 2003; orig. Eng. ed., 1962) • G. FACKRE and M. ROOT, *Affirmations and Admonitions: Lutheran Decisions and Dialogue with Reformed, Episcopal, and Roman Catholic Churches* (Grand Rapids, 1998) • W. GRIEVE, ed., *Between Vision and Reality: Lutheran Churches in Transition* (Geneva, 2001) • E. W. GRITSCH, *Fortress Introduction to Lutheranism* (Minneapolis, 1994); idem, *A History of Lutheranism* (Minneapolis, 2002) • THE LUTHERAN WORLD FEDERATION and THE ROMAN CATHOLIC CHURCH, *Joint Declaration on the Doctrine of Justification* (Grand Rapids, 2000) • E. C. NELSON, *The Rise of World Lutheranism* (Philadelphia, 1982); idem, ed., *The Lutherans in North America* (rev. ed.; Philadelphia, 1980) • W. G. RUSCH and D. F. MARTENSEN, eds., *The Leuenberg Agreement and Lutheran-Reformed Relationships: Evaluations by North American and European Theologians* (Minneapolis, 1989) • J. H. SCHJØRRING, "Church Identity in the Nordic Countries—an International Perspective," *For All People: Global Theologies in Contexts* (ed. E. M. W. Pedersen, H. Lam, and P. Lodberg; Grand Rapids, 2002) 109-27; idem, ed., *Nordiske folkekirker i opbrud* (Århus, 2001) • J. H. SCHJØRRING, P. KUMARI, and N. A. HJELM, eds., *From Federation to Communion: The History of the Lutheran World Federation* (Minneapolis, 1997) • O. TJØRHOM, ed., *Apostolicity and Unity: Essays on the Porvoo Common Statement* (Grand Rapids, 2002) • V. VAJTA and H. WEISSGERBER, eds., *The Church and the Confessions: The Role of the Confessions in the Life and Doctrine of the Lutheran Churches* (Philadelphia, 1963) esp. A. M. Lumbantobing, "The Confession of the Batak Church," 119-47.

E. THEODORE BACHMAN† and NORMAN A. HJELM

Lutheran World Federation

The Lutheran World Federation (LWF), constituted by 49 churches in Lund, Sweden, in 1947, is the result of efforts to bring together the → Lutheran churches of the world on the basis of a common confessional allegiance (→ Confession of Faith). Although antecedent organizations included the General Council of the Evangelical Lutheran Church in North America (1867) and the General Evangelical Lutheran Conference in Germany (1868), the most immediate and important precursor to the LWF was the Lutheran World Convention (LWC), founded in Eisenach in 1923. In Paris in 1935 the LWC laid the groundwork for a more permanent confederation. In spite of difficulties, work continued during World War II and accelerated rapidly in light of the challenges both of assisting European Lutherans to overcome the war's devastation and of caring for orphaned missions. The highly effective → relief program for Europe shaped the Lutheran World Service, which continues to account for a major portion of LWF staff and financial resources.

In 2002 the LWF numbered 136 member churches in 76 countries. It represents 61.7 million of the 65.4 million baptized Lutherans in the world. Some churches, though not all, which are associated with the American-based Lutheran Church–Missouri Synod remain outside the LWF.

LWF history can be traced through official reports from its nine international assemblies, the federation's highest authority: Lund 1947, Hanover 1952, Minneapolis 1957, Helsinki 1963, Evian 1970, Dar es Salaam 1977, Budapest 1984, Curitiba, Brazil, 1990, and Hong Kong 1997. The tenth assembly is scheduled for Winnipeg in 2003.

World Lutheranism's confessional basis is articulated in the LWF constitution, revised in 1990: "The Lutheran World Federation confesses the Holy Scriptures of the Old and New Testaments to be the only source and norm of its doctrine, life and service. It sees in the three Ecumenical Creeds and in the → Confessions of the Lutheran Church, especially in the unaltered → Augsburg Confession and the Small Catechism of Martin → Luther, a pure exposition of the Word of God" (art. 2). The constitution also identifies three tasks of the LWF: it "furthers the united witness to the Gospel of Jesus Christ and strengthens the member churches in carrying out the missionary command and in their efforts towards Christian → unity worldwide; furthers worldwide among the member churches diaconic action, alleviation of human need, promotion of → peace and human → rights, social and economic justice, care for God's creation and sharing of resources; furthers through cooperative study the self-understanding and the communion of member churches and helps them to act jointly in common tasks" (art. 3).

Echoing the LWC, the LWF in 1947 described itself as "a free association of Lutheran churches." Already then, however, a debate about the ecclesial character of world Lutheranism was underway, which laid the theological groundwork for a common declaration of pulpit and altar fellowship.

At its Dar es Salaam assembly in 1977, the LWF took the distinctly ecclesial step of declaring a → status confessionis regarding the effects of apartheid at the Lord's Table (→ Eucharist). At Budapest in 1984 the LWF suspended two white churches in southern Africa because of such apartheid, a suspension lifted in 1991. Increasing ecumenical involvement also put the ecclesial question to the LWF, whose member churches more and more understood themselves to be a united fellowship. Added to the theological groundwork, these factors led to two significant actions in Budapest 1984: amending the constitution by adding the sentence, "The member churches of the LWF understand themselves to be in pulpit and altar fellowship with each other," and adopting statements on self-understanding and unity, both of which use the terminology "Lutheran communion."

At the 1990 assembly in Curitiba this intensified ecclesial understanding was embodied in the adoption of a new constitution. The LWF was now defined as "a communion of churches which confess the triune God, agree in the proclamation of the Word of God and are united in pulpit and altar fellowship." The assembly also agreed to set up a council of 48 persons charged with leadership of the federation between assemblies. Notably, membership on this council is equally divided between representatives of member churches from the Northern and Southern hemispheres, and at least 40 percent of its members are women, a figure also applicable to voting members of the assembly itself. Such structural decisions have been seen within the LWF as direct implications of its self-understanding as a communion of churches. In 2002 the council of the LWF, meeting in Wittenberg, Germany, went a step further, endorsing a proposal that would make this understanding explicit in the very name of the organization: "The Lutheran World Federation: A Communion of Churches."

The self-application to the LWF of stronger ecclesial language is consonant with a fundamental ecumenical commitment. Like other → Christian World Communions, the Lutheran communion is committed both to the multilateral approach of the → World Council of Churches (WCC) and to bilateral approaches to church unity. The LWF's ecumenical priority is uniquely expressed in the Institute for Ecumenical Research, established in Strasbourg, France, in 1963.

The federation's → dialogue with the → Roman Catholic Church began in 1957 and in 1999 brought about the ecumenically highly significant → Joint Declaration on the Doctrine of Justification, an agreement affirming that the 16th-century condemnations by each tradition of the other concerning the article of → justification by → grace through → faith are no longer applicable or church dividing. Even as dialogue between the churches of the LWF and the Roman Catholic Church continues regarding other issues, the two bodies are together involved in conversations with representatives of various Protestant traditions in the hope that the applicability of the Joint Declaration will be widened. The LWF also has had or is having bilateral dialogues with the → Anglican Communion, → Baptist World Alliance, → Orthodox churches, Seventh-day Adventist Church (→ Adventists), → World Alliance of Reformed Churches, and → World Methodist Council. These bilateral relationships extend also to joint efforts in witness and service.

Programmatically, the LWF has three departments: World Service, → Mission and → Evangelism, and → Theology and Studies. Its secretariat includes offices responsible for ecumenical relations, political affairs and human rights, and communication services. In 1995 the LWF and the WCC together formed ACT — Action by Churches Together — as a means of responding more immediately and effectively to major emergencies throughout the world. The LWF has its headquarters in Geneva; a plan to create regional offices to serve member churches has thus far resulted in the establishment of offices in Africa, Asia, Europe, and North America. The Geneva staff numbers close to 100 persons, and field staff in service, relief, and development projects number approximately 4,000.

Bibliography: E. L. BRAND, *Toward a Lutheran Communion: Pulpit and Altar Fellowship* (Geneva, 1989) • S. GRUNDMANN, *Der Lutherische Weltbund. Gründung, Herkunft, Aufbau* (Cologne, 1957) • E. C. NELSON, *The Rise of World Lutheranism: An American Perspective* (Philadelphia, 1982) • J. H. SCHJØRRING, P. KUMARI, and N. A. HJELM, eds., *From Federation to Communion: The History of the Lutheran World Federation* (Minneapolis, 1997) • K. SCHMIDT-CLAUSEN, *Vom Lutherischen Weltkonvent zum Lutherischen Weltbund. Die lutherische Kirche, Geschichte und Gestalten* (vol. 2; Gütersloh, 1976) • V. VAJTA, *From Generation to Generation: The LWF, 1947-1982* (Geneva, 1983) • B. WADENSJØ, *Toward a World Lutheran Communion: Developments in Lutheran Cooperation up to 1929* (Uppsala, 1970).

EUGENE L. BRAND and NORMAN A. HJELM

Lutheranism

1. Term
2. Emergence of the Movement
   2.1. Political Dimension
   2.2. Book of Concord
   2.3. Orthodoxy and Pietism
3. Expansion
   3.1. Europe
   3.2. North America
   3.3. Third World
      3.3.1. Africa
      3.3.2. Asia
      3.3.3. Latin America
4. The Future of Lutheranism

1. Term

The term "Lutheranism" may be used in a variety of ways: as describing the form of Christianity that developed from the 16th-century → Reformation at Wittenberg and most particularly from the teachings of its leader, Martin → Luther (1483-1546); as describing the theological and confessional tradition based on the documents of the Book of Concord; or as describing the self-understanding and/or the identity of church bodies throughout the world that claim agreement with Luther's teaching.

Luther himself, however, decried the use of his name: "I ask that [people] make no reference to my name; let them call themselves Christians, not Lutherans. What is Luther? After all, the teaching is not mine. Neither was I crucified for anyone. St. Paul, in 1 Corinthians 3, would not allow the Christians to call themselves Pauline or Petrine, but Christian. How then could I — poor stinking maggot-fodder that I am — come to have [people] call the children of Christ by my wretched name? Not so, my dear friends; let us abolish all party names and call ourselves Christians, after him whose teaching we hold" (*LW* 45.70-71).

The term was first used in 1520 in the traditional way of naming a heresy after its head. Thus the writings of Johann Eck (1486-1543), Jerome Emser (1477-1527), and Desiderius → Erasmus (1469?-1536) contain designations such as "Lutherani," "Lutheranism," and "Lutherana secta." Groups of Lutherans themselves began to use the term in controversies in the mid-16th century in order to demarcate their positions from those of their opponents, such as "Gnesio-Lutherans" from "Philippists," or Lutherans from the followers of John → Calvin. Only after 1586 does the term "Lutheran Church" appear, in Württemberg and Saxony in Germany. In 1597 the theological faculty at Wittenberg began using this name in order to identify the "true church" as the one based solely on the pure doctrine of the → gospel as formulated by Luther. In the 17th century Lutheran → orthodoxy (§1) used "Lutheranism" in opposition to Calvinists, Roman Catholics, and radical enthusiasts. Not until the 19th century did Lutheranism, again in controversy — against → rationalism and the formation of Union churches in Germany — become a central term of identity.

2. Emergence of the Movement

The origins of Lutheranism in German-speaking Europe may be dated to either 1521 or 1530. The Edict of Worms in 1521 formally excommunicated Luther and his followers, a decree that remained in effect until the Peace of Augsburg in 1555 (→ Augsburg, Peace of). This latter settlement gave fundamental legal significance to the → Augsburg Confession, or Confessio Augustana (CA), of 1530, the document that remains basic today to the confessional self-understanding of Lutheran churches throughout the world. The CA, whose chief architect was Philipp → Melanchthon (1497-1560), agrees with the theological position of Luther in defining the → church in terms of its doctrine and confession (→ Confession of Faith). The CA thus provides substance to the theological claims that at that time were distinctive to Lutheranism, claims that are often gathered under the three Reformation "solas" — *sola gratia* (grace alone), *sola fide* (faith alone), and *sola Scriptura* (Scripture alone as authority; → Reformation Principles).

The CA, however, does not understand the movement of reform for which it speaks as formative of a new church. The movement was shaped by a claim to evangelical catholicity, that is, it sees its mission as an interim one working for the renewal of the one, holy, catholic, and apostolic church by the gospel. In a certain sense, therefore, Lutheranism is to be viewed as a movement that proposes a particular evangelical understanding of the gospel to the entire church catholic.

Lutheranism emerged as a distinctive unit of the Reformation in reaction to the positions of independent reformers like Ulrich → Zwingli (1484-1531), Heinrich Bullinger (1504-75), Johannes Oecolampadius (1482-1531), Martin → Bucer (1491-1551), and others. Largely as a result of the eucharistic controversies after 1525, those whose views were in line with Luther's joined and gradually took on an ecclesial identity demarcated not only from the Roman Catholics but also from the Swiss reformers, → Anabaptists, and others. Subsequently, a conservative approach to changes in church practice on the part of the Wittenberg Lutherans — for example, in respect to the understanding of the → Mass, liturgical forms, and the admissibility of statues and → images — was combined with Luther's central view of the gospel of → justification by → grace alone through → faith to place the Lutheran movement in a middle ground between Roman Catholicism, on the one side, and Zwinglianism (→ Zwingli's Theology), → Calvinism, and the Anabaptists, on the other. This arrangement found institutional expression in 1528-33 in new → church orders influenced by Johannes Bugenhagen (1485-1558), Melanchthon, and Andreas Osiander (1496/98-1552), orders that were integrally associated with Luther's doctrinal views. Simultaneously, Luther's Large and Small → Catechisms of 1529 received wide circulation, making a strong impact on popular → piety and thus increasing the self-consciousness of the Lutheran movement.

The initial causes of the growth of the Lutheran movement were not uniform. There had been reform movements before Luther — for example, at the levels of mystical piety and of the generally critical view of the church taken by humanists. Furthermore, the direct influence of Luther himself was quickly mediated and modified by other reformers such as Calvin, Zwingli, and Bucer, and even by such "Lutheran" colleagues as Melanchthon, Osiander, Bugenhagen, Johann Brenz (1499-1570), and Johann Agricola (1494-1566). The way in which Luther's initial originality was transmitted by others made Lutheranism at an early stage the pluriform entity it remains to this day. On the one hand, dogmatic and confessional Lutheranism was dependent on some of Luther's basic views, even as it developed independent positions. On the other hand, the study of Luther (→ Luther Research) has consistently led to new orientations and reforms, sometimes nearly breaking the boundaries of the movement.

Thus we can say that Lutheranism's self-understanding rests on agreement with → Luther's theology in its fundamental theses, not all of which were unique to Luther — for example, the doctrine of justification ("the doctrine by which the church stands and falls," *articulus stantis et cadentis ecclesiae*), → Christology ("communication of properties," *communicatio idiomatum*), the doctrine of the → Eucharist (the "real presence" of Christ "in, with, and under" the bread and wine), and also his views on → law and gospel, the → two kingdoms, original sin, and → freedom of the will and → predestination. Furthermore, in respect to ecclesiology, Luther held that there are seven "marks" (*notae ecclesiae*) of the true church: → proclamation, → baptism, the Eucharist, the office of the keys, → ordination, → catechesis, and → discipleship ("On the Councils and the Church," *LW* 41.148-68).

Whether or not Lutheranism — as its theology and ecclesiology has developed — has fully and critically appropriated these basic convictions of Luther is, perhaps, an open question.

2.1. *Political Dimension*

The Lutheran movement did not, however, emerge as a phenomenon of pure religion or theology. From the beginning it was inextricably bound up with the political realities of the → Roman Catholic Church, the empire, and Germany.

For example, the CA itself was the result of Charles V (emp. 1519-56) agreeing to provide a forum at which the Lutherans could be heard, the Diet of Augsburg of 1530. Luther, as a condemned heretic, was not allowed to participate, so Melanchthon, a layman, was designated to write a statement of Lutheran belief that was subsequently signed by seven German princes and two city councils. The emperor called immediately for a Roman Catholic response, which was prepared largely by Johann Eck, the Confutation. (In response to this reply, Melanchthon in 1531 wrote his Apology of the Augsburg Confession.) Nevertheless there was a call for a number of concessions by the Lutherans and also for the enforcement of the Edict of Worms, by which Luther and his followers had been excommunicated and the initially conciliatory tone of the diet was changed. Luther himself, as recorded in a "table talk" of 1530, commented, "We [Lutherans and Roman Catholics] will never again get as close together as we did at Augsburg" (WA.TR 4.495.7-9, no. 4780).

Even more, the growth in power of the German states directly affected the character of the Lutheran movement. In 1544 Pope Paul III (1534-49) warned Charles V that his gradual toleration of Lutheran territories violated → church law; at the same time, the pope offered the emperor 12,500 mercenaries and financial support for a war against the Lutheran princes who had formed the Schmalkaldic League. Not until 1555 at the Peace of Augsburg were adherents of the Augsburg Confession allowed territorial rights in accordance with the principle of → *cuius regio eius religio,* by which the established church of a territory was determined by the faith of its ruler.

While Lutheranism emerged initially in Germany, it was not long before the movement spread to other parts of Europe, the Nordic countries and beyond. The spread northward was determined largely by the specific political circumstances of the royal Union of Kalmar, which united Denmark, Sweden, and Norway from 1397 to 1523. From each of these countries, however, there were also direct contacts with Wittenberg: through students such as the Swedish Petri brothers Olaus (1493-1552) and Laurentius (1499-1573), through appeals for assistance in developing higher education such as that initiated by Christian II (1513-23) of Denmark in 1520, and through requests for direct assistance in ecclesiastical reorganization in accord with Lutheranism, such as the request by Christian III (1534-59) of Denmark that Johannes Bugenhagen assist in restructuring and ordinations. Ecumenically significant, as it has turned out, has been the fact that the Lutheran Churches of Sweden and Finland maintained the historic succession of the → episcopate, while those of Denmark and Norway did not.

Subsequent growth of Lutheranism during the first half of the 16th century, on a more limited scale, changed the religious landscape throughout the rest of Europe. This growth was perhaps most notable in the Baltic lands (Estonia, Latvia, Lithuania) but was evident also in eastern Europe (Poland, Czechoslovakia, Hungary, Romania) and even, to an extremely limited degree, in Austria, Italy, and France.

2.2. Book of Concord

In the period after the 1555 Peace of Augsburg, Lutheranism solidified its position in Europe but was marked by internal controversy and conflict. History has identified no fewer than six controversies within Lutheranism during this period. Four of them dealt with the proper understanding of justification by faith (the → Antinomian, Majoristic, Osiandrian, and → Synergist Controversies), one with the proper relationship between Lutheranism and Roman Catholicism (the Adiaphorist Controversy), and one with relations to the Reformed in respect to the understanding of the Lord's Supper (the → Crypto-Calvinist Controversy). Mediation, led particularly by Melanchthon, failed to unite the Lutherans until finally in 1577 the → Formula of Concord, signed by 8,000 theologians and at least 85 political leaders, united the German Lutherans for the first time since the controversies within Lutheranism over → adiaphora, stirred up by the 1548 Interims of Augsburg and Leipzig.

The Formula of Concord was followed in 1580 by publication of the Book of Concord, later subtitled "The Confessions of the Evangelical Lutheran Church." This imposing volume, over 750 pages in its latest English edition (R. Kolb and T. J. Wengert), is regarded by many Lutheran churches throughout the world in its totality as the confessional norm for Lutheranism; other Lutheran churches give pride of place to the CA and Luther's Small Catechism, regarding the remainder of the Book of Concord as a worthy commentary on these two statements. The work comprises the three ecumenical creeds (Apostles', Nicene, Athanasian; → Confessions and Creeds), the Augsburg Confession (1530), Apology of the Augsburg Confession (1531), the Schmalkaldic (or Smalcald) Articles (1537), Treatise on the Power and Primacy of the Pope (1537), Luther's Small and Large Catechisms (1529), and the Formula of Concord (1577). This collection of 16th-century documents and statements — regarded as enduringly normative — has given Lutheranism its character as a "confessional movement."

2.3. Orthodoxy and Pietism

Lutheran orthodoxy in the 17th century established confessional identity, largely over against the growing influence of Calvinism, by way of a scholastic dogmatic system that worked out the specifics of Lutheranism on the basis of agreement between the biblical witness and Luther's teaching. The "Scripture principle" was thus oriented to the confessional writings. Furthermore, the doctrine of the person of Christ was seen as the sole basis for the doctrine of redemption. Fundamental also were teachings on the → order of salvation (ordo salutis) and on the → Word of God and the → sacraments as the → means of grace. In a rather unhistorical way, orthodox Lutherans treated Luther as a dogmatic authority.

During this period the term "evangelical Lutheran" — describing both church and doctrine — came to be used largely to differentiate Lutheranism from both Calvinism and Roman Catholicism. The failure of doctrinal conversations designed to overcome these cleavages strengthened the confessional establishment of Lutheranism. Many scholars have taken the position that with the predominance of Lutheran orthodoxy, the Lutheranism that emerged in the 16th century lost its original and distinctive profile. Also, many contend that this original profile was further eroded by the subsequent movement of → Pietism and by the later → Enlightenment. However, the orthodox Lutheranism that developed after the Book of Concord still found respectable champions up to the end of the 18th century.

The movement of Pietism, which can best be dated from 1675 to the early 19th century, was related to Lutheran orthodoxy "as medieval mysticism was related to medieval scholasticism" (J. Wallmann). Some orthodox theologians were aware of the danger of "dead orthodoxy," notably Johann Gerhard (1582-1637), who founded a "school of piety" (schola pietatis) in 1622 in an attempt to combine scholastic dogma with a piety of the emotions. But Pietism itself became a crucial part of Lutheran life with the publication in 1675 of Pia desideria (Pious desires) by Philipp Jacob Spener (1635-1705). After a diagnosis of the degeneration of the church, this work — which reads like a political manifesto — offered a reform program of six steps: a richer presence of the Word of God, a revival of the common priesthood of all believers, a conviction that Christianity consists more of practice than of knowledge, the avoidance of unnecessary theological controversies, a thorough reform of → theological education, and the practice of simple, edifying → preaching.

These two strains — orthodoxy and Pietism — have marked Lutheranism's life and experience throughout its history. It is, for example, not possible to understand or fully to appreciate the music of Lutheranism's greatest composer, Johann Sebastian Bach (1685-1750), apart from an awareness of how both orthodoxy and Pietism influenced his music. As Lutheranism expanded — to North America and to the Third World — "the head and the heart" have characteristically each maintained positions of great importance.

3. Expansion
3.1. Europe

The Lutheran movement in the 19th century became widely diverse. Lutherans, like all others, were deeply influenced by the industrial revolution and by enormous changes in communication and commerce (→ Industrial Society). The American Declaration of Independence (1776) and the French Revolution (1789) raised questions of individual and national → rights. The Congress of Vienna (1814-15) condemned the tyranny of Napoléon yet affirmed the "holy alliance" of England, Prussia, Austria, and Russia. Karl → Marx (1818-83) battled for economic change. In Germany, largely in opposition to rationalism and under the influence of both → Romanticism and revivalism, "neo-Lutheranism" stressed maintaining a firm hold on classic Lutheran elements.

Wilhelm Loehe (or Löhe, 1808-72) in Neuendettelsau practiced a catholic ecclesiology in his parish and also organized a diaconal center of hospitals, homes, and educational institutions that ultimately had global influence. Theologians at Erlangen led the development of a neo-Lutheran theology, stressing the → regeneration of the individual believer through the church and its means of grace and contending that Lutheranism and its confessions have preserved authentic orthodox Christianity.

Lutheranism in Scandinavia retained its close relationship to the state. It also, however, was marked by awakenings and → revivals that were not strictly confessional but were influenced by both German Pietism and neo-Lutheranism. In Denmark N. F. S. → Grundtvig (1783-1872), prodigious scholar, author, theologian, and educator, led a churchly renewal movement that has left an enduring mark on Danish society. In Norway Hans Nielsen Hauge (1771-1824) and in Sweden Carl Olof Rosenius (1816-68), both laymen, promoted revivals that influenced, not least, immigrants to North America from those countries. In Finland the itinerant preacher Paavo Ruotsalainen (1777-1852) led an awakening that has marked the Lutheran Church in Finland and, indeed, the entire nation to the present day.

All of these European Lutheran movements were also marked by a strong sense of mission. The 19th century was the time of the establishment of missions and mission societies (→ Mission; German Missions). Loehe wrote that "mission is nothing but the one church of God in motion, the actualization of the one universal, catholic church" (p. 59). Lutheran missionaries, beginning in most cases in the 19th century, brought their movement to all corners of the globe.

3.2. *North America*

Lutherans, however, were present in the Americas earlier than the 19th century. A group of German Lutheran immigrants founded a short-lived settlement in what is now Venezuela in 1528. The name "Lutheran" appeared in Florida in 1564, but it was in reality applied to French Huguenots by Spanish Catholics, who regarded all Protestants as Lutherans. In 1638, however, when Sweden and Holland established colonies in Delaware and what was to become New York, Lutheran churches were also established. The Church of Sweden initially supported Swedish congregations in what was to become Delaware, Pennsylvania, and New Jersey. In the early 19th century, however, just a few years before the large Swedish immigrations to the United States, these parishes were transferred to the Episcopal Church.

The father of American Lutheranism must be regarded as Henry Melchior Muhlenberg (1711-87), who was sent to the United States in 1742 directly from Halle, a center of Lutheran Pietism. Muhlenberg came largely in order to create peace among various factions of German Lutheran immigrants. He is best remembered, however, for his extensive work in establishing congregations in the eastern United States. (His personal motto was *ecclesia plantanda*, "the church must be planted.")

The many Lutheran church bodies in the United States, which were commonly viewed as immigrant and non–English speaking, had great difficulty assimilating to the American cultural and theological scenes. A significant attempt to establish a distinctively American Lutheran theology was made by Samuel Simon Schmucker (1799-1873), founder and president (1826-64) of the Lutheran Theological Seminary at Gettysburg, Pennsylvania. He sought to have Lutherans agree to a revision of the Augsburg Confession in order to create an "American Lutheranism." This attempt failed, however, leading to considerable bitterness and division between Lutheran bodies. Not until 1918 and the formation, from a number of German synods, of the United Lutheran Church in America did unity between Lutherans begin to take shape. This achievement was followed by mergers with Scandinavian bodies, leading to the establishment in 1988 of the Evangelical Lutheran Church in America (ELCA), a thoroughly American and ecumenical church of some five million members. The ELCA has taken notable ecumenical strides in reaching, although not without internal controversy, relations of "full communion" with the Episcopal Church, the American church bodies that are members of the →

World Alliance of Reformed Churches, and the → Moravian Church.

Yet Lutheranism in North America is still not fully united. The Lutheran Church–Missouri Synod (LCMS), a body of more than two million members, had its origins in the 1839 migration of 700 Lutherans from Saxony to Missouri in the United States. The migration was an act of protest against the rationalism that marked the German Lutheranism of the time. Giving the strongest leadership to this group was C. F. W. Walther (1811-87), whose goal also became in large measure to preserve Lutheranism from being Americanized. The extremely conservative LCMS has remained apart not only from ecumenical relationships but even from other Lutheran bodies in the United States and from the Lutheran World Federation (LWF). Nevertheless, a 12-member Committee on Lutheran Cooperation between the ELCA and the LCMS does exist, and in 2003 it agreed to future substantive discussions designed to explore theological differences between the two bodies.

Lutheranism in North America is still in the process of formation. Not until after World War II did Lutherans really become something other than a German and Scandinavian immigrant group marked by racial, cultural, and theological isolation. Now, to be sure, ecumenical Lutheranism is both contributing to and learning from the highly pluralistic cultural and religious scene that marks both the United States and Canada. Perhaps its greatest challenge, however, is to retain a distinctive and classic Lutheran profile — in contrast to much of North American mainline → Protestantism — even as it takes its place among those who offer a united Christian witness to North American society.

3.3. *Third World*

The initial commitment of German Pietism to global mission was strengthened by the migration to North America, as well as by the revival and → Inner Mission movements in European Lutheranism. Moreover, the 19th century has been seen as the century of expansion for virtually all Christian groupings. It was a time of considerable optimism for the future of the Christian world. While that optimism is now often seen as having been largely misplaced — the missionary movement, which in effect exported Christian disunity, was often a handmaid to imperialism and → colonialism — Lutheranism during this time did become a global movement.

3.3.1. *Africa*

Lutheranism was first planted in Africa in the empire of Ethiopia by Peter Heyling (1607/8-ca. 1652), a German physician and lawyer who held a position in the Ethiopian royal court. Heyling translated part of the NT into Amharic, one of the many languages in Ethiopia. In 1837 further work was carried on by another German, Johannn L. Krapf (1810-81). Subsequently, mission groups from the Church of Sweden played crucial roles. The Ethiopian Evangelical Church Mekane Yesus (Abode, or Dwelling-Place, of Jesus), formed in 1959, is one of the fastest-growing Lutheran churches in the world, now numbering over 3,350,000 members. Pietistic in character, it has struggled with some success to establish ecumenical contact with the far larger → Ethiopian Orthodox Church, although there has also been serious friction between the two bodies. It has also taken a serious role in the social reconstruction of Ethiopia after the nation's difficult period under Communist domination (1975-91).

As Africa has become an increasingly Christian continent, Lutheranism has played a growing role. Major growth has taken place in Tanzania, Madagascar, Namibia, and South Africa. The churches of the LWF have established coordinated programs of theological education throughout the continent, and significant ecumenical developments have taken place particularly with Anglicans in eastern and southern Africa.

Perhaps of greatest historical, social, and theological significance for Lutheranism in the 20th century in Africa — and beyond — was the celebrated → *status confessionis* debate and action within the LWF in respect to the stance of two relatively small white churches in southern Africa regarding the practice of apartheid in South Africa and what is now Namibia (→ Racism). These churches failed to open up in fellowship to the far larger black Lutheran churches. A debate began within the LWF as early as 1970, and most vigorously at the 1977 assembly of the LWF in Dar es Salaam, Tanzania, as to whether the practice of these churches was actually compromising the fundamental confession of the gospel, that is, a *status confessionis*. In 1984 at its assembly in Budapest, the LWF suspended the membership of the two churches. This suspension was lifted only in 1991 after the abolition of apartheid in southern Africa and after a lengthy process of pastoral care, visitation, and evaluation.

The suspension of membership has been crucial within global Lutheranism, for it demonstrated the ecclesial role of the LWF itself in disciplining churches within the Lutheran communion. Furthermore, it resulted in the charge that the LWF was establishing socioethical or political strategies to judge faithfulness to the gospel. As its response, the LWF in its sixth assembly at Dar es Salaam issued a statement that has taken on great significance for any understanding of the ecclesial character of Lutheranism's life in the world: "Confessional subscription is more than a formal acknowledgment of doctrine. Churches which have signed the confessions of the church thereby commit themselves to show through their daily witness and service that the gospel has empowered them to live as the people of God. They also commit themselves to accept in their worship and at the table of the Lord the brothers and sisters who belong to other churches that accept the same confessions. Confessional subscription should lead to concrete manifestations in unity in worship and in working together at the common tasks of the church" (*In Christ — A New Community* [Dar es Salaam, 1977] 179).

3.3.2. *Asia*

The first → missionaries from Halle, the center of German Pietism, were Bartholomew Ziegenbalg (1682-1719) and Heinrich Plütschau (1677-1752), who in 1706 went to the Danish colony in Tranquebar, India, to start work among Tamil-speaking Indians. In this endeavor Ziegenbalg based his work on five principles of mission: (1) the education of children in parochial schools should concentrate on the Bible (→ Mission Schools); (2) the Word of God must be available in the native language (→ Bible Versions); (3) the gospel must be presented in ways that conform to the culture of the people (→ Acculturation); (4) the aim of mission is personal → conversion; and (5) a church must be organized as quickly as possible. In 1733 the first Indian pastor was ordained, a convert from → Hinduism. This mission led to the formation of the Tamil Evangelical Lutheran Church, a body also supported in its earliest years by the Church of England (Anglican). The first U.S. missionary to India was John C. F. Heyer (1793-1873), who, assisted by Anna S. Kugler, an American medical doctor, took over a small mission in Rajahmundry from its founders, the Bremen Missionary Society.

In 1861 Lutheranism took hold in northern Sumatra, Indonesia, under the leadership of German missionary Ludwig I. Nommensen (1834-1918). This work was concentrated among the Batak people. The missionary principle in Sumatra centered not so much on individual conversion but on mass conversion of the people. The result has been the establishment of what amounts to an Indonesian Lutheran folk church (→ People's Church [Volkskirche]), now numbering several million members in several different bodies. Interestingly, these bodies applied for membership in the LWF, beginning in 1952, and were ultimately admitted not on the basis of adherence to the Augsburg Confession but on the basis of their own "Confession of Faith of the Huria Kristen Batak Protestan," which was deemed consistent with the classic Lutheran document.

Lutheran work in China began in the 19th century when German missionaries came in the wake of other Christians — Roman Catholic, Orthodox, Dutch Reformed, and Anglicans — who had started work in the 17th century. A number of Lutheran churches were formed. With the establishment of the People's Republic of China in 1949, these discrete church bodies went out of existence. Whatever conscious Lutheranism persists in China is now expressed within the China Christian Council, officially recognized by the government and also a member of the → World Council of Churches, and in the countless underground Christian movements.

3.3.3. *Latin America*

There has been only a small Lutheran presence in Latin America, particularly in historic comparison to the domination of Roman Catholicism and, in recent years, to the rapid growth of Pentecostalism throughout the continent (→ Pentecostal Churches; Assembleias de Deus no Brasil). The oldest settlement of Lutherans was the result, not of mission work, but of immigration to Brazil in 1823 by 5,000 German Lutherans. When many more Germans came to Brazil, the German Lutheran churches organized them into → congregations, and ultimately a number of regional → synods were formed. In 1954 these synods took the name Igreja Evangélica do Confissão Luterana no Brasil (Evangelical Church of the Lutheran Confession in Brazil). Only in the latter decades of the 20th century did this church — now more than 700,000 members, larger than all other Latin American Lutheran churches combined — begin to be something other than a German church that happened to be in Brazil. Its outreach and witness now extend increasingly and vigorously to all sectors of Brazilian society, including not least the landless and others who are victims of an extremely imbalanced and difficult social situation. Significantly, Brazilian Lutheranism has reflected soberly on the possible relationship between Luther and Lutheranism, on one hand, and Latin American → liberation theology, on the other. The saga of this church illustrates well the difficulty that Lutheranism has had in moving from the lands of the Reformation and from North America to new cultures and indigenous social situations.

An important chapter in global Lutheranism was the last-minute decision of the LWF in 1970 to move its scheduled fifth assembly from Porto Alegre, Brazil, to Évian-les-Bains, France. This decision was taken — not without opposition — on the basis of the political situation in Brazil, rife as it then was with human rights abuses. Had the assembly taken place in Brazil, it would have been the first large global gathering of Lutherans outside the North. That happening had to wait until the next assembly in 1977, in Dar es Salaam. In 1990 the LWF did hold its eighth assembly in Curitiba, Brazil. Increasingly, world Lutheranism has begun to see that major decisions have sociopolitical contexts and consequences. It has not always been clear, however, that such issues must, in the Lutheran tradition, be seen in theological and ecclesiological perspective, nor has historic Lutheran → "quietism" in matters of social and political ethics been easy to overcome.

Smaller Lutheran churches also came with German immigrants — to Argentina, Chile, and Paraguay. Even earlier, Danish immigrants to the Virgin Islands had established Lutheran congregations from 1666. A phenomenon centered in Latin American Lutheranism, but also found in other places (most notably, the United Kingdom), is the existence of separate congregations. Over the course of time, such bodies using their native European languages came to exist alongside small and in some cases unrelated local Lutheran bodies, notably in Bolivia, Colombia, Costa Rica, Ecuador, Guatemala, Mexico, and Peru.

4. The Future of Lutheranism

It would not be adequate to an understanding of Lutheranism to treat the subject solely within either a historical or a demographic framework. If, as here initially described, the movement is one proposing "a particular evangelical understanding of the gospel to the entire church catholic," it must continually face issues about its self-understanding or identity, the forms of its expression, the shape of its local and global witness, and its relations with all others who claim the name "Christian."

Lutheranism throughout the world is manifestly pluriform. The road from Wittenberg to North America and then to the Third World has not been a direct one, and in some instances a common Lutheran identity is difficult to discover. The modern ecumenical movement, geopolitical realities, and countless changing contexts raise difficult questions about the identity and mission of Lutheranism.

In 1991 a Lutheran journal devoted an entire issue to the question "Whither Lutheranism?" In his introduction to the issue, editor J. L. Boyce noted that "in many ways this is a new day for Lutherans. . . . On [North America] the fledgling yet monstrous ELCA struggles with institutional and financial constrictions as it seeks to define its mission for the 21st century. The ethnic identities of its predecessor bodies no longer serve to define or uphold the loyalties of its membership as before. On the world scene, Lutheran global expansion in the two-thirds world has surfaced a whole new range of perspectives for Lutherans to consider. At the very least these include issues of global economics, ecology, and justice. But they include, too, ecumenical concerns for future relations of Lutherans to Christians of other traditions, as well as of Lutheran mission to non-Christian faiths. . . . In the face of such realities and questions, the issue of the nature of Lutheran identity and confessional subscription has become pressingly real. What does it mean to be a confessional Lutheran in a day of ecumenical awareness and commitment?" (p. 240).

A decade later this paragraph is still to the point. The social and political realities of a globalized world challenge Lutheranism to continue coming out of its shell of social quietism. New ecumenical realities — the → *Joint Declaration on the Doctrine of Justification by Faith* (1999), signed by the LWF and the Roman Catholic Church, and also agreements such as the → Porvoo Common Statement (1992) between Lutheran and Anglican churches in Nordic and Baltic lands and in the United Kingdom — question the persistence of Lutheran denominationalism. Religious pluralism on every continent calls for the development of a new approach to interfaith relations. In this respect, Lutheranism must progress further in its historically tainted relations with the Jewish people (→ Jewish-Christian Dialogue).

All of these issues — sociopolitical, ecumenical, interfaith — require fresh theological and ecclesiological reflection. How the convictions of Reformation Lutheranism are to be given substance and applied in the 21st century remains an unanswered question facing the Lutheran communion of churches.

→ Denomination; Ecumenism, Ecumenical Movement; Lutheran Churches

Bibliography: General and historical: C. BERGENDOFF, *The Church of the Lutheran Reformation: A Historical Survey of Lutheranism* (St. Louis, 1967) • J. BODENSIECK, *Encyclopedia of the Lutheran Church* (3 vols.; Minneapolis, 1965) • C. E. BRAATEN, "Lutheranism," *The Oxford Companion to Christian Thought: Intellectual, Spiritual, and Moral Horizons of Christianity* (ed. A. Hastings, A. Mason, and H. Pyper; Oxford, 2000) 401-3 • W. ELERT, *The Structure of Lutheranism* (St. Louis, 2003) • G. GASSMANN, D. H. LARSON, and M. W. OLDENBURG, *Historical Dictionary of Lutheranism* (Metuchen, N.J., 2001) • E. W. GRITSCH, *Fortress Introduction to Lutheranism* (Minneapolis, 1994); idem, *A History of Lutheranism* (Minneapolis, 2002) • E. LUND, ed., *Documents from the History of Lutheranism, 1570-1750* (Minneapolis, 2002) • E. C. NELSON, ed., *The Lutherans in North America* (rev. ed.; Philadelphia, 1975).

Theological: W. ALTMAN, *Luther and Liberation: A Latin American Perspective* (Minneapolis, 1992) • C. E. BRAATEN, *Principles of Lutheran Theology* (Philadelphia, 1983) • G. GASSMANN and S. HENDRIX, *Fortress Introduction to the Lutheran Confessions* (Minneapolis, 1999) • E. W. GRITSCH and R. W. JENSON, *Lutheranism: The Theological Movement and Its Confessional Writings* (Philadelphia, 1976) • R. KOLB, *Confessing One Faith: Reformers Define the Church, 1530-1580* (St. Louis, 1991); idem, *Luther's Heirs Define His Legacy: Studies on Lutheran Confessionalization* (Brookfield, Vt., 1996) • R. KOLB and J. A. NESTINGEN, eds., *Sources and Contexts of the Book of Concord* (Minneapolis, 2001) • R. KOLB and T. J. WENGERT, eds., *The Book of Concord: The Confessions of the Evangelical Lutheran Church* (Minneapolis, 2000) • W. H. LAZARETH, *Christians in Society: Luther, the Bible, and Social Ethics* (Minneapolis, 2001) • W. LOEHE, *Three Books about the Church* (Philadelphia, 1969) • B. LOHSE, *Martin Luther's Theology: Its Historical and Systematic Development* (Minneapolis, 1999) • J. PELIKAN, *Bach among the Theologians* (Philadelphia, 1986) • E. SCHLINK, *Theology of the Lutheran Confessions* (Philadelphia, 1961) • P. J. SPENER, *Pia desideria* (Philadelphia, 1964) • T. G. TAPPERT and J. W. DOBERSTEIN, eds., *The Notebook of a Colonial Clergyman: Condensed from the Journals of Henry Melchior Muhlenberg* (2d ed.; Minneapolis, 1998).

Contemporary: E. T. BACHMANN and M. B. BACHMANN, *Lutheran Churches in the World: A Handbook* (Minneapolis, 1989) • J. L. BOYCE, ed., *Whither Lutheranism?* (= WW 11/3 [1991]) • W. GRIEVE, ed., *Between Vision and Reality: Lutheran Churches in Transition* (Geneva, 2001) • W. GRIEVE and P. N. PROVE, eds., *A Shift in Jewish-Lutheran Relations? A Lutheran Contribution to Christian-Jewish Dialogue, with a Focus on Antisemitism and Anti-Judaism Today* (Geneva, 2003) • E. C. NELSON, *The Rise of World Lutheranism: An American Perspective* (Philadelphia, 1982) • J. H. SCHJØRRING, P. KUMARI, and N. A. HJELM, eds., *From Federation to Communion: The History of the Lutheran World Federation* (Minneapolis, 1997).

WOLF-DIETER HAUSCHILD and NORMAN A. HJELM

Luther's Theology

The theology of Martin → Luther (1483-1546) arose out of his work as an interpreter of the Bible and out of his involvement in the debates of the → Reformation era. After his appointment as professor of Scripture (→ Exegesis, Biblical) at the University of Wittenberg in 1512, his most important theological works were frequently his lectures on biblical books, for example, on Galatians (1531 lectures, pub. 1535) and Genesis (1535-45). His polemical writings were also theologically significant — Luther claimed he would never have become a good theologian if he had not been attacked by his opponents (*LW* 34.287).

1. Structure and Influences

Luther provided no comprehensive account of his own theology. It has therefore been a matter of debate whether such an account should be systematic or historical (B. Lohse 1986, 1999). Another fundamental question is whether Luther's theology has a central theme and, if so, what that theme is (H. Junghans). In 1532 Luther described the main themes of theology as human beings condemned as sinners and God the redeemer who justifies them. His treatment of these themes and others can best be seen from a combination of historical and systematic approaches.

Luther's education influenced his theology but does not fully explain its origin. He called himself a → nominalist, and his allegiance to this school of late medieval thought taught him to value the power of the → Word and to respect the distinction between philosophy and theology. → Mysticism showed him the importance of religious → experience and → suffering. Although he was not strictly trained in → humanism, he learned to value biblical languages, and his movement attracted many young humanists of his era. His early years in the monastery (→ Monasticism) seemed repressive because of the requirement of penance and his own scrupulosity, but they also gave him a deep familiarity with Scripture. → Augustine (354-430; → Augustine's Theology) had the strongest influence on him as an interpreter of → Paul (L. Grane). In line with theologians of his order (→ Augustinians 3) like Gregory of Rimini (ca. 1300-1358) and his own teacher and mentor Johann von Staupitz (1468/69-1524), he stressed the prevenience of the → grace of God in the justification of sinners, though we cannot speak with certainty of an Augustinian school that had a direct impact on Luther.

2. Development, 1513-19

Three factors moved Luther beyond the above starting points: his early work as an expositor of the Bible, his break with scholastic philosophy and theology, and controversy over the practice of indulgences.

2.1. Early Biblical Exposition

Most important was Luther's work on Scripture. From 1513 to 1519 he lectured on Psalms, Romans, Galatians, and Hebrews and then returned to the Psalms. The content of these books opened up the question of the → righteousness of the sinner before God the judge, a question that caused internal conflicts over his own worthiness (→ Assurance of Salvation; Temptation). According to the preface to the Latin edition of his works in 1545, Luther made his Reformation discovery during this period. He perceived that divine righteousness was the gift of a gracious God to sinners through → faith in Christ and not simply an attribute of the divine judge (→ Justification; Last Judgment). This new understanding of Rom. 1:16-17 is found in the early lectures, but Luther did not stress it there. Hence the dating and specific content of Luther's Reformation discovery are still debated (→ Luther Research). It is certain that the Reformation breakthrough occurred during a process of wrestling with Scripture, with the demands of monastic life, and with the piety and theology of his age.

2.2. Break with Scholastic Theology, 1515-18

In a letter dated May 18, 1517, Luther speaks of "our theology and St. Augustine" as having dethroned Aristotle (384-322 B.C.; → Aristotelianism) in

Wittenberg. In the Romans lectures of 1515-16 he began his attack on → scholastic theology. In public disputations he won over students and colleagues like Andreas Carlstadt (ca. 1480-1541), Nikolaus von Amsdorf (1483-1565), and Philipp → Melanchthon (1497-1560) for the new Wittenberg theology (K. Bauer).

Luther's defense of Augustine against Aristotle emerged clearly in the 1517 disputation against scholastic theology. Luther argued against Ockhamism that without the grace of God the human will could not follow the direction of → reason and thereby merit justification. Against all of Scholasticism he asserted that grace was not simply an aid or condition required to fulfill the → law and to merit salvation. Instead, much as Augustine had taught, grace justified and renewed people so that now for the first time they could truly obey the law without concern for merit. Already in the Romans lectures Luther stressed that → sin remained in believers even after they were baptized.

In the Heidelberg Disputation of 1518 Luther continued his attack on Scholasticism by means of a theology of the cross (→ Theologia crucis). It is a matter of debate how central this concept was for Luther's theology — the expression occurs only five times in his works, four times alone in early 1518 — yet M. Lienhard and G. Forde see in this concept a key to Luther's entire theology, maintaining that the cross discloses our attempts to become righteous on our own as nothing but sin. Meanwhile, the action of God against our sin, clothed in the humiliation of the cross, points the way to life. Hence true knowledge of God is knowledge of the redeemer hidden in the humiliation of the cross, not arbitrary speculation about God that ignores the cross and focuses on the works of creation (the *theologia gloriae*, or "theology of glory"; → Analogy).

2.3. Indulgence Controversy

The → indulgence controversy that began with the 95 theses of October 31, 1517, forced Luther to develop his insights on the sacrament of penance and to defend them publicly, for example, in 1518 before Cardinal Thomas de Vio Cajetan (1469-1534) in Augsburg. During this controversy the main themes of Luther's new theology were confirmed and sharpened.

True penance was not limited to a sacrament but was rather a daily repentance that arose from serious wrestling with the power of sin. Forgiveness of sins did not have its basis in the quality of → penitence but in faith that relied on the → promise of → forgiveness in the → Word of God. Faith was not a human achievement but the gift of God through the

work of the → Holy Spirit, which was not to be equated with the sacramental infusion of → grace (§3.2).

To defend this new understanding of justification, Luther appealed to the → authority of Scripture. In the Leipzig disputation with Johann Eck (1486-1543) in 1519, he explained that the divine Word had supreme authority in the church, above even pope or council. Luther could also appeal to the → church fathers, → tradition, and the right use of → reason as authorities, but only to the extent that they did not conflict with the clear message of the → gospel in Scripture.

3. Reformation Theology, 1520-21

When the church → hierarchy threatened Luther with → excommunication in 1520 (→ Church Discipline), he formulated a new understanding of the Christian life for the ordinary person and worked out a concept of church and sacrament that would be independent of the Roman hierarchy.

3.1. *Freedom of a Christian*

"A Christian is a perfectly free lord of all, subject to none. A Christian is a perfectly dutiful servant of all, subject to all" (*LW* 31.344). These lines from Luther's *Freedom of a Christian* (1520) summarized the significance of justification by faith for the Christian life.

Justification implied first a radical → freedom, since the → soul could do without everything but God's Word, which contained the promise of the gospel that called for appropriation in faith. "God our Father has made all things depend on faith so that whoever has faith will have everything, and whoever does not have faith will have nothing" (*LW* 31.349). For Luther, therefore, the strengthening of faith was the purpose of Christian teaching and community.

The Christian life, however, involved more than faith and the strengthening of the soul. All his life Luther had to combat the misunderstanding that because good works (→ Ethics) did not contribute to justification, they were unnecessary. In his *Treatise on Good Works* (1520), Luther united faith and works by calling faith in Christ, which is a work of the Spirit, the "first and highest and noblest of all good works," the fulfillment of the first commandment (→ Decalogue). In explaining the other commandments, Luther distinguished between the truly good works of loving one's neighbor, which proceeded from faith, and the false works of religious satisfaction, which contradicted faith because they did not seek justification and forgiveness from Christ but tried to merit it on their own.

Even works done in faith, however, cannot justify, for sin always clings to them, and all who are justified solely by the alien righteousness of Christ are still sinners. The justified person, in Luther's view, is at once righteous and sinful (*simul iustus et peccator*). The Christian life is an ongoing fight against sin; sin is constantly forgiven by faith in Christ but never fully uprooted. This interpretation of Luther has been challenged by Finnish scholars (esp. T. Mannermaa, S. Peura, and R. Saarinen) who claim that Luther also defined justification as a union with Christ that initiates a process of divinization (→ Theosis). In their view, the believer is not simply reckoned righteous but actually becomes righteous through the presence of Christ in faith (C. E. Braaten and R. W. Jenson).

3.2. *Church and Authority*

Luther stated his new concept of church and sacrament in three other works of 1520: *On the Papacy in Rome, Address to the Christian Nobility of the German Nation,* and *The Babylonian Captivity of the Church.*

At the beginning of the *Address,* Luther contested the claim of the clergy to exclusive spiritual status (→ Clergy and Laity) by asserting that all believers belonged to a common priesthood (→ Priest 4). All Christians, he said, truly belong to the spiritual estate; the only distinction among them is one of office (→ Ministry, Ministerial Offices). The doctrine of the priesthood of believers validated the → responsibility of civil authorities to reform the church. It also meant that the laity could interpret Scripture and exercise authority in the church. The German Bible (→ Bible Versions), which Luther began to translate in exile at the Wartburg in 1521/22, supported these new roles for laity by giving many more people access to Scripture.

As early as 1519 Luther had written tracts on the sacraments of penance, → baptism, and the → Eucharist. In *The Babylonian Captivity of the Church* he retained at first all three, but at the end he excluded penance because it had only one of the constitutive features of a sacrament, the word of promise, and not the other two, a visible sign and a divine command. Furthermore, strictly understood, penance was an ongoing return to the baptismal promise. The authentic sacraments for Luther became baptism and the Lord's Supper; they were visible and effective signs of the divine promise and were instituted to evoke and confirm faith.

In his first lectures on the Psalms (1513-15), Luther described the → church unpolemically as the communion of the faithful. In 1520 he used this definition to distinguish the true church from the hierarchically constituted → Roman Catholic Church. Since he believed the Roman hierarchy had falsified the Christian life, he had to show that the church was independent of Rome and could exist without its bishop. Thus he arrived at an expressly ecumenical concept of the church, according to which the true church was present wherever the Word of God was taught, evoking genuine faith through proclamation and sacrament. The true church was also spiritual and hidden in the sense that it could not be equated exclusively with a single human form or hierarchy. It was present in any → congregation where the Holy Spirit awakened faith through the gospel.

4. Controversial Issues, 1522-28

By 1522 the main themes of Luther's theology (i.e., promise, justification by faith alone, priesthood of believers, authority of Scripture, the redefinition of church and sacraments) were already in place. As the different Reformation groups clarified their positions, however, Luther had to take a stand on new issues. These debates added important features to his theology.

4.1. *Ministry*

In 1523 when the formation of what were to be "Protestant" churches was underway, Luther began to shape his views on the office of ministry. The ministry of Word and sacrament (→ Proclamation) was instituted by God, but the congregation was responsible for calling suitable ministers to this office. The urgency of the early days of the Reformation led Luther to assure congregations they had this right even against the resistance of Roman authorities. In principle, Protestant bishops might also appoint clergy, but not without congregational assent. Luther probably envisioned an episcopal model of church governance (→ Bishop, Episcopacy), but almost no Roman bishops went over to the Reformation. Furthermore, Luther found in Scripture divine warrant only for the pastoral office, not for a specific pattern of → church government.

4.2. *Civil Authority*

In debates over civil and religious authority during the Peasants' War of 1524/25 (→ Church and State), Luther developed his controversial concept of → two kingdoms. God ruled the world through two types of government. He ruled spiritually through the proclamation of the gospel, and he exercised secular rule through application of the law by civil government (the first, or political, use of the law). Christians should obey divinely instituted civil authorities except when the authorities hindered the proclamation of the gospel or ordered Christians to break the divine law. When Christians suffered injustice at the hands of civil rulers, they could take comfort in the gospel but not use the gospel as the basis of insurrection. To prevent misuse of the gospel as law and to support the secular authorities, Luther drew a sharp line between the two kingdoms. Although he affirmed the secular realm as ruled by God, this sharp distinction made it difficult for some of his followers to apply the gospel to the lives of Christians in the world (→ Lutheranism).

4.3. Word and Spirit

In the controversies with Carlstadt and others who opposed the external mediation of divine salvation, Luther had to declare more explicitly the external means of the Spirit's work. In his view the Spirit worked only through outward means, since in God's activity the outward always preceded the inward. Hence, forgiveness won at the cross did not come to believers through → meditation on the cross, as in → mysticism, but solely through Word and sacrament. This emphasis on Word and sacrament as the outward → means of grace emphasized the importance of worship and community, and it distinguished Luther's theology from individualistic mystical and spiritualist systems (→ Spiritualism).

4.4. Bondage of the Will

To rule out all human merit Luther accorded no power to the human will to decide either for or against God's grace. As he saw it, from the time of the fall the will had been under the dominion of sin and hence could not decide for God as if it were starting from a neutral position. Instead, God had to decide for us, and this initiative of God was the most important issue at stake for Luther. In the act of justification the will was freed from servitude to sin and set under the lordship of the Spirit. In his 1525 treatise *The Bondage of the Will*, written in answer to → Erasmus (1469?-1536, esp. his tract *On the Freedom of the Will*), Luther stressed the sole working of God (→ Predestination) to such an extent that both supporters and antagonists saw in his position a tendency toward determinism.

4.5. Eucharist

The controversy with Ulrich → Zwingli (1484-1531; → Zwingli's Theology) concerning the real presence of Christ's body and blood in the eucharistic bread and wine contributed to the splitting of the Protestant movement. Luther's endorsement of the real presence followed from his insistence on the absolute reliability of the words of institution. These words of promise, he thought, declared to all the presence of Christ's body or human nature in and under the elements.

In the debate with Zwingli Luther also introduced the controversial notion of the → ubiquity of the body of Christ. Zwingli had argued that Christ's body could not be present on many altars at one and the same time, since after the ascension it was restricted to one location at God's right hand. Luther replied that the personal union of the divine and human natures in Christ (the "communication of attributes"; → Christology 6.3) made it possible for the human body of Christ to be present wherever *(ubique)* the divine nature was present. The point for Luther was not an abstract doctrine of ubiquity but the assurance of Christ's bodily presence at the Eucharist according to his promise.

Luther emphasized that the same human nature that won salvation at the cross was now present at the imparting of salvation in the supper. He labeled as *Schwärmer* (enthusiasts, fanatics; see 4.3) those opponents who insisted on separating the divine from the human nature of Christ as well as salvation from the external means of salvation.

4.6. Law and Gospel

In drawing up theological guidelines for Protestant pastors and congregations, Luther stood with Melanchthon against the → antinomians, as he called Johann Agricola (1494-1566) and others. They both insisted that the law must be preached as well as the gospel. Already in 1520 Luther had stated that in Scripture a distinction must be made between commands and promises. Later he claimed that the ability to distinguish between → law and gospel made one a theologian.

The law had to be preached for two reasons: first, to bring sin to light (the second use of the law) so as to summon to repentance and to readiness for the gospel, and, second, to teach true good works by means of the commandments. This second reason for preaching the law has led W. Wagner and other scholars to maintain that Luther taught the so-called third use of the law, that is, its use as a guide to the Christian life for justified believers. Luther's exposition of the Ten Commandments in his Large and Small Catechisms of 1529 may support this view, but W. Lazareth prefers to speak of a "parenetic function of the Gospel" in Luther's theology.

5. Trinitarian Basis of the Christian Life

At the end of his *Confession concerning Christ's Supper* of 1528, Luther affirmed the "sublime article of the majesty of God, that the Father, Son, and Holy Spirit, three distinct persons, are by nature one true and genuine God, the Maker of heaven and earth" (*LW* 37.361). The early church's → dogma of the → Trinity underpinned Luther's theology (Lohse 1985, 1999) and served in his later years as the framework of what he said about the Christian life.

5.1. Life in God's Creation

In his doctrine of → God Luther emphasized the creature's dependence on God the Creator. In the Large → Catechism he states that "none of us has life . . . from ourselves, nor can we by ourselves preserve any of [the gifts of creation], however small and unimportant" (The Creed, §16). As Creator, God is not just the first cause but also the preserver of all things and is present and active everywhere without ceasing (→ Creation). God uses creatures as "masks" through which to accomplish his creative work. This participation of creatures in God's work takes place through three structures of the created order: the ministry, → marriage and family, and civil government. Luther believed that these structures were divinely instituted but not sacrosanct in the sense of being beyond criticism from the side of the gospel or the spiritual kingdom.

This dynamic picture of creation is more characteristic of Luther's doctrine of God than the distinction between the hidden God *(Deus absconditus)* and the revealed God *(Deus revelatus)*. This latter distinction emphasizes the hiddenness of God's majesty and summons creatures who are intimidated by the hidden God to turn to the divine grace and love revealed in the cross of Christ.

5.2. Life in the Presence of Christ

In sermons on the Gospel of John (1528-32, 1537-40), Luther expounded the union of Christ's two natures in one person as the basis of faith. Both natures of Christ were necessary for the act of → reconciliation. Christ overcame the devil by virtue of his divine nature, and the second person of the Trinity made satisfaction for sin by virtue of his human nature (→ Atonement).

Christ is also present in justification. Faith does not justify because it is a human ability or achievement but only because it lays hold of Christ and makes him present in the heart. In justification believers not only receive Christ's righteousness but experience a certain union with the second person of the Trinity through which his attributes become theirs and their sin is transferred to him.

5.3. Life in the Spirit

The Holy Spirit was for Luther true God, yet a distinct person of the Godhead who is sent in two ways: first, visibly at Pentecost, then by the Word into the hearts of believers. This twofold sending is a major theme in Luther's theology because the Spirit plays a crucial role. It nourishes justifying faith by Word and sacrament and gives strength in the daily fight against sin, making Christ present in believers' hearts. From a Trinitarian and soteriological standpoint the work of the Spirit is no less central than Christology in Luther's theology.

6. Luther's Place in the History of Theology

The medieval background of Luther's theology may be seen in its preoccupation with issues from the third article of the creed: forgiveness of sin by the work of the Spirit through Word and sacrament in the Christian community. His concepts of God and creation, however, and his attention to the struggle between faith and despair, or God and the devil (H. Oberman), also address modern and postmodern concerns about human existence and meaning (→ Modern Period; Modernity; Postmodernism). In addition, because Luther's reform movement sought to recover and preserve the best of catholic Christianity, his theology has become quite ecumenically significant (→ Ecumenical Dialogue; Ecumenism, Ecumenical Movement).

Bibliography: General: P. ALTHAUS, *The Theology of Martin Luther* (Philadelphia, 1966) • G. EBELING, *Luther: An Introduction to His Thought* (Philadelphia, 1970); idem, "Luthers Theologie," *RGG* (3d ed.) 4.495-520; idem, *Lutherstudien* (3 vols.; Tübingen, 1971-85) • G. W. FORELL, *Martin Luther: Theologian of the Church* (St. Paul, Minn., 1994) • F. GOGARTEN, *Luthers Theologie* (Tübingen, 1967) • E. GRITSCH, *Martin–God's Court Jester: Luther in Retrospect* (Philadelphia, 1983) • S. HENDRIX, "American Luther Research in the Twentieth Century," *LQ*, n.s., 15 (2001) 1-23 • R. HERMANN, *Luthers Theologie* (Göttingen, 1967) • K. HOLL, *Gesammelte Aufsätze zur Kirchengeschichte,* vol. 1, *Luther* (Tübingen, 1923) • H. J. IWAND, *Luthers Theologie* (Munich, 1974) • J. KITTELSON, "Luther the Theologian," *Reformation Europe* (St. Louis, 1992) 21-46 • B. LOHSE, "Zur Struktur von Luthers Theologie," *JGNKG* 83 (1985) 41-53 • J. LORTZ, "Martin Luther. Grundzüge seiner geistigen Struktur," *Reformata Reformanda* (vol. 1; Münster, 1965) 214-46 • O. H. PESCH, *Hinführung zu Luther* (Mainz, 1982) • L. PINOMAA, *Faith Victorious: An Introduction to Luther's Theology* (Philadelphia, 1963) • R. WEIER, *Das Theologieverständnis Martin Luthers* (Paderborn, 1976).

Historical development: U. ASENDORF, *Lectura in Biblia* (Göttingen, 1998) • K. BAUER, *Die Wittenberger Universitätstheologie und die Anfänge der Deutschen Reformation* (Tübingen, 1928) • O. BAYER, *Promissio. Geschichte der reformatorischen Wende in Luthers Theologie* (Göttingen, 1971) • L. GRANE, *Modus loquendi theologicus. Luthers Kampf um die Erneuerung der Theologie (1515-1518)* (Leiden, 1975) • M. HARRAN, *Martin Luther: Learning for Life* (St. Louis, 1997) • S. HENDRIX, *Ecclesia in Via: Ecclesiological Develop-*

ments in the Medieval Psalms Exegesis and the "Dictata super Psalterium" (1513-1515) of Martin Luther (Leiden, 1974) • B. Hoffman, *Luther and the Mystics: A Reexamination of Luther's Spiritual Experience and His Relationship to the Mystics* (Minneapolis, 1976) • J. Köstlin, *The Theology of Luther in Its Historical Development and Inner Harmony* (2 vols.; Philadelphia, 1986) • B. Lohse, *Luther's Theology: Its Historical and Systematic Development* (Minneapolis, 1999) • K.-H. zur Mühlen, *Nos extra Nos. Luthers Theologie zwischen Mystik und Scholastik* (Tübingen, 1972) • S. Ozment, *Homo spiritualis* (Leiden, 1969) • W. Russell, *The Schmalkald Articles: Luther's Theological Testament* (Minneapolis, 1995) • D. Steinmetz, *Luther and Staupitz: An Essay in the Intellectual Origins of the Protestant Reformation* (Durham, N.C., 1980) • J. Wicks, *Luther's Reform* (Mainz, 1992).

God and Trinity: K. Bornkamm, *Christus–König und Priester* (Tübingen, 1998) • C. E. Braaten and R. W. Jenson, eds., *Union with Christ: The New Finnish Interpretation of Luther* (Grand Rapids, 1998) • J. Dillenberger, *God Hidden and Revealed: The Interpretation of Luther's Deus Absconditus and Its Significance for Religious Thought* (Philadelphia, 1953) • C. Helmer, *The Trinity and Martin Luther* (Mainz, 1999) • R. Jansen, *Studien zur Luthers Trinitätslehre* (Bern, 1976) • M. Lienhard, *Luther: Witness to Jesus Christ* (Minneapolis, 1982) • R. Prenter, *Spiritus Creator* (Philadelphia, 1953) • E. Seeberg, *Luthers Theologie,* vol. 2, *Christus* (Stuttgart, 1937) • I. D. K. Siggins, *Martin Luther's Doctrine of Christ* (New Haven, 1970) • P. S. Watson, *Let God Be God! An Interpretation of the Theology of Martin Luther* (Philadelphia, 1947).

Ethics: P. Althaus, *The Ethics of Martin Luther* (Philadelphia, 1972) • F. E. Cranz, *An Essay on the Development of Luther's Thought on Justice, Law, and Society* (2d ed.; Mifflintown, Pa., 1998) • P. Frostin, *Luther's Two Kingdoms Doctrine* (Lund, 1994) • W. Lazareth, *Christians in Society: Luther, the Bible, and Social Ethics* (Minneapolis, 2001) • W. Wagner, "Luther and the Positive Use of the Law," *JRH* 11 (1980) 45-63.

Cross: G. O. Forde, *On Being a Theologian of the Cross: Reflections on Luther's Heidelberg Disputation, 1518* (Grand Rapids, 1997) • A. McGrath, *Luther's Theology of the Cross* (Oxford, 1990) • J. Vercruysse, "Luther's Theology of the Cross at the Time of the Heidelberg Disputation," *Greg.* 57 (1976) 523-48.

Other specific topics: B. Gerrish, *Grace and Reason: A Study in the Theology of Luther* (Oxford, 1962) • K. Hagen, *Luther's Approach to Scripture* (Tübingen, 1993) • J. Headley, *Luther's View of Church History* (New Haven, 1963) • H. Junghans, "Die Mitte der Theologie Luthers," *ZdZ* 37 (1983) 190-94 • R. Kolb, *Martin Luther as Prophet, Teacher, and Hero* (Grand

Rapids, 1999) • D. Löfgren, *Die Theologie der Schöpfung bei Luther* (Göttingen, 1960) • J. Trigg, *Baptism in the Theology of Martin Luther* (Leiden, 1994).

Biographical: R. Bainton, *Here I Stand* (New York, 1950) • M. Brecht, *Martin Luther* (3 vols.; Philadelphia and Minneapolis, 1985-93) • M. Edwards, *Luther's Last Battles* (Ithaca, N.Y., 1983) • H. Haile, *Luther: An Experiment in Biography* (Garden City, N.Y., 1980) • S. Hendrix, *Luther and the Papacy* (Philadelphia, 1981) • J. Kittelson, *Luther the Reformer* (Minneapolis, 1986) • B. Lohse, *Martin Luther: An Introduction to His Life and Work* (Philadelphia, 1986) • R. Marius, *Martin Luther: The Christian between God and Death* (Cambridge, Mass., 1999) • H. Oberman, *Luther: Man between God and the Devil* (New Haven, 1989).

Scott Hendrix

Lux Mundi

Lux Mundi belongs to a series of essay volumes that have punctuated the theological history of the Church of England for the past 150 years: *Essays and Reviews* (1860), *Lux Mundi* (1889), *Foundations* (1912), *Essays Catholic and Critical* (1926), *Soundings* (1962), and *Radical Orthodoxy* (1999). *Lux Mundi* is probably the most significant volume among them. A. M. Ramsey considered that this book inaugurated "an era in Anglican theology" that lasted 50 years. It also represented what might perhaps be called the most characteristic tendency within the pluriform Anglican tradition (→ Anglican Communion), namely, a "conservatively critical" stance, or "liberal Catholicism" (not → "modernism"!), in which an insistence on the "Catholic" substance of Scripture and → tradition accompanied a more "liberal" concern with mediating between the Christian faith and contemporary culture (→ Mediating Theology).

All the members of the *Lux Mundi* team were associated with Oxford University, and the regular intellectual exchange between these friends provided a unified perspective for the symposium itself. Against the background of (Greek) → patristics and the idealist philosophy of T. H. Green (1836-82; → Idealism), the 11 scholars produced a volume described by its own subtitle as "studies in the religion of the incarnation." Its goal was "to put the Catholic faith into its right relation to modern intellectual and moral problems," and to this end two lines of inquiry were especially important: the Darwinian theory of → evolution and the historical-critical method as applied now to Holy Scripture (→ Exegesis, Biblical).

The authors insisted that the incarnate Jesus (→ Incarnation) was precisely the Logos (→ Christology), who was and is everywhere at work in both → nature and → culture, so that "we can conceive no phase of progress which has not the Incarnation for its guiding star" (J. R. Illingworth). This assertion did not just apply to theories in the natural sciences; in politics as well, → democracy and → socialism served the → progress of → truth in the world. (Author H. S. Holland [1847-1918] was one of the founders of "Christian socialism" in England; → Religious Socialism.)

At the time, the most provocative essay in *Lux Mundi* was "The Holy Spirit and Inspiration," by editor Charles Gore (1853-1923). Gore addressed the question of scriptural → inspiration only after exploring the work of the Spirit in the history of Israel and the church and in the history of humankind in general. An even more troubling feature was Gore's incidental remark that in dealing with the OT writings, Jesus himself "never exhibits the omniscience of the bare Godhead in the realm of natural knowledge, such as would be required to anticipate the results of modern science or criticism." In asserting that "God declares his almighty power most chiefly in his condescension, whereby he beggared himself of divine prerogatives, to put himself in our place," Gore presaged the → kenotic theory that he developed in his later book *The Incarnation of the Son of God* (1891), which found both positive and negative echoes in English theology during the following decades. Although the kenotic theory prompted H. P. Liddon (1829-90) to declare that this Oxford group had betrayed their fathers, namely, the Tractarians (→ Oxford Movement), the chapters on the → church and the → sacraments were clearly shaped by Anglo-Catholic concepts. Indeed, the chapter on the sacraments, from the hand of the later bishop of Oxford Francis Paget (1851-1911), brings beautifully together the creational, incarnational, and eschatological dimensions of his subject.

Charles Gore himself became successively bishop of Worcester, Birmingham, and Oxford. During this period he defended over against modernism the enduring validity of the → creeds of the early church, within whose firm framework the *Lux Mundi* authors had developed their critical and progressive reflections from the outset. Gore insisted that the → virgin birth as well as the bodily → resurrection of Christ were to be understood as historical events, though he did believe that the statements "he came down from heaven" and "he sits at the right hand of God" are to be understood more in the "symbolic" sense.

After he retired, Gore wrote *Reconstruction of Belief* (3 vols., 1921-24). He always thought that → miracles, among which the incarnation was preeminent, were a "necessary" corrective to human → sin. Unlike J. R. Illingworth (1848-1915) in *Lux Mundi*, however, Gore never underestimated the cross (→ Theologia Crucis). Just so, one of the heirs of *Lux Mundi* on the liberal side, namely, William Temple (1881-1944), realized toward the end of his life that a theology of "explanation" must yield first place to a theology of "redemption."

Bibliography: R. MORGAN, ed., *The Religion of the Incarnation: Anglican Essays in Commemoration of* Lux Mundi (Bristol, 1989) • A. M. RAMSEY, *From Gore to Temple: The Development of Anglican Theology between* Lux Mundi *and the Second World War, 1889-1939* (London, 1960; U.S. ed., *An Era in Anglican Theology* [New York, 1960]) • G. WAINWRIGHT, ed., *Keeping the Faith: Essays to Mark the Centenary of* Lux Mundi (Philadelphia, 1989).

GEOFFREY WAINWRIGHT

Luxembourg

	1960	1980	2000
Population (1,000s):	314	364	430
Annual growth rate (%):	1.11	0.15	0.74

Area: 2,586 sq. km. (999 sq. mi.)

A.D. 2000

Population density: 166/sq. km. (430/sq. mi.)
Births / deaths: 1.23 / 0.98 per 100 population
Fertility rate: 1.83 per woman
Infant mortality rate: 5 per 1,000 live births
Life expectancy: 77.2 years (m: 73.9, f: 80.5)
Religious affiliation (%): Christians 93.8 (Roman Catholics 92.1, Protestants 1.9, marginal 1.1, other Christians 1.5), nonreligious 3.8, Muslims 1.1, other 1.3.

1. Geography and Legal Foundations
2. Churches
    2.1. Roman Catholic
    2.2. Protestant
    2.3. Expatriate Congregations
    2.4. Free Churches
3. Ecumenical Relations
4. Non-Christian Religions

1. Geography and Legal Foundations

The Grand Duchy of Luxembourg, a constitutional monarchy (declared a neutral independent state by the Treaty of London, May 11, 1867), is bounded by

Belgium on the north and west, Germany on the east, and France on the south. Its population in the year 2000 included over 140,000 expatriates, or about one-third of the country's total residents. Because Luxembourg was hardly affected by the → Reformation, the majority of its population is Roman Catholic. In 1982 the country entered into a convention with the Protestant Reformed Church, and in 1997 agreements were reached with the → Roman Catholic Church, the Protestant Church of Luxembourg, the Greek → Orthodox Church, and the Jewish cultic community (→ Judaism).

In 1802 Napoléon I (1769-1821) issued the law of "18 germinal an X [= April 2, 1802] relative à l'organisation des cultes," a law that still governs the relationship between → church and state. The Articles Organiques des Cultes Protestants forms the basis of the state's relationship with the Protestant churches. The state itself is responsible for schools and other social institutions. The constitution of 1868 guarantees the rights and freedom of citizens, including their full religious → freedom. Archbishops, bishops of the Greek Orthodox Church, *pasteurs titulaires* of the two indigenous Luxembourg Protestant churches, and chief rabbis are all considered "chefs du culte." The state's own prerogatives with regard to their appointment and installation are covered by the agreements of 1982 and 1997.

2. Churches

2.1. *Roman Catholic*

The → Concordat of 1801 and various later decrees, resolutions, and laws constitute the legal basis of the Roman Catholic Church in Luxembourg. A → diocese was established in 1873, and since 1908 it has been directly responsible to the pope (→ Exemption), with a 1981 law bestowing upon the diocese the status of a legal person. In 1988 a papal bull elevated the Luxembourg diocese to the status of an archdiocese. The Roman Catholic Church in Luxembourg encompasses 14 deaneries with 274 parish churches; it also supports its own seminary for → priests (founded in 1845 for ecclesiastical and theological education). Catholic religious life is shaped especially by → Jesuit activities (since 1594) and by the popular veneration of Mary (→ Mary, Devotion to). From the mid-1970s active membership in the Roman Catholic Church began to diminish.

2.2. *Protestant*

Protestantism in Luxembourg is made up of a small but traditionally minded minority (in A.D. 2000, only 8,000 members). Its history begins in the early 19th century, since before that time Protestants were rarely allowed to settle in the country, and especially not in the capital. The purely Roman Catholic population viewed the arrival of Protestants as a "sundering of the unity of faith" that for centuries had united Luxembourgers in one spirit "at the foot of the altar." Although they viewed the acceptance of Protestants as a "destruction of peace and quiet," this attitude ultimately did not prevent Protestants from settling in the country.

After the Congress of Vienna (1814-15), the purely Roman Catholic Duchy of Luxembourg became a grand duchy closely associated with the German House of Nassau and with the German Confederation. A Prussian garrison was stationed in the grand duchy to ensure its neutrality, creating the need for pastoral services for the Protestant soldiers, officials, and their families, as well for the initially small number of Protestant inhabitants in the country; this need was met with the support of the ruling house itself and by the engagement of military and court pastors.

After the Prussian garrison departed in 1867, Protestant inhabitants established civilian congregations in both the city and the surrounding countryside. During the period of industrialization (→ Industrial Society), Protestant skilled workers, factory owners, craftsmen, and merchants along with their families settled especially in the southern part of the country in the canton of Esch. There thousands of people found work in the ore pits, at the iron and steel works, and with the railroad. Over a third of the inhabitants came to be concentrated in canton Esch, which occupies only a tenth of Luxembourg's entire area. Industrial workers began depending on the Protestant church for help with their problems and concerns, and as a result Protestant women's groups emerged to provide → social services.

A private Protestant religious community developed under the protectorate of Saxony-Weimar, and in 1894 the Protestant Grand Duke Adolf (1817-1905) granted legal recognition to this religious community with its inclusion of Lutheran, Reformed, and Unitarian traditions. In 1982 the state entered into a convention with the Protestant Reformed Church of Luxembourg, effectively granting it independent status. Similar agreements followed in 1997.

Commensurate with Napoleonic law all "cultic servants" such as → pastors, auxiliary pastors, and theological secretaries are paid by the state; there is no church tax or denominational distribution of taxes. Individual denominations are themselves responsible for carrying out their work and as such are completely dependent on the voluntary support of their members. Hence the Protestant Reformed Church is responsible for its church building in Esch, while the Protestant Church is similarly responsible for its family house in Luxembourg City and in Obercorn. The state owns the Trinity Church in Luxembourg City, which it has put at the disposal of the Protestant Church.

2.3. Expatriate Congregations

Members of the European Union established foreign congregations in Luxembourg, including several with their own pastoral offices. German officials and their families have been served by Protestant pastors since the end of the 1950s, and a contractual relationship has been in effect since 1973 between the German-speaking Protestant church, headquartered in Luxembourg Belair, and the Evangelische Kirche in Deutschland. The Dutch Protestant Church was established in the mid-1960s. The English-speaking church community has included both the → Anglicans and the Reformed Church of Scotland since 1964; since 1997 it has had its own pastoral headquarters. The Greek Orthodox Church conducts worship services in the section of the city known as Pulvermühle. A small → Russian Orthodox Church has been in existence since 1928. Since 1994 the Danish Church in Luxembourg has had its own pastor and pastoral headquarters. The Francophone Protestant Parish was incorporated into the Protestant Church of Luxembourg in 2001 and is now served by that pastor in an arrangement of personal union. The pastors also serve as religion teachers in the Europa School.

2.4. Free Churches

Free churches and other religious communities enjoy the same nonprofit legal status as do the foreign religious communities. A law passed on April 21, 1928, requires all such organizations to be nonprofit, provide the addresses of their members, make full financial disclosure, and publish such materials in the *Mémorial,* the official journal of the Grand Duchy of Luxembourg. → Free churches with an evangelical orientation include the Free Evangelical Church (→ Mennonite, since 1843) and the → Pentecostal Church. They have attracted Catholics and religiously unaffiliated persons. The New → Apostolic Church was established in 1933. Finally, the → Jehovah's Witnesses have grown, especially through attracting resident Portuguese workers.

3. Ecumenical Relations

Relationships among the various Protestant groups in Luxembourg improved considerably during the 1990s. The newly formed Alliance of the Protestant Churches in Luxembourg (1993) includes the Protestant Church of Luxembourg, the Protestant Reformed Church, the Francophone Protestant Parish, the German-Speaking Protestant Church, the Dutch Protestant Church, and the Danish Church in Luxembourg (→ National Councils of Churches). Together, these member churches engage in public service, adult education, youth ministries, and social and mission services. In 2000 this cooperative work resulted in the First Protestant Church Conference. The alliance is also a founding member of the Council of Christian Churches in Luxembourg (1997). Both indigenous Protestant churches are members of the → Conference of European Churches and of the Leuenberg Church Association, while the Protestant Reformed Church is also a member of the → World Alliance of Reformed Churches and of the → Reformed Alliance.

The confession of sin and petition for forgiveness formulated by the Archdiocese of Luxembourg, following the lead of the Holy See in its mea culpa of March 12, 2000, was directed to both the Jewish and the Protestant communities among others and provided considerable impetus to ecumenical cooperation.

4. Non-Christian Religions

The Jewish community was decimated during the → Holocaust and numbers fewer than 1,000 members today. Jews are attested in Luxembourg since 1276. After a bloody persecution in 1349 Emperor Charles IV of Luxembourg (1316-78) took them under his imperial protection. There are two → synagogues, one in Luxembourg City and one in Esch.

An Islamic center was established in Mamer during the 1990s, and an additional group is centered in the northern part of the country (→ Islam). Both → Buddhism and the → Baha'i religion have a few adherents in Luxembourg, albeit without any cultic center.

Bibliography: Archdiocèse de Luxembourg, *Annuaire 2000/2001* (Luxembourg, 2000) • D. B. Barrett et al., eds., *WCE* (2d ed.) 1.461-63 • J. Christophory, *Luxembourg* (rev. ed.; Oxford, 1997) • J. Hansen, *Secondary Education in Luxembourg* (Strasbourg, 1997) • J. Newcomer, *The Nationhood of Luxembourg: Eight Essays on the Grand Duchy* (Echternach, Lux., 1999) • J. Schoos, "Luxemburg," *TRE* 21.626-30 • R. Tiburzy, *Luxemburg* (Cologne, 1997) • N. van Werveke, *Kulturgeschichte des Luxemburger Landes* (Esch, Lux., 1983).

Karl Georg Marhoffer

M

Macao → Hong Kong and Macao

Macarisms → Beatitudes

Maccabees → Hasmonaeans

Macedonia

	1960	1980	2000
Population (1,000s):	1,392	1,795	2,233
Annual growth rate (%):	1.25	1.38	0.64

Area: 25,713 sq. km. (9,928 sq. mi.)

A.D. 2000

Population density: 87/sq. km. (225/sq. mi.)
Births / deaths: 1.44 / 0.80 per 100 population
Fertility rate: 1.90 per woman
Infant mortality rate: 20 per 1,000 live births
Life expectancy: 73.3 years (m: 71.1, f: 75.7)
Religious affiliation (%): Christians 63.4 (Orthodox 60.6, Roman Catholics 1.7, other Christians 1.2), Muslims 29.7, nonreligious 5.6, atheists 1.3, other 0.1.

1. Geography and Independence
2. History
3. Religions
3.1. Macedonian Orthodox Church
3.2. Islam
3.3. Roman Catholics and Protestants

1. Geography and Independence

Macedonia is a land-locked South Slavic country in the central part of the Balkan Peninsula, bordering on Kosovo and Serbia to the north, Bulgaria to the east, Greece to the south, and Albania to the west. In 1994 ethnic Macedonians accounted for 66.6 percent of the population, ethnic Albanians 22.7 percent, ethnic Turks 4.0 percent, Roma 2.2 percent, and Serbs 2.1 percent. More than a quarter of the population lives in the capital city of Skopje. The boundaries of the state are the same as those defined in 1945, when Macedonia became a constituent republic of the Communist-ruled federation of Yugoslavia as that federation's southernmost entity. Although it was the only republic that gained its independence peacefully, its territory, language, and ethnic identity — and therefore its international status and recognition — were intensely disputed by its neighbors.

Macedonia's first multiparty elections for its 120-seat national parliament, the Sobranje, were held in December 1990. Following its declaration of independence from Yugoslavia in November 1991, the Macedonian quest for international recognition met fierce objections from Greece over the legitimacy of the use of the name "Macedonia," which corresponds with the name formerly used for the northern Greek province and the larger ancient state. International mediation led to the compromise name "Former Yugoslav Republic of Macedonia," under which the newly independent country was admitted to the → United Nations in 1993.

Since the resolution of the difficult dispute with Greece, Macedonia has been in the news because of substantial interethnic unrest and civil → war caused by an uprising of the growing Albanian minority. Armed confrontations were stopped and relative stability achieved in 2001 thanks to the relentless efforts of the European Union. This development resulted in constitutional amendments granting broader → rights to the growing Albanian minority, → disarmament of the warring factions, and the presence of an international peacekeeping force.

2. History

The wider region known traditionally as Macedonia has a complex and turbulent history. (This larger region comprises Pirin Macedonia, now part of Bulgaria; Aegean Macedonia, in Greece; and Vardar Macedonia, the present nation, named after the Vardar River, which flows southeast through the country into Greece.) The territory has been severely contested and controlled successively by the Greeks, Romans, Byzantines, Bulgarians, Turks, and Serbs. Historically, Macedonians first appeared about 700 B.C. By about 400 they adopted the → Greek language and began to build a kingdom that was significantly enlarged by the conquests of Alexander the Great (336-323). Macedonia became a Roman province in the second century B.C.

According to the NT, Christian evangelization of the area began with a missionary journey of the apostle → Paul to Macedonia as described in some detail in Acts 16:10–17:15. A second visit by the same apostle is recorded in Acts 20:1-6, and frequent references to Macedonia are made in other NT texts (e.g., Acts 18:5; 19:21-22; Rom. 15:26; 2 Cor. 1:16; 11:9; Phil. 4:15; 1 Tim. 1:3). The first convert of Paul in Europe was Lydia, "a dealer in purple cloth" (Acts 16:14), in the Macedonian city of Philippi.

Macedonia came under Byzantine domination after the division of the → Roman Empire in A.D. 395. By the fifth century the Christian church in Macedonia was well organized, with several bishoprics and well-known metropolitan residences in Thessalonica and Skopje. Several Christian → basilicas date to this time.

Following devastation by the Goths and Huns, the territory of Macedonia was settled by Slavic tribes in the 6th and 7th centuries. Their Christianization began in the 9th century under the influence of the well-known "apostles of the Slavs," the brothers Cyril and Methodius, who came from Thessalonica. The intensive missionary and educational activity of their disciples Clement and Naum (→ Mission) made Macedonia one of the leading centers of Slavic → literacy and led to the establishment of a strong Ohrid archbishopric, which was elevated to the level of an autocephalous patriarchate during the rule of the powerful czar Samuel in the 11th century.

The Bogomils, a medieval Bulgarian Christian movement that was theologically → dualistic, gained a significant foothold in the region in the 10th century and subsequently spread from Macedonia to Serbia, Bosnia, and Dalmatia. It is claimed that the movement's founder was an Orthodox priest from Macedonia by the name of Bogomil, a Slavic translation of Gk. *theophilos*, "beloved of God." Because of its semi-Manichaean doctrines and its rejection of the established church with its rituals, the Bogomils were severely persecuted by the → Orthodox Church and, later in Bosnia, the → Roman Catholic Church, as well as by secular forces.

After the temporary breakup of the Byzantine Empire in 1204 during the Fourth Crusade (→ Byzantium), the Macedonian territory was again bitterly contested, alternately ruled by Byzantines and Bulgars until Stephen Dušan the Mighty (ruled 1331-55) conquered it and made Skopje his capital. After the Ottoman Turks conquered the Serbian Empire, they ruled Macedonia from 1395 to 1912. These five centuries of political oppression by the Turks and ecclesiastical domination by the Greeks severely weakened the sense of Macedonian national and cultural identity.

In the context of the 19th-century national revivals in the Balkans and various claims on Macedonia by its neighbors, Macedonian independence was promoted by the increasingly powerful Internal Macedonian Revolutionary Organization (IMRO), which was officially founded in 1893. At the end of the 1912-13 Balkan Wars, which drove out the Turks, Macedonia was divided between Greece, Serbia, and Bulgaria. Following World War I the region of Vardar Macedonia became part of the new "Kingdom of Serbs, Croats, and Slovenes," which was in turn renamed Yugoslavia in 1929.

Hostilities and deep distrust continued during the period between the world wars. Attempts to assimilate Macedonians as "Southern Serbs" and to dominate the region as "Southern Serbia" led to much anti-Serbian resentment, national and cultural countermovements, and → terrorism by the IMRO, including complicity in the assassination of the Serbian king Alexander of Yugoslavia in 1934 in Marseilles.

During World War II Macedonia was divided between Bulgaria, an ally of the Axis, and Italian-allied Albania. In August 1944 foundations for an independent Macedonia were laid by the partisan resistance movement at the historic session of the Antifascist Assembly of the National Liberation of Macedonia. The postwar federal and socialist Yugoslavia constituted Macedonia as one of its six republics and recognized the Macedonian people as a distinct nationality.

3. Religions

3.1. *Macedonian Orthodox Church*

Throughout Macedonia's turbulent history a beleaguered Macedonian Orthodox Church has played a significant role in preserving national identity, literacy, and culture. Its roots are ancient, and it claims that the Archbishopric of Ohrid, established by Sts. Clement and Naum, was the first autocephalous Slavic church. This 800-year-old archbishopric was abolished in 1767 by the Turkish sultan Mustafa III, and its ecclesiastical territory was annexed to the → Ecumenical Patriarchate of Constantinople. In the meantime, several efforts to restore the archbishopric and the autonomy of the Macedonian church were made, without success.

With the creation of Yugoslavia following World War I, Macedonian Orthodox believers came under the jurisdiction of the Serbian Orthodox Church. External conditions for the restoration of → autocephaly were created during World War II, and in 1944 an Initiative Board for the organization of the Macedonian Orthodox Church was formed. In March 1945 the First Clergy and People's Synod met in partisan-held Skopje and adopted a resolution to restore the Archbishopric of Ohrid as the Macedonian Orthodox Church. The Serbian Orthodox Church, however, rejected this decision and obstructed other attempts at independence.

Meeting in 1958, the Second Clergy and People's Synod took a decisive step toward autocephaly by reestablishing the Archbishopric of Ohrid, electing Bishop Dositej Stojković, a Serb, as archbishop of Ohrid and metropolitan of Macedonia. These moves were publicly supported by the Communist Macedonian government and by the people. Tensions increased with the Serbian Orthodox Church, which again denied the request for autocephaly.

The Macedonian Orthodox Church then acted unilaterally, proclaiming its autocephaly and independence from the Serbian Orthodox Church at its third synod, which met in Ohrid in 1967, the bicentennial anniversary of the abolition of the Archbishopric of Ohrid. The Serbian Holy Synod denounced the decision and condemned the clergy as schismatic. Even today, more than a decade after the independence of the Macedonian state and despite various Orthodox and ecumenical efforts, the autocephaly of the Macedonian Orthodox Church is not recognized by other national Orthodox churches in deference to the Serbian opposition.

Macedonia has about 1,200 churches organized in six eparchies, whose → bishops make up the Holy Synod of Bishops, headed by the archbishop of Ohrid and Macedonia. Affirming again its own status, the Holy Synod at its session in June 1994 stated that "the autocephalous status of the Macedonian Church and the interest of the Macedonian people and state are holy and inalienable values, which it has no intention of ever giving up." The church gives special attention to the preservation of the national identity and its cultural traditions among Macedonian expatriates in Western countries. The Australian Eparchy and the Canado-American Eparchy comprise 44 churches and two monasteries.

3.2. *Islam*

→ Islam was introduced in Macedonia during the long Ottoman rule, when there were large numbers of Turkish settlers. Today more than half a million Muslims, nearly 30 percent of the population — mostly Albanian but also including 120,000 Macedonians — worship in some 425 → mosques. Both the Orthodox and Islamic communities have secondary religious schools in Skopje, which is also the seat of the Orthodox Theological College for the training of clergy. The Albanians established a university in Tetovo in 1994, the funding and recognition of which have been matters of much dispute.

3.3. *Roman Catholics and Protestants*

A small Macedonian Roman Catholic diocese with a bishop based in Skopje has approximately 40,000 members.

Protestant work in Macedonia dates from the efforts in 1873 of the American Board of Commissioners for Foreign Missions in European Turkey. The best-known missionary of the period was Helen Stone, who was captured and held hostage by Macedonian rebels for six months until a ransom was paid for her by the Turkish government. Methodists represent the oldest and largest Protestant group, with about 2,000 members in ten congregations. They received national attention in 1999 when one of their leaders, Boris Trajkovski, was elected president of Macedonia, thus becoming the first Protestant head of state in a post-Communist country.

There are about 40 other smaller but growing free-church and independent local congregations, the majority of which belong to evangelical, Pentecostal, Congregational, or Baptist denominations. Most of the younger generation of Protestant ministers have been trained at the Evangelical Theological Faculty in Osijek, Croatia. Their humanitarian work and creative outreach to university students, → Roma, and prisoners (→ Prison Ministry) and their publishing and broadcasting activities have received considerable public attention, as well as open Orthodox opposition.

There are presently several dozen foreign → missionaries active in Macedonia, although their legal status has not been fully regularized. Although the Macedonian constitution and the 1997 Law on Religious Communities and Groups guarantee full freedom of religious affiliation and activity (→ Religious Liberty), religious minorities frequently complain about government favoritism toward the Orthodox Church, which obstructs their work.

There are two translations of the NT into Macedonian. Only recently has the whole Bible become available in this modern South Slavic language (→ Bible Versions 4.6).

Bibliography: M. Apostolski, D. Zografski, et al., eds., *Istoria na makedonskiot narod* (3 vols.; Skopje, 1969) • J. K. Cowan, ed., *Macedonia: The Politics of Identity and Difference* (London, 2000) • V. Georgieva and S. Konechni, *Historical Dictionary of the Republic of Macedonia* (Lanham, Md., 1998) • J. M. Halpern, *Bibliography of English Language Sources on Yugoslavia* (Amherst, Mass., 1969) • N. G. Hammond, *The Macedonian State: The Origins, Institutions, and History* (Oxford, 1990) • J. J. Horton, comp., *Yugoslavia* (Santa Barbara, Calif., 1990) • D. Illevski, *The Macedonian Orthodox Church: The Road to Independence* (Skopje, 1973) • J. R. Lampe, *Yugoslavia as History: Twice There Was a Country* (2d ed.; Cambridge, 2000) • P. Mojzes, "A History of the Congregational and Methodist Churches in Bulgaria and Yugoslavia" (Diss., Boston University, 1965) • H. T. Norris, *Islam in the Balkans: Religion and Society between Europe and the Arab World* (Columbia, S.C., 1993) • S. Palmer and R. R. King, *Yugoslav Communism and the Macedonian Question* (Hamden, Conn., 1971) • H. Poulton, *Who Are the Macedonians?* (Bloomington, Ind., 1995) • S. Pribechevich, *Macedonia: Its People and History* (Philadel- phia, 1982) • J. Shea, *Macedonia and Greece: The Struggle to Define a New Balkan Nation* (Jefferson, N.C., 1997).

PETER KUZMIČ

Madagascar

	1960	1980	2000
Population (1,000s):	5,367	9,072	17,395
Annual growth rate (%):	2.56	3.24	3.04
Area: 587,041 sq. km. (226,658 sq. mi.)			

A.D. 2000

Population density: 30/sq. km. (77/sq. mi.)
Births / deaths: 3.91 / 0.87 per 100 population
Fertility rate: 5.21 per woman
Infant mortality rate: 68 per 1,000 live births
Life expectancy: 60.5 years (m: 59.0, f: 62.0)
Religious affiliation (%): Christians 50.8 (Roman Catholics 22.4, Protestants 20.7, unaffiliated 3.0, indigenous 2.9, Anglicans 1.6, other Christians 0.2), tribal religionists 46.6, Muslims 2.0, other 0.6.

1. General Situation
2. Religious Situation
   2.1. Christianity
   2.2. Tribal Religions
   2.3. Islam

1. General Situation

The Republic of Madagascar, off the coast of southeast Africa, is the world's fourth largest island. The Arabs knew it from the ninth century. In 1506 the Portuguese became the first Europeans to reach it; in 1896 it became a French colony (→ Colonialism), achieving independence in 1960. A military regime took over in 1972, soon thereafter imposing a ban on multiparty politics that lasted until the presidential and National Assembly elections of 1992-93. By the constitution of 1998, the country has a federal form of government, with each of the six provinces responsible for adopting its own laws.

The island has a central hilly spine, dwindling to an arid zone in the south and southeast. Offshore fishing is strongest in the northwest and southwest sectors. The land is divided between pasture (41 percent), forests (40 percent), agriculture (5 percent), and other (14 percent), including some specialized mining operations. The most important export products are shrimp, coffee, cotton fabrics, cloves and clove oil, and vanilla. Ethnically, the main group is the Malagasy (98.6 percent), which comprises 18 main ethnic subgroups derived from a mixture of Indonesian, African, and Arabic roots.

2. Religious Situation
The main religions of Madagascar are Christianity and → tribal religions; there are also a small number of Muslims (→ Islam).

2.1. *Christianity*
→ Missionaries (→ Dominicans?) began work in Madagascar in 1587. Portuguese → Jesuits and French Lazarists (→ Religious Orders and Congregations) unsuccessfully endeavored to establish themselves in the southeast during the 17th and 18th centuries. In the accompanying French expeditions massacres took place on both sides.

Welsh Congregationalists (→ Congregationalism; Reformed and Presbyterian Churches) of the London Missionary Society (→ British Missions 1.2.1) established themselves under the protection of King Radama I (1810-28) from 1818. Despite heavy mortality they converted and educated thousands of young people from noble families. Radama's widow, Queen Ranavalona I (1828-61), expelled the missionaries and killed many converts, whom the church has remembered as → martyrs. Under her son, who wanted modernization, the situation again reversed. Many conversions followed, but with fierce rivalry between Roman Catholic and Protestant missions.

The Anglican Mission (→ Anglican Communion) opened in 1864, the Norwegian Lutherans (→ Lutheran Churches; Scandinavian Missions) in 1866, and the Quakers (→ Friends, Society of) in 1869. Lutherans from the United States (→ North American Missions) began work in the southeast in 1892. In 1869 the marriage of the prime minister (hitherto neutral) and the Protestant Queen Ranavalona II led to further Protestant advance. The number of Protestants quadrupled in a year, and virtually the whole ruling elite became Protestant. Roman Catholics were clearly at a disadvantage.

With the increase of French power a dangerous politico-religious tension became obvious. After the French conquest in 1896 the Holy Ghost Fathers replaced the Jesuits in the north, and the Lazarists replaced them in the south. British Protestants were in a delicate position and ultimately asked the Société des Missions Évangéliques (→ French Missions) for support. The rivalry between Roman Catholics and Protestants became only slightly more balanced as a result, something evident in the juxtaposition of Roman Catholic and Protestant churches in almost every village. In the coastal areas the people remained much less receptive to Christian → mission,

perhaps in part because of memories of the brutal and discouraging experiences they endured in the 17th century.

After the mass movements of conversion in the 19th century, Christianity grew more slowly. In 1900 Christians were estimated at 39 percent of the total population in 1970 it was up to 49 percent. The → Roman Catholic Church ordained the first native bishop in 1936, the first native archbishop in 1960. In 2000 the church had three archdioceses and 17 dioceses. It has oriented its work toward the mass of peasants and the coastal regions, sponsoring hundreds of schools and dozens of orphanages. Through its schools, it has begun to penetrate some of the higher classes. Personally, many Roman Catholic believers continue to participate also in the Malagasy cult of the dead (→ Syncretism).

The largest two Protestant churches are the Church of Jesus Christ in Madagascar (resulting from a union in 1968 of groups stemming from British Friends and from the Paris Mission, with 2.5 million adherents in 1995) and the Malagasy Lutheran Church (from work begun in 1866 by Norwegian Lutherans and in 1895 by U.S. Lutherans, with 852,000 adherents in 1995), both members of the → World Council of Churches. Since 1960 primarily the → Pentecostal churches and fundamentalist groups (→ Fundamentalism; Evangelical Movement) have recorded significant growth.

In 2000 there were 25 → Independent Churches functioning in Madagascar.

Overall, the churches see it as their primary task to develop seminary education, run clinics, promote social development, and support economic projects. After the restoration of democracy in the early 1990s, relations between → church and state have been neutral. Legally, → religious liberty has been guaranteed since 1861.

The largest interdenominational organization is the Christian Council of Churches in Madagascar (→ National Councils of Churches), founded in 1980 and recognized officially by the state in 1985, to which most of the Protestant churches, plus the Roman Catholic and Anglican churches, belong. It has a commission to study church → unity (→ Ecumenism, Ecumenical Movement). A common theological college exists in addition to denominational seminaries. There is also a mixed theological commission with which the Roman Catholic → bishops' conference is linked through a commission for → ecumenism. Some churches in Madagascar belong also to the → Lutheran World Federation and the Association of Evangelicals of West Africa and Madagascar (headquartered in Nairobi, Kenya).

2.2. Tribal Religions

For all their differences, the various native religions show much uniformity. Central is a belief in life after death and a relation between the living and the dead. The main Malagasy names for God are "Andriamanitra" (King/Prince with good fragrance, thus inviting worship) and "Zanahary" (Creator). Traditional doctors and diviners are common, as well as the practice of sorcery and witchcraft. The cult of the → dead is an important element of religious beliefs and practices. Elaborate and costly tombs were constructed in many areas. In the Merina rituals for "the return of the dead," the remains were removed from the tomb, paraded in a dancing → procession, and wrapped in new raw silk shrouds and mats before being restored to the tomb. Paradoxically, the accumulated collective dead constituted a force for fertility, so that women desirous of children sought contact with them. Among the Betsileo and Sakalava the cult of royal ancestors goes hand in hand with the cult of the dead.

2.3. Islam

Traces of Islamic belief and practice, sometimes in very unorthodox forms, are found especially among many of the coastal people from the northwest to the southeast. The orthodox (Sunni) Islamic Afro-Arab Swahili-speaking peoples of the east coast of Africa founded settlements on the northwest coast of Madagascar in the Middle Ages, which the Portuguese largely destroyed when they arrived. The 20th century then saw a large migration of Afro-Arabs from the overpopulated Comoros to the northwest coast and the establishment there of a new population of Muslims.

→ African Theology

Bibliography: D. B. Barrett et al., eds., WCE (2d ed.) 1.466-69 • M. Brown, A History of Madagascar (Ipswich, 1995) • J. Cole, Forget Colonialism? Sacrifice and the Art of Memory in Madagascar (Berkeley, Calif., 2001) • Ø. Dahl, Meanings in Madagascar: Cases of Intercultural Communication (Westport, Conn., 1999) • B. A. Gow, Madagascar and the Protestant Impact: The Work of the British Missions, 1818-95 (New York, 1979) • R. Huntington and P. Metcalf, Celebrations of Death (Cambridge, 1979) • K. Middleton, Ancestors, Power, and History in Madagascar (Leiden, 1999) • L. W. Ramambason, Missiology: Its Subject-Matter and Method. A Study of Mission-Doers in Madagascar (Frankfurt, 1999) • A. W. Southall, "White Strangers and Their Religion in East Africa and Madagascar," Strangers in African Societies (ed. W. A. Shack and E. P. Skinner; Berkeley, Calif., 1979) 211-26 • P. Tyson, The Eighth Continent: Life, Death, and Discovery in the Lost World of Madagascar (New York, 2000).

Aidan W. Southall

Magic

1. Term and Meanings
2. Paradigms
   2.1. J. G. Frazer
   2.2. L. Lévy-Bruhl
   2.3. B. Malinowski
   2.4. E. E. Evans-Pritchard

1. Term and Meanings

The term "magic" derives by way of Lat. magia and Gk. mageia from OPer. magu-, a word of uncertain etymology denoting a priestly clan. In antiquity the term came to denote the more general practice of magic. Supernatural ability, rituals (→ Rite), automatic writing, and secret information were its stock-in-trade. Despite Christian opposition, it persisted in the Christian era. The study of comparative religion (→ Religious Studies) made the concept a basic category in the 19th century, treating magic as no less fundamental than → religion.

In 1931 B. Malinowski (1884-1942) classically formulated the separate spheres of magic and religion. As he saw it, religion gives rise to ultimate values and reaches its ends directly, while magic makes use of acts that have practical value and are only means to ends. Historical and ethnographic research (→ Ethnology), however, does not support so clear-cut a distinction, for magic and religion are closely related both in outlook (→ Worldview) and in ritual acts. Nor may we oversharply differentiate magic and science by defining science as action that reaches its goals with rational means and magic as action that uses symbolic means (J. Goody; → Symbol). Since all definitions of magic are imprecise, we may simply mention certain paradigms.

2. Paradigms

2.1. J. G. Frazer

J. G. Frazer (1854-1941) directed attention to the → sanctuary of the goddess Diana in Ariccia, near Rome. Here the officiating priest-king attained to his position by smiting his predecessor with the branch of a certain tree. The same fate finally awaited him too (Strabo Geog. 5.3.12). Frazer found the explanation in the magical thinking of ancient peoples. An allegedly primitive view of nature postulates it as a law that things act on one another by a secret sympathy; like produces like. The destruction of an image brings about the destruction of what it depicts (imitative, or homeopathic, magic). Destroying things associated with a person (e.g., fingernail clippings) destroys the person (contagious magic). By means of this law believers hoped to gain control over natural events or processes. The magician exercised this control. The priest-king of Aricia, as well as the Shilluk king in Sudan, used this type of magic and stood in an inner relation to nature. When the vitality of his magic waned, so did the fertility of nature.

E. E. Evans-Pritchard (1902-73) refuted this thesis and set the murder of the priest-king in a context, not of primitive thinking, but of the politics of a segmentary society. He also found it mistaken to interpret magic as an unsuccessful attempt to explain nature (by confusing imagined connections with actual ones), which to him was an impermissible psychologizing of the processes of thought.

2.2. L. Lévy-Bruhl

L. Lévy-Bruhl (1857-1939) was interested as a philosopher in the functions and laws of so-called primitive thinking and inferring. In his view a different law underlay such thinking (mentalité), namely, the law of mystical participation. In support of this law he cited the Bororo Indians of southern Brazil, who were reported as stating that they were red parrots. For the primitive mind, so he thought, people could easily be both themselves and something else.

This thesis, however, could not be sustained. The Bororos expected that after → death their → souls would become parrots, but only because they and the birds were both manifestations of the same essence. Clearly, we do not have here a different form of thinking. We have instead a soul-related symbolism that identifies the symbol (the bird) with what it symbolizes (the soul).

2.3. B. Malinowski

Empirical testing of Frazer's theories began with Malinowski. Ethnographic research showed that magic and religion are independent of one another. Magic has a compensatory function and optimistically (→ Optimism and Pessimism) thinks it can control nature, even when it cannot. In opposition to Frazer's theory of development, we should view magic, religion, and science as three independent but synchronous modalities of action.

2.4. E. E. Evans-Pritchard

If Malinowski offered the classic example of nature magic, Evans-Pritchard did the same for social magic. His study of → witchcraft among the Azande tribes in southern Sudan describes the people's efforts to find who is responsible for human misfortune. Witchcraft, oracles, and magic form a coherent system of actions, even though their presuppositions are irrational. The relation to nature might be seen, for example, in the collapse of a granary and a resultant death due to termites. Although we would see here a causal connection, believers in magic trace it to witchcraft, which explains why the two things happened at the same time. Oracles show who is responsible, while magic opposes the perpetrator(s). The study darkens the picture of magic. It is not here a fine example of human optimism but a bad example of a conspiracy theory.

→ Alchemy; Animism; Astrology; Divination; Exorcism; Fetishism; Occultism; Spiritism; Superstition; Taboo; Totemism

Bibliography: B. R. CLACK, *Wittgenstein, Frazer, and Religion* (Basingstoke, 1999) • F. H. CRYER, *Divination in Ancient Israel and Its Near Eastern Environment: A Socio-historical Investigation* (Sheffield, 1994) • E. E. EVANS-PRITCHARD, "The Divine Kingship of the Shilluk of the Nilotic Sudan," *Essays in Social Anthropology* (London, 1962) 66-86; idem, "The Intellectualist (English) Interpretation of Magic," *BFA(C)* 1 (1933) 282-311; idem, *Nuer Religion* (New York, 1980; orig. pub., 1956); idem, *Witchcraft, Oracles, and Magic among the Azande* (Oxford, 1987; orig. pub., 1937) • J. G. FRAZER, *The Golden Bough: A Study in Magic and Religion* (3d ed.; London, 1966) • J. GOODY, "Religion and Ritual: The Definitional Problem," *BJS* 12 (1961) 142-64 • F. GRAF, *Magic in the Ancient World* (Cambridge, Mass., 1997) • H. G. KIPPENBERG and B. LUCHESI, eds., *Magie. Die sozialwissenschaftliche Kontroverse über das Verstehen fremden Denkens* (2d ed.; Frankfurt, 1995) • H. G. KIPPENBERG and G. G. STROUMSA, eds., *Secrecy and Concealment: Studies in the History of Mediterranean and Near Eastern Religions* (Leiden, 1995) • C. LÉVI-STRAUSS, *Totemism* (London, 1964) • L. LÉVY-BRUHL, "Das Gesetz der Teilhabe," *Religions-Ethnologie* (ed. C. A. Schmitz; Frankfurt, 1964) 30-50 • B. MALINOWSKI, *Magic, Science, and Religion, and Other Essays* (London, 1982; orig. pub., 1948); idem, "The Role of Magic and Religion" (1931), *Reader in Comparative Religion: An Anthropological Approach* (ed. W. Lessa and E. Vogt; 3d ed.; Evanston, Ill., 1972) 63-72 • P. SCHÄFER and H. G. KIPPENBERG, *Envisioning Magic: A Princeton Seminar and Symposium* (Leiden, 1997).

HANS G. KIPPENBERG

Magic Square → Word Square

Magisterium → Teaching Office

Magnificat → Canticle

Mahabharata

The Mahabharata (Skt. *Mahābhārata,* "Great History of the Bharata Dynasty") comprises, together with the Purana-like Harivamsa (*Harivaṁśa,* or genealogy and life of Krishna), over 100,000 Sanskrit stanzas, composed presumably between the fourth century B.C. and the fourth century A.D. The core of the epic is the conflict between the Pāṇḍavas (Pāṇḍu's sons, including the Dharma-king Yudhiṣṭhira and Krishna's friend Arjuna) and their hostile cousins, the Kauravas (descendants of Kuru), with whom they were contesting the sovereignty of North India.

Of the 18 books of the Mahabharata, books 6-10 are taken up with the great and decisive battle in Kurukshetra (near Delhi), book 11 contains the lamentations of the women after the battle, and 12 and 13 primarily discuss questions of dharma (i.e., the principles of correct secular and religious conduct). The shorter final books give an account of the subsequent fate of the victorious Pāṇḍavas and their ally Krishna, who, in the sixth book, as Arjuna's charioteer, had solemnly proclaimed the → Bhagavad Gita. Besides the main plot the Mahabharata contains numerous episodes and legends, including a brief résumé of the other Sanskrit epic, → Ramayana.

The compilers of the Mahabharata were obviously intent on creating a kind of → encyclopedia of the traditional knowledge of the period. Thus the Mahabharata, whose authority in questions of dharma is still recognized by Indians today, is, together with the (later) → Puranas, the most important source for a knowledge of classical → Hinduism. Its religious orientation is predominantly Vaishnava, especially in the philosophical treatises (e.g., the Bhagavad Gita, in which Krishna reveals himself to Arjuna as the god Vishnu).

→ Bhakti; Karma; Krishna Consciousness, International Society for; Upanishads

Translations: J. van BUITANEN (Chicago, 1973-78) bks. 1-5 only • K. M. GANGULI (ed. P. C. Roy; 4th ed.; Calcutta, 1981; orig. pub. 1883-96).

Bibliography: V. BHAWALKAR, *Woman in the Mahabharata* (Delhi, 1999) • J. L. BROCKINGTON, *The Sanskrit Epics* (Leiden, 1998) • A. HILTEBEITEL, *Rethinking India's Oral and Classical Epics: Draupadī among Rajputs, Muslims, and Dalits* (Chicago, 1999); idem,

The Ritual of Battle: Krishna in the Mahabharata (Ithaca, N.Y., 1976) • E. W. HOPKINS, *Epic Mythology* (Delhi, 1974; orig. pub., 1915); idem, *The Great Epic of India* (Delhi, 1969; orig. pub., 1901) • J. W. LAINE, *Visions of God: Narratives of the Theophany in the Mahabharata* (Vienna, 1989) • B. van NOOTEN, *The Mahabharata* (New York, 1971) • S. SØRENSEN, *An Index to the Names in the Mahabharata* (Delhi, 1963) • N. SUTTON, *Religious Doctrines in the Mahabharata* (Delhi, 2000).

RENATE SÖHNEN-THIEME

Malachi, Book of

1. Name, Author, Form
2. Contents
3. Date

1. Name, Author, Form

"Malachi" is not the name of a prophet but simply means "my messenger" (see 3:1). We do not know, then, the name of the author. The work consists of six discussions setting out a thesis, stating the arguments against it, then establishing it and drawing out the implications. This form influenced later scribal disputations (→ Scribes) in early → Judaism.

2. Contents

The book deals with the people's offering of worthless → sacrifices and reduced → tithes, divorce and mixed → marriages, and proclamation of the day of God's judgment. Many scholars view the exhortation to obey the law in 4:4 and the announcement of the return of → Elijah in 4:5-6 as additions closing the whole prophetic canon. In addition, 2:11b–13a is sometimes thought to be an addition. K. Elliger and A. Renker postulate considerable editorial revision.

3. Date

We can only guess at the date of the work. The postexilic → temple already exists, and with it the regulated ritual, abuse of which the Book of Malachi criticizes. The work probably originated in the fifth century B.C. A. E. Hill's use of recent linguistic research suggests a date of around 500 B.C.

→ Literature, Biblical and Early Christian, 1; Minor Prophets; Prophet, Prophecy

Bibliography: Commentaries: A. DEISSLER (NEchtB; Würzburg, 1988) • A. E. HILL (AB; Garden City, N.Y., 1998) • D. L. PETERSEN (OTL; Louisville, Ky., 1995) • P. L. REDDITT (NCBC; Grand Rapids, 1995) • H. GRAF REVENTLOW (ATD; Göttingen, 1993) • E. SCHULLER

(NIB: Nashville, 1996) • R. L. Sмith (WBC; Waco, Tex., 1984).

Other works: B. Glazier-McDonald, *Malachi: The Divine Messenger* (Atlanta, 1987) • R. Mason, *Preaching the Tradition: Homily and Hermeneutics after the Exile* (Cambridge, 1990) • J. M. O'Brien, *Priest and Levite in Malachi* (Atlanta, 1990) • A. Renker, *Die Tora bei Maleachi. Ein Beitrag zur Bedeutungsgeschichte von Tora im Alten Testament* (Freiburg, 1979) • K. W. Weyde, *Prophecy and Teaching: Prophetic Authority, Form Problems, and the Use of Traditions in the Book of Malachi* (Berlin, 2000).

Winfried Thiel

Malankara Orthodox Syrian Church →
Syrian Orthodox Churches in India

Malawi

	1960	*1980*	*2000*
Population (1,000s):	3,529	6,183	10,984
Annual growth rate (%):	2.38	3.17	2.51
Area: 118,484 sq. km. (45,747 sq. mi.)			

A.D. 2000

Population density: 93/sq. km. (240/sq. mi.)
Births / deaths: 4.53 / 2.03 per 100 population
Fertility rate: 6.18 per woman
Infant mortality rate: 130 per 1,000 live births
Life expectancy: 42.5 years (m: 42.2, f: 42.8)
Religious affiliation (%): Christians 76.9 (Protestants 24.6, Roman Catholics 21.4, indigenous 17.3, unaffiliated 10.6, Anglicans 1.8, marginal 1.3), Muslims 14.6, tribal religionists 7.8, other 0.7.

1. General Situation
2. Christian Churches
3. Other Religions

1. General Situation

The Republic of Malawi is a landlocked country of East Africa, bordered on the east, south, and southwest by Mozambique, by Zambia on the west, and by Tanzania on the north. It stretches 900 km. (560 mi.) along Lake Malawi (or Lake Nyasa), most of which is part of Malawi territory.

Bantu tribes migrated into the area in the 16th century, with Arab slavers appearing in the 19th century (→ Slavery). In 1891 the area became the British protectorate of Nyasaland (→ Colonialism), which achieved its independence in 1964. The country was under the rule of Hastings Banda

from independence until 1994, when multiparty elections were allowed and a new constitution promulgated.

Malawi is one of the world's poorest countries, with its economy depending on a substantial amount of outside economic assistance. Its troubles were compounded in 1992, when it absorbed over a million refugees from Mozambique. It further struggles with a rapid increase in the number of cases of HIV/AIDS present among its people.

2. Christian Churches

The history of the Christian church in Malawi goes back to the time of David Livingstone (1813-73), who in 1858 made an appeal to the Universities of Cambridge and Oxford to start work in central Africa. The Anglican Church (→ Anglican Communion), the first to respond to this appeal (1861), is now organized in Malawi into two → dioceses, with centers at Chilema and Lilongwe, the country's capital. The Church of Central Africa, Presbyterian (1926; → Reformed and Presbyterian Churches), by far the largest Protestant church in Malawi, comprises three synods: Livingstonia (1875), Nkhoma (1889), and Blantyre (1876).

The → Roman Catholic Church was represented in the country from the late 16th and early 17th centuries by → Jesuits, although effective missionary work began only in 1889 with the arrival of the Missionaries of Africa (White Fathers). In 1997 the church comprised six dioceses.

Besides these mainstream churches many other denominations are present, including the Seventh-day → Adventists (from 1891), Providence Industrial Mission (1900), Church of Christ (1907), → Churches of Christ (1909), Assemblies of God Mission (1945), and Pentecostal Fellowship (1978; → Pentecostal Churches). There are also over 200 → Independent Churches that have broken away from mainstream churches.

The churches' main activities are education, medical work, and → evangelism. Various churches provide primary and secondary education and education in farming and technical skills. Medical work continues to be in the forefront of the churches' program. Hospitals, outstation clinics, and medical training centers have been built. Most important of all, churches are engaged in vigorous evangelical work. As a result, over three-fourths of the population are Christians. To enhance their impact, theological colleges and Bible centers have also been provided. Presently many churches are largely staffed by African clergy and strive to be self-supporting.

All churches in Malawi, as well as non-Christian

religious institutions, work together to improve the spiritual and socioeconomic life of their people. The most important ecumenical institutions are the Christian Council of Malawi (→ National Councils of Churches), Christian Service Committee, Catholic Commission for → Ecumenism, and the lay training centers at Chilema, Nkhota-Kota, and Ekwendeni. The relationships between → church and state are cordial. There is cooperation between them in the socioeconomic development of the country as a whole. The state fosters freedom of religion at all levels (→ Religious Liberty).

3. Other Religions

Besides Christianity other religious faiths are present in Malawi. The largest is → Islam, introduced during the 1840s, which is strongest among the Yao. In recent times there has been an Islamic revival in education and proselytizing.

→ Tribal religions, which are still strong in Malawi, are based in a strong belief in God and respect for the ancestral spirits (→ Ancestor Worship). Nyau male secret societies, plus the Mbona, Bimbi, and Chikang'ombe cults, are still active. These cults are believed to enhance the agricultural prosperity of the land, which is the backbone of the Malawian economy.

Bibliography: J. N. Amanze, *The Bimbi Cult* (Blantyre, Mal., 2002) • D. B. Barrett et al., eds., *WCE* (2d ed.) 1.470-73 • J. C. Chakanza and K. R. Ross, eds., *Religion in Malawi: An Annotated Bibliography* (Blantyre, Mal., 1998) • P. A. Kalilombe, *Doing Theology at the Grassroots: Theological Essays from Malawi* (Gweru, Zim., 1999) • I. Linden, *Catholics, Peasants, and Chewa Resistance in Nyasaland* (London, 1974) • J. McCracken, *Politics and Christianity in Malawi, 1875-1940* (Cambridge, 1977) • J. M. Mfutso-Bengo, *In the Name of the Rainbow: Politics of Reconciliation as a Priority of Pastoral Care in South Africa and Malawi* (New York, 2001) • S. C. Muyebe, *The Catholic Missionary within and beyond the Politics of Exclusivity in Colonial Malawi, 1901-1945* (Lewiston, N.Y., 1999) • M. E. Page and A. Woods, *The Creation of Modern Malawi* (Boulder, Colo., 1998) • K. R. Ross, *Here Comes Your King! Christ, Church, and Nation in Malawi* (Blantyre, Mal., 1998); idem, ed., *Faith at the Frontiers of Knowledge* (Blantyre, Mal., 1998) • J. Schoffeleers, *Guardians of the Land* (Gwelo, 1979); idem, *In Search of Truth and Justice: Confrontations between Church and State in Malawi, 1960-1994* (Blantyre, Mal., 1999) • A. Woods and M. E. Page, *The Creation of Modern Malawi* (Boulder, Colo., 2000).

James N. Amanze

Malaysia

	1960	1980	2000
Population (1,000s):	8,140	13,763	22,299
Annual growth rate (%):	3.09	2.60	1.74

Area: 330,442 sq. km. (127,584 sq. mi.)

A.D. 2000

Population density: 67/sq. km. (175/sq. mi.)
Births / deaths: 2.21 / 0.47 per 100 population
Fertility rate: 2.86 per woman
Infant mortality rate: 9 per 1,000 live births
Life expectancy: 73.2 years (m: 71.1, f: 75.5)
Religious affiliation (%): Muslims 47.6, Chinese folk religionists 23.5, Christians 9.0 (Roman Catholics 3.4, Protestants 2.9, unaffiliated 1.1, other Christians 1.5), Hindus 7.4, Buddhists 6.7, tribal religionists 3.0, new religionists 1.5, other 1.3.

1. General Situation
2. Religious Situation
  2.1. Roman Catholic Church
  2.2. Protestant Churches
  2.3. Ecumenical Relations
  2.4. Church and State

1. General Situation

Malaysia lies in the tropics north of the Equator. It embraces two areas separated by approximately 600 km. (375 mi.) across the South China Sea: the Malay Peninsula and parts of the island of Borneo (Sarawak and Sabah) to the north outside the sultanate of Brunei. The Malaysian peninsula is bordered on the north by Thailand and on the south by Singapore. The country's capital is Kuala Lumpur.

The Malaysian peninsula has 43 percent of the total area but 83 percent of the total population of the country. At first Malaysia, which gained sovereignty from the colonial power Britain in 1957 (→ Colonialism), covered only the peninsula. In 1963 Britain added the Borneo territories and Singapore, but Singapore left the federation in 1965. Ethnic diversity marks Malaysia, with estimates in 1999 showing 58 percent Malay and other indigenous people, 26 percent Chinese, and 7 percent Indian. The remaining 9 percent include the Dayak, Iban, and Kadazan peoples in Sarawak and Sabah. The social structure varies, too, according to the differences in language and culture. The existence of three different subcultures with their own traditions, norms, languages, and religions forms an obstacle to integration. Along with economic conflicts the country faces cultural, educational, and linguistic tensions.

Malaysia is a constitutional federation with a

Parliament-elected monarchy and a two-chamber legislative system. At the head of 9 of the 13 federated states is a sultan. The sultans, who are also the religious heads of their states, form the Conference of Rulers, from whose members a king is elected for a five-year term. The king is also head of the Islamic community of the country.

2. Religious Situation

In 2000 nearly half of the people of Malaysia were Muslims (→ Islam), and about one-quarter were Chinese folk-religionists. Others, depending on their ethnic background, were followers of → Buddhism or → Hinduism. Most of the Christians were Chinese, a few were Indians, but practically none were Malays.

Regionally, most of the Christians are found in Sarawak (where 34 percent of the population were Christian in 1990) and Sabah (30 percent), with few in peninsular Malaysia (3 percent). This imbalance is due to there being more indigenous peoples in Sarawak and Sabah (esp. the Iban, Dayak, and Kadazan peoples), who in part were animists (→ Animism; Tribal Religions). The colonial past of Borneo also had an impact.

2.1. Roman Catholic Church

The first Christians came to completely Muslim Malaya along with the conquering colonial powers of Portugal, Holland, and Britain. The Portuguese occupation of Melaka (or Malacca) in 1511 formed a first base for the → Roman Catholic Church, which set up a → diocese there. In 1953 this diocese became the first one located in Singapore, which became a separate archdiocese in 1972. Ethnically, most of the Roman Catholics are Indian. Others are Chinese, and most of the Eurasians are Roman Catholic.

In Sarawak and Sabah most of the Roman Catholics are either indigenous or Chinese. Sarawak has the larger Chinese population, and it has papal representatives. In Sabah, however, there is some repression of Roman Catholics, as papal representatives are limited in their pastoral visits to Kota Kinabulu, the state capital, and then for only two weeks a year. Between 1969 and 1977 no Protestant missionaries were allowed in Sabah. Unlike the Protestants, the Roman Catholics have not been able to set up national ministers who could replace the foreign missionaries.

2.2. Protestant Churches

When the Dutch took over Melaka in 1641, the first Protestant missionaries came to Malaya, but at first they ministered only to Europeans. Active missionary work began only when Britain became the colonial power at the beginning of the 19th century. The

London Missionary Society (→ British Missions) sent the first → missionary in 1814, though Malaya was mostly used as a base for missionary work in China.

In 1995 the Methodist Church in Malaysia (→ Methodist Churches) was the largest Protestant church in Malaysia, with 230,000 adherents in 300 congregations. Deriving from the work of American missionaries who came to Singapore in 1885, it became independent with the election of its first national → bishop in 1968. The Sarawak Annual Conference was set up in 1965, and the Sarawak Iban Provisional Annual Conference in 1962. The Methodist church also has secondary and primary schools, which are increasingly coming under state control, as well as medical facilities, along with community programs for the Ibans in Sarawak and a community center in Kuala Lumpur.

The Evangelical Church of Borneo, founded in 1928, counted 190,000 adherents, in 500 congregations. It resulted from the work of the Australian Borneo Evangelical Mission (→ Evangelical Missions).

The Anglican Church (→ Anglican Communion), which originated in North Borneo in the early 19th century, has three dioceses in Malaysia under the Archbishop of Canterbury, numbering 180,000 in 300 congregations. It does evangelistic, educational, and medical work among the Chinese, Indian Tamils, and Sea Dayaks. It runs primary and secondary schools and clinics, as well as an agricultural program in Kuching, Sarawak. Since 1974 it has been a member of the Council of the Churches of East India.

Among other Protestants are the Seventh-day → Adventists, who are concentrated in Sabah. We may also mention many independent churches that arose with the migration of Chinese and Indian people to Malaysia, including the True Jesus Church and the Bible Presbyterian Church (→ Reformed and Presbyterian Churches). Other churches are the Orthodox Syrian Church and the Mar Thoma Syrian Church (→ Syrian Orthodox Churches in India).

There are four → Lutheran Churches in Malaysia: the Basel Christian Church of Malaysia in Sabah, the Evangelical Lutheran Church in Malaysia (most of its members are Tamils), the Lutheran Church in Malaysia and Singapore (mostly Chinese), and the Protestant Church in Sabah. In 1947 the Evangelical Lutheran Church joined with the Anglicans and Methodists to set up a center for theological students in Kuala Lumpur, which became the Malaysian Theological Seminary in 1979. The four Lutheran bodies united in 1977 to form the Federation of Evangelical Lutheran Churches in Malaysia and Singapore.

2.3. Ecumenical Relations

A feature of the Malaysian Protestant churches is a regional, linguistic, and ethnic diversity similar to that of the population as a whole. This diversity hampers close cooperation, as does the restrictive policy of the government regarding missionary work among the Malays. In addition, considerable conflict has arisen between churches who favor → ecumenism and those who oppose it, especially the conservative Chinese Protestants. Up to 1948 the churches belonged to the Council of Churches of Malaysia and Singapore, with 11 regional councils. In 1975, however, they split into two independent councils of Malaysia and of Singapore (→ National Councils of Churches).

Another attempt at cooperation came with the establishment of the Christian Federation of Malaysia in 1985. With headquarters at Kuala Lumpur, this body includes the Roman Catholic Church, the National Council of Churches of Malaysia, and the National Evangelical Christian Fellowship. It was officially recognized and registered as a federation in 1986 and acts on behalf of Christians in negotiations with the government.

2.4. Church and State

As regards → church and state relations, article 3 of the constitution defines Islam as the state religion. Other groups enjoy → religious liberty, but the government actively promotes Islam in the schools and universities. At the same time some of the states, which have the right to regulate religious affairs, have passed laws forbidding the proclamation of non-Islamic beliefs among Malays.

→ Asian Theology; Christian Conference of Asia

Bibliography: S. E. ACKERMAN and R. L. M. LEE, *Heaven in Transition: A Non-Muslim Religious Innovation and Ethnic Identity in Malaysia* (Honolulu, 1988) • D. B. BARRETT et al., eds., *WCE* (2d ed.) 1.473-78 • T. DORAISAMY, *The March of Methodism in Singapore and Malaya, 1885-1980* (Singapore, 1982) • T. P. C. GABRIEL, *Hindu and Muslim Inter-religious Relations in Malaysia* (Lewiston, N.Y., 2000) • V. KASCH, "Malaysia," *Handbuch der Dritten Welt*, vol. 7, *Süd- und Südostasien* (ed. D. Nohlen and F. Nuscheler; Hamburg, 1983) 386-406 • R. L. M. LEE and S. E. ACKERMAN, *Sacred Tensions: Modernity and Religious Transformation in Malaysia* (Columbia, S.C., 1997) • H. MUTALIB, *Islam and Ethnicity in Malay Politics* (New York, 1990) • J. ROONEY, *Khaber Gembira [The good news]: A History of the Catholic Church in East Malaysia and Brunei (1880-1976)* (London, 1981) • J. W. ROXBOROGH, *A Bibliography of Christianity in Malaysia* (Kuala Lumpur, 1990); idem, *A Short Introduction to Malaysian Church History* (Kuala Lumpur, 1986) • G. SAUNDERS, *Bishops and Brookes: The Anglican Mission and the Brooke Raj in Sarawak, 1848-1941* (New York, 1992).

VOLKER KASCH

Maldives

	1960	1980	2000
Population (1,000s):	99	158	302
Annual growth rate (%):	2.01	2.99	3.23
Area: 298 sq. km. (115 sq. mi.)			

A.D. 2000

Population density: 1,014/sq. km. (2,628/sq. mi.)
Births / deaths: 3.85 / 0.63 per 100 population
Fertility rate: 6.02 per woman
Infant mortality rate: 40 per 1,000 live births
Life expectancy: 66.7 years (m: 67.7, f: 65.8)
Religious affiliation (%): Muslims 99.1, other 0.9.

1. General Situation
2. Religious Situation

1. General Situation

The Republic of Maldives, comprising a pencil-shaped cluster of 26 atolls, lies in the Indian Ocean to the southwest of India. Only about 200 of its 1,190 islands are permanently inhabited. No island is over 13 sq. km. (5 sq. mi.) in area; the highest point in any of them is only 2.4 m. (8 ft.) above sea level. Maldives is important geopolitically because of its location astride or along major sea lanes in the Indian Ocean.

Ethnically, Maldivians are a mixture of South Indians, Sinhalese, and Arabs; the official language is Dhivehi, of Sanskrit origin. The nation's leading source of income is → tourism, providing 60 percent of the country's foreign exchange receipts, followed by fishing.

The archipelago was inhabited from at least the fifth century B.C. by settlers from India and Sri Lanka. The Portuguese were the first → colonialists in the Maldive Islands (1558-73), followed by the Dutch (17th cent.) and then the British (late 18th cent.), who formalized a protectorate agreement in 1887. Maldives gained its independence from Britain in 1965.

2. Religious Situation

In 1153 the islands, originally → Buddhist, converted to → Islam as the result of trade, Arab immigration, and the work of → missionaries from new Muslim territories in India. The islands, even when under the Dutch and the British, were governed as a sultanate until 1953. Attempts were then made to initiate progressive social legislation, but Muslim traditionalists prevailed, and the sultanate was restored. In 1968 the sultan was deposed, and a republic established. An initial constitution of 1964, revised in 1968 and most recently in 1998, recognizes Islam as the only religion of the nation. The constitution provides for individual rights, which, however, must not contradict Islam. The legal system is based on → Shariʿa (→ Law and Legal Theory).

Historically, there is evidence that St. Thomas Christians from India were once on Maldives, and some Christian links come from → Roman Catholic establishments in Sri Lanka. In recent centuries, however, Christian → mission, including Christian literature, has never been allowed. There are no resident Christian clergy or parish structures. Since 1965 Christian observances have been permitted only in private households.

→ Islam and Christianity

Bibliography: C. Baxter, "Nepal, Bhutan, and the Maldives," *Government and Politics in South Asia* (3d ed.; Boulder, Colo., 1993) 361-75 • J. England, *The Hidden History of Christianity in Asia: The Churches of the East before the Year 1500* (Delhi, 1996) 66 • T. Heyerdahl, *The Maldive Mystery* (London, 1986) • C. H. B. Reynolds, comp., *Maldives* (Oxford, 1993) • L. Vilgon, *Maldive Islands and Minicoy Bibliography* (Stockholm, 2000) • H. Yajima, ed., *The Islamic History of the Maldive Islands* (2 vols.; Tokyo, 1982-84).   The Editors

Mali

	1960	1980	2000
Population (1,000s):	4,375	6,863	12,559
Annual growth rate (%):	2.36	2.85	2.91
Area: 1,248,574 sq. km. (482,077 sq. mi.)			

A.D. *2000*

Population density: 10/sq. km. (26/sq. mi.)
Births / deaths: 4.44 / 1.53 per 100 population
Fertility rate: 6.10 per woman
Infant mortality rate: 138 per 1,000 live births
Life expectancy: 50.0 years (m: 48.3, f: 51.7)
Religious affiliation (%): Muslims 82.4, tribal religionists 15.5, Christians 2.0 (Roman Catholics 1.0, other Christians 1.0), other 0.1.

1. General Situation
2. Religious Situation

1. General Situation

The Republic of Mali, in the interior of western Africa, is one of the largest countries of Africa. It stretches 1,500 km. (930 mi.) from the central Sahara (the traditional salt mines of Taoudenni) to the Sahel area southwest of the Niger River. Between Tombouctou (traditionally spelled "Timbuktu") and Ségou, in the Macina region, the river branches into a large inland delta, an area of lakes and swamps, once a single lake, that the ever-encroaching desert threatens.

Astride important north-south trans-Saharan caravan routes and the west-east routes of the Mecca pilgrimage, Mali has been the site of medieval African empires (Mali in the 12-13th cent., Songhai in the 14th cent.) unknown to the West till the recent surge of research on African history. Since the 11th century, towns like Tombouctou have been centers of West African Islamic culture, and the traditional loam → mosques of this part of the Sahel zone are recognized as cultural monuments of international importance.

The French colonial conquest began in 1883, and from 1895 present-day Mali was part of Afrique Occidentale Française. French colonial policy (→ Colonialism) included a strong drive toward the assimilation of local educated elites, but also a harsh intervention in rural life through the taxation and forced labor of the Office du Niger. In 1946 the Rassemblement Democratique Africain was founded in French West Africa, with a Malian section, the Union Soudanaise, which aimed at independence.

Independence was achieved in 1960 under Modibo Keita (1915-77), who attempted a radical course linked to policies pursued by Kwame Nkrumah (1909-72) in Ghana and Sékou Tourée (1922-84) in Guinea. Mali abandoned the franc zone and other special relationships with France and attempted to build up a new industrial base for the → economy, with support from the Eastern European socialist bloc. These policies were reversed by a military coup in 1968, which brought Moussa Traoré to power, who ruled until the next coup, in 1991. The country's first democratic elections were held in 1992.

The modern state, which is very sparsely populated, embraces a wide palette of famous African cultures (e.g., Bambara, Dogon, and Tuareg). In 1995 the literacy rate was estimated at only 31 percent for people over age 15 (39 percent for males, 23 percent for females).

Mali is extremely weak economically, with 65 percent of its land area desert or semidesert. Its gross domestic product per capita (est. at $850 in 2000) is among the lowest in the world. About 80 percent of the labor force is engaged in farming and fishing. Major agricultural products are cereals, fruits and vegetables, cotton, tobacco, and tea. In the late 1990s the government took steps to develop the country's gold-mining operations, which, along with adherence to a path of economic reform, have the potential to provide needed growth and stability.

2. Religious Situation

Mali is the site of one of the classic expositions of African traditional religions (M. Griaule; → Guinea 2; Tribal Religions). In the 20th century people identifying themselves with → Islam grew from 30 percent to over 80 percent of the population. Sufi brotherhoods (Tijānīyah and Qādirīyah; → Sufism) have been expanding their influence.

The first Roman Catholic missions (→ Mission) began work in the area in 1895; the first Malian → priest was ordained in 1936, the first Malian → bishop consecrated in 1962. The first Protestant → missionaries were Americans who entered the country in 1919 with the Gospel Missionary Union, and in 1923 with the → Christian and Missionary Alliance (→ North American Missions). Churches stemming from these efforts were the largest Protestant churches in 1995: respectively, the Evangelical Protestant Church of Mali (24,000 adherents) and the Christian Evangelical Church of Mali (42,000 adherents).

Although → religious liberty is guaranteed under the 1960 constitution and Roman Catholic schools since 1973 have had a special status vis-à-vis the government, the Christian → minority amounts to only 2 percent of the population, almost equally divided between Catholics and Protestants. There are especially significant Christian populations among the Dogon, Senufo, and Bwa peoples.

→ African Theology

Bibliography: D. B. BARRETT et al., eds., *WCE* (2d ed.) 1.480-82 • R. J. BINGEN, D. ROBINSON, and J. M. STAATZ, eds., *Democracy and Development in Mali* (East Lansing, Mich., 2000) • L. BRENNER, *Controlling Knowledge: Religion, Power, and Schooling in a West African Muslim Society* (Bloomington, Ind., 2001) • A. F. CLARK, *From Frontier to Backwater: Economy and Society in the Upper Senegal Valley* (Lanham, Md., 1999) • M. GRIAULE, *Conversations with Ogotemmêli: An Introduction to Dogon Religious Ideas* (London, 1975; orig. pub., 1948) • J. O. HUNWICK, ed., *Timbuktu and the Songhay Empire: Al-Sa'di's Ta'rīkh al-Sūdān down to 1613, and Other Contemporary Documents* (Leiden, 1999) • P. J. IMPERATO, *Buffoons, Queens, and Wooden Horsemen: The Dyo and Gouan Societies of the Bambara of Mali* (New York, 1983) • E. SILLA, *People Are Not the Same: Leprosy and Identity in Twentieth-Century Mali* (Oxford, 1998).

PAUL JENKINS

Malta

	1960	1980	2000
Population (1,000s):	312	324	378
Annual growth rate (%):	-0.45	1.21	0.59
Area: 316 sq. km. (122 sq. mi.)			

A.D. *2000*

Population density: 1,197/sq. km. (3,100/sq. mi.)
Births / deaths: 1.41 / 0.83 per 100 population
Fertility rate: 2.10 per woman
Infant mortality rate: 6 per 1,000 live births
Life expectancy: 77.7 years (m: 75.4, f: 79.9)
Religious affiliation (%): Christians 98.4 (Roman Catholics 96.9, other Christians 1.5), other 1.6.

1. Christian Mission
2. Churches
3. Church and State
4. Other Religions

1. Christian Mission

It is commonly agreed that the → apostle → Paul himself brought Christianity to Malta when he was shipwrecked on the island on his way to Rome (Acts 27–28). Ancient Christian remains, especially → catacombs, bear witness to an established church there in the 3d century. Little is known about the history of Christianity in Malta in the next seven centuries, but we have evidence of a substantial Christian presence after the 11th century.

Today most of the people of the Republic of Malta belong to the → Roman Catholic Church. The constitution recognizes this fact as a basis of Maltese society. In 1996 there were 942 priests, 89 brothers, and 1,318 sisters in Malta serving over 350,000 members. Many priests, monks, nuns, and laypersons are also at work in Malta as → missionaries (→ Mission). The church supports a wide network of pastoral and social activities, including parishes, schools (→ School and Church), which serve a third of the pupils in Malta, homes for children and senior citizens, and several other benevolent institutions.

2. Churches

The Anglicans (→ Anglican Communion), Methodists (→ Methodist Churches), and Scottish

Presbyterians (→ Reformed and Presbyterian Churches) came to Malta when Britain took control of the island in the early 19th century. They constitute very small communities of mostly British residents. There is also a small Greek Orthodox Church (→ Orthodox Church). An ecumenical group (→ Ecumenism, Ecumenical Movement) representing all the churches meets regularly to discuss doctrinal issues (→ Ecumenical Dialogue) and church relations and to hold times of common prayer.

3. Church and State

Under the three periods of Socialist rule (1971-87), tensions and conflicts marked relations between → church and state. Efforts were also made, however, to settle disputes such as that regarding church → property and Roman Catholic schools. The new regime after 1987 set out to end all remaining conflicts. Agreements were signed (→ Concordat) on the reintroduction of the faculty of theology to the state university, on the government financing of Roman Catholic schools, on church supervision of religious instruction (→ Religious Education) in state schools, and on the transfer of church property to the state.

4. Other Religions

The Muslim community (→ Islam) in Malta is small but has a new → mosque with regular worship. There is also a very small Jewish presence (→ Judaism).

Bibliography: D. B. Barrett et al., eds., *WCE* (2d ed.) 1.483-85 • W. C. Berg, *Historical Dictionary of Malta* (Lanham, Md., 1995) • A. Bonnici, *History of the Church in Malta* (3 vols.; Valletta, Malta, 1967-75) • J. J. Cremona, *The Maltese Constitution and Constitutional History since 1813* (2d ed.; Marsa, Malta, 1997) • A. Koster, *Prelates and Politicians in Malta: Changing Power-Balances between Church and State in a Mediterranean Island Fortress, 1800-1976* (Assen, 1984) • A. Luttrel, ed., *Medieval Malta: Studies on Malta before the Knights* (London, 1975) • J. S. C. Riley-Smith, *Hospitallers: The History of the Order of St. John* (London, 1999) • H. J. A. Sire, *The Knights of Malta* (New Haven, 1995) • B. A. Zammit, *The Power of the Cross* (Atlanta, 1999).

George Grima

Mandaeans

1. Term
2. Basic Views
3. Development
4. Literature

1. Term

The term "Mandaean" is used for a → Gnostic-type baptismal fellowship (→ Baptism) that existed on the eastern borders of Syria and Palestine in the first century A.D. and that is the only one of such representatives of the → syncretism of antiquity to survive to this day. Modern Mandaeans, some 15,000 in number in the late 1970s, live in the marshy delta region of the Tigris and Euphrates, in the Iranian province of Khūzestān, and in the Iraqi cities of Baghdad and Basra. Since the Iran-Iraq War of 1980-88 we have not had reliable statistics about their numbers.

Within East Aramaic the Mandaeans developed their own literary language with its own script and produced an extensive religious literature. The term "Mandaean" (Aramaic for "Gnostics") is a late one. The Mandaeans called themselves Nasoreans (i.e., observants). In the → Qur'an (2:62; 5:69), under the name "Sabaeans," they are grouped with Christians and Jews as "people of the book," that is, members of a book religion (→ Tolerance).

2. Basic Views

The Mandaeans belong to the emanative type of Gnosticism, according to which the existence of the world and humanity is by a preexistent descent or step-by-step downward movement of the divine (→ Emanation). The Mandaeans, however, never gave systematic form to this basic view. Their mythological ideas (→ Myth, Mythology), which we find in many different parts and layers of their writings, form no clear pattern. Most impressive in their writings is the sense of being strangers in the world.

The central cultic acts — baptism *(maṣbūtā)* and the ascent of the → soul *(masīqtā)* — serve before death as a liberation from bondage to the world and after death as the return of the soul to the realm of light. Baptism brings a substantial union of believers with the world of light, while the second ritual guarantees the soul a smooth return through the planetary spheres to that world. Baptism is by immersion in running water (the "Jordan"). Since it is designed to ensure lasting union with the world of light, it is repeated every Sunday and is not just a one-time act of → initiation.

3. Development

Mandaean religion went through developments that are hard to follow in detail. It obviously originated among heretical Jewish baptismal sects. The early view that its first home was Babylon has now been abandoned. The date of the exodus from the Babylonian area is open to dispute (1st, 2d, or 3d cent.).

As it developed, the religion took on Iranian (→ Dualism; Iranian Religions) and Babylonian (astral mythology and the related → magic) elements, though not from Hellenism. The baptismal rite adopted some aspects of → Nestorian baptism. Its original rootage in → Judaism and the OT turned into hatred of Judaism and the OT God and polemics against them.

The relation to Christianity was also polemical. → Jesus Christ, viewed as a false prophet, was contrasted with Enosh-Uthra, the true Mandaean redeemer. → John the Baptist was not a forerunner of Christ but his opponent. Forms of the Mandaean → salvation history adopted baptism from John. In general, the traditions relating to Jesus and John seem to be of later origin.

4. Literature

Mandaean writings include mythological tractates, sermons, catechisms, liturgical and cultic texts, commentaries, legends, and divans (illustrated scrolls). There are also magic texts and amulets. The poetry is of a distinctive type within Semitic poetry. The writings were collected and compiled in an attempt to show Muslims that the Mandaeans were "people of the book" (see 1). The most important texts were translated by M. Lidzbarski (1868-1928) between 1905 and 1925 (Book of John, liturgies, *Ginza* [Treasure]) and Lady E. S. Drower (1879-1972; the canonical prayerbook and the historically important legendary *Haran Gawaita*, which describes the wanderings of the Mandaeans to "inner Haran").

The uncoordinated character of the writings as compilations and the peculiarities of the external tradition make it hard to determine exactly their historical development. An important chronological point of reference was achieved with the discovery by T. Säve-Söderbergh that some parts of the literature were worked over in the → Manichaean Psalms of Thomas (dated between 240 and 276).

Bibliography: D. COHN-SHERBOK, *Rabbinic Perspectives on the NT* (Lewiston, N.Y., 1990) • N. DEUTSCH, *The Gnostic Imagination: Gnosticism, Mandaeism, and Merkabah Mysticism* (Leiden, 1995) • E. S. DROWER, trans., *The Canonical Prayerbook of the Mandaeans* (Leiden, 1959); idem, trans., *The Haran Gawaita and the Baptism of Hibil-Ziwa* (Vatican City, 1953) • E. S. DROWER and R. MACUCH, *A Mandaic Dictionary* (Oxford, 1963) • S. GÜNDÜZ, *The Knowledge of Life: The Origins and Early History of the Mandaeans and Their Relation to the Sabians of the Qur'an and to the Harranians* (Oxford, 1995) • E. LUPIERI, *The Mandaeans: The Last Gnostics* (Grand Rapids, 2002) • R. MACUCH, *Handbook of Classical and Modern Mandaic* (Berlin, 1965) • T. NÖLDEKE, *Mandäische Grammatik* (Darmstadt, 1964; orig. pub., 1875) • S. A. PALLIS, *Essay on Mandaean Bibliography, 1560-1930: Chronologically Arranged, with Annotations and an Index; Preceded by an Extensive Critical and Historical Introduction on the Mandaean Research up to 1930* (Amsterdam, 1974; orig. pub., 1933); idem, *Mandaean Studies: A Comparative Enquiry into Mandaeism and Mandaean Writings and Babylonian and Persian Religions, Judaism and Gnosticism, with Linguistic and Bibliographic Notes and References* (2d ed.; Amsterdam, 1974; orig. pub., 1926) • K. RUDOLPH, *Die Mandäer* (2 vols.; Göttingen, 1960-61); idem, "Problems of a History of the Development of the Mandaean Religion," *HR* 8 (1969) 210-35 • T. SÄVE-SÖDERBERGH, *Studies in the Coptic Manichaean Psalm-Book: Prosody and Mandaean Parallels* (Uppsala, 1949) • E. SEGELBERG, *Maṣbūtā: Studies in the Ritual of Mandaean Baptism* (Uppsala, 1958) • G. WIDENGREN, *Die Mandäismus* (Darmstadt 1982). See also the bibliography in "Gnosis, Gnosticism."

PETER NAGEL

Manichaeanism

1. Religious Type and Features
2. Ethics and Community Life
3. Writings
4. Spread
5. Relation to Christianity

1. Religious Type and Features

Manichaeanism, named after its founder, the Persian Mani (A.D. 216-76/77), is a Gnostic-type → dualistic religion of redemption, though by its origin and in its manifestations it differs in many respects from Syrian and Egyptian → Gnosis. It is (1) a religion founded by a historical personage, (2) a universal religion with a world mission, and (3) a book religion with a canon of sacred writings. Structurally, it involves a hierarchically ordered church, which it views as a means of salvation. We do not find here the free conventicles, or "reading circles," of older Gnosticism. It shares with Gnosticism the basic understanding of humanity as ontologically the product of an illegitimate mixing of light and darkness and metaphysically the site of conflict between → good and → evil, between the divine Pneuma and hylic (or material) concupiscence (→ Ontology; Metaphysics).

The theme and goal of Manichaean teaching are the need and the real possibility of releasing the light enclosed in humanity and the world, but its explanation of the sorry situation differs radically from that of Syrian and Egyptian Gnosis. Light did not become darkness through the descent of the divine but through the antigodly rebellion of a second principle (darkness, *hylē* [lit. "matter"]) that is trying to penetrate into the harmony of the world of light. All action in the world of light is reaction to this attack.

The first defensive measure is the calling of primal man to fight against the rebellion. Primal man is the savior *(salvator)* insofar as he repels the attack, and he is the victim *(salvandus)* insofar as he finally falls in the battle and loses one part of his substance of light. The goal of what follows is the restoration of primal man and the part of light that is lost. In Manichaeanism this process is not merely described on the levels of cosmogony, anthropogenesis, → soteriology, and → eschatology but is made possible for those who open themselves to the Manichaean message as a repetition of the → archetypical redemption of primal man.

2. Ethics and Community Life
The soteriology of Manichaeanism actively takes us up into the process of redemption. By following → ascetic norms of life, especially the "three seals" (*tria signacula* — of mouth, hands, and genitals), and by nurturing plants that contain light, we can be the means of liberating light. The idea that in all matter there is a cross of light that must be kept intact leads to a minimalizing of all life's relations, including a prohibition of agriculture and all manual → work apart from calligraphy, trade, and money-changing. These restrictions lead to poor social relations. Rigorous keeping of the commands is possible only for the elect, who are supported by the hearers *(auditores)*.

Community life involves → worship, instruction, penance (→ Penitence), and → fasting. The high point is the annual Bema feast (*bēma*, "raised place," signifies the focus of Mani's presence). This event takes place in February or March, which honors the martyrdom of Mani (→ Martyrs). Mythical ritual practices include the holy → kiss, the → laying on of hands, and the extending of the right hand; there are no → sacraments.

3. Writings
Manichaeanism produced an extensive literature, but because of constant persecution (see 4), only fragments survive. Seven (or, by another account, five) of Mani's own works are regarded as canonical. Especially common are didactic works, psalms, prayers, apocalypses, biographical and hagiographic texts, edifying moral tales and parables, and martyr stories. Taken over from Christianity are the Gospels (in the form of the Diatessaron), the epistles of Paul, and several apocryphal Acts (→ Apocrypha 2.2). The OT is rejected.

4. Spread
Within a few decades Manichaeanism spread all over the → Roman Empire and into central and eastern Asia. It survived in China until the 14th century. Except in the first years of brief promotion or toleration, it came under persecution in all the countries and among all the religions in which it did missionary work, though from 762 to 840 it was the state religion of the Uighur kingdom in central Asia. Its missionary successes were due to skillful adaptation to existing religions (→ Acculturation; Syncretism). Different views exist regarding the survival or metamorphosis of Manichaeanism in the dualistic → sects of the Middle Ages (→ Cathari).

5. Relation to Christianity
Manichaeanism viewed itself as summing up, transcending, and completing all previous religions, especially Christianity. Mani saw in → Jesus his greatest predecessor. Adopting the Pauline formula, he described himself as the → apostle of Jesus. He early separated himself from his religious model, the Jewish-Christian sect of the Elkesaites, though he selectively adopted their traditions. His followers revered him as the promised end-time Paraclete of John 14, an idea that Christians opposed as blasphemy. Manichaeanism became the permanent enemy of Christianity.

→ Augustine's Theology; Iranian Religions 10

Bibliography: Collections of texts: A. ADAM, *Texte zum Manichäismus* (2d ed.; Berlin, 1969) • A. BÖHLIG, *Die Gnosis,* vol. 3, *Der Manichäismus* (Zurich, 1980) • S. CLACKSON, E. HUNTER, and S. N. C. LIEU, comps., *Dictionary of Manichaean Texts,* vol. 1, *Texts from the Roman Empire (Texts in Syriac, Greek, Coptic and Latin)* (Turnhout, 1998).

Greek MS: R. CAMERON and A. J. DEWEY, trans., *The Cologne Mani Codex (P. Colon., inv. nr. 4780) "Concerning the Origin of His Body"* (Missoula, Mont., 1979) • A. HENRICHS and L. KOENEN, "Ein griechischer Mani-Codex," *ZPE* 5 (1970) 92-216; idem, "Der Kölner Mani-Kodex (P. Colon. inv. 4780)," ibid. 19 (1975) 1-85; 32 (1978) 87-199; 44 (1981) 201-318; 48 (1982) 1-59.

Coptic MSS: C. ALLBERRY, *A Manichaean Psalm-Book* (pt. 2; Stuttgart, 1938) • I. GARDNER, ed., *The Kephalaia of the Teacher: The Edited Coptic Manichaean Texts in Translation with Commentary* (Leiden, 1995) • S. GIVERSEN, *The Manichaean Coptic Papyri in the Chester Beatty Library* (fac. ed.; 4 vols.; Geneva, 1986) • P. Nagel, *Die Thomaspsalmen des koptisch-manichäischen Psalmenbuches* (Berlin, 1980) • H. J. Polotsky, *Manichäische Homilien* (Stuttgart, 1934).

MSS in Middle Persian and other languages: M. Boyce, *A Catalogue of the Iranian Manuscripts in Manichaean Script in the German Turfan Collection* (Berlin, 1960) • A. V. W. Jackson, *Researches in Manichaeism, with Special Reference to the Turfan Fragments* (New York, 1932) • H. Schmidt-Glintzer, *Chinesische Manichaica* (Wiesbaden, 1987) • W. Sundermann, *Ein manichäisch-soghdisches Parabelbuch* (Berlin, 1985); idem, *Mitteliranische manichäische Texte kirchengeschichtlichen Inhalts* (Berlin, 1981); idem, *Mitteliranische und parthische kosmogonische und Parabeltexte der Manichäer* (Berlin, 1973); idem, ed., *Iranian Manichaean Turfan Texts in Early Publications (1904-1934): Photo Edition* (London, 1996) • D. Weber, ed., *Iranian Manichaean Turfan Texts in Publications since 1934: Photo Edition* (London, 2000) • P. Zieme, *Manichäisch-türkische Texte* (Berlin, 1975).

Secondary works: J. P. Asmussen, *Manichaean Literature: Representative Texts Chiefly from Middle Persian and Parthian Writings* (Delmar, N.Y., 1977) • Augustine, *The Catholic and Manichaean Ways of Life*, FC 56 • J. BeDuhn, *The Manichaean Body: In Discipline and Ritual* (Baltimore, 2000) • A. Böhlig and C. Markschies, *Gnosis und Manichäismus: Forschungen und Studien zu Texten von Valentin und Mani sowie zu den Bibliotheken von Nag Hammadi und Medinet Madi* (Berlin, 1994) • G. Filoramo, *A History of Gnosticism* (Cambridge, Mass., 1990) • K.-L. Lee, *Augustine, Manichaeism, and the Good* (New York, 1999) • S. N. C. Lieu, *Manichaeism in Central Asia and China* (Leiden, 1998); idem, *Manichaeism in the Later Roman Empire and Medieval China* (2d ed.; Tübingen, 1992) • P. Mirecki and J. BeDuhn, eds., *Emerging from Darkness: Studies in the Recovery of Manichaean Sources* (Leiden, 1997) • E. Rose, *Die manichäische Christologie* (Wiesbaden, 1979) • S. Runciman, *The Medieval Manichee: A Study of the Christian Dualist Heresy* (Cambridge, 1982; orig. pub., 1955) • G. Widengren, *Mani and Manichaeism* (London, 1965).

PETER NAGEL

Manipulation

1. Term

The word "manipulation" derives from Lat. *manus* (hand) and *plero* (fill). Semantically, it is akin to handling, but with the negative connotation of illegitimate or doubtful modes of handling. Though it may be used with reference to → nature, it refers primarily to acts relating to people, whether physical, psychological, or social. One might define it as a deliberate influencing of individuals and → groups that are not aware of being influenced or given any option in the matter. It thus differs from → *authority* (consciously experienced and legally recognized influencing) and *compulsion* (consciously experienced and resisted influencing).

2. Manipulation of Nature

As regards the manipulation of nature, at issue are invasions of nature that are open to ethical criticism (→ Ethics), for example, gene technology (→ Medical Ethics). Opinions differ on the permissibility of such invasions. We must not label a → technology manipulation simply because it is new. History offers many instances of invasions that seemed at first to be against nature but today are universally accepted. Ethically, the question is whether there is a natural order that we must never disrupt for any reason, a view that many ethicists reject. They seek a → norm for such invasions in their significance for humanity and ultimately for the → environment (→ Environmental Ethics), not primarily in the natural order.

3. Manipulation of People

As regards the manipulation of people, the problem is different, for here → freedom is at issue.

3.1. *Physical*

Physical manipulation involves bodily invasions that might attack or change the personality (→ Person), as in the case of some forms of brain surgery or psychological medications. In this category also is technology as it affects the genes or the embryo.

3.2. *Psychological*

Psychological manipulation is a way of influencing people by implanting desires or ideas, often unconsciously. In extreme cases such intrusion can enfeeble the mind, putting people in a state of disorientation by isolating them socially or sensorially, and confusing them. When handled in this way, people are much more ready to adopt the desired ideas or patterns of → behavior in the hope of being accepted again by those around them. In many cases a change of personality may result. The effect can be heightened by making the manipulated persons "helpers of the helpers," that is, by giving them a share in the manipulation of others, which they will often do to unload their frustrations.

Less intensive but more common practices include public examinations of → conscience, public admissions of guilt, or mutual criticisms and accusations in order to achieve conformity. Totalitarian → societies are familiar with these methods, but sensitivity training uses them in a milder form.

3.3. Social

Social manipulation rests on the fact that we cannot live alone and our conduct is largely shaped by the group in which we live (→ Socialization). If manipulation can bring people into a desired setting (e.g., by forbidding them to join other → organizations), then they can be influenced in the direction of specific modes of conduct or ideas.

Membership of the group and the associated conformity can be stronger if it involves a structure with ranks and functions, so that the members can all advance at least a few stages and thus feel that they are valuable members (→ Hierarchy). Also helpful are collective rituals, ceremonies, songs, banners, and the like, all of which have great powers of suggestion. We have only to think of the Nürnberg rallies of the National Socialist Party (→ Fascism; Radicalism of the Right). Finally, the → aggression of group members may be oriented to outside objects (i.e., scapegoats).

We might also mention propaganda. In its crudest form it consists of lies, half-truths, and misleading images that are set before people. It may also take subtler forms by not expressly presenting the ideas that it seeks to communicate but packaging them in many changing concrete messages in which they are always present as the unexpressed presupposition and may thus be taken for granted. We find all these methods not only in totalitarian societies but also in some modern → sects that especially aim at young people (→ Youth Religions). In a milder and relatively innocent form they are always present, too, where integration into a group is sought (e.g., English public schools, seminaries, military academies, even → congregations).

4. Ethics

Ethically, it will be seen from the above discussion that deliberate manipulation of others is always wrong because it is a form of influencing behavior that takes place without the awareness or consent of those concerned. It is an assault upon their freedom and their basic → rights; any who seek power over them should first secure their agreement. We are of-

ten tempted to justify manipulation on the ground that life in modern → industrial society demands a good deal of discipline, so that some compulsion is unavoidable, even though it may be disliked and resisted. This line of thinking thus helps the authorities to use manipulation (the so-called manipulating of consent) and in this way to evade opposition. The method itself, though, is still undemocratic (→ Democracy) and abhorrent.

5. Defenses

We are not wholly defenseless against psychological and social manipulation. With a strong sense of norms and a powerful → faith, we can resist the practices of persuasion. The training of a critical sense and the maintaining of original group relations are also good weapons against unwanted influencing. Knowing the possibilities of manipulation and its methods is the most important means of defense.

Bibliography: J. A. C. Brown, *Techniques of Persuasion* (Harmondsworth, 1983; orig. pub., 1963) • J. Habermas, *The Structural Transformation of the Public Sphere* (Cambridge, Mass., 1989; orig. pub., 1962) • B. Häring, *Ethik der Manipulation* (Graz, 1977) • L. R. Jacobs, *Politicians Don't Pander: Political Manipulation and the Loss of Democratic Responsiveness* (Chicago, 2000) • G. S. Jowett and V. O'Donnell, *Propaganda and Persuasion* (3d ed.; Newbury Park, Calif., 1999) • W. B. Key, *The Age of Manipulation: The Con in Confidence, the Sin in Sincere* (Lanham, Md., 1993) • A. Koestlers, *Darkness at Noon* (London, 1940) • M. T. Singer and J. Lalich, *Cults in Our Midst* (San Francisco, 1995) • C. R. Smith, *The Quest for Charisma: Christianity and Persuasion* (Westport, Conn., 2000) • D. Tannen, *The Argument Culture: Moving from Debate to Dialogue* (New York, 1998).

JAKOB M. M. DE VALK

Manuscripts, Biblical → Bible Manuscripts and Editions

Mar Thoma Church → India 3; Syrian Orthodox Churches in India

Marcionites

1. Marcion
2. Doctrines
3. Relation to Gnosticism
4. Significance

1. Marcion

Marcion (d. ca. A.D. 160) was a shipowner from Pontus in Asia Minor (from ancient Sinope?). Under Emperor Antoninus Pius (138-61) he tried to win over the Roman church to his understanding of the Christian message. When he failed, he founded his own church (in 144?). His followers called themselves Marcionites.

2. Doctrines

Marcion taught that there are two gods. The anthropomorphic god of the OT is the creator (demiurge) of the world and humanity, with all their faults (→ Creation). As the lawgiver, he is the Just One. The true and essentially good god, the Other, has revealed himself for the first time in → Jesus Christ. By the death of Christ he redeems believers from the power of the demiurge. The OT knows nothing of the good god and should not be read Christologically (→ Allegory). In keeping with the → dualism of the creator and the good god is a negative view of matter and the flesh, also a → Docetic → Christology and a demand for strict → asceticism. Only → souls receive → salvation.

→ Paul was the only → apostle to understand and uphold the → truth. Since Marcion did not accept the OT and regarded church tradition as falsified in a Jewish sense, a new norm of faith had to be found. He found it in Paul's epistles (without the Pastorals) and the → gospel that Paul transmitted directly from Christ, which is in Luke. Even these texts, however, had to be purged of falsifications. With his collection of authoritative Christian writings, Marcion set up the first NT → canon (§2.2). He expounded his teachings in *Antitheses,* a work now lost.

3. Relation to Gnosticism

Marcion's doctrine of two gods and abhorrence of the world linked him to → Gnosis, but his rejection of oral → tradition was a point of difference. His criticism of the OT god and depiction of the good god were under philosophical influence. Marcion, then, can hardly rank as a scriptural theologian. Marcion's most important pupil, Apelles, turned back to monotheism and increased the merging of Marcionite doctrine with Gnosticism and philosophy.

The Marcionites formed a church with an episcopal constitution. At first they offered the catholic church serious competition, but they declined after the third century and survived only in the east, and only up to the fifth century. → Manichaeanism probably absorbed part of them.

4. Significance

Marcion was the first "reformer" in church history. His criticism of the OT and reduction of Christian teaching to a dismembered Paulinism forced the church to defend the OT and to establish its own NT canon. The fight against the Marcionites produced a stricter differentiation from → heresy and a tightening of church teaching and → organization.

→ Early Church

Bibliography: B. ALAND, "Marcion. Versuch einer neuen Interpretation," *ZTK* 70 (1973) 420-47 • D. L. BALÁS, "Marcion Revisited: A 'Post-Harnack' Perspective," *Texts and Testaments* (ed. W. E. March; San Antonio, Tex., 1980) 95-108 • E. C. BLACKMAN, *Marcion and His Influence* (London, 1948) • H. VON CAMPENHAUSEN, *The Formation of the Christian Bible* (London, 1972) 147-65 • D. W. DEAKLE, "The Fathers against Marcionism: A Study of the Methods and Motives in the Developing Patristic Anti-Marcionite Polemic" (Diss., St. Louis, 1991) • H. J. W. DRIJVERS, "Marcionism in Syria: Principles, Problems, Polemics," *SecCent* 6 (1987/88) 153-72 • K. GRESCHAT, *Apelles und Hermogenes. Zwei theologische Lehrer des zweiten Jahrhunderts* (Leiden, 2000) • A. VON HARNACK, *Marcion: The Gospel of the Alien God* (Durham, N.C., 1990; orig. pub., 1923) • G. MAY, "Marcion in Contemporary Views: Results and Open Questions," *SecCent* 6 (1987/88) 129-52 • U. SCHMID, *Marcion und sein Apostolos. Rekonstruktion und historische Einordnung der marcionitischen Paulusbriefausgabe* (Berlin, 1995).

GERHARD MAY

Marginalized Groups

1. Definitions
2. Examples
3. The Role of Institutions
4. Causes
5. The Role of the Church
   5.1. Scripture, Justice, and the Marginalized
   5.2. The Credibility of the Church
   5.3. Church Statements

1. Definitions

Communities or groups are described as marginalized or marginal because of their distance from the centers of political or economic → power or influence, or because of their limited access to the decision-making processes that affect their lives.

Almost every modern-day document on justice refers to the "marginalized," a term used by sociologists and politicians alike. Rapidly expanding international networks of financial power linked to political influence — dramatically demonstrated, for example, by the World Economic Forum, usually held annually in Davos, Switzerland — may have produced a host of new elites, but their growth has been paralleled by an expanding number of marginalized people, those who have little or no financial or political power (→ Economic Ethics).

Who are the marginalized? Decades ago they would have been described as → minorities or unfortunate groups — the poor, the homeless, the vagrants, or dropouts from regular society. Increased social consciousness in the 1960s and 1970s, however, brought new aspects of meaning to the word. Drug addicts (→ Substance Abuse), → homosexuals, → refugees, foreign workers, and the unemployed or unemployable (→ Unemployment) became more evident in Western societies. Few church documents would then have referred to these people as marginalized, even though they were widely known as such in the → mass media and in ordinary conversation. Only women in those decades were beginning to describe themselves as marginalized, leading to the gradual spread of the term to include social and political dimensions.

In the late 1970s and early 1980s these groups began to articulate their situations to wider audiences, most often through the media. No longer were they merely known about; they now were heard. They had their own spokespersons, some of whom achieved international recognition, with their own claims and demands. Their self-description came to be "marginalized."

The nongovernmental forum preceding the U.N. World Conference against → Racism, held in Durban, South Africa, September 2001, has come to be regarded as one of the greatest meetings ever of marginalized people. Participants ranged from indigenous peoples to Dalits from India, from Palestinians to African-Americans, gays and lesbians to trade unionists, disabled African women to refugees and descendants of African slaves. The vast scope of their pleas for justice caused representatives of governments some consternation.

There is a difference between marginal groups and marginalized groups. The former have usually chosen to live on the edge of society. They include young people rejecting a community's social mores, people with political objections to the current administration of a country, or people who choose a → lifestyle that sets them apart (e.g., the Amish). In contrast, the marginalized regard themselves as victims, pawns in other people's political or social games, discarded or ignored.

The link between marginalized groups and mi-

nority groups is interesting. At one time the two words were regarded as synonymous — marginalized groups were thought by definition to be minorities. Not so today. For instance, within the current world economic order the marginalized, the poor, are certainly not the minority. In fact the minority are the ever-diminishing band of wealthy elite.

Some marginalized groups have been created quite deliberately, for example, by government legislation that limits their access to education, social benefits, or housing. Some are marginalized because of attitudes and actions of the majority, a process often carried out, or reinforced, by societies' institutions, including the church and the media.

2. Examples

For a group in a society to be labeled marginalized by those in powerful positions has the effect of rejecting that group, of pushing it to the edges of society. To label oneself marginalized can be a statement of fact, protest, or provocation. It can also be an indication of a deep-seated feeling of powerlessness or unworthiness, as, for instance, when a community or social group knows it is marginalized but chooses to do nothing about it because the people in it feel paralyzed and powerless. As the late South African anti-apartheid activist Steve Biko said, "The greatest weapon in the hands of the oppressor is the mind of the oppressed."

An example of this oppression comes from the history of India. For centuries the so-called Untouchables (who now claim the more positive title "Dalits," meaning "oppressed") actually believed the Brahmins, who decreed that the Untouchables were not worthy to be included within the → caste system (→ Hinduism). Religious injunctions and social mores reinforced this view to the point where, despite the many Dalits who are part of the renaissance of Dalit identity in the last two decades, millons of them still believe they are indeed inferior, deserving of their place at the bottom of the social ladder (→ Class and Social Stratum).

Each → society has a range of marginalized groups, though marginalization because of → poverty is a common feature. There are marginalized people in communities with a high standard of living. Women have historically been marginalized, most often having been denied access to decision-making forums. Other groups are clearly pushed aside, such as people with different sexual orientation from the majority, or people with what are regarded as extreme political views. There are even ironic twists in the understanding of who is marginalized. In South Africa, for example, the majority of the population is in fact marginalized. Ever since the collapse of apartheid there has been an urgent need for increased affirmative action — in education, employment, and economic levels — on behalf of the black majority in order to reverse the imbalance of power and redress the economic control exercised by the white minority.

3. The Role of Institutions

Marginalized groups are created by the majority (or by a powerful minority) who have decided to exclude them. The institutions of society often have a pivotal role in this process, either by imposing or reinforcing the marginalization. For example, a police force that concentrates its patrols in low-income areas, or places where "unacceptable" people live, typically reports a higher percentage of arrests in these places, which become known as high-crime areas. In most Western societies, however, white-collar crime, corporate fraud, and embezzlement are the fastest-growing categories of crime. In 1977 it was estimated that street crime cost the United States $3-4 billion, while white-collar crime cost more than $40 billion; in 1991 a U.S. Justice Department report stated that white collar crime cost up to 25 times more than street crime. Furthermore, it has been pointed out that the American justice system itself often reinforces marginalization: higher sentences for the same crime are frequently given to persons from low-income groups than to persons from a majority or an elite group; white-collar criminals are more likely to receive probation and less likely to receive prison sentences than are criminals from marginalized groups (→ Law and Legal Theory).

Similarly, social welfare institutions often subject marginalized groups to rigorous investigation when determining rights to benefits or privileges, while at the same time making such access easy for middle-class members. Again, local community authorities who decline to translate important legal documents into the languages of the various ethnic groups in the community are almost certainly helping create gaps in society that will lead to some being marginalized.

Since 1997 the British government has been trying to improve its relationship with voluntary groups. A "compact code" was introduced in May 2000, laying down principles for closer consultation regarding matters of public policy between government and community groups. The relationship has improved, but nevertheless there is evidence that black and ethnic groups are still marginalized. The most common complaint has been that groups have not been involved at the earliest stages of consultation.

4. Causes

Sometimes a dramatic or sudden event can trigger the reinforcement of marginalization. The so-called war on terror declared by the United States after the tragic events of September 11, 2001, when powerful symbols of that country were attacked with large loss of life, quickly created an environment of suspicion and discrimination against people, particularly Muslims, from the Middle East. Despite clear statements by government leaders against such discrimination, antagonism has reached a point where families and individuals — many of whom have lived in the United States for many years and who had rarely had a day of fear in their lives — have suddenly experienced uncertainty, pushing them to the edges of their communities.

Sometimes marginalization occurs because of the inability of people within a nation to face up to their own history. Attitudes to indigenous peoples, most often marginalized in their own societies, are a case in point. The marginalization of indigenous peoples went hand in hand with the rejection of their spiritual links and historical memory, even to the point that sometimes the history was rewritten to distort or ignore the role of the indigenous. For example, in Aotearoa–New Zealand most history books before the 1970s portrayed the indigenous Maori as warlike and irresponsible in their dealings with the white settlers. Later histories have more accurately portrayed the Maori as a people who had accepted the Christian gospel call for peace and hospitality to the stranger but who were forced to defend their land and resources under the onslaught of imperial troops and the greed of British settlers. Similarly, historical analysis has shown that the land courts set up by the white settlers to adjudicate land disputes became, in effect, a means for the settlers to confiscate Maori land, since the Maori were rarely able to provide sufficient evidence of their prior ownership of the land. Thus began the history of the marginalization of the Maori in their own land. Modern descendants of the white settlers were never exposed to the realities of this history, and thus the gap between the two races widened, and the marginalization of the Maori in the land that was once their own was increased.

A major, and usually easily recognizable, marginalized group in all societies are → persons with disabilities. Studies in Canada, Great Britain, and the United States have shown that 60 percent of disabled people live below the poverty line, either because state support for them is inadequate or because they have not had access to education or training in skills sufficient for them to be financially independent.

5. The Role of the Church

The → church itself often reinforces the process of marginalization. While affirming the need to help the poor, even using phrases such as "God's preferential option for the poor," churches rarely seek to change their own structures to reflect that priority. Even though the church may seldom create marginalization, it frequently acts in a way that reinforces it by not standing against it or using its prophetic voice to condemn injustice. Marginalized people struggle on two fronts: for access and equality within society, and for their own self-esteem and pride. Churches in all communities have a potentially significant role to play in both areas.

5.1. *Scripture, Justice, and the Marginalized*

The churches' understanding of the marginalized is clearly to be guided by Scripture. The OT understanding of justice is of right relationships with God and with all humankind. → Yahweh is the one who sets the oppressed free, who is with the poor, protecting and defending them. Humans are required to act justly toward each other (Mic. 6:8).

Jesus gave new meaning to this imperative, interpreting the search for and achievement of justice as the expression of God's love for the world and all humankind: "Truly I tell you, just as you did not do [a needed act of justice] to one of the least of these, you did not do it to me" (Matt. 25:45). God's kingdom is revealed as a kingdom of justice, and the church is to be the visible sign of that kingdom, the sign of God's acceptance and love for all people.

These gospel directives clearly indicate that the churches' search for renewal and → unity must be bound up with a similar desire for justice in which none are despised or rejected. "In the context of covenant, justice is not a forensic term having to do with the right behavior of the covenant community. The acid test of right behavior is whether or not the justice due to the poor and oppressed is secured" (P. Niles, 70).

5.2. *The Credibility of the Church*

Cruel realities, however, have interrupted the church in its fulfillment of this vocation. In some countries the church is a political force or influence, embracing large sections of the population. Yet its own hierarchical structure has fostered pride and ambition, and in many instances its missionary outreach has been an ally of the process of colonization or even enslavement (→ Colonialism and Mission). Often, despite good intentions, church actions have been at the side of the powerful, and it has shown too little concern to relate to the poor and marginalized.

Most churches face a huge credibility gap: proclaiming solidarity with the poor, while building cathedrals "to the glory of God"; standing alongside the oppressed, while dining with the oppressors; bringing words of comfort to the homeless and the unemployed, while failing to challenge those within its own membership involved in trade deals, property speculations, or commodity transactions that widen the gap between rich and poor. The churches' understanding of their relationship to the marginalized, in their many different contexts, is a test of their commitment to genuine church renewal.

5.3. *Church Statements*

Official statements of the churches regarding their relationship to the marginalized have been unambiguous. The Second → Vatican Council's Pastoral Constitution on the Church in the Modern World, *Gaudium et spes* (1965), forcefully condemns a number of crimes and attacks against human life. "All violations of the integrity of the human person, such as mutilation, physical and mental torture, undue psychological pressures; all offenses against human dignity, such as subhuman living conditions, arbitrary imprisonment, deportation, slavery, prostitution, the selling of women and children, degrading working conditions where [people] are treated as mere tools for profit rather than free and responsible persons: all these and the like are criminal. They poison civilization; and they debase the perpetrators more than the victims and militate against the honor of the creator" (§27). The same condemnation was repeated in John Paul II's 1995 encyclical *Evangelium vitae*.

Several years earlier, in 1948, the First Assembly of the → World Council of Churches (WCC), meeting in Amsterdam, understood those same sentiments. In its founding statement it asserted, "We have to learn afresh together to speak boldly in Christ's name, both to those in power and the people, to oppose terror, cruelty and race discrimination, to stand by the outcaste, the prisoner and the refugee. We have to make the church in every place a voice for those who have no voice and a home where everyone will be at home."

In 1986 at a world consultation in Larnaca, Cyprus, the churches of the WCC faced the challenge of how best to share their resources. They concluded, "On every continent — at a time of increased terrorism and violence — the people are now struggling for life, for justice and for peace . . . the polarisation and fragmentation which we see in many forms on all continents threatens the survival of us all. . . . We recognise that justice will not be given by the powerful until and unless the powerless stand together. We know that God is with those

401

struggling for justice and peace, and we know in our hearts — if not in our actions — that our place must be with them."

These commitments culminated in the WCC's eighth assembly, held in 1998 in Harare, Zimbabwe. The message of this assembly noted, "We are challenged by the vision of a church that will reach out to everyone, sharing, caring, proclaiming the good news of God's redemption, a sign of the kingdom and a servant of the world. . . . We are challenged by the vision of a church, the people of God on the way together, confronting all divisions of race, gender, age or culture, striving to realize justice and peace, upholding the integrity of creation."

In a homily preached in Johannesburg in 1995, John Paul II emphasized solidarity with marginalized peoples. "Solidarity must be fostered among States, but also within every society where a process of de-humanization and the disintegration of the social fabric undeniably aggravates racist and xenophobic attitudes and behavior. This negative process results in the rejection of the weakest, be it the foreigner, the handicapped or the homeless. Solidarity must be based upon the unity of the human family, because all people, created in the image and likeness of God, have the same origin and are called to the same destiny." These words were repeated in 2001 in the Vatican statement to the U.N. World Conference against Racism.

Many individual congregations and parishes continue to provide help to marginalized groups. There are outstanding examples of Christian witness in programs of congregational support for the homeless, for victims of social abuse, for those with HIV/AIDS, and for uprooted people in conflict situations. Few churches, however, have successfully initiated movements to bring about dramatic change in the status of the marginalized — to restore or reassert their place in the societies that have pushed them to the margins. The role of the church as servant, a gospel imperative, may be understood in a sermon, a soup kitchen, a church welfare agency, or a truckload of emergency aid. But it continues to need interpretation in the councils of the churches that exclude the marginalized from their own decision-making structures.

Bibliography: S. AMIRTHAM, *Stories Make People: Examples of Theological Work in Community* (Geneva, 1989) • J. ANDRÉ, *The Stranger within Your Gates: Uprooted People in the World Today* (Geneva, 1986) • M. ELLINGSEN, *The Cutting Edge: How Churches Speak on Social Issues* (Grand Rapids, 1993) • E. G. FERRIS, *Beyond Borders: Refugees, Migrants, and Human Rights in the post–Cold War Era* (Geneva, 1993) • D. B. FORRESTER, *On Human Worth: A Christian Vindication of Equality* (London, 2001) • H. JUSSILA, R. MAJORAL, and F. DELGADO-CRAVIDÃO, eds., *Globalization and Marginality in Geographical Space: Political, Economic, and Social Issues of Development in the New Millennium* (Aldershot, 2001) • C. MILLS and G. COLES, eds., *Life on the Edge: Human Settlement and Marginality* (Oxford, 1998) • P. NILES, *Resisting the Threats to Life: Covenanting for Justice, Peace, and the Integrity of Creation* (Geneva, 1989) • K. RAISER, *To Be the Church: Challenges and Hopes for a New Millennium* (Geneva, 1997) • M. VINCENT and B. R. SORENSEN, eds., *Caught between Borders: Response Strategies of the Internally Displaced* (London, 2001).

BOB SCOTT

Mariavites

1. Origin and History
2. Distinctives

The Mariavites (from Lat. *qui Mariae vitam imitantur,* "who imitate the life of Mary") stress veneration of the Virgin.

1. Origin and History

In Płock in 1893 Felicia Kozlowska (1862-1921), of the order of the Poor Clares (→ Franciscans) and at the instigation of priest Jan Kowalski (1871-1942), founded an order of secular → priests who did extensive social work (→ Religious Life). Persecuted by the → hierarchy and proscribed by Rome, the group, calling itself Mariavites, formed an independent church in 1906. In 1909 it joined the Utrecht Union of → Old Catholic Churches, and later that year Kowalski was consecrated bishop.

In 1924, because of scandal about the group's teaching on "mystical" marriages of priests and nuns and its reinterpretation of the → Mass, the Utrecht Union severed relations. In 1935 the General Synod deposed then archbishop Kowalski.

Since that time two organizations have survived: the Old Catholic Church of the Mariavites (or Old Catholic Mariavite Church in Poland), which did not follow Kowalski but returned to the original principles (25,000 members in the year 2000), and the Catholic Mariavite Church, Kowalski's supporters (5,000 members).

2. Distinctives

The Old Catholic Church of the Mariavites confesses the original, unaltered, universal faith and church order of the ancient, undivided church of the first century. Special attention is paid to the → Eucharist and to invocation of the mother of God and her unfailing help, both of which it regards as the source of church revival. It recognizes the dogma of the immaculate conception of → Mary (→ Mariology). It finds no place for auricular confession (→ Penitence), priestly → celibacy, or → relics. In 1969 it became a member of the → World Council of Churches, and after 1972 it came into limited communion with the Utrecht Union.

The Catholic Mariavite Church honors Felicia Kozlowska as the bride and spouse of Christ. For several years it has been ordaining women priests and bishops.

Bibliography: O. CHADWICK, *A History of the Popes, 1830-1914* (New York, 1998) 529-32 • K. P. FELDMANN, *Die Altkatholische Kirche der Mariaviten* (Płock, 1940) • J. PETERKIEWICZ, *The Third Adam* (London, 1975) • B. STASIEWSKI, "Mariavites," *NCE* 9.217-18 • W. WYSOCZAŃSKI, "Die altkatholische Kirche," *Ökumene in Polen* (East Berlin, 1982) 34-48.

KAROL KARSKI

Mariology

1. Content and Problems
    1.1. Devotion to Mary and Mariology
    1.2. Traditions of Mariology
    1.3. Mariological Dogmas
    1.4. Vatican II
    1.5. Ecumenical Problems
2. Historical Development
    2.1. Early Church
    2.2. Middle Ages
    2.3. Reformation and Protestantism
    2.4. Post-Tridentine Roman Catholicism
    2.5. Vatican II
    2.6. Orthodox Church
    2.7. Mariology in Ecumenical Dialogue

1. Content and Problems

1.1. Devotion to Mary and Mariology

The NT witness names Mary as the mother of → Jesus of Nazareth (see Matt. 1:16, 18, 20; 2:11, 13; 12:46; 13:55; Mark 3:31; 6:3; Luke 1:26-56; 2:4-7, 16, 19, 34, 48, 51; 8:19; John 2:1, 3, 5, 12; 6:42; 19:25-26). In the Roman Catholic tradition, believers' devotion to Mary finds expression in acts of trust, thanksgiving, praise, invocation, and intercession, as well as in liturgical actions and canticles, statues, other artistic and literary representations, feast days and shrines, and imitation of her exemplary life (→

Mary, Devotion to). To be distinguished from these expressions are the theological reflections that seek to anchor popular → devotion in the church's teaching and that issue in binding dogmatic statements that are designed to safeguard "Marian truth." The upshot of these reflections is a comprehensive presentation of Mary in Roman Catholic systematic theology.

1.2. Traditions of Mariology

Often in the tradition of Reformation theology Mary is featured as a submissive and serving figure. She is acknowledged as the mother of Jesus and calls forth attention because of her significance for the person and work of the Son of God, as we read in the → Apostles' Creed (". . . born of the Virgin Mary"). While High Church movements, especially in the → Anglican tradition, offer some praise to Mary along with the beginnings of a doctrine of Mary, there is also widespread rejection of Marian devotion and a basic suspicion of any special Mariology or Marian dogmas (see 2.3).

In the Orthodox doctrinal tradition statements about Mary have no direct dogmatic function (→ Orthodox Church; Orthodox Christianity). Mary has a place only within reflection on the mystery of the → incarnation and the communion of the → church on earth with the church in heaven. As the God-bearer *(theotokos)*, she has a prominent position in the event of salvation, and to the communion of saints she, as the all holy *(panagia)*, offers an example of faith, love, humility, and → obedience (see 2.2).

In Roman Catholic teaching, however, the doctrine of Mary became an independent locus in → dogmatics that methodically sets forth Marian truth and links it to such other doctrinal statements as those concerning Christ, the church, → grace, and the consummation. Mariological systematics articulates the inner connection between Mariological belief and the whole cosmos of the faith. The Marian dogmas that it unfolds rank as inerrant exposition of the revelation in Christ. Both materially and structurally, they articulate the essential mysteries of faith, so that Mary can be regarded as the supreme exhibiter of Catholic belief.

In contrast, Latin American → liberation theology profiles Mary as embodying the prototype of creation as it is liberated by Christ. The Magnificat (Luke 1:46-55) thinks along the lines of the oppressed poor and inspires us to give concrete shape to the messianic reality (→ Mary, Devotion to, 3).

In → feminist theology, reflection on the person and significance of Mary offers critical starting points for a fresh understanding of the faith, for a creative attitude of faith, and for the overcoming of traditional patriarchal structures in thinking and church life. The protest of a liberation Mariology owes much to the Magnificat. Mary's "fiat" in Luke 1:38 ("let it be [Vg *fiat*] with me according to your word"; → Mary, Devotion to, 2) motivates a break from fixed roles in thought and action and a move toward a future inspired by a life-giving prophetic vision.

1.3. *Mariological Dogmas*

Roman Catholic Mariology rests on four Marian dogmas: (1) the divine motherhood *(theotokos)* of Mary (Council of → Ephesus, 431; DH 252); (2) the virgin conception and Mary's perpetual virginity (Gk. *aeiparthenos,* Lat. *semper virgo,* Second Council of Constantinople, 553; DH 422; → Councils of the Church); (3) Mary's immaculate conception and sinlessness (→ Pius IX, 1854; DH 2803); and (4) her bodily assumption into heaven (Pius XII, 1950; DH 3903).

1.3.1. Mary is called the God-bearer, or Mother of God, because according to the flesh the incarnate divine Logos was born of her (DH 252). As the physical mother of Jesus, Mary was the human presupposition for the union of the human and the divine in the person of Christ (→ Christology). She thus has a part in the mystery of the incarnation. Her unique relation to the event of the incarnation serves to show how the supernatural has taken concrete form in the natural (→ Grace 3). It sets forth the embodiment of → salvation, the reality of God's saving work in history, and the need for a free human response to that grace (→ Soteriology).

As the handmaiden of the Lord who receives grace (Luke 1:38) and as the first of the redeemed, Mary has a twofold soteriological function. As "mediatrix" (*Lumen gentium* [*LG*] 62.1), she has a part in the work of the Redeemer, although the use of this term "neither takes away anything from nor adds anything to the dignity and efficacy of Christ the one Mediator" (ibid.). Second, as a "preeminent and . . . wholly unique member of the church" (§53), Mary represents (→ Representation) the fellowship of the redeemed (→ Church 3.2.2). By virtue of her privileged position and significance in → salvation history and the → order of salvation, Mary is, on the one hand, a type of the historically mediated saving work of Christ (the Christotypical Mary) and, on the other hand, a type of the historically lived-out motherhood of the church (the ecclesiotypical Mary). The one way of looking enhances Mary, the other the church.

1.3.2. The doctrine of the virginity of Mary combines three elements: the biological condition (Luke 1:34), the spiritual attitude as one of exclusive dedication to God (1:38), and the bestowal of conception by the Spirit without a human father (Matt. 1:18-25). This Marian mystery can be interpreted as an event in salvation history and also symbolically. In describing her perpetual virginity, tradition speaks of Mary's virginity before, in, and after the birth of Jesus *(ante partum, in partu, post partum).* In combination, these various aspects produce an understanding of the virgin conception as the beginning of the new creation, the event of a fresh start in salvation history, the sign of the absolute openness and surrender of the creature to the Creator, and the expression of active reception of salvation.

In the typology of Mary and the church, the virginity relates both spiritually and physically to the church. Spiritual virginity, a total dedication of faith, is imitated and continued by the church as it keeps its faith intact and gives birth to Christ in the hearts of believers. The physical virginity, the supreme gift of grace (*LG* 42.3), finds expression in a → celibate lifestyle (Marriage and Divorce 1.5.1; Vow) among priests, monks, and nuns and in restraint at every level (1 Cor. 7:32-34). Along with motherhood, virginity is a paradigm of faith and → discipleship. It shapes the Marian faith of the church and supplements the hierarchical structure (→ Hierarchy).

1.3.3. The immaculate conception, which sheds further light on the Marian mystery, asserts that at the very first moment of her conception, Mary remained pure of every stain of sin (DH 2803). It involves Mary's liberation from original → sin from the moment of her conception in the womb of her mother, as well as her preservation from the dominion of sin all her earthly life. The biblical texts offer no basis for this thesis. It rests on the consideration that in accordance with the primacy of grace, Mary's redemption must precede her life in grace, since otherwise there could be no original relationship to God. The thesis makes it possible to regard Mary as in a special Trinitarian relationship (→ Trinity). Hence the fact of biological motherhood is less prominent than the idea that from eternity God chose Mary as the medium of the incarnation of Christ (*LG* 61).

In the typology of Mary and the church, the perfect sinlessness of Mary functions as a prototype and model for the church. In the Blessed Virgin the church has already reached perfection, and believers in Christ are to make every effort to increase in holiness (*LG* 65).

1.3.4. The dogma of the assumption relates to

the end of Mary's temporal existence. It states that at the end of her earthly course, Mary was assumed body and soul into heavenly glory (DH 3902). Most closely related to her divine Son as his helper (*socia*, DH 3900, 3902), Mary reached the goal of the redemptive work of Christ in salvation history before others. This thesis, which also has no biblical basis, derives logically from the first three, and especially from the third, which relates to the sinless beginning of Mary's life (see Rom. 6:23).

Ecclesiologically, the glorified Mary points to the eschatological character of the church, through which union with God and the renewal of the world go forward (*LG* 48.1-2). This thesis establishes the union of the pilgrim church with the heavenly church, the beatified, and the → saints (§4, *LG* 49-50). It confirms "certain hope and comfort to the pilgrim people of God" (§68).

1.4. *Vatican II*

The dogmatic constitution *Lumen gentium* of → Vatican II integrates Marian doctrine into a presentation of the nature and universal mission of the church (§§52-59). This first comprehensive statement of the magisterium on the theme of Mary and Mariology lays down the basic points of systematic Mariology: the position and task of Mary in the economy of salvation, her predestination, the mysteries of her life, and the relation between Mary and the church. The Marian dogmas are set within the total context of salvation history and linked in such a way to Christological and ecclesiological statements that the dogmatic attributes of Mary shed light on the mystery of Christ and the church.

Bibliography: W. BEINERT and H. PETRI, eds., *Handbuch der Marienkunde* (Regensburg, 1984) • J. B. CAROL, *Mariology* (3 vols.; Milwaukee, Wis., 1955-61) • Y. CONGAR, *Christ, Our Lady, and the Church: A Study in Eirenic Theology* (Westminster, Md., 1957) • D. DONNELLY, ed., *Mary, Woman of Nazareth: Biblical and Theological Perspectives* (New York, 1989) • I. GEBARA and M. C. BINGEMER, *Mary, Mother of God, Mother of the Poor* (Maryknoll, N.Y., 1989) • G. MIEGGE, *The Virgin Mary: The Roman Catholic Marian Doctrine* (Philadelphia, 1953) • H. A. OBERMAN, *The Virgin Mary in Evangelical Perspective* (Philadelphia, 1971) • J. PELIKAN, *Mary through the Centuries: Her Place in the History of Culture* (New Haven, 1996) • E. SCHILLEBEECKX and C. HALKES, *Mary: Yesterday, Today, Tomorrow* (New York, 1993) • O. SEMMELROTH, *Mary, Archetype of the Church* (New York, 1963) • M. THURIAN, *Mary, Mother of the Lord, Figure of the Church* (London, 1963).

ERWIN FAHLBUSCH

1.5. *Ecumenical Problems*

The two Roman Catholic Marian dogmas of 1854 (immaculate conception) and 1950 (bodily assumption) complicate → ecumenical dialogue on Mary. However, the teaching of John XXIII that the deposit of faith may be expressed in a variety of dogmatic formulas opens the way to the reception of the truths they are meant to undergird by other means. Thus British Methodists, in their dialogue with Roman Catholics, have taken the position that they can accept the truths regarding Mary about grace for a unique vocation and eschatological destiny that the dogmas are meant to illuminate, even though they are unable to subscribe to the dogmas as stated because of the lack of a clear, biblical basis. Joseph Cardinal Ratzinger, since 1981 prefect of the Vatican's Congregation for the Doctrine of the Faith (→ Curia 1.2.2), has taken the position that the Orthodox are not obliged to accept these two dogmas in the precise Roman form adopted after the Great Schism of 1054. Other Roman Catholics, however, might take a stronger line in insisting on the reception of the two disputed dogmas.

Ecumenical objections to these two dogmas are various. The Orthodox object to their having been defined by Rome in separation from → councils of the whole church. Additionally, they do not share the understanding of "original sin" that led to the theologoumenon and later → dogma of the immaculate conception. The Orthodox, however, frequently do invoke the prayers of the "Mother of God," believe her to be "all holy," and hold her in the highest esteem (→ Orthodox Church).

Protestants affirm the credal statements of the → virgin birth as scripturally based, but many question belief in the perpetual virginity of Mary as apparently contradicting the teaching of Scripture about the "brothers" (or even, in Alexandrinus and Bezae, "brothers and sisters") of the Lord (Mark 3:32 and par.). They also contest the dogmas of the immaculate conception and the bodily assumption as lacking any clear scriptural witness or even attestation in the earliest levels of → tradition. Many Protestants fear that Roman Catholic teaching and, even more, popular devotion to Mary obscure the sole mediatorship of Christ. They are particularly worried by suggestions in some contemporary circles that the pope should solemnize Mary as "Mediator of all Graces" or even as "Co-Redemptrix." At a congress of Mariologists in Częstochowa, Poland, in 1996, Orthodox, Anglican, and Protestant participants warned of the ecumenical danger of any such solemn definition. This view was echoed by most of the Roman Catholics present.

In recent years many Protestants have conceded that the traditional Protestant reaction against Marian piety has led to the opposite danger of neglecting the few but highly significant points that the NT itself makes in presenting Mary as one who is a paradigm of → obedience to the Word of God (Luke 1:38), as a true contemplative (2:19, 51), and as one whom "all generations will call . . . blessed" (1:48). Two recent dialogues (Catholic-Methodist in England and Catholic-Reformed in France) have pointed to the possibility of a convergent Marian piety that fully recognizes her role in → salvation history and her significance as a paradigm of obedience while at the same time safeguarding the unique mediatorship of Christ and affirming that all in Mary is of God's grace. She is as much in need of → salvation as anyone else, a point that Roman Catholics say is affirmed by the dogma of the immaculate conception, according to which she receives the gift of salvation in advance of the atoning death of her Son.

Ecumenical dialogue on Mary relates to many of the key issues that have traditionally divided Roman Catholics from other churches, namely, Scripture and tradition, the nature of the church's → teaching office, and anthropological questions of → sin and → grace. Despite remaining difficulties linked to all such questions, there is no doubt that today Roman Catholics understand Protestant reservations about excessive Marian piety, and Protestants understand the Christological basis of Catholic Marian doctrine, considerably more clearly than was once the case.

Bibliography: R. E. BROWN, K. P. DONFRIED, J. A. FITZMYER, and J. REUMANN, eds., *Mary in the NT: A Collaborative Assessment by Protestant and Roman Catholic Scholars* (Philadelphia, 1978).

DAVID CARTER

2. Historical Development

The history of piety and the development of doctrine give evidence of the historical character of Marian theses and dogmas. According to the sources, methods, and goals that are selected, the doctrine of Mary may be called biblical, patristic, scholastic, positive, academic, or popular. Mariological ways of thinking tend to be either Christotypical, in which case Mary has her own saving function, or ecclesiotypical, in which case she is a prototype and model for the → church.

2.1. *Early Church*

The biblical witness mentions Mary only in relation to the mystery of Christ (Gal. 4:4-5; Mark 3:31-35; 6:1-6; Matt. 1:18-25; 2:11; Luke 1:26-56; 2:1-35, 41-51; 11:27-28; John 2:1-11; 19:25-27; Acts 1:14; →

Mary in the New Testament). The first Christian references stress Mary's role in the economy of salvation as the counterpart to that of Eve, → Justin Martyr (ca. 100-ca. 165) speaking of a kind of recapitulation of what happened in Eden (*Dial.* 100), and → Irenaeus (ca. 130-ca. 200) describing a "recirculation" from Mary back to Eve (*Adv. haer.* 3.22.4). From the time of the Council of → Nicaea in 325, we increasingly find the title *theotokos,* "God-bearer," for Mary. The first known instance is in Alexander of Alexandria (d. 328) in 325 (*PG* 18.568C, see also 82.908A), though an earlier version of the antiphon *Sub tuum praesidium* (ca. 300, the oldest known prayer to Mary), entitled *Theotokos,* is very close to a text that could well be older.

→ Origen (ca. 185-ca. 254; → Origenism), Basil (ca. 330-79), Gregory of Nazianzus (329/30-389/90; → Cappadocian Fathers), John → Chrysostom (ca. 347-407), and → Cyril of Alexandria (ca. 375-444) all speak of Mary's moral imperfection (vanity and lack of faith). Epiphanius (ca. 315-403) in 377 sharply censures the female priesthood of the Collyridians (from *kollyris,* "little bread, cake") for offering bread to Mary in pagan fashion (*PG* 42.735-54).

Along with general belief in conception by the → Holy Spirit, some Fathers and authors found in Mary a model for families with many children in order to counter the → Manichaean thesis that → marriage is evil. → Tertullian (ca. 160-ca. 225) and → Jerome (ca. 345-420) emphasize the normal character of Mary's marriage in answer to the teaching of the → Docetists that Christ had only the appearance of a body. Statements about Mary thus stand in the service of → Christology. From the fifth century onward we find no doubts as to Mary's being a virgin even in her giving birth (*virginitas in partu*). Greek and Latin authors extol it as a truth that serves orthodox faith in the incarnation as God's work.

From the time of the Council of Ephesus in 431 to the Gregorian reforms of 1050, many feasts to Mary were established. The first in the East was that of the Theotokos (4th cent.). The number soon grew to include feasts for the conception of Mary, on December 8 (from the end of the 7th and beginning of the 8th cents.); her birth, on September 8 (early 6th cent.); her dedication, on November 21 (end of 7th cent.); and her assumption, on August 15 (5th cent.). In the West the first feast, that of the God-bearer, dates from between the end of the 5th and the beginning of the 7th century (last Sunday in Advent, December 18, or January 1). Later, other feasts were taken over from the East (→ Church

Year 2.1-2): the purification, on February 2; the assumption, on August 15; the annunciation, on March 25; and the birth of Mary, on September 8.

In the liturgical context of church life, theological reflection flourished regarding Mary as the Lord's mother, as the extraordinary saint, as the one who was assumed into heaven, and as the one who helps brothers and sisters in the Lord. Orthodoxy and Roman → Catholicism both testify to the prominence of this liturgical Mariology that resulted from the church's faith.

In the fourth century, perhaps even the third, invocation of Mary began, as we see from the text beginning "Under thy protection. . . ." After the Council of Ephesus the role of Mary relative to the role of humankind received increasing stress. Gregory of Nazianzus was the first to call martyrs mediators (*mesiteuousi*, in *Or. theol.* 11.5, to Gregory of Nyssa [*PG* 35.837C]). Among the company of holy mediators the Fathers gave Mary a place of special prominence. The first sure instance of the use of "mediator" for Mary is in Andrew of Crete (ca. 660-740), who referred to Mary as the "Mediatrix [*mesitis*] of the law and grace" and stated that "she is the mediation between the sublimity of God and the abjection of the flesh" (*PG* 97.808B, 865A).

2.2. *Middle Ages*

In the West theological reflection on Mary focused more on Mary alone, and it took a more speculative turn than one focused more on → prayer or → liturgy. In the early 9th century, Pseudo-Jerome (likely Paschasius Radbertus [ca. 790-ca. 860]) questioned the growing belief in the bodily assumption of Mary into heaven (*Ep.* 9). In the middle of the century the book *Mediatrix* came out as a Latin translation of the Greek original *Life of Theophilus*, written by Paul the Deacon (ca. 720-ca. 800), but gained wide circulation only in the 12th century.

The idea of spiritual motherhood occurs sporadically in the 5th century, but only in the indirect sense that Mary is the mother of believers as the mother of Christ, the Head (→ Augustine), and the mother of the living only as she bore Christ, our life (Peter Chrysologus). In the 10th century there appeared for the first time the title *mater misericordiae,* Mother of Mercy (John of Salerno, *Vita Sancti Odonis* 2.20 [*PL* 133.724B]), which relates to the divine motherhood (the Mother of Christ the Merciful) or the spiritual motherhood (Merciful Mother). In the 10th century the Litany of the Saints, which was of French origin and which occurs in the Psalter of Salisbury Cathedral, contained for the first time the title "Redemptrix," which was, however, not widely adopted.

From the time of the Gregorian reforms in 1050 to the Council of → Trent in 1563, we find more clearly the Mariology of preachers as well as the Mariology of theologians. Theologians plainly differentiated the mediatorship of Christ as a redemptive and completely independent mediatorship (*mediator redemptionis*) from that of creatures, among them Mary, which influences the disposition and is thus a dispositive and serving mediatorship (*mediatio dispositive et ministerialiter*) and is always dependent on the one Mediator, being wholly subject to him (*mediatores secondarii*). Preachers, however, disseminated a teaching and piety that were barely compatible with the truth of the one perfect Mediator. They took it that Mary shared in the sufferings of the cross and championed the efficacy of her merciful intercession, often in contrast with the severity of Christ the Judge (e.g., Bernard of Clairvaux and Bernardine of Siena).

→ Bernard (1090-1153), → Thomas Aquinas (ca. 1225-74; → Thomism), Bonaventure (ca. 1217-74), and most medieval theologians rejected the immaculate conception of Mary as irreconcilable with the universal nature of original → sin and redemption (→ Reconciliation). The introduction of the idea of a more perfect redemption by the preservation of Mary from the fall into original sin (so Duns Scotus [ca. 1265-1308]) helped to spread the doctrine, which → Pius IX (1846-78) finally promulgated as a dogma in his bull *Ineffabilis Deus* in 1854.

From the time of → Anselm of Canterbury (1033-1109), the father of → Scholasticism, an academic Mariology developed, but it did not endow Mary with any independent significance. In Peter Lombard (ca. 1100-1160), Aquinas, Bonaventura, and Duns Scotus (→ Scotism), Mariology became the crown of Christology.

2.3. *Reformation and Protestantism*

The Reformers protested against what they regarded as the abuse of Mariology. Martin → Luther (1483-1546; → Luther's Theology) neither greatly venerated Mary nor opposed her veneration. He accepted the biblical testimonies to Mary, writing an exposition of the Magnificat (*LW* 21.295-355). He also accepted the Mariological statements of the early creeds and the Council of Ephesus. It was an incontestable and abiding merit of the Reformers to point decisively to the Christological basis of both Mariology and devotion to Mary, and to stress the exemplary nature of Mary's faith (ecclesiotypical model).

The Protestant attitude to the mother of the Lord gives evidence of *particulae exclusivae* (i.e., thinking in mutually exclusive terms; → Reformation Principles) and of → polemics against Romanism. It usually does not oppose Eastern Orthodoxy, however, even though in many ways (e.g., in the theology of → icons) Orthodoxy goes further than Roman Catholicism (→ Orthodox Christianity). → Protestantism rejects the dogmas of the immaculate conception and the bodily assumption of Mary into heaven as unbiblical and as incompatible with the principles of grace alone and faith alone. It finds no place for cultic veneration of Mary, though admitting that we should deeply respect and extol her and follow the example of her faith. Mary is not to be invoked because the Bible does not tell us to do so and because the practice easily gives rise to abuses. Some Protestants might say something more positive about Mary and show more devotion to her if they had their own hagiology (M. Lackmann), if Roman Catholics did not put them off by exaggerations, and if they had more concern to testify to the truth than to protest against Roman Catholics (R. Schimmelpfennig, H. Asmussen; → Denomination 5).

2.4. Post-Tridentine Roman Catholicism

In the period after the Council of Trent, Roman Catholic Mariology was polemical as developed by the first great → Jesuit theologians in Spain: Alfonso Salmerón (1515-85) and Francisco Suárez (1548-1617), who published the first systematic Mariology in 1590. Similar writings appeared in Italy by Robert → Bellarmine (1542-1621), in Germany by Peter Canisius (1521-97), and in Poland by Justyn of Miechau (d. 1689). Much earlier John Gerson (1363-1429) in his "Epistola cancellarii Parisiensis de susceptione humanitatis Christi allegorica et tropologica" (Opera 1 [Paris 1606] 451ff.) had raised the question of a basic principle of Mariology from which one might deduce the other theses and thus construct a logical and coherent tractate on Mary.

In the 17th century, the so-called golden age of Mariology, F. Q. Salazar (1575-1646) developed the thesis of Mary's active participation in redemption. The French school, with the more sober Cardinal Pierre de Bérulle (1575-1629), the more emotional Jean-Jacques Olier (1608-57), and Jean Eudes (1601-80), helped to develop a "Mariology of the heart" and the so-called Marian piety. In much the same direction we find the idea of becoming slaves of Mary (F. S. Fenicki, Mariae mancipium [1632]; Bartholomaeus de los Rios, De hierarchia mariana [1641]). The popular revelations of Maria de Agreda (1602-65, La mystica ciudad de Dios [1670]) contained many apocryphal elements (→ Popular Catholicism). The doctrine of the mediatorship and divine motherhood gained ground, although protests against excesses came from Ludovico Antonio

Muratori (1672-1750) under the pseudonym Lamindus Pritanius and from A. Widenfeld (Monita salutaria [1673]), who came under sharp criticism for supposed disrespect for Mary. In the spirit of the Monita, → Jansenism replaced the annunciation with a feast for Christ, as Vatican II would later do as well.

Less circumspect was the promotion of an extreme Mariology of the heart by Jacques Bénigne Bossuet (1627-1704) and Louis-Marie Grignion de Montfort (1673-1716), whose tractate on full devotion to Mary (1842) still inspires people to become slaves of Mary and to commit themselves wholeheartedly to her (Polish World War II martyr Maximilian Kolbe and John Paul II are two modern examples). In his Le glorie di Maria (1750) Alphonsus Liguori (1696-1787) proclaimed a maximalist, popular Mariology based on belief in a general mediation of grace through her. This work was used by preachers up to Vatican II, with over 1,000 editions in many different languages. It evoked further serious reservations among Roman Catholic theologians and sharper protests from Protestants.

The dogma of the immaculate conception that Pius IX promulgated in 1854 holds that the Blessed Virgin Mary "was, from the first moment of her conception, by the singular grace and privilege of almighty God and in view of the merits of Jesus Christ the Savior of the human race, preserved free from all stain of original sin." Whereas earlier this dogma was interpreted as a marvelous privilege for Mary, it is now regarded as the perfect triumph of redemptive grace in her (sola gratia).

The first half of the 20th century was marked by a vigorous movement for a proclamation of the mediatorship (esp. urged by Cardinal D. Mercier) and the assumption (esp. by C. Balić) of Mary. In 1950, then, in the apostolic constitution Munificentissimus Deus, Pius XII (1939-58) promulgated the dogma of the assumption of Mary — that after the completion of her earthly life, she was assumed, in body and soul, into heavenly glory. This maximalist Mariology placed "a new jewel in Mary's crown," while ecclesiotypical Mariology found testimony to the glory of redemptive grace. There has been completed in Mary that to which the pilgrim church has not yet attained.

2.5. Vatican II

→ Vatican II, after rejecting those who wanted a separate and more developed Marian decree, placed Mariology in Lumen gentium, the Dogmatic Constitution on the Church (chap. 8, "Our Lady"). It deals with Mariology from the standpoint of salvation history rather than conceptually, in the context of the mystery of Christ and the church. It handles the doctrine of mediatorship with great caution, warning against excesses in both teaching and practice. The council tried to harmonize a Christotypical Mariology, which stresses Mary's similarity to Christ, with an ecclesiotypical Mariology, which presents Mary as a prototype of the church.

Paul VI (1963-78), in his apostolic exhortation *Marialis cultus* (1974), laid down principles for a renewing of devotion to Mary: it must have a Trinitarian character, must point to Christ and the Holy Spirit, must stimulate imitation of the faith of Mary and lead to the Christian life (ecclesiotypical aspect), must be clearly subject to the Bible and the liturgy, and must take note of contemporary → anthropology and the demands of → ecumenism. In his encyclical *Redemptoris Mater* (1987) John Paul II defended traditional Marian piety but also showed along what lines one must correct the doctrine of mediatorship (maintaining mediatorship in Christ and the Holy Spirit).

2.6. Orthodox Church

The Mariology of Eastern Orthodoxy is doxological (→ Doxology), not academic. It comes to expression in praise, as in liturgical poetry (→ Hymnology), and in the art and veneration of icons. An example of the linking of Christology and Mariology, the hymn → Acathistus focuses on the mystery of the incarnation. More recent Orthodox Mariology underlines the close link between Mary and the Holy Spirit. Sergius Bulgakov (1871-1944), for example, calls Mary *pneumatophora*, or "Spirit-bearer." The → church fathers play a prominent role in Orthodox Mariology. The churches of the East highly venerate her who was conceived immaculately and assumed into heaven (the "dormition," or falling asleep [Lat. *dormitio*]), but they do not acknowledge the Roman Catholic dogmas of 1854 and 1950.

Bibliography: R. Bäumer and L. Scheffczyk, eds., *Marienlexikon* (6 vols.; St. Ottilien, 1988-94) • W. Beinert and H. Petri, eds., *Handbuch der Marienkunde* (Regensburg, 1984) • S. Benko, *The Virgin Goddess: Studies in the Pagan and Christian Roots of Mariology* (Leiden, 1993) • P. Boyce, ed., *Mary: The Virgin Mary in the Life and Writings of John Henry Newman* (Grand Rapids, 2001) • W. Delius, *Geschichte der Marienverehrung* (Munich, 1963) • H. Graef, *Mary: A History of Doctrine and Devotion* (2d ed.; London, 1985) • R. Laurentin, *Queen of Heaven: A Short Treatise on Marian Theology* (Dublin, 1956) • B. Leahy, *The Marian Profile in the Ecclesiology of Hans Urs von Balthasar* (New York, 2000) • S. M. Manelli, *All Generations Shall Call Me Blessed: Biblical Mariology* (New Bedford, Mass., 1995) • A. Nachef, *Mary's Pope: John Paul II, Mary, and the Church since Vatican II* (Franklin, Wis., 2000) • S. C. Napiórkowski, "The Present Position in Mariology," *Spirituality and Politics* (ed. C. Duquoc; London, 1967) 52-62 • N. A. Nissiotis, "Mary in Orthodox Theology," *Mary in the Churches* (ed. H. Küng and J. Moltmann; Edinburgh, 1983) 25-39 • G. Schimmelpfennig, *Die Geschichte der Marienverehrung im deutschen Protestantismus* (Paderborn, 1952).

Stanisław Celestyn Napiórkowski

2.7. Mariology in Ecumenical Dialogue

Strong Protestant reaction against Roman Catholic Marian devotion and teaching in the past meant that many ecumenists regarded these themes as particularly difficult subjects for → ecumenical dialogue (→ Mary, Devotion to). Accordingly, it was felt that these issues should be left until other, less contentious subjects had been resolved. In the wake of Vatican II, however, an English Roman Catholic layman, Martin Gillett, founded in 1967 in Great Britain the Ecumenical Society of the Blessed Virgin Mary. He believed, in contrast to others, that common discussion of the role of Mary could advance the cause of → ecumenism. The society soon gained support from elements in all main Christian traditions and became a key focal point in English for common study of Mary, its congresses and local meetings producing an impressive number of papers — historical, theological, ecumenical, and devotional.

Since the end of World War II, there have been 20 international Mariological congresses, the most recent held at Kevalaer, Germany (1987), Huelva, Spain (1992), Częstochowa, Poland (1996), and Rome (2000). At these meetings Anglicans, Lutherans, Reformed, Orthodox, and Roman Catholics have attempted to reach agreements on the question of the place of Mary in Christian → worship and the communion of saints. Participants in these congresses have seen the Mariological problem as methodological (the Bible and → tradition), anthropological (→ sin and → grace), and ecclesiological (the communion of → saints, the character of the → teaching office, and the role of the → Holy Spirit in leading the church into all truth [John 16:12-15]).

Three main dialogues have addressed the questions of Marian piety and doctrine. The first was an American dialogue between Lutherans and Roman Catholics that in 1978 produced the landmark study *Mary in the NT: A Collaborative Assessment by*

Protestant and Roman Catholic Scholars. It was followed by a consideration of Mary in the context of the mediatorship of Christ and the saints, *The One Mediator, the Saints, and Mary* (1990). A second has been the British Roman Catholic–Methodist Dialogue, its conclusions recorded in *Mary: Sign of Grace, Faith, and Holiness* (1995). Third, the most recent and detailed study is by the technically unofficial but highly regarded French Groupe des Dombes, who produced the two-volume text *Marie dans le dessein de Dieu et la communion des saints* (1997-98). It should also be noted that the Anglican–Roman Catholic International Commission has also now begun discussions concerning Mary and her role in faith and the church.

Albeit with differing nuances and emphases, these dialogues all point to an emerging consensus on Marian doctrine and devotion that could help resolve fundamental differences over synergy and the nature of the human response to divine grace. The Groupe des Dombes, in particular, emphasizes both the priority of divine grace and the necessity of human response, a response that is characterized by an act of "letting go in order to let God act." It also speculates as to whether, within growing → unity, divergences in piety, emphasis, and even doctrine might be tolerated within certain limits. All three dialogues emphasize Mary as a model disciple, always within the church and never above or detached from it, a point that, if safeguarded, makes it possible in some sense to speak of Mary as a model for the church.

Bibliography: H. G. Anderson, J. F. Stafford, and J. Burgess, eds., *The One Mediator, the Saints, and Mary* (Minneapolis, 1992) Lutherans and Catholics in Dialogue 8 • D. Carter, "Ecumenical Dialogue on Mary," *Maria* 2 (2001) 105-20 • W. McLoughlin and J. Pinnock, eds., *Mary Is for Everyone: Essays on Mary and Ecumenism* (Leominster, 1997) • A. Stacpoole, ed., *Mary and the Churches* (Dublin, 1987); idem, ed., *Mary's Place in Christian Dialogue* (Wilton, Conn., 1983) • L. Vischer, "Mariology in the Ecumenical Movement," *Mid-Stream* 17 (1978) 1-12.

David Carter

Mark, Gospel of

1. Origins
2. Structure and Contents
3. Compositional Features
4. Theological Themes
5. Purpose

1. Origins

According to ancient writers, the Gospel of Mark was composed in Rome. These witnesses include Papias (ca. 60-130), whose otherwise lost text is quoted by the fourth-century historian Eusebius (*Hist. eccl.* 3.39.14); → Irenaeus, writing late in the second century (*Adv. haer.* 3.1.1); and Clement of Alexandria, writing about the same time, as recorded by Eusebius (*Hist. eccl.* 6.14.5-7). Moreover, these writers identify the writer as a person named Mark, who is called an "interpreter" of the apostle → Peter. According to Clement, the gospel was written during Peter's lifetime; according to Papias and Irenaeus, it was composed after the apostle's death. The evangelist has often been identified as John Mark of Jerusalem (Acts 12:12), an ascription without clear basis. The name "Mark" (Gk. *Markos*, Lat. *Marcus*) was common in the first century.

The location of writing the gospel, its authorship, and the date of its composition have been investigated in modern scholarship in light of evidence within the gospel itself. The gospel was written for a Greek-speaking community, who needed translation of Aramaic terms (3:17; 5:41; 7:11, 34; 15:22, 34). The community no doubt consisted at least in part of → Gentiles: there is a need to explain Jewish feasts (15:42) and purification rites (7:1-8); traditional dietary regulations are set aside (7:18-19); the → Sabbath is not observed strictly (2:23-28; 3:1-5); Jesus ministers to Gentiles (5:1-20; 7:24-30); and a Gentile mission is commanded (13:10). It is a community in which the moral teachings of Israel's Scriptures are to be maintained (10:17-22; 12:28-34).

The author has only a vague picture of Palestinian geography: at 7:31 he has Sidon between Tyre and the Sea of Galilee and locates that sea in the Decapolis, but neither is correct; and at 5:1 he has the "country of the Gerasenes" on the shore of the Sea of Galilee, but it is actually over 50 km. (30 mi.) to the southeast. (These details make it less likely that John Mark of → Jerusalem was the author.) At 13:2, 14 it appears that the Jerusalem → temple has either been destroyed (which took place in A.D. 70) or will be soon (some of the terminology is from Dan. 9:27; 11:31; 12:11). At 10:30 and 13:9-13 it is evident that persecution — religious, but especially political — has been, or is being, experienced. Simon of Cyrene is called "the father of Alexander and Rufus" at 15:21. Is this the Rufus of Rom. 16:13, who lived in Rome in the mid-50s and perhaps later?

A plausible conclusion from the data is that this gospel was written in a Greek-speaking, non-

Palestinian setting after Roman → persecution under Nero had taken place (64-65) and while war was raging in → Palestine (66-70); it was for a Christian community that was composed primarily, but not necessarily exclusively, of Gentiles. The locale of composition may well have been Rome, but Galilee and Syria have been suggested by modern scholars as well; the date of composition was between 66 to 70, or shortly thereafter.

The author, whose alleged connection with Peter has not fared well in critical scholarship, is now generally regarded as unknown. The Gospel of Mark is widely considered the earliest of the four canonical gospels and a source for the Gospels of Matthew and Luke (→ Synoptics).

2. Structure and Contents

The gospel opens, not with Jesus' nativity or early years, but with his baptism by → John the Baptist and his temptation in the wilderness (1:1-13). Thereafter follows a narration of Jesus' ministry in Galilee (1:14–8:26), including conflicts with scribes and → Pharisees, → parables, and the working of → miracles. Attention turns to Jerusalem in the next section, which contains many teachings about Jesus' coming → passion, death, and → resurrection, plus teachings on → discipleship (8:27–10:52). The narrative of Jesus' ministry in Jerusalem, including his suffering and death, unfolds over the duration of his last week in that city (11:1–15:47).

The gospel concludes with a brief resurrection narrative in which only the promise of seeing the resurrected Jesus is made; in contrast to the other canonical gospels, an actual appearance to his disciples is not narrated (16:1-8). In the judgment of most scholars, the Gospel of Mark ended at 16:8. The material in 16:9-20, which appears in the KJV (→ Bible Versions), is not present in the earliest MSS.

3. Compositional Features

The contents of this gospel are presented in ways distinctive to the writer. First, the evangelist has put together traditions of similar form and contents. He places five stories in a row that portray Jesus in conflict with the scribes and Pharisees (2:1–3:6), and later several consecutive accounts of conflict with the Jerusalem authorities (11:27–12:37). Parables and sayings about the → kingdom of God are collected together in 4:1-34, as are small units having to do with → marriage, children, and possessions in 10:1-22. Unless there had been a passion narrative already in existence and at hand for the writer, as some scholars have suggested, Mark created his own

— and presumably the first — passion narrative (14:1–15:47), as others scholars claim.

A second feature distinctive to this writer's presentation is intercalation, or the insertion of stories within stories. For example, 5:25-34 is inserted into 5:22-43, and 11:15-19 into 11:12-21. He thereby links passages that interpret each other.

Finally, it is characteristic of this writer to use certain words (e.g., *euthys,* "immediately," used 40 or 41 times, but only 10 times in the rest of the NT) and stylistic touches (e.g., the "historic present" tense, used 151 times in 661 verses) that give his account a sense of urgent movement.

Although this gospel stresses Jesus' role as a teacher, the most vivid impression comes from Jesus' activities and the busy course of his life and ministry (e.g., his miracles, his travels around Galilee and then to Jerusalem, and his suffering and death there).

4. Theological Themes

In 1892 M. Kähler referred to the Gospels as "passion narratives with extended introductions." That is a particularly fitting description of the Gospel of Mark, in which 6 of 16 chapters relate to Jesus' last week in Jerusalem. Moreover, the gospel anticipates Jesus' suffering and death before his arrival there by three passion predictions (8:31; 9:31; 10:33-34) and other notices throughout the narrative (3:6; 9:9-10, 12; 10:38, 45). The shadow of the cross falls backward upon Mark's story of Jesus.

Another notable feature of Mark is the so-called messianic secret, a term made famous in 1901 in the work of W. Wrede based primarily on the gospel's portrayal of Jesus as preventing demons from revealing his identity (1:25, 34; 3:12), commanding his disciples to silence (8:30; 9:9), and also commanding silence of those who have witnessed his miracles (1:43-45; 5:43; 7:36; 8:26). While Wrede thought that Jesus did not consider himself the Messiah, it is nevertheless clear that the traditions that Mark received were impregnated with Christological features. The evangelist therefore imposed upon the material the view that Jesus kept his messiahship a secret during his earthly ministry, revealing it from time to time to his disciples, although being misunderstood by them. True comprehension came about only after his resurrection. The messianic secret is therefore to be seen as a theological construct, not a matter of historical reporting. Others have interpreted the messianic secret differently, such as in the view that when Mark strung pericopes together, he had to tone down the miraculous. Readers should not be so taken in by the manifestations of divine power in Jesus that they see him primarily as a miracle worker. The true identity of Jesus is clear only in light of the cross and resurrection (9:9; 15:39; → Theologia crucis).

The → Christology of Mark's gospel has received extensive treatment by scholars. The major Christological titles are used (Christ, Lord, Son of God, Son of Man), and Jesus is portrayed as a mighty worker of miracles. He is also shown as a redemptive figure who came to give his life as a "ransom for many" (10:45). The background for this thought is Isa. 53:10-11, where the Servant who bears iniquities dies as a means of → atonement for many. The theme of ransom here emphasizes liberation (i.e., the effect of giving a ransom), not the party receiving it (God, the devil, etc.). Jesus' resurrection from death certifies the atoning work; what he promised (10:45) has indeed happened, thus vindicating him and his word.

Another theme of the gospel is discipleship. The disciples of Jesus are unperceptive (4:41; 6:51-52; 8:14-21), seek glory (9:33-34; 10:35-41), betray Jesus (14:10-11), desert him (14:50), and deny him (14:66-72). Moreover, there is no postresurrection reconciliation. In contrast, no matter how inadequate the disciples are, Jesus remains faithful in the worst of times. After choosing them (1:16-20; 2:13-14; 3:13-14), he considers them family (3:34-35) and promises them a renewed relationship with himself after the resurrection (14:26-28; 16:7). Discipleship and Christology, moreover, are related. As Jesus went to the cross, so must the disciple take up the cross and follow him (8:34). At any time and place discipleship is difficult and may be marked by failure and even death.

5. Purpose

In the ancient view, the Gospel of Mark was written overtly to transmit the → preaching of the apostle Peter. In modern times scholars have made various other proposals. For some, the author wrote this work primarily for catechetical purposes (→ Catechesis). Others see its purpose as mainly theological, especially for combating erroneous Christological views.

The enigmatic statement that opens the book — "the beginning of the good news of Jesus Christ" — perhaps provides a clue to the meaning of the gospel as a whole. What follows in 1:2–16:8 provides an account of the *beginning* of the gospel that has been and is being preached orally in the church, an account the author may have sensed the community needs so that it can face the present in light of the past.

Bibliography: Commentaries: P. J. Achtemeier (ProcC; 2d ed.; Philadelphia, 1986) • R. T. France (NIGTC; Grand Rapids, 2002) • R. H. Gundry (Grand Rapids, 1993) • M. Hooker (BNTC; Peabody, Mass., 1991) • J. Marcus (AB; New York, 2000) • R. Schnackenburg (NTSR; 2d ed.; New York, 1971) • E. Schweizer (Richmond, Va., 1970) • V. Taylor (2d ed.; New York, 1966).

Other works: M. Kähler, *The So-Called Historical Jesus and the Historic Biblical Christ* (Philadelphia, 1964; orig. pub., 1892) • W. H. Kelber, ed., *The Passion in Mark* (Philadelphia, 1976) • J. D. Kingsbury, *The Christology of Mark's Gospel* (Philadelphia, 1983) • W. Marxsen, *Mark the Evangelist* (Nashville, 1969) • C. Tuckett, ed., *The Messianic Secret* (Philadelphia, 1983) • T. J. Weeden, *Mark–Traditions in Conflict* (Philadelphia, 1971) • W. Wrede, *The Messianic Secret* (London, 1971; orig. pub., 1901).

Arland J. Hultgren

Maronites → Uniate Churches

Marranos

A Marrano is a Christianized Jew or Moor of medieval Spain, especially one who converted only to escape persecution (→ Conversion 1).

From the 11th century Spanish Jews (→ Judaism), showing that they too had to avoid things, borrowed from the Arabs the term *maḥram* (something prohibited), which, in its Castillian form *marrano,* they used to refer to pigs. The *reconquistadores* then took over the word and applied it to the Jews themselves. When baptism was forced on the Jews, it became a common term of contempt for those thus baptized (they called themselves *'ănûsîm,* "coerced ones"), who were always suspected of clinging to their original faith.

The term took hold when persecutions of Jews became more common (→ Anti-Semitism, Anti-Judaism) after 1391, and especially with the → Inquisition after 1480 and the expulsion of Jews from Spain in 1492 and Portugal in 1496. The Marranos who remained or who emigrated to Goa, Lima, Mexico, and Cartagena formed congregations whose life and character diverged from what might be found in Christian Europe. The term could also be used elsewhere (e.g., Italy in the 13-15th cent.) when Jewish loyalty was maintained or restored in conflict with forced conversions (also to → Islam in eastern Persia in the 19th cent.).

Many thinkers in the early modern period, including Isaac de La Peyrère (1596-1676) and Baruch Spinoza (1632-77; → Spinozism), were perhaps forced by the ambiguity of their background as Marranos to achieve unusual clarity about what is true and false in faith and thought.

Bibliography: M. ALPERT, Crypto-Judaism and the Spanish Inquisition (Basingstoke, 2001) • D. M. GIT-LITZ, Secrecy and Deceit: The Religion of the Crypto-Jews (Philadelphia, 1996) • R. L. MELAMMED, Heretics or Daughters of Israel?: The Crypto-Jewish Women of Castile (New York, 1999) • B. NETANYAHU, The Marranos of Spain: From the Late Fourteenth to the Early Sixteenth Century, according to Contemporary Hebrew Sources (3d ed.; Ithaca, N.Y., 1999); idem, Toward the Inquisition: Essays on Jewish and Converso History in Late Medieval Spain (Ithaca, N.Y., 1997) • E. PARIS, The End of Days: A Story of Tolerance, Tyranny, and the Expulsion of the Jews from Spain (Amherst, N.Y., 1995) • N. ROTH, Conversos, Inquisition, and the Expulsion of the Jews from Spain (Madison, Wis., 1995) • D. M. SWETSCHINSKI, "Marranos," EncRel(E) 9.210-18.

CARSTEN COLPE

Marriage and Divorce

1. Dogmatics and Ethics

1.1. Historical Data

Historical research has never been able to establish the original form of marriage — monogamy or polygamy (polygyny or polyandry) — or whether one form developed into the other. Yet it is striking that in so-called primitive cultures, as well as more civilized ones, we always find a religious or cultural understanding of marriage and weddings. Behind or "above" the institutionally regulated and celebrated uniting (not merely monogamously) of a man and a

woman, which is also a uniting of clans (both in [endogamy] and outside [exogamy] the tribe), of ancestors, of possessions, and of rights, there obviously stands in many cases the sense or myth of a "heavenly marriage" of the gods. This holy wedding expresses the union of opposites, of male and female (of yin and yang, etc.), and human marriage ceremonies thus participate in this primal event. Sexual union has a symbolic character, bringing to pass something that already is.

Both adultery and divorce are viewed in the light of this participation. Protective incantations, blessings, and oracles help the married couple and their families and clans against dangers and evil spirits that might destroy this participation. Research into the → history of religion teaches us that this participation in a divine event apparently consistently takes precedence in marriage contractions over the procreation of children.

1.2. Biblical Data

It is hard to establish directly from OT and NT texts a theological basis for monogamous marriage as a lifelong partnership. Polygamous practice, the patriarchal tradition, and considerations regarding offspring and the maintenance of possessions are all too often to the fore in the OT.

In the NT what is said about marriage in the Epistles is not easily harmonized with modern Christian ideas of marriage. The basic theological thrust (if we can even speak of such a thing) is toward monogamous marriage as the will and creation of God, which reflects his own inviolable partnership with → Israel or the → church, and with the human race as a whole. But only biblically grounded theological reflection, rather than individual texts, provides the basis for this view. The differences that emerge here find expression only too clearly in the different → denominational concepts of marriage.

1.2.1. In the impact of the Hebrew Bible on the church, the statements about man and woman in Gen. 1:27 and 2:21-24 acquired primary significance. The stories of the polygamy of the patriarchs (Genesis 12–50; → Patriarchal History) completely faded by comparison, as did those regarding the judges (Gideon), the kings (→ David and → Solomon), what was said about Levirate marriage (Deut. 25:5-10), the right of a childless married man to have children by a slave, the practice of divorce or expulsion by the husband's fiat, and the definition of adultery as the sexual relationship of a married woman with any man but of a married man only with a married woman. (This favoring of the husband lived on in the American South and in South Africa, with direct reference to the Bible, and with less direct reference to general Euramerican culture.)

Undoubtedly, the excessively metaphoric OT statements about the divinely willed equal regard and → love and → faithfulness between husband and wife as a reflection of the divine → covenant proved to be significant and theologically relevant for later church teaching about marriage, even if it also reflected the primacy of securing posterity and ultimately patriarchalism. The uniform OT view that the death of a partner ends a marriage also remained influential (in distinction, e.g., from what Eastern cultures such as India believe).

1.2.2. The OT statements in Gen. 1:27 and 2:21-24 plainly lie behind what the NT says about marriage. The central sayings of Jesus are in Matt. 5:27-32 (which radicalizes adultery as lusting after a married woman by a married man) and Matt. 19:4-6, 8-9. The → Pharisees (v. 3), in view of different teachings about divorce (the more lenient view of Hillel and the stricter view of Shammai), had asked Jesus whether he regarded "any cause" as permissible. His reply that there should be no divorce "except for unchastity *(porneia)*" later gave rise to different interpretations in the church.

→ Paul referred to this saying in 1 Cor. 7:10, but his argument is complicated by his naming an unbelieving partner as a reason for divorce in certain circumstances (vv. 12-16). He recommends that the believer maintain the marriage, since the unbelieving partner is "made holy" by the believing partner, and the children are "holy" (v. 14). But if the unbelieving partner breaks off the marriage, so be it (v. 15). Paul is here reaching back to one part of the OT and Jewish tradition in which mixed marriages with non-Israelites are dissolved or prohibited. Later the assumption in the church that all are believers ruled out this argument.

Paul's statements about marriage become clearer in the light of the two opposing movements that had already become influential in the churches: the rejection of marriage as such (see 1 Tim. 4:3) and a religious fear of → sexuality (1 Cor. 7:1-9, 36-38). In reply to both tendencies he refers to the freedom of the gospel. What moves him is not a theory of orders of creation but a belief in divine calling (1 Cor. 7:17) in full freedom either to be fully married or, in view of "the impending crisis" (v. 26), to remain unmarried as he himself does. We can hardly take too seriously the way in which → eschatology (→ Parousia) cuts across his admonitions to the churches about marriage. We find something of the same in the Gospels and ultimately in the many texts that compare the church to a bride going to meet her bridegroom

(Matt. 9:15; 22:1-14; 25:1-13; Luke 12:35-38; also John 3:29).

The consummation of the community takes place in this "wedding," which is still ahead and which is not viewed as a divine drama (see 1.1 above) in which human marriage participates. Instead the community is itself a partner in this wedding (the unfaithful community is "adulterous," a comparison that we find already in the OT). Thus human marriage can no longer be something "eternal." It is legitimate, however. Indeed, it is in truth a reflection of divine love and self-giving. Yet it may be forgone in the hot fervor of eschatological expectation.

Ephesians 5:22-23, which also quotes Gen. 2:23-24, is the central passage for all church doctrines of marriage. It gives full expression to the nature of marriage as a reflection. The relation to life in Christ shows members of the community the meaning of the "mystery" (Eph. 5:32, Gk. *mystērion*, Lat. *sacramentum*) of marriage between husband and wife. Here are the roots of later sacramental teaching (→ Sacrament).

The NT does not offer any strict doctrine of marriage. Beyond what it says about the divinely willed union of husband and wife, which is in principle an indissoluble, lifelong, loving, and total partnership both of body and soul as a reflection of the union between Christ and the church, its statements about the social roles of husband and wife are conditioned by the age and the background.

1.3. *In Christian History*

A hasty sketch of the history of ideas of marriage, primarily those in the church, shows how broad are the possibilities of expounding the OT and NT statements about it. Naturally, general cultural, economic, ethnic, ecclesiastical, and juridical factors play an important part. Only in a critical retrospect can we disentangle them from the strictly biblical and theological factors.

1.3.1. Worth noting is the → Talmudic tradition (→ Judaism) in its exposition of OT texts about marriage. Marriage is divinely willed and lifelong, but it may be dissolved if it breaks down. It is not a "private" act of those becoming wed, yet it is also not given too exalted a religious-metaphoric significance, although the acceptance of the bride by the bridegroom can be viewed as a symbol of God's acceptance of Israel. In the constitution of Jewish marriage and in the law of divorce, the man plainly has priority, yet Jewish law also protects the wife. In marriage and the → family the wife has more influence than an outside critic might suspect.

The church developed its understanding without

any direct contact with Judaism. In the → early church resistance to religious movements hostile to marriage and a concern to understand spiritual chastity in relation to physical sexuality came to the fore (→ Asceticism; Monasticism). Many problems arose concerning divorce, rules for the remarriage of widowed officebearers (1 Tim. 3:2), marriage with unbelievers, the reconciliation of partners who were at fault, and the question whether marriage or divorce in the "old life" before → should be viewed differently. In the fourth and fifth centuries two rules still in force today became firmly established in the → Orthodox Church: first, that priests must enter into marriage before ordination, and second, that → bishops must not marry but be monks. Sometimes widowed priests and deacons are allowed to remarry (e.g., if there are little children to care for), but this permission is by *oeconomia* (→ Economy [Orthodox Theology]), not by doctrinal *akribeia* (strictness, rigidity).

In the Orthodox Church marriage is still a sacrament that the priest dispenses. In principle it is indissoluble, but because it is a sign of divine → grace and the mystery of love, and this sign takes precedence over the ideal of permanence, it may be dissolved. In exceptional cases a believer may be allowed to contract a third marriage.

In contrast to the East, the church in the West developed the doctrine of marriage only by a slow process of legalizing and sacramentalizing. For a long time there were secular as well as church marriages. Only in the High Middle Ages did the church demand marriage by a priest, and it was only in the 13th century that marriage became one of seven sacraments. It cannot be administered without a priest, but it is also not administered by him. The married couple administer it to one another by their consent and seal it by bodily union. Marriage dispenses grace and is indissoluble. In church law dissolution simply ratifies the fact that a marriage is nonexistent or invalid.

The Council of → Trent confirmed the sacramental view that had been shaped in the Middle Ages. In this whole process Eph. 5:32 played a decisive role as regards the sacramental aspect, as did the sayings of Jesus in Matt. 19:6 as regards indissolubility.

→ Celibacy for ecclesiastical officeholders is a legalized form of the eschatological expectation of believers (see 1.2.2) in the virgin church, now applied specifically to officeholders (along with monks and nuns). Unmarried priests were preferred from the beginning of the fourth century, and then the celibacy of bishops was required and only unmarried

priests were ordained. After 1139 all marriages of priests were declared invalid.

1.3.2. When U. → Zwingli and M. Bucer (1522), and later M. → Luther (1525), married, they were protesting not simply against celibacy but against the exalting of monasticism. They were also rediscovering the divinely given freedom of all people to accept marriage, sexuality, natural love, and the procreating and rearing of children as a calling or → vocation. The thesis of Luther (1483-1546) that marriage is a "worldly thing" (a wording that critics have often misunderstood) is obviously putting the public estate of marriage under the jurisdiction of the "authorities" (→ Two Kingdoms Doctrine). It views marriage, not as a sacrament that dispenses grace, but as a divinely willed, "holy," and "blessed" estate, an order set up by the word of the Creator. Marriage denotes the "sacrament of your dear Son Jesus Christ and the church, his bride" (concluding prayer of the baptismal order of 1529 [*LW* 53.110-15]). In this fallen world marriage as an "estate" is wholly dependent on grace and → forgiveness. Yet, as in the tradition, it is also a help against → sin and concupiscence.

The main difference from Roman Catholic teaching does not lie so much in the denial of the sacramental aspect (which is more important in J. → Calvin; note the polemic in *Inst.* 4.19.36) or in the concept of orders of creation (which many Lutherans emphasize today) but in the more general doctrine of → creation, which no longer accepts the scholastic view that grace transcends → nature (→ Luther's Theology). Marriage (or the sacrament of marriage) does not confer grace. God himself gives grace and → blessing to faithful, penitent, and fallible married couples. Marriage is indissoluble by institution but dissoluble in practice. Courts must see to this distinction, and the church must stick to its pastoral duty.

The → Reformers did not differ radically in their views of marriage. P. → Melanchthon (1497-1560) worked out precise criteria for divorce, and Zwingli (1484-1531) concerned himself with the duties of the Zurich council in this regard, and with other practical matters, as did also H. Bullinger (1504-75). Calvin (1509-64), whose statements in *Inst.* 4.19 are characterized especially by a sharp rejection of the Roman Catholic sacramental view, emphasized in his preaching, commentaries, and especially in his practical work in Geneva the fact that as an order, marriage is a gift of God to the partners and to the family that they establish. He took a more restrictive view of divorce than the other Reformers.

Although all the Reformers thought about marriage in terms of → natural law, they did not reflect upon these possibilities as capable of being sacramentally elevated and consummated. Bucer (1491-1551) came closest to later ideas of marriage in describing it in personal terms or as a partnership.

1.3.3. With this epoch in Western history the unity of the cultural and ecclesiastical understanding of marriage came to an end. Lutheran and Reformed → orthodoxy still aimed at a certain legalizing of marriage and its purpose, and the → Anglican Communion attempted a complete exclusion of divorce, but with the → Enlightenment movement of civil → emancipation there developed, if not a rationalistic, at least an autonomous, understanding of marriage. One may rightly see in J. Locke (1632-1704), C. Thomasius (1655-1728), and some proponents of natural law the authors of the newer concept of marriage as a union for partnership and procreation. It is worth noting that the Restoration → Book of Common Prayer (1662), harking back to canon law, advanced as the three purposes of marriage (1) the procreation and nurture of children, (2) the avoidance of sin, and (3) mutual help and comfort, doing so much more clearly than did earlier versions. As such, it offers a religious version of the early Enlightenment understanding of marriage.

There has been much criticism of I. Kant's (1724-1804) very formal definition of marriage as the union of two persons and the sharing of their sexual attributes (*Metaphysik der Sitten* §24). But this formulation must be put in the context of the intentionally formal legal language of §22 and the concession in §23 ("the most personal"). It must also be seen in connection with the total purpose of securing the equality and correlation of the marriage partners. Nevertheless, it is still cold and unsatisfying. Kant's readers at the end of the century of Enlightenment must have longed for a religious reference — whether that of Ephesians 5 or some other mystery. They found this dimension abundantly in → Romanticism.

This movement relating the earthly to the eternal had forerunners in England (E. Young and indeed J. Milton), and references back to N. → Zinzendorf (1700-1760; → Pietism), classical → mysticism, the troubadours, and the thinking of the Far East seemed meaningful. Marriage was now more than ever a private affair, and love was marriage even without a wedding (F. Schlegel's *Lucinde* [1800]). It unites the lovers with one another, and with → time and eternity, reality and the superterrestrial. In love they touch infinity. Marriage seals what is inseparable and is indissoluble. The ideal of harmony is dominant, and it can go hand in hand with a long-

ing for death (Novalis). The later F. D. E. → Schleiermacher (1768-1834), who regarded marriage as a social and family institution, still rejected divorce on these grounds.

1.4. *Current Concepts of Marriage*

Romanticism offered the last more broadly influential religious, but only in part theological, basis for marriage in Western culture. The partly romantic movement of restoration in the Victorian-Wilhelmian era produced conservative, prudishly antisexual, and supposedly Christian conventions in marriage and family, but it also suppressed the beginnings of feminine emancipation in the later Enlightenment and Romanticism. A truly theologically influential conception of marriage did not come until the 20th century.

Toward the middle of the 20th century, important theological books on marriage — whether practical, like those of T. Bovet (1948) and J. Fischer (1956), or academic-theological — referred in many cases to the Romantic view and its critics as well as to the Reformers and to the Bible. Roman Catholic authors also refer to Romanticism (it was not for nothing that a number of leading Romantics in the 19th cent. became Roman Catholics) but also to the relevant → encyclicals, to Trent, to medieval teaching, to → Augustine (→ Augustine's Theology), and to the Bible.

In the Protestant sphere one can easily distinguish the authors who argue in terms of the orders (P. Althaus, W. Elert, H. Thielicke, and E. Brunner) and those who think along covenant lines, or with a focus on the hope of establishing the kingdom (K. → Barth, A. de Quervain, H. van Oyen, P. L. Lehmann). H. Dombois heightened the tension with his new theological concept of the → institution, as did E. Wolf.

Modern writers are no longer fundamentally controlled by the typical German Protestant debate about → law and gospel, as may be plainly seen in what H. Ringeling says about marriage, in the sections on marriage in T. Rendtorff's *Ethics*, and in the works of H.-J. Thilo (1978) and the Roman Catholic moralist F. Böckle (in dialogue with Protestant authors and debate with the Catholic tradition). But for all the careful discussion of the theological issues, a definitive Protestant book on marriage has yet to be written.

In the English-speaking world academic theologians and ethicists have seldom produced larger works on marriage. The influential books on the subject are practical and come from the educational divisions of the various churches. Surprisingly, the Anglican world often refers uncritically to Roman

Catholic canon law (e.g., in handbooks and instructional manuals). In ecumenical contacts with the earlier missionary churches (→ Mission), the partial toleration of polygamous family structures presents problems for theological justification if dual partnership is lacking in polygamy. Conservative churches in the Anglo-Saxon area continue to wrestle with these problems, which must also be seen in connection with the universalizing of → medical ethics. Christians in the churches of the → Third World (→ Third World Theology) cling for the most part to the Euramerican ideal of marriage.

1.5. Tasks Remaining

Theological → ethics does not presume to control the marriages of millions of Christians, nor by looking at the historical development of marriage does it claim to describe the history of actual marriages across the centuries. Nevertheless, one should not underestimate its tasks and possibilities in an age that is seeking direction and models. The younger generation in the industrialized world vacillates a good deal in its readiness for the institution of marriage and family. We have no more control over the → anxieties that are at work here than over the reasons for the great number of broken and dissolved marriages, which are such a negative example to young people. An official statement by the Church of England (1999) offers counseling and encouragement in the light of these difficulties, although permitting a second marriage only in special cases.

Drawing on its rich tradition, and borrowing responsible information from → sociology and → psychotherapy, theological ethics must at least constructively examine the following questions and find a valid solution for them.

1.5.1. The first question is that of *celibacy.* From Matt. 19:10-12 and 1 Corinthians 7 there developed a specifically Christian tradition of celibacy that admittedly also often incorporated the ascetic ideals of the day. In Protestantism the reaction against overestimating monasticism became so strong that a dubious valuing of marriage alone ensued. At many points this reaction reminds us of the rejection that unmarried (and childless) women suffered in ancient Israel and Judaism.

Modern problems among the succeeding generation of priests amid the upholding of celibacy (esp. severe in Latin America) have even strengthened these traditional feelings on the Protestant side. Attention needs to be given to new → communities and to individuals that voluntarily renounce marriage either for a period or for life. Their vocation can also shed light on those whose celibacy is due to fate and not to choice.

1.5.2. The second problem is that of *denominationally → mixed marriages* (see 3). Invitations to a biblical grounded understanding of marriage will remain extremely burdened in the realm of → pastoral care as long as convinced Christians in a denominationally mixed marriage cannot worship and celebrate Communion together, and will lack credibility among those outside the church.

1.5.3. The *social dimension of marriage* is a further question. Common in the younger generation is the ideal of a purely private union, which makes the "institution" dispensable. New thinking on the social as well as the divine dimension is thus urgently needed. Existing answers and formulas are at most useful only among those who know that they are in solidarity with the church and also have the spiritual maturity to tolerate traditional concepts.

1.5.4. The increasing number of *couples living together without being married* (esp. in central and northern Europe) has prompted many thoughtful theological statements and publications but has left most churches in a passive mood and in helplessness. The churches have responded similarly to *homosexual couples* desiring a divine service of blessing, though a number of Scandinavian and German-speaking denominations have come forth with liturgies for such services.

1.5.5. Another question is that of *setting up a family.* The Catholic stress on procreation of children as an end often comes under criticism, but there is great wisdom in it. If it does not depreciate the marital partnership, and if sexuality is not related solely to procreation, the human ability to create new → life carries with it a great responsibility. Face-to-face with the anxieties of the day — destruction of the → environment (→ Ecology), the shortage of resources, and nuclear destruction (→ Weapons) — theological ethics must still encourage married couples to create new life, yet also to engage in → birth control. At this point the Christian churches must work out serious differences.

1.5.6. A final question is that of *the age for marriage.* Present-day orientation, especially in the media, to young and healthy people has also influenced the → anthropology of theological ethics and the practical manuals. But theological ethics must also take into account the sexuality of older people and their experience of → partnership in its many dimensions. In cooperation with medicine and sociology it must also consider the rights of the sick and → persons with disabilities to sexuality and partnership.

Bibliography: R. BAINTON, *What Christianity Says about Sex, Love, and Marriage* (New York, 1957) •

K. Barth, *CD* III/4 • F. Böckle, H. Ringeling, et al., "Ehe und Familie," *HCE* 2.117-209 • U. Bögers-hausen, *Die konfessionsverbindende Ehe als Lehr- und Lernprozeß* (Mainz, 2001) • T. Bovet, *A Handbook to Marriage and Marriage Guidance* (London, 1958; orig. pub., 1946) • Church of England, House of Bishops, *Marriage* (London, 1999) • R. F. Collins, *Divorce in the NT* (Collegeville, Minn., 1992) • J. Fischer, *Ehe und Elternschaft* (Hamburg, 1956) • A. Hastings, *Christian Marriage in Africa* (London, 1973) • L. I. Kopp, *Nichteheliche Lebensgemeinschaften versus Ehe? Eine theologisch-ethische Auseinandersetzung mit der Sinnhaftigkeit angemessener Lebensformen der Geschlechterbeziehung* (Münster, 2000) • P. L. Lehmann, *Ethics in a Christian Context* (Westport, Conn., 1979; orig. pub., 1963) • C. H. Ratschow et al., "Ehe / Eherecht / Ehescheidung," *TRE* 9.308-62 • T. Rendtorff, *Ethics* (vol. 2; Minneapolis, 1989) 6-80 • H. Ringeling, *Ethik des Leibes* (Hamburg, 1965); idem, *Theologie und Sexualität* (2d ed.; Gütersloh, 1969) • F. D. E. Schleier-macher, *Die christliche Sitte* (2d ed.; Berlin, 1884) • H. Thielicke, *The Ethics of Sex* (New York, 1964) • H.-J. Thilo, *Ehe ohne Norm? Eine evangelische Eheethik in Theorie und Praxis* (Göttingen, 1978) • B. Wannen-wetsch, *Die Freiheit der Ehe. Das Zusammenleben von Frau und Mann in der Wahrnehmung evangelischer Ethik* (Neukirchen, 1993) • E. Wolf, "Dic Institution Ehe," *Sozialethik* (ed. T. Strohm; Göttingen, 1975) 180-96.

Dietrich Ritschl

2. Marriage and the Family in Western Tradition
→ Family 2

3. Church Law
3.1. *History*
Church law regarding marriage became important toward the end of the first millennium. Up to then Christians married according to tradition and secular law. The NT had given new emphasis to married life but left the form of marrying unchanged. In the → early church there is only sparse testimony to its influence on the form (→ Ignatius, → Tertullian) but many more references to the moral demands in marriage. From the fourth century a → blessing was added at the → wedding. In the East this feature became the legal basis of marriage and hence obligatory (before 896, in a *novella* of Emperor Leo VI). At the same time, church principles became important in marriage law, as may be seen in controversies about the legitimacy of imperial marriages (Constantine VI [780-97], at the time of Empress Irene [780-802]; also the four marriages of Leo VI [886-912]).

From about 1200 the church in the West clericalized the Roman and Teutonic forms (emphasizing, respectively, consent and copulation). Consent, which had been informal in Roman jurisprudence, became basic. This factor influenced the recognition of occasional lay marriages (up to the 14th cent.) and secret marriages. The councils of Verona (1184) and Lyons (1274) defined marriage as a → sacrament.

The → Reformation broke this line of development, but it continued in the → Orthodox Church and was essentially confirmed in the → Roman Catholic Church at the Council of → Trent, which fixed the law of marriage and made a decisive change by introducing an obligatory form.

3.2. *Roman Catholic Church*
In the Roman Catholic Church the 1917 → Codex Iuris Canonici codified marriage law, and then 1983 CIC 1055-1165 made some significant changes, which in part were foreshadowed in the pastoral constitution *Gaudium et spes* of → Vatican II. Marriage of two persons is regarded as "a partnership of their whole life" (can. 1055). The 1917 CIC stressed the elements of contract and purpose (progeny), but these features are less prominent in 1983. So long as there are no impediments, marriage is valid through a mutual declaration of will *(causa efficiens)*. The bond of marriage between baptized persons (whether Roman Catholics or not) is a sacrament. An idea that has been in vogue since the age of → Scholasticism, namely, that the couple themselves dispense the sacrament, is qualified by a reference to the need for the church's cooperation. All Roman Catholics (except in cases of defection, can. 1124; → Church Membership 5) must follow the set form: a church wedding celebrated by the local priest (or his delegate) before two witnesses. A new point is that in special cases laypeople may serve as delegates (can. 1112).

It is debated whether civil marriages on the part of Roman Catholics are invalid or irregular and can lead to exclusion from the → Eucharist (can. 915). In exceptional cases there may be a → dispensation from the form, for example, in denominationally mixed marriages, which even though they may be civil marriages, or marriages in some other church, are regarded as regular and sacramental because the church cooperates by way of the dispensation. This dispensing from the obligatory form is to be distinguished from the duty of getting a license for a → mixed marriage (can. 1124). A marriage that is invalid because of an impediment may become valid by a renewal of consent when the impediment is removed (cans. 1156-60). Marriages that are invalid for other reasons may be made good by the Holy See or in some cases by the diocesan bishop (by a *sanatio in radice* [healing in the root] dispensation, cans. 1161-65).

In a valid marriage a bond is created between the spouses that is "permanent and exclusive" (can. 1134) but that in some cases church courts can nullify (see cans. 1671-91). A valid marriage between two unbaptized persons, if one of them is later baptized, can be dissolved in accordance with the so-called Pauline privilege (1 Cor. 7:12-15, cans. 1143-50). The 1983 CIC, with reference to the special problems of Christians in the → Third World, issued a statement on polygamy (can. 1148) decreeing that men who are living in polygamy, but are then baptized, must decide for one of the wives but also make economic provision for the others. The pope can dissolve a marriage for good reason if it is valid but was never consummated (cans. 1697-1706).

3.3. Orthodox Church

In the Orthodox Church, with some regional differences, the validity and sacramental character of a marriage are related to the consent of the two partners, their promise of fidelity, and the rite of coronation by the priest. Civil marriage is of no significance ecclesiastically. The principle of the indissolubility of marriage has been broken by a canonical recognition of some grounds for divorce. Even a second or third marriage may be a sacrament, but a fourth is forbidden. The partners must both belong to the Orthodox Church. In keeping with current practice, however, the Second → Pan-orthodox Conference (1982) proposed sanctioning marriage between an Orthodox and non-Orthodox partner, "in clemency and charity," so long as the children are baptized and brought up in the Orthodox Church. It is left to the → autocephalous churches to decide what to do about the marriage of an Orthodox partner to a non-Christian or unbeliever.

3.4. Protestant Churches

M. → Luther (1483-1546), for pastoral reasons, opposed medieval → canon law and the abuses of his time in what he had to say about marriage. The church must give its blessing and → pastoral care. Luther did not accept the sacramental character of marriage, modified the concept of impediments, confirmed consent as the basis of marriage, and permitted divorce in some cases.

The other → Reformers — P. → Melanchthon, U. → Zwingli, J. → Calvin, J. Brenz, M. Bucer, and J. Bugenhagen — did not view marriage as a sacrament and left legal questions to the temporal powers. Yet the church still had a say in the matter of marriage, especially as church weddings were basic for the people.

When the elector set up a consistory in 1539, Luther recognized its authority in marriage questions as a secular court with church members. He resisted its development into a church court for secular marriage questions. In the period that followed, the regional consistories claimed competence in both spiritual and secular questions, which they decided according to canonical and territorial law, with regard for Reformation insights (the doctrine of *causa mixta*). Only in the → Enlightenment did the state take over marriage legislation, and even then it left the celebration of marriages to the church. The legal act and the ecclesiastical act were one and the same. But the state's exercise of sovereignty in marriage matters paved the way for separation. This came in Germany in 1875 with the law of civil marriage and did not leave the church any legal role.

The territorial churches in Germany make their own rules about weddings on the presupposition that there has first been a civil ceremony. In general they demand that at least one of the partners be Protestant and that a pastoral interview precede the wedding. They decide on the authorization of the wedding or on reasons for refusing it. There are special rules when the partners belong to different denominations, when one of them does not belong to a church, or in the case of divorced persons.

The earlier, almost self-evident, prohibition of marriage with a non-Christian was relaxed in the 1970s. The → Arnoldshain Conference recommended a similar procedure. Some churches stress the difference between the liturgical act and the wedding. A special register is to be kept for such weddings, the same rules being applied to marriages with those who have left the church or who are not baptized.

On a Protestant understanding, the indissolubility of marriage in the NT is based on the will of the Creator (Matt. 19:6; Mark 10:9), but it need not be applied as human law. God protects marriage. Divorce runs contrary to his will, but so too does a marriage in which the command of love no longer directs the partners to one another. Thus Protestant churches allow divorce only when by human judgment the partnership has been definitively destroyed.

German Protestant churches have certain rules for the marriage and divorce of clergy: notice of engagement and intended marriage must be given; the spouse must normally be a member of the Protestant Church, with the possibility of dispensation; and church leaders may forbid an intended marriage if it is prejudicial to the ministry. During a divorce proceeding, a minister may be granted a leave of absence, but he or she will no longer be dismissed if the divorce is granted, and some ministers are now at work with Roman Catholic spouses. The authorities must give their approval if a divorced minister wants to remarry. These rules presuppose a link between life and witness in all Christians, but they may reflect too much what the congregation expects of its ministers and can easily become too stringent ethically. What ought to count is not the pastor as a role model but the authenticity of witness, which includes the witness of those who have incurred guilt.

3.5. Anglican Communion

In the → Anglican Communion, too, marriage is not a sacrament, but the Church of England strongly maintains its indissolubility and is opposed to the remarriage of divorced persons. Since the state took up the matter of divorce reform in the Divorce Reform Act of 1969, there have been efforts to make possible remarriage after divorce in certain cases. An archbishop's commission set up by the Convocation of Canterbury issued a report *Marriage, Divorce, and the Church* in 1971 with a proposal to this effect, but like similar efforts up to early 1985, it was not successful. Yet many → bishops have given their clergy freedom whether or not to remarry divorced persons, the issue being complicated by the fact that according to state law they cannot refuse their churches for the purpose, though they themselves are not required to conduct the ceremony.

→ Church Law; Law and Legal Theory

Bibliography: M. G. LAWLER, "Marriage," *OCCT* 408-11 • C. H. RATSCHOW et al., "Ehe / Eherecht / Ehescheidung," *TRE* 9.308-62.

On 3.1: C. N. BROOKE, *The Medieval Idea of Marriage* (Oxford, 1989) • D. G. HUNTER, ed., *Marriage in the Early Church* (Minneapolis, 1992) • P. L. REYNOLDS, *Marriage in the Western Church: The Christianization of Marriage during the Patristic and Early Medieval Periods* (Leiden, 1994) • K. RITZER, *Formen, Riten und religiöses Brauchtum der Eheschließung in den christlichen Kirchen des ersten Jahrtausends* (2d ed.; ed. U. Hermann and W. Heckenbach; Münster, 1981) • E. WESTERMARCK, *The History of Human Marriage* (5th ed.; 3 vols.; London, 1921) • J. WITTE, *From Sacrament to Contract: Marriage, Religion, and Law in the Western Tradition* (Louisville, Ky., 1997).

On 3.2: L. S. CAHILL, "Marriage," *NDCST* 565-70 • P. HEGY and J. MARTOS, eds., *Catholic Divorce: The Deception of Annulments* (New York, 2000) • *HKKR,* esp. M. Kaiser, "Grundfragen des kirchlichen Eherechts," 730-46 • J. KAMAS, *The Separation of the Spouses with the Bond Remaining: Historical and Canonical Study with Pastoral Applications* (Rome, 1997) • L. ÖRSY, *Marriage in Canon Law: Texts and Comments, Reflections and Questions* (Wilmington, Del., 1986).

On 3.3: P. EVDOKIMOV, *The Sacrament of Love: The Nuptial Mystery in the Light of Orthodox Tradition* (New York, 1985) • D. FORD, *Women and Men in the Early Church: The Full Views of St. John Chrysostom* (South Canaan, Pa., 1996) • J. MEYENDORFF, *Marriage: An Orthodox Perspective* (3d ed.; Crestwood, N.Y., 1984).

On 3.4: H. DIETERICH, *Das protestantische Eherecht in Deutschland bis zur Mitte des 17. Jahrhunderts* (Munich, 1970) • J. F. HARRINGTON, *Reordering Marriage and Society in Reformation Germany* (Cambridge, 1995).

On 3.5: *Anglican Marriage in England and Wales* (London, 1992) • *The Canons of the Church of England* (6th ed.; London, 2000) • *Marriage, Divorce, and the Church: The Report of a Commission Appointed by the Archbishop of Canterbury to Prepare a Statement on the Christian Doctrine of Marriage* (London, 1972).

ALFRED BURGSMÜLLER

3.6. North American Churches

The separation of → church and state that is underwritten in the Constitution of the United States, the proliferation of religious bodies, and the → secularization of its culture all make it difficult to give a clear picture of marriage procedures as they are actually practiced. As in many parts of western Europe, civil marriage before a registrar is both easy and simple; unlike the churches in western Europe, however, those in North America are often strong and vigorous in their observance of marriage procedures and liturgies, even when marriage before the church *(coram ecclesiae)* after one (or more) divorce(s) is the norm.

The mainstream churches of the United States and Canada all make certain administrative requirements that even in practice are more demanding on couples than the various provisions laid down (for example) by the legislatures of each state or province. Roman Catholics, in the renewed pastoral practice that has followed → Vatican II, impress upon couples the importance of → Christian education in marriage before the marriage celebration itself. Such "pre-Cana weekends" group couples together, so that by instruction, discussion, and interaction in other ways, they may reflect on the meaning of marriage. Other churches are following suit, and the majority of pastoral manuals and service books emphasize to the pastor, the couple, and the wider community the important step being undertaken.

Another recent development has been the considerable enrichment of marriage liturgies. (Many of the old rites in use in the United States were paltry by comparison.) The Roman Catholic Ordo Celebrandi Matrimonium (1969), which was a great step forward from the service contained in the Rituale Romanum (1614) from a theological point of view as well as in the rich content of the prayers, has helped to encourage other churches to revise their marriage rites. Notable among these rank the Episcopal (i.e., Anglican) rite of the → *Book of Common Prayer* (1979), which brings Thomas → Cranmer's positive approach to marriage into contemporary language and form, and the United Methodist *Service for Christian Marriage* (1979), which is similarly rich, innovative, yet traditional (→ Methodist Churches). The Consultation on Common Texts produced a text for ecumenical use (1985) that is itself a symptom of the current age, in which Christians share together in the *mysterium* of marriage across traditional denominational boundaries (→ Mixed Marriages), even (if they wish) celebrating the → Eucharist together when doing so. This particular rite, like the two others mentioned, stresses the role of the → families and → congregation in prayerful support of the marriage and also gives a prominent place to the solemn → blessing of the couple. Thus the partners' mutual consent, so central of old, still retains its importance, but it takes on a more ecclesiological dimension when set within the context of the church community at prayer. → Liturgy and life dialogue obliquely because rite expresses aspiration, which falls short of reality. But these developments say something about the need for the church to undergird, in different ways, the institution of marriage within society.

Many churches allow marriage after divorce, in one way or another. Sometimes the local → pastor decides; sometimes there is a local or central policy. The → Roman Catholic Church retains the medieval concept of nullity as the official way of dealing with this phenomenon. Other churches tend to adopt a modern version of the traditional Byzantine teaching, that the marriage no longer exists because it has "died"; and there are even a few unofficial liturgies to ritualize the termination of a marriage, though these are not celebrated frequently. Increasing anxiety at the divorce rate has led some to question what appears to be the churches giving in to the spirit of the age. Others, however, seek a return to the primitive practice of (1) separating betrothal from marriage and (2) making marriage part of the life and concern of the local congregation. Such a realignment (which the Roman Catholic Church did with adult → baptism in 1972 by the restoration of the catechumenate) has indeed much to commend it, relying as it does on a notion of marriage catechumenate that would serve to strengthen marriage in society and in the church at a time when it is under great stress.

Bibliography: J. H. ABRAHAM, *From Courtship to Courtroom: What Divorce Law Is Doing to Marriage* (New York, 1999) • K. B. HACKSTAFF, *Marriage in a Culture of Divorce* (Philadelphia, 1999) • T. MACKIN, *Divorce and Remarriage: Marriage in the Catholic Church* (New York, 1984) • M. SEARLE and K. W. STEVENSON, *Documents of the Marriage Liturgy* (Collegeville, Minn., 1992) • K. W. STEVENSON, *Nuptial Blessing: A Study of Christian Marriage Rites* (London, 1982); idem, *To Join Together: Celebrating Christian Marriage* (New York, 1987) • A. THATCHER, ed., *Celebrating Christian Marriage* (Edinburgh, 2001) • M. K. WHYTE, ed., *Marriage in America: A Communitarian Perspective* (Lanham, Md., 2000).

KENNETH W. STEVENSON

4. Practical Theology

Practical theology has an increasingly vital role to play in marriage and divorce. Couples want to know how to develop strong unions in a culture of marital instability. Pastors must perform weddings involving a complex combination of ritual, spiritual inspiration, social and legal bonding, and practical guidance. Communities and states desire new ways to help balance the private nature of marriage with its public advantages for children, health, the workplace, and the common good. Church leaders need fresh visions for interpreting therapeutic and social scientific perspectives on marriage and divorce in relation to their theological traditions.

In the Middle Ages → practical theology focused significantly on issues of → property and → sexuality, especially fidelity to spouses, paternity of children, and consent to the marriage vow. The → Reformers were particularly interested in questions of social utility and legality: rights and responsibilities of couples before the state, protection of children and inheritance, and appropriate grounds for divorce. Theologians in the modern period developed an increasing concern for individual liberties: to choose one's own spouse, to dissolve the union, to find in marriage a sense of personal and spiritual fulfillment. These legacies have contributed to complex tensions within marriage today among its private, public, legal, and spiritual dimensions, producing profound practical theological differences on the true nature and meaning of marriage, as well as on the → ethics of divorce.

These challenges must be met by the → pastor and the church (→ Congregation) on a variety of levels. Theologically, it is more important than ever to retrieve the rich religious understandings of marriage that have so profoundly influenced the meaning of this institution in the West, and to reinterpret this heritage creatively in relation to the current marriage situation. Whether one agrees or not that marriage today is in decline, it is indisputable that there is a crisis in its meaning and purpose, and as in other such periods (such as the → Reformation), new theological perspectives need to be forged. Pastors can effectively help marriages only when they have robust hermeneutical resources for addressing its current privatization, → secularization, and utilitarianism. Biblical and theological perspectives can help couples and society understand marriage as not just a business contract but also a sacred and edifying union, not just an expression of romance but also a bond of transforming and committed love, not just a joining of two individuals but also a covenant of significance to the larger community.

Socially, marriage and divorce concern a range of stakeholders. First and foremost, → Judaism and Christianity have always tied marriage to children (even if they have valued nonchildbearing marriages as well). → Augustine, for example, classically defined the three "goods," or purposes, of marriage as fidelity, children, and sacrament. Even in traditions that sanction divorce, religious leaders have insisted that the welfare of children is a fundamental and not merely secondary priority (→ Childhood). Second, churches are increasingly confronted with the question of how marriage should be defined, including equality of roles between genders, unions between gays and lesbians (→ Homosexuality), and rights of long-term cohabiters. And third, especially since John → Calvin, marriage has been understood as a vital concern of → society as a whole. Not only is → family the primary crucible within which the next generation learns important social values, but stable and lasting marriages bring structure and support to neighborhoods, communities, the economy, and the state. This connection has been clearly recognized in cities around the United States that have adopted Community Marriage Policies, in which religious institutions, businesses, counselors, and government leaders have created a united effort to help marriages succeed. (This program, which began in 1986 in Modesto, Calif., had spread to over 150 cities by 2002.) Many churches are learning to hold up marriage as a valuable social institution without stigmatizing members who divorce.

Therapeutically, pastors and church leaders should take seriously their role as marriage educators. This role includes → counseling in times of crisis and intervention and referral in cases of abuse. But it also should involve the use of programs like PREP (The Prevention and Relationship Enhancement Program, started in the 1990s by Howard Markman and Scott Stanley) and PAIRS (Practical Application of Intimate Relationship Skills, founded in 1975 by Lori Gordon) to help couples build and sustain healthy relationships in the first place. Because pastors are typically present at the formation of a marriage, they are uniquely situated to teach couples the lifelong communication and conflict-resolution skills they will need (→ Pastoral Care). They are also in a position to connect newlyweds with established couples in their congregations to serve as marriage mentors. All these steps should be taken within the context of exploring important relational values like equal regard, mutual commitment, gender equity, agapic → love, and → hope. Herein lie opportunities for pastors to move beyond merely providing a wedding ritual to engaging prospective spouses in reflection on the larger relational, social, and spiritual meaning of their union. In addition, marriage education can take place effectively in youth groups and in programs for continued marriage enrichment, and it should be a factor in providing guidance around divorce, remarriage, and stepfamilies.

Bibliography: D. S. Browning, *Marriage and Modernization: A Realistic, Constructive Look at Modern Threats to Married Life* (Grand Rapids, 2003) • D. S. Browning, B. J. Miller-McLemore, P. D. Couture, K. B. Lyon, and R. M. Franklin, *From Culture Wars to Common Ground: Religion and the American Family Debate* (2d ed.; Louisville, Ky., 2000) • A. Thatcher, *Marriage after Modernity: Christian Marriage in Postmodern Times* (New York, 1999) • J. Wall, D. S. Browning, W. J. Doherty, and S. Post, eds., *Marriage, Health, and the Professions: If Marriage Is Good for You, What Does This Mean for Law, Medicine, Ministry, Therapy, and Business?* (Grand Rapids, 2002) • J. Witte Jr., *From Sacrament to Contract: Marriage, Religion, and Law in the Western Tradition* (Louisville, Ky., 1997).

John Wall

Martyrs

The Christian church has always had its martyrs, but the model comes from the → early church. In the middle of the second century the *Martyrdom of Polycarp* provided the first example and the terminology. The martyr is a → disciple and imitator of Christ (→ Discipleship 2) who, in a situation of → persecution, holds fast the confession of Christ and thus comes under sentence of death. Death seals faith in Christ as the witness (Gk. root *martyr-*) of blood, that is, martyrdom. Only those who give up their lives can be called martyrs. Those who survive persecution and torture were called confessors. The early martyrs included many women.

The term "martyr" originally was a legal one denoting the witness in a trial. In the NT we find both the legal use and a new use for witnesses to the resurrection who bear testimony to their faith in word and deed (Acts 1:8). The first martyrdom, that of Stephen in Acts 6:8–8:3, is the result of witness to Christ, though we do not find here any developed theology of martyrdom. The meeting of Christian usage with Jewish (2 Maccabees 7) and Hellenistic traditions (→ Hellenism) and the theological interpretation of increasing experiences of persecution (→ Apocalypticism) created the specifically Christian understanding of martyrs as blood witnesses. Alongside the increasing honoring of martyrs as real witnesses, we also find in the Middle Ages warnings against any longing for martyrdom. The fourth century also saw a spiritualizing of the concept as ascetics came to be seen as disciples of the martyrs and → asceticism was venerated as a daily martyrdom.

Throughout the centuries, to the present, there have been actual martyrs in the church. We may simply recall the Russian Orthodox theologian and scientist Pavlov Florensky (b. 1882), who lost his life in a labor camp in 1937 (or 1943?), or Dietrich → Bonhoeffer (b. 1906), whom the Nazis executed in 1945 (→ Church Struggle; Fascism), or Archbishop Oscar Romero (b. 1917), who was murdered in El Salvador in 1980. Even though the last two finally had to die for their political opinions, they still offer examples of Christian martyrdom as illustrations of vital Christian discipleship. Remembrance of the life and death of martyrs binds Christians of different denominations together inasmuch as martyrdom points to the one Christ.

→ Lapsi; Martyrs, Acts of the; Saints, Veneration of

Bibliography: G. A. Bisbee, *Pre-Decian Acts of Martyrs and Commentarii* (Philadelphia, 1988) • G. W. Bowersock, *Martyrdom and Rome* (Cambridge, 1995) • D. Boyarin, *Dying for God: Martyrdom and the Making of Christianity and Judaism* (Stanford, Calif., 1999) • W. H. C. Frend, *Martyrdom and Persecution in the Early Church* (Grand Rapids, 1981; orig. pub., 1965) • B. S. Gregory, *Salvation at Stake: Christian Martyrdom in Early Modern Europe* (Cambridge, 1999) • U. Kellermann, *Auferstanden in den Himmel. 2 Makkabäer 7 und die Auferstehung der Märtyrer* (Stuttgart, 1979) • P. A. Marshall, with L. Gilbert, *Their Blood Cries Out: The Untold Story of Persecution against Christians in the Modern World* (Dallas, 1997) • R. Royal, *The Catholic Martyrs of the Twentieth Century: A Comprehensive World History* (New York, 2000) • J. S. Scott, *Christians and Tyrants: The Prison Testimonies of Boethius, Thomas More, and Dietrich Bonhoeffer* (New York, 1995) • J. Sobrino, *Companions of Jesus: The Jesuit Martyrs of El Salvador* (Maryknoll, N.Y., 1990) • N. M. Vaporis, *Witnesses for Christ: Orthodox Christian Neomartyrs of the Ottoman Period, 1437-1860* (Crestwood, N.Y., 2000) • E. Weiner and A. Weiner, *The Martyr's Conviction: A Sociological Analysis* (Atlanta, 1990).

Ruth Albrecht

Martyrs, Acts of the

→ Persecutions in the → early church resulted in a specific literary genre, the acts of the martyrs. We find two types. The first consists of a record of the trials of martyrs, for example, that of → Justin Martyr in Rome about 165 *(Martyrium Sancti Iustini et Sociorum),* or that of the 12 martyrs of Scillium (near Carthage?), North Africa, in 180 (H. Musurillo, 86-89), or that of → Cyprian of Carthage in 258 *(Acta Proconsularia,* Musurillo, 168-75). The second type consists of a report of events before and during the imprisonment and then of the execution of the death sentence. Examples are the *Martyrdom of Polycarp,* bishop of Smyrna in about 166 *(ApF[L]* 2.312-45), or that of Perpetua and Felicity in Carthage in 203 (Musurillo, 106-31). The non-Christian *Acta Alexandrinorum* parallels the first form.

The theological interpretation of martyrdom as → discipleship of Christ (→ Martyrs) forms the basis of the honoring of martyrs and then the veneration of → saints. In the oldest account, that of Polycarp's martyrdom, we also find the beginnings of a cult of → relics and of annual commemorations. The early acts of martyrs, which after persecutions ended were imitated in the legends of martyrs, influenced the development of Christian hagiography as a whole (→ Literature, Biblical and Early Christian, 3).

Bibliography: G. A. Bisbee, *Pre-Decian Acts of Martyrs and Commentarii* (Philadelphia, 1988) • H. Delehaye, *Les passions des martyrs et les genres littéraires* (2d ed.;

Brussels, 1966; orig. pub., 1921) • D. G. KYLE, *Spectacles of Death in Ancient Rome* (London, 1998) • H. MUSU-RILLO, ed., *The Acts of the Christian Martyrs* (Oxford, 1972) • J. E. SALISURY, *Perpetua's Passion: The Death and Memory of a Young Roman Woman* (New York, 1997) • M. A. TILLEY, trans., *Donatist Martyr Stories: The Church in Conflict in Roman North Africa* (Liverpool, 1996).

RUTH ALBRECHT

Marx, Karl

Karl Heinrich Marx (1818-83), a German philosopher, sociologist, economist, and political theoretician, was the creator of historical → materialism. "Marxism" was named after him. Marx was the son of a lawyer of Jewish lineage who converted to Protestantism. In 1835, after a carefree bourgeois youth, he passed the *Abitur* (secondary school examination) in his hometown of Trier. From 1836 he studied → philosophy and history in Bonn and Berlin, where he was strongly influenced by Hegel's philosophy (→ Hegelianism) and initially felt drawn to the left-wing Hegelians. He received his doctorate at the University of Jena in 1841.

Prompted by his liberal political views, Marx began a career as a journalist and in 1842 became the coeditor of the left-leaning bourgeois/democratic *Rheinische Zeitung* in Cologne, where his colleague Moses Hess introduced him to socialist ideas (→ Socialism). After encountering problems with the censor, he decided to emigrate to Paris together with his wife, Jenny of Westphalia, whom he had married shortly before and whose family belonged to the Prussian nobility. Beginning in 1844 in Paris, Marx published *Die Deutsch-Französichen Jahrbücher* (The German-French yearbooks) and also became acquainted with Friedrich Engels (1820-95), who became a lifelong friend and collaborator and even helped Marx financially.

In 1845 Marx emigrated to Brussels after being expelled from France; there he and Engels wrote *Die deutsche Ideologie* (The German ideology, 1845-46), in which they adopted L. Feuerbach's critique of → religion. In *Misère de la philosophie* (The poverty of philosophy, 1847), an ironic reversal of a work subtitled *Philosophie de la misère* (The philosophy of poverty, 1846) by the French utopian socialist P.-J. Proudhon, Marx took issue with the latter's ideas and developed in response his own economic interpretation of history, postulating a just system of social organization issuing of necessity from the laws of history itself.

Both Marx and Engels participated more actively in the following years in international politics, becoming members of the Communist League in 1848, at the initiative of which they wrote the *Communist Manifesto* in the same year, a platform for the league summarizing all the theses of socialist philosophy. Because of the German revolution, Marx and Engels returned to Cologne and published the *Neue Rheinische Zeitung,* an undertaking that, after the failure of the revolution a year later, resulted in trial and emigration again. Marx's path took him by way of Paris to London, where he lived until his death in 1883.

Marx's experiences in practical politics and in journalism had confronted him with concrete social reality. In London he thus began an intensive study of political → economy, and his attempts to articulate the basic laws of the → capitalist economy came to expression in his *Kritik der politischen Ökonomie* (Critique of political economy, 1859) and especially his most important work, *Das Kapital* (1867). Engels published the second and third volumes of *Kapital* in 1885 and 1894. Beginning in 1864, Marx was active in leadership roles in the General Council of the International Working Men's Association.

The central element in Marx's philosophy is the philosophy of G. W. F. Hegel, which he strongly criticized and reversed and yet whose dialectical method and rational schematism he himself adopted (→ Dialectic). In the process the Hegelian concept of → bourgeois society became the argumentative center of his philosophizing, with dialectics a revolutionary principle. Marx considered older materialism to be static, undialectical, and thus unhistorical. He applied the dynamic principle of dialectics to life and to societal relationships in the form of dialectical materialism; in the form of historical materialism, it then became the heart of his philosophical view of things. Like Hegel, Marx saw in the totality of world history a process that followed specific laws in moving toward its goal; for just that reason, Marx believed that the historical sciences could be studied like any other natural science.

Bibliography: Primary sources: K. MARX and F. ENGELS, *Collected Works* (vols. 1-47; New York, 1975-95); idem, *Werke [von] Karl Marx, Friedrich Engels* (40 vols. in 43; Berlin, 1972-74).

Secondary works: D. C. HODGES, *The Literate Communist: 150 Years of the Communist Manifesto* (New York, 1999) • D. McLELLAN, *The Thought of Karl Marx* (2d ed.; London, 1980) • F. MEHRING, *Karl Marx: The Story of His Life* (London, 1948; orig. pub., 1918) • A. H. NIMTZ, *Marx and Engels: Their Contribution to*

the Democratic Breakthrough (Albany, N.Y., 2000) •
W. A. SUCHTING, *Marx: An Introduction* (New York,
1983).

MICHAEL LÖBL

Marxism

1. Historical Development
  1.1. Place in History
  1.2. Sequence of Marxisms
    1.2.1. Marx and Marxist Theory
    1.2.2. Marxism in the Nineteenth Century
    1.2.3. Marxism in the Epoch of the World Wars
    1.2.4. Third World Derivatives
    1.2.5. Marxisms after World War II
  1.3. Theories and Doctrinal Positions
    1.3.1. Proletariat
    1.3.2. Socialism and Communism
    1.3.3. Middle-Class Society and Capitalism
    1.3.4. Philosophy
2. Marxism and Ethics
  2.1. Ethics and Class Consciousness
  2.2. Justice
  2.3. Work
  2.4. Threefold Alienation
  2.5. Economy and Ethics
  2.6. Family
  2.7. Ideological Criticism
  2.8. Categorical Imperative
  2.9. Critical Questions
3. Present Situation

1. Historical Development

Marxism is the social doctrine that the disciples of Karl → Marx (1818-83) — especially F. Bernstein, K. Kautsky, A. Bebel, F. Mehring, and G. V. Plekhanov, in partnership with F. Engels (1820-95) — developed in the 1880s and 1890s from various elements of thought that they regarded as the essence of Marx's teaching. Marx himself disliked being called a Marxist, and we cannot really view him as the founder of Marxism. His revolutionary theories were not meant to be doctrines but, in the strict sense, merely an account of a real movement of history (*MECW* 6.498). The fact that from the very first his followers inaugurated what we might call a Marxist confession was an ideological anomaly (→ Ideology) based on the precarious makeup of the mass movement of socialist workers.

1.1. *Place in History*

The thought of Marx and the sequence of Marxisms that followed denote a crisis in middle-class, capitalist European society in the late 19th and early 20th centuries. In an increasingly precarious way Marxism itself was caught up in this crisis. From a Marxist standpoint the crisis was (1) a final systemic crisis in the capitalist means of production (→ capitalism), (2) a social crisis in class relations that was due to the antagonism between capitalists *(bourgeoisie)* and workers *(prolétariat),* (3) a crisis resulting in class war, and (4) a crisis that would be resolved by social revolution on the part of the proletariat.

This perspective took the doctrinal and confessional form of Marxism when it became increasingly open to questions as it became clear that (1) middle-class society (→ Bourgeois, Bourgeoisie) and its capitalistic means of production showed no signs of being in decay but merely subject to intermittent disruptions, (2) economic potential increased, (3) nationalism (→ Nation, Nationalism) and military might (→ Power 1) brought imperial rivalry between the states, and (4) the warlike age of modern imperialism resulted. These developments did not at all represent the crisis that Marx had expected and that would allow of a productive resolution. The true crisis was not a limitation of the capitalist means of production but a *lack* of limitation in respect to the imperialist mobilization that overtook European nations and society as they entered upon the age of high industrialization (→ Industrial Society).

1.2. *Sequence of Marxisms*

In its variety, Marxism went through a series of very different forms. The Marxisms of political parties formed the center. Accompanying and counterbalancing the Marxisms of officials and workers was that of academic intellectuals (also para-Marxisms such as → critical theory, the philosophy of hope, and Heideggerian Marxism). It is questionable whether we can reduce the mass of Marxist traditions to a single or minimal concept. Marxism is best defined by looking at the problems that gave rise to it. Its characteristic response to those problems is to think and act in terms of class positions and class struggles.

1.2.1. *Marx and Marxist Theory*

The "historical" Marx was himself an exception to Marxism. He was definitely a middle-class republican who admired Prometheus, who suffered under an authoritarian state, and who even before 1848 had begun to have strong doubts about the republican initiatives of the middle class. He thus developed the bold vision of a rising industrial proletariat with the revolutionary power to bring about liberation and unification in world history. His first approach, in "Contribution to the Critique of Hegel's Philosophy of Law: Introduction" (1844; *MECW* 3.175-87), was a purely theoretical one that used the → anthropology of L. Feuerbach (1804-72), the dialectic of G. W. F. Hegel (1770-1831; → Hegelianism), and even the ethics of I. Kant (1724-1804; → Kantianism; Categorical Imperative). It was disciplined by the insight that an idea of → emancipation can become a reality in people's lives only when it corresponds to their actual "radical needs."

In practical association with the workers' movement of emancipation, Marx turned more to → empiricism and → realism, in contrast to his former attachment to postulates and norms. In 1844-45 he began a close working relationship with Engels. Historical realism found a "disciplinary matrix" in the interpretation of history and criticism of ideology that Marx and Engels wrote in 1845-46 (*The German Ideology* [*MECW* 5.21-539]). Even those who produce ideas must recognize their manifold dependence on various practical authorities. Consciousness simply expresses the true life process and an ability to put it into actual social practice (pp. 39-40). It is always conditioned by a basis of material achievement or a power of productivity on the part of the individuals concerned (pp. 41-43). Social upheavals occur when new and higher powers of mass productivity are fashioned that cannot be freely developed in the traditional orders of production and society but rather burst open these orders.

The proletarian movement, or Communism, was conceived as a real movement that took its life, not from the inspiration of ideas, but from their practical social energies and interests of workers. The concept is Hegelian — the rational is real — rather than an idealistic focus on postulates and norms.

In the *Communist Manifesto*, written on the eve of the 1848 → revolution, Marx and Engels set forth a program based on the expectation that they were at the start of a great revolutionary period, in the course of which the proletariat would triumph over the middle class. Communism was not meant as a doctrine to be expressed in theoretical propositions but as an account of the "actual relations springing from existing class struggle, from a historical movement going on under our very eyes" (*MECW* 6.498, also 6.177).

In Paris the 1848 revolution certainly bore witness to conflict between the proletariat and the middle class, but it also showed that the conflict was only in its initial stages. The Parisian Communists disbanded in 1850; the capitalist means of produc-

tion had plainly not yet exhausted its potential. A long period of drought followed for Marx in which he wrote only small pieces, especially for Horace Greeley's *New York Weekly Tribune,* and began for the first time to study more radically the movement of capitalist production. The result was the first volume, in 1867, of his gigantic work *Das Kapital.* Marx expected the work to make a greater impact on the world of civil servants than on the workers (*MECW* 42.360-61).

When finally in the 1860s socialist workers' organizations were founded on a larger scale, Marx served on the London General Council of the International Working Men's Association, founded in 1864, until it dissolved in 1872. At the end of the Franco-Prussian War (1870-71), the Paris Commune, made up of various worker factions, arose and rekindled Marx's revolutionary fire, and the rise of a popular revolutionary movement in Russia kept it bright. After the publication of the first volume, work on *Das Kapital* slowed down (vols. 2 and 3 appeared only in 1885 and 1894, after Marx's death, through the efforts of Engels), and little more light was shed on the future of the capitalist means of production.

1.2.2. *Marxism in the Nineteenth Century*
The first, classic Marxism of the late 19th century was still within the horizon of Marx's expectations. It was tied to the political force of the new workers' movement, which was one of social reform rather than revolution. Ideologically, it looked beyond the modest political and parliamentary successes of this movement to real power and the ultimate goal of the future, a socialist society.

The term best describing the Marxism of the 1880s and 1890s is Kautskyism. It finds expression chiefly in the *Erfurt Program,* authored by K. Kautsky (1854-1938) and adopted by the German Social Democrats in 1891. Like the *Communist Manifesto,* this document predicted economic crises that would become more and more extensive and devastating and that would result in the necessity of changing the means of production (→ Property) from capitalist to socialist.

At the turn of the century Kautskian Marxism stood in need of revision. E. Bernstein (1850-1932) signaled a new direction by rejecting expectations of a catastrophic collapse of the capitalist means of production, the impoverishment of the proletariat, and ensuing revolutionary upheavals.

The practice of reform and its expectations for the future now came under the pressure of the enormous demands of the imperial age and the related world wars. In the collisions of this epoch the older

Marxist movement played itself out, abandoning its revolutionary outlook and its orientation toward final goals. The classic form of German Marxism lasted from the 1880s to World War I; in the interwar period it survived only in pockets, ending with the death of R. Hilferding (1877-1941) in a Gestapo prison in Paris.

1.2.3. *Marxism in the Epoch of the World Wars*

The second form of Marxism developed during the period of the 20th-century world wars, taking place for the most part on the periphery of industrial Europe. Its expectations were different from those of the earlier Marxism. In prerevolutionary Russia V. I. Lenin (1870-1924) promulgated a Marxism of strict obligations anchored in demands for doctrinal recognition: "Those who recognize only class conflict are not true Marxists. True Marxists also recognize the dictatorship of the proletariat" (*Werke* 25.424). Under Lenin Marxism became absolute, total, and autocratic. The doctrine of Marx is all-powerful (*vsesil'nyi*) because it is true (19.3) and has fully taken into itself all relevant human knowledge (31.276).

After the outbreak of war in 1914, the revolutionary wing of Social Democracy split with the antiwar wing. The history of Marxism took an unusual turn at the time of the 1917 October Revolution in Russia. The revolution, a product of the war that itself arose not from a crisis in the capitalistic means of production but from the transformation of the imperialist war into a civil war, aimed to take control of the state by force. "Socializing" the means of production meant placing them under the centralized state formed by a "dictatorship of the proletariat." The "building up of socialism" meant in effect a continuation of the world war and civil wars by very similar means.

Soviet Marxism, having begun with the first Russian revolution of 1905, thus came to play an active part in the imperialism and militarism of the age. It may be divided into the era of Lenin (up to 1924), the interregnum of factional infighting (1925-29), and then the era of J. Stalin (1929-53), during which Soviet socialism was changed from revolutionary dictatorship into individual despotism. After the death of Stalin (1879-1953), a long crisis of disintegration began.

Historical Marxism has since 1924 been known as Marxism-Leninism, but in fact it was under the stronger influence of Stalin. As the champion of Marxist opposition to Stalin, L. Trotsky (1879-1940) was exiled in 1929 and later assassinated in Mexico. The two competing Leninisms came to be known as Stalinism and Trotskyism.

1.2.4. *Third World Derivatives*

The Marxism of the Russian revolution was already a secondary Marxism. The revolutionizing of the Asian East, envisioned early by Lenin, produced there and in Latin America and Africa, regions in which society and civilization were even less like the industrial West than Russia, more remote forms of Marxism. From the outset we have here little more than a liturgical use of the term. The Marxist provenance, visible as social conflict between a class of "haves" and an exploited class of the working poor, became the focus of a political grouping (→ Third World). In the 1920s and 1930s Chinese Bolshevism and Maoism, along with the expositions they evoked, formed secondary and tertiary forms of Marxism.

1.2.5. *Marxisms after World War II*

After World War II Soviet Marxism dealt with both social stagnation in the USSR and the extreme challenge of integrating other countries imperially (Titoist Yugoslavia broke away in 1949) by an enormously exaggerated ideological production. It expressed itself in campaigns of polemic and in a late Marxist-Leninist encyclopedism with state-demanded systematic compendiums on every aspect of Marxist doctrine.

Alongside the stagnation, decline, division, and eventual dissolution of Soviet Marxism, there were serious efforts in the West to oppose a critical neo-Marxism to both late Stalinism and late capitalism. The principal advocates of philosophical Marxisms and para-Marxisms in this period were G. Lukács (1885-1971), E. Bloch (1885-1977), M. Horkheimer (1895-1973), H. Marcuse (1898-1979), T. W. Adorno (1903-69), and J.-P. Sartre (1905-80), who with their writings old and new staged a brief revival for Marxism in the 1960s and 1970s.

1.3. *Theories and Doctrinal Positions*

We can think of historical Marxism only in terms of a genealogy of Marxisms. The range of Marxisms are a confused web of what is Marxist and what is either related to Marxism or removed from it. The historical nature of the Marxisms leaves little room for a Marxist systematics.

1.3.1. *Proletariat*

As Lenin saw it in 1913, the most important task of Marxist teaching was to clarify the world-historical role of the proletariat in creating the socialist society (*Werke* 1.69). Apart from its doctrinaire form, this statement admirably sums up the heart of Marxism. Without the proletariat there could be no Marxism. With it, however, one is entangled in the most taxing conceptual and practical problems, and as time went by, it became more doubtful whether Marxism could persist. even with the proletariat.

Marx's early hailing of this coming "emancipator" (*MECW* 3.187) was a forced and speculative act, and the attempt to integrate the proletarian revolution into the concept of a revolution in the development of society and civilization (5.86-89) created difficulties (→ Aporia). These difficulties increased with the prospect of a workers' revolution. There is in fact an antinomy between a revolution in which the working class releases the already hatched out elements of a higher society (22.335) and one in which it must first rid itself of the old rubbish (5.88). Marx first had the idea of a dictatorship of the proletariat in 1850-52 when the Communist League collapsed. The problem came to light both in the double character of social and political revolution (3.205-6) and in the way in which Marx and Engels put less emphasis on the idea of a workers' revolution during the turbulence of the Crimean War and other conflicts. They began to see in Europe the possibility of a mixed social and cultural revolution on the part of the people, even to the point of anticipating a "Russian 1793."

The real proletarian movement did not have a revolutionary profile at all. The supposed revolutionary proletariat was a precarious substitute for the real proletariat.

At the turn of the century Bernstein expressed doubts about the higher potential of the proletariat, doubts that occasioned his break with Marxist orthodoxy. As he said in 1899 in his *Voraussetzungen des Sozialismus* (The preconditions of socialism), "We cannot expect of a class that is poorly housed and badly educated, and that has no sure or adequate income, the high intellectual and moral standing that the establishing and maintaining of a socialist society presuppose" (pp. 255-56).

The most determined, orthodox opponents of revisionism replied that in their policy they were less concerned about the limits of proletarian effectiveness and more concerned to show the proletariat its historical duty. The Marxism that became doctrine (i.e., that of Lenin) was a Marxism of strict duty — thus Lenin's *Task of the Proletariat in the Revolution*. With its doctrines and aims and principles, this tool became the ideological means of imposing duties on the proletariat. In it the mission of the proletariat became something forced, a matter of faith that had about it more of the *quia absurdum* (because it is absurd) than of uncertain confidence.

The idea of the proletariat underwent a normative change under the extreme doubts and pressures of world war, as we see from the statement of R. Luxemburg (1871-1919) that if the proletariat does not fulfill its class duty and establish socialism, then ruin threatens all of us (*Ausgewählte Reden und Schriften* [1955] 2.666).

The situation differed in Russian Marxism, where an ambitious and aggressive revolutionary party authoritatively imposed its minority discipline on the proletariat. By educating the workers' party, Marxism educated the avant-garde of the proletariat, which was capable of seizing power and leading the whole people to socialism, a belief Lenin expressed in his *State and Revolution* (*Werke* 25.416). At the extreme pole of this shift in balance and purpose, an absolutist party leadership could say of itself that it actually was the proletariat. Ultimately it was an ideological myth of Soviet socialism that the proletariat was the creator of a socialist society. The proletariat became a pseudonym for a very different entity.

1.3.2. *Socialism and Communism*

What Marx and Engels at first saw very unclearly, on the margin, as the general result of the proletarian movement and the class war (i.e., a higher society) became the Archimedean point of Marxism, its goal or "final goal." While the breakthrough to socialism either never took place or failed in Western Europe, it did become — in an unforeseen and very irregular way on the periphery of modern European civilization — the proximate goal of a politically victorious and socially very heterogeneous and defective social revolution. The Marxist prognostications of the *Communist Manifesto*, the communes, and the 1875 program, which had proved to be false, were now brought to a forced fulfillment. In the process, the reality of the social revolution in Russia burst through the conceptual framework of Marxist traditions. The activists of this revolution developed their own revolutionary Marxism, which used slogans or pseudonyms for the very different realities of their revolution.

1.3.3. *Middle-Class Society and Capitalism*

Along with attachment to the proletariat, Marx bequeathed to Marxism his predictions regarding the collapse of the capitalist means of production, and with their demise the end of modern middle-class society. For two main reasons Marx and Engels expected the capitalist means of production to come to a quick end. The first was the intolerable nature of the tyrannical and exploitative wage system. The second was the recurrence of devastating economic crises (→ Economy). As time went on, however, the first reason proved to be less provocative, the second less persistent.

The movement of modern society, which is more than merely that of capitalist production, did not produce a final economic crisis and an attendant social revolution but, instead, an era of developing nationalist and imperialistic power. Face-to-face with a confusion of economic and political effects, both domestic and international, the concept of the capitalist means of production lost much of its pregnancy and gave way to the complex but less distinctive title "capitalism." In 1916 Lenin saw in imperialism the final stage of capitalism, a stage marked by monopoly capital, finance capital, export capital, → colonial policies, the carving up of the world by capitalist industrial powers, and strife over these new divisions. The result was to heighten the guilt of the system. Finally there arrived on the scene the terrorist regimes of → fascism as the dictatorship of the most reactionary circles of finance capital. The later Marxist title "capitalism" thus became even more imprecise. By focusing on the antagonism between the middle class and the workers, it became the mother of a faulty → sociology of modern middle-class society.

1.3.4. Philosophy

Marxist philosophy is not a uniform complex of thought. Instead, it is a sequence (often disparate) of thought experiments that are meant to offer a general framework within which to conceive of past and future historical movement. The first attempt at coordination, that of a philosophy of → freedom, may be found in the works of Marx published between 1842 and the so-called yearbooks of 1844. The second, which contains reflections on the dimensions of human fulfillment and alienation, may be found in the Paris MSS of 1844. The third, the *Analysis of Practical Life-Processes,* which also deals with the polarity of ideology and reality, followed quickly in 1845-46. Finally, we can see another basic philosophy behind *Das Kapital,* that of an objective logic of social movement. How far these various attempts represent Marxist philosophy as a possible totality is a matter of debate. Trying to synthesize such a philosophy out of them poses basic problems.

After he abandoned his early Hegelianism, Marx himself never did much in the way of constructing systematic philosophical positions. It was Engels who became the father of the philosophy of Marxism both by systematizing historical materialism (*MECW* 27.283; see Marx's summary of the 1859 preface) and by sketching the basic outlines of a materialistic → dialectic that would include the realm of → nature. In Russian Marxism Engels's approaches at first gained great prominence as a general "worldview," and later, in the Marxism of Lenin and of the Soviets, they even achieved logical and didactic priority as the first item in a twofold system

of "dialectical and historical materialism." By focusing on the world's "being in itself" and therefore its "objectivity," Engels gave later Marxist philosophy its objective orientation and immunized it against transcendental criticism (→ Transcendental Philosophy). In his attack on "empirio-criticism" Lenin gave his dubious → materialism an objectivist theory of knowledge. In Russian and Soviet Marxism, unlike that of Marx and Engels, the scientific → worldview assumed importance as a weapon against → religion (→ Religion, Criticism of).

Soviet Marxist philosophy gained a definitive systematic form after Stalin's victory over his opponents between 1931 and 1938, when a little catechism *Of Dialectical and Historical Materialism* came out under Stalin's own name. With its general worldview, based on seven basic features of dialectical method and materialistic theory as transcribed from Engels, all Soviet thinking was brought under ideological supervision.

1.3.4.1. With the basic tenet of *dialectical materialism,* Marxist-Leninist philosophy is at its furthest remove from the tradition of Marx himself. Marx's perspective was not cosmic but anthropocentric and praxis-centered (→ Anthropology 4-5). The abstraction of a world of pure objectivity (matter as "objective reality") was alien to him, though not to Engels (→ Subjectivism and Objectivism). It was Engels who created a school with dogmatic principles in which he tried to answer the basic philosophical question as to the relation between thinking and being (→ Ontology) and between spirit and nature: "Which is primary, mind or nature?" (*MECW* 26.366). Engels's solution was that matter is not a product of mind but that "the mind itself is merely the highest product of matter" (p. 369). "The real unity of the world consists in its materiality, and this is proved not by a few juggled phrases, but by a long and wearisome development of philosophy and natural science" (25.41).

By bold deduction (*MECW* 25.11-12) and an attempted empirical verification, Engels added an objective dialectic to his concept of the material world. Dialectic, he said, is "nothing more than the science of the general laws of motion and development of nature, human society and thought" (p. 131).

The dialectical materialism of Soviet Marxism became a self-serving commentary on these ideas. In the special context of authoritarian party rule, this scholasticism in its abstractness and formalism took on an essentially political and disciplinary significance. The thematic subordination of everything specific to something universal symbolized the social subordination of all individuals to the will of the supreme leadership. We have here the formula of a logic of submission and unconditional → obedience to law. This basic note persisted in the post-Stalin decades and may be seen as well in the final writings of Marxist philosophers in the former East Germany (e.g., W. Eichhorn).

1.3.4.2. The system of *historical materialism* in the philosophy of society and history (→ Philosophy of History) goes back to Marx's *Résumée* of 1859, which already represents a departure from his basic thinking of 1845/46, in which he referred to the conscious being of actual life-processes. The main focus now is on the functional integration of the various segments or spheres of the social process or social relations: being/consciousness, economy/politics/intellectual life, basis/superstructure, and forces of production/relations of production. In such abstraction from the reality of interactive processes, historical materialism has achieved an unhistorical formalism. It rests on treating as a dubious totality that which in Marx had only restricted methodological significance.

Lenin's approach gave the whole complex a specific shift of accent. Whereas Marx was interested in the way in which we can enter into social relations according to our productive powers, Lenin started with given material relations and linked them to the ideological relations that correspond to and reflect them. His social thinking was controlled by material relations, material conditions, and the objective laws that obtain between them.

The general trend in post-Lenin historical materialism has been to transpose interpersonal relations into institutionally or situationally defined "things" and then to treat the correlative movement of these things as a process that operates according to objective law. The subjective and practical side is not primary and constitutive but secondary and executive. The result is the loss of any human immediacy. Along these lines an East German compendium of Marxist-Leninist philosophy (1979, 1982) states that social relations and processes are indeed due to the activities of conscious individuals who have their own purposes, but in them a social being develops that is independent of the social consciousness of individuals and that is reflected by it.

The materialism that has this conceptual profile is one of relations and conditions, not one of social being defined as the reality of the life process. It has thus become in every way an unwieldly construct. Marx would have fresh cause today to argue that materialism is hostile to humanity, as it was for Thomas Hobbes. Above all for Marx, "we must avoid postulating 'society' again as an abstraction

vis-à-vis the individual" (*MECW* 3.299), which is precisely what his successors have done with both their system and their method.

Those who control the objective functionalism of the concept of society in historical materialism have made of it the typical mode of thinking of officials and functionaries. As a sociology related to the present, historical materialism systematically blocks more profound or vital self-understanding of socialist society.

1.3.4.3. Marx and Engels's criticism in *Die deutsche Ideologie* was not criticism of one ideology (bourgeois or petit bourgeois) in the name of another (proletarian) but a *rejection of all ideology*. Positively, it was an effort to set aside the language of ideas and ontology and to find, even for the higher concerns of world history, a language of actual life that would express an "understanding of practice." The Marxism of their successors, however, is again ideological, although it retains the form of Marxism. Logically, then, the most powerful 20th-century Marxism, that of Lenin, abandoned the criticism of ideology, which is often labeled false consciousness, and set up its own ideology in conflict with others, the socialist ideology of the working class, which calls itself a logically scientific ideology.

The concept of interaction between the primary conditions of material life and secondary but relatively independent social consciousness means that for institutional Marxist-Leninist ideologues, their ideological work is an important factor in shaping socialist society. By means of a gigantic ideological apparatus, the ideology becomes in practice ideomagic.

The power of this apparatus, the exercise of power by professional ideologues, and the ritual appeals to Marxism on the part of rulers all favor the view abroad that the ideology with its programmatic prognostications is really the center of power in the Communist system, which may thus be seen as an ideocracy. Yet criticism of ideology in the school of Marx would find in conceptual constructs only the symbolic expression of practice, and in especially lofty constructs the symbols of a practice that has not yet found any certain path and is constitutionally defective, a precarious combination of power and weakness.

Bibliography: Primary sources: E. BERNSTEIN, *The Preconditions of Socialism* (Cambridge, 1993; orig. pub., 1899) • W. EICHHORN, M. BUHR, et al., eds., *Marxistisch-leninistische Philosophie* (East Berlin, 1979) • K. KAUTSKY, *The Road to Power* (Chicago, 1909); idem,

Terrorism and Communism: A Contribution to the Natural History of Revolution (Westport, Conn., 1973; orig. pub., 1919) • V. I. LENIN, *Collected Works* (London, 1960-70); idem, *Materialism and Empirio-criticism: Critical Comments on a Reactionary Philosophy* (Moscow, 1947); idem, *The State and Revolution: Marxist Teaching of the State and the Task of the Proletariat in the Revolution* (2d ed.; London, 1925); *Werke* (45 vols.; Berlin, 1968-78) • R. LUXEMBURG, *The Russian Revolution* (1918), and *Leninism or Marxism?* (Westport, Conn., 1981) • K. MARX and F. ENGELS, *Collected Works* (vols. 1-47; New York, 1975ff.) • G. V. PLEKHANOV, *Fundamental Problems of Marxism* (London, 1929; orig. pub., 1908) • J. STALIN, *Problems of Leninism* (Beijing, 1976; 11th Russ. ed., 1952) • L. TROTSKY, *Terrorism and Communism: A Reply to Karl Kautsky* (Westport, Conn., 1986; orig. pub., 1920).

Histories, biographies, dictionaries: I. BERLIN, *Karl Marx: His Life and Environment* (4th ed.; Oxford, 1978) • T. BOTTOMORE, ed., *A Dictionary of Marxist Thought* (2d ed.; Oxford, 1991) • J. C. DOCHERTY, *Historical Dictionary of Socialism* (Lanham, Md., 1997) • R. A. GORMAN, ed., *Biographical Dictionary of Marxism* (Westport, Conn., 1986) • A. J. GREGOR, *The Faces of Janus: Marxism and Fascism in the Twentieth Century* (New Haven, 2000) • L. KOLAKOWSKI, *Main Currents of Marxism: Its Rise, Growth, and Dissolution* (Oxford, 1978) • M. RUBEL, *Marx-Chronik. Daten zu Leben und Werk* (Munich, 1968) • J. WILCZYNSKI, *An Encyclopedic Dictionary of Marxism, Socialism, and Communism* (Berlin, 1981).

Collections of texts: I. FETSCHER, ed., *Der Marxismus. Seine Geschichte in Dokumenten* (5th ed.; Zurich, 1989; orig. pub., 1962) • N. HARDING, ed., *Marxism in Russia: Key Documents, 1879-1906* (Cambridge, 1983) • W. OELMÜLLER, ed., *Weiterentwicklungen des Marxismus* (Darmstadt, 1977) • H. J. SANDKÜHLER and R. DE LA VEGA, eds., *Marxismus und Ethik. Texte zum neukantianischen Sozialismus* (Frankfurt, 1974).

Other secondary works: J. H. BILLINGTON, *Fire in the Minds of Men: Origins of the Revolutionary Faith* (New York, 1980) • E. BLOCH, *On Karl Marx* (New York, 1971) • G. A. COHEN, *Karl Marx's Theory of History: A Defence* (Princeton, 2001) • I. FETSCHER, *Marx and Marxism* (New York, 1971); idem, *Von Marx zur Sowjetideologie* (22d ed.; Frankfurt, 1987) • H. FLEISCHER, *Marx und Engels. Die philosophischen Grundlinien ihres Denkens* (Freiburg, 1970); idem, *Marxism and History* (London, 1973) • J. HABERMAS, "Zur philosophischen Diskussion um Marx und der Marxismus," *Theory and Practice* (Boston, 1974) • J. R. T. HUGHES, *Ecology and Historical Materialism* (Cambridge, 2000) • B. KAGARLITSKY, *New Realism, New Barbarism: Socialist Theory in the Era of Globalization* (London, 1999) • K. KORSCH,

Karl Marx (New York, 1963; orig. pub., 1938) • A. F. MCGOVERN, "Marxism," *NDCST* 570-79 • B. MAGNUS and S. CULLENBERG, eds., *Whither Marxism? Global Crises in International Perspective* (New York, 1995) • E. MANDEL, *Marxist Economic Theory* (New York, 1969); idem, *The Place of Marxism in History* (Atlantic Highlands, N.J., 1994) • M. MERLEAU-PONTY, *Adventures of the Dialectic* (Evanston, Ill., 1973; orig. pub., 1955) • R. MUNCK, *Marxism at 2000: Late Marxist Perspectives* (New York, 2000) • R. PANASIUK and L. NOWAK, eds., *Marx's Theories Today* (Amsterdam, 1998) • G. PETROVIC, *Marx in the Mid-twentieth Century: A Yugoslav Philosopher Considers Karl Marx's Writings* (Garden City, N.Y., 1967) • J.-P. SARTRE, *Critique of Dialectical Reason* (2 vols.; London, 1982-91; orig. pub., 1960) • S. SIM, *Post-Marxism: An Intellectual History* (London, 2000) • E. M. WOOD, *Democracy against Capitalism: Renewing Historical Materialism* (Cambridge, 1995).

HELMUT FLEISCHER

2. Marxism and Ethics
2.1. Ethics and Class Consciousness

According to Karl → Marx (1818-83), morality or → ethics is not a phenomenon that may be deduced from higher eternal principles but is simply a reflection of the prevailing ideological superstructure (→ Ideology). According to this philosophical approach, the priority of social being over consciousness is what determines the emergence of the individual out of historical determinism (*MECW* 5.262-63). That priority also shows morality to be class conditioned (→ Class and Social Stratum). As Marx says, "The Communists do not preach *morality* at all. . . . They do not put to people the moral demands: love one another, do not be egoists, etc.; on the contrary, they are very well aware that egoism, just as much as selflessness, *is* in definite circumstances a necessary form of the self-assertion of individuals" (p. 247).

This derivation of morality from economic conditions and the related reduction of its content may well have contributed to the fact that neither in Marx nor in his pupils or successors do we find any theoretical conceptions of morality worthy of the name. They see morality either as a necessary weapon in the class conflict (V. Lenin) or as a means to give → legitimation to the rule of the party, which morally embellishes its demand for submission. Already in the 19th century, however, many theoretical anarchists opposed this dogmatic restriction (→ Anarchy). At the same time, the thesis of an implicit ethics of Marxism may well be advanced, as the following sections indicate.

2.2. *Justice*

The commitment of Marx and F. Engels (1820-95) and other leading Marxists like K. Liebknecht (1871-1919) and R. Luxemburg (1871-1919) to the socially disenfranchised and disadvantaged, that is, to the victims of an expansion-oriented → capitalism, need not be viewed merely as a reflection of their economic interests — they all came from well-situated middle-class families — but as the product of a deeply moral sense of justice (→ Righteousness, Justice). Their influence on state-supported legal measures to better the lot of the → proletariat is just as demonstrable as their impact on Latin American → liberation theology and its basic "option for the poor."

2.3. *Work*

Marx's analysis of → work as a central element in human → society and the concrete phenomena of alienation led him to a passionate complaint against a system in which "all family ties among the proletarians are torn asunder, and their children transformed into simple articles of commerce and instruments of labor" (*MECW* 6.502). Political involvement in the struggle against exploitation and disenfranchisement and on behalf of better conditions of life and work played a central part in the organization of labor unions and Social Democratic parties. In the years that followed, the goal was taken up in milder form by church groups and Christian parties. For both the present and the future, these same issues remain a basic political challenge in different cultural and economic contexts.

2.4. *Threefold Alienation*

With the analysis of triple human alienation — from → nature, from others, and from work — and with the utopia of the overcoming of this alienation in a Communist society (see "Estranged Labor" [1844], *MECW* 3.270-82), Marx refused to accept the segmenting of the different spheres of → life as an unalterable fate. He began with the view that life, both in its beginning and in its future, is a totality (5.44-46, 85-87). For the present, however, life is rent asunder and disrupted because most people are forced to sell their labor and find material security under unworthy conditions. The movement toward repetitive piecework still goes on, but its removal is an inalienable postulate of Marxism.

2.5. *Economy and Ethics*

The key role of the → economy and the antagonism in capitalism between social production and private → property are themes in the discussion of social justice (→ Economic Ethics). The concentration of economic power and private property in the hands of a few contradicts the principle of sharing, as

would be stated a century later in the 1948 Universal Declaration of Human → Rights (→ Human Dignity). The degrading of people into dispensable cogs in a gigantic process of production and the resultant understanding of goods as fetishes (*MECW* 35.81-87) fundamentally violate human dignity and its characteristic features of uniqueness, personality, and inviolability. The possibility of humane work and criticism of a system that is defined only in terms of efficiency are a permanent legacy of Marxism. The phenomenon of brutal exploitation has been lessened in developed → industrial societies thanks to the struggles of unions and state legislation, but it has been exported in full force to → Third World countries.

2.6. *Family*

The destructive structural conditions of labor — stress, alienation, and exploitation — affect the → family, including its reproductive function. Often this pressure involves a fixing of roles for the sexes. The man will work at his job, the woman does unpaid housework and raises children. Criticizing this stereotyping in principle is a concern of feminist theorizing (→ Feminist Theology). A common complaint is that Marxism itself has not sufficiently analyzed the injustice of this tradition or fought against it with adequate passion.

2.7. *Ideological Criticism*

Marxist criticism of ideology makes it possible to view morality and ideology as historically and socially mediated (*MECW* 3.141-44). They thus gain in transparency and lose the character of fixed necessity. Over against modern theories of the autonomy and self-grounding of systems, their theoretical unmasking (37.813-18) and the postulate of their historical alterability preserve a place for human → freedom. Criticism of ideology became a concern also in many 20th-century theological and philosophical approaches.

2.8. *Categorical Imperative*

Marx's → "categorical imperative" — namely, to "overthrow all relations in which man is a debased, enslaved, forsaken, despicable being" (*MECW* 3.182) — grew out of his philosophical controversies with G. W. F. Hegel (1770-1831; → Hegelianism) and L. Feuerbach (1804-72; → Religion, Criticism of). Marx formulated a vision of free and self-determined people that L. Tolstoy (1828-1910) broadened from the standpoint of acting on behalf of the lowly and deprived. This vision found different forms of expression in E. Bloch's (1885-1977) utopia of upright conduct, in H. Marcuse's (1898-1979) plea against one-dimensional humanity, in the protest of → critical theory against capitalist-deformed → culture, and in the literary work of B. Brecht (1898-1956).

2.9. *Critical Questions*

Marx's statement that "man is the highest being for man" (*MECW* 3.182) is ethically ambivalent. First, blindness to the relation to God and to the → environment involves a factual claim to domination and exploitation. The former socialist states have suffered from the consequences of this blindness, which has not put a stop to the plundering of the Third World. Second, loss of a sense of our own creatureliness (→ Creation) and relativity legitimates a claim to mastery that does justice neither to nature nor to other people. Finally, the subsuming of morality under the category of superstructure conceals its → dialectic and its creativity. It overlooks the fact that in given situations people are not just victims but doers and that material relations do not automatically absolve them from their own → responsibility.

→ Christians for Socialism; Church in a Socialist Society

Bibliography: S. ARONOWITZ, *The Crisis in Historical Materialism: Class, Politics, and Culture in Marxist Theory* (2d ed.; Minneapolis, 1990) • G. BRAKELMANN, *Abschied vom Unverbindlichen. Gedanken eines Christen zum demokratischen Sozialismus* (Gütersloh, 1976) • H. GOLLWITZER, *Die kapitalistische Revolution* (rev. ed.; Tübingen, 1998) • I. HALFIN, *From Darkness to Light: Class, Consciousness, and Salvation in Revolutionary Russia* (Pittsburgh, 2000) • J. M. LOCHMAN, *Encountering Marx: Bonds and Barriers between Christians and Marxists* (Philadelphia, 1977) • S. LUKES, *Marxism and Morality* (Oxford, 1985) • R. W. MILLER, *Analyzing Marx: Morality, Power, and History* (Princeton, 1984) • R. G. PEFFER, *Marxism, Morality, and Social Justice* (Princeton, 1990) • E. STARKE, "Moral und Moralkritik im 19. Jahrhundert," *Ethik in der europäischen Geschichte,* vol. 2, *Reformation und Neuzeit* (ed. S. H. Pfürtner; Stuttgart, 1988) 102-24 • L. WILDE, *Ethical Marxism and Its Radical Critics* (New York, 1998).

EKKEHARD STARKE

3. Present Situation

It is abundantly clear that for more than a century and a half, Marxism has provided a political, economic, and philosophical stimulus to global developments of great importance. A number of nations have used Marxism as their guiding ideology; other nations have been forced into Marxist structures in respect to both → politics and economics. At the beginning of the last decade of the 20th century, however, with the collapse of the Soviet Union and its satellite nations in Eastern Europe, the whole situation changed. Whether that collapse was caused primarily by political developments stimulated by the West or by weaknesses inherent to the Marxist system is for history to judge. The fact remains that Marxism seems no longer to be a viable political, economic, or intellectual option.

To be sure, Marxist voices are heard within the academic world, sometimes under the guise of other ideologies or schools of thought. The influence of Marxist ideas, many congruent with democratic and even Christian convictions, is not to be lost. Moreover, in 2001 a few nations still claimed officially to be Communist: China, where economic developments have long since deserted the system of Marx and Lenin, as well as Cuba, Laos, and Vietnam (*The World Factbook, 2001* [Washington, D.C.]; North Korea's government is "authoritarian socialist; one-man dictatorship"). Other nations, primarily in the Third World, perhaps look to Marxist ideas in their struggle for liberation and prosperity. Yet clearly an era in the world's geopolitical, economic, and ideological realities has come to a close.

THE EDITORS

Marxism and Christianity

1. Sources of Conflict
   1.1. The Marxist Critique of Religion
   1.2. Political Tensions and Accommodations
2. Christian Positions
   2.1. Roman Catholicism
   2.2. Protestantism
3. Dialogue in Europe
4. Dialogue in North America
5. Dialogue in Latin America
6. Conclusion

1. Sources of Conflict

1.1. *The Marxist Critique of Religion*

Karl → Marx (1818-83), especially in his younger period, took the view that the task of criticizing religion had already been effectively concluded by German philosophers, especially Ludwig Feuerbach (1804-72), who had attempted to base → religion and especially Christianity exclusively in anthropology (→ Criticism).

Although Marx himself never used the expressions "historical → materialism" or "dialectical materialism," his approach to history was nevertheless materialist as he sought to equate the truth of a belief with its historical origin and social function. On this basis, Marx saw religion as a factor contributing to general political and economic alienation in secular society. He believed that this general alienation, expressed in capitalist exploitation, would ultimately disappear, taking both religion and the → state with it. Until that time, Marx viewed religion as aiding in the stabilization of social oppression and dependency.

These fundamental ideas were taken over by colleagues and followers of Marx — most notably Friedrich Engels (1820-95), K. E. Dühring (1833-1921), and ultimately V. I. Lenin (1870-1924) — and religion came increasingly to be seen, in Lenin's phrase, as "spiritual alcohol," which aided the slaves of → capitalism to deny their → humanity and to thwart their quest for a worthwhile human existence. While religion was seen as being purely a private matter in the eyes of the state, the party had the duty to combat the defective consciousness, ignorance, and obscurantism that lay hidden behind faith. It was thus the party's task to propagate → atheism. Yet Lenin, like Marx before him, did not think that propaganda alone would banish religion. Religious oppression was, for him, a product and reflection of economic oppression in society. The comfort given by priests prevents people from taking revolutionary action. Religion therefore had to be rooted out, just as the society that gives rise to → poverty must be extirpated.

1.2. *Political Tensions and Accommodations*

The Soviet Union implemented Lenin's abhorrence of religion. While the party often claimed that religion was to be combated primarily by the spread of the party's "scientific" worldview, in reality the oppression of religion was fostered by prohibition, violence, and general → persecution. In other Communist countries — the nations of Eastern Europe, China, Southeast Asia, and to some extent still in Cuba — there was a general attempt to put down all forms of religious expression. Even now, more than a decade after the fall of Communism, the story of this persecution of religion and its institutions has not been fully told.

It remains true, however, that in the years leading to the upheavals of the late 1980s and early 1990s, even countries in which → Marxism was state doctrine were beginning to recognize the reality of increasing coexistence between Marxists and especially Christians. Communists were beginning to shift in their appraisal of Christian history. Marx himself somewhat grudgingly gave a certain amount of credit to religion for its protest against human suffering. His descendants, however, were exploring the possibility of finding a more positive

place for religion, even under fully developed Communism.

2. Christian Positions
2.1. *Roman Catholicism*

For the most part, Christianity found itself in tension with Marxism during almost the whole course of their common history. Up to the early 20th century, Christianity encountered Marxism primarily as an economic theory (→ Economy), since most of the writings of the young Marx were not known until the third and fourth decades of the century. Leo XIII (1878-1903) studied the "socialist solution" and rejected it in his encyclical *Rerum novarum* (1891) because of its denial of the right to private → property and its tendencies toward → anarchy. In two encyclicals — *Quadragesimo anno* (1931) and *Divini redemptoris* (1937) — Pius XI (1922-39) described Communism as "essentially perverse," although he attributed the development of its doctrines as due in large part to failures of Christian social responsibility.

Nevertheless in the postwar period, especially in largely Roman Catholic France and Italy and among those who struggled for social reform, Marxism had considerable attraction. Some took the view that Marxist economic theory — not its philosophical basis and surely not its atheism — might be viable. This conclusion set off vigorous debates with others who saw the economic categories of Marx as integrally related to his philosophy. Similarly, there were debates between those who attempted to separate Marxist social analysis from its atheistic philosophy and those who saw them bound together. These discussions engaged both Roman Catholic and Protestant intellectuals.

2.2. *Protestantism*

In assessing Protestant reactions to Marxism, especially in Germany, where the reactions quite naturally began, distinctions must be drawn between (1) the adoption of individual concepts and motifs of Marxism that are seen as theologically fruitful, such as Paul → Tillich's (1886-1965) interpretation of → sin as alienation or Karl → Barth's (1886-1968) criticism of "religion," and (2) the debate with Marxism as a doctrine or system. Account must also be taken of the ambivalence of such terms as "Marxism," "socialism," and "Communism"; clear conceptual distinctions between these terms is often not possible.

In the 19th century Protestants encountered an imperfectly known Marx largely under the impact of Marxism's (minimal) influence among workers. At this point Protestant reaction to Marxism was mainly at the point of the latter's criticism of religion and the church. During this time fundamental → dialogue with Marxism was largely limited to the work in Germany of R. Todt (1839-87), who accepted Marx's economic analysis of the class society but opposed the antichurch trend and the atheism both of Marxism and of the Social Democracy movement.

In the face of a → proletariat suffering under rampant industrialization (→ Industrial Society), Protestants began to face social issues, although mostly in terms of philanthropy. In the main, however, it was only in the 20th century that serious debates concerning Marxism began, mostly in respect to variant forms of → socialism. Some theologians became passionate supporters of certain of these forms, even asserting that, in the contemporary world, one could not be merely a Christian but must also be a socialist. This support of socialism was best typified by the establishment of the movement known as → religious socialism in 1906 in Switzerland. Important leaders of this movement were Christoph Blumhardt (1842-1919), Hermann Kutter (1863-1931), and Leonhard Ragaz (1868-1945), all of whom stressed the importance of Christian → eschatology in dealing with the social problems of the day, relating a strict rejection of the omnipotent state to the struggle for social justice. Both Barth, when he was a pastor in a Swiss working-class parish, and Tillich in Germany pressed for political expressions of socialist and Marxist demands, though they both rejected any equation of the → kingdom of God with a future "classless society."

Nazism and the resultant World War II put a rapid end to these lively debates in Germany. Many theologians, including some who were politically liberal, either left Germany (e.g., Barth and Tillich) or were imprisoned for their opposition to the Nazis (e.g., Paul Schneider and Dietrich → Bonhoeffer, both of whom were executed). However, the vehement anti-Communist propaganda of the National Socialist regime and its broad racist ideology did find broad support in church circles, especially among the → German Christians but also among such Lutheran theologians as Paul Althaus (1888-1966), Friedrich Gogarten (1887-1967), and, above all, Emanuel Hirsch (1888-1972). Many of these regarded themselves as nonpolitical and were not inclined to criticize political or ideological systems. There was, during this time, neither practical dialogue nor theoretical discourse between Christianity and Marxism.

After the defeat of German → fascism, the Evan-gelical Church in Germany sought new beginnings, as typified in the Stuttgart Declaration of Guilt (1945) and the subsequent → Darmstadt Declaration (1947), both of which were marked by penitent self-criticism (→ Germany 2.2.1). In such a spirit Protestant theologians in Germany renewed, in many forms, the debate with Marxism. Christians and Marxists formed alliances for political action, for example, in respect to controversies over German rearmament, and basic theological and ideological conversations also began to take place. A massive obstacle to such dialogue, particularly in the German Democratic Republic and other Eastern European nations, was the atheistic propaganda and church persecution carried to alarming levels by Josef Stalin (1879-1953). This action prevented free discussion in those lands or, at great risk to Christians, pushed discussion underground. Additionally, this program provided ideological fodder for Western cold war attitudes.

3. Dialogue in Europe

The debate between Christianity and Marxism reached new profundity in the postwar period as the actual philosophical writings of Marx, discovered largely in the 1930s, came to be more and more familiar. Additionally, the critical work of scholars like Nikolai Berdyaev (1874-1948), a Russian who had settled in France, came to be known. Although not dealing with Marx as a philosopher, Berdyaev nevertheless drew attention to the kind of secular → messianism that was typical of Marxism and even stronger in Russian Communism.

In the West there was theoretical engagement with Marxism, for example, in the work of Helmut Gollwitzer (1908-93). In Eastern Europe the contact was largely practical. As early as the constituting assembly of the → World Council of Churches (1948), the Czech theologian Josef Hromádka (1889-1969) declared that although Christians must resist → totalitarianism, they must also not fail to see the potential for human liberation that is present in Communism. In West Germany an ecumenical commission on Marxism worked on various themes up to 1972: the dialogue between world religions and Marxism, property, → ideology, anthropology, conflicts between economic systems, truth, tolerance, and the development of Marxist systems in different cultural contexts.

The work of the Paulus-Gesellschaft (the Society of Paul), founded in 1956 by the Bavarian priest Erich Kellner in 1956, was for a significant period of time perhaps the most important vehicle for Marxist-Christian dialogue in Europe. This society, founded largely by Roman Catholics but open to persons of all faiths or of no faith, was an international, interdenominational organization that conducted interdisciplinary seminars, conferences, dialogues, and action projects. In 1969 it formally became the Paulus-Gesellschaft Internationale, with members in North and South America as well as Europe.

In 1964 the society held two conferences, in Munich and Cologne. At the Cologne meeting, although no Marxists were present, three papers were considered: by the Marxist philosopher Ernst Bloch (1885-1977), delivered in absentia, the theologian Karl → Rahner (1904-84), and the ethnologist Konrad Lorenz (1903-89). Subsequently, between 1965 and 1978, the Paulus-Gesellschaft held six formal Christian-Marxist conferences: in Salzburg, Austria, on the topic "Christianity and Marxism — Today" (1965); Herrenchiemsee, West Germany, "Christian Humanity and Marxist Humanism" (1966); Mariánské Lázně (Ger. Marienbad), Czechoslovakia, "Creativity and Freedom in a Humane Society" (1967); Florence, Italy, "Man: Guide of the Evolutionary Process" (1975); Salzburg, "A Democratic and Social Europe of Tomorrow" (1977); and Düsseldorf, West Germany, "Marxist Philosophy and Christian Values Today" (1978).

Three works from this period, by Marxists from both Western and Eastern Europe, typify the opening up of new conversations and dialogues between Marxists and Christians in the 1960s and 1970s: the French Marxist Roger Garaudy's work *From Anathema to Dialogue* (Eng. ed., 1966), the title of which perhaps sums up the new spirit of these conversations; the Czech Vitézslav Gardavský, *God Is Not Yet Dead* (Eng. ed., 1973); and the Czech Milan Machovec, *A Marxist Looks at Jesus* (Eng. ed., 1976).

Writing in respect particularly of how Marxist-Christian dialogue was carried out in Eastern Europe, the scholar and participant Paul Mojzes in 1981 described six types of dialogue and the countries in which each type prevailed:

1. total absence of dialogue, annihilation of churches by the Communist government: Albania;
2. avoidance of dialogue, coexistence and political accommodation leading to limited cooperation: USSR, Bulgaria, Romania;
3. practical dialogue despite official disclaimers: East Germany;
4. carefully managed dialogue in order to facilitate cooperation, recognition of each other's strength: Hungary, Poland, International Peace Symposia;
5. critical involvement in dialogue, pluralism of ex-

pectations and attitudes: Czechoslovakia, Yugoslavia, Paulus-Gesellschaft congresses; and
6. dialogic engagement in freedom, unprivileged position of either partner: some dialogues of the future? (p. 39).

In spite of the variety of expressions of dialogue that took place in Europe in the 1960s and 1970s, after the forces of the Warsaw Pact countries moved into Czechoslovakia in 1968 to suppress the liberation movement led by Alexander Dubček, Marxist-Christian dialogue declined rapidly. Later, to be sure, conversation was resumed in some cases. For example, in 1984 in Budapest, Christians and Marxists entered into unofficial conversations that were followed by a symposium sponsored by the Hungarian Academy of Science and the Roman Catholic Secretariat (later Pontifical Council) for Dialogue with Nonbelievers (since 1993 merged with the Pontifical Council for Culture) on ethical values in society, the shaping of such values by society, and changes in both society and ethical values. The issue of this symposium was to see how far coexistence between Marxists and Christians is possible despite differences concerning these issues.

Although the results of the several dialogues between European Christians and Marxists should not be underestimated, the fact remains that at the downfall of Communism in Europe in the early 1990s, the fundamental rejection of Christianity by Marxism still prevailed within both the political and the intellectual communities. Christian faith in a personal God revealed in history was rejected as an atavism that undermines human → autonomy.

4. Dialogue in North America

Socialism — either in a moderate sense or in a stricter Marxist framework — has never taken hold in North America, certainly not in the United States. A variety of reasons explain this fact, including the relative absence, in contrast to Europe, of sharp class distinctions; the "American dream" that every hardworking person can become an owner of property; and the willingness of the labor movement to work for incremental concessions for workers rather than for fundamental societal change. Before the 1960s the churches in America, with certain exceptions, were negatively disposed to socialism. The → Roman Catholic Church took the lead in this attitude, despite the movement centered on the *Catholic Worker*, which began in 1933 under the inspiration of Dorothy Day (1897-1980) and Peter Maurin (1877-1949). There was a somewhat greater openness in American Protestantism to socialism and even Communism, typified perhaps by Henry F. Ward of Union Theological Seminary and the Methodist Federation for Social Action, both supporters of a number of Communist causes. Reinhold → Niebuhr (1892-1971) in the 1930s made a strong case for Marxist analysis and reportedly even referred to himself as a Christian Marxist (G. Harland, *The Thought of Reinhold Niebuhr* [New York, 1960] 236), a position he later vigorously and famously disavowed.

Three types of Marxist-Christian dialogue took place in North America between 1965 and the mid-1980s. From 1965 to 1972 there were dialogues on Christian and Marxist worldviews at, among other places, the University of Notre Dame, the University of Santa Clara, and the Chicago Theological Seminary. Lectures at the last institution by Jürgen Moltmann, Charles West, Sidney Lens, and others were published as *Openings for Marxist-Christian Dialogues* (1968). The American Marxist Herbert Aptheker (1915-2003), who felt that this work misrepresented Marxist views concerning religion, countered with *The Urgency of Marxist-Christian Dialogue* (1970). During this time European Marxists — for example, Garaudy, Gardavský, and Machovec — were brought to North America for conversations with Christians. The U.S. Committee for the Christian Peace Conference, founded in 1965, was instrumental in bringing Machovec to America; it also worked with offices of the Presbyterian Church in making such arrangements.

A second type of North American dialogue took place between 1972 and 1977, dealing largely with action in opposition to capitalism. These dialogues were heavily influenced by perceptions of the socioeconomic situation in Latin America, which had instigated → liberation theology in that continent. A movement called Christians for Socialism was founded in Chile in 1972 and in North America in 1974. Its followers perceived "capitalism imperialism" as their enemy and argued that Marxist social analysis could be used without embracing Marxist atheism or philosophical materialism. Christians for Socialism described itself as theologically rooted in the biblical tradition and ideologically in the Marxist criticism of both capitalism and religion.

The third type of dialogue, which took place from 1977 to 1984, centered on questions of → peace and justice. Paul Mojzes arranged a conference on peace at Rosemont College in Pennsylvania in 1977 at which the principal Christian speaker was Charles West of Princeton Theological Seminary and the main Marxist speaker was Yuri Zamoshkin of the Soviet Union. Participants in the conference came from North America, Canada, Eastern and Western Europe, and the Soviet Union. Other North American

dialogues during these years focused on U.S. socioeconomic problems (Rosemont College, 1978), on dehumanization (Dayton, Ohio, 1980), and on the nature of work (Washington, D.C., 1982).

In addition to discussing religious-philosophical issues, Marxist-Christian dialogues in North America from the early 1970s to the 1980s also concentrated on anthropological and sociological issues (esp. → sexism and → racism), economic and political issues, and international questions. Since the mid-1980s and after the fall of Communism, dialogues on these and other such issues have continued, but without a specific Marxist-Christian focus.

5. Dialogue in Latin America

The Christian dialogue with Marxism in Latin America has been decidedly less theoretical and more concrete and practical than in other parts of the world. In 1978 the Cuban Methodist biblical scholar Israel Batista Guerra indicated that rather than "dialogue," the preferred term was *encuentro* (encounter): "The theoretical has not been the fundamental fact in our experience. We have lived and moved under the impulse of praxis" (*Cristo vivo en Cuba* [ed. S. A. Martínez et al.; San José, C.R., 1978] 81).

Perhaps the most telling influence of Marxism on Latin American Christians has been in the development of liberation theology. In the early 1970s the "political theology" associated largely with the Germans Johannes Metz and Jürgen Moltmann stimulated theologians in Latin America to turn toward a Marxist analysis of society. The principal motivation for this turn was the moral reaction to the vast and collective suffering of the Latin American poor. The signal work was *A Theology of Liberation* by the Peruvian Roman Catholic Gustavo Gutiérrez, published first in 1971. Gutiérrez understood the task of theology as "critical reflection on praxis," using the tools of Marxist analysis. Other theologians followed suit, among them the Roman Catholics Leonardo Boff, Clodovis Boff, Enrique Dussel, and Jon Sobrino, as well as the Argentinian Methodist José Míguez Bonino.

In 1984 and 1986 the Vatican, through instructions of its Congregation for the Doctrine of the Faith, reacted strongly to liberation theology, noting an "insufficiently critical" use of such Marxist concepts as class struggle and warning against a reduction of faith to politics. Nevertheless, in 1986 John Paul II affirmed in a letter to Brazilian bishops the "useful and necessary" character of liberation theology.

Another important Latin American development in Christian-Marxist relations took place in

Cuba when Fidel Castro, in a wide-ranging conversation with Frei Betto, indicated that while fundamental philosophical differences remain, there is basis for serious dialogue and common action between Christians and Marxists. These published reflections have generally been taken as another sign of the willingness of many to reconsider traditionally dogmatic Marxist views concerning religion and Christian faith.

6. Conclusion

In sum, one might say that there has been no full reconciliation between Christianity and Marxism, even though the relation is now much less tense than in the period of Soviet ascendency. For Christians, full reconciliation would require the surrender of their belief in transcendence and of their view that beyond every determinism, humans have → freedom and bear responsibility for their actions. Yet the points of contact between Christianity and Marxism remain deep. Christians, both Roman Catholics and Protestants, have used such Marxist ideas as alienation and exploitation. Even John Paul II, notably in his 1987 encyclical *Sollicitudo rei socialis,* made use of Marxist concepts. It would be difficult to understand the work of many Christian theologians since World War II without taking into account the dialogue that has taken place with the descendants of Marx.

Bibliography: H. APTHEKER, *The Urgency of Marxist-Christian Dialogue* (New York, 1970) • G. BAUM, *The Church for Others: Protestant Theology in Communist East Germany* (Grand Rapids, 1996) • A. J. VAN DER BENT, *The Christian-Marxist Dialogue: An Annotated Bibliography, 1959-1969* (Geneva, 1969) • N. A. BERDYAEV, *Christianisme, marxisme. Conception chrétienne et conception marxiste de l'histoire* (Paris, 1975); idem, *The Origin of Russian Communism* (London, 1955) • F. BETTO, *Fidel Castro and Religion* (New York, 1987) • J.-Y. CALVEZ, *La pensée de Karl Marx* (Paris, 1970; orig. pub., 1956) • J. ELLUL, *Jesus and Marx: From Gospel to Ideology* (Grand Rapids, 1988) • R. GARAUDY, *From Anathema to Dialogue: A Marxist Challenge to the Christian Churches* (New York, 1966) • V. GARDAVSKÝ, *God Is Not Yet Dead* (New York, 1973) • H. GOLLWITZER, *The Christian Faith and the Marxist Criticism of Religion* (New York, 1970) • G. GUTIÉRREZ, *A Theology of Liberation: History, Politics, and Salvation* (rev. ed.; Maryknoll, N.Y., 1988) • P. HEBBLETHWAITE, *The Christian-Marxist Dialogue: Beginnings, Present Status, and Beyond* (New York, 1977) • D. R. JANZ, *World Christianity and Marxism* (New York, 1998) • A. KEE, *Marx and the Failure of Liberation Theology* (London, 1990) • A. J. KLINGHOFFER, *Red Apocalypse: The Religious Evolution of Soviet Communism* (Lanham, Md., 1996) • N. LASH, *A Matter of Hope: A Theologian's Reflections on the Thought of Karl Marx* (Notre Dame, Ind., 1982) • J. M. LOCHMAN, *Christ and Prometheus? A Quest for Theological Identity* (Geneva, 1988); idem, *Church in a Marxist Society: A Czechoslovak View* (London, 1970); idem, *Encountering Marx: Bonds and Barriers between Christians and Marxists* (Philadelphia, 1977) • A. McGOVERN, *Marxism: An American Christian Perspective* (Maryknoll, N.Y., 1980) • M. MACHOVEC, *A Marxist Looks at Jesus* (Philadelphia, 1976) • J. MÍGUEZ BONINO, *Christians and Marxists: The Mutual Challenge to Revolution* (London, 1976); idem, *Doing Theology in a Revolutionary Situation* (Philadelphia, 1975) • J. P. MIRANDA, *Marx and the Bible: A Critique of the Philosophy of Oppression* (Maryknoll, N.Y., 1974) • P. MOJZES, *Christian-Marxist Dialogue in Eastern Europe* (Minneapolis, 1981); idem, ed., *Varieties of Christian-Marxist Dialogue* (Philadelphia, 1978) • T. OGLETREE, ed., *Openings for Marxist-Christian Dialogue* (Nashville, 1968) • N. PIEDISCALZI and R. G. THOBABEN, eds., *From Hope to Liberation: Towards a New Marxist-Christian Dialogue* (Philadelphia, 1974); idem, eds., *Three Worlds of Christian-Marxist Encounters* (Philadelphia, 1985) • W. STUMME, ed., *Christians and the Many Faces of Marxism* (Minneapolis, 1984).

JEAN-IVES CALVEZ, EKKEHARD STARKE, and
NORMAN A. HJELM

Mary, Devotion to

1. General
    1.1. History
    1.2. In Liturgy and Prayer
    1.3. In Literature, Music, and Art
    1.4. Religious Orders
    1.5. Theology
    1.6. Orthodox Church
    1.7. Protestant Churches
2. Feminist Theology
    2.1. Criticism of Mariology
    2.2. Current Directions
    2.3. Theological Issues
3. Latin America
    3.1. Legacy of the Conquest
    3.2. Religious Orders
    3.3. Liberation Theology

1. General

Devotion to Mary plays an important role in the → Orthodox Church and the → Roman Catholic

Church. To be distinguished from praise of Mary is the appeal for her intercession before God in every need. Devotion to Mary originated in the spontaneous → piety of believers (→ Popular Religion), although pagan influences (→ Syncretism) and psychological factors (→ Psychology of Religion) probably helped to generate and shape it. An important influence has been a changing perception of Mary's role in obtaining divine blessings, including those of → salvation.

1.1. *History*

Elements of → devotion to Mary appear, arguably, in Luke and John (→ Mary in the New Testament). → Justin (ca. 100-ca. 165) and → Irenaeus (ca. 130-ca. 200) developed the parallel between Eve and Mary. The first Greek invocation of Mary ("under thy protection . . .") came from the early fourth century. From the time of → Athanasius (ca. 297-373) and Ambrose (ca. 339-97; → Church Fathers), Mary was treated as a model. Severian (fl. ca. 400), bishop of Gabala in Syria, bears witness to praise of Mary as a daily practice. In the West → Augustine (354-430; → Augustine's Theology) discussed her. In the East we find feasts of Mary from at least the fifth century, feasts adopted in the West in the seventh century (→ Church Year 2.1-2).

The Council of → Ephesus (431) was an important spur to devotion to Mary with its support for the title *theotokos*, "God-bearer," for Mary. In the period that followed, increasing stress fell on Mary's transcendent role in the present as heavenly lady, queen, and intercessor. Specific themes developed in the High → Middle Ages, especially Mary as Mother of Sorrows or Mother of Mercy. Debate regarding the immaculate conception helped to increase devotion to Mary. → Bernard of Clairvaux (1090-1153) commended unconditional trust in Mary and emphasized her mediatorial role.

The → Catholic Reform and Counterreformation made much of Mary. Especially devoted to Mary in the 17th century were Francis de Sales (1567-1622) and John Eudes (1601-80), who championed devotion to the heart of Mary (→ Sacred Heart of Jesus). Louis-Marie Grignion de Montfort (1673-1716) propagated full-scale devotion to Mary, and Alphonsus Liguori (1696-1787) was also influential with his work *The Glories of Mary* (1750). After the → Enlightenment → Romanticism revived the veneration of Mary. In 1854 the raising of the immaculate conception to dogmatic rank by → Pius IX (1846-78) further increased devotion to Mary. A series of appearances at → Lourdes (1858) and → Fatima (1917) helped to establish and spread it.

The 20th-century popes continued the process.

Leo XIII (1878-1903) repeatedly commended the praying of the → rosary. Pius XII (1939-58), sometimes called the Marian pope, promulgated the dogma of the bodily assumption of Mary in 1950. → Vatican II affirmed a legitimate devotion to Mary but, partially in the interests of → ecumenism, warned against false and exaggerated practices.

1.2. *In Liturgy and Prayer*

1.2.1. The → liturgy is the official setting of the veneration of Mary, even though she is in fact rarely mentioned in the main Roman eucharistic liturgies, in contrast to her frequent invocation in many Eastern liturgies. In the canon of the → Mass (→ Eucharistic Prayer), Mary is mentioned along with other saints as an expression of the fellowship of the whole church. Proper prefaces refer to the election of Mary, and her intercession is sought in other texts and in prayers at the administration of the → sacraments. Feasts of Mary developed first in relation to the birth of → Jesus (e.g., the annunciation). Soon also, however, came commemoration of Mary's divine motherhood. Events in her life (birth and death) and beliefs regarding her (the immaculate conception and bodily assumption) also became the occasions of feasts. Liturgical reform after Vatican II, especially during the pontificate of Paul VI (1963-78), attempted to correct mistaken developments and to set devotion to Mary within the larger mystery of Christ.

Altars to Mary and pictorial representations illustrate Mary's importance for → faith and promote devotion to her. From the fourth century churches were dedicated to Mary, and → monasteries also bore her name (→ Patron Saint). Geographic areas and whole countries were dedicated to Mary; in 1942 Pius XII consecrated the world and the church to the immaculate heart of Mary, and some predominantly Roman Catholic countries followed suit. This act of consecration was repeated by John Paul II in 1983.

1.2.2. Popular devotion to Mary comes to expression in a series of typical but extraliturgical → prayers (→ Popular Catholicism). These prayers include the → Ave Maria and the Angelus, which is a reminder of the annunciation and the incarnation and which closes with a petition. We might also note the rosary, the Salve Regina, and the Litany of Loreto. The months of May and October are specifically devoted to Mary.

→ Pilgrimages (individually or in groups) are especially important. Devotion is offered to pictures or statues at the sites of reported → miracles. New places of pilgrimages are associated with appearances (Lourdes, Fatima). Votive offerings are for special needs and for giving thanks for the help received.

1.3. *In Literature, Music, and Art*

The promotion and expression of devotion to Mary in literature is widespread in medieval legends and miracle stories, many of which are based on the life of Mary as described in the *Protoevangelium of James,* a second-century apocryphal text. The most widely distributed book on Mary in modern times is Liguori's *Glories of Mary.* In 1833 Clemens Maria Brentano (1778-1842) published a life of Mary based on the visions of Anna Katharina Emmerick (1774-1824). Mention may also be made of liturgically used → hymns, antiphons, and sequences. Mary is still an important literary theme.

Musical expression of the praise of Mary appears in the settings of prayers and in popular or more formal songs, including a number of operatic arias. Almost all the great composers have written works for liturgical use, including works with a Marian theme or works dedicated to Mary.

Marian iconography is a widespread theme in Christian art (→ Images). The enthroned Theotokos, or "Virgin in Majesty," is a dominant theme in church apses (→ Church Architecture). She sometimes shares the throne with her Son. We also find Mary with the Christ child in her arms (the Hodegetria and the Eleusa), and in medieval art she is often shown in the company of her mother, Anne, and other female saints, or with her protecting cloak encompassing groups of believers (→ Devotional Images). Other images include Mary as intercessor (the Deesis), as the Pietà holding the crucified body of Christ, at the annunciation, at her assumption into heaven, as the immaculate conception or the immaculate heart, and as the Mother of Sorrows (with one or more swords in her heart). Some modern Marian art is based on apparitions such as those at Lourdes and Fatima. Many cycles depict events in the life of Mary such as the marriage of her parents, Joachim and Anne, the nativity of the Virgin, and her dormition, or "falling asleep," at the end of her life.

1.4. *Religious Orders*

→ Religious orders and congregations have given a special form to Marian piety. They see in Mary a model of the Christian → life according to the evangelical counsels (→ Sermon on the Mount 4). Many orders attribute their origins to the stimulation and help of Mary and view themselves as participating in her work. Belief in her actual role in shaping the world for Christ gives a special Marian orientation to orders and societies with an apostolic and missionary goal (→ Catholic Missions).

Members of lay Marian congregations such as the Marian Congregation of 1563, the Legio Mariae, and the Rosary Crusade promote a specifically Marian → spirituality as a form of → discipleship of Christ. Typical in such groups are personal devotion to Mary and apostolic commitment.

1.5. *Theology*

Theologically, devotion to Mary rests on her election and readiness to be the mother of Jesus Christ. Her free and positive response in Luke 1:38 and her close relation to Christ are viewed as an exemplary actualizing of faith, so that in all things Mary can rank as a model of Christian life. Insofar as she actively cooperated in the work of her Son, she is also regarded as a type of the → church (§3.2). Vatican II set Mary in this ecclesiological context and thus opposed making devotion to Mary an independent phenomenon. With John Paul II the Roman Catholic Church has stressed the significance of the work of Mary for the church today.

The invocation of Mary rests on her role in the work of salvation and on belief in the communion of saints. Marian spirituality always has had strong emotional components that tend toward exaggeration and one-sidedness. Rightly understood and integrated, however, devotion to Mary is not meant to threaten the divine glory or the significance of Christ. Pius X (1903-14) found in it a pointer to Christ. Clearly, God alone is to be worshiped. Theology identifies the honor that should be paid to Mary as *hyperdoulia* (lit. "more than veneration"; cf. *d[o]ulia,* the honor given to angels and saints). The Council of → Trent commended veneration of all the → saints (DH 1821), and both the Second Council of → Nicaea (DH 600) and Trent (DH 1823) ruled in favor of veneration of images of Christ, Mary, and the saints, holding that to honor the image is to honor the person.

1.6. *Orthodox Church*

In the Orthodox Church devotion to Mary has a special form linked to the significance of the liturgy and → icons in the life of the church and believers. Praise of Mary comes to expression in liturgically used hymns such as the → Acathistus. Mary is lauded at the → Eucharist after the epiclesis; stress thus falls on her closeness to the mystery that is celebrated but also on her connection with the whole church.

The ruling of Nicaea II (787) is quoted in support of the veneration of icons. A kind of mystical identity is postulated between original and copy (→ Platonism). Icons of Mary have a prominent place on the → iconostasis, which separates the sanctuary from the nave. In Orthodoxy August is Mary's special month. Special emphasis in devotion to Mary falls on the "salvation-bringing *theotokos*," the "all-holy and perpetual virgin," and the "merciful intercessor and mediatrix with the Almighty."

1.7. Protestant Churches

In Protestant churches (→ Protestantism) devotion to Mary plays a meager role because from the outset it was seen to be incompatible with the fundamental principles of the → Reformation (→ Reformation Principles). Direct appeal to Mary for intercession and aid does not take seriously the mediatorship of Christ and the mercy of → God. The attitude of Martin → Luther (1483-1546) to the veneration of Mary, however, has been variously interpreted. He undoubtedly found in Mary a model of faith and → humility, but he attacked the misunderstandings behind devotion to Mary. A true comprehension of → justification makes the veneration of saints superfluous. Ulrich → Zwingli (1484-1531) retained a high view of Mary but did not promote devotion to her.

In recent years some Protestants have come to accept that asking the prayers of Mary is no more illegitimate than asking for those of other faithful Christians. Others remain deeply suspicious of any form of Marian piety.

Roman Catholic veneration specifically attracts criticism, less so that of the East. Mary undoubtedly needs to be a theme of ecumenical → dialogue, but thus far that dialogue has only just begun (→ Mariology 1.5 and 2.7). Since attitudes toward the veneration of Mary seem to reflect particular understandings of faith, agreement on the matter can be reached only in the context of comprehensive theological discussion.

→ Catholicism (Roman)

Bibliography: R. Bäumer and L. Scheffczyk, eds., *Marienlexikon* (6 vols.; St. Ottilien, 1988-94) • W. Beinert and H. Petri, eds., *Handbuch der Marienkunde* (Regensburg, 1984) • J. B. Carol, *Mariology* (3 vols.; Milwaukee, Wis., 1955-61) • M. P. Carroll, *The Cult of the Virgin Mary: Psychological Origins* (Princeton, 1992) • Y. Congar, *Christ, Our Lady, and the Church: A Study in Eirenic Theology* (Westminster, Md., 1957) • W. Delius, *Geschichte der Marienverehrung* (Munich, 1963) • D. Donnelly, ed., *Mary, Woman of Nazareth: Biblical and Theological Perspectives* (New York, 1989) • H. Düfel, *Luthers Stellung zur Marienverehrung* (Göttingen, 1968) • H. Graef, *Mary: A History of Doctrine and Devotion* (2d ed.; London, 1985) • R. Laurentin, *Queen of Heaven: A Short Treatise on Marian Theology* (Dublin, 1956) • M. O'Carroll, *Theotokos: A Theological Encyclopedia of the Blessed Virgin Mary* (Wilmington, Del., 1983) • J. Pelikan, *Mary through the Centuries: Her Place in the History of Culture* (New Haven, 1996) • H. Petri, ed., *Christsein und marianische Spiritualität* (Regensburg, 1984) • K. Rahner, *Mary, Mother of the Lord: Theological Meditations* (New York, 1963) • G. Schimmelpfennig, *Die Geschichte der Marienverehrung im deutschen Protestantismus* (Paderborn, 1952) • L. J. Suenens, *Mary the Mother of God* (New York, 1959) • W. Tappolet, ed., *Das Marienlob der Reformatoren. Martin Luther, Johannes Calvin, Huldrych Zwingli, Heinrich Bullinger* (Tübingen, 1962).

Heinrich Petri

2. Feminist Theology

2.1. Criticism of Mariology

Feminist theologians criticize → Mariology for its patriarchal bias in Roman Catholic theology, and for the exclusion of the maternal feminine dimension of the Christian faith associated with Mary from Reformation theology. Some reject her as a hopelessly androcentric figure. The traditional Mary is seen by feminists as an idealized and asexual virgin who is passively related to God, who has no significance of her own, and who, as a projection of male fears and fantasies, defines the role of Christian womanhood as that of the servile, sexually passive, and sacrificing wife and mother with a subordinate role in both → church and → society.

2.2. Current Directions

While some feminists dismiss Mary altogether, others are reclaiming dimensions of the Marian tradition that are seen to offer a more positive and life-affirming image of womanhood. This endeavor tends to go in two directions.

2.2.1. First, women working within the Christian tradition look beyond the usual picture of Mary for alternative symbols of motherhood and female → discipleship, often by appealing to the insights of → liberation theology (I. Gebara and M. C. Bingemer, C. J. M. Halkes). The Magnificat is seen as a central text in expressing God's option for the poor and in affirming the salvation of women and their liberation from social and sexual oppression. This song from the lips of a woman is a thanksgiving to God for granting her a share in the work of → salvation. In this context the *fiat* (let it be) of Luke 1:38 is not the passive surrender of a humble maiden to God's will but the free decision of a woman who defies the conventions of patriarchal society by agreeing to become the mother of God without male tutelage or intervention. Mary conceives her Savior-Son through the → Holy Spirit (1:35; the OT term, *rûaḥ*, is fem.) as a fruit of her → faith. For women, then, she is a sister in faith and an example of woman's courage and integrity before God and the world.

In addition to liberation theology, other Christian feminists look to historical dimensions of Marian theology and → devotion as resources for a revitalized theology of women's salvation. Some see in patristic and medieval devotion, theology, and art (→ Christian Art) a more potent and redeeming image of maternal femininity than in modern representations (T. Beattie, S. J. Boss, S. Cunneen).

2.2.2. The second direction taken by feminist studies of Mary is informed by scholarship in the → history of religion and the history of symbolism. It tends to focus on Mary's potential as a goddess figure (A. Baring and J. Cashford). These scholars argue that the human mother of → Jesus has the attributes of a goddess (like the goddesses of Sumer, Babylon, or Egypt), for example, as the virgin mother of God who suffers for her slain Son, as the queen of heaven, and as the helper in need. Since Christianity gave no symbolic expression to the processes of fertility and renewal in nature and in the cosmos, and since it repressed the consciousness that the goddess symbolized, these features found expression in the cult of Mary — sometimes in perverted form. (Note the autonomy of virginity in sexual asceticism.) Thus it is argued that symbols of the divine feminine are inalienable factors in human life and development that cannot be completely eradicated from patriarchal → monotheism.

Some feminists who have done research into goddesses see in them the roots of genuine female identity. The virgin mother, the goddess who is not defined in relation to the male, is a model that can help women free themselves from patriarchal images. At this point the two approaches — liberation theology and studies of the goddess (thea-logy) — have something in common, even though those who take the goddess approach do not believe that the weak biblical picture of Mary alone can help women to liberation.

2.3. Theological Issues

A point of convergence between feminist Marian theology and thealogy lies in the question of whether or not the divine likeness of women as well as of men is anchored and protected in the Christian view of → God. Some would argue that it is not enough simply to accord Mary the status of a goddess, but rather that there must be greater understanding of the psychological as well as the religious functions of maternal divinities and goddess figures. Thus we must ask to what extent Christianity has projected onto the figure of Mary the maternal fem-

inine qualities that should more properly be attributed to God. Only by exploring such lines of inquiry will it become possible to discover the contours of a theological vision in which Mary can become an authentic expression of faith for both women and men.

→ Feminism; Feminist Theology

Bibliography: A. Baring and J. Cashford, *The Myth of the Goddess: Evolution of an Image* (London, 1993) • T. Beattie, *God's Mother, Eve's Advocate: A Marian Narrative of Woman's Salvation* (London, 2002) • S. J. Boss, *Empress and Handmaid: On Nature and Gender in the Cult of the Virgin Mary* (London, 2000) • C. Christ, *The Laughter of Aphrodite: Reflections on a Journey to the Goddess* (San Francisco, 1987) • S. Cunneen, *In Search of Mary: The Woman and the Symbol* (New York, 1996) • M. Daly, *Beyond God the Father: Towards a Philosophy of Women's Liberation* (Boston, 1973) • J. Gatta, *American Madonna: Images of the Divine Woman in Literary Culture* (New York, 1997) • I. Gebara and M. C. Bingemer, *Mary: Mother of God, Mother of the Poor* (Maryknoll, N.Y., 1989) • C. J. M. Halkes, *Gott hat nicht nur starke Söhne* (Gütersloh, 1980) • M. Kassel, "Maria. Urbild des Weiblichen im Christentum? Tiefenpsychologisch-feministische Perspektiven," *Was geht uns Maria an?* (ed. E. Moltmann-Wendell et al.; Gütersloh, 1988) 142-60 • R. R. Ruether, *Mary: The Feminine Face of the Church* (Philadelphia, 1977) • L. Schottroff, *Let the Oppressed Go Free: Feminist Perspectives on the NT* (Louisville, Ky., 1993) • M. Warner, *Alone of All Her Sex: The Myth and the Cult of the Virgin Mary* (rev. ed.; New York, 2001).

Tina Beattie and Maria Kassel

3. Latin America

3.1. *Legacy of the Conquest*

Devotion to Mary has made a great impact on Latin America, expressing itself in many different ways in the various countries. Some authors even speak of an earlier, precolonial cult of Mary (R. M. Huber). Undoubtedly, however, → devotion to Mary is a legacy of the Spanish and Portuguese conquerors. The discovery and conquest of the continent (→ Colonialism) were regarded to be under the protection of Mary. Thus the ship in which Christopher Columbus (1451-1506) landed in Latin America was the *Santa Maria,* and before sailing he placed himself under the protection of the Lady of Rábida. He reached land on October 12, 1492, the feast day of Our Lady of Pilar. After returning to Spain, he made a → pilgrimage of gratitude to the shrine of Our Lady of Guadalupe.

The conquerors, too, were devotees of Mary. Francisco de Pizarro (ca. 1475-1541) was accustomed to praying the office of Mary, and he carried a statue of the Divine Mother of Victory, the patron saint of his birthplace, Trujillo. Diego de Almagro (1475-1538) had a picture of Mary painted on his banner and arranged to be buried in the → monastery of La Merced in Cuzco. Vasco da Gama (ca. 1460-1524) held a vigil before an → altar of Mary before setting out on his journey of conquest. Ferdinand Magellan (ca. 1480-1521) placed himself under the protection of the Mother of the God of Victory. Pedro de Valdivia (ca. 1498-1553) conquered Chile with a statue of Mary on his saddlebow. Juan de la Cosa (1460?-1510) placed Mary in the compass card of the first map of the world.

As a result of the appearance in 1531 in Mexico of the Mother of God to the Indian Juan Diego, whom John Paul II canonized in Mexico in 2002, devotion to Mary took deep roots in the continent. Mary, known as the Virgin of Guadalupe, bore Indian features and spoke the language of the Indians. At their general conference in Puebla in 1979 (→ Latin American Councils 2.5), Latin American bishops stated that devotion to Mary belongs to the innermost identity of the Latin American people.

In struggles for independence as well as in the history of the conquest, devotion to Mary played a significant role. Mary was often invoked as the patron saint of the independence movements and as the woman who "brought down the powerful from their thrones" (Luke 1:52). This attitude has been largely on the level of → popular Catholicism, but rulers also often misused devotion to Mary along the lines of patriarchal Catholicism in order to protect the social status quo.

3.2. Religious Orders

The various → religious orders made an important contribution to the veneration of Mary in Latin America in their own distinctive forms. The → Dominicans promoted the → rosary, the → Franciscans veneration of the immaculate conception, and the Augustinians invocation of the Mother of God of Mount Carmel. Every conqueror added veneration of his local patron saint, so that we find in Latin America Our Lady of Montserrat, Covadonga, Aranzazu, Rocío, Macarena, Dolorosa, and others. Native Indians had female deities like Pacha Mama (mother earth; → Nature Religion) and often adopted new names to give new forms to their older devotion (→ Acculturation). Popular → piety expressed itself in many ways that are still found today, including → pilgrimages, feasts, religious → dances,

lay brotherhoods (→ Lay Movements), novenas, and Marian months.

Each Latin American country has a national shrine in honor of Mary and a national form of invocation (e.g., Our Lady of Guadalupe in Mexico, of Copacabana in Bolivia, of Maipú in Chile). In the 19th and 20th centuries the dedication of countries to statues of Mary, and of the whole continent to the Virgin of Guadalupe, expressed the will of the → Roman Catholic Church to maintain itself against the inroads of → Protestantism.

3.3. Liberation Theology

Latin American → liberation theology also finds a place for devotion to Mary. This theology has drawn attention to the sociological dimension of → Mariology and devotion to Mary, and it presents Mary as a prophetess on behalf of the poor. It is precisely the poorest of the poor who show the most → love for Mary. The Roman Catholic Church in Latin America has again found itself in Mary, seeing in her a picture of peoples living in → poverty. She thus offers a model of integral liberation, with the Magnificat orienting → spirituality to liberation.

Bibliography: L. Boff, *El Ave María. Lo femenino y el Espíritu Santo* (4th ed.; Santander, 1996); idem, *The Maternal Face of God: The Feminine and Its Religious Expressions* (San Francisco, 1987) • D. A. Brading, *Mexican Phoenix: Our Lady of Guadalupe. Image and Tradition across Five Centuries* (Cambridge, 2001) • L. M. Burkhart, *Before Guadalupe: The Virgin Mary in Early Colonial Nahuatl Literature* (Albany, N.Y., 2001) • D. Heath, *Contemporary Cultures and Societies of Latin America: A Reader in the Social Anthropology of Middle and South America* (Prospect Heights, Ill., 1988) • R. M. Huber, "Pre-Columbian Devotion to Mary in the Testimony of the Kensington Stone," *AEcR* 117 (1947) 7-21 • H.-J. Prien, *Die Geschichte des Christentums in Lateinamerika* (Göttingen, 1978); idem, "Volksfrömmigkeit in Lateinamerika," *NZM* 42 (1982) 28-43 • R. Vargas Ugarte, *Historia del culto de María en Iberoamérica y de sus imagenes y santuarios más celebrados* (3d ed.; 2 vols.; Madrid, 1956).

Eduardo Cano

Mary in the New Testament

Overview
1. Matthew
2. Luke-Acts
3. John
4. Other References

Overview

Of the seven Marys mentioned in the NT, this article considers only Mary the mother of → Jesus, and only in light of the biblical record. (See the articles "Mariology" and "Mary, Devotion to" for further perspectives.)

Mary is mentioned by name only in the Gospels of Matthew, Mark, and Luke and in the Acts of the Apostles. → Paul has indirect references to Mary (see 4). Her significance is further developed in early Christian writings outside of the NT and, especially, in subsequent theological reflection.

Little can be said of the historical person. According to the Gospels, her name was Mary (anglicized form of Gk. *Maria[m]*, from Heb. *Miryām*); she was a resident of Nazareth at the time of Jesus' conception; she was betrothed to Joseph, whom she eventually married and with whom she had other children (unless Jesus' siblings are regarded as Joseph's from an earlier marriage); she and Joseph were both pious and poor; and she was in some way related to Elizabeth, mother of → John the Baptist. Outside the NT writings, we have no evidence from the first century regarding her person or life.

1. Matthew

In terms of the canonical shaping of the NT, the first witness to Mary is the Gospel of Matthew, where her role is developed in relation to Joseph and, more so, to Jesus. Several references to Mary occur in the first two chapters, where Matthew's biography grounds Jesus' life in the history and hope of God's historic engagement with → Israel (§1). Mary participates in the identification of Jesus with the grand story of God's interaction with Israel when she appears alongside other women in Jesus' genealogy (Matt. 1:1-17). Each in her own way, the others (Tamar, Rahab, Ruth, and the wife of Uriah) belong to enigmatic stories and seem ill-suited to serve as ancestors of the Messiah. In each account, however, obstacles are overcome, security is found, and the line of David is preserved.

These precursors both anticipate and help to interpret Mary's appearance in Matt. 1:18-25. Matthew takes care to present Joseph as Jesus' legal, but not biological, father, a fact from which emerges the enigma and potential impropriety of Mary's own story. In a dream, however, Joseph receives assurance that Mary's child was conceived by the → Holy Spirit, that this child will save his people, and that his birth fulfills prophecy. In fact, the message Joseph receives ties Mary herself into Isaianic prophecy, as the "virgin" who would "conceive and bear a son" (Matt 1:23; see Isa. 7:14). Although this message does not remove the possibility of perceived scandal, since the baby is not his biological progeny, Joseph nonetheless responds in a way that draws Mary and her child into his family, thus securing both them and the Davidic lineage of Jesus. Subsequently, in Matthew 2, Mary neither acts nor speaks but is continuously with Jesus (vv. 11, 13, 14, 20, 21), highlighting the degree to which her life and fate are intertwined with that of her child.

Mary appears also in Matt. 12:46-50 and 13:54-58, where issues of identity are in view. In the first text Jesus identifies his mother, brothers, and sisters as those who do "the will of my Father in heaven" (→ Obedience), a criterion that serves at an explicit level neither to include nor to exclude Mary as a member of Jesus' new family. In the latter, Jesus is identified as a member of Mary's family by way of those who disparage his prophetic status.

2. Luke-Acts

Luke-Acts contributes the most to the NT portrait we have of Mary, which is due largely to the significant role Luke gives to his account of the birth and childhood of Jesus, where Mary is a prominent actor in her own right. Throughout his narrative, Luke mentions Mary by name 13 times (Luke 1:27, 30, 34, 38, 39, 41, 46, 56; 2:5, 16, 19, 34; Acts 1:14) and refers to her directly, without mentioning her name, an additional three times (Luke 2:41-52; 8:19-21; 11:27-28). In his portrayal of a young woman in ways often at odds with the conventions of her world, Luke presents Mary as an exemplar of the new reality being actualized in the advent of Jesus (→ Incarnation).

2.1. Mary appears first in Luke 1:26-38, the account of the annunciation of Jesus' birth. Here she is a young girl, perhaps 12-13 years old, not yet or only recently having achieved puberty, a resident of a town far removed from the Jewish and Roman centers of purity and power. Her family of origin is never mentioned. She is betrothed to Joseph but has not yet joined his household and thus has no claims to his status. Hence, unlike others in Luke's birth account (cf. 1:5-7), she is not introduced in any way that would commend her to us as one deserving of honor. At this juncture her insignificance seems to be her primary contribution to the Lukan narrative.

Mary, however, is granted the highest status: an honorable greeting by the archangel of the Lord and an invitation to participate in the restoration of Israel. Gabriel announces the birth to Mary of a son of greatly exalted rank who will be "holy" and will be called "Son of the Most High" and "Son of God" (1:32-35; → Christological Titles). Mary's reply is memorable on its own terms, "Here I am, the slave of the Lord; let it be to me according to your word" (v. 38, author's translation). Mary thus shows herself to be one who hears and embraces God's word, submits herself to the divine purpose, and claims a place in God's own household. In a world where personhood was measured in relatedness to others, Mary defines herself with reference to God's family.

Mary's response is strange insofar as it diverges from conventional wisdom and practice, but also because it is presented to us as the deliberate act of a young woman whose behavior departs from acceptable norms. Rather than following the normal script of submission to father or husband, she exhibits purposeful resolve and thus lives according to the peculiar rhythms of the new era being ushered in by God. In doing so, she portends the appearance of others in this gospel whose behavior departs from the conventional but is nonetheless regarded as exemplary — for example, a centurion who invites Jesus' beneficence (7:1-10), a woman who expresses authentic hospitality to Jesus (7:36-50), and a widow who relentlessly pursues justice (18:1-8).

2.2. The encounter between Mary and Elizabeth immediately ensues, with Elizabeth pronouncing two forms of blessing on her younger kinswoman (Luke 1:39-45). The first highlights Mary's motherhood, while in the second she is declared fortunate on account of her faith. This exchange within the Lukan birth account emphasizes God's gracious initiative, which leads to Mary's response. Luke makes it clear that the divine favor shown to Mary is not because of Mary's motherhood. Her state of pregnancy is the consequence of her blessedness, not its cause. Her role in the actualization of God's saving plan is thus highlighted, but, again, this role is the result of divine blessing, not its impetus.

This scene is coupled with another, Luke 11:27-28, where an unnamed woman pronounces a blessing on Mary on account of her having given birth to Jesus. This announcement presumed two widely held views regarding women: (1) that a woman finds her place in traditional society in terms of her relatedness to her man, typically to her father or husband or, if widowed, to her son; and (2) that she finds value in childbearing and may be regarded as blessed through being the mother of a son who is granted great honor. Jesus' response to the woman ("Blessed rather are those who hear the word of God and obey it"; cf. 8:19-21) is a corrective that coheres with Luke's earlier presentation of Mary as one who hears and reflects on the divine word, embraces that word positively, and even proclaims the word in the fashion of a → prophet (1:26-38, 46-55; 2:19, 51).

This emphasis anticipates Luke's final testimonial to Mary, Acts 1:14, where she is explicitly counted within the community of Jesus' faithful → disciples.

2.3. Luke's opening chapters highlight the importance of Mary in three additional ways. First, especially in her response to divine blessing, Mary's Song (or the Magnificat, Luke 1:46-55), the portrayal of Mary is tied up with that of Israel. The song interweaves images and language from Israel's Scriptures in order to celebrate and give definition to the mighty and merciful activity of God in bringing his → covenant to fruition in Jesus. In Mary's representation, the Mighty One acts on behalf of the lowly, with whom Mary identifies both herself and her people, Israel. Similarly, Simeon's prophetic oracle to Mary (2:34-35) associates the division of Israel over Jesus with the sorrow Mary will experience on account of his fate.

Second, along with Joseph, Mary is presented as one who is guided in God's purpose by → Torah and whose devotion to Torah is unambiguous. This portrait portends the larger concern of Luke-Acts to situate the restoration of Israel within the ongoing story of faithful Israel, not in opposition to it.

Third, as illustrative of authentic discipleship as her response to Gabriel might be, and as insightful as Mary's Song might be into the character of God's work, Mary herself does not appear to grasp fully the significance of what God is doing. She gives herself to mulling over the meaning of these things, then at one point fails altogether to comprehend the consequence of Jesus' filial relationship with God (Luke 2:19, 48-50, 51). Here is poignant testimony to how radical a → conversion (§1) is required for those who would give themselves to, and participate fully in, → discipleship.

3. John

Although she is never named in the Gospel of John, Mary appears as Jesus' mother in two scenes: the wedding at Cana (John 2:1-11) and Jesus' crucifixion (19:25-27). The interaction between Jesus and his mother at the wedding feast has puzzled interpreters, who question its coherence or wonder at Jesus' apparent rudeness to his mother. The account itself gives no reason to think that Jesus has replied to his mother in a hostile way, however, and the developing narrative, with its emphasis on Jesus' "hour," urges the view that their conversation is designed to raise early on the question of Jesus' aims. Against the backdrop of the opening of the gospel (1:1-18), with its profound emphasis on Jesus' identity with God, Mary's appearance in this scene testifies to Jesus' humanity as one with a physical, earthly family.

In his account of the crucifixion, John introduces Mary a second time but gives her neither words to speak nor actions to perform. Instead, Jesus' references to his mother from the cross highlight again his humanity and remind John's readers that this is the "hour," his reason for coming, about which Jesus had spoken at Cana.

4. Other References

Paul refers to Mary only indirectly by way of underscoring Jesus' having been born to a Jewish woman (Gal. 4:4; Rom. 1:3) or as a human being (Phil. 2:6-7).

The Gospel of Mark contains two references to Mary. In the first she, together with Jesus' brothers, is presented among those who are outside the family of those who do God's will and who therefore oppose his ministry (Mark 3:31-35). At this point Mark's presentation stands in opposition to that of Luke and, to a lesser degree, that of Matthew. In the second, Jesus is identified in relation to his mother, brothers, and sisters by way of casting doubt on his prophetic status (6:3).

In Revelation 12 we find a vision of a woman "clothed with the sun, with the moon under her feet, and on her head a crown of 12 stars" (v. 1) who gives birth to the Messiah. Some interpreters find a reference to Mary here, but vv. 2-6 suggest rather that the woman symbolizes the faithful → people of God.

Among early Christian writings outside the NT, the most important for subsequent theological reflection on Mary and iconographic representation of her is the second-century *Protevangelium of James*. Unlike the NT gospels, with their treatment of Mary only in relation to Jesus, it focuses centrally on Mary, narrating her parentage, birth, childhood, purity, perpetual virginity, and marriage to the older Joseph (a widower with children). Scholars generally agree that this work preserves nothing of independent historical value concerning Mary.

→ Feminist Theology

Bibliography: R. E. BROWN et al., eds., *Mary in the NT* (Philadelphia, 1978) • J. A. FITZMYER, "Mary in Lucan Salvation History," *Luke the Theologian: Aspects of His Teaching* (New York, 1989) 57-85 • B. R. GAVENTA, *Mary: Glimpses of the Mother of Jesus* (Philadelphia, 1999) • B. R. GAVENTA and C. L. RIGBY, eds., *Blessed One: Protestant Perceptions of Mary* (Louisville, Ky., 2002) • J. B. GREEN, "The Social Status of Mary in Luke 1,5–2,52: A Plea for Methodological Integration," *Bib* 73 (1992) 457-71.

JOEL B. GREEN

Mary Magdalene

1. NT
2. Patristic Conflations
3. Gnostic Literature
4. Feminist Reconstructions of Earliest Christianity

1. NT

The NT includes 12 references to Mary Magdalene, all of which occur in the Gospels. She is differentiated from other biblical Marys by reference to what was apparently her hometown, the city of Magdala on the northwest shore of the Sea of Galilee. Luke 8:1-3 and Mark 15:40-41 both name Mary Magdalene among a group of women who followed → Jesus throughout Galilee and provided for him out of their resources. Luke adds that Jesus had cast seven → demons out of Mary Magdalene, a detail included also in the longer ending of Mark.

All remaining NT references to Mary Magdalene appear in the context of the crucifixion, burial, and → resurrection of Jesus. Her name appears in the list of women who witness the crucifixion (Matt. 27:55-56; Mark 15:40; John 19:25) and who see where the body of Jesus is laid (Matt. 27:61; Mark 15:47). On Easter morning Mary Magdalene arrives at the tomb, either alone (John 20:1-18) or with other women (Matt. 28:1; Mark 16:1; Luke 24:10), where she is met first by angels and then, according to Matthew and John, by Jesus himself.

In the NT Mary Magdalene's character is most fully developed in the Gospel of John. In John, Mary Magdalene goes to the tomb alone. Finding it empty, she runs to tell → Peter and the beloved disciple, who return with her. They look inside the tomb and confirm that it is empty except for the grave cloths, but the two men return home without witnessing the resurrection. Mary Magdalene stays in the garden, where she encounters first angels and then Jesus himself. Initially, she mistakes Jesus for the gardener, recognizing him only after he calls her by name. When Mary hears her name, she responds by calling Jesus "Rabbouni" (i.e., "Teacher"). The Teacher sends Mary to the disciples to announce the news of his resurrection and → ascension. This commission from Jesus has earned Mary Magdalene the title *apostolorum apostola*, "apostle to the apostles."

Although all of the gospels report Mary Magdalene as the first, or among the first, to witness the resurrection, she is not included in the list of witnesses in 1 Cor. 15:5-8. There the apostle → Paul fails to mention her or any women at the tomb when he reminds the Corinthians of the teaching he received and handed on concerning the appearances of the risen Christ.

2. Patristic Conflations

Several NT stories became associated with Mary Magdalene, even though her name appears nowhere in them. For instance, she is not named as the woman who anoints Jesus, either when he is at table with Simon the Pharisee in Galilee (Luke 7:36-50) or when he is nearing → Jerusalem and his death (Mark 14:3-9; Matt. 26:6-13; John 12:1-8). In John's account, it is Mary of Bethany, the sister of Martha and Lazarus, who anoints Jesus shortly before his death. Neither is Mary Magdalene named as the Mary who, during his Galilean ministry, sits at Jesus' feet and listens to his teaching while her sister, Martha, would like help from her (Luke 10:38-42). Nor is Mary Magdalene named as the woman caught in adultery whom Jesus rescues from stoning (John 8:2-11). Nowhere in the biblical witness is Mary Magdalene referred to as a sinner or a prostitute, yet her association with NT stories featuring sinful women and/or women who overtly display their devotion to Jesus has led to her depiction in art, literature, and film as a penitent prostitute.

A composite sketch of Mary Magdalene, including pieces of each of these NT stories and the distinct women featured in them, is dramatically drawn in a sermon preached by Pope → Gregory the Great (590-604), dating from the late sixth century. In his sermon Gregory identifies Mary Magdalene with Mary of Bethany, as well as the female sinner of Luke 7 and the Mary (of Galilee?) who listens intently to Jesus while he teaches. This composite gained popularity, and Mary Magdalene became not only a model of pious devotion to Jesus and a herald of the resurrection but also a contemplative, listening at the feet of Jesus, and a symbol of true repentance (→ Penitence), the sinner who has been forgiven much and thus loves much. For centuries, the → Roman Catholic Church recognized elements of Gregory's conflation in its configuration of feast days. Not until the 1969 reform of its liturgical calendar were different feast days appointed in the West for Mary of Bethany and Mary Magdalene.

3. Gnostic Literature

In several of the documents included in the → Nag Hammadi library, Mary Magdalene plays a major role among the disciples. The writings that mention Mary date from the second to the fourth centuries and are written from a → Gnostic point of view. Elements of the canonical witness are present in their portrait of Mary, including her being a disciple of Jesus in Galilee and a witness to the resurrection.

These documents, however, further develop Mary into a disciple who is particularly loved and honored by Jesus. She is both a companion to Jesus and a conversation partner, so treasured that the male disciples, particularly Peter, become jealous. In *Pistis Sophia,* a Gnostic document found prior to the discovery of the Nag Hammadi library, Mary is the chief dialogue partner of Jesus, asking 39 of 64 questions. Competition between Peter and Mary surfaces in the *Gospel of Thomas,* the *Gospel of Mary (Magdalene)* and *Pistis Sophia.* The *Gospel of Philip* (63, 34-37) includes the observation that "the Savior loved her more than all the disciples." Gnostic literature generally associates the feminine with that which is perishable, earthly, and imperfect (see M. Meyer, 565), and Gnostic writers routinely contrast the feminine with the preferred spiritual, heavenly, perfect male (see *Gospel of Thomas* 114). In these documents, however, Mary herself is never cast in a negative light.

4. Feminist Reconstructions of Earliest Christianity

While Gnostic writers focused on Mary's role as disciple and companion of Jesus, patristic writers drifted in another direction (→ Church Fathers). From the early centuries of Christianity, Mary Magdalene has been regularly identified in the West with the sinful woman who anoints Jesus in Luke 7. Moreover, that woman's sin has been assumed to be sexual — most often it is imagined as → prostitution, although Luke does not name any particular type of sin for which the woman is forgiven.

Recent studies of Mary Magdalene point out that the Western church's way of speaking about Mary Magdalene has been greatly at odds with the way the Evangelists portray her. In the NT, Mary is not a pitiable, repentant sinner; rather, the NT Mary Magdalene is an honorable model of discipleship and apostleship. She is more faithful than either Peter, who repeatedly denies Jesus, or Paul, who actively persecutes the church before his encounter with the risen Jesus. In contrast to these male apostles, Mary follows Jesus throughout Galilee and to Jerusalem; she is present at the → cross when other disciples have largely fled; it is she to whom Jesus appears on → Easter morning, and at his command she carries the central message of Christianity — the news of Christ's resurrection — to others.

Reflecting on the discrepancies between the NT and Gnostic witnesses on the one hand, and the traditional church portrait of Mary Magdalene on the other, feminist exegetes and historians conclude that the transformation of Mary from → disciple and → apostle into repentant whore is representative of a far-reaching patriarchal revision of earliest Christian history. That is, a church that quickly established within itself a → hierarchy of male leadership also systematically misrepresented its own earliest traditions in order to conceal the role that women played as leaders among the first followers of Jesus. Studies of Mary Magdalene since 1975 aim to reread ancient sources in order to recover Mary as "the true feminine model, one which, according to the gospels, embodies strength, courage and independence, all feminine qualities which the Church has attempted to suppress" (S. Haskins, 393).

→ Feminist Theology; Men; Women

Bibliography: E. de Boer, *Mary Magdalene: Beyond the Myth* (Harrisburg, Pa., 1997) • R. Collins, "Mary," *ABD* 4.579-81 • S. Haskins, *Mary Magdalene: Myth and Metaphor* (New York, 1994) • K. L. Jansen, *The Making of the Magdalene: Preaching and Popular Devotion in the Later Middle Ages* (Princeton, 2000); idem, "Mary Magdalena: *Apostolorum Apostola,*" *Women Preachers and Prophets through Two Millennia of Christianity* (ed. B. M. Kienzle and P. J. Walker; Berkeley, Calif., 1998) 57-96 • I. Maisch, *Mary Magdalene: The Image of a Woman through the Centuries* (Collegeville, Minn., 1998) • A. Marjanen, *The Woman Jesus Loved: Mary Magdalene in the Nag Hammadi Library and Related Documents* (Leiden, 1996) • M. Meyer, "Making Mary Male: The Categories 'Male' and 'Female' in the Gospel of Thomas," *NTS* 31 (1985) 554-70 • J. M. Robinson, ed., *The Nag Hammadi Library in English* (3d ed.; San Francisco, 1988) • J. Schaberg, "How Mary Magdalene Became a Whore," *BibRev* 8 (1992) 30-37, 51-52 • P. Thimmes, "Memory and Re-Vision: Mary Magdalene Research since 1975," *CR.BS* 6 (1998) 193-226.

Mary Hinkle

Masons

1. Values and Organization
2. History
3. Relations with the Churches

1. Values and Organization

The Masons, or Freemasons, compose the world's largest fraternal organization. Advocating human dignity, → tolerance, free development of the personality, brotherhood, and universal love, they assume that human → conflicts can be resolved without destructive consequences, which requires relationships of trust between those of different convictions. Freemasonry is strongly oriented to the individual and has a concern for moral perfection but otherwise has no ethical principles of its own, since on its view moral → norms are in constant flux. Its rituals do not merely reflect the spiritual foundations of the Masons but also give them figurative and symbolic expression. The ritual is a dynamic → symbol of cosmic happenings whereby participants are integrated into the order of the universe. Special symbols are the badges, aprons, and white gloves, all of which unite the members and form the core of the movement in symbols and symbolic acts.

The lodges are societies, but there is no worldwide organization. There are no secret leaders, nor is there secret knowledge. Secrecy is a condition of mutual trust. The whole teaching lies in the three grades of "entered apprentice," "fellow of the craft," and "master mason." To deepen and develop the teaching is the concern of the higher grades, which are organized in different rites (e.g., Scottish, Royal Arch, or York). There are also research lodges (Quatuar Coronati), which are devoted to the academic investigation of Freemasonry. The oldest was founded in London in 1886. The regular lodges in a country are linked in a grand lodge or in various federations. The president of a lodge is elected by the members; the presidents form a council at meetings of the grand lodge.

The number of Masons worldwide peaked in the 1950s. In 2000 there were approximately five million members worldwide, with roughly half in the United States. Other countries with sizable numbers of Masons include the United Kingdom, Sweden, Germany, Norway, and Denmark. Masons are not tolerated in totalitarian systems because they are a secret society and champion freedom and toleration.

2. History

The term "freemason" appeared for the first time in 1376 in a London document, where it referred to a qualified mason or stonemason who could work skillfully with freestanding stone. The word "lodge" occurred first in 1278 with reference to a wooden building in which construction workers could work and converse. Later the term was used for groups of masons working together on a large building. An important change came at the end of the 16th century and the beginning of the 17th, when first in Scotland and then in England many who were not engaged in building became members ("gentleman masons" in Scotland, and "accepted masons" in England).

Two developments gave rise to the esoteric symbolism of Freemasonry: the constitutional writings of the English masons, and the "masons' word" (used for recognition) of the Scottish masons. It seems that the symbolism was then changed by the lodges of accepted masons in the 17th and early 18th centuries and took its present form in the 1730s. In 1723 the "old charges" of James Anderson (d. 1739) developed out of the general and specific duties of the English constitutional writings.

Freemasonry spread first in the British Isles and then to France, Holland, Germany, and Austria. The first grand lodge was founded in England in 1717, with the French grand lodge being founded in 1736, and the German in 1737. The German lodge accepted the Prussian crown prince and later king Frederick II (1740-86) as a member.

Rationalists found a home in the secret society of the Illuminati, a Masonic sect founded in Ingolstadt in 1776 by Adam Weishaupt (1748-1830). In spite of strong personal links, there were essential differences between the Masons and this society. Freemasonry was ultimately an esoteric (→ Esotericism) society with no ideology, whereas the Illuminati constituted a rational system with specific ideological and political aims.

The first lodge "aux trois canons" was founded in Vienna in 1742. Holy Roman Emperor Francis I (1745-65) had already been received into the Masons when an English deputation visited The Hague. The Austrian grand lodge was founded in 1784 with six provincial lodges, which Emperor Joseph II (1765-90) placed under police supervision in December 1785. The next emperor, Leopold II (1790-92), tried to use Freemasonry for his own political ends. Under the final emperor, Francis II (1792-1806), most of the lodges dissolved, having been declared illegal in 1795. The union with Hungary in 1867 altered the situation, for Austrian Masons could now carry out their rituals in Hungary. A grand lodge was again formed after the collapse of the Hapsburg monarchy in 1918.

In the 20th century Erich Ludendorff (1865-1937) sharply criticized the Masons, and A. Hitler (1889-1945) proscribed them in 1933, launching some persecution and confiscating their property. After reconstitution in 1945, the German lodges came together in the united grand lodges of Germany in 1958.

3. Relations with the Churches

Since the 18th century there has been an almost unbridgeable gulf between Freemasonry and the church. The church has condemned especially the humanistic and → deistic ideas of the Masons. From the outset, Masons found themselves exposed to suspicion, hindrances, and persecution. Even before the first papal → bull against them, publications appeared that strongly opposed the movement. In 1738 Clement XII (1730-40) issued the bull *In eminenti*, condemning Freemasonry, which was published and came into force only in the Papal States, Spain, Portugal, and Poland. Renewed condemnation came in 1751 under Benedict XIV (1740-58), in 1814 under Pius VII (1800-1823), in 1825 under Leo XII (1823-29), in 1864 under → Pius IX (1846-78), and in 1884 under Leo XIII (1878-1903).

Today the → Roman Catholic Church finds greater variety in the Masonic movement and has entered into a → dialogue, the first visible result of which is the elimination from → church law of the → excommunication of Freemasons (cf. 1917 CIC 2335 with 1983 CIC, which does not mention the Masons). Nevertheless, the German bishops have issued a declaration of incompatibility that, with the express consent of John Paul II, along with a commentary by Cardinal Ratzinger, prefect of the Congregation for the Doctrine of the Faith (→ Curia), has been made binding on the whole church.

Freemasonry assesses a person's worth not according to confession of a → dogma but according to personal integrity. It uses for the final authority the symbol of "the supreme master builder of the universe." Such a phrase expresses the desire of Masons to achieve a form in which there can be human unity without dogmatic assertions.

Many Protestant ministers, particularly among those who espouse Enlightenment theology, personally belong to lodges. Many of the denominations, however, regard a religion in which all unite along the lines of Freemasonry as the product of a rational, deistic faith. As such, they see the view of humanity in Freemasonry as irreconcilable with the NT view of humanity with its stress on the grace of the triune God.

The ideas, rituals, and symbols of the Masons have been presented in many songs, plays, operas, and novels (e.g., by M. Claudius, J. H. Voss, F. von Schiller, J. W. von Goethe, W. A. Mozart, E. Schikaneder, and G. E. Lessing).

Bibliography: S. C. Bullock, *Revolutionary Brotherhood: Freemasonry and the Transformation of the American Social Order, 1730-1840* (Chapel Hill, N.C., 1996) • M. C. Carnes, *Secret Ritual and Manhood in Victorian America* (New Haven, 1989) • L. Dumenil, *Freemasonry and American Culture, 1880-1930* (Princeton, 1984) • M. C. Jacob, *Living the Enlightenment: Freemasonry and Politics in Eighteenth-Century Europe* (New York, 1991)

• H. Neuberger, *Freimaurerei und Nationalsozialismus* (2 vols.; Hamburg, 1980) • A. Piatigorsky, *Freemasonry: A Study of a Phenomenon* (London, 2000) • H. Reinalter, *Die Freimaurer* (Munich, 2000) • J. G. Ridley, *The Freemasons: A History of the World's Most Powerful Secret Society* (New York, 2001) • J. J. Robinson, *A Pilgrim's Path: Freemasonry and the Religious Right* (New York, 1993) • H. Vorgrimler, *Kirche und Freimauer im Dialog* (Frankfurt, 1975) • W. J. Whalen, *Christianity and American Freemasonry* (3d ed.; San Francisco, 1998).

Helmut Reinalter

Masorah, Masoretes

1. In a broad sense the term "Masorah" refers to the notes and signs used by scribes in the transmission and preservation of the Hebrew text of the OT and its pronunciation, including the vowel signs and accent marks. In the narrower and more customary sense, the term refers to the informational and text-critical notes about the text written in the margins and at the end (and sometimes the beginning) of biblical books. The Masorah is an external accompaniment to the text. The exact meaning and origin of the term remain uncertain; it derives either from the verb *msr*, "hand down" or "count," or from *'sr*, "bind" — most likely the former in the sense of "count." The Masoretes, then, were those who counted the letters, words, and verses of the Bible (→ Bible Manuscripts and Editions 1).

2. The Masoretes, who functioned from about A.D. 500 to 950, compared MSS, debated readings, and progressively eliminated (sometimes incorporating) variants in the text. They continued and systematized the work already begun by the earlier → scribes (*sopherim*; see *Meg.* 3a; *Ned.* 37b; *Gen. Rab.* 36).

Three schools or traditions of Masorah developed: the Babylonian, Palestinian, and Tiberian, with the last dominating in the West. Among the Tiberian Masoretes, the families of ben Asher and ben Naphtali were most prominent, with the textual traditions traced back to these two showing little significant variation. The Babylonian and Palestinian Masoretes became submerged in the Middle Ages and have been rediscovered only in modern times.

3. The Masoretic notes on the text are preserved in what are designated the *Masorah marginalis* and the *Masorah finalis*. The former is divided into two categories: the *Masorah parva* (or *qĕṭannâ*), the small

Masorah, and the *Masorah magna* (or *gĕdôlâ*), the large Masorah. In the Tiberian system, the *Masorah parva* (Mp) was written in the side margins. Utilizing extreme brevity and abbreviations, it supplies information about word frequency, spelling particularities, modifications to be made in reading (the *qere* and *ketib*), and so forth. A systematized reproduction of the Mp of the Leningrad Codex B19a (L) is printed in the margins of the *Biblia Hebraica Stuttgartensia* (BHS). The *Masorah magna* (Mm), written in the top and bottom margins of the page, reproduces and expands on the information contained in the Mp but does not repeat the *qere-ketib* information or the unique reading notations. The Mm of L has been published by G. E. Weil and referenced in the first apparatus of BHS.

The *Masorah finalis* appears at the end of biblical books and provides statistics on word counts; like all the Masorah, it seeks to preserve the integrity of the text. For example, at the end of Deuteronomy we are told that the sum of verses in the Torah is 5,845, the sum of paragraphs *(sedarim)* is 167, the total number of words is 79,856, and the number of letters is 400,945.

→ Exegesis, Biblical, 1; Canon 1; Hebrew Language; Literature, History of, 1

Bibliography: J. Barr, *The Variable Spellings of the Hebrew Bible* (Oxford, 1989) • A. Dotan, "Masorah," *EncJud* 16.1401-82 • S. Frensdorff, *The Massorah Magna*, pt. 1, *Massoretic Dictionary; or, The Massora in Alphabetical Order* (New York, 1968) • P. H. Kelley, D. S. Mynatt, and T. G. Crawford, *The Masorah of Biblia Hebraica Stuttgartensia: Introduction and Annotated Glossary* (Grand Rapids, 1998) • S. Z. Leiman, ed., *The Canon and Masorah of the Hebrew Bible* (New York, 1974) • B. B. Levy, *Fixing God's Torah: The Accuracy of the Hebrew Bible Text in Jewish Law* (New York, 2001) • D. S. Mynatt, *The Sub Loco Notes of the Torah in Biblia Hebraica Stuttgartensia* (Fort Worth, Tex., 1994) • J. D. Price, *The Syntax of Masoretic Accents in the Hebrew Bible* (Lewiston, N.Y., 1991) • E. Tov, *Textual Criticism of the Hebrew Bible* (rev. ed.; Minneapolis, 1992) • G. E. Weil, "La Masorah," *REJ* 131 (1972) 5-104; idem, *Massorah Gedolah* (vol. 1; Rome, 1971) • I. Yeivin, *Introduction to the Tiberian Masorah* (trans. E. J. Revell; Chico, Calif., 1980).

John H. Hayes

Mass

1. Term
2. History in the West
   2.1. To Gregory the Great

1. Term

The Christian term "mass" (Lat. *missa*) initially referred to the dismissing of a gathering, the sense being that the church was sent into the world at the conclusion of its gathering for worship (→ Blessing). From the fourth century the term came to be used for the whole service of → worship, and from the fifth and sixth centuries exclusively for what is now called the Mass. The reason for the change in usage is that increasingly the whole of worship, especially the → Eucharist, came to be seen as an action that dispenses God's blessing.

In content the term "mass" covers all the essential parts of the celebration — the introduction, the ministry of the Word, the Eucharist (preparation of offerings, → eucharistic prayer, and communion), and the conclusion. The Mass, Lord's Supper, or divine → liturgy is in all churches a central liturgical celebration that is done at the command of → Jesus and in memory of him until he returns (1 Cor. 11:23-26).

2. History in the West

In the first centuries after Christ one could not speak of a Western form of the Mass, or of forms used only in the Western Empire and its territories. The clear distinction between East and West that gradually resulted in lasting separation began only as antiquity came to an end.

2.1. *To Gregory the Great*

2.1.1. *Apostolic and Postapostolic Period*

In the apostolic and postapostolic period, there was a basic schema for the whole service and a framework for the important prayers, especially the eucharistic prayer. The detailed structure and formulation, however, depended not on any sharing of experiences among the churches but on their respective situations, including their religious and cultural background (e.g., Syrian-Palestinian for → Jewish Christians, Hellenistic for → Gentile Christians) and the rhetorical and celebrative gifts of the leaders (see *Did.* 10; → Justin Martyr *1 Apol.* 65, 67; Hippolytus *Trad. apos.* 9; → Elder). The small number of participants and the location in houses allowed scope for spontaneous development. All who were present naturally received the Eucharist, the requirements for which were → baptism and a Christian life (see *Did.* 9.5; Justin Martyr *1 Apol.* 66.1). The day for celebration was Sunday or its vigil (Acts 20:7; *Did.* 14.1; Justin Martyr *1 Apol.* 67.7).

In many areas, even before the Council of → Nicaea, there were larger congregations with church buildings (→ Church Architecture). There the Eucharist would be celebrated on Sundays and feast days under the presidency of the → bishop in the form that we find in Justin Martyr (ca. 100-ca. 165), which has the basic structure of the later Mass. It included the ministry of the Word and the Eucharist separate from the meal, which as the agape feast lived on after the second century with a religious, social, and later a charitable character.

There were also occasions for celebrations apart from those on Sunday. They were held in smaller circles, such as at tombs, in private houses, or in prison cells. Already by the end of the second century, however, they had assumed a congregational character (e.g., in commemoration of → martyrs), as indeed some of them had been from the very first (e.g., the Mass on Saturday and on the so-called station days, Wednesday and Friday).

2.1.2. *Regional Variations*

From the fourth and fifth centuries the various political and social conditions within the early imperial church led to the rise of forms of celebration corresponding to the larger numbers of church members and the status of church leaders as publicly and legally recognized dignitaries. As → patriarchs came to supervise ecclesiastical areas, regional uniformity began to mark the celebrations. Theological controversies and conciliar decisions on Christological and Trinitarian issues (e.g., at → Ephesus in 431 and → Chalcedon in 451; → Christology; Trinity), along with their ecclesiastical consequences in such matters as language, helped to form regionally uniform though distinct liturgical traditions.

In the East we find the East Syrian (→ Nestorians, Chaldeans, and Malabars), West Syrian (Antiochians, Maronites, Byzantines, and Armenians; →

Antiochian Theology), and Alexandrian branches (Copts and Ethiopians; → Alexandrian Theology; Liturgy 2). In the West we find different Latin liturgical families, including those in North Africa and Rome, Milan and Aquileia, Spain and Gaul, and among the Celts (→ Liturgy 1, 3). The development of these Latin traditions is obscure. Apart from the Ambrosian liturgy in Milan and remnants of the old Spanish liturgy, they all perished between the 8th and 12th centuries; no more than traces remain in the Roman Mass that absorbed them.

2.1.3. *The Mass in Rome*

For the fourth to the sixth centuries we know the Mass of the city of Rome, celebrated in Latin, only from occasional reports and from later sources in the form of the episcopal liturgy. It began with an introit (an antiphonal psalm) or → procession to the church where the Mass was to be celebrated. Then came the Kyrie, the Gloria, and the Oratio (collect). The liturgy of the Word followed, probably a lesson, responsive psalm, gospel, and, on Sundays and feast days, a → sermon. The general prayer followed, not the dismissal of catechumens and penitents as in other liturgies.

The eucharistic part began with the offerings (not yet liturgically stylized) and thanksgiving. By the sixth century the great → prayer had achieved the form that it still has as Prayer I in the current Roman Mass book: a variable preface with the Sanctus-Benedictus and a fixed canon (formally related to the Alexandrian tradition) in which prayers and the thought of sacrifice are predominant and the commemorative extolling of God's saving acts that figures so largely in Eastern (and non-Roman Western) liturgies is less prominent. Communion, in distinction from its celebration in the East, is simple: the breaking of the bread (without accompanying Agnus Dei), the → kiss of peace (not before the general prayer, as in other churches, esp. in the East), the → Lord's Prayer, the dismissal of the many noncommunicants, communion in both kinds to the accompaniments of responsive psalms, and the concluding prayer *(oratio ad complendum)*. The benediction *(oratio super populum)* brought the whole service to an end.

2.2. *Middle Ages*

2.2.1. *Liturgical Development*

In the → Middle Ages the decisive development was the fusing of the tradition of the city of Rome with that of Gaul and Germany to form the Roman-Frankish Mass. This fusion occurred because of the growing importance of Christianized peoples north of the Alps after the fall of the Western → Roman Empire and the desire, in honor of the seat of Peter

and for the sake of unity, to make the Roman liturgy a liturgy for the Frankish imperial church in place of the many non-Roman liturgical traditions. The extant Roman liturgical books (e.g., the papal sacramentary sent by Hadrian I to Charlemagne in 790) were incomplete and had to be supplemented by national traditions.

Germanic → piety and legal and social structures, as well as theological developments, thus led to a process of inculturation, and a mixed Roman and Germanic liturgy resulted. Rome accepted this development, and after A.D. 1000 the result became *the* Roman liturgy. It characterizes the ordinary of the Mass (the *Ordo Missae*), which arose between the 8th and 11th centuries and which differs from the old Roman Mass at various points. Thus we find preparatory prayers at vesting (→ Vestments), as well as a thanksgiving within the celebration. Processions on entry, on reading the gospel, on preparing the offerings, and at communion now became ritually more elaborate. The priestly bringing of the gifts has become an offering (later called the little canon; → Sacrifice). Like the communion, it involves many silent priestly prayers. Gestures like bowing and the → sign of the cross enrich the canon. At communion only the priest's Host is broken, and the people communicate only infrequently and with little Hosts. The Lord's Prayer is put immediately before the fraction, and the Agnus Dei is sung at the kiss of peace or at communion (→ Church Music).

In following years this "clergy liturgy" underwent few essential changes. Kneeling, prayers, and singing accompanied the elevation from the 13th century. A relatively independent preaching portion also developed, often apart from the Mass. The cup was withheld from the laity. A more radical departure from the early Middle Ages was the addition of the silent Mass, without congregation (e.g., the votive Masses, or the Mass for the departed). In this Mass the → priest himself would read the lections and chant the canticles. The people's missal arose in this connection, integrating from the 13th century onward the formerly separate sacramentary, lectionary, and gradual. The → Franciscans took over and popularized the silent Mass of the Roman → curia. It became the basis of the pre-Tridentine Mass books (→ Liturgical Books) and of the reform of the Mass at the Council of → Trent.

2.2.2. *Theology and Piety*

A theology of mystery was determinative in the → early church. Anamnesis of Christ involved the actual presence of the pascha of Christ (→ Passover). Thus the real somatic presence was the medium of communion with the Lord and in the church as his body. The Middle Ages lost this sense of an event. Interest focused instead on the "how" of the real presence. The doctrine of transubstantiation resulted, according to which the priest changes the substance of bread and wine, which retain their accidents, into the Lord's body and blood. In the church's name he offers the Lord Jesus Christ to the Father, who is thus present in the → sacrament. He repeats (more rarely, represents) his sacrifice on the cross for the → salvation of the world, for the living and the dead.

This act can and should take place frequently, since the "fruits" of the Mass are limited, for the Mass is the church's offering. Concentration on the event of consecration means that the priest acts in isolation, makes the change the heart of the action, and posits the real presence as the goal. Communicating, already rare, retreats even further into the background. It is in any case only in one kind (the bread). Contemplating the Host at its elevation ("communion with the eyes") largely replaces it.

Eucharistic piety came to expression in the frequent celebration and endowing of masses. It found strong support in the allegorical explanations that became popular from the early Middle Ages (e.g., Amalarius of Metz [ca. 780-ca. 850]), especially in commemorative allegorizing (→ Allegory) that depicted the rites (not the text) as a presentation of the → suffering and glorifying of Christ. During the Middle Ages these factors led to a considerable appreciation of the Mass, but also to an accumulation of increasingly diverse interpretations, that is, to a multiple view of the Mass that was at one and the same time clerical, individualistic and private, and historicizing and mimetic. The result was exaggeration and defects, which made reformation imperative.

2.2.3. Luther

Criticism by Martin → Luther (1483-1546) concerned among other things the dubious sacrificial character of the medieval Mass (→ Luther's Theology). He succeeded little better than his opponents, though, in recapturing the biblical and early-church concept of commemorative representation that sees the Mass as an event and safeguards the uniqueness of the justifying sacrifice of Christ. He rejected the sacrificial character of the Mass, seeing it as a pure gift of God. In virtue of the words of institution, however, he retained the real presence *in usu* (i.e., in the actual celebration) and in the sense of eating with the mouth *(manducatio oralis),* on the basis of which participating in the body and blood of Christ can be for forgiveness, but also for judgment (in the case of the eating by the wicked, or *manducatio impiorum).*

Luther did reject as unscriptural any Mass without congregation or common communion. The result was reform oriented to the congregation, including congregational singing and using the local vernacular language. Luther omitted the preparation of the offerings, since the texts emphasized the church's sacrifice. For similar reasons he reduced the eucharistic prayer to the dialogue and preface, the institution, the Sanctus, and the Benedictus, sung at the elevation, which he retained. As a result of these reforms, early Reformation churches were frequently marked by the celebration, every Sunday, of an evangelical Mass with strong congregational participation. Such experience of the evangelical Mass influenced the subsequent development of Lutheran and Reformed liturgies. Later, Pietism and rationalism led to a considerable decline in this practice and a return to medieval individualism.

2.3. *Trent to Vatican II*
2.3.1. *Roman Missal (1570)*

Recognizing that many abuses existed, the Council of Trent nevertheless wanted to defend the sacrifice of the Mass. It stressed among other things the role of the priest and the offering (of Christ), arguing that this unbloody offering by the priest has atoning power, though without impugning the uniqueness of the sacrifice of Christ. It argued that the Mass without congregation or communion, or with communion in only one kind, does not run contrary to the institution by Jesus. It left reform of the liturgy to the → pope. Reform should follow "the norm of the Fathers." In fact, however, the sources at the disposal of the church allowed consultation only of the Roman-Frankish texts of the 11th century.

The order of the pre-Tridentine noncongregational Mass, which had been developed at the Roman curia, underlay the new liturgy. The Roman Missal, which Pius V (1566-72) published in 1570, was to be binding on all orders and congregations that did not have their own tradition reaching back more than 200 years (→ Religious Orders and Congregations), and it was to be unalterable. With few exceptions it was universally received, and the modern missionary movement spread it all over the world. Attempts at reform and → acculturation in the 17th and 18th centuries (esp. in France, Italy, Germany, and the Rites Controversy in China) met with no success. Concurrent with the unchangeable clerical Mass in Latin, a eucharistic → devotion (as in the Middle Ages) arose among the faithful, and also a musical form that paid little heed to the texts or structure (the polyphonic mass or orchestral mass; → Mass, Music for).

2.3.2. *The Liturgical Movement and Vatican II*
From the 16th to the 20th century, editions of sources and biblical, patristic, and liturgical studies (→ Liturgics) deepened and altered the knowledge and understanding of the Mass. The 20th century brought the → liturgical movement and a new view of the church and its liturgy that aimed at overcoming the clericalist Mass and at encouraging active participation by the congregation. Already before → Vatican II this movement resulted in partial reforms and in approximations of the Roman Mass, in both theology and practice, to that of other churches.

Vatican II took up this movement. In articles 47-58 of *Sacrosanctum concilium,* the Constitution on the Sacred Liturgy, it named the following basic components: active and conscious celebration by all, richer Bible readings, the homily, the "prayer of the faithful," use of vernacular languages, general prayer, communion by all in both kinds, and concelebration. In keeping with the general principles of reform laid down in articles 21-40, it pointed out that the Mass should have a congregational character (i.e., that its basic form should be congregational), that it should be simple, understandable, and visible, and that it should be adjusted to local cultural requirements.

3. After Vatican II

3.1. *Roman Missal (1970)*
Exactly 400 years after Pius V published the Tridentine Missal, which had remained intact for the most part, despite a few changes in detail, the new Roman Missal of Paul VI (1963-78) appeared in 1970. In keeping with a principle adopted by the council, this is not a full missal but consists of a sacramentary for the celebrant, a lectionary (1970; 2d ed., 1981), and a gradual for → lectors and singers (1974). These books are for universal use in Latin and are also to serve as models that the bishops may adapt in the national languages or, in the case of the music, replace.

On the basis of changes ordered by *Sacrosanctum concilium* (see 2.3.2), an explanation of the order is given in the general introduction. Noteworthy is the inclusion of three new eucharistic prayers that follow the early and Eastern traditions.

3.1.1. *Congregational Mass*
The general structure of the congregational Mass (with options in parentheses) is as follows. The congregation gathers. The *introduction* contains the introit; greeting of the → altar (incense); greeting of the congregation (with introductory words); gen-

eral confession of sin in three possible forms, including the Kyrie; and collect of the day.

The *liturgy of the Word* follows (with introductory words), with the first reading and a responsive psalm, second reading (Sundays and feast days) plus Alleluia (gospel procession and incense), reading of the gospel, the homily and creed (Sundays and feast days), and general prayer.

Next comes the *Eucharist*, with three subparts: preparing of the gifts, the great prayer, and the communion itself. The preparing of the gifts includes the bringing of the gifts (procession and song), offering of the bread and prayer, preparation of the cup, bringing of the cup and prayer (incense: censing of altar, offerings, priest, and people), washing of the hands and prayer, and offertory prayer.

The great prayer comprises the eucharistic prayer in four forms; the preface with Sanctus and Benedictus; the post-Sanctus and epiclesis; the words of institution, with elevation and acclamation by the people; the anamnesis prayer and communion epiclesis; intercession for the church, the living, and the departed; and the concluding doxology.

Communion itself then follows, including the Lord's Prayer, followed by embolism and → doxology; the prayer for peace, then the wish and kiss of peace; the fraction and mingling, with singing of the Agnus Dei; Behold the Lamb of God (invitation to communion); reception with accompanying singing (cup also to the laity); thanksgiving, either silent or sung; and concluding prayer.

The *conclusion* consists of announcements (prayer for the people), benediction (closing prayers), and dismissal and exit.

3.1.2. *Settings*
The Roman Missal of Paul VI contains the texts of prayers, lections, and canticles for the Mass on feast days and festal seasons and on Sundays and midweek throughout the → church year, also for commemorations of saints, for special feasts and special occasions, and for votive masses and masses for the dead. Forms include those provided by the bishop or priest, forms for concelebration, and, when there are good reasons, forms for masses without congregation. As far as possible, → deacons, acolytes, lectors, and cantors ought to serve at the Mass. The faithful take part in common prayers and singing, also by listening, acclamation, responses, gestures, and actions (standing, sitting, kneeling, offering, and going up to communion).

3.1.3. *Special Forms*
An instruction in 1969 of the Congregation for Divine Worship regulates the Mass for special groups (the group Mass or house Mass). A further direction

in 1973 from the same congregation regulates the Mass for children, which has its own great prayer and lectionary. Special forms of the Mass are also available for → persons with disabilities.

3.2. The Churches
Where political or economic circumstances did not hamper it, the missal of Paul VI was soon translated into many languages and adapted in many different ways. Adaptation — we can hardly speak of profound acculturation — applied mainly to gestures, postures, vestments, vessels, and music. Many books also contain so-called euchological texts (orations and prayers) that are not in the Latin original. Thus the basic structure remains the same, but after four centuries of Latin uniformity, relatively independent regional traditions have arisen, and liturgical exchanges have begun to take place among the churches.

3.3. Ecumenical Perspectives
Research into the history and theology of liturgy has led to considerable transdenominational approximations taking place between Eastern Orthodox, Protestants, and Roman Catholics as regards the theology and form of the Mass (→ Ecumenism, Ecumenical Movement; Ecumenical Theology; Liturgical Movement). These studies formed an important foundation for the Mass reforms of Vatican II, as well as for the earlier eucharistic revivals in many Reformation churches (e.g., the restoration of the eucharistic prayer and the rejoining of the liturgies of Word and sacrament). Paul's missal takes note of Eastern traditions (e.g., in the eucharistic prayers), and there are also many other parallels in Protestant liturgy, visible in the → Book of Common Prayer of the North American Episcopalians (1979), the *Lutheran Book of Worship* (1979) of Lutheran churches in the United States and Canada, and the *Book of Common Worship* (1997) of the Presbyterian Church (U.S.A.). These books were themselves the fruit of the widespread ecumenical liturgical movement of the 20th century.

As an important witness to developing unity, we may point to the Lima Declaration, *Baptism, Eucharist, and Ministry* (1982) of the → World Council of Churches (Faith and Order), and the ecumenical celebration of the Eucharist at Lima on January 15, 1982. There is good reason to think that we shall move further toward ecumenical → consensus regarding the doctrine and celebration of the Eucharist and in this way toward the visible → unity of the church of Jesus Christ. In the process, the principle of *Sacrosanctum concilium* (37-38) should be adopted that speaks against "a rigid uniformity" in favor of legitimate diversity.

→ Gregorian Chant; Hymn; Hymnal

Bibliography: Sources: M. ANDRIEU, *Les Ordines Romani du Haut Moyen-Age* (5 vols.; Louvain, 1931-61) • *Apostolic Constitution (Missale Romanum) of Pope Paul VI* (trans. C. Howell; London, 1973) • J. DESHUSSES, *Le sacramentaire Grégorien, ses principales formes d'après les plus anciens manuscrits*, vol. 1, *Le sacramentaire, le supplément d'Aniane*; vol. 2, *Textes complémentaires pour la messe* (Fribourg, 1971-75) • K. GAMBER, ed., *Codices liturgici latini antiquiores* (2 vols.; Fribourg, 1968; supp., 1988) • A. HÄNGGI and I. PAHL, eds., *Prex eucharistica. Textus e variis liturgiis antiquioribus selecti* (2d ed.; Fribourg, 1978) • A. HUGHES, *Medieval Manuscripts for Mass and Office: A Guide to Their Organization and Terminology* (Toronto, 1995) • *Lectionary for Mass: English Translation* (New York, 1970) • *Liber Sacramentorum. Romanae Aeclesiae ordinis anni circuli (Cod. Vat. Reg. lat. 316/Paris bibl. Nat. 7193, 41/56) (Sacramentarium Gelasianum)* (Rome, 1968) • H. MEYER and L. VISCHER, eds., *Growth in Agreement: Reports and Agreed Statements of Ecumenical Conversations on a World Level* (New York, 1984) • *Missale Romanum. Editio princeps (1570)* (Vatican City, 1998) • *Missale Romanum. Lectionarium* (3 vols.; 2d ed.; Vatican City, 1981) • I. PAHL, ed., *Coena Domini*, vol. 1, *Die Abendmahlsliturgie der Reformationskirchen im 16./17. Jahrhundert* (Freiburg, 1983) • *The Rites of the Catholic Church* (2 vols.; New York, 1990-91).

Other works: T. F. BEST and D. HELLER, eds., *Eucharistic Worship in Ecumenical Contexts: The Lima Liturgy–and Beyond* (Geneva, 1998) • P. F. BRADSHAW, *The Search for the Origins of Christian Worship* (New York, 1992) • Y. BRILIOTH, *Eucharistic Faith and Practice: Evangelical and Catholic* (London, 1965; orig. pub., 1930) • C. CASPERS and M. SCHNEIDERS, eds., *Omnes circumadstantes: Contributions towards a History of the Role of the People in the Liturgy* (Kampen, 1990) • L. DEISS, *Celebration of the Word* (Collegeville, Minn., 1993) • S. J. P. van DIJK and J. H. WALKER, *The Origins of the Modern Roman Liturgy: The Liturgy of the Papal Court and the Franciscan Order in the Thirteenth Century* (London, 1960) • J. A. JUNGMANN, *The Mass of the Roman Rite: Its Origins and Development (Missarum sollemnia)* (rev. ed.; New York, 1959; orig. pub., 1948) • E. J. KILMARTIN, "The Catholic Tradition of Eucharistic Theology: Towards the Third Millennium," *TS* 55 (1994) 405-57; idem, *The Eucharist in the West: History and Theology* (Collegeville, Minn., 1998) • E. MAZZA, *The Celebration of the Eucharist: The Origin of the Rite and the Development of Its Interpretation* (Collegeville, Minn., 1999) • H. B. MEYER, *Eucharistie. Geschichte, Theologie, Pastoral* (Regensburg, 1997); idem, "Liturgie in lebenden Sprachen. Das 2. Vatikanum und die Folgen," *Die Feier der Sakramente in der Gemeinde* (ed. M. Klöckener and W. Glade; Kevelaer, 1986) 331-45 •

N. Mitchell, *Real Presence: The Work of Eucharist* (Chicago, 1998) • D. N. Power, *The Eucharistic Mystery: Revitalizing the Tradition* (New York, 1992) • K. Rahner and A. Häussling, *The Celebration of the Eucharist* (London, 1968) • M. Rubin, *Corpus Christi: The Eucharist in Late Medieval Culture* (Cambridge, 1991) • R. Sokolowski, *Eucharistic Presence: A Study in the Theology of Disclosure* (Washington, D.C. 1994) • F. West, *Scripture and Memory: The Ecumenical Hermeneutic of the Three-Year Lectionaries* (Collegeville, Minn., 1997) • World Council of Churches, *Baptism, Eucharist, and Ministry* (Geneva, 1982).

Hans Bernhard Meyer

Mass Media

1. General
2. Historical Differences
3. Alternative Systems
4. Theory of Effect
5. Mediators of Reality and Agents of Socialization
6. Social Functions of Media: Responsibility and Accountability
7. Importance for the Church and Religions
8. Communication Revolution and Information Society: Current Trends

1. General

1.1. The collective term "mass media" refers to the several different technologies that have been developed into institutional forms for the large-scale dissemination of information and → culture. These technologies are better known by their familiar names as the press, radio, television, film, and so forth. The use of a single term, however, reflects the fact that all these means of mass communication share some basic features. Together they belong to what is now virtually a separate social institution, on a par with longer established institutions such as → education, religion, → family, and → politics.

1.2. Institutional status implies a set of organized and interrelated activities and relationships, governed by a set of distinctive purposes, rules, conventions, and → norms. The mass media, in general, have acquired this status de facto, both on account of their growth into a major industry (→ Industrial Society) and public service (→ Service Society) and because they have come to serve many significant functions in the life of developed societies and in the → everyday life of most individuals. We can speak of a media institution pertaining to each national society, but also of a global network of mass → communication.

1.3. Premodern (→ Modernity) forms of → society were also characterized by society-wide networks of communication, usually in the hands of church or → state. The mass media are different in several respects, more than just in their involving new technologies for the reproduction and dissemination of "messages." The difference is captured by the use of the term "mass communication," which refers to the typical communication process of the mass media.

This process is characterized by a great scale of production, with the potential to reach very large numbers of scattered individuals; a highly organized form of production of communication; a largely impersonal relationship between sender and receiver, since the receiver is usually anonymous and unable to respond to the communicator; and a relationship that, for similar reasons, is typically voluntary, calculative, and nonmoral. Mass communication also typically belongs to and sustains the public sphere of the life of society — its messages are in principle freely available and accessible to all, often deal with matters of public interest, and have a function in the public life of society in matters of politics, opinion, and public morality. Central to ideas of mass communication and mass media is the concept of the "mass" as a historically new form of collectivity, composed of large numbers of mutually anonymous and unorganized individuals, physically separated from and united with each other only by the chance of their giving attention to some common object of interest or attraction made available by the media to each individual simultaneously.

Mass communication must be carefully planned and organized as an industry, as well as a creative enterprise, which introduces features of mass production into the communication process that have effects on the content produced and disseminated. This content tends to be patterned and standardized and is often predictable. It is governed by what has been called a media logic that accentuates and prioritizes the "culture" of media organizations and professions. This ethos is manifested in an attraction to famous or infamous persons, as well as a liking for immediacy, drama, and popular appeal. According to some critics, the combination of demands of organizational routine and sensationalist values works against the reflection of social reality and even against genuine communication (in the sense of the transmission of meaning). On these grounds the media have recently been blamed for the devaluation of politics and for a decline in political trust and participation.

2. Historical Differences

While it is normal and convenient to refer to all the mass media by one term, there are important differences between the separate media, each of which has its own history. The sequence of the development of media was from book to newspaper, to film, to radio and sound recording, to television, and now to new telematic, computer-based media and media for video making, recording, and playback. We can perceive a continuing process whereby each new medium has caused the existing media to adapt and to change their functions and significance in society.

The first *books* were printed in the mid-15th century and for some time did not depart far from the familiar contents of manuscript production. However, new forms, a different culture, and new ideas were gradually introduced and played a key part in the → Renaissance, the → Reformation, and later the → Enlightenment.

The *newspaper* began during the 17th century as a means of communication for the town-based → bourgeois class, with essential functions for commerce and politics. In its definition and functions it was primarily secular (→ Secularization) and related to the economic, political, and social concerns of the moment (→ Social History). It helped to promote → democracy and social change and to undermine the dominance of established institutions of the → church, landed class, and autocratic state.

The *film* medium, appearing at the end of the 19th century, was defined largely as a means of popular entertainment for the urban masses, drawing its content from popular literature and the theater. At times, however, film has also been used as a means of national propaganda (→ Nation, Nationalism), as a device for popular education, and as an art form in its own right.

Since the 1930s *radio and television* broadcasting have come to be regarded as the major mass media because of their greater reach than any other media and the multiplicity of their functions. Their verbal and visual character allows them to overcome barriers of education, culture, class, and literacy, and their technologies can cross large distances and national frontiers. For this reason they have been viewed as important means for promoting change within developing countries and mediating relations between developed and less developed regions.

The potential for increased and transnational flow of television and radio was much increased by the expansion of cable and satellite transmission from the late 1970s onward. Current technological changes, especially those based on telecommunications and computer technology, have the potential for revolutionizing mass communication by way of converging technologies. The initial effect has been the addition of a new "mass medium" to the spectrum, currently represented by the *Internet and World Wide Web*. This is a mass medium in the sense of having a large and rapidly increasing diffusion and in taking over some of the functions of traditional media. It is also different, however, in being an interactive rather than a one-way medium and having a capacity to deliver very diverse and even personalized content. At the time of this writing its uses have not crystallized into a clear pattern; a process of social and commercial experimentation is taking place rapidly and on a large scale.

3. Alternative Systems

It is important to differentiate not only between different historical periods and different kinds of mass media technology, but also between different sorts of media systems. The differences are primarily related to the type of social and economic systems, the relations between media and the state, the functions that the media are expected to serve in the society (often a matter of differences of history and culture), and the level of economic development. Most national media systems are of a mixed character, but most can also be characterized as belonging predominantly to one or another of the three types described below.

In an earlier phase of mass media, at mid-20th century, the differences between types of social systems were quite pronounced and led to the proposition that there are different normative theories of the press (F. S. Siebert, T. Peterson, and W. Schramm; J. Nerone). The rapid decline in the influence of Communism in the world, the development of new information and communication technologies, and the related trend toward the deregulation of telecommunications and other media have reduced the intersystem differences. Nevertheless, alternative models remain, as follows.

3.1. The main features of the *competitive, or free market, system* are private ownership of the media, removal of the media from government control, and the goal of making a profit by meeting the wishes of the potential audiences. Such a system is thought to satisfy the needs of society by way of meeting individual demands and also by making access to channels of communication, freely or for payment, to the main institutions of society. The chief advantages of this model are its freedom and openness to diverse cultural expression, information, and opinions, as well as in its dynamic tendency to develop new technological potential. The chief dangers lie in monopoly ownership, political bias (in influence and → ideology), and the subordination of informational and cultural values to commercial imperatives (→ Manipulation).

3.2. The *public utility, or social responsibility, model* is typified by the public-service broadcasting institutions of western Europe and other parts of the world, where society allocates a wide range of functions in the sphere of education, information, culture, and entertainment to public bodies that are accountable to society for what they do, usually by way of elected representatives. Public funding provides a form of control and accountability, protection against commercial or sectional interest, and a guarantee that the basic communication needs of society will be met. The chief advantage is the serving of the public interest or general welfare. The main dangers stem from lack of independence from the state, possible bureaucratization (→ Bureaucracy), and lack of responsiveness to popular demand.

3.3. Systems of the Third World, which can be referred to as a *development model* of mass media, are usually characterized by limited capacity and reach and by a strong attachment to the primary goal of economic and social → development. Third World media normally either accept or are given this central task and are less free to choose their own goals, which often involves a subordination to government or state authority. The main benefits of the model are usually found in the careful and planned use of limited national resources for essential purposes, including the fostering of cultural and political identity. The limitations, aside from the question of resources, lie in the frequent lack of true freedom of expression. Quite often journalists are subject to arbitrary penalties and even personal danger.

3.4. Actual media systems are more varied and complex than this simple tripartite division might suggest. In some countries restrictions are religious rather than political. In others, as in many parts of the former Soviet Union, the characteristics of mass media stem from the combined effect of the legacy of Communism, new liberalism, lack of resources, and a poorly functioning social and legal system.

A feature of media systems that has been growing in significance is the trend toward internationalization (or globalization), both because of new technology and because of the increasing reach of the global capitalist economic system. This trend has been interpreted both positively and negatively. On the one hand, it may be a precondition for the rise of a global civil society. On the other, it may reduce diversity and impose the cultural values and political influence of the developed world on the rest of the world. In practice, the greater part of media experience for most people, whether in more developed or in less developed countries, remains to a large extent "national" in every respect, or filtered through national "gatekeepers."

4. Theory of Effect
Early ideas about the effects of mass media were much influenced by the notion of the → masses and by the historical examples of the use of mass media for propaganda, advertising, social control, and social change in the era before television. The masses, viewed as a large number of isolated individuals, were thought to be especially vulnerable to persuasion (→ Rhetoric) and manipulation. The most frequently postulated effects were a breakdown of the individual moral order and a greater collective power to mobilize populations, often for irrational or dubious ends. It now appears more correct to view the mass media, in either their early or later versions, as having a potential for both positive and harmful ends. The characteristics of mass media and the history of their use allow us to identify certain basic alternative possibilities.

First, there is the potential either for uniting and unifying or for fragmenting and individualizing communities or societies. The first tendency flows from the mass media providing common objects of attention, a common culture, and a supply of similar information to large numbers of otherwise separated individuals and households. It can be argued that in the rapidly changing modern society, the media more than any other institution, especially the dominant media of television and the national press, now provide the main force for integration on a day-to-day basis. A tendency to fragmentation may, however, also be stimulated by the media through the greater self-sufficiency of individuals and households, a more calculative and secular attitude, greater mobility and change, a decline in older beliefs and → values that have held societies together, and a reduction in the amount of personal social contact.

Another dimension of assessment concerns → power and control, and here we are offered two quite different models. In one, the central → authority or a dominant → class controls the "message systems" that reach into every home; in the other, mass media are seen as offering a diverse and varied response to the demands and wishes of their scattered audience members and a service to pluralistic politics.

A third main dimension for alternative assessment has been according to the relative weight given to the mass media or to society as a force for change. Some view the mass media simply as a reflection of changes and tendencies in society, especially dependent on the social structure or on economic and political factors, while others see the mass media as having a strong causal influence on society either because of their distinctive technologies or because of their typical contents and culture. Those who emphasize the technologies as determinant are likely to expect many changes in society when the dominant technology of communication changes, for instance, in the shift from print to radio, then to television, and now to more interactive, computer-based media of communication. The Internet, because of its interactive and more individual character, should tend to increase the heterogeneity of society and also the pace of change. It should also make it more difficult for centralized mass propaganda to be effective.

Early theory of media effects emphasized the capacity of mass media to disseminate information and to influence opinion and attitude on a large scale. There were also fears of harm caused, especially to the young, by the media presentation of violence and immorality. Gradually, however, it was recognized that the influence of mass media is filtered through other social networks and depends on many factors, especially the motivations and predisposition of audiences, as well as the trust and authority attaching to media sources and "mass communicators." The general trend in research and theory has been to emphasize the power of the audience to resist unwanted influence and to interpret messages differently. The message as sent is by no means the same as the message received or understood. It is not easy to link behavior directly to media as a cause.

5. Mediators of Reality and Agents of Socialization

There is wide agreement that the mass media should be considered as of great potential significance for society, even if they do not have the absolute power of persuasion or influence on behavior as originally supposed. Much of our knowledge, in the widest sense, comes not from direct personal experience but by way of the mass media. Contact with society and the world is to a large extent indirect, mediated by technological and organizational systems that provide information about remote parts of the world or the inner workings of institutions to which we may have no access (governments, business, military institutions, etc.). Such systems also inform our ideas about the personal → experience of other individuals or groups in society or about situations that we may not yet have personally encountered. This function has implications, for instance, for our relations with others and for anticipating many possible experiences of our own life, such as → marriage, parenthood, divorce, illness, and old age.

The mass media have a major role as agents of → socialization by making available models of behavior for possible imitation or avoidance, versions of experience and ideas, a symbolic (→ Symbol) world of fact and fiction that extends far beyond the immediate world of household, locality, or workplace. This symbolic world offers many more options, it can often be summoned or chosen at will, and it is almost impossible to limit or control its availability, its content, or its possible effects. If the media have a socializing role, then it is logical to suppose that they can have a desocializing role as well (i.e., one that undermines other, more positive influence). This issue is particularly relevant to the agencies that are traditionally responsible for the upbringing and forming of the young (→ Youth Work), especially families, → schools, and churches.

6. Social Functions of Media: Responsibility and Accountability

The mass media have gradually acquired an increasing range of social functions, including a number of tasks that do not fall clearly within the realm of the family, education, politics, religion, or other social institutions. These tasks include providing information, helping to integrate and make sense of experience (→ Meaning), ensuring cultural continuity, providing relaxation and entertainment, and mobilizing people toward certain goals. All these functions are essential in any society to secure cooperation, adaptation to change, adequate control, continuity over time, and the achievement of various collective ends. They are also based on first serving individual needs for information, guidance, security, relaxation, and so on. The mass media are often expected to support other social institutions by giving access to channels of supplementary communication. They have even taken over some of these functions, leading to increasing dependence on the mass media.

A general problem has arisen, especially in liberal media systems, in that society needs the contribution or cooperation of the mass media but has less possibility for ensuring this support. For cultural and political as well as technological reasons, it is increasingly difficult to control and regulate media, to allocate responsibilities, or to call media to account for meeting the expectations of society on the basis of an agreed "public interest." The forces of cultural liberation, as well as those of commerce, often militate against meeting the social, cultural, and informational needs of society. Nevertheless, the system contains certain built-in mechanisms for gaining some compliance with social needs, in addition to certain areas that are still subject to law and regulation, especially where clear evidence exists of harm to society or individuals.

Other means of accountability include the normal working of the audience and advertising market, the pressure of public opinion, the various forms of self-regulation that have developed, and the growth of professionalism in certain areas. The last area has led to the formulation of professional codes of → ethics and conduct, as well as some voluntary forms of accountability to the public. Nevertheless, the tension between freedom and accountability is inescapable, and the relation between media and society requires constant monitoring and negotiation. Despite the regulatory trends, there is an increasing attention to issues of media ethics and normative theory.

7. Importance for the Church and Religions

The case of the different churches and religions exemplifies the situation of increased dependence on the media. On the one hand, many churches, for different reasons, have lost much of the direct regular contact with many individuals that they often enjoyed in the past. On the other hand, the mass media offer the potential of reaching many more individuals in their own homes than the churches can or ever could by their own direct means. Many churches see here both an opportunity and a duty to use the means of mass communication for their particular mission. Virtually all organized religions try to do so, often supported by special media training programs and expert advice (→ Electronic Church; Christian Publishing).

The chances for getting access to mass media channels vary widely according to the nature of the system, as outlined above. Under the free market model many churches buy their own broadcasting time or stations, especially in North America, while under the public broadcasting model there is often some form of institutionalized access for organized religion. In the Third World the situation is quite variable, although international bodies such as the → Lutheran World Federation, the → World Coun-

cil of Churches, agencies of the → Roman Catholic Church, and the World Association for Christian Communication help to bring together the aims of churches and the development aims of Third World countries.

One of the potential dangers of close involvement of this kind is that the message of the institution may be diluted or distorted by the need to conform to the requirements and standards of successful mass communication. Not only the churches face such a risk, but also politicians and educators. It must also be kept in mind that the general lessons of media research and theory concerning effective communication also apply to religious communication. The audience must be "available" (reachable) and well motivated, and the communication source must earn respect and trust. Much depends on the situation rather than on the technological means.

8. Communication Revolution and Information Society: Current Trends

The mass media are, as we have seen, on the point of another significant departure because of the growth of new electronic media, especially in their online forms and currently best exemplified by the World Wide Web (Internet). A major consequence has been a shift away from centralized uniform media distribution reaching large numbers with the same message and toward a more abundant, interactive, and diversified supply that can be chosen according to personal interest or need. In what has been called the emerging information society, communication of all kinds is increasing in importance, and the boundaries between mass media and other channels, networks, and types of communication are becoming increasingly blurred.

The pace and nature of change are difficult to predict and will vary according to the different models described above. Certain trends, however, are already fairly clear at the start of the 21st century. First, there is an accelerating speed, as well as an increased volume and diversity, of communication of all kinds, with accompanying problems of "overload" and difficulty of selection. Second, there is a gradual increase in internationalization, or globalization, of all kinds of communication flows, personal as well as public. Third, there is less social control and accountability at the national level. Fourth, communication has become a much bigger business because of links with information and communication technology (ICT) industries, and a higher proportion than ever is concentrated within the control of a limited number of large and often global corporations. Finally, the proliferation of media has led to an increased fragmentation of audience attention, raising doubts about the future of so-called mass communication. There is still much evidence, however, that a great deal of the same content now reaches most people, albeit by more numerous distribution channels.

These trends reflect forces at work in society and technology that cannot really be held back. Also, however, they highlight the increased salience of social and ethical considerations that arise in relation both to "old" mass media and to new forms of communication.

Bibliography: J. H. ALTSCHULL, *Agents of Power: The Role of the News Media in Human Affairs* (New York, 1984) • C. CHRISTIANS and M. TRABER, eds., *Communication Ethics and Universal Values* (Thousand Oaks, Calif., 1997) • G. COMSTOCK et al., *Television and Human Behavior* (New York, 1978) • J. CURRAN and M. GUREVITCH, eds., *Mass Media and Society* (3d ed.; London, 2000) • L. GROSSBERG, E. WARTELLA, and D. C. WHITNEY, *Mediamaking: Mass Media in a Popular Culture* (Thousand Oaks, Calif., 1999) • H. HARDT, *Social Theories of the Press: Early German and American Perspectives* (Beverly Hills, Calif., 1978) • S. MCBRIDE et al., *Many Voices, One World: Communication and Society Today and Tomorrow* (London, 1980) • D. MCQUAIL, *Theories of Mass Communication* (4th ed.; London, 2001) • J. NERONE, ed., *Last Rites: Revisiting Four Theories of the Press* (Urbana, Ill., 1995) • F. S. SIEBERT, T. PETERSON, and W. SCHRAMM, *Four Theories of the Press* (Urbana, Ill., 1956).

DENIS MCQUAIL

Mass, Music for the

1. Origins
2. The Ordinary of the Mass
3. The Proper of the Mass
4. Monophony
5. Polyphony
6. Settings of the Proper
7. Settings of the Ordinary
8. The Requiem Mass
9. After the Reformation
10. Other Post-Reformation Traditions
11. Other Forms

1. Origins

"Mass" is one of the Western names for the central → worship service of the church. Rooted in the Latin words of dismissal — *Ite, missa est* (lit. "Go, it is the dismissal" or "Go, you are dismissed") — the → Mass highlights the sending of the people into

the world to be the body and blood of Christ, whom they receive in Word and at table.

Fragmentary sources before Hippolytus (ca. 170-ca. 236) indicate that Christian worship revolved around the Word and the sacraments of → baptism and the Lord's Supper, or → Eucharist. A daily evening celebration of the supper, derived from the Last Supper and postresurrection meals with Jesus at Emmaus, became a weekly event on Sunday morning, a weekly → Easter. A service of the Word, derived from synagogue worship, was originally separate from the supper. The two were joined, and by the second century the Word and table sequence of the Mass was set: the people gather and hear Scripture lessons "opened" in proclamation, followed by intercessory → prayer; they bring bread and wine, which, after a prayer of intercession including Jesus' "words of institution" from the Last Supper, are received by them as the body and blood of Christ, whereupon the assembly is sent into the world in blessing, service, and mission.

The Western church gravitated to two cycles: the Mass on Sundays and festivals, and prayer offices on the other days. As these gatherings occurred throughout the year and in annual remembrances of → martyrs and → saints, what ordinarily happens at each service was distinguished from what changes with specific days and seasons. The former is the *ordinary,* the latter the *proper.*

2. The Ordinary of the Mass

The ordinary of the Mass includes the Kyrie, Gloria, Credo (i.e., the Nicene Creed), Sanctus, and Agnus Dei. Kyrie Eleison ("Lord, have mercy"), introduced by the fourth century with a → litany, stood alone by the end of the eighth century as "Kyrie eleison, Christe eleison, Kyrie eleison," each cry usually repeated three times.

The Gloria in Excelsis Deo ("Glory to God in the highest") has its kernel in Luke 2:14. Present in the Mass by the late fourth century, it became a regular feature of the gathering portion of the Mass.

The Nicene Creed was introduced in the sixth century as a response of the people to the proclamation of the Word (→ Niceno-Constantinopolitan Creed). Unless the form of its expression is restricted to simple recitation, its length and potential for musical complexity have led to many choral settings.

The Sanctus ("Holy, holy, holy") may date from the time of the apostles. Following the ancient dialogue — Sursum Corda ("Lift up your hearts"), Habemus ad Dominum ("We lift them up to the Lord"), and the preface, which calls the congregation to give God thanks and praise — the assembly acknowledges God's coming in holiness in Christ. Derived from Isa. 6:3 and joined with the Benedictus ("Blessed [is he who comes]"), from Matt. 21:9, this central congregational component of the Mass persisted in simpler musical settings as late as the 12th or 13th century, when other parts of the congregation's musical office had been taken over by the → choir.

The Agnus Dei ("Lamb of God [. . . have mercy on us]"), derived from John 1:29 and introduced in the 7th century, accompanies the breaking of the bread for distribution and serves as a → hymn during communion. The number of repetitions was set at three around the middle of the 9th century. In the 10th and 11th centuries "grant us peace" was substituted for "have mercy on us" in the last petition.

3. The Proper of the Mass

The proper of the Mass includes the introit, → gradual and Alleluia (which is replaced, during Lent, with the tract), and offertory and communion verses — all probably originally complete psalms or portions of psalms reduced over time to single verses with antiphons. The gradual and communion are the earlier of these components, present by the fifth century. The gradual is related to the readings for the day, while the other parts of the proper accompany liturgical actions. The music of the graduals, which is more responsorial (i.e., involving alternation between a soloist and a group) and melismatic (having extended melodic passages sung on one syllable), has an interpretive character. Tropes (words or musical phrases added to or inserted into preexistent chants) and sequences (tropes on the final *a* of the gradual's "Alleluia" developed into separate "hymns"), sometimes considered part of the proper, came later.

4. Monophony

The church derived its musical practice from the → synagogue and assumed singing by the participants without instruments. Lessons, prayers, and all of worship were intoned in unaccompanied monophony. The interpenetration of Jewish and Hellenistic streams led to what is called → Gregorian chant. At first congregational, it ultimately became more choral.

Gregorian chant in its present form can be traced to around 800 but is dependent on layers that preceded that date. By 750 perhaps 650 melodies were formed out of a congregational base. The most accessible source today for Gregorian chant in relation to the Mass is the *Liber usualis.*

In the 9th century new forms and styles appeared in tropes and sequences. Troping began with such parts of the proper as the introit or the offertory and moved to the ordinary. They were sung in place of the gradual or after it and the Alleluia, between the Epistle and Gospel. Sequences began around 850 and reached their peak with Adam of St.-Victor (12th cent.). By the 16th century there were perhaps as many as 5,000 sequences, one or more for almost every day of the church year. The Council of → Trent (1545-63) suppressed all but 4 of these sequences. Lutherans pared them down somewhat less extensively.

5. Polyphony

An early form of polyphony called organum was employed for tropes and sequences. The Mass, which had stimulated monophonic congregational song, now stimulated polyphonic choral music. Both monophonic chant and polyphonic elaborations flowed together in alternation.

Sequences tied to the gradual and Alleluia were first set in parallel organum in the 9th and 10th centuries. By the time of the Winchester Troper, an 11th-century English MS, troping had moved to the Kyrie and Gloria. In the first half of the 12th century, the school of St. Martial in southern France elongated the notes of the original chant tunes as sustained structural pillars to support another voice, which moved in shorter notes above it.

The process continued later in the 12th century with Léonin (fl. late 12th cent.) and then Pérotin (d. 1238?), both traditionally associated with the Cathedral of Notre Dame of Paris. In the *Magnus liber organi* (Great book of organum), known now only in altered 13th- and 14th-century versions, Léonin is reputed to have set in two-voice organum the solo parts of the graduals, Alleluias, and responsories for the major festivals of the whole church year. Pérotin is credited with shortening and improving them.

The broad outlines of the history are clear. People like Guido of Arezzo (ca. 991-1050) developed a system of staff notation to avoid having to learn the chant by memory. Notation made it possible to sing unknown chants at sight and to write out improvisatory polyphony. This step gradually stimulated increased compositional complexity. Léonin and Pérotin wrote out "improvised" rhythmic modes, and Pérotin moved from two-voice to three- and even four-voice polyphony.

As in St. Martial, the original chant voice served as a structural pillar to support lengthy and rhythmic melismas. These embellishments could set off the readings in bold relief, but they also could take center stage. The conductus and motet, both at first related to the readings, not surprisingly became independent entities. The conductus apparently began as "walking music" to accompany the entrance and exit of the person doing the readings. In the 13th century the → motet eclipsed it. Motets, which may have begun as polyphonic parts of the gradual, were spun off as independent compositions in place of the gradual for use elsewhere in the Mass, such as at the offertory, or as secular pieces performed outside eucharistic worship.

6. Settings of the Proper

Both the ordinary and the proper of the Mass have been given polyphonic settings. Settings of the proper by various composers are found in the Jena Choirbooks that Frederick the Wise (1463-1525) assembled for the Castle Church at Wittenberg on the eve of the → Reformation. The high point of such compositions came with Heinrich Isaac (ca. 1450-1517), the first to compose a complete group of polyphonic settings of the proper for the entire church year. Commissioned by the Cathedral of Constance in 1508, Isaac wrote about 100 proper cycles, found in his massive Choralis Constantinus.

Many composers wrote music for parts of the proper, but none on the scale of Isaac. William Byrd (1543-1623) wrote two books of graduals with propers for every feast. Giovanni Palestrina (ca. 1525-94) wrote 68 offertories covering the whole liturgical year. Michael Haydn (1737-1806), the younger brother of Franz Joseph, composed a set of graduals for the whole → church year and offertories for most of it.

7. Settings of the Ordinary

Mass composition tended more toward settings of the ordinary, and thus "mass" as a musical term refers today to the ordinary of the Mass. These settings comprise a vast repertoire from the 14th century to the present, most of it from between 1450 and 1600, when ordinary cycles were the chief compositional form.

Machaut (ca. 1300-1377) is credited with writing the first complete polyphonic setting of the ordinary, the Messe de Nostre Dame. Composing around the 1360s for his home → cathedral in Rheims, Machaut employed four voices rather than three like the Tournai Mass compilation from the first half of that century, which he may have known. He used isorhythm (repetition of a rhythmic pattern) and chant melodies in the tenor for the Kyrie, Sanctus, Agnus Dei, and Ite missa est, setting the lengthier Gloria and Credo more freely. (The tenor

was the part that "held" the preexistent melody, or cantus firmus; in four-part textures like Machaut's, it was directly above the bass.) Only for the final → amens did he employ extreme hocket (a back-and-forth interruption of two or more parts by the insertion of rests). This style produced a climax but skillfully avoided "violence to the words," as called for in the decree De vita et honestate clericorum (1324-25) of John XXII (1316-34).

Attempts to unify movements by musical means were made by Leonel Power (d. 1445), John Benet (fl. ca. 1420-50), and John Dunstable (ca. 1390-1453). They employed a cantus firmus in the tenor with sacred tunes not from the chant of the ordinary, anticipating the more mature mass cycles after 1450.

Guillaume Dufay (ca. 1400-1474) wrote one of the first of the cantus firmus masses that unified the whole by use of a secular tune, "Se la face ay pale" (If my face is pale [the reason is love]). He also used the tune "L'homme armé" (The armed man), most favored by composers until the end of the 16th century. In the so-called motto mass, or head-motif mass, the same musical figure or motif begins each movement, as in the Missa "Mi-mi" by Jean d'Ockeghem (ca. 1430-95). Ockeghem wrote 13 settings of the ordinary. One of them, the Missa Prolationum, skillfully uses imitation, another technique that characterizes mass settings. His intricate canons yield not math, however, but music. In the Sanctus, when two new voices enter in strict imitation, the piece flowers into sonic breadth.

Josquin des Prez (ca. 1440-1521) wrote almost 20 ordinaries, plus individual movements in a wide variety of styles. He employed sacred and secular tunes with cantus firmus techniques, continued Ockeghem's imitative example in the Missa ad Fugam. In his Missa "Mater Patris" he followed yet another common practice, fashioning preexistent polyphonic works into "parody masses" (a phrase referring, without satirical intention, to masses reworked from existing material).

The Western Wynde Mass of John Taverner (ca. 1490-1545) is a set of 36 variations. Other works based on the same secular tune were written by Christopher Tye (ca. 1505-ca. 1572) and John Sheppard (ca. 1515-ca. 1560). Taverner's work is constructed with consummate skill; its simplicity is perhaps a response to Protestant pressures in England.

Orlando di Lasso (1532-94) and Palestrina are the most important late 16th-century composers of Mass ordinaries. Lasso wrote about 70 ordinaries, 50 of them parody masses with material from his own compositions. Palestrina, the most resourceful and prolific, wrote over 100. His Missa Papae Marcelli stands out, partly because of the apocryphal story that it convinced the Council of Trent to save polyphony, but mostly because its masterful polyphony yields happily to homophony as necessary to make the text clear.

The 17th century saw the addition of instruments and double choruses, like the mass in the second Symphoniae Sacrae (printed posthumously in 1615) of Giovanni Gabrieli (ca. 1554-1612) or the Missa gantz Teudsch (1619) of Michael Praetorius (1571-1621). In 1621 Claudio Monteverdi (1567-1643) used instruments alone for the first time in a → requiem (i.e., a musical setting for the Mass for the dead; see 8) at the → funeral of Cosimo II de' Medici. A century later Johann Sebastian Bach (1685-1750) naturally employed instruments in five missae breves (or short masses, i.e., Kyries and Glorias only, not, as in the 15th and 16th centuries, brief settings of the whole ordinary), parody masses on movements from his → cantatas. Like his five settings of the Sanctus, these compositions were for parish use.

Tonal and instrumental developments in the 18th century made longer forms possible. Bach's Mass in B Minor broke out of liturgical constraints. Well over two hours in length, even the three to four hours of the Sunday morning masses in Leipzig could not accommodate this setting of the ordinary. It is a major musical gift to the world, spawned by the Mass.

Composers continued to push beyond liturgical limits. Franz Josef Haydn (1732-1809) wrote 6 large-scale masses between 1796 and 1802. Wolfgang Amadeus Mozart (1756-91) wrote 16 complete Mass settings, of which 9 are short because the mass at Salzburg was not to last more than 45 minutes. His unfinished Mass in C Minor from Vienna is longer, even with its missing parts. The Missa Solemnis of Ludwig van Beethoven (1770-1827) is like Bach's B Minor, as is the Mass in D by John Knowles Paine (1839-1906). Franz Schubert (1797-1828) wrote six settings of the Mass, and Franz Liszt (1811-96) and Anton Bruckner (1824-96) also wrote large settings.

John Baptist Singenberger (1848-1924) filtered the ideals of the Caecilian movement (a Roman Catholic effort to reform church music by emphasizing chant and Renaissance polyphony) through a 19th-century idiom in 23 masses, a requiem, and 40 graduals for parish use. With 20th-century angularity, Igor Stravinsky (1882-1971), Johann David (1895-1977), Ernst Pepping (1901-81), and Hugo Distler (1908-42) also wrote liturgical masses.

8. The Requiem Mass

The funeral Mass, or requiem, attained its shape by the 14th century as

> introit (which begins *Requiem aeternam dona eis, Domine,* "Give them eternal rest, O Lord," hence the name of this Mass),
> Kyrie,
> gradual *(Requiem aeternam)* and tract *(Absolve, Domine,* "Absolve, Lord"),
> sequence *(Dies irae,* "Day of → wrath"),
> offertory *(Domine Jesu Christe,* "O Lord Jesus Christ"),
> Sanctus and Benedictus,
> Agnus Dei,
> communion *(Lux aeternam,* "[May] eternal light"), and
> responsory *(Libera me,* "Deliver me").

Musical settings have drawn from both the ordinary and the proper.

Ockeghem was the first to compose a polyphonic setting, using only the introit, Kyrie, gradual *(Si ambulem,* "Though I walk" [Ps. 23:4]), and tract *(Sicut cervus,* "As the deer" [Ps. 42:1]), with pre-Tridentine alternate texts. Antoine Brumel (ca. 1460-ca. 1515), the pacemaker of classic and romantic requiems before the Council of Trent, wrote the first requiem with the Dies Irae. The second requiem of Tomás Luis de Victoria (ca. 1548-1611), composed with characteristic Spanish brightness for the funeral of Empress Maria of Austria in 1603, is one of his finest works and the epitome of 16th-century settings.

The requiems by Mozart, Giuseppe Verdi (1813-1901), and Hector Berlioz (1803-69) are concert pieces, especially the latter two, which are in the style of 19th-century opera. Gabriel Fauré's (1845-1924) is shorter and quieter; Maurice Duruflé's (1902-86) is something of the same style, written on Gregorian chant themes. The War Requiem of Benjamin Britten (1913-76) intersperses Wilfred Owen's poetry in response to the horror of World War II.

Every musical offering with the title "requiem" is not necessarily related to the Mass. Johannes Brahms's (1833-97) German Requiem, a collection of biblical texts, is in reality an → oratorio. Brahms was probably influenced by the Musikalische Exequien (1636) of Heinrich Schütz (1585-1672), which is not a requiem but a missa brevis plus a motet and a Nunc Dimittis on which is superimposed the text Brahms later used, "Blessed are the dead."

9. After the Reformation

After the Reformation, one stream — including Roman Catholics and Lutherans (→ Roman Catholic

Church; Lutheran Churches) — preserved the Mass with access to its historic musical repertoires; another did not. Lutherans sang the ordinary in both choral and congregational forms, the latter often metrical and in the vernacular. The proper continued as the choir's responsibility, although it shifted to congregational hymns in place of the introit, a single unchanging verse with an Alleluia or a motet in place of the gradual, one or two congregational options or motets at the offertory, and anthems and hymns in place of the communion psalmody.

For Anglican usage Thomas → Cranmer (1489-1556) created the → Book of Common Prayer by editing the Sarum usage of the Latin Mass into English. John Marbeck's (d. ca. 1585) Book of Common Prayer Noted (i.e., with musical notes) provided monophonic and syllabic music for the ordinary. The choral and congregational practice of Anglicans kept the Mass and all its music available (→ Anglican Communion).

John → Wesley's (1703-91) Sunday Service of the Methodists in North America (1784) was a conservative revision of the Anglican Mass for use every Sunday, shortened and spoken, with hymn singing assumed, especially at communion. Methodists generally moved away from the Mass, despite Wesley's intentions. Choral or congregational settings of the ordinary have not been part of Wesleyan practice (→ Methodism).

John → Calvin (1509-64) kept the Word and table sequence but not the Mass. Reformed churches lost the historic ordinary, proper, and their music. Unison metrical psalms became the liturgy in Geneva (→ Calvinism).

Ulrich → Zwingli (1484-1531) obliterated the Mass and all music. Unlike → Luther and Calvin, who wanted a weekly celebration of Holy Communion, Zwingli's denial of Christ's presence at communion led to a → preaching service for 48 Sundays of the year and a communion service for the other 4, with no music for either. For Calvin the creative link between worship and music that the Mass had facilitated was restricted; for Zwingli it was destroyed.

10. Other Post-Reformation Traditions

→ Anabaptists, English → Baptists, and Quakers (→ Friends, Society of) abandoned the Mass. Lutheran Pietists (→ Pietism), after the 18th century, moved in a Reformed direction but seldom completely severed their roots in the Mass.

Recoveries of 19th-century confessional and liturgical forms undergirded the Second → Vatican Council (1962-65) and its move from the use of Latin to the vernacular. A remarkable ecumenical consensus, associated with the modern → liturgical movement, emerged concerning the outlines of the Mass. Many traditions, following the example of the → early church and their own reasoning, gravitated to its shape and to weekly eucharistic celebration. With this convergent development came a multiplication of congregational settings of the ordinary. Some were quite outstanding, including settings with striking African or South American features. Consciously popular settings often imitated the culture, reversing the mind-set of the 15th and 16th centuries that assumed that → church music would function like a filter in "cleansing" secular tunes.

11. Other Forms

From the earliest days of the church, readings were proclaimed by music. Polyphony expanded the possibilities, as in 14th- and 15th-century Italy and Germany or 16th-century Spain. Later Schütz set to music biblical texts that could take the place of readings or, more characteristically, like Bach's cantatas, could join the sermon. Innumerable anthems and motets fit this mold.

Passions were tied to specific days in Holy Week, formalized in the 5th century when → Leo I assigned the singing of the passion story in the Gospel of Matthew to the Mass on Palm Sunday. They ultimately became separate passion plays and vespers but never lost their moorings in the Mass. For centuries a single singer sang the passions in three ranges: the Evangelist's words at midrange, Jesus' words lower, and everybody else (the *turba*, "crowd") higher. In the 13th century three singers took these parts, and then polyphony expanded the possibilities to choral settings (→ Passion Music).

Psalm settings represent a massive repertoire, not only in the proper, but as complete psalms and other excerpts employed ubiquitously. Motets and anthems used as introits, offertories, or communion anthems make up another huge repertoire. Not precisely settings of readings or psalms and different from a cantata, they mix texts in a variety of ways related to the day and its theme.

→ Hymnody, apart from the hymnlike music of the ordinary, is not as native to the Mass as to the prayer offices, but the Pliny-Trajan correspondence at the end of the first century may point to its early presence there too. Hymns or psalms or both may have been used in the early church. Centuries later a line of development may be traced not only from the Alleluia of the gradual to sequences and motets but also to congregational *Leisen* (medieval German folk hymns with some variant of Kyrie eleison or Alleluia at the end of each stanza) and the hymn of the day. After the Reformation, hymns used in the Mass at various points — beginning, end, between lessons, with the sermon, at the offering, at communion — multiplied greatly.

→ Organ music has been used before and after the Mass and as preludes to parts of the ordinary, the proper, and hymnody. No other instrument has such a large repertoire of church-related music. Much of that repertoire, like so much other music, has been generated by the Mass.

→ Church Musicians

Bibliography: W. Apel, Gregorian Chant (Bloomington, Ind., 1958) • M. Bangert, "Mass," Key Words in Church Music (ed. C. Schalk; St. Louis, 1978) 236-45 • F. Blume, Protestant Church Music: A History (New York, 1974) • P. F. Cutter, Musical Sources of the Old-Roman Mass (Neuhausen-Stuttgart, 1979) • K. A. P. Duffy, "The Jena Choirbooks: Music and Liturgy at the Castle Church in Wittenberg under Frederick the Wise, Elector of Saxony" (Diss., Chicago, 1995) • E. Foley, Foundations of Christian Music: The Music of Pre-Constantinian Christianity (Bramcote, Nottingham, 1992); idem, From Age to Age: How Christians Celebrated the Eucharist (Chicago, 1991) • D. Hiley, Western Plainchant: A Handbook (Oxford, 1993) • J. A. Jungmann, The Mass: An Historical, Theological, and Pastoral Survey (Collegeville, Minn., 1975) • The Liber usualis, with Introduction and Rubrics in English (Tournai, 1953; repr., Great Falls, Mont., 1997) • LW 53, Liturgy and Hymns (Philadelphia, 1965) • J. W. McKinnon, The Advent Project: The Later-Seventh-Century Creation of the Roman Mass Proper (Berkeley, Calif., 2000) • NGDMM • B. Thompson, Liturgies of the Western Church (Cleveland, 1961) • P. Westermeyer, Te Deum: The Church and Music (Minneapolis, 1998).

Paul Westermeyer

Masses, The

1. Term
2. Main Use
3. Freud to Mao
4. Industrialized Society
5. Mass Culture
6. Recent Usage

1. Term

"The masses" is a term deriving from Lat. massa and Gk. maza, meaning a kneaded lump. It has the sense of a heap or aggregation or unorganized assembly. Used first for things, from the → Middle Ages onward it came to be used also for people.

In the → modern period "the masses" tends to have a negative nuance, as in reference to plebeians, a crowd, or a mob. Between 1890 and World War II political sociology employed it for uncontrollable forces in → society, not a class (→ Class and Social Stratum) or → group, but a socially restless mob that could be easily → manipulated. After World War II we find it more positively in such combinations as "mass → communications," → "mass media," "mass → consumption," and "mass → culture."

After 1945 the term "mass society" became common. This imprecise usage covers such things as the influencing of society by the media, the loss of individuality (→ Person), the collectivizing of consciousness, the sense of isolation vis-à-vis anonymous urbanization (→ Anonymity; City), and a majority in society that the usual political → institutions do not represent — a conglomerate that has varying roles (→ Self). After 1960 the term became less significant, being replaced by slogans referring to the post-industrial society or to the computer and information society (→ Industrial Society; Information).

2. Main Use

The term's greatest importance occurred between 1890 and 1950. Against a criminological background (e.g., as developed by C. Lambroso and S. Sighele), G. Le Bon (1841-1931) and G. de Tarde (1843-1904) used it psychologically and sociologically (→ Psychology; Sociology). It became a negatively nuanced, defensive concept for a middle-class elite. It characterized the lower classes that were seeking → emancipation (→ Equality), the mediocre, uncultured, and dissentious masses that had become the defenseless victims of hotheads (such as the → socialists).

3. Freud to Mao

Between World War I and World War II attempts were made at more careful definition. S. Freud's (1856-1939) psychoanalytic hypothesis (→ Psychoanalysis) described those belonging to the masses as psychologically immature (→ Development 2). As a consequence, they attempted to identify with a substitute → father (→ Identity).

In his Being and Time (1927) M. Heidegger (1889-1976; → Existentialism) internalized the masses as one. Against the background of the distinction between authentic and inauthentic existence, he defined ordinary people as mass people. In principle this description fits all of us; only a few can take the burden of authenticity upon themselves. Heidegger thus combined the negative and structural features of the masses.

→ Fascism and Communism (→ Marxism 1) shared a low view of the masses but understood their mobilization very differently. V. I. Lenin (1870-1924), J. Stalin (1879-1953), and Mao Zedong (1893-1976) saw in them revolutionary potential that the party could influence and harness (→ Revolution). For B. Mussolini (1883-1945) and A. Hitler (1889-1945), however, they were merely social particles to be recruited for the *squadristi* or storm troopers, with a view to seizing → power. They thus became an instrument of repression that compliantly applauded the Führer.

4. Industrialized Society
In highly industrialized societies we find a very different development in the understanding of "the masses." Around 1920 H. Ford (1863-1947) introduced so-called mass production, with mass consumption as the goal. With increased purchasing power average citizens in the United States, then in Western Europe, could buy things that in earlier times had been reserved for the upper and middle classes.

5. Mass Culture
Parallel with mass consumption and the associated higher standard of living came mass culture. Goods and services are also values and personal status → symbols; as such, they are a form of expression. They thus shape the form that → leisure takes. H. Marcuse (1898-1979), M. Horkheimer (1895-1973), and E. Morin (b. 1921) judged this development negatively, but liberal thinkers in the United States took a more moderate view of consumer attitudes resulting from marketing and advertising.

6. Recent Usage
The classifying of late industrial society as a mass society (H. Freyer, P. de Man, H. Arendt, C. W. Mills, D. Riesman) rests on the phenomena of mass consumption and mass culture. In its negative evaluation it is a reaction to times of war and crisis. When general prosperity returned and → democracy began to take root, the negative and romantically influenced appraisal lost its hold. Today the term "mass" most often occurs in such combinations as "mass communications" and "mass media."

Bibliography: H. ARENDT, *The Origins of Totalitarianism* (new ed.; New York, 1973) • D. BELL, *The End of Ideology: On the Exhaustion of Political Ideas in the Fifties* (Cambridge, Mass., 2000; orig. pub., 1960) • J. R. BENIGER, *The Control Revolution: Technological and Economic Origins of the Information Society* (Cambridge, Mass., 1986) • A. A. BERGER, *Manufacturing Desire: Media, Popular Culture, and Everyday Life* (New Brunswick, N.J., 1996) • E. CANETTI, *Crowds and Power* (New York, 1981; orig. pub., 1960) • M. HEIDEGGER, *Being and Time* (Albany, N.Y., 1996; orig. pub., 1927) • M. HORKHEIMER and T. W. ADORNO, *Dialektik der Aufklärung* (Frankfurt, 1981; orig. pub., 1944) • G. J. KASZA, *The Conscription Society: Administered Mass Organizations* (New Haven, 1995) • G. LE BON, *The Crowd: A Study of the Popular Mind* (New York, 1960; orig. pub., 1895) • R. MARCHAND, *Advertising the American Dream: Making Way for Modernity, 1920-1940* (Berkeley, Calif., 1985) • C. W. MILLS, *The Power Elite* (New York, 1959) • D. RIESMAN, *The Lonely Crowd: A Study of the Changing American Character* (New Haven, 1950) • R. ROSENBLATT, ed., *Consuming Desires: Consumption, Culture, and the Pursuit of Happiness* (Washington, D.C., 1999) • W. W. ROSTOW, *The Stages of Economic Growth: A Non-Communist Manifesto* (3d ed.; New York, 1990).

KEES BERTELS

Materialism

1. Term
2. Earliest Greek Views
3. Seventeenth-Century Materialism
4. French Enlightenment Materialism
5. German Debates
6. Variants

1. Term
Materialism, which is one of the basic philosophical positions (→ Worldview), traces all reality to a single explanatory principle. In distinction from subjective and objective types of → idealism, it monistically (→ Monism) finds the basis of all reality, including intellectual and moral, in physical matter, with its attributes, states, causal products, and functions.

The concept of materialism is usually attributed to R. Boyle (1672-91). In the German sphere it was formulated in 1726 by J. G. Walch (1693-1775) and distinguished from mechanism, which dualistically (→ Dualism) leaves a place for a nonmaterialist explanatory principle.

Two types of materialism exist, a theoretical and a practical. We may subdivide the former into scientific, physiological, social, or historical materialism, according to the relevant sphere of reality and the underlying forms of material reality. The term can also function methodologically as the regulative principle of a final material explanation. Practical materialism rests on a rule governing behavior that determines what goals are worth pursuing for the satisfaction of individual or social needs or for the achieving of material welfare along → hedonistic or → utilitarian lines.

2. Earliest Greek Views

The modern schema of interpretation has resulted in debate whether the pre-Socratics, or Ionian nature philosophers (→ Greek Philosophy), espoused a law-oriented, organic, and materialistic explanation of the cosmos and the human → soul (→ Anthropology) in the form of hylozoism (the view that matter is intrinsically alive). For Thales (6th cent. B.C.) water was the principle of being, for Anaximander (610-546/45) *apeiron* (the boundless), and for Anaximenes (fl. ca. 545) air. Heraclitus (ca. 540-ca. 480) ascribed the same function to the *logos,* as living fire.

Open to similar debate is the common materialistic and mechanistic interpretation of the philosophy of Leucippus (5th cent. B.C.) and Democritus (ca. 460-ca. 370), who used the hypothesis of unchangeable and eternal atoms to explain the problem of change. In the process they viewed the soul as composed of especially mobile atoms and determined by mechanistic laws.

3. Seventeenth-Century Materialism

Epicurus (341-270 B.C.) adopted the atomistic and mechanical understanding of spirit advocated in Democritus, as we see from Lucretius (d. 55 B.C.) in his *De rerum natura* (On the nature of things). He related this understanding to his hedonistic view of the good. Here was the basis of the modern materialism of the 17th century, which found at least indirect support in the quantitative methodology of modern physics (esp. in Galileo, R. Descartes, and I. Newton).

This materialism underwent development at the hands of P. Gassendi (1592-1655), for whom atoms, empty space, and movement were principles of → nature, the soul being a material cause of movement, as well as immaterial and immortal (→ Immortality). T. Hobbes (1588-1679) applied the basic concept of mechanistic materialism to his theory of human action and moral values such as → law and the → state.

4. French Enlightenment Materialism

In the French philosophy of the 18th-century → Enlightenment, the → atheistic thrust of materialism, which is often latent, came to open expression. E. B. de Condillac (1715-80), often wrongly viewed as a materialist, defended a sensationalism that al-

lows for an immaterial sensing subject along the lines of → Cartesianism. This position was in contrast to the popular materialism of P. J. Cabanis (1757-1808), which viewed consciousness as strictly a material product.

Over against this view the naturalism of D. Diderot (1713-84; → Encyclopedia 1) had → pantheistic features. For him the cosmos was not dependent on a transcendent essence (→ Immanence and Transcendence). Rather, he understood it organically as composed of molecules, to which he attributed eternal activity and sensibility and which can move beyond animal life to consciousness.

More radically than Diderot, J. O. de La Mettrie (1709-51) developed his materialistic theory of → identity, which views thought and consciousness as a quality of organic matter, so that there can be no difference between a machine and animal life, between psychological or moral phenomena. La Mettrie, who limited the function of morality to a mechanism of → happiness, did little to advance philosophical criticism of → theism.

D. d'Holbach (1723-89), who also explained all things in terms of mechanistically determined particles of matter, combined his materialism with an aggressively atheistic criticism of religion (→ Religion, Criticism of) and → ethics. He attempted to explain egoistic interests physically and to link up with a social utilitarianism. For C.-A. Helvétius (1715-71) putting this ethics into practice was a task for → education and state legislation.

5. German Debates

In reaction against collapsing → idealism and on the basis of mechanistic science, a materialism arose in the 19th century in Germany that set the theory of → evolution in opposition to belief in → creation and adopted an understanding of the soul in terms of brain physiology. In the battle concerning materialism that broke out in Germany in 1854, the physiologist R. Wagner (1805-64) defended the Christian thesis of a created soul against K. Vogt (1817-95), who reduced all activities of the soul to functions of the brain. In this conflict materialism found advocates in J. Moleschott (1822-93) and L. Büchner (1824-99), whose *Kraft und Stoff* (Force and matter, 1855) made materialism an influential worldview. By the end of the century materialism had made an even wider impact through the Spinozist-materialistic (→ Spinozism) philosophy of E. Haeckel (1834-1919), especially in his popular *Die Welträtsel* (The riddle of the universe, 1899), which was a development of Darwinism.

Rooted in left-wing → Hegelianism (e.g., as developed by L. Feuerbach), the historical and dialectical materialism of K. → Marx (1818-83; → Marxism 1; Dialectic) and F. Engels (1820-95) used materialism as a general model of explanation for reality as a whole (i.e., natural events) and specifically for history (→ Philosophy of History). It defended the thesis that the social processes of meeting human needs (i.e., the means of production) determine the course of history in virtue of their regular antitheses, thus leading to the praxis of social → revolution.

6. Variants

Variants of materialism might be found also in neo-Marxism (E. Bloch; → Critical Theory) and in → analytic philosophy, where it takes a functional, eliminative, and physicalist form, involving a theory of identity.

→ Kantianism; Ontology; Realism; Science; Science and Theology

Bibliography: E. BLOCH, *Das Materialismusproblem, seine Geschichte und Substanz* (Frankfurt, 1972) • J. BRANNIGAN, *New Historicism and Cultural Materialism* (Basingstoke, 1998) • A. GIDDENS, *A Contemporary Critique of Historial Materialism* (2d ed.; Basingstoke, 1995) • F. GREGORY, *Scientific Materialism in Nineteenth-Century Germany* (Dordrecht, 1977) • S. GUTTENPLAN, ed., *A Companion to the Philosophy of Mind* (Oxford, 1994) • P. HITCHCOCK, *Oscillate Wildly: Space, Body, and Spirit of Millennial Materialism* (Minneapolis, 1999) • J. R. T. HUGHES, *Ecology and Historical Materialism* (Cambridge, 2000) • K. NICHOLSON, *Body and Soul: The Transcendence of Materialism* (Boulder, Colo., 1997) • R. PANASIUK and L. NOWAK, eds., *Marx's Theories Today* (Amsterdam, 1998) • G. REY, *Contemporary Philosophy of Mind* (Oxford, 1997) • R. C. VITZTHUM, *Materialism: An Affirmative History and Definition* (Amherst, N.Y., 1995) • B. A. WALLACE, *The Taboo of Subjectivity: Toward a New Science of Consciousness* (Oxford, 2000).

WILHELM LÜTTERFELDS

Matthew, Gospel of

1. Origin
2. Relation to Judaism
3. Composition
4. Contents
5. Theology

1. Origin

The Gospel of Matthew was written about A.D. 90 for a community of Greek-speaking Christians of both Jewish and Gentile origin. On this view the Jewish War and the destruction of Jerusalem were events of the past (22:7). If the traditional ascription is discounted, the author was possibly a → Jewish Christian of the second generation after → Jesus. While it appears that he enjoyed rabbinic training (13:52), his language was Greek, and his theological outlook universal (4:19; 28:19). The place of writing was perhaps → Antioch of Syria, for the social conditions reflected in the gospel are those of a prosperous, urban area with a large population of both Jews and Gentiles.

Organizationally, Matthew's community had already broken with → Judaism (21:43; 28:15). In calling itself the → church (16:18), it understood itself to be a fellowship of the children of God and the → disciples of Jesus (13:38; 23:8-10), and it regulated matters of doctrine and discipline (16:18-20; 18:15-20). Because Matthew's community engaged in vigorous missionary activity (→ Mission), it experienced → persecution at the hands of both Jews and Gentiles (5:10-12; 10:17-18; 23:34-36; 24:9-14).

2. Relation to Judaism

The struggle between Matthew's community and contemporary Judaism was particularly fierce. Matthew characterizes the Jewish leaders as evil ("brood of vipers," 3:7; 12:34; 23:33) and pictures Jesus as pronouncing a series of seven woes against them (23:13-36) and declaring that God will take his kingdom from them (21:43). Also, Matthew describes "the people as a whole" (i.e., Israel as God's chosen nation) as declaring under oath that they are responsible for the death of Jesus (27:25). Ultimately, however, Matthew's intention with these harsh words and pictures is not to condemn the Jews but to evangelize them (23:37; 28:19).

3. Composition

In writing his gospel, the author made use of oral and written traditions he had inherited. From Mark he derived the general outline of his story of Jesus. In the source → Q he found numerous sayings of Jesus. And he appropriated oral and written materials (called M; → Synoptics) not available to the other evangelists.

In taking over these traditions, the author also edited them. He arranged his sources to create, for example, the five great discourses of Jesus (chaps. 5–7; 10; 13; 18; 24–25). Some materials he abridged (cf. 9:18-26 with Mark 5:21-43), clarified (cf. 13:10a with Mark 4:10), substituted (cf. 13:24-30 with Mark 4:26-29), and even omitted (Mark 3:20-21, missing in Matt. 12:22-32).

4. Contents

Using such traditions and techniques, the author composed his gospel-story of the life and ministry of Jesus. The temporal setting for this story is → salvation history, in which the "time of prophecy" gives way to the "time of fulfillment" (→ Promise and Fulfillment), which is also the "time of (the earthly and exalted) Jesus."

The formula "from that time (on) Jesus began . . ." occurs at 4:17 (". . . to proclaim") and 16:21 (". . . to show his disciples"), dividing this story into the following three parts:

1. the presentation of Jesus (1:1–4:16);
2. the ministry of Jesus to Israel and Israel's repudiation of Jesus (4:17–16:20); and
3. the journey of Jesus to Jerusalem and his → suffering, death, and resurrection (16:21–28:20).

Embedded within the second and third parts of this story are the five great discourses of Jesus.

5. Theology

Through his story of Jesus, the author proclaims the "gospel of the kingdom" (4:23; 9:35; 24:14). This → gospel is the good news that in Jesus Messiah, his Son, God in his → eschatological rule has drawn near to dwell to the end of time with his people, the church, thus inaugurating the age of salvation (1:23; 28:20; → Soteriology). On Matthew's view, this good news is to be proclaimed first to Israel (15:24) and then to all nations (24:14; 28:19). Those Jews and Gentiles who accept this proclamation enter into the gracious sphere (→ Grace) of God's eschatological rule; they become disciples of Jesus, submit to → baptism, and keep Jesus' teaching (28:19-20). Jesus' teaching is strongly ethical and eschatological in nature. Ethically, Jesus' disciples are to exhibit in their lives a → righteousness that "exceeds that of the scribes and Pharisees" (5:20). They are to love God (→ Love) with heart, soul, and mind and to love the → neighbor as one's self (22:37-40).

Eschatologically, Jesus' disciples are to remain faithful to him no matter what the cost, to carry out the worldwide mission he has entrusted to them, and to be watchful and ready for his return at the consummation of the age. Then he will carry out the final judgment of salvation or condemnation (24:3–25:46).

→ Exegesis, Biblical; Lord's Prayer; Miracle

Bibliography: Commentaries: W. D. Davies and D. C. Allison Jr. (ICC; 3 vols.; Edinburgh, 1988-97) • H. Frankemölle (2 vols.; Düsseldorf, 1994-97) • J. Gnilka (HTKNT; 2 vols.; Freiburg, 1986-88) • D. A. Hagner (WBC; 2 vols.; Dallas, 1993-95) • C. S. Keener (Grand Rapids, 1999) • U. Luz (EKKNT; 3 vols.; Neukirchen, 1985-97); idem (3 vols.; Minneapolis, 1989-2002) on chaps. 1–7, 8–20, and 21–28.

Other works: W. Carter, *Matthew and the Margins: A Sociopolitical and Religious Reading* (New York, 2000) • B. Gerhardsson, *The Mighty Acts of Jesus according to Matthew* (Lund, 1979) • D. R. Hare, *The Theme of Jewish Persecution of Christians in the Gospel according to St. Matthew* (Cambridge, 1967) • J. D. Kingsbury, *Matthew: Structure, Christology, Kingdom* (Philadelphia, 1975); idem, *Matthew as Story* (2d ed.; Philadelphia, 1988) • U. Luz, *Matthew in History: Interpretation, Influences, and Effects* (Minneapolis, 1994); idem, *The Theology of the Gospel of Matthew* (Cambridge, 1995) • J. H. Neyrey, *Honor and Shame in the Gospel of Matthew* (Louisville, Ky., 1998) • J. Riches, *Matthew* (Sheffield, 1996) • G. N. Stanton, *A Gospel for a New People: Studies in Matthew* (Edinburgh, 1992) • G. Strecker, *Die Bergpredigt* (Göttingen, 1984); idem, *Der Weg der Gerechtigkeit* (Göttingen, 1962) • W. G. Thompson and D. E. Aune, eds., *The Gospel of Matthew in Current Study* (Grand Rapids, 2001) • E. M. Wainwright, *Towards a Feminist Critical Reading of the Gospel according to Matthew* (Berlin, 1991).

Jack Dean Kingsbury

Mauritania

	1960	1980	2000
Population (1,000s):	991	1,551	2,580
Annual growth rate (%):	2.02	2.60	2.47
Area: 1,030,700 sq. km. (398,000 sq. mi.)			

A.D. 2000

Population density: 3/sq. km. (6/sq. mi.)
Births / deaths: 3.65 / 1.19 per 100 population
Fertility rate: 4.66 per woman
Infant mortality rate: 83 per 1,000 live births
Life expectancy: 55.5 years (m: 53.9, f: 57.1)
Religious affiliation (%): Muslims 98.7, other 1.3.

1. General Situation
2. Religious Situation

1. General Situation

The Islamic Republic of Mauritania, a former French colony (→ Colonialism), is a desert state in West Africa. It opens onto the Atlantic on the west, with neighbors Senegal to the south, Mali to the south and east, Algeria to the northeast, and Western Sahara to the north and northwest. Ethnically, mixed Arab-Berber and Maur (Moor)/black constitutes 40 percent of the population, with the remainder divided equally between Maurs and blacks. Agriculture is possible only in the south, but during past decades droughts have restricted it severely. Along with agriculture and herding, iron ore and fishing are important sectors of the economy. → Development programs in 1988 included a dam on the Senegal River in the south in concert with Mali and Senegal. Together with political decisions in other fields (e.g., Arabization in schools, concentration of economic and political power in the hands of the Maurs), it contributed to ethnic tensions by inducing further socioeconomic changes in favor of the Maurs and led to racial unrest in 1989.

Mauritania became independent in 1960 and adopted a one-party system in 1964. After ruinous participation in the Western Sahara War (beginning 1976), an effort to annex the southern third of the former Spanish Sahara, a military regime took over in 1978.

Growing protest against the racial policy of the regime and its international isolation as a result of the support of Iraq during the 1990 Gulf War generated protests at home and forced the transition to a formal multiparty democracy in which the previous political leadership under Maaouya Ould Sid Ahmed Taya managed to retain power. The political opposition as well as the press found themselves persecuted on an ongoing basis. The enduring institution of slavery within Mauritanian society also increasingly became a topic of discussion. Economically, the country has cooperated closely with the IWF and the World Bank.

2. Religious Situation

The state religion is → Sunnite → Islam of a Malikite stamp. Family and social law correspond to the Shari'a. Since independence the government has found in Islam the only tie among the various ethnic groups. About 60 percent of the people belong to the → Sufi orders of Tijānīyah and Qādirīyah and their subdivisions. A few cling to traditional practices that existed from before the arrival of Islam.

The few members of the → Roman Catholic Church are either Europeans (French and Spanish) or from other African states. Since → conversion from Islam is not possible, the work of the church is entirely among these foreign workers. They are entrusted to the → diocese in the capital, Nouakchott. This diocese, which has existed since the beginning of the 20th century, is the only Christian organization. The diocese has representatives also in Nouadhibou, Atar, Zouérate, Rosso, and Kaédi, and

it is a member of the Conférence Episcopal de Sénégal-Mauritanie, centered in Dakar, the Senegalese capital. It also belongs to the Conférence Plénière des Ordinaires de L'Afrique Occidentale and to the Symposium of Episcopal Conferences of Africa and Madagascar. There is no official state relation with the → Vatican, but there is an apostolic delegate in Dakar. Nuns work in government social centers.

After an unsuccessful attempt at entry in 1965 by the Worldwide Evangelization Crusade, the Protestant churches have withdrawn all their → missionaries.

→ African Theology

Bibliography: D. B. BARRETT et al., eds., *WCE* (2d ed.) 1.488-90 • P. MARCHESIN, *Tribus, ethnies et pouvoir en Mauritanie* (Paris, 1992) • M. OULD-MEY, *Global Restructuring and Peripheral States: The Carrot and the Stick in Mauritania* (London, 1996) • A. G. PAZZANITA, *Historical Dictionary of Mauritania* (2d ed.; London, 1996) • U. P. RUF, *Ending Slavery: Hierarchy, Dependency, and Gender in Central Mauritania* (Bielefeld, 1999) • S. C. STEWART and E. K. STEWART, *Islam and Social Order in Mauritania: A Case Study from the Nineteenth Century* (Oxford, 1974) • R. WEGEMUND, "Die Militärregierung in Mauretanien. Zwischenbilanz nach zehn Jahren," *Afrika-Spectrum* 23 (1988) 293-314.

REGINA WEGEMUND

Mauritius

	1960	1980	2000
Population (1,000s):	659	964	1,177
Annual growth rate (%):	2.64	1.00	1.05
Area: 2,040 sq. km. (788 sq. mi.)			

A.D. 2000

Population density: 577/sq. km. (1,493/sq. mi.)
Births / deaths: 1.79 / 0.64 per 100 population
Fertility rate: 2.21 per woman
Infant mortality rate: 13 per 1,000 live births
Life expectancy: 72.7 years (m: 69.5, f: 76.1)
Religious affiliation (%): Hindus 42.9, Christians 32.8 (Roman Catholics 26.9, Protestants 11.5, other Christians 1.7), Muslims 17.0, nonreligious 3.1, Baha'is 2.0, Chinese folk religionists 1.4, other 0.8.

1. General Situation

The Republic of Mauritius lies 800 km. (500 mi.) east of Madagascar in the Indian Ocean, with the island dependency of Rodrigues a further 800 km. to the east. The country's capital is Port Louis.

The Portuguese discovered Mauritius in 1505. The Dutch occupied it in 1598, followed by the French in 1721 and the British in 1810 (→ Colonialism). Since achieving independence in 1968, Mauritius has enjoyed a fairly stable democracy and has attracted considerable foreign investment. The main products for export are sugar and molasses, with tourism and textiles the mainstays of the economy at the turn of the new millennium.

2. Religious Situation

Of all religions found in Mauritius Christianity was the first to be introduced — at the end of the 16th century. → Hinduism and → Islam subsequently arrived when succeeding colonial powers brought in indentured laborers and slaves (→ Slavery) from the Indian subcontinent, Madagascar, and the East Indies. → Buddhism began with the wave of immigration of Chinese entrepreneurs in the 20th century.

2.1. *Churches*

The arrival in 1598 of the first occupying colonial power, the Dutch, marked the start of the Reformed tradition. Its proud inheritor is the Presbyterian Church in Mauritius (→ Reformed and Presbyterian Churches). Although the church offers parish ministry only in three localities, it maintains strong ties with Protestant churches in Scotland, France, and Switzerland.

The roots of the → Roman Catholic Church in Mauritius go back to French rule in 1721. Now part of the Bishops' Conference of the Indian Ocean, the church in 2001 included 47 parishes, served by 97 priests. Its main activities include charity work, community assistance, medical service, and diocesan schools.

The Anglican Church in Mauritius (→ Anglican Communion) had its origin in the beginning of the British colonial period. Today it is part of the Province of the Indian Ocean. It sponsors programs and ministry among the aged, the blind, youth (→ Youth Work), and delinquents. It also runs two high schools and has an active women's association. In 2001 the church had 16 parishes and 12 priests.

The Seventh-day → Adventist Church was founded in 1914 by a French missionary. The Christian → Brethren Church was officially registered in 1942, but its subsequent activities remain unknown. The New (Jerusalem) Church began in 1907. →

Christian Science has been present since 1950, the → Jehovah's Witnesses since 1951.

In 2000 the largest non-Catholic church was the → Assemblies of God. Other groups included → Pentecostals, independent churches (the largest were Voice of Deliverance and Christian Church), and Presbyterians. Many of these groups have refused to be categorized in the official census. The rise of these Christians is essentially a post–World War II phenomenon, the result of immigration and arrival of missionaries from Europe, Australia, South Africa, China, and Taiwan. They emphasize → evangelism and conversion.

2.2. *Ecumenical Tendencies*

There is no ecumenical organization in Mauritius, though talks of starting a council of churches have regularly been voiced (→ National Councils of Churches). The Anglicans, Assemblies of God, Presbyterians, and Roman Catholics collaborate in promoting the work of the Bible Society.

Representatives of all faiths gather on special national occasions to commemorate or celebrate events. Otherwise there is little contact or official → dialogue.

2.3. *Church and State*

Freedom of religion and conscience is guaranteed under article 2 of the constitution. All religions now enjoy government subsidies on a per capita membership basis. Some churches, however, have refused to accept the subsidy because of their doctrinal conviction regarding separation between → church and state.

→ African Theology

Bibliography: R. B. ALLEN, *Slaves, Freedmen, and Indentured Laborers in Colonial Mauritius* (Cambridge, 1999) • D. B. BARRETT et al., eds., *WCE* (2d ed.) 1.490-93 • P. R. BENNETT, comp., *Mauritius* (Oxford, 1992) • F. VON BULOW, *Mauritius* (Munich, 2000) • M. CARTER, *Servants, Sirdars, and Settlers: Indians in Mauritius, 1834-1874* (Delhi, 1995) • W. K. STOREY, *Science and Power in Colonial Mauritius* (Rochester, N.Y., 1997).

VICTOR W. C. HSU

Meaning

Overview
1. Meaning in Philosophy
    1.1. General and Continental Philosophy
    1.2. Analytic Philosophy
2. Meaning in the Social Sciences and Cultural Studies
3. Meaning in Theology

Overview

"Meaning" has diverse senses in everyday language and in various scientific and cultural disciplines. The context is crucial for clarification in each particular instance.

In general, finding meaning concerns the ability to recognize salient features of the world and to employ that recognition as a framework of understanding or as information useful for accomplishing a specific purpose. Theories differ as to whether meaning resides primarily in thought, in a person's linguistic expression or act, in some feature(s) of the world, or perhaps in some relation of these elements to one another. They also differ as to whether the ability to recognize, express, and create meaning is limited to human beings or is also possessed by other species or by devices with artificial intelligence.

We can inquire about the meaning of individual words, phrases, or sentences, or about the meaning of whole texts, consisting of many words and complex ideas. We can ask about the meaning of actions and of socially shared beliefs, values, and practices. We can consider entire → worldviews and ponder whether there is overall meaning to our individual lives, or indeed to history and the cosmos as a whole.

Hermeneutics is methodical interpretation to disclose meaning. In the early modern period it emerged in the new historical-critical approach to the Bible. Manuscripts on → hermeneutics by Friedrich → Schleiermacher (1768-1834) set forth principles and methods for interpreting not only the Bible but also classical texts, for he was both a theologian and a translator of Plato into German. Following his lead, Wilhelm Dilthey (1833-1911) broadened the scope of hermeneutics to embrace all historical and cultural areas of study. The issue is how one enters into a past era and culture not one's own by discerning accurately the meaning of its texts and artifacts. Various disciplines subsequently formed their own approaches to questions of meaning, so the nature and uses of hermeneutical practices are now quite diverse.

1. Meaning in Philosophy

1.1. General and Continental Philosophy

In the popular mind, → philosophy is the quest for the meaning of life or of the world as a whole. That view should not surprise us, for some of the best-known philosophers (Plato, Aristotle, the Stoics) speak of such things. Some modern philosophers, however, have seriously doubted that such a broad inquiry is itself a "meaningful" undertaking. → Ni-

hilists such as Friedrich → Nietzsche (1844-1900) deny any objectively given meanings in life, accepting only those freely affirmed or created by human beings themselves. His lineage extends in part to the 20th-century existentialist Jean-Paul Sartre (1905-80; → Existentialism) and humanist Albert Camus (1913-60; → Humanism).

The phenomenological method of Edmund Husserl (1859-1938; → Phenomenology) underlies the hermeneutical strand of 20th-century Continental philosophy. Martin Heidegger (1889-1976) held that since we inescapably find ourselves concretely situated (*geworfen*, "thrown") in the world, the meaning we discover, perhaps in conversation with other cultures and ages, is inevitably circumscribed by the "hermeneutical circle" constituted by our own life situation. Hans-Georg Gadamer (1900-2002), the leading theoretician of hermeneutical philosophy, engaged more directly the issues raised by Schleiermacher and Dilthey. Paul Ricoeur (b. 1913) dwelt increasingly on → language, and particularly on narrative as the medium through which we encounter and appropriate meaning.

1.2. Analytic Philosophy

In the 20th century → analytic philosophy narrowed the scope to language. It sought to clarify linguistic meaning, to explicate the meanings of words or word-complexes, showing how they point to things other than themselves. John Locke (1632-1704), a distant forerunner of analytic philosophy, proposed an *ideational* theory of meaning: language conveys our thoughts, and thus words are "sensible marks of ideas." His theory assumes, some think erroneously, that thought is independent of language and that each expression has a definite idea associated with it.

The *referential* theory of meaning, also a forerunner, takes proper names as paradigmatic and finds a term's meaning in its referent (the thing it names), or else in the relation between the term and its referent. Gottlob Frege (1848-1925), a logician and mathematician, showed the difficulty with the referential theory in his famous distinction between the sense (*Sinn*) of a name or term and its reference (*Bedeutung*). "The Morning Star is identical with the Evening Star" expresses two different senses or cognitive values, each of which refers to the same object (Venus). Another difficulty is that "syncategorematic" terms such as "if" and "and" evidently do not refer at all but function in a different way in the logic of language.

Bertrand Russell (1872-1970) offered a *propositional* theory according to which the meaning is the propositional (cognitive) content that a statement intrinsically has in virtue of its linguistic and logical structure. A similar view appears in *Tractatus Logico-Philosophicus,* an early work of Ludwig Wittgenstein (1889-1951).

Some analytic philosophers turned to the context of → communication, the *use* that language has, which may differ from its formal meaning derived from ideas or logical characteristics. The later Wittgenstein of the *Philosophical Investigations* called attention to diverse "language games" employed within distinct communities. His view of meaning as context-dependent, lacking universality and metaphysical import, led to revisionist views of → philosophy of religion and → theology. J. L. Austin (1911-60) examined the behavior of speakers, what he called their illocutionary acts, as the key to meaning in a given context. His "performative" approach influenced emotivist theories of → ethics and analyses of liturgical uses of language.

Subsequent analytic philosophy of language continued the debate about meaning and use with great technical detail and in varied positions that intersect with → linguistics and cognitive psychology. Students of artificial language treat meaning as determined by explicit rules. Those with a social-contextual perspective treat it as a matter of convention, of regularities in usage.

An influential offshoot of the logical positivism of the 1930s was the *verification* theory of meaning, based on a model from the natural sciences. It held that the meaning of a statement consists in the conditions under which it is verifiable. Statements not in principle (i.e., scientifically) verifiable are thus meaningless. Its most influential proponent, A. J. Ayer (1910-89), put religious and ethical statements in the unverifiable, hence meaningless, category. A refinement, the *falsifiability* criterion, said a statement need not be directly verifiable (indeed, some accepted scientific theories are not), but to be meaningful it must at least specify conditions that, if they were to occur, would disprove it. Challenges based on this falsifiability criterion of meaning influenced debates about the "death of God" theologies of the 1960s (→ God Is Dead Theology) and continue to affect treatment of the → theodicy problem in theology and philosophy of religion.

2. Meaning in the Social Sciences and Cultural Studies

Some psychologists treat mental and emotional disorders by helping individuals to recognize overarching patterns of meaning in their lives. From experiences with the → Holocaust, Viktor Frankl (1905-97) devised logotherapy as a regimen for recovering a comprehensive orientation in a modern world beset by → pluralism, uncertainty, and the threat of meaninglessness. C. G. Jung (1875-1961) formulated a theory of → archetypes residing in the collective unconscious mind, a reservoir of archaic, mythic-religious patterns accessible in → dreams and vital to appropriate in contending with problems of personal growth and the construction of a mature selfhood. Joseph Campbell (1904-87), a literature scholar, popularized similar archetypal themes in widely read books on comparative → mythology.

Anthropologists and sociologists address meaning at the level of whole cultures or their social subunits. Premodern societies are typically structured so that members of a particular group experience a wholeness to life in their immediate surroundings, whereas modern societies typically differentiate themselves internally into distinct domains and specialized functions, with the individual having a number of roles across these domains (→ Modern Period). As a result, a modern person can experience the world as unduly complex, unintelligible as a whole, with disconnected patterns of meaning dispersed among discrete spheres and perhaps concentrated in a few intersubjective relationships. Theologian Harvey Cox depicted the resulting anomie (→ Aporia) in *The Secular City.* Peter Berger and other social scientists developed the theory underlying such analyses. The functional system theory of the → social sciences often regards religion as a way of coping with the apparent contingency of human life that threatens our wish for security and certainty. Religious → symbols and practices aid in constructing a worldview in which complexity can be grasped and that eliminates the fear that all could be meaningless. So construed, however, religious belief might seem valuable as a tool for giving meaning to life, yet not be something true or important in its own right.

Various movements in the latter half of the 20th century — → structuralism, deconstruction, → postmodernism — rooted in the social sciences and philosophy found their center of gravity in literary studies, sometimes called cultural studies, and developed their own versions of hermeneutics. One influential view, that a culture's representations of reality and meaning are social constructs of those holding positions of power, has led to a criticism and "unmasking" of received texts, artifacts and social-political structures in order to open the way for alternative expressions of meaning, hence for alternative social realities.

3. Meaning in Theology

Meaning in classical Christian theology principally concerns biblical interpretation. Patristic and medieval theology distinguished the literal-historical meaning of biblical texts from three spiritual senses. → Allegory (Gk. *allēgoria,* "veiled language," or description of one thing under the image of another) locates the truths of the faith in the symbolic content of biblical narratives. The tropological (Gk. *tropos,* "turning") sense of passages instructs in Christian conduct, through lessons about → obedience and disobedience to God and their consequences. The anagogical (Gk. *anagōgē,* "leading up") sense conveys mystical or eschatological messages about otherworldly states or events to come. This fourfold pattern of → exegesis sought to extract from the words of Scripture all dimensions of meaning thought to be revealed by God.

The major Protestant → Reformers denounced use of the three spiritual senses as placing Scripture under the control of human understanding and ecclesiastical authority. Their Scripture principle instead invoked a direct encounter of the reader with the → Word of God by confining theological study to the literal-historical meaning of the biblical text. Lutheran and Reformed scholastics elaborated the exegetical procedures following from this principle, procedures that dominated → Protestantism until challenged by the historical-critical methods of Enlightenment-era liberals and the new hermeneutics of Schleiermacher, after which diverse approaches to theological meaning have marked the Protestant landscape.

Much 20th-century theology, especially Protestant theology, can be viewed as an explicit or implicit struggle with questions of meaning. Rudolf Bultmann (1884-1976) utilized themes from Heidegger in his → existentialist theology of the NT, which was designed to establish connections between the message of and about Christ and the self-understanding and quest for meaning of persons in the modern scientific world. Through his influential sermons as well as formal theology, Paul → Tillich (1886-1965) presented religious → faith (ultimate concern) as the remedy for the existential → anxiety of civilization in the wake of the two world wars. Dietrich → Bonhoeffer (1906-45) grappled personally with the Nazi threat and the task of finding and expressing meaning in a "religionless Christianity." Jürgen Moltmann directed the quest for meaning to the future in his *Theology of Hope.*

In Roman Catholic thought with its traditional linkage between theology and → metaphysics, meaning continues to be viewed in large measure as something objectively given in features of the → creation. This approach underlies sacramental theology, in particular the understanding of the → liturgy and symbolism of the → Mass, the doctrine of the real presence (→ Eucharist). Other issues of theological meaning have elicited strong debate in the → Roman Catholic Church. One concern is how the declaration of papal → infallibility proclaimed by the First → Vatican Council (1869-70) is to be construed, the circumstances to which it properly applies, and its limits. Another, arising from Vatican II (1962-65), concerns flexibility in the meaning of the traditional doctrine *extra ecclesiam nulla salus est* (outside the church there is no → salvation), in light of increasing → ecumenism and debates as to where the boundaries of "church" are to be drawn. Also, in exegesis many Catholic scholars are now equaling, if not surpassing, their Protestant counterparts in the extent to which they employ the historical-critical method to establish the primary meanings of biblical texts.

→ Language and Theology; Literary Criticism

Bibliography: On 1: J. L. Austin, *How to Do Things with Words* (London, 1962) • W. Carl, *Frege's Theory of Sense and Reference* (Cambridge, 1994) • R. Carnap, *Meaning and Necessity* (Chicago, 1947) • D. Davidson, *Inquiries into Truth and Interpretation* (New York, 1984) • G. Frege, "On Sinn and Bedeutung" (1892), *The Frege Reader* (ed. M. Beaney; Oxford, 1997) • H.-G. Gadamer, *Philosophical Hermeneutics* (Berkeley, Calif., 1976); idem, *Truth and Method* (New York, 1975) • C. Misak, *Verificationism: Its History and Prospects* (New York, 1995) • A. Moore, ed., *Meaning and Reference* (New York, 1993) • C. Ogden and J. Richards, *The Meaning of Meaning* (New York, 1938) • W. Quine, *The Roots of Reference* (LaSalle, Ill., 1973) • H. Reiner, *Der Sinn unseres Daseins* (Tübingen, 1960) • P. Ricoeur, *Conflict of Interpretations: Essays in Hermeneutics* (Evanston, Ill., 1974) • B. Russell, *An Inquiry into Meaning and Truth* (New York, 1940) • A. Schutz, *The Structures of the Life-World* (Evanston, Ill., 1973) • L. Wittgenstein, *Philosophical Investigations* (Oxford, 1953); idem, *Tractatus Logico-Philosophicus* (New York, 1961).

On 2: P. Berger, *The Sacred Canopy: Elements of a Sociological Theory of Religion* (New York, 1969) • P. Berger and T. Luckmann, *The Social Construction of Reality* (Garden City, N.Y., 1966) • J. Campbell, *The Masks of God* (4 vols.; New York, 1959-68) • H. Cox, *The Secular City* (New York, 1967) • V. Frankl, *Man's Search for Meaning: An Introduction to Logotherapy* (4th ed.; Boston, 1992; orig. pub., 1963) • J. Hospers, *Meaning and Truth in the Arts* (Chapel Hill, N.C., 1948)

• C. Jung, *Modern Man in Search of a Soul* (London, 1933) • N. Luhmann, *Funktion der Religion* (Frankfurt, 1977) • H. Putnam, *Meaning and the Moral Sciences* (London, 1978).

On 3: D. Bonhoeffer, *Letters and Papers from Prison* (London, 1959) • R. Bultmann, *Jesus Christ and Mythology* (New York, 1958) • J. Moltmann, *Theology of Hope* (New York, 1967) • J. Robinson and J. Cobb Jr., eds., *The New Hermeneutic* (New York, 1964) • F. Schleiermacher, *Hermeneutics: The Handwritten Manuscripts* (ed. H. Kimmerle; Missoula, Mont., 1977) • P. Tillich, *The Courage to Be* (New Haven, 1952).

Robert F. Brown and Werner Schwartz

Means of Grace

The so-called means of grace (*media gratiae,* or, sometimes among Lutherans, *organa gratiae et salutis,* "instruments of grace and salvation") are the means by which, revealed in the power of the → Holy Spirit, God offers → grace in Jesus Christ and awakens and strengthens → faith. When we refer to these means, we think especially of the symbolic and sensory manifestation of grace in the Word and in the reality of the world, the external Word (i.e., Holy Scripture) as the presupposition of the understanding of the internal Word (i.e., of the Holy Spirit). If, then, what is said about the means of grace is primarily bound up with the theology of the → sacraments, in this sense the sacraments, as means of grace, will also include the Bible, the proclamation of its message, and absolution (→ Penitence). As Christ is proclaimed in the → congregation and the sacraments are administered, the triune God himself imparts his grace (Matt. 28:18-20; Acts 2:42, 46-47; Rom. 10:17; 1 Cor. 11:26). Throughout the course of church history various groups of enthusiasts and mystics-spiritualists (e.g., Montanus, Joachim of Fiore, and the → Anabaptists) have protested against a materialistic, ritualistic understanding of the imparting of grace.

In the tradition of the → Orthodox Church, the church has the character of mystery as a fellowship of believers. Its → liturgy is sacred action by which the redeeming power of the Holy Spirit works upon participants. → Salvation is actualized in the liturgy by uncreated divine energies. The Holy Spirit is the "purely personal mediator of salvation," and pneumatology is understood as the exposition of the total revelation of the triune God (N. A. Nissiotis).

In Roman Catholic theology the seven sacraments are means of grace by which the → priest, who is commissioned by the church, imparts to individuals the grace that Christ has merited and that makes them capable of → faith and → discipleship ("habitual grace" in → baptism, confirmation, and ordination; "actual grace" in the other sacraments). In a broader sense there is also reference to → sacramentals, especially in connection with the Word, and to → prayer, though the latter lacks the externality that is essential to the means of grace. After → Vatican II Roman Catholic theology began to regard the Bible and church proclamation as more significant for faith and the spiritual life (see *Dei Verbum* 22), and → preaching came to be viewed as also a means of grace. For K. → Rahner (1904-84) God's word of revelation to the world has fundamentally a sacramental character, and the church that bears this Word thus becomes itself "a basic sacrament of the salvation of the world" (E. Jüngel and Rahner, 75).

Lutheran doctrine also regards preaching and the sacraments (esp. baptism and the → Eucharist) as means of grace because the → Word of God is at work in them. The means of grace protect faith against fanatical self-deception (so M. → Luther against Carlstadt and U. → Zwingli) and maintain the primacy of the gift of salvation over the subjective act of faith. They do so by disclosing the embodiment of salvation as it comes to individuals and takes them up into the community. This is the communicative aspect of the means of grace. Nevertheless, the means of grace must be received with a readiness for faith, as against an attitude that looks primarily at *opus operatum* (the work performed). The Holy Spirit may also give direct illumination and faith.

For J. → Calvin the church is one of the external means by which → God invites us to fellowship with Christ. In the Reformed tradition, however, the doctrine of God's sovereignty and → predestination can work against an → assurance of salvation based on the means of grace. The receiving of salvation in a subjective act of faith is more decisive in this tradition. The sacraments serve as a reminder and confession; in the context of discipleship they are viewed as a seal of calling. In a broader sense the → law is also understood as a means of grace (→ Church Discipline; Sanctification).

Decisive in ecumenical → dialogue is the point that in the church's work the revelation of God in Jesus Christ should be proclaimed, acknowledged, and believed as grace, in invocation of the Holy Spirit and according to Holy Scripture and the apostolic tradition. In relation to world religions and the modern secular world, which do not know the historical context of Christianity and the ecclesiological setting of the means of grace, a distinction must be made between the means of grace and other manifestations of the Spirit of grace. Such distinction allows one to recognize that Christ's rule extends to the world as a whole.

Bibliography: G. AULÉN, *The Faith of the Christian Church* (Philadelphia, 1948) • E. BENZ, *The Eastern Orthodox Church, Its Thought and Life* (Garden City, N.Y., 1963) • G. C. BRAY, *Sacraments and Ministry in Ecumenical Perspective* (Oxford, 1985) • S. DUFFY, *The Dynamics of Grace: Perspectives in Theological Anthropology* (Collegeville, Minn., 1993) • G. EBELING, *The Problem of Historicity in the Church and Its Proclamation* (Philadelphia, 1967); idem, *Word and Faith* (London, 1963) • E. JÜNGEL and K. RAHNER, *Was ist ein Sakrament? Vorstöße zur Verständigung* (Freiburg, 1971) • H. H. KNIGHT, *The Presence of God in the Christian Life: John Wesley and the Means of Grace* (Metuchen, N.J., 1992) • E. B. KOENKER, *Worship in Word and Sacrament* (St. Louis, 1959) • J. MACQUARRIE, *A Guide to the Sacraments* (New York, 1997) • N. A. NISSIOTIS, *Die Theologie der Ostkirche im ökumenischen Dialog* (Stuttgart, 1968) • K. RAHNER, *The Church and the Sacraments* (New York, 1964) • H. SCHWARZ, *Divine Communication: Word and Sacrament in Biblical, Historical, and Contemporary Perspective* (Philadelphia, 1985) • P. TILLICH, *Systematic Theology*, vol. 3, *Life and the Spirit: History and the Kingdom of God* (Chicago, 1963) • R. L. UNDERWOOD, *Pastoral Care and the Means of Grace* (Minneapolis, 1993) • P. S. WATSON, *The Concept of Grace* (Philadelphia, 1959) • J. F. WHITE, *The Sacraments in Protestant Practice and Faith* (Nashville, 1999).

BERNHARD MAURER

Medellín → Latin American Councils 2.4

Media → Mass Media

Mediating Theology

1. "Mediating theologians" are attested in the history of dogma of the → early church (→ Christology 2.1-2.2; Trinity), during the Middle Ages (→ Sacrament 2.3; Scholasticism), as well as during the Reformation and in connection with more recent British and 19th-century → North American theology (§§3-5). Not every such theologian, however, has sought a genuine *mediation* between opposing positions or intellectual currents. The ideals of unity

and harmony (e.g., G. Calixtus [1586-1656]; later, e.g., S. T. Coleridge [1772-1834], the so-called early Oriel school, the liberal F. D. Maurice [1805-72], and the Scottish discussion concerning faith and the natural sciences) were more important than a rigorous → theology of genuine argumentative mediation between apparently or genuinely irreconcilable positions with regard to → revelation and nature (→ Science and Theology), revelation and history, historical-critical biblical exegesis (→ Exegesis, Biblical), the atoning death of → Jesus and → reconciliation, and so on.

The same applies to → transcendentalism in the United States (→ Transcendentals) and, with some qualification, to the so-called Mercersburg theology of J. W. Nevin (1803-86) and P. Schaff (1819-93; see in this regard J. H. Nichols), which, despite its considerable ecumenical relevance, has been largely forgotten today. The latter resembles German mediating theology, which to a certain extent also influenced it.

2. Although many examples can be found throughout the history of theology (including within the Roman Catholic tradition) of theologians who genuinely built bridges and avoided extremes while integrating opposing positions, the expression "mediating theology" *(Vermittlungstheologie)* is generally reserved for the broad theological movement after F. D. E. → Schleiermacher (1768-1834; → Schleiermacher's Theology), which developed the basic concern of mediation programmatically (→ Theology in the Nineteenth and Twentieth Centuries 1.5). Although the contours of this theology are not clearly defined, it represented a significant theological current alongside the other two influential movements during the first 60-70 years of the 19th century, namely, early → liberal theology and (confessional) → restoration theology. It was more, however, than merely mediation between these other two.

The deeper concern of all mediating theology is to provide a theologically sound mediation between the concept of scientific knowledge in modernity (→ Modern Period) and the "uniquely Christian spirit" (F. Lücke), that is, the Spirit of God active within the human spirit as proclaimed in revelation. Mediating theology did not really articulate, however, whether it was equating modern → science and → culture, on the one hand, and, on the other, revelation and God's supernatural activity. This ambivalence prompted criticism from various quarters and shows that Schleiermacher's influence did not reach mediating theology quite intact and that the latter's roots, if only indirectly, can also be found in → Romanticism.

3. In 1828 "mediating theology," so named by F. Lücke (1791-1855), acquired as its primary voice the periodical *Theologische Studien und Kritiken,* though it came to expression in other periodicals as well (including *Jahrbuch für deutsche Theologie*) and numerous works on → systematic theology (e.g., by A. Twesten, A. Schweizer, C. Ullmann, K. I. Nitzsch, Lücke, and others), practical theology (Nitzsch), and especially biblical exegesis and historical works (e.g., by C. Weizsäcker, K. von Hase, A. Neander, and K. R. Hagenbach). Because even into the later period of mediating theology Schleiermacher's influence exerts itself alongside, rather than together with, accompanying speculative systems influenced by Hegelian thinking (e.g., I. A. Dorner and R. Rothe; → Hegelianism), one cannot really speak of a synthesis of Schleiermacher and Hegel (1770-1831). Instead, various representatives of mediating theology were sooner able to combine elements of the personal faith of the → revivals (§2.5) with their own positions, the most impressive example being that of A. Tholuck (1799-1877).

4. Just as mediating theology does not exhibit the clearly discernible contours of a theological school, so also is it difficult to determine just when its activities came to an end. Its representatives continued to be interested in God's revelation in Jesus Christ (contra D. F. Strauss [1808-74]), in responsible historical-critical exegesis, in the Reformational foundation of Christian doctrine, in the institutions of the → state and of the "pan-cultural ethical function of the church" (F. W. Graf), and generally in supporting the Evangelische Kirche der Union. Although these issues continued to be of concern within the Ritschlian school, one cannot really identify that school as "mediating theology" in the strict sense.

The influence of mediating theology on British and American theological authors is also noteworthy, though these authors were more likely to share the idealist and revivalist presuppositions than was the German-language historical and systematic theology that developed after about 1870.

Bibliography: J. P. CLAYTON, *The Concept of Correlation: Paul Tillich and the Possibility of a Mediating Theology* (Berlin, 1980) • H. F. GEISSER, "Phänomen Vermittlungstheologie. Evangelisch–Katholisch–Ökumenisch," *Evangelisch und Ökumenisch* (ed. G. Maron; Göttingen, 1986) 512-31 • F. W. GRAF, *Profile des neuzeitlichen Protestantismus* (vol. 1; Gütersloh, 1990) • R. HOLTE, *Der Vermittlungstheologie. Ihre theologischen Grundbegriffe kritisch untersucht* (Uppsala, 1965) • G. VON KLOEDEN, *Evangelische Katholizität. Philip Schaffs Beitrag zur Ökumene* (Münster, 1998) • J. L. NEVE, *History of Protestant Thought* (Philadelphia, 1946) 197-296 • J. H. NICHOLS, *Romanticism in American Theology* (Chicago, 1961) • C. WELSH, *Protestant Thought in the Nineteenth Century* (2 vols.; New Haven, 1985).

DIETRICH RITSCHL

Medical Ethics

1. Problem
2. Methodology
   2.1. Competence
   2.2. Isolation
   2.3. Universalization
   2.4. Framework and Basis of Decisions
3. Present-Day Tasks
   3.1. Centers and Institutes
   3.2. Research
   3.3. Patient-Related Problems
4. Future Therapeutic Ethics

1. Problem

Medical ethics (or ethics in medicine) is not a special ethics but the application of ethical theories, principles, and processes of decision (→ Ethics) to the themes and problems that in the broadest possible sense arise in relation to → health and illness, health policy, → suffering, → healing, research, and the → responsibility for the health of future generations. Hence it is not merely "doctors' ethics," as it was in ordinary parlance and literature up to a few decades ago. Distinct but overlapping fields cover (1) the doctor-patient relation, that is, the dual relation between those who offer care and individual patients, often including their families and important contact persons. The problems associated with the pharmaceutical industry and research arise here — that is, the whole sphere of interactional relations. The fields then cover (2) health policy and health care, hospitals, financing, advances in research, and responsibility to the → Third World countries regarding the exporting of medical technology and drugs — that is, the whole structural sphere. Finally, the fields cover (3) the expectations and actual practices of the population in relation to health, including hygiene, addictions (→ Substance Abuse), pain, sickness, and → death — that is, the whole sphere of health and culture.

The three fields overlap after the manner of concentric circles. In the first circle physicians and health workers seem to have the decisive voice; in the second, lawyers and health planners and experts; in the third, parents, schools, churches, and the media (→ Mass Media). Recent research, however, shows that the movement is from (3) to (1) rather than from (1) to (3). The expectations of the population determine the health system, which in turn influences the actual practice of those who deliver health care or pharmaceuticals to the patients or customers. At the same time, the amazing → progress of medical technology, which seems to make the impossible possible and health attainable, does raise new and at times irresponsible expectations.

2. Methodology

Although reflection on medical ethics is still a young discipline, the following may be said regarding the methodology and basis.

2.1. Competence

In courses ethics may be a matter for experts, but all mature and responsible people can and should make ethical decisions (including in medical ethics), so long as they see the complexity of the ethical problem, strive for nonpartisan objectivity, and at the same time are ready to accept the consequences of the decisions they make. Ruled out, then, is the idea that medical ethics is a matter for experts alone, as though only doctors and specialists on commissions were competent in this area. Also ruled out, however, is the arbitrary subjection of medical ethics to subjective preferences and emotional judgments or to the mere wishes of patients. Ruled out, too, is the pseudoscientific reduction of medical and therapeutic action to an uninvolved and ethically neutral imparting of information (a particular danger in genetic counseling).

The new interest in medical ethics (first in the United States and the Netherlands, then in Australia, Great Britain, France, and German-speaking countries) gives evidence of this broad understanding of the discussion-based decision-making process both in the larger problems and in the specific patient-related questions of medical ethics. Already in the Nürnberg trials of 1945-46 (→ Fascism), the prosecution of criminal medical acts showed how necessary it is to stake out the area of medical ethics. If we do not do so, ethical discourse in the area lacks concrete orientation, for it is clearly not enough merely to orient it to what is criminal (→ Punishment). From the time of the Nürnberg Code of 1947 (on experimenting with people), many international declarations have been made on specific problems of medical ethics, for example, those of the World Medical Association, the Council of International Organizations of Medical Science, and the Christian Medical Commission of the → World Council of Churches. We may also mention the declarations of many national academies along with medical groups and churches. These declarations (on such matters as defining the point of death, organ transplants, biomedical research on people, therapeutic → abortion, reproductive medicine, genetics, help in dying, hospital patients, and many other topics) are largely oriented toward the U.N. Universal Declaration of Human → Rights (1948) and toward the resultant pacts, which have thereby achieved central importance for medical ethics.

2.2. Isolation

The reduction of medical ethics to doctors' ethics, which was common in the days of paternalistic medicine and which related solely to physicians, made no solid distinction between the scientific and ethical components of problems in medical ethics. In fact a distinction of this nature is necessary, for most of the problems in medical ethics are complex. Questions of diagnosis and prognosis are associated in a very complicated way with financial, legal, psychological, social, and indeed ethical questions, and also with the interests of research, so that careful consideration is imperative. The ethical aspects must be named and isolated as clearly as possible, though not to the neglect of their relation to other aspects of the problem. Only then can we make a genuine ethical decision that is not simply a disguised prognostic evaluation, financial judgment, psychological preference, or the like. Being a member of the medical profession or of a body that formulates health-care policy may make the differentiating of the ethical aspects easier, on the one hand, because of previous experience. On the other, however, experience can also make more difficult an unprejudiced differential diagnosis of a problem in medical ethics.

2.3. Universalization

For the → United Nations, which is supposed to be ethically neutral but which does speak concretely about medical ethics through the agency of the World Health Organization (WHO), as well as for the Christian churches, a burning issue is that of the transcultural validity of general standards and international declarations on the subject, even if for different reasons. Are there tendencies toward a universal medical ethics, at least in principle? In the long run can we overcome specific cultural differences in such matters as attitudes to the body and sickness and death, the position of → women, and the size and structure of the family? Even today, these differences are not just geographic in nature, for with the influx of foreign workers into industrialized countries (→ Industrial Society), patients there are culturally and religiously heterogeneous, so that these countries are already acquainted with the problem of the universalizing of medical ethics within their own territories.

At this point we undoubtedly have an important future task for medical ethics, whether in terms of Christian theology or of → philosophy. East Asian traditions are also beginning to play a significant role in the discussion. The trend is clearly toward (further) internationally agreed basic maxims of medical ethics. At the forefront of the process is a global concern to recognize and establish human rights (→ Human Dignity).

2.4. *Framework and Basis of Decisions*

The international declarations mentioned above (see 2.1) and various state laws (e.g., on gene technology, reproductive medicine, the trade in embryos, experiments on humans and on animals, laws regulating pharmaceuticals) form a framework — at least in the negative sense of prohibitions — for all decisions in medical ethics. But this framework offers no more concrete answers to specific problems than do the positive demands based on the principles derived from human rights (e.g., the dignity of the → person, the → autonomy of the patient, the avoidance of harm [*nihil nocere*, "harm nothing"], justice, and the right to participate) when it comes to direct solutions to specific problems. These principles or criteria, which expand on the Hippocratic Oath, are widely accepted today. There is some tension between them, but they do help clarify the presuppositions for basic decisions. It is because of the complexity of most of the problems in medical ethics and the uniqueness of each human life and destiny that direct inferences from overriding ethical principles are seldom possible.

Argument is normally needed in order to establish a basis for decision. The argumentative process must be transparent and rational. It must be open to review and testing by the participants. These are lofty demands, but medical ethics must accept them. In practice, then, it often takes the form of criticism of set routine and an appeal to the previously neglected professional ethical sense of the different medical groups, hospitals, → institutions, research teams, and political authorities. In so doing, it also encounters opposition and is misunderstood as operating primarily negatively and critically. Nevertheless, in insisting on the argumentative character of reaching ethical decisions and on a new and more nuanced professional sense, most of the different schools of medical ethics are agreed. Subjective emotional judgments and reliance on slogans thus no longer have any place in medical ethics today.

The basic → norms and maxims derived from human rights recur in theological discussions. The final reference here, however, is to our divinely conferred dignity, divine likeness, and uniqueness. Clearer and more deliberate articulation is given to this fact than in philosophical medical ethics, though we also find it there, especially in the United States. At the same time, the logical-ethical conclusions for medical ethics that are drawn from this principle are not always the same among Roman Catholics and Protestants, as we see from the different positions regarding, for example, → birth control or in vitro fertilization. Interdenominational debate is in full swing, however, and we should not overestimate the differences except as regards contraception. For an ethics of principle (→ Deontology) operates more abstractly and removed from the actual situation of the patient than a theological ethics that is more oriented to a narrative, future-oriented teleological ethics of responsibility, that is, a successful life and death for those beset by medical problems. Increasingly today, then, we find in theological medical ethics a combination of a future-oriented teleological approach with what is called a "rule utilitarianism," often advanced in the United States — that is, a → utilitarianism in the sense of a striving for a high quality of life within certain guidelines (→ Ethics 1).

We may illustrate the task of reaching decisions by the example of the demand for a humane death — or, better, a death in dignity, intensely debated in the late 1990s in Australia and the Netherlands and, after 2000, throughout Europe as a whole. Even though recognition of the guidelines forbids actively putting a severely ill patient to death, problems remain. A purely utilitarian position will seek to reduce the suffering as much as possible while still preserving life. Experimenting on the patient is also forbidden (per the Nürnberg Code). Attempts to heal by means of new medications are permitted, though so-called randomization (selection by lots) and blind and double-blind experiments can become subcategories of the problem. When ought efforts to prolong life be abandoned? Secular utilitarianism is vague on this point. Clinical practice approves more readily in the case of older patients.

Measures to alleviate pain, even though they do not cure, are generally regarded as justified. Clinical practice tends to permit "dying on request" more for older patients. In this matter a biblically based medical ethics can offer certain correctives, provided a basic understanding of the arguments is also present. Life and death free from pain are not part of the biblical promise, nor is prolonging life at all costs the goal. To a biblically oriented medical ethics deciding for or against prolongation when death is sure and imminent should hardly be related to age. We must consider and accept freedom to withhold such measures even in the case of younger patients who are dying. In this matter theological medical ethics serves as a corrective. In other matters it can lead to open conflict and contradiction.

3. Present-Day Tasks

In addition to the broad ethical tasks that arise in health policy, the following challenges call for attention.

3.1. *Centers and Institutes*

Medical ethics needs to be taught. Many medical schools in the United States have required courses on the subject. In Europe they appear more as elective courses, though such teaching also takes place in numerous special events and courses, de facto also in patient-history groups and Balint Society groups, in the media, and in books that are read by others as well as those in the medical profession. The teachers and authors in these activities are mostly philosophers, theologians, medical historians, medical psychologists, general practitioners, more rarely lawyers, and ideally all these specialists working in teams. Particularly receptive students and readers include young medical students, practitioners and clinicians over 40, and those who do counseling (psychologists, theologians, and social workers). Through publications, the media, and the churches, the circle of interested parties needs to be extended to cover the whole public and especially to reach teachers and parents.

Research in the area is also demanded. This research is not just a matter of working over old problems historically and seeing how they arose and were solved. We require a rational, argumentative analysis of prototypical, real, and hypothetical (i.e., worst-case, e.g., in human gene technology, health policy) situations and difficulties, clarification of their relation to existing → law, and the initiating of new legislation. Research takes place in institutions that are either solely (like some in the United States and France) or partly (as normally in German-speaking countries) dedicated to this task. The work is also done among individual academics and in small centers, conferences, and symposia in universities and churches. The Academy for Ethics in

Medicine was founded in 1986 in Göttingen for Germany, Switzerland, and Austria, and similar influential groups are active elsewhere in Europe and the United States. They not only do research but also interface with the public and offer advice to governments, ministries of health, and parliamentary commissions, which often must decide on difficult questions of medical ethics that jurists alone cannot answer.

3.2. *Research*

The historic ethical coresponsibility of physicists for the atom bomb (→ Weapons) often serves as a parallel today to that of those who do genetic research with its unforeseeable and potentially disastrous consequences for people, animals, and plants. Even if no one seriously wants another Galileo case (with the literal forbidding of research by moral courts or the churches), the serious ethical problems raised by what seems to be neutral research pose an unusually complex dilemma (see H. Jonas and many others). At issue is not merely genetic research but natural science as a whole (→ Science and Theology), including a great deal of medical and pharmaceutical research. If Reformation theology in particular has favored free and progressive scientific investigation, the demand laid upon theology and the church today is to insist as strongly and intelligently as possible that no research or technological progress is ethically neutral.

3.3. *Patient-Related Problems*

When we look more closely at the many problems in medical ethics that directly affect patients, we can reduce them to a relatively small number of basic issues, even though each patient's medical concerns and life story are ultimately unique and can be compared to those of others only with difficulty. The great questions include the beginning of life (issues relating to pregnancy and abortion, prenatal diagnostics and screening), the end of life (death with dignity and → euthanasia), the obligation of full disclosure, telling the → truth, selection (triage) or rejection of patients in times of emergency or disaster, proxy decisions for others (including compulsory hospitalization), → manipulation (e.g., blind and double-blind experiments with new drugs), teaching how to live a restricted life because of chronic illness or handicaps (→ Persons with Disabilities), and death. Although these problems have been present for a long time, at least from the beginning of modern medicine, they were known in their basic forms much earlier.

The striking advances in medicine have given some of these problems a drastically greater urgency — for example, the beginning of life as a result of genetics and reproductive medicine, the end of life by intensive care and life-prolonging therapies, and the duty of full disclosure by difficulties of prognosis because of the introduction of complex therapies. We may also refer to problems of determining the time of death in the case of organ donors. The use of palliative but not curative measures in the case of those severely ill has given rise to fresh discussion about the quality of life. The indication here too is that the thrust toward quantification is irresistible, as though we could establish verifiable criteria as to what is a life worth living or not worth living. We cannot dismiss this concern, for medical technology has temporally extended the problem phases in the process of dying in such a way that we seem to need quantifiable criteria. Transferring the idea of quality of life to those with disabilities, however, or to children whom we expect to be severely handicapped leads us into immediate proximity with the criteria by which the National Socialists decided that a life is of no value (→ Holocaust).

4. Future Therapeutic Ethics

The many links between the themes and tasks of medical ethics and the ethics of science and technology, or even of social and political ethics, suggest especially to Christians that in medical ethics we have a paradigm for ethics in general: conscious acceptance of responsibility for present and future life, a readiness to heal and to comfort, openness to new possibilities in critical distinction from unscrupulous Prometheans and their promises of success and progress, and, not least, a basic therapeutic consciousness in all personal, vocational, and public matters.

Underlying all these features of responsible ethics (→ Diakonia) is a convinced respect for life. Grateful respect for life extends to nonhuman life as well. Thus → animals (who are the subjects of millions of necessary, as well as avoidable, experiments in research and related fields) come within the bounds of medical ethics and therapeutic responsibility. In medical ethics we have a supreme example of what is increasingly seen to be an acute global problem in responsibility to sick humans, animals, and plants. On the basis of the Bible Jews and Christians may establish and articulate respect for life differently from those of other traditions and convictions; no one, however, on good grounds can evade the demand for a basic therapeutic ethical attitude.

Bibliography: Reference works and periodicals: British Medical Association, *Philosophy and Practice of Medical Ethics* (London, 1988) • A. Eser and M. von Lutterotti, eds., *Lexikon Medizin, Ethik, Recht* (Freiburg, 1989) • *Hastings Center Report* (Hastings-on-Hudson, N.Y., 1971-) • *Journal of Medical Ethics* (London, 1975-) • *Journal of Medicine and Philosophy* (Dordrecht, 1976-) • W. Korff, L. Beck, and P. Mikat, eds., *Lexikon der Bioethik* (3 vols.; Gütersloh, 1998) • W. T. Reich, *Encyclopedia of Bioethics* (rev. ed.; 5 vols.; New York, 1995) • *Zeitschrift für Ethik in der Medizin* (Heidelberg, 1989-).

General works: B. M. Ashley and K. O'Rourke, *Health Care Ethics: A Theological Analysis* (St. Louis, 1982) • T. L. Beauchamp and J. F. Childress, *Principles of Biomedical Ethics* (5th ed.; New York, 2001) • A. Bondolfi and H. Müller, eds., *Medizinische Ethik im ärztlichen Alltag* (Basel, 1999) • D. Callahan, *Setting Limits: Medical Goals in an Aging Society* (Washington, D.C., 1995) • J. M. Gustafson, *The Contributions of Theology to Medical Ethics* (Milwaukee, Wis., 1975) • S. Hauerwas, *Suffering Presence: Theological Reflections on Medicine, the Mentally Handicapped, and the Church* (Notre Dame, Ind., 1986) • H. Jonas, *Technik, Medizin, und Ethik* (Frankfurt, 1985) • S. E. Lammers and A. Verhey, eds., *On Moral Medicine: Theological Perspectives in Medical Ethics* (Grand Rapids, 1987) • K. Lebacqz, *Professional Ethics: Power and Paradox* (Nashville, 1985) • R. A. McCormick, *Health and Medicine in the Catholic Tradition* (New York, 1984); idem, *How Brave a New World? Dilemmas in Bioethics* (Washington, D.C., 1985) • M. E. Marty, *Health and Medicine in the Lutheran Tradition* (New York, 1983) • W. F. May, *The Physician's Covenant: Images of the Healer in Medical Ethics* (Philadelphia, 1983) • G. Meilander, *Bioethics: A Primer for Christians* (Grand Rapids, 1996) • E. D. Pellegrino and D. C. Thomasma, *For the Patient's Good: The Restoration of Beneficence in Health Care* (New York, 1988) • P. Ramsey, *Ethics at the Edges of Life: Medical and Legal Intersections* (New Haven, 1978); idem, *The Patient as Person: Explorations in Medical Ethics* (New Haven, 1970) • D. Ritschl, *Konzepte. Ökumene, Medizin, Ethik* (Munich, 1986) • K. L. Vaux, *Health and Medicine in the Reformed Tradition* (New York, 1984).

Dietrich Ritschl

Medical Missions

4. Devolution
5. Current Issues
   5.1. Primary Health Care
   5.2. The Church as a Healing Community

Medical missions have been an ancillary service from the beginning of the missionary movement (→ Mission). Only in the 20th century did they come to be viewed as an independent task. This background is important as missionary societies relinquish medical missions in favor of the medical work of churches in the → Third World. A new understanding of medical missions has become necessary.

1. Background
In obedience to the command of Jesus to "cure the sick" (Matt. 10:8), early Christians cared for those who were ill. That ministry belonged in the first centuries (A.D. 100-400) to → deacons and deaconesses, who were to report sick people to the local → bishop. Upon the establishment of Christianity in the Constantinian era, the erection of Christian hospitals began. With the foundation of → religious orders from the 6th century onward, a network of → monasteries offering health care spread throughout western Europe. In the late → Middle Ages (13th-14th cents.) some hospitals owned by church orders passed into the hands of municipal governments.

During the age of maritime discovery (ca. 1420-1600), members of religious orders, predominately → Franciscan friars and → Jesuits, offered simple medical care as part of their missionary apostolate. Some hospices and hospitals for the sick were begun in South America and Africa. Although these pioneer efforts did not survive into the modern era because of the low quality of medical care, they were the first attempts at medicine practiced transculturally.

Few missionary doctors and nurses were sent to the mission fields before 1800. The first Protestant physician sent out to do missionary work was a Dutchman, Justus Heurnius, who served in the East Indies until 1638 (→ Dutch Missions). A century later, concerned for the health of mission personnel, the Danish-Halle Mission sent Dr. Kaspar Gottlieb Schlegemilch to Tranquebar, India, in 1730 (→ German Missions). In 1735 Count Nikolaus → Zinzendorf sent a Dr. Grothaus to St. Croix, West Indies, for similar care of → Moravian missionaries.

Dr. John Thomas (1757-1801) reached India while serving the East India Company as a ship's doctor. Moved by the physical and spiritual needs of the Bengali people, he stayed in India from 1787 to 1791, living in a simple bamboo hut where he ministered to the sick and learned the Bengali language. Upon his return to England in 1792, he not only was accepted by the new Baptist Missionary Society as their first → missionary but also influenced William Carey to accompany him.

2. Expansion
Dr. John Scudder (1793-1855), with degrees in both theology and medicine, went to Ceylon (now Sri Lanka) from the United States in 1819, and later to India. His enthusiasm for serving God through missionary medicine influenced five sons, one daughter, three grandsons, and a granddaughter, Ida S. Scudder, to become medical missionaries (→ North American Missions).

The first usage of the term "medical missions" is associated with the pioneer work of Dr. Peter Parker (1804-88). Trained both as a doctor and as a Presbyterian minister, Parker was sent to China in 1834 by the American Board of Commissioners for Foreign Missions. Having gained an outstanding reputation as a physician in Canton, Parker founded the Medical Missionary Society in China in 1836 as an auxiliary for newly arriving medical missionaries. Exiled during the first Opium War, Parker visited Great Britain, where he rallied support for medical missions. The first European association furthering medical missions, the Edinburgh Association for Sending Medical Aid to Foreign Countries, owes its inception to him. Two years later it became the Edinburgh Medical Missionary Association (→ British Missions). Returning to China, Parker was the first doctor in that country to use an anesthetic agent during surgery. In 1845 he began to teach five full-time Chinese medical students, thus founding China's first modern medical education program.

The year 1841 was a banner year for medical missions. In response to Parker's challenge, the Christian Medical Society was formed in Edinburgh. In that same year David Livingstone (1813-73) sailed for Cape Town, South Africa, under the London Missionary Society. Although his major accomplishments were in exploration, in opening up Africa to trade and → education, and in speeding the end of → slavery, the inspiration of his life and death motivated hundreds, including medical missionaries, to serve in Africa.

One influenced by Livingstone's death was Dr. Robert Laws (1851-1934) of Aberdeen, Scotland. Trained in theology and medicine, he followed the trail of Livingstone to central Africa under the Free Church of Scotland. Before British → colonialism reached Nyasaland (now Malawi), Laws combined

→ evangelism, the teaching of various building trades at the Overtoun Institute, and medicine, including the building of 13 hospitals.

Protestant Christianity in Korea began with medical missions. Horace Allen (1858-1932), a Presbyterian doctor, won the confidence of the ruler of Korea by saving the life of the king's nephew when local doctors could not stop the bleeding from a deep wound. The respect for Allen that followed permitted Horace Underwood and Henry Appenzeller, a Presbyterian and a Methodist, to enter Korea in 1884 as the first missionaries. Laws were subsequently changed to allow Korean citizens to become Christians.

Most esteemed among 20th-century pioneers is Albert → Schweitzer (1875-1965). A native of Alsace, Schweitzer earned doctorates in music, philosophy, theology, and medicine. Acclaimed as a theologian and interpreter of Bach, he captivated the world in 1913 by dedicating himself to serve the poor and needy in Africa. From age 30 until his death he served as a medical missionary at Lambarene Hospital in Gabon, French West Africa. In 1952 he was awarded the Nobel Peace Prize.

3. Concentration
3.1. *Mission Hospitals*
Medical missionaries in the 19th century sought to introduce the latest scientific knowledge for the treatment of diseases and to develop hospitals as centers for medical care. Compassionate concern not only for the soul but also for the body prompted Christians to respond to physical needs to the best of their ability and medical knowledge. The more medicine became a scientific art, the more effectively it alleviated diseases that had formerly been scourges in human history, including cholera, leprosy, tuberculosis, malaria, yellow fever, and tetanus.

This effect expanded greatly in the last half of the 19th century, with the encouragement of colonial authorities. In 1849 there were just 40 missionary doctors around the globe. In 40 years that number grew sixfold. The Centenary Conference on the Protestant Mission of the World (London, 1888) celebrated the growth of medical missions. In 1887 there were about 260 medical missionaries, with 116 from Great Britain, 112 from the United States, and 4 from Canada.

Development of Roman Catholic medical missions paralleled that of Protestants, although on a much smaller scale. In 1910 there were 69 Catholic hospitals in South Asia and 7 in Siam, plus 99 dispensaries on the islands of the Pacific.

The pace of mission hospital preeminence in-creased in the early 20th century. The Christian Medical Society of Scotland by 1915 included in its work 54 hospitals worldwide with 4,000 beds and a combined staff of 86 missionary physicians, 69 missionary nurses, and 230 indigenous doctors and nurses.

The 1920s marked the high point of Protestant medical missions. The *World Missionary Atlas* (London, 1925) enumerated 1,157 missionary medical doctors (801 men, 356 women) serving in mission hospitals alongside 614 national physicians. Finally, there were 5,458 additional trained medical personnel serving in mission hospitals and in 1,686 dispensaries.

The 1950s and 1960s, while known as the postcolonial era, did not diminish the importance of medical missions in many countries. In many Third World nations, Christian missions continued to provide a significant percentage of the total curative medicine available. In 1968, for example, church-related hospitals and clinics carried out 43 percent of the medical work in Tanzania, 40 percent in Malawi, 34 percent in Ghana, 26 percent in Taiwan, 15 percent in India, 13 percent in Bangladesh, 12 percent in Indonesia, and 9 percent in Zaire/Congo.

3.2. *Missions and Medical Education*
Of the various ways that medical missions influenced medical education around the world, the foremost was the contribution made in formal training in scientific medicine. It began in China as Peter Parker, soon after opening his hospital in Canton in 1835, began private tutoring of his first three Chinese assistants. Next came the translation of medical textbooks into Chinese, first by Dr. Benjamin Hobson (1816-73), a graduate of Guy's Hospital, London, working with the London Missionary Society in 1850. An LMS missionary, Dr. Kenneth Mackenzie (1850-88), founded the first Chinese medical school in 1881. By the turn of the century mission boards had launched 32 medical schools in China, with a total enrollment of 270 students (227 male, 43 female). In 1906 British and American mission societies united in founding the Peking Union Medical College, a project supported and staffed from 1915 by the Rockefeller Foundation by means of the China Medical Board (→ Mission Schools).

In India, as in China, medical education under the missions began informally. In formal training, however, British authorities developed the Indian Medical Service, with medical missions complementing the training offered by the government in scientific medicine. Nevertheless, the missions founded three important centers for medical training. The Miraj Medical School, begun in 1892 by Dr. W. J. Wanless (1865-1933) of the American Board, trained assistants for mission hospitals. Ludhiana in the Punjab began in 1894 as a joint mission medical school for Christian women under the leadership of Dr. Edith Mary Brown (1864-1956). In 1952 it became coeducational as the Christian Medical College, Ludhiana. The most famous of the mission medical colleges, Vellore in South India, began in 1918 under the leadership of Dr. Ida Scudder (1870-1960) as the Union Missionary Medical School for Women. Today, as an affiliated college to Madras University, it ranks at the top of India's institutions for medical education, offering over 60 degree programs on graduate and postgraduate levels, with special emphasis on rural and public-health ministries.

Medical education in Korea and Japan followed German patterns. The prestigious Yonsei University College of Medicine, Seoul, is an offshoot of Severance Union Medical College, founded in 1904. Since the 1920s St. Luke's International Hospital in Tokyo has offered training for nurses, with special emphasis on public-health programs.

Two creative projects in the Near East deserve mention. The Syrian Protestant College in Beirut (1863), which in 1920 became the American University of Beirut, included a medical department as early as 1867. Although Roman Catholic priests were impeded in the exercise of medicine, surgery, and obstetrics by → canon law until 1936, Cardinal Charles M. A. Lavigerie (1825-92), archbishop of Algiers, founded in 1881 a medical training course on Malta for freed slaves who were enrolled in the medical school of La Valetta, with practical training for medical mission service in Africa.

The first systematic medical education on the island of Madagascar, the Royal Medical Missionary College, began as a joint endeavor by Norwegian and British missionaries in 1887. It ceased to exist when the French took over political control in 1895. Most missions in Africa designed their training programs for medical assistants. However, Dr. Albert Cook (1870-1951), medical missionary of the Church Missionary Society, founded the Mengo Medical School in Uganda in 1917, the forerunner of Makerere University's medical school. Medical missionaries in the Congo began the École Agrée d'Infirmiers at the Baptist Mission Hospital at Yasuku in 1921, as well as a sister institution at Sona Bata that in 1951 became the Institut Médical Evangélique at Kimpese.

The *World Missionary Atlas* in 1925 listed 19 Christian medical colleges offering a full medical course, with 914 medical students enrolled. In addition there were 1,932 nursing students enrolled in the 66 nursing schools run by missions.

3.3. *Women in Medical Mission*

From the middle of the 19th century, Roman Catholic missions tended to provide basic care for the sick through dispensaries rather than hospitals. An exception took place in Hawaii in ministry to lepers. While Father Damien de Veuster (1840-89), a Belgian, devoted his life from 1873 to 1899 to lepers on the island of Molokai, Franciscan sisters administered the leprosarium, took full charge of the hospital in 1884, and set up the first hospital on Maui in the same year.

Elevating the condition of women grew as a missionary motivation in the early 20th century, including, for Catholics, education for → birth control. Dr. Anna Dengel (1892-1980), a native of Austria, trained for missionary nursing in Lyons, France, and studied medicine at Cork University in Ireland. Five years (1920-24) of work among women at a small hospital staffed by the Franciscan Missionaries of Mary in Rawalpindi, India, convinced her of the need for a religious congregation devoted to medical missions. Approval to form the Society of Catholic Medical Missionaries was not obtained until 1936, when Propaganda Fide published *Constans et sedula*, which lifted the centuries-old ban on religious sisters doing surgical and obstetric work. In 1937 the Medical Missionaries of Mary was formed.

During the same period Maryknoll Sisters pioneered in medical missions. The first eight sisters to China included two nurses. While nursing was an acceptable occupation for women, Mother Mary Joseph, Maryknoll's foundress, desired to send a sister-doctor overseas. Elizabeth Hirschboeck, upon graduation from Marquette University medical school in 1928, began her spiritual formation with Maryknoll as Sister Mercy. Hers was a long and distinguished career as mission doctor in Korea (beginning in 1931), Bolivia (1943), and the United States. Her passion for medical missions inspired others. In 1984 it was estimated that over a third of all Maryknoll Sisters had engaged in some type of medical work.

Mission as → diakonia received new emphasis for women in mission in recent years in many countries. It was from the medical mission sisters that Mother Teresa (1910-97) of Calcutta learned how to care for the sick and dying among the poor.

In contrast to Catholic missionary sisters, Protestant women missionaries were free to serve as medical missionaries. By 1925 the world total of missionary nurses reached 1,007. Many single missionaries served as deaconesses.

Clara Swain (1834-1910) was the world's first woman missionary doctor. In 1870 in Bareilly, northern India, she founded the first hospital for women in Asia. Fanny Jane Butler (1850-89) was the first English missionary woman doctor. In 1880 she sailed for India under the Church of England Zenana Missionary Society and served in mission hospitals in Bengal, Bihar, and Kashmir until her untimely death. Missionary doctor Anna Sarah Kugler (1856-1930), an American Lutheran, founded in 1897 the Kugler Hospital at Guntur, Andhra Pradesh, considered one of the best in India. Mary Reed (1854-1943), an American Methodist, contracted leprosy yet returned to supervise a leper asylum at Chandag, India, from 1891 to 1938. The first woman missionary doctor of the Mennonite Brethren, Katharina L. Schellenberg (1870-1945), specialized in treating outpatients for 40 years (1906-45) in the Hyderabad area. Eva Lombard (1890-1978), the first woman missionary doctor of the Basel Mission, worked with the Kanarese Mission in Mysore, South India, from 1920 to 1957.

Noteworthy also are the pioneer women medical missionaries in China. Methodist Lucinda L. Coombs (1849?-1919) opened the first hospital for women in China in Peking (Beijing) in 1875. Leonora Howard (1851-1925), also a Methodist medical missionary, opened the Isabella Fisher Hospital in Tientsin in 1881. Elizabeth McKechnie (1845-1939) served as a missionary nurse at a third hospital established to serve women and children exclusively — the Margaret Williamson Hospital, which opened in 1885 in Shanghai.

Mary Pierson Eddy (1864-1923), born in Sidon of missionary parents, returned to Lebanon after medical training to establish in 1903 a hospital and sanatorium for tuberculosis patients. Sarah Rebecca Parrish (1869-1952), sent to the Philippines by the Methodist Episcopal Woman's Foreign Missionary Society and the first Protestant woman medical missionary in that country, founded in 1908 the Mary Johnston Hospital and School of Nursing in Tondo, a slum district of Manila.

3.4. Supporting Structures

The World → Missionary Conference at Jerusalem in 1928 emphasized the place of medical missions in the work of the church. It held that medical work "should not be thought of as only a pioneer of evangelism or as merely a philanthropic agency . . . . there ought to be a closer co-operation that often exists in this work between the medical profession and the ministers of the Christian Church" (Report,

8.197). In support of these missions were 14 medical missionary associations, each having its own local network of supporters.

Catholic medical missions experienced a parallel mobilization of resources in the sending churches. In 1925 the Catholic Hospital Association in the United States stimulated interest in organizing the Catholic Medical Mission Board. Their purpose was to collect and distribute medicines and supplies to Catholic missionaries on the field. By 1934 they had shipped 23,000 surgical instruments to almost 900 mission stations, assisting the work of 95 religious congregations.

4. Devolution

In the first half of the 20th century, primarily in Asia rather than in Africa, the goal was established of transferring responsibility for the care of the sick to national Christian workers. It was realized on pragmatic grounds that hospitals that remained the permanent responsibility of mission boards would become their future liability. Two alternatives were considered to avoid this problem: either the state would take over the hospitals, or they would become adjuncts of the church to be administered and staffed by that body. Both alternatives were tried in the postcolonial era that followed.

Only a few models exist of medical missions initiatives from the Third World. By 1929 both the National Missionary Society of India and the Anglican Church in Ceylon had launched medical mission work.

The → World Council of Churches led in the 1960s in rethinking the role of the Christian church in → healing ministries. Pivotal were the conclusions of two consultations held in Tübingen in 1964 and 1967. The first affirmed, "The Christian ministry of healing belongs primarily to the → congregation as a whole" (Healing Church, 8). The second focused on the key theological issue of → health and salvation. In 1968 the WCC created its Christian Medical Commission, renamed in 1992 as the Churches' Action for Health. It led in health planning as a new discipline, an unexplored field in the pioneering stage of medical missions. It addressed its concerns to the churches rather than to mission agencies.

During the same decade → Vatican II brought a radical change for Roman Catholics by redefining the concept of evangelization. Salvation was not only spiritual but also physical. Formerly, missionaries sought to open the door of salvation by medical work done for indigenous peoples. Now they were encouraged to work with the people in providing access to health care generally, in addition to providing treatment for specific medical needs.

5. Current Issues
5.1. *Primary Health Care*
At its establishment in 1947, the World Health Organization identified "Health for All by the Year 2000" as one of its objectives. Priority was given to the attainment of a level of health for all that will permit people to lead socially and economically productive lives. Primary health care, rather than curative medicine, was to be the priority.

Medical missions have shifted programs in response to this new priority. In 1961 the American Baptist Mission Hospital in Vanga, Zaire, consisted of a small rural hospital and two isolated dispensaries. In 1986 a 200-bed, five-doctor hospital received referrals from a network of 50 primary health centers serving over 200,000 people. Most primary health centers are located close to Christian churches. Government leaders from the Ministry of Health to village development committees are involved and committed to the program. From Haiti to India to Ecuador, such programs have achieved a close partnership between church and government, utilizing both the hospitals and local health centers.

Some mission agencies have changed their deployment of medical personnel. Maryknoll Sisters today focus not on maintaining expensive hospitals but on finding innovative ways to meet the health-care needs of the poor, directly involving the people themselves.

5.2. *The Church as a Healing Community*
In 1985 the International Association for Mission Studies launched a study project entitled "The Church as a Healing Community." It affirmed that healing is the process of bringing about a dynamic state of well-being of the individual and society; of physical, mental, emotional, spiritual, economic, political, and social well-being; and of harmony and healing in community, with the environment, and with God. Recognition of the contributions of traditional medicine, of faith healing, and of action programs to heal the earth have taken place in many cultural contexts.

The era of medical missions, led by expatriate agencies and personnel, has largely ended. The core of its mission — the Christian ministry of healing — continues to be needed in international health care.

→ Colonialism and Mission

Bibliography: CHRISTIAN MEDICAL COMMISSION, *Healing and Wholeness: The Churches' Role in Health* (Geneva, 1990) • S. M. CRANE, *A Legacy Remembered: A Century of Medical Missions* (Franklin, Tenn., 1998) • A. DRIES, *The Missionary Movement in American Catholic History* (Maryknoll, N.Y., 1998) • C. DURAISINGH, ed., *Health and Healing in Mission* (= *IRM* 83/329 [April 1994] 223-311) • D. M. EWERT, ed., *A New Agenda for Medical Missions* (Brunswick, Ga., 1990) • C. GRUNDMANN, *Gesandt zu heilen. Aufkommen und Entwicklung der ärztlichen Mission im neunzehnten Jahrhundert* (Gütersloh, 1992); idem, "The Role of Medical Missions in the Missionary Enterprise: A Historical and Missiological Survey," *MisSt* 2 (1985) 39-48 • G. JANSEN, "Christian Ministry of Healing on Its Way to the Year 2000: An Archaeology of Medical Missions," *Miss.* 23 (1995) 295-307; idem, "The Tradition of Medical Missions in the Maelstrom of the International Health Arena," *Miss.* 27 (1999) 377-92 • J. C. McGILVRAY, *Quest for Health and Wholeness* (Tübingen, 1981) • J. PIROTTE and H. DERROITTE, eds., *Églises et santé dans le tiers monde. Hier et aujourd'hui = Churches and Health Care in the Third World: Past and Present* (Leiden, 1991) • S. R. THURMAN, "The Medical Mission Strategy of the Maryknoll Sisters," *Miss.* 30 (2002) 361-73 • D. E. VAN REKEN, *Mission and Ministry: Christian Medical Practice in Today's Changing World Cultures* (Wheaton, Ill., 1987) • D. WHITEMAN, ed., "Medicine, Health, and Mission," *Miss.* 21 (1993) 275-341, 379-83 • S. WIESINGER, ed., *Licht für die Welt. Ein Bericht über die weltweite christliche Missionsdiakonie an Lichtlosen* (Stuttgart, 1982) • WORLD COUNCIL OF CHURCHES, *The Healing Church* (Geneva, 1965).

NORMAN E. THOMAS

Meditation

1. Meaning
2. Eastern Religions
3. Aid to Faith
4. Aid to Health

1. Meaning
Meditation involves an inner perception that defies definition and can be understood only as it takes place. Nevertheless, abandoning the attempt to explain it conceptually does not mean that we can say nothing intelligible or helpful about it. According to O. Haendler (1890-1981), all healthy people meditate. When we know astonishment or wonder, when a word or event grips us, when we look at a picture or at something beautiful and it touches us (→ Aesthetics), we have an experience close to meditation. Haendler views meditation as "the living activity of

our most inward mental and spiritual organs, with which we apprehend life's reality and achieve the depth and power and essentiality of our own being" (p. 13). W. Massa comes close to a definition when he describes meditation as "an understanding perception that avoids any directed thinking or willing," adding that in it "the I as the guiding function of the everyday consciousness is reduced to passivity, to quiet attention, all outward perceptions being excluded" (G. Ruhbach, 11).

We more easily grasp what meditation is when we consider that there are two approaches to the perceiving of reality: logical understanding (→ Logic) and → reason looking at things in their totality. The understanding, which is associated with an oriented will, tries to comprehend reality with the help of counting and measuring, experimenting and analyzing; reason, however, whose basic element is meditative knowledge, grasps that which encounters it as a whole (→ Experience 2). It does not first dissect and then put together again but accepts the validity of what is not dissected (V. von Weizsäcker). In contrast to rational comprehension, meditative perception is not at the disposal of the will but takes place spontaneously. We cannot force it any more than we can sleep. We can simply let it come.

Meditation is close to → contemplation. Plotinus (ca. A.D. 205-70; → Platonism) said of contemplation that in it the spirit remains unmoved, sunk in beholding (*Enn.* 5.5.8). The same might be said of meditation. The only difference is in application. Contemplation has in it something of the way of mystical salvation. Meditation covers a wide spectrum in both → religion and art (→ Christian Art). In → mysticism meditation is the transition from ascetic purification (→ Asceticism) to → mystical union.

2. Eastern Religions

The objection often arises that an Indian element entered Christianity with meditation, since meditation resembles Yoga. Against this concern we must insist that meditation and Yoga are not identical and that a tradition of Christian meditation reaches back to the very origins of Christianity. The term "meditation" and related words do not occur in the NT, but the activity itself is present. Meditation was practiced in → monasticism and developed in → mysticism. Experiences of meditation have also influenced → prayer and → hymnody.

At the same time, we cannot deny that the encounter with → Buddhism and → Hinduism helped to revive meditation in the Protestant churches. As regards physical exercises, elements of Yoga and → Zen have sometimes been part of instruction for

Christian meditation; these elements are free from suspicion only when they are detached from their philosophical background (→ Worldview). The difference between Christian meditation and Buddhist meditation is that the former is oriented to an object (the encounter of the perceptible world and the self-revealing God; → Revelation), whereas the latter expressly has no object.

Although a basically rationalistic mood has long prevailed in → Protestantism (→ Rationalism), the practice of meditation retained its vitality in the → Roman Catholic Church. The *Exercises* of → Ignatius of Loyola (1491-1556; → Jesuits; Spirituality) greatly helped to promote it. In the → Orthodox Church also, → piety has always been influenced by the meditative character of its → liturgy.

3. Aid to Faith

Meditation is an aid to → faith because it is an important approach to the understanding of biblical texts. OT and NT statements are framed in such a way that they disclose themselves more readily to total perception than to discursive thinking. "Holy Scripture is itself meditative, and only by meditation is it entirely accessible. . . . This means for us that in Holy Scripture everything we perceive meditatively gains in vitality and opens itself up to us" (Haendler, 54).

Meditation is also an aid to faith insofar as it is an important means of giving depth to → prayer (→ Devotion). We must not think of prayer and meditation as alternatives or of meditation as replacing prayer. It simply prepares the way for it. It is not itself prayer, but all profound prayer takes place in an attitude of meditation (Haendler, 55).

Furthermore, meditation is an aid to living. As an "exercise in authentic being" (K. Tilmann, 23), it works against distraction and confusion (→ Anonymity). By opening up for us the way to the self, it offers us control and freedom in antithesis to compulsion (p. 50).

Meditation is also very important for relations with others. As contact from heart to heart, it completes and heals our human encounters. Seeing people in depth, we can know them afresh and in love, and we can meet them in inner freedom. The more we meditate, the more deeply we experience, the more genuinely we love, and the more we can overcome our own hatred and that of others (Haendler, 34).

4. Aid to Health

By reducing tensions and situations of tension, meditation is an essential means of spiritual hygiene. According to K. Thomas, more than half of those who are sick could be cured by meditation as it spreads its peace and harmony across the autonomic nervous system to every cell in the organism (Ruhbach, 36).

→ New Religions; Spirituality

Bibliography: D. Boleman, *The Varieties of the Meditative Experience* (Irvington, N.J., 1977) • F. Dorff, *Simply Soul Stirring: Writing as a Meditative Practice* (New York, 1998) • O. Haendler, *Meditation als Lebenspraxis* (Göttingen, 1977) • F. C. Happold, *Prayer and Meditation* (Baltimore, 1971) • H. R. Jarrell, *International Meditation Bibliography, 1950-1982* (Metuchen, N.J., 1985) • T. Keating, *The Better Part: Stages of Contemplative Living* (New York, 2000); idem, *Open Mind, Open Heart: The Contemplative Dimension of the Gospel* (New York, 1995) • M. B. Pennington, *Centering Prayer: Renewing an Ancient Christian Prayer Form* (Garden City, N.Y., 1980) • G. Ruhbach, ed., *Glaube, Erfahrung, Meditation* (Munich, 1977) • K. Thomas, *Meditation in Forschung und Erfahrung in weltweiter Beobachtung und praktischer Anleitung* (Stuttgart, 1973) • K. Tilmann, *Die Führung zur Meditation* (Zurich, 1972) • H. F. de Wit, *Contemplative Psychology* (Pittsburgh, 1991); idem, *The Spiritual Path: An Introduction to the Psychology of the Spiritual Traditions* (Pittsburgh, 1999).

Walter Saft

Megilloth

"Megilloth" (Heb. *mĕgillôt,* "rolls, scrolls") is a technical term referring to the five scrolls that were brought together from the 6th century A.D., each being read in the → synagogue during a festival (or fast). From the 12th century the sequence was Song of Songs, for → Passover; Ruth, for the Feast of Weeks (→ Pentecost); Lamentations, for the fast on the ninth of Av, commemorating the destruction of → Jerusalem by the Babylonians and later by the Romans; Ecclesiastes, for the Feast of Booths (Tabernacles); and Esther, for Purim (→ Jewish Practices 2).

The unusual content of three scrolls — Song of Songs, Ecclesiastes, and Esther — provoked objection in some circles to their inclusion in the Hebrew → canon (§1). The erotic features of Song of Songs, the skepticism of Ecclesiastes, and the introduction of a post-Mosaic festival in Esther were bothersome, but the first and last of these books, too popular to be rejected, were allegorized and devotionalized respectively, and a secondary epilogue blunted the force of the skepticism of Ecclesiastes.

Bibliography: H. E. Clem, "Megilloth," *ABD* 4.680 • S. W. Crawford, "Five Scrolls," *EncDSS* 1.295-97 • A. Schwartz and Y. Schwartz, *The Megilloth and Rashi's Commentary, with Linear Translation* (New York, 1983) • B. G. Webb, *Five Festal Garments* (Downers Grove, Ill., 2000).

James L. Crenshaw

Melanchthon, Philipp

Philipp Melanchthon (1497-1560) was the most significant German reformer after Martin → Luther. Melanchthon was born in Bretten, Palatinate, as the son of the armorer George Schwarzerdt. After attending the distinguished Pforzheim Latin School, he matriculated in Heidelberg in 1509 at the early age of 12. (That year also his surname was changed from Schwarzerdt to the Greek equivalent, Melanchthon [black earth].) He received his bachelor of arts in 1511 and from 1512 studied in Tübingen, where he earned his master of arts in 1514. In both cities he made important contacts with later reformers, including Johannes Oecolampadius and Thomas Blarer. Intensive studies in the humanities resulted in publications of Melanchthon's own poetry, of editions of others (e.g., of the Latin poet Terence in 1516), and of a Greek grammar (1518), all of which contributed to his scholarly renown.

At the recommendation of his relative Johannes Reuchlin, Melanchthon, then only 21 years old, accepted a newly established professorship in Greek in 1518 at the University of Wittenberg, where he remained professionally active until his death. In 1519 he attained the status of a *baccalaureus biblicus* and thenceforth lectured on the Bible in the school of → theology. His lectures attest to his openness to Luther's theology and form the foundation for his numerous significant commentaries on books of the Bible. His exegetical work on the Book of Romans gave rise to his *Loci communes theologici* (Common topics of theology, 1521, with many later editions, the last in 1559), which was meant to replace the *Sententiarum* of Peter Lombard. Melanchthon's relationship with Luther was one of intensive collegial friendship; despite occasional crises, that → friendship was sustained by profound mutual respect and formed the essential personal prerequisite for the considerable ecclesiastical changes effected by Reformation theology.

From 1525 Melanchthon was one of the leaders in the Reformational reorganization of → church government in electoral Saxony, and his Visitation

489

Articles (1528) profoundly influenced Reformational church organization. From 1529 he participated as a theological counsel for electoral Saxony in diets, religious dialogues, and the negotiations of the Schmalkaldic League. His ability to articulate the theological concerns of the Reformation without resorting to polemical language enhanced his position in confrontations with opponents of the Lutheran doctrine of the → Eucharist (e.g., at the Concord of Wittenberg [1536]) and with representatives of Roman Catholicism (e.g., at the Conferences of Hagenau, Regensburg, and Worms [1540-41]).

Melanchthon's scholarly work influenced the entire system of schools and universities in nascent Protestantism and firmly established the connection between the → Reformation and the educational culture of → humanism. In his capacity as the author or chief architect of standard Protestant confessional writings (e.g., the → Augsburg Confession [1530], Apology of the Augsburg Confession [1531], and Treatise on the Power and Primacy of the Pope [1537]) and of influential biblical commentaries, as the author of significant doctrinal compendiums of Reformational theology (Loci communes, Examen ordinandorum), and finally as the personal mentor of significant Protestant theologians of the "second generation," Melanchthon exerted greater influence than any other reformer on the emergent formation of the church and on the basic theological orientation of confessional → Lutheranism. In his broad correspondence, he emerges as a theological and religio-political counselor and scholar of genuinely European proportions. At Wittenberg Melanchthon taught in both the humanistic and theological schools, reshaped the educational organization of both schools, and embodied the intimate connection between historical-philological, scientific-mathematical, and theological scholarship.

The last decade of Melanchthon's life was shaped by the inner-Lutheran disputes with the → Gnesio-Lutherans (formed in 1548). Because of certain concessions Melanchthon made in worship rites after the military defeat of the Schmalkaldic League, concessions dealing with what in his opinion were non-essential "middle issues" not affecting confessional identity (i.e., → adiaphora), he became a profoundly disputed figure tainted by the notion of heresy. All the same, this acute crisis did not prevent Melanchthon's life work from exerting an enduring influence on academic theological education of orthodoxy and on the ecclesiastical organization of Lutheranism itself on an international scale.

Bibliography: Primary sources: C. G. BRETSCHNEIDER and H. E. BINDSEIL, eds., Philippi Melanchthonis opera quae supersunt omnia (28 vols.; Frankfurt, 1963; orig. pub., 1834-60) • R. KEEN, trans., A Melanchthon Reader (New York, 1988) • S. KUSUKAWA, ed., Philip Melanchthon: Orations on Philosophy and Education (Cambridge, 1999) • P. MELANCHTHON, Loci communes (1521; 3d ed., 1543) (trans. J. A. O. Preus; St. Louis, 1992) • H. SCHEIBLE and W. THURINGER, eds., Melanchthons Briefwechsel (10 vols.; Stuttgart, 1977-98) • Supplementa Melanchthoniana (5 vols.; Frankfurt, 1968; orig. pub., 1910-29).

Bibliographies: L. C. GREEN, ed., Melanchthon in English: New Translations into English, with a Registry of Previous Translations (St. Louis, 1982) • VD 16 M 2330-4425.

Secondary works: G. FRANK, ed., Der Theologe Melanchthon (Stuttgart, 2000) • K. HARTFELDER, Philipp Melanchthon als Praeceptor Germaniae (Nieuwkoop, 1972; orig. pub., 1889) • J. HAUSTEIN, ed., Philipp Melanchthon. Ein Wegbereiter für die Ökumene (Göttingen, 1997) • S. KUSUKAWA, The Transformation of Natural Philosophy: The Case of Philip Melanchthon (Cambridge, 1995) • J. LOEHR, ed., Dona Melanchthoniana. FS Heinz Scheible (Stuttgart–Bad Cannstatt, 2001) • E. P. MEIJERING, Melanchthon and Patristic Thought: The Doctrines of Christ and Grace, the Trinity, and the Creation (Leiden, 1983) • H. SCHEIBLE, Philipp Melanchthon. Eine Biographie (Munich, 1997); idem, ed., Melanchthon in seinen Schülern (Wiesbaden, 1997) • T. J. WENGERT, Human Freedom, Christian Righteousness: Philip Melanchthon's Exegetical Dispute with Erasmus of Rotterdam (New York, 1998); idem, Law and Gospel: Philip Melanchthon's Debate with John Agricola of Eisleben over "Poenitentia" (Grand Rapids, 1997).

THOMAS KAUFMANN

Melchites

The Orthodox in the Middle East who remained in communion with the Ecumenical Patriarchate of Constantinople following the Council of → Chalcedon (451), who did not follow the → Monophysites, were originally called Melchites (i.e., royalists, from Syr. melk, "king" [cf. Heb. melek, Arab. malik]). It was a term of defamation for their adherence to the Byzantine emperor of → Byzantium.

As a result of the Islamic conquest (→ Islam), the three Melchite patriarchates of → Antioch, → Alexandria, and → Jerusalem were often vacant. In 960-1085 restoration of Byzantine rule brought relief to Antioch and a closer link to Constantinople. The

Orthodox Melchite hierarchy and people suffered greatly from the → Crusades, the Mamlukes of Egypt, and the Mongols from 1250 to 1516. Finally, they were under Ottoman rule from 1516 to 1918. The Churches of Alexandria and Jerusalem then had Greek hierarchs. Together with the Antioch native → patriarchs, they were always closely tied to the ecumenical patriarch of Constantinople, their "first among equals" (primus inter pares).

Some Antiochian hierarchs and people tried not to break total and official fellowship with the → Roman Catholic Church. Accordingly, and under the efforts of Roman Catholic missions, they formed in 1724 the so-called → Uniate Greek Catholic Church, which since then has existed alongside the Greek Orthodox churches. The Ottoman Turkish authorities did not recognize this development, and only in 1838 did Patriarch Maximos Mazlum gain recognition for the Uniate Greek Catholic Church. Since then, there have been three Greek Orthodox churches (of Antioch, Alexandria, and Jerusalem), each with its patriarch, and a Greek Catholic Church, with its own patriarch of Antioch. The seat of the two patriarchs of Antioch is Damascus. The Greek Catholic patriarch of Antioch is also responsible for the Greek Catholics of the Alexandrian and Jerusalemite territories. It is to this latter Greek Catholic Church of Antioch that the term "Melchite" is now most often applied. In November 2000 its head became Patriarch Gregory III (Laham), who replaced the ailing Maximos V Hakim.

Whether Melchite Orthodox, as they were called, or the Melchite Catholics united to Rome, as they are now called, members can be found today not only in the Near East but also overseas. Their liturgy has been Byzantine since the → Middle Ages. The liturgical languages (→ Liturgy) are Greek and Arabic, along with the national languages of their parishes abroad.

→ Ecumenical Patriarchate; Orthodox Church; Orthodoxy 3

Bibliography: C. Charon, *History of the Melkite Patriarchates (Alexandria, Antioch, Jerusalem), from the Sixth Century Monophysite Schism until the Present (1910)* (3 vols.; ed. N. Samra; Fairfax, Va., 1998) • C. Descy, *The Melkite Church* (Newton, Mass., 1993) • A. Hage, "Melchite Rite," *NCE* 9.627-30 • D. Thomas, ed., *Anti-Christian Polemic in Early Islam: Abū ʿĪsā al-Warrāq's "Against the Trinity"* (Cambridge, 1992).

ADEL THEODOR KHOURY

Men → Sexuality 5

Mendicant Friars → Dominicans; Franciscans

Menno Simons

1. From Priest to Anabaptist Leader
2. Writings
3. Conflict and Assessment

Menno Simons (1496-1561) was an → Anabaptist reformer who gave leadership to the nonviolent wing of the Anabaptist movement in the Low Countries. Adherents of → Mennonite bodies throughout the world recognize him as one of their primary founders.

1. From Priest to Anabaptist Leader

Only a few details are known concerning Menno Simons's background. He was born in the village of Witmarsum in the Dutch province of Friesland. His parents were farmers, his father, Simon, coming from the neighboring village of Pingjum. Menno may have received some private education, attending one of the cloister schools in Bolsward near Witmarsum, or he may have enrolled in a Latin town school. A few years of Latin, → rhetoric, → logic, and → church music would have been sufficient to attain the necessary requirements for the consecrated office. Having completed his theological examinations, he was → ordained in Utrecht in 1524 and became vicar in Pingjum, having been nominated by the parishioners themselves, a privilege of the Frisian Roman Catholics.

Even in his first year as vicar, perhaps under the influence of the Sacramentarian ideas of early Dutch reformers, Menno had doubts concerning the church's teaching on transubstantiation. His misgivings were not alleviated when in 1526 he began to read the NT for the first time and could not find the doctrine clearly supported in Scripture. In 1531 he received news that a certain Sikke Freeriks was executed in Leeuwarden for accepting rebaptism, which led him to question the church's practice of infant → baptism. His continuing study of the → church fathers, Protestant → reformers such as Martin → Luther, Martin → Bucer, and Heinrich Bullinger, and further biblical studies did not ease Menno's reservations concerning the church's practice of baptizing infants.

In 1532 Menno Simons accepted a new appointment as parish → priest in his home village of Witmarsum and was likely in contact with Anabaptists for the first time the following year. Anabaptism had emerged in Switzerland and southern Germany in 1525, in the context of Zwinglian reform and German peasant uprisings. Anabaptist ideas found their way to the Low Countries through the erstwhile radical Lutheran reformer Melchior Hoffman. In 1529 Hoffman had encountered Anabaptism in Strasbourg and in 1530 had brought his brand of Anabaptist reform to the northern German city of Emden. While Hoffman returned to Strasbourg in 1533 and soon after was imprisoned for his Anabaptist activities, his ideas found acceptance in Amsterdam, Leeuwarden, Münster, and surrounding environs.

Menno Simons was sympathetic to the Anabaptist teachings that Melchior Hoffman brought to the Low Countries, although he opposed the positions of some Hoffman followers whose excessive → apocalyptic views included the belief that the city of Münster was the new Jerusalem and that the kingdom of Christ should be ushered in by force. In February 1534 radical Anabaptists took control of Münster, defying the authority of both the → state and the established church. In April 1535 several hundred Anabaptists also captured the Oldeklooster monastery near Bolsward, Friesland. After a brief siege, the Anabaptists were overtaken; most were killed or captured. Among those slain was a Pieter Simons, possibly a brother to Menno. This incident had a profound affect on Menno Simons, who was appalled both by the violent radicalism of the Anabaptists and by the strong show of force exerted by the authorities. He expressed his opposition to the Münsterite use of the sword by composing a tract against the Münsterite leadership entitled "The Blasphemy of Jan van Leyden." Since Münster was defeated in June 1535, however, Menno did not publish the tract, and it appeared only in 1627.

The following months were a time of deep questioning and indecision. After much conflict of conscience Menno left the priesthood at the end of January 1536 and joined the Anabaptist cause. A year later in Groningen he was ordained → elder by the Anabaptist leader Obbe Philips. During this time he also married Geertruyd, a Beguine nun.

After the Münster defeat in 1535, the Anabaptist movement fell into disarray and was reduced to a number of smaller factions. Attempts in 1536 to unite the various groups at Bocholt, Westphalia, failed, although the spiritually minded David Joris emerged as the primary leader. His increasing spiritualization of the gospel, however, led him to drop the outward Anabaptist practices of → baptism and the Lord's Supper. By 1544 he left the Netherlands

for Basel, and Menno Simons emerged in the Low Countries as leader of the Anabaptist cause.

As elder of Anabaptist congregations, Menno Simons spent much of his life as a hunted individual. A 1545 decree mentions his followers as *Mennisten* (hence Mennonites), although in the Netherlands, Anabaptist groups decades later would prefer to call themselves *doopsgezinden* (baptism-minded). He lived in various regions — East Friesland (1537-44), the Lower Rhine region close to Cologne and Bonn (1544-46), and in cities along the Baltic coast (1546-54). His final years were spent at Wüstenfelde near Oldesloe in Schleswig-Holstein (1554-61). Although some 1,000 adherents of Anabaptism paid the ultimate price of martyrdom during his time as Anabaptist leader, the former priest of Witmarsum died naturally under the protection of the nobleman Bartholomaeus von Ahlefeld.

2. Writings

Menno Simons was not a schooled theologian, and his writings cannot be compared to the systematic writings of some of the other 16th-century reformers. Some of his theology was developed in the context of dialogue with Protestant theologians (e.g., Gellius Faber, John Laski, Martin Micron). Most of his writings, though, came from the standpoint of a fugitive and church leader with pastoral concerns for scattered congregations located in regions along the Lower Rhine, the Netherlands, the Baltic coast, and eastward to the Prussian city of Danzig (Gdańsk).

Menno Simons's most significant work was the *Fundamentboek* (Foundation of Christian doctrine), published in 1539, revised in 1558, and reprinted many times thereafter. The *Fundamentboek* aims at a reformation of faith and church practice based on Scripture. Its themes reflect the interests that the reformer had throughout his career: repentance; the new birth; → regeneration; a blameless life among all Christians, including the clergy; rejection of the "real presence" of Christ in the → Eucharist in favor of the celebration of the supper as a memorial meal; renunciation of infant baptism in favor of believers', or adult, baptism; and concerns that the state govern justly.

3. Conflict and Assessment

Menno Simons has sometimes been given credit for bringing about unity to the Anabaptist movement in the Low Countries, but his own theological views and ecclesiological assumptions frequently brought him into conflict with his coreligionists. He clashed, for instance, with David Joris and his followers, whose excessive spiritualization of the gospel allowed for compromises. He came into conflict with other Anabaptists over issues related to → Christology and the doctrine of the → Trinity. Menno's own Christology, a departure from Chalcedonian Christology, was shaped by the views of Melchior Hoffman, who maintained that Christ's flesh was heavenly in origin and did not originate from Mary. Adam Pastor of Westphalia challenged Menno's perspectives and argued for an anti-Trinitarian perspective. When Pastor could not be dissuaded, he was banned by Menno's colleague Dirk Philips.

Perhaps the most serious conflict that Menno Simons encountered came in his final years, when the Anabaptists in the Low Countries could not agree on practices of → church discipline. Along with his colleagues Leenaert Bouwens and Dirk Philips, Menno emphasized that the true church was a voluntary gathering of believers "without spot or wrinkle" who lived in faithful obedience to the teachings and example of Christ. Those who did not live up to the standards of the community were to be disciplined; unrepentant sinners were to be → excommunicated, which often implied a complete severing of ties between the community and the sinner. Some Anabaptist groups, such as the Waterlanders and the High Germans, were critical of Menno's strict application of church discipline, although his own colleagues Dirk Philips and Leenaert Bouwens felt that his position was too lax.

While the ability of Menno Simons to lead the Anabaptist community through such internal disagreements has been variously assessed, scholars generally recognize him as one who gave significant leadership to the Anabaptist movement in the Low Countries and, through his writings, influenced the development of Anabaptism and Mennonitism throughout the centuries.

Bibliography: *Primary sources: Complete Writings* (trans. L. Verduin; ed. J. C. Wenger; Scottdale, Pa., 1956; repr., 1992) • *Opera omnia theologica* (Amsterdam, 1681).

Secondary works: C. BORNHÄUSER, *Leben und Lehre Menno Simons. Ein Kampf um das Fundament des Glaubens (etwa 1496-1561)* (Neukirchen, 1973) • G. R. BRUNK, ed., *Menno Simons: A Reappraisal* (Harrisonburg, Va., 1992) • C. J. DYCK and W. KLAASSEN, eds., *MennQR* 62 (July 1988) papers from the international colloquium "Spiritual Renewal and Social Change" • T. GEORGE, *Theology of the Reformers* (Nashville, 1988) • E. GRISLIS, "The Doctrine of the Incarnation according to Menno Simons," *JMS* 8 (1990) 16-33 • I. B. HORST, *A Bibliography of Menno Simons* (Nieuwkoop, 1962); idem, *The Dutch Dissenters: A Critical Companion to Their History and Ideas* (Leiden, 1986) • W. E. KEENEY, *Dutch Anabaptist Thought and Practice, 1539-1564* (Nieuwkoop, 1968) • W. KLASSEN, "Menno Simons Research, 1937-1986," *MennQR* 60 (1986) 483-96 • C. KRAHN, *Menno Simons, 1496-1561. Ein Beitrag zur Geschichte und Theologie der Taufgesinnten* (Newton, Kans., 1982; orig. pub., 1936) • P. VISSER and M. SPRUNGER, *Menno Simons: Places, Portraits, and Progeny* (Altona, Man., 1996) • S. VOOLSTRA, *Menno Simons: His Image and Message* (North Newton, Kans., 1997).

KARL KOOP

Mennonites

1. History
   1.1. Genesis
   1.2. Development
   1.3. Immigration
   1.4. Organization
   1.5. Current Trends
2. Theology and Ethics
   2.1. Pastoral Writing
   2.2. Growth of Theology

1. History

The Dutch and German term "Mennists," used in derision to designate the followers of the Dutch Anabaptist leader → Menno Simons (1496-1561), was translated into English as "Mennonites," which is used in most countries today as their name. Similarly, the term → "Anabaptist" was originally one of derision. In the 6th-century Justinian Code "Anabaptist" described dissident religious movements that "rebaptized" people who had received infant → baptism. Justinian's ancient laws against them were invoked against the new dissidents of the 16th century.

1.1. *Genesis*

The origin of Anabaptism predates Menno's ministry, for visions for radical reform were circulating widely in central Europe in the early 16th century. Protests from peasant circles joined with those of intellectuals in seeking a restoration of the church that would regain an inner affinity with the teachings of → Jesus and the practice of the apostolic church (→ Early Church).

This impulse first crystallized as a distinct and organized movement in Zurich in 1525. There the more radical followers of Ulrich → Zwingli (1484-1531) protested his willingness to accept the city council as the arbiter of reform. The definitive distinctive of the radicals was their ecclesiology, for they believed that the → church is to be composed only of those who profess personal faith in Christ. Believers' baptism is the door into the church, the Lord's Supper (→ Eucharist) the ongoing means by which the community is re-created, and → church discipline (culminating in the ban) the means of keeping it pure. Jesus' teaching, whose heart is the → Sermon on the Mount and whose apex is love of one's enemy, constitutes the → norm for → discipleship. God rules and protects the church directly through the Bible and the → Holy Spirit. The church does not rely on the state to order its outward life or to compel people's assent to the Christian creed by means of infant baptism or a military crusade. Since only those are Christians who have come to an existential faith and become part of a → congregation, all others are to be evangelized.

Recent scholarly debate has emphasized the polygenesis and heterogeneity of Anabaptism. Hans-Jürgen Goertz offers a minimalist statement of its core: believers' baptism and anticlericalism. Arnold Snyder contends that there were many variations in theology and practice, yet a common theological and ethical core to Anabaptism wherever it emerged — across the Netherlands, in southern and northern Germany, in pockets of Moravia, Tirol, and beyond.

1.2. Development

1.2.1. There is general agreement that no single leader or geographic setting determined the development of Anabaptism. In each region leaders with different religious backgrounds and reform agendas emerged. Thus their development of Anabaptist impulses varied.

Conrad Grebel (ca. 1498-1526), in Zurich, began as a disciple of Zwingli; his distinctive concern was the freedom of the church from the state. Hans Denck (ca. 1495-1527), in southern Germany, was a mystic; he championed the inward illumination of the Spirit. Balthasar Hubmaier (1485-1528), a South German who received a doctorate in theology under Johannes Eck from the University of Ingolstadt in 1512, tried to create an Anabaptist mass church and made the case for defensive warfare. Pilgram Marpeck (ca. 1495-1556) was a Tyrolian engineer by profession and a self-taught, eclectic theologian by → vocation. He articulated a *via media* for Anabaptism between legalism and → spiritualism. One of the unique fruits of this middle way was a sacramental theology set within a believers' church, yet rooted in the larger Christian tradition.

Menno himself, a Frieslander, began as a → priest. He was a tenacious apologist for the move-

ment and a fearless shepherd of the scattered sheep. His compatriot Dirk Philips (1504-68), steeped in pre-Reformation sacramentarianism, championed a fusion of → dogma, → hierarchy, and spiritualism. Then there was Peter Riedemann (or Rideman, 1506-66), for whom → community of goods was indispensable to an inner affinity with the NT. Finally, there were countless preachers, women and men, who believed themselves called by the Holy Spirit to preach the hard way of Christ and, often, to denounce those who saw the matter differently from themselves (A. Snyder and L. Hecht).

1.2.2. Fierce → persecution followed the Anabaptist refusal to conform to the → state churches in the regions they lived in. In Flanders, for example, they were wiped out. In Switzerland they survived, but only above the tree line. In rural enclaves in the Alsace, southern Germany, Prussia, and eventually southern Russia, they found refuge on the condition that they not missionize or inspire dissent in their neighbors. A movement that had largely begun in cities thus increasingly retreated to remote rural regions across central Europe.

Over time, the Mennonite witness changed. It lost its eschatological passion and became one of orderly and diligent community, appealing for exemption to military service for itself but not daring to do so for others. After the Netherlands' wars of liberation from Spain (1568-1648), Mennonites gradually shared in the → tolerance that characterized Dutch society. They flourished spiritually, producing a vast devotional literature, and economically, joining the movement to the cities and to entrepreneurship (A. Hamilton, S. Voolstra, and P. Visser).

Hutterianism was the communal expression of Anabaptism, in which all things were held in common. Hutterites believed that other Anabaptists fell short of apostolic Christianity at the point of their unwillingness to make economic community one of the marks of the faithful church. It emerged in 1529 but was solidified as a movement in 1533 under the leadership of Jakob Hutter in Moravia. The → Hutterites were subject to separate waves of persecution over two and a half centuries, which decimated their spirit and numbers. At one point they were reduced to a mere 19 intrepid souls in a corner of Hungary (*Chronicle of the Hutterian Brethren*).

1.2.3. As church life became more settled, congregations developed an ordered existence. In the first generation there had been ministers but also → prophets, both men and women, whose call by God was direct. By the second generation it was almost universal to have a threefold ministry of elder (the term used for → bishop), minister, and → deacon.

They were chosen (by lot or vote) by the congregations or districts they served. Most of them were farmers by profession and remained so. In the Netherlands medical doctors became common candidates for ministry because they, like farmers, were masters of their own schedule.

→ Worship in early Anabaptism took the form of a simple service, commonly modeled on 1 Corinthians 12–14. Not only the preachers but any worshiper inspired by the Spirit was given freedom to speak. By the third generation this practice was reserved to the ordained (→ Ordination; Ministry, Ministerial Offices). Singing was the enduring form of congregational participation in worship. → Preaching was the heart of worship, but it was not, for the most part, set over against the Lord's Supper. Although there had been early attempts to restore frequent communion, the Mennonites fell back into the medieval practice of a once- or twice-yearly celebration, with a preparatory service the week before and → foot washing right before or after the breaking of bread.

Baptism was practiced according to local custom and took the forms of pouring, sprinkling, or immersion. As congregations became insular and the church as a whole stagnated, it became harder and harder to base baptism on an inner → conversion (§1), and it often became merely an act of religious and social conformity. The church, which found itself unable to carry out missionary work among families that were not already Mennonites, increasingly received children raised in the church on the basis of their assent to Mennonite doctrine rather than their personal act of trust in Christ as Savior and Lord. In some settings inheriting land depended on being a church member, and so there was pressure to baptize people whether or not a living faith was evident. This state of affairs was seen as tragic by many faithful Mennonites. Such feelings have led to renewal movements throughout Mennonite history, like the Mennonite Brethren in Russia, who emerged in 1860 with the goal of building up the church on the basis of a transformative encounter with Christ.

1.2.4. Because of external persecution and internal splits, individuals and groups were constantly being dislocated. As communities found a more settled existence, they tried to forge harmony out of a multitude of theological backgrounds and interpretations of the moral life. One way of building unity was to go through the exercise of writing a → confession of faith. One of the earliest is the Concept of Cologne from 1591, which expresses the basics of Trinitarian theology and a believers' church. Typi-

cally, however, there are also articles on → ethics. For example, merchants are urged to live modestly and to deal fairly with their customers. One senses here and in many of the confessions that followed across the centuries a pastoral concern for an unashamed profession of faith and → obedience, but also some freedom for local interpretation. The Dordrecht Confession of 1632 and the High German Confession of 1660 are the mother confessions of the various families of Mennonites (H. Loewen).

1.2.5. As these congregations sought to be a church "without a spot or wrinkle" (Eph. 5:27), their striving for holiness of life frequently led to bitter disputes and separations. Indeed, factionalism has been called the Mennonite sickness.

The most famous of these separations was led by Jacob Amman (ca. 1644-ca. 1730), an elder in the Alsace and father of the Amish. He denounced what he saw as compromises the congregations across the Swiss border had made, especially in fraternizing with members of the state church. Ten years of mutual accusations led to a breach that has never been healed. The Amish thus became the first of several "Old Order" movements among Mennonites that sought to restore a lost simplicity of life. Starting in the late 19th century, this impulse included a wariness of modern → technology.

1.3. Immigration

There were two major waves of immigration to flee conscription and other restrictions in civil society, such as laws against further land acquisition for Nonconformists. From the late 17th to the early 19th century, Swiss, Alsatian, and South German Mennonites migrated to North America. Their first home was in William Penn's Quaker colony (now Pennsylvania), where they flourished for the first time. From there they spread to other parts of the United States and Canada.

For about 50 years, beginning with the end of the 18th century, Mennonites from Prussia settled in the newly conquered Russian territory of the Ukraine. The condition for their immigration was that they form farming villages isolated from their neighbors. They developed a commonwealth, a Christian society that regulated every aspect of life. Like Hubmaier's short-lived experiment, it was increasingly based on the anomaly of a mass believers' church. In the 1870s members who were convinced that their way of life, including → conscientious objection, was threatened migrated to North America. Another wave of immigrants did so after the revolution of 1917, after 1945, and again after 1990. Now the Mennonite Church in Russia is a struggling remnant.

The most flourishing groups of Mennonites with the largest numbers and most vigorous community life emerged from these migrations, first to North America, and later also to Central and South America. Living mostly in open societies, these Mennonites have thrived economically, regained their missionary impulse, built schools, written → theology, and engaged their host culture. Beginning with the initiative of the Dutch in 1850, the Russians in 1870, and the North Americans in 1890, these communities planted churches in Asia and Africa. With → evangelism came → education and → social services. Every Mennonite conference (i.e., geographic grouping) has an active mission board. Representatives of these conferences joined together to form the Mennonite Central Committee in 1920, bringing about partnerships with local agencies in relief, → development, and peacemaking in 60 countries.

1.4. *Organization*

In 1925 the first Mennonite World Conference was held, primarily to link European and North American believers, but it also received reports of emerging churches abroad. Since then the World Conference, based in Strasbourg, has held a world assembly every six years and sponsors joint missionary and theological work. Of the 1.2 million baptized Mennonites around the globe in 2001, over 600,000 live outside the North Atlantic world. The largest populations are in Congo (Zaire), Ethiopia, Indonesia, and India. Some of these conferences have a vision for → mission and an intensity of → faith that have led them to assume more and more of the international leadership role formerly held by North American groups.

Many Third World Mennonite conferences have a charismatic, if not fully Pentecostal, piety and church order. Some of them are attracted to the cluster of historic Mennonite traits, often demonstrating more of an affinity for first-generation Anabaptists than for contemporary Mennonites in the West. Particularly those in settings of civil conflict have made a renewed engagement with → pacifism, which some fundamentalistically formed North American Mennonites had left behind when they went abroad as → missionaries.

1.5. *Current Trends*

In North and Latin America the Old Order movements preserve a realm of separatistic enclaves. Some of them nourish a robust sense of community and a grounded faith in a fractured society. They are growing more rapidly than their mainstream kin, mostly through their large families. Others are in the grip of legalism to the point of disintegration. The mainstream continues to assimilate into Canadian and United States society out of both economic opportunity and social responsibility.

Historically, the peace teaching had a definitive role in shaping congregations; it was widely considered the litmus test of faithfulness in two respects. First, it made them wary of nationalism and → warfare. Second, it made it clear that peacemaking was as essential to the mission of the church as was evangelism — both were invitations to accept God's offer of → reconciliation.

At present a host of liturgical, theological, and political influences is reshaping congregations, church institutions, and the loyalties that underlie them. Forms of worship vary from the isolated traditionalism of the Old Order communities to a moderately liturgical style, to a full-fledged → church-growth approach.

Out of a desire to reformulate their convictions in a rapidly changing church and society, the two largest mainstream groups in North America — Mennonite Church U.S.A. and Mennonite Brethren Church — each commissioned a new confession of faith (published in 1995 and 1999, respectively). The former is more indebted to mainline churches and the latter to evangelical ones, but both confessions reflect an integration of wider Christian theological insight with an affirmation of Anabaptist ecclesiology and the ethic that flows from it. This struggle to learn from the wisdom of the larger church yet hold critically to an Anabaptist vision of the gospel is reflected in the work of two of the most significant systematic writers: James Reimer, who advocates a greater identification with historic orthodoxy, and Denny Weaver, who warns against it.

2. Theology and Ethics

The Mennonite marriage of theology and ethics as two realms of Christian expression is exemplified in a strand of Balthasar Hubmaier's eucharistic theology. He says that in the Holy Supper, in a single unbroken motion, I remember in gratitude Christ's laying down his life for me and pledge to lay down mine for my neighbor. Anabaptism was an existential form of Christianity whose heart was individual and collective → sanctification, a life conformed to that of Jesus. With other Protestants, Anabaptists shared the conviction that → salvation comes by → grace alone through faith; with Roman Catholics and John → Calvin (*Inst.* 3.16.1), they believed that → justification and sanctification are inseparable and that true faith always issues in → love.

The goal to "gain Christ," "be found in him," and know "the sharing of his sufferings" (Phil. 3:8-10) was the heartbeat of the movement (*Spiritual Life in*

Anabaptism; → Pietism). Theology was seen as a sometimes useful and often perverse handmaiden in that undertaking. The early Anabaptists included apocalypticists, for whom larger theological reflection was peripheral. Also, there were → perfectionists, so engrossed in regulating every aspect of behavior that their theology was mostly ethics. Most Anabaptists, however, grounded their doctrine and discipleship in the authority of the Bible from a Trinitarian perspective. Who interpreted this canon? Three impulses vied with one another: the authoritative teacher (as with Philips), the Spirit-indwelt believer (as with Denck), and the congregation (and larger church) collectively as a hermeneutical community, in which sisters and brothers gather in the power of the Spirit to lay out the Scriptures together (as with Grebel, Hubmaier, Marpeck, and Sattler).

Anabaptism as a whole was anticlerical. It aspired to Spirit-led leadership, holding that the gifts of the Spirit are variously distributed. At the same time, in the heat of battle a new authoritarianism overtook some communities with surprising speed.

2.1. *Pastoral Writing*

Most Anabaptist leaders wrote for their communities out of situations of persecution and controversy. Michael Sattler (1490?-1527), the author of the Schleitheim Confession of 1527, the first confession of faith, wrote it and his other writings largely as pastoral instruction for a scattered flock. Out of markedly different intellectual backdrops, mystic Hans Denck and Hutterite disciplinarian Peter Riedemann did the same. Menno Simons and his colleague Dirk Philips were pastoral writers, spelling out Anabaptist beliefs and practices while warning against the interpretations of magisterial theologians, to say nothing of other Anabaptists!

Pilgram Marpeck, an eclectic thinker and irenic spirit, might best be termed a pastoral theologian. In his writings he usually began with a point of controversy but dwelled on it long enough to provide a fuller theological frame of reference. For example, Marpeck concluded that the spiritualistic impulse (the turning inward in a church that had for centuries been preoccupied with the outward) needed to be balanced by a positive teaching of the → incarnation. Without it, → individualism would undermine the church as the body of Christ and the Bible as its authority. Dealing with the life of the congregation, he developed a theology of sacraments to counter the spiritualists' suspicion of physical reality (J. Rempel).

As prophetic Anabaptism turned into pastoral Mennonitism in the final quarter of the 16th century, the era of great figures came to an end. Yet pastoral writing remained the style of writing native to Mennonite consciousness. The 17th century was the age of confessions of faith, martyr tales, prayer books, and → catechisms. The 19th century was the age of minister's manuals, preserving and altering the implicit theology preserved in the church's ritual life. It is noteworthy that much of this theological reflection was collective — either directly, as in the case of confessions of faith, or indirectly, in the form of martyr stories, which were taken up from one volume to the other within a new framework of moral exhortation, while old prayers were adapted and added to new volumes, generally without specifying the individual author.

2.2. *Growth of Theology*

In the 18th century there were great Mennonite preachers, like Jacob Denner (1659-1746). Books of their sermons were published for use in personal devotion (→ Devotional Literature) and as instruction for aspiring preachers. Not until the 20th century, however, did systematic theological reflection emerge as a discipline. At first it was carried out by historians who sought to establish doctrinal and moral norms from first-generation Anabaptism. The most famous of these writers is the American Harold S. Bender (1897-1962). The next generation, led by the German Hans-Jürgen Goertz (b. 1937), insisted on the necessity of unimpeded historical inquiry as a descriptive science.

The preeminent transitional figure in the shift from history to theology as the canonical discipline among Mennonites is John Howard Yoder (1927-97), the most prolific and formative Mennonite thinker of our time. He placed core Anabaptist beliefs under biblical and historical scrutiny, took what withstood the test, and addressed it to burning intellectual and social issues in the North Atlantic and the developing world *(Politics of Jesus).* More than most Mennonite thinkers in North America, Yoder also engaged the ecumenical movement in dialogue about the foundational assumptions of Christian orthodoxy and unity *(Royal Priesthood).*

The favored medium of theological reflection among Mennonites remains the pastoral rather than the systematic. The work of many pastoral writers speaks to and for the various Mennonite groups they represent. Biblical studies remains the core Mennonite discipline on both the popular and the scholarly level. Practical concerns, such as evangelism and peacemaking, dominate. Sometimes these topics become rival ways of focusing mission, pulling the church toward either an uncritical evangelicalism or an uncritical → pluralism. The fusion of evangelical impulse and peace vision characterizes much Mennonite writing from Third World countries that reaches the West in English translation.

The most extensive theological undertaking among Mennonites at the turn of the 21st century is the five-volume Global Mennonite History Project, edited by John A. Lapp. A volume interpreting the life and work of Mennonites on each continent (except Australia) is being written by a scholar from that continent and critiqued by an international team. This project is an immense investment in identity by a → denomination seeking a faithful future in a pluralistic world.

→ Ecumenism, Ecumenical Movement; Peace Churches; Protestantism

Bibliography: Primary sources: The Chronicle of the Hutterian Brethren (vol. 1; trans. Hutterian Brethren; Rifton, N.Y., 1987) • B. Hubmaier, *Balthasar Hubmaier, Theologian of Anabaptism* (trans. H. W. Pipkin and J. H. Yoder; Scottdale, Pa., 1989) • P. Marpeck, *Writings* (trans. W. Klassen and W. Klaassen; Scottdale, Pa., 1978) • Menno Simons, *Complete Writings* (trans. L. Verduin; ed. J. C. Wenger; Scottdale, Pa., 1956) • D. Philips, *Writings* (trans. C. Dyck, W. Keeney, and A. Beachy; Scottdale, Pa., 1992) • P. Riedermann, *Peter Riedemann's Hutterite Confession of Faith* (trans. J. Friesen; Scottdale, Pa., 1999) • *Spiritual Life in Anabaptism* (trans. C. Dyck; Scottdale, Pa., 1995).

Secondary works: H. Bender et al., eds., *MennEnc* (vols. 1-4, Hillsboro, Kans, 1969; vol. 5, Scottdale, Pa., 1995) • H.-J. Goertz, *The Anabaptists* (London, 1996; orig. pub., 1980) • A. Hamilton, S. Voolstra, and P. Visser, eds., *From Martyr to Muppie* (Amsterdam, 1994) • H. Loewen, *One Lord, One Church, One Hope, and One God* (Elkhart, Ind., 1985) • J. Reimer, *Mennonites and Classical Theology* (Kitchener, Ont., 2001) • J. D. Rempel, *The Lord's Supper in Anabaptism* (Scottdale, Pa., 1993) • A. Snyder, *Anabaptist History and Theology* (Kitchener, Ont., 1995) • A. Snyder and L. Hecht, *Profiles of Anabaptist Women* (Waterloo, Ont., 1996) • D. Weaver, *Anabaptist Theology in Face of Postmodernity* (Telford, Pa., 2000) • J. Yoder, *The Politics of Jesus* (Grand Rapids, 1992); idem, *The Royal Priesthood* (Scottdale, Pa., 1998).

John D. Rempel

Messiah → Christological Titles 3.1

Messianism

1. Religious Aspects
2. Messianic Movements
3. Rituals

1. Religious Aspects

The term "Messiah" derives from the biblical title *māšîaḥ*, "the anointed." → Anointing confers legitimacy upon a person as king or → high priest.

The Jewish view rested on the divine → promise of an eternal kingship to the descendants of → David (2 Sam. 7:12-16; → Monarchy in Israel). When → Israel came under foreign rule in the sixth century B.C., this promise lay behind the hope that Zerubbabel of the house of David might be the king of the age of salvation (see Hag. 2:20-23; Zech. 3:8; 6:12-13). The promise was handed down up to the rise of Christianity (e.g., *Pss. Sol.* 17; → Qumran).

The early Christians took up the promise (Rom. 1:3-4), but it soon became marginal (*Barn.* 12.10-11). Throughout Christian history individuals have claimed to be the Messiah and have promised redemption from → evil in the present world (→ Soteriology).

For → Islam as well as Judaism, "Messiah" was a reinterpreted title of lordship denoting not merely the rights of the ruler but the claims of his potential subjects to liberation. The Arabic *Mahdī* (lit. "one rightly guided") refers to the divinely directed ruler who fills the world with righteousness and to whom his subjects owe unconditional → obedience.

We also find messianism in → Buddhism and → tribal religions. Expectation of a world without → suffering or injustice goes hand in hand with hope of liberation from foreign rule.

2. Messianic Movements

If devotees of → apocalyptic look for an otherworldly order, messianists have in view a charismatic person (→ Charisma) who will set up an order in this world. The person may be either present or absent and may or may not be represented by a → prophet or envoy. When people are convinced that the Messiah is present or is coming, they go into action, often attacking the centers of → power.

W. E. Mühlmann saw in messianic movements a step back to unreflecting emotionalism, which slowly yields to reflection and stabilization. A messianic movement derives its strength from the personal closeness of the adherents to the savior. It thus remains small. The emotional temperature rises in messianism. The lower down the social ladder we go, the more radical the forms that the drive for salvation assumes when it begins to take hold (M. → Weber). The representative of the Messiah may also become the Messiah, as in Babism (→ Baha'i).

Messianic movements may result in a new dynasty. They have thus been called unstable points of transition on the way from segmentary to class societies (M. I. Pereira de Queiroz). The basic problem of all messianic movements is that "the messianic fact is faced less with a dilemma (to succeed *or* to fail) than with a destiny (to succeed *and* to fail)" (H. Desroche, 39).

3. Rituals

Messianic hopes find actualization in movements, but they also find expression in rituals (→ Rite) that embody this expectation. Jewish recollection of the deliverance from Egypt lived on in the → Passover as the promise of repetition in the end time. → Samaritans expected the Taheb on Passover night. We find something of the same in Shiite Islam (→ Shia, Shiites), in which the Mahdi is expected on the day of the defeat of Ḥusayn ibn ʿAlī at Karbala in 680, a day celebrated in a rite of rebellion.

→ Charismatic Movement; Christology; Christological Titles; Future; Millenarianism; New Religions; Revelation; Utopia; Youth Religions

Bibliography: M. Ayoub, *Redemptive Suffering in Islām: A Study of the Devotional Aspects of ʿĀshūrāʾ in Twelver Shiism* (The Hague, 1979) • W. Beuken, S. Freyne, and A. Weiler, eds., *Messianism through History* (London, 1993) • F. Bowie, with C. Deacy, eds., *The Coming Deliverer: Millennial Themes in World Religions* (Cardiff, 1997) • J. H. Charlesworth, H. Lichtenberger, and G. S. Oegema, eds., *Qumran Messianism: Studies on the Messianic Expectations in the Dead Sea Scrolls* (Tübingen, 1998) • H. Desroche, *Sociologie de l'espérance* (Paris, 1973; ET *The Sociology of Hope* [London, 1979]) • F. Dexinger, *Der Taheb. Ein "messianischer" Heilsbringer der Samaritaner* (Salzburg, 1986) • W. E. Mühlmann, *Chiliasmus und Nativismus. Studien zur Psychologie, Soziologie und historische Kasuistik der Umsturzbewegungen* (Berlin, 1961) • J. Neusner, W. S. Green, and E. S. Frerichs, eds., *Judaisms and Their Messiahs at the Turn of the Christian Era* (Cambridge, 1987) • M. I. Pereira de Queiroz, *Réforme et révolution dans les sociétés traditionelles* (Paris, 1968) • K. Pomykala, *The Davidic Dynasty Tradition in Early Judaism: Its History and Significance for Messianism* (Atlanta, 1995) • H. G. Reventlow, ed., *Eschatology in the Bible and in Jewish and Christian Tradition* (Sheffield, 1997) • A. A. Sachedina, *Islamic Messianism: The Idea of the Mahdi in Twelver Shi'ism* (Albany, N.Y., 1981) • P. Smith, *The Babi and Baha'i Religions: From Messianic Shi'ism to a World Religion* (Cambridge, 1987) • A. Sponberg and H. Hardacre, eds., *Maitreya, the Future Buddha* (Cambridge, 1988) • V. Turner, *The Ritual Process: Structure and Anti-structure* (Ithaca, N.Y., 1969) • M. Weber, *Economy and Society: An Outline of Interpretive Sociology* (2 vols.; Berkeley, Calif., 1978; orig. pub., 1922) • B. R. Wilson, *Magic and the Millennium: A Sociological Study of Religious Movements of Protest among Tribal and Third-World Peoples* (London, 1973).

Hans G. Kippenberg

Metaethics

1. Metaphysical Issues
2. Epistemological Issues

Moral philosophy comprises not only → ethics as such — namely, systems of rules or beliefs that govern human conduct, or ought to — but also their underlying bases. The latter sphere, metaethics, concerns the philosophical status, internal logic, and ultimate justification of systems of ethical → norms, beliefs, and discourse. It wrestles with such issues as whether ethical principles derive from empirical study of the natural world or from rational cognition of an autonomous domain of → value. Put differently, do judgments of value derive from facts about the world, does "ought" derive from "is"? Some metaethical positions hold that ethical discourse functions in ways quite apart from the terms of this debate.

1. Metaphysical Issues

Much metaethical inquiry in the history of → philosophy addresses the metaphysical status of such properties as → good, → evil, right, and wrong, when these are ascribed to moral or immoral character or behavior. Protagoras (ca. 485-ca. 410 B.C.), a famous Sophist, apparently espoused the *subjectivist* view that ethical properties have no independent reality in things but are just expressions of the mental attitude of the speaker or individual subject who ascribes them to things. Most later philosophers of a skeptical orientation incline toward → subjectivism in ethics.

Plato (427-347 B.C.; → Platonism), a critic of Protagoras, held the *realist* view that ethical properties have objective being in the realm of ideas, independent of our thinking or ascriptions. Aristotle (384-322; → Aristotelianism) proposed a different brand of → realism for which ethical properties are grounded in, or reducible to, objective features of the perceived, empirical world. From a metaphysical standpoint many metaethicists can be characterized as either subjectivists or realists.

2. Epistemological Issues

Metaethical inquiry in the modern era mainly addresses epistemological concerns. What do ethical concepts mean, and what is their justification? Are they → autonomous, or are they derived from some other cognitive domain? Do moral judgments have universal validity? Several different approaches stand out.

The older → *rationalism* found its metaethical epitome in I. Kant (1724-1804; → Kantianism), who located our sense of moral obligation in a noumenal realm distinct from that of theoretical reason, one that is a priori, autonomous, and universal in validity. Kant's ethics is a formalism in which moral principles are laws that our → reason legislates for itself. B. Blanshard (1892-1987), also a rationalist, acknowledged a dialectical tension between moral reason and the domain of feeling (→ Dialectic). Along with Kantian → deontology, the following three approaches are typical of more recent metaethics.

For *naturalism*, ethical concepts derive from our experience of the natural world. Hence ethics is one of the sciences dealing with knowledge of the natural characteristics of things, a subcategory of → empiricism. Naturalistic ethics should be objective and universal, subject to verification in the manner of the natural sciences. The → utilitarians J. Bentham (1748-1832) and J. S. Mill (1806-73) fit into this camp, as do other ethical philosophers, such as J. Dewey (1859-1952), who have strong affinities for the methodologies of the empirical social sciences. Naturalism, contrary to rationalism, tends to derive value from fact, "ought" from "is."

Intuitionism has a link with rationalism in regarding morality as autonomous, rooted in a directly apprehended, nonnatural, objective domain. But an intuitionist in ethics can be an empiricist in other respects, as was G. E. Moore (1873-1958), for whom "good" is a primitive, undefinable, and unanalyzable ethical term that refers to a directly cognizable objective reality, distinct from the empirical features of natural phenomena. Intuitionists have difficulty showing that a moral term such as "good" refers to a property of something, even a nonnatural property, rather than having some other function in moral discourse.

Noncognitivism is the stance that moral concepts and discourse do not in the main, or even at all, have a theoretical, property-ascribing function. Diverse views fall under this heading. A. J. Ayer (1910-89) denied that moral discourse consists of factual statements, hence it cannot be either true or false, for ethics is "emotive," consisting of "mere pseudo-concepts." R. M. Hare (1919-2002) shifted the emphasis from emotivism ("X is good" means "I like X") to prescriptivism ("one ought to do X"). Noncognitivist positions concentrate attention on

how ethical discourse actually functions in expressing one's views or emotions and in recommending, exhorting to, or discouraging certain sorts of attitudes and behaviors. Critics of noncognitivism see it as undercutting the possibility of objectivity or universality in ethics.

Metaethics was central to mid-20th-century discussions of ethical theory in the English-speaking world. Thereafter major attention of moral philosophers turned to applied ethics.

Bibliography: A. J. AYER, *Language, Truth, and Logic* (London, 1936) • B. BLANSHARD, *Reason and Goodness* (New York, 1961) • R. BRANDT, *Facts, Values, and Morality* (Cambridge, 1996) • R. M. HARE, *Sorting Out Ethics* (Oxford, 1997) • J. RACHELS, ed., *Ethical Theory* (Oxford, 1998) • C. STEVENSON, *Ethics and Language* (London, 1946) • G. WARNOCK, *Contemporary Moral Philosophy* (London, 1967) • B. WILLIAMS, *Ethics and the Limits of Philosophy* (Cambridge, Mass., 1985).

ROBERT F. BROWN

Metaphor

Since Aristotle (384-322 B.C.; → Aristotelianism), the metaphor (Gk. *metaphora*, "transfer") has been understood as a rhetorical stylistic device involving the replacement of one term or group of words by another that is more illustrative — for example, "evening of life" for "old age" (→ Rhetoric). The replacement is taken out of its normal semantic context and transferred into the place of the term with which it is comparable in some decisive sense, though without that comparison being articulated explicitly. The most frequent form of metaphors involves use of the genitive, as in "light of the world." The tradition of metaphors has especially valued the transfer of animate notions onto inanimate ones ("you are my morning star").

While awareness of our → language determines which transfers are semantically appropriate, our awareness of objects (so G. Kurz) determines what can function representatively as a → symbol of the universal. Metaphors can also appear when a given language lacks certain expressions (*inopiae causa,* Cicero); as such, they render various semantic content communicable (→ Communication).

Discussions involving the meaning of metaphors have led to the emergence of two fundamental perspectives. Opponents of the metaphor, often adopting a rationalistic and positivistic position (→ Rationalism; Positivism), view it as a mere stylistic rhetorical device, as figurative or veiled language capable of being replaced at any time by the actual or nonfigurative terms (substitution theory, M. Bunt-fuss's "weak theory of metaphor"). On this view, philosophical and scientific language should studiously avoid metaphors because they constitute illusion (Voltaire), linguistic deception (F. Kainz), or nonsensical speech (the early L. Wittgenstein; → Analytic Philosophy).

By contrast, certain literary styles such as Mannerism, → baroque, and surrealism, along with certain contemporary movements, view metaphoric expression as the more expressive and original language of humankind, as a mode of expression that must be consciously fostered as a sign of artistic creativity. Moreover, metaphors render information accessible that is otherwise incommunicable (thesis of irreplaceability). Its meaning emerges only from the context (M. Black's interaction theory; Buntfuss's "strong theory of metaphor"). On this view, the metaphor is a multilayered phenomenon.

This positive understanding of metaphors is attested as early as the 18th century in the thinking of G. Vico (1688-1744) and J.-J. Rousseau (1712-78), and in Germany especially in that of J. G. Hamann (1730-88), who understood speech itself as a metaphoric reflection of the divine. Later, during the 1950s, a lively discussion emerged within → linguistics concerning the various grammatical forms of metaphors, the accompanying shifts in meaning in semantic fields, textual rules of determination, and rhetorical considerations.

In → theology, this understanding of the metaphor focused especially on → parables. Around the turn of the last century A. Jülicher (1857-1938) understood the metaphor as figurative, veiled language and as a precursor of the allegory, to be distinguished from the concrete, didactically oriented language of parables. By contrast, E. Jüngel and P. Ricoeur believe that precisely the analogical character of metaphor makes it capable of expressing the divine message adequately (→ Analogy); indeed, it is only figuratively, through the use of metaphor, that that message can be expressed at all. The parable narrative as a whole is understood as a metaphor for God's reign and differentiated thus from the → allegory, in which individual features are themselves interpreted metaphorically. Many fascinating metaphors originate in religious language, where they articulate transcendent experiences and various ways of understanding God. In any event, the question of how such metaphors are to be interpreted and how one deals with them appropriately is a central concern of religious thinking (R. Bisschops and J. Francis).

Within philosophical discussion at the end of the 1970s, the dispute concerning metaphors between Ricoeur and J. Derrida also shows that an "apparently old topic" or "used up person" could return and become the emphatic focus of attention (Derrida). During the past two decades, interest in metaphors has soared, prompted not least by the discussion of → postmodernism and constructivism in philosophy and by what might be described as a narrative turn in theological thinking. One generally accepted finding of modern theories of metaphor is that the increasing complexity of our own reality itself makes metaphoric speech necessary. According to G. Lakoff and M. Johnson, a secure orientation in daily life requires the engagement of metaphorically structured concepts deriving from our empirically experienced understanding of reality, together with the connotative elements attaching to that reality. Anyone wishing to become acquainted with the lives, cultures, and religions of other people should turn to a study of their metaphors.

Commensurate with this view, behavioral research examines the extent to which those interested in manipulating opinions use carefully chosen metaphors to influence behavior or to promote one-dimensional thinking (H. Marcuse; → Mass Media).

→ Psychoanalysis examines metaphors to uncover dominant themes in the unconscious psyche to aid in bringing repressed psychological issues to light. Various psychotherapeutic procedures today focus on metaphors. For example, when ineffective or burdensome metaphors affect a person's understanding of reality ("I feel as heavy as a stone"), the introduction of new metaphors can help a person learn new ways of dealing with life and of easing life's burdens (strategic therapy).

Bibliography: P. d. L. Avis, *God and the Creative Imagination: Metaphor, Symbol, and Myth in Religion and Theology* (London, 1999) • S. Bacon, *The Conscious Use of Metaphor in Outward Bound* (Denver, 1998) • R. Bernhardt and U. Link-Wieczorek, eds., *Metapher und Wirklichkeit. Die Logik der Bildhaftigkeit im Reden von Gott, Mensch und Natur* (Göttingen, 1999) • R. Bisschops and J. Francis, *Metaphor, Canon, and Community: Jewish, Christian, and Islamic Approaches* (Bern, 1999) • M. Black, *Models and Metaphors: Studies in Language and Philosophy* (Ithaca, N.Y., 1981; orig. pub., 1962) • M. Buntfuss, *Tradition und Innovation. Die Funktion der Metapher in der theologischen Theoriesprache* (Berlin, 1997) • A. C. Danto, *Die Verklärung des Gewöhnlichen. Eine Philosophie der Kunst* (3d ed.; Frankfurt, 1996) • B. Debatin, T. R. Jackson, and D. Steuer, eds., *Metaphor and Rational Discourse*

(Tübingen, 1997) • J. Derrida, "White Mythology: Metaphor in the Text of Philosophy," *Margins of Philosophy* (Chicago, 1982) 207-71 • R. W. Funk, *Language, Hermeneutic, and the Word of God: The Problem of Language in the NT and Contemporary Theology* (New York, 1966) • W. Harnisch, *Die Gleichniserzählungen Jesu. Eine hermeneutische Einführung* (2d ed.; Göttingen, 1990) • A. Haverkamp, ed., *Die paradoxe Metapher* (Frankfurt, 1998) • F. Kainz, *Über die Sprachverführung des Denkens* (Berlin, 1972) • G. Kurz, *Metapher, Allegorie, Symbol* (4th ed.; Göttingen, 1997) • G. Lakoff and M. Johnson, *Metaphors We Live By* (Chicago, 1980) • S. McFague Teselle, *Speaking in Parables: A Study in Metaphor and Theology* (Philadelphia, 1975) • K. Müller-Richter and A. Larcati, *Kampf der Metapher! Studien zum Widerstreit des eigentlichen und uneigentlichen Sprechens. Zur Reflexion des Metaphorischen im philosophischen und poetologischen Diskurs* (Vienna, 1996) • A. Ortony, ed., *Metaphor and Thought* (2d ed.; Cambridge, 1993) • P. Ricoeur, *The Rule of Metaphor: Multi-disciplinary Studies of the Creation of Meaning in Language* (London, 1994; orig. pub., 1975) • P. Ricoeur and E. Jüngel, *Metapher. Zur Hermeneutik religiöser Sprache* (Munich, 1974) • H. Weder, *Die Gleichnisse Jesu als Metaphern* (4th ed.; Göttingen, 1990).

Elisabeth Schwarz

Metaphysics

1. Term and Concept
2. History
   2.1. Ancient and Medieval Thought
   2.2. Modern Period
   2.3. Twentieth Century
3. Issues for Theology

1. Term and Concept

The term "metaphysics" derives from the Gk. expression *ta meta ta physika* (lit. "the things that come after physics"), which stands as the title of a work by Aristotle (384-322 b.c.; → Aristotelianism). The name was long attributed to a bibliographic accident, to placement of the book after the *Physics* in the Aristotelian canon. But the name in fact fits the sequence that knowledge takes according to Aristotle. In controversy with the earlier Ionian and Eleatic philosophies, Aristotle speaks of the *archē*, or ground of being, the first principles that in the order of things precede physical nature and determine both *what* it is and *that* it is. Aristotle begins his inquiries in the *Physics* and related writings with → nature as such, but then proceeds in the *Metaphysics*

to what is, in the order of being, prior to nature — that on which nature depends, the principles underlying it, the topics of what Aristotle calls "first philosophy." René Descartes (1596-1650; → Cartesianism) employed the same term in the title of his most famous work on the ultimate basis of our knowledge, the *Meditations on First Philosophy*.

In recent times popularization of the adjective "metaphysical" embraces all sorts of allegedly paranormal, occult, or supernatural phenomena. It is important to realize that this usage has little if anything to do with the nature of metaphysics in mainstream → philosophy, where it seeks to be a focused, rational inquiry, at the most general level, into the basic nature and structure of reality.

Some metaphysicians are → *dualists*, holding that reality consists of two distinct kinds of things (matter, bodies, or "extended substance" vs. minds or other nonphysical substances), and they often have difficulty showing how the two are related or interact. Some metaphysicians are → *materialists*, who hold that reality is exhausted by matter and energy, or *naturalists*, who hold that only what the empirical sciences can investigate counts as real. Some are → *idealists*, who say all reality is ultimately mental or spiritual (i.e., nonphysical), or at least that physical reality is actually a manifestation of what is ultimately nonphysical. *Epiphenomenalists*, in contrast, view mind as an outgrowth of, and as existing in dependence on, body.

2. History
2.1. *Ancient and Medieval Thought*

For the pre-Socratics and for Plato and Aristotle, "first philosophy" points to a wisdom underlying ordinary knowledge. Whoever grasps ultimate principles and causes does not merely possess incidental information about the world but is more deeply informed about its ground and is therefore "wise." Plato (427-347 b.c.; → Platonism) called such a wise person an *epoptēs*, the term for an initiate into the highest level of the mystery cults (→ Mystery Religions), suggesting one who has attained the highest level of earthly → happiness.

Metaphysics, or "first philosophy," inquires into the most general features of being as such. It embraces disciplines later called ontology (a term coined in the 17th cent. from a participial form of the Gk. verb "to be") and theology, where it inquires into the ultimate ground of being. This inquiry is nowadays called philosophical theology. Aristotle's *Metaphysics* discusses such topics as the various senses of "being," unity and multiplicity, substance and accident, form and matter, potentiality and actuality, motion or change, causality, mathematical objects, and ideas. It also discusses the highest or divine principle, the unmoved mover, on which all other beings depend and to which they are responsive. As such, metaphysics is a theoretical science that one pursues for the sake of understanding rather than for some practical purpose.

For Aristotle as for Plato, this theory is philosophical practice of the highest sort, the vision of the supreme ground of all things, the thinking of the divine being, a practice that is intrinsically valuable. For the Neoplatonism of Plotinus (ca. A.D. 205-70) and Proclus (410 or 412-85), → ontology that embraces both physical and nonphysical realms became decidedly hierarchical, and metaphysics moved even more into the service of → contemplation and → mysticism.

The efforts of religious thinkers to reconceive the impersonal divine principle of → Greek philosophy in light of the personal attributes of the biblical God altered the nature of metaphysics. Even with modifications, for → Thomas Aquinas (ca. 1225-74) metaphysics retained a twofold character. In his *Commentary on the Sentences* he refers to the object of metaphysics both as God and as the essence and principle of actual being *(ratio entis)*. Some of his formulations explicitly present actual being itself *(ens simpliciter)* as the content of metaphysics. But for Thomas an inquiry into being always also includes God as its Creator. In this sense he designates metaphysics as "divine science" *(theologia sive scientia divina)* because it views God as the ultimate cause of being, in contrast to revealed theology *(theologia sacrae scripturae),* which treats God in his specific acts of self-impartation.

Metaphysics in the Christian Middle Ages was not done uniformly. Duns Scotus (ca. 1265-1308) departed from the Thomistic framework by seeking in the divine will a new grounding for the relationship of the contingent or possible existence of creatures to the necessary existence of infinite being. Henry of Ghent (ca. 1217-93) denied the undisputed preeminence of metaphysics over all other sciences and instead gave the primacy to → theology. William of Ockham (ca. 1285-1347) dethroned classical metaphysics by affirming that metaphysics as such has no object (as distinct from individual beings themselves) and by his assessment that → logic has a more universal character than does metaphysics — a view not held in the same way by certain other → nominalists.

2.2. *Modern Period*
Metaphysics felt the impact of the shift in emphasis from ontology to → epistemology. Descartes's use

of the term "first philosophy" challenged classical metaphysics. He still accepted God as the supreme ground of being, and in turn as the supreme ground of knowledge, but these points are not self-evident. The self-certainty of "I am thinking" precedes all other knowing, even our knowledge of God. The "I" alone is the unshakable foundation. The distance from ontological metaphysics became even more noticeably pronounced in subsequent thought.

In his *Leviathan,* Thomas Hobbes (1588-1679) called classical metaphysics "vain philosophy," thereby expressing a → skepticism about it that became widespread in the Anglo-Saxon philosophy of John Locke (1632-1704) and his empiricist successors. In §1 of his *Enquiry concerning Human Understanding,* David Hume (1711-76) declared that much of metaphysics is not science and that we "must cultivate true metaphysics with some care, in order to destroy the false and adulterate." This full-blown turn to epistemology on the part of British empiricism was already in place before Kant.

Also in place and in debate with one another were the substantive metaphysical systems of the great rationalists Baruch Spinoza (1632-77; → Spinozism) and G. W. Leibniz (1646-1716). Spinozists affirmed a → pantheistic metaphysics in which all actual beings are ultimately instances embraced within the two modes, thought and extension, of the one, all-inclusive, divine being. Leibnizians, in contrast, affirmed the independent reality of the individual monads or unitary beings, centers of conscious or potentially conscious existence that coexist with one another and with God, the supreme monad.

In his effort at a reconceptualization of metaphysics, Immanuel Kant (1724-1804; → Kantianism) began, not as did his predecessors with the question of the first principles of being, but with the prior question concerning the possibility of knowing such principles. Before the structure of being can be presented, the concepts and principles of our thinking must be examined with respect to their competence for such a task. It is first necessary to make → reason itself the object of the inquiry and, as in the *Critique of Pure Reason,* to determine its limits. The *archē* of metaphysical inquiry here is constituted not by being but by reason itself, "the faculty that supplies the principles of a priori knowledge" (B24).

Kant's predecessor, Christian Wolff (1679-1754), had called ontological metaphysics *metaphysica generalis* and theological metaphysics *metaphysica specialis.* The latter he explicated in a threefold form as psychology, cosmology, and theology, based on his view that any philosophical determination concerning the world or human beings that goes beyond the givens of empirical knowledge has a metaphysical character. Kant, however, believed he could show that this *metaphysica generalis,* or ontology, presupposes the three "objects" of *metaphysica specialis,* namely, rational psychology, rational cosmology, and their unity in rational theology. His *Critique of Pure Reason* rebutted the pretensions of these three to constitute knowledge and thus claimed to dismantle the Wolffian and classical types of metaphysics.

Kant's German idealist successors deemed metaphysics of this sort to have been discredited. J. G. Fichte (1762-1814) replaced it with his *Wissenschaftslehre* (science of knowledge), and G. W. F. Hegel (1770-1831; → Hegelianism), in speaking in deprecating tones of metaphysics as such, usually is referring to the developments from Descartes to Wolff. For Hegel, metaphysics in a positive sense refers to the science of logic or pure speculative philosophy, since for him logic and metaphysics are not distinct but coincide. F. W. J. Schelling (1775-1854), alone among the German idealists, sometimes seems to engage in classical metaphysics, but only in a qualified way.

Other 19th-century views of metaphysics were many and varied. The anti-Hegelian materialism of Ludwig Feuerbach (1804-72) became one of the foundations of → Marxism, also influenced by Hegel, which in its various forms tends to dismiss all nondialectical types of philosophizing as metaphysics (→ Dialectic). Søren → Kierkegaard (1813-55) attacked Hegel from a different angle, treating his speculative philosophy as in effect a metaphysics that does away with "the existing individual." Auguste Comte (1798-1857) denied that we can ever have knowledge of unobservable or nonphysical objects and so denounced metaphysics as ungrounded speculation to be replaced by a system of "positive philosophy" (→ Positivism). Darwinism forced a reconsideration of metaphysical conceptions of human nature and of the natural-history dimensions of cosmology (→ Evolution 2). F. H. Bradley (1846-1924) advanced an absolute idealism that denied the reality of relations. Friedrich Nietzsche (1844-1900) regarded past metaphysical systems as idols to be smashed in his striving for the production of new systems of → values.

2.3. *Twentieth Century*

Edmund Husserl (1859-1938), founder of the movement known as → phenomenology, empha-

sized the role of intentionality in knowing and replaced classical metaphysical analysis with eidetic → intuition as the route to grasping the essences of things. Martin Heidegger (1889-1976), influenced by both Husserl and Kierkegaard (→ Existentialism), sought by reinterpreting the pre-Socratics to recover an ethos prior to the reputed origins of metaphysics in ancient Greek thought. In so doing, he became in his later writings a persistent critic of the "onto-theology" that he held has, in the intervening millennia, disastrously infected thought about God, the world, and human nature.

Alfred North Whitehead (1861-1947) developed a complex "process metaphysics" that drew upon developments in the physical and life sciences for a new cosmology based on organic rather than mechanistic models, on creative possibilities and novelty rather than deterministic causation, one embracing not just the system of nature but God and social existence as well. Charles Hartshorne (1897-2000) expounded the implications of process metaphysics for philosophical theology, in particular for the ontological proof and for conceptions of the divine attributes (→ God, Arguments for the Existence of, 2.1; Process Philosophy).

On the side of → analytic philosophy Rudolf Carnap (1891-1970), a central figure in the logical positivism of the Vienna Circle, treated metaphysical issues as "pseudoproblems" and dismissed metaphysical statements as unverifiable and thus meaningless. This approach began an extended debate that spilled over into epistemology and ultimately into → philosophy of religion, for Carnap's "verificationism" holds that to be meaningful a statement must be formally either true or false, as are the statements of logic and mathematics, or else must make some claim that is empirically testable as to its truth or falsity. The equation of metaphysics with meaninglessness was soon shown to be dubious and false; the statement that all statements that are not formally true or false or empirically verifiable are metaphysical and thus meaningless is itself a metaphysical statement.

Ludwig Wittgenstein (1889-1951) contended in his later writings and lectures that statements, including metaphysical propositions, have their meaning and role within the conventions of the "language games" of diverse communities and so lack reference or universality in other, wider contexts. On the one hand, the idea of language games offers a basis on which the metaphysical game, taking pragmatic form as it is played, carries its own conviction, which makes superfluous any further reflection on its meaning or claim to → truth. On the other hand, Wittgenstein emphasized that it is the task of grammar, and certainly of depth grammar as a reflective process of demonstration, to bring to light all the conditions for comparing a statement with reality, that is, all the conditions for the understanding of meaning (*Schriften* 4.13.45).

Not only where philosophy today deals with the original question of the unity of all being, but also where an effort is made to do without metaphysics or even philosophy itself, it is hard to abandon a metaphysical approach, though metaphysics might not involve either theoretical or practical philosophy in Aristotle's sense. In epistemology not all the constitutive presuppositions can be offered by empirical research. To the fore here are fundamental conceptions of being that determine the basic constitution of all objects. In → ethics, too, metaphysics arises when it is maintained that the distinction between → good and → evil cannot be reduced to normative theses because this distinction itself is tied to nonnormative conditions of validity.

In the latter half of the 20th century, metaphysics took up an increasingly complex set of issues. P. F. Strawson advocates "descriptive metaphysics," which takes the metaphysical task to be an account not of how reality is but of how our thinking about reality or the world is actually structured. *Realists* take issue with this approach, for they think that our perceptual knowledge delivers to us reliable information about existing spatiotemporal objects that have the properties they do independently of our knowing them, and that any more general or metaphysical reflection that is legitimate is to be done on this basis. *Antirealists*, in contrast, engage in metaphysics on a Kantian or a Strawsonian foundation, holding that we have no direct access to a world existing independently of our knowing it, hence metaphysics is a study of how our conceptual apparatus, or the language we learn, structures the world as it is presented to us. Metaphysicians of either stripe debate with great technical refinement issues such as the relation of an entity to its properties and to its relations with other entities, whether entities are enduring substances or just transient complexes in the temporal series, what an identity of two or more things consists in, and whether alternative "possible worlds" have any metaphysical import.

Bibliography: On 1: J. GRACIA, *Metaphysics and Its Task: The Search for the Categorical Foundation of Knowledge* (Albany, N.Y., 1999) • D. HAMLYN, *Metaphysics* (Cambridge, 1984) • M. LOUX, *Metaphysics: A Contemporary Introduction* (London, 1998).

On 2.1: ARISTOTLE, *Metaphysics* (trans. W. Ross; Oxford, 1924) • THOMAS AQUINAS, *Commentary on the Metaphysics of Aristotle* (trans. J. P. Rowan; Chicago, 1961).

On 2.2: F. H. BRADLEY, *Appearance and Reality* (2d ed.; Oxford, 1930; orig. pub., 1893) • R. DESCARTES, *Discourse on the Method, and Meditations on First Philosophy* (ed. D. Weissman; New Haven, 1996; orig. pub., 1637 and 1641) • G. W. F. HEGEL, *Science of Logic* (trans. A. V. Miller; London, 1969; orig. pub., 1812-16) • T. HOBBES, *Leviathan* (ed. J. C. A. Gaskin; Oxford, 1996; orig. pub., 1651) • D. HULL, *The Metaphysics of Evolution* (Albany, N.Y., 1989) • D. HUME, *An Enquiry concerning Human Understanding* (Chicago, 1900; orig. pub., London, 1748) • I. KANT, *Critique of Pure Reason* (trans. P. Guyer and A. W. Wood; Cambridge, 1998; orig. pub., 1781; rev., 1787) • J. SECADA, *Cartesian Metaphysics: The Late Scholastic Origins of Modern Philosophy* (Cambridge, 2000) • C. WOLFF, *Vernünftige Gedanken von Gott, der Welt und der Seele des Menschen* (Halle, 1751).

On 2.3: G. BERGMANN, *The Metaphysics of Logical Positivism* (New York, 1954) • R. CARNAP, *The Logical Structure of the World: Pseudoproblems in Philosophy* (trans. R. A. George; Berkeley, Calif., 1967; orig. pub., 1928) • C. HARTSHORNE, *The Logic of Perfection, and Other Essays in Neoclassical Metaphysics* (LaSalle, Ill., 1962); idem, *Omnipotence and Other Theological Mistakes* (Albany, N.Y., 1984) • M. HEIDEGGER, *Introduction to Metaphysics* (trans. G. Fried and R. Polt; New Haven, 2000; orig. pub., 1953) • H. HOFMEISTER, *Philosophisch denken* (2d ed.; Göttingen, 1997); idem, *Truth and Belief: Interpretation and Critique of the Analytical Theory of Religion* (Dordrecht, 1990) • E. HUSSERL, *Cartesian Meditations: An Introduction to Phenomenology* (trans. D. Cairns; The Hague, 1960; orig. pub., 1931) • P. STRAWSON, *Individuals: An Essay in Descriptive Metaphysics* (New York, 1959) • A. WHITEHEAD, *Process and Reality* (New York, 1929) • L. WITTGENSTEIN, *Philosophical Investigations* (Oxford, 1953).

HEIMO HOFMEISTER and ROBERT F. BROWN

3. Issues for Theology

Martin → Luther (1483-1546) adamantly opposed the scholastic theology of his day, largely erected on an Aristotelian foundation, and in so doing set the tone for Protestant theology's general hostility to philosophical metaphysics. Although there were striking exceptions, many Protestant theologians in subsequent centuries sought to distance their work from any systematic engagement with metaphysical issues, philosophically considered. This tendency holds true, not only for "fundamentalist" versions of the *sola Scriptura* principle and for the neo-orthodoxy of Karl → Barth (1886-1968), but also for "liberalisms" that draw heavily on the natural or social sciences or on antimetaphysical philosophies for their tools. The latter is perhaps a questionable stance, since one might wonder how intelligible reflection about theological issues can proceed without drawing upon a fund of consistent and defensible conceptions of God, the world, and human nature, the sort of interrelated concepts about fundamental reality that are regarded as metaphysics. Many would deny that the Bible itself supplies a systematic metaphysics of a sort needed to undergird theology.

Wolfhart Pannenberg is one systematic theologian who has called for a renewed recognition of the role of metaphysics in theology. → Process theology, most notably that of John B. Cobb Jr. and David Ray Griffin, has brought the metaphysics of Whitehead and Hartshorne into active engagement with theological concepts. Recent interest in "Anselmian theology" on the part of some Protestant philosophers of religion has brought that brand of metaphysics into discussions of God's being and of the relation between God and world.

Roman Catholic theology, in contrast with the theologies of Protestantism, has never tried to cut itself off from metaphysics, as typified by theologians of the 20th century such as Karl → Rahner (1904-84), who wrestled most seriously with Heidegger's thought. This continuity is in part owing to the efforts of Joseph Maréchal (1878-1944) and others to promote a positive engagement of → Thomism with the currents of modern thought, as well as to the ongoing influence of a more metaphysical brand of Augustinianism than that appealed to by the Protestant Reformers (→ Augustine's Theology). It is also owing to a much greater theological openness to both sides of the reason-revelation distinction and to their mutual correlation, and in turn to greater openness to cultural influences, of which philosophical metaphysics is one instance.

Bibliography: J. B. COBB JR., *God and the World* (Philadelphia, 1969) • J. DONCEEL, trans., *A Maréchal Reader* (New York, 1970) • D. GRIFFIN, *Reenchantment without Supernaturalism: A Process Philosophy of Religion* (Ithaca, N.Y., 2001) • W. PANNENBERG, *Metaphysics and the Idea of God* (Grand Rapids, 1990) • K. RAHNER, "Theos in the NT," *Theological Investigations* (vol. 1; Baltimore, 1961) 79-148 • R. SCHARLEMANN, *The Being of God: Theology and the Experience of Truth* (New York, 1981).

ROBERT F. BROWN

Methodism

1. Origins and Spread
2. Ecclesial Characteristics
   2.1. Koinonia
   2.2. Leitourgia
   2.3. Martyria
   2.4. Diakonia
3. Soteriological Concentration
4. Doctrinal Norms
   4.1. Holy Scripture
   4.2. Church Tradition
   4.3. Experience
   4.4. Reason
5. Ecumenical Spirit

1. Origins and Spread

Having its origins in Anglicanism (→ Anglican Communion), Methodism ranks among the most recent of the larger ecclesial communities; in 2000 it numbered some 70 million members and adherents worldwide. Through its own pneumatological emphases it contributed — at least indirectly — to the rise of the even younger family of → Pentecostal churches.

The beginnings of Methodism lie in the movements for revival and renewal within the Church of England in the 18th century, especially in the evangelistic work of the Wesley brothers, John (1703-91) and Charles (1707-88), both of whom were and remained Anglican priests. Distancing themselves both from the → Moravians, who had been instrumental in quickening their personal faith (the "evangelical conversions" of Pentecost 1738), and from the Calvinist stream represented by George → Whitefield, the Wesleys took what they came to call an → Arminian direction in their → preaching. From 1740 John → Wesley became the great organizer of the Methodists, whose parachurch structures made their separation from the Anglican fold possible and — after their founder's death — practically inevitable. In North America the ecclesiastical independence of Methodism followed already in 1784 on the political independence of the United States from the English crown. Charles Wesley was the poet of Methodism, whose → hymnody impressed itself most deeply on the → spirituality of the movement.

In the 19th century the work of overseas missions from Britain and America took Methodism chiefly to Africa, India, and China (→ British Missions). The further spread of Methodism resulted also from emigration of British Methodists to Australia, South Africa, and Canada, as well as from the return to continental Europe and Scandinavia of some who had discovered Methodism in the United States.

2. Ecclesial Characteristics

2.1. *Koinonia*

In Methodism the most characteristic and intense experience of the Christian life is found in small groups. From the start, Methodist communities figured — like their Pietist predecessors — as *ecclesiolae in ecclesia* (little churches within the church). Moreover, every local "society" was itself divided into "classes" of 12 members, each with a layperson as its pastoral leader; the more advanced also met in "bands" of 4 or 5 for mutual encouragement.

As Methodism's character shifted from the societal to the churchly, the most intimate forms of fellowship were largely lost; but the continuing sense of need for closer contact in → faith and life has led to the repeated emergence of small-group structures in Methodism, even if of a looser kind than those of early Methodism. Methodists themselves reckon "fellowship" — which admittedly may degenerate into mere coziness — as a characteristic of Methodism.

2.2. *Leitourgia*

For the original Methodists worship consisted principally in participation in the services of the Anglican parish churches (morning and evening prayer and, where possible, Holy Communion; → Eucharist). These services were supplemented by the Methodists' own gatherings for preaching and → prayer. At a time when the Lord's Supper was observed only three or four times a year in the average parish, John Wesley himself celebrated or received Holy Communion some 70 to 90 times annually, and he exhorted his followers to "constant communion." In 1784 he recommended the elders in North America to "administer the Supper of the Lord on every Lord's Day." On the American frontier, however, the preaching service became the norm. In England, even though the desire of the Methodists to receive the sacrament from the hands of their own preachers was a factor in the separation between them and the Church of England, eucharistic frequency declined in the 19th century, partly perhaps as a result of Methodism's self-assimilation to the free churches in reaction to Anglo-Catholicism.

In the 20th century, Methodists in both the American and the British traditions participated, if somewhat hesitantly, in the broader → liturgical movement, with its eucharistic renewal, and thereby rediscovered the Wesley brothers' *Hymns on the Lord's Supper* (1745). The more general *Collection of Hymns for the Use of the People Called Methodists* (1780), with a preponderance of texts by Charles Wesley, was structured "according to the experience of real Christians" and claimed to be "a little body of experimental and practical divinity" containing "all the important truths of our most holy religion." More recent Methodist hymnals have a broader ecumenical range in both time and space and are often shaped more by ecclesial creed and calendar than by the spiritual life of the believer. Special services in the Methodist tradition have been love feasts, watch nights, and an annual service for "such as would renew their covenant with God."

2.3. *Martyria*

The chief verbal form of the church's witness is preaching. In April 1739 John Wesley began his career as a traveling preacher — often in the open air — which carried him some 385,000 km. (240,000 mi.) in the next half century. The first four volumes of his *Standard Sermons* belong to the doctrinal norms of all Methodist churches. Methodists historically regard → evangelism as the primary task laid upon their particular community.

2.4. *Diakonia*

Love of neighbor, which finds its first expression in the good works of the individual believer, led John Wesley also into concern for → education, health care (e.g., dispensaries for the poor), → prison visitation and reform, and the abolition of → slavery. Social engagement is a lasting characteristic of Methodism (although the political Left often claims it for their monopoly).

3. Soteriological Concentration

In varying formulations John Wesley often said that "our main doctrines, which include all the rest, are three, that of repentance, of faith, and of holiness" (*The Principles of a Methodist Farther Explained* [1746]). The negative background was original → sin; the positive, the saving work of God through Christ and the Holy Spirit. → Justification by faith brought as "the common privilege" of believers the → assurance of sins forgiven for the sake of Christ and the direct witness of the → Holy Spirit to our status as children of God (see Rom. 8:15-16). This → salvation, however, might be forfeited through unbelief or persistent wickedness; Wesley rejected Calvinistic teaching concerning the unconditional perseverance of the elect. → Regeneration is the beginning of → sanctification, which is the work of the Holy Spirit in the believer, but the believer must actively cooperate by prayer and effort. The believer is expected to strive for "entire sanctification," which consists in "perfect love" toward God and neighbor, although this concentrated affection does not exclude the "mistakes" to which a fallen human nature, not yet fully healed, remains prone. Salvation may be understood as the spiritual and moral restoration of the human being to the — Christologically defined — image of God ("having the mind of Christ" and "walking as Christ walked").

It must be emphasized that Wesley grounds this → soteriology in the Trinitarian being of God, in the God-man Jesus Christ and the universal sufficiency and scope of his objective work of redemption, and in the all-enabling power of the Holy Spirit, who comes as prevenient, convicting, converting, and transforming → grace. The Wesleyan soteriology can be viewed as Pelagian only by those who would deny all active character — even that of "reception" — to the human appropriation of salvation, which is not the catholic or the orthodox faith. In 20th-century British Methodism the anthropological aspect of soteriology was pedagogically formulated as: "All need to be saved; all can be saved; all can know they are saved; all can be saved to the uttermost" (J. M. Turner 1985, 45).

4. Doctrinal Norms

Four factors shape and test Methodist doctrine, although they are not to be seen as on an equal footing or fulfilling identical functions. The designation of Scripture (→ Word of God), → tradition, → reason, and → experience as "the Wesleyan quadrilateral" — popular in United Methodism for some decades in the late 20th century — has been recognized as a misnomer, as should have been clear already from the nuanced statement in the *Discipline* of 1972 that for "the Methodist pioneers" the "living core" of Christian truth stood "revealed in Scripture, illumined by tradition, vivified in personal experience, and confirmed by reason."

4.1. *Holy Scripture*

Wesley characterized himself as "a man of one book," in the sense that the Bible constituted "the center of gravity in his thinking," though not a "boundary of his reading" (T. C. Oden, 82). Scripture contains "all things necessary to salvation" (Articles of Religion). Methodism's recognition of the primacy of Scripture maintains the → Reformation principle of Scripture as the supreme norm of doctrine.

4.2. *Church Tradition*

In his "Letter to a Roman Catholic" (1749), Wesley set out "the faith of a true Protestant" as an expansion upon the → Niceno-Constantinopolitan creed. He esteemed the early Fathers. He appealed to the English Reformation as expressed especially in the → Book of Common Prayer and in the official Homilies. For the North American Methodists Wesley prepared an abridgment of the Thirty-nine Articles that holds a constitutionally inviolable place in the United Methodist Church. All Methodist churches use the ancient ecumenical creeds and acknowledge the *Standard Sermons* of John Wesley as a subordinate norm of doctrine.

4.3. *Experience*

"Experience" refers chiefly to the "Christian experience" of believers, although the term can include also the experience of → everyday life. In neither case is experience, in a Wesleyan perspective, a source of doctrine but rather its proving ground.

4.4. *Reason*

Living in the age of the → Enlightenment, Wesley valued the human capacity for rational thought, while placing it in the service of religion (see his two "Appeals" to "Men of Reason and Religion"). According to R. E. Chiles, American Methodism underwent a long-term "theological transition" in which what had been secondary poles in a Wesleyan ellipse assumed the greater importance: the emphasis shifted from → revelation to reason, from sinful man to moral man, and from free grace to free will.

5. Ecumenical Spirit

Wesley favored "a catholic spirit" that, in distinguishing between essential "doctrines" and permitted "opinions," allowed for friendship and cooperation between Christians of different communities as long as their differences did not "strike at the root of Christianity" (see Wesley's sermon "Catholic Spirit" and his tract *The Character of a Methodist*). The more precise distribution of themes between the categories of "doctrine" and "opinion" is debatable, for Wesley himself could vary over time and with circumstance in his estimate of → "predestination" on the one hand and "perfection" on the other; and Methodists have shown a corresponding flexibility in doctrinal conversations with other bodies. Generally, Methodists do not consider that differences in ministerial and governmental structures should be church-dividing.

Methodists of British origin — remembering perhaps their own "provisional" character — have in several places entered into "organic union" with Christians of other denominations (e.g., the → Church of South India in 1947, the United Church of Zambia in 1965, the Church of North India in 1971, the Uniting Church in Australia in 1977), and the Methodist Church in Great Britain in 1969 and 1972 approved a joint plan for reunion with the Church of England that the Anglicans twice declined. Methodists of American origin are more inclined to an → ecumenism of "reconciled diversity" that does not call for organizational unity (as with the agreements for pulpit and table fellowship between Methodists and Lutherans in Germany, Austria, Sweden, and Norway in the 1980s and 1990s and the continuing participation of Methodist denominations in the United States in the Consultation on Church Union and its sucessors).

The → World Methodist Council conducted successful bilateral dialogues with the → Lutheran World Federation (1979-84; *The Church: Community of Grace*) and with the → World Alliance of Reformed Churches (1986-87; *Together in God's Grace*). The global dialogue with Anglicanism, in its report *Sharing in the Apostolic Communion* (1996), called for mutual recognition between Anglican and Methodist churches as belonging to the one church of Jesus Christ, but this recommendation was not fully received by the Lambeth Conference of Anglican bishops in 1998. Since 1967 the World Methodist Council has been in dialogue with the → Roman Catholic Church through the Pontifical Council for Promoting Christian Unity; the Joint Commission produces quinquennial reports, of which the most mature have been *The Apostolic Tradition* (1991), *The Word of Life: A Statement on Revelation and Faith* (1996), and *Speaking the Truth in Love: Teaching Authority among Catholics and Methodists* (2001). Since 1990 a preparatory commission has been working to initiate official dialogue between the World Methodist Council and the → Orthodox churches.

Bibliography: T. Berger, *Theology in Hymns? A Study of the Relationship of Doxology and Theology according to "A Collection of Hymns for the Use of the People Called Methodists" (1780)* (Nashville, 1995) • T. A. Campbell, *John Wesley and Christian Antiquity: Religious Vision and Cultural Change* (Nashville, 1991); idem, "The 'Wesleyan Quadrilateral': The Story of a Modern Methodist Myth," *MethH* 29 (1990/91) 87-95 • R. E. Chiles, *Theological Transition in American Methodism, 1790-1935* (Nashville, 1965) • K. J. Collins, *The Scripture Way of Salvation: The Heart of John Wesley's Theology* (Nashville, 1997) • A. Coppedge, *John Wesley in Theological Debate* (Wilmore, Ky., 1987) • R. E. Davies, *Methodism* (2d ed.; London, 1976) • M. Hurley, ed., *John Wesley's Letter to a Roman Catholic* (London, 1968) • S. J. Jones, *John Wesley's Conception and Use of Scripture* (Nashville, 1995) • W. Klaiber and M. Marquardt, *Gelebte Gnade. Grundriß einer Theologie der Evangelisch-methodistischen Kirche* (Stuttgart, 1993) • T. A. Langford, *Methodist Theology* (London, 1998); idem, *Practical Divinity,* vol. 1, *Theology in the Wesleyan Tradition;* vol. 2, *Readings in Wesleyan Theology* (rev. ed.; Nashville, 1998) • R. L. Maddox, "John Wesley and Eastern Orthodoxy: Influences, Convergences, Differences," *AsbTJ* 45 (1990) 29-53; idem, *Responsible Grace: John Wesley's Practical Theology* (Nashville, 1994) • M. D. Meeks, ed., *The Future of the Methodist Theological Traditions* (Nashville, 1985); idem, ed., *What Should Methodists Teach?* (Nashville, 1990) • T. C. Oden, *Doctrinal Standards in the Methodist Tradition* (Grand Rapids, 1988) • H. D. Rack, *Reasonable Enthusiast: John Wesley and the Rise of Methodism* (London, 1989) • M. Schmidt, *John Wesley: A Theological Biography* (2 vols.; London, 1962-73) • J. M. Turner, *Conflict and Reconciliation: Studies in Methodism and Ecumenism in England, 1740-1982* (London, 1985); idem, *Modern Methodism in England, 1932-1998* (London, 1998) • G. Wainwright, "Methodism's Ecclesial Location and Ecumenical Vocation," *The Ecumenical Moment* (Grand Rapids, 1983) 189-221; idem, *Methodists in Dialogue* (Nashville, 1995); idem, *On Wesley and Calvin: Sources for Theology, Liturgy, and Spirituality* (Melbourne, 1987) • J. Weissbach, *Der neue Mensch im theologischen Denken John Wesleys* (Stuttgart, 1970) • K. Westerfield Tucker, *American Methodist Worship* (New York, 2001); idem, ed., *The Sunday Service of the Methodists: Twentieth-Century Worship in Worldwide Methodism* (Nashville, 1996) • C. W. Williams, *John Wesley's Theology Today* (Nashville, 1960).

Geoffrey Wainwright

Methodist Churches

1. Origins
2. Churches
   2.1. England
   2.2. United States
   2.3. Divisions
   2.4. Unions
3. Doctrine and Church Life
   3.1. Common Foundations
   3.2. Distinctives
   3.3. Doctrinal Basis
4. Patterns of Worship, Discipline, and Discipleship
   4.1. Organization
   4.2. Mission
   4.3. International Bodies
   4.4. Ecumenism

1. Origins

The beginnings of → Methodism may be traced to the experience and work of John → Wesley (1703-

91) and his brother Charles (1707-88) in England. After studying at Oxford, the two brothers crossed the Atlantic in 1735 to serve as → missionaries in the American colony of Georgia, but they returned feeling that their mission was a failure. Later back in London, both brothers in May 1738 made the discovery of God's → grace and received an → assurance of faith that launched them on a revival that spread throughout England and finally had worldwide repercussions (→ Revivals). In this period the Wesleys, George → Whitefield (1714-70), and others set out to declare to all who would listen "the glad tidings of salvation." Charles Wesley became England's greatest hymnist, composing more than 6,000 → hymns, many of which literally carried the movement forward in song.

The name "Methodist" was first used when the Wesleys, Whitefield, and others were at Oxford and met regularly for study and → prayer. This group of young men was subject to derision and was variously called "The Holy Club," "The Bible Moths," "The Reforming Club," or "Methodists." The nickname "Methodists" stuck, perhaps because it best described the disciplined lives of the members.

First in Bristol in 1742, then in London, and then in time throughout England, awakened persons were organized into "class" meetings (→ Pastoral Care). The whole group, or "society," in a given place would be divided into companies or classes, in which at first the various leaders undertook the task of collecting contributions. It was soon apparent to John Wesley that the classes might also be instrumental in providing pastoral oversight for the growing number of Methodists. This insight was the beginning of a decisive feature of Methodism.

Wesley took the idea of "bands" from the → Moravian Brethren. These were smaller groups than the classes, in which members of a society were drawn together for more intimate union with one another. The bands met three times each week. The bands were the inner cells, or the core, of the societies.

In contemporary practice, where Methodism has been shaped by the British tradition, societies are still known, but the band is little known. In the American tradition, Methodists have neither societies nor bands, although a variety of contemporary programs aimed at achieving the goals envisioned by both has developed.

Contemporary Methodists hold that vital faith leads to transformation of life, and this transformation leads to active discipleship. In seeking to follow the teachings of Jesus Christ, they share their faith with others and are eager to move beyond the Christian community with those who live in their com-

munities and beyond, possessing a concern for people in other parts of the world. Methodists also see themselves as a part of the universal church belonging to all Christians.

2. Churches

John Wesley did not intend to organize a new → denomination. He was an ordained minister in the Church of England (→ Anglican Communion) and sought to channel the Methodists into the established church. It became apparent over the decades of the awakening, however, that the church could not assimilate the increasing numbers of new Christians coming into the faith. Parish lines were inflexibly drawn (→ Congregation), and many of the new converts (→ Conversion 1) felt excluded.

2.1. *England*

A "deed of declaration" written and adopted in 1784 led to the formation of the Methodist Church in Britain. Following Wesley's death in 1791, a variety of separate ecclesial groups developed in England, including the British Wesleyan Methodist, Primitive Methodist, New Connection Methodist, Wesleyan Reformed Union, United Free Methodist, Bible Christians, and Calvinistic Methodist Churches.

2.2. *United States*

The first organized Methodist church was the Methodist Episcopal Church in America, which was founded at the Christmas Conference of 1784 in the city of Baltimore. It was instituted by John Wesley, who passed the torch to the colonies by sending Francis Asbury (1745-1816) and Thomas Coke (1747-1814) to superintend the work in the New World. In England, Wesley → ordained Coke superintendent (later, against Wesley's preference, called bishop) and then instructed Coke to ordain Asbury in America. These appointments by Wesley paved the way for independent Methodism. In addition, Methodist emigrants from Ireland helped plant and nurture churches in New York and other eastern cities of the United States.

2.3. *Divisions*

In America, the church developed amid the frontier conditions of a population moving west. Circuit-riding preachers conducted evangelistic services (→ Evangelism) and camp meetings, drawing people into newly formed churches and leaving clusters of new Christians in every place. The Methodist circuit riders were in the vanguard of the spreading American population. At one point in American history it was observed that every place that had a U.S. Post Office also had a Methodist church.

The African Methodist Episcopal Church traces its beginning to the experience of racial discrimination at Old St. George's Church, Philadelphia, in 1786 (→ Racism). Its organizing conference was held in 1816. The African Methodist Episcopal Zion Church began in New York City when black Methodists left John Street Church in the latter part of the 18th century. It was officially organized in 1820.

In 1844 the Methodist Episcopal Church divided over the issue of → slavery into the Methodist Episcopal Church and the Methodist Episcopal Church, South. In 1870, following the American Civil War, the African American members of the Methodist Episcopal Church, South, organized themselves as an independent denomination, the Colored Methodist Episcopal Church, changing this name in 1954 to the Christian Methodist Episcopal Church. Wesleyan and Free Methodist Churches organized in the later 19th century to stress Wesley's emphasis on → sanctification and holiness of life. The → Church of the Nazarene, which recently joined the World Methodist Council, was organized in the early 20th century.

In 1760 there were 600 Methodists in America, a number that had mushroomed to 120,000 in 1805 and to 1.38 million in 1865. Today the U.S. Methodist churches have a combined membership of more than 15 million.

2.4. Unions
Significant unions of the separate English Methodist churches occurred in 1932, and the union of three Methodist churches in the United States in 1939 made the Methodist Church the largest Protestant Church in America at the time. In 1968 the Methodist Church and the Evangelical United Brethren Church united to become the United Methodist Church.

Where church unions have occurred, creating new national entities like the United Church of Canada, the Uniting Church in Australia, and the United Church of Zambia, the Methodist contribution is found within these united churches. Worldwide, of the 74 separate denominations that bear the name "Methodist," many are organized along national or regional lines, for example, the Methodist Church in Kenya; the Methodist Church, Brazil; the Methodist Church, Korea; the Methodist Church of Southern Africa; and the Free Wesleyan Church, Tonga.

3. Doctrine and Church Life
3.1. Common Foundations
In doctrine (→ Dogma) Methodists share with other Christians belief in the triune God — Father, Son and Holy Spirit (→ Trinity); faith in the redeeming → love of God revealed in → Jesus' life, teachings, atoning death, → resurrection, triumph over the powers of evil and → death, and promised return (→ Eschatology; Last Judgment; Promise and Fulfillment); and the activity of the → Holy Spirit in personal experience and in the community of believers. Methodists understand themselves to be a part of Christ's universal church, recognizing the reign of God as both a present and a future reality (→ Future; Kingdom of God). In the words of the historic creeds, they express belief in the one holy, catholic, and apostolic → church and the → unity of the body of Christ (→ Confession of Faith).

3.2. Distinctives
Only on the broad basis of the common foundations can special Wesleyan emphases be highlighted. Distinctive accents in Methodist teaching include a belief in God's prevenient grace, which precedes conscious human impulses and gives the first glimmer of understanding concerning God's will (→ Law) and the awareness of having sinned against God (→ Sin). Methodists believe that this grace goes before saving grace, awakening the longing for deliverance from sin and death and moving persons toward repentance and faith. Methodists believe it is by faith that persons receive justifying grace and are forgiven and restored to God's favor (→ Righteousness, Justice; Forgiveness; Reconciliation). They may also expect to receive the assurance of present salvation as the Holy Spirit is active in "bearing witness with our spirit that we are children of God" (Rom. 8:16).

The little understood Methodist emphasis on → sanctification and → perfection, simply stated, is that through the power of the Holy Spirit persons are enabled to increase in knowledge and in love for → neighbor. The new birth not only means → regeneration but is the first step toward sanctification, leading to what Wesley described as a heart "habitually filled with the love of God and neighbor" and the experience of "having the mind of Christ and walking as he walked." Methodists have also defined sanctification as "perfect love," although they have seen it more in terms of perfect intention than perfect performance (→ Perfectionists). For Methodists, faith and good works belong together within an all-encompassing theology of grace, flowing from God's gracious love "shed abroad in our hearts by the Holy Ghost" (Rom. 5:5 KJV).

Repentance, according to John Wesley, was to be accompanied by "fruits meet for repentance" (Matt. 3:8 KJV). Methodists therefore hold that personal salvation leads to Christian mission and to service in the world, in a unity of evangelical witness and Christian social action. Following the example of

John Wesley and George Whitefield, Methodists through the years have established colleges, universities, theological schools, homes for children and the aging, hospitals, and social service centers in many nations. These emphases find their place in Methodist churches as expressions of basic Christianity already affirmed by the universal church.

3.3. *Doctrinal Basis*

The basis for Methodist doctrine in England originally consisted of the Thirty-nine Articles of the Church of England, the Books of Homilies, and the → Book of Common Prayer. The Bible constituted the final → authority in all doctrinal matters. As the movement grew, Wesley provided his people with sermons and a biblical commentary for their doctrinal instruction. John Wesley's published *Sermons on Several Occasions* (1746-60) and his *Explanatory Notes on the NT* (1755) became the guide for Methodist biblical → exegesis and doctrinal interpretation.

Wesley recognized that in America the situation was different. In place of the Thirty-nine Articles and the Book of Common Prayer, he sent a revision of the Church of England Articles and a Sunday Service (→ Worship) for use in the churches. The *Sermons* and *Notes on the NT* were well known to American Methodists and were understood to be included in the established standards of doctrine.

4. Patterns of Worship, Discipline, and Discipleship

In the 21st century local congregations often seek to blend traditional → hymnody and worship with elements of contemporary music and worship. Some of these congregations conduct both traditional and contemporary services during a given week as they seek to serve a wider constituency. Methodists see active discipleship as an important goal, with its basis of vital faith and experience the primary motivation for witness and outreach. Partnership in pursuing common goals is also important for evangelism and witness.

4.1. *Organization*

British Methodism and churches in the British Methodist tradition vest authority in the Conference, which meets annually. Representatives are elected from the churches as members of Conference. The president of Conference is elected to head the church for one year, during which time he or she itinerates extensively in the interests of the church and as its primary representative. The chief administrative officer, known as the secretary of Conference, serves for a longer term and may be reelected for additional terms.

In American Methodism the task of superintending the church resides in the office of → bishop and extends to the district → superintendent. The bishop appoints district superintendents to serve in overseeing the work in geographic areas known as districts. The bishop and the superintendents work closely together in the appointment of ordained ministers.

Churches organized through the mission of British Methodism, although today independent and autonomous, tend to reflect British Methodism, while those developing from American missionary activity bear the marks of American Methodism. This pattern is especially seen in church governance.

The highest authority in the Methodist Church in America is the General Conference, which meets every four years. To cite one example, the large United Methodist Church is organized into five regional jurisdictions, each containing a large number of conferences. The year before the General Conference, the 66 conferences of the United States and all the international central Conferences that are connected with the U.S. church elect delegates to the church's Quadrennial Conference. Here legislation is made for the church and a new Book of Discipline is published, containing any changes enacted within the past four years. The General Conference is composed of 1,000 delegates. A few weeks following the General Conference, five jurisdictional conferences meet. Here bishops are elected and, through appointed committees, are assigned to the episcopal areas they shall serve, which may have one or more conferences. In America bishops are elected for life, but some churches with roots in the American tradition in other parts of the world have term episcopacy.

4.2. *Mission*

From its inception Methodism has been a missionary movement and has been in the forefront as a missionary-sending church. Agencies centered in London, New York, and Nashville have sent missionaries to every part of the world. Through this missionary enterprise Methodist churches were quickly established in southern and central Africa, Australia, India, China, South America, Oceania, and other world regions.

In the 40 years between 1956 and 1996, the growth of Methodist churches worldwide was very uneven. During this period membership in Africa grew 449 percent, in Asia 690 percent, and in Latin America 783 percent. In North America, however, membership declined by 4 percent, and in Europe by 41 percent (*World Methodist Council Handbook of Information* [1997]). Trends in growth and loss of membership since 1996 have followed a similar pattern.

Some denominations belonging to the → World Methodist Council are international in character. These bodies are the United Methodist Church, Wesleyan Church, Free Methodist Church, Church of the Nazarene, and three historic black denominations — the African Methodist Episcopal, African Methodist Episcopal Zion, and Christian Methodist Episcopal Churches. Each of these churches has congregations in more than one region of the world.

In other cases, churches once connected with a parent body have become fully independent. The British Methodist Church, for example, has 17 partner churches in all parts of the world that are the result of British Methodist mission endeavor but today are fully independent. Once receiving missionaries, these churches now have their own programs of missionary outreach.

4.3. International Bodies

Over the past 50 years "families" of Christian churches have assumed an important place in world Christianity. Officially known as → Christian World Communions, these families of churches include Adventists, Anglicans, Baptists, Brethren, Friends, Lutherans, Mennonites, Methodists, Moravians, Orthodox, Reformed, Roman Catholics, Salvation Army, and others. More than 20 such families are represented in the the Annual Conference of Secretaries of Christian World Communions, which has met every year since 1958.

The world communion for Methodists was conceived and began with a historic first "Oecumenical Methodist Conference," held at historic Wesley's Chapel, London, in 1881. At this conference 400 representatives from 30 separate churches from around the world met to assess the Methodist movement over the past 100 years and to look toward the future. From that time the Oecumenical Methodist Conference has met at regular intervals. Coinciding with the birth of the → World Council of Churches in 1948, the Methodist body changed its name to the World Methodist Council, believing the word "ecumenical" should belong rather to the World Council of Churches. The World Methodist Council has its international headquarters at Lake Junaluska, North Carolina. It also maintains a secretary and office in the Ecumenical Center in Switzerland.

As a World Communion the World Methodist Council seeks to link its member churches — 78, as of 2001 — in areas of common concern and work; spread the good news of Jesus Christ through world evangelism; support human reconciliation, seeking to create conditions that foster human community

and world → peace; and pursue unity in the faith through engagement and → dialogue with other Christian World Communions, believing that the faith Methodist people share with other Christians is greater than the differences that separate Christians. Congregations belonging to the council's member denominations are found in 130 countries of the world. These churches have 36 million members with a constituency of more than 70 million persons.

4.4. Ecumenism

Methodist and World Methodist Council–related United Churches are known for their participation in and support for other Christian churches and councils. Methodist churches were founding members of the World Council of Churches and have participated in the organization of local ecumenical councils. Prominent Methodists have also served as presidents of the World Council of Churches, and two have been elected WCC general secretaries.

In ecumenical organizations Methodists generally bear a proportionate or larger share of the financial support and take an active part in the implementation of agreed upon ecumenical goals and objectives.

Bibliography: Reference works: N. B. HARMON, ed., *Encyclopedia of World Methodism* (2 vols.; Nashville, Tenn., 1974) • J. A. VICKERS, ed., *A Dictionary of Methodism in Britain and Ireland* (Peterborough, Eng., 2000) • C. YRIGOYEN and S. E. WARRICK, eds., *Historical Dictionary of Methodism* (Lanham, Md., 1996).

John Wesley: K. J. COLLINS, *A Real Christian: The Life of John Wesley* (Nashville, 1999) • R. P. HEITZENRATER, *The Elusive Mr. Wesley* (2 vols.; Nashville, 1984); idem, *Wesley and the People Called Methodists* (Nashville, 1995) • T. C. ODEN, *John Wesley's Scriptural Christianity: A Plain Exposition of His Teaching on Christian Doctrine* (Grand Rapids, 1994) • *The Works of John Wesley* (35 vols.; ed. F. Baker et al.; Nashville, 1984) the "Bicentennial Ed."

History: D. ANDREWS, *The Methodists and Revolutionary America, 1760-1800: The Shaping of an Evangelical Culture* (Princeton, 2000) • F. A. DREYER, *The Genesis of Methodism* (Bethlehem, Pa., 1999) • D. HEMPTON, *The Religion of the People: Methodism and Popular Religion, c. 1750-1900* (London, 1996) • J. E. KIRBY, *The Episcopacy in American Methodism* (Nashville, 2000) • R. E. RICHEY, *Early American Methodism* (Bloomington, Ind., 1991); idem, *The Methodist Conference in America: A History* (Nashville, 1996) • J. M. SCHMIDT, *Grace Sufficient: A History of Women in American Methodism, 1760-1939* (Nashville, 1999) • A. G. SCHNEIDER, *The Way of the Cross Leads Home: The Domestication of*

American Methodism (Bloomington, Ind., 1993) • J. H. WIGGER, *Taking Heaven by Storm: Methodism and the Rise of Popular Christianity in America* (New York, 1998).

Other works: T. CAMPBELL, *Methodist Doctrine: The Essentials* (Nashville, 1999) • J. CRASKE and C. MARSH, eds., *Methodism and the Future* (London, 1999) • J. E. KIRBY, R. E. RICHEY, and K. E. ROWE, *The Methodists* (Westport, Conn., 1996) • T. A. LANGFORD, *Methodist Theology* (London, 1998) • W. B. LAWRENCE, D. M. CAMPBELL, and R. E. RICHEY, *The People(s) Called Methodist: Forms and Reforms of Their Life* (Nashville, 1998) • R. L. MADDOX, ed., *Rethinking Wesley's Theology for Contemporary Methodism* (Nashville, 1998) • R. E. RICHEY, D. M. CAMPBELL, and W. B. LAWRENCE, *Connectionalism: Ecclesiology, Mission, and Identity* (Nashville, 1997) • G. S. WAKEFIELD, *Methodist Spirituality* (London, 1999).

JOE HALE

Mexico

	1960	1980	2000
Population (1,000s):	36,945	67,570	98,881
Annual growth rate (%):	3.10	2.21	1.42
Area: 1,958,201 sq. km. (756,066 sq. mi.)			

A.D. *2000*

Population density: 50/sq. km. (131/sq. mi.)
Births / deaths: 2.22 / 0.51 per 100 population
Fertility rate: 2.49 per woman
Infant mortality rate: 28 per 1,000 live births
Life expectancy: 73.4 years (m: 70.4, f: 76.4)
Religious affiliation (%): Christians 96.0 (Roman Catholics 93.0, indigenous 3.3, Protestants 3.1, marginal 2.2, unaffiliated 1.2, other Christians 0.1), nonreligious 3.3, other 0.7.

1. General Situation
2. Christian Churches
   2.1. Roman Catholics
   2.2. Protestants
   2.3. Pentecostals
3. Ecumenical Aspects
4. Church and State
5. Non-Christian Religions

1. General Situation

The United Mexican States is the second largest and second most populated country in Latin America, behind Brazil. Mexicans are an ethnic mix (Sp. *mestizaje*) of whites, native Indians, and blacks. There is also a white minority, as well as indigenous minorities (e.g., Mayas, Otomís, Tojolobales, Chamulas, Lakandones, Tzotziles, Tzeltales, and Huicholes) who make up between 10 and 20 percent of the population. Politically, Mexico is a federal republic with 31 states and 1 federal district. It became a parliamentary democracy when the Partido Revolucionario Institucional (PRI, Institutional Revolutionary Party) took over the government in 1929. In the 1988 presidential election the PRI for the first time failed to gain an absolute majority.

The PRI's increasing loss of political influence accelerated during the following years, beginning when several of the federation states came under the control of opposition parties, including the Partido Acción Nacional (PAN, National Action Party). The serious economic crisis accompanying the end of the six-year term of Carlos Salinas de Gortari in 1993, along with a Zapatista rebellion in Chiapas, accelerated these developments, leading to the victory of PAN and its candidate, Vicente Fox, in the presidential elections of July 2000. This election signaled the end of a hegemony that had lasted 71 years and the beginnings of political pluralism.

The history of Mexico is usually divided into the following epochs: pre-Spanish cultures (up to 1521), Spanish colonial period (1521-1821; → Colonialism), and federal republic (1821 to the present), with the empires of Iturbide (1822-23) and the French Hapsburg Maximilian (1864-67) as interludes. Two significant developments under the republic were the liberal reforms of Benito Juárez (1806-72) in 1857, which produced a constitution and guaranteed fundamental rights, and the collapse of the oligarchic regime of Porfirio Díaz (1830-1915) in 1911, which initiated a middle-class democratic → revolution. The revolution reached a climax in 1917, with a constitution that included progressive articles on property and labor.

To understand modern Mexico, we must grasp the nationalist → ideology that since the revolution has been oriented to the concept of the *mestizaje,* the mixture of three cultures (native, Roman Catholic Creole, and lay republican), and that has found expression in the art of the revolution, especially the muralists (Diego Rivera, Clemente Orozco, and David Siqueiros), and the literature (Carlos Fuentes, Octavio Paz, and Juan Rulfo).

2. Christian Churches

At the coming of the Spaniards the territory of modern Mexico was a mosaic of contending ethnic groups, among whom the Aztecs and their capital, Tenochtitlán, played the leading part. With the capture of the Aztec capital in 1521 by Hernán Cortés

(1485-1547), the way opened for comprehensive Christianizing of these peoples by the → missionaries who accompanied the conquerors (→ Mission). Churches were built on the pyramids, and Christianity strengthened the spiritual and political unity of New Spain. During the colonial period and even after independence from Spain up to the victory of → liberalism under Juárez, Roman Catholicism was the only permitted religion. Since the introduction of → religious liberty by the law of December 4, 1860, new religious fellowships, mainly Protestant, have gradually established themselves.

2.1. *Roman Catholics*

The first missionaries to New Spain were the → Franciscans, soon followed by → Dominicans (1526), → Augustinians (1533), Mercedarians (1537), and → Jesuits (1585). Conflicts between the regular clergy (who were Erasmians) and the secular clergy at both the parish and the diocesan level marked the early period. A colonial church finally resulted (→ Colonialism and Mission). Crown control by means of → patronage helped to shape the structure and hierarchy (decided in the Mexico City councils, 1555-85; → Latin American Councils 1; Diocese). At first some → bishops defended the Indians, especially Bartolomé de Las Casas (1484-1566) in Chiapas and Vasco de Quiroga (1470-1565) in Michoacán, but by the 17th and 18th centuries the bishops were defending the colonial order and helping the Spanish and white minority to maintain control over the Creoles, mestizos, and Indians.

The colonial regime promoted the building of churches and → monasteries. The church sponsored schools, hospitals, and philanthropic work and also had an influence on → culture both among the people with the cult of the Virgin of Guadalupe (based on four appearances in 1531 to the Indian Juan Diego; → Mary, Devotion to, 3) and among the educated with the work of scholars like Sister Juana Inés de la Cruz (1651-95).

The Roman Catholic leadership opposed the fight for independence, but members of the lower clergy like Miguel Hidalgo (1753-1811) and José María Morelos (1765-1815) became advocates and instigators. When the republic was set up, the church profited from the right of patronage, which now went to the independent state. The Liberals then began to attack autonomous bodies like the army, Indian communes, and especially the Roman Catholic Church as a political and economic power. Reforming laws passed between 1856 and 1860 brought separation between → church and state and weakened the power of the church, but they left intact its intellectual and cultural influence. As a result of the

politics of reconciliation under Porfirio Díaz between 1876 and 1911, the church succeeded in rebuilding its organization and establishing afresh its position. The solemn crowning of the Virgin of Guadalupe in 1895 climaxed this development.

At the same time, on the basis of the encyclical *Rerum novarum* of Leo XIII (1878-1903), the church in Mexico began social work among the working classes and the rural population. Several social congresses followed in the early 20th century. The strongly anticlerical and Jacobinic elements in the revolution found expression in the 1917 constitution and led later to the Cristero Rebellion (1926-29) as a reaction of the people to the anticlericalist regime of Elías Calles (1924-28). Even under Lázaro Cárdenas (1934-40) attacks on the church continued with an attempt to introduce a socialist and atheistic school system.

After 1940 the church won back the political and social ground that the revolution had contested. Mutual respect between church and state became the rule and until the present contributes to the social and political stability of the country. The bishops of Chiapas, Tehuantepec, Tarahumara, and Morelos have radicalized their work under the influence of → liberation theology, while the majority hold the reforming position advocated by the former primate of Mexico, Cardinal Corripio Ahumada (archbishop of Mexico City, 1977-94).

2.2. *Protestants*

The historic Protestant churches in Mexico are the product of North American missionary efforts (→ North American Missions), which began in 1869. There were hopes at the time of a Roman Catholic schism on the basis of the unsuccessful struggles in 1861 and 1867 of a small group of Mexican priests who supported the liberal constitution of 1857. (These priests were later excommunicated and established a Mexican Catholic church independent of Rome.) By making common cause with existing leaders and breakaway congregations, the missionary societies of the great North American denominations set up Methodist (→ Methodist Churches), Baptist (→ Baptists), Presbyterian (→ Reformed and Presbyterian Churches), Congregational (→ Congregationalism), and Episcopal churches. These churches recruited members from mobile social groups (wage earners, casual workers, and small property owners of the Liberal tradition). They offered educational programs for the children (primary and secondary schools), plus trade schools and theological seminaries.

The formation of an elite by → education and the vital Liberal tradition favored the growth of

Protestant groups, which were against the policy of reconciliation under Porfirio Díaz and joined the Liberal opposition. This fact explains the strong participation of Protestant leaders in the revolution and the recruiting of these groups by the regimes of Venustiano Carranza (1914-20) and Elías Calles, especially for the Department of Education with Andrés Osuna (1872-1955), a Methodist, and Moisés Sáenz (1888-1941), a Presbyterian. By 1910 this historic Protestantism had some 100,000 members and sympathizers. Despite attempts at unity and compromises with the social programs of the revolution, however, it grew thereafter only very slowly. It still had some importance because of its leading role, but it ultimately came to represent only a minority among Protestants, who for the most part are politically and socially → conservative.

Several → faith missions began work in Mexico between 1920 and 1930 as missions to the Indians. We may note especially the Pioneer Mission Agency in the district of Huasteca and the Instituto Ligüístico de Verano (Summer Institute of Linguistics, in conjunction with the Wycliffe Bible Translators), who came in 1935 with the support of the regime of General Cárdenas. Along with its linguistic work and translations into the native languages, this latter group engaged in missionary activity that came under severe criticism from anthropologists in the 1970s and resulted in the government canceling the contract that allowed it to do educational work among the Indians. From the 1960s onward new faith societies arose, especially those working among students (e.g., the Cruzada Estudiantil para Cristo, the Mexican branch of the U.S.-based Campus Crusade for Christ). Like their predecessors, these missions had strong fundamentalist and anti-Communist tendencies (→ Fundamentalism; Evangelical Missions).

2.3. Pentecostals

→ Pentecostal churches arrived in Mexico in 1910 with agricultural workers returning from the southern United States, but they made little impact before the 1950s. Then, however, the settling of thousands of peasants in the cities as the result of comprehensive economic changes by the government favored the spread of the movement, which seemed to hold out an answer to the feeling of loss of → identity and → anonymity among these → marginal suburban groups.

Today some 80 percent of Mexican Protestants belong to Pentecostal churches (Assemblies of God, Church of God, Church of the Light of the World, Apostolic Church, and others). Their success may be traced to (1) their use of healing rites and of → glossolalia, which resemble traditional → shamanistic

practices, and (2) their → millenarianism and their opposing of the traditional village caciques (i.e., persons of great local, regional, or national influence gained through common-law authority because of family or status). A further factor has been the destruction of the political, economic, and ideological monopoly anchored in the system of popular Roman Catholic festivals.

Official statistics show that Protestantism (including the Pentecostals) is growing proportionately faster than the population as a whole. From a mere 0.38 percent of the population in 1900, the percentage of Protestants roughly doubled by 1930 (0.79 percent) and then by 1960 (1.66 percent) had doubled again. The next 30 years saw a nearly threefold growth (to 4.89 percent).

3. Ecumenical Aspects

The North American missionary societies have used different ways of trying to correct the critical situation resulting from competition and Roman Catholic opposition (e.g., the Protestant conferences of 1888 and 1892). It was only after the Congress on Christian Work in Latin America, meeting in Ancon, Panama, in 1916, that Mexico was divided into specific areas of work. Common theological institutions and press organs were created, thus lightening the financial burden. These first beginnings were followed by discussions on the creation of an evangelical Mexican church, though without success. In 1929 the Concilio Evangélico de México was founded, with the limited function of defending Protestant interests in cases of conflict or persecution. Protestants today are split up into dozens of groups, and there is no serious attempt at unity.

Relations between Protestants and Roman Catholics have been tense ever since Protestantism first entered the country with Liberal support. The hierarchy tends to denounce the propaganda of other Christian groups, whom it labels sects, and whose increasingly active presence it sees as a threat to its own claim to hegemony. Some radicalized Protestant groups (including some Anabaptist-type groups, plus those sympathetic to the ecumenical movement) have linked hands with radicalized Roman Catholic groups in liberation theology, though their significance is small compared to that of the Protestant and Roman Catholic leadership.

4. Church and State

From the time that Liberals took over (1856) and during the active years of the revolution (1914-40), relations between the Roman Catholic Church and the state were tense. After 1940 a modus vivendi was achieved that facilitates mutual respect. Relations between Protestants and the state have always been good. They were especially so in the phases of emphatic state anti-Catholicism and Jacobinism (1914-40).

Without calling into question the secular state, diplomatic relations were reestablished in 1992 with the Vatican, and the constitution's discriminatory anticlerical articles were modified. An office of undersecretary of religion was created that immediately demonstrated the state's provision for voluntary regulation in religious matters in a context of increasing religious pluralization. In the meantime, now that PAN has access to power, the Roman Catholic Church seems to have recovered a certain public presence that, during the hegemony of the PRI, had been threatened and kept in check. An element of religious intolerance in ethical matters relating to sexuality and the family in particular has emerged.

5. Non-Christian Religions

Various non-Christian groups have established themselves in Mexico. The most important are the → Mormons, with settlements in Chihuahua from 1920. Others include → Jehovah's Witnesses, → Bahai'is, Hare → Krishna, and the → spiritism of Allan Kardec. Among the rural population we also find forms of religious → syncretism linking pre-Hispanic religions to → popular Catholicism. One such cult is that of the priestess María Sabina in the Sierra Mazateca in the state of Oaxaca. In addition, at the end of the 20th century various neoindigenous cults (e.g., neo-Aztec and neo-Mayan) have emerged, sometimes with considerable followings, especially in historical locales associated with the pre-Columbian period.

→ Latin American Theology

Bibliography: History, culture, politics: A. A. Alves, Brutality and Benevolence: Human Ethology, Culture, and the Birth of Mexico (Westport, Conn., 1996) • C. Esteva-Fabregat, Mestizaje in Ibero-America (Tucson, Ariz., 1995) • R. Hassig, Time, History, and Belief in Aztec and Colonial Mexico (Austin, Tex., 2001) • G. M. Joseph, A. Rubenstein, and E. Zolof, Fragments of a Golden Age: The Politics of Culture in Mexico since 1940 (Durham, N.C., 2001) • J. Lafaye, Quetzalcóatl y Guadalupe. La formation de la conscience nationale au Mexique (Paris, 1974) • M. C. Meyer and W. L. Sherman, The Course of Mexican History (4th ed.; New York, 1991) • L. Stephen, Zapata Lives: Local Histories, Nation Views, and Politics in Southern Mexico (Berkeley, Calif., 2001).

Religion, churches: J. Adame Godard, El pensi-miento político y social de los católicos mexicanos (Mexico City, 1981) • D. J. Baldwin, Protestants and the Mexican Revolution: Missionaries, Ministers, and Social Change (Urbana, Ill., 1990) • D. B. Barrett et al., eds., WCE (2d ed.) 1.494-500 • J.-P. Bastian, Los disidentes. Sociedades protestantes y revolución en México, 1872-1911 (Mexico City, 1989); idem, Protestantismo y sociedad en México (Mexico City, 1984) • K. Bowen, Evangelism and Apostasy: The Evolution and Impact of Evangelicals in Modern Mexico (Montreal, 1996) • D. A. Brading, Mexican Phoenix: Our Lady of Guadalupe. Image and Tradition, 1531-2000 (New York, 2001) • K. D. Gill, Toward a Contextualized Theology for the Third World: The Emergence and Development of Jesus' Name Pentecostalism in Mexico (Frankfurt, 1994) • G. W. Grayson, The Church in Contemporary Mexico (Washington, D.C., 1992) • T. G. Powell, "Priests and Peasants in Central Mexico: Social Conflict during 'La Reforma,'" Hispanic American Historical Review 57 (1977) 296-313 • R. E. Quirk, The Mexican Revolution and the Catholic Church, 1910-1929 (Westport, Conn., 1986) • R. Richard, "Church-State Relations and the Mexican Constitutional Congress, 1916-1917," JChS 20 (1978) 73-80.

Jean-Pierre Bastian

Micah, Book of

1. Man and Date
2. Contents and Redaction
3. Theology and Message

1. Man and Date

Micah was from Moresheth-gath in the Judean hill country. He was also active in → Jerusalem. He was a younger contemporary of Isaiah, and his message is similar. He prophesied between 734 and 712 B.C. Nothing is known of his status. He has been described as a poor farmer, a worker on the land, and a village landowner or elder (H. W. Wolff).

2. Contents and Redaction

The book is divided into three parts (chaps. 1–2, 3–5, 6–7) and carries a message structured according to the schema of disaster and → salvation. Scholars dispute how much comes from Micah himself. They agree as to the sayings in chap. 1 (at least from v. 6), chap. 2 (apart from vv. 12-13), and chap. 3. Most of the material in chaps. 4–7 derives from later periods. Even the Micah traditions in 1–3 underwent → Deuteronomistic revision and updating during the exile (J. Jeremias, Wolff). All the → promises of salvation in chaps. 4–5 are from this period.

Perhaps the liturgical editing was influenced by liturgical laments from the context of exilic or postexilic celebrations in Jerusalem in which prophets of salvation performed (Wolff). Although the accusations and announcements of disaster in 6:1–7:7 pick up on themes used by Micah, they probably date from the postexilic period and reflect abuses of that time. The conclusion, a → liturgy or psalm-sequence (7:8-20), contains the response of the community. It can be traced to a final liturgical redaction.

3. Theology and Message

The primary message of Micah is almost exclusively one of judgment, first against Samaria, then especially against Judah and Jerusalem. Social criticism predominates the accusations. As an advocate of the socially weak, Micah, like Amos and Isaiah, attacks their oppression by the upper classes, especially as regards land rights. The social complaint culminates in the announcement of the devastation of Jerusalem (3:12), which was quoted in Jeremiah's day (Jer. 26:18). Exilic interpreters who had themselves experienced that judgment now introduced their own expectations of salvation into the book. Postexilic redaction updated Micah's social message for its own situation.

→ Minor Prophets; Prophet, Prophecy

Bibliography: Commentaries: E. Ben Zvi (FOTL; Grand Rapids, 2000) • A. Deissler (NEchtB; Würzburg, 1984) • D. R. Hillers (Hermeneia; Philadelphia, 1984) • R. Kessler (HTKNT; Freiburg, 1999) • W. McKane (Edinburgh, 1998) • D. J. Simundson (NIB; Nashville, 1996) • H. W. Wolff (BKAT; Neukirchen, 1982); idem (Minneapolis, 1990).

Other works: M. Broshi, "The Expansion of Jerusalem in the Reigns of Hezekiah and Manasseh," *IEJ* 24 (1924) 21-26 • J. Jeremias, "Die Deutung der Gerichtsworte Michas in der Exilszeit," *ZAW* 83 (1971) 330-54 • I. Willi-Plein, *Vorformen der Schriftexegese innerhalb des Alten Testaments* (Berlin, 1971).

WINFRIED THIEL

Middle Ages

1. Church History

1.1. *Terminology*

In his → theology of history Joachim of Fiore (d. 1202) referred to his own age as the *media aetas* (middle age) of the Son of God, between the past age of the Father and the coming age of the Spirit. Not until → humanism, however, do we find the idea, albeit negative, of a period between antiquity and → renaissance. Johannes Andreae of Aleria (1417-75) spoke of the *media tempestas* (middle time) in a 1469 letter. Christopher Cellarius (1638-1707), especially in his *Historia medii aevi* (1688), gave the concept wider circulation. The more negative "Dark Ages" derived from philology (the decay of Latin), Protestant historiography (the decline of

Christianity), and the → Enlightenment. In contrast, → Romanticism idealized medieval life and → religion.

In the 19th century historical studies focused especially on national history and the editing of diplomatic and historiographical sources, for which special institutions and series (e.g., Monumenta Germaniae Historica, Rerum Britannicarum Scriptores) were established. By the end of the century this field was well mined, and attention shifted to economic, social, and cultural history. Under French influence in particular, scholarly inquiry turned to the history of mentalities.

Despite the negative connotation that still clings to the term "medieval" in everyday usage, there has been an enhanced interest in the period, visible in the success of medieval themes in literature and cinema (e.g., Umberto Eco's *Name of the Rose*), the acceptance of works in the field as textbooks, the interest in medieval music, and so forth. The division into early, high, and late Middle Ages, which follows a biological model of growth, blossoming, and decay (→ Evolution), corresponds to a pervasive attraction to triads in characterizing epochs. We might just as well speak of two periods, with the vast material and intellectual changes of 1050-1150 serving as transition. Essential economic, social, and intellectual features of the Middle Ages also persisted into the 18th century, and thus other writers use such terms as "Old Europe" or "age of feudalism" to characterize an even longer span of premodern Europe.

1.2. Early Middle Ages (late 4th–mid-11th cent.)

1.2.1. Foundations

With the end of the tribal migrations, new kingdoms arose in Europe introducing different forms of life and settlement. In southern and western Europe the original Mediterranean unity had been disrupted, and the cities declined in size. Yet the influence of the comprehensive organization of the Roman Empire and urban civilization lingered as ethnic and cultural fusion took place between the subjugated Romans and Celts and the victorious Germanic tribes. In the rural eastern and northern regions, there were isolated and, for the most part, economically autonomous settlements. The population shrank, then slowly rose again (est. at around 17 million in A.D. 300, down to 12 million in 600, up to 24 million in 1000). The spread of Roman Christianity (→ Mission 3), along with the cultural legacy of Rome, was a determinative factor in a relatively uniform Western development, with Latin as the medium of communication.

1.2.2. Political Development

With the Merovingian and Carolingian dynasties, the Frankish kingdom became the most important political force, taking over the empire with the crowning of Charlemagne (ruled 768-814) in A.D. 800. Frankish rule extended from what is modern-day northeastern Spain to Denmark, the Danube, and central Italy. In the so-called Carolingian renaissance some centers such as Aachen and Reichenau saw a flowering of art and culture, with the building of palaces and monasteries. After the death of Charlemagne in 814, the empire fragmented, and the east (modern-day Germany) took the lead politically and militarily, with power centered in a dukedom embracing Saxony, Bavaria, Swabia, and Lotharingia.

After 919 the kings came from the Saxon house (the Ottonian dynasty); after 1024 the Frankish Salians ruled. Incursions into Italian politics, power struggles between the nobility and the elected monarchy, and conflicts with Slavic subjects and neighbors dominated political engagements in this period. In the western Frankish kingdom the later Carolingians and Capetians (after 987) struggled to hold their own against the great feudal lords. In Anglo-Saxon England, which was partly under Danish rule, Alfred the Great, king of Wessex (871-99), played a role like that of Charlemagne, staving off the Danes and fostering the arts and religion.

Until the 10th century Europe was still prey to invasions that church sources (the only extant testimony) refer to as incursions of the heathen (→ Gentiles; Gentile Christianity) into *Christianitas*. Beginning in the late 8th century, the Vikings from the north not only landed on the coasts but also sailed inland up the rivers, attacking London in 841 and coming to the gates of Paris in 887/88. The Norman Vikings took over whole territories — Normandy, then England, southern Italy, and Russia — but they assimilated themselves quickly after accepting Christianity. In the south Arabs subjugated the Iberian Peninsula after 711. They came as far as Poitiers in 732 and St. Moritz in 940 and ruled Sicily from 827 to 1091. The Magyars started coming east in the 9th century, reaching Orléans in 937, but after a decisive defeat by Otto I (emp. 936-73) at Lechfeld in 955, they embraced Christianity in 1000. Only at the beginning of the second millennium did the situation begin to settle down as the Peace of God movement, which limited warfare to combatants and to specific periods (→ Peace 2.2.3), helped to check the innumerable domestic feuds.

These upheavals, the constant conflict between local lords, the pressure of state claims (e.g., to military service), and the general sense of insecurity all contributed to the development of feudal networks. Free peasants swore allegiance to counts or abbots in order to secure protection and often received land in lease. As vassals they had to perform services and make payments. Most of the population came under this system by the end of the early Middle Ages. Independent nobles also swore allegiance to the kings. The remnants of the Roman senatorial class and officeholders under the Germanic kings constituted a new nobility subject to the kings or dukes, who, by acclamation and Christian → consecration, were regarded as divinely appointed (sacral kingship).

1.2.3. *Church*

The nobles appointed the ecclesiastical → hierarchy of → bishops, → abbots, and abbesses (among whom were almost all the early medieval saints). The nobles founded churches, appointed dependents as → priests, and took over the titles that were due them. Proprietors could sell, donate, or share → churches with their lands. Pope Eugenius II (824-27) sanctioned the → proprietary church system in 826. Emperors and kings also invested bishops, often their own relatives, wherever they could. This system, especially under Otto and his successors, functioned by the emperor's enlarging the holdings of imperial bishops and abbots in return for their pledges of military and financial services. The archbishop of Mainz held a particularly exalted position within the system as supreme chancellor.

The Carolingian alliance with the papacy in overthrowing the Merovingians (and thus the substitution of Christian consecration for blood relationship in imperial succession), the efforts of Archbishop Boniface of Mainz (722-54) to link the Frankish church closely to Rome, and the creation of the Donation of Constantine (Constantine's supposed handing over of all the imperial insignia and the Western empire to the → pope) would suggest the power of the papacy in this period. Yet, popes could hardly make good any claims to dominion. In 754 Pope Stephen II (752-57) sought Pepin's aid because, left in the lurch by Byzantium, the pope could not protect himself against the Lombards.

The Italian campaigns of Pepin, which established the → Papal States, began a series of Roman campaigns that influenced the relationship between the empire and the papacy. In 799 Pope Leo III (795-816) fled to Charlemagne at Paderborn, and in 800 he did homage on his knees to the emperor, whom he crowned. In theological controversies Charlemagne's opinions carried more weight than the pope's (e.g., in the Iconoclastic Controversy over → images in 790-94 and the *filioque* controversy in

809). Even the proclamation of the pope as lord of the earth in the mid-9th century in the Pseudo-Isidorian Decretals forged at Rheims (→ False Decretals), which sought to make Frankish bishops independent of metropolitans, → synods, and secular powers, could not prevent the Ottonians or the Salians and their armies from deciding who would ascend the chair of Peter and what policies he would follow. In 1046 Emperor Henry III deposed three rival popes and appointed a reformist successor.

Anglo-Saxon England came under papal jurisdiction with its conversion in the sixth century and the assimilation of the north at the Synod of Whitby in 664. The Viking raids to some extent broke the link with Rome after 793, however, and brought about a decline — except for the period under Alfred — until reform efforts in the tenth century. The Norman Conquest of 1066 was supported by Pope Alexander II (1061-73), who defended the legality of William's claim to the English throne. William (d. 1087) invaded England under the banner of St. Peter, and after replacing the Anglo-Saxon hierarchy by Normans, he linked the English church more closely to Rome, though with firm reservations regarding royal prerogatives.

1.2.4. *Everyday Life*

Everyday life was not deeply permeated by church ideals and practices. Parishes north of the Alps were large. As late as the 11th century, cities the size of Cologne or Antwerp ranked as single parishes. Since the conversion of many of the peoples was not by individual decision but at the command of rulers (the Franks) or by force (the Saxons; → Germanic Mission), attachment to pre-Christian notions remained strong. Conciliar documents and penitentials are full of complaints about this matter, as are the letters of Boniface. Whether Charlemagne's efforts to intensify the religious life of the people had as much success as his efforts on behalf of court schools is open to question. He required on pain of punishment that everyone should at least know the → Lord's Prayer and the creed. Monastic lay abbacies were the decisive cultural force in the early Middle Ages — testimony to the fact that → sacred and profane had not yet been sharply divided along clergy/lay lines.

1.3. *High Middle Ages*
(*mid-11th–early 13th cent.*)
1.3.1. *Foundations*

More favorable weather, better agricultural → technology, and the end of raids from outside brought about a substantial increase in the population of Europe (60 million est. in 1200), which enabled expansion in the High Middle Ages. The nobles organized the clearance of land for new settlements, and Germanic settlers moved into Slavic territory (→ Slavic Mission). In Spain the Muslims were pushed back in the *reconquista,* and the land was resettled by Christians. Cities developed rapidly, especially in Italy and the Netherlands, either by denser settlement or by extension. Other economically progressive developments include the practices of the → Cistercians: their property management by monks and conversi, exchanging experiences at the General Chapter, exact bookkeeping, granges, water and mining technology, and trading in the cities (→ Monastery).

Society became more integrated and complex. From the 10th century on, service at court or as administrators enabled possibilities of upward mobility for the formerly not free or not noble (e.g., castellans and the German officials of the great lords). With professional warriors active and civilians forbidden to bear arms, a knightly class developed with its own lifestyle. With the → Crusades and the establishment of military orders, the church tried with some success to imbue this class with Christian ideals. Citizens, many of them organized in guilds, freed themselves from city rulers (bishops or counts) by revolts or purchase, coming more closely under the direct rule of the Crown. The academic systematizing of theology (→ Scholasticism) and → canon law, which gave it no less force than the gospel (Hugh of St.-Victor, *Quaest. in ep. Pauli* 295 [*PL* 175.504]; Gratian's *Decretum* [1140]; → CIC), consolidated the status of the clergy as a separate → class. Monastic life was diversified with the establishment of new orders for men and women in the 11th to the 13th centuries (→ Religious Orders and Congregations).

1.3.2. *Political Development*

In general, states became more territorial and less personal than in the early Middle Ages. The → Investiture Controversy, further battles between the spiritual and secular powers, rivalry between the nobility and the Crown, and German interference in Italian politics all contributed to constant political tension. The Hohenstauffen (1137-1254) were particularly involved, most of all Frederick I Barbarossa (emp. 1152-90). After Emperor Frederick II (1215-50), who concentrated on Italy, and an interval without an emperor, the German states increased their power at the expense of the central authority. With Rudolf I (1273-91) the Hapsburgs rose to power; they reigned, with breaks, until 1806.

Along with the empire the national states in the West became stronger. The French kings systematically built up royal holdings. They were often at war with the English kings, who had extensive feudal territories on the Continent. Louis VII (ruled 1137-80), the "most Christian king," supported the pope and to this end achieved control over the national church. Louis IX (1214-70), or St. Louis, made France a flourishing state with good law and well-organized government.

England, under Norman rule since 1066, had its own investiture conflict (William Rufus [1087-1100] and → Anselm). The Plantagenets came to power in 1154, and in trying to bring the clergy under criminal law, Henry II (ruled 1154-89) entered into the struggle with Thomas Becket, which he lost with the latter's assassination. The misrule of John (1199-1216) resulted in the enhanced power of the barons and a declaration of the liberties of the English church at the signing of the Magna Carta in 1215. John's capitulation to the papacy, however, opened the door to a period of unrest that pitted church and barons against Crown and papacy.

1.3.3. *Church*

The long-expected split between the churches of East and West finally occurred in 1054 when the → patriarch of Constantinople and papal legates excommunicated each other (→ Byzantium; → Heresies and Schisms 3). Strengthened by imperial interference (Synod of Sutri, in 1046), monastic reforming ideals (→ Cluny, Order of) took root in the papacy; a decree was promulgated in 1059 that tried to limit the role of the Roman nobility and the emperor in the election of popes. Gregorian reforms mandated priestly → celibacy, which had been long prescribed, and forbade simony and lay investiture. Resistance to these efforts shattered the ancient unity of the church and the world (→ Empire and Papacy).

The (unpublished) *Dictatus papae* of 1074/75 reflects the views of → Gregory VII (1073-85) on the supremacy of his papal office vis-à-vis both the empire and the bishops. He claimed automatic sanctity for each properly ordained successor of Peter, the subjection of all secular powers and all other bishops to the Roman pontiff, papal exemption from any other jurisdiction, the infallibility of the Roman church, and other prerogatives. This unenforceable line of thinking was taken up again by → Innocent III (1198-1216), then by Boniface VIII (1294-1303), and finally by → Pius IX (1846-78, esp. in the → infallibility [§3] dogma of 1870).

Monastic reform in the 12th century produced many important popes, but the ideals of the influential Bernard of Clairvaux (1090-1153) never fully came into practice. In his *De consideratione* (3.11) to Pope Eugenius III (1145-53), Bernard stated plainly that the apostles prohibited ruling and commanded serving. The papacy, however, did not restrict itself to spiritual matters. It found in legal administration an important means of regulating temporal matters as well. Already under Eugenius III, and more so under Alexander III (1159-81), the → curia became the setting for innumerable lawsuits that brought both petitioners and money from all parts of Christendom to Rome.

Innocent III styled himself as "less than God and more than man." He claimed dominion not only over the universal church but also over all the earth. Under him the actual power of the papacy reached its height. The kings of Aragon, Sicily, England, Poland, and Portugal became his lieges. He also frequently intervened in matters such as the succession to the empire. The church's hierarchy was still largely drawn from the nobility, but now increasingly from the administrative class as well. Within the politically ambitious and bureaucratically complex church, new models of holiness developed, including → discipleship through → poverty and union with Christ through → mysticism.

The attempt of Boniface VIII in the late 13th and early 14th centuries to repeat the successes of Innocent III resulted in disaster. His stand on the matter of clergy taxation brought him into conflict with the powerful kings of England and France. His bull *Unam sanctam* of 1302, which asserted dominion over the temporal as well as the spiritual sphere and made salvation dependent on union with Rome, precipitated the crisis of 1303, when he was arrested, imprisoned, and discredited.

The Crusades took many aggressive younger men to the Holy Land, where they established crusading states from 1099 to 1291. As a result, some pacification came to Europe, and new cultural contacts were made. These "armed pilgrimages" failed because of conflicts between the participating nations, an early symptom of the emergence of nationalism as a historical force (→ Nation, Nationalism). After 1102, when Paschal II (1099-1118) called for a crusade against Emperor Henry II, the popes also began to use the *militia Christi,* or army of Christ, as a weapon against Christians whom they declared to be heretics. In 1204 Venice diverted the crusade to Constantinople, conquered it, and set up a Latin kingdom and patriarchate there that lasted until 1261.

1.3.4. *Laity*

Despite hostilities toward clergy created by strife between church and state, after the Investiture Controversy everyday life came increasingly under clerical influence. → Marriage is a case in point. Long a civil matter, it came under the norms of → moral theol-

ogy (consent and indissolubility) and was associated with the church's blessing. Also, by the 12th century the parish system had come into full operation. Replacing most proprietary churches, the parishes were under the authority of the bishops. Parishioners became responsible for tithes, fees, and oblations (→ Church Finances). In 1215 Lateran IV (→ Councils of the Church) demanded annual penance and communion (→ Eucharist), important factors in the new literature written for parish clergy to promote a deeper level of Christian education and practice among the laity. A few surviving sources (e.g., a vision of the Holstein peasant Gottschalk in 1189) show how far pre-Christian ideas had amalgamated with Christian theology in the faith of the people.

Social concern beyond parish boundaries had religious motivation. In the first half of the 12th century, the 300 or so monks at Cluny cared for over 10,000 poor people a year, and as many deceased were remembered in prayer. Hospitals reached a peak in about 1200. → Beguines, noncloistered religious laywomen active in the Low Countries and Germany, were often dedicated to care for the sick, the dying, and the dead.

As prosperity increased in both church and society, religious movements reacted by calling for apostolic poverty (Acts 2:41-45), for "the naked following the naked Christ." The wealth publicly demonstrated by monks in art and → liturgy (such as at Cluny) evoked criticism. The Cistercians claimed that the Benedictine Rule should be strictly observed. Reforming and mendicant orders, as well as lay movements such as the Beguines, advocated apostolic poverty. The dubious lifestyle of the hierarchy, which Bernard of Clairvaux openly attacked, promoted a readiness to seek religious alternatives based on other (Eastern and dualistic) traditions. For two or three generations there were competing churches in Latin Christendom. Southern France, Upper Italy, the Rhineland, and Austria saw interpretations of the message of salvation that advocated extreme poverty and radical dualism.

The → Cathari and → Waldenses were urban phenomena. Valdès (or Peter Waldo, d. before 1218) was a merchant who, like the later St. → Francis, rejected his wealth and wanted to preach. The Waldensian commitment to lay preaching, and not the members' embrace of poverty or any major doctrinal divergence, was condemned by the church. In the 12th century, doctrinal issues were not rigidly fixed (e.g., the number of → sacraments). Discussions were held with Jews and heretics (→ Judaism). In the 13th century the boundaries of the Christian community were consolidated as dogma became more firmly fixed (see Lateran IV, chap. 1 against the Albigenses and the Cathari, and chap. 3 on heretics [i.e., the Waldenses]), heretics came under persecution, Jews were restricted (Lateran IV), and debates were forbidden.

While the 12th-century reforming orders traditionally saw their chief goal in contemplative self-sanctification, the early 13th-century preaching orders, or mendicants (→ Dominicans; Franciscans), aimed to counter heresy by catechetical work in the cities. The mendicants, however, were not fully successful, and in 1208/9 a crusade was launched that almost completely extirpated the Albigenses. The → Inquisition was established as part of this effort. The mendicants took charge of it, and they also dominated the university study of theology. The connection between inquisition and study can be seen in the founding of the University of Toulouse in 1229 to combat heresy.

1.4. Late Middle Ages
(early 13th–late 15th cent.)
1.4.1. Foundations

The 13th century had seen great growth in material prosperity, cultural achievement, and the institutionalizing of dogma (→ Summa). This growth was checked in the 14th century by the famine of 1316/17 and the Black Death of 1348/50, to which a third of the population of Europe fell victim. The consequent recession lasted into the 15th century. Thus the estimated population of Europe in 1340 was 54 million, but by 1440 it had fallen to only 37 million. The recession was linked to an ongoing agrarian crisis, peasant revolts, and constant currency devaluations.

Cities became more important because of trade, crafts, and flight from the countryside. Thus Germany had some 3,500 cities, 90 percent of them under 2,000 inhabitants. Cologne was the largest, with a population of 40,000 in the 15th century. City leagues (e.g., the Hanseatic) exercised important economic and political power. Trades were becoming specialized, and banking families like the Fuggers dominated trading and financial enterprises. Bookkeeping and secretarial organization developed. Bloody struggles often took place for control of city government. The city in general pointed ahead to the future with its social differentiation, its early capitalistic economy (→ Capitalism), its intellectual life (universities), and its form of government. Kings and nobles, first in Italy, also took up residence in cities. With economic and technical military innovations, knights gradually became obsolete. The situation of peasants (90 per-

cent of the population) varied from region to region but greatly worsened both economically and legally, leading to an increased readiness to rebel.

1.4.2. Political Development

The centrally organized states on Europe's borders gained in importance compared to the politically divided empire, whose rulers had real influence only when they had sufficient domestic power. The ineffectually excommunicated Louis IV the Bavarian (1314-47) gathered antipapal intellectuals at his court (notably Marsilius of Padua [ca. 1280-ca. 1343] and William of Occam [ca. 1285-1347]; → Nominalism) and neutralized papal influence in imperial elections, but he failed because of his reckless domestic policy. The anti-king Charles IV of Luxembourg (1346-78), who was also king of Bohemia, made Prague his brilliant seat (the university was founded in 1348) and established the procedure for imperial elections (seven electors) in the Golden Bull of 1356 (the basic law until 1806). Under Frederick III of Hapsburg (cmp. 1440-93) the empire became more a confederation of independent states.

In contrast, the French monarchy promoted centralization. Despite the Hundred Years' War with England (1339-1453) and social revolts, royal power increased under Charles V of Valois (1364-80) with the help of his taxation policies. The English occupied Paris from 1422 to 1436, but northern France was reconquered by 1453 under the charismatic leadership of Joan of Arc. The main unresolved problem was rivalry with Burgundy.

In England the nobility and middle class successfully reduced the power of the Crown, with Parliament reorganized in 1265. The agitators behind the Peasants' Revolt of 1381 (against the poll tax) took up the call of John → Wycliffe (ca. 1330-84) for reform. The Wars of the Roses (1455-85) destroyed the competitors from both Lancaster and York, and the more despotic Tudor dynasty began with the victory of Henry VII (1485-1509) over Richard III (1483-85) at Bosworth.

In the Iberian Peninsula the Islamic states were vanquished. Around 1200 Aragon, Castille, and Portugal had occupied only the northern half, but Granada, the last Muslim possession, fell in 1492. Portuguese explorers made important overseas discoveries, such as the Azores in 1431 and the Cape of Good Hope in 1487.

Poland was engaged in long struggles with the German Knights but established itself especially by union with Lithuania in 1386.

1.4.3. Church

The conflict with the French crown shattered Boniface VIII (1294-1303) when in his *Unam sanctam* he tried to make obedience to the papacy necessary to salvation. Philip IV the Fair (1285-1314) denounced Boniface as a heretic and had him imprisoned. The ensuing move of the papacy to Avignon (1309-77) and the Great Schism (1378-1417; → Heresies and Schisms 3) marked a decline in the prestige and power of the papacy. It was no more able than the empire to organize a new crusade or to prevent the capture of Constantinople by the Turks (1453). → Conciliarism (as developed by the Councils of Constance [1414-18] and Basel [1431-49]; → Councils of the Church 3) also proved a failure. Papalism replaced it from the time of Pope Eugenius IV (1431-47). Nobles still held the highest papal offices, but the middle classes were gaining positions in the hierarchy. → Asceticism, mysticism, and scholarship became influential factors in new models of sanctity.

In the later Middle Ages religiously motivated intolerance increased. With the plague, lepers and Jews became scapegoats (→ Anti-Semitism, Anti-Judaism), and there were both spontaneous pogroms and officially organized attempts at expulsion or extirpation. Later both ecclesiastical and secular courts made witches, seen as members of heretical → sects or increasingly as servants of Satan, the main target of persecution (→ Witchcraft). The *Hammer of Witches,* a handbook for persecuting witches that became normative in the 17th century, may be traced back to the (forged) findings of Cologne University and the (authentic) bull *Summis desiderantes* (1484) of Innocent VIII (1484-92). From 1492 to 1496 the Inquisition drove all Jews out of Spain and Portugal.

By means of the Inquisition the papacy also suppressed monastic movements that aimed at radical spirituality and poverty (e.g., the Fraticelli; → Franciscans 2). Often so-called religious aberration was a pretext for material enrichment. In 1209-29 the French monarchy gained control over the rich and autonomous south by means of the Albigensian Crusade. In 1307-12 it suppressed the Templars and seized their property. We find similar incidents in Germany in innumerable pogroms and witchcraft trials.

1.4.4. *Everyday Life*

Everyday life reveals both superstition and intense Christian devotion. The laity embraced monastic → hours, increasingly went on → pilgrimages, and developed the cult of Mary (→ Mary, Devotion to, 1). Much of this devotion was due to the popular preaching of the mendicants, who had great influence especially on city life (e.g., Vincent Ferrer, Bernardino of Siena, John of Capistrano, Savona-

rola). Unusual forms of religious excitement, whether in mysticism, in the partially heretical flagellant movement, or in popular piety (with calls for repentance, local pilgrimages, religious drama, etc.), attest to the creativity of Christians in adapting devotional practices to their diverse needs.

The universal cry for church reform was generated by the perceived moral inadequacy — especially avarice — and incompetence of the clergy, the successful preaching of the ideals of chastity and poverty, the divergent lifestyles of the orders, the hunt for benefices, the misuse of church penalties (→ Excommunication), the granting of → indulgences for financial reasons, the abused immunizing of clergy from secular law, and the prohibition of reading the Bible in the vernacular (→ Bible Versions). Attempts to remedy the evils were not satisfactory. Conciliarism and reform failed at the Councils of Constance and Basel; the papacy and the national churches were invested in maintaining practices that were often viewed as degraded. Successful monastic innovations were confined to the orders (e.g., among the Benedictines), and living saints like Nicholas of Flüe and Lucia of Narni set good examples but did not generate widespread movements of reform.

Heretical deviations — often sharing concerns articulated within orthodox circles — were numerous, from little-known ones like the attempt of Guglielma of Bohemia (d. 1281) in Milan to establish a church led by a woman pope and women cardinals, to the famous pioneers of the Reformation. Jan → Hus (ca. 1372-1415) built on the demands of John Wycliffe. Religious, social, and nationalist motivations were so successfully blended here that the many crusading attempts to subjugate the → Hussites failed, and only internal division defeated them.

In Reformation regions popular religious life underwent fundamental change. In Roman Catholic areas many later medieval practices continued, but with greater clerical control, until the → Enlightenment, and some still survive or have been revived (→ Catholicism [Roman]), reaching a high point in the "popular baroque" (→ Popular Catholicism).

2. Culture

2.1. *General Features*

It is impossible to reconstruct any epoch in its total history. For the Middle Ages the sources constitute a particular problem. Most of the written tradition in the early Middle Ages, and also much of the written evidence from the high and late Middle Ages, comes from church authors and thus reflects the views of only one section of the educated elite. Only fragments of the early and even later oral lay tradition still survive. Perspectives of the ecclesiastical elite also informed material sources, such as art and architecture.

Nevertheless, the following general features of medieval culture can be seen. The society and economy were largely agrarian, with a strong regional thrust. The forms of government were mostly monarchical (kings, princes, abbots, generals of orders), though with oligarchic components (councils, diets, chapters). Family life was strictly patriarchal. The mentality was profoundly religious, whether under hierarchical instruction according to prevailing theological and canonical developments, or with a mingling of pre- and extra-Christian elements (→ Religion; Religion, Personal Sense of, Syncretism). As a result, most artistic, literary, and musical achievements were rooted in the religious sphere.

2.2. Early Middle Ages
(late 4th–mid-11th cent.)
2.2.1. *Change in Worldview*

The cultural styles of the migrating Germanic peoples with their less-developed → individualism and their emphasis on the tribe, as well as similar tendencies among provincial peoples in the → Roman Empire itself long before its military and political collapse, led to basic changes in the → worldview that had dominated classical antiquity.

After the legalization and subsequent imperial support of the Christian religion, efforts at evangelizing were reoriented. No longer did cultivated city dwellers have to be converted, but missionary efforts were directed to non-Christians outside the empire (→ Mission), and pagan, Germanic, and Celtic religious beliefs and practices were confronted. Classical education was no longer necessary for civic life, and pagan authors were deliberately set aside. In the West in the early Middle Ages, few people could still read Greek. Language and art were popularized along barbarian models: Latin became the spoken language, with some Celtic and German additions; classical aesthetic norms were replaced by those of folk art, such as loss of three-dimensionality and natural proportions, as well as the geometricizing of ornaments.

After the fall of the Roman upper classes, → monasticism became the chief force in maintaining Latin culture. However, in spite of Cassiodorus (ca. 490-ca. 585), who included liberal arts in his curriculum at the cloister Vivarium, and in spite of the learning of the Irish monks, much of the literature of antiquity was not preserved. Books were no longer valued simply as textual media; they also became cultic or prestige objects because of their elaborate decoration, their use in liturgy, and their rarity.

2.2.2. *Structures of Mentality*

The early medieval mentality inclined to the concrete and the transcendent. → Augustine (354-430; → Augustine's Theology), → Gregory the Great (590-604), and other thinkers of late antiquity dealt more with persons than → institutions and preferred supernatural explanations to natural. These traits were common to the whole period, as we see in the belief in miracles or the idea of the state as a union of persons. In late Roman antiquity as well as the Germanic kingdoms, earthly orders and legal hierarchies (→ Law) were traced directly to God. Trial by → ordeal, though prohibited in the later Middle Ages, reveals a fundamental confidence in God's direct intervention in daily life.

In the *Leges barbarorum* (tribal legal collections), no account was taken of the motives of malefactors, suggesting the emphasis on concrete occurrence rather than subjective states. In the Benedictine Rule (though not in John Cassian), right conduct rather than right thinking receives primary, albeit not exclusive, attention. In the oblate system, by which most Benedictines were recruited, the actual prayer of a child and not the child's will or aptitude formed the basis of the child's offerings. In narrative literature such as the historical and hagiographic works of Gregory of Tours (538/39-94), the seemingly disorderly mass of graphic details also illustrates the attention to concrete activities. In his popular rendering of Boethius's *Consolation of Philosophy*, King Alfred (849-99) replaced personified → nature by God, an ambiguous move in terms of the concrete/abstract dynamics but clearly showing a preference for making religious expression most explicit.

What was essential was → authority — for example, that of the nobility or → church fathers — not individual will or thought. The priority of the hierarchical extended to the upper world. Christ was not a Brother, as in the High Middle Ages, but the remote royal Judge (e.g., in *Muspilli*, an OHG poem on the last judgment). Of his two natures the divine received the greater emphasis (→ Christology). Even on the cross, Christ was depicted as the living and triumphant Ruler with the kingly crown, not as the one who suffers and dies (→ Theologia crucis).

The personal sphere of the emotions also exhibited marked differences from antiquity. We no longer find the emotion of → love depicted as the life-determining force that so fascinated the poets of the late Republic (e.g., Catullus, Propertius). Love lyrics were not written in either Latin or the vernacular languages. Nor was there mystical literature (→ Mysticism 2) that presupposed an individual, loving, emotional relationship with a personal God; likewise, theological works offer little reflection on God's love.

2.3. High Middle Ages
(mid-11th–early 13th cent.)
2.3.1. Differentiation

The obvious rise in European population after the 11th century, which was the result of better climate and better economic and political conditions, went hand in hand with greater affluence and a greater differentiation of forms of life. We see this trend in agriculture (clearing of forests) and the development of → cities, a revival in former Roman areas, a new wealth that spawned poverty movements both in the church (the mendicant orders) and in opposition to it. The result was a new → pluralism with differing possibilities of urban, monastic, and rural culture. People were able to move about more freely and became more socially mobile. Crusades, pilgrimages, and colonizing brought new contacts. One person could participate in many social systems at the same time (e.g., as knight, courtier, and citizen). The same differentiation manifested itself in the proliferation of monastic orders (e.g., Carthusians, Premonstratensians), in art (e.g., the Gothic groined vault and the rose window with stained glass panels), and in music (the polyphony of parallel voices found a place alongside Gregorian-style plainsong; → Gregorian Chant).

2.3.2. Spiritual and Secular Spheres

Another process reached a climax in the 11th and 12th centuries, namely, the division of an originally unitary worldview into that of religious and secular spheres. This process can be seen in the Investiture Controversy. As a result, emperors and kings lost much of their sacral character, while the church became a superior clerical system more sharply distinguished from the laity (note the rood loft) and with its own ritual specialists (priests) and theoreticians (university theologians and canonists; → Clergy and Laity). The simultaneous development of an independent lay culture using vernacular languages was another aspect of this process.

2.3.3. Rationalism

The conflicts between the secular and spiritual kingdoms forced both sides to rationalize their ideologies. Sharpened critical abilities (→ Criticism) and techniques of analysis and argumentation produced a polemical literature. What medieval authors extolled as *discretio* (discernment) and *ingenium* (cleverness, genius) gained in importance. These developments involved far-ranging, complex, and refined thinking. Logical discourse as a method took its place alongside associative and allegorical monastic theology and led to the development of Scholasticism. Arguments became increasingly this-worldly, and less importance was assigned to direct divine intervention (→ Immanence and Transcendence). Berengar of Tours (ca. 1010-88) could appeal in his theological controversies to "reasons of nature."

The same trend led finally to official suppression of the trial by ordeal in the 12th century. The primary social centers of the new → rationalism were the → universities, which began to replace the monasteries as the main institutions of learning. Rationalism was also manifest in art and architecture as Gothic architecture replaced the Romanesque style of combining cubic and cylindrical components with a systematic, uniform structural framework using buttresses and rib vaults.

2.3.4. Individualism

The dissolution of the earlier medieval outlook brought with it a new sense of the "I," as distinct from the hitherto dominant "we." Initially, this change was true of only small elites at court or in the cities and monasteries. Although identification with one's group (*ordo* or *status*) still carried significant weight, a new concern for individual agency can be seen in the construction of an essentially more personal morality based on feelings and a sense of guilt, as in Peter Abelard (1079-1142) and Bernard of Clairvaux (→ Penitence). Abelard could even argue — although without persuading most of his contemporaries — that those who put Christ to death were innocent so long as they acted in good faith.

Another religious example of individualism was the development of an extensive (mostly Cistercian) literature reflecting profound introspection (knowing oneself) as the premise of spiritual progress. "I" instead of "we" in prayer became more common, as did claims of mystical experience and speculation about it (→ Mysticism 2). The first autobiographical account of a → mystical union seems to be that of the Benedictine historical theologian Rupert of Deutz (ca. 1075-1129, *Commentary on Matthew* 12). Early forms of passion mysticism appear in Peter Damian (1007-72), and Anselm of Canterbury (1033-1109) taught mystical prayer in his *Meditations*.

In the women's religious movements from the 12th century on, there were many mystically gifted Beguines and nuns (e.g., Marie of Oignies, Lutgard of Tongeren, Hadewijch, Mechthild of Magdeburg, and Angela of Foligno). Bridal and passion styles of mysticism that presuppose an individual's relation to God are merely the most striking manifestation of a more general humanizing, not in the sense of creating a more humane society, but as an increasing subjectivity on the part of humans, who see themselves as the center of creation. The term *humanitas* again took on its originally positive significance after having denoted frailty in the early Middle Ages. God and Christ were now depicted in more human dimensions and with more human qualities, such as the Man of Sorrows with the crown of thorns. Theological and devotional works contained more reflection on the human nature of Christ.

The secular sphere also showed signs of a reflective individuality. Romances, for example, include internal monologue, and lyrics describe the special situation of the lover (the poet or a fictional "I"). Suffering was no longer seen as an externally imposed fate but as arising from within (e.g., Parcival). In history, individual features replaced stereotypes. Linked to these trends is a renewed appreciation of classical antiquity; in Latin poetry, for example, antiquity was praised with references to the *aetas Virgiliana* or *Ovidiana*.

These developments are also manifest in the sphere of art. Beginning in the 11th century, attempts were made at portraits of ecclesiastical and secular lords on monuments (relief or etching), for example, that of Rudolf of Rheinfelden (ca. 1080). With the 12th-century renaissance came Gothic and the full plastic representation of people in their natural proportions, drawing on models of antiquity (e.g., Reiner of Huy's baptismal font, 1107/18). Sculpture gradually broke free from architecture with full figures, another gain in realism (Chartres, Porte Royale, ca. 1150).

2.3.5. *Emotion*

The High Middle Ages saw the rediscovery of love as a dominant factor in human life. In the 11th century the nobility of southern France — for example, William IX of Poitiers (1071-1127) — advanced ideals that soon captured all the aristocracy of Europe. The developed individual now sought a partner, the ideal mistress of the troubadours, or one who was marked by special character or conduct. The result was the exclusive focusing on one person that gave rise to the story of Tristan and Isolde (Gottfried von Strassburg) or the letters of Héloïse to Abelard (whether genuine or the work of a 13th-cent. fabricator).

A typical figure in court poetry was the knight who finds himself on a false path or a way of adventure, as in the Arthurian cycle (Chrétien de Troyes,

Hartmann von Aue, Wolfram von Eschenbach). The knight is now alone, not the leader of an army of vassals, and his experiences are a personal possession that he dedicates to his lady rather than acts performed in the service of his lord, as had been the style in older epics (Roland, Nibelungenlied, Cid).

2.3.6. *Consensus Thinking*

With rationalism and individualism we also find a certain tendency to disparage the hierarchy and to prefer consensus thinking. The reforming Cistercian order with its renunciation of oblates set itself under the leadership of the chapter of abbots, with emphasis upon the Ciceronian ideal of friendship (esp. Aelthelred of Rievaulx [ca. 1110-67]). A similar tendency marked the founding of guilds. Christ, no longer simply Lord, was now imaged as Brother and Beloved (e.g., by Bernard of Clairvaux).

2.3.7. *Desacralizing of the World*

One result of the Investiture Controversy was the desacralizing of the world. Abelard could understand Genesis as natural history, not → salvation history. The popularity of Fortuna in the literature and art of the 12th century points to the replacement of the causal chain that begins in the supernatural by one that is purely natural. The this-worldliness of lay culture inspired the composition of court romances, troubadour lyrics, farces, and other forms — all new genres in which the religious element is minimal or absent altogether. Furthermore, the end of life in this world became a theme of reflection in a way hitherto unknown, and personified death appeared in poetry from 1200 on (e.g., Hélinand of Froidmont, "Vers de la mort").

2.3.8. *Summary*

Thus there are characteristic differences between the mentality of the early Middle Ages and that of the High Middle Ages: authority versus experience, external law versus inner norm (→ Conscience), hierarchy versus partnership, supernatural causation versus natural causation, absence of "romantic" emotionalism versus emotional awakening. Aspects of the earlier mentality lingered on (and still do) but never regained dominance.

In spite of the distinction into religious and secular spheres, many developments were analogous in both periods because of the close ties between court and cloister. Restructuring of both the material and the intellectual culture of the Middle Ages was the result, and its essential features would persist until the 18th century. In this sense one may speak of the older Europe or, in socioeconomic terms, of the age of → feudalism. The period from around 1050 to 1150 was that of the most important break in mentality before the Enlightenment, for which the High

Middle Ages laid the foundations by developing discursive theology and philosophy.

2.4. Late Middle Ages
(early 13th–late 15th cent.)

2.4.1. Crisis

In general, the trends in mentality and culture that had emerged in the High Middle Ages continued in the late Middle Ages. A period of political and cultural consolidation that lasted to the middle of the 13th century was followed by an age of more frequent and violent crises. Wars, earthquakes, famines, and scarcities seemed to be more widespread than before. Agricultural problems multiplied in the late Middle Ages. Fewer grain crops were grown. Farms and villages were deserted and became derelict. The Black Death, the plague that afflicted Europe from 1348 to 1350, swept away a third of the population and was a traumatic experience for those who survived.

Uncertainty was also increased by the many social revolts (France in 1358, Florence in 1345 and 1378, England in 1381), also by the Hundred Years' War between France and England (1339-1453), in which sieges and plundering soldiers caused more death and poverty than open warfare. In other areas too, wars, feuds, and violence were the order of the day. With anxiety came aggression. The search for scapegoats found expression in the common persecuting of lepers and Jews, and the beginning of witchhunts.

The crisis in the normative authority of the papacy (the move to Avignon and the Great Schism) was also destabilizing. For a time all Christendom was excommunicated as rival popes excommunicated each other and each other's adherents. Antagonism between papacy and empire flared repeatedly, such as the strife between John XXII (1316-34) and Louis IV the Bavarian (1314-47), who was supported by the progressive philosophers Marsilius of Padua and William of Ockham, who propagated secular views of state and society.

Secular court and city culture flourished, patronizing such achievements as the *Manesse-Handschrift* of Heidelberg and late Gothic city council houses, as well as many churches and their furnishings, books of hours, and others. Leading in the same direction was early humanism, with its ideals that were sometimes quite independent of any religious system of reference.

2.4.2. Death

The fatal onslaughts of pestilence from 1348 on broadened and intensified the process by which dying became a central theme of reflection and meditation, as we see in the *ars moriendi* (the art of dying [well]), the → dance macabre, and the 14th-century English morality play "Everyman." The OT depiction of a wrathful God took on new life after having been less prominent during the preceding centuries. The need to find protection came to figurative expression in the common theme of the protective mantle of → Mary and Sebastian (→ Saints, Veneration of), which wards off the arrows of pestilence shot by God, as well as the stress on intercession and the ladder of salvation, with the Mother and the Son of God begging divine grace for mortals.

Personifying → death became yet more common in poetry and art. Death was now one of the last things along with judgment, heaven, and hell. The increasing importance of the hour of death and the growth of a secular outlook seem to be directly related. Remembering death fostered an increased savoring of life and was thus one of the factors that would produce our modern secularized worldview. The macabre might often be linked to the lesson of the vanity of the world, but it was a this-worldly, rather than an otherworldly, motif.

2.4.3. Lay Religious Culture

An important lay religious culture developed involving meditations in the vernacular, house altars, small devotional pictures, and the sacralizing of the countryside by wayside shrines with popularized mystical motifs (e.g., passion piety). Movements like the *devotio moderna* and the mendicant orders with their enhanced preaching (the → pulpit now became a fixture in churches; → Preaching) responded to the religious needs of the laity.

2.4.4. Philosophy

Counteracting the trend to greater inwardness, philosophical consideration of the natural world claimed new attention (→ Philosophy), undoubtedly a result of the fuller acceptance of Aristotle (384-322 b.c.; → Aristotelianism) that began with the assimilation of Arabic (esp. Avicenna and Averroës, the normative commentator) and → Jewish philosophy. Attention shifted from the intangible world of ideas in Plato (427-347; → Platonism) to that of concrete individual things in Aristotle.

The Franciscan William of Occam, the most important thinker of the *via moderna*, separated → faith and knowledge, theology and philosophy. Unlike Thomas Aquinas (ca. 1225-74; → Thomism), who tried to relate Christian doctrine rationally to Aristotelian philosophy, Occam did not regard theology as a science. Doctrines like → monotheism, the → Trinity, the → incarnation, and the → immortality of the → soul, which Thomas had not regarded as contrary to → reason, Occam declared to be nonrational, since they can only be believed and not proved. Proof depends upon a sensory grasp and experience of things, not on general ideas. All that is real is individual.

These considerations were basic steps in separating faith from knowledge, the sacred from the profane, and also in the further development of individualism. They were steps that, by way of the Enlightenment, → materialism, and Romanticism, finally led to the secularized outlook of today's world. The principle that in explaining the world, all unnecessary hypotheses should be cut away (Occam's razor) would finally lead many people in the → modern period to dispense with the hypothesis of God, and hence to turn to → atheism.

2.4.5. Piety

In addition to its connection to rationalism, nominalism also related to a direction of late medieval → piety that seemed to strive increasingly after the bodily and concrete and perceptible. Pilgrimages became more common, and some laity even felt a need for daily communion. Piety was visually oriented. Reliquaries originally closed now had windows so that the bones they contained could be seen (→ Relics). Salvific power was attributed to seeing the host elevated (→ Eucharist; Mass). Ostensories, monstrances, and tabernacles came into use as liturgical vessels.

2.4.6. Mysticism

With the division of spiritual and secular rule, a retreat to the inner realm was still a possibility, even for the laity. The late Middle Ages saw such a flowering of mystical expressions, especially associated with 14th- and 15th-century women, that one might almost speak of a mystical invasion, with outstanding examples such as Bridget of Sweden (ca. 1303-73) and → Catherine of Siena (1347-80).

The often provocatively formulated "essence mysticism" of Meister → Eckhart (ca. 1260–ca. 1328), shaped by the emphatic intellectualism of the Dominicans and the currents of women's piety that Eckhart encountered in his pastoral work, is not typical of the total panorama of the epoch, which was characterized more by the passion piety exemplified in the Franciscan Meditationes vitae Christi of Pseudo-Bonaventura (ca. 1300). Eckhart's closest disciples Henry Suso (ca. 1295-1366) and Johann Tauler (ca. 1300-1361) tried to blunt his teaching, which gained only limited acceptance, and harmonize it with more traditional models.

2.4.7. Realism

As in philosophy, so in popular literature a trend developed toward realism (in the modern sense), represented by Giovanni Boccaccio (1313-75) in his Decameron and Geoffrey Chaucer (ca. 1343/44-

1400) in his Canterbury Tales. Secular humor became part of the spiritual drama, often with an inclination toward satirical and skeptical depictions (e.g., Heinrich Wittenweiler's Ring [ca. 1410]). We find the same in translations. Early New High German renderings of Latin texts are in general more vivid and objective than the originals (e.g., offering more precise indications of time).

It is striking, however, that in contrast to this greater realism, allegory in both religious and secular poetry reached a prolonged highwater mark at the very same time and to some extent in the same authors (→ Allegory). After the initial Roman de la rose (1230-80) of Guillaume de Lorris and Jean de Meun, the most famous works of this genre almost all date from the 14th century, beginning with the Divine Comedy of Dante (1265-1321), followed by the works of Albertino Mussato (1261-1329) and Petrarch (1304-74) in Italy, Guillaume de Digulleville (1295?-1380) and Philippe de Mézières (ca. 1327-1405) in France, and William Langland (ca. 1330-ca. 1400), John Gower (1330?-1408), and Chaucer in England. Germany produced little along this line, one example being the Buch von den neuen Felsen of Rulman Merswin (1307-82).

The emergence of realism in Western cognition was no less obvious in the fine arts. The portrait was developed first in the French court in the middle of the 14th century. The turn of the century brought the verism of the sculpted heads of Claus Sluter (ca. 1340/50-1405/6), which was developed fully in his Moses Well in Dijon. Realism also enlivened the works of Konrad Witz (ca. 1400-ca. 1445), who painted the first topographically accurate landscapes. Again there was a counterthrust, this time the "soft style" of Gothic (ca. 1400), with madonnas of idealized beauty. The fact that realism finally prevailed by the middle of the century was perhaps a sign of the future direction of European cultural and intellectual history.

Bibliography: International Medieval Bibliography (Leeds, 1967ff.) • ORB: The Online Reference Book for Medieval Studies (httn://orb.rhodes.edu/) • L.-J. PAETOW, Guide to the Study of Medieval History (New York, 1981) • M. SCHAUS, ed., Feminae: Medieval Women and Gender Index (http://www.haverford.edu/library/reference/mschaus/mfi/essays.html) • J. R. STRAYER, ed., Dictionary of the Middle Ages (13 vols.; New York, 1982-89).

Church history: General: G. BARRACLOUGH, The Medieval Papacy (London, 1968) • J. BRUNDAGE, Medieval Canon Law (London, 1995) • E. DUFFY, Saints and Sinners: A History of the Popes (New Haven, 1997) •

F. Eyck, *Religion and Politics in German History: From the Beginnings to the French Revolution* (New York, 1998) • J. Gilchrist, *The Church and Economic Activity in the Middle Ages* (London, 1969) • L. Glick, *Abraham's Heirs: Jews and Christians in Medieval Europe* (Syracuse, N.Y., 1999) • B. Kienzle, ed., *The Sermon* (Turnhout, 2000) • C. Lawrence, *Medieval Monasticism: Forms of Religious Life in Western Europe in the Middle Ages* (London, 1989) • J. Lynch, *The Medieval Church: A Brief History* (London, 1992) • J. McNamara, *Sisters in Arms: Catholic Nuns through Two Millennia* (Cambridge, Mass., 1996) • *New Cambridge Medieval History* (7 vols.; Cambridge, 1995-2000) • H. Ridder-Symoens, ed., *Universities in the Middle Ages* (Cambridge, 1992) • R. W. Southern, *Western Society and the Church in the Middle Ages* (Middlesex, 1970).

Church history: Early Middle Ages: U. Blumenthal, *The Investiture Controversy: Church and Monarchy from the Ninth to the Twelfth Century* (Philadelphia, 1988) • P. Brown, *The Rise of Western Christendom: Triumph and Diversity, A.D. 200-1000* (Cambridge, Mass., 1977) • R. Collins, *Charlemagne* (Toronto, 1998) • P. Geary, *Before France and Germany: The Creation and Transformation of the Merovingian World* (New York, 1988) • R. McKitterick, *The Frankish Church and the Carolingian Reforms, 789-895* (London, 1977) • R. MacMullen, *Christianizing the Roman Empire* (New Haven, 1984) • R. Markus, *Gregory the Great and His World* (Cambridge, 1997) • H. Mayer-Harting, *The Coming of Christianity to Anglo-Saxon England* (London, 1972) • T. Noble, *The Republic of St. Peter: The Birth of the Papal State, 680-825* (Philadelphia, 1984) • P. Riché, *The Carolingians: A Family Who Forged Europe* (Philadelphia, 1993) • J. Wallace-Hadrill, *The Frankish Church* (Oxford, 1983).

Church history: High and Late Middle Ages: P. Biller and A. Hudson, eds., *Heresy and Literacy, 1000-1530* (Cambridge, 1994) • J. Bossy, *Christianity in the West, 1400-1700* (Oxford, 1985) • G. Constable, *The Reformation of the Twelfth Century* (Cambridge, 1996) • H. Cowdrey, *Pope Gregory VII, 1073-1085* (Oxford, 1998) • J. Given, *Inquisition and Medieval Society: Power, Discipline, and Resistance in Languedoc* (Ithaca, N.Y., 1997) • M. Lambert, *Medieval Heresy: Popular Movements from Bogomil to Hus* (London, 1977) • C. Lawrence, *The Friars: The Impact of the Early Mendicant Movement on Western Society* (London, 1994) • R. Moore, *The Formation of a Persecuting Society: Power and Deviance in Western Europe* (Oxford, 1987) • C. Morris, *The Papal Monarchy: The Western Church from 1050 to 1250* (Oxford, 1989) • M. Newman, *The Boundaries of Charity: Cistercian Culture and Ecclesiastical Reform* (Stanford, Calif., 1996) • J. Riley-Smith,

The Crusades: A Short History (New Haven, 1990) • I. S. Robinson, *The Papacy, 1073-1198: Continuity and Innovation* (Cambridge, 1990) • G. Tellenbach, *Church, State, and Christian Society at the Time of the Investiture Contest* (New York, 1959) • B. Tierney, *The Crisis of Church and State, 1050-1300* (Toronto, 1988) • A. Winroth, *The Making of Gratian's Decretum* (Cambridge, 2001).

Church history: Non-English works: A. Angenendt, *Geschichte der Religiosität im Mittelalter* (Darmstadt, 1997) • B. Calati, R. Grégoire, and A. Blasucci, *La spiritualità del medievo* (Rome, 1988) • P. Dinzelbacher, *Angst im Mittelalter* (Paderborn, 1996); idem, *Christliche Mystik im Abendland* (Paderborn, 1994); idem, *Handbuch der Religionsgeschichte im deutschsprachigen Raum*, vol. 2, *Hoch- und Spätmittelalter* (Paderborn, 2000) • P. Dinzelbacher and D. Bauer, eds., *Volksreligion im hohen und späten Mittelalter* (Paderborn, 1990) • A. Fliche, *Histoire de l'église* (vols. 6-10; Paris, 1946) • R. Frenken, *Kindheit und Mystik im Mittelalter* (Frankfurt, 2002) • D. Iogna-Prat, E. Palazzo, and D. Russo, eds., *Marie. Le culte de la Vierge dans la société médiévale* (Paris, 1996) • F. Rapp, *L'église et la vie religieuse en Occident à la fin du Moyen Âge* (Paris, 1971).

Culture: General: H. Belting, *Likeness and Presence: A History of the Image before the Era of Art* (Chicago, 1994) • J. Brundage, *Law, Sex, and Christian Society in Medieval Europe* (Chicago, 1987) • M. Carruthers, *The Book of Memory: A Study of Memory in Medieval Culture* (Cambridge, 1990); idem, *The Craft of Thought: Meditation, Rhetoric, and the Making of Images, 400-1200* (Cambridge, 1998) • M. Colish, *Medieval Foundations of the Western Intellectual Tradition, 400-1400* (New Haven, 1997) • R. Crocker, *An Introduction to Gregorian Chant* (New Haven, 2000) • U. Eco, *Art and Beauty in the Middle Ages* (New Haven, 1988) • R. Emmerson and B. McGinn, eds., *The Apocalypse in the Middle Ages* (Ithaca, N.Y., 1992) • J. Ferrante, *Women's Roles in the Composition of Medieval Texts* (Bloomington, Ind., 1997) • A. Gurevich, *Medieval Popular Culture: Problems of Belief and Perception* (Cambridge, 1988) • R. Kieckhefer, *Magic in the Middle Ages* (Cambridge, 1990) • M. Labarge, *A Small Sound of the Trumpet: Women in Medieval Life* (Boston, 1986) • C. Lawrence, *Medieval Monasticism: Forms of Religious Life in Western Europe in the Middle Ages* (London, 1989) • J. Leclercq, *The Love of Learning and the Desire for God: A Study of Monastic Culture* (New York, 1961) • B. McGinn, *The Presence of God: A History of Western Christian Mysticism* (4 vols.; New York, 1991-98) • J. C. Schmitt, *Ghosts in the Middle Ages: The Living and the Dead in Medieval Society* (Chicago, 1998) • R. W. Southern, *The Making of the Mid-*

dle Ages (New Haven, 1953) • A. VAUCHEZ, The Laity in the Middle Ages: Religious Beliefs and Devotional Practices (Notre Dame, Ind., 1993).

Culture: Early Middle Ages: H. FICHTENAU, Living in the Tenth Century: Mentalities and Social Orders (Chicago, 1991) • V. FLINT, The Rise of Magic in Early Medieval Europe (Princeton, 1991) • Y. HEN, Culture and Religion in Merovingian Gaul, A.D. 481-751 (Leiden, 1995) • J. HERRIN, The Formation of Christendom (Princeton, 1987) • K. JOLLY, Popular Religion in Late Saxon England (Chapel Hill, N.C., 1996) • R. McKITTERICK, The Carolingians and the Written Word (Cambridge, 1989) • R. MacMULLEN, Christianity and Paganism in the Fourth to Eighth Centuries (New Haven, 1997) • V. ORTENBERG, The English Church and the Continent in the Tenth and Eleventh Centuries: Cultural, Spiritual, and Artistic Exchange (Oxford, 1992) • P. RICHÉ, Education and Culture in the Barbarian West (Columbia, S.C., 1976) • J. RUSSELL, The Germanization of Early Medieval Christianity (New York: 1994).

Culture: High and late Middle Ages: R. BENSON and G. CONSTABLE, eds., Renaissance and Renewal in the Twelfth Century (Oxford, 1982) • T. BESTUL, Texts of the Passion: Latin Devotional Literature and Medieval Society (Philadelphia, 1996) • R. BRITNELL, ed., Daily Life in the Late Middle Ages (Stroud, Eng., 1998) • C. BYNUM, Holy Feast and Holy Fast: The Religious Significance of Food to Medieval Women (Berkeley, Calif., 1987) • G. DUBY, The Age of the Cathedrals: Art and Society, 980-1420 (Chicago, 1981) • E. DUFFY, The Stripping of the Altars: Traditional Religion in England, 1400-1580 (New Haven, 1992) • H. GRUNDMANN, Religious Movements in the Middle Ages (Notre Dame, Ind., 1995) • B. HOLSINGER, Music, Body, and Desire in Medieval Culture: Hildegard of Bingen to Chaucer (Palo Alto, Calif., 2001) • J. HUIZINGA, The Autumn of the Middle Ages (Chicago, 1996) • C. JAEGER, The Envy of Angels: Cathedral Schools and Social Ideals in Medieval Europe, 950-1200 (Philadelphia, 1994) • R. KAEUPER, Chivalry and Violence in Medieval Europe (Oxford, 1999) • C. MORRIS, The Discovery of the Individual, 1050-1200 (New York, 1972) • B. NEWMAN, From Virile Woman to Woman Christ (Philadelphia, 1995) • M. RUBIN, Corpus Christi: The Eucharist in Late Medieval Culture (Cambridge, 1991) • S. WAUGH and P. DIEHL, eds., Christendom and Its Discontents: Exclusion, Persecution, and Rebellion, 1000-1500 (Cambridge, 1996).

Culture: Non-English works: P. DINZELBACHER, Das hohe Mittelalter. Kultur und Mentalität (Darmstadt, 2003); idem, ed., Europäische Mentalitätsgeschichte (Stuttgart, 1993); idem, ed., Sachwörterbuch der Mediävistik (Stuttgart, 1992) • P. DINZELBACHER and H.-D. MÜCK, eds., Volkskultur des europäischen Spätmittelalters (Stuttgart, 1987) • J. LE GOFF and J.-C. SCHMITT, eds., Dictionnaire raisonné de l'Occident médiéval (Paris, 1999) • F. HEER, Aufgang Europas. Eine Studie zu den Zusammenhängen zwischen politischer Religiosität, Frömmigkeitsstil und dem Werden Europas im 12. Jahrhundert (Vienna, 1949); idem, Die Tragödie des Heiligen Reiches (Vienna, 1952) • J. A. VAN HOUTTE, ed., Handbuch der europäischen Wirtschafts- und Sozialgeschichte (vol. 2; Stuttgart, 1980) • H. MARTIN, Mentalités médiévales (Paris, 1996) • Renovación intelectual del Occidente Europeo (siglo XII) (Pamplona, 1998) • G. SCHNÜRER, Kirche und Kultur im Mittelalter (3d ed.; Paderborn, 1936) • F. SEIBT, ed., Europa im Hoch- und Spätmittelalter (Stuttgart, 1987); idem, ed., Handbuch der europäischen Geschichte (vol. 2; Stuttgart, 1987).

PETER DINZELBACHER, with ANNE L. CLARK

Middle Axioms

Preparing for the world conference on practical Christianity at Oxford in 1937, the ecumenist and social thinker Joseph H. Oldham (1874-1969) described "middle axioms" as guidelines for the action of Christians in specific political situations, guidelines to which non-Christians could also subscribe out of their own moral convictions. Such axioms could not be deduced directly from higher Christian principles ("broad criteria," e.g., → love), but they are in harmony with them and are more concrete, though not so concrete as actual directives for action, or programs. They thus occupy "middle" ground. In line with Oldham's thinking, the concept of the responsible society in the form of middle axioms played an important role at the first meeting of the → World Council of Churches at Amsterdam in 1948 and in the ensuing ecumenical work in social ethics (→ Ecumenism, Ecumenical Movement).

By way of the writings of the American ethicist John C. Bennett (1902-95) on social and foreign policy, the term made its way into fundamental ethical discussion. As an example, racial integration was cited as a common guideline for both Christians and non-Christians. Paul L. Lehmann (1906-93) and others found in the concept, however, a methodological ambiguity from the standpoint of ethical theory, and also an unhealthy closeness to the tradition of → natural law. The choice of the word "axiom" for something that stands in the middle rather than at the beginning also came in for varied criticism (e.g., by P. Ramsey). The term was not adopted in European discussion, though what it was trying to denote was present in different forms (→ Ethics 4-5).

Bibliography: J. C. BENNETT, *Christian Social Ethics in a Changing World: An Ecumenical Theological Inquiry* (New York, 1966) • T. F. BEST and M. ROBRA, eds., *Ecclesiology and Ethics: Ecumenical Engagement, Moral Formation, and the Nature of the Church* (Geneva, 1997) • P. L. LEHMANN, *Ethics in a Christian Context* (New York, 1963) 149-59 • L. S. MUDGE, *The Church as a Moral Community: Ecclesiology and Ethics in Ecumenical Debate* (New York, 1998) • P. RAMSEY, *Basic Christian Ethics* (Louisville, Ky., 1993) • W. A. VISSER 'T HOOFT and J. H. OLDHAM, *The Church and Its Function in Society* (London, 1937).

DIETRICH RITSCHL

Middle Class → Bourgeois, Bourgeoisie

Middle East Council of Churches

1. Formation
2. Membership
3. Assemblies and Themes
4. Aims
5. Recent Tasks
6. Structure

1. Formation

After lengthy ecumenical efforts on the part of the Orthodox and Protestant churches of the Middle East, the Middle East Council of Churches (MECC) was founded in 1974 as the successor of the largely Protestant Near East Christian Council, which had been founded in 1964. In 1990 the seven Roman Catholic churches of the region became members of the MECC, making it the ecumenical representative of the great majority of the 12 to 14 million Christians of the region. The MECC headquarters are in Beirut, with liaison offices in Cairo, Jerusalem, and Limassol, Cyprus. The geographic area it covers stretches from Morocco to Iran and from Turkey to the Arabian Gulf.

2. Membership

MECC membership includes four "families" of churches: the → Oriental Orthodox churches (Coptic, Armenian, and Syrian of Antioch), the Eastern → Orthodox churches (Patriarchates of → Antioch, → Alexandria, and → Jerusalem and the Archbishopric of Cyprus), the → Roman Catholic churches (Maronite of Antioch, Syrian of Antioch, Coptic, Armenian of Cilicia, Latin of Jerusalem, Chaldean of Babylon, Greek Catholic of Antioch [→ Melchites]), and the Protestant and Episcopal

churches (National Evangelical Synod of Syria and Lebanon, National Evangelical Union of Lebanon, Coptic Evangelical Church Synod of the Nile, the Evangelical Presbyterian Church of Iran, Union of the Armenian Evangelical Churches in the Near East, Evangelical Church in Sudan, Presbyterian Church in Sudan, Evangelical Lutheran Church in Jordan, the Episcopal Church in Jerusalem and the Middle East, the Episcopal Church in Sudan).

The MECC is organized according to the concept of families of churches rather than on the basis of individual church membership. This concept designates churches that have a common ecclesial tradition and are in communion with one another.

3. Assemblies and Themes

To date, the MECC has convened seven General Assemblies, following a variety of themes:
1. 1974, "Our Common Christian Mission Today";
2. 1977, "He Gave Us the Service of Reconciliation";
3. 1980, "His Kingdom Come";
4. 1985, "The Living Hope";
5. 1990, "To Keep the Unity of the Spirit in the Bond of Peace";
6. 1994, "Peace I Leave with You, My Peace I Give You"; and
7. 1998, "Jesus Christ, the Same Yesterday, Today, and Forever."

The fourth assembly was of special significance, being preceded by a historic meeting of the patriarchs of the Oriental and Eastern Orthodox churches, as well as leaders of the Roman Catholic and Protestant churches of the region. The fifth assembly was important as the occasion when the Roman Catholic churches of the Middle East were accepted into the MECC as the fourth family of churches. The eighth General Assembly is planned for late 2003.

4. Aims

The aim of the MECC is to promote dialogue between the churches of the Middle East, aiming at helping them recover their unity and common witness within → monotheism. According to its constitution, the MECC is a regional expression of the global ecumenical movement. For that reason, it has established particularly important cooperation with the → World Council of Churches.

5. Recent Tasks

During recent years, the MECC has worked to ensure the continuity of the Christian presence in the Middle East. In this connection, efforts have been made to enable Christians to live in this region in freedom and to participate with other communities in together developing nations and societies. The council also cooperates with the churches for spiritual renewal through dynamic education programs aiming at enabling them, in the midst of tension and suffering, to continue to live and witness the incarnation and resurrection of Jesus Christ.

The MECC works toward restoring God's gift of → unity to the churches of the Middle East and, through them, toward contributing to Christian unity in the whole world. Such efforts are particularly significant in the Middle East, which was the site of the earliest → heresies and divisions in the church. In this connection the MECC has always emphasized that church unity is not to result in a coalition against other religious communities or groups.

Furthermore, the MECC facilitates the witness of churches through humanitarian service to the poor, oppressed, and → refugees. It promotes constructive → dialogue and cooperation with other religions, fostering a common commitment to justice and peace in the Middle East and the world at large. It seeks to make the international community aware of the life of Christians in the Middle East (present there continuously since Pentecost) and to encourage global solidarity with their witness to love, freedom, equality, justice, and peace. Finally, the council interprets through publications and magazines the life of the local churches and their witness on behalf of the universal Christian faith.

6. Structure

The MECC organization consists in a General Assembly, an executive committee elected by the General Assembly, and program units divided into specialized departments. All these structures are coordinated and served by a general secretariat. The four MECC presidents, representing the four families of churches, and the general secretary are elected by the General Assembly, which usually meets every four years.

→ Ecumenism, Ecumenical Movement

Bibliography: B. J. BAILEY and J. M. BAILEY, *Who Are the Churches in the Middle East?* (Grand Rapids, 2003) • L. EKIN, *Enduring Witness: The Churches and the Palestinians* (Geneva, 1985) • "Jerusalem, a Shared Trust," *MECC Perspectives,* no. 8 (July 1990) • M. C. KING, *The Palestinians and the Churches: 1948-1956* (Geneva, 1981) • *Unity in Service with the Palestinians: Consultation on Service to Palestine Refugees, Called by the Middle East Council of Churches . . .* (Nicosia, Cyprus, 1980) • "Who Are the Christians of the Middle East?" *MECC*

Perspectives, no. 6/7 (October 1986). MECC produces periodicals in Arabic (the *Al-Muntada Monthly* and the quarterly *Al-Muntada Magazine*), English (the quarterly *NewsReport Magazine*), and French (the thrice-yearly *Courrier oecuménique du Moyen Orient*).

LEOPOLDO NIILUS and GABRIEL HABIB

Midrash

The term "midrash" (pl. midrashim), first found in 2 Chr. 13:22; 24:27, comes from Heb. *dāraš*, which in the Bible means "seek, inquire, search out" (Judg. 6:29; Deut. 4:29), especially "seek and read from the book of the LORD" (Isa. 34:16), to set one's heart "to study the law [*tôrâ*] of the LORD" (Ezra 7:10; cf. at Qumran 1QS 5:11 and 6:6). In the → Mishnah the main meaning is "explain" or "expound" a verse of Scripture (*m. Šeqal.* 1:4).

The understanding of prerabbinic interpretation (e.g., in the Bible itself or at → Qumran) as midrash is debated, but in rabbinic literature (→ Rabbi, Rabbinism) midrash is (1) the general act of investigation and exposition (*m. 'Abot* 1:17), (2) the exposition of a specific verse (*m. Šeqal.* 6:6), and (3) a collection of expositions, the so-called midrashim. There is still no universally accepted definition, but an attempt has been made to identify the "functional form" that is midrash, which underlies all of its literary actualizations. By means of a variable hermeneutical operation (→ Hermeneutics), a statement is made about some lemma of Scripture. Thus midrash, as an exposition that mainly interprets linguistic or graphic marks of Scripture, is distinguished from a commentary, which explains the events described.

The midrash collections are traditionally classified by chronology (Tannaitic, Amoraic), by content (→ Halakah; Haggadah), or by genre (verse-by-verse exposition, homiletic exposition related to the pericopes for Sabbaths and feast days). These criteria, however, will hardly stand up to criticism. Important midrashim include *Mekilta* on Exodus; *Sipra* on Leviticus; *Sipre* on Numbers, *Sipre* on Deuteronomy, and Midrash *Rabbah* on the → Torah and → Megilloth; *Tanḥuma* on the Sabbath pericopes; and *Pesiqta de Rab Kahana* and *Pesiqta Rabbati* on the festal pericopes.

→ Exegesis, Biblical; Scribes; Talmud

Bibliography: A. R. E. AGUS, *Hermeneutic Biography in Rabbinic Midrash: The Body of This Death and Life* (Berlin, 1996) • H. W. BASSER, *In the Margins of the Midrash: Sifre Ha'azinu Texts, Commentaries, and Re-*

flections (Atlanta, 1990) • A. GOLDBERG, *Rabbinische Texte als Gegenstand der Auslegung* (Tübingen, 1999) esp. pts. 4, 8-11 • R. HAMMER, *The Classic Midrash: Tannaitic Commentaries on the Bible* (Mahwah, N.J., 1995) • J. NEUSNER, *Introduction to Rabbinic Literature* (New York, 1994) esp. pts. 2-3; idem, *Invitation to Midrash: The Workings of Rabbinic Bible Interpretation* (Atlanta, 1998); idem, *Tradition as Selectivity: Scripture, Mishnah, Tosefta, and Midrash in the Talmud of Babylonia* (Atlanta, 1990); idem, *What Is Midrash? and, A Midrash Reader* (Atlanta, 1994) • H. L. STRACK and G. STEMBERGER, *Introduction to the Talmud and Midrash* (Minneapolis, 1992).

MARGARETE SCHLÜTER

Military Chaplaincy

1. General
2. National Developments
   2.1. Europe
   2.2. United States
3. Problems

1. General

Military chaplaincy has a centuries-long tradition in the churches of both East and West. In the main Protestant churches the → Reformation age set the guidelines for → worship in the armed forces and for the work of military chaplains (→ Pastor, Pastorate; Protestantism).

For various reasons military chaplaincy has undergone considerable changes in recent decades. Changes in relations between armed forces, → church, and → state; the religious neutrality of most states; political changes, especially in the formerly socialist countries (→ Socialism); → ecumenical dialogue; and the monstrous potential of modern forces for destruction (→ Weapons) have confronted military chaplaincy with a new situation that shows itself in the search for new tasks, in wrestling with questions of work for → peace, and in the switch from military to ethical problems.

The task of the military chaplaincy is to counsel members of the forces in matters of faith during both war and peace. Chaplains also give advice on → lifestyle and → ethics. In the ordering of religious practice they have a free hand, but they are expected to show respect for the spirit of → religious liberty and ecumenicity (→ Ecumenism, Ecumenical Movement).

In times of peace chaplains must deal with → conscientious objectors. By demanding personal → responsibility and stressing → human dignity in the armed forces, they can make a contribution to peace. In times of → war or crisis they serve on active duty. Chaplains are primarily responsible for pastoral care, but their duties include more than → proclamation. International experience shows that they have more chances to give individual help than do officers, though other experts like psychologists, psychiatrists, and social workers are now being increasingly used in the forces.

2. National Developments

2.1. *Europe*

Not all countries have church-state treaties governing military chaplaincy. Predominantly → Roman Catholic countries like Italy, Spain, and Portugal have a Roman Catholic military chaplaincy that is closely linked to the forces. Most of the population of Austria is also Roman Catholic, so that the traditional military chaplaincy serves Roman Catholics, but spiritual care is also provided for others. In this regard there is cooperation between the Protestant churches. In Austria the → bishop of the Evangelical Church of the Augsburg and Helvetic Confessions names a general military superintendent, who supervises Protestant work in the Ministry of Defense.

In *Germany* military chaplaincy has been regulated by arrangements with the churches. As regards Roman Catholics, article 27 of the 1933 → concordat put the chaplaincy under a military bishop outside normal church structures. As regards Protestants, the 1957 agreement between the government and the Evangelische Kirche in Deutschland (EKD, Evangelical Church in Germany) set the military chaplaincy on a new legal basis. Chaplains have an official relation to the state: those of higher rank for life, the rest for 6-12 years. Each Landeskirche, or provincial church, has a military office that is administratively under the Ministry of Defense and spiritually under the military bishop. Territorially, the chaplaincy follows divisions in the forces. The six districts and the fleet all have their own deans, as do the divisional staffs. The work is done either in military → congregations or, more commonly, at a personal level in civilian congregations. The Ministry of Defense regulates instruction given about lifestyle, which takes place each month, divided according to rank or denomination. Themes and materials are decided centrally by the two church ministries in connection with the Ministry of Defense.

In *France* Roman Catholics, Protestants, and Jews all share in the official military chaplaincy. There are too few Orthodox for their own chaplain, and the French constitution does not give → Islam any legal right of practice. Each group has an *aumônier des armées,* with an assistant in each branch. As the armed forces have changed into professional armies, the need for the military chaplaincy has decreased, although the overall organization of chaplains has stayed basically the same. In the year 2000 there were approximately 200 Roman Catholic chaplains, 50 Protestant, and fewer than 40 Jewish.

Full-time Catholic and Protestant military chaplains are active in the armed forces of *Netherlands* and *Belgium.* In Netherlands their number has included humanistic chaplains. Similar developments are also taking place in Belgium, which could lead to a decrease in the amount of work done within the religious communities.

The change toward a professional army has also had an effect on the number of chaplains in the *United Kingdom,* where the chaplaincy system itself has been little changed. In the year 2000 there were still almost 200 military chaplains active. Two-thirds of the chaplains were Anglican (→ Anglican Communion), with 10 percent belonging to the Church of Scotland and 15 percent to the Roman Catholic Church. Others included representatives of the → Baptists, Methodists (→ Methodist Churches), and other → free churches. The organization of the forces includes a Royal Army Chaplains' Department. The chief chaplain, an Anglican, and the assistant chaplains, representing other Protestant bodies, are on the general staff and command the whole corps of chaplains apart from Roman Catholics. The latter are under the principal Roman Catholic chaplain, who has a colonel's rank. Each church has its own organ for testing applicants for the chaplaincy. Administratively, the chaplains are under the forces, but in matters of life and teaching, they are responsible to their own churches.

In Scandinavia we find different arrangements and standing. In *Sweden* the church and the state were legally separated from each other in 2000, with the work of the military chaplaincy being governed by an agreement drawn up between the church and the armed forces. Both sides contribute to the funding of the work. Full-time military chaplains have been assigned to the chief headquarters and to each of the garrison districts.

In *Denmark* the high command of the defense forces controls the military chaplaincy, but in practice it is very much a matter for the local churches (→ Congregation 3) and their ministers. The war provost is also the senior minister of a church in Copenhagen. The various forces have their own provosts. Because of the relatively short terms of duty and the form of organization, local churches bear responsibility for the care of draftees.

In *Norway* the high command has a military provost who is paid by the defense forces and appointed by the bishop of Oslo, who oversees the Corps of Military Chaplains. The number of full-time military chaplains has decreased slightly because of a recent reorganization of the armed forces, but the system and the structure of chaplaincy have remained similar within the army. Pastors not of the national Lutheran Church may also be chaplains if their own churches recognize them and if they are prepared to minister to members of the national church (→ People's Church [Volkskirche]).

A distinctive feature in *Finland* is that since the period of Russian rule in the 19th century, there has been an Orthodox as well as a Lutheran military chaplaincy. The chaplains paid by the state today are thus either Lutheran or Orthodox (→ Orthodox Church). The military bishop, who is on the staff, is always a minister of the Evangelical Lutheran Church of Finland. He has no → diocese but is a member of the → Synod. Another regular chaplain is also on the staff. A provost is responsible for each area. In the year 2000 there were 26 full-time chaplains and dozens who served part-time.

The most noticeable difference in military chaplaincy has taken place in the post-Communistic countries of eastern Europe. In *Russia* and *Ukraine,* the Orthodox and the Protestants have each concluded formal agreement with the armed forces. Under these new arrangements, for example, dozens of new churches have been built in Russian army garrisons.

In *Poland* in the year 2000 there were over 200 active Roman Catholic military chaplains, as well as 25 Orthodox and 12 Protestant. In *Romania* 56 Orthodox military chaplains were active, plus a few Catholic and Protestant chaplains. The smaller countries of eastern Europe likewise have instituted military chaplaincies since 1990.

Bibliography: M. Bock, *Religion within the Armed Forces: Military Chaplaincy in an International Comparison* (Munich, 1998) • S. E. Cheston and R. J. Wicks, ed., *Essentials for Chaplains* (New York, 1993) • D. R. Herspring, *Soldiers, Commissars, and Chaplains: Civil-Military Relations since Cromwell* (Lanham, Md., 2001) • R. J. Wicks, R. D. Parsons, and D. Capps, eds., *Clinical Handbook of Pastoral Counseling* (exp. ed.; 2 vols.; New York, 1993).

Markku Heikkilä

2.2. *United States*

In the American Revolutionary War 179 chaplains served with the Continental army and the state militias. Navy chaplains were even recruited in France to serve the French peasants who under John Paul Jones made up the crew of the *Bon Homme Richard.* Early chaplains had no rank and received only modest compensation. Later, during the Civil War, large numbers of civilian clergy, including an Episcopal bishop, enlisted as regular fighting members of the armed forces.

A staggering 96 percent of U.S. citizens profess religious → faith. It was thus inevitable that after World War II the military chaplaincy should grow as the military itself increased and was deployed around the world. Each generation has witnessed charges that clergy are serving two masters — church and state — but the status of chaplains has nevertheless become more secure.

In 1979 a suit was filed in New York federal court challenging the constitutionality of the military chaplaincy, appealing to the so-called establishment clause of the First Amendment to the Constitution, which states that Congress may make no law that "establishes" religion. The legal defense of the military acknowledged that while the chaplaincy, strictly interpreted, was religious in nature, it did not violate the First Amendment because that same amendment also required that "the free exercise" of religion be guaranteed, with military chaplains being charged with that responsibility. Two lower courts decided in favor of the military, and the case was withdrawn before reaching the Supreme Court. In the United States, therefore, we could say that the military chaplaincy has the sympathies of both the legislative and the judicial branches of government. (See I. Drazin and C. B. Currey, *For God and Country.*)

As of 2000 the armed forces of the United States, both active duty and reserve, were served by over 5,000 chaplains, with 3,000 on active duty. Of this number 67 percent were → Protestant (representing more than 50 denominations), 30 percent → Roman Catholic, 3 percent Jewish (→ Judaism). In recent years a number of Muslim clerics (4 in the navy alone) have also been appointed. All chaplains have officer rank, from first lieutenant to major general. Each branch of service has its own chief of chaplains, with offices in or near the Pentagon in Washington, D.C. Together they form the Armed Forces Chaplains Board. Each chaplain must be certified by his or her own → denomination before applying for Armed Forces chaplaincy. Chaplains of the navy support the Marine Corps and the Coast Guard in addition to service to the fleet. Chaplains of all services support military families as part of their role of serving the military individual.

Some chaplains are pacifists (→ Pacifism), but like all members of the military they are required to refrain from political expression of their sentiments. Chaplains today are bound by the Geneva Conventions to be noncombatants.

Bibliography: J. W. BRINSFIELD JR., *Encouraging Faith, Supporting Soldiers: The United States Army Chaplaincy, 1975-1995* (Washington, D.C., 1997) • R. M. BUDD, *Serving Two Masters: The Development of American Military Chaplaincy, 1860-1920* (Lincoln, Nebr., 2002) • I. DRAZIN and C. B. CURREY, *For God and Country: The History of a Constitutional Challenge to the Army Chaplaincy* (Hoboken, N.J., 1995) • C. M. DRURY, comp., *The History of the Chaplains Corp, United States Navy* (9 vols.; Washington, D.C., 1948-85) • R. J. HONEYWELL, *Chaplains of the United States Army* (Washington, D.C., 1958) • R. G. HUTCHESON JR., *The Churches and the Chaplaincy* (Atlanta, 1975) • A. I. SLOMOVITZ, *The Fighting Rabbis: Jewish Military Chaplains and American History* (New York, 1999).

EDGAR G. ADAMS

3. Problems

3.1. Practices in the military chaplaincy raise many fundamental questions and problems. In Germany central structural problems resulted from Prussian military and ecclesiastical politics that shaped military chaplaincy during the 19th and 20th centuries. The military and the military chaplaincy became intimately associated, and the church exercised increasingly less influence on the orientation of the chaplaincy. The consequences of these structural problems manifested themselves in the role of military chaplaincy during the two world wars, a role the military found convenient for serving its own interests.

The same tendencies are still evident in Germany today. Military chaplains are involved in military training and exercises, civilian church authorities and the military → bishop exercise little or no influence on Protestant church offices, and synodical courts exercise no significant power over the influential administrative apparatus (→ Synod). There is no evidence of any critical dialogue between leading military chaplains and the politicians and officers who continue to formulate policy based on what is clearly an instrumental view of the military chaplaincy.

3.2. The approaches of the military chaplaincy to ethical questions such as the justification of defensive → war, of the use of → force, and of thinking in terms of friend and foe (→ Enemy) move wholly within a framework that is under the shadow of the military. The traditional structural weaknesses in the military chaplaincy are sharpened by the ethical demands made on soldiers in the nuclear age. A separate structure for military chaplains was set up at a time when the calculation that → war might serve political ends seemed to be a rational one, which is no longer the case. In a future war between equally armed powers, the cost would far outweigh any gain; the loss of life and property would stand in no relation to the result. War is thus irrational in principle, for the extinction of humanity has become a technical possibility.

The dilemma facing the military chaplaincy in Europe, then, is whether it represents the church → consensus that the use of nuclear → weapons is illegitimate or whether it accepts the NATO doctrine that envisions their possible use. Conflicting statements from the sphere of the military chaplaincy give evidence of the danger that justification might be found for prevailing political conceptions.

Along with the global nature of the military risk, the increasing ecumenicity of the church also makes a military chaplaincy seem obsolete when it is financed and organized by ministries of defense with military and political goals. Hardly less significant for the future of the military chaplaincy is the dissolution of the Warsaw Pact, which was formerly NATO's potential adversary. If it is the task of the remaining forces to help establish a security system for Europe, the traditional interests of a separate military chaplaincy no longer apply, and another reason for retaining the existing structure falls to the ground.

3.3. German reunification in 1990 brought a turning point for military → pastoral care, in two respects. First, the dissolution of the Warsaw Pact, which followed quickly thereafter, created a completely new situation. While the pact existed, the mandate of the Bundeswehr (federal armed forces) was to prevent war by its very existence. Since the 1990s, however, German troops have again become involved in international conflicts for the first time since World War II — in Kosovo, Macedonia, and Afghanistan. This situation has expanded the engagement of those responsible for pastoral care in the military and also made it necessary to reflect anew on the legitimacy of each engagement and thus to define its own self-understanding, something that has only begun to take place.

Second, reunification has also raised the question of the validity of the 1957 Militärseelsorgevertrag (MSV, agreement governing military pastoral care) in the new German states. The adoption of the MSV was deemed not acceptable by the state churches (Landeskirchen) of the former East Germany. The pastoral care of soldiers (*Soldatenseelsorge,* the East German expression) had to be carried out only by → pastors also engaged in parish service.

The East German churches had been shaped in a situation in which → church and state were strictly separated; their experience had been the changing of Volkskirchen, or → people's churches, into a Christian minority (→ Germany 2.2). In this process, the churches of the former East Germany also developed a more rigorous → peace ethic than that which marked the churches of West Germany. They stated clearly in September 1987, "In obedience to the triune God, we have expressed our renunciation of the spirit, logic, and praxis of deterrence" (Decree of the Synods of the Alliance of Evangelical Churches [Bund Evangelischer Kirchen]).

After considerable controversy, the EKD synod, the reunified German church, reached a compromise in 1994. The pastoral care of the military was to be the responsibility of the EKD in the new (eastern) federal states until 2003, while the MSV system was to remain in place in the former West Germany. Recent suggestions point to the transfer of military pastoral care completely to the churches. However, given the strong interest both of the Lutheran state churches and the government's Ministry of Defense in maintaining the MSV, it is doubtful whether these suggestions will be realized in the foreseeable future.

3.4. During this period of trying to reconcile different experiences of military chaplaincy, it might be the time to consider seriously a suggestion that Martin → Niemöller (1892-1984) made in private correspondence in 1951. As he saw it, the pastoral care of the forces should be put back in the hands of the → congregations, and independent structures should be abandoned. To be sure, organizational measures cannot fully protect the church against being used for political ends. Nevertheless, the church has its own mission, as all the participants can recognize. As it credibly lives out its ministry of reconciliation among soldiers, it can make a small contribution toward the required reversal of their thinking. At any rate, such a proposal would remove pastors from military staffs and from participating in training and maneuvers. Any loss they suffer would be only in outward status.

→ Conscientious Objection

Bibliography: I. Drazen and C. B. Currey, *For God and Country: The History of a Constitutional Challenge to the Army Chaplaincy* (Hoboken, N.J., 1995) • F. van Iersel, *Religion and Ethics in the Context of the Armed*

Forces: Exploring the Road to the Renewal of Military Chaplaincy (Tilburg, 1996) • J. MÜLLER-KENT, *Militärseelsorge im Spannungsfeld zwischen kirchlichem Auftrag und militärischer Einbindung* (Hamburg, 1990) • I.-J. WERKNER, *Soldatenseelsorge versus Militärseelsorge* (Baden-Baden, 2001).

JENS MÜLLER-KENT

Millenarianism

1. NT
2. Early Church
3. Islam
4. Western Middle Ages
5. Reformation
6. Western Modern Period

Millenarianism, or chiliasm, was originally the expectation of a thousand-year reign of salvation in which the elect would reign with Christ before the end of world history. It has now become a comprehensive term for programs with a religious origin or reference that aim at a final future salvation within the world.

1. NT

The term "millenarianism" took its origin from the solution that the Book of Revelation proposed for the contradictions that early Christians were experiencing: they were facing severe tribulations, yet they believed in the presence of God's rule. God would shortly gain the victory over his enemies and give to → martyrs, and to all who resisted ungodly power, a new life that no "second," or definitive, → death could ever end. For a thousand years they would reign with God and Christ in priestly closeness before Satan would be granted another short space of time at the end of history (20:4-6, 7-10).

This conception of historical → eschatology was new in primitive Christianity; there are no other instances of the idea of an intervening messianic reign on earth (including 1 Cor. 15:20-28), and it maintains its independent status even over against related traditions in Judaism (e.g., 4 Ezra 7:26-33; *2 Apoc. Bar.* 29–30). There might be some relation to Persian eschatology, which in late antiquity formulated the hope of a thousand-year restoration of the beginning after a final battle between good and evil (*Bahman Yasht* 3.61), and to Plato *Plt.* 10.614-16. In its distinctive form, however, Rev. 20:4-6 is an innovation in religious history. It precedes even Christian speculation about a world-week in which each day counts as a thousand years (*Barn.* 15.4-5).

2. Early Church

The program of Revelation, along with the sensuous millenarianism of Cerinthus (fl. ca. 100), quickly found a reception in the early church and was filled out by ideas of salvation taken mainly from the OT tradition (see → Justin *Dial.* 80-81, → Irenaeus *Adv. haer.* 5.32, → Tertullian *Adv. Marc.* 3.24). Variations arose (see *Apoc. Paul* 21). Finally, Lactantius around 310 achieved an integration with the Greek and Roman idea of a → golden age (*Div. inst.* 7.14-26).

Millenarianism never gained acceptance by the whole church. When the → persecution of Christians ended in the fourth century, it ran into a crisis from which only spiritualizing and reinterpretation could save it. The Byzantine tradition largely robbed it of its edge by advancing the idea of a fulfilled prolongation of the existing state. In the West the solution of → Augustine (354-430) in *City of God* 20.7-9 became normative. He found in the thousand years an open period and related it to the history of the church viewed as the earthly → kingdom of God.

3. Islam

Millenarianism had little importance in Christianity up to the 11th century, but it assumed a distinctive form in → Islam. From the 8th century there arose among the oppressed Shiites (→ Shia, Shiites) expectations of a Mahdi who would bring → righteousness. The Twelver Shiites (in Iran) identified him with the 12th imam, who had been living in hiding from 873/74 and who was represented by specific scholars up to the time of his reappearing. The Sunnites (→ Sunni, Sunnites) then took up the idea but awaited a last caliph of the house of the Prophet. Mahdist movements maintain considerable influence even today.

4. Western Middle Ages

From the beginning of the 12th century, new messianic expectations arose in the West, though Augustine's interpretation of Revelation remained normative. Even Joachim of Fiore (ca. 1135-1202) tried to come to terms with it and used speculations about ages and generations rather than Revelation 20 as the basis of his expectation of a spiritual state of the world that → monasticism would bring in by 1260 as the age of the Spirit succeeding that of the Father and the Son. With this idea he opened up a new line of millenarianism that would initiate social criticism when further developed by the Spiritual Franciscans, popular movements, and Cola di Rienzo (1313-54). The idea also made an impact on the Taborites, whose millenarianism went back to

Revelation 20 and took the dynamic form of social revolution.

5. Reformation

In the 16th century the tradition of millenarianism was particularly influential on the left wing of the → Reformation. In T. → Müntzer (ca. 1489-1525), intensified by mystical → spirituality, it led to the use of force against rulers who were felt to be ungodly. It came to a head and collapsed in the Anabaptist kingdom at Münster. The mainline reformers, Lutheran, Reformed, and Anglican, sharply rejected millenarianism (CA 17; Calvin *Inst.* 3.25.5; Forty-two Articles, art. 41).

6. Western Modern Period

Nevertheless, millenarianism blossomed again in the 17th and 18th centuries, its growth promoted by a new, biblicist regard for the Book of Revelation. In England it reached a climax in the revolutionary period around 1650. On the Continent it emerged in Swabian → Pietism and surrounding circles (J. A. Bengel, F. C. Oetinger, J. H. Jung-Stilling). In North America it became an essential motif in the Great Awakening (→ Revivals) in the 18th century.

By contrast, the → Enlightenment condemned a sensory, biblicist millenarianism (H. Corrodi). The new optimism, however, found it easy to divide world history into periods. Thus G. E. Lessing (1729-81), drawing on Joachim of Fiore, articulated his certainty that an age of fulfillment was coming by describing epochs of humankind (*The Education of the Human Race,* §§85-90). A philosophical millenarianism arose that influenced early → Romanticism. The later F. W. J. von Schelling (1775-1854) gave this view an ecumenically Christian character when he looked forward to a → unity of the church in the age of John, which would follow the ages of Peter and Paul (*Philosophy of Revelation,* lect. 37, esp. p. 324).

In the 19th century various lines ran alongside one another, one of them influencing early → socialism. Theological millenarianism, however, persisted. By way of J. C. (1805-80) and C. F. (1842-1919) Blumhardt and L. Ragaz (1868-1945), it made its way into → religious socialism. A third line made a great impact on such new sects as → Jehovah's Witnesses.

After prior intimation in H. Ibsen (1828-1906, *Emperor and Galilean* [1873]) and preparation of the ground by A. Moeller van den Bruck (1876-1925), the chiliastic idea of the third empire was finally taken up by National Socialism. National Socialist propaganda failed to convince of this usage, however, and ceased to use it after 1939. E. Bloch's (1885-1977) proposal to rescue chiliastic traditions by correctively integrating them into the → utopia of → Marxism met with no success. In 1944 the Roman → curia rejected millenarianism (DH 3839), and it remains largely discredited today.

Bibliography: O. BÖCHER, G. G. BLUM, R. KONRAD, and R. BAUCKHAM, "Chiliasmus," *TRE* 7.723-45 (bibliography) • B. S. CAPP, *The Fifth Monarchy Men: A Study in Seventeenth-Century English Millenarianism* (London, 1972) • N. COHN, *The Pursuit of the Millennium: Revolutionary Millenarians and Mystical Anarchists of the Middle Ages* (London, 1993; orig. pub., 1957) • S. HUNT, ed., *Christian Millenarianism: From the Early Church to Waco* (Bloomington, Ind., 2001) • *Millenarianism and Messianism in Early Modern European Culture* (Dordrecht, 2001) vol. 1, *Jewish Messianism in the Early Modern World* (ed. M. Goldish and R. H. Popkin); vol. 2, *Catholic Millenarianism: From Savonarola to the Abbé Grégoire* (ed. K. A. Kottman); vol. 3, *The Millenarian Turn: Millenarian Contexts of Science, Politics, and Everyday Anglo-American Life in the Seventeenth and Eighteenth Centuries* (ed. J. E. Force and R. H. Popkin); vol. 4, *Continental Millenarians: Protestants, Catholics, Heretics* (ed. J. C. Laursen and R. H. Popkin) • J. MOLTMANN, *The Coming of God: Christian Eschatology* (Minneapolis, 1996) esp. 129-256 • W. NIGG, *Das ewige Reich. Geschichte einer Sehnsucht und einer Enttäuschung* (Erlenbach, 1944; 3d ed., 1967) • M. REEVES and W. GOULD, *Joachim of Fiore and the Myth of the Eternal Evangel in the Nineteenth Century* (Oxford, 1987) • E. R. SANDEEN, *The Roots of Fundamentalism: British and American Millenarianism, 1880-1930* (Chicago, 1970) • F. W. J. SCHELLING, *Philosophie der Offenbarung* (vol. 2; Darmstadt, 1966) • R. SCHWARZ, *Die apokalyptische Theologie Thomas Müntzers und der Taboriten* (Tübingen, 1977) • T. P. WEBER, *Living in the Shadow of the Second Coming: American Premillennialism, 1875-1982* (exp. ed.; Chicago, 1987) • H.-A. WILCKE, *Das Problem eines messianischen Zwischenreichs bei Paulus* (Zurich, 1967).

MARTIN KARRER

Ministry, Ministerial Offices

1. Roman Catholicism
2. Orthodoxy
3. Protestantism
4. Scripture
5. Current Issues
    5.1. Ministry, Ministries
    5.2. Ordination
    5.3. Candidates

5.4. Oversight, episkopē
5.5. Apostolic Succession, Historic Episcopate
5.6. Papacy

Ministry, carrying forth Christ's mission in the world, is fundamentally the task of the church, the whole → people of God, and is conferred on each Christian in → baptism. Certain persons, however, are called and ordained to ministries of leadership within the church itself. These ordained ministries, sometimes referred to as offices or holy orders, are understood differently in the various branches of the Christian church.

1. Roman Catholicism
The → Roman Catholic Church now has three levels of holy orders, in contrast to the seven orders that existed until → Vatican II: the → episcopate, presbyterate/priesthood, and diaconate. Since Vatican II the diaconate again constitutes a permanent ecclesiastical office, although candidates for the priesthood are still ordained first as → deacons. Beyond these offices, the laity can also perform the ministries of lector and acolyte, the bestowal and at least temporary exercise of which are also prerequisites for becoming a deacon (1983 CIC 230, 1009.1, 1035.1, 1050).

Ordination as → bishop confers the "fullness of the sacrament of orders" (*Lumen gentium* [*LG*] 21), bishops having previously been ordained as deacons and presbyters (→ Elder). The papacy, Bishopric of Rome and Patriarchate of the West, is not a separate order but is distinguished from other bishops by its primacy of jurisdiction over the Roman Catholic Church as a whole. Primacy also includes doctrinal → authority, which under certain conditions is considered → infallible. The bishops stand in apostolic succession — the uninterrupted chain of consecrations going back to the → apostles. In the Roman Catholic understanding, a bishop's legitimacy and validity depend on this succession and on being in communion with the bishop of → Rome. Episcopal ministry involves the threefold functions of teaching, sanctifying (esp. with regard to the Eucharist), and leadership. The bishop is the → pastor of the local church (diocese). Bishops possess the authority to ordain, imparting to the ordained a specific and indelible mark *(character indelibilis)*. They are members of the college of bishops under the leadership of the → pope. This collegium embodies the communion of the local churches and thus the → unity of the church.

Presbyters/priests extend the bishop's ministry of proclaiming the good news, guiding the commu-

nity, and presiding at the → Eucharist in parishes within the → diocese. Deacons also extend the bishop's ministry, serving the people of God in → liturgy, word, and → charity in conjunction with the presbyterate (*LG* 29). Since the 12th century the Latin church has admitted only celibate males to the priesthood and the episcopacy. Permanent deacons may be married.

2. Orthodoxy
The → Orthodox Church understands ministry, as does Roman Catholicism, as exhibiting unbroken continuity with the → early church. It is based on the threefold division of bishops, presbyters/priests, and deacons. It sees the unity of the church in the episcopal collegium, whose teaching authority has been expressed in the original ecumenical → councils of the church. Though Orthodoxy acknowledges the traditional primacy of the bishop of Rome, it rejects the Roman understanding of the supreme jurisdictional and doctrinal authority of the papacy.

Orthodox bishops constitute episcopal synods and the → Pan-Orthodox Council, and they take their orientation from the authority of metropolitans and → patriarchs, while acknowledging the → ecumenical patriarch of Constantinople as primus inter pares. The relation of these two episcopal ministries of oversight (synods/council and metropolitans/patriarchs) is not clearly defined.

The decisive features of the Orthodox understanding of ministry are the focus on pneumatic elements — in a profound sense → ordination is an invocation of the Spirit and not a juridical conferral of authority — and an orientation toward the eucharistic community. According to Orthodox understanding, there can be no truly ecumenical councils until the schism of 1054 is healed and their bishops are again in full communion with Rome. Orthodox churches admit married men to the priesthood, but bishops must be celibate, usually coming from monastic communities (→ Monasticism).

3. Protestantism
The → Reformation understood the notion of ordained ministry as service, especially as public or open proclamation of the Word and administration of the → sacraments (e.g., 2 Cor. 5:18). This understanding does not take its orientation from any spiritual quality attaching to the officebearer. Protestant churches discontinued the Latin church's requirement of → celibacy for ordination.

3.1. Martin → Luther (1483-1546) characteristically spoke about ministries *(Ämter)* in the plural, taking as his point of departure the NT apostles, gospel writers, and → prophets (WA 50.634.13), all of whom fostered God's Word and work. He discussed two lines of understanding the origin of ministries. On the one hand, he focused on the problem of → organization (and the corresponding apostolic instructions) that make it necessary for certain individual Christians to take over functions that in principle are given to all Christians as part of the universal priesthood. On the other hand, he understood that Christ himself commissioned, by means of charismatic calling, certain persons with special gifts as described in Eph. 4:11.

By contrast, Philipp → Melanchthon (1497-1560) spoke about the *one* ministry of (public) → proclamation and administration of the sacraments, an office established by God and bestowed upon certain persons through ordination. Articles 5 and 14 of the → Augsburg Confession especially make this point, which also influences the overall understanding of the church as expressed in the CA (art. 7). The understanding of the office of bishop in the CA (art. 28; see also Melanchthon's *Treatise*) assumes that from the perspective of their basic functions and thus also according to divine law, no distinction exists between bishops and pastors.

Because in the Reformation the bishops in Germany and adjacent areas remained faithful to Rome, → Lutheran churches there developed without bishops. The ministry of oversight was given to → superintendents, and the governance of the churches often devolved on the princes. In Scandinavian countries, in contrast, churches accepted the Reformation intact, and thus the episcopal structures were retained. In this respect, the Scandinavian Lutheran churches resemble the churches of the → Anglican Communion.

3.2. According to John → Calvin (1509-64), ministry in the church exists according to God's will in four different forms: shepherds, teachers, elders, and deacons. Calvin adopted this doctrine from Martin → Bucer (1491-1551) and at the same time modified elements of the threefold ministerial structure of the early church. On this view, the basic ministry is that of the shepherd, or pastor, and the other offices participate in that ministry. The pastor proclaims the → gospel, administers the sacraments, provides leadership in the local → congregation, and addresses issues of → church discipline, being supported by the elders especially in matters of discipline. Like Luther, Calvin did not see the ministry as being derived from the universal priesthood. Within the congregation, ministers represent God himself. Nor did Calvin believe that a separate

episcopal ministry was a necessary part of God's plan for the → church.

Calvin's understanding of ministries variously influenced the → church orders and → confessions of faith in the Reformed churches. The Second → Helvetic Confession (pub. 1566), for example, specifically underscores the equal spiritual rank of the various ministries.

3.3. Yet another understanding of ministerial offices and their structure is found in the Anglican churches. The church in England went through the Reformation with its structures intact, adopting the early church threefold structure of bishops, presbyters/priests, and deacons. Anglicanism thus more closely resembles the Roman Catholic structure than do the other Reformation traditions. Especially the office of bishop is, by virtue of divine law, of fundamental importance for the church; it derives from the apostles themselves and is bestowed through the → laying on of hands. This Anglican understanding has been of particular importance in recent ecumenical discussions. Anglican churches are restoring a permanent diaconate, though being ordained deacon is still a prerequisite for ordination to the priesthood.

3.4. Since the Reformation, critical voices have appeared, including Socinianism, → spiritualism, and → Pietism. They have emphasized the notions of universal priesthood and of the various charismata mentioned in the letters of Paul (e.g., in 1 Cor. 14:26-33; → Charisma), though they have not entirely abandoned the notion that certain individual Christians may well be commissioned for special ministry. Lutheran → orthodoxy (§1), in contrast, developed the doctrine of ordained ministry beyond that of the Reformers themselves and added to it a doctrine of → hierarchy applicable to the various offices (e.g., J. Gerhard).

→ Methodism also has a well-developed understanding of the office of pastor over against the congregation. Because of John → Wesley's (1703-91) reluctant decision to perform ordinations himself, however, Methodist preachers lack various features attaching to Anglican priests, and Methodist bishops, derived from the office of superintendents, are not understood as standing in historic apostolic succession.

Disputes arose during the 19th century within Lutheran confessional theology regarding the question of ministry. One side emphasized the distinction between the ministry and the congregation (A. Vilmar, W. Löhe, T. Kliefoth), while the other understood ministry as a function of the congregation that the latter transfers to certain individuals

(J. Höfling, A. Dieckhoff). After the dissolution of the system of territorial → church government in Germany and adjacent areas in the early 20th century, many European Protestant churches introduced the office of the territorial bishop. The Reformed and several united and uniting churches have the leadership office of → preses (Ger. *Präses,* from Lat. *praeses,* "guard, president, ruler").

The various Protestant systems of ministry developed in Europe were transplanted to the immigrant churches of North and South America and the Pacific and also were introduced in the missionary churches of Africa and Asia (→ Mission 3).

4. Scripture

4.1. The NT uses the term *hiereus* (priest) mainly in referring to the sacrificial ministry of → Jesus himself or in narratives referring to priests of the temple. But the whole company of the redeemed can also be called priests (Rev. 1:6; 5:10; 20:6), and in 1 Pet. 2:5, 9 all those who have been baptized are called a holy or a royal priesthood (see 5.1). The NT picture of ministries within the church constitutes a clean break with the sacerdotal priesthood of the OT. Instead, early Christian congregations had various specific, permanent offices that → Paul qualifies Christologically as *diakoniai* (ministries) or *leitourgia* (service, 2 Cor. 9:12). The Pastoral Epistles attest that these leadership ministries became increasingly important in the sense of a pastoral or episcopal office in which an individual leads through service to Word and sacrament.

There is also concern for preserving apostolic tradition or even for representing Christ to the worshiping assembly. Such an understanding is anticipated in Phil. 1:1 and 1 Pet. 5:1-5, and an early form might even be intended in the *proïstamenoi* ("[those who] have charge of you," NRSV; "your leaders and counsellors," NEB) of 1 Thess. 5:12, corresponding to the *presbyteroi* (elders) of the Jewish Christian communities. Such a development was certainly commensurate with the altered situation of the early church, which was experiencing an increase in the size of congregations, an increase in the temporal distance from the original events and the apostles, and problems of community identity.

In the course of this development — possibly even during the NT period itself — it is understandable that the leaders of the communities began taking initiative for the eucharistic meal and assuming responsibility for baptism. Furthermore, there may well be legitimate reasons for the emergence of the "monarchical episcopate" and of the regional bishopric, and thus for the emergence of the early

church's threefold understanding of ministry. Although the idea of apostolic succession in the sense of a historical continuity of apostolic doctrine and ministry doubtless became an important consideration, its subsequent form as a transmission of apostolic office as such cannot be derived from the NT.

4.2. The various understandings of ministry and the attendant structures discussed in the sections above need to be examined against the biblical evidence. Any attempt to develop an understanding of office for the church must deal with the variety of orders and polities in the early church. A view of ministry as ordained office, for example, must deal with the complex charismatic structure of ministries as attested in the Pauline communities. Binding the administration of sacraments to a particular ministry, a connection that seems self-evident to both Roman Catholic and Reformation understandings, is not explicitly supported by the NT itself. The Lutheran concept of the one ministry must stand up against the variety of community ministries witnessed to in the NT.

Only at the end of the NT period do the Pastoral Epistles begin differentiating offices involved in congregational leadership to be conferred by ordination. Mention is made, however, only of groups involved in congregational leadership. What is known as the monarchical episcopate (i.e., the bishop as head of the college of presbyters and deacons of a local church) and, even more, the concept of regional bishoprics were not developed until the post-NT period. The same applies to the idea of apostolic succession. Jesus himself expresses no intentions concerning congregational organization; he only chooses and sends forth → disciples.

In light of these findings, questions concerning the nature of ministry and which forms apply to the church by "divine right" are more difficult than earlier thought. None of the historic views of ministry can be derived directly from biblical evidence; conversely, the various concepts of ministry here outlined do not contradict the biblical testimonies. The rediscovery by biblical scholars of the variety of ministries in the NT has stimulated the ecumenical discussions of recent times (→ Ecumenical Dialogue).

5. Current Issues

5.1. *Ministry, Ministries*

The emphasis in Vatican II on the church as the people of God (*LG* chap. 2), together with a rediscovery in the Protestant churches of the NT concept of the church as the priesthood of all believers, has led to a declericalization of the concept of ministry. By virtue of their baptism all Christians are called to proclaim the gospel, and it is the entire congregation that celebrates the sacraments.

Yet, as the Reformers taught (see 3.1-2), and according to today's ecumenical consensus, a ministry exists within and for the sake of the people of God that by ordination is charged with the spiritual leadership of the church through preaching and teaching the gospel and presiding at the celebration of the sacraments. This ordained ministry must maintain unity and adherence to apostolic doctrine and must speak and act in the name of the whole community. These ministers stand *with* the community but also *before* it as representatives of Christ. Besides the ordained ministry there are many other ministries and ecclesial vocations in the church (e.g., → lectors, ministers of communion, teachers, → catechists, social workers, administrators) that exist in their own right. Often persons appointed to such ministries are recognized as such by a rite of conferral. Still under discussion is how these ministries relate to a permanent, ordained diaconate.

5.2. *Ordination*
There is general ecumenical agreement that the church ordains persons for the special ministry/ministries of leadership within the community of the faithful. Ordination actualizes the calling, sending, and blessing for the ministry conferred, with the calling involving an established process that culminates in the liturgical act. Ordination involves the laying on of hands with the invocation of the → Holy Spirit. It lays claim to the entire person and cannot be repeated, though persons may have their ministry withdrawn or may themselves withdraw from office.

The issue here is validity. For an ordination to be valid, the Roman Catholic/Orthodox tradition requires that it be performed by bishops who stand within the historic episcopate (see 5.5 below); ordinations not so performed are said to be defective. In Protestant churches ordination is normally performed by ministers of the regional *episkopē,* which for some churches is the historic episcopate (see 5.5) and which for others is the succession of apostolic doctrine.

5.3. *Candidates*
Until recently, candidates for ordination were always males, which remains the case in the Roman Catholic and Orthodox churches. Today, however, many Protestant churches also ordain women. Pressure to do so has come from the movements in society for equal rights for women (→ Women's Movement), but the theological justification for such ordinations is the renewed understanding of the church as an eschatological community where gender differences no longer apply (Gal. 3:26-28).

Very recently the ordination of noncelibate → homosexuals has become an issue in many churches. It is not yet clear whether being "one in Christ Jesus" (v. 28) will be seen to apply to such persons as well.

5.4. *Oversight, episkopē*
The ministry of oversight — that is, caring for the apostolicity of the church's life and teaching — has traditionally been exercised by bishops. This essential ministry, which transcends congregations and thus becomes a focus for unity, was not lost in the Protestant churches deprived of bishops. Either they continued a personal form of the ministry through superintendents or presidents, or they provided for oversight in collegial ways through presbyteries or classes. In Lutheran churches there has been a tendency to replace church presidents with bishops, thus keeping the *episkopē* a personal ministry, for which → Reformed and Presbyterian churches prefer a collegial form. A variety of titles are given to those who exercise oversight in larger or smaller divisions (e.g., archbishop, presiding bishop, metropolitan, bishop suffragan, bishop coadjutor, superintendent, dean).

5.5. *Apostolic Succession, Historic Episcopate*
How the church is apostolic and how ordained ministry is involved in apostolicity is one of today's most difficult ecumenical questions. Vatican II, with its emphases on the church as the people of God and on the → collegiality of the → teaching office, together with → Faith and Order's historic document *Baptism, Eucharist, and Ministry* (1982), evidences a rethinking of what constitutes the apostolicity of the church. According to the latter document, "The primary manifestation of apostolic succession is to be found in the apostolic tradition of the Church as a whole. The succession is an expression of the permanence and, therefore, of the continuity of Christ's own mission in which the Church participates. Within the Church the ordained ministry has a particular task of preserving and actualizing the apostolic faith" ("Ministry," par. 35).

The historic episcopate — the unbroken chain of ordinations from the apostles to the present day — is now generally seen as a sign, though not a guarantee, of apostolicity. In historic declarations of full communion between Anglicans and Lutherans, signatories of the → Porvoo Common Statement (the British and Irish Anglican churches and the Nordic and Baltic Lutheran churches, 1992), the Called to Common Mission agreement (the Episcopal Church, U.S.A., and the Evangelical Lutheran Church in

America, 2001), and the Waterloo Declaration (the Anglican Church of Canada and the Evangelical Lutheran Church in Canada, 2001) have been able to reconcile their respective ordained ministries on the basis of such a distinction. Following the earlier Niagara Report (1987), Anglicans have been able to recognize in Lutheran ministries "a succession in the presiding ministry of a church" (par. 94), and Lutherans have been able to accept (where necessary) the historic episcopate as "a valuable symbol of unity and continuity in the Church" (par. 92).

Discussions between Protestants and Roman Catholic or Orthodox churches have so far not been as fruitful. They may yet, however, find a way to apply a renewed understanding of apostolicity to resolve the problem of the *defectus* in ordinations (see 5.2 above).

5.6. *Papacy*

One of the most difficult ecumenical problems is the papacy as it is presently understood in the Roman Catholic Church. In this case also, the emphasis of Vatican II on the collegiality of teaching authority is more acceptable to others than the developments initiated by Vatican I. Orthodox churches and even some Protestant churches are prepared to accept the bishop of Rome as primus inter pares but find the full Roman doctrine of the papacy — including infallibility — unacceptable. Recognizing the impasse, John Paul II in the encyclical *Ut unum sint* (1995) has invited other church leaders to a "patient and fraternal → dialogue" on "a way of exercising the primacy which, while in no way renouncing what is essential to its mission, is nonetheless open to a new situation" (pars. 96, 95).

→ Ecumenism, Ecumenical Movement

Bibliography: Roman Catholicism: B. COOKE, *Ministry to Word and Sacrament: History and Theology* (Philadelphia, 1980) • *LTK,* supp. vols. 1-3 (texts of Vatican II, with detailed commentaries) • P. PASTERCZYK, *Theologie des kirchlichen Amtes. Das priesterliche Amt in den Dokumenten des 2. Vatikanischen Konzils und in der nachkonziliaren Theologie* (Frankfurt, 2002).

Orthodoxy: N. NISSIOTIS, *Die Theologie der Ostkirche im ökumenischen Dialog* (Stuttgart, 1968) • C. H. RATSCHOW, "Amt / Ämter / Amtsverständnis VIII," *TRE* 2.596-600.

Protestantism: I. ASHEIM and V. R. GOLD, eds., *Episcopacy in the Lutheran Church? Studies in the Development and Definition of the Office of Church Leadership* (Philadelphia, 1970) • W. BRUNOTTE, *Das geistliche Amt bei Luther* (Berlin, 1959) • U. KÜHN, *Kirche* (Gütersloh, 1980) • H. A. LIEBERG, *Amt und Ordination bei Luther und Melanchthon* (Berlin, 1962).

Scripture: D. L. BARTLETT, *Ministry in the NT* (Minneapolis, 1993) • J. BURTCHAELL, *From Synagogue to Church: Public Services and Offices in Earliest Christian Communities* (Cambridge, 1992) • E. SCHWEIZER, *Church Order in the NT* (London, 1961).

Bilateral reports: ANGLICAN-LUTHERAN INTERNATIONAL COMMISSION, "The Diaconate as Ecumenical Opportunity" (1995), *Growth in Agreement II: Reports and Agreed Statements of Ecumenical Conversations on a World Level, 1982-1998* (ed. J. Gros, H. Meyer, and W. G. Rusch; Geneva, 2000) 38-54 (see other ecumenical statements in this volume) • EASTERN ORTHODOX–ROMAN CATHOLIC DIALOGUE, "The Sacrament of Order in the Sacramental Structure of the Church" (1988), ibid., 671-79 • P. C. EMPIE and T. A. MURPHY, eds., *Papal Primacy and the Universal Church: Lutherans and Catholics in Dialogue V* (Minneapolis, 1974) • LUTHERAN–ROMAN CATHOLIC JOINT COMMISSION, *Church and Justification* (Geneva, 1994) esp. §4.5 • ROMAN CATHOLIC–LUTHERAN JOINT COMMISSION, "The Ministry in the Church" (1981), *Growth in Agreement I: Reports and Agreed Statements of Ecumenical Conversations on a World Level* (ed. H. Meyer and L. Vischer; Geneva, 1984) 248-75 • SWEDISH LUTHERAN–ROMAN CATHOLIC DIALOGUE, *The Office of Bishop* (Geneva, 1993).

Current issues: P. C. BOUTENEFF and A. D. FALCONER, eds., *Episkopé and Episcopacy and the Quest for Visible Unity: Two Consultations* (Geneva, 1999) • M. KANYORO, ed., *In Search of a Round Table: Gender, Theology, and Church Leadership* (Geneva, 1997) • G. KRETSCHMAR, *Das bischöfliche Amt. Kirchengeschichtliche und ökumenische Studien zur Frage des kirchlichen Amtes* (Göttingen, 1999) • J. H. REUMANN, *Ministries Examined: Laity, Clergy, Women, and Bishops in a Time of Change* (Minneapolis, 1987) • E. SCHILLEBEECKX, *Ministry: A Case for Change* (London, 1981) • M. THURIAN, *Priesthood and Ministry: Ecumenical Research* (London, 1983) • WORLD COUNCIL OF CHURCHES, *Baptism, Eucharist, and Ministry* (Geneva, 1982).

EUGENE L. BRAND and ULRICH KÜHN

Minor Prophets

The Minor Prophets, or Book of the Twelve (Gk. *Dōdekaprophēton;* Lat. *Prophetae Minores,* first so designated by → Augustine, *De civ. Dei* 18.29), conclude the second part of the → canon (§1) in the Hebrew Bible, namely, the Prophets. Unlike the tradition of the → Reformation, the older tradition understands the 12 writings as a single book (see Sir. 49:10; *B. Bat.* 14b/15a) and organizes them according to a chronological principle. The first group includes the prophets dating (either actually or allegedly) to the eighth century: Hosea, Joel, Amos, Obadiah, Jonah, and Micah; the second group, those dating to the seventh century: Nahum, Habakkuk, and Zephaniah; and the final group, the postexilic prophets Haggai, Zechariah, and Malachi.

The LXX orders the minor prophets differently. The first six (Hosea, Amos, Micah, Joel, Obadiah, Jonah) are arranged according to length, with Jonah last presumably because of its narrative character. The organizational variation in the LXX shows that the process of collecting and organizing these writings into a single book had a lengthy history. (Except for the Leningrad Codex, Hebrew texts have only a single concluding Masorah.)

The collection itself includes writings dating to different periods (8th-3d cent. B.C.) and with varying content. It was probably begun during the postexilic period and concluded during the third century B.C. Even though Zechariah 9–11, 12–14, and Malachi come from the hand of different authors, these sections were condensed down to only two books, showing that the redactors consciously organized these writings according to the → number 12 (commensurate with the 12 → tribes of Israel). This organization also reflects the redactors' own angles of vision insofar as the connecting element is a reflection on → Israel's historical experiences with its God, a reflection found in all 12 books and conducted amid a consciousness of past judgment and in anticipation of future → salvation. To these reflections, the prophets as messengers of God added their own judgments. Despite the various differences between the prophets, the redactors considered prophecy in Israel to be a unified witness (→ Prophet, Prophecy, 2), whose end coincided with the end of the Minor Prophets.

→ Bible Manuscripts and Editions 1

Bibliography: Commentaries: E. R. ACHTEMEIER (NIBC; Peabody, Mass., 1996) • M. H. FLOYD (FOTL; Grand Rapids, 2000) pt. 2.

Other works: A. O. BELLIS, *Many Voices: Multicultural Responses to the Minor Prophets* (Lanham, Md., 1995) • T. COLLINS, *The Mantle of Elijah* (Sheffield, 1993) 59-87 • P. R. HOUSE, *The Unity of the Twelve* (Sheffield, 1990) • B. A. JONES, *The Formation of the Book of the Twelve* (Atlanta, 1995) • K. KOCH, *The Prophets* (2 vols.; London, 1982-83) • J. LINDBLOM, *Prophecy in Ancient Israel* (Philadelphia, 1980; orig. pub., 1962) • J. D. NOGALSKI, *Redactional Processes in the Book of the Twelve* (Berlin, 1993). See also the bibliographies in the separate articles on each of the Minor Prophets.

PETER MOMMER

Minorites → Franciscans

Minorities

1. In Sociological Perspective
2. Variations
3. Discrimination and Tolerance
4. In Theological Perspective

The basic definition of a minority is numerical. It is the smaller number of persons or the smaller part of a group, as in the lesser number of persons voting for a choice not selected in a democratic process of decision.

1. In Sociological Perspective

"Minority" is often used in a sociological sense, usually for a group that is a numerical/statistical minority within a larger → society and that has identifiable characteristics (such as age, giftedness, religion, social behavior, skin color, ethnic or racial heritage, language, immigrant status, sexual orientation, or disability; → Sociology). Members of such a minority may feel closely bound together because of distinguishing features or heritage that is shared in common or because of treatment from the society at large.

Occasionally (e.g., because of giftedness), the treatment from society may generally be positive and sometimes laudatory. Often, however, societal treatment is negative or is experienced as discriminatory by members of the minority. Sometimes a distinguishing characteristic of the minority is emphasized by the wider society, while other features of the minority are ignored; such experience can be the basis of stereotypes and → prejudice against the minority. Minority individuals and groups may receive unequal treatment on the basis of features that are of no objective significance in the given situation, such as employment or housing. Both overt and more disguised forms of discrimination serve to perpetuate the minority situation and to marginalize the minority group (→ Marginalized Groups; Class and Social Stratum).

Whether a group is considered a minority in the sociological sense may be defined either by the society at large or by the group itself. Sometimes a group that is actually a statistical majority will consider itself or be considered by society as a minority because it finds itself in a subordinate position or experiences oppression in society. (For example, women are sometimes referred to as a minority because of societal oppression, even though statistically they may in fact be a slight majority in the population.) Technically, such a group is more correctly referred to as marginalized rather than as a minority. In contrast, some groups that may be a statistical minority object to being referred to as a minority because they perceive it to be a pejorative label; they prefer instead to be referred to by ethnic identity or by another distinguishing characteristic they have chosen.

The majority in a society usually has a certain → power and can restrict the possibilities of minorities. Some minorities (e.g., persons who are disabled, older persons), however, have been able to use political systems, lobbies, demonstrations, writing, and other means to raise public awareness of their needs and concerns, to address discriminatory behavior, and to achieve levels of power.

2. Variations

In some parts of the world, national minorities live in regional or local concentrations. In other places, minorities have no particular locale but may be linked by meetings, publications, media programs, or → technology (e.g., women, persons who are gifted).

In countries that have large immigrant populations — in a sense, many minority groups in one population (e.g., Latino Americans in the United States) — the minority groups may eventually adopt the dominant culture. In such cases, the features that distinguished them may live on in family or local traditions and celebrations, or as a subculture with some institutions of its own, such as → education, religious traditions, and political views. In other cases, minority groups may resist adopting the dominant culture and seek to keep their recognizable identity.

3. Discrimination and Tolerance

Discrimination against minorities is often deeply ingrained and takes many years to deal with effectively. Law-abiding strategies include granting equal → rights, exposing and condemning discrimination, and approving measures that enable minorities to improve their social situation, including financial and educational measures.

Integration and → pluralism demand some → tolerance of those who think differently. This quality is difficult to achieve when → ideologies are present that claim absoluteness, and therefore those who work for tolerance must radically question such absolute claims. Those working for tolerance usually do so on several fronts: developing reconciling/peacemaking strategies, galvanizing persons to be outspoken protectors of human rights, and highlighting the values of diversity.

4. In Theological Perspective

From a theological point of view, all baptized persons are equal in the → kingdom of God and in the → church on earth. Discrimination and hierarchies are done away with by the cross — as Paul says, in the church there is no longer Jew or Greek, slave or free, male or female; we are all one in Christ Jesus (Gal. 3:28). All are equally persons for whom Christ died and therefore equally reconciled with him and (potentially and rightfully) with one another. The → gospel turns upside down the standards and behavior patterns of the world, so that those who are first become last, and those who are last become first. The lowly are raised up, and the haughty are put down. And all of Jesus' followers are called to be servants of one another (→ Discipleship).

There will be no minorities or majorities in God's kingdom in the *eschaton*. The eschatological hope is shared equally by all believers, regardless of race, gender, age, giftedness, religion, social behavior, and so forth. If the church is to be a proleptic people in the world, a sign and foretaste of the eschatological age, then it must witness to that reality in the present by treating all baptized persons as equals (J. Moltmann).

God's Word awakens faith in us, in which we trust ourselves to Christ and receive from him the gift of community as church. Trust in God is also the source of trust in one another within the Christian community. Mutual trust and respect and love are signs of the → people of God, and so we seek by the power of the Spirit to overcome discrimination and prejudice within the body of believers. Such trust and love include living with differences and rejoicing in the diversity within the church on earth, through the fellowship of the Holy Spirit. The church is called to live such a witness in the world. The experience of sociality in the → congregation and in the church at all levels, national and international, is essential to living out the witness of the gospel.

At the same time, the church must keep vigilance in the world. In the realm of worldly social order and judicial systems, the church must recognize where discrimination and unfair practices exist and must work for justice in society so that all voices are heard and all persons are treated fairly, justly, and with respect. The church is called to name injustice and prejudice and to work for human rights and equal treatment of all human beings.

→ Nation, Nationalism; Racism; Refugees

Bibliography: R. S. APPLEBY, *The Ambivalence of the Sacred: Religion, Violence, and Reconciliation* (New York, 2000) • G. BAUM and H. WELLS, eds., *The Reconciliation of People: Challenge to the Churches* (Maryknoll, N.Y., 1997) • J. MOLTMANN, *The Spirit of Life* (Minneapolis, 1992) chap. 11 • M. Y. RIGGS, *Awake, Arise, and Act: A Womanist Call for Black Liberation* (Cleveland, 1994) • P. SCHMIECHEN, *Christ the Reconciler: A Theology for Opposites, Differences, and Enemies* (Grand Rapids, 1996) • M. VOLF, *Exclusion and Embrace: A Theological Exploration of Identity, Otherness, and Reconciliation* (Nashville, 1996) • H. WALTON JR., *African American Power and Politics: The Political Context Variable* (New York, 1997) • C. WEST, *Prophetic Thought in Postmodern Times* (Monroe, Maine, 1993) • W. WINK, *Engaging the Powers: Discernment and Resistance in a World of Domination* (Minneapolis, 1992).

MARGARET A. KRYCH

Minster

The word "minster" (Ger. *Münster*) derives from the ecclesiastical Lat. *monasterium* (Gk. *monastērion*) by way of OEng. *mynster*. It originally denoted a monastery church or a → monastery. It came to be applied to → cathedrals that were monastic foundations (e.g., York, Lincoln, Lichfield, also in southern Europe). But since monastic churches could also serve as parish churches, it might also have a more general use, especially when houses for the clergy surrounded the church in the monastic style.

From the early → Middle Ages we also find a use for colleges of secular canons, that is, clergy living under rule. In southern Germany a link has been seen between the use for a city parish church and the cathedral style (e.g., in Freiburg and Ulm). Such use has also been construed as an expression of the claim of citizens for emancipation within the church (→ Clergy and Laity).

Bibliography: E. BADSTÜBNER, *Klosterkirchen im Mittelalter. Die Baukunst der Reformorder* (2d ed.; Munich, 1985) • F. G. BLACKLOCK, *The Suppressed Benedictine Minster, and Other Ancient and Modern Institutions of the Borough of Leominster* (rev. ed.; Leominster, 1999) • W. BRAUNFELS, *Monasteries of Western Europe: The Architecture of the Orders* (London, 1993) • A. ERLANDE-BRANDENBURG, *The Cathedral: The Social and Architectural Dynamics of Construction* (Cambridge, 1994) • A. WILLEY, *York Minster* (London, 1998).

GERLINDE STROHMAIER-WIEDERANDERS

Miracle

1. Basic Considerations
   1.1. Distinctions
   1.2. Concept
   1.3. Approach
   1.4. Criterion and Interpretations
   1.5. Definition
   1.6. Limitations
   1.7. Miracle Workers and Witnesses
2. NT
   2.1. Jesus
   2.2. Apostles
   2.3. The Devil and His Servants
   2.4. Theological Meaning
3. Practical Theology
   3.1. Personal Piety
   3.2. Tension
   3.3. Reformulation
   3.4. Church Practice

1. Basic Considerations

1.1. *Distinctions*

No systematic hermeneutical examination of miracles in the larger sense can avoid articulating exactly which elements are to be addressed as objective facts and which as part of the concept itself. Because arguments on the two sides can no longer be adduced in support of one another, the modes in which the two aspects are examined necessarily also diverge.

The remaining conceptual content prompts even further distinctions, depending on whether one is dealing with a simple or a complex concept. Only simple concepts must derive directly from reality and are able to illuminate some part of the latter and make it more comprehensible. Complex concepts do not need to be commensurate with reality.

The remaining factual content also requires further distinctions, depending on whether one is dealing with an alleged or an actual fact. Only the alleged fact must be articulated conceptually such that the perception of its extraordinary features does not degenerate into an inability to see what is genuinely at hand. An actual fact, however, need only be confirmed by perception.

1.2. *Concept*

The authentic concept of miracle is complex. From the very outset, this concept also includes products of the → imagination, of misunderstanding, and so on, and retrospectively it ends up including even more such phenomena. Hence any alleged simple concept that might emerge alongside this complex concept cannot be an authentic concept of miracle. Not accepting this distinction condemns conceptual discussion to an exercise with tautologies and concepts contrary to → logic. The simple concept can attest only something that genuinely has taken place or can take place. Such, however, would no longer be a miracle. By contrast, → fundamentalism has developed its own, ontologically affirmative concept of miracles that it then uses for self-confirmation.

The circumstances attaching to authentic miracles are an alleged fact. Any contrary insistence on genuine facticity leads directly to → occultism and → parapsychology, which are treated under a separate heading.

1.3. *Approach*

These phenomena of miracles can be addressed systematically only by rationally reconstructing how a simple concept becomes a complex one and how the alleged fact joins or replaces an actual one (e.g., how can thunder become an interpretive or commanding heavenly or divine voice?). This undertaking simultaneously constitutes a critique of miracles.

1.4. *Criterion and Interpretations*

Phenomenally, the borders between the simple (inauthentic) and complex (authentic) miracle concept are fluid. One criterion by which one can identify the latter is how well that concept lends itself to addressing questions of → faith, of a religious interpretation of the world, and the like. Symbolic scriptural interpretation (→ Exegesis, Biblical, 2), which is already at work in the later NT strata, understands miracles (specifically → Jesus' healings and exorcism of → demons, or unclean spirits) exclusively as → signs of the kind of faith Jesus intended or that the biblical writers themselves already had.

The interpretations (→ Meaning) attaching to both alleged and actual facts of miracles often overlap and thus may be difficult to distinguish empirically. Indeed, the latter's accessibility to experience depends not least on the extent to which the fact in question can be verified historically in the first place.

1.5. *Definition*

The best definition of miracle must do justice to the following criterion: The degree to which the authentic concept of miracle can be employed depends on the degree to which the fact constituting the miracle is assigned to allegation, on the one hand, and to reality, on the other. If the acceptance of a miracle from a written account is utterly arbitrary, then the allegedly factual miracle in that account must also be considered utterly beyond explanation. The easier it is to impose arbitrary interpretations on accounts of healing miracles, the more difficult should it also be to assume that the miracle can be explained by reference to autosuggestion or hypnosis.

The definitions suggested by J. W. von Goethe (1749-1832) and I. Kant (1724-1804; → Kantianism) fulfill the criteria mentioned here and in the previous section. "The miracle is faith's favorite child" (Goethe, *Faust* 1, "Night"). Kant suggests that "miracles are phenomena whose causes and causal laws are and must remain utterly unknown." He classifies them as (1) theistic and (2) demonic miracles, with the latter further subdivided into angelic (agathodemonic) and diabolical (kakodemonic) miracles (AA 6.119). Theistic miracles include the creation of the world, → revelation in the larger sense, → conversion, and the → resurrection of the dead (pl.!). Angelic miracles (→ Angel) include rescue from mortal danger, while diabolical miracles (→ Devil) include the effects of a → curse and malevolent → magic.

1.6. *Limitations*

One cannot simply call everything a miracle that elicits astonishment or amazement. Such an interpretation strains the concept of miracle because such elements can constitute the entire interpretive content of a religion, from the "great miracle" of cosmic creation to the "small miracles" of the → rabbis, → apostles, → saints, and → Sufis.

One can define a miracle only within a series of relationships (1) between the cognitive status and psychological type of the miracle worker and the observer, (2) between the miracle object and the intentional content of the miracle experience, and (3) between the "object" miracle and its concept, the latter of which as a complex concept can be either particular or total.

The object of a miracle is a phenomenon that elicits a miraculous experience and remains the focus of that experience. The experience of a miracle can itself become the object of a miracle if, on its own, it elicits yet another miraculous experience. Factors predisposing a person to have miraculous experiences include agitation, astonishment, amazement, fright, and faith either in something or in someone specific.

1.7. *Miracle Workers and Witnesses*

A miracle generally includes a miracle worker. Similarly, a miracle would be nothing without witnesses who see it or without those in need on whose behalf it is performed. These persons either become the most enthusiastic proponents of the phenomenon "miracle," or they classify it under secret discipline (as in → Buddhism). Their exaggerated written accounts of miracles can make critical examination necessary (see above), at which point the literary (genre) history of miracle literature begins. A history of miracles is possible only as a conceptual history.

Bibliography: P. R. L. Brown, *The Cult of the Saints: Its Rise and Functions in Latin Christianity* (Chicago, 1981) • H. Clavier, "Wunder," *BHH* 3.2188-2291 (good overview) • U. Forell, *Wunderbegriffe und logische Analyse* (Göttingen, 1967) • R. M. Grant, *Miracle and Natural Law in Graeco-Roman and Early Christian Thought* (Chicago, 1952) • G. Mensching, *Das Wunder im Glauben und Aberglauben der Völker* (Tübingen, 1957) • A. Schimmel, *Mystische Dimensionen des Islam* (Cologne, 1985) 284-302 • R. Swinburne, *The Concept of Miracle* (New York, 1970) • G. Theissen, *The Miracle Stories of the Early Christian Tradition* (Philadelphia, 1983) • M. Waida and M. Kelsey, "Miracles: An Overview, Modern Perspectives," *EncRel(E)* 9.541-56.

Carsten Colpe

2. NT

The multiplicity of Greek equivalents for the general concept of miracle in the NT — *dynameis,* "deeds of power"; *sēmeia,* "signs"; *terata,* "outrageous phenomena"; and *thaumasia,* "remarkable things" — shows that these miracle accounts were not primarily concerned with a mere abrogation of natural laws. The appearance in the miracle either of God's own activity or of diabolical powers always functions rather as a → sign (§2) that must be interpreted theologically. Modern → exegesis was the first to inquire (also) concerning the credibility or the historical core of miracle accounts.

2.1. *Jesus*

The Gospels (→ Gospel 1) attribute about 30 miracles to → Jesus. To the extent these miracles can be traced back to the historical Jesus, they can be viewed as the symbolic acts of a → prophet (§3). Such is the case with all the healing miracles (Mark 2:1-12 and par.; 3:1-6 and par.; 5:25-34 and par.; 7:31-37; 8:22-26, etc.), and especially with Jesus' → exorcisms, that is, with the → healing of those "possessed" by → demons (Matt. 9:32-34; 12:22-24 and par.; 15:21-28 and par.; Mark 1:23-28 and par.; 5:1-20 and par.; 9:14-29 and par.).

According to Mark 5:1-20 and parallels, accounts of healing exorcisms include finding a demon at an impure or uninhabited area, an emphasis on its power, an encounter between the demon and the exorcist, the demon's attempt at countering the exorcist, a command to depart, the query concerning the name, acknowledgment of the exorcist's superiority, exorcism of the demon, a demonstration of its destructive power, and an expression of fear or amazement from the crowd (see R. Bultmann 1931, 236-41). Jesus shared the ancients' understanding of illness as being caused by demons (see Matt. 12:43-45

and par.). Commensurate with that view, his own healing methods are of a wholly magical nature (→ Magic), as are the demon's own threats (Mark 1:25 and par.; 9:25 and par.; Luke 4:39, etc.), the use of spittle or spittle paste (Mark 7:31-37; 8:22-26; John 9:6-7), and touching or the → laying on of hands (Matt. 8:15 and par.; 9:29; 20:34; Mark 7:32-33; 8:22-26; see also Mark 5:41 and par., though also Mark 5:27-29 and par.; 6:56 and par.).

Jesus fully acknowledged the success of other (Jewish) miracle workers (Matt. 12:27 and par.) and differed from them in interpreting his own miracles eschatologically (→ Eschatology 2.1). His exorcisms, performed by the "finger of God" (Luke 11:20; or "Spirit of God," Matt. 12:28), are prophetic acts symbolizing the inbreaking of the → kingdom of God (Matt. 12:28 and par.). The abrogation of the power of the → devil and his demons anticipated by Jewish eschatology (1QS 3:24-25; 4:20-22; 1QH 3:18; 1QM 1:10-11, etc.) begins with Jesus' own acts, and his miraculous healings fulfill prophetic hopes and predictions (Matt 11:4-6 and par., according to Isa. 29:18-19; 35:5-6; 61:1).

One such symbolic prophetic act was Jesus' cursing of the fig tree (Matt. 21:18-19a and par.), which only during the post-Easter period was transformed into a nature miracle (Matt. 21:19b and par.) or a → parable (Luke 13:6-9). The background to Jesus' raising of the dead is also prophetic (see 1 Kgs. 17:17-24; 2 Kgs. 4:32-37); at least one such raising is well attested (and quite early; Mark 5:21-24, 35-43 and par.). As the temporal distance from the earthly Jesus increased, interest in spectacular demonstrations of his power over → death also increased (Luke 7:11-17; John 11:17-44). His miraculous feeding of the multitude has a similar background (Mark 6.32-44 and par.; 8:1-10 and par.; John 6:1-15), recalling the table fellowship of the prophets and yet grotesquely surpassing the literary model (2 Kgs. 4:42-44). Post-Easter → Christology (§1) also characterizes Jesus' other four nature miracles (Matt. 17:24-27; Mark 4:35-41 and par.; 6:45-52 and par. = John 6:16-21; Luke 5:1-11 and par.; cf. John 21:1-11).

2.2. *Apostles*

Jesus' → disciples and → apostles also performed miracles in which God or Jesus Christ was thought to be at work (Acts 4:30; Rom. 15:19; 2 Cor. 12:12). Jesus himself, in whose name even outsiders could perform exorcisms (Mark 9:38-40 and par.; cf. Acts 19:13-17), taught his followers this art (Matt 10:8 and par.; Mark 3:15 and par.; 6:13; Luke 10:17-20). Even though both the success (Luke 10:17) and failure (Mark 9:18 and par.) of Christian exorcisms were probably projected back into the time of Jesus, there is no reason to doubt that the apostles (Acts 3:1-10; 5:15-16; 14:8-11; 16:18; 19:11-12; see also 2:43; 5:12; 14:3; 15:12) and Stephen (Acts 6:8) performed miracles. Both → Peter (Acts 9:36-43) and → Paul (Acts 20:9-12) are alleged to have raised someone from the dead, and their miracles or curse and chastisement (Peter in Acts 5:1-11; Paul in Acts 13:6-12) correspond to Paul's order to the Corinthian congregation to hand over the man guilty of incest to Satan "for the destruction of the flesh" (1 Cor. 5:5).

2.3. The Devil and His Servants

The devil and his servants (demons, pseudo-messiahs, pseudoprophets, the antichrist) also perform "great signs and omens" that lead people astray into apostasy and idolatry (Matt 24:24 and par., according to Deut. 13:2-4; 2 Thess. 2:9; Rev. 13:13-14; 16:14; 19:20) and that are considered to be characteristics of the end time. Satan and the demons also function as God's chastising agents, causing both illness and death (Acts 12:23; 1 Cor. 5:3-5; 10:10; 2 Cor. 12:7-8; 1 Tim. 1:20; see also Rev. 11:3-6).

2.4. Theological Meaning

Even the NT itself has difficulty interpreting miracles theologically. Mark introduces the commandment of silence (the so-called messianic secret, see Mark 1:34, 44; 3:12; 5:43; 7:36, etc.) to address the question of why outsiders do not acknowledge who Jesus is, based on his miracles. The Synoptic gospels distinguish between Jesus' healing miracles, referring to them as either *dynameis* (demonstrations of power) or *sēmeia* (spectacular signs) designed to support his otherworldly claims.

Jesus rejects such signs, which were demanded, for example, by the devil (Matt. 4:1-11 and par.) and by the Jews (Matt 12:38 and par.; 16:1 and par.; Luke 11:16; see also Luke 23:8) as a manifestation of unbelief (Matt 12:39 and par.; 16:4 and par.). Paul also rejects this (Jewish) demand for "signs" (1 Cor. 1:22); → glossolalia is a "sign" for unbelievers (1 Cor. 14:22).

Nonetheless, the NT also views healing miracles as signs. Especially in the Gospel of John and the Acts of the Apostles, they serve as divine confirmation of Jesus as the Messiah and Son of God (→ Christological Titles). Through them, Jesus was attested to his own contemporaries (John 4:48; Acts 2:22), and they were then committed to writing in order to facilitate faith among those who came later (John 20:31). Although → John the Baptist reportedly did not perform such signs (John 10:41), "wonders and signs" were performed by Christian charismatics (1 Cor. 12:10) and apostles (Acts 2:43;

Rom. 15:19; 2 Cor. 12:12) as part of → discipleship. Through such acts, God "added his testimony" and support to Christ's followers (Heb. 2:4).

Bibliography: H. D. Betz, "Jesus as Divine Man," *Jesus and the Historian* (FS E. C. Colwell; Philadelphia, 1968) 114-33 • B. Blackburn, *Theios Anēr and the Markan Miracle Traditions: A Critique of the "theios anēr" Concept as an Interpretative Background of the Miracle Traditions Used by Mark* (Tübingen, 1991) • O. Böcher, *Christus Exorcista. Dämonismus und Taufe im Neuen Testament* (Stuttgart, 1972); idem, "Exorzismus I," *TRE* 10.747-50 • R. Bultmann, *Die Geschichte der synoptischen Tradition* (2d ed.; Göttingen, 1931; ET *The History of the Synoptic Tradition* [Oxford, 1963]); idem, "The Question of Wonder," *Faith and Understanding* (ed. R. W. Funk; New York, 1969) 247-61 • W. Cotter, *Miracles in Greco-Roman Antiquity* (London, 1999) • W. Kahl, *NT Miracle Stories in Their Religious-Historical Setting* (Göttingen, 1994) • H. C. Kee, *Medicine, Miracle, and Magic in NT Times* (Cambridge, 1986); idem, *Miracle in the Early Christian World* (New Haven, 1983) • B. Kollman, *Jesu und die Christen als Wundertäter. Studien zu Magie, Medizin und Schamanismus in Antike und Christentum* (Göttingen, 1996) • J. P. Meier, *A Marginal Jew*, vol. 2, *Mentor, Message, and Miracles* (New York, 1994) • W. Nicol, *The Sēmeia in the Fourth Gospel: Tradition and Redaction* (Leiden, 1972) • S. J. Scherrer, "Signs and Wonders in the Imperial Cult: A New Look at a Roman Religious Institution in the Light of Rev 13.13-15," *JBL* 103 (1984) 599-610 • G. Stählin, "Die Gleichnishandlungen Jesu," *Kosmos und Ekklesia* (FS W. Stählin; Kassel, 1953) 9-22 • G. Theissen, *The Miracle Stories of the Early Christian Tradition* (Philadelphia, 1983) • G. H. Twelftree, *Jesus the Miracle Worker* (Downers Grove, Ill., 1999) • W. Weiss, *"Zeichen und Wunder." Eine Studie zur Sprachtradition und ihrer Verwendung im Neuen Testament* (Neukirchen, 1995) • D. Wenham and C. Blomberg, ed., *The Miracles of Jesus* (Sheffield, 1986).

Otto Böcher

3. Practical Theology

3.1. Personal Piety

From the perspective of → practical theology, the question of miracles emerges as a problem of daily → piety and can be understood only in connection with the attendant social and historical background. Miracles are an accepted part of practical → everyday life in traditional societies (→ Society). Miracle healings generate the traditions associated with places of → pilgrimage (e.g., → Lourdes); miracle healers are consulted (esp. in Africa and the Caribbean); and the stories of miracles associated with the lives of such models are passed down (note the many legends of → saints).

This unaffected belief in miracles collapses, however, in modern pluralistic societies. Pluralization (→ Pluralism) of → worldviews and of one's practical life orientation also brings with it a process of "cognitive contamination" (P. Berger) insofar as these worldviews and orientations mutually relativize and devalue one another. Moreover, the worldview of the natural sciences and of → technology excludes miracles from the outset, especially given the claim that miracles operate outside → natural laws.

Today, however, an opposing tendency is also emerging. Pluralistic Western societies do not merely disassociate themselves from traditional forms and notions of faith in miracles; they also create new forms of belief in miracles, doing so for clearly discernible reasons. The abrogation of → tradition that takes place within the overall cultural process, together with the pluralization of values that is both hastened and radicalized by the increasingly multicultural nature of these societies, simultaneously creates a need for new, binding points of orientation. Fundamentalist currents (→ Fundamentalism) and the yearning for more coherence and cohesion within fractured social surroundings have created the conditions favorable to the emergence of a new belief in miracles, one that has also come to concrete expression in connection with the → New Age movement. Traditional forms and witnesses to faith in miracles are critically examined, while at the same time new forms of such faith (esp. from pre-Christian contexts and the Far East) are often adopted without the slightest critical examination. In view of this development, a considered theological examination of miracles and faith in miracles has become an indispensable necessity for practical theology.

3.2. Tension

Today faith in miracles generates tension in people's lives that neither can nor should be resolved. The most obvious tension is the cognitive tension between faith in miracles and essential elements of the modern worldview. This particular tension also represents an objection to the predominant mechanistic worldview and the colossal claims made regarding the accessibility and malleability of all conceivable relationships (→ Materialism; Monism). Faith in miracles also generates existential tension in which spiritual experiences compete with the familiar experiences of a technological world. Legitimate Christian faith will seek to preserve precisely these fields of tension. Neither a fundamentalist faith in miracles

that classifies all questions of worldview traditionally nor a purely psychological explanation of experiences associated with miracles can do justice to the biblical material or to the tradition of Christian experience with miracles.

3.3. Reformulation

This situation makes it necessary to reformulate our understanding of miracles to do justice both to the biblical and Christian tradition and to concrete daily life. Such a reformulation and theologically considered Christian understanding must take the following dimensions into consideration. Christian belief in miracles must be based on a comprehensive culture of attentiveness; that is, those who believe in miracles are those who are still open to the unexpected in the world around them. A world without belief in miracles ultimately withers internally.

Christian belief in miracles is also sustained by trust in God's own creative and formative power, a trust that also touches on the ethical dimension insofar as a person cannot believe in this power of God and at the same time contemplate endangering the world through human actions (→ Ethics; Environment).

Finally, Christian belief in miracles is always accompanied by anticipation (→ Hope), which in its own turn is accompanied by the knowledge that not all expectation must come to fulfillment (→ Promise and Fulfillment). Both → spirituality and → prayer can be the concrete expression of such expectation.

3.4. Church Practice

Such reformulated, theologically considered faith in miracles will doubtless not simply emerge on its own and must instead acquire the reflected form of church praxis. The fruitful tensions that modern faith in miracles generates can be addressed in → preaching, and the "symbolic language of faith" (G. Theissen) can connect these tensions with the concrete experiential world of believers. Preaching should never shy away from addressing the question of miracles; schools, church instruction, and adult education can address systematically the question especially of the cognitive dimension of belief in miracles, though such forums do require reflected and sophisticated didactic methods (note in this regard G. Scholz).

Particularly in the context of → pastoral care, however, the question of miracles might constitute the central focus. In view of the multifarious experiences to which people are exposed in today's world (A. Grözinger), the paradigm of miracles can provide help both in cognitive and in existential questions. All such suggestions, however, depend on taking into consideration concrete human existence and experience in daily life, and on then discovering miracles in the midst of life itself and its attendant experiences.

Bibliography: P. L. BERGER, *A Far Glory: The Quest for Faith in an Age of Credulity* (New York, 1992); idem, ed., *The Desecularization of the World: Resurgent Religion and World Politics* (Washington, D.C., 1999) • A. GRÖ-ZINGER, *Differenz-Erfahrung. Seelsorge in der multi-kulturellen Gesellschaft* (Waltrop, 1994) • G. SCHOLZ, *Didaktik neutestamentlicher Wundergeschichten* (Göttingen, 1994) • C. T. TART, ed., *Altered States of Consciousness* (3d ed.; New York, 1990) • G. THEISSEN, *The Sign Language of Faith: Opportunities for Preaching Today* (London, 1995) • B. WENISCH, *Geschichten oder Geschichte? Theologie des Wunders* (Salzburg, 1981).

ALBRECHT GRÖZINGER

Misereor → Relief and Development Organizations

Mishnah

"Mishnah," deriving from Heb. *šānâ,* "repeat, learn," means (1) a single item of learning (pl. Mishnayot); (2) the teachings of an individual Tanna; and especially (3) the collection of traditional material, mainly → Halakic, of Tannaitic → Judaism, which attained quasi-canonical authority soon after its final redaction about A.D. 200, on which all the later decisions of religious and civil → law are founded, and which forms the basis of the → Talmud. Originally given orally, the Mishnah as oral teaching stands equally beside the written → Torah, or Miqra (from *qārā',* "read"), which is read. Its Halakot supplement, expand, and make current the statutes of the Torah, but unlike the halakic → Midrash, the Halakah of the Mishnah is not, for the most part, linked to the Bible. We find Halakah derived from the Bible, independent of the Bible, and originally independent but secondarily linked to the Bible.

In spite of the Mishnah's reception as a legal codex, we are still not sure what its original purpose was. It has been explained as a source collection, a textbook, a legal book, or a linguistically ritualized substitute for the temple cult. The course of its evolution is also obscure. Tradition traces its beginnings, if not considered given along with the written Torah at Sinai, to the "men of the great synagogue" and its completion to the redaction of Judah ha-Nasi (ca. 135-ca. 220) on the basis of earlier collec-

tions. The traditional material incorporated in the Mishnah comes from several generations, especially from the periods when the center of Jewish learning was at Jamnia (= modern Yavne, ca. 70-135) and then at Usha (near Haifa, ca. 135-75). During these periods the → rabbis, as the dominant group in Palestinian Judaism after the loss of → Jerusalem as the political and cultic center, tried to steer a course between conservation and a new beginning. The Mishnah found its final formulation and redaction in the generation of Judah ha-Nasi.

The Mishnah has a predominantly thematic arrangement in six orders *(sĕdārîm),* which together comprise 63 tractates *(massektôt).* The first order, *Zera'im* (Agriculture), discusses benedictions, agricultural laws, and temple levies. The second, *Mo'ed* (Appointed times), offers rules for the → Sabbath and feasts. The third, *Našim* (Women), deals with marriage and → vows. The fourth, *Neziqin* (The order of damages), covering civil and penal law and idolatry, contains the famous tractate *'Abot* ([Sayings of] the Fathers). The fifth, *Qodašim* (Holy things), deals with → sacrifices and the temple cult. The sixth, *Ṭoharot* (Purities), takes up various matters of → cultic purity and impurity.

→ Pharisees; Scribes

Bibliography: J. NEUSNER, *Introduction to Rabbinic Literature* (New York, 1994) esp. pt. 2; idem, *Judaic Law from Jesus to the Mishnah: A Systematic Reply to Professor E. P. Sanders* (Atlanta, 1993); idem, *Judaism: The Evidence of the Mishnah* (Chicago, 1981); idem, *The Judaism behind the Texts — The Generative Premises of Rabbinic Literature,* pt. 1, *The Mishnah* (3 vols.; Atlanta, 1993-94); idem, *The Mishnah: A New Translation* (New Haven, 1988) • E. NODET, *A Search for the Origins of Judaism: From Joshua to the Mishnah* (Sheffield, 1997) • S. SAFRAI, ed., *The Literature of the Sages,* pt. 1, *Oral Tora, Halakha, Mishna, Tosefta, Talmud, External Tractates* (Philadelphia, 1987) 211-62 • E. P. SANDERS, *Jewish Laws from Jesus to the Mishnah* (Philadelphia, 1990) • H. L. STRACK and G. STEMBERGER, *Introduction to the Talmud and Midrash* (Minneapolis, 1992).

MARGARETE SCHLÜTER

Missio → Relief and Development Organizations

Missio canonica

In → Roman Catholic usage *missio canonica* (canonical sending) is formal ecclesiastical commissioning for the permanent discharge of ecclesiastical offices (→ Ministry, Ministerial Offices) or for some specific functional activity as a special ministry.

1. In Roman Catholic → canon law *missio canonica* denotes the jurisdictional commissioning of clergy relative to specific tasks and ministries, but also the orderly calling of all church members (→ Clergy and Laity) to responsible cooperation in the church's ministry of sanctification, proclamation, or leadership (1983 → CIC 129-44). It is granted by the → pope or diocesan → bishop on the basis of the material or personal fitness of the candidate and is revocable at any time. The calling of clergy or laity to work in schools takes place in the specific form of a *mandatum docendi* (mandate to teach; 1983 CIC 229.3).

With regard to teaching, canon 812 requires that those who teach theological disciplines in any institution of higher education whatsoever must have a *mandatum* from the competent ecclesiastical authority (→ Theological Education). Such a requirement was reiterated by John Paul II's apostolic constitution *Ex corde ecclesiae* (1990). The use of *mandatum* rather than *missio canonica* implies that the mandate to teach is neither a delegation of jurisdiction nor a granting of an ecclesiastical office. In 1999 the Catholic bishops of the United States approved *The Application of "Ex corde ecclesiae" for the United States*, which had the force of particular law on May 3, 2001. The *mandatum* is described in the *Application* as "an acknowledgment by the church authority that a Catholic professor of a theological discipline is a teacher within the full communion of the Catholic Church" (art. 4.4.e.i).

2. As a central element in church self government, *missio canonica* has national recognition in many countries according to the prevailing constitution or → concordat (→ Church and State). Germany, for instance, sees in it the canonical criterion used by the church in appointing its clergy. Those who have *missio canonica* may legally exercise their office. If it lapses or is withdrawn, deprivation follows (→ Teaching Office 1), and there can be no recourse to civil law.

Bibliography: CATHOLIC THEOLOGICAL SOCIETY OF AMERICA, *Report of the CTSA Committee on the Profession of Faith and the Oath of Fidelity* (Washington, D.C., 1990) • J. CONN, *Catholic Universities in the United States and Ecclesiastical Authority* (Rome, 1991) • A. GALLIN, ed., *American Catholic Higher Education: Essential Documents, 1967-1990* (Notre Dame, Ind., 1992) • J. KEENAN, "Compelling Assent: Magisterium, Conscience, and Oaths," *IThQ* 57 (1991) 209-27 • J. LANGAN, ed., *Catholic Universities in Church and Society: A Dialogue on "Ex corde ecclesiae"* (Washington, D.C., 1993) • D. O'BRIEN, *From the Heart of the American Church: Catholic Higher Education and American Culture* (Maryknoll, N.Y., 1994) • L. ÖRSY, *The Church: Learning and Teaching* (Wilmington, Del., 1987); idem, *The Profession of Faith and the Oath of Fidelity: A Theological and Canonical Analysis* (Wilmington, Del., 1990).

BERND T. DRÖSSLER and PETER C. PHAN

Missiology

1. Roots
2. Formal Study
3. Nonacademic Contributions
4. Redefinition
5. Networking

Missiology is systematic reflection on the work of mission (usually Christian mission), including the mission or sending of God *(missio Dei)*, of Jesus Christ, of the apostles, of the church, or of other mission organizations. In the broadest sense it includes the study of the theology of mission (foundation, goal, and means; → Mission 1-2), particular mission theories, mission principles and practice, and the social, cultural, or political aspects of mission. As an academic discipline, it includes research, writing, teaching, and publication related to the study of world or global mission.

1. Roots

The study of missiology dates back at least to the Roman Catholic missionary martyr Ramón Llull (ca. 1233-ca. 1315; → Llullian Method), who went on four preaching missions to North Africa and the Near East. He devoted his life to preaching and debating with Muslims and advocated the establishment of a college at Majorca for the training of missionaries in the Arabic language and Muslim religious background. Reflection on mission was advanced by the Spanish Dominican Bartolomé de Las Casas (1484-1566), who denounced abuses of Indians in the New World and later received the title "Protector of the Indians." In the 16th century a Jesuit missionary to Peru, José de Acosta (1540-1600), further developed missiological reflection in his treatise *On Procuring the Salvation of the Indians* (1588). In the same period Thomas a Jesu (1564-1627), a Carmelite theologian, wrote *On Procuring* the Salvation of All Peoples (1613), in which he advocated the founding of a Roman congregation for the propagation of the faith, which came about in 1622 with the establishment of the Propaganda Fide under Gregory XV. This action was followed five years later by the founding, under Urban VIII, of Urban College (now Pontifical Urbaniana University), a college for the training of missionaries from all nations (→ Missionary Training).

On the Protestant side, missiological reflection and writing goes back to several 17th-century Dutch Reformed theologians, especially Gisbertus Voetius (1589-1676), Justus Heurnius (1587-1652), and Johannes Hoornbeeck (1617-66), who wrote about the biblical obligation to do missionary work and dealt with missionary problems in the Dutch East Indies. Scattered reflections on missionary methods can also be found in the writings of the Lutheran Pietist promoter of missions August Hermann → Francke (1663-1727), who was instrumental in publishing the missionary letters of the first Protestant missionary in India, Bartholomäus Ziegenbalg (1682-1719).The founder of Moravian missions, Count Nikolaus Ludwig von → Zinzendorf (1700-1760), gave his followers explicit missionary guidelines for their mission work in the Caribbean, Greenland, and elsewhere (→ Moravian Church). The English Baptist lay preacher William Carey (1761-1834), founder of the Serampore Mission in India, is regarded as the father of modern Protestant missions (→ British Missions). In 1792 he published a missiological treatise, *An Enquiry into the Obligations of Christians to Use Means for the Conversion of the Heathens,* which helped to ignite the modern era of Protestant missions. The above examples — both Roman Catholic and Protestant — all belong to a less formal, initial period of missiological reflection.

2. Formal Study

Missiology as a formal academic discipline arose in the 19th century in response to a variety of factors: the worldwide spread of → missionary activity among both Protestants and Roman Catholics, a rapid increase in the number of new mission societies and boards for mission, the rise of young mission churches in the → Third World as the result of missionary activity, the close linkage between overseas missions and Western colonial expansion (→ Colonialism and Mission), growing familiarity with living world religions and study of the history of religions, and, above all, the needs of missionaries and mission agencies for greater clarity about the missionary task in changing situations. In 1835 Prince-

ton Theological Seminary took steps to make instruction in missions a required part of the academic curriculum. A few leading American Protestant seminaries followed the example. Later Rufus Anderson (1796-1880), pioneer American missiologist, began giving lectures entitled "Foreign Missions: Their Relations and Claims" at Andover and other seminaries in the eastern United States (→ North American Missions).

In Europe the immediate occasion for creating university-related lectureships and studies in mission was the need to validate and support mission work as the legitimate and necessary task of mission agencies and, by implication, of Western Christian society. Perhaps the first to lecture on the subject was Friedrich → Schleiermacher (1768-1834), who treated mission as an aspect of → practical theology. Karl Graul (1814-64), director of the Leipzig Mission (→ German Missions), was committed to a thorough academic and linguistic training for missionaries, enabling them to work on a solid theological basis and with a contextual approach (→ Contextual Theology). In 1864 he proposed in a public lecture that the scientific study of missions be initiated as a legitimate academic discipline at the university level. Graul himself was granted qualifications as a lecturer in missiology at the University of Erlangen, but his untimely death the same year prevented him from following through. The renowned Scottish missionary to India Alexander Duff (1806-78) wrote books and lectured widely in Great Britain on missions in India, advocating a strong educational approach to influence Hindu society. In 1867 he was named professor of evangelistic theology at New College, Edinburgh, becoming the first university lecturer on missions. Also in 1867 Karl H. C. Plath (1829-1901) launched a scheme to establish chairs of mission in German universities.

Of still greater importance was the work of Gustav Warneck (1834-1910), pastor and professor of missions at Halle (1897-1908) and now generally regarded as the father of the systematic study of missions. In 1874 he began editing the first general missiological magazine, the *Allgemeine Missions-Zeitschrift.* Between 1892 and 1903 he produced *Evangelische Missionslehre,* a five-volume compendium on mission policy and practice, which became a standard reference work. Warneck promoted popular → missionary conferences, fostered cooperation among German mission societies, and wrote books dealing with the history of Protestant missions and with various aspects of mission policy in the colonial age (→ Colonialism; Mission 3).

Warneck's pioneering work was closely followed

by that of the Roman Catholic missiologist Joseph Schmidlin (1876-1944), professor of missions at the Catholic University of Münster, who founded the journal *Zeitschrift für Missionswissenschaft* in 1911. Schmidlin advocated → proclamation and evangelizing (→ Evangelism) as the main emphases in Catholic missiology, whereas Pierre Charles (1883-1954), a Belgian missiologist at Louvain, saw the planting of the indigenous church where it did not already exist as the central task. Catholic missiology later flourished in university faculties in Germany, the Netherlands, Switzerland, and Rome.

On the Protestant side, chairs for missiology were created in many theological faculties in Germany, Netherlands, and Scandinavia (→ Scandinavian Missons). The chair of world missions was sometimes linked to the teaching of comparative religions, and sometimes to church history. In the 1920s and 1930s many American seminaries added full- or part-time professorships of missions and began requiring at least one course in the field. A few seminaries or divinity schools with graduate programs — including Yale, Hartford, Union Theological Seminary in New York, Princeton, and Chicago — offered degree programs in world missions and encouraged the writing of master's theses and doctoral dissertations on subjects pertaining to missions.

In North America, missiology as a formal academic discipline made great strides in the second half of the 20th century, especially as organizations for missiological study gained recognition alongside other learned societies. The dramatic entry of → evangelicals in missiological education after the 1960s and the ability of conciliar Protestants, evangelicals, and → Roman Catholics to merge their efforts in order to engage in extensive networking were responsible for this advance. At the same time, new methodological approaches, critical viewpoints, and specialized fields were incorporated into the discipline of missiology. Along with the study of Bible, church history, and world religions, the tools of the → social sciences were employed, especially those of cultural anthropology. The "mission of God" was seen not simply as a phenomenon to be interpreted theologically but also as a human activity to be critically advanced with the help of these tools.

Several American theological faculties in the evangelical tradition developed "schools of world mission," offering multiple approaches and both professional and academic degree programs (e.g., Fuller Theological Seminary, Pasadena, Calif.; Trinity Evangelical Divinity School, Deerfield, Ill.; Asbury Theological Seminary, Wilmore, Ky.).

Among Roman Catholics, the Maryknoll Fathers and Brothers, the Maryknoll Sisters, and the Catholic Theological Union have promoted mission study and mission resource and publication programs.

3. Nonacademic Contributions

Missiological reflection has by no means been confined to university or seminary faculties. Important contributions to mission theory have been made by mission administrators and practitioners. Among these were Henry Venn (1796-1873), general secretary of the Anglican Church Missionary Society; Rufus Anderson, senior secretary for the American Board of Commissioners for Foreign Missions, who, along with Venn, is credited with developing the "three-self" formula for church development (from their inception, mission churches should be self-governing, self-supporting, and self-propagating); John L. Nevius (1829-93), Presbyterian missionary to China, now best known for his influence on church planting in Korea; Roland Allen (1868-1947), British missionary to China with the Society for the Propagation of the Gospel who wrote a radical critique of Western missionary paternalism; Donald A. McGavran (1897-1990), India missionary and founder of the American "church growth" school of missiology (→ Church Growth 5); Bishop Stephen Neill (1900-1984), prolific writer on many aspects of mission and → ecumenism; Max Warren (1904-97), former general secretary of the Church Missionary Society and missiological observer; and Lesslie → Newbigin (1909-98), India missionary, bishop of the → Church of South India, ecumenical administrator, and passionate advocate for the movement of mission in unity.

Significant contributions to missiology were also made in connection with major Protestant missionary conferences both before the Edinburgh World Missionary Conference of 1910 and after that event in ecumenical meetings organized by the → International Missionary Council (IMC, founded 1921) and, after 1961 when the council integrated with the → World Council of Churches, by the WCC's Commission on World Mission and Evangelism. Issues dealt with included the Christian approach to other faiths and to → secularism (Jerusalem, 1928), the Christian message to the world and the evangelistic task of the local church (Tambaram, India, 1938), global missionary partnership (Whitby, Canada, 1947), "The Missionary Obligation of the Church" (Willingen, West Germany, 1952), the need to integrate mission into the life of the church (Accra, Ghana, 1958), "Witness in Six Continents" (Mexico City, 1963), "Salvation Today" (Bangkok, 1973),

"Your Kingdom Come" (Melbourne, 1980), "Mission in Christ's Way" (San Antonio, Tex., 1989), and "The Gospel in Diverse Cultures" (Salvador, Brazil, 1996). Key to this global discussion was the WCC Central Committee's seven-point "Ecumenical Affirmation: Mission and Evangelism" (1982).

The 1910 Edinburgh conference gave impetus to the launching of the first international English-language journal of missiology, the *International Review of Missions* (1912, in 1969 its last word was changed to *Mission*), and to special mission research libraries, mission training programs, institutes for the study of mission, and other mission publication projects. In many countries national missionary councils collaborated with the IMC and WCC in mission research and critical reflection.

The Second → Vatican Council (1962-65) stimulated fresh missiological reflection among Roman Catholics, producing the Decree on the Church's Missionary Activity *(Ad gentes divinitus),* Declaration on the Relationship of the Church to Non-Christian Religions *(Nostra aetate),* and Decree on Ecumenism *(Unitatis redintegratio).* Post–Vatican II papal pronouncements (e.g., Paul VI's 1975 apostolic exhortation *Evangelii nuntiandi,* on evangelization in the modern world, and John Paul II's 1991 encyclical *Redemptoris missio,* on the permanent validity of the church's missionary mandate), as well as statements from bishops' synods and reports from regional Catholic episcopal conferences (esp. in Latin America, Africa, and Asia) have dealt with → liberation theology, → base ecclesial communities, inculturation, interreligious → dialogue, the "preferential option for the poor," gospel and justice, human → development, and other topics related broadly to missiology. Roman Catholic and ecumenical mission study institutes in India, the Philippines, Papua New Guinea, South Korea, and Brazil have made significant national contributions, as have meetings of the → Ecumenical Association of Third World Theologians.

Among evangelicals, international congresses convened by the Lausanne Committee on World Evangelization (LCWE), above all the first Lausanne Congress (1974), stimulated careful formulation of evangelical positions on mission theology and practice. The Lausanne Covenant of 1974 stands as a benchmark statement for worldwide evangelical missionary cooperation (→ Lausanne Movement). It includes an unwavering commitment to "the uniqueness and universality of Jesus Christ" (§3). LCWE cooperated with the theological commission of the World Evangelical Fellowship in developing further statements on gospel and culture, homogeneous units, simple lifestyle, social responsibility, social transformation, and other topics.

4. Redefinition

Traditional seminary courses in world missions tended to be informative, motivational, and promotional rather than critical. Such courses were designed to accompany and support the continuing growth of American Protestant and Roman → Catholic missions. They provided a modicum of prefield training for missionary candidates and worked to develop a supportive climate for missions in local parishes.

The decade of the 1950s, however, witnessed a massive attack on older, colonialist assumptions, leading both to the demise of the ancient "Christendom" mentality and to a loss of certainty about alleged Western superiority. Sharply critical attacks were directed at Western imperialism by leaders of Third World churches, spokespersons for other world religions, Marxists, and many Western Christians. It became urgently necessary for the missiological community to redefine aims and goals and to respond to political, cultural, economic, and other attacks on the mission enterprise. Answering the question "Why missions?" became a crucial priority.

The redefinition of mission was based on the cardinal assumption that the triune → God, rather than the → church, is the author of mission (hence the phrase *missio Dei*). Proclaiming the kingdom and not church extension is the primary task in God's mission. Churches and mission agencies acquire the right to engage in God's mission as servants and faithful followers of Jesus Christ. From this new perspective such issues as evangelization, global partnership, resource sharing, relations of dominance and dependence, gospel and culture, gospel and social justice, and the proper approach to other faiths all demand rethinking. Although total agreement on the definition of mission — and corresponding mission priorities — has not been possible, there now exists wide agreement concerning a more holistic and ecumenical approach. The missionary task in the new era of "mission in six continents" is understood as *the whole church with the whole gospel for the whole world.*

5. Networking

Many broad-based resources and facilities for mission study have arisen in recent decades, illustrating the trend toward increased missiological networking and ecumenicity. In North America the binational U.S.-Canadian Association of Professors of Missions was formed in 1952, followed by several regional groupings. The tripartite American Society for Missiology (ASM), linking academics, administrators, and practitioners, came into existence in 1973 as a joint venture of conciliar Protestants, Roman Catholics, and evangelicals or independents. Also in 1973 the ASM began publication of its own quarterly, *Missiology;* its monograph and dissertation series now numbers more than 30 volumes. The Evangelical Missiology Society was organized in 1990, superseding the Association of Evangelical Professors of Mission. On the initiative of scholars from Europe and North America, the International Association for Mission Studies (IAMS) was organized in 1972, linking individual scholars and missiological associations from North America, Germany, the United Kingdom and Ireland, Scandinavia, the Netherlands, South Africa, India, and elsewhere. Since 1974 IAMS has published *Mission Studies.*

The independent Overseas Ministries Study Center, founded in 1922 and now located in New Haven, Connecticut, is publisher of the *International Bulletin of Missionary Research* and combines a residential study program with mission research; it has also facilitated missiological research grants underwritten by foundations. The evangelical William Carey Library in Pasadena, California, and Orbis Books, publishing arm of the Maryknoll Fathers, both specialize in publishing mission study books (→ Christian Publishing). Scholarly study aids such as Gerald Anderson's *Biographical Dictionary of Christian Missions* (1998), the *Evangelical Dictionary of World Missions* (2000), and David Barrett's *World Christian Encyclopedia* (1982; 2d ed., 2001) are other valuable tools for missiologists.

Missiology stands ready to offer to the church guidance and direction for its task of global mission. It plays a vital role as a handmaid to biblical and theological studies, reminding the church of its essential missionary nature and recalling the church to its primary vocation of bearing witness to God's → salvation in the entire world. Missiology has struggled to overcome false, inauthentic, or outmoded missionary images, strategies, and relationships. It aims to make the → gospel relevant and contextual in every society and culture and to fashion a Christian community reflecting the totality of God's gifts.

Bibliography: G. ANDERSON, *Biographical Dictionary of Christian Missions* (New York, 1998) • D. B. BARRETT et al., eds., *WCE* (2d ed.) • J. H. BAVINCK, *An Introduction to the Science of Missions* (Philadelphia, 1960) • D. J. BOSCH, *Transforming Mission* (Maryknoll, N.Y., 1991) •

J. A. B. JONGENEEL, *Philosophy, Science, and Theology of Mission in the Nineteenth and Twentieth Centuries: A Missiological Encyclopedia* (2 vols.; New York, 1995-97) • A. S. MOREAU, ed., *Evangelical Dictionary of World Missions* (Grand Rapids, 2000) • K. MÜLLER, T. SUNDERMEIER, S. B. BEVANS, and R. H. BLIESE, eds., *Dictionary of Mission: Theology, History, Perspectives* (Maryknoll, N.Y., 1997) • O. G. MYKLEBUST, *The Study of Missions in Theological Education* (2 vols.; Oslo, 1955-57) • W. R. SHENK, *Changing Frontiers of Mission* (Maryknoll, N.Y., 1999) • J. STOTT, ed., *Making Christ Known: Historic Mission Documents from the Lausanne Movement, 1974-1989* (Grand Rapids, 1996) • J. VERKUYL, *Contemporary Missiology* (Grand Rapids, 1978).

JAMES A. SCHERER

Mission

1. Theology of Mission: Historical Development
   1.1. Definition
   1.2. Biblical, Patristic, and Medieval Perspectives
   1.3. Early Modern Approaches
2. Theology of Mission: A Maturing Scientific Discipline
3. History of Mission
   3.1. Methodology
   3.2. Mediterranean Development and Asian Outreach
   3.3. Western Concentration and Expansion
   3.4. Global Spread and Differentiation
   3.5. Crisis and Transformation: End of the Twentieth Century and After

1. Theology of Mission: Historical Development
1.1. *Definition*

As a branch of → missiology, the theology of mission is a discipline of faithful questioning that focuses on the basis, methods, and purpose(s) of Christian witness in all its forms. Most theologians of mission consider Scripture to be the normative text from which the proper foundation of mission should be drawn. In some traditions, definitive guidance for contemporary reflection on mission is also sought from → patristic sources and/or magisterial statements. Theories of mission become theologies of mission when abstract theses, definitions, and strategies are tested against the imperatives of the → gospel. Depth and authenticity are added as the history of actual missionary practice is rigorously evaluated. Such theology must also be responsive to contextual factors if it is to be relevant for particular communities of faith. The adequacy of any theology of Christian mission will be determined by its inner coherence, its capacity to guide faithful practice, and its ability to inspire courageous and creative witness to the God whom Christians believe became incarnate in Jesus Christ.

The complex relationship of missiology to the entire discipline of → theology is reflected in the various approaches taken to the theology of mission. Many missiologists in the modern period have understood mission to be a specialized set of pastoral activities undertaken with respect to non-Christians in exotic circumstances. In this case, the practical dimensions of mission theology tend to be highlighted and the techniques or special challenges of cross-cultural mission work take center stage. When, however, the theology of mission is conducted as a form of → systematic theology, Christian efforts to communicate and demonstrate the gospel to non-Christians are connected to long-standing dogmatic interests. Engaged from this angle, mission theology is more likely to take up subjects like the universality of the Christ-event, the salvific value of non-Christian religious traditions, or the theological significance of human history and culture. Here also arise questions about the status of mission as an essential characteristic of the church's fundamental nature.

The unavoidable tension indicated by a diversity of still-active methodological approaches to the theology of mission need not be resolved. Like theological ethics, the theology of mission quite rightly encompasses both theoretical and practical concerns. This orientation to the subject invites critical reflection on the means of mission, which are never theologically neutral. By the same token, serious consideration is given to the outworking of foundational convictions and crucial assumptions about proper missionary motives and aims. A comprehensive theology of mission will thus attend to the methods used to effect Christian witness, as well as mission's foundation and goal(s).

1.2. Biblical, Patristic, and Medieval Perspectives

Missiology did not become a scholarly discipline in its own right until the latter part of the 19th century. Yet, it would be a mistake to assume that earlier patterns of Christian mission did not also issue out of particular theological frameworks that might be regarded as implicit or not completely developed theologies of mission. D. Bosch has drawn attention to a series of underlying theological "paradigms" that have defined mission in distinctive ways since the time of the → apostles. The pluriform character of

mission theology thus identified is significant in itself. The work of Bosch and others also serves to recollect the earliest roots of what would in the late modern era become a more scientific endeavor.

1.2.1. Biblical reflection on the nature of mission begins in the OT. There one finds often vivid descriptions of the human condition that are not essentially modified by the witness of the NT. Humankind is lost, disoriented, bent on self-destruction, and in desperate need of → conversion (§1). God creates the possibility of fundamental reorientation by entering into human history. In part the OT recounts the story of God's mighty acts as a way to define Israel's origins and peculiar identity. At the same time, this history has a missiological function. It describes the character of the deity who repeatedly intervenes to rescue → Israel (§1). Significantly, we learn that God is concerned not only for the welfare and ultimate destiny of this one people but for "all the families of the earth" (Gen. 12:3). Equally important, God makes known Israel's responsibilities as God's own covenant partner. Ethical obligations laid down at Sinai — reiterated frequently by the prophets — serve both to differentiate Israel from the nations and to distinguish Israel's God from every rival divinity then recognized in the ancient Near East. To the extent that Israel can be true to its corporate vocation as the → people of God, its presence in the midst of the nations becomes a missionary existence and its actions a reannouncement of God's intentions for the whole created order.

The NT affirms, clarifies, and extends this approach to mission. The same God who dispatched liberators and prophets on behalf of the Jewish nation now sends the Son and the Spirit into the world. The community that gathers in the name of Jesus, like Israel of old, understands itself to be a people set apart. God's care for the Jews is not thereby put aside. Jesus' example and the disciples' practice of mission confirm that the old → covenant retains its validity. Even → Paul, the "apostle to the Gentiles" (Rom. 11:13), will insist that God's earlier promises to Israel still stand, "for the gifts and the calling of God are irrevocable" (v. 29). This conviction leads him to expect Israel's eventual → salvation, albeit by means of a fact entirely unknown to the OT: Christ crucified.

The whole of the NT likewise challenges the theologian of Christian mission to underscore the radical newness of the age inaugurated by Jesus' appearance, while respecting the continuity of God's purposes. Thus, the idea of election endures, but the gospel is shown to break through every ethnocentric, racial, or social boundary that threatens to artificially restrain its scope. Similarly, the → church that assembles in the aftermath of the → resurrection willingly embraces the core of Israel's moral code but freshly interprets it through the law of → love. Most important, the Great Commission texts of the Gospels (Matt. 28:16-20 and par.) make plain that the ultimate privilege of covenant membership in the new era is to participate in God's outreach to the nations here and now. In this way, the NT actualizes a latent regard for the → Gentiles, already expressed in the OT but largely reserved there for the future, by linking their fate to the church's very identity. Following → Pentecost, the disciples' response to Jesus' call represents the initial stage of a specifically Christian missiological consciousness that continues to evolve today.

1.2.2. In the immediate postapostolic period, the early church laid additional conceptual foundations on which to base its missionary approach to the world. Paul's theological breakthrough to the Gentiles, for example, led to a profound engagement with Hellenistic culture. The significance of this move for the theology of mission cannot be overestimated. Crossing the Jewish-Gentile frontier meant that Christianity's Jewish roots were thereby relativized, as L. Sanneh has observed. Henceforth, no culture — not even Jesus' own — could sustain a claim of special affinity with the gospel or convincingly purport to capture its full meaning for all people in every social and historical location. Coincidentally, as Sanneh further noted, Hellenistic culture was effectively destigmatized, suggesting that Christianity could not shun any social matrix as innately "unclean" without compromising its inherent openness to cultural difference. An unlimited license to translate the good news across cultures, not yet expired, was thus granted.

Some of the second-century → apologists went on from this insight to explore the question of God working in revelatory fashion outside the biblical realm. This possibility was admitted, most notably by → Justin Martyr, whose concept of the *logos spermatikos* (seed-logos, or seminal Word) continues to be a touchstone for the → theology of religions. The arguments of Justin and others succeeded in winning a choice place for → philosophy at the table of Christian theology, but the welcome extended in this premodern age was still equivocal; only fragments of the truth were thought to lie within philosophy's ken. The church recognized no sure path of salvation outside of itself (*extra ecclesiam nulla salus*). At best, a philosophical quest or an alternative religious tradition might prepare one to receive the gospel, but neither could serve as a substitute for saving faith in Jesus Christ.

Purposeful, self-confident witnessing, unafraid of the martyr's death but just as eager to connect the gospel with life, led the way to tremendous growth for the Christian community within the Greco-Roman cultural sphere. In particular, works of benevolence impressed many in the wider population and drew new adherents to the church. An ironic tribute to the effects of Christian charity may be heard in the lament of the pagan emperor Julian (360-63) that "the impious Galileans maintain our poor in addition to their own" (*Ep.* 84). Christians themselves often preferred to point to the transforming effect of miracles on pagan hearts and minds in order to explain the gospel's extraordinary progress (R. MacMullen). Not surprisingly, one of the most renowned evangelists of the early church came to be remembered as Gregory the Wonderworker.

A change in Christianity's civil status, from persecuted sect to the official religion of the empire by the end of the fourth century, added the power of state patronage to the church's missionary toolbox. Naturally, theological approaches to mission worked out subsequently had to adjust to this momentous shift in social context. The church by no means abandoned its commitment to diaconal service, its respect for martyrdom, or its faith in the miraculous, but room was nevertheless made in its theology of mission for the use of secular inducements or even force to advance the cause of Christianization.

1.2.3. Medieval theologians, especially in the West, took for granted that truly Christian rulers would be zealous evangelizers. In a number of celebrated cases, this role was enthusiastically embraced (e.g., by the kings of the Franks) and the reach of Christianity was significantly extended, but the fusion of royal desires with missionary purpose carried a heavy philosophical price. Diminishing enclaves of Eastern Christians under → Islam aside, medieval Christianity came to be experienced largely as a territorial religion with recognized centers and elastic peripheries (→ Middle Ages 2). In these circumstances warfare, not preaching, usually determined large-scale changes in religious demography, a paramount fact of history that demanded theological reflection.

By the 13th century, in light of Charlemagne's successful wars in Saxony, the reconquest of Spain, and countless → Crusades in the East, the canonist lawyer Pope Innocent IV (1243-54) would articulate a position already held broadly in the West with respect to coercion and mission: forced → baptisms were invalid, but the papacy could authorize the use of the sword to assist Roman Catholic → missionaries or to defend the interests of Christian people (see J. Muldoon, B. Kedar). In the centuries to come, such thinking, or its moral equivalent, paved the way for not a few leading theologians, both Protestant and Catholic, to fold the facts of European colonial expansion into their understanding of God's providence (T. Christensen and W. R. Hutchison; → Colonialism; Colonialism and Mission). A relatively few, but courageous voices of protest (e.g., that of Bartolomé de Las Casas in 16th-cent. Spanish America) dared to question the true cost of doing mission within the protective sway of raw imperial power.

1.3. *Early Modern Approaches*

However liberating in other respects, the → Reformation movement spearheaded by Martin → Luther (1483-1546) and John → Calvin (1509-64) failed almost entirely to remove the medieval leg-iron of territoriality from the ankle of European Christianity. As a result, mission in the early modern period continued to be incorporated into, and was repeatedly subordinated to, larger schemes of political and military hegemony. On this basis, for example, the governments of Portugal and Spain directly sponsored efforts to extend Christianity to their colonial dominions in the New World, Africa, and Asia. Likewise, Catholic and Protestant rulers in Europe lent crucial support to vigorous campaigns of reevangelization within their own and neighboring realms in order to produce subject populations that more closely reflected the doctrinal orientation of those who governed them (L. Châtellier).

The peaceful → Anabaptists of the Reformation era stood almost alone in their commitment to mission as a spiritual exercise rather than a means to define space in sectarian terms. The marginality of the Anabaptist position was made manifest, however, when they were left out of the political and religious settlements drawn up at Augsburg (1555; → Augsburg, Peace of) and Westphalia (1648; → Thirty Years' War) on the basis of territorial confessionalism, the logic of which was summed up in the principle → *cuius regio eius religio* (whose the region, his the religion).

The often overwhelming effect of geopolitics on modern missions cannot be ignored, but recognition must also be given to other trends in the theology of mission that began to emerge in the 17th century. One of these was an intention to connect missionary work more directly to the church's self-understanding, that is, to see mission as an issue of ecclesiology. For → Roman Catholic Christianity, an unmistakable step in this direction was taken with the establishment of the Vatican's Congregatio de Propaganda Fide (Congregation for the propagation of the faith) in 1622 (→ Curia). The Propaganda represented, among other things, an assertion by the papacy that mission was primarily a function of the church rather than a tool of statecraft. By means of this novel instrument of organization, the magisterium attempted to recover for the church its prerogative to initiate, plan, coordinate, prioritize, and evaluate all Catholic missionary activity.

An accompanying shift took place with respect to thinking about the primary goal of mission. Many began to consider the church not only the proper subject of mission but also its special object. Mission became the task of *plantatio ecclesiae* (church planting), which meant in this instance the extension of the church's hierarchical structures into new locations where enterprising Christian powers might or might not be dominant or even active. For Reformed Protestants, Gisbertus Voetius (1589-1676) advocated a similar move toward ecclesiastical mission, arguing that Christ's command both authorized and obligated congregations or groups of churches to send missionaries and plant churches but that the command clearly did not so empower governments (J. Jongeneel 1991).

Voetius's appeal apparently fell on deaf ears in his own generation, but by the middle of the 19th century a more ecclesiocentric approach to mission had become the norm for Protestants. Two names in particular are usually connected with this development in Protestant mission theology: Henry Venn (1796-1873) and Rufus Anderson (1796-1880). As administrators of the two largest Protestant mission-sending organizations of the 19th century (the Church Missionary Society and the American Board of Commissioners for Foreign Missions, respectively), each was committed to the goal of creating independent churches ("self-governing, self-supporting, and self-propagating") in the lands where their missionaries were active. An influential contemporary of Venn and Anderson was the Lutheran Karl Graul (1814-64), founding director of the Leipzig Mission, whose own theological approach focused on the church as the beginning and end of mission.

The agencies headed by Venn, Anderson, and Graul in the 19th century themselves represent the mature stage of a second major development in thinking about mission by Protestants in the early modern period. The idea of a private voluntary association dedicated to the cause of mission seems to have appeared first in the writings of the 17th-century Lutheran layman Justinian von Welz (1621-

ca. 1668, J. Scherer 1969; → Voluntarism). Welz's plans bore rather meager fruit in the short term, but his proposal anticipated in some respects the parachurch groupings through which → Pietists and → Moravians would launch in the 18th century an extensive series of far-flung Protestant efforts to evangelize the world outside of Europe. William Carey (1761-1834) then refined the form, advising in his 1792 *Enquiry* that the commercial trading company offered a model of organization particularly well suited to meet the logistic challenges of global mission (A. Walls 1988). Somewhat incongruously, this extraecclesial social structure became the preeminent mechanism by which for more than two centuries Protestants created countless congregations and churches in foreign lands. Certainly, the missionary society proved to be an efficient and flexible means of evangelization, constituting for Protestants the practical equivalent of the Roman Catholic monastic order (→ Evangelism; Religious Orders and Congregations).

2. Theology of Mission: A Maturing Scientific Discipline

Working near the end of the long 19th century, Gustav Warneck (1834-1910) probably did more than anyone else to establish a scientific basis for the study of mission. This effort put the theology of mission on an entirely new footing, not least because Warneck the missiologist was willing to engage a broad range of scholarship that went well beyond the strictly theological, while thinking comprehensively and critically about his subject. A substantial part of Warneck's influence on the field was mediated through the pages of the first scholarly journal devoted to mission, the *Allgemeine Missions-Zeitschrift*, whose founding editor he became in 1874. Another major contribution came in the form of a multivolume handbook of Protestant mission theology, his *Evangelische Missionslehre* (1892-1903). On the whole, Warneck's theological conclusions appear to be less creative than his groundbreaking approach to methodology, which also directly affected the development of Roman Catholic missiology through J. Schmidlin (1876-1944). Warneck assumed a Western-centered Christendom as the home base of foreign missions. He also held conventional views on the likelihood of Christianity's swift triumph over all its religious rivals.

Warneck stood squarely in the *Volkskirche* (folk church, or → peoples' church) tradition of German missiology, which reached back at least as far as Graul. This perspective accounts for his focus on evangelization as a task of church planting that pays

utmost respect to indigenous social structures, ethnic consciousness (sometimes expressed in terms of national feeling), and presumed factors of race (T. Yates, W. Ustorf). Bruno Gutmann (1876-1966) and Christian Keysser (1877-1961) applied and developed further the idea of *Volkschristianisierung* through their work in East Africa and New Guinea, respectively. The "homogeneous unit principle" of church growth missiology (D. McGavran; → Church Growth 5) represents a more recent and peculiarly American appropriation of this continental European pathway to the theology of mission.

After World War I the field of missiology developed rapidly but unevenly as a scientific discipline, with new voices beginning to ask probing questions about the history and future of Christian mission. Some persistent patterns of inquiry may be detected against a busy and somewhat confusing backdrop. For example, one finds almost constant attention being paid to issues of → culture. This interest meant, first of all, new analyses of the relationship between the Christian "message" and the highly industrialized, aggressive cultures of those who had been carrying it from West to East or North to South. In the interwar years especially, uncritical assumptions of the compatibility between the gospel and Western culture (J. R. → Mott) yielded to a sense of wariness about the values that ruled modern societies. Earlier German suspicions that the root of the problem lay in the activist overconfidence of Anglo-Saxon missionary thinking — epitomized by the Student Volunteer Movement slogan "the evangelization of the world in this generation" — were superseded by more general doubts about the character of the emerging world civilization that relentlessly emanated outward from its North Atlantic center.

The Jerusalem meeting of the → International Missionary Council (IMC) in 1928 identified → secularism as Christianity's most serious rival and called for a theological response that could challenge its presuppositions. A decade later at the IMC meeting in Tambaram, India, Hendrik Kraemer (1888-1965) described a set of interlocking crises that menaced the whole of what he considered a non-Christian world. Ironically, he saw a vigorous, increasingly globalized Western civilization spawning new forms of idolatry in Europe through fascism, Communism, and National Socialism, even as it ceaselessly eroded the cultural foundations of traditional Eastern religions. In Kraemer's view, following the lead of Karl → Barth (1886-1968), the cross of Christ stood in opposition to all human aspirations, whether religious or secular. He therefore called for Christian mission to be grounded in a theology of antithesis, with the missionary acting as a living "point of contact" between God and the human part of a fallen natural order (→ Dialectical Theology).

In ecumenical circles after World War II, Kraemer's bleak appraisal of → modernity did not carry the day. A far stronger impulse took hold that combined a more positive and hopeful view of humanity's capacity to improve itself with a growing willingness to see God's active presence outside the church. The first part of this outlook was not entirely new to the theology of mission. Belief in the possibility of evolutionary human development had already drawn thousands of volunteers into mission during the → Social Gospel era, eager to empower civilizing "uplift" through → education. Mission in this case was a matter of bringing light into benighted citadels of ignorance, both domestic and foreign.

William Earnest Hocking built on this foundation of benevolent good works but also proposed expansion into new conceptual territory by calling on the next generation of Christian missionaries to cooperate with progressive forces of reform around the world (as C. F. Andrews had done with Gandhi). Once Hocking's most fundamental point had been accepted — that Christianity had no monopoly on the truth to which the followers of Christ were bound to give witness — a thoroughgoing reevaluation of the church's missionary situation had to follow. By the end of the 20th century, a number of long-settled positions connected to the theology of mission had been completely overturned or were subject to severe challenge.

The principal results of what has been since 1945 an intense and fruitful season of contemporary theological reflection on the meaning of Christian mission may be summarized under four headings.

2.1. First, few missiologists working today assume *the territorial principle of Christendom* that so many generations before them had taken for granted in their approach to mission theology. One therefore rarely encounters now the once common notion that mission can be undertaken simply or primarily as a process of expansion from Christian countries and cultures to non-Christian areas (see K. S. Latourette). The Mexico City meeting of the Commission on World Mission and Evangelism of the → World Council of Churches (WCC) in 1963 gave a clear signal that the sharp line separating mission-sending and mission-receiving regions had begun to disappear when it declared that people on all six continents needed the gospel. Fresh investiga-

tions of a multidirectional process of "contextualization" followed and eventually displaced older language that described how foreign missionaries "accommodated" or "adapted" the gospel from Western to non-Western cultures (→ Contextual Theology).

Since the 1970s especially, sustained scholarly attention has been trained on the dynamics of faith transmission across every kind of cultural boundary (e.g., Walls 1996), with particular interest being paid to how recipients of the gospel actively shape the outcome of missionary encounters when they formulate local theologies (R. J. Schreiter) or inculturate their new faith by means of → popular religion (T. Bamat and J.-P. Wiest). Meanwhile, in the lands of old Christendom, the work of L. → Newbigin (1989) has stimulated an energetic program of research that seeks to understand the complicated relationship of the gospel to postmodern Western culture (e.g., D. Guder, J. A. Kirk, and K. J. Vanhoozer).

2.2. A second major shift in missiological thinking after World War II to be noted here concerns *the relationship of church to mission*. The figure of Johannes Hoekendijk looms large in this discussion. With devastating effect he accused the modern Protestant missionary movement of having traded its apostolic birthright for a shallow ministry of propaganda too easily satisfied by the replication of existing institutional forms. The crux of the problem, according to Hoekendijk, was the sin of ecclesiocentrism, a form of idolatry that placed the church and its worldly interests in the middle of a much too narrowly conceived missiological universe.

Alternative concepts began to surface as early as the 1952 IMC meeting at Willingen, West Germany, in response to this critique, the most enduring of which has been the expression *missio Dei* (mission of God). Soon it became the convention for ecumenical Protestants to speak of a single Christian mission whose Author was the triune God, in contrast to the plural and often competing missions of the churches. When the *International Review of Missions* eliminated the final "s" from its title in 1969, a telltale marker of the new perspective had been laid down for all to see.

Not as much movement is evident among Roman Catholics on this issue, in part because the problem of denominationalism does not present itself in quite the same way in that tradition. Yet, one can observe already in the documents of → Vatican II (e.g., *Lumen gentium* 1) an emerging view of the church that prefers to see it as a "sacrament — a sign and instrument" of God's reign, rather than the single most important product of mission.

For their part, Eastern Orthodox theologies of mission have consistently assumed a Trinitarian basis for all the church's missionary activity (I. Bria 1986; → Orthodox Church; Orthodox Missions).

2.3. The interesting history of the concept *missio Dei* leads directly to a third key issue that has dominated much of late-20th-century missiology: *the meaning of salvation.* As H. H. Rosin has shown, not only did *missio Dei* serve to identify God as the genuine subject of Christian mission, but the phrase became a means to enlarge substantially the horizon of salvation itself; the proximate and ultimate aims of God's mission were redefined in various ways. Hoekendijk, for example, urged the church to disregard its earth-bound instinct for self-preservation in order to be captured by the soaring eschatological vision of biblical *shalom* and the promise of God's kingdom. Others preferred to talk about humanization as the most comprehensive goal of mission, as at the Uppsala Assembly of the WCC in 1968.

After the Medellín Conference of Latin American Bishops (1968; → Latin American Councils 2.4; Latin America Council of Bishops), liberation became the rallying cry for many Catholics and Protestants who yearned to see the full implications of God's good news realized in the lives of those most in need of deliverance from sin's deadly grasp on material reality: the poor. The call for salvation as liberation has received a mixed reception. On the one hand, a vibrant array of → liberationist theologies has arisen since the 1970s all around the world (e.g., → black theology, *mujerista* theology, *dalit* theology). The → Ecumenical Association of Third World Theologians is dedicated to this line of approach toward theology and mission (V. Fabella and R. S. Sugirtharajah). On the other hand, many Western evangelicals have been reluctant to follow this thread from the story of *missio Dei* to its probable end if it means designating particular secular causes as the work of God in history (A. Glasser and D. McGavran).

Despite obvious differences in emphasis, one can still perceive lasting effects from this discussion that continue to influence reflection on mission across the theological spectrum. Chief among these is the fact that one now hears the language of justice spoken even among those who tend otherwise to eschew radical politics (e.g., see Lausanne I and II, J. Stott; → Lausanne Movement).

2.4. A fourth and final cluster within current research revolves around the problem of *interfaith witness.* Some of the most difficult arguments waged recently among Christians themselves have centered on this area of mission theology. An earlier conviction, almost a consensus among Western Christians a century ago, that Christianity could be proved to be the final or absolute religion of all humanity in an objective or scientific sense has been largely abandoned, in no small part due to the work of Ernst → Troeltsch (W. R. Burrows). At the same time, the need for → tolerance in a religiously plural world has become more and not less acute, especially in places where sectarian extremism has threatened civil order or the freedom of religious expression.

Consequently, the theology of mission has had to contend with two imperatives, not easily reconciled. One demands humility and requires Christians to confront a history of missionary outreach that has compromised the gospel more than once by resorting to coercion and violence. The other recognizes that commending faith in Jesus Christ to others is still an indispensable component of a fully realized Christian existence. While some have argued for a thoroughly relativist understanding of the world's religions in the interest of peaceful coexistence (e.g., J. Hick and P. F. Knitter; → Relativism), few believe that a vital theology of mission that is distinctively Christian can be built on such a foundation.

In the last quarter century, a way forward for interfaith encounter has been sought through → dialogue, with some impressive gains achieved along the way. These advances include a renewed appreciation for the importance of personal relationships as living contexts for the sharing of faith. Many Christians have also discovered in the experience of dialogue that people of other faiths may well desire to give witness to commonly held values in a world often dominated by a secular and materialist point of view. This insight has led to a variety of significant interreligious initiatives for joint action in mission, from the local to the international level (H. Küng). What remains to be resolved is the → postmodern dilemma of 21st-century Christians who sincerely respect the authenticity of non-Christian faith but still believe that God acted decisively and uniquely for the salvation of the whole world through the life, death, and resurrection of Jesus Christ.

Bibliography: On 1: D. J. BOSCH, *Transforming Mission: Paradigm Shifts in Theology of Mission* (Maryknoll, N.Y., 1991) • L. CHÂTELLIER, *The Religion of the Poor: Rural Missions in Europe and the Formation of Modern Catholicism, c. 1500-c. 1800* (New York, 1997) • T. CHRISTENSEN and W. R. HUTCHISON, eds., *Mission-*

ary Ideologies in the Imperialist Era: 1880-1920 (Århus, 1982) • J. A. B. JONGENEEL, "The Missiology of Gisbertus Voetius: The First Comprehensive Protestant Theology of Missions," *CTJ* 26 (1991) 47-79; idem, *Philosophy, Science, and Theology of Mission in the Nineteenth and Twentieth Centuries: A Missiological Encyclopedia* (2 vols.; Frankfurt, 1995-97) • B. Z. KEDAR, *Crusade and Mission: European Approaches toward the Muslims* (Princeton, 1984) • R. MACMULLEN, *Christianizing the Roman Empire* (New Haven, 1984) • J. MULDOON, *Popes, Lawyers, and Infidels: The Church and the Non-Christian World, 1250-1550* (Philadelphia, 1979) • L. SANNEH, "Theology of Mission," *The Modern Theologians: An Introduction to Christian Theology in the Twentieth Century* (ed. D. F. Ford; 2d ed.; Oxford, 1997) 555-74; idem, *Translating the Message: The Missionary Impact on Culture* (Maryknoll, N.Y., 1989) • J. A. SCHERER, ed., *Justinian Welz: Essays by an Early Prophet of Mission* (Grand Rapids, 1969) • B. STANLEY, ed., *Christian Missions and the Enlightenment* (Grand Rapids, 2001) • T. SUNDERMEIER, "Theology of Mission," *DMiss* 429-51 • A. F. WALLS, "Missionary Societies and the Fortunate Subversion of the Church," *EvQ* 88 (1988) 141-55.

On 2: T. BAMAT and J.-P. WIEST, eds., *Popular Catholicism in a World Church: Seven Case Studies in Inculturation* (Maryknoll, N.Y., 1999) • R. C. BASSHAM, *Mission Theology, 1948-1975: Years of Worldwide Creative Tension, Ecumenical, Evangelical, and Roman Catholic* (Pasadena, Calif., 1979) • I. BRIA, *The Liturgy after the Liturgy: Mission and Witness from an Orthodox Perspective* (Geneva, 1996); idem, ed., *Go Forth in Peace: Orthodox Perspectives on Mission* (Geneva, 1986) • W. R. BURROWS, "The Absoluteness of Christianity," *DMiss* 1-6 • J. DUPUIS, *Toward a Christian Theology of Religious Pluralism* (Maryknoll, N.Y., 1997) • V. FABELLA and R. S. SUGIRTHARAJAH, eds., *Dictionary of Third World Theologies* (Maryknoll, N.Y., 2000) • A. F. GLASSER and D. A. MCGAVRAN, *Contemporary Theologies of Mission* (Grand Rapids, 1983) • D. L. GUDER, ed., *Missional Church: A Vision for the Sending of the Church in North America* (Grand Rapids, 1998) • J. HICK and P. F. KNITTER, eds., *The Myth of Christian Uniqueness: Toward a Pluralistic Theology of Religions* (Maryknoll, N.Y., 1987) • W. E. HOCKING, *Re-thinking Missions: A Laymen's Inquiry after One Hundred Years* (New York, 1932) • J. C. HOEKENDIJK, *The Church Inside Out* (Philadelphia, 1966) • J. A. KIRK and K. J. VANHOOZER, eds., *To Stake a Claim: Mission and the Western Crisis of Knowledge* (Maryknoll, N.Y., 1999) • H. KRAEMER, *The Christian Message in a Non-Christian World* (London, 1938) • H. KÜNG, ed., *Yes to a Global Ethic* (New York, 1996) • K. S. LATOURETTE, *A History of the Expansion of Christianity* (7 vols.; New York, 1937-45) • D. A. MCGAVRAN, *Understanding Church Growth* (Grand Rapids, 1970) • J. R. MOTT, *The Decisive Hour of Christian Missions* (New York, 1910) • J. E. L. NEWBIGIN, *The Gospel in a Pluralist Society* (Grand Rapids, 1989); idem, *The Open Secret: An Introduction to the Theology of Mission* (2d ed.; Grand Rapids, 1995) • H. H. ROSIN, *"Missio Dei": An Examination of the Origin, Contents, and Function of the Term in Protestant Missiological Discussion* (Leiden, 1972) • R. J. SCHREITER, *Constructing Local Theologies* (Maryknoll, N.Y., 1985) • J. STOTT, ed., *Making Christ Known: Historic Mission Documents from the Lausanne Movement, 1974-1989* (Grand Rapids, 1996) • W. USTORF, *Sailing on the Next Tide: Missions, Missiology, and the Third Reich* (Frankfurt, 2000) • A. F. WALLS, *The Missionary Movement in Christian History: Studies in the Transmission of Faith* (Maryknoll, N.Y., 1996) • G. WARNECK, *Evangelische Missionslehre. Ein missionstheologischer Versuch* (5 vols.; Gotha, 1892-1903) • T. YATES, *Christian Mission in the Twentieth Century* (Cambridge, 1994).

Other works: G. H. ANDERSON, ed., *Biographical Dictionary of Christian Missions* (Grand Rapids, 1999) • C. E. BRAATEN, *The Flaming Center: A Theology of the Christian Mission* (Philadelphia, 1977) • J. A. KIRK, *What Is Mission? Theological Explorations* (London, 1999) • K. MÜLLER, *Mission Theology: An Introduction* (Nettetal, 1987) • J. A. SCHERER, *Gospel, Church, and Kingdom: Comparative Studies in World Mission Theology* (Minneapolis, 1987) • C. VAN ENGEN, D. S. GILLILAND, and P. PIERSON, eds., *The Good News of the Kingdom: Mission Theology for the Third Millennium* (Maryknoll, N.Y., 1993) • F. J. VERSTRAELEN et al., eds., *Missiology: An Ecumenical Introduction. Texts and Contexts of Global Christianity* (Grand Rapids, 1995).

STANLEY H. SKRESLET

3. History of Mission

3.1. *Methodology*

3.1.1. The history of mission has been written with different objectives in mind. Luke composed the Acts of the Apostles as a sequel to his gospel to show that God's → salvation was open to → Gentiles as well as to Jews (→ Judaism). He also wished to document the movement of gospel preaching and of the church from → Jerusalem to → Rome. Eusebius, bishop of Caesarea, wrote his magisterial *Ecclesiastical History* at the time of Emperor Galerius's Edict of Toleration (311) to set forth the missionary activities of the apostles and their successors and to prove that the entire process had been guided by God, despite → persecution and martyrdoms (→ Martyrs).

The history of mission has to do with the church of God in its movement in the world (W. Loehe), with the moving out of the gospel message to the nations (J. Ratzinger), and with participation in God's existence in the world (P. Schuetz). Properly speaking, church history would include mission history as a major dimension. Yet much church history emphasizes doctrines, institutions, controversies, conflicts, or schisms to the neglect of the story of → evangelism and the growth of the → church. Mission history is written, then, to supply a missing dimension or component of church history.

3.1.2. Histories of mission have been written to edify, inspire, instruct, or simply to provide an account (→ Historiography). In the modern period, histories of mission have often been written to burnish the reputation of a particular mission society or to record the missionary contribution of a denomination. More recently, the history of mission has been undertaken from a nonsectarian and scholarly point of view as a panoramic record of the mission activities of → missionaries, mission agencies, and churches everywhere (K. S. Latourette). Historians and historical associations in Asia, Africa, and Latin America are now beginning to write the history of the church and mission in their own regions from the perspective of their own experience and critical judgment.

3.1.3. Two considerations, one theological and the other demographic, are methodologically significant. Theologically speaking, it matters whether mission history is written as an expression of the one "mission of God" *(missio Dei)* or as the record of human mission agencies. Mission in the spirit of *missio Dei* will attempt to transcend distinctions of mission agency, denomination, or nationality in order to provide a unified ecumenical picture of the mission of God (→ Ecumenical Mission 1).

From a demographic standpoint, Western mission writers from the age of discovery until the era of Western colonialism viewed mission as the process of Christian expansion from the Western Christian heartland into the non-Christian world. A post-Christendom approach, in which the West is also viewed as a field for mission or reevangelization, sees mission as the task of the local church in each place, on all six continents. Such mission may involve crossing local frontiers with the → gospel, or it may include participation in mission activities in remote areas. When mission is understood as the task of every local church, it also includes recognition that the majority of practicing Christians are now living in the lands of Asia, Africa, and Latin America. Mission histories written in the future are certain to differ from those written in the 19th and 20th centuries.

3.2. *Mediterranean Development and Asian Outreach*

3.2.1. The history and theology of primitive Christianity are the history of mission and the theology of mission (M. Hengel). In this sense early Christianity was like the religions around it (→ Hellenistic-Roman Religion). It was also forced thereby into self-critical examination and delimitation. The first Christians did not seek to win → proselytes in the sense of duplicates of themselves. They aimed to bring the gospel to the people and thus to have them respond to the call to → faith. Their mission was to both Jews and Gentiles. → Paul in his work established a chain of churches that he seems to have envisioned as reaching to Spain (C. Burchard).

After Paul, Christian mission accepted the same task, which it tried to discharge by simple Christian presence as well as by evangelistic service, often in charismatic independence of the churches (→ Charisma). The variety of ministries was so great that we cannot reduce them to a single model. Lists of officeholders at the time of the emerging church → hierarchy do not mention a missionary ministry as such. The understanding of the apostolic office (→ Apostle, Apostolate) seems to have shown more interest in the preservation of → tradition than in missionary dynamic.

Beginning in the second century, the → apologists developed a new form of address to educated non-Christians by expounding Christian wisdom, which intended to prove its superiority in philosophical controversy, thus fulfilling in principle the task of making → disciples of all nations. The martyrdom of → Justin (d. ca. 165) shows that at this period the spread of the faith took place both by the witness of Christian life in → persecution and by dying for the gospel.

3.2.2. Centers of expansion in the → Roman Empire were → Palestine, Syria (with → Antioch as a base for the mission to Asia Minor), Greece, and Rome. Some Christians were also present in Gaul and Spain. In the western part of North Africa the first Latin-speaking churches consisted more of colonists than of the native Berbers. This feature was a reason for the → Donatist schism and provided a cause for the later extinction of the church by → Islam. The origins of Christianity in Egypt are obscure (→ Coptic Orthodox Church). The development there of → monasticism introduced a factor that would be very important for later mission.

The entry of Christianity into new linguistic and cultural spheres outside the empire began already at the onset of the second century in the city-state of Edessa, which also produced an extensive Christian literature in Syriac. Southeast of Edessa, across the Tigris, Arbela (or Arbīl) was a Christian center. Northeast, in Armenia, with the end of Persian rule and Zoroastrianism (→ Iranian Religions 6-7), Christianity became for the first time a state religion (→ Oriental Orthodox Churches).

3.2.3. The change under Constantine in the fourth century (→ Church and State) could have made mission serviceable to imperial power politics. Constantine himself (emperor 306-37) and his successors, however, did not do much to exploit it. The church for its part did not want to attach to its mission the odium of state compulsion, the more so as new heretical groups (→ Heresies and Schisms) were contesting the field with their own missionary activity. Orthodox Christianity gained a foothold in Ethiopia in the fifth century, but soon, from western Syria, → Monophysitism replaced it (→ Ethiopian Orthodox Church). Nubia had two missions, first a Diophysite mission sponsored by Justinian (527-65), then a Monophysite mission sponsored by Empress Theodora (527-48). With the help of Coptic monks the latter finally prevailed.

Similarly, tensions accompanied missionary work in northern Europe. The missionary bishop Ulfilas (d. 383) saw to it that the Goths were converted to → Arianism, but the Frankish king Clovis (481-511) decided for Nicene Christianity (→ Germanic Mission), though not under papal authority. The most northerly Nicene bastion was the monastic Celtic church in Ireland. The church in England arose out of a two-pronged Nicene movement from north and south. Aidan (d. 651) initiated the work in Northumbria, and Augustine of Canterbury (d. between 604 and 609), sent by → Gregory I (590-604) at the head of a missionary group, served in Kent, where Ethelbert the king was baptized in 597. The latter mission is a striking example of a mission "from above" in which the adoption of Christianity does not necessarily mean its true acceptance.

3.2.4. The → Nestorian mission to India began the work in Far East Asia, though the origins of this mission are not wholly clear. It seems that around A.D. 300 some immigrant Christians from Mesopotamia established churches in Malabar (South India) with a Syrian language and → liturgy. In the course of a volatile history, the modern → Syrian Orthodox Church in India is the result.

We find no continuity, however, in the occasional Orthodox, Monophysite, and Nestorian missionary ventures into the Arabian Peninsula. It is worth not-

ing that the one-time Christians there have become "the best Muslims" (C. D. G. Müller).

Another fact worth pondering is that in 635, at much the same time as the rise of the prophet Muhammed (ca. 570-632), the Nestorians reached China under the monk Alopen and, under imperial protection, attempted Christianizing along the lines of → acculturation. With a change of dynasty, however, this venture came to an abrupt end in 845.

3.3. Western Concentration and Expansion

3.3.1. The Arab Islamic conquests either obliterated Christianity in the southern and eastern areas of the Mediterranean (i.e., North Africa) or reduced it to a → minority that was subject to discrimination. There was some compensation for these losses in Europe, first as a result of the work of the Irish-Scottish mission, which penetrated to Burgundy, the area around Lake Constance, and northern Italy. Anglo-Saxon missionaries in the service of Rome (Willibrord, Boniface, Pirminius) then reached out across the Netherlands to central Germany and Bavaria, establishing → monasteries and bishoprics. Saxony, too, received the gospel from Anglo-Saxon missionaries.

The use of force against the Saxons by Charlemagne (768-814) was counterproductive. Success came only from the neighboring bishoprics, in which Frankish settlers and returning Saxon hostages who had been converted played a part. A base was thus set up for missionary work to the north. After sporadic beginnings Anskar (801-65), later archbishop of Hamburg and Bremen, led the way, but resistance had to be overcome, sometimes by force. For example, in Iceland in the year 1000 the Althing, or legislative assembly, made a democratic decision for Christianity, and the Christianizing of Greenland followed.

3.3.2. → Byzantium initiated the → Slavic mission in the beginning of the eighth century. Two Greek brothers sent by the emperor, Cyril (ca. 827-69) and Methodius (ca. 815-85), then worked in Moravia, using the national language, translating parts of the Bible, and putting the → liturgy into a script of their own invention. They saw to it that their mission received recognition from Rome. No national church emerged, however, either in Moravia or among the East Slavs.

Vladimir, the grand prince of Kiev in Russia (980-1015), decided for Byzantium and had himself baptized there in 988. The Greek Orthodox tradition of faith flourished in his kingdom (→ Orthodox Church), along with the Slavic cultural inheritance. Here as elsewhere the spread of the faith was closely tied to power politics, but the link was of almost unparalleled intensity in the mission to the North Slavs. (Gregory I had authorized "indirect" warfare on → pagans as an aid to mission, and Charlemagne came close to direct warfare against the Saxons.) The conflict with the North Slavs (Wends), which lasted for two centuries, made war on pagans a program, even to the point of the Wend Crusade, which → Bernard of Clairvaux (1090-1153) called for in 1147 with the slogan "Conversion or Death."

The → Crusades to conquer the Holy Land in the 11th and 12th centuries had no direct missionary aims. They fostered the ideology of the holy → war, however, and created among Muslims a hostile picture of Western Christian aggressiveness that persists to the present day.

3.3.3. The church never lost sight of the alternative of peaceful mission. This approach gained new vitality among the mendicants (→ Religious Orders and Congregations) under the lead of → Francis of Assisi (1181/82-1226; → Franciscans), who made the idea of mission an inalienable part of the apostolic life for himself and his order. Ramón Llull (ca. 1233-ca. 1315; → Llullian Method) gave the practice of sending a methodological basis.

Missionary companies of mendicants aiming at Asia labored to burst through the Islamic barrier. Temporarily, the Roman hierarchy even established itself in China. Its eventual failure was due in part to its opposition to the Nestorians, who flourished among several Turkic peoples and the Mongols in China and central Asia (→ Mongolian Mission) until the rise of → Buddhism and Islam. Finally, the rise of religious → syncretism in the centers of the Silk Road put an end to the total Christian presence in the Far East, reducing the Nestorians to a national Assyrian church and giving the impression to some that Christianity is Western.

3.4. Global Spread and Differentiation

3.4.1. The beginning of the → modern period toward the end of the 15th century was also the time when the identification of Christianity and the West became determinative for the further spread of the faith, which was still under the influence of the medieval idea of the *orbis Christianus* (→ Middle Ages 2), but now in the context of the new nation-states (→ Nation, Nationalism) and in confrontation with the cultures of America and Africa. Furthermore, mission would now be increasingly hampered by division in Christendom and, in turn, in the West, which cast doubt on the credibility of the message.

The Iberian switch from internal reconquest to external conquest led to the apportioning of the New World between Spain and Portugal and, for both of them, the papally controlled interfacing of colonial patronage and missionary work (→ Colonialism; Colonialism and Mission). The agents of mission were again the orders, with the newly founded → Jesuits very quickly at their head. On the ruins of the Aztec and Inca empires, a new system of oppression arose that exploited the Indians, treated pagans as rebels, and used mission as a means of domestication. Efforts to forge a colonial ethics did as little to change things as did the → reductions, essentially paternalistic reservations for Christianized Indians, or the vehement protests of B. de Las Casas (1484-1566) and others of like mind. How high the price of missionary expansion really was in the age of colonialism, only time would show.

We find different emphases in the Roman → Catholic mission to Asia. This effort too had to operate in close touch with the colonial power (i.e., the Portuguese). But Portugal was more interested in trade than in actual colonizing. Evangelistic work thus had more room, whether in the form of the rapid evangelization practiced by F. → Xavier (1506-52) in India, neighboring Southeast Asia, and Japan, or according to the strategy of accommodation that R. de Nobili (1577-1656) adopted in India and M. Ricci (1552-1610) in China, which gave rise to the prolonged Rites Controversy (→ Rite). In India the mission itself became an obstacle when it tried to bring the Malabar Christians under the jurisdiction of Rome, with only temporary and partial success. The hopeful establishing of the church in Japan came to a rapid end within a century with terrible persecution, but the new beginning in China lasted into the 18th century. The most lasting was the work in the Philippines, which under Spanish rule became the one and only predominantly Christian country in Asia.

The → curia itself made a late but important attempt to reform the system of colonial mission by founding the Congregation for the Propagation of the Faith in 1622 (after 1967, the Congregation for the Evangelization of Peoples). This step was an important one on the path toward the founding of native churches, though conflicts with colonial mission were still a threat.

3.4.2. Surprisingly, the Protestant → Reformation at first took a halfhearted defensive position in relation to mission. M. → Luther (1483-1546; → Luther's Theology) did indeed shatter the traditional system in principle with his "grace alone" and "Christ alone" (→ Reformation Principles) and his grounding of the church once more in the Word. His followers, however, for the most part stressed only defensive implications under the influence of the domestic concerns of the church leaders and such theological arguments as the ancient teaching that the apostles had finished the work of evangelizing or that the end of the world was imminent.

J. → Calvin (1509-64; → Calvin's Theology; Calvinism) basically followed Luther but added his own emphasis by linking the *regnum Christi* to the duty of mission. He cooperated in the first Protestant missionary venture by sending some Genevans on a Huguenot colonial venture in Brazil in 1557, an experiment that eventually failed. When the Dutch Reformed in Indonesia and the English colonists in North America took up their missionary responsibility on a broader basis in the 17th century, it was at the cost of renewing the old colonial model.

The different example set by the Puritan J. Eliot (1604-90; → Congregationalism) with his native Indian church in Massachusetts hardly lasted more than a generation. Already in Germany the Austrian Lutheran layman J. von Welz (1621-ca. 1668) had issued in vain a call for mission to the heathen.

3.4.3. New missionary impulses could hardly be expected among the Orthodox. In its expansion to the east, Moscow asserted its spiritual authority as the third Rome, but with a political linking of the evangelization of non-Christians to spiritual care for the colonists.

3.4.4. For Roman Catholic missions the 18th century was largely one of decline. Among Protestants, however, a new beginning came with the Lutheran Danish-Halle Mission (→ German Missions 1) in Tranquebar in South India (1706), which made a great impact by way of example and, with English support, quickly forged relations with other Christian groups. This mission was initiated but not directed by the Danish crown. Deriving its inspiration from the → Pietism of A. H. → Francke (1663-1727), it brought together the two concepts of awakening and → development. It found a powerful agent in the pioneer missionary B. Ziegenbalg (1682-1719; → Lutheran Churches 9.2.1). Having a goal of a linguistically and culturally independent church, it spread its witness essentially through national workers and laity. At the same time, it did not neglect → dialogue with → Hinduism and Islam.

The Halle Mission exerted worldwide influence through N. L. von → Zinzendorf (1700-1760) and his Moravian Mission (1732; → Moravian Church), the → Methodism of the brothers C. Wesley (1707-88) and J. → Wesley (1703-91; → Methodist Churches), the missionary initiatives of the American → revivals among the Indians (→ Modern Church History 2), and the broad stream of the early 19th-century awakenings. First in England and then in Continental Europe and America, these revivals generated a whole host of missionary societies.

3.4.5. If we are not simply to give a list, we might offer a typological survey. The *independent missions of the awakening,* which arose in the British sphere and were close to a more enlightened imperialism and to humanitarian efforts, followed the example of the Baptist pioneer missionary and former shoemaker W. Carey (1761-1834) and his program of world mission, for which he offered a model in the Danish settlement of Serampore near Calcutta, in express association with the Tranquebar Mission. As Serampore became a center for Bible translation throughout Asia, tract and → Bible societies in Europe and America become auxiliary agents in providing "the Word for the world." Denominationalism was at first less important than the great cause of global work for the → kingdom of God.

The later Congregationalist London Missionary Society (LMS), founded in 1795 as simply "The Missionary Society" (→ British Missions), became the model for many later agencies. One was the Evangelical Missionary Society founded at Basel in 1815, which saw itself as transnational and transdenominational. From the beginning it felt a close affinity with England. It had a network of auxiliary agencies, some of which acted as separate societies.

The relation of these societies to the church varied, and not all were apart from the churches. Anglican Evangelicals (→ Anglican Communion) separated from the LMS in 1799 and gathered their supporters into the Church Missionary Society (known before 1812 as the Society for Missions to Africa and the East). What primarily held these societies together was an ardent desire to show Christian love to the pagan world, a legacy that necessarily included missions.

3.4.6. Not in antithesis but to some extent by way of correction, specifically *church missionary organizations* were founded. England had already had such an organization since 1701 in the Society for the Propagation of the Gospel in Foreign Parts (SPG). At some point this agency was unable to restrict its work to British colonies. Under the influence of D. Livingstone (1813-73), it was joined in 1857 by the (Anglican) Universities' Mission to Central Africa.

On the Continent the coming together of neo-Pietism and Lutheran → orthodoxy (§1) resulted in the founding of denominational missions such as the Dresden-Leipzig Mission (1836) and the Hermannsburg Society (1849). We find similar developments in Scandinavia and America under the catchword that mission is "the church itself in its missionary activity" (L. A. Petri). The result was an expansion of the range and effect of mission, although it also led to some denominational restriction in the understanding of it.

In reaction and in an attempt to maintain the revivalist thrust, we also find one-man undertakings such as that of K. Gützlaff (1803-51) to China, which made a great impact in Europe, or that of the charismatic J. E. Gossner (1773-1858), though in this case a society resulted. Gützlaff provided a model for the → China Inland Mission (CIM) of the medically trained Englishman J. H. Taylor (1832-1905), who aimed at the rapid evangelizing of millions of Chinese with the help of a host of workers from many denominations, many of them women — a pattern for later → women's missions. Eschatological tension and a careful concern for Chinese language and culture formed a synthesis in the CIM that would last until the Communists took over in 1949, and it served as a model for many similar organizations.

3.4.7. The *colonialist missions* in China (apart from the CIM), at the time of what the Chinese called the "unequal treaties," showed how harmful the effects were of the dubious imperialist entanglement of the Western powers. In black Africa as well, which was only gradually opened up to Christianity, colonialism and mission repeatedly went together, helping one another, though in very different ways. In the German sphere the Evangelical Missionary Society for East Africa (1886) was the only mission founded with explicit colonial goals. Friedrich von Bodelschwingh (1831-1910) preserved it from dissolution, and it found a new future as the → Bethel Mission. Cultural goals, often associated with secularized eschatology, played a role in → North American missions and in the work of some Protestants in East Asia.

3.4.8. The true gains of the period came where missions resisted the temptations of power politics and became *missions working for the development of national churches* and, more rarely, for the political and social → emancipation of the peoples. In the process there were unavoidable conflicts and reverses. The tensions were especially severe in Africa, as we see from Uganda, South Africa, Congo, and Madagascar. Livingstone's fight against → slavery strengthened missionary motivation, but in a different way it favored colonialism by encouraging further British intervention for the "good" of the native population.

In Asia the focal points of mission were India, Indonesia, and the Philippines; in the Pacific it was New Guinea, Hawaii, and other island groups. Latin America was predominantly a Roman Catholic sphere. In North America work among Indians and blacks ranked as home missions. The → Russian Orthodox Church had a new outburst of missionary energy that for the first time reached the parts of its empire in the Far East, as well as China and Korea.

In Russia as elsewhere Islam was a barrier to the spread of the faith that was hard to overcome. Against expectations, the gradual bringing of Islamic countries under political subjugation to the West did little to change the situation.

3.5. *Crisis and Transformation: End of the Twentieth Century and After*

3.5.1. The second half of the 20th century confronted the world Christian mission with massive challenges and changes. Among the major reasons were the collapse of the older Christendom as a consequence of two major world wars and the spread of Communism; decolonization in Asia and Africa, and with it the disappearance of the protective colonial umbrella in countries where Western missions had been active; and the resurgence of major world religions, especially Islam and Hinduism, and the parallel emergence of powerful new ethnic or national identities in former mission areas. Accompanying these changes was the massive decline in active Christian membership and participation among both Protestants and Roman Catholics, especially in European countries, with a resultant decline of interest in, and resources for, global mission. Ironically, as the West underwent → secularization and dechristianization, Christian communities in Africa south of the Sahara, Latin America, and parts of Asia grew by leaps and bounds in the latter part of the 20th century.

3.5.2. Western mission agencies and their partner churches were confronted by major challenges in the aftermath of World War II. In 1949 the revolutionary People's Republic of China demanded the expulsion of all foreign mission personnel and the cutting off of financial and fellowship ties with overseas churches and missions. Countries such as India and Burma restricted visas and work permits for new missionary personnel. → Conversions (§1) to Christianity were banned in most Muslim countries, and mission activities were restricted to education and medicine (→ Medical Missions). Hindus issued strong condemnations against conversion and labeled Christian missionary work as proselytism. In many places Christians suffered from discrimination and persecution. Communal riots and attacks of Muslims against Christians and vice versa broke out in Nigeria and Indonesia. Overall, isolated Christian churches, deprived of the colonial umbrella, lived a precarious existence.

3.5.3. Such discouraging circumstances were the context and catalyst for remarkable numerical growth, individuality, and maturity among → Third World churches. Africa south of Sahara became predominantly Christian. Latin America, long a Roman Catholic stronghold, experienced fresh growth, especially among Pentecostals. China, with a Protestant population not exceeding 1 million in 1949, grew to as many as 50 million (some estimates are considerably higher) in both registered and unregistered churches in all regions and provinces by 2000. Chinese Catholics, despite special problems, also continued to grow. In many cases growth in numbers was matched by increased zeal for mission and evangelism. Asian countries, led by India, Korea, the Philippines, and overseas Chinese, sent out their own cross-cultural missionaries. In Africa, Nigeria and Kenya were outstanding for their missionary contributions. Regional Catholic bishops' conferences in Asia, Africa, and Latin America laid down guidelines for inculturation, liturgical experimentation, and dialogue with non-Christians. → The Ecumenical Association of Third World Theologians promoted lively exchange among theologians. Leadership training was a priority everywhere.

3.5.4. Mission agencies in the West regrouped and sought new solutions to the issue of mission purpose and identity. The → International Missionary Council (1921), successor to the Edinburgh World Missionary Conference (1910), provided constructive leadership and guidance to conciliar mission agencies and their partner churches through research and the holding of periodic world mission conferences. After 1961, when the IMC was integrated into the → World Council of Churches, meetings of the WCC Commission on World Mission and Evangelism continued to provide such leadership.

In 1974 conservative evangelical mission groups, particularly the Interdenominational Foreign Mission Association of North America (founded 1917) and the Evangelical Foreign Missions Association (1945), in conjunction with several "parachurch" organizations, sensing a decline in commitment on the part of ecumenical or conciliar mission agencies, formed the Lausanne Committee on World Evangelization (LCWE). Its aim was to mobilize evangelicals for mission, engage in needed research, and provide a solid theological platform (via its Lausanne Covenant) for evangelical missionary cooperation. A secondary effect of LCWE was to give rise to proposals for "reaching the unreached" and planting churches among unevangelized people groups.

Among Roman Catholics, → Vatican II (1962-65) gave rise to important new missionary statements and provided the impetus for new mission strategies and experiments (e.g., → base communities, → liberation theologies, preferential option for the poor, and an emphasis on human → rights). Inculturation and the practice of → dialogue, along with evangelization and advocacy of justice, became preeminent marks of Catholic mission activity.

A severe decline in numbers of career missionaries sent out by Western mission agencies, especially conciliar Protestants and Catholic mission congregations, was partially offset by a tremendous growth in numbers of Third World missionaries and mission organizations. Meanwhile, urban revival movements, Christian youth encounters, and efforts to reclaim lapsed Christians were by now a typical part of the mission identity of Christian bodies in the West.

3.5.5. As a new millennium begins, no prediction regarding the future shape of world Christianity, or a global strategy for Christian mission, can be hazarded. Suffice it to say that the most recently Christianized areas of the earth may be expected to take the lead, perhaps supplanting the lands of traditional Christendom. The agents and methods will be newly developed for the task, supplementing and even supplanting the methods and practices of mission societies and denominational boards developed in the 19th century. Ultimately, the precise outline of future mission history belongs to the mystery of *missio Dei.*

Bibliography: G. H. ANDERSON, ed., *Biographical Dictionary of Christian Missions* (Grand Rapids, 1999) • D. B. BARRETT et al., eds., *WCE* (2d ed.) • D. B. BOSCH, *Transforming Mission* (Maryknoll, N.Y., 1991) • A. VON HARNACK, *The Expansion of Christianity in the First Three Centuries* (trans. J. Moffatt; 2 vols.; London, 1904-5) • K. S. LATOURETTE, *A History of the Expansion of Christianity* (7 vols.; New York, 1937-45) • A. F. WALLS, *The Cross-Cultural Process in Christian History* (Maryknoll, N.Y., 2002); idem, *The Missionary Movement in Christian History* (Maryknoll, N.Y., 1996).

HANS-WERNER GENSICHEN† and
JAMES A. SCHERER

Mission Schools

1. History

1.1. *Goals*

Schools have been highly valued in Protestant and Roman Catholic → mission (→ Catholic Missions; School and Church), even if only as aids to mission (→ Literacy). They make minimal knowledge possible in preparation for → baptism, and they serve to train national workers for pastoral work and → proclamation. They also create the conditions for discharge of the missionary task. Denominational, linguistic, and geographic reasons have been used as reasons for the various missions to maintain their own schools.

American Presbyterians working in Brazil around the turn of the 20th century suggested five goals for their educational institutions: (1) aid in the propagation of the gospel; (2) prepare believers for life on a higher economic scale, which would enable them to support the → church and exert greater influence on → society; (3) provide a greater moral and spiritual environment for → education than that of the public schools; (4) train church leaders; and (5) contribute to the culture and development of the nation (P. Pierson, 108). It was assumed that in the West the church and school had worked together to establish what was considered a Christian culture and that the same process could occur also in various mission fields. Another assumption was that Western-style education was the indispensable basis for → progress. Especially in the 19th century, mission schools were welcomed by many in Asia and Latin America, even by those who were not otherwise interested in the Christian message.

1.2. *Protestant Schools*

Various types of educational institutions have been a part of Roman Catholic and Protestant missions since their beginning. Early in the 18th century B. Ziegenbalg (1682-1719) of the Danish Halle Mission (→ German Missions 1) established schools for both boys and girls in Tranquebar, India. While the primary goal of these schools was evangelistic, they were also designed to lead to socioeconomic change, especially for the lower → castes. Other Protestant schools were set up on a broad basis early in the 19th century by Anglo-Saxon, especially British, societies as part of their work in India, Africa, and the Pacific (→ British Missions).

The difference in mission schools in India in the 19th and 20th centuries reflected the variety of answers to the problem that affected the first missionaries there, namely, whether the mission school as a direct means of mission could on its own help the mission and the young Christian church to discharge fully their shared responsibility for → salvation and well-being, for ministering to both soul and body, in the educational realm.

G. Warneck (1834-1910) put the arguments for and against the mission schools into the wider context of his concept of national Christianization. In so doing, he offered orientation to the mission schools of continental Europe. But he ran up against doubters in mission circles at home who regarded the time and money spent on such schools as a diversion from the "real" task of → evangelism.

The various mission societies eventually established many primary and secondary schools in Asia, Africa, and Latin America. → Universities and specialized institutions to train medical personnel and church leaders were established primarily in Asia and Latin America.

1.3. *Roman Catholic Schools*

J. Schmidlin (1876-1944) dealt expressly and critically with the practices in Roman Catholic mission schools, largely in agreement on this point with Warneck. The agreement was hardly surprising, for in the use of schools as an aid to mission, the methods were much the same as those of Protestants, perhaps under their direct influence. The decline and restarting of Roman Catholic missions stood in causal relation to the very inadequate attempts to train a national clergy, due in part to the lack of an infrastructure of education for the laity (→ Clergy and Laity).

On the basis of the reports of apostolic vicars on the positive effect of schools on the success of Protestant missions, Roman Catholic missionary authorities issued a series of instructions that resulted in the abandoning of earlier methods, for example, a warning in 1845 not to neglect popular education in trying to train a native clergy but to teach secular themes in primary and secondary schools. Other instructions related to statistics (1861), support by the state (1868), and the opening of schools for both boys and girls (1869).

Bibliography: J. EGGERT, "The School Policy of the German Protestant Missions in Tanzania before the First World War," *Missionary Ideologies in the Imperialist Era, 1880-1920* (ed. T. Christensen and W. R. Hutchison; Århus, 1982) 200-207 • K. S. LATOURETTE, *A History of the Expansion of Christianity* (7 vols.; New York, 1937-45) • P. E. PIERSON, *A Younger Church in Search of Maturity* (San Antonio, Tex., 1974) • J. SCHMIDLIN, "Die Schule in der Mission," *ZMR* 27 (1937) 19-31 • "Missionsschule I/II," *LMTG* 302-12.

JOHANNA EGGERT and PAUL E. PIERSON

2. Operation

2.1. *Finances*

The role of schools was never without controversy in missionary communities, both Roman Catholic and Protestant. Questions arose primarily over their effectiveness in aiding evangelization and over the resources required for their maintenance. Financial problems were greater than anticipated. Hopes for local financial aid were usually disappointed, and schools generally failed to become self-supporting. Mission schools could thus continue to exist only by charging tuition, which often eliminated the enrollment of the poorer students they were intended to help. The need for students who could pay tuition brought increased numbers of non-Christians into student bodies, and the drive for academic excellence often led to the employment of non-Christian teachers. These factors diluted the Christian ambience of these schools. In the British colonies the governments subsidized mission schools, but this relationship led to a problematic association of the Christian faith with → colonialism.

2.2. *Priorities*

There was also a constant tension over whether to assign the limited numbers of missionary personnel to educational or to evangelistic ministries. Often two different philosophies of mission lay behind this debate, especially in Asia. While some advocated direct → evangelism (often of the poor) as the focus of the missionary task, others believed that the introduction of Western-style education would lead the most influential people to adopt the Christian faith, which would in turn move nations to embrace Christian values. Some went so far as to suggest that "civilizing the heathen" was a necessary preliminary step toward their → conversion. With the growth of theological → liberalism and the → Social Gospel in the West, however, the call to evangelism often became muted.

2.3. *Statistics*

Despite controversies and problems, there were impressive achievements. By 1910 the various Protestant missions worldwide had established 30,000 elementary and village schools with 2.1 million students, and 740 → kindergartens with 27,000 students. Boarding schools on the secondary level and normal schools for teacher training were also established; in 1923 there were 55,000 girls in high schools and 3,000 in normal schools.

2.4. *Emphases*

2.4.1. *Universities*

Universities on occasion grew from small beginnings. A school for three street children started in 1870 by Mary Chamberlain, the wife of a Presbyterian missionary, in her home in São Paulo, Brazil, became in 1871 the Escola Americana (with 44 students), which ultimately developed into the Mackenzie Institute (1940), at one time the largest private university in Brazil. A school for girls established in 1886 by a Methodist missionary in Seoul, Korea, eventually became Ehwa, which now, with 20,000 students, is the largest women's university in the world. Nearby is Yonsei, a men's university and the oldest university in Korea, established by Presbyterians. A number of other colleges and universities were established for men and women, primarily in India, China, Korea, Japan, and the Middle East.

→ Benedictines established Fu Jen Catholic University, the first Roman Catholic college in China, in 1925; four years later it included separate colleges of liberal arts, education, and the natural sciences. In 1930 Benedictine sisters followed by founding the first Catholic women's college in China. The curricula in these schools usually combined Christian teaching, traditional Western subjects including the sciences, mathematics, and geography, with the languages and cultures of the host countries.

2.4.2. *Education of Women*

The education of girls and women soon received special attention from women's missionary societies in the sending countries. In nearly every mission field women were typically abused and thought to be incapable of learning. In India, for example, until well into the early 20th century, most Hindu fathers were bitterly opposed to the education of their daughters. Gradually, however, the education of women became not so much a strategy for evangelization as an instrument for social change. One writer has concluded that "education was the key for the liberation of women around the world" (D. Robert, 160).

2.4.3. *Training of Church Leaders*

Training schools for church leaders, both men and women, were important. Although women were rarely if ever ordained, in a number of Asian and Middle Eastern countries they were employed as evangelists or catechists and known as Bible women. A number of schools for the training of such women were established in India and China. Bible schools and theological institutions for men, ranging from the primary level to the university and graduate levels, were often established to prepare persons for leadership in the churches.

2.4.4. *Medical Schools*

Another major area of specialization was medical education (→ Medical Missions). Missionaries introduced Western medicine to Asia and Africa and often to interior areas of Latin America. Medical care for women, often forbidden by culture or religion to male physicians, became especially important. By 1900 there were medical classes for men and women in several parts of China, India, and Japan. By 1910 there were 37 schools of nursing sponsored by American missions in Korea, Japan, India, China, Syria, the Philippines, Brazil, Mexico, and Puerto Rico. Many of these schools were the product of cooperative efforts undertaken by a number of missionary enterprises. Perhaps the best-known missionary medical institution was — and remains — at Vellore, India. Established in 1918 by Dr. Ida Scudder and supported by a number of denominations, it has received international recognition.

2.4.5. *Professional and Trade Schools*

Additionally, trade schools of various kinds were established by missions. By 1900 at least 50 such schools were functioning. There were also agricultural schools in Ghana, Brazil, and elsewhere. The Gammon Institute, founded by Presbyterians in 1908, became one of the most notable university-level schools of agriculture in Brazil.

3. Present Situation

With the passing of time, many mission schools were closed, taken over by governments often hostile to Christianity, or they simply became secularized (→ Secularization). Others have continued to maintain a strong Christian character. In some cases, as educational opportunities provided by governments have increased and improved, many of the original reasons for the establishment of mission schools are no longer valid.

A contemporary approach to mission schools is seen in the work of the missions of the Assemblies of God in Central America. Based on a strong, growing church among the poor, its strategy is to change conditions that perpetuate → poverty for children by establishing a new educational system within the region's current infrastructure. Such help is clearly needed, for "one-third of all children in Central America are denied access to public educa-

tion. Of the remaining two-thirds who begin primary school, only 26 percent finish the sixth grade" (D. Peterson, 151). In a manner similar to mission schools of the 19th century, leaders of missions in these countries see education as a program of social action designed to reform unjust social structures. In 1993 this program had 117 primary and 45 secondary schools with 42,000 students.

→ Colonialism and Mission

Bibliography: R. P. BEAVER, *American Protestant Women in World Mission* (rev. ed.; Grand Rapids, 1980) • A. DRIES, *The Missionary Movement in American Catholic History* (Maryknoll, N.Y., 1998) • P. HILL, *The World Their Household: The American Woman's Foreign Mission Movement and Cultural Transformation, 1870-1920* (Ann Arbor, Mich., 1985) • D. PETERSON, *Not by Might nor by Power: A Pentecostal Theology of Social Concern in Latin America* (Oxford, 1996) • D. ROBERT, *American Women in Mission* (Macon, Ga., 1996).

PAUL E. PIERSON

Missionary

1. Biblical Usage
2. Early Church to World War II
3. Changes after World War II
4. Present Situation
5. Other Religions

The understanding of the term "missionary" depends on semantic usage, theological interpretation, and historical context. Derived from Lat. *mitto* (send) or *missus* (sent), the word "missionary" has traditionally designated someone sent on a religious → mission — by God (Jesus Christ as representative of the *missio Dei*) or by a church, a mission society, or another sending body to propagate faith or carry out a mission task. A close relation exists between the aim, intention, and authority of the sender, the credentials of the person or persons (missionaries) sent, and the actual nature and purpose of the mission. In recent years, emissaries of non-Christian faiths (esp. Buddhists and Muslims) have sometimes been referred to as missionaries. In today's more secular parlance, "mission" is often used to describe the organized effort of a commercial, diplomatic, military, or other type of entity, though the designation "missionary" is not often used in this connection. The label, however, is often popularly applied to any person zealously committed to a particular cause. This article focuses on the religious and mainly Christian usage of the term.

1. Biblical Usage

The word "missionary" does not appear in the Bible. Moreover, it is not a precise equivalent of NT words that denote authorized sending or the status of a commissioned messenger (e.g., *apostellō*, *apostolos*, *pempō*). It cannot be said that the missionary of modern times is, despite many similarities in task or function, the equivalent of the NT → apostle, for in each case the authority of the sender is different. While the early church had no missionary office as such, missionary functions (e.g., witness, service, church planting, and leadership training) were performed not only by Jesus' apostles and by Paul but also by NT → deacons (Philip and Stephen), itinerant evangelists (Apollos; → Evangelism), prominent converts (Barnabas), helpers of Paul (Timothy, Silvanus, Titus, Mark, and others), and anonymous lay believers. The NT apostolate was a unique phenomenon that cannot be equated with missionary vocation in later times.

2. Early Church to World War II

After the time of Constantine the Great (ruled 306-37), the first Christian Roman ruler, missionary excursions across the frontiers of the → Roman Empire into pagan areas were undertaken by monks and clergy. Their purpose was to extend orthodox Christianity into unevangelized border regions.

During the Middle Ages we hear of missionaries in the West attempting to Christianize France (Martin of Tours [ca. 316-97]), Ireland (Patrick [mid or late 5th cent.]), Anglo-Saxons (Augustine of Canterbury [d. 604]), Germans (Boniface [ca. 675-754]; → Germanic Mission), and Scandinavians (Anskar [801-65]). Celtic monks were known for their missionary peregrinations (Columbanus [ca. 543-615]). On the eastern frontier, missions were directed to central Asia and China by the → Nestorian Church of the East (ca. 781), to the Slavs by Cyril (ca. 827-69) and his brother Methodius (ca. 815-85; → Slavic Mission), to Kerala in South India by Syrian missionaries, and to Ethiopia by Frumentius (4th cent.), sent by Bishop → Athanasius of Alexandria.

Not until the late 15th and 16th centuries, the so-called age of exploration, were the terms "mission" and "missionary" used to designate sending overseas. The eminent Spanish Jesuit Francis → Xavier (1506-52), after preliminary visits to Goa and the Moluccas, undertook the first major evangelistic mission in Japan and died in an effort to penetrate China. He was followed in India by the Jesuit Robert de Nobili (1577-1656) and in China by another Jesuit, Matteo Ricci (1552-1610).

The overseas conquests of Spain and Portugal and the discovery of unevangelized lands in the Americas, Africa, and Asia led to missions by → Jesuits, → Dominicans, → Franciscans, and other religious orders. Sent out on ships bearing Iberian conquistadores under the *Patronato Real* (royal patronage) of Spain and Portugal, missionaries were given the task of Christianizing indigenous tribes and peoples. Unfortunately, their collaboration with plantation and mine owners under the encomienda system often led to the widespread oppression and enslavement of native peoples and Africans (→ Latin America and the Caribbean 1.3; Reductions). While exceptions to this pattern existed, missions in the age of exploration bore in large part the stamp of Western imperialism in its cultural, economic, political, and ecclesiastical forms (→ Colonialism).

By the early 18th century Protestant missionaries, working partly under colonial auspices — for example, the → Puritan missionary John Eliot (1604-90) among Native American tribes in New England, the Danish-Halle missionary Bartholomew Ziegenbalg (1682-1719) in Tranquebar, South India (→ German Missions 1), and → Moravian exiles from Herrnhut (after 1732) working in diverse fields — began to develop a distinctively Protestant missionary profile.

In 1792 the modern missionary movement may be said to have begun with the sending of William Carey (1761-1834), an English Baptist lay preacher and missionary advocate, to the British East India Company and later to the Danish colony at Serampore in India. Carey and his colleagues introduced many valuable innovations (e.g., intensive language study, Bible translations, self-supporting enterprises, and ecumenical ventures) that contributed to the effectiveness of Western missions.

→ Biographies and autobiographies of 19th-century missionary heroes and heroines, often bordering on hagiography, stimulated faith and commitment on the part of mission supporters, educated them in the customs and folkways of exotic peoples, and informed them of scientific advances and geographic discoveries. Missionaries such as Robert Morrison (1782-1834), Adoniram Judson (1788-1850), David Livingstone (1813-73), and J. Hudson Taylor (1832-1905) became popular celebrities. Today only Mother Teresa (1910-97) of Calcutta has such instant name recognition.

The 19th century, often called the great century of Christian expansion, saw an enormous multiplication of Protestant mission societies and Roman Catholic missionary orders in Europe and in North America. In the United States newly formed Protestant mission societies were generally integrated into denominational structures as church mission boards; Catholic mission congregations, while remaining independent, were related to diocesan structures. The expansion of Western mission agencies coincided with the rising fortunes of Western imperialism and the acquisition of overseas colonies (→ Colonialism and Mission).

Spiritual awakening movements such as the Student Volunteer Movement for Foreign Missions, founded in 1886, aroused popular interest and led to the recruitment of astonishing numbers of young mission volunteers. Women, especially single women, now began to predominate in the ranks of missionaries as mission roles were expanded to include not merely preachers and evangelists but also teachers, doctors, nurses, social workers, and administrators (→ Women's Missions; Medical Missions). Until the end of World War II, missionaries from the West held a virtual monopoly over what were designated "foreign missions."

3. Changes after World War II

With the coming of movements for national independence in Asia and Africa and the withdrawal or expulsion of former colonial powers after World War II, the situation changed. Western missions and missionaries were now seen, retrospectively, as having been too closely allied to colonial expansionism and were accused by their critics of cultural imperialism, → proselytism, or ethnic genocide. The missionary image was now viewed as badly tarnished and in need of rehabilitation. Native churches founded by mission efforts were put down as spiritual colonies or replicas of Western churches or seen as little more than religious departments of former colonial powers. Around the middle of the 20th century, books written under suggestive titles such as *Missionary, Go Home!* were common. A moratorium on the sending of Western missionaries was even proposed. In 1949 the People's Republic of China expelled all Western missionaries, and other Asian countries denied them entry or restricted visas and work permits. → Third World churches, products of missionary effort, strove to overcome the stigma of inferiority or foreignness and worked to accentuate marks of their own spiritual autonomy and cultural identity. The new situation represented a crisis for Western mission agencies. In time, most problems were resolved through → ecumenical dialogue, but the transition was painful for churches in both North and South.

The morphology of Western missionary vocation underwent drastic changes. In the early colonial period, European missionaries had been typically pioneer evangelists, Bible translators, and church founders. A generation or two later, as national converts grew and younger churches came into being, missionaries assumed roles as → bishops, managers, or heads of institutions such as schools and hospitals, mission treasurers, or liaison officers between the home board and the young church. Still later, in the period of national independence, missionaries were considered to be invited guests, serving at the pleasure of national churches and under their authority. Stripped of authority roles and now working as experts or specialists in theological training or other ministries, they were sometimes said to be "needed but not wanted." Expendable and coming as invited guests rather than as authorized messengers, some Western missionaries began to question the validity of their roles. A few mission boards substituted the term "fraternal worker" for "missionary." For a time it became necessary to reinvent the missionary role according to circumstances.

Gradual changes occurred in relationships between overseas mission boards or societies and the emerging churches. The shift from a dependent relationship to one of independence, and subsequently to interdependence, took place slowly. A wholesome change occurred as formerly dependent churches discovered their own organizational autonomy and spiritual independence. Third World churches now began to claim the right and duty to do mission in their own name and to send out their own missionaries, sometimes to neighboring territories but sometimes even to their own erstwhile mother churches.

Within the ecumenical missionary movement new slogans were heard such as "partnership in obedience," "mission in six continents," and "mission from everywhere to everywhere." Church and mission leaders were recovering the older missionary terminology but with new meaning. The church was now understood as missionary by its very nature, with every local church becoming a church in mission. Global mission was now understood as mutual, multilateral, and multidirectional. Every local church was challenged to engage in mission both in its own neighborhood and at the ends of the earth.

By a strange irony of history, this ecumenical reinterpretation of the meaning of mission and missionary was occurring at a time when Western Christianity — especially in Europe, whose spiritual tone was eroded by acids of → secularism and scientific → humanism — was suffering from "loss of nerve" and experiencing deep numerical attrition.

The old balance between "Western Christendom" and the "non-Christian world" was irrevocably altered. Christians in the South now outnumbered those in the North. In sub-Saharan Africa, Latin America, and parts of Asia, the Christian church underwent explosive growth, while in Europe anxious voices were calling for the reconversion or re-evangelization of Christendom.

4. Present Situation

By the last two decades of the 20th century, the world map of Christianity had decisively changed. With it there emerged a new identity for the Christian missionary. He or she is now likely to be a person of color, male or female, ordained or lay, full-time or voluntary, serving in the evangelistic outreach of a Third World church. A recent survey reveals that 1,600 non-Western mission organizations in Africa, Asia, Latin America, and Oceania are sending out an estimated 88,000 cross-cultural workers who now serve in the missions of non-Western churches. The profile of Western missionaries has also changed decisively.

In Africa the Christian population has grown from roughly 9 million believers in 1900 to over 350 million, or nearly 50 percent of the total population, in 2000. African churches, especially those of Nigeria, Kenya, and Uganda, have sent out missionaries from more than 100 mission organizations. African → Independent Churches also continue to multiply. The Ethiopian Evangelical Church Mekane Yesus, for example, established in 1959 as a merger of Lutheran and Reformed churches and a member of the → Lutheran World Federation, has grown from fewer than 50,000 members in 1960 to more than 3.3 million in the first years of the 21st century, even in the face of severe challenges to church and society such as rapid urbanization, internal migration (→ Refugees), civil wars, drought, and the spread of AIDS.

In Asia and the Middle East, home to major faiths such as → Hinduism, → Buddhism, and → Islam, the Christian population remains relatively small, but there are areas of dramatic growth. Indian evangelistic bands are actively working among tribal and hill populations. Tribal churches of Myanmar, deeply rooted among Kachin, Karen, Chin, and other tribes, are working to complete the evangelization of their own peoples. Overseas Chinese mission bodies from Taiwan, Hong Kong, and Singapore zealously reach out to overseas Chinese communities. Professing Christians constitute roughly one-eighth of the population of Indonesia.

Perhaps the greatest explosion of Asian Christian growth is occurring in the People's Republic of China where, since 1980, the Christian population has swollen from one or two million to a minimum of 50 million Christians, Protestant and Roman Catholic, in both registered and unregistered churches. The exact numbers (which some have asserted are much higher) cannot be easily discerned. This growth has taken place through the efforts of Chinese → clergy and lay workers working without the aid of outside mission organizations. In South Korea, where the growth of the church has been phenomenal, mission bodies and local congregations are said to be supporting more than 10,000 cross-cultural workers outside the country.

In 2000 Latin America was the most Christianized continent on earth. The evangelical community in particular has experienced rapid growth, from 50,000 in 1900 to upwards of 60 million in 2000, with unusual strength in Chile, Brazil, El Salvador, and Guatemala (→ Evangelical Movement). Independent neo-Pentecostal churches with grassroots lay participation are committed to evangelism and church planting. Among Roman Catholics the → base Christian communities have furthered renewal and reached out to the poor and marginal. The missionary function has been effectively performed by entire communities.

In North America there has been a precipitous decline in the number of long-term or career missionaries (persons fluent in the language and able to live in local cultures) sent out by mainline churches. The conciliar mission boards — usually affiliated with the U.S. → National Council of Churches of Christ and/or the Canadian Council of Churches — until 1953 were responsible for sending out the large majority of North American Protestant missionaries, reaching a peak of 12,000 in 1968 and then experiencing a steady and lasting decline in numbers. U.S. → Catholic mission societies similarly peaked at 9,655 missionaries (including priests, brothers, and sisters) in 1968 before beginning a decline.

Evangelical missionaries related to the Interdenominational Foreign Mission Association of North America (founded 1917) and the Evangelical Foreign Missions Association (1945) surpassed conciliar missionaries in numbers during the 1970s and 1980s. They in turn were overtaken by personnel of several newer independent or unaffiliated mission bodies, which now account for the majority of North American cross-cultural workers. Today the Southern Baptist Convention leads in numbers of overseas personnel serving more than four years, followed by the Wycliffe Bible Translators, the New Tribes Mission, and the Assemblies of God (→ Evangelical Missions).

Concurrently, there has been steady growth in numbers of short-term (defined as serving from two months to two years) missionaries and mission volunteers from North America. Recruitment of teachers, agricultural or development experts, builders, doctors, dentists, and other specialists for short-term service under church or mission auspices has vastly increased and helps to compensate for the lack of career missionaries. Short-term personnel, however, are not expected to master local languages or learn local customs and cultures. They contribute their services and enrich the global experience of churches to which they return. Youth-oriented missions such as Youth with a Mission (YWAM) and similar groups annually send out thousands of youth on short-term evangelistic encounters.

As noted, there has been a dramatic increase in the sending out of missionaries by Third World churches or congregations. Some work cross-culturally among bordering tribes; others go to Europe or North America for study, teaching, and service; while still others participate in "South-South" exchanges with Third World churches. Mission structures include both independent mission societies and church mission departments. Missiological studies incorporating prefield encounters with people of other faiths, resources from the → social sciences, and methods of cross-cultural communication normally form a part of → missionary training programs. Ideally, prefield preparation, field training, especially in languages, and furlough study proceed according to an integrated plan. Programs of mission study offering advanced training in → contextualization, inculturation, mission theology, → spirituality, → dialogue, and relations with other living faiths are available in a number of seminaries and universities. Many Third World seminaries now include → missiology in their curricular requirements.

Some evangelical groups advocate, in contrast to ecumenical partnerships with Third World churches, a strategy of returning to an earlier style of missionary pioneering. Proponents of this approach focus efforts on "reaching unreached peoples" so as to complete the task of world evangelization. Individual mission agencies are encouraged to adopt a particular unreached people and focus on that group. Such movements reject the notion that the missionary task is essentially completed, calling for mission agencies to deploy more workers for the completion of the unfinished task.

Occasional tensions have existed between the personal messenger and the religious community as bearer of the missionary message, and between lay volunteers and full-time professionals (→ Lay Movements). The vocation of the missionary has been reinvented over and over again, and the term "mission" itself has been reminted with fresh content, depending on the time and context. The age of the Western missionary is definitively over, yet missionaries in all lands and cultures will need to discover and perform their tasks, in obedience to the Lord, "until he comes again." In that sense, *mission* and *missionary* will endure as indispensable components of what it means to be the church of Jesus Christ living in the world.

5. Other Religions

Mission activities are no longer a monopoly of Christian churches. For a century or more, adherents of other religions, envying earlier successes of Christian overseas missions and philanthropic activities, have studied and adapted the methods used and have begun sending their own missionaries to the West. Followers of Hare → Krishna and of the → Unification Church ("Moonies") can now be found in many Western urban centers. Mosques in western Europe and North America, originally intended for the worship of immigrant populations, are being transformed into "cultural centers" that propagate Islam to lapsed Christians. Islam and Buddhism are inherently missionary faiths, and over time they will change from foreign diaspora communities to groups actively recruiting Westerners.

Bibliography: G. H. ANDERSON, ed., *Biographical Dictionary of Christian Missions* (Grand Rapids, 1999) • O. DEGRIJSE, *Going Forth: Missionary Consciousness in Third World Catholic Churches* (Maryknoll, N.Y., 1984) • A. DRIES, *The Missionary Movement in American Catholic History* (Maryknoll, N.Y., 1998) • M. T. HUBER and N. C. LUTKEHAUS, eds., *Gendered Missions: Women and Men in Missionary Discourse and Practice* (Ann Arbor, Mich., 1999) • P. JENKINS, *The Next Christendom: The Coming of Global Christianity* (New York, 2002) • J. K. MANDELBAUM, *The Missionary as a Cultural Interpreter* (New York, 1989) • J. A. SIEWERT and D. WELLIVER, eds., *Mission Handbook: U.S. and Canadian Christian Ministries Overseas, 2001-2003* (18th ed.; Wheaton, Ill., 2000).

JAMES A. SCHERER

Missionary Conferences

1. Early History
2. Ecumenical Conferences
3. Evangelical Conferences

1. Early History

Early requests for a worldwide missionary conference on the part of Protestant → missionaries and mission leaders from English- and German-speaking areas (such as by W. Carey in 1810) met with no success. Only with the development of Protestant churches at the end of the 19th century did large-scale missionary conferences become possible at the turn of the 20th century. The development of these churches involved a rapid increase in the number of evangelical and fundamentalist missionary societies in the United States and Europe (→ Evangelical Missions; Fundamentalism), the increasing fragmentation of the Protestant world and the growing desire for visible → unity (though only within Protestant Christendom), the heightened expectation of the → parousia in many Protestant circles, and all in conjunction with an optimistic belief in progress (→ Optimism and Pessimism), yet at the same time a sense of the looming crisis of the Western world.

The 19th century had known three types of mission conferences. First, the home churches had organized missionary conferences for the dissemination of information and for enlisting recruits. Then there had been regional, national, and even continent-wide conferences for mission leaders. Third, area conferences had been convened in Asia, Africa, and Latin America. A pattern is visible (with some exceptions) of a movement from conferences of mission leaders to the assembling of delegates from all the churches of the world, at which missionary leaders and scholars (→ Missiology) would simply be advisers.

Regular area conferences took place in India (from 1855), China (1877), Mexico (1888), and South Africa (1904). These meetings (predominantly gatherings of white males) attempted to coordinate mission work in each area, reduce tensions, and settle disputes.

The mission meetings at Liverpool (1860), Bremen (1866), London (1878 and 1888), and New York (1900) combined business sessions for mission leaders and missionaries with mass evangelistic rallies. The New York Ecumenical Mission Conference (1900), with estimated attendance of 160,000 to 200,000 over ten days, plus 2,500 official delegates representing 160 mission boards, was the largest sustained formal religious event in the history of the United States, and the largest mission conference ever held.

The desire for closer cooperation (e.g., as proposed by G. Warneck in 1888 and F. Ellinwood in 1900) was that gatherings of mission leaders would evolve into cooperative mission organizations called conferences. In Saxony Warneck (1834-1910) combined various missions into a single Saxon mission conference (1879). In 1897 he was able to unite 14 missionary societies in Der Ausschuß der deutschen evangelischen Missionsgellschaften (Standing committee of the German Protestant missionary societies).

2. Ecumenical Conferences

Edinburgh, 1910. Inspired by the watchword of the Student Volunteer Movement, "The evangelization of the world in this generation," this mission gathering was the first to call itself a *world* missionary conference. It was the first great global conference of Protestant mission to include High Church Anglicans (→ Anglican Communion), who had previously stayed aloof. Key leaders in the preparatory work were J. H. Oldham (1874-1969, executive secretary of the conference) and J. R. → Mott (1865-1955, chairman), who imbued the conference with his eschatological optimism. The delegates, who were almost exclusively Western (of the 1,200 participants, only 17 were from the → Third World), defined mission only as the → preaching of the → gospel to the heathen (→ Gentiles; Gentile Christianity). Enthusiasm for the use of → technology in the service of mission, as well as the uncritical linking of the gospel to so-called Christian civilization, reflected the spirit of the 19th century. The striving for church unity was made concrete by referring to Jesus' missionary commission, which led to urgent demands for ecumenical cooperation (→ Ecumenical Dialogue): there should be proportionate and official representation; all denominations should be represented, and there must be an uncompromising adherence to the essential Christian convictions (but which ones?). Out of the conference came the *International Review of Missions* (from 1912, with Oldham as its first editor) and, in 1921, the founding of the → International Missionary Council (IMC).

Jerusalem, 1928. This inaugural meeting of the IMC was the first globally representative consultation of Protestant missions. Of the 251 delegates 52 were from the younger churches. This conference could look back, not only on the great crisis of Western civilization in World War I, but also on the founding of two great ecumenical movements: → Life and Work (launched in a "universal Christian conference" in Stockholm in 1925, led by Archbishop N. Söderblom and Oldham) and → Faith and Order (begun in a "world conference" in Lausanne in 1927, led by Bishop C. Brent, with then bishop W. Temple drafting the final statement). Jerusalem dealt with social questions and the problem of → secularism. A clear-cut rejection of "social Christianity" and of questions from the history of religions led to an emphasis on → Christology (Temple). M. Schlunk (1874-1958), K. Hartenstein (1894-1952), and H. Kraemer (1888-1965) criticized the compromise that, while acknowledging Jesus Christ as "the message of the church to the world," also found elements of truth and certain saving values in other religions (→ Salvation).

Tambaram/Madras, 1938. This conference was held under the influence of the global economic crisis, militant neopaganism (→ Communism; Fascism), and the growing threats to world peace. More than half of the 471 delegates, who came from 69 countries, were from the younger churches. They discussed the church as the agent of the message of the gospel (H. Kraemer). In his preparatory study, *The Christian Message in a Non-Christian World* (1938), Kraemer, influenced by K. → Barth, promoted the claim of Christianity to absoluteness, as well as its discontinuity with non-Christian religions. Delegates from the Third World stressed the need for visible unity of the church for the sake of missionary witness. Mission was seen as the task of the local church — a critical milestone on the way to the independence of the younger churches. In the same year preliminary steps were taken toward the founding of the → World Council of Churches (WCC), with which it was planned the IMC would be in association, though remaining independent.

Whitby, Canada, 1947 ("Christian Witness in a Revolutionary World"). Held shortly after World War II, this third IMC ecumenical conference brought together 112 delegates from 40 countries. There had now been a generational shift in the IMC, for Oldham retired in 1938, and Mott in 1942. The theme was global evangelization, still with the former optimism, though not now in the sense of a → conversion of the world. The conference again identified mission in a given area as the exclusive responsibility of the local churches in that place, who would proceed in a "partnership in obedience." In doing so, it abandoned the distinction between mother churches and young churches. The founding of the WCC in Amsterdam in 1948 confirmed the strong emphasis on church unity and the sense that church and mission belong together — not least, thanks to personal links.

Willingen, West Germany, 1952 ("The Missionary Obligation of the Church"). The 190 delegates assembled discussed "the end of the Christian era" but could formulate no new solutions. This conference highlighted the idea of the *missio Dei* (G. Vicedom) — the mission of the triune God (→ Trinity) in and for the world, in which the church participates. This concept replaced the ecclesiocentric notion of the mission of the church as the norm. Familiar themes of the role and training of missionaries, the role of the mission societies, and the forms of missionary work also came under discussion.

Accra, Ghana, 1958. At this fifth and last general conference of the IMC, it was decided to integrate the IMC into the WCC, which took place in New Delhi in 1961 at the Third Assembly of the WCC. It was a step that set the course for the full equality of the churches of Africa, Asia, and Latin America in the ecumenical movement, but it also led to the increasing organizational separation of evangelical and fundamentalist societies from the mainline Protestant missionary movement. L. → Newbigin (1909-98) became president of the IMC, and W. Freytag (1899-1959) vice president.

Mexico City, 1963 ("Witness in Six Continents"). This conference was the first sponsored by the WCC Commission on World Mission and Evangelization after the integration, and the first missionary conference in which Roman Catholic observers took part. The → Russian Orthodox Church had now joined the WCC, and John XXIII (1958-63) had established the Secretariat for Promoting Christian Unity (1960) and had convened → Vatican II (1962-65). Most of the former colonies in Africa had achieved independence (→ Colonialism). Protestant and Orthodox delegates at Mexico City stressed that each church is in mission wherever it is, and that each has the task of telling the gospel to people today. At issue was common action in mission. The emphases at the later mission conferences were shaped by two subsequent WCC conferences: the World Conference on Church and Society, held at Geneva in 1966, which dealt with revolutionary change in the world (→ Revolution); and the WCC's 1968 Uppsala Assembly, which addressed the social → responsibility of the church (→ Social Ethics) and called for church aid in → development.

Bangkok, 1973 ("Salvation Today"). This was the first missionary conference at which Third World delegates were in a majority. It deplored the gap between the rich North and the poor South (→ Poverty). It dealt with the relation between individual and collective salvation and with questions of inculturation (→ Acculturation) and → contextual theology. The issue of the right of all humans to maintain their cultural → identity led inevitably to → dialogue with Buddhists (→ Buddhism). The search for genuine → partnership produced various proposals, among them (though not endorsed) a moratorium on the use of Western personnel and money for a limited period in some regions. Lively debates took place on these proposals.

Melbourne, 1980 ("Your Kingdom Come"). This conference, which gathered 600 participants, including 250 official observers (mostly from the North), discussed the gospel as good news for the poor and as judgment for the rich. Proclamation, which was emphasized as the responsibility of the whole church and of every member, included the crossing of frontiers and the call to conversion. Missionary proclamation and activity, however, was no longer the only theme but was integrated into the problems of the churches. Vocal expression was given to → liberation theology and to the theology of the compassionate God (J. Esquivél). The question of how far the church should take part in the struggle to liberate the oppressed, since God wills their freedom, was discussed vigorously.

San Antonio, Texas, 1989 ("Your Will Be Done: Mission in Christ's Way"). This conference included 270 voting delegates (40 percent of them women), plus almost 500 additional participants. In the presence of more than 20 non-Christian observers, and with a view to dialogue, the question was raised whether Jesus Christ is the only way to salvation. Most of those present agreed that he is. Central themes included the credibility of mission, the close connection between mission and dialogue, the special role of the poor, the → solidarity of the church with those who are suffering, and → responsibility for the earth (→ Ecology; Environment). Other matters of emphasis were the key role of Third World missionaries in the overall world mission, the responsibility of the church in each place for world mission, and the rejection of all forms of → proselytism. More than previously, conciliatory gestures were made toward priorities for evangelicals in mission (as later expressed in Manila 1989; see 3).

Salvador, Brazil, 1996 ("Called to One Hope: The Gospel in Diverse Cultures"). Attended by 574 participants from about 100 countries, this world missionary conference highlighted the issue of culture in ecumenical and missiological thinking as developed in the WCC's three-year study "Gospel and Cultures." Delegates affirmed the dynamic interaction between gospel and culture in which the gospel illuminates and transforms cultures, while cultures illuminate and incarnate the gospel. Syncretism and proselytism evoked sharp debate. Affirming the catholicity of the church, the conference warned against aggressive evangelism that does not respect the culture of a people. L. Newbigin spoke with pas-

sion of the urgency to bear Christian witness to those of other faiths and secular worldviews, but this theme was muted in the conference reports.

3. Evangelical Conferences

Wheaton, Illinois, 1966 ("The Church's Worldwide Mission"). Sponsored by the Interdenominational Foreign Missions Association and the Evangelical Foreign Missions Association, the conference was attended by 938 delegates from 71 countries. This congress produced the Wheaton Declaration as a distinctive evangelical theory and strategy of mission in contrast with that of the ecumenical movement. Delegates pledged to seek "the mobilization of the church, its people, its prayers, and resources, for the evangelization of the world in this generation."

Berlin, 1966 ("One Race, One Gospel, One Task"). In the same year the evangelical journal *Christianity Today* sponsored a World Congress on Evangelism in Berlin, Germany. The congress, with Billy Graham as honorary chairman and *Christianity Today* editor C. F. H. Henry as executive chairman, was attended by 1,100 conservative evangelical leaders from more than 100 countries. A basic commitment to the authority of the Bible and to evangelism united the participants. The congress gave a new sense of identity and strength to the worldwide evangelical community. The concern expressed by Graham over a "basic crisis in mission" received polemical expression in West Germany in the Frankfurt Declaration on the Fundamental Crisis in Christian Mission (1970). A broadening to include more attention to social issues occurred in the Chicago Declaration of Evangelical Social Concern (1973).

Lausanne, Switzerland, 1974 ("Let the Earth Hear His Voice"). Called at the initiative of Billy Graham, the International Congress for World Evangelization assembled 2,700 participants (calling themselves brothers and sisters, not delegates) from over 150 nations. Intentionally, 50 percent of both participants and speakers were from the Third World. The Lausanne Covenant, drafted by J. Stott of Great Britain, went far beyond traditional evangelical affirmations to affirm that "evangelism and sociopolitical involvement are both part of our Christian duty" (par. 5).

Pattaya, Thailand, 1980 ("How Shall They Hear?"). Beginning in 1974, the → Lausanne Movement, led by the Lausanne Committee for World Evangelization (LCWE), became a major expression of evangelical concern for evangelism and, increasingly, social responsibility. Sponsored also by World

Vision and the Billy Graham Association, the Pattaya conference was designed as a follow-up to Lausanne I. The more than 800 delegates worked in 17 miniconsultations to develop strategies for presenting the gospel to unreached peoples of various religious and cultural backgrounds. In 1984 the Lausanne Committee and the World Evangelical Fellowship (WEF; → World Evangelical Alliance) arranged an international consultation in Wheaton to continue discussion of the relation of church and mission, as well as the problems of social justice that had not thus far been aired by evangelicals.

Manila, 1989 ("Calling the Whole Church to Take the Whole Gospel to the Whole World"). The second International Congress on World Evangelization (or Lausanne II) took place in the Philippines, with over 3,000 participants from 170 countries. Worth noting were the efforts to clarify the relation between charismatic evangelicals (→ Charismatic Movement) and those more inclined to pietism or fundamentalism. This congress also addressed many of the problems under ecumenical discussion, including the role of women, the credibility of mission, mission as a task of the local congregation, the role of the poor, responsibility for → creation, dialogue with non-Christian religions, prophetic witness (→ Prophet, Prophecy) against → force and against apartheid (→ Racism), and contacts with the Orthodox and Roman Catholics. The hope was repeated of reaching the world for Christ before the century's end. A distinctive evangelical statement was made on the theology of mission regarding Christ as the one way to salvation, the importance of Holy Scripture, and expectation of Christ's return.

Singapore, 1989. This gathering was called the Global Consultation on World Evangelization (GCOWE). In 1987 Thomas Wang, then international director of the LCWE, presented the fact that there were hundreds of separate global plans to reach the world for Christ by the year 2000. Less than two years later he convened the first GCOWE in Singapore, bringing together 314 mission leaders from 50 countries. The result was the birth of the AD2000 and Beyond movement, with a commitment to establish a church-planting movement within every unreached people group (down to all groups with as few as 6,000 members). In the following years evangelical Christians in more than 100 countries started national initiatives.

Seoul, South Korea, 1995. This conference, called GCOWE II, brought together over 4,000 delegates from 186 countries, making it the largest and most widely represented international Christian gathering in history. Its focus was on reaching every unreached people by the year 2000, with priority given to 1,700 people groups each with over 10,000 population, less than 5 percent Christian, and less than 2 percent of their population evangelical.

Pretoria, South Africa, 1997. In July some 4,000 mission leaders and supporters of the AD2000 project met to strategize the final push toward A.D. 2000 goals. Fully 80 percent of those attending were non-Westerners who had paid their own way to the conference, demonstrating the growing maturity of the global evangelical community.

Bibliography: General: R. C. BASSHAM, *Mission Theology, 1948-1975: Years of Worldwide Creative Tension, Ecumenical, Evangelical, and Roman Catholic* (Pasadena, Calif., 1979) • M. LEHMANN-HABECK, "Die Weltmissionkonfcrenzen, ihr Beitrag zur Missionstheologie," *Warum Mission?* (ed. H. Fries, F. Köster, and F. Wolfinger; Munich, 1984) 2.23-48 • N. E. THOMAS, "World Mission Conferences: What Impact Do They Have?" *IBMR* 20 (1996) 146-54.

On 1: T. A. ASKEW, "The New York 1990 Ecumenical Missionary Conference," *IBMR* 24 (2000) 146-54 • W. R. HOGG, *Ecumenical Foundations: A History of the International Missionary Council and Its Nineteenth-Century Background* (New York, 1952) • T. WETTACH, "Der Auftrag der Missionskonferenzen heute," *JbM* 19 (1987) 147-63.

On 2: (Edinburgh) *World Missionary Conference* (9 vols.; New York, 1910) • (Jerusalem) *Report of the Jerusalem Meeting of the International Missionary Council* (8 vols.; London, 1928) • (Tambaram/Madras) *The Tambaram Series: Following the Meeting of the International Missionary Council at Tambaram, Madras, Christmas 1938* (7 vols.; London, 1939) • (Whitby) *The Witness of a Revolutionary Church* (New York, 1947) • (Willingen) *Missions under the Cross* (ed. N. Goodall; London, 1953) • (Accra) *The Ghana Assembly of the International Missionary Council* (ed. R. K. Orchard; London, 1958) • (Mexico City) *Witness in Six Continents* (ed. R. K. Orchard; London, 1964) • (Bangkok) *Salvation Today* (ed. P. Potter; Geneva, 1973) • (Melbourne) *Your Kingdom Come: Mission Perspectives* (Geneva, 1980) • (San Antonio) *The San Antonio Report: Your Will Be Done. Mission in Christ's Way* (ed. F. R. Wilson; Geneva, 1990) • (Salvador) *Called to One Hope* (ed. C. Duraisingh; Geneva, 1998).

On 3: R. T. COOTE, "A.D. 2000 and the 10/40 Window: A Preliminary Assessment," *IBMR* 24 (2000) 160-66 • (Lausanne I) *Let the Earth Hear His Voice* (ed. J. D. Douglas; Minneapolis, 1975) • (Lausanne II) *Proclaim Christ until He Comes* (ed. J. D. Douglas; Minneapolis, 1990) • J. STOTT, ed., *Making Christ Known: Historic*

Mission Documents from the Lausanne Movement, 1974-1989 (Grand Rapids, 1996).

THEO WETTACH and NORMAN E. THOMAS

Missionary Geography → Geography of Religion

Missionary Training

1. Protestant
   1.1. Europe
   1.2. United States
        1.2.1. Mainline Denominations
        1.2.2. Evangelicals
        1.2.3. Mission Centers
   1.3. Third World
2. Roman Catholic
3. Orthodox

1. Protestant

1.1. *Europe*

In Germany missionary training has an honored history (→ German Missions). A. H. → Francke (1663-1727) founded the University of Halle in 1702 to train missionaries for India. In 1722 Count N. → Zinzendorf (1700-1760) began an intentional community on his estate at Herrnhut of those who in the 1740s would go out as the first → Moravian missionaries.

The 19th century saw the flowering of mission studies in German universities. Karl Graul (1814-64), director of the Leipzig Mission, advocated a missionary professorship in each theological faculty and the sending of university-trained missionaries overseas. Gustav Warneck (1834-1910) became internationally renowned as professor of mission at the University of Halle (1897-1908), the first chair of its kind in Germany.

In Germany the territorial churches support primarily the missionary schools in Hermannsburg, which Ludwig Harms (1808-65) founded in 1849. The Leipzig and Hermannsburg Missions sponsored it, and the churches of Hanover, Brunswick, and Schaumburg-Lippe now support it. Training men and women for overseas service over a six- or seven-year period, it offers courses in → theology and → missiology and a half-year practicum overseas. After the completion of studies new missionaries complete a period of overseas assistantship.

In Scotland Alexander Duff (1806-78), following distinguished mission service in India as an educa-

tor (1830-63), proposed in 1866 that a missionary professorship be established. It would be accompanied by the study of Asian and African languages and cultures, a vision partly inspired by Propaganda Fide in Rome (→ Curia). In 1867 Duff was appointed to a new chair of evangelistic theology at New College, Edinburgh, the first such professorship anywhere. Although no successor was appointed upon Duff's death, the University of Edinburgh would resume leadership in mission studies in the late 20th century under the leadership of Andrew Walls (b. 1928).

The most comprehensive ecumenical center for training Christian leaders is the Selly Oak Colleges in Birmingham, England. In 1922 the Cadbury Trust gave land, buildings, and endowment to five colleges (later expanded to eight). Four of them were founded by British missionary societies and churches (Anglican, Methodist, Baptist, and Reformed; → British Missions). The Department of Mission, with an international faculty, offers courses to British missionary candidates and students from more than 50 countries. Advanced degrees are provided through association with the University of Birmingham. Special programs include Islamic studies and the Center for New Religious Movements.

In the Netherlands ten missionary societies founded a joint missionary training school in Rotterdam in 1905. In 1917 it moved to Oegstgeest in proximity to the University of Leiden, whose professors gave courses in theology, Oriental languages, ethnology, and Islam. Since 1946 a bachelor's degree in theology has been required for entrance into the mission school (→ Dutch Missions).

In Scandinavia the Stavanger School of Mission in Norway prepares missionaries for service, with support by Norwegian missionary societies and the Church of Norway (Lutheran). Olav Guttorm Myklebust (1905-2001) founded the Egede Institute for Missionary Research in Oslo in 1946, and from 1939 to 1976 he taught missions to many future missionaries at the Norwegian Lutheran School of Theology in Oslo. In Sweden Peter Fjellstedt (1802-81) was instrumental in founding a missionary training institute that in 1862 became the Fjellstedtska School in Uppsala, which also trained clergy. In the 20th century Uppsala University included an Institute of Mission Studies and a professorship in church history (with the history of mission) held by Bishop Bengt Sundkler (1909-95) from 1949 to 1974 (→ Scandinavian Missions).

In Switzerland Werner Bieder (b. 1911) became director of missionary education for the Basel Mission in 1955. In that year Basel terminated its five-year seminary course for men and began to offer an intensive mission education program for both men and women who had completed their professional training.

In Paris both the Reformed and Lutheran churches support the Faculté Libre de Théologie Protestante de Paris, which maintains close contacts with the nearby Société des Missions Évangéliques de Paris. It is affiliated with the Comunidad Evangélica de Acción Apostólica, an international consortium of 30 churches in Africa, Asia, and Europe (→ French Missions).

1.2. United States

1.2.1. Mainline Denominations

Throughout the 19th century in the United States, student initiatives were often at the forefront of missionary motivation and training. At its founding in 1810 Andover Seminary was a hotbed of evangelicalism and missionary concern. S. J. Mills (1783-1818) and other students lobbied for the establishment of the American Board of Commissioners for Foreign Missions in 1810, and the following year they organized their student Society of Inquiry on the Subject of Missions. The missionary drive of the various societies of inquiry passed to the new collegiate → YMCAs beginning in 1858, then to the Inter-Seminary Missionary Alliance, and from 1886 to the Student Volunteer Movement, with its watchword, "The evangelization of the world in this generation." These student organizations motivated missionary candidates and led voluntary classes for mission study (→ North American Missions; World's Student Christian Federation).

Princeton Theological Seminary holds the distinction of being the first school in the United States to provide mission courses. Charles Breckenridge was appointed professor of → practical theology and missionary instruction in 1836. Three years later he left to become secretary of the Presbyterian Board of Foreign Missions, and no successor was provided. Nevertheless, the nurturing of the missionary spirit continued. In its 1912 centennial year, Princeton announced that it had sent 410 students into foreign missions, or one of every 13 alumni.

Before the World → Missionary Conference in Edinburgh in 1910, only four North American seminaries had professorships in missions: Omaha (Presbyterian), in Nebraska; Southern Baptist (1899), in Louisville, Kentucky; Yale Divinity School (1906), in New Haven; and Episcopal Divinity School (1907), in Cambridge, Massachusetts. In the decade following the conference six new professorships were established, including those at Union Theological Seminary in New York and at Princeton Seminary, and at Boston, Emory, and Drew Universities, with 11 more being added in the 1920s. The Hartford School of Missions (1911), later known as the Kennedy School of Missions of the Hartford Seminary Foundation (1913), became the premier training center for mainline Protestant missionaries and mission scholars, including a Ph.D. in missions, but the seminary closed that program in 1960. Lutherans, Baptists, Mennonites, and many other denominations added professors of missions in subsequent decades.

Mount Holyoke (Mass.) Female Seminary, founded by Mary Lyon (1797-1849) in 1837, became by 1887 the preferred training center for over 20 percent of missionary women connected with the American Board. In 1881 the Woman's American Baptist Home Missionary Society founded the Baptist Missionary Training School in Chicago. Lucy Rider Meyer (1849-1922) founded the Chicago Training School of City, Home, and Foreign Missions in 1885. It remained the premier training center for Methodist women missionaries until its 1934 merger with Garrett, in Evanston, Illinois, a Methodist theological seminary. Its function was later taken over by the Scarritt College for Christian Workers in Nashville under the sponsorship of the Women's Division of the Methodist Board of Missions.

In the 1950s several mainline Protestant denominations united in preservice training for missionaries at the Missionary Orientation Center in Stony Point, New York. It closed in the early 1970s as the numbers of new missionaries declined.

1.2.2. Evangelicals

By the end of the 19th century, much of the missionary training in North America was occurring in various Bible institutes that had been established with a specific focus on missions. A. B. Simpson (1843-1919) founded the Missionary Training Institute in 1883. The missionary agency that he established, known from 1897 as the → Christian and Missionary Alliance, later established the Jaffray School of Missions (now Nyack College and Alliance Theological Seminary). A. J. Gordon (1836-95) founded the Boston Missionary Training Institute in 1889, which later evolved into Gordon College and Gordon-Conwell Theological Seminary. A Bible school later named the Moody Bible Institute was established in Chicago in 1889 (→ Moody, Dwight L.), and the Toronto Bible Institute was founded in 1894. Others followed these models.

Most missionaries in the → faith missions trained at such institutes. By 1960 there were 250 Bible institutes and colleges with a total of 25,000 students. The colleges have been sources of missionary vocation, while the institutes have trained missionary candidates. For example, between 1890 and 1976 over 5,400 graduates of Moody served as missionaries in 108 countries, mostly in faith missions. These institutions eventually offered standard bachelor's degrees but differed from other colleges in having a strong focus on the Bible and practical subjects related to various Christian ministries.

Southwestern Baptist Theological Seminary in Fort Worth, Texas, is the largest seminary in the world. Since its founding in 1908 the seminary's heart has been personal → evangelism and world missions. The seminary's master of divinity program requires every student to take eight semester hours of evangelism and missions. The outcome has been that Southwestern trains 50 percent of the missionary force of the Southern Baptist Convention.

Columbia (S.C.) International University, originally Columbia Bible College, established a graduate school in 1936 that was renamed the Graduate School of Bible and Missions in 1947. Donald A. McGavran (1897-1990; → Church Growth 5) established the Institute of Church Growth at Northwest Christian College in Eugene, Oregon, in 1961. In 1965 his institute moved to Fuller Theological Seminary in Pasadena, California, where it became the School of World Mission. By the 1980s this school had developed into the largest graduate faculty of missiology in North America. Other evangelical institutions — for example, Asbury Theological Seminary (Wilmore, Ky.), Biola University (La Mirada, Calif.), and Trinity International University (Deerfield, Ill.) — also established schools or strong departments of mission. These programs functioned at both master's and doctoral levels (including a doctor of missiology degree after 1986) and accepted students both before and during their period of missionary service, with a growing number coming from abroad. Today, a number of other institutions offer programs in missions and missiology.

Not all missionary training has followed the academic model. Youth with a Mission, founded in North America in 1960 by Loren Cunningham, launched in 1969 its first School of Evangelism, a 14-month missionary preparation course that emphasized both character development and missionary skills. In 1976 in the United States, YWAM began the more basic Discipleship Training School. This six-month program combines a lecture phase with from two to four months of missions experience in a cross-cultural setting of poverty. By 2002 its headquarters were in Lausanne, Switzerland, and

it had expanded its program to over 800 locations in 135 countries, with over 20,000 full-time and affiliated workers. Missions with specialized ministries focus training programs on unique needs, such as a linguistic training provided by Wycliffe Bible Translators.

The major characteristic of the newer missionary training institutions is their evangelical theology, which considers mission and evangelism to be an essential task of the church, joined to the use of the social sciences, especially cultural anthropology. Desiring to learn from the past, they attempt to balance high views of Scripture and the uniqueness of the Christian faith with a positive attitude toward other cultures, both Western and non-Western. This commitment results in a desire for authentic contextualization in the receptor culture, and the search for elements within that culture that can be used to communicate the Christian faith. At the same time, they recognize that every culture, including one's own, is in need of constant transformation by the gospel (→ Evangelical Missions; Lausanne Movement).

1.2.3. *Mission Centers*

The Overseas Ministries Study Center (1967) originated in 1922 as the Houses of Fellowship for furloughing missionaries. By 1983 some 8,000 missionary adults, plus 4,000 missionary children, had been hosted. A program of continuing education in world mission, begun in 1967 for residents, expanded under the directorships of R. Pierce Beaver (1906-87) and Gerald H. Anderson (b. 1930) to serve a broad national constituency. Relocation in 1987 from Ventnor, New Jersey, to New Haven, Connecticut, resulted in the expansion of its year-long program of mission seminars to reach seminarians, international mission leaders, North American missionaries, and mission executives, with access to the mission library at Yale University.

In 1976 Ralph D. Winter (b. 1924), of Fuller Seminary, established the U.S. Center for World Mission in Pasadena, California. It coordinates studies and strategies for reaching unreached peoples with the gospel — also called frontier missions.

1.3. *Third World*

With the explosive growth of the missionary movement originating in the so-called → Third World, training institutions have been established in many countries. By 1995 more than 200 missionary training centers were at work in Third World countries, many of them established in the previous 20 years. Costa Rica, Peru, Kenya, Singapore, and the Congo each have two or more such centers.

Indian Protestants pioneered in Third World

missions. V. S. Azariah (1874-1945) led in establishing the Indian Missionary Society in 1903 and the National Missionary Society in 1905. All Indian theological schools have been involved in the training of leaders for mission service, primarily within India itself. Union Biblical Seminary in Pune and the South Asia Institute for Advanced Christian Training in Bangalore offer master's-level work in missions, and there are many other programs at the bachelor's and postbaccalaureate levels. The Indian Institute for Cross-cultural Communication is run by the India Missions Association, a national coordinating body for all indigenous missions. It offers training in → linguistics, Bible translation (→ Bible Versions), and → literacy in unwritten languages. The Yavatmal College for Leadership Training began in 1984 with nine sponsoring denominations and mission agencies, and trainees from 20 different missionary societies. It was one of the first training colleges to offer a bachelor of missions degree.

From just 93 in 1979, the number of Korean overseas missionaries grew to 2,576 in 1992 and then to 10,745 in 2002. They work with 136 mission agencies in 162 countries. Official Korean missionary training began in 1973 through the initiative of the Asia Missions Association. The East-West Center for Missionary Research and Development was the first training program established to carry on this work. The first accredited mission faculty in Korea was the School of World Mission at the General Assembly Presbyterian Seminary in Seoul; now there are many others. Special training for cross-cultural mission is provided by training centers and institutes. The Global Ministry Training Center, founded in 1986, provides training both for missionaries who will work as independent pioneers in church planting and for those who will partner with international mission agencies. Trainers and trainees live together for nine months in intentional community, giving special attention to issues of interpersonal relationships and family life.

The number of Latin American missionaries and mission agencies has risen dramatically since 1972. In that year there were 61 indigenous missionary societies on the continent; by 1988 there were 150. During the same period the number of missionaries rose by nearly 400 percent, with two-thirds coming from Brazil. The Antioch Mission, founded in 1975, offers training on its "Valley of Blessing" campus outside São Paulo, Brazil. It provides for missionary candidates both seminary training for the bachelor of theology degree and an 11-month missionary training program, which includes fieldwork. Many graduates serve as missionaries in Portuguese-speaking Africa, Europe, and different parts of Asia. The Evangelical Center for Missions in the state of Minas Gerais, founded in 1982, was the first graduate-level institution in Brazil to offer training for cross-cultural vocational or tent-making missionaries.

Nigerian Protestants grew in concern for unreached peoples within their country during the past 25 years. In 1981 Bayo Famonure, then traveling secretary for the Nigerian Fellowship of Evangelical Students, led in founding the first missionary training center in West Africa. Called the Calvary Ministries School of Missions, it offers short courses on its campus near Jos, in the Plateau State, both in a Discipleship Training School and in a School of Missions. Five years later, in 1986, the Evangelical Mission Society of Nigeria, with Panya Baba as director, began specialized training for Nigerian missionaries. Initially the Nigeria Evangelical Missionary Institute attracted a wide range of missionary candidates from all over Nigeria. Besides its 11-month training program, the institute produces textbooks and other materials for use by other African missionary training schools.

2. Roman Catholic

The origins of Roman Catholic missiology are usually dated from the inauguration of the chair of missiology at the University of Münster in 1914 (→ Catholic Missions). Kaiser Wilhelm II (1888-1918), in setting up the Protestant chair at Halle and the Catholic chair at Münster, envisioned missiology as a way to help manage the religious dimension of colonial life (→ Colonialism). A lively debate took place in the ensuing years between the theological centers of Münster, Louvain, and Rome.

In the United States the Society of the Divine Word opened St. Joseph's Technical School in Techny, north of Chicago, in 1909. It became the first Catholic foreign mission seminary in the United States. In 1911 the bishops approved the formation of the Catholic Foreign Mission Society of America, popularly known as the Maryknoll Fathers and Brothers. The formation and education of Maryknoll priest and brother candidates includes one year of spiritual discernment and study at the formation center in Maryknoll, New York, followed by accredited theological and ministry studies. Ministry preparation includes a supervised two-year internship overseas in a Maryknoll mission.

The first American Catholic community for women devoted exclusively to foreign missions began in 1912 as a group of laywomen who volunteered to assist James A. Walsh (1867-1936), founder of the Maryknoll Fathers. In 1920 they received canonical recognition as the Foreign Mission Sisters of St. Dominic, known as the Maryknoll Sisters. From the very beginning, the Maryknoll Sisters were open to membership by Catholic women of all nationalities who were seeking to follow a call to cross-cultural mission. Their preparation for ministry parallels that of Maryknoll Fathers and Brothers.

Historically, each Catholic → diocese organized its own novitiate and seminary for the training of → priests, and each → religious order followed the same structure. Following → Vatican II, a consolidation of training institutions took place between 1966 and 1970. Major changes included establishment of the Catholic Theological Union in Chicago in 1967 by joint sponsorship of provinces of several religious orders. In 1969 a similar arrangement came into force in Washington, D.C., as the Washington Theological Union. In Berkeley, California, the → Franciscan, → Dominican, and → Jesuit theological faculties became associated with the Graduate Theological Union and the University of California. Each consortium included an enhanced program in missiological studies.

In the Netherlands, in contrast to Protestant missionaries, Catholic priest-missionaries received no specific academic training in missiology. Each missionary order provided a kind of on-the-job training through mission clubs and contact with missionaries on furlough. Religious brothers and sisters received professional training in their particular fields, including teaching, health care, and agriculture.

3. Orthodox

The dominant characteristics of Orthodox missionary training can be traced to the pioneer Byzantine missionaries to the Slavs, Cyril (ca. 827-69) and Methodius (ca. 815-85). They introduced three key elements in authentic Eastern Orthodox missions: use of the vernacular in → worship, indigenous clergy, and the responsible selfhood of the churches. Indigenization was stressed in the tutoring of both priests and monks. These same principles characterized Orthodox missions that brought the faith to Russia in the ninth century, as well as the training of priests for ministry among the Oriental churches of the Middle East, India, Egypt, Ethiopia, and elsewhere.

The Russian Revolution (1917) effectively halted mission outreach from that country to Japan and China. Fresh starts began in Europe after World War II. Mission interest rekindled in Greece primarily through Poreuthentes, an inter-Orthodox center for mission founded in 1960 by Anastasios Yannou-

latos (b. 1929). As a professor at the University in Athens, he was instrumental in establishing the Center of Missionary Studies and a chair in missiology (1976).

In the United States the primary concern in theological education initially was for ministries to the Orthodox in → diaspora. The 1960s and 1970s saw the emergence of concern for evangelism among the non-Orthodox, as well as for support for the rebuilding of the church in Albania and for a seminary in Kenya for the African Orthodox Church, an African Initiated Church (→ Independent Churches). Active participation in the ecumenical movement stimulated leaders to articulate an Orthodox mission theology useful in theological training. In contrast to both Protestants and Roman Catholics, the Orthodox have not developed specialized institutions for the training of mission personnel (→ Orthodox Missions).

→ Ecumenism, Ecumenical Movement; Mission

Bibliography: R. P. BEAVER, "The American Protestant Theological Seminary and Missions: An Historical Survey," *Miss.* 4 (1976) 75-87 • V. L. BRERETON, *Training God's Army: The American Bible School, 1889-1940* (Bloomington, Ind., 1990) • A. DRIES, *The Missionary Movement in American Catholic History* (Maryknoll, N.Y., 1998) • D. HARLEY, *Preparing to Serve: Training for Cross-Cultural Mission* (Pasadena, Calif., 1995) • R. E. HEDLUND, "Missionary Training in the Indian Context," *Indigenous Missions in India* (ed. R. E. Hedlund and F. Hrangkhuma; Madras, 1980) • W. R. HOGG, "The Teaching of Missiology: Some Reflections on the Historical and Current Scene," *Miss.* 15 (1987) 487-506 • O. G. MYKLEBUST, *The Study of Missions in Theological Education* (2 vols.; Oslo, 1955-57) • D. ROBERT, *American Women in Mission: A Social History of Their Thought and Practice* (Macon, Ga., 1996) • J. STAMOOLIS, *Eastern Orthodox Mission Theology Today* (Maryknoll, N.Y., 1986) • W. E. TAYLOR, ed., *Internationalising Missionary Training: A Global Perspective* (Exeter, 1991) • R. WINDSOR, ed., *World Directory of Missionary Training Programmes* (2d ed.; Pasadena, Calif, 1995) • J. D. WOODBERRY, C. VAN ENGEN, and J. E. ELLISTON, eds., *Missiological Education for the Twenty-first Century* (Maryknoll, N.Y., 1996).

NORMAN E. THOMAS

Mixed Marriage

1. In Roman Catholic → canon law a mixed marriage is a → marriage between Christians of different denominations. Canon 1124 of → CIC 1983 de-

fines it as a marriage between baptized persons (→ Baptism), one of whom belongs to the → Roman Catholic Church and the other to "a church or ecclesial community not in full communion with the Catholic Church." In this sense a mixed marriage differs from a marriage with an unbaptized person, which poses an obstacle that only a → dispensation can remove (cans. 1086.2, 1127.2).

2. For a mixed marriage Rome demands "the express permission [*licentia*] of the competent authority" (1983 CIC 1124). The permission can be granted only when the Roman Catholic partner declares that "he or she is prepared to remove dangers of defecting from the faith" and makes "a sincere promise to do all in his or her power in order that all the children be baptized and brought up in the Catholic Church." Furthermore, the non–Roman Catholic partner must be "truly aware of the promise and of the obligation of the Catholic party." Both partners must accept instruction about "the purposes and essential properties of marriage" (can. 1125).

The canonical form that is essential to the validity of a marriage, except in the case of marriage with an Orthodox Christian (→ Orthodox Christianity), may in individual cases be dispensed with by the → bishop as long as there is "some public form of celebration" (can. 1127.2). Individual bishops' conferences fix the details, for example, whether the local situation warrants the granting of permission, or whether the Roman Catholic partner makes a written promise (as in Germany and Austria) or merely an oral promise (as in Switzerland, England, and Wales). Personal reasons must be given for dispensing with the form. Recognition of Protestant marriage is possible only if the wedding included a declaration of intent.

→ Lutheran churches and → Reformed churches impose no conditions or restrictions on mixed marriages. Some churches, however, make → ordination dependent on the partner being a Protestant (→ Ministry, Ministerial Offices).

Orthodox churches abroad handle their prohibition of mixed marriage (can. 72 of the Trullan Synod, in 692) in pastoral adjustment to the situation according to the principle of → economy.

3. Jewish religious law formally forbids religious mixed marriages and will not allow rabbis to participate in them. Because of their view of marriage and their concern to perpetuate → Judaism, Orthodox, Conservative, and most Liberal rabbis refuse cooperation even today. Nearly half of the Reform rabbis in the United States, however, cooperate for the very same reasons, especially when the children will be brought up as Jews. Since the Jewish character of such marriages is contested even outside the Orthodox rabbinate in Israel, this practice is a source of division. A particular challenge for Jewish communities in Europe is the integration of Jewish immigrants, many of whom are in religiously mixed marriages.

4. In the worldwide ecumenical → dialogue of the Christian churches about marriage and mixed marriage, an Anglican and Roman Catholic Commission in 1975 reached "full agreement on the creaturely and sacramental nature of marriage" (→ Sacrament); in regard to the regulation of mixed marriages, however, it ran up against a "central theological difficulty of an ecclesiological character." The Roman demand that children be brought up as Roman Catholics came under criticism as an unecumenical ecclesiological claim showing a lack of sensitivity to the → conscience of the other partner and the nature of the married relationship. The proposal to replace the promise by instruction from the → priest met with only partial success. After the unecumenical guidelines of 1977 were superseded by the detailed norms of the Bishops' Conference of England and Wales in 1990, an oral assurance to make a "serious" effort to raise the children as Roman Catholics "within the framework of the partnership" sufficed. Thus far the commission's hope that the special relation between Rome and the → Anglican Communion would allow recognition of Anglican marriage has not materialized.

Dialogue in 1976 between Roman Catholics and the Lutherans and the Reformed about the theology of marriage and the problem of mixed marriage focused on the question of church legislation. For Rome "church laws are a function of theology and an expression of → pastoral care." Protestant members of the commission, however, regarded Rome's marriage laws as an ecumenical obstacle and doubted whether they could fully or appropriately express pastoral concern. Local dialogues between Protestants and Roman Catholics, while affirming a possible agreement on the sacramentality of marriage, either have evaded the ecclesiological aspect that accounts for the problems of Catholic canon law with mixed marriage (Germany, 1986) or simply highlight the differences still outstanding in the self-understanding of each church (Australia, 1999).

5. Mixed marriages are common in Germany. Each church may in some cases provide an officiant.

Double marriages are not accepted. Pastoral care aims to make the common Christian → faith fruitful for life in marriage and in the → family but also to make the partners at home in one or the other denomination. Experience shows, however, that Christian and church commitment is weaker in a mixed marriage than when the family belongs to the same denomination. The mixed marriage can be an ecumenical bridge only when the partners deliberately see it as such and on their own initiative develop it in connection with other forms of fellowship in faith and worship. Self-help organizations to this end are, for example, the Foyers Mixtes in France and the Association of Interchurch Families (founded in England in 1968), with related groups in Ireland, Switzerland, Scandinavia, Germany, the United States, Canada, and Australia. These groups present the concerns of mixed families to the churches and take part in ecumenical consultations (e.g., at a global conference in Geneva in 1998).

Conflicts arise because local churches do not offer adequate opportunities for common religious practice, but also because, despite protested agreement in basics, at important points in individual and family life and worship the churches remain divided and immovable. Thus the idea of a "double belonging," which the above organizations developed for children of mixed marriages, ran up against reservation on the part of the church authorities (Bishops' Conference of England and Wales 1990). The idea that the mixed marriage as a "house church" demands sacramental fellowship has also failed thus far to receive official recognition from the Roman Catholic side as a matter of pastoral urgency that would justify eucharistic fellowship (but see 1983 CIC 844).

→ Local Ecumenism

Bibliography: M. BARD, *Whom God Hath Joined* (Great Wakering, 1987) • R. BEAUPÈRE, "Marriage, Mixed," *DEM* (2d ed.) 739-42 • J. S. COHEN, *Intermarriage and Conversion: A Halakhic Solution* (Hoboken, N.J., 1987) • J. C. HAWXHURST, ed., *Interfaith Wedding Ceremonies: Samples and Sources* (Kalamazoo, Mich., 1996) • S. HELL, *Die konfessionsverschiedene Ehe. Vom Problemfall zum verbindenden Modell* (Freiburg, 1998) • A. HERON, *Two Churches–One Love* (Dublin, 1997) • R. ISRAEL and A. AXELRAD, "Intermarriage and Conversion," *The Third Jewish Catalog: Creating Community* (ed. S. Strassfeld and M. Strassfeld; Philadelphia, 1980) 254-62 • G. KILCOURSE, *Double Belonging: Interchurch Families and Christian Unity* (New York, 1992) • J. A. ROMAIN, *Till Faith Do Us Part: Couples Who Fall in Love* *across the Religious Divide* (London, 1996) • A. C. VRAME, *Intermarriage: Orthodox Perspectives* (Brookline, Mass., 1997).

WALTER SCHÖPSDAU

Moderator

In modern usage "moderator" (Lat. *modero*, "restrain, direct") denotes the (neutral) president of an assembly or leader of a radio or television colloquy. It has been in use since the Middle Ages for the one charged to chair a council.

The 1983 → CIC has the term for the lead priest in multiple parishes or parish unions (can. 517) and also for a vicar-general whose function is to coordinate diocesan administration (can. 473). We also find the term for leaders in → religious orders and congregations.

Among the Reformed, Presbyterians (→ Reformed and Presbyterian Churches), and Congregationalists (→ Congregationalism), the moderator is the elected president of a presbytery, synod, or assembly. The moderator is first among equals, with limited personal functions between sessions. The main Reformed use of the term is in Scotland (from 1563), the United States, Canada, and South Africa; the equivalent in western Europe is Ger. *Präses* (Eng. "preses"), or president of the synod. We find *Moderator* in Germany, however, for the president of the → Reformed Alliance and the Confederation of Evangelical Reformed Churches in Lower Saxony.

Bibliography: J. S. GRAY and J. C. TUCKER, *Presbyterian Polity for Church Officers* (3d ed.; Louisville, Ky., 1999) • D. W. HALL and J. H. HALL, *Paradigms in Polity* (Grand Rapids, 1994) • J. KENNEDY, *Presbyterian Authority and Discipline* (Edinburgh, 1960) • E. R. LONG, *Patterns of Polity: Varieties of Church Governance* (Cleveland, Ohio, 2001).

HERBERT FROST†

Modern Church History

1. Europe
   1.1. Seventeenth Century
      1.1.1. Absolutism
      1.1.2. Pietism
      1.1.3. Puritanism, Precisianism, Jansenism
   1.2. Eighteenth Century: Enlightenment
      1.2.1. Britain
      1.2.2. France
      1.2.3. Germany
      1.2.4. Roman Catholicism

1. Europe

1.1. Seventeenth Century

The → Thirty Years' War (1618-48), which ultimately became a struggle for hegemony in Europe on German soil, also formed the apogee of the period of confessionalism (→ Denomination 4) and its many crises. The Peace of Westphalia (1648) at once gave modern Europe its basic law (F. Dick-

mann) and the new era a new outlook. A period of greater stability was created, resting on greater rationality in both foreign and domestic affairs and resulting in more power for absolute rulers and the reduction of the influence of the churches, though not of Christianity. This process was not restricted to any single country or church but covered all Europe, a result that church historians have thus far largely ignored. The same applies to the impact of economic and social phenomena in the broad sense on both the churches and Christianity, even to the point of the forming of differing collective mentalities or states of consciousness. We can appreciate the distinctiveness and also the variety of modern Christianity only when we see the full breadth of these traditions from a comparative and socio-historical standpoint (→ Social History).

1.1.1. Absolutism

From the 17th century onward absolutism was politically dominant over much of Europe. It shaped the whole political and social fabric inasmuch as everything focused on the ruler. A profound change in relationships took place in the sense of more rational organization, though with detachment from roots and traditional law. The churches were adjusted to state control (→ Church and State). A feature of this development was that lawyers now played the prominent role alongside rulers that court preachers had previously exercised. The churches came to be seen largely as agencies to impose social discipline on the population, and their representatives as aids to the rulers in achieving their political ends (→ Orthodoxy 1).

1.1.2. Pietism

A result of this trend was the increasing interest of some more committed Christians in mystical texts (→ Mysticism 2.5) and radical writings. Authors like V. Weigel (1533-88), J. V. Andreae (1586-1654), and especially J. Böhme (1575-1624) found adherents among individuals as well as eager like-minded groups. The inner and sometimes outer separation from the state churches, which clearly had so little of the spirit of Christ and followed so poorly the example of the → primitive Christian community, went hand in hand with this development. Many elements deriving from these experiences and moods flowed into the movement of German → Pietism.

P. J. Spener (1635-1705) gave this movement a Lutheran form (→ Lutheranism 3.2). In the tradition of the piety of J. Arndt (1555-1621), it aimed at promoting a living personal faith, criticizing the existing state of the church yet also offering proposals for radical reform. Reform would no longer depend on the cooperation of rulers and church representatives. Pietism would build up the whole church on the local → congregation by the renewal of individuals and their association with others of like persuasion. As Spener saw it, a revived faith of this type could be certain that Christ's millennial kingdom (→ Apocalypticism 4.4) would shortly be set up on earth. Here lay his well-known hope for better times for the church.

Though Spener's theological insights and goals retained their fundamental importance for this kind of Pietism, the movement as a whole was broader. Varied spiritual, social, and political circumstances gave it different forms. In Württemberg Pietism joined in opposition to the absolute ruler, but in Brandenburg-Prussia, under the direction especially of A. H. → Francke (1663-1727) in Halle, Pietism worked hand in hand with absolutism against the alliance of the estates with orthodox Lutheranism. L. von → Zinzendorf (1700-1760) gave it yet another form, harking back in a unique way to the preabsolutist period but also looking ahead to a society no longer organized in estates. At the same time, even those who went their own way like G. Arnold (1666-1714) or J. K. Dippel (1673-1734), who are usually called radical Pietists, did belong essentially to the movement, which united people of all classes. Initially, city patricians and aristocrats predominated, but later, and fully so after 1740, the lower middle classes and even peasants also supported it.

1.1.3. Puritanism, Precisianism, Jansenism
Making the churches a functional part of the modern state was something that took place all over Europe. But a piety related to that of Pietism took different forms in Britain, Holland, and Roman Catholic France. The term → "Puritans" came into use in England under Elizabeth I (1558-1603) for Christians who wanted to reform the state church in accordance with the principles of → Calvinism. The Puritans were strict in their observances, scrupulous in self-examination, and critical of luxury and dissipation. Seeking a close relationship with God, they aimed to obey his commands to the letter. Prominent champions included W. Perkins (1558-1602) and W. Ames (1576-1633). Their thinking, and that of like-minded believers, gained broad support in opposition to the ecclesiastical and political absolutism of the Stuarts.

This antiabsolutist and Puritanical potential for resistance finally culminated in the civil war, when, with Scottish support, the monarchy and state church were overthrown, and O. Cromwell (1599-1658) emerged as the leading figure. The final development was accompanied by a potent religious radicalism characterized by inclinations to indepen-

dence, → millenarianism, and exorbitant, fanatical goals. The excesses were followed by a sobering disillusionment. After the Restoration (1660) a concentration on the nurturing of inner piety in withdrawn circles replaced the active concern to Christianize the world. Puritanism also underwent an important development in the English colonies in North America (see 2).

Many spiritual and personal links connected Puritanism and the contemporary Precisianism in Holland. Here again the aim was a profound Christianizing of society under the aegis of devout individuals. After 1650 the emphasis shifted from the whole people to a smaller and truly Christian group. An outstanding representative of the movement was G. Voetius (1589-1676). The whole movement was rich in personalities and ideas. We might refer, for example, to J. Cocceius (1603-69), G. Tersteegen (1697-1769), or J. de Labadie (1610-74). Beginning as a Jesuit in the south of France, Labadie did his main work in Holland as a preacher, pastor, and church reformer, ending his life as a separatist. His life well illustrates the spread of piety across confessional barriers.

In fact, we can find the same structural features in Roman Catholicism, namely in the → Jansenists, who were primarily in France and Belgium. The movement took its name from Bishop C. Jansen (1585-1638), who in his *Augustinus*, published posthumously in 1640, firmly set → Augustine's strict doctrine of sin and grace in opposition to the prevailing spirit in the church and the Jesuits as its representatives. Since the Jansenists were also critics of absolutism, they came under persecution by the Crown, as well as by the official church. In 1710 Louis XIV (ruled 1643-1715) had their center at Port-Royal destroyed. Then in 1713 Clement XI condemned the thinking of Jansen and the mystical biblical exposition of P. Quesnel (1634-1719). Early Jansenism had a special attraction for a brilliant intellectual elite, best represented by B. → Pascal (1623-62).

All these movements of piety were expressions of an era of upheaval in which older forces mingled with new. We see this mixture in the basic concept of a renewal of genuine Christianity and the focus on the devout individual. We see it also in the grounding of truth in experience, in criticism of the church, and in the willingly accepted role of being the outsider within a nominally Christian world. This attitude, however, could not persist for long, for even in the churches the spirit of the → Enlightenment was increasingly coming into conflict with this kind of piety.

1.2. *Eighteenth Century: Enlightenment*

Many traditions and factors contributed to the rise and finally to the triumph of the Enlightenment in Europe in the middle of the 18th century. The → Renaissance and → humanism revived the thinking of antiquity (→ Greek Philosophy), especially neo-Stoicism (→ Stoicism). Absolutist politics and the → economy displayed an increasing rationality. A third factor was overseas expansion (→ Colonialism 2.3), which brought comparisons with political, social, and religious relations at home. Also, from the 17th century onward numerous technical and scientific discoveries and inventions promoted pragmatic rationality (→ Science and Theology; Technology). Especially important was the rapid increase in the population of Europe from the middle of the 17th century, a development seen as the expression of a change for the better that formed the root of the new vitality and the new confidence in life voiced by many thinkers of the time, even to the point of simplistic → optimism. Progress now seemed possible and feasible in every area of life.

Everywhere, however, → progress demanded the rejection of older authorities, whether in → science, literature, or → theology. The demand was for → empiricism, for individual testing and knowing, versus merely accepting a theory of tradition. The relation to the → environment also underwent a change. The intellectual elite of Europe no longer saw itself as a part of → nature but in contrast with it. In this respect R. Descartes (1596-1650; → Cartesianism) conceptualized the age's understanding of itself. We must realize, however, that around 1750 only the upper classes of Europe — no more than 10 percent of the population — were affected and filled with the spirit of the Enlightenment. We may also see a considerable cultural decline from West to East.

1.2.1. *Britain*

The Enlightenment first took broader hold in Britain. In an economy that social and political measures had freed and that was thus flourishing, the theological and ecclesiastical differences between Roman Catholics and Nonconformists came to count for less. The state church was dominated by the Latitudinarians, whose attitude was one of dogmatic breadth with an emphasis on the rationality of Christianity. The essentials were all simple and perspicuous; Christian faith formed the climax of the religion native to all people.

The writings of J. Locke (1632-1704) on politics, anthropology, and Christianity enjoyed extraordinary success because of his stabilizing a piety of sound common sense. As he saw it, → reason and →

revelation agree that there is one God, that his providence is wise, and that we must live virtuously so as to attain happiness on earth and more fully in eternity.

How greatly Locke's dismissing of basic theological problems corresponded to prevailing ideas may be seen in the public reactions of the deists. Mostly laypeople, the deists wanted a purely rational Christianity; in every sphere of life, including religion, reason must rule. The majority of the people, however, did not accept the writings of J. Toland (1670-1722), M. Tindal (1656-1733), or other deists. These thinkers failed to present a Christianity that could be modernized without being relativized. The defense of traditional Christianity in their apologies often enough did little more than raise new questions. If their ideas still made an impact, it was largely through their propagation in French and German translations.

1.2.2. *France*

No less a figure than Voltaire (1694-1778) played a part in the spread of → deism. In France the economic and social conditions for the adoption of such ideas had long since been present. Rationality dominated at court, in the army, and in the government. At the same time, absolutism offered targets enough for growing criticism on many levels. Literary leaders were the philosophes, who argued for their ideal of a better society that would be more humane, rational, and hence enlightened. The great → encyclopedia that was edited from 1781 onward by D. Diderot (1713-84) and J. d'Alembert (1717-83) summed up their comprehensive desire to instruct and educate. Their supporters came mostly from their own ranks, the middle and upper urban classes. After 1770, however, they began to make a wider appeal, though still not reaching the majority of the people, even in Paris.

Naturally, criticism was aimed also at the → Roman Catholic Church, for anticlericalism had a long tradition in France. The oppressive measures taken by Louis XIV against the → Huguenots, → quietists, and Jansenists had strengthened the conviction that the church was a support and arm of the absolute state that was under attack. For the reforming of society, then, it had to be destroyed. "Écrasez l'infâme" (Crush the infamy [i.e., Christianity]) was the slogan of Voltaire.

P.-H. d'Holbach (1723-89) went even further and advocated militant → atheism, which was going too far for the ruling classes. At that time, though, there was a clear abandonment of the church and even of Christianity. Secular themes crowded out religious themes in literature. A new ideal of humanity and society had great fascination, especially in the form in which J.-J. Rousseau (1712-78) presented it. Part of the new ideal was a natural, humane, and rational religion that would bring peace and harmony, as distinct from what the churches, which were under such sharp attack, could offer.

1.2.3. Germany

As Enlightenment views spread from France to Germany, criticism of the church found a home, albeit primarily in the circles around Frederick II (1740-86) of Prussia, although such criticism was not a basic feature of the German Enlightenment. In the empire the universities largely had the function that the educated middle-class public had elsewhere in the West. In the main, enlightened professors cooperated closely with enlightened absolutism, as we see essentially in state movements toward reform. C. Thomasius (1655-1728) and C. Wolff (1679-1754), both of Halle, illustrate this cooperation. The Enlightenment was seen as having a task of popular education in which the churches would also play their part. The primary task was the promotion of tolerance and the ending of confessionalism, not political → emancipation.

The main form of the Enlightenment in Protestantism was → neology (in this period generally a term of reproach), which stressed the rational character of Christianity and the need for moral action. Court preachers like A. F. W. Sack (1703-86), J. F. W. Jerusalem (1709-89), and J. J. Spalding (1714-1804) represented this trend, along with professors of theology like J. G. Töllner (1724-74), W. A. Teller (1734-1804), and the influential J. S. Semler (1725-91), as well as laity like the Berlin writer and bookseller F. Nicolai (1733-1811). The common aim was to show the value of doctrines for ethics. The neologists strongly attacked original sin on the ground that it seemed to impugn human worth.

The German Enlightenment also had its radicals, even in → Protestantism. But men like J. C. Edelmann (1698-1767) and C. F. Bahrdt (1741-92) were intellectual and social outsiders. The great Hamburg scholar H. S. Reimarus (1694-1768) carefully concealed his radical deism while he lived. After his death it was left to G. E. Lessing to publish extracts from his *Apology* as *Anonymous Fragments*.

1.2.4. Roman Catholicism

If possible, the Roman Catholic Enlightenment in Germany and southern and eastern Europe made even stronger common cause with enlightened absolutism. For that reason it was often politically sponsored, as in southern Bavaria and then in Austria under Joseph II (1780-90). Along with Jansenism, which here and elsewhere was not just a theo-

logical movement but also a cultural and political position, it resisted → baroque Catholicism and its extravagance, as well as its massive popular piety. Joseph II wanted the church to be an educational instrument in the development of a modern centralized state. But the failure to make the reforms popular and the insensitivity of the bureaucracy in labeling popular piety as → superstition provoked unrest and genuine uprisings. Influential circles among the clergy and the middle classes undoubtedly supported the Enlightenment, but they were too few in number to bring any greater success.

With differences only in detail, the same process repeated itself in northern and southern Italy, Spain, and Portugal, where the state tried, but failed, to install Enlightenment principles. Poland was a special case, for here Russian troops hampered the development of Enlightenment thinking in 1792. In Russia itself the Enlightenment played no part.

1.3. Modernity

The early modern period ended in western and central Europe in about 1770, and → modernity began. Liberalization and reform in the various economic and social spheres characterized the new development, along with increasing rationality and a thrust toward more secular humanity. The decades between the last third of the 18th century and the first of the 19th have been called the "saddle period" (R. Koselleck) linking the old Europe to the new. How decisive was the change even in mentality may be seen from the coining of new political and social terms at the time.

The most significant phenomena were the industrial → revolution in Britain and the great French Revolution. Napoléon's (1769-1821) armies carried the ideals and goals of the latter across Europe, which explains why the Congress of Vienna in 1815 could not restore the prerevolutionary situation. It resulted, though, in the suppression of emancipatory, liberal, and national thinking in the name of legitimacy and Christianity. European conservatives rallied around this banner (→ Conservatism 1.2.2), but they found it hard to achieve political stability. Unrest and revolt toppled governments, with the 1830 and 1848 revolutions as their climax. The older powers triumphed, but forward-looking policies had to make compromises with new forces and ideas.

1.3.1. Churches around 1800

The churches in the Europe of 1800 represented a force that we can hardly overestimate. They could do so because they undertook to revive and modernize Christianity. Roman → Catholicism offers a good example of a process that took place in all nations and denominations. France confiscated church property in 1789, and in 1803 church territories were taken over in Germany. Disendowment resulted in comprehensive and conscious defeudalization (→ Feudalism). A new clergy came into being that served the church unselfishly, often at the cost of other concerns. These men did not seek or find support for their work in the state but in Rome. There thus developed an intense new orientation and attachment to the → pope and the → curia, and → Ultramontanism was born. At the same time, Roman Catholics in many countries experienced a new intensity of faith and a new love for their church, and many devout activities resulted. The orders blossomed (→ Religious Orders and Congregations), and the number of → priests swelled. In many cities spiritual circles were formed, and pastoral and diaconal work flourished.

Contemporary → revivals in Protestantism exhibited many parallels. Some churches underwent profound change (e.g., in Germany, Württemberg, Franconia, Berlin, Lower Rhine, parts of Westphalia, Hamburg, Bremen, Schleswig-Holstein, Silesia, East Prussia, and Pomerania). Religious awakenings took place also in Britain. In England → Methodism swept the country and formed a new church. Influential Evangelical circles came into being within the Church of England as well (→ Evangelical Movement 2). The Calvinistic → free churches were deeply changed by the new spirit. In Scotland the 1843 Disruption brought into being the Free Church of Scotland, with strong concern for evangelism, scholarship, and mission (→ British Missions). The revival movement also made its mark in French-speaking Switzerland both in Geneva and in Vaud, where in 1845 the Free Church of Vaud Canton came into being. The movement then spread to France and Holland. Finally, we may note the culturally influential revivals in the Lutheran state churches of Scandinavia.

1.3.2. Social Context

We can understand the confusing variety of such religious upheavals and revivals when we consider the larger social context, which makes it clear that we have here a modernizing of Christianity, focusing on its liberation and on a new concern for the individual. In both Roman Catholicism and Protestantism subjective experience figured largely in the new piety. The contents of traditional church teaching were impressively exploited in the interests of individual devotion. An essential feature in this regard was that now there was no longer any difference in principle between the religious life of the laity and that of theologians. Nontheologians had achieved

central importance. A feature of the age was the commitment of innumerable men and women of every class to Christianity as a primary concern, and to a life in keeping with it. Finally, we note that these people were organizing themselves in the modern form of societies (→ Voluntarism). In these societies members who were equal in principle voluntarily banded themselves together to achieve common goals.

1.3.3. Industrialization

Around the middle of the 19th century, a process of industrialization increasingly began to take hold in western and central Europe. Up to this point most of those who had taken part in the revivals were conservative, for anticlerical statements and excesses during the 1830 and 1848 revolutions had helped to keep them so. In both Roman Catholicism and Protestantism religious zeal coincided with antiliberal thinking. Attacks might be made on such slogans as "The Marriage of Throne and Altar" (e.g., by Ultramontanists), but even those who made the attacks were consciously attached to the slogan. In consequence, Christianity lost much of its intellectual and religious power to wrestle innovatively with the profound social and mental changes that were now taking place.

Christians ultimately looked to the saving work of the church to solve all problems (→ Salvation History), undertaking their many charitable activities primarily with this end in view (→ Diakonia 4; Inner Mission). Only slowly and partially did a change occur in the paternalistic structures of the many societies and unions that all the churches and denominations had formed to help solve all manner of problems, as now the needy themselves began to take more responsibility for making their own decisions. At the same time, the → ideology of → liberalism was triumphing, belief in progress was dominant, and the findings of science were achieving the rank of revelation.

In the final third of the 19th century, nationalism (→ Nation, Nationalism) joined forces with a strong imperialism, the expression of increasing uncertainty and division in Europe in both domestic and foreign policies. The various social classes drifted apart both spatially and intellectually, with the industrial → proletariat in particular creating its own subculture.

Here and elsewhere Christianity was relegated to the margins. In many European states and societies faith and science were discussed as alternatives, although in reality science had won the day. As industrialization eroded the established world through the course of the century, Christianity lost its cogency. It could no longer accompany, support, or regulate life in any full sense at the new points of cultural and intellectual contest.

1.3.4. Church Reactions

Church reactions covered the whole range from anxious retreat to self-conscious activity. Emerging movements in Roman Catholicism, Protestantism, and Anglicanism stressed the sacred role of the church and therefore the power of the Eternal, which is not subject to change. The → Oxford Movement, Ultramontanist Catholicism, and confessional Protestantism all sought to master the problems of the industrial age. But they clearly revealed an instinct, when faced with the confusing problems of the new day, to form their own subculture in every sphere of life.

This feature was especially strong in Ultramontanism around 1900. In the fight against what was called → modernism, which Rome viewed as a multifaceted and dangerous replacement of church teaching by modern ideas, from 1910 all priests were forced to take the → Anti-Modernist Oath. With less power at their disposal, other churches also sought to limit the influence of modern biblical → exegesis and the spirit of criticism. And everywhere there was a concern about the increasing unchurching of people and secularization of society.

In the final decades of the 19th century, highly regarded and influential figures in industrial countries sought with great vigor and skill to foster a new form of Christian social order (→ Social Ethics). Prominent in this effort were Leo XIII (1878-1903), Albert de Mun (1841-1914), and Léon Harmel (1829-1915) among Roman Catholics, and A. Stoeker (1835-1909) among Protestants. All such leaders were concerned to unite the church and to promote its work through societies and congresses (→ Societies and Associations, Ecclesiastical), using lectures and other means of public discourse. They realized that religious themes were no longer enough to mobilize the masses; social issues had to be tackled, and, directly or indirectly, the church had to enter the political arena.

Stoeker's work offers a vivid illustration of the concept, its possibilities, and its problems. It won over lower-middle-class Protestants, not least by → anti-Semitic agitation, a tactic that was not peculiar to Protestants. Around 1900 nationalism, anti-Semitism, and other ideologies assumed for many people the rank of saving truths. These attempts at re-Christianization clearly promoted the church's self-awareness and traditional churchmanship, but they hardly won over new groups or strata. There were indeed exceptions. In the industrial areas of Britain, for example, both Evangelicals and Anglo-Catholics formed many flourishing congregations in working-class areas, and the newly forming Labour Party drew much of its early strength from Nonconformist church circles.

1.3.5. Christian Unions

The various church societies also had an influence in other ways. British Protestantism cultivated a special enthusiasm for overseas → mission. Young people went in great numbers to Japan, China, India, and Africa, and many voluntary societies were formed to support the → missionaries, both economically and spiritually. The variety and vitality of such societies characterized all denominations in all the industrial countries. They organized people of all kinds, very often in terms of a specific vocation, age group, or gender.

Christian labor unions also came into being, along with guilds and associations. Congresses and conferences were organized to try to find theoretical and practical solutions to the problems of the "social question" that the churches were now so actively debating (→ Social Movements). Impressive Roman Catholic organizations in Germany, Belgium, and elsewhere sought to protect their members against falling away from the church and to help them master the many difficulties they faced in the industrialized world. Finally, political parties sprang up in many lands (e.g., the Roman Catholic Center Party in Germany and the Reformed Anti-Revolutionary Party in Holland).

Groups had developed in the churches that defined themselves politically, as well as theologically and ecclesiastically, and that might be called conservative, liberal, or social democratic. The conservative position, undoubtedly the dominant one in every church, was responsible for most of the activities. But alternatives existed. They derived for the most part from a conviction that the conditions of other social classes needed more radical treatment, especially those of the working classes. On the eve of World War I considerable religious, ecclesiastical, and theological → pluralism characterized every church and nation.

1.4. Twentieth Century

With the outbreak of World War I in August 1914, an epoch ended, and a new age began that featured revolutions and ideological wars. The years from 1914 to 1945 constitute in some sense a single unit. Then came the cold war between the two superpowers, the United States and the USSR, a war that was fought also on European soil.

Instead of bringing stability or understanding to Europe, the 1919 Paris Peace Conference gave a new thrust to nationalism. Irreconcilable differences, national prejudices, and hostile stereotypes dominated the thinking and actions of many politicians and thus served the cause only of incompatibility and division. Reparations and inflation shattered economies and had destabilizing sociopsychological consequences. The Allied victory was regarded as a victory for → democracy, but democracy actually took root in only a few countries. The League of Nations was unfortunately a failure. People became accustomed to hatred, hostility, and the thirst for revenge in both domestic and foreign policy. These forces were especially virulent, along with anxiety and fear, in the reaction to Communism (→ Marxism; Socialism). In contrast, both the Right and the Left initially largely underrated the phenomenon of → fascism.

1.4.1. *Churches*

In this period the churches became more deeply involved than ever before in national and ideological conflicts. During World War I they loudly and passionately supported the goals of their own governments, proclaimed God as an ally who would guarantee victory, and in his name called for endurance both at home and at the front. This militant spirit alienated much of the population even further from the churches and Christianity. Naturally, all churches vociferously and emphatically protested against the persecution of Christians in the Soviet Union.

Less convincing was the common equation of Communism with evil as such. B. Mussolini (1883-1945), A. Hitler (1889-1945), and even F. Franco (1892-1975) gained much help and support from the churches along such lines.

1.4.2. *Ecclesiastical and Religious Developments*

Not so prominent but no less important were the efforts of many European churches to secure freedom from the state so that they could engage in internal reforms that would revive church life and could mount a more intensive attack on the many problems of the modern world. Despite reverses, the ideal of a Christian world order still played an important part, for which Pius XI (1922-39) was an important advocate. He set up → Catholic Action to mobilize the laity with this goal in view. He also issued → encyclicals in the various fields of individual and social ethics that gave clear directions for the struggle. Finally, he pursued a wide-ranging policy of → concordats to give the church as much influence as possible (e.g., in Germany and Italy). Other churches followed a similar course in principle. In Germany O. Dibelius (1880-1967) argued that the church alone could aggressively defend the

foundations of society against liberalism, socialism, a nonreligious state, and especially Communism.

Between the wars, however, in a climate of striking intellectual and cultural innovation, new approaches were pursued in devotional life and in theology. French Roman Catholicism turned openly to the humanitarian and political ideals of the 1789 revolution. In German Roman Catholicism the → liturgical movement influenced a whole generation. In German Protestantism we also find the multifaceted → dialectical theology and the Luther renaissance (→ Luther Research 1), with their efforts to return to the core of the biblical message. Finally, Protestantism also produced the forward-looking ecumenical movement, which affected other continents as well.

After the World Missionary Conference at Edinburgh in 1910, committed Christians turned their attention to the search for basic agreement in matters of → faith and order as well (→ Missionary Conferences 2). The way would prove to be difficult, however; only at Lausanne in 1927 did coordination of the various efforts take place. In the meantime the conviction had grown up among other Protestant groups and circles that it would be easier to reach understanding on a practical level. Thanks to activists like N. Söderblom (1866-1931), the → Life and Work conference at Stockholm in 1925 was a great success. Protestant Christianity now began to move away from its national and denominational divisions toward a new age of → ecumenism. This development proved to be most important because only a few years later much of Europe came under the sway of totalitarian regimes.

1.4.3. *National Socialism*

Roman Catholics and Protestants in Germany at first showed great enthusiasm for the national revolution and the new National Socialist state, which was quickly replaced by more sober thoughts and then disillusionment. The → church struggle, a complicated attempt full of inner tensions, began to resist the grip of the totalitarian state on the churches. Roman Catholics had to learn that the concordat offered them no protection against the incursions of the regime. Protestants who had counted on the establishment of a Christian social order had to learn that the creation of a national church by the → German Christians, which they accepted in principle, was being used as a cover for the subjugation of the church to National Socialist ideals.

In the face of this development many Protestants refused to cooperate. Under the leadership of M. → Niemöller (1892-1984), the Pastors' Emergency League was formed. Free synods were held opposing the German Christian authorities. Barmen I (1934) issued the → Barmen Declaration — largely the work of K. → Barth (1886-1968) — with its strict Christological orientation and clear statement of implications. Only a minority participated in the Confessing Church, yet this minority had the force that would determine the future of the Evangelical Church in Germany. At first, however, both Roman Catholics and Protestants had to engage in exhausting conflicts with the totalitarian regime.

Many Christians retreated into a private devotional life or into church life. They learned with horror and paralysis of events of injustice and violence, such as the pogrom of November 9/10, 1938, the so-called *Reichskristallnacht* (Night of the broken glass). Neither Catholics nor Protestants made any public protest against this outrage, or against the countless other crimes in World War II and the systematic extermination of the Jews (→ Holocaust). Nor did the churches take part in political resistance against National Socialism. Only individual Christians like D. → Bonhoeffer (1906-45) played a more direct role in the resistance. The way was clearer for other European churches during World War II, for the battle against National Socialism coincided with national interests in their case. Hence Christians of every denomination joined in military or political opposition to the regime.

Neither Christians nor churches, however, left an impression of heroism. Alongside many inspiring examples of loyalty and courage, we find much cowardice, anxiety, halfheartedness, and resignation. Nevertheless, despite the timidity and divided interests of Christians in Germany, many Christians at this time had a strong sense of togetherness, a new feature that emerged during those terrible years. At the end of the war the ecumenical movement could build on this foundation.

1.4.4. *Late Twentieth Century*

In trying to identify significant trends in churches in western and eastern Europe during the latter part of the 20th century, one must first admit that relatively little came of the forward-looking ideas and convictions of the last years of World War II. At the same time, Christians in many western European countries in all denominations did try to assume political responsibilities. We thus find Christian and in part interconfessional parties in Italy, Belgium, Austria, Germany, and France. We can hardly overestimate the influence of these practical Christians on domestic and foreign affairs for at least a decade. But as the first enthusiasm waned, immobility, consumer thinking, and militant anti-Communism took over. These years, however, saw no attempt at a

mere restoration of older relations, not even in the churches.

New questions arose, which unmistakably had an effect. Unless we take them into account, we can hardly understand the profound upheavals in Europe during the 1960s and beyond. Led by a new generation and supported by an unprecedented economic upturn, modernization took place on a vast scale, not just socially and economically but also intellectually, culturally, and in self-awareness. What had been taking place under cover now came out into the open. A secular, permissive, and decisively pluralistic society came into being. Nourished by a sense of common Christian responsibility, ecumenical thinking came to be taken for granted. Existing positions came under intense criticism, and many sociopolitical tasks were accepted by the churches. A special commitment was made to the integrity of → creation, → peace in the world, and a just solution to the problems of the North-South conflict. The age of Eurocentricity had ended, in the churches as elsewhere. The European churches have hardly or not yet grasped the magnitude of the new task of trying to solve global problems by offering responsible help in shaping a united Europe.

→ European Theology (Modern Period); Orthodoxy; Theology in the Nineteenth and Twentieth Centuries

Bibliography: Comprehensive: K. ALAND, *A History of Christianity,* vol. 2, *From the Reformation to the Present* (Philadelphia, 1986) • C. DAWSON, *Christianity and European Culture* (ed. G. J. Russello; Washington, D.C., 1998) • M. GRESCHAT, ed., *GK,* esp. vols. 7-12 • H. JEDIN and J. DOLAN, *HCH* • K. NOWAK, *Geschichte des Christentums in Deutschland* (Munich, 1995) • S. POLLARD, *Peaceful Conquest: The Industrialization of Europe, 1760-1970* (Oxford, 1981) • F. M. L. THOMPSON, ed., *The Cambridge Social History of Britain, 1750-1950* (3 vols.; Cambridge, 1990) • W. R. WARD, *The Protestant Evangelical Awakening* (Cambridge, 1992).

Seventeenth and eighteenth centuries: A. CABANTOUS, *Entre fêtes et clochers. Profane et sacré dans l'Europe moderne, XVII-XVIII siècle* (Paris, 2002) • W. J. CALLAHAN and D. HIGGS, eds., *Church and Society in Catholic Europe of the Eighteenth Century* (Cambridge, 1979) • T. A. CAMPBELL, *The Religion of the Heart: A Study of European Religious Life in the Seventeenth and Eighteenth Centuries* (Columbia, S.C., 1991) • O. CHADWICK, *The Popes and European Revolution* (Oxford, 1981) • F. DICKMANN, *Der Westfälische Frieden* (6th ed.; Munich, 1992; orig. pub., 1959) • S. JÜTTNER and J. SCHLOBACH, eds., *Europäische Aufklärung(en)* (Hamburg, 1992) • H. LEHMANN, *Das Zeitalter des Absolutis-*

mus (Stuttgart, 1980) • W. MÜLLER, *The Church in the Age of Absolutism and Enlightenment* (New York, 1981) • E. R. NORMAN, *Church and Society in England, 1770-1970* (Oxford, 1976) • R. PORTER and M. TEICH, eds., *The Enlightenment in National Context* (Cambridge, 1981) • W. R. WARD, *Christianity under the Ancien Régime, 1648-1789* (Cambridge, 1999).

Nineteenth century: R. AUGERT, *The Church in the Industrial Age* (New York, 1981) • J. GADILLE and J.-M. MAYEUR, eds., *Die Geschichte des Christentums*, vol. 11, *Liberalismus, Industrialisierung, Expansion Europas (1830-1914)* (Freiburg, 1997) • P. GERBOD, *L'Europe culturelle et religieuse de 1815 à nos jours* (Paris, 1977) • M. GRESCHAT, *Das Zeitalter der Industriellen Revolution* (Stuttgart, 1980) • R. KOSELLECK, *Critique and Crisis: Enlightenment and the Pathogenesis of Modern Society* (Cambridge, Mass., 1988); idem, "How European Was the Revolution of 1848/49?" *1848—a European Revolution? International Ideas and National Memories of 1848* (ed. A. Körner; New York, 2000) • R. LIEDTKE and S. WENDEHORST, eds., *The Emancipation of Catholics, Jews, and Protestants: Minorities and the Nation State in Nineteenth-Century Europe* (Manchester, 1999) • K.-E. LÖNNE, *Politischer Katholizismus im 19. und 20. Jahrhundert* (Frankfurt, 1986) • T. NIPPERDEY, *Deutsche Geschichte, 1866-1918* (vol. 1; Munich, 1990); idem, *Germany from Napoleon to Bismarck, 1800-1866* (Princeton, 1996; orig. pub., 1983).

Twentieth century: G. ADRIÁNYI, *The Church in the Modern Age* (New York, 1981) • T. BUCHANAN and M. CONWAY, eds., *Political Catholicism in Europe, 1918-1965* (Oxford, 1996) • O. CHADWICK, *The Christian Church in the Cold War* (London, 1992) • A. LINDT, *Das Zeitalter des Totalitarismus. Politische Heilslehren und ökumenischer Aufbruch* (Stuttgart, 1981) • J.-M. MAYEUR, ed., *Histoire du Christianisme*, vol. 13, *Crises et renouveau, de 1958 à nos jours* (Paris, 2000) • K. MEIER, ed., *Die Geschichte des Christentums*, vol. 12, *Erster und Zweiter Weltkrieg, Demokratien und totalitäre Systeme (1914-1958)* (Freiburg, 1992) • S. P. RAMET, *Nihil obstat: Religion, Politics, and Social Change in East-Central Europe and Russia* (Durham, N.C., 1998) • R. J. WOLFF and J. K. HOENSCH, eds., *Catholics, the State, and the European Radical Right, 1919-1945* (Boulder, Colo., 1987).

MARTIN GRESCHAT

2. United States
2.1. *Survey*
The development of Christianity in the United States is similar to, yet dissimilar from, that in Europe. Religious uniformity and establishment were impossible to maintain, and → pluralism reigned, so that within two centuries of the first European settlements, → religious liberty prevailed. → Voluntarism, lay leadership (→ Clergy and Laity), intense activism, and denominationalism (a new form, neither → church nor → sect) marked American Christianity. Denominations maintained their particular doctrines but cooperated in → revivals, reform, → mission, and a sense of being part of a chosen nation, as → Protestantism as a whole supplied the nation with themes, → language, and symbols.

2.2. *Colonial Era*
2.2.1. *Spanish and French Colonialism*
Spanish and French Roman Catholics (→ Catholicism [Roman]) were the first in North America, but they did not colonize with their own people. Religious expansion followed conquest by their military forces through the missionary activities of the → Franciscans and → Jesuits. The Spanish left an enduring mark through their Indian work in what is now the U.S. Southwest, Florida, and California, as did the French in Northeast Canada, the U.S. Midwest, and the Mississippi River valley to New Orleans.

2.2.2. *Church of England, Puritanism, and Denominational Pluralism*
2.2.2.1. The future of the United States, including its religion, was in the hands of the British, whose practice was to establish large colonies of their own people (→ Colonialism). The Virginia Company founded Jamestown in 1607. Though hampered by the absence of a → bishop, the Church of England became the established church in the southern colonies (→ Anglican Communion), as well as in Maryland, where the Roman Catholic Lord Baltimore (1580?-1632) had originally founded a colony based on religious → tolerance. The laity emerged as the controlling power through elected vestries that appointed and paid clergy. Anglicanism also replaced the Dutch Reformed (→ Reformed Churches) in parts of New York when it was conquered. Beginning in 1689, the bishop of London appointed commissaries to exercise part of his → power (§3).

Under the leadership of Thomas Bray (1656-1730), the Society for the Propagation of the Gospel (SPG) was founded in England (1701) to send missionaries to the Indians and colonists (→ Colonialism and Mission), as was the Society for Promoting Christian Knowledge (SPCK, 1698) to supply prayer books, Bibles, and literature. Under this new impetus Anglicanism slowly spread throughout the colonies, and sporadic efforts were made to missionize the Indians and the black slaves, who first arrived in

Virginia in 1619 (→ British Missions 1.1.1). In all Anglican colonies other religious groups were present and largely tolerated.

2.2.2.2. To the north → Puritans became the established church. A small group of Separatists (→ Separatism), cut off from the Church of England over → liturgy, ecclesiology, and → ethics, fled to Holland and then to New England in 1620 (→ Pilgrim Fathers) under the leadership of Elder William Brewster (1567-1644) and Governor William Bradford (1590-1657). Each → congregation, founded on a → covenant between God and members, was a complete church with all power in itself.

Pilgrims were soon absorbed by the large, powerful group of Puritans led by John Winthrop (1588-1649), John Cotton (1585-1652), and Thomas Hooker (1586-1647), who settled Massachusetts Bay in 1629, fleeing the persecutions of Archbishop William Laud (1573-1645). Engaged in a holy experiment as God's chosen people, an idea bequeathed to the United States, they founded a "due form of government both civil and ecclesiastical" in a "city upon a hill" for the entire world to see (Winthrop sermon "A Modell of Christian Charity" [1630]). Only visible saints, those who testified before the church as to their valid → conversion (§1) and → regeneration experience, could vote in this holy commonwealth.

Within ten years 20,000 people arrived, Harvard College was founded (1636), and Indians were Christianized. Though only the Puritans ruled, they could not destroy dissent. Roger Williams (ca. 1603-83) was banished in 1636; Anne Hutchinson (1591-1643) was driven out in 1637; Quakers (→ Friends, Society of) were whipped, and four were executed in the late 1650s. In 1662 a Half-Way Covenant was adopted, allowing church members' baptized offspring who lacked a personal conversion experience to present their children for baptism and partial membership. The Puritan → Congregationalists retained control and establishment into the early 19th century.

2.2.2.3. The middle colonies of Pennsylvania, New York, New Jersey, and Delaware began with religious toleration, a prelude for the American system. Pennsylvania, dominated initially by its Quaker founders, experienced at once a flood of German Lutherans (→ Lutheran Churches; Lutheranism), Reformed (→ Calvinism), and sectarians, Scotch-Irish Presbyterians, English → Baptists, Anglicans, and Roman Catholics. In all the middle colonies competing → denominations came to terms with toleration and lived in peace. Pennsylvania grew to be a great political and religious center in the colonies.

2.2.3. *The Great Awakening*
Jonathan → Edwards (1703-58) was astonished when a powerful revival broke out in 1734 in his congregation in Northampton, Massachusetts. Revivalism, the most important religious movement in American history, combined both Puritanism and European → Pietism in insisting on the necessity and certainty of a personal experience of the new birth. Small-scale "seasons of renewal" had not been unknown in the colonies. The Great Awakening swept the colonies under the powerful preaching in 1739 of a young Anglican, George → Whitefield (1714-70; → Methodism), transforming the style of preaching, forms of worship, and ethics; emphasizing → millenarianism; and reshaping the churches and ministry. Eventually it thrust the Methodists and Baptists into American dominance, and it became the spiritual home of America's blacks.

2.3. American Revolution and Religious Tolerance

When the American Revolution broke out in 1775, the churches were vigorous supporters except for the SPG missionaries and a few of John → Wesley's (1703-91) Methodist preachers (→ Methodist Churches). The → Enlightenment views of religious toleration reflected in Thomas Jefferson's (1743-1826) Declaration of Independence (1776) agreed with the de facto religious toleration then current throughout the colonies (→ Rights, Human and Civil; Human Dignity). It was also supported by revivalists and secured by statute in several of the colonies.

The significance of the constitutional separation of church and state became clear in the 19th century, when the churches entered a period of great activism dedicated to the evangelization of the West, the sending of → missionaries worldwide, the emerging struggle against → slavery, and a variety of other reform movements. The churches followed westward migration, while by the 1830s the eastern cities began to show the effects of Roman Catholic immigration.

2.4. Revival and Sects
2.4.1. *Second Great Awakening*
A fresh revival broke out in New England and on the Kentucky frontier in the late 1790s, continuing in various phases up to the Civil War (1861-65). Frontier camp meetings emphasized extempore → preaching and → prayer, "protracted meetings," a new populist hymnody (→ Hymn), heightened emotionalism, the "anxious bench," and millennial themes (→ Apocalypticism; Eschatology). The revivalistic denominations flourished in the South and West, especially the Baptists and Methodists.

The strongly restorationist Disciples of Christ emerged under the leadership of Alexander Campbell (1788-1866) and later joined with the Christian Church of Barton W. Stone (1772-1844).

The premier evangelist before the Civil War was Charles G. → Finney (1792-1875), whose activism and moral perfectionism (→ Law) inspired a generation of reformers who supported temperance (→ Substance Abuse), prison reform, an end to slavery, and a host of other causes. Revivalism advocated cooperation among fellow revivalistic churches. They participated in the Evangelical Alliance (1846; → Evangelical Movement 2; World Evangelical Alliance), but they also promoted schism and controversy in disagreements with nonrevivalists.

2.4.2. Sects

The majority of 19th-century American Protestants were postmillennialists, optimistic and deeply committed to building the → kingdom of God on earth as the first step toward inaugurating the reign of Christ. Postmillennialism in its religious and secular forms continued to grow in strength through the 19th century, as shown in the great proliferation of reform groups, new denominations, and → utopian communists.

But dissenting movements were organizing on the margins of the evangelical consensus. A diverse Unitarianism (→ Unitarians) emerged from New England Congregationalism led by William Ellery Channing (1780-1842). Ralph Waldo Emerson (1803-82) relinquished his Unitarian pastorate in favor of the highly individual, semimystical ethicism of → transcendentalism (→ Individualism; Mysticism 2). The Shakers grew on the frontier of western New York and in the Ohio River valley, and other communitarian groups such as the Rappites and the → perfectionist group of John Humphrey Noyes (1811-86) in Oneida, New York, flourished (→ Oneida Community). In the 1830s Joseph Smith (1805-44) started the Church of Jesus Christ of Latter-day Saints (→ Mormons). After Smith's death Brigham Young (1801-77) led the faithful on an epic pilgrimage into the wilderness of Utah, where the group flourished. The followers of William Miller (1782-1849), who predicted the return of Christ in 1844, expected the reign of Christ to be preceded by terrible destruction and judgment. Those who remained faithful after that date were gathered to form the → Adventists, later the Seventh-day Adventists.

2.5. Consequences of the Civil War

Earlier efforts at antislavery by followers of Jonathan Edwards and Quakers such as A. Benezet (1713-84) and J. Woolman (1720-72) were replaced by those of Finney converts, led by Theodore D. Weld (1803-95) and William Lloyd Garrison's (1805-79) Liberator (1831), whose work culminated in the American Anti-Slavery Society (1833). In the South, earlier Methodist and Baptist opposition to slavery gave way first to a reluctant embrace of the system, with a valiant effort of conversion of slaves, then to the belief that slavery was the foundation of a Christian society.

Denominations were split regionally by the Civil War. Each side blessed its cause as alone justified in the eyes of God, and revivals swept the armies of both North and South. President Abraham Lincoln (1809-65), virtually alone, transcended the simple identification of God and nation by affirming that God's will is beyond either side, so that each must go on to do the right as he or she sees it, "with malice toward none and charity for all" (Second Inaugural Address).

2.6. Nineteenth and Twentieth Centuries
2.6.1. Challenges of the Modern Period and Fundamentalism

After the war America was vastly different — slaves were set free, Northern manufacturing developing as its urban centers flourished, railroads spanned the nation, and the westward movement accelerated (→ Industrial Society; Technology).

The successful revival movement of Dwight L. → Moody (1837-99) exemplified the response of American evangelicalism to the challenges of the Gilded Age: immigration, industrialization, → evolution, and biblical criticism (→ Exegesis, Biblical). Resurgent premillennialism signaled the gradual split in the American evangelical → consensus, as conservatives intensified millenarian revivalism, while liberals concentrated on cooperative ventures and social problems as tasks in building the kingdom of God. Moody supported foreign missions through international cooperative groups such as the Student Volunteer Movement (1888) and the → YMCA (→ North American Missions) and founded a new generation of conservative reform groups and educational institutions. A host of professional traveling evangelists followed Moody, but none could match him, not even Billy Sunday (1862-1935).

The eschatological focus and cultural pessimism of conservative Protestants led to a confrontation with liberal Protestantism and the broader American culture in the first quarter of the 20th century. The militant conservatives, called fundamentalists (→ Fundamentalism), sought control of denominations, mission boards, and educational institutions, but following losses in the denominations and the public humiliation of the Scopes trial (1925), fundamentalism retreated from the public arena, establishing an alternative system of Bible institutes, mission boards, radio stations, denominations, and professional organizations.

The period after World War II saw fundamentalism reencounter the broader culture, led by the successful revivals of Billy Graham (b. 1918) from the 1940s onward and by the effective use of radio and television (→ Mass Media), by which revivalism was joined to an aggressive political agenda through the Moral Majority of Jerry Falwell, Pat Robertson, and many others beginning in the 1970s (→ Electronic Church). Opposed to liberal Christianity and liberal politics, contemporary fundamentalism again began to contend for the faith in the public arena. Though premillennial, it affirms America as God's chosen people fighting godless Communism (→ Marxism; Marxism and Christianity) and is utterly opposed to mainline Protestants and Roman Catholics who, for example, led in criticism of the Viet Nam War, though it is allied to Roman Catholics on issues such as → abortion.

2.6.2. *Christian Science and Related Movements*
Though revivalism remains the preference of a clear majority of American Protestants, it did not go unchallenged. As early as the 1870s it gave birth to Mary Baker Eddy's (1821-1910) → Christian Science as representative of a host of similar groups. Built on revivalistic biblicism, mesmerism, and an affirmation of optimistic → idealism (→ Optimism and Pessimism), groups emerged such as Unity, → New Thought, → spiritualism, and the "positive thinking" movements.

2.6.3. *Liberal Protestantism*
The rise of the → Social Gospel movement from within revivalism expressed a different response. It adopted biblical criticism, employed and transformed evolution to express Christian faith, attacked the problems of urbanization and the industrial revolution with an effort to reform the social structures responsible, and expressed a progressivistic optimism in the unfolding of the kingdom of God on earth. Led by Washington Gladden (1836-1918), George Herron (1862-1925), and Walter → Rauschenbusch (1861-1918), the Social Gospel captured the major Northern schools of religion and the mainline denominations. The modernist wing of → liberalism provoked the attacks of fundamentalists, while the main liberal tradition marched on, organizing an array of ecumenical organizations, including the Federal Council of Churches (1912) and the → World Council of Churches (1948; → Ecumenism, Ecumenical Movement).

Following World War I (→ War) and the Great Depression, a dissenting movement arose within liberalism, associated with European neoorthodoxy (K. Barth) and the theology of crisis (→ Dialectical Theology). Led by Reinhold → Niebuhr (1892-1971), neoorthodoxy blended a sharply self-critical political analysis with biblical symbols stressing human sinfulness (→ Sin). Following World War II, the Protestant denominations became deeply involved in → politics and social issues (→ Social Ethics).

2.7. *Black Churches*
The black Protestant denominations remain a major carrier of revivalism in American life. Nurtured among the Baptists and Methodists, most major black denominations were founded after the Civil War. Discrimination and prejudice (→ Racism) were the fate of blacks in American society, and the first genuinely creative steps were not taken until the mid-20th century. Led by the civil rights efforts of Martin Luther → King Jr. (1929-68; → Civil Rights Movement) in the 1950s and 1960s, and by a 1954 Supreme Court decision against segregated education, a steady but slow march against discrimination commenced. A new self-consciousness among black denominations and an increasing role in shaping American Christianity resulted (→ Black Theology; Liberation Theology).

2.8. *Roman Catholic Church*
Fed by the 1840s flood of Irish immigration, the → Roman Catholic Church became the largest single Christian group in America by the 1870s. A violent outbreak of anti-Catholicism and nativism resulted, and antipopery (→ Pope, Papacy) marked American culture until the mid-20th century. Roman Catholicism fought back, creating its own schools and constructing hospitals and colleges. Its stand on state aid for parochial schools continued to agitate the church-state question in America. The election in 1960 of the first Roman Catholic president, John F. Kennedy (1961-63), as well as the Second → Vatican Council, drastically changed the role and acceptance of Roman Catholicism in the United States. Along with opposition to the Supreme Court abortion decision of 1973, Roman Catholicism has provided the strongest Christian critique of government policy in the areas of nuclear warfare, economics, and U.S. involvement in Latin America.

2.9. *Prospect*
The present power and position of Roman Catholicism in American culture, the rapid rise and expansion of conservative Christianity, the continuing vitality of the denominations, the presence of perhaps up to 1,000 individual denominations (though 90 percent of all U.S. Christians belong to less than 10

denominational families) — all these factors point to the continuation and expansion of pluralism, activistic voluntarism, revivalism, and the role of the laity as the distinguishing characteristics of Christianity in the United States.

Bibliography: S. E. AHLSTROM, *A Religious History of the American People* (New Haven, 1972) • C. L. ALBANESE, *America: Religions and Religion* (Baltimore, 1981) • G. C. BRAUER, *Protestantism in America* (Philadelphia, 1965) • J. BUTLER, G. WACKER, and R. BALMER, *Religion in American Life* (New York, 2003) • E. S. GAUSTAD, ed., *A Documentary History of Religion in America* (2d ed.; Grand Rapids, 1993) • E. S. GAUSTAD and P. L. BARLOW, *New Historical Atlas of Religion in America* (New York, 2000) • N. O. HATCH, *The Democratization of American Christianity* (New Haven, 1989) • C. H. LIPPY and P. W. WILLIAMS, eds., *Encyclopedia of the American Religious Experience* (New York, 1988) • G. M. MARSDEN, *Religion and American Culture* (San Diego, Calif., 1990) • M. E. MARTY, *Pilgrims in Their Own Land* (Boston, 1984) • D. C. MATHEWS, *Religion in the Old South* (Chicago, 1977) • S. E. MEAD, *The Lively Experiment* (New York, 1963) • H. R. NIEBUHR, *The Kingdom of God in America* (New York, 1937) • M. A. NOLL, *The Old Religion in a New World: The History of North American Christianity* (Grand Rapids, 2002) • A. J. RABOTEAU, *Slave Religion* (New York, 1978) • D. G. REID, R. D. LINDER, B. L. SHELLEY, and H. S. STOUT, eds., *Dictionary of Christianity in America* (Downers Grove, Ill., 1990) • H. S. STOUT and D. G. HART, eds., *New Directions in American Religious History* (New York, 1997).

GERALD C. BRAUER†

3. Eastern Churches

3.1. Orthodox Church

The capture of Constantinople by the Ottoman Turks in 1453, which brought to an end the (Eastern) Christian Roman Empire, involved profound changes for the whole of the Orthodox Church. We may thus date the beginning of the modern history of the Orthodox Church to this event, especially as we cannot regard the fall of the capital as an isolated happening but must view it in connection with other basically contemporaneous developments, such as the subjugation of other independent Orthodox states to the Ottoman Empire (Serbia, Bulgaria) and the growing importance of Russia as the only free Orthodox country that could offer protection to Orthodoxy (→ Orthodox Christianity).

3.1.1. Ecumenical Patriarchate

Most directly affected by the end of the Eastern empire was the Ecumenical Patriarchate. Its existence in the Ottoman Empire meant a certain degree of legal insecurity, since the Sublime Porte, often because of the intervention of Roman Catholic or Protestant powers, would sometimes depose or even execute patriarchs that were out of favor, or they sometimes made changes simply to collect the special fees that came with a change of office. (Between 1453 and 1821 patriarchs held office an average of only three years.)

The sultans, who assumed some of the rights of the former emperors in the regulation of church affairs, also made the patriarch the ethnarch (Turk. *millet başı*) of all Orthodox Christians in their empire, putting Christians under them even in matters of civil law. This organization of all the Orthodox as a single "Roman [i.e., Greek] nation" (*Rum milleti*) gave a certain precedence to Greek culture that would later find expression in the abolition of the independent Slavic patriarchates in Serbia and Bulgaria and in the promotion of Greek rather than Slavonic as the liturgical language in the Balkans.

Because of this feature of Turkish government, the fight for the independence of Greece and other Balkan countries in the early 19th century had a considerable effect on the Ecumenical Patriarchate. The Sublime Porte, for example, treated the patriarchate as responsible for the revolts, murdering Patriarch Gregory V on April 10, 1821 (Easter). Again, newly kindled Slavic nationalism (→ Nation, Nationalism) resulted in the expulsion of many Greek bishops and priests from what had now become independent (autocephalous) churches. The search for national independence led several Orthodox churches to unilaterally declare themselves autocephalous, which the Ecumenical Patriarchate later accepted, although a synod held in Constantinople in 1872 radically condemned phyletism (i.e., the doctrine that within the territory of another nationality, a nationally defined church should exist as an independent body).

The movement of the Greeks of Pontus and Asia Minor out of Turkey after the war between Turkey and Greece in 1922-23 considerably reduced the number of Orthodox dioceses of the Ecumenical Patriarchate in Turkey. Then in 1926 the introduction of Swiss civil law deprived the patriarchate of its last legal privilege, that of controlling the marriages of Greeks in Turkey. Since the Turks identified the patriarchate with Greek policies, the Greek Orthodox churches in Constantinople often became the target of anti-Greek pogroms, especially in connection with the crisis in Cyprus. The result was a steady decline in the Greek population in Turkey. From 3 million in 1913, the number of members of the Orthodox Church in Turkey itself shrank to only

10,000 in 1995, with about 4,500 in İstanbul (the name, since 1930, of ancient Constantinople).

Emigration in the 20th century, however, gave the patriarchate a number of new Greek and other dioceses in America, Australia, and western Europe. It also has a leading role in world Orthodoxy, a role already uncontested at the inter-Orthodox meeting of 1923 (Constantinople), and especially at the Pan-Orthodox Conferences (beginning in Rhodes in 1961) and in preparations for the "Great and Holy Council." It was challenged only by the Moscow Patriarchate, which made brief attempts to enter into competition after World War II.

3.1.2. *The Other Ancient Patriarchates*
In numbers, the Orthodox Patriarchate of *Alexandria* was always small in the days of Arab rule, and then Ottoman and Mameluke rule, right up to the 19th century. Nevertheless, it produced several figures of significance for all Orthodoxy, including Patriarchs Meletios I Pegas (1590-1601) and Metrophanes Kritopoulos (1636-39). The situation improved for the patriarchate with the settlement of Greek families, first in Egypt, then throughout Africa, during the 19th century. As a result the patriarch, who under the *millet* system had for centuries resided in Constantinople in some dependence on the Ecumenical Patriarchate, moved back to Alexandria in 1846 and was able to infuse more vitality into congregational life. After the fall of the Egyptian monarchy in 1952, however, Greeks began to leave Egypt again. Today the main focus of the Alexandrian patriarchate is its successful missionary work, for example, in East Africa (esp. Uganda and Kenya) and among Greek residents throughout the continent.

During Ottoman days the patriarchs of *Antioch* lived in Armenian Cilicia, then in 1375/86 they moved to Damascus. Though most believers came under increasing Arab influence, the Greek element remained preponderant (by a privilege granted in 1724) until, after contested elections, Russian influence helped to give the church an Arab patriarch in 1899. From that time all the patriarchs in Antioch have been Arabs, and the Christian Arab tradition has been strong in this patriarchate. Antioch has also done much to foster lay participation, such as the Mouvement de la Jeunesse Orthodoxe (Orthodox youth movement), founded in 1942/51. Emigration to the United States and western Europe has also produced overseas dioceses. There are also congregations of converts with a purified Roman → rite. A deanery formed of former Anglican parishes has recently emerged.

The existence of pilgrimage sites within the Patriarchate of → *Jerusalem* has given this patriarchate a unique system of government, namely, a monastic system: the Brotherhood of the Holy Sepulchre, which is made up solely of Greeks. This order has the twofold task of caring for the Arab Orthodox population in the land and of protecting the holy sites for Orthodox worship. From the days of the → Crusades, and under Ottoman rule from 1517 to 1917, the Jerusalem Patriarchate had to resist incursions from Roman Catholics and also from some Protestants (from the 19th century onward) who tried to proselytize the Orthodox (→ Proselytism) and to take over the holy sites.

3.1.3. *Russian Orthodox Church*
When the unsuccessful attempt at union with the Roman Catholic Church at Ferrara-Florence in 1438/39 (→ Councils of the Church 3) brought to light the internal weakness of the Byzantine state and church, the Russian Orthodox Church declared itself to be autocephalous in 1448. In 1589, in the presence of Ecumenical Patriarch Jeremias II (1572-79, 1580-84, 1587-95), it then proclaimed its elevation to a patriarchate, which all the other patriarchs recognized by 1593. Moscow was given the fifth place in the traditional order of precedence among patriarchates, after Jerusalem. The new self-awareness found expression in the ideology of Moscow as the Third Rome (developed by the monk Philotheus [or Filofei] of Pskov in a letter to the czar in 1510), in the independent courses pursued in art and literature (as determined at the Stoglav [i.e., "hundred-chapter"] church council of 1551), and in the increasing part that Russia now came to play in protecting the beleaguered Orthodox of the Near East and the Balkans against Islamic rule and Western proselytizing.

During the next centuries intense missionary activity enabled the Russian church to spread across all Siberia and to China, Japan, and even America (from 1792; → Orthodox Missions). In the confused days of 1605-13 the church took a leading part in the national struggle against Polish occupation. After liberation this role gave it great influence in secular affairs. Conflict, however, about the need and shape of liturgical reform under Patriarch Nikon (1652-66) then resulted in the schism of a large group of so-called → Old Believers (or Old Ritualists) and led indirectly to the weakening of the church.

Czar Peter I the Great (1682-1725) was able to exploit this situation when he forbade the election of a new patriarch in 1700 and in 1721 abolished the office altogether in favor of a Spiritual College, or Most Holy Synod, which after the Protestant pattern meant collegial government under a state official, the chief procurator, and the transformation of the church into a kind of state department for religious affairs. This restriction of the church in its eternal activities, however, brought with it a turning to → spirituality, as in the → starets (lit. "venerable old man"; pl. startsy) movement. In the 18th and 19th centuries the church's official theology, art, and music were under very heavy Western influence.

When the czarist regime fell in March 1917, a council that had been wanted for many years could at last be held, and it restored the patriarchal office in November 1917. But the October → Revolution brought with it 70 years of oppression by Communist governments that were hostile to religion, with periods of government hampering, illegality, and bloody persecution. Declarations of loyalty to the Soviet regime and a patriotic role in the war of 1941-45 brought relief for a time, but the religious legislation of 1929 allowed only liturgical acts in church buildings and no public activity of any kind, even purely social. Only after 1988 did a discernible change come in the situation. Within three years the number of priests and congregations then doubled, and the church began to make an unexpected impact on public life.

More liberal legislation in 1990 allowed the Russian church to build many new monasteries and churches and to organize social work anew. But the emergent national and political conflicts in the Soviet Union also brought both old and new tensions. In the Ukraine, for example, a part of the Orthodox Church again proclaimed itself autocephalous, and many of the people in western Ukraine returned to the → Uniate Church.

3.1.4. *Younger Autocephalous Churches*
Serbia. When the Turks overran Serbia after the battle of Kosovo in 1389, the Serbian church first came under the Greek-Bulgarian patriarchate in Ohrid, and the Peć Patriarchate was abolished. In 1557 Peć was restored, however, and the church could be reorganized. At the end of the 17th century some Serbs emigrated to Slovenia and southern Hungary under the Hapsburgs. In these territories a Serbian church for "Hungarian" Serbs was set up, elevated to the Patriarchate of Sremski Karlovci by Emperor Francis Joseph in 1848. The older Patriarchate of Peć was suspended anew in 1766. When Serbia became a principality in 1830 (a kingdom after 1882), the metropolitan district of Belgrade achieved autonomy in 1831 and became autocephalous in 1879. But a single church organization for all Serbs came only after World War I with the metropolitan of Belgrade at its head as patriarch. The churches in

Montenegro and Dalmatia were also integrated into this new organization. The division of Yugoslavia in 1941 shattered the Orthodox structure and brought various anti-Orthodox measures, many of them gruesome, including murders and forced conversions to Roman → Catholicism in Croatia. After restoration in 1947 the Serbian Orthodox Church gave itself a new central organization, but this change did not satisfy the desire of the church in Macedonia for more autonomy. In 1967 the Macedonian Orthodox Church declared itself autocephalous, which up to now no other autocephalous church has been willing to recognize.

Romania. Walachia was the first Romanian principality to come under Ottoman rule (1391), followed by Moldavia (1513). The unreliability of the vassal rulers, however, finally forced the Sublime Porte in 1711 and 1716 to put Greek nobles on the throne. The result was to make Romanian Orthodoxy more Greek. The rest of Orthodox Romania was under Hungarian rule from the 11th century, came under the Turks from 1541 to 1691, then under Austria up to 1867, then again under Hungary from 1867 to 1918. It had to be constantly on guard against the Roman Catholic influence exerted by Hungarian and Polish feudal lords. A decree of toleration in 1572 ensured full religious liberty for four confessions but merely tolerated the Orthodox. Only with unification in 1862 did the way open up for an autocephalous Romanian Orthodox Church. The metropolitan of Bucharest became the primate of this church in 1865. The Ecumenical Patriarchate recognized its → autocephaly in 1885, and all Romanians became part of it in 1918/19. A patriarchate was set up and recognized in 1925.

Bulgaria. Abortive uprisings in Bulgaria in 1595 and 1688 resulted in the higher clergy becoming more Greek and finally in the abolition of the autonomy of the archbishopric of Ohrid in 1776. In the 18th century the monasteries of Rila and Chilander (a Serbian institution on Mount Athos) initiated self-reflection. The first Bulgarian school was established in Gabrovo in 1835. The national movement (the so-called Bulgarian renaissance) opposed both Ottoman rule and Greek spiritual leadership. The unilateral establishment by the sultan of an ethnically oriented independent exarchate for all Bulgarians in the Ottoman empire (1870/72), with its seat in Istanbul up to 1913, then in Sofia, resulted in the expulsion of Greek clergy and in schism. Only in 1945 was agreement reached with the Ecumenical Patriarchate. In 1953 the former exarch then became a patriarch.

Others. The founding of new states in the 19th

and 20th centuries brought with it changes in church order and expansion of the Orthodox family. The *Church of Greece* was the first to become autocephalous in 1833, recognized by the Ecumenical Patriarchate in 1850. With the takeover of former Turkish areas by Greece, the metropolitans in these districts came under the Church of Greece (1928). But Crete, the Dodecanese, and Mount → Athos retained their essentially direct relation to the Ecumenical Patriarchate. Autocephalous churches emerging from World War I also sought pan-Orthodox recognition. Constantinople accorded autocephaly to the *Church of Poland* in 1924 (Moscow followed in 1948) and to the *Church of Albania* in 1937 (after a unilateral declaration in 1929). Autocephaly was acknowledged by Moscow for the *Church of Georgia* in 1948, by the Ecumenical Patriarchate in 1990. The roots of the Georgian church go back to the fifth and sixth centuries.

In 1923 the Ecumenical Patriarchate accorded autonomy to the *Church in Czechoslovakia,* and then autocephaly in 1998. The Moscow Patriarchate accorded the church autocephaly in 1951, as it did the *Orthodox Church in America* in 1970, although the former decision regarding autocephaly has been recognized more widely. In 1923 the Ecumenical Patriarchate recognized the autonomy of the *Church of Finland* and the *Church of Estonia,* as did Moscow, respectively, in 1957 and 1923.

3.2. *Interchurch Relations*
3.2.1. *With Roman Catholics*
Rome must have recognized that the attempt at union at Florence in 1438/39, which brought the whole of the Orthodox Church under the headship of the → pope, formally failed with its repudiation at Constantinople in 1584. Even under Ottoman threat the Orthodox still refused to give up their own faith.

Roman Catholic → missionaries, however, still aimed to detach at least some portions of the Orthodox world from the whole and to bring them into union with the Roman Catholic Church, finally using political means to this end. Thus in Roman Catholic states some bishoprics and some parts of the churches united with Rome, for example, in Polish Lithuania in 1595/96, when some bishops in Brest Litovsk, in the metropolitan area of Kiev, decided to make common cause with their Roman Catholic counterparts. We find similar developments in Transcarpathia in 1646/55 and 1689 and in Romania in 1697/1700.

In the Near East, under the influence of Portugal and France, unions with the Orthodox (Melchite Greek Catholic Patriarchate of Antioch, 1709/24)

and the → Oriental Orthodox churches (Ethiopia, 1628; India, 1661/1923; Syrian Catholic, 1760; Chaldean, 1830; Armenian Catholic, 1845; Coptic Catholic, 1895) also enjoyed some success. Political power usually played a part in such unions. When the larger political situation changed, the unions frequently dissolved, again often under political influence, such as happened in Russia in 1772/95, 1839, and 1875, the Ukraine in 1946-50, and Romania in 1948. They were reinstated, however, after the fall of Communism in the 1990s.

Developments in western Ukraine and Romania since 1989/90 brought a serious crisis in relations between the Orthodox and the → Roman Catholic Church, since they showed that despite the declarations of → Vatican II, the Vatican still seemed to be hoping to promote papal primacy with the help of Uniate churches. This development has presented a threat to ongoing bilateral → dialogues, which had already produced some agreement.

3.2.2. *With Protestants*
From the 16th century onward the Orthodox Church and its theology came into unavoidable confrontation with the Protestant churches. Already in 1557 in Moscow a disputation took place with Swedish Lutherans regarding the veneration of → icons and fasting, and in 1575 the → Augsburg Confession reached the Ecumenical Patriarchate. These conversations, however, were in the main just as fruitless as later discussions with the Anglican Nonjurors in 1712-25.

More momentous was the contact with the → Reformation made by Ecumenical Patriarch Cyril Loucaris (in office seven times between 1612 and 1638). The confession that he issued in 1624, which showed the influence of → Calvinism, was condemned by many synods (1638, 1642, 1672, 1691), and the confessions of the Kiev metropolitan Peter Mogila (1632-46) and the Jerusalem patriarch Dositheus (1669-1707) were set in opposition to it, though these two did rely heavily on Roman Catholic models. At this point counterreformation ideas (→ Catholic Reform and Counterreformation) were in part misunderstood as authentically Orthodox. A "pseudomorphosis" (G. Florovsky) of Orthodox and especially Russian theology began, namely, its alienation by Western thinking.

3.2.3. *Involvement in Ecumenism*
During the 19th century renewed reflection took place on true Orthodox identity, along with more intensive research into history and the Fathers (→ Patristics). Neopatristics in particular occupied the Orthodox Church and enabled it as one of the first Christian churches to make a special theological

contribution of its own in conversations with other confessions.

The ecumenical question (→ Ecumenism, Ecumenical Movement) stirred Ecumenical Patriarch Joachim III in 1902, and in 1920 the Ecumenical Patriarchate issued a pioneering encyclical with far-reaching ecumenical demands for an end to proselytizing and the restoration of Christian love between the churches. Orthodoxy thus played an important role in the early phase of the ecumenical movement, though for political reasons the churches in the Soviet bloc were unable to participate and were even forced into opposition (e.g., at the Moscow Conference of 1948).

Some Orthodox churches were founding members of the → World Council of Churches, and all autocephalous churches have been members since 1961. Many bilateral dialogues have also taken place, that with the → Old Catholic Church, initiated as early as 1874/75 in Bonn, having reached satisfactory conclusions. Good strides have also been made in dialogue with the Oriental Orthodox churches (esp. at Chambésy in 1990 and 1993).

→ Ecumenical Dialogue; Orthodox Church; Theology of the Nineteenth and Twentieth Centuries

Bibliography: A. S. ATIYA, *A History of Eastern Christianity* (rev. ed.; London, 1980) • S. K. BATALDEN, ed., *Seeking God: The Recovery of Religious Identity in Orthodox Russia, Ukraine, and Georgia* (DeKalb, Ill., 1993) • J. CHRYSOSTOMUS, *Kirchengeschichte Rußlands der neuesten Zeit* (3 vols.; Munich and Salzburg, 1965-68) • W. HELLER, ed., *Tausend Jahre Christentum in Rußland* (Göttingen, 1988) • J. MEYENDORFF, *The Orthodox Church: Its Past and Its Role in the World Today* (Crestwood, N.Y., 1981) • S. RUNCIMAN, *The Great Church in Captivity: A Study of the Patriarchate of Constantinople from the Eve of the Turkish Conquest to the Greek War of Independence* (London, 1968); idem, *The Orthodox Churches and the Secular State* (Auckland, 1971) • B. SPULER, *Gegenwartslage der Ostkirchen in ihrer nationalen und staatlichen Umwelt* (2d ed.; Frankfurt, 1968); idem, *Die morgenländischen Kirchen* (Leiden, 1964) • N. THON, *Quellenbuch zur Geschichte der Orthodoxen Kirche* (Trier, 1983).

NIKOLAUS THON

4. Mission and Third World Churches

→ Colonialism and Mission; Contextual Theology; Culture and Christianity; Ecumenism, Ecumenical Movement; Liberation Theology; Mission; Missionary Conferences; Nation, Nationalism; Third World; Third World Theology

Modern Period

1. Basic Structures
2. Political Aspects
3. Economic Aspects
4. Social Aspects
5. Ecclesiastical and Religious Aspects

1. Basic Structures

The term "modern period" (Ger. *Neuzeit*), which has been in general use only since the mid-19th century, refers to the period from the end of the → Middle Ages to the present. Since the 16th century it has also been accompanied by the consciousness of belonging to a new epoch. In discussion from the time of the → Enlightenment, independence and self-assertion are thus basic features. Independence indeed does not exclude the late medieval or Renaissance and Reformation roots. But the basic independence of the modern period can be reduced to those conditions only by ignoring the understanding of self and the world that has developed in the modern period. There is a difference between the conditions of origin of this period and its true basis.

In terms of this difference we may also differentiate between the early modern period and → modernity. The early modern period, which began in about 1500, was dependent on → tradition, even where actually independent of its own origin. The transitional period to modernity was the second half of the 18th century. With its → revolutions in philosophy, politics, and industry, this period created the conditions that underlie the manifestation of autonomy. The constitution of the modern way of dealing with the self and the objective and social ways of dealings with the world constantly bring with it accelerating changes that, despite the irreversibility of → progress, do not rule out significant influences from the past.

As a process of modernization, and in view of the cleft between disillusioning → experiences and new expectations, the modern era is open to the → future. Hence, though there is a trend toward a global society, no conclusive empirical answer can be given to the question of whether humanity will actually achieve a planetary universality (→ Universalism and Particularism).

Expanding geographically, the modern spirit has moved out from Europe and America. Its European rationality (→ Rationalism) has been exported through its principles of change and development. The principle of subjectivity in its many forms, which is related to a sense of threat and independent self-preservation, finds expression in subjective relations to the self, objective relations to the world, and intersubjective relations to others. As knowledge of the objective world and its laws (→ Science) builds on the achievements of a subjectivity that studies the cosmos in time-space categories and thinks in linguistic categories, a basis is found for the existence of inner and outer → freedom, moral (self-)regard, and social and legal relations, in the → autonomy of the free will.

All the same, the whole project, committed to theoretical and practical → reason since the Kantian Copernican revolution (→ Kantianism), plunged into ambivalence. An objective and social world with a one-sided rational aim and rule (→ Technology) that is dominated by the imperatives of scientific and technical innovations, growth in economic productivity (→ Economy), and the expansion of → bureaucracy has come under the sway of the rationalistic culture of a calculating, quantifying outlook. The systemic self-preservation of depersonalized societies by money and → power seems to foster the material and social reproduction of the human species, quite apart from the natural needs, theoretical insights, and practical self-determination of individuals. The dialectic of the Enlightenment that characterizes modernity (→ Critical Theory 2.2) is based on a correspondence between the dominion over external → nature and the self-dominion over the inner nature of the individual. With this dialectic, however, the ambivalence of the principle of subjectivity becomes a matter of discussion. The legacy of natural self-preservation seems also to affect human history by means of rationally constituted relations to the world and society.

2. Political Aspects
The centralizing of political powers in the early modern period, strengthened by the divisions in Western Christianity (→ Denomination), produced national and territorial states under the rule of absolute monarchs (→ Nation, Nationalism). These states monopolized military power, finance, and government (→ Modern Church History). Though rational doctrines of → natural law were at first invoked to justify this absolutism, the same doctrines also offered grounds on which to criticize it. Individuals in private, often in secret circles, discussed such matters on the basis of a distinction between public politics and private morality. In this way public opinion began to be formed.

With the American and French revolutions, human and civil → rights found an anchor in rational law (→ Law and Legal Theory). Organized along the lines of a division of powers and → democracy, the constitutional state that is based on law came into being. Guaranteeing the subjective rights of citizens, it also gave legal safeguards to an economically based society of citizens separate from the political state.

These legal principles of the political revolution made their way only slowly across Europe, so that the process of establishing modern legal democracies was only provisionally completed after two world wars (→ War). The slowness of the process may be seen in eastern Europe, where bureaucratic → socialism began to break up only at the end of the 20th century. This development helped to ensure world peace, but democratic states cannot guarantee that the idea of a constitutional state will coincide with the reality. This tension results primarily from the fact that the transition from a democratic constitutional state to a social and welfare state tends to strengthen existing bureaucratic tendencies.

3. Economic Aspects
Beginning in Britain in the second half of the 18th century, the industrial revolution transformed the older European subsistence states, which simply met basic needs, into states with a private capitalistic market economy (→ Capitalism). Its success depended upon a middle-class society different from the political state but ruled by private law. Constant innovation sped up productive capacity and, along with the opposing interests of capital and labor, brought revolutionary changes to public and private life.

In the 19th century private control of the means of production conflicted with contractually regulated labor, which was nonetheless subject to the instability of supply and demand, a conflict characterizing Western society during the 19th century. Although organized labor and state legislation affecting labor, social issues, and entrepreneurship to some extent defused the conflicts in the 20th century, the market economy nonetheless has the constitutive tendency, with its unending gains in productivity and profit, to commercialize all spheres of private and public life. This tendency will no doubt increase in strength with the discrediting of the planned economies of socialism.

The limitless gains in productivity have an even more serious effect on the environment, which is not independent of the means of production that are used. So long as neoclassical economic theory, which supports the capitalist market economy, treats ecological damage merely as an external effect, environmental destruction will not be reversed, despite an awakening ecological awareness and state controls (→ Ecology; Environment). Only strong international action can turn the tide.

Similarly, only a basic change in the economic order can reduce the growing division between the expanding economies of the North and the economically dependent countries of the South (→ Dependence). The latter in many cases bear the burden of being "liberated" colonies (→ Colonialism) of Euramerican imperialism.

4. Social Aspects

The process of modernization has introduced social change by replacing the hierarchical societies of → feudalism and absolutism with functional differentiation (→ Functionalism). Modern society breaks up into a variety of → social systems with specific and unique functions. Correspondingly, there is cultural → pluralism (→ Culture), especially as no social system can unite and integrate society. Yet functional differentiation and philosophical pluralism are subject to an opposing trend toward dedifferentiation.

The economy, governed by omnipresent → money as a means of communication, so invades other areas of life that cultural goods are produced and offered as items for sale. As the industries of culture and leisure expand, strengthened by the → mass media, and as bureaucratic agencies also expand, modern individual culture increasingly becomes an ambivalent phenomenon (→ Individualism). Shut out of social systems that tend to dehumanize, individuals wander into psychological niches in which it is hard to distinguish between protest and idiosyncracy (→ Counterculture; Youth Religions).

The situation of the nuclear → family, which is a result of the industrial revolution, resists this trend. The increase in adolescent crises that express disruptive → narcissism (→ Youth) is an indication that family → socialization is at odds with social role expectations.

5. Ecclesiastical and Religious Aspects

At different times in different countries, political modernization has brought separation between the state and specific churches and denominations (→ Church and State). The functional differentiation of modern society has also changed profoundly the social position of the Christian → religion. Churches that focus on spiritual → communication and → diakonia must act within increasingly secularized societies. → Secularization, which is not the same as the transforming of religious into secular contents (for which there is little evidence in intellectual history), means that social systems have no religious functions outside those of communities of faith.

In principle, quite apart from any continuing relations between church and state, religion is a matter of individual decision. Involved here is → religious liberty based on basic human rights, which is in keeping with the character of the Christian religion. Yet it also intensifies for Christianity the crisis of validity and relevance that is caused by criticism of religion and → ideology. The shifts of mood that are called → postmodern obscure rather than clarify the situation. Technological and economic rationality has its own crisis as the expression of a modernity that is shaped by quantifying rather than qualitative reason. Against this background the Christian crisis is best met, not by the mobilizing of sensory and more physical feelings and → intuitions, but by the strengthening of attempts at cognitive → education.

Bibliography: H. BLUMENBERG, The Legitimacy of the Modern Age (Cambridge, Mass., 1983) • H. EBELING, ed., Subjektivität und Selbsterhaltung (Frankfurt, 1996; orig. pub., 1976) • J. HABERMAS, The Philosophical Discourse of Modernity (Cambridge, Mass., 1987); idem, The Structural Transformation of the Public Sphere (Cambridge, Mass., 1989; orig. pub., 1962) • M. HORKHEIMER and T. W. ADORNO, Dialectic of Enlightenment (New York, 2000; orig. pub., 1944) • P. KONDYLIS, Die Aufklärung im Rahmen des neuzeitlichen Rationalismus (Hamburg, 2002; orig. pub., 1981) • R. KOSELLECK, Critique and Crisis: Enlightenment and the Pathogenesis of Modern Society (Cambridge, Mass., 1988; orig. pub., 1959); idem, Futures Past: On the Semantics of Historical Time (Cambridge, Mass., 1985; orig. pub., 1979) • N. LUHMANN, Gesellschaftsstruktur und Semantik. Studien zur Wissenssoziologie der modernen Gesellschaft (4 vols.; Frankfurt, 1980-95); idem, Observations on Modernity (Stanford, Calif., 1998) • F. WAGNER, Geld oder Gott? Zur Geldbestimmtheit der kulturellen und religiösen Lebenswelt (Stuttgart, 1985).

FALK WAGNER†

Modernism

1. Term, Contents, Goals
2. Range
   2.1. Germany
   2.2. France
   2.3. Britain
   2.4. Italy
   2.5. Austria, Bohemia, Moravia

3. Antimodernism
  3.1. Integralists
  3.2. Pius X
  3.3. Germany

1. Term, Contents, Goals

In the history of the → Roman Catholic Church, "modernism" refers to a broad movement around the turn of the 20th century that sought to reconcile Catholic teaching and practice with modern science and the modern world. The movement was condemned by Pius X (1903-14) in his 1907 encyclical *Pascendi,* which called modernists the church's worst enemies because they were inside it. The stern judgment and punishment (→ Church Discipline) of the widely varying thought and writing of philosophers and theologians in several different countries on the count of modernism shows that this word became quite a catchall term. "Modernism" and "antimodernism" also became terms by which to describe a particular period in the church's history.

Modernists championed a broad spectrum of goals: reforms in theology and the church, the adjusting of the church to science (→ Science and Theology) and → democracy, critical Bible → exegesis, development of the science of religion (→ Religious Studies), the use of national languages in the → liturgy, the ending of compulsory → celibacy for the priesthood, the improvement of → religious education, the repudiation of political → Catholicism, the strengthening of the church's social involvement, common labor unions with other denominations, and increased development of the lay apostolate (→ Clergy and Laity). Most modernists were devout Roman Catholics, which we can see from the submission of the majority to papal sanctions after *Pascendi* condemned modernism (→ Teaching Office 1).

Although modernism was bitterly opposed and widely suppressed by the efforts of Pius X, it ultimately triumphed at Vatican II. At many essential points in its constitutions, the council adopted modernist positions, thus largely vindicating the earlier efforts.

2. Range

2.1. *Germany*

Among the most important German Roman Catholics who favored reform were the Freiburg church historian F. X. Kraus (1840-1901), the Würzburg professor of → apologetics and comparative religion H. Schell (1850-1906), the patristic scholar A. Ehrhard (1862-1940), and the literary critic

C. Muth (1867-1944). Kraus, though neither a liberal nor a modernist, criticized sharply in several anonymous articles, and especially in his *Spectator-Briefen* (Spectator letters) in the *Allgemeine Zeitung* (1896-1900), the fanaticism of the → Ultramontanists, who were putting the → church above → religion.

Schell demanded that the church make common cause with → progress in every form and, for the sake of renewal, enter into dialogue with the world. His works *Der Katholizismus als Prinzip des Fortschritts* (Catholicism as the principle of progress, 1897) and *Die neue Zeit und der alte Glaube* (The new age and the old faith, 1898) were put on the Index in 1898 (→ Censorship). He submitted and was thus allowed to continue teaching.

In 1901 Erhard published *Der Katholizismus und das 20. Jahrhundert im Licht der Kirchlichen Entwicklung der Neuzeit* (Catholicism and the 20th cent. in light of the ecclesiastical development of the modern era). In it he pointed out that the → conflict between Roman Catholicism and modern thought (→ Modern Period) could be overcome if the latter would abandon its anti-Christian → prejudices and the former would stop absolutizing the → Middle Ages.

A Catholic literary debate between Muth's journal *Hochland* and the journal *Der Gral* of the Austrian R. von Kralik (1852-1934) centered on the question whether literature should be judged by its own artistic standards (Muth) or by Roman Catholic moral standards (Kralik).

2.2. *France*

In France the modernism crisis arose from → philosophy, and especially biblical criticism. M. Blondel (1861-1949) related transcendence (→ Immanence and Transcendence) more closely to human actualization and thus emerged as an advocate of immanentism, the view that religious dogma is ultimately a product of human needs. (At least Blondel's adversaries charged him with holding this position.)

The Parisian church historian L. Duchesne (1843-1922) taught historical criticism to young theologians, including A. Loisy (1857-1930), a teacher at the *Institut Catholique* in Paris, and M.-J. Lagrange (1855-1938), who founded the Jerusalem Bible School in 1890 and edited the *Revue biblique* from 1892 onward. Loisy, an outstanding scholar and publicist, was convinced that there was no full agreement between the concept of the → gospel when interpreted critically and the various forms of historical Christianity, especially church → dogma and the institutional church (*L'évangile et l'église* [The gospel and the church, 1902]). In the massive controversy that followed, Loisy defended his position in *Autour d'un petit livre* (Author of a small book, 1903). The → curia condemned his main works in December 1903. At first he submitted, but in 1908, after his express renunciation of Christian faith, he was → excommunicated.

Special attention was claimed by Pius X's condemnation of "Sillonism" in a letter to the French bishops in 1910. This thinking grew out of a study circle Le Sillon (The furrow) founded around 1900 by M. Sangnier (1873-1950) of the Paris Polytechnic. The goal of this group was, through a variety of educational efforts, to prepare Roman Catholics in different ways for exercising personal democratic responsibility and to reconcile again the church and the ideals of the French republic. The curia condemned this effort as social modernism.

2.3. *Britain*

Though Roman Catholics were a minority in Britain, British modernists were extremely important. After becoming a Roman Catholic and joining the → Jesuit order (→ Conversion 2), G. Tyrrell (1861-1909) came to know biblical criticism and neo-Kantianism (→ Kantianism) through F. von Hügel (1852-1925), who promoted modern theological developments. When Tyrrell began to use the methods of criticism himself, he soon came to doubt the → authority of the church's → hierarchy and the dogma of the church. He tried to show that Christ did not come as a teacher of orthodoxy and that dogma was only a human attempt to express the perceived power of God in intellectual formulas (→ Christology). French and Italian modernists received his works, at first published under a pseudonym, with great enthusiasm. When forced to disclose his identity, Tyrrell was expelled from the Society of Jesus in 1906. In 1906 and 1907 he published two more moderate works in which he tried to mediate between the exaggerated dogmatism of theologians and the → pragmatism of some philosophers. His strong protests against *Pascendi* in leading English newspapers were punished at once by excommunication. He died without submitting in 1909.

2.4. *Italy*

Movements of church reform in Italy were for the most part instituted from outside. The influence of Tyrrell, von Hügel, and Duchesne, who lived in Rome after 1895, caused younger priests to try to infuse new life into Italian theology, to establish a cultural basis for Christian democracy, and to build a bridge between the church and the world. The laity also took part in these efforts.

In theology we might mention E. Buonaiuti (1881-1946), professor of church history at the Roman Seminary, whose *Rivista storico-critica delle scienze teologiche* (Historical-critical review of theological science, 1905) tried to strike a middle way between progressivism and → conservatism, but with critical inquiry into the history of the church and its dogmas. Excommunicated in 1921 and 1924, he remained in the church until 1926 as *vitandus* (one to be avoided).

The Barnabite G. Semeria (1867-1931), who was a mediator in the sphere of the early history of Christianity (→ Early Church) and the → philosophy of religion, was driven into exile in Belgium in 1912 as a result of the reaction against modernism.

S. Minocchi (1869-1943), professor of → Hebrew language and literature at Florence and Pisa, published the journal *Studi religiosi* from 1901 onward. Adopting some of the thinking of Loisy and Tyrrell, this journal was devoted especially to study of the Bible. The curia ordered its suspension in 1907, and in 1908, after a sermon in which Minocchi denied the historicity of the biblical → creation story, he was forbidden to dispense the → sacraments and that year ceased to exercise his priestly functions (→ Civil Law and the Church; Priest, Priesthood).

The leader of Italian social modernism, R. Murri (1870-1944), who edited *Cultura sociale* and founded the Lega Democratica Nationale, a democratic Roman Catholic party, was also suspended (1907) and excommunicated (1909).

2.5. *Austria, Bohemia, Moravia*

In Austria at the turn of the century, Roman Catholicism was exposed to a movement seeking freedom from Rome (→ State Churches). Perhaps for this reason there was no reforming activity worth mentioning in German-speaking Austria. The Innsbruck canonist L. Wahrmund (1861-1932), who was transferred to Prague in 1908 because of his sharp attacks on the papacy (→ Pope, Papacy), was at best only a sympathizer with German reform Catholicism.

Not so well known are the strivings for reform in the Slavic portions of the Austrian Empire. The critical book *Nostra culpa* (Our guilt) by the Carinthian pastor A. Vogrinec (1873-1947) was put on the Index in the year of its publication (1904). Vogrinec immediately submitted.

In Bohemia and Moravia groups of priests were friendly to reform, such as the Katholische Moderne (Catholic modernity), a group founded in Olomouc in 1895. Its third congress, held in Prerau, along with the annual congress of Jeduota (a clergy union in Bohemia), led in 1906 to the issuing of a pastoral letter by the bishops to the clergy that anticipated the condemnation of *Pascendi.* The latter resulted in a superficial suppression of Czech modernism.

3. Antimodernism

The term "antimodernism," which is just as imprecise as "modernism," embraces conservative adherents of an unchangeable church and persecutors of reforming movements.

3.1. *Integralists*

The so-called integralist Catholics used verbal and written means, including spying and denunciation, to combat modernism. In Italy, France, Belgium, the Netherlands, and Poland they controlled and financed their own journals, reporting the news of sanctions imposed against modernists. Suppression increased after the publication of *Pascendi,* reaching its height in 1912/13.

Vienna was a major center in the fight against modernism. At work there were the dogmatician E. Commer (1847-1928); the papal historian L. von Pastor (1854-1928), Austria's envoy to the → Vatican from 1920 to 1928; and A. Mauss (1868-1917), who taught religion in Vienna and edited the Austrian *Katholisches Sonntagsblatt.*

Mauss served as an informant for the most powerful of the integralists, the Italian priest U. Benigni (1862-1937), who from 1906 to 1911 was papal undersecretary for church affairs abroad and who in 1909, with the knowledge and help of Pius X, set up a secret antimodernist network, the Sodalitium Pianum (SP, "Solidarity of Pius"). This group published *Correspondance de Rome* and confidential bulletins. It never had more than 50 members throughout Europe as a whole, but with the help of other informants and hierarchical patrons, it was able to spread a net of suspicion and denunciation over all European Catholicism.

3.2. *Pius X*

Pius X was undoubtedly an important pope in view of his contributions to pastoral work, church music (→ Liturgical Movements), → mission (→ Catholic Missions), and even Bible scholarship. But already as bishop of Mantua (1884-93) and patriarch of Venice (1893-1903), he came out as a resolute opponent of the new Christianity. He was not made an antimodernist by Benigni or others in his confidence but used these men in his battle against modernism, which became more intense as he grew older. Already in his first months as pope he put the main works of Loisy on the Index (December 1903). In his 1904 encyclicals *Ad diem illum* and *Iucunda sane accidit,* he warned against scholars who were throwing doubts on Christian origins. In July 1907 the decree *Lamentabili sane exitu* condemned 65

theses after the pattern of the → Syllabus of → Pius IX (1846-78), 50 of them from the works of Loisy. The climax of his condemnation of modernism came in September 1907 with his *Pascendi.* Although nearly all modernists submitted, the hostility against them only increased. In 1910 all ordained officeholders and teachers of theology were forced to take the → Anti-Modernist Oath.

Finally, the bishops and cardinals personally asked the pope to halt the hunting down of modernists. The French Jesuit journal *Les Études* came out publicly against the integralists. Benedict XV (1914-22) was elected to succeed Pius X by the votes of cardinals who expected and requested him to put an end to the persecution. He worked assiduously to achieve this end, and in 1921 the SP was disbanded.

3.3. *Germany*

Germany managed to avoid enforcement of the ban on modernism, and reform Catholicism continued, even though Pius X especially feared German theologians, the Center Party, and nonintegralist scholars. Pius accepted compromises as far as Germany was concerned, conceding under pressure from the bishops that German theologians at state universities need not take the Anti-Modernist Oath, that the antimodernist encyclical of May 1910, *Editae saepe Dei,* need not be read from German pulpits, and that reform Catholics might participate in the work of confessionally mixed labor unions.

Bibliography: Sources: AAS 36-37 (1903-4) and esp. 40-41 (1907-8) • M. BLONDEL, "Histoire et dogme. Les lacunes philosophiques de l'exégèse moderne" (1904), *Les premiers écrits de Maurice Blondel* (Paris, 1956) 145-228 • E. BUONAIUTI, *Il modernismo cattolico* (Modena, 1943); idem, *Pellegrino di Roma* (Rome, 1945) • A. EHRHARD, *Katholisches Christentum und moderne Kultur* (Munich, 1906); idem, *Der Katholizismus und das 20. Jahrhundert im Lichte der kirchlichen Entwicklung der Neuzeit* (Stuttgart, 1901); idem, *Liberaler Katholizismus? Ein Wort an meine Kritiker* (Stuttgart, 1902) • A. FOGAZZARO, *Der Heilige* (Munich, 1906) • A. GAMBARO, *Il modernismo* (Florence, 1912) • A. HOUTIN, *Histoire du modernisme catholique* (Paris, 1913) • F. VON HÜGEL, *Selected Letters* (London, 1932) • R. VON KRALIK, *Tage und Werke* (Vienna, 1922) • A. LOISY, *Autour d'un petit livre* (Paris, 1903); idem, *The Birth of the Christian Religion* (London, 1948; orig. pub., 1933); idem, *The Gospel and the Church* (Buffalo, N.Y., 1988; orig. pub., 1902); idem, *Memoirs pour servir a l'histoire religieuse de notre temps* (3 vols.; Paris, 1930-31) • E. MOMIGLIANO, *Tutte le encicliche dei sommi pontifici* (Milan, 1959) • C. MUTH (Veremundus, pseud.), *Steht die katholische Belletristik auf der Höhe der Zeit?*

(Mainz, 1898) • M. D. PETRE, *Alfred Loisy: His Religious Significance* (Cambridge, 1944); idem, *Autobiography and Life of G. Tyrrell* (2 vols.; New York, 1912) • P. SABATIER, *Les modernistes* (Paris, 1909) • H. SCHELL, *Der Katholizismus als Prinzip des Fortschritts* (Würzburg, 1897) • G. TYRRELL, *The Programme of Modernism: A Reply to the Encyclical of Pius X* (New York, 1908); idem, *Through Scylla and Charybdis; or, The Old Theology and the New* (London, 1907); idem, *Tradition and the Critical Spirit: Catholic Modernist Writings* (comp. J. C. Livingston; Minneapolis, 1991) • A. VERMEERSCH, *De modernismo acta S. Sedis, 1907-08* (Brugge, 1908) • W. WÜHR, ed., *L. von Pastor: Tagebücher–Briefe–Erinnerungen* (Heidelberg, 1950).

Secondary works: R. S. APPLEBY, *"Church and Age Unite!" The Modernist Impulse in American Catholicism* (Notre Dame, Ind., 1992) • L. BARMAN and C. J. T. TALAR, eds., *Sanctity and Secularity during the Modernist Period: Six Perspectives on Hagiography around 1900* (Brussels, 1999) • G. DALY, *Transcendence and Immanence: A Study in Catholic Modernism and Integralism* (Oxford, 1980) • G. FORNI, *The Essence of Christianity: The Hermeneutical Question in the Protestant and Modernist Debate (1897-1904)* (Atlanta, 1995) • J. J. HEANEY, *The Modernist Crisis: Von Hugel* (Washington, D.C., 1968) • D. JODOCK, ed., *Catholicism Contending with Modernity: Roman Catholic Modernism and Antimodernism in Historical Context* (Cambridge, 2000) • L. R. KURTZ, *The Politics of Heresy: The Modernist Crisis in Roman Catholicism* (Berkeley, Calif., 1986) • T. M. LOOME, *Liberal Catholicism, Reform Catholicism, Modernism: A Contribution to a New Orientation in Modernist Research* (Mainz, 1979) • T. G. McCARTHY, *The Catholic Tradition: The Church in the Twentieth Century* (2d ed.; Chicago, 1998) • M. R. O'CONNELL, *Critics on Trial: An Introduction to the Catholic Modernist Crisis* (Washington, D.C., 1994) • M. RANCHETTI, *The Catholic Modernists: A Study of the Religious Reform Movement, 1864-1907* (London, 1969) • H. G. REVENTLOW and W. FARMER, eds., *Biblical Studies and the Shifting of Paradigms, 1840-1914* (Sheffield, 1995) • D. G. SCHULTENOVER, *A View from Rome: On the Eve of the Modernist Crisis* (New York, 1993) • C. J. T. TALAR, *(Re)reading, Reception, and Rhetoric: Approaches to Roman Catholic Modernism* (New York, 1999) • E. WEINZIERL, ed., *Der Modernismus. Beiträge zu seiner Erforschung* (Graz, 1974).

ERIKA WEINZIERL

Modernity

1. The Term: History and Problems

The term "modernity" is a relatively new one related to the adjective "modern." It obviously stands opposed to antiquity, though more in the sense of contrasting with the obsolete → classicism of the 19th century. There is thus an implied rejection of an outdated past and an orientation to the future. ("Modernity" is considered here primarily in its reference to the arts, esp. literature. The related word → "modernism," which is often used in similar contexts, refers more exclusively in this encyclopedia to particular theological tendencies and disputes.)

1.1. *The Adjective*

The force of the noun "modernity" derives from the prior use of the adjective. The LLat. *modernus* (from the adv. *modo*, "now, right now," first found in the 5th cent.) is the opposite of *antiquus* (coming before) and may denote the cyclic interaction of old and new. When Christian authors used it for themselves as distinct from pre-Christian authors, however, the idea was one of superiority in virtue of faith, and there was a resultant historicizing, with the idea that an advance had been made over an outmoded antiquity. The same thought occurred in later → Scholasticism, when we find the *via moderna* (→ Nominalism) contrasted with the *via antiqua.*

Antiqua, however, could also denote a normative and exemplary past as opposed to which modern phenomena were disparaged (e.g., Gothic architecture as opposed to that of antiquity at the time of the → Renaissance). The debate entered a decisive stage with the famous literary controversy known as the *Querelle des anciens et des modernes* (Quarrel of the ancients and the moderns, after 1687). Over against the *Anciens,* who recognized the permanent, normative → authority of antiquity, C. Perrault (1628-1703) took the view that contemporary literature was not only as good as that of antiquity but better. He thus transferred to literature the concept of →

progress that had been present in learning from the time of R. Descartes (1596-1650; → Cartesianism). The result of the conflict was the recognition that the modern age is autonomous relative to antiquity, that there can be no repeating a past epoch, and that the course of history is irreversible.

The discussion of the concept of modernity by F. Schiller (1759-1805), F. Schlegel (1772-1829), J. W. F. Schelling (1775-1854), and G. W. F. Hegel (1770-1831; → Hegelianism) simply repeated the theme of the *Querelle* but with added depth from the standpoint of the → philosophy of history. For Schelling, the model of ancient and modern epochs was embedded in a concept of the universe as history.

During the 19th century the antithesis "ancient/modern" lost some of its importance. The modern was no longer that which was opposed to the ancient but that which broke away from the more immediate past. This understanding meant a more limited span for the modern, namely, the time of one's own generation, the present, what is current — not necessarily what is in vogue but, more to the point, that which accords with the spirit of the age yet also has significance for the future.

1.2. *Denoting an Epoch*
It is thus along the lines indicated by the use of the adjective that we are to understand the term "modernity." In Germany E. Wolff (1863-1929) helped to fashion the equivalent *Moderne,* which, with some modifications, was then taken up by the Viennese writer and essayist H. Bahr (1863-1934). It then became a kind of slogan between 1890 and 1910.

More narrowly than the adjective, the noun denotes an epoch. In order to use it, though, we must be able to define the epoch chronologically, to say what phenomena it embraces, and to see what essential features distinguish it from other epochs. Thus far there has been no agreement on these points.

The initial restriction to a period between 1890 and 1910 is typically accompanied by an extension that makes modernity equal to the → "modern period." The broader the concept is, however, the harder it is to find a common denominator for the varied phenomena. We can thus understand why many argue that "modernity" is a term that defies precise definition and does not permit of any "objective, encyclopedic" description (H. Holländer). We also find the vague term "postmodernity," which presupposes a clear idea of what modernity is as something that may be surveyed and left behind. The only solution to the riddle of definition is to make a clear distinction between the different concepts.

2. Modernity around 1900
2.1. *Literature*
If we use the word "modernity" for the literature at the turn of the 20th century, the beginning came with the rise of naturalism about 1870 (with French novelist É. Zola) or 1885 (in Germany). Modernity as represented around 1890 by the *Freie Bühne* (Free stage) of the Berlin Fischer Verlag took the offensive under the banner of plays by H. Ibsen (1828-1906) and G. Hauptmann (1862-1946).

For Bahr, however, naturalism was only the first phase of modernity. In his essay "Zur Kritik der Moderne" (On criticism of modernity, 1890), explaining that the → truth naturalism demanded was "truth as each of us experiences it," he was already offering a formula for the → impressionism that he presented as the second phase of modernity. Modernity, though, reached its goal only in the third phase, when beauty became the leading concept instead of truth and it was no longer a matter of reality (or its subjective reflection) but of the autonomous production of a dream world (*Die Überwindung des Naturalismus* [Overcoming naturalism, 1891]). At this point a transition took place to the not very clearly differentiated art nouveau, symbolism, and neoromanticism.

At its core Bahr's understanding was thus antinaturalist. In this regard he was influenced by the French *décadence* movement (P. Bourget, J.-K. Huysmans, M. Maeterlinck). Similarly, H. von Hofmannsthal (1874-1929) developed his concept of modernity in debate with European "decadence" (esp. in his 1893 d'Annunzio Essay). A sense of crisis may be detected in the adoption of this tradition. The I feels that it is forced into reflection, threatened with a loss of → identity, and impotent against the reality that it detests. In reaction it thus tries to create its own artificial reality and, by way of this "beauty," gain access to a rather ill-defined transcendence (→ Immanence and Transcendence). We find these elements already in C. Baudelaire (1821-67), who might thus be called the true ancestor of this aesthetic modernity.

Although the "Vienna modernity" took the lead in thus reorienting the naturalistic "Berlin modernity," in Berlin too, as in German literature in general, there was a move away from naturalism, though now, in distinction from Vienna, under the sign of F. → Nietzsche (1844-1900). In defining modernity, Nietzsche also went back to the French *décadence* he knew through Bourget (*Der Fall Wag-*

ner [The case of Wagner, 1888]), but he sought to rise above this modernity by means of a life lived at a level of intoxication. A feature of R. Dehmel (1863-1920), who followed him, was thus an antidecadent vitalism (→ Philosophy of Life).

Quite apart from the negative evaluation of modernity, as in the equation of "modern" and "sick," Nietzsche's diagnosis was basic to its understanding. Thus the close linking of modernity to the theater, with R. Wagner (1813-83) as an example, was a basic motif in the whole work of the brothers Heinrich (1871-1950) and Thomas (1875-1955) Mann, and it remained paradigmatic even later, as in T. Lessing, G. Simmel, and others. For the rest it corresponds to an insight into the brokenness of the modern ego that W. Benjamin (1892-1940) found already in Baudelaire: "The modern hero is not a hero but a portrayer of heroes."

The last phase of literary modernity around the turn of the last century was → expressionism, which was a counterthrust against aestheticism. In many ways — especially in the problem of identity and the deforming of reality — expressionism was its radicalized continuation.

2.2. *Other Spheres*
The movement of modernity in literature up to the outbreak of World War I had its counterpart in other spheres. No field was unaffected. In the *theater* a first new feature was the naturalistic → realism of O. Brahm (1856-1912), which later was replaced by the stylized art of M. Reinhardt (1873-1943). In the *plastic arts* modernity began with the impressionists, but more strictly with the vanquishing of impressionism by P. Cézanne (1839-1906), who (as in literature) radically rejected mimetic procedures. In his view, "Art does not copy nature but is a harmony parallel to it." It is thus anti-illusionist. The stylization of art nouveau, cubism, and expressionism, which deforms perceived reality, led to an autonomy of artistic means and eventually to abstraction, as for example in 1910 in the first abstract pictures of W. Kandinsky (1866-1944).

In *architecture* and *design* art nouveau achieved international importance (H. van der Velde, P. Behrens). In the logical artistic fashioning of things in everyday use, a tendency toward the aestheticizing of all life emerged. In *music,* with the exhausting of prior approaches to harmony and tonality, the atonality of A. Schoenberg (1874-1951) and his followers A. Berg (1885-1935) and A. Webern (1883-1945) brought with it a wholly new idiom (after 1908).

2.3. *Essential Features*
There are two essential features of modernity around 1900. First, the old is replaced by the new, for which the adjective "modern" is used. We have here what has been viewed since Bahr as a law of the epoch of modernity itself. Compared to what happened in the past, the replacement now of established positions comes with increasing speed.

Second, the thought of → progress, which is inseparably linked to the adjective, has in modernity a contradictory relation to the sense of a continued crisis.

3. Modernity from Baudelaire to the Present
3.1. *Links with Tradition*
The advantage of limiting modernity to the time at the turn of the 20th century (and before 1914) is that despite its variety, we can think of it as a unity. Against such a restriction it may be argued that although the age after World War I was marked by a plurality of divergent traditions, it was still a continuation of the pluralism of styles in modernity around 1900 and may be seen as a result of the thrust that modernity had toward innovation from the very outset.

In many areas we find an unmistakable linkage of tradition. Thus in music Schoenberg stood behind the transition from atonality to 12-tone music (around 1920) and "serial music" (after 1950). In the plastic arts we find a similar ongoing line from 1910 to 1959 and then on to 1969. The architecture of L. Mies van der Rohe (1886-1969) would hardly be conceivable without that of P. Behrens (1868-1940). The thesis of H. Friedrich (1904-78) regarding the structural unity of the modern lyric from Baudelaire to the middle of the 20th century is still convincing. The determinative features of 20th-century modernity — loss of identity, collapse of the ego, depersonalization (→ Person), orientation to an empty transcendence, break with conventions of perception, openness and decomposition of artistic work, high regard for experimentation, an inclination for the absurd, shock as an intentional effect, artistry, an expansion of art into the sphere of reality and its influence on everyday life — appear already in the modernity of 1900 or may be traced back to early beginnings at that time, just as discoveries in science that would shatter the prevailing view of things were already being made at that time (e.g., by A. Einstein and S. Freud). Likewise, the social presuppositions of cultural modernity, the world of the big city as distinct from the province, and the problems of modern → industrial society were already significant before 1900.

From the outset modernity was marked by conflict between avant-garde art and the broad public, which, oriented to existing conventions, reacted against modern art with misunderstanding, resistance, and aggression. The antimodernity trends that sought to preserve or restore traditional attitudes and values (such as the *Heimatkunst* [regionalism] movement after 1890) became stronger under National Socialism (→ Fascism), and a war of extermination developed between those who regarded themselves as "healthy" against "sick" or "decadent" modernity (e.g., the public burning of books in 1933 and the exhibition of "degenerate art" in 1937). As a result, modernity had to be rediscovered in Germany after 1945.

Since modernity called the traditional Christian view of things into question, most Christians opposed it, as in *Verlust der Mitte* (Loss of the center, 1948), the widely circulated work of art historian H. Sedlmayr (1896-1984). The specifically Christian literature of the time (e.g., by R. A. Schröder and R. Schneider) adopted traditional forms of presentation. Nevertheless, modern experiences were close to Christian experiences. Radical → dialectical theology is specifically modern. Modernity has also had considerable influence on → church music and → church architecture.

3.2. Classical and Avant-Garde Modernity

To try to divide modernity into classical and avant-garde periods does not work very well, since modernity was avant garde from the very first, and the border between the two emphases constantly shifted. A new avant garde made the old avant garde classical. Thus movements that called themselves avant garde — futurism, cubism, expressionism, dadaism, surrealism, nouveau roman, concrete poetry — were already being called classical by others.

In discussing postmodernity, we must ask whether indeed the constant and accelerating movement of modernity from one avant garde to another has not played itself out and come to an end. The postmodern relation to the past would then be radically different from that of modernity to the past; according to U. Eco, it involves an ironic citing of the past instead of negation and the replacing of the old by the new.

4. Modernity as an Enlightenment Project

4.1. Essential Features

Postmodernity usually presupposes in some way a much broader concept of modernity. It traces the origin of modernity to the → Enlightenment and defines its content accordingly.

Essential marks of this modernity are the development and extension of science according to the principle of rationality (→ Rationalism) as Descartes first formulated it; the translating of the results of natural science into → technology, which makes possible increasing mastery of → nature; the conviction that relentless scientific and technological advance is for the good of humanity as a whole; the shaping of social life (in → law, government, and → economy) on rational principles; → tolerance and → democracy as principles of political culture; and liberation from all irrational dependence (→ Freedom) and the → autonomy of the individual (→ Individualism), which is seen as equivalent to the promise of happiness.

4.2. Countertrends

It is also a feature of this type of modernity, however, that very early it contained tendencies contrary to the program of a scientific and technological civilization. In his *Discours sur les sciences et les arts* (A discourse on the sciences and the arts, 1750), J.-J. Rousseau (1712-78) contradicted the optimism of the Enlightenment with his thesis that scientific and technological progress would lead us to alienation from our own nature (→ Anthropology). Removing this alienation has been a constant theme of modernity. Aesthetic modernity since Baudelaire (see 2.1) is to be viewed as essentially an answer to the experience of alienation, as a movement of protest against the supremacy of science and technology in the industrial society.

The consensus regarding progress that gives unity to that society came into a deep crisis only when it threatened to bring about an ecological catastrophe (→ Ecology; Environment). The rationalism of the Enlightenment finds itself exposed to radical doubt precisely because, founded on the hope of modernity for the race as a whole, it is revealed as the cause of a total disaster. This doubt is strengthened by the fact that the peoples of the → Third World have often seen their expectations disappointed when they sought modernization after the manner of industrialized countries. The result has been the rise of fundamentalist movements, which, for all their diversity, are one in their aggressive rejection of Enlightenment modernity (e.g., the → fundamentalism of → Islam).

From 1980 J. Habermas (→ Critical Theory) has opposed the postmodernity tendency, which either results from or exploits the changed awareness, to declare the project of the Enlightenment dead. Taking up again the concerns of T. W. Adorno (1903-69) and M. Horkheimer (1895-1973; see his *Dialektik der Aufklärung* [Dialectic of the Enlightenment, 1947]), Habermas supported the intentions of the Enlightenment, despite the need for criticism of instrumental reason. Oriented to the utopian hopes of the Enlightenment (→ Utopia), and in contrast to the representatives of postmodernity, he found in modernity an incomplete project that we must continue to promote.

4.3. Christianity and Modernity

The relation of Christianity to Enlightenment modernity is divided and also varies by → denomination or confession. Rationalizing, a dominant feature of modernity, is the same as a demystification of the world (see M. → Weber), which was introduced, and has been promoted, by the Christian faith itself but which has now turned against it as science increasingly offers its own explanations. In one field after another → emancipation has been taking place from the tie to Christianity (see E. → Troeltsch, "Das Wesen des modernen Geistes" [The essence of the modern spirit, 1907]; → Secularization).

4.3.1. Protestantism

The special relation of → Protestantism to modernity is essentially determined by the fact that the autonomy sought by the Enlightenment rested on the overthrow by M. → Luther (1483-1546; → Luther's Theology) of the dependence of individual Christians on the official church (→ Hierarchy). The advocates of Enlightenment modernity themselves viewed the → Reformation as the historical prelude to modernity. At the same time, Protestantism failed to oppose modernity too strongly, being more often in danger of too broad an adjustment to it (→ Culture Protestantism; Liberal Theology). Accepting the scientific concept of modernity, Protestant theology undertook the critical examination of the texts of the Bible (from D. F. Strauss and L. Feuerbach to R. Bultmann's idea of → demythologizing; → Exegesis, Biblical), though without abandoning the claim made by the text that it demands from us a decision of → faith.

A new systematic approach like that of F. Wagner in 1990 still did not infer from the crisis of modernity that Christianity should define itself in opposition to it. Instead, the experience of modernity has been adopted into theological thinking with a view to achieving a new definition of Christian faith. We see here the expectation that Christianity and modernity, both in crisis, might mutually promote one another.

Yet a decided antimodernity did arise in Christianity at the end of the 19th century, especially in American fundamentalism, which clings to an understanding of the Bible as the direct → Word of God (→ Biblicism) and often arrives at views that stand opposed to the conclusions of science and history (→ Science and Theology).

4.3.2. Roman Catholicism

Unlike Protestantism, Roman → Catholicism reacted against the Enlightenment with radical repudiation, and Enlightenment modernity responded by seeing in it a hostile force resistant to progress (→ Conservatism). For many decades, with results still apparent today, Roman Catholicism insulated itself against modernity (→ Kulturkampf) and took disciplinary measures against modernist trends within the church (→ Anti-Modernist Oath). Strictly opposing the consciousness of modernity, it sought to preserve a particular life and consciousness of the faithful (→ Worldview).

At the same time, the demand of H. Küng (e.g., in Christ sein [On being a Christian, 1974]) for an unprejudiced openness to modernity perhaps expressed the self-understanding of many Roman Catholics and pointed the way to the future. As Küng saw it, the Christian answer to the challenge of the crisis of modernity is not to abandon modernity's hope of progress but to realize that this progress is not as secular modernity thinks of it, for it demands a → new self in the sense of the biblical message.

Bibliography: R. J. BERNSTEIN, The New Constellation: The Ethical-Political Horizons of Modernity/Postmodernity (Cambridge, Mass., 1992) • M. CALINESCU, Five Faces of Modernity: Modernism, Avant-Garde, Decadence, Kitsch, Postmodernism (Durham, N.C., 1987) • T. EAGLETON, The Illusions of Postmodernism (Oxford, 1996) • D. S. FERRIS, Silent Urns: Romanticism, Hellenism, Modernity (Stanford, Calif., 2000) • C. GEFFRÉ and J.-P. JOSSUA, The Debate on Modernity (London, 1992) • G. von GRÄVENITZ, ed., Konzepte der Moderne (Stuttgart, 1999) • C. E. GUNTON, The One, the Three, and the Many: God, Creation, and the Culture of Modernity (Cambridge, 1993) • J. HABERMAS, "Modernity: An Unfinished Project," Habermas and the Unfinished Project of Modernity: Critical Essays on "The Philosophical Discourse of Modernity" (ed. M. Passerin d'Entrèves and S. Benhabib; Cambridge, Mass., 1997) 38-58; idem, The New Conservatism: Cultural Criticism and the Historians' Debate (ed. S. W. Nicholsen; Cambridge, Mass., 1989); idem, The Philosophical Discourse of Modernity (Cambridge, Mass., 1987) • H. HOLLÄNDER and C. THOMSEN, eds., Besichtigung der Moderne. Bildende Kunst, Architektur, Musik, Literatur, Religion. Aspekte und Perspektiven (Cologne, 1987) • S. LASH, "Reflexive Modernization: The Aesthetic Dimension," Theory, Culture, and Society 10 (1993) 1-24 • Modernism/Modernity (Baltimore, 1994–) journal of the Modernist Studies Association • H. J. PIECHOTTA et al., eds., Die literarische Moderne in Europa (3 vols.; Opladen, 1994)

• H. Sedlmayr, *Verlust der Mitte: Die bildende Kunst des 19. und 20. Jahrhunderts als Symptom und Symbol der Zeit* (1th ed.; Salzburg, 1998) • S. Vietta, *Ästhetische Moderne in Europa. Grundzüge und Problemzusammenhänge seit der Romantik* (Munich, 1998) • F. Wagner, "Christentum und Moderne," *ZTK* 87 (1990) 124-44 • P. A. Ward, ed., *Baudelaire and the Poetics of Modernity* (Nashville, 2001) • W. Welsch, *Unsere postmoderne Moderne* (3d ed.; Weinheim, 1991).

JÜRGEN VIERING

Moldova

	1960	1980	2000
Population (1,000s):	3,004	4,010	4,458
Annual growth rate (%):	2.10	1.00	0.22

Area: 33,700 sq. km. (13,000 sq. mi.)

A.D. 2000

Population density: 132/sq. km. (343/sq. mi.)
Births / deaths: 2.29 / 1.85 per 100 population
Fertility rate: 1.80 per woman
Infant mortality rate: 24 per 1,000 live births
Life expectancy: 68.8 years (m: 65.0, f: 72.5)
Religious affiliation (%): Christians 74.1 (Orthodox 48.3, indigenous 19.5, Protestants 2.6, Roman Catholics 2.4, other Christians 1.4), nonreligious 15.9, Muslims 5.6, atheists 3.4, Jews 1.0.

1. General Situation
2. Religious Situation

1. General Situation

In June 1990 a "bridge of flowers" was formed between Moldovia and Romania, as all 12 crossing points across the long-closed border were opened. The former renamed itself Moldova, declaring its sovereignty on August 27, 1991. When the USSR was dissolved at the end of 1991, Moldova became an independent state but remained part of the → Commonwealth of Independent States (CIS), which all but the Baltic republics of the former USSR eventually joined (→ Soviet Union). Politically and economically, Moldova has continued to hover between post-Communist Romania and the CIS, and its religious history is still shaped by that tension.

Romanians, including Moldovans, see themselves as descendants of the ancient kingdom of Dacia, which Rome conquered in A.D. 106. After first having become Christian through → Byzantium as far back as the fourth century, the principalities of Moldovia and Walachia united as Romania

in 1859, but they remained under the Ottoman Empire until they were taken over by the Russians in 1878. In that process, Russia annexed southern Bessarabia, the area now referred to as Moldova. As late as 1897 it was referred to as the Siberia of the West, for it was isolated and backward, with a → literacy rate of only 16 percent.

The Moldovan language is virtually identical to Romanian, a Romance language written traditionally in the Latin script. In modern history language has been used as a tool of political and religious submission in the struggle for control of the area. The Orthodox churches and monasteries in Moldova were forced to conduct services in Russian (1781-82), and from 1944 to 1989 the Soviets required use of the Cyrillic alphabet in writing Moldovan.

Independent Moldova did not project a promising future to its citizens. During the 1990s its total population actually declined because so many Moldovans immigrated to Romania, where they were received as full citizens. The → Orthodox Church remained part of the Russian Patriarchate, and Russia, with its doctrine of protecting Russian nationals in the "near abroad" (i.e., the newly independent countries formerly part of the USSR), continued to assert its right to intervene. Economically, overall output in Moldova dropped by 40 percent during its first decade, and the average monthly salary of workers in 1998 was only 437 lei ($90), or 40 percent below the → poverty line.

2. Religious Situation

2.1. In 1850 the province of Bessarabia was already quite mixed religiously. There were hundreds of Orthodox churches serving Russians, Moldovans, and Orthodox schismatics, as well as 17 synagogues and 6 → Lutheran and 4 → Roman Catholic churches. In 1782 there had been 608 churches using only Russian and 417 using Moldovan. The Bessarabian church, organized in 1813 as the Kishinev Eparchy (i.e., → diocese), was made subordinate to the Moscow Patriarchate in 1820. As of 1912 it comprised 1,089 churches, 22 → monasteries (16 male, 6 female), 612 church schools for clergy children, a school for nuns, and a seminary. At its height in the late 19th century, six brotherhoods of laity had been organized, as well as a candle factory and branches of the → Orthodox Missionary Society (founded 1870) and the Imperial Orthodox Palestine Society (1882). In 1917 a Moldovan National Party called for → autocephaly of the Bessarabian church, but then the Paris Peace Conference (1919-20) affirmed Bessarabia's reunification with Romania.

When Moldova was occupied by the USSR in

1940 and made the Moldovian SSR in 1944, drastic Sovietization measures were introduced. In keeping with the basic antireligious policy, the Orthodox cathedral in the capital, Kishinev (now Chişinău), was turned into a central exhibition hall, 20 monasteries were closed, and hundreds of churches were left to fall into ruin. In his survey of the gradual reopening of Orthodox churches, Nathaniel Davis reports that for the 2.5 million Orthodox in Moldova, there were only 546 "working" churches in 1958, before the antireligion campaign under N. Khrushchev (1959-64) reduced the number to 223. By 1986 that number had declined further to only 198 churches open. Then came the changes signaled by M. Gorbachev's perestroika and the eventual independence of Moldova as state. In the short space of five years, the number of Orthodox churches in the Kishinev Eparchy jumped to 650.

2.2. The Evangelical Christians–Baptists and Pentecostals of Moldova have a short but fascinating history. In three independent instances in the early 20th century, persons linked to a family of Orthodox clergy and to a family of Molokans (Bible-centered Christians descending from so-called Spiritual Christian Russian peasants who refused to join the → Russian Orthodox Church in the 1600s) became convinced about believers' → baptism through their own studies of the Bible. Their number increased, and once ties had developed to existing churches in nearby Odessa, Ukraine, churches began being organized in 1908.

During the interwar years, when Moldova was part of the Kingdom of Romania, a union of Evangelical Christians and Baptists (ECB) was formed (1927) called the Bessarabian Union of ECB. It claimed 200 churches and a membership of 10,000 by 1939. Then came the occupation by the Soviets. The Kishinev pastors were arrested, and church buildings were converted into other uses.

Upon the resumption of church life as part of the Soviet Union in 1945, the Moscow union of ECBs sent a plenipotentiary to oversee the integration of the Moldovan ECBs into the union, including the joining of → Pentecostals after 1945. Pentecostals had emerged in Moldova in the 1930s, and two-thirds of them participated in the union with the ECB churches after 1945. Not until 1982 were they permitted to form their own union.

In 1945 there were only 88 ECB churches, with 3,085 adult members. By 1988 this number had increased to 104 registered churches, with 28 more awaiting registration. In addition, there were 7 autonomous congregations, plus 27 affiliated with the unregistered ECB union that had also emerged in Moldova at the time of the Khrushchev antireligion campaign.

When the USSR broke apart in 1991, the Moldovan Union of ECB became part of the Euro-Asiatic Federation of ECBs and in other ways cooperated with those church unions. The relationship with Romanian → Baptists, however, with whom they are closer linguistically, has not developed because of the minimal connections over the past century. Also, less than half of the ECB members in Moldova are ethnic Moldovans.

2.3. Although the present state of Moldova has also been more tolerant of religious diversity, there has been a shift toward greater control, as is true across the former USSR. In Trans-Dniestria, a region in eastern Moldova and southwestern Ukraine where a Slavic separatist movement, supported by the Russian army, has proclaimed a breakaway republic, two → Methodist congregations have repeatedly been refused registration since 1997. The local Methodist leader finally appealed for help to the Organization for Security and Cooperation in Europe. In this case Moldovan authorities argued in response that "the state is Orthodox, and no sectarians are allowed here — especially Methodists!" In another case in late 2001, police, working closely with a top official of the Tiraspol Orthodox diocese, threatened an unregistered Baptist congregation in Tiraspol with demolition of its meeting facility.

In a more politically related matter, the Bessarabian Orthodox Church of the Romanian Patriarchate, also known as the Church of the True Orthodox–Moldova, left the jurisdiction of the Moscow Patriarchate in 1997 and requested separate registration. When the government denied this request, the church appealed, eventually taking its case to the European Court of Human Rights, which ruled in its favor. In May 2002 the Moldovan Supreme Court supported the European court decision, ordering the Moldovan government to pay compensation of 15,000 lei (then worth $1,100). More recently, the leader of the Spiritual Organization of Muslims in Moldova, representing 3,000 faithful, lodged a complaint with the European court over the government's refusal to grant it the status of a registered faith (→ Islam). The Moldovan legislature began considering a new law on religion that would transfer the responsibility of registering faiths to the State Service for the Affairs of Cults, potentially making the process more transparent and less political.

Bibliography: N. Davis, *A Long Walk to Church: A Contemporary History of Russian Orthodoxy* (Boulder, Colo., 1995) • N. Dima, *From Moldavia to Moldova:*

The Soviet-Romanian Territorial Dispute (Boulder, Colo., 1991) • *Istoriia evangel'skikh Khristian–Baptistov v SSSR* (Moscow, 1989) • KESTON INSTITUTE, *Keston News Service* (Oxford, 1971-) • C. KING, *The Moldovans: Romania, Russia, and the Politics of Culture* (Stanford, Calif., 2000) • D. D. LAITIN, *Identity in Formation: The Russian-Speaking Populations in the Near Abroad* (Ithaca, N.Y., 1998) • W. SAWATSKY, *Soviet Evangelicals since World War II* (Scottdale, Pa., 1981).

WALTER SAWATSKY

Molinism

1. Theology of Molina
2. Debate about Grace

1. Theology of Molina

The term "Molinism" refers to theological systems like that of Spanish Jesuit Luis de Molina (1535-1600), who, in his *Concordia liberi arbitrii cum gratiae donis* (The harmony of free will with gifts of grace), highlighted the role of human cooperation over that of God's sovereignty in the salvific operation of divine grace.

The doctrine of grace as formulated by the Council of → Trent (1545-63) is open to interpretation. It clearly postulates a cooperation of divine → grace and the human will as constitutive to → salvation (→ Synergism), but it does not give theological precision to the postulate. In the last third of the 16th century there thus arose a debate about grace. Inflamed by Molina's *Concordia*, → Dominicans and → Jesuits struggled intensely over the issue for more than three centuries.

Tradition either could not or would not solve the problem of reconciling the particularity of eternal salvation with the universality of God's will to save (1 Tim. 2:4) except by either making salvation dependent on ourselves or by presupposing an inscrutable divine decree of → predestination. The Middle Ages made a fresh effort to ensure the preponderance of divine grace but without eliminating constitutive human cooperation.

1.1. Molina held that without grace, though under the general working of God that obtains for us even after the fall (→ Sin), we can achieve the theological cardinal → virtues of → faith, → hope, and → love on our own. The saving quality of such human acts depends on a prevenient grace that is, however, only sufficient *(gratia sufficiens)*; it becomes efficient to save us *(gratia efficiens)* only with our own cooperation and consent. Molina did not

advocate a particular predestination that depends on God alone.

1.2. This → Pelagian doctrine of grace is modified by Molina's assumption of "middle knowledge" *(scientia media)*. On the basis of his omniscience God allegedly knows all potential world orders with a "natural knowledge." Not only does God foreknow all the situations of the world order created by him and all free human decisions and reactions in this actually created world, but he also, with a "middle knowledge," knows all potential human reactions and decisions in all potential world orders and situations, even though these potentials might never exist or come to pass. With this knowledge God knows how each of us will act in each world. But since free decision regarding the actual world order and its concrete situations lies with God alone, Molina could attribute it solely to God's will that the particular world exists in which, for example, Peter uses his human → freedom positively for the attainment of salvation and Judas uses it for sinning. Molina thought that such a distinction protected both our own freedom for salvation or perdition and the freedom of God, who, by deciding on the actual world order, determines what decision we will in fact make in our freedom.

On the ground of these deliberations Molina confidently rejected the charge raised against him of Pelagianism. His theory, however, clashed with a countertheory developed by Domingo Báñez (1528-1604). Building on → Thomas Aquinas's teaching on grace (→ Thomism), Báñez sharply reduced human cooperation in achieving salvation by tracing it back to a grace that works physically *(gratia efficax, praemotio physica)*.

2. Debate about Grace

Already in the 1560s at the Collegium Romanum the Jesuit Francisco Toledo (1532-96) had espoused a synergistic doctrine of grace against the wishes of his own order, and 20 years later in Lyons the Jesuit Leonhard Lessius (1554-1623) had done the same over the protests of the Lyons faculty. Against this background it is understandable that Molina, whose work had overcome the first hurdle of the Spanish → Inquisition and was already being printed in 1588, should go over to the offensive when Báñez and the Mercedarian Francesco Zumel (1541-1607) were charged with Lutheranism (→ Luther's Theology) and there was a call for fresh examination of Molina's *Concordia* (→ Censorship).

Public disputations and an exchange of pamphlets and resolutions between the Dominicans and the Jesuits sharpened the conflict, and Clement VIII (1592-1605) took up the matter in Rome in 1597. A papal commission set up in 1597-1601 recommended the condemnation of 20 propositions of Molina (→ Curia; Teaching Office). In disputations in 1602-6 in which the pope participated, however, the Jesuit Robert → Bellarmine (1542-1621), with well-considered arguments, succeeded in bringing the teaching of the Dominicans under scrutiny as well and hence in achieving a balance in the argument.

Though the majority was against Molina, difficult substantive questions and political considerations prevented the pope from making a clear decision. In 1607 Paul V (1605-21) forbade further debate with his ruling that the doctrine of the Dominicans was not Calvinistic (→ Calvinism) and that of the Jesuits was not Pelagian. The complexity of the issues, however, meant that this prohibition was easily circumvented. Since the congruent middle positions of Bellarmine and Francisco Suárez (1548-1617) did not find acceptance in their order, the Jesuits soon came to be seen as Molinists. As the Lyons theologians had opposed Lessius, so in the 17th century the → Jansenists tried to defend the Augustinian doctrine of grace against the Pelagianism of the Jesuit Molinists (→ Augustine's Theology).

The controversies flared up again at various times in the 18th and 19th centuries, the latest after the promulgation of the encyclical *Aeterni Patris* (1879, DH 3135-40), when Jesuits (e.g., G. Schneemann) and Dominicans (e.g., M. A. Dummermuth) debated the accuracy of Molina's interpretation of Thomas.

→ Catholic Reform and Counterreformation; Catholicism (Roman); Justification; Reformation

Bibliography: Primary sources: A. J. FREDDOSO, trans., *On Divine Foreknowledge: Part IV of the Concordia* (Ithaca, N.Y., 1988) • L. DE MOLINA, *Concordia liberi arbitrii cum gratiae donis, divina praescientia, providentia, praedestinatione et reprobatione* (Lisbon, 1588; 2d ed., Antwerp, 1595; repr., Madrid, 1953).

Secondary works: W. S. ANGLIN, *Free Will and the Christian Faith* (Oxford, 1990) • D. BASINGER, W. HASKER, and E. DEKKER, eds., *Middle Knowledge: Theory and Applications* (New York, 1999) • J. BRODERICK, *The Origin of the Jesuits* (Chicago, 1997; orig. pub., 1940) • W. L. CRAIG, "'Lest Anyone Should Fall': A Middle Knowledge Perspective on Perseverance and Apostolic Warnings," *IJPR* 29 (1991) 65-74; idem, *The Problem of Divine Foreknowledge and Future Contingents from Aristotle to Suarez* (Leiden, 1988) • E. DEKKER, *Middle Knowledge* (Louvain, 2000) • R. DOUBLE, *The Nonreality of Free Will* (New York, 1991) • T. P. FLINT, *Divine Providence: The Molinist Account* (Ithaca, N.Y., 1998) • H. GAYRAUD, *Thomisme et Molinisme* (2 vols.; Toulouse, 1890-92) • B. HAMILTON, *Political Thought in Sixteenth-Century Spain* (Oxford, 1963) • W. HASKER, D. BASINGER, and E. DECKER, eds., *Middle Knowledge: Theory and Applications* (Frankfurt, 2000) • M. OCAÑA GARCÍA, *Luis de Molina (1535-1600)* (Madrid, 1995) • M. G. WHITE, *The Question of Free Will: A Holistic View* (Princeton, 1993).

MANFRED BIERSACK

Monarchianism → Christology; Trinity

Monarchy in Israel

1. Israelite Monarchies
2. Ideology and Theology of Monarchy
3. Ideas of the Kingdom of God
4. Messianic Expectations

1. Israelite Monarchies

There were various monarchies in ancient → Israel (§1). Israel itself was originally made up of → tribes, with monarchy not native to it. The monarchy was introduced and adopted only with further developments, dependent in part on the overall political situation in the Middle East. The main source for the history of monarchy in Israel is the OT (Judges; 1-2 Samuel; 1-2 Kings; 1-2 Chronicles; the Prophets). Light is also shed by contemporary annals and inscriptions (see *TGI* [3d ed.], *ANET*, and *TUAT* 1). We might refer as well to 1 Maccabees and Josephus *Ant.*

Purely episodic was the setting up of a Canaanite city monarchy at Shechem by Abimelech son of Jerubbaal (Judges 9), which had no basis in the tribal federation. It is an open question whether things were different when monarchy was ascribed to Gideon (8:22-23), as the reference in v. 22 to "the men of Israel" (RSV) might suggest.

Saul's monarchy (ca. 1012-1004 B.C.) was a military monarchy deriving from his function as charismatic leader of the host under pressure from foreign enemies — Moabites, Ammonites, Edomites, kings of Zobah, Amalekites, and especially the → Philistines (1 Sam. 14:47-48). The new institution was contested (chaps. 8–12). With Saul we find the first beginnings of a royal residence (Gibeah), a court, and a dynasty. Though Saul was of the tribe of Benjamin, he occasionally led the whole tribal army (Judah alone being sometimes absent). The Philistine wars destroyed his monarchy (chap. 31).

The monarchy of → David (ca. 1004-965) was a complex imperial construct that David himself created and that centered on himself. It included the city monarchies of Ziklag and → Jerusalem ("the city of David," 2 Sam. 5:6-7, etc.), the kingdoms of Judah and Israel (Saul's sphere of rule), and a number of more or less closely related vassal states. The kingdom of David was a territorial state on the scale of an ancient Near Eastern empire — "from the river of Egypt to the great river, the river Euphrates" (Gen. 15:18; also 1 Kgs. 4:21). It was held in balance by the person of David, with the beginnings of a domestic structure (court, administration, and army) but with no organic unity.

Solomon (965-926) was the first to set the kingdom on a firmer basis, but he lost much of David's empire. His policy of consolidation laid the foundations of a monarchically ruled state. He built the capital buildings with the → temple at Jerusalem (1 Kings 6–8) as the site of the state religion. He also strengthened dynastic rule (see the royal promise of 2 Sam. 7:11-16 and the royal ritual of Psalms 2; 72; 110).

The kingdom was wrecked by the claim to central government (1 Kings 12), with two small monarchies resulting from the split: Judah-Jerusalem in the south, Israel in the north. The 19 northern kings ruled until 722, when Israel fell before the attack of the Assyrians. Judah survived for more than a century longer because of its strong dynasty, its Solomonic institutions, and its favorable geographic situation. Altogether 19 kings and 1 queen directed the destiny of the small nation of Judah. Though it did not fall to the Assyrians in 701 (see Isa. 1:8), it was conquered by the Babylonians in 597 and 587.

Only in the Maccabean period did an independent monarchy emerge again. Beginning with Alexander Jannaeus (103-76), the → Hasmonaeans bore the title "king" until the coming of the Romans in 63 B.C.

2. Ideology and Theology of Monarchy
The introduction of monarchical structures aroused debate early as to their legitimacy. The fable of Jotham (Judg. 9:7-15) is an impressive indictment of monarchy. Discussion of the validity of monarchy (1 Sam. 8:10-18) reached a climax with the composition of the royal documents in the age of David and Solomon. The story in 2 Samuel 7 laid a foundation for the structure. The royal ritual shows how the system functioned. Essential elements were → anointing — a legal act of appointment to vassal status (probably of Egyptian origin), the giving of the throne name after the Egyptian model (see Isa.

9:6-7), enthronement at God's "right hand" (Psalm 110), and adoption as God's son (Psalm 2). An ideology of sacral monarchy developed in Judah, though not in the north, as far as we know, where older factors of charismatic leadership were important. A comparison between Psalm 72 and the royal law in Deut. 17:14-20 shows the difference.

The → prophets took a critical stance against both monarchies (including → Elijah, → Elisha, Micaiah son of Imlah, Amos, Hosea, Isaiah, Micah, Zephaniah, Jeremiah, and Ezekiel). The view is for the most part negative in the → Deuteronomistic history, as the kings are blamed for the disasters that befall Israel and Judah.

The Hasmonaean monarchy was not uncontested, being set up by popular resolve "forever," or "until a trustworthy prophet should arise" (1 Macc. 14:41).

3. Ideas of the Kingdom of God
The rise of a "God as King" theology, resting on ancient Near Eastern ideas of the divine king, was one of the most significant of all developments in Israel. It found its clearest expression in the so-called Zion tradition (Psalms 24; 93–99) and especially in the idea of the royal court (1 Kings 22; Isaiah 6; Ezekiel 1–3; note esp. the title $YHWH$ $Ṣ ĕbā ̂ôt$; → Yahweh). The theologoumenon of $YHWH$ mlk (Yahweh is King), which later scholarship associated with an enthronement festival (S. Mowinckel), became a confessional statement in various forms in hymns to Yahweh as King (Psalms 29; 47; 93–99). Scattered references (Num. 23:21; Deut. 33:5; Isa. 41:21; 43:15; 44:6; Zeph. 3:15; Ps. 5:2; 10:16; 145:1; 149:2, etc.) and ideas like the monarchy, kingdom, or royal rule of Yahweh (Ps. 22:28; 103:19; 145:11-13; 1 Chr. 29:11; Dan. 4:3, 34) show that the thought was widespread, even though it might not always be expressly developed.

4. Messianic Expectations
Inherent in the Judean royal ritual was the notion of Yahweh's anointed (*mašîaḥ*, whence Eng. "Messiah"; → Messianism) as God's enthroned vice-regent. Occupying contemporary theologians (note the royal psalms; → Historiography), this concept became a theme in Judean prophecy. A message of judgment might be pronounced against the Jerusalem court and king (Isaiah 7; Jeremiah 21–22; Ezekiel 17; 19, etc.), but a future king was promised in the context of a message of → salvation (Isa. 9:6-7; Mic. 5:2-5a; Amos 9:11-15; Jer. 23:5-8; Ezek. 34:11-31; 37:21-28, etc. [with doubts at times about the authenticity]). The existing monarchy was ignored, and attention

focused on the office of the anointed one, with all that it implied (most clearly stated in Isa. 9:6-7).

The thought of David redivivus gave color to the picture (see Mic. 5:2-5a). With the collapse of the monarchy, the ongoing → hope of fulfillment of the dynastic → promise (note Nathan's prophecy to David in 2 Samuel 7) became messianic expectation. This hope, too, might be disappointed (see Haggai 2 and Zechariah 4), and it underwent considerable prophetic modification. In Deutero-Isaiah (→ Isaiah, Book of, 3) the Persian king Cyrus II the Great (558-529 B.C.) can be called the anointed of Yahweh (Isa. 45:1).

In Haggai and Zechariah the mention of Zerubbabel, of the line of David, calls for notice. Zechariah revises the idea through mention of a doubled messianic expectation ("two anointed ones," 4:14; cf. chap. 6). Ezekiel (or his school) revives the idea of a tribal head, or prince (nāśî', Ezek. 34:11; 37:25). In the late Deutero-Zechariah David is contrasted with the world emperor Alexander the Great (336-323 B.C.; see Zech. 9:9). Messianic expectation became a fixed part of early Jewish → eschatology.

→ Ark of the Covenant

Bibliography: W. H. BARNES, Studies in the Chronology of the Divided Monarchy of Israel (Atlanta, 1991) • J. CAMPONOVO, Königtum, Königsherrschaft und Reich Gottes in den frühjüdischen Schriften (Fribourg, 1984) • F. CRÜSEMANN, Der Widerstand gegen das Königtum (Neukirchen, 1978) • W. DIETRICH, Die frühe Königszeit in Israel. 10. Jahrhundert v. Chr. (Stuttgart, 1997) • H. FRANKFORT, Kingship and the Gods: A Study of Ancient Near Eastern Religion as the Integration of Society and Nature (Chicago, 1984; orig. pub., 1948) • V. FRITZ and P. R. DAVIES, eds., The Origins of the Ancient Israelite States (Sheffield, 1996) • M. GÖRG, Gott-König-Reden in Israel und Ägypten (Stuttgart, 1975) • B. HALPERN, The Constitution of the Monarchy in Israel (Chico, Calif., 1981) • T. N. D. METTINGER, In Search of God (Philadelphia, 1988); idem, King and Messiah (Lund, 1976) • S. MOWINCKEL, He That Cometh (Oxford, 1956) • H. M. NIEMANN, Herrschaft, Königtum und Staat. Skizzen zur soziokulturellen Entwicklung im monarchischen Israel (Tübingen, 1993) • J. J. M. ROBERTS, "In Defense of the Monarchy: The Contribution of Israelite Kingship to Biblical Theology," Ancient Israelite Religion (ed. P. Miller et al.; Philadelphia, 1987) 377-96 • A. SCHOORS, Die Königreiche Israel und Juda im 8. und 7. Jahrhundert v. Chr. Die assyrische Krise (Stuttgart, 1998) • K. SEYBOLD, Das davidische Königtum im Zeugnis der Propheten (Göttingen, 1972) • S. TALMON, King, Cult, and Calender in Ancient Israel (Jerusalem, 1986) • W. I. TOEWS, Monarchy and Religious Institution in Israel under Jeroboam I (Atlanta, 1993) • T. VEIJOLA, Die ewige Dynastie. David und die Entstehung seiner Dynastie nach der deuteronomistischen Darstellung (Helsinki, 1975) • E. ZENGER, "Herrschaft Gottes / Reich Gottes," TRE 15.176-89. See also the bibliography in "Israel 1."

KLAUS SEYBOLD

Monastery

1. Term
2. Development
3. Architecture
4. Function
5. Legal Status
6. New Trends

1. Term

There are monasteries not only in Christianity but also in → Buddhism, → Taoism, → Jainism, and Islamic → Sufism.

The monastery separates monks and nuns from the world (→ Monasticism). After they have taken their → vows, it opens up for them an ongoing, secluded monastic life of either → contemplation or action within the rules of the order, the aim being a life that is holy and well-pleasing to God in fulfillment of the so-called counsels of perfection, or evangelical counsels (i.e., → poverty, chastity, and → obedience).

2. Development

In the → early church → anchorites (from Gk. anachōreō, "separate oneself, withdraw") withdrew from the world and lived a solitary life, seeking by means of → asceticism to lead a life of dedication to God in huts and caves. This type of monasticism, illustrated by hermits and → stylites, or pillar saints, never completely died out.

Cenobitic (Gk. koinobios, "living in a community") monasticism is traced back to Pachomius (d. 346), who founded his first monastery in Egypt in about 320. Eastern monks (→ Orthodox Church), who mostly follow the rule of Basil of Caesarea (ca. 330-79), built cenobitic establishments, or cenobies, in cities (esp. → Byzantium and → Jerusalem) and isolated places. Monastic villages, cities, and even provinces (Thebais in Egypt) and a monastic republic (Mount → Athos) served their self-sufficient lifestyle. Within the delimiting and protective walls a set of buildings stood alone with at least an entrance gate, a church, cells for living, a common room, and a council chamber. In Syria, with its strict division between solitary and communal monasticism, the architecture ministered more to the holy and to needs of pilgrims than to the common life of the monks (e.g., the Qal'at Sim'ān, or "mansion of Simeon," the huge edifice near Aleppo built in honor of Simeon Stylites).

In the West monks first lived in individual cells that, with walls around them, were like kraals (Tours, ca. 400) or were grouped to form a monastic community (Lérins, a Cistercian monastery founded ca. 410). Irish monks for the most part opted for the solitary life. Only with the rule of → Benedict of Nursia (ca. 480-ca. 547) did a common life in monasteries become the prevailing monastic lifestyle. The detailed instructions for the → Benedictines' daily program are appropriate to a life in community. The *Rule* (66.6-7) provides for most of the rooms that would be found in the later monastery.

The rule of Basil allowed for combined monasteries of monks and nuns. Byzantium forbade this arrangement in the 9th century, but such monasteries remained a normal feature in Armenia, Palestine, and Egypt up to the 14th century. They could be found in the West from the 6th to the 9th century and might often be under the rule of an abbess (→ Abbot, Abbess). They reappeared in the 12th century in the early years of the Premonstratensian order (→ Religious Orders and Congregations), as well as in the orders of Fontevrault (abbey founded 1100), Sempringham (established early 1100s), and the Bridgettines (approved 1370).

3. Architecture

The Western monastery in its developed form followed the Carolingian plan of the St. Gallen monastery, founded in about 719 on the site of the hermitage of St. Gall (d. ca. 650). According to this ideal plan, the monastery was a kind of polis of impressive rationality and perfection. There were four main divisions. In the center was the church, with the *claustrum* (enclosure) adjoining, the *dormitorium* to the east, the *refectorium* (dining hall) to the south, and the *cellarium* (storeroom) to the west, all connected by cross passages. As yet there was no chapter house.

The *claustrum*, a kind of monastery within the monastery, was reserved for the monks alone. Another area to the north of the church contained a building for prominent guests, the school, the abbot's house, and adjoining buildings. In the baroque period this area developed into the prelate's court. The area to the east of the church contained the hospital and novices' quarters, while to the south and

west were service buildings, stables, workshops, and gardens. The whole design was a model of an autonomous organism.

3.1. Like no other, the Benedictine monastery of → Cluny in the 11th and 12th centuries influenced monastic lifestyle and architecture.

The architecture of the → Cistercians, who, unlike the Cluniacs, aimed afresh at an authentic interpretation of the Benedictine Rule in true asceticism, was impressively uniform. The monastery was usually located in a desolate place at the entrance to a valley and was completely surrounded by a wall. It was built to last, stern and simple, according to architectural rules laid down by the General Chapter. Adornment on the capitals and in the windows was at first totally forbidden, and later mostly so. The aim was to keep to the schema set forth in the rule. The church had no tower, only a place for the little → bells. It served simply as a monastery church and was usually situated on an elevated site. Around the cloister in the east, the monk's choir was followed by the more richly decorated colonnade and the monk's chamber; above, in the upper story, was the monk's dormitory. In the west wing was the *cellarium*, along with the refectory and dormitory for the conversi, or lay brothers. In the south was the monks' refectory, with well, kitchen, and warming room. The pattern may be seen excellently at surviving monasteries in France (Fontenay [Côte d'Or]) and Germany (Maulbronn [Württemberg] and Eberbach [Rhinegau]).

3.2. The Carthusians, founded in 1084 at La Grande Chartreuse, near Grenoble, developed their own style. They aimed to combine the hermit life with the cenobitic. They were to have only 12 monks with a prior (later extended to 24). Guigo I (1083-1136), fifth prior of the Grande Chartreuse, developed the ideal charterhouse in his rule *Consuetudines domus Carthusiae* (1127). There were three functionally related living areas: the cloister, with 12 individual houses for the monks; the common rooms, including refectory, chapter house, library, and church, along with the prior's cell; and the administrative court. The individual houses had three rooms: a heated anteroom, the sparsely furnished cell, and a chamber. They constituted small residences with gardens.

3.3. In contrast to the older architecture was the urban architecture of the → Dominicans and → Franciscans. Their monasteries would usually be on the city outskirts close to the walls, and they might sometimes also have a defensive function. The buildings were adapted to the sites. Usually they followed the Benedictine pattern, though the constitution and lifestyle of the orders made some structures superfluous (e.g., the abbot's house, administrative court, or separate buildings for priests and laity). The introduction of individual cells in the late 14th and 15th centuries was an innovation with implications for both architecture and living conditions. This development resulted architecturally in the two-storied cloisters, though the character of the monasteries also changed.

To a large extent the monasteries and their buildings and furnishings were civil foundations. Because of the work of the orders in → preaching, → pastoral care, and care for the sick, the churches and even the community rooms assumed a public or semipublic character. The mendicant churches were preaching stations and were favored as burial sites by patricians. The rooms were furnished with paintings and statues with subjects chosen from → salvation history or the history of the order. The refectories carried depictions of the Last Supper, such as the famous *Last Supper* (1495-98) by Leonardo da Vinci (1452-1519) at the Santa Maria delle Grazie church in Milan. Fra Angelico (d. 1455) did all the paintings for the Dominican monastery San Marco in Florence.

3.4. The great princely → baroque abbeys in Bavaria, Swabia, Austria, and Switzerland represent as a group another architectural highpoint. They are normally symmetrical with two wings (e.g., the Benedictine abbey at Einsiedeln). Symbolizing perfection, they seek to be actualizations of the city of God on earth (e.g., Weingarten Abbey, near Ravensburg). Like castles, with a secular architectural orientation, they reflect the political situation and economic power of the monasteries, but they were also significant as centers of research and scholarship. They included gardens, reception rooms, orangeries, summer cottages, museums, and art galleries.

3.5. Baroque abbeys were also built in Italy, Spain, and Portugal. In Italy with its many cities, landowning monasteries were less common and never acquired political influence. In Spain and Portugal the link to the Crown was decisive from an early period. Many monasteries were fortresses and residences, within which kings built their palaces. The classic example is the Escorial (1563-84), a vast structure northwest of Madrid that has served as the burying ground of almost all Spanish kings.

Building continued in the centuries that followed. A modern example of successful monastic architecture is the Dominican La Tourette, near Lyons, France, built in 1960 by Le Corbusier (1887-1965).

4. Function

In the course of church history monasteries have had different functions and significance, varying with time, place, and order. In different ways they have fulfilled their general task of doing God's work.

We can say the same regarding their architecture. None of the great orders laid down specific rules; the monasteries built were functional, serving their respective rules and reflecting the lifestyle of the orders.

4.1. Especially in the West the monasteries from an early time, and especially before the founding of → cities, were crystallization points of social life. They opened up and planned new areas. They were also bases for → mission, political institutions, imperial and royal residences, care centers for the nobility, burial sites for founders and supporters, places of pilgrimage, and hospices for pilgrims, guests, the poor, and the sick. Especially from the land they provided many services for the local population.

We can hardly overestimate the importance of the monasteries as centers of → culture, scholarship, and → education. Almost exclusively we owe to them the handing down of the culture of antiquity. In the early → Middle Ages literacy was inseparably linked to them. Scholars were trained in their schools. They copied MSS, which were preserved in their libraries. They creatively nurtured → liturgy and → church music.

4.2. The monasteries were and are also important economically. The monks and nuns, often of noble birth, brought considerable property to them. Endowments and bequests increased their possessions in both land and money. Besides contributing to agriculture, the residents were skilled in crafts and made important innovations in the history of crafts and → technology. As profitable, self-standing concerns, the monasteries looked after their own tenants and entered into various economic relations with their neighbors.

5. Legal Status

The legal position of the monasteries has varied across the years. A monastery typically was under the local diocesan bishop, but there were many attempts to break free of this relation (→ Exemption).

The 1917 → CIC dealt with monasteries in the section "Government of Religious" (pt. 3, chap. 6, cans. 487-537). In the 1983 CIC they are covered in book 2, part 3, "Institutes of Consecrated Life and Societies of Apostolic Life." The canon law offers norms for the organization of monastic communities, the conduct of their members, their direction, and their relation to other forms of church → authority.

6. New Trends

In missionary lands outside Europe monasteries have been founded since the end of the 19th century, though Benedictines from Portugal came to Brazil in the 16th century. In 1973 there were 91 monasteries in Latin America, 60 in Africa, and 53 in Asia. The → Roman Catholic Church is promoting the growth of monastic communities, believing that the reception of Christian life into the native culture can become modeled in the contemplative life (→ Acculturation; Culture and Christianity).

Since → Vatican II there has been lively discussion of monastic life, of the place of the contemplative life in the church, of active participation in the apostolic task as distinct from a symbolic life lived according to the evangelical counsels, and of new forms of economic self-sufficiency and the independent shaping of community life. By way of the ancient rule of hospitality, the monasteries have opened their doors to temporary visits, in this way rendering meaningful service by offering a share in their life.

In Reformation countries theological criticism of monasticism and the desire to use monastic possessions more effectively led to the almost complete dissolution of the older monasteries, many of them being converted into either schools or hospitals. More recently, Protestant → communities have arisen that are ecumenically oriented, in their community life harking back to monastic forms of life and architecture.

→ Christian Art; Church Architecture

Bibliography: M. ANSTETT-JANSSEN, *Maulbronn Monastery* (Munich, 1999) • E. BADSTÜBNER, *Klosterkirchen im Mittelalter. Die Baukunst der Reformorder* (2d ed.; Munich, 1985) • W. BRAUNFELS, *Monasteries of Western Europe: The Architecture of the Orders* (London, 1993) • J. T. CLAPPI, "An Urban Benedictine Monastery: Boston, Massachusetts" (Thesis, Bristol, R.I., 1995) • P. J. GREENE, *Medieval Monasteries* (Leicester, 1994) • Y. HIRSCHFELD, *The Judean Desert Monasteries in the Byzantine Period* (New Haven, 1992) • J. KAMIL, *The Monastery of St. Catherine in Sinai: History and Guide* (Cairo, 1991) • M. W. MCCLELLAN, *Monasticism in Egypt: Images and Words of the Desert Fathers* (Cairo, 1998) • T. MAUDE, *Guided by a Stone-Mason: The Cathedrals, Abbeys, and Churches of Britain Unveiled* (London, 1997) • J. OETGEN, *Mission to America: A History of St. Vincent Archabbey, the First Benedictine Monastery in the United States* (Washington, D.C., 2000) •
C. PLATT, *The Abbeys and Priories of Medieval England* (New York, 1984).

JOHANNES SCHILLING

Monasticism

1. Definition, Range

In the history and sociology of religion (→ History of Religion; Sociology of Religion), the term "monasticism" is used to refer to the form of life involving separation from most of the members of a → religion for → asceticism and → prayer, with a view to achieving religious → perfection. We find it in almost all the higher religions — that is, besides Christianity, in → Jainism; all forms of → Buddhism, including Lamaism (→ Tibetan Religions) and → Zen Buddhism; → Taoism; and → Islam (among the dervishes) — though not in → Judaism except for a short period with the Essenes in Palestine and the Therapeutae in Egypt (→ Qumran). In most religions monasticism is predominantly a male phenomenon, but in Lamaism and especially in Christianity, particularly in the West, there is an important tradition of monasticism among women.

2. Christian Monasticism

As compared to monasticism in general, the characteristic feature of Christian monasticism is that this form of life is understood as full → discipleship of Jesus and is traced back to the NT. In about 900 the triad of → poverty, chastity, and → obedience (the "evangelical counsels") became seen as traits defining the basis of the religious life (→ Sermon on the Mount 4), and personal commitment developed into → vows. In pursuit of these ideal traits various forms of premonastic asceticism preceded monasticism itself, especially the itinerant asceticism of the hinterland of Syria and Palestine and the congregational asceticism of widows, virgins, and male ascetics (i.e., family asceticism).

We can speak of monasticism only when ascetics separated themselves from other Christians and formed their own world outside the → congregation. Nor can we apply the term "monasticism" to all further developments. Not all → religious orders are monastic in the true sense, for in some cases new forms of life and new goals have arisen that differ from the original aim of religious perfection (see 5.2 and 5.3).

3. Rise

3.1. *Motives*

The transition to asceticism outside the congregation took place in the second half of the third century A.D. It did not simply derive from earlier forms but may be explained by the changed situation in the church (→ Early Church). The tightening organization of the congregations under → bishops left increasingly less room for lifestyles that were not oriented to the functioning of the whole and could not be integrated into the common order, while the greater numerical and organizational strength of the churches now permitted individuals and groups to separate. The trend toward a mass church, which became visible in the third century, meant that the church was no longer in opposition to the world, as it had been since the beginning. Now in fact the church increasingly seemed to be part of the world, from which one had to withdraw (→ Sacred and Profane) if one was really to follow Christ (→ Perfection).

We also must not undervalue the pessimistic attitude (→ Optimism and Pessimism) to → society and its orders that was widespread in many social, religious, and philosophical forms in late antiquity, which could make common cause with the Christian urge to flee the world. Whether monastic organizations in non-Christian religions (e.g., the Therapeutae or the Qumran community) and → Greek philosophy had any direct influence is questionable, though there can be no doubt as to the importance of philosophical theories for the theology of monasticism. Of decisive significance finally was the person of the father of monasticism, Anthony (see 3.2.1), along with his biography, the *Vita Antonii* of → Athanasius (ca. 297-373; see 3.2.3).

3.2. *Egyptian Beginnings*

Monasticism had its beginnings in Egypt in the two main types: anchoritic, or eremitic (from Gk. *anachōreō*, "separate oneself, withdraw," and *erēmos*, "desert"), and cenobitic (Gk. *koinobios*, "living in a community," from *koinos bios*, "common life").

3.2.1. *Anchorites*

Withdrawal from the congregations led the Egyptian ascetics — mostly men, but also some women — into the desert. Not the first of these, but the most important for his influence and later impact, was Anthony (251?-356). Each hermit lived alone in ascetic style, practicing sexual abstinence, → fasting, and mortifications of various kinds, prayed constantly, and engaged in light → work, with a view to warding off all external influences and demonic passions (→ Demons) and achieving perfect → penitence and discipleship. Isolation was not total, for loose eremitic communities came into being (many between Cairo and Alexandria, including in the Nitrian Desert and at Scete and Kellia). In these communities practical needs were regulated, and weekly services were held when possible.

Most important, these groups were clustered around a spiritual father (Aram. *abba*) or mother (Gk. *amma*), who instructed their "children" and offered → pastoral care until their charges attained to the spiritual ripeness of a *bios angelikos* (angelic-type life). The spiritual directions of these "parents" took literary form in the *Apophthegmata Patrum* (Sayings of the Desert Fathers).

3.2.2. *Cenobites*

The cenobitic style of monasticism arose about 320, particularly under Pachomius (ca. 290-346). The new feature was more, and more highly valued, common life. A walled compound, the → monastery, replaced the looser colony, and an → abbot with unrestricted lifelong → authority replaced the more informal spiritual leader. Following a common rule replaced the emphasis on individual spiritual development. Thus there developed a uniform lifestyle with common meals, set → hours of prayer, and prescribed dress. Light work was replaced by obligatory group work, with an allocation of tasks according to the needs of the whole community. Individuals no longer handled the minimum resources they needed themselves, for → property belonged now to the monastery, which allowed members to renounce all their possessions. Instead of an individual pursuit of the highest possible ascetic achievement, unconditional obedience became the norm. Reception into the community was also regulated.

A motive force behind the change might well have been the experience that the anchorite ideal was beyond the reach of most of those who attempted it, along with the insight that human society is not just a means to individual perfection but also the appropriate sphere for spiritually perfected Christians. The monastery was to realize the ideal of the → primitive Christian community of Acts 4:32-35. → Koinonia became a key concept for the monastic life.

Pachomius founded several monasteries with hundreds of monks as members (first at Tabennisi, on the banks of the Nile in Upper Egypt; then a second at Pabau, near Thebes; ultimately, seven more). Two cloisters for women developed under the leadership of his sister. Around 400 these institutions fell victim to their numbers and wealth. Yet new cenobitic foundations followed, such as the White Monastery of Athribis, where Shenoute became the superior in about 388. Monasticism became the most powerful force in the Egyptian church. It still has an important role in the → Coptic Orthodox Church, enjoying recently a definite renaissance.

3.2.3. Spread

Egyptian monasticism in both its forms spread to all areas of Christianity through personal acquaintance (esp. mass pilgrimages to Egypt and the migration of Egyptian monks) and literary testimonies (esp. Palladius's *Historia Lausiaca*, Athanasius's *Vita Antonii*, the *Historia monachorum in Aegypto* [ET *The Lives of the Desert Fathers*], the *Apophthegmata Patrum*, and the rule of Pachomius). Not all early monasticism, however, was an offshoot of that of Egypt. The Egyptian influence encountered many different regional situations and traditions, and many different types of monasticism resulted.

4. Eastern Monasticism
4.1. *Palestine*
The eremitic monasticism of Egypt had a direct influence on Palestine, where notables such as Sil-

vanus, Hilarion of Gaza, and Epiphanius of Salamis built monasteries. The desert around Jerusalem, however, became the site of a monasticism from Asia Minor that developed into the lavra type of community, midway between the eremitic and cenobitic (→ Monastery 2). It consisted of a group of anchorites who lived in separate huts but who were subject to a single abbot. Chariton built the first such monastery at Pharan, a few miles outside the city.

Important monasteries and lavras arose in the fifth century, notably the large Mar Saba lavra. Built into the rock overlooking the Kidron Valley east of Bethlehem, it became a center of spiritual, liturgical, and theological life for the whole Christian East. It was founded by Sabas (439-532) in 478; the theologian → John of Damascus (ca. 655-ca. 750) became a monk there in about 725.

Jerusalem had its own development, shaped by its position as a place of → pilgrimage and the resultant internationalism. Egyptian influence predominated, but it was linked to Western tradition, for the most important houses were founded by Christian women from → Rome (Melania the Elder, Melania the Younger, and Paula [in Bethlehem], in each case with houses both for women and for men). The significant part that theologians like → Jerome (ca. 345-420; → Church Fathers) and Rufinus of Aquileia (ca. 345-410) played here made these monasteries centers of scholarship and theological debate. Like all the early Palestinian foundations, they eventually became Byzantine (see 4.6).

Western monasteries were constantly founded at the holy sites, and most Western orders established their own houses. The → Oriental Orthodox churches also founded their own communities, so that to this day Palestine has the greatest variety of monastic forms in the Christian world.

4.2. *Syria*
Premonastic asceticism played a special part in Syria, which accounts for the tendency toward extremes that characterized Syrian monasticism. The transition to monastic asceticism seems at first to have been made independently, but then we find Egyptian influence, especially in the cenobitic sphere. Whether and how far Persian and → Manichaean influences were also at work is debated.

The first stage was anchoritic. In many cases it manifested special ascetic achievements, such as going without sleep for long periods, being walled up, and lifelong living on pillars (esp. Simeon Stylites [ca. 390-459]; → Stylites). At the end, cenobitic monasticism and mixed forms prevailed.

In every form, even the most radical, early Syrian

monasticism displayed missionary ardor (→ Mission); the monasteries also engaged in diaconal activities. Its ideals were spread beyond Syria by John → Chrysostom (ca. 347-407). From Syria fanned out the barely tolerated → Acoemetae ("those who do not sleep"), who demanded a renunciation of sleep in favor of unceasing prayer, and the ultimately condemned Messalians, or Euchites ("those who pray"), who prescribed asceticism and constant prayer as a means to expel the demon that dwells in all of us and to attain to the palpable presence of God.

4.3. *Asia Minor*

The start of monasticism in Asia Minor was the movement initiated by Eustathius (ca. 300-after 377), bishop of Sebaste in Pontus. The extreme program of this group, which called for the complete rejection of → marriage and property and was condemned at the Council of Gangra in Paphlagonia around 341, caused church-recognized monasticism to draw a clear line against such imbalance.

A key figure in this regard was Basil of Caesarea (ca. 330-79; → Cappadocian Fathers), who under Egyptian and Syrian influence set up monasteries in Pontus and Caesarea. With these organizations and the injunctions ("rules") that he composed for them, Basil laid the foundations of all cenobitic monasticism in the → Orthodox Church. Basil would accept only the cenobitic form, for he believed that true Christian living is possible only in community, where we find the help we need by complementing each others' gifts of → grace and through the fellowship of love.

The bedrock of fellowship is perfect obedience to the leader (*proestōs* [masc.] or *proestōsa* [fem.]), who is to be the spiritual father or mother, the teacher and physician of the soul of the brothers or sisters. As a therapeutic tool Basil developed → confession of sin. For monastic life he prescribed a fixed rhythm of prayer, Bible reading, common worship, and → work. Pursuing his ideal, Basil established a monastery in his own city and allotted to it social tasks on behalf of both church and society (including hospital, school, and relief of the poor).

4.4. *Constantinople*

Toward the end of the fourth century, monasticism came into and around Constantinople (→ Byzantium), and new foundations followed constantly in the city until the collapse of the empire in 1453. Most important was the Studios monastery, with its reforming of cenobitic life along the lines of a strict monarchical community (esp. under Theodore of Studios [d. 816]).

The program of Studios became the basis for the foundation in 961 of the first monastery at Mount → Athos, later known as the Great Lavra (a cenobitic institution, in spite of its name), which marked the beginning of the rise of Athos as a center of Orthodox monasticism. Athos, a monastic republic, contained cenobitic features, but they quickly became less significant. → Hesychasm, which flourished on Athos in the 13th and 14th centuries, gave spiritual expression to the upsurge of the anchorite ideal.

4.5. *Balkans and Russia*

With the coming of Christianity, monasticism also entered the Slavic Balkans and Russia. The strictly cenobitic cave monastery at Kiev came into being in about 1050 under the influence of Athos. The Mongol hoard destroyed most Russian monasteries in the 13th century. The flight of many monks and restoration in the 14th century led to new monastic regions: the wilder parts of northern Russia and the area around Moscow (e.g., the Trinity Monastery). Here we find cenobitic, eremitic, and mixed forms alongside one another; Joseph of Volokolamsk (d. 1515) represented the cenobitic form, Nil Sorsky (d. 1508) the eremitic.

→ Secularization in the 18th century reduced the number of Russian monasteries considerably. The 19th century, however, brought a new upsurge (e.g., the Optina Pustyn monastery; → Starets). The 1917 → revolution left only a few monasteries intact, which were put under strict state control. The Communist collapse opened the door to new developments.

4.6. *Relations to Church and Society*

4.6.1. *Monasticism and the Church*

The importance of monasticism made it imperative to clarify its position in the organization of the church. The Council of → Chalcedon (cans. 4 and 8) placed monasteries under the local bishops. The legislation of Justinian I (527-65) strengthened church integration by allowing only the cenobitic and the lavra as acceptable monastic forms. Yet the coexistence of the cenobitic and the anchorite types, often in extreme form, as well as mixed monastic types, persisted throughout the history of Byzantine and Slavic Christianity (→ Orthodoxy 3). Integration was ever only partial. Those who seek spiritual perfection do not bow easily to church authority. Variety also reigns among the cenobitic. They orient themselves to the "rule" of Basil, but the charter (typicon) of each monastery does so in its own way. There are no orders as such, only groups of monasteries under common leadership.

4.6.2. *Basic Orientation*

Overall, the orientation of Orthodox monasticism is

→ contemplative. If it plays any role outside the monasteries, it is that of pastoral care, for which it seems to possess greater spiritual authority than the regular church offices (e.g., Simeon the New Theologian, very prominent in Byzantium as a mystical writer). Where social engagement does occur, it is not in the hands of the monks or nuns. Eastern monasticism never had nor sought the charitable and cultural significance that monasticism had in the West.

5. Western Monasticism

In the West, too, monasticism developed out of congregational asceticism, doing so in the second half of the fourth century. The influence of Eastern monasticism was decisive. We find anchoritic forms (wandering ascetics and hermits), but mostly cenobitic. From the outset, monasticism in the West took on specific features. Aristocratic circles played a great part (esp. in Rome and Gaul), so that there was a link to education and → culture. After the collapse of the → Roman Empire in the West, monasticism thus became the natural guardian of this legacy.

Bishops and monasteries were often closely linked. Bishops spread the monastic ideal and founded monasteries. Often they themselves were monks and associated their → basilicas with cloisters. As a result, they adopted a monastic lifestyle for clergy (with → celibacy and canonical life), and monasticism in turn was integrated into the church. It stood in the church's service, changing with the church's needs and having less of a world-denying, contemplative character than it did in the East.

5.1. Organization and Reform

5.1.1. Forms and Rules

Here again we find many different regions of monasticism at first, each with their own characteristics (Italy; southeast Gaul: the Rhone Valley and Lérins; northwest Gaul: Tours; Ireland, etc.). Of special importance for all Western monasticism were the theories and organizational forms developed by → Augustine (354-430; → Augustine's Theology) in North Africa. His rule (there are several, and authorship is disputed) views the monastery as a fellowship of love *(caritas)* grounded in God and oriented to him. This principle governs the common life of monks and nuns. In this spirit Augustine founded not only a lay fellowship of the traditional kind but also, as bishop, a monastic house for clergy. In this way he linked the monastic ideal to the church's ministry (→ Augustinians).

In the fifth and sixth centuries many different rules emerged. By a long process that came to completion only in the tenth century, one of these rules emerged as the standard for all monasticism in the West, namely, the *Rule* of → Benedict of Nursia (ca. 480-ca. 547; → Benedictines). Thanks to the organizational stability given by the monks' permanent attachment to a place *(stabilitas loci)* and a fixed → hierarchical order, and thanks also to the high value accorded to common prayer (the monastic hours) and → work during the day *(ora et labora)*, the Benedictine houses were a constant factor during the Völkerwanderung (or great migration of Germanic peoples), serving as guardians of culture for the emerging medieval world (esp. in agriculture, education, and the transmission of texts).

5.1.2. Reform Movements

The resulting role of monasteries in public life led to a secularizing that provoked reactions consistent with the general tendency to reduce integration into state and society (whence the reforms of → Gregory VII; → Church and State; Middle Ages). In the 10th and 11th centuries came the monastic reform movement of → Cluny and other centers such as Gorze, Hirsau, and Fruttuaria. Then in the 11th century new communities arose that tried to incorporate eremitic ideals, which had been only marginally practiced in the West. More loosely associated eremitic settlements were founded, such as the Camaldolese (Romuald of Ravenna [ca. 950-1027]) and the Carthusians (Bruno of Cologne [ca. 1032-1101]), as well as houses that as a whole chose the way of isolation and radical → poverty. The most important fruit of this revival was the order that dominated monastic life in the 12th century, the → Cistercians, who saw themselves as the true successors of Benedict.

New in this whole development from the 10th to the 12th centuries was not only the tremendous growth of monasticism but the fact that the reforms and new foundations brought fixed unions of houses with a common lifestyle and leadership. On the one hand, this development broke up the unity of monasticism in the West; on the other, it fostered the emergence of orders.

5.2. Differences in Monasticism

Monastic differentiation increased with the emergence of new types of fellowships that diverged in many respects from the traditional pattern.

1. In the spirit of Gregorian reform the canons regular and canonesses regular combined a canonical life with monastic elements under rule on the basis of the injunctions of Augustine. Two such groups were the Augustinian Canons (11th cent.) and the Premonstratensians (12th cent.).
2. Orders of knights were founded in connection with the → Crusades.

3. In the 13th century came the mendicant orders (e.g., the → Dominicans, → Franciscans, Carmelites, and Augustinian Hermits), who had no fixed location and were attached to no single house but to the order as such. They called their houses convents rather than monasteries. These new city orders, which were better adjusted to the development of city life and the new mobility of late medieval society (→ Middle Ages 1.4), became more prominent than traditional monasticism, which was located far from centers of population.

4. Another movement was that of the → Beguines.

5. As church life declined in the 14th and 15th centuries, so did monasticism, and a fresh call for reform was heard. Reforming congregations arose in almost all the orders, and among the mendicants the Observants set themselves against the traditional branches.

The lay societies of "brothers and sisters of the common life" practiced the ideals of poverty and fellowship intentionally not within the traditional monastic framework. They exerted great influence, however, on attempts at reform in the orders. On the whole, however, decay continued, and it provoked the criticism of early reformers such as J. → Wycliffe and then of the Reformation itself, which went beyond criticism of abuses and rejected monasticism in principle.

5.3. Monasticism under the Sign of Confessional Catholicism

After the enormous losses the Reformation had brought to monasticism, → Catholic reform and counterreformation founded new orders and stabilized the older ones. The orders themselves became the most important agents of the Counter-Reformation.

5.3.1. New Societies

Typical of the age was the new kind of order that deviated even more widely from traditional monasticism, namely, that of clerks regular who gave up not only stability of place but also the canonical hours in order to be available for the work of the church in the world. Thus we find the Theatines (founded 1524), the Barnabites (1530), and especially the → Jesuits (1540). The same ideals and principles activated the newly independent women orders of the Ursulines (1535) and of the English Ladies (Institute of the Blessed Virgin Mary), though the former had to give up its original program, and the latter took hold only in the 18th century. Out of this new type came the 19th-century congregation, which had a specific purpose and linked its members only by simple vows (→ Religious Orders and Congregations 2.3).

5.3.2. Renewal and Decline of Classic Monasticism

Among the older orders only the Carmelites experienced new growth at first, with the emergence of the Discalced Carmelites (esp. under → Teresa of Ávila [1515-82]), though the new development took place only among women.

The Council of → Trent (sess. 25) laid the foundations for a renewal of the older orders in the 17th century, in which France took the lead. There the Benedictines and Cistercians (esp. in the form of the new, strongly ascetic, and purely contemplative Trappists, who became an independent order in 1892) enjoyed a fresh blossoming. An upsurge came in other Catholic countries too in the 17th century and first half of the 18th (e.g., the Baroque monasteries at Melk, Zwiefalten, and Weingarten).

Decline followed again, however, in the second half of the 18th century as inner decay and → Enlightenment criticism came together. Even under the old regime church and state authorities in Austria, France, and Germany began to disband monasteries (→ Secularization). The French Revolution completed the process with total secularization. Italy and Spain followed suit, and to a large extent Germany did likewise in a law of the empire in 1803.

5.4. Monasticism in the Nineteenth and Twentieth Centuries

With the post-Napoleonic → restoration came a fresh promotion of monasticism on the part of Roman Catholic states (e.g., France, Bavaria) and the Roman Catholic Church. The reviving religious life of the 19th century brought a host of new congregations and some renewal of the orders. The movement, which included non-European countries, lasted until the middle of the 20th century.

In the 20th century a new form of common life with monastic elements was the → secular institute (e.g., → Opus Dei, the Schoenstatt Fathers, the Schoenstatt Sisters and Brothers of Mary), whose members accept the evangelical counsels but stay "in the world" and in most cases seek no ongoing life in common. The latter part of the 20th century saw an attempt to renew the orders to meet changed situations (→ Vatican II) but also a rapid decline in numbers that might be described as the biggest process of self-dissolution since the age of the Reformation.

5.5. Monasticism in Uniate Churches

Monasticism in the → Uniate churches, which represents the Eastern monastic traditions within the framework of the Roman Catholic Church, developed its own separate branch. Important representatives include the → Basilian monks and the Antonites, who are found especially in Lebanon.

5.6. *Monasticism according to Vatican II*

Vatican II presented the theological evaluation of monasticism according to the official Roman Catholic teaching today. It defined monasticism as an estate *(status)* that is a necessary element of the life and holiness of the church, the basis for which is the vow of the evangelical counsels. Monks and nuns thereby receive "a special → consecration, which is deeply rooted in their baptismal consecration," but is "a fuller expression of it" (*Perfectae caritatis* 5). They dedicate themselves "wholly to God," devote themselves more intimately to his service, desiring to "derive still more abundant fruit from the grace of [their] baptism" than baptism alone provides (*Lumen gentium* 44).

The legal aspects of the life of orders are dealt with in the 1983 → CIC 573-730 (→ Church Law). These canons deal with the foundation of monasteries, the role of heads, reception into orders, the novitiate, vows, withdrawal and release, duties, laws of institutes and members, and financial matters.

6. Reformation and Monasticism

6.1. *Continuities*

The → Reformation questioned monasticism in principle and, where it triumphed, led to its end. With many former monks (→ Reformers) as leaders, however, the Reformation is related in many ways to monasticism and its ideals. Monasticism provided the context for the rediscovery of the proclamation of → justification solely by → faith in Christ, since the monk Martin → Luther (1483-1546; → Luther's Theology) came across this biblical teaching through his striving (albeit unsuccessfully) for perfection; this link remained in the basic theological structuring of → law and gospel. Monasticism also provided the lasting norm insofar as the ideal of perfect discipleship was not abandoned but was now claiming, not monks alone, but all Christians, though on the new basis of the justification received by faith alone.

6.2. *Criticism of Monasticism*

Criticism of monasticism focused on the idea that it claims to represent a higher form of the Christian life than life in the world. Such thinking devalues the Christianity of the baptized as such and suggests that they need not seek perfection. Objection also arose against the meritoriousness of the monastic life, which contradicts justification by faith. Irrevocable vows were also rejected because they limit the → freedom of faith by imposing ties that Holy Scripture does not prescribe.

The one irrevocable vow from which there is no conceivable dispensation is that of → baptism. This sacrament, however, is fulfilled in many different ways, possibly even in the monastic life when we evaluate it correctly and do not declare it to be irrevocable. (See *The Judgment of Martin Luther on Monastic Vows* [*LW* 44.243-400]; CA and Apol. 27, "Monastic Vows"; and J. → Calvin *Inst.* 4.13, "Vows, and How Everyone Rashly Taking Them Has Miserably Entangled Himself.")

6.3. *Social and Religious Consequences*

With the publication of Luther's *De votis monasticis* in September 1521, a mass exodus from monasteries and convents began, and the houses that still remained in Protestant areas were later in large part dissolved. The result was a great upheaval: for society and → economy, since so many people and so much property had been tied in with the orders; for the church, since so many of its tasks had been fulfilled by the orders; for religious and ethical attitudes, since being a Christian in the world was now upgraded enormously (→ Vocation), with full discipleship as the standard for every believer.

6.4. *Forms of Protestant Monasticism*

Beginning in the 19th century, in some Protestant churches there was a reconsideration of basic elements of the monastic life. Several communities have been founded with many of the features of monasticism, including no private property, celibacy, and various forms of common life (e.g., deaconess houses, various brotherhoods and sisterhoods, Jesusbruderschaft, Grandchamp Community, → Taizé Community, and → Iona Community; → Oxford Movement). The aim is to establish Protestant communities that would nevertheless adhere to the theological and ecclesiastical guidelines established by the Reformation. Revoking the obligations would not be seen as affecting → salvation or incurring → punishment by the church. Nor would this kind of life be regarded as meritorious or as containing greater fullness or being more complete than that of the rest of the baptized. Rather, it would serve as a sign in the form of a one-sided and radical outworking of certain features of the Christian life that all believers share.

Bibliography: General: M. DE DREUILLE, *From East to West: A History of Monasticism* (New York, 1999) • N. FOLEY, ed., *Journey in Faith and Fidelity: Women Shaping Religious Life for a Renewed Church* (New York, 1999) • K. S. FRANK, *Grundzüge der Geschichte des christlichen Mönchtums* (Darmstadt, 1963) • W. M. JOHNSTON, ed., *Encyclopedia of Monasticism* (2 vols.; Chicago, 2000) • P. KING, *Western Monasticism: A History of the Monastic Movement in the Latin Church* (Kalamazoo, Mich., 1999) • D. KNOWLES, *Christian*

Monasticism (London, 1969) • P. Levi, *The Frontiers of Paradise: A Study of Monks and Monasteries* (New York, 1990) • *Le millénaire du Mont Athos, 963-1963. Études et mélanges* (2 vols.; Venice and Chevetogne, 1963-64) • I. Smolitsch, *Russisches Mönchtum. Entstehung, Entwicklung und Wesen, 988-1917* (Würzburg, 1953).

Early church: D. J. Chitty, *The Desert a City: An Introduction to the Study of Egyptian and Palestinian Monasticism under the Christian Empire* (New York, 1977) • M. Dunn, *The Emergence of Monasticism: From the Desert Fathers to the Early Middle Ages* (Oxford, 2000) • K. S. Frank, *Askese und Mönchtum in der Alten Kirche* (Darmstadt, 1975) • J. E. Goehring, *Ascetics, Society, and the Desert: Studies in Early Egyptian Monasticism* (Harrisburg, Pa., 1999) • K. Holl, *Enthusiasmus und Bußgewalt im griechischen Mönchtum* (Hildesheim, 1969; orig. pub., 1898) • A. Holmes, *A Life Pleasing to God: The Spirituality of the Rules of St. Basil* (Kalamazoo, Mich., 2000) • D. Knowles, *From Pachomius to Ignatius: A Study in the Constitutional History of the Religious Orders* (Oxford, 1966) • C. Leyser, *Authority and Asceticism from Augustine to Gregory the Great* (Oxford, 2000) • B. Lohse, *Askese und Mönchtum in der Antike und in der Alten Kirche* (Munich, 1969) • P. Rousseau, *Pachomius: The Making of a Community in Fourth-Century Egypt* (Berkeley, Calif., 1999) • J. Thomas and A. C. Hero, eds., *Byzantine Monastic Foundation Documents: A Complete Translation of Surviving Founders' Typika and Testaments* (5 vols.; Washington, D.C., 2000) • A. Vööbus, *History of Asceticism in the Syrian Orient* (3 vols.; Louvain, 1958-88).

Middle Ages: C. H. Berman, *The Cistercian Evolution: The Invention of a Religious Order in Twelfth-Century Europe* (Philadelphia, 2000) • J. E. Burton, *The Monastic Order in Yorkshire, 1069-1215* (Cambridge, 1999) • G. Constable, *Cluny from the Tenth to the Twelfth Centuries* (Aldershot, 2000) • G. Coppack, *The White Monks: The Cistercians in Britain, 1128-1540* (Stroud, 2000) • H. E. J. Cowdrey, *The Crusades and Latin Monasticism, Eleventh–Twelfth Centuries* (Aldershot, 1999) • S. Foot, *Veiled Women* (2 vols.; Aldershot, 2000) • M. Innes, *State and Society in the Early Middle Ages: The Middle Rhine Valley, 400-1000* (Cambridge, 2000) • D. Knowles, *The Monastic Order in England: A History of Its Development from the Times of St. Dunstan to the Fourth Lateran Coucil, 940-1216* (2d ed.; Cambridge, 1976) • C. H. Lawrence, *Medieval Monasticism: Forms of Religious Life in Western Europe in the Middle Ages* (3d ed.; New York, 2001) • T. Nyberg, *Monasticism in North-Western Europe, 800-1200* (Aldershot, 2000) • N. B. Warren, *Spiritual Economics: Female Monasticism in Later Medieval England* (Philadelphia, 2001).

Modern Period: Orthodox: J. Leroy, *Moines et monastères du Proche-Orient* (Paris, 1958) • T. Špidlík,

"Das östliche Mönchtum und das östliche Frömmigkeitsleben," *Handbuch der Östkirchenkunde* (vol. 3; ed. W. Nyssen, H.-J. Schulz, and P. Wiertz; Düsseldorf, 1997) 24-50.

– Roman Catholic: R. Lemoine, *Le droit des religieux du Concile de Trente aux Instituts Séculiers* (Paris, 1956) • H. Leyser, *Hermits and the New Monasticism: A Study of Religious Communities in Western Europe* (New York, 1984) • W. Seibrich, *Gegenreformation als Restauration. Die restaurativen Bemühungen der alten Orden im Deutschen Reich von 1580 bis 1648* (Münster, 1991) • J. M. White, ed., *The American Catholic Religious Life: Selected Historical Essays* (New York, 1988).

– Anglican: P. F. Anson, *The Call of the Cloister: Religious Communities and Kindred Bodies in the Anglican Communion* (rev. ed.; London, 1964) • M. Hill, *The Religious Order: A Study of Virtuoso Religion and Its Legitimation in the Nineteenth-Century Church of England* (London, 1973) • S. Mumm, *Stolen Daughters, Virgin Mothers: Anglican Sisterhoods in Victorian Britain* (London, 1998).

– Protestant: Communauté de Taizé, *Rule of Taizé: In French and English* (Taizé, 1965) • J. Halkenhäuser, *Kirche und Kommunität. Ein Beitrag zur Geschichte und zum Auftrag der kommunitären Bewegung in den Kirchen der Reformation* (Paderborn, 1978) • B. Lohse, *Mönchtum und Reformation. Luthers Auseinandersetzung mit dem Mönchsideal des Mittelalters* (Göttingen, 1963) • D. Wendebourg, "The Wittenberg Reformation and Monasticism," *Retrieving the Pearl* (ed. E. Farrugia; Rome, 2002).

Dorothea Wendebourg

Money

Money is generally understood as a "universal means of exchange" and therefore as a quasi-natural economic instrument (see 1). Along with → capitalism, industrialization, and modernization, money has spread across the whole world and promotes such things as the division of labor, freedom, and → culture. Yet it is not just an economic instrument. It also promotes the development of a comprehensive intellectual and social power, as may be seen in its contacts with other spheres, for example, in the way a subject directs abstract thought toward an object (with such forms as identity, space, and time), autonomous individuals are detached from the world around them and other individuals (individual → ethics, competition, the pressure to achieve and to save), and the legal subject is engaged with → property, contractual relations, relations between capitalists and the labor force, centralized political and bureaucratic organization (→ Bureaucracy). Religious and ethical reservations regarding money, especially → usury and interest, have sensed something of all these aspects (see 2).

1. Economic theory usually ascribes three functions to money: (1) it is a means of exchange, which it facilitates by splitting the direct exchanging of goods or services into the two acts of buying and selling; (2) it is a measure expressing the value or price of an article; and (3) it is a means of preserving value (e.g., a means of payment in the case of goods already delivered, a means of bridging past and future).

As regards the basis of money there are three groups of theories, based on the aforementioned functions. According to the first, money is itself a commodity that is the product of → work (gold, coins, "metalism"; see Aristotle, classic economists from John Locke on, and the close connection to the objective view of value, i.e., value from work). Second, there are conventional or → nominalist theories according to which money has an agreed or decreed value but no intrinsic value (Plato and → Thomas Aquinas). Finally, there are functional theories, according to which money as a means of exchange receives its value in market transactions. Here again we have the transition from an objective to a subjective doctrine of value by which value equals rate of exchange, fixed by the free acts of those who play a part in the market, possibly also driven by a need for liquidity or a desire to conserve value.

The criticism of money in the thought of Karl → Marx (1818-83) relates to these theories. It analyzes the form of money as an expression of social relations that have passed beyond conscious human control. It thus takes up motifs from the tradition depicted under 2 below and from L. Feuerbach's (1804-72) criticism of religion. It views capital as the modern idol (→ Fetishism) that in some respects resembles the Christian God. Money is a form for Marx because it expresses a contradictory content. The contradiction in a commodity (barter) is between its utility (the result of useful labor) and its nature as a bearer of value (exchange value, the result of abstract work). Goods take on this twofold identity once they are exchanged in the marketplace. The human relations (working and social) that by way of the market enter into a relationship are no longer perceived as such, but to those operating there they seem to be a thing that they can control (objectification, perversion of object to subject, money as the real community).

This fetishism (where, as in → nature religions, a manufactured but alienated object controls us) becomes truly significant when money as capital functions as an automatic subject. As money has the twofold nature of a commodity, so according to Marx capital and its relation to labor can be seen to "develop" out of the contradictions of money, being logically necessary. Finally, the contradictory nature of money may be seen in the crisis-ridden character of capitalist production as such, in the polarization of ignorance and expert knowledge, of → poverty and riches, and so forth.

While theories of money long formed a central economic theme, in the 20th century pragmatic considerations pushed them to the margin. In a rapidly expanding specialization the theory of money is now concerned about the cycle of goods and money, money markets, and the demand for money, whereby increasing importance has been acquired recently by international money and capital markets that are accessible in only a limited fashion to political influence. In fiscal policy (i.e., economic control by way of state budgets; see Keynesian economics), there were hopes of limiting the proneness of capitalism to crises. In the 1970s the central bank (M. Friedman) replaced this type of control. For monetarism the domestic price index depends directly on the money supply. An appropriate expansion of the statistically determined "money basis" of an economy permits the simultaneous establishment of price stability and economic growth. Externally, there is a close relation between domestic prices and the balance of payments. This theory underlies the monetarist approach used by foreign exchanges and the International Monetary Fund.

2. The suppression of controversial debate about money is itself a sign of the ideological establishment of capitalist → industrial society as the only conceivable possibility. But it seems to set aside 3,000 years of rejection and criticism of money in the Bible, in Greek and Latin literature, and in Christian theology. In the resistance especially of lower classes ("heretics," e.g., the → Waldenses), this criticism went hand in hand with the new expansion of a money economy in the High Middle Ages, that is, the growth of trade both at home and abroad, especially the development of precious-metal coins, trading with these coins, and the payment of interest ("usury").

A money economy must be plainly distinguished from the much older direct exchanging of gifts, which seeks to reestablish reciprocal social relations, allowing no abstract, socially indifferent relations between buyer and seller. The capitalist economy that developed in western Europe during only the last two centuries is of the money type, with its commensurately abstract and material organization of production (the industrial revolution) and other social spheres (management).

In the increasingly independent concern for pure acquisition of money (profiteering, avarice), critics perceive the destructive effects it had on the traditional social organization. Money destroys even cities, said Sophocles in *Antigone*. It drives people from their homes. It teaches them to do evil. It makes them capable of anything. Plato (427-347 B.C.) and Aristotle (384-322) wanted to restrict money strictly to its "useful" function as a means of exchange, and in spite of economic expansion, this remained the dominant view of antiquity. The rejection of money and interest (forbidden among the Jews) is prominent in the Hellenistic portions of the OT, less so in earlier portions when they were of less practical significance. → Jesus was for the most part plainly antagonistic. A disciple betrayed him to the "thieves" for money.

Against the → Manichaeans → Augustine (354-430) insisted that money and wealth are not evil as such; what is evil is their misuse and the cupidity that underlies it. As a money economy developed in the → cities from the time of the High Middle Ages, more tolerant views emerged in the course of debate and in opposition to radical social revolutionaries, but the churches, especially M. → Luther, have remained critical right up to the present day, as have many lay authors (e.g., J.-J. Rousseau, Marx).

→ Achievement and Competition; Consumption; Dependence; Development; Economic Ethics; Marxism; Materialism; Socialism; Third World

Bibliography: J. K. GALBRAITH, *Money: Whence It Came, Where It Went* (rev. ed.; Boston, 1995) • D. S. LANDES, *The Wealth and Poverty of Nations: Why Some Are So Rich and Some So Poor* (New York, 1998) • K. MARX, *Capital: A Critique of Political Economy* (New York, 1977) • R. W. MÜLLER, *Geld und Geist. Zur Entstehungsgeschichte von Identitätsbewußtsein und Rationalität seit der Antike* (2d ed.; Frankfurt, 1981) • M. NEARY and G. TAYLOR, *Money and the Human Condition* (New York, 1998) • R. H. NELSON, *Economics as Religion: From Samuelson to Chicago and Beyond* (Philadelphia, 2001) • J. R. SCHNEIDER, *The Good of Affluence: Seeking God in a Culture of Wealth* (Grand Rapids, 2002) • M. L. STACKHOUSE, D. P. McCANN, S. J. ROELS, and P. N. WILIAMS, eds., *On Moral Business: Classical and Contemporary Resources for Ethics in Economic Life* (Grand Rapids, 1995) • F. WAGNER, *Geld oder Gott? Zur Geldbestimmtheit der kulturellen und religiösen Lebenswelt* (Stuttgart, 1985) • E. D. ZINBARG, *Faith, Morals, and Money: What the World's Religions Tell Us about Money in the Marketplace* (New York, 2001).

RUDOLF WOLFGANG MÜLLER

Mongolia

	1960	1980	2000
Population (1,000s):	959	1,663	2,736
Annual growth rate (%):	2.63	2.76	2.00

Area: 1,566,500 sq. km. (604,800 sq. mi.)

A.D. 2000

Population density: 2/sq. km. (5/sq. mi.)
Births / deaths: 2.60 / 0.60 per 100 population
Fertility rate: 2.98 per woman
Infant mortality rate: 46 per 1,000 live births
Life expectancy: 67.7 years (m: 66.1, f: 69.4)
Religious affiliation (%): nonreligious 31.4, tribal religionists 30.0, Buddhists 23.0, atheists 8.8, Muslims 5.1, Christians 1.3, other 0.4.

1. General Situation
2. Religious Situation
3. State and Religion

1. General Situation

Geographically, Mongolia is a region in central Asia comprising an independent republic that until the 1990s maintained close ties with the Soviet Union (Outer Mongolia) and Nei Monggol (Inner Mongolia), an autonomous region within China. Modern Mongolia draws its identity from the empire of Ghengis Khan (ca. 1162-1227), which at its zenith extended from China to central Europe.

With the backing of the Soviets, Mongolia declared its independence from China in 1911. In 1924 a Communist regime was established, with the capital in Urga (subsequently renamed Ulaanbaatar, meaning "Red Hero"). After the fall of the Soviet Union, the former Communist Mongolian People's Revolutionary Party (MPRP) gradually relaxed its control of power. Losing the elections of 1996 but regaining power in the 2000 elections, the MPRP has focused on social welfare and issues of public order.

Ethnically, the people of Mongolia in 2000 were primarily Mongols (85 percent, predominantly Khalkha), with smaller numbers Turkic (7 percent, mainly Kazakhs), Tungusic (5 percent), and other (3 percent, including Chinese and Russian).

Mongolia's economy has traditionally been based on agriculture and the breeding of livestock. In 1998 its chief exports were mineral products, wool, cashmere products, wool, hides, and leather goods. Political instability, a series of natural disasters, and the Asian financial crisis of 1998-99 have combined to stall economic growth.

2. Religious Situation

Beginning in the 7th century, → Nestorian missionaries from China made contact with Mongolians, but by the 10th century their work had disappeared (→ Mission; Missionary). Roman Catholic influence through Franciscan and Dominican sources began in the 13th century (→ Mongolian Mission).

During the 15th century, Mongolia was torn apart with dissension and strife. Tibetan → Buddhism was introduced in Mongolia beginning in 1575. It included the naming of the Jebtsun Damba Khutukhtu, or "Living Buddha," who filled a role roughly analogous to that of the Dalai Lama in Tibet.

In 1911 a group of Mongol princes proclaimed an autonomous republic under Bogd Gegen, the eighth Living Buddha. When Bogd Gegen died in 1924 following the Communist takeover in Outer Mongolia, the Soviets forbade a continuation of the institution, and a successor, the ninth incarnation, was never installed.

The lack of any significant presence of Christianity or Islam in Mongolia since the Middle Ages is due mainly to the continual strong predominance of Lamaism. By the 1920s the movement controlled over 2,600 temples and lamaseries and provided support for 120,000 lamas and 85,000 disciples of the Living Buddha.

In the late 19th century various → Scandinavian and other Protestant missions had attempted work in Outer Mongolia (Khalkha), which was then under Chinese rule, but without success. In the 20th century Roman Catholic → missionaries (→ Catholic Missions) entered Inner Mongolia, but with no greater success. Urga had a → Russian Orthodox Church, but primarily for Russian residents. All missions were closed down when the Communists took over in Outer Mongolia and China.

The Gandan lamasery in Ulaanbaatar is the center for the current Buddhist revival in Mongolia. Mongolians continue to follow the Tibetan version of Lamaism (→ Tibetan Religions), respecting the Dalai Lama as the supreme theocratic leader.

Mongolian folk religion is a mixture of Lamaism and → shamanism with Lamaist features. The modern significance of shamanism is hard to estimate, for it has no public temples or ceremonies. It is still influential, however, being centered in family worship.

3. State and Religion

In the 1930s the Communist regime in Mongolia broke the hold of Lamaism in the country. Except for the Gandan lamasery, all → monasteries were closed down, and temple properties were seized (→ Secularization). The → clergy were partly liquidated and partly imprisoned, among other things for real or alleged collaboration with the Japanese. Most of the monks were integrated into economic and social life. The constitution guaranteed → religious liberty, but it was hard to claim in practice.

Relations between Lamaism and the state began to relax in the 1960s. The Gandan temple complex now includes a seminary for the training of Buddhist priests. Other monasteries have been restored as museums of national culture. The clergy participate regularly in Buddhist conferences and international peace gatherings. Mongolian Buddhists receive financial support from India, which is coordinated by the Indian ambassador to Mongolia.

The 1992 constitution recognizes Buddhism, shamanism, and Islam as the country's main religions, with all people having certain religious rights. Other religions may be restricted, however, insofar as their practice is seen as a threat to national security.

Bibliography: C. R. BAWDEN, *Confronting the Supernatural: Mongolian Traditional Ways and Means* (Wiesbaden, 1994); idem, *The Modern History of Mongolia* (London, 1989) • B.-O. BOLD, *Mongolian Nomadic Society: A Reconstruction of the "Medieval" History of Mongolia* (New York, 2001) • D. CHRISTIAN, *A History of Russia, Central Asia, and Mongolia* (Oxford, 1998) • M. EVEN, "The Shamanism of the Mongols," *Mongolia Today* (ed. S. Akiner; London, 1991) 183-205 • M. C. GOLDSTEIN and C. M. BEALL, *The Changing World of Mongolia's Nomads* (Berkeley and Los Angeles, 1994) • W. HEISSIG, *The Religions of Mongolia* (Berkeley, Calif., 1980) • S. KOLKIN and B. A. ELLEMAN, eds., *Mongolia in the Twentieth Century: Landlocked Cosmopolitan* (Armonk, N.Y., 1999) • N. T. NAMZHIM, *The Economy of Mongolia: From Traditional Times to the Present* (Bloomington, Ind., 2000) • J. NORDBY, comp., *Mongolia* (Santa Barbara, Calif., 1993) bibliography • R. A. RUPEN, *How Mongolia Is Really Ruled: A Political History of the Mongolian People's Republic, 1900-1978* (Stanford, Calif., 1979) • S. SOUCEK, *A History of Inner Asia* (Cambridge, 2000).

KLAUS HESSE

Mongolian Mission

The Mongolian mission was originally part of the broader mission to central Asia of the Apostolic Church of the East (→ Nestorians). The base for the mission was sixth-century Merv (now Mary, Turkmenistan), south of the Oxus (now Amu Dar'ya) River. Nestorian Christianity spread along the market towns of the Silk Road to the eastern German and Turkish tribes and south of the Aral Sea, with the principal agents being Christian merchants, clergy, and monks. The mission gathered strength in the ninth century, especially under Timothy I (patriarch 780-823). Christianity reached all social strata but did not cover whole areas except for villages that became totally Christian.

At the beginning of the 11th century Mongol tribes had extended south of Lake Baikal, and some princes of the Kereits had Christian names. Through these tribes others were won over, including the Merkit, Öngüt, and Khitan, a tribal union led by the Mongols who ruled the Liao kingdom (907-1125) in northern China. When this kingdom collapsed at the hands of the Juchen, a seminomadic Tungusic people, the Khitan founded West Liao in western Turkestan with a Christian ruling house. A Christian of the Naiman tribe was the last prince before its destruction by the Mongols in 1218.

Nestorian work spread also to the western Mongol kingdom. Temüjin (ca. 1162-1227), like his father, was first in the service of Keraite Christian princes before subjugating that tribe and the Naiman. In 1206 he received the name "Genghis Khan" (i.e., supreme lord). Kereit and Naiman nobles had a strong influence on this regime, for the wives and mothers of the great khans were Christians.

After → Islam destroyed Christianity in west central Asia, and during the Mongol invasions, the apostolic church was able to intensify its work among the khans. By the beginning of the 14th century it had 72 → dioceses in the kingdom.

Sporadic persecution took place in Iran. Before the adoption of Sunnite Islam (→ Sunni, Sunnites) in 1295 by Ghāzān, the Mongol ruler of Persia, a monk of the Öngüt tribe became the Nestorian → catholicos Jabalaha III (1281-1307).

After the consolidation of the Mongol kingdom by the son of Genghis Khan, the papacy (→ Pope, Papacy) and France made attempts to convert the ruling Mongol houses of Iran and China (the Yüan Dynasty [1279-1368]) to Christianity or to set up a missionary church in competition with the Nestori-

ans. The background of what were at first only diplomatic moves was the loss of → Jerusalem in 1244, along with the crusading plans (→ Crusades) of Innocent IV (1243-54) and Louis IX of France (1226-70), which were to include an alliance with the Mongols. In pursuit of that plan a number of fruitless approaches were made to Iran (Lawrence of Portugal was sent in 1245, the Dominican Ascelin in 1247) and to Genghis Khan's capital Karakorum, in the center of what is now Mongolia (Willem van Ruysbroeck in 1253-55).

Going essentially as a missionary, not an ambassador, the Franciscan John of Monte Corvino (1247-1328) did work among the Mongols and in Cambaluc (now Beijing). Clement V (1305-14) appointed John archbishop (the first of Beijing), as well as → patriarch of the Orient. The overthrow of the Yüan Dynasty by the Ming shattered Latin missionary work in China. The campaigns of Timur (1336-1405) then reduced the Nestorian missionary church in west-central Asia and Iran to a few remnants.

A fresh start was made in the 19th century with the setting up of the Roman Catholic vicariate in 1840. Statistics list five bishoprics. No vital influence has been registered by the missionary efforts of the London Mission Society (active in Mongolia after 1817; → British Missions), the Irish Presbyterians (→ Reformed and Presbyterian Churches), the Scandinavian Alliance Mission, or other → Scandinavian mission agencies.

After the Mongolian Communist Party relinquished its hold on power in 1990, the country realized a measure of religious freedom. A new translation of the Bible in Mongolian was printed in 2000, when rapid gains were also noted in the number of Protestants.

→ Mission 3

Bibliography: C. R. Bawden, *Confronting the Supernatural: Mongolian Traditional Ways and Means* (Wiesbaden, 1994); idem, *Shamans, Lamas, and Evangelicals: The English Missionaries in Siberia* (London, 1985) • C. Dawson, *The Mongol Mission* (London, 1955; repr., Toronto, 1992) • M. Hoàng, *Genghis Khan* (New York, 1991) • S. Soucek, *A History of Inner Asia* (Cambridge, 2000). See also the bibliography in "Nestorians."

Gernot Wiessner†

Monism

C. Wolff (1679-1754) brought the term "monism" into use in the academic philosophy of the German

→ Enlightenment. It describes theories that trace all things back to one substance (e.g., the rational pantheism of B. Spinoza [1632-77]; → Spinozism) versus those that do not (e.g., the system of R. Descartes [1596-1650], which began with two substances — the *res cogitans*, "thinking substance," and the *res extensa*, "extended substance"; → Cartesianism). The opposite concept is → dualism. German → idealism did not use the term "monism," but it came into general use after G. W. F. Hegel (1770-1831, → Hegelianism).

The term also found a very different use in the second half of the 19th century relative to epistemological trends accompanying the emancipation of natural science. Toward the end of the century it was connected with a movement that, from 1890, found its most important organ in the journal *The Monist*. It promoted a unitary → worldview having no religious reference. This monistic movement rapidly lost its importance after World War I.

The philosophical problem of whether to accept one, two, or several basic principles reaches back to antiquity (→ Greek Philosophy). Parmenides (ca. 540-after 480 B.C.) took the view that thought and being are one and the same, a single → absolute. His later follower Zeno (d. ca. 263 B.C.) supported this theory by showing what great difficulties we inevitably encounter if we replace the One by the Many. Along the lines of the German Enlightenment one might thus say that Parmenides was a monist.

In his dialogue *Parmenides* Plato (427-347; → Platonism) showed that if we assume the One, the existence of the Many must follow, and that if we presuppose the Many, we are forced to conclude that there is only the One. This conclusion is contradictory. Plato was thus the author of → dialectic (see *Par.* 166C). J. G. Fichte (1762-1814) and Hegel took up this dialectical concept. For Hegel too the alternative of monism or dualism was a false one; a philosophy was dualistic that stopped at → antinomies without tracing them back to their original unity.

Bibliography: J. W. Cooper, *Body, Soul, and Life Everlasting: Biblical Anthropology and the Monism-Dualism Debate* (Grand Rapids, 1989) • E. Craig, "Monism," *REPh* 6.474-75 • P. Curd, *The Legacy of Parmenides: Eleatic Monism and Later Presocratic Thought* (Princeton, 1998) • W. James, *A Pluralistic Universe* (Cambridge, Mass., 1977; orig. pub., 1909) • D. Loy, *Nonduality: A Study in Comparative Philosophy* (New Haven, 1998) • B. P. McLaughlin, "Philosophy of Mind," *CDP* 597-606 • S. H. Phillips, "Monism, Indian," *REPh* 6.475-79.

HANS-DIETER KLEIN

Monogram of Christ

The oldest MSS tradition offers contractions of the divine names, especially $\overline{IC}$ for Jesus (= IHCOYC) and $\overline{XC}$ or $\overline{XPC}$ for Christ (= XPICTOC). These contractions, which might be understood as ciphers for the → salvation achieved in Christ (→ Christology), are also found to some extent in monogrammatic form (e.g., as the chrismon, or Chi-Rho) in the → Middle Ages in introductions to letters and documents.

From around 200 we also find the common symbol ⳨, the staurogram (→ Cross 3), which is made up of the superimposed letters tau (T) and rho (P) as an abbreviation for *stauros / stauroō* (cross / crucify). It is a → symbol of the cross of Christ denoting the saving event. At the beginning of the fourth century the apologist Lactantius (d. ca. 325) called the staurogram "the heavenly sign of God" (*De mort. pers.* 44.5), and Constantine (306-37) had it fixed on the shields of his soldiers before the crucial battle against Maxentius (306-12) at the Milvian Bridge in 312.

After 315 Constantinian coins carried the Christogram ☧, made up of chi (X) and rho (P), the first two letters of XPICTOC. The symbol had been in secular use, but it had never previously been used for the name "Christ"; its similarity with → syncretistic sun symbols (✳ and ✴) might have played a role for Constantine. Since X may also be written +, it is not always easy to differentiate ⳨ and ☧. What is not clear, in spite of Lactantius, is which symbol Constantine actually used in 312.

After approximately 324 the symbol ☧, surrounded by a wreath of victory, crowned imperial standards, which were paid cultic honors. This so-called labarum, which probably had a → magical function, became the imperial sign of victory and a symbol of state. After Constantine it found its way in various forms into all spheres of → Christian art (✳ and ✴, from IX = IHCOYC XPICTOC), especially in a funerary context. On so-called passion sarcophagi, along with the wreath and the cross understood as a symbol of victory, it was also in many cases flanked with → doves (→ Immortality) or the → apocalyptic A and Ω (→ Alpha and Omega).

In the second half of the fourth century, ☧ became common along with ⳨, and the two could be combined as ⳨. By the end of the fifth century, though, they were increasingly replaced by the cross as a symbol.

Bibliography: P. Brunn et al., eds., *Sylloge inscriptionum christianarum veterum Musei Vaticani* (pt. 2; Helsinki,

1963) • H. CHILD and D. COLLES, *Christian Symbols, Ancient and Modern: A Handbook for Students* (New York, 1972) • J. DANIÉLOU, *Primitive Christian Symbols* (Baltimore, 1964) • R. KOCH, *Christian Symbols* (San Francisco, 1996; orig. pub., 1932) • G. H. L. F. PITT-RIVERS, *The Riddle of the "Labarum" and the Origins of Christian Symbols* (London, 1966) • E. REES, *Christian Symbols, Ancient Roots* (London, 1992) • W. WISCH-MEYER, "Christogramm und Staurogramm in den lateinischen Inschriften altkirchlicher Zeit," *Theologia crucis–signum crucis* (ed. C. Andresen and G. Klein; Tübingen, 1979) 539-50.

HANNS CHRISTOF BRENNECKE

Monolatry

The term "monolatry," a combination of Gk. *monos* (one) and *latreia* (worship), refers to the religious practice of worshiping one → God. → Monotheism, in holding that only one God exists, is necessarily monolatry. → Polytheism may be, insofar as its worshipers choose one of several deities as their sole object of worship. Over time, however, polytheists can change their worship from one deity to another, perhaps depending on which one seems more meaningful. → Hinduism illustrates such a practice, for example, with its concentration on Krishna. Social, political, and geographic factors play a role in the development of monolatry.

There is a strong practice of monolatry in the Jewish Scripture, even if at times it is a struggle against "foreign" gods. The NT and Christian practice have introduced the doctrine of the Holy → Trinity, so that worship is rendered simultaneously to One-God-in-Three and Three-in-One. → Islam stands firmly on the pillar of worshiping the one God, Allah. Many → tribal (indigenous) religions have monolatrous practices, particularly in times of crisis, such as among African, (tribal) Indian, Pacific, and American Indian societies.

In the Jewish Scripture attention to the one God is regularly made by outstanding figures such as → Moses, Joshua, → Elijah, and other prophets. See, for example, Exod. 20:5; 34:14 and the great Jewish creed in Deut. 6:4 (→ Confession of Faith). Sometimes monolatry is cast in a struggle with other gods and goddesses like Baal (1 Kgs. 18:16-40) or Astarte, Milcom, Chemosh, and Molech (11:5, 7, 33).

In the Christian Scripture monolatry is taken for granted, since the same God is at work in both testaments. → Jesus goes further and names this God Father, whose rule on earth he came to bring.

→ Henotheism; Phenomenology of Religion; Religion

Bibliography: J. BARR, *The Concept of Biblical Theology: An OT Perspective* (Minneapolis, 1999) • M. BECK, *Elia und die Monolatrie. Ein Beitrag zur religionsgeschichtlichen Rückfrage nach dem vorschriftprophetischen Jahwe-Glauben* (Berlin, 1999) • E. O. JAMES, *The Concept of Deity: A Comparative and Historical Study* (London, 1950) • J. PAKKALA, *Intolerant Monolatry in the Deuteronomistic History* (Göttingen, 1999). See also the bibliography in "Monotheism."

JOHN MBITI

Monophysites

1. Origin
2. Theology
3. Development

1. Origin

The Monophysites, in opposition to the conclusion of the Council of → Chalcedon (451), view Christ as having one *(monos)* divine → nature *(physis)* after the → incarnation, not two (→ Christology). Arising in the fifth century as a movement against Chalcedon, the Monophysites became a potent force in Eastern theology and → politics (→ Byzantium).

2. Theology

Theologically, Monophysite doctrine grew out of the Alexandrian Christological tradition (→ Alexandrian Theology), which focused on the redemptive activity of the → Word of God becoming incarnate. Drawing on statements by → Cyril of Alexandria (ca. 375-444), Eutyches (ca. 378-454) in 448 rejected the Ephesus formulary of 433 and taught that Christ was "one nature after the union." His teaching was opposed by → Leo I of Rome and Antiochian theologians (→ Antiochian School) at Chalcedon. Christians in Egypt and Palestine, however, rejected Chalcedon as untrue to the teaching of Cyril and the early church, preferring the language "out of two natures" rather than "in two natures" to protect the "one nature of the incarnate Word of God" — a phrase coined by Apollinaris (ca. 310-ca. 390) against adoptionist or divisive Christologies.

In the centuries after Chalcedon, Monophysite theology developed in many forms amid controversy with Chalcedonians. Severus (ca. 465-538) used a Platonic → analogy (→ Platonism) of body and → soul to express the one-nature definition, which underlined the unity of Christ and the reality but also dependence of the humanity on Christ's divinity. For Severus one incarnate nature ensured one source of activity. In contrast, Julian of Halicarnassus (d. after 518) taught a more extreme version in which the body of Christ was incorruptible before the → resurrection. Other extreme Monophysites defined the humanity of Christ as an illusion (→ Docetism).

3. Development
Ecclesiastically and politically, the Eastern church (→ Orthodoxy 3; Orthodox Church) struggled to remain one (→ Unity) despite the fierce theological controversy, as emperors sought to enforce orthodoxy and ensure the loyalty of Egypt and Syria. The *Henoticon* of 482 (→ Union), sponsored by Emperor Zeno (474-91), condemned both Nestorius (d. ca. 451; → Nestorians) and Eutyches, but it was unsuccessful as a moderating measure.

After a series of failed synods (→ Councils of the Church), Severus, patriarch of Antioch, was condemned in 536 by a synod at Constantinople. He authorized the → ordination of Monophysite → bishops as well as lower clergy, which led to a separate church (→ Heresies and Schisms). Persecution of Monophysites followed. Justinian's (527-65) further attempts at reconciliation (esp. in 553 at the Second Council of Constantinople) also failed.

Monophysite missionaries spread this doctrine to Ethiopia and Armenia in the sixth century, leading to the organization of the present-day → Oriental Orthodox churches: in Armenia, Egypt, Eritrea, Ethiopia, India, and Syria.

→ Armenian Apostolic Church; Coptic Orthodox Church; Ethiopian Orthodox Church; Syrian Orthodox Church; Syrian Orthodox Churches in India

Bibliography: R. C. CHESNUT, *Three Monophysite Christologies: Severus of Antioch, Philoxenus of Mabbug, and Jacob of Sarug* (New York, 1976) • W. FREND, *The Rise of the Monophysite Movement* (Cambridge, 1972) • P. GREGORIOS, W. LAZARETH, and N. NISSIOTIS, eds., *Does Chalcedon Divide or Unite?* (Geneva, 1981) • A. GRILLMEIER, *Christ in Christian Tradition,* vol. 2, *From the Council of Chalcedon (451) to Gregory the Great (590-604)* (2d ed.; Louisville, Ky., 1996) • J. N. D. KELLY, *Early Christian Doctrines* (New York, 1959) • B. MEUNIER, *Le Christ de Cyrille d'Alexandrie. L'humanité, le salut et la question monophysite* (Paris, 1997) • A. VAN ROEY and P. ALLEN, eds., *Monophysite Texts of the Sixth Century* (Louvain, 1994) • I. R. TORRANCE, *Christology after Chalcedon: Severus of Antioch and Sergius the Grammarian* (Norwich, 1988) • A. VÖÖBUS, "The Origin of the Monophysite Church in Syria and Mesopotamia," *CH* 42 (1973) 17-26 • K. P. WESCHE, trans., *On the Person of Christ: The Christology of Emperor Justinian* (Crestwood, N.Y., 1991).

J. REBECCA LYMAN

Monotheism

1. Term
2. Historical Definitions
3. Monotheism as a Normative Concept
4. Monotheism in Religious History
5. Monotheism as a Total Outlook

1. Term
Monotheism is a religious, theological, or philosophical position whose normative feature is recognition of only one God.

Those who use the term "monotheism" in either confession or research are differentiating between different views of God. Like other isms, this term also tends to denote a movement, sphere, or epoch in which, whether the respective inhabitants or contemporaries use the term or not, a specific outlook or opinion prevails. Whether those who define their own position claim the validity of their logic from a foreign source, or whether they take the validating proof from their own tradition, a semantic antinomy can arise.

We see such antinomies as "monotheism" used in interfaith → dialogue, among the participating theologians, in the study of religion, and in philosophical affirmations (→ Worldview) of different provenance. For the most part, the semantic problem is not perceived. Resolution of the contradictory uses is needed if "monotheism" is to be more than a polemical concept, as it often is. Obstacles are the fact that a theology can invoke the term to give universal or final validity to its central view or teaching (→ God 3-5), but also that → religious studies uses the term in an extended way for even nonreligious subjects that might be called monotheistic, or makes statements that merge into others with the same truth-value (→ Truth). The difficulty is the greater in that neither theology nor religious studies can claim exclusive title to the term.

2. Historical Definitions
Since the term "monotheism" is a Christian one, we might expect to find it in antiquity. But the only approximation to it is *monotheia,* "sole deity" (*Narratio de rebus Persicis,* 5th or 6th cent.). The term is in fact a modern one, first used by the Cambridge

Platonist Henry More (1614-87; → Platonism), whose aim was to distinguish the Christian worship of God from that of others. For him pagan worship was not monotheistic, and Jewish worship only unwittingly so.

Henry St. John Bolingbroke (1678-1751) found monotheism fairly clearly in Thales (6th cent. B.C.; → Greek Philosophy) and among the ancient Egyptians (→ Egyptian Religion 1.3). David Hume (1711-76) then found it among Semitic peoples (Babylonians as well as Jews; → Babylonian and Assyrian Religion). Such development proved that it would have a history involving persecution and restoration. I. Kant (1724-1804; → Kantianism) claimed that "not reflection or profound speculation but common sense" led to monotheism, and that "there were glimmerings of it among all peoples, even in the darkest polytheism" (*Critique of Pure Reason*).

G. W. F. Hegel (1770-1831) showed the flexibility of the term, contrasting it with → pantheism, not → polytheism. Monotheism thus took on the many meanings in religious studies that it had already as used by G. F. Creuzer (1771-1858), the most prominent Romantic advocate of such studies.

3. Monotheism as a Normative Concept

3.1. A concept that takes *monos* strictly to exclude plurality does not express a self-evident claim to absoluteness, such as confession of the one God represents. Nor is such a concept basic to a supernatural divine absoluteness (→ Absolute, The) that also posits unity independently of the multiplicity of the earthly, of ethical forces and human speculations. It is itself a product of the same rational absolutizing in virtue of which all extra- or preChristian truth is a remnant of the original revelation (→ Innocence, State of) or a work of the Logos, who became incarnate in Christ (› Incarnation). In the case of monotheism, the resultant normativity (→ Norms) has translated itself into a readiness to find monotheism even outside Christianity, but with the natural need to qualify it, when found, with further attributes.

3.2. These qualifications mean a recognition that the norm posited by Christianity is satisfied, with the reservation that it is satisfied only to a certain extent. We can evaluate both the recognition and the reservation in two ways according to the two disciplines involved. For → natural theology the satisfying of the norm might be a positive sign of an original or continuing → revelation, and reference might then be made (though wrongly, both historically and conceptually) to an original monotheism. Alternatively, autonomous religious studies

might critically find here a relativizing of the claim to absoluteness and refer (rightly, at least phenomnologically) rather to → henotheism or → monolatry.

As regards the reservation, theology might positively understand it as a religious validation or additional demonstration of its claim to absoluteness, though in reality it refrains ideologically from so uncertain a procedure. Religious studies might show by the use of such qualifications to monotheism as monarchical, mystical, exclusive (tautological!), trinitarian (the number three is not important), inclusive, pluriform, ethical, intellectual, philosophical, emotional, or personal that if we are not prejudiced, we can find something of high religious value anywhere. In reality, however, the use is restricted, and the theological norm is unwittingly accepted.

4. Monotheism in Religious History

Along with Christianity, which still adds historical qualifications, → Judaism (→ Jewish Theology) and → Islam plainly count as monotheistic religions, now that the theologically induced western European spirit, wrestling with both religions for different reasons and at different times, poses the question of the truth of the view of God independently of its acceptance. The result is that Jews and Muslims can have a part in the diagnosing and claiming of monotheism. If this openness relates to the concept and not to the traditional confession, semantic antinomies arise — *monos* implies unity, which takes a different form in each of these three religions.

4.1. The Jewish Shema, "Hear!" in Deut. 6:4 calls → Yahweh "one" (MT 'eḥād, LXX *heis*, Vg *unus*) and differentiates him in many ways from any "one" God of whom the Egyptians or Sumerians might speak. In 32:12, in the related Song of Moses, it is Yahweh "alone" (*bādād, monos, solus*) who leads Israel, not a foreign God. The → rabbis were the first to establish the uniqueness of God by the use of *yiḥud* (unification); they allowed no room for any other god. Judaism as a whole, though, never made of monotheism an epochal, cultural, intellectual, or confessional system with the uniqueness of God at the center.

4.2. Jesus confirmed the Deuteronomistic confession in the same words in Mark 12:29, and a hymnic confession in 1 Tim. 1:17 includes the phrase "to . . . the only God" (*monō theō, soli Deo*). Differentiation from other gods in the world around is implied. But the thrust toward *ter unus* (thrice one) or *trinus* (three together) that resulted from the Trinitarian controversies (→ Trinity), which became the distinguishing mark of Christianity, stood in the way of *unicus* (one, only).

4.3. Islam interpreted this Christian terminology tritheistically, opposing to it its *tawḥīd* (unity, making one, declaring to be a unity). In the process the view of God of the Prophet, Muḥammad (ca. 570-632), which is not described by this term or any related root in the → Qur'an, makes use of a confessional and theologico-philosophical concept that has many senses covering the unity of Allah, his uniqueness, and the necessity of his distinctive existence (→ Islam 5).

5. Monotheism as a Total Outlook

Monotheism, then, is a total worldview that contains a (tendentiously at least) plain idea or conviction (→ Faith) of the oneness of God. An approach to the conceptualizing of the latter phenomenon may be found in the (hypothetical) Yahweh-alone movement in OT Israel, in the doctrine of God that the → early church formulated with the help of ruler ideology (→ Emperor Worship), and in the *mu'tazilah* teaching that early Islam developed (→ Islamic Philosophy 2) with the help of Hellenistic philosophy. Such implications, however, still need rational and historical-psychological verification, a task that scholarship must take up if there is to be a conceptually sober explication of this very complex phenomenon.

→ Christology; Creation; Phenomenology of Religion; Religion; Theism

Bibliography: W. F. ALBRIGHT, *From the Stone Age to Christianity: Monotheism and the Historical Process* (2d ed.; Baltimore, 1957) • J. ASSMANN, *Moses, the Egyptian: The Memory of Egypt in Western Monotheism* (Cambridge, Mass., 1997) • R. BAUCKHAM, *God Crucified: Monotheism and Christology in the NT* (Grand Rapids, 1999) • M. P. CHRISTANAND, *The Philosophy of Indian Monotheism* (Delhi, 1979) • S. FREUD, *Moses and Monotheism* (London, 1974; orig. pub., 1939) • P. HARTILL, *The Unity of God: A Study in Christian Monotheism* (London, 1952) • L. W. HURTADO, *One God, One Lord: Early Christian Devotion and Ancient Jewish Monotheism* (Philadelphia, 1998) • P. LAPIDE and J. MOLTMANN, *Jewish Monotheism and Christian Trinitarian Doctrine: A Dialogue* (Philadelphia, 1981) • T. M. LUDWIG, "Monotheism," *EncRel(E)* 10.68-76 • J. S. MBITI, *Concepts of God in Africa* (London, 1970) • W. SCHMIDT, *Der Ursprung der Gottesidee* (12 vols.; Münster, 1912-55) • H. SHANKS and J. MEINHARDT, *Aspects of Monotheism: How God Is One* (Washington, D.C., 1997) • R. STARK, *One True God: Historical Consequences of Monotheism* (Princeton, 2001) • E. TROELTSCH, *The Absoluteness of Christianity and the History of Religions* (London, 1972; orig. pub., 1901). See also the bibliography in "Jewish Theology."

CARSTEN COLPE

Montanism

1. Oracles
2. Prophecy
3. Decline

Montanism arose around A.D. 172 in Phrygia, Asia Minor. It was founded by Montanus, a recent convert to Christianity, who in trances uttered oracles predicting the imminent descent of the heavenly → Jerusalem at the village of Pepuza in Phrygia (→ Ecstasy; Eschatology; Prophet, Prophecy). He urged devotees to assemble there, to practice rigorous → fasting, and to give money to a common fund.

1. Oracles

The oracles of Montanus claim the → authority of → revelation (e.g., "It is I, the Lord God Almighty, who am present in a man" or "Behold, man is like a lyre, and I hover over him like a plectrum; man sleeps but I watch. Behold, it is the Lord who makes men's hearts ecstatic and gives them [new] hearts"). Two oracles express rigorism by refusing repentance for sin after → baptism ("The church can remit sins, but I will not do so lest others also sin") and by promoting martyrdom ("Do not hope to die in bed or in abortion or in languishing fevers but in martyrdom, so that he who suffered for you may be glorified"; → Martyrs).

2. Prophecy

Two prophetesses, Maximilla and Priscilla (or Prisca), joined Montanus to receive the → Holy Spirit. Maximilla herself claimed → inspiration: "The Lord sent me as a devotee, revealer, interpreter of this labor and promise and covenant; I was forced, willing or not, to learn the knowledge of God" (cf. 1 Cor. 9:16). Her prophecies included → apocalyptic messages (e.g., "There will be wars and revolutions" and "After me there will be no more prophecy, but the end"). An anonymous critic noted that in the 13 years after her death, there had been no wars, a comment that allows us to place her death before the reign of Commodus (176-92). Maximilla aroused controversy with words such as "I am driven from the sheep like a wolf; I am not a wolf but utterance, spirit, and power." Her admirers had to prevent orthodox → exorcists from attacking her.

Priscilla uttered "saving words as clear as they are mysterious." She accused the orthodox of being "flesh but hating the flesh." Her vision of Christ was all-important: "Appearing as a woman clothed in a shining robe, Christ came to me; he put wisdom into me and revealed to me that this place [Pepuza] is sacred, and here Jerusalem will come down from heaven." Details of the oracle come from apocalypses. The Book of Revelation supplies the shining robe (19:7-8) and the new Jerusalem from heaven (21:2); 2 Esdras provides the woman with shining face, replaced by the new Zion (10:25-27), which is a sacred place with a city (vv. 53-54), and perhaps also the identification of Zion with Ardab (9:26 Aram.; cf. Montanus's native Ardabau in Phrygia, Eusebius *Hist. eccl.* 5.16.7).

Montanists claimed forerunners among the prophesying daughters of Philip (Acts 21:9), of whom two were buried at Hierapolis in Phrygia (*Hist. eccl.* 5.24.2). Papias, bishop of Hierapolis, was fascinated by oral tradition and bizarre apocalyptic, which he ascribed to Jesus (Irenaeus *Adv. haer.* 5.33.3-4 = *2 Apoc. Bar.* 29:5). The Montanists were conservative in theology (→ Christology; God), as an oracle shows: "God brought forth the Word as a root brings forth a tree, and a spring a river, and the sun a ray." → Tertullian (ca. 160-ca. 225), the most famous Montanist, held that Jerusalem would in fact be found in Palestine, not Phrygia. Yet the Montanists' emphasis on prophecy, minimized in postapostolic times, threatened episcopal → authority (→ Bishop, Episcopate), as well as the tenuous accord between → church and state (→ Persecution of Christians).

3. Decline

→ Synods were held against Montanism under Apollinaris, bishop of Hierapolis (ca. 161-80, Eusebius *Hist. eccl.* 5.19.2). The Roman church also became involved. The Roman bishop Zephyrinus (198-217) may have been intending to recognize Montanist prophecies, but a certain Praxeas reminded him of negative decisions by earlier Roman bishops and made him recall letters of peace already issued (Tertullian *Adv. Prax.* 1.5). In the same period the Montanist Proclus debated with the "learned presbyter" Gaius and forced him to ascribe the Gospel of John, with its Paraclete, and the Apocalypse, with its heavenly Jerusalem, to the shadowy heretic Cerinthus (see *Hist. eccl.* 3.28.2). Cyril of Jerusalem (d. 386?) claimed that Montanists killed and ate an infant in their mysteries (*Cat.* 16.8). The code of Emperor Theodosius (379-95) imposed penalties on them.

By the fourth century the danger had waned. Never strong numerically, the Montanists gradually died out, despite their having established a → hierarchy of bishops, presbyters, and → deacons.

Bibliography: T. D. BARNES, "The Chronology of Montanism," *JTS* 21 (1970) 403-8 • R. M. GRANT, *Heresy and Criticism: The Search for Authenticity in Early Christian Literature* (Louisville, Ky., 1993) • R. E. HEINE, *The Montanist Oracles and Testimonies* (Macon, Ga., 1989) • E. C. HUBER, *Women and the Authority of Inspiration: A Reexamination of Two Prophetic Movements from a Contemporary Feminist Perspective* (Lanham, Md., 1985) • P. DE LABRIOLLE, *Les sources de l'histoire du montanisme* (Fribourg, 1913) • D. RANKIN, *Tertullian and the Church* (Cambridge, 1995) • A. STROBEL, *Das heilige Land der Montanisten* (Berlin, 1980) • W. TABBERNEE, *Montanist Inscriptions and Testimonia: Epigraphic Sources Illustrating the History of Montanism* (Macon, Ga., 1997) • C. TREVETT, *Montanism: Gender, Authority, and the New Prophecy* (Cambridge, 1996).

ROBERT M. GRANT

Moody, Dwight L.

Dwight Lyman Moody (1837-99) was the best-known and most influential American evangelist of the late 19th century. His influence on American revivalism and → Protestantism, especially evangelicalism (→ Evangelical Movement), continued well into the 20th century.

Moody was born in Northfield, Massachusetts. His father died when he was four. As one of nine children, Moody grew up in humble circumstances and with the equivalent of a fifth-grade education. At the age of 17 the ambitious Moody left rural Massachusetts to find work in Boston, where a year later he had a → conversion experience. Shortly thereafter, Moody moved to Chicago to work as a shoe salesman.

In Chicago Moody succeeded in business but became increasingly committed to Christian work. He began a → Sunday school class for immigrant children in 1858 (from which Moody Memorial Church eventually emerged). Two years later he quit shoe-selling to devote himself full-time to → YMCA and Sunday school work. A tireless promoter, Moody attracted children and adults to his religious services, and he proved adept at soliciting financial support from leading Chicago businessmen such as John Farwell and Cyrus McCormick.

Moody's star rose rapidly in the YMCA. By the late 1860s he was president of the Chicago YMCA and a popular speaker at YMCA conventions in the United States and England. The Chicago Fire of 1871, however, destroyed much of the YMCA infrastructure in Chicago and prompted Moody to pursue full-time traveling → evangelism. In 1873 he embarked on a wildly successful two-year tour of Great Britain, and he returned to the United States as a household name. Over the next two decades he conducted revival campaigns in many of the major American cities and again in Britain (1881-84). Crusades in New York City (1876) and Boston (1877) were especially noteworthy, and his Chicago campaign during the 1893 World's Fair drew unprecedented crowds.

While continuing evangelistic work in the 1880s and 1890s, Moody shifted his emphasis to → education. In 1880 he established the Northfield Conference in his Massachusetts hometown, which attracted visitors each summer for several years. The 1886 Student Conference at Northfield was notable for the 100 young people who volunteered there for foreign missionary service, the number including J. R. → Mott, who had such an impact later on international missionary and ecumenical efforts (→ Ecumenism, Ecumenical Movement). Also in Massachusetts he established the Northfield Seminary for Young Women (1879) and the Mount Herman School for Young Men (1881). In 1887 he established the Bible-Work Institute of the Chicago Evangelization Society, a school that took the name of Moody Bible Institute upon his death in 1899.

Moody's influence continued long after his death. Concerning revivalism, he furthered the trend toward simplified theology, emotionalized religion, and an emphasis on organizational technique. Unordained and largely self-educated, Moody eschewed complicated theology in his evangelistic campaigns. His simple and straightforward sermons emphasized the "three Rs" — ruin, redemption, and → regeneration. Moody also pioneered the use of music in evangelism; indeed, much of the credit for the popularity of his → revivals can be attributed to his song leader, Ira Sankey (1840-1908). Moody's warm-hearted sermons and Sankey's → gospel songs epitomized the sentimentalized Protestantism of the Victorian era.

Moody also applied modern business methods to revivalism. His campaigns relied on promotion in the → mass media, door-to-door canvassing of area residents, cooperation from local churches, and financial support by business leaders. In all, Moody paved the way for the modern mass evangelism of Billy Sunday (1862-1935) and Billy Graham (b. 1918).

Moody also played a key role in foreign missions. He toured college campuses speaking on the importance of spreading the gospel, and in 1886 his Northfield Conference launched the Student Volunteer Movement. Taking as its motto "the evangelization of the world in this generation," this organization eventually inspired an estimated 20,000 college students to become Christian → missionaries.

Moody was also an important forerunner to Protestant → fundamentalism. At a time when postmillennial views generally prevailed, Moody ascribed to and helped popularize the belief in Christ's premillennial, imminent, and supernatural return to earth (→ Millenarianism; Parousia). Such a view led Moody to deemphasize social and political action in favor of individual conversion, an emphasis that became common among conservative evangelicals for much of the 20th century.

Moody helped lay the institutional foundation for 20th-century fundamentalism. He played a key role in the formation of summer Bible and prophecy conferences. These meetings nurtured personal networks among conservative Protestants of various → denominations. Chicago's Moody Memorial Church became an important fundamentalist congregation, and the Moody Bible Institute became the flagship institution of interdenominational fundamentalism in the 20th century.

Though a father to fundamentalism, Moody himself retained an irenic spirit that sometimes troubled later conservatives. He included on his revival platforms theistic evolutionists such as Henry Drummond (1851-97), and he sought to downplay divisive doctrinal issues among his associates, hoping in vain that a focus on evangelism could serve to unify increasingly divergent points of view among theological liberals and conservatives. While his Chicago enterprises found their way into the fundamentalist camp, his Northfield schools generally moved toward mainline liberal Protestantism after his death.

→ Conservatism; Liberal Theology; Mission 3.5

Bibliography: L. DORSETT, *A Passion for Souls: The Life of D. L. Moody* (Chicago, 1997) • J. FINDLAY, *Dwight L. Moody: American Evangelist, 1837-1899* (Grand Rapids, 1969) • W. MCLOUGHLIN, *Modern Revivalism: Charles Grandison Finney to Billy Graham* (New York, 1959) • J. POLLOCK, *Moody* (New York, 1963).

RICHARD S. OSTRANDER

Moonies → Unification Church

Moral Argument → God, Arguments for the Existence of

Moral Education

1. Definition
2. History
3. Current Status

1. Definition

Moral education is what schools do, consciously and unconsciously, to help the young think about issues of right and wrong, to help them desire the social good, and to help them behave ethically (K. Ryan, 3406). "Character education" and "values education" are terms often used synonymously with "moral education."

Although all social institutions bear some burden for instruction in morality, the public expects schools to play a central role in the development of character. In the United States only a few states, however, have educational standards that address character education directly in their curricular standards, although 46 states do address character education indirectly through outcomes statements. No state codes of education or standards outlaw, forbid, or in any way discourage → education in → ethics.

Moral education is considered an interdisciplinary field of study and, in a comprehensive program, will be emphasized across the academic disciplines as well as in all extracurricular aspects of a student's education. Sustained efforts in moral education appear much stronger in countries that include compulsory → religious education (e.g., the United Kingdom, Norway) than in countries that do not (e.g., the United States).

2. History

Moral education leading up to the founding of the new American republic was thoroughly Calvinist (→ Calvinism) and was supported principally by the → family and local → church. Instruction in → piety, as well as instruction in reading and writing in order to read the Holy Scriptures (→ Literacy), was first mandated in Massachusetts in 1671. Texts such as the *New England Primer,* initially published in 1690, became the leading schoolbook for Protestants for the next 100 years. The promotion of Christian → virtue through the teaching of academics was continued throughout the colonial era.

The 19th century marked a transitional period in the nature of moral instruction. Horace Mann (1796-1859), one of the most influential figures in American education, advocated for common schools. These free public schools, while primarily educating poor urban children to become good citizens, moved moral instruction away from the home and churches to state-sponsored institutions (→ School and Church). In order to accommodate growing numbers of immigrant Catholics and Jews, the Protestant nature of the common school curriculum became more general in order to teach basic religious and ethical principles common to all creeds. By the end of the 19th century, 41 of the 46 states had passed statutes forbidding sectarian influence within the public schools.

In the early years of the 20th century, the public school curriculum continued to include instruction in citizenship and character development. Between 1930 and 1950, however, the content of moral education changed noticeably to an overall concern for the child's → happiness and self-regard rather than continuing to rely on any specifically religious or conventional idea of character development. The major educational influence here was John Dewey (1859-1952), who argued that morality was not to be imposed on a child. He called for teaching that emphasized a rational approach to moral decisions, believing that if students understood what was right, they would choose to act properly. This progressive philosophy, coupled with rapidly changing social mores in American society, radically changed the moral curriculum of the American schools. Instruction became largely detached from any substantive traditions, beliefs, or ritual practices of particular faith communities.

The USSR's successful launch of Sputnik in 1957 brought a distancing from progressive educational philosophy as well as traditional character education. Educational theorists began to focus more on promoting academic achievement in → science, math, and foreign languages rather than dealing with moral education. Then in *Engel v. Vitale* (1962) the Supreme Court ruled that → prayer and Bible reading in public schools were unconstitutional. Next, a series of national and local laws explicitly removed the promotion of character education from the schools. In the new rational, scientific age, moral educators gradually became less committed to propagating any objective moral content. Rather, a focus on a variety of programs emphasizing values clarification, decision making, and moral reasoning became the pedagogy of choice in the schools.

The values clarification program was begun largely as an alternative to more traditional approaches to moral education, which were sometimes perceived as inculcating a certain set of values, or moralizing. Relying on a set of key questions, values clarification strategies generally encouraged students to think more critically about their own values. In *Values and Teaching* (1966; 2d ed., 1978) Louis Raths and others argued that since young people live in a complicated world of competing (and thus presumably confusing) value perspectives, they should learn to act based on their own freely chosen values, beliefs, and feelings. The teachers' job was not to teach particular ethical ideas but to help students "clarify" their own values. In the end, however, values clarification made the mistake of treating children like mature adults who needed only to clarify values that were already sound, ignoring the need of children for help in developing sound values in the first place (T. Lickona, 11; → Values, Ethics of).

Two leading psychologists were persuasive in urging teachers to be nonjudgmental in teaching about values while encouraging students to be responsible for their own decisions. In *Schools without Failure* (1969) William Glasser (b. 1925) denigrated any "preaching" of moral truths, encouraging teachers to totally accept the young people as they are in order to help students learn to improve themselves. And Lawrence Kohlberg (1927-87) proposed a series of teacher-led discussions about moral dilemmas that required students to make difficult real-life decisions. These ethical dilemmas were intended to move the students away from any objective framework of right and wrong and toward determining their own, situational morality. Each of the reasoning or cognitive development methods implied that learners could struggle their way toward good moral decisions "without bothering to acquire moral habits or strength of character" (W. Kilpatrick, 18).

3. Current Status

While self-esteem as a concept lost some currency in the 1990s, other related ideas took its place. One of these, "emotional intelligence," attained prominence for its affective approach to moral education. The dominant strategy of moral education in the public schools at the turn of the 21st century emphasized individual moral choices along with the centrality of developing positive self-esteem. Research, however, has shown little or no association between psychological well-being and moral conduct, and no substantive research has supported the idea that programs focused on self-esteem have any positive effect on moral behavior (J. D. Hunter, 268-71).

Many programs of character development focus on improving responsible decision-making through

a study of current societal concerns such as → sex education, → conflict resolution, peacekeeping (→ Peace Education), and drug abuse (→ Substance Abuse). Some ethicists maintain that the public schools are slowly reawakening to what has historically been one of their most essential tasks, namely, a more traditional view of character development: teaching students to know, love, and do what is → good (K. Ryan and K. E. Bohlin, 5, 23).

Overall, moral education programs continue to reflect a multiplicity of core values and a strong reluctance to impart particular normative ideals and virtuous habits to students. This attitude is the result of little general agreement as to what the content of moral education ought to be in a public school system that serves a diverse society. Some scholars have argued for a study of the classical virtues or a universal human canon. Others have suggested that public schools in a → democracy ought to emphasize the virtues of citizenship. Theologians and religious scholars, curiously, have paid slight attention to the educational dimensions of morality. Despite little public agreement as to either the content or the methodology of moral education, public opinion polls continue to reveal widespread support for character development as a central goal of the public schools (H. Sockett, 543).

Bibliography: J. L. Elias, *Moral Education: Secular and Religious* (Malabar, Fla., 1989) • J. D. Hunter, *The Death of Character: Moral Education in an Age without Good and Evil* (New York, 2000) • W. Kilpatrick, *Why Johnny Can't Tell Right from Wrong, and What We Can Do about It* (New York, 1992) • T. Lickona, *Educating for Character: How Our Schools Can Teach Respect and Responsibility* (New York, 1989) • J. L. Nolan, "Public Education," *The Therapeutic State* (New York, 1998) • M. S. Pritchard, *Reasonable Children: Moral Education and Moral Learning* (Lawrence, Kans., 1996) • K. Ryan, "Moral and Values Education," *International Encyclopedia of Education* (vol. 6; New York, 1985) 3406-13 • K. Ryan and K. E. Bohlin, *Building Character in Schools* (San Francisco, 1999) • H. Sockett, "The Moral Aspects of the Curriculum," *Handbook of Research on Curriculum* (ed. P. W. Jackson; New York, 1992) 543-69.

Muriel M. Radtke

Moral Rearmament

Moral Rearmament (MRA) is a religious renewal movement initiated by American Lutheran pastor Frank N. D. Buchman (1878-1961). When conferences for international → disarmament failed after

World War I, Buchman concluded that → peace must begin with total human change. This conviction impelled him to start a worldwide revival movement to be marked by daily hearing of the → Word of God (quiet time) and living according to four absolutes based on the radical norms of the → Sermon on the Mount: honesty, purity, unselfishness, and → love. In 1921 he described the movement as "a program of life issuing in personal, social, racial, national, and supernatural change."

From various movements of → piety Buchman learned the need for personal → conversion and international responsibility (esp. influential were the → World's Student Christian Movement, John → Mott, and the → YMCA and → YWCA). Also significant were encounters that acquainted him with social Christianity, such as with F. von Bodelschwingh, A. Stoecker, and P. Le Seur (→ Social Movements). Beginning in England, the movement was registered in 1939 under the name "Oxford Group." From England the group, which was drawn from all social strata, carried its concern especially by personal witness to many other countries, where it became internationally known as Moral Rearmament.

The original movement gained influence in Germany in the early 1930s, affecting pastors and theologians. Political pressure, however, severed international links after 1937, and no proper development then was possible. During a stay in Germany, Buchman developed the essential program of MRA beginning in 1938. He found in moral and spiritual rearmament a Christian alternative to military armaments and set his ideology in opposition to that of National Socialism (→ Fascism) and Communism (→ Socialism). With the motto "Through changed people one can change the world," he sought a new world community. MRA later was often able to contribute to solving what seemed to be insoluble problems in interpersonal and especially sociopolitical matters (e.g., social problems in India and racial problems in South Africa). From the outset it was one of the few movements combining personal piety and social commitment.

Since 1946 the MRA has had a center at the former Caux-Palace near Montreax on Lake Geneva. By means of lectures, drama, and films, its teams spread its ideology of moral and spiritual renewal. Caux became the site of open encounters at the highest level and served the cause of → reconciliation in the broadest sense. For example, it was the scene of an important meeting of German and French leaders soon after World War II, headed respectively by Konrad Adenauer and Robert Schu-

man. Later it set up centers in other countries, including India, Japan, and Brazil.

The impact of the movement may still be seen in many church societies and communities, such as in the form of the quiet time, → confession of sins, and teamwork. A direct offshoot of MRA in Germany was the Marburg Circle (1957), with its specific concern for → mission and → pastoral care and a greater openness to other cultures and → religions.

Bibliography: F. Buchman, *Remaking the World* (rev. ed.; London, 1961) • W. H. Clark, *The Oxford Group: Its History and Significance* (New York, 1951) • P. Howard, *Frank Buchman's Secret* (London, 1961) • G. Lean, *Frank Buchman: A Life* (London, 1985) • E. Luttwak, "Franco-German Reconciliation: The Overlooked Role of the Moral Rearmament Movement," *Religion: The Missing Dimension of Statecraft* (ed. D. Johnson and C. Sampson; Oxford, 1994) 47-63 • T. Spoerri, *Dynamic out of Silence: Frank Buchman's Relevance Today* (London, 1976).

Ingrid Reimer

Moral Theology

1. Term
2. Content
3. Basis
4. Christian Content
5. Universal Relevance
6. Sin

1. Term

Moral theology, today often called theological ethics, is a discipline in Roman Catholic → dogmatics that deals with human → freedom and → responsibility (→ Anthropology) and with the foundations and principles of moral action. It is the doctrine of the Christian → lifestyle and the glorious liberty of the children of God (Rom. 8:21). Its theonomous basis differentiates it from → ethics and moral philosophy. The central Christian beliefs of → creation, the fall (→ Sin), the → incarnation, redemption in Jesus Christ, and the → promise of an eschatological → salvation (new heaven, new earth; → Resurrection; Eschatology) provide the claim and goal for human action, though with no specifically Christian catalog of → norms.

In Roman Catholic theology moral theology emerged from dogmatics as an independent discipline only toward the end of the 16th century. Then up to the middle of the 20th century it occasionally linked up with → pastoral theology (§2) and →

canon law, from which it received, as training for the practice of penance, a restrictive legalistic and casuistic dilution (→ Casuistry). It has thus frequently come to be seen as merely a doctrine of sin and moral duties, with ascetic theology as a separate discipline offering positive teaching on the life of → virtue and → perfection. Fresh reflection on the biblical basis has been needed to loosen it from this dubious alliance and to provide a more salvation-oriented personal view of → law and gospel.

2. Content

The content of moral theology is arranged according to the basic statements of fundamental morals (general ethics), which deals especially with the themes of freedom and responsibility, the biblical foundations of morality (the ethos of the OT → prophets and → Decalogue, the → Sermon on the Mount and Pauline ethics), → conscience, the basic decisions and motivations of human action, but also the problem of norms (→ Natural Law), sin and → guilt, → conversion (→ Penitence), and → reconciliation. In special ethics the issue is the religious sphere of human action, for example, questions of protecting life, sex and → marriage (→ Sexual Ethics), → truth and truthfulness. → Social ethics now deals with the problems of justice, → economic ethics, and sociopolitical action.

3. Basis

The basis and structure of moral theology depend essentially on the underlying worldview and anthropology. As Christians see it, all that exists depends on the creative → Word of God. Hence all creation has a rational structure that has not been lost, even through the obscuring of human knowledge as a result of the fall. The Bible tells us that we are made in the image of God (Gen. 1:27). Endowed with reason, we bear responsibility and are thus summoned to act rationally.

In virtue of our freedom, the related personality, and our social and natural ties, we have dominion over creation, charged to shape it but not to exploit it (→ Human Dignity). Biological, psychological, and social factors may limit our freedom, but it does not mean that everything is predetermined. We are still open to the world and may intervene in the evolutionary process of → nature. These controlling interventions are legitimate so long as they serve human well-being and success both individually and socially. With our reason, though we are implicated in nature, we are also apart from it, so that nature as such cannot be a norm of ethical conduct.

We have moral responsibility in virtue of our ra-

tional and emotional character as persons. This responsibility is not something forensically imposed upon us from without. In a very inward way it constitutes the development of our freedom. To act morally is thus to act rationally. Here is something intrinsic to our very being. Our approach to moral theology, then, must be rational. To that extent moral theology is closely connected to philosophical ethics.

4. Christian Content

If we inquire into what is specifically Christian in theological ethics, we cannot understand the answer as a mere superstructure of Christian values (→ Ethics of Values) or norms added to what is purely human. The Christian element coincides with a humane fulfilling of what is human. Christian faith, then, expresses what applies to each of us inwardly, what will enable us to truly develop our humanity and its freedom. In our freedom and openness we know that we are called to give shape to the world. We must set up the concrete norms of action and declare obligatory the values that are in keeping with our divine commission to achieve a just and peaceful world. This moral → autonomy is not in conflict with the Christian element. Indeed, it reaches a climax and finds its true theological basis, a theonomous basis, in → faith.

5. Universal Relevance

The tremendous technological innovations (→ Technology) of the past century brought → progress, but they also brought disastrous economic, social, political, and ecological development (→ Ecology; Environment) and conjured up new perils. Our epoch is characterized by very dangerous borderline experiences because of the increase in population, the use of nuclear energy, genetics, artificial insemination, and communications technology. The possibility of the self-destruction of all human life on earth, which was never previously present, poses a new challenge to human responsibility.

This possibility has also occasioned a paradigm shift in ethics today. Responsibility no longer relates merely to the immediate, current sphere of the personal life of individuals and those around them. We must extend it globally and universally to the fate of all people, of all → life on our planet — indeed, for the whole cosmos. The future of the earth is in our hands. For a preventive ethics the ecological dimension plays a special role. For Christians, responsibility means responding to God's prior gracious action (→ Grace). We see this point already expressed in the prologue (Exod. 20:1-2) to the Decalogue.

6. Sin

Our own sin and shortcomings make responsible action difficult. Sin does not simply mean offending God. It is more of an assault on human well-being. Moral action takes place in this world and among people, not apart from it. In that sense there is a justifiable → secularism. In Jesus as the Word of God, God himself has become man in this world. Responsible Christian action thus must take the world seriously. The deeper meaning and purpose of this world that is as yet unredeemed is not plain to see. It is closed to us. The loss of transcendent meaning shows itself in the unrelatedness of things and people.

Nevertheless, the salvation of the world is manifest in Jesus Christ. The foundation of Christian faith and → hope lies in his proclamation of the → forgiveness of guilt to those open to it and his promise of a better world. Faith looks to an absolute → future that includes the world's own future. Despite the disasters and → evil that constantly afflict us, Christian hope orients itself to a final form of humanity that has already been initiated. This orientation is the ultimate reason for the → optimism that is distinctively Christian.

→ Catholicism (Roman); Roman Catholic Church

Bibliography: L. S. Cahill, *Sex, Gender, and Christian Ethics* (New York, 1996) • C. E. Curran, *American Catholic Social Ethics: Twentieth-Century Approaches* (Notre Dame, Ind., 1982) • L. K. Daly, ed., *Feminist Theological Ethics: A Reader* (Louisville, Ky., 1994) • J. Gründel, *Normen im Wandel* (4th ed.; Munich, 1984) • J. M. Gustafson, *Ethics from a Theocentric Perspective,* vol. 1, *Theology and Ethics;* vol. 2, *Ethics and Theology* (Chicago, 1981-84) • S. Hauerwas, *The Hauerwas Reader* (ed. J. Berkman and M. Cartwright; Durham, N.C., 2001) • K. E. Kirk, *Conscience and Its Problems* (London, 1927) • H. Küng, *Global Responsibility: In Search of a New World Ethos* (London, 1991) • J. C. Murray, *We Hold These Truths: Catholic Reflections on the American Proposition* (New York, 1960) • H. R. Niebuhr, *The Responsible Self: An Essay in Christian Moral Philosophy* (New York, 1963) • R. Niebuhr, *The Nature and Destiny of Man,* vol. 1, *Human Nature;* vol. 2, *Human Destiny* (New York, 1941-43) • O. O'Donovan, *Resurrection and the Moral Order: An Outline for Evangelical Ethics* (Grand Rapids, 1986) • W. Rauschenbusch, *Christianity and the Social Crisis* (New York, 1907) • H. Ringeling, ed., *HCE* • J. A. Ryan, *Distributive Justice: The Right and Wrong of Our Present Distribution of Wealth* (3d ed.; New York, 1942; orig. pub., 1919) • J. H. Yoder, *The Politics of Jesus* (Grand Rapids, 1972).

Johannes Gründel

Moralism

We first find the term "moralism" in the works of J. G. Fichte (1762-1814; → Idealism 5), who argued that it is the same as what philosophy is formally and idealistically (*Wissenschaftslehre* 2.6.196). Building on the teaching of I. Kant (1724-1804; → Kantianism) and Fichte that the moral is autonomous (→ Autonomy 2), moralism is often taken to denote a morality that has no links to God or to the orders of → creation but that, as practical → reason, defines → good and → evil on its own. F. → Nietzsche (1844-1900) criticized this type of moralism as an attempt to establish a new → ethics after the collapse of Christianity. When we dismiss God, he said, we cling the closer to belief in morality. "It is thought that a moralism without religious background will suffice, but this is the road to → nihilism" (*Kritische Gesamtausgabe* 8/1.326).

"Moralism," however, may also denote the view that sees morality as the one and only absolute principle of action and tries to eliminate all other aspects in advance as morally irrelevant. In the same pejorative sense "moralism" might be used for an outlook that reduces morality to legalism and narrows ethical action to the observance of laws, commands, and prohibitions. Immoralism is not the opposite of moralism but expresses an antithesis to morality, examining it and seeking to overcome it. We see this position in Nietzsche when he repeatedly called himself an immoralist. His aim was to attack what he thought to be a life-negating feature of morality (→ Life 2) and to unmask it as a lie.

Bibliography: J. G. Fichte, *Die Wissenschaftslehre* (Bonn, 1834; ET *Science of Knowledge* [ed. P. Heath and J. Lachs; New York, 1970]) • J. Haroutunian, *Piety versus Moralism: The Passing of the New England Theology* (Hamden, Conn., 1964) • R. B. Louden, *Morality and Moral Theory: A Reappraisal and Reaffirmation* (New York, 1992) • K. W. Thompson, *Moralism and Morality in Politics and Diplomacy* (Lanham, Md., 1985).

Heimo Hofmeister

Moravian Church

1. Ancient Moravian Church, 1457-1621
2. Decline, 1621-1721
3. Renewed Moravian Church, 1722-Present
    3.1. Zinzendorf
    3.2. Names
    3.3. Ecumenical Relations

The name "Moravian" was not used by the Moravian Church before the 18th century but has come to be utilized primarily as the church developed within the English-speaking world. The church itself is an international body dating from 1457 and presently consisting of 19 provinces and various institutions. Since the Second World War former mission provinces have been granted a status equal to those in Europe, England, and North America, and now each province of the church governs its own affairs except for matters of doctrine, → mission, and interprovincial concern (→ Church Government), which are decided by a Unity Synod of the whole church that meets every seven years. Each province has its own liturgical tradition, part of which it shares internationally. The Moravian Church remains small in continental Europe, Great Britain, and North America; its largest provinces are in southern Africa, Tanzania, and the Caribbean. In the year 2000 its worldwide membership numbered 800,000.

1. Ancient Moravian Church, 1457-1621

The Moravian Church is the result of almost 550 years of history in various contexts. Its earliest roots are in the Hussite movement, which took shape on the basis of the preaching of Jan → Hus (ca. 1372-1415), who was martyred at the Council of Constance. Moderate (Utraquist) and radical (Taborite) branches of this movement reached accord in 1420 on the Four Articles of Prague: (1) the Word of God should be preached freely, (2) Communion should be administered in both kinds to → clergy and laity, (3) worldly possessions of the clergy should be abolished, and (4) public sins should be exposed and punished (→ Hussites 2; Church Discipline).

At a conference in Cheb in 1432, delegates from various Hussite groups concluded that "the law of God, the practice of Christ, of the apostles, and of the primitive church" would be used to determine truth. Roman Catholics joined with the Utraquists to defeat the more radical reformers in 1434. The Four Articles were then modified extensively and became known as the Compactata of Basel. Failure to realize the goals of reform frustrated many followers, as did the constant use of military power.

A major contributor to the Hussite reformation was Peter Chelčický (ca. 1390-ca. 1460), a follower of John → Wycliffe (ca. 1330-84) who opposed all forms of power and secular authority and sought a return to what he understood as pre-Constantinian, primitive, egalitarian Christianity. His teachings were expressed in 1440 in *Šít víry* (Net of the faith).

From these struggles came, in 1457, what historians call the Ancient Moravian Church — originally called "Brethren of the Law of Christ," affirming its special allegiance to Jesus' → Sermon on the Mount as an expression of the Christian life. It later gave itself the name "Unitas Fratrum," or Unity of the Brethren. In seeking a true Christianity, the Brethren at first separated themselves from society, a decision lasting until 1495, when the group ended their more radical forms of Christian life.

In 1467 the Unitas Fratrum instituted an apostolic ministry, receiving → ordination from the → Waldenses. During the period of decline the last remaining → bishops of the Ancient Moravian Church ordained the first bishops of the Renewed Church, thus preserving the continuity of ministerial orders.

One of the distinctive elements of the theology of the Ancient Moravian Church was a division of the elements of Christian faith and life into *essentials, ministerials* (that which serves the essential), and *incidentals* (the different ways things are done). The single essential is to respond to the triune God in faith, love, and hope, which the church has affirmed throughout its history. Matters such as ecclesiology (→ Church), → sacraments, and → preaching are considered ministerials, serving the essential, while different styles of → worship and organization are incidentals.

At the time of the → Reformation, the Moravian Church established relationships with the → Reformers. In 1533, for example, Martin → Luther (1483-1546) was asked to write a preface to the German version of the Bohemian Confession of 1532; he also wrote a preface to the Latin version of the confession of 1535. In Poland the Consensus Sandomiriensis (or Concord of Sandomierz) was concluded in 1570 among the Moravians, Reformed, and Lutherans. While the earlier orientation was stronger toward Luther, during its last 50 years the Ancient Moravian Church was increasingly drawn toward the Reformed. Though the group had initially affirmed separation from world, nobility came to be welcomed, schools were established, and ascetic attitudes were relaxed. In 1579-94 the six-volume Kralice Bible (equivalent in the Czech language to Luther's German translation) was published (→ Bible Versions).

2. Decline, 1621-1721

The → Thirty Years' War (1618-48) devastated the Moravians, as the Hapsburg ruler Ferdinand II (ruled Bohemia 1617-19 and 1620-27) drove → Protestantism out of all Bohemian territories. Indeed, for 100 years the Moravians were forced to continue their life primarily as a "hidden seed" in their homelands. Only in Poland could congregations function publicly.

The key person during this time of decline was the brilliant Moravian bishop Johannes Amos Comenius (1592-1670). Considered to be among the fathers of modern education (→ Kindergarten 1.1), Comenius argued for the education of all to a universal wisdom, advocating a new school system extending from family to university, including an academy of the sciences to pool all learning. For Comenius, faith in Christ as king was central, soon to be expressed in what he believed was the imminent end of time. In 1662 Comenius published the last confession of the Unitas Fratrum.

Dogged by war, plague, and countless personal losses, Comenius was a tireless servant of the Unity. His grandson later consecrated the first bishop of the Renewed Moravian Church, thus preserving a thread of continuity with the Ancient Moravian Church. Ultimately, Comenius preserved the old Unitas Fratrum for persons like Count Nicholas von → Zinzendorf (1700-1760), who later rediscovered that heritage partially through Comenius's writings.

3. Renewed Moravian Church, 1722-Present
3.1. *Zinzendorf*
In 1722 a group of refugees from Moravia was given permission to settle on the estate of Zinzendorf in Saxony, where what historians call the Renewed Moravian Church was formed. This group later gave the name "Moravian" to the church, although Zinzendorf initially intended it to be a kind of diaspora society within the Lutheran Church, according to the pietistic principle of *ecclesiolae in ecclesia* (little churches within the church). For the latter half of the 18th century, as an expression of its understanding of the church, the Moravians were divided into three *Tropi* (indicating different ways of teaching): Moravian (the "way" from the Ancient Moravian Church in Moravia), Lutheran, and Reformed (→ Lutheranism; Calvinism). These three ways, functioning as one church, accepted both the Lutheran → Augsburg Confession (1530) and the Ten Theses of the Reformed Synod of Berne (1528).

Zinzendorf, a count of the Holy Roman Empire, was educated in the → Pietist school at Halle and the → orthodox (§1) Lutheran University of Wittenberg. Deeply influenced by the theology of the early Luther, challenged by the views of the → Enlightenment, nourished by contacts with religious leaders, including Roman Catholic and Reformation figures, and driven by a vision of Christ

for the world, Zinzendorf hoped for a renewal of the church and its world mission. The Renewed Moravian Church that developed at Herrnhut (the name given to the colony on Zinzendorf's lands) and its growing awareness of mission provided Zinzendorf with a laboratory for his views and concerns. A profoundly spiritual, communal experience on August 13, 1727, carried this vision forward.

Zinzendorf's ecumenical vision was particularly expressed in a one-year visit to North America, beginning in December 1741, when he added his voice to the "Associated Brethren of Skippack," a group working together in eastern Pennsylvania to find ways of addressing the religious needs of the area's German-speaking settlers. What began in January 1742 as a conference of Lutherans, Reformed, Moravians, Quakers (→ Friends, Society of), → Mennonites, → Baptists (including the Ephrata Cloister and those now known as the Church of the Brethren), Schwenkfelders, Separatists, Hermits, Inspired, and others ended by June of that year with the establishment of an ecumenical German-speaking church, the "Congregation of God in the Spirit." This cooperative venture provided for the retention of particular identities and traditions. Involvement in mission to the West Indies, Surinam, and the North American Indians was discussed, and a school was begun in Philadelphia's Germantown section. This experiment did not survive because of opposition from various Lutheran and Reformed leaders who restored traditional European church patterns to North America, with the interesting exception of the Union Church often developed by Lutherans and Reformed.

Zinzendorf understood the NT references to the role of Christ in creation as an indication that all religious experience is actually that of the Savior, who is also Creator (→ Christology). The character of God as person indicates that the Creator/Savior works in personal and contextual ways, thus legitimizing diversity. In the various contexts of life and history, one meets not just the truth of God but the God of truth, in whose person all is embraced that may not yet be understood. The "essential" of religion is a personal relationship with the Savior, through whom the whole Godhead relates to the world. The crucial issue for a church is not to solve all the problems of its tradition but to raise the question of whether the Savior can be met in its midst. The Savior thus met must be the wounded Savior, who chooses to carry his wounds eternally — as does the resurrected Christ (John 20:27) — and renounces the exercise of coercive power.

After the death of Zinzendorf the Moravian Church adjusted to more conventional norms. Radical social experimentation within Moravian communities ceased. Women and the laity returned to more conventional social roles, and → synods established order and doctrine. Persons such as Friedrich → Schleiermacher (1768-1834), who attended Moravian schools and called himself "a Moravian of a higher order," were particularly critical of these developments.

A renewed interest in Zinzendorf developed by the late 19th century. Since 1960 there have been 70 volumes and reprints of his works published, and in 1998 the first systematic English-language treatment of his theology appeared.

3.2. Names

Though such terms as "Moravian Brethren" and "Herrnhuters" were applied to the Renewed Moravian Church, it preferred the name "Brüdergemeine" (Community of Brethren), which was in a sense a translation of "Unitas Fratrum," the name of the → early church. While "Brüdergemeine" is still used in the Continental European Province, both "Moravian Church" and the Latin "Unitas Fratrum" are used today in English-speaking areas.

As a consequence of the separation of the Continental European Province from other Moravian provinces during the Second World War, and as an expression of a conscious decision by the international synod of 1957, "Unity" became the term of preference for the international Moravian Church. At the same time the most recent doctrinal expression of the Moravian Church, accepted in what is called the "Ground of the Unity," also fully recognizes the value of other creeds from both the early and the Reformation eras of church history.

3.3. Ecumenical Relations

In the 18th century the Moravian churches were largely established as settlements, some termed "pilgrim," which were especially involved in mission. Moravian congregations became examples of social reform, women were ordained, laity played leadership roles, and congregations were divided into age and status groups for the purpose of spiritual care. Ecumenical from the very beginning, Zinzendorf's concern for mission made it necessary to interact with churches serving potential mission areas, such as the Lutheran Church in Denmark and the → Anglican Church in England.

The Moravian Church joined the → World Council of Churches at its founding in 1948 and also belongs to various national and regional councils of churches. Since 1975 the Moravian Church in South Africa has been a full member of the → Lu-

theran World Federation. In the United Kingdom the Fetter Lane Common Statement was accepted by the Anglican and Moravian Churches in 1995 against the background of the 1749 parliamentary recognition of the Moravian Church as an ancient episcopal church. Later the Church of Ireland also recognized this statement. In 1998 the Moravian Church entered into full communion with the Evangelical Lutheran Church in America, a relationship now being explored with the Episcopal Church.

The internationally known Moravian devotional publication *Daily Texts* (Ger. *Die Losungen*), in use since 1731, is now circulated globally in 50 languages and dialects. Approximately 1.5 million copies are printed annually (→ Devotional Literature 3).

Bibliography: German sources: E. BEYREUTHER, *Die große Zinzendorf-Trilogie. Der junge Zinzendorf, Zinzendorf und die sich all hier beisammenfinden, Zinzendorf und die Christenheit* (Marburg, 1988) • E. BEYREUTHER and G. MEYER, *Nikolaus Ludwig von Zinzendorf. Hauptschriften* (6 vols.; Hildesheim, 1962-63); idem, *Ergänzungsbände zu den Hauptschriften* (14 vols.; Hildesheim, 1964-85) • E. BEYREUTHER, G. MEYER, and A. MOLNAR, *Nikolaus Ludwig von Zinzendorf. Materialien und Dokumente* (47 vols.; Hildesheim, 1971-) • D. MEYER, ed, *Bibliographisches Handbuch zur Zinzendorf-Forschung* (Düsseldorf, 1987).

Secondary works: K. M. FAULL, *Moravian Women's Memoirs: Their Related Lives, 1750-1820* (Syracuse, N.Y., 1997) • A. J. FREEMAN, *An Ecumenical Theology of the Heart: The Theology of Count Nicholas Ludwig von Zinzendorf* (Bethlehem, Pa., and Winston-Salem, N.C., 1998) • G. L. GOLLIN, *Moravians in Two Worlds: A Study of Changing Communities* (New York, 1967) • "Ground of the Unity: Church Order of the Unitas Fratrum" (1995), *Ecumenical Theology of the Heart,* Freeman, 314-18 • J. T. HAMILTON and K. G. HAMILTON, *History of the Moravian Church: The Renewed Unitas Fratrum, 1722-1957* (Bethlehem, Pa., and Winston-Salem, N.C., 1967) • K. G. HAMILTON, ed., *The Bethlehem Diary,* vol. 1, *1742-1744* (Bethlehem, Pa., 1971) • A. J. LEWIS, *Zinzendorf the Ecumenical Pioneer* (Philadelphia, 1962) • C. PODMORE, *The Moravian Church in England, 1728-1760* (New York, 1998) • R. RICAN, *The History of the Unity of the Brethren* (Bethlehem, Pa., and Winston-Salem, N.C., 1992) • E. A. DE SCHWEINITZ, *A History of the Unitas Fratrum, from Its Overthrow in Bohemia and Moravia to Its Renewal at Herrnhut, 1627-1722* (Bethlehem, Pa., 1877) • B. P. SMABY, *The Transformation of Moravian Bethlehem: From Communal Mission to Family Economy* (Philadelphia, 1988) • M. SPINKA, *John Amos Comenius: That Incomparable Moravian* (Chicago, 1943);

idem, *John Hus: A Biography* (Princeton, 1968) • W. H. WAGNER, *The Zinzendorf-Muhlenberg Encounter: A Controversy in Search of Understanding* (Nazareth, Pa., 2001) • J. R. WEINLICK, *Count Zinzendorf* (Bethlehem, Pa., and Winston-Salem, N.C., 1989; orig. pub., 1956) • J. K. ZEMAN, *The Hussite Movement and the Reformation in Bohemia, Moravia, and Slovakia (1350-1650): A Bibliographical Study Guide* (Ann Arbor, Mich., 1977).

ARTHUR J. FREEMAN

Mormons

1. Rise and Development
2. Propagation and Organization
3. Self-Understanding
4. Special Teachings
    4.1. Understanding of God
    4.2. Salvation and Exaltation
    4.3. Temple Rituals
5. Assessment

1. Rise and Development

The religious fellowship of the Mormons, which calls itself the Church of Jesus Christ of Latter-day Saints, was founded by Joseph Smith (1805-44) in April 1830 in Fayette, New York. Beginning in 1820, Smith had a series of remarkable experiences and → visions. In his youth Father God and Jesus Christ once appeared to Smith and told him, in answer to a question, that all the → confessions of faith of all the churches, including the → free churches, were an abomination to the deity. Smith later inferred from this message that he had the task of founding a new religious community. In 1827 the angel Moroni, who had often come to Smith, handed him the supposedly centuries-old golden plates that had been hidden on Hill Cumorah, near Palmyra, New York. Smith's translation, with the aid of special glasses, of the ancient Egyptian hieroglyphics engraved on the plates became the Book of Mormon.

The unusual Mormon teachings and practices generally met with violent opposition wherever the Mormons moved and resulted in a steady flight westward and even in the death of "prophet" Smith himself in prison in Illinois in June 1844. The carpenter Brigham Young (1801-77), who succeeded Smith as president of the church, led the Mormons in 1846/47 on the migration to the Great Salt Lake Desert in Utah.

In decades that followed, the settlers transformed the desert into a cultivated area, with Salt Lake City as the center. When in 1890, after a long period of controversy, the Mormons gave up polygamy (→ Marriage and Divorce), which they had officially taught and practiced, the Mormon territory became eligible to achieve statehood, entering the Union in 1896 as Utah.

2. Propagation and Organization

By very active → mission the Mormons have spread to almost every country on earth. Thus in Germany the first Mormon → baptism took place in the Elbe at Hamburg in 1851. In 2000 the church reported a membership of 11.1 million persons worldwide, in 26,000 congregations; 5.2 million of this number are in the United States, 5.9 million in other countries. The basic church curriculum has been translated into 175 languages.

The community is strongly hierarchical. At the head is the president and prophet, who is assisted by two counselors. These three constitute the First Presidency, which is assisted by the Quorum of the Twelve Apostles. Helping the apostles are the First and Second Quorums of Seventy, who serve in various locations around the world. We find this system of presidencies and quorums at every level (e.g., area, stake, district) and down to the local congregation, or ward.

3. Self-Understanding

The Mormons see themselves as a community that did not arise by sectarian division (→ Sect) but by direct divine intervention. The idea of restoration plays a large part in this regard. Mormons believe that by his prophet Joseph Smith, God has fully restored the original church, which was supposedly totally corrupted by a falling away from faith in the postapostolic age, so that the church now exists again as in OT and NT times with its laws, → revelations, rituals, and offices. The Mormons thus believe today that they are the only true church on earth.

4. Special Teachings
4.1. *Understanding of God*

The Mormons teach that all being and becoming is subject to a supreme cosmic principle, the law of constant → progress. Even God himself is not exempt from this law. For aeons, then, God was a normal human who worked his way to deity by study of cosmic laws. He still has a body of flesh and bone, has the outward appearance of a man, and resides on the planet Kolob in the star system Kokaubeam. Rejection of the → Trinity goes hand in hand with this view of God. The Mormons believe in three independent divine persons — the Father, the Son (Jesus the physical son of God, begotten of a heavenly mother), and the Holy Spirit — each of whom can be in only one place at one time (→ Ubiquity).

4.2. Salvation and Exaltation

The Mormons distinguish between → salvation and exaltation (i.e., becoming a god). The former is by the atoning death of Christ, which leads to → resurrection for all. The door of → immortality is open to them.

Salvation is only the beginning of the path to exaltation, for which each person bears responsibility. Only those who follow all the Mormon teachings and laws on earth and keep all the temple rituals reach the highest level of deification. All others must be content with lower levels of existence in the hereafter.

4.3. Temple Rituals

"Baptisms for the dead" are among the most strictly observed rituals, also the "sealing of marriages for time and eternity," "endowments" (the handing over of secret instructions, passwords, and handshakes), and the "second anointing," by which a few high-ranking Mormons are anointed already on earth as gods. The marriage sealings and the endowments, which were taken in part from the → Masons, are a special help to later deification (cf. → theōsis).

5. Assessment

On the basis of the many teachings that come by special revelation and are not compatible with the biblical testimony, along with the non-Christian temple rituals, the Mormons — despite their own understanding of themselves — are not counted among the many Christian churches and communions (→ Ecumenism, Ecumenical Movement). They are to be rated as a new, separate, syncretistic (→ Syncretism) religion.

Bibliography: L. J. ARRINGTON and D. BITTON, The Mormon Experience: A History of the Latter-day Saints (New York, 1979) • P. L. BARLOW, Mormons and the Bible: The Place of Latter-day Saints in American Religion (New York, 1991) • D. BITTON, Historical Dictionary of Mormonism (Metuchen, N.J., 1994) • R. HAUTH, Tempelkult und Totentaufe. Die geheimen Rituale der Mormonen (Gütersloh, 1985) • D. H. LUDLOW, ed., Encyclopedia of Mormonism: The History, Scripture, Doctrine, and Procedure of the Church of Jesus Christ of Latter-day Saints (4 vols.; New York, 1992) • B. R. MCCONKIE, Mormon Doctrine (2d ed.; Salt Lake City, 1966) • A. L. MAUSS, The Angel and the Beehive: The Mormon Struggle with Assimilation (Urbana, Ill., 1994) • R. V. REMINI, Joseph Smith (New York, 2002) • J. SMITH, Selected Sermons and Writings (ed. R. L. Millet; New York, 1990).

RÜDIGER HAUTH

Morocco

	1960	1980	2000
Population (1,000s):	11,525	19,254	28,854
Annual growth rate (%):	2.73	2.21	1.54
Area: 458,730 sq. km. (177,117 sq. mi.)			

A.D. 2000

Population density: 63/sq. km. (163/sq. mi.)
Births / deaths: 2.18 / 0.60 per 100 population
Fertility rate: 2.55 per woman
Infant mortality rate: 41 per 1,000 live births
Life expectancy: 68.6 years (m: 66.8, f: 70.5)
Religious affiliation (%): Muslims 98.2, nonreligious 1.0, other 0.8.

1. General Situation
2. Religious Situation
   2.1. Muslims
   2.2. Christians
   2.3. Jews and Others
   2.4. Church and State

1. General Situation

The Kingdom of Morocco, bordering the North Atlantic Ocean and the Mediterranean Sea, lies between Algeria and the Western Sahara. In the 11th and 12 centuries it was the center of a Berber empire ruling much of Spain and northwest Africa. Spanish rule came in the 19th century, then French in the 20th century (→ Colonialism); independence was achieved in March 1956. Later that year Tangier (which had been internationalized in 1923) was turned over to the new country.

In the 1970s Morocco annexed the Western Sahara (formerly the Spanish Sahara), beginning a long period of costly armed conflict with the Polisario Front, which seeks independence for the region. Not until 1991 was a cease-fire reached, administered by the United Nations. Plans were announced for a referendum on self-determination, which by 2001 still had not occurred.

In 2000 the people of Morocco were divided ethnically and linguistically between Moroccan Arabs (two-third) and Berbers, or Imazighens (one-third), who speak a variety of languages. Phosphate mining, along with agriculture and tourism, is an important element of the Moroccan economy (70 per-

cent of the world's phosphate reserves are in
Morocco and the Western Sahara). Significant oil
deposits were recently discovered in Morocco.

2. Religious Situation
2.1. *Muslims*
Almost all the people of Morocco are Muslims (→
Islam), Sunnites of the Malikite rite. Islamic expansion drove out the Romans in Morocco in the late
seventh century. In 740 Berbers revolted against
Umayyad rule from Damascus and began to develop
their own version of Islam. Centuries of conflict and
shifting control followed.

Sunni Islam is presently the state religion of Morocco.

2.2. *Christians*
2.2.1. For centuries, mercenaries and their chaplains serving with the sultans, along with traders
and pirates' prisoners, constituted a Christian presence in Morocco. → Francis of Assisi (1181/82-
1226) sent disciples to Morocco. Portuguese, British,
and Spanish colonialism on the coast (e.g., at Es-
saouira, Tangier, and Ceuta) brought with it Christians and Christian churches. Under French and
Spanish rule traders and settlers spread Christianity
throughout the country, and churches, schools, clinics, and social centers were established. White Russians, Greek farmers, and traders followed.

The → Roman Catholic Church did organized
mission work by means of influence in the educational, medical, and social sectors, Anglicans (→
Anglican Communion) worked among Jews and
Muslims. → Faith missions were also active. With
the coming of independence, however, missionary
work became illegal, and most → missionaries were
expelled. As most of the Europeans left, church
structures also decayed.

2.2.2. Most of the Christians in Morocco today
are descendants of the colonial era, along with development agents, technicians, representatives,
tourists, U.S. soldiers at military bases, and Christian students, especially from the rest of Africa.

The Roman Catholic Church has archbishops at
Tangiers and Rabat, also a pronuntius (→ Nuncio).
It maintains a discreet Christian presence that seeks
a clear break with the colonial past and avoids neo-
colonialism. The priests are mostly Franciscans.
Poor Clares and Little Brothers and Sisters of Jesus
(→ Religious Orders and Congregations) are also at
work.

There are two Anglican congregations, in Tangiers and Casablanca.

The Église Évangélique au Maroc (EEM) is a
transnational and interdenominational church re-

lated to the Église Reformée de France (→ Reformed and Presbyterian Churches), from which it
had to separate in 1956. It has pastors in Casablanca
and Rabat.

Of the two very small Russian Orthodox congregations, the one in Rabat is under the Moscow →
patriarch, while the one in Casablanca is independent. The Greek Orthodox congregation also has its
seat in Casablanca (→ Orthodox Church).

D. Barrett has estimated that in addition there
may be as many as 120,000 isolated "radio believers"
scattered across Morocco, with an additional 10,000
secret converts from Islam (→ Conversion 1) who
have chosen to remain outwardly Muslim in their
religious practices.

The Roman Catholics, EEM, Anglicans, Russian
Orthodox in Rabat, and Greek Orthodox Church in
Rabat all have representatives on the Conseil des
Églises du Maroc (→ National Councils of
Churches). They also belong to the → Middle East
Council of Churches. The Roman Catholic bishops
are on the North African Bishops' Conference, while
the EEM belongs to the → World Alliance of Reformed Churches and is related to its mother church
in France by the Commission des Églises Évangéliques d'Expression Française a l'Étranger.

The aims and self-understanding of the church
have changed significantly since 1956. The missionary agencies formerly active in Morocco (esp. North
African Mission, Gospel Missionary Mission, Emmanuel Mission; → Missionary Structures) no longer have any direct influence. Mission is now done
from outside by radio, ship, correspondence
courses, and a little through missionaries entering
as tourists. The EEM does no missionary work but
offers pastoral care to foreigners.

2.3. *Jews and Others*
In 2000 Morocco was home to 17,000 Jews (→ Judaism), dramatically reduced from 156,000 in 1900. In
addition, among the foreigners we find adherents of
→ Hinduism, → Buddhism, and traditional religions. The Baha'is enjoyed some success in the
1960s but are now forbidden to do missionary
work.

2.4. *Church and State*
The state is committed to preserving Islam as the religion of all Moroccans. Officials are either Muslims
or Jews. A Moroccan cannot officially be a Christian.
A Christian cannot marry a Muslim, and any child
born to a Christian woman and a Moroccan man is
considered a Muslim. The government allows public
worship by the country's Christian or Jewish minorities, who are strictly forbidden to proselytize or
even discuss Christianity with Moroccans.

→ African Theology

Bibliography: D. B. Barrett et al., eds., *WCE* (2d ed.) 1.510-13 • R. Bourqia and S. G. Miller, eds., *In the Shadow of the Sultan: Culture, Power, and Politics in Morocco* (Cambridge, Mass., 1999) • M. M. Charrad, *States and Women's Rights: The Making of Postcolonial Tunisia, Algeria, and Morocco* (Berkeley, Calif., 2001) • V. J. Cornell, *Realm of the Saint: Power and Authority in Moroccan Sufism* (Austin, Tex., 1998) • A. M. Findlay and A. M. Findlay, comps., *Morocco* (rev. ed.; Santa Barbara, Calif., 1994) bibliography • M. Gershovich, *French Military Rule in Morocco: Colonialism and Its Consequences* (London, 2000) • D. M. Hart, *Tribe and Society in Rural Morocco* (London, 2000) • M. M. Laskier, *North African Jewry in the Twentieth Century: The Jews of Morocco, Tunisia, and Algeria* (New York, 1994) • H. Munson Jr., *Religion and Power in Morocco* (New Haven, 1993) • C. R. Pennell, *Morocco since 1830: A History* (New York, 2000) • M. Schatzmiller, *The Berbers and the Islamic State* (Princeton, 2000).

The Editors

Moses

1. Name
2. Career
3. Historicity
4. Roles
5. Interpretations

1. Name
Exod. 2:10 explains the name "Moses" with a philologically impossible Hebrew etymology (deriving it from *mšh*, "draw out"). In fact, the name is the short form of an Egyptian name such as "Thutmose" (from *mśy*, "bear"), without the theophoric element.

2. Career
In the OT Moses is the central figure in the early history of → Israel (§1). Commissioned by → Yahweh, he rescued the people from oppression in Egypt, proclaimed the → law to them at → Sinai, led them through the desert, and died immediately before their entry into West Jordan. Though perhaps theologically questionable, the sequence of events in Exodus to Deuteronomy by which Israel believed it had been constituted the → people of God can quite legitimately be called the Mosaic history. These biblical books do not offer a biography of Moses per se but a many-layered and many-voiced presentation of his mediatorial work and of the way in which he

carried out that work. We see the greatness of his task from the special circumstances at both the beginning and end of his life — the miraculous deliverance of a Hebrew boy by an Egyptian princess (Exod. 2:1-10) and the burial (by Yahweh?) at an unknown site of an old man whose "vigor had not abated" (Deut. 34:5-7).

Moses received his call from Yahweh (or Yahweh's angel) in the land of Midian (Exod. 3:1–4:17, which is framed by 2:11-25 and 4:18-26, giving the account of Moses' stay in Midian and his marriage there). He first had to overcome Pharaoh and Egypt in carrying out his task, but eventually the power of Egypt was broken at the Red Sea (or Sea of Reeds), and Israel was free (5:1–15:21). Although in the ensuing march through the desert there were battles with other tribes and peoples (the Amalekites in Exod. 17:8-16, the Amorites in Num. 21:21-25, the Midianites in Numbers 31, etc.), the true conflict of Moses was with his own people, to whom he gave its future form of government at Sinai (Exod. 19:1–Num. 10:11) but who constantly revolted against his leadership and direction (murmuring in Exodus 16 and elsewhere, making the golden calf in chap. 32, the revolt of Korah in Numbers 16–17, etc.). Some passages even suggest that Moses himself (with his brother Aaron) was not totally faithful to his commission (Num. 20:12; 27:13-14; Deut. 32:50-52). In a great farewell discourse he recapitulated all that had happened and repromulgated the law (Deuteronomy 1–30).

The OT often refers to Moses in connection with the law in a formal way (Josh. 1:7 etc.). Apart from that reference, however, he is mentioned surprisingly seldom (e.g., Judg. 1:16; 4:11; 18:30; 2 Kgs. 18:4; Ps. 99:6; 105:26; 106:23; Isa. 63:11-12; Jer. 15:1; cf. Hos. 12:13).

3. Historicity
It is only by way of Pentateuchal criticism that one can say anything about the historical figure of Moses (→ Pentateuch). Since the → Enlightenment such criticism has arrived at many negative results but has produced no uniform, generally acceptable alternative picture. It has questioned Moses' authorship of the Pentateuch as first advanced by postbiblical Jewish tradition (Philo, Josephus, and the rabbis, who spoke of the "five books of Moses"). Though scholars have repeatedly advanced the authorship of Moses for various documents, today even the → Decalogue is viewed largely as a product of the Deuteronomic-Deuteronomistic movement, which 500 years after Moses undertook a reform of Israel in his name. General consensus thus holds

that we are largely dependent on traditions *about* Moses, traditions that W. L. de Wette (1780-1849), however, categorized in 1807 as historically unverifiable → myth. Subsequent scholars, however, did suggest that additional distinctions be made. In 1805 de Wette dated the Deuteronomic law, which had traditionally been understood as "the inheritance of Moses," to the seventh century B.C.

During the rest of the 19th century, scholars focused on extracting both the narrative and the legislative parts of the Priestly document from the rest of the Pentateuch material, ultimately dating it even later (J. Wellhausen). These findings effectively eliminated any possibility of accepting as historical the Moses depicted by the final version of the Pentateuch, namely, as the lawgiver who shaped the history of ancient Israel. Because the earlier Pentateuch sources, regardless of how one might date them, similarly emerged only long after Moses' own time, scholars used the methods of form and genre criticism and tradition history (→ Exegesis, Biblical) to examine the preliterary stage of development; this process primarily suggested or confirmed the elimination of some of the typical individual elements of the narrative (such as the birth legend, which is found in similar form outside Israel as well).

The best-known thesis is that of M. Noth (1902-68), who drew on work already done by E. Meyer (1855-1930). Noth suggested that what we have are in fact several originally independent themes (exodus from Egypt, guidance in the wilderness, revelation at Sinai, entry into the land); however, because Moses could not possibly have been an original part of each of these stories, the task is to determine those from which he can be eliminated only with difficulty and those into which the figure of Moses was only subsequently introduced. Noth himself opted for placing Moses in the entry, since the remark concerning Moses' grave in East Jordan in Deut. 34:5-6 seemed to bear the marks of an authentic local tradition.

By contrast, most scholars believe the name "Moses" is the most integral or least derivative element within the Moses tradition, suggesting that it represents evidence of a geographic origin from Egypt rather than of ethnic background. On this view, Moses was the leader of the exodus and then also during the ensuing events, which cannot easily be isolated from one another. The personal incident involving his marriage in Midian similarly fits, since it too does not seem invented and would certainly account for the special position and destiny Moses enjoyed among his people.

4. Roles

The OT, along with the postbiblical tradition and modern scholarship, offers different depictions of Moses that are in analogy to other, generally better-known figures or types. Philo (d. A.D. 45-50, *De Vita Mosis* 2) surveys the possibilities by presenting Moses as king, philosopher, lawgiver, prophet, and priest. Moses certainly was not a king in the strict sense but a charismatic leader (→ Charisma) of Israel in the days before it became a state. He ranks as a philosopher or theologian on the not very likely premise that he might have learned an early → monotheism in Egypt (under Akhenaton?). Modern Pentateuch criticism has cast doubt on his role as a lawgiver, but this function predominates in the OT and in the later view of Moses. He is depicted as a prophet in the Deuteronomic-Deuteronomistic tradition (Deut. 18:15, 18; 34:10; cf. Hos. 12:13 and Num. 12:6-8). His alleged priesthood derives from his belonging to the tribe of Levi (Exod. 2:1; 6:20; cf. Judg. 18:30).

M. Buber (1878-1965), drawing attention to the almost inconceivable stature of such a figure, presented a portrayal hardly influenced by Pentateuch criticism.

5. Interpretations

Postbiblical → Judaism added many legends to the depiction of Moses, with Hellenistic Judaism often magnifying him as an ideal human being for apologetic reasons (→ Apologetics). The → rabbis viewed him mainly in terms of his role in → salvation history as lawgiver and as prototype of the Messiah (→ Messianism).

In NT Christianity and thereafter Moses is the premier representative of the OT and Judaism, the attitude toward which is reflected in one's attitude toward Moses. He predicted Christ (John 1:45), and his → faith is a model (Heb. 11:23-28). The gift that Christ brought, however, stands in contrast to Moses' law (John 1:17; → Law and Gospel).

Bibliography: J. ASSMANN, *Moses the Egyptian: The Memory of Egypt in Western Monotheism* (Cambridge, Mass., 1997) • E. AURELIUS, *Der Fürbitter Israels. Eine Studie zum Mosebild im Alten Testament* (Lund, 1988) • L. L. BELLEVILLE, *Reflections of Glory: Paul's Polemical Use of the Moses-doxa Tradition in 2 Corinthians 3:1-18* (Sheffield, 1991) • M. BUBER, *Moses: The Revelation and the Covenant* (Amherst, N.Y., 1998; orig. pub., 1946) • G. W. COATS, *Moses: Heroic Man, Man of God* (Sheffield, 1988) • G. W. COATS and H. T. C. SUN, *The Moses Tradition* (Sheffield, 1993) • J. COHEN, *The Origins and Evolution of the Moses Nativity Story* (Leiden,

1993) • J. JEREMIAS, "Μωϋσῆς," *TDNT* 4.848-73 •
J. KIRSCH, *Moses: A Life* (New York, 1998) • E. MEYER,
Die Israeliten und ihre Nachbarstämme (Halle, 1906) •
M. NOTH, *A History of Pentateuchal Traditions* (Chico,
Calif., 1981; orig. pub., 1948) • D. T. OLSON, *Deuteron-
omy and the Death of Moses: A Theological Reading*
(Minneapolis, 1994) • W. H. C. PROPP, *Exodus 1–18*
(New York, 1999) • W. H. SCHMIDT, *Exodus, Sinai und
Mose* (2d ed.; Darmstadt, 1995) • R. SMEND, *Das
Mosebild von Heinrich Wald bis Martin Noth* (Tü-
bingen, 1959) • J. VAN SETERS, *The Life of Moses: The
Yahwist as Historian in Exodus–Numbers* (Louisville,
Ky., 1994) • J. WELLHAUSEN, *Prolegomena to the History
of Israel* (Atlanta, 1994; orig. pub., 1878).

RUDOLF SMEND

Mosque

The term "mosque," designating the Islamic place of
worship, comes from Arab. *masjid,* via a borrowing
from Aramaic. Islam distinguishes between the
jāmiʿ, which is a place of worship in the narrower
sense (i.e., a place of gathering for obligatory worship on Friday and the two festival services, a sacred
building of distinctive structure), and the *masjid,* a
cultic site in the broader sense (i.e., a place where
one casts oneself down for → prayer). The term
jāmiʿ, which does not occur in the Qur'an, results
from domestic liturgical disputes. But the *masjid* belongs intrinsically to the → monotheism of developing → Islam. In the → Qur'an it is the equivalent
of what were initially heterogeneous cultic sites like
Solomon's → temple (17:1, 7), the Kaaba (17:1), and
general Christian and Jewish places of worship
(18:21; 22:40). Only later was it reserved for the Islamic cult (9:17-18). A narrow, particularist understanding ran counter to prophetic traditions, which
emphasize the fact that the special privilege of
Muḥammad (ca. 570-632), as compared with other
→ prophets, was that the whole earth served as his
masjid. The need for a special cultic site was purely
pragmatic.

The prophet had no special place of worship in
Mecca. The little groups of believers held their
twice-daily *ṣalāh* (prayer) and their lengthy vigils in
private houses. The situation changed fundamentally in Medina, where ritual prayer soon took the
form of a regulated → liturgy. As the fellowship of
prayer grew, not only for Friday worship, a larger
place of worship, the *masjid,* such as Jews and Christians have, became necessary. The entrance to the
prophet's residence served the purpose. Tradition
tells us that it was an open court with covered galleries to the north and south. While prayer was offered
facing Jerusalem, the north gallery was used first,
and later the south.

With the spread of → Islam (§2) the Medina
model was adjusted to new situations. In newly
founded or conquered cities the main place of gathering, the *jāmiʿ,* had to be able to accommodate the
whole garrison. Since all adult Muslims must attend
Friday worship, the early mosques had an important
socializing function. Religiously undisciplined
nominal adherents learned that a religious ceremony had to precede political addresses. In the
eighth century the Islamic cult conformed itself increasingly to Jewish and Christian patterns. The
Umayyads (661-750) and their lieutenants made a
point of coming into the mosque with the insignia
of their dignity. The older Arab judge's seat, the
minbar of the prophet, became a princely throne
from which the caliph gave his Friday addresses and
which he took with him on journeys. The *miḥrāb*
(niche indicating the direction of Mecca) and
maʿdhana (minaret) were introduced in assimilation to the Christian apse and bell tower.

By the end of the eighth century the cultic function of the mosque had gained precedence over the
political function. By about 790 all Egyptian mosques
had pulpits for sermons. In the ninth century the
main types of mosques had developed. Along with
the Medina type we find the hypostyle court style
(e.g., the Umayyad mosque in Damascus), the basilica style (e.g., Al-Aqsa Mosque in Jerusalem), and the
iwan style of Mesopotamia and Persia (a rectangular
building with arches opening onto a court, the central structure being primarily a memorial mosque,
e.g., the Dome of the Rock in Jerusalem).

The chief mosque stands at the city center.
Nearby is the bazaar, where goods can be bought to
meet specific cultic needs, as well as public foun-
tains and baths, which make it possible to attain the
requisite → cultic purity. For centuries the mosque
was the only place of both religious and secular
learning, though from the 11th century it had to
share this role with other institutions (e.g., Sufi
monasteries). Today the mosque is no longer the
natural city center or center of learning. Yet it retains its main function as the site of the Friday liturgy and still has political influence. Its important
role, then, is still to be a guardian of Islamic identity
at a time when Muslims are unsettled by crises in
the Islamic world.

Bibliography: A. M. BARBAR, *The Architecture of the
Mosques in North Africa: A Bibliography* (Monticello,

Ill., 1979) • S. S. Blair and J. M. Bloom, *The Art and Architecture of Islam, 1250-1800* (New Haven, 1994) • J. E. Campo et al., "Mosque," *OEMIW* 3.133-51 • S. S. Damluji, ed., *The Architecture of the Prophet's Holy Mosque Al-Madinah* (London, 1998) • R. Ettinghausen and O. Grabar, *The Art and Architecture of Islam, 650-1250* (New Haven, 1994) • F. B. Flood, *The Great Mosque of Damascus: Studies on the Making of an Umayyad Visual Culture* (Leiden, 2001) • "Mosque," *DArt* 22.191-96.

Angelika Neuwirth

Motet

The term "motet" generally indicates an unaccompanied choral composition (→ Choir) based on a sacred text for use in the liturgical service of Christian → worship. The specific meaning of the term has varied considerably from its origin in the 13th century as a polyphonic extension of the Gregorian repertory.

The 13th-century use of the term derived from the addition of words (Fr. *mot,* "word") to the *duplum,* or upper part of compositions known as clausulae, in the period of Pérotin (d. 1238?). The *duplum* with added text was called *motetus,* "the worded part," from which the entire form took its name. The classic 13th-century motet was polyphonic (usually in three parts), polyrhythmic (usually employing a different rhythmic mode in each part), often polytextual (employing one or two different texts in the upper parts, in addition to the Latin text of the tenor), and sometimes polyglot (employing several languages simultaneously).

During the 14th century, the period of the *ars nova* (new art), motet composition fell more and more under the domination of isorhythms, reaching its culmination in the works of G. de Machaut (ca. 1300-1377). With J. de Ockeghem (ca. 1430-95), Obrecht (1452-1505), Dufay (ca. 1400-1474), and other 15th-century composers, the motet moved toward a greater freedom, expanding to four (and sometimes five and six) voices, gradually moving away from the use of isorhythms, and slowly decreasing its dependence on tenors borrowed from the → Gregorian repertory.

The motet was usually introduced into the service at the offertory (→ Mass), at the elevation, during → processions, and during other ceremonies for which the → liturgy did not prescribe a particular text to be sung.

The 16th century saw such great motet composers as Palestrina (ca. 1525-94) and Orlando di Lasso (1532-94), together with a host of composers in the Reformation tradition who gradually substituted the chorale melodies of the early Lutheran church for the Gregorian cantus firmus (lit. "fixed song," a melody forming the basis of a polyphonic composition), thus giving rise to the development of the chorale-motet. In the English tradition the term "motet" was usually employed for the older Latin compositions, the term "anthem" being used for similar compositions in English, although there are exceptions to this practice. At this time the phrase *cantiones sacrae* (sacred songs) became a widely prevalent description for collections of motets intended for use in the services of the church.

In the baroque period it becomes increasingly difficult to draw the line between the motet and other forms of church music, as the older ideal of the motet gives way to the concertato style. In Italy the motet developed as a form for solo voice(s), while in Germany it remained largely a choral form, reaching its highest development in the six great motets of J. S. Bach (1685-1750). In the post-Bach period the motet, together with church music generally, experienced a dramatic decline, becoming a vehicle for insignificant works by a variety of lesser composers.

In the 19th century the motet regained a small measure of its former prominence through the compositions of Felix Mendelssohn (1809-47), Franz Liszt (1811-96), Johannes Brahms (1833-97), and Max Reger (1873-1916). The 20th century has seen a rebirth of the older chorale-motet and freer non–cantus firmus motet forms in the works of such men as Johann Nepomuk David (1895-1977), Ernst Pepping (1901-81), Hugo Distler (1908-42), and — more recently — John Taverner, Arvo Pärt, and others. Today the term is applied to a wide variety of accompanied and unaccompanied choral compositions for use in the church.

→ Church Music; Mass, Music for the; Theology and Music

Bibliography: F. Blume, *Protestant Church Music: A History* (New York, 1974) • J. E. Cumming, *The Motet in the Age of Du Fay* (Cambridge, 1999) • H. Leisentritt, *Geschichte der Motette* (Leipzig, 1908) • F. Matthiassen, *The Style of the Early Motet* (New York, 1966) • D. R. Melamed, *J. S. Bach and the German Motet* (Cambridge, 1995) • E. H. Sanders, *French and English Polyphony of the Thirteenth and Fourteenth Centuries: Style and Notation* (Aldershot, 1998) • E. H. Sanders et al., "Motet," *NGDMM* 12.617-47 • C. Schalk, "Motet," *Key Words in Church Music* (ed. C. Schalk; St. Louis, 1978) 257-61.

Carl Schalk

Mother Goddesses

1. History

In a special way the mother is a figure in whom people see great power. The result in religion has been the worship of mother goddesses.

1.1. *Early Paleolithic and Ancient Greece*

Already in the European and Near Eastern Early Paleolithic (40,000-25,000 B.C.), the ability to give → life found expression in many female figures with heavily emphasized sexual features, as well as in snake and bird deities (→ Serpent; Sexuality). By 6000 B.C. we find the Anatolian Great Mother, or Magna Mater.

In the early Greek period we find her in the form of a female deity worshiped primarily in grottoes. The Olympus period shows traces of this early time in the worship of Artemis, Aphrodite, Athena, and the earth goddesses (→ Greek Religion). The best known of the mountain goddesses of Asia Minor was the Phrygian Cybele. In the → mystery religions, after the pattern of the earth goddess Demeter of Eleusis, the cult spread across the → Roman Empire and, with the rite of blood baptism, became popular in reaction against Christianity (→ Roman Religion).

1.2 *Ancient Near East*

Mother goddesses played an important part in ancient Near Eastern kingdoms. The Sumerian Inanna was viewed as the queen of → heaven and earth and as the power that generates → love, growth, and order. We also find the female → demon Lilith and Ereshkigal, goddess of the underworld. The goddess Ninhursag appears as the mother of all children. Inanna's aggressive character also made it possible to equate her with the Semitic Venus deity Ishtar and the West Semitic Astarte.

In Canaanite → Ugarit in the 15th-13th centuries, we find many of these same traits in the triad Astarte, Anath, and Asherah. In Babylonian myth (→ Babylonian and Assyrian Religion; Myth, Mythology, 1), conflict with Sumerian culture may be seen in the behavior of Marduk, the national god of Babylonia, who carves up the universal primal mother Tiamat. In Egypt Hathor was worshiped as the tree goddess and heavenly cow. Nut was the goddess of the night heaven, Neith the patroness of weapons and weaving, Isis the goddess of wisdom and the throne, the rule of birth, life, and → death, and the goddess of the stars (→ Egyptian Religion).

1.3. *Hinduism*

In India we see continuous development from the pre-Indo-European period till the present. Each village has its local mother goddess, who is feared and worshiped with blood → sacrifices. The mother goddesses of the forest are less universally acknowledged. National groups like the Tamils link their identity as a people to pure virgin motherhood, which is symbolized in → Hinduism by Kannaki, the goddess of chastity. The whole subcontinent is regarded as holy as the goddess "Mother India." Since the earth is viewed as the common womb of all living things, the earth goddess Prithvi is only one of its forms.

A later trend in Hinduism affirms the existence of a single great goddess Mahadevi, or goddess Devi, who is manifested in many different forms. Her common designation as the power (Skt. *śakti*, "life force") of all deities has in view her inexhaustible creative forces. The goddess of → nature and fertility (Uma), whom we do not find in the Veda, developed as the Shakti of the pre-Aryan Siva. In the north she was the mountain goddess Parvati. In later Brahmin Hinduism she was equated with the divine cow, like the Indo-European Laksmi. We may also mention Sarasvati, prototype of the later river deities; Durga, who protects and upholds the cosmic order; and Kali, the cosmic mother and nurse.

1.4. *Other Eastern Religions*

In other religions integration has left little place for the separate experience of mother goddesses. In → Taoism assimilation to the mother of the world is the last stage before attaining to the supreme Te, the return to childhood.

Theravada → Buddhism worships the mother goddess Pattini, an idealized mother figure prominent in Sri Lanka. In Mahayana Buddhism Tara, the perfection of knowledge, is a female bodhisattva, and in Tibetan and Mongolian Tantric Buddhism (→ Tibetan Religions), she is exalted as the mother of all Buddhas and the Shakti of the primal cosmic Buddha. Many mother goddesses have male partners. In Chinese Buddhism the mother goddess Kuan-yin as bodhisattva became the goddess of grace and the first teacher able to save from suffering and danger.

1.5. *Judaism*

As regards → Judaism, the biblical tradition tells us that after the settlement of → Israel (§1) in Canaan, the pole of Asherah stood alongside the massebah, or pillar, of the God of Israel, and that King Manasseh in the seventh century even put a carved image of Asherah in the → temple at Jerusalem (2 Kgs. 21:7). Solomon worshiped Astarte as well as → Yahweh (1 Kgs. 11:33). Astarte had plainly been linked very firmly in Israel to the idea of fertility and life. Even in exile in Egypt Israel had a cult to her or to some other goddess as the queen of heaven (Jer. 44:15-19). In the fifth century at Elephantine in Egypt, Jews worshiped Anath (also spelled "Anat"), West Semitic goddess of love and war, as well as Yahweh.

With the establishment of → monotheism in Israel, mother goddesses were no longer complementary to Yahweh but were venerated in Yahweh himself. The language of the cult of mother goddesses was adopted to express the dying and rebirth (→ Regeneration) of the land, but it was applied morally to the relation between God and his people. The Song of Songs may have had its roots in songs about the love of the goddess for the king, but it was expounded as an → allegory of Israel's marriage to God, the → covenant that God has set up with Israel as his chosen creature. The female element in God came to expression especially in the hypostatizing of two phenomena in which God is close to us: Wisdom (ḥŏkmâ, esp. Proverbs 7–8) and Dwelling (šekînâ, cf. Exod. 40:34-38). The → rabbis saw Israel as a collective entity and the → Sabbath as a maternal mediatrix.

In → Gnostic thought Wisdom was the divine being by which entanglement in the world came about, but in many Gnostic systems it was also the mediator of redemption. In later Jewish Zohar → mysticism (→ Judaism 3) the šekînâ, like the old mother goddesses, was characterized both by virginity and promiscuity, by motherliness and bloodthirstiness.

1.6. Christianity
In Christianity God's mercy took concrete form in a material-earthly → incarnation for the sake of redeeming what is natural or derives from nature; this incarnation became the "most pure Mother" (→ Mariology). Mary is the incorporation of Israel and the affianced of God who breaks out in jubilation at the expected liberation (Luke 1:46-55).

→ Gentile Christians transferred to Mary what they worshiped in mother goddesses. She is depicted as Aphrodite with a star-studded mantle, or standing on a sickle moon like Artemis, or with an ear of corn like Ceres, or a dove like Ishtar. Like Isis, she is invoked for the healing of the sick, and from her womb the child Jesus takes over world rule. From the fifth century on, her feasts were celebrations of planting and harvest. She was venerated for the aid she could give in natural crises and confinements. The Roman Catholic → dogma of the assumption also proclaims Mary as a heavenly protectress.

Ancient Syrian Christianity attributes the features of mother goddesses to the → Holy Spirit, the word for "spirit" being a feminine noun in Semitic languages. The church is described similarly.

2. Sociocultural Context
Consideration of mother goddesses is a burning issue in the women's liberation movement (→ Feminism; Women; Women's Movement). In 1861 J. J. Bachofen (1815-87), in his work *Das Mutterrecht* (Mother right), viewed myths about mother goddesses as a living expression of an earlier stage in human cultural development, the matriarchal. His work, however, failed to prove that the presence of mother goddesses is evidence of matriarchy, that the matrilineal and the matriarchal necessarily go together, or that matrilineal societies are the remnants of a matriarchal era. Today matriarchy might be understood simply as a mother principle. Stress on the eternal feminine in deity or on the mother goddess thus depends on the natural ability of the woman to be a mother and more generally on the relation to nature.

The complexity of the sociocultural relations may be seen in India and China. The different poles of mother goddesses in India — passive and nourishing in the cow, fearful and vengeful in Kali, with the Parvati type in between — are linked to experiences of the mother and the mother-in-law in the extended family, or to the well-wishing faithful wife of the father. In China, however, the idea that led to the honoring of the divine as mother goddess was simply that of the woman as the honorable mother of her children.

→ God; Nature Religion; Phenomenology of Religion; Religion; Tribal Religions

Bibliography: J. J. BACHOFEN, *Das Mutterrecht* (6th ed.; Frankfurt, 1985; orig. pub., 1861; partial ET *Myth, Religion, and Mother Right* [Princeton, 1973]) • L. GOODISON and C. MORRIS, eds., *Ancient Goddesses: The Myths and the Evidence* (Madison, Wis., 1999) • E. O. JAMES, *The Cult of the Mother-Goddess: An Archaeological and Documentary Study* (London, 1959) • D. R KINSLEY, *The Goddesses' Mirror: Visions of the Divine from East and West* (Delhi, 1995) • E. NEUMANN, *The Great Mother: An Analysis of the Archetype* (2d ed.; London, 1963) • C. OLSEN, ed., *The Book of the Goddess* (New York, 1983) • R. PATAI, *The Hebrew Goddess* (3d ed.;

Detroit, 1990) • J. J. Preston et al., "Goddess Worship," *EncRel(E)* 6.35-59; idem, ed., *Mother Worship: Theme and Variation* (Chapel Hill, N.C., 1982) • L. E. Roller, *In Search of God the Mother: The Cult of Anatolian Cybele* (Berkeley, Calif., 1999) • R. R. Ruether, *Women-Church: Theology and Practice of Feminist Liturgical Communities* (San Francisco, 1985) • M. Vermaseren, *Cybele and Attis: The Myth and the Cult* (London, 1977) • D. Wolkenstein and S. N. Kramer, *Inanna: Queen of Heaven and Earth* (New York, 1983).

Christoph Elsas

Mother of God → Mariology; Mary, Devotion to

Motive, Ethics of

1. Term
2. Problems
   2.1. Implicit
   2.2. Explicit

1. Term

The expression "ethics of motive," which came to be used as a philosophical term during the 20th century, refers to a basic ethical disposition that looks for the ethical qualification of actions in a reference to their underlying intention, while remaining indifferent toward any actual consequences such actions may have. One can show that E. → Troeltsch (1865-1923) also used the term in this sense in his characterization of Kantian ethics as ethics not oriented — as was objective-theological ethics — toward the result of actions (p. 626).

2. Problems

2.1. *Implicit*

The antithesis between this view and an ethics of result or → responsibility became a problem in ethics after I. Kant (1724-1804), who had specifically stressed the importance of the motivation and → conscience if a moral act was to be performed. Something of the antithesis appeared in Plato (427-347 B.C.; → Platonism) and Aristotle (384-322; → Aristotelianism), but it had not been a factor in the basic concepts of the → ethics of antiquity, for example, in the concept of justice. Only in → Augustine (354-430; → Augustine's Theology), on the basis of the admonition of Jesus that we should not make a show of our own righteous works, do we find the suggestion that a work is pleasing to God,

not as a work, but in virtue of the disposition (*animus*) and intention (*intentio*) with which it is performed. P. Abelard (1079-1142) found in the NT statement about the sinfulness of mere desire a basis for the function of motivation in moral action. In pre-Kantian ethics the same question regarding the relationship between motivation and ethics also took the form of the question as to the significance of conscience.

2.2. *Explicit*

The frequently negative assessment of this expression today derives from M. → Weber (1864-1920), who criticized Christian ethics as merely one of motivation in which a Christian "does what is right and places the outcome in God's hands." As he saw it, on this view the intrinsic value of an act sufficiently justifies it (*Gesammelte Aufsätze,* 505). Over against an understanding of morality that acknowledges only a person's motivation or conviction as determinative for the moral character of action, and against the idea that the possible outcome of an act has no bearing on its moral character, he advanced an ethics of responsibility in which "one must answer for the (foreseeable) *consequences* of one's actions" ("Profession," 360). He recognized that achieving good ends might often involve questionable means, and also that we cannot rule out undesirable side effects, but in contrast to an ethics of motives that is concerned only for "the flame of pure conviction," an ethics of responsibility wrestles with the diabolical forces that lurk in every field of power, becoming thereby fully aware of their presence and not falling helplessly victim to them, as is often the case in an ethics of motive (pp. 366-68).

M. Scheler (1874-1928) distinguished between a false and a true ethics of motive and viewed himself as a representative of the latter. He defined a false theory as one for which the goal of volition is revealed by motivation instead of action being directly oriented to the actualizing of a specific value. Kant seemed to have reached this boundary in his assertion that the truly good person, for example, when providing assistance, is concerned only with doing his duty without considering the reality of the other person's well-being (*Formalismus,* 136). Scheler recognized the intrinsic worth of a moral disposition but, in opposition to Kant, stressed that although moral worth lies primarily in motivation, value attaches also to the other stages of volition and action (intention, project, decision) that call for consideration. Scheler's material specification of motive goes hand in hand with this assertion. In keeping with this perspective, he found the goodness of an action in the actualizing of the higher of many positive values, while an → act was bad if it involved the choice of a lower or negative value (pp. 45-46). Scheler developed this view in contrast to an ethics of results that in his definition makes the value of a person or volitional act, or indeed conduct in general, dependent on its practical consequences in the real world (p. 127). He pointed out that this theory ignores the intrinsic worth of moral purpose and motivation, though he could not say how far he accepted the validity of Kant's distinction between *Moralität* (abstract morality) and *Sittlichkeit* (morality grounded in custom).

Questions concerning the relation between motive, intention, and result in human action enter contemporary debate in tandem with a theological emphasis on Christian → love *(agapē)* conceived as motivation. This position accents the underlying reason an agent acts; → euthanasia, for example, might be killing justified by a motive of love. Or, love is the "fundamental orientation" of the agent to God in life's actions. With its focus on matters of the heart, this picture ties back to Kant, and arguably to → Augustine and → Jesus. Yet in Roman Catholic debates, attention has returned to Thomistic distinctions between motive, result, and intention in an action and the object by which it is named. As John Paul II (b. 1920) holds, good motives matter, yet they cannot make an evil act good.

Bibliography: G. E. M. Anscombe, *Intention* (Oxford, 1963) • D. Baumgardt, "Gesinnungsethik oder Erfolgsethik?" *PhSt(B)* 1 (1949) 91-110 • J. Fuchs, *Human Values and Christian Morality* (Dublin, 1971) • John Paul II, *Veritatis splendor* (London, 1993) • G. Outka, *Agape: An Ethical Analysis* (New Haven, 1972) • C. Pinches, *Theology and Action* (Grand Rapids, 2002) • H. Reiner, "Gesinnungsethik und Erfolgsethik," *ARSP* 40 (1953) 522-26 • M. Scheler, *Der Formalismus in der Ethik und die materiale Wertethik* (5th ed.; Bern, 1966; ET *Formalism in Ethics and Non-formal Ethics of Values* [Evanston, Ill., 1973]) • M. Slote, *Morals for Motives* (Oxford, 2001) • E. Troeltsch, *Gesammelte Schriften* (vol. 2; 2d ed.; Tübingen, 1922) • M. Weber, *Gesammelte Aufsätze zur Wissenschaftslehre* (Tübingen, 1922; 3d ed., 1968); idem, "The Profession and Vocation of Politics," *Writings* (Cambridge, 1994) 309-69.

Heimo Hofmeister

Mott, John R.

John Raleigh Mott (1865-1955) was one of the most influential persons in the formation of the modern ecumenical movement. Born in Purvis (Livingston Manor), New York, on April 25, 1865, he was the son of a prosperous lumber merchant. His was a pious Methodist family, and he remained a Methodist layman his entire life. Soon after his birth, the family relocated in Postville, Iowa, where Mott remained until his college years.

Mott experienced an evangelical → conversion during his years at Cornell University in Ithaca, New York. He was deeply influenced both by English evangelist J. E. K. Studd (1858-1944) and by U.S. evangelist Dwight L. → Moody (1837-99), whom he met in 1886. For Mott the slogan "The evangelization of the world in this generation," associated with the Student Volunteer Movement (SVM), took on special meaning and became a driving force for his life as he came to develop a profound sense of the mission of the → church, which he combined with exceptional skills of organization. This conversion experience also led Mott to combine in his own life all the dimensions of → ecumenism: the themes addressed by the → Life and Work and the → Faith and Order movements, as well as → mission.

Mott served as student secretary of the International Committee of the → Young Men's Christian Association (YMCA, 1888-1915) and then as YMCA general secretary (1915-31). In 1888 he became chair of the Executive Committee of the Student Volunteer Movement, a position he held until 1920. From 1891 onward, the year of his first trip to Europe, Mott played a key role in the formation of the → World's Student Christian Federation (WSCF). He was a participant in the meeting at Vadstena, Sweden, in 1895 that led to the establishment of the federation, and he became its general secretary (1895-1920) and then chairman (1920-28). In connection with his work on behalf of the SVM, YMCA, and WSCF, Mott traveled extensively in Europe, Asia, and Australia between 1891 and 1909.

Mott's passion for the mission of the church led him to active involvement in the planning for the World Missionary Conference in 1910 in Edinburgh, an event that is often described as the birth of the modern ecumenical movement. He chaired the first preparatory committee, presided at most of the sessions in Edinburgh, and was elected the chairman of the Edinburgh Continuation Committee. This conference established Mott as a preeminent Christian leader in the world and in the ecumenical movement. His role as chair and J. H. Oldham's (1874-1969) as secretary were viewed as decisive.

In 1921 at Lake Mohonk, New York, the → International Missionary Council (IMC) was formally constituted. This council succeeded the Edinburgh Continuation Committee, which Mott had helped to keep alive during the difficult years of World War I. Together with Oldham, Mott was a major force in the creation of the IMC, serving as its chair from 1928 until 1946.

As early as 1890 Mott had met the Swedish theologian and ecumenist Nathan Söderblom (1866-1931), who in 1914 was chosen archbishop of Uppsala. Over the years the Swedish primate and the American layman became fast friends. When Söderblom took the leadership in organizing the Universal Christian Conference on Life and Work, which took place in Stockholm in 1925, Mott recognized the critical nature of a Christian witness on issues of → peace and justice. Throughout the 1920s Mott's addresses and sermons often turned to the question of applying Christianity to the current world scene.

In 1917 Mott had taken part in a U.S. government mission to Russia, a country he had first visited in 1899 in connection with his student Christian work. In the 1920s and 1930s Mott continued his early travels, visiting virtually every corner of the world.

In his early years of ecumenical activity, Mott showed little concern for the unity of the church. After Edinburgh, however, Mott had a growing realization that ecumenism must mean more than simply cooperation between churches, a view that his increasing contacts with the → Orthodox churches reinforced. Being a proponent of → evangelism thus led Mott also to become an advocate of Christian unity. In 1927 Mott was an American Methodist delegate to the First World Conference on Faith and Order in Lausanne, Switzerland. Illness in Lausanne, however, prevented him from actually participating in the conference.

Ten years later, in 1937, Mott was present at both the Oxford Conference on Life and Work and the Conference on Faith and Order in Edinburgh. At Oxford, Mott was the chair of the business committee and presided at a number of conference sessions. In Edinburgh, Mott shared the general chairmanship with three others. At both events he expressed his strong support for a "world council of churches." From the early 1930s Mott had encouraged Faith and Order and Life and Work to draw closer together, and in these efforts he was in close contact with his old friend Oldham and the Dutch ecumenist Willem A. → Visser 't Hooft (1900-1985), who later became the first general secretary of the → World Council of Churches. Beginning in 1937, Mott served on the committee charged with designing the structure for the emerging World Council of Churches.

In 1946 Mott, like Söderblom before him, was awarded the Nobel Peace Prize for his many contributions to peace and concord among nations. Before that time he had received countless academic and public awards for his leadership and contributions to church and state.

In 1948 Mott was present in Amsterdam for the council's first assembly. He was the preacher at the opening service, and at the conclusion of the assembly he was elected honorary president in recognition of his unique services to the ecumenical movement.

On January 31, 1955, after a brief hospitalization, Mott died in Evanston, Illinois, at the age of 89. He remains widely acknowledged as one who, perhaps more than any other, personally engaged and wove together all the various strands of the ecumenical movement.

Bibliography: Primary sources: Addresses and Papers of John R. Mott (6 vols.; New York, 1946-47) • *Confronting Young Men with the Living Christ* (New York, 1923) • *The Decisive Hour of Christian Missions* (New York, 1910) • *The Evangelization of the World in This Generation* (New York, 1900) • *Liberating the Lay Forces of Christianity* (New York, 1932). Mott's papers are at the Divinity School of Yale University, New Haven, and in the YMCA Library, New York City.

Secondary works: C. H. HOPKINS, *John R. Mott, 1865-1955: A Biography* (Grand Rapids, 1979) • B. MATTHEWS, *John R. Mott: World Citizen* (London, 1934).

WILLIAM G. RUSCH

Motu proprio

Motu proprio (Lat. "by one's own impulse") is a canonical ruling (→ Polity, Ecclesiastical) issued by the → pope on his own accord. Along with the apostolic → constitution it is an important form of proclamation in papal legislation. A favorable ruling (rescript) has great force when issued in this form (→ CIC 1983).

Bibliography: R. R. GAILLARDETZ, *Teaching with Authority: A Theology of the Magisterium in the Church* (Collegeville, Minn., 1997).

BERND T. DRÖSSLER

Mourning → Grief

Mozambique

	1960	1980	2000
Population (1,000s):	7,461	12,095	19,563
Annual growth rate (%):	2.22	2.26	2.47

Area: 812,379 sq. km. (313,661 sq. mi.)

A.D. 2000

Population density: 24/sq. km. (62/sq. mi.)
Births / deaths: 4.06 / 1.59 per 100 population
Fertility rate: 5.62 per woman
Infant mortality rate: 101 per 1,000 live births
Life expectancy: 48.9 years (m: 47.5, f: 50.4)
Religious affiliation (%): tribal religionists 50.4, Christians 38.3 (Roman Catholics 15.6, Protestants 11.3, indigenous 9.0, unaffiliated 1.7, other Christians 0.9), Muslims 10.5, other 0.8.

1. General Situation
2. Religious Situation
   2.1. Roman Catholic Church
   2.2. Protestant Churches
   2.3. Ecumenical Contacts
   2.4. Islam

1. General Situation

The Republic of Mozambique lies on the east coast of Africa, bordered by Tanzania on the north; Malawi, Zambia, and Zimbabwe on the west; and Swaziland and South Africa on the south. African peoples (almost 98 percent of Mozambique's population) comprise 11 major ethnic groups, the largest of which are the Makhuwa (6.8 million) and Lomwe (2.0 million) in the north, the Sena-Podzo (1.1 million) and Shona (1.0 million) in the center, and the Tsonga-Changana (1.9 million) and Tswa (1.1 million) in the south, all of whom speak very different languages. The capital is Maputo, formerly called Lourenço Marques.

Arab traders were followed in the 16th century by the Portuguese at the ports, and Portugal made Mozambique a colony in 1569 (→ Colonialism). The Portuguese penetrated to the interior only after 1880, where they met with prolonged resistance. The → slave trade flourished until around 1900, mainly with Brazil. Forced labor continued until 1970.

In 1962 E. Mondlane united liberation movements into the Frelimo (Front for the Liberation of Mozambique), and began to retake the country from Portugal. Mozambique became independent in 1975 and adopted a democratic constitution under Frelimo leadership. Lack of support from the West contributed to the adoption of Marxism, which was formally abandoned in 1989. In 1990 a new constitution provided for a multiparty system and a free-market economy.

A brutal civil war devastated most of the country throughout the 1980s and until 1992. Social and economic mismanagement exacted a further heavy toll, and by 1994 Mozambique had become one of the world's poorest countries. By 1995 approximately 1.7 million Mozambican → refugees had been repatriated. Economic reforms, a low rate of inflation, and cancellation of a large part of its external debt have combined to give the country some much-needed economic growth.

The economy is agrarian, the main crops being cashews, cotton, sugar, corn, cassava, and tea. In 2000 the main exports were prawns, other foods and beverages, machinery and transport equipment, and cotton, most of which were shipped to the European Union or to South Africa. Mozambique has commercial ports on the Indian Ocean for Malawi, Zimbabwe, and the Transvaal.

2. Religious Situation

Catholicism came to Mozambique from Portugal in 1505, and Protestant → missionaries began work in 1879 with the help of nationals converted in neighboring countries. About half of the people are tribal religionists (→ Guinea 2), with Christianity and → Islam the next largest groups. Between 1975 and 1982 it was the government's official policy to eliminate the church. The new constitution of 1990 guaranteed → religious liberty (→ Church and State).

2.1. *Roman Catholic Church*

In the 16th century the → Jesuits were at work in the kingdom of Monomotapa, between the Zambezi and Limpopo Rivers. The → Dominicans replaced them, but the Jesuits returned in 1881. In 1891 the → Franciscans took up work in Beira. Until 1940 only Portuguese orders were permitted (→ Religious Orders and Congregations), and they were under the → patronage of the Portuguese king or state, not Rome. They enjoyed enormous privileges for → mission, → education, and health work. The → Roman Catholic Church spread out from the administrative centers, using priests from abroad. In 2000 there were 9 → dioceses.

Until 1974 close ties existed to Portugal, but in the 1970s the White Fathers and the Burgos Fathers voiced criticism, which led to increased church-state tensions. Ultimately, however, Mozambican bishops and other churchmen became official mediators in talks ending the war in 1992. After independence Maputo had a Mozambican national as archbishop.

2.2. Protestant Churches

Only tiny Protestant churches and fellowships were able to establish themselves under the Portuguese. Their variety is based more on history, geography, and language than on denominational factors. The Presbyterians, United Methodists, Free Methodists, Anglicans, and Reformed all maintain important educational, medical, and social work.

In 1995 the largest Protestant group was the United Baptist Church of Mozambique (400,000 persons affiliated; → Baptists). It stems from a merger in 1970 between the Evangelical Baptist Church and the Scandinavian Baptist Mission.

Next largest are several → Assemblies of God groups. The group "Assemblies of God" (380,000 affiliates in 1995) was founded in 1960 and is related to the U.S. Assemblies of God. The Pentecostal Assemblies of God (150,000) arose in 1938 from work by the Canadian Assemblies. The African Assemblies of God (70,000) began in 1970 as a result of efforts from Zimbabwe.

The Presbyterian Church (100,000 in 1995; → Reformed and Presbyterian Churches) derives from missionary work done in 1880 in the Limpopo Valley (Gaza Province) by J. Mhalamhala, who came from a refugee settlement in South Africa. It was built up by the Swiss missionaries P. Berthoud, H. A. Junod, and others in Ricatla, then Maputo. A school for evangelists was founded in Ricatla in 1907, and one for pastors in 1917. Schools, hospitals, social work, and training for women continued in spite of repression. The church became independent of the mission in 1970. After independence the church took up an attitude of critical loyalty to the socialist regime. A related church is the Igreja de Cristo em Manica e Sofala (15,000), from 1965, with headquarters in Beira.

The Anglican Diocese of Lebombo (95,000; → Anglican Communion) owes its origin to nationals who had been converted in South Africa to the south and in Malawi (Niassa Province). In 1908 the → Seamen's Mission was set up in Maputo.

Seventh-day → Adventists (82,000) date from 1933 in Mozambique.

The United Methodist Church (60,000; → Methodist Churches), of American origin (→ North American Missions), developed after 1884, first in Inhambane, then in Maputo, Gaza, and Beira. The United Congregational Church (7,000; → Congregationalism) in the south is an offshoot. The Wesleyan Methodist Church (16,000) was started by R. N. Machava in 1885 with support from the Methodist Church of South Africa. The Free Methodist Church (20,000) in Inhambane, which derives from the work of two American missionaries in 1885, has spread in the south and in Beira.

2.3. Ecumenical Contacts

In 1948 the Christian Council of Mozambique (→ National Christian Councils) was formed by the Presbyterians, Methodists, and Anglicans. In 1958 it established the United Seminary for theological training in Ricatla, open to all denominations. A common secondary boarding school was founded in Maputo in the 1960s for students from abroad, as was a center to train hospital workers.

→ Solidarity grew with independence, brought in the Roman Catholics, and resulted in the adoption of common positions in relation to the state, in the women's day of prayer, in theological → dialogue, and finally in 1989 in the first steps toward ending the civil war. Some churches belong to denominational alliances (→ World Methodist Council; World Alliance of Reformed Churches), to the Communauté Évangélique d'Action Apostolique, to the → All Africa Conference of Churches, and to the → World Council of Churches. Since 1993 the Evangelical Association of Mozambique has served the groups representing the nearly 12 percent of the population that are evangelical.

2.4. Islam

Islam was first introduced into Mozambique by Arab and Persian traders who reached the northern coast around 1000. From that period until the Portuguese arrived in the 16th century, Muslim sultans ruling from Zanzibar controlled the Mozambican coast. The Yao people (450,000 in 2000), who since the 19th century were traders between Lake Malawi and Kilwa Kivinje, Tanzania, are 80 percent Muslim, the only interior tribe south of the equator to have undergone mass conversion to Islam.

→ African Theology

Bibliography: C. Alden, *Mozambique and the Construction of the New African State: From Negotiations to Nation Building* (New York, 2001) • H. Assefa and G. Wachira, eds., *Peacemaking and Democratization in Africa: Theoretical Perspectives and Church Initiatives* (Nairobi, 1996) • D. B. Barrett et al., eds., *WCE* (2d ed.) 1.513-17 • M. L. Bowen, *The State against the Peasantry: Rural Struggles in Colonial and Postcolonial Mozambique* (Charlottesville, Va., 2000) • J. M. Cabrita, *Mozambique: The Tortuous Road to Democracy* (New York, 2000) • M. Hall and T. Young, *Confronting Leviathan: Mozambique since Independence* (Athens, Ohio, 1997) • A. Helgesson, *Church, State, and People in Mozambique: An Historical Study, with Special Emphasis on Methodist Developments in the Inhambane Region* (Uppsala, 1994) • J. K. Mandelbaum, *The Missionary as a Cultural Interpreter* (New York, 1989) • M. D. D. NEWITT, *A History of Mozambique* (Bloomington, Ind., 1995).

SIMÃO CHAMANGO and CHARLES BIBER

Müntzer, Thomas

Little is known about the early life of the radical reformer and theologian Thomas Müntzer (ca. 1489-1525), who was born in Stolberg, Thuringia. The first reliable witness to his life is his 1506 matriculation entry at the University of Leipzig. He was definitely enrolled in the University of Frankfurt an der Oder in 1512, from which he probably graduated. After ordination in the Halberstadt Diocese, he was active as a minister in Brunswick, though he also had a sinecure in Aschersleben. He apparently studied at the University of Wittenberg between 1517 and 1519. The educational basis of his later Reformational activity likely included, in addition to his regular studies there, intensive → humanistic studies, an extensive study of the → church fathers, and an acquaintance with medieval → mysticism.

While remaining in close contact with the Wittenberg circle, particularly with Carlstadt, Müntzer occupied several positions in quick succession, including in Jüterbog, where he attacked the ecclesiastical → hierarchy while engaged in intense discussion with the → Franciscans. In May 1520 he accepted a position representing the Zwickau pastor Johannes Egranus, then finally received his own preaching position at the Church of St. Catherine. Müntzer, who had close contact with spiritualistic, → apocalyptic circles influenced by pre-Reformational → Hussite traditions, came into conflict with other Reformational or traditional groups, prompting the Zwickau city council in April 1521 to dismiss him.

Müntzer went to Prague, where he was active as a preacher, but he could not stay there long. His *Prague Manifest* (1521) is a kind of stylized confession and the first significant witness for his apocalyptic and spiritualistic theology, whose basic theme — the mystical purification of the elect through suffering → discipleship and in → obedience to the living voice "in the abyss of the soul" — remained a dominant theological theme of Müntzer's life.

After a period of setbacks, restless wandering, and personal → suffering, Müntzer in April 1523 settled into a pastoral position in Allstedt, Thuringia, where for the first time he was able to participate in ecclesiastical change, for example, by introducing worship services in the vernacular; he also composed hymns during this period. Because of a refusal of → tithes by his congregation, which Müntzer himself covered, serious conflicts arose between Müntzer and the territorial rulers of Saxony, prompting him to flee secretly in 1524. He was able to resume his ministry for a few weeks in the imperial city Mühlhausen; his goal, sealed in an "eternal covenant," was to establish a "conciliar regiment" oriented toward God's Word. The attempt failed, and Müntzer was expelled.

In October 1524 Müntzer arrived in Nürnberg, where he published two writings in which he not only broke definitively with M. → Luther but also renounced the secular authorities, whose government the rule of the elect was to bring to an end. He also spent time in Basel, where he met Oecolampadius, then also in Klettgau and Hegau, where he came into closer contact with rebellious peasants.

In February 1525 Müntzer returned to Mühlhausen and gradually became a leader and agitator in the nascent Thuringian → peasant war. He interpreted this struggle apocalyptically and, on the basis of a vision, assured the peasants of God's help. On May 15 he was captured by territorial troops; on May 27, after a hearing and torture, he was executed.

Although Müntzer's theology can be reconstructed only in part, its central elements include a mystical-spiritualist hermeneutic of the inner word, an emphasis on conformist suffering with Christ's own suffering, and a demand for separating the elect from the wicked. These elements, cast within the horizon of heightened apocalyptic expectation, generate a revolutionary vision with radical explosive power but limited historical viability. Precisely this relationship between → theology and → revolution constitutes a fundamental problem for any interpretation of Muntzer. As a result, he has become a hotly disputed figure, especially in connection with his adoption by Marxist historians.

→ Reformation

Bibliography: Primary sources: M. G. BAYLOR, ed., *Revelation and Revolution: Basic Writings of Thomas Müntzer* (Bethlehem, Pa., 1993) • G. FRANZ, ed., *Schriften und Briefe* (Gütersloh, 1968) • P. MATHESON, ed., *The Collected Works of Thomas Müntzer* (Edinburgh, 1988).

Secondary works: U. BUBENHEIMER, *Thomas Müntzer, Herkunft und Bildung* (Leiden, 1989) • A. FRIESEN, *Thomas Muentzer, a Destroyer of the Godless: The Making of a Sixteenth-Century Religious Revolutionary* (Berkeley, Calif., 1990) • H.-J. GOERTZ, *Thomas Müntzer: Apocalyptic, Mystic, and Revolutionary* (Edinburgh, 1993) • E. W. GRITSCH, *Reformer without a Church: The Life and Thought of Thomas Müntzer, 1488(?)-1525*

(Philadelphia, 1967); idem, *Thomas Münt-zer: A Tragedy of Errors* (Minneapolis, 1989) • B. LOHSE, *Thomas Müntzer in neuer Sicht. Müntzer im Licht der neueren Forschung und die Frage nach dem Ansatz seiner Theologie* (Hamburg, 1991) • T. SCOTT, *Thomas Müntzer: Theology and Revolution in the German Reformation* (London, 1989) • G. SEEBASS, "Müntzer, Thomas," *TRE* 23.414-36.

THOMAS KAUFMANN

Munus triplex → Office of Christ

Music, Musicians → Church Music; Church Musicians; Mass, Music for the; Theology and Music

Myanmar

	1960	1980	2000
Population (1,000s):	21,746	33,821	49,342
Annual growth rate (%):	2.11	2.09	1.61

Area: 676,577 sq. km. (261,228 sq. mi.)

A.D. *2000*

Population density: 73/sq. km. (189/sq. mi.)
Births / deaths: 2.49 / 0.88 per 100 population
Fertility rate: 3.00 per woman
Infant mortality rate: 65 per 1,000 live births
Life expectancy: 62.6 years (m: 61.0, f: 64.3)
Religious affiliation (%): Buddhists 72.2, tribal religionists 12.7, Christians 8.4 (Protestants 5.9, Roman Catholics 1.3, other Christians 1.1), Muslims 2.1, Hindus 1.8, Confucianists 1.6, other 1.2.

1. General Situation
2. Religious Situation
   2.1. Buddhists
   2.2. Christians
       2.2.1. Roman Catholics
       2.2.2. Protestants
   2.3. Ecumenical Relations
   2.4. Church and State

1. General Situation

The Union of Myanmar (known up till 1989 as Burma) is an Asian country between South and Southeast Asia on the Bay of Bengal. Britain subdued the country between 1824 and 1885 through three Anglo-Burmese wars (→ Colonialism). British rule was followed by Japanese control during World War II, and then independence in 1948.

Free elections took place in 1960, and then not again until 1990, when the main opposition party won decisively. As of 2001, however, the ruling military junta has refused to hand over power. A key opposition leader is Aung San Suu Kyi, recipient of the Nobel Peace Prize in 1991, whom the rulers put under house arrest from 1989 to 1995 and, from September 2000 to May 2002, under formal arrest.

Myanmar, once the richest country in Southeast Asia, has become one of the world's poorest nations, largely through the greed and mismanagement of its rulers. After many years of pursuing a policy of international isolationism, its leaders have had difficulty in attracting needed foreign investment (→ Economy).

2. Religious Situation

2.1. *Buddhists*

Theravada → Buddhism, also known as Hinayana (i.e., "lesser vehicle") Buddhism, reached Myanmar early in the Christian era. It absorbed some aspects of local traditional religion and became the dominant religion by the ninth century. The University of Pali, established in 1950 with state assistance, includes among its goals the training of Buddhist missionaries. In 1954-56 the sixth world synod of Buddhism was held in Myanmar. One of the most important pagodas in all Buddhism is the Shwe Dagon in Rangoon.

Mahayana (i.e., "great vehicle") Buddhism is practiced by some of the Chinese community (approximately 3.5 percent of the population). Chinese who are assimilated into the local population, however, are more likely to be Theravada Buddhists.

2.2. *Christians*

2.2.1. *Roman Catholics*

The Portuguese Franciscan P. Buonfere initiated Roman Catholic missions in 1554. By the end of the 16th century the Portuguese Jesuit N. Pimenta had established the first congregation. Bayingyis — Eurasians of Portuguese and Burmese ancestry — shaped the first churches. From 1856 various missions were at work (esp. the Paris Mission, Irish Sisters of the Good Shepherd, later American → Jesuits; → Catholic Missions). Roman Catholic work was institutionalized in 1866.

At the end of the 19th century there were upwards of 70,000 Roman Catholic Christians, a number that had increased by 2000 to well over half a million, 90 percent of whom were among the ethnic Karens, Kachins, Chins, and Shans. Special ministries include leprosy centers, orphanages, and aid for the elderly (→ Medical Missions).

2.2.2. *Protestants*

A. Judson of the American Baptist Mission (ABM) was the first Protestant missionary to Myanmar (1813). In 1826 he produced a Burmese dictionary that is still highly regarded, and in 1834 a translation of the Bible in Burmese (→ Bible Versions). The founding of churches, however, progressed slowly. When Judson died in 1850, there were 63 Baptist congregations, 62 ABM missionaries, 267 → Baptists among the Burmese, and 7,750 among the Karens. Missions to the Chins began in 1845 and to the Kachins in 1876.

The Burma Baptist Convention was founded in 1865. After national independence in 1948 the convention achieved increasing autonomy from the American Baptist Convention, and definitively so in 1966, when the government of General Ne Win expelled all Protestant and most Roman Catholic missionaries from the country. In 1995 there were 3,500 Baptist congregations, especially among the Karens, Kachins, and Chins, with 1.75 million adherents overall, making it by far the largest single Christian group in Myanmar. Special activities included cooperative work and → continuing education in the villages.

Along with the → Baptists the first Anglo-Burmese War (1824-26) brought Anglican → military chaplains as missionaries. To the Burmese these chaplains seemed to represent the interests of the British crown, especially when the work of the Society for the Propagation of the Gospel increased after the annexation of Burma as a province of British India in 1853 and the British colonial regime ceased to recognize Buddhism as the state religion in 1885. The → Anglican Church of Burma was founded in 1877 with the appointment of the first → bishop of Rangoon. By 1995 this church had 57,000 members.

Other larger denominations in Myanmar are the → Assemblies of God (223,000 adherents in 1995, begun in 1924 by Lisu Christians from China), Church of Christ (104,000, mostly refugees from China, from work started by the → China Inland Mission), Methodist Church of Upper Burma (70,000, a product of → British missions), Presbyterian Church of Myanmar (50,000, mostly migrants from the Mizo Presbyterian Church in Assam), with smaller groups of Lutherans, Congregationalists, and → Salvation Army. Besides these recognized groups, D. Barrett estimates that Myanmar also was home in 1995 to 192,000 secret Buddhist believers and 70,000 in isolated "radio churches."

2.3. *Ecumenical Relations*

The Regional Council for Burma, founded in 1914 as part of the National Christian Council of India, was at first essentially an alliance of Baptist, Anglican, and Methodist missionary societies. At the end of World War II the All Burma Christian Youth League, which united such Christian youth and student organizations as the → YMCA, the → YWCA, and the Student Christian Movement, encouraged ecumenism within Burma with a view to uniform direction for all the denominations and cooperation with Buddhists in "nation building." In 1949 the Regional Council became the Burma Christian Council (BCC), which was independent of the missions. In 1975 it reconstituted itself as the Burma Council of Churches. It is a member of the → Christian Conference of Asia, and several of its churches belong to the → World Council of Churches.

2.4. *Church and State*

The government of U Nu, the first prime minister of independent Burma (1948-58, 1960-62), gave to Buddhism and the Sangha, or fellowship of monks, increased legal and financial support as compared to other religious groups. In 1961 Buddhism became the state religion (→ Church and State).

In contrast, the government of Ne Win (1958-60 and 1962-88) exercised restraint in religious matters, no longer recognized Buddhism as the state religion, and granted equal rights to all religious groups. The "Burmese way to → socialism," the basis of the new one-party state, involved the nationalizing of all the churches' social, medical, and educational institutions and the expulsion of foreign missionaries. The churches of the BCC accepted the moratorium as an opportunity to achieve spiritual independence and to strengthen relations with the Buddhists, especially in the area of development. After 1975 Buddhists and Christians worked together in the BCC's → Urban and Rural Mission (→ Buddhism and Christianity).

Bibliography: C. ANDERSON, *To the Golden Shore: The Life of Adoniram Judson* (Grand Rapids, 1972) • D. B. BARRETT et al., eds., *WCE* (2d ed.) 1.517-21 • J. BECKA, *Historical Dictionary of Myanmar* (Metuchen, N.J., 1995) • P. CAREY, ed., *Burma: The Challenge of Change in a Divided Society* (New York, 1997) • M. GRAVERS, *Nationalism as Political Paranoia in Burma: An Essay on the Historical Practice of Power* (2d ed.; Richmond, Surrey, 1999) • M. MAUNG, *The Burma Road to Capitalism: Economic Growth versus Democracy* (Westport, Conn., 1998) • S. D. SAY, "A Brief History and Development Factors of the Karen Baptist Church of Burma (Myanmar)" (Thesis, Pasadena, Calif., 1990) • M. J. SMITH, *Burma: Insurgency and the Politics of Ethnicity* (rev. ed.; Dhaka, 1999) • M. E. SPIRO, *Buddhism and Society: A Great Tradition and Its Burmese Vicissitudes* (2d ed.; Berkeley and Los Angeles, 1980); idem, *Burmese Supernaturalism: A Study in the Explanation and Reduction of Suffering* (2d ed.; Philadelphia, 1978); idem, *Gender Ideology and Psychological Reality: An Essay on Cultural Reproduction* (New Haven, 1997) • D. I. STEINBERG, *Burma, the State of Myanmar* (Washington, D.C., 2001) • B. VICTOR, *The Lady: Aung San Suu Kyi, Nobel Laureate and Burma's Prisoner* (Boston, 1998).

WOLFGANG GERN

Mystery Religions

1. Term
2. Phenomenology
3. History
4. Types
5. Relation to Judaism and Christianity

1. Term

Mystery religions are secret cults of the ancient Greco-Roman world that offered initiates an experience other than that of the official religions. The mysteries center on a time of sacred events, a festival related to fertility in the yearly cycle and involving rites aimed at the common welfare. Cultic formulas are used, and the eyes are closed (Gk. *myō*) with a view to experiencing what takes place in the dark. The participants enter into direct bodily and spiritual relations of sympathy with certain suffering deities whose divine fate is the subject of → myth. Individual → initiation confers special privileges, promises → salvation, and guarantees → happiness both here and hereafter.

2. Phenomenology

The mystery religions all grew out of the religions of peoples that had lost their political organization. The members recognized the → Roman Empire as the state that comprised almost all the civilized world and aimed to provide a religious home for anyone, no matter what their origin. They thus formed societies apart from the public cult, partly supported by the state, partly by themselves.

The existence of classical mysteries (→ Greek Religion) suggests that we treat the idea of broad Eastern influence with skepticism. The Athenians celebrated these mysteries exclusively in sacred Eleusis at a specific time and in close relation to the city municipality (i.e., to the free males of Athens), though women, slaves, and aliens could also be consecrated. The mysteries were also connected with the military and with craft unions as secret organi-

zations. In some mysteries, consecration could take place at any time and in any place.

→ Processions, public → sacrifices, and musical presentations provided a setting for the consecrations. Two points were constitutive. The first and main focus was the contemplation of certain divine things, which granted a kind of entry into the divine world. The second focus was the way to this entry, namely, by the observance of rites as preconditions. After a period of → fasting and mortification (→ Asceticism) came purification by expiatory sacrifices. An → oath was taken to keep silent about all that was seen and heard in the course of the ceremonies. The initiates then learned the esoteric meaning of the myth of the cult's origin and received a → revelation of the true point of the divine drama. Then, strengthened by a ritual meal (→ Cultic Meal), they received imitative integration into the cult.

We do not know the nature or content of the vision. Initiates belonged to the circle of those who did know, and there was no greater offense than that of disclosing the mysteries to the uninitiated. Initiation, expressed as a descent into the underworld, was a very dangerous moment, and woe to those who, unworthy, sought to move unguided through the rites to a knowledge of the mysteries of existence! In the night initiates passed back through the natural emergence of life and ultimately to the realization that the light is, as it were, born from this emergence. Presumably, it was through the *drōmena* (from *draō*, "perform mystical rites"), the external cultic acts prescribed by the → liturgy of the sacred drama; the *deiknymena* (*deiknymi*, "show"), or presentation of the sacred symbols by the hierophant, or priest of the mysteries, which gave expression to the holy; and the *legomena* (*legō*, "say, tell"), the accompanying cultic formulas, that initiates came to an awareness of the deity and of a divine event. They thus gained confidence that in the future they could build on this knowledge of the divine and count on the benevolence of the deity.

Along with the function of initiation we find agrarian, sexual (→ Sexuality), and mythical aspects that involved stimulating intoxicants, sexual prowess that begets the future, and sacred stories of divine examples of the overcoming of suffering. In every case ancient rites were performed that evoked a sense of the uniqueness of the event and thus dispelled uncertainty as to salvation.

Initiation into the mysteries brought an irrevocable change of status. The holiness of initiates corresponded to the preceding purifications and stood in direct contrast to what was yet to be done in the initiation ritual. Sacred *myēsis* (initiation) was the decisive step. The drama simply repeated, renewed, and deepened what was passively allowed to happen.

3. History

We may agree with → ethnology in classifying the mystery religions as initiatory rites. The Vienna culture-history school found an important root in male initiations. The mystery religions reflect the matriarchal state, beginning with the introduction of agriculture in the Mesolithic Age. The males organized themselves in secret societies, whose rites — even with the repudiation of the underlying → culture (§3), worship of → mother goddesses, and matriarchy — evidently retained the initial link to agriculture. On this view, the influencing or ensuring of the harvest could well be the ancient substratum of what are mostly cyclically structured rites.

It is to be noted, however, that the Egyptian Osiris had an early relation to sheepherding, and interpretation of the mystery religions in terms of initiation points back to the ritual of hunter sacrifices. All the same, the tests of courage and the sexual and orgiastic features seem to derive mainly from an agrarian context.

The morphological school of ethnology of A. E. Jensen (1899-1965) traces the mystery religions back to the early stages of the cultivation of foods among ancient planters and their cult of the slain deity (the *dema* complex, first discovered in New Guinea), which with its death is the source of cultivated plants that give sustenance. This theory, however, is not wholly convincing. The sources at least suggest that the mystery religions took specific shape in Greece, where in the seventh and sixth centuries B.C. they gave developing Greek → individualism a religious form that individuals could freely choose.

4. Types

Important mystery religions were the Eleusis mysteries, which we can trace back to the 15th century B.C. (→ Hellenistic-Roman Religion 4). From the 7th century onward the mysteries held at Agrai, near Athens, were celebrated each year in February in preparation for the great Eleusis mysteries in September, whose various ceremonies lasted eight days. Because of their age and fame the Eleusis mysteries were obviously the model for the mystery religions in general, though there developed great differences in content.

Along with goddess mysteries, significant mysteries from the 5th century onward were the myster-

ies of the "great gods" on the island of Samothrace in Greek Thebes. Originally probably related to smiths, these mysteries featured warlike orgiastic elements and promised protection, especially in perils at sea.

More significant were the secret rites of Dionysus, which we also know from the 5th century B.C. This cult, which was spread throughout Greece by itinerant priestesses and also had centers in southern Italy, Asia Minor, and Egypt, related to life as a whole and offered a comprehensive disclosure of the secret of the link between life and death.

Already by the 5th century Orphism was influencing the mystery religions, and the legendary musician Orpheus was considered the general founder of initiation. With the penetration of Greek culture (→ Hellenism) there then arose the mysteries of Isis (Demeter) and Osiris (Dionysus), as well as Sarapis and Antinous (→ Egyptian Religion).

After A.D. 140 the mysteries of Mithras, a new system of astral and cosmic mysteries, spread with Roman soldiers and officials in the Roman provinces, earlier in Rome itself. We also find the Great Mother, or Magna Mater, cult of Cybele in Asia Minor. This orgiastic ritual was a mystery religion in the broad sense. The terminology of mystery religions was also adopted by Pythagorean Platonic and Stoic philosophers in describing the philosophical path to knowledge of true being (→ Platonism; Stoicism).

5. Relation to Judaism and Christianity

5.1. In Hellenistic → Judaism we find a polemical emphasis on the mysteries of God in opposition to the mystery religions but also an adaptation to the latter (Wis. 2:22; 6:22; 8:4, contra 12:3-5). Philo of Alexandria (b. 15-10 B.C., d. A.D. 45-50) went back to the mystery metaphors of philosophy, rejecting the rituals by employing the terms as a means to put Jewish teaching in Hellenistic garb. Among the Essenes (→ Qumran) the linking of an → oath, definitive acceptance, a first meal, and an arcane discipline remind us of the mystery religions. Otherwise it is especially the story *Joseph and Asenath* that depicts the Jewish cultic meal as a mystery meal intended to win → proselytes. From the time of Daniel the term *mystērion* was also used to denote a divinely controlled eschatological secret (→ Eschatology), whose disclosure by an → angel as mystagogue is the uniform theme of Jewish → apocalyptic.

This rootage in very different supernatural soil, as distinct from the view of the mystery religions as arising naturally in human existence, is still claimed when the term "mysteries" occurs in the writings of Christian Gnostics and → church fathers. But whereas, according to the belief in divinization (→ Theosis), we become what we were not before, redemption for → Gnostics consists of becoming God again.

5.2. Many analogies in church writings and rites may be explained by the similar conditions throughout the Roman Empire under which religions spread from the East. This insight relativized historical investigations (→ History of Religion), which at the beginning of the 20th century sought to prove genetic dependence in such concepts as → regeneration and imitation of the cult hero (e.g., R. Reitzenstein, W. Bousset, A. Loisy, and S. Angus; → History of Religions School). In Roman Catholicism the mysteries theology of O. Casel (1886-1948) argued that in virtue of common features as regards the cultic presence of the redemptive act, the mystery religions offered a schooling for Christianity. According to the → anthroposophy of R. Steiner (1861-1925), there has been poured out upon the Christian community, with the mystery of Golgotha and through the conviction that the divine is given with the Word that is now present, that which was poured out upon initiates in the cult.

5.3. The Christian *mystērion* is also a secret revelation because it is disclosed only to → faith, but unlike all esotericism it is to be proclaimed to all people "from the housetops." On the one side, the church fathers increasingly followed Hellenistic Judaism by displaying "the mysteries of the Logos" (Clement of Alexandria *Protr.* 12.119-20) to people of Greek culture in images familiar to them. On the other hand, the → apologists fought the mystery religions as "devilish imitations" of Christian → truth.

The First Epistle to the Corinthians points out the danger of sacramental certainty (where *sacramentum* becomes the equivalent of *mystērion*) and of a magical understanding of → baptism by church members. The Corinthians were perhaps misinterpreting → Paul along the lines of the mystery religion known to them (e.g., that of Dionysus). Paul did not use the terms of the mystery religions in sacramental texts but, like the NT as a whole, used them only for the eschatological mysteries of God. By prevailing ideas the → Eucharist could easily be related to the meal of the mystery religions, especially the Dionysiac-Orphic theophagy. The difference was that, like baptism, it did not offer a depiction of natural events. The story of Christian initiation does not refer back to a timeless mythical past but refers to an attested historical event, looks

ahead to the eschatological new creation that is based upon it, and hence puts the accent very differently on personal and ethical obligation.

→ Phenomenology of Religion; Religion; Sacred and Profane

Bibliography: S. Angus, *The Mystery-Religions and Christianity: A Study in the Religious Background of Early Christianity* (London, 1925) • U. Bianchi, *The Greek Mysteries* (Leiden, 1976) • G. Bornkamm, "Μυστήριον, μυέω," *TDNT* 4.802-28 • W. Burkert, *Ancient Mystery Cults* (Cambridge, Mass., 1987) • J. Ferguson, *Encyclopedia of Mysticism and Mystery Religions* (New York, 1982) • J. Finegan, *Myth and Mystery: An Introduction to the Pagan Religions of the Ancient World* (Grand Rapids, 1989) • J. Godwin, *Mystery Religions in the Ancient World* (San Francisco, 1981) • M. W. Meyer, ed., *The Ancient Mysteries: A Sourcebook. Sacred Texts of the Mystery Religions of the Ancient Mediterranean World* (Philadelphia, 1999) • R. Reitzenstein, *Hellenistic Mystery-Religions: Their Basic Ideas and Significance* (Pittsburgh, 1978; orig. pub., 1910) • K. Rudolph, "Mystery Religions," *EncRel(E)* 10.230-38.

Christoph Elsas

Mystical Union

1. Experience
2. Theological Reflection
   2.1. Roman Catholic
   2.2. Protestant
   2.3. Orthodox

1. Experience

In religion mystical union *(unio mystica)* is an ecstatic → experience (→ Ecstasy) of perfect union with God. We meet it in various religions, including → Hinduism and → Islam. In Christianity it has the form of ontological union, bridal mysticism, and passion mysticism. The biblical root lies in the metaphor of union with Christ in both Paul (e.g., Gal. 2:20; 3:27) and John (e.g., John 15:4, 7; 17:22). We may also refer to the divine indwelling of the Spirit (Rom. 8:8-11).

The East pointed the way to a union in love, especially → Origen (ca. 185-ca. 254; → Origenism), Gregory of Nyssa (ca. 330-ca. 395; → Cappadocian Fathers), and Diadochus of Photike (mid-5th cent.). Union with Christ became a central theme in Greek → Christology (§3) and → soteriology (§2.1; → Theosis). In the West → Bernard of Clairvaux (1090-1153), in his series of sermons on the Song of Songs, spoke of mystical union in the form of the kiss that denoted the inflowing of the Holy Spirit. The ecstasy is a → death that brings new → life (→ Mysticism 2.4.1). Mystical union rules out sensory experience. In this life we can have union only with the Son of Man; we cannot attain to union with the most high God.

From the 12th century onward mystical union was also a theme in religious lyrics (e.g., Pseudo-Bernard's hymn *Jesu dulcis memoria,* popular in English as "Jesus, the Very Thought of Thee," and works by John of the Cross [1542-91] and Angelus Silesius [1624-77]). Hagiography (→ Lives of the Saints) and the literature of revelation tell of many ecstatic experiences of union from the 13th century onward, especially in women's mysticism (e.g., Hadewijch of Antwerp [13th cent.], Beatrice of Nazareth [1200-1268], Mechthild of Magdeburg [ca. 1207-ca. 1282], → Catherine of Siena [1347-80], and → Teresa of Ávila [1515-82]; → Mysticism 2.3.1).

Erotic mystical union experienced as kissing and embracing is usually accompanied by a feeling of both spiritual and bodily sweetness (Gertrude "the Great" [1256-ca. 1302], "the union which is sweetness, the sweetness which is union with [Christ]," in *Leg.* 2.2). It may also involve somatic reactions (e.g., Dorothy of Montau [1347-94], Bridget of Sweden [ca. 1303-73], who spoke of mystical pregnancies and other experiences). Mystical union is not so common among men, but see Roger of Provence (d. ca. 1310), whose soul merged *unitissima* (in most complete union) with God, and John of the Cross, whose inflamed soul was deified as wood is changed by fire into heat and light.

2. Theological Reflection
2.1. *Roman Catholic*
Among Roman Catholics theological reflection on mystical union rests on Neoplatonic conceptions (→ Platonism 3) mediated by Dionysius the Pseudo-Areopagite (ca. 500) and focusing mystagogically on describing the stages of → spirituality that lead to mystical union and on evaluating it ontologically. An example of this tradition is the *Scala perfectionis* (Scale of perfection), the principal work of W. Hilton (ca. 1343-96), which teaches that by → contemplation and renouncing the world, we can attain to an infused experience of → grace (3.2) that culminates in mystical union.

In defining mystical union, the stress regularly falls on the dogmatic issue that only by grace can the → soul become what God is by nature, and that mystical union cannot as yet reach the → perfection of eschatological union. Thus, for example, J. Ger-

son (1363-1429) said that Bernard was contradicting church doctrine by saying that in mystical union the soul is transformed into the being of God. Many mystagogues like J. Tauler (1300-1361) or J. van Ruysbroeck (1293-1381; → Mysticism 2.4.2) could offer poetic descriptions of mystical union, and Meister → Eckhart (ca. 1260-ca. 1328) could also describe mystical union as the birth of God and an awakening.

The claim that mystical union might be permanent was regarded as a sure sign of heresy, and so too were → pantheistic interpretations. A normative theological definition was that reached by Carmelite mystics in Spain in the 16th century.

2.2. *Protestant*
Protestant theology engaged in a full reinterpretation of mystical union. It is no longer an isolated ecstatic experience for some but the union with Christ and "deification" that comes for all believers through → faith. M. → Luther (1483-1546; → Luther's Theology) stated that union with Christ is by faith, in which Christ's being has become ours before God (WA 5.144.17ff.); faith links the soul to Christ like a bride to her bridegroom (*LW* 31.351). In faith Christ and the Christian do not confront one another as Thou and I (as in "historical" faith) but are so "cemented" *(conglutinatio)* that they are "as one person" (*LW* 26.168). In Lutheran → orthodoxy (§1) mystical union is part of → justification. → Pietism regarded it as one of the five pillars of the Christian life (→ Order of Salvation 2.2). According to P. J. Spener (1635-1705), every Christian can say, "I am Christ."

Nor did Reformed theology ignore the mystical union. J. → Calvin (1509-64; → Calvin's Theology) related it not merely to justification but also to sanctification. He laid stress on the ministry of the Holy Spirit bringing us to faith in Christ and inward renewal. He too could refer to sacred marriage *(agglutinavit),* and to the *unio mystica* (*Inst.* 3.11.10; 4.12.24). In support he could appeal to Bernard. The Reformed Church also had its mystical Pietists. Simplifying the older order of salvation, F. D. E. → Schleiermacher (1768-1834; → Schleiermacher's Theology) could equate the forgiveness of → sins and Christ's indwelling. In the 20th century K. → Barth (1886-1968) gave a new emphasis to union with Christ in *CD* IV/3, 539-54, though pointing out that we may use the phrase "mystical union" only with a very careful definition of the term "mystical" that gives the preeminence to Christ and the Holy Spirit.

2.3. *Orthodox*
Orthodox theology (→ Orthodoxy 3) is impregnated with mystical elements. *Theōsis,* objectively

accomplished in Christ, is the climax of the divine economy. With the cooperation of the Holy Spirit it makes possible a mystical ascent of believers to God that reaches its goal in ecstatic deification. Orthodox hymnology and its festal calendar constantly express the longing after perfection (→ Liturgy 4; Order of Salvation 1.1; Salvation 3; Worship 3).

→ Devotional Literature 2; Discipleship 2.1; Spirituality 1.2; Visions

Bibliography: A. M. ALLCHIN, *Participation in God: A Forgotten Strand in Anglican Tradition* (Wilton, Conn., 1988) • P. DINZELBACHER, *Christliche Mystik im Abendland. Ihre Geschichte von den Anfängen bis zum Ende des Mittelalters* (Paderborn, 1994); idem, "Die Gottesbeziehung als Geschlechterbeziehung," *Personenbeziehungen in der mittelalterlichen Literatur* (ed. H. Brall et al.; Düsseldorf, 1994) 3-36; idem, *Mittelalterliche Frauenmystik* (Paderborn, 1993); idem, "Die Psychohistorie der unio mystica," *JPsHF* 2 (2001) • GERTRUDE OF HELFTA, *The Herald of Divine Love* (trans. M. Winkworth; New York, 1993) • M. IDEL and B. McGINN, eds., *Mystical Union in Judaism, Christianity, and Islam: An Ecumenical Dialogue* (New York, 1996) • B. McGINN, *The Foundations of Mysticism* (New York, 1991) • I. MARCOULESCO, "Mystical Union," *EncRel(E)* 10.239-45 • N. PIKE, *Mystical Union: An Essay in the Phenomenology of Mysticism* (Ithaca, N.Y., 1992) • J. VAN RUUSBROEC, *The Adornment of the Spiritual Marriage; The Sparkling Stone; The Book of Supreme Truth* (London, 1951) • L. B. SMEDES, *Union with Christ: A Biblical View of the New Life in Jesus Christ* (2d ed.; Grand Rapids, 1983) • D. E. TAMBURELLO, *Union with Christ: John Calvin and the Mysticism of St. Bernard* (Louisville, Ky., 1994) • G. WREDE, *Unio mystica. Probleme der Erfahrung bei Johannes Tauler* (Stockholm, 1974).

PETER DINZELBACHER

Mysticism

1. History of Religion

1.1. *Definition in Religion*

1.1.1. *General Definition*

The word "mysticism" has an etymological link to Gk. *myō, myeō, mystērion* (shut [eyes, mouth], initiate [into the mysteries], mystery), words connoting absorption, → esotericism, → faith, and relation to the hidden ground of being. A general definition of the term might be "an individual, emotional sense of identification with no specific expressible content in which → language points beyond itself to an → experience of something that can be indicated only in → paradoxes and that transcends all empirical content as ultimate reality."

Agreeing with this statement are some formal elements of mysticism, including the desire for union with, and integration into, a higher reality by direct contact with the ground of being, which embraces the whole person and, by the suspension of → time in eternity in the "superconsciousness," reintegrates a state of creation that removes the distinction between the particular and the universal. We thus have the "logic" of the concurrence of opposites and a feeling of liberation from restraint and unattainability by an overpowering intellectual enlightenment that fills a person with joyous certainty. From the convergence point of time and eternity, this enlightenment gives a knowledge of the → truths of what is → future, distant, and → metaphysical, making it possible to read them in hearts and texts and → nature. In the process the dialectical use of negation as a higher form of affirmation (→ Dialectic) finds a parallel in the denial of the finite → self in order to attain to all-encompassing life.

1.1.2. *Physiology, Psychology, Theory of Perception*

Physiologically, psychologically, and from the standpoint of the theory of perception, mysticism, like similar states of consciousness differing from ordinary experience, belongs to the right side of the brain, which cannot express itself in words. What is actually experienced is the unity of the empirical self in the stream of consciousness. The experience of unity that involves broad control and inner strengthening, which holds firm vis-à-vis the inner world, is lacking in the case of schizophrenia. Mysticism is thus part of the primal thrust of divided human nature to burst through the limits of one's own personality and to achieve unity, as may be achieved also through the sex drive or through intoxication.

The content of the mystical experience reflects the stimuli in virtue of which the experience may be happy, satanic, revealing, or psychotic. The prior model and the whole spirit of the mystical search shape the experience itself by the interpretations involved, which enable us to perceive what the senses receive in different ways (L. Wittgenstein's "seeing as"), retroactive interpretations included. All mystical "sense impressions" might thus be actually the same, but the conscious perceptions differ. While, however, the mystical experience is ineffable during the experience itself, the two different modes of consciousness can be contrasted later in reflection and verbal expression, once the situation of distinction over against the One must be established. Taught and classified as "phases of the mystical life" (E. Underhill) are the vision of unity, inner vision, → ecstasy, surrender, immediacy to God or oneness with him, and mysticism of the infinite or of the personal life.

1.1.3. *History of Religion*

In the → history of religion — though one might differentiate mysticism and the → contemplative life from devotionalism, sacramentalism, and prophetism (→ Prophet, Prophecy), as N. Smart does — mysticism and organized → religion tend to be interwoven because both are looking to the infinite and share the emotions that belong to the holy (R. Otto; → Sacred and Profane). In a very special way, then, mystical experiences are a product of interaction with a religious background, so that the study of mysticism must start in that context (S. T. Katz), even though we cannot show strict dependence.

Mystics often confirm → tradition with experiences, but they may also transcend it. For their experiences may take the place of what → authority lays down just because the experiences seem to derive from that authority but lead to seeing old values with new eyes (G. Scholem). Mystics may thus be scriptural theologians but with their own insight into what is taught, so that it becomes inward to them (→ Meditation), taken from Scripture but independently of the will (Otto). The cleft that divides from the historic biblical faith is thus bridged as suprahistorical mysticism reinterprets outward → salvation history into a timeless process of → salvation that takes place in the inward → soul.

Confirming the inner and internalizing meaning, we also find criticism of any lifestyle or religion that remains too external. But because mysticism uses all its powers on behalf of the inner life, it must adhere to existing social forms (F. Heiler). Constantly stressing the unusual in contrast to familiar statements, it may be convinced that its ideas are truer to reality than others around it, even those of other mystical traditions.

1.2. *Main Trends in Religious History*

1.2.1. *Native Cultures of America and of Northern and Central Asia*

Mystical experiences were widespread among the hunters, fishers, and herders of America and of northern and central Asia through their lifelong participation in sacred speech, rites, and traditions pertaining to the world of nature. In this comprehensive setting it was expected of the Indians of the prairies and plateaus that with the attainment of sexual maturity, and after rites of purification, they would spend days alone, fasting in a search for → visions, and thus achieve mastery over the elements by this exposure (→ Initiation Rites). In → shamanism a mystical death and the ensuing ecstatic flight of the soul, with the breaking through of levels in the center of the world, represent an early and basic form of → mystical union.

1.2.2. *Indus Culture*

Besides this technique of going beyond oneself (i.e., ecstasy), we find among the peasants and townsfolk of the Indus culture (→ Hinduism) another archaic form of mystical experience — that of → Yoga, or "union" in the technique of going into oneself (i.e., "enstasy"). Similar to both ecstasy and enstasy is the producing of a kind of inner heat by rhythmic breathing and often also the use of drugs with a view to escaping from time and attaining to an unconditioned state. The theistic Yoga tradition includes not only a purely magical process that addresses only the will and individual forces of the →

ascetic but also → devotion to a divine Lord (Skt. *Īśvara*).

If enstasy (*samādhi*, "state of deep concentration") is reached in this way with the help of an object or a thought, it is said to be supported or differentiated because an inner function still meditates on the object. But if it is reached without outer or inner connections, all consciousness vanishes apart from the impressions that are left over from the previous inner functioning of the spirit and that make possible a return to consciousness. Such a *samādhi* is unsupported *(asamprajñāta)*, which has no cause or express preparation. It is a spontaneous enlightenment of wisdom that effects absolute isolation for life as one who is "freed in life" *(jīvanmukta)*.

1.2.3. Hinduism

Mysticism developed in → Hinduism with reflection on the → sacrifice that upholds the world. The syllable *om,* which is central here, and the word *brahman,* which shapes sacred verses, are viewed as the essence of the sacrifice and therefore of humanity and the world. Forms of meditation on them are thus acceptable substitutes, with an emphasis on what is inward as true reality.

The → Upanishads know the experience of the transcendence of space and of time (→ Immanence and Transcendence), the two converging in an experience of absolute oneness that expresses itself in a → negative theology (*neti neti,* "neither this nor that") and that even transcends the difference between → good and → evil. On a monistic interpretation (→ Monism) this state must be absolute truth, beyond which one cannot go. In the impersonal mysticism of identity, the union of the individual soul (*ātman*) with the universal principle (*brahman*) removes all → duality, as in the doctrine of nondualism (*advaita*).

The mystical self-isolation of Sāṁkhya-Yoga knows no absolute One beyond the individual spirit, so that liberation here is the opposite of being absorbed in a transcendental self. For the → Bhagavad Gita this state is in some sense only a beginning. It is followed by loving surrender (*bhakti*) to the deity and a selfless fulfillment of duty in the context of pure → spirituality beyond space and time and also the One.

1.2.4. Chinese Mysticism

Chinese mysticism arose separately from oracles whose signs all aimed finally at union with the Tao (→ Taoism and Chinese Popular Religion), the cosmic order that comprehends all things. The true Tao mysticism, linked especially to Lao-tzu (6th cent. B.C. as the author of the *Tao-te Ching* (Classic of the way of power), finds in Tao the ultimate ground

of being, cosmic reason, the → absolute, the godhead — with which we are to achieve harmony by renouncing all external interests and active interfering. Immersion in nature brings illumination, but drugs, → alchemy, and magical incantations also help. In → Confucianism, however, family unity mediates mysticism socially.

1.2.5. Buddhism

Though → Buddhism is → atheistic and skeptical regarding the soul, it knows something similar to mystical unity in the sequence of trance states that led the Buddha to nirvana by way of *samādhi,* which, all aiming at a state of rest, are the main components of Buddhist meditation. Nirvana is a timeless state that, not being composite, is one and unifying, so that the Buddha, being enlightened, has unrestricted insight. In Mahayana the supreme mystical state is Buddhist emptiness, which leads by analysis to a new mode of human action. Meditation on the mandala, which reflects the cosmos, aims at union with Buddha, who is identified with the universe, thus resulting in full mutual integration and total conversion, in which the Yogi breaks through the level of the cycle of birth and mystically shares in Buddha's transcendent body of teaching. This status of illumination (*bodhi*) embodies a supreme ideal of sympathy combined with insight. As in Hinduism, there is not only a monistic but also a theistic form (i.e., Amida Buddhism).

Both forms are also possible in Japanese → Zen, since supreme inwardness carries with it no necessary content of knowledge as regards absolute reality. It even rejects the common goal of all "enstatic" trends, namely, the step from plurality to undifferentiated unity, since such unity still remains part of an antithesis. Zen relies on the unexpected and violent irruption of something new that does not derive from prior states. An aid to this development is a paradox *(kōan)* for which a higher meaning must be found beyond customary thinking or even extraordinary hallucinatory experiences. This higher meaning takes place in illumination (*satori*) as the ability to see the real as it is and to be active in it, unhampered by passions.

1.2.6. Greece

In Greece the Dionysus cult (→ Mystery Religions) contained orgiastic rites aimed at achieving the presence of the god himself in his intoxicated adherents. This cult was linked to Orphism in the Pythagorean-Platonic tradition (→ Hellenism; Hellenistic-Roman Religion), which Plotinus (ca. 205-70) developed into a mysticism that exerted great influence on Judaism, Christianity, and Islam. Its starting point was the idea that the One, which is immanent in all the hypostases deriving from it and which exists in an incomparably positive transcendence, can be expressed ultimately only in negations. The mystical process consists of a return of the spirit to the One by contemplation (Gk. *theōria*) of intelligible forms. The forms play a decisive role because each → emanation relates to the preceding higher state as a reflection.

The One does not specifically reveal itself by address to us. Rather, we must turn to it, for it is present to us as a creative force in suprapersonal → love. Eros alone always remains of the human personality as it waits quietly until the One appears like the rising sun to the human spirit that returns to it. Then we have our being in God *(enthousiasmos),* and ecstasy (i.e., going outside of ourselves) becomes stasis, the state in which the divine and human centers cover each other.

In this respect the self is not totally erased but is raised to supreme fulfillment and thereby changed, because it is taken in possession by God. We constantly seek to attain this deification by ascetic striving for ecstatic unification, which is basically possible for anyone. Along with the desired inward unification, as opposed to a purely monistic interpretation, the essential otherness of the supraempirical basis remains. The reflective capacity of the finite, by which there can be mediation of the ascent to the One, preserves this otherness.

1.2.7. *Judaism, Christianity, and Gnosis*

In contrast, → Judaism, Christianity, and → Gnosis begin with a voluntary election in salvation history by which the transcendent comes to us, and mystical knowledge in these frameworks has → eschatological features. Typically Jewish is the stress on the permanent distance between creature and Creator (→ Creation). In spite of Hellenistic influences and the internalizing of salvation history by → allegory, part of ecstasy even in Philo (d. A.D. 45-50) is that the human is submerged when the divine enters the ecstatic but then returns after possession. In Judaism, however, the term closest to mystical unification is *devekut* (holding, clinging), and ecstatic features are recognized only as those that manifest themselves in the constant relation of the human will to the divine will at work in worldly reality.

In Gnosis, however, we find a mysticism that views the elect individual soul as identical with the power behind the all. Despite the eschatological reservation that the full union of all earthly spiritual powers with those in the spirit world will come only in the future, theistic mysticism is here a monistic mysticism of the isolation of the spirit when the Gnostic has the character of full divinity and everything cosmic is simply a futile obstacle. Church mysticism escapes such views as it relates to the world more in Greek or more in Jewish fashion.

In Judaism early Merkavah mysticism shows closeness to Gnosis. Following Ezekiel's vision of the throne chariot of God, it consists of striving by contemplation to overcome intervening spheres and to attain to pure transcendence. Hasidism, in contrast, was a popular movement that stressed → prayer and spiritual practice based on Halakah law. It taught that the first manifestation of the Shekinah (presence) of God mediates between his hidden essence and his fully manifest creation, and does so even down to the level of the everyday. The accompanying esoteric teaching of the → cabala is close to Neoplatonic and Gnostic speculation. After expulsion from Spain, this teaching became strongly eschatological. It saw in the mystical return to original creation an anticipation of the messianic age.

1.2.8. *Christianity and Islam*

In Christianity and → Islam, under the influence of Syrian → monasticism on → Sufism and of Muslim culture on Spanish culture, there were many similarities between the female mystics Rābi'ah al-'Adawīyah (713?-801) and → Teresa of Ávila (1515-82) and between the men al-Junayd of Baghdad (d. 910) and John of the Cross (1542-91), who were more under the influence of Plotinus. The Islamic technique of concentration by rhythmic thinking about God (*dhikr*, "mention, remembrance") is related in some sense to the Christian "prayer of the heart." Love in Sufism, which engages the whole personality and comes before contemplation of any image, stimulated Christian love mysticism.

The aim of all Islamic mysticism is return to the experience of the → covenant of God with the humanity that recognizes him as Lord, even before their creation. For its "way" (*tarīqa*) Muhammad (ca. 570-632), as a vessel for the word of God who was void of intellectual knowledge (*ummī*), is the first link in the chain of tradition (*silsile*), and his ascent to the divine presence (→ Qur'an 17) is a prototype of the spiritual ascent of the mystic to intuitive knowledge of God (*ma'rifah*).

A difference from the Christian doctrines of the unmixed and unseparated union of the divine and human natures in Christ (→ Christology 2) and of the integrating of believers by the → Holy Spirit is that Islam treats any talk of unification or → identity with suspicion, as though it were putting something else alongside the one God. In justification of mystical experience nothing can have existence apart from God. After trust in God and renunciation, our human existence falls away (*fanā'*), and

God alone remains (*baqā'*, "subsistence"). Then after the unconscious ecstasy of the self that is emptied for the indwelling *(ḥulūl)* of God, the personality returns to a life according to God's will in the "second soberness."

Bibliography: P. C. ALMOND, *Mystical Experience and Religious Doctrine: An Investigation of the Study of Mysticism in World Religions* (Berlin, 1982) • L. DUPRÉ, "Mysticism," *EncRel(E)* 10.245-61 • M. ELIADE, *Yoga: Immortality and Freedom* (London, 1989; orig. pub., 1954) • C. ELSAS, *Neuplatonische und gnostische Weltablehnung in der Schule Plotins* (Berlin, 1975) • F. HEILER, *Die Bedeutung der Mystik für die Weltreligionen* (Munich, 1919) • M. IDEL and B. MCGINN, eds., *Mystical Union in Judaism, Christianity, and Islam: An Ecumenical Dialogue* (New York, 1996) • W. JAMES, *The Varieties of Religious Experience* (Cambridge, Mass., 1985; orig. pub., 1902) • S. T. KATZ, ed., *Jewish Neo-Platonism* (New York, 1980); idem, ed., *Mysticism and Philosophical Analysis* (London, 1978); idem, ed., *Mysticism and Sacred Scripture* (Oxford, 2000) • D. KNOWLES, *What Is Mysticism?* (new ed.; London, 1979) • A. KNYSH, *Islamic Mysticism: A Short History* (Leiden, 2000) • I. MARCOULESCO, "Mystical Union," *EncRel(E)* 10.239-45 • R. OTTO, *The Idea of the Holy: An Inquiry into the Non-rational Factor in the Idea of the Divine and Its Relation to the Rational* (2d ed.; London, 1970); idem, *Mysticism East and West: A Comparative Analysis of the Nature of Mysticism* (New York, 1932) • A. SCHIMMEL, *Mystical Dimensions of Islam* (Chapel Hill, N.C., 1975) • G. SCHOLEM, *Major Trends in Jewish Mysticism* (3d ed.; New York, 1961); idem, *On the Kabbalah and Its Symbolism* (New York, 1996; orig. pub., 1960) • N. SMART, *The Yogi and the Devotee: The Interplay between the Upanishads and Catholic Theology* (London, 1968) • W. T. STACE, *Mysticism and Philosophy* (Los Angeles, 1987; orig. pub., 1960) • E. UNDERHILL, *Mysticism: A Study in the Nature and Development of Man's Spiritual Consciousness* (New York, 1974; orig. pub., 1911) • F. G. WALLNER, ed., *Science, Humanities, and Mysticism: Complementary Perspectives* (Vienna, 2000) • R. C. ZAEHNER, *Concordant Discord: The Interdependence of Faiths* (Oxford, 1970); idem, *Hindu and Muslim Mysticism* (Oxford, 1994; orig. pub., 1960); idem, *Mysticism: Sacred and Profane* (Oxford, 1957).

CHRISTOPH ELSAS

2. Church History
2.1. *Concept and Research*
Mysticism is a fundamental religious phenomenon that aims at direct → intuition of the experience of God. Conceptual apprehension of the phenomenon depends on the given historical and religious con-

text and its theological, philosophical, or psychological interpretation. There are two constant types of mysticism — evasion mysticism and introversion mysticism, depending on whether the soul's center (→ Soul; Person) is ecstatically taken up from outside into the transcendent divine reality or the reality is experienced in the center (→ Immanence and Transcendence).

Toward the end of the 18th century J. H. Jung-Stilling (1740-1817) drew attention to the importance of mysticism in devotional and spiritual history. This emphasis resulted in a beginning of academic research into mysticism in the 19th century. J. Görres (1776-1848), J. Hamberger (1801-85), F. Pfeiffer (1815-68), W. Preger (1827-96), and others were active on the historical side, and R. Otto (1869-1937), F. Heiler (1892-1967), F. R. Merkel (1881-1955), and others on the side of the history and → philosophy of religion (→ History of Religion). A. Deissmann (1866-1937), A. → Schweitzer (1875-1965), and M. Dibelius (1883-1947) studied mystical elements in the NT, while F. W. Wentzlaff-Eggebert (b. 1905), J. Bernhart (1881-1969), E. Seeberg (1888-1945), H. Bornkamm (1901-77), and others devoted themselves to their historical interpretation and arrangement. A. Ritschl (1822-89) in the 19th century and → dialectical theology (esp. K. → Barth, E. Brunner, and F. Gogarten) in the 20th century adopted a critical approach to mysticism. Interest revived in it, however, as an experience of transcendence that embraces all human → life and as a corrective to a one-dimensional, externally oriented → technological world.

2.2. *NT*
In the NT, as in the OT, the biblical belief in → revelation leaves no place for autonomous and nonhistorical mysticism. God does not work directly in the inner soul but indirectly through the historical sending and word of Jesus Christ (→ Christology), to which the response is → faith rather than sight (2 Cor. 5:7; 1 Cor. 13:12; John 14:9-10; 1 Pet. 1:8). This faith has the character of eschatological → hope (Rom. 8:24-25; John 3:2-3; → Eschatology).

→ Paul and John thus hold aloof from what is autonomously mystical (1 Cor. 4:8; 13:11-12; 2 Cor. 12:1-11; John 1:18; 5:37; 6:46; 1 John 4:12). In both, however, we may speak of mystical elements based on the presence of Jesus Christ through the Spirit in his people (Gal. 2:10) and on the ontic relation between Christians and Christ (2 Cor. 4:10-11). Both these truths occur in faith and await eschatological consummation. Paul's experiences in 2 Cor. 12:2-10 bear a close resemblance to mystical ecstasy, but he does not generalize them or boast about them. Paul prefers the intelligent language of faith to ecstatic → glossolalia (1 Corinthians 14). In John the immanence formula of our abiding in Christ and his abiding in us (e.g., John 6:56-57) does not mean mystical identity but relates to the abiding of faith in the Word of Christ that is freely granted (15:3-11).

Faith shares with mysticism the intention of expounding human existence in its totality. Its eschatological character, though, differentiates it from what autonomous and nonhistorical mysticism says about being.

2.3. Early Church

2.3.1. Postapostolic Era

Statements in the → early church about the pneumatically understood ontological relation between Christians and Christ became stronger in the postapostolic period (e.g., by Ignatius of Antioch [d. ca. 107]). Believers are in Christ, and Christ is in them. The power of this fellowship is the divine → love that will consummate it eschatologically. → Irenaeus (d. ca. 200) also stressed union with Christ and, against → Gnosticism, affirmed its eschatological character. Clement of Alexandria (d. ca. 215; → Alexandrian Theology) and → Origen (d. ca. 254; → Origenism) explained this union ethically as an agreement of will with the Logos revealed in Christ, seeing in it the presupposition of end-time redemption of the psyche.

2.3.2. Eastern Church

In the Eastern church especially of the Byzantine period (→ Byzantium), more of the elements of autonomous mysticism invaded the Christian faith. Evagrius Ponticus (346-99), against the background of Origenist and Neoplatonic (→ Platonism) ideas, developed a system of Christian mysticism in which the human spirit returns by several stages to union with the divine Spirit and finds there what he called essential knowledge (→ Epistemology). This knowledge involves an intellectual vision of the Trinitarian mystery and a related beatific vision. In 553 the Second Council of Constantinople condemned this teaching because it threatened to erase the boundaries between the exalted Christ and believers.

Elements of mysticism may also be seen in Basil of Caesarea (ca. 330-79; → Cappadocian Fathers) and his directions for the monastic life (→ Monasticism). Gregory of Nyssa (ca. 330-ca. 395) saw in → prayer an ascent to the eternal and, in an endless process, a participation by creaturely life in the divine life. Noetically, he preserved the distinction between the two by the way of negation. John Climacus (ca. 570-ca. 649) in his Ladder of Paradise drew on the mysticism of Evagrius, describing in 30 → ascetic steps the extirpation of passions that

chain the soul to the earthly. He also saw here an ascetic ascent of the soul to the divine ground of being. Ephraem Syrus (ca. 306-73) and Maximus the Confessor (ca. 580-662) recommended flight from the world as the prerequisite of spiritual freedom and mystical experience.

Dionysius the Pseudo-Areopagite (ca. 500) developed the mystical thinking of Gregory of Nyssa in his → apophatic theology. In his four extant works — Celestial Hierarchy, Ecclesiastical Hierarchy, Divine Names, and Mystical Theology — Dionysius attempted a synthesis between Neoplatonism and Christianity. He distinguished between positive (his "cataphatic") and negative (apophatic) statements of theology. The mystical ascent of the soul to → God takes place in three stages — purification, enlightenment, and union — which links the soul to the transcendent God, who dwells in obscurity. In the description of this way positive statements about God are transcended, which is the via negationis (way of negation). To this ascent of the soul there corresponds a Neoplatonically conceived hierarchical ranking of all being (→ Hierarchy).

In the Byzantine church mystical thinking took a new turn in the theology of Simeon the New Theologian (949-1022). In his thinking and especially in his → hymns, Simeon aimed at a vision of the → light-encircled → Trinity. Ultimately, the Christ who is seen in the vision of light totally fills the soul and brings it spiritual rest and joy. In the High → Middle Ages the thoughts of Simeon were developed in → Hesychasm, especially by Gregory Palamas (ca. 1296-1359; → Palamism), into a specific technique of prayer in which the vision of divine light might be reached by prayer and silence.

2.3.3. Western Church and Augustine

The father of mysticism in the West was → Augustine (354-430; → Augustine's Theology), who saw it in terms of a mysticism of knowledge and will. Augustine pointed the soul away from all outward things to the inner realm, where divine grace illumines the intellect and lovingly perfects the will. In this way the longing for the vision of God is rightly oriented proleptically, though eschatological fulfillment is still ahead. → Gregory the Great (pope 590-604) also supported the idea of a contemplative certainty of God, though with no immediacy. Faith will achieve sight only in the eschaton.

2.4. Middle Ages

Following Augustine and Gregory, and under Eastern influence, the Middle Ages in the West developed the mystical knowledge of God essentially in relation to → Anselm's statement credo, ut intelligam (I believe in order that I might understand).

Such knowledge typically took the form of purification, enlightenment, and union.

2.4.1. *Early*

In the early period the main influence apart from Augustine was Dionysius, as he was known in the Latin translation of John Scotus Erigena (ca. 810-ca. 877). The Victorines in Paris united the two traditions. Hugh of St.-Victor (1096-1141) used the negative way to distinguish mystical → contemplation from other modes of experience and knowledge, linking them in a hierarchy of knowledge leading up from the rational to the suprarational. Richard of St.-Victor (d. 1173) taught a mystical → experience in which the human spirit attains to the purity and immediacy of contemplation of God. The decisive prerequisite of this mysticism, however, is divine → grace, which lays hold of the soul and ecstatically enlightens it.

→ Bernard of Clairvaux (1090-1153) described mystical contemplation along similar lines. After the soul has taken the steps to the truth of humility and then love of neighbor, it achieves contemplation of the divine essence by following the crucified Christ (→ Discipleship). In exegeting the Song of Songs, Bernard developed his characteristic bride mysticism, according to which love as an expression of divine grace unites the bridegroom Christ to the soul, or the church, as his bride. We find the influence of Bernard affecting the very personal modes of expression of the great women mystics of the 12th and 13th centuries such as → Hildegard of Bingen (1098-1179), Elizabeth of Schönau (1129-64), Mechthild of Magdeburg (ca. 1207-ca. 1282), and Mechthild of Hackeborn (1241-99).

2.4.2. *High*

The great mendicant orders of the 12th and 13th centuries finally linked mysticism to → Scholasticism in the High Middle Ages. In *Itinerarium mentis in Deum* (Journey of the mind into God), the → Franciscan Bonaventure (ca. 1217-74) speculatively described the way of the soul to God. In orientation to Augustine and the Victorines and seizing on the charismatic experiences of Francis of Assisi (1181/82-1226), Bonaventure outlined a process of turning aside from the external world and, with the help of grace, ecstatically mounting above one's own inwardness to God.

→ Thomas Aquinas (ca. 1225-74; → Thomism), on account of his Aristotelian epistemology, discussed mystical experiences only in the context of the seven gifts of the Spirit. After Thomas, however, → Dominican mysticism developed in Theodoric of Freiburg (ca. 1250-1310) and Nicholas of Strasbourg (ca. 1300), and particularly in the German

mysticism of Meister → Eckhart (ca. 1260-ca. 1328), who by preaching and pastoral care influenced the Upper German mysticism of women Dominicans.

We find in Eckhart's mysticism a return to the Neoplatonic image of the soul-fire, according to which the human soul has a place within it where the gap between creature and Creator can be bridged. Eckhart called this place the spark or ground of the soul, where the eternal divine Logos is born spiritually. This Logos unites the soul to God when, in surrender and disengagement, it breaks free from ties to outward, worldly things and then, in spiritual → freedom and renewal of → virtue, turns afresh to the world. Since Eckhart gave enthusiastic descriptions of this mystical union in his German sermons (→ Preaching), he was suspected of erasing the distinction between Creator and creature (→ Pantheism) and was thus condemned by the bull *In agro dominico* (1329).

Eckhart's pupils J. Tauler (ca. 1300-1361) and Henry Suso (ca. 1295-1366) propagated his ideas without speculative exaggeration. Tauler, too, found in detachment from the world a necessary condition of the gracious birth of the divine Logos in the ground of the soul. Suso found in emotional → meditation on the cross of Christ an essential prerequisite of the spiritual birth of the divine Logos in us. In Nicolas of Cusa (1401-64) we still see the impact of Eckhart's view of God. In God as absolute and infinite being (→ Ontology), all the contradictions that determine creaturely and finite being are transcended or removed. God as the Infinite One is the transcending or coinciding of opposites.

2.4.3. *Late*

The later Middle Ages saw a strong movement toward practical → piety. The → Brethren of the Common Life, founded by G. Groote (1340-84), and the Devotio Moderna (Modern devotion), which was so influential in this movement, set as the goal a passivity before God that came to expression in humble renunciation of all self-will (→ Humility) and a following of Christ even to the point of resignation to hell, that is, assent to God's verdict of damnation. The mystical union that follows upon humility is understood as the harmony of the will with Christ's will, or conformity to Christ.

The classic expression of the Devotio Moderna was the four books of the *Imitation of Christ*, ascribed to Thomas à Kempis (1379/80-1471). Others writers in the same tradition were Jan van Ruysbroeck (1293-1381), Gerhard Zerbolt of Zutphen (1367-98), Wessel (ca. 1419-98), John of Wesel (ca. 1400-1481), and John of Goch (1400-1475). Closely related to these works were the *Theologia Deutsch*

(German theology) of a priest of the Frankfurt German Order (end of the 14th cent.) and meditations on the passion by Ludolf of Saxony (ca. 1300-1378) and by John Mauburnus of Brussels (ca. 1460-1501).

We find a special link between the Devotio Moderna and → humanism in → Erasmus (1469?-1536). Jean Gerson (1363-1429) and Pierre d'Ailly (1350-1420) sought to relate → nominalism to mysticism by showing how God meets us in the inner emotional experience of the heart but cannot be reached by theoretical reason in outward experience apart from revelation. We find important phenomena of visionary mystical experience during the 14th and 15th centuries in Bridget of Sweden (ca. 1303-73), → Catherine of Siena (1347-80), and Catherine of Genoa (1447-1510).

2.5. *Protestantism*
Various medieval traditions of mysticism found partial critical reception in → Protestantism.

2.5.1. *Luther and the Reformation Era*
From the perspective of the Christian belief in revelation, M. → Luther (1483-1546; → Luther's Theology) was critical of the immediacy attaching to mysticism, although in his earlier period he took a positive view of some of its intentions. Already in his Romans lectures of 1515/16 he rejected a path of mystical knowledge that bypasses the incarnation of the Logos (*LW* 25.287-88). In the first Psalms lectures (1513-15), however, he showed a certain sympathy for the negative theology of Dionysius the Pseudo-Areopagite over against the garrulity of the Scholastics (WA 3.372.8ff.), but he soon repudiated speculation that goes beyond the limits of revelation (*LW* 36.109-11). He was equally critical of Bonaventure on this count (WA 23.732.8-9). In his Romans lectures he approved of the mysticism of Tauler, which stresses human passivity (*LW* 25.367-68). Indeed, he praised Tauler at first as a German theologian who is superior to the Scholastics (*LW* 31.128-29).

Luther's sympathy for Tauler waned after he came into conflict with the mysticism of A. Carlstadt (ca. 1480-1541) and T. → Müntzer (ca. 1489-1525), who appealed to Tauler. Luther now began to emphasize the self-linking of the divine Spirit (→ Holy Spirit) to the outward, revealed Word. He retained a special sympathy for the bride mysticism of Bernard of Clairvaux (*LW* 25.267), though relating the union between the Bridegroom and the soul to faith rather than to mystical love. Against the scholastic idea of habitual grace (*gratia habitualis*) as a quality poured into the soul, he used mystical language in teaching that justifying faith (→ Justifi-

cation 2), not the ecstatic love of mysticism, sets people *extra se* (outside themselves) in the → righteousness of Christ (*LW* 26.387). Luther shared with mysticism an interest in our passivity before God and in the character of theological knowledge as experiential cognition (WA 9.98.21), but he had no place for an autonomous mysticism apart from the event of the → Word of God and faith.

U. → Zwingli (1484-1531; → Zwingli's Theology) and J. → Calvin (1509-64; → Calvin's Theology) remained aloof from mysticism except insofar as their acceptance of ideas from Augustine introduced mystical elements.

2.5.2. *Heterodox Protestants*
Carlstadt and Müntzer did little to promote mysticism, but the impact of an autonomous mysticism was strong in some left-wing Protestants. C. Schwenckfeld (1490-1561), for example, championed a new immediacy. Partially following and partially deviating from Luther, he taught the union of deity and humanity in the flesh of Christ and, on this basis, the deification of believers (→ Theosis) and their participation in the divine nature of Christ (2 Pet. 1:4). S. Franck (ca. 1499-ca. 1542) interpreted mystical statements along the lines of → spiritualism by teaching a direct participation of the human spirit in the invisible eternal Logos and a spiritual church as opposed to the externalizing of the mainline → church (§2). In the reflections of Paracelsus (1493-1541) on the relation between God, Christ, humanity, world, and life, he saw a unity of the human spirit and corporeality.

V. Weigel (1533-88) gave an inward turn to Luther's doctrine of → penitence along the lines of Tauler and the *Theologia Deutsch*. He argued that theological knowledge must be based on the "inner book" (i.e., inner knowledge). In penitence the Christ in us effects → forgiveness. After 1579 Weigel, adopting the spiritualism of Paracelsus, opposed to the outward church with walls the inward church of the spirit, which in the Eucharist partakes of the new "heavenly flesh" of Christ. Weigel influenced J. Böhme (1575-1624), who adopted Neoplatonic ideas and developed a theosophy according to which the all-embracing life that emanates from God dialectically includes God's "fiery will of love" and his "dark will of wrath." By → regeneration we may attain to a share in the positive power of divine love against evil. Faith is a piercing through to the positive power of the divine essence.

Borrowing from Paracelsus, Weigel, and Böhme, J. V. Andreae (1586-1654) and J. A. Comenius (1592-1670) modified Protestant mysticism into a pansophy that aims at a heavenly and spiritual knowledge and speech versus something merely natural and rational. Pansophy reached a climax in the "sacred philosophy" of F. C. Oetinger (1702-82), who on the basis of the concept of incarnation worked out a comprehensive philosophy of life. By the flesh that is transfigured in Christ, God dwells in the creature with his glory and is all in all. Divine grace redeems us from the life of self-alienation, which is the consequence of sin.

2.5.3. Orthodoxy and Pietism
Even Lutheran → orthodoxy (§1) could adopt the idea of a mystical union, though only as one element in the → order of salvation, which is based on justification. Mystical ideas became more significant in the reforming J. Arndt (1555-1621), who in his *True Christianity* tried to give new life to an ossifying orthodoxy by adopting the mystical ideas of Bernard and Tauler. Arndt saw in the human person an image of God from creation (→ Anthropology) that had been lost through → sin but could be regained by the grace of regeneration. The soul ascends to God by self-denial in penitence, the crucifying of the old self, and the → resurrection of the → new self.

Arndt's thinking influenced German → Pietism, especially P. J. Spener (1635-1705) and A. H. → Francke (1663-1727), who related the thought of crucifixion of the old self to the penitential conflict. N. L. von → Zinzendorf (1700-1760; → Moravian Church) expressed similar views. In Lutheran Pietism, however, the doctrine of justification held in check any tendency toward an autonomous mysticism.

This tendency was stronger in G. Tersteegen (1697-1769) in the sphere of Reformed Pietism. Tersteegen accepted Tauler's idea of the birth of the divine Logos in the ground of the soul. In his main work, the three-volume *Auserlesene Lebensbeschreibungen heiliger Seelen* (Selected biographies of saints, 1733-53), biographies of Roman Catholic mystics, he also adopted some of the ideas of Catholic quietist mysticism (see 2.6), which also found an echo in Francke and Zinzendorf.

2.5.4. Enlightenment to the Twentieth Century
The → Enlightenment pushed mysticism into the background with its interest in → rationalism. In the 19th century, however, German → idealism and the awakening (→ Revivals) showed a fresh interest in mystical ways of thinking. J. G. Fichte (1762-1814) in his *Anweisung zum seligen Leben* (The way toward the blessed life, 1805) advocated an ethical mysticism, while F. W. Schelling (1775-1854) and G. W. F. Hegel (1770-1831; → Hegelianism) went

back to Oetinger and took up mystical features into their systems. The → liberal theology of A. Ritschl and → dialectical theology in the early 20th century were critical of all mystical identity thinking, as already noted, but interest in mysticism revived with increasing technology.

2.6. Roman Catholicism from the Sixteenth to the Twentieth Century
Medieval mysticism found a direct successor, and underwent further development, in the → Roman Catholic Church from the 16th to the 20th century. Specifically, Spanish and French mysticism in the 16th and 17th centuries drew notably from medieval mysticism. The Devotio Moderna particularly influenced the Spanish mysticism of the Counter-Reformation (→ Catholic Reform and Counterreformation) and also had an impact on the *Spiritual Exercises* of → Ignatius of Loyola (1491-1556) and his ascetic training of the will.

A new factor in Spain and France was → quietism, which was heavily influenced by the Franciscan Peter of Alcántara (1499-1562) and by → Teresa of Ávila (1515-82). In dialogue with John of the Cross (1542-91), Teresa formulated in *Las moradas* (The interior castle *or* The mansions) seven levels of prayer through which the soul may mount up to God. On the seventh and highest level the soul has direct awareness of the presence of the three divine persons and enters into a mystical → marriage with the deity. The presupposition of this ascent to God is concentration and rest in prayer.

Francis de Sales (1567-1622) was dependent on Teresa. In his *Traité de l'amour de Dieu* (Treatise on the love of God, 1616), he described the fulfilling of the will by the love that is passively received and that actively corresponds to God. Miguel de Molinos (1628-96; → Jansenism) also promoted quietism in Spain and influenced Madame Guyon (1648-1717) and F. Fénelon (1651-1715) in France, as well as Pietism in Germany.

In Germany in 1687 Francke published a Latin translation of two works of Molinos under the title *Manducatio spiritualis* (Spiritual eating). In 1699, because of the relativizing of the → sacrament of penance, 23 propositions of Fénelon were condemned, and quietism was repressed in the Roman Catholic Church. It made an impact in the Netherlands through the French former Jesuit Jean de Labadie (1610-74), who had gone over to → Calvinism in 1650.

Notwithstanding the critical trends of the Enlightenment, mystical elements remained in Roman Catholicism through the *Spiritual Exercises*. We find mysticism in Germany in the writings of A. K. Emmerick (1774-1824), J. M. Sailer (1751-1832), and others.

2.7. Theological Appraisal

In appraising mysticism theologically, we must state that the Christian belief in revelation strictly rules out all elements of an autonomous and timeless mysticism that aims at immediate knowledge of God and that threatens to detach redemption from the once-for-all historical revelation in Jesus Christ, making it the content of individual self-education. The suppression of eschatology in favor of mystical identity is also excluded in the name of the God who defines and imparts himself in his revelation, who has redeemed us outside ourselves *(extra se)* in Christ, and who will bring us to fulfillment in the *eschaton.* Since this redemption is already at work through the Holy Spirit in faith, it is not just to be understood noetically as a pure act of knowledge but must be seen as an eschatological event that embraces the whole person. This event contains mystical elements to the extent that justification involves our passivity before God and therefore a basic difference between being and having — a difference that suits mystical thinking.

Although historical revelation critically excludes a nonhistorical, autonomous mysticism, the event of salvation that takes place in it, which aims eschatologically at the whole person, pneumatologically confers on mystical elements a right to exist in the Christian faith if the knowledge of faith is to be that of a new life and not to harden into mere doctrine.

Bibliography: C. BUTLER, *Western Mysticism: The Teaching of SS. Augustine, Gregory, and Bernard on Contemplation and the Contemplative Life* (London, 2000; orig. pub., 1924) • L. DUPRE and J. A. WISEMAN, eds., *Light from Light: An Anthology of Christian Mysticism* (2d ed., New York, 2001) • S. FANNING, *Mystics of the Christian Tradition* (New York, 2001) • M. FOX, *Passion for Creation: The Earth-Honoring Spirituality of Meister Eckhart* (Rochester, Vt., 2000) • É. GILSON, *The Mystical Theology of St. Bernard* (New York, 1940) • V. LOSSKY, *The Mystical Theology of the Eastern Church* (London, 1957) • A. LOUTH, *The Origins of the Christian Mystical Tradition from Plato to Denys* (New York, 1981) • B. McGINN, *The Mystical Thought of Meister Eckhart: The Man from Whom God Hid Nothing* (New York, 2001); idem, *The Presence of God: A History of Western Christian Mysticism* (3 vols.; New York, 1991-98) • K.-H. ZUR MÜHLEN, *Nos extra nos. Luthers Theologie zwischen Mystik und Scholastik* (Tübingen, 1972) • R. OTTO, *The Idea of the Holy: An Inquiry into the Non-rational Factor in the Idea of the Divine and Its Relation to the Rational* (2d ed.; London, 1970; orig.

pub., 1917) • E. A. PEERS, *Studies of the Spanish Mystics* (2d ed.; 3 vols.; London, 1951-60) • C. PEPLER, *The Three Degrees: A Study of Christian Mysticism* (London, 1957) • R. R. POST, *The Modern Devotion: Confrontation with Reformation and Humanism* (Leiden, 1968) • B. REYNOLDS and P. HEINICKE JR., *The Naked Being of God: Making Sense of Love Mysticism* (Lanham, Md., 2000) • A. SCHWEITZER, *The Mysticism of Paul the Apostle* (Baltimore, 1998; orig. pub., 1930) • D. SOLLE, *The Silent Cry: Mysticism and Resistance* (Minneapolis, 2001) • B. WINDEATT, ed., *English Mystics of the Middle Ages* (Cambridge, 1994).

KARL-HEINZ ZUR MÜHLEN

Myth, Mythology

1. Forms
    1.1. Term
    1.2. Time and Place
    1.3. Presentation of the Ground of Being
2. Relations to Religion, Society, and Knowledge
    2.1. Myth and Religion
    2.2. Myth and Society
    2.3. Myth and Knowledge
3. Demythologizing, Symbolic Function

1. Forms

1.1. *Term*

Various definitions of myth are offered, depending on whether myth is viewed as a lack of → truth from the standpoint of → rationality (→ Enlightenment) or whether it is regarded as a lost center over against an unredeemable claim of → reason and scholarship. → Romanticism resulted in research into mythology. Myth was first explained in terms of experienced forces of → nature and misuse of → language. Examination of complexes of myth made possible a reconstruction of the history of individual myths and their variants. → Ethnology observed that myths are handed down orally as common history.

According to the basic meaning of the Greek term, speech, mime, and gesture all have a place in myth. Myth puts feeling into a presentation that develops imaginative power as the principle of its immanent → logic. The aim is to anchor understandable order, presuppositions, and divine guarantees of order, and to relate and systematize them. The stories make no claim to universal validity, for myth is simply an expression and partial aspect of known religious truth. The mythical may be irrational, but myth has a *logos,* or at least a *ratio* (C. Colpe). The mythical offers us an experience of power as a primal or final event controlled by a superhuman being, or as a reality that concerns the present and the → future; as the offering of this experience is sensed, myths arise. If the mythical power is not there, we see ourselves as distant from the event that myth reports, and myth is then only a story conveying an insight. People close to nature are also aware of this distinction.

A myth is a traditional story that is not, however, represented by any single text and, rather, can have widely differing variations. One is frequently not justified in concluding causal relations from temporal succession or spatial proximity. Myths receive their typical compactness and complexity from the fact that they developed in illiterate cultures, in which stories are the primary form of → communication and instruction. To become a permanent legacy over many generations, they must take literary and historical form. The whole corpus of myths in a given tradition is known as mythology, a term also used for the study of myths.

Part of the mythological is the contemporary clothing and adornment that help to give it relevance. But the mythological also points to the abiding mythical content that is to be rediscovered. Psychologically, the suprapersonal structural elements that build up myths have been seen as → archetypes in the collective unconscious (C. Jung). Structurally and ethnologically, the remarkable similarity of myths to one another has been seen as pointing to supraindividual laws of structure (C. Lévi-Strauss; → Structuralism).

1.2. Time and Place

There is no flow of time in myth (K. Hübner). Myth knows no Now. Events stand still, as it were, from eternity to eternity, though earlier and later differ. In the repeated recounting of powerful events that are exemplary, typical, and eternal and thus outside all temporality (→ Time and Eternity), myth is cultic action paralleling ritual gestures (→ Rite) that gives knowledge of the world a narrative form in the eternal, mythical present. In each culture we thus must define more precisely what is the relation between the narrative and the ritual action. Myth has neither absolute time nor absolute place. Place is always relative as an aura of the manifestation, so that, illogically, many places are the center of the world, gods and things can be in many places at once (→ Ubiquity), and things distant in space can be thought of as together.

1.3. Presentation of the Ground of Being

By communicating a revelation of the being of things that can only be experienced and not appre-

hended in thought, myth differs from other forms of speech by presenting and not arguing. Unlike types of narrative that distinguish between the time of the narrative (erzählter Zeit) and the time of the narration (Erzählzeit), myth forms a frame first for reality and then for all further narration. The creation of the world and other key scenes can function as myths in this way.

In myth the relation between type and copy is ontological (→ Ontology), not ethical. Where copying becomes following and imitating, we have legend. The statements of myth are not meant to educate and have only a secondary reference to what is of collective significance. Myth, then, is unlike fable, which is meant to be applied. The understanding of time, which in myth is totally different from what we experience, differentiates myth from the fairy tale, which also records wonderful events connected with nonhistorical beings but puts them in our time and is thus oriented to what takes place in the world. Tellers of legends and sagas, in which the idea of time corresponds to our historical time, record what is valid and permanent in the garb of history, so that they basically draw on the mythical but localize and individualize it. The fact that the same motif can take the form of myth, saga/legend, or fairy tale, and that the story can be told and received in any of these forms, shows that the differences between them are not too precise. In religious literature the consciously literary rendering can lead to the religious novel, and the understanding of myth as historical cloaking of universal concepts can lead to → allegory. Myths and mythological references in great epics are to be viewed as part of a program of education and are thus probably already the sign of a process of → secularization.

2. Relations to Religion, Society, and Knowledge

2.1. Myth and Religion

We may characterize myth as a symbolic form that maintains the unity of word and being, of signifier and signified, yet still retains within itself the basis of the ongoing differentiation that underlies → religion, which uses sensory symbols and → signs but knows them to be such (E. Cassirer). Hence myth is a way of expressing the content of → revelation; it is the → symbol, made up of elements of reality, for the unconditioned that is at issue in the religious act (P. → Tillich). The holy takes concrete form in figures or deities depicted as persons, and holy people and things are the bearers of mediated sanctity. In the process of symbolizing, not only the point of reference but the symbolic element itself is sanctified and therefore absolutized if the myth is religious and not just a myth of Oedipus or some other cultural hero or heroine. Even if enactment of the myth is not seen as a free act of the will but the myth magically has its own effect, we may still speak of nonreligious myth. In → prayers of thanksgiving for a deliverance, we may also have nonmythical religion. But appropriating the religious content by anchoring it in a worldview and its communication can be done only in mythical forms.

In the process the divine and human realms are related, with only a difference of degree and not of principle in divine conduct (→ Polytheism). Myths in all their variety are an answer to the void that is left when God and the world are separated.

2.2. *Myth and Society*

Myth brings system into history and gives it → meaning. Constantly referring back to the first beginning in the cultic presentation, it gives assurance of → salvation and erases intervening disasters. The beginning becomes the present as messianic personalities (→ Messianism) in myths tell of a paradisiacal time or country (→ Paradise) that we may regain by doing certain things (Colpe). Hence myth does not necessarily justify the given order.

In times of social change or evolution, myth may be disintegrative for society and functional only for a subsystem. Changes in the social structure through → war or migration give rise to an ideological superstructure for those who newly attain to wealth or power, which is of a mythological type if it is given the traditional mythical form.

Social institutions may also be changed to bring them into line with prevailing mythical models, thus making them more legitimate. As a model for future structures, myth may take a utopian form (→ Utopia) and anticipate the future. → Marxism can accept myth in this sense.

2.3. *Myth and Knowledge*

Myth forms the total horizon of history. The mythical archetype is the prototype, which, since it is fulfilled once and for all, reduces the validity of each succeeding act to that of likeness, since only repetition gives reliability and security. In the "myth of the eternal return" (M. Eliade), even historical suffering can be made bearable by reference to its superhistorical meaning, and so also incomprehensible → guilt, so that we can find shelter in the cosmic order, and there can be confirmation of consent to the laws to which we feel subject.

As language on a very lofty plane, myth tries to master theoretically the contradictions that beset society by constantly orienting itself to what is intended. In the process conservative social forces (→ Conservatism) are inclined parasitically to exploit

the meaning as form (R. Barthes) so as to transform what has taken place historically into supposedly unalterable constants of nature. Only a consciousness of the → "dialectic of enlightenment" (M. Horkheimer, T. Adorno) can prevent enlightenment with the positivistic principle of → immanence (→ Positivism), the explanation of each event as repetition, from regressing into the "myth of what is actually the case." Myth can have positive influence in the form of appropriating reality, but it can also be an obstacle to pushing on to reality by being hid and withdrawn from discussion as an unattainable mystery, in this way securing control over people.

If, relative to the prevailing reality, the contents of the mythical consciousness are lost and yet, in virtue of the intellectual function that gave rise to them (Cassirer), they still give orientation as to the knowledge of things, new myths develop, and myth thus shows itself to be a form of life that is needed to express what reality demands for the mastering of life's problems. Implicit myths in this regard are the emotional and experiential elements (→ Experience) of a possible mythical story that can serve as a basis for certain fundamental assumptions in the life of a society or a person.

3. Demythologizing, Symbolic Function

Since gods, people, and things are not precisely differentiated in myth, one form can easily change into another. But experience of the absolute transcendence of the Creator (→ Creation) and Lord of history in the → monotheistic religion of revelation breaks free from this dreamlike stage. Only where the Creator is thought to be imperfect like the world does myth remain in force or acquire new validity in the antithesis between the Creator and the supreme, supercosmic principle (→ Gnosis, Gnosticism). Myth is also "broken" by the idea of a historical aeon, and rejection of the idolizing of creatures means rejection of myths as human fiction, even though myth may be retained as a religious category (Tillich).

The existential interpretation (→ Existentialism) of R. Bultmann (1884-1976) led to → demythologizing. In this interpretation self-understanding is by → faith alone, and explanations of the world in myth are a mere scaffolding that modern science has outdated.

Yet mythical explanations are not subject to rationality. They have a totality that gives them a claim to validity (W. Pannenberg) in any culture or cultic community. Israel was an exception only because the history of God's action was not presented as a basic history but as a history that goes on to the present and beyond, so that its consummation, which surpasses anything that has yet taken place, can come only with a new act of God in the future. For Christians anticipation of this eschatological kingdom of God (→ Eschatology) in Jesus Christ again functions as a mythical archetype. Whereas the epiphanies of mythical archetypes can take place multiple times, the Christian concept of the → incarnation, by contrast, claims a definitive once-for-allness.

In a very broad sense one might describe as myths the biblical accounts of the history of Israel and that of Jesus as the Son of God inasmuch as they are far removed from any historical-critical reconstruction. But the → salvation history that relates to real historical persons plainly differs from myth in the sense of the myth-and-ritual school and its idea of a periodic enactment of the myth of the divine kingship in the faith of Israel (S. H. Hooke).

Over against the inclination to articulate myth stands the prohibition of images, which will not allow the delimiting of the God of Israel from other numinous entities by means of a specific form. At the same time, because God's action was experienced in history, the story of it involved a certain mythicizing of history. For this reason even monotheistic belief expresses itself in broken myth rather than history in the narrow sense of historical criticism; myth is more meaningful than history insofar as symbols make us think (P. Ricoeur).

We cannot agree with Bultmann and his attempted demythologizing in thinking of myth along Enlightenment lines as merely a pedagogically motivated allegory or parable conveying truth that might just as well be grasped in nonmythical form. We are able to think truth properly only as we constantly move on past myth and come back to it.

→ Dualism; God; Heaven; Hell; Immortality; Mother Goddesses; Philosophy; Psychology; Theogony; Worldview

Bibliography: P. D. L. Avis, God and the Creative Imagination: Metaphor, Symbol, and Myth in Religion and Theology (London, 1999) • R. Barthes, Mythologies (New York, 1972; orig. pub., 1957) • K. W. Bolle, "Myth," EncRel(E) 10.261-73; idem, "Myths and Other Religious Texts," Contemporary Approaches to the Study of Religion (vol. 1; ed. F. Whaling; Berlin, 1984) 297-363 • R. Bultmann, NT and Mythology, and Other Basic Writings (Philadelphia, 1984; orig. pub., 1918) • R. Buxton, ed., From Myth to Reason? Studies in the Development of Greek Thought (Oxford, 1999) • E. Cassirer, The Philosophy of Symbolic Forms (4 vols.; New Haven, 1953-96; orig. pub., 1923-29) • C. Colpe, Theologie, Ideologie, Religionswissenschaft (Munich, 1980) • W. G. Doty, Mythography: The Study of Myths and Rituals (2d ed.; Tuscaloosa, Ala., 2000) • A. Dundes, ed., Sacred Narrative: Readings in the Theory of Myth (Berkeley, Calif., 1984) • M. Eliade, Cosmos and History: The Myth of the Eternal Return (New York, 1959; orig. pub., 1949) • R. S. Ellwood, The Politics of Myth: A Study of C. G. Jung, Mircea Eliade, and Joseph Campbell (Albany, N.Y., 1999) • J. Gould, Myth, Ritual, Memory, and Exchange: Essays in Greek Literature and Culture (Oxford, 2001) • S. H. Hooke, Myth, Ritual, and Kingship: Essays on the Theory and Practice of Kingship in the Ancient Near East and in Israel (Oxford, 1958) • K. Hübner, Die Wahrheit des Mythos (Munich, 1985) • C. G. Jung, On Mythology (ed. R. A. Segal; Princeton, 1998) • G. S. Kirk, Myth—Its Meaning and Functions in Ancient and Other Cultures (Berkeley and Los Angeles, 1970); idem, The Nature of Greek Myths (Harmondsworth, 1974) • B. Malinowski, Myth in Primitive Psychology (Westport, Conn., 1972; orig. pub., 1926) • H. M. Olson, ed., Myth, Symbol, and Reality (Notre Dame, Ind., 1980) • P. Ricoeur, The Symbolism of Evil (New York, 1967; orig. pub., 1960) • H. Wiebe, Art, Myth, Religion, and Ritual: The Subversive Artist. Invoking Archetypal Roots (Kitchener, Ont., 1998).

Christoph Elsas

—N—

Nag Hammadi

1. Discovery and General Features
2. Types
3. Literary Genres and Relation to the NT

1. Discovery and General Features

Nag Hammadi (Arab. Naj' Ḥammādī, near the site of the ancient town of Chenoboskion) is a town in Upper Egypt about 80 km. (50 mi.) northwest of Luxor and the Valley of the Kings. In 1945 some Coptic MSS were discovered nearby, at the base of a boulder near the foot of a mountain called the Jabal al-Tarif. The corpus contains 12 codices, plus leaves from a 13th, with 52 tractates in all (including six doublets).

The collection dates anywhere from early to late fourth century A.D. All the works were translated from earlier Greek versions. The Coptic texts had been produced between the second century and the early fourth century. For the most part, they are original Gnostic texts, which has provided research into Gnosticism with a new source-base. With the *Gospel of Thomas* they have given us some possibly authentic sayings of → Jesus not previously known (→ Jesus Seminar 2.1).

The texts are now in the Coptic Museum in Old Cairo, where an international body has been entrusted with the task of editing them. Editing began slowly, but after 1966 it proceeded more rapidly un-der the patronage of UNESCO and under the leadership of James M. Robinson, who headed the technical committee for the facsimile edition. Nag Hammadi research is now international.

2. Types

The reason for the collection and the immediate causes of hiding the MSS are unclear. The works might have been linked to a group of heretical monks connected with Pachomius (ca. 290-346), but this hypothesis is not provable. The works cover a broad Gnostic spectrum. On the one hand, some trends are evident that relate to the heretical schools known to us from the → church fathers (→ Heresies and Schisms). On the other hand, the writings represent the various stages and developments of Gnosticism.

Some works are plainly Valentinian, such as *Gospel of Truth* (I, 3 [the numbers showing codex and number within the codex]), *Treatise on Resurrection* (I, 4), *Tripartite Tractate* (I, 5), *Gospel of Philip* (II, 3), and *A Valentinian Exposition* (with subgroups, XI, 2). Some tractates are Sethian in orientation (including Barbelo-Gnostic), such as *Apocryphon of John* (in four versions), *Gospel of the Egyptians* (III, 2 and IV, 2), *Apocalypse of Adam* (V, 5), and at least five other writings (VII, 5; VIII, 1; IX, 1, 2; and XIII, 1). The range of what is or might be Gnostic runs from genuine Gnostic texts (*Paraphrase of Shem* [VII, 1]) to secondary Christian Gnostic texts

(*Eugnostos the Blessed* [V, 1] and *Sophia of Jesus Christ* [III, 4]) and Christian works with a Gnostic tinge (*Exegesis on the Soul* [II, 6]).

A basic question is whether the types reflect the inner development of → gnosis. Writings VI, 6-8 belong to Hermetic Gnosticism. *Sentences of Sextus* (XII, 1) and *Teachings of Silvanus* (VII, 4) are Hellenistic Christian → Wisdom writings. A poor Gnostic rendering of Plato's *Republic* 588B-589B appears in VI, 5.

3. Literary Genres and Relation to the NT

The Nag Hammadi tractates are in many genres: apocalypses (→ Apocalyptic), acts, gospels, epistles, revelation monologues, dialogic didactic works, sayings, → prayers, and polemical tractates. Other genres may be found within individual works or complexes, including → hymns, → parables, admonitions, → blessings, and → curses. A surprising point is that the gospels — *Thomas* (II, 2), *Philip* (II, 3), and *Truth* — do not have the same literary form as the NT → gospels, although *Apocryphon of James* (I, 2) is close to the → Synoptic gospels from a literary standpoint. The revelation monologues are in the style of *egō eimi*, "I am" (esp. *Thunder, Perfect Mind* [VI, 2] and *Trimorphic Protennoia* [XIII, 1], as well as some individual sections). From a form-critical point of view they are close to what is found in John's Revelation, but extreme caution is needed in any attempt to show chronological and genetic dependence (e.g., between *Trimorphic Protennoia* and the Johannine Prologue).

Questions of the relationship and dependence between the NT and the Nag Hammadi texts are just as complex as similar questions regarding gnosis and early Christianity. We must weigh the matter separately for each text and group of texts. A thorough comparison of primitive Christian and Gnostic literary forms should precede any attempt at genetic historical constructions.

→ Apocrypha 2; Literature, Biblical and Early Christian

Bibliography: C. A. Evans, R. L. Webb, and R. A. Wiebe, *Nag Hammadi Texts and the Bible* (New York, 1993) • B. Layton, *The Gnostic Scriptures* (Garden City, N.Y., 1987) • J. M. Robinson, *Nag Hammadi: The First Fifty Years* (New York, 1996); idem, ed., *The Facsimile Edition of the Nag Hammadi Codices* (12 vols.; Leiden, 1972-84); idem, ed., *The Nag Hammadi Library in English* (3d ed.; San Francisco, 1988) • K. Rudolf, *The Nature and History of Gnosticism* (San Francisco, 1983) • D. M. Scholer, *Nag Hammadi Bibliography, 1948-1969* (Leiden, 1971); idem, *Nag Hammadi Bibliography, 1970-1994* (New York, 1997). See also the Nag Hammadi codices printed in the Coptic Gnostic Library series (New York, 1989-).

Peter Nagel

Nahum, Book of

The prophet Nahum came from Elkosh (site unknown). He was active between the capture of Thebes (or No-Amon, see 3:8) by the Assyrians in 664/663 B.C. and the fall of Nineveh in 612. The essential content of his book is intimation of the collapse of Assyria and of future → salvation for → Israel (§1). These themes and the liturgical forms used are generally taken to suggest that Nahum was a Jerusalem cult prophet.

The work begins with a fragmentary acrostic psalm (1:2-8) that Nahum himself, it is widely thought, did not perhaps formulate. After a word of comfort for Judah (1:9-15; 2:2), three well-crafted sayings against Assyria follow (2:1, 3-13; 3:1-7; 3:8-19), which might be prophetic liturgies.

J. Jeremias was of the view that the work underwent redaction in the later exile and then took on its present form. H. Schulz dated it from the same period but regarded it as pseudepigraphic.

→ Minor Prophets; Prophet, Prophecy

Bibliography: Commentaries: A. Deissler (NEchtB; Würzburg, 1984) • K. Elliger (ATD; 7th ed.; Göttingen, 1975; orig. pub., 1949) • F. O. Garcia-Treto (NIB; Nashville, 1996) • F. Horst (HAT; 3d ed.; Tübingen, 1964; orig. pub., 1936) • J. J. M. Roberts (OTL; Louisville, Ky., 1991) • O. P. Robertson (NICOT; Grand Rapids, 1990) • W. Rudolph (KAT; Gütersloh, 1975) • K. Spronk (HCOT; Kampen, 1997).

Other works: K. J. Cathcart, "Nahum, Book of," *ABD* 4.998-1000 • J. Jeremias, *Kultprophetie und Gerichtsverkündigung in der späten Königszeit Israels* (Neukirchen, 1970) • H. Schulz, *Das Buch Nahum. Eine redaktionskritische Untersuchung* (Berlin, 1973) • K. Seybold, *Profane Prophetie. Studien zum Buch Nahum* (Stuttgart, 1989).

Winfried Thiel

Namibia

1. General Situation
2. Missionary Churches
3. Independent Churches
4. Ecumenical Situation
5. Church and State

	1960	1980	2000
Population (1,000s):	624	1,030	1,733
Annual growth rate (%):	2.30	2.71	2.35

Area: 825,118 sq. km. (318,580 sq. mi.)

A.D. 2000

Population density: 2/sq. km. (5/sq. mi.)
Births / deaths: 3.44 / 1.09 per 100 population
Fertility rate: 4.55 per woman
Infant mortality rate: 54 per 1,000 live births
Life expectancy: 57.1 years (m: 56.2, f: 58.2)
Religious affiliation (%): Christians 92.3 (Protestants 54.8, Roman Catholics 25.1, indigenous 12.1, Anglicans 6.4, unaffiliated 5.2, other Christians 0.5), tribal religionists 5.7, nonreligious 1.3, other 0.7.

1. General Situation

The Republic of Namibia, in Southwest Africa on the coast of the Atlantic Ocean, has been independent only since 1990. In 1968 the United Nations gave the area its present name, from the Namib Desert, which extends about 1,300 km. (800 mi.) along the coast. Namibia is the fourth largest African exporter of nonfuel minerals. It is a major source of the world's uranium and of gem-quality diamonds.

Germany annexed the Namibian area in 1885, naming it German Southwest Africa ($\rightarrow$ Colonialism). South Africa seized the territory during World War I, renamed it South-West Africa, and introduced apartheid there in 1948 ($\rightarrow$ Racism). In 1966 the U.N. mandate was withdrawn, and decades-long negotiations began with a view to independence. Also in 1966 a Marxist group, the South-West Africa People's Organization (SWAPO), launched a guerrilla war for independence. Only in 1990 did South African administration of the country end. Free elections were held that year, with SWAPO (having renounced Marxism) gaining a majority.

Ethnically, Namibia in 2000 embraced five major groups and 28 languages. The largest ethnic groups were the Ovambo (870,000), Kavango (166,000), and Herero (138,000). Others include the Khoisan (9 percent), mixed race (7 percent), the Damara (6 percent), and Europeans (5 percent, mainly Afrikaners, Germans, and English speakers).

2. Missionary Churches

2.1. In 1805 the London Missionary Society ($\rightarrow$ British Missions 1.2) started the first $\rightarrow$ mission (§3) to Namibia, establishing a mission station in the south under Abraham and Christian Albrecht. J. H. Schmelen (1776-1848), the first missionary to the Hereros, persuaded the Rhenish Mission (founded 1829; $\rightarrow$ German Missions 1) to begin mission work in the territory. H. Hahn (1818-95), who worked for the mission after 1842, was instrumental in concluding various treaties between different groups. At his request Finnish missionaries were sent after 1870 to Ovamboland, in the north, while the German missionaries worked in the south. Two African Lutheran Churches developed out of this work.

The Evangelical Lutheran Ovambokavango Church (ELOC) was the result of Finnish mission work. It became independent in 1954 and elected its first indigenous bishop in 1963. In 1995 it numbered 423,000 persons. The Evangelical Lutheran Church in Namibia (ELCIN, known as the Rhenish Mission Church until it became independent in 1957) developed out of German mission work. The first indigenous leader, called (according to German tradition) the $\rightarrow$ preses, was elected in 1972. This church now has an episcopal structure. In 1995 there were 150,000 persons affiliated with it.

2.2. The $\rightarrow$ Roman Catholic Church began missionary work in Namibia in 1879 with an expedition of the apostolic prefect C. Duparquet (1830-88), the first Catholic missionary to the interior of central Africa. The mission was not at first successful. The vicariate of Keetmanshoop (after 1896) resulted from the work of the Salesians. Between 1906 and 1960 the Roman Catholics built 17 mission stations. Along with its spiritual work the church also offers educational and medical services. The members are mostly black, but the clergy are almost all white.

2.3. The $\rightarrow$ Anglican Communion made some early missionary efforts, but it met with modest success only from 1898 onward. World War I hampered its work, but the situation improved after the Treaty of Versailles (1919), by which Germany renounced its right to overseas possessions. In 1995 the Diocese of Damaraland, part of the Province of South Africa, had an indigenous bishop overseeing the 30,000 persons affiliated with the church.

2.4. Methodist work ($\rightarrow$ Methodism; Methodist Churches) began in the early 19th century but was not at first successful. In 1995 approximately 3,000 persons belonged to the Methodist Church of South Africa, most of whom were Afrikaans speaking. The strongest concentration was in the area around the town of Rehoboth. An influx of refugees from Angola increased the number of Methodists in Kavango, the region bordering on Angola to the north. Programs include care of refugees, soup kitchens, gardening projects, crèches, and women's programs.

3. Independent Churches

Of the 52 Independent Churches in 1995, we may mention a few. In 1955 upheavals among the Herero people led to the founding of Oruuano (meaning "community"), the Herero Church (with 10,000 people affiliated in 1995). The Protestant Unity Church (29,000) and the Church of Africa (4,000) followed; in 1959 the Independent Rhenish Mission of South Africa was formed (15,000). In 1946 some Nama Hottentots broke off from the Rhenish Mission and became part of the African Methodist Episcopal Church, a denomination from the United States that began work in South Africa in 1892. This church, with 11,000 affiliated, is strong in central Namibia and south of Windhoek, the nation's capital.

As a result of missionary work in Namibia, traditional religions (→ Guinea 2) have outwardly decreased. They are still present, however, surfacing especially in times of crisis.

4. Ecumenical Situation

In 1971 the two Lutheran churches — the ELCIN and the ELOC — united as the United Evangelical Lutheran Church of South-West Africa (later, Namibia). In 1977 the German Evangelical Lutheran Church (10,000 affiliated in 1995) joined the church. It formed several commissions to serve the cause of unity, including those on theology and proclamation, mission and → evangelism, social and diaconal work, and literature and communication.

The Council of Churches in Namibia (→ National Councils of Churches) derives from the Christian Centre, set up in 1975 as an ecumenical meeting place for black workers in Windhoek. The real aim was to found the Namibian Council of Churches, which followed in 1978. Its members include the African Methodist Episcopal Church, Anglican Church, ELCIN, ELOC, Evangelical Reformed Church in Africa (→ Reformed and Presbyterian Churches), German Evangelical Lutheran Church, Methodist Church of Southern Africa, Roman Catholic Church, and United Congregational Church in Southern Africa. The council strives for closer cooperation among its members and is also involved in various humanitarian activities through its departments and committees, such as for → diaconate, theology, local and regional → ecumenism, → development, and alternative education. Help is given to political prisoners and their families; other programs address the problems of → hunger and drought.

5. Church and State

In 1971 the leaders of the United Evangelical Lutheran Church in South-West Africa voiced their opposition to apartheid in a memorandum. In an open letter of the same year the Lutheran bishops came out in support of independence. These actions and others convinced SWAPO that clergy and laity with church responsibilities could be regarded as part of the Namibian → revolution.

Relations between → church and state increasingly worsened, and many church leaders from various denominations suffered imprisonment or expulsion. The churches were trying to promote reconciliation between the people and the colonial rulers, and they thus found it hard to arrive at a definite political position or to speak out clearly against economic exploitation by South Africa. After independence, however, the churches played a unique role as bridges between local Namibians and their former rulers.

As of 2000, all citizens enjoy freedom of religion. Christian denominations, as well as all other religious groups, have access to the media and to participation in schools.

→ African Theology

Bibliography: D. B. Barrett et al., eds., WCE (2d ed.) 1.521-24 • L. Cliffe, The Transition to Independence in Namibia (Boulder, Colo., 1994) • R. F. Dreyer, Namibia and Southern Africa: Regional Dynamics of Decolonization, 1945-1990 (London, 1994) • R. J. Gordon and S. S. Douglas, The Bushman Myth: The Making of a Namibian Underclass (2d ed.; Boulder, Colo., 2000) • S. Groth, Namibia–the Wall of Silence: The Dark Days of the Liberation Struggle (Wuppertal, 1995) • J. W. Hofmeyr and K. E. Cross, A History of the Church in Southern Africa: A Select Bibliography of Published Material (2 vols.; Pretoria, 1986) • L. C. W. Kaela, The Question of Namibia (New York, 1996) • S. Nambala, History of the Church in Namibia (= LQ, n.s., 8 [1994]) • M. Norval, Death in the Desert: The Namibian Tragedy (Washington, D.C., 1989) • S. Schoeman and E. Schoeman, comps., Namibia (rev. ed.; Santa Barbara, Calif., 1997) bibliography • T. Widlok, Living on Mangetti: "Bushman" Autonomy and Namibian Independence (Oxford, 1999).

Engelhard !Nôabeb

Narcissism

H. Ellis (1859-1939) first coined the term "narcissism" in → psychiatry to denote → homosexuality, then regarded only as sexual perversion (→ Sexuality). The idea was that of people loving their own reflection, like Narcissus in the Greek → myth (→ Love). S. Freud (1856-1939) distinguished between primary narcissism as a general stage in psychological → development (§2), in which subject and object are symbolically united, and secondary narcissism, by which psychological energies (→ Libido) are deflected from the object and possess the self, as is often observed in → psychosis (e.g., in Freud's famous Schreber case). For Freud the power that pathologically involves a loss of reality is, as primary narcissism, the basis of ego development, since the I constitutes itself by repressing object-relations. Only when we learn to break free from external objects and to form an inner image of them can we be alone without being lonely.

At this point we arrive at the further development of → ego psychology, which defines narcissism as a focusing of psychological interests on the → self and which H. Kohut (1913-81) built up into a history of the development of the self independently of impulses. In the process Kohut shattered the negative image of narcissism. He stressed its ability, through the → imagination, to project creative alternatives to the existing world of objects; through means of empathy, to soften the boundaries between subject and object; and through means of wisdom and → humor, to face the limitation of personal life. He thus gave positive shape to narcissism instead of supressing it.

C. Lasch applied theories about narcissism to social relations (→ Society), in which the general climate is shaped therapeutically rather than religiously and → bureaucracy makes social inconveniences into personal problems that need therapeutic treatment. Increased narcissistic phenomena among young people might thus be regarded as a new type of → socialization (T. Ziehe).

At the same time, a pre-oedipal psychology of religion opened up the possibility of achieving a better understanding of some factors in the tradition, such as → mysticism and → miracle stories, as "cosmic empathy" (K. Hoppe). On this basis a new and more fruitful round of discussion between → theology and → psychoanalysis could be initiated in which → analogies could be shown in basic → anthropological ideas and the focus could be on problems of creative imagination (H. G. Heimbroack) and health as → joy in oneself. Along these lines narcissistic forces need not bifurcate into fantasies of greatness or → aggression.

→ Lifestyle; Partnership; Pastoral Psychology; Psychotherapy

Bibliography: S. BACH, *Narcissistic States and the Therapeutic Process* (New York, 1985) • J. COOPER and N. MAXWELL, eds., *Narcissistic Wounds: Clinical Perspectives* (Northvale, N.J., 1995) • J. FISCALINI and A. L. GREY, eds., *Narcissism and the Interpersonal Self* (New York, 1993) • S. FREUD, *On Narcissism: An Introduction* (ed. J. Sandler et al.; New Haven, 1991; orig. pub., 1914) • H. KOHUT, *The Search for the Self: Selected Writings of Heinz Kohut, 1950-1978* (2 vols.; New York, 1978) • C. LASCH, *The Culture of Narcissism: American Life in an Age of Diminishing Expectations* (New York, 1978) • P. W. PRUYSER, "Narcissism in Contemporary Religion," *JPC* 32 (1978) 219-31 • E. F. RONNINGSTAM, ed., *Disorders of Narcissism: Diagnostic, Clinical, and Empirical Implications* (Washington, D.C., 1998) • J. SCHARFENBERG, "Narzißmus, Identität und Religion," *Psy.* 27 (1973) 949-66 • L. SHENGOLD, *Delusions of Everyday Life* (New Haven, 1995).

JOACHIM SCHARFENBERG†

Narrative Theology

1. The Nature of Narrative
2. Frei and the Eclipse of Biblical Narrative
3. Ricoeur and the Phenomenology of Human Experience

1. The Nature of Narrative

Narratives are stories. Stories become theological when they involve → God, that is, when one of the characters active in them, implicated in their plots, whose character and nature are revealed by the actions recounted in the story, is God. Stories involving God are of different orders.

The first instance is the stories of the Bible in which God is depicted directly as a character in the persons of God, Jesus, and the Holy Spirit. Other stories recount individual lives in their fullness, including the interaction between individuals and God. And there are stories of communities, churches, and nations, collective stories with God as implicit or active participant. The common element in these stories is the narrative form, which organizes incidents and details along a temporal frame, links incidents to form a plot, establishes movement toward a perceptible telos, or ending, and intertwines plot and character in such a fashion that actions reveal character and characters advance plot.

No line of demarcation separates the different orders of narrative. Narrative has the remarkable power to draw together the biblical stories, the life of the individual, and the shared life of communities in a complex and nuanced, yet unified, whole. A rich and profoundly honest article by Renita Weems, "A Mistress, a Maid, and No Mercy," illustrates this ability. Weems weaves together a retelling of the biblical account of Hagar and Sarah with her own individual story as an upwardly mobile daughter of a domestic worker in order to tell the collective story of African-American women in modern America. Narratives, well illustrated by Weems, represent the thickness of → experience, its multilayered quality, and create coherence without reduction of complexity.

Narrative theology, a broad and disparate movement within the discipline of → theology, is marked by a unifying appreciation for the ability of narrative to represent the relationship between God and human beings and by a sense of the fittingness of that representation. Narrative theology marks the congruence, sometimes only partial, of many lines of interest and development. Weems's article grows out of an unbroken tradition of biblical story-telling within the African-American church (→ Black Churches). James Cone has stressed the importance of that story to the survival of the African-American community and to its resistance to oppression — the interweaving, for instance, of the Exodus story with the story of the African-American struggle for freedom and dignity in America (→ Racism; Civil Rights Movement).

Similarly, → Judaism preserved an unbroken relationship to its ancestral stories alongside its continuous engagement with the nonnarrative forms of the → Torah. Jewish literary scholars such as Robert Alter and Meir Sternberg have continued and enriched that narrative tradition by using the insights of modern literary theory (→ Literary Criticism). It would be wrong to suggest that these unbroken traditions were completely unreflective on their practice. However, the power of the narratives, particularly the biblical narratives, in those religious communities was not dependent on or translated into reflective language. The narratives spoke directly and in their own unaltered form to the circumstances of the communities, shaping their common lives, the lives of individuals within the communities, and their relationship with God.

2. Frei and the Eclipse of Biblical Narrative

2.1. In large sectors of Western Christianity, especially those strongly influenced by European academic institutions, the tradition of direct and unproblematic reading of the biblical narratives as the theological foundation of Christian faith and life has been "eclipsed," in the wording of Yale theologian Hans Frei (1922-88). In a careful and detailed study (Eclipse), Frei found that beginning in the 18th century, the meaning of the biblical narratives progressively came to be identified not with the ob-

vious explicative sense of the biblical stories but, rather, with the historical events and incidents to which these stories seemed to refer. The shift from conceiving the meaning of the text as a function of the narrative coherence of the story itself to a matter of the historical reference of the story was largely driven by a concern for → truth.

Before the shift, the truth of the biblical narratives was a self-evident implication of the meaningfulness of the narratives themselves. Few sources of outside information about such matters as creation and ancient history were available to challenge that coherence. The rise of the age of exploration, however, increasingly produced independent sources of information by which to reconstruct the ancient world. The truth of the biblical narratives thus came to be identified with their correspondence to reconstructions of history grounded in extrabiblical data and articulated by rational argument (→ Enlightenment; Rationalism). The meaning of the texts depended on that truth. The result, Frei argued, was the displacement, or eclipse, of the most obvious sense of the biblical narratives and its replacement by increasingly tentative and fragmentary reconstructions of actual history. Alternately, the truth of the biblical narratives was defended by translating biblical stories into the terms of broad philosophical or anthropological systems. Again, the result was the eclipse of the biblical narrative in which Christian faith had been traditionally grounded.

2.2. Frei's image of the eclipse of biblical narrative suggested that narrative might again emerge to illumine the theological landscape. A number of forces, most of them apparent in the work of Frei himself, converged to bring narrative out of eclipse. First to mention is the influence of neoorthodox theology, particularly the exegetical method of Karl → Barth (1886-1968). Although Barth took some account, often negative, of the results of historical-critical study of the Bible, his theological method most frequently began with → exegesis of the narrative form of the biblical accounts, as David Ford has documented. If Barth's theological program was essentially that given him by → Anselm (1033-1109), namely fides quaerens intellectum (faith seeking understanding), then the fides was the witness of the biblical narratives to Jesus Christ and the intellectum was inner-Christian reflection on the coherence of that witness. Reflection never displaced the primacy of the narratives themselves, nor could the witness of the narratives be considered dependent on any nonbiblical foundation for either truth or coherence. In America Barth's emphasis on the biblical narrative was taken up by H. Richard Niebuhr

(1894-1962), who located → revelation in the biblical stories.

Developments within the fields of literary theory, together with the practice of interpreting literary texts, also influenced narrative theology. In America so-called New Criticism insisted that the text itself rather than anything outside the text (i.e., author or readers) was the proper object of literary → interpretation. New Criticism's model for the practice of interpretation, close reading, paid attention to such matters as plot and character and their mutual implication. Character was immediately read from the narrative as a natural implication of the actions of prominent actors, and simultaneously character determined the course of events as the narrative unfolded the characters' intentions. The interaction of characters and actions in the plot revealed the concrete identity of the characters, not as abstract essences that could be borne by a number of interchangeable individuals, but as embodied, or "emplotted," intentions within a specific narrative.

2.3. For Frei (see his *Identity*) this dialectic between character and plot made narrative the fit form of literature to reveal the unique identity of → Jesus Christ as truly incarnate God and to display the unity between Jesus' intentions and those of God. For other theologians such as the ethicist Stanley Hauerwas, the mutual implication in narratives of action and character is simply the basic mode of human life, drawing together the individual's and the community's life stories with the normative story of the Bible and other formative stories to form individual character or a community of character.

Still more specifically, Frei supported his understanding of the nature of biblical narrative by drawing on *Mimesis* (1969), the classic work in literary theory by Erich Auerbach (1892-1957). Using the biblical story of the sacrifice of Isaac, Auerbach describes a genre he calls realistic narrative, which organizes events along a chronological line, locates events in realistic settings, follows recognizable canons of human causality, and, in Auerbach's famous phrase, is "fraught with background" — that is, conveys a sense of depth and complexity commensurate with the human experience of reality. Frei renamed the genre, as applied to the biblical narratives, "history-like narrative" in order to draw attention to the nature of Christian claims about the → incarnation of Jesus Christ in human history. In designating the genre history-*like,* Frei seemed to beg the question of the relationship of this narrative genre to history as reconstructed by independent historians. That question may in fact have been begged, but for

Frei himself in the *fides quaerens intellectum* tradition of Anselm and Barth, the biblical narratives constitute the normative witness to the nature of the world and to God's actions in the world's history, to which "independent" history must be adjusted. Adjusting the narrated world of the Bible to the autonomous world of history or nature had led to the eclipse of biblical narrative as normative witness. Frei and the narrative theologians who followed him have sought to reverse this adjustment.

3. Ricoeur and the Phenomenology of Human Experience

3.1. Not all narrative theology is rooted in the neoorthodox assumptions characteristic of Hans Frei's work. An equally prominent starting point for many narrative theologians has been a → phenomenology of human experience that stresses the parallels between the structure of human experience and the structure of narrative. For Paul Ricoeur (b. 1913), who offers the fullest articulation of this approach, narratives, whether historical or fictional, possess a unique ability to reveal possible forms of human existence, possibilities that can be grasped by individuals in order to guide the project that is an actual human life. The power of narrative to present genuine possibilities of existence is grounded in the correspondence between narrative and the human experience of existence.

Of particular importance is the identity between the representation of → time in narratives and our experience of time. Ricoeur begins his magnum opus, *Time and Narrative* (3 vols., 1984-88), with an extended consideration of → Augustine's meditation on time in books 10 and 11 of the *Confessions.* Augustine was confounded by time and its → paradoxes. The past no longer exists, the future does not yet exist, and the present is a mere ephemeral point in time. For Ricoeur, narrative shares with experience the same movement from that which is no longer, into that which is not yet, through the present; narrative gives form to the unity of the human experience of time by recording in the present moment memory of things past and anticipations of things to come. In rendering time, narrative organizes the welter of human experiences into meaningful patterns and orients them toward a telos, a sense of a fit ending or goal. Narratives have the power to influence and indeed shape the course of human experience because of a perfect coincidence between narrative and lived experience. Other literary forms do not share this congruence with human experience, which is a powerful argument for resisting all attempts to convert sacred stories into any other form.

Ricoeur's interpretive program is strongly oriented toward actual texts. Close, disciplined study of the structure of narrative texts reveals the world of the text in all its concreteness. The textual world in turn reveals genuine possibilities for human existence, whether the narratives are historical or fictional in character. Ricoeur's direct predecessor in phenomenological analysis, Martin Heidegger (1889-1976), had held that authentic human possibilities are bounded by human mortality. Ricoeur, however, held that narratives point beyond death, so that human life could be lived with → hope. In looking beyond death and seeing the possibility of hope, Ricoeur became a theologian of narrative.

3.2. The often controversial relationship between theologians of narrative rooted in the neoorthodox tradition and those whose starting point is a phenomenological analysis of human existence can indicate some of the continuing lines of discussion within the broad movement of narrative theology.

Theologians of the Frei school have offered a number of challenges to Ricoeur's work. First, they charge Ricoeur with foundationalism, grounding the truth of Christian claims — the possibilities of existence embodied in the narratives — in an antecedent philosophical tradition. In turn, the Ricoeur school has suspected Frei's approach of fideism, a displacement of truth claims by the demands of → faith. The issue joined is how to conceive of the truth of the narratives.

Frei's school has also charged Ricoeur with denying the uniqueness of the Christian stories and, as a result, of undermining traditional Christian claims for the one-time incarnational character of the story of Jesus Christ. Many narratives could reveal genuine possibilities of human existence. Indeed, in principle nothing is unique about the narrative account of the life and death of Jesus — other narratives might be substituted. But the substitutability of other stories denies the heart of the central Christian claim, that God became incarnate in one particular individual, whose life and death uniquely embodied the presence of God among people.

3.3. David Tracy, Ricoeur's colleague at the University of Chicago, responds by in part granting the point. Many narratives could reveal genuine possibilities of existence. A → pluralistic age requires us to acknowledge this fact if we are not to disvalue or even dismiss the stories of religions other than our own. Tracy then introduces a qualitative difference among narratives. Although no single story can make a unique claim for revealing the only possibilities of existence, some narratives — ones Tracey

calls classics — "so disclose a compelling truth about our lives that we cannot deny them some kind of normative status" (p. 108). That truth is not the contingent truth of narrated or historical events (the problematic claims of Frei's approach) but universal, permanent truths of human possibility. *Christian* classics reveal determinate possibilities of existence that are characterized by trust in the graciousness and love of God. These possibilities are not unique — other religious classics offer different possible forms of existence — but neither are they indeterminate or infinitely substitutable.

The issue joined is absolutely fundamental and concerns the true referent of the biblical narratives. For Frei, the narrative refers to the characters and events that are recounted in it, events that continue to shape our lives. For Ricoeur and Tracy, the reference of the text is finally to a world of existential possibilities that only the narrative can reveal.

3.4. The controversy between the Frei and Ricoeur schools reveals deep issues that continue to occupy narrative theologians. The informal practice of narrative theology in the churches, the simple reading of biblical stories and correlation of those stories with the life stories of individuals and the community, has recently been strengthened. Despite Frei's concern for the eclipse of biblical narrative in much of the Western church, it must be said that even within those churches most affected by the identification of the meaning of the biblical texts with its historical referent, the tradition of straightforward narrative never died out. Support for that tradition of reading has recently also come from within historical-critical study of the Bible. Increasingly, Bible scholars are concerned with the final form of the text. In the case of narratives this focus leads to a holistic reading of blocks of narrative material that bears some relationship to traditional readings. The influence of the canonical criticism of Brevard Childs on this holistic reading is immense.

Furthermore, and from a less historical side, the impact of reading strategies drawn from the study of secular literature has been enormous in recent years. The influence of New Criticism has been mentioned, but more recent trends such as reader-response → criticism and, to a lesser extent, → structuralism have supported attention to the narrative form of the text itself and its interaction with the community of interpretation, precisely the concerns that characterize narrative theology. From all indications, it seems that this practical base of narrative theology will continue to develop and define the movement.

→ Canon; Hermeneutics; Language and Theology; Linguistics; Meaning

Bibliography: R. ALTER, *The Art of Biblical Narrative* (New York, 1981) • E. AUERBACH, *Mimesis: The Representation of Reality in Western Literature* (Princeton, 1969) • K. BARTH, *Anselm: Fides Quaerens Intellectum* (London, 1960) • B. CHILDS, *Biblical Theology of the Old and New Testaments: Theological Reflections on the Christian Bible* (Minneapolis, 1990) • J. CONE, *God of the Oppressed* (New York, 1975) • D. FORD, *Barth and God's Story: Biblical Narrative and the Theological Method of Karl Barth in the "Church Dogmatics"* (Frankfurt, 1981) • H. FREI, *The Eclipse of Biblical Narrative: A Study in Eighteenth and Nineteenth Century Hermeneutics* (New York, 1974); idem, *The Identity of Jesus Christ: The Hermeneutical Bases of Dogmatic Theology* (Philadelphia, 1974) • S. HAUERWAS, *A Community of Character: Toward a Constructive Christian Social Ethic* (Notre Dame, Ind., 1981) • H. R. NIEBUHR, *The Meaning of Revelation* (New York, 1941) • P. RICOEUR, *Essays on Biblical Interpretation* (Philadelphia, 1980); idem, *The Rule of Metaphor* (London, 1978); idem, *Time and Narrative* (3 vols.; Chicago, 1984-88) • M. STERNBERG, *The Poetics of Biblical Narrative: Ideological Literature and the Drama of Reading* (Bloomington, Ind., 1985) • D. TRACY, *The Analogical Imagination: Christian Theology and the Culture of Pluralism* (New York, 1981) • K. J. VANHOOZER, *Biblical Narrative in the Philosophy of Paul Ricoeur: A Study in Hermeneutics and Theology* (Cambridge, 1990) • R. J. WEEMS, "A Mistress, a Maid, and No Mercy," *Just a Sister Away: A Womanist Vision of Women's Relationships in the Bible* (San Diego, Calif., 1988) 1-16.

ROBERT B. ROBINSON

Nation, Nationalism

1. Concept and Development
   1.1. Concept
   1.2. Social and Historical Development
2. Nation and Nationalism
   2.1. Before 1989
   2.2. After 1989
3. Nationalism and Theology

1. Concept and Development

1.1. *Concept*

Underlying the concept of the nation is the idea of differences. Various notions are presupposed that confirm the existence and solidarity of a given human → group in distinction from all that is alien to it (→ Foreigners, Aliens). Consent thus arises as to what a nation is. It carries with it the thought of a → future, the guarantee for which seems to be power. In other words, it is a component of social reproduction as a continuation of the past, as well as a form of common life in harmony with laws that defined the existence of earlier generations (→ Society 2.3; Tradition).

1.2. *Social and Historical Development*

Serious differences of opinion exist as to how the nation arose in → society and history. The *patria* of antiquity was the land of one's ancestors, one's birthplace, a view that prevailed up to the → Middle Ages. The *patria* constituted a territorial society. It was the *pagus* (village, country district; Fr. *pays*), the area containing the property of the feudal lords (→ Feudalism) or the city where one lived. The inhabitants of the *patria,* subject to its territorial law (the *consuetudo patriae,* "custom of the *patria*"), defined themselves in opposition to foreigners *(extranei).* The *patria propria* (one's own *patria*), which as such was precisely defined, remained cohesive in the Middle Ages, despite the universal sense of belonging to the *patria communis,* the Christian world.

In Europe the Peace of Westphalia (1648) instituted the nation as the subject of international law, and through the breakup of the Holy Roman Empire, the balance between nations became the explicit framework of the European political game. On this occasion the first modern definition of the nation as the union of a prince or a state or a religious framework was posed (→ Cuius regio eius religio).

During this whole period the term "nation" had a narrow sense, in keeping with its etymology (from *nasci,* "be born"). It denoted a human group that has a common origin or to which such an origin is ascribed. Gradually, however, the accent shifted back to place. In 1694 the French Academy defined the nation as the sum of those inhabiting the same → state or land, living under the same laws, and speaking the same → language. In the 18th century the middle class came to have an increasing share in a government (→ Enlightenment 1-2; Modern Period), which led to a sense of national dynamic. Soon the rights of the nation came to be proclaimed in opposition to the supreme and unshared power of the king. The 1789 French Revolution sanctified the nation as the one subject of law, the only valid power, since → authority rested on it alone. Attempts were then made in the 19th century to explain the rise of nations, for example, by B. Disraeli (1804-81) in England and J.-E. Renan (1823-92) in France.

The French and American revolutions mitigated,

but did not finally eliminate, the religious basis of the concept of nation. The French republic eventually put forward a nonreligious model of the nation through the progressive secularization of the notion of citizenship (emancipation of the Jews in 1789-91, separation of → church and state in 1905). In the United States, through the recognition of Christian pluralism and on account of a different relationship between the state and civil society, the revolution weakened the religious basis of the state but not that of the nation and its foundational myths.

In Europe the secularization of the concept of nation led to its redefinition in Germany and France. On the debris of the Holy Roman Empire, the nation, now divided into multiple state traditions, was defined according to the concept of *ius sanguinis* (right of blood, i.e., allegiance based on one's parents), which favored a cultural, historical, and, above all, linguistic unity that was destined to transcend the political frontiers. In contrast, the French conception, which stems from a territory or a centralized state, was based on *ius soli* (right of the soil, i.e., allegiance based on one's place of birth), which founds the nation in the meeting place between a geographic space and a universalist project. In fact, the religious aspect of the concept of nation has not disappeared, and in France the tension between national Catholicism and republican universalism has remained a constant element up to the present.

2. Nation and Nationalism

2.1. *Before 1989*

From the 19th century onward the feeling of national adherence gave rise to new aspects of international relationship. Alliances were formed to support ethnic groups in their struggle for independence (→ Emancipation 2) or to keep them under the tutelage of an established state power. This situation lasted into the late 20th century (→ Colonialism; Minorities).

With the recognition of national → identity came radicalization by nationalism. Since nationalism must bear at least some responsibility for the murderous conflicts that have afflicted the world since 1914, efforts at avoiding such conflicts in the future have sought to offset the disintegrating effect of claims to national exclusiveness. Paradoxically, the → institutions that have resulted from such efforts — the League of Nations and the → United Nations — have the term "nation" in their titles, even though it was and is their aim to limit the element of power in mutual state relations.

The paradox is resolved if we understand by "na-

tions" the peoples whose readiness for → peace stands in contrast to the aggressiveness of states (→ Aggression). These institutions also condemn the idea that the nation can ultimately claim to be the sole criterion of what is of use or value in foreign policy decisions. Nations must thus avoid thinking of themselves as separate and hermetically sealed entities. By integrating themselves into a broad international union, they can perhaps give up their own distinctive traits. Experience thus far shows, however, that in fact nationalism is not so easily set aside.

2.2. *After 1989*

2.2.1. With the collapse of the Soviet empire, the 1980s and especially the 1990s saw the construction of the European Union and the failure of Arab nationalisms. The period saw a critique of national legitimacy, a return of traditional nationalisms, and an evolution of the notion of nation.

Linked to the state structures of the Eastern bloc, a movement has pushed since 1989 for the return to understanding "nation" as founded as a political framework, beyond religion and language, on the concept of ethnicity. The conflicts in the former Yugoslavia and in Chechnya in Russian Caucasia largely stemmed from this movement. The movement, however, has not been limited to the former USSR but has also touched countries in Africa (e.g., Rwanda and Ivory Coast) and Asia (e.g., Indonesia and the area of Kurdistan). The nation is, then, a coherent and specific whole that hinges on myths, a sublimated history, and a project tending to preservation. The emergence of new nation-states is not bereft of tensions; the legitimacy of emerging states is often contested, and the very nature of the nations they administer, as in central Asia, has yet to be defined.

2.2.2. The return of a religious conception of the nation is another current at work at the turn of the 21st century. Such a view can share the framework with a multinational state in the ethnic sense and serve to create unity, as in the case of the Hindu nationalist Bharatiya Janata Party (Indian people's party), which has been in power in India since 1998. It can, on the contrary, deny the legitimacy of state structures, perceived as "ungodly," and elevate the concept of nation to a bloc that is religiously united. Such a negation of the state and of the nation has found its expression especially in the Iranian Islamic and the Sunni fundamentalist projects.

Without denying the legitimacy of the nation-state, another religious current insists on the pertinence of "civilizing airs" as true spaces for the management of politics, identity, and power, both throughout history and for the future. The nation becomes a subdivision of minor importance within a larger bloc whose unity is largely a result of practice and religious culture. This arrangement holds for religious and cultural minorities that occupy a discrete territory within a state, such as Bretagne in France, Wales in the United Kingdom, and some linguistic regions as defined by the European Parliament.

2.2.3. In the last place, a dual model is perceptible on both sides of the Atlantic in the relationship between ethnic and cultural communities. The current American model places the community, defined by cultural and linguistic markers, as the intermediary point between the individual, the state, and the nation within the framework of a global project. In contrast, the European model of the nation, whether based on "blood" or on "soil," is traditionally lived as an end in itself, the nation being the ultimate political framework of the individual.

Within such a model the European Union, emerging as a political actor and, in the longer term, as a provider of identity, considers itself the place for a profound reflection on the concept of nation, in particular in its articulation with that of citizenship. The construction of a European citizenship not proceeding exclusively from the nation-state poses the problem of having to adjust the concept of nation. The recognition of a common European heritage through Brussels — a cultural, spiritual, and historical heritage whose transmission was previously based on the national community — is forcing Europeans to rethink the uniqueness of the nation as a creator of identity and political legitimacy.

2.2.4. The nation and its counterpart, nationalism, are in the midst of a profound redefinition. Their very nature — ethnic, cultural and linguistic, religious, or political — is affected, as well as their place in the global scheme of things. That place is either a source of legitimacy or, on the contrary, merely a receptacle of a higher religious, cultural, or political legitimacy. The oscillation between these two political modalities goes back to the old tension between the nation and the community, the extended family, and the nation project, which transcends and unites the differences of its participants.

3. Nationalism and Theology
Certain parallels exist between nation and nationalism, on the one side, and → religion and theology, on the other. In Christianity, and even more so in → Judaism and → Islam, nationalism can an-

chor itself in religion. When Christianity roots out non-Christian religions (→ Colonialism and Mission), the suppressed religious energies still persist in the form of affected → piety or → superstition.

Christian peoples have always yielded to the need to base their sense of nationhood on religion. The military → oath, saluting the flag, and public commemorations remind them of this close connection (→ Military Chaplaincy). The unconscious and indirect links between the two phenomena are perhaps closer than those that are direct and institutionalized. In the recognition of national heroes, and especially of → martyrs, those who have made a → sacrifice of their life for the nation, and in various other customs and practices, we see at one and the same time an ethnic, ethical, and religious sense. Expectation of the Messiah (→ Eschatology; Messianism), which may nourish nationalism and erase the distinction between the political leader and the savior of the → masses, shows to what extent religious and national feelings are able to permeate one another.

On the American continent we see a direct relation between the spread of → capitalism in industrial centers (→ Industrial Society) and the increasingly apparent relation of ruler and ruled between the North and the South, and the growing underdevelopment (→ Development 1) and sharpening of class conflict (→ Class and Social Stratum) in dependent countries (→ Third World). This interdependence has caused the battle for national liberation to take a single course as the battle against underdevelopment, the Creole middle class, and the capitalist system that opposes → socialism. This special situation in dependent and underdeveloped capitalist countries helps us to explain the period 1930-60 in Latin America, the crisis of populist (→ Populism) and nationalist movements, and the political radicalization of the 1960s and 1970s. In this setting → liberation theology (→ Contextual Theology) tried to create a Christian worldview that would be in accord with the building up of Latin American socialism within the → dialectic of the → Roman Catholic Church in defining national entities, a role challenged by the proliferation of Protestant → sects and indigenous movements (→ State Churches).

Nationalism south of the Sahara is different. It neither finds nor leaves any complex local culture (→ Afro-American Cults). It gives no singular popular culture the rank of a new literary or politically sanctioned culture as the Europeans did. Black Africa (→ Africa 1) also deviates from the principle of drawing political boundaries along ethnic lines. African nationalism was developed by intellectuals who united on the basis, not of a specific culture, but of mutual agreement. It is thus the bringing together of an aggregate of individuals belonging to a territory that has been arbitrarily defined historically. The only common feature of these individuals is that they are black, not white. There is thus a great gulf between their traditional roots and the technical and institutional construct that is imposed on them from outside. Since the indigenous cultures vary so much within the state, it is hard to avoid having to use a foreign language as the nation's official language. It has been said that for these reasons African groupings, which adopted a literary culture as a result of → conversion to Christianity or → Islam, are inclined to develop a true nationalism. Christianity, however, seems to be more exposed to tensions between external and indigenous factors than caught up in a process of identification with nation-states.

Such tensions, for example, include the opposition between magic, the mentality of which is directed to limited and individual problems, and the teaching of the churches, which emphasizes the sharing of material and spiritual goods beyond ethnocultural differences and an independence with regard to supernatural forces in the structuring of social life. In addition, some points of dogma are not well received (e.g., papal infallibility among Catholic Tutsi). No less serious is the clash between local African customs in the financial management of religious goods and the norms of churches of North American or European origin.

In short, to the extent that nationalism developed out of historical distinctiveness, it did so in hidden tension between a desire for ethnic and territorial separateness and the acceptance of otherness (→ Tolerance). It included within itself the different forms of collective existence, especially religion, perhaps particularly in the form of ethnic-religious → socialization.

→ Racism

Bibliography: Nationalism and religion: T. G. JELEN, The Political Mobilization of Religious Beliefs (New York, 1991) • M. JUERGENSMEYER, The New Cold War? Religious Nationalism Confronts the Secular State (Berkeley, Calif., 1993) • G. KEPEL, Jihad: The Rise and Fall of Islamic Extremism (London, 2001); idem, The Revenge of God: The Resurgence of Islam, Christianity, and Judaism in the Modern World (University Park, Pa., 1994) • Religions and Nationalisms: Canada and Quebec (= SocComp 31 [1984]) 328-443.

Case sudies: H. BANNERJI, The Dark Side of the Nation: Essays on Multiculturalism, Nationalism, and Gender (Toronto, 2000) on Canada • R. BRUBAKER, Citizenship and Nationhood in France and Germany (Cambridge, Mass., 1992) • A. DJILAS, The Contested Country: Yugoslav Unity and Communist Revolution, 1919-1953 (Cambridge, Mass., 1991) • A. R. MOMIN, "Conflict of Law and Religion in Contemporary India," SocComp 33 (1986) 223-36 • P. RICHARD, Death of Christendoms, Birth of the Church: Historical Analysis and Theological Interpretation of the Church in Latin America (Maryknoll, N.Y., 1987) • M. TEICH and R. PORTER, eds., The National Question in Europe in Historical Context (New York, 1993).

Other works: M. L. COTTAM and R. W. COTTAM, Nationalism and Politics: The Political Behavior of Nation States (Boulder, Colo., 2001) • R. G. FOX, ed., Nationalist Ideologies and the Production of National Cultures (Washington, D.C., 1990) • D. FROMKIN, The Independence of Nations (New York, 1981) • E. GELLNER, Nations and Nationalism (Oxford, 1996) • E. J. HOBSBAWM, Nations and Nationalism since 1780: Programme, Myth, Reality (2d ed.; Cambridge, 1992) • S. P. HUNTINGTON, The Clash of Civilizations and the Remaking of World Order (New York, 1996) • G. JUSDANIS, The Necessary Nation (Princeton, 2001) • M. OLSON, The Rise and Decline of Nations: Economic Growth, Stagflation, and Social Rigidities (New Haven, 1982) • J. RUPNIK, ed., Le déchirement des nations (Paris, 1995) • A. D. SMITH, The Ethnic Origins of Nations (Oxford, 1987); idem, The Nation in History: Historiographical Debates about Ethnicity and Nationalism (Hanover, N.H., 2000); idem, Nationalism and Modernism: A Critical Survey of Recent Theories of Nations and Nationalism (London, 1998) • C. TILLY, ed., The Formation of National States in Western Europe (Princeton, 1975).

PAUL-ANDRÉ TURCOTTE

National Association of Evangelicals

1. Origins
2. Growth
3. Current Issues

The National Association of Evangelicals (NAE) is a voluntary association founded in 1942 that represents U.S. evangelical denominations, organizations, institutions, congregations, and individuals. In 2001 it represented an estimated 43,000 → congregations from 51 member → denominations (totaling nearly 5 million members), individual congregations from 27 additional denominations, and hundreds of independent churches. Including over

250 schools and parachurch organizations in its membership, the NAE calculates that its core constituency numbers about 15 million, with a "service constituency" of more than 27 million Americans. Also in 2001 its World Relief arm (→ Relief and Development Organizations), with an annual operating budget of over $46 million dollars, was active in 38 countries. The NAE's headquarters are located in the Los Angeles suburb of Glendora, with an additional office of governmental affairs in Washington, D.C.

1. Origins

The NAE arose out of the fundamentalists' growing dissatisfaction in the 1930s with the liberal-leaning Federal Council of Churches and its status as the unofficial voice of American Protestantism. The NAE's organizational roots can be traced to a series of cooperative meetings and initiatives of the New England Fellowship (NEF), a diverse group of moderate New England → fundamentalists. Central to this development was J. Elwin Wright, a Pentecostal-turned-Congregationalist whose conference center in Rumney, New Hampshire, served as the focal point for NEF efforts.

An initial exploratory meeting for the formation of a national evangelical body was held in October 1941 at the Moody Bible Institute in Chicago. Those in attendance included Wright and prominent fundamentalist figures such as radio evangelist Charles E. Fuller, Moody president Will Houghton, Ralph Davis, head of the Africa Inland Mission, and William Ward Ayer, pastor of New York City's Calvary Baptist Church. Also in attendance was the New Jersey–based fundamentalist activist Carl McIntire, head of the newly created American Council of Christian Churches (ACCC; → International Council of Christian Churches). McIntire attempted to persuade the meeting's conveners to join the ACCC. Wright and the others, however, balked at the ACCC's ultraseparatist mind-set and sought a more positive organizing principle than McIntire's focus on opposing the Federal Council.

The actual formation of the NAE occurred at a gathering held in St. Louis in April 1942, when delegates mapped out plans for the new organization and elected Boston Congregationalist pastor Harold J. Ockenga as its interim president, with Wright in the role of promotional secretary. A constitutional convention in Chicago in May 1943 was attended by nearly 1,000 delegates representing a variety of independent institutions and organizations, as well as 50 Protestant denominations from across a broad spectrum of theological traditions, including the Southern Baptists, the Presbyterian Church, U.S. (Southern), the Lutheran Church–Missouri Synod, and several Wesleyan Holiness (→ Holiness Movement), → Pentecostal, "peace church," and European ethnic denominations.

The group settled on a broad seven-point doctrinal statement that affirmed biblical inerrancy, substitutionary → atonement, and — important for Pentecostal participants — "the present ministry of the → Holy Spirit." To accommodate the vast number of independent organizations and institutions within conservative ranks and to serve as a resource for conservative factions in more liberal denominations, the group decided to offer a multitiered membership, and to do so for individual congregations within the Federal Council as well. Denominations that wished to join NAE, however, were required to drop their membership in the Federal Council.

2. Growth

A headquarters office was established in Boston as well as a public affairs office in Washington, D.C. Despite the promise its early organizing efforts generated, it soon became clear that the NAE was in many ways limited by the inherent theological, regional, and ethnic diversity that marked the evangelical mosaic. By 1945 only 15 smaller denominations representing a mere 500,000 evangelicals — a tiny fraction of those represented at the 1943 Chicago convention — had officially joined the NAE. Many larger conservative bodies such as the Southern Baptist Convention (→ Baptists) and the Missouri Synod Lutherans (→ Lutheranism) saw no major benefits in NAE membership. Other sympathetic denominations, including the Presbyterian Church, U.S. (Southern), and the Reformed Church in America (→ Reformed and Presbyterian Churches), could not accept the NAE stipulation that its member denominations could not belong also to the Federal Council (later extended to its successor, the → National Council of the Churches of Christ in the U.S.A. [NCCC]).

Although the NAE failed to embody the emerging evangelical coalition in its official membership, the organization did serve an important function as an organizing body for various special-interest groups that more closely mirrored the larger evangelical community. In 1944 the NAE facilitated the founding of the National Religious Broadcasters and the Evangelical Press Association (→ Christian Communication). The Church School Commission created at the 1943 NAE convention became the National Sunday School Association in 1945, a year which also saw the organization of the Evangelical Foreign Missions Association (→ Evangelical Missions). In 1947 the National Association of Christian Schools grew out of the NAE. Several key NAE personnel were also major contributors to the planning and discussions surrounding the creation of the → World Evangelical Alliance in 1951.

Through the late 1940s and the 1950s the NAE sharpened its role as a voice for evangelicals in the public sphere. This role included marshaling of traditional Protestant opposition to Roman Catholic influence in the government, first in objecting to President Harry Truman's attempts to appoint an ambassador to the → Vatican (1951), and then in raising concerns about John F. Kennedy's candidacy for president (1960). By 1960 the NAE had expanded its membership to include 32 denominations representing 1.5 million adherents.

Amid the U.S. racial turmoil of the 1960s (→ Civil Rights Movement), the tiny African-American presence within NAE shrank with the establishment in 1963 of the National Negro Evangelical Association (later the National Black Evangelical Association [NBEA]). Although fraternal ties and communication existed between the two bodies, the split through the years provided objective fodder for both black and white detractors to characterize the NAE as a "white evangelical" organization. NAE also found itself thrust into the midst of the Vietnam conflict because evangelicals made up the bulk of the Protestant missionary presence in Southeast Asia. The visibility of its World Relief arm, until then a relatively minor operation, grew significantly, and by 1972 it was estimated to be caring for nearly 100,000 Vietnamese → refugees.

By the late 1970s evangelicals' growing concerns about the national moral, cultural, and political climate made the NAE a strategic tool for the larger movement. The importance of the NAE and its constituency to a resurgent → conservative political movement was clear. President Ronald Reagan made a particular effort to court the NAE, twice addressing its conventions, delivering his famous Evil Empire speech before delegates at the 1983 meeting. As a result, budgets increased, as well as its Public Affairs Department in Washginton, D.C. Such was the newfound visibility and influence of the NAE that during the 1980s a total of 15 new denominations (including the → Church of the Nazarene in 1984, the largest group to join the NAE since the → Assemblies of God in 1943) joined the organization, boosting its total denominational membership more than 65 percent, to 4.5 million.

In the late 1980s the NAE had to cope with the televangelist scandals (→ Electronic Church), and then in 1993 with the new administration of President Bill Clinton, which was less inclined to cater to the evangelical vote. At the same time, the NAE again battled its traditional funding problems, an aging core membership, and the perception that it represented only middle-class, white, Republican evangelicals.

In 1998 NAE headquarters moved to California, with the vision of influencing the entertainment industry as well as the political establishment. Efforts were made to cultivate a stronger minority presence through working with the NBEA and the growing Hispanic evangelical body, the Alianza de Ministerios Evangélicos Nacionales (AMEN). And in an effort to recognize evangelical movements within mainline Protestantism, the board made the controversial decision to allow member organizations to belong also to the NCCC. A blow came in the spring of 2001 as the National Religious Broadcasters decided to quietly sever its connections with the NAE.

3. Current Issues

The NAE has played an important part in creating, and giving shape to, the → evangelical movement in the period since World War II. It has been especially useful in serving as an incubator for new evangelical interest groups and umbrella organizations. The broad alliance that has typified it since its beginnings, particularly its openness to the full acceptance and participation of Pentecostals, has been a crucial factor in fostering wider alliances and an overall tone of cooperation and civility within evangelical circles.

The NAE, however, has been continually hamstrung by a variety of factors. First, serving as a centralized, representative organization for a decentralized, diverse, and amorphous evangelical movement is inherently difficult. The problems intensify insofar as evangelical effort and identity have been increasingly bound up in the flexible, innovative ministries of individual evangelists and parachurch organizations, not denominational hierarchies or bureaucracies.

Second, since it is an agency built on strictly voluntary membership, funding even its most basic operations has been a perpetual burden.

Third, the NAE has had difficulty adjusting the nature and scope of its mission as the religious, cultural, and political landscape has changed over the years. Initially formed as a counterweight to liberal Protestant councils, the NAE has seen this function largely disappear as mainline Protestant constituencies continue to erode. The NAE's ombudsman role in Washington, D.C., as a voice for evangelical concerns on federal policy serves a valuable function for the larger movement. That role, however, is fraught with the burden of partisan politics and has increasingly been usurped by other evangelical interest groups as well as by the subculture's innate proclivity for creating grassroots crusades.

The NAE's response to these problems and a crystallization of its mission will be key in determining whether it will continue to play a major role within evangelicalism in the 21st century.

Bibliography: J. A. CARPENTER, *Revive Us Again: The Reawakening of American Fundamentalism* (New York, 1997) • E. M. EVANS, *The Wright Vision: The Story of the New England Fellowship* (Lanham, Md., 1990) • *Evangelical Action! A Report of the Organization of the National Association of Evangelicals* (Boston, 1942) • G. M. MARSDEN, *Reforming Fundamentalism: Fuller Seminary and the New Evangelicalism* (Grand Rapids, 1987) • A. H. MATTHEWS, *Standing Up, Standing Together: The Emergence of the National Association of Evangelicals* (Carol Stream, Ill., 1992) • J. D. MURCH, *Cooperation without Compromise: A History of the National Association of Evangelicals* (Grand Rapids, 1956) • *United . . . We Stand: A Report of the Constitutional Convention of the National Association of Evangelicals* (Boston, 1943).

LARRY ESKRIDGE

National Church Movements → State Church

National Council of the Churches of Christ in the U.S.A.

1. Origins
2. Self-Understanding
3. Function and Funding
4. Members

The National Council of the Churches of Christ in the U.S.A. (NCCC) is the largest ecumenical organization in the United States. In 2002 its 36 member churches — Protestant, Orthodox, and Anglican — had a combined membership of more than 50 million Christians.

1. Origins

The most obvious predecessor to the current NCCC was the Federal Council of Churches, formed in 1908 as a forum for consultation among its 33 member denominations and as an instrument for cooperative social service. The Federal Council also assisted, over the next four decades, in the formation of state and local councils of churches in nearly every part of the country (→ Local Ecumenism). This same period also saw the birth or growth of numerous specialized ecumenical agencies (generally representing denominational boards), including the International Council of Religious Education, the Foreign Missions Conference, the Home Missions Council, the National Protestant Council on Higher Education, the United Stewardship Council, the United Council of Church Women, and Church World Service. By 1933 several of these bodies were addressing common concerns through a permanent interagency group; the ecumenical picture, though, was still extraordinarily complex.

In 1941 a study conference recommended a single corporate structure designed to integrate the work of various interdenominational agencies, including the Federal Council, and thus to give more visible and coherent expression to the growing fellowship among the churches. A plan was ready by 1944, and after six years of study and debate, the NCCC was inaugurated in November 1950. The new council represented the merger of 12 former agencies. A total of 29 churches, ranging from Quaker (→ Friends, Society of) to Eastern Orthodox (→ Orthodox Church), voted to become constituting members.

2. Self-Understanding

Given this background, it is understandable that the NCCC was initially conceived as an instrument of interchurch cooperation made up of largely autonomous program units with distinct purposes and constituencies. The → Faith and Order goal of promoting visible church → unity, so central to the conception of the → World Council of Churches, has historically been a minor theme of the NCCC.

In 1981, however, the NCCC Governing Board voted to change the council's self-description, found in the preamble to its constitution, from "a cooperative agency for the churches" to "a community of Christian communions" that "covenant with one another to manifest ever more fully the unity of the church." Attempts were made, throughout the 1980s and 1990s, to embody this vision in the council's structure, especially by strengthening the relationship between the program units and the governing assembly and by increasing the participation of the member churches in the governance, funding, and interpretation of the NCCC. Such efforts were made more urgent by a funding crisis at the end of the century.

3. Function and Funding

The current NCCC has two arms — (1) Faith, Justice, and Education Ministries and (2) Church World Service (CWS) — under one General Assembly. Leaders hope that this arrangement will ease historic tensions over financial matters, while still allowing for cooperation between CWS and the rest of the council.

Historically, about 70 percent of the NCCC's budget has been disbursed by CWS. The council is also well known for such things as its sponsorship of the Revised Standard Version, and later the New Revised Standard Version, English translations of the Bible (→ Bible Versions); its sponsorship of visits by groups of U.S. Christians to churches in the former Soviet Union; and its public support of human and civil → rights. During the first decade of the 21st century, the NCCC plans to focus major attention on a "mobilization" to alleviate → poverty in the United States.

The council is largely dependent on member churches for its income. Most funds received through denominational sources are designated for specific programs or projects. The NCCC's budget thus fluctuates from year to year, depending on the needs to which the council responds.

4. Members

The NCCC includes a wide range of Protestant and Orthodox communions. → The Roman Catholic Church, while not a member, works closely with various NCCC program units. The council's membership generally does not include Holiness (→ Holiness Movement), → Pentecostal, and conservative → evangelical or → fundamentalist churches (including the Southern Baptist Convention and the Lutheran Church–Missouri Synod), although several of these groups participate through individual representatives in the work of NCCC's Commission on Faith and Order. Discussions began in 2001 and were aimed at creating a new ecumenical forum that would include a wider array of churches.

Bibliography: H. G. ANDERSON, "Ecumenical Movements," *Altered Landscapes: Christianity in America, 1935-1985* (ed. D. W. Lotz; Grand Rapids, 1989) • S. M. CAVERT, *The American Churches in the Ecumenical Movement, 1900-1968* (New York, 1968) • J. F. FINDLAY, *Church People in the Struggle: The National Council of Churches and the Black Freedom Movement, 1950-1970* (New York, 1993) • NCCC, triennial reports (1952-) • N. VANDERWERF, *The Times Were Very Full* (New York, 1975).

MICHAEL KINNAMON

National Councils of Churches

1. Definition
2. History
3. Issues
   3.1. Membership
   3.2. Function
   3.3. Ecclesiological Significance
   3.4. Ecumenical Significance

1. Definition

A council of churches is a voluntary association of separated Christian churches through which its members seek to manifest their fellowship with one another (→ Koinonia), to engage in common activities of witness and service, and to advance toward the ecumenical goal of greater visible → unity. A council of churches can be distinguished from a temporary church coalition in that its members make a long-term commitment to one another. It can be distinguished from a clergy association or Christian service organization in that its members are not individuals but churches, and from an interfaith council in that its self-understanding includes shared confession of Jesus Christ.

National councils of churches are composed of churches from a given country, bringing together representatives named by the national structures of the churches. Councils of churches also exist in many local settings (e.g., cities, states, or provinces), as well as internationally (e.g., the → All Africa Conference of Churches, the → World Council of Churches). These councils, though linked by common participation in the ecumenical movement, are not structurally related; their constituent members are churches, not other councils.

The English word "council" can be confusing, since it conveys two distinct meanings. Many European languages have one term (e.g., *concilium, Konzil, concile*) that stands for the ecumenical councils of the ancient church (in which authoritative decisions were made regarding matters of faith, practice, and witness), for the governing bodies of some contemporary churches, or for the "conciliar fellowship" sometimes envisioned as the goal of the ecumenical movement. A second term (e.g., *consilium, Rat, conseil*) is used for the associations or fellowships described in this article. The authority of these latter councils is only that accorded them by their members. In some settings the problem is avoided by using such terms as "conference" or "association" instead of "council."

2. History

Councils of churches in their various forms are products of the modern ecumenical movement. The desire to substitute cooperation for competition in overseas missions led to the establishment of missionary councils both in Europe (e.g., the German Missionary Council [1885] and the British Missionary Society [1912]) and in the mission fields of Asia and Africa (e.g., the National Missionary Council of India, Burma, and Ceylon [1912]). As their name implies, these councils were composed primarily of mission agencies and were intended to coordinate action for the spread of the gospel.

The Edinburgh World Missionary Conference of 1910 gave considerable impetus to the establishment of national missionary councils in colonized regions (→ Colonialism and Mission). In 1910 there were 2 national councils through which limited cooperation was possible. By 1928, the year of the Jerusalem meeting of the → International Missionary Council, there were 23 such councils.

This same period also saw important changes in the self-understanding and terminology of councils. India is a good example of these changes. In 1922 the National Missionary Council became the National Christian Council of India, Burma, and Ceylon, a designation that reflected the increasing role played by Asian Christians. The new body also expanded its range of activities to include famine relief, agricultural education and village improvement, literature promotion, and → youth work — although → evangelism remained the council's primary purpose.

The development of missionary councils, however, does not tell the whole story. The first national councils in which churches were constituent members appears to have been the Protestant Federation of France (1905), a loose association created to enable mutual consultation and to carry out common tasks. This group was followed in 1908 by the Federal Council of the Churches of Christ in America, which by 1910 included 31 denominations representing the majority of U.S. Protestants. These organizations reflected a growing sense that the voluntary principle was inadequate: the churches needed to be together in council. But the emphasis was still on cooperative programming, not growth in unity.

By the middle of the 20th century, however, a new understanding was beginning to emerge, along with new terminology. In 1950, for example, the Federal Council was reborn as the → National Council of the Churches of Christ in the U.S.A. In India the Christian Council became the National Council of Churches in 1956, its constitution specifying that "only organized church bodies are entitled to direct representation in the council," a pattern repeated in other parts of the world.

There were two primary reasons for these changes. First, national independence in countries such as India contributed to the indigenization of the churches and to the realization that the membership of foreign mission agencies in national Christian councils undermined the relationship of these bodies to the national community and obscured their true purpose, now increasingly understood as the promotion of Christian fellowship in each place. Second, the birth of the World Council of Churches (WCC) in 1948 deeply affected ecumenical organizations around the world. The WCC is defined in its basis as a "fellowship of churches" whose first purpose is "to call the churches to the goal of visible unity." Councils, that is to say, are not simply instruments for cooperative service and evangelism but fellowships through which the churches seek to grow in deeper unity with one another.

In recent years new models of conciliar life have been developed in such places as the United Kingdom and Australia. In the "classic" model, representatives of the member churches meet periodically in order to decide how to carry out tasks on behalf of the churches. The danger is that the council, guided and staffed by ecumenical enthusiasts, will assert its own agenda alongside of, or even over against, that of the churches. In the new "churches together" model, the council is seen, not as an organization that does things for the churches, but as the place where churches act together. Practically speaking, this view means that the council does not act unless there is a consensus among the member churches to do so and that church leaders play a more prominent role in decision making.

Other councils (e.g., the → Middle East Council of Churches and the Christian Council of Sweden) have structured themselves according to families of churches, that is, Roman Catholic, Orthodox, and Protestant. This model allows for representation that is not solely based on the size and resources of individual churches.

3. Issues

The meaning and purpose of national councils of churches have received considerable attention during the last generation of the ecumenical movement, including three world consultations sponsored by the WCC (1971, 1986, and 1993). These discussions can be summarized under four headings.

3.1. Membership

The outstanding recent development with regard to national councils is certainly the increasing participation in them of the → Roman Catholic Church. There was no Roman Catholic membership in national councils before → Vatican II (1962-65). At the time of the 1971 world consultation referred to above, 10 national councils had full Roman Catholic membership. By 2000 this number had grown to 55, thanks in part to the encouragement offered in several Vatican documents.

→ Orthodox churches are active members in numerous councils, although their involvement in the WCC has been under serious review since the Harare Assembly in 1998. With a few exceptions, Pentecostal and evangelical Protestants are not conciliar participants and in some places have developed parallel cooperative organizations (→ Pentecostal Churches; Evangelical Movement; Lausanne Movement).

The question of membership raises an important tension between comprehensiveness and focus. Councils of churches generally desire, on the one hand, to include the broadest possible spectrum of churches. But their effectiveness also depends, on the other hand, on a clear, common vision of what → ecumenism requires and on a commitment to live out that vision through common activities — objectives that are often more difficult to achieve as membership expands.

Another issue concerns the meaning of membership in a council of churches. Since the WCC's Toronto Statement of 1950, "The Church, the Churches, and the World Council of Churches," it has been acknowledged that membership need not mean "that each church must regard the other member churches as churches in the true and full sense of the word." A 1975 Vatican report observes, however, that membership in a council implies recognition of the other members as "ecclesial communities"; it is at least a first step, in other words, in a deepening mutual recognition that all belong to Christ.

3.2. Function

An obvious function of national — and local — councils is to serve as channels for practical cooperation between the churches in such fields as disaster relief, → development, social justice, public-policy advocacy, → education, → communication, and the distribution of interchurch aid. In performing these tasks, councils are, in one sense, instruments of the churches. Recent discussions, however, also emphasize the responsibility of councils to push beyond what the churches may identify as their common agenda. Councils can, and frequently do, take "prophetic" stances and actions on public issues and in the process work closely with groups that are marginal to the official decision-making structures of the churches.

The three world consultations sponsored by the WCC also stressed that the cooperative work of national councils should not be separated from discussions of → Faith and Order or from acts of common → worship. Councils are not simply service and development agencies but instruments for promoting unity and common witness. Thus, while they leave actual union conversations to the churches involved, councils can stimulate a growing recognition among the churches, foster multilateral discussion of divisive theological issues, provide a climate for → reception of ecumenical agreement, and build essential trust.

3.3. Ecclesiological Significance

The phenomenon of now-separated churches committing themselves to one another in the fellowship of a council is a relatively new one, and thus the ecclesiological character of these bodies has been the subject of much interest and debate. It can be argued that the unity, holiness, catholicity, and apostolicity of the church shine forth more clearly when churches engage through councils in common witness, service, and worship than when they do these things in isolation (→ Church 3.1.2). Councils of churches generally do not claim, however, to be adequate manifestations of Christ's one church. Their ecclesiological significance resides in their ability to promote growing unity among their members and to anticipate that unity, however partially, in their present life. Conversely, the greatest problem that councils face is the often low commitment of their members to one another and the sense that actions taken in a council have little claim on the "persons in the pews."

3.4. Ecumenical Significance

According to the world consultations referred to above, the ecumenical significance of councils of churches depends upon their self-understanding. If, on the one hand, councils regard themselves as permanent cooperative agencies, as structures alongside the churches that enable the churches to do some things together, then they may actually serve to institutionalize present divisions, making the pressure for unity and renewal less urgent. If, on the other hand, they see themselves as steps on the way toward deeper fellowship, councils are indispensable instruments of ecumenical growth. Lukas Vischer has expressed the hope of many ecumenists: "Christian councils are, so to speak, the thorn in the flesh of the churches. They are a constant reminder to the churches of the anomalous situation in which they live. They prod the churches to expose themselves continually to the power of the Holy Spirit. They constitute the setting, created by the churches themselves, within which the promise of renewal may be heard, within which the churches can share their experiences and gradually establish a common tradition, and within which they can also face together and overcome together the crises to which they are exposed."

Bibliography: T. F. Best, "Councils of Churches: Local, National, Regional," *DEM* 231-38; idem, ed., *Instruments of Unity: National Councils of Churches within the One Ecumenical Movement* (Geneva, 1988) • D. Kessler and M. Kinnamon, *Councils of Churches and the Ecumenical Vision* (Geneva, 2000) • World Council of Churches, *The Council of the Ancient Church and the Ecumenical Movement* (Geneva, 1969).

Michael Kinnamon

National Socialism → Fascism

Natural Law

1. Term
2. History
   2.1. In Antiquity
   2.2. In Christianity
   2.3. Modern Period and Critical Natural Law
3. Knowledge, Content, and Basis
   3.1. Knowledge
   3.2. Content
   3.3. Basis
4. In Protestantism
5. In Roman Catholicism
6. Recent Critique and Constructions

1. Term

The term "natural law" is used for the ethical theory of what is truly right (→ Ethics). The discipline differs from that of positive (i.e., prescribed) law by positing an order of what is right that is inherent in our human nature and that is known to us intrinsically. Natural law is thus the epitome of that order. It denotes that which is right by nature (Gk. *physei dikaion,* Lat. *ius/lex naturae*) rather than by statute

(Gk. *nomikon diakaion*). In consequence of the modern empirical restriction in the use of the term "nature," however, "natural law" and "law of nature" have now become predominantly scientific terms (→ Empiricism; Modern Period). Tradition speaks of an essential human nature that we may know by inward insight, and by linking law and ethics it makes this nature a pre-positive and super-positive → norm and critical court in legal culture (→ Law and Legal Theory).

2. History
2.1. *In Antiquity*
The pre-Socratics (→ Greek Philosophy 2) viewed law as the order that governs the whole cosmos. The Sophists were the first to take as their point of departure the notion of justice as the state of human → society as, on the basis of → culture, it actually exists and has been elevated to the status of law, a notion of justice identical with the obtaining of positive law.

In opposition to this positivism Plato (427-347 B.C.; → Platonism) developed natural law as a doctrine of justice and as a criterion of positive law. Through the participation of → reason in the world soul by means of the *orthos logos,* political legislation acquires a true paradigm and insight into the nature and correctness of → laws.

Aristotle (384-322; Aristotelianism) in his *Nicomachean Ethics* divided political law into natural and statutory (5.7.1134b18-1135a5). In distinction from the particular law laid down by us, natural law is universal, original, and independent of human opinion. Yet it may take different forms, according to historical political reality and moral insight.

After Aristotle the → Stoics advocated a cosmic natural law that lacked political consequences. Cicero (106-43) ultimately reunited Stoicism with the classical tradition of natural law and related Roman law and jurisprudence to it. → Nature, custom, and law (Gk. *physis, ethos,* and *nomos*) were the three legal spheres according to origin and temporal sequence. A law of reason is the basis of law in human society, which is institutionalized among nations as *ius gentium.*

2.2. *In Christianity*
In tracing back cosmic natural law to the divine Creator (→ Creation), Stoicism influenced the → early church philosophically. The first high point in Christian teaching on natural law came with → Augustine (354-430; → Augustine's Theology), who saw God's reason and will behind the natural order as an eternal law. The moral law of nature is a reflection of this eternal law in human reason. It is for-

mulated materially in the → Decalogue or the → Golden Rule.

→ Thomas Aquinas (ca. 1225-74; → Thomism) was the first great systematizer. His system covered the eternal law, then the moral law of nature, and then positive law, which had its own, yet not unintegrated, significance. We see the importance of inner experience for natural law from his appeal to indwelling (natural) inclinations (*Summa theol.* I of II, q. 94, art. 2). With the exception of the basic moral principles, this law is changeable and adaptable.

The eternal law becomes a law of reason in virtue of the ability of human reason to distinguish between → good and → evil (I of II, q. 91, art. 2). In the ontic order of things reason thus has a mediating role between the eternal law and that which is according to nature in all its reality and specificity (→ Ontology). Nature enters into the judgment made by reason as to what is ethical and right. The natural order is thus an order that we know in the light of reason by participation in the eternal law, not one that we read off from nature itself. The theonomy of law does not simply replace nature but completes it.

Recognition has now been earned by late Spanish Scholasticism (F. de Vitoria, F. Suárez) and its achievements in this tradition. For H. Grotius natural law was a source of the right in → international law.

2.3. *Modern Period and Critical Natural Law*
In the modern period natural law lost its basic link with theology. Instead of the Creator's will in the natural order, the will and insight of individuals became the starting point. Increasingly, nature came to be viewed only empirically and mechanistically. The basis of law and the → state ceased to be sought in morals. From the time of T. Hobbes (1588-1679) a contract theory began to take center stage.

Natural law reached full flower in the 18th century, as the → Enlightenment saw in it the secularized law of reason (→ Secularization; Secularism), which is always valid and can be concretely constructed. Natural law thus became civil law (C. Wolff). Rationalistic natural law (→ Rationalism) inspired the American and French Revolutions and attained its greatest influence in the great legislative achievements around 1800.

Philosophically, the climax came with I. Kant (1724-1804; → Kantianism). As he saw it, nature as the basis of natural law cannot be an object of → experience. The sole standard of natural law lies in practical reason, which is valid a priori. The common basis of law and ethics in the law of custom

does not mean that materially the right is dependent on this law. The right, though, is materially the same as positive law, so that law and morality are not the same.

From this criticism of natural law the 19th century inferred the emptiness of the concept. A rapidly pioneering legal positivism recognized as law only the compulsory law of the state. According to K. Bergbohm (1849-1927) nature and reason, ethos and religious law, can never be a valid basis for legal norms but can only explain them. In Britain → utilitarianism (J. Bentham) shaped legal positivism. Despite various revivals of natural law, especially in neo-Thomism (L. Taparelli, V. Cathrein), legal positivism remained dominant. H. Kelsen (1881-1973) labeled natural law as → ideology.

The 20th-century experience of totalitarianism (→ Fascism) brought a renaissance of natural law after 1945 (G. Radbruch). E. Bloch (1885-1977) put a critical natural law in place of the traditional one, relating it to our common human dignity. In the principle of hope he found anticipation of a better existence. The U.N.'s Universal Declaration of Human → Rights (1948; see also the Basic Law of the Federal Republic of Germany in 1949) shows the influence of natural law thinking.

Materially, natural law has been rehabilitated today in legal policy. In political ethics the idea of justice has come to life with the help of the contract theory (J. Rawls). Like ethics, legal philosophy offers an important basis for law. Rationally critical and analytically transcendental considerations also play a part (O. Höffe). In critical discussion, natural law still retains its relevance (R. Dreier).

3. Knowledge, Content, and Basis
3.1. *Knowledge*
The history of natural law and its basis is also the history of its knowledge. The normative power of reason finally depends on our relation as moral subjects to an objective ontic reality. The attempt to postulate a basic knowledge of right and wrong along purely transcendental and anthropological lines can never be more then formal (→ Anthropology). A material ethics of the right must break out of the subject-object circle (the self and the world of experience) by ontic insight and epistemological certainty. Neither a formal imperative (such as the → categorical imperative) nor statutes on an empirical basis can alone form a starting point for reason. Working back to our ontological nature as a superior normative basis is the main task of natural law teaching, though it must not fall into mere naturalistic essentialism.

3.2. Content

We know the claims of the right (i.e., authorities of universal validity) through our → conscience. From our inner moral experience we know that self-fulfillment is required of us, that we must satisfy bodily and intellectual needs for the attainment of existential ends (J. Messner). The moral a priori of the natural law tradition thus goes back to concrete experiences in common life, to synthetic principles. This empirical path to natural law rests on our human constitution and is not a mistaken naturalistic inference from what is to what should be. The reality we experience, our nature as it is understood and explained, opens the door to absolutely valid insights in the form of the rights and duties of true human existence, even though the material formulation and actual acceptance may still be dependent on relationships.

In this regard human beings in particular are referred to the social realm. Initially, this social dimension means fellowship in the → family, within which, in the struggle for self-fulfillment, social modes of conduct came to be obligatory (→ Socialization), including mutual respect, → love, truthfulness, and especially justice. Natural law thinking may thus seem to be autonomously posited in us, even though any link between the natural order and the order of creation may be denied.

3.3. Basis

Over against the strict separation of law and ethical theory in legal positivism, the question of what is truly right constantly arises from the experience of legal reality and its material claim. Existing systems of norms cannot deprive basic principles of their validity, even when the former contradict the latter (G. Radbruch). Structurally, superpositive legal principles are immanent in all positive legal systems (R. Dworkin). In political practice a sense of the right proves to be a progressive force (→ Progress) for the improvement of law (→ Peace) and for the creation of new law as new questions of environmental preservation (→ Ecology; Environment) pose new demands.

In the 1970s the English-speaking world faced up more radically than before to the issue of justice in the matter of social welfare (J. Rawls). Höffe could speak of a critical natural law. Natural law thus proved to be stronger than all political → power (→ Resistance, Right of) as a criterion of truth and righteousness.

Without being anchored in morality, law loses its obligatory character. As a → virtue, justice relates to people and → values and cannot be reduced to a utilitarian contract. All problems of what is right are not also moral problems, nor can all be solved by law. Right and morality are related but not identical. Establishing this relation is the task of natural law.

4. In Protestantism

The → Reformers (→ Reformation) found natural law teaching in the late scholastic tradition (→ Scholasticism) but opposed to it their understanding of → revelation by the Word, of → grace, and of natural and rational knowledge. In arguing in his → two-kingdoms doctrine that natural law belongs to the secular kingdom, M. → Luther (1483-1546; → Luther's Theology) taught and promoted the modern detheologizing of natural law. J. → Calvin (1509-64; → Calvin's Theology) derived subjection to the authorities directly from God's will. Nevertheless, this approach did not entail any denial of a divine order of creation, ignoring of the material problems of natural law, or exclusion of any possibility of their solution. In P. → Melanchthon (1497-1560) Aristotelian natural law still had a place. As he saw it, reason can recognize the first principles and natural order in human relations.

The → Enlightenment view of natural law, however, as well as the later positivist concept of law and the essentialist teaching of → neoscholasticism on the topic, strengthened the trend away from natural law and the turning toward a moral basis of law in Scripture or a Christological basis (→ Christology). Thus → dialectical theology (see K. → Barth and his influence on the → Confessing Church) sought a starting point in the biblical revelation, claiming to proceed along the lines of → salvation history rather than abstract philosophy. Yet the existential situation still had some relevance. For E. Brunner (1889-1966) a link existed to → natural theology, yet with Scripture as the norm.

Protestant ethics saw many phases and trends in the encounter of the Christian and the secular (C. Frey) as it evaluated practical reason and drew the line between the practice of faith and the secular ethos. A distinctive, materially Christian practice was united in various ways with a normative basis in transcendental anthropology. Without having to clarify the question of the relation between a basis of the legal ethos in Christology or in natural law and the knowledge of this ethos, the Protestant law of love for God and the new creation expected in the *eschaton* (H.-D. Wendland; → Eschatology) offered a critical starting point for Christian → responsibility for the world. Some advocates of a Protestant → social ethics (e.g., F. Karrenberg, M. Honecker) appealed to natural law and the adoption of the methods of → sociology. In cooperation with non-

Christians, and in attempts to arrive at a proper ethical evaluation of → technology and problems of peace and the environment, natural law came to play a varied role. In the ecumenical movement, especially in common work for peace, justice, and the integrity of → creation, there developed a necessary openness to natural law arguments in the light of the gospel (→ Ecumenism, Ecumenical Movement).

5. In Roman Catholicism

Finally, the natural law tradition underwent a revival in Roman Catholic moral philosophy in opposition to legal positivism. Already in the middle of the 19th century, L. Taparelli (1793-1862) had sought a natural law based on experience. As distinct from many champions of neo-Thomism, who with an appeal to "eternal law" advocated a legal morality, and with a concern to answer criticism of natural law, J. Messner (1891-1984) took note of the historical and sociological conditioning of natural law.

In the 1960s a crisis in natural law thinking arose among those who espoused Roman Catholic → moral theology. For a time use of the term "natural law" was replaced even in church documents by theological argumentation. The application of natural law principles and inferences from them became a point of debate in → sexual ethics (e.g., → birth control) more so than in problems of social ethics.

In the modern → pluralism of → worldviews, the → teaching office and theologians then began to seek open → dialogue by means of natural law in what was after → Vatican II a more personal and dynamic understanding. In the arguments the systematic theological study of natural law plunged more deeply into the question of what is distinctively Christian. Within the church basic personal rights (→ Human Dignity) commanded greater respect. Trends developed in Roman Catholic moral theology that laid more stress on the ontic equality of human action and that opted for an operational understanding of what is right by nature (R. Spaemann). Other trends along the lines of formal transcendental philosophy showed how ill-adapted the human is to play a regulatory role (Höffe). Argumentation became broader and more dynamic. It thus came into line with new developments in critical thinking about natural law and justice.

→ Democracy; Legitimation

Bibliography: D. J. M. BRADLEY, *Aquinas on the Twofold Human Good: Reason and Happiness in Aquinas's Moral Science* (Washington, D.C., 1997) • R. DREIER, *Studien zur Rechtstheorie* (2 vols.; Frankfurt, 1981-91) • J. FIN-NIS, *Natural Law and Natural Rights* (2d ed.; Oxford, 1982) • O. HÖFFE, *Political Justice: Foundations for a Critical Philosophy of Law and the State* (Cambridge, 1995); idem, "Recht und Moral," *NHP* 17 (1979) 1-36 • M. HONECKER, *Sozialethik zwischen Tradition und Vernunft* (Tübingen, 1977); idem, *Wege evangelischer Ethik. Positionen und Kontexte* (Fribourg, 2002) • B. HOOSE, ed., *Christian Ethics: An Introduction* (Minneapolis, 1998) • R. M. McINERNY, *Ethica Thomistica: The Moral Philosophy of Thomas Aquinas* (rev. ed.; Washington, D.C., 1997) • A. C. MacINTYRE, *After Virtue: A Study in Moral Theory* (2d ed.; Notre Dame, Ind., 1984) • J. MESSNER, *Das Naturrecht. Handbuch der Gesellschaftsethik, Staatsethik und Wirtschaftsethik* (7th ed.; Berlin, 1984; orig. pub., 1950) • M. NOVAK, *On Two Wings: Humble Faith and Common Sense at the American Founding* (San Francisco, 2002) • E. SCHOCKENHOFF, *Natural Law and Human Dignity: Universal Ethics in an Historical World* (Washington, D.C., 2003).

RUDOLF WEILER

6. Recent Critique and Constructions

Within the field of theological → ethics, most recent work on natural law, Protestant as well as Roman Catholic, has been connected to the earlier tradition of natural law reflection by way of the natural law ethic associated with early modern Catholic → moral theology. Very often the relevant connection is one of repudiation rather than affirmation, but the connections are clear nonetheless. For that reason, if we are to understand contemporary theological approaches to natural law, we must look first at the modern natural law ethic that provides the context, and usually the foil, for these approaches.

On this view, moral → norms are grounded in the processes and inclinations of the human person, including sensual, rational, and spiritual inclinations, which are seen as being intrinsically purposive and thus normatively binding. The fundamental principle of natural law, so understood, is that the human → person should act in accordance with the normative functions of human nature, as they are discerned through intelligent observation of human life. Typically, this principle was further specified by reference to the purposes intrinsic to biological faculties or organs, which, it was said, set parameters for their legitimate exercise or use.

This view of natural law began to be criticized by Roman Catholic theologians in the early decades of the 20th century, well before the Second → Vatican Council called for a more theological and scripturally oriented approach to moral theology. One important line of criticism can be traced to the writings of the German theologian Herbert Doms, who argued that the → sexual ethic implied by the then-current understanding of natural law was unsatisfactory. Rather than speaking in terms of primary and secondary "ends" of → marriage, he argued, we must understand marriage first of all in terms of the mutual orientation of the spouses to personal union with one another. This widely influential argument gave rise to an alternative approach to moral reflection that came to be known as personalism, which might be defined broadly as an account of morality that gives priority to the well-being of the human person, comprehensively considered. This approach became particularly influential among English-speaking moral theologians, thanks especially to the influence of Richard McCormick, Charles Curran, and Lisa Cahill.

This personalist approach to moral reasoning was reinforced by a more general line of criticism developed (in somewhat different forms) by Karl → Rahner and Bernard Lonergan. According to both, the traditional account of natural law is inadequate because it represents a "static" or "classical" view of human nature. The more we become conscious of the ways in which the expression of our human nature is historically conditioned, the less we are prepared to draw moral conclusions from our own ideas of the supposedly permanent structures of that nature; or so the argument goes.

Yet very few Catholic theologians have been prepared to dismiss the idea of natural law altogether. By the middle of the 20th century, many (perhaps most) Catholic theologians had rejected the idea that the natural processes of human life set moral constraints, independently of the personal or historical contexts within which those processes are expressed and rendered meaningful. Yet there was a widespread desire to retain what were seen as the valid insights of the older approach, especially its moral → realism and its commitment to finding a framework for moral dialogue for all men and women of goodwill. For this reason, Catholic theologians increasingly adopted a view according to which natural law should be equated, more or less straightforwardly, with → reason operating practically. This is the view taken, for example, by John Courtney Murray, whose analysis of the U.S. Constitution in natural law terms had such an impact at Vatican II. Murray does affirm the metaphysical foundations of natural law in a teleological account of → nature. However, he also appears to equate human nature more or less completely with the human capacity for rationality; hence, his explanations of the way in which natural law functions emphasize

the operations of practical reason, in such a way as to minimize or even to deny the normative force of nature understood in any wider sense.

Jacques Maritain might seem to offer an exception to the general tendency in this period to equate natural law straightforwardly with the deliverances of practical reason. In contrast to many of his peers, Maritain asserts clearly the metaphysical foundations of natural law. And yet, even though Maritain grounds natural law in a robustly metaphysical conception of nature, this conception has little direct normative significance; in contrast to most of his contemporaries, Maritain does not consider natural law, considered as a source for moral norms, to be accessible to human reason (→ Metaphysics). Rather, our knowledge of the norms of natural law comes through our inclinations toward the → good. This mode of knowledge, which depends on our connaturality to what is good, provides a starting point for intellectual reflection on moral matters, but in itself it is obscure and unsystematic. Hence, even though Maritain does construe natural law in such a way as to preserve the connection between natural law and a robust conception of human nature, he denies that natural law has any direct, cognitively accessible normative force.

In addition to the moral and theological objections mentioned above, the older Catholic idea of natural law was also undermined by the influence of arguments against the so-called naturalistic fallacy. That is, the claim that moral conclusions can be derived from factual premises undoubtedly played some role in the widespread identification of natural law with the operations of practical reason. This line of argument was particularly important for Germain Grisez and John Finnis, Catholic philosophers who jointly developed one of the most important recent theories of natural law, widely known as the "new theory of natural law." On this view, moral norms are grounded in the rational apprehension of certain basic goods, which are known to be such as soon as they are apprehended. These apprehensions, in turn, are given meaning and directedness through the first principle of practical reason, that the good is to sought and done and the bad is to be avoided, and through modes of responsibility that further specify the ways in which the good is to be pursued. These principles, operating from the starting point of rational apprehension of the basic goods, are claimed to generate a comprehensive and rationally compelling set of moral norms, which compose natural law. This account of natural law has been widely influential in English-speaking circles, and it is beginning to influence Continental thinkers as well, as we see, for example, in the recent work of the German Catholic theologian Martin Rhonheimer.

At the same time, Protestant criticisms of natural law were not forestalled by the extensive rethinking of natural law going on in Catholic circles. In the early 20th century Karl → Barth powerfully reformulated the traditional Protestant criticism that natural law moralities represent an effort to establish human righteousness apart from God's → law and God's → grace. Somewhat later, Reinhold → Niebuhr forcefully defended the claim that the pervasive reality of human sinfulness has decisively undermined our knowledge of a natural moral order (→ Sin). More recently, Stanley Hauerwas has argued that the doctrine of natural law, at least in its usual formulations, provides an insufficiently theological basis for a Christian ethic.

At the same time, we would have a one-sided view of Protestant approaches to natural law if we considered nothing but these criticisms. Over the past 30 years Protestant theologians have increasingly turned to the natural law tradition as a source for their own moral reflection. Indeed, in English-speaking circles one of the most influential advocates of a reconsideration of the theological significance of nature has been Reformed theologian James Gustafson. Admittedly, Gustafson's own constructive proposal does not take the form of a retrieval of a classical account of natural law. Rather, drawing heavily on the work of H. Richard Niebuhr, Gustafson proposes an ethic of responsiveness to, and responsibility in the light of, the transpersonal forces that both sustain and threaten human life, including both natural forces, understood in a wide range of ways, and broad social forces. In his view, Christians should respond to all such forces with an attitude of → piety, construing them as expressions of divine agency. Correlatively, piety is put into action through a process of discerning how best to respond to divine agency as expressed through these forces.

Gustafson's emphasis on nature as a comprehensive context for human discernment and responsibility has had a wide appeal. And its appeal is by no means limited to Protestant scholars; the distinguished Catholic moral theologian Charles Curran, who was one of the most influential critics of traditional Catholic versions of natural law in the middle decades of the last century, has recently developed a Catholic moral theology within the framework of an ethic of responsiveness along the lines sketched above. Even more strikingly, we see similar ideas expressed in more recent Protestant retrievals of a nat-

ural law ethic that, on the surface, are very different from Gustafson's liberal and pragmatic approach; see, for example, recent work by the Lutheran theologian Reinhard Hütter.

Finally, we are seeing renewed interest in retrieving some elements of earlier approaches among younger theologians, mostly but not only Catholics. For example, Stephen Pope has recently argued that Aquinas's theory of natural law and contemporary work on sociobiology can be brought into fruitful correlation; Cynthia Crysdale has attempted to extend the insights of Bernard Lonergan into an approach to natural law that takes account of contemporary → science; Christina Traina has argued that Aquinas's natural law ethic is more open to feminist insights than is commonly realized; and Jean Porter has suggested the possibilities of retrieving the scholastic concept of natural law as a basis for a contemporary theological ethic. These approaches may or may not prove to be fruitful lines of research, but the ubiquitous influence of the natural law tradition and its obvious relevance to so many contemporary concerns guarantee that theories of natural law will continue to play an important role in theological ethics for the foreseeable future.

Bibliography: Early modern formulations and critiques: K. BARTH, *CD* II/2 • H. DOMS, *The Meaning of Marriage* (New York, 1939) • B. LONERGAN, "A Transition from a Classicist Worldview to Historical Mindedness," *Law for Liberty: The Role of the Law in the Church Today* (ed. J. E. Biechler; Baltimore, 1967) 126-33 • J. MARITAIN, *Man and the State* (Chicago, 1951) • J. C. MURRAY, *We Hold These Truths* (New York, 1960) • R. NIEBUHR, *The Nature and Destiny of Man,* vol. 2, *Human Destiny* (New York, 1943) • K. RAHNER, "Naturrecht," *LTK* 7.827-28; idem, "Theology and Anthropology," *Theological Investigations* (23 vols.; Baltimore, 1961-92) 9.28-45.

Contemporary reappraisals: L. CAHILL, *Sex, Gender, and Christian Ethics* (Cambridge, 1996) • C. CRYSDALE, "Revisioning Natural Law: From the Classicist Paradigm to Emergent Probability," *TS* 56 (1995) 464-84 • C. CURRAN, *The Catholic Moral Tradition Today: A Synthesis* (Washington, D.C., 1999); idem, *Contemporary Problems in Moral Theology* (Notre Dame, Ind., 1970) • J. FINNIS, *Aquinas: Moral, Political, and Legal Theory* (Oxford, 1998); idem, *Natural Law and Natural Rights* (Oxford, 1980) • G. GRISEZ, *The Way of the Lord Jesus,* vol. 1, *Christian Moral Principles* (Chicago, 1983) • J. GUSTAFSON, *Ethics from a Theocentric Perspective,* vol. 1, *Theology and Ethics;* vol. 2, *Ethics and Theology* (Chicago, 1981-84) • S. HAUERWAS, *A Community of Character: Towards a Constructive Social Ethic* (Notre

Dame, Ind., 1981); idem, *With the Grain of the Universe: The Church's Witness and Natural Theology* (Grand Rapids, 2001) • R. HÜTTER, "The Twofold Center of Lutheran Ethics: Christian Freedom and God's Commandments," *The Promise of Lutheran Ethics* (ed. K. L. Bloomquist and J. R. Stumme; Minneapolis, 1998) 31-54 • R. McCORMICK, *Corrective Vision: Explorations in Moral Theology* (New York, 1994) • S. POPE, *The Evolution of Altruism and the Ordering of Love* (Washington, D.C., 1994) • J. PORTER, *Natural and Divine Law: Reclaiming the Tradition for Christian Ethics* (Grand Rapids, 1999) • M. RHONHEIMER, *Natur als Grundlage der Moral* (Innsbruck, 1987) • C. TRAINA, *Feminist Ethics and Natural Law: The End of the Anathemas* (Washington, D.C., 1999).

JEAN PORTER

Natural Theology

1. Term
2. Function
   2.1. In the History of Thought
   2.2. Reception in the Church
   2.3. Contemporary Ethics
3. Problem

1. Term

What is called natural theology is not an independent theme but an ongoing, urgent problem in Christian theology relating to the question of → truth. Natural theology wants to show that God is self-evident and that he does not serve merely as a deus ex machina in the world. It thus claims the adjective "natural" in two ways. The first reference is to *the natural sphere in the concrete world order* (→ Nature) as the natural horizon against which God appears. It is as natural beings that humans are under God's impact and summoned to know him. The world itself has a theological witness, namely, in natural laws and the way they meet life's demands. Crises and disasters, however, also carry a reference to the God of → revelation, as Paul tells us in Rom. 1:19-21, traces of which are evident in creation. In this sense "natural" is the opposite of "historical" or "positive." God acts *before* all → tradition and constantly shows himself *after* all tradition. A radiance of originality, perspicuity, and legitimacy surrounds him (known in so-called natural religion).

Since we can see this evidence only by sensory or intellectual observation, the term "natural" also applies to *the faculty of human knowledge* and links up with the thesis of an inborn knowledge of God by rational insight (→ Epistemology). From the days of the → Enlightenment, natural theology has been upheld as a possibility of doing theology with the aid of natural powers alone.

In either case the knowledge of God programmatically breaks free from the event and claim of special revelation and gives the term "God" a universal claim to truth that → philosophy itself can also raise.

2. Function

2.1. *In the History of Thought*

Both linguistically and materially, natural theology goes back to the days of Middle → Stoicism, which divided theology into mythical, natural, and political (or civil). By way of → Augustine (354-430; → Augustine's Theology) and → Thomas Aquinas (ca. 1225-74, *Summa theol.* II of II, q. 94, art. 1; → Thomism), this division lasted up to the beginnings of the Enlightenment (H. Grotius, P. Bayle). Within the triad natural theology had a distinctively critical function. Over against polytheism it had to assert the unity and uniqueness of the deity. It represented philosophical theology (→ Philosophy and Theology), and its main historical achievement was to show that God is a necessity of thought. For a long time after I. Kant (1724-1804; → Kantianism), however, the traditional proofs of God were regarded as definitively refuted. Today, though, they have enjoyed an astounding revival on the basis of postclassical → logic (→ God, Arguments for the Existence of).

Especially important is the link between natural theology and the ancient concept of → natural law (→ Greek Philosophy). We see this link reflected in M. → Luther's (1483-1546) extolling of → reason (→ Luther's Theology), which does not need revelation in secular government, in making agreements, or in buying a field (→ Two Kingdoms Doctrine). In neo-Lutheranism (→ Lutheranism) this teaching led to the fateful identifying of historical orders (e.g., → marriage, people, race) with the will of God. Hence it is not wholly unproblematic, for the actual or underlying interrelationship of God, world, and humanity had lost its basis with the Enlightenment. The law of nature became the law of reason, but enlightened reason rested on human subjectivity and could no longer appeal to experiences of God. Between Luther and the present stands → nihilism, the experience that nature, which discloses reason, bears witness only to the "death" of God (B. → Pascal, F. → Nietzsche; → God Is Dead Theology).

2.2. *Reception in the Church*

The → reception of natural theology in the church, which took place in a wrestling with Greek thinking, brought it about that Christian faith learned to understand itself in terms of philosophy. Natural theology thus took over the function of testing the truth of the confession (the → rule of faith; → Confession of Faith) in the sphere of → experience and thought. It wanted to be understood as an attempt to relate positively all knowledge of God in the world of culture to the → salvation of God revealed solely in Christ. Its specifically Christian form thus involved a distinction between natural and supernatural revelation corresponding epistemologically to that between reason and faith (the double order of knowledge of DH 3015; → Vatican I and II).

While the Enlightenment could reckon with two sources of knowledge, on the Roman Catholic view nature could not be the epitome of a separate order of being but had to be related to the revelation present in it. This relation is the point of the much quoted saying that "grace does not destroy nature but perfects it" (*Summa theol.* I, q. 1, art. 8, ad 2). As → grace presupposes nature, faith takes natural reason into its service. Hence Vatican I could make only the possibility, and not the reality, of a rational knowledge of God a binding doctrine (DH 3004). It thus gave natural theology a new and different function, that of giving primordial orientation in the light of revelation.

It was around this definition that the long battle in modern → Protestantism concerning the validity and limits of natural theology raged. On the Reformation view grace is linked exclusively to the → gospel. But then it would seem that the attempt to relate grace to some natural capacity, to advance reason or → responsibility as a point of contact for it (E. Brunner), amounts to a denial of "Christ alone." If, then, the → Barmen Declaration (1934), which K. → Barth (1886-1968) saw as the primary document of a confessional wrestling with the problems of natural theology, states in its first thesis that Jesus Christ is the binding standard of Christian knowledge of God, it disputes the rank of natural theology as a source of church → proclamation, though not, of course, denying its possibility as such.

2.3. *Contemporary Ethics*
The expository power of natural theology has reemerged in contemporary → ethics. Thus the obligatory nature of commands rests on the "appeal structure of received life" (T. Rendtorff). There are some "spontaneous utterances of existence" (K. E. Løgstrup) — for example, truthfulness or → faithfulness — that make a kind of mute demand on us in every human relationship that we should → trust one another or show mercy to one another. Insofar

as we may claim that these "utterances" are a self-interpretation of → creation, natural theology arises with the aim of showing that the demands of Jesus have universal validity. But we must certainly distinguish these efforts from the classical program of considering nature, history, or reason an independent source of revelation.

3. Problem
In Anglo-Saxon scholarship the universality of the truth claim of natural theology is what makes it an attractive challenge. The tradition of the Gifford Lectures, which promote "natural theology in the broadest sense of the term" (the founder mentioned "the true knowledge of God, that is, of the being, nature, and attributes of the Infinite, of the All, of the First and the Only Cause" and expressed his concern to further the knowledge of "the relations of man and of the universe to Him") has been resumed and continued today in → dialogue with contemporary science and the → philosophy of religion on a newly defined methodological level (T. F. Torrance, A. Peacocke; → Evolution). In the background is a recognition that criticism of natural theology need not be in opposition to the legitimate questions of a theology of nature. For the criticism was aimed at natural theology as → metaphysics, at the metaphysical evidences (regarding omnipotence, omniscience, etc.) to which it subjected the question of God. Natural theology indeed has identified problems that have remained unavoidable themes in theological reflection.

One of the unmastered problems is the challenge of the phenomenon of human religion. Another today is the newly experienced transparency of nature to the mystery of God's creation.

If we seek a dogmatic expression for what must be handled better and differently here, the issue is that of the connection and the material order between faith in God the Creator and faith in the incarnate Reconciler (→ Incarnation). As long as Christian faith holds fast to the NT equation of truth with the person of Jesus Christ, it can meet this problem only by expounding the singular NT definition of truth (John 14:6) according to its truly worldwide scope, as Barth did with his doctrine of parables of the kingdom of heaven or as American → process theology tries to do (dubiously!) with its idea of "creative transformation" (J. B. Cobb). The NT's concern with the self-evident nature of God needs to be reappropriated and reestablished beyond traditional metaphysical concepts of nature, and against the horizon of history, given the nearness of God that is manifest in Christ.

Bibliography: J. Barr, *Biblical Faith and Natural Theology* (Oxford, 1993) • K. Barth, *CD* II/1, IV/3 • J. B. Cobb and D. R. Griffin, *Process Theology: An Introductory Exposition* (Philadelphia, 1976) • A. Farrer, *Faith and Speculation: An Essay in Philosophical Speculation* (Edinburgh, 1988) • J. Gustafson, *Ethics from a Theocentric Perspective,* vol. 1, *Theology and Ethics;* vol. 2, *Ethics and Theology* (Chicago, 1981-84) • S. Hauerwas, *With the Grain of the Universe: The Church's Witness and Natural Theology* (Grand Rapids, 2001) • E. Jüngel, "Das Dilemma der natürlichen Theologie und die Wahrheit ihres Problems," *Entsprechungen. Gott–Wahrheit–Mensch* (Munich, 1980) 158-77 • N. Kretzmann, *The Metaphysics of Creation* (Oxford, 1999); idem, *The Metaphysics of Theism* (Oxford, 1997) • C. Link, *Die Welt als Gleichnis. Studien zum Problem der natürlichen Theologie* (2d ed.; Munich, 1982) • R. McInerny, *Characters in Search of Their Author* (Notre Dame, Ind., 2001) • K. Rahner, "Observations on the Problem of the Anonymous Christian," *Theological Investigations* (23 vols.; Baltimore, 1961-92) 14.280-94 • R. Swinburne, *The Coherence of Theism* (rev. ed.; Oxford, 1993).

CHRISTIAN LINK

Nature

1. History of the Term
   1.1. Greek Philosophy
   1.2. Christian Thinking
   1.3. Humanism and the Renaissance
2. Modern Understanding
3. Theological Significance

1. History of the Term

The term "nature" clearly is used in many different ways, in both everyday speech and technical language. This imprecision makes its meaning versatile but problematic in relation to such concepts as → life, → experience, and reality. The flexibility and imprecision mark its whole history (→ Philosophy of Nature), in which we find all the meanings that it has in common parlance. Common to them all is the idea that "nature" stands for the sphere of the given.

1.1. Greek Philosophy

Physis in → Greek philosophy is more a forerunner than an equivalent of "nature." In the pre-Socratics it is simply reality, and in terms of its root *phy-* (bring forth, produce), which implies growth (whence *phyton, phyteia,* "a plant"), it denotes an organized unity with a known essence. Out of this basic idea three variants developed: the process of

becoming, the result, and the essence manifested in it. The last of these led to the idea that knowledge of the nature of a thing is synonymous with knowledge of its → truth.

In the medical tradition we find emphasis on the natural as the healthy. In the Sophists this emphasis resulted in criticism of convention, with "natural" acquiring normative rank. As a result, the natural came to be defined as the opposite of human achievements. Plato (427-347 B.C.; → Platonism) tried to overcome this antithesis by seeking to show that human productivity, insofar as it is in accord with the truth, is related to the divine productivity that brings forth *physis.*

Aristotle (384-322 B.C.; → Aristotelianism) was the first to view *physis* as a separate field of objects that can be understood as nature in the modern sense (→ Modern Period). In him, though, "nature" appeared mainly in the sphere of theoretical → philosophy. The → Stoics stressed the ethical implications (→ Ethics) by uniting nature and reason in the thought of an all-permeating world → soul. Such a view brought to light the latent → pantheism in the concept of *physis.*

1.2. Christian Thinking

The use of the term "nature" in Christianity was ambivalent from the very first. When it was viewed as the state of the world and humanity (→ Anthropology) under → sin, nature had to be disparaged. But the combination of Platonic, Aristotelian, and Stoic elements in → Hellenism made the term an attractive one for Christianity in interpreting → creation. This point was an important one in the struggle with the → dualism of → Gnosis.

In the theology of → Augustine (354-430) the concept of nature handed down from antiquity was adapted in a distinction between, on the one hand, God himself as creating nature and, on the other, created nature itself. → Evil was no part of the nature that God had created. Augustine saw in the nature that we know by the senses a divinely given book in which we can find the → revelation of God as we do in the book of Scripture. This symbolic understanding of nature became stronger in the → Middle Ages.

With the reception of Aristotle in the 13th century, however, nature came to be seen increasingly as the world of objects with its own laws discernible in physics. The relation between nature and → grace then inevitably became a problem, for God's action in the sphere of nature means intervention in the laws. → Thomas Aquinas (ca. 1225-74; → Thomism) taught the → autonomy of nature in order to emphasize the greatness of grace. He still found an inherent → teleology in nature. With the turning aside from this framework in late → Scholasticism (→ Nominalism), a mechanistic view of nature arose.

With his rejection of Aristotelian → ontology M. → Luther (1483-1546; → Luther's Theology) had no interest in a cosmological concept of nature. He focused instead on the observation of individual created things that reveal the goodness of the Creator. Later, however, such a cosmological concept became dominant, even in → Protestantism.

1.3. Humanism and the Renaissance

→ Humanism and the → Renaissance abandoned the idea of nature as a sign of God, stressing instead its autonomy. The mastering of nature by developing → technology gave rise at the same time to an understanding of nature itself as a mechanism. The full autonomy of nature made its relation to God problematic. Two answers that commanded support were *pantheism,* which denied the distinction between God and the world, and → *deism,* which made it absolute. In both, however, God was ultimately superfluous for an understanding of nature (→ Materialism).

Against his own intentions this conclusion might be seen in R. Descartes (1596-1650; → Cartesianism). The distinction he made between *res extensa* (extended substance) and *res cogitans* (thinking substance) was influential as an antithesis between nature and spirit. B. Spinoza (1632-77; → Spinozism) tried to overcome this dualism by viewing nature and spirit as two moments in the divine. Here, God and nature were synonymous.

I. Kant (1724-1804; → Kantianism) gave the term "nature" its distinctive, modern sense by defining it as the existence of things insofar as they are governed by universal laws. But the reason that knows nature is then a logical presupposition of what is said about it. The world and nature thus part company. The subject lives in the world, and nature is dependent on the subject's thinking. Reason takes God's place as nature's opposite.

Although Kant stressed against → rationalism the reality of the *Ding an sich,* the related thesis of its unknowability meant its complete overshadowing by reason. J. G. Fichte (1762-1814; → Idealism) drew from this position the conclusion that the I posits the non-I. G. W. F. Hegel (1770-1831; → Hegelianism) and F. Schelling (1775-1854), protesting against this view, sought the unity of nature and spirit, but largely without success as the various individual disciplines developed separately. Even F. Nietzsche's (1844-1900) objection — that the view of nature in idealism, no less than that of sci-

ence, aimed at its mastering and subjection — had at first little influence. This objection, which → critical theory took up and developed, demands further thought in view of the ecological crisis (→ Ecology; Environment).

2. Modern Understanding

The modern scientific view of nature contains two irreconcilable aspects. On the one hand, nature is the objectivity that is independent of us; on the other, it is that which conforms to the laws of nature (though these laws, as Kant showed, are an achievement of reason). The linking of the two aspects means that, notwithstanding the experimental method (→ Empiricism), direct experience plays little part in the understanding of nature.

A view of nature that embodies the motifs of → Romanticism exists independently alongside the prevailing scientific view. Both agree in setting nature in antithesis to → culture, technology, and history (→ Philosophy of History). In this regard nature is normative, for what is against it seems to be illegitimate or impossible. Or nature is the threatening, or the better counterpart, of culture or reason. Either way, an appeal to nature replaces further argument.

We see here that the philosophy of nature still determines thinking about it and therefore observation of it, though little express discussion is devoted to this theme. In the concept of nature the decisions of classical → metaphysics live on, though without the ontological connection. New discussions between theology and postclassical physics (e.g., by T. F. Torrance and J. C. Polkinghorne) might open the door, however, to a changed concept of nature that would avoid the problems that now exist.

3. Theological Significance

In view of the many different definitions of nature, theology faces the question whether it may speak legitimately of nature at all, especially as nature, when used to interpret creation, inevitably raises difficulties (→ Aporia). The dualism inhering in the antithetical function of the concept of nature is incompatible with belief in creation. When the Greek notion of equating nature with the divine crowds out the belief in creation, which makes the world dependent on God, that notion's religious side presumably comes to the fore anew. We see the same side in the search for new orientations with the remythifications (→ Myth, Mythology) resulting from the ecological crisis (→ New Age), but also in nature itself, when speaking of nature as subject is no longer taken metaphorically (→ Metaphor).

Self-reflection in natural science and → epistemology shows how hard it is to argue along these
lines and might suggest that there can be no general
view of nature; indeed, science makes little use of it
in practice. The methods and basic theories of science, however, are rooted in the metaphysical concept of nature. The results of science cannot, then,
be equated with reality itself.

This insight stands behind K. Barth's (1886-1968;
→ Dialectical Theology) admonition to theology
that it must develop a genuine understanding of creation. Like Barth's rejection of → natural theology,
this admonition was misunderstood as a negation of
nature. What → Barth was really emphasizing, however, was that before or alongside revelation there
can be no clear knowledge of either God or nature.

A cosmological and universal concept of nature
such as obtains in traditional ontologies and their
actual derivates proves to be theologically dubious.
Nor does the attempt of A. N. Whitehead (1861-
1947) and the ensuing → process philosophy and
theology to overcome the diastasis of nature and
spirit offer any well-founded alternative.

Starting with individual experience might offer
an alternative to the dominant concept of nature,
without losing connection with everyday usage of
the term. A place would also be found along these
lines for the emotional and → aesthetic implications
of the theme. In bodily experience we see our dependence on vital → communication with the human
and nonhuman world around us. Reflection on the
fact that human life is a part of nature can thus express an essential element in the belief in creation.

→ Power 2; Science and Theology

Bibliography: J. Cornwell, ed., Nature's Imagination:
The Frontiers of Scientific Vision (Oxford, 1995) • D. C.
Lindberg and R. B. Numbers, eds., God and Nature:
Historical Essays on the Encounter between Christianity
and Science (Berkeley and Los Angeles, 1986) • C. Link,
Die Welt als Gleichnis (2d ed.; Munich, 1982) • C. Mer-
chant, The Death of Nature: Women, Ecology, and the
Scientific Revolution (New York, 1980) • G. Picht, Der
Begriff der Natur und seine Geschichte (4th ed.; Stutt-
gart, 1998) • J. C. Polkinghorne, Faith, Science, and
Understanding (New Haven, 2000) • L. S. Rouner, On
Nature (Notre Dame, Ind., 1984) • J. Torrance, The
Concept of Nature (Oxford, 1992) • T. F. Torrance, Re-
ality and Scientific Theology (Edinburgh, 1985).

Wolfgang Schoberth

Nature, Philosophy of → Philosophy of Nature

Nature Religion

The term "nature religion" has been used in a great
variety of senses, of which seven are distinguished
here.

Philosophical. In the second and first centuries
b.c. (later, the → Stoics), and also in the 18th century (D. Hume), early doctrines of human nature
came to completion with the observation or postu-
lation of a disposition that in the → modern period
would be called religious.

Theological. In the light of the → revelation of the
true knowledge of God, such a religious disposition
became a problem for the second-century Christian
→ apologists. Various terms were used to describe
and control it, the clearest being → "natural theology," which we find from → Augustine (354-430, De
civ. Dei 6.5-10; → Augustine's Theology) to → Scholasticism and on to → Vatican I (DH 3015-29).

Epistemological. In the age of English → deism
Herbert of Cherbury (1583-1648) traced back special revelation to a natural religion resting on five
common notions: a supreme being, the need to
worship this supreme being, virtue and piety as specific parts of this worship, a horror of wrongdoing
(including the need to expiate it by penitence), and
reward and punishment after this life.

Anthropological. In the age of overseas discovery
explorers found "natural religion" among peoples in
a so-called state of nature. In the → Enlightenment
such religion was seen to take historical shape
among the Chinese.

Chronological. → Evolutionist religious studies,
and those critical of Christianity, tried to derive
from the supposed coincidence of historical and
constitutive initial manifestion the reality and concept of a primal religion that makes true divinity
known to us through → creation (or → nature) or
→ conscience. F. D. E. → Schleiermacher (1768-
1834; → Schleiermacher's Theology) dismissed this
position.

Psychological. In the 19th century the investigation and philosophy of nature produced the theory
that primitive humanity was under a compulsion to
use nature for its own ends. This compulsion taught
it to distinguish between what is helpful in nature
and what stands in the way. A childlike feeling for
nature related the good and beneficial effects to
states of human awareness. Natural events were thus
personified. The worship and service of nature that
give access to its forces form the origin of all nature
religion, that is, the deification of nature as a whole,
of the forces at work in it, and even of some of its
products.

Classificatory. By means of such phenomena religions came to be divided into nature religions, moral religions, and religions of redemption, though only the latter would count as true religions, since that which nature religions have to offer — the sustaining, ordering, and enhancing of life — is conceivable and attainable without their mediation.

Today the term "nature religion" carries with it all the above senses, though each requires its own methodology. The result has been the disappearance of "nature religions" as an invariable entity and concept. No longer having to use the term in an unvarying sense brings with it the advantage of being able to take the phenomena grouped in textbooks under this head and to relate them to more meaningful structures and to more specific historical and geographic situations. We can then see in greater depth and more culture-specifically the symbolism of cosmic nature and the specificity of human nature in the religions.

→ Religion

Bibliography: C. L. ALBANESE, *Nature Religion in America: From the Algonkian Indians to the New Age* (Chicago, 1990) • P. BYRNE, *Natural Religion and the Nature of Religion: The Legacy of Deism* (London, 1989) • R. S. CORRINGTON, *Nature's Religion* (Lanham, Md., 1997) • HERBERT OF CHERBURY, *Pagan Religions* (trans. J. A. Butler; Ottawa, 1996) • D. HUME, *"Dialogues concerning Natural Religion"* (1779) and *"The Natural History of Religion"* (1757) (ed. J. C. A. Gaskin; Oxford, 1993) • H. R. HUTCHESON, ed., *Lord Herbert of Cherbury's "De religione laici"* (New Haven, 1944) • K.-H. KOHL, *Abwehr und Verlangen. Zur Geschichte der Ethnologie* (Frankfurt, 1987) esp. 103-22, "Naturreligion. Zur Transformationsgeschichte eines Begriffs" • J. PEARSON, R. H. ROBERTS, and G. SAMUEL, eds., *Nature Religion Today: Paganism in the Modern World* (Edinburgh, 1998).

CARSTEN COLPE

Nazarene

1. The term *ho Nazarēnos* occurs in the NT in apposition to the name → "Jesus" to show that the Jesus meant is the man of Nazareth (Mark 1:24; 10:47; 14:67; 16:6). Matthew does not have the term but replaces it by *ho Nazōraios* in 26:71, also using that term in 2:23. We find both terms in Luke (the former in 4:34; 24:19; the latter in 18:37), but only the latter in Acts (6 times). John uses the latter term, but only in the passion story (18:5, 7; 19:19). The idea that this form of the name derived from a suppos-

edly pre-Christian sect (the Nazaraioi) is mistaken, as is the idea that the → Mandaeans used it for themselves.

Derivation from the Heb. *nāzîr* (→ Nazirites), meaning one who is dedicated to God (see Num. 6:2-21; Judg. 13:5, 7 LXX), is not wholly satisfying either linguistically or substantively (see Matt. 11:19 = Luke 7:34-35). Matt. 2:23 carries a reference to prophecy, but passages such as Isa. 11:1; 40:3; 49:6 and Jer. 31:6 do not offer any very clear explanation. It would seem that Matthew's reference to the native city of Jesus is in fact the true derivation. The form *Nazor* would bridge the philological difficulty. Matthew with his better knowledge of Scripture was the first to see a connection with the Messianic Branch *(nēṣer)* of Isa. 11:1.

2. → Jewish Christians are called Nazarenes in Acts 24:5, and we also find *nozerim* in the so-called blessing of apostates in the Prayer of Eighteen Benedictions according to the Cairo MS (→ Genizah). → Tertullian (ca. 160-ca. 225) and → Jerome (ca. 345-420) tell us that the Jews called all Christians Nazarenes. In distinction from "Christians," however, which was also a name given to believers by others (Acts 11:26), "Nazarene" came to denote only a specific group.

Epiphanius (ca. 315-403), Jerome, and Augustine (354-430) show that by the fourth and early fifth centuries, some Jewish Christians called themselves Nazarenes. They lived in and around Beroea in Coele-Syria. They read their gospel (the Gospel of the Nazarenes) in Hebrew, that is, in Aramaic or Syriac, fragments of which may be found in Jerome and medieval MSS of Matthew (→ Apocrypha 2.1.2). Jerome also quotes from a Nazarene commentary on Isaiah. From the reports, which do not wholly agree among themselves, it seems that the Nazarenes kept the Mosaic → law but rejected the Pharisaic → Halakah. Their → Christology was close to that of the mainline church. They called Jesus the Son of God (→ Christological Titles 3.3), accepted his virgin birth, but rejected his preexistence as God. They recognized the existence of the → Gentile church and → Paul as its → apostle. Their gospel was close to the canonical Matthew; one may see in it a fictionally expanded and corrected version. Hegesippus (2d cent.) perhaps knew this gospel, which would be testimony to the early age of the group.

→ Ebionites; Primitive Christian Community

Bibliography: A. F. J. KLIJN, "Jerome's Quotations from a Nazorean Interpretation of Isaiah," *RSR* 60 (1972) 241-

55 • A. F. J. Klijn and G. J. Reinink, *Patristic Evidence for Jewish-Christian Sects* (Leiden, 1973) • H. Kuhli, "Ναζαρηνός / Ναζωραῖος," *EDNT* 2.454-56 • R. A. Pritz, *Nazarene Jewish Christianity: From the End of the NT Period until Its Disappearance in the Fourth Century* (Leiden, 1988) • H.-P. Rüger, "ΝΑΖΑΡΕΘ / ΝΑΖΑΡΑ ΝΑΖΑΡΗΝΟΣ / ΝΑΖΩΡΑΙΟΣ," *ZNW* 72 (1981) 257-63 • P. Vielhauer and G. Strecker, "Jewish-Christian Gospels" and "The Gospel of the Nazaraeans," *NT Apocrypha* (2d ed.; 2 vols.; ed. W. Schneemelcher; Louisville, Ky., 1991-92) 1.134-65.

HELMUT MERKEL

Nazarenes → Church of the Nazarene

Nazirites

The term "Nazirite" is from Heb. *nāzîr,* "one who is consecrated, devoted [to the Lord]." The laws regarding Nazirites (Num. 6:1-21) include abstinence from wine (or any other product of the grapevine) and other strong drinks (→ Dietary Laws; Asceticism), from cutting one's hair or beard, and from touching a corpse. Both men and women could become Nazirites. One could be a Nazirite for a specified period of time, during which, if the → vow was broken, there was a means for purification and restoration (vv. 9-12). There was also a ritual for leaving at the end of the time of consecration in order to return to normal life (vv. 13-20). Some OT persons were, to be sure, lifelong Nazirites. Before their births, Samson was designated a Nazirite for life by an angel (Judg. 13:3-5), and Samuel was dedicated for lifetime service as a Nazirite by his mother, Hannah (1 Sam. 1:11).

In the eighth century B.C. the → prophet Amos accused the people of Israel of having forced Nazirites to drink wine (Amos 2:11-12).

The origins of Nazirite customs cannot be determined, but they persisted into the New Testament era. Scenes in the Acts of the Apostles portray the apostle → Paul as having completed a Nazirite vow (18:18; 21:23-24). The → Mishnah tractate *Nazir* codifies Nazirite law.

Bibliography: T. W. Cartledge, "Were Nazirite Vows Unconditional?" *CBQ* 51 (1989) 409-22 • W. Eichrodt, *Theology of the OT* (2 vols.; Philadelphia, 1961) 1.303-6 • W. H. C. Propp, "Was Samuel a Nazirite?" *BibRev* 14 (1998) 2 • H.-J. Stipp, "Samson, der Nasiräer," *VT* 45 (1995) 337-69 • R. de Vaux, *Ancient Israel* (Grand Rapids, 1997) 466-67.

ARLAND J. HULTGREN

Necrology

A necrology is a list of people's names arranged according to date of death for the use of members of parishes, → religious orders, and spiritual → communities in intercession or remembrance. We also find necrologies in secular societies. In → monasteries the names may often be read out on the appropriate day. Older necrologies are often primary historical sources.

Bibliography: M. M. Sheehan, "Necrology," *NCE* 10.296-97.

ALBERT MAUDER†

Negative Theology (Western)

"If we cannot say what God is, we can at least say what he is not" (→ Athanasius *Ep. mon.* 2). As an attempt conceptually to show forth the transcendence (→ Immanence and Transcendence) of the divine essence by means of human → reason, Christian negative theology rests on the premise of God's absolute unknowability in himself, together with God's full self-communication to humanity in the → incarnation. The resulting unity of concealedness and → revelation stands at the heart of Christian negative theology, which seeks to explore the possibilities of speaking about and to God in the light of this → paradox.

The classical roots of negative theology lie primarily in the Platonic tradition, as it developed through Plotinus (ca. 205-70) and Proclus (410 or 412-85), and it is here, in the concept of the *nous,* that we find the emergence of a type of transcendental cognition that is innate to the human mind. The early Greek Christian tradition set the unknowability of → God within the ecclesiological contexts of → liturgy and Scripture (→ Apophatic Theology). In the hands of Dionysius the Pseudo-Areopagite (ca. 500), negative theology assumed its classic threefold shape as affirmation, negation, and eminence. Through his influence, principally the *Mystical Theology,* negative theology came to the West.

Many of the leading theologians of the Middle Ages commented on the writings of Dionysius, and most, including Bonaventure (ca. 1217-74) and → Thomas Aquinas (ca. 1225-74; → Thomism), were deeply influenced by his thinking. The Dominican Meister → Eckhart (ca. 1260-ca. 1328) was one of the most radical negative theologians of the period, but he too can be seen to use negativity as a corrective to complacency in matters of → language and God, in the light of the intense religious positivism of his age.

Medieval theology constantly returned to the theme of the unknowability of God, but figures such as the author of the *Cloud of Unknowing*, Walter Hilton (ca. 1343-96) or Jan van Ruysbroeck (1293-1381), wrote with outstanding invention and skill of the radical unknowability of God as a modality of the divine presence. Indeed, if the negative theology of the patristic and medieval tradition was chiefly reflection upon the divine unknowability and the paradox of Christian language, then the late mystics, including figures such as John of the Cross (1542-91) and → Teresa of Ávila (1515-82), can be said to have developed new forms of speaking that incorporated the paradox into language itself in the articulation of a new, dialectical expressivity.

Although Martin → Luther (1483-1546; → Luther's Theology) was initially attracted by negative theology through his reading of Johannes Tauler (ca. 1300-1361, a student of Meister Eckhart), he came to view it with suspicion, as a false form of the *theologia gloriae* (theology of glory).

In modern times negative theology has seen a revival, not only in terms of a widespread fascination with → mysticism and the mystical, but also on account of the turn to "otherness" and "negation" in contemporary → philosophy. With respect to the latter, the debates have centered on the work of Jacques Derrida, who writes in depth of the tradition of negative theology as a possible precursor of (and competitor to) his own philosophy of *différance*. We observe here a convergence of the radical → skepticism that inheres in ancient ways of conceiving of our knowledge of God with the new "critical" skepticism that has emerged from the "postmodern" questioning of the authority of scientific reason and the "rational." This turn to negativity can be seen to be a counterbalance to the wide-scale attempts to achieve a rapprochement between the modes of reasoning that are characteristic of natural → science and the postulates of revealed or → natural theology.

→ Postmodernism

Bibliography: M. DE CERTEAU, *The Mystic Fable* (Chicago, 1992) • O. DAVIES, "Thinking Difference: A Comparative Study of Gilles Deleuze, Plotinus, and Meister Eckhart," *Deleuze and Religion* (ed. M. Bryden; London, 2001) 76-86 • O. DAVIES and D. TURNER, eds., *Silence and the Word: Negative Theology and Incarnation* (Cambridge, 2002) • J. DERRIDA, "How to Avoid Speaking: Denials," *Derrida and Negative Theology* (ed. H. Coward and T. Foshay; New York, 1992) • B. A. GERRISH, "'To the Unknown God': Luther and Calvin on the Hiddenness of God," *JR* 53 (1973) 263-92 • S. T. KATZ, ed., *Mysticism and Language* (New York, 1992) • B. McGINN, *The Mystical Thought of Meister Eckhart: The Man from Whom God Hid Nothing* (New York, 2002) • M. A. McINTOSH, *Mystical Theology* (Oxford, 1998) • M. A. SELLS, *Mystical Languages of Unsaying* (Chicago, 1994) • D. TURNER, *The Darkness of God: Negativity in Christian Mysticism* (Cambridge, 1995).

OLIVER DAVIES

Nehemiah → Ezra and Nehemiah, Books of

Neighbor

1. Biblical Teaching
2. Lifestyle
3. Basic Human Relation
4. Christian Usage

1. Biblical Teaching

In the biblical tradition the Christian concept of the neighbor finds its chief place in the twofold commandment of → love (Matt. 22:35-40; Mark 12:28-34; Luke 10:25-37), which brings together two OT commandments (Deut. 6:4-5 and Lev. 19:18). The concept of the neighbor overlaps and impinges on that of the brother. In OT → ethics it includes special protection for aliens. The aim of the so-called second table of the → Decalogue is to secure the rights of the neighbor. Prophetic proclamation (→ Prophet, Prophecy, 1) also champions rights and righteousness in favor of the neighbor (Jeremiah 9). Regard for the neighbor is inseparably bound up with love of God and the knowledge of God (see Hos. 4:1).

In his preaching Jesus juxtaposes love of → enemies antithetically to love of neighbor (Matt. 5:43-48 and par.). He presents both in the light of his proclamation of the → kingdom of God and the corresponding lifestyle. In answer to the question "Who is my neighbor?" he tells the story of the Good Samaritan (Luke 10). In this story he changes the question from one of definition to one of action: the neighbor is the one who self-sacrificially helps another person in distress. As the Gospels see it, when Christians become neighbors to others, they are Christ to them (M. → Luther).

2. Lifestyle

Being a neighbor is the mark of a lifestyle in which one person relates to another in the love that God himself gives. Love and obedience to God and love of neighbor are inseparable (see John 13:34; 14:21). The law that God establishes includes that of the neighbor (E. Wolf). Here the tradition (e.g., the → Heidelberg Catechism) saw the relation between the two tables of the Decalogue. In the Christian community the fellowship of brothers and sisters bears witness to neighborliness. It is a Christian duty to show love to all people (Rom. 13:8).

3. Basic Human Relation

In the → theology and → philosophy that since German → idealism, and in debate with it, sought to develop what it means to be a subject or a person, neighborliness is a basic human relation. It is viewed simply as the relation of the I to the Thou (i.e., another person). In theology the philosophy of personalism and its concept of dialogic existence (see M. Buber; → Dialogue; Existential Theology) has been influential.

4. Christian Usage

In Christian parlance the neighbor always means one who is entrusted to the Christian, who is to be accepted in his or her need (see Luther's *Freedom of a Christian* [LW 31.333-77]). The Christian must serve and protect this neighbor and see to his or her rights. Ethically, then, love of neighbor is not just a turning to others. It expresses itself in the tasks that Christians undertake in the world.

In all that they do, including in their → vocation, Christians serve God and neighbor. The ethics of vocation tried to relate the two concepts (A. Ritschl). The problem arose, however, of distinguishing Christian service from a world of (gainful) employment. A distinction thus came to be made between specifically serving one's neighbor and work (K. → Barth). Love of neighbor expresses itself specifically in service, not least in the → diakonia of the Christian community. Work too, though, has the protection and welfare of the neighbor in view. A comprehensive social ethics thus had to be attempted. Social orientation is a feature of all action. The neighbor's welfare is always also a concern of the larger society (i.e., the state).

In the tradition of biblical exposition, receiving and serving one's neighbor does not depend on the nearness to or distance from that neighbor. In some cases distant neighbors, even though far off, need direct intervention. Being a neighbor means concrete human encounter. This view is in keeping with the ethics of the "near horizon" (W. Schulz), which aims at close togetherness, in distinction from the far horizon, which sponsors broad responsibilities.

Thinking out the relation between the two is a necessary ethical task, especially in view of the increasing awareness of global human relations.

Love of neighbor finds ethically articulated expression in regulations and rights that protect neighbors and their welfare. Neighbors cannot depend solely on the ethical acts of individuals, even though the spontaneity of such acts is indispensable. For this reason we must speak of the rights of neighbors, in which we see a mark of the order and constitution of the Christian community as a living family (see the → Barmen Declaration, thesis 3). In Christian social ethics turning to others also means sharing the lives of those who are in need. In this regard there has been in Christian ethics an increasing stress on → solidarity with the poor (→ Poverty) and needy. A place has also been found for the idea of a common political practice focusing on the political conditions of neighborliness that make participation and social action possible. This idea has been developed and tested especially in → liberation theology.

Bibliography: K. Barth, *CD* I/2, 401-54 • J. Bloechl, *Liturgy of the Neighbor: Emmanuel Levinas and the Religion of Responsibility* (Pittsburgh, 2000) • D. Bonhoeffer, *Ethics* (ed. E. Bethge; New York, 1965) • M. Buber, *I and Thou* (trans. W. Kaufmann; New York, 1996; orig. pub., 1923) • G. Gutiérrez, *A Theology of Liberation: History, Politics, and Salvation* (Maryknoll, N.Y., 1988) • G. Hallett, *Christian Neighbor-Love: An Assessment of Six Rival Versions* (Washington, D.C., 1989) • T. W. Ogletree, *Hospitality to the Stranger: Dimensions of Moral Understanding* (Philadelphia, 1985) • K. Rahner, *The Love of Jesus and the Love of Neighbor* (New York, 1983); idem, "Reflections on the Unity of the Love of Neighbor and the Love of God," *Theological Investigations* (vol. 6; New York, 1969) 231-49 • W. Schrage, *The Ethics of the NT* (Philadelphia, 1987) 68-87 • R. Spaemann, *Happiness and Benevolence* (Notre Dame, Ind., 2000; orig. pub., 1989) • J. A. Vela-McConnell, *Who Is My Neighbor? Social Affinity in a Modern World* (Albany, N.Y., 1999) • E. Wolf, *Das Recht des Nächsten. Ein rechtstheologischer Entwurf* (2d ed.; Frankfurt, 1966).

Hans G. Ulrich

Neo-Kantianism → Kantianism

Neology

1. Term
2. Historical Development

3. Dogmatic Position
4. Supporting Factors
5. Theological Significance

1. Term

Originally coined to denote linguistic and literary innovation, "neology" came to be used from about 1770 as a term of reproach against theologians who were viewed as proposing new doctrines. The orthodox who were critical of the Enlightenment adopted it, but so too did many supporters (e.g., G. E. Lessing). The reference today is to the middle phase of Enlightenment Protestant theology after 1740. Advocates used it of themselves only rarely and with reservations, preferring "Enlightenment." Nor is the meaning always uniform. It is influenced by the contested theological evaluation of the → Enlightenment.

2. Historical Development

Recognizable after the historical publications of S. J. Baumgarten (1706-57) and the *Bestimmung des Menschen* (The vocation of man, 1748) of J. J. Spalding (1714-1804), a theological group arose that deviated from the dogmatics of confessional orthodox (→ Orthodoxy 1-2) but also from → Pietism and theological Wolffianism. It began with the individual inner → experience of Christians, which it explained in the framework of the rationality of the philosophy of religion (→ Reason; Philosophy of Religion). The group oriented theological and pastoral work once again to individual → edification and social well-being. Naturally, pious emotion derived from the working of the → Word of God, but in its authentic simplicity it permitted and promoted critical testing of the authoritative claim of church dogmas and even of the Bible as a supposedly verbally inspired → canon.

What had thus far been no more than a broad historical interest now became historical criticism. The criterion was religious and moral plausibility, on whose basis → tradition could be related to essential Christianity in a way that relativizes historical conditioning (→ Denomination). Through its appeal to religious maturity, neology represents Enlightenment emancipation.

3. Dogmatic Position

The advocates of this theological Enlightenment formed a group that was decidedly Protestant and that appealed to M. → Luther (1483-1546; → Luther's Theology) as the hero of freedom of → conscience. It adopted the Dutch and British model of denominational → tolerance, as well as Shaftes-

bury's Platonism. (Antideistic theology and moral philosophy had preceded the German neology in England and Scotland.) Among its church leaders in this sense were A. F. W. Sack (1703-86), Spalding, W. A. Teller (1734-1804), and J. F. W. Jerusalem (1709-89). Neological ideas were influential on the faculties at points where they did not impinge on confessional adherence, such as in the historical field, illustrated by the work of J. A. Ernesti (1707-81), J. G. Toellner (1724-74), J. S. Semler (1725-91), J. J. Griesbach (1745-1812), L. T. Spittler (1752-1810), and A. H. Niemeyer (1754-1821). It finally replaced dogmatic claims upon history with the idea of a generic "dogmatic history" (esp. Jerusalem and Semler). In keeping with this historicizing was a systematic, biblical, or (more accurately) practical simplification of dogmatics that could link it more directly to → ethics and make religion a guide in ordinary life (Spalding).

The revision of the "doctrine of faith," as it often came to be called, involved criticism (of the belief in → demons, Christ's vicarious atonement, original sin, justification, the → Trinity, and confessional allegiance), but it could also be constructive (e.g., work by E. J. Danov, J. F. Gruner, and J. C. Döderlein), often in expressly popular and practical dogmatics (e.g., by Griesbach, G. Less, and J. A. Nösselt). Most effective was the didactic preaching of neological pastors, who made happiness and betterment the goal. So too was the neological revision of prayer books and hymnbooks for use in → school and church (in Berlin in 1760 and 1780, in Leipzig in 1765).

4. Supporting Factors

Neology owed its success not least of all to the fact that theologically important historical research did not fall under the censure of the primary theological faculties (→ University) and could be taken up increasingly in philosophical faculties as well (e.g., by J. D. Michaelis, J. G. Eichhorn, and J. A. Eberhard). For the first time, too, the formation of religious opinion became a public matter through publications such as the *Allgemeine Deutsche Bibliothek* (Universal German library, 1765-96, in 118 vols.) and literary works that were not subject to church control, such as the four-volume poem *Messias* (The messiah, 1748-73) of F. G. Klopstock (1724-1803) or the three-volume novel *Sebaldus Nothanker* (1773-76) of C. F. Nicolai (1733-1811).

5. Theological Significance

Neology set itself the task of detaching → theology from blurring metaphysical-cosmological and eschatological-apocalyptic settings (→ Metaphysics; Eschatology; Apocalypticism) and seeking the transformation of the Christian tradition into the free subjectivity of Enlightenment piety (→ Self 1). Its concept of a liberal academic theology different from the religious practice of theologians (as in Semler's *Versuch einer freiern theologischen Lehrart* [Attempt at a freer manner of theological instruction, 1777]) implied distancing itself from existing authoritarian traditions but also unavoidable interest in the future form of the → kingdom of God. The thought of the perfectibility of Christianity was still linked in this regard to the criterion of divine providence (i.e., accommodation and the education of the race) but also to the principle of the scriptural → kerygma.

Over against the → deistic and naturalist opposing of reason to history and → revelation, its apologetic fought for the independence of supernatural → religion. In the debate about the Reimarus *Wolfenbüttel Fragments* (1774/78), the neologians for good reasons rejected the deistic, critical position of H. S. Reimarus (1694-1768). It is thus incorrect to regard neology as a halfway stage to → rationalism.

Nevertheless, the neological concept of private religion brought to light ecclesiological weakness. Reaction to a 1788 religious edict promoted by J. C. Wöllner seeking to purge the clergy of → freethinkers showed that the church as a statutory institution could no longer be clearly distinguished from state authorities and their interests (→ Church and State). Tying even autonomous religion to external mediation was thus the point at which the theologians J. G. → Herder (1744-1803) and F. E. D. → Schleiermacher (1768-1834; → Schleiermacher's Theology) left neology behind (→ Theology in the Nineteenth and Twentieth Centuries).

→ Dogma, History of; Kantianism; Modernism; Natural Theology; Physicotheology; Protestantism

Bibliography: K. BARTH, *Protestant Theology in the Nineteenth Century: Its Background and History* (London, 1972; orig. pub., 1947) 33-173 • E. HIRSCH, *Geschichte der neuern evangelischen Theologie* (5 vols.; Gütersloh, 1949-54) 4.3-119 • G. HORNIG, "Neologie," *HDThG* 3.125-46 • W. SPARN, "Vernünftiges Christentum," *Wissenschaft im Zeitalter der Aufklärung* (ed. R. Vierhaus; Göttingen, 1985) 18-57 • T. YASUKATA, *Lessing's Philosophy of Religion and the German Enlightenment* (New York, 2001).

WALTER SPARN

Neopietism → Pietism

Neoplatonism → Platonism

Neoscholasticism

1. Neoscholasticism is a movement in philosophical theology that sought to revive Roman Catholic theology — after the shocks of → rationalism, the → Enlightenment, and → revolution — by the adoption of → Scholasticism, particularly as taught by → Thomas Aquinas (ca. 1225-74; → Thomism). Often the term carries a polemical undertone, referring to its → Ultramontanism (esp. in F. Michelis) and Jesuitism (→ Jesuits). Its rise in the 19th century may be understood against the background of the decline of romantic (e.g., the Tübingen school) and idealistic (G. Hermes, A. Günther) attempts to revitalize theology, as well as the vacuum in theological teaching. Various centers in Italy and Spain with strong apologetic interests were most influential.

In Germany the older scholastic tradition of B. F. L. Liebermann (1759-1844) was developed, which found religious and ecclesiastical expression in the Mainz Circle. The concern came out clearly in the ten-volume *Dogmatische Theologie* of J. B. Heinrich (1816-91), who offered a rational understanding of the faith, stressing Scripture and → tradition, excluding speculative subleties, achieving clarity of terms, and offering a good conceptual arrangement of the contents.

2. A definite new start came only with J. B. Franzelin (1816-86) and M. J. Scheeben (1835-88), in whom (according to K. Eschweiler) neoscholasticism came to full flower. Most typical was J. Kleutgen (1811-83), who based theology on a precise → *philosophia perennis*, which recognized and adopted the Platonic elements in Aquinas (→ Platonism). Kleutgen included both positive and speculative features in his rational handling of the faith (→ Speculative Theology). Following in the philosophical tracks of F. J. Clemens (1815-64) and H. E. Plassmann (1817-64), and wrestling with the errors and misinterpretations of Scholasticism, he sought a restoration and reappropriation of Thomistic philosophy that would also bring with it development and relationship with all the gains of modern scholarship.

Even though defensiveness regarding the thinking of the day hampered Kleutgen in carrying out this program, and brings him under Roman Catholic criticism today, his basic thoughts were propagated by A. Stöckl (1823-95) and, in Austria, by K. Werner (1821-88). They then achieved a full breakthrough with the help of the encyclical

Aeterni Patris (1879) of Leo XIII (1878-1903), which, rejecting the idea of mere repristination, recommended that what was old should be developed and perfected by every profitable discovery. The commending of Aquinas, which would recur in many papal documents up to the decree of → Vatican II on the training of priests (*Optatam totius* 16), was not meant exclusively, so that Bonaventure (ca. 1217-74) and Duns Scotus (ca. 1265-1308) also enjoyed a renaissance in neoscholasticism.

The movement found fruitful soil in Belgium (D. Mercier) but also affected research into the literary and intellectual history of the → Middle Ages, involving a number of scholars, editions, institutions, and periodicals. It thus played a part in such fields as apologetics, ecclesiology (→ Church 3.2), and → Mariology, even though originally the main concern was historical and hermeneutical (→ Hermeneutics).

Note should also be taken of neo-Thomism in France and Belgium at the turn of the 20th century (esp. P. Rousselot and J. Maréchal), in which opposition to the contemporary thinking of I. Kant gave way to more open dialogue and an attempted synthesis. In the process, some elements of German → idealism came into philosophical theology, which was aiming to overcome what was regarded as the → agnostic criticism offered by later → phenomenology and → existential philosophy (→ Nouvelle théologie). This approach also affected the understanding of Thomas, with more stress being laid on the Platonic intentions. In the process the term "neoscholasticism" lost much of its content, though the movement as such remained historically important as a pointer for a theology that was pledged to tradition and yet also opened up to historical thinking.

Bibliography: V. B. Brezik, ed., *One Hundred Years of Thomism: Aeterni Patris and Afterwards* (Houston, Tex., 1981) • R. T. Ciapalo, ed., *Postmodernism and Christian Philosophy* (Mishawaka, Ind., 1997) • E. Coreth, W. M. Neidl, and G. Pfligersdorffer, eds., *Christliche Philosophie im katholischen Denken des 19. Jahrhunderts* (vol. 2; Graz, 1988) • D. A. Gallagher, ed., *Thomas Aquinas and His Legacy* (Washington, D.C., 1994) • D. W. Hudson and D. W. Moran, eds., *The Future of Thomism* (Mishawaka, Ind., 1992) • J. F. X. Knasas, *The Preface to Thomist Metaphysics: A Contribution to the Neo-Thomist Debate* (New York, 1990) • G. A. McCool, *From Unity to Pluralism: The Internal Evolution of Thomism* (New York, 1989); idem, *The Neo-Thomists* (Milwaukee, Wis., 1994) • J. L.

Perrier, *The Revival of Scholastic Philosophy in the Nineteenth Century* (New York, 1909) • M. J. Scheeben, J. Wilhelm, and T. B. Scannell, *A Manual of Catholic Theology: Based on Scheeben's "Dogmatik"* (4th ed.; 2 vols.; London, 1908-9) • L. Scheffczyk, ed., *Theologie in Aufbruch und Widerstreit* (Bremen, 1965) • J. S. Zybura, *Present-Day Thinkers and the New Scholasticism* (St. Louis, 1926).

                                                    Leo Scheffczyk

Neo-Thomism → Thomism

Nepal

	1960	1980	2000
Population (1,000s):	9,263	14,498	24,347
Annual growth rate (%):	1.95	2.59	2.39

Area: 147,181 sq. km. (56,827 sq. mi.)

A.D. 2000

Population density: 165/sq. km. (428/sq. mi.)
Births / deaths: 3.35 / 0.96 per 100 population
Fertility rate: 4.47 per woman
Infant mortality rate: 70 per 1,000 live births
Life expectancy: 59.8 years (m: 60.1, f: 59.6)
Religious affiliation (%): Hindus 76.2, tribal religionists 9.4, Buddhists 8.2, Muslims 4.0, Christians 1.6 (indigenous 1.5, other Christians 0.1), other 0.6.

1. General Situation
2. Religious Situation
   2.1. Christianity
   2.2. Other Religions

1. General Situation

The Kingdom of Nepal, lying along the slopes of the Himalayas, is bordered on the north by China (Tibet) and on the other three sides by India. Altitudes range from a few meters above sea level to the highest point on earth. The variety of elevations gives the country a range of climatic zones from the subtropical jungle to the arctic conditions of the high Himalayas and the arid zone of the Tibetan plateau.

The political unit known as modern Nepal has existed since the latter part of the 18th century, when the first king of the present dynasty, starting from a small kingdom in central Nepal, united the petty kingdoms across the hills into one country. Over the centuries this hill area has provided a haven for people from north and south, so that the present racial makeup of the country is a mixture of various Asian elements.

Nepal is one of the least developed countries in the world, with a per-capita gross domestic product of $1,100 (1999 est.), 42 percent of the population below the → poverty line (1995-96 est.), and an adult → literacy rate of only 27.5 percent (1995 est.). Few Nepalese have access to unpolluted water or basic health care. Nepal is also faced with rapid population growth, a relatively narrow resource base, extreme inaccessibility of many parts of the country, a landlocked position, and, since 1991, an inherently unstable government.

2. Religious Situation

2.1. *Christianity*

Except for a Roman Catholic mission that flourished in the 18th century (→ Catholic Missions), Christianity did not penetrate Nepal in any organized way until 1951, when American → Jesuits working in Bihar, India, were invited to open a high school for boys. In 1955 sisters from Germany (I.B.V.M.; → Religious Orders and Congregations) came to open a high school for girls. In 2001 the → Roman Catholic Church operated several schools, two centers for retarded children, a social service center, a research center, and an alumni center. Mother Teresa's sisters minister to destitute, dying, and abandoned children. The Roman Catholic Church in Nepal, which began as a part of an Indian → diocese, became an apostolic prefecture in 1997 with the appointment of Anthony Sharma of Darjeeling as apostolic prefect.

Protestant efforts in Nepal began in 1953, when two American missionary families, Methodist (→ Methodist Churches) and Presbyterian (→ Reformed and Presbyterian Churches), were invited to open a hospital. They sought the cooperation of other Protestant groups and in 1954 founded the United Mission to Nepal (UMN), an interdenominational organization that still functions as the main organ of Protestant efforts. In 2001 the UMN had 33 member bodies and 20 affiliated members, that is, foreign churches of various denominations who contribute personnel and support. None of the member bodies exists in Nepal. The UMN is the largest missionary body, with 272 expatriate personnel working in various parts of the country and engaged in a variety of health, educational, and purely developmental works. In addition to the UMN, the Seventh-day → Adventists opened a hospital in 1957, the Evangelical Alliance Mission (→ Evangelical Missions) is engaged in medical work, and the International Nepal Fellowship is engaged in leprosy control. In Kathmandu, the capital, there are several native Protestant communities, three with membership in excess of 400, and a number of smaller groups across the country. Except for one community affiliated with the → Assemblies of God, all of these communities are independent, with no denominational affiliation.

2.2. *Other Religions*

→ Hinduism is the official state religion of Nepal. There are small numbers of Buddhists (→ Buddhism) and Muslims (→ Islam), with an even smaller number of Christians. → Religious liberty is guaranteed by the constitution but is defined to mean that people are free to practice the religion into which they are born. Proselytizing and → conversion of Hindus and Buddhists is forbidden by law (→ Proselytism).

→ Asian Theology

Bibliography: G. N. FLETCHER, *The Fabulous Flemings of Kathmandu: The Story of Two Doctors in Nepal* (New York, 1964) • D. N. GELLNER, J. PFAFF-CZARNECKA, and J. WHELPTON, eds., *Nationalism and Ethnicity in a Hindu Kingdom: The Politics of Culture in Contemporary Nepal* (Amsterdam, 1997) • J. LINDELL, *Nepal and the Gospel of God* (Kathmandu, 1979) • R. P. PARAJULEE, *The Democratic Transition in Nepal* (Lanham, Md., 2000) • L. PETECH, *Il nuovo Ramusio,* vol. 2, *I missionari italiani nel Tibet e nel Nepal* (pts. 1-4; Rome, 1952) • N. R. SHRESTHA, *In the Name of Development: A Reflection on Nepal* (Lanham, Md., 1997) • UNITED MISSION TO NEPAL, *Introducing Nepal and the UMN* (Kathmandu, 1986) • F. VANNINI, *Christian Settlements in Nepal during the Eighteenth Century* (New Delhi, 1976) • A. VERGATI, *Gods, Men, and Territory: Society and Culture in Kathmandu Valley* (New Delhi, 1995) • J. C. WATKINS, *Spirited Women: Gender, Religion, and Cultural Identity in the Nepal Himalaya* (New York, 1996).

JOHN K. LOCKE, S.J.

Nestorians

1. Founding and Expansion
2. Situation Today
3. Theology and Worship

1. Founding and Expansion

The so-called Nestorians, who also called themselves the East Syrians or, from a political standpoint, the Persian church, derived primarily from Christianity on the Tigris. After a treaty with Emperor Jovian (363-64), the final loss to the Romans of the city of Nisibis (modern Nusaybin, Turk.), and the flight of refugees to Edessa, the church continued its development outside the → Roman Empire.

There were Christians in the Adiabene by the second century, with an early → mission (§3) penetrating southern Mesopotamia and then the Persian sphere. A loose episcopal organization arose in the third century. Christians could be found on the southern shore of the Caspian Sea and eastward on the Upper Oxus. Prisoners of war from the West played a significant role in this mission.

We see the distinctiveness of Christian life in the region, and its lack of dogmatism, from Aphrahat (early 4th cent.), known as the Persian Sage, the first significant theologian of the East. In 424 under the → catholicos Dadisho‘, when political conditions were favorable, an autonomous Church of Persia was formed (→ Autocephaly). It was plainly separate from Christianity in the Roman Empire and rejected → patronage.

It was left to Barsumas (d. before 496), who with the Persian school was driven from Edessa to Nisibis as a Nestorian, to finalize a confession for the Persian church, which he accomplished at the Synod of Beth Lapat in 484. He also founded a theological and academic center for Nestorianism in Nisibis that for many years gave the church a highly trained clergy. Here the theology of the → Antiochian school found a home.

Not Nestorius (d. ca. 451) but his theological teacher, Theodore of Mopsuestia (ca. 350-428), set the theological norm and provided authoritative biblical exegesis. The adoptionist trends of Antioch thus found their way into Nestorian → Christology. Nestorius had called → Mary the Christ-bearer rather than the God-bearer (→ Mariology 2). In so doing, he had given expression to the belief that the Logos merely dwelt in the man Jesus but did not deify him. The Council of → Ephesus in 431 condemned Nestorius, but the Formula of Union in 433 softened the dogmatic statement, though after 436 Nestorius was banished to Upper Egypt. The victory of a more moderate Christology at → Chalcedon in 451 failed to bring peace.

The Nestorians went their own way, and Constantinople II in 553 even condemned Theodore of Mopsuestia. In 543/44 Justinian I condemned the Three Chapters — the writings of Theodore, Theodoret (ca. 393-ca. 460), and Ibas of Edessa (d. 457), which embodied the Nestorian heresy for the West. In these works the Savior's human nature is perfect and linked to the Logos, but by an independent decision. This inner union is the Savior's privilege but rules out mingling.

The leader of the Nestorians was the catholicos in the twin city Seleucis-Ctesiphon on the Tigris (from the 8th cent., in Baghdad), who finally came to style himself the → patriarch of the East. From this center the far-flung church was governed. Following the trade routes, its mission took it to central Asia, to China (documented by a pillar from 781 found at Xi'an; → Mongolian Mission), and south to India, where it embraced the Mar Thomas Christians (→ Syrian Orthodox Churches in India). The Mongol invasions and the victory of the Egyptian Mamluks at Ain Jalut in 1260 put an end to the expansion and reduced the Nestorians to their present dimensions.

The Nestorians achieved lasting significance by their educational work, especially the School of Nisibis, which flourished until the seventh century, and the "hospital" (i.e., school) at Jundishapur. Of particular importance was their mediating of Greek learning to the Arabs, especially the works of Aristotle and Galen, who for their part then became the instructors of the West (→ Aristotelianism 2.2).

Bibliography: A. S. ATIYA, *A History of Eastern Christianity* (2d ed.; Millwood, N.Y., 1980) • N. G. GARSOIAN, T. F. MATHEWS, and R. W. THOMSON, eds., *East of Byzantium: Syria and Armenia in the Formative Period* (Washington, D.C., 1982) • W. HAGE, *Syriac Christianity in the East* (Kottayam, Kerala, 1988); idem, "Der Weg nach Asien. Die ostsyrianische Missionskirche," *Kirchengeschichte als Missionsgeschichte* (ed. K. Schäferdiek; vol. 2/1; Munich, 1978) 360-93 • C. D. G. MÜLLER, *Geschichte der orientalischen Nationalkirchen* (Göttingen, 1981) • W. SELB, *Orientalisches Kirchenrecht*, vol. 1, *Die Geschichte des Kirchenrechts der Nestorianer. Von den Anfängen bis zur Mongolenzeit* (Vienna, 1981) • A. R. VINE, *The Nestorian Churches: A Concise History of Nestorian Christianity in Asia from the Persian Schism to the Modern Assyrians* (New York, 1980; orig. pub., 1937) • A. VÖÖBUS, *History of the School of Nisibis* (Louvain, 1965) • W. G. YOUNG, *Patriarch, Shah, and Caliph: A Study of the Relationships of the Church of the East with the Sassanid Empire and the Early Caliphates up to 820 A.D.* (Rawalpindi, 1974).

C. D. G. MÜLLER

2. Situation Today

With the political upheavals of the 14th and 15th centuries, the multinational Nestorian church became a tribal church centered on the mountains of Kurdistan in northern Mesopotamia. Rivalries, especially after the 15th century regarding the inheriting of the patriarchate from uncle to nephew, resulted in splits in the 16th century, one branch being the Chaldaean Church, which today has some 500,000 members and is in communion with Rome (→ Uniate Churches).

Inroads made by American Presbyterians, Anglicans, and Russian Orthodox further weakened the church in the 19th century. Finally, World War I and the ensuing political reconstruction of the Near East had a disastrous effect on the Nestorian church, whose members were scattered across the continents.

The Nestorian church — the Holy Apostolic Catholic Assyrian Church of the East — joined the → World Council of Churches at its founding in 1948 and has been able to consolidate, but questions of church reform resulted in a schism in 1968 (→ Heresies and Schisms). The estimated 150,000 members (in Iraq and the Near East, South India, United States, and Australia) owe allegiance in more or less equal numbers to the catholicos-patriarch in Tehran (with seven metropolitan bishoprics) and to the catholicos-patriarch in Baghdad (with four).

3. Theology and Worship

Confessionally the Nestorian church is fully independent. It finds the basis of its unchanged orthodoxy in the fact that during its long history it was never under Christian rulers who might have influenced its dogmatic development. This, at least, was the argument made in about 800 by the catholicos-patriarch Timotheos I.

In fact the Nestorian church did not develop any comprehensive or universally binding doctrinal system. It accepts only the first two ecumenical councils (→ Nicaea I, in 325, and Constantinople I, in 381) with their Trinitarian creeds (→ Niceno-Constantinopolitan Creed; → Trinity). As distinct from the later councils, it accepts Christ only according to the Dyophysite tradition of Antioch, that is, as a truly divine and a truly human person (→ Christology 2.2.3).

The Nestorian church has no doctrine of original → sin but practices infant → baptism. A distinctive feature is the lack of → images in the churches, though this rule has arisen only in modern times. The → liturgy (in East Syriac or, as in India, in national languages) follows three → anaphoras, the primary one being that of the apostles Addai and Mari, the traditional founders of Christianity in Mesopotamia.

Bibliography: G. BADGER, *The Nestorians and Their Rituals* (London, 1987) • J. F. COAKLEY, *The Church of the East and the Church of England: A History of the Archbishop of Canterbury's Assyrian Mission* (Oxford, 1992) • W. HAGE, "Apostolische Kirche des Ostens (Nestorianer)," *Konfessionskunde* (ed. F. Heyer; Berlin, 1977) 202-14 • J. JOSEPH, *The Modern Assyrians of the Middle East: A History of Their Encounters with Western Christian Missions, Archaeologists, and Colonial Powers* (Leiden, 2000) • B. SPULER, "Die nestorianische Kirche," *HO* 8/2.120-69 • A. THOTTAKARA, ed., *East Syrian Spirituality* (Rome, 1990) • D. WILMSHURST, *The Ecclesiastical Organization of the Church of the East, 1318-1913* (Louvain, 2000).

WOLFGANG HAGE

Netherlands

	1960	1980	2000
Population (1,000s):	11,480	14,144	15,871
Annual growth rate (%):	1.37	0.49	0.25
Area: 41,526 sq. km. (16,033 sq. mi.)			

A.D. *2000*

Population density: 382/sq. km. (990/sq. mi.)
Births / deaths: 1.06 / 0.91 per 100 population
Fertility rate: 1.55 per woman
Infant mortality rate: 6 per 1,000 live births
Life expectancy: 78.5 years (m: 75.8, f: 81.2)
Religious affiliation (%): Christians 79.9 (Roman Catholics 36.1, Protestants 27.8, unaffiliated 12.8, indigenous 2.3, other Christians 0.9), nonreligious 12.7, Muslims 4.1, atheists 1.4, other 1.9.

1. Religious and Social Trends
2. Protestant Churches Uniting
   2.1. Netherlands Reformed Church
   2.2. Reformed Churches in the Netherlands
   2.3. Evangelical Lutheran Church
   2.4. "Together on the Way"
3. Other Protestant Denominations
   3.1. Reformed
      3.1.1. Christian Reformed Churches
      3.1.2. Old Reformed Congregations
      3.1.3. Reformed Churches (Liberated), Dutch Reformed Churches
      3.1.4. Remonstrant Brotherhood
      3.1.5. Covenant of Free Evangelical Congregations
   3.2. Non-Reformed
4. Roman Catholic Church
5. Old Catholic Church
6. Migrant Churches
   6.1. Moravian Church
   6.2. Moluccan Evangelical Church
   6.3. Indonesian-Dutch Christian Church
   6.4. Samen Kerk in Nederland
7. Ecumenical Agencies
   7.1. Council of Churches in the Netherlands
   7.2. Netherlands Missionary Council
   7.3. Interchurch Contact in Government Affairs

8. Church and State
9. Other Religious Groups

1. Religious and Social Trends

In the Eighty Years' War (1568-1648) the Dutch rebelled against their Spanish masters, struggling not just for national independence but also for (Protestant) → religious liberty. Because the Reformed were protagonists in that struggle, the Reformed Church became the privileged church of the new state and remained so for over two centuries. Only Reformed could hold official positions. Only they could worship in official church buildings; members of other → denominations could worship only in buildings that did not look like churches (the *schuilkerken,* "hiding churches," some of which have survived). This situation ended in 1798 with a change in the Dutch constitution granting freedom of religion.

Until 1900, however, the Reformed continued to be the largest group in the Dutch population. In 1816 the old Reformed Church became the Netherlands Reformed Church (Nederlandse Hervormde Kerk). Subsequently, a number of schisms and separations occurred, creating a host of new churches, all calling themselves some variety of Reformed (→ Reformed and Presbyterian Churches).

At the beginning of the 20th century, Dutch society still had a strong Calvinist stamp (→ Calvinism). In 1899 fully 48 percent of the population belonged to the Netherlands Reformed Church; only 2 percent belonged to no church at all. The century saw a dramatic change in both figures. By 1930 the percentage belonging to the Netherlands Reformed Church had dropped to 35, and subsequently to 20 (1966), 17 (1979), and 13 percent (1999). During the same period the percentage of Dutch citizens belonging to no church rose to 14 (1930), 33 (1966), 44 (1979), and then 63 percent (1999). These figures point to a certain → secularization, yet many people who are not officially church members still consider themselves religious.

Dutch society is characterized by a strong tendency of → individualism. And increasingly, since the 1960s, it has become multicultural, with many Third World immigrants settling in the Netherlands. At first these strangers were welcomed as guest workers. Later their presence became increasingly a matter of concern and a source of social tension. Much discussion has taken place regarding integration, which has been the official aim of government policy. So far, however, this policy has not been very successful, for in many cases immigrants live in poor conditions in isolated groups, fostering their own cultural and religious customs and hardly able to communicate in the Dutch language. The authorities have tried to reduce the number of → refugees that obtain a permit to stay by admitting only political, but not economic, refugees. In many cases, however, such a distinction is far from clear.

Some figures may serve as an illustration. In 2000 about 1.5 million of the over 15 million inhabitants of the Netherlands were from non-European countries or belonged to families that only recently had immigrated. The majority of this number came from Turkey or Morocco; others arrived from the former Dutch colonies Indonesia (esp. the Moluccas) and Suriname, or from the Netherlands Antilles (the Caribbean islands that are still part of the Kingdom of the Netherlands).

About half of these immigrants are Muslims, making → Islam the nation's second largest religion. All over the country there are now some 400 → mosques or other prayer centers. According to official projections the number of immigrants will increase to 2 million by 2015, when half of the population of each of the four largest cities (Amsterdam, Rotterdam, The Hague, Utrecht) will have their roots in → Third World countries. Already in these cities the majority of all schoolchildren are from immigrant families. Currently, 43 percent of the residents of Amsterdam are immigrants; citywide, 13 percent are Muslims, versus 10 percent Roman Catholic and 5 percent Netherlands Reformed. Besides continued immigration, a relatively higher birth rate explains the growing percentage of Muslims in the Netherlands.

Especially since the terrorist attacks in the United States on September 11, 2001, the Dutch have registered certain feelings of uneasiness about the growing Muslim presence in Dutch society. After a period in which the Netherlands had developed into a liberal, ideologically neutral society and in which, as a consequence of the separation of → church and state, religion and religious values had been socially marginalized, the Dutch have shown renewed interest in the question of the identity of Dutch culture. Western values like → democracy, women's emancipation, freedom of speech and of religion, so characteristic of Dutch society, suddenly have seemed to be in danger and in need of defense. In this context, there is also a new interest in matters of moral standards and of → religion. These changes have not resulted in an increase of → church membership, although they did lead to new political success for the Christen Democratisch Appèl (CDA, Christian Democratic Appeal). This centrist political party, which had been the most powerful political factor in the Netherlands for decades but since the elections of 1994 had suffered heavy losses, suddenly reemerged as a political power in the elections of May 2002.

2. Protestant Churches Uniting

2.1. Netherlands Reformed Church

In the 19th century and in the first half of the 20th century, the Netherlands Reformed Church was hardly more than an administrative institution holding together parties of very different, if not conflicting, orientations (modernists, orthodox, defenders of the ethical [i.e., existential] character of truth, etc.). As a consequence of the experiences during and immediately after the Second World War, however, a new sense of community across party differences developed. A new, presbyterial-synodical → church order was introduced in 1951 that captured the church's view of being a missionary confessing church in the midst of society, confessing, as it is said, "in community [*not* agreement!] with the confession of the Fathers." Since the war this new sense has come to expression in many synodical statements, publications, and reports on faith issues, as well as on social and political issues. The church has its roots in the Reformed (Calvinist) tradition but at the same time feels strongly connected to the Dutch nation and its history.

As of 2002 the Netherlands Reformed Church had 1.9 million members in 1,316 local → congregations, with 1,785 → pastors. Each local congregation is led by a consistory of ordained officeholders (pastor, → elders, and → deacons). → Ordination always takes place within the congregation. Elders (who do pastoral care) and deacons (who do social care) are elected church members; the pastor, who must have completed special training, is called from elsewhere. The church exists in 73 classes (sing. "classis"), or regions. Each local consistory is represented in the regional assembly, which in turn delegates one representative to the General Synod. Delegates serve a five-year term. Every year a new *moderamen* (executive committee) is elected.

The 13 Walloon (French-speaking) congregations, dispersed around the country and with less than 1,000 members in all, have a special place in the church. This number is all that is left today of the 200,000 → Huguenots who fled to the Netherlands from France in the 17th century. They send one delegate to the General Synod.

2.2. Reformed Churches in the Netherlands

The Reformed Churches in the Netherlands (Gereformeerde Kerken in Nederland) originated in 1892 as the result of the merger of two 19th-century separation movements from the Netherlands Reformed Church. These secessions were motivated by objections against the then dominant liberal tendency in the latter church and by a desire to concentrate anew on the traditional Reformed confessional documents. The first split (the Afscheiding, "separation") occurred in 1834, the second (the Doleantie, "grieving"), much larger, under the inspiration of Abraham Kuyper (1837-1920), in 1886; in this second separation objections against the national character of the Netherlands Reformed Church were also emphasized. The very name of this group (with pl. "churches") indicates an emphasis on the relative → autonomy of the local congregation. This feature reflects a sensitivity often still characteristic today of smaller Reformed communities: their aversion to any synodical centralism.

Since the 1960s the Reformed Churches in the Netherlands has become an increasingly open community — both to → ecumenism and to modern views generally. This shift has brought it closer to the Netherlands Reformed Church and made possible its participation in a process of unification (see 2.4), the more so as this church, in its renewal during and immediately after the Second World War, officially had begun taking more seriously its own Reformed tradition.

The Reformed Churches in the Netherlands (660,000 members, 859 local congregations, 1,119 pastors) is organized in much the same way as the Netherlands Reformed Church. Here again each local congregation is led by a consistory of ordained officeholders (pastor, elders, and deacons). There are 73 classes, whose borders coincide with those of the classes of the Netherlands Reformed Church, and each classis again has one representative in the General Synod. Under the influence of the unification process, some structural changes in the operation of the General Synod and the duties of the *moderamen* have been introduced.

2.3. Evangelical Lutheran Church

The Evangelical Lutheran Church in the Kingdom of the Netherlands (Evangelisch-Lutherse Kerk in het Koninkrijk der Nederlanden), like the Netherlands Reformed Church, has roots going back to the 16th century. In Dutch Calvinist society, Lutherans have always been a minority. In 1791 a group of orthodox Lutherans separated and formed its own denomination because of objections against rationalist tendencies that had become dominant in the Lutheran Church. In 1952 this separation ended in a reunification.

The structure of the Evangelical Lutheran

Church (15,000 members, 60 local congregations, 46 pastors) has been strongly influenced by → Calvinism. Each congregation is led by the local pastor, together with a group of elected members, called (as in the Reformed Church) elders and deacons, although they are not formally ordained as such. There is no regional structure. On the national level, the church is represented by the → Synod. Half of the Synod's members are pastors, half are laypeople, each elected for four-year terms (→ Clergy and Laity). The head of the Synod is the president (not "bishop"), who ordains all new pastors before they are introduced into their respective local congregations.

2.4. "Together on the Way"

For several decades the Netherlands Reformed Church, the Reformed Churches in the Netherlands, and the Evangelical Lutheran Church have been involved in a process of church unification called Samen op Weg, "Together on the Way." The process began officially in 1969 as a bilateral process of the two Reformed Church communities. Since 1973 their General Synods have held combined meetings. In 1986 the General Synods issued a common statement declaring the unification process to be irreversible.

Also in 1986 the Evangelical Lutheran Church became an official partner in the process. There were two primary reasons for the Lutherans to take this step: (1) a conviction that the → Lutheran Church had become too small a community to be able to survive on its own in the long run, and (2) a recognition that the Reformed and the Lutheran traditions, both rooted in the 16th-century Reformation, have much in common, as has been articulated by the → Leuenberg Agreement (1973), a Lutheran/Reformed document adopted by the large majority of European Lutheran and Reformed churches. The Lutherans are concerned, however, that their specific tradition (e.g., their special emphasis on worship → liturgy) not disappear in the midst of the overwhelming majority of Reformed.

In 1990 a first combined meeting of the three synods took place. Meanwhile, combined synod meetings have become more the rule than the exception; the business of each of the synods has become more and more common matter, and the respective synodical executive committees function together as a common committee. In 1992 the first draft of a new common church order could be submitted, and in 2002 the final text, which safeguards a special position for Lutherans (e.g., through the continuing existence of a separate Lutheran synod), was adopted. It is intended to replace, and continue,

the existing church orders of the three participating churches after the final resolution on church unification is passed (due by November 2003).

It is planned that the new, united church — the Protestant Church in the Netherlands — will begin functioning in 2004. Its church order, based on the Lutheran and the Reformed traditions together, mentions in its first article both the Lutheran and the Reformed confessional documents. Already in 1999 the several boards and offices of the three partner churches were brought together into one common organization, located in Utrecht.

Since the 1970s, interim regulations have made it possible for local congregations of these three communions to join in a federation with their partner congregations. So far 260 such federations have been established, generally involving only Reformed congregations. In the united church these federations may or may not become fully united congregations; there will also be room for Netherlands Reformed, Reformed, and Lutheran congregations to continue their separate existence, attached to their own specific tradition, either Lutheran or Reformed. On the regional level (the classis level), however, separate structures will not be maintained.

In the long unification process traditionalist groups, especially in the Netherlands Reformed Church, have loudly and repeatedly voiced their objections. Primarily, they have defended the Reformed tradition and the identity of the old Reformed Church as uniquely connected to the Dutch nation and its history, a heritage they view as being sacrificed to the "Together on the Way" process. Though unification deliberations have been conducted with much openness and sensitivity, it is to be expected that a few pastors and (parts of) their congregations will not accept the ultimate decision of unification and will stay outside the united church.

3. Other Protestant Denominations

3.1. Reformed

In this subsection we consider five more of the many other Reformed churches in the Netherlands.

3.1.1. Christian Reformed Churches

The Christian Reformed Churches in the Netherlands (Christelijke Gereformeerde Kerken in Nederland) has its roots in the Afscheiding of 1834. When in 1892 most of the adherents of that separation movement joined with the adherents of the Doleantie of 1886 to form the Reformed Churches in the Netherlands, a number of them preferred to stay apart and to constitute their own denomination. More than the Doleantie adherents, the Christian

Reformed Churches emphasizes the element of personal experience of → salvation. As of 2002 the denomination had 75,000 members, 187 local congregations in 13 classes, and 203 pastors.

3.1.2. Old Reformed Congregations

Some local congregations that originated in the 1834 separation movement initially stayed apart but later formed their own separate denomination, called the Old Reformed Congregations in the Netherlands (Oud Gereformeerde Gemeenten in Nederland). This group shares the Christian Reformed emphasis on the element of personal experience of salvation. It is also characterized by a strong → quietism, a strict avoidance of any contact with the modern world, and a cultural → conservatism. It has about 140,000 members.

3.1.3. Reformed Churches (Liberated), Dutch Reformed Churches

In 1944 a group of protesters against synodical centralism, especially in matters of doctrine, separated from the Reformed Churches in the Netherlands and formed the Reformed Churches (Liberated) (Gereformeerde Kerken [Vrijgemaakt]). Their rigid claim of being exclusively "true Reformed" caused some of their members to leave this new denomination in 1967 and choose their own independent position. This step led to the origin of the Free Reformed Churches (Independent) in the Netherlands, now called the Dutch Reformed Churches (Nederlands Gereformeerde Kerken). Together, these denominations now have 155,000 members.

3.1.4. Remonstrant Brotherhood

On the left wing of Reformed Protestantism is the Remonstrant Brotherhood (Remonstrantse Broederschap), a denomination originating at the beginning of the 17th century out of controversies within the Reformed Church. It derives its name from the remonstrance, or public manifesto, issued by followers of Jacobus Arminius (1560-1609; → Arminianism), in which the Calvinist doctrine of → predestination (understood as determinism) was rejected and a revision of the official Reformed confession of faith was requested. At a meeting in Dordrecht in 1618-19, the General Synod of the Reformed Church, however, confirmed the Calvinist doctrine of predestination, rejected the remonstrance, and → excommunicated its authors, the Remonstrants. The latter established their own denomination, which was at first persecuted, then later tolerated.

The Remonstrant Brotherhood has been characterized by its openness to humanist views in the line of Desiderius → Erasmus and by its nondogmatic, modernist attitude regarding issues of faith (→ Hu-

manism; Modernism). It stresses → human dignity and responsibility. In 1988 the Remonstrant Brotherhood became an observer in the "Together on the Way" church unification process. In 1993, however, it decided to end its participation, viewing the draft church order for the intended united church as too traditional and confessionalist.

In the Remonstrant Brotherhood baptized children are not considered members. There is also the possibility of becoming an official friend of the brotherhood. In 2002 there were 8,000 members and friends, in 46 congregations, served by 25 pastors. The General Assembly, consisting of delegates from each of the congregations and from the convent of pastors, is the highest administrative body (although the local congregations are to a large extent autonomous).

3.1.5. Covenant of Free Evangelical Congregations

As a result of 19th-century revival movements within the Netherlands Reformed Church, several free evangelical congregations originated, which joined together in 1881 in the Covenant of Free Evangelical Congregations in the Netherlands (Bond van Vrije Evangelische Gemeenten in Nederland). In the spirituality of these congregations, elements of evangelicalism (→ Evangelical) blend with elements of the Reformed tradition. In 2002 there were 9,000 members (including baptized children) in 45 congregations, with 28 pastors. Each local congregation is fully autonomous. There is no synod to which the group submits, only a committee to deal with matters of common interest.

3.2. Non-Reformed

Entering the Netherlands early in the 16th century, Anabaptism (as it was called by outsiders) was characterized by its rejection of infant baptism and by its ardent desire for renewal in church and society. The number of → Anabaptists, soon called → Mennonites, remained small. Local congregations existed as independent entities, dispersed over the country. This autonomy still survives, although in 1811 the General Mennonite Society (Algemene Doopsgezinde Sociëteit) was established. This society has the task of fostering the sense of unity among Mennonites and of dealing with matters of common interest. Influenced by → Enlightenment thinking and by the ideals of the French Revolution, it rejected confessional orthodoxy and refrained from accepting a common written confession as its basis. (This spirit survives in the practice today of asking those coming for → baptism to write down their own private → confession of faith rather than express their agreement with any existing confession.) The society included 133 local congregations in 2002, with 12,000 (adult, confessing) members.

→ *Baptists*, like Mennonites, reject infant baptism. Unlike Mennonites, however, they represent an evangelical mind and have a zeal for → evangelism. The first Dutch Baptist congregation was founded in 1845. In 1881 several congregations, without giving up their local autonomy, united in the Union of Baptist Congregations. In 2002 there were 90 member congregations with altogether 12,000 (adult, confessing) members and 53 pastors.

The Religious Society of → *Friends* (Quakers), which originated in England in 1652, has a membership in the Netherlands of only a few hundred. The Dutch society was founded in 1932.

The → *Salvation Army* has been in the Netherlands since 1887. In 2002 it had approximately 80 corps, 6,500 soldiers, and 500 officers. The army runs several youth centers, social centers, houses for children and for the elderly, nursing homes, and rescue centers. It is also well known for its aid work in emergency situations.

In 2002 the → *Anglican Church* in the Netherlands had 10,000 members, most of them with their roots in English-speaking countries. They are officially members of a diocese of the Church of England, with their own clergy.

Seventh-day → *Adventists*, who have been in the Netherlands since 1898, had 12,000 members, 50 local congregations, and 30 pastors in 1997.

4. Roman Catholic Church

After the beginning of national independence, born out of the Eighty Years' War, there was no effective Roman Catholic episcopal hierarchy in the Netherlands for over two centuries. Like any other non-Reformed denomination, the → Roman Catholic Church was not allowed to be openly present in society. Roman Catholic → worship was permitted only in the "hiding churches." Roman Catholic Church life was administered by apostolic vicars, later by papal → nuncios. The new constitution, introduced in 1848, finally made possible the restoration of the Roman Catholic episcopal → hierarchy, which occurred in 1853.

Before the Second World War the Roman Catholic Church in the Netherlands was characterized by a spirit of docility vis-à-vis Rome. To Roman Catholics the period 1850-1950 was a period of gradual emancipation, of regaining social influence. The Second → Vatican Council then made possible a breakthrough for critical and more open voices. A pastoral council of the Dutch church province met from 1968 to 1970 in order to discuss the results of

Vatican II and to apply them to the Dutch situation. Lay representatives, delegated by the several dioceses, as well as ecumenical observers, were invited to express as motions their views and desires regarding the church (e.g., on ministry, priesthood, → celibacy, → authority in the church, the position of women in the church). These motions were adopted by the council and passed on to the complete bishops' conference. The resolutions were not legally binding on the → bishops, yet the bishops declared themselves willing to take them seriously and bring them up in discussions with Rome.

In 1967, on behalf of the Dutch bishops' conference, the *Nieuwe Katechismus* (New catechism) was published. This book aimed at presenting faith in a new, understandable way to modern adults. Because of its nonconventional, nondoctrinal, lively language, as well as its acceptance of modern life as a starting point and its use of biblical stories, it became extremely popular, and not just among Roman Catholics. Vatican authorities later criticized certain paragraphs (e.g., on the divine nature of → Jesus, on Mary, and on the → Eucharist) as being not fully orthodox and demanded their revision. The revision was published as a separate volume.

One of the signs of renewal of the Roman Catholic Church was its new ecumenical openness. In 1967 it concluded a bilateral agreement with the Netherlands Reformed Church on the mutual recognition of baptism, and in 1968 it reached similar bilateral agreements with the Reformed Churches in the Netherlands and the Evangelical Lutheran Church. Also in 1968 it became a member of the Council of Churches in the Netherlands (see 7.1). Concerning the granting of → dispensations for → mixed marriages, the bishops took a stand that was more pastoral than legalistic. In 1971 the Roman Catholic Church, along with several Protestant churches, issued a joint declaration, according to which the → priest or pastor of the other church involved is allowed to officially participate in the wedding ceremony upon invitation by the host church.

Since the beginning of the 1970s, however, the tendency of renewal has stopped. Rome intervened, especially using the appointment of conservative bishops to reverse the ecumenical openness, which, in the view of the Vatican, was in danger of going too far. A polarization became manifest in the church between an increasingly conservative episcopate and the priests, who, working at the local level, wanted to continue in the spirit of the 1960s. In 1980 a special meeting of the Dutch bishops took place in Rome, under the presidency of the → pope, aiming at regaining unity among Dutch Roman Catholics. This effort had only limited success. When the pope announced that he would make an official visit to the Netherlands in May 1985, and when it became clear that he would be kept away from dissenting voices during that visit, critical Roman Catholics organized a demonstration under the motto "The other face of the church." This demonstration, which occurred on the eve of the pope's arrival, was the start of the Acht Mei Beweging (8th of May Movement), which for many years sponsored an annual mass meeting. Recently, however, it was decided to stop this initiative, and now the polarization seems to have lost its edge.

The → ecumenical dialogue has continued over the years, in several phases. Since 1992 a dialogue committee of theologians representing the Roman Catholic, Old Catholic, Lutheran, and Reformed Churches focused on issues of ecclesiology, such as have been discussed in world-level ecumenical dialogues. The committee discussions have resulted in the publication of two volumes, *From Roots to Fruits: Protestants and Catholics towards a Common Understanding of the Church* (1998; orig. in Dutch, 1994) and *Of All Times and of All Places: Protestants and Catholics on the Church Local and Universal* (2001). Whereas these volumes contain essays written personally by members of the committee, the committee as a whole recently produced a common document *The Local and the Universal Dimension of the Church,* which highlights the so-called in-between level, between the local and the universal. It argues that taking seriously the essentially ecclesiastical character of such in-between church structures on the national or regional levels could open new ecumenical possibilities.

The Dutch Roman Catholic hierarchy includes an archdiocese (Utrecht, the seat of the first bishop, Willibrord, since 695) and, since 1955, six → dioceses: Haarlem, Rotterdam, Breda, 's Hertogenbosch, Roermond, and Groningen. Countrywide, there are 1,670 local parishes. In the pastoral care on the local level, some 1,480 priests, 130 deacons, and 386 pastoral workers (a third of them women) are active. Because of the relatively high birth rate of Roman Catholic families, since the first half of the 20th century the Roman Catholic Church has been the largest church community in the Netherlands. Its constituency has decreased over the last decades, however, though less drastically than that of the Netherlands Reformed Church. In 1996 Dutch Roman Catholics numbered 5.2 million.

5. Old Catholic Church

The → Old Catholic Church claims to be the continuation of the pre-Reformation Catholic Church.

The church originated in the Utrecht schism of 1723, the result of both the increasing Roman centralism and the influence of → Jansenism in the Roman Catholic Church. The schism developed when the decision of the Utrecht chapter to elect Cornelis Steenoven (1662-1725) bishop was rejected by Rome. Steenoven was ordained anyway, and his followers constituted their own church community.

When the First Vatican Council (1870) adopted its dogmatic decisions on the primacy and → infallibility (§3) of the pope, protests against these decisions led to the origin of other Old Catholic movements elsewhere in Europe, later also in the United States. The Old Catholic Church in the Netherlands is part of the Union of Utrecht, established in 1889 as an alliance of these like-minded churches and movements. In the union the International Bishops' Conference is the most important forum for discussion, in which the Old Catholic archbishop of Utrecht has the function of moderator. Since 1931 the Old Catholic Churches have church fellowship (full communion) with the Anglicans.

The Old Catholic Church in the Netherlands has always been a small community. Since 1982 it has two bishops: in Utrecht (archbishop) and Haarlem. There are 8,000 members in 25 local parishes, with 40 priests, working part-time on altogether 14 full-time positions. The administrative structure of the church is synodal-episcopal. The synod, a consultative body consisting of representatives of the parishes as well as of the clergy, meets once each year. Important decisions are taken by the Collegial Board, of which the bishops are members.

6. Migrant Churches

The multicultural influx of the last decades has included the immigration of a multitude of non-indigenous Christians to the Netherlands. Precise figures are not available, but their number is estimated to be about 800,000. The majority of these Christian immigrants are Roman Catholic, with smaller numbers of Protestants and Orthodox (→ Protestantism; Orthodox Church). Roman Catholic Church policy is to promote full integration of the Roman Catholic immigrants into Dutch Roman Catholicism. Establishing particular parishes for specific national and language groups is considered only an interim phase and a step in that direction.

In contrast, Protestant and Orthodox immigrants remain much more on their own. They have typically constituted their own religious communities, which have been called migrant churches. Their number includes groups from English- and French-speaking Africa, Spanish-speaking Latin America, other European countries, and Asian countries, especially the Philippines, Sri Lanka, Indonesia, and Japan. Most of these churches exist in the center of the larger Dutch cities. They often meet for worship in temporary quarters such as garages. The meetings are held in the native languages, using elements of the home culture. Worship services are usually less formal than Dutch-language services. An estimated 350 such Protestant or Orthodox migrant churches exist, in and through which the gospel is preached and God is praised in altogether over 75 languages.

The phrase "migrant churches" covers a diverse reality. Some of these churches represent a mainstream Christian tradition. Also called historic migrant churches, they have existed in the Netherlands for a fairly long time, are well known in Dutch society, and have contacts with Dutch churches and church networks. A second category includes churches that were established in the Netherlands by churches in the members' home country. For the most part, such churches have little contact with Dutch church life. A third category is independent churches, established by migrant groups themselves, generally around a charismatic leader. Most of their members have entered the Netherlands only recently. Again, these churches stand outside Dutch church life.

6.1. Moravian Church

One of the historic migrant churches is the → Moravian Church (Evangelische Broedergemeente), which has its background in the work of Count Nikolaus Ludwig von → Zinzendorf (1700-1760), with its center in Herrnhut, Germany. Moravians (Herrnhuters) came to the Netherlands in the 18th century, founding their first settlement in Zeist, near Utrecht. The Moravians did much mission work, including in Suriname, a Dutch colony in South America that became independent in 1975.

Many Surinamese opted for Dutch citizenship and immigrated to the Netherlands. As many of them were Moravian Christians, this immigration meant an explosive increase of Moravian membership in the Netherlands. In 2002 there were seven autonomous regional congregations, with a total membership of 20,000. On the national level the work is coordinated by the Central Council, in which all congregations are represented. Each congregation is led by a council of elders elected by the congregation members. Ministry has three degrees: deacon, presbyter, and bishop.

The Moravian Church plays an important role in supporting its members in investigating their own roots and identity, as well as in finding their own place in society. It reminds Dutch society of its own, not at all glorious, colonial past (→ Colonialism) — for example, by keeping the theme of former → slavery on the agenda. (In Suriname, slavery was not abolished until 1863.)

6.2. Moluccan Evangelical Church

Another historic migrant church is the Moluccan Evangelical Church (Molukse Evangelische Kerk). Its members are descendants of the 4,000 people from the Moluccas (or Spice Islands) who served in the Dutch colonial army in Indonesia and who, in the 1950s, after the end of the Dutch colonial regime, were brought to the Netherlands for a (temporary!) stay, hoping for an independent political status of their home area, the Moluccas, that would allow them to return. Fully 90 percent of these Moluccan immigrants were Protestants of the Reformed tradition. Fairly quickly, however, the Moluccan mother church in Indonesia accepted the political situation in the new, independent Republic of Indonesia, which caused the Moluccans in the Netherlands much bitterness. In 1952 they felt compelled to break their ties with the mother church and to establish their own church in the Netherlands.

In 2002 the church had 65 local congregations, brought together in four classes. The national center is at Houten, near Utrecht. Worship is usually in Malaysian, although recently, in view of the younger generation, there has been more room for use of Dutch. The relation to the Moluccas, as well as to the rest of Indonesia and to the churches there, remains high on the agenda. In recent years relations have improved. For the members of this church, the civil war that broke out on the Moluccas in 1999 is a matter of grave concern.

The Moluccan Evangelical Church recently became a member church of the Council of Churches in the Netherlands. Over the past decades, because of differences of opinion on how to be Christian in Dutch exile, several Moluccan groups separated from the Moluccan Evangelical Church and established their own denominations; the various groups, however, maintain contact with each other. Together they have 35,000 members, of which 25,000 belong to the Moluccan Evangelical Church.

6.3. Indonesian-Dutch Christian Church

A third historic migrant church is the Indonesian-Dutch Christian Church (Indonesisch-Nederlands Christelijke Kerk). It was instituted in 1985 as a church of the Reformed tradition to accommodate Indonesians who had migrated to the Netherlands but did not feel at home in the Dutch churches because of the differences in culture, language, and religious climate. Its members also include Dutch who lived in Indonesia and who still feel especially connected to that country. There is an official membership of 600; many more, however, participate in church activities.

6.4. *Samen Kerk in Nederland*

In 1992 the three migrant churches mentioned in this section established the Platform of Non-indigenous Churches, which later became an association known as Samen Kerk in Nederland (SKIN, lit. "together church in the Netherlands," or "a way of being church together in the Netherlands"). Based in Amersfoort, this platform aims to promote interaction and communal action of all its member churches and so to strengthen their presence in Dutch society. In recent years it has become the unofficial mouthpiece of its member churches vis-à-vis the government. SKIN has taken steps to improve theological training facilities for migrant church leaders and also helps to open the labor market for migrants. In 2002 the association included 44 member churches, with a total membership of 60,000.

7. Ecumenical Agencies

7.1. *Council of Churches in the Netherlands*

The Council of Churches in the Netherlands in its present form was founded in 1968. The 13 member churches are the Anglican Church, Evangelical Lutheran Church, Mennonite Brotherhood, Moluccan Evangelical Church, Moravian Church, Netherlands Reformed Church, Old Catholic Church, Reformed Churches in the Netherlands, Remonstrant Brotherhood, Roman Catholic Church, Salvation Army, Society of Friends (Quakers), and → Syrian Orthodox Church in the Netherlands. These churches together represent over 90 percent of Dutch Christianity. Five other churches are "candidate members" of the council, including the Covenant of Free Evangelical Congregations and the Seventh-day Adventists. Absent from the council are the right-wing Reformed churches and most of the migrant churches.

The council sees as its task, among others, "to consider the unity of the churches in worship celebration, witness, and service and to make this unity concrete by initiating and promoting all that some or all participating churches can do together" and "to discuss questions on Christian faith, church, and society and to promote discussion of these questions within the churches." In implementing this task, the council organizes each year a broad ecumenical consultation to which representatives of other churches and ecumenical organizations are also invited.

The council has established several consultation groups (Faith and Ecclesial Community, Worship Celebration, Interreligious Encounter, Justice and Integrity of Creation, Missionary Presence, Ethical Issues) and project groups (Violence and → Peace, Migration and → Development, → Poverty in the Netherlands, Church and → Environment, Refugees). Other subgroups oversee preparation of the annual Week of Prayer for Christian Unity, the publication of a quarterly with liturgical indications for every Sunday, and discussion of issues relating to a just international financial system.

The Council of Churches has become an important mouthpiece of its member churches on social and political issues. In recent years, however, the larger churches have increasingly shown a tendency to decide, speak out, and take action for themselves.

7.2. *Netherlands Missionary Council*

The Netherlands Missionary Council, established in 1929, is a national platform of encounter and consultation, reflection and cooperation, in which a number of ecumenical and evangelical missionary organizations and church bodies take part. One of the council's tasks is to represent its member bodies in the missionary work of the → World Council of Churches.

Member bodies include missionary organizations of the three "Together on the Way" churches, the Covenant of Free Evangelical Congregations, the General Mennonite Society, the Moravian Church, the Old Catholic Church, the Remonstrant Brotherhood, the Union of Baptist Churches, as well as organizations like the Netherlands Bible Society. The missionary bodies of the Christian Reformed Churches and the Roman Catholic Church have observer status.

7.3. *Interchurch Contact in Government Affairs*

The Interchurch Contact in Government Affairs (Interkerkelijk Contact in Overheidszaken) is a special form of interchurch cooperation involving (as of 2002) 22 denominations, including three Jewish groups. It had its origin during World War II, when Christian churches joined together in their resistance against the German occupation authorities, protesting against the Nazi persecution of the Jews. Its aim is to keep in touch with the government and political parties, especially when issues of religious freedom are at stake.

8. Church and State

Since 1798 equal treatment of all religious groups and denominations has been a principle of the Dutch constitution. Separation between church and state was fully introduced in 1848, and the state refrains from intervening in internal church affairs.

The present constitution of the Kingdom of the Netherlands, introduced in 1983, states in its article 1, "All persons in the Netherlands shall be treated equally in equal circumstances. Discrimination on the grounds of religion, belief, political opinion, race, or sex or on any other grounds whatsoever shall not be permitted." This wording makes clear the principle of equal treatment of all religious groups and denominations. Article 6 is also especially important: "Everyone shall have the right to manifest freely his religion or belief, either individually or in community with others, without prejudice to his responsibility under the law." The constitution mentions no church, and there is no → concordat with the Roman Catholic Church. There is no provision for a church or religious community to register with the state. Each church is governed by its own constitution, insofar as it does not contradict civil law.

In 1981 the state ended all subsidizing of pastors' salaries and pensions, although it does pay for pastoral care by chaplains in the army and in prisons (→ Military Chaplaincy; Prison Ministry), and it funds the restoration and maintenance of church buildings considered as national monuments (→ Church Finances). Also the state pays for the theological training of pastors of all churches, subsidizes youth work and cultural work (tasks considered of public importance), and makes television and radio broadcast time available to the churches. Public hospitals and homes for the elderly may fund pastoral care if they choose to include it in their budget (→ Pastoral Care of the Sick). Municipal authorities are likewise free to subsidize religious and humanist/ philosophical teaching in public schools, a matter that is implemented differently from place to place.

9. Other Religious Groups
In 2002 there were upwards of 700,000 *Muslims* in the Netherlands, a group that is becoming increasingly prominent and significant in Dutch society (see 1).

Especially since the 1970s, *Hindus* have been present in the Netherlands in significant numbers (→ Hinduism). Many immigrants from Suriname are Hindu. In 2002 the total number of Hindus was estimated to be 120,000.

There are as many as 50,000 *Buddhists* in the Netherlands, mainly refugees from China and elsewhere in East Asia. The Dutch have shown much interest in → Buddhism, dating back to the 1960s and 1970s, when many people, feeling uneasy about Western culture, embraced Eastern forms of religion. In 2000 a Buddhist temple was opened in Am-

sterdam — the first Buddhist temple in western Europe. There are several Buddhist organizations, with constituencies varying between a few dozen and a few thousand.

Jews have long lived in the Netherlands, especially since the 16th century, when (even with a dominant Calvinism) there was relative freedom of religion. In May 1940, at the time of the German invasion in the Second World War, Netherlands was home to 140,000 Jews. The Nazi occupation authorities transported more than 104,000 Jews to concentration and death camps, where few survived. This → Holocaust experience had, and continues to have, a great impact on Dutch society, including the churches. Dutch theologians developed the view that Nazi → anti-Semitism resulted from centuries of Christian anti-Judaism. Dutch mainstream churches today consider their relation to Jews to be properly one of → dialogue, not mission (→ Jewish-Christian Dialogue; Jewish Mission; Judaism). In 2002 there were only 28,000 Jews living in the Netherlands, of which some 12,000 were members of one of the three existing Jewish communities (two of them orthodox, one liberal). In 1981 the Overlegorgaan van Joden en Christenen (OJEC, Council of Jews and Christians) was founded, which includes the three Jewish groups, as well as several Christian churches. Its aim is primarily to combat anti-Semitism, not to promote theological dialogue.

A variety of sects and marginal Christian groups are active in the Netherlands. The largest is the → Jehovah's Witnesses, with 50,000 adherents. These movements, however, remain marginal phenomena within Dutch society.

→ Dutch Missions; United and Uniting Churches

Bibliography: J.-J. BAUSWEIN and L. VISCHER, eds., "The Netherlands," *The Reformed Family Worldwide* (Grand Rapids, 1999) 383-97 • J. W. BECKER, J. DE HART, and J. MENS, *Secularisatie en alternatieve zingeving in Nederland* (Rijswijk, 1997) with English summary • J. W. BECKER and R. VINK, *Secularisatie in Nederland, 1966-1991* (Rijswijk, 1994) with English summary • K. BLEI, "Ecumenical Relationships in the Netherlands," *Mid-Stream* 35 (1996) 311-26; idem, *The Netherlands Reformed Church* (Grand Rapids, 2003) • M. E. BRINKMAN and H. WITTE, eds., *From Roots to Fruits: Protestants and Catholics towards a Common Understanding of the Church* (Geneva, 1998) • G. DEKKER, J. DE HART, and J. PETERS, *God in Nederland, 1966-1996* (Amsterdam, 1997) • S. C. DEN DEKKER–VAN BIJSTERVELD, *De verhouding tussen kerk en staat, in het licht van de grondrechten* (Zwolle, 1988) • K. FERRIER, *Migrantenkerken. Om vertrouwen en aanvaarding*

(Kampen, 2002) • W. Goddijn, J. Jacobs, and G. van Tillo, *Tot vrijheid geroepen. Katholieken in Nederland, 1946-2000* (Baarn, 1999) • E. G. Hoekstra and M. H. Idenburg, *Wegwijs in religieus en levensbeschouwelijk Nederland. Handboek religie, kerken, stromingen en organisaties* (3d ed.; Kampen, 2000) • J. I. Israel, *The Dutch Republic: Its Rise, Greatness, and Fall, 1477-1806* (Oxford, 1995) • L. J. Koffeman, "Survey of Church Union Negotiations: The Netherlands," *ER* 54 (2002) 385-90 • L. J. Koffeman and H. Witte, eds., *Of All Times and of All Places: Protestants and Catholics on the Church Local and Universal* (Zoetermeer, 2001) • A. J. Rasker, *De Nederlandse Hervormde Kerk vanaf 1795* (3d ed.; Kampen, 1986) • S. Schama, *The Embarrassment of Riches: An Interpretation of Dutch Culture in the Golden Age* (London, 1991).

KAREL BLEI

Neurosis

1. Definitions
2. Forms, Structures, Genesis
    2.1. Classic Conflict Neuroses
    2.2. Postclassic Neuroses
3. Treatment
4. Neurosis and Christian Faith

1. Definitions

The term "neurosis" really means nervous sickness, but from the days of S. Freud (1856-1939) it has taken on the sense of psychoneurosis. Disturbances in → development (§2) at specific phases, as well as unconscious → anxieties and their defense, result in a → conflict between the claims of impulse (→ Libido) and a constitutionally and biographically weakened ego that manifests itself in certain symptoms and character distortions. More importance is now attached to the role of early pathology of the → self.

In behavior therapy neurosis is seen as the result of emotional conditioning under circumstances of anxiety that can be produced experimentally (→ animal neurosis). Divergent psychological and anthropological systems result in a lack of terminological precision, but "neurosis" has now irrevocably acquired a psycho-genetic-dynamic sense.

2. Forms, Structures, Genesis

2.1. *Classic Conflict Neuroses*

Symptoms of neurosis like hysteria, phobia, compulsion, or depression are seen as unsuccessful attempts to resolve unmastered oedipal conflicts. Thus Freud believed. According to the timing and

severity of infantile traumatizing in psychosexual development (→ Sexuality) and the way it is handled inwardly (e.g., through imagination or so-called screen memory), acute crises induce a selective and mostly reversible regression, or temporary reversion, to early points of fixation and models of defense that were appropriate to that state of development but not to the present stage. The infantile conflict is thus revived inwardly. In the face of the strong claims of the superego and ideals, the demands of the id lead to the ego's anxiety and repression. In spite of many distortions and misinterpretations of reality, the relation to reality is not lost, as in → psychosis.

Neurotic symptoms that are felt to be alien to the ego — hysterical paralysis, impairment of the senses, compulsive ideas and actions, or various forms of anxiety (e.g., acrophobia, claustrophobia) — represent ego compromises between the satisfying of infantile impulses and self-punishment by the superego. At once a symbolically clothed expression of unconscious conflicts and an appeal for help to those around, the hidden meaning of the symptoms can be understood only in terms of neurotic personality development. Oral, anal, phallic (dominant male) character structures are more or less specific variations of the normal, but in character neuroses (schizoid, depressive, hysterical) the pathogenic effect of the defense is emphasized (e.g., W. Reich's "compulsive-neurotic character armor"). In neurotic relations (collusions) repressed conflicts are interpersonally acted out and dramatized (e.g., family neuroses).

2.2. *Postclassic Neuroses*

There are also postclassic (pre-oedipal, ego-disturbed) neuroses. In contrast to diagnosis of oedipal-authoritarian conflicts at the time of Freud, the most common forms today are character disturbances, → narcissistic and psychosomatic disturbances (so-called organ neuroses), and forms of addiction. They are due to interrupted upbuilding of the self, accompanied by social changes. Disruptions of identity in a fatherless society rest on a lack of father-models with which to identify and which to idealize (P. Kutter).

Narcissistic symbiotic neuroses point to a disturbed mother-child relation at the time of separation. The core complex is the separation conflict. The symbiotically attached "false self" (D. W. Winnicott) remains dependent on the ideal object.

Defective motherliness leads to fragile identity, incapacity for conflict, and disintegration anxiety; to apathy and problems of work, social contact, and sex; to hidden forms of depression ("masked depression"); and to vegetative dystonia, that is, states of nervous unrest and tension that have no physical cause, as well as problems of the heart and circulation. Early disturbances of this kind might be called neuroses of emptiness (M. Boss), existence neuroses (V. von Gebsattel), or "noogenic" neuroses (broadly, arising from existential frustration; V. Frankl).

3. Treatment

If neurosis as a defense against conflict causes a loss of autonomous self-development, analytic therapy (psychoanalysis, group therapy, short therapy, analytically oriented → counseling) is indicated in order, by means of → interpretation, to make it rationally and emotionally possible for the ego, strengthened by instruction and insight, to master inner conflicts and weaknesses as these are relived in transference. Insofar as neurotic conduct is learned emotional reaction to external events, behavior modification can extinguish anxieties by means of classical conditioning (systematic desensitizing) and can reconstruct missing alternatives (reinforcement, modeling) according to the aims of the client.

4. Neurosis and Christian Faith

The thesis that neuroses are grounded in repressed religion (Jung et al.) or that religion is of itself neurotogenic oversimplifies the complex relations between religious → socialization and the sickness that has been called religious neurosis. It does seem that moralistic "Christian" instruction that is hostile to one's impulses can have a pathogenic role. "Ecclesiogenic neuroses" (E. Schaetzing) include sexual disturbances, depression, → suicidal tendencies, masochistic self-punishment, and general life-restriction. Some speak further of "ecclesiogenic disturbances of the development of identity and the self," which may also have sociopolitical and cultural effects. One cannot say a priori, however, that religious faith has a prophylactic function relative to neuroses (Freud); it can be shown only in dialogic practice.

The possibilities and limits of pastoral care for those who suffer from neuroses became clearer only in the latter part of the 20th century (→ Pastoral Psychology). Pastoral aid must have no illusions that it can heal (→ Healing) but must aim only at competence. Diagnostic knowledge of depth psychology, insight into one's own needs and attitudes that is gained from analytic self-experience (e.g., noticing a "helper syndrome"), and insight also into neurotic transference (e.g., in depressive helplessness) can protect against overevaluation of the self and harmful action or cooperation. It is essential

that there should be links to church → counseling centers and professional supervision. A variety of methodological concepts and rules have been developed for pastoral dialogue and counseling.

→ Psychoanalysis; Psychology; Psychotherapy

Bibliography: M. Bassler, ed., *Psychoanalyse und Religion* (Stuttgart, 2000) • G. F. Drinka, *The Birth of Neurosis: Myth, Malady, and the Victorians* (New York, 1984) • S. Freud, *New Introductory Lectures on Psychoanalysis* (trans. J. Strachey; New York, 1965) • V. P. Gay, *Reading Freud: Psychology, Neurosis, and Religion* (Chico, Calif., 1983) • J. W. Jones, *Contemporary Psychoanalysis and Religion* (New Haven, 1991) • H. Kohut, *The Restoration of the Self* (New York, 1977) • R. F. Lax, ed., *Essential Papers on Character Neurosis and Treatment* (New York, 1989) • W. Loch, ed., *Die Krankheitslehre der Psychoanalyse* (6th ed.; Stuttgart, 1999; orig. pub., 1967) • G. S. Reed, *Transference Neurosis and Psychoanalytic Experience* (New Haven, 1994) • D. Shapiro, *Dynamics of Character: Self-regulation in Psychopathology* (New York, 2000) • R. P. Snaith, *Clinical Neurosis* (2d ed., Oxford, 1991) • D. W. Winnicott, *The Family and Individual Development* (London, 1968).

Heribert Wahl

New Age

New Age thinking began in the 1960s, especially in the United States in California. A product of the global social and ecological crisis, it involves new thought and action in every sphere of life, from diet to → science and → politics. It also involves a commensurate new awareness of self and the world. It calls itself holistic and spiritual, though not religious (in contrast to traditional religions like Christianity; → Spirituality). It opposes the dualistic, rationalistic, and mechanistic worldview that has been common from the days of R. Descartes (1596-1650; → Cartesianism). Instead, it advocates a → worldview that integrates science and → mysticism, → nature and humanity, man and woman, God and the world (→ Immanence and Transcendence).

New Age is clearly in agreement with (1) the prognostications of esoteric → astrology, which see the now-dawning Age of Aquarius (one of peace and spiritual advancement) as synthetic, androgynous, and mystical in spite of every threat; (2) belief in the immanence of the divine in the wisdom traditions of the → philosophy perennis, the world religions, → esotericism, → occultism, → theosophy, and → anthroposophy; (3) the hypotheses of evolutionary and holistic physicists, biologists, and psychologists (cf. P. Teilhard de Chardin, C. F. von Weizsäcker, C. Bresch, D. Bohm, R. Sheldrake, and K. H. Pribram) regarding the spiritual dimension of depth appertaining to all reality; and (4) the attempts of neo-Romantic writers and artists to express this dimension in their works (e.g., P. Handke, B. Strauss, J. Beuys, F. Hundertwasser, and K.-H. Stockhausen).

Though not organized, the New Age movement has evoked a wide response through the commercial interest of the media (→ Mass Media), public discussion of its theses, and lectures and courses. In this regard an important part is often played by ancient esoteric techniques that are not public and that aim at new experiences of the self, partners, and the world, including tarot, → meditation (→ Zen), physical exercises (→ Yoga), breathing, self-healing, and → sexuality. J. Redfield's best-seller *Celestine Prophecy* has spawned a set of related texts and a new movement, the New Civilization Network, which (esp. in Europe) has been referred to as the Next Age.

The New Age movement has come under criticism, on the one hand, from intellectuals, who oppose its flight from social and political → responsibility and its abandonment of the gains of the → Enlightenment, and, on the other hand, from the churches, which note its highly individualistic approach and anti-institutionalism, and which see in its spirituality a pseudoreligion with a vague, pantheistic view of God (→ Pantheism), Gnostic and syncretistic ideas of the world (→ Gnosis, Gnosticism), a hedonistic value-system (→ Hedonism), and a naturalistic belief in self-redemption. Along with the student revolts of the 1960s, from which some of its leaders came, the feminist movement (→ Feminism), which partly overlaps it, and the ecological movement (→ Counterculture), into which it seems to be heading, the New Age movement was undoubtedly one of the symptoms of crisis in the latter part of the 20th century. As the ultimate reason for the crisis, it pointed to the spiritual vacuum in → industrial society and thus brought back into discussion the religious aspect of humanity *(homo religiosus).* People, it argued, need religious experiences and are capable of them. They need traditional religions only insofar as these forms are necessary. Though not itself a → religion, it demands that the religions critically ask what their own contribution is to a spiritual holism.

Along with the New Age movement → fundamentalism has also experienced a resurgence, and there has been rediscovery of mystical traditions in the Christian churches. To some it seems that mysti-

cism, as a religious experience that can build interdenominational, interreligious, and intercultural bridges, might offer a positive and critical solution to the problems to which the New Age has given expression.

Bibliography: J. BORYSENKO, *Fire in the Soul: A New Psychology of Spiritual Optimism* (New York, 1993) • M. FOX, *The Coming of the Cosmic Christ: The Healing of Mother Earth and the Birth of a Global Renaissance* (San Francisco, 1988) • O. HAMMER, *Claiming Knowledge: Strategies of Epistemology from Theosophy to the New Age* (Leiden, 2001) • W. J. HANEGRAAFF, *New Age Religion and Western Culture: Esotericism in the Mirror of Secular Thought* (Leiden, 1996) • P. HEELAS, *The New Age Movement: The Celebration of the Self and the Sacralization of Modernity* (Oxford, 1996) • K. LEDERGERBER and P. BIERI, *Was geht New Age die Christen an? Brücken zum gegenseitigen Verständnis* (Freiburg, 1988) • J. LEWIS and J. G. MELTON, eds., *Perspectives on the New Age* (Albany, N.Y., 1992) • J. G. MELTON, J. CLARK, and A. KELLY, eds., *New Age Encyclopedia* (Detroit, 1990) • J. REDFIELD, *The Celestine Prophecy* (New York, 1994) • M. ROTHSTEIN, ed., *New Age Religion and Globalization* (Århus, 2001) • G. SCHIWY, *Der Geist des neuen Zeitalters. New-age-Spiritualität und Christentum* (Munich, 1987); idem, *Der kosmische Christus. Spuren Gottes ins Neue Zeitalter* (Munich, 1990) • J. SUDBRACK, *Mystik im Dialog. Christliche Tradition, ostasiatische Tradition, vergessene Traditionen* (Würzburg, 1992).

GÜNTHER SCHIWY

New Apostolic Church → Apostolic Churches

New Church → Swedenborgianism

New Media → Mass Media

New Religions

1. The term "new religions" refers to religious movements of fellowship, faith, or → salvation, whether of a Christian or a non-Christian slant, that for the most part arose as a result of the global changes and upheavals of the 19th and 20th centuries. Partly on the basis of older religions, partly on that of apparently still-powerful precolonial traditions and → tribal religions, these new religions feed on an → irrationalism that the → reason of the

European → Enlightenment had once decisively combated but that the unparalleled process of → secularization that it unleashed, with its devastating worldwide consequences, stirred into life again.

Hardly one of the new religions is really as new as it claims to be. Their thoroughgoing → syncretism, which usually appeals to a new → revelation, in part uses the arsenal of traditional wisdom and in part dresses itself up in pseudoscientific jargon. It shrewdly extols itself as a synthesis, even where clearly antithetical interests clash with one another, always giving new embodiment to the → sacred.

These features show that we have here second-hand religions. The mixture includes anachronisms in modern garb, conflicts, archaic forms of → manipulation, regress on the one hand, progress on the other. The goal, unfortunately, is not the → autonomy of the subjects, who are only too ready to be sucked into the swamp.

2. The process of forming new religions continues apace, but with no clear direction. It is impossible to offer any classification of the phenomenon from the standpoint of the history of culture, for the actual conditions that produce the new religions differ radically across the globe. Thus we cannot relate the rise of the → Mormons and the many other religious groups in the New World to the existence of thousands of → Independent Churches among the Africans in South Africa alone. It may be that the Black Muslims among African-Americans, the Ghost Dance movement and Peyote cults among native Americans, and the → voodoo practices in Haiti share some typical colonial features with the → Umbanda religion in Brazil or → cargo cults in Melanesia, but they all arose separately and independently, as did the → Baha'i religion in the middle of the 19th century in Persia, → anthroposophy in Germany at the beginning of the 20th century, and the hundreds of new religions *(shin-shūkyō,* or "newly born religions," *shinkō-shūkyō)* in Japan with the dissolution of the official state Shinto after the 1945 defeat.

In modern states a factor that favors new religions is → religious liberty, but the real reasons for their emergence are complex. Even atheistic states (→ Atheism) are not completely free from the development of new religions. Meant to be bulwarks against demonized older powers, they themselves have set up new gods and certainly contributed to modern wars of religion.

The number of new religions throughout the world is now legion. It would be a massive undertaking to list them, in view of their often being linked with self-styled → prophets and saviors, whose rise and fall they faithfully share if they have no firmer anchor. The so-called → youth religions in the West (e.g., the → Children of God), which spread rapidly in the 1960s, are just a few examples of the many new developments, whose number and variety are almost beyond comprehension. A prominent feature of new religions is their exotic nature, as though we were at a postcolonial masked ball in the centers of former global rule.

3. So long as people see themselves forced to take refuge in → illusions because otherwise they cannot tolerate social relations (→ Society), there will continue to be new religions. → Science can offer only partial protection against them, having only a limited claim to → truth.

We cannot take seriously the truth claims that the new religions imperiously make. What we really see in them is an addressing of practical needs. When the promises of a religious upsurge work against inhuman relations, they point to a more worthwhile human existence (→ Human Dignity). The fight against oppression and the → utopia of a better life then wrap themselves in the garb of religion, as especially in chiliastic-nativist movements (→ Millenarianism). In fact the schema of new religious development is often shockingly banal. Mostly in the context of fervent expectations (a "charismatic milieu," R. Otto), a person with some prophetic gifts appeals to visions, voices, or → dreams in which divine revelation is imparted. Followers and confidants quickly group around this person. Opposition also arises, tension grows, fronts form. Miraculous → healings take place, spirits and the departed (→ Dead, Cult of the) are conjured up, gods are on the scene. Finally, a fellowship of the elect forms around the prophet.

Spontaneous appearances, ceremonies, and gatherings then become fixed rituals (→ Rite) that call for permanent or periodic repetition and objectify themselves. The fascination of the holy may be reliably felt at specific times and places, and it may always be perceived in the person of the founder, who either in life or after death is deified, and whose words and/or writings are canonized. Disciples are called, often by the founder, and the central events are recalled with endlessly new promises. A sense of individual calling and collective expectation accompany one another. The → masses thirst for the message and its prophet. The prophet would be nothing if not needed. The model often resembles that of the conspiracy or even the gang, whose members are emotionally bound together. An emotionally volatile climate is usually favorable. Individuals are thus caught up in a vortex that they cannot resist. They change, and they see themselves as born anew or awakened (→ Regeneration).

The religious process is commonly aligned with political upheaval. In so-called → crisis cults there is a solid amalgam of political and religious mission. Nationalism itself (→ Nation, Nationalism) has not scorned to pose as a movement of religious salvation, as we see not least of all in National Socialism (→ Fascism), with its messianic leader, its ideological promises of salvation, its cultic rites to appeal to the masses, and its hosts of convinced and inspired followers. People are dazzled by such movements. For better or worse, they have to plunge into the frenzy of the movement. This pattern holds especially where we have a fanaticism that leads inevitably to terror.

Hardly a single → worldview might not be regarded as a new religion. They all give their supporters an answer to the constant question as to the → meaning of life. They offer security against the vacillations of a capricious fate. They give adherents a new → identity that promises to remove the tormenting contradictions of existence. Through the worldview supporters finally feel eternally safe. The collective anxieties and hopes that lie behind new religions and movements of salvation, and that find a focus in them, can no more be reduced to a schema than can the concrete social conditions that give rise to them. An analysis is required that goes beyond mere description and takes all conditions into account, including the needs and longings that embody themselves in the new religions.

→ Adventists; Ānanda Mārga; Cao Dai; Divine Light Mission; EST; Jehovah's Witnesses; Kitawala; Krishna Consciousness, International Society for; Spiritism; Taiping Rebellion; Theosophy; Transcendental Meditation; Unification Church

Bibliography: D. V. BARRETT, *Sects, Cults, and Alternative Religions: A World Survey and Sourcebook* (London, 1996) • S. BRUCE, "The New Religions of the 1970s," *Religion in the Modern World* (Oxford, 1996) 169-95 • G. D. CHRYSSIDES, *Exploring New Religions* (London, 1999) • C. COLPE, "Synkretismus, Renaissance, Säkularisation und Neubildung von Religionen in der Gegenwart," *HRG* 3.441-523 • O. EGGENBERGER, G. SCHMID, and G. O. SCHMID, eds., *Die Kirchen, Sondergruppen und religiösen Vereinigungen. Ein Handbuch* (7th ed.; Zurich, 2001) • I. HEXHAM and K. POEWE, *New Religions as Global Cultures: Making the Human Sacred* (Boulder, Colo., 1997) • S. HUNT, "The New Religions– Issues and Controversies," *Religion in Western Society* (New York, 2002) 162-77 • J. R. LEWIS, *Peculiar Prophets: A Biographical Dictionary of New Religions* (St. Paul, Minn., 1999); idem, ed., *The Encyclopedia of Cults, Sects, and New Religions* (2d ed.; Amherst, N.Y., 2002) • A. J. RUDIN and M. R. RUDIN, *Prison or Paradise? The New Religious Cults* (Philadelphia, 1980).

FRIEDRICH STENTZLER

New Self

1. Presuppositions
2. Biblical and Theological Bases
3. Secular Analogies and Psychoanalysis
4. Personal Identity

1. Presuppositions

To speak about the new self presupposes that we are people of → time. Time, however, is experienced not in individual, separated moments but in the nexus of past, present, and → future. It is the future and its relation to the past that defines the new self. A further premise is that we are not to be understood merely as we are in ourselves — that is, as substances (see Aristotle's doctrine of categories) — but in relations that determine our existence.

2. Biblical and Theological Bases

2.1. Biblically, a new time is granted that resists → death, both in the midst of life and at its end. This time relates to the prophetic → promises of a new → covenant that brings a new heart, the center of life, and a new spirit (Jer. 31:33; Ezek. 18:31). To these promises Jesus linked the message of the imminent → kingdom of God (Mark 1:15; → Eschatology).

Paul explained this reality in terms of two spheres of life (aeons): the old, which is in principle already past, and the new, which is dawning but already determinative. The new age will refashion the creature as God meant it to be (2 Cor. 5:17). Other passages contrast explicitly the "old self" and the "new self" (Eph. 4:22-24; Col. 3:9-10). From Romans 5 it can be seen that these two spheres are equated with the reality of life in → Adam and in Christ (→ Christology 1). Col. 1:15 and 2 Cor. 4:4 thus see Christ as the true image of God (see Gen. 1:26; Heb. 1:3), which eschatologically transcends the original perfection of the creature.

2.2. In terms oriented to the central idea of substance (Aristotle's *ousia*), medieval theology tried to conceptualize the new, as distinct from the old, and to see in it a state. The renewing Spirit of God was depicted as infused → love (Peter Lombard).

Though the → Reformers did not totally break with Aristotle, for them the doctrine of → justification was the criterion of the new self, who lives in virtue of the relation that God has one-sidedly restored. M. → Luther (1483-1546; → Luther's Theology) abandoned the trichotomy of body, soul, and spirit. For him all the personal elements in life are renewed in the heart. (K. → Barth took this view pregnantly, defining the human spirit [which for him is the real one — in Christ] as permission to live.) P. → Melanchthon (1497-1560) took over from → humanism a doctrine of emotions that determine the will. With the restoration of the image of God, the will is given → freedom by → grace. J. → Calvin (1509-64), who viewed the image of God as the immortal soul (→ Immortality), thought more dualistically. The new self is oriented to life with God, but the justification that we are given shows itself here and now in the → sanctification of life in the body.

2.3. Systematic theology understands the new self in terms of the relationship initiated by the Trinitarian God (→ Trinity). First, the norm and goal lie in the image derived from the Creator. The image includes the freedom for participative responsibility (esp. in taking dominion over the creation) and communication (note the creation as male and female). Second, Christ restored the relation to God that was broken at the fall. → Soteriology discusses the reconciling act of God that makes us one with God again. Third, the work of God's Spirit includes both justification and sanctification, the former never without the latter teleologically, the latter never without the former in practice (Barth). The life of the new self is in Christ, and the subject of the new self is defined from outside the self. According to Reformation → catechisms, the new self expresses itself in daily → penitence, faith, a comforted → conscience, → prayer, living → hope, and the freedom or gratitude that brings both a new practical direction and conduct in keeping with it.

→ Revelation, word, and justification are correlated in this constantly renewed event. We cannot adequately define the new self conceptually but only in narrative (note Luther on justification by faith; → Narrative Theology; Reformation Principles). Revelation confers no secret knowledge (→ Occultism); rather, it grants a relation to God and initiates life-giving action. Its character as word prevents us from thinking of the new self in terms of fixed habit. The contested question of a point of contact for the →

Word of God (E. Brunner) does not point to the old self as a solid basis for renewal; rather, what we bring with us as creatures of God is redefined. → Creation, then, is not arbitrarily viewed nature but that which brings natural life in all its limitation to success.

3. Secular Analogies and Psychoanalysis

In → utopias and projections we find secular analogies to the new self. For K. → Marx (1818-83; → Marxism) the human being, embedded in a deterministic history, was a being primarily with economic interests who was to find true humanity both in the right to that which was produced in common and in the ability to deal with the objects of his or her labor. Under the conditions of class society, however, workers were denied this right. By doing away with the ownership of the means of production and with a market and monetary economy, alienation (from self, others, and nature), so it was held, would be vanquished in the realm of freedom (→ Economic Ethics; Economy). The new society would produce the new self, which, despite the continued need to work to sustain life, would be the social subject of history. For Marx, communism was the solution to the riddle of history and knew itself to be such.

→ Psychoanalysis seeks to replace regression (to early stages of life) by the possibility of dealing with problems through the challenges of present-day life and a progressive synthesis of impulse and reality. In this way the disruption of life by the unconscious might be overcome. In the work of S. Freud (1856-1939) more emphasis falls on conscious acceptance of the limits of one's own possibilities (→ Grief) than on synthesis. Death means regress to the initial id (of organic, preconscious life). No answer is thus given to the question whence to derive courage and hope for further life, or even for new life.

Christian theology can learn from secular ideas, especially concerning the material conditions of renewed human life. But as theology based on the Bible, it will cling to the future of God, which initiates, directs, and limits our human future, for the possibilities of the history and interpretation of life are not exhausted by human programs of life and history. Christian → ethics can thus learn from the nonprogrammatic way in which → Jesus taught and acted so that, similarly, we may first question and therefore liberate human concepts of reality that restrict the possibilities of human conduct (e.g., note the new possibilities for behavior in loving one's enemies).

4. Personal Identity

The new self does not replace the created person; rather, it gives time to redefine the person's identity (P. → Tillich). Since we never know ourselves, we must take the disciplines of the humanities seriously (→ Science and Theology). Concretions of the new self are not possible on reductionist views, such as stimulus-reaction schemata that fail to make intelligible either → responsibility or the question of → meaning. The new self is overestimated if by liberating action a person actualizes himself or herself without regard to → guilt and retrospective responsibility. Theological → anthropology will thus favor the realism of hope and see both the acts and the projects of the new self as → signs in the tension between the ultimate and the penultimate (D. → Bonhoeffer).

Bibliography: Sources: K. Barth, *CD* III/2, IV • D. Bonhoeffer, *Discipleship* (Minneapolis, 2001); idem, *Ethics* (New York, 1955) • E. Brunner, *Man in Revolt: A Christian Anthropology* (Philadelphia, 1939) • CA 6, 20; CA Apol. 4 • J. Calvin, *Inst.* 3 • Formula of Concord, SD 5-6 • S. Freud, *Gesammelte Werke* (vol. 11; 3d ed.; Frankfurt, 1961) • Heidelberg Catechism (1973) • M. Luther, "The Disputation concerning Man," *LW* 34.133-44; idem, Large Catechism, art. 3 • K. Marx and F. Engels, *MECW* • P. Melanchthon, *Werke in Auswahl* (vol. 2; Gütersloh, 1952-53) 2/1.8-17, 85-140, 236-53; 2/2.360-415, 762-80 • W. Pannenberg, *Theology and the Kingdom of God* (Philadelphia, 1969) • Peter Lombard, *III Sent.*, dist. 25-32 • F. D. E. Schleiermacher, *The Christian Faith* (2 vols.; New York, 1963; orig. pub., 1821-22) §§91-95, 100-101, 106-12, 121-25 • P. J. Spener, *Der neue Mensch* (ed. H. G. Feller; Stuttgart, 1966) • P. Tillich, *Systematic Theology* (3 vols.; Chicago, 1951-63).

Secondary works: D. Browning, *Religious Thought and the Modern Psychologies* (Philadelphia, 1987) • G. Ebeling, *Dogmatik des christlichen Glaubens* (Tübingen, 1979) 1.334-414; 3 • C. Frey, *Arbeitsbuch Anthropologie. Christliche Lehre vom Menschen und humanwissenschaftliche Forschung* (Stuttgart, 1979); idem, *Theologische Ethik* (Neukirchen, 1990) • R. L. Hart, *Unfinished Man and the Imagination: Toward an Ontology and a Rhetoric of Revelation* (New York, 1968) • P. E. Hughes, *The True Image: The Origin and Destiny of Man in Christ* (Grand Rapids, 1989) • R. Niebuhr, *The Nature and Destiny of Man* (New York, 1953) • W. Pannenberg, *Theology and the Kingdom of God* (Philadelphia, 1969) • L. Stevenson and D. L. Haberman, *Ten Theories of Human Nature* (3d ed.; Oxford, 1998) • C. Taylor, *Sources of the Self: The Making of Modern Identity* (Cambridge, Mass., 1989).

Christopher Frey

New Testament Era, History of

1. Term, Tasks, Limits
2. Basic Features
   2.1. Seleucids and Hasmonaeans
   2.2. Romans
   2.3. The Years of Jesus
3. Missionary Presuppositions in the Diaspora
4. Double Historical Effect of Destruction of the Temple

1. Term, Tasks, Limits

As a historical discipline or literary genre, the history of the NT era is linked to the name of Matthias Schneckenburger (1804-48), though in many respects it existed earlier. In his lectures on the subject, which appeared posthumously in 1862, Schneckenburger formulated the tasks and intentions of this branch of research in a way that is still influential. He also drew attention implicitly to the problems in historical theology that still call for attention.

In studying the NT era or background, the national, cultural, and religious relations must be depicted into which → Jesus came, along with the movement he started and the churches that quickly developed. The relevant social conditions must also be described. The depiction, however, relates only to what helps to cause, or helps us to explain, what we find in the NT. Ethnologically, then, what is needed is an oriented but theologically impartial account of the political, social, and religious situation of the Jewish people, then of the Greeks and Romans (→ Hellenism; Roman Empire).

Chronologically, the period covers the span from the Maccabean wars (from 166 b.c.) to the revolt of Simeon bar Kokhba (a.d. 132-35). The two limits are both relative, however, since the events and consequences of the Maccabean period presuppose the Hellenization of the Near East from the fourth/third century b.c., and many of the literary witnesses that we need for specific groups and movements in the NT era are much later than Bar Kokhba (→ Gnosis, Gnosticism; Judaism; Rabbi, Rabbinism; Samaritans). The history of the NT era is designed to help us gain a historical understanding of Jesus, of early Christianity, and of the → gospel as its center.

2. Basic Features

For Judaism the age that includes the NT era was that of the second temple. Better than any other, this title focuses on the center of all historical movements in Judaism, whether in → Israel itself or the → diaspora, from the beginning of the building of the temple (520 b.c.) to its destruction (a.d. 70) and beyond. The Second Jewish War began when Emperor Hadrian (117-38) set about to transform shattered → Jerusalem into a pagan city with a temple to Jupiter Capitolinus, and in this way to destroy all hopes for rebuilding the → sanctuary.

As the place of the presence of God and daily priestly worship before him, where the people assembled three times a year in his presence for the feasts and experienced his grace as atonement was made for their → sins in the → sacrifices, the temple at Jerusalem, with the related → Torah that went forth from it, was the very heart of postexilic Israel. The temple at the center gave Jerusalem its rank as the religious and political metropolis, the seat of the Sanhedrin with the officiating → high priest at the head, the economic and cultural center, and the main place of learning. Every Jew had an indissoluble relation to the temple (including cult, offerings, tax, and end-time expectation). The temple was the point of decision, whether directly or indirectly, and often with messianic motivation (→ Messianism).

2.1. Seleucids and Hasmonaeans

The first deep-seated division was that between the Jews and the Samaritans. Its origins are obscure, but we see its effects in the NT, and it persists to our own day. It manifested itself in the founding (the date is contested) of a Samaritan sanctuary on Mount Gerizim.

The early apocalyptic movement with its burning expectation of end-time divine rule (→ Apocalypticism; Eschatology) and the Maccabean revolt with its religio-political aims were triggered when the Seleucid Antiochus IV Epiphanes (175-164 B.C.) desecrated the temple and imposed the death penalty for observance of the religious law. After the collapse of the anti-Seleucid coalition of apocalyptics and Maccabeans soon after the recapture of the temple and its reconsecration (164 B.C., still celebrated as Hanukkah, "dedication"), three religious parties began to crystallize: the Essenes (→ Qumran), → Sadducees, and → Pharisees. These groups would have an essential influence on the life of Israel up to A.D. 70, though to different and changing degrees. The relation to the temple and the Torah marked their identity.

Under the leadership of the Zadokite Teacher of Righteousness, the Essenes moved to the Dead Sea because they thought that under the Maccabean-Hasmonaean high priesthood (Jonathan, 160 or 152-143 B.C.), which they regarded as illegitimate, the temple was unclean, and because they regarded the official exposition of the law (e.g., the fixing of the religious calendar and its ramifications) as erro-

neous. Their understanding of themselves as a spiritual temple went hand in hand with broad expectation of a new temple at Jerusalem.

The Sadducees found recruits among the leading priestly and aristocratic families in Jerusalem and supported the Hasmonaean high priests, who, having gained independence from the Seleucids under Simon (143-135 B.C.), were also political leaders. They remained dominant until well on in the first century B.C. and beyond. They held little brief for postbiblical apocalyptic eschatology or for customs and practices that had developed outside the priestly domain. They had their own extensive oral tradition (e.g., the šĕmaʿ yiśrāʾēl), the work of biblical and legal scholars (→ Scribes). But they did not give this tradition a role in any way comparable with that of Scripture.

The Pharisees, a lay movement, recognized the Jerusalem temple and priesthood but were in partial competition with priestly circles. On the basis of Exod. 19:6, they voluntarily accepted the laws of → cultic purity that appertained to the → priests. They also adopted and stressed inherited practices and traditions, which, as oral Torah received from Moses at Sinai, they put on a par with the written tradition (the Bible). With the support of the people they were sometimes able to hold their own against the Sadducees and their traditions.

In the → synagogue, whose origins are obscure, but which was the place of → prayer (with many links to the temple; → Worship), of the reading and exposition of Scripture, and of the handling of tradition as a whole, the Pharisees and their scribes had an institution at their command that guaranteed their influence not only in Jerusalem but throughout Israel and the diaspora. The synagogue was also an essential basis for the work of Jesus and for Jewish and early Christian → mission to the nations. It would also be a basis for the survival and reconstruction of Judaism after the destruction of the temple.

2.2. Romans

When Pompey (106-48 B.C.) subjugated the eastern Mediterranean in 63 B.C. and put an end first to the Seleucids, then to the Hasmonaeans (whose remnants lasted till 37 B.C.), the NT era in the narrower sense began from the standpoint of world politics. Directly or indirectly, the Romans would now rule the country that was part of the eastern bastion of the empire. The new age began shakily with the sacrilege that Pompey committed by entering the temple. Messianic expectations, which would constantly be rekindled in the days that followed, were intensified as a result (*Pss. Sol.* 17).

The fate of the country then fell into the hands of Herod the Great and his lesser successors. By the grace of Rome and in Roman interests, Herod was king de jure from 40 B.C. (de facto from 37) to 4 B.C. Friendly to Rome, politically adroit, and ruthlessly tyrannical, Herod pursued the policy of a Hellenistic ruler, both developing and exploiting the country's agriculture and commerce. He founded Caesarea on the coast and Sebaste in Samaria in honor of his friend Augustus (27 B.C.–A.D. 14), promoted other Hellenistic cities in the land, and from 20/19 B.C. engaged in the lengthy and magnificent rebuilding of the temple, even though he himself was an Idumean with only a loose attachment to Judaism.

At Herod's death, and after a vacuum characterized by messianic revolts, the Romans at his wish divided the land among his sons: *Archelaus* (4 B.C.–A.D. 6), who took over the ethnarchy of Judea, Idumea, Samaria, and the coastal regions; *Herod Antipas* (4 B.C.–A.D. 39), who ruled the tetrarchy of Galilee and Perea; and *Philip* (4 B.C.–A.D. 34), the governor of the tetrarchy of Batanea, Trachonitis, Auranitis, Gualanitis, Panea, and Ulatha; also Philip's sister *Salome* (d. A.D. 10), whose rule covered the cities of Azotus/Ashdod, Jamnia, and Phasaelis. Archelaus was replaced in A.D. 6 because of intolerable misrule, and his ethnarchy became a Roman province, a prefect under the Syrian legate being at its head, with coastal Caesarea as his capital.

Swift political change came under Tiberius (A.D. 14-37) with the ruthless government of Pontius Pilate (26-36), who established peace but was finally replaced by the Syrian legate Vitellius. Under Caligula (37-41) the desecration of the temple plunged the land into bloody conflict. Under Claudius (41-54) Agrippa I (10 B.C.–A.D. 44, popularly known as Herod in the NT) ruled in part (37-40), and then fully (41-44), as a Herodian king, friendly to Judaism and hostile to Christianity (Acts 12). After his early death the country again became almost totally a Roman province. His son Agrippa II (50-100) had to be content with control over the temple and a minikingdom between Lebanon and Anti-Lebanon (Chalcis), later also the tetrarchies of Philip and Antipas. Agrippa II retained this position until the First Jewish War, and was indeed tolerated by the Romans until his death.

The war broke out when Judean procurator Gessius Florus (64-66) carried his misrule to the point of plundering the temple treasures and uniting the most diverse groups — apart from → Jewish Christians and some rabbis like Johanan ben Zakkai — in a tense and in many ways self-destructive alliance against Rome. The war ended when the siege begun by Emperor Vespasian (69-79) ended with the capture of Jerusalem by his son Titus (emperor 79-81) and the destruction of both city and temple (70). Remaining fortresses were gradually reduced (Masada finally in 74).

Jerusalem became the headquarters of the Tenth Legion, and the whole country after 67 was made an independent province with a legate at Caesarea. Among other penal measures the Jews were forced to pay the former temple tax to the temple of Jupiter Capitolinus at Rome. Under Trajan (98-117) devastating revolts broke out among diaspora Jews who had hardly been affected by the war (115-17). Finally came the Bar Kokhba revolt of 132-35 for the reasons already specified.

2.3. *The Years of Jesus*

Comparable in many ways to the period of the Maccabean revolt, the time of unrest after the death of Herod the Great and during the Roman occupation produced resistance groups of different kinds (the Sicarii; → Zealots) and initiated movements of renewal of an end-time nature that provoked conflicts among the Jews. Appealing to prophetic and apocalyptic proclamation, the leaders of these movements called for conversion in the face of coming judgment (esp. → John the Baptist) or of the present (Jesus' → parables) or future (Jesus' title "Son of Man"; → Christological Titles 2) rule of God and its message of salvation for the socially and religiously outcast and solitary (→ Jesus). The prophetic message found concrete expression in symbolic actions like → baptism (John), → exorcisms, and table fellowship (Jesus; → Eucharist; Signs).

If surprisingly often the tracks of such movements lead us to Galilee or East Jordan, it is because here there were socially deep-seated antagonisms of the periphery against the center, of the farming hinterland against the priestly dominated metropolis, though we must not make too much of these antitheses in view of John's priestly origins. The leaders' sense of mission, which was more or less messianic, and which was especially marked in conversion movements, explained the distinctive lifestyle they adopted, whether as the bold preacher in the wilderness or as the itinerant charismatic in Galilee. It also explained, in the case of Jesus, the freedom with which he treated both people and traditions, including the written as well as the oral Torah, for example, in matters relating to the Sabbath and purity (→ Halakah). The political alarm caused by even these peaceful movements may be seen in the violent deaths that both John and Jesus suffered.

Warned by the Pharisees (Luke 13:31) of the mortal danger under which he stood from Herod Antipas, Jesus did not finally die because of Halakic conflicts with the scribes and Pharisees (though see, e.g., Mark 3:6) but because of his symbolic action in the temple, which was aimed at the Sadducean priestly temple aristocracy. As a reflection of his sense of mission, this action might have been aimed in some sense against the temple itself (John 2:19; Mark 14:57-58 and par.). The accusations brought against Jesus by the temple aristocracy resulted in his condemnation to crucifixion under Pontius Pilate (→ Jesus 2.3). → Christology on the basis of the → resurrection, as well as the rapid spread beyond the borders of the country of what G. Theissen has called the Jesus movement, freed Jesus from the stigma of being an alleged political agitator, as we see in a way that we can hardly overestimate in the formation of the primitive Christian tradition, and especially in the genre that we call gospel.

3. Missionary Presuppositions in the Diaspora

The sayings in criticism of the temple were taken up by the first community. When Stephen, one of their leaders, suffered martyrdom in consequence (Acts 6:14; see also 21:13; → Martyrs), members of the Greek-speaking circle around him in Jerusalem launched a mission to Samaria and the diaspora.

A whole host of conditions contributed to the success of this mission (and later also → Paul's) among both Jews and Gentiles:

- the use of Koine Greek as the common language of the empire (→ Greek Language);
- the political unity of the Mediterranean world under Roman rule;
- relative legal security under the Roman policy of religious toleration, though this security was less available in Israel;
- a wide-ranging transportation system that made possible relatively quick communication by letter (Paul);
- among Jews, the attractiveness that proclamation of the coming of the Messiah had always had;
- the presence of large Jewish communities in world-class cities like → Antioch, → Alexandria, and → Rome, but also in medium-sized and smaller Mediterranean cities;
- a long teaching tradition in the Hellenistic synagogue that accommodated essential features of Jewish religion to Greek Hellenistic thinking (Philo et al.);
- non-Jewish sympathizers who attended the syna-

gogues and felt the attraction of Jewish → monotheism, including women of every stratum;
- the pull of small groups that in a macrosociety offered shelter and → identity;
- acquaintance with key concepts and expectations of the Hellenistic world, including → freedom, → peace, knowledge, and redemption;
- the → hope of a personal Savior *(Sōtēr)* in various forms (→ Emperor Worship; Gnosis, Gnosticism; Mystery Religions) or of a redemptive knowledge of salvation *(sōtēria)* that would open up the way to participation in a transcendental life; and
- the attraction of a holy book like the OT in its Greek translation (LXX; → Bible Versions) and the ability that acquaintance with the written and oral tradition gave to prove that the community was anchored in this ancient Scripture and to formulate a binding ethical lifestyle by appeal to it (see M. → Weber; → Ethics).

4. Double Historical Effect of Destruction of the Temple

When the message of the resurrection of the crucified Messiah spread into Jewish diaspora communities, it inevitably caused conflicts and rivalries, as we see from the work of Paul (2 Cor. 11:23-27) and from churches outside his sphere of operation (edict of Claudius in Rome in A.D. 49, Acts 18:2). These conflicts also arose in Israel (Acts 21:18-21) from the Sadducee and priestly circles and resulted in → persecutions and executions, the latter, however, only in individual cases (Stephen, → James the son of Zebedee, James the brother of Jesus).

The war against Rome brought a decisive change. By refusing to take part in the war, Jewish Christians broke ranks and thus came under suspicion of being traitors. With the destruction of the city and temple they also lost, with their center, what had thus far been regarded (as is clear for Paul) as their central ecumenical importance. The center moved unavoidably from Jerusalem, the spiritual capital, to Rome, the political capital. By relating the destruction of Jerusalem to the death of Jesus, Christians tacitly came to see in it a divine judgment on the city, temple, and people.

For the Christian → congregations, however, the destruction still confirmed their OT legacy. In their → proclamation they constitutively and comprehensively referred to Jewish written and oral traditions and also to Jewish Christian traditions. We see this pattern in the Gospels (cf. Matt. 23:2-3). We see it in Luke and Acts, in spite of their Hellenistic → historiography. We see it in epistles like Hebrews, with its understanding of Jesus as the messianic high priest. We see it in Revelation, perhaps written under Domitian (81-96), when after some first beginnings under Nero (54-68) Christians came into conflict with Roman rule as the Jewish people had constantly done (see the Book of Daniel).

The further the origins in Israel receded chronologically and geographically into the background, the more the traditions became an expounded → tradition whose → reception was nourished by the theological inheritance of the Hellenistic synagogue. In following years this inheritance increasingly became that of the → church as rabbinic Judaism, after the destruction of the temple, consolidated the house of Israel on Hebrew and Aramaic foundations. The history of Christianity and the history of Judaism had now begun to go their separate ways as they developed out of the circumstances of the first century A.D.

→ Apocrypha; Apostolic Fathers; Early Church; Hellenistic-Roman Religion; Literature, Biblical and Early Christian; Primitive Christian Community

Bibliography: J. Ådna and H. Kvalbein, eds., The Mission of the Early Church to Jews and Gentiles (Tübingen, 2000) • P. W. Barnett, Jesus and the Rise of Early Christianity: A History of NT Times (Downers Grove, Ill., 1999) • C. K. Barrett, The NT Background: Writings from Ancient Greece and the Roman Empire That Illustrate Christian Origins (San Francisco, 1995) • H. Conzelmann, History of Primitive Christianity (Nashville, 1973) • F. G. Downing, Making Sense in (and of) the First Christian Century (Sheffield, 2000) • E. Ferguson, Backgrounds of Early Christianity (2d ed.; Grand Rapids, 1993) • J. S. Jeffers, The Greco-Roman World of the NT Era: Exploring the Background of Early Christianity (Downers Grove, Ill., 1999) • H. C. Kee, The Origins of Christianity: Sources and Documents (Englewood Cliffs, N.J., 1973) • H. Koester, Introduction to the NT (2 vols.; 2d ed.; New York, 1995) • B. Reicke, The NT Era: The World of the Bible from 500 B.C. to A.D. 100 (Philadelphia, 1968) • C. J. Roetzel, The World That Shaped the NT (Atlanta, 1985) • C. Rowland, Christian Origins (Minneapolis, 1985) • M. Schneckenburger, Vorlesungen über neutestamentliche Zeitgeschichte (ed. T. Löhlein; Frankfurt, 1862) • E. Schürer, The History of the Jewish People in the Age of Jesus Christ (175 B.C.–A.D. 135) (ed. G. Vermes and F. Millar; 3 vols.; Edinburgh, 1973-87) • H.-A. Wilcke, Neutestamentliche Umwelt und Zeitgeschichte (Essen, 1996). See also ANRW and CRINT.

Peter von der Osten-Sacken

New Theology → Nouvelle théologie

New Thought

1. The New Thought movement began with the American healer Phineas P. Quimby (1802-66), who laid the foundations for its spread with his great success in spiritual → healing. His "science of health and life" and "mental science" were attractive because they allowed of direct practical application in treating the sick, and they quickly gained followers. In his Varieties of Religious Experience (1902), William James called it "the religion of healthy-mindedness."

2. Helping the rapid spread of the movement was the work of early writers like W. F. Evans (1817-89), H. Wood (1834-1909), P. Mulford (1843-91), O. S. Marden (1850-1924), H. W. Dresser (1866-1954), and R. W. Trine (1866-1958) in systematizing the teaching and giving it literary and aesthetic shape. In 1889 "New Thought" was adopted as the title at the instigation of the Swedenborgian W. Halcombe (→ Swedenborgianism).

In 1895 development came quickly with Divine Science in the United States, the Higher Thought in Britain, Oomoto in Japan, and similar movements in India, China, Korea, Australia, Brazil, and Africa. It also spread in Germany from 1900 onward; in 1923 the pandenominational Neugeistbund united various theosophical (→ Theosophy), spiritist (→ Spiritism), mystical (→ Mysticism), and neo-Gnostic (→ Gnosis, Gnosticism) groups, with 3,500 chapters formed by 1935. The organ of the movement in Germany was Die weiße Fahne (The white flag), edited by K. O. Schmidt (1904-77) from 1924 to 1966. Though reconstruction was slow after World War II, the movement acted as a positive ferment in almost all new religious and spiritual ventures, and most of its thinking may be seen in → New Age.

The International New Thought Alliance (1914) is the umbrella agency for some 600 active groups of New Thought, with a combined millions of members, though exact numbers are hard to come by, since the boundaries with related religious organizations like → Christian Science and the Unity School of Christianity are difficult to fix.

3. The New Thought movement sees God as impersonally good and spiritual, with universal world love as the central force of all reality (→ Pantheism). Christ is the first representative of New Thought ideas. Humans as part of the divine spirit can achieve harmony with the Infinite by systematic spiritual self-training and thus attain to the higher

divine energies, stable → health, and spiritual balance. The strong positive thinking that leads to this result derives from an absolute acceptance of known → truth by the human spirit. Dominion of spirit over matter follows, as well as a new divinity of → nature.

New Thought seeks reforms in medicine (using → laying on of hands, distance healing, and healing through → prayer), diet (vegetarianism, no narcotics), clothing, housing, → education, → sexuality, and labor. Modern machine-humanity is rejected. Deification is the goal of cosmic development (cf. → theōsis).

Bibliography: Primary sources: H. W. DRESSER, *History of the New Thought Movement* (New York, 1919) • W. F. EVANS, *The Mental Cure* (Boston, 1869) • E. S. HOLMES, *The Science of Mind* (New York, 1966; orig. pub., 1926) • P. P. QUIMBY, *The Quimby Manuscripts* (ed. H. W. Dresser; New York, 1921) • R. W. TRINE, *Higher Powers of Mind and Spirit* (New York, 1917).

Secondary works: C. S. BRADEN, *Spirits in Rebellion: The Rise and Development of New Thought* (Dallas, 1963) • G. M. HARLEY, *Emma Curtis Hopkins: Forgotten Founder of New Thought* (Syracuse, N.Y., 2002) • H. MYNAREK, *Ökologische Religion. Ein neues Verständnis der Natur* (2d ed.; Munich, 1990); idem, *Religios ohne Gott?* (2d ed.; Munich, 1989); idem, *Die Vernunft des Universums* (Munich, 1988) • G. T. PARKER, *Mind Cure in New England; from the Civil War to World War I* (Hanover, N.H., 1973).

HUBERTUS MYNAREK

New Zealand

	1960	1980	2000
Population (1,000s):	2,372	3,113	3,760
Annual growth rate (%):	2.05	0.84	1.10

Area: 270,534 sq. km. (104,454 sq. mi.)

A.D. *2000*

Population density: 14/sq. km. (36/sq. mi.)
Births / deaths: 1.52 / 0.78 per 100 population
Fertility rate: 2.10 per woman
Infant mortality rate: 6 per 1,000 live births
Life expectancy: 78.0 years (m: 75.5, f: 80.5)
Religious affiliation (%): Christians 84.7 (Protestants 26.8, Anglicans 21.3, Roman Catholics 14.1, unaffiliated 13.7, indigenous 5.2, marginal 3.5, other Christians 0.2), nonreligious 11.4, other 3.9.

1. Pre-Christian
2. Early Mission Period
3. White Settlement and the Churches
4. Maori Religion after 1840
5. Other Twentieth-Century Developments

1. Pre-Christian

The peoples now called Maori came to New Zealand from eastern Polynesia, perhaps in the late 14th century. Long isolation produced a distinctive culture with developed hierarchies, arts, technology, and oral literature. The Maori universe was full of spirits, divided into complementary spheres of light (Te Rangi) and darkness (Te Po). Adepts in the highest spiritual and mythical knowledge (→ Myth, Mythology, 1) formed a class of experts *(tohunga)* who had access to the higher spirit beings *(atua)* and delivered prophetic oracles *(karakia)*. If a pre-Christian cult of the supreme God existed (and this is disputed), it was very restricted. Most Maori dealt only with the lower atua. These were local divinities and ancestral spirits (→ Ancestor Worship), spiritual guardians contacted by tohunga for prediction, diagnosis, or healing. The most important religious activity was the observance of *tapu* (→ Taboo), a system of ritual prohibition associated with power and its possession. War was frequent; revenge *(utu)* for offenses against kin was a social obligation.

European contact began in 1769, but the Maori reputation for ferocity and → cannibalism deterred permanent settlement. European vessels stopped for supplies, bringing disease, prostitution, and an appetite for firearms and other metal goods.

2. Early Mission Period

Samuel Marsden (1764-1828), chaplain of the British colony of New South Wales, persuaded the Church Missionary Society (CMS; → British Missions) to begin a mission in New Zealand in 1809. Maori initially valued the mission only as a source of foreign goods. A Wesleyan mission, also influenced by Marsden, arrived in 1822. Until the late 1830s response to both missions remained slight. By 1840, however, 40,000 Maori were estimated to be attending services, and the Maori NT was circulating widely. The Roman Catholic mission, under vicar apostolic of western Oceania J. B. F. Pompallier (1801-71), who arrived in 1838, had hundreds of hearers within a year. Christianity was now self-propagating.

The move toward Christianity was associated with increasing revulsion from the endemic warfare, now intensified by the use of European firearms. Adoption of Christianity facilitated escape from the utu system, which perpetuated → war by insisting on revenge. It entailed exclusive allegiance to the atua Jehova (the name used in the Maori Bible), and a new tapu system of commands and prohibitions. → Literacy spread quickly, as Maori strove to learn and fulfill the biblical requirements.

Christianity promoted the idea of brotherhood transcending tribe. This value, together with the now constant presence of *pakeha* (i.e., non-Maori, esp. white people), helped to foster Maori (as distinct from tribal) identity. Peace, however, encouraged the arrival of large numbers of European settlers, who were subject to no control. Unable to prevent the colonizing of the country, the missionaries persuaded the Maori to accept British sovereignty as a means of controlling white settlers. The Treaty of Waitangi (1840), which established British rule, guaranteed Maori land rights, but as immigration increased (pakeha outnumbered Maori from 1858), Maori lost much of their lands and became powerless to influence events (→ Colonialism).

3. White Settlement and the Churches

In origin, New Zealand Christianity was a Maori institution. The arrival of so many new settlers, however, transformed the dynamics of the church. G. A. Selwyn (1809-78), appointed → bishop of New Zealand by the Crown in 1840, set out to create a comprehensive Anglican church embracing both Maori and pakeha, with a college training a local ministry drawn from both communities. He met opposition from CMS missionaries about the extent of his authority, from European settlers because of his frequent espousal of Maori rights, and from many Maori over his identification with the government (i.e., pakeha) cause in the Maori wars.

Immigrants — especially the more disciplined "respectable" settlers who succeeded the earlier adventurers — brought ideals and church structures from Britain. Thomas Burns led Free Church of Scotland migrants in founding Dunedin in 1848, producing a Presbyterian church order, college, and education system on Scottish lines (→ Reformed and Presbyterian Churches). An Anglican plan (with provision for a bishop, cathedral, and college) guided the group that founded Christchurch in 1851. English → Methodists, including farm workers driven out by the agricultural depression of the 1870s, brought their traditions of vigorous → evangelism and lay ministry, which enabled them to set up churches among the new scattered rural communities. The high numbers of Irish immigrants caused the → Catholic mission, established for the Maori, to accord them priority. (New Zealand became an ecclesiastical province in 1877.) Other migrants introduced other structures: Congregational (1840), Baptist (1851), Christian Brethren (1853).

Imported church structures were sometimes modified under colonial conditions. Most notably, Selwyn oversaw the birth in 1859 of a self-governing Anglican church free of the colonial state, with synodical government in which bishops, priests, and laity were represented. This model influenced Anglican polity elsewhere, and eventually the Church of England itself (→ Anglican Communion). Consolidation took place in denominations that were fragmented in their places of origin; union of the diverse Methodist bodies was initiated in 1883 and completed in 1913, nearly 20 years before their union in Britain. Settlers from all the Scottish churches, as well as Irish, Welsh, and English Presbyterians, joined the Presbyterian Church of New Zealand. The first presbytery was organized in Auckland in 1856, while the Presbyterian Church of Otago and the Southland (operating south of the Waitaki River) continued the Free Church of Scotland traditions of Burns and the Dunedin settlers. → Union of these churches, briefly achieved in 1861, was concluded in 1901.

The older churches, which had begun as missions to the Maori, attempted to serve both Maori and pakeha. In practice, the Maori became an appendage to institutions that were constructed and dominated by pakeha. The period of alienation that issued in the Maori king movement and the wars accelerated this tendency; the old missions declined, and of the new churches only the → Mormons (1853) had much attraction for Maori. A partial reconciliation after the wars, when missions were invited into the territory controlled by the Maori king, brought partial recovery, and the newer churches (notably the Presbyterians in 1895) began Maori missions. The CMS handed over its Maori mission to the New Zealand Anglican Church in 1883.

4. Maori Religion after 1840

The Treaty of Waitangi, despite good intentions, was circumvented in practice and did not protect Maori interests. The election of a Maori king in 1857 was followed by open wars against the British government in the 1860s. Neither the king movement nor the war movement was in principle anti-Christian (some warriors even followed the injunction to give one's enemy food), but defeat and intensified land seizure forced most Maori to choose between breaking with pakeha society completely or living on its margins.

Meanwhile missions merged into churches organized on British lines. Maori clergy became distanced from Maori life. Alcoholism (→ Substance Abuse), diseases of alienation (including *mate*

Maori, "Maori disease," a depressive condition in which the sufferer pined away), and the lower forms of tohungaism became common. Some Maori returned to what could be recovered from the dislocated pre-Christian tradition, but even this heritage was combined with use of the one indubitably Maori Christian institution: the Maori Bible.

The prophet Te Ua combined Maori cosmology, biblical rhetoric, and a protective tapu system called Pai Marire or Hau Hau, which helped to prolong the wars until1867. Later Pai Marire theology identified Jehova with Io, the (assumed) pre-Christian name of the Supreme Being. Te Kooti (ca. 1814-93), founder of the Ringatu Church, preached allegiance to Jehova, a tapu system based on OT law, and coming deliverance for the Maori. Rua Kenana (1869-1937) developed the futurist elements in Ringatu, which is still a significant Maori church.

In 1918 T. W. Ratana (1876-1939), until then a nominal church member, had a vision and emerged as Mangai (Mouthpiece) of Jehova. Crowds responded to his preaching and healings. Most mainstream pakeha clergy, at first favorable, became concerned that → angels (perhaps continuing the functions of the pre-Christian "guardians") were playing too great a part in Ratana's theology, and Christ too little. The Ratana revival recalled the Maori to Jehova, and away from alcoholism, tohungaism, and alienation. It also reasserted Maori identity and led to social renewal and political consciousness. Ratana said, "In one of my hands I hold the Bible; in the other is the Treaty of Waitangi." From 1932 the political impact of the movement grew with the election of Ratana supporters as Maori members of Parliament. The Ratana Church, which arose from the movement, remains an important religious force.

5. Other Twentieth-Century Developments

The first fruit of Christian → ecumenism in New Zealand was the National Missionary Council, formed in 1926 to promote cooperation in overseas missions. It was later absorbed into the National Council of Churches (NCC), established in 1961. The Ratana and Ringatu Churches are associate members. The Catholic Bishops' Conference has a commission on ecumenism and a joint working group with the NCC.

New Zealand has shared the secularizing influences that have affected many Western countries, with consequent decline in active Christian profession (→ Secularization). The Catholic Church has known tensions over state education, which has been determinedly secular. In the late 20th century

the Protestant churches experienced major controversies about the status of traditional Christian doctrines, → sexuality, and other topics. The most significant religious factors have come from demography. The Maori have steadily increased as a proportion of the population; they have a strong urban presence (esp. in Auckland), and there has been large-scale immigration from elsewhere in Polynesia, particularly the Cook Islands and Samoa. Church policy has progressively recognized the bicultural nature of New Zealand society and seeks to reflect this reality in ecclesiastical structures, leadership, and hierarchy.

Bibliography: J. C. ANDERSEN, *The Maori Tohunga and His Spirit World* (New York, 1977) • E. BEST, *Maori Religion and Mythology* (Wellington, 1924; repr., New York, 1977) • A. K. DAVIDSON, *Selwyn's Legacy: The College of St. John the Evangelist, 1843-1992. A History* (Auckland, 1996) • A. K. DAVIDSON and P. J. LINEHAM, *Transplanted Christianity: Documents Illustrating New Zealand Church History* (Auckland, 1987) • J. H. EVANS, *Churchman Militant: George Augustus Selwyn, Bishop of New Zealand and Lichfield* (London, 1964) • J. M. HENDERSON, *Ratana: The Origins and the Story of the Movement* (Wellington, 1963) • J. IRWIN, *Introduction to Maori Religion* (Bedford Park, 1984) • L. KEYS, *The Life and Times of Bishop Pompallier* (Christchurch, 1957) • P. J. LINEHAM and A. R. GRIGG, *Religious History of New Zealand* (Palmerston North, 1984) bibliography • H. MOL, "New Zealand," *Western Religion: A Country by Country Sociological Inquiry* (ed. H. Mol; The Hague, 1972) 365-79; idem, *Religion and Race in New Zealand* (Christchurch, 1966) • C. NICHOL and J. A. VEITCH, *Religion in New Zealand* (Wellington, 1980) • J. M. R. OWENS, *Prophets in the Wilderness: The Wesleyan Mission to New Zealand, 1819-27* (Auckland, 1974) • L. M. ROGERS, ed., *The Early Journals of Henry Williams* (Christchurch, 1961) • K. SINCLAIR, *History of New Zealand* (5th ed.; London, 2000) • H. M. WRIGHT, *New Zealand, 1769-1840* (Cambridge, Mass., 1967).

ANDREW F. WALLS

Newbigin, J. E. Lesslie

By his personal stature and the range of his activities, Lesslie Newbigin (1909-98) stands out as a father of the ecumenical church in the 20th century. Raised an English Presbyterian, he was ordained by the Church of Scotland in 1936 for missionary service in India, where he represented his denomination in the final rounds of negotiation toward the organic union of Anglicans, Presbyterians, Methodists, and Congregationalists in the → Church of South India (1947). Consecrated as one of the first bishops in the CSI, Newbigin presided over the Diocese of Madurai and Ramnad until 1959 and attained international prominence through his contributions to the first and second assemblies of the → World Council of Churches (WCC), at Amsterdam (1948) and Evanston (1954). Active also at the Willingen meeting of the → International Missionary Council in 1952, he was released to serve as general secretary of that body at the time of its integration with the WCC, and then as the first director of the new Division of World Mission and Evangelism (1959-65). He returned to India as → bishop in Madras until retirement in 1974. Back in Britain, he then taught mission and ecumenics for five years at the Selly Oak Colleges in Birmingham, before taking on for most of his eighth decade the pastorate (→ Pastor, Pastorate) of a local congregation of the United Reformed Church in the racially and religiously mixed inner suburb of Winson Green. Even in his third retirement in South London, Newbigin continued to preach, lecture, and write, concentrating on the task of Christian → apologetics that he had seen to be increasingly necessary since his final settlement in an intellectually and spiritually apostate West.

From the time of his vision of a cross "spanning the space between heaven and earth . . . with arms that embraced the whole world" that was given to him one night in the summer of 1929 while he worked at a social center for unemployed coal miners in South Wales, Newbigin was committed to belief in the atoning will and work of God — a belief that was theologically consolidated by his study of James Denney's commentary on Romans. His obedient → discipleship to Christ led him into direct → evangelism, whether in student missions or selling gospels at an anna apiece in the streets of Kanchipuram. As a pastoral bishop, Newbigin traveled his first rural → diocese with his fellow workers and organized training schools for → catechists; and then later in metropolitan Madras he gathered his presbyters around him for monthly services of Word and table as well as encouraging the participation of laypeople in civic and industrial life. Newbigin was a man of → prayer, deeply steeped in the Scriptures, a preacher with a strong sacramental sense.

Described by one of his Indian episcopal colleagues as a bishop on the run, Newbigin was also an energetic writer. His defense of the South Indian pattern of organic → unity in *The Reunion of the Church* (1948) blossomed into a full-blown ecclesiology in *The Household of God* (1953), which sought to integrate not only the "protestant" and "catholic" but also the "pentecostal" dimensions of the church; and his comprehensive vision found condensed expression in the famous description of "the unity we seek," which he drafted for the third assembly of the WCC, at New Delhi (1961). The recovery of pneumatology made possible also the genuinely Trinitarian theology of mission that Newbigin presented in mature form in *The Open Secret* (1978). His → missiology combined global, cross-cultural, and local elements in an understanding and practice of the church as "God's embassage in the world." His brief flirtation with so-called secular theology in the early 1960s found a worthier expression in his later concern for the → gospel as "public truth"; in fact, from his Bangalore lectures of 1941 ("The Kingdom of God and the Idea of Progress") onward, he had known the importance of distinguishing between the divine reign and human achievement. While history could be the scene and vehicle of God's redemptive action, the best that humans could contribute was "acted prayers," out of which God would preserve for the final day what had been entrusted to him (see 2 Tim. 1:12).

Given the crisis of the Christian faith in the West at the very time when Western culture and rapacity were spreading globally through → technology, Newbigin devoted the last 25 years of his life to the question of a "reconversion of the West," a "missionary encounter with → modernity." In *Foolishness to the Greeks* (1986) and *The Gospel in a Pluralist Society* (1989), he emphasized the intellectual character of the task. A Cartesian epistemology of → doubt had to be countered by a recognition of the fiduciary character of all knowledge, such as Newbigin was helped to articulate by the writings of the Hungarian practitioner and philosopher of science Michael Polanyi (esp. his *Personal Knowledge* [1958]). Just as → Athanasius and → Augustine had supplied European culture for over a millennium with a Trinitarian basis, so now, without a reversion to Constantinianism in its aspect of enforcement of the faith, Christian thinkers had the task of bringing the cross and resurrection of Christ to bear in the face of "plausibility structures" — whether ancient or modern → monisms or postmodern → nihilisms — into which they cannot be accommodated. On the world scene, Newbigin foresaw → Islam and free-market economics as the chief rivals of the gospel in the 21st century.

→ Ecumenism, Ecumenical Movement

Bibliography: T. F. FOUST, G. R. HUNSBERGER, J. A. KIRK, and W. USTORF, eds., *A Scandalous Prophet: The*

Way of Mission after Newbigin (Grand Rapids, 2002) includes a full list of Newbigin's works • G. R. HUNS- BERGER, *Bearing the Witness of the Spirit: Lesslie Newbigin's Theology of Cultural Plurality* (Grand Rapids, 1998) • L. NEWBIGIN, *The Light Has Come: An Exposition of the Fourth Gospel* (Grand Rapids, 1982); idem, *Unfinished Agenda: An Autobiography* (London, 1985; updated ed., Edinburgh, 1993) • G. WAIN- WRIGHT, *Lesslie Newbigin: A Theological Life* (New York, 2000).

GEOFFREY WAINWRIGHT

Newman, John Henry

John Henry Newman (1801-90), leading theologian of the → Oxford Movement, was initially an Angli- can but in midlife joined the → Roman Catholic Church, becoming a → priest and, in 1879, a → car- dinal. Newman grew up with five siblings in a → bourgeois London family in which he often felt mis- understood and lonely, finding solace in the Bible and other religious and theological works. In the au- tumn of 1816 he experienced an "inner → conver- sion," convincing him he was one of the chosen and was destined for a life without marriage. In 1817 he began studying law at Oxford, quickly changed to theology, became a fellow in 1822 and a tutor in Oriel College in 1826, and finally became → pastor at St. Mary and university preacher in 1828 (the lat- ter until 1843).

During a trip to the Mediterranean in 1832, Newman realized that because of liberal trends at home he had a mission to fulfill in England. Upon returning, he resolved with his friends John Keble and Edward B. Pusey to try to bring the Church of England into harmony again with the → early church and with the doctrines of the → church fa- thers. To this end, the group published *Tracts for the Times* (90 tracts, 1834-41), for which they were ac- cordingly called Tractarians. Here the group advo- cated faith in the visible church, episcopal → au- thority, sacramental → grace, and the high integrity of → penitence, and they also tried to present the → Anglican Church as a *via media* between Roman Ca- tholicism and the churches of the → Reformation. In this capacity they also shaped the identity of the "Society of Friends of the Church" (→ Oxford Movement).

Public indignation and severe criticism of his own Catholicizing interpretation in Tract 90 (1841) of the Church of England's Thirty-nine Articles prompted Newman to resign his offices and to retire to a semimonastic life. In his *Essay on the Develop-* *ment of Christian Doctrine* (1845), Newman argued that the dogmas God entrusted to the church un- derwent historical development but still maintained their basic identity. He recanted his earlier "harsh words" against the Church of Rome and decided to → convert to Roman Catholicism. In October 1845 Newman made the Catholic confession of faith, was baptized (*sub conditione*) and confirmed, and in 1846 went to Rome, where the next year he was or- dained priest and joined the Oratorians of St. Philip Neri. He returned to Birmingham and founded an → Oratory there in 1848, where he dealt with issues of a largely pedagogical nature until his death, inter- rupted only by his tenure as rector of the Roman Catholic University in Dublin (1851-58).

In his lectures (from 1852) Newman endorsed strengthened intellectual education for Catholics and demanded free scholarship under the auspices of theology (*Idea of a University* [1852]). Newman was prompted to defend his religious development in his *Apologia pro vita sua* (1864) by the mistrust and suspicions spread especially by Henry Manning (also a convert, whom the pope appointed arch- bishop of Westminster in 1865), who tirelessly and militantly propagated → Ultramontanism in En- glish Catholicism and opposed what he considered to be Newman's excessively liberal views on educa- tion, and by public doubt in the sincerity of Newman's own conversion and even by suspicions of heresy.

Newman initially took a rather reserved view of the dogmas of primacy issued by → Vatican I, but then he vehemently defended them once protest arose in England and diplomatic consequences were demanded (*Letter to the Duke of Norfolk* [1875]). He developed his view of the unconditional adherence to church → dogma in his *Essay in Aid of a Grammar of Assent* (1870), in which he distinguished real or "incarnate knowledge" from merely "conceptual un- derstanding and assent" and advocated the status of such knowledge as an independent act of reflection.

Alongside Newman's scholarly publications, his poetic work also attracted considerable attention, for example, "Lead, Kindly Light" (1833), a popular hymn, and "Dream of Gerontius" (1865), which Ed- ward Elgar set to music. In his sermons (13 vols., 1870-79), Newman accentuated faith's concrete en- counter with the living reality of God's revelation. His own life was characterized by → asceticism, → prayer, and a pastoral ethos. The influence and sig- nificance of his philosophical and theological think- ing are reflected in the so-called Newman Renais- sance, which gained momentum after World War II and assessed his work from a variety of perspectives.

Bibliography: Primary sources: *Apologia pro vita sua: Being a History of His Religious Opinions* (ed. M. J. Svaglic; Oxford, 1967) • *An Essay in Aid of a Grammar of Assent* (ed. I. T. Ker; Oxford, 1985) • *The Idea of a University Defined and Illustrated* (ed. I. T. Ker; Oxford, 1976) • *The Works of Cardinal Newman* (41 vols.; London, 1874-1921).

Secondary works: D. GOSLEE, *Romanticism and the Anglican Newman* (Athens, Ohio, 1996) • S. L. JAKI, *Newman's Challenge* (Grand Rapids, 2000) • I. T. KER, *John Henry Newman: A Biography* (Oxford, 1988) • T. MERRIGAN, *Clear Heads and Holy Hearts: The Religious and Theological Ideal of John Henry Newman* (Louvain, 1991) • D. NEWSOME, *The Convert Cardinals: John Henry Newman and Henry Edward Manning* (London, 1993) • A. NICHOLS, *From Newman to Congar: The Idea of Doctrinal Development from the Victorians to the Second Vatican Council* (Edinburgh, 1990) • J. R. PAGE, *What Will Dr. Newman Do? John Henry Newman and Papal Infallibility, 1865-1875* (Collegeville, Minn., 1994) • W. WARD, *The Life of John Henry, Cardinal Newman* (2 vols.; Farnborough, 1970; orig. pub., 1912).

ERWIN FAHLBUSCH

Nicaea, Councils of

1. Geography and History

As early as A.D. 112 the Province of Bithynia in northwest Asia Minor, on the east coast of the Bosporus, contained many Christians, both urban and rural, as we learn from the salutation of 1 Peter and a famous letter of Governor Pliny (ca. 61-113) to Emperor Trajan (98-117). In this province, some 50 km. (30 mi.) southwest of the imperial seat of Nicomedia (modern Turk. İzmit), lay Nicaea (modern İznik), which, as we know from the council in 325, had its own bishop. The nearness to Nicomedia and the large number of Christians explain why there were so many → martyrs at Nicaea during the Diocletian → persecution beginning in 303.

2. First Council (325)

Nicaea has secured a place in the history of Christian theology (→ Dogma, History of) and world history because Constantine I (306-37) decided to move to Nicaea the council that had been planned for Ancyra (modern Ankara) in early 325.

2.1. *Occasion*

The occasion of this first ecumenical → council was a doctrinal dispute from about 319 between Alexander of Alexandria (bishop 312-28) and his theologically and philosophically highly trained presbyter Arius (ca. 280-336; → Arianism) regarding the relation of the deity of the Father and the Son to all → creation (→ Trinity). Alexander excommunicated Arius and explained his action in a dogmatic statement. The dispute centered on the exposition of Prov. 8:22 but was affected by the schism (→ Heresies and Schisms) between Peter of Alexandria (bishop 300-311) and Melitius of Lycopolis in Egypt (d. ca. 325) that resulted from the Diocletian persecution. Never properly settled, that dispute broke out with new passion when Arius refused to side with either party.

The situation deteriorated when Arius won over to his support the powerful bishop of the imperial seat, Eusebius of Nicomedia (d. ca. 342). The most erudite theologian of the day, Eusebius of Caesarea (ca. 260-ca. 340), also had misgivings about Alexander's proceedings against his presbyter (→ Elder). An episcopal synod at Antioch early in 325 supported Alexander. Eusebius of Caesarea and two of his party called for reconsideration and summoned a council to Ancyra to see if other affected areas of the church would endorse Antioch's decision. At this point the emperor, who had thus far underestimated the controversy as a mere strife of words of no more than local significance, proposed that the council should be shifted to Nicaea. He himself would see to the travel arrangements for the bishops and play a part in the proceedings.

2.2. *Decisions*

The council opened on June 19 (or May 20, the traditional opening date), 325. In his *Life of Constantine* Eusebius of Caesarea vividly portrayed the emperor's entry without weapons or bodyguard. The best account of the dogmatic part of the proceedings is to be found in a letter that Eusebius sent back to his → diocese and that → Athanasius (ca. 297-373) handed down to posterity. From this letter we learn that Constantine and Eusebius were the dominant participants.

Eusebius put the discussion on a new dogmatic basis when, diverging from precedent, he proposed that the rule of faith underlying baptismal instruction (→ Confession of Faith) should serve as a ground of action, and that the council, instead of anathematizing Arius specifically, should condemn any deviation from this Trinitarian formula as heresy. Constantine agreed to this proposal, but in an address moved that a reference to the essential unity *(homoousia)* of the Father and the Son should be added to the creed. The opponents of Arius in Alexandria and Antioch, however, succeeded in having express condemnations attached that would follow the decision reached at Antioch but be in agreement with the theological orientation of Constantine and Eusebius. The majority accepted and subscribed to the resultant statement on July 25.

Only Eusebius of Nicomedia and Theognius of Nicaea (d. before 342) refused to agree to the condemnation of Arius and the deposing of his two episcopal supporters in Egypt. These two, however, were granted time for reconsideration.

2.3. Results

We can hardly overestimate the impact of this council on the history of both church and empire. With Nicaea a new instrument of government — the council — was created that profoundly changed the constitution of both the one and the other.

The → law set forth in the canons of Nicaea would have legal force in the empire (→ Church and State), as we see from canons relating to bishoprics and the election of → bishops (can. 4) and to the rights of such ancient churches as Alexandria, Rome, Antioch, and Jerusalem (cans. 6 and 7; → Patriarch). The creed itself, at the instigation of Eusebius and Constantine, went far beyond the original dispute and became a confession of the → identity of God in the consubstantiality of Father and Son ("God from God, light from light, true God from true God"). It became a document of primary importance not merely in church history and the history of doctrine but in religious history as a whole, for it formulated a Christologically (→ Christology) defined → monotheism that in principle replaced all special ethnic and local cults.

One unfortunate consequence was the exclusion and rejection of → Judaism as a rival form of monotheism. The rule for fixing the date of → Easter (in principle still valid today) on the first Sunday after the vernal full moon was also designed to make a break with the Jewish → Passover (→ Church Year).

3. Second Council (787)

The Second Council of Nicaea was the seventh ecumenical council; like Nicaea I it dealt with a Christological question. Convened in 787, it took up the issue, debated from the seventh century, of the depiction of Christ on → icons (→ Images; Images of Christ). A council meeting in Hieria in 754 and

claiming to be ecumenical had rejected the legality of such depictions but had brought down on itself passionate attacks from the people, who venerated icons, and from the monks (→ Monasticism; Popular Religion). Nicaea II sanctioned the depiction of Christ, → Mary, → angels, and → saints on icons. This decision, attacked again in the early ninth century, was confirmed in 843, and the veneration of icons hereafter became a fixed part of Eastern → Orthodoxy (§3).

→ Ecumenical Symbols; Niceno-Constantinopolitan Creed

Bibliography: V. Burrus, *"Begotten, Not Made": Conceiving Manhood in Late Antiquity* (Stanford, Calif., 2000) • A. Giakalis, *Images of the Divine: The Theology of Icons at the Seventh Ecumenical Council* (Leiden, 1994) • J. N. D. Kelly, *Early Christian Creeds* (3d ed.; New York, 1972) 205-62 • P. L'Huillier, *The Church of the Ancient Councils: The Disciplinary Work of the First Four Ecumenical Councils* (Crestwood, N.Y., 1996) • B. J. F. Lonergan, *The Way to Nicea: The Dialectical Development of Trinitarian Theology* (London, 1976) • C. Luibhéid, *The Council of Nicaea* (Galway, 1982) • N. P. Tanner, ed., *Decrees of the Ecumenical Councils* (2 vols.; London, 1990) 1.1-19, 131-56 • E. Timiadis, *The Nicene Creed: Our Common Faith* (Philadelphia, 1983).

Wolfgang Ullmann

Nicaragua

	1960	1980	2000
Population (1,000s):	1,493	2,790	4,694
Annual growth rate (%):	3.19	2.77	2.41
Area: 131,670 sq. km. (50,838 sq. mi.)			

A.D. 2000

Population density: 36/sq. km. (92/sq. mi.)
Births / deaths: 3.02 / 0.53 per 100 population
Fertility rate: 3.35 per woman
Infant mortality rate: 39 per 1,000 live births
Life expectancy: 69.7 years (m: 67.3, f: 72.1)
Religious affiliation (%): Christians 96.2 (Roman Catholics 92.0, Protestants 15.1, indigenous 3.9, marginal 1.3, other Christians 0.7), nonreligious 1.5, spiritists 1.4, other 0.9.

1. Colonial Age
2. Political Emancipation
3. Sandinista Revolution and the Roman Catholic Church
4. Protestantism
5. Ecumenical Relations

Nicaragua is the second largest of the eight countries considered by the United Nations to be part of "Central America" (after Mexico). Its population, however, is relatively small, giving it the second lowest population density (after Belize).

1. Colonial Age

After the Spanish conquest (1523) the original inhabitants of Nicaragua suffered under the tyranny of various governors, including Pedrarías Dávila and Rodrigo de Contreras. By forced labor in the encomienda system (e.g., in agriculture and in gold mines; → Latin America and the Caribbean 1.3), illegal enslavement, and the export of → slaves, the population dropped from 600,000 to 70,000, so that already by 1527 the Crown found itself compelled to send the clergyman Diego Alvarez Osorio (ca. 1485-1536, bishop from 1531), who was named protector of the Indians. Despite great efforts, however, Osorio enjoyed only partial success because of the opposition of the authorities and the colonists.

In 1536 Bartolomé de Las Casas (1484-1566) was prosecuted on account of his support for the Indians, and in 1550 there followed the murder of Antonio de Valdivieso (bishop 1544-50), who after 1544, helped by a few → Dominicans, → Franciscans, and secular clergy, had tried to build up the → church, promote its → mission, and care for the Indians. From the 17th century onward the church developed along more peaceful lines. → Evangelization was primarily in the hands of the Franciscans.

2. Political Emancipation

With the end of the United Provinces of Central America (1823-39), Nicaragua achieved its independence. The Conservative forces that ruled it from 1857 to 1893 concluded a → concordat with Rome in 1862, making Roman Catholicism the official religion and giving it many privileges. J. S. Zelaya, the first Liberal president (1893-1909), introduced a new constitution in 1894 that separated → church and state and guaranteed religious freedom. Protestant → mission now became possible, but sharp conflicts arose with the → Roman Catholic Church. In the period of Conservative → restoration (1911-28), Roman Catholics regained their social preeminence. They set up new schools, founded new dioceses, and met the growing respect for → Protestantism apologetically.

In the 19th and 20th centuries the independence of Nicaragua was constantly exposed to the threat of intervention or invasion with support from either the Conservatives or the Liberals. From the 18th century onward the Atlantic coast was a British protectorate as a result of treaties with the Miskito Indians. In 1860, however, Britain accepted Nicaraguan sovereignty.

The United States tried to oust the Liberal president Zelaya by supporting a Conservative revolt. When it failed, the threat of massive military intervention forced Zelaya out in 1909 for refusing to concede to the United States perpetual rights to a canal and to military bases. The United States secured these rights in 1916 with the Bryan-Chamorro Treaty, but only after suppressing a Liberal drive for independence in 1912 with American troops, which were stationed in Nicaragua until 1925. When the Liberals achieved military success in 1927, American marines landed again, but the worker-general Augusto César Sandino (1895-34) waged a successful campaign against them up to 1933.

In 1934, however, Sandino was murdered by the American-supported National Guard under Anastasio Somoza García (1896-1956), and the way was clear for the Somoza dictatorship, which was continued in the second generation by his sons Luis Anastasio Somoza Debayle (ruled 1957-63) and Anastasio Somoza Debayle (1963-79). Nicaragua became an economic preserve of the Somoza clan and the officers of the National Guard that guaranteed it militarily. When the economic situation, already poor because of mounting foreign debts and an oil crisis, worsened after a devastating earthquake in 1972 and the regime largely misappropriated the international contributions to earthquake relief, civilian resistance grew, with the murder of editor Pedro Joaquín Chamorro in 1978 the most dramatic event. Finally, in 1979 the war of liberation waged since 1961 by the partly Marxist and partly Christian Frente Sandinista de Liberación Nacional (FSLN, the Sandinista National Liberation Front) managed to topple Somoza.

3. Sandinista Revolution and the Roman Catholic Church

The Government Junta of National Reconstruction took over the government. In 1980, after three junta members had paid a visit to Pope John Paul II, a national literacy campaign received support from the Roman Catholic Church under Archbishop Miguel Obando y Bravo. In 1979 the Nicaragua Bishops' Conference, in a pastoral letter entitled "Revolution and Christian Faith," had unexpectedly expressed approval of the revolutionary process. In October 1980, in a communiqué on religious liberty, the leadership of the FSLN stated that the free exercise of religion is an inalienable human right in the full sense.

The basis of the church's positive attitude was the process of church renewal triggered by → Vatican II and Medellín (→ Latin American Councils 2.4). In this process many of the clergy pledged support for the poor. The result was stronger cooperation between the → clergy and laity, the founding of church → base communities, and the making of ecumenical contacts. From 1969 onward Christians from these circles had played a part in the FSLN's revolutionary struggle for liberation (→ Revolution). In 1979 four → priests held ministerial posts. This Christian involvement caused the bishops to begin distancing themselves from the Somoza dictatorship after 1970. In a series of important pastoral letters they made violations of human and civil → rights public, even though condemning the revolutionary struggle of the FSLN along with the oligarchy.

Important socioeconomic reforms came with the revolution. In education the literacy campaign was accompanied by free education at school and university and the promotion of popular culture. In health care, inoculation campaigns were undertaken, and a network of health-care centers was established for the poor. In housing both public housing and private ownership were advocated. In agriculture land reform went ahead, over two million hectares (five million acres) were redistributed, and cooperatives were founded.

In 1980 the FSLN imposed its majority in the State Council. The result was a middle-class exodus and official church withdrawal of support for the regime. In 1981 the United States ceased to give economic aid and imposed a trade embargo, at the same time giving support to the Contras in Honduras. The civil strife involved the death of some 25,000 people, the uprooting of another 35,000 on the Atlantic coast, and damage estimated at $12 billion. In the emergency conditions after 1982 the Miskito Indians were forcibly resettled to secure the border with Honduras, attacks were made upon the supporters and forms of traditional Roman Catholic piety by so-called *turbas divinas* (divine mobs), and priests were expelled.

The Roman Catholic Church itself did not suffer persecution. At first there was simply church-internal strife between (1) base communities, agrarian parishes, and their priests, who were all oriented to → liberation theology and favored the Sandinistas, and (2) the predominantly conservative episcopate, which received support from middle-class adherents of the → charismatic movement, new catechumens, most of the secular clergy, the → Latin American Council of Bishops (CELAM), and the → pope.

The introduction of conscription in 1983 sharp-ened the conflict with the official church. The pope's visit in the same year strengthened the hands of the bishops, who already in 1980 had demanded that the priests in the cabinet should resign. The struggle reached a climax in 1986 with the expulsion of ten priests and the president of the bishops' conference.

After the release of all political prisoners, free elections were held in 1990. They were won by a mixed opposition group of 15 parties under Violeta Chamorro, widow of the slain editor, who was elected president by popular vote. The election defeat took the FSLN completely by surprise. Agrarian reform was not secured by the issuing of property titles, nor were the houses of functionaries secure. Before the transfer of power there was a hectic appropriation of public goods (the "Piñata," or transfer of properties), which tainted the FSLN with the smell of corruption.

A stormy transition period followed under the presidency of Chamorro (1990-96). General Humberto Ortega was left as head of the armed forces in order to reduce and depoliticize the 100,000-member army. Far more difficult was the demobilization of the Contras, who were difficult to integrate and who repeatedly resorted to armed confrontation to emphasize their demands. Moreover, the exile lobby now pressed for a return of all property expropriated under the Sandinistas, property largely belonging to those who profited from the Somoza dictatorship.

The FSLN leadership refused any democratic openness with regard to both internal and external affairs (refusing dialogue with the civilian society) and clung instead to authoritarian centralism. When open dialogue was disallowed at the party congress of 1994 as well, dissatisfaction was so intense that the party split. The FSLN suffered defeat also in the election of 1996.

Despite strikes, the national economy was privatized, resulting in a dramatic increase in unemployment. Between 1990 and 1999 the number of agricultural cooperatives decreased from over 3,500 to fewer than 900. Although large property owners returned, they recovered only 25 percent of their property. The remaining property was given back to the demilitarized or transferred to workers. The FSLN supported the new government, not least in order to avoid an investigation of the transactions of the Piñata.

In 1996 right-leaning Arnoldo Alemán was elected, with the help of dissatisfied constituents of the FSLN. Then in October 1998 Hurricane Mitch decimated Nicaragua. It was the second-worst hurricane on record, affecting one-third of the country, injuring a million inhabitants, and killing thousands. This disaster exposed the enormous incompetence and corruption in the Alemán government and his Liberal Party (PLC), with its extreme neo-liberal politics. The general apathy of the political classes toward the fate of the masses was exposed when even the FSLN offered no effective plan for reconstruction.

The FSLN made gains in the local elections of November 2000 by joining forces with the Unidad Social Cristiana, although it lost the 2002 presidential elections.

4. Protestantism

The 1972 earthquake proved to be an intellectual turning point for Protestants that strengthened their identity. It gave them a social, national, and, to some extent, revolutionary awareness, with 15-20 percent supporting the revolution, 25 percent radically rejecting it, and 55 percent withholding judgment.

The strongest Protestant churches are the → Pentecostal churches, all with U.S. roots, led by the → Assemblies of God (220,000, founded 1912, independent from 1936; all figures that follow are based on estimates for persons affiliated in 1995; → Assembleias de Deus no Brasil), Church of God (Cleveland, 40,000), United Pentecostal Church (Jesus Only, 30,000), and Church of God of Prophecy (24,000).

Also significant are the Seventh-day → Adventists, founded in 1904, with almost 100 congregations and 52,000 members.

The Iglesia Morava (→ Moravians), founded in 1849, independent after 1974, is an Indian church. The Miskito and Rama comprise some 70 percent of the estimated 37,000 members. It is notable for medical and educational work but suffered very severely in the civil war of the 1980s. When the war ended, reconstruction went ahead vigorously to make good the previous losses.

The → Baptists, founded in 1917, independent after 1974, are leaders among Protestants in the social field. The National Baptist Convention of Nicaragua, which in 1995 had approximately 20,000 persons affiliated in 150 congregations, sponsors a seminary, a hospital, a residence for senior citizens, and five schools. The International Baptist Church also has 42 congregations with 9,000 members.

Among other churches of historic Protestantism are the Episcopal Church, with 7,300 affiliated, and the Evangelical Central American Mission (1900), with 5,800 affiliated. There are also churches comprising groups of Salvadoran refugees.

5. Ecumenical Relations

For ecumenical cooperation between Roman Catholics and Protestants, we must turn to progressive forces, such as the Antonio Valdivieso Ecumenical Center (with its journal *Amanecer* [Dawning], theological study, education, communications, and development projects), in which the hierarchy sees a "political ecumenism." The Evangelical Commission to Promote Social Responsibility (CEPRES, from 1980) gave largely uncritical support to the revolutionary process. Protestant cooperation after 1972 (earthquake relief) took institutional form in the Evangelical Committee for Development Aid (CEPAD). In 1990 this organization comprised 51 churches or congregations and 9 groups of pastors. It then assumed the character of an ecumenical institution, calling itself the Church Council for a Denominational Alliance. Its critically positive attitude to the revolution resulted in the 1989 withdrawal of the Assemblies of God, which for a long time had not been actively participating.

The National Committee of Evangelical Pastors (CNPEN) came into being to represent evangelicals and to distribute American financial aid. It increasingly took up a negative position vis-à-vis the revolution. The Interchurch Center for Theological and Social Studies (CIEETS), founded in 1985 by 30 Protestant communions and pastors' committees, serves the cause of pastoral training for the various Protestant churches. In 1988 the theological journal *Xilotl* was started, and in the same year the pastoral journal *Misión Evangélica*. CIEETS exerts itself to stimulate political and social involvement on the part of pastors; at a conference in 1986 it distributed a document entitled *The Central American Kairos*.

→ Latin American Theology

Bibliography: General situation: T. C. Brown, *The Causes of the Continuing Conflict in Nicaragua: A View from the Radical Middle* (Stanford, Calif., 1995); idem, *The Real Contra War: Highlander Peasant Resistance in Nicaragua* (Norman, Okla., 2001) • T. Cabestrero, *Blood of the Innocent: Victims of the Contras' War in Nicaragua* (New York, 1985) • D. Close, *Nicaragua: The Chamorro Years* (Boulder, Colo., 1999) • L. J. Enríquez, *Agrarian Reform and Class Consciousness in Nicaragua* (Gainesville, Fla., 1997) • E. Griffin-Nolan, *Witness for Peace: A Story of Resistance* (Louisville, Ky., 1991) • L. Horton, *Peasants in Arms: War and Peace in the Mountains of Nicaragua, 1979-1994* (Athens, Ohio, 1998) • K. Hoyt, *The Many Faces of Sandinista Democracy* (Athens, Ohio, 1997) • I. Lundgren, *Lost Visions and New Uncertainties: Sandinista "profesionales" in Northern Nicaragua* (Stockholm,

2000) • J. M. Paige, *Coffee and Power: Revolution and the Rise of Democracy in Central America* (Cambridge, Mass., 1997) • T. W. Walker, ed., *Nicaragua without Illusions: Regime Transition and Structural Adjustment in the 1990s* (Wilmington, Del., 1997).

Religious situation: R. Aragón and E. Löschke, *La iglesia de los pobres en Nicaragua* (Managua, 1991) • J. E. Arellano, *Breve historia de la iglesia en Nicaragua (1523-1979)* (2d ed.; Managua, 1986) • H. Belli, *Breaking Faith: The Sandinista Revolution and Its Impact on Freedom and Christian Faith in Nicaragua* (Westchester, Ill., 1985) • D. Berrigan, *Steadfastness of the Saints: A Journal of Peace and War in Central and North America* (New York, 1985) • B. Cortés, "Introducción a las periodizaciones históricas del protestantismo nicaragüense," *Reforma y conquista. América Latina 500 años después* (Managua, 1989) 165-82 • M. Dodson and L. N O'Shaughnessy, *Nicaragua's Other Revolution: Religious Faith and Political Struggle* (Chapel Hill, N.C., 1990) • D. Haslam, *Faith in Struggle: The Protestant Churches in Nicaragua and Their Response to the Revolution* (London, 1987) • C. Jerez, *The Church and the Nicaraguan Revolution* (London, 1984) • J. M. Kirk, *Politics and the Catholic Church in Nicaragua* (Gainesville, Fla., 1992) • R. N. Lancaster, *Thanks to God and the Revolution: Popular Religion and Class Consciousness in the New Nicaragua* (New York, 1988) • J. Mulligan, *The Nicaraguan Church and the Revolution* (Kansas City, Mo., 1991) • C. C. O'Brien, *Gott und der Prozeß der Befreiung. Kirche, Staat und Krieg in Nicaragua* (Hamburg, 1987) • H.-J. Prien, "Die Haltung der nichtkatholischen Kirchen zum Revolutionsprozeß in Nikaragua," *Das Evangelium im Abendland und in der Neuen Welt* (Frankfurt, 2000) 537-72; idem, "Zehn Jahre Christen und Revolution," *dü* 25 (1989) 68-71 • D. Sabia, *Contradiction and Conflict: The Popular Church in Nicaragua* (Tuscaloosa, Ala., 1997).

Hans-Jürgen Prien

Niceno-Constantinopolitan Creed

The term "Niceno-Constantinopolitan Creed" was first used in the 17th century (by J. B. Carpzov I) with a view to fixing the key dates in the development of what is commonly called the Nicene Creed (→ Confessions and Creeds). Early church → tradition found in this creed a confirmation and expansion of the dogmatic decision made at the Council of → Nicaea (325) and linked it to what took place when the "Synod of 150 Fathers" met at Constantinople in 381.

Neo-Protestantism (e.g., A. von Harnack [1851-1930]; → Protestantism), following the research of F. J. A. Hort (1828-92), questioned the tradition in two ways: by contesting the continuity between Nicaea and Constantinople and by finding in the Niceno-Constantinopolitan Creed an earlier symbol that the council in 381 simply accepted. Further textual study, however, especially of the records of → Chalcedon (451), rehabilitated the earlier view (E. Schwartz), and modern scholars, though with differing emphases, follow this line. The main decisions, it is believed, were taken already at → Alexandria in 362, at → Antioch in 379, and in the edict *Cunctos populos* of Theodosius in 380. The Council of Constantinople then found in Nicaea a standard of orthodoxy, but with a rejection also of any questioning of the deity of the → Holy Spirit (→ Trinity). Chalcedon validated this decision ecumenically.

More firmly than Nicaea, Constantinople took up the concern of Eusebius of Caesarea (d. ca. 340) that the common baptismal creed, rather than academic theses, should be the dogmatic → norm. For this reason the anathemas were dropped in 381, being put in a separate statement.

The Niceno-Constantinopolitan Creed follows the basic outline of the old Roman confession familiar to us as the → Apostles' Creed. It takes over from this confession the beliefs concerning the → incarnation and the passion, but it adds the *homoousion* statements of Nicaea, though leaving out "of the substance of the Father" (→ Christology), as was necessary now that a more precise distinction had been made between "substance" and → "person" in the Trinity. An addition is that the Holy Spirit, "who proceeds from the Father," is to be worshiped and glorified together with the Father and the Son.

The Niceno-Constantinopolitan Creed came into use in the Eucharist in 511 in the East, after 809 in Aachen, and from 1014 onward in Rome.

The addition "and from the Son" (→ Filioque), with reference to the proceeding of the Holy Spirit, was accepted by the Toledo Council of 589, Paulinus of Aquileia (ca. 730-802) in 796, and Charlemagne (800-814) and his theologians at the Synod of Aachen in 809. It triggered a Trinitarian controversy between Latin and Byzantine theology. The → popes at first opposed it, and attempts at reunion at Lyons (1274) and Florence (1439; → Union) proposed its elimination. In spite of modern reservations in the West, however, it still retains its place in Western usage.

Bibliography: T. A. Campbell, *Christian Confessions: A Historical Introduction* (Louisville, Ky., 1996) • J. N. D.

KELLY, *Early Christian Creeds* (3d ed.; New York, 1972) • M. H. MICKS, *Loving the Questions: An Exploration of the Nicene Creed* (Cambridge, Mass., 1993) • J. STEVENSON, ed., *Creeds, Councils, and Controversies: Documents Illustrating the History of the Church*, A.D. 337-461 (rev. ed.; London, 1989) • N. P. TANNER, ed., *Decrees of the Ecumenical Councils* (2 vols.; London, 1990) 1.21-36 • T. F. TORRANCE, *The Trinitarian Faith: The Evangelical Theology of the Ancient Catholic Church* (Edinburgh, 1988) • WORLD COUNCIL OF CHURCHES, *Confessing the One Faith: An Ecumenical Explication of the Apostolic Faith as It Is Confessed in the Nicene-Constantinopolitan Creed (381)* (Geneva, 1991).

WOLFGANG ULLMANN

Niebuhr, Reinhold

Karl Paul Reinhold Niebuhr (1892-1971), a North American → social ethicist, was born in Wright City, Missouri, the third child of German immigrants Gustav Niebuhr, a pastor, and his wife, Lydia (née Hosto). He studied theology at Elmhurst College near Chicago (1907-10), at Eden Theological Seminary in St. Louis (1910-13) — both of which were institutions of his denomination (which became part of the United Church of Christ) — and finally at the Divinity School of Yale University (1913-15). After his father died in April 1913, Niebuhr spent five months overseeing the latter's congregation in Lincoln, Illinois. His early sermons exhibit the kind of distance from theological doctrine typical of liberal Protestantism, a pronounced interest in social and economic problems, and a certain affinity for the → Social Gospel movement.

After earning his B.D. in 1914 and his M.A. in 1915, Niebuhr, supported by his mother, oversaw the Bethel Evangelical Church in Detroit until 1928. Worship services in this rapidly growing → congregation, whose members came largely from the middle class, were conducted in German until 1919, the language with which Niebuhr had grown up. During World War I Niebuhr helped with the Americanization of his German-American congregation.

Niebuhr debated issues associated with the social consequences of drastic production changes in Detroit, the center of the U.S. automobile industry. His varied activities were also undertaken under the influence of racial conflicts caused by the massive influx of workers. His works during this period include a diary published in 1929 under the title *Leaves from the Notebook of a Tamed Cynic,* as well as numerous newspaper articles. His first book, *Does Civilization Need Religion?* (1928), addresses the inability of liberal Protestantism to deal with modern class conflicts, whose complexity Niebuhr believed could be understood only through the establishment of conditions more congenial to mutual understanding.

In 1928 Niebuhr accepted an appointment from the Union Theological Seminary in New York City to a newly established chair for "applied Christianity." It was here that in 1930 he met his future wife, Ursula Keppel-Compton, a teacher of religion at Barnard College, also in New York. Niebuhr's book *Moral Man and Immoral Society* (1932) was understood as a renunciation of his → pacifist colleagues. Despite his intensive social activity, he distanced himself from the idea that human intervention could actualize God's reign. Niebuhr's lectures on W. → Rauschenbusch were published in 1935 under the title *An Interpretation of Christian Ethics.* In 1939 he delivered the Gifford Lectures at the University of Edinburgh; the lectures, published in 1941 and 1943 as *The Nature and Destiny of Man,* are considered by many to be his most important theological work. Later publications such as *The Irony of American History* (1952), *The Self and the Dramas of History* (1954), and *The Structures of Nations and Empires* (1959) attest Niebuhr's interest in American foreign policy and in a → theology of history. After a series of strokes in 1952, Niebuhr had to curtail his activities and in 1960 retired from teaching.

Niebuhr's assessment of religion, politics, and society attracted attention even outside the church because of its combination of political realism and a fine sense for the possibilities and limitations of human existence. He was a founder of Fellowship of Socialist Christians (1931), for which he founded the periodical *Radical Religion* (later renamed *Christianity and Crisis*), and also, after World War II, a founder of Americans for Democratic Action (1947).

Niebuhr was a popular preacher and speaker at church, academic, and political events, and he participated extensively in the founding of the → World Council of Churches. The differences between Niebuhr and Karl → Barth involve primarily issues of church politics. Niebuhr's theological significance derives from his having completed and even transcended American cultural Protestantism; in developing his own understanding of → sin and → grace as part of this endeavor, he also drew on the theology of → Augustine and the → Reformation. In America itself, his position in comparison to theological → liberalism might be described as neoorthodoxy, though one can understand it only with some qualification as an American counterpart of European → dialectical theology.

Bibliography: C. C. Brown, *Niebuhr and His Age: Reinhold Niebuhr's Prophetic Role in the Twentieth Century* (Philadelphia, 1992) • K. Durkin, *Reinhold Niebuhr* (London, 1989) • R. W. Fox, *Reinhold Niebuhr: A Biography* (New York, 1986) • L. B. Gilkey, *On Niebuhr: A Theological Study* (Chicago, 2001) • G. Harland, *The Thought of Reinhold Niebuhr* (New York, 1960) • R. W. Lovin, *Reinhold Niebuhr and Christian Realism* (Cambridge, 1995) • L. Rasmussen, ed., *Reinhold Niebuhr, Theologian of Public Life* (Cleveland, 1991) • D. B. Robertson, *Reinhold Niebuhr's Works: A Bibliography* (Lanham, Md., 1983) • R. H. Stone, *Professor Reinhold Niebuhr: A Mentor to the Twentieth Century* (Louisville, Ky., 1992).

Caroline Schröder

Niemöller, Martin

Martin Niemöller (1892-1984), a German Lutheran pastor, theologian, and ecumenist, grew up in Lippstadt and Elberfeld as the son of a pastor influenced by nationalistic Protestant ideas. After completing his secondary school education, he became an officer in the navy. During World War I he saw action in various capacities and at the end of the → war was a submarine commander. After the war he began an agricultural apprenticeship but then in 1919 began studying → theology in Münster. In 1920 Niemöller participated voluntarily in putting down the revolt of the so-called Red Army of the Ruhr. After passing his church examinations, he became the manager of the Westphalian → Inner Mission in 1924, and in 1931 he accepted a pastoral position in Berlin-Dahlem.

Niemöller consistently rejected the creation of the Weimar Republic and voted for the National Socialists as early as 1924, welcoming Hitler's seizure of power in 1933 and remaining loyal to Hitler even later. Nonetheless, from the beginning he opposed the efforts of the → German Christians to bring the Protestant church into organizational and ideological conformity, doing so publicly beginning in May/June 1933 as a member of the board of the Young Reformation Movement and as adjutant of the designated Reich bishop Friedrich von Bodelschwingh.

After the victory of the German Christians, Niemöller founded the Pastors' Emergency League in September 1933, whose more than 3,000 members (up to the end of 1933) rejected the "Aryan paragraphs" in the church as being contrary to the confession, pledging themselves instead to base

their own proclamation exclusively on the Bible and the confession. This Emergency League formed one of the most important sources for the emerging → Confessing Church, within which Niemöller represented the uncompromising position of complete dissociation from the Reich church, which was dominated by the German Christians, in accordance with the resolutions of the Dahlem Synod, held by the Confessing Church in October 1934. As such, and as the leading representative of those known as the Dahlemites, he came into conflict not only with the church policies of the state but also with those in the Confessing Church who were prepared to make confessional concessions to the politics of mediation advocated by Hanns Kerrl, Reich minister for church affairs (from 1935). The result was a split in the Confessing Church itself.

Despite his increasing isolation, Niemöller felt increasingly prompted to criticize the church policies of the Nationalist Socialist regime (→ Fascism), and thus he became a symbolic figure of church resistance. He was arrested in 1937, and although he was also quasi-acquitted in 1938, he nonetheless remained in custody in the concentration camp Sachsenhausen as a "personal prisoner" of Hitler, with whom he had already had an argument during a reception of German church representatives in January 1934. Niemöller unsuccessfully applied for active military service in 1939, and for a time even considered converting to Roman Catholicism because of the inner turmoil among Protestants. Apparently as an incentive to do so, he was transferred to Dachau in 1941 to be with three Roman Catholic priests. In 1945 Niemöller was liberated from the hands of a liquidation commando in South Tirol.

Niemöller occupied various positions of leadership in the newly formed Evangelical Church in Germany, including deputy council head (1945-49) and head of the Foreign Office (1945-56), but he was thwarted by confessional and territorial inertia in his attempt to implement a basic structural reform. From 1947 to 1964 he was president of the Hesse-Nassau regional church. He undertook numerous trips on behalf of ecumenical concerns and international understanding and in 1961 was elected one of the presidents of the → World Council of Churches. Despite this international recognition, however, Niemöller remained a disputed figure, especially because of his persistence in pursuing the topic of guilt commensurate with the Stuttgart Declaration of Guilt (1945) and the → Darmstadt Declaration (1947), his occasional polemical critique of the escalating cold war and of the nuclear arms race, and his trips to Communist countries.

Niemöller, who changed from a militaristic national Protestant into a → pacifist ecumenist, kept a certain distance from academic theology, considering simply → piety and straightforward → discipleship oriented toward the → Sermon on the Mount to be much more important. He considered the → Barmen Declaration (1934) to be a kind of summation of theology, against which confessional peculiarities were either secondary or anachronistic.

Bibliography: J. BENTLEY, *Martin Niemöller* (New York, 1984) • J. S. CONWAY, "The Political Theology of Martin Niemöller," *German Studies Review* 9 (1986) 529-46 • H. G. LOCKE, ed., *Exile in the Fatherland: Martin Niemöller's Letters from Moabit Prison* (Grand Rapids, 1986) • H. G. LOCKE and M. S. LITTELL, eds., *Remembrance and Recollection: Essays on the Centennial Year of Martin Niemöller and Reinhold Niebuhr and the Fiftieth Year of the Wannsee Conference* (Lanham, Md., 1996) • C. NICOLAISEN, "Niemöller, Martin," *BBKL* 6.735-48 • M. NIEMÖLLER, *"God Is My Fuehrer," Being the Last Twenty-eight Sermons by Martin Niemöller* (trans. J. Lymburn; New York, 1941) • M. SCHREIBER, *Martin Niemöller* (Reinbek, 1997).

THOMAS MARTIN SCHNEIDER

Nietzsche, Friedrich

Friedrich Nietzsche (1844-1900), a German philosopher and classical philologist, profoundly influenced generations of theologians, philosophers, psychologists, and writers through his attempt to expose the roots and motives of traditional Western → religion, moral thinking, and → philosophy. After the death of his father, who was a pastor, Nietzsche grew up surrounded by women and by the spirit of Protestant → piety. While studying classical philology in Bonn and Leipzig from 1864 to 1868, he became friends with the philologist Erwin Rhode and was introduced to Arthur Schopenhauer's philosophy. He was also drawn to the music of Richard Wagner, with whom he had spoken personally in Leipzig.

In 1869, after Nietzsche had published several smaller philosophical works, his teacher Friedrich Ritschl recommended him for a special professorship in Basel, where he had considerable contact with Wagner, the historian Jakob Burckhardt, and the theologian Franz Overbeck. The Franco-German war of 1870-71 abruptly interrupted Nietzsche's Basel period. He participated in the war as a medical orderly and never completed recovered from an illness he had during this period.

The *Birth of Tragedy out of the Spirit of Music* was published in 1872, a work in which Nietzsche thought he was able to establish the Apollonian (the harmonious, restrained) and the Dionysian (the irrational, passionate) as the driving principles in the life and art of antiquity. Reacting against Germany's acquisition of power after the war, in *Untimely Meditations* (4 vols., 1873-76) and *On the Use and Misuse of History* (1874) he turned against the prevailing spirit of the time, which he considered tainted by → historicism and cultural philistinism.

Nietzsche's break with Wagner in 1878 over the latter's *Parsifal* marks the transition to his second period. After extolling the ideal of excellence, he now engaged in radical → criticism, one witness to which is his writing *Human, All-Too-Human* (1878-80), which he dedicated to Voltaire. He received early retirement in 1879 as the result of a life-threatening illness, the recovery from which influenced his writing *The Dawn of Day* (1881) and *The Gay Science* (1882). After leaving Basel, he lived primarily in northern Italy. During this period, he wrote his main work, *Thus Spoke Zarathustra* (pts. 1-3, 1883-84; pt. 4, 1891), a poetic rendering of his own philosophical ideas. He was unable to complete the planned systematic presentation of his philosophy, which was to be called *The Will to Power: Attempt at a Revaluation of All Values.*

Nietzsche's last years were characterized by increasing isolation; the constant physical and psychological strain culminated dramatically in 1889 in Turin in a paralytic shock. Death brought an end to his semiconscious state in 1900 after his mother and sister had cared for him selflessly for 12 years.

In his main work Nietzsche developed the notion of the *Übermensch* (superman), a person who acknowledges the death of God and accepts the task of eliminating everything that is sickly, insincere, and hostile to life. This philosophy was supposed to replace → nihilism, which Nietzsche sensed would be the result of contemporary thinking. He thus directed his efforts against Christianity, which he felt produced only a "slave morality"; against the → bourgeoisie, whose morality he felt was profoundly insincere; and against the herd (→ Masses, The), which was a threat to everything that was noble and of higher value. He came to the basic conclusion that everything that is, is actually a manifestation of the will to → power. That is, there is no absolute being as such; being is found only in becoming, understood as an eternal recurrence of the same (→ Existentialism). Nietzsche was a brilliant stylist, a subtle psychologist, and a biting critic and pamphleteer. Putting himself philosophically on the side of feeling, instinct, will, and life, he exerted a profound influence in a variety of areas on those who came after him.

→ God Is Dead Theology

Bibliography: Primary sources: Basic Writings of Nietzsche (trans. W. Kaufmann; New York, 1968) • *The Birth of Tragedy* (trans. D. Smith; Oxford, 2000) • *The Complete Works of Friedrich Nietzsche* (18 vols.; ed. O. Levy; Edinburgh, 1909-13) • *Thus Spoke Zarathustra: A Book for All and None* (trans. W. Kaufmann; New York, 1978) • *Werke. Kritische Gesamtausgabe* (ca. 40 vols.; ed. G. Colli and M. Montinari; Berlin, 1967–).

Secondary works: S. D. HALES and R. WELSHON, *Nietzsche's Perspectivism* (Urbana, Ill., 2000) • R. HAY-MAN, *Nietzsche: A Critical Life* (New York, 1980) • A. J. HOOVER, *Friedrich Nietzsche: His Life and Thought* (Westport, Conn., 1994) • L. H. HUNT, *Nietzsche and the Origin of Virtue* (London, 1991) • W. KAUFMANN, *Nietzsche: Philosopher, Psychologist, Antichrist* (4th ed.; Princeton, 1974) • B. MAGNUS and K. HIGGINS, eds., *The Cambridge Companion to Nietzsche* (Cambridge, 1996) • H. W. REICHERT and K. SCHLECHTA, eds., *International Nietzsche Bibliography* (2d ed.; Chapel Hill, N.C., 1968) • R. SCHACHT, ed., *Nietzsche's Postmoralism: Essays on Nietzsche's Prelude to Philosophy's Future* (Cambridge, 2000) • R. C. SOLOMON and K. M. HIGGINS, *What Nietzsche Really Said* (New York, 2000).

MICHAEL LÖBL

Niger

	1960	1980	2000
Population (1,000s):	3,028	5,586	10,805
Annual growth rate (%):	3.79	3.36	3.17
Area: 1,287,000 sq. km. (496,900 sq. mi.)			

A.D. 2000

Population density: 8/sq. km. (22/sq. mi.)
Births / deaths: 4.68 / 1.52 per 100 population
Fertility rate: 6.54 per woman
Infant mortality rate: 105 per 1,000 live births
Life expectancy: 50.5 years (m: 48.8, f: 52.2)
Religious affiliation (%): Muslims 91.2, tribal religionists 8.1, other 0.7.

1. General Situation
2. Religious Situation

1. General Situation

The Republic of Niger, a landlocked country in West Africa, borders on Algeria and Libya to the north, Chad to the east, Nigeria and Benin to the south,

and Burkina Faso and Mali to the west. Europeans first entered Niger in the late 18th century, with the French making Niger part of French West Africa in 1904 (→ Colonialism). It became a colony within French West Africa (1922), an overseas territory of France (1946), an autonomous republic within the French community (1958), and an independent nation in 1960. After a military coup in 1974, Parliament was dissolved and a military council took over.

Niger held its first free elections in 1993. A Libya-backed Tuareg insurgency in the north, which began in 1990, was finally settled in 1995. Coups in 1996 and in April 1999 were followed by a return to civilian rule in December 1999.

The country suffered crippling droughts between 1967 and 1973, during which half of the nation's cattle were wiped out. The economy still has not recovered from this devastation.

In 1994 only 3 percent of the land was under permanent cultivation, 8 percent was meadows and pastures, and 2 percent was forests. The remaining 87 percent was largely desert. The economy is mainly agrarian, the main products being peanuts and vegetables. Uranium is Niger's principal export, though a collapse in the world uranium market in the 1980s has forced the government to develop other products. In 1999 they were primarily livestock (mostly cattle, sheep, and goats) and cowpeas.

Ethnically, Niger is home to three dozen different groups, the main ones being Hausa (56 percent), Djerma (22 percent), Fula (9 percent), and Tuareg (8 percent). In 1995 the literacy rate for persons 15 years of age and older was estimated at only 14 percent overall–21 percent of males and 7 percent of females.

2. Religious Situation

The main religion of Niger is → Islam (mostly Sunnis; → Sunna), which reached Niger from Dahomey (modern Benin) by the 11th century. Next most numerous are the adherents of traditional African religions (→ Guinea 2), who are found mostly in the south.

Christians form a very small → minority in Niger, where, alone in sub-Saharan Africa, their numbers have actually declined since 1960 (largely because of French expatriates leaving the country after independence). The → Roman Catholic Church gained a footing in 1931 and formed a → diocese in 1961. Some 95 percent of the Roman Catholics are foreigners, mainly from Europe, North America, Lebanon, Togo, Benin, and Burkina Faso. The largest group of Protestants, the Églises Évangéliques du Niger (5,500 affiliated in 1995), is a product of the work of the Sudan Interior Mission, which entered Niger in 1923. The Protestants operate a large hospital, a leprosarium, several clinics, and schools, as well as various other social service programs.

Under the 1993 constitution, Niger is a nonconfessional state and guarantees considerable freedom of religion. Missions encounter few legal restrictions.

→ African Theology

Bibliography: D. B. Barrett et al., eds., *WCE* (2d ed.) 1.546-48 • R. B. Charlick, *Niger: Personal Rule and Survival in the Sahel* (Boulder, Colo., 1991) • B. M. Cooper, *Marriage in Maradi: Gender and Culture in a Hausa Society in Niger, 1900-1989* (Portsmouth, N.H., 1997) • F. Fuglestad, *A History of Niger, 1850-1960* (Cambridge, 1983) • C. Lund, *Law, Power, and Politics in Niger: Land Struggles and the Rural Code* (Hamburg, 1998) • A. M. Masquelier, *Prayer Has Spoiled Everything: Possession, Power, and Identity in an Islamic Town of Niger* (Durham, N.C., 2001) • P. Stoller, *Embodying Colonial Memories: Spirit Possession, Power, and the Hausa in West Africa* (New York, 1995); idem, *Fusion of the Worlds: An Ethnography of Possession among the Songhay of Niger* (Chicago, 1989) • L. F. Zamponi, comp., *Niger* (Santa Barbara, Calif., 1994) bibliography.

THE EDITORS

Nigeria

	1960	*1980*	*2000*
Population (1,000s):	42,305	72,024	128,786
Annual growth rate (%):	2.80	2.85	2.73
Area: 923,768 sq. km. (356,669 sq. mi.)			

A.D. 2000

Population density: 139/sq. km. (361/sq. mi.)
Births / deaths: 3.97 / 1.25 per 100 population
Fertility rate: 5.48 per woman
Infant mortality rate: 70 per 1,000 live births
Life expectancy: 54.4 years (m: 52.8, f: 56.0)
Religious affiliation (%): Christians 45.8 (indigenous 17.6, Protestants 12.7, Roman Catholics 11.1, Anglicans 9.0, other Christians 0.7), Muslims 44.0, tribal religionists 9.9, other 0.3.

1. General Situation
2. Religious Situation
   2.1. Traditional Religion
   2.2. Islam
   2.3. Christianity
       2.3.1. Roman Catholic Church
       2.3.2. Protestants
       2.3.3. African Independent Churches
   2.4. Ecumenism and Dialogue
   2.5. Church and State

1. General Situation

The Federal Republic of Nigeria is the most populous country in Africa. Situated on the west coast of Africa, Nigeria is bounded on the north by Niger, on the east by Chad and Cameroon, and on the west by Benin; in the south it opens onto the Gulf of Guinea in the Atlantic Ocean. The original capital was Lagos, on the southwest coast, but in December 1991 the capital was officially moved to Abuja, in the center of the country.

English is the official language of administration. Nigerian languages number 520, corresponding to the 520 ethnicities. The main languages are Hausa, Yoruba, Igbo, Efik, Annang, Tiv, Kanuri, Ijaw, Beni, and Fulani.

British diplomatic links with Nigeria began in 1849, and in 1861 Lagos became a crown colony (→ Colonialism). The two protectorates of Northern and Southern Nigeria emerged in 1900, but they amalgamated in 1924 to form a single Nigeria. Nigeria became a federation in 1954, gained independence in 1960, and became a republic in 1963. Military rule obtained from 1966 to 1979, civilian rule from 1979 to 1983, then military rule again until 1999.

In 1999 Nigeria's external debt was a staggering $29 billion. Because Nigeria pays 20 percent of its earnings to creditor nations, and also because of the incompetence and corruption of past administrations, the massive income from crude oil and other petrochemical products has generally left untouched the poverty of most Nigerians. The agricultural sector, once producing enough food to feed the country, has failed to keep up with the rapid population growth and now must import foodstuffs.

2. Religious Situation

The main religions of Nigeria are the traditional tribal religions, → Islam, and Christianity. Sects include → Jehovah's Witnesses.

2.1. *Traditional Religion*

Traditional religions, followed by most Nigerians before Christianity and Islam, continue to be influential among both Muslims and Christians. The central belief is in the Supreme Being, for whom the tribes have different names. The best known are Olodumare (Yoruba), Chukwu (Igbo), Abasi Ibom (Efik, Annang, Ibibio), Soko (Nupe, Gbari), Kashiri (Binawa, Butawa, Dungi), and Owo (Igala). Tribal divinities (→ Tribal Religions), who are in constant relationship with the Supreme Being, stand in high regard with the people. Ancestral spirits (→ Ancestor Worship) occupy a third place in the theocratic governance of the universe. Each clan has a distinguishing → totem symbol. Traditional religion places special emphasis on consultation of ancestors and divinities in times of crisis. It is now being studied in Nigerian universities.

2.2. *Islam*

Islam is practiced mostly in the north of Nigeria, but it also influences the West and the middle belt. Entering Nigeria in the 9th century from North Africa, Islam became the official state religion in the north by the end of the 14th century. It enjoyed a peaceful spread until the Fulani emigrants launched a jihad lasting from 1803 to 1831, which established Fulani hegemony in the north (lasting till today), unified the Hausa states, and made Sokoto the caliphate and the focal point of Islamic religion and politics in Nigeria.

The Islamic leadership influences government decisions in Nigeria. The government supports pilgrimages to Mecca and has established Shariʿa courts for Muslims. Islam strives for the cultural unity of the tribes under its control and influences government decisions. The Universities of Zaria and Kano are cultural centers for its spread. Sunni Muslims of the Malikite rite are the most prevalent (→ Sunna), though Shiites (→ Shia, Shiites) are present as well. The three Sufi brotherhoods of Qādirīyah, Tijānīyah, and Aḥmadīyah are also influential.

In the 19th century all the north was forcibly Islamized, and from 1963 to 1965 the northern state government enforced Islam in other states. Islamic schools are active in the winning of converts (→ Conversion), and → mosques have been built throughout Nigeria. Abuja, the new capital, is the declared center for Islam in Africa.

2.3. *Christianity*

A little less than half of all Nigerians practice Christianity. In the year 2000 a total of 2,079 different denominations existed in Nigeria (*WCE* [2d ed.] 2.839), the majority of which are → Independent Churches.

2.3.1. *Roman Catholic Church*

The → Roman Catholic Church came to Nigeria first. Already in 1487 Portuguese missionaries had visited Benin and Warri, but success came only in the 19th century. The Société des Missions Africaines sent missionaries from Lyons to Lagos in 1861, the Holy Ghost Fathers landed in the east in 1885, and the St. Patrick Irish Fathers joined them in 1932.

The church suffered severe setbacks in the civil (Biafran) war of 1967-70, which involved massacres of Ibo in the north, Biafra's declaration of independence in the east, army intervention, and the final capitulation of Biafra. Many Roman Catholics were among the 30,000 who were slaughtered in the north and the million who fled to the east.

→ Catholicism forms the single largest Christian denomination in Nigeria. In 1997 there were 32 dioceses, grouped in three metropolitan provinces. The 25 male and 40 female congregations (→ Religious Orders and Congregations), in cooperation with diocesan clergy and religious, are outstanding in social and educational services. In 1990 there were 416 → missionary priests, 1,477 local clergy, 1,361 brothers in orders, and 354 missionary sisters at work in Nigeria. The Nigerian church itself is now a missionary-sending church.

2.3.2. *Protestants*

The percentage of Anglicans (→ Anglican Communion) in Nigeria is the second highest among all African countries (behind only Uganda). In 1845 the Church Missionary Society (CMS; → British Missions) started work in Badagry, near Lagos. It extended its work to the north in 1857. In 1893 the Sudan Interior Mission sent missionaries from Britain under CMS auspices, but they met with dogged opposition from the emirs and British administrators. In 1888 the CMS moved to Onitsha on the Niger River, with Samuel Adjai Crowther (ca. 1807-91) as bishop. The Anglophone West African Province of the CMS was formed in 1952, and in 1979 the Nigerian Province was created with 11 dioceses under local bishops.

Methodists (→ Methodist Churches) came to Nigeria in 1842. With the arrival of Primitive Methodists at Calabar in 1893 from the Spanish island of Fernando Póo, they extended their work to the south. The Methodist patriarch resides in Lagos and is overall head of the church in Nigeria. All the bishops are indigenous.

The Southern Baptists (→ North American Missions) came to the Yoruba region from the United States in 1850. The Yoruba Baptist Association, now the Nigerian Convention, was formed in 1914. Like the CMS and the Methodists, the → Baptists serve Nigeria not only with → evangelism but also with schools, hospitals, and social agencies.

The work of the Belfast Interdenominational Mission led to the founding of the Qua Iboe Church. Calabar was the first port of arrival of the Jamaican Presbyterian missionaries (→ Reformed and Presbyterian Churches) in 1846. The United Presbyterian Church of Scotland soon followed, and the Canadian Presbyterians joined them in 1954. An

Irish missionary to Nigeria, Hope Waddell (1804-95), and Mary Slessor (1848-1915), a great name in Nigerian and Scottish circles, who stopped the killing of twins in Nigeria, have made the Presbyterians warmly cherished.

Many smaller Protestant agencies poured into Nigeria, including the above-mentioned Sudan Interior Mission (1893), which established the Evangelical Church of West Africa, the Sudan United Mission (1903), the Seventh-day → Adventists (1914), the → Salvation Army (1920), the Lutherans (1931; → Lutheran Churches), the Apostolic Church from Britain (1931), the Assemblies of God (1939), and the Church of Jesus Christ (1953).

2.3.3. African Independent Churches

In the year 2000 the African Independent Churches, with a strong emphasis on → healing, → dreams, and Pentecostal features (→ Pentecostal Churches), represent over one-sixth of the total population of Nigeria. An early example was the Native Baptist Church, which broke away from the Southern Baptist Church in Lagos in 1888. In 1901 the African Church left the CMS over the replacement of an African bishop by a European CMS bishop. The Christ Army Church followed in 1915. The United African Methodist Church split off from the Methodists in 1917. The Aladura churches started in 1914 as praying bands to counteract the influenza that was then ravaging West Africa.

Independents have been most numerous in Protestant environments, especially among the Annang and Ibibio. Numerous American denominations are widely present. The Church of the Lord (Aladura) is a member of the → World Council of Churches.

2.4. Ecumenism and Dialogue

→ Ecumenism has promoted interchurch → dialogue and cooperation. The Christian Council of Nigeria (→ National Councils of Churches) was formed in 1930 by the main Protestant churches, the Christian Association of Nigeria in 1976 by Protestants and Roman Catholics, the Nigerian Association of the Aladura Churches in 1960, and the Fellowship of Churches of Christ in Nigeria in 1955 for Independent Churches.

Ten interreligious dialogues between Christians and Muslims took place between 1957 and 1982 (→ Islam and Christianity). At the university level, Christian and Muslim intellectuals formed the Nigerian Association for the Study of Religions, which meets yearly for interreligious dialogue and publishes the journal *Religions*.

The Shari'a crises in the country (see 2.5) led to the formation in 1999 of the Nigeria Inter-religious Council, cochaired by the sultan of Sokoto and the president of the Christian Association of Nigeria. Composed of 25 Christians and 25 Muslims, the council aims to promote communication and dialogue between the country's two main, rival religions. Plans exist for establishing the council at the state and local government levels.

The two religions often behave like uncomfortable bedfellows, with a period of peaceful coexistence followed all too often by serious religious riots. In March 1998 the pope met with Muslim leaders during his visit to Nigeria, and peace was seemingly assured. Before long, however, the nation was plunged into the Shari'a crisis, with the attendant protests and deaths.

2.5. Church and State

After the civil war (1967-70) many Christian missionaries were expelled from eastern Nigeria, and the entry of new ones was restricted. After 1988, however, the entry of missionaries was permitted, though it was regulated on a quota basis per denomination. Over half of Nigerian primary and postprimary schools are related to Christian missions. Missions opened the schools and ran them with government permission and partial subsidy. After the civil war, however, schools were nationalized in the east and west and parts of the north.

Christians feel that the government does not treat all religions equally. They cite the refusal of permission to build Christian churches in the north, the biased appointments to top government posts, and Nigeria's membership in the Organization of Islamic Conferences (OIC). The OIC issue created such tension that the federal government in 1987 set up an Advisory Council on Religious Affairs composed of Christians and Muslims, but with only an advisory competence.

The Nigerian constitution of 1999 guarantees → religious liberty, including the freedom to change one's religion and to propagate it, though with certain restrictions. Respect for religious liberty suffered in 2000 and 2001, however, through the implementation of an expanded version of Muslim Shari'a law in several northern states. Riots in Kaduna State that cost the lives of 3,500 people resulted from this action.

Shari'a was made compulsory in key states in the north for Muslims. In Zamfara State, for example, convicted thieves have had a hand amputated, and women convicted of immoral sexual relations have been flogged. Christians have complained of discriminatory treatment that the new constitution expressly forbids, and many have left the states with Shari'a for other, nonbelligerent parts of the country. So far, the federal government has been unable to persuade the northern states to abandon Shariʿa.

A nettlesome issue at the turn of the century is the fact that Nigeria's democratically elected president, Olusegun Obasanjo, is a Christian, the first such elected to the highest office since independence (exclusive of the period during the Biafran war). Previous leaders, both civilian and military, have all come from the north. Many see the Shariʿa issue as an attempt by the Muslim north to destabilize Obasanjo's administration.

→ African Theology

Bibliography: On 1: A. ADEDEJI, Nigeria: Renewal from the Roots? The Struggle for Democratic Development (London, 1997) • J. F. A. AJAYI, Tradition and Change in Africa (ed. T. Falola; Trenton, N.J., 2000) • T. FALOLA, Culture and Customs of Nigeria (Westport, Conn., 2001); idem, Development Planning and Decolonization in Nigeria (Gainesville, Fla., 1996); idem, The History of Nigeria (Westport, Conn., 1999) • J. O. IHONVBERE and T. M. SHAW, eds., Illusions of Power: Nigeria in Transition (Trenton, N.J., 1998) • U. B. INAMETE, Foreign Policy Decision Making in Nigeria (Selinsgrove, Pa., 2001) • P. E. LOVEJOY and P. A. T. WILLIAMS, eds., Displacement and the Politics of Violence in Nigeria (Leiden, 1997) • J. OKPAKA, ed., Nigeria: Dilemma of Nationhood. An African Analysis of the Biafran Conflict (New York, 1974) • E. E. OSAGHAE, Crippled Giant: Nigeria since Independence (Bloomington, Ind., 1998) • J. PETERS, The Nigerian Military and the State (London, 1997).

On 2.1: E. I. METUH, ed., The Gods in Retreat: Continuity and Change in African Religions (the Nigerian Experience) (Enugu, Nigeria, 1986).

On 2.2: D. S. GILLILAND, African Religion Meets Islam: Religious Change in Northern Nigeria (Lanham, Md., 1986) • R. LOIMEIER, Islamic Reform and Political Change in Northern Nigeria (Evanston, Ill., 1997).

On 2.3: J. F. A. AJAYI, Christian Missions in Nigeria, 1841-1891: The Making of a New Elite (London, 1965) • E. A. AYANDELE, The Missionary Impact on Modern Nigeria, 1842-1914: A Political and Social Analysis (London, 1966) • E. P. T. CRAMPTON, Christianity in Northern Nigeria (3d ed.; London, 1979) • P. N. DOM NWACHUKWU, Authentic African Christianity: An Inculturation Model for the Igbo (New York, 2000) • K. ENANG, African Experience of Salvation (2d ed.; London, 1987); idem, Nigerian Catholics and the Independent Churches (Immensee, 2000) • N. KASTFELT, Religion and Politics in Nigeria: A Study in Middle Belt Christianity (London, 1994) • M. C. KITSHOFF, ed., African Independent Churches Today: Kaleidoscope of Afro-Christianity (Lewiston, N.Y., 1996) • A. O. MAKOZI and G. J. A. OJO, eds., The History of the Catholic Church in Nigeria (Lagos, 1982) • G. C. OOSTHUIZEN and I. HEXHAM, eds., Empirical Studies of African Independent/Indigenous Churches (Lewiston, N.Y., 1992) • E. B. UDOH, Guest Christology: An Interpretative View of the Christological Problem in Africa (Frankfurt, 1988).

On 2.4: V. CHUKWULOZIE, Muslim-Christian Dialogue in Nigeria (Ibadan, 1986) • S. O. ILESANMI, Religious Pluralism and the Nigerian State (Athens, Ohio, 1997).

KENNETH ENANG

Nihilism

The background of "European nihilism" (F. → Nietzsche) is first the biblical doctrine of → creation ex nihilo by the God who remains faithful to his word, and then the nihil privativum of → mysticism. Medieval metaphyics understood the annihilatio of all things as a purely conceptual notion in the sense of God's absolute power. With the recasting of knowledge in mathematics (e.g., see R. Descartes), the scientific reconstruction of the world from → numbers, figures, and movement became a political project (T. Hobbes). It is worth noting that this recasting of knowledge was accompanied by the introduction of zero, the Indian-Arabic null symbol, or cipher (MLat. cifra, from Arab. ṣifr, "empty").

I. Kant (1724-1804; Kantianism) suggested that the entirety of the world in and for itself is nothing except to the extent it exists through the will of an other. F. H. Jacobi (1743-1819) opposed this revolutionary position (held also by J. G. Fichte), which effectively reduces all of reality to a construction of the ego. In his history of → philosophy, G. W. F. Hegel (1770-1831; → Hegelianism) posits an → "atheism of the moral world" based on the mystical experience of absolute nothingness in the liberated, purified "unhappy consciousness" that → God is dead.

Nihilism as a manifestation of excessive self-relatedness and self-gratification soon became the ironic and frivolous worldview attributed to the social outsiders portrayed in literature from F. Hölderlin (1770-1843), the anonymous Nachtwachen des Bonaventura (The night watches of Bonaventura, 1805), F. Schlegel (1772-1829), L. Tieck (1773-1853), to E. T. A. Hoffmann (1776-1822). Jean Paul (1763-1825) diagnosed a type of artistic nihilism concerned solely with the "sphere of free-play within nothingness." Soon, however, the dark side of this interim sphere between being and nonbeing began to emerge, since "where there are no gods, ghosts rule" (Novalis). A kind of "therapeutic nihilism" developed in medicine that sought healing in (anatomical) research rather than in a traditional course of treatment (Joseph Dietl in Vienna, ca. 1845). A critique of the Bible and of religion alongside a growing trust in → science formed the background for an increasingly radical, social-revolutionary pathos that in Russia generated a revolutionary movement from within a literary-critical discussion carried on since Pushkin (cf. I. S. Turgenev's *Fathers and Sons* [1862]). F. M. Dostoyevsky (1821-81) exemplifies a disposition obsessed by the "demon of irony."

The pessimism of A. Schopenhauer (1788-1860; → Optimism and Pessimism), often called → pantheistic nihilism and shaped by his sense of the emptiness and suffering of life, provided one of the points of departure for Nietzsche's understanding of the death of God. The unnerving realization that "there is no truth" results in a "devaluation of the ultimate values" and thence to the "no of action," the ecstatic overcoming of nihilism in an attempt to "revalue all values." The "absurd negation" of what is, of being as such in Nietzsche's "perfect nihilism," leads M. Heidegger (1889-1976) to recognize the essence of nihilism in history, where being itself is nothing. Heidegger demands that one consider the "absence of being in precisely that which it claims to be from within itself" (→ Existentialism).

After World War I nihilism is experienced as a "value vacuum" (H. Broch); in response, attempts are made to rouse a consciousness of → responsibility (W. Rathenau). An increasing number of thinkers view nihilism as the normal state of affairs. G. Benn (1886-1956) places his hopes in a "feeling of form," while C. Schmitt (1888-1985) puts his faith in decision "born from nothingness"; E. Jünger (1895-1998) considers it imperative that we experience the "enormous power of nothingness" in ourselves. In response to S. Beckett, T. Adorno (1903-69) defends "what is reproached as nihilism" against the false attempt to overcome it.

Nihilism became the guiding notion, an (architectural) project in aestheticism from *l'art pour l'art* (art for art's sake) to a dadaist admixture of art and life to the seemingly demonic self-annihilation of the totalitarian-political dimension. Associations have long been made between absurdity, boredom, ennui, demoralization, emptiness, and the feeling of incapacity attaching to loneliness. The seemingly circular "computational rationality" generated a widespread consciousness of → progress having gone astray. Nihilism triumphs in its "sociopolitical incarnation," which makes one unable to acknowledge that there is a world beyond humankind (H. Corbin). In view of the unique destructive capacity that characterized the 20th century (most pointedly in the → Holocaust) and its society trapped in → historicism and mathematical precision, recourse is found only in the notion of a "solidarity of the distressed" (J. Patocka).

→ Anarchy; Idealism; Materialism; Skepticism

Bibliography: T. W. ADORNO, *Negative Dialectics* (New York, 1973; orig. pub., 1966) • D. BONHOEFFER, "Inheritance and Decay," *Ethics* (ed. E. Bethge; New York, 1965) 88-109 • M. CACCIARI, *Architecture and Nihilism: On the Philosophy of Modern Architecture* (New Haven, 1993) • H. CORBIN, *Le paradoxe du monothéisme* (Paris, 1981) • P. E. DEVINE, *Relativism, Nihilism, and God* (Notre Dame, Ind., 1989) • J. C. EDWARDS, *The Plain Sense of Things: The Fate of Religion in an Age of Normal Nihilism* (University Park, Pa., 1997) • F. J. EVANS, *Psychology and Nihilism: A Genealogical Critique of the Computational Model of Mind* (Albany, N.Y., 1993) • M. A. GILLESPIE, *Nihilism before Nietzsche* (Chicago, 1995) • A. GLUCKSMANN, *Dostoiewski à Manhattan* (Paris, 2002) • M. HEIDEGGER, "Das Wesen des Nihilismus," *Gesamtausgabe* (vol. 67/2; Frankfurt, 1999) • E. JÜNGER, *Über die Linie* (Frankfurt, 1952) • I. KANT, *Versuch den Begriff der negativen Größen in die Weltweisheit einzuführen* (Königsberg, 1763) • R. KAPLAN, *The Nothing That Is: A Natural History of Zero* (New York, 2000) • H. K. KOHLENBERGER, "Annihilation," *HWP* 1.333-34 • R. RORTY, *Contingency, Irony, and Solidarity* (Cambridge, 1989) • J.-P. SARTRE, *Being and Nothingness: A Phenomenological Essay on Ontology* (New York, 1966; orig. pub., 1943).

HELMUT KOHLENBERGER

Nineteenth- and Twentieth-Century Theology → Theology in the Nineteenth and Twentieth Centuries

Noah

Noah is a widely attested legendary figure from → primeval history (Genesis 1–11) of unknown, pre-Israelite origin. The Priestly Adamite genealogy in Genesis 5 introduces him in tenth position as the son of Lamech (→ Pentateuch). A non- or pre-Priestly redactor in Gen. 5:29 interprets his name as meaning "one who brings relief" (from *nḥm* Pi., "comfort"), though a connection with the verb *nwḥ*, "rest," seems more likely. The original etymology is probably irretrievable.

Noah's most important role is found in the flood narrative (Genesis 6–8). There he is the "righteous man" (6:9, also 7:1) who, together with his family, is saved from destruction and thus ensures the continuation of → life after the flood. Although the legendary material has been fused together by Yahwistic and Priestly redactors into the present account, it originally comes from Mesopotamia, where it is attested in cuneiform witnesses, including especially the older Epic of Atrahasis and the later Gilgamesh Epic (tablet 11), the flood hero being Atrahasis or Utnapishtim. The Priestly redactor theologically enhances the end of the flood narrative into a great new beginning by introducing the Noachian → covenant (9:1-17; cf. the Yahwistic version in 8:21-22). The renewal of the → blessing of → creation and the permission to eat the meat of properly slaughtered → animals is underscored by God's eternally valid → promise, symbolized by the rainbow, never again to devastate the world through a flood.

The ensuing legend of Noah as the first vintner and simultaneously as the first victim of inebriation lacks both substantive and literary unity and derives from a different (earlier?) tradition documenting the bestowal of primeval blessing and → curse upon the peoples of Israel (Shem, Japheth) and Canaan (Ham; Gen. 9:18-27). The original Yahwistic version of primeval history probably included neither this nor the earlier figure of Noah with the accompanying legends. Not surprisingly, the figure of Noah did not exert much influence in the rest of the OT (mentioned only in Isa. 54:9; Ezek. 14:14, 20; 1 Chr. 1:4).

Bibliography: L. R. BAILEY, *Noah: The Person and the Story in History and Tradition* (Columbia, S.C., 1989) • N. R. C. COHN, *Noah's Flood: The Genesis Story in Western Thought* (New Haven, 1996) • T. FRETHEIM, "The Book of Genesis," NIB 1.319-674 • V. HAMILTON, *The Book of Genesis, Chapters 1–17* (Grand Rapids, 1990) • W. G. LAMBERT and A. R. MILLARD, *Atra-ḫasīs: The Babylonian Story of the Flood* (Oxford, 1969) • C. OCHS, *The Noah Paradox: Time as Burden, Time as Blessing* (Notre Dame, Ind., 1991) • J. B. PRITCHARD, ed., ANET (3d ed.) 93-97, 104-6, 265-317, 512-14 • G. VON RAD, *Genesis* (Philadelphia, 1961) • E. A. SPEISER, *Genesis* (Garden City, N.Y., 1964) • C. WESTERMANN, *Genesis* (3 vols.; Minneapolis, 1984) vol. 1.

HERMANN SPIECKERMANN

Nomads

1. Definition

The → word "nomad" is derived from Latin through Gk. *nemō*, meaning either "pasture" or "distribute." The simplest definition of a nomad is a person who must keep moving to gain basic life sustenance. Nomadism is usually the product of a sparse → environment, weather patterns (sometimes seasonal), or economic or political shifts making mobility essential for survival. It does not properly apply to immigrants, those who move from one dwelling place to another for convenience, promotion, or escaping unpleasantness. Nor is it appropriate as the term for → refugees, those who are forcibly expelled from their homes by → war or political oppression. True nomads are wanderers who have no fixed home; the constant mobility defines their title.

2. Major Types

Modern studies indicate three major types of nomads. Our most ancient ancestors were *nomadic hunters or gatherers.* Forced by the availability and patterns of wild game, wild herbs, roots, fruits, and nuts to forage and hunt for food wherever the supplies could be located, Paleolithic, Mesolithic, and Neolithic nomads largely were of this type. The most ancient nomads followed the food as the Ice Age formations melted. The retreating ice allowed plant growth and fodder to occur further north from the ice's former southern extremities. Depending on the climate and location, they may have moved daily; in more lush climates, seasonally or semiannually. Their shelter was largely natural cave formations or overhangs of cliffs. Their tools for hunting and food preparation were largely stone implements — spear points, knives, and scrapers, with an occasional grinder for preparations of wild grain found en route.

A second type is *pastoral nomads,* who appear when the first domestication of animals is successful. Their herds — first sheep and goats, later cattle — needed forage and water to survive. The nomadic routes were planned to find forage, water, and some kind of haven wherever they moved. The range of a day's travel was limited to the duration the animals could tolerate, still feed, and not suffer. Among modern tribes of such nomads, such as the Bedouin populations of the Middle East, territorial claims have developed, especially for good water sources. If water flow from a spring or well is dependable year-round, it tends to be a prime site for village settlement. Nomads, though, may still stop there for nourishment on their route, as they do in parts of the Middle East. Biblical accounts suggest that the patriarchal period of Israelite history especially reflects such mobility patterns (see 3).

A third type is *tinker or trader nomads*. These people lived on the fringes of larger societies because of their access to specialized materials (e.g., metal ore) that they crafted into products desired by members of the more stable societies. They traveled between two poles: the sources of their raw materials, and the populations willing to pay for their products. The availability of copper, silver, tin, and gold was limited to sparse sources in the Middle East. Similarly with the development of bronze as an alloy and iron tools, which were superior to bronze for both military and agricultural purposes, the sources and the markets governed the nomadic routes. While barter was the primary mode of early trade, exchange of goods yielded to token currency within a zone in which it was acceptable. Capacity to trade in more than one medium simply extended the nomadic capacity to provide goods to broader territory. Their value in providing labor may have followed seasonal crop life, as with modern migrant farm laborers, or rotated along a regular pattern where either crop or animal care required seasonal labor to accomplish certain tasks before losses were incurred.

Biblical texts reflect aspects of all three major types. The main type evident is the pastoral nomad. They are portrayed as → family or clan organizations, moving flocks of sheep, goats, or donkeys. The animals provided food, material for tents, milk and cheese, and transport or (in the case of donkeys) trade. From about 1200 B.C. camels were acquired, allowing much further travel across forbidding desert terrain. The partnership of families on such nomadic travels was partly to enhance security (no one makes it alone in the desert), partly to share labor (children learned to tend flocks at early ages), and partly to preserve domestic identity. The elder male of the tribe would be responsible not only for managing defense and finding the routes to needed sources of food, water, and shelter but also for transmitting the identity of the tribe through the stories of historical exploits, hazards endured, heroic performances, villainous behavior, and unique occasions of blessing or difficulty.

The requisites of mobile housing, easily portable on donkeys or camels, meant that baggage was kept to a minimum and focused on what was essential for defense, food preparation, and trade. Tribal alliances could be struck to meet severe threats by opponents, but the genius of nomadic life was the freedom to move when and where one decided, unless hostility required emergency measures.

3. Modifications

The most conspicuous modification of the purely nomadic life in biblical times continues in use today in the Middle East and in other regions of the world. Anthropologists have called it the dimorphic nomadic life, referring to the combination of temporary settled existence with a seasonal wandering. We thus read stories of the → patriarchs settling down for a time, with a base of operations from which they depart either seasonally or with some other regularity (e.g., the experiences of Abraham and Lot around Bethel, Gen. 13:1-12).

In their settled state, as with some modern Bedouin, such nomads may live in a modest stone or mud-brick house near a cave or other shelter for their flocks during the cold and rainy seasons of late fall and early spring. They may even plant a crop of winter grain on some convenient plot, but their main life support is the flocks of the pastoral nomadic root. With the heat that ripens the grain for harvest by May comes the diminishing of grass for grazing and the likely shortage of water from springs that dry up as the rainy season ends. This change leads the family to pack for travel in the hot summer months to a variety of locations where they can find grazing for their flocks, water for the flocks and themselves, and some refuge in case of hostilities. Otherwise they live in the open in their tents, moving their flocks as the grazing runs out; in this way they preserve life another year.

The nomads' travels may also take them to the fringes of settled agricultural communities, especially after the grain there is cut. They will negotiate the rights to have their flocks graze the stubble fields, providing the landowner with the benefit of natural fertilizer left as the grazing herd moves through. For the nomads, the benefit is doubled by the access to communal water supplies (springs, wells, or cisterns) that do not dry up. Traveling by night, with moonlight to guide, and camping by morning on agreed and permitted locations meant that tents would appear one morning, stay a few days or a week, and then disappear overnight, as the needs to move drove them. Even such brief encampments allowed social life, like a wedding, to occur during a stop. The new familial lines would then be reflected in who did the packing and who formed living partnerships for the balance of the trip.

4. Contemporary Manifestations

Nomadic life still exists in various countries around the world, including Africa (notably in Ethiopia, Mauritania, and Somalia), Asia (esp. in India, Mongolia, and Russia), northern Europe (the Lapps in northern Scandinavia), the Middle East (in Saudi Arabia, Iran, Iraq, and Jordan), North America (some Apache groups), and South America (e.g., shellfish gatherers in Chile; hunters, gatherers, and fishermen in Paraguay and Brazil; forest hunters and gatherers in Bolivia, Paraguay, and Brazil; and aquatic nomads such as the Guató in Paraguay).

Bibliography: D. BRADBUND, "Nomads and Their Trade Partners: Historical Context and Trade Relations in Southern Iran," *American Ethnologist* 24 (1997) 895-919 • A. M. KHAZANOV, *Nomads and the Outside World* (2d ed.; Madison, Wis., 1994) • R. B. LEE and I. DEVORE, eds., *Man the Hunter* (Chicago, 1968) • A. RAO, ed., *The Other Nomads: Peripatetic Minorities in Cross-Cultural Perspective* (Cologne, 1987) • P. ROBBINS, "Nomadization in Rajasthan, India: Migration, Institutions, and Economy," *Human Ecology* 26 (1998) 87-112 • M. SAHLINS, *Stone Age Economics* (London, 1974) • E. R. SERVICE, "Nomadic Societies," *NEBrit* (1986 ed.) 16.881-83 • N. THAYER, "Nomad's Land: Herdsmen Confront New Economic Order," *Far Eastern Economic Review* 160 (1997) 21-22.

ROGER S. BORAAS

Nominalism

1. Origin and Nature of Nominalism
2. Nominalism in Philosophy
3. Nominalism in Theology

1. Origin and Nature of Nominalism

The original use of the term "nominalism" was in the context of disputes in medieval → Scholasticism about the metaphysical status of universals and about the epistemological status of universal terms and their correlative concepts. Issues raised there are perennial ones that also played a part in philosophical debates both before and after the scholastic era, though they are not always defined exactly as they were by the nominalists and their opponents.

Aristotle (384-322 B.C.) in his *Categories* discussed how we use names or terms to speak of subjects or substances and their characteristics. Porphyry (ca. 232-ca. 303) wrote his *Isagoge* (Introduction) to this text, which Boethius (ca. 480-524) translated into Latin with commentary (→ Aristotelianism 2). This material, which passed into later European philosophy as it rediscovered the Aristotelian corpus, raised a number of crucial issues. Do species and kinds subsist on their own, or do they just exist in the mind of the knower? If they do have being apart from the mind, is it physical or non-

physical being, and is it a subsistence separate from perceived objects or only an existence in them?

Early medieval thought distinguished Platonic realism (*universalia ante rem*, "universals before the thing") from Aristotelian realism (*universalia in rebus*, "universals in the thing"). In → Platonism the ideas that the mind knows are eternal — distinct from, and ontologically prior to, the things that come to exist in space and time and that instantiate, or "participate in," them. In Aristotelianism universals, ontologically considered, are kinds of constituent features shared by similar individual things and recognized by the mind as such.

"Nominalism" became the medieval label for the anti-Platonic view, more extreme than Aristotle's, that universals are mere "names" *(nomina)* and do not refer to the features of perceived objects as such, as independent of our thinking and language about them (as so "named"). Roscelin of Compiègne (ca. 1050-ca. 1125) is said to have attributed no independent existence to universals and so is regarded as one of the first nominalists.

The main alternative to nominalism in the early Middle Ages was → realism of the Platonic variety, with William of Champeaux (ca. 1070-1121) its most extreme defender. "Conceptualism" is a label sometimes given to a modification of nominalism by Peter Abelard (1079-1142), who held that universals exist in the mind as concepts but do reliably name features of existing things, although the universals are not themselves things in anything like the realist sense. Abelard's view was later displaced by more sophisticated accounts better acquainted with the Aristotelian texts that treat general concepts as abstractions from the shared features of objects of sense experience.

2. Nominalism in Philosophy

Early medieval nominalists and their opponents debated complex issues of → ontology, → epistemology, and semantics. There were numerous positions, and in some cases it is difficult to assign individuals with precision to particular schools. The *Metalogicon* of John of Salisbury (ca. 1115-80), a student of Abelard, is an example of texts that attempt to sort through the early authors and positions (→ Philosophy).

Most influential of the later nominalists was William of Ockham (ca. 1285-1347), whose ontology is closely linked to his philosophy of → language. His theory of the different types of terms (syncategorematic, categorematic, absolute, connotative) proposes an analytic method for reducing complex statements to ones that are simple and directly verifiable. Ockham took from Duns Scotus (ca. 1265-1308; → Scotism) the view that we have intuitive knowledge of the existence and presence to us of individual things. For Ockham, everything real pertaining to the world is a particular individual. From direct knowledge of individual existents and their attributes, and from our intellect's logical operations in constructing general concepts and statements, we grasp the world as objective reality. The concepts we form in doing so are the only universals. In keeping with this nominalist epistemology, Ockham's → philosophy of nature avoids the teleological explanations of Aristotelian substance metaphysics, and his → ethics is → deontological.

Many late medieval nominalists were followers of Ockham. With increasing emphasis on semantics and → logic — on the distinction between logical and real necessity and possibility — one could be a nominalist in a broader sense, without subscribing to the ontological nominalism of the earlier movement. Nominalism that rejected traditional → metaphysics and focused on logical analysis of language and concepts was embraced in the *via moderna,* or "new way" of interpreting Aristotle. Major nominalist philosophers included Jean Buridan (ca. 1300-1358 or after), Marsilius of Inghen (ca. 1330-96), and the 14th-century group known as the Oxford Calculators.

Philosophers after the medieval period who have received, or have claimed, the label "nominalist" include Thomas Hobbes (1588-1679) and the 20th-century figures Nelson Goodman (1906-98) and Willard V. Quine (1908-2000). The latter two hold that predicates do not name abstract entities, for they have meaning only as parts of sentences whose referents are to be determined by designation of concrete individuals or by tying the terms to universal quantifiers or to existential quantifiers. These recent versions of nominalism, unlike their medieval predecessors, can fit with a conventionalist or a relativist epistemology.

3. Nominalism in Theology

Medieval nominalism was momentous for → theology because controversy about the relation of concepts to being also called into question the concept of God. → Anselm of Canterbury (1033-1109) thought that a consequence of Roscelin's nominalism was his tritheistic → heresy, which held that it is impossible to affirm one divine being in the three persons of the → Trinity. Abelard too was suspect, but for the opposite error of Sabellianism (→ Christology 2.1.2). In treating the Trinity, Ockham drew attention to our incomplete knowledge of Trinitarian terms and thus restricted the use of syllogistic reasoning in theology, invoking instead the element of → faith. Such a fideist position is typically nominalist. Ockham himself did not entirely reject → natural theology, but some followers, such as Robert Holcot (d. 1349), advocated a consistently nominalist-fideist approach to theology.

Duns Scotus had distinguished logical from real modalities and had applied his modal insights to the traditional distinction between God's absolute, unconditioned power *(potesta absoluta)* and God's actually employed or ordained power *(potesta ordinata).* Ockham and his theological followers made extensive use of this paradigm, with a consequent stress on divine transcendence (→ Immanence and Transcendence) and → freedom, together with affirming the utter contingency of the world and of its particular contents. The theme of divine sovereignty pervades Ockham's doctrine of → justification, according to which God by → grace accepts human good works as meritorious.

The nominalist theology of Gregory of Rimini (ca. 1300-1358) emphasized divine grace more strongly and so became the basis for late medieval Augustinianism (→ Augustine's Theology). In his *Collectorium* Gabriel Biel (ca. 1420-95) compiled the theological teachings of nominalism and the *via moderna* and so influenced the theological development of Martin → Luther (1483-1546; → Luther's Theology 1). The theology of the *via moderna* entered the thinking of John → Calvin (1509-64; → Calvin's Theology) at the Collège de Montaigu in Paris, probably through the teaching of the Ockhamist theologian John Major (1469-1550).

→ Middle Ages

Bibliography: Primary sources; John of Salisbury, *The Metalogicon* (trans. D. D. McGarry; Berkeley, Calif., 1962) • William of Ockham, *Predestination, God's Foreknowledge, and Future Contingents* (2d ed.; trans. M. M. Adams and N. Kretzmann; Indianapolis, 1983); idem, *Ockham's Theory of Propositions: Part II of the Summa Logicae* (trans. A. J. Freddoso and H. Schuurman; Notre Dame, Ind., 1980); idem, *Ockham's Theory of Terms: Part I of the Summa Logicae* (trans. M. J. Loux; Notre Dame, Ind., 1974).

Secondary works: M. Adams, *William Ockham* (2 vols.; Notre Dame, Ind., 1987) • L. Alanen and S. Knuuttila, "The Foundations of Modality and Conceivability in Descartes and His Predecessors," *Modern Modalities* (ed. S. Knuuttila; Dordrecht, 1988) 1-69 • R. Eberle, *Nominalistic Systems* (Dordrecht, 1970) • M. Gosselin, *Nominalism and Contemporary Nominalism: Ontological and Epistemological Implica-*

tions of the Work of W. V. O. Quine and of N. Goodman (Dordrecht, 1990) • G. LEFF, *William of Ockham: The Metamorphosis of Scholastic Discourse* (Manchester, 1975) • A. McGRATH, *The Intellectual Origins of the European Reformation* (Oxford, 1987) • C. NORMORE, "The Tradition of Medieval Nominalism," *Studies in Medieval Philosophy* (ed. J. Wippel; Washington, D.C., 1987) 201-17 • H. OBERMAN, *The Dawn of the Reformation: Essays in Late Medieval and Early Reformation Thought* (Edinburgh, 1986); idem, *The Harvest of Medieval Theology: Gabriel Biel and Late Medieval Nominalism* (rev. ed.; Grand Rapids, 1967) • J. PELIKAN, *The Christian Tradition*, vol. 3, *The Growth of Medieval Theology (600-1300)* (Chicago, 1978) • J. PINBORG, *Logik und Semantik im Mittelalter* (Stuttgart, 1972) • P. SPADE, ed., *The Cambridge Companion to Ockham* (Cambridge, 1999) • W. STEGMÜLLER, *Glauben, Wissen und Erkennen. Das Universalienproblem einst und jetzt* (Darmstadt, 1974).

SIMO KNUUTTILA and ROBERT F. BROWN

Nonconforming Church → Free Church

Nonviolence → Force, Violence, Nonviolence

Norms

1. Definitions
2. Philosophical Norms
3. Moral Norms
4. Theological Norms

1. Definitions

A norm (from Lat. *norma*, "carpenter's square," later "rule, measure, regulation") may be theoretical (in descriptive natural and social → sciences) or practical (in normative sciences, such as → logic, → aesthetics, → ethics, and → theology). In common speech norms denote (1) average values by which to measure what is normal or abnormal, and in technical or pragmatic usage, (2) conventional units of measurement or rules by which to classify things or behavior (e.g., traffic laws).

Norms in the various descriptive and theoretical sciences describe a variety of relations and behaviors. In physics they designate (3) the regular interrelationship of objects and events (natural laws) as established by empirical observation and its interpretation. In → psychoanalysis they denote (4) the limits of a sound psyche as known from what is ab-

normal (→ Soul). In → law and legal theory they are (5) factually valid precepts of law and custom, independent of their origin, form, or content. And in → sociology norms are (6) standards of → behavior that are valid in typical situations as we know them empirically in a given social system, including social → institutions in which what is said (→ Language) is linked to expected action (e.g., in promises). In all these spheres norms are descriptive but may readily have prescriptive connotations (i.e., be "normative") as regards their regulative function within the various domains.

→ Philosophy, in its divisions of logic, aesthetics, and ethics, as well as theology, deals with norms. Logical norms are (7) rules of thought that guarantee consistency and freedom from contradiction; they are constitutive for all forms of thinking. Aesthetics norms — for example, (8) judgments about harmony, rhythm, and beauty — claim validity for all works of art but are obviously dependent on social and historical conventions. Ethical norms are (9) rules of action (→ Action Theory) that can claim moral justification. Finally, we speak of norms in theology with reference to (10) the ultimately regulative theses of a specific → faith.

Even descriptively, it is hard to say for certain what is normal about a given phenomenon or process. Reference may be made to a statistical average, in terms of which we may speak of abnormal deviations. The situation is even more difficult in normative disciplines, since there is no comparable standard by which to decide.

2. Philosophical Norms

The term "norms" took on significance in practical philosophy in discussion of I. Kant's (1724-1804) → categorical imperative as a purely formal definition of what is moral. The issue here was defining the moral not merely by such criteria as the universal validity and necessity of custom. Concepts such as → virtue and → duty were subsumed under that of norms as authoritative precepts (W. Wundt). Norms as concretions of ideal contents of what is right came to be seen as dependent on values (E. Husserl, M. Scheler, N. Hartmann; → Value, Ethics of).

Discussion then focused on such questions as (1) whether behind norms that are directly oriented to action there are valid moral principles such as benevolence, or some basic norm that can be shown to be universal and universally valid; (2) how we are to test, establish, and justify norms, whether by a model of transsubjective counseling (P. Lorenzen, O. Schwemmer, F. Kambartel), on a transcendental-pragmatic basis (K. O. Apel), or by a universal speech ethics using the logic of practical discourse (J. Habermas); and finally (3) whether an ultimate philosophical establishment of moral norms is necessary, possible, or feasible. In the late 20th century situation ethics raised the further question (4) whether the specificity of the situation does not decide what is moral quite apart from any norms (J. Fletcher).

3. Moral Norms

Legal norms are fixed by agreement and enforced by institutionalized threats and sanctions (→ Punishment). Moral norms, however, must secure recognition by rational arguments that prove the → autonomy of morality and do not rely merely on a heteronomy that grounds its validity in authoritative precepts (→ Authority) or the will of God. (Cf. the dilemma of Euthyphro in Plato: Is the good good because God wills it, or does God will it because it is good?) If we finally find norms in values that must be attained (e.g., the → Good), we come into the sphere of → teleology. If we first assume that certain norms, at least to some extent, have a compulsory character because otherwise our common life makes no sense, we move into the sphere of → deontology as the model for a theoretical grounding of ethics.

In need of clarification in ethical theory is the question how to relate moral norms to a given situation. Can we deduce directions for concrete action immediately from norms (→ Casuistry), or is there a nuanced interplay of moral norms, nonmoral value judgments, and purely factual judgments in any given moral decision? In the latter case we must strictly differentiate between prescriptive and descriptive elements in reaching a decision so as to avoid a mistaken derivation of moral or value judgments from factual judgments. Possibly we cannot make a simple distinction between judgments of what is and what ought to be. In this case we must find the ultimate basis of moral judgments in reference to a coherent → worldview that includes prescriptive and descriptive elements already indissolubly related (→ Analytic Ethics).

4. Theological Norms

Descriptive and prescriptive elements are both undoubtedly present in religious faith. Theology, in its attempt to give a systematic account of a specific faith and to show its inner coherence, develops norms that give direction to faith as it is lived out. In Christian theology we find such norms in → revelation, → grace, → faith, → hope, → love, → justification, → sanctification, and → law and gospel. In specific periods theological → axioms of this kind, often summarizing complex biblical materials, in different combinations and with different degrees of emphasis, have directed the thinking and faith of Christians and their talk about God (e.g., the → Reformation principles).

As a comprehensive view of the world that makes a lofty claim to authority, religious faith tends to absolutize its own position. For this reason almost all religions make a claim to absoluteness (→ Absolute, The). Theological analysis may clarify the normative elements in various religions (→ Phenomenology of Religion) that are at least structurally comparable, and in this way reach a nuanced view of them. With the help of perspectives from practical → experience, such insight may then help to open up fruitful interreligious → dialogue, absolute claims notwithstanding.

Bibliography: D. Chong, *Rational Lives: Norms and Values in Politics and Society* (Chicago, 2000) • H. M. Clor, *Public Morality and Liberal Society: Essays on Decency, Law, and Pornography* (Notre Dame, Ind., 1996) • D. Copp, *Morality, Normativity, and Society* (New York, 1995) • W. J. FitzPatrick, *Teleology and the Norms of Nature* (New York, 2000) • J. Fletcher, *Situation Ethics* (Philadelphia, 1966) • M. Hechter and K.-D. Opp, eds., *Social Norms* (New York, 2001) • E. A. Posner, *Law and Social Norms* (Cambridge, Mass., 2000) • D. Ritschl, *The Logic of Theology* (Philadelphia, 1987) • W. Schwartz, *Analytische Ethik und christliche Theologie* (Göttingen, 1984) • J. D. Wallace, *Ethical Norms, Particular Cases* (Ithaca, N.Y., 1996) • G. H. von Wright, *Handlung, Norm und Intention. Untersuchungen zur deontischen Logik* (Berlin, 1977); idem, *Norm and Action: A Logical Enquiry* (London, 1963).

Werner Schwartz

North American Missions

1. Background
2. Beginnings
3. New Developments
4. Since 1950

1. Background

North American missions originated in work among American Indians. In the colonial period some colonists, especially New England → Puritans and → Moravians in the Middle States, engaged in missionary outreach to their Native American neighbors. John Eliot (1604-90) of Massachusetts was probably the first North American to engage in missions when he began preaching to Indians near Boston in 1641. David Zeisberger (1721-1808), working in New York, Pennsylvania, and Ohio, was known as the Moravian "apostle to the Indians." After American independence in 1776, with the surge of nationalism, westward migration, and the enthusiasm of the Second Evangelical Awakening (→ Revivals), American Protestants founded an amazing number of new missionary societies to work among Indians, African slaves, new immigrants living on the frontier, and eventually also non-Christians in foreign lands.

2. Beginnings

North American foreign missions grew out of this soil. As churches were touched by the evangelical awakening, and as they saw British and Continental evangelicals embarking on world missions (→ British Missions; German Missions; Scandinavian Missions), they became convinced that they too should launch out. The first organization for foreign missions was the American Board of Commissioners for Foreign Missions (Boston, 1810), primarily an effort of → Congregationalists. Soon American → Baptists organized a mission agency (1814), followed by Methodists (1819), Episcopalians (1821), Presbyterians (1837), and Lutherans (1837; → Methodist Churches; Reformed and Presbyterian Churches; Lutheran Churches). In contrast to the practice in Europe, where mission work was left to independent societies, in the United States churches began taking over responsibility for missionary work by incorporating free mission societies into the structure of many → denominations as boards for → mission. Canadian missions followed the same pattern when they came into being in the latter half of the 19th century.

The motives of American missions in their early days were, in addition to obedience to the Great Commission, usually a belief in universal benevolence, a concern for the souls of the lost and dying, and a desire to sacrifice for the work of God. National interests entered very little into the motivation, especially since early overseas missions concentrated on India, Burma, the Middle East, and China, where the United States initially had few national interests and Canada had none. The Hawaiian Islands, evangelized by American Congregationalists from 1819, were an exception, insofar as mission work and trade contributed to eventual annexation by the United States, which occurred in 1898. In that same year, during the Spanish-American War, the United States broke with its anti-imperial tradition by annexing Puerto Rico and the Philippine Islands, both of which quickly became fields of missionary outreach. European colonial rivalry over China, especially after the Boxer Uprising (1900), also led to heavy American missionary involvement in that country.

During the middle decades of the 19th century, a long-standing desire to find a solution to the American → slavery problem led to the formation of numerous African colonization societies for the peaceful repatriation of African Americans. The success of these societies was limited, but they led to the sending of American → missionaries to West Africa. Black American churches also began sending their own missionaries to Africa. Toward the end of the 19th century, American colonial interests began to coincide with mounting evangelical enthusiasm and humanitarianism to promote a dramatic expansion of North American missions into Asia, Africa, and Latin America (→ Colonialism and Mission).

During the final decade of the 19th century and the first decade of the 20th century, American overseas missions seemed to come of age. As the United States moved onto the world stage as a global power, missions enjoyed temporary popularity in society as a whole as a vehicle for expanding American cultural influence. Many people, including several American presidents, saw America as capable of making an impact on the world not through military power or selfish imperial interests but by spreading its religious faith and values. America could fulfill its old Puritan vision of being a beacon to the nations, a "city set on a hill." Where, as in the Philippines, America was quite directly becoming politically imperialistic, this humanitarian tendency helped to justify the newly acquired but unaccustomed colonial role (→ Colonialism).

American college and university students were now particularly caught up in zeal for missions, becoming a powerful vehicle for evangelical activism. In 1888 the Student Volunteer Movement for Foreign Missions was founded as a direct result of summer Bible conferences for collegians held on the campus of Dwight L. → Moody's (1837-99) school at Mount Hermon, Massachusetts. This student movement — marked by its watchword, "the evangelization of the world in this generation" — swept the country, forcing denominational mission boards to expand their missionary recruitment. From it came the Missionary Education Movement and the Laymen's Missionary Movement for promoting → education and funding for overseas missions. From the ranks of the student volunteers came such outstanding missionary statesmen as John R. → Mott (1865-1955), Robert E. Speer (1867-1947), and others who stirred enthusiasm, promoted missionary planning, and also created new structures for missionary and ecumenical cooperation.

Women now also began to assume greater leadership roles in mission. Protestant women had originally been sent out only as wives of missionaries, but now many single or unmarried women received an independent commission. The result was that women, including wives, now constituted 60 percent of the American missionary force. Missionary work offered women an opportunity to break out of the stereotyped roles to which they had been largely confined. They began organizing mission-sending societies of their own, beginning with the Women's Union Missionary Society of America (1861). By 1900 they had established 41 such bodies in the United States and 7 in Canada. Some of these societies, organized for the recruitment and support of women missionaries, became quite wealthy and influential; most were later absorbed into church boards.

3. New Developments

Even before the turn of the 20th century, fresh developments in the pattern of sending began changing the overall mission picture. Important new nondenominational mission societies were organized, including the Evangelical Missionary Alliance (1887, which merged with the Christian Alliance in 1897, forming the → Christian and Missionary Alliance), Central American Mission (1890), the Sudan Interior Mission (1893), and the Africa Inland Mission (1895). Such new missions were deeply influenced by the pattern of the nondenominational and international → China Inland Mission, a → "faith mission" founded in 1865 by J. Hudson Taylor (1832-1905), with a strong following and participation in both the United States and Canada. These evangelical mission societies focused more exclusively on → evangelism and church planting than their denominational predecessors, who began to move increasingly in the direction of societal transformation.

The older denominational mission efforts, while not abandoning evangelism, moved increasingly toward → social services and education, establishing schools (from the primary to the collegiate level), clinics, and hospitals (→ Medical Missions). These projects became popular expressions of mission, helping to promote societal uplift and enjoying the support of wealthy North American patrons. Social services to underprivileged → masses now became one mark of the growing liberal attitude found within denominational missions, especially between 1900 and 1930.

Accompanying this emphasis on Christian service to the unfortunate was a new appreciation and respect for other cultures and religions. An important layman's survey of Protestant missions was *Rethinking Missions* (1932, known as the Hocking Report), by Harvard philosopher William Ernest Hocking (1873-1966), who maintained that missions should abandon efforts toward → conversions to Christianity and work with other world religions for the mutual improvement of societies and the world. The conclusions of this report were widely repudiated both by evangelicals and by others within the major denominations. Such trends in time led → evangelical mission supporters in conservative denominations, as well as in "parachurch" and nondenominational missions, to part company with the mainline Protestant missionary movement.

The North American Protestant missionary efforts among mainline denominations in the United States and Canada, particularly after 1900, began moving in the direction of ever closer missionary cooperation. Mission board secretaries joined in the joint Foreign Missions Conference of North America (1895), which led eventually to the Division of Overseas Ministries of the → National Council of the Churches of Christ in the U.S.A. (1950) and the Commission on World Concerns of the Canadian Council of Churches (1948). Mission executives in both countries were active in the → International Missionary Council (IMC, 1921-61) and later in the Commission on World Mission and Evangelism of the → World Council of Churches.

The conciliar missionary movement, however, began to generate negative reactions on the part of conservative evangelicals, which led many of them to withdraw from conciliar mission organizations in order to form their own conservative mission associations. Already in 1917 leaders of nondenominational faith missions had founded the Interdenominational Foreign Mission Association (IFMA) as their own cooperative agency. In 1945 conservative and mostly smaller evangelical denominations formed the Evangelical Foreign Missions Association (EFMA). By midcentury the North American Protestant world missionary movement was badly split.

Roman Catholics in North America, which until 1908 was considered a mission territory and the object of missionary endeavors by Catholic mission societies from Europe, rapidly advanced toward maturity. Efforts in the 19th century had been directed toward recent immigrants, frontier people, African Americans, and Native Americans. In 1911, partly in response to the impetus of Protestant missions but also challenged by issues connected with the Spanish-American War, American Catholics organized the first distinctively American sending body, the Catholic Foreign Mission Society of North America (Maryknoll Mission), to promote → Catholic missions overseas. Priests and religious serving overseas before that time normally did so under the auspices of existing international mission institutes. These international mission orders, both men's and women's, organized their own sending branches in North America. In 1901 Catholics began holding mission congresses and formed mission extension societies and diocesan branches of the Society for the Propagation of the Faith. East Asian countries were the initial focus of Roman Catholic overseas missions. After 1950 Latin America received massive attention, followed by Africa.

Men's → religious orders that sent the most personnel overseas were the Jesuits, Maryknoll Fathers and Brothers, Franciscans, Redemptorists, and the Divine Word Missionaries. Leading women's religious congregations included the Maryknoll Sisters, Marist Missionaries, Medical Mission Sisters, School Sisters of Notre Dame, and Sisters of Mercy. In addition to religious priests, brothers, and sisters, a considerable number of diocesan priests and laypersons were also involved in Roman Catholic missions. In 2001 the total number of U.S. Catholic missioners deployed overseas or engaged in cross-cultural mission in the United States was 6,108 (180 diocesan priests, 1,784 religious priests, 349 religious brothers, 2,589 religious sisters, 15 seminarians, and 1,191 laypersons). By region the largest number were engaged in cross-cultural mission within the United States (2,682), followed by Latin America (1,247, esp. Brazil, Mexico, and Peru), Asia (734, esp. the Philippines and Japan), and Africa (704, esp. Kenya and Tanzania). Smaller numbers were at work in Eurasia, the Middle East, Oceania, and Europe. By ministry activity approximately one-half were engaged in either education or pastoral work. The total number of U.S. Catholic missionaries peaked at 9,655 in 1968, declining gradually thereafter. In recent years a sharp decline in religious priests has been offset by a marked rise in numbers of lay missioners, including families.

4. Since 1950

The second half of the 20th century produced striking changes in this overall picture. The Protestant denominational missions belonging to the conciliar movement, which had set the pace from the 19th century through the middle of the 20th century,

now gradually declined in terms of numbers of missionaries sent and yielded leadership to the conservative evangelicals. The period is characterized by a vast increase in new mission agencies, the formation of competing groupings of mission associations, the rise of divergent mission theologies and strategies, and a multiplication of programs for mission study and research.

In contrast to the 56 U.S. Protestant mission agencies that existed before 1900, by 1999 there were no fewer than 693 U.S. and 121 Canadian Protestant mission agencies, the overwhelming majority of which were founded in the period 1960-90. More than half of these new missions were "nondenominational," with Baptist and Pentecostal/charismatic groups also prominent. These 814 North American agencies employed approximately 120,000 full-time persons located in 197 countries, two-thirds of whom were nationals of the countries in which the agencies worked. The number of fully supported long-term North American missionaries serving overseas remains around 33,000. Short-termers and volunteers (serving two weeks to two years) add several hundred thousand more.

U.S. Protestant mission agencies with more than 500 workers in 2000 included the Southern Baptist Convention (4,562), Wycliffe Bible Translators (2,930), Youth with a Mission (1,817), Assemblies of God (1,543), and New Tribes Mission (1,514). Total income for all agencies approached $3 billion. These mission agencies are fairly evenly distributed by numbers between the regions in which they serve: Latin America (305), Asia (301), Africa (235), Western Europe (187), Eastern Europe (184), and Oceania (87). In numbers of full-time U.S. missionaries serving in each region, Latin America leads (10,711), followed by Asia (9,772) and Africa (7,091). Countries with more than 50 U.S. agencies each include Mexico (176), India (153), Philippines (142), Brazil (131), Kenya (116), Russia (111), and Japan (102).

By 1960 the missionary movement from North America had divided into two competing streams: the conciliar, or ecumenical, stream, represented by larger mainline denominational missions; and a newer alliance of smaller denominations and evangelical parachurch organizations identified with the → Lausanne Movement. The conciliar mission movement traces its descent from the Edinburgh World Mission Conference (1910) and the initiatives of the IMC, which in 1961 was integrated into the World Council of Churches. Following integration, many evangelicals felt excluded and no longer represented by that movement. The Lausanne

Movement, formally organized in 1974 at the International Congress on World Evangelization and officially known as the Lausanne Committee for World Evangelization (LCWE), is the successor to several earlier evangelical mission conferences sponsored by the EFMA, the IFMA, and the journal *Christianity Today*.

Billy Graham took the lead in convening the Lausanne group. As an umbrella organization for worldwide evangelical missions, its aims are to mobilize evangelicals for cooperative missionary effort, to base mission work on biblical norms, to engage in strategic planning, and to call for united → prayer. Its major achievement has been the adoption of the Lausanne Covenant, a joint declaration of evangelical principles upholding the uniqueness of Jesus Christ. The LCWE has sponsored other important congresses (at Pattaya, Thailand, in 1980; and Manila, 1989) and convened evangelical consultations on policy issues.

Ecumenical mission agencies, in partnership with sister churches in Asia, Africa, and Latin America, exchange resources (personnel, project aid, and scholarships) for mission and seek to overcome relationships of dominance and dependence. They agree on the need to replace the older Western missionary expansionist model with one that expresses a global missionary → partnership between churches on six continents. They join with partner churches in supporting development projects and in advocating justice, liberation, human → rights, and debt relief. They train specialists capable of engaging in interfaith dialogue, especially with Muslims. The ecumenical missionary vision largely tracks major themes of ecumenical missionary conferences held at Bangkok (1972), Melbourne (1980), San Antonio, Texas (1989), and Salvador, Brazil (1996) — dialogue, option for the poor, proclaiming the kingdom, mission in Christ's way, common witness, and authentic witness within each culture.

Evangelicals, meanwhile, have held miniconsultations on taking the gospel to people of other religions and people groups (Pattaya, 1980) and, in the two congress themes of the 1989 Manila conference, reaffirmed an eschatological note ("Proclaim Christ until He Comes") and embraced wholeness in mission ("Calling the Whole Church to Take the Whole Gospel to the Whole World"). Some parachurch groups have committed themselves to various kinds of pioneer mission. They seek out lost, unreached, or unevangelized communities and work toward the planting of viable churches among all such groups.

Conversations between representatives of the two streams have brought about greater understanding and narrowed differences between them, but there appears to be little prospect of uniting the two streams into a single missionary movement.

In the area of missionary research and publication, however, there has been remarkable and sustained cooperation between all confessional groups. In contrast to the first half of the 20th century, when the teaching of missions, training of missionaries, and research into missionary problems were limited to the Kennedy School of Missions (Hartford, Conn.) and several East Coast seminaries, the second half has seen an explosion of academic programs, special institutes, organizations, and publications for mission research. In 1952 the Association of Professors of Missions in North America was launched, linking several regional associations. The academic study of missiology gained official recognition in 1972 with the organization of the American Society of Missiology (ASM), a tripartite organization of Roman Catholics, conciliar Protestants, and "independents" (i.e., evangelicals). The ASM publishes its own quarterly journal, *Missiology*, and has undertaken a series of mission monographs as well as a dissertation series. Doctoral programs in mission studies and "cross-cultural evangelism" are offered in a number of seminaries, chiefly by evangelicals but also by Roman Catholics and mainline Protestants. Among those enrolled are many international students. Under the auspices of the Pew Charitable Trusts, research enablement grants have been made available for North American and Third World scholars.

The *International Bulletin of Missionary Research*, since 1977 a quarterly publication of the Overseas Ministries Study Center (New Haven, Conn.), has become an indispensable tool, as are successive editions of the *Mission Handbook*, published originally by the Missionary Research Library and more recently by the Mission Advanced Research Center, or MARC. The *World Christian Encyclopedia* (1982; 2d ed., 2001) presents a massive survey of churches and religions in the modern world. The *Biographical Dictionary of Christian Mission* (1998) contains over 2,400 entries on missionaries since NT times. Electronic bibliographies on every conceivable missionary subject are now available online. At no time in the past has so much information about the state of the modern mission enterprise been recorded and made available.

At the beginning of the third millennium, North America remains the dynamic center of global mission sending, planning, research, and information. At the same time, the North American component has been globalized in such a way that it cannot easily be distinguished from contributions and resources provided by other regions, which increasingly challenge North American dominance. The divided and competitive character of the North American scene remains a problem. History shows, however, that each new generation has a way of creating its own response to the missionary challenge.

Bibliography: G. H. ANDERSON, ed., *Biographical Dictionary of Christian Missions* (New York, 1998) • D. B. BARRETT et al., eds., *WCE* (2d ed.) • R. P. BEAVER, ed., *American Missions in Bicentennial Perspective* (Pasadena, Calif., 1977) • A. DRIES, *The Missionary Movement in American Catholic History* (Maryknoll, N.Y., 1998) • D. L. ROBERT, ed., *Gospel Bearers, Gender Barriers: Missionary Women in the Twentieth Century* (Maryknoll, N.Y., 2002) • J. A. SCHERER and S. B. BEVANS, eds., *New Directions in Mission and Evangelization,* vol. 1, *Basic Statements* (Maryknoll, N.Y., 1992) • J. A. SIEWERT and D. WELLIVER, eds., *Mission Handbook: U.S. and Canadian Christian Ministries Overseas, 2001-2003* (18th ed.; Wheaton, Ill., 2000) • J. STOTT, ed., *Making Christ Known: Historic Mission Documents from the Lausanne Movement, 1974-1989* (Grand Rapids, 1996) • U.S. CATHOLIC MISSION ASSOCIATION, *Mission Handbook 2002* (Washington, D.C., 2002).

CHARLES W. FORMAN and JAMES A. SCHERER

North American Theology

1. Theology as a Practical Discipline
2. Calvinism: Reactions and Defense
3. Rational Orthodoxy
4. Critical Reactions
5. New Theological Approaches
6. Conservative Developments
7. Theological Realism
8. Secular Theologies
9. Christian Thought in the Secular World
10. Theologies of Particularity
11. Theological Study and Publication

For three centuries, theologians in North America maintained a deep interest in the reasonableness of Christianity, a conception of → theology as a practical enterprise, and a close linkage to the → denominations. They divided as well into alignments that reflected not only traditional disputes over doctrine but also social location and cultural identity. The 20th century brought transformations in all of these tendencies (→ Modern Church History 2).

1. Theology as a Practical Discipline

The accent on the practical found initial expression among the Reformed theologians of colonial New England, who defined theology as "the doctrine of living to God," by which they meant that the primary aim of theology is knowledge of God not as an end in itself but for the sake of salvation. For such → Puritans as Thomas Hooker (1586-1647) and Thomas Shepard (1605-49), the chief goal was to clarify matters of → soteriology, → ethics, and the ordering of the → congregation. Impressed by the → logic of Petrus Ramus in France and by the distinction originally drawn by Zacharias Ursinus in Germany and Dudley Fenner in England between God's natural → covenant (or covenant of works) with Adam and God's covenant of → grace with Abraham, they developed a federal *(foedus)* theology (→ Orthodoxy 2.3; Covenant 3) through which they defined the → church, interpreted the social order (→ Society), and described the stages in the → order of salvation *(ordo salutis)*.

1.1. The systematic summation of this covenant theology came in Samuel Willard's *Complete Body of Divinity* (1726), compiled from lectures in Boston between 1687 and 1705. On most issues Willard (1640-1707) represented a conservative voice; he still argued that theology was a practical discipline designed to promote eternal → happiness as well as God's glory. In slightly expanding the scope of → natural theology, however, he pointed toward a trend that would attain prominence in early 18th-century New England. For some Congregational theologians after the turn of the century, the emphasis would fall on the → virtuous life in a rational and orderly universe overseen by a benevolent God.

1.2. Jonathan → Edwards (1703-58), the most gifted theologian America has produced, opposed this anthropocentric impulse with a sophisticated theocentric → Calvinism. He also redefined Reformed theology, however, by elaborating the theme of the divine beauty, describing the complexity of the religious affections, and exploring with great subtlety the theological implications of philosophical → idealism. Convinced of the harmony between → reason and → revelation, he drew, with critical selectivity, on Locke, philosophical idealism, and the Cambridge → Platonists, but he insisted in his *Nature of True Virtue* (1765) that the natural moral sense (so admired by Francis Hutcheson in Scotland) and the natural reason lack the capacity for a truly virtuous "consent to Being." In his treatise *Freedom of the Will* (1754), a critique of → Arminian indeterminism, he defined the issues of a debate that lasted over a century.

1.3. Subsequent realignments within American Calvinism formed largely in response to Edwards. His disciples, especially Samuel Hopkins (1721-1803) and Joseph Bellamy (1719-90), known as the New Divinity theologians, emphasized divine sovereignty (→ God), a governmental theory of → atonement, an intricate view of the will designed to justify revivalist exhortation, and a conviction that regeneration produces a selfless "disinterested benevolence." They would admit only the regenerate to membership in the New England churches.

Their opponents, the Old Calvinists, led by Moses Hemmenway (1735-1811), questioned Edwards's → metaphysics, criticized the Edwardsean defense of → revivalism, and expressed reservations about Edwardsean views of the means of grace. They found the New Divinity restrictions on → church membership unduly rigorous.

1.4. An alternative to both forms of Calvinism could be found in a nascent liberal movement led by the Boston minister Charles Chauncy (1705-87), whose notions of divine benevolence and universal salvation clashed with the prevailing ideas of divine sovereignty (→ Universalism and Particularism). For ministers drawn to Chauncy's thought, the practicality of theology is to be found largely in the guidance it provides for the moral life.

2. Calvinism: Reactions and Defense

By the late 18th century, Calvinist ideas came under fire not only from colonial Arminians, who rejected the doctrine of → predestination, but also, more radically, from → deists like Thomas Paine (1737-1809), whose *Age of Reason* (1794) debunks belief in a biblical revelation. Equally important, the proliferation of religious denominations, sometimes linked to divisions in social class, began to define theological identities. By the early 19th century the establishing of seminaries intensified divisions even within the Calvinist traditions.

2.1. One approach, diverse in expression, was to reject the Calvinist tradition altogether. In Boston William E. Channing (1780-1842) and Andrews Norton (1786-1853) led a Unitarian movement that claimed that a rational interpretation of Scripture (→ Exegesis, Biblical) results in views of human nature (→ Anthropology) as capable of moral virtue and spiritual perfection, of Christ as a unique but not divine savior, and of God as a unitary and benevolent Father.

→ Unitarians, however, were not the only critics. The Episcopalian William White (1748-1836) helped define a theological alternative in the Episcopal Church that brought ecclesiological issues to the forefront and found in sacramental theology a counterweight against both revivalist and Calvinist ideas and practices.

The rejection of Calvinism often bore traces of a populist sentiment that highly educated Calvinist theologians had distorted biblical truth and that self-educated theologians and ordinary laypeople could interpret the Bible for themselves. Such sentiments appeared in the early universalist movement, led by John Murray (1741-1815), who introduced Americans to notions of universal salvation that were also circulating in England. Methodist theologians like Thomas Ralston (1806-85) employed a similar populist rhetoric as they resurrected older notions of prevenient grace to bolster their argument that salvation is a universal possibility, even though many will reject it.

The rhetoric of → populism also infused the theology of a "Christian" movement that rejected denominational labels and sought to restore primitive Christian practice and belief. This primitivist appeal had its ablest defender in the "restorationist" Alexander Campbell (1788-1866), founder of the Disciples of Christ, who argued that the NT promises salvation to all who believe the essential biblical truths and express their belief by seeking baptism by immersion (→ Christian Church [Disciples of Christ]). But the primitivist impulse could lead beyond conventional Protestant boundaries, and groups like the Shakers, Hicksite Quakers (→ Friends, Society of), and → Mormons appealed to immediate revelation as well as Scripture to ground alternative theological visions.

2.2. A second approach was to preserve Calvinism but revise it. In reaction to the Unitarians, Nathaniel William Taylor (1786-1858) at Yale Divinity School redefined both sinfulness and → regeneration so as to magnify the gravity of human choices without surrendering divine sovereignty. This "New Haven theology," which influenced the "New School" party in the Presbyterian and Congregational churches, drew critical replies from Bennet Tyler (1783-1858) at the Theological Institute of Connecticut (later Hartford Seminary) and Leonard Woods (1774-1854) at Andover Seminary, both of whom defended more traditional Calvinist doctrines.

A more radical effort to redefine Calvinism from within marked the writing of Charles G. → Finney (1792-1875), revivalist and professor at Oberlin College, who argued in *Lectures on Systematic Theology* (1846) that the idea of divine moral government implies a human capacity for repentant response to grace. For revivalist theologians of the Finneyite variety, theology is practical in that it formulates the doctrines of repentance, → conversion (§1), and → sanctification (→ Practical Theology).

2.3. The main defense of Calvinist tradition came from Archibald Alexander (1772-1851) and Charles Hodge (1797-1878) at Princeton Seminary. Hodge's three-volume *Systematic Theology* (1872-73) defines theology as an inductive → science that rests on a verbally inspired Scripture. An admirer both of the scholastic Francis Turretin in Geneva (→ Scholasticism) and of the inductive method proposed by Francis Bacon, Hodge argues that Reformed theology consists of accurate theoretical generalizations from the collecting of scriptural facts. His form of Calvinist theology also teaches that Adam is the representative figure through whom all humanity fell into sin, that the fall entrapped the will within bonds of sinfulness, and that Christ is the divine-human representative whose sacrificial death redeems only God's elect.

2.4. The Calvinist issues never completely monopolized debate. In the → Lutheran church, Samuel Simon Schmucker (1799-1873) generated controversy when he called for revision of the → Augsburg Confession to make it more compatible with revivalist piety and ecumenical cooperation (→ Ecumenical Dialogue). Among Roman Catholics, Martin John Spalding (1810-72) epitomized the resurgence of neo-Thomist thought (→ Neoscholasticism) in the service of denominational polemics, and the leading Catholic theologian of the era, Francis Patrick Kenrick (1796-1863), expressed in his *Theologia dogmatica* (1839-40) the theological positions that had been formulated at the 16th-century Council of → Trent.

3. Rational Orthodoxy

Underlying all the disagreements, however, was a remarkable consensus. From roughly 1790 to 1860 one dominant strand in virtually all American theological positions was a confidence that rational proofs can demonstrate the truth of Christian revelation. Despite confessional and denominational divisions, most theologians affirmed a "rational orthodoxy" that promoted a specific form of harmony between reason and revelation. Through natural theology, they contended, reason prepares the mind to receive the scriptural revelation; through both external arguments (from → miracle and → prophecy) and internal evidences (from consistency), reason proves the authenticity and uniqueness of the Christian revelation; and through the "grammatical interpretation" advocated by J. A. Ernesti in Germany and Moses Stuart in America, reason can

rightly interpret the revealed message. Catholic theologians differed from the Protestant majority only insofar as they contended that the evidences also prove the authority of the → Roman Catholic Church as the repository and interpreter of the revelation.

This striving for rational proof and explanation helps to explain the hegemony of Scottish common-sense → realism in antebellum American theology. By certifying the validity of cognitive perceptions and of an innate moral sense, the philosophy of Thomas Reid (1710-96) in Glasgow and Dugald Stewart (1753-1828) in Edinburgh fortified this pious → rationalism. Americans also admired the inductive → epistemology of Francis Bacon, for it provided a check on speculative excess.

4. Critical Reactions

The prevalence of rational orthodoxy stimulated critical reactions against it, especially on the part of theologians influenced by either liberal or conservative forms of → romantic thought. These theologians often turned to a different conception of theological rationality as participation in an eternal Reason, discerned through an intuition of reason's own presuppositions.

4.1. The → transcendentalists, especially Ralph W. Emerson (1803-82), employing S. T. Coleridge's revision of I. Kant's epistemology (→ Kantianism), claimed that the orthodox remained within the realm of mere understanding rather than appreciating the insights of intuitive reason. As part of the transcendentalist ferment Theodore Parker (1810-60) introduced German idealism along with Wilhelm M. DeWette's biblical criticism.

4.2. Reaction against a Baconian rational orthodoxy could also assume traditional forms. The Roman Catholic convert Orestes Brownson (1803-76), for example, challenged the naïveté of rationalist → biblicism.

4.3. The "Mercersburg theologians" — John W. Nevin (1803-86) and Philip Schaff (1819-93), who taught at the German Reformed seminary in Mercersburg, Pennsylvania — said that rational orthodoxy missed the deeper rationality of tradition and overlooked the transmission of Christ's "Life" through the church's sacramental and catechetical history. Influenced by I. A. Dorner and J. A. W. Neander in Germany, Nevin interpreted J. → Calvin through the lenses of an idealistic philosophy in which the universal precedes the particular (so that the church precedes the individual) and an incarnational theology in which the coming of Christ alters generic humanity.

The Lutheran confessionalists C. F. W. Walther (1811-87) and Charles P. Krauth (1823-83), admirers of 17th-century German → dogmatics, contended that rational → orthodoxy (§1) had fallen prey to a shallow conception of reason.

4.4. Particularly influential as a critic of the orthodox rationalists was the Congregationalist theologian Horace Bushnell (1802-76) in Hartford, Connecticut, whose *God in Christ* (1849) contends that religious → language is → metaphoric and poetic, not literal, and that scientific theological proofs and systems are therefore unattainable. Redefining doctrines of the → Trinity, the → atonement, and the Christian life, Bushnell became an inspiration for early American theological → liberalism, and his doctrine of Christian nurture as a gradual process within the setting of the → family influenced Protestant ideas about religious formation for more than a century. Bushnell's contentions about language mean that the truthfulness of theology is to be discerned through observation of its success in deepening the religious life.

4.5. The struggle in America over → slavery dealt a blow to a confident rational orthodoxy, as some theologians used the Bible to support slavery, while others used it to call for abolition. Antebellum black preachers such as Henry H. Garnet (1815-82) deplored the compatibility between conventional theology and Southern slavery. For theologians of the postwar generation, moreover, it became necessary to rewrite theology in response to innovations in biology, history, and biblical criticism.

5. New Theological Approaches

5.1. One result was the so-called new theology, which gradually redefined both reason and revelation and placed ever greater emphasis on theology as a form of practical thought. Proponents of this theology — such as Newman Smyth (1843-1925), whose book *The Religious Feeling* (1877) recalled the innovations of Dorner and F. D. E. → Schleiermacher (→ Schleiermacher's Theology) in Germany — still sought like their predecessors to show the reasonableness of Christianity, but they appealed now to religious and moral → experience more than to the external evidences that had drawn the attention of the antebellum Baconians.

5.2. Following the social and economic struggles of the 1880s, when laboring people clashed repeatedly with → capitalists over wages and living conditions, a small group of theologians, Protestant and Catholic, elaborated a theology for a → "social gospel" that called even more of the older presuppositions into question. The Catholic Americanists and

the Protestant Christian Socialists insisted, in different ways, on the importance of the social location of theological reflection. John Ireland (1838-1918), the first archbishop of St. Paul, contended in *The Church and Modern Society* (1903) that the church could meet the challenges of the new age only if it identified itself with the battle for social justice, a position developed with greater detail in the social teachings of John A. Ryan (1869-1945), a professor of → social ethics at Catholic University in Washington, D.C., who argued that proper ideas of God express themselves in such mundane ways as support for a living wage for working people.

The Baptist theologian Walter → Rauschenbusch (1861-1918) of Rochester Seminary, impressed by the historical understanding of the → kingdom of God promoted by Albrecht Ritschl in Germany, argued that social conditions always generate the theological conceptions adapted to them. He urged a theology fitted to a democratic political and economic order.

5.3. American philosophers joined in subjecting the older conception of reason in theology to criticism. Josiah Royce (1855-1916) at Harvard, a student of Kantian and Hegelian idealisms, argued that Baconian → empiricism fails to uncover and secure the logical presuppositions required for the possibility of theology. The → pragmatist William James (1842-1910) insisted that any rationalism, including Royce's, distorts the data of religious experience and fails to conceive properly of thought as a tool to guide experience rather than mirror reality. John Dewey's (1859-1952) instrumentalist view of thinking influenced a small number of liberal theologians after World War I.

5.4. The → liberal theologies resulting from such revaluations assumed diverse forms. One group, including William Newton Clarke (1841-1912) and William Adams Brown (1856-1943), located the authority for theological claims in "experience" as well as Scripture. Clarke, who taught at Colgate Seminary, refurbished an ethical idealism; Brown, who taught at Union Seminary in New York, adopted the Ritschlian view of theological statements as value judgments rather than propositions that explained in the manner of the physical sciences.

Another group, led by Borden P. Bowne (1847-1910) at Boston University, defended on philosophical grounds a personalist theology that defines reality as a network of → persons with a supreme Person at its head. Personalists emphasized the moral correlates of theology, but they opposed any suggestion that pragmatic criteria alone could define theological truth. Their attraction to metaphysics distinguished their form of rationality from the earlier empirical Baconian style.

A third group proposed an empirical theology that would respect the restraints imposed by scientific method. D. C. Macintosh (1877-1948) at Yale used the empirical approach to define God as a reality that produces predictable results when made the object of a right religious adjustment. More important, the theologians of the University of Chicago, especially H. N. Wieman (1884-1975), sought theological formulations attuned to scientific descriptions of the world. Wieman developed a theological naturalism that sought to discover the dynamic process operative in nature that acts to generate value. He introduced the → process philosophy of A. N. Whitehead (1861-1947) at the University of Chicago.

6. Conservative Developments

By the end of the 1920s, the → conservative wing of Protestant theologians intensified a counterattack against the liberals.

6.1. J. Gresham Machen (1881-1937), who represented → Calvinism and commonsense philosophy at Princeton seminary, defined Christianity and liberalism in 1923 as two distinct religions. By that time, some of the conservatives had coalesced into a → fundamentalist party marked by adherence to biblical inerrancy and premillennial → dispensationalism.

This position found detailed expression in the *Systematic Theology* (1947-48) of Lewis S. Chafer (1871-1952) of Dallas Theological Seminary. Fundamentalist theology flourished by identifying itself with the populist strand in American theology, criticizing elite universities as secular institutions, and casting its lot with newly founded Bible schools that advertised their concern for extending → Christian education to groups on the economic and cultural margins.

6.2. Not all conservative theologians adopted dispensational views. C. F. H. Henry (b. 1913) at Fuller Theological Seminary criticized the liberals by arguing that only an intelligible supernatural revelation gives theological discourse its meaning and that revelation is necessary to an informed reason. In some forms of Protestant conservatism, the evidentialist traditions of the early 19th century found a renewed currency.

6.3. Other evangelicals, however, used a different apologetic strategy. Cornelius Van Til (1895-1987) at Westminster Seminary took the position advanced earlier by Abraham Kuyper (1837-1920) in the Netherlands that Christian theology can accept no autonomous reason (→ Autonomy) divorced from scriptural revelation and that the task of Christian → apologetics is to show that only the presupposition of biblical → theism can support any truly rational view of the world.

7. Theological Realism

7.1. Quite a different critique of liberalism came from the group known as theological realists. While acknowledging a debt to liberal biblical and historical scholarship, they found in the European theology of crisis, especially as formulated by Emil Brunner (1889-1966) and Paul → Tillich (1886-1965), a vocabulary that exposed the extent to which theology had become captive to a shallow modern → culture. H. Richard Niebuhr (1894-1962) at Yale criticized the pragmatic tendency, which he found even in the empiricism of his mentor D. C. Macintosh, to use cultural values as criteria in defining God. His brother Reinhold → Niebuhr (1892-1971) at Union Seminary in New York recovered the import of the doctrine of original sin as a presupposition of a social ethic. As an immigrant to America from Germany, Tillich became almost a celebrity during his years on the faculties of Union Seminary, Harvard University, and the University of Chicago.

By the mid-1960s Karl → Barth's theology also made deep inroads in American theological faculties, and Barth's critique of natural theology challenged both liberal and conservative American assumptions about the meaning of theological rationality. Rather than assume that reason and experience could provide proofs of Christian truth claims, the Barthians thought of theology as faith's effort to understand itself (→ Dialectical Theology).

7.2. Although the realist critique proved influential in the mainline seminaries and denominations, it hardly monopolized the attention of all theologians. In the writing of Dom Virgil Michel (1890-1938), especially *The Liturgy of the Church* (1937), the Roman Catholic Church found an inspiration for liturgical reform that combined historical awareness (→ Liturgical Movement), an organic sense of both the church and society, and a passion for social justice. The Catholic theologian John C. Murray (1904-67) explored the grounds for → religious liberty in an increasingly diverse American culture. His influence extended beyond the American scene when he became a primary contributor to *Dignitatis humanae,* the Declaration on Religious Liberty, of the Second → Vatican Council (1962-65).

An influential group of liberal Protestants, moreover, countered the Barthian critique by defending a more positive linkage between theology and metaphysics. Charles Hartshorne (1897-2000), Bernard Loomer (1912-85), and D. D. Williams (1910-73) at the University of Chicago continued to press the assertions of a → process theology that accented the continuities between Christian truth claims and a rationally coherent view of reality.

8. Secular Theologies

The cultural turmoil of the 1960s engendered a new array of theological options. The radical theology of Thomas J. J. Altizer (b. 1927) combined insights from Barth, metaphysics, and a poetic imagination influenced by the visions of William Blake to argue that the → incarnation entails the immanence of the sacred within the secular. While few were drawn to Altizer's image of the "death of God" (→ God Is Dead Theology), a larger company of theologians, ranging from Protestants Harvey Cox (b. 1929) and Paul van Buren (1924-88) to Roman Catholics Leslie Dewart (b. 1922) and Gregory Baum (b. 1923), attempted to speak to a secular consciousness for which older distinctions between a natural and a supernatural realm no longer made sense.

9. Christian Thought in the Secular World

These secular theologies inscribed new lines of division in American Christianity, and after 1965, as Americans faced civil unrest in cities torn by racial division (→ Civil Rights Movement), a war in Vietnam that fragmented the nation, political assassinations, and a scandal that forced a president from office, the divisions intensified.

9.1. A new public awareness of → evangelical pieties in popular Protestantism (→ Popular Religion) helped evangelical theologians like Donald Bloesch (b. 1928) make the case that the secularity of the 1960s had never been as widespread as its proponents believed. Evangelical theologians agreed on the authority and historical reliability of Scripture and the necessity for explicit confession of faith in Christ as Savior, but they themselves divided over biblical inerrancy, Pentecostal piety, and the proper relation between evangelical faith and American culture.

9.2. Some American theologians tried to take secularity seriously but also subject it to criticism. No one did this with greater sophistication than the Canadian Jesuit Bernard Lonergan (1904-84), whose *Insight: A Study of Human Understanding* (1957) still stands as a landmark effort to correlate theology and the human sciences. An effort to understand the nature of understanding itself, the book maintains continuity with tradition (which

for Lonergan meant a revised → Thomism) while entering into a learned conversation with the natural and social sciences, an enterprise that Lonergan continued in his *Method in Theology* (1972).

9.3. Lonergan influenced, among many others, the Catholic theologian David Tracy (b. 1939) at the University of Chicago, who sought in his *Blessed Rage for Order* (1975) to bring → secularism and Christian faith into → dialogue. Similar projects flourished in the two decades after the Second Vatican Council.

Avery Dulles (b. 1918) spoke for more conservative Catholic theologians when he argued in 1977 that such "revisionist" projects surrendered essential Catholic truths. Some American Catholic contributors to the 1980 volume *Consensus in Theology?* conceded that → consensus even within the Catholic tradition seemed impossible to reach.

9.4. Among Protestants, the continued effort at dialogue between theology and secular thought appeared especially in the appeal of process philosophy to theologians like John Cobb (b. 1925) and Schubert Ogden (b. 1928), who mounted conversations with Continental philosophy, natural science, and non-Christian religions. But the realism of the Niebuhrs also won defenders, and the students of H. Richard Niebuhr, in particular, remained prominent among theologians interested in dialogue with other disciplines.

Gordon Kaufman (b. 1925) at Harvard saw theology as a discipline whose concern with symbolizing the grounds and limits of human experience has the primary aim of nurturing the distinctively human. James Gustafson (b. 1925), who taught at Yale, Chicago, and Emory, argued for a "theocentric ethic" in which human flourishing remains secondary to a larger good. Both believed, however, that a responsible theology must recognize the cognitive weight of natural science as well as of Christian tradition.

By the early 1980s, scientific interests led some, like Sallie McFague (b. 1933) at Vanderbilt, to explore the relationships between theology, religious language, and efforts to preserve the earth's → ecology (→ Environment).

9.5. For other Protestant theologians, it was more important to define a distinctively Christian identity than to engage in a dialogue with secular thought. Among these theologians, none had more influence than Hans Frei (1922-88) at Yale, whose *Eclipse of Biblical Narrative* (1974) initiated his effort to discern how one might depict the identity of Christ by reading the Gospels through the methods of the New Criticism in literary theory. Frei's enterprise helped stimulate a movement of → "narrative theology" in which the primary concern is the internal coherence of the "Christian story" and the way in which it forms the identity of the believer.

Frei's colleague George Lindbeck (b. 1923) continued the project in his *Nature of Doctrine* (1984), in which he explored how the distinctive grammar of Christian language might provide the interpretive schemes that guide communal formation and ecumenical conversation.

9.6. In a related movement, Catholic theologian Aidan Kavanagh (b. 1929) of Yale Divinity School and Protestants Geoffrey Wainwright (b. 1939) of Duke University and Don Saliers (b. 1937) of Emory University found in Christian liturgical practice a source for reflection on Christian → identity and formation.

9.7. Finally, theologians who spoke explicitly from historic traditions joined in the effort to define Christian identity, including especially such theologians as Carl Braaten (b. 1929) and Robert Jenson (b. 1930), whose Trinitarian theologies bear the mark of their allegiance to the Lutheran tradition, and George Florovsky (1893-1979) and John Meyendorff (1926-92), who brought the insights of Russian Orthodoxy (→ Orthodox Church) to theology in America.

10. Theologies of Particularity

By the time Lindbeck advanced his argument for attention to the particular logic and grammar of Christian discourse, however, other assertions of particularity, rooted in social movements that began in the 1960s, had captured the imagination of numerous younger American theologians.

10.1. In 1969 James Cone (b. 1938) published *Black Theology and Black Power.* More than any other book, it gave rise to a distinctive → black theology in which the corporate experience of African Americans becomes the interpretive lens for reading Scripture and writing theology. The aim of such a theology is manifestly practical, namely, to empower blacks and undermine white → racism. Subsequent black theologians retained this practical intention as they debated the tension between liberation of blacks and reconciliation with whites, appropriated black cultural forms for theological expression, explored black history, and related black thought to other forms of → liberation theology, especially in Latin America.

10.2. Spurred by the rise of → feminism and the growing visibility of theologies of liberation, → feminist theologians began as early as 1960 to call

for revisions that might also free theology from its blindness to a distorting masculine bias. In 1968 the Catholic theologian Mary Daly (b. 1928) of Boston College published *The Church and the Second Sex.* Daly soon left the church, but her desire to rethink theological language and to use theology for the liberation of women attracted supporters, none more influential in the early stages of the movement than Rosemary Radford Ruether (b. 1936), who attempted to show in her *Liberation Theology* (1972) how sexism reflects a habit of → dualistic thinking that needs theological criticism.

Feminist theologians proceeded from a critique of patriarchy and exclusively masculine language to a broad effort to recover the experience of women in Christian tradition, to give voice to women's experience, to reform the church, and to recover Christian insight into the nature of human and divine relatedness, often informed by Trinitarian reflection. But the demand for particularity raised questions about the ability of any one perspective to represent the multiplicity of women's voices.

Drawing on the language of the novelist Alice Walker in 1983, Katie Geneva Cannon (b. 1950) and others began to write as "womanist" theologians, intent on speaking from the perspective of African American women. In a similar way, Hispanic theologians, both men and women, began to speak from their cultural locations, while other writers found in sexual orientation or conditions of disability an experience that provides a distinctive theological point of view.

10.3. These voices of particularity recovered the view of the earlier social gospel that theology bears the imprint of its social context. But the multiplicity of these voices, often cast against competing alternatives, signified that theologians in America at the turn of the 21st century differed profoundly about the methods, the subject matter, and the purpose of their discipline. Few shared 19th-century assumptions that theological claims should appear convincing to any reasonable person. Most still described theology as a practical discipline, but they now differed as well about what its practicality entailed.

11. Theological Study and Publication

For almost two centuries, American theologians resided mainly in local parishes. The founding of Andover Seminary in 1808 began a transition in which theology became the monopoly of seminary faculties, and the seminaries at Yale, Harvard, Princeton, Union in New York, and the University of Chicago occasionally became synonymous with specific movements of thought (→ Theological Education). The American separation between → church and state kept theological departments out of the state universities. Even now, when state universities foster strong departments of → religious studies, theology as such remains located primarily in the denominational and interdenominational seminaries.

While university presses often publish theological works, the main agencies of theological publication have been such houses as Abingdon, Eerdmans, Fortress, and Westminster/John Knox, which are devoted primarily to religious publication. In the 19th century such journals as the *Biblical Repertory and Reformed Review* at Princeton and the *Mercersburg Review* at Mercersburg Seminary exemplified the publishing activity of the seminaries, while each of the larger denominations also published important theological journals. Prominent journals — the *Harvard Theological Review, Journal of Religion* (University of Chicago), and *Theology Today* (Princeton Seminary) — still retain an association with specific schools, but the growing importance of scholarly guilds, such as the American Academy of Religion, which sponsors the *Journal of the American Academy of Religion,* and the Society of Biblical Literature, with its *Journal of Biblical Literature,* marked a change in theological publication (→ Christian Publishing).

Bibliography: General: S. E. AHLSTROM, "Theology in America: A Historical Survey," *The Shaping of American Religion* (ed. J. W. Smith and A. L. Jamison; Princeton, 1961) 232-321; idem, ed., *Theology in America: The Major Protestant Voices from Puritanism to Neo-orthodoxy* (Indianapolis, 1967) • P. W. CAREY, ed., *American Catholic Religious Thought* (New York, 1987) • D. W. FERM, *Contemporary American Theologies* (New York, 1981) • E. B. HOLIFIELD, *The Rise of American Theology: Revelation, Reason, and Faith, 1636-1865* (New Haven, 2003) • M. A. NOLL, *America's God: From Jonathan Edwards to Abraham Lincoln* (New York, 2002) • T. W. TILLEY, ed., *Postmodern Theologies: The Challenge of Religious Diversity* (Maryknoll, N.Y., 1995) • M. TOULOUSE and J. O. DUKE, eds., *Makers of Christian Theology in America* (Nashville, 1997).

On 1: T. D. BOZEMAN, *To Live Ancient Lives* (Chapel Hill, N.C., 1988) • C. CHERRY, *Nature and Religious Imagination: From Edwards to Bushnell* (Philadelphia, 1980); idem, *The Theology of Jonathan Edwards* (New York, 1966) • J. CONFORTI, *Samuel Hopkins and the New Divinity Movement* (Grand Rapids, 1981) • N. FIERING, *Moral Philosophy in Seventeenth-Century Harvard* (Chapel Hill, N.C., 1981) • F. H. FOSTER, *A Genetic History of the New England Theology* (Chicago, 1907) • A. C. GUELZO, *Edwards on the Will: A Century of American Theological Debate* (Middletown, Conn., 1989) • J. HAROUTUNIAN, *Piety versus Moralism: The Passing of the New England Theology* (New York, 1932) • E. B. HOLIFIELD, *The Covenant Sealed: The Development of Puritan Sacramental Theology in Old and New England, 1570-1720* (New Haven, 1974) • T. HOOKER, *The Application of Redemption* (London, 1648) • S. H. LEE and A. C. GUELZO, eds., *Edwards in Our Time: Jonathan Edwards and the Shaping of American Religion* (Grand Rapids, 1999) • P. MILLER, *The New England Mind: The Seventeenth Century* (New York, 1939) • T. SHEPARD, *The Sincere Convert* (London, 1657) • W. K. B. STOEVER, *A Faire and Easie Way to Heaven: Covenant Theology and Antinomianism in Early New England* (Middletown, Conn., 1978) • S. WILLARD, *A Complete Body of Divinity* (Boston, 1726).

On 2: W. E. CHANNING, *Unitarian Christianity* (Boston, 1819) • P. K. CONKIN, *The Uneasy Center: Reformed Christianity in Antebellum America* (Chapel Hill, N.C., 1995) • C. HODGE, *Systematic Theology* (3 vols.; New York, 1872-73) • D. W. HOWE, *The Unitarian Conscience* (Middletown, Conn., 1970) • S. MEAD, *Nathaniel William Taylor* (Chicago, 1942) • M. NOLL, *Princeton and the Republic, 1768-1822* (Princeton, 1989); idem, ed., *The Princeton Theology* (Grand Rapids, 1983) • M. SPAULDING, *Lectures on the Evidences of Catholicity* (Louisville, Ky., 1848).

On 3: T. D. BOZEMAN, *Protestants in an Age of Science* (Durham, N.C., 1978) • E. B. HOLIFIELD, *The Gentlemen Theologians: American Theology in Southern Culture, 1795-1860* (Durham, N.C., 1978) • T. PARKER, *A Discourse on the Transient and Permanent in Christianity* (Boston, 1841).

On 4: O. A. BROWNSON, *Selected Writings* (ed. P. W. Carey; New York, 1991) • H. BUSHNELL, *God in Christ* (Hartford, Conn., 1849) • W. R. HUTCHISON, *The Transcendentalist Ministers* (New Haven, 1959) • C. P. KRAUTH, *The Conservative Reformation and Its Theology* (Philadelphia, 1871) • J. W. NEVIN, *The Mystical Presence* (Philadelphia, 1846) • J. H. NICHOLS, *Romanticism in American Theology* (Chicago, 1961) • R. W. PRICHARD, *The Nature of Salvation: Theological Consensus in the Episcopal Church, 1801-1873* (Urbana, Ill., 1997) • P. SCHAFF, *The Principle of Protestantism* (Philadelphia, 1845) • T. TAPPERT, ed., *Lutheran Confessional Theology in America, 1840-1880* (New York, 1972) • C. F. W. WALTHER, *The Proper Distinction between Law and Gospel* (St. Louis, 1929; orig. pub., 1897).

On 5: B. P. BOWNE, *Studies in Theism* (New York, 1879) • W. A. BROWN, *Christian Theology in Outline* (New York, 1906) • K. CAUTHEN, *The Impact of Ameri-*

can *Religious Liberalism* (New York, 1962) • W. N. CLARKE, *An Outline of Christian Theology* (Cambridge, Mass., 1894) • J. DEWEY, *A Common Faith* (New Haven, 1934) • R. T. HANDY, ed., *The Social Gospel in America* (New York, 1966) • W. R. HUTCHISON, *The Modernist Impulse in American Protestantism* (Cambridge, Mass., 1976) • W. JAMES, *Pragmatism* (New York, 1907); idem, *The Varieties of Religious Experience* (New York, 1902) • D. C. MACINTOSH, *Theology as an Empirical Science* (New York, 1919) • W. RAUSCHENBUSCH, *Christianity and the Social Crisis* (New York, 1907); idem, *A Theology for the Social Gospel* (New York, 1917) • J. ROYCE, *The Problem of Christianity* (New York, 1913) • N. SMYTH, *The Religious Feeling* (New York, 1877) • H. N. WIEMAN, *Religious Experience and Scientific Method* (New York, 1926) • D. D. WILLIAMS, *The Andover Liberals* (New York, 1941).

On 6: L. S. CHAFER, *Systematic Theology* (8 vols.; Dallas, 1947-48) • C. F. H. HENRY, *God, Revelation, and Authority* (6 vols.; Waco, Tex., 1976-83) • J. G. MACHEN, *Christianity and Liberalism* (New York, 1923) • G. MARSDEN, *Fundamentalism and American Culture* (New York, 1980); idem, *Reforming Fundamentalism: Fuller Seminary and the New Evangelicalism* (Grand Rapids, 1987) • D. WELLS, ed., *Reformed Theology in America* (Grand Rapids, 1997).

On 7: W. D. DEAN, *American Religious Empiricism* (Albany, N.Y., 1986) • R. LOVIN, *Reinhold Niebuhr and Christian Realism* (Cambridge, 1995) • J. C. MURRAY, *We Hold These Truths* (New York, 1960) • H. R. NIEBUHR, *The Meaning of Revelation* (New York, 1941); idem, *Radical Monotheism and Western Culture* (New York, 1960) • R. NIEBUHR, *Moral Man and Immoral Society* (New York, 1934); idem, *The Nature and Destiny of Man* (New York, 1949).

On 8: C. CROCKETT, ed., *Secular Theology: American Radical Theological Thought* (London, 2001).

On 9: J. B. COBB, *A Christian Natural Theology, Based on the Thought of Alfred North Whitehead* (Philadelphia, 1965) • S. HAUERWAS and L. G. JONES, eds., *Why Narrative? Readings in Narrative Theology* (Grand Rapids, 1989) • R. W. JENSON, *Systematic Theology* (2 vols.; New York, 1997-99) • A. KAVANAGH, *On Liturgical Theology* (New York, 1984) • G. LINDBECK, *The Nature of Doctrine* (Philadelphia, 1984) • S. McFAGUE, *Models of God* (Minneapolis, 1987).

On 10: K. CANNON, *Womanism and the Soul of the Black Community* (New York, 1995) • R. CHOPP and M. L. TAYLOR, *Reconstructing Christian Theology* (Minneapolis, 1994) • J. CONE, *God of the Oppressed* (New York, 1975) • E. JOHNSON, *She Who Is* (New York, 1992) • R. R. RUETHER, *New Woman, New Earth* (San Francisco, 1975).

E. BROOKS HOLIFIELD

North Korea

	1960	*1980*	*2000*
Population (1,000s):	10,525	17,666	23,913
Annual growth rate (%):	2.73	1.39	1.22
Area: 122,762 sq. km. (47,399 sq. mi.)			

A.D. *2000*

Population density: 195/sq. km. (504/sq. mi.)
Births / deaths: 1.78 / 0.56 per 100 population
Fertility rate: 2.10 per woman
Infant mortality rate: 19 per 1,000 live births
Life expectancy: 73.2 years (m: 70.1, f: 76.1)
Religious affiliation (%): nonreligious 55.8, atheists 15.6, new religionists 12.6, tribal religionists 12.3, Christians 2.3 (indigenous 2.0, other Christians 0.3), Buddhists 1.5, other 0.1.

1. General Situation
2. Religious Situation
   2.1. Non-Christian Religions
   2.2. Roman Catholics
   2.3. Protestants
   2.4. Ecumenical Contacts

1. General Situation

The Korean Peninsula was provisionally divided along the 38th parallel in 1945 by mutual agreement between the United States and the USSR, whose combined forces had defeated the Japanese army, bringing an end to Japan's 35-year imperial rule. In 1948 the government of the Republic of Korea (ROK) was formed in the South under the leadership of Syngman Rhee (1875-1965), followed shortly thereafter by the proclamation of the Democratic People's Republic of Korea (DPRK) in the North under Kim Il Sung (1912-94). Military confrontations along the line of division multiplied, leading finally to the outbreak of the Korean War (1950-53). Masses fled the war — and the Communist regime — in the North during this period, and many Southerners were trapped in the North when the border was sealed by the 1953 armistice agreement, leaving an estimated ten million families separated.

Initial hopes and intentions of Korean independence and reunification fell victim to cold war tensions. The South developed under the dominant influence of the United States, while the North strengthened its relationships with the Communist world. Both sides developed in a militarist mode, increasing tensions and solidifying the division, which became a primary symbol of cold war confrontation. Kim Il Sung's *juché* ideology (self-reliance, Koreans first) took hold in the North, emphasizing self-reliance in politics, economics, defense, and ideology. This orientation led the DPRK away from Soviet influence in 1955, and in the 1960s it declared its independence from both Moscow and Beijing. A strong personality cult developed around Kim Il Sung, who assumed an identity as the Great Leader, with mythical powers, and North Korea became one of the world's most closed and rigidly structured societies.

North Korea's economy suffered a severe setback with the collapse of the Soviet Union and Communist regimes in Eastern Europe from 1989. Cut off from vital oil supplies and major trading partners, Kim Il Sung sought a new opening of North-South dialogue before he died in 1994. These changes raised new hopes for progress toward the long-postponed goal of reunification by peaceful, independent means, which had been jointly declared by the two Korean governments on July 4, 1972.

After a long period of official mourning, his son Kim Jong Il assumed power and signaled his willingness to pursue this policy. Significant signs of progress began to appear, however, only after a series of devastating floods and consequent famine that occurred in the North in the mid-1990s prompted the government to appeal to the international community for massive economic and material assistance. The generous response of the United Nations and both governmental and nongovernmental donors contributed to a new openness to the outside world.

In the South, Kim Dae Jung, a democratic leader committed to reunification, was elected in February 1998, and he soon declared a new "Sunshine Policy" with respect to the DPRK. In June 2000 he traveled to P'yŏngyang, the North Korean capital, for a historic meeting with Kim Jong Il and later that year was awarded the Nobel Peace Prize for his initiatives. A promising, far-reaching joint declaration was issued by the two Korean governments soon after, on June 15, 2000. These steps, combined with the recent normalization of diplomatic relations with the DPRK by key Western governments, contributed to increasing rapprochement with South Korea, which led to new agreements on family reunions, tourism, and economic cooperation.

2. Religious Situation

Until very recently, less has been known about religion in North Korea than in almost any closed society other than Albania and Mongolia before the global collapse of Communism after 1991. Hard facts on the conditions of religious believers after 1945 are still difficult to come by, making assessments necessarily approximate. As more international observers have been granted access to the DPRK in recent years, more information is gradually coming to light, which the following paragraphs reflect.

Korea has a long history of repression of → religion, especially of religious beliefs of foreign origin. Christianity was especially resisted after it first appeared on the peninsula in the late 18th century, and it was systematically attacked under Japanese imperial domination from 1910 (→ Persecution of Christians). Japanese rulers severely persecuted all religious believers during the 1930s when they sought to impose → Shinto as the national religion. Since 1945 the leadership of North Korea adopted the aggressive → atheism of Stalinist Communism and engaged in systematic repression of religious ideas and organizations, especially between 1946 and 1958.

Despite this history, Christianity flourished in Korea, and by 1945 a larger portion of the population called themselves Christians than in any other Asian country except the Philippines. Since the end of World War II efforts were made in the North to eliminate or rigidly control religion, and a large number of churches and other places of worship were destroyed. After 1945 the Communist leadership of the North created organizations to manage and seek to control the activities and religious practices of religious groups. In 1983, however, Kim Il Sung declared limited religious freedom, allowing these organizations a degree of latitude in contacting and organizing their members. Until very recently there were widespread doubts in South Korea and elsewhere about the existence of churches in North Korea. It now becomes increasingly clear that the practice of religion, including Christianity, continued and that in some places it is again on the rise.

2.1. Non-Christian Religions

→ Confucianism, → Buddhism, and → shamanism all have deep historical roots in Korea and continued to be widespread in North Korea after 1945, though Buddhists were especially sharply repressed after that time. One estimate suggests that the number of shamanists in 2000 could be as high as 2.2 million. Shamanism is so deeply rooted in Korean culture that a number of its practices and holidays have been adapted into secular life. The indigenous Korean religion, Ch'ŏndogyo (Religion of the heavenly way), which emerged among Korean peasants in 1860, is estimated to have some two million followers in North Korea today, approximately the same as in 1945. The cult established around the "Great Leader" constitutes another modern form of religion; his elevation to "eternal president" in 1998 was intended to guarantee continued adoration after his death.

2.2. Roman Catholics

Christianity first came to Korea from China through a Roman Catholic convert in the late 18th century, nearly a century before the arrival of Protestant missionaries. The Roman Catholic converts were badly persecuted, and many of them were martyred, but by 1884 it is estimated that there were 18,000 believers in the church.

In 1945 North Korea had two suffragan → dioceses of Seoul and a third related to the church in China. Half of Roman Catholic Christians and all their priests and administrators are said to have fled to the South after 1945, leaving an estimated 25,000 in the North.

From the late 1980s there have been visits to Catholic Christian communities by both ecumenical delegations and → Roman Catholic Church hierarchs, and in 1988 the Changchun Roman Catholic "cathedral" was erected in P'yŏngyang. Though there are still no ordained → clergy to serve the scattered communities, South Korean → priests and → bishops and Vatican officials regularly visit and conduct mass in this church.

2.3. Protestants

The earliest Protestant missions in North Korea were the Presbyterian and Methodist, the former being by far the stronger in 1945. Small Christian minorities belonged to the → Holiness and Seventh-day → Adventist churches and the → Salvation Army. Many of their members fled to the South when the Communist government came into power in 1945, and many more joined the mass emigration during the Korean War. The ruling party of North Korea created the Korean Christians Federation (KCF) in 1946, grouping together all Protestant Christians without reference to their former → denominations.

The KCF estimates its membership at 100,000 persons worshiping together in some 10,000 → house churches around the country. Some of these groups have been visited by foreign church delegations. In the mid-1980s the KCF reconstituted a Protestant theological seminary and gained permission to build two churches, Bongsu and Chilgol, in P'yŏngyang, with 400 and 150 members respectively. They are the only parishes today permitted the privilege of public worship. Well-informed visitors to the DPRK put the present numbers of practicing Protestant Christians in North Korea at a much lower levels than those used by the KCF, suggesting a total of 13,000, grouped together in some 675 house churches, mostly along the west coast, served by some 40 trained pastors and 20 ordained lay leaders.

2.4. Ecumenical Contacts

Despite reports to the contrary from the few church-related individuals who visited North Korea between 1981 and 1985, there were widespread and serious doubts about the existence of a living Christian community in that country. In an attempt to reach out beyond their borders, the KCF wrote to the → World Council of Churches (WCC) in 1974 to inquire about possible membership, but there was no reliable means to maintain subsequent communication. The KCF did join the → Christian Peace Conference in 1976, however, and sent representatives to some of its meetings in Eastern Europe. In November 1984 the WCC organized the world consultation "Peace and Justice in North-East Asia: Prospects for Peaceful Resolution of Conflicts" in Tozanso, Japan. The main item on the consultation agenda was the threat posed by the continuing division of the Korean Peninsula. The KCF was invited but could not attend, although it did send a message welcoming the ecumenical initiative and wishing it success.

In early 1985 the → National Council of the Churches of Christ in the U.S.A. (NCCC) was invited to send a delegation of church representatives to North Korea, the first in more than 40 years. They met with senior state officials and representatives of the KCF and worshiped with house church congregations in P'yŏngyang and Kaesŏng. Later that year two senior staff members of the WCC received an official invitation to visit North Korea and proposed to the leadership of the KCF that they consider joining in a face-to-face meeting with leaders of the South Korean National Council of Churches in Korea (NCCK).

This invitation was reiterated by an official delegation of church leaders from the NCCC that paid a second visit to the DPRK in April 1986. In September of that year the WCC convened "Seminar on the Biblical and Theological Foundations of Christian Concern for Peace" in Glion, Switzerland, in which four representatives of the KCF and six from the NCCK participated, providing the first opportunity for Christians from North and South to meet one another since Korea was divided in 1945. This historic ecumenical gathering gave rise to two further WCC-sponsored North-South Christian encounters in Glion: one in 1988, when the KCF and NCCK developed a common prayer for peaceful reunification in North and South that was also used by churches elsewhere, and another in 1990. Similar conferences took place also in Kyoto, Japan (1995), and in Macao (1996).

The confidence built in these gatherings provided a framework, called the Tozanso Process, within which representatives of the KCF traveled four times to the United States between 1989 and 1997 for official → dialogue meetings with U.S. church counterparts. All these visits outside the DPRK, and several more later to Germany, Canada, and elsewhere, provided opportunities for encounter and planning for joint initiatives to promote reunification between representatives of the KCF and the NCCK. Toward the end of the 1990s representatives of the NCCK were able for the first time to travel to the DPRK for meetings with their Northern counterparts on the Korean Peninsula itself; these visits have since continued and become more frequent.

As a result of these ecumenical efforts, DPRK officials made their first request for international humanitarian assistance for flood victims to the WCC, and churches were among the first to provide help. The fact that this aid was given through the KCF significantly broadened the role and recognition of this Christian body in North Korean society. Goods produced by its noodle factory and bakery, both built with international church assistance, and its distribution to the broad public around the country of food, clothes, medical supplies, and other essentials provided by church and ecumenical partners abroad were known and appreciated.

Bibliography: On 1: B. CUMINGS, *Korea's Place in the Sun: A Modern History* (New York, 1997) • N. EBERSTADT and R. J. ELLINGS, eds., *Korea's Future and the Great Powers* (Seattle, Wash., 2001) • C.-H. KANG and P. RIGOULOT, *The Aquariums of Pyongyang: Ten Years in a North Korean Gulag* (trans. Y. Reiner; New York, 2001) • *Managing Change on the Korean Peninsula* (New York, 1998) • D. OBERDORFER, *The Two Koreas: A Contemporary History* (Reading, Mass., 1997) • S.-K. YI, *Inside the Hermit Kingdom: A Memoir* (Toronto, 1997).

On 2: D. B. BARRETT et al., eds., *WCE* (2d ed.) 1.558-60 • CHRISTIAN CONFERENCE OF ASIA, *Reunification: Peace and Justice in the 1980s* (Hong Kong, 1988) • A. D. CLARK, *A History of the Church in Korea* (Seoul, 1971) • COMMISSION OF THE CHURCHES ON INTERNATIONAL AFFAIRS, *Peace and Justice in North East Asia: Prospects for Peaceful Resolution of Conflicts* (Geneva, 1985) •

PARK K. S., *Reconciliation-Reunification: The Ecumenical Approach to the Korean Peninsula* (Hong Kong, 1998) • E. WEINGARTNER, ed., *Peace and the Reunification of Korea* (Geneva, 1990).

DWAIN C. EPPS

Northern America

1. United States–Canada–Mexico
2. North American Distinctives
   2.1. Space
   2.2. The Bible
   2.3. Race and Ethnicity
   2.4. Pluralism
   2.5. Significance of Region
3. Canadian Counterpoint
4. Ecumenism and Mission

[*Note:* In current U.N. usage "Northern America" comprises the United States and Canada, plus the island dependencies of Bermuda (U.K.), Greenland (Den.), and St. Pierre and Miquelon (Fr.). The U.N.'s "Latin America and the Caribbean," then, includes Mexico and all of Central America, the West Indies, and South America. In its discussion here of the United States and Canada, with brief reference also to Mexico, this article uses throughout the more common phrase "North America."]

1. United States–Canada–Mexico

Spiritual as well as geographic orientation for the history of religion in North America, and especially of the Christianity that has been so dominant in both the United States and Canada, is provided readily by comparisons with the religious history of Mexico. In all three nations, modern religious history bears the stamp of early modern Europe, but in very different ways.

Mexico was marked in its beginning by the comprehensive Roman → Catholicism characteristic of southern European regimes during the → Renaissance and the Catholic Counter-Reformation (→ Catholic Reform and Counter-Reformation). Canada, by contrast, developed under the necessity of accommodating in a single nation both Quebec, a traditional Old World colony with church and state linked together organically, and English-language societies in Upper Canada and the Atlantic Provinces shaped by both British Protestant paternalism and the American separation of → church and state. For its part, the United States carried Protestant tendencies toward → voluntarism and democratic polity to their logical conclusions (and sometimes beyond).

Throughout its entire history, the tensions dominating religion in Mexico have been those characteristic of Roman Catholic Europe; they feature the clash between anticlerical liberal → rationalism and → Ultramontane Catholic → conservatism. In the United States the tensions are mostly the result of differences over how best to apply modern → individualism to church and society. In Canada a mixture of patrician conservatism and multicultural → democracy has dominated religious history.

The religious border between the United States and Mexico was defined by the antagonism that existed in the 16th and 17th centuries between the Iberian Catholic Hapsburgs and the English Protestant Tudors. The border between the United States and Canada was defined by the strife between Catholic France and Protestant Britain in the 18th century. Yet after Britain, with its Protestant institutions, completed the conquest of Canada, it set the stage for a much freer religious exchange between the United States and Canada than has existed between the United States and Mexico. The one exception to that generalization is the fairly recent flow of migration from Mexico to the United States, which now represents a bridge between the two countries for both Catholic and Pentecostal Protestant history.

2. North American Distinctives
Regarded against the background of world Christian history, religious history in North America has been unusual in at least five particulars — the physical space involved, the role played by the Bible, the mixing of racial and ethnic groups, the fact of unusual → pluralism, and the significance of region.

2.1. *Space*
In the first instance, religious history is affected by North America's being so much bigger than Europe. This huge geographic expanse gave churches the kind of breathing room that simply had not existed before, it allowed European religious antagonists to drift apart, and it gave creative souls every possible opportunity to propose new versions of Christianity, as well as other religions.

The scale of North America is suggested by the fact that the distance between London and Moscow, with all the thickly packed church history encountered between these two cities, is less than the distance between Montreal and Denver, or Montreal and Houston — distances that traverse a much thinner ecclesiastical history. The physical space bounded by Rome, Geneva, and Wittenberg would fit easily into Arizona or five other American states, not to mention being swallowed up in the land area of seven individual Canadian provinces.

2.2. *The Bible*
The Christian history of Canada and the United States differs also from that of Europe in the magnified role that the Bible has played in North America. It is not so much that North American Christianity honors the Bible more than European Christianity, but rather that religious authorities other than Scripture have been much weaker in North America. Neither a centralized → state church nor a hierarchical professoriat nor a tradition of deferential → worship supports the use of Scripture in North America. Rather, the Bible is a book of the people that has regularly been employed against such traditional supports.

The public role of the Bible is everywhere on view throughout American history. From the famous words in President Abraham Lincoln's Second Inaugural Address of 1865 claiming that "both [North and South] read the same Bible, and pray to the same God," to continued quotation by political leaders up to the present day, the Bible looms large in American public life. Representatives of religious minorities also regularly recognize, even celebrate, the Bible.

From 1860 to 1925, a period that could be described as the height of American biblical civilization as defined by intense Protestant loyalty to the Authorized, or King James, Version (KJV), American publishers brought out at least 136 non-KJV English-language editions of 42 separate translations of the Scriptures. The Douay-Rheims-Challoner translation for Roman Catholics was most prominent among these versions, but it was hardly by itself, even among Catholic Bibles. During the same period American publishers also issued at least 279 editions of complete Bibles in 39 languages other than English. Of these, an even 100 were complete German-language Bibles, another 10 editions each were of the Bible in Danish and Dakota, another 4 editions each were in Finnish, Gilbertese, Polish, and Zulu.

In Canada the centrality of the Bible has not been as obvious as in the United States, but Canadian Christianity has also been more directly shaped by a concentration on Scripture than much of European Christianity. During the 19th century, Canadian Protestants were almost as prone to employ biblical imagery as their neighbors south of the border. When the Dominion of Canada was formed in 1867, it seemed only natural for the Methodist Leonard Tilley of New Brunswick to apply the words of Ps. 72:8 to his country ("He shall have dominion also from sea to sea," KJV).

Northern America in A.D. 2000: Demography

	Population (1,000s)	Annual Growth Rate (%)	Population Density (per sq. km. / mi.)	Births / Deaths (per 100 pop.)	Fertility Rate (per woman)	Infant Mortality Rate (per 1,000 live births)	Life Expectancy (years)
World total	6,091,351	1.27	45 / 116	2.13 / 0.86	2.66	51	66.9
Northern America[a]	308,636	0.71	14 / 37	1.30 / 0.86	1.93	6	77.6
Canada	30,679	0.75	3 / 8	1.15 / 0.78	1.68	6	79.4
United States	277,825	0.71	29 / 76	1.32 / 0.87	1.96	6	77.4

[a]Figures include Bermuda (U.K.), Greenland (Den.), and St. Pierre and Miquelon (Fr.).

2.3. Race and Ethnicity

From the beginning, settlement in North America by Europeans was attended also by settlement by Africans. Even if the latter were the enslaved victims of kidnapping, the intermingled black-and-white character of society is a permanent part of the American experience. Almost as soon, North America witnessed a mingling of the various British nations — English, Scottish, Irish, and Welsh. In the region that became Canada, French and English settlement coexisted from the early 18th century. During the great era of European migration to North America that began in the 1830s, northern Europeans of all kinds streamed across the Atlantic, soon to be followed by great numbers of eastern and southern Europeans as well. Before the start of the 20th century, immigrants from Asia were added to the North American mix, and by the middle decades of the 20th century a great influx from the Hispanic world (Cuba, Mexico, Puerto Rico, Central and South America) was added as well. The religious effect of these migrations was to populate North America with a far greater range of ethnic churches than existed in any one nation of Europe, Asia, or Latin America.

The most important ethnic contribution to the history of North American Christianity remains African American. Most slave owners were not eager to have their slaves hear the Christian message. When slaves nonetheless succeeded in learning something about Christianity and then even formed churches for themselves, a remarkable transformation was underway (→ Black Churches). African American denominations emerged from humble northern beginnings around 1800 and received a major boost from emancipated slaves after the Civil War. Notable Christian leaders among African Africans — like Richard Allen, founder of the African Methodist Episcopal Church; the theologian-bishops of the 19th-century AME Daniel Payne and Henry McNeal Turner; or the Baptist Martin Luther → King Jr. in the 1950s and 1960s — decisively altered the history of their times. The most notable development, how-

ever, was the willingness of countless slaves, freed slaves, and those threatened by → slavery to find dignity, purpose, and resolution in a religion they had received so grudgingly from the slave masters.

2.4. Pluralism

To visitors from overseas, the stupendous array of churches, parachurch agencies, and non-Christian religious bodies has long been one of the most striking features of North American religious life. For all of Europe's traditional confessional → denominations, moving to the New World meant at least two new realities — multiple schisms (→ Heresies and Schisms) and ecclesiastical competition. Schism is far from unknown in Europe, but it has flourished as never before in North America. Whether the Polish National Catholic Church from Roman Catholicism, the → Churches of Christ from → Presbyterianism, the Lutheran Brethren and the Lutheran Free Church from the main ethnic → Lutheran churches, the Reformed Episcopalians from the Episcopal Church in the United States, the Protestant Reformed Church from the largely Dutch-American Christian Reformed Church, the Ukrainian Orthodox Church of the U.S.A. from the Ukrainian Orthodox Church in America (→ Orthodox Church), or the many, many others, the list of such divisions is virtually endless.

To be sure, North American forces have also worked in the other direction. Within all major religious traditions, ecclesiastical amalgamations have taken place that were unthinkable in Europe. Again the list is very long, whether seceding splinters rejoining larger Presbyterian churches; Finns, Danes, Swedes, and Norwegians joining Germans and Slovaks in multiethnic Lutheran churches; or jaded evangelicals joining recent immigrants from the Middle East in the Antiochian Orthodox Church. However significant these ecumenical forces have been, however, the forces of individualization have been greater.

European churches in North America also had to learn how to compete democratically if they wanted to survive. After the creation of the United States

Northern America in A.D. 2000: Religious Affiliation (as percentage of population)

	Christians	Muslims	Hindus	Non-religious	Chinese Folk Religionists	Buddhists	Tribal Religionists	Atheists	New Religionists	Sikhs	Jews	Spiritists	Other
World total	33.1	20.0	12.8	12.7	6.3	5.9	4.1	2.4	1.6	0.4	0.2	0.2	0.3
Northern America[a]	84.9	1.4	0.4	8.7	0.3	0.8	0.1	0.5	0.2	0.2	1.9	0.1	0.5
Canada	80.5	1.1	1.0	9.8	2.5	0.8	—	1.7	0.1	1.0	1.3	—	0.2
United States	85.4	1.4	0.3	8.6	—	0.8	0.2	0.3	0.3	0.1	2.0	0.1	0.5

Note: A dash represents a value of less than 0.05 percent. Because of rounding, horizontal totals may not equal 100.0.
[a]Figures include Bermuda (U.K.), Greenland (Den.), and St. Pierre and Miquelon (Fr.).

with substantial freedom of religion (as mandated by the U.S. Constitution), churches found themselves thrown back onto their own ingenuity. In these circumstances the denominations that were slow to adjust — especially → Congregationalists and → Anglicans/Episcopalians — found themselves rapidly outstripped by → Baptists and → Methodists, the denominations that knew best how to frame their message in the ethos of American democracy. Congregationalists and Anglicans were the largest denominations at the time of the American founding in 1776. Within less than 50 years, however, they had been far outstripped by the Methodists and Baptists, and they had been matched by the rapid growth of the "Restorationist" movement, consisting of Churches of Christ and Disciples of Christ.

For all American churches it has been necessary to use American concepts to communicate about themselves in the American environment. Among the most striking examples in accepting the need to "speak American" in the public square have been the Quakers, Mennonites, and other pacifists, who have diligently presented their convictions to governmental authorities during times of war. Another example is the skill with which public representatives of the → Roman Catholic Church — from Bishops John Carroll and John England in the early decades of the United States to John Courtney Murray and the editor Richard John Neuhaus in recent decades — have defended Catholic convictions with republican rhetoric. For Canada a parallel situation has obtained where, especially since World War II, leaders in the United Church, Roman Catholics, spokespersons for the Evangelical Fellowship of Canada, and still other groups have become expert at using the language of Canadian public discourse to express the distinctive convictions of their religious traditions.

North American pluralism explains why Ernst → Troeltsch's famous distinction between established *churches* that support the status quo and pietistic or mystical *sects* that seek a pure church barely survives in the United States and has only slightly more validity in Canada. Even the archetypal European church, Roman Catholicism, has in many places and at various eras acted in America like a → sect. The most prominent example is the Catholic sponsorship of private schools, which remove Catholic children from America's so-called public education. No American denomination has ever enjoyed the churchly prerogatives and responsibilities of a European state church. The American pattern is rather *denominationalism,* which encourages American churches to exhibit both sectarian traits (they constitute themselves, they exist without state financial assistance, they compete for adherents) and churchly traits (some enjoy high social status, many exert direct or indirect influence on public mores or public policy, almost all accept relief from taxation). The denomination, in the North American sense, is a singular product of an environment defined by great space, the absence of formal church-state ties, and competition among many ecclesiastical bodies.

In the 20th century, American pluralism developed well beyond the traditional Christian denominations. Offshoots of Christianity, like the Church of Jesus Christ of Latter-day Saints, or → Mormons, have flourished in this atmosphere. Over the last century the Mormons became a major missionary force, with about two-thirds of the denomination's 15 million adherents now located outside the United States. Mormons have emerged as leaders in the politics of several states in the U.S. West, in education with Brigham Young University, and in a host of other institutions, sports, the arts, and some high-tech industries. Mormon concern for family life, use of the King James version of the Bible, and defense of traditional morals draw them closer to conservative Protestants, even as loyalty to the distinctive teachings of Joseph Smith's *Book of Mormon* keeps them a separate religious people.

By the end of the 20th century, two other mono-

Northern America in A.D. 2000: Church Affiliation (as percentage of population)

	Total Christians	Roman Catholics	Indigenous	Protestants	Orthodox	Unaffiliated	Anglicans	Marginal
World total	33.1	17.6	6.2	5.8	3.7	1.5	1.0	0.5
Northern America[a]	84.9	24.5	26.7	23.5	1.6	10.8	1.0	3.9
Canada	80.5	45.4	6.6	12.9	2.1	9.5	2.6	1.4
United States	85.4	22.2	29.0	24.7	1.6	10.9	0.8	4.1

Note: Because of rounding, horizontal totals of the individual Christian groups may not equal the total percentage of Christians. Also, Christians in some countries are counted in more than one category, in which case the total of the individual groups may exceed the overall percentage of Christians.

[a]Figures include Bermuda (U.K.), Greenland (Den.), and St. Pierre and Miquelon (Fr.).

theistic faiths — Judaism and Islam — enjoyed a significant presence in North America. → Judaism had come to flourish in many ways, especially as an object of vigorous study in yeshivas, Jewish universities, and many secular campuses. All the major expressions of Jewish ethnic and religious life (and each with several subgroups) had assumed a heightened visibility — Reform, which now allowed for women rabbis; Conservative, which balanced fidelity to Judaic tradition with life in a modern industrial state; and Orthodox, which clung most tenaciously to the study of the Talmud and the culture of the shtetl. American Jews also experience a full range of uncertainties, with mounting worry over intermarriage and cultural assimilation, along with internal division over the kinds and degree of support to offer the State of Israel, including the claim of the Orthodox rabbinate in Israel to exercise sole authority on the question of who is a Jew.

→ Islam, though newer to America, has grown very rapidly since the 1960s, with large-scale immigration from Pakistan, Iran, Egypt, and Turkey joining the smaller communities of Lebanese, Syrian, and various other Arab groups that had existed in the United States throughout the century. Most of the three-plus million Muslims in the United States at the end of the 20th century were Sunnis. The African American Nation of Islam is a small but visible group that under Wallace D. Muhammad, son of Elijah Muhammad, has found increasing acceptance in the worldwide Muslim community.

2.5. *Significance of Region*

Although the pluralism of Christian — and also non-Christian — religious organizations certainly pertains to North America as a whole, it is not necessarily the same story for each of its regions. North America's great cities do usually provide a home for many varieties. Outside the cities, however, the churches tend to be clumped together into strong regional concentrations. It has always been that way. At the end of the colonial period in the 1770s, the largest denomination in the new United States was the Congregationalists, who were located almost exclusively in New England, and the second largest was the Church of England (soon to be known as Episcopalians), which was overwhelmingly concentrated in the southern colonies.

Strikingly different regional strengths remain to the present. In the four large U.S. census areas (Northeast, South, Midwest, and West), Protestants are overrepresented in the South and Midwest and underrepresented in the Northeast and West. Conversely, Roman Catholics are overrepresented in the Northeast and Midwest and underrepresented in the South. Although the South has only slightly more than one-third of the nation's population, over one-half of all African-American Protestants live in that region. The number of conservative, evangelical, fundamentalist, or pentecostal Protestants is also considerably higher in the South than in the nation as a whole. The American West is home to the largest concentration of the nonchurched population. In Canada, Protestants are overrepresented in the Western and Atlantic Provinces, while Catholics are overrepresented in Quebec.

Region also makes a large difference in the distribution of individual denominations. In the late 20th century, Baptists made up the largest sector of the churched population in 14 southern and mid-South states. In another 6 states of the Southwest and West, where they were outnumbered by Catholics, Baptists were the most numerous Protestant denomination. Outside of the broad southern third of the country, however, Baptists are a much smaller part of the population. In the upper Midwest — including Wisconsin, Iowa, Minnesota, North Dakota, South Dakota, Nebraska, and Montana — Lutherans are the most numerous Protestant body. Methodists are especially strong in a band running from Delaware (the state with the highest concentration of Methodists in the country) through Nebraska. The main denominations of the Restorationist movement (Churches of Christ, Disciples of Christ, and → Christian Churches) are likewise strong in the lower Midwest and upper South. Roman Catholics predominate in New York and New England, around the shores of Lake Michigan, in the Southwest, and in the far southern portions of Texas, Louisiana, and Florida.

In Canada, nominal Roman Catholic allegiance remains very high in Quebec, but it also reaches levels in Ontario and the Atlantic Provinces found in only a few subregions of the United States. The United Church of Canada remains strong in Saskatchewan and Manitoba, with considerable allegiance also in Ontario, Alberta, and British Columbia. Anglicans are still a force in Toronto, as well as in other parts of Ontario and the Western provinces. Of the smaller Protestant bodies, Lutherans and Mennonites are well represented in Alberta and British Columbia, Presbyterians retain significant loyalty in British Columbia and Ontario, and Baptists and Pentecostals are strong in the Maritimes and a few western sections. The highest concentration of Canadian Jews is found in and around Toronto and Montreal.

3. Canadian Counterpoint

With a history sharing much with the United States, Canada, like its much more populous neighbor, has also experienced close connections between religion and public life, though not in the same way or for the same reasons. Canada's modern history began in the early 17th century with French settlements in what is now Quebec. By contrast to the United States, Catholicism was politically important from the first. The corporate conception of civic life that characterizes Roman Catholic societies has exerted an especially strong influence in Quebec, even to the present, when levels of religious practice in that province have fallen dramatically.

A religious factor loomed large in almost all major Canadian developments until recent times. After the Treaty of Paris (1763), when Britain took control of Quebec, British success at accommodating the province's Roman Catholic establishment prepared the way for Catholic loyalty to the Crown during the American → Revolution. When patriots invaded Canada in 1775, Bishop J.-O. Briand of Quebec labeled support for the Americans heresy, and most of his fellow religionists took the message to heart. In the Maritimes a much smaller, more Protestant population also refused to join the patriot cause. In that case, at least part of the reason was the apolitical → pietism fostered by Henry Alline and other leaders of the revivalistic "New

Light Stir," which began about the same time as the war (→ Revivals).

A great stimulus to the creation of an anti-American Canadian nationalism was the War of 1812 (→ Nation, Nationalism). When undermanned militia and British regulars repelled the attacks of American troops in the Niagara peninsula and on the Great Lakes in 1813 and 1814, Canadian ministers hailed God's providential rescue of his people from tyranny with the same assurance that Americans had employed after their struggle against Britain a generation before. Loyalty to the king and trust in God constituted the Canadian "Shield of Achilles" that frustrated the despotic plans of the American democratic mob.

The tragic career of Louis Riel, who twice attempted to set up quasi-independent governments for the métis (mixed bloods of French-Canadian and Indian parentage) in Manitoba, also involved religion in several ways. When Riel was executed in 1885 following his second failed rebellion, it fueled bitter conflict between Protestants eager to extend a British religious hegemony and French-speaking Catholics who felt Riel had been wronged. Ill will generated by the Riel episode came to an end only when Wilfrid Laurier, the Liberal Party's candidate in the 1896 national election, successfully assuaged the wounded sensibilities of both sides. In passing, it is worth noting that Laurier, a Catholic from Quebec who won widespread affection from all Canadian regions during his lengthy tenure (1896-1911), became his nation's prime minister more than three decades before a Catholic was even nominated for president by a major American party and more than six decades before a Catholic was elected to that office.

Even with the easing of Catholic-Protestant antagonism over the last half century, Catholicism still makes a difference in Canadian electoral politics. In the mid-1980s Catholic-Protestant differences explained electoral variance better than any other social-structural trait; moreover, these differences were not just a reflection of anglophone-francophone differences. In the Quebec separation plebiscite of 1995, active francophone Catholics were much less likely to vote in favor of sovereignty than were nominally Catholic or secular Quebecois.

Canada's deliberate choice to maintain European ties encouraged a spirit that several scholars, most famously Seymour Martin Lipset, have described as the critical element in Canadian politics. It is not as though the individualism, free-market advocacy, and democratic principles that have meant so much in the United States are absent in Canada. Rather, in

Canada → liberalism has always been balanced by corporate visions of the Left and the Right, and often with significant religious support. As examples, the fundamentalist preacher William "Bible Bill" Aberhart embodied populist and communitarian principles in Alberta's Social Credit Party, which he led to power in the 1930s. A Baptist minister and contemporary of Aberhart, Tommy Douglas, exploited principles from the → Social Gospel in organizing the Cooperative Commonwealth Federation in the Prairies during the same depression years. That movement eventually was transformed into the New Democratic Party, Canada's socialist alternative to the Liberals and Progressive Conservatives, which has held power in several provinces at various times since the 1960s. The redoubtable Christian philosopher George Parkin Grant was only the most forceful of several prominent spokespersons in the 1950s and 1960s for a kind of statist conservatism that excoriated Canada's drift into American economic, political, and intellectual orbits.

Catholic corporatism and several varieties of Protestant loyalism have together encouraged a different approach to questions of church and state than has developed in the United States. The Catholic establishment in Quebec, where the school systems, hospitals, and labor organizations were once exclusively ecclesiastical enterprises, has given way only since the end of the Second World War. In the Maritimes and Ontario, the Anglican and Presbyterian churches never received quite the level of endowed support that their established counterparts enjoyed in England and Scotland, but direct forms of aid to the churches did not end until the Clergy Reserves (land set aside for the use of the churches) were secularized in 1854. Even after that contentious event, indirect government support continued for many religious agencies. Denominational colleges, for instance, were folded into several of the major provincial universities, so that to this day a few such colleges exist as components of the universities. In addition, varying kinds of aid are still provided to at least some church-organized primary and secondary schools in every Canadian province. As late as 1997 the Newfoundland school system was still operated on a denominational basis, but with changes underway that set up a fully "public system" for the first time.

One of the most important reasons for structural religious differences between the two nations arises from the varied proportions of religious adherence. A major cross-border survey by the Angus Reid Group in October 1996 revealed about the same proportion of each population adhering to mainline churches (15 percent in the U.S. vs. 16 percent in Canada), but in the United States a much higher proportion of adherents to conservative Protestant churches (26 percent vs. 10 percent) and to African-American Protestant churches (9 percent vs. less than 1 percent). By contrast, a higher proportion of Canadians were adherents to the Roman Catholic Church (26 percent to 20 percent), and a much higher proportion were secular or only nominal in religious attachments (40 percent to 20 percent).

Contrasts between Canada and the United States are intriguing, precisely because the two nations coexist with so many similarities. Modern polling suggests that the process of → secularization has moved more rapidly in Canada than in the United States, but even in this modern period it is obvious that on questions of religion Canadians and Americans share many attitudes and experiences. Even as free trade and the spread of American → mass media draw the two nations closer together, differences in religious history continue to make at least something of a difference.

4. Ecumenism and Mission

Since World War II the most visible ecumenical activities in the United States and Canada have been carried out by agencies aiming directly at increased interdenominational cooperation. Of these groups, the → National Council of the Churches of Christ has played an especially prominent part. Not surprisingly, given the relative decline of the older Protestant denominations, the council in which these groups have been prominent also suffered through difficult financial times in the last decades of the 20th century.

In 1960 nine mainline Protestant denominations created the Consultation on Church Union (COCU), which looked forward toward organic union. It has since evolved into the Churches Uniting in Christ (CUIC), which seeks not so much merger as a common Christian dialogue and a testimony against racism in American society and around the world.

During these same decades, a number of American church bodies, including Roman Catholic and Orthodox, have been engaged in bilateral → theological dialogues. Aims of these dialogues have varied, with some seeking simply to increase mutual understanding with higher degrees of cooperation, and others pursuing "full communion," a relationship that mutually acknowledges theological and ecclesial integrity, sacraments, and ministries. Notable among the latter have been agreements between Eastern and Oriental Orthodox churches, the *Formula of Agreement* between the Evangelical Lutheran Church in America (ELCA) and the three American member churches of the World Alliance of Reformed Churches — the Presbyterian Church (U.S.A.), the Reformed Church in America, and the United Church of Christ (1997), between the ELCA and the Moravian Church in America (1999), and *Called to Common Mission* between the ELCA and the Episcopal Church, U.S.A. (2001). The United Church of Christ and the Christian Church (Disciples of Christ) have also reached the stage where full ecclesial life is being shared. Additionally, the Anglican Church of Canada and the Evangelical Lutheran Church in Canada have reached an agreement of full communion.

A wide range of other ecumenical activity has also taken place beyond the mainline Protestant churches. → The National Association of Evangelicals (founded in 1942), the National Religious Broadcasters (which spun off the NAE in 2001), the Christian Holiness Partnership (a successor of the National Camp Meeting Association for the Promotion of Holiness, founded in 1867), and the Pentecostal Fellowship of North America (established in 1948) are examples of lower-keyed organizations that have each contributed measurably to cooperation among individual churches and individuals.

The most significant breakthrough of recent decades has been the increasing level of contact between Roman Catholics and Protestants, since to achieve even a measure of engagement it has been necessary to overcome the antagonism of centuries. As a result of the Second → Vatican Council (1962-65), Catholics abandoned their church's historic assumptions about the need for a Christendom uniting the interests of church, state, and society. In the wake of the council, mandates from the Vatican encouraged → dialogue with many Protestant and Orthodox churches. Of these discussions the most important took place with the Lutherans and centered on → justification by → faith, a critical issue that had been contested since the → Reformation. Early in the 1980s the official dialogue between American Lutherans and Catholics led to a joint statement of substantial agreement on this most important Christian doctrine (humans rely completely on God's grace for salvation, but it is necessary for all Christians to pursue good works diligently). After another 15 years that American agreement became the basis for a broader statement of reconciliation on this issue by the Vatican and the Lutheran World Federation, the → Joint Declaration on the Doctrine of Justification (1999).

In the United States a great stimulus to Catholic-evangelical cooperation has been provided by the Evangelicals and Catholics Together (ECT) initiative, which in the 1990s blossomed from personal conversation between Charles Colson, an evangelical politician turned prison reformer, and Richard John Neuhaus, who had been active in the → civil rights movement as a minister of the Lutheran Church–Missouri Synod before he became a Catholic and a leading spokesman for culturally conservative causes. The ECT has led to three noteworthy, if also ad hoc, nonecclesial, statements: "Evangelicals and Catholics Together: The Christian Mission in the Third Millennium" (1994), "The Gift of Salvation" (1997), and "Your Word Is Truth" (2002). The three statements have generated extensive discussion, especially in the evangelical world, and by no means all of it positive. Yet by finding common ground on many contemporary cultural issues, as well as by outlining substantial areas of theological agreement (while acknowledging important areas of remaining theological disagreement), ECT suggests a remarkable alteration in Catholic-Protestant interchange over just the last half century.

American influence in world Christianity rests on direct, as well as indirect, influence, and the most direct influence is mediated by American → missionaries. The American proportion of the worldwide Protestant missionary force rose rapidly at the start of the 20th century, continued to grow until reaching about two-thirds of the world total in the early 1970s (roughly 52,000 out of 80,000), but now, while continuing to grow numerically, is making up a decreasing proportion of world Christian missionaries because of the recent surge in volunteers from other countries.

Within the American missionary force, the number of evangelicals has risen steadily. Missionary activity of the mainline Protestant denominations dominated American missionary efforts at the start of the century, remained strong into the 1950s, and then trailed off significantly since that time. Roman Catholic missionary work began only in the early years of the century, rose steadily in number of participants until the late 1960s, and then has declined gradually since that time. By contrast, evangelical (and Mormon) missions have continued to expand until they now constitute all but a small fraction of American missionary efforts.

Especially in the last half of the century, nondenominational evangelical missionary societies have grown much more rapidly than denominational agencies (→ North American Missions; Evangelical Missions). This development is significant because the nondenominational agencies tend to be even more aggressively conversionistic than the mission groups from evangelical denominations. In addition, funding for the nondenominational societies is completely entrepreneurial — those who want to be missionaries make contact with their own friends and with individual local churches and from these personal connections gather funds for their own financial support. The one major exception is the mission board of the Southern Baptist Convention, which maintains distinctly evangelical standards and funds its missionaries from a centralized budget.

The American missionary programs that have been the most conversionistic in their message are also the most voluntaristic in their methods. Precisely such mission societies have come to dominate the American missionary force over the course of the last half century. Examples include World Vision, an evangelical → relief and development agency founded in 1950 to assist orphans in Korea and elsewhere in Asia. During 2001 World Vision raised $964 million, with about 55 percent coming from American sources. For comparison, this total was over 30 times as large as the entire budget of the → World Council of Churches.

For sheer scale and reach, however, there has never been anything yet to compare with Campus Crusade for Christ's "Jesus" film project. Following the lead of Bill Bright, the founder of this evangelistic organization, Campus Crusade in the 1970s sponsored the production of a movie by John Heyman, a Jewish filmmaker, which depicted the life of Christ as found in the Gospel of Luke. It then set about dubbing the movie into national languages and showing it on the screen (and then through videos and the Internet) wherever it could find an audience. Over the last 20 years, through a wide network of American and non-American workers and a steady flow of primarily American donations, the film has been produced in over 700 different languages, with another 300 translations in preparation. It has been viewed by over five billion people in 236 countries. The most active promoters of the film have been the mission boards of two American evangelical denominations (Southern Baptist Convention and → Church of the Nazarene), two American interdenominational agencies (World Vision and Operation Mobilization), and the Roman Catholic Church.

Even as North American mission outreach continues to grow, however, the explosion of Christian groups in the non-Western world means that the North American place in world Christianity needs to be reconsidered. The expansion of evangelical- or Pentecostal-type movements elsewhere in the world usually does not arise from American influence. It is rather that religious movements in other regions are flourishing in conditions that in some ways parallel the innovative, open, and nontraditional social and ecclesiastical environment that has marked North America for over 500 years.

Bibliography: American religion in the world: D. H. BAYS and G. WACKER, eds., *The Foreign Mission Enterprise at Home: Explorations in North American Cultural History* (Tuscaloosa, Ala., 2003) • C.-J. BERTRAND, *Les églises aux États-Unis* (Paris, 1975) • P. A. ESHLEMAN, "The 'Jesus' Film," *IBMR* 26 (2002) 68-72 • P. JOHNSTONE and J. MANDRYK, *Operation World: Twenty-first Century Edition* (Carlisle, Eng., 2001) • D. MARTIN, *Pentecostalism: The World Their Parish* (Oxford, 2002) • M. B. POWELL, ed., *The Voluntary Church: American Religious Life, 1740-1860, Seen through the Eyes of European Visitors* (New York, 1967) • D. L. ROBERT, *American Women in Mission* (Macon, Ga., 1996) • L. O. SANNEH, *Abolitionists Abroad: American Blacks and the Making of Modern West Africa* (Cambridge, Mass., 1999) • A. SIEGFRIED, *America Comes of Age: A French Analysis* (New York, 1927) • A. F. WALLS, "The American Dimension of the Missionary Movement," *The Missionary Movement in Christian History* (Maryknoll, N.Y., 1996).

Religion and public life: T. J. CURRY, *The First Freedoms: Church and State in America to the Passage of the First Amendment* (New York, 1986) • P. GLEASON, *Keeping the Faith: American Catholicism Past and Present* (Notre Dame, Ind., 1987) • D. W. HOWE, *The Political Culture of the American Whigs* (Chicago, 1979) • J. C. MURRAY, *We Hold These Truths: Catholic Reflections on the American Proposition* (New York, 1960) • M. A. NOLL, ed., *Religion and American Politics* (New York, 1989) • J. T. NOONAN JR., *The Lustre of Our Country: The American Experience of Religious Freedom* (Berkeley, Calif., 1998) • A. DE TOCQUEVILLE, *Democracy in America* (trans. H. C. Mansfield and D. Winthrop; Chicago, 2000; orig. pub., 1835-40) • R. A. WELLS, ed., *The Wars of America: Christian Views* (Mercer, Ga., 1991) • J. F. WILSON and D. L. DRAKEMAN, eds., *Church and State in American History* (2d ed.; Boston, 1987) • J. WITTE JR., *Religion and the American Constitutional Experiment* (Colorado Springs, Colo., 2000).

Canada: T. FLANAGAN, *Louis "David" Riel: Prophet of the New World* (2d ed.; Toronto, 1996) • G. P. GRANT, *Lament for a Nation: The Defeat of Canadian Nationalism* (Princeton, 1965) • J. W. GRANT, *The Church in the Canadian Era* (2d ed.; Burlington, Ont., 1988) • R. JOHNSTON, "The Reproduction of the Religious Cleavage in Canadian Elections," *Canadian Journal of Political Science* 18 (1985) 99-114 • S. M. LIPSET, *Continental Divide: The Values and Institutions of the United States and Canada* (New York, 1990) • T. MURPHY and

R. Perin, eds., *A Concise History of Christianity in Canada* (Toronto, 1996) • G. A. Rawlyk, ed., *Aspects of the Canadian Evangelical Experience* (Kingston and Montreal, 1997); idem, ed., *The Canadian Protestant Experience* (Burlington, Ont., 1990) • M. Van Die, ed., *Religion and Public Life in Canada* (Toronto, 2001) • W. Westfall, *Two Worlds: The Protestant Culture of Nineteenth-Century Ontario* (Kingston and Montreal, 1989).

American religious history: S. A. Ahlstrom, *A Religious History of the American People* (New Haven, 1972) • R. Baird, *Religion in America* (New York, 1844) • T. E. Fulop and A. J. Raboteau, eds., *African-American Religion: Interpretive Essays in History and Culture* (New York, 1997) • E. S. Gaustad and P. L. Barlow, *New Historical Atlas of Religion in America* (New York, 2000) • P. C. Gutjahr, *An American Bible: A History of the Good Book in the United States, 1777-1880* (Stanford, Calif., 1999) • N. O. Hatch, *The Democratization of American Christianity* (New Haven, 1989) • J. Hennesey, *American Catholics: A History of the Roman Catholic Community in the United States* (New York, 1981) • D. E. Jones et al., *Religious Congregations and Membership: 2000* (Atlanta, 2002) • R. S. Keller and R. R. Ruether, eds., *In Our Own Voices: Four Centuries of American Women Religious Writers* (San Francisco, 1996) • C. H. Lippy and P. W. Williams, eds., *Encyclopedia of the American Religious Experience* (3 vols.; New York, 1988) • G. M. Marsden, *Fundamentalism and American Culture, 1870-1925* (New York, 1980) • M. E. Marty, *Pilgrims in Their Own Land: Five Hundred Years of Religion in America* (New York, 1984) • H. R. Niebuhr, *The Kingdom of God in America* (New York, 1937) • M. A. Noll, *A History of Christianity in the United States and Canada* (Grand Rapids, 1992); idem, *The Old Religion in a New World* (Grand Rapids, 2002) • A. J. Raboteau, *Canaan Land: A Religious History of African Americans* (New York, 2002) • D. G. Reid et al., eds., *Dictionary of Christianity in America* (Downers Grove, Ill., 1990) • J. D. Sarna, ed., *The American Jewish Experience* (2d ed.; New York, 1997); idem, ed., *Minority Faiths and the American Protestant Mainstream* (Urbana, Ill., 1998) • H. S. Stout and D. G. Hart, eds., *New Directions in American Religious History* (New York, 1997) • G. Wacker, *Heaven Below: Early Pentecostals and American Culture* (Cambridge, Mass., 2001).

MARK A. NOLL

Northern Ireland → United Kingdom

North-South Conflict → Third World

Norway

	1960	1980	2000
Population (1,000s):	3,581	4,086	4,407
Annual growth rate (%):	0.78	0.32	0.27
Area: 323,878 sq. km. (125,050 sq. mi.)			

A.D. 2000

Population density: 14/sq. km. (35/sq. mi.)
Births / deaths: 1.29 / 1.06 per 100 population
Fertility rate: 1.95 per woman
Infant mortality rate: 5 per 1,000 live births
Life expectancy: 78.1 years (m: 75.3, f: 80.9)
Religious affiliation (%): Christians 94.3 (Protestants 91.1, indigenous 3.4, Roman Catholics 1.3, other Christians 1.0), nonreligious 1.8, Buddhists 1.6, Muslims 1.0, other 1.3.

1. Evangelical Lutheran Church (Den norske Kirke)
  1.1. Reformation to 1814
  1.2. Basic Order
    1.2.1. Reform
    1.2.2. Since 1984
    1.2.3. Organization
  1.3. Church Movements
  1.4. Theology
  1.5. Practice
2. Other Churches
  2.1. Religious Legislation
  2.2. Specific Groups
3. Interchurch Relations
4. Non-Christian Religions

1. Evangelical Lutheran Church (Den norske Kirke)

The overwhelming majority (86 percent) of the total population of Norway belongs to the Evangelical Lutheran Church, which is officially named the Church of Norway (Den norske Kirke; → Lutheran Churches), though earlier it tended to be called the state religion or the state church.

1.1. *Reformation to 1814*

The church province of Norway was largely independent in the Middle Ages under the archbishopric of Nidaros (modern Trondheim). As a result of the 1536/37 → Reformation, however, it came under the territorial jurisdiction of the Danish king. Although the first Lutheran → church order (Kirkeordinansen, September 2, 1537) clearly gave the congregations the right to choose their own → pastors and to set up a Protestant episcopate (→ Bishop, Episcopate), the king took over the supreme government of the church. According to → Reformation principles, he expressly understood himself to be only the helper and overseer of the → church, but very quickly the church, with its bishops and pastors, came to be viewed as simply an ecclesiastical department of state (→ Church and State).

In 1604 the Norwegian bishops attempted unsuccessfully to set up their own church law and to secure greater autonomy for their church. The royal administration gained increasing influence over church affairs (→ Church Government), culminating in religious legislation that effectively gave it absolute control. The royal law of 1665 became the basis for both Danish law in 1683 and Norwegian law in 1687. This law formally adopted as a confessional basis the three ancient creeds (→ Confessions and Creeds), the unchanged → Augsburg Confession, and Martin → Luther's (1483-1546) Small Catechism (→ Luther's Theology; Lutheranism). Within the confines of this confessional uniformity (→ Confession of Faith), there was no place for → religious liberty before the 19th century except in areas where for economic reasons the adherents of other faiths were tolerated (e.g., the → Huguenots).

Church administration was in the hands of the royal chancellery, and in Norway especially it was strongly centralized. The king appointed the bishops, recruiting them mainly from the Danish clergy. In the age of → Pietism (from 1736) a Norwegian, Peder Hersleb (1689-1757), was the leading bishop (of Copenhagen). An attempt to establish a Pietist form of church administration through a special college of theologians and jurists failed. Ultimately, it took → Enlightenment impulses to loosen the confessional monopoly and finally bring religious freedom.

With its new constitution of 1814 the newly elected Norwegian parliament (the Storting) introduced a comparatively modern instrument resting on the principles of representative → democracy. The religious clauses, however, simply ratified the ancient legal basis of the church (→ Church Law), agreeing almost word for word with the previous absolutist formulations. Even the express desire of the framers of the constitution to secure religious liberty found no fulfillment in the church clauses. Not until 1891 was universal freedom of religion guaranteed constitutionally.

By the Treaty of Kiel in 1814 Denmark ceded Norway to Sweden. In the same year Norway forged a new union with Sweden, but with express provision for the retention of the new Norwegian constitution. The church in Norway could now go its own way. Spiritually and culturally, however, Danish influence was still detectable. In contrast, the church tradition of Sweden had little effect on religious life in Norway right up to the ending of the union in 1905.

1.2. Basic Order

The religious clauses of the 1814 constitution, which for the most part are still valid, stated that "the Evangelical Lutheran religion is the official religion of the state" (§2). It was assumed that the people would confess this religion and desire religious instruction for their children. To be sure, this clause is no longer viewed as the basis of the general religious instruction offered in the schools (→ Religious Education; Moral Education; Church and School).

The church remained a territorial church, and the king had to be a Lutheran. The same restriction applied to members of the government (since 1884 at least half were required to belong to the church).

Church administration was in the hands of the king, who possessed both *ius ecclesiasticum* and *ius liturgicum*. With these strict provisions the church in Norway was almost completely untouched by democratic tendencies for the next 150 years.

1.2.1. Reform

In 1920 a *menighetsråd* (church council) was officially set up for each parish. Members were popularly elected, with all baptized adults in the congregation having a vote. Only after World War II, however, did the Storting revise the basic church law. This revision resulted in the introduction of a synodical form of government (→ Synod; Presbyterianism). The revised church law of 1953 provided for this structure, giving to the diocesan councils (→ Diocese) set up in 1933 the power to hold sessions every fourth year to offer advice on common tasks. Finally, in 1969 a central Church Council was formed, and in 1984 a General Synod, with advisory competence but also the power to legislate touching mainly internal and some external matters. Even though the question of the church's ties to the state continues to be an issue, a new, revised church constitution brought this ecclesiastical legislation to a provisional end in 1996.

The long and often tension-laden relation between church and state, which had caused many schisms, seemed now to have become one of constructive cooperation in which the church can increasingly become an independent partner. In 2002 a church commission studying the relationship of church and state recommended disestablishment of the state church. Political parties are increasingly agreeing that such a step is urgently needed.

1.2.2. Since 1984

The General Synod has 85 members, consisting of the 11 diocesan councils (each with 7 members) and

3 others chosen at large by the Synod. In addition, there are 3 members from the Sami (Lapp) minority population, plus the 2 chairpersons of central councils for foreign relations and for Sami matters. The three theological faculties of the church have observers at the Synod, which meets annually for a week. Diocesan councils consist of the bishop, a pastor, a nonordained → church employee, and four lay members (→ Clergy and Laity), a composition that guarantees a clear lay majority in the Synod. In light of their Sami minority population, the three northern dioceses have an additional member each.

A doctrinal commission was also set up consisting of 20 persons, including the 11 bishops. The central church office works under the constant supervision of the Church Council, which is made up of 15 members of the General Synod. The Bishops' Conference (set up in 1917) meets three times a year to give advice and adopt positions on relevant topics. The elected preses has no independent position of leadership in the church. At the state level church matters are dealt with by the church department in the Ministry of Church and Education. In 1989 state appointment of pastors was replaced by appointment by the diocesan councils. The government still appoints bishops and regional deans.

1.2.3. *Organization*

The Church of Norway is divided into 624 parishes, some of which have many small preaching centers. In the year 2000 there were 93 deans and 11 bishops, about 1,100 congregational ministers, and another 300 men and women who are chaplains in hospitals (→ Pastoral Care of the Sick), other → institutions, and the military services (→ Military Chaplaincy). Financially, the Church of Norway depends on state and local taxes; it has no authority of its own to impose taxes. Church buildings belong to the → congregations, but the local communities are responsible for their construction and upkeep. The church councils present budgets locally, and regional and central committees do so at the national level; church expenses are part of the municipal and national budgets (→ Church Finances).

1.3. *Church Movements*

The Norwegian church is particularly distinguished by a strong, often Pietist → lay movement. Hans Nielsen Hauge (1771-1824), son of a peasant, was the spiritual leader of a → revival throughout Norway that brought renewal to the life of the church and also to that of the nation. This revival, which was at its height around 1800, motivated the formation of small groups for the edifying of the congregations. These groups were also fertile soil for the missionary movement and → inner mission. Church of Norway

pastors often supported the lay movements, which promoted independence from official church government and strengthened congregational life under spiritual direction. Resting on the Pietist idea of *ecclesiola in ecclesia,* a little church within the church (→ Pietism 2.3), they offered an alternative to the strict form of a state church. This aspect found expression in the formation of church → societies, some 26,000 of which are at work on behalf of mission both at home and abroad. They publish informational materials with a circulation of some 250,000 copies (→ Christian Communication).

Lay initiative is especially visible in → mission. From the 1840s onward many missionary societies came into being; the founding of the Norwegian Missionary Society in 1842 (→ Missionary Structures) brought the task of mission to the notice of the whole people. More than 500 Norwegian → missionaries are at work in the service of the Evangelical Lutheran Church (2000 est.; → Scandinavian Missions). At great personal sacrifice the societies have a total budget in excess of the normal expenditure of the church. Norwegian missionaries are at work in all continents, but especially in Africa and Asia. In view of the large Norwegian merchant fleet, there are about 30 seamen's churches (→ Seamen's Mission) around the world. They serve various purposes and care increasingly for Norwegian emigrants and guest workers.

1.4. *Theology*

The Pietist lay movement greatly influenced the Norwegian church theologically. From the founding of the University of Oslo in 1811, the theological faculty felt the impact of revivals more than that of the various European theological schools (→ Theology in the Nineteenth and Twentieth Centuries). A conservative Lutheran confessionalism was dominant in the 19th century. As representatives of → liberal theology gained a footing in the faculty around 1900, however, the NT professor, Sigurd Vilhelm Odland (1857-1937), gave up his professorship in order to devote himself to building up a private, theologically conservative faculty, which began in 1908 as Menighetsfakultetet (lit. "Congregation's faculty"), now the Norwegian Lutheran School of Theology. Later theological development up to World War II was characterized by polarization between the two faculties, though relations now are more cooperative. On the rapidly growing and officially recognized private faculty, the normative → theology moved from one of → experience after the Erlangen pattern to Lutheran confessionalism, in which the Luther renaissance plays a part (→ Luther Research). The theology of the university faculty reflected the various trends in modern theology, mostly German. Neither K. → Barth nor → dialectical theology, however, found any large following.

The training of pastors (→ Theological Education) takes place at the two schools and at the Misjonshøgskole (Missionary training college) at Stavanger, founded in 1843. Women have come increasingly into the ministry (→ Women's Movement) since the church opened the door to them in 1961 (→ Ordination). → Catechists and → deacons are trained at the church's own colleges.

1.5. *Practice*

The national church situation largely affects congregational life in Norway (→ People's Church [Volkskirche]). Membership remains stable, with 82 percent of infants still being baptized, although only 5 percent of the members are present at → worship services on a given Sunday. The parochial structure presupposes that all baptized members belong to a parish, but the number of churches is far from adequate. A pastor may have to care for an average of up to 3,500 members, and on account of the great distances worship may not be held in every church or chapel every Sunday. The meager weekly attendance contrasts sadly with the percent baptized, the 72 percent confirmed (→ Confirmation), and the 95 percent who are buried at a church service (→ Funeral).

It is generally understood that the stability of membership is because the Church of Norway is a national church and there are no special church taxes. → Secularization and new religious trends in the → modern period seem not to threaten the basic traditional attachment of the population to the church and its rites. Church aid programs and diaconal services (→ Diakonia) find generally positive acceptance and support, and the media take notice of the church and its activities. The founding of the Christian Democratic Party in 1933 (→ Political Parties) greatly influenced the political climate, though the party itself has attracted no more than 15 percent of the votes.

The form of worship has been greatly influenced by German and Danish Lutheranism. The latest revisions (→ Liturgical Books) remained faithful to this tradition while deliberately adopting some ecumenical features (→ Ecumenism, Ecumenical Movement). The new 1985 hymnal made a place in worship for hymns of the revivalist tradition, often of Anglo-Saxon inspiration (→ Hymnal 1.3; Hymnody 5). A new translation of the Bible in 1978 (→ Bible Versions), which the Norwegian Bible Society (founded 1816) edited, has enjoyed widespread regard and distribution.

2. Other Churches
2.1. *Religious Legislation*

Most of the → denominations have found an entry into Norway. A special law passed in 1969 regulates the relations among denominations and non-Christian religions according to the principles of human and civil → rights. Public financial support is given to all groups according to the number of their members. They also may give their own religious instruction, and their ministers have the right to officiate at weddings (→ Marriage and Divorce).

2.2. *Specific Groups*

The largest → free church is the Pentecostal (since 1906; → Pentecostal Churches), with 45,000 members in 2000 and an active missionary outreach (350 missionaries). The → Roman Catholic Church was reestablished in Norway only in 1843. It set up an apostolic vicariate in 1892 but grew only in the later 20th century, mostly through immigration. It now has 43,000 members in three dioceses (Oslo, Trondheim, and Tromsø), plus several monastic orders. Methodists (13,000 members; → Methodism; Methodist Churches) and → Baptists (10,000 members) have been active in Norway since the middle of the 18th century. The Evangelical Lutheran Free Church of Norway (since 1876) has 21,000 members. We also find some Free Evangelical congregations, which are strongly inclined to → congregationalism. The → Salvation Army has been active in Norway since 1888.

In sum, 6-7 percent of the population belong to the free churches, within which the meaning and nature of church membership differ widely. Most of these churches are members of the Norwegian Free Church Council.

A special feature of spiritual life in Norway is the existence of the Human Ethical Union (68,000 members in 2000), an active group that seeks to persuade people to leave the church. It comes legally under the law regarding faith communions, although members regard themselves as nonreligious → agnostics (→ Atheism).

3. Interchurch Relations

Though strongly Lutheran, the Church of Norway is ecumenically open. It is a founding member of both the → Lutheran World Federation and the → World Council of Churches. Bishop Eivind Berggrav (1884-1959), renowned as a leader in the church struggle in Norway during World War II, was one of the first presidents of the WCC and did much to promote ecumenical thinking. The Church of Norway also belongs to the → Conference of European Churches. It cooperates strongly in the work of the

Nordic Ecumenical Council, and the bishops take part in the informal conference of Nordic Lutheran bishops, which meets every three years. It has especially close ties to the Evangelical Lutheran Church in America, which was greatly influenced by 18th-century Norwegian immigrants.

The Interchurch Council, acting under the General Synod, deals with ecumenical questions. On the national level the Church of Norway established the Christian Council of Norway in 1992 (→ National Council of Churches), which encompasses almost all churches, including the Roman Catholic Church, though so far no representatives of the Pentecostal churches. The General Synod ratified the → Porvoo Common Statement in November 1994, as well as the Leuenberg Agreement in November 1999, and in 1997 it established church communion with the United Methodist Church in Norway.

4. Non-Christian Religions

General liberty of religion came to Norway only in the 20th century. Before World War II some 1,000 Jews (→ Judaism) lived in Norway, but the → Holocaust reduced their numbers to about 200. They have a → synagogue in Oslo. In 2000 Orthodox Jews in Norway numbered 1,000.

Other religious groups are also small. The largest, swollen by immigration, mostly from Pakistan and the Near East, is the Muslim (→ Islam). In 2000 it had 56,000 adherents, both Sunnite and Shiite (→ Shia; Sunna), in registered and unregistered communities. There were 7,000 registered Buddhists (→ Buddhism) and less than 2,000 each of → Sikhs and Hindus (→ Hinduism).

Other non-Christian groups and representatives of the so-called → new religions press their views, especially among young people, but with only limited success.

Contacts are maintained between church workers among emigrants in the cities and the various religious groups, generally in the context of exercising diaconal responsibility. A semiofficial interreligious council fosters dialogue and cooperation. In 2000 the Faculty of Theology at the University of Oslo announced plans to develop a program of interreligious studies and → dialogue.

Bibliography: A. AARFLOT, "Neueste Entwicklungen im Verhältnis von Staat und Kirche in Norwegen," *ZEvKR* 29 (1984) 570-78; idem, *Norsk kirke i tusen år* (Oslo, 1978); idem, *Trossamfunn og folkekirke* (Oslo, 1999) • R. DANIELSEN, *Norway: A History from the Vikings to Our Own Times* (Oslo, 1995) • J. T. FLINT, *Historical Role Analysis in the Study of Religious Change: Mass Educational Development in Norway, 1740-1891* (Cambridge, 1990) • T. GREIPSLAND, *Olav V: A King and His Church* (Oslo, 1987) • P.-O. GULLAKSEN, *Stat og kirke i Norge* (Oslo, 2000); idem, "Das Verhältnis von Staat und Kirche in Norwegen," *ZEvKR* 45 (2000) 277-92 • B. LØVLIE, *Kirke, stat og folk i en etterkrigstid* (Oslo, 1996) • D. R. MATTHEWS and H. VALEN, *Parliamentary Representation: The Case of the Norwegian Storting* (Columbus, Ohio, 1999) • E. H. ROBERTSON, *Bishop of the Resistance: A Life of Eivind Berggrav, Bishop of Oslo, Norway* (St. Louis, 2001) • W. R. SHAFFER, *Politics, Parties, and Parliaments: Political Change in Norway* (Columbus, Ohio, 1998).

ANDREAS AARFLOT

Nouvelle théologie

The phrase *nouvelle théologie* refers primarily to a theological controversy in France beginning in the mid-1940s involving the Jesuit theologians of the Fourvière school on the one side and the Dominicans of the St. Maximin school on the other. The former, founders of two series published in Paris — Sources Chrétiennes (Éditions du Cerf) and Théologie (Aubier) — favored a return to biblical and → patristic sources as opposed to an anachronistic neoscholasticism. The latter, guardians of a strict → Thomism, stressed the dangers of developing historical relativism, against which not only Thomistic theology and the teaching of the church's "universal doctor" offered protection, but also → dogma itself. Yet it would be wrong to see here merely a further conflict between → Jesuits and → Dominicans. The concern of the *nouvelle théologie* brings to light a basic controversy regarding the relation between → truth and history that affected Roman Catholic theology in the years leading up to → Vatican II.

One of the most influential theologians at the Roman → curia was the Dominican R. Garrigou-Lagrange (1877-1964), a professor at Angelicum University. In a very polemical article entitled "La nouvelle théologie, où va-t-elle?" (Where is the new theology leading us? *Ang.* 23 [1946] 92-114), he used the phrase to describe the works of H. Bouillard (esp. his *Conversion et grâce chez saint Thomas d'Aquin* [Conversion and grace in St. Thomas Aquinas, 1944]) and H. de Lubac (*Surnaturel* [The supernatural, 1946]), the → evolutionism of P. Teilhard de Chardin (1881-1955), and the "philosophy of action" of M. Blondel (1861-1949). P. Parente had already used the term *nouvelle théologie* (in *OR*, February 9/10, 1942) to characterize the works of M.-D. Chenu and L. Charlier, which had been banned a few years before. And in September 1946 Pius XII (1939-58) also referred expressly to the *nouvelle théologie* when warning the Jesuits against new trends on the occasion of their electing a new general at Rome (→ Modernism).

Despite protests (e.g., by J.-G. Saliège and B. de Solages), the theologians at Rome (e.g., C. Boyer and J.-B. Janssens) would not let the matter rest. A tendentious process began, aimed in July 1950 against the Jesuit faculty of theology at Lyon-Fourvière (→ Censorship). The Jesuit general removed five faculty members for "pernicious errors regarding essential parts of dogma" (→ Heresies and Schisms). Cardinal de Lubac and Father Bouillard bore the brunt of this attack. Those concerned neither were told what errors they had been charged with nor were allowed to discuss the accusations publicly.

In fact the Fourvière theologians had never proposed to develop a new theology (de Lubac 1989, 362). Instead, they had introduced a new way of doing → theology, noting that from the 16th century onward there had usually been a destructive separation between theology and → spirituality, or theology and history, in the prevailing theology and pointing out that a living theology of the Christian community of faith cannot ignore either spiritual or historical → experience. This fundamental appeal to a common Christian → hermeneutics apparently worried the representatives of a narrow and nonhistorical Thomism, who suspected that those who were trying to take seriously the historicity of theological systems (→ Systematic Theology) and even of dogmatic formulas were guilty of → relativism and → subjectivism.

The final act of this painful episode in French theology came in August 1950 with the promulgation of the → encyclical *Humani generis*. In this work Pius XII firmly warned against dangerous tendencies and condemned actual errors he saw in modern theology regarding the immutability of dogmatic truths, supernatural grace, original → sin, and the real presence of Christ at the → Eucharist (§3.2). This encyclical was seen as a brilliant victory for the conservatives at Rome over the advocates of the *nouvelle théologie* (→ Conservatism 2). Paradoxically, however, one may cite whole passages from it which are in full accord with the arguments of the theologians whom it brings to order when, in opposition to a neoscholasticism that is detached from the sources, it insists on the necessary mediation of history for a proper understanding of the mystery of the Christian faith (cf. DH 2314).

In this way the path was prepared for Vatican II, especially in such matters as → revelation *(Dei Verbum)* and the mystery of the church *(Lumen gentium)*. Nor did Paul VI (1963-78) hesitate fully to rehabilitate such advocates of the *nouvelle théologie* as de Lubac and Y. Congar, who were appointed official experts *(periti)* of the council (→ Councils of the Church).

Because of this controversy it is difficult to use a phrase like *nouvelle théologie* to describe new movements in contemporary French theology. Common features in such movements include a serious effort to destroy the metaphysical basis of theological discourse (→ Metaphysics), a willingness to engage in promising → dialogue with other disciplines and the various forms of French structuralism (note the challenge of J. Derrida's program of language deconstruction to theological debate), and the lively attention paid to bridging the gap between speaking and acting. The most promising trend is perhaps to be found in a specific hermeneutical theology that, under the influence of Paul Ricoeur, rings in the hermeneutical age of → reason but also finds a place for the insights of → structuralism in faithful textual exposition of the biblical narratives and the derived traditions. Such a theology, however, is not content to regard itself merely as a new interpretation of Christianity. It takes concrete history with all seriousness and normally issues in action, in specific Christian practice, in changing the social attitudes of those who await the coming → kingdom of God.

→ Theology in the Nineteenth and Twentieth Centuries

Bibliography: H. U. von Balthasar, *The Theology of Henri de Lubac: An Overview* (San Francisco, 1991) • Y. Congar, *Journal d'un théologien, 1946-1956* (ed. É. Fouilloux; Paris, 2000) • É. Fouilloux, *Une église en quête de liberté. La pensée catholique française entre modernisme et Vatican II, 1914-1962* (Paris, 1998) • F. Gaboriau, *Théologie nouvelle. Ouvrir le débat* (Paris, 1985) • C. Geffré, "Silence et promesses de la théologie catholique française," *RTP* 114 (1982) 227-45 • B. Lauret, "'Theology, New' (Roman Catholic *théologie nouvelle*)," *DEM* 1000-1001 • F. Leprieur, *Quand Rome condamne* (Paris, 1989) • H. de Lubac, *Mémoire sur l'occasion de mes écrits* (1989; ET *At the Service of the Church: Henri de Lubac Reflects on the Circumstances That Occasioned His Writings* [San Francisco, 1993]); idem, *The Mystery of the Supernatural* (New York, 1998; orig. pub., 1965); idem, "Le problème du développement du dogme," *RSR* 35 (1948) 130-60 • R. J. O'Connell, *Teilhard's Vision of the Past: The Making of a Method* (New York, 1982).

Claude Geffré

Nuclear Weapons → Weapons

Number

1. A sense of number seems to be an inherent part of human life and property. All cults and religions have understood number in much the same way. The Babylonians (→ Babylonian and Assyrian Religion), using 60 as the basis, oriented their numerical system to the heavenly bodies. The Pythagoreans (→ Greek Philosophy 2.2) equated the cosmos with pure mathematics. For them the odd numbers were masculine and positive. Their views influenced Judaism, Christianity, and → Islam. The strictly arithmetic theories (esp. of Euclid [4th cent. B.C.]), which were not under Pythagorean influence, were also developed further.

2. *Zero* was borrowed from the Arabs, who, following the Indians, gave us our "arabic" numerical system.

One does not count as a real number, for it is the basis of everything else. The one God became recognizable in the encounter with a cognitive being.

Two as a polarity comes in with → creation, for without male and female, yin and yang, breathing in and breathing out, no life is possible. As lines both divide and connect, two may be both positive and negative, and it involves dissonance.

Three overcomes and releases the tension. The triangle is the first geometric figure. Since the world is three-dimensional, human beings live in the past, present, and → future. They see → sky, earth, and water. They experience beauty, goodness, and truth, and they are taught thesis, antithesis, and synthesis (→ Dialectic). Many three-headed or three-shaped deities are also found (→ Trinity); fables and proverbs tend to use groups of three. The sayings of → Jesus often go in threes. Three has played its part in → church architecture, including the triptych.

Four was the concluding number for the Pythagoreans and pointed to order: four directions, four elements, four quarters of cities. And we have 4/4 march time.

Five is linked to flowers rather than crystals and has a sensory connotation; it is the number of Ishtar and Venus, though note the five wise and five foolish virgins and the five secrets of Mary. In ancient China five was central, the middle of the magic square, common also in the West. Note also → Manichaeanism and Islam, with their five "pillars" and five daily prayers.

Six is the number of the world; a star with six sides symbolizes the micro- and macrocosm.

Seven was important for the Semites and Iranians (→ Iranian Religions). It was the number of the planets, as well as of the days of the week. Seven ages of humankind have been postulated. Seven steps often lead to a goal, whether in Ishtar's journey or the *Seven Steps* of Jan van Ruysbroeck (1293-1381) or the *Seven Valleys* of Farīd od-Dīn ʿAṭṭār. Seven, as a combination of the spiritual three and the material four, is an ideal number for groupings. Thus we find seven → sacraments, seven deadly sins, seven virtues, seven liberal arts, and so forth. The OT contains many sevens. But seven may be ambivalent. Babylon regarded the seventh day as dangerous and tried to avoid it (cf. the → Sabbath rest).

Eight represents the beginning of eternity (→ Time and Eternity) and brings good fortune. → Circumcision was on the eighth day. There are eight beatitudes (→ Sermon on the Mount), and the → baptismal font was octagonal.

Nine (the third power of the holy three) played a large role in the Turco-Mongolian and Celtic worlds. In the West the influence of the Mithra cult (→ Mystery Religions 4) and of Christianity often prompted the nine to be changed into seven.

Ten, which encompasses a decade, is the sum of the first four numbers. It is the ordering principle of dynastic, military, and legal orders. There are ten commandments (→ Decalogue).

Counting higher, 11 destroys perfections; it is an unlucky number. The number 12, the sign of the zodiac, is the number closing the circle. There are 12 → tribes of Israel and 12 → disciples. For Christians 13 became an unlucky number at a rather late stage (with reference to the number present at the Last Supper), but for → Judaism it was holy (e.g., the riddle of the → Passover Haggadah; 13 virtues in the Book of Exodus). The number 14 denotes half a lunar period. Also, in a probable borrowing from Egypt, there are 14 "auxiliary → saints."

Among the larger numbers, 40 points to testing and preparation (the flood, the wilderness wanderings, Christ's temptations in the desert, the period of → fasting, seclusion of the → Sufis, etc.). After childbirth women were unclean for 40 days (Mary's 40 days after Christmas celebrated as Candlemas). It can also represent a boundary number, for example, with regard to punishment (Deut. 25:3; 2 Cor. 11:24). Islam treats 40 as a round number (Ali Baba and the 40 thieves). At 40 one also reaches the age of discretion.

The number 70 or 72 is used for larger groups. Jesus sent out 70 disciples, as did Confucius. Muslims refer to 72 sects, and we often read of 70 or 72 martyrs (see the LXX; → Bible Versions 2).

3. Since the letters of the Semitic alphabets also have numerical value (→ Hebrew Language), many attempts were made to read off mystical meanings from these biblical numbers, and gematria flourished.

Literary works may be structured in numerically significant ways, such as the threefold overall division and the terza rima of Dante's (1265-1321) *Divine Comedy*, which points to the Trinity. The same is true of → church music, especially in the oeuvre of J. S. Bach (1685-1750).

→ Church Year 3.2 and 4.1

Bibliography: C. C. Clawson, *Mathematical Mysteries: The Beauty and Magic of Numbers* (New York, 1996) • M. J. Gazalé, *Number: From Ahmes to Cantor* (Princeton, 2000) • R. M. Haralick, *The Inner Meaning of the Hebrew Letters* (Northvale, N.J., 1995) • A. Schimmel, *The Mystery of Numbers* (New York, 1994).

Annemarie Schimmel

Numbers, Book of

1. Title
2. Contents
3. Meaning and Role

1. Title

The title "Numbers" derives from the Latin name of the fourth book of the → Pentateuch, which is from the Greek title *Arithmoi* (Numbers). The lists contained in the book account for this designation. The Hebrew name derives from one of the first words in the book, *bĕmidbar*, "in the wilderness [of Sinai]."

2. Contents

The Book of Numbers can be divided into three sections.

2.1. The first part (1:1–10:10) is generally ascribed to the Priestly source (P). Chap. 1 describes the census (cf. chap. 26), chap. 2 the marching orders for the various tribes, followed by an enumeration of the Levites (3–4) and by various laws concerning impurity, compensation, and the → Nazirites. The Aaronic → blessing appears in 6:22-26. Chaps. 7–8 deal with various types of → sacrifice, 9–10 with the date of the → Passover celebration, as well as with the cloud and the trumpets.

2.2. The second part, which is primarily narrative (10:11–22:1), contains considerable material from the Yahwist (J) and Elohistic (E) sources. (It is not easy, however, to distinguish between the two.) The departure from Sinai is described in 10:11-28, with vv. 29-32 mentioning → Moses and Hobab and vv. 33-36 presenting the battle cry of the → ark. Chap. 11 also contains material mixed from P and preserves traditions concerning the murmuring of the people, the pouring out of the spirit that was on Moses onto the elders, and the miraculous feeding with the quails (par. Exod. 16:12-13). Chap. 12 recounts the rebellion of Miriam and Aaron against Moses. Chaps. 13–14 contain Calebite traditions (with some material from P) regarding the possession of Hebron, as well as the accounts of the spies and the rebellion of the people. Chap. 20 contains the story about Moses getting water from the rock (par. Exod. 17:1-7), 21:1-3 recounts the battle and defeat at Hormah, 21:4-9 the story of the bronze → serpent, and 21:33–22:1 the story of the battle with King Og of Bashan.

The poems in 21:14b, 18, 27b-30, which in part are quite old, are not to be ascribed to the sources J and E, as is usually done (J. A. Soggin). P is generally credited for the marching orders (10:11-27), various ordinances concerning sacrifice and the → atonement of unintentional → sins (chap. 15), the revolt of Korah and the episode with Dathan and Abiram (chap. 16), as well as various regulations (chaps. 17–19, e.g., those concerning the ceremony of the red heifer).

2.3. In the third part (22:2–36:13) two passages are ascribed to JE: the legend of Balaam (22–24, here too without the poetic passages) and the tradition of Baal of Peor (25:1-15). To P scholars generally ascribe chap. 26 (par. chap. 1); chap. 27, concerning the inheritance rights of daughters and the installation of Joshua as Moses' successor; chaps. 28–29, with additional laws concerning sacrifice, the → Sabbath and new moon, unleavened bread, Passover, the Festival of Weeks, and the Festival of Booths; and chap. 30, with its treatment of → vows.

Chaps. 31–36 are an addendum. In 31:1-12, 15-54 we have secondary material from P, while chaps. 32 and 34–36 constitute a series of parallels to Joshua 13–21. E. Cortese is probably correct in ascribing them to P. The material deals with the tribal boundaries of Reuben, Gad, and the half-tribe of Manasseh (chap. 32) and with the division of Canaan (33:50-56), its boundaries (chap. 34, par. Joshua 14–19), and the Levitical cities and the cities of refuge (chap. 35, par. Joshua 20–21). Chap. 33, which gives an account of the different stages of the exodus from Egypt, includes various place names not contained in earlier traditions. The conclusion again contains laws concerning the inheritance rights of married women (chap. 36).

3. Meaning and Role

The Book of Numbers traces Israelite life from the escape from Egypt to the threshold of the people's occupation of Canaan. As such, it is partly the story of learning to live free under the covenant. Its subsequent place as the fourth book in the Pentateuch makes it a bridge to the description of new life that Israel experienced under both Mosaic and a developing priestly leadership, seen in Aaron. It might be called the Charter of Freedom Tale, for Israel's experiences of threat and of promise relayed in its stories show both regrets at having left the "safe" life in Egyptian slavery and the exultant episodes in which God openly fulfilled his promises to provide for, protect, and guide his people.

Bibliography: Commentaries: T. R. Ashley (NICOT; Grand Rapids, 1993) • E. W. Davies (NCBC; Grand Rapids, 1995) • T. B. Dozeman (NIB; Nashville, 1998) • B. A. Levine (AB; 2 vols.; Garden City, N.Y., 1993-2000) chaps. 1–20 and 21–26 • J. Milgrom (JPSTC; Philadelphia, 1990) • M. Noth (OTL; Philadelphia, 1968) • D. T. Olson (IBC; Louisville, Ky., 1996) • W. Riggan (DSB; Philadelphia, 1981) • K. D. Sakenfeld (ITC; Grand Rapids, 1995) • N. H. Snaith (NCBC; London, 1967).

Other works: D. Kellermann, *Die Priesterschrift von Numeri 1,1 bis 10,10 literarkritisch und traditionsgeschichtlich untersucht* (Berlin, 1970) • G. E. Mendenhall, "The Census Lists of Numbers 1 and 26," *JBL* 77 (1958) 52-66 • J. R. Neusner, *Sifre to Numbers* (Atlanta, 1998) • M. Noth, *Überlieferungsgeschichte des Pentateuch* (Stuttgart, 1948) • H. Rouillard, *La péricope de Balaam (Nombres 22–24)* (Paris, 1985) • J. A. Soggin, "Ancient Israelite Poetry and Ancient 'Codes' of Law, and the Sources 'J' and 'E' of the Pentateuch," *VTSup* 28 (1975) 185-95.

J. Alberto Soggin

Numismatics → History, Auxiliary Sciences to, 5

Nunc Dimittis → Canticle

Nuncio

Nuncios, also apostolic nuncios, are permanent papal legates, that is, plenipotentiary envoys of the → pope with a twofold function: ecclesiastical and governmental. With respect to the church, their task is one of oversight over the parts of the church (→ Diocese) to which they have been sent. They inform the papacy about the situation and events in these areas, assist the → bishops with advice and action (though without any direct intervention in their diocesan jurisdiction), foster close relations with the bishops' conferences and report their agendas and findings to the papacy, propose candidates for the episcopate, and give information about their suitability. As diplomats, nuncios represent the pope as the supreme head of the → Roman Catholic Church. Their task in this capacity is to foster relations between the papacy and state authorities (→ Church and State) and to protect the interests and rights of the church, asking the bishops for advice and giving them information when the circumstances warrant.

Nuncios are chosen, appointed, and dismissed by the pope according to the norms of church law. They are always clergy, usually with the titular rank of archbishop. They normally must retire at age 75. They act on instructions from the cardinal secretary of state and are directly responsible to him. "Nuncio" is their title when they have the rank and right (recognized at the Congress of Vienna in 1815) to be doyen of the diplomatic corps; since 1965 the title "pronuncio" has been used in states where this right is not recognized, though in the late 1990s the Vatican began to phase out its use. The title "internuncio" was used before the 1983 → CIC to denote a rank of extraordinary envoy and plenipotentiary minister.

In the 15th and 16th centuries nuncios were mainly political, but after the Counter-Reformation (→ Catholic Reform and Counterreformation) they increasingly acted within the church, for example, to implement the decisions of the Council of → Trent. In the 18th century conflicts with local bishops resulted, for example, with German archbishops regarding a nunciature established in Munich (which led in 1786 to the Congress of Ems and the antipapal decrees known as the Punctation of Ems). Overall, nuncios help to establish the central power of the papacy. → Vatican II tried to restrict their competence, but without success.

The papal right to send nuncios is considered a *ius nativum,* that is, derived from divine right. Paul VI (1963-78) based this idea on the 18th-century doctrine of the Roman Catholic Church as a perfect society (→ Church 3.2). For the law, see 1983 CIC 362-67 and Paul's → motu proprio *Sollicitudo omnium ecclesiarum* of June 24, 1969.

→ Hierarchy

Bibliography: AAS 61 (1969) 473-84 • M. Oliveri, *The Representatives: The Real Nature and Function of Papal Legates* (St. Paul, Minn., 1981).

Werner Böckenförde

O

Oath

1. Concept and Origin

An oath is either a solemn assertion or a promise. We find this form of enhancing reliability in almost all cultures. Oaths perhaps arose from the attempt to link gestures, acts, words, and the reaction of the world around in such a way as to reduce any doubt as to the validity of a → communication. Thus raising the hand at an oath might originally have been a gesture of peace. The beginning of an oath — "If I do this, may it be so" — conveys the tone of agreement and trustworthiness. The differentiated development of → culture conferred sanctity on certain places (→ heaven, earth, springs, stones), on plants and animals (herbs, trees, bears, tigers), on people (ancestors, children, kings), and on social acts (eating and drinking, → friendship, → war and → peace), each of which became the basis of oaths.

Lying and unfaithfulness led to the question, What happens if an oath is broken? The original answer was that the harmony of the world is broken and that the perjurer has forfeited his or her life. The oath thus became a conditional self-cursing (e.g., "May the earth swallow me up"). Then in a later development there emerged behind holy things and actions the powers that became personal gods, who were now invoked in an oath. At a trial the deity pronounces sentence in the → ordeal, but it is conditionally suspended by a sworn promise. This form of oath is used at peace treaties, alliances, the establishing of friendship, legislation for a family or tribe, a royal accession, the swearing of allegiance, and individual contracts. In court a plaintiff, defendant, or witness may make statements on oath.

2. Greece and Rome

The Olympian gods swore by the Styx, the river of the underworld, and therefore by a deity that was worshiped at an earlier stage and that had power over death. Thus the sacred things and gods by which the Greeks swore changed. The Greeks themselves reflected the change and tried to check an inflation of oaths by restricting and strengthening them (e.g., mythical King Rhadamanthys imposed oaths in settling disputes). They suspended the oath and then reintroduced it (Solon). Their conclusion was that the gods do not punish promptly and that keeping oaths is in many cases unreasonable and immoral. Sophocles also perceived, however, that an oath makes people watch what they say or promise.

Roman law recognized several oaths in court proceedings. Very early, officials were pledged to the well-being of the *res publica.* To strengthen the validity of individual laws, officials also had them sworn (*iusiurandum in legem,* "oath into law"). Finally, taking an oath to the republic was also taking an oath to its laws. In the imperial period an oath was sworn by the genius of the emperor.

3. OT

Various formulas occur in the OT: the oath of exculpation (Exod. 22:10-11), the ordeal at trials (Num. 5:12-31), Saul's oath of revenge (1 Sam. 14:44), and Abner's assertion by the life of the king (1 Sam. 17:55). Oaths must be kept, since they "bind the soul," though fathers or husbands may release women from oaths (Numbers 30). The → prophets criticize those who swear "by those who are no gods" (Jer. 5:7). Neighboring peoples should learn from the way that Israel swears (12:16). Swearing "as the Lᴏʀᴅ lives" is a confession (4:1-2).

God himself swears. His → promise to → Abraham in Gen. 24:7, to Abraham, → Isaac, and → Jacob in 50:24, and to → David in Ps. 89:3-4 is said to be an oath. God also swears that he will punish his unfaithful people (Amos 4:2; 6:8). But he takes pity again and calls upon the people to bear witness to his faithfulness (Isaiah 43). Yahweh is faithful to himself, to his → creation (Gen. 8:2-3; 9:8-17), and to his people in such a way that his oath does not bind him formally. With him reality and promise are inseparable, so that absolute → faithfulness and absolute → freedom go together. When Israel says that God takes an oath, it means that he is astonishingly faithful.

4. NT

Matt. 23:16-22 is an attack on making overly subtle distinctions in what one swears by. → Jesus says that we must not deceive ourselves, for whenever we swear, we have God to deal with. Matt. 5:33-37 develops the thought. When we swear, we try to make sure of something that is not under our control. Hence it is best not to do so.

In Matt. 26:63 the high priest adjures Jesus "before the living God" to say whether he is the Christ. Jesus answers with a threat: From now on the Son of Man will meet you only as Judge. Shortly thereafter → Peter swears three times that he does not know Jesus (Matt. 26:69-75).

→ Paul fights for recognition as an → apostle and for the content of the → gospel. He thus swears, calling God to witness (Rom. 1:9; 2 Cor. 1:12-23; 11–12; Phil. 1:8; 1 Thess. 2:5). In Heb. 6:13-20 God alone cannot swear by anyone higher than himself. Jas. 5:12 refers to the saying of Jesus in Matt. 5:33-37 and demands a simple Yes, Yes or No, No, as does Paul in 2 Cor. 1:17-19. This response might have been a formula used by the early community, like → "Amen."

In the first centuries Christians refused to take an oath of allegiance to the → state and were thus persecuted as traitors (→ Persecution of Christians). In 535 Justinian ordered officials to swear by God and the gospels that they would honestly serve him and his wife, Theodora. The church now became a pillar of the state.

5. Judaism

The → Talmud discusses judicial oaths. Frivolous oaths are almost as bad as false ones. The basis of every oath is God's oath to → Noah that he will sustain life. In medieval courts up to the beginning of the 19th century, Jews had no way to swear in public courts without bringing dishonor on themselves.

6. Middle Ages

In medieval courts Teutonic law gave prominence to the witness, not as a witness to facts, but as a witness to the reliability of the plaintiff or the defendant. In their battle for supremacy emperors and popes swore fidelity to one another (→ Empire and Papacy). Feudalism demanded an oath of fidelity on the part of the lord and an oath of allegiance on the part of the subject. In the cities citizens formed legal corporations in which the council and citizens swore to perform their respective duties (→ City). Federations might be directed against feudal overlords (e.g., in Switzerland and in episcopal cities). The → Cathari, → Waldenses, Lollards, and others refused the oath and as a result suffered bloody persecution from both the church and rulers.

7. Church Doctrine

7.1. *Roman Catholic Church*

The → Corpus Iuris Canonici, → Thomas Aquinas (ca. 1225-74), and the → Codex Iuris Canonici (cans. 1316-21) agree essentially that an oath rests on faith in the true God. Those who swear must know what they are swearing and must do so honestly, without mental reservation. The subject of the oath must also be morally permissible (→ Moral Theology). A sworn promise is related to what is sworn; it cannot be binding in a purely formal sense.

The → pope and → bishops can grant a dispensation from a sworn promise if it is forced or is given in some impossible situation. The Roman Catholic view considers society's need for reassurances (also the church's) but also seeks to protect those who swear from immoral obligations. (The oath to A. Hitler, for example, lost its binding force the moment Hitler pursued wicked aims.)

7.2. *Protestant Churches*

The → Augsburg Confession (art. 16) grants secular governments the right to demand oaths (→ Two Kingdoms Doctrine). Martin → Luther (in the Larger Catechism) thought an oath might serve the ends of truth, peace, and one's neighbor. God will punish false oaths and oath-breaking. The Geneva Catechism and → Heidelberg Catechism permit oaths to back up truth and to uphold love and concord. The Anglican Thirty-nine Articles permit an oath when the civil authorities demand it, "in a cause of faith and charity, so it be done . . . in justice, judgment, and truth" (art. 39). The South German Anabaptists (Schleitheim Confession) rejected the oath on the ground that we must not bind ourselves absolutely except to Christ. The Dutch → Anabaptists (→ Menno Simons), followed by the → Mennonites, rejected the oath on the ground that Christians are always pledged to truthfulness.

8. Modern Law

In the course of → secularization oaths became less common, and written documentation made many oaths superfluous. Witnesses are still sworn in court proceedings, and oaths of office are demanded, but in many countries religious formulas are not enforced. Both civil and religious rites of matrimony can be viewed as special instances of oath taking (→ Law and Legal Theory).

The → Roman Catholic Church still demands official and judicial oaths but no longer enforces the → Anti-Modernist Oath. In his motu proprio *Ad tuendam fidem* (May 1998), however, John Paul II amended the CIC and the Code of Canons of the Eastern churches to require, in effect, an oath of allegiance to all "definitive" teachings of the magisterium.

Protestant churches may also demand pledges of loyalty and the swearing of witnesses in disciplinary cases.

9. Problems

The oath to Hitler temporarily brought swearing into religious discredit in Germany. Though comparative studies are not available, certain tendencies may be detected. Technological development has made circumstantial evidence more important, while psychology has relativized the reliability of the statements of witnesses, and consequently of the oath. The oath has thus lost much of its importance as a means of proof. Yet the revival of religion in many lands, and especially the need of governments to ensure the loyalty of civil servants and the armed forces, has helped the oath to survive in secular societies. Conditional self-imprecation is then replaced by more serious penalties for perjury. Some nonofficial movements, like doctors opposed to nuclear war, also appeal to an oath. The problem arises, not with the form of the oath, but with its function. The churches grant that the state has a right to demand oaths but only within the limits of law and morality.

Certain questions remain: Should religion support, tolerate, or reject the quasi-religious rites of the state? When a person in power demands an oath, is that person bringing a power-relation to bear on the → conscience of those who swear it? What is the relation of the military oath to a commitment to → peace? If Jesus did not totally forbid oaths, he demanded that we ask ruthlessly what we are doing when we swear an oath. Solemn assurances must serve both personal integrity and the social need for confidence.

Because of the need to trust a person unconditionally, on the one hand, and the justified doubt in the human capacity for trustworthiness, on the other, societies will probably always make use of ceremonial asseverations in which a person pledges honor, money, or freedom as assurances of trustworthiness.

Bibliography: S. BOORER, *The Promise of the Land as Oath: A Key to the Formation of the Pentateuch* (Berlin, 1992) • T. W. CARTLEDGE, *Vows in the Hebrew Bible and the Ancient Near East* (Sheffield, 1992) • P. R. GLAZEBROOK, "Oaths, English Post-Reformation," *NCE* 10.596-99 • R. HIRZEL, *Der Eid* (New York, 1979; orig. pub., 1902) • L. M. ORSY, *The Profession of Faith and the Oath of Fidelity: A Theological and Canonical Analysis* (Wilmington, Del., 1990) • M. A. PAULEY, *I Do Solemnly Swear: The President's Constitutional Oath: Its Meaning and Importance in the History of Oaths* (Lanham, Md., 1999).

JOACHIM SCHWARZ

Obadiah, Book of

The Book of Obadiah opens with the phrase "The vision of Obadiah," a superscription obviously intended to reflect the prophetic functions of Obadiah, about whom we know nothing. Although the name may have been a fictitious one attached to an originally anonymous collection of oracles against Edom, an actual individual may be behind the book, someone generally identified as a cult prophet who was active shortly after the fall of → Jerusalem in 587 b.c. (see vv. 11-14). H. W. Wolff suggests he may have been a cult → prophet who appeared at early-exilic laments in Jerusalem, where he updated and interpreted older, orally transmitted oracles against Edom (1b-4, 5-14, 15b).

The book consists of only 21 verses. Although the demarcation of individual oracles is disputed, a tripartite structure is clearly discernible in 1b-14, 15b; 15a,16-18; and 19-21, the final saying (possibly multilayered) representing an addendum. Vv. 1b-6, 8 find word-for-word or thematic parallels in Jer. 49:14-16, 9, 10, 7, suggesting either literary borrowing from the Book of Obadiah itself or access to common oral tradition (so Wolff).

The content involves a message of judgment against Edom prompted by the hostility of the Edomites during the fall of Judah in 587. The book expands this message into an announcement of the day of → Yahweh "against all the nations" (v. 15), a day from which Zion, however, is spared.

→ Minor Prophets

Bibliography: *Commentaries:* A. Deissler (NEchtB; Würzburg, 1984) • R. Mason (OTGu; Sheffield, 1991) • S. Pagán (NIB; Nashville, 1996) • P. R. Raabe (AB; New York, 1996) • W. Rudolph (KAT; Gütersloh, 1971) • A. Weiser (ATD; 8th ed.; Göttingen, 1985; orig. pub., 1950) • H. W. Wolff (Minneapolis, 1986).

Other works: E. Ben Zvi, *A Historical-Critical Study of the Book of Obadiah* (New York, 1996) • R. A. Martin, S. Scorza, and R. E. Whitaker, *Obadiah: Computer Generated Tools for the Study of Correlated Greek and Hebrew Texts of the OT* (Wooster, Ohio, 1995).

Winfried Thiel

Obedience

1. Concept
2. Biblical Views
3. From the Patristic Period to the Counter-Reformation
4. Modern Ethical Reflection

1. Concept

Obedience is a central but much debated concept in the Christian tradition. At the heart of the tradition is the idea that life should be lived in obedience to God's will as expressed in God's Word (→ Word of God). As the divine Word is always mediated or embodied in creaturely forms, however, discussion about obedience to God necessarily involves decisions about where and to what extent the ways, purposes, and commands of God may be discerned in creaturely and fallen reality. Thus, while Christian thinkers will in general agree with Peter's statement "We must obey God rather than men" (Acts 5:29 RSV), there is much disagreement about obedience because the precise form the commands, ways, and Word of God take depends on assumptions made about the nature of → revelation, biblical interpretation (→ Exegesis, Biblical; Hermeneutics), → Christology, the work of the → Spirit, the nature of the → church, → eschatology, and the extent to which God's purposes for human life are presently mediated through ecclesial → authority, the → state, the → family, and human → reason (→ Kingdom of God). Obedience to God has often been understood to involve obedience to creaturely mediators or embodiments of God's Word.

Further complicating matters, the term "obedience" is variously used to point to a spectrum of human actions ranging from "blind" obedience and outward conformity to a law or authority, to a thoughtful and freely given following-after such as is experienced in the learning process, to a mystical participation or solidarity with patterns of thinking, willing, acting, and feeling stemming from God. Thus the precise understanding and evaluation of what is entailed in obedience depend upon understandings about → anthropology, human selfhood and identity, and metaphysical assumptions about God's relationship to → creation in general.

While obedience to church, state, teachers, and family has typically been considered a virtue within the tradition, bitter experiences with totalitarian systems, authoritarian modes of thinking, and oppressive lifestyles have led to a many-faceted antiauthoritarian movement that has questioned the status of obedience within Christian culture. Consequently, theological reflection on obedience often takes place at a critical distance.

2. Biblical Views

2.1. In Hebrew, as in many other languages, both Semitic and Indo-European, the word for obedience stems from words meaning "hear" or "hearken." While the semantic range of the Hebrew word includes a use that simply indicates the passive reception of sound, other uses imply a more active response of faithful obedience. A prime example of the latter is Deut. 6:4, "Hear, O Israel. . . ."

In the OT Israel's hearkening or not hearkening

to the "voice" or "word" of → Yahweh is a central motif. God speaks his Word through chosen representatives and through the → covenants God makes with his people, the most important being the Mosaic covenant instituted on Mount Sinai (Exod. 19:5; Deuteronomy 4–5). The obedience required of Israel is not merely an outward conformance to laws and ordinances (→ Law) but, more critically, is an inward hearing and response, as the prophets often remind the people: "To obey is better than sacrifice, and to heed than the fat of rams" (1 Sam. 15:22; see also Isa. 1:11-17; Hos. 6:6).

2.2. In the NT → Jesus Christ is the exemplar and fulfillment of true human obedience (Rom. 5:18-21). He is the type of obedience, as Adam is the type of disobedience (v. 19). Christ's obedience, an obedience even to "death on a cross" (Phil. 2:8), is clearly tied to the mystery of redemption (see Heb. 5:8-9).

But while Jesus is the type of obedience to God, his reactions to human authority and tradition are varied. While often obedient to Jewish custom, family, religious authorities, and the demands of the Roman Empire, his relativization of the authority of all those institutions is quite striking. He came to fulfill the law and not abolish it (Matt. 5:17; cf. 4:1-11), and yet his frequent setting aside of Sabbath observance (e.g., John 5:1-18; Mark 3:1-6; 7:1-23) and reinterpretation of the law (Matt. 5:21-48) imply that he embodied and called for a new kind of relationship to the Word of God.

For Jesus' followers, obedience to God now means a new kind of "faith-obedience" (Rom. 1:5) or "faith-hearing" (Gal. 3:2), a "hearing" of Jesus (John 10:27) in faith made possible by the Spirit (1 Pet. 1:2; John 14:25-26; cf. Mark 4:11-12). Obedience becomes → discipleship and life lived according to the Spirit (Gal. 5:16-26; → Sanctification). Christian discipleship includes respect for orders such as family, community, and state (Eph. 6:1, 5; 2 Cor. 7:15; Col. 3:20, 22; Phlm. 21; Heb. 13:17; Rom. 13:1-2; Titus 3:1). Yet there is no unconditional obedience to human authorities, for obedience to them has its limit in obedience to God (Acts 5:29).

3. From the Patristic Period to the Counter-Reformation

Patristic thought is strongly marked by the idea that obedience and every grace involve human participation in the divine life, a participation that has been realized in history in Christ and is mediated by him. → Augustine (354-430) called obedience the mother and guardian of all → virtues. In → monasticism it became a central → vow. The monastic resolve to

obey the evangelical counsels (chastity, → poverty, and obedience) in detachment from worldly concerns was viewed and worked out as a liberating possibility, even though it meant subordination to a superior. According to the Benedictine Rule, monks renounced their own wills and unhesitatingly obeyed the command of a superior, observing it as though it were the command of God (see §5 of the rule). For → Thomas Aquinas (ca. 1225-74), the act of commanding is an act of the intellect, and the virtue of obedience can be understood to involve sharing in another's practical wisdom, which shares to a greater extent in that of God (*Summa theol.* II of II, qq. 47, 104).

In the → Reformation, there was an extensive questioning and rethinking of the place of obedience in the Christian life. While obedience to church and civil authorities was not rejected in principle, all human authority, especially ecclesial, was called to be judged according to the standard of the Scriptures (J. → Calvin *Inst.* 4.9.12); it was frequently judged to be lacking. Obedience to the papacy was rejected. Monasticism also was rejected, insofar as it was understood as a more perfect expression of Christian life or a form of works-righteousness, and contemporary corruptions within it were condemned (M. → Luther, *On Monastic Vows* [*LW* 44.251-400]).

J. → Hus (ca. 1372-1415) had found that Scripture, and especially the words and deeds of the apostles, taught him not to obey the rulings of authorities. The Czech Reformation and Anabaptist groups went much further than Luther (1483-1546) and Calvin (1509-64) in questioning obedience to civil authorities. Yet for the → Bohemian Brethren, obedience to the community rule was the motive power of a God-fearing and therefore liberated life (B. Seifferth).

In the Counter-Reformation obedience occupied an important place, especially in works on → spirituality and → moral theology, tractates that made a strong impact on the church. → Ignatius of Loyola's (1491-1556) view of obedience decisively influenced the development of Roman Catholic theology in the 17th century. This view combined medieval monastic obedience with ecclesiastical obedience (→ Jesuits). It found institutional illustration in the so-called vow of the fourth order (i.e., special obedience to the pope in going on missions). As A. Müller points out, stress on the official priesthood and the hierarchy, as well as the assimilation of the hierarchical structure of the church to the mystical-religious ideal of obedience, brought new vitality to Christian life and thinking.

Ignatius's letter "On Prompt and Blind Obedience" (1550) distinguished for the first time between thinking obedience and blind obedience. In it the → virtue is for the first time a basic attitude of will rather than of intellect. This view is not to be viewed as the consequence of a voluntarist → anthropology (→ Voluntarism) but as an ecclesiological-mystical position. Superiors are to be obeyed, not because of their well-considered judgments or goodness, but because they are indirect representatives of Christ. This Christological anchoring of obedience may be seen at three levels. At the first level, where there is no obedience in the proper sense, commands are simply executed. At the second, persons try to make the will of the superior their own. At the third (and perfect) level, persons subject their own intellect to that of the superior. Francis de Sales (1567-1622) also stressed the ascetic dimension of obedience in the relation between → humility and obedience.

4. Modern Ethical Reflection

In → modernity the category of obedience has undergone profound changes. In the → Enlightenment, obedience was increasingly loosed from its Christological and mystical moorings on the basis of the general abandonment of a metaphysical notion of a hierarchical order of being, the individualization of notions of human personhood, and new interpretations of the nature of revelation (P. Baelz, 15). While the vocabulary remained constant (note the parallels between Frederick the Great of Prussia [1712-86] and Ignatius Loyola that F. W. Kantzenbach has documented), secularized notions of obedience were tied instead to universal reason, history, or notions of human society. I. Kant (1724-1804) viewed obedience as correlative to ethical → duty (→ Kantianism). It is not opposed to the principle of the → autonomy of the will because it represents agreement between one's own will and the moral law.

German → idealism (J. G. Fichte, G. W. F. Hegel) expressly sanctioned religion's role in strengthening obedience, claiming that the logic of history harmonizes with the will of God. Obedience expresses subjective assent to this identity. S. → Kierkegaard (1813-55) protested against such notions and sought to separate obedience to the "life-pattern" of Christ from mere obedience to the moral law. Others have attacked the role religion has played in promoting unquestioning obedience to authorities, a crucial factor behind the diffuse defamation of the concept in the 20th century.

In 20th-century theology various emphases are found in discussions of obedience. Karl → Barth (1886-1968) decisively retheologized the category.

He saw in obedience a readiness given by God to receive God's Word (CD II/2, 233-34) and gave it a specific, Christocentric dimension (pp. 568-69; → Dialectical Theology). Emil Brunner (1889-1966) emphatically affirmed the theological orientation but stressed that obedience is achieved in the relative autonomy of the various spheres of life.

Roman Catholic theology up to the middle of the 20th century dealt with obedience under → church law. Theologically debatable in this regard is the customary and self-evident equation of church rulings with ethical commands and the structural subordination of the laity to the clergy (→ Clergy and Laity; see esp. 1983 → CIC 188-89). After → Vatican II Roman Catholic theology began to discuss the relation of obedience to autonomy. Moral theology in the German sphere (see A. Auer) and → Latin American theology (see C. Boff; → Liberation Theology) used the term "relational autonomy" in an attempt to expound afresh the voluntary relationship of obedience between God and humans. In criticism of obedience modern Roman Catholic theology also took up impulses from → critical theory, which pointed out the danger of ideologizing obedience when it is viewed as forced subjection to ruling → authority.

In view of the historically significant ambivalence of the term, theology must ask whether it is appropriate to consider obedience as a central concept. Is it in keeping with the truth of Jesus that broken concepts should constantly be restored by fresh interpretations (D. Sölle)? The question is understandable. Nevertheless, contemporary theologians, especially those engaged in Trinitarian theology and reconceived notions of human personhood, are seeking to understand obedience in ways that both resist authoritarianism and open up a decisive dimension of Christian → freedom and → grace.

→ Catholic Reform and Counterreformation; Conscience; Deontology; Emancipation; Ethics; Father; Responsibility

Bibliography: On 2-3: P. Althaus, *The Ethics of Martin Luther* (Philadelphia, 1972) • R. Fisichella, "Obediential Potency," *Dictionary of Fundamental Theology* (ed. R. Latourelle and R. Fisichella; New York, 1994) 741-42 • F. W. Kantzenbach, "Blinder Gehorsam. Variationen des Gehorsamsbegriffs (1600-1945)," *ZRGG* 38 (1986) 208-30 • G. A. Lee, "Hear; Hearken; Listen; Obey," *ISBE* 2.649-50 • J. Miller, "Zur ignatianischen Gehorsamslehre," *TPQ* 104 (1956) 193-213 • A. Müller, *Obedience in the Church* (Westminster, Md., 1966) • B. Seifferth, *Church Constitution of the Bohemian and Moravian Brethren* (London, 1886) •

W. Tyndale, *The Obedience of a Christian Man* (London, 2000; orig. pub., 1528) • C. Walther, "Gehorsam," *TRE* 13.148-57 • E. Wolf, *Sozialethik* (Göttingen, 1975) • F. W. Young, "Obedience," *IDB* 3.580-81.

On 4: A. Auer, "Christianity's Dilemma: Freedom to Be Autonomous or Freedom to Obey?" *Moral Formation and Christianity* (ed. F. Böckle; New York, 1978) 47-55 • P. Baelz, *Christian Obedience in a Permissive Context* (London, 1973) • K. Barth, *CD* II/2, IV/4 • C. Boff, "Towards an Ethic of Critical-Social Obedience," *Christian Obedience* (ed. C. Duquoc and C. Floristán; New York, 1980) 53-58 • D. Bonhoeffer, *Dietrich Bonhoeffer Works*, vol. 4, *Discipleship* (Minneapolis, 2001) • W. Brueggemann, *Interpretation and Obedience* (Minneapolis, 1991) • E. Brunner, *The Divine Imperative* (Philadelphia, 1947) • B. Dewey, *The New Obedience: Kierkegaard on Imitating Christ* (Washington, D.C., 1968) • E. Jüngel, *God as the Mystery of the World* (Grand Rapids, 1983) • N. Lash, *Voices of Authority* (Shepherdstown, W.Va., 1976) • J. M. Lochman, *Signposts to Freedom: The Ten Commandments and Christian Ethics* (Minneapolis, 1982) • H. McCabe, "Obedience," *NBl* 65 (1984) 280-87 • J. Moltmann, *The Church in the Power of the Spirit* (New York, 1977); idem, *The Trinity and the Kingdom* (San Francisco, 1981) • K. Rahner, "Christ as the Exemplar of Clerical Obedience," *Obedience and the Church* (Washington D.C., 1968) 1-18; idem, *Hearer of the Word* (New York, 1994) • E. Schillebeeckx, "Secular Criticism of Christian Obedience and the Christian Reaction to That Criticism," *Christian Obedience*, ed. Duquoc and Floristán, 10-21 • D. Sölle, *Creative Disobedience* (Cleveland, 1995) • A. von Speyr, *Das Buch vom Gehorsam* (Einsiedeln, 1966).

Alberto Bondolfi and David L. Stubbs

Oberammergau

1. History
2. Anti-Judaism
3. Reform
   3.1. The 1984 Play
   3.2. The 2000 Play

1. History

According to tradition, a plague that swept Germany in 1633 spared the Bavarian village of Oberammergau, and in gratitude for their deliverance the townspeople promised to honor God by performing a play the following year that depicted the death of Jesus (→ Passion, Account of the; Religious Drama). In following years the town repeated the play, and now, almost four centuries later, it still continues to do so every ten years.

The 2000 production involved six months of performances that attracted nearly 500,000 viewers from all parts of the world. The elaborate production, nearly six hours in length, is produced, directed, staged, and performed solely by the residents of Oberammergau, a project that in 2000 engaged more than 2,000 of its 5,300 inhabitants. The majority of playgoers come from outside Germany, with Americans constituting the largest group.

The Oberammergau Passion Play has its textual roots in the earliest surviving dramas about the death of Jesus, presented in Latin beginning in the 12th century. In time, passion plays were performed in hundreds of European communities; between the 14th and 16th centuries over 300 villages in Germany and Austria alone reenacted the passion. The actual text currently used at Oberammergau, revised for the 2000 play, was prepared between 1850 and 1860 by Joseph Daisenberger.

2. Anti-Judaism

Almost from their inception such passion plays, including the Oberammergau production, unfortunately contained a large number of anti-Jewish elements. Indeed, the plays generally portrayed the Jews as bloodthirsty, intent on killing Jesus. The priestly class was a special target of scorn, although the plays also focused on the Jewish crowd that clamored for the crucifixion of Jesus. The plays minimized the fact that first-century Judea was occupied by the Romans, and they softened the pivotal role played in the death of Jesus by the Roman procurator Pontius Pilate. In some productions it was scarcely mentioned that crucifixion was a Roman method of capital punishment. The portrayed enemies of Jesus — and, by extension, of Christians and Christianity — were the Jewish people.

Bloody reactions against European Jews often followed performances of these passion plays. In 1338 the councillors of Freiburg banned the performance of anti-Jewish scenes in that town's play, and because of such anti-Jewish representations the Jewish → ghetto in Frankfurt received special protection in 1469. Similarly, a passion play in Rome in 1539 was banned after one production led to violent attacks against the city's Jewish residents. The anti-Jewish message of Oberammergau was not lost on Adolf Hitler, who in 1934 called the play a "precious tool" in his fight against the Jews, commending the play because "never has the menace of Jewry been so convincingly portrayed."

3. Reform

After the end of World War II, and in light of both the → Holocaust itself and the positive teachings of → Vatican II, many Christian and Jewish leaders publicly called for a radical reform of the Oberammergau play's script, music, and staging that would eliminate its negative portrayal of Jews. Because of the play's long history of anti-Jewish bias, two major American Jewish organizations — the American Jewish Committee and the Anti-Defamation League — have been heavily involved since 1960 in dealing with questions raised by the play. Each group has made a number of specific recommendations to the Oberammergau authorities regarding changes in the production.

At an episcopal conference in Rome in March 1982, John Paul II gave support to such reforms by declaring that Roman Catholic teaching in all forms should present Jews and Judaism "not only in an honest and objective manner, free from prejudices and without any offenses, but also with full awareness of the heritage common [to Jews and Christians]." In 1988 the Bishops' Committee for Ecumenical and Interreligious Affairs of the U.S. National Conference of Catholic Bishops published a strongly worded document, *Criteria for the Evaluation of Dramatizations of the Passion,* urging that "extraliturgical depictions of the sacred mysteries conform to the highest possible standards of biblical interpretation and theological sensitivity." Great caution was advised in using biblical passages that "seem to show the Jewish people in an unfavorable light."

In the 1980s and 1990s Jewish and Christian scholars held a series of conferences, consultations, and symposia focusing on the reform of the Oberammergau play. These scholars agreed that the production was clearly anti-Jewish, marred by a fundamentally flawed anti-Semitic orientation. The goal of these events was the removal of all anti-Jewish elements from the play. It was the judgment of these scholars that since the Oberammergau Passion Play is the "grandparent" of many similar plays throughout the world, the anti-Jewish bias of the production is a significant obstacle to positive Christian-Jewish relations.

3.1. *The 1984 Play*

Critics who attended performances of the Oberammergau play after World War II, including its 1984 production, which marked the drama's 350th anniversary, argued that the production clearly conveyed the belief that the Jewish people then — and now — are guilty of Jesus' death and as a result must endure collective → punishment from God. They further charged that the play was strongly supersessionist,

conveying the view that Christianity and the church are theologically successor to, and triumphant over, Judaism and the synagogue.

Christian and Jewish critics were especially stunned by the virulent → anti-Semitism conveyed by the judgment scene at Oberammergau in 1984, in which 250 men, women, and children were shouting, on the large outdoor stage, for Jesus' crucifixion: "We take his blood upon us and upon our children." This chilling curse from Matthew 27:25 was subsequently removed from the 1990 and 2000 performances.

3.2. *The 2000 Play*

Many reforms of the Oberammergau text took place as a result of a referendum in Oberammergau in the mid-1990s in which Otto Hüber and Christian Stückl were authorized to rewrite and direct the 2000 production. Changes included a new emphasis on the dynamic Jewish religious world in which Jesus lived and a more accurate portrayal of Pilate as the venal governor who was responsible for Jesus' death. In the new text Jesus is repeatedly called → rabbi, and he recites a Hebrew prayer that reflects his Jewishness, a feature omitted from earlier Oberammergau productions.

Also in 2000 the Jewish crowd, hitherto portrayed as monolithically clamoring for Jesus' death, reflects the various divisions that existed within → Judaism during the lifetime of Jesus. Of critical importance was the removal from the play of the word → "Pharisee," meaning "religious separatist" in Hebrew, which has traditionally been a pejorative frequently used within the church to vilify Jews and Judaism. Similarly, the despised figure of Judas — traditionally clothed in yellow, the same color as the Star of David Jews were forced to wear during the era of the Holocaust — has now been recast as a highly complex person, no longer the one-dimensional traitor of past productions.

Despite these positive changes, many critics still see the Oberammergau Passion Play as flawed, with definite anti-Jewish elements, a conclusion reached unanimously by a panel of eight American scholars of religion — three Roman Catholics, two Protestants, and three Jews — who analyzed the 2000 script at the request of the American Jewish Committee (AJC). While recognizing the constructive changes made, these scholars expressed disappointment that the play continues to present a theologically harsh and historically inaccurate view of Jews and Judaism at the time of Jesus. The following comments (in AJC archives, New York) by three of the members illustrate their overall concerns.

John T. Pawlikowski of the Catholic Theological

Union in Chicago expressed deep disappointment at the 2000 text. It "fails to take into account what biblical scholars are saying today." Furthermore, it shows "little or no scholarly sensitivity for the complexity of the Gospel accounts . . . [e.g.,] the Jewish priests are portrayed as totally wicked and ultimately responsible for Jesus' death." He concludes, "All in all I do not feel the 2000 version of the play should be supported. While one can detect some effort to make it more acceptable to the current canons of the Christian-Jewish relationship, it is far too minimal. Christian visitors deserve something better."

Franklin Sherman, formerly professor at the Lutheran School of Theology in Chicago and subsequently an interfaith relations associate for the Evangelical Lutheran Church in America, expressed a more positive view of the 2000 text: "On the whole, the improvements to the traditional text are impressive and go a long ways towards eliminating the elements of 'the teaching of contempt' that marred the previous versions. The elements that remain are, unfortunately, in the NT text and hence difficult to remove." Along with his positive view of the text, however, Sherman criticized it for being strongly supersessionist, particularly in its opening proclamations.

Michael J. Cook, professor of Judeo-Christian studies at Hebrew Union College–Jewish Institute of Religion in Cincinnati, expressed concern that although improvements were made in the 2000 text, some of them substantial, yet there is little evidence of the "fundamental rethinking" necessary to "exorcise the anti-Jewish conceptual structure of the presentation." Cook observes that, although "some party must personify Evil, that function came to devolve solely upon the Jewish authorities and the Jews as a people — now the foil against which the purity and innocence of Jesus can be juxtaposed in stark contrast." For Cook that juxtaposition results in a "dreadful" drama in which the Jews are the collective losers. Indeed, Cook is fearful that, despite the more subtle changes made in the text, "the inference by the [2000] audience will be essentially no different from that in previous years." Since for many in the audience the Oberammergau Passion Play represents "gospel truth" about the life, trial, and death of Jesus, the play, without deeper changes, has the potential to continue the transmission of negative perceptions and attitudes toward Jews and Judaism.

→ Jewish-Christian Dialogue

Bibliography: S. S. FRIEDMAN, *The Oberammergau Passion Play: A Lance against Civilization* (Carbondale, Ill., 1984) • E. LANE and I. BRENSON, eds., *The Complete Text in English of the Oberammergau Passion Play* (London, 1984) • G. R. MORK, " 'Wicked Jews' and 'Suffering Christians' in the Oberammergau Passion Play," *Representations of Jews through the Ages* (ed. L. J. Greenspoon and B. F. Le Beau; Omaha, Nebr., 1996) 153-70 • *The Passion Play: 2000, Oberammergau* (Munich, 2000) • J. S. SHAPIRO, *Oberammergau: The Troubling Story of the World's Most Famous Passion Play* (New York, 2000).

A. JAMES RUDIN

Objectivism → Subjectivism and Objectivism

Observance

The term "observance" (Lat. *observo,* "observe, watch, follow, keep") is used legally with reference to custom or to mere tradition that has not yet reached the stage of custom. In Roman Catholic → religious orders it is the effort to follow exactly the original rule without any later relaxations. In the Franciscan controversy regarding poverty in the 13th and 14th centuries (→ Franciscans), the reformers called themselves Observantines or Observants. Favoring a strict observance among → Cistercians are the Trappists (known officially since 1902 as the Order of Cistercians of the Strict Observance [O.C.S.O.]).

In → religious studies (→ Phenomenology of Religion) "observance" denotes a mode of life that outwardly seems to be religious and that thus in some sense stands related to legalism (→ Law) and → taboos.

→ Church Law

Bibliography: K. S. FRANK, "Observanten," *LTK* (3d ed.) 7.968-69 • L. J. LEKAI, *The rise of the Cistercian Strict Observance in Seventeenth Century France* (Washington, D.C., 1968) • D. NIMMO, *Reform and Division in the Medieval Franciscan Order: From St. Francis to the Foundation of the Capuchins* (Rome, 1987) • M. B. PENNINGTON, *The Cistercians* (Collegeville, Minn., 1992).

BRUNO PRIMETSHOFER

Occasional Services

1. Development
   1.1. Early Church and Middle Ages
   1.2. Reformation to the Present
2. Theological Problem
3. Insights from the Humanities
4. Pastoral Responsibility

1. Development

The church's "occasional services" are called such not because they are used infrequently but because they are rites that have been developed for specific occasions. The term is thus comparable to the variety of poetry called occasional verse.

Occasional services are often seen as a special form of ordinary → worship. Instead of assembling because of the weekly rhythm or the cycle of the → church year, the → congregation meets because one of its members is crossing a threshold from one stage of life to another. As it does for its regular services, the assembly puts this occasion also under the → Word of God.

1.1. *Early Church and Middle Ages*

One occasional service developed very early in the church's history as a response to a need felt throughout the church: Holy Baptism. This ritual → initiation into the Christian faith and life and incorporation into the body of Christ is essential to Christianity and is central to the faith. The action of → baptism as well as baptismal formulas are given in the NT (Acts 2:38; 8:35-38; 9:17-19; Matt. 28:19). Details concerning the method of baptismal washing appear in the late-first-century *Didache* and in the writings of → Justin Martyr (d. ca. 165). As early as the beginning of the third century we find a developed baptismal rite in the *Apostolic Tradition* (ca. 215).

→ Ordination can in certain ways be related to baptism, and there is a developed form for ordination as practiced in Rome in the *Apostolic Tradition*. Again, this sacramental action is essential for the work of the ministry of the church, and so it is not surprising that such a rite took shape early in the church's life.

The development of all the other occasional services is more haphazard and generally occurred much later in church history. Early Christian burial rites consciously opposed the pervading gloom of pagan rites, so certain customs were established, such as lights and songs and white clothing, but actual rites and texts were much slower to develop (→ Funeral). By the time of the Reformation there was as yet no consensus.

→ Marriage reflected secular customs and the right of civil authorities to regulate marriage. Christians therefore respected indigenous traditions and the powers of the → state, though they insisted on one thing: the free consent of those who were to be joined in marriage. By the time of the → Reformation, the marriage → liturgy still varied considerably from place to place and was not yet conducted entirely within the church building.

The → consecration of a church was originally effected simply by celebrating the → Eucharist within its walls, thus using it for the purpose for which it was built. In later centuries, as symbolism of the place and the building developed, more specific acts of consecration were devised. But these rites too, like all others of the church, varied from place to place and from → diocese to diocese until they were codified in the latter 16th century.

1.2. *Reformation to the Present*

At the time of the Reformation, Lutherans and Anglicans, in preparing their church orders and service books, drew upon prevailing local customs for the occasional services. Not until 1614 was the Roman Ritual, the manual for priests, codified for the entire → Roman Catholic Church. Although this ritual of Pope Paul V was the official and authorized book, local and regional customs and variants continued. The Roman Ritual continues as *De Benedictionibus,* in English translation for the United States called *Book of Blessings* (1989).

By the early 20th century the liturgical churches had recovered and collected a number of orders dealing with individuals and groups within the church, including those for baptism, → confirmation, confession (→ Confession of Sin), visitation and communion of the sick, commendation of the dying, burial, marriage, ordination, installation, laying of a church cornerstone, dedication of a church, and the opening and closing of synods.

By the middle of the 20th century, a desire began to be apparent in many denominations to mark everything, every object, every event with some sort of "liturgical" rite, some fixed set of words. In 1926, for example, the newly elected president of the venerable Lutheran Ministerium of Pennsylvania simply began work in his new office without ceremony, even though pastors were regularly installed in their parishes with a specific rite. His successor in 1943, however, was formally inaugurated into his office with a service of installation. That change in → piety was even more evident in the development of forms for the blessing of objects used in worship — → crosses, candles, communion vessels, → vestments, Bibles, even service books and → hymnals. The blessing, even the "baptism," of → bells had a long tradition in the church, for bells were understood to be creatures with a voice that publicly proclaimed what the church was doing. The blessing of objects such as books, however, was a novelty.

The Roman Catholic *Book of Blessings* is the most comprehensive collection of occasional services available in any denomination. It is organized in six parts: (1) blessings pertaining directly to persons (families and members of families, the sick, → missionaries, catechists and catechumens, teachers and students, meetings and organizations, pilgrims and travelers); (2) blessings related to buildings and forms of human activity (homes, schools, hospitals, factories, gymnasiums, animals, the activities of fields and flocks); (3) blessing of objects for use in churches (fonts, repository for oils, bishop's chair, lectern, doors, → images, bells, → organ, chalice and paten, → cemetery); (4) blessing of articles meant to foster the devotion of Christian people (religious articles, → rosaries, scapular); (5) blessings related to feasts and seasons (Advent wreath, manger, Christmas tree, houses, throats [on the feast day of St. Blaise, to cure or prevent diseases of the throat], ashes on Ash Wednesday, food and drink); and (6) blessings for various needs and occasions (readers, servers, parish officers).

The Lutheran *Occasional Services* (1982) for North America and the Episcopal *Book of Occasional Services* (1988) for the United States are also rather full compilations and are more wide-ranging than their predecessors.

Bibliography: M. HATCHETT, *Commentary on the American Prayer Book* (New York, 1981) • P. H. PFATTEICHER, *Commentary on the Occasional Services* (Philadelphia, 1983) • W. H. WILLIMON, *Worship as Pastoral Care* (Nashville, 1979).

PHILIP H. PFATTEICHER

2. Theological Problem

2.1. Occasional services have become a problem since, with → secularization, church attendance has decreased in many countries, but participation in occasional services remains constant or is even increasing. More and more members thus have contact with church life only through these occasional services. As a result, such services tend to lose contact with the congregation, becoming in effect family festivals, particularly in the case of private baptism.

The problem comes to light when a → confession of faith is required of participants. In confirmation, seen as a recollection, renewal, or completion of baptism, the confirmands must make such a confession and a → vow to live a life of → discipleship. But the subsequent manner of life followed by most does not conform to the vow — and in fact unmasks it as a lie. Infant baptism is also shown to be a problem when the parents promise to give the child a Christian upbringing, as the → liturgy prescribes, but in reality are neither able nor ready to do so. A funeral is also a problem when the deceased and the bereaved are religiously indifferent, even atheists.

2.2. The churches have sometimes tried to solve this problem by imposing moral or religious conditions on occasional services (e.g., refusing to marry divorced persons, or refusing to offer a church funeral in cases of cremation or → suicide). Where tried, these measures have not proved practicable and have ultimately been abandoned.

Another solution is to view occasional services in the context of the church's calling to → mission. As many unchurched people gather on these occasions, the → gospel can be preached to them as neopagans (→ Evangelism). They can ideally be shown that their → faith implies, and leads to, church fellowship.

In a polemical work of 1960 R. Bohren advanced an opposing thesis. He argues that such missionary efforts are counterproductive, for the rite obscures the → kerygma (see §3). The church's sacred ministry simply puts a religious face on natural processes and thus makes a Baal out of Christ. It produces outward Christians who are living without Christ. With his rejection of occasional services, Bohren at least has the radical summons of Jesus to discipleship on his side (see Matt. 8:22).

The theological problem, however, is not just that of improving present practice by reserving occasional services only for those who belong to the core congregation. The real question is whether the church as it now is, is truly the church. The issue is how to evaluate theologically why many who are in fact far from the church nevertheless participate in occasional services.

3. Insights from the Humanities

Since most church members and adherents do not want to go through life's transitions without these occasional services, there would seem to be a function for them. Various sociological hypotheses explain the desire for occasional services and their effects. Points of transition involve psychological crises for an intimate group because, as in the case of a birth or a death, a new balance must be found between the group's members. These transitions also involve personal psychological crises requiring the mastering of feelings that are both extreme (→ grief, sense of loss, etc.) and ambivalent (coexistent → love and hate). Points of passage also raise questions about the value and meaning of → life and about the → future. All religions have rites of passage that ease these transitions.

The church itself offers help in such crises by means of ritual, that is, by unchanging interactions accompanied by words and attendant → symbols. By its fixed form, ritual contributes to emotional stability, integrating those concerned into a fellowship of people with the same experiences and thus lessening the sense of loneliness. Ritual thus represents the transition symbolically and helps persons achieve familiarity with it. Symbols make it possible to identify and work out the psychological → conflicts. By rite and speech they also answer the question of → meaning. They give validity to existence, which the occasion has made precarious; through their apotropaic character they overcome → anxiety about the future; and they encourage → hope by their reference to transcendence (→ Immanence and Transcendence). Help comes through the performance of the rite, not necessarily through the meaning of the words recited. In this respect there is a certain tension between ritual and kerygma.

4. Pastoral Responsibility

In the historical development of occasional services, → pastors have been given the leading role. If they are not to fail the weary and heavy-laden who need the help of the ritual, they must also acknowledge a diaconal and pastoral task in relation to these persons (→ Pastoral Care; Deacon, Deaconess). Whether they fulfill this task depends on their understanding of the church — specifically, on their not regarding the NT statements about the church as limiting narrowly the true form of the church but, rather, being open to other forms that the church might take in changed circumstances. They may find themselves unable to judge unequivocally who does or does not belong to the church of Christ. They also may affirm that even for those at a distance from the church, transitional situations raise questions that correlate with the answers of the gospel. The question of meaning may thus be viewed as a hidden search for the Father of Jesus Christ. In the need of these people for → legitimation, pastors will hear a longing for faith.

The fact that persons in need are first stabilized by ritual and not by the meaning of the recited texts is because the redeeming work of God in Christ does not invalidate God's creation and act of blessing. If pastors in celebrating the rites accompany and support those concerned without inner hesitation or resistance, a relation of trust can develop that favors pastoral care and → proclamation. This relation will begin already in the preparation of the service if it is done sympathetically. Because of the context, however, the → sermon in the occasional service will often be seen as merely part of the ritual: the preacher and hearers are playing assigned roles, and the words will seem to have no great relevance to → everyday life. The sermon will leave the

sphere of the rite only if it succeeds in expressing in unconventional terms what the hearers feel and in setting those feelings in the light of God's love. Later conversations (e.g., when visiting the bereaved at home) are not under the same pressure of ritual.

Weddings and funerals, insofar as they involve elements of life transition, can readily be seen as correlating with questions and divine answers in the gospel. The doctrine of baptism for most churches has fixed the meaning of infant baptism. In this regard the occasional element relates to the experience of the parents, a motif to which the → prayers and sermon should relate.

→ Church Growth

Bibliography: F. AHIUS, *Der Kasualgottesdienst. Zwischen Übergangsritus und Amtshandlung* (Stuttgart, 1985) • R. BOHREN, *Unsere Kasualpraxis. Eine missionarische Gelegenheit* (5th ed.; Munich, 1979; orig. pub., 1960) • A. KAVANAGH, *Confirmation: Origins and Reform* (New York, 1988); idem, *The Shape of Baptism: The Rite of Christian Initiation* (New York, 1978) • P. H. PFATTEICHER, *Commentary on the Occasional Services* (Philadelphia, 1983) • E. RAMSHAW, *Ritual and Pastoral Care* (Philadelphia, 1987) • R. RUTHERFORD, *The Death of a Christian: The Rite of Funerals* (New York, 1990) • M. SCHIBILSKY, *Alltagswelt und Sonntagskirche* (Munich, 1983) • S. A. STAUFFER, ed., *Baptism, Rites of Passage, and Culture* (Geneva, 1999) • K. W. STEVENSON, *To Join Together: The Rite of Marriage* (New York, 1987).

WALTER NEIDHART†

Occultism

From Lat. *occultus,* "secret, hidden," the term "occult" has reference to phenomena, processes, and practices in → nature, the spiritual world, or the extraterrestrial sphere that point to hidden forces that escape both normal sensory observation and the knowledge that rests on it. From the end of the 19th century, the term "occultism" came into use primarily for practical or theoretical dealings with transcendental phenomena of this kind. Today it is usually related to the occult → worldview that is based on these occult forces, which does not conform to a scientific outlook and which often has a religious accent. For rational and methodologically conducted research into the field, the terms that are gaining currency are → "parapsychology" or, more generally, "pararesearch." Since occult phenomena are ascribed here to inner psychological powers, → spiritism is no longer classified as occultism.

Despite intensive study the nature of occult phenomena is still a mystery. Phenomenologically, it seems best to arrange them according to their relation to familiar spheres of knowledge. → Alchemy, → astrology, materializations, radiesthesia, ghosts, table rappings, voices, automatic writings, and other such phenomena transcend or contradict the laws of physics. Other phenomena such as → miracles of → healing, paranormal healing, iris- and aura-diagnostics, and → stigmatization similarly transcend or contradict biological laws. Suprasensual perception and psychokinesis are the central parapsychological phenomena. In a broader sense we may also include the phenomena of → mysticism, → reincarnation, and various forms of contact with the beyond. Yet even if the normal laws of physics are frequently transcended in the previous classifications, we cannot meaningfully classify the broad complex of → magic because physical, biological, and psychological elements inseparably permeate one another there.

The growing interest in occultism is only one aspect of the rehabilitation of phenomena that prevailing worldviews, especially the scientific view, have crowded out. Theology can hardly link occult phenomena solely to deception and fraud or charge them, as O. Prokopp does, with being a crime against science. T. W. Adorno (1903-69; → Critical Theory) also goes too far when he defines occultism simply as the metaphysics of the simple. It is also much too harsh to say, as H. Stadelmann does (p. 48), with an appeal to the Bible, that in horoscopes, the consulting of cards, conjurations, pendulums, and so forth, we see the guilty involvement of humanity that results in a state under divine judgment and takes the form of a collective bewitchment. Parapsychological abilities are part of the order of → creation that, like all created things, may be used in opposition to God's express will, as, for example, in protective or sexual magic. Only when all other explanations fail may we refer to demonic or satanic influences (→ Devil), from which believing Christians must keep their distance.

→ Immanence and Transcendence

Bibliography: A. F. Aveni, *Behind the Crystal Ball: Magic, Science, and the Occult from Antiquity through the New Age* (New York, 1996) • B. J. Gibbons, *Spirituality and the Occult: From the Renaissance to the Twentieth Century* (London, 2001) • A. C. Lehman and J. E. Myers, *Magic, Witchcraft, and Religion: An Anthropological Study of the Supernatural* (4th ed., Mountain View, Calif., 1997) • P. G. Maxwell-Stuart, ed., *The Occult in Modern Europe: A Documentary History* (New York, 1999) • O. Prokopp and W. Wimmer, *Der moderne Okkultismus* (Stuttgart, 1976) • H. Stadelmann, *Das Okkulte* (2d ed.; Giessen, 1984) • G. G. Stroumsa, *Hidden Wisdom: Esoteric Traditions and the Roots of Christian Mysticism* (Leiden, 1996).

Karl Hoheisel

Oceania

Overview
1. Background
2. Church and Society
3. Church Expansion
4. Church Independence
5. Ecumenical Relations
6. Relation to Other Religions

Overview

"Oceania" is the U.N. term for the major area encompassing Australia, New Zealand, and the Pacific Islands. The last are divided into Micronesia, Melanesia, and Polynesia. (For information on Australia and New Zealand, see the separate articles.)

The region of *Micronesia,* the westernmost of the three island groups, lies mostly above the equator. Among others, it includes the following territories and independent nations, listed here in approximate west-to-east order (information in parentheses shows the current or last colonial power [→ Colonialism] and, as applicable, the date of independence):

Republic of Palau (U.S., 1994)
Northern Mariana Islands (U.S.)
Guam (U.S.)
Federated States of Micronesia (U.S., 1991)
Republic of the Marshall Islands (U.S., 1991)
Republic of Nauru (Austral., 1968)
Republic of Kiribati (U.K., 1979).

The territories and countries of *Melanesia* lie to the south of Micronesia, below the equator. Among others, they include the following, listed again in approximate west-to-east order:

Papua New Guinea (Austral., 1975)
Solomon Islands (U.K., 1978)
Republic of Vanuatu (Fr./U.K., 1980)
New Caledonia (Fr.)
Republic of Fiji (U.K., 1970)

The region of *Polynesia* lies generally east of Melanesia. Its countries and territories include the following ten, arranged west-to-east:

Tuvalu (U.K., 1978)
Wallis and Futuna Islands (Fr.)
Tokelau (N.Z.)
Samoa (formal name: the Independent State of
    Western Samoa; N.Z., 1962)
Kingdom of Tonga (U.K., 1970)
American Samoa (U.S.)
Niue (N.Z.)
Cook Islands (N.Z.)
French Polynesia (Fr.)
Pitcairn Island (U.K.)

1. Background

In the 19th century all the islands except Tonga came under colonial rule. By the year 2000 many had gained their independence; some were self-governing, with a former colonial power responsible for foreign affairs (e.g., Niue); and others were still colonies.

Farming and fishing are the main economic resources in most of the islands. Economic problems result from the low productivity of subsistence farming, population growth, and limited exports. Fishing fleets from Japan, South Korea, and Taiwan exploit and destroy the fishing grounds with their drift nets (esp. for tuna). In 1989 the states in the South Pacific banned this type of fishing and closed their ports to ships engaging in it. U.S. nuclear experiments in the South Pacific in the 1940s and 1950s (at Bikini and Enewetok atolls, in the Marshall Islands; → Weapons) and after 1966 by the French (at Mururoa atoll and underground, in French Polynesia) have caused enormous ecological damage by radiation and fallout, imperiling resources necessary to human life (→ Ecology; Environmental Ethics). A new threat is that of global change of climate through the greenhouse effect and too much carbon dioxide in the atmosphere.

2. Church and Society

Christian churches were established in all the island territories before the coming of colonial rule. In those precolonial times, kings and village leaders formed a close relation with Christianity, and → church and state worked in cooperation at both the national and the village levels. Local ministers normally sat on village councils or served as advisers of chiefs. Though Christianity introduced many changes in island culture, it gradually became completely incorporated into the modified culture that then emerged. The church became guardian of village traditions and the island way of life.

After colonial rule was established, the church stood as a link to the past, representing a continuing national identity. Where independence has been restored, the churches have rejoiced, and cordial relations have usually been established between church and state. The only significant conflicts have been in those places where colonial governments have resisted the independence movements while the churches have supported them. In Vanuatu Christian ministers were the ones leading the struggle for independence. In French-controlled New Caledonia the struggle for independence has had a denominational aspect, since some of the people are Protestant and favor independence, while others are Roman Catholic and are more favorable to the French connection.

3. Church Expansion

The religious geography of the Pacific Islands follows a clear pattern (→ Geography of Religion). In almost every country there is one predominant church, the one begun by the → missionaries who were first on the scene.

3.1. The pioneer mission for the Pacific was that of the Roman Catholics (→ Catholic Missions), who came from the Philippines to the Mariana Islands in 1668. Since then the Marianas have been predominantly Roman Catholic (→ Roman Catholic Church). Some early efforts were also made by the Roman Catholics in the Caroline Islands, but they were more sporadic, and the population of the Carolines has been only partly Roman Catholic.

The Roman Catholics, after their early start in Micronesia, were late in coming to the other parts of the Pacific. Hence they are only a → minority, though a significant minority, in French Polynesia (begun 1834), Tonga (1842), Samoa (1845), and the Cook Islands (1894), all in Polynesia; and in Fiji (1844), Vanuatu (1887), and the Solomon Islands (1898), all in Melanesia. The only territories in which they predominate are the Marquesas, Wallis and Futuna Islands, and New Caledonia, all French areas. On the main island of New Caledonia, the majority of the population is Roman Catholic, but in the entire territory of New Caledonia and the Loyalties, the indigenous population is equally divided between Catholic and Protestant.

The principal Catholic mission in the South Pacific has been that of the Marist Order, which still maintains missionaries in nearly all the lands that have been mentioned. In French Polynesia, however, the missionaries have been provided by the Congregation of the Sacred Hearts (formerly known as the Picpus Fathers), and in Kiribati they have come from the Missionaries of the Sacred Heart, originating in Issoudun, France. In Micronesia mission

Oceania in A.D. 2000: Demography

	Population (1,000s)	Annual Growth Rate (%)	Population Density (per sq. km. / mi.)	Births / Deaths (per 100 pop.)	Fertility Rate (per woman)	Infant Mortality Rate (per 1,000 live births)	Life Expectancy (years)
World total	6,091,351	1.27	45 / 116	2.13 / 0.86	2.66	51	66.9
Oceania	30,254	1.32	4 / 9	1.76 / 0.76	2.42	22	74.8
Australia–New Zealand[a]	22,598	1.05	3 / 7	1.38 / 0.77	1.92	6	78.7
Australia	18,832	1.04	2 / 6	1.35 / 0.77	1.89	6	78.8
New Zealand	3,760	1.10	14 / 36	1.52 / 0.78	2.10	6	78.0
Melanesia[b]	6,489	2.13	12 / 31	2.93 / 0.79	3.95	47	62.9
Fiji	848	1.58	46 / 120	2.16 / 0.47	2.54	17	73.7
Papua New Guinea	4,612	2.15	10 / 26	3.05 / 0.90	4.23	55	59.9
Solomon Islands	444	3.05	16 / 41	3.42 / 0.38	4.57	19	72.8
Micronesia[c]	539	2.18	197 / 511	2.76 / 0.49	3.70	30	70.4
Polynesia[d]	627	1.49	126 / 327	2.20 / 0.52	2.96	29	72.0

Note: Because of rounding, population figures for the regions and the major area as a whole may not equal the sum of their constituent parts.
[a]Figures include Christmas Island, Cocos (Keeling) Islands, Norfolk Island (all Austral.). [b]Figures include Bougainville (P.N.G.), New Caledonia (Fr.), Vanuatu. [c]Figures include Guam (U.S.), Kiribati, Marshall Islands, Micronesia (Federated States of), Nauru, Northern Mariana Islands (U.S.), Palau. [d]Figures include American Samoa (U.S.), Cook Islands (N.Z.), French Polynesia, Niue (N.Z.), Pitcairn (U.K.), Samoa, Tokelau (N.Z.), Tonga, Tuvalu, and Wallis and Futuna Islands (Fr.).

work is done by the → Jesuits from the United States. The number of foreign missionaries maintained by the Roman Catholic Church in the Pacific Islands continues to be much higher than that maintained by the major Protestant churches. It should also be noted that in most islands the introduction of Protestantism was by Pacific people themselves, while Catholicism was introduced by French missionaries.

3.2. The first Protestant mission to the Pacific was that of the London Missionary Society (LMS) in 1797 (→ British Missions), which began its work in Tahiti and adjacent islands. The people of these islands became, and have remained, predominantly Protestant. Since 1863 their international connections have been not with the LMS but with the Paris Evangelical Missionary Society (→ French Missions), and their church is named the Evangelical Church of French Polynesia. The LMS's subsequent labors led to the formation of the Cook Islands Christian Church, the main church in the Cooks (begun 1821), and the Congregational Christian Church in Samoa (→ Congregationalism), the largest Samoan church (1830). The Congregationalists in American Samoa broke away from this body in 1980 to launch their own Congregational Christian Church.

3.3. Beyond Samoa, the LMS was involved in the Tuvalu Church (1861), which has a practical monopoly of religious life in Tuvalu; the Kiribati Protestant Church (started by Americans in 1857),

which divides Kiribati in approximately equal shares with the Roman Catholics; and the Evangelical Church of New Caledonia and the Loyalty Islands (1841). This last body, like the Protestants of Tahiti, switched its international affiliation to Paris rather than London, though not till the turn of the 20th century.

3.4. Aside from the LMS the most widespread Protestant missions — and churches — have been those of the Methodists (→ Methodist Churches). They were the first to establish continuing work in Tonga (1826) and in Fiji (1835), where still today the Methodists are by far the largest Christian group. In the case of Fiji they are in one church, the Methodist Church in Fiji, but in Tonga they have been seriously divided, the largest group being in the king's church, the Free Wesleyan Church of Tonga, and smaller groups in the Free Church of Tonga and the Church of Tonga, divisions arising from political struggles of earlier years. The Methodist Church of Samoa (1835) is also a significant body, and in the western part of the Solomon Islands the major body of Christians is Methodist in origin (1902), though now it is named the United Church.

3.5. Three other Protestant churches are important. The Presbyterians (→ Reformed and Presbyterian Churches) have been from the beginning (1848) the largest church of Vanuatu, the only country in which they are found. The Anglicans (→ Anglican Communion) were the first to establish

Oceania in A.D. 2000: Religious Affiliation (as percentage of population)

	Christians	Muslims	Hindus	Non-religious	Chinese Folk Religionists	Buddhists	Tribal Religionists	Atheists	New Religionists	Sikhs	Jews	Spiritists	Other
World total	33.1	20.0	12.8	12.7	6.3	5.9	4.1	2.4	1.6	0.4	0.2	0.2	0.3
Oceania	83.0	0.9	1.2	10.7	0.2	1.0	0.8	1.2	0.2	—	0.3	—	0.5
Australia–													
New Zealand[a]	80.5	0.9	0.3	14.1	0.1	1.2	0.3	1.5	0.2	—	0.4	—	0.5
Australia	79.7	1.0	0.3	14.6	0.1	1.3	0.3	1.7	0.2	—	0.5	—	0.3
New Zealand	84.7	0.2	0.6	11.4	0.2	0.9	0.5	0.9	0.1	—	0.1	—	0.4
Melanesia[b]	89.9	1.0	4.3	0.7	0.1	0.2	2.8	—	0.1	0.1	—	—	0.8
Fiji	57.1	6.8	32.9	1.4	0.4	—	—	—	—	0.7	—	—	0.7
Papua New Guinea	95.1	—	—	0.3	0.1	0.2	3.4	—	—	—	—	—	0.9
Solomon Islands	95.8	0.1	—	0.3	—	0.3	3.0	—	—	—	—	—	0.5
Micronesia[c]	93.3	—	—	1.1	0.7	1.2	1.2	—	0.4	—	—	—	2.1
Polynesia[d]	92.8	—	—	1.6	3.0	0.1	0.1	—	—	—	—	—	2.4

Note: A dash represents a value of less than 0.05 percent. Because of rounding, horizontal totals may not equal 100.0.

[a]Figures include Christmas Island, Cocos (Keeling) Islands, Norfolk Island (all Austral.). [b]Figures include Bougainville (P.N.G.), New Caledonia (Fr.), Vanuatu. [c]Figures include Guam (U.S.), Kiribati, Marshall Islands, Micronesia (Federated States of), Nauru, Northern Mariana Islands (U.S.), Palau. [d]Figures include American Samoa (U.S.), Cook Islands (N.Z.), French Polynesia, Niue (N.Z.), Pitcairn (U.K.), Samoa, Tokelau (N.Z.), Tonga, Tuvalu, and Wallis and Futuna Islands (Fr.).

continuing work in the Solomon Islands (1851), and they are still the largest church in those islands, using the name "Church of Melanesia." They reach out to the Santa Cruz Islands, the Banks Islands, and the northern three islands of Vanuatu. The only important church begun by a nondenominational mission (1904) is the South Seas Evangelical Church. Its strength is chiefly on the island of Malaita, the most populous island in the Solomons.

3.6. Papua New Guinea received a succession of missions, starting with the LMS in 1873. Each mission — LMS, Methodist, Anglican, Lutheran, and Roman Catholic — settled in a distinct area along the coast, and as a result distinct area churches exist today. In the interior the highlands were not effectively reached till after World War II, when religious freedom reigned, and consequently a large number of churches share the region.

3.7. North of the equator, in the Marshall Islands and the eastern Carolines, the dominant church is the United Church of Christ, which arose from the work (from 1852) of the American and Hawaiian Congregationalists. In the western Carolines the chief Protestant body is related to the Liebenzell Mission (1907; → German Missions).

3.8. There has been some influx of sectarian groups. The Mormons began their mission work in 1844 by coming to the Pacific, and they have shown much recent growth particularly in Tonga, Samoa, American Samoa, and Niue, where in 2000 they were the second or third largest Christian group in each place. The Seventh-day Adventists have spread

to all the countries, but always as a small minority. Baha'is, Assemblies of God, and some other Pentecostal bodies are found in several lands.

4. Church Independence
Missionary control lingered longer in the Pacific than in other parts of the world, but by 1977 all of the major Protestant churches had become completely independent, managing their own affairs and requesting foreign help only on their own terms. The Protestant ministry has long been almost totally indigenous, and the churches have been in large part self-supporting. Each country has had its own theological college, and since 1966 there has been a cooperative college — the Pacific Theological College — operating on a higher level, located in Suva, the capital of Fiji.

In 1966 the islands were removed from the jurisdiction of the missionary arm of the Vatican and became normal → dioceses. Since then, most bishops have been Islanders rather than foreigners, and the number of indigenous priests has grown considerably. As has been noted, however, there is still a heavy reliance on foreign priests and on foreign funds. All the Roman Catholic dioceses in the countries covered here are brought together in the Episcopal Conference of the Pacific (CEPAC), based in Suva.

5. Ecumenical Relations
Comity agreements established by the early missions ensured harmonious, if distant, relations between most Protestant churches. Between the Roman Cath-

Oceania in A.D. 2000: Church Affiliation (as percentage of population)

	Total Christians	Roman Catholics	Indigenous	Protestants	Orthodox	Unaffiliated	Anglicans	Marginal
World total	*33.1*	17.6	6.2	5.8	3.7	1.5	1.0	0.5
Oceania	*83.0*	26.2	7.7	23.3	2.7	14.2	17.5	1.8
Australia–New Zealand[a]	*80.5*	24.5	8.3	16.7	3.6	17.4	21.4	1.8
Australia	*79.7*	26.6	8.9	14.7	4.3	18.2	21.5	1.4
New Zealand	*84.7*	14.1	5.2	26.8	0.2	13.7	21.3	3.5
Melanesia[b]	*89.9*	29.2	6.5	42.1	—	7.7	7.0	0.8
Fiji	*57.1*	10.7	9.1	46.5	—	0.5	0.9	2.0
Papua New Guinea	*95.1*	31.1	5.9	43.6	—	10.2	5.6	0.5
Solomon Islands	*95.8*	13.5	5.6	38.5	—	1.9	35.1	1.1
Micronesia[c]	*93.3*	60.8	4.2	34.4	—	1.6	0.3	3.0
Polynesia[d]	*92.8*	29.3	4.0	57.0	—	4.7	0.2	11.4

Note: A dash represents a value of less than 0.05 percent. Because of rounding, horizontal totals of the individual Christian groups may not equal the total percentage of Christians. Also, Christians in some countries are counted in more than one category, in which case the total of the individual groups may exceed the overall percentage of Christians.

[a]Figures include Christmas Island, Cocos (Keeling) Islands, Norfolk Island (all Austral.). [b]Figures include Bougainville (P.N.G.), New Caledonia (Fr.), Vanuatu. [c]Figures include Guam (U.S.), Kiribati, Marshall Islands, Micronesia (Federated States of), Nauru, Northern Mariana Islands (U.S.), Palau. [d]Figures include American Samoa (U.S.), Cook Islands (N.Z.), French Polynesia, Niue (N.Z.), Pitcairn (U.K.), Samoa, Tokelau (N.Z.), Tonga, Tuvalu, and Wallis and Futuna Islands (Fr.).

olics and Protestants, however, relationships were competitive and acrimonious, producing tensions that the ecumenical movement of the past generation has removed. Protestants have been brought into close relationship with each other and into friendly cooperation with Roman Catholics. → National councils of churches, called by various names, have been set up in most of the countries. The principal organ of ecumenical activity is the → Pacific Conference of Churches (PCC), which was inaugurated in 1966. In 1976 it was joined by CEPAC, representing the Roman Catholic Church; the Pacific, thus, has been a pioneer in Protestant–Roman Catholic cooperation.

The greatest contribution of the PCC has been in awakening the churches to their social responsibilities on a regional level. It has made the churches aware of the harmful effects of colonialism, → tourism, nuclear-bomb testing, and multinational corporations (see 1). It has conducted studies of these problems and has spoken out on behalf of the churches.

The PCC has also been a link to the rest of the world. Pacific church leaders are now involved in global ecumenical activity, no longer remaining isolated as they were for so long. The ecumenical movement has become a force for modernization.

6. Relation to Other Religions

Only in Fiji are there significant numbers of people of other faiths. Indian immigration, which began in the late 19th century as a way of securing indentured labor for the sugar plantations, has resulted now in close to 40 percent of the population of Fiji being either Hindu (→ Hinduism) or Muslim (→ Islam). For a long time the relation between Christians and these others was cool, for the Fijians resented the introduction of Indians by the British and feared for the loss of their land. In recent years there has been some violent conflict, but also some rapprochement. In 1960 the Methodist schools became interracial, and the Methodist Church united its small Indian division with its large Fijian organization. Some interfaith conversations have also taken place.

→ Cargo Cults; Ecumenism, Ecumenical Movement

Bibliography: General situation: D. DENOON, with S. FIRTH, eds., *The Cambridge History of the Pacific Islanders* (Cambridge, 1997) • D. DENOON and P. MEIN-SMITH, *A History of Australia, New Zealand, and the Pacific* (Oxford, 2000) • J. M. FITZPATRICK, ed., *Endangered Peoples of Oceania: Struggles to Survive and Thrive* (Westport, Conn., 2001) • K. R. HOWE, *Nature, Culture, and History: The "Knowing" of Oceania* (Honolulu, 2000) • B. V. LAL and K. FORTUNE, eds., *The Pacific Islands: An Encyclopedia* (Honolulu, 2000) • J. M. MAGEO, ed., *Cultural Memory: Reconfiguring History and Identity in the Postcolonial Pacific* (Honolulu, 2001) • D. NOHLEN and F. NUSCHELER, eds., *Handbuch der Dritten Welt* (vol. 8; 3d ed.; Bonn, 1994) • P. J. STEWART and A. Strathern, eds., *Identity Work: Constructing Pacific Lives* (Pittsburgh, 2000) • R. Torrence and A. Clarke, eds., *The Archaeology of Difference: Negotiating Cross-Cultural Engagements in Oceania* (London, 2000) • J. Wassmann, ed., *Pacific Answers to Western Hegemony: Cultural Practices of Identity Construction* (Oxford, 1998) • G. M. White and L. Lindstrom, eds., *Chiefs Today: Traditional Pacific Leadership and the Postcolonial State* (Stanford, Calif., 1997).

Religious situation: J. Barker, ed., *Christianity in Oceania: Ethnographic Perspectives* (Lanham, Md., 1990) • D. B. Barrett et al., eds., *WCE* (2d ed.) • I. Breward, *A History of the Churches in Australasia* (Oxford, 2001) • C. W. Forman, *The Island Churches of the South Pacific: Emergence in the Twentieth Century* (Maryknoll, N.Y., 1982) • J. Garrett, *Footsteps in the Sea: Christianity in Oceania to World War II* (Geneva, 1992); idem, *To Live among the Stars: Christian Origins in Oceania* (Geneva, 1982); idem, *Where Nets Were Cast: Christianity in Oceania since World War II* (Geneva, 1997) • T. Hiney, *On the Missionary Trail: A Journey through Polynesia, Asia, and Africa with the London Missionary Society* (New York, 2000) • T. Otto and A. Borsboom, eds., *Cultural Dynamics of Religious Change in Oceania* (Leiden, 1997) • T. Swain and G. Trompf, *The Religions of Oceania* (London, 1995) • A. Tippett, *Solomon Islands Christianity: A Study in Growth and Obstruction* (London, 1967) • H. Whitehouse, *Arguments and Icons: Divergent Modes of Religiosity* (Oxford, 2000) religion in Melanesia.

CHARLES W. FORMAN

Office of Christ

From the days of the → early church, with a view to interpreting the title "Christ," it was the tradition, unformulated doctrinally, to speak of Christ's priestly office *(munus sacerdotale)* and his kingly office *(munus regium).* The question was left open whether we should speak instead of a *triplex munus* by adding the prophetic office *(munus propheticum).* J. → Calvin took this view in *Inst.* 2.15, though not in all his writings. So did the → Catechismus Romanus 1.3.7, Lutheran → orthodoxy, and, even more so, Reformed orthodoxy. What was in view was a threefold office rather than three distinct offices. There was no arbitrary exegeting of biblical passages but, rather, the insight that the three anointings of the OT (of kings, priests, and prophets) came together to fulfillment in the Messiah. Yet the doctrine tended to result in a systematizing that offered no adequate protection against a separation of Christ's person and work. In *CD* IV/1-

3, however, K. → Barth (1886-1968) offers a reconstruction that places the doctrine within a more comprehensive framework.

→ Christological Titles; Christology

Bibliography: H. Ott, *Die Antwort des Glaubens* (3d ed.; Berlin, 1981) 303-12 • W. Pannenberg, *Jesus, God and Man* (2d ed.; Philadelphia, 1977) 208-25 • O. Weber, *Foundations of Dogmatics* (2 vols.; Grand Rapids, 1981-83) 2.169-77 • D. T. Williams, *The Office of Christ and Its Expression in the Church: Prophet, Priest, King* (Lewiston, N.Y., 1997).

DIETRICH RITSCHL

Offices

The word "offices," derived from Lat. *officium* (office, duty), is used in two main senses in the → Roman Catholic Church.

1. "Office" denotes an ecclesiastical office (→ Ministry, Ministerial Offices). The reference is to a divinely or ecclesiastically ordained ministry and the acceptance of a spiritual mission (see 1983 → CIC 145.1). In the broad sense the whole of the Christian way of faith constitutes the ministry, all believers being called "to exercise the mission which God entrusted to the Church" (can. 204.1) and pledged to participation in it (cans. 208-23).

In the Roman → curia, the supreme authority in matters of faith and morals is the Congregation for the Doctrine of the Faith, known from 1908 to 1965 as the Congregation of the Holy Office.

2. Liturgically, "offices" is a common term for (1) daily Bible readings or → devotions (→ Liturgical Books); (2) the canonical → hours that the clergy must observe; (3) services in honor of → Mary, consisting of Psalms and other materials and used in particular by female) orders and devotional societies (→ Religious Orders and Congregations); and (4) the → requiem at the burial of the dead (→ Funeral) or in remembrance either of a dead person or of all the deceased, especially on All Souls' Day.

Bibliography: S. E. Donlon and A. A. Reed, "Office, Ecclesiastical," *NCE* 10.652-54.

HEINER GROTE†

Offices, Ecclesiastical → Ministry, Ministerial Offices

Official Principal

In the → Anglican Communion the official principal is the person entrusted by a bishop with the exercise of judicial authority. The same function is discharged by the chancellor or commissary general of the Consistory Court. The → Orthodox Church has no comparable office, since the bishop himself exercises jurisdiction. Nor is there any place for an office of this kind in the jurisdiction of Protestant churches.

In the → Roman Catholic Church the *officialis,* or judicial vicar *(vicarius iudicialis),* represents the diocesan bishop in ecclesiastical jurisdiction. The 1983 → CIC 1419-27 emphasizes that jurisdiction is an episcopal function. The judicial vicar shares in it as the → vicar-general does in the direction of the → diocese and the bishop's vicar in the work of the diocese, but since the bishop makes judgments through the judicial vicar, there can be no appeal from him to the bishop. The judicial vicar must be a → priest and trained in canon law. The bishop must appoint him for a specific period and can discharge him only for serious cause. He is not to be also the vicar general. He appoints adjudicators for specific cases and presides either in person or through an assistant except when the bishop handles the case himself. A single judicial vicar may be appointed for several smaller dioceses.

Bibliography: E. G. Moore, *Introduction to English Canon Law* (3d ed.; Oxford, 1992) • J. S. Quinn, "Officialis (Judicial Vicar)," *NCE* 10.657-58 • N. Timms and K. Wilson, eds., *Governance and Authority in the Roman Catholic Church: Beginning a Conversation* (London, 2000).

Albert Stein†

Oikoumene

The term "oikoumene," from the present passive participle of the Gk. verb *oikeō,* "inhabit," and used from the time of Herodotus (d. between 430 and 420 B.C.), means "the inhabited earth." In the 20th century the Swedish archbishop N. Söderblom (1866-1931) was the first to use the term to describe the work of reconciling and uniting the separated churches (→ Reconciliation). The term caught on and resulted in its present use in the ecumenical movement (→ Ecumenism, Ecumenical Movement).

In a basic study of the history and meaning of the term "ecumenical" (1953), W. A. → Visser 't Hooft (1900-1985) pointed out that historically there have been seven uses: for the whole (inhabited) earth, for the (→ Roman) empire, for what belongs to or represents the whole → church, for what has universal validity in the church, for what pertains to global → mission, for what concerns the relation between churches or Christians of different → denominations, and for the intellectual approach toward membership of the church's worldwide fellowship that manifests a readiness to work for the → unity of Christ's church.

The LXX uses *oikoumenē* fairly often in the sense of "world" (esp. in the Psalms), with NT usage referring to the church's sphere of work (e.g., Luke 2:1; Matt. 24:14). In Heb. 2:5 the word refers to the unity of humankind with God in the *eschaton* (→ Eschatology).

In the → early church the ecclesiastical and political meanings merged in the equation of the oikoumene with the Christian empire under Constantine (312-37) and his successors (→ Historiography 3.2; Church and State). Synods and → councils played a key role in this respect as an expression of the desire for unity. The ecumenical became that which is universally accepted (→ Ecumenical Symbols).

The → Reformation had the same point in view when it called the early creeds catholic and ecumenical (Book of Concord [1580]; → Formula of Concord). In this regard "oikoumene" denotes the unity of the church as earthly Christianity illumined and assembled by the → Holy Spirit. The idea that the church is ecumenical because it takes the → gospel to the world and is thus worldwide was developed further in the → revival movements (note esp. Count → Zinzendorf and the → Moravians). The adjective "ecumenical" ties together the concept of mission and the global outlook, as at the founding conference of the Evangelical Alliance in 1846 (→ Worldwide Evangelical Alliance).

Early in the 20th century the ecumenical movement first used the phrase "universally Christian," but "ecumenical" gradually replaced it. The oikoumene denotes the development and self-understanding of this movement as it finds expression, for example, in the → World Council of Churches (WCC). At issue here is the oikoumene as the divinely given unity of the church and also as the church's ministry to the world, its worldwide sending (ideas developed in the Oxford Life and Work Conference in 1937). The term "secular ecumenism" (→ Secularization) signifies the church's total involvement in the secular world for reconciliation and humanization, and to ecumenical concern for the unity of all people. The understanding, tasks, and problems that the word "oikoumene" indicates receive special emphasis in interchurch contacts at the local level (→ Local Ecumenism).

→ Ecumenical Dialogue; Ecumenical Learning; Ecumenical Mission; Ecumenical Theology

Bibliography: K. Raiser, "Oikoumene," *DEM* (rev. ed.) • H. J. Urban, ed., *HÖ* • W. A. Visser 't Hooft, *The Meaning of Ecumenical* (London, 1953); idem, "The Word 'Ecumenical'–Its History and Use," *A History of the Ecumenical Movement* (4th ed.; ed. R. Rouse and S. C. Neill; Geneva, 1993) 735-40.

André Birmelé

Old Age

1. Perspectives
2. Aging as a Lifelong Process
3. Questions for the Future
4. An Opportunity for the Church

1. Perspectives

1.1. In the OT the position of the elderly was one of honor (Lev. 19:32). Understanding is to be found only in the aged (Job 12:12 RSV), and righteousness and judgment are best preserved in the older generation (see Dan. 7:22). Old age and → experience are synonymous (Sir. 25:6).

The NT develops the same ideas. At 12 years of age → Jesus was said to be increasing "in wisdom and in years, and in divine and human favor" (Luke 2:52). Eph. 4:13 sets as the goal of all → perfection "maturity, to the measure of the full stature of Christ." The NT sees → life and → death in the light of the relationship with God. There is life with God both now and hereafter, regardless of the biological course of one's life (Ps. 23:6).

Threats from → war, → hunger, epidemics, and lack of biochemical medications limited life expectancy in ancient Egypt and Greece to around 27 years. The life span of monks (→ Monasticism) in the → Middle Ages averaged closer to 35 years by adherence to a regular diet, freedom from military service, and psychological stability. Old age was seen as a divine gift and thus called for great respect. The preindustrial period was marked by high regard for the → experience of the elderly, which could be passed on in a world that went through little change.

1.2. Current concern over old age, becoming older, or aging as a negative experience seems to be firmly rooted in Western culture. We see this concern especially in the United States, where an undue emphasis on → individualism and competition (→ Achievement and Competition) has warped a capi-

talist economy into a powerful force of economic development, though with certain negative consequences. We see it also in the widespread emphasis on → sports as a paradigm for living. Competitive sports form the model for a good life. To win at any cost has become the goal for living. The individual person is valued only in terms of physical attributes of strength and beauty, and aging is feared as a loss of ability, strength, and value. In this milieu, as a person begins to decline physically, the individual's sense of self-worth and value depreciates quickly. Aging staff members of a company, treated like aging products, once useful, are now to be discarded as of little or no value.

In contrast, most other world cultures continue to respect the accomplishments of older persons, according elders with honor and seeking them out for advice and counsel. The older person is regarded as one who has a unique contribution to make to the lives of the younger members of society. Elders have lived, survived, learned how to adapt, and are now a source of security and wisdom for younger individuals of the same society. Nevertheless, as the global nature of human society intensifies, prejudice against elders is beginning to appear in these other cultures. Younger persons, observing the nature, values, and results of Western culture, eagerly accept change, often to the detriment of elders and families alike. This situation presents Christianity with an incredible opportunity to demonstrate the importance of individuals throughout their entire life span as beloved persons enjoying God's gifts as they live and serve their Creator.

Bibliography: H. Feiereis and H.-J. Thilo, *Basiswissen Psychotherapie* (Göttingen, 1999; orig. pub., 1980).

Hans-Joachim Thilo and John A. Jorgenson

2. Aging as a Lifelong Process

Significant scholarly research concerning various factors of aging has been pursued in Europe and North America. As a result of these studies elders are no longer being written off as being senile or disengaging with life. The aging process is much more complex than early concepts suggest.

Some studies have examined biological factors included in the process of aging. Other studies have explored sociological factors affecting the older person. That which was once defined as disengagement is now seen as part of a complex reorientation at this stage of life. Psychological factors that impact the older person as an individual and in respect to relationships have been defined and assessed. A variety of specific dementias have replaced the more generic concept of senility. Cultural differences have been analyzed in several recent studies.

Theological factors in aging are just now beginning to be explored, and the significant impact of → spirituality on life satisfaction has been addressed by several disciplines. For example, medical researchers have recently defined the significant effect spirituality has on both the status of health and the recovery rate from disease or major surgery, especially among elders. Similarly, sociological gerontologists have identified spirituality as an important coping mechanism for elders confronting loss of one kind or another.

These investigations have resulted in a much more comprehensive awareness of what the aging process includes. Some researchers have even suggested that more aging occurs prior to birth than after if one defines aging as a comprehensive developmental process that begins with conception and continues until → death.

Research has also demonstrated the importance and the variety of interactions that occur between the stages or phases of the aging process. What persons do as children predetermines a significant part of later life in a variety of areas, including spirituality. Furthermore, the importance of relationships as coping mechanisms throughout the span of life has also been demonstrated. Elders who have persons who care about them tend to survive serious medical procedures at a rate of 2 to 1 over elders who are alone; also they recover more quickly than those who are alone.

Serious reflection concerning spirituality has identified its positive role in quality of life and survival among older persons. In 1995 the Fetzer Institute joined the National Institute on Aging in a study of elders *(Multidimensional Measurement)* and defined several factors in spiritual development, a study that has encouraged further research. Harold Koenig in 1994 identified 14 spiritual factors that determine quality of life and recovery among elders facing serious medical challenges or end-of-life issues. In 1995 Melvin Kimble and colleagues produced a most useful resource both for studying the impact of spirituality among elders and for responding to this growing opportunity to Christian → ministry.

Overall, this more profound attitude toward aging has several components that have developed over the past century. For example, changes in nutrition have affected physical health. Balanced diet and a wide variety of foods have significantly improved the quality of health in all people, especially those who are older. Similarly, the development of new and effective vaccines to counteract childhood diseases has increased the number of individuals surviving into adulthood. These developments have resulted in a lengthening of the average life span: in 1900 the average life span in the United States was 47.3 years; in 2000 that average had increased by over 60 percent to 77.4 years. Worldwide during the same century, the average more than doubled, rising from approximately 30 years to 66.9 years.

The quality of life for individuals has also increased. Most Americans enjoy relatively good health until they die, ultimately succumbing to one or another age-related condition. In addition, current research suggests that a genetic-based means of extending an individual's life span may be possible in the near future.

3. Questions for the Future

The future presents a dilemma. The issues related to a growing percentage of older persons in the population are rapidly becoming a worldwide concern. World Health Organization research suggests that many of the issues currently being addressed by Western cultures that have the economic resources to meet these challenges will confront most of the developing world within the next 30 years as the percentage of elders in the population worldwide increases.

The challenge faced by these developing countries will include caring for a growing population of elders without having access to adequate funding for basic human needs such as minimum health care, subsidized housing, adequate nutrition, and other elder requirements. Another major issue is responsibility for such elder care. Some cultures give the responsibility to the oldest son; other cultures prefer to have a daughter or the youngest sibling provide the care, with this person ultimately inheriting the family resources. What role government plays in the future as younger persons adopt Western patterns of life and as cultures change has not been resolved.

→ Health concerns play a growing part of an older person's life. Having sufficient resources for basic living, concerns about debilitating illnesses, mental health issues, maintaining independence, and not being a burden to one's family, friends, or an institutional staff all create frustrating concerns that can be demeaning for many elders. Who determines what is to be done when life is challenged: the elder, the family, the doctor, the government, technology, or available funding? Are increasingly available heroic measures to extend life for elders good stewardship of limited health resources?

The role that a growing number of elders — with their experience, resources, and abilities — might play in a community has not been addressed widely. Recognition of the contribution elders do make in raising grandchildren, providing care for other elders, and providing volunteer support for community service activities has been neglected, if not ignored. Some innovative programs aimed at involving older persons in community life have been suggested, and some initial experiments are being conducted in certain places by interested organizations.

End-of-life issues are beginning to be addressed seriously in the American culture. → Euthanasia and physician-assisted → suicide are topics of growing concern as the medical profession, the judicial branch of government, and various humanitarian and faith-related organizations debate moral concerns related to the end of life. For example: at what point is a person defined as being dead? Medical definitions may not agree with moral or legal reasoning.

Additionally, the relationship needs of single adults are often not well addressed. This factor is increasingly a serious concern as these individuals grow older often with no significant source of caring and concerned persons to assist them with the changes of life brought about by aging. Moreover, debate concerning the morality of sexual preferences further aggravates these relationship needs, as prejudices impact gay and lesbian elders when they seek the community's care and support (→ Homosexuality).

A new issue that holds a significant amount of concern for elders is that of stem-cell research. The potential benefits of such research for elders has barely been suggested, especially with relation to addressing such diseases as Parkinson's, Alzheimer's, diabetes, mental disorders, arthritis, and other physical conditions related to an older body. Questions of how to fund such research while maintaining adequate moral and legal safeguards to avoid abuse, but also while adequately investigating the possibilities of long-lasting benefits, are complex and difficult.

4. An Opportunity for the Church

In the midst of these issues related to aging, the potential benefit of a new paradigm for Christian congregational ministry may be worthy of consideration. Such a paradigm would empower laity to initiate and maintain a ministry with elders. In this approach the role of → clergy would become more that of a coach or mentor than a leader. Issues to be addressed include the following:

How might a parish address the concerns of lifetime spiritual development in an effective manner? (Answering this question would optimally unite two populations in our society who have not been heard — youth and our elders.)

What are the dimensions of stewardship that might be explored in such a new model for parish life?

What might be the measures of growth appropriate to each of the stages in one's lifetime? How might → congregations or parishes respond to the needs expressed?

What is the role of → faith in motivating persons, especially elders, in this new paradigm?

Aging can be seen as a pragmatic, God-given gift to us with which to address the future. In this light, aging becomes an exciting potential, hardly worthy of the negative prejudices often encountered.

Bibliography: V. L. Bengston and K. W. Schaie, eds., *Handbook on Theories of Aging* (New York, 1999) • E. C. Bianchi, *Aging as a Spiritual Journey* (New York, 1999) • R. H. Binstock and L. K. George, *Handbook of Aging and the Social Sciences* (5th ed.; Orlando, Fla., 2001) • J. E. Birren and K. W. Schaie, eds., *Handbook of the Psychology of Aging* (5th ed.; Orlando, Fla., 2002) • D. Callahan, *Setting Limits: Medical Goals in an Aging Society* (New York, 1987) • M. A. Kimble, S. H. McFadden, J. W. Ellor, and J. J. Seeber, eds., *Aging, Spirituality, and Religion: A Handbook* (Minneapolis, 1995) • H. A. Kiyak and N. R. Hooyman, "Aging in the Twenty-first Century," *Hallym International Journal of Aging* 1 (1999) 56-66 • L. D. Knutson, *Understanding the Senior Adult: A Tool for Wholistic Ministry* (Bethesda, Md., 1999) • H. Koenig, *Aging and God* (Binghamton, N.Y., 1994) • J. E. Lukens, ed., *Affirmative Aging* (Harrisburg, Pa., 1994) • E. J. Mansoro and S. N. Austad, eds., *Handbook on the Biology of Aging* (5th ed.; Orlando, Fla., 2001) • L. E. Missinne, *Reflections on Aging: A Spiritual Guide* (Liguori, Mo., 1990) • *Multidimensional Measurement of Religiousness/Spirituality for Use in Health Research: A Report of the Fetzer Institute, National Institute on Aging Working Group* (Kalamazoo, Mich., 1999) • B. Payne and E. Brewer, eds., *Gerontology in Theological Education: Local Program Development* (New York, 1998) • Z. Schachter-Shalomi and R. Miller, *From Age-ing to Sage-ing* (Northvale, N.J., 1994) • C. W. Tilberg, ed., *The Fullness of Life: Aging and the Older Adult* (New York, 1980) • A. S. Wimberley, ed., *Honoring African Elders: A Ministry in the Soul Community* (San Francisco, 1997).

John A. Jorgenson

Old Believers

"Old Believers" (Russ. *Raskolniki,* "Schismatics") is the name given to those Christians in the → Russian Orthodox Church who in the mid-17th century opposed the liturgical reforms of the Moscow patriarch Nikon (1605-81). They themselves took the name "Old Ritualists" or "Old Orthodox," claiming to be the only ones to continue true Orthodoxy (→ Orthodox Christianity; Orthodox Church). Those reforms were avowedly to restore ancient uses but were in point of fact an importation of contemporary Greek practices instead of the ancient Russian tradition established at the landmark Council of the Hundred Chapters (1551). The Old Believers, who believed that the Greek church had compromised itself at the Council of Florence (1431-ca. 1445; → Councils, Ecumenical) by seeking reunion with the → Roman Catholic Church, saw Nikon's reforms as a betrayal of genuine Orthodoxy and, by implication, heretical.

The Old Believers kept alive a pre-Nikonian version of the liturgical texts, an austere liturgical chant, and a distinctive manner of → icon painting, pectoral crosses, even at times of dress. A main point of contention was the way of holding the fingers in making the → sign of the cross. The Greeks at the time were using three fingers rather than two, denoting the → Trinity instead of the two natures of Christ (→ Christology). The Russians had at first stayed with two fingers but later developed a five-finger sign combining the two → dogmas.

When it was ruled that the Greek custom should replace the Russian, the suspicion spread that the three-finger cross related to the beast of Revelation 12 and 19:17-21, that the three fingers stood for dragon, beast, and false prophet. In view of the brutality with which these reforms were enforced, Archpriest Avvakum (1620/21-82), a leader of the Old Believers, felt that the suspicion was justified. When imprisoned, the Old Believers could not be forced even by torture to use the three-fingered cross, which led to threats of death. Fearing that they might give way under torture, some Raskolniki burned down their wooden churches with themselves inside. Peter the Great (1672-1725) offered them limited toleration but at the price of double taxation. An 1883 law granted them the right of private religious practice, but only with the edict of toleration issued in 1905 by Czar Nicholas II (1868-1918) did they secure full → religious liberty (→ Tolerance).

Different solutions to new issues produced differences among the Old Believers. Many contested matters, however, were cleared up and divisions over-come. An unbridgeable gulf, however, has separated the Popovtsy (priestly sects) and the Bezpopovtsy (priestless sects), the former seeking means of having their own → priests, the latter denying that the priesthood is possible any longer. In 1846 a → hierarchy was established for the largest group of Popovtsy in Bukovina by the deposed metropolitan Ambrose of Bosnia, and in 1923 for another group by Archbishop Nicholas of Saratov. Subsequently, archbishoprics have been established in Moscow (Old Ritualist, the metropolitan see) and Novozybkov (Old Orthodox). The concern of the approximately three million Old Believers — in Russia, Estonia, Latvia, Lithuania, Belarus, Ukraine, Romania, and other countries — is to keep the old Russian worship and lifestyle in their totality and to maintain separation from the world (→ Separatism).

Bibliography: P. AVVAKUM, *Archpriest Avvakum, the Life Written by Himself* (trans. K. N. Bostrom; Ann Arbor, Mich., 1979) • F. C. CONYBEARE, *Russian Dissenters* (Cambridge, Mass., 1921) • C. LANE, *Christian Religion in the Soviet Union* (London, 1979) • N. LUPININ, *Religious Revolt in the Seventeenth Century: The Schism of the Russian Church* (Princeton, 1984) • P. MEYENDORFF, *Russia, Ritual, and Reform: The Liturgical Reforms of Nikon in the Seventeenth Century* (Crestwood, N.Y., 1991) • T. ROBBINS, "Apocalypse, Persecution, and Self-Immolation: Mass Suicides among the Old Believers in Late-Seventeenth-Century Russia," *Millennialism, Persecution, and Violence: Historical Cases* (ed. C. Wessinger; Syracuse, N.Y., 2000) 205-19 • R. R. ROBSON, *Old Believers in Modern Russia* (De Kalb, Ill., 1995) • T. WARE, *The Orthodox Church* (new ed.; New York, 1993).

PETER HAUPTMANN

Old Catholic Churches

1. Self-understanding
2. Ecumenical Experience
3. History
4. Doctrine
5. Practice
6. Statistics

1. Self-understanding

The Old Catholic Churches are a group of autonomous, episcopal, and synodal churches that confess the pluriformity and the essential doctrines and institutions of the church through its first millennium. They arose in various reforming movements and in resistance to the growing centralized power of the papacy in the → Roman Catholic Church (→

Pope, Papacy). As distinct from the modern Roman Catholic self-understanding, they stress the following axioms:

1. The test of catholicity is "what has been believed everywhere, always, and by all" (Vincent of Lérins).
2. "In essentials, unity; in nonessentials, liberty; in all things, charity" (Augustinian medieval tradition).
3. "What concerns all should be discussed and decided by all" (medieval law).

The churches view catholicity qualitatively (in orientation to what is whole and original). As they see it, local churches have considerable freedom to relate to each age and culture. The church is for them a spiritual fellowship resting on individual conviction. All → authority in it is responsible to the people of God and under the control of the corresponding bodies.

2. Ecumenical Experience

2.1. Like the → Anglican churches, with which they are in full communion, the Old Catholic Churches take a path in → ecumenical dialogue that is midway between Roman Catholicism and the churches of the Reformation, and also between East and West. They view the unity of the church as an act of the whole people of God that cannot be achieved primarily by arrangements between leaders but only by the Spirit-filled involvement of all Christians. The goal is a conciliar fellowship that will first come about between Christians locally (→ Local Ecumenicity) and then lead to closer relations between local churches. Ecumenical theology should press back to the doctrine of the universal church before disruption, in light of which the various points of controversy should be studied.

2.2. Ignaz von Döllinger (1799-1890), president of the Old Catholic Union Commission, organized two union conferences in Bonn in 1874-75, attended by Anglican, Orthodox, and Protestant theologians, which have been considered the most important religious conversations of the 19th century. From 1893 further steps were taken toward uniting denominations. Old Catholics also worked in the → Faith and Order movement from the very first (→ Ecumenism, Ecumenical Movement). Six of their churches are members of the → World Council of Churches: the Catholic Diocese of the Old Catholics in Germany, Old Catholic Church of Austria, Old Catholic Church of Switzerland, Old Catholic Church of the Netherlands (or, Church of Utrecht), Old Catholic Mariavite Church in Poland, and Polish National Catholic Church (U.S.A.).

The conference of Old Catholic theologians in 1983 endorsed the congruence declarations of Lima (1982) and expressed a wish for conversations about unity with all the churches that stand on this basis.

2.3. The Old Catholic Churches also support bilateral conversations as long as they serve the cause of unity and do not set up new obstacles. As Döllinger said in 1872, to heal one rift, we must not deepen another. A model is the full communion with the Anglicans that some churches approved in the 19th century and that found official recognition in the Bonn Agreement of 1931. In the text of the agreement the Old Catholic Churches and the Anglicans recognize each other's catholicity and express the conviction that each holds all the essentials of the Christian faith (→ Eucharist 5). Full communion was reached also with the Philippine Independent Catholic Church in 1965.

The efforts to achieve unity with the → Orthodox Church, which have been going on for 100 years, reached the point of a mixed commission in 1974, though the texts of the commission still need revision at some points.

After → Vatican II there were discussions with the Roman Catholic Church with a view to a pastoral agreement about limited intercommunion and recognition of each other's marriages. But Rome did not approve the text put out by the bishops' conferences in 1974.

In Germany discussions started with the Evangelische Michaelsbrüderschaft in 1968 and with the Evangelical Lutheran Church in Bavaria in 1981. At the local and national levels the Old Catholic Churches have taken part in many ecumenical initiatives (ecumenical texts of the Bible and hymns, Bread for the World [→ Relief and Development Organizations], working fellowships, student councils, common services). They practice eucharistic hospitality toward all Christians who share with them a belief in the reality of the Eucharist.

3. History

The oldest of the Old Catholic Churches is the Archbishopric of Utrecht (founded by St. Willibrord [d. 739]). After the Reformation it was in a precarious position, for it was essentially a secret church whose bishops had to have foreign titles. After it protected the so-called → Jansenists, and when after 1702 Rome would not appoint an archbishop, the Chapter of Utrecht chose C. Steenoven, who in 1723 was consecrated by the missionary bishop D. M. Varlet, with the consent of five other Roman Catholic bishops. Between 1870 and 1925 this church moved from its → Gallican, late

Jansenist ecclesiology to a stronger Old Catholic position.

In Germany and Switzerland after 1850 the schools of J. M. Sailer (1751-1832), A. Günther (1783-1863), and Döllinger came under attack from the Vatican → Syllabus (1864), from indexes, from the ban on theological conferences, and from the introduction of the so-called church *venia legendi* (right to teach). Resistance to the Vatican I dogmas of papal infallibility and supreme jurisdiction led by way of congresses at Munich, Cologne, Constance, and Olten (1871-76) to the founding of independent local churches that received episcopal succession through Utrecht. Döllinger made a vital contribution to the Old Catholic movement with his conciliar writings and ecumenical initiatives, always confessing himself to be an Old Catholic. In Bavaria, on the basis of Gallican principles, he worked within a mediating position that did not recognize Vatican I, which lasted until his death in 1890. During the → Kulturkampf the Old Catholics achieved a secure legal position in Prussia, Baden, Hesse, and several Swiss cantons.

In the United States A. Kozlowski and F. Hodur formed a Polish Catholic Church in 1897, in which immigrants fought for their national religious independence. A daughter church was then founded in Poland in 1922, and a bishopric in Canada in 1967. The liturgy was put into English as well as Polish in 1958. There are also smaller Old Catholic Churches in the Czech Republic and Yugoslavia, and some parishes in France, Italy, and Sweden.

4. Doctrine

The Old Catholic Churches formed the Utrecht Union in 1889, with the Declaration of Utrecht as its basic document. It confesses the faith of the undivided church of the first millennium, with its creeds and seven ecumenical councils. It repudiates the dogmas of papal → infallibility (1870) and the immaculate conception of Mary (1854; → Mariology). It also repudiates the Syllabus and the bulls *Unigenitus* (1713) and *Auctorem Fidei* (1794), evoked by the late Jansenist movement. It accepts the decisions of the Council of → Trent, but only insofar as they agree with the teaching of the early church. In the doctrine of the Eucharist it holds fast to the real presence but regards the eucharistic sacrifice, not as a repetition of the offering of the cross (→ Sacrifice), but as a representation of the heavenly offering (Heb. 9:11-12, 24). Finally, it stresses theological work as the way to unity, and toleration in the spirit of J. M. Sailer.

The Old Catholic Churches reject the Roman Catholic doctrine of merit and indulgences (1874 Union Congress). As regards → grace and → justification, they take a middle position that now stresses above all the cooperation of grace and → freedom. They repudiate eternal → predestination to perdition. They grant → tradition an authoritative character, finding it partly in the consent of great ecclesiastical bodies and partly in the great writings of all centuries as we know them through theological scholarship. They accept theological development (→ Dogma) only in the sphere of the unconditionally necessary implications of Christ's teaching, with which that development stands or falls. What many have rejected as → heresy cannot become dogma (Döllinger). The Old Catholic Churches recognize seven sacraments, but → baptism and the Eucharist are the chief sacraments.

5. Practice

In practice there is stress on the small group as an accepting fellowship. Decisions regarding church law are made by collegial bodies (e.g., representative → synods, congregational meetings, church boards), on which → bishops and → priests have an important role. Since the 19th century the → liturgy has been in the national language and has found a place for the modern forms suggested by the → liturgical movement. Both priests and bishops may marry, which the churches find promotes → pastoral care and the spirituality of → marriage. The consecration of women as deaconesses has been approved since 1982.

6. Statistics

Worldwide, there are eight Old Catholic Churches, with a total of 866,000 adherents in 1995. There is full communion with the Philippine Independent Catholic Church, which was founded in 1902 and has two million members.

Not to be confused with the Old Catholics are the small groupings around what are called *episcopi vagantes* (men, rarely also women, who have irregular episcopal orders), who maintain a purely formal episcopal succession.

Bibliography: J. J. I. von Döllinger [Janus, pseud.], *The Pope and the Council* (Boston, 1870) • G. Huelin, ed., *Old Catholics and Anglicans, 1931-1981* (Oxford, 1983) • *Ignaz von Döllinger (1799-1890)* (= MTZ 50/4 [1999]) 312-83 • *IKZ* (Bern, 1911-) quarterly periodical • C. B. Moss, *The Old Catholic Movement: Its Origins and History* (2d ed.; London, 1964) • J. M. Neale, *A History of the So-Called Jansenist Church of Holland* (London, 1970; orig. pub., 1853) • P. Neuner, *Döllinger*

als Theologe der Ökumene (Paderborn, 1979) • K. PRU-
TER, *The Old Catholic Church: A History and Chronol-
ogy* (2d ed.; San Bernardino, 1996) • K. PRUTER and
J. G. MELTON, *The Old Catholic Sourcebook* (New York,
1983) • B. WIELEWINSKI, ed., *Polish National Catholic
Church: Independent Movements, Old Catholic Church,
and Related Items. An Annotated Bibliography* (Boulder,
Colo., 1990).

CHRISTIAN OEYEN

Old Roman Creed

"Old Roman Creed," or "Romanum," is the scholarly name for the earlier and shorter form of the →
Apostles' Creed as we have it in its original Greek
(with probably also a simultaneous Latin edition) in
Marcellus (d. ca. 374) and Rufinus (ca. 345-411) and
three MSS from the early Middle Ages. It was evidently the baptismal creed of the early Roman
church (→ Baptism). The baptismal questions that
have come down to us from Hippolytus (d. ca. 236)
at the beginning of the third century are an almost
exact prototype of this creed.

Dating of the Old Roman Creed is difficult. A
starting point is the fact that baptismal questions
are not attested before the end of the second century. The declaratory baptismal confession, however, is part of the → rite of *traditio* (delivery —
from teacher to catechumen) and *redditio* (returning or reciting — at baptism) of the confession (→
Confession of Faith), which came at the end of
catechetical instruction and which we find only at
the beginning of the third century (→ Catechism).
The interrogative form developed, then, at the turn
from the second century to the third, and the declaratory form probably only in the fourth century.

The baptismal questions themselves give evidence of a complex process of development, the
main features of which we can reconstruct from several formulas that preserve an earlier stage of tradition. In the many versions we note how more specific attributes, titles, and further statements were
added to the original three articles, while an express
confession of Christ that was originally independent made its way into the second article. It is debated whether its pronounced two-membered
structure intends to explicate the preceding titles of
majesty "the only begotten Son of God" and "our
Lord" (after Luke 1:35 and Phil. 2:1-11), but it seems
certain that the creed does not contain any express
→ Christology of preexistence.

On the basis of the corresponding statements of
the → rule of faith, we could say that we have here

the basic content of Christian faith in a compendium of community theology, cast in the form of a
fixed confession.

→ Christological Titles; Confessions and Creeds

Bibliography: J. N. D. KELLY, *Early Christian Creeds* (3d
ed.; New York, 1972) 100-166 • B. J. F. LONERGAN, *The
Way to Nicea: The Dialectical Development of Trinitarian Theology* (Philadelphia, 1979) • F. M. YOUNG, *The
Making of the Creeds* (London, 1991).

DIETMAR WYRWA

Oman

	1960	1980	2000
Population (1,000s):	558	1,130	2,717
Annual growth rate (%):	2.46	4.64	3.90
Area: 306,000 sq. km. (118,150 sq. mi.)			

A.D. 2000

Population density: 9/sq. km. (23/sq. mi.)
Births / deaths: 4.20 / 0.39 per 100 population
Fertility rate: 6.63 per woman
Infant mortality rate: 21 per 1,000 live births
Life expectancy: 72.0 years (m: 70.1, f: 74.5)
Religious affiliation (%): Muslims 88.4, Hindus 5.9,
Christians 3.7 (Roman Catholics 2.0, other Chris-
tians 1.8), other 2.0.

1. General Situation
2. Religious Situation

1. General Situation

The Sultanate of Oman, with Muscat (or Masqat)
as its capital city, lies in the southeast corner of the
Arabian Peninsula, strategically located at the entrance to the Persian Gulf. Over 80 percent of the
population lives in urban areas, the balance inhabiting largely desert areas. As early as the third century B.C., Oman (known before 1970 as Muscat
and Oman) was an important and prosperous
trading site, a harbor on routes to Vietnam and Indonesia. Since the settling of Arab tribes in Oman
in the second century A.D., the population has
been mostly Arab, with Persian, Baluchi, Indian,
and African → minorities. The Arabs today are
grouped mostly in sedentary tribes; there are
300,000 foreign workers.

In the middle of the 7th century, the country
was under the rule of the Umayyads (ruled 661-
750), whose capital was Damascus. The Umayyads
were for a short time leaders of the Arab Muslim
world but were overthrown by the Abbasids (ruled

750-1258), whose capital became Baghdad. In the 8th century the Omanis rebelled against the Umayyads, expelling them from their country, and thereafter were able to maintain relative independence from the Abbasid caliphate. In about 1507 the Portuguese captured Muscat, maintaining a presence on the coastline of Oman until they were expelled in 1650.

In the 18th century Oman itself again became a leading sea power, becoming a trading force in the Indian Ocean and extending its possessions both to South Asia and to Zanzibar in East Africa. In 1891 Oman became a British protectorate as the result of a series of treaties that increasingly gave control of the nation to Great Britain. The expansion of British power, the coming of steamships, the opening of the Suez Canal, and the loss of the slave trade all contributed to the decline of Oman toward the end of the 19th century. An internal struggle for power led to the division of Oman in 1920, but it was reunited in 1955 as a result of British pressure (→ Colonialism).

Under Sultan Said bin Taimur (1932-70), Oman became an extremely reactionary country. Quasi-medieval conditions kept its people isolated from outside influences. In July 1970 the sultan was deposed, and with British support, his son, Qaboos bin Said, became the new ruler. With help from British officers and Iranian troops, Qaboos resisted a revolt in the southern province of Dhofar by the Popular Front for the Liberation of Oman, a force that had the support of Marxist South Yemen. In order to make Oman more progressive, Qaboos adopted a comprehensive program to build up infrastructure and develop the economy. Aided by oil revenues, this program has had considerable success.

Oman's form of government is autocratic. A consultative council was summoned in 1983 for legislative purposes, even though it had no political power. In 1996 Qaboos issued a royal decree establishing an advisory bicameral legislature and guaranteeing basic civil liberties for Omani citizens (→ Rights, Human and Civil). Foreign policy has been marked by close ties with Western powers, especially the United States, which has a military base on the Omani island of Maṣīrah.

2. Religious Situation

Oman was one of the first countries to be converted to → Islam. Today Muslims compose nearly 90 percent of the population, with slightly more than half belonging to Ibadi Islam. The remainder follow various → Sunni (Wahhabi, Shafiʿite, or Hanbalite)

and Shiite beliefs. Unlike more extreme Islamic groups, the Ibadi have allowed non-Ibadi people to retain their allegiances. However, since the Ibadi version of Islam does not regard the imamate as hereditary but rather as an elective office, conflict has periodically broken out between the sultan and the imam and the latter's followers. Since the elected imam must also be an ʿālim, or Islamic scholar, Qaboos could not lay claim to that office.

Christianity is thought to have come to Oman with the Portuguese in 1507-8 and also to have departed with them. The → Roman Catholic Church reestablished itself in the area in 1841 with the assignment of personnel to Aden, Yemen. That work grew until in 1889 the Vicariate of Arabia was formed, now administered from Abu Dhabi in the United Arab Emirates and responsible for Roman Catholics in Oman.

The arrival in Oman in 1889-90 of James Cantine and Samuel Zwemer of the American Arab Mission led to sponsorship of Protestant work in 1894 by the Reformed Church in America. That church founded a hospital in Muscat, which was for many years an important Christian presence in Oman (→ Medical Missions). The present Protestant Church in Oman, still served by personnel from the Reformed Church in America, includes Christians of a number of denominations. The sultan has granted to the church parcels of lands in several Omani locales.

In recent years a number of Christian communities have emerged among the expatriate population in Oman. Besides the Roman Catholics, the strongest are → Anglican congregations, under the jurisdiction of the Episcopal Church in Jerusalem and the Middle East, and smaller groups of both Orthodox and Pentecostal Christians, largely from India. The Evangelical Alliance Mission is perhaps the strongest of the more conservative Christian groups.

Bibliography: C. H. ALLEN JR. and W. L. RIGSBEE II, *Oman under Qaboos: From Coup to Constitutions, 1970-1996* (London, 2000) • D. B. BARRETT et al., eds., *WCE* (2d ed.) 1.567-69 • T. BIERSCHENK, *Religion and Political Structure: Remarks on Ibadism in Oman and the Mzab (Algeria)* (Bielefeld, 1983) • R. EL-SOLH, ed., *The Sultanate of Oman, 1918-1939: External Affairs* (Reading, U.K., 2000) • J. A. KECHICHIAN, *Oman and the World: The Emergence of an Independent Foreign Policy* (Santa Monica, Calif., 1995) • A. H. AL-MAAMIRY, *Oman and Ibadhism* (2d ed.; New Delhi, 1989) • C. J. RIPHENBERG, *Oman: Political Development in a Changing World* (Westport, Conn., 1998).

THE EDITORS

Oneida Community

The premier American example of a communal society based on perfectionism was the Oneida Community, founded by John Humphrey Noyes (1811-86). As the result of a visionary experience in 1834, Noyes came to believe that human beings could live lives without → sin. This faith in the possibility of sinlessness became the basis for his communitarian ventures (→ Perfection; Perfectionists). In 1841 he converted a small group of friends and family in Putney, Vermont. By 1845 this group, living together, formally adopted "Bible communism," that is, the full sharing of all → property. Local hostility to the community's sexual practices, however, led to the group's dissolution in 1847. By 1848-49 the Putney group relocated on land near Oneida, in central New York State. The Oneida Community eventually grew to about 250, with about 50 others at various branch communities.

Sexual patterns at Oneida continued and developed the scheme of "complex → marriage" first used at Putney. Such a marriage was based upon the belief that in a sinless existence, each person should be deemed to be married to every other person of the opposite sex. Sexual affiliations were temporary and were governed by concepts of "ascending and descending fellowship," the belief that sexual relations assisted spiritual growth if they paired persons of lesser and greater spiritual maturity. The practice of male continence prevented conception. Stable male-female pairings ("special love") were strongly discouraged as antithetical to communal feeling. Beginning in 1879, Noyes added the practice of "stirpiculture," according to which some children were deliberately conceived by the systematic selection of parents. This → eugenic experiment lasted a decade. Social cohesion at Oneida was reinforced by the practice of "mutual criticism," in which each individual's maturity and spirituality were ruthlessly analyzed by an examining committee.

Oneida was one of a large number of social experiments and → millenarian movements in the United States during the 1830s and 1840s (→ Apocalypticism; Modern Church History 2.4.1). They were responses to broader social forces, in particular the economic upheavals associated with the Panic of 1837 and the breakdown of traditional patterns of village and family life during the Jacksonian period (1829-37).

Noyes believed the second coming of Christ (→ Parousia) had occurred in A.D. 70. He appears to have associated Oneida's practices with the millen-

nial age, although his eschatological views remain obscure and contradictory.

The Oneida Community formally dissolved in 1881, when it was converted into Oneida Community, Ltd., a joint stock company. The name was later changed to Oneida, Ltd., and is commonly known as Oneida Silversmiths.

→ Apostolic Churches

Bibliography: M. BARKUN, *Crucible of the Millennium: The Burned-Over District of New York in the 1840s* (Syracuse, N.Y., 1986) • L. FOSTER, *Religion and Sexuality* (Urbana, Ill., 1984) • T. M. HERRICK, *Desire and Duty at Oneida: Tirzeh Miller's Intimate Memoir* (ed. R. S. Fogarty; Bloomington, Ind., 2000) • S. KLAW, *Without Sin: The Life and Death of the Oneida Community* (New York, 1993) • I. L. MANDELKER, *Religion, Society, and Utopia in Nineteenth-Century America* (Amherst, Mass., 1984) • ONEIDA COMMUNITY, *Handbook of the Oneida Community, 1867 and 1871: Bound with Mutual Criticism* (New York, 1976) • R. D. THOMAS, *The Man Who Would Be Perfect: John Humphrey Noyes and the Utopian Impulse* (Philadelphia, 1977).

MICHAEL BARKUN

Ontological Argument → God, Arguments for the Existence of

Ontology

1. Term and Concept
2. Ontology in the History of Philosophy
3. Ontology and Christian Theology

1 Term and Concept
Ontologia is a term coined in the 1600s, from Gk. *ta onta* (existing things) and *logos* (reason, doctrine). Its first use may have been in the *Lexicon philosophicum* (1613), compiled by Rudolf Goclenius the Elder (1547-1628). With the meaning "doctrine of being," some authors used the term synonymously with "metaphysics." Others treated ontology as one branch of → metaphysics, alongside the other two branches, cosmology and rational or philosophical → psychology.

2. Ontology in the History of Philosophy
The topic of ontology (without the name) appears early in the philosophical tradition. In fact, any metaphysical reflection upon the nature of being, the kinds of being, and their relations to one another could be called ontology. Aristotle's *Meta-*

physics and his *Categories* contain the elements of a systematic ontology that proved to be extremely influential for medieval and subsequent thinkers, both philosophical and theological, in the Jewish, Christian, and Islamic traditions (→ Aristotelianism).

The church fathers (→ Patristics) and the → Scholastics adopted the terminology of antiquity, but as altered and transcended in their treatment of issues of Christian theology (→ Creation; Incarnation; Trinity). In the Trinitarian context Augustine (354-430; → Augustine's Theology) challenged the logical categorization of Aristotelian ontology and replaced the category of substance, which does not sufficiently value relations, with the concept of → person (*De Trin.* 5.5-6).

For the Scholastics the decisive issues of ontology included the relation of divine or necessary being to created or contingent being, the way in which creatures share in the divine perfections, the hierarchy of kinds of beings (embracing God and the universe), and → analogical reasoning as the way to understand and express such relationships. Reflection on creatureliness led to a distinction (unknown in antiquity) between being *(esse)* and essence *(essentia)*. In various ways essence now became the central theme of medieval and modern ontology.

In Thomas Aquinas (ca. 1225-74; → Thomism) being is the perfection of perfections (*De pot.* q. 7, art. 2, ad 9), in which each creature shares according to the measure of its essence. Among the basic features of being are the transcendentals (which surpass the other attributes of particular beings in that they alone apply to all instances of being), consisting of unity, truth, goodness, and beauty. From this perspective God is mainly envisaged not as a separate Supreme Being but as the subsistent fullness of being as such.

Under the impact of later medieval → nominalism, ontological questions came to be viewed as properly issues of grammar and formal → logic, thus weakening or breaking entirely the ancient link between logical reasoning and ontology. In the → modern period emphasis on subjectivity displaced concern with being as such (→ Subjectivism and Objectivism), so that existent things came to be regarded as mere objects. Possible thought as freedom from contradiction became the determinative factor, with affirmation of being itself relegated to the status of mere existence *(Dasein),* or a "being posited," an actual presence of something that is possible for thought. Hence a contingent being is one whose existence is indifferent with respect to its essence, or "what" it is. We see a trend in this direction in the late Scholastic Francisco Suárez (1548-1617),

and Christian Wolff (1679-1754) completed the process.

In his *Philosophia prima, sive ontologia* (1729), Wolff treated ontology as a deductive science of what is possible for thought. General metaphysics, as distinct from special metaphysics, discusses the causes of the actual existence of what is possible (treating the world and the soul, which is grounded in God). Thus Wolff's a priori ontology, grounded in the principle of noncontradiction and the principle of sufficient reason, as influenced by the rationalist philosopher G. W. Leibniz (1646-1716), deduced a series of necessary truths about beings as such, general truths that have their basis, and are known, quite apart from other sorts of knowledge that we have concerning the existence and contingent features of actual beings. In this way ontology and philosophical theology parted company.

Immanuel Kant (1724-1804; → Kantianism) effectively sought to put an end to scholastic or deductive approaches to ontology by showing, in the antinomies in his *Critique of Pure Reason* (1781), that deductive arguments can be framed for mutually opposed rationalist theses (such as that the world has a beginning in time, or that it hasn't), with the result that they cancel each other out rather than yielding knowledge of being. Kant's inquiry into the transcendental subject, namely, the ground of the appearance of all that is — the "subject" in the Latin sense of "that which underlies" — replaced the older rationalistic ontology. He exhibited the conditions in the finite subject or knower that are constitutive of the reality of the objects that it apprehends. For Kant, "being" is not a predicate. Our assertion of being (or nonbeing) in the particular case does not function as do genuine predications made concerning objects. Instead, it declares (or denies) the actual existence of the conceived or constituted object with its predicates (B 626), for knowledge of actual existence always involves sense experience, not just conceptions of properties or predicates.

Many of the various post-Kantian philosophies involve ontological issues, though often discussed under the rubric of metaphysics. → Neoscholastic movements in the 19th century and beyond sought to perpetuate versions of classical, usually Aristotelian, ontology. The *Science of Logic* of G. W. F. Hegel (1770-1831; → Hegelianism), in a new form of → idealist ontology, systematically presents the pure thoughts that are the basic determinants of being.

Of particular interest in 20th-century discussions of ontology are Heidegger and Quine. The early work of Martin Heidegger (1889-1976), *Being and Time* (1927), sought to provide an existential analysis of human being — the being that can pose the question of being — prior to addressing the ontological issue as such. But the later Heidegger abandoned entirely the project of ontology as an errant path taken by Western philosophers from Plato onward, reverting instead to pre-Socratics, who antedated the fundamental error.

Willard V. Quine (1908-2000), a prominent philosopher in the analytic tradition (→ Analytic Philosophy), treated ontological issues in relation to the explanatory power of theories. Acceptance of a given theory commits one to belief in certain kinds of beings. From this perspective, beings are the values given to variables within a particular theoretical context. Diverse ontologies are thus closely linked with alternative logics, and so ontology cannot be a single universal or deductive system.

3. Ontology and Christian Theology

The → church fathers and the scholastic theologians saw a direct connection between ontology as such and philosophical → theology. For them the essence or being that ontology studies in particular beings is in the first instance a feature of God or divine being, and only secondarily extended, by "participation" or in some other fashion, by God to created beings. These theologians thus took over ontological terminology and concepts from ancient philosophy but, in doing so, adapted them to the theological task.

Stoic conceptions of the *logos* antecedent to, and pervading, the creation (→ Stoicism) underwent modification as applied to the Word of God. In the Trinitarian thought of → Augustine (354-430; → Augustine's Theology) and others, concepts of Father, Son, and Spirit as "persons" engaged in eternal as well as temporal relations better fit beliefs about divine being than did Aristotelian categories of substance and accidents, or matter and form. Theological reflection on the status of creatureliness led to new ways of distinguishing being, essence, and existence.

Some Protestants, including Martin → Luther (1483-1546) and Karl → Barth (1886-1968), strongly opposed use of philosophical ontology in the explication of Christian faith, instead regarding confessional statements (→ Confessions and Creeds) as grounded solely in → revelation and → grace, and perhaps as inherently paradoxical. Catholic theologians such as Hans Urs von Balthasar (1905-88) and Karl → Rahner (1904-84) saw use of philosophical ontology as an essential tool in expounding central theological themes of → creation and redemption,

→ sin and → grace, as well as the underlying and basic conceptions of God and world. Some Protestant theologians (e.g., Paul → Tillich, Wolfhart Pannenberg, Gerhard Ebeling, and Heinrich Ott) have come to similar conclusions.

Bibliography: Primary sources: G. W. F. Hegel, *Science of Logic* (trans. A. V. Miller; London, 1969; orig. pub., 1812-16) • M. Heidegger, *Being and Time* (trans. J. Stambaugh; Albany, N.Y., 1996; orig. pub., 1927) • I. Kant, *Critique of Pure Reason* (trans. P. Guyer; Cambridge, 1998; orig. pub., 1781; rev., 1787) • C. Wolff, *Philosophia prima, sive ontologia* (Frankfurt, 1729).

Secondary works: É. Gilson, *Being and Some Philosophers* (2d ed.; Toronto, 1952) • N. Hartmann, *New Ways of Ontology* (Chicago, 1953) • W. Marx, *Heidegger and the Tradition* (Evanston, Ill., 1971) • J. Owens, *The Doctrine of Being in the Aristotelian Metaphysics* (Toronto, 1951) • W. V. Quine, *From a Logical Point of View* (2d ed.; Cambridge, Mass., 1964).

Günther Pöltner and Robert F. Brown

Optimism and Pessimism

1. Origin and Meanings
2. Conceptual Problems
3. Philosophy and Metaphysics
4. Theology and Religion

1. Origin and Meanings

The terms "optimism" and "pessimism" originated in the philosophical polemics of the 18th century (e.g., Voltaire's satire *Candide; or, Optimism* [1759], written against G. W. Leibniz). At issue was evil in the world, in → nature, and in human possibilities. Optimism finds in the world the best possible world, which justifies its Creator (→ Creation; Justification 2; Theodicy). Pessimism views the world as a flawed world that is without God or that defies him (→ Atheism; Sin). A special form of optimism is the belief in → progress as an attempt to give → meaning to what takes place in the world. In common usage the two terms denote → everyday attitudes to life.

2. Conceptual Problems

Optimism and pessimism retain their polemical character when applied to individuals, epochs, nations, and religions. Their systematic use in basic matters of → philosophy and → religion thus gives rise to problems. Philosophy, religion, and related disciplines have tried to find answers to questions of → hope and failure that will not just explain but will transcend optimism and pessimism as elementary prejudices regarding the world, humanity, its history, → culture, and morality (H. Blumenberg).

3. Philosophy and Metaphysics

Plato (427-347 B.C.; → Platonism) related human instability, which engenders optimism and pessimism, to the problems of God and → immortality (*Phd.* 107C). Theodicy achieved prominence in the Christian tradition, which postulates the divine origin of the world, in spite of all its evil. → Augustine's hamartiology characterizes human beings as unconditionally sinners (→ Augustine's Theology).

Since optimism and pessimism could find no other points of orientation, they emerged as specific concepts only at the end of the → baroque, with the comprehensive → secularization of thought. They are closely linked to 18th- and 19th-century philosophy. Leibniz (1646-1716) saw the world as a harmony of body, spirit, and → grace, thus concluding that is was "the best of all possible worlds." He was thus in the theodicy tradition. Thinkers who followed him, however (esp. Voltaire and I. Kant), broke radically with that tradition.

A new basis was found for optimism on such very different principles as → aesthetics (third earl of Shaftesbury, German → classicism), → dialectic (G. W. F. Hegel, K. → Marx), the "invisible hand" of the market (A. Smith), and → pedagogics and the ability to solve problems (the → Enlightenment and Anglo-Saxon → pragmatism from the time of J. Dewey). In this respect optimism and pessimism are part of a view of reality: optimism is mentioned particularly in the evaluation of → progress, while pessimism allows that society may blossom under threat (T. Hobbes) or that it is possible only through private depravity (B. de Mandeville).

A. Schopenhauer (1788-1860), under Brahman influence (→ Hinduism), was the first to make of pessimism a principle that, in the eternal antithesis of idea and phenomenon, prompts the will to strict → asceticism. F. → Nietzsche (1844-1900), in contrast, spoke of the "pessimism of strength," which empowers us to cross all barriers. → Existentialism also claims to occupy a position beyond both optimism and pessimism, while discussion of values opens up completely other dimensions of evaluation (→ Values, Ethics of).

4. Theology and Religion

In spite of its message concerning the divine likeness and redemption through Jesus, Christianity has often been linked to pessimism because of its doctrines of original sin and → predestination and its eschatological expectation (→ Apocalypticism). This judgment overlooks its message of grace, the justification of sinners, the → kingdom of God, and the dawning consummation of creation (→ Eschatology). Optimism and pessimism are not suitable terms for characterizing theological concerns and trends.

The same applies in other religions as well. → Islam's stress on submission to God's control embraces both optimism and pessimism. Likewise, the regulation of a common life in cultic fellowship such as we find in → Judaism, Hinduism, and → Shintoism cannot be subsumed under these categories.

Bibliography: E. C. CHANG, ed., *Optimism and Pessimism: Implications for Theory, Research, and Practice* (Washington, D.C., 2001) • K. GOLDAMMER and H. BLUMENBERG, "Optimismus und Pessimismus," *RGG* (3d ed.) 4.1660-64 • B. DE MANDEVILLE, *The Fable of the Bees; or, Private Vices, Publick Benefits* (New York, 1962; orig. pub., 1714) • L. A. RUPRECHT, *Tragic Posture and Tragic Vision: Against the Modern Failure of Nerve* (New York, 1994) • VOLTAIRE, *Candide* (Boston, 1999; orig. pub., 1759).

JÜRGEN STEIN

Opus Dei

1. Origin and Development
2. Structure and Leadership
3. Work and Goals

The Roman Catholic organization Opus Dei (Lat. "work of God") has since 1982 been the only personal → prelature in the → Roman Catholic Church. Its head is a → bishop whose seat is in Rome, and its ecclesiastical basis is the Codex Iuris Particularis Operis Dei, issued by the → pope in 1982. The current internal regulations established by Opus Dei (1984-90) are not accessible to the public, though they include the Latin writings *De Spiritu et de piis servandis consuetudinibus* (125 arts.) and *Regulae internae pro administrationibus* [*administrationes* = section for women] (75 arts.), as well as the Spanish writings *Glosas* (5 vols.) and *Vademecum* (7 vols.). The Opus Dei refers to itself as a "battle troop with the most rigorous disciplines" and as "mancipium of the church" (*De Spiritu* 64 and 22). Theologically and as regards ecclesiastical politics, it is part of the movement of Catholic integralism (→ Modernism 3); it is one of the most powerful and influential of the more recently formed Catholic societies.

1. Origin and Development

In 1928 the Spanish priest Josemaría Escrivá de Balaguer y Albás (1902-75, beatified in 1992) founded the Opus Dei, which attracted parts of the anti-Marxist elite during the Spanish Civil War. Although membership was initially restricted to males, in 1930 the organization began accepting women. In 1943 clerics in the men's section were incorporated in a sacerdotal society. In the same year the Opus Dei established itself in Portugal. In 1947 Rome became its headquarters; by 2001 it had established ecclesiastical representation in 61 countries.

According to the 2001 *Annuario Pontificio,* the prelature encompassed 1,684 churches and pastoral establishments. Its 84,598 members include 2,155 clerics (with 1 cardinal and 12 bishops in Latin America, 2 bishops in Rome, 1 bishop in the United States, and 1 bishop in Austria). Even though the names of the lay members are generally kept secret, one can reliably say that approximately 60,000 of all members of the Opus Dei minister in Spain and in the Spanish cultural sphere in Latin America. Probably about 5,000 others are active in Italy and another 3,000 each in the Philippines and in the United States. Overall, half the members are women.

2. Structure and Leadership

The sections for men and women are kept strictly separated (see *Regulae*). In each section members are divided into three groups. One is the → celibate "numeraries": professional academics who are expected to have an academic title (with the exception of "numeraries auxiliaries" in the women's section, who do domestic chores in the centers of the two sections). Numeraries include the clerics of the prelature, who constitute the Sacerdotal Society of the Holy Cross, with an unknown number of associated diocesan clerics. Only male numeraries may advance to leadership positions in the Opus Dei, and only → priests into the highest of those positions. The other two groups are celibate "associates," from all professions and classes, and the "supernumeraries," which includes all members who since 1950 have been permitted to marry. The Opus Dei also has "cooperators," who in part include non-Catholics and even non-Christians.

Numeraries live in centers that form the point of orientation for the remaining members. The course of each member's day is rigidly shaped by numerous spiritual exercises. Daily, for example, celibate members are to wear a cilice, or spiked chain, around a thigh for at least two hours and are to scourge themselves once weekly with a discipline, or cordlike whip (*De Spiritu* 125; → Asceticism). In his main

work, *Camino,* whose translations have occasionally failed to convey the harshness of the original, Escrivá demands "blind → obedience to superiors" and "holy coercion." The *Glosas* and *Vademecum* describe in detail how each individual member is controlled, including → censorship of any works authored by the person and of the books and electronic media the person is allowed to receive and of any private correspondence and university attendance. Refusal of this censorship results in expulsion (*Vademecum*).

Quite independent of one another, former members in several different countries have recounted harsh indoctrination procedures and even injuries from sectlike practices. Global criticism has been directed against the Opus Dei for its use of penitential instruments for indoctrination even in the case of young people. In the United States former members and parents have established the self-help initiative Opus Dei Awareness Network, Inc. (Pittsfield, Mass.).

3. Work and Goals

The Opus Dei seeks to aid its members in incorporating Christianity into their daily lives and in sanctifying their work. Lay members instructed by the numeraries-priests are generally engaged in secular professions. A small number of lay numeraries are engaged in leadership and educational positions. Cooperators are to pray and work for the prelature and to support it financially through → tithing. Non-Christian cooperators are also to be led to the "light of faith" and to a "Christian disposition" (Codex 16.2). The Christian world is divided into Catholics and those "who call themselves Christian but often do not know Christ" (*De Spiritu,* Spanish annotations, no. 16).

According to *Crónica,* the leadership periodical of the male section, God created the "holy, unchangeable, and everlasting" Opus Dei "in the heart of his church" to protect the Roman Catholic Church from error, a weakening of discipline, and disintegration. In 1979 the Opus Dei offered its services to the Holy See as a "mobile corps" and has since then been able to enhance its influence in the church, especially within church leadership. Today 1 of every 17 priests in the Opus Dei occupies an office or bears a title bestowed by the pope, whereas during the 1970s only 1 of every 100 enjoyed such distinction. In the year 2001 members of the Opus Dei occupied at least 51 offices in the Roman Curia.

The *Crónica* states that another goal of the Opus Dei is to Christianize all social institutions. Strategic points of departure for this "apostolate" are especially the elite groups (Codex 2.2 and 116), in which members participate in disproportionately large numbers. In largely Catholic countries such as Spain during the rule of F. Franco and in Latin American military dictatorships, members have also been able to occupy politically influential positions. Members also cooperate with nonmembers in establishing "apostolic corporate works," including youth clubs, scientific institutes, and universities. The *Vademecum* also enjoins them to help finance the Opus Dei centers by establishing foundations "with or without legal personality," which are to cover possible deficits through donations.

Since the mid-1970s a network close to Opus Dei has been established consisting of corporate works, foundations, and banks. Because these works have no formal legal connection with the Opus Dei as a religious prelature, their association with the Opus Dei is not always evident to outsiders. Evidence of such a clandestine network emerged in 1986 in a financial scandal surrounding the Spanish industrialist José María Ruiz-Mateos, a supernumerary. During the 1990s considerable financial subventions were found to be flowing from national and transnational establishments, in this case especially from the European Union, into projects attaching to the corporate works and other foundations of the Opus Dei.

→ Authority; Clergy and Laity; Religious Orders and Congregations

Bibliography: P. BERGLAR, *Opus Dei: Life and Work of Its Founder, Josemaría Escrivá* (Princeton, 1994) • J. ESCRIVÁ, *The Way* (Chicago, 1954; orig. pub., 1939) • J. ESTRUCH, *Saints and Schemers: Opus Dei and Its Paradoxes* (New York, 1995) • P. HERTEL, *"Ich verspreche euch den Himmel." Geistlicher Anspruch, gesellschaftliche Ziele und kirchliche Bedeutung des Opus Dei* (4th ed.; Düsseldorf, 1991) • R. A. HUTCHISON, *Their Kingdom Come: Inside the Secret World of Opus Dei* (New York, 1999) • M. DEL CARMEN TAPIA, *Beyond the Threshold: A Life in Opus Dei* (New York, 1997) • D. LE TOURNEAU, *What Is Opus Dei?* (Dublin, 1987) • G. URQUHART, *Opus Dei: The Pope's Right Arm in Europe* (Washington, D.C., 1997).   PETER HERTEL

Oratorio

An oratorio is a multisectional, accompanied choral work (→ Choir) presenting a dramatic situation, usually religious, without staging or costumes. It includes a narrator (who reads the *testo*, "text"), soloists representing characters or virtues, and choruses reflecting on the drama. Accompaniments range from continuo (→ organ/harpsichord) to full orchestra. *La rappresentazione di anima e di corpo* (Representation of soul and body, 1600), by E. de' Cavalieri (ca. 1550-1602), is considered the first oratorio; the term itself appeared in 1640.

The roots of the oratorio are medieval liturgical drama, monody, the vernacular dialogues and lauda of 16th-century Italy (e.g., as sung in the devotional exercises of the Oratory of St. Philip Neri), madrigal and → motet (→ Church Music), and 17th-century Italian opera (using secco and accompanied recitative, and the da capo aria). Latin oratorios flourished in 17th-century ecclesial foundations (e.g., under G. Carissimi in Rome, later G. Charpentier in France), but vernacular oratorios replaced Latin in the 17th century. Carissimi's student A. Scarlatti (1660-1725) drew upon Neapolitan opera (which highlighted the orchestra's role and da capo arias). Accompaniments became a constituent part of the dramatic presentation.

German composers introduced the Italian style. H. Schütz's (1585-1672) Christmas and Easter *Histories* are typical. J. A. Hasse (1699-1783) of Dresden continued the Italian practice in the 18th century, but J. S. Bach's (1685-1750) oratorios remain → cantata collections. G. F. Handel's (1685-1759) English oratorios emphasize the chorus and, like J. Haydn's (1732-1809), expand the orchestra's role, serving as models thereafter.

→ Enlightenment influence moved the oratorio from church to theater (Haydn's *Creation* and *The Seasons*). Amateur choral societies in the 19th century provided a ready market for F. Mendelssohn (1809-47, *Elijah* and *St. Paul*), J. Brahms (1833-97, *German Requiem*), and others.

Popularity waned by the 20th century, but several major composers (e.g., H. W. Parker, A. Schoenberg, A. Honnegger, W. T. Walton, I. Stravinsky, and K. Penderecki) contributed notable works. Handel's *Messiah* has retained pride of place in the English-speaking world.

→ Liturgy; Passion Music; Requiem; Worship

Bibliography: F. BLUME, *Protestant Church Music* (New York, 1974) • D. R. HURLEY, *Handel's Muse: Patterns of Creation in His Oratorios and Musical Dramas, 1743-1751* (Oxford, 2001) • H. MCCONNELL, "Motet," *Key Words in Church Music* (ed. C. Schalk; St. Louis, 1978) 272-74 • K. PAHLEN, *The World of the Oratorio: Oratorio, Mass, Requiem, Te Deum, Stabat Mater, and Large Cantatas* (Portland, Oreg., 1990) • H. E. SMITHER, *A History of the Oratorio* (3 vols.; Chapel Hill, N.C., 1977-87) • E. WIENANDT, *Choral Music of the Church* (New York, 1965).   ROBERT D. HAWKINS

Oratory

The term "oratory" is used for a small chapel for private devotions with only restricted liturgical functions. In this sense it may denote the → chapel of a hospital or castle. The → Cistercians called their churches oratories (→ Monasticism). Architecturally the oratory was designed for more intimate worship as distinct from more expansive churches (→ Church Architecture). The Oratorians (→ Religious Orders and Congregations) also preferred a church with a single nave.

From 1983 → CIC 1223-29 there is a distinction between an oratory and a private chapel: the oratory is a place where a society or a specific circle of believers may meet for worship with the permission of the ordinary, whereas the private chapel is a place where individuals worship with the ordinary's consent. Oratories and private chapels are consecrated with the same → rites.

Among → Protestants the term was used in the 17th century for the prayer rooms of patrons (→ Patronage) and princes.

→ Devotion, Devotions; Monastery

Bibliography: E. BADSTÜBNER, *Kirchen der Mönche* (Berlin, 1980) • A. H. FELDHAUS, "Oratories, Canon Law of," *NCE* 10.714-15 • D. HOWARD, "Oratorians," *DArt* 23.472-74 • J. S. WEISZ, *Pittura e misericordia: The Oratory of S. Giovanni Decellato in Rome* (Ann Arbor, Mich., 1984).

GERLINDE STROHMAIER-WIEDERANDERS

Ordeal

"Ordeal," deriving from OEng. *ordāl*, "judgment," refers to a procedure in sacred law in which, for lack of witnesses or other rational means of proof, → priests or other experts (see Deut. 17:8-13) try to establish → guilt or innocence by a divine proof. The accused person is subjected to a duel or to trial by poison, fire, water, and so forth, in which failure supposedly denotes guilt. Ordeals are common in African → tribal religions but have also figured in more advanced societies, for example, in Israel and other ancient Near Eastern cultures and, under Germanic influence, the Middle Ages.

In the OT, associated with the practice of pronouncing oracles (Numbers 17; 1 Sam. 10:17-25), we find the casting of lots by the priests, which served to identify the guilty person out of a number of suspects (Joshua 7; 1 Sam. 14:24-26; see also Exod. 28:30; Lev. 8:8; Prov. 16:33). We also find a

corresponding ordeal in Egypt in which the image of God singles out the guilty party.

The ordeal by cursing or trial (→ Curse) intensified or expunged the guilt of a suspect. Closely linked to this procedure was the → oath of purging, with an associated self-cursing (Exod. 22:8, 10-11; Lev. 6:2-3), all of which had to take place at the holy site in God's presence (Exod. 22:9; 1 Kgs. 8:31; note also the prayers of the accused in Psalms 5; 7; 17; 26–27, etc., which might be linked to the ordeal). In Mesopotamia and neighboring territories such as Elam and Asia Minor, we find the river ordeal (see the Code of → Hammurabi §§2, 132). If, when the accused was thrown into the water, the river god gave that person back again, innocence was established. In Israel up to the middle of the first century A.D. (*m. Soṭa* 9:9b), a wife suspected of adultery was subjected in the Jerusalem → temple to a drink ordeal, which was linked to a curse offering (Num. 5:11-31).

In the Middle Ages we find the duel, the lot, trials by iron and water, and specific Christian ordeals such as trials by the cross and the Eucharist. In 1215 Lateran IV (→ Councils of the Church) finally banned the duel and also the participation of the clergy in ordeals. Ordeals lived on into the 16th and 17th centuries in → witch trials.

Bibliography: A. S. AHMED, "Trial by Ordeal among Bugtis," *Marginality and Modernity: Ethnicity and Change in Post-colonial Balochistan* (ed. P. Titus; New York, 1997) 51-77 • R. BARTLETT, *Trial by Fire and Water: The Medieval Judicial Ordeal* (Oxford, 1986) • A. DESTRO, *The Law of Jealousy: Anthropology of Sotah* (Atlanta, 1989) • E. A. DOUMATO, "Engaging Spirits: Prophylaxis, Witchcraft, Exorcisms, Trial by Ordeal, and Zar," *Getting God's Ear: Women, Islam, and Healing in Saudi Arabia and the Gulf* (New York, 1999) 147-84 • T. HEAD, "Saints, Heretics, and Fire: Finding Meaning through the Ordeal," *Monks and Nuns, Saints and Outcasts: Religion in Medieval Society* (ed. S. Farmer and B. H. Rosenwein; Ithaca, N.Y., 2000) 220-38.

WILLY SCHOTTROFF†

Order of Salvation

1. General Sense
   1.1. Eastern Developments
   1.2. Western Developments
2. Particular Sense
   2.1. Lutheran Orthodoxy
   2.2. Pietism
   2.3. The Nineteenth and Twentieth Centuries

1. General Sense

The concepts of the order and economy of salvation refer generally to the hidden decree and plan of God for the salvation of the world. They refer as well to all that God has done, and does, between the beginning and the end of the times to fulfill his saving purpose (see Eph. 1:10; 3:9), that is, salvation events in history (→ Salvation History), the sum of saving acts, and saving education in → faith.

1.1. *Eastern Developments*

The Greek → church fathers worked out their theology in reflection on the mysteries of the divine → economy. This economy embraces the realities of creation and redemption, the unfolding of salvation in the time of the church, and the consummation in the *eschaton* (see → Irenaeus *Adv. haer.* 3 and 4). In its unity it is a work of the triune God (→ Chrysostom). Objectively considered, it consists of the redemption of the human race by the incarnate Son of God. Subjectively, it includes the personal appropriation of salvation through the energy of the → Holy Spirit.

The two aspects come together in the deification of all created things (→ Theosis), encompassing nature and humanity (→ Christology 3). This deification is the goal of God's saving order. With mystical incorporation into Christ, believers participate in the sanctifying phases of the life of the God-Man (crucified, dead, and raised with him, Gregory of Nazianzus). Deification is the gift of God, given in → grace. But it is decided by our free will as we open ourselves to grace, do not obstruct the saving work, love the good, set aside passions, strive for renewal in spiritual wrestling, and ascend to the beatific vision of God (Basil the Great; Maximus the Confessor described growth in the spiritual life as the result of purification, illumination, and union [*De eccl. hier.* 5.3]). To the achieved states of sanctification there correspond progressive stages of glory in the heavenly kingdom. The work of grace on the way of salvation is owed to the deifying power of the Holy Spirit. By the Spirit believers partake of the divine nature and are changed into a new life (Basil, → Cyril of Alexandria, Irenaeus, et al.).

The divine economy thus finds reflection in the existential experience of salvation (personalist economy of salvation). It takes shape in the → church as the mystical body of Christ and the organ of the Holy Spirit. It comes to light in cultic events (→ Worship) and may be seen in → icons. Its mysteries control Orthodox → spirituality (→ Palamism) and give Orthodox dogmatics its structure.

1.2. *Western Developments*

In the Western Latin doctrine of salvation, a strictly comprehensive view was not maintained. The independent development of a doctrine of grace from the time of → Augustine (→ Augustine's Theology) broke the connection between → Christology and → soteriology that had been a controlling element in patristic theology. The workings of the divine acts of salvation were increasingly viewed and described within theological → anthropology, the doctrine of the → sacraments, and the problem of → justification.

As a result of the anthropological approach (Augustine) and an interest in the rational explanation and ethical articulation of the reality of redemption, the doctrine of → sanctification became especially important. Western dogmatic structures put grace at the center (the new order of salvation); placed the treatment of → God and the → Trinity, → creation and → sin, Christ and his redeeming work before grace as its presupposition; and then in conclusion dealt with the church, the sacraments, and → eschatology as the development of grace.

2. Particular Sense

The order of salvation (*ordo salutis*) took on special meaning after the → Reformation in the development of doctrine in Lutheran and Reformed dogmatics and in → Pietism. It became a classic expression for the steps by which individuals come to participate in the salvation given by God.

2.1. *Lutheran Orthodoxy*

In the interests of a more precise definition of the Christian belief in salvation, Lutheran → orthodoxy (§1) developed a doctrine that analyzes and systematizes God's turning to humans in the Holy spirit (*gratia Spiritus Sancti applicatrix,* "the applicative grace of the Holy Spirit"). Lutheran dogmaticians coordinated the divine works of grace and human religious → experience and offered a description of the activity of the Holy Spirit (see Luther's Small Catechism, art. 3: "calls, gathers, enlightens, and makes holy"). They set this work in a conceptually orderly schema, as, for example, J. A. Quenstedt (1617-88) in *Theologia didactico-polemica sive systema theologiae* (1685): calling, regeneration, → conversion, justification (penitence and confession), mystical union with God, and renewal. A somewhat similar *ordo* was proposed by N. Hunnius (1585-1643) in *Epitome credendorum* (1625): calling, repentance, justification, conversion, renewing, new birth, and union with Christ.

Reformed dogmaticians worked out similar orders, but with more attention to the practical effects of election (→ Predestination) on the life of believers between mortification and vivification, as, for example, William Ames (1576-1633) in his *Medulla theologiae* (The marrow of theology, 1623). Typical elements were effectual calling, regeneration, faith, justification, sanctification, and glorification.

2.2. Pietism

In the 18th-century theology that led up to Pietism, the concept of the *ordo salutis* covered both the operations of God and the spiritual changes in humans. J. F. Buddeus (1667-1729) and J. Carpov (1699-1768) used the expression as a technical term describing the states corresponding to the Spirit's working as stages in the Christian life. E. J. Danovius (1741-82) and F. V. Reinhard (1753-1812) found five stages: vocation, illumination, conversion, sanctification, and mystical union. The Pietists thought in terms of stages through which believers must pass and which are consciously to be distinguished. We participate in the saving transition from a state of sin to a state of grace by self-examination and preparation for the reception of grace. According to A. H. → Francke (1663-1727), we must be able to give concrete information concerning the time, place, and circumstances of our conversion.

J. A. Bengel (1687-1752) corrected the overemphasis on an individual order of salvation by considering the steps in the development and chronological unfolding of God's saving work in history (the divine economy), asserting that the community of the Lord can know where it stands (*Ordo temporum* . . . [1741]). With Francke's concern for a pedagogical commitment to "amendment of life," there was associated — in pietistic → millenarianism — a desire to change the world and the confidence to do it. At issue here was the effect of the order of salvation within history.

J. → Wesley (1703-91) found the climax of the process of personal salvation, which begins with regeneration and conversion and aims at perfection, in sanctification as a visible and controllable demonstration and development of appropriated salvation. Sanctification as an expression of the cooperation (interaction) of God and humans represents the Spirit of Christ in life. Sanctification issues in evangelistic witness and social action, governs the discipline and structuring of the life of the congregation as a fellowship of the sanctified, and points the way to world consummation (→ Methodism). After Lutheran dogmaticians had systematized the detailed workings of grace and Pietism had changed them into acts and moments in personal → piety (the *ordo salutis* as personal experience), the essential elements in the order of salvation came to be regarded more in terms of the condition and possibility of making the → kingdom of God visible in all spheres of human life.

2.3. The Nineteenth and Twentieth Centuries

After criticism by → Enlightenment theology, F. → Schleiermacher (1768-1834) formulated a simpler form of the older doctrine, distinguishing only between regeneration as the beginning and sanctification as the continued progress of the life of communion with Christ. Confessional Lutheran theology, however, maintained the traditional view up to the middle of the 20th century (E. Wacker). In and even beyond the revivalist theology of the 19th century (→ Revivals), the acts and moments of the *ordo salutis* were paradigmatic for the piety of the awakened believer. Personal experience was a basic theme, but the theology of the day was turning to a broader concept of experience, and the order of salvation as such aroused little interest. Attention was paid, however, to individual aspects (e.g., justification). K. → Barth (1886-1968) criticized the psychological and biographical restrictions and the salvation egoism that had come to mark the order of salvation, explicating justification and sanctification under the theme of vocation as the community's ministry of witness (*CD* IV/3).

In ecumenical circles conversion is the goal of → evangelism, while sanctification is a program of Christian world change, and God's saving address culminates in Spirit-effected freedom (→ Liberation Theology; Political Theology).

This historical sketch, by taking the order of salvation, *ordo salutis*, as an example, shows how in the broad stream of Reformation Christianity God's incalculable self-demonstration can be rationalized, psychologized, and applied in faith. As a paradigmatic attempt to conceptualize objective salvation for the subject and to bring it under control in the subject's activities, the order of salvation is one of many denominationally different models for discussion of the problem of God's relation to humanity and the world.

Bibliography: On 1: J. Feiner and M. Löhrer, eds., *MySal* 1, also 3/2, 4/2 • J. Gross, *La divinisation du chrétien d'après les Pères grecs, contribution historique à la doctrine de la grâce* (Paris, 1938) • G. W. H. Lampe, "Christian Theology in the Patristic Period IX: Salvation, Sin, and Grace," *A History of Christian Doctrine* (ed. H. Cunliffe-Jones; Philadelphia, 1980) 149-69 • V. Lossky, *The Mystical Theology of the Eastern Church* (Crestwood, N.Y., 1976) • W. Lowe, "Christ and Salvation," *Christian Theology: An Introduction to Its Traditions and Tasks* (2d ed.; ed. P. C. Hodgson and R. H. King; Philadelphia, 1985) 222-48 • G. I. Mantzaridis, *The Deification of Man: St. Gregory Palamas and the Orthodox Tradition* (Crestwood, N.Y., 1984) • P. Nel-

LAS, *Deification in Christ: The Nature of the Human Person* (Crestwood, N.Y., 1987).

On 2: J. BAUR, *Salus Christiana. Die Rechtferti-gungslehre in der Geschichte des christlichen Heils-verständnisses* (Gütersloh, 1968) • W. ELERT, *The Structure of Lutheranism* (2 vols.; St. Louis, 1962) • P. C. ERB, ed., *Pietists: Selected Writings* (New York, 1983) • E. GRITSCH, *A History of Lutheranism* (Minneapolis, 2002) • N. HUNNIUS, *Epitome credendorum* (1625, selections), *Documents from the History of Lutheranism, 1517-1750* (ed. E. Lund; Minneapolis, 2002) 241-44 • R. R. NIEBUHR, *Schleiermacher on Christ and Religion: A New Introduction* (New York, 1964) • W. PANNENBERG, *Systematic Theology* (vol. 3; Grand Rapids, 1998) • D. N. J. POOLE, *Stages of Religious Faith in the Classical Reformation Tradition: The Covenant Approach to the Ordo Salutis* (Lewiston, N.Y., 1995) • F. E. STOEFFLER, *German Pietism during the Eighteenth Century* (Leiden, 1973); idem, *The Rise of Evangelical Pietism* (Leiden, 1965) • P. DE VRIES, *John Bunyan on the Order of Salvation* (New York, 1994) • E. WACKER, *Ordo Salutis. Die Heilsordnung* (new ed.; ed. M. Pörksen; Breklum, 1960; orig. pub., 1898).

ERWIN FAHLBUSCH

Order of Service → Liturgy

Orders and Congregations → Religious Orders and Congregations

Orders, Theology of → Two Kingdoms Doctrine

Ordinary of the Mass → Mass

Ordination

1. Terminology
   1.1. Latin
   1.2. Greek
   1.3. Germanic Languages
2. Ecumenical Dialogues
3. Juridical Interpretations
   3.1. Enfeoffment
   3.2. Delegation
   3.3. Recognition
   3.4. The Calling of the Church
4. Epicletic/Sacramental Interpretations
   4.1. Middle Ages
   4.2. Ecumenical Developments
5. Ordination Rites
   5.1. Imposition of Hands
   5.2. Symbols
   5.3. Vestments
   5.4. Anointing
   5.5. The Ordinator
6. Effects of Ordination
   6.1. Absolute and Relative Ordination
   6.2. Succession
7. Validity of Ordination
   7.1. Defectus
   7.2. Reordination
   7.3. Recognition of Ordinations
   7.4. Ordination of Women
8. Ordination as an Ecclesial Act
   8.1. Baptism
   8.2. Priesthood of All Baptized Believers

1. Terminology

The term "ordination" is complex, not least because of inconsistent or even contradictory usage among Christian traditions throughout church history and at the present time. One example of this terminological complexity is the differentiation between the "consecration" of → bishops, the "ordination" of presbyters/priests (→ Elder; Priest, Priesthood), the "making" of → deacons, and the "admitting" to minor orders (a term also used, on occasion, in Anglicanism in respect to deacons). All of these terms refer to what are now most commonly known as ordinations. Interestingly, in French the same word, *consécration,* is used for the ordination of both priests and bishops, perhaps following the fifth-century Sacramentarium Veronense, in which bishops and priests were "consecrated," and the → rite for conferring holy orders on a deacon was seen as a → "blessing" *(benedictio super diaconos).* Churches like the Church of Sweden have tried to solve the problem by the use of a consistent terminology: it "ordains" bishops, priests, and deacons by the imposition of hands by the bishop; it "sends out" → missionaries; it "appoints" persons (lay or ordained) to specific tasks; and parishes and dioceses "receive" ordained persons into their communities.

The 1982 → Faith and Order document *Baptism, Eucharist, and Ministry* summarizes what now seems to be a general convergence position concerning ordination: "The act of ordination by the laying on of hands of those appointed to do so is at one and the same time invocation of the Holy Spirit *(epiklesis);* sacramental sign; acknowledgment of gifts and commitment" ("Ministry," par. 41).

1.1. *Latin*

"Ordination" (Lat. *ordinatio*), a term found first in → Tertullian (d. ca. 225), comes from *ordo* (order, rank). *Ordo* was incorporated into ecclesial language on the basis of its use in Roman law, where it designates a corporate body or a state over against the *populus* (the people). A related term is "ordinal," which is the manual for the performance of ordinations.

Similarly, "ordinary" (from *ordinarius*), which in some traditions designates the officeholder, normally the diocesan bishop, is derived from *ordo*, as is "ordinator," the one who ordains. At the beginning of the fifth century, → Jerome (ca. 345-420) used *ordinatio* as a synonym for Gk. *cheirotonia*.

1.2. *Greek*

The idea of ordination is usually traced back to Gk. *cheirotonia* (lit. "stretching out of hands," hence "voting [by show of hands], appointment") as used in the *Apostolic Tradition* of Hippolytus (ca. 170-ca. 236), where its main content has to do with the → laying on of hands *(cheirothesia)*. The related verb *cheirotoneō* is used in 2 Cor. 8:19 for the appointment of Titus to travel with Paul. According to modern patristic research the term *cheirothesia* in the early church normally is associated with a blessing, while *cheirotonia* refers to sacramental ordination.

These usages from the → early church have been preserved in the churches of the Byzantine Rite. The frequent translation "set apart" seems not to be in accordance with the fundamental idea of the handing over of a person to the church as its servant.

1.3. *Germanic Languages*

In the Scandinavian countries the national churches after the → Reformation retained the vernacular usage of the early Germanic *Wīh*, "holy," which connoted the rite by which, in a specified way, a person or a thing was consecrated to God (e.g., Swed. *vigning* and Norw. *vigsling*). Though retained in the Roman Catholic tradition, Ger. *Weihe* was avoided by the 16th-century Continental → Reformers.

2. Ecumenical Dialogues

Ordination is a fundamental ecclesiological practice that has a structuring and identity-shaping function in the process of discerning what the → church actually is. That ordination is a rite for admission into the public ministry of Word and sacrament (→ Word of God) is universally agreed upon, although issues of both form and content remain divisive. Differences exist not only between churches and ecclesial communities but also within these bodies — both over time and at any given moment —

which shows that theological boundaries are increasingly being drawn not only between churches but within them. Thus it is that ordination has become an object for ecumenical study and dialogue.

This dialogue has highlighted the challenges of identifying the difference between ordination as such and kindred acts of admission to the public ministry of the church, the content of ordination, the identity of those who should or should not be ordained, and the identity of those who have the task of ordaining. Such challenges are made difficult because what in one tradition is perceived as a rite of ordination may have the same content as a rite in another tradition that is *not* intended to be an ordination. A difficult ecumenical task is to discern what in form and content is an ordination, compared, on the one hand, with acts of → benediction and installation for lifelong positions and, on the other, with ordinations that are understood as being for a limited time only.

Changes in many traditions concerning their views of ordination have coincided, over the past 30 years, with progress in → ecumenical dialogue. Perhaps the most signal document indicating such change is *Baptism, Eucharist, and Ministry*. Particular churches that have changed or clarified their understanding of ordination include the Evangelical Lutheran Church of America, which has begun to consecrate (the term "ordination" is not used) bishops to the historic episcopacy; the Church of Sweden, which has clarified the meaning of ordination to the diaconate; and the Roman Catholic Church, which since → Vatican II has both ceased ordination to minor orders and taken the position that ordination to the episcopate has a sacramental character.

Research on the meaning and performance of ordination is comprehensive. In many cases, however, research results have been forced together into normative positions that serious scholarship cannot support. This flaw is obvious both in the extensive debate, spanning centuries of scholarship, concerning ordination in the early church and in reflections on varying ideas about ordination from the 16th-century reformations. For example, Martin → Luther's (1483-1546) various written comments on ordination, made over a span of 30 turbulent years, clearly cannot be harmonized into a consistent position. Researchers who claim otherwise have simply ignored the respective contexts of Luther's words on the subject (→ Luther's Theology).

The ecumenical dialogues have necessitated sober and nuanced scholarship regarding ordination and the ordained → ministry. These dialogues today demonstrate a certain tension between juridical and epicletic/sacramental interpretations of ordination, although recent developments in ordination liturgies reveal a tendency to keep these two perspectives together. The early church also seems to have sought a balance between the two aspects, as the rite for the ordination of bishops in the *Apostolic Tradition* well illustrates in its prayer of consecration: "So now pour upon this chosen one that power which is from you, the governing Spirit whom you gave to your beloved Son, Jesus Christ, the Spirit given by him to the holy apostles, who founded the Church in every place to be your temple for the unceasing glory and praise of your name." This prayer has been used in the Orthodox tradition since the third century and in the Roman Rite since Vatican II. Other traditions also reflect its influence in their ordination rites.

3. Juridical Interpretations

Juridical views of ordination, in their effort to focus on power, may ignore the gifts of the → Holy Spirit conveyed in ordination. In these views differences between ordination, inauguration, installation, and related acts sometimes become formal in nature as different churches define ordination in light of the tasks assigned to the person being ordained, with scant consideration of the meaning of ordination itself. These juridical views can be differentiated into four fundamental positions: enfeoffment, delegation, recognition, and "the calling of the church."

3.1. *Enfeoffment*

The medieval idea of enfeoffment (i.e., investing with a fief or estate) that characterized feudal societies — and therefore also the medieval Western church — has survived in traditions and theologies dominated by a juridical concept of ordination. For this position the central meaning of ordination is the conferring of power (esp. the *potestas ordinis*, "power of order," i.e., the power to sanctify through Word and sacrament). This view is predominant in the *Pontificale* of William Durandus, bishop of Mende (ca. 1230-96), an extremely influential document of the Middle Ages that emphasizes reception into the → hierarchy more than the making of ministers for the church. Power *(potestas)* and the commission of the priesthood are explicitly handed over to the ordinand, an emphasis adopted by Lutheran-Melanchthonian traditions.

In the Swedish Church Ordinance of 1571, for example, the bishop proclaims after the → vows of the ordinand and before the prayer of consecration (the Our Father with imposition of hands): "And I, by the authority entrusted to me on God's behalf by his church for this purpose, commit unto thee the

office of priest. In the name of the Father, and of the Son, and of the Holy Spirit. Amen." This proclamation had an equivalent formulation in the English Reformation, represented in the 1662 → Book of Common Prayer, when the bishop says: "Take thou authority to preach the Word of God, and to minister the holy sacraments in the → Congregation, where thou shalt be lawfully appointed thereunto." Enfeoffment places power in the hands of the ordinator, who in turn conveys power to the ordinand.

Lutheran → orthodoxy (§1) of the 17th century rooted ordination not only in NT but also in OT teaching (including Genesis 48; Num. 8:5-26; 27:15-23). During this period the idea of a specific power given in ordination was stressed, accompanied by the Melanchthonian view of the ordained ministry as a → teaching office over against the congregation of listeners. Furthermore, at this time the idea dominated of ordination as an entrance to an order, the body of ministers and elders *(ministerium)*, who functioned as a representative of the church *(ecclesia repraesentativa)*.

3.2. *Delegation*

Another fundamentally juridical theory of ordination views the congregation as the source of the rights and therefore the power conferred in ordination, which in this case usually designates certain tasks. In some traditions that attribute great significance to a particular understanding of "the priesthood of all believers," ordination is a delegation by the congregation of power given to the church. This view can be found in some Baptist and Congregationalist traditions, and it was important in 19th-century German Protestant theology (with its *Übertragungstheorie,* or theory of transference).

3.3. *Recognition*

A third type of juridical theory views ordination as the public recognition of a personal → vocation. This idea can be found in → Pietism and also in → Congregationalist, Baptist, and Pentecostal traditions (→ Baptists; Pentecostal Churches). It is based on the position that the → grace that fits a person for the ministry is given immediately and directly by God and is recognized, but not conferred or given, in ordination.

3.4. *The Calling of the Church*

The juridical view of ordination has long dominated in the Lutheran-Melanchthonian and Reformed traditions. The imposition of hands, in these traditions, has symbolized the empowerment or right to proclaim the → gospel and administer the sacraments. In practice, other rights have also been added, such as the right to lead a parish. One could designate this position "the calling of the church."

This tradition directly countered the late medieval view that ordination conferred on priests certain personal qualities that transformed them into qualitatively better or fuller Christians in comparison with the laity, the common people of God (→ Clergy and Laity). Thus the concept of calling *(vocatio)* — including (1) selection of a candidate *(electio),* (2) testing the candidate's suitability *(examinatio),* (3) confirmation of fitness *(confirmatio),* and (4) ordination *(ordinatio)* — seems best to characterize classical Lutheran-Melanchthonian views of ordination. In some churches the congregation was involved in the first three stages of the process; in others the whole process was limited to the bishops, magistrates, or → superintendents, depending on the structures of the church. At times the term "ordination" was used as the overall concept and thus as a synonym to "calling." In its treatment of church order, the → Augsburg Confession (1530) requires that persons admitted to public teaching and the administration of the sacraments must be "properly called" *(rite vocatus)* (CA 14), which includes ordination.

4. Epicletic/Sacramental Interpretations

The sacramental view of ordination is epicletic in character, emphasizing the act of → prayer for the Holy Spirit and the bestowal of the Spirit's gifts on the ordinand. Juridical aspects are subordinated to, and integrated into, the epicletic event of ordination.

In the Orthodox tradition this view of ordination has spanned the centuries; its ecclesiology views ordination, especially of bishops, as a realization of the promise of Christ to be present in the hierarchical structure of the church as Head and Body. Ordination, in this view, is primarily not an act of power but an act that structures the church as a royal priesthood (1 Pet. 2:5, 9). Ordination as a → sacrament or a sacramental act can thus be defined as one that effects what it symbolizes, namely, priesthood as an effective instrument for Christ's proper work of indwelling his church.

4.1. *Middle Ages*

In his influential work *Sentences* Peter Lombard (ca. 1100-1160) delineated a theology of seven sacraments, one of which is ordination. This teaching was accepted by the Council of Florence in 1439 (→ Councils of the Church 3). It is important to note that ordination in general was not thus sacramentally defined, but specifically ordination to the priesthood *(sacerdotium).*

During the → Middle Ages the Western church defined the sacraments by referring to the scholastic categories of *matter* (the material elements used in the rite) and *form* (the words spoken during the rite). Since, over centuries, a large number of ceremonial acts have been added to the rite of ordination, questions of what is matter and what is form have arisen and been disputed by theologians. Some have held that the → investiture, or handing over of → vestments, is the necessary element (see 5.3); others, the handing over of symbols or symbolic acts, such as giving the chalice, anointing with oil, or laying on of hands.

The Reformers, who defined sacraments according to the medieval teaching of the "greater sacraments" *(sacramenta maiora),* virtually without exception denied that ordination is a sacrament. The Augsburg Confession, written by Philipp → Melanchthon (1497-1560), provides only corrections to earlier sacramental practice and does not deal with the identity of the sacraments. The Apology of the Augsburg Confession (1531, also by Melanchthon), however, admits to the possibility of regarding ordination as a sacrament (13.11-13). When some Lutheran scholars argue that not only Melanchthon but also Luther himself could attribute a sacramental meaning to ordination (defined in terms of the gift of the Holy Spirit), they base their argument on a view of the ordained ministry as an instrument of Word and sacrament. In this view ordination cannot be considered an → adiaphoron, a category that was developed later in the Reformation period.

In Anglicanism the Thirty-nine Articles refer to five "commonly called sacraments," including ordination, "which are not to be counted for sacraments of the Gospel" (1571, art. 25). John → Calvin (1509-64; → Calvin's Theology) could conceive of the laying on of hands as a sacramental element in ordination (*Inst.* 4.19.31). Nevertheless, he too concluded that there were only two sacraments ordained by Christ (4.19.1, 4, 19, 28)

4.2. *Ecumenical Developments*

Ecclesial traditions and theologians that advocate a view of ordination as a sacrament or as sacramental hold that not only ordination to the priesthood but also ordination to deacon and bishop are sacramental. The ongoing ecumenical quest for a common understanding of the concept of sacrament — a quest that attempts to overcome both the static concern with the number of sacraments and the deficiencies in many historical definitions — has opened new possibilities for understanding. "Today it is possible for us to have a better understanding of various traditional elements in the doctrine of the office of the ministry. . . . We see more clearly than before that the question of whether ordination is a sacrament is chiefly a matter of terminology" (H. Meyer and L. Vischer, "Report of the Joint Lutheran–Roman Catholic Study Commission on 'The Gospel and the Church'" [1972, the "Malta Report"], §59).

Another dialogue states that ordination can be interpreted as a sign and effective instrument through which a person receives the gifts of the Holy Spirit for a specific office or order in the church and through which that person becomes a gift to the church for life. "The liturgical validation at the time of the act of ordination includes the invocation of the Holy Spirit ('epiclesis') with the laying on of hands by other ordained ministers. . . . The laying on of hands is an efficacious sign which initiates and confirms the believer in the ministry conferred" (Meyer and Vischer, "The Presence of Christ in Church and World: Final Report of the Dialogue between the World Alliance of Reformed Churches and the Secretariat for Promoting Christian Unity" [1977], §98).

Sacramental ordination thus becomes an expression of the *sola gratia,* the unmerited grace of God given to a person and to the church. "In this sacramental act, the gift of God is bestowed upon the ministers, with the promise of divine grace for their work and for their sanctification . . . and the Spirit seals those whom he has chosen and consecrated" (Anglican–Roman Catholic Conversations, *Ministry and Ordination* [1973, the "Canterbury Statement"], §15).

5. Ordination Rites

Rites of ordination differ mainly on the basis of whether ordination is looked upon as instrumental or expressive. An instrumental view holds that appropriate gifts of the Holy Spirit are conferred on the ordinand by prayer and the imposition of hands and that thereby the ordained becomes himself or herself a gift to the church for life. An expressive view of ordination holds that ordination itself does not convey any specific lifelong gifts but is rather a recognition by the church by its prayer for the person being ordained; the ordination is not seen as adding anything to the person's → baptism or prior personal calling.

The first known rite of ordination is that in the *Apostolic Tradition.* Several rites have survived from the fourth century, including the Liturgy of St. Serapion (d. after 360, bishop in Egypt) and those in the compilations known as the *Apostolic Constitutions* (ca. 350-80). From the fifth century, the *Statuta ecclesiae antiqua* (Ancient statutes of the church) has been preserved. The traditional view

originating in these rites is that the ordinand must be baptized and confirmed, must be male (see 7.4), and must fulfill certain personal standards of morality and education.

5.1. *Imposition of Hands*

Throughout the history of the church, the laying of hands on the ordinand's head has normally been at the center of ordination, although a number of other acts have also been included. The imposition of hands is based on Acts 6:1-6; 13:1-3; 1 Tim. 4:14; 5:22; and 2 Tim. 1:6. Calvin's *Ecclesiastical Ordinances* (1541) provided for abstention from the imposition of hands because of "superstition in the past," an unusual position among Reformed traditions. The Westminster Form of Presbyterial Church Government (1645) provides that "every minister of the word is to be ordained by imposition of hands and prayer, with → fasting, by those preaching presbyters to whom it doth belong." In some Congregationalist traditions — contrary to, for example, the Savoy Declaration (1658) — the extension of the "right hand of fellowship" or the imposition of hands on the shoulder has occasionally been substituted for the laying on of hands on the head.

5.2. *Symbols*

In various traditions a handing over of symbols of office was gradually introduced into ordination rites. Ordination to minor orders, from the middle of the fifth century, was conferred without the imposition of hands but by the handing over of instruments.

During the 10th century and through the → pontifical (liturgical book) of 1485, new rites that obscured the laying on of hands were introduced. → Thomas Aquinas (ca. 1225-74) and others held that the "tradition of the instruments" (*traditio* or *porrectio instrumentorum,* i.e., the solemn delivery to ordinands of instruments characteristic of their ministry) was an essential matter of the sacrament of ordination. This view was corrected by the main teachings of the 16th-century Reformers and, within Roman Catholicism, by *Sacramentum ordinis,* a 1948 apostolic constitution of Pius XII.

The practice vanished during the 16th century but has been reintroduced in Anglicanism and parts of → Lutheranism in the 19th and 20th centuries. In most episcopally ordered churches of the West today, the bishop is given miter, ring, and staff (crosier); the priest is given the chalice and paten, as prescribed in the Roman Catholic rite and as followed in some others. The giving of the Bible to priests is also a part of the tradition, and in churches with a threefold ordering of ministry, the book of the Gospels is given to deacons. The giving of a Bible is also increasingly a part of Protestant and free church ordination ceremonies.

Historically, the importance of the giving of these symbols of office was highlighted in the Investiture Controversy of the 11th and 12th centuries. It was the claim of the emperor and of princes that they had authority to appoint bishops and to invest them with ring and staff. The papacy, primarily in a decree of Urban II (1088-99), condemned the practice and reclaimed the authority of appointment.

5.3. Vestments

The giving of liturgical vestments to the ordinand occupies a central position in many rites of ordination. In many traditions the stole is given, and in other traditions several other liturgical vestments are also handed over. The stole, known in Eastern rites as the orarion, was originally the vestment of the deacon but today has been widely and ecumenically accepted as a sign of ordination; it is frequently described as a sign of the "yoke of Christ."

In the early church the ordinand also likely received vestments proper to particular orders: the chasuble (i.e., outermost garment, also known as planeta) for the priest, and the stole for the deacon. In the Byzantine Rite a priest is vested at ordination with the orarion, the zone (i.e., a beltlike cincture), and the phelonion (equivalent to the chasuble).

Both the practice and the importance of the handing over of instruments and vestments in the rite of ordination accelerated enormously when Frankish and German customs were integrated into church life. In the Roman Rite the conveyance of instruments and vestments had been a simple act preceding the consecration, but when Gallic and Germanic attitudes toward ceremony were accepted, the handing over of instruments and vestments was incorporated into the act itself. In the ordination of a bishop the miter was handed over; in a deacon's ordination, the dalmatic (i.e., overtunic) was given.

5.4. Anointing

The ordination rites of some traditions include anointing of the hands of priests, which expresses the sacerdotal character of priesthood. This anointing of the priest's hands is probably of Irish or Anglo-Saxon origin, appearing first in the Missale Francorum (6th or 7th cent.). The bishop is anointed on his head, a custom of Gallican origin probably introduced during the 9th century. This practice is intended to be a visual expression of the prayer for the charisms of the Holy Spirit. The pontificals of the 13th century also introduced the anointing of the bishop's hands, a custom originally part of the ordination to the episcopate of deacons who had not first been ordained priests.

5.5. The Ordinator

The identification of the proper person to perform ordinations — the ordinator — varies among Christian traditions. The questions involve who has been given the authority to ordain, and by whom. While early church practice seems to have differed in local churches, for Hippolytus the bishops (as a college?) are to be the sole ordinators of bishops, with no one else, not even presbyters, participating in the imposition of hands. In the seventh-century Gelasian Sacramentary presbyters are ordained by the bishop and other presbyters, similar to earlier practices. This practice perhaps reflects a lost collegiality of presbyters. Deacons were originally ordained by the bishop alone.

In churches today that hold to the historic succession of the episcopate, the only recognized ordinator is the bishop. The bishop is held to be a necessary and effective sign both of the apostolicity of the office conveyed and of the apostolicity of the church itself. The conviction is that apostolic teaching is exercised and embodied in persons specifically ordained by Christ and by the church (i.e., → apostles, bishops). The bishop is thus the embodiment and instrument of both Christ and the church (both in persona Christi and in persona ecclesiae).

The Evangelical Lutheran Church in America (ELCA), in its ecumenical agreement of full communion with the Episcopal Church, U.S.A. ("Called to Common Mission," implemented in 2001), calls for all new ELCA bishops to be consecrated in historic succession and for all → pastors to be ordained by bishops. There is considerable controversy over this point within the ELCA, and in a postagreement action the ELCA has provided for the possibility of exceptions, whereby a person, for reasons of confessional interpretation and conscience, may obtain permission to be ordained by a designated pastor instead of by bishops. During the last part of the 20th century, most of the larger Lutheran churches in Africa and Asia have had their bishops ordained in historical episcopal succession.

The idea that the → episcopacy is not itself a distinct order in the ministry of the church is of medieval origin; the → pope could then entrust to an → abbot the right to perform the ordination of priests. Normally, however, bishops with papal authorization ordained. During the 12th century Hugh of St. Victor (d. 1141) and Peter Lombard introduced a distinction between ordo and dignitas (dignity, honor), the latter being reserved to bishops. This distinction, coupled with the earlier view of Jerome (ca. 345-420) that there is no fundamental difference between bishops and priests, later became decisive for various strains within the 16th-century Reformation, which held that priests and bishops hold the same office.

In the Lutheran-Melanchthonian reformation of Germany, the Reformers recognized the authority of (Roman Catholic) bishops to ordain. But since these bishops refused to ordain "Lutherans," the first presbyterial ordinations were performed by the theological faculty at Wittenberg in 1535. Princes, however, even when they acted as emergency bishops, never performed ordinations. Nevertheless, the 16th-century Lutheran confessional documents profess a desire to maintain historic, or episcopal, order: "It is our greatest desire to retain the order of the church and the various ranks in the church — even though they were established by human authority. We know that → church discipline in the manner described by the ancient canons was instituted by the Fathers for a good and useful purpose" (CA Apol. 14.1).

In other → Lutheran churches, as in the Nordic countries, diocesan bishops have remained the persons possessing the power to ordain. In traditions that hold that the bishop is a presbyter with extended rights (e.g., to ordain), the juridical view (see 3) is usually dominant. This is still the case in some Lutheran traditions (Germany) and some Reformed traditions, even though the one exercising *episcopē* is called superintendent, president, or moderator.

In → free church traditions, following the Congregationalist reformation of the 17th century, the local congregation itself is the ordinator. In principle, ordination can be performed by any member of the local church, although the power to ordain is usually conveyed to a pastor.

6. Effects of Ordination

From the time of → Augustine (354-430) baptism, → confirmation, and ordination were held to bestow lasting effects described as *character* and ultimately as *character indelibilis,* or an indelible mark on, or quality of, the soul. These three sacraments can therefore be received but once, with the qualification that since ordination is not to an abstract ministry but to particular orders (deacon, priest, bishop), a person could receive three ordinations. This doctrine, explicitly formulated by Augustine and elaborated by the later Scholastics, can actually be traced back to → Cyprian of Carthage (ca. 200-258), who applied to baptism the expression "the Lord's seal" (*Ep.* 72.9), an expression in turn based on NT passages such as Eph. 1:13.

Most churches, even those that deny that ordination effects a *character indelibilis,* in practice hold that ordination is for life, a view not founded on a single theory but reflecting various interpretations either of the gift of the Spirit as given in ordination or the lasting effect of vows or oaths taken at ordination. The international Methodist–Roman Catholic conversation, in its "Dublin Report" (1976), well illustrates convergence: "Roman Catholics affirm that orders are indelible. Through the sacrament of orders, the ordained minister is sealed by the Holy Spirit and configured to Christ the Priest; he receives a permanent gift. . . . Methodists do not normally speak of the indelibility of ordination. But in the → Methodist Church, if a minister resigns from the exercise of his ministry . . . or is suspended or dismissed from it . . . his ordination is not repeated, and his orders are in this sense irremovable" (§§99-100).

6.1. *Absolute and Relative Ordination*

The term "absolute ordination" indicates that a person ordained to one of the three orders (deacon, priest, bishop) is ordained for life. The act cannot be repeated, even if the person's opportunities for exercising ministry are withdrawn. If subsequently the person is again appointed to the ministry, he or she will not be reordained. The person thus retains the office into which he or she has been ordained, even if the office is not exercised or the person is employed outside the church.

In contrast, the term "relative ordination" refers to the requirement that no one should be ordained without a "title of ordination," an assignment of the ordinand to a specific parish or congregation. The term is also used in those traditions, mostly Pentecostal, that ordain a person each time he or she takes up ministry in a local parish. In similar circumstances, other traditions "install" a person into specific ministry on the basis of prior ordination.

6.2. *Succession*

Succession in ordination, or apostolic succession *(successio apostolica),* is usually viewed as having three elements: the laying on of hands *(successio manibus);* the succession of bishops at the same seat, or place *(successio sedis);* and continuity in faith and doctrine *(successio doctrina).* Each of these elements is integrated into the ordination of bishops. Some traditions have focused succession on one of the three elements, but the idea of apostolic succession actually refers not to the ordination of deacons or presbyters/priests but to that of bishops.

In the early church the bishop was ordained by at least three fellow bishops, as testified by the *Apostolic Tradition* and the *Apostolic Constitutions.* Apostolic succession has been marked by the imposition of hands in ordination, attesting to fellowship in the apostolic faith, and the subsequent placing of the bishop on the *cathedra* (throne), or official seat. These rites have often been accompanied by other liturgical acts such as a deacon holding the book of the Gospels over the head of the candidate for the episcopacy, an epicletic act demonstrating the bishop's participation in apostolic teaching.

7. Validity of Ordination

In ecclesial traditions that take seriously the question of the validity of orders, the notion of validity refers to an action that can be canonically assured and controlled. To a large extent debates concerning the mutual recognition of ministries between churches are canonically rooted. In recent ecumenical debates, at least since the Faith and Order Assembly at Lausanne in 1927, this fact has been theologized, with the result that necessary distinctions between → theology and → church law have been overlooked. The question of the validity of ordinations arises from the question of a valid → Eucharist, such as the view of Ignatius of Antioch (ca. 35-ca. 107) that a valid Eucharist could be celebrated only by a priest authorized by a bishop (*Smyrn.* 8.1). In the Western church ever since Augustine, it is commonly held that even a heretical or schismatic bishop or priest can validly administer the sacraments, including, for such a bishop, ordination (→ Heresies and Schisms).

The 16th-century Reformers emphasized the validity of the sacraments more than that of office; indeed, the sacraments were held to be valid, "even though administered by unrighteous priests" (CA 8.2). Nevertheless, the clear assumption of the 16th-century confessional writings is that only ordained persons are to administer the sacraments. There were, however, two exceptions: → emergency baptism and absolution. In the 18th-century controversies between Lutheran orthodoxy and Pietists, the Pietists held that ordination must be completed by special gifts of the Spirit, including personal → conversion (§1), some taking the position that such conversion is the ground for the validity of the ministry of Word and sacrament. The orthodox countered by stressing that the grace given in ordination, rather than the personal qualities of the clergy, is sufficient for ministry in the church.

7.1. *Defectus*

The Decree on Ecumenism of Vatican II, *Unitatis redintegratio* (1964), asserts that there is a deficiency in the orders of all "separated churches and ecclesial communities in the West" (heading to §§19-24). The point is made that from the Roman Catholic perspective, Protestant churches and communities

"have not preserved the proper reality of the eucharistic mystery in its fullness, especially because of the absence of the sacrament of Orders [*sacramenti ordinis defectum*]" (§22). The nature of this "defect" has been intensively discussed in subsequent dialogues: from the view that nonsacramental ordination in non–Roman Catholic churches is totally lacking in theological significance, to the view that because Christian unity has not yet been actualized, all orders — including Roman Catholic — must therefore be regarded as defective. In practice, all churches and ecclesial communities that are not in full communion with each other are involved in this discussion.

7.2. *Reordination*

One of the most burning questions affecting the unity of the church, already raised by the → Donatist controversy at the beginning of the 4th century, is the matter of reordination. The issue became especially acute in Western churches after the reformations of the 16th century, for reordination was by no means a theoretical question when a member of the clergy converted from one church to another. Solutions depend on the criteria for valid ordination held by the receiving church. Additionally, proposals for "conditional ordinations" *(sub conditionis)* have at times been made under which a second ordination would be performed in such a way that it becomes clear that the ordaining church simply is not sure of the validity of the first ordination.

There is an obvious lack of mutuality in respect to the validity of ordinations. For example, the Roman Catholic Church accepts priests ordained by → Orthodox churches, but the Orthodox do not accept Roman Catholic priests. Also, the bull *Apostolicae curae* (1896) of Leo XIII went so far as to condemn Anglican orders as invalid through defect of both form and intention. Anglican churches, however, accept priests ordained in the Roman Catholic Church, though not, for example, Baptist ordinations. The question of reordination is especially crucial at present in conversations between uniting churches.

7.3. *Recognition of Ordinations*

The term "recognition of ordinations" was, in the modern meaning of the phrase, first used at the founding of the → Church of South India in 1947, a merger of Anglican, Methodist, and Congregational churches. For the first time a church in historic episcopal succession united with nonepiscopal churches. Ordinations in the previous church bodies were mutually recognized, and it was agreed that all ordinations in the new church would be performed by bishops together with pastors.

In the United States in 1989 the Consultation on Church Union (COCU), since January 2002 known as Churches Uniting in Christ, proposed liturgical orders for recognition or reconciliation of the ministries of bishops, presbyters, and deacons. Additionally, the ELCA-Episcopal agreement "Called to Common Mission" (see 5.5) provides for the acknowledgment or recognition by the Episcopal Church of the ministries of pastors/priests and bishops of the ELCA by a temporary suspension, in this one case only, of the 17th-century restriction that "no persons are allowed to exercise the offices of bishop, priest, or deacon in this Church unless they are so ordained, or have already received such ordination with the laying on of hands by bishops who are themselves duly qualified to confer Holy Orders" ("Preface to the Ordination Rites," Book of Common Prayer [1979]). Subsequent ordinations/consecrations to the episcopacy in both churches are to be mutual, so that over time the ELCA will have adopted historic succession.

The recognition of ordinations presupposes agreement by churches on the form and content of ordination. Still relevant to the issue and still debated are questions such as, To what extent do the wordings of official teachings from past history remain normative today? and Are there limits to a pluriform system of ministries in a communion of churches?

7.4. *Ordination of Women*

An ecumenical issue of considerable importance is rooted in divergences between churches in respect to the ordination of women and, by extension, in respect to the validity of ordinations performed by women bishops. The debate is largely a 20th-century phenomenon, and the discussion has been focused mainly on the ordination of women to the ministry of Word and sacrament. In this debate, the fact that women were ordained to the diaconate in the early church, at least in some local churches of the West and in the Byzantine tradition, has surprisingly aroused little interest, probably because of a longstanding focus on ordination to the presbyterate.

Arguments against the ordination of women to the presbyterate and episcopate center on Christ's appointing only men as his apostles, a restriction that has been tradition for more than 19 centuries. The ordination of women into the presbyterate and episcopate is seen as destroying the unity and catholicity of the church. Arguments in favor of such ordination center on a conviction that unity and catholicity are defective unless they reflect complete inclusiveness in relation to the ministry; to inhibit women from ordained ministry on grounds of their gender only extends the historical suppression of women. Proponents on both sides of the question underline their arguments by reference to Scripture, to tradition (esp. the early church), and to the authoritative teachings of the churches. Those in favor of the ordination of women also often use arguments based on modern sociological and anthropological research.

The first ordination of a woman as a minister in a recognized denomination took place in 1853 in the Congregational Church in New York State, although the ordinand was dismissed a year later. By the end of the 19th century, American women had been ordained in the Disciples of Christ (→ Christian Church [Disciples of Christ]), the Methodist Protestant Church, some Baptist churches, and the Congregational Church. Congregationalists in England and Wales started to ordain women in 1917. Among the churches with a more catholic view of ordination, the Church of Sweden began to ordain women to the priesthood in 1960. A woman was ordained priest in the → Anglican Communion in Hong Kong in 1944, an action condemned by the Lambeth Conference in 1948, which caused the ordinand to cease functioning as a priest until 1970. Starting with the Province of Hong Kong, most Anglican churches today ordain women as deacons and priests and increasingly as bishops. The first women bishops were ordained or consecrated in the Methodist (1980), Anglican (1989), and Lutheran (1992) traditions. Also, some → Old Catholic churches in Germany, Switzerland, and Austria ordain women as deacons and priests, a practice not accepted by other Old Catholic churches.

The Roman Catholic Church has taken the position that it has no mandate to break tradition by ordaining women (*Inter insignores* [1976] of Paul VI, *Ordinatio sacerdotalis* [1994] of John Paul II, and "Inadmissibility of Women to the Ministerial Priesthood" [1995] of the Congregation for the Doctrine of the Faith). This position is also held strongly by Eastern and → Oriental Orthodox churches. Most Pentecostal and many → evangelical churches take a similar position. Indeed, most Christians in the world today belong to churches that do not ordain women.

8. Ordination as an Ecclesial Act

Ordination is clearly an ecclesial act. There is ecumenical agreement that "it is God who calls, ordains and sends the ministers of Word and Sacrament in the church. He does this through the whole people, acting by means of those who have been given authority so to act in the name of God and of the whole church" (Anglican-Lutheran Conversation, "Pullach Report" [1973], §78). Ordination is thus a structural factor in ecclesiology and basic to the self-understanding of each particular tradition. It thus involves the whole church, including the laity. In his first letter to the Corinthians (ca. 96), Clement of Rome advanced the idea of historic succession, commenting that ordination presupposes the approval of the church (*1 Clem.* 44.3). The same idea can be found in the *Apostolic Tradition.*

During the late Middle Ages, however, the church was represented by the clergy, and the priesthood was exclusively restricted to priests and bishops; in this way the congregation lost any meaningful role. One of the main demands of the Lutheran and Calvinist reformers of the 16th century was that ordination should take place in the worshiping community, a proposal that was not always implemented in Lutheran-Melanchthonian churches. Today the participation of the whole church is assumed in all traditions but made concrete in a variety of ways.

To view ordination as an ecclesial act is thus to oppose the functionalist conception of ordination of the 18th century, according to which the "usefulness" of the ordained ministry was fundamental. The perception of ordination as an ecclesial act also contradicts the idea, developed during the 19th century, of the ministry as a profession, as well as subsequent views, influenced by certain psychological theories, that define ordained ministry in terms of the concept of role.

8.1. *Baptism*
In modern theology and ecclesiology baptism has often been presented as the fundamental rite of ordination in the church. Thus, for example, the *COCU Consensus* (1985) maintains, despite its epicletic and sacramental view of ordination (7.37), that "as persons are initiated into the faith, they are, in a true sense, ordained to a caring priesthood" (7.28).

This idea, however, also used in Orthodox theology, lacks support from both the NT and the early church. Nor can it be found in the 16th century in Luther. To be sure, when Luther tried to revive the idea of the church as "a royal priesthood" (1 Pet. 2:9), he did say that the ordained minister also is consecrated, anointed, and born in baptism. To Luther this wording does not mean, however, that a person is ordained in baptism, since baptism does not constitute being rightly called by the church (WA 12.178). Baptism, however, remains constitutive of the church, the essential and necessary element for all ministries in the church.

8.2. *Priesthood of All Baptized Believers*
One of the main questions discussed in almost all Christian traditions is the relation between the priesthood of all baptized believers and ordination to the ministry of Word and sacrament. In his early writings Luther appealed to the "general priesthood" but subsequently made little or no reference to it; Melanchthon generally avoided the idea. The view — now often widely cited — that ordination and the ordained ministry are rooted in the priesthood of all believers is not supported by the ordination rites of the 16th century.

Ordination to the office of the church is essentially different from an act of consecration — for which Luther used the term *Weihe* — which is to be seen as reception into the general priesthood of the church. It is notable, however, that since the 19th century, traditions that reject the idea of a sacrificial ordained ministry or of a ministerial priesthood still ground ordained ministry in a sacrificial category, namely, the church as a royal priesthood. Today, the participation of the whole church in ordination is present in all traditions, although made concrete in a variety of ways.

Bibliography: D. L. BARTLETT, *Ministry in the NT* (Minneapolis, 1991) • P. C. BOUTENEFF and A. D. FALCONER, eds., *"Episkopé" and Episcopacy and the Quest for Visible Unity: Two Consultations* (Geneva, 1990) • S.-E. BRODD, *Diakonatet. Från ecklesiologi till pastoral praxis* (Uppsala, 1992) • J. A. BURGESS and J. GROS, eds., *Growing Consensus: Church Dialogues in the United States, 1962-1991* (New York, 1995) • J. N. COLLINS, *Are All Christians Ministers?* (Newtown, Austral., 1992) • B. COOKE, *Ministry to Word and Sacraments: History and Theology* (Philadelphia, 1976) • L. W. COUNTRYMAN, *The Language of Ordination: Ministry in an Ecumenical Context* (Philadelphia, 1992) • L. ECKERDAL, *"Genom bön och handpåläggning." Vignings-jämte installationshandlingar–liturgiska utvecklingslinjer* (Stockholm, 1985) • J. H. ELLIOTT, *The Elect and the Holy: An Exegetical Exmination of 1 Peter 2:4-10* (Leiden, 1966) • P. C. EMPIE and T. A. MURPHY, eds., *Lutherans and Catholics in Dialogue*, vol. 4, *Eucharist and Ministry* (Minneapolis, 1979) • K. K. FITZGERALD, *Women Deacons in the Orthodox Church: Called to Holiness and Ministry* (Brookline, Mass., 1999) • J. GROS, H. MEYER, and W. G. RUSCH, eds., *Growth in Agreement II: Reports and Agreed Statements of Ecumenical Conversations on a World Level, 1982-1998* (Geneva and Grand Rapids, 2000) • G. KRETSCHMAR, *Das bischöfliche Amt. Kirchengeschichtliche und ökumenische Studien zur Frage des kirchlichen Amtes* (Göttingen, 1999) • A. MAFFEIS, *Il ministero nella chiesa. Uno studio del dialogo cattolico-*

luterano (1967-1984) (Rome, 1991) • H. MEYER and L. VISCHER, eds., *Growth in Agreement [I]: Reports and Agreed Statements of Ecumenical Conversations on a World Level* (New York and Geneva, 1984) • J. F. PUGLISI, *The Process of Admission to Ordained Ministry: A Comparative Study* (3 vols.; Collegeville, Minn., 1996-2001) • J. H. P. REUMANN, *Ministries Examined: Laity, Clergy, Women, and Bishops in a Time of Change* (Minneapolis, 1987) • E. SIGURBJÖRNSSON, *Ministry within the People of God: The Development of the Doctrines on the Church and on the Ministry in the Second Vatican Council's "De Ecclesia"* (Lund, 1974).

SVEN-ERIK BRODD

Organ, Organ Music

1. The Pipe Organ
2. History
3. Music

The organ is a keyboard instrument that produces sound by forcing air through flue and reed pipes (pipe organ), over metal reeds (harmonium), by electromagnetic pulses (Hammond Organ), or by computer-analyzed electronics. Prototypes include the water-driven *hydraulus,* as well as the bellows-driven *portative* (easily transported), *positive* (larger, often stationary), and *regal* (reed instrument). We also have composite, multimanual, and pedal instruments consisting of several positives and pedal divisions.

1. The Pipe Organ
Since the invention of the pipe organ in 250 B.C. by Alexandrian engineer Ktesibios, building technique has greatly evolved. The church's liturgical demands (→ Liturgy) further influence building style. Common traits shared by all pipe organs are (1) one or more sets (ranks) of sounding pipes, (2) a windchest to store air, (3) a mechanical or electric pump or bellows to supply air, and (4) a keyboard to direct the air into pipes (see J. Perrot, xix).

2. History
The hydraulus was popular in the → Roman Empire for court and civic functions, as well as for circuses. In the mid-5th century the less cumbersome portative and the larger positive entirely replaced the hydraulus. The sacking of Rome in A.D. 410 and the empire's move to → Byzantium ended for a time the organ's development in the West. Though still built in the East, the organ remained technically unim-

proved. Western interest was sparked again during the Carolingian period. An 11th-century priest, Georgius, built several instruments, paving the way for the organ's acceptance by the church. The church, previously skeptical in view of the profane usage of the instrument, shifted its critique to the noisy bellows and action, prompting further refinements.

In the 15th century stop mechanisms allowed the organist to play one rank of pipes at a time (tone-channel chest, trackers). Until then the entire ensemble of pipes sounded (Blockwerk) when the organ was played. Until the 13th century flue (simple whistle) pipes were the norm. Reed pipes (metal or wood vibrating slat) appeared in Dijon in the 13th century, enlarging the tonal resources. Multirank, reed portatives (Regal) were common by the 15th century, comprising imitative stops (vox humana, ranket, etc.). Positives of flues and/or reeds accompanied or played in alternation with the choir. Mechanical coupling and transfer action (15th cent.) made possible the combining of several positives into one multimanual instrument placed in the nave or west gallery. The old Blockwerk became the great organ (Hauptwerk). Other divisions included a positive at the organist's back (Rückpositiv), immediately above the manuals (Brustwerk), and others above, beside, and behind the main division (Oberwerk, Seitenwerk, Hinterwerk, Unterwerk, Kronwerk, Echo, Schwellwerk). Some divisions contained characteristic stops (Hornwerk, Bombarde). Organ pedals, which originally pulled down notes from a manual, eventually controlled separate divisions (16th cent.), often placed as towers on either side of the case. Builders in the 17th and 18th centuries (esp. E. Compenius, A. Schnitger, G. Silbermann, J. M. Stumm, and C. J. Riepp) brought the organ to mature design. The → baroque period saw the proliferation of novelty stops imitating thunder, birds, and drums (J. Gabler, esp. his fully restored organ at the basilica of Weingarten, 1737-50).

The 19th and early 20th centuries introduced technological refinements (e.g., the Barker lever, crescendo), developing an instrument in keeping with → Romantic ideals (Cavaillé-Coll). Pneumatic, electropneumatic, and finally electric action made possible gargantuan instruments engulfing the → congregation or audience. Builders interested in symphonic style made possible a subtle increase or decrease of sound and numerous contrasting effects achieved by electric stop action. The tonal integrity of individual stops within the overall ensemble, the foundation of design during the golden age of the 16th-18th centuries, was sacrificed for massive effects and flexibility.

Substantially unaltered older instruments displayed the merits of classic design in their voicing, action, and complementary divisions. Organists wished a more intimate, immediate control of performance. A. → Schweitzer (1875-1965), C.-M. Widor (1844-1937), and others, familiar with earlier organs by F.-H. Cliquot (1732-90), A. Schnitger (1648-1719), and Andreas (1678-1734) and Gottfried (1683-1753) Silbermann, renewed interest in organ design in the 1920s (the Orgelbewegung, or organ movement). An organ built in 1922 following specifications by M. Praetorius (1571-1621) in his *Syntagma musicum* (1617, vol. 2 of *De organographia*) demonstrated the merits of such instruments. Increasing numbers of builders adopted principles of construction rediscovered during the movement, which composers such as P. Hindemith (1895-1963) and H. Distler (1908-42) applied in compositions.

3. Music

The first printed keyboard music was generic, suitable for organ as well as other instruments. Organ settings of choral works *(intablature)* and newly composed accompaniments for the cantus firmus *(organisare)* were popular. Early collections contained → motet intabulations, → mass versets, and → dances (e.g., Robertsbridge Codex, 14th cent.; Faenza MS, 15th cent.; C. Paumann, *Lochamer Liederbuch,* 15th cent.; *Buxheimer Orgelbuch,* ca. 1470).

Roman Catholic influence on organ building in Italy (esp. in the Ambrosian ceremonial) resulted in organs consisting almost exclusively of choruses of flue (as opposed to reed) stops. Compositions included ricercare and canzone versets (mass, Magnificat), preludes *(intonazioni)* to the mass, and toccatas (free chordal and scalar passage work) for specific moments (e.g., the elevation). Leading composers were G. Gabrielli (ca. 1554-1612), C. Merulo (1533-1604), and G. Frescobaldi (1583-1643). C. Antegnati (1549-1624), G. Diruta (ca. 1554-after 1610), and others published appropriate registration formulas for "affects."

Spain, France, and southern Germany, subject to similar liturgical demands, produced strikingly different instruments and music. Spanish organs had few manuals but built up large families of contrasting flues and reeds on divided keyboards (different stops drawn for the top and bottom of the same keyboard). Compositions include *diferencias* (variations), *tientos* (like the ricercar), mass and Magnificat versets, and Office hymns (A. de Cabezón, J. Cabenilles). Aggressive batteries of reeds prompt-

ed pieces imitating battles. France developed reeds and mutations (e.g., tierce, nazard, cornet) displayed in suites of "couplets." J. Titelouze (ca. 1563-1633), N. de Grigny (1672-1703), F. Couperin (1668-1733), N. A. Lèbegue (ca. 1630-1702), and L.-C. Daquin (1694-1772) wrote settings for the Mass and Office, as well as variations on popular noels. Southern Germany drew on Italian and French models, producing organs with modest pedal divisions. J. J. Froberger (1616-67) produced liturgical pieces, free toccatas, and praeambula.

In the 16th century the → Reformation had a profound and immediate effect on organ building and music. U. → Zwingli (1484-1531) and J. → Calvin (1509-64) raised theological objections to the use of instruments in public worship, with Zwingli banning even singing (→ Hymnody). Dutch churches housed large organs purchased with civic funds and played before and after worship. J. P. Sweelinck (1562-1621) wrote variations and toccatas for such concerts. He taught numerous other composers, including S. Scheidt (1587-1654), H. Scheidemann (ca. 1596-1663), and the Englishman J. Bull (1562/63-1628).

Influenced by Continental → Calvinism, English → Puritans banned elaborate liturgical music, including organ music. The Lutheran reform supported instrumental and choral music, often based on the congregational hymn. Chorale preludes (with the tune in manual or pedal, figuration or fugal writing for accompaniment) or partitas (variations on the chorale) introduced hymns and provided alternations. G. Böhm (1661-1733), V. Lübeck (1654-1740), D. Buxtehude (1637-1707), J. Pachelbel (1653-1706), and J. S. Bach (1685-1750) are among the most notable composers. Freely composed, occasionally sectional praeambula ending with a fugal section (Buxtehude, Bach), trio sonatas of three independent voices on two manuals and pedal, and concerti transcriptions were written as teaching, liturgical, and concert pieces (Bach, J. L. Krebs, J. G. Walther).

Further developments included symphonic treatment of chorale tunes (M. Reger) and, in the 19th and 20th centuries, rhapsodic works such as symphonies, suites, and sonatas (Reger, Widor, A. Guilmant, L. Vierne, M. Duruflé). Avant-garde techniques have brought music beyond the limits of traditional notation, harmonies, and technique.

→ Church Music; Church Musicians; Theology and Music

Bibliography: P.-G. ANDERSEN, *Organ Building and Design* (Oxford, 1969) • J. FESPERMAN, *Two Essays on Or-*

gan Design* (Sunbury, 1975) • J. Perrot, *The Organ from Its Invention in the Hellenistic Period to the End of the Thirteenth Century* (Oxford, 1971) • R. N. Roth, comp., *Wond'rous Machine: A Literary Anthology Celebrating the Organ* (Lanham, Md., 2000) • N. Thistlethwaite and G. Weber, eds., *The Cambridge Companion to the Organ* (Cambridge, 1998) • D. G. Türk, *Daniel Gottlieb Türk on the Role of the Organist in Worship (1787)* (ed. M. A. G. Woolard; Lanham, Md., 2000) • P. Williams, "Organ," *NGDMM* 13.710-79 • P. F. Williams, *The European Organ, 1450-1850* (Bloomington, Ind., 1966); idem, *The King of Instruments: How Churches Came to Have Organs* (London, 1993); idem, *The Organ in Western Culture, 750-1250* (Cambridge, 1993).

Robert D. Hawkins

Organism

1. Term
2. Biology and Natural Philosophy
3. Political and Religious Analogies

1. Term

The term "organism" (from Gk. *organon* and Lat. *organum,* "instrument, sensory organ"), in common use since the 18th century, denotes an integrated, self-reproducing whole that in view of its inner teleology is more than the sum of its parts, even though the process of self-realization is possible only through the functions of the parts. In the biological and philosophical sense (→ Nature; Philosophy of Nature), "organism" has the basic sense of the structure of a living creature with all its individual phenomena (→ Life 2). We find an analogous use in politics (→ Society; State) and religion (→ Church). Although causal and mechanistic interpretations (→ Causality) are still applied to the notion of organism as the quintessential definition of living beings, the focus in philosophy is → teleology, so that today organism is seen in antithesis to causal mechanism.

2. Biology and Natural Philosophy

2.1. The teleological view of organism goes back to Aristotle (384-322 b.c.; → Aristotelianism). Taking issue with the pre-Socratic idea of a cyclic balance of elementary ontic antitheses (*isonomia;* → Greek Philosophy), Aristotle developed his doctrine of the immaterial → soul as that which gives movement, purpose, and essence to the living body, whose "entelechy" it is (i.e., it actualizes the soul's potential). Because of the soul we may think of nat-

ural bodies as purposeful instruments (organs). After the analogy of nature and → technology, the parts of a living being are also organs insofar as they discharge specific functions for the superior whole. (But, for example, a hand that has been severed has only the name "hand.")

The biology and medicine of antiquity continued to think along Aristotelian lines. As modified by → Stoicism and Neoplatonism, this doctrine lived on into medieval → Scholasticism, which saw in living creatures a graded → revelation of the Creator.

2.2. In the → modern period, under the impact of empirical research in the later Middle Ages, the teleological interpretation of "organism" gradually lost ground to a mechanistic understanding. For R. Descartes (1596-1650; → Cartesianism) corporeal organisms were automatic machines whose movements arose from the clocklike arrangement of their organs. On the basis of the dualism of thought and extension, human beings alone, in virtue of their → reason, occupy a special position in the kingdom of mathematically calculable creatures. Over against this view vitalism saw the *anima* as vitalizing the body (G. E. Stahl).

G. W. Leibniz (1646-1716) formulated a compromise between teleological and mechanistic views in his doctrine of "preestablished harmony" between the mechanistic world of the body and the goal-oriented world of the soul. For him bodily organisms down to the smallest parts are machines, but the related souls, or entelechies, are higher, indivisible monads that individually display the principles of finality in the universe. With the question of the development of organisms, however, the basic difference of approach flared up afresh.

2.3. I. Kant (1724-1804; → Kantianism) linked the divergent principles of natural philosophy by locating them in the knowing subject. In the *Critique of Pure Reason* he set up a framework of categories for causal natural science, but in the *Critique of Judgment,* with the concept of a natural end, he formulated a regulative principle, valid only subjectively as a maxim of reflection, for the evaluation of the products of nature, which are both cause and effect. This teleological self-reference is basic to Kant's understanding of the organism as not merely a machine. As in the organism the parts in both their form and their existence are possible only in virtue of their relation to the whole and to one another, so the whole rests on the relation to the parts and the relation of the parts to one another. In the organism everything is both end and means. The inner teleology that obtains in self-organization rules out creation by an outside artist. The organism is an analog of life, though naturally with an → epistemological caveat.

2.4. Along with matter (→ Materialism), organism was a central category in the nature philosophy of F. W. J. Schelling (1775-1854; → Idealism). For the sake of → freedom, and as the premise of self-consciousness, Schelling first used the concepts of → transcendental philosophy, then those of the philosophy of identity, to make a unifying absolute out of ideality and reality. He linked the Kantian definition of organism to the contrary principles of irritability and sensibility, the self-reproduction of the whole and sexual distinction, the unity of the vital process and infinite individuation, so that the organism lives on in a cyclic balance of ever new antitheses. As an expression of nature in God and God in nature, and as the point of contact with spirit, the organism logically takes precedence over what is inorganic and mechanistic; it is a mode of freedom in the sphere of natural necessity. The Romantic philosophy of nature (C. G. Carus, K. F. Burdach, L. Oken) came under Schelling's influence.

2.5. The philosophy of nature of G. W. F. Hegel (1770-1831), which presents the idea in its otherness, contains a triad of structured organisms, of which the highest, the animal, exists as subjectivity in an inner integration and unity. The life of the organism in stages is determined by the logical → categories: *morphological individuality* as an inner relation, *assimilation* as an outer relation, and *relation to the species* as a self-relation through others. Included in the last of these is the → death of the natural individual and the possibility of transition to the concrete universality of spirit.

2.6. Helped by the great forward steps in empirical knowledge, a mechanistic view of life established itself in the 19th century (H. Lotze, J. Moleschott, E. Haeckel). This view found support in evolutionary insights into the importance of mutation and selection (C. Darwin; → Evolution), which, with the idea of organism as a combination of power-seeking forces (F. → Nietzsche), were applied to the conflict of the parts of an organism (W. Roux). Yet vitalistic and holistic voices (respectively, H. Driesch and A. Meyer-Abich) were also heard as the 19th century gave way to the 20th. An a priori theory, however, defined the irreducible quality of the organism in terms of the relation to its limit and what lay beyond (H. Plessner).

In the commonly accepted view of the organism as a graduated structure of open systems in a fleeting harmony that minimizes an increase in entropy (L. von Bertalanffy), mechanistic and cybernetic approaches combined, supplemented by a theory of "bionomous" complexes aiding the working of the organs (K. E. Rothschuh). The arising of self-organization, along with mutation and metabolism, is presently seen by biochemists and biophysicists as determined, but individual and historical forms remain indeterminate (M. Eigen). → Chance and necessity were thus combined. The cybernetic formula "self-organization," which has a causal origin, also finds a place for "teleonomous" elements because the purpose cannot be separated from the → self. Accelerated advances in genome research have expanded the basic philosophical question of the relationship between efficient and final causes, a question discussed in many variations, by adding the question of just how one is to conceive or understand the materiality of the life process together with the genetic information that programs that very process.

3. Political and Religious Analogies

3.1. Although a teleologically oriented, metaphoric use of "organism" in politics dates only from the later 18th century, analogies between living bodies and social structures may be found already in antiquity. Going back to the admonitory *homonoia* literature of the fifth century B.C. (e.g., the fable of Menenius Agrippa, recounted by Livy, about the revolt of the members against the stomach), the analogy of the body and the state is common in Plato (427-347 B.C.; → Platonism) and Aristotle, though they use it for different purposes.

In Plato the state and its larger structure resemble, on a smaller scale, individuals and their organizing of the spheres of the soul. Aristotle, however, criticized the idea gained from individual life that the state is a unity, since this view does not allow for the multiplicity of state members, which are all different, although functionally related. Under Stoic influence the analogy of the organism came to be applied to humanity as a whole (Cicero) and even to the universe (Seneca). Roman thinking about the state (→ Roman Empire) related the *corpus*, viewed as an organism, to the *civitas, res publica, imperium, regnum*, political estates, and *collegia*. The stress fell on the unity of the members under the leadership of a head.

3.2. For → Paul the → congregation is the body of Christ, integrated according to the gifts of grace. It is meaningless to rank the members of the body, for they all belong to Christ. Since Christ constitutes the body, the emphasis lies on unity, on the precedence of the whole, and on obligation to the weak. In the deutero-Pauline tradition Christ is the head, to which the body is to grow in → eschatological development. Church history later witnessed a → hierarchical structuring of the institutional church on this basis (→ Church 2.2.4-6).

3.3. → Augustine (354-430; → Augustine's Theology) took up the ideas of Paul and Greco-Roman antiquity and passed them on to the → Middle Ages in his doctrine of the two cities at war with one another in → salvation history. The disparagement of autonomous secular rule that we find in Augustine became even stronger as time passed.

For the early Middle Ages *regnum* was part of the one mystical body of Christ under the *sacerdotium*. In the High Middle Ages the conflict between the two authorities resulted in the idea of two separate corporations. John of Salisbury (ca. 1115-80) was the first to measure the hierarchically integrated state by the standard of the human organism as God had created it.

→ Thomas Aquinas (ca. 1225-74; → Thomism) related the organism of state and the spiritual fellowship by a hierarchy of ends. The supremacy of the soul over the body supported that of the spiritual and temporal authorities over the people, but Marsilius of Padua (ca. 1280-ca. 1343) equated citizen legislators with the soul and found in rulers the organ that serves them.

3.4. With the mechanizing of the concept of organism in the early modern period, the → state was compared metaphorically to a machine. According to T. Hobbes (1588-1679), the state is like an artificial person whose soul is the sovereign, and individuals, who threaten one another in a state of nature, subject themselves to it by contract. The metaphor of the machine came into German thinking by way of S. Pufendorf (1632-94) and had a great impact upon 18th-century political theory. We find it in absolutist thought, though it indirectly limited the freedom of the sovereign.

3.5. In antithesis to the metaphor of the state as machine, the French → Revolution introduced the concept of → organization. The people set up the government and aim at popular participation. Kant clarified this concept, which involves the interaction of part and whole, by pointing to the organized products of nature. Along these lines J. G. Fichte (1762-1814) figuratively described a state constituted by a contract that protects the individual. Since without a state it is uncertain who will first be attacked by whom, each person necessarily commits what is theirs to the state. The state, then, is a true and not merely a theoretical totality, grounded in itself.

3.6. The younger Schelling and Hegel sought to depose the machinelike state, which is hostile to liberty. Schelling first conceived of the "absolute organism" in the form of a state that, like a work of art, would combine freedom and necessity in something real, but later he doubted the feasibility of a state of this kind. Hegel (→ Hegelianism) described as an organism a state (and its constitution) that would be characterized by separation of powers. In virtue of its self-reference, such a state would not be exclusively oriented to the protection of individuals. As a permeating unity of universality and individuality, it would be the reality of the moral idea.

The main concepts in the ethics of F. D. E. → Schleiermacher (1768-1834; → Schleiermacher's Theology) rest not only on the duality of individuality and fellowship but also on the distinction between organizing activity, which makes nature an organ of reason, and symbolizing activity, by which reason represents itself in nature. The organism stands for the limiting value of the complete interrelation of the two factors.

3.7. → Romanticism (A. Müller, F. von Baader) sharply opposed natural law theories and revolutionary theories that regard the state as the product of merely human activity. It found in the organism of the state a historical totality that developed historically, that resulted from the formations of people and → nation, that was hierarchically integrated, that was above individuals, and that involved a balancing of opposites. Personalized in the monarch, the state derived from nature (religiously understood), and it was theologically transfigured after the medieval model.

3.8. In both the Roman Catholic Tübingen school (J. S. Drey, J. A. Möhler) and some branches of neo-Lutheranism (T. Kliefoth), the organism embodied a model of church history and dogmatic history that, in antithesis to ideas of decay, progress, and consummation (→ Philosophy of History), projected a thought of development. In conservative, antiliberal neo-Lutheranism "organism" also became a central ecclesiological concept. On the one hand, the church, objectified in the ministry and the confession, was viewed as an organ of divine action (F. J. Stahl). On the other hand, "organism" stood for the common activity of the faith of the community (F. W. J. Höfling). Both views rejected an understanding of the church as the sum of its individual members. They were finally mediated in the concept of the church as an organism that embraces office and community and in which Christ, the Head, gives himself a living body (T. Harnack; → Theology in the Nineteenth and Twentieth Centuries).

3.9. In constitutional discussions in 19th-century Germany, the leading idea was that of the state as a moral and spiritual organism (J. C. Bluntschli). French and English → sociology, however, preferred the biological model for describing the consensus of the whole, which, despite an advanced division of labor, is needed for self-preservation (A. Comte). The biological model was also used for linking together differentiation and integration in a figure of general and self-regulating dependence after the pattern of the theory of selection (H. Spencer).

In the 20th century the concept of system absorbed that of social organism (T. Parsons). A social system that involves membership and that produces specific achievements and modes of conduct came to be called an organization (N. Luhmann).

3.10. In German sociology during the first half of the 20th century, the distinction between a fellowship *(Gemeinschaft),* regarded as a living organism, and a society *(Gesellschaft),* understood as a mechanical artifact (F. Tönnies), still exerted an influence. Also, an anti-individualistic → universalism viewed all society as a spiritual superorganism graded according to values (O. Spann; → Values, Ethics of). The organism analogy, however, did not prevail. A leading reason was its closeness to National Socialist ideology (P. Krannhals; → Fascism), made possible by its irrational placing of the whole above the individual and the understanding of organism in biological and racial terms.

The fact that "organism" can have so many figurative meanings also made its use in sociology difficult. Historically, it can denote the clocklike functioning of the totality, the political participation of citizens, or the subjection of citizens to tutelage in the name of the people as a whole.

Bibliography: D. Des Chene, *Spirits and Clocks: Machine and Organism in Descartes* (Ithaca, N.Y., 2001) • M. Eigen, *Steps toward Life: A Perspective on Evolution* (Oxford, 1992) • H. Haken, A. Karlquist, and U. Svedin, eds., *The Machine as Metaphor and Tool* (Berlin, 1993) • H. Jonas, *The Phenomenon of Life: Toward a Philosophical Biology* (New York, 1966) • R. C. Lewontin, *The Triple Helix: Gene, Organism, and Environment* (Cambridge, Mass., 2000) • E. Mayr, *The Growth of Biological Thought: Diversity, Evolution, and Inheritance* (Cambridge, Mass., 1982) • M. M. Murphy and L. A. J. O'Neill, eds., *What Is Life? The Next Fifty Years: Speculations on the Future of Biology* (Cambridge, 1995) • K. E. Rothschuh, *History of Physiology* (Huntington, N.Y., 1973) • A. I. Tauber, ed., *Organism and the Origins of Self* (Dordrecht, 1991).

Jörg Dierken

Organization

"Organization," a term with many meanings, derives from Gk. *ergon/organon* by way of Lat. *organum* and *organisatio.* Two related and complementary meanings now hold the field: (1) a dynamic, process-oriented sense that stresses the intentional establishment of an order, structure, or system and that sees in organization an instrument; and (2) a more static and structural sense that stresses the established order, structure, or system (i.e., the result of organizing). Either way, the term may be either descriptive or analytic. In the static sense it may denote a group of people who work together to achieve a common goal (e.g., an enterprise, business, institute, society, → church, or → political party). It may also denote a system of action (→ Action Theory), an institutionally regulated nexus of social interactions reflecting a certain regularity of social action.

In view of the complexity of what is called organization, scholars use various competing or supplementary perspectives, approaches, and theoretical models taken, for example, from → social ethics, → theology, and → sociology. On such views organizations are collectives that, independently of persons, function like persons for action, study, the assembling of → information, guidance, and the making of decisions. In this regard they differ from groups, which can act only through individuals who use them as their instruments.

In sociological analysis the best approach seems to be that which understands organization as a special type of social structure or system founded by specific people for the achievement of specific ends, in a specific form, with a → hierarchical constitution, complex, relatively long-lasting, and structured. It is made up of people of different origin and only partially agreed interests who work with one another in different roles, who look to a common center of control and decision, who keep cooperation within an institutionally (→ Institution) regulated framework, and whose activities and their results may be ascribed to the collective as agent or legal person. The structure is the complex result of a variety of related rational actions on the part of the individuals who as leaders, supporters, or honorary members, whether temporarily or permanently, belong either directly or indirectly to the organization, take part in its activities, and profit from them.

Such an approach makes it possible to analyze not merely ecclesiastical or social organizations, to take into account as well the theological aspects, yet also to deal with the problematic interrelation of roles and individuality in an organization, paying special attention to the spheres and forces of action and the functions and consequences of membership. Also on this view one may set up a typology of organization, for example, according to the principle of cui bono (lit. "to whose advantage?" i.e., societies with special aims, business enterprises, service organizations, welfare organizations; see W. R. Scott) or in terms of the compliance of the members (through force, utility, or values).

→ Class and Stratum; Mass; Organism; Politics; Society; Sociology of Churches, State

Bibliography: G. BÜSCHGES and M. ABRAHAM, Einführung in die Organisationssoziologie (2d ed.; Stuttgart, 1997) • P. A. CLARK, Organisations in Action: Competition between Contexts (London, 2000) • S. R. CLEGG and C. HARDY, eds., Studying Organization: Theory and Method (London, 1999) • R. H. HALL, Organizations: Structures, Processes, and Outcomes (6th ed.; Englewood Cliffs., N.J., 1996) • M. MAURICE and A. SORGE, eds., Embedding Organizations: Societal Analysis of Actors, Organizations, and Socio-economic Context (Amsterdam, 2000) • W. R. SCOTT, Organizations: Rational, Natural, and Open Systems (4th ed.; Upper Saddle River, N.J., 1998).

GÜNTER BÜSCHGES

Oriental Orthodox Churches

1. Background and Beliefs
2. Ecumenical Relations

1. Background and Beliefs

The Oriental Orthodox churches, part of the worldwide family of Eastern Christians, comprise the → Armenian Apostolic Church (Catholicate of Holy Etchmiadzin and Catholicate of Sis), → Coptic Orthodox Church, Eritrean Orthodox Church (→ Eritrea 2), → Ethiopian Orthodox Church, Malankara Orthodox Syrian Church (sometimes referred to as the Indian Orthodox Church; → Syrian Orthodox Churches in India), and the → Syrian (Syriac) Orthodox Church of Antioch (including the Catholicate of India). These churches are sometimes referred to as the Ancient Orthodox churches, Lesser Eastern churches, Non-Chalcedonian churches, or Pre-Chalcedonian churches. The title "Monophysite" (from Greek words meaning "[only] one nature [of Christ]") is often applied to this family of Eastern Christians but is vehemently rejected by the churches concerned because of the term's heretical implication. Though these churches profess a common faith, each one reflects specific national and cultural identities that have played a major part in their historical development.

These churches have undergone periods of → persecution and difficulties at the hands of both Chalcedonian Christians and non-Christian groups. Over the centuries this pressure has resulted in a dramatic reduction in the number of Oriental Orthodox adherents. Though precise figures are unavailable, it is estimated that in 2002 Oriental Orthodox Christians numbered approximately 52 million worldwide.

All of the Oriental Orthodox churches embrace and profess the teachings of the first three ecumenical → councils, namely the Council of → Nicaea (325), condemning → Arianism and defining → Jesus Christ as consubstantial with the Father; the Council of Constantinople (381), upholding the divinity of the → Holy Spirit; and the Council of → Ephesus (431), condemning → Nestorianism. As such, the Oriental Orthodox employ the → Niceno-Constantinopolitan Creed as a profession of faith. These churches, however, reject the Christological definition formulated by the Council of → Chalcedon (451) that the one person of Christ is divided into two distinct natures, human and divine. The position held by the Oriental Orthodox churches regarding Jesus Christ is that of → Cyril of Alexandria (ca. 375-444), which states that Christ is "one incarnate nature" that is both fully human and fully divine, without confusion, diminution, or commixture. Though often referred to as → Monophysites, the Oriental Orthodox churches condemn Eutychianism, which affirms one nature in Christ, but only one of divinity, not humanity. These churches likewise profess that the Virgin Mary is truly the Mother of God and not simply the mother of another human being (→ Mary in the New Testament; Mary, Devotion to). The churches concerned are all of an established hierarchical structure, each having a synodal governing body.

The six churches known as Oriental Orthodox are of diverse liturgical traditions, reflecting both that of Antioch (in the case of the Armenians, Malankarese, and Syrians) and that of Alexandria (the Coptic Church and the churches of Eritrea and Ethiopia). Moreover, these churches maintain their own liturgical languages and have contributed significantly to the patristic witness of the Holy Church. In addition, the Oriental Orthodox churches have played a leading role in the foundation of Christian → monasticism. The Coptic and Syrian (Syriac) churches have been especially instrumental in this regard. The life of solitude experienced by the hermits of the Egyptian desert and the Syrian ascetics of Mesopotamia, together with the cenobitic life first established in the wilderness of Egypt, has greatly influenced the spirituality of the Oriental Orthodox churches. Such individual ascetics as Anthony the Great (d. 356), Pachomius (d. 346), Ephraem Syrus (d. 373), Gregory of Narek (d. 1003), and Tekla Haymanot (d. 1313) are of special note in this matter (→ Asceticism).

2. Ecumenical Relations

The Oriental Orthodox churches have likewise played a major role in the ecumenical life of the Christian church in recent decades. In 1965 the member churches of Oriental Orthodoxy met in Addis Ababa at the invitation of the late Emperor Haile Selassie I. The impetus of this meeting, together with the results of the first unofficial consultation between Eastern Orthodox and Oriental Orthodox theologians, held the previous year in Århus, Denmark, provided the incentive for Oriental Orthodox Christendom to enter into formal → dialogue with various other Christian churches, including the Eastern Orthodox churches, the → Roman Catholic Church, the → Anglican Church, and members of the Reformed churches. In addition, since 1971 a series of nonofficial consultations have been held between theologians of the Oriental Orthodox churches and the Roman Catholic Church under the auspices of the Viennese ecumenical foundation Pro Oriente (→ Ecumenical Dialogue).

In January 2003 members of the Preparatory Committee for the Catholic Church–Oriental Orthodox Churches International Joint Commission for Dialogue met in Rome to establish the rules for membership in the joint commission, as well as to set up the commission's work plan, agenda, procedures, methodologies, and timetable. The purpose of the dialogue is to foster a better understanding between the Catholic and Oriental Orthodox churches by addressing issues of common concern. During an audience with the members of the preparatory committee, Pope John Paul II affirmed that "essential clarifications have been reached with regard to traditional controversies about Christology, and this has enabled us to profess the faith we hold in common" (OR[E], February 5, 2003, 5).

Oriental Orthodox churches are also active participants in both international and national ecumenical bodies such as the → World Council of Churches, the → All Africa Conference of Churches, the → Middle East Council of Churches, and the → National Council of the Churches of Christ in the U.S.A. Within the United States the Oriental Ortho-

dox have formed the Standing Conference of the Oriental Orthodox Churches of America, which has an ongoing consultation with the United States Conference of Catholic Bishops as well as a joint commission with representatives of the Standing Conference of Canonical Orthodox Bishops in the Americas, an official body of various Eastern Orthodox jurisdictions. Moreover, in recent years a series of symposia have been held at St. Vladimir's Orthodox Theological Seminary in Crestwood, New York, bringing together representatives of both Eastern and Oriental Orthodox churches. These symposia have been cosponsored by St. Nersess Armenian Seminary of New Rochelle, New York, and St. Vladimir's.

Within the framework of the official relationships described above, individual Oriental Orthodox churches have established special relations with churches outside the Oriental Orthodox family, as in the case of the Syrian (Syriac) Orthodox Church with Rome and the Greek Orthodox Patriarchate of Antioch. In their Common Declaration of 1984, Syrian patriarch Ignatius Zakka I and Pope John Paul II affirmed: "It is not rare, in fact, for our faithful to find access to a priest of their own Church . . . impossible. Anxious to meet their needs and with their spiritual benefit in mind, we authorize them in such cases to ask for the sacraments of Penance, Eucharist and Anointing of the Sick from lawful priests of either of our two sister Churches, when they need them." The two church leaders emphasized that such cooperation be undertaken "to widen the horizon of their brotherhood and affirm herewith the terms of the deep spiritual communion which already unites them." In 1991 the leadership of both the Syrian (Syriac) Orthodox Church and the Greek Orthodox Patriarchate of Antioch agreed that both their ancient patriarchates profess one common faith and that all efforts and endeavors should be made to manifest the oneness of the Holy Church of Antioch.

→ Orthodox Church

Bibliography: A. S. Atiya, A History of Eastern Christianity (new ed.; Millwood, N.J., 1991) • B. J. Bailey and J. M. Bailey, Who Are the Churches in the Middle East? (Grand Rapids, 2003) • A. Fortescue, The Lesser Eastern Churches (London, 1913; repr., Piscataway, N.J., 2001) • P. Gregorios, W. H. Lazareth, and N. A. Nissiotis, eds., Does Chalcedon Divide or Unite? Towards Convergence in Orthodox Christology (Geneva, 1981) • Oriental Orthodox–Roman Catholic Interchurch Marriages and Other Pastoral Relationships (Washington, D.C., 1995) • R. Roberson, The Eastern Christian

Churches (6th ed.; Rome, 1999) • K. Sarkissian, *The Council of Chalcedon and the Armenian Church* (London, 1967) • R. F. Taft, ed., *The Oriental Orthodox Churches in the United States* (Washington, D.C., 1986) • M. Zibawi, *Eastern Christian Worlds* (Collegeville, Minn., 1995).

JOHN P. MENO

Origen

The early Greek church leader Origen (ca. 185–ca. 254) grew up in the syncretistic milieu of the cosmopolitan city of → Alexandria, the son of Leonidas, an educated convert to Christianity who died a → martyr's death in 202. Having received a solid Greek and Christian education, Origen made his living as a teacher of grammar until queries from pagans interested in Christianity prompted him to provide instruction in Christianity as well (other Christian teachers had fled Alexandria during persecutions). His enthusiasm for the → ascetic ideals of his age prompted him to interpret Matt. 19:12 literally and thus to become a eunuch "for the sake of the kingdom of heaven." During this early period of teaching, he also studied → philosophy with Ammonius Saccas, later the teacher of Plotinus.

Origen's school, for which he alone was responsible, became officially associated with the church only at a later period and through episcopal appointment for catechetical instruction (→ Catechesis). His colleague Heraclas probably gave the instruction in elementary Christianity from the outset, while Origen himself taught the more gifted and advanced students. Instruction at the school was rigorous and included the curriculum of the higher → sciences of the day, from geometry and arithmetic to philosophy; it sought to enlist these disciplines in the service of Christian → theology, the culmination of which was scriptural → exegesis. The school attracted not only mainstream Christians but also many philosophically inquisitive → pagans and Christian heretics. One of Origen's students was Ambrose of Alexander, whom Origen had converted from Valentinian → Gnosticism and who ultimately became the patron of his increasingly famous teacher, making it possible for Origen to pursue extensive scholarly and literary projects.

One significant caesura in Origen's life was his apparently forced move from Alexandria to Caesarea (Palestine) in 231 or 233. Because Origen was consecrated as a presbyter (→ Elder) while in Palestine, Bishop Demetrius had him condemned at two different Egyptian → synods. Heraclas now took over the catechetical school in Alexandria, while Origen established a successful school in Caesarea, where he was able to implement without opposition his program of providing Christian education for gifted students. As his reputation grew as a representative of church theology, he was called upon to counter heretical views at various synods and to persuade errant Christians to return to the fellowship of the church. The papyri of Toura (near Cairo) contain the protocol of such a synod.

Because Origen was a prominent Christian, he was imprisoned and severely tortured during → persecutions under Emperor Decius (249-51). After his release, he apparently continued his life as a venerated representative of the Christian faith until complications from his torture caused his death around 254.

Origen's voluminous lifework is largely a reflex of his work as a theological pedagogue. His primary systematic work, *De principiis* (On the fundamental doctrines), which he composed while still living in Alexandria, presents the basic features of an imposing independent system based on a synthesis of traditional Christian, Platonic, and Gnostic ideas. It provides considerable insight into the peculiarities of Origen's own thinking; even as a systematician, Origen always focused on addressing specific theological problems and pedagogical issues, his ultimate goal being to lead his students cautiously and systematically to a more profound understanding of Christian doctrine. The heart of Origen's theology is always scriptural exegesis; in the fourth book of *De principiis* he became the first Christian theologian to reflect systematically on its hermeneutical method (→ Hermeneutics), discussing the threefold meaning of Scripture.

Among Origen's many exegetical works, his monumental commentary on John is especially noteworthy. His *Hexapla* is an edition of the OT synoptically juxtaposing the Hebrew text alongside his own Greek transcription and the four current Greek translations (→ Bible Manuscripts and Editions). In his apology *Contra Celsum* Origen exhaustively refutes the attack of the Platonist Celsus against Christianity. His homilies, which he had transcribed only during his later years, reveal a more exoteric Origen, one who is keen on accommodating his message to the intellectual level of his listeners.

→ Church Fathers

Bibliography: Primary sources: ANF 4, pt. 4 • *Contra Celsum* • (trans. H. Chadwick; Cambridge, 1965) • GCS • *On First Principles; Being Koetschau's Text of the De*

principiis (trans. G. W. Butterworth; New York, 1966) •
PG 11-17.

Secondary works: H. S. Benjamins, *Eingeordnete
Freiheit. Freiheit und Vorsehung bei Origenes* (Leiden,
1994) • H. Crouzel, *Bibliographie critique d'Origène*
(Steenbrugis, 1971; supps., 1982, 1996); idem, *Origen*
(San Francisco, 1989) • B. E. Daley, "Origen's De
Principiis: A Guide to the Principles of Christian Scrip-
tural Interpretation," *Nova and vetera* (ed. J. Petroc-
cione; Washington, D.C., 1998) 3-21 • R. P. C. Hanson,
*Allegory and Event: A Study of the Sources and Signifi-
cance of Origen's Interpretation of Scripture* (Richmond,
Va., 1959); idem, *Origen's Doctrine of Tradition* (London, 1954) • J. C. Smith, *The Ancient Wisdom of Origen*
(Lewisburg, Pa., 1992) • H. Strutwolf, *Gnosis als System. Zur Rezeption der valentinianischen Gnosis bei
Origenes* (Göttingen, 1993) • J. W. Trigg, *Origen* (London, 1998); idem, *Origen: The Bible and Philosophy in
the Third-Century Church* (Atlanta, 1983).

Holger Strutwolf

Origenism

1. Term
2. Origen
   2.1. Life and Work
   2.2. Exegesis
   2.3. Theology
   2.4. Spirituality
3. Later Origenism
   3.1. A Disputed Legacy
   3.2. Origen and Monasticism

1. Term

"Origenism" denotes a nexus of dogma, exegesis,
and spiritual teaching that goes back to → Origen
(ca. 185-ca. 254) and that developed in both East
and West after his death.

2. Origen

2.1. *Life and Work*

Born in → Alexandria, Origen received baptismal
instruction there and then became a teacher of
grammar and Christian philosophy. In approximately 232 he left Alexandria for Caesarea in Palestine, where he continued his teaching ministry as an
ordained → priest. He died there as a result of torture suffered during the Decian → persecution of
Christians.

Only about a fourth of Origen's extensive literary
output has survived. We know many of these works
only in the Latin translations made around 400 by
Rufinus of Aquileia (ca. 345-411) and → Jerome (ca.
345-420). Apart from letters his works fall into two
main groups: exposition of Holy Scripture (commentaries, homilies, and scholia; → Exegesis, Biblical) and systematic treatises (dogmatic, devotional,
and apologetic). Unhappily, we have lost his most
important commentaries (esp. on Genesis), but
even more severe is the loss of many of his great
treatises, some of which were the subject of contention even in his own lifetime (e.g., *On the Natures,
Dialogue with Candidus, Stromateis,* and *On the Resurrection*). Among works that have been fully or
partially preserved are the *Homilies* on Genesis, Exodus, Joshua, and Canticles; the *Commentaries* on
Canticles, Matthew, John, and Romans; plus *De
principiis* and *Contra Celsum.*

Well versed both biblically and philosophically
(→ Greek Philosophy; Hellenism; Stoicism), Origen
wrote for Christians who sought intellectual, moral,
and spiritual perfection. His most persistent and
liveliest attacks were on → Gnosis and the → Marcionites. Yet he was prepared for → dialogue with
the Gnostics, as also with → Judaism and → Platonism. He was introduced to Judaism by a Hebrew
teacher and possibly to Platonism by the philosopher Ammonius Saccas (ca. 175-242), the teacher of
Plotinus.

2.2. *Exegesis*

The Bible, the source of all wisdom, was the main
theme in Origen's work. He dealt with it variously as
philologist, grammarian, and theologian. The
Hexapla — an edition of the OT in six columns (the
Hebrew text, a transliteration of the Hebrew into
Greek, and four Greek translations: Aquila, Sym-
machus, the LXX, and Theodotion; → Bible Versions
2) — displays his liking for textual criticism. This extraordinary work brought out more clearly the differences between the Hebrew text that Jews used and
the Greek version (LXX) that Christians used.

Origen is better known, however, for his theory
of → hermeneutics and his practice of →
allergorical exegesis. As a disciple of Philo (d. A.D.
45-50) and Clement of Alexandria (d. ca. 215; → Alexandrian Theology), he defended the view that the
true content of Scripture is spiritual. Readers must
have the Spirit of Christ if they are to get beyond the
letter to the meaning that the Spirit has set in the
text. Origen worked out rules to make it possible to
perceive this mysterious spiritual content, which
deals with the triune God, the intelligible world, and
the end of the ages.

2.3. *Theology*

In his *Principles* Origen projected and executed a
theological program that had no precursor or com-

petitor among the → church fathers. On the basis of the confession and Holy Scripture (→ Confessions and Creeds), he presented a comprehensive doctrine of → God, humanity (→ Anthropology), and the world (→ Creation). The desire for coherence led him to hypotheses that were later rejected, such as the preexistence of souls, a sequence of worlds until all spiritual beings freely return to God, and the complete equality of the last state with the first (→ Apocatastasis).

In Origen's system decisive roles are played by the goodness of God (→ Good, The) and human → freedom. The fall was the result of a misuse of freedom by the → angels, the first spiritual beings to be created, but the same freedom, being taught and supported by divine → providence, will enable all of us to attain to a perpetual vision of the triune God (→ Contemplation). Origen also took a crucial step forward in developing the doctrine of the → Trinity, especially in what he said about the → Holy Spirit as an individual substance with two modes of operation, the charismatic (→ Charisma) and the → epistemological.

The → Christology of Origen is complex. For him the Son is both subordinate to the Father and equal with him. The Son has many functions as revealer and mediator, which come to expression in the terms by which he is known in Scripture (the *epinoiai*, "conceptions, purposes"). Before the → incarnation he already assumed unfallen humanity. His incarnation became a saving event in the sense of bringing a full → revelation of God and offering a model of the full and free obedience of the human will to God (→ Soteriology).

2.4. *Spirituality*
We attain to the knowledge and vision of God by a spiritual understanding of Scripture and by imitation of the incarnate Christ (→ Discipleship 2). Since we are composed of spirit, → soul, and body, we are at odds with ourselves. The soul, the seat of free will, is subject to passions through the influence of the body, but the spirit, sharing the divine Spirit, draws it to God. The conflict does not take place only within us. It is directly related to that of angels and demons, the background of which is Christ's struggle with Satan. → Asceticism, → prayer, and practical → virtue are the weapons with which we can win the victory in the fight.

The decisive weapons, however, are the power, the → light, and the → love that Christ brings to us as the image of the invisible God when he comes to dwell and to grow in us. Christ gives us a share in the qualities that are proper to him as God's express image. Believers increasingly develop to spiritual perfection. By union with Christ they attain to the vi-

sion of God, but they are never completely perfect on earth. Origen's ideal was perhaps mystical, yet his writings contain no plain references to mystical or ecstatic experiences per se (→ Mysticism 2).

3. Later Origenism
3.1. *A Disputed Legacy*
During his lifetime and afterward Origen was both attacked and defended. The *Principles* often stood at the heart of the controversy. Among partly thoughtful and enthusiastic admirers were Pamphilius (d. 310, author of an important apology), Eusebius of Caesarea (ca. 260-ca. 340), → Athanasius (ca. 297-373), Hilary (d. ca. 367), Didymus (d. 398), the three → Cappadocian Fathers, Evagrius Ponticus (346-99), Ambrose (339-97), Rufinus, Jerome (at first), and much later → Bernard of Clairvaux (1090-1153) and → Erasmus (1469?-1536; → Humanism). Among opponents were Methodius of Olympus (d. ca. 311), Eustathius of Antioch (d. ca. 337), Peter of Alexandria (d. 311), Epiphanius (d. 403), Theophilus of Alexandria (patriarch 385-412), and Jerome (in his later period).

The debates that broke out in the fourth century were complex. They often related to hypotheses of Origen (regarding the preexistence of souls, apocatastasis, subordinationism, his doctrine of resurrected bodies, eternal creation, and excessive allegorizing) but attached alien and even contradictory elements to his thought. High points in the controversy were Jerome's switching from defense to opposition (ca. 400) and the condemnation under Justinian (527-65) of Origen and Origenism — first in 543 and then in 553 at Constantinople II. The loss of about three-quarters of his literary output was the result of these condemnations.

It should be stressed that Origen still influenced the theology of the East, indirectly through theologians like Gregory of Nazianzus (329/30-389/90) and Gregory of Nyssa (ca. 330-ca. 395), and directly through the authors of the → catenae, first of all Procopius of Gaza (ca. 475-ca. 538). Throughout the Middle Ages the West was primarily influenced by the exegetical principles of Origen as they were used and handed down by Hilary, Ambrose, and Jerome.

3.2. *Origen and Monasticism*
Origen's thinking not only had an impact on later exegetical and theological work. It also enjoyed development in monastic circles. As we can see from Athanasius's *Life of St. Anthony*, Egyptian → monasticism of the anchoritic type was influenced from the very first by the spirituality of Origen (involving asceticism, spiritual conflict, warring against → demons, etc.). The monks of Nitria and Kellia in-

cluded many Origenists who in the late fourth century engaged in highly intellectual speculation and triggered controversies by ruling out any external piety or bodily concept of God. In this regard Evagrius Ponticus worked out a complete theological system (see esp. his *Gnostic Centuries*) on the basis of Origen's hypotheses regarding the creation of intelligences by God and the final restoration of original unity. This type of Origenism found supporters among Palestinian monks in the first half of the sixth century. To deal with these developments Justinian in 543 and 553 condemned an Origenism that was closer to the teaching of Evagrius than to that of Origen himself.

Bibliography: Primary sources: ANF 4 • GCS 1-12 • *PG* 11-17.

Secondary works: BiPa 3 • E. A. CLARK, *The Origenist Controversy: The Cultural Construction of an Early Christian Debate* (Princeton, 1992) • H. CROUZEL, *Bibliographie critique d'Origène* (Steenbrugis, 1971; supps. 1982, 1996); idem, *Origen* (San Francisco, 1989); idem, *Théologie de l'Image de Dieu chez Origène* (Paris, 1956) • J. F. DECHOW, *Dogma and Mysticism in Early Christianity: Epiphanius of Cyprus and the Legacy of Origen* (Macon, Ga., 1988) • A. GUILLAUMONT, *Les "Képhalaia Gnostica" d'Évagre le Pontique et l'histoire de l'origénisme chez les Grecs et chez les Syriens* (Paris, 1962) • R. P. C. HANSON, *Allegory and Event* (London, 1959); idem, *Origen's Doctrine of Tradition* (London, 1954) • C. KANNENGIESSER and W. L. PETERSEN, eds., *Origen of Alexandria: His World and His Legacy* (Notre Dame, Ind., 1988) • R. J. LYMAN, *Christology and Cosmology: Models of Divine Activity in Origen, Eusebius, and Athanasius* (Oxford, 1993) • A. MONACI CASTAGNO, *Origene predicatore e il suo pubblico* (Milan, 1987) • ORIGEN, *Dizionario* (Rome, 2000) • L. B. RADFORD, *Three Teachers of Alexandria–Theognostus, Pierius, and Peter: A Study in the Early History of Origenism and Anti-Origenism* (Cambridge, 1908) • J. N. ROWE, *Origen's Doctrine of Subordination: A Study in Origen's Christology* (New York, 1987) • K. J. TORJESEN, *Hermeneutical Procedure and Theological Method in Origen's Exegesis* (Berlin, 1986) • J. W. TRIGG, *Origen* (London, 1998); idem, *Origen: The Bible and Philosophy in the Third-Century Church* (Atlanta, 1983). See also the *Actes* of the seven international congresses on Origen: *Origeniana* 1 (Bari, 1975), 2 (Rome, 1980), 3 (Rome, 1985), 4 (Innsbruck, 1987), 5 (Louvain, 1992), 6 (Louvain, 1995), 7 (Louvain, 1999).

ERIC JUNOD

Original Sin → Sin

Orthodox Christianity

1. Eucharistic Ecclesiology
2. Scripture
3. Tradition
4. The Teaching Office
5. Theological Anthropology and Christology
6. The Importance of Images
7. The Hesychast Controversy
8. The Holy Trinity
9. Current Trends

Christian → faith is the faith of a community that began with the group of → disciples gathered by → Jesus himself and that received the gift of the Spirit at → Pentecost after the → resurrection (Acts 2). This Spirit is the Spirit of Christ, the Spirit of → truth, who "abides with you, and he will be in you" (John 14:17) and who, in spite of all the shortcomings and imperfections of both individuals and historical groups, speaks in and through that community gathered "in Christ." Particularly when it celebrates the → Eucharist (§3.1.3), the community is an eschatological gathering (→ Eschatology) at which the → kingdom of God can be experienced in anticipation of the → parousia. The → Orthodox Church sees itself as having maintained a vision of → salvation that is fundamentally consistent with the original Christian → revelation, and as having maintained its ecclesiological, anthropological (→ Anthropology), and Trinitarian implications.

1. Eucharistic Ecclesiology
As used by modern Orthodox theologians, the term → "eucharistic ecclesiology" implies a certain interpretation of the early (apostolic and postapostolic) understanding of the Christian community. It also serves to explain the particular ecclesiological stand of the Orthodox Church vis-à-vis Western Christendom.

In its use of the term *ekklēsia*, "church" (→ Church 2.1), the NT designates primarily a local assembly gathering at a particular place (e.g., "the church of God that is in Corinth," 1 Cor. 1:2), although it can acquire, for instance in Ephesians and Colossians, a cosmic dimension. Individually, Christians are "members," but together they are the "body" — not a partial manifestation of it but the whole body, with Christ as the head. This wholeness does not imply a geographic concept of universality. It is manifested locally whenever "two or three" are gathered in Christ and is the primary meaning of the eucharistic celebration. Since Christ himself is the head of the body, every local eucharistic assembly is a cosmic and eschatological event. According to an expression of Ignatius of Antioch (ca. 35-ca. 107; → Apostolic Fathers), "Wherever Jesus Christ is, there is the catholic church" (*Smyrn.* 8.2). Each local church therefore manifests the wholeness, or catholicity, of the body.

Wherever Christianity spread, it formed local eucharistic communities. By the end of the second century, a practically uniform structure existed in all of them: a → bishop presided, with presbyters and → deacons around him. This identity of structure was determined by the "eucharistic unity" of each local church; specifically, the eucharistic assembly required a *proïstamenos,* "leader," who was seen as the image of the Lord himself, as teacher, shepherd, and → high priest. The "catholicity" of each local church implied identity and continuity with both the original apostolic preaching (the *kērygma*) and the teaching (the *dogma*) of all the churches (→ Teaching Office).

Identity with the apostolic preaching was expressed in the continuity of the episcopal ministry with that of the → apostles (Clement, → Irenaeus), whereas unity of faith between all the churches required the participation of several neighboring bishops in the → ordination of each new bishop (Hippolytus), as well as regular consultation on matters of faith between local churches, particularly in the form of → councils. This ecclesiology, based on the sacramental (→ Sacrament) and eschatological identity of all eucharistic assemblies, and therefore all local churches, implied equality between all the holders of the episcopal office. Each bishop was seen, at the eucharistic assembly, as sitting on a teaching chair, the "chair of Peter" (→ Cyprian), and the highest sign of truth during a doctrinal controversy would be the agreement of a large number of bishops sitting in council.

Against this background, it is obvious that the gradually developing concept of a Roman bishop possessing the exclusive privilege of being the "successor of Peter" would create tensions leading eventually to schism (→ Heresies and Schisms) between the East and the Latin West. In practice, the East departed also from the original ecclesial structure in that most bishops became administrative heads of several eucharistic communities (or parishes headed by presbyters); furthermore, bishops of major cities acquired privileges of leadership (as archbishops, metropolitans, or patriarchs) over their brother bishops. The actual power of bishops was thus not really measured any longer by their place in the local eucharistic assembly. These developments, however, were interpreted ad hoc and were seen as a matter of

practicality, not → dogma. They were defined by the church and subject to its control and to constant change.

Historically, the Orthodox Church remained a fellowship of local churches, equal in dignity and united in faith, as distinct from the Western centralization around → Rome (→ Roman Catholic Church). In the light of this ecclesiological approach, one can understand the Orthodox approach to Scripture, → tradition, and doctrinal authority.

2. Scripture

For the original Christian community the only "scriptures" were those included in the Jewish canon. Progressively, however, the writings that were preserved by some local churches and considered apostolic were also read at the eucharistic assemblies and eventually were accepted into a NT canon. There were hesitations as to the status of the books of the OT that were not part of the "shorter" Hebrew → canon, and also about some writings claiming to be apostolic. As late as the fourth century, for example, the Book of Revelation was rejected by the church of → Antioch and the → Cappadocian Fathers, but it was eventually included in the canon by the Trullan Synod (692), which also accepted the "longer" OT canon, including 3 Maccabees but excluding Wisdom, Tobit, and Judith.

Since the East was not involved in the bitter debates about the canon that marked the → Reformation and the Counter-Reformation (→ Catholic Reform and Counter-Reformation), the issue even today retains some fluidity in the consciousness of the Orthodox Church. The longer canon, as it exists in the Septuagint, the standard version of the Orthodox Church, is used in the liturgy, but the books that are not included in the Hebrew canon are generally referred to as deuterocanonical. Significantly, the modern Russian Synodal translation of the OT is based on the Hebrew original.

3. Tradition

The dispassionate attitude toward the issue of canonicity reflects the Orthodox understanding of tradition. The liturgical use of the Gospels, the regular Scripture readings, the biblical character of most → patristic writings, and hymnography all show that Scripture is considered as the primary and essential → Word of God. But the Bible remains the book of the church. There is an awareness that the same Spirit who inspired the authors who guided the church in defining the scriptural canon and in rejecting numerous → apocryphal writings also speaks in and through the church, preserving its fidelity to the faith "once for all entrusted to the saints" (Jude 3)

The concept of holy tradition expresses this particular function of the Spirit. It should not be confused with simple → conservatism. The living tradition, guided by the living Spirit, is called to answer new questions and settle new issues. For precisely this reason the theology of the early councils and the church fathers includes concepts and notions taken from the philosophical systems of their day (e.g., the term *homoousios* in the Nicene Creed; → Philosophy and Theology; Nicaea, Councils of, 2). There were objections against such an "unscriptural" approach, but the Fathers were able to show that the use of new concepts and new terminology is often the best way to be consistent with Scripture; the mere repetition of scriptural terms is not a guarantee of orthodoxy.

4. The Teaching Office
The normal way to express the apostolic tradition is — as Irenaeus (fl.180) and → Tertullian (ca. 160- ca. 225) showed — for the bishops to maintain it in their eucharistic → preaching and to settle disputes at councils. Historical experience, however, shows innumerable examples of heretical bishops and pseudocouncils proclaiming false doctrines. There are even extreme cases in which a single individual — for example, Maximus the Confessor (ca. 580-662) — remained faithful to the truth when all the bishops accepted heresy. For this reason the Orthodox Church does not recognize that any person or → institution can be infallible *ex sese* (from itself). Not even a council convened as ecumenical, the most authoritative exponent of the truth, possesses automatic → infallibility. A council must be the object of discernment by the whole church, guided by the Spirit.

To be properly understood, Scripture must be read under the guidance of the Spirit, who inspired the writers, and in the context of the church's experience. This approach allows for critical interpretation of literary genres present in Scripture (→ Literature, Biblical and Early Christian, 1-2) and, in general, for proper use of modern critical methods of Bible → exegesis, since the guidance of the Spirit is open to scholars as well as to the simple reader.

Liturgical texts and practices (→ Liturgy 2) are among the surest criteria of tradition, not only because, as Irenaeus wrote, "our doctrine conforms to the Eucharist" (*Adv. haer.* 4.18.5), but because they reflect the continuity of the apostolic faith through the ages. They too, however, require historical discernment — even more carefully than Scripture —

so that their real and authentic meaning might be properly understood.

5. Theological Anthropology and Christology
Eucharistic ecclesiology and the notion of tradition in Orthodoxy have meaning only within a Christological context that itself is inseparable from a theocentric understanding of human nature (→ Anthropology 3.3). For the Eastern patristic tradition the human being, as conceived and created by God, is not autonomous: its very existence implies communion with the Creator, since it was created "in the image of God" (Gen. 1:27). Since God "alone has → immortality" (1 Tim. 6:16), human beings live only by sharing in God's life. They may decide in favor of self-determination (→ Autonomy) and self-sufficiency, but such a decision, expressed in the biblical story of the fall of Adam and Eve (Genesis 3), implies corruption and → death because humans do not possess → life in themselves.

This Eastern understanding of human origin and destiny is clearly distinct from the prevailing trends of Western thought as expressed in the Augustinian tradition (→ Augustine's Theology), and later in → Scholasticism and the → Reformation. It does not involve a clear opposition between → nature and → grace, since human nature — our very existence — implies participation in God (i.e., in grace). Without communion with God, human beings lose their very humanity. Furthermore, the sin of → Adam and Eve is not interpreted as transmissible → guilt, requiring retribution. Rather, their rebellion resulted in their mortality and that of their children, as well as in a new cosmic situation in which the → serpent has usurped God's power and human beings no longer enjoy full → freedom but have become dependent upon the requirements of a constant struggle for survival. Indeed, "death exercised dominion from Adam to Moses, even over those whose sins were not like the transgression of Adam" (Rom. 5:14). Fallen humanity is an enslaved, rather than a guilty, humanity; in conditions of fallenness, however, sin becomes inevitable.

Salvation (→ Soteriology) from this condition of mortality, dependence, and servitude comes in Christ. It is interpreted more in terms of healing, restored communion, and new life than in terms of → justification. The assumption by the Son of God of the mortal human condition, including death itself, was followed by his → resurrection and glorification. By being "buried with him in baptism" (Col. 2:12), humans receive divine life again, because in him divinity and humanity were reunited; human life recovers its "theocentricity," for which it was originally created. Since Christ died and rose again, our life "is hidden with Christ in God" (Col. 3:3); through faith, though, it also becomes accessible in the mystery of the church on earth.

Such an approach to human destiny and salvation, although patristic authors never found it necessary or possible to express it in a philosophically coherent system, was based on the personal divine identity of Christ, which was indeed the main issue in the interminable Christological controversies from the fourth to the eighth centuries. On the one hand, only God and no creature could vanquish death and be the Savior. Consequently, Jesus was God, "of the same substance" *(homoousios)* with the Father, and his mother, Mary, was "Mother of God" *(theotokos)*. He, being personally God, died in the flesh (Theopaschism). On the other hand, he had to assume humanity because "what is not assumed is not saved," that is, the fallen, mortal humanity that needed salvation. In this humanity he died and was assumed into heaven. The Chalcedonian → Christology of A.D. 451 (→ Chalcedon, Council of) thus affirmed two natures in Christ, united in the one "hypostasis," or person, of the divine Logos.

This "high" Christology, which is proclaimed in Orthodox → hymnody as well as in patristic theology, is often criticized as being cryptomonophysitic (→ Monophysites). Is there not a danger, when one emphasizes the divine identity of Christ, of underestimating his humanity? This is not the case, however, if the theocentric anthropology, mentioned earlier, is taken seriously. In being assumed by the Logos, the humanity of Jesus becomes more human, not less. Indeed, it is separation from God that constitutes fallenness and dehumanization, whereas Jesus, being the Son of God, is also the "new Adam," the true Man. Furthermore, the Chalcedonian formula affirms that "the characteristic properties" of humanity were preserved in Jesus, and later Orthodox theology is specific in affirming that those properties include the condition of fallenness, particularly corruptibility and mortality. The heresy of Aphthartodocetism, which affirmed the incorruptibility of Christ's humanity after his birth (→ Docetism), was firmly rejected. The Word, wrote → John of Damascus (ca. 655-ca. 750), "assumed the ignorant and subjected nature" *(De fide orth.* 3.21 [*PG* 94.1084BC]). The natural growth of Jesus from infancy to adulthood and his entire life were those of a human being, except for sin. Being personally God, he nevertheless died on the cross in the fallen, corruptible nature that he had assumed. But because that death was the voluntary "death of God," it was followed by a resurrection in a renewed, incor-

ruptible, and glorified human nature — comparable to that of Adam before the fall.

In → baptism and the Eucharist, the renewed and transfigured humanity of Christ, through the Holy Spirit, is made accessible to those who believe. This presence of Christ in the church, which is his body, is a memorial of his death but also an anticipation of his second coming and eschatological presence. Characteristically, the eucharistic canon, attributed to John → Chrysostom (ca. 347-407; → Church Fathers), commemorates together the death and resurrection of Jesus, as well as his coming again, as if these events were already all accomplished: "all that is come for us: the cross, the tomb, the resurrection on the third day, the ascension into heaven, and the second and glorious coming." This dimension of "realized eschatology" is very much the foundation of what one might call the Orthodox spiritual experience. Two major episodes in the history of Orthodox Christianity can serve as examples: the iconoclastic crisis of the 8th and 9th centuries and the so-called → Hesychast controversy of the 14th.

6. The Importance of Images

The iconoclasts, who wanted to suppress the veneration of → images in the church, based their arguments on the Mosaic prohibition against "any graven image" (Exod. 20:4 KJV). In Christianity, as in the OT, there can be no "image" of the transcendent God (→ Transcendental Theology). The response of the Orthodox consisted of proclaiming the reality of the → incarnation: God became man and has become visible through the humanity of Jesus Christ. The image of Christ is therefore a confession of faith in the incarnation; it shows his glorified humanity, as seen by his eyewitnesses, the apostles.

The same transfigured humanity, however, can also be contemplated in the images of the → saints, who in their lives have restored the "fallen image" to its "former beauty." The veneration of images, or → icons, in the Orthodox Church has thus become an important element in → worship and an affirmation that the image of God has been restored in Jesus Christ and, through him, in the holy persons of his mother and all the saints.

7. The Hesychast Controversy

The theological debates of the 14th century were an extension of these same theological presuppositions. They were concerned particularly with the notion of deification, or → *theōsis*. In Greek patristic thought from the time of Irenaeus and → Athanasius (ca. 297-373), this term served to designate the participation of humanity in divine life in Christ. In the monastic tradition (→ Monasticism) known as Hesychasm, the possibility of "knowing" and "seeing" God was understood as the goal of the Christian life. The → vision of God "within the heart" of the baptized, in the form of → light — identified with the light seen by the apostles on the Mount of Transfiguration (Matt. 17:1-8 and par.) — was defined as a real experience of God, not a → symbol or an intellectual image, as the adversaries of Hesychasm asserted. In order to maintain, at the same time, the absolute transcendence of divine essence, the Byzantine theologian Gregory Palamas (ca. 1296-1359; → Palamism) affirmed the distinction in God between the invisible and unattainable divine essence and the "energies" of God, which make possible the "deification" of creatures and their real communion with the Creator.

8. The Holy Trinity

Orthodox Christology is not really understandable without a full perception of the role of the Holy Spirit in the "economy" of salvation, which is a manifestation of God as → Trinity. "The Father does all things by the Word in the Holy Spirit," wrote Athanasius (*Ep. Serap.* 1.28 [*PG* 26.596A]). Salvation did indeed occur through the historical event of the death and resurrection of Jesus Christ, but the appropriation, the catholic acceptance of salvation, occurs when each human person receives in his or her heart the Spirit, who cries "Abba! Father!" (Gal. 4:6). Through the Spirit, therefore, the body of Christ ceases to be limited to the one historical individual, Jesus, but unites in him all those who believe. This role of the Spirit in the "new creation" is based upon his participation in the original → creation as well. The cosmic dimension of redemption is strongly emphasized in the Orthodox liturgical texts, for instance, the prayer for the blessing of water on Epiphany (January 6).

In the Eastern patristic tradition, the restoration of communion between God and humans implies "cooperation" *(synergeia)* between divine grace and human freedom, and the most specific function of the Spirit consists precisely of "meeting" the personal human response to grace. The eucharistic communion *(koinōnia)* is par excellence the gift of the Spirit. Every sacramental act, beginning with baptism, includes in the Eastern liturgical tradition a specific invocation of the Spirit, and the eucharistic canon culminates with the epiclesis (the anaphora of Basil the Great).

Addressed to the Father and recalling the creative and redemptive act of the Son, the eucharistic prayer is sealed by the invocation of the Spirit, manifesting the true nature of the church as a free gathering of believers who become, through the Spirit, the true body of Christ for the salvation of the world.

Clearly expressed in the eucharistic prayer, the Trinitarian character of the faith can be seen in all aspects of spirituality. "No sooner do I conceive of the one," writes Gregory of Nazianzus (329/30-389/90), "than I am illumined by the splendor of the three; no sooner do I distinguish them than I am carried back to the one. When I think of any one of the three, I think of him as the whole, and my eyes are filled, and the greater part of what I am thinking escapes me" (*Or. theol.* 40.41 [*PG* 36.417BC]). The Trinity, therefore, is not a matter of philosophical speculation but, rather, the primary existential and soteriological content of the Christian revelation. The faith begins with the recognition of Jesus as the Messiah and the Son of God (see Peter's confession in Matt. 16:16). This recognition itself is the work of the Spirit because "no one can say 'Jesus is Lord' except by the Holy Spirit" (1 Cor. 12:3), and communion in the Spirit leads one to the Father.

To describe the three divine persons the Cappadocian Fathers used the Greek term *hypostasis,* "concrete reality." The doctrine of three hypostases appeared to many as a de facto tritheism, and the Fathers had to explain that the community of essence *(ousia)* between the three persons was an affirmation of divine unity, that it implied a "co-inherence" *(perichōrēsis)* of the three persons, a perfect unity of action, without mixture or coalescence. This unity without confusion is best expressed in the Johannine definition that "God is love" (1 John 4:8). An absolute → monotheism, without the Trinitarian dimension, would not allow this definition. It is because God is perfect → love that the three hypostases are indeed one God, whereas three created hypostases — for example, three men — are three distinct beings, not one man. But they too, through love, can become "one" in Christ.

At this point, it is appropriate to recall another basic aspect of Greek patristic thought: its → apophatic character. The Trinitarian reality, which expresses the very essence of God, is transcendent and different from all created categories. It can therefore be best expressed negatively, by saying what God is not (→ Negative Theology [Western]). Nevertheless, God manifests his Trinitarian being, particularly through the incarnation, and opens it up for participation: "I in them and you in me, that they may become completely one" (John 17:23). The perfect love that unites the Father, the Son, and the Holy Spirit is also offered to creatures, which justifies a dictum that became current among 19th-century Russian theologians: "The Trinity is our social program." This approach is justified, however, only if one also keeps in mind God's transcendence, for he can never be simply imitated, but only participated in. Within the community of the church, believers can only be "stewards of God's mysteries" (1 Cor 4:1).

9. Current Trends

Contemporary Orthodox thought and its ethos have inevitably been influenced by historical trends, such as the late Byzantine and medieval cultural forms and the impact of Western thought and secular → "enlightenment" (note the nationalism of the peoples of modern eastern Europe). However, the fundamental Orthodox vision of Christianity remains the one that was shaped in the classic period of Greek patristic thought. This vision is enshrined particularly in the cycles of the liturgy, in hymnody, and in spirituality. The use of different liturgical languages only strengthens this unity of spiritual perception, a unity that comes from early Christianity and that is, in principle, accessible to all different cultures and civilizations.

Since Orthodox ecclesiology did not allow for the existence of a permanent infallible → institution like the papacy (→ Pope, Papacy), the responsibility for an Orthodox integrity in faith and experience rests with the church as a whole, and the liturgy is perceived as the most authentic and reliable expression of tradition. Actually, during the centuries of Muslim rule in the Middle East, Orthodox communities survived without regular preaching or intellectual leadership, primarily through continuous liturgical life. The theology and spiritual wealth of the Byzantine liturgy made this survival possible. The liturgy played a similar role in countries of eastern Europe, when normal theological development was made impossible by the political circumstances of the 20th century.

Similarly, the continuity of the monastic tradition, with its emphasis on a personal experience of God as the goal of all spiritual efforts, has maintained the → authority of individual spiritual leaders (Gk. *gerontes;* Slav. *startsi;* → Starets), who, without challenging the doctrinal and canonical authority of the bishops, often represent a prophetic witness, the authenticity and → power of which was recognized, for instance, by Fyodor Dostoyevsky (1821-81) and by intellectuals attracted to Orthodox Christianity in modern Russia.

Since the 17th century, however, Orthodox theology has been placed in an inevitable confrontation with the West. This confrontation resulted sometimes in an artificial adoption of Western → catego-

ries and ideas, as in the case of Patriarch Cyril Lucar of Constantinople (1570-1638), who in 1624 published a basically Calvinistic confession of faith (→ Calvin's Theology; Calvinism). A similar phenomenon occurred in the case of the academy established in Kiev, where the ideas of the Latin counter-reformation were often accepted as Orthodox. This inoculation of Western ideas, however, eventually led to a revival of Orthodox identity, expressed in categories of modern thought. This reviving occurred, on the one hand, with the emergence in the 19th century of a system of theological education based on developed historical and patristic scholarship. On the other hand, particularly in Russia, there emerged several schools of lay theology (→ Clergy and Laity) that, by their very existence and success, illustrate the point, apparent throughout the history of the Christian East, that the whole church, not limited to an authoritative magisterium, is responsible for the faith.

Alexis Khomiakov (1804-60) and Ivan Kireevsky (1806-56), known as the older Slavophiles, developed the corporate and conciliar dimensions of ecclesiology (the notion of *sobornost*). In the first decades of the 20th century the more philosophical and speculative school of Vladimir Sergeevich Solovyov (1853-1900), which included authors like Pavel Florensky (1882-1937), Sergei Bulgakov (1871-1944), and, in part, Nicolas Berdyaev (1874-1948), attempted a more questionable synthesis of Orthodoxy with German → idealism, which provoked a "neopatristic" reaction (Georges Florovsky, Dumitru Staniloae). Also influential were authors developing a eucharistic ecclesiology (Nicolas Afanassieff, John Zizioulas).

Orthodox communities are present in most Western and Third World countries, and Orthodox theologians are involved in most aspects of the ecumenical movement. The Orthodox tradition is itself a direct challenge to contemporary thought, even as it is being challenged by such thought. After centuries of continuous history in societies that were themselves — at least nominally — Christian and Orthodox, Orthodoxy must meet a test of its catholic authenticity as it confronts the pluralistic and secularized world of the later 20th and early 21st centuries (→ Pluralism; Secularization).

Bibliography: Survey: V. Lossky, *The Mystical Theology of the Eastern Church* (Crestwood, N.Y., 1976); idem, *Orthodox Theology: An Introduction* (Crestwood, N.Y., 1989) • J. Meyendorff, *The Orthodox Church: Yesterday and Today* (3d ed.; Crestwood, N.Y., 1981) • J. Pelikan, *The Christian Tradition: A History of the*

Development of Doctrine, vol. 2, *The Spirit of Eastern Christendom (600-1700)* (Chicago, 1974) • T. Spidlik, *The Spirituality of the Christian East: A Systematic Handbook* (Kalamazoo, Mich., 1986) • T. Ware, *The Orthodox Church* (new ed.; London, 1993); idem, *The Orthodox Way* (New York, 1979)

Other works: N. Afanassieff, *L'église du Saint-Esprit* (Paris, 1975) • H. G. Beck, *Geschichte der orthodoxen Kirche im byzantinischen Reich* (Göttingen, 1980) • G. Florovsky, *Bible, Church, Tradition* (Belmont, Mass., 1972) • A. Jensen, *Die Zukunft der Orthodoxie* (Cologne, 1986) • G. I. Mantzaridis, *The Deification of Man: St. Gregory Palamas and Orthodox Tradition* (Crestwood, N.Y., 1984) • J. Meyendorff, *The Byzantine Legacy in the Orthodox Church* (Crestwood, N.Y., 1982); idem, *Catholicity and the Church* (Crestwood, N.Y., 1983); idem, *Christ in Eastern Christian Thought* (Crestwood, N.Y., 1975); idem, "Christ's Humanity: The Paschal Mystery," *SVTQ* 31 (1987) 5-40; idem, *Living Tradition: Orthodox Witness in the Contemporary World* (Crestwood, N.Y., 1978); idem, *Orthodoxy and Catholicity* (New York, 1965); idem, *A Study of Gregory Palamas* (2d ed.; Crestwood, N.Y., 1974); idem, ed., *The Primacy of Peter: Essays in Ecclesiology and the Early Church* (Crestwood, N.Y., 1992) • A Monk of the Eastern Church, *The Jesus Prayer* (Crestwood, N.Y., 1987) • P. Nellas, *Deification in Christ: The Nature of the Human Person* (Crestwood, N.Y., 1987) • Orthodox Center of the Ecumenical Patriarchate, *L'église locale et l'église universelle* (Chambésy, Switz., 1981) • L. Ouspensky and V. Lossky, *The Meaning of Icons* (Crestwood, N.Y., 1982) • A. Schmemann, *For the Life of the World* (rev. ed.; Crestwood, N.Y., 1973); idem, *Introduction to Liturgical Theology* (Crestwood, N.Y., 1986) • D. Staniloae, *Theology and the Church* (Crestwood, N.Y., 1980) • L. Thunberg, *Man and the Cosmos: The Vision of St. Maximus the Confessor* (Crestwood, N.Y., 1985) • P. Valliere, *Modern Russian Theology–Bukharev, Soloviev, Bulgakov: Orthodox Theology in a New Key* (Grand Rapids, 2000) • N. Zernov, *The Russian Religious Renaissance of the Twentieth Century* (New York, 1963) • J. Zizioulas, *Being as Communion: Studies in Personhood and the Church* (Crestwood, N.Y., 1985).

John Meyendorff†

Orthodox Church

1. Terminology and Self-Understanding

In keeping with their flexible and liberal spirit, which opposes defining the concept of → orthodoxy (§§1-2) as a doctrinaire rigidity of binding belief, the Orthodox churches have no required term for themselves. The many terms used are to be understood in their historical contexts as reactions against church developments that at various times required emphases on identity and uniqueness and authenticity of this or that particular expression of the original Christian → revelation. The various terms are thus complementary inasmuch as they express specific aspects of ecclesiological identity that retain their sharp contours within the confessional totality and that make it plain how the church understands its own nature.

1.1. Names

Orthodox Church is the most common name for the family of churches that in their eucharistic fellowship (→ Eucharistic Ecclesiology) manifest in various ways the one → faith of the undivided → church. The future → Pan-Orthodox council will be called "The Holy and Great Council of the Orthodox Church." The designation "orthodox," which at first was current beyond the East, established itself with the East-West split as the preferred term in the East, the West opting for "catholic," which the East also uses. We find "Orthodox Church" in the famous Confession (1638) of Peter Mogila (1596-1646), the metropolitan of Kiev; in the replies in 1718 of the → patriarchs of four of the five ancient Orthodox centers (i.e., all but Rome; see 2.1) to the Nonjurors (→ Anglican Communion); in replies to the call for → union issued by Pope → Pius IX (1846-78) in 1848; and in the reaction of Ecumenical Patriarch Anthimus VII (1895-97) to a fresh call for union with Rome in 1894/95. Finally, the designation is common in contemporary → ecumenical dialogue, especially in statements made by Orthodox delegates to full assemblies of the → World Council of Churches (WCC).

Orthodox Catholic Churches is an expanded form that, by adding "Catholic," the oldest predicate of the authentic church, excellently expresses the ecclesiological reality of Orthodoxy. Many eminent theologians prefer it for this reason. In controversy with Rome it was used in 1484 by the Constantinople Synod of Orthodox Patriarchs and sometimes in responses to Roman calls for unity (e.g., that of the Moscow Congress of 1948).

Eastern Orthodox Church, another expansion that relates to the original distinction between East and West, underlines geographic and cultural aspects. Denominational studies use it, as do many theologians. It was also used in the reply to the Nonjurors and by the Constantinople Synods of 1836, 1838, and 1895. Finally, Orthodox participants at the Seventh Assembly of the WCC, at Canberra in 1991, used it in their "Reflections of Orthodox Participants," which expressed concerns of "the Eastern Orthodox and Oriental Orthodox delegates."

Eastern Church is a relative term that goes back to the division of the → Roman Empire in 395 and denotes the church that developed in the Eastern branch and that engaged in → mission beyond its borders. After the schism it came to be synonymous with Orthodoxy, in distinction from the Latin church of the West. It had this sense for the Constantinople Synods of 1638, 1642, 1691, 1836, and 1838, as well as for the Jerusalem Synod of 1672, the confessional writings (→ Confessions and Creeds) of Patriarch Metrophanes Critopoulos (1636-39) of Alexandria and Patriarch Dositheus (1669-1707) of Jerusalem, and also the Orthodox patriarchs in their response to the Nonjurors. It is also common in the → liturgy, yet since neither the Eastern nor the Western church is an ecclesial unity, "Eastern Church" seems to be outdated in its original geographic sense.

Greek Orthodox Church is a term that, notwithstanding the multinational structure of Orthodoxy, stresses the common basis of all Orthodox churches to the degree that the Greek cultural tradition influenced the development and shaping of their theology, structure, and → spirituality. Culturally and theologically, one may call all Orthodox churches "Greek" without challenge to their national identity. In keeping are the early terms used for the → autocephalous churches of the various nationalities. The Orthodox delegates to the → Faith and Order conference at Lund in 1952 used this designation. New terms that stress national homogeneity and jurisdictional → autonomy can give rise to the misunderstanding that Greek is a nationalistic concept. But the name "Greek Church," which was the predominant name used in older literature and which is a parallel to "Latin Church," is now outdated and meaningless.

Catholic Church was the name preferred by the older councils and → church fathers. It stresses the continuity of the ancient, authentic, Christian → revelation in the Orthodox Church insofar as the → early church regarded itself as catholic, not merely in the sense of universal, but in the sense of orthodox in distinction from → heresies and schisms and as such the bearer of the → truth in its profound totality. Participation in this totality makes the church catholic throughout the world and therefore in the Eastern church, in which the whole of the salvation event, not just a part, is a reality. This designation was chosen by Patriarch Photius I the Great (858-67, 877-86) in his controversy with Rome, by Antioch patriarch Theodore Balsamon (d. after 1195), by the Synods of Constantinople of 1351, 1484, 1691, and 1727, by the Jerusalem Synod of 1672, by the confessional writings of Patriarchs Metrophanes Critopoulos and Dositheos II, by Constantinople patriarchs Gennadius II Scholarius (1453-56, 1458, 1462-63) and Jeremias III (1716-26, 1732-33), and by the patriarchs in their reply to Pius IX. The term "catholic" has now been paired with "orthodox" in order to indicate the divergent ecclesiological developments and understandings that divide Orthodox Catholics from Roman Catholics.

One, holy, catholic, and apostolic church is the comprehensive term that fixes the identity of the Orthodox Church apologetically, as at synods of 1836 and 1838 and in the replies to Pius IX and his successor, Leo XIII (1878-1903). But since the → Niceno-Constantinopolitan Creed sanctioned this doxological description in an ecumenical confession of faith, it cannot be used to define the identity of the Orthodox Church in particular.

We find variations of the above titles as various predicates are used to state controversial aspects, the most common being

Catholic and Apostolic Church
Catholic, Apostolic, Eastern Church
Church of Christ
Eastern Catholic Church
Eastern Orthodox and Apostolic Church
Eastern Orthodox and Catholic Church of Christ
Eastern, Orthodox, Catholic, and Apostolic Church
One, Holy, Catholic, and Apostolic Orthodox Church of Christ
Orthodox, Catholic, and Apostolic Church of Christ
Orthodox Church of Christ

Note that "Greek Catholic" is used for the so-called Eastern Catholic churches (→ Uniate Churches).

1.2. *Meaning*

As the sources show, many of these titles are used alongside one another in an attempt to offer an authentic description of the church by hendiadys. The term "orthodox" is predominant, an adjective that etymologically expresses two ideas: "right thought, belief, teaching" (from Gk. *orthos*, "straight, right," + *dokeō*, "think") and "right worship" (*orthos* + *doxazō*, "praise").

In this connection correct faith is not abstract doctrine but the true praise of God, which manifests itself continuously in the church's life as → doxology, as thanksgiving for the experience of → salvation, and as revealed truth in history. The identity of Orthodoxy is not to be found in a doctrinal system of sure truths or in a system of organization but in its liturgy, in which → creation experiences communion with its Creator.

1.3. *Approach*

Orthodoxy as a living organism expressed in liturgy cannot be studied solely on the basis of accepted scholarly criteria and analyses, for in its essence it is a multifaceted → life in which there is participation in an existential process that calls more for feeling and sensibility than for rationality. Examining special issues by means of objective academic criteria can give a knowledge of facts but not a knowledge of the essence itself, a knowledge best attained through the liturgical life of Orthodoxy.

Genuine Orthodox theology is a discipline apart, a liturgical discipline, → apophatic in approach. Theological research is done with an awareness that what is to be known transcends human understanding, which at the height of its knowledge plunges into the deep darkness of the divine incomprehensibility and, with a sense of gracious encounter, must articulate doxologically the truth that is experienced. Many misunderstandings and prejudices concerning the Orthodox Church thus go back to a wrong approach as students try to form, merely with the help of sources and scholarship, a picture of Orthodoxy, which is not really doctrine but a way of life, with its own → system-related criteria and thought forms.

1.4. *Singular versus Plural*

In view of the autocephalous structure of the Orthodox Church, the plural "Orthodox *churches*" is commonly used in the West, though in the context of Western ecclesiology and structures it does not accord with the Orthodox view of the church. Thus for Roman Catholic theologians the plural implies a defect as regards the unity of the church, whereas for the Orthodox unity rules out the singular in the sense of a church with a centralized structure (→ Pope, Papacy). Protestants, too, think that the plural denotes a variety that contradicts the agreement in faith, liturgy, and canonical order that exists as the basis of eucharistic fellowship among the Orthodox churches.

The question of singular or plural is of no relevance for the Orthodox inasmuch as → unity in diversity is a concrete reality, and diversity displays the catholicity of essential unity. Thus both the singular and the plural are correct. From the purview of systematic ecclesiology the singular is needed when the → ontology of → Orthodox Christianity, its one essence, is in view. But the plural is appropriate from the historical and empirical standpoint, when what is in view is the concrete form of the church, which manifests itself as a plurality with concrete organizational ramifications.

2. History

In church history the year 1054 is regarded as the official date of the schism between East and West, a date of comparable importance to 1517, when the great split in the Western church began (→ Reformation). Roman Catholic theologians speak in this regard of "the Eastern schism," while Orthodox theologians refer to "the schism of the Roman Church," finding in Orthodoxy continuity with the → early church and blaming the split entirely on Rome.

On December 7, 1965, Pope Paul VI (1963-78) and Ecumenical Patriarch Athenagoras (1948-72), with his synod, abrogated the anathemas of 1054 and in so doing showed that the issue in 1054 was neither mutual → excommunication nor a process of laying the blame on one church alone. Nevertheless, ancient prejudices remain, so that the rise of the Orthodox churches is often dated from that year.

Along such lines the relations between the churches are often depicted in terms of a trunk with its root in Christ, which is the one church, and the branches, which are the divided churches. It is a crass error, however, to view the Orthodox churches along similar lines, as though the autocephalous churches were separated churches.

2.1. *Structural Development*

Christianity at first was a Jewish religious movement that, despite fierce opposition, soon spread across and beyond the Roman Empire. As the mother of all the churches, → Jerusalem merited a place of honor throughout the Christian world; as cultural, political, and economic centers of the empire, however, → Rome, → Alexandria, and → Antioch became the main structural bastions of the early church. When → Byzantium in 330 was given the name of its imperial founder Constantine I (ruled 306-37) and became the new imperial capital, it quickly also became a cultural and political center more important than Rome itself. The Council of Constantinople in 381 recognized this fact by making the former suffragan of Byzantium the bishop of Constantinople and by giving the "new Rome" second ranking after the old (→ Ecumenical Patriarchate).

Later ecumenical → councils confirmed this structure, which in the first instance was a matter of practical organization. They also confirmed the special position of the metropolitan bishops as → patriarchs. In view of the historical importance of Jerusalem, the Fourth Ecumenical Council (Chalcedon, in 451) gave its bishop too the title of patriarch, but it used the title → "catholicos" for metropolitans outside the empire. Within the empire five centers of church organization and authority — ranked in the order Rome, Constantinople, Alexandria, Antioch, and Jerusalem — gave stability to the church. This concept of a → pentarchy became the principle of pluralist church structure and organization. Rome, however, strove for centralization, against which the East, at the Council of Sardica in 342, protested strongly.

It is striking that in the West, Rome, the only patriarchate, finally achieved centralization as the collapse of the empire brought political variety. In the East, where political unity was preserved, however, the dominant principle was that of inculturation, that is, of variety in organization, theology, and liturgy. The political fate of the Eastern Empire, with the loss of its eastern territories in the seventh century, obviously contributed to this development. The Church of the East split off from the imperial church after the Council of Ephesus (→ Nestorians; Ephesus, Council of), as did the → Oriental Orthodox churches after the Council of → Chalcedon in 451. The result of all these developments was that different ecclesiological positions in different cultural and historical contexts led to alienation, and to ultimate schism between East and West.

2.2. New Horizons

The painful loss to → Islam of Alexandria, Antioch, and Jerusalem was alleviated by → missionaries from Constantinople who spread the gospel to the Slavs, a development that would decisively shape European culture (→ Slavic Mission). Church history views the patriarchate of Photius largely from the standpoint of the controversy with Pope Nicholas I (858-67), setting less store on the powerful missionary work of the Thessalonian brothers Cyril (ca.

827-69) and Methodius (ca. 815-85), work that took place during his patriarchate and in accord with his church policies.

The attempt to found an independent Slavic church in Moravia with its own liturgical language failed under pressure from the neighboring Latin church, but the work was not without outstanding success. The disciples of the two brothers, when driven out of Moravia, brought Christianity to the Southern Slavs on the Danube and in the Balkans and, by means of the Cyrillic script, laid the foundations of an independent Slavic liturgy.

Finally, the baptisms at Kievan Rus (988) brought a vast area to the faith in the Greek Orthodox form developed at Constantinople and also introduced Russia into Europe, although the church there remained a metropolitan district under the Patriarchate of Constantinople until the 15th century. With the help of Rome, Bulgaria, which was also under Constantinople, tried to achieve both ecclesiastical and political sovereignty in the 9th century, a development that further soured the already strained relations between Rome and Constantinople.

2.3. The East-West Schism

In accordance with → Paul's missionary principle of a pluriform religion, the Greek and Latin churches — in tension from the outset for political, sociological, ethnological, psychological, and anthropological reasons — developed two dominant expressions of Christianity. Over a long period of increasing alienation, an antithesis between the two resulted, based on the absolutizing of the two forms, that constricted the faith and shattered all chances of agreement. Certain events marked this historical development. Up to 732 Illyricum, Calabria, and Sicily had been under the Roman Patriarchate. At that time, however, Byzantine emperor Leo III (717-41) placed them under Constantinople in order to bring ecclesiastical and political boundaries into line.

An expression of the realignment of Rome came when Pope Stephen II (752-57) crossed the Alps in November 753 to visit Pepin III the Short, king of the Franks (751-68), in search of a treaty of protection (→ Middle Ages 2). Pope Leo III (795-816) continued this policy when at Christmas in 800 he crowned Pepin's son Charlemagne (768-814) emperor, thus committing treason in the eyes of Constantinople.

Finally, in an atmosphere of mistrust and hatred, Cardinal Humbert of Silva Candida (d. 1061), on July 16, 1054, served a → bull of excommunication on the patriarch of Constantinople, Michael I Cerularius (1043-58), and his followers at the altar of Hagia Sophia. Eight days later the patriarch replied in turn by excommunicating the cardinal and his followers. This bitterness reached a climax when in 1204 the Fourth Crusade, which was meant to liberate the holy sites, ended instead with an invasion of Constantinople and the establishment of a Latin kingdom and patriarchate (→ Crusades). Later attempts at union (at councils in Lyons in 1274 and at Ferrara-Florence in 1438-39) were foredoomed to failure.

2.4. Reorientation and Restructuring

In July 1261 the Latin kingdom collapsed and the national dream of the Greeks was fulfilled, but the empire never could be recovered, and on May 29, 1453, it fell to the Turks. As the invention of printing (ca. 1450), the discovery of America (1492), and the beginning of the Reformation (1517) were initiating a new age in the West, Orthodoxy was suffering great catastrophe. The Ottoman Empire rose on the ruins of the Eastern Roman Empire, and all the Eastern patriarchates came under its political rule.

The only remaining independent Orthodox power was Moscow, which now became the new guardian of Orthodoxy. Negotiations concerning union between the Greek and Roman churches at Florence in 1439 had, in the eyes of the Russians, deprived Constantinople of its moral authority, and consequently the Russian church became independent of Constantinople in 1448. Then in 1589 Moscow was made a patriarchate by Ecumenical Patriarch Jeremias II (1572-79, 1580-84, 1587-95), which was confirmed by synods in 1590 and 1593. All these developments were the logical outcome of the shift of power in the Orthodox world.

As Moscow, the "third Rome," became the heir of Constantinople, the sultan, according to the Turkish millet system, made the ecumenical patriarch the spiritual head and, in civil law, the secular head of all the Orthodox subjects of his Ottoman Empire, which by the end of the 15th century stretched from Mesopotamia to the Adriatic. The independent development of the Moscow Patriarchate, which was still in a tense mother-daughter relation with the Ecumenical Patriarchate, experienced the maturing of an individual spirituality and a growth that manifested itself in missions as far afield as Siberia and Alaska (→ Orthodox Missionary Societies).

The liberation of Orthodox nations from Turkish rule in the early 19th century resulted in a new wave of autocephaly, for the churches of the new states could not tolerate being under a head, the ecumenical patriarch, who was still subject to the former tyranny and thus an obstacle to the development of strong national identities. The Ecumenical Patriarchate met this development with the principle of "economy" (→ Economy [Orthodox Theology]), a principle that for centuries has played a crucial role in the Orthodox Church and that will be generally agreed on by consensus at the Pan-Orthodox council being planned for the 21st century. By means of this principle binding rulings could be reached on open questions such as the canonical status of the present Orthodox Church in America.

2.5. The Diaspora

The expansion of Christianity inevitably raised the problem of the → diaspora, a problem that unexpectedly confronted the Orthodox churches in the late 19th and early 20th centuries, when for political and economic reasons many Orthodox left their homogeneous motherlands to seek new homes in the United States, Canada, Australia, and western Europe. National, linguistic, cultural, and denominational differences — made worse by prejudice — hindered the integration of these communities of Orthodox in their new lands. In consequence, in respect to church life, bishoprics attached to home churches were created. The ecumenical movement, which helped set aside mistrust and foster mutual regard, both eased the path of Orthodoxy as it sought to incarnate itself in strange settings and also made → dialogue possible between the Orthodox Church and the churches of the West (→ Ecumenism, Ecumenical Movement).

The jurisdictional status of the diaspora bishops hampered the achievement of an identity for Western Orthodoxy, since such bishops, while working alongside one another, remained linked primarily to their mother churches. The danger was of an overemphasis on national identity at the expense of the catholicity and ecumenicity common to Orthodoxy in every nation. Reasonable pastoral measures on the part of the mother churches had to be in keeping with the spirit of the canonical ordering of the Orthodox Church, which organized local churches territorially rather than nationally and did not permit parallel jurisdictions in the same area. The Standing Conference of Canonical Orthodox Bishops in the Americas was founded in 1960 (with parallel councils in France, Australia, and Sweden) in an attempt to meet this concern, which the future Pan-Orthodox council will ultimately address.

2.6. Orthodoxy and the Oikoumene

Christ prayed that his disciples "may all be one" (John 17:21). At the end of the epiclesis (→ Eucharistic Prayer; Eucharist 3.1.3), the Orthodox liturgy urgently prays that God will put an end to divisions.

The need for this petition points to a human weakness that already confronted the → primitive Christian community. Divisions occurred after the Councils of Ephesus in 431 and Chalcedon in 451, and the patriarchs and emperors in Constantinople took the initiative in attempts to overcome them, though without lasting success. To the Reformation split in the West the Ecumenical Patriarchate reacted with a readiness for dialogue that reached a high point in the exchange of letters between Lutheran theologians from Tübingen and Ecumenical Patriarch Jeremias II in 1573-81. Though the difficulties were severe, the dialogue did not end with strife but with a farewell to the "sagacious Germans."

The patriarchate resumed ecumenical dialogue at the beginning of the 20th century — first of all in a 1902 encyclical in which the Orthodox Church called for cooperation in meeting the problems of the churches and the world, and then in a 1920 encyclical, prepared largely by Germanos Strenopoulos, later archbishop of Thyateira, and addressed to "the churches of Christ everywhere," which emphasized the need for fellowship between all churches. This Orthodox summons was the Magna Carta of the subsequent ecumenical involvement of the Orthodox churches in the World Council of Churches. The Ecumenical Patriarchate, the Churches of Greece and Cyprus, and the Romanian Orthodox Episcopate in America were founding members of the WCC in 1948, followed by the Orthodox churches of Eastern Europe in 1961. Orthodox have also taken part — and continue to take part — in official bilateral theological dialogues with the Anglicans, Lutherans, Old Catholics, Oriental Orthodox, Reformed, and Roman Catholics.

In sometimes styling themselves the "one, holy, catholic, and apostolic church," the Orthodox may seem not to recognize the ecclesial reality of other churches, and we find a reflection of this tension in the two texts from November 1986 proposed for the third Pan-Orthodox Conference on the relation between the Orthodox Church and the rest of the Christian world and on the Orthodox Church and the ecumenical movement. Orthodox history shows that strict order has not governed the Orthodox churches, but rather the principle of economy (see 2.4), that is, of a merciful love for others and of freedom. This attitude was recognized by the First Preparatory Commission for the Pan-Orthodox Council when it stated that the Orthodox Church shows considerable freedom in applying economy to other brothers in Christ and that in Orthodoxy this economy will govern the future relations of the Orthodox Church to other churches and denominations.

Bibliography: Survey: E. Benz, *The Eastern Orthodox Church, Its Thought and Life* (Chicago, 1963) • J. Binns, *An Introduction to the Christian Orthodox Churches* (New York, 2002) • D. J. Constantelos, *Understanding the Greek Orthodox Church: Its Faith, History, and Practice* (New York, 1982) • A. Kallis, "Kirche V: Orthodoxe Kirche," *TRE* 18.252-62; idem, *Orthodoxie. Was ist das?* (6th ed.; Mainz, 1999; orig. pub., 1979) • J. Meyendorff, *The Orthodox Church: Its Past and Its Role in the World Today* (trans. J. Chapin; 3d ed.; Crestwood, N.Y., 1981) • N. D. Patrinacos, *A Dictionary of Greek Orthodoxy* (New York, 1984) • T. Ware, *The Orthodox Church* (new ed.; London, 1993).

History: Archbishop Pitirim of Volokolamsk, with F. Mayer, *The Orthodox Church in Russia: A Millennial Celebration* (New York, 1982) • V. Clark, *Why Angels Fall: A Journey through Orthodox Europe from Byzantium to Kosovo* (New York, 2000) • Y. M.-J. Congar, *After Nine Hundred Years* (New York, 1959) • N. Davis, *A Long Walk to Church: A Contemporary History of Russian Orthodoxy* (Boulder, Colo., 1995) • J. Fennell, *A History of the Russian Church to 1448* (London, 1995) • G. Florovsky, "The Orthodox Churches and the Ecumenical Movement prior to 1910," *A History of the Ecumenical Movement, 1517-1948* (3d ed.; ed. R. Rouse and S. C. Neill; Geneva, 1986) 169-215 • G. Mastrantonis, trans., *Augsburg and Constantinople: The Correspondence between the Tübingen Theologians and Patriarch Jeremiah II of Constantinople on the Augsburg Confession* (Brookline, Mass., 1982) • J. Meyendorff, *Byzantium and the Rise of Russia* (Cambridge, 1981); idem, *Living Tradition: Orthodox Witness in the Contemporary World* (Crestwood, N.Y., 1978); idem, *Rome, Constantinople, Moscow: Historical and Theological Studies* (Crestwood, N.Y., 1996) • J. Meyendorff and R. Tobias, eds., *Salvation in Christ: A Lutheran-Orthodox Dialogue* (Minneapolis, 1992) • J. M. Neale, *A History of the Holy Eastern Church* (5 vols.; London, 1847-73) • D. V. Pospielovsky, *The Orthodox Church in the History of Russia* (Crestwood, N.Y., 1998) • S. Runciman, *The Eastern Schism* (Oxford, 1955); idem, *The Great Church in Captivity: A Study of the Patriarchate of Constantinople from the Eve of the Turkish Conquest to the Greek War of Independence* (Cambridge, 1968) • A. Schmemann, *The Historical Road of Eastern Orthodoxy* (New York, 1963) • L. Simeonova, *Diplomacy of the Letter and the Cross: Photios, Bulgaria, and the Papacy, 860s-880s* (Amsterdam, 1998) • N. M. Vaporis, *Witnesses for Christ: Orthodox Christian Neomartyrs of the Ottoman Period, 1437-1860* (Crestwood, N.Y., 2000) • N. Zernov, "The Eastern Churches and the Ecumenical Movement in the Twentieth Century," *History of the Ecumenical Movement,* ed. Rouse and Neill, 645-74.

Theology and spirituality: J. BRECK, *Scripture in Tradition: The Bible and Its Interpretation in the Orthodox Church* (Crestwood, N.Y., 2001) • S. N. BULGAKOV, *The Orthodox Church* (Crestwood, N.Y., 1988; orig. pub., 1935) • G. FLOROVSKY, *Collected Works* (10 vols.; Belmont, Mass., 1972-87) • V. LOSSKY, *The Mystical Theology of the Eastern Church* (London, 1957); idem, *The Vision of God* (2d ed.; London, 1973) • J. A. MCGUCKIN, *Standing in God's Holy Fire: The Byzantine Tradition* (Maryknoll, N.Y., 2001) • G. A. MALONEY, *A History of Orthodox Theology since 1453* (Belmont, Mass., 1976) • J. MEYENDORFF, *Byzantine Theology: Historical Trends and Doctrinal Themes* (2d ed.; New York, 1979); idem, *Christ in Eastern Christian Thought* (New York, 1975) • A. NICHOLS, *Theology in the Russian Diaspora: Church, Fathers, Eucharist in Nikolai Afanasev (1893-1966)* (Cambridge, 1989) • J. PELIKAN, *The Christian Tradition: A History of the Development of Doctrine* (vols. 1-2; Chicago, 1971-74) • A. SCHMEMANN, *Introduction to Liturgical Theology* (2d ed.; New York, 1975); idem, *Sacraments and Orthodoxy* (New York, 1965) • T. SPIDLIK, *The Spirituality of the Christian East: A Systematic Handbook* (Kalamazoo, Mich., 1986) • H. WYBREW, *The Orthodox Liturgy: The Development of the Eucharistic Liturgy in the Byzantine Rite* (Crestwood, N.Y., 1990).

ANASTASIOS KALLIS

Orthodox Missions

1. Early Efforts
2. Decline
3. Russian Contributions
4. Archbishop Yannoulatos

The missionary tradition of the Eastern Orthodox Church is often unknown in Western circles, despite the outstanding contribution of its many exemplary → missionaries. Throughout the 2,000-year history of the Orthodox, their mission efforts often differed from those of their contemporary Western counterparts.

1. Early Efforts
The → Orthodox Church sees the missionary legacy of the apostolic church continuing in the fourth century and beyond through such stalwart missionaries as Gregory the Illuminator of Armenia (ca. 240-332), Nino (or Nina) of Georgia (4th cent.), Frumentius of Ethiopia (4th cent.), Hilarion of Gaza (ca. 291-371), and Alexander the Syrian (d. ca. 430), who organized a group of 150 of his most able monks to evangelize the lands around the Euphrates River. From the fourth through the sixth centuries, the Byzantine church actively evangelized the many pagans within the empire, while also sending out missionaries to Syria, Mesopotamia, Persia, Armenia, Phoenicia, Arabia, Nubia, Ethiopia, India, Mongolia, and China, as well as westward to the Goths, Huns, and Iberians.

The most famous of the Byzantine missionaries were the brothers Cyril (ca. 827-69) and Methodius (ca. 815-85) of Thessalonica, who evangelized the Slavic peoples of Moravia (→ Slavic Mission). Although Frankish missionaries had been working in this area for 50 years before their arrival, Cyril and Methodius were the first to create a Slavic alphabet and translate Holy Scriptures, Divine Services, and writings of the → church fathers into the language of the people. Despite fierce opposition from their Frankish counterparts, they received the blessing for their methods and work from the churches of both Rome and Constantinople. They labored in this region for 20 years, leaving behind more than 200 trained, indigenous clergy. Although little trace of their work survived in the regions of Moravia during the years of Frankish → persecution following their deaths, their disciples carried their legacy into the southern Slavic lands, doing evangelistic work and spreading the gospel in the lands of Serbia, Bulgaria, Moldavia, and eventually Russia.

2. Decline
The fall of Constantinople in 1453 initiated a period of missionary decline in the Orthodox lands of the Balkans and the Middle East. Islamic law forbade any proclamation of the gospel to those outside the Christian faith, while → conversion to → Islam was greatly encouraged and sometimes forced upon the subjugated Christians. For more than 400 years the church in these lands was thus generally prevented from participating in any missionary activity.

One exception was that of Kosmas of Aitolos (Kosmas the Aetolian, 1714-79). Kosmas, a monk from Mount → Athos, left his → monastery after 19 years to reevangelize hundreds of villages in what is modern-day northern Greece and Albania. His 20-year missionary effort helped to create more than 200 schools, whose main goal was to enable people to read Holy Scripture and writings of the church fathers. His missionary efforts were ended by martyrdom in 1779 (→ Martyrs).

3. Russian Contributions
3.1. While the Orthodox churches in the Balkans and the Middle East struggled greatly during this period, the church in Russia actively began participat-

ing in significant missionary outreach throughout the lands north and east of Kiev from the 14th century onward (→ Russian Orthodox Church). The most famous missionary of this era was Stephen of Perm (1340-96), the evangelizer of the Zyrian people of northwestern Siberia from 1378 to 1396. He followed the missionary model of Cyril and Methodius, creating an alphabet with ancient Zyrian runes and translating Holy Scripture and liturgical services for the people, training and ordaining indigenous clergy, and establishing a strong local church.

From the 16th to the 18th century the Russian church's missionary outreach faltered under the hostile policies of the state, yet it nevertheless recorded some advances. In the mid-16th century Bishop Gurii (d. 1563) evangelized the peoples of Kazan and helped convert thousands of Muslims (→ Islam). Centuries later the famous Academy of Kazan would become an important center of missionary and linguistic research and training. Other noteworthy missionaries of this period were the layman Trifon of Novgorod (d. 1584), who proclaimed the gospel to the Lapp people, and Bishop Filofei of Tobolsk (1650-1727), who evangelized and helped convert 40,000 indigenous peoples in various parts of Siberia. In 1714 the first official Orthodox mission began in Peking.

3.2. Missionary activity reached its apex in the 19th century, when a great spiritual renewal swept across Russia, bringing about a renewed apostolic zeal. Since most of the missions of this period took place among the numerous ethnolinguistic groups within the vast boundaries of the Russian Empire, the achievements of these outstanding missionaries generally attracted little attention outside of Orthodox circles.

The philologist Makarii Glukharev (1792-1847) spent 14 years in the rugged Siberian Altai Mountains proclaiming the gospel among warrior nomads and seminomads. Although the numerical fruit of his work was limited, he set an example and paved the way for the following generation of missionaries. By the end of the 19th century, 25,000 out of the 40,000 nomads in this area became Christian. During his years as a missionary, Glukharev published a significant book entitled *Thoughts on the Methods to Be Followed for a Successful Dissemination of the Faith among Mohammedans, Jews, and Pagans in the Russian Empire*. He became an important catalyst for Russian missions by formulating a working theory of → missiology within his church.

3.3. What is perhaps the most famous Russian missionary effort began when a group of ten monks from the Valaam monastery in what is now the Karelia Republic went to Alaska in 1792. Although the group witnessed promising numerical success in the early years, various tragedies and deaths reduced the original missionary group to one simple lay monk, Herman (ca. 1756-1837). Herman persevered, however, living a holy life and offering a witness of love to the indigenous peoples, often defending them from the oppression of Russian traders and exploiters. Although Herman never translated any materials or engaged in active missionary outreach, he drew people to Christ and is revered today as the father of Orthodoxy in Alaska.

Missions continued in Alaska and beyond largely through the long ministry of Innocent Veniaminov (1797-1879). Innocent began his apostolic efforts in 1823 as a married → priest working among the Fox-Aleut tribes of Alaska. During his ten years among this group, he created an alphabet and translated parts of Holy Scripture and Divine Services into their language, as well as training numerous indigenous leaders. From 1834 to 1839 he began work among the neighboring Tlingit peoples, once again creating a new writing system and translating parts of Holy Scriptures and liturgical services into their language. After the death of his wife in 1841, Innocent was elevated as a missionary → bishop and served in newly created dioceses in the Alaskan and eastern Siberian lands for the next 27 years. He traveled thousands of miles yearly by primitive means in order to reach the furthest regions of his dioceses.

Innocent's ministry culminated in his election as metropolitan of Moscow in 1868, in which capacity he served for the last 10 years of his life. During this time he established the Russian Orthodox Mission Society, whose goal was to prepare, support, and send out missionaries; raise missionary awareness among local churches; and create materials for various missions. By the turn of the century, the society was overseeing the work of more than 16,000 members within 55 diocesan committees. It helped to send hundreds of missionaries throughout the vast lands of Siberia and the eastern end of the Russian Empire, as well as to Alaska, Japan, China, and Korea. It also published more than 2 million copies of works translated into 20 languages for various missions. The Bolshevik revolution in 1917 ended the work of this society.

3.4. Another exemplary Russian missionary was Nicholas Kasatkin (1836-1912), whose apostolic effort took place in Japan from 1861 to 1912. He entered Japan when the country was still considered one of the most xenophobic and unevangelized countries in the world. At the end of his 50-year ministry, the Orthodox Church of Japan numbered more than 33,000 Christians within 266 communities and included 43 clergy and 121 lay preachers. Another part of Nicholas's legacy was his translation into Japanese of the NT and most of the OT, as well as most of the liturgical services of the church.

Again, the Bolshevik revolution abruptly disrupted all missionary activity coming out of Russia, enslaving Orthodoxy's largest and most active church, while the Orthodox churches in the Balkans were still recovering from their centuries under oppressive Ottoman rule. These circumstances kept the Orthodox Church inactive in external missions during the first half of the 20th century.

4. Archbishop Yannoulatos

In the late 1950s a missionary awakening began within the international Orthodox youth movement Syndesmos (lit. "uniting bond"). Anastasios Yannoulatos (b. 1929), a Greek theologian, led this revival, establishing the missionary magazine *Poreuthentes* (Go forth; from Matt. 28:19). Published in Greek and English, it sought to reawaken the Church of Greece and the international Orthodox community to its missionary responsibility. Yannoulatos established the inter-Orthodox mission center Poreuthentes in Athens in 1960 for the purpose of training and sending out cross-cultural missionaries. After a serious bout of malaria ended his first missionary endeavors in East Africa in the 1960s, Yannoulatos pursued further studies, eventually becoming professor of world religions at the University of Athens (1972-91). He made a significant contribution to the Orthodox and larger Christian world with his original missiological writings. In 1980 he founded and edited *Panta ta Ethne* (All nations), the first official mission magazine of the Church of Greece.

Yannoulatos turned next to actual missionary work, serving as acting archbishop of East Africa (1981-91) and then archbishop of Albania (from 1991). In East Africa he followed the Orthodox missionary tradition by opening the first Orthodox seminary in Africa and training and ordaining 62 indigenous clergy and 42 specialized → catechists. He also oversaw the translation of liturgical services in seven languages, while establishing 67 new churches and building numerous medical clinics and primary schools.

In Albania Archbishop Anastasios organized a holistic outreach in → evangelism, → education, health care, → development, culture, and the → environment. His first effort was to establish a seminary, which has trained and ordained 125 clergy over the past 12 years. He has built 85 new churches and rebuilt or repaired another 200. His missionary

and humanitarian efforts have been recognized throughout the Orthodox world and beyond, solidifying his position as the leading contemporary voice of Orthodox missions. Through his influence numerous other mission societies have begun in Greece. His work has also bolstered the missionary efforts of the Orthodox Church in Finland, as well as Orthodox churches in America.

The most visionary mission center today among the Orthodox churches worldwide is the Orthodox Christian Mission Center in St. Augustine, Florida, established in 1985. This center, a Pan-Orthodox mission effort under the auspices of the Standing Conference of Canonical Orthodox Bishops in the Americas, sends out long-term missionaries and sponsors ten short-term mission teams every year. It supports the indigenous work of missions in 25 countries, educates students from mission countries, and helps generally to raise the missionary consciousness of Orthodox churches in America.

→ Mission

Bibliography: G. Afonsky, *A History of the Orthodox Church in Alaska (1794-1917)* (Kodiak, Alaska, 1977) • I. Bria, *The Liturgy after the Liturgy: Mission and Witness from an Orthodox Perspective* (Geneva, 1996); idem, ed., *Martyria/Mission: The Witness of the Orthodox Churches Today* (Geneva, 1986) • J. Forrest, *Resurrection of the Church in Albania: Voices of Orthodox Christians* (Geneva, 2002) • P. Garrett, *St. Innocent, Apostle to America* (Crestwood, N.Y., 1979) • G. Lemopoulos, *Your Will Be Done: Orthodoxy in Mission* (Geneva, 1989) • G. P. Liacopulos, *Lights of the Modern World: Orthodox Christian Mission and Evangelism in the United States* (Minneapolis, 2000) • M. Oleksa, *Orthodox Alaska: A Theology of Mission* (Crestwood, N.Y., 1993); idem, ed., *Alaskan Missionary Spirituality* (New York, 1987) • J. Stamoolis, *Eastern Orthodox Mission Theology Today* (Maryknoll, N.Y., 1986) • A. Tachiaos, *Cyril and Methodios of Thessalonica* (Crestwood, N.Y., 2002) • P. Vassiliadis, *Eucharist and Witness: Orthodox Perspectives on the Unity and Mission of the Church* (Geneva, 1998) • L. Veronis, *Missionaries, Monks, and Martyrs: Making Disciples of All Nations* (Minneapolis, 1994) • A. Yannoulatos, *Facing the World: Orthodox Christian Essays on Global Concerns* (Crestwood, N.Y., 2003).

Luke Veronis

Orthodoxy

1. Lutheran Orthodoxy
   1.1. Epoch
   1.2. Political Context

1. Lutheran Orthodoxy

1.1. *Epoch*

The term "Lutheran orthodoxy" (sometimes "old Lutheran orthodoxy" or "old Protestant orthodoxy") is ill adapted to describe this specific form of Reformation Christianity, which extended between the → Reformation and the → Enlightenment. Radical → Pietism called the period orthodox because of (1) its interest in pure doctrine alone and not also in a holy life in devout fellowship and (2) the alliance between ecclesiastical and secular government. But this summary was a caricature. Again, "old Lutheran Orthodoxy" was used to distinguish the epoch as premodern (E. → Troeltsch).

The more common term used today to describe the epoch is simply "early → modern period," which sees Lutheran orthodoxy as one element in a whole social process of modernization in which traditional and dynamic factors constituted once more a relatively homogeneous world. Because this world had a religious center ("religion" here meaning "confession"; → Confession of Faith), this age has rightly been called the confessional age. It began between 1530 and 1577/80 (→ Formula of Concord), then after 1675 it was challenged by new religious, social, and scientific developments. It finally came to an end around 1740.

1.2. *Political Context*

In contrast to countries with state churches (e.g., in Scandinavia) or those with a distinction between political rule and religion (e.g., Netherlands, Poland up to 1658/1717), the Holy Roman Empire was divided by the Peace of Augsburg (1555) into religious as well as political units (→ Augsburg, Peace of; Cuius regio eius religio). Except in a few imperial cities, the authorities (mostly consistorial) guaranteed a system of church government that tied the church closely to the state, increasingly so along the lines of a developing absolutism, which Lutheran pastors opposed in exercise of their "office of oversight" (cf. the episcopal system, in which the prince was only "the first among the church members"). Even defenders

of a princely state relativized its claim to sovereignty by giving to the exercise of political power a character of ministry and calling. At the same time, some Pietist and humanistic motifs worked in favor of absolutism or state church territorialism. The activities of the Lutheran churches were aimed to encourage individuals who were bound to the state and, after 1648 (→ Thirty Years' War), to restore prosperity and → peace. → Church discipline, itself only moderately effective, was not subordinated to the social discipline imposed by the state.

1.3. *Cultural Aspects*

Lutheran Orthodoxy is a specific confessional expression of the cultural developments known as later → humanism, Mannerism, and the → baroque. It involved great variety and also great cultural and linguistic tensions, but it maintained an abiding confidence in cosmic order and a saving purpose for the world (→ Salvation History). The confessional culture of → Lutheranism was especially fruitful in linguistic reform, in spiritual and secular poetry (N. Frischlin, *Hebraeis* [1590]; J. M. Meyfart, *Das himmlische Jerusalem* [1627]; Gryphius, tragedies, odes, and sonnets [1646ff.]; P. von Zesen, *Assenat* [1670]), in the theater, in religious music and music for the court and the home (M. Praetorius, H. Schütz, D. Buxtehude, J. S. Bach, the Dresden opera), in architecture and church furnishings (Wolfenbüttel, the altar of St. Mary's Church in Marburg), and in libraries and scholarship (new universities and academies such as Jena, Hamburg, Coburg, and Stettin; new disciplines such as → metaphysics [C. Martini, A. Calovius]; the development of natural science and a rejection of existing theories [J. Maestlin, J. Kepler, V. Weigel]; and the encouraging of polymathy [D. G. Morhof]).

1.4. *Piety and Theology*

1.4.1. *Piety*

Albrecht Ritschl wrongly saw Lutheran orthodoxy as purely academic doctrine, when in fact it tapped many resources to give training in Christian faith and life in conformity with the → gospel. → Worship (→ preaching, → hymns, → church music, eucharistic piety), → pastoral care (penance, church discipline, → occasional services, funeral sermons), domestic piety (→ catechism, → devotional literature), and public rituals also shaped the Christian life (seen as *militia Christiana*), pardoned sinners both actively and passively under the sign of the cross (→ Theologia crucis), provided assurance of God's direction in such misfortunes as want, sickness, → war, and → death, which were always at hand particularly for women and children (meditation on death and expectation of the → Last Judgment), and aided in the giving of praise and thanksgiving to the Creator for his goodness to his creatures. Widely read devotional books, such as the best-selling *Four Books of True Christianity* by Johann Arndt (1555-1621), bear witness not only to the inner appropriation of the belief in → justification (§2) but also to a pervasive sense of weakness in the emotional and moral grasping of the message of faith.

It would be wrong to describe the many attempts to overcome distinctions of doctrine and life as a reforming orthodoxy set in opposition to a "dead" institutional church. The only truth to that verdict is the fact that criticism often had a spiritualistic motive (Weigel, as well as Arndt and J. V. Andreae). Despite some reservations, the whole church accepted the criticism and the demand for a more deeply individual faith (J. Gerhard, B. Meisner). Thus there developed in Lutheranism a → mysticism — by no means "recatholicizing" — that applied the Christological communication of attributes to Christians (P. Nicolai) without replacing Christ with pious inner experience. Conflict arose only in the controversy with a programmatic Pietism.

The development of → piety had its crises. The assaults of personal sinfulness (→ Sin) were viewed along narrower moralistic lines that were also overlaid with the experience of futility. Independence was claimed for the external communication of faith by preaching, Scripture, the → sacraments, and the → church, but along with this element went apocalyptic anxieties or hopes (e.g., expressed in → astrology or reading comets; → Apocalypticism 4.4), a sense of the mysteriousness of life (and thus → alchemy, → magic, and → witchcraft), and the theosophical modification of Christian mysticism (J. Böhme, also G. W. Leibniz; → Theosophy). Before the 18th century, Lutheran piety shunned deistic tendencies, despite its efforts to distinguish one's relation to God from one's relation to the world (i.e., morality).

1.4.2. *Theology*

The high regard for academic theology in Lutheran orthodoxy was primarily because the organizing and controlling of scholarship was still seen as a matter for the discipline that deals with eternal salvation. Theology was the primary university faculty, enjoyed the highest social esteem, had the most students among all the higher faculties, and produced the most scholarly works. It took a strong interest in other arts faculties, for theological propaedeutic was grounded in the study of languages, history, and philosophy (including → ethics, → logic, → metaphysics, physics, and → rhetoric). Theologians al-

ways began their studies in philosophy. There were material and personal rivalries, but only during the 17th century did reflection that was independent, though not critical, of → revelation make more radical efforts to free itself from its allotted role. For its part, theology with an ontological claim resisted the competing → ontologies of the new and autonomous philosophies that incorporated → theology either methodologically (R. Descartes, C. Wolff) or pantheistically (B. Spinoza). By the end of the 17th century, theology had lost its primacy over law and philosophy.

An essential feature of Lutheran orthodoxy was a view of theology not as a taught system but as a *habitus,* a frame of mind that must be achieved by scholarly effort, even though it is divinely given, since its source is the revelation of salvation in Holy Scripture. This habitus was understood practically as the ability to lead sinners to salvation. For this pastoral goal doctrine, built up by demonstration from Scripture as the epistemological principle in theology (Gerhard), has an instrumental character. Theological work was thus primarily seen as soteriological → exegesis, homiletics, → pastoral theology, and polity (→ Church Government). The special presentation of the contents of dogma (in tractates, confessional expositions, disputations, loci, and systems) had as its essential aim confessional integration.

This understanding of theology as a habitus required clarification of the relation between theological scholarship and personal faith. One solution insisted on a close relation between vocation and saving faith in a theology of regeneration (D. Hofmann, Arndt, and Pietism generally). Another solution, a humanist position, distinguished between academic theology and piety (G. Calixtus, later also Enlightenment theology). A third, or middle, view hoped for personal union between the habitus and saving faith but did not insist on it (Meisner, Gerhard, Calovius, J. A. Quenstedt).

1.4.3. *Doctrinal Development*

Doctrinal development began negatively in conscious distinction from Tridentine Roman Catholicism (→ Catholic Reform and Counter-Reformation, 2.2) and the Philippist and Calvinist interpretations of Reformation teaching. In a first phase, up to the 1590s (M. Chemnitz, T. Kirchner, L. Hutter) and even when the Formula of Concord had become current, the dominant theme was expounding the relation between motifs in M. → Luther (1483-1546; → Luther's Theology) and P. → Melanchthon (1497-1560; → Reformers), along with replies to → Crypto-Calvinism.

In a second phase, up to 1630, interest focused on theological method and the use of Aristotelian tools and metaphysics, and also on a universal doctrine of election in response to → Calvinism and in continuation of themes in Melanchthon. → Christology, however, owed its inspiration to Luther and Johann Brenz (1499-1570). On the basis of article 8 in the Formula of Concord, "The Person of Christ," Christological reflection was refined in about 1625 by the Tübingen theologians Theodore Thumm and Lukas Osiander II. They opposed their understanding of Christ being the presence of God to all humankind against the Giessen view that the God-man is present only to the devout. It also stood in antithesis to the Helmstedt Christology of T. Hesshusen, which would assign dominion only to the exalted Lord, and it contrasted sharply with the lack of Christological interest in the school of Georg Calixtus (1586-1656), also at Helmstedt.

In keeping with the Tübingen view of the person and work of Christ as concrete communion between divinity and humanity (God neither sparing his Son death nor denying his presence to humanity) was the new doctrinal locus, *unio mystica,* or "mystical union" (e.g., taught by Nicolai and Meisner). This union, together with the forensic doctrine of justification, became a central element in →) soteriology, considered largely in terms of the appropriating grace of the Holy Spirit, with later emphasis on the → order of salvation. Other dogmatic innovations were methodological, including the definition of theology, the transition from writing works such as Melanchthon's *Loci* to a pastorally oriented analytic method (B. Mentzer), the doctrine of fundamental articles (N. Hunnius, J. Hülsemann), and the doctrine of Scripture, which as a result of controversy led to a formulation of an objective doctrine of the → inspiration of the biblical text that was later caricatured as mechanical. In opposition to → spiritualism (H. Rathmann), the unity of Scripture and Spirit was upheld, though with hermeneutical reflection on the work of exposition (J. K. Dannhauer).

In the third phase, after 1640/50, the previous achievements were consolidated, largely by Quenstedt (1617-88), and stress fell on the acceptance of the common Christian tradition, that is, on a Lutheran catholicity. There was, however, opposition to the reductive traditionalism of the Calixtus school (→ Syncretistic Controversy). At the same time, the doctrine of the → Trinity was defended as rationally plausible in answer to Socinianism (A. Kessler, Calovius; → Natural Theology; Physicotheology). → Deism and → atheism, which were now developing, were also combated (J. Musaeus, V. E. Löscher). In the process, agreed arguments from natural theology came to be taken for granted, at the expense of revelation. The need for the latter was found in relation to problems of the Christian life and the demands of society; a separation of ethics from dogmatics resulted, first in Calixtus. For dogmatics, a term first found in 1659, the role was theoretical and then historical as it came under the impact of eclectics (→ Dogma, History of). After 1700 a change increasingly took place in dogmatics with Pietism, which Lutheran orthodoxy at first supported, and after 1720 with the work of Christian Wolff (1679-1754). In the practice of piety and the theory of religion, a gulf separated Lutheran orthodoxy from the → neological criticism of dogmas, which dated from 1750.

→ Lutheran churches today owe their common Christian basis, their Reformation profile, and not least their theological precision largely to the work of Lutheran orthodoxy. Not the selective attempt to go back to this orthodoxy as in the German restoration movement of the 19th century but the relevant recalling of the period as a whole is a necessary prerequisite if Lutheranism is to retain its theological competence and ecumenical profile.

→ Modern Church History 1

Bibliography: Primary sources: J. ANDREAE, *Disputationes theologicae, de praecipuiis doctrinae Christianae capitibus* (Montbéliard, 1593) • J. ARNDT, *True Christianity* (1605-9) (ed. P. Erb; New York, 1979) • *The Book of Concord: The Confessions of the Evangelical Lutheran Church* (ed. R. Kolb and T. J. Wengert; Minneapolis, 2000) • M. CHEMNITZ, *Examination of the Council of Trent* (trans. F. Kramer; 4 vols.; St. Louis, 1971-86); idem, "Free Will" and "Sin," *The Doctrine of Man in Classical Lutheran Theology* (ed. H. A. Preus and E. Smits; Minneapolis, 1962); idem, *Loci theologici* (Frankfurt and Wittenberg, 1653); idem, *The Lord's Supper* (1570) (trans. J. A. O. Preus; St. Louis, 1979); idem, *The Two Natures in Christ* (1578) (trans. J. A. O. Preus; St. Louis, 1971) • D. CHYTRAEUS, *Opera* (Leipzig, 1594) • M. FLACIUS, *Clavis Scripturae sacrae* (Copenhagen, 1695) • J. GERHARD, *An Explanation of the History of the Suffering and Death of Our Lord Jesus Christ* (trans. E. M. Hohle; St. Louis, 1999); idem, *Loci theologici* (Tübingen, 1763) • D. HOLLAZ, *Examen theologicum acroamaticum* (Rostock and Leipzig, 1718) • P. MELANCHTHON, *Melanchthon on Christian Doctrine: Loci Communes* (1555) (trans. C. L. Manschreck; New York, 1965) • J. A. QUENSTEDT, *Theologia didactico-polemica, sive systema theologiae* (Leipzig, 1702) • "Theology in the Age of Orthodoxy (1580-

1700)," *Documents from the History of Lutheranism, 1517-1750* (ed. E. Lund; Minneapolis, 2002) 216-44.

Secondary works (English): R. G. CLOUSE, *The Church in the Age of Orthodoxy and the Enlightenment: Consolidation and Challenge from 1600 to 1800* (St. Louis, 1980) • W. ELERT, *The Structure of Lutheranism* (2 vols.; St. Louis, 1962) • E. FARLEY, *Theologia: The Fragmentation and Unity of Theological Education* (Philadelphia, 1983) • E. W. GRITSCH, *A History of Lutheranism* (Minneapolis, 2002) • E. F. KLUG, *From Luther to Chemnitz: On Scripture and the Word* (Grand Rapids, 1971) • R. KOLB, *Andreae and the Formula of Concord: Six Sermons on the Way to Lutheran Unity* (St. Louis, 1977); idem, *Luther's Heirs Define His Legacy: Studies on Lutheran Confessionalization* (Brookfield, Vt., 1996) • C. P. KRAUTH, *The Conservative Reformation and Its Theology: As Represented in the Augsburg Confession, and in the History and Literature of the Evangelical Lutheran Church* (Philadelphia, 1871) • C. L. MANSCHRECK, *Melanchthon: The Quiet Reformer* (New York, 1958) • J. PELIKAN, *From Luther to Kierkegaard* (2d ed.; St. Louis, 1963) • J. A. O. PREUS, *The Second Martin: The Life and Theology of Martin Chemnitz* (St. Louis, 1994) • R. D. PREUS, *The Theology of Post-Reformation Lutheranism* (2 vols.; St. Louis, 1970-72) • H. SCHMID, *The Doctrinal Theology of the Evangelical Lutheran Church, Verified from the Original Sources* (3d ed.; Philadelphia, 1875) • R. VIERHAUS, *Germany in the Age of Absolutism, 1648-1763* (Cambridge, 1988).

Secondary works (German): J. BAUR, *Luther und seine klassischen Erben* (Tübingen, 2000); idem, *Die Vernunft zwischen Ontologie und Evangelium. Eine Untersuchung zur Theologie Johann Andreas Quenstedts* (Gütersloh, 1962) • M. GRESCHAT, ed., *Orthodoxie und Pietismus* (Stuttgart, 1982) • M. HECKEL, *Deutschland im konfessionellen Zeitalter* (Göttingen, 2001) • H. KLUETING, *Das konfessionelle Zeitalter, 1525-1648* (Stuttgart, 1989) • W. MAURER, *Der junge Melanchthon zwischen Humanismus und Reformation* (2 vols.; Göttingen, 1967-69; repr., 1996) • C. H. RATSCHOW, *Lutherische Dogmatik zwischen Reformation und Aufklärung* (2 vols.; Gütersloh, 1964-66) • W. SPARN, *Wiederkehr der Metaphysik. Die ontologische Frage in der lutherischen Theologie des frühen 17. Jahrhunderts* (Stuttgart, 1976).

JÖRG BAUR and WALTER SPARN

2. Reformed Orthodoxy

2.1. *General Character*

The term "Reformed Orthodoxy" can be understood either confessionally or historically. From the confessional perspective, it indicates the "right teaching" of the Reformed faith, as determined by its historical confessional documents, at any time since the → Reformation of the 16th century (→ Confession of Faith). Understood historically, however, the term refers restrictively to the confessional theology of the era immediately following the Reformation — roughly from 1565 to 1725. After 1725, confessionally orthodox theology tended to fragment and ceased to be the dominant intellectual movement that it was in the 17th century, but its history can be traced in somewhat more rationalistic forms through the 18th century. It is the latter, historical sense that concerns us here.

The religious and theological developments that occurred during this era evidence patterns of institutionalization that mirror what social historians have termed the "confessionalization" and "deconfessionalization" of Protestant Europe. In the second part of the 16th and the first part of the 17th centuries (ca. 1565 to 1640), the era of early orthodoxy, the Reformed not only developed the patterns of confessional orthodoxy that defined the spiritual and intellectual existence of Reformed → Protestantism, but they also participated in the rise of Protestant → universities and theological faculties where, in contrast to the era of the Reformation, professors who had been trained as Protestants themselves trained Protestant clergy, in the context of fairly strict confessional subscription. During the remainder of the 17th century, that confessional orthodoxy developed and elaborated its teachings under increasing pressure from changes in philosophy, in biblical interpretation, and in the politics of European religion — changes that, in the early 18th century, led to a decline of Protestant orthodoxy as an intellectual movement and as a unified confessional model within the Protestant nations of Europe.

The → theology of the Reformed churches in the era of orthodoxy stands in relative continuity with the thought of the Reformers, developing largely within the bounds of the established confessions, yet also with elements of discontinuity that arose because of the altered contexts of polemic against Rome and the Lutherans (→ Roman Catholic Church; Lutheranism) and various new confessional adversaries, namely, → Arminians and Socinians (→ Unitarians), because of major shifts in → philosophy leading to the new → rationalisms of the 17th and 18th centuries, and because of shifts in the ecclesial and academic cultures of the era. It is certainly a mistake to attempt to measure these developments and changes by identifying a single author in the era of the Reformation (e.g., John → Calvin [1509-64]) and comparing him with another individual author in the 17th century (e.g., Gisbertus Voetius [1589-

1676]), or by selecting a single author or, indeed, a single document as the cause of change (e.g., Theodore → Beza's [1519-1605] *Tabula praedestinationis* of 1555).

Similarly, it is a mistake to reduce this rather variegated and diverse movement to the development of a single doctrine, like → predestination, or to a purportedly antithetical development of two doctrines, namely predestination and → covenant, as if the theologians of the era based entire bodies of doctrine on a single dogmatic notion. In the time of Calvin the movement was already so complex and varied in its confessions and in its major thinkers (in addition to Calvin, such writers as Heinrich Bullinger [1504-75], Wolfgang Musculus [1497-1563], Andreas Hyperius [1511-64], and Peter Martyr Vermigli [1500-1562]) as to defy identification with the thought of a single individual. So too was the doctrinal or confessional basis of the movement so broadly catholic as to preclude deductive development of "central dogmas." Given the diversity, the term "Reformed" is preferable to the term "Calvinist."

If the thought of the Reformed orthodox was the product of training in the confessional milieu established by the → Reformers, it was also a theology steeped in the linguistic and philological tools of the → Renaissance and presented in academic forms of disputation, topical discussion, and refined distinction that evidenced a "scholastic" method grounded in medieval forms and altered significantly by humanistic concerns in → logic and → rhetoric. From a philosophical perspective, this orthodox and scholastic theology was rooted in the long tradition of Christian → Aristotelianism — a highly eclectic philosophy modified by recourse to patristic materials of a more Platonic tendency (notably → Augustine), by the medieval doctors who drew heavily on non-Aristotelian sources like Augustine and Pseudo-Dionysius, by the Renaissance reappropriation of Aristotelian thought and other classical philosophies, and by the Reformed orthodox themselves in interaction with skeptical philosophy, with the beginnings of → deism and, in the course of the 17th century, with the thought of René Descartes (1596-1650), Thomas Hobbes (1588-1679), Nicolas Malebranche (1638-1715), Baruch Spinoza (1632-77), and others. Given the diversity of its theological roots in the Reformation, the breadth of its confessional statements, its emphasis on → exegesis, and the diversity of influences exerted on it, whether polemical or more positive, whether intellectual or cultural, Reformed orthodoxy cannot be reduced to a neat, monolithic theological system, much less to

the logical development of a single → dogma such as predestination.

2.2. Early Orthodoxy (ca. 1565-1640)

2.2.1. The era of early orthodoxy can be identified as extending, roughly, from the time of the deaths of the major second-generation codifiers of the Reformation and of the publication of the major national confessions of the Reformed churches, to the time of the deaths of the more senior voices of the Synod of Dort (1618-19). It is the era during which the major institutionalization and confessionalization of the Reformed faith took place and, accordingly, the era of the primary development of a full-scale academic theology, both in the establishment of a tradition of biblical interpretation in critical texts, translations, and commentaries and in the more systematic forms of *Loci communes, Compendia theologiae,* and sets of academic *disputationes.*

Still, the process of institutionalization and the theology that it generated ought not to be viewed as rigid or monolithic. Major formulators like Beza, Zacharias Ursinus (1534-83), Caspar Olevianus (1536-87), Lambert Daneau (1530-95), Girolamo Zanchi (1516-90), Franciscus Junius (1545-1602), Amandus Polanus (1561-1610), William Perkins (1558-1602), Bartholomaus Keckermann (1571-1609), and Johann Heinrich Alsted (1588-1638) evidence a fairly wide variety of formulations, as well as an interplay of varied appropriations of exegesis, the older tradition, and philosophy in their thought. Their method, moreover, tended to bind doctrinal formulation to exegesis: the Reformed orthodox carried out the method developed by Philipp → Melanchthon (1497-1560), Martin → Bucer (1491-1551), Calvin, Bullinger, Vermigli, and others, according to which topics, or *loci,* were extracted from Scripture in the course of exegesis and then subsequently linked together in a series suitable to teaching.

2.2.2. The doctrinal development, considered largely as an expansion and elaboration of the teachings of the Reformers, can be described both positively and polemically. The positive development can be described as the effort of later Reformed theologians to present their teachings in fully academic or scholastic form for the sake of teaching in the university setting and to develop Reformed doctrine with clearer reference to the patristic and medieval materials underlying the Protestant tradition. On the latter point, the Reformed orthodox were just as concerned as the Reformers themselves to identify the catholicity of the Protestant faith and somewhat more ready than the Reformers to state clearly the positive elements of the medieval tradition. This use of medieval models is evident in the thought of such writers as Zanchi and Daneau. A primary manifestation of this academic retrieval of the broader tradition was the development of theological prolegomena — notably by Franciscus Junius (1545-1641), Amandus Polanus (1561-1610), and Johann Heinrich Alsted (1588-1638) — for the sake of defining the task of theology both in the university and in the church.

The majority of the Reformed understood theology as either primarily or entirely practical, a discipline oriented toward the church and tending toward the goal of salvation. In its method this theology was "scholastic," but it was a scholasticism modified by Renaissance → humanism and, in particular, by the logic and rhetoric of Pierre Ramus (1515-72) and Giacopo Zabarella (1532-89). Nor, indeed, can this Reformed orthodoxy be labeled "rationalist": in contrast to the rationalist philosophies of the day, it continued to assume the priority of → revelation over → reason and the ancillary status of philosophy in relation to theological discourse.

2.2.3. The polemical side of the development consisted in the careful definition of the Reformed faith over against alternatives such as Socinianism, aspects of the Radical Reformation, and, most significantly, against Roman Catholicism as codified by the Council of → Trent and defended by such writers as Robert → Bellarmine (1542-1621) and Cardinal J. Perronius (1556-1618). Bellarmine in particular must be counted as a major influence on Protestant doctrinal development, given the detail and cogency of his → polemic. In the early orthodox era, he was answered by such writers as William Ames (1576-1633), Lucas Trelcatius the younger (1573-1607), and Festus Hommius (1576-1642). Their rebuttals of Bellarmine often included refinements of Protestant doctrine. This polemic, together with the institutionalization of Reformed thought in the academic context, resulted in large-scale reconsideration and adaptation of philosophical categories and of the precise distinctions of the older → Scholasticism for the sake of arguing such doctrines as the divine essence and attributes (→ God), the → Trinity, the person of Christ, and predestination.

2.3. High Orthodoxy (ca. 1640-1725)

2.3.1. The "high orthodox" era was the time of the final flowering of Reformed orthodoxy, characterized by a large-scale development of exegetical study, positive theological system, and codified polemic. It is also the era of the flowering of two significant forms of Reformed piety or spirituality, that of the → Puritans in England and of the *Nadere*

Reformatie in the Netherlands. These developments in spirituality were indebted to each other and profoundly interrelated with the orthodox or scholastic theology of the era. Whereas among the German Lutherans, a relatively clear and often antagonistic distinction has frequently been made between the Pietists and the orthodox, neither the Puritans nor the proponents of the *Nadere Reformatie* argued a → piety in antithesis to scholastic Reformed orthodoxy. In fact, many of the most influential proponents of this Reformed piety were also the teachers of the scholastic theology of the era, concerned to manifest the connection between the academic disciplines of theology and the life of the church.

Notable evidences of this balance of orthodoxy and piety are found in the thought of Voetius, Johannes Hoornbeeck (1617-66), John Owen (1616-83), and Richard Baxter (1615-91). Voetius exemplifies the technical use of scholastic method in the university, and Hoornbeeck the codification of polemic, yet both were also deeply involved in catechetical work and the encouragement of what can be called vernacular piety for the life of the congregation. Owen is remembered as one of the most erudite opponents of Arminianism and Socinianism but also as a → catechist, a significant preacher, and the author of the most extended study ever produced on the work of the → Holy Spirit. Baxter, remembered primarily as the author of works on → spirituality like *The Saints' Everlasting Rest* (1650) and *The Reformed Pastor* (1656), was deeply read in scholastic theology and wrote several massive technical treatises, including a theological system.

2.3.2. The high orthodox era is also known for several heated controversies that took place within the bounds of Reformed confessionalism — the controversies generated in large part by the theologians of the Academy of Saumur, Louis Cappel (1585-1658), Moyse Amyraut (1596-1664), and Joshua La Place (ca. 1596-1665); by ongoing recrimination among proponents of the supra- and infralapsarian definitions of predestination; and by developments in covenant theology, primarily in the thought of Johannes Cocceius (1603-69) and his followers. Three of the controversies were over issues remaining after the doctrinal condemnation of the Arminians at the Synod of Dort, namely, debate over Amyraut's "hypothetical universalism," over the supra- and infralapsarian definitions of predestination, and over La Place's theory of the "mediate" imputation of → sin.

Arguably, all of the theologians involved understood themselves as Reformed orthodox proponents of a fully confessional theology. Amyraut, whose teaching had precedent in the thought of several of the delegates at Dort — Alsted, John Davenant (1572-1641), and Matthias Martinius (1572-1630) — held that the infinite sufficiency of Christ's death (a point on which all were agreed) implied the possibility of universal salvation and a "hypothetical" divine intention to accomplish it, if all would come to faith in Christ. His opponents, notably Pierre du Moulin (1568-1658), Friedrich Spanheim the elder (1600-1649), Francis Turretin (1623-87), and Johann Heinrich Heidegger (1633-98), denied the hypothetical intention to save all and emphasized a single divine intentionality, namely, to save the elect.

La Place, against similar opposition, argued that the imputation of Adam's sin to all of humanity was not an immediate, purely forensic act on the part of God but a mediate — or mediated — divine act grounded on the hereditary fact of human sinfulness. Opponents like Turretin argued that this view was problematic inasmuch as it removed the perfect forensic balance between the immediate imputation of Adam's sin to all and the immediate imputation of Christ's righteousness to the faithful. Both Amyraut and La Place were eventually condemned in the Formula Consensus Helvetica (1675), in which the authors carefully defined the Saumur theologies as mistaken but not heretical.

2.3.3. Debate between supra- and infralapsarians — over the question of whether the objects of God's eternal willing ought to be considered as *creabilis et labilis* (possibles to be created and permitted to fall) or as *creatus et lapsus* (actuals created and fallen) — also arose in the aftermath of Dort, where an infralapsarian majority had framed the canons, albeit without any condemnation of the supralapsarian definitions. A failed older scholarship has read this debate as a battle between metaphysically speculative, "rigid" predestinarians (the supralapsarians) and thinkers who were less speculative and less rigid (the infralapsarians). Given that both sides held that the decrees of God are eternal and not grounded in foreknowledge of the temporal order, that neither view enlarged the number of the elect, and that the supralapsarians tended to define theology as fundamentally "practical" and argued that their definitions were intended to exclude all merit of any sort from the divine elective willing, this older explanation cannot hold.

Rather, the debate was over such issues as the character of the → creation (and the fall), namely, whether, as in the supralapsarian perspective, they ought to be viewed primarily as means to the end

of election and reprobation, and over the certainty of the end or goal willed by God for humanity, a point pressed by the supralapsarians. Resolution of the debate, in a late-17th-century writer like Petrus van Mastricht (1630-1706), consisted in the recognition that the two definitions were actually compatible readings of the same issues from different but equally legitimate perspectives on the divine knowing: God knows both all possibility and all actuality.

2.3.4. The controversy over Cocceian federalism had several dimensions. First, it is important to state that the controversy did not pit a covenantal, historical biblicism against an a priori, predestinarian scholasticism. All parties, whether Cocceian or Voetian, were orthodox Reformed predestinarians, all approved of the then-standard Reformed assumption of a prelapsarian covenant of works or nature and a postlapsarian covenant of → grace, and all used the scholastic methods of the era. Within these boundaries, the debate was framed by the Cocceian assumption of a gradually abrogated covenant of works and a gradually inaugurated covenant of grace that, in the Voetian view, undermined the equal authority of the OT on such issues as Sabbath observance and offered a problematic view of → salvation under the OT, namely, as lacking the absolute fulfillment given in the NT. There was also a philosophical overtone to the controversy, given that several of the Cocceians — for example, Abraham Heidanus (1597-1678) and Franz Burman (1632-79) — manifested → Cartesian tendencies. Controversy diminished in the early 18th century both because of the rapprochement of the parties and because of the civil acknowledgment of the right of each party to professorships and pastorates.

2.4. *The Close of the Era of Orthodoxy*

The last decades of the 17th century saw the beginnings of changes that would render orthodoxy a somewhat marginalized intellectual movement in the 18th century. The older philosophy, an eclectic Christian Aristotelianism, finally gave way to alternative patterns of thought. Orthodoxy itself had begun to adapt to Cartesian rationalism, only to find that philosophy modified or set aside in the → natural theology of early deism and in the rationalistic systems of Spinoza, Gottfried Wilhelm Leibniz (1646-1716), and John Locke (1632-1704). At the same time, the biblical criticism of Richard Simon (1638-1712), buttressed by reflection on the nature of religion and religious writing by Spinoza and Lodewijk Meijer (1629-81), began a transformation of biblical interpretation that would undermine the precritical exegetical models of the Reformation and the era of orthodoxy and would feed into the deist critique of biblical revelation in the next century.

By the end of the first quarter of the 18th century, Protestant orthodoxy, together with the older philosophy and logic and the precritical models of biblical exegesis, ceased to occupy the mainstream of intellectual life. A highly eclectic, somewhat rationalist, and often confessionally indifferentist theology replaced strict confessional orthodoxy in many of the centers of Protestant thought. The Swiss Reformed writers Jean Alphonse Turretin (1671-1737) and Jean Frédéric Ostervald (1663-1747) advocated less strict confessional subscription and a more rationalist form of Reformed theology.

Other Reformed thinkers of the 18th century, notably Daniel Wyttenbach (1706-79) and Johann Friedrich Stapfer (1708-75), attempted to produce a new form of orthodoxy grounded in the rational → metaphysics of Christian Wolff (1679-1754) and formulated on the assumption that natural theology provided the necessary rational foundation on which a theology of supernatural revelation could be based. It became characteristic of 18th-century theological systems to begin with an entire exposition of natural theology, including discussions of natural revelation, the essence and attributes of God, and morality, prior to discussing, in a separate portion of the theology, the revealed truths of the Trinity, → Christology, and human salvation.

Still, there remained in the 18th century a series of writers who defended the older models. In Britain, Thomas Ridgley (1667-1734), John Gill (1697-1771), Thomas Boston (1677-1732), and John Brown of Haddington (1722-87) continued to write theology in the older orthodox patterns, although Brown adopted the natural/supernatural model of his era. Among the Continental writers, Aegidius Francken (1676-1743) and Bernhardus de Moor (1710-65) can be counted as more traditional orthodox thinkers. The latter's massive commentary on the late-17th-century *Compendium theologiae* of Johannes Marckius (1656-1731) stands as a definitional and bibliographic testimony to the depth and detail of the older orthodox achievement.

Where the more academic, scholastic, and philosophically patterned orthodoxy began to fade, its child — the → Pietism of the Puritans, English Dissent, and the Dutch *Nadere Reformatie* — continued to flower as an ecclesial movement. But while there was often a hostile relationship between Lutheran Pietism and Lutheran orthodoxy, the piety of the Puritans and of the *Nadere Reformatie* remained bound to traditional Reformed orthodoxy. Thus, the more inward-looking religion of piety remained committed, in such writers as Johannes Beukelman (1704-57), Abraham Hellenbroeck (1658-1731), and Alexander Comrie (1706-74), to orthodox Reformed doctrine, albeit without the philosophical underpinnings characteristic of the older orthodoxy.

Bibliography: B. ARMSTRONG, *Calvinism and the Amyraut Heresy: Protestant Scholasticism and Humanism in Seventeenth-Century France* (Madison, Wis., 1969) • W. J. VAN ASSELT, *The Federal Theology of Johannes Cocceius (1603-1669)* (Leiden, 2001) • W. J. VAN ASSELT and E. DEKKER, *Reformation and Scholasticism: An Ecumenical Enterprise* (Grand Rapids, 2001) • W. J. VAN ASSELT, P. L. ROUWENDAL, et al., *Inleiding in de Gereformeerde Scholastiek* (Zoetermeer, 1998) • O. FATIO, *Méthode et théologie. Lambert Daneau et les débuts de la scholastique réformée* (Geneva, 1976) • C. GRAAFLAND, *Van Calvijn tot Comrie. Oorsprong en ontwild ontwikkeling van de leer van het verbond in het Gereformeerd Protestantisme* (3 vols.; Zoetermeer, 1992-94) • H. HEPPE, *Reformed Dogmatics Set Out and Illustrated from the Sources* (rev. ed.; London, 1950; repr., Grand Rapids, 1978) • R. A. MULLER, *After Calvin: Studies in the Development of a Theological Tradition* (New York, 2003); idem, *God, Creation, and Providence in the Thought of Jacob Arminius: Sources and Directions of Scholastic Protestantism in the Era of Early Orthodoxy* (Grand Rapids, 1991); idem, *Post-Reformation Reformed Dogmatics: The Rise and Development of Reformed Orthodoxy, ca. 1520 to 1725* (4 vols.; Grand Rapids, 1987-2003) • O. RITSCHL, *Dogmengeschichte des Protestantismus. Grundlagen und Grundzüge der theologischen Gedanken- and Lehrbildung in den protestantischen Kirchen* (vols. 1-2, Leipzig, 1908-12; vols. 3-4, Göttingen, 1926-27) • C. TRUEMAN and R. S. CLARK, eds., *Protestant Scholasticism: Essays in Reassessment* (Carlisle, U.K., 1999) • H. E. WEBER, *Die philosophische Scholastik des deutschen Protestantismus in Zeitalter der Orthodoxie* (Leipzig, 1907); idem, *Reformation, Orthodoxie und Rationalismus* (2 vols. in 3; Gütersloh, 1937-51; repr., Darmstadt, 1966).

RICHARD A. MULLER

3. Eastern Orthodoxy
→ Orthodox Christianity; Orthodox Church

Our Father → Lord's Prayer

Outcasts → Caste; Pariahs

Oxford Movement

1. Background
2. Significance
3. Periods
4. Legacy

1. Background

The Oxford Movement began in 1833 with a sermon preached by John Keble (1792-1866) to the judges and the justices of the peace in Oxford. It signaled the beginning of the Catholic revival in the Church of England. An understanding of this movement is necessary in order to understand the pluriformity of the Church of England (→ Anglican Communion).

After the English → Reformation the Church of England preserved more of the traditional catholic structure (e.g., the episcopate; → Bishop, Episcopate) than did most Reformation churches. After the Calvinistic interregnum (→ Calvinism) in the 1640s and 1650s, however, the Church of England fell into → deism and Latitudinarianism (→ Enlightenment; Modern Church History 1). It recovered as the result of three → revivals: (1) the Methodist, led by the → Wesley brothers John (1703-91) and Charles (1707-88; → Methodism; Methodist Churches); (2) the Evangelical, which gathered strength at the time of the French → Revolution; and (3) the Catholic, in the 1830s and 1840s, which was brought about by Keble, E. B. Pusey (1800-1882), and J. H. → Newman (1801-90). After these three revivals the Church of England emerged as a pluriform church with three distinct pillars: one Evangelical, one Catholic, and one Broad Church, consisting first of Anglicans who accept the Thirty-nine Articles, then liberals, and finally "cultural Anglicans," who receive → baptism, → marriage, and burial (→ Funeral) according to the church's → rites and ceremonies.

2. Significance

Initially, the Oxford Movement was a protest against Erastianism in the Church of England (→ Church and State), for example, in allowing the state to abolish a number of dioceses in Ireland. But it was also a manifestation of → Romanticism, that is, as a translation of Romanticism's organistic thinking into ecclesiastical terms (→ Church; Organism).

The first main goal of the Oxford Movement was the restoration of the Church of England according to the teachings of the early → church fathers. Though not a movement in the direction of Rome, it was distinctly anti-Protestant. The ideal was Anglo-Catholicism — a form of Christianity that was neither Roman nor Calvinistic. But hostility such as that of Thomas Arnold (1795-1842), who spoke of the "Oxford malignants," drove some of the leaders of the Catholic revival into the → Roman Catholic Church. Newman, for example, became a Roman Catholic in 1845. He thus confirmed the worst fears of those who had already understood the Oxford Movement as a Romanizing movement.

3. Periods

We may divide the Oxford Movement into four distinct periods. First was the Tractarian period (1833-41), when the leaders of the movement presented their ideas in the form of popular tracts. This period ended in 1840 after Tract 90, an explanation of the Thirty-nine Articles in a Roman Catholic sense, had been condemned.

Next was the period of ritualism, which lasted until 1870. During this time, often in defiance of episcopal discipline, Roman Catholic rituals were reintroduced into the Church of England, including the use of candles (→ Light), → vestments, → incense, auricular confession, and statues (→ Images)

During the period from 1870 to 1960 Anglo-Catholicism, combining scholarship and intensive pastoral and missionary work, became a dominant part of the Church of England. Part of it came to terms with liberal theology (see esp. the volume → Lux Mundi [1889]) and influenced the Broad Church segment via the weekly → Eucharist and the so-called parish and people movement (1950-70).

The final period came after → Vatican II and the radical 1960s, when the Oxford Movement entered a state of uncertainty, if not disarray. The Roman Catholic Church encouraged *aggiornamento* authoritatively through its conciliar documents (→ Councils of the Church; Teaching Office). Anglo-Catholics went through a similar experience but had no Vatican Council to determine either the outcome or their future policies. Paradoxically, they divided into what we may call pre– and post–Vatican II Anglo-Catholics. Evangelicals also became stronger than they had been since the Victorian period (→ Evangelical Movement). In the 1960s, moreover, radicals and liberals in the Church of England became more vociferous, as seen in controversy surrounding the book *Honest to God* (1963) by J. A. T. Robinson, the bishop of Woolwich. Some Anglo-Catholics even supported the liberals and radicals.

4. Legacy

The most enduring legacy of the Oxford Movement was its reemphasizing of many Catholic doctrines and rituals that had retained a place in the Church of

England but had been almost forgotten in the 17th and 18th centuries, such as the apostolic succession (→ Ministry, Ministerial Offices) and ecclesiology. The movement also revived → monasticism, which had been suppressed in 1536 and 1539 under Henry VIII (1509-47). Bishop Samuel Wilberforce (1805-73) promoted the founding of women's orders in the 1840s and 1850s. Men's orders, apart from the Cowley Fathers, came only in the 1890s (→ Religious Orders and Congregations). Another stress of the movement was on holiness (→ Sacred and Profane), though this emphasis had been anticipated in the 18th-century Wesleyan Revival, as had also that on more frequent Communion.

The influence of the Oxford Movement on the ecumenical movement was paradoxical. It opened the road toward → dialogue with Rome (→ Ecumenism, Ecumenical Movement) while shutting off that which led to the → free churches, especially the Methodist denominations.

Bibliography: C. ANGELL, A Ritual Controversy in the Victorian Church of England (Rome, 1983) • O. CHAD-WICK, The Spirit of the Oxford Movement: Tractarian Essays (Cambridge, 1990); idem, The Victorian Church, pt. 1, 1829-1859 (New York, 1966) chaps. 3 and 6 • R. W. CHURCH, The Oxford Movement: Twelve Years, 1833-45 (London, 1891) • I. CLUTTERBUCK, Marginal Catholics. Anglo-Catholicism: A Further Chapter of Modern Church History (Leominster, 1993) • L. N. CRUMB, The Oxford Movement and Its Leaders: A Bibliography of Secondary and Lesser Primary Sources (Metuchen, N.J., 1988; supp., 1993) • R. S. EDGECOMBE, Two Poets of the Oxford Movement: John Keble and John Henry Newman (Madison, N.J., 1995) • P. J. JAGGER, A History of the Parish and People Movement (Bedfordshire, 1978) • E. JAY, ed., The Evangelical and Oxford Movements (Cambridge, 1983) • P. B. NOCKLES, The Oxford Movement in Context: Anglican High Churchmanship, 1760-1857 (Cambridge, 1994) • M. R. O'CONNELL, The Oxford Conspirators: A History of the Oxford Movement, 1833-45 (New York, 1969) • P. VAISS, ed., From Oxford to the People: Reconsidering Newman and the Oxford Movement (Leominster, 1996).

PETER STAPLES